THE
SCIENCE OF SOCIETY

THE
SKETCH OF SOCIETY

PUBLISHED UNDER THE AUSPICES OF THE SUMNER CLUB
ON THE FOUNDATION ESTABLISHED
IN MEMORY OF
PHILIP HAMILTON McMILLAN OF THE CLASS OF 1894
YALE COLLEGE

THE
SCIENCE OF SOCIETY

BY

WILLIAM GRAHAM SUMNER

*Late Professor of Political and Social Science
in Yale University*

ALBERT GALLOWAY KELLER

*Professor of the Science of Society
in Yale University*

AND

MAURICE REA DAVIE

*Professor of Sociology
in Yale University*

VOLUME IV

NEW HAVEN

YALE UNIVERSITY PRESS

LONDON: HUMPHREY MILFORD: OXFORD UNIVERSITY PRESS

COMPLETE TABLE OF CONTENTS OF VOLUMES I, II, III, AND IV

THE *table of contents for this volume (Volume IV) consists of the topics in the general table of contents, listed below, which are designated by asterisks. The general table is repeated here by way of furnishing a perspective of the whole treatment.*

VOLUME I

Preface.

PART I

INTRODUCTORY

* An asterisk after a section-number indicates that there is in the *Case-Book* a section corresponding to that number.

PART II

SELF-MAINTENANCE: INDUSTRIAL ORGANIZATION

PART III

SELF-MAINTENANCE: REGULATIVE ORGANIZATION

VOLUME II

PART IV

SELF-MAINTENANCE: RELIGION

VOLUME III

PART V

SELF-PERPETUATION

VOLUME IV

PREFACE

In this *Case-Book* the student is introduced, as it were, to the workshop. The following instances have been set down with little comment, though they are arranged in a certain geographical order, as explained in the Note to the Index; and they are less closely classified than the citations in the text. Categories have been allowed to run together to a certain degree; in some cases topics have not been broken into subdivisions; in general, the evidence has been permitted to appear in a guise somewhat resembling the original accumulation. It is hoped that this relative looseness of classification will assist the student to understand the complexity and endless interrelations of the materials, in that he will be obliged to do some classifying for himself. He will readily see that the evidence for the evolution of societal institutions is never wholly consistent, and that hard and fast lines of demarkation between man-made categories do not exist. He will note variations and survivals of all sorts; especially will he encounter, here as well as in the text, numerous excerpts from contemporary journals which will exhibit the persistence of mores sometimes assumed to be extinct. In any case, he has before him an extensive and representative sample of unselected evidence, from which will appear the typically inductive character of our treatment, much as the inductive processes of modern law-teaching are revealed by the legal case-method. He is advised to make a practice of scanning the following collections, under the several topics, prior to inspection of the text and its conclusions.

There has been yet another consideration which has led to the attachment of a *Case-Book* to the body of this book. Much of the evidence employed in arriving at the conclusions in preceding volumes has been excluded from the text by necessities of exposition; many of the cases listed below, though originally in the body of the book, have been removed as constituting an excessive weight on presentation. We have been unwilling, however, simply to set them aside. They have been collected with diligence and care over a number of years, chiefly by the senior author; and among them are variants and contradictories which the reader ought to see. By scrutiny of the bulk of the evidence he will be in a position to criticize our conclusions more intelligently and doubtless often to improve upon the interpretations adopted by us. Considerations of space have forced no little contraction of our extracts, together with the omission of numbers of them altogether; but we believe that these collections, added to the evidence presented in the text, constitute a fair and reasonably full representation of the materials used.

It is our good fortune that Professor Davie joins us in the composition of this volume.

A. G. KELLER.

§9. Primitive Atomism.

THE account of Homer[1] concerning the Cyclopes, the representatives to him of utter savagery, is typical of atomism: "Each rules his consorts and children, and they pay no heed to one another." Says Curr[2] of the Australians: "Sorcery makes them fear and hate every man not of their own coterie, suspicious of every man not of their tribe; it tends to keep them in small communities, and is a great bar to social progress. . . . It is a singular fact that very few, if indeed any, of the Australian tribes celebratè any event with a feast or take a meal in common. . . . One of the leading characteristics of the Australian Black is that he entertains an intense hatred to every man and child of his own color, outside of those tribes with which he is personally acquainted, and longs to satisfy it with blood."

The Papuan of New Guinea lacks all political organization and common feeling; "everyone claims for himself unlimited freedom of action and movement, and the same purely individualistic principle finds its somewhat extended application in the family and village community."[3] "To the primitive man," comments Hagen,[4] "one's own self comes first. . . . Compassion, charity, gratitude, all are concepts unknown to him." Krieger[5] says that the people of villages a few kilometers apart cannot understand each other's language, owing to the great number of dialects in New Guinea. They cannot form a unit larger than a village for this reason and because of mutual distrust, the latter being due in good part to fear of sorcery; the natives are suspicious, shy, cowardly, and untrustworthy. The average distance over which a language extends is from eight to ten kilometers and often each village has a separate dialect; the only means of communication over stretches is pidgin-English. Slave-raiding and head-hunting expeditions are always expected, and they do not dare cross a frontier. Seligmann[6] corroborates these facts and says that a different language or dialect occurs every twenty or thirty miles. Neighboring tribes possessing identical physical characteristics and having many cultural features in common may yet present strange divergences. A part of the Gazelle Peninsula, though only thinly populated, is divided into twenty districts in each of which a different dialect is spoken; all of these differ so much that while two inhabitants of neighboring districts may be able to converse, those of localities a little farther removed have difficulty in understanding each other.[7] Anxiety about imaginary ill is the prevailing tone, with distrust as an immediate consequence. The smallest islands have divisions which hold no intercourse. Difference of language is a badge of hostility. It would seem that uncivilized men tend constantly to differentiate language, which in turn keeps them uncivilized. It takes

---

1 *Odyssey*, IX, 114.
2 *Aust. Race*, I, 49, 50, 82, 101.
3 Blum, *Neu-Guinea*, 23.
4 *Papua's*, 266.

5 *Neu-Guinea*, 141, 193, 206, 209, 413.
6 In JAI, XXXIX, 246.
7 Von Pfeil, in JAI, XXVII, 183; Finsch, *Samoafahrten*, 109.

high civilization, with communication and literature, to suppress dialects and unite masses of men. Pidgin-English in Melanesia, as in eastern Asia and western Africa, testifies to the need of overcoming the obstacle of language if the work of civilization is to go on.[8] A similar situation existed in New Caledonia, where "the people knew of no native name embracing the entire island, but all was divided into separate districts and villages, with distinct names for each. War there was the rule, peace the exception."[9]

Among the Bushmen of South Africa, "families alone form associations in single small hordes." The only uniting force is the sentiment of sex, parenthood, or relationship. Hordes keep at a distance from one another "since the smaller the number the more easily is a supply of food procured. Even families have to break up in order to procure food."[10] Nowadays the Bushmen sometimes form little villages, but only temporarily and accidentally. They have no chiefs but only the temporary leadership of some person who wins influence.[11] Von Schkopp[12] mentions certain Pygmy tribes in Cameroons as being timid and cautious, seldom meeting with other natives and being especially anxious to avoid encountering Europeans. The African Pygmies in general are reported as being very anti-social; they apparently have no ties of family affection, such as those of mother and son or sister and brother, and seem to be wanting in all social qualities, asking only to be let alone, to "live and let live." They preserve their freedom, of which they are intensely jealous, and hold themselves entirely aloof from other natives, among whom they neither marry nor are given in marriage.[13] "As a result of the universal employment of fetiches in African tribes, there is no confidence between man and man. Every one is in distrust of his neighbor; every man's hand against his fellow. . . . Because of this lack of confidence, the natural affections and the duties of the dearest relations are perverted. Wives afraid of husbands, and husbands afraid of wives; children afraid of parents, and parents afraid of children; the chief of the village uncertain of his people; and the entire community that must live and eat and associate together, living and eating and associating with a constant secretly entertained suspicion of each other."[14]

Furness[15] thinks that "possibly there is no portion of the world of an equal area where so many dialects are spoken" as in eastern Assam, some of them being totally different. The Abors of that region are said to be like tigers; two cannot dwell in one den. Their houses are scattered singly or in groups of twos and threes over an immense extent of mountainous country. If they come together, quarrels and feuds speedily disperse them.[16] Among the Nagas of India united action by one village is spoken of as an impossibility; if a village decreased in numbers, the larger ones demanded annual tribute or they plundered and ruined it. "We thus see a community of some hundreds perched on a hill, and depending almost exclusively on their own resources, constantly fighting others similarly located, on all sides, yet thoroughly able to maintain themselves. Perhaps in no other part of the world can so complete a tribal isolation be seen, and subdivision carried to such an extreme."[17] Of one people in Borneo it is said that they neither eat rice nor salt and "do not associate

8 Von Pfeil, *Südsee*, 130, 135, 289.
9 Turner, *Samoa*, 240.
10 Lichtenstein, *S. Afr.*, II, 469, 194.
11 Fritsch, *Eingeb. S.-Afr.*, 444.
12 In *Globus*, LXXXIII, 284.

13 Burrows, *Pigmies*, 177-179, 182; Junker, *Afrika*, III, 91.
14 Nassau, *Fetichism*, 268-269.
15 In JAI, XXXII, 446.
16 Gomme, in JAI, XVII, 128.
17 Godden, in JAI, XXVII, 24, 16.

with each other but rove about the woods like wild beasts."[18] In northeast Celebes the inhabitants of the several villages are distinct tribes, each under its own chief, speaking languages unintelligible to each other, and almost always at war.[19] Very averse to association are the Kubus of Sumatra; in their wild state they live in a deep forest, making temporary dwellings, if their rude shelters can be so called, where they stay for a few days at a time, gathering food. They are so timorous and shy that it is a rare circumstance for anyone to see them, and of course an extremely rare one for any white man; Forbes[20] thinks it doubtful if any white man has ever seen the Kubu, except as one sees the hind-quarters of a startled deer. In the Pelew Islands all show distrust and are on guard, with fixed countenances, all the time. The visitor who receives betel and food wants his host to taste of it first, to guard against being poisoned.[21]

"The most conspicuous characteristic of the Seri [American Indian] tribe as a whole is isolation. The geographic position and physical features of their habitat favor, and indeed measurably compel, isolation; their little principality is protected on one side by stormy seas and on the other by still more forbidding deserts; their home is too hard and poor to tempt conquest, and their possessions too meager to invite spoliation; hence, under customary conditions, they never see neighbors save in chance encounters on their frontier or in their own predatory forays—and in either case the encounters are commonly inimical. The natural isolation of the habitat is reflected in modes of life and habits of thought; and during the ages the physical isolation has come to be reflected in a bitter and implacable hereditary enmity toward aliens—an enmity apparently forming the strongest motive in their life and thought, and indeed grown into a persistent instinct. . . . The great fact remains that not a single mixed-blood Seri is known to exist, and that no more than two of the blood . . . now live voluntarily beyond the territorial and consanguineal confines of the tribe. . . . The Seri antipathy is at once deepened into an obsession and crystallized into a cult; the highest virtue in their calendar is the shedding of alien blood; and their normal impulse on meeting an alien is to kill unless deterred by fear, to flee if the way is clear, and to fawn treacherously for better opportunity if neither natural course lies open.[22]

One of the most conspicuous traits of certain backward Alaskans is independence. "What he wants to do he will do, as a rule. He lives for the present, and gratifies the desires of the hour, no matter what it may cost him. . . . Nothing galls him like being 'bossed' or controlled. To him it is a species of slavery, and the slave is the lowest of all beings, in his estimation."[23] It is said, with reference to the disintegration of certain Amazon tribes, that "a whole race of men is wasting away before the eyes of the world, and no power of philosophy or Christianity can arrest its proudly gloomy progress towards a certain and utter destruction."[24] Von Martius[25] remarks on the curious division of the Brazilian tribes into almost innumerable groups, opposed and exclusive, "in which American mankind appears as a huge ruin." In Matto Grosso the tribes live scattered about family-wise, with pronounced jealousy of feeling toward each other. The land is overflowed for months and they have to live in

18 Roth, in JAI, XXIV, 237.
19 Wallace, Malay Archip., 242.
20 In JAI, XIV, 121-122.
21 Semper, Palau-Ins., 235; Kubary, Pelauer, 73, 90.

22 McGee, in BAE, XVII, pt. I, 130*, 132*.
23 Jones, Thlingets, 92.
24 Markham, in JAI, XXIV, 237.
25 Beiträge, I, 137, 244, 245, 247, 534, 535.

boats, which accounts somewhat for this isolation. Nevertheless these peoples show a marked intelligence. The Miranhas live in an unbroken stress of mutual hostility, practising robbery, murder, and man-hunting, and exhibiting deep savagery and cannibalism. Of the Tehuelches of Patagonia, Fitzroy[26] wrote: "When mutually convenient all assemble at one place but if food becomes scarce or quarrels happen each party withdraws to its own territory. At such times one party will encroach on the hunting grounds of another and a battle is the consequence." Brinton,[27] speaking of the isolated man who lives "alone with his wife, his children around him, his household goods and gods all within his lonely lodge," notes that "that man's monogamy, his sense of property, his feelings of duty and responsibility, of association and independence, can in no way be assimilated to those of the man who is the free product of the state, developed through countless generations of gradual culture."

§18. Folkways and Mores.

LANGUAGE well illustrates the conception of the folkways and mores; much of the following is taken from a work by one of the authors.[1] Language is one of the most original and characteristic phenomena of societal evolution; it is not possible to classify it as a science, art, invention, or fashion. It contains the ultimate germs of all these classes. It was the first of those agencies of "exchange"[2] which both held and universalized culture. Prior to its development and that of writing, a discovery—for instance, of the use of metals—might have been made and forgotten over and over again as the users moved from the vicinity of the deposits.[3]

Language is a product of the folkways which illustrates their operation in a number of most important details; it meets the need of coöperative understanding in all the work and in connection with all the interests of life. It is a societal phenomenon, being necessary in war, the chase, and industry so soon as these interests come to be pursued coöperatively. Each group developed its own language which then held that group together and sundered it from others.[4] All are now agreed that, whatever may have been the origin of language, it owes its form and development to usage. "Men's usage makes language. . . . The maxim that 'usage is the rule of speech' is of supreme and uncontrolled validity in every part and parcel of every human tongue."[5] "Language is only the imperfect means of men to find their bearings in the world of their memories; to make use of their memory, that is, their own experience and that of their ancestors, with all probability that this world of memory will be like the world of reality."[6]

Whitney[7] said that language is an institution, meaning that it is in the folkways or mores. He adds: "In whatever aspect the general facts of language are viewed, they exhibit the same absence of reflection and intention. . . . No one ever set himself deliberately at work to invent or improve language,— or did so, at least, with any valuable and abiding result. The work is all ac-

26 *Beagle*, II, 131.
27 In *Smithson. Rep.*, 1893, 597.
1 Sumner, *Folkways*, §§135, 137, 141.
2 Keller, *Starting-Points*, ch. VII.
3 Lippert, *Kgchte.*, II, 223.

4 Gumplowicz, *Soc. und Pol.*, 93.
5 Whitney, *Language*, 37, 40.
6 Mauthner, *Kritik der Sprache*, III, 2 (quoted); II, 184, 186, 278, 403, 426, 427.
7 *Language*, 48, 51, 46, 44, 23, 14.

complished by a continual satisfaction of the needs of the moment, by ever yielding to an impulse and grasping a possibility, which the already acquired treasure of words and forms, and the habit of their use, suggest and put within reach. . . . Every single item of alteration, of whatever kind, and of whatever degree of importance, goes back to some individual or individuals who set it in circulation, from whose example it gained a wider and wider currency, until it finally won that general assent, which is alone required in order to make anything in language proper and authoritative." The fact that Whitney's statements, if applied to any of the folkways, would serve to describe and define them, shows to what an extent language is a case of the operation by which mores are produced; they are always devices to meet a need, which are imperceptibly modified and unconsciously handed down through the generations. The ways, like the language, are incorporeal things; they are borne by everybody and nobody, and are developed by everybody and nobody. Everybody has his little peculiarities of language, his peculiarities of accent or pronunciation, and his pet words or phrases; each is suggesting all the time the use of the tricks of language which he has adopted. "Nothing less than the combined effort of a whole community, with all its classes and orders, in all its variety of characters, circumstances, and necessities, is capable of keeping in life a whole language. . . . Every vocable was to us [as children] an arbitrary and conventional sign; arbitrary, because any one of a thousand other vocables could have been just as easily learned by us and associated with the same idea; conventional, because the one we acquired had its sole ground and sanction in the consenting use of the community of which we formed a part." "We do not, as children, make our language for ourselves. We get it by tradition, all complete. We think in sentences. As our language forms sentences, that is, as our mother-tongue thinks, so we learn to think. Our brain, our entire thought-status, forms itself by the mother-tongue, and we transmit the same to our children."8

Nature-men have only petty coins of speech; they can express nothing great nor can they compare, analyze, and combine. They are overwhelmed by a flood of details, in which they cannot discern the ruling idea, and the material and sensual constitute their limits. If they move they have to get a new language. The American languages are a soft mass which changes easily if tribes separate, or as time goes on, or if they move their habitat. Sometimes measures are adopted in order to make the language unintelligible, as the Dushmen insert a syllable in a word to that end. "The language of nature peoples offers a faithful picture of their mental status. All is in flux. Nothing is fixed or crystallized. No fundamental thoughts, ideas, or ideals are present. There is no regularity, logic, principles, ethics, or moral character. Lack of logic in thinking, lack of purpose in willing or acting, put the mind of a nature man on a plane with that of our children. Lack of memory, anti-logic, paradox, fantasy in mental action, correspond to capriciousness, levity, irresponsibility, and the rule of emotions and passions in practical action."9

What we see in the cases of primitive dialects is that, if we suppose men to have joined in coöperative effort with only the sounds used by apes and monkeys, the requirement of their interests would push them on to develop languages such as we now know. The isolating, agglutinative, incorporative, and

8 Schultze, *Naturvölker*, 96.   9 Schultze, *Naturvölker*, 86, 89, 91; Schultze, in *Am Urquell*, II, 22, 48.

inflectional languages can be put in a series according to the convenience and correctness of the logical processes which they embody and teach. The Semitic languages evidently teach a logic different from that of the Indo-European. It is a different way of thinking which is inculcated in each great family of languages. They represent stages in the evolution of thought or ways of thinking. The instance is one of those which best show us how folkways are built up and how they are pulled down. The agglutination of words and forms sometimes seems like a steady building process; again, the process will not go forward at all. "In the agglutinative languages speech is berry jam. In the inflectional languages each word is like a soldier in his place with his outfit."[10] The accidental errors of pronunciation which may be due to very slight individual variations in the form of the vocal organs are cases of individual contribution to the development of language. The baby words and individual mispronunciations which are taken up by a family and its friends, but never get further, show us how dialects grow. There are changes in language which are, "in their inception, inaccuracies of speech. They attest the influence of that immense numerical majority among the speakers of English who do not take sufficient pains to speak correctly, but whose blunders become finally the norm of the language."[11] In analogy things which are alike are embraced in a single term; in metaphor two or more things which seem alike, but may not be so, are grouped together and are embraced in a single term. All these modes of change in language attest the work of individuals on language. Sometimes there is extension of influence to a group; again, the influence is only temporary and is rejected again; again it falls in with a drift of taste or habit, when it is taken up and colors the pronunciation or usage of the population of a great district, and becomes fixed in the language. All this is true also on the negative side, since usage of words, accent, timbre of the voice, and pronunciation expel older usages. Language therefore illustrates well all the great changes of folkways under the heads of coöperation and antagonism. There is an excellent chance to study the operation in the case of slang. A people who are prosperous and happy, optimistic and progressive, will produce much slang; it is a case of play; they amuse themselves with the language. One may think the new words and phrases vulgar and in bad taste, or senseless and ridiculous; but though he may eschew them, the masses will decide whether they shall be permanently rejected or not. The vote is informal. The most confirmed purist will by and by utter a new slang word when he needs it. One's objections are broken down; his taste is altered by what he hears. We are right in the midst of the operation of making folkways and can perceive it close at hand.

Malinowski's *Crime and Custom in Savage Society* comes to hand too late for our text to profit by it. This is regrettable—the more so in view of the esteem we accord to all the other publications of this author with which we are familiar.

The thesis of the book is, broadly, that too much attention has been given to the power of customs, taboos, and group-solidarity in general and too little to the variations about group-norms: evasions, reconciliations, atonements. The author wants to see life as it is actually lived, and he finds the outlines of all the general patterns indistinct and frayed out into threads. He is far from denying the essential control of custom; what he is protesting against is really a form

---

10 Schultze, *Naturvölker*, 93.   11 Whitney, *Language*, 28.

of the "category-fallacy."[12] He does not like such concepts as "group-respon-sibility," "group-justice," "group-property," and "communism," and protests against "the dogma of the absence of individual rights and liabilities among savages. . . . Underlying all these ideas was the assumption that in primitive societies the individual is completely dominated by the group—the horde, the clan or the tribe—that he obeys the commands of his community, its tradi-tions, its public opinion, its decrees, with a slavish, fascinated, passive obedience. This assumption, which gives the leading tone to certain modern discussions, upon the mentality and sociality of savages, still survives . . . in most American and German works and in some English writings." In particular there has been no real study of primitive law; the assumption has been that individuals did not diverge from the paths laid down for their treading. "This lacuna in modern anthropology is due, not to any over-sight of primitive le-gality, but on the contrary to its over-emphasis. Paradoxical as it sounds, it is yet true that present-day anthropology neglects primitive law just because it has an exaggerated, and I will add at once, a mistaken idea of its perfection."

The contentions of the book are arrived at inductively from the author's col-lections assembled during his residence among the Melanesian Trobriand Is-landers. The latter do not reveal any "communism" in their economic life, but "we are met by law, order, definite privileges and a well-developed system of obligations." Economic obligations exert a binding force, and there exists a real system of reciprocity, to which is attributed the dual organization. Self-interest and social ambition enforce mutual obligations. There is a legal side even to religious acts, not to mention marriage. The principle of give-and-take pervades tribal life. In short, reciprocity is the basis of social structure. Speak-ing of his brief classification of the rules of custom, the author continues: "Though in my survey attention has naturally been mainly focussed on the legal machinery, I was not intent on proving that all social rules are legal, but on the contrary, I wanted to show that the rules of law form but one well-defined category within the body of custom. . . . It scarcely needs to be added that 'law' and 'legal phenomena,' as we have discovered, described and defined them in a part of Melanesia, do not consist in any independent institutions. Law represents rather an aspect of their tribal life, one side of their structure, than any independent, self-contained social arrangements. Law dwells not in a special system of decrees, which foresee and define possible forms of non-fulfil-ment and provide appropriate barriers and remedies. Law is the specific result of the configuration of obligations, which makes it impossible for the native to shirk his responsibility without suffering for it in the future. . . . There is no doubt that custom is not based only on a universal, undifferentiated, ubi-quitous force, this mental inertia, though this unquestionably exists, and adds its quota to other constraint. There must be in all societies a class of rules too practical to be backed up by religious sanctions, too burdensome to be left to mere goodwill, too personally vital to individuals to be enforced by any ab-stract agency. This is the domain of legal rules, and I venture to foretell that reciprocity, systematic incidence, publicity and ambition will be found to be the main factors in the binding machinery of primitive law."

It is a pity that this book must perforce be dismissed with such perfunctory attention—the recital of a few of its chapter-headings and the reproduction of several passages. Most of the author's instances are quotable. As regards the

12 §456, of the text.

thesis of the volume, it is probable that systematic works have been inclined to lay too little stress upon variations around types. We have stated often enough that such variations exist, and that the process of adjustment could not take place without them; that the individual is the producer of variations, and so the lead-off factor in societal evolution. But it is true, as Malinowski says, that the field-men themselves have only lately arrived at the point where they report such commonplaces. His book cannot but assist in the effort to see primitive life whole. The only possible quarrel which we could have with him is that which always impends between the field-observer and the "arm-chair systematist."

§28. The Collection Stage.

THE collection stage, as was mentioned in the text, is largely inferential. There are a few instances, however, of peoples approaching this condition and living in large part at least upon foodstuffs which they collect. The Bushmen of South Africa are a classic example of a lowly stage of development. Livingstone[1] says of them: "The Bushmen never cultivate the soil or rear any domestic animal, save wretched dogs. The chief subsistence of the Bushmen is the flesh of game, but this is eked out by what the women collect of roots and beans, and fruits of the desert." Curr[2] gives a description of the march of a native Australian family spreading over a front of half a mile to a mile and a half, so as to collect food. Certain peoples of the Malay States are said to have "subsisted entirely on the root of the tapioca plant, wild herbs gathered by the women, and animals trapped or killed with the aid of the blow-pipe by the men. . . . They attempted nothing in the way of agriculture, except the wild tapioca previously mentioned. Indeed, their extreme nomadic habits would hardly permit it, for . . . they changed camping ground at least three or four times in the course of a year. They had no system of chieftainship, nor did they look up to any single person as their head."[3] One of the most important causes which contribute to the periodical migrations of the wild tribes of the Malay Peninsula is their great love of fruit, especially that of the durian. They spend their entire lives in the hunt for wild roots, fruit, and game.[4] It is said of the Shoshones of the Salt Lake Desert that they were more improvident than birds and more brutal than beasts. Some tribes, it is stated, had neither arms nor utensils and but rarely ate cooked food.[5] The Indians of the Rocky Mountains, according to Schoolcraft,[6] planted nothing and lived only by the indigenous productions, on fish, game, and roots. They existed in small detached bodies and single families, and changed their locations so widely that they seemed to have no particular claim to any portion. Among the Firelanders, "women are sometimes sent for fuel into the forest, but not often. They pick the berries, but the men gather the fungi, for which they have to climb trees."[7] Certain Orinoco tribes did not cultivate their lands at all. "They were always traveling from river to river collecting wild fruits; never built houses, and had no shelter from sun or rain. Indeed, it is probable that their

---

1 *Miss. Trav.*, 49.
2 *Aust. Race*, 242.
3 Knocker, in JAI, XXXIX, 146.
4 Skeat and Blagden, *Malay Penin.*, I, 521, 522.

5 Cognetti de Martiis, *Forme Primitive*, 156.
6 *Tribes U.S.*, pt. I, 224.
7 Bridges, *Voice for S. Amer.*, XIII, 207.

nomadicity saved them from extermination."[8] Further evidence of the original condition of self-maintenance is presented in §49, on Original Destitution.

§30. The Pastoral Stage.

RATZEL[1] gives considerable attention to the pastoral economy. He cites several causes of nomadism: the pastures are not rich enough to suffice more than a short time; the rainfall makes one pasturage better at one time, another at another; quarrels over pasturage keep the weaker peoples on the move. In one case the pastures have to be deserted when they are at their best on account of the flies that injure the camels; the herds must retire to the forests. This author distinguishes three ways in which the transition from nomadism to settled life has come about: where a wandering race has been compulsorily confined within limits so narrow that roaming was out of the question, for example, in the case of the invaders of the Greek peninsula; where herds have been lost in war or by pestilence; or where the desire for comforts and luxuries has overcome the love of freedom. "Only he can fully understand the power of trade as a civilizer who has seen its operation in the steppes." Tea, opium, spirits, fine clothes, and weapons will corrupt the hardiest nomad. Trade arouses and creates wants and then meets them until the nomad sees that he cannot satisfy them any longer unless he (that is, his wife and daughters) goes to work at agriculture or industry. China has been able to accomplish little against the Mongols with the sword; even if its armies had had great success, they would not have been nearly so efficacious as the operations of trade, to reduce them to poverty and weakness and, in a measure, to diligence and active industry.

The difficulty in making the transition to settled life is well shown in the case of the Bashkirs. They used to have flocks and herds and horses, but now they have not. They draw wood from the forest, get honey, hunt with falcons, catch fish, and work in the factories and mines; they do not like agriculture. Their economic position is extremely poor; their only forms of property are shirts full of holes and bast shoes. It is possible to meet them in summer going to work shirtless, barefooted, bareheaded, with only a few rags wound round the body; in winter they put on the single over-garment. Their food is bad, especially in winter; in summer when the cattle can get grass they get on pretty well, but in winter the cattle and the people alike suffer hunger and there are days together when they get nothing to eat. Their unfortunate condition is said to be due to a transition from nomadic life. The allotments of land to them, fifteen dessiatine (40.5 acres) each, would be sufficient for a good farmer, but not for them with their mode of life; hence they have fallen into poverty and sold their land.[2]

All civilized people, according to Ratzel,[3] have a common interest against nomadism. China and Russia in Central Asia are in fact allies encompassing the nomads from both sides. The Russians suppress the Turkish tribes and the Chinese the Mongolians. Both crowd out the nomads, the Russians more energetically, the Chinese more slowly, depriving them first of their plunder-

8 Roth, in BAE, XXXVIII, 214-215.
1 *Vkde.*, III, 36, 47, 57; Lippert, *Kgchte.*, I, 478-479.
2 *Russian Ethnog.* (Russ.), II, 110.
3 *Vkde.*, III, 54.

territory, then of their pastures, until they must migrate or settle. Vámbéry is quoted to the effect that the destiny of nomads is to be driven into the barrenest parts of the deserts and steppes, there to sink into misery and die out. "Civilization strengthens him who bends beneath it and weakens him who resists it. The Mongols conquered China and then were absorbed and conquered by Chinese civilization. All conquerors must assume the duties of conquest and of the height in world importance to which they have arisen." They must make permanent states and establish strong institutions fit for a great state, or fall. "The nomads conquer with a rush. Then this necessity comes upon them. If they bend to it, nomadism is sacrificed. If they resist it, they decline again." Nomadism flourished in Asia so long as Siberia was open as a retreat. Thence the nomads made their excursions, and when repelled, thither they retreated; the wild tribes there were no barrier against them. The conquest of Siberia by Russia put an end to this, and the effect for Europe was as great as the effect for Asia of the conquest of Mongolia by China. Though in north Africa and west Asia nomadism has been restrained by the Mediterranean and the states bordering on it, it has been protected by the Arabian and African deserts until now the Sudan states, built out of nomads, are setting bounds to it.[4]

There are really several kinds of nomadism: first, that of the Bushmen and Australians, wandering hunters and collectors; second, that of shepherds and herdsmen, such as the Masai and Arabs; and third, the type presented by horsemen, of which there are several varieties—the Patagonians, Abipones, Kirghis. As an example of nomadism not related to pastoral economy, may be cited the tendency of the inhabitants of nearly all the Pacific Islands to wander from place to place in their large canoes, so that at times an island would appear to be thickly peopled, and at others scarcely an individual was to be found.[5] But the term is chiefly applied to cattle-raising, for herding and nomadism go together. The desert is preferred if it gives more room, so that in Namaqualand fruitful oases are avoided by the population.[6] The nomadic Tungus are cattle-breeders, and change their habitat according to the season of the year. Each clan has its own region assigned to it, land over which they can wander at will and where no strangers are allowed to settle.[7] Typical pastoral people are the Soyots, reindeer nomads of the upper Yenesei. They systematically capture wild reindeer which are tamed and crossed with the tame ones, so that the tame reindeer stand in type quite near the wild. The tame ones go out and mingle with the wild and the Soyots regard it as very favorable that the two shall cross. The wild ones when associated with men speedily become fully tame. The reindeer like salt and the Soyots put it out for them; this is one of the ways in which they are attracted to man. The tame ones that go off with the wild return after two or three weeks. They are taken by hand; no lasso is used except for horses. The Soyots regard the herds as their chief property and pay no attention to agriculture; all animals are specially marked. Meat is often eaten raw or merely warmed; raw blood is seldom drunk. The reindeer are used in riding and as beasts of burden.[8] The Todas raise buffaloes and, like other pastoral peoples, are often on the move. "There are two chief reasons for these movements of the buffaloes, of which the

4 Ratzel, *Vkde.*, III, 52, 51, 55.
5 Williamson, *Cent. Polyn.*, I, 325.
6 Ratzel, *Vkde.*, III, 36; I, 58.

7 Czaplicka, *Aborig. Siberia*, 53.
8 Olsen, *Primitivt Folk*, 51, 54, 55, 57, 66, 70, 78.

most urgent is the necessity for new grazing-places. During the dry season, lasting from December to March, the pasturage around the villages where the Todas usually live becomes very scanty, and the buffaloes are taken to places where it is more abundant. . . . The other chief reason for the migrations is that certain villages and dairies, formerly important and still sacred, are visited for ceremonial purposes, or out of respect to ancient custom."9

Africa shows how nomadic or semi-nomadic life hinders the growth of the arts by constant change of place and restlessness; nomadic tribes of Africa manufacture scarcely any tools but obtain them through trade.10 Before European intervention changed the conditions of life in Africa, it was the dweller in the plains and the fertile plateaux, and not, as in Europe, the dwellers in the mountains, who were the virile and fighting races. "The natural wealth of the African consists of live stock, and it is the ambition of the labourer and the peasant to buy one or two head of cattle and several wives. . . . Though as a rule the desires of the pastoral tribes are limited to the acquisition of grazing lands, and they were indifferent to territorial sovereignty, it would seem that small sections were otherwise minded. Thus in South-East Africa the cattle-owning Zulus founded in Zululand the dynasty of Tchaka, and further north the Wahima became kings of Uganda, Unyoro, and Ankole. In the west the Fulani pastorals in like manner became the dominant race. The Masai and the Somalis, on the other hand, though they held undisputed sway over the greater part of East Africa, founded no dynasties. But though in these instances the pastorals created the governing caste over the settled agriculturists, the bulk of the tribe remained as semi-nomad pastorals, completely out of touch with their aristocratic kinsmen, socially less advanced than the settled and urban population, but maintaining by rigorous ordeals and tests a high standard of personal courage and endurance."11

The warlike and predatory element is generally characteristic of nomadic life; nomads often rob and destroy and hinder orderly growth. "When the horses come in strong from the pasture and the second shearing of the sheep is over the nomad calls to mind whatever raids for booty or revenge he has postponed. His staff turns easily into a weapon. Avenger, hero, and robber are the three steps through which the young men go. The two motives are the desire for the wealth reported to be accumulated in more civilized regions and the love of adventure and romance."12 Lippert13 calls this the Beduin mode of existence, the term signifying a desert or steppe people with horses or camels and some cattle, who live not so much by peaceful grazing as by fighting and plundering. Nomadic peoples are usually warlike.

The Hottentots are a herding people or at least in the transitional stage between hunting and herding. A kraal in Namaqualand sometimes has a hundred huts made of mats upon a framework of branches, with as many as ten or twelve persons in a hut. The cattle form one big herd in which, however, each one owns his share; the kraal is set in a ring, and the cattle are herded at night inside the ring, each pair having the hind legs tied together.14 The Akamba have no legend as to the origin of cattle and other domesticated animals, but say that there was a time when the tribe possessed no cattle but only hunted game. They do not brand the cattle except those sent away to pay for a wife

9 Rivers, *Todas*, 123.
10 Ratzel, *Vkde.*, I, 429.
11 Lugard, *Brit. Trop. Africa*, 73-74.

12 Ratzel, *Vkde.*, III, 50.
13 *Kgchte.*, I, 183; II, 71.
14 Ratzel, *Vkde.*, I, 98.

or those surrendered as blood-money for a death.[15] Among the Wahima and Masai, a few herdsmen suffice to keep together herds of several hundred; "one or two Wahima, whistling through their teeth in a very peculiar way, place themselves at the head of a herd which follows them like dogs, even though long stretches are to be covered at a trot or the way is over difficult hilly ground and through water.[16] Herding is not practised much between the Congo and the Niger, perhaps on account of the *tsetse*-fly.[17] Diseases which affect cattle are often a source of difficulty; "thirteen years ago [1879] the cattle plague, which devastated so much of East Central Africa, swept through Ankole and carried off three-fourths of the cattle. The Bahima, who then depended almost exclusively on their cattle for food, perished from starvation in great numbers, and the following year still more of them died from a visitation of smallpox, which proved very fatal to them in their weakened condition. Lieutenant Mundy states that from the information given to him by intelligent Bahima, he believes the Hima population and their stock of cattle at the present day to be not more than a third of what they were fourteen years ago."[18]

On account of the passion of the Upper Nile negroes for cattle, the slave-dealers, in order to offer them their heart's desire, robbed others of their stock. The destruction of the herds is used as a political means of subjugation.[19] Seligmann[20] gives a vivid picture of pastoral life in the Sudan. "In Northern Kordofan the life of the nomad Arabs, though pastoral like that of the Beja of the Red Sea Province, differs from the latter on account of the severity of the dry season and the organized effort that is required to meet it. The movements of families are no casual wanderings, nor are independent groups of tents to be found scattered over the country, but all movements take place *en masse*. Nothing is left to chance, no 'here to-day and gone to-morrow,' no tents shifted silently in the night as is so often supposed. The whole life of the tribe is regulated by the supply of grass and water for men and cattle, and it is only during the short wet season that there is a complete freedom of movement within the tribal boundaries. . . . At the close of the wet season the Sheykh of each section sends out scouts to find out where there is most water. There are certain known *fula*, slight depressions with a clayey bottom, in which the water lies for some time, though in none of these . . . does the water last throughout the dry season, and in most of the sandy wadies the surface water disappears as soon as the rains are over. Great care must be exercised in choosing the summer quarters, so that there may be reasonable hope of sufficient water for the dry season. . . . In the middle of January, cows and goats were being watered every third day, sheep every fifth, horses every day, and camels, kept for convenience near the *feriq*, only drank once in ten days." At the end of the season the camp is shifted, each *da'n* keeping together. "A *da'n* consists of a man and wife or wives, children, and retainers, including all slaves and freed men under his protection. The cattle are driven in front, then follow the camels bearing the women, each of whom, if her husband is rich enough, reclines in her *utfa*. . . . The baggage camels plod along, while the men mounted on their trotting camels superintend the caravan. . . . The march is usually continued

---

15 Hobley, *A-Kamba*, 22.
16 Weiss, in *Globus*, XCI, 158.
17 Ratzel, *Vkde.*, I, 558.

18 Johnston, *Uganda*, II, 627.
19 Ratzel, *Vkde.*, I, 511.
20 In JAI, XLIII, 627-628, 629.

for about ten hours without a break, but with heavily laden camels the pace is slow. This mode of travel continues until the winter quarters are reached."

Before the arrival of Europeans in America there were no pastoral peoples. Following the introduction of the horse a few peoples in the southern pampas developed in the direction of nomadism.[21] To-day, owing largely to the encouragement given by the United States Indian Service, a considerable number of American Indians are cattle-raisers.[22] The ancient Egyptians succeeded in taming some kinds of cattle without having passed through any real stage of nomadism.[23] "The chief pursuit of the Israelites was breeding, especially of goats, sheep and cattle. With them property and cattle meant the same thing. The life of the shepherd and the yield of the herd were extolled in innumerable phrases, the love and faith of Jehovah being likened to the care of the shepherd."[24] There were two seasons among the Aryan herders: one, when the cattle could live out of doors, and another when they must be penned.[25] Common to all inhabitants of Germany, said Strabo,[26] "is their readiness to migrate —a consequence of agriculture in the proper sense—and their custom, instead of laying in stores of provisions, of living in huts and providing only for the needs of the day. They derive most of their food from their cattle like the Nomads; and imitating them they load their goods and furniture on wagons, and move with their cattle wherever they like."

We cannot infer from the use now made of an animal that it was first domesticated with that utility in view. The horse and camel, thinks Ratzel,[27] were originally domesticated for milk and only later became beasts of burden. The element of comradeship, not only with respect to dogs but other animals as well, must also be included. There can be no sentiment about agriculture as there is in Africa about cattle, which are for the negro the "basis of life, fountain of joy, measure of property, means of winning all other desirable things, above all women and finally even money;" for him the cattle may come to be even a brake on progress, for he will not give them up to advance in civilization. Naturally, people can be reduced to utter misery through having their cattle stolen; the Nubians ruined the Dinka in this way, and the Basuto were also overthrown by the same expedient. Cattle also excite cupidity and occasion war; how they affect the whole life of the tribe will be shown in §98.

Cattle are more valuable to the negroes of East Africa as beasts of burden than for milk or meat. Here is found the custom of bleeding the cattle at intervals and drinking the blood; from a strong ox the negroes will take about a liter of blood, repeating the operation in a month. They drink it raw or mixed with milk.[28] The Bageshu are very fond of bleeding the bulls and cooking the blood, which is considered a great delicacy. "The mode of drawing the blood is to tie a cord tightly round the animal's neck until the artery swells out, and shoot an arrow, which has a guard on it to prevent it from going in too deeply, into the artery. They draw off two or three pints of blood which they boil and make into a pudding. The animal soon recovers from its loss and is apparently none the worse for it."[29] The milch-cow of south-east Africa is said to give milk only as long as the calf needs it and to permit herself to be

---

21 Grosse, *Familie*, 90.
22 *Rep. Com. Ind. Affairs*, 1920.
23 Lippert, *Kgchte.*, I, 198.
24 Maurer, *Vkde.*, I, 17.
25 Schrader, *Aryans*, 300.

26 *Geog.*, ch. XXIX.
27 *Vkde.*, I, 57.
28 Ratzel, *Vkde.*, I, 205, 208.
29 Roscoe, in JAI, XXXIX, 192.

milked only when the calf is standing near by.[30] The tribes of British Central Africa use milk but little, and eat the flesh only when an animal dies.[31] With the Bahima milk is the chief diet. "When milk is plentiful they drink it warm from the cow early in the morning, and what is over they drink at noon. They never allow the milk to stand after noon or to go sour; what they cannot drink they give to their servants. When cattle are few and milk is scarce, the men drink the morning milk, and the women the evening. . . . vegetables are, however, tabu to both men and women under ordinary circumstances; the person who eats vegetables ought not to drink milk."[32] Milk must never be boiled for food; they believe it causes the cows to fall ill and die. The herding tribes amongst the negroes generally despise other food than milk, fat, and meat, and everything concerned with milk and milking is sacred. They scarcely ever take milk when sweet. The receptacles are never washed nor is the milk ever allowed to touch metal for fear of harming the cow.[33]

§31. The Agricultural Stage.

ALTHOUGH agriculture leads to a settled life, primitive peoples who cultivate the soil are sometimes not highly sedentary. As compared with hunters and cattle-raisers, they show a much greater attachment to one locality, but in comparison with more civilized conditions there is still considerable wandering. This is largely because of the nature of primitive agriculture and the warlike conditions of the times. Thucydides[1] says that "the country which is now called Hellas was not regularly settled in ancient times; the people were migratory, and readily left their homes whenever they were overpowered by numbers. There was no commerce, and they could not safely hold intercourse with one another either by land or sea. The several tribes cultivated their own soil just enough to obtain a maintenance from it, but they had no accumulations of wealth, and did not plant the ground with trees; for, being without walls, they were never sure that an invader might not come and despoil them."

Among primitive peoples today conditions exist similar to those described by Thucydides. Certain clans of Manipur "fell a piece of jungle and, when sufficiently dry, burn it and then dibble in the seed, and seldom cultivate the same piece of land for more than two years in succession. They therefore need much room, and the desire for new land, coupled with the fear of stronger clans, has led to the whole race adopting a more or less vagabond mode of life, which has been made fatally easy by the wide-spread growth of the bamboo, which makes house building, of a certain kind, very simple."[2] Similar conditions of agriculture exist in Ceylon. "The Culture-Veddah is distinguished from the Nature-Veddah through the cultivation of grain alongside of hunting, the gathering of honey and the digging of yams. When he moves into his summer quarters he fells a suitable piece of forest and burns it down in the intervals between hunting. When the rains come he builds a dry hut on the open place and sows seeds on the charred areas; he then leaves his family there with a stock of provisions and makes for several days toward the high grounds for the purpose of stag-hunting, during which time he lives in caves. When the

30 Weiss, in *Globus*, XCI, 156.
31 Stannus, in JAI, XL, 324.
32 Roscoe, in JAI, XXXVII, 100-101.

33 Ratzel, *Vkde.*, I, 207.
1 *Hist.*, I, §21; Schrader, *Aryans*, 281.
2 Shakespear, in JAI, XXXIX, 371-372.

weather clears and the grain ripens, he returns and proceeds to gather the harvest. Small presents are given to other less provident companions who during his absence have presented small pieces of meat and the like to his family. After the harvest, and now in the dry season, the family goes to a district where lizards are to be found. The Culture-Veddah makes his hut tighter than the Nature-Veddah and does not, like the latter, take his family with him to the high grounds; however, he has not yet learned how to make his clearance of land into a field or garden, or his six-months' hut into a permanent home."[3]

The negroes are said by Ratzel[4] to be the best tillers of all nature-people. He also says that although they are good agriculturists and have copious resources, they are almost nomadic and change the site of their villages from generation to generation. Many of them plant hedges round their fields, loosening the ground with a wooden hoe, since superstition prevents some from using iron tools. The plow is as yet almost unknown to negroes. They have great difficulty in storing food from one year to another: in the region of the tropical rains and the white ants the granaries consist in huts or other arrangement raised on posts, while the Bechuanas use vessels of pottery, located in the open field.[5] Johnston[6] has emphasized the improvident nature of negro agriculture: "It is this wasteful habit of the African," he says, "whose only idea of manuring the soil is, when he first clears it, to cut down and burn to ashes all the brushwood and trees, afterwards digging the ashes into the soil—which has done so much to turn Africa from a land of forest into one of prairie, steppe, and even desert. As a Negro tribe flourishes and increases in numbers, so it gradually destroys all the forests in its country by extending its clearings for agricultural purposes and abandoning each plantation as the soil becomes exhausted after the first few crops." Weeks[7] describes a similar situation in the Upper Congo district: "Large farms were made around the towns. The men did the clearing of the bush, felling the trees, and cutting down the undergrowth: the women worked with them, heaping up the grass and brushwood ready for burning, and helping generally. As a rule, the women did the hoeing, planting and weeding, but the men did not so despise this work as never to do it. . . . Their mode of hoeing never allowed them to go deeper than 4 or 5 inches into the ground, consequently a farm was played out after three or four seasons, and then it was allowed to lie fallow, another piece was cleared and hoed."

Some of the American Indians were agriculturists, especially those in the east and south, who combined tillage with fishing and hunting and resided for the greater part of the year in villages.[8] Their agricultural development was checked by the lack of domesticated animals; when the American aborigines first saw oxen plowing they pitied them and blamed the Spaniards for laziness in putting work on animals.[9] Agriculture led the Shingu tribes of Brazil to a sedentary life. Though these tribes had been reduced to a partially settled existence by fishing, still the fish were plentiful only at particular seasons when the river was full; and so they remained more or less nomadic until the women had learned to plant, make pottery, and prepare meal.[10] Hunting and fishing

3 Sarasin, *Weddas*, 491.
4 *Vkde.*, I, 200, 60.
5 Ratzel, *Vkde.*, I, 200.
6 *Uganda*, II, 675.
7 In JAI, **XXXIX**, 128-129; Dundas, C., in JAI, **XLIII**, 499.

8 Morgan, in *Smithson. Contr. Knowledge*, **XVII**, 141.
9 Bourdeau, *Forces*, 99.
10 Von den Steinen, *Zent.-Bras.*, 219.

and seeking fruits in the woods are, next to war, the chief occupations of the men among the Guaycurus of Brazil, while the business of the women is to prepare the flour from the roots of the mandioca plants and the manufacture of cotton stuffs and pottery.[11] Neither bananas nor mandioca are cultivated by the Botocudo, for, with an eye to the produce of the chase, he moves out of the district before those plants have time to ripen; maize, beans, and pumpkins, which promise a yield within a few months, are cultivated by the women. Even the maturity of the maize is often not waited for, but the half-ripe kernels are roasted in the fire. The women gather edible roots, palm-cabbage, the different fruits of the forest, and honey.[12] In Paraguay, each horde has a definite place near a stream which never dries up, whither they always return, and where they cultivate a little maize, mandioca and a kind of pumpkin; otherwise they live by hunting and fishing.[13]

The history of the development of agriculture among the Araucanians is instructive. "Up to the present time the Araucano only takes to agriculture in a desultory fashion, and to provide the mere necessities of life. Their methods are of the most primitive. Probably the principal reason why the barbarian tribes take to agricultural life with such distaste is the difficulty of inadequate implements, and the consequent amount of labour entailed by such work, especially before the introduction of domestic animals. The Araucano, for instance, could see no use in working hard to obtain what the earth gave spontaneously; and as a consequence, so long as his liberty to roam at will was uncurtailed, he showed himself refractory to such a mode of life."[14] There have been two foreign invasions which have left their indelible mark on the development of the Araucanians: the first by the Incas and the second by the Spaniards, both of which afford striking illustration of the influence of war as a factor in societal evolution. "The former first brought the Araucano into touch with civilisation. From this epoch date his knowledge of domestic animals, of the elements of agriculture, and of such arts as weaving and metal working. This period also sees him first begin to adopt a more sedentary life, constructing rude huts instead of the usual *toldo* or skin tent. As Humboldt has so justly remarked, 'the most difficult and the most important event in the history of human society is perhaps the change from a nomadic to an agricultural life.' This change among the Araucanos was not brought about by any compulsory conditions, but seems to have been adopted gradually by the race on seeing the advantages accruing from the new mode of life, and at first only in a very desultory way. The Spanish conquest brought with it knowledge of new cereals and plants, other domestic animals, a fuller use of metals, and a considerable change in the tribal government, owing to the necessity of continued union to repel the invader. . . . The Incas introduced the llama and vicuña into the country, and from that time weaving became a recognised art among the northern tribes, although farther south the possession of a few of these animals was considered as a sign of considerable wealth. But the wearing of woollen clothing did not become generalized till the introduction of sheep during the Spanish occupation."[15]

This section may be concluded with a few examples of the attitude with which agriculture is regarded, especially by pastoral nomads. The agricultural class

11 Spix and Martius, *Brazil*, II, 76.
12 Von Martius, *Beiträge*, I, 323.
13 Koch, in *Globus*, LXXVIII, 219.

14 Latcham, in JAI, XXXIX, 343.
15 Latcham, in JAI, XXXIX, 334-335, 336.

among the Huns, we are told, was despised by its fellows, and the term "wheat-eater" expressed the contempt or envy of the carnivorous Highlander. Certain tribes of western Asia have no cattle or sheep, "those animals being looked down upon as the peculiar property of tribes who have forgotten their independence and degraded themselves by the cultivation of the soil." The Kirghiz too look down with contempt on those engaged in agriculture.[16] The Mongols more than almost any other race despise agriculture; therefore, though they occupied the plain, they did not cultivate it.[17] The negroes of the Gold Coast regard agriculture as slavish, though this may be a notion imported from America. These sentiments reflect the antagonism of herders and tillers; especially in Africa are the former a scourge to the latter.[18] In this country the tillers and the herders have fought with each other in the legislatures of many of our States; at different periods of time the rights of these two parties have been construed very differently.

§32. Degrees of Density in Population.

It seems to be impossible to reach a conclusion as to the density of the native Australian population; one explorer made an estimate which would give 70 square miles per soul, a large part of the territory being inaccessible to them so that they were confined to the rivers. Smyth,[1] making corrections, reached the conclusion that "each aboriginal" had 28 square miles. The estimated population of Gippsland would give ten and one-third square miles per soul.[1] In the Alice Springs district of Australia there were, in 1899, forty souls on one hundred square miles—and this is probably a case of overpopulation.[2] Brown[3] states that "prior to 1820 the Narrinyeri probably numbered about 3000 to 4000 with a density of 1 to 1-3 to the square mile; that they certainly could not have numbered less than 1800, and that it is very improbable that they were more than 6000. Comparing these figures with what we know of other parts of Australia, it appears that this district must have been one of the most densely populated of the whole continent." The average number of persons in the horde is given by the same author as being about sixty; it can hardly have been over 100 or less than 25. "Taking Taplin's figure of 800 fighting men on the south side of the lakes, and taking it that there were 40 clans or hordes all told, we have an average of 20 fighting men to the clan." Dornan[4] says of the Tati Bushmen: "I have seldom seen more than four families, numbering twenty-two individuals together, and this was a camp at permanent water."

The population on the whole east coast of Greenland, in 1884, reached 548 souls.[5] Among the Eskimo south of Hudson Strait the individual requires 120 square miles.[6] The Smith Sound tribe consists of slightly over 35 families—about 200 men, women, and children—who wander along six hundred or more miles of coastline. "They usually travel in groups of three or four families. Greater concentration of numbers would be dangerous on account of the scar-

16 Roth, in JAI, XVI, 103.
17 Huntington, *Pulse of Asia*, 313.
18 Ratzel, *Vkde.*, I, 632, 410.
1 *Vict.*, I, 31 ff.
2 Spencer and Gillen, *Nat. Tr. Cent. Aust.*, 9.
3 In JAI, XLVIII, 230, 231.

4 In JAI, XLVII, 47.
5 Holm, *Ethnol. Skizze*, 159.
6 Report of Robert Flaherty, explorer of Ungava, from letter of L. A. Chase of the Keeweenaw Historical Society; Green, in New York *Times*, Oct. 10, 1926.

city of food." Jefferson[7] estimated the Virginia Indian population as about one to the square mile, and census-figures cited by Peschel, as of 1825, report the ratio among hunting-tribes as one to one and three-quarters square miles— the same figures being given for certain Papuans of New Guinea.[8] School- craft[9] states that "from some data that have been employed it is doubtful whether an area of less than 50,000 acres, left in the forest state, is more than sufficient to sustain by the chase a single hunter." In another place he says that a family of five Indians needs 40,000 acres and, as predatory nomadic bands, 50 square miles to the family. These estimates, though they are no more than that, lend some concreteness to the statements about population-conditions among hunters.

Stanley saw the densely populated banks of the Congo River in Africa and estimated the population at some 40 millions; further exploration brought the estimates down to 20 or 30 millions; then, in 1911, the Belgian census reported eight and one-half millions, though some of the decrease may have been due to the harsh treatment of the natives.[10] Nogueira[11] estimated the population of Portuguese West Africa (1880) as about two and a half per square mile; of Portuguese East Africa as three-eighths of one per square mile. An unusual condition exists in the Shilluk territory, which lies upon the White Nile and has an extent of 2000 square miles; when its population is compared with that of the populous districts of Europe, we are justified in reckoning from 600 to 625 a square mile. In 1871 the Egyptian government took a census of this territory, the result of which would indicate such a density. "No known part of Africa, scarcely even the narrow valley of the Nile in Egypt, has a density of population so great; but a similar condition of circumstances, so favorable to the support of a teeming population, is perhaps without a parallel in the world. Everything which contributes to the exuberance of life here finds a concen- trated field—agriculture, pasturage, fishing, and the chase. Agriculture is rendered easy by the natural fertility of the soil, by the recurrence of the rainy seasons, by irrigation effected by the rising of the river, assisted by numerous canals, and by an atmosphere ordinarily so overclouded as to moderate the radiance of the sun, and to retain throughout the year per- petual moisture. There is plenty of fishing. Across the river there is a free and open chase over wildernesses which would advantageously be built upon, but for the hostility of the neighboring Dinka."[12] By way of sharp contrast, sev- enty miles away from the Shilluk territory is the land of the Bongo, where there are not over 12 to the square mile.[13]

Ratzel[14] has a very significant table of the density of population of various groups as related to the type of self-maintenance:

Inhabitants per (English) Square Mile

Hunting and fishing tribes in the outermost regions of the inhabited
world (Eskimo) 0.005-0.015
Hunting tribes of the steppe regions (Bushmen, Patagonians, Australians) 0.005-0.025

7 *Writings*, III, 195.
8 Peschel, *Races*, 193; Krieger, *Neu-Guinea*, 150.
9 *Ind. Tribes*, I, 433; V, 485.
10 Morel, *Black Man's Burden*, 109.
11 *Raça Negra*, 183.

12 Schweinfurth, *Heart of Afr.*, I, 85-86.
13 Ratzel, *Vkde.*, I, 508.
14 *Anthropogeog.*, II, 264-265; Semple, *Geog. Env.*, 65; Supan, "Bvlkg. d. Erde," in *Petermann's Mitth.*, Ergänzheft. 135, 1901.

Hunting tribes with some agriculture, or deriving support from tillers (Indians, Dyak, Papuans, poorer Negro tribes, Batwa)	0.5-2
Fisher-tribes on coasts and rivers (Northwest Americans, inhabitants of small Polynesian islands)	up to 5
Nomadic herdsmen	2-5
Tillers, with the beginnings of crafts and trade (inner Africa, Malay Archipelago)	5-15
Nomads with agriculture (Kordofan, Sennaar)	10-15
Mohammedan countries in western Asia and the Sudan	10-25
Fisher-tribes practising agriculture (Pacific islands)	up to 25
New countries with European agriculture, or climatically disadvantaged European countries	25
Purely agricultural regions of central Europe	100
Purely agricultural regions of southern Europe	200
Regions of commingled agriculture and manufacture	250-300
Purely agricultural regions of India	over 500
Regions of European large-scale manufacture	over 750

§37. Limitation of Numbers.

In South Australia, no mother will bring up more than two children. They would interfere with her duty to her husband in the matter of providing food.[1] The West Australians ate every tenth child born as "necessary to keep the tribe from increasing beyond the carrying capacity of the territory"[2]—a motive original, probably, in the recounter's mind. There is a legend that the first settlers of an African oasis ordered that there should never be more than eighty adult males; if there were one old man, one woman, and one child for each of the eighty, the population would be 320, which is a third of the density of other Libyan oases.[3] In Madagascar, "the superstition of the people, causing them to put their children to death if born on certain unlucky days, was a means of keeping down the population in all parts of the island, and still causes the destruction of a fourth of all the children new-born in some of the tribes."[4] In Bengal, "nothing can be more curious than the results of a low assessment, whether fixed forever or not. In one large district, at least, where a low assessment was secured for thirty years, the result has been, not that a wealthy class has arisen, but that simply all restraint has vanished, and the poor population has multiplied to such an extent that the wealth accumulated is not more able to support the increased mass of people than the former resources were to feed the then existing numbers."[5] "Though the Dyaks marry young, they do not have large families. It is not often that one meets a family of over three or four children, and I have only known of one case where a woman had seven children. The conditions are favourable, one would think, to a rapid increase of population. They have plenty of good plain food, and the climate is healthy. There are none of the principal checks to population mentioned by Malthus among savage nations—starvation, disease, war, infanticide, or immorality. What, then, is the cause of the small number of

1 Smyth, *Vict.*, I, 46.
2 Whitmarsh, *World's Rough Hand*, 178.
3 Ratzel, *Vkde.*, III, 43.
4 Sibree, *Great Afr. Isl.*, 139.
5 Baden-Powell, *Brit. Ind.*, I, 346, note.

births? Climate and race may have something to do with it, but I think the
main cause of it is the infertility of the women. This is no doubt brought about
by the hard work they do, and the heavy loads they often carry. A Dyak
woman sometimes spends the whole day in the field, and carries home at night
a heavy load, often walking for several miles over hilly paths. In addition to
this, she has to pound the rice, a work which strains every muscle of the body.
I have often been told by Dyak women that the hardest work they have to do
is this rice-pounding. This kind of hard labour begins at an early age, and
never ceases until the woman is too old or too weak to work."[6] A number of
cases occur, in tribes which seem to be in decline, where the doctrine prevailed that the old men should have the young wives and the young men the
older.[7] For other instances see Ch. LIV of the text.

§49. Original Destitution.

THAT people living in a state of nature do not enjoy ease and plenty is amply
illustrated, especially in the case of those tribes which inhabit the more in-
hospitable districts. The problem of water-supply is a difficult one in the peninsula of Carpentaria, Australia, and forces the natives to be ever on the move.
"In dry times the rock-holes and most of the springs become dry, and the
natives are compelled to keep in the vicinity of the rivers and watercourses;
but as soon as the rain comes in sufficient quantities to replenish the rock-holes
and revive the springs, the people make an exodus into the back country and
remain there as long as the water lasts, because that is the only time they can
pursue the game and obtain other foods in those parts of their hunting grounds.
They proceed first to where the water is known to disappear most rapidly;
then they go to those places in rotation where it remains longer, and in this
way utilize their water supply to the greatest advantage."[1] Bassett-Smith[2]
says that the aborigines of northwest Australia, having no means of shelter,
at night would light a number of small fires and crouch, six or seven of both
sexes, around the fire, together with absolutely naked children. In the wet
season they put up a few branches for protection. This section is four hundred
feet above sea-level and suffers from intense heat; it is possible to work only
early and late in the day. The wind is scorching, the glare is blinding; only the
hardiest can live there. The natives are hard pressed for food; the writer once
saw a boy creep into a water-hole, swim across under water, and stealthily
get among the reeds on the other side, where he seized a sleeping duck. He
carried it about for a short time hugging it, and then, plucking it alive, he put
it in the ashes to cook. A man finding a bandicoot's hole, thrust in his arm and
pulled the animal out, singed it in the fire, bit open the abdomen, removed the
entrails, and thrust it in the ashes again for a short time. He then ate it, tail
first. The writer had a fish which he was anxious to keep in perfect condition,
but the native spied it and seized it with his teeth just behind the head, dividing
the backbone, which is the usual way in that section of killing a big fish. The
natives of Australia are generally described as omnivorous; "there is nothing
in the nature of food, or of substances which can by any possibility contribute

---

6 Gomes, *Sea Dyaks*, 104.
7 Von den Steinen, *Zent. Bras.*, 331; §§354,
428, of the text.

1 Mathews, in AA, II, 501.
2 In JAI, XXIII, 325, 327.

to the maintenance of life, that they will not eat."[3] The southeast Australians eat great quantities of roasted moths. These, which are thickly congregated in the crevices of the rocks, are stifled with smouldering brush; then, being roasted on the hot ashes, they are shrivelled to about the size of a grain of wheat.[4] It is necessary for a tribe in Victoria to move very frequently from place to place, always keeping within the boundaries of the country which it calls its own—"now to the spot where eels can be taken in the creeks; often to the feeding-grounds of the kangaroo; sometimes to the thicker forests to get wood suitable for making weapons; to the seacoast continually for fish of various kinds; and at the right season, to the lands where are found the native bread, the yam, and the acacia gum. Constantly under the pressure of want, and yet, by travelling, easily able to supply their wants, their lives lack neither excitement nor pleasure." In a wild state, a black did little more than attend to the wants of his stomach. There is a small plant on the root of which the children chiefly subsist. "As soon almost as they can walk, a little wooden shovel is put into their hands, and they learn thus early to pick about the ground for these roots and a few others, or dig out the larvae of the ant-hills . . . the work necessary to obtain a mouthful even of such indifferent food being thus really more than would be sufficient for the cultivation of the earth according to the more provident arrangements of civilized men."[5]

The Bushmen are a very primitive race which has been subject for centuries to a bad environment. Fritsch[6] thinks them normal and undeveloped. They never cultivate the soil nor rear any domestic animals save wretched dogs. "Their chief subsistence is the flesh of game, but that is eked out by what women collect of roots and beans and fruits of the desert."[7] Fritsch[8] describes the Bakalahari as equally miserable or worse, for while he thinks the Bushmen are undeveloped and not degraded, he asserts that the Bakalahari are a heterogeneous collection of vagabonds and outcasts of the neighboring tribes. Büttner[9] describes the Bergdamara as a race of slaves and vagabonds who support existence on anything which seems possibly edible.

In the Sahara and the Sudan, when camels and goats cease to give milk and the seed of grass is used up, there ensues a long despairing period of need, when the natives live on dum-palm fruit not fit for human food; even the Teda say that it is not possible to support life for more than a short time on that alone.[10] A Tuareg, on being asked how his people got a living, replied: "When the female camel has her young and can give no milk we go to Ghat and there we eat dates, ghusup, and bread, if we can get it. When the camel once more gives milk we come back, drink the milk and lie around on the side of the road."[11] Junker[12] says of the natives on one branch of the Nile that even though their wants are very slight, they are very poor and experience a severe struggle for existence. He found no evidence whatsoever of conditions of equality and abundance which the utopians have pictured as the state of nature peoples. The only purpose in life of the natives in south-west Africa, writes Büttner,[13] is to fill their bellies with something that looks edible; they eat

3 Smyth, *Vict.*, I, 183.
4 Howitt, *S.E. Aust.*, 693.
5 Smyth, *Vict.*, I, 123, 48, 49.
6 *Eingeb. S.-Afr.*, 397; Ranke, *Mensch*, II, 114.
7 Livingstone, *Mission. Tr.*, 55; Hahn, in *Globus*, XVIII, 85.

8 *Eingeb. S.-Afr.*, 407.
9 *Walfischbai*, 229; Serpa Pinto, *Africa*, II, 167.
10 Nachtigal, *Sahara*, I, 267.
11 Ratzel, *Vkde.*, III, 38.
12 *Afrika*, I, 258.
13 *Walfischbai*, 229.

gum arabic, the pounded roots of trees, steal grass seed from ants, and regard a swarm of locusts as a blessing. "No race in central South Africa understands better than the Barwa and the Masarwa how to secure water in the driest places, how to catch the scent of wild animals, and how to approach stealthily and outwit them. Because they have been harshly treated by the Bechuanas, they are very distrustful, even toward the whites. . . . I might say that among the south African races they are what the carrion-vulture is among birds and the jackal among mammals."[14]

The Yakuts, who live in a difficult environment, experience a severe struggle for life; by far the greater number, says Sieroshevski,[15] live at the limit of existence. So cold is the climate that in winter no ax can cut wood, which freezes as hard as stone. From a more southern habitat, where they lived on horses for all purposes, the Yakuts moved northward; then, cattle superseded the horses and hay became a great consideration because of the cold climate and the need of housing the animals in the winter. Hay is now the central factor of their existence. In the southern regions they also raise a little grain. They are in a transition from being a nomadic horse-using people through cattle-herding to agriculture; the horse is passing; cattle, though requiring hay for the winter, are becoming the mainstay; while grain-tillage is just beginning. Some subsistence is obtained through fishing which, however, operates to the disadvantage of the people, for fishing and cattle-breeding are antagonistic modes of livelihood; when they have good fishing, they pursue it and let the grass grow old and dry before they cut it. Coöperation is not in their mores; when it was proposed to them, they said: "For that people must be angels"; "People differ in industry and honesty"; "We quarrel over the division of gains at cards; we should tear each other in pieces if we tried to share hay, milk, butter and wages." The best Yakut mower with two female rakers can get in, according to the season, from twenty to thirty tons of hay, which will carry twelve or fifteen head of cattle through the winter. This is the limit; with less power, labor must be hired, hay bought, or the cattle partly starved. Even in good years part of the Yakuts suffer hunger. The commonest industrial group consists of four persons: two grown laborers, one youthful person, and one boy or old man, such a group being held by them to need ten head of cattle for its support. Above that number is ease; below it, poverty. They are well off with ten, when there is good fishing or hunting; but where no incidental support exists, as in the north with its longer winter and poorer meadows, fifteen or twenty are needed. In the south where tillage is available and there are subsidiary winter-occupations, six head of cattle, or one and one-half per soul, suffice to maintain the group, though on the verge of distress and privation. The variation is from six to twenty head per group, or from 120 to 400 rubles (about $90-$300) in capital. Any loss reduces such a household to misery; any luck raises it to ease. The great mass are at the limit, one and one-half head per soul being the limit of life-support. Sieroshevski knew of but one Yakut who had 500 head of cattle; a few have 100 or 200. In one district of three hundred households, 23 have no cattle, 55 have less than one per soul, 27 have one, 72 have one and one-half, then the numbers taper off, one with twelve and one-fifth and one with thirty-two and one-half per soul. Increase of wealth in cattle is limited by lack of wage-laborers and by communal owner-

14 Holub, *S.-Afr.*, I, 434-435.   431; Sieroshevski-Sumner, in JAI, XXXI, 79-
15 *Yakuts* (Russ.), 273 ff., 415, 418, 423 ff.,   80.

ship of land. A family of three, four, or five workers and three head of cattle per soul can get along without hired laborers. After describing the budget of families on the limit of subsistence, the writer says that if they plant grain and it prospers, they win comfort, but that half are not up to that level and live in constant distress. Their dependence on luck is tragic; if prices rise a little or if one is overreached by a neighbor or gets cheated in weight by the merchant, or loses calves, these are heavy blows to the barely balanced budget. To escape ruin, they sell their products, which are in good demand, and go hungry. Salt, vodka, tobacco, and sugar go first; then grain and tea give way to substitutes, and clothes become rags. The people cannot work for hunger, the cattle grow lean and give less milk, and the family falls into a vicious circle from which only a stroke of luck can free them. Two-thirds of the Yakut families are in debt, half of them only to a slight extent, from one ruble to five per head of cattle, which they pay in due time, the rest hopelessly, so that all their industry goes to pay interest.

On account of the severe struggle for existence among the Yakuts, their numbers are kept down, especially through a high infant mortality. According to their own assertions, the fecundity of their women is, on the average, ten children for one husband; sometimes they bear twenty or even more. The author quoted knew of one case of twenty-two births, another of twenty, and another of nineteen. In most cases the number varies between five and ten. But with this high birth-rate goes the high rate of infant mortality. The author gives a case of a woman married at twenty, who lived with her husband thirty years, bearing him nine children, of whom seven died in childhood, one was born dead, and only one grew up. Another woman had nine children, all of whom died; another eight and lost them all. In other cases two were brought up out of ten, five out of twenty, seven out of nineteen, one out of six. Ivanowski[16] mentions a case in Mongolia where a population of 500 families—some 6772 souls—gained only 58 births over deaths in ten years, the cause being an "enormous infant mortality." The effect of an unfavorable environment on children is depicted by another author[17] in the case of a tribe in Central Asia. The people live in rude cane huts, even though the winters are hard and the temperature drops down to –36°F. There is often lack of food and fearful famines result when the men fail to catch enough fish. In summer there are myriads of gnats and flies. The writer does not see how the little naked children stand it; day and night they are surrounded by stinging insects.

A long digging-stick, with which they dig up the roots of the wild yam, is the only agricultural implement of the least civilized Veddahs. "Wild bread-fruit and bark mixed with honey are the vegetable side-dishes with the flesh of animals slain by arrow (deer, apes, large lizards) and of fish procured through poisoning the water. The Veddah has attached the dog to himself as an attendant and aid in hunting."[18] Of certain natives of Borneo we learn: "Like the animals of the bush they pass a rambling life, caring only for the satisfaction of their subsistence-needs. They remain where nature affords them for a time sufficient sustenance, later to seek out new sources of existence. With tillage of any sort whatsoever they are wholly unacquainted; for food they use all sorts of animals, even the most loathesome, together with sago and

16 *Mongolei*, 2.
17 Prjevalski, *Forskningsresor*, 140.

18 Schmidt, *Ceylon*, 277, 180; Marsden, *Sumatra*, 41; Anon., in *Globus*, XXVI, 44; Forbes, in JAI, XIV, 121.

wild fruits. They do not want salt and believe that fatal sicknesses rise from the use of it."[19]

One is impressed, in the Gilbert Islands, by the incredibly small quantity of food needed to maintain life. "At the time of my visit," writes Finsch,[20] "a large part of the inhabitants of Maraki had nothing but *pandanus,* unripe cocoanuts, palm-sap, and small fish. A handful of the latter, together with a cocoanut-shell full of palm-sap, morning and evening, sufficed for the nourishment of an adult. The three-edged point of the green, unripe nuts, which did not yet contain any kernel, was knocked off, torn into four pieces and eaten. Although the famine had lasted a long time, over a year and perhaps more, these people still appeared tolerably well. To be sure, there were also at that time pitiful sights, but they were nothing in comparison with the pictures of human misery which I came to know so well in Tarawa or the famine types of Banaba. Here the few inhabitants abandoned their poor island following a famine, woebegone if not dreadful figures of skin and bones."

The standard of living of certain natives of Alaska is very low. "The wealthiest count only the following vessels and utensils in their subsistence department: one to three large kettles, one tea-kettle, one frying-pan, several wooden trays (native), several knives (generally home manufacture), horn spoons and two or three cups." Furniture was observed in only one place, that being a peculiar box in which to put tea-cups. "The average head of the family dispenses with all the above save one kettle, one or two wooden trays, a knife or two, and possibly a small cup, which he invariably carries whilst travelling."[21] Nelson[22] found villages among the Bering Strait Eskimo on the verge of famine; they had not provided sufficiently for the winter, hoping to be able to fish; then the winter turned out to be very severe and they could not fish. The same author states that in the winter of 1879-1880 famine and disease caused the death of at least two-thirds of the population on St. Lawrence Island in Bering Strait. He mentions another instance where the natives, getting whisky from a ship, had an orgy of intoxication at the time of the run of walrus, thereby neglecting to get their winter supply. Over one thousand died; the corpses lay all about two years later when he visited the place.

In McGuire's[23] *Ethnology in the Jesuit Relations* occurs the statement that "notwithstanding these periods of plenty, hunger and disease were constant visitors, and it is difficult to say which caused the greater mortality. When the snow was deep the moose was easily tracked by means of snow-shoes; but when the ground was bare or the snow was light, starvation was common, and after eating their skin clothing, and even the lacings of their shoes, the natives ate one another." Each year a period comes, just before the harvest time, when the Sia Indians must deal out their food in such limited portions that the elders go hungry in order to satisfy the children; "the expression of the men changes to a stoical resignation, and the women's faces grow a shade paler with the thought that in order to nourish their babes they themselves must be nourished. And yet, such is their code of hospitality that food is always offered to guests as long as a morsel remains."[24] Of one of the tribes of California Indians it is said: "They eat all creatures that swim in the

19 Schwaner, *Borneo,* I, 229-230.
20 *Ethnol. Erfahr.,* III, 50.
21 Allen, in *Smithson. Rep.,* 1886, pt. I, 262.
22 In BAE, XVIII, 258, 269, 298.
23 In AA, III, 264.
24 Stevenson, in BAE, XI, 12.

waters, all that fly through the air, and all that creep, crawl, or walk upon the earth, with a dozen or so exceptions.[25] Another Indian tribe used for food crows, ants' eggs, and the like, because of great economic distress;[26] still another "subsisted mainly on roots and seem never to have enjoyed plenty except in the season of the prickly pears. They ground the bones of fish, mixed the dust with water, and used the paste as food."[27] Fish are the staff of life of the tribes on the Amazon River; when they fail in one place the natives move their dwellings to another. The recent decline in the abundance of fish has meant a decline in the Indian population.[28] So severe is the struggle for existence in Paraguay that a nervous apprehensiveness is said to be the chief characteristic of the natives.[29]

Reversion to the original state of destitution has occurred many times, through famine, among the ancient civilized peoples and in the modern era. The cases show how precarious has been the footing won by the race in its ascent from destitution. The stories of the Old Testament furnish familiar illustrations. Three famines are mentioned in the book of Genesis: one each in the days of Abraham, of Isaac, and of Jacob; in the last case, there was a general famine beginning in Egypt but subsequently spreading and continuing for a period of seven years. Another famine in the land of Canaan which lasted for a period of ten years is mentioned in the book of Ruth, and several others are recorded in later periods of Biblical history.[30]

There was a famine in Rome in 436 B.C., so severe that the starving people are reported to have thrown themselves by the thousands into the Tiber. There was a great famine in Egypt in 42 A.D. In 650 A.D. there was a severe and general famine throughout India. In 879 suffering and starvation were so general that the year has come to be known as the period of the universal famine. In 941, 1022, and 1033 there were famines in India so terrible that entire provinces were depopulated and the practice of cannibalism became common. There were ten famines and thirteen epidemics in France in the tenth century. About the year 1000 there occurred a five-year famine throughout the Roman world, during which catastrophe people ate each other, and 1005 was a famine year in England. There was a ten-year famine in Egypt beginning in 1064. Famines were a regular occurrence in Europe during the eleventh and twelfth centuries. The one in Germany in 1125 is said to have destroyed one-half the population. In 1505 Hungary was devastated and children were eaten by their parents without official interference or censure. "All through the Middle Ages it was the practice of the city authorities to expel the neediest inhabitants to perish, and this was in accord with the public opinion of the time." Famines continued to be a common affliction in Europe to the middle of the seventeenth century and even occurred during the eighteenth. In Germany the last period of shortage so severe and uncontrolled as to be designated a famine occurred in 1817. It is often said that previous to the nineteenth century there was never a decade in which famines did not occur, while during

25 Powers, in *Contr. to N. Amer. Ethnol.*, III, 348.
26 Sapir, in HAI, II, 872.
27 Fletcher, in HAI, I, 805.
28 Von Martius, *Beiträge*, I, 605, note; Spix and Martius, *Bras.*, 12, 68.

29 Ehrenreich, in *Globus*, LXXIII, 74.
30 Gen., XII, 10; XXVI, 1; XII, 54-57; Ruth, I, 1-5; II Sam., XXI, 1; I Kings, XVIII, 1, 2; II Kings, VI, 24-29; VIII, 1; XXV, 3; Jer., XXXVIII, 9; LIII, 6; Lam., II, 20; IV, 10; Joel, I, 4-20.

that century there took place the potato famine in Ireland and numerous periods of distress in India and China.[31]

How the mores tend to break down during such a calamity may be further illustrated by the following excerpt from a thirteenth-century Russian chronicle: "We were all in a fury of irritation; a brother rose against his brother, a father had not pity for his son, mothers had no mercy for their daughters; one denied his neighbors a crumb of bread. There was no charity left among us; only sadness, gloom and mourning dwelt constantly within and without our habitations. It was a bitter sight, indeed, to watch the crying children, begging in vain for bread and falling dead like flies."[32]

§53. Labor.

PRIMITIVE people rarely show any of the discipline and prolonged application to a task characteristic of more advanced races. Labor is disliked by the aborigines of Victoria, and "unnecessary labor is to them simply impossible."[1] Work does not go off lively with the Kanaka; "they are not diligent and nothing induces them to hurry up with their work."[2] The Africans actually do not understand what it means to be in a hurry; "the characteristic condition of the modern, busy, civilized man, who 'never has time,' is entirely beyond their comprehension, and while we fix the hour or indeed the exact minute for the beginning of our work, it is incomprehensible to the African how one can keep at an appointed task for days and even for weeks. They always have 'time' and never anything to put off."[3] The Indians of our Southwest and of northern Mexico really do considerable work, though they seldom hurry; like most primitive peoples they do not care to work for long stretches at a time.[4] The Seminoles are said to be industrious, but by industry the author does not mean the persistent and rapid labor of the northern white men; he means only that these Indians are workers and not loafers.[5]

If the savage had more incentive to labor, he would undoubtedly apply himself to a greater extent. Somerville[6] says of the natives of the Solomon Islands that "the people seem to make no use of their wealth; the mere fact of possession is sufficient, and *kalo* (whales' teeth), shell rings, calico, clothes—any article of European clothing is a great prize—are simply stored up, and scarcely worn or used at all. Neither is the desire for wealth very strong, certainly not strong enough to overcome laziness, except in rare instances." On the other hand, there are instances where savages will persist in work that appeals to them. This impulse is common to all the Indians of Brazil; "it is evidenced . . . by the lengthy and painful task of covering the entire body with tattoo marks, many of which are completed only in the later years of manhood, and by the care taken in the mummification of corpses; and . . . through the manufacture, extremely fatiguing on account of the lack of suitable tools, of dwellings, weapons and ornaments. With indefatigable persistence they cut the beams and sheathing for their huts with stone axes, be-

31 Reuter, *Pop. Problems*, 121-124; Biot, *Esclavage*, 318; Glaber, *Chronicle*, 227; Lamprecht, *Franz. Wirthschaftslebens*, 118; Schultz, *Höf. Leben*, I, 102.
32 Morgulis, in *Sci. Mo.*, XVI, 65.
1 Smyth, *Vict.*, I, 407.

2 Von Pfeil, *Südsee*, 85.
3 Von Götzen, *Afrika*, 121.
4 Hrdlička, in BAE, Bull. XXXIV, 29-30.
5 MacCauley, in BAE, V, 503.
6 In JAI, XXVI, 405.

fore the whites brought them hatchets and knives, and with incredible assiduity they sorted feather after feather and worked them together with pitch and palm or cotton thread into elaborate scepters or fitted them into the meshwork of their head-bands and hats. The Indian is lazy where there is no personal interest in the work, but restless and industrious where work means the attainment of a satisfaction."[7] Abel[8] says that in his normal condition the Papuan is indolent, "but if you happen to catch him when he is in the mood for labor, and when he is working in company with his fellows, his activity and endurance will strike you as phenomenal." When work is made into a sort of game, the primitive man, like the child, displays perseverance. A sea-captain who saw much of the Eskimo says that they often make invention a part of their sport; they go out to certain difficult places, and having imagined themselves in certain straits, they compare notes as to what each one would do; they actually make experiments, setting one another problems in invention.[9] The child of nature, who seems so care-free, nevertheless has his troubles; one ethnographer believes that he has many more cares than the civilized industrial worker.[10]

The savage does not like work for its own sake, for the stimulation it gives, for the sheer joy of striving, or for the satisfaction of accomplishment. The latter idea is really ultra-modern. An Australian once said: "White fellows work, not black fellows; black fellow gentleman."[11] A somewhat similar notion was quite common in antiquity,[12] excepting always the sentiments of the Jews. The Jewish God was a worker, not a reveler like Jupiter nor a loafer like Buddha; the rules regarding agriculture were considered as precepts emanating from God himself.[13] In Proverbs appears an exhortation against idleness, which is mentioned as the cause of poverty and want.[14] Young men should work for their support; he that will not work should not eat.[15] In Rabbinical literature occur such dicta as these: "No work, however offensive, is as degrading as idleness"; "Idleness imperils life"; "Seven years a famine may last; but it will not enter the door of the artisan."[16]

In some instances primitive lack of industry is owing to the fact that the people, by reason of the exuberance of nature, have no incentive to labor. Laziness is said to be the heritage of all Pacific races—the result of the extreme fertility of a land which gives them no occasion to work in order to live.[17] Consider, for instance, the bread-fruit tree, whose melon-like fruit weighs one and a half to two kilograms, and is the chief food-supply. Capt. Cook once stated: "If a man, in our harsh climate, works the whole year through, to plow, sow and harvest enough to support himself and his children and to save a little with great pains, he does not fulfil his duty to his family, after all, any better than a South Sea Islander who has planted ten bread-fruit trees and never done another thing."[18] Such conditions tend naturally to idleness. Easy existence is also afforded by the sago palm and with the same result. Wallace[19] has said that "the effect of the cheapness of food is decidedly preju-

7 Von Martius, *Beiträge*, I, 405-406.
8 *New Guinea*, 46-48.
9 Mason, *Invention*, 23.
10 Kubary, *Karolinen-arch.*, 3.
11 Hale, *Ethnog.*, 109.
12 Schmidt, *Monde Romain*, 67-69.
13 Buhl, *Israeliten*, 66; Jer., XXVIII. 24 ff.

14 Proverbs, XXIV, 30.
15 II Thess., III, 10; Eph., IV, 28.
16 *Jewish Encyc.*, VII, 590.
17 Somerville, in JAI, XXVI, 411.
18 Ratzel, *Vkde.*, I, 326.
19 *Malay Archip.*, 381.

dicial, for the inhabitants of the sago countries are never so well off as those where rice is cultivated. Many of the people here have neither vegetables nor fruit, but live almost entirely on sago and a little fish. Having few occupations at home, they wander about on petty trading or fishing expeditions to the neighbouring islands; and as far as the comforts of life are concerned, are much inferior to the wild hill-Dyaks of Borneo, or to many of the more barbarous tribes of the Archipelago." Two men can convert into food the trunk of the sago tree, which is often over 20 feet high and four or five feet in circumference, in five days, and two women will bake the whole into cakes in five more days, though the raw sago will keep very well and can be baked as wanted. This will give food enough to maintain a man for a whole year,—a year's maintenance for ten days' labor! If a man does not possess sago trees of his own, he must pay about seven shillings and sixpence for one; "and as labor here is five pence per day, the total cost of a year's food for one man is about twelve shillings." In spite of, or rather because of, the abundance and cheapness of one kind of food, the inhabitants are poverty-stricken. The people live in "that abject state of poverty that is almost always found where the sago-tree is abundant. Very few of them take the trouble to plant any vegetables or fruit, but live almost entirely on sago and fish, selling a little tripang or tortoise-shell to buy the scanty clothing they require."[20] Poor despite the bounty of nature, indolent because of it—such is also the situation in the Caroline Archipelago. Though the island Sonsol is covered with rich vegetation, coconut trees are not numerous and therefore do not suffice for the maintenance of the population, especially since the custom prevails of using the nourishment of the palm not in the form of the fruit but in that of palm wine. This substance, taken three times a day, is their chief sustenance. The bread-fruit trees yield their usual two harvests a year, at which time a relative superfluity, instead of the more general want, ensues. "It is unfortunately true that the indolence of the people is the cause of their general destitution. No effort is made to put by a store of provisions." Though the island is extremely fertile, so that a number of nutritious plants thrive there, yet they are not cultivated. The inhabitants look upon St. David Island as Eldorado, because there is to be found an abundance of coconuts.[21] A cheap food-supply in other places is the banana. According to Humboldt,[22] the productivity of the banana is to corn as 133 is to 1, and to potatoes as 44 is to 1. In the New World, the Arawak Indians had little stimulus to industry and trade, for three or four months' labor in the field produced supplies for the year;[23] Hostmann[24] says that for the negro of ordinary physical powers "two hours' work a day is more than sufficient to support himself, a wife, and several children, more or less."

Existence is easy in the Chin Hills of India. "It is commonly supposed that the Chin is a wretched, half-starved, over-worked and generally unhappy being. The reverse is the case, and if his labor in agriculture be analyzed, which is his hardest work, it is found that in reality he has an easier time than the farmers in the west of America and in the colonies. . . . The one hardship that attends agriculture in the hills is that the Chin has to work in

20 Wallace, *Malay Archip.*, 381, 529.
21 Kubary, *Karolinen-arch.*, 80, 83, 84, 85.
22 *Nouvelle Espagne*, II, 362; Letourneau, *Soc.*, 17.

23 Von Martius, *Beiträge*, I, 692.
24 *Beschaving*, II, 228.

very heavy rain for some months. His constitution is, however, hardened to this, and it does not affect his health in any way. The Chin instead of being pitied is to be congratulated that he can make his living so easily, and that he has not to stack straw and hay, build outhouses for cattle and machinery, and protect his cattle from the weather; he has no great heat and no terrible winter to contend with, and he always has three meals a day, a roof over his head, and all the clothing he needs."[25] It is largely, however, because of his easy living that the Chin is undeveloped; cheap food is not always a blessing. In Kashmir "it seems as though the ease with which a living can be made were the chief cause of the reputed idleness and laziness of the people; and laziness, aided, perhaps, by the opportunities for dishonesty afforded by the large amount of local traffic and barter which the abundant waterways foster, may be responsible for much of the untrustworthiness which is said to be so prominent a trait of the Kashmiris." Lack of incentive is characteristic of the Chanto, another Asiatic native. "There is nothing to tempt him out of his small oasis; nothing to waken him or to arouse determined effort. His work in summer may be hard for a time, but it rarely hurries him, or causes him anxiety. He knows that the water will be turned into his ditch on such a day; his crops must be cut at such a time, and all the family must work, but bad weather never seriously interrupts the harvest, and a delay of a day or two will do no harm. And so year after year, and generation after generation, the Chanto goes his care-free, monotonous way, and grows gentle and mild and weak of will. He has no contact with the world outside his own oasis, and therefore fears whatever is new or strange. The Chanto's mind is so habitually idle,—that is, it receives so little stimulus from his ordinary surroundings,—that new sights and new ideas do not interest him, and he is strangely free from curiosity, nor does his easy, quiet life often tempt him to quarrel. In winter, he sits idle with nothing to occupy his thoughts, and naturally eating and drinking and the pampering of his body become the chief things in life. It would be strange indeed, if, under the given physical conditions, the Chanto were other than the courteous, submissive, self-indulgent creature that he is."[26]

Apropos of the incitement to labor residing in spirituous drinks, Dr. Harvey[27] remarks upon the sailor of aforetime. Fortunes were made in shipping by reason of the low wages paid to seamen, especially by Scandinavian, German, and even English owners. Shipmasters almost invariably had to put to sea with drunken crews. At the end of a long voyage in a sailing-vessel, the common sailor quickly disposed of his small and hard-won earnings in one or two wild drinking-bouts and was then obliged to go to sea at once at whatever wage an unscrupulous sea-master might choose to offer. With the advent of steam-ships, quicker voyages, and better wages, conditions have changed and the sailors' standard of living has risen. The crew work harder than was usually the case in sailing-vessels, and hold on tighter to what they get.

§67. Specialization in the Food-Quest.

WHEN all things were ready, runs a legend in the Solomon Islands, the *figona* bore a child, who grew up to be a man, but he was helpless in such matters as

---

25 Carey and Tuck, *Chin Hills*, 213.   27 Personally communicated.
26 Huntington, *Pulse of Asia*, 28, 235-236.

cooking, making a fire, and weeding a garden. When the *figona* saw this he gave birth to another child, a girl, who grew up to be a woman and understood these matters: "Be it your part," said the *figona* to the woman, "to get food and prepare it by cooking and distribute portions of it." And so it has been ever since.[1]

Woman's share in the food-quest naturally differs according to the stage of development of the tribe. Among hunters, such as the American Indians, she gathered and stored the edible roots, seeds, berries, and plants for future use, and dried and smoked the meats brought by the hunters. To the men fell the important task of supplying the tribe with meat and most of the materials for clothing. We are told in some instances of hunters who go out accompanied by their wives to visit the hunting-ground.[2] Women often aid in fishing. In Tasmania the women were accustomed to dive for shell-fish, which they placed in a rude basket tied round the waist.[3] Among the Papuans, "the duty of catching crabs is entirely that of the women, and men consider it derogatory to do so."[4]

More significant in primitive household economy is woman's work in agriculture. In the legend which recounts the coming of the Caddo from the underworld it is related: "First an old man climbed up, carrying in one hand fire and a pipe, and in the other a drum; next came his wife with corn and pumpkin seeds."[5] In southeast Papua, the men clear the land for cultivation and dig the ground for yam-planting; the women then plant the seed and weed the garden. As the seed sprouts the men fix the poles for the vines to climb upon. The women harvest, store, and look after the supplies. Men are not supposed to take a yam from the storehouse, even if hungry, without the consent of the women. "The highest attribute ascribed to a woman is that of being 'arawata,' which means that she is a good gardener, and strong in caring for the food supplies. To be the possessor of a large supply of good yams in the storehouse, when the new crop is growing, is the best sign of character."[6] To help support the male portion of a family, a young Papuan girl will be early espoused to a boy and be required to provide food for her little prospective husband. "The Papuan women are slaves or beasts of burden in the family, but the Malay-Polynesian females are treated with considerable deference and regard."[7] Among the Shendoos of India, by way of exception, "field labor as a general rule, is performed by the men; only the wives of very poor men labor in the fields."[8] Among the Semang tribes of the Malay Peninsula who have reached the agricultural stage, the men do the felling and heavy clearing, whilst the women do the lighter clearing and lopping of branches, as well as the sowing and reaping, and not infrequently the tilling of the soil, if the scratching of its surface with a pointed stick can be so called. The men, again, do most of the hunting and trapping, but the women take a large share in the fishing and in the collecting of roots and fruits.[9]

That monotonous duties like weeding more commonly fall to the woman is

1 Fox and Drew, in JAI, XLV, 140.
2 Hewitt, in HAI, II, 969; Harrington, in AA, XV, 221-222; Boas, in BAE, XXXI, 421.
3 Barnard, in AAAS, 1890, p. 603.
4 Lyons, in JAI, LI, 436. For other cases of women fishing, see Bromilow, in AAAS, 1909, 472; Skeat and Blagden, *Malay Penin.*,

I, 374-375; Jenness and Ballentyne, *D'Entre-casteaux*, 200-201; HAI, II, 499.
5 Fletcher, in HAI, I, 181.
6 Bromilow, in AAAS, 1909, 472.
7 Ella, in AAAS, 1887, 488.
8 Lewin, *S.E. India*, 283.
9 Skeat and Blagden, *Malay Penin.*, I, 374-375.

seen in the following quotation: "The girl too plants and weeds her plot. Her brother or a near kinsman will do the heavy work for her, will fell the scrub and build a fence; for this is the man's work always. In return she will do the woman's work for him, and weed his garden in addition to her own. For almost the only man who weeds is the solitary widower."[10] Women do the weeding among the Tupis of Brazil, the Baganda of Central Africa, the Tibetans, the Micronesians, and others.[11]

When a Zulu household makes a new settlement, the men clear up the land; subsequent cultivation is the affair of the women, except that the heavier field-labors are carried on together. At the harvest, men, women, and children all work together.[12] Among the Wachaga of East Africa, men take a greater share in field-labors than is usual among Africans; they keep the irrigation-canals in repair and in general attend to the irrigating, and they break the new ground.[13] With the Ba-Huana, the clearing is done by the men; the rest of agriculture is left to the women.[14] Fields for millet are roughly dug by both men and women towards the end of the dry season, with the Bageshu, and directly the rain comes the grain is sown. "Both sexes take part in the sowing; . . . both men and women go out to reap it and bring in each night what they reap. . . . Both men and women work amongst the plantains, but the weeding of the grain crops devolves upon the men."[15] "Among the Sungu all work connected with agriculture is performed by women; this is not so among the forest-dwelling northern Batetela, where the superior strength and skill of the men is necessary to remove the trees."[16] The Baganda women do all work on the plantain-trees, which is not heavy, once the ground has been broken up and the young trees planted; the girls are trained to garden from six years old; even ladies and princesses doing it. It is a great honor to have a good garden, a disgrace to have a bad one.[17] The Baganda men are the hut-builders, the women being given over to agricultural pursuits,[18] while in the Upper Congo district it is said that "the food belonged to the woman who cultivated the farm, and while she supplied her husband with the vegetable food, he had to supply the fish and meat and share them with his wife or wives."[19] As among nearly all African tribes, the Akamba women do all the work in the fields and are also hewers of wood and drawers of water.[20]

In America, the unwarlike California Indians treated their women well and shared their work.[21] It would seem here that when man's characteristic specialty of war is in abeyance, strict sex-division of labor tends to disappear. Among the southern and western tribes, the men helped in the field-work; among the Natchez, "the ground was cultivated and prepared by the warriors alone, and the women were not allowed to take any part in the work at any stage." As the crop in this extreme case was destined for a harvest festival, such an exclusion of woman probably goes back to some religious taboo.[22]

10 Jenness and Ballentyne, *D'Entrecasteaux*, 94.

11 Varnhagen, *Brasil*, I, 114; Ratzel, *Vkde.*, I, 458, II, 162; Bishop, *Tibetans*, 96.

12 Ratzel, *Vkde.*, I, 250; Holub, *Capstadt*, II, 47, 74.

13 Abbott, in USNM, 1891, 387-388.

14 Torday and Joyce, in JAI, XXXVI, 281.

15 Roscoe, in JAI, XXXIX, 193.

16 Torday, in JAI, LI, 378.

17 Roscoe, in JAI, XXXII, 56, 57.

18 Johnston, *Uganda*, II, 714.

19 Weeks, in JAI, XXXIX, 117-118.

20 Tate, in JAI, XXXIV, 136.

21 Powers, in *Contrib. N. Amer. Ethnol.*, III, 405.

22 Ratzel, *Vkde.*, II, 626; Carr, in *Smithson. Rept.*, 1891, 528.

Among the Attacapa, "the women alone were charged with the labors of the field and of the household."[23] Mason[24] states that the aid received by Indian women in tilling the soil varied, "being greater among the tribes south of the Ohio and less among the Iroquois or Six Nations." The latter had a strong military system and their women possessed considerable influence and organization. Among the Omahas, "the women had an equal standing in society, though their duties differed widely from what we imagine they should be. On cold days, when the husband knew that it was difficult for the woman to pursue her usual occupations, he was accustomed to go with her to cut wood, and he used to assist her in carrying it home. But on warm days, the woman used to go alone for the wood. . . . When a woman was strong, she hoed the ground and planted the corn; but if she was delicate or weak, her husband was willing to help her by hoeing with her. The woman did the work which she thought was hers to do. She always did her work of her own accord. The husband had his share of the labor, for the man was not accustomed to lead an idle life."[25] Much of this primitive division of labor was forced by the exigencies of life; the case of the Pima Indians is illustrative: "The men may be forgiven for allowing the women to perform certain tasks in the cultivation of the crops that are usually considered the portion of the stronger sex when it is learned that this plan was necessary in order to maintain pickets constantly for long periods, and that an armed guard was the sole guaranty of safety to the village. Every three or four days small parties of five or ten would come to steal live stock or to kill any individual that might have gone some little distance from the villages. Larger war parties came once or twice a month, though longer periods sometimes elapsed without a visit from the Apaches."[26]

It has been noted that when minute specialization comes about, it is likely to leave man in charge of the more interesting activities. In Efate (New Hebrides) man and wife work on the plantation together, each having a special plant, and a share in one that is cultivated jointly.[27] In this case, there is no specification as to the identity of the plants, but in Micronesia it is the betel and tobacco, that is, the luxuries, which occupy man, while the women cultivate the commonplace taro.[28] Similarly, among the Shingu Indians, the man raises the tobacco, which the woman does not use;[29] and in Massachusetts the men cultivated tobacco, the women the rest.[30]

"To the modern mind it is surprising to find the processes of agriculture conducted in the main by women, and mirroring themselves in the figures of women-goddesses. But in days when man was mainly concerned with hunting and fighting it was natural enough that agriculture and the ritual attendant on it should fall to the women. Moreover to this social necessity was added, and still is among many savage communities, a deep-seated element of superstition. 'Primitive man,' Mr. Payne observes, 'refuses to interfere in agriculture; he thinks it magically dependent for success on woman, and connected with child-bearing.' 'When the women plant maize,' said the Indian to Gumilla, 'the stalk produces two or three ears. Why? Because women know how to produce children. They only know how to plant corn to ensure its germinating. Then let them plant it, they know more than we know.' Such seems to have

23 Hewitt, in HAI, I, 114.
24 *Woman's Share*, 148.
25 Dorsey, in BAE, III, 266.
26 Russell, in BAE, XXVI, 200-201.

27 Macdonald, in AAAS, 1892, 725.
28 Ratzel, *Vkde.*, II, 162.
29 Von den Steinen, *Zent. Bras.*, 214.
30 Williams, in *Mass. Hist. Soc.*, III, 208.

been the mind of the men of Athens who sent their wives and daughters to keep the Thesmophoria and work their charms and ensure fertility for crops and man."[31]

§68. Specialization in Handicrafts.

Food-Preparation. Cooking and preparing food are traditional feminine occupations, and among hunters and fishers it is often woman's task to fetch whatever game or fish the men may have caught, cut it up, clean it, and prepare it. Cooking is found to be woman's prerogative among such scattered peoples as the Araucanians, the Guiana Indians, the Baganda and Atharaka˙ of Africa, tribes of the Malay Peninsula, and others.[1] In some instances, men share this task with women. In Southeast Papua, "the men make sago and do most of the work in the preparation of special puddings. The women prepare the ordinary meal by boiling, the men being allowed to roast yams or bananas,"[2]— the more special or interesting things being, again, the activities of the men. In Eastern Polynesia the cooking is performed chiefly by the males; even chiefs will take part in the culinary operations. "A great variety of tasty dishes are prepared by them, and both the preparation and the cooking are very cleanly. . . . The Papuans leave the cooking and all its preparations to the females of the family. . . . Here the food is cooked in a hotch-potch manner,—fish, fowls, vegetables and fruit are baked in one large bundle, and very little care is taken in cleansing anything."[3] Among the Wataveita, near Kilima Njaro, men alone make fire by friction; the process is a secret from women;[4] by the Banziri, women are taken along in the boats to do the cooking and to keep a fire always burning on an earthen hearth.[5] In the Egyptian Sudan, the men are quite willing to cook, but not to grind the meal; they prefer rather to eat the durrha-grains unground, simply roasted over the fire,[6] not being able to bring the woman's work of grinding into consonance with their masculine dignity.

Among the Palaungs of Farther India, "the mixing of the ingredients to make the different curries, and the cooking of the vegetables and the leaves of trees with curried gravies is usually done by the mother; if meat is added to the mixture, the cooking is generally done by the father himself. Many Palaung women do not eat meat in any form, and it is not often given to children."[7] In Rotuma, however, the men make the fires and cook the food, an operation never performed for them by the women.[8] In the Pelew Islands cooking is the specialty of men; in the Mortlock group, of women;[9] and in the New Hebrides women may not cook or even touch their husbands' food.[10] Again, men are not at all ashamed of cooking and every man knows how to do it just as well as a woman.[11] The Shingu men roast their own fish and meat, while the women bake cakes, boil drinks and fruits, and roast palm-

31 Harrison, *Gh. Relig.*, 272.

1 Latcham, in JAI, XXXIX, 341; Roth, in BAE, XXXVIII, 235; Roscoe, in JAI, XXXII, 52; Champion, in JAI, XLII, 80; Skeat and Blagden, *Malay Penin.*, I, 374-375.

2 Bromilow, in AAAS, 1909, 472.

3 Ella, in AAAS, 1887, 490-491.

4 Johnston, in JAI, XV, 10.

5 Clozel, in PSM, XLIX, 674.

6 Junker, *Afrika*, II, 217.

7 Milne, *Eastern Clan*, 46-47.

8 Gardiner, in JAI, XXVII, 421.

9 Ratzel, *Vkde.*, II, 166.

10 Leggatt, in AAAS, 1892, 698.

11 Finsch, *Samoafahrten*, 269.

nuts; the men roast food, but never boil.[12] By contrast, among the Lapps, "all boiling of meat is, according to old tradition, the affair of the house-father. The mother must attend only to other kinds of boiling, the roasting of meat and fish, preparation of soup, coffee, and the like, and the making of cheese."[13] And finally, to take the evidence of a survival, Roman women prepared bread for feasts and house-sacrifices; they alone celebrated the festivals of Vesta, and their sacrifice was bread. Men, on the other hand, prepared the meat that was sacrificed on occasion.[14]

Clothing, etc. Both sexes share in the preparation of skins and other materials and the making of clothes, though the following cases indicate that such tasks more commonly fall to the men.

Among the Teda, a tribe of robbers in the Sahara, "the business of sewing is exclusively in the hands of the men."[15] In East Central Africa the men do all the sewing on their own and on the women's garments.[16] On the Loango coast the men alone weave; no woman may lay hand on the cloth before it is clipped.[17] In Tibet, the men invariably knit the coarse woollen socks that are in common use; "whether in the house or journeying, the men are never seen without the distaff. They also weave, and make the clothes of the women and children!" Rockhill,[18] who thus reports on the Tibetans, goes on: "It is no unusual thing, in Mohammedan countries, for men to knit. The writer has noticed it in Algeria, the Friar Odoric, speaking of the people of Huz, in Persia, says of them: 'and 'tis the custom for the men to knit and spin, and not the women.'" Among some of the American tribes skin-dressing, the weaving of suitable fibers into fabrics and other articles of necessity, the making of clothing and of mats and mattresses were done by the women. In other tribes, both men and women performed these tasks, either each sex making its own clothing or the heavier part of such tasks as weaving being done by the men, the lighter by women.[19] In still other instances—and these are more numerous—skin-dressing, sewing, weaving, and the manufacture of clothing are men's occupations. Among the Hopi Indians, the women do not make the garments and blankets, but the men; a Hopi woman does not make even her own moccasins; the men do all the sewing and embroidery.[20] Among the Navajo, and in some of the Pueblos, men are among the best weavers.[21] The greater part of the buckskin clothing, including leggings and moccasins, for both sexes, was made by the men.[22] Since weaving, among the Jibaro Indians of Ecuador, was an industry exclusively incumbent on the men, they always made the clothes of their wives.[23] The Bororo men, in Brazil, did the spinning, so that the house of the men was the spinning-room.[24]

Among the Pacific islanders, women generally weave the mats; near Torres Straits the men consider it derogatory to do women's work, and refer to the making of mats as such.[25] Among the Australians, the women chewed the grass-roots of which fishing-nets were made, to render them soft; but the

12 Von den Steinen, *Zent. Bras.*, 214.
13 Wiklund, *Lapparne*, 31-32.
14 Lippert, *Kgchte.*, II, 138.
15 Nachtigal, *Sahara*, I, 344.
16 Macdonald, in JAI, XXII, 102.
17 Bastian, *Deut. Exped.*, II, 34, note.
18 Rockhill, in USNM, 1893, 746; Bishop, *Tibetans*, 96.

19 Fletcher, Hough, and Mooney, in HAI, I, 301, 310, 750, resp.; Hewitt, in HAI, II, 969.
20 Dorsey, in PSM, LV, 745-747.
21 Mason, *Woman's Share*, 10.
22 HAI, I, 750; II, 284, 323.
23 Karsten, "Jibaro," BAE, Bull. LXXIX, 62.
24 Von den Steinen, *Zent. Bras.*, 488.
25 Haddon, in JAI, XIX, 342.

men made the mats.[26] Andamanese women make all ornaments, whether for themselves or their relatives.[27]

Transportation and Trade. Primitive women are commonly the pack-animals. The Samoan woman carries her husband's reserve of arms to war.[28] This is but a type of the subsidiary services of the sex at such a time. Similarly in hunting. Among the Eskimo, "when a man brings home a seal in tow, on reaching the land he pays no heed to anything but himself and his weapons, which he carries to their places above high-water mark. They do not even look at their booty as it lies on the shore. The rest is all the affair of the women." It is beneath dignity for an Eskimo to have to do with the woman's boat, the *oomiak.* It is a freight-boat; he occupies the light hunting-craft, the *kayak.*[29] In one Algonquin tribe, "the women perform all domestic work, including the transportation of game, fetching the fuel, erecting the tipis, hauling the sleds when traveling, etc.; the men are the providers."[30] The Coroado women are virtual slaves; in their wandering excursions they load themselves with everything necessary, like beasts of burden. They even fetch from the forest the game killed by the men.[31] This last duty is not uncommon among hunting tribes; and in general, the women have to find and carry the fuel; an exception is where, among the Dyaks, "one of the first duties of a husband is to provide this, or he gets into bad odor with his wife or mother-in-law."[32] A typical picture of a primitive family on the march would show, as among the Pima Indians, the male proceeding first, unencumbered save for his weapons and sometimes mounted, while his wife laboriously followed afoot with her child and a heavily laden burden-basket and on her back most of the family's possessions.[33] The man must be free and ready to protect his family at a moment's notice. The Kagoro of Nigeria never voluntarily carried anything other than his hoe or his weapons; all loads are borne by women.[34]

In the matter of trade, women often discharge a special function.[35] East African women, besides tilling the soil and carrying loads, also attend markets and play spy and intermediary between provinces even in war.[36] Among the Northwest Indians, "originally the chiefs conducted the trade of the tribe, but in time the natural abilities of the other sex in driving bargains has resulted in the predominance of the influence of the women in such matters."[37] Similarly, it is reported of the natives of Nicaragua that the women pursued trade, while the men cared for the domestic labors; at the slightest provocation the man was expelled from the house of the woman;[38] while Herodotus[39] says that among the Egyptians "the women buy and sell, the men abide at home and weave."

Miscellaneous Cases. The heavier tasks connected with house-building are commonly performed by the men; it is their job to cut, haul, and set the heavy posts and beams. The lighter tasks, such as thatching, are woman's work.

26 Ratzel, *Vkde.*, II, 52.
27 Man, in JAI, XII, 330, note.
28 Ella, in AAAS, 1892, 628.
29 Nansen, *Esk. Life,* 71, 192; Cranz, *Grönland,* 199.
30 HAI, II, 31.
31 Spix and Martius, *Brazil,* II, 246-247.
32 Roth, *Sarawak,* I, 363.

33 Hodge, in HAI, II, 252; Russell, in BAE, XXVI, 140-141.
34 Tremearne, in JAI, XLII, 147.
35 §§384, 386, of the text.
36 Mason, *Woman's Share,* 149.
37 Niblack, in USNM, 1888, 239.
38 Bancroft, *Nat. Races,* II, 685.
39 *Hist.,* II, 35.

Where the hut or tent is made solely of skins, as the Indian tipi, the women may do all the work.[40]

The Papuan men make the canoes, and "in the last stages of the making of a war-canoe the women were not allowed even to go into the shed where the work was approaching completion."[41] Again, only the men ever carve; "some are naturally more skilful than others, and are consequently often engaged by their neighbours to carve their canoe-heads. . . . Women are unable to carve, simply because they never make use of the adze; it is as typically the tool of the men as the shell knife is of the women."[42] In Samoa, "all objects made by men, and the tools in making them, were called *oloa,* and those made by women were called *tonga.* . . . *Oloa* included houses, house utensils, boats and boat utensils, weapons, tools, nets used for fishing and pigeon catching, certain ornaments, and all foreign articles obtained from other islands, including in more recent times white men's productions. *Tonga* included mats of different sorts, bark cloth, fans, combs, baskets, etc."[43] This case is very typical and needs only to be expanded to include, among the male occupations, those which border on the ornamental and artistic and in some instances the religious. Thus, among the Omaha "all rituals and religious rites were in charge of men; therefore the painting and tattooing of symbols devolved on them."[44] With the Guiana Indians, all musical instruments were the perquisites of the sterner sex.[45]

Pottery is generally made by the women.[46] Serpa Pinto[47] records, as an exception to the general custom of the region, that in Cangamba it is the men who make the cooking-pots. On the Zanzibar coast the women shape the pottery and color it with graphite; in Guiana, even though the women make all the pottery, yet the ornamentation is as often the work of men as of women; in New Guinea the Papuan women do none of the ornamentation—are thought, in fact, by a competent observer, inapt for the function.[48] In Mashonaland, women are the great brewers and "a good wife is valued according to her skill in this department."[49]

Shaving, curiously enough, is regarded as a feminine occupation in the Andaman Islands, the men shaving each others' heads only when the services of a woman are not available; every woman is supposed to be proficient in shaving, tattooing, and scarifying, and tattooing is almost invariably performed by women.[50] The same custom prevails in Africa among the Becwana, who hold that men are but bunglers at shaving.[51]

The above cases depict the usual sex-differentiation in regard to the handicrafts, indicating that the domain of each sex is fairly well marked. A case striking in its exceptionality is that of the Seminole Indians: "There is little

40 Skinner, in AA, XVI, 83-84; HAI, pt. I, 41; pt. II, 323; Roth, in BAE, XXXVIII, 689-692; Fletcher and LaFlesche, in BAE, XXVII, 97-98; Bromilow, in AAAS, 1909, 472; Skeat and Blagden, *Malay Penin.*, I, 374-375; Jenness and Ballentyne, *D'Entrecasteaux*, 200; Williamson, *Cent. Polyn.*, II, 379.

41 Bromilow, in AAAS, 1909, 472.

42 Jenness and Ballentyne, *D'Entrecasteaux*, 200; Skeat and Blagden, *Malay Penin.*, I, 374-375; Furness, *Head-Hunters*, 9; Hewitt, in HAI, II, 969.

43 Williamson, *Cent. Polyn.*, II, 379.

44 Fletcher and LaFlesche, in BAE, XXVII, 97.

45 Roth, in BAE, XXXVIII, 903.

46 Ratzel, *Vkde.*, I, 379; Latcham, in JAI, XXXIX, 339; Fletcher, in HAI, I, 301.

47 *Africa,* 256.

48 Ellis, *Man and Woman*, 6, note, 316.

49 Bent, *Mashonaland*, 55.

50 Man, in JAI, XII, 78, 328, 331, 335.

51 Willoughby, in JAI, XXXIX, 242.

difference of function in either family or tribe. Men hunt, women take care of the house; both work the fields. Men sometimes do the housework and women field work. Men hunt and women fish. Both are tailors, shoemakers, flour-makers, cane-crushers and syrup-boilers, wood-hewers and bearers, and water-carriers. There are but few domestic functions which belong exclusively to one or the other."[52]

§72. Rudimentary Specialization.

AMONG some of the Melanesians, canoe-makers formed a distinct craft. "The canoe-makers may belong to any division and the occupation is hereditary, the art passing usually from father to son, though others may learn the craft. The Tikopians make very good models of canoes and a man who wishes to become a canoe-maker will make such a model. If the people approve this model the beginner will be encouraged to make the real article which he must do alone in the bush, and if it is well made he will probably be asked sooner or later to act as a *tufunga* and make one professionally. There is no formal instruc-tion and nothing of the nature of apprenticeship. When a man is making a canoe on trial he has to cut down the tree single-handed and the labour of doing this is so great that it deters all except those who are very much in earnest. . . . Tumeric-making . . . like canoe-building is hereditary but may be taken up by others who learn the necessary procedure . . . The third class of people who are called *tufunga* are the tattooers. The occupation may be combined with canoe-making and dyeing or may be practised separately."[1]

The Polynesians had a highly developed division of labor. In Hawaii there were boat-builders, carvers, house-builders, and even roofers.[2] In Samoa, be-sides tillers, there were carpenters, canoe-builders, makers of fish-nets and hooks, surgeons, and tattooers, the functions of the last two being strict monopolies of certain families. These specialists also had assistants: those who cut wood and plaited sinnet for the carpenters, prepared cord for net-makers, and sought herbs for doctors.[3] House-building here was a distinct trade and on an average one among every three hundred men was a master-carpenter. "Whenever this person went to work he had in his train some ten or twelve, who followed him, some as journeymen, who expected payment from him, and others as apprentices, who were principally anxious to learn the trade."[4] Wil-liamson[5] makes the following general comments on specialization in Poly-nesia: "*Tufunga* was a term applied . . . to a carpenter, and a tattooer; but it seems to have had the wider meaning of an artisan, skilled in the making of certain articles or the doing of certain things. Stair gives a list of thirty-one different occupations of this character, the name of each of which begins with *o le tufunga,* and we shall find that in parts of Polynesia a corresponding term was used for a priest—that is, I imagine, a person skilled in the art of prayer . . .carpentry and tattooing were, in the main, specially esteemed. . . . Some of the occupations were common to all places and parties, but others were confined to certain localities, and practised by fraternities, who guarded zealously their privileges from any infringement. . . . None of these occupa-tions was strictly hereditary, though certain families, the members of which

52 MacCauley, in BAE, V, 503.   3 Ella, in AAAS, 1892, 635.
1 Rivers, *Melan. Soc.*, I, 326-328.   4 Turner, *Samoa*, 157.
2 Ratzel, *Vkde.*, II, 172.   5 *Cent. Polyn.*, II, 377-379.

had practised the several trades for many generations, acquired a special prestige. . . . Each principal trade or employment . . . and each trade . . . had its presiding god. . . . Even some of the chiefs were accustomed to engage in the different handicrafts common to the people, . . . there was no degradation attached to work, and the most skilful man, whatever his position might be, was always the one most sought after for work."

Among the Indians of the northwest coast, "different men and women acquire adeptness in different arts and industries, and devote their leisure to their trade. Some of the men are expert house-carpenters, canoe-builders, basket-makers, tanners of hides, hewers of wood, metal workers, carvers of stone, horn, bone, slate, wood, manufacturers of metal implements, ornaments, household utensils, etc., and are regularly paid for their services. This is especially true of the wood-carvers, who make and paint the totemic and mortuary columns. Others enjoy prestige as successful hunters of certain animals or expert fishermen. Some of the women are expert basket-makers, carvers of house-utensils, weavers of cloaks and mats of cedar bark and wood, and makers of dance and ceremonial costumes. Generally the men are carvers and the women weavers."[6] There was no special class of craftsmen in Peru; "trades were pursued along with agriculture and cattle-raising. But some persons among the villagers had gained a certain especial dexterity in one, and others in another branch of industry; some were reported to be weavers, others as good potters or metal-workers."[7] The stone graves of Tennessee contain sets of tools of various artisans, from which may be inferred a considerable specialization.[8] Most of the Indian tribes had men who were experts at stone-chipping and could decide instantly on the best mode of flaking a particular stone. It is a work of no little care and skill to make even so rude an instrument as an arrow-head, and only the most expert were very successful at the business.[9]

Among more advanced peoples specialization was still rudimentary. The case of the Homeric Greeks may be taken as typical. A craftsman important enough among them to bear a designation, though of a vague order, was the "builder." The term was a broad one; for this functionary made articles whose basis was wood, handling, like the smith, any accessory materials. The whole craft of wood-working was little specialized within itself; the builder regularly went to the mountain for the stuff he needed, and cut it down himself, though sometimes wood-cutters appear to have been a separate class. There was a qualitative distinction between skilful and less skilful builders, a fact which indicates that a number of men were engaged in the occupation; but the lord of a house and even of a people may appear as his own master-workman. The builder was also ship-builder and made even the sails; he constructed chairs and worked in ivory and gold in decorating them; and he was the regular house-builder. The chariot-maker was not called builder, and seems to have been a separate craftsman; he did the work in iron and leather which chariot-making required. A prince is found working at his own chariot. Stone-work seems to have been done by unspecialized workmen. A shield-cutter is mentioned; but most leather-work and sewing were domestic. Grain was crushed in hand-mills by female slaves. Pottery and the potter came in for little atten-

---

6 Niblack, in USNM, 1888, 254.
7 Cunow, *Verf. d. Inkareichs*, 100, note.
8 Thruston, *Antiq.*, 3.

9 Sellers, in *Smithson. Rep.*, 1885, pt. I, 874, 875; Holmes, in BAE, XV, 61; Montelius, *Sver. Hist.*, I, 42; Powers, in *Contr. N. Amer. Ethnol.*, III, 374-375.

tion. Basketry, rope-twisting, tanning, and minor operations show no specialization; all the industries might be grouped under home-manufacture, smithery, and building. There were no special merchants, sailors, or oarsmen among these Greeks; the word sailor refers to a sea voyager rather than to a professional seaman. The function of pilot, steersman, and steward was of no special significance; it took a prophet to guide the ships to Troy. Those steered or piloted who were the most adept at it, but it was not a profession. There was a class of fishermen among the poor, who became carriers when the chance offered; and there were divers who got shell-fish and sponges. Naturally no strong or consistent social distinction had had time to grow up and surround certain specializations with the distinction of class, much less of caste. The social specialists, or workers for the community, are listed as seer, physician, builder of timbers, and bard.[10]

The Smith. Most important among primitive craftsmen, and certainly most interesting, is the smith. His position is generally peculiar; he is revered in some places, despised in others. Most of the evidence concerning the primitive smith comes from Africa. African smiths often form a special class or even caste, and their function is in many cases hereditary. They are honored as skilled men by most of the tribes and their craft is regarded as a noble or at least a very important and useful profession, which frequently confers special social and political rights; in some places the blacksmith is called "the iron doctor."[11] In Kaarta the smiths form a privileged caste, and, along with the royal family, are not liable to capital punishment.[12] With the Atharaka "the smiths are regarded as distinguished men . . . and their portion of the meat is always the shoulder. They are permitted to marry as they please, and there are no restrictions imposed on them in this respect, as I gather is not infrequently the case amongst other African tribes."[13] The smith is commonly regarded as a neutral, is not killed in war, and may be induced by the victor to settle in the latter's district and there ply his trade.[14] He often lives outside of the village, near the iron mines, and his smithy is sometimes a meeting-place.[15] In a few instances we find him a political leader.[16] Among the Tuareg of the Sahara the smiths are much esteemed, coming immediately after the nobles in the social classification; and the same obtains in certain central African states founded by the Berbers.[17] Among the Arabs they are exempt from taxation and even get some customary dues in kind, in exchange for gratuitous services to particular men.[18]

On the other hand, the African smith is sometimes regarded as an outcast, or is feared and hated. No free Somal sets foot in a smithy, shakes hands with a smith, takes a wife from among them, or gives his daughter to one.[19] Among the Galla and other tribes of Africa the smiths form a subjugated and despised

10 Keller, *Hom. Soc.*, 80-84.

11 Letourneau, *Soc.*, 163; Torday and Joyce, in JAI, XXXV, 406-407; Stuhlmann, *Mit Emin*, 117; Ratzel, *Vkde.*, I, 369; Bastian, *Deut. Exped.*, I, 157-158; Burrows, in JAI, XXVIII, 42; David, in *Globus*, LXXXVI, 195; Weeks, in JAI, XXXIX, 107; Nachtigal, *Sahara*, II, 178; Lockyer, in *Smithson. Rep.*, 1893, 102.

12 Letourneau, *Soc.*, 439, 442; and *Morale*, 227.

13 Champion, in JAI, XLII, 79-80; Barton, in JAI, LI, 88.

14 Volkens, *Kilimandscharo*, 245.

15 Stuhlmann, *Afrika*, 794; Serpa Pinto, *Africa*, I, 108, 109.

16 Junker, *Afrika*, III, 47, 48; Büttner, *Walfischbai*, 28-29; Foureau, *D'Alger*, 302.

17 Letourneau, *Guerre*, 263.

18 Letourneau, *Polit.*, 475.

19 Ratzel, *Vkde.*, I, 434.

caste, though in some instances they are held in bondage on account of their skill.[20] In the Sahara, the smith is to a certain extent a pariah. "To call anyone a smith is an offence which can be atoned for only by blood. No one gives his daughter in marriage to a smith; no one lets his son learn such a trade; no one keeps up friendly relations with this outcast. The craft is transmitted from father to son and, since the children of smiths marry only among themselves, the caste remains pure and unmixed. Moreover, there is much to indicate that this contempt is mingled with another feeling. For example, no one would make bold to injure a smith, so deep is the scorn with which he is regarded; even to raise weapons against him is viewed as a very great dishonor. Despite the fact that the Mohammedan negroes have many legends to the effect that formerly a smith covered the entire craft with eternal ignominy through offending against the faith and betraying the Prophet, the custom of regarding him as a strange, unprotected, and outlawed creature is certainly of pre-Islamic origin; for a similar ostracism of the smith, whether it be that they are revered as wise men or feared as evil sorcerers, occurs among the heathen tribes of Africa, as in less civilized lands generally and even in places where Islam has never played a rôle."[21]

The different sentiments with which the smith is regarded are really not contradictory, any more than are the concepts "holy" and "unclean." As the text explains, he is a sort of fetish-man; his art, being beyond the comprehension of primitive people, is mysterious or supernatural and himself a magician or sorcerer. How the two views of the smith blend and unite may be seen in the following quotations: "The smith's trade was highly esteemed in the Congo, as being of royal origin, while among the Mandigoes it is so despised that the people have no intercourse with this class of craftsmen. Among most of the warlike tribes the position of the smith is an exceptional one and in the skirmishes of the Kabyles his life is spared if he is recognized on the battlefield, for his person, on account of his serviceableness, is sacred, like that of the physician among other nations. Elsewhere the metal-worker is persecuted as a wizard. These different points of view are explained easily enough in the nature of the case. If a worthy art has been acquired from a more highly civilized and friendly people, it would naturally be admired or taken under the protection of the kings themselves. If, on the contrary, a conquering people finds it in the subjugated land, it will similarly be utilized, although relegated to a subordinate position—all the more so if the people believe they have reason to fear it on account of its mysterious nature."[22] Among the Teda, "the utterances of the smith's wife are held to be oracular, and in case of sickness if there is no physician or medicine-man at hand, recourse is had to the sword-cutler. To strike or kill a smith is regarded as a great crime or rather as an act of cowardice. But—strange contradiction!—no Teda would eat with an armourer or sleep under his roof or marry his daughter. To call a Teda 'armourer' is one of the grossest insults, which can only be wiped out by blood. I have searched in vain for the cause of this peculiar position of the smith

20 Paulitschke, *Nordost-Afr.*, I, 211; Ratzel, *Hist. Mankind*, II, 494; III, 143; Macdonald, in JAI, XXII, 118, note; Yule, *Cathay*, 555.

21 Nachtigal, *Sahara*, I, 443-444; Ratzel, *Vkde.*, III, 170; Letourneau, *Prop.*, 146; Paulitschke, *Nordost-Afr.*, I, 202; Leo, *Island*, 520.

22 Bastian, *Afrik. Reisen*, 161.

among the Teda, which appears to be based, on the one hand, upon great reverence, and, on the other, upon just as great contempt."[23]

The blacksmith in Abyssinia is looked upon with mingled dread and superstition. He is supposed to be able to communicate the devil to whomsoever he will, and to be able to turn into a hyena and commit ravages on his enemies;[24] all through Africa, but particularly in the East, smiths are suspected of lycanthropy, their souls being supposed to leave their bodies at night, enter beasts, and practise cannibalism.[25] The Masai of East Africa regard smiths as unclean.[26] By the Kikuyu it is thought that if one sleeps in a smith's house, illness or even death will supervene. Smiths are believed to possess magical powers which they obtain from the tools of their trade—from the fire, the iron, the bellows, and the anvil; if, for instance, a smith is forging a weapon and when it is white hot he plunges it into water, saying, "May such and such a village cool as this iron is cooling," evil effects will fall on the village. Only that smith or another can remove the spell; a medicine-man has no power over a smith's magic.[27] Owing to his association with iron, the blacksmith among the Hausa is a person to be avoided, "for this metal usually makes his breath smell badly. If not, beware lest the breath should burn your clothes and even your flesh. No females, except young girls, are allowed near smelting works or forges, for the iron would never harden if women were present. . . . The butcher and barber also are dangerous persons, for they are just as much in contact with blood as the blacksmith is with iron; and both are *harum*, almost meaning *tabu*. All these classes are despised, and should be made to marry amongst themselves."[28] A worker in iron is looked upon by the Dinkas as particularly likely to possess the evil eye; "he is believed to injure cattle by looking at them, and so unpopular is he, that he finds it very expensive to buy a wife and very difficult to dispose of a daughter." The Jurs, who are great iron-workers, are believed by all their neighbors to be very malevolent and greatly skilled in witchcraft.[29] Other negroes believe that if a person in whose family the smith's art is not hereditary should build a workshop, he will die. Why? "Because the hammer of the smith is a godhead, and it can not calmly see such bungling work; the deity will afflict such a person with sickness and bring him to his death."[30] In West Africa, the smith's trade is to a certain extent holy and permitted only to chiefs, and the smith has certain priestly functions; upon him devolves the duty of making the nails which are put in idols to prevent or detect theft. This is true not only of the Congo peoples but of the negroes in the river-basin of the Ogowe as well. Among the Fan the smith is also a priest, and some tribes, not familiar with smithery, hang the peculiarly constructed bellows, which are common to all equatorial Africa, in their fetish-houses as objects of reverence.[31] Rather generally in Africa the smith functions as priest, while certain ceremonies are consecrated with his hammer.[32]

The fetish-character of the smith is clearly seen in the case of the Yakuts. "Smiths stand in a close and peculiar relation to shamans. Popular sayings

23 Rohlfs, "Reise," in *Petermann's Mitth.*, Ergänzheft. 25, 30.

24 Bent, *Ethiopians*, 212.

25 Lippert, *Kgchte.*, II, 410.

26 Singer, in *Globus*, LXXXVI, 267.

27 Hobley, in JAI, XLI, 436; and in XL, 432.

28 Tremearne, in JAI, XLV, 44.

29 Cummins, in JAI, XXXIV, 159-160, 166.

30 Spiess, in *Globus*, LXXV, 63.

31 Lenz, *Westafrika*, 87, 184.

32 Bastian, *Deut. Exped.*, II, 217; Thomas, in JAI, XLVII, 182; Clodd, *Magic*, 71 ff.

are: 'Smiths and shamans come out of one nest.' 'Smiths and shamans stand on the same plane.' 'The wife of a shaman is to be respected; the wife of a smith is worthy of honour.' Smiths also are able to cure diseases, to give counsel and to make predictions; yet their dexterities lack any magical character; they are only clever men who know a great deal, and whose fingers are expert. Smiths, especially in the north, generally transmit the craft from father to son. In the ninth generation a smith obtains almost supernatural qualities; and the more of a man's ancestors were smiths, the more real these qualities are. In the legends, mention is often made of smiths; they are called an honoured band. Spirits are, above all, afraid of the clink of iron and of the roar of the bellows in activity. In the Kolymsk Ulus, a shaman was not willing to perform until the author should take out from the hut his box of instruments, and after the shaman had failed, he explained to the bystanders that the spirits are afraid of the smith (the author), and therefore will not come at the call. Only in the ninth generation can a smith without danger for himself forge the iron ornaments of the shaman's professional dress and drum, or the brazen breastplate with the figure of a man, which represents the tutelary spirit of the shaman and is put on when he is about to perform. The saying is: 'If a smith who has forged the decorations of a shaman has not enough of the qualities of his own smith-ancestors, if the sound of their hammers and the flash of their fires do not surround him on every side, then birds with crooked claws and beaks will tear his heart.' Amongst such venerated hereditary smiths, the tools have acquired souls, so that they can give out sounds of themselves."[33]

The Buryats of Siberia believe there are two kinds of smiths: white smiths who cure disease and protect and are of heavenly origin; and black smiths who are evil—as the color black usually is. If the latter makes a model of a man out of iron and strikes it with his hammer, the man whom the model represents shortly dies.[34] Among the hill tribes of Central India the iron-founder is supposed to be a sacred or uncanny person; and the same feeling shows itself in the very common use of iron, copper, or brass to exorcise demons.[35] In Burma, food is offered at least once a year to the spirit of Min Magayi, "the mighty blacksmith who watches over every house in the country; and an offering to the same divinity is placed at the top of the first post erected for a monastery."[36] Among the Tibetans, the blacksmiths walk in the funeral procession ahead of the corpse, with a drum which they beat during the burning of the body.[37] In the Hindu Kush we find a situation more common to Africa: smiths are regarded as natural bondsmen and are sometimes brought for sale to the Mussulmen of the valleys.[38]

While the blacksmiths in Abyssinia are considered to be were-wolves, the Apache look upon them as being allied to the spirits, and call the smith the witch, spirit, or ghost of the iron.[39] In Iceland, blacksmiths were regarded as wild rude men using bars of iron instead of weapons. In the Sagas, no person of esteem is a smith. The smiths live in caves and underground houses like elves and dwarfs, and are clever people existing in loneliness and want, de-

33 Sieroshevski-Sumner, in JAI, XXXI, 104 (italics removed).
34 Melnikow, in Globus, LXXV, 133; Czaplicka, Aborig. Siberia, 285.
35 Crooke, in JAI, XXVIII, 231.

36 Brown, in JAI, XLV, 356
37 Bishop, Tibetans, 106.
38 Yule, Cathay, 555.
39 Bourke, in BAE, IX, 459.

fending their liberty by courage and activity. Often men who are free-born, but of slave mothers, become smiths.[40]

Among the Indo-Europeans of ancient times also the smith possessed fetishistic qualities. "As the amazement of man at the marvellous art of melting the hard metal in the fire and fashioning things of price out of it caused its invention to be ascribed to supernatural beings, so its exercise by mortal beings could not be conceived without the assistance of mysterious and magical means. This view prevailed throughout all Europe. . . . The note of mysticism characteristic of the smith's art appears in the element of treachery and fraud, found in common in the best works of Greek and German smith sagas. This conception has been most characteristically developed by the ancient Germans. "Among them Wieland gradually became the deceitful, treacherous magician, and it was inevitable when the Christian world procured the northern countries the acquaintance of the devil that the priests should eagerly avail themselves of the person of the malevolent smith to illustrate the Christian idea of the Evil One to their heathen flocks. It is beyond all doubt that the old German conceptions of the smith and the devil have many features in common. The devil is the *swarze* master of soot-begrimed hell, he smithies and works like Wieland, above all he is *hinkebein* [lame]. . . . The transference of the art of smithying from divine and supernatural beings to men, and the gradual growth of a special guild of smiths, are best illustrated from Teutonic antiquity. Although, so far as is known, no hero or demi god is mentioned by name as making his sword or his shield for himself, in classical tradition, yet among the Germans we find numerous heroes of noble birth who know how to work at the smithy for themselves. Wealthy men erected smithies in their forests, the remains of which are still to be traced in Iceland and in the west of Germany by the charcoal and slag. In Ireland too, the most ancient smithies were placed in the most sequestered woods. . . . There were times when the smith, like the gypsies in later years, travelled from one place to another, prepared to set up his workshop at any place. A contrast to this, but one which points equally to the primitive condition of the times, is afforded by the public smithies open to all in the Middle Ages in Germany, where every man did his own bit of work for himself. . . . If the smith is credited with the highest degree of skill possible to man, it is easy to understand that other arts were also ascribed to him. Mention must be made of his skill in medicine, as well as in poetry, music, and the dance. . . . To no idea are the words smith and smithying so often applied as to that of poetry and song, and even in the later Middle Ages poet-smiths are known." Not infrequently, among later Indo-Europeans, the smith was also the physician.[41]

Among the Homeric Greeks the smith was apparently a foreigner, and combined inn-keeping with his regular occupation. He appears, in one instance, to have been a retainer. He was respected as other craftsmen were, but, strangely enough, was not included among the *"demioergoi."* "Mention of mortal smiths is rare; from what is said of them, and from the study of the god Hephæstus, no evidence appears to indicate that the smith was regarded as a sorcerer or utter alien. The smith was not confined to the vicinity of ore-deposits, nor were such folk-movements prevalent as would surround him from time to time with a strange population. Hephæstus presents the figure

---

40 Leo, *Island*, 520.   41 Schrader, *Aryans*, 163, 164, 166, 167; Ratzel, *Vkde.*, II, 542.

of a . . . respected, though not influential god, quite under the maternal domination."[42]

The occupation of the swordsmith was in old days in Japan the most sacred of crafts. "He worked in priestly garb, and practised Shinto rites of purification while engaged in the making of a good blade. Before his smithy was then suspended the sacred rope of rice-straw . . . which is the oldest symbol of Shinto: none even of his family might enter there, or speak to him; and he ate only of food cooked with holy fire."[43] Even today in Japan, "the occupation of a swordsmith is an honourable profession, the members of which are men of gentle blood. In a country where trade is looked upon as degrading, it is strange to find this single exception to the general rule. The traditions of the craft are many and curious. During the most critical moment of the forging of the sword, when the steel edge is being welded into the body of the iron blade, it is a custom which still obtains among old-fashioned armourers to put on the cap and robes worn by the Kugé, or nobles of the Mikado's Court, and, closing the doors of the workshop, to labour in secrecy and freedom from interruption, the half gloom adding to the mystery of the operation. Sometimes, the occasion is even invested with a certain sanctity, a tasselled cord of straw, such as is hung before the shrines of the Kami, or the native gods of Japan, being suspended between two bamboo poles in the forge, which for the nonce is converted into a holy altar."[44]

It is interesting to note that a common occupation of gypsies, especially in Europe, is smithery.

§75. Conditions of Group-Specialization.

The tribes of Central Australia come from miles around to a place where there is a good deposit, in order to secure stone for making knives.[1] Seligmann[2] cites many instances of tribal division of labor and a good deal of trade in various parts of Melanesia. The natives of one section of New Guinea have industries divided among the several districts, each with its own. One makes pots, another wooden spoons, others basketwork, still others do wood-cutting, and so forth. The chief trade is in the hands of islanders, who cover great distances and are independent and self-sufficient, even with Europeans. The coast tribes will not allow them, however, to come into direct relations with the people of the interior.[3]

Stigand[4] reports an incident from his travels in Africa which throws another light on the relationship. "I produced some calico with which to pay the chief for his services," he writes, "but he waived it aside, dashed into the village, and threw himself head foremost into one of the hovels, and a miserable specimen of a chicken hopped out through one of the many holes in the dwelling. It was finally caught, and the chief ran back and, throwing himself on the ground, presented the anaemic fowl to me. The laws of hospitality demanded that he should first make a present to the stranger before accepting my calico. Very useful does the traveller find this almost universal law as, on

42 Homer, *Odyssey*, XVIII, 328; Keller, *Hom. Soc.*, 272; Schrader, *Aryans*, 160, 164; Seymour, *Hom. Age*, 116; Justi, *Persien*, 31-32.

43 Hearn, *Japan*, 139.

44 Mitra, in JASB, VI, 121-122.
1 Horne and Aiston, *Cent. Aust.*, 91, 96.
2 *Melanesians*, chs. VII and XL.
3 Schmidt, *Deut. Kolonien*, II, 342.
4 *Elephant*, 222, 223.

arrival in a new village, he is practically certain of a chicken at least. In many places it may take him a couple of days' bargaining before he can buy another, or he may find it almost impossible to obtain anything else, but the first present is always forthcoming." The ideas of trade of the Atharaka are said to be very one-sided, and the prices they demand for goats, wax, hides, etc., are ludicrous. "The trouble at present is that they are not in want of rupees, so that they can afford to stand by their price or return with their produce. The attempt made to introduce trade, using the rupee as a medium, was in consequence a complete failure; a most lively trade could, however, be carried on in beads and wires with great advantage to the traders. At present the Akamba are exchanging their cast-off beads and ornaments for the Tharaka produce, which the wily Akamba in turn sell to the traders."[5] Letourneau[6] has a number of instances of the vague idea of barter found among backward tribes.

There are many additional instances in the New World of the conditions out of which arise group-specialization and trade. As the redwood grows only along the lower Klamath River, the Indians of that section have a monopoly of making canoes; a lively industry has grown up and consequently a good deal of trade with other tribes.[7] Fabulous stories were told years ago of the abundance and beauty of the pearls found in Florida, Louisiana, and Virginia. They were eagerly sought by barter and by plundering the graves of the natives where they had been buried with the dead.[8] An extensive trade in salt, taken from the great inland lagoons, was formerly conducted by the Papago, the product finding ready sale at Tubac and Tucson.[9] The Avavares "bartered bones, which the Mariames ground and used for food;"[10] while pounded salmon flesh formed an important article of trade among the Chinooks.[11]

Roth[12] gives information additional to that contained in the text on tribal division of labor and barter among the Guiana Indians. He also states that "the Indian knights of the road do not hesitate to puff and advertise their wares to the best advantage on lines similar to those employed by their more civilized brethren. Thus, in the well-established trade and barter carried on between the Saluma and Trio, the former tells the latter that the glass beads which they are selling them grow on bushes which they themselves plant. In Surinam, de Goeje states that when making a purchase the buyer will put some turalla, a vegetable talisman, between his lips to prevent the seller overreaching him." The giving of presents among some of these tribes is somewhat related to barter. If the Uaupes Indians show one hospitality in the way of cassava, smoked fish, etc., they expect something in exchange, and often show themselves very exacting in this respect. "At the Patamona village of Karikaparu the chief's brother upon seeing me walk in lame and weak on arrival gave me a long hardwood stick to help support myself. About a week later, when opening my 'trade,' he saw some knickknack that took his fancy; he asked me for this, reminding me of his previous present to me of the stick."

5 Champion, in JAI, XLII, 69.
6 Commerce, chs. I-IX.
7 Mason, in Smithson. Rep., 1886, pt. I, 230.
8 Holmes, in HAI, II, 219.
9 Hodge, in HAI, II, 200.

10 Fletcher, in HAI, I, 118.
11 Sapir, in HAI, II, 917.
12 In BAE, XXXVIII, ch. XXXII, especially §§818, 822, 823-827.

§76. Trade and War.

SINCE primitive women are often beasts of burden, it may be that their employment in trade developed from their service in carrying goods to market.[1] Women become traders also because of their aptitude in this respect, as seems to have been the case with the Indian tribes of the northwest coast, for "in all the commercial transactions the women took a very principal part, and proved themselves by no means unequal to the task. Nor did it appear that either in these or in any other respects they were inferior to the men; on the contrary, it should rather seem that they are looked up to as the superior sex, for they appeared in general to keep the men in awe and under subjection."[2] It may also be that women engaged in trade along with their duties for the sake of "pin-money," as is asserted to be the case in Togo, though this sounds quite modern.[3] A more pertinent explanation is that in the state of constant intertribal hostility only women could safely trade. In Northeast Africa the women alone do the trading, for they alone enjoy immunity. Among the Somals and Galla, the entire business of trade is in the hands of women who are regarded as neutrals and in a certain respect sacrosanct.[4] Though markets are held on fixed days in Nubia, there is danger of trouble and lack of security. Unarmed men from each side come together to trade; but the rest, under arms, survey the transactions and are ready to intervene. Ambush by one of the parties often concludes the affair. To avoid all this, among the Masái, the women do the exchanging even in time of war.[5] We find this custom of using women as intermediaries to prevail in Tartary, in West Africa, in the Kilimanjaro region, among the Tibetans, in Nicaragua, and elsewhere.[6] Instances of other intermediaries, such as the Jews, who are tabooed or privileged persons and carry goods between hostile or warring tribes, parallel the case of the women and help to explain it. Heyd[7] states that as early as the ninth century the Jews covered the entire area between France and China as traders and that this had a great effect on the dissemination of culture.

§77. Transitional Forms between War and Trade.

To the classic example of silent barter mentioned by Herodotus, where he describes the traffic of the Carthaginians with certain Africans, may be added several others in Africa and a number among the natives of other countries. An early seventeenth century writer has the following to say with reference to the Gold Coast: "Neere unto those are certaine Negros, which suffer not themselves to bee seene of any, nor to bee heard speake: but have excellent gold which they exchange with other Negros, which bring unto them Salt, such as the mineral Salt of Tagazza, and leaving the same, they goe away from thence halfe a dayes journey: the Negros come downe in certaine Barkes, and lay at every heape of Salt a quantitie of gold, and goe their wayes. When the Salt-Merchants returne, if they like the summe, they take it; if not, they leave the

1 Cayley-Webster, *New Guinea*, 87.
2 Niblack, in *Smithson. Rep.*, 1888, 337; Vancouver, *Voyage*, II, 409.
3 Klose, *Togo*, 259.
4 Paulitschke, *Nordost-Afr.*, I, 298.
5 Letourneau, *Commerce*, 76.

6 Letourneau, *Soc.*, 157; Schmidt, *Deut. Kolonien*, II, 162, 171; Volkens, *Kilimandscharo*, 239; Mason, *Woman's Share*, 222; Bancroft, *Nat. Races*, II, 737; Geijer, *Svensk. Hist.*, 385; Letourneau, *Commerce*, 18, 76, 224.
7 *Levantehandel*, I, 139-140.

gold still with the Salt, and goe their wayes: and then the other returne, and what heapes of Salt they finde without gold, they take for their owne: the other, either they leave more gold for, or else leave altogether. This seemeth hard to beleeve, but many of the Arabians and Azanhagi testified it to our Author for truth."[1] Another writer mentions silent barter on the lower Niger, while the same sort of thing prevails on the Loango coast.[2] In the sixth century A.D., the Abyssinians used this method of trade with the Somals, while the precautions taken at a later date by the Turkish merchants in dealing with the Tcherkesses recall the same transitional state of affairs between war and trade. The merchants did not land, nor did they let the natives on board until hostages had been given. The landing was always made by armed men; the goods were displayed from the distance. It is supposed that the ancient Persians had similar mores.[3]

An excellent case of silent barter is reported from Sumatra. In the small trade carried on between the Kubus and the Malay traders, the transactions are performed without the one party seeing the other. "The Malay trader, ascending to one of their places of rendezvous, beats a gong in a particular way to give notice of his arrival. On hearing the signal, the Kubus, bringing out what forest produce they may have collected, and depositing it on the ground at this place, hastily retire into close hiding, beating a gong as a signal that all is ready. The trader then slowly and cautiously approaches, lays down on the ground the cloth, knives, and other articles of barter he has brought, to the amount which he considers an equivalent exchange, beats a gong, and in like manner disappears. The Kubus proceed then to examine the barter offered; if they consider the bargain satisfactory they remove the goods, beat their gong and go away; while the trader packs up the produce he finds left lying on the ground. If the bargain is not considered by them sufficiently advantageous, they set on one side a portion of their produce, to reduce it to what they consider the value of the barter offered; and thus the affair see-saws till finally adjusted or abandoned."[4] Of the Toála of South Celebes, Sarasin[5] writes: "In earlier times they did not trade directly with the Buginese, but carried on a secret barter. They deposited their wares upon a way traversed by the Buginese, whereupon the passer-by took them and, upon his own estimate of their value, left certain articles in exchange. They did this in order not to be seized and enslaved; now, however, it no longer occurs," that exigency being no longer to fear. The Veddahs of Ceylon got arrow-points from the smith of a more advanced tribe by deposit barter,[6] while one of the first and greatest Chinese travelers, Fa-hsien, recorded the following concerning Ceylon, which he visited between 399 and 414 A.D.: "This country was not originally inhabited by human beings, but only by devils and dragons, with whom the merchants of the neighbouring countries traded by barter. At the time of the barter the devils did not appear, but set out their valuables with the prices attached. The merchants then gave goods according to the prices marked and took away the goods they wanted. And from the merchants going backwards and forwards and some stopping there, the attractions of the place

1 Purchas, *Pilgrimage*, bk. VI, ch. XIV, 810.

2 Lauder, *Expéd. au Niger*, III, 180, quoted in Letourneau, *Commerce*, 78; Bastian, *Deut. Exped.*, I, 139-140.

3 Letourneau, *Commerce*, 314, 409.

4 Forbes, in JAI, XIV, 122; Skeat and Blagden, *Malay Penin.*, I, 225-226.

5 In *Globus*, LXXXIII, 278.

6 Letourneau, *Commerce*, 12.

became widely known, and people went thither in great numbers, so that it became a great nation."[7]

Trust and mistrust are shown in the trade by deposit among the Indians of the American northwest coast, "The stranger began by depositing his goods on the bank, then withdrew; the Indian afterwards came and placed by the side of the first deposit what he thought a fair exchange and then went away. The stranger then came back and carried off the Indian's goods if they seemed to him of sufficient value; if not, he simply withdrew again, and waited till something else was added. If they did not come to an agreement, each took back his goods."[8] In Chile there once existed an amelioration of the deposit system. The people on coming to town to trade would warn the chief, who thereupon summoned his subjects with trumpets. The people would take what suited them of the merchandise offered, and then retire into the houses. When the merchants were ready to go, the chief would summon those who took the merchandise and they would bring objects in exchange.[9] The Indians of New Mexico, in their exchanges with the Spanish soldiers, would plant on the road between Chihuahua and Santa Fé little crosses to which they suspended a leather wallet with a little venison; they then placed at the foot of the cross a buffalo-skin. This signified: "We wish to make exchanges with the worshipers of the cross." The soldiers would take the skin and leave salted meat.[10] Other cases of silent barter have been collected.[11]

There is further evidence of the warlike origin of trade in various efforts to overreach the alien. In the seventeenth century the Pima Indians sent well-armed bands through the Apache cordon to trade at the Spanish and Mexican settlements of Sonora. Later American traders appeared among them. "Some Pimas sometimes try to turn the tables on the traders by offering damp wheat that of course overweighs. More frequently they put a quantity of sand in the middle of the wheat sacks, which are furnished by the trader and not ordinarily emptied when the wheat is brought in. Rarely, the best wheat is put on top and an inferior quality lies concealed beneath."[12] This quotation emphasizes a phase of primitive trade which is related to hostility, in that strangers are generally regarded as enemies, so that practices are approved in dealing with them which would not have the sanction of the mores if applied to fellow group-members. The Eskimo regard strangers as being outside the law; it is honorable to deceive and steal from them. The Polynesians stole from the Europeans; never among themselves. The Tuareg respect the rights of strangers but little, yet live in the closest union themselves. The Africans are generally suspicious of strangers, who are supposed to have hostile intentions until the opposite is proved. Caravans are stopped at the boundaries and the equipage examined. The Somals and Gallas make the merchant sit down outside the village until a deputation of old men introduce him with ceremony into the village. A case is mentioned of a Carthaginian ship voluntarily wrecking itself on a false route, so as to mislead a Roman ship. This act was highly approved and compensation accorded.[13] The different mores surrounding inter-

7 Giles, *Travels of Fa-hsien*, 66-67.
8 Bancroft, *Nat. Races*, I, 63-64.
9 Letourneau, *Commerce*, 168.
10 Humboldt, *Nouvelle Espagne*, II, 108-109.
11 Grierson, *The Silent-Trade;* Lindsay,

Hist. Merchant Shipping, I, 21, 22; Letourneau, *Commerce*, 11-13, 16, 42, 149, 159, 314, 528-529.
12 Russell, in BAE, XXVI, 94.
13 Letourneau, *Commerce*, 16, 160, 286, 62, 373.

group as contrasted with intra-group relations are evidenced in the Jewish custom of allowing usury with strangers.[14] As the result of suspicion, a curious custom exists among the Bangala. When counting, they use fingers and hands in the usual way; they add and subtract under ten with their fingers, and for larger numbers use palm nuts and the like. "This was not because they were incapable of adding and subtracting mentally, but because they were always so suspicious of each other that they wanted an ocular proof that the sum was right, and that neither was getting the better of the other."[15] Piracy was also closely connected with trade, being found among the Malays, Chinese, Phœnicians, and others, while commerce and conquest have been the policy of nations within more recent times.[16]

§78. Exchange in the Industrial Organization.

TRADE has operated in many places and at different times to supplant conditions of war with those of peace, and accordingly has led to the advancement of civilization. Hagen[1] says of the Papuans of New Guinea that in ages past they have traded only when absolute need broke up their laziness. Certain festival market-days were established in rotation, and then the step to the fabrication of rough wares was not difficult and presently there were centers of manufacture of various products such as boats, clay vessels, and smoked fish. Some Papuans are even regular tradesmen who buy to sell, going about to all the markets; these are mainly islanders, some of whom go to considerable distances, and they are jealous of infringement upon their "beats." The people of Bilibili even have special traders who know the languages of various districts; in fact, these islanders, among them, understand and speak all the many languages of New Guinea. Trade is mainly along the coasts, for the coast-peoples will not permit penetration of the interior, they themselves wishing to act as middlemen. The custom of trade-friendship is highly developed; no one man of one tribe can trade with all of another group; each family has trade-friends who are guest-friends while business is being done. Such friends often settle for years in their hosts' villages. Sons of chiefs go on trading-voyages for purposes of education. Such sojourners may marry and remain; thus the loose organization of the tribes is strengthened and the barriers of a multitude of languages are done away with. "Speech and trade are the chief factors which determine the 'external relations' . . . and regulate them, and only so far as these reach does the Papuan state exercise its influence." It cannot extend very far, according to our criteria, because the population is so sparse. They have few needs and trade is chiefly in food-products and "ethnographic articles." Naturally the exchange is no more than barter. "The Papuan trades and goes to market only to satisfy his personal needs."

Competent judges have declared that trade was the first step toward civilization among the negroes of the west African coast, in spite of the missionaries and philanthropists. The tribes in the interior of Africa have been kept from European civilization by the people of the coast, who interpose themselves as middlemen. The market, among the trading negroes, is the center of all active

---

14 Deut., XXIII, 19.
15 Weeks, in JAI, XXXIX, 419, 420.

16 Maspero, *Hist. Anc.*, I, 752; Letourneau, *Commerce*, 238, 256, 377, 446, 453, 505.
1 *Papua's*, 216-221.

life, and "attempts to civilize them succeed best by seizing upon this peculiarity."[2] Markets are especially common in Kabylic, where they are public
property belonging to one or more tribes. The intertribal markets are founded
with the consent of tribes in time of peace; each tribe establishes such as it
wishes in time of war. Custom makes of their markets a neutral place, under
a taboo—*anaia* or protection. Everybody who goes to market is inviolable as
long as he does not leave the territory of the tribe to which the market belongs.
People of hostile tribes, even in time of war, may meet with impunity at the
market. In time of peace the market is a place having something of sanctity;
every misdemeanor committed there acquires exceptional gravity and is severely punished. Theft on the market is a capital offense; the thief is likely
to be stoned to death on the spot; at the very least he is stripped, his beard and
eyebrows are shaved, and he is expelled under a shower of stones.[3] The Bataks
of Sumatra come to their markets with green branches as a sign of peace, and
on these occasions all hostility ceases.[4] A similar stress toward peace is
present in those instances of peaceful access, as when, among the natives of
Victoria, strangers coming to the quarries are treated not as enemies but as
guests,[5] while among the American Indians, tribes meeting their enemies at
the quarries were obliged to treat them as friends, under an injunction of
the Great Spirit.[6]

The civilizing influence of trade is seen in the development of a trade-lan-
guage. One such jargon in America—the Mobilian—was based upon Choctaw,
but borrowed also from all the neighboring dialects and even from the more
northern Algonquian languages. It was spoken and understood among all the
tribes of the Gulf states, probably as far west as Matagorda bay and northward along both banks of the Mississippi to the Algonquin frontier about the
entrance of the Ohio. "It was called Mobilienne by the French, from Mobile,
the great trading center of the Gulf region. Along the Mississippi it was
sometimes known also as the Chickasaw trade language, the Chickasaw being
a dialect of the Choctaw language proper. Jeffreys, in 1761, compares this
jargon in its uses to the lingua franca of the Levant, and it was evidently by
the aid of this intertribal medium that De Soto's interpreter from Tampa Bay
could converse with all the tribes they met until they reached the Mississippi.
. . . The Mobilian trade jargon was not unique of its kind. In America, as in
other parts of the world, the common necessities of intercommunication have
resulted in the formation of several such mongrel dialects, prevailing sometimes over wide areas. In some cases, also, the language of a predominant
tribe serves as the common medium for all the tribes of a particular region.
In South America we find the lingoa geral, based upon the Tupi language,
understood for everyday purposes by all the tribes of the immense central
region from Guiana to Paraguay, including almost the whole Amazon basin.
On the northwest coast we find the well-known 'Chinook jargon,' which takes
its name from a small tribe formerly residing at the mouth of the Columbia, in
common use among all the tribes from California far up into Alaska, and
eastward to the great divide of the Rocky Mountains. In the southwest the
Navaho-Apache language is understood by nearly all the Indians of Arizona

2 Ratzel, *Vkde.*, I, 593, 5, 193.
3 Letourneau, *Commerce*, 282, 292, 293;
Hanoteau and Letourneux, *Kabylie*, II, 81.
4 Letourneau, *Commerce*, 238.

5 Smyth, *Vict.*, I, 359.
6 Donaldson, in *Smithson. Rep.*, 1885, pt.
II, 102.

and New Mexico, while on the plains the Sioux language in the north and the Comanche in the south hold about the same position. In addition to these we have also the noted 'sign language,' a gesture system used and perfectly understood as a fluent means of communication among all the hunting tribes of the plains from the Saskatchewan to the Rio Grande."[7]

While the development of the mechanism of exchange will be discussed below, mention might be made here of a primitive device of accounting: "Various bunches of sticks may be seen over any front door of a chief of a household. When a trade is made and partial payment accepted, a stick four or five inches long is taken and notches cut into it to represent the quantities of what is proffered in payment. The stick is then cut or split in two pieces. Each of the two parties to the trade takes a stick. When they again meet for settlement, these sticks must match to complete the notches which were made in the stick of which they are a part. Any tampering with either half of the stick is thus easily discovered. Sticks have different kinds of notches cut into them, some to represent cloth, some tobacco and other articles."[8] A similar practice was in vogue during the Middle Ages, and it is likely that the word "stock" originally had this significance.

The effect of trade on primitive society may be indicated by the case of the Omaha. "With the coming of the trader and the introduction of iron implements and other articles for daily use, new conditions confronted the Indians; they were no longer obliged to make all the articles required for use and the time formerly occupied by the long and wearisome process of chipping and rubbing stone was now left free." The iron implements were acquired by bartering pelts. Barter was not new to the Indians, but up to the time of the coming of the white trader no Omaha had slain animals merely for commercial purposes. Trade thus gave rise to hunting for gain. "The quest of game for profit introduced new motives for hunting and also of cultivating the soil, motives not consonant with the old religious ideas and customs; consequently under their influence such customs slowly but inevitably fell into disuse." This tended to weaken the power of ancient beliefs and to introduce new standards, commercial in character. The stimulation of hunting as an avocation weakened the influence of the old village life, created different standards of wealth, enhanced the importance of the hunter, and greatly increased the labors of the women in preparing pelts and skins for the market. "There is good reason to ascribe to the last-named condition an impetus to the practice of polygamy among the Omaha."[9]

It is difficult to pass over, in considering trade, so remarkable an adjustment as money; but this topic has been treated with considerable fullness by one of the authors[10] and we refer to that treatment without seeking to reproduce it here. The same may be said of weights and measures; and here we refer to the excellent volume of Ridgeway, who likewise considers the evolution of coinage. It is hard to realize the opposition which this author met in the endeavor to treat such subjects by the inductive method.[11]

"In 1892 I published my *Origin of Metallic Currency and Weight Standards,* in which I fully developed the anthropological method of dealing with the

---

7 Mooney, in BAE, XIX, pt. I, 187-188.
8 Peet, in *Int. Cong. Anthrop.,* 1893, 201.
9 Fletcher and LaFlesche, in BAE, XXVII, 614-615.

10 Sumner, *Folkways,* §§142-155.
11 *Origin of Metallic Currency and Weight Standards:* Ridgeway, in JAI, XXXIX, 14-15, 11-13.

problem of the origin of weights of coinage and coin types. I had already converted some political economists and a few classical scholars, but on the appearance of my book the conversion of the historians of trade and money was completed, and ever since, both in Germany and in this country, the soundness of the method has been recognised by scientific students of history. Yet there are still some Greek numismatists . . . [who are not persuaded]. Still less will they believe that the tunny fish was ever a unit of barter or account in those towns, as the dried cod-fish, still the badge of Iceland, was and is still the unit of exchange in that island, and as the beaver, still seen on certain coins and stamps of Canada, represents the beaver whose skin formed, down to our time, the unit of account throughout all the Hudson Bay Company's territory. Nor will they believe that when gold or silver coins were struck there was any relation between the old barter unit and the new silver, although we know from good ancient authority that when Solon struck the first silver drachm at Athens, he equated his new drachm to the sheep and the goat, the old units of account. These, down to his day, had continued, along with the cow, to be the unit of account in the laws of Draco, the old Athenian legislator. It will thus be seen how difficult it is to get the old school of archaeologists weaned from their love of *a priori* speculation and to yield obedience to the inductive method of anthropology, and at the same time to the voice of history. Some of the old school, however, have long since modified their position, and whilst abusing the author have not scrupled to adopt his ideas."

The author goes on to consider the reasons for the opposition he encountered. "What was the cause of this repugnance to a new theory based on a wide induction? The fact is that classical scholars and archaeologists in this country were entirely given up to *a priori* methods, which gave every scope for the play of wild speculation untrammelled by any restraint of solid facts. They proposed emendations in sound texts without ever dreaming of inspecting a single manuscript of the author whose sentiments they proposed to correct. They slavishly followed their German brethren and had settled down, as already said, into a comfortable conviction that not only the culture and art of Greece and Rome stood on a different platform from all other studies, but that it might be pursued with a looseness of method which was banned in all scientific inquiries. They further held that this culture was in the main derived from the East and Egypt, *lux ex Oriente* being their leading axiom. It was a matter of faith that the Greeks had no weight standards nor any means of weighing gold or silver, and did not employ weight in any form until they borrowed weights and weight systems from Babylonia. . . . The orthodox school of archaeologists, when I began to write, held that all weight standards that were used in the world, no matter where found, from Ireland to China, were derived from Babylonia. . . . The talent was supposed to be the first weight unit fixed. Yet investigation shows that all over the world, wherever men have discovered gold and use it, they quickly weigh it with the seeds of plants, which nature has placed as weights of great accuracy ready to hand. Thus the Incas of Peru had scales, and used seeds for weights. The West Africans used the Tacoo or Crab's eye, and the Damba, for weighing gold dust, long before any European had traded with them. The Assyrians themselves used a grain as their lowest unit, which I have shown from its weight to be a wheat grain. The wild tribes of Laos use grains of rice to weigh the gold dust from their streams, and as they value each little hoe which forms their lowest unit in a system of barter, which ranges from the hoe to the buffalo as the regular higher unit, and to the slave as the occasional higher unit, they have no difficulty in appraising in gold the value of any one of their commodities, whether slave, buffalo, earthenware jar, or piece of cloth. . . . So far, then from the Greeks starting with the Babylonian heavy talent as their unit, they had as their smallest weight (on no less authority than that of Theophrastus) the barley corn. In other words, they were just in the same position as ourselves, for our own troy grain, as I have shown, is only the barley corn. . . . By the statute of Henry VII it was enacted that all the weights of the kingdom should be based on the penny sterling, and that 'the penny sterling or pennyweight should be of the weight of thirty-two grains of wheat, dry and taken out of the midst of the ear of wheat after the ancient laws of the realm.' This statute was really but a re-enactment of laws in use since Anglo-Saxon times. Now an experiment showed me that four grains of wheat regularly equal three grains of barley, and as I found in an ancient Roman metrology that four grains of wheat equal three grains of barley, and as four to three is the relation between the wheat grains of Henry VII and the troy grain introduced from France, there can be no doubt that the troy grain is the barley corn, which we know was used as well as the wheat grain in certain districts of the Roman empire, as well as in Greece."

§80. Primitive Improvidence and Thrift.

SAVAGES very commonly take no thought for the morrow; "when chance brings them a hearty meal, they lie down to digest it and do not stir till they are goaded out of their laziness by the return of hunger."[1] When times are favorable, the Australian black fellow is as light-hearted as possible. "He has not the slightest thought of, or care for, what the morrow may have in store, and lives entirely in the present."[2] So impatient is the Papuan that he will not wait until the betel-nuts are ripe, but eats them green.[3] It is stated of a group of Melanesians that the pump-drill for making holes was constructed whenever the need arose and then carelessly thrown aside, though it could be used not only for wood but for shell as well.[4]

The African Bushman has been referred to as the unfortunate child of the moment. He is destructive and careless, because he is governed in any decision or action by the impulse of the moment.[5] Foresight is not characteristic of the Akamba, who will not cultivate anything beyond what is required for their immediate use; "despite the frequency of famines no Mkamba thinks of ever sowing more than is necessary to carry him on to the next rains."[6] Stigand[7] makes the following interesting comment on the African: "The improvidence of the savage is wonderful. He is an optimist of the highest order. Never does he learn by experience. Cheerfully will he eat all his remaining food, perhaps sharing it with others, quite oblivious of the fact that there are several days' journey in front of him and no possibility of obtaining more

1 Letourneau, *Prop.*, 110.
2 Spencer and Gillen, *Nat. Tr. Cent. Aust.*, 53.
3 Von Pfeil, *Südsee*, 123.
4 Jenness and Ballentyne, *D'Entrecasteaux*, 184.

5 Fritsch, *Eingeb. S.-Afr.*, 418-419; Lichtenstein, *S. Afr.*, II, 50; Ratzel, *Vkde.*, I, 56; Lippert, *Kgchte.*, I, 39, 40.
6 Dundas, C., in JAI, XLIII, 499.
7 *Elephant*, 207-208.

until the journey's end. His sharing his food is not real generosity; he sees that he has got enough and to spare for the meal, and never thinks of the morrow. It is too much trouble to tell the others to go away, so he just lets them eat with him. On a trek in North Eastern Rhodesia, I watched my porters, day after day, cutting the strips of bark with which their loads were tied up, to save the trouble of unknotting them. This happened nearly every day for a month; on arrival in camp they whipped out a knife and cut the last strips. Every morning they had to sally forth and cut and prepare new strips before we could proceed. They never learnt any better, not even at the end of the trek; they are probably still doing it."

Certain natives of Borneo are very improvident; "when they have rice they hold a succession of feasts until it is finished." Garrett,[8] who reports this, continues: "When I was there the daughter of the Patinggi (head of the village) had just been married. A great feast had been held and everything eaten up, with the result that the men had to go into the jungle to get rotan and rubber, with which to buy rice, without any food: even the children had had nothing to eat the day I met them." The Hindu who has enough for the day is contented and will work no more; this is one reason for the dead level of poverty in India.[9]

The Greenlander is characterized by "a lightminded carefreeness which brings it about that he is inclined to live only a life for the day, to satisfy the moment's wants, without the least thought for the future. 'When the day comes, counsel will come.' He lives according to that rule, swells about and starves in constant succession. With so generous a hand does nature at certain times of the year distribute her gifts that it should be quite easy for the majority to provide for themselves a not inconsiderable winter-supply, but only the wiser provide themselves with enough to meet about half the winter's needs."[10] The Tlinkit lives for the present; "if given his choice whether to accept five dollars at once or fifty dollars a year hence, although reasonably certain that he could have the fifty dollars, he would accept the five, and be done with it. The NOW appeals to him. . . . A white man thinks twice before he throws up his job. Not so with the Thlinget. His desires, more than his needs, control him."[11] With the Indians of British Guiana, "the need of the moment demands satisfaction, the next hour lying beyond their mental reckoning";[12] while the Arawaks lack foresight because they lack incentive to labor. Three or four months' work suffices to maintain one of these Indians a whole year; the rest of the time he spends in hunting, fishing, visiting, drinking, and dancing. "His life is a life of indulgence, and only with reluctance will he renounce the pleasures of the present to bestir himself for the future."[13] With such instances as these in mind, one readily realizes that the development of foresight is prerequisite to the advancement of civilization.

The picture of primitive thrift cannot be so amply illustrated. A rudimentary type of foresight practised by the West Australians is to re-insert the head of a wild yam, so as to be sure of a future crop; but beyond this they do absolutely nothing which may be regarded as a tentative in the direction of cultivating plants for their use.[14] The provident father in New Britain

---

8 In JAI, XLII, 54.
9 Barnett, in *Fortnightly Rev.*, LIV, 207-217.
10 Fries, *Grönland*, 126.

11 Jones, *Thlingets*, 92.
12 Schomburgk, *Brit.-Guiana*, I, 162-163.
13 Von Martius, *Beiträge*, I, 692.
14 Roth, in JAI, XVI, 120.

plants some coconut trees when his son is born; in seven or eight years they support the boy, who, as soon as he can do anything, has a grove of his own.[15] Thrift among the Somals takes the form of capital in livestock; the only poor persons are the cripples and outcasts.[16] The Akus of Sierra Leone are thrifty and industrious, "extremely parsimonious and consequently wealthy," and are making great advances in civilization; while the Kru are hard-working, intelligent men whose great ambition is to save money and return to their native country, there to enjoy a plurality of wives and live at ease without labor.[17]

More numerous examples of thrift are found among the American Indians, especially those practising agriculture. All the tribes east of the Mississippi were more or less agricultural, which is in itself an evidence of foresight, while the storing of food was common; to the natives' provision for the future, indeed, the white colonists in a number of instances owed their preservation from famine.[18] The "instinct" of frugality was strong enough to assert itself now and then among the wild-rice gatherers of the Upper Lakes. The Winnebago women contrived to save, by hiding, some of their food in time of abundance; they often buried rice and maize in the ground to keep them from being stolen, while throughout Wisconsin the grain was deposited in the ground to be taken out when needed for food. The Minnesota Indians gathered sufficient wild rice for winter consumption and in some instances saved the grain for an entire year.[19] The Indians of the Southwest practised a rude sort of forest-conservation, for while they had the whole forest to work on, they very seldom, if ever, entirely girdled the yellow pine tree, but always left sufficient bark to keep it alive. The Indians removed the dry outer bark of the trees by means of stone hatchets, after which they found it easy to strip off the inner bark which, when dried and pounded, was used as a substitute breadstuff to eke out the scanty supply of corn raised in the little valleys.[20] The many uses to which the Salish tribes put the cedar tree are evidence at once of foresight and of adaptability. The cedar was to the Indian what the coconut-palm was to the South Sea Islander. "From its outer bark he constructed ropes and lines, coverings for his dwelling, his slow matches, or 'travelling fire,' and many other things. From its inner bark his wife wove garments for herself and children, made their beds and pillows, padded her children's cradles, and fashioned the compressing bands and pads for deforming their heads, and also the insignia of their secret societies, their headdresses and other ceremonial decorations, besides applying it in a multitude of other ways. From its wood he built the family and communal dwellings, made such furniture as he used—tubs, pots, kettles, bowls, dishes, and platters,—fashioned his graceful and buoyant fishing and war canoes, his coffin, his treasure chests, his ceremonial masks, his heraldic emblems, his commemorative columns, his totem poles, and a host of other objects. From its branches he made his most enduring withes and ties, and from its split roots his wife constructed the beautiful basketry of this region. There was practically no part of this remarkable tree which he did not apply to some useful purpose or other. He even resorted to it for food in times of scarcity and famine: his wives and daughters robbing the squirrels and chipmunks of their stores of its cones for the nutriment they contained.

15 Danks, in AAAS, 1892, 618.
16 Paulitschke, *Nordost-Afr.*, I, 323.
17 Griffith, in JAI, XVI, 301, 303.
18 Carr, in *Smithson. Rep.*, 1891, 507, 508, footnotes, 526.

19 Jenks, in BAE, XIX, 1071-1072, 1086, 1088.
20 N.Y. *Times*, Jan. 26, 1923.

One can hardly imagine what the condition of the natives of this region would have been without this tree, no other of the country lending itself to such a variety of useful purposes."[21] The Indians of the Northwest Coast have a keen appreciation of the value of money, work for wages, and have considerable business judgment. "It would seem that with their ideas of acquiring wealth, we have little to teach them in habits of thrift."[22]

§81. Motives to Accumulation.

EVEN when they have fertile land and good agriculture, natives are found suffering from hunger, as on the African west coast, because they have remained otherwise on a lower stage and lay up no store of provisions.[1] By contrast there appear manifestations of foresight, like that of the Banar of Farther India, who lay up their seed-supply immediately from the first of the harvest, and keep it sacred, believing that the spirits will punish them with death for selling any of it.[2] Here appears the sanction of religion upon the mores. A striking instance of capital-formation is the planting of a tree or trees at the birth of a child, to be his future capital.[3] Pliny[4] says the branches of the cypress tree were so valuable for use as poles and props that it was once a saying among the Romans that a cypress-wood was a dowry for a daughter.

Cases illustrative of non-inheritance are numerous. Of the Andamanese it is stated that since all their possessions consist of goods that have to be replaced, there is no accumulation of the labors of former generations. They are not tied by any law of inheritance; as a matter of sentiment the nearest of kin takes charge of all the effects left by a deceased person, and often they are distributed among those who seem in need of them. Part of them become a sort of common property.[5] Codrington[6] reports from Florida Island that "when they hang up the dead man's arms on his house, they make great lamentations, all remains afterwards untouched, the house goes to ruin." In the region of the Nyanzas, if a chief dies the whole village is abandoned; among the Unyamwesi the oxen of a dead chief are consumed in monthly feasts on his grave, often until all are gone.[7] At Quillengues, West Africa, "at the feasts of the dead there is an enormous slaughter of cattle, for the heir feels the necessity of killing the whole flock to regale the populace and content the soul of the departed."[8] Of the Pimas of Arizona it is reported that "the custom of destroying all the property of the husband when he dies impoverishes the widow and children and prevents increase of stock."[9] Among the Copper River natives of Alaska, the wives and children are always left in destitute circumstances at the husband's death, however wealthy he may have been. This arises from the habit of distributing among the tribe at his death the property, the accumulation of which seems to be a matter of great pride, because the demonstration at the obsequies is in proportion to the deceased's wealth. Here is a case involving posthumous ostentation.

Vanity plays its salient rôle in furthering wastefulness as well as in pro-

21 Hill-Tout, in JAI, XXXIV, 28-29.
22 Niblack, in Smithson. Rep., 1888, 239.
1 Waitz, Anthrop., II, 82.
2 Bastian, Bilder, 124.
3 Andree, Eth. Parallelen, 21.
4 Nat. Hist., bk. XVI, ch. LX.

5 Man, in JAI, XII, 340.
6 Melanesians, 255.
7 Stuhlmann, Mit Emin, 99, 310.
8 Serpa Pinto, Africa, I, 54.
9 Yarrow, in BAE, I, 99.

moting accumulations. "Every family incident in a Hindu household is attended with ceremonies—ceremonies at puberty, ceremonies at birth, ceremonies at marriage, and ceremonies at funerals. In fact, the life of a Hindu is emphatically one of ceremonies. Savings of ages, hoarded by dint of thrift and frugality, are dissipated in a day or in a few days to meet the expenses concomitant to some ceremonial that is proposed to be performed."[10] Among the Northwest Indians, "the self-denial of comforts and even necessaries exercised for many years in the accumulation of property by man and wife is very remarkable, but, in their estimation, is amply repaid on the occasion of a distribution of the same and the erection of a decorative column, which in many instances stands in front of an unfinished lodge frame as a visible monument of the owner's folly and extravagance. . . . The owner probably lives in the lodge of some relative, or perhaps is dead. It has been beyond his means to finish his house, but for that he cares little; his vanity has been gratified; his pride satisfied. On the day when he stood presiding over his pile of goods and chattels, previous to their distribution amongst his eager and expectant guests, he had reached the summit of his ambition. . . . He is thenceforth a petty chief of the village."[11]

§88. The "Taming of Fire."

When we encounter the natural inquiry as to the source in nature from which fire was derived, we are thrown back on inference. Legends and survivals may lend support to this or that theory but they are not conclusive in themselves. Certain theories are inherently improbable, for instance, those that assign the derivation of fire to what must have been rare and incidental occurrences, such as the rubbing together of bamboo-stems in a high wind.[1] What one acute and experienced observer[2] of primitive life says of this theory is pertinent to much which we shall encounter later on. He rejects it with contempt remarking that, while incidents have often instructed men, to do that they must be such as occur repeatedly and do not demand any effort at analysis. Those in which he can participate, thereby acquiring a process leading to an end in view, or a method, are the ones that have instructed him. The primitive man is strictly practical; he is not a philosopher or an inventor. What has lent a spurious significance to the above friction-theory is the fact that man's earliest known process of generating fire was by friction. The source of fire must have been in some frequently repeated and very widespread natural phenomenon.

Among origins may be reckoned volcanic activity. It is to be understood that the savage did not dally about for scientific research in the vicinity of an erupting crater, for to him the frightful sights and sounds, formidable enough in themselves, were manifestations of the supernatural, and were thus fraught with a special terror. If the eruption-period were the only time during which he could have appropriated fire from volcanoes, we could rule out this source forthwith. But the cooling lava-streams, with their crevices reaching down to the red-hot strata of the underflow, might well have given early man a chance to experiment with the lighting of dry sticks. However, it will be noted that this source of fire is not one universally available.

The derivation of fire from electric storms seems to us the most simple and

10 Husain, in JASB, III, 140.   1 Mason, *Invention*, 87.
11 Niblack, in USNM, 1888, 308.   2 Von den Steinen, *Zent. Bras.*, 222.

reasonable theory. Doubtless the savage felt the same terror in the vicinity of electric discharges that he did in the presence of volcanic disturbances, although the relative frequency of the storm would have enlisted the element of familiarity to reduce his fear. But a fire started by lightning might smolder on for days and months, no longer attended by terrifying outbursts of natural force. Prairie and forest fires and the smoldering of punk and peat are observable occurrences. Here would be a chance for observation and experiment. Further, the wide prevalence of electric storms, especially in the warmer zones—two hundred per annum in Togoland, West Africa, and over one hundred and fifty in Java, as against twelve in New England[3]—in which man must have taken his immediate origin, would allow of the independent appropriation of fire in a number of widely separated localities. The extraordinary extension of the use of fire over both space and time is more readily explained upon this latter hypothesis than by any other single theory. Doubtless it was attained in some localities in an exceptional way, or in several ways; but the thunderstorm looks to be the chief source of derivation.

Local evidence sometimes hints at the volcanic or the electric origin. The Andamanese cannot produce fire, and there is no tradition that their ancestors could do so; but, as they live near two islands, one of which contains an extinct and the other an active volcano, it is reasonable to suppose that their acquaintance with fire was first made through these sources.[4] Again, "the Golas of West Africa put out all the fires in a village when lightning ignites any substance and immediately kindle new fires therefrom,"[5]—as if utilizing a fresh supply from a stock source.

When one comes to the interpretation of fire-myths, he enters upon still more difficult and insecure ground. The Caroline Islanders have a legend of an evil spirit, a sort of Prometheus, who was thrown from the sky for rudeness, but who brought fire, till then unknown, to men.[6] Not only among the Melanesians but among the Polynesians as well, occur fire-myths which represent fire as brought to earth against the will of the gods.[7] "The early vacillation of the myth between the heavenly and the earthly divinity," writes Lippert,[8] discussing the mythical sources from which fire was derived or stolen, "reflects quite significantly the two possibilities of fire-derivation. Hesiod and those who followed him made the Titan pilfer the fire of heaven from the lightning-hurling Zeus, but Æschylus has Prometheus kindle a narthex-stalk at the volcano Mosychlos on the island of Lemnos, and thus purloin the fire from Hephæstus." Fire-myths, where they deal with the first derivation of the element, always very significantly refer to the bringing of the first fire from some place or direction; we learn little or nothing in the way of direct evidence as to its original appropriation out of nature. Rather do the myths refer to a second stage, where fire was "kept" and carried. A few examples of such myths follow.

There is a legend among the Boloki people of the Congo that they bought their first fire from another tribe in exchange for a young woman. Previously they cooked their food in the sun, or ate it quite raw.[9] If one believes their own statements, the Batetela were ignorant of the art of producing fire before they

---

3 Gregory, Keller, and Bishop, *Phys. and Com. Geog.*, §108, note.
4 Man, in JAI, XI, 272.
5 Mason, *Invention*, 87.
6 Montero y Vidal, *Filipinas*, I, 468.

7 Ratzel, *Vkde.*, II, 306.
8 *Kgchte.*, I, 257 (quoted), 254-255; Æschylus, *Prometheus*, 109; Plato, *Protagoras*, ch. XI.
9 Weeks, in JAI, XL, 376.

came to their new home. The Sungu maintain that they learned it from the Basongo Meno; the Olemba to this day import their fire-sticks from the Bahamba. Both tribes aver that in former times perpetual fires were kept in all the villages.[10] The Hausa believe that long, long ago an old female devil brought sticks to a certain town in order to sell them, but, as the people there had no use for them, they naturally would not buy them. "The old devil then rubbed two sticks together, and, having lighted them, made a fire, and warmed herself, and, on seeing this, the people bought her stock readily and learned the use of fire. The original fire was never allowed to go out, and many people in Hausaland still preserve the ancient flame."[11] The Semas of India have a tradition of a time when fire was not known, and believe that men then had long hair like apes to keep out the cold; but investigation has failed to disclose any notion as to how fire was discovered.[12] In some parts of India the remarkable idea is prevalent that fire is produced from water. In the Veda, fire is called "son of the waters," and this name is also once applied to the sun. "Doubtless the idea arose from the apparent production of lightning from rain-clouds."[13] A myth which has some bearing on the appropriation of fire out of nature is common to the Samoans, who say there once was a time when their ancestors ate everything raw, but that later a fire-bringer secured it from the earthquake god who had fire always burning in his subterranean region. On De Peyster's Island they say that fire was discovered by seeing smoke rise from the friction of two crossed branches of a tree shaken by the wind.[14] How mankind learned to ignite fire is told in a curious and interesting legend common to many of the Polynesians: "The Maori Prometheus, Maui, who was a great practical joker, having extinguished all existing fires, his mother directed the servants to go and ask the goddess Mahuika to give them fire to cook with, but they were all too terrified to obey her. Maui then offered to go himself. His parents warned him not to play any tricks on the old lady, and he promised to be careful. But on reaching the abode of the Goddess of Fire, and obtaining what he asked for, he went aside and extinguished it, and presented himself again. The fire was obtained by the goddess from the root of her nails, which she tore out to obtain it. Maui kept on extinguishing the fire given, and asking for more, till he thoroughly exasperated the Fire Goddess, who, when reduced to her last toe-nail, pulled it out and dashed it on the ground, when everything caught fire. Maui changed himself into a hawk, and flew with rapid flight; but the earth and sea caught fire, and Maui narrowly escaped destruction. The fire was extinguished by the aid of the God of Storms. But before the fire was all lost the Fire Goddess saved some sparks, which she threw into the kaikomako and a few other trees, where they are still cherished. Hence men rub portions of the wood of these trees together when they wish to ignite a fire."[15] One may be permitted to read into this legend the electric storm as the source of derivation; it illustrates also the second stage, the "keeping" of fire.

The preservation of fire and some of the effects of fire on social organization may be illustrated by the following scattered instances. In the D'Entrecasteaux Islands "there is always at least one fire alight in the hamlet from which brands

10 Torday, in JAI, LI, 378.
11 Tremearne, in JAI, XLV, 31-32.
12 Hutton, *Sema Nagas*, 42.
13 *Rig-Veda*, I, 22, 6, in Monier-Williams, *Brāhmanism*, 346.

14 Turner, *Samoa*, 209, 211, 285-296.
15 Stack, in AAAS, 1891, 374-375; N.Y. *Times*, July 16, 1907.

can be taken by any one to kindle a fire for himself. In travelling, the natives sometimes carry a fire-stick, sometimes put in at a hamlet and get one. Should it be necessary, however, almost any native can kindle a fire with two dry sticks and some shavings."[16] Hagen[17] cites a case in New Guinea where a village lost its fire and had to send to an island to get more, as there was war with neighboring villages. A high price was charged. A rather incredible case of fire-making method is the one reported from central Australia, where the native rubs up some dung, which he places on the back of a shield; then he takes a throw-stick and rubs it backwards and forwards for a few strokes, the dung being said to catch alight almost at once, and being fed with leaves and grass.[18] A symbolic employment of fire is mentioned in the case of the Baganda of Africa. In front of the hut which faces the royal enclosure is a hole in the ground where, every night, fire from the hut is placed and kept burning brightly, even during a rain-storm, until daybreak, when it is removed to the hut again. When the king journeys the fire goes with him, and when he dies it is extinguished. The death of the king is in fact announced to the nation by words meaning "the fire has gone out."[19]

Among some of the aborigines of Siberia the common fire is a symbol of the unity of the clan. "The chief owner of the fire," whom they imagine as an old woman, is not only a good spirit who bestows the use of fire on living clansmen, but also an intermediary between the living and the departed ancestors who are the heroes of the clan. By being burned the dead are given to the "owner of the fire," who has the power of choosing some of them to become also "owners" of the clan-fire. "Only a clansman has the right to kindle fire on the hearth of a fellow clansman, or to take fire out of his *yurta* [tent]. If a man from another clan lights his pipe in the *yurta,* he must finish smoking it before he goes out. Any infringement of these customary rules will bring misfortune on the clan, and the alien clansman who has brought it about may have to pay a fine in consequence. Each clan has its own firebrand, kept by the eldest of the clan, and only from this firebrand can the fire be made at which the bear meat is cooked at the bear festival. When a clan divides, the eldest of the clan breaks the firebrand in two, giving a half to the eldest of that portion of the clan which is removing. Then only is the clan regarded as formally divided." The same people furnish an illustration of the use of fire in betrothal and in the wedding ceremony. The following is a description of a betrothal: "The bridegroom's father takes a small sword, and, placing it in the hands of the father of the bride, says: 'This sword is a pledge of betrothal; take it and worship. Do thou pray to the goddess of fire.' Then, having received the sword, he worships the fire, saying: 'We have here and now settled to marry our son and daughter; therefore, O thou goddess of fire, hear thou and be witness thereto. Keep this couple from sickness, and watch over them till they grow old.' The bridegroom's father then receives the sword, and worships in like manner." During the marriage ceremony occurs the "sacrifice to the fire," which is strictly observed even by Christian Yakut. The bride approaches the fire from the north, and throwing into it three sticks brought from her own *yurta,* and a piece of butter, pronounces these words: "I come as mistress to rule the hearth." Then she bows to her father-in-law and mother-

---

16 Jenness and Ballentyne, *D'Entrecas-teaux,* 194.
17 *Papua's,* 204.

18 Horne and Aiston, *Cent. Aust.,* 94.
19 Roscoe, in JAI, XXXII, 51-52.

in-law, and the feast begins. Finally, there is the use of fire in the ceremony of "blessing the bride," which takes place before the girl leaves her own *yurta*. During this ceremony a bright fire is burning, before which she must bow. When she reaches the *yurta* of the groom she must bow before his hearth-fire too, and place in it a piece of meat and some butter."[20]

It is plain that the idea of kinship lay at the basis of a number of forms visualizing societalization. The use of fire and water, or the imparting of them, are actual and symbolical means of intensifying the integration of the kin-group. In 1694 the Delawares said: "We reckon ourselves all one because we drink one water," although they lived some on one side of the river and some on the other.[21] Among the Chukchi "generally the fire of a strange family is regarded as infectious and as harboring evil spirits. Fear of pollution extends also to all objects belonging to a strange hearth, to the skins of the tent and the sleeping-room, and even to the keepers and worshippers of strange penates. The Chukchi from far inland, who travel but little, when they come to a strange territory, fear to sleep in the open air and to subsist on their own scant food supply. On the other hand, an unknown traveler, coming unexpectedly to a Chukchi camp, can hardly gain admittance to a tent, as the writer himself experienced. . . . Every family is hampered by prohibitions, the most important being the taboo of interchange of fire (even of partly burnt fuel), which causes much inconvenience on the cold and timberless tundra. It is worthy of note that no such taboo is recognized in their relations with neighboring peoples." Nearest male relations form a union pledged to assist one another. "This union is cemented by the community of fire, by consanguinity (which is admitted for the male side), by the identity of the signs painted on the face with the blood of sacrifice, and by hereditary ritual songs."[22]

An old Maori method of keeping fire is described by a native in these words: "If I wanted to carry fire when on the march through the bush, I would cut a short piece of the hollow *rata* vine and set fire to one end of it; it would burn away slowly inside, and all I had to do was to stuff up the ends and wrap up the *rata* in moss and it would smoulder away slowly for hours. Thus, when it was time to camp, we could quickly get a fire for warmth and cooking without the trouble of hunting for a dry *kaikomako* and sweating over it with a rubbing-stick."[23] Before the Cheyenne Indians had flint and steel, they used sticks. After cutting them, "the maker held them up to the sun and prayed over them, asking that they might be blessed and might prove useful"; but fire was difficult to produce and so the Indian carried it, using dry buffalo-chip as punk.[24] In the tent and in the earth lodge of the Omaha, the fire was always in the center and was the point from which certain lines of etiquette were drawn. "The guest on entering must never pass between his host and the fire. When the guest was seated no one, not even a child, would pass between him and the fire. If by any chance it became necessary to do so, notice was given to the person passed and an apology made. This etiquette applied to the members of the family as well as to guests."[25] Among the natives of Guiana, fire has seldom to be lighted afresh, for it is kept constantly burning in every

20 Czaplicka, *Aborig. Siberia*, 44-45, 103, 110, 115, 116; Mucke, *Horde*, 241.
21 *Minutes of the Provincial Council of Pennsylvania*, I, 447.
22 Bogoras, in AA, III, 97, 101.

23 Cowan, *Maoris*, 202.
24 Grinnell, *Cheyenne*, I, 53, 54; Skinner, in AA, XVI, 81.
25 Fletcher and LaFlesche, in BAE, XXVII, 334.

house, and even on long canoe journeys a large piece of smoldering timber is usually carried. "Even when walking across the savanna an Indian sometimes carries a firebrand. On the Rio Tiquie at the present time the Bará carry with them from stream to stream a box made from a segment of bamboo-reed, with a hole drilled through its base, to allow the air to fan the glowing tinder within, a substance obtained from a certain ant's nest. In this way they are provided with the means of lighting a new fire without much trouble."[26]

§92. Fire and Religion.

WE have encountered only one case where the "vestal fire" is asserted to have had no religious significance, but to have been kept up in the protection of caves purely for the sake of convenience, the flame being "as carefully watched and attended as the celestial fire."[1] The fetishistic quality is usually implicit, even when not explicitly expressed. We are told, for example, that when the king of Sparta went forth on a campaign, he first sacrificed; "then the fire-bearing attendant, taking fire from the altar, leads the way to the borders of the country." After sacrificing again, "he passes the boundaries of the country. Fire from these sacrifices leads the way, never to be extinguished." A priest was chosen for this function, and its religious character was revealed also by the fact that this priest enjoyed general immunities and privileges. The Persians likewise and the Germans carried fire to war; it was commonly used as a summons and as a signal. The Scandinavians, when they went out to get land, took fire with them—whence the custom of taking possession of property in land by the use of fire.[2]

Paulitschke[3] reports a case where it would appear that fire was kept burning for the sake of ostentation or vanity; but he notes that it is an ancient and sacred custom to perform all important transactions of the household by the hearth-fire, and thinks there is fire-worship behind it all. On the Isle of Man each family kept a fire constantly burning, no one daring to be without a thing so important, or to depend on the care of others for it. This looks like un-adorned worldly caution; but the account goes on to say that it was believed that inconceivable calamities would ensue if all the fires on the island went out at once.[4] The religious element generally enters quite clearly. It is suc-cinctly indicated in such a statement as that of Ratzel,[5] who says that every Herero village has its holy fire, which is the middle point, economically, politi-cally, and in all other respects, of the society. Similar instances appear in numbers in Frazer's encyclopædic work.[6]

The belief that a new fire must on occasions be lighted, in order to escape sickness or other misfortune, is illustrated especially clearly among certain Africans. Among the Wagogo of East Africa, fire is as a rule always kept burning, but in case of sickness the medicine-man causes all fires in the patient's house to be extinguished and the embers to be cast out at the west end of the dwelling; then he lights his own fire. All fires are put out when the rain-doctor comes to operate, and when the medicine-man comes to charm

26 Roth, in BAE, XXXVIII, 71.

1 Thomson, in USNM, 1889, 472.

2 Xenophon, Lacedæmon, XIII; Herodo-tus, Hist., VIII, 6; Vergil, Æneid, II, 296-297; Haug, Parsis, 165; Lippert, Kgchte., I, 261-262; Dasent, Burnt Njal, xxxvii.

3 Nordost-Afr., I, 145.

4 Gomme, Village Life, 97.

5 Vkde., I, 331.

6 The Golden Bough, especially pt. I, vol. II; pt. VII, vols. I and II.

away wild beasts or infectious diseases.[7] In British Central Africa, where fire is carried from hut to hut in the form of a smoldering log and blown into flame with the breath, all fires are extinguished after the death of anyone in the village, fresh fire is made outside the dead man's house, and from this fire is taken to every hut.[8] When the natives of the Upper Congo wanted to make a new fire, as they did under certain conditions, they took a piece of Mopumbu tree for the lower stick and any kind of wood for the upper one. The top stick was not twirled but rubbed up and down the lower stick. This fire was called by a term meaning "newly originated fire," not a fire lighted from another one; fetish-fire was made by this process. "Some people would have their food cooked only by such a fire for fear of witchcraft." Fire was extinguished either by pouring water on it, or by dividing the burning logs; but the "new fire" was never voluntarily allowed to go out; should the rain put it out, either another new fire was made by rubbing the sticks together or it was procured from a healthy person. Under no circumstances would it be taken from one who was being treated by the medicine-man, "for to do so would be to run the risk of catching the sickness from which the patient was suffering." If frequent sickness visited a house or family, the fires were extinguished and a new fire started. "The idea at the root of thus extinguishing all the family fires and starting new ones was to procure a new lease of health by removing the probable cause of their bad health—a polluted fire." These people also have a ceremony of purification by fire, which is performed in the case of persons who have had to do with the preparation of a corpse for burial, those who attend upon a very sick person, and also those to whom the moon is taboo.[9] Amongst the Nigerian head-hunters, if any tree or house were set on fire by lightning, all the people would at once quench their fires and hasten to the spot with bundles of grass to get new. "To neglect this would show that the person so doing possessed black magic, and did not want to change his fire."[10]

The fire-board of the Siberian aborigines is shaped roughly to resemble a human being. "The consecration of a new fire-board to the office of protector of the hearth and herd is accompanied with the sacrificing of a reindeer to The Master-on-High, the anointing of the fire-board with the sacrificial blood and fat, and the pronouncing of an incantation over it."[11] This object is very clearly a fetish. It is a village custom among a group in Indo-China that once a year all the village fires must be extinguished and new fires made. "A man and a woman are chosen, who rub two pieces of wood together in order to get fire by friction. All the other fires in the village are lit from this source."[12] The Cherokee Indians kept a fire-maker in charge at the burial mound and the town-house built upon it, whose duty it was to keep the fire always smoldering. At the annual feast a new fire was kindled from this fire-pit, and all the fire in the different houses was obtained from the fire-maker at the town-house[13]— such fire possessing a religious quality. The American Indians were accustomed at the green-corn dance and other ceremonious occasions to generate a new fire.[14]

The close connection between fire and religion may be further illustrated

7 Cole, in JAI, XXXII, 315.
8 Stannus, in JAI, XL, 326.
9 Weeks, in JAI, XXXIX, 456-457, 113-114.
10 Tremearne, in JAI, XLII, 164.

11 Czaplicka, Aborig. Siberia, 265.
12 Milne, Eastern Clan, 207.
13 Peet, in Int. Cong. Anthrop., 1893, 184.
14 Catlin, Eight Years, I, 186.

in a variety of ways. In Fanti-land it is thought that a wizard can make fire whenever and wherever he likes;[15] in Rotuma, fire could always be obtained from the spirit-house.[16] Some diseases are thought by the Mongols in North Siberia to be due to the wrath of fire at the violation of some of the regulations in its honor. Conflagrations have the same origin; it is wrong to vex the divinity by opposing means; let him satisfy and quiet himself.[17] Among the Nagas of India the fire-stick is used less often for lighting fires than for taking omens. "Fire is occasionally almost personified. The village of Seromi was at one time repeatedly burnt down. At last an old man got burnt. It was at once said that now that a victim had been obtained the village would not be burnt for a very long time. This was many years ago, but no serious conflagration has taken place since."[18] The children of a Palaung clan are solemnly taught that they must always treat the fire with respect. "No one should spit into it, nor should dirty water be thrown on it to extinguish it, though clean water may be used. Stale vegetables may be thrown into it, but no rice, unless as a charm. . . . It is considered very wrong to step upon a fireplace even when there is no fire, so no one may toast his toes on a cold day within the four pieces of wood that form the square and keep the sand and ashes in place. There are fire-spirits, but no offering is made to them unless some one living in the house has painful spots at the corner of the mouth or on the lips. . . . It is not necessary to bring fire from an old home to a new one, and the first fire should never be lighted with matches, but with flint and steel or by the friction of wood."[19] Although the ancient fire-worship and sacrificial ritual have almost disappeared among the Brahmans of India, yet at Benares and other strongholds of Brahmanism a certain number who are orthodox still offer daily oblations in a sacred fire which they maintain in their own houses. Among them the sacred fire is regarded as the "brilliant guest" who lives in the midst of the family, the divine mediator who bears the savor of daily offerings toward heaven, the golden link of union between men on earth and the celestial denizens of air and sky.[20] One of the oldest and best-known folk-deities of the Chinese pantheon was the kitchen-god or "hearth-prince." He resembles Agni (Ignis) of the Aryan Vedas, god of fire, and is a messenger of heaven.[21] Among the Maori the sacred fire was the protecting power of the village home. A portion of a bird would be suspended over the sacred fire and afterward buried in the ground, where it would act as a protecting genius of the land; "by its subtle power witchcraft would be warded off and prosperity retained; the life of man was preserved by such means."[22]

To the Seri Indians, a very backward tribe, fire is a beast, not a physical phenomenon; and the production of fire is thought to be like animal reproduction.[23] In Mexican hieroglyphics the fire-drill was the symbol of fecundity,[24] and in the Nagualistic rites "it was regarded as the primal element and the immediate source of life."[25] Among some tribes of Mongols, bride and groom worship fire on their wedding-day.[26] Fire is supposed in the Zend-Avesta and the Vedas to be spread everywhere as the cause of life; while a variant of the

15 Conolly, in JAI, XXVI, 150.
16 Gardiner, in JAI, XXVII, 421.
17 Shchukin, *Shamanism* (Russ.), 33.
18 Hutton, *Sema Nagas*, 42, 43.
19 Milne, *Eastern Clan*, 46, 180.
20 Monier-Williams, *Brāhmanism*, 392, 365-366.

21 Chamberlain, in AA, X, 692.
22 Best, in AAAS, 1898, 771; Gomes, *Sea Dyaks*, 166.
23 McGee, in BAE, XVII, pt. I, 199.
24 Preuss, in *Archiv. f. Anth.*, XXIX, 150.
25 Brinton, *Nagualism*, 43.
26 Shchukin, *Shamanism* (Russ.), 31.

Romulus legend represents Romulus as born of a spark from the hearth, which was an altar.[27]

The Buryats do not like to give fire at all;[28] the White Russian peasant will not give it to anybody on a holiday—everything belongs to the spirits at the holy time—this going with the belief that it is a great sin to work on Friday.[29] In Ireland, on no account would either fire or water—but above all things a coal of fire, even for the kindling of a pipe—be given for love or money out of a house during May Day.[30] Where, as in ancient Scandinavia, land was taken possession of by fire, that could not be done by a woman. She might not handle the sacred element, but was allowed to take as much land as she could walk around in a spring day, from sunrise to sunset, leading a two-year old cow or a half-grown steer.[31] Women must not have to do with the holy things, especially at certain periods of their lives; among some Pacific coast tribes girls at puberty are kept out of the sunlight and away from the fire; it is a disgrace to parents if they see fire or the sun.[32]

§96. Artificial Selection.

GALTON'S[1] specifications regarding qualities in animals conducive to domestication repay criticism. He states: "1. they should be hardy; 2. they should have an inborn liking for man; 3. they should be comfort-loving; 4. they should be found useful to the savages; 5. they should breed freely; 6. they should be easy to tend." Several of these items are accepted in the text, as corresponding to Darwin's specifications, and need not be discussed.

Consider, however, the statement that the animal suitable for domestication must be hardy, so that it may thrive if neglected. This condition seems to us superfluous. If an animal will not thrive under neglect, how was it getting on before it received any attention at all? The very object of domestication soon comes to be the protection of a plant or animal against the competition existing in nature and which, up to the time of domestication, it had to meet for itself. It would be difficult to imagine an animal that was not hardy at the time of its first domestication.

Galton's second condition is unquestionably well taken if it means a relatively friendly disposition, and the illustrations are convincing. "The young bison will try to dash out its brains against the tree to which it is tied, in terror and hatred of its captors." Instances might be found to contravert any specific example;[2] but yet there must be recognized, in animals, a variation of disposition as well as corporeal variation, and a selection under nature of such dispositional variations. Otherwise we could not explain the craftiness of the fox, the blind fury of the rhinoceros, or the industry of the beaver. It can scarcely be believed, however, that any animals really cherished a "fondness for man" prior to domestication. They felt toward him as toward other competitors. The nature of the struggle for existence pursued by the several animals

27 Pater, *Marius the Epicurean*, 12; Haug, *Parsis*, 155; Jackson, *Zoroaster*, 61; Justi, *Persien*, 76; Schrader, *Keilinschriften*, 418, 419.
28 Bastian, *Bilder*, 400.
29 *Russian Ethnog.* (Russ.), I, 103.
30 Gomme, *Village Life*, 98.
31 *Landnamabok*, IV, 10.

32 Bancroft, *Nat. Races*, III, 152; I, 197.
1 *Human Faculty*, 261 ff.
2 For instance, as regards the bison, see Hornaday, in *Smithson. Rep.*, 1887, pt. II, 454 ff.; "Buffalo" Jones, "The 400 of the Plains," in the *Illustrated American*, Mar. 23, 1895, 374-376.

which were later to be domesticated may have rendered them less savage or timorous than other animals were; but to compare the dog with the ox or sheep, as Galton does, or to ask, after instancing man's power over the dog in consequence of which a smile or a frown may inspire calmness or fear, "Who, for instance, ever succeeded in frowning away a mosquito, or in pacifying an angry wasp by a smile?" seems to us irrelevant. Long ages of domestication and selection have bred into the dog a disposition which cannot justly be compared with that of animals domesticated much later, or not at all. It is the negative quality of less timorousness rather than the positive one of fondness for man which was doubtless often determinative at the beginning.

These qualities are all of a piece: "desire for comfort" means to us nothing more than unconscious recognition of alleviation of the struggle for existence, as assured under domestication. Man surrounds domestic animals and plants with an artificialized environment affording protection against hardships and, in particular, against competition. He plucks out of the garden-bed all such hardy competitors as he is pleased to call "weeds." It seems certain that animals differ in their disposition to take advantage of this easement in living. Bees will use wax provided for them and thus economize on effort to make their own. In general, it would seem that the more highly organized animals tend to fall into this line of less resistance, while lower forms of life submit themselves in few respects to the human régime, however much it would guarantee them of safety and comfort. The matter seems to be one of power of adaptation; if the demands of adjustment to man's presence and control outweigh those of the struggle for existence in the open, the "desire for comfort" does not appear, whereas if the line of least resistance lies in submission, the animal in question may be said to be "comfort-loving." And the comfort-loving ones were not killed off like the recalcitrant, and so had a chance to pass on their complaisant disposition.

It must not be forgotten that during the earlier stages of domestication captivity was enforced, so that the animals had time to adapt themselves to the new order, if they could, just as they would have had time to adjust to some hypothetical necessity of wild life—such as, for example, living in an enclosed valley after falling over a cliff. Hence we regard Galton's second and third conditions as phases of adaptability. And the last condition, that animals should be easy to tend, falls under the same category—the adaptability of the animal to a régime agreeable to man.[3]

§98. Pastoral Society.

How cattle take hold of the imagination of people and influence the entire societal structure is best illustrated among the Africans. The fruits of the field are never anywhere in Africa beloved to such an extent as cattle. Although the Zulus plant and cultivate grain, their chief business is herding; they ride on cattle and even race with them, make them carry burdens, use the milk as daily food and the meat on great occasions, consider the fat the greatest luxury, also grease themselves with it, and make cloaks, shields, and straps of the hides. The herds are their capital, their pride, and their luxury, while the fields serve their necessities. He who has no cattle is a proletarian, no matter how

3 For examples of primitive methods of taming wild animals, see Lippert, *Kgchte.*, II, 486; Roth, in BAE, XXXVIII, 551, 555; Grinnell, *Cheyenne*, I, 55.

much corn he has, for only by means of cattle can he buy things beyond the first necessity. With cattle alone can he buy a wife or make the sacrifices by which diseases are healed and funerals celebrated. The king is the administrator of the national stock, consisting of these herds, and considers the keeping of cattle as a noble sport; every morning the state of the herds is reported to him and he reviews them. Plundering expeditions are made to get more. The Bechuana, who have done something in the way of developing varieties of cattle, are extremely fond of them, play with them, and ornament them. The men who hate every other kind of work are good herdsmen. The chief is buried in his cattle-yard, and the herd is driven over his grave. Since possession of cattle is the source of power of both Bechuana and Zulu chiefs, the acquisition of herds by the common people, through wages earned among the whites, has tended to lessen their influence. Among the Damara, children form little herds and flocks from the animals given to them by relatives, which property grows as they themselves grow. The family is indissolubly connected with the herd; if a man dies and leaves a widow with infant children, the next powerful man in the relationship inherits the entire family in the Roman sense; he steps into the place of the deceased in every respect. Like the Herero, the Damara live entirely upon cattle, which form the chief topic of conversation; men of the highest rank consider it an honor to tend cattle.[1]

Among the Bechuana of South Africa cattle have the nature of totem-animals and form a central point in the religious life of the natives. The cattle-kraal is in close connection with the place of public assembly, where the public business of the tribe is transacted and all the religious rites are held. At the time of a great drought and after all other rituals had failed, there was still another that could be depended upon—a ritual too sacred to be used except in an emergency—the sacrifice of an ox on the grave of a chief. Nor is this the only occasion which needs the sacrifice of an ox; there is an elaborate ritual at the founding of a new town, in preparing an army for battle, in the purification of warriors, and in other ceremonies, in which the ox takes a conspicuous part. The warrior to be purified is smeared by the medicine-man with the contents of the stomach of an ox, into which certain powdered roots have been mixed; and while the thought of such a thing is repulsive to us, the native looks at it in a very different light; indeed, it is a common thing for the men to wash their hands and occasionally their faces with cow-dung, a practice which the recently initiated boys lose no opportunity in imitating, for it is a sign of manhood. The marriage-settlement, which the bridegroom's father hands over to the custody of the bride's family, consists exclusively of cattle, while during the marriage ceremony the sheet of fat that is around the entrails of the ox is rubbed with appropriate "medicine" and laid on the bride's shoulders. At death, the correct thing is to tie up the corpse in an ox-skin. Then, before burial, an ox-bone is held toward the dead man, and then is placed at his head in the grave; a milking-thong, a nose-cord of an ox, and a milk-bowl are shown to the deceased in the same way. After this the peculiar whistle of the herd-boy is imitated, finally some dry cow-dung is thrown into the grave, and the deceased is on his way to the happy herding-grounds. Cattle, in short, take the central place in all the ritual of the greater ceremonies, which Willoughby,[2] who reports all this, believes can be explained only by assuming that the ritual

---

1 Ratzel, *Vkde.*, I, 58, 251, 293, 207, 335, 333; Büttner, *Walfischbai*, 228 ff.

2 In JAI, XXXV, 301, 302-303, 303-305, 306, 307, 308, 310-311, 314.

came from a far-distant past when the ox was the totem of the people. If this is so, it is not hard to feel the significance of the Bechuana saying, "The person who has no cattle is nothing at all of a person," or the custom of greeting a chief as "master of cattle" or "one who came forth from cattle." "It is not only that the cattle are the chief wealth of the people, though that counts for much, but it is that they were the clan-god of their fathers."

To a Mkamba, "his greatest pride and joy are his cattle, nothing else has the same value in his eyes; I fear even a wife is a second consideration to these, for after all she is only valued as a portion of the herd." To part with a cow, excepting for the purchase of a wife, is too painful to be considered. Dundas[3] continues: "I shall never forget the horror displayed by a native who complained that he was starving, when I suggested that he should slaughter a cow; such a thing is inconceivable to the Mkamba; bulls may on occasion be sacrificed, but cows never; neither will he ever think of selling a cow, even if he is on the verge of starvation. The manner in which a Mkamba regards his cattle is thus more in the light of family heirlooms; they also tell the position of the family and are a record of its past. It is conceivable, then, what a calamity cattle disease is to them. I know an old man whose cattle were dying of disease, and the sight was so heartrending to him that he could not stand it and went to stay elsewhere until the calamity should be past." The chief occupation of the Bahima is herding cattle; "they form warm attachments for the animals, some of them they love like children, pet and talk to them, coax them, and weep over their ailments; should a favourite die their grief is extreme, and cases are not unknown in which men have committed suicide on the loss of a favourite animal." Time of day among these people is reckoned in terms of cattle; for example, 6 A.M. is milking-time, 1 P.M. the time to draw water for cattle. As in so many other instances, women are not permitted to tend the stock.[4]

The Dinka and Bari are as passionate herdsmen as the South Africans. "The possession of cattle is the great ambition, and the tending of them the chief occupation of the Dinka. . . . Nothing confers such prestige and position as the possession of large herds, and the authority of a Beng (Sheik) who loses his cattle is usually impaired." The Dinkas consider milk to be the best of all foods, and drink very largely of it. They also use the urine of cattle for washing themselves, and smear their bodies with the ash of burnt dung. Cattle are currency in any transaction, as for instance the purchase of a wife or the payment of reparation for an injury. "In the absence of money, cattle may be regarded as the 'root of all evil' in the Dinka country. Every raid has for its object the acquisition of stock, and for its justification, the story of some former raid by the enemy upon the intending raiders. Every quarrel and dispute is nearly or remotely traceable to the same origin, and if the proverb *Cherchez la femme* applies, the woman is only reckoned in terms of cattle. . . . If, however, the vices of the Dinkas are derived from their greed of cattle, they owe their virtues also to the same source. With them this passion seems to replace, in some measure, the ideals and aspirations to which the European has recourse as foils to the materialism of life." The Dinka displays reckless gallantry in attempts to rescue or defend his herds, while as a cattle-master he exhibits a gentleness and kindness foreign to him in other respects. "In

---

3 In JAI, XLIII, 501-502; Hobley, in   4 Roscoe, in JAI, XXXVII, 94-96, 114, 100.
JAI, XLI, 424.

the tending of cattle he never tires. Such labour is to him a labour of love. To feast his eyes on fat kine, feel their sleek coats, drink of their milk, and adorn himself with the ashes of their dung, no Dinka would ask a happier life. His songs, his stories, his rude modelling in clay, and, in fact, all his progressions in the direction of art, are inspired by his one absorbing interest—cattle."[5] High consideration for cattle, though lacking the picturesqueness of the Dinkas, is found among the Masai, Somals, and other tribes of northeast Africa.[6]

The Kirghis of the Russian steppes live entirely by their herds, and this governs all the details of their lives.[7] The Todas of India have the highest possible regard—amounting almost to reverence—for the cow. The milking and churning operations of the dairy form the basis of the greater part of their religious ritual. "The lives of the people are largely devoted to their buffaloes, and the care of certain of these animals, regarded as more sacred than the rest, is associated with much ceremonial. The sacred animals are attended by men especially set apart who form the Toda priesthood, and the milk of the sacred animals is churned in dairies which may be regarded as the Toda temples and are so regarded by the people themselves. The ordinary operations of the dairy have become a religious ritual and ceremonies of a religious character accompany nearly every important incident in the lives of the buffaloes. . . . At the present time the buffaloes are tended entirely by males, and males only are allowed to take any part either in the work of the dairy or in those dairy operations which are performed in the house."[8]

The Indo-European was a cattle-breeder; his herds were his wealth, the object for which he fought, and the source of his food and clothing.[9] In the *Iliad* pastoral nomads are called the most righteous of men.[10] Not only was the value of the full grown cow in gold the Greek standard, but it was also that of the ancient Egyptians, whose oldest gold unit is termed "ox-gold," and so also was it over all Asia and Europe. "Investigation showed that the value in gold of a full grown cow during a period of one thousand years from India to Ireland only varied from 140 to 120 troy grains of gold. This has for us a peculiar significance since our own gold unit, the sovereign, weighs 120¼ grains. It is really descended from the ancient gold unit based upon the cow, the primitive chief unit amongst all cattle-keeping communities in all periods of the world."[11]

§99. The Dog.

As was stated in the text, one must confine himself to generalities respecting the societal effects of animal-fetishism unless he cares to enter into lengthy detail in the effort to exhaust the subject. Such cannot be the object in a general treatise on the science of society.[1] Hence, in conformity with our method of selection of types, we shall seek to indicate the concrete background to a

5 Cummins, in JAI, XXXIV, 154-155; Ratzel, *Vkde.*, I, 510.

6 Barton, in JAI, LIII, 42, 45; Paulitschke, *Nordost-Afr.*, II, 100; Murray, in JAI, LIII, 420.

7 *Russ. Ethnog.* (Russ.), II, 149.

8 Rivers, *Todas*, 38, 49; Reclus, *Prim. Folk*, 217.

9 Tacitus, *Germ.*, ch. V; Schrader, *Aryans*, 259.

10 Homer, *Iliad*, XIII, 3.

11 Ridgeway, in JAI, XXXIX, 13-14.

1 Lippert, in his *Kulturgeschichte* (I, 478 ff.; II, 390 ff.), presents considerable detail illustrative of the topic before us.

number of the positions taken, by rehearsing in its salient aspects the history of what was in all probability the first domesticated animal, the dog.

Protracted selection has much transformed this animal once appropriated in the form of several wild species.[2] Weismann[3] distinguishes seven main breeds of dog, with numerous sub-breeds; forty-eight sub-breeds are guardians of the house; thirty have silk-like hair; there are twelve of terriers, thirty-five of sporting-dogs (ranging from the deerhound to the pointer), nineteen of bulldogs, thirty-five of greyhounds, six of naked or hairless dogs. Many of these could not have survived had they existed in nature. The range of the domesticated dog in space and time, which is very great, supports the preceding evidence that he has been long under domestication; for he was unquestionably taken to all corners of the earth by man. His bones are found with those of prehistoric man,[4] and but few aboriginal peoples have not possessed him. Yet there are a number of cases which reveal the animal but partially tamed.

The Australian dingo would not sleep or take shelter under the roof of his master; in watching he was vigilant and fierce, and would fly at the throats of visitors. He was trained to hunt, which was his principal use.[5] In Homer[6] we read of a breed of large, fierce dogs which were like wild beasts and would tear a stranger to pieces; the shepherd himself carried a spear, "a defender from dogs and men," and kept them off a stranger only by stoning them. It is noteworthy that these half-wild animals, in addition to their other wolf-like characteristics, do not bark but howl, thus exhibiting again the marks of their origin; the Indians showed great fear of the Spanish bloodhounds, especially when they bayed.[7] The wildness of the strain is kept up, in the case of some Indian dogs, by frequent interminglings with wolves.[8]

The treatment which dogs receive tends, in some cases, to keep them in a savage state. The Greenlanders handle their sledge-dogs in barbarous manner, cutting them up with their heavy whips and feeding them poorly; of the East Greenlanders, we read: "In summer, when they have no use for dogs, they leave them on a little desert island, whence one can hear at a very great distance their piercing howls."[9] Among the Indians they "are worked very hard, have hard blows and hard fare; in fact, they are treated just as this fine animal is treated among the Esquimaux."[10] Contrasts of course occur: the Canoeiros Indian women of Brazil even gave the breast to young dogs, which were often granted preference to children in the matter of food and drink; while the Guiana women suckled dogs and other young mammals as they would their own children.[11]

Speculation as to how the dog was brought into a status of even semi-domestication is probably fruitless; Lippert's[12] conjecture that he probably followed the hunter to get the refuse of the game, and that thus man became

2 Darwin, *Orig. of Species*, ch. I.
3 *Evol. Theory*, I, 32.
4 Ranke, *Mensch*, II, 456.
5 Dawson, *Aust. Aborig.*, 89.
6 *Odyssey*, XIV, 29-38; Keller, *Hom. Soc.*, 38.
7 Lichtenstein, *S. Afr.*, II, 272; Strong, in JAI, XLIX, 300; Roth, in BAE, XXXVIII, 552; Friederici, in *Globus*, LXXVI, 361; Von

Martius, *Beiträge*, I, 460, 672, 673; Kerr, *Gen. Hist. of Voyages*, III, 62.
8 McGee, in BAE, XV, 203; Allison, in JAI, XXI, 307.
9 Holm, *Ethnol. Skizze*, 31.
10 McGee, in BAE, XV, 345.
11 Von Martius, *Beiträge*, I, 261, note; Roth, in BAE, XXXVIII, 551.
12 *Kgchte.*, I, 491.

acquainted with him and cultivated his society, seems as satisfactory as any other.

Utilities of the dog. One eminent anthropologist[13] considers it "most probable that the dog was long the only domesticated animal"; and he enumerates the uses to which the dog was put as follows: "The Esquimaux forced him to draw the sledge; the Chinook kept him for the sake of his wool; the South Sea Islanders, having no game, bred the dog for food; the Chonos Indians taught him to fish." His utility has run all the way from the slightest to the greatest—to several Arctic peoples his presence is almost a condition of human existence. For a short time, and if the cold is not too intense, the dogs of the Hyperboreans will cover sixty to ninety miles in a day, while those of Kamtchatka will draw three persons and their baggage about twenty-five miles a day on bad roads and over fifty on good ones.[14] What Arctic exploration has owed to the dog is well known.[15] The service of the dog as a draught-animal elsewhere than in the Arctic regions is sometimes overlooked; the gesture for "dog" in the Indian sign-language—two fingers extended and drawn along a surface—indicates the traditional utility of this animal among them.[16]

Dog-Eating. The various utilities of the dog do not call for rehearsal; it is to his most primitive and therefore unfamiliar service that a word should be given. It has been stated in the text that the primary incentive to the domestication of both plants and animals lay in the food-interest; animals that have ceased, in some cases altogether, in others locally, to afford food to man, were unquestionably at one time of great importance in just this particular. It is not difficult to believe that early man was practically omnivorous; and ethnographic instances and survivals preserved in the cult unite to support such a conviction. The case of the dog is in point.

The Nicobarese have practised the eating of dog's flesh from remote times.[17] In Korea, dog-flesh is in much demand at certain seasons and dogs are extensively bred for the table;[18] it is no uncommon event in China to see such meat displayed in the market. Among some tribes of northern Peru, dog-flesh passed for the greatest delicacy.[19] Among the Dakotas, "*shun-ka*, or dog, cannot be called a domestic dish; it is only eaten in cases of dire necessity, and is considered too delicate for ordinary consumption. It is usually eaten at a special feast in honor of warriors of renown, to whom, as the highest courtesy, the head is given."[20] This and the following cases reveal a special significance, of a magical or religious order, attached to the eating of the dog. Among certain Central Africans dog's flesh is much prized, but women are forbidden to eat it. After such a meal a bath must be taken before returning to the house; and the husband must not touch his wife, even with his finger, for a day thereafter.[21] Some tribes of Nagas, instead of burying his dog with the deceased, cut up the dog and distribute its flesh to all guests at the funeral

---

13 Lubbock, *Prehist. Times*, 586, 558.
14 Ratzel, *Vkde.*, II, 745; *Russian Ethnog.* (Russ.), II, 562.
15 Captain T. F. Hall (*Has the North Pole Been Discovered?* chs. II, III, and *passim*) collates the records of dog-teams employed by Peary and others.
16 Tylor, *Anth.*, 118.

17 Man, in JAI, XVIII, 369.
18 Bishop, *Korea*, 154.
19 Cunow, *Verf. d. Inkareichs*, 88.
20 Beckwith, in *Smithson. Rep.*, 1886, pt. I, 255; Donaldson, in *Smithson. Rep.*, 1885, pt. II, 341.
21 Brunache, *Cent. Afr.*, 69.

who are not of the same clan as the dead man.[22] An ancient Irish hero is represented as having lost power and life because he had eaten of dog's flesh against a Druid's command.[23]

In one of the dancing-ceremonies of the Haida, the performer would snatch up the first dog he could find, kill it, and tearing pieces of its flesh, eat them.[24] We are plainly told that the Sioux ate "ceremonially" the dogs which they kept for their flesh; and the inference is that dog-eating had become for them a thing of the past retained as a cult-survival.[25] In the Sioux sun-dance stewed puppy was eaten together with wild turnips—with which practice may be compared the eating of boiled puppy in ancient Rome, which was done at intervals by the highest civil and ecclesiastical dignitaries.[26] In any case the dog was often the animal of sacrifice, from which it may be inferred that he was formerly eaten. One case of sickness is recorded in which three dogs were hung to the door of the house as an offering for recovery.[27] One of the most important religious festivals of the Iroquois was the cremation of the white dog, whose soul was employed as a sort of messenger to the Great Spirit. This dog must be healthy, and without blemish, and snow-white. It was strangled in such manner as not to spill any blood nor break any bone, decorated in a certain manner, and hung in the fork of a pole for a certain time prior to the solemn sacrifice.[28] "The missionary Kirkland witnessed among the Seneca a ceremony lasting seven days, in which two white dogs were strangled, painted, decorated, and hung up in the center of the village on the evening preceding the beginning of the rites; and after the performances had lasted several days, the dogs were taken down and placed on a pyre, and when nearly consumed one was removed and placed in a kettle with vegetables and eaten. This shows that as late as 1760 the flesh of the victim was ceremonially eaten among the Iroquois."[29] This instance falls into line with those of the Apis-bull and the white elephant and opens the topic of the dog as a fetish.

The Dog-Fetish. That the half-wild dogs not infrequently "buried" the dead by devouring their bodies is a fact of ethnography and history. But, under such conditions, the dog was well-started on his fetish career.[30] There is also that about the actions of the dog which would have caught the attention of minds saturated with the ghost-theory—all the more so since the dog was, in all probability, the first domestic animal, and so the first beast to which consistent, intimate attention was given. His alertness and ability to scent danger where even the sharpened senses of the savage perceived none; his tendency to growl at or challenge unseen things at night, to "bay the moon"— these were characteristics which led primitive man to assign him a sort of second-sight. And so the belief grew that the dog could see spirits where men could not; and that he did not fear them—for did he not snatch at the leavings of meals, so often sacred to the ghosts, and worry them out of the very clutches of the dread beneficiaries? The spirits, at any rate, were believed to be frightened away by his snarling. Like fire and water,[31] the dog came thus

22 Hutton, *Sema Nagas*, 246.
23 Von Pflugk-Harttung, in *Trans. Roy. Hist. Soc.*, VII, 70.
24 Dall, in BAE, III, 110.
25 McGee, in BAE, XV, 170.
26 Bourke, in BAE, IX, 519.
27 Swanton, in HAI, II, 405.

28 Morgan, *League of Iroq.*, 207-222; Hale, in *Amer. Antiquarian and Oriental Jour.*, VII, 7-12; Movers, *Phoen.*, I, 405 ff.; Hewitt, in HAI, II, 939-944.
29 Hewitt, in HAI, II, 940.
30 §§247, 248, 256, of text.
31 §276 of text.

to be a protector against the assaults of the unseen world—a restrainer of spirits.

First, as to the power of seeing spirits: Hindu villagers believe that dogs perceive spirits and by their barking or moaning warn their masters while passing at night from one village to another.[32] The Nagas believe "the spirits of the dead are not visible to human eyes; but dogs can see them, and if a dog howls or barks when no stranger is near, they believe that the souls of the dead are hovering about."[33] The dog, in Homer, saw spirits when men could not see them, or could see them only with divine aid. When Athena came into the courtyard of Odysseus, only he to whom she revealed herself, and the dogs, saw her; and the dogs did not howl, but whined and fled.[34] The Cheyenne Indians believe that dogs are the first to become aware of ghosts.[35] According to certain folktales, and, indeed, popular superstition, the nocturnal howling of the dog betokens a visitation of death in or from the indicated direction; that is, the dog sees the approach of the death-dealing spirit.[36] According to the Araucanians, "when a dog bayed by night, it was a demon prowling round, on the look-out to occupy somebody whose owner . . . was away, that is dreaming; and those that heard it woke their companions, to avoid such a misfortune."[37] Says the dog in the Indian legend: "I will be her dog and see that no disease approaches her. If an invisible spirit approaches, I will bark."[38] Moslem tradition urges the believer: "When at night ye hear a dog bark or an ass bray, then flee before Satan to God, for they have seen the invisible."[39] They have seen "the invisible": but to the primitive there is but one category to cover all invisible forces—the ghosts and spirits.

Strikingly enough, the dog is found in several cases to be the agency that both protects the ghosts and keeps them from issuing out of the spirit-world. In the New Hebrides the ghost of a dog can scare away the ferocious spirit of the lower world, Sara;[40] while in the Solomon Islands it is believed that dogs help men against the terrible snake-spirits.[41] The Greenlanders bury a dog's head with a child "so that that wise animal may show the little uninstructed soul the way to the happy land."[42] Then, again, the watch-dogs of the spirit-world must be considered and given a "sop": twelve cakes are taken by the soul to pacify the twelve dogs of hell.[43] At the entrance to the underworld, think some Siberian aborigines, are found dogs as guardians, and "a person who used to beat his dog during his life on earth will be stopped by them, though, in order to propitiate the guardians, he can carry in his mittens the fins of fishes, of which they are very fond." One of these tribes, the Gilyak, believe that besides his principal soul or souls each man has a lesser soul which continues to live for some time in the best-beloved dog of the deceased, which is especially cherished and cared for.[44] Among the Sema Nagas, "a favourite dog is usually killed when its owner dies. It is killed just as its body is lowered into the grave that its soul may accompany his. In the case of a

32 Sukthankar, in JASB, I, 370.
33 Furness, in JAI, XXXII, 463.
34 To readers of Greek this passage (Homer, Odyssey, XVI, 159-163) will be seen to lay significant linguistic and metric emphasis upon the normality of such powers in the dog. Keller, Hom. Soc., 169 and note 5.
35 Grinnell, Cheyenne, II, 101, 102.
36 Lippert, Kgchte., I, 492.

37 Latcham, in JAI, XXXIX, 350.
38 Boas, in USNM, 1895, 402.
39 Hammer-Purgstall, Geisterlehre, 25.
40 Macdonald, in AAAS, 1892, 728.
41 Fox and Drew, in JAI, XLV, 150.
42 Fries, Grönland, 121.
43 Rehatsek, in JASB, I, 306.
44 Czaplicka, Aborig. Siberia, 150 (quoted), 273.

man who has killed a tiger, leopard, or bear, such action is necessary, and if he possesses no dog at the time of his death, a dog is bought for the purpose in order that its soul may go with that of the dead man and guard him on his way to the village of the dead from the attacks of the beasts he has killed and whose souls are lying in wait for his."[45] The way to the world of the dead was thought by the Vedic Indians to be guarded by two dogs.[46] Among the Dyaks "the narrow road to Elysium is guarded by a ferocious double-headed dog . . . to whom it is necessary to present a valuable bead."[47] The dog was already the animal of the dead among the Mexican Indians; when the ancient inhabitants of Anahuac burned a corpse they killed a red dog and laid it beside the dead body. They thought that four years after death this dog had to carry the soul over the "ninefold stream" that flows around the innermost hell, the final abode of the dead.[48] The Tlinkit never took dead bodies through the door, but through a hole made in the side of the house or through the aperture in the roof, and a dog was taken along with the corpse. "If the dog were not taken they believed that some one of the family would surely die, but if the spirit of the deceased entered the dog it would not return to the injury of any member of the household."[49] In these views we see a strange parallel to the Greek conception of Cerberus who restrains the spirits once across the stream from the possibility of return. Rationalization of such cases leads to the theory that the dog is needed by the soul of the "just" man as a protector in order to make a safe crossing into the spirit-world, just as he is needed by the living man under many sets of circumstances.[50]

The Dog in Religion. The dog keeps off the ghosts from living man and so preserves him. Hence the Persian conviction that it is through the understanding of the dog that the world persists. "When the dog, together with the cock, strive against Darudji—the evil Ahriman-spirit—they take away the strength from him who otherwise would cause pain to men and cattle. And so the saying goes that through him (the dog) are all enemies of the good man overcome. His voice destroys the evil." So valuable an ally in the struggle man must meet receives the best of care; we see "the old cult-significance of the matter in that the care of the dog is set on a par with the guarding of the holy fire."[51] In D'Entrecasteaux there is a myth concerning the acquisition of fire, in which the dog is effective.[52] The idea is now not so far off that the dog himself, or at least some peculiarly marked animal—a "white dog"—is a spirit. Among the old clans in Manipur eclipses are generally ascribed to the sun and the moon being either caught by, or hiding from, Pathian's dog, which was set on them, because they stole his master's tobacco, or scattered his rice.[53] "Among the primitive Guarani heathens [of South America] an eclipse was called *yagua,* meaning dog in their tongue, from their fable that a great dog roamed about among the stars and now and again tried to swallow the sun or moon." One who predicted eclipses was called "friend of the dog."[54] A war god in a number of Samoan villages is incarnate in a dog—a white one usually. "When he wagged his tail, barked, and dashed ahead in sight of the

45 Hutton, *Sema Nagas,* 71.
46 Schrader, *Aryans,* 422.
47 Roth, *Sarawak,* I, 140.
48 Beyer, in AA, X, 419.
49 Jones, *Thlingets,* 151.
50 Lippert, *Kgchte.,* I, 499.

51 Lippert, *Kgchte.,* I, 497 (quoting from the *Vendidad*); II, 392.
52 Jenness and Ballentyne, *D'Entrecasteaux,* 156-157.
53 Shakespear, in JAI, XXXIX, 385.
54 White, *El Supremo,* 98.

troops of the enemy, it was a good sign; but to retreat or howl was a bad omen."[55] There are some American Indian tales of people being descended from dogs.[56]

In Persia there was a dog-cult. It succumbed to the fire-cult and the religious significance of the dog dropped away, leaving, however, many a survival in custom to explain. The original and evolutionary relation having now lapsed into oblivion, there is developed a rationalization of the facts which not seldom bears but a grotesque likeness to the historical actuality: for example, that the dog is well treated because if he is beaten, the evil deeds of wolves and robbers increase; or, as a still more rationalized version, that the dog is honored because his hide was the first clothing of man.[57] Similarly in Egypt the dog was a fetish, and was mummified. The god Anubis bore the head of a dog and the Romans called him the Latrator (barking) Anubis; he was the "protector of graves." In Homer,[58] Scylla is referred to as "barking Scylla"—a sort of personification of threatening calamity. In both Persia and Egypt the religious respect accorded the dog demanded a corresponding treatment and implied a peculiar form of domestication. Later the religious character wears away into symbolism. Homeric royalty was generally attended by white dogs, which were, like the scepter, a sort of symbol of authority.[59]

§102. Slavery and Herding.

In parts of Africa, slave-hunts are chiefly for wives, and a slave is not of himself valuable, unless there is a sufficient demand for labor. In the tales of some of the Siberians there is mention of the capture of numbers of herdsmen along with the herds taken in war. These herdsmen were enslaved, being particularly valuable in that "they knew their own herds better than the victors!" By the Chukchee, "captive women were hard-worked, and were made the wives of their masters. Sometimes they were sold from one camp to another; but, on the whole, their position was little different from that of the Chukchee women."[1] Rockhill[2] does not believe that slavery exists in the greater part of Tibet, and certainly not among the pastoral tribes, beyond a mild form of domestic serfdom; yet in some of the outlying districts where there is a large non-Tibetan population, regular slavery prevails. The herding nomads of East Africa cannot use slaves, who would merely increase their numbers, and they therefore make war to steal cattle only. Negro herdsmen whose herds have a certain size can feed and use no more slaves and so kill their captives; but others can use slaves and do not kill prisoners. Peoples who have a good market, on account of their connection with the Arabs on the coast, carry on war to win slaves whom they sell, for the most part, to the coast people.[3] Here the slave has become a ware in commerce, this carrying us beyond the stages of extractive industry, but illustrating how the development of civilization alters the conditions and form of slavery. These run parallel with the several phases of the industrial organization; thus, the later-developed cotton-

55 Turner, *Samoa*, 49.
56 HAI, I, 14; pt. II, 744. The dog-motive is found in Bornean art; Haddon, in JAI, XXXV, 113.
57 Lippert, *Kgchte.*, I, 498-500.
58 *Odyssey*, XII, 85, 122 ff., 245 ff.

59 Keller, *Hom. Soc.*, 38; Lippert, *Kgchte.*, I, 502; Maspero, *Hist. Anc.*, I, 588; Lehmann, *Overtro*, I, 63.
1 Czaplicka, *Aborig. Siberia*, 27; *Russian Ethnog.* (Russ.), II, 492.
2 In USNM, 1893, 680.
3 Ratzel, *Vkde.*, I, 554, 449, 83.

industry and the invention of the gin determined them in America and else-where.[4]

A few miscellaneous cases, varying about the normal, may fill in the outlines of pastoral slavery. Among the Bechuanas live a group of Bushmen whose status is not well defined and who seem to receive no remuneration for their service in tending the former's flocks and herds.[5] "Since the Matabele devote themselves entirely to war, do not carry on any agriculture or handicraft, do not make their own assegais, do not even chop their own wood, they need a number of slaves."[6] Again, "because there is little scope for slave-labor under the exploitation of female labor-force and in the presence of the pariahs, the slave-trade is but insignificant" among the tribes in the eastern horn of Africa. Suahili slaves are acquired and set to work in the towns, but they are of no use to the nomadic cattle-peoples. We may note, by way of anticipation, that the presence of agriculture has immediate results on slavery. Even among prevailingly pastoral tribes, to whom slaves are of little use, "there is an exception in the case of tillers . . . who have their farm-land attended to by slaves."[7] In each district of the herding Bahima are settlements of slaves who are agriculturists; "the chiefs and various clans claim from them servants of both sexes to do their menial work, and men for building the more per-manent kraals, and for carrying the baggage from place to place, when they move to new pasturage."[8] Until the tribes have advanced beyond the strictly pastoral economy there is small utility in slavery. A few examples of the servitude of group to group are found among the negroes, Arabs, and others;[9] while Justi[10] mentions certain agricultural Scythians who were held as slaves by other Scythians for the sake of having the land cultivated. "The Germans who, according to the description of Cæsar,[11] confirmed by Tacitus, concerned themselves little with agriculture but passed their whole lives in the hunt or in warlike exercises, laid the weight of tillage upon the dependent classes."

§104. Slavery as an Adjustment.

SLAVERY prevailed everywhere in Melanesia, says Ratzel,[1] originating either in war or debt; sometimes it was hard, sometimes not. Yet in his book on the Melanesians, Codrington[2] affirms "there is no such thing as slavery properly so called. In headhunting expeditions prisoners are made for the sake of their heads, to be used when occasion requires, and such persons live with their captors in a condition very different from that of freedom, but they are not taken or maintained for the purpose of slaves." The fact seems to be that slavery is not a developed institution in this region, but exists sporadically in connection with certain religious and even cannibalistic practices. In San Cristoval of the Solomon group, beside children who are bought, there are "real slaves, people guilty of serious offences who are sold away to places at a distance, and people captured in war. Such slaves were kindly treated, but could be killed if a human sacrifice were needed in building a new house,

4 Grant, Memoirs, I, 225.
5 Dornan, in JAI, XLVII, 38-39.
6 Müller, Land u. Leute, 117.
7 Paulitschke, Nordost-Afr., I, 260.
8 Roscoe, in JAI, XXXVII, 98.
9 Sumner, Folkways, §272; Lippert, Kgchte., II, 539; Wellhausen, Arabern, 464.

10 Persien, 97.
11 Bel. Gall., VI, 29, 21, 35; Kowalewsky, Ök. Entw., I, 51, 74.
1 Ratzel, Vkde., II, 279.
2 Melanesians, 346.

launching a new canoe, or at the death of a chief."[3] Slaves in New Georgia are
kept chiefly for their heads, which are taken suddenly and unexpectedly, when
occasion calls for them, the victim first being killed by a tomahawk from an
ambush. He has no warning, which is merciful. Aside from this hazard, conditions are so mild that it is scarcely possible to distinguish master from man.[4]
In Fiji "there used to be slaves, treated, often eaten, like beasts kept for
labor and butcher's meat";[5] while among the cannibals of New Britain "one
may find even to-day [written in 1898] chiefs who keep slaves for the purpose
of food, and who are in the habit of killing them every few days to satisfy their
diabolical tastes."[6] Conditions among the eastern blacks are so primitive and
the self-maintenance organization so undeveloped that slavery as an institution
can hardly be said to exist. When we turn our attention to the western blacks
we find a totally different situation.

The Africans have enslaved and been enslaved since time immemorial. Slavery
still exists in some sections; Junker[7] says the negro does not understand new
laws like the one to abolish house-slavery. In some respects, as in transportation, slavery is a necessary adjustment. "Africa is covered with a network of
roads of a kind—native paths, leading from village to village, formed by the
naked feet of many generations of villagers, but only broad enough to admit
of a single file. Beasts of burden are of course scarcely possible on such tracks,
and as a matter of fact, over the great part of Africa the native himself is
the only beast of burden."[8] In the far interior pack-animals can be employed,
but they cannot traverse belts infested by the tsetse fly or survive in the coast
regions and were unknown in Uganda and Nyasaland. These conditions favor
slavery on the one hand and, on the other, retard the development of commerce.[9] War also has been an important factor in accounting for African
slavery, along with the organized slave trade that was developed under European and Mohammedan influence.

Slavery has helped to keep the Kaffir tribes in perpetual unrest and barbarism
by destroying the germs of civilization and preventing its growth.[10] Among
the Nama, the Bechuana, and others are found despised groups like the Hill-
Damara and Bushmen who are virtually slaves and receive bad treatment; but
the real bondsmen are those who have been taken prisoner in war or forced
into serfdom through poverty. The Nama women mistreat the slaves, though
this is not usual in South Africa, where the women are themselves reckoned
among the servants. To treat a slave brutally or even to kill him is not a
punishable offense.[11] Among the Wachagga there are two kinds of slaves: the
house slaves and those of the chief, the first being women and children taken in
raids and belonging to the warriors and counselors as their share of the booty,
and the others being such natives as have fallen into debt and been sold to the
chief as field-workers, or minors who have committed an offense for which
their relatives have not paid compensation. Both kinds of slaves, who may not
be sold over again, can regain their freedom—the children when they become
of age and when they have worked off the value of the goods stolen or de-

3 Fox, in JAI, XLIX, 123; Williamson,
Cent. Polyn., II, 392; Weiss, Chatham Isl.,
24.
4 Somerville, in JAI, XXVI, 400, 402.
5 Letourneau, Prop., 75.
6 Cayley-Webster, New Guinea, 75.
7 Afrika, III, 477.

8 Keltie, Partition of Afr., 482.
9 Lugard, Brit. Trop. Afr., 461; Oetker,
Deut. in Afr., 40.
10 Frere, in JAI, XII, 266.
11 Fritsch, Eingeb. S.-Afr., 364; Holub,
S.-Afr., II, 331, 536.

stroyed. In all cases, what the slave earns belongs to the master; on the other hand, as he disposes of the property of the master like one of the members of the family, the desire to be free is not very pressing. Children of slaves are the property of the owner.[12] Considerate treatment is accorded the slaves among the Hovas, where they are generally members of the family, though of a somewhat lower rank; "often the master furnishes them a life which many a freeman might envy."[13]

Slavery is very common and even profitable in Central Africa. "There are places in Africa," writes Macdonald,[14] referring especially to the east central section, "where three men cannot be sent on a journey together for fear two of them may combine and sell the third." Slavery makes the Central African much more gloomy than the free man of the South; it adds danger and uncertainty to life. It appears to be economically profitable to buy slaves and put them to work; "they are living money and every man tries to see how much of it he can amass."[15] The economic value of slaves operates to assure them fair treatment: "the head of a village may, under the African law, kill his slave, but only a fool would do so, as he would simply impoverish himself by the value of his chattel in the open market. . . . Domestic slaves have a quasi right to any property they may accumulate while they stay with the masters under whom they gather it; but if sold, the property remains the master's. Most Africans like to see their slaves grow rich. They consider them in a way their own children. . . . A slave's wives and children belong to his master and may be sold at any time. A headman in debt sells first his slaves, then his sisters, then his mother, and lastly his free wives, after which he has nothing left."[16] Slaves, who do much of the agricultural work in Uganda, are well treated as members of the family;[17] while in the case of the Ba-Mbala, "they do not work harder than freemen, are usually provided with wives by their master, can possess property and other slaves, and can purchase their freedom if their estate of slavery is acquired and not congenital." Among the Ba-Yaka, on the other hand, where slaves form about fifty per cent of the total population, they receive very little consideration, are often ill-treated, cannot possess property, and therefore have no chance of redeeming themselves. The Ba-Huana also are harsh in the treatment of their slaves,[18] while the northern Batetela will eat their slaves, "but as no one for whom the slave has worked may partake of the meal, it is usual to buy a slave specially for cannibalistic purposes and to kill him at once before he has worked for his new master."[19] This case is alignable with the exemption of the work-animal from sacrifice. In general, slaves are very well treated among the natives of Central Africa, comments Brunache,[20] who adds significantly, "where they have not been contaminated by contact with the whites."

In East Africa the slave generally lived in peace and ease. "In most tribes he could acquire property of his own, and though his master may have a right to such property, this right is rarely made use of. . . . The European will as a rule hardly be able to distinguish the slave from his master, so much do they

12 Volkens, *Kilimandscharo*, 248.
13 Ratzel, *Vkde.*, II, 513.
14 In JAI, XXII, 103, 109.
15 Letourneau, *Prop.*, 98, 83, 84; *Soc.*, 444.
16 Macdonald, in JAI, XXII, 101.
17 Stuhlmann, *Afr.*, 186; Johnston, *Uganda*, II, 620.

18 Torday and Joyce, in JAI, XXXV, 411, and in JAI, XXXVI, 46, 286.
19 Torday, in JAI, LI, 373-374; §284, of text and *Case-Book*.
20 *Cent. Afr.*, 111.

live as equals, and ordinarily one would take the slave to be a child, son, or wife of the master. The great distinction here is that the slave may as a rule be sold to another man. On the other hand, the master is as a rule liable for the debts and misdeeds of his slave."21 To the northeast, among the Galla and Somal, although there exists an extensive traffic in slaves, the latter are well treated and cannot even be called poor. The power of the owner over his slaves is not absolute; even if the slave commits murder he is not killed but receives corporal punishment or is re-sold. The slaves themselves know that they are kept less for their work than for their children, who are objects of sale. Their masters usually give them patches of ground which they cultivate for themselves; also cattle and occasionally presents.22 Numbers of young natives often voluntarily attach themselves to the Nubians, and are highly delighted to get cotton shirts and guns of their own. "They will gladly surrender themselves to slavery, being attracted also by the hope of finding better food . . . than their own native wilderness can produce. The mere offer of these simple inducements in any part of the Niam-Niam lands would be sufficient to gather a whole host of followers and vassals."23 The Tuareg slaves are at the mercy of their masters, but the latter take care not to kill the goose that lays the golden eggs. The situation of these captives may be compared to that of vassals; in certain groups it is miserable, in others it is even enviable. "As a general thing, the Tuaregs are rather kind to their servants, rarely use them brutally, do not sell them, and are intimate with them."24 In spite of the mild form which slavery takes in East Africa, it is the bane of the district and precludes any steady and secure advance, on account of the slave trade and the incursions of the Somal and Galla, while the Arabs are the greatest curse of all.25 "In the Mohammedan field, the slave who survives the horrors of the raid and of the caravan journey to the coast, and who safely reaches his destination in the house or in the fields of a Mohammedan master, may deem himself happy when he recalls the frightful scenes he has witnessed, but his lot is far from enviable. Although it is an exaggeration to say that the Koran teaches and encourages slavery and slave trade, it is bad enough that it allows these evils; even in recommending mild treatment Mohammed was not in advance of the moralists of his age. On the whole, slavery among Mohammedans is severer than among untutored Africans in the same measure as the Mohammedan culture surpasses that of the heathen, yet it seems to be less cruel than European slavery."26

On the west coast more than in any other part of Africa has slavery flourished, and it was here that the Europeans came for the human cargo destined to work the plantations of the New World. But even here slaves were on the whole well treated by the natives.27 Along the Congo, slaves worked for their master at anything he set them to do, although they were often allowed some choice; all that the slave earned belonged to the master. "The master had to house his slave, feed him, clothe him, look after him in sickness, protect and help him in trouble, and find a wife for him when old enough to marry. . . . The children were slaves and belonged to their master. A slave

---

21 Dundas, C., in JAI, LI, 264-265.
22 Paulitschke, Nordost-Afr., I, 323; II, 139, 140, 152, 153.
23 Schweinfurth, Heart of Afr., II, 421-422.
24 Zeltner, in JAI, XLIV, 355; Letourneau, Prop., 181.

25 Ratzel, Vkde., I, 443.
26 Chatelain, in Illust. Afr., Mar., 1896.
27 Elliot, in JAI, XXIII, 81; Nassau, Fetichism, 15.

might be sold at any moment to pay his master's debts, and so be separated from his wife and children, or he might be killed to accompany his deceased master, or to carry a message to his master's ancestor. Except for these two great disabilities, his lot was not hard; he cost too much, and escape was too easy to other masters in distant towns, for ill-treatment to be prudent." Though the writer has known a few slaves to run away, he has seen more than a few treated like members of the family.[28] In order to keep a hold on the slaves in Togo, they are soon married; then they establish their own household, working, as soon as children come, only four days a week for their masters. The rest of the time they can use to their own advantage. Usually the slave is free from all labor when his children are old enough to work in his place the customary number of days of the week for the master. The older slaves even have slaves of their own, who replace them in bondage. Slaves are usually inherited from father to son, but after the death of their second master they are free; female slaves become free through marriage with a free man, and the children of such a marriage are also free and can attain even to royal dignities. Children of a slave father and free mother are free but they cannot come into the council. In short, slavery, at least in Bassari, is only a condition of service in which the slave is reckoned with the family.[29] In southern Cameroons the slaves live with the master's family; children of a slave-marriage may not be sold and are already half free. While the master may beat his slave, cut off his ears if he runs away, or sell him, he may not kill him even though he has slain one of the master's relatives. If a slave is continually mistreated, he can run away and go to another master who must protect him from the former one and not return him. If one slave buys another and gives him to his master, he becomes half free.[30] In Nigeria the slaves, who were usually war-captives, were well treated although the chief had power of life and death over his slave and sometimes killed him when vexed. Cases occurred here where slaves rose to be kings and chiefs.[31] A system of internal slavery existed in Sierra Leone, "but it is mainly of a very mild character, and unless in war-times, slaves seldom desert their masters."[32] In Ashanti, barring the liability of being sent at any moment to serve his master in the next world, the lot of a slave is not generally one of hardship. "As a general rule, the slave is considered a member of the family, and, if he be native-born, succeeds in some cases, in default of an heir, to the property. He intermarries with his master's children, eats with him from the same dish, and shares in all his amusements. Slaves of all kinds are allowed to acquire property of their own, which they can use as they please, as long as they continue to serve their masters. It not unfrequently happens that the slave acquires slaves of his own, and sometimes he attains wealth and a position superior to that of his master. . . . The slave addresses his master as 'my father,' and is himself addressed as 'my son'; and their mutual relations are very well expressed by these terms."[33] The same general situation prevails with the neighboring Ewe-speaking peoples, among whom, as in West Africa generally, the

28 Weeks, in JAI, XXXIX, 429, 422-423, 424-425.

29 Klose, in Globus, LXXXIII, 314.

30 Conradt, in Globus, LXXXI, 334-335; Schmidt, Deut. Kolonien, II, 24.

31 Tremearne, in JAI, XLII, 175; Kingsley, W. Afr. Studies, 479.

32 Griffith, in JAI, XVI, 306.

33 Ellis, Tshi, 290-291.

condition of slavery is not regarded as degrading and a slave is not considered an inferior being.[34]

From the foregoing account it should be clear that domestic slavery as practised by the Africans is a thing quite different from the wholesale enslavement, forced labor on plantations, and harsh treatment which Europeans have meted out to the less civilized races, and to the negroes in particular. Sir Charles Dundas[35] discerningly remarks: "However we may condemn the practice of slavery among Africans, it affords a striking illustration of comparatively speaking humane instincts in these primitive people, for the terrors of slavery as practised by white men not much more than a century ago were never known to the Africans. It is often difficult for the European to distinguish marriage from slavery in Africa, but this is due less to the lowly position of women than to the surprisingly liberal treatment of slaves."[36] With the arrival of Europeans on the west coast of Africa began a traffic in slaves to the New World which did not end until many millions had been transported; with them also began the slave raids, the depopulating of villages, and the death of countless natives either through the hardships connected with the march to the coast or the overcrowded, neglected conditions of the slave-ships. Livingstone estimated that for every slave actually exported, nineteen others died on the way.[37] Klose[38] has remarked that, while native slavery meant no special hardships, the slave raid brought horror with it and involved the domestic ruin of Africa. "Murder and arson are the rule in this business. Great villages and tracts of land were laid waste and depopulated through the slave hunts. Although to-day the black human merchandise cannot be sent overseas, the Mohammedan courts still use a large number of slaves." Most of the European nations took part in the slave-trade, the Portuguese being the first and probably the greatest of the traders. Some of the coast negroes, in particular the Dahomans, acted as intermediaries, and waged war to get captives for sale to the whites; war became through the slave trade an important source of income and one exploited with regularity.[39] Africa then and for the first time became acquainted with slavery as a developed system of exploitation. In some respects the slave trade ameliorated conditions among the natives in Africa, for it placed a value on human life by making a person a marketable commodity and thereby checked the slaughter of prisoners of war and the practice of human sacrifice, while contact with the whites introduced certain cultural advantages, but on the other hand it added to the sum total of human misery and was the greatest destructive force to orderly and peaceful development. The worst form of slave labor was that endured on plantations owned by the more civilized nations. Despite prohibitions, slavery, slave-raids, slave-markets, and the slave-trade still continue in Abyssinia, French, British, and Italian Somaliland, Eritrea, Egypt, Tripoli, the Libyan Desert, Morocco, Rio de Oro, Liberia, the Soudan, the Hedjaz, Arabia, Afghanistan, Tibet, in most independent Mohammedan states, and in several other territories. This statement is based upon the report presented to the League of Nations in September, 1925, by its Temporary Slavery Commission, which was composed of British,

34 Ellis, *Ewe*, 219-220.
35 In JAI, LI, 265-266.
36 In JAI, LI, 266.
37 Nassau, *Fetichism*, 240.
38 *Togo*, 383.

39 Schurz, *Ztsft. f. Soc.*, I, 46; Chatelain, in *Illust. Afr.*, Mar., 1896; Kingsley, *W. Afr. Studies*, 480; Ratzel, *Vkde.*, I, 531; Chamberlain, in AA, X, 689; Phillips, in JAI, XVII, 225; Margry, *Nav. Fran.*, 18; Johnston, *The Negro in the New World*.

French, Belgian, Portuguese, and Dutch officials who had had much experience in colonial administration.[40]

Though Africa affords the classic example of all types of slavery, evidence from other parts of the world, especially as related to domestic servitude, may be considered so as to round out the survey of this important institution. The Ossetes of Transcaucasia have slaves whom they treat as members of the family.[41] In the Chin Hills a man had the same right to kill or sell his slave as his dog, but the bad treatment of slaves was rare and on the whole their lives were far from what the term slavery would lead one to expect. "Among the Siyins it was a point of honor not to ravish Burmese captives, and the women who lived with Chins as their wives usually consented to do so. The Siyins themselves look on a slave-holder who is cruel to his slaves in the same way that we look upon a bully. . . . A slave has naturally to work for his living, but his day's work is neither long nor arduous; all that he earns belongs to his master; his food is the same as his master's, except in times of scarcity, when he fares badly and has to subsist on what roots he can find in the jungle and on the roots of the plantain tree. At feasts he drinks with the chiefs and, when drunk, will knock them down as readily as any freeman."[42] In the Chittagong Hills slavery is a recognized institution, the slaves being chiefly captives taken in war. "It is considered wrong for a master to take advantage of a female slave in his house. A master's slaves are his children, and they are always treated well. If a man's wife dies, he may marry one of his slaves, but by doing so he at once raises her to the position and privileges of a free woman."[43] In earlier times in southern India fifteen species of slaves were recognized, of which four types could never obtain their liberty without the consent of their owners, while the others might obtain their freedom under stipulated conditions; slave women, however, bearing sons to their masters, became free. The British had great difficulty in suppressing the traffic in slaves, especially as related to the agricultural class and the children who were sold by famine-stricken parents.[44] Slavery has never been an important factor in China except in connection with the custom of selling children. The law requires the owners of domestic slaves to provide husbands for their females, and prohibits the involuntary or forcible separation of husband and wife, or parents and children, when the latter are of tender age. "It is worthy of note," comments Williams,[45] "how few have been the slaves in China, and how easy has been their condition in comparison with what it was in Greece and Rome. Owing chiefly to the prevalence of education in the liberal principles of the Four Books, China has been saved from this disintegrating element." In Korea there have been two classes of slaves: government slaves and those belonging to the nobility. "They are very well treated and rarely evince any desire to become freemen. Indeed Coreans frequently offer themselves and their families as slaves to the richer nobles. Slavery, however, is fast dying out."[46] All told, slavery in Asia has never meant what Europe and America have made

---

40 Hostmann, *Beschaving*, I, 194 ff., 340-343; II, 168-171, 413; Warnshuis, "Slavery in 1926," in *Survey*, LVI, 485.

41 Von Haxthausen, *Transkaukasia*, II, 28.

42 Carey and Tuck, *Chin Hills*, 203, 204.

43 Lewin, *S.E. India*, 194, 91, 235.

44 Thurston, *S. India*, 441-443, 445-446, 447; Wilken, *Vkde.*, 421.

45 *Middle Kingdom*, I, 413, 277; Cognetti de Martiis, *Forme Primitive*, 273; Medhurst, in *Trans. Roy. Asiatic Soc.*, pt. IV, 17-18; Eitel, in *Ch. Rev.*, X, 283-284; Letourneau, *Prop.*, 167.

46 Saunderson, in JAI, XXIV, 307.

of it. "It is a curious consequence of this humanity of custom that the word 'slave' cannot be made to sting the Asiatic consciousness, as it does the European."[47]

A part of the domestic establishment of a chief in central Borneo consists of slaves who are prisoners of war or their descendants. "The relations between master and man are such that one must have mingled for a long time among the Kayans in order to know who of them are slaves." Some are better off than free men; they may even be sent for months at a time to trade among other tribes, with a share in the profits; while some get to be priests and priestesses and win wide influence.[48] In British North Borneo slaves were divided into two groups, the indoor and the outdoor, and their status carefully regulated. Among other things, "no master can refuse permission to his slave to free him or herself, or his or her children, whether indoor or outdoor, nor can he refuse permission to a slave to seek a new master, but he can complain to the courts if he has reason to think anyone has endeavored to entice away his slave."[49] Any slave may be free on paying a value of four pounds, "but in most cases they have been brought up as ordinary members of the family, and have no wish to leave their home. Cases of unkind treatment are very few and far between."[50] On the east coast of Borneo, the relation was rather that of follower and lord than of slave and master, and slavery was so much in the mores that an English settler could not get men to work for him for wages: they deemed it degrading to do so, but said they would work for him if he would buy them.[51] The Dusuns will not have slaves, nor will they sell their children, nor will they give up runaway slaves.[51] "The slaves of the Sea-Dyaks do not in general appear to be hardly treated, as in their wars only such as are young are taken captive; these, after living with their captors for some years, lose the remembrance of their families, or, perhaps, only recollect that they were destroyed, and consequently fall into the customs and practices of the people amongst whom they live, and from whose power they soon lose all hope of deliverance. In many instances, children who have been taken from the Land-Dyaks become so endeared to their conquerors that these latter adopt them as their own, and they are then admitted to all the privileges of the free-born of the tribe, and intermarry with the sons and daughters of the other inhabitants of the village. . . . In the villages the slaves are not distinguishable from their masters and mistresses, as they live all together, and fare precisely the same, eating from the same dish and of the same food."[51] Slaves among the tribes of Timor are not treated harshly; their manumission can be obtained at any time by paying a fixed fee, when the slave rises to his former master's rank. "Slaves rarely seem to care for their freedom. Their livelihood is more secure with their masters."[52]

Among the aborigines of North America the condition of the bondman seems generally to have been little inferior to that of his master, whom he assisted in paddling, fishing, and hunting, even in making war on neighboring tribes. Usually he was a prisoner of war, though in the western section there was a rather active traffic in slaves, largely in the hands of the Chinook. "The distinction between the slave and the free man was especially sharply drawn in

47 Nivedita, *Indian Life*, 69.
48 Nieuwenhuis, *Borneo*, I, 170-171.
49 Roth, *Sarawak*, II, 212, 210; in JAI, XXII, 32.

50 Cator, *Head-Hunters*, 198.
51 Roth, *Sarawak*, II, 209, 210, 215; Gomes, *Sea Dyaks*, 94, 95.
52 Forbes, in JAI, XIII, 417.

all ceremonial practices, from which slaves were rigidly excluded, and generally also with regard to marriage, for the slave usually could not mate with a free man or woman."[53] Since the Indians subsisted mainly by hunting and fishing, slavery was not a developed institution among them.

In Mexico the lot of the slave was easy, though if incorrigible he could be sold or used for sacrifice; he could have other slaves and devote some time each day to his own affairs, while his children were free.[54] Slaves among the Paraguay Indians were well treated though held to be an inferior race.[55] The servitude of Indian slaves to other Indians in Guiana—a condition of affairs which exists up to the present day—was "almost invariably of the nature subsisting between friend and friend rather than one of master and servant. . . . This good treatment meted out by Indians to Indians was well known to the older writers." But while the practice of enslaving one another had existed among the Indians from the earliest times, it was of a nature very different from the servitude which they later came to know at the hands of the whites. After the conquest, the trade in slaves was encouraged and abetted by the Europeans, the religious, military, and civil authorities all lending their countenance and furnishing assistance. "The Spanish Jesuits, unlike the Franciscan, Dominican, and Augustinian monks, earned an unenviable notoriety for the drastic measures they resorted to in their so-called conquest of souls," while "the Dutch made no secret of their slave raids among the natives, and openly pursued the trade, either directly or indirectly, through other Indians, notably the Carib."[56] Failure to enslave the Indians extensively gave impetus to the importation of negroes from Africa, from which there developed the great slave trade of modern times.

There is evidence among the civilized peoples of antiquity of the existence of slavery as an institution and, in some instances, of harsher treatment than was usual among less advanced groups. In the Code of Hammurabi the status of the slave is well-defined: if he marries a free wife, the children are free and may inherit property from the mother; if he strikes the man's son or disputes ownership, his ear may be cut off; if he is killed, he is to be replaced (being viewed as property, not as a human life); a native slave may not be sold to a foreigner; if such sale is proved, the slave is freed.[57] The Jewish laws about slaves come first among the laws in the "Book of Covenants." A male slave, with his wife, is to be freed in the seventh year, unless he prefers to remain a slave. A man may sell his daughter into slavery, *i.e.*, to be a concubine. The female slave is also set free in the seventh year, and persons so freed are to be given gifts when they depart. The slaves were war-captives, or bought persons, or criminals. The lot of slaves was not hard: the owners had not the power of life and death; the slave could acquire property; if the slave was an Israelite he was protected by especial restrictions on the master in behalf of fellow-countrymen.[58] Among the Avesta people, captured enemies were utilized as servants and slaves and apparently received humane treatment.[59] The two great classical states, more especially Rome, built their

53 Henshaw, in HAI, II, 598; Parkman, *Old Régime*, 24; Mason, in USNM, 1894, 589; Farrand, in AA, III, 242; Russell, in BAE, XXVI, 197.

54 Letourneau, *Morale*, 247; Cognetti de Martiis, *Forme Primit.*, 355.

55 Boggiani, *Caduvei*, 100.

56 Roth, in BAE, XXXVIII, 597, 598, 599-600.

57 Harper, *Hammurabi*, 136.

58 Exod., XXI; XXII, 2; Deut., XV, 12-18; Levit., XXV, 39-46, 49; Buhl, *Israeliten*, 35, 106.

59 Geiger, *Ostiran. Kultur*, 481.

power on slavery. "Both states pursued their interests with little care for the pain they might inflict on others, or the cost in the happiness of others. The Roman state began by subjugating its nearest neighbors. It used its war captives as slaves, increased its power, conquered more, and repeated the process until it used up all the known world." In Homer three main classes of servants exist: slaves by descent, born in the household; captives in war; and bought slaves; but one class does not seem inferior to another either in privileges or in social estimation. Female captives were often taken as concubines. At Athens slaves enjoyed great freedom of manners and conduct. "They dressed like the poorest freedmen. No one dare misuse the slave of another simply because he was a slave. If the master abused a slave, the latter had an asylum in the temple and could demand to be sold. Slaves could pursue any trade which they knew, paying a stipulated sum to their owners, and could thus buy their manumission. Their happiness, however, depended on the will of another. In the law they were owned as things were, and could be given, lent, sold, and bequeathed. They could not possess property, nor have wives in assured exclusive possession against masters. Their children belonged to their masters."[60] It is in ancient Rome that we find slavery most thoroughly developed, and the slaves most harshly treated. Mommsen says that compared with those of the Roman slaves the sum of all the negro ills is but a drop. Free laborers disappeared when conquest rendered slaves numerous and cheap. "They were systematically worked as hard as it was possible to make them work, and were sold or exposed to perish when too old to work. Such was the policy taught by the elder Cato. The number on the market was always great; the price was low; it was more advantageous to work them so hard that they had no time or strength to plot revolts. This is the most cynical refusal to regard slaves as human beings which can be found in history."[61] Among the ancient Germans, slaves, who were usually prisoners of war, counted for nothing politically, were regarded as domestic animals, could be sold or killed.[62] Slavery continued in the Christian empire until it was removed in the Teutonic lands through a different legal form, *viz.*, bond-service.[63]

§105. Slavery for Debt and Crime.

THE means employed in East Africa for compelling a debtor to pay are various and curious, and commonly terminate in enslavement. Among some tribes a man may surround his debtor's house with fire until he pays; in another district he may be given permission by the chief to extinguish his debtor's fire time after time until the latter is compelled to pay lest he starve; in many parts the creditor may plunder his debtor entirely, or take what he pleases, or what he is owed; in still other districts the creditor has the right to enslave the debtor or his wife and children; while among another group a creditor may hinder the burial of his debtor's corpse until the debt is paid.[1] In the Upper Congo the methods of collection are just as strange to us and as drastic: "To recover

60 Sumner, *Folkways*, §§285 ff.; Seymour, *Homeric Age*, 262, 271; Letourneau, *Prop.*, 237-239; Letourneau, *Morale*, 247.

61 Sumner, *Folkways*, §286; Letourneau, *Prop.*, 273-274; Grupp, *Röm. Kaiserzeit*, I, 301; Dill, *Nero*, 281; Dobschütz, *Chr. Life*, 119.

62 Cæsar, *Bell. Gall.*, VI, 13; Letourneau, *Polit.*, 40; Holt, in JAI, XXVIII, 161.

63 Dobschütz, *Chr. Life*, 384, 385; Maitland, *Domesday*, 26-36; Letourneau, *Morale*, 357; Letourneau, *Prop.*, 202, 302-303.

1 Dundas, C., in JAI, LI, 277, 264; Torday and Joyce, in JAI, XXXVI, 46.

a debt a creditor would first dun the debtor until he was tired, then he would break the pots and saucepans and anything he found outside the debtor's house, and tell him that on a certain day he would call again for the money. If the debtor then failed to pay, the creditor would call a few of his friends together and would lie in ambush near the farms until the wife of the debtor came along, when they would pounce upon her and take her to their town. The woman would be lightly tied and well treated. The debtor would hear of the capture, and, supposing he owed 1,000 brass rods, he would get the money together as soon as possible and take it and 500 extra rods, which he would have to pay his creditor to compensate himself and friends for the trouble of tying up the woman and cost of feeding her. . . . If the debt is not paid the creditor can keep the woman or women as his own wives, if they are free women, or keep them or sell them if they are slave women. If a man has no wives, then a member or members of his family may be tied up on the same principle as shown above. Sometimes a creditor would seize people of the same town as his debtor, but this was rarely done except in cases of hostility between towns."[2] Interest, in East Central Africa, is enormous, "amounting to cent. per cent. at three months, and the debtor usually stays with his creditor until the debt is paid off. If eventually he cannot pay he becomes the slave of his creditor. Slave-children, slave-wives, slaves, and cattle of the debtor can be seized by the creditor, but the latter's chief usually interferes and lends him money at a tremendous rate of interest to pay off the debt; thus it often happens that the greater number of the inhabitants of a village become the slaves of their chief. If a debtor dies, his brother must discharge the debt; there is no claim on the corpse. War often follows the non-payment of debts, and traders of the same tribe as the debtor are seized and often killed."[3]

Many Africans have been made slaves by famine. Not many Jekris, in the Niger Protectorate, are free; generally it is only the chiefs and their families, the rest of the people being slaves. Fathers who are hard pressed will sell or pawn a son, who is for the time being a slave, but is redeemable. A pawn is a person placed in temporary bondage to another, by the head of the family or, in the case of a pawned slave, by the owner, either to pay a debt or to obtain a loan. The head of a family has the right, with certain limitations, to pawn any of his relations. Also a man or woman can pawn himself or herself for a loan and by repayment become free again.[4] Among the Ewe, "the pawn remains in the service of the creditor till the debt, with interest, is paid by the pawner, services to the creditor counting nothing toward the liquidation of the debt. If a pawn should die, the person who pawned him is bound to replace him by another, or else pay the debt."[5] In Togoland debt-slavery is common and the whole family must answer for the debts of any member;[6] while in south Cameroons a man who cannot pay his debts must go to the creditor and work for him until he or his relatives have paid up, his work for the creditor not counting as payment; the debtor can also settle his debt through his wife or daughter, who may become the property of the creditor; his son may also be given as a pledge but can be held only until the account is paid.[7]

Under the system of pawning, especially since the interest-rate on the original

2 Weeks, in JAI, XXXIX, 423.
3 Torday and Joyce, in JAI, XXXV, 408.
4 Granville and Roth, in JAI, XXVIII, 118; Tremearne, in JAI, XLII, 175.

5 Ellis, Ewe, 220, 294-295.
6 Klose, in Globus, LXXXIII, 314.
7 Conradt, in Globus, LXXXI, 334-335.

debt may be fifty per cent or more,[8] many persons are condemned to life-long bondage. The pawns are in some cases never redeemed; they are servants but not slaves.[9] In the Lower Congo region, litigation between families ultimately takes the form of debt, "and as it frequently happens that payment is delayed, or even impossible, these dependents remain all their life under the authority of the new master. Their condition is, however, not worse than before, and they are indifferent as to their ownership. The only claim on them is a part of their earnings, which in any case they would have to make over to somebody or other."[10] In the Upper Congo districts the same custom prevailed, the status of the pawn being somewhat higher than that of a slave in that he might be redeemed and thus become again a free person. "Such pawns never run away, as the whole of their family connections are in the neighbourhood."[11]

In the Chin Hills of India, a man who had accumulated debts which he could not pay, applied to some well-to-do man to pay them for him, and consented to become his slave until he repaid the debt, which he often failed to do.[12] Among the Kuki-Lushai clans "orphans or destitute people could join the chief's household, getting food, shelter and protection in return for their labour; these could purchase their freedom by the payment of one *mithan,* that is a tame bison."[13] Debt-slavery was common in the Chittagong Hills, among some of the outlying districts of Tibet, and in South India; in the last case there were included those given up as a pledge for money borrowed, those fed and kept alive in famine times, those binding themselves for money borrowed, and those unable to pay gambling debts.[14]

The above cases are typical, but the East Indies have formed, perhaps, the classic ground for debt-slavery. Wilken[15] shows how, when the regulative system is still undeveloped, individual settlement of difficulties of all sorts still obtains; and among these settlements is the seizure for debt of an individual or one of his kin. This may be carried even to the seizure of his corpse. The author cites numerous examples, chiefly from the people of the Archipelago, and states that interest on debts is often 100 per cent. " 'Qui non habet in aere, luat in corpore' is, then, a rule that is found everywhere." Among the Malays, a common way of getting into debt-slavery is through gambling, to which they are wholly devoted.[16] In the essence of the thing, says Perelaer,[17] *pande-lingschap* (being in pawn for debt) and slavery are perfectly identical; and "the free Dyak cherishes the deepest contempt for the *pandeling.*" And he goes on to describe the manner in which unscrupulous wealthy men play on the baser passions of the unwary, pressing money upon them, which they promptly spend, and then fall into their sad lot—hard labor and many blows at slight provocation. In Borneo the term *budak* is generally applied to an indebted person who has lost social standing thereby and is to all intents and purposes a slave. The owner is entitled to kill his *budaks* on the occasion of the religious feasts, taking for this purpose those who are of low descent and who cannot boast of free family relatives. The final settlement of such a person's debt, when he has succeeded in wiping it off, is accompanied by a great many expenses; on

8 Letourneau, *Commerce,* 131, 267-269, 295, 316, 367, 401-403, 416, 430, 462, 474, 485.
9 Nassau, *Fetichism,* 14.
10 Phillips, in JAI, XVII, 224.
11 Weeks, in JAI, XXXIX, 425, 427-428.
12 Carey and Tuck, *Chin Hills,* 203-204.
13 Shakespear, in JAI, XXXIX, 374.

14 Rockhill, in USNM, 1893, 680; Lewin, *S.E. India,* 235; Thurston, *S. India,* 441-442, 443.
15 "Pandrecht," in VG, II, 391 ff.; 398 (quoted), 400, 411; Wilken, *Vkde.,* 421-427.
16 Ratzel, *Vkde.,* II, 446.
17 *Dajaks,* 157.

the other hand, a badly disposed owner has hundreds of ways, if he so desires, of keeping the pawn in debt and therefore in servitude, as for instance by fining him for innocent little transgressions. In some districts there are no real *budaks,* but those who at the end of three years, being unable to pay their debts, become slaves, or *samboat;* "then they are bound to obey their creditors and to work for them without being allowed their freedom, not even in case they possess the necessary means to satisfy their debt. They remain with their children and grandchildren forever in a state of subjection."[18]

How a traffic in debt-slaves may develop is illustrated in the case of the island of Nias. A Malay trader buys a number of slaves or war-captives from a chief and takes them on his ship to another island; he then goes to a Chinese and states that these people, who are willing to work there, are in debt to him for their passage. The Chinese takes over the people in Nias who are supposed to be in debt, and settles their account; he then sells them clothing and other things at a high price and occasionally gives them an advance so that they may satisfy their passion for gambling. He keeps this up until the debt of the men has grown to a large sum. As the rate of pay agreed upon is very little, while the interest on the advances is extortionate, the debt gradually mounts until the debtor is unable to settle it and becomes a slave.[19]

In Sumatra the debtors seem to be less miserable. They are allowed subsistence and clothing, although the product of their labor is not applied to the diminution of their debt. "Their condition is better than that of pure slavery, in this, that the creditor cannot strike them, and they can change their masters, by prevailing on another person to pay their debt, and accept of their labor on the same terms. Of course, they may obtain their liberty, if they can by any means procure a sum equal to their debt; whereas a slave, though possessing ever so large property, has not the right of purchasing his liberty." But descent to pure slavery is possible. If the creditor formally demands the amount of his debt three separate times, and the debtor cannot persuade anyone to redeem him, he becomes a real slave, upon the creditor's giving notice to the chief of the transaction. "This is the resource he has against the laziness or untoward behavior of his debtor, who might otherwise . . . be only a burthen to him. . . . The simple manners of the people require that their servants (debtors) should live, in a great measure, on a footing of equality with the rest of the family, which is inconsistent with the authority necessary to be maintained over slaves, who have no principle to restrain them but that of personal fear, and know that their civil condition cannot be altered for the worse."[20] Debt-slavery exists also in Celebes,[21] while in the Philippines most of the slaves have lost their liberty because they were not able to pay debts contracted by themselves or their fathers, with the result that, even when the debt was insignificant, a man passed easily from freedom to servitude.[22]

When a Tlinkit loans another money, he expects twice as much in settlement, whether the borrower pays the sum back within a week or ten years.[23] Among some of the Indians in Oregon, children of very poor parents were sometimes

18 Roth, *Brit. N. Borneo,* II, clxxxiv, clxxxv, ccv; Schwaner, *Borneo,* II, 149, 205 ff.; Bock, *Borneo,* 78; Perelaer, *Dajaks,* 158-159.
19 Raap, in *Globus,* LXXXIII, 174.

20 Marsden, *Sumatra,* 252, 253, 259-260.
21 Riedel, in *Bijd.,* 1886, 82.
22 Montero y Vidal, *Filipinas,* I, 49-50.
23 Jones, *Thlingets,* 199.

taken and sold to pay debts,[24] while in Mexico such children made up one of the classes of slaves.[25]

In all the ancient states the rate of interest was excessive. Usury was forbidden between Jews, and entirely by the Koran, while legislation in Egypt fixed the amount as not exceeding the principal, and the laws of Manu specified the interest-rates in detail. A debtor among the Israelites was not to be a slave, but to give service until the year of jubilee. A widow tells Elisha that her husband's creditors will come and take her two sons to be bondmen; again, the man who could not pay was to be sold with his wife and children.[26] In the Avesta time a free man could lose his independence by pawning himself, while in Rome, where the laws were especially severe, the creditor could put the debtor to death or sell him to strangers.[27]

Enslavement for crime. Enslavement as a punishment for crime is not so common as debt-slavery. The Marutse of South Africa are generally free from servitude, but they can be forced to it if arraigned and sentenced for some offence or if they incur the disfavor of the king.[28] Among the Wachaga, the punishment set for crimes against property is "that the thief shall pay double the worth of what is stolen, in cattle or products of the field. If he cannot, restitution is made through the sale of his wife or his children. If he is unmarried, he must pay his debt as a slave in the service of the injured party."[29] "It is noteworthy that the negroes at first gave up [for enslavement] only their criminals and those convicted of witchcraft." That in this slavery was the alternative to death, as in many primitive societies, is indicated by the rest of the quotation: "Since this deportation is no longer possible, the latter [witches] are killed."[30] Miss Kingsley[31] reports of the coast negroes that a man condemned to death for murder or adultery can give a slave to be executed for himself. In Ashanti, a man and woman discovered *in delicto* in the bush, or in the open air, are by custom the slaves of the person who discovers them, but are redeemable by their families.[32] Among the Ewe-speaking peoples an important class of native-born slaves consists of those who have been condemned to slavery for crimes or misdemeanors.[33]

In northeast Africa, the thief caught in the act, or one proved a thief by the evidence of theft, falls into slavery; "and this Draconian severity is made use of, in other tribes too, by the Galla chiefs, for they favor this kind of punishment. And so it comes about, for example, in Djimma and its neighborhood, that half of the population languishes in conditions of slavery, although sale into foreign parts is relatively uncommon."[34] Of a people of Madagascar it is said that "they or their ancestors have become slaves either from having been sold for debt, or as a punishment for political offences or for certain crimes. The cruel code of native laws up to about sixteen years ago demanded not only death for many offences, but also reduced the culprit's wife and children to

24 Farrand, in AA, III, 242.
25 Prescott, *Hist. Conq. Mex.*, bk. I, ch. II, 18.
26 II Kings, IV, 1; Matt., XVIII, 25.
27 Exod., XXII, 25; Levit., XXV, 39; *Koran*, II, III, 130; Letourneau, *Prop.*, 222, 262, 272, 352-358; de Martiis, *Forme Primit.*, 349; Bühler, *Manu*, VIII, 140-152; Kohler and Peiser, *Bab. Rechtsleben*, III, 13; Maspero, *Hist. Anc.*, I, 750; Geiger, *Ostiran.*,

Kultur, 481; Bousset, *Relig. des Judentums*, 102-103; Heusler, *Deut. Privatrecht*, I, 103.
28 Holub, *Süd-Afr.*, II, 331.
29 Volkens, *Kilimandscharo*, 250.
30 Pechuël-Lösche, *Loango*, 4.
31 *W. Afr. Studies*, 497.
32 Ellis, *Tshi*, 285.
33 Ellis, *Ewe*, 218.
34 Paulitschke, *Nordost-Afr.*, II, 139.

slavery."[35] In the Chin Hills of India, if a man was caught stealing, he gave his daughter or son into slavery, until he paid some twenty times the value of what he had stolen.[36] In Ceylon, a sentence for theft, incendiarism, and other crimes meant slavery.[37]

"In the old days, according to the old Dyak laws, people who were careless enough to set a house on fire rendered themselves liable to become slaves to those who had been burnt out, and this may have gone as far as two or three generations, so that the grandchildren were slaves by birth."[38] Murderers and other offenders were condemned to perpetual slavery.[39] In the East Indies generally, punishment for wrongdoing, along with debt, are the usual causes of slavery, and since fines are common, debt may follow from crime.[40] In Timor-laut, if a man steals and cannot restore, or owes and cannot pay debts, he becomes a slave of the man from whom he has stolen or borrowed. The parallelism between debt-slavery and slavery in consequence of crime is here self-evident. If a man accuse another falsely of being a thief, or speak ill without a cause, so as to bring anyone to shame before the village, he may become his victim's slave. In any of these cases he may be redeemed for a heavy ransom.[41]

Present-day barbers in China compose a peculiar class of society. They are descendants of criminals of the Sung dynasty (900-1200 A.D.) who, on condemnation, have lost their civil rights and have passed their disabilities down to their offspring. Born a barber, a person must labor as a barber, and remain as such ineligible for literary examination—that is, for an official career.[42] In Japan, finally, degradation to slavery was a common punishment in early times; debtors became the slaves of creditors and thieves of those they had robbed.[43]

§113. The Rôle of Vanity and of Ghost-Fear in Property-Formation.

THE motives of hunger, love, vanity, and ghost-fear lead to the acquisition of many familiar forms of property that do not need rehearsal. Why men make property out of material things that are useful in self-maintenance is clear enough to anyone. That a wife and children, or a slave, may be property is not difficult to understand—certainly not, when one has informed himself upon the primitive family relations.[1] Vanity is in any age a determinative of the identity and nature of property. The motive of ghost-fear produces what are to us odd forms of property and property-tenure. A few selected examples of primitive forms of property should help to get the lowest terms of the institution before us.

It is interesting to review the brief inventory of the effects of a savage who has almost no property at all. The traveller Holub[2] lists the possessions of an old Bushwoman and her son. She was lying on a skin between thornbushes, which represented shelter. They had one block of wood for a head-rest, another for a chair, a turtle-shell for a water-holder, a rude pot, and a flat stick; these

35 Sibree, *Great Afr. Isl.*, 181 (pub. in 1880).
36 Carey and Tuck, *Chin Hills*, I, 203-204.
37 Schmidt, *Ceylon*, 273.
38 Roth, *Sarawak*, II, 213.
39 Perelaer, *Dajaks*, 153-155.
40 Wilken, *Vkde.*, 421-427.

41 Forbes, in JAI, XIII, 15.
42 Personally communicated by Dr. E. D. Harvey.
43 Hearn, *Japan*, 258.
1 §§380, 419, of the text.
2 *Capstadt*, I, 267; Ratzel, *Vkde.*, I, 60-75, and cuts.

articles "completed the property of these two unexacting mortals who, except
as they sometimes felt hunger, made no demands on life or man." But the
Bushmen generally have more property than this: bows and arrows, ostrich-
eggs, gourds, tortoise-shells, rough earthen pots, and dogs. They wear amulet-
trophy-ornaments and some clothing, and possess a weighted root-digger, fire-
sticks, a rude musical instrument, a sun-umbrella to protect children, and a
clapper for games.[3] Fritsch[4] reports the Bushman as "the true philosopher,"
very indifferent to property.

The Australian's bag of private effects contains round stones, with which
he works sorcery upon enemies, and the fat of someone he has killed, all carefully wrapped in bark and painted with red ocher. His wife carries, besides
the rude domestic implements, the leg of a native bear, the head of a kangaroo,
and often the hands of some defunct member of the tribe—a friend or perhaps
a former husband.[5] The little pouch carried by the Papuan contains knife,
tobacco, and lighting materials, and is hung at the head of his grave.[6] In New
Guinea, the chief man's ornament, given a youth by his father right after the
circumcision-ceremony, is an arm-ring, called *tsánë;* and this word "is at the
same time also the word for possession or property, *par excellence.*"[7]

"Chignon [false hair] and cattle-herds form the highest earthly fortune
among the common Maschukulumbe; and chignon, cattle-herds, and human
skulls among their chiefs. Next to these comes the pipe." They "spare no sacrifices" to get a certain shell-talisman which is thought to afford protection
against all possible evils, sickness, mishaps, wiles of wild beasts or enemies,
and even the bullets of the white men.[8] The pursuit of the local form of property becomes a passion; among the Fan "ivory is everywhere an evil thing
before which the quest for gold sinks into a parlour game."[9] On the Loango
Coast rings of iron and copper serve "partly for decoration, partly as fetish-
amulets."[10]

Certain tribes of Borneo set their hearts on brass in any shape; a local sultan
had a jar which gave oracles of death by moaning. It was put away covered
with gold-embroidered brocade. The owner said that no offer would tempt him
to part with it.[11] To the Pelew Islander the hand-basket in which he carries
about his betel is very sacred; "nobody may touch it, step over it, or take anything out of it."[12]

Among the Kwakiutl Indians a peculiar kind of dance is a property, or a
personal attribute; there are strict rules of descent by which it devolves from
one man to another, by marriage or by killing the former owner.[13] Family
names were as much private property as other of the belongings of the Salish,
and in the old days no one would dream of taking a name from another person's family. "These names were never mere tags or labels to distinguish one
person from another but were always connected with the family legends, and
had reference to some true or fancied incident in the life of the ancestors of
the family possessing them."[14] Among the Wyandots "each individual has the
exclusive right to the possession and use of a particular amulet."[15] Of the

3 Lichtenstein, *S. Afr.*, II, 43.
4 *Eingeb. S.-Afr.*, 419.
5 Smyth, *Victoria*, I, 130-131.
6 Von Rosenberg, *Geelvinkbaai*, 92.
7 Hagen, *Papua's*, 170.
8 Holub, *Capstadt*, II, 212, 92.
9 Kingsley, *Travels W. Afr.*, 325.

10 Bastian, *Deut. Exped.*, I, 152.
11 Roth, *Sarawak*, II, 234, 286.
12 Kubary, *Karolinen-arch.*, I, 90-91.
13 Boas, in USNM, 1895, 421.
14 Hill-Tout, in JAI, XXXIV, 322.
15 Powell, in BAE, I, 65.

Seri stone implement, the chief one used by this very primitive people, McGee[16] writes: "Though initially a natural pebble chosen nearly at random from the beach, it eventually becomes personal property, acquires fetishistic import, and is buried with the owner at his death." This is a strong piece of evidence as to the simplest form of appropriation and its sequels. "Among the Miranhas," says Von Martius,[17] "there was one who wore a necklace of very large ounce-teeth. In vain did I offer him several axes for it. His pride withstood every temptation . . . for that trophy of a brave hunting-encounter exalted him in the eyes of his fellow-tribesmen."

A few additional cases may be added to those in the text on the potlatch—the reckless distribution of property for the purpose of self-glorification. Jones[18] describes the custom among the Tlinkits as follows: "The man who gives one receives honour and public esteem for himself and his family in proportion to the amount he gives away. He is the most renowned who has given the greatest or the greatest number of potlatches. A man who is ambitious to give a potlatch will save and stint for years, even to the extent of denying himself and family the necessities of life, that he may give as big a one as possible. The members of his family contribute their quota and endure the privations it entails. From two to five thousand dollars worth of goods are sometimes given away in a single potlatch. Men absolutely impoverish themselves and families, but their poverty is patiently endured for the name that has been established. Henceforth the man is an honoured member of the community, however low he was before he gave the potlatch. He and his will be given a seat of honour in all public functions and a liberal share of what is distributed in every feast to which they are invited." Among the Salish, blankets were not regarded as garments or bedding; they were the measure of a man's wealth. "It was the ambition of most men to amass a number of these and then distribute them by means of a potlatch, and so acquire social distinction and make a profitable investment at one and the same time."[19] Every important event in life was celebrated by the Tsimshians with a feast and potlatch. "An essential feature of the Tsimshian potlatch and of that of the tribes farther to the south is the opportunity it gives for the public announcement of events that are important for the social standing of the individual. The public announcement gives the legal claim to the social advance made at the time; and the higher the honor claimed, the wider must be the circle of witnesses or the degree of publicity." Among the various occasions on which potlatches were given was the public bestowal of a name, for each person had different names as his social position was advanced in the course of his life. A man who gives many potlatches becomes a great chief. "Thus it is," comments Boas,[20] from whose account these facts have been taken, "that there is a vast amount of dead stock accumulated in the camp doomed never to be used, but only now and then to be transferred from hand to hand for the mere vanity of the thing. There is another way, however, in which property is disposed of even more foolishly. If a person be insulted, meet with an accident, or in any way suffer an injury, real or supposed, either of mind or body, property must at once be sacrificed to avoid disgrace.

16 In BAE, XVII, 245.
17 *Beiträge*, I, 89.
18 *Thlingets*, 140-141, 142-143.
19 Hill-Tout, in JAI, XXXIV, 334.

20 In BAE, XXXI, 440, 510-512, 537, 542; HAI, pt. II, 884; a story in the *Saturday Evening Post*, Dec. 15, 1923, sub-titled "The Adventure of the Sewing-Machine Potlatch," is based on this custom.

A number of blankets, shirts, or cotton, according to the rank of the person, is torn into small pieces and carried off." It is astonishing what they will do or suffer in order to establish or maintain dignity.

§114. Communal Property.

THAT food is often regarded by primitive peoples as the common possession of the group is evidenced in the following instances. In Atjeh, "when the fish are on the bank you always see persons who have actually had nothing to do with the fishing . . . appropriate a couple of handfuls or a little basketful and go off without paying anything or without any one taking notice of it. To me, also," the author[1] goes on, "some fish were often offered, and at last I noticed that it was not agreeable . . . when I refused the gift." The native feels it a duty, "which indeed has its origin in self-interest, that he shall give a small part of the fish he brings to the shore to anyone who happens to be present." Among the Maori "the taking of whales, seals, etc., was very tapu [taboo], and woe betide the man who cut up or tasted one of these creatures till the ceremony of making the animal 'common' had taken place."[2]

As late as 1845 the Dyaks of Borneo knew nothing about payment and barter with regard to the common articles of livelihood; "they, therefore, unless they do it from the start without asking, cannot be brought to do what is wanted by means of presents and . . . on the contrary find it quite right if one allows one's people to take as many fowls and as much fruit as one requires. In the same way they know nothing about theft and do not hesitate to help themselves to the fruits in your garden or to the tobacco in your hand as much as they are immediately in need of. They never take more."[3] On Easter Island, in the Marquesas group, and elsewhere in Polynesia joint-households are found; one could come in and share from the pot, and then go without thanks, just as Morgan describes the case among the Six Nations.[4] The Marquesas Islander carried no provisions on a journey; if he was hungry he went into some hut and, without asking permission, dipped his hand into the tub of bread-fruit paste. He was only exercising a right, and needed neither to ask leave or give thanks.[5] In Tahiti "a man divided everything in common with his friend, and the extent of the word friend was, by them, only bounded by the universe; if he was reduced to his last morsel of bread, he cheerfully divided it with the friend." Laws introduced by the missionaries to protect private property were submitted to with reluctance. Community of ownership in such things prevailed to a greater or less degree in the Society Islands, as it did in Samoa and Tonga; "request for a wife or child, or any other precious thing had to be complied with 'subject to reciprocity.'" In another of the Polynesian group "the common uncultivated pandanus was regarded as the property of every one, even if it grew in a man's own plot"; and among some of the Melanesians it was allowable for a hungry man to take and eat bananas from another man's garden.[6] Various writers draw attention to the hindrance to advancement which the Polynesian system involved, for "no sooner did one man successfully strike an independent line of industry of his own, than down came upon him a

1 Jacobs, *Groot-Atjeh*, II, 94-95.
2 Tregear, in JAI, XIX, 109.
3 Roth, *Sarawak*, II, 232, note.
4 Letourneau, *Soc.*, 393.

5 Letourneau, *Prop.*, 62.
6 Williamson, *Cent. Polyn.*, III, 270-271, 278, 317; Seligmann, *Melanesians*, 133.

swarm of his relations, insisting by all family ties and country customs upon a division of the fruits of his labour. Brown says that stealing from the plantation of a relative was not considered wrong, and in fact was not called stealing; it was simply a part of the communistic system under which no man could rise above the level of his fellows. The industrious man might work, whilst the lazy relative helped himself from the fruit of his labours."[7]

In East Greenland all present share in a seal, and in the case of the first one of the season, even if they do not belong to the village.[8] Nansen[9] says that there are but few kinds of animals which the hunter can keep for himself and his family; he gets a comparatively small part of even a walrus killed without help; and "if there is a famine in the village he must after all this give a feast or share with others so that they are not at the hazard each one of each day's take." This last remark is very significant. The Central Eskimo too shares widely when food is scarce; while in times of plenty only the housemates receive part of the quarry.[10] Many of the Tlinkits own no home personally, but move about from house to house among the tribe. "They are never at a loss to find some place in which to stay, and that without cost. If the owner is not at home any of his tribe may go in and make themselves at home, and stay as long as they please."[11]

Among many of the Indians of both North and South America there was practical community in the matter of food; "a man who was hungry need never suffer;" he could go in anywhere and have food set before him.[12] Some of the Indians, as the Mandans, had no regular or stated times for their meals; the pot was always boiling over the fire, and any one who was hungry had a right to order it taken off, and to fall to eating as he pleased. "Such is an unvarying custom amongst the North American Indians. . . . He, however, who thus begs when he is able to hunt, pays dear for his meat, for he is stigmatized with the disgraceful epithet of a poltroon and a beggar."[13] On the Orinoco, the fishermen leave their canoes without touching a fish in them and proceed to their houses to rest; the women and boys load up the fish and heap it before the doors of the captains, who divide the spoil in due proportion among the heads of families, according to the number of children.[14] Among the Coroados of Brazil, "the inhabitants of the hut, or any neighbor or individual of the same tribe, who happens to be present, takes part in the meal; every one without regard to precedency pulls off a piece of the meat [and] squats down with it."[15] Among the Fuegians, those who first find a dead whale have the right to distribute it. They try to evade the duty of sharing; as long as a party can safely keep a whale to themselves they take care not to spread the news. They hoard the blubber for months, by burying it in mud or under a run of fresh water. If the monopolizers are found out, the rush of people, coming too late, in their disappointment either force a partition or resort to violence.[16]

The ancient Jews were allowed to pluck corn and grapes on another's property and eat them then and there, but not to carry them away.[17] In the house-community of the South Slavonians, Dalmatians, and others, "every member

7 Williamson, *Cent. Polyn.*, III, 234 ff.
8 Holm, *Ethnol. Skizze*, 35.
9 *Esk. Life*, 108.
10 Boas, in BAE, VI, 582.
11 Jones, *Thlingets*, 49.
12 Grinnell, *Cheyenne*, I, 170.

13 Donaldson, in *Smithson. Rep.*, 1885, pt. II, 83, 84.
14 Roth, in BAE, XXXVIII, 235.
15 Spix and Martius, *Travels*, II, 259, 260.
16 Bridges, in *A Voice for S. Amer.*, XIII, 201.
17 Deut., XXIII, 24, 25.

of the body has an absolute right to be maintained, housed, and clothed out of the common fund."[18]

The various shadings of communalism in things other than food are brought out in the cases which follow. "The organization of the Australian horde is essentially communistic. Personal property consists merely of such weapons and tools as each man can carry with him on his wanderings."[19] In Australia the stones for axes were procured in special localities, which were the property of local groups of men without the permission of whom the stone could not be removed.[20] Definite communism of property still flourishes in one form or another throughout Melanesia.[21] In one of these island groups, even a work-boy's trade is not his personal property; "it belongs to all the family in common, and as many as can will gather round to see it opened out. Besides the loin-cloth and the belt and knife that the lad is wearing—these he is usually allowed to keep, at least for a time—he will probably bring a mirror and a pair of scissors, a second knife perhaps, and red shell ear-pendants manufactured by the whites. One thing is never lacking, the stick-tobacco varying from ten to thirty pounds in weight according to the time that he has served at work. His elder brother presides over the distribution of all this wealth, and the rest of the kinsfolk aid him with copious suggestions; as for the boy, he must content himself with looking on, and take with proper gratitude the tiny fraction of all his gains that may be allotted to him."[22]

In West Africa private property constantly merges into public property on the death of its individual owner, but tribal and family property cannot become private.[23] Among the Kabyles the goods in a family are not divided up, and the income is used for the sustenance and support of all members without distinction. The community gives every one the tools for labor, a gun, and the capital for business or trade; but the recipient has to dedicate his labor to the community and pay his earnings completely into the hands of the family head.[24]

In theory, at least, a woman may belong to the group: among certain Alfurs of Buru and Ceram the bride-price is paid or received by the members of the family-group as a whole. This is "the best proof of the most intimate economic solidarity. The woman so bought is thereafter the property of the whole group and is assigned to her husband, as it were, only for use during the period of his life. After his death each member of the group has the right to court the widow without paying a bride-price." The same situation occurs in Timor. These house and village communities show at the same time a community of property and industry; above all is land the common property of the group.[25]

Nansen[26] says of the Eskimo that with respect to the right of property there is a certain communism within three widening groups: first, the family, second the housemates and kinsfolk, and third the village. Private property is most fully recognized in the hunting-boat and hunting-weapons which belong to the hunter alone and which no one else may touch. Snow-shoes are also implements of the chase, but as they were introduced by Europeans, they have

---

18 Maine, *Early Law*, 245.
19 Evans, in PSM, LII, 30.
20 Spencer and Gillen, *Nat. Tr. Cent. Aust.*, 590.
21 Rivers, *Melan. Soc.*, II, 146 ff.
22 Jenness and Ballentyne, *D'Entrecasteaux*, 95-96.

23 Kingsley, in JAI, XXVIII, 195.
24 Hanoteau et Letourneux, *Kabylie*, II, 4, 6, 469, 471.
25 Wilken, in VG, I, 340-341, 344, 383-384; Rivers, *Melan. Soc.*, II, 144.
26 *Esk. Life*, 108.

become private property in a lesser degree; while an Eskimo seldom or never touches another's weapons, he will not scruple to use another's snow-shoes without leave.

Next to clothes and hunting-implements come the tools used in the houses, such as knives, saws, and skin-cutters. Many of these, and especially the women's sewing-materials, are altogether private property. Other household-implements are the common property of the family or even of all the occupants of the house. The woman's boat and the tent belong to the father of the family, or to the family as a whole. The house belongs to all its inmates. Although they have no private property in land, there is a recognized rule that no one shall pitch a tent or build a house at a place where people are already settled, without obtaining their consent. Also where dams have been built in a salmon river to collect the fish, it is regarded as wrong for strangers to interfere with the dam or to fish in that water. Drift-wood belongs to the first finder; to establish a right he must drag it above high-water mark and if possible mark it. Under such conditions no one will touch it, even for years; one who did would be regarded as a scoundrel. If a man borrows a thing and harm comes to it, he must make it good. They never borrow if they can help it; and if a debtor dies, the creditor never makes any claims. If anyone has a surplus, he is held bound to share it with the others. Among the Bering Strait Eskimo, "if a man borrows from another and fails to return the article, he is not held to account for it. This is done under the general feeling that if a person had enough property to enable him to lend some of it, he has more than he needs. The one who makes the loan under these circumstances does not even feel justified in asking a return of the article, and waits for it to be given back voluntarily."[27] Rink[28] finds that "the right of any individual to hold more than a certain amount of property was, if not regulated by law, at least jealously watched by the rest of the community, and that, virtually, the surplus of any individual or community—fixed by the arbitrary rate which tradition or custom had assigned—was made over to those who had less."

The Eskimo evidence seems to form a consistent story; but the tribes at Point Barrow afford a clear exception, for there the idea of individual ownership is much more strongly developed.[29] All of these Arctic cases are significant. The conditions of life, especially of the Eastern and Central Eskimo, are such that they mold the mores perforce, all along the line.[30] Where industrial organization, war, government, law, and class-restrictions are no more than rudimentary, differentiation in forms of property could not be expected. The mores here reveal the "strain of consistency" characteristic of them.[31] Under such conditions of the natural environment, combined with such a degree of isolation, doubtless the immediate adjustment lay in the direction of communalism. Evidently the field for the display of individualism was limited.

As for the American Indians, we have the broad generalization that "the basis of the Indian social organization was the kinship-system. By its provisions almost all property was possessed in common by the gens or clan. Food, the most important of all, was by no means left to be exclusively enjoyed by the individual or the family obtaining it."[32] In all the eastern part of North America, in a great part of the northwest and in many districts of

---

27 Nelson, in BAE, XVIII, pt. I, 294.
28 *Tales*, 29-30.
29 Murdoch, in BAE, IX, 429.

30 Keller, *Soc. Evol.*, 262 ff.
31 Sumner, *Folkways*, §5.
32 Powell, in BAE, VII, 34.

South America, female descent and inheritance prevailed; and under such circumstances an individual man had no property but his clothes and weapons. He did not inherit, but the clan, rather, inherited from him. There was, therefore, scarcely anything but clan-property, and private property was but sparsely represented.[33] Among the Omahas, household-property "consisted of the right of occupancy of a common dwelling, the right of persons to shares of fish, game, etc., acquired by any member of the household."[34] "Proprietory rights with reference to the eagle inhere in the clan rather than in the individual; nests, eaglets, and adult eagles are owned by the whole clan, not by any one member." The Hopi have corporate charms and talismans, which are the palladia of the group.[35] The Tupinambas of South America seem to have provided a favorable field for Franciscan teaching, "since their goods and whatever they have is common to all those in the house, likewise the iron tools—the things they value highest—as well as the clothing."[36]

Strabo[37] says of the ancient Arabs that they had property common among the relations, administered by the eldest; it was correlative with communalism in women; so the Basques have communal property inside the family.[38] Such general statements could be matched from many other places and times. One of the many instances of communism in practice is the following reference to colonial Virginia; this colony had been managed from the beginning on the community plan, all sharing the work and such provisions as were at command. Governor Dale, on his arrival, "allotted all the settlers private gardens," and "gave each man three acres of cleared ground to farm for himself and his family, and we are informed that when they were 'fed out of the common store and labored jointly together, glad was he that could slip from his labor, or slumber over his taske, he cared not how, nay the most honest among them would hardly take so much paines in a weeke as now for themselves they will doe in a day.' As a result, a declining Colony, that had lost about 80 per cent. of its founders largely through lack of provisions and supplies, was turned into a flourishing one."[39]

§117. Land as a Maintenance-Area.

THE general principle to be illustrated is that the concept of property in land, at first either wanting or vaguely defined, acquired definiteness, proceeding from communalism toward individualism along with advance in the self-maintenance organization.

Among the backward tribes of West Australia, "the country of a local group, with all its products, animal, vegetable, and mineral, belongs to the members of the group in common. Any member has the right to hunt over the country of his group at all times. He may not, however, hunt over the country of any other local group without the permission of the owners." Hunting or collecting vegetable products on the country of another local group constitutes an act of trespass. While tribal boundary lines are thus rather closely defined, there is no evidence among them of the individual ownership of any part of the soil or any of its products.[1] On the D'Entrecasteaux Islands each

33 Ratzel, *Vkde.*, II, 629.
34 Dorsey, in BAE, III, 366.
35 Fewkes, in AA, II, 693; III, 214.
36 Oliveira Martins, *Quadro*, 79.

37 *Geog.*, XVI, ch. IV, §25.
38 Buschan, in *Globus*, LXXIX, 118.
39 Stanard, *Colonial Virginia*, 30.
1 Brown, in JAI, XLIII, 146.

district is the common possession of the natives who inhabit it, and trespass on hunting-grounds constitutes an infringement of right.[2] Elsewhere in Melanesia each group or clan laid claim to hunting-grounds or certain reefs for fishing, on which any member, but no outsider, might hunt or fish.[3] The Alfurs of Buru enforce rights to the sea, to a certain distance from shore; strangers must get permission of the district to fish, and pay for it.[4]

In the Upper Congo district the boundaries of a town are well defined, the islands belonging to it being well known to all the other villages in the neighborhood. "If an animal is killed on ground owned by a town other than that to which the huntsman belongs he has to send a portion—generally the head—to the chief of the town that claims that ground."[5] In East Central Africa communal hunts take place yearly, when the game is driven by setting fire to the dry grass. "It is considered the greatest offence against a village to burn its grass, otherwise no strict bounds are observed."[6] Originally, "every family of the Nature-Veddahs had its separate hunting-ground, which was recognized by the others. Infringement upon the hunting-ground seldom occurred and then, for the most part, had serious consequences."[7]

Among the North American Indians the hunting-territory was generally regarded as the common property of the whole tribe,[8] while in South America many peoples, lacking fixed dwellings, had no exclusive territory save the tribal hunting-ground. Such districts were tacitly recognized by neighbors: "any encroachments on these lands lead to quarrels, which are usually settled by a sort of duel between the champions of the respective factions, but which often end in a free fight all around."[9] The staple food of the Araucanians was the fruit of the pine, which was, of course, not cultivated; "every year during the autumn months excursions are made by the whole tribe to the pine forests, where they remain until they have collected sufficient for the following year. Each tribe has its own district, inherited by custom from generation to generation and inviolate, by unwritten law, from other tribes, even in time of warfare. This harvest was formerly of such supreme importance, that all intertribal quarrels and warfares were suspended by mutual accord during this period."[10]

Among herders, again, since interest lies in the use rather than in the possession of land, pasturages are generally common property. Among the pastoral Bahima of Africa, land is not regarded as of any value except for grazing purposes; "neither king nor people ever speak of the land as having any value, nor is it carefully delimitated as in Uganda." At the same time it is roughly divided up among nine leading chiefs, who have control over their districts in the matter of pasturage. Though they care little for the land, still "they adhere to natural boundaries for their districts and do not trespass into other districts for grazing purposes."[11] Among the Akamba "no particular area is set apart for grazing and no title to grazing land is acknowledged. In former days when they could not take their cattle into the plains for fear of the Masai, they were very cramped for grazing ground and it was the

2 Jenness and Ballentyne, *D'Entrecasteaux*, 39-41.
3 Seligmann, *Melanesians*, 468.
4 Wilken, in VG, I, 44.
5 Weeks, in JAI, XXXIX, 123.
6 Torday and Joyce, in JAI, XXXV, 405-406; and in JAI, XXXVI, 42.

7 Sarasin, *Weddas*, 480-481.
8 HAI, II, 819.
9 Keane, in JAI, XIII, 207; Von Martius, *Beiträge*, I, 85-86, 325; Ehrenreich, *Vkde. Brasil.*, 57; Wied, *Brasilien*, I, 370.
10 Latcham, in JAI, XXXIX, 341.
11 Roscoe, in JAI, XXXVII, 98.

practice to fence certain areas in among the cultivated districts which were set apart as commonage for grazing."[12] There are considerable areas in Africa under the domination of nomadic tribes, such as the Masai of British East Africa, who have established a grazing right for their cattle but claim nothing beyond that. The desire of the agricultural tribes for land is replaced among these nomadic pastorals by the ambition to own cattle. "In other regions—such as Bornu in Nigeria—the poverty of the soil, and the migratory habits of the people, lead to the frequent transfer of villages from one site to another, and consequently to a similar absence of any rigid system of land tenure. Elsewhere we find wandering tribes of pastorals traversing the lands occupied by the settled tribes, who accord to them rights of grazing for their cattle."[13]

The tendency toward more rigid definition of property in land is clearly marked among agricultural groups, though there are cases where farming-land is still regarded as the property of the community. Although individual property in land exists at present in Melanesia, communal ownership used to be the rule and traces of it are still to be found. Land in some sections is the property of the whole hamlet, not of any individual or family; within an area belonging to the district as a whole each hamlet holds a tract in usufruct, the various portions of which are cultivated in turn. Over the non-cultivated tracts, retained by the district, all may range in search of fish, game, or fruit. On some of the islands each man has his share in the garden-land, which descends to his children. This land is assigned to him by the clan chief, after discussion with the elders, and the whole clan turns out to help in the work of clearing it. In the old days land was never sold; when heirs to any given area failed, it reverted to the clan. "Garden making on another man's land is frequent, his permission being first obtained, and a portion of the crop being given him in return."[14]

Among the agricultural peoples of British Tropical Africa land is wanted for its usufruct, and though there may be private property in that respect there is none in land itself. "The produce of the land is the property of the occupier, and he may own trees planted by himself, either on unoccupied land or on land occupied by another. He may sell or pawn the crops on his land, or trees owned by him, but not the land itself. He may be ousted from his holding for offences against the community. . . . A chief acts as trustee for the tribe in regard to land. He is joint owner with his people, and he cannot exercise any proprietary rights without the co-operation of his people." The fundamental characteristic of land tenure here seems to be an individual holding derived from the common stock at the disposal of the tribe or family. Evidence is available that such a tenure tends to develop rapidly into individual ownership. "The conception of individual ownership," the author[15] remarks significantly, "is promoted by the cultivation of permanent crops which take long to mature, such as cocoa, rubber, etc. It is remarkable with what tenacity the native mind holds to the idea of private ownership, or at least of the absolute right to tenure in perpetuity."

In the case of the Bangala, "within the boundary the people of the town were free to make their farms and build their houses where they liked, provided the land was not already occupied by someone else. Priority of occupation is the

12 Hobley, A-Kamba, 83.   Rivers, Melan. Soc., II, 146-148; Jenness and
13 Lugard, Brit. Trop. Africa, 286-287.   Ballentyne, D'Entrecasteaux, 71-72.
14 Seligmann, Melanesians, 87, 467, 468;   15 Lugard, Brit. Trop. Afr., 284-286.

only title to a piece of land."[16] Among the Lumbwa there is no individual property in land, though growing crops are objects of inheritance and sale.[17] The same general considerations apply widely in East Africa: in Ukamba "wherever a man cultivates or builds a village on virgin soil he acquires a right to that land, and no one can cultivate or settle there without his permission." The title to the land never lapses, yet "ownership relates only to the right to build on or cultivate the land. Grazing, timber and water are common property everywhere." In Kikuyu all untilled land is free to anyone to use for grazing and timber; the tribe has a collective interest in the land, even though that which is cultivated is private. Among the Wachaga every clan has its own area, but within this each member's particular banana-grove is his own property, as must be the case where permanent cultivation exists. The land on which maize and other crops are cultivated is distributed by the chief. No title is therewith conveyed, for the cultivator has a right to the crop only. By the Wadigo coco-plantations are cultivated extensively and are to all intents and purposes private lands; but according to local law it is only the trees which are owned, not the land. Among a number of tribes ownership is acquired by cultivation but is lost by disuse during several years. Land is not and really cannot be sold; any payment is regarded only as a recompense for the labor expended on clearance by the first owner.[18]

In Central Polynesia title to land was by occupation. Land was the common property of the septs or families, though there was individual ownership in a sense, because a title could be acquired by cultivation and sons inherited fathers' land; but no land-owner could devise his holding to anyone outside the limit of his sept, and in default of heirs the land reverted to the head of the sept for assignment to other members of it. In the case of the more permanent crops the tendency toward exclusive possession was strong: "The planting of yams or plantains by permission conferred no title, but the planting of coconuts did so; thus, there being no boundary marks, encroachment by planting these trees was a continual cause of friction."[19] The tendency toward exclusive appropriation was also manifest in the case of the American Indians who planted their corn in the same places each year and those who made an extensive investment for irrigating.[20]

The primitive notion of property in land appears clearly in the matter of alienation. To the native mind, uninfluenced by foreign ideas, land is an unsalable thing. The East African says that all land belongs to God and that to sell it amounts to stealing. In recent years Arabs and other aliens have purchased plantations in this section, but the native himself never comprehends a complete sale of land: "to him it is never more than a mortgage, and therefore he obstinately claims the right to reacquire his plantation at any time by merely refunding the purchase price, deeming that the purchaser has had good value for his money, in that during the interval he had the produce of the plantation." The most striking and consistent feature of the Bantu law is that land is unsalable.[21] "We have power to dispose of the land; we cannot sell the land; no chief can sell the land," said a Lagos chief in evidence before the Supreme Court in British Tropical Africa. "If an alien requires land, whether he be a

---

16 Weeks, in JAI, XXXIX, 424.
17 Barton, in JAI, LIII, 78.
18 Dundas, C., in JAI, XLV, 296-297, 300, 273, 274-275.

19 Williamson, *Cent. Polyn.*, III, 304, 234-240.
20 Thomas, in HAI, pt. I, 25, 26.
21 Dundas, C., in JAI, LI, 275.

native stranger who desires to cultivate, or a European who desires to trade or mine, the question to the native mind would be, whether or not the stranger's presence is desirable and to the benefit of the community. If it is, he is given land rent-free. He may or may not give a part of his profits or produce in return for the favour conferred upon him. If he does, it has no connection with the land, and is not in proportion to its area. Similarly if the Government takes land for a recognised public purpose, no payment would be demanded, but any person dispossessed would obtain land elsewhere through the chiefs."[22] Compare this with the custom in Celebes where the right of the individual to the land occupied by him is, over against that of the district, no property-right but only a right of usufruct. The *jus domini* of the district is recognized in that no one has the right to alienate the land outside the district.[23] In this connection the statement by Letourneau[24] with reference to eminent domain may be mentioned: "no matter how it may be understood or used, the right of eminent domain may be looked upon as a survival of primitive communal property."

The selling of land, in the sense of parting forever with the ownership of it for a consideration paid down or otherwise received, does not appear to have been an indigenous practice in Polynesia. Difficulty attended sales of land to white men because the people did not know how far the buying went; "their idea was that it only involved the acquisition of the title of the owner chief, and that the right to use the plantation would still remain to them; just as they had possessed it under the selling chief."[25]

Neither the individual, among the American Indians, nor the family possessed vested rights in land. "The land belonged to the tribe as a whole, but individual families and clans might appropriate for their own use and tillage any portion of the tribe's unoccupied domain. Hence it was impossible for a chief, family, clan, or any section of a tribe legally to sell or to give away to aliens, white or red, any part of the tribal domain, and the inevitable consequence of illegal sales or gifts was bad feeling, followed often by repudiation of the contract by the tribe as a whole."[26] Grinnell[27] says that "until within comparatively recent times, all land sales and all treaties have been made by the Indians on the theory that they were passing over to the white people certain rights of occupancy—were lending them the use of the land. These rights in a general way were to live on the land, to pass over it, to cultivate it, to use its waters, the animals that lived on it, the birds that flew over it, and the fish in the streams; yet the Indians looked forward to a time at the end of the loan when the land should be returned to them, when nature would heal the scars made by the white man, when the animals and the birds would reëstablish themselves and the fish would increase in the rivers." The author has heard of Indians complaining of mining operations carried on in territory which they had passed over to the whites, "their grievance being that when they thus lent the land they understood that only its surface was to be used, and that while the whites had the right to plow the soil and turn it over for cultivation, their rights of excavation did not go beyond this. They had no right to bore into the ground and to carry away the minerals." Our governmental policy of civilizing the Indians has been based primarily on the owner-

22 Lugard, *Brit. Trop. Afr.*, 305-306.
23 Wilken, in VG, II, 383-384.
24 *Prop.*, 203.

25 Williamson, *Cent. Polyn.*, III, 243, 278.
26 Henshaw, in HAI, II, 283.
27 In AA, IX, 4, 5-6, 7-11.

ship of land in fee simple, a concept foreign to the Indian and one which he has had great difficulty in grasping.

§119. Family-Holdings.

THE apportionment of land to families, and the transition thereby afforded to private property in land, are observable among the Papuans, of whom it is said: "The land which a tribe has taken into its possession is divided among the several families, and every family-member then gets his portion assigned by the family-head for his use." The tribal land is mostly under allotment, and since the ranges of other tribes join immediately on the tribal boundaries, it is not easily possible to extend the plantations. To this population-land situation there develops an adjustment, rather exceptional for backward peoples, of sale and rent of land to members of another tribe. The rent is paid by a portion of the harvest.[1] The family-holding is clearly defined by permanent land-marks, such as trees, swamps, and small hills. The male head of the family partitions it at the commencement of each annual planting-season.[2] In Southeast Papua, five classes of land are distinguished: village land; village site, abandoned but claimed by the original owners; garden plot; clump of trees; and land without an owner. "Land is divided amongst families, and every individual has his own portion. Land is never sold, and cannot be alienated. It can be loaned for a term. A person dying may bequeath a portion to one not of his family, but the land returns to the family on the death of the legatee." The boundaries are marked by small stones, which indicate each person's property. Inheritance of land is in the female line.[3]

In British Tropical Africa "the tribal land at the disposal of the chief might be allotted either to families which had outgrown their family lands, or to strangers who desired to settle among the tribe, provided that they paid the customary tribute and dues. Family lands are at the disposal of the head of the family, and every member of the family has a right to a share in the land—a right which is not forfeited even by prolonged absence. The holder and his descendants have undisturbed possession in perpetuity, and all rights of ownership, except that they cannot alienate the land so as to deprive the chief of his ultimate control over it. The occupier's title is held by virtue of his membership of the family, and perpetuates in the name of its head."[4] The same general situation prevails in East Africa, and although the senior member of the family is designated as the owner, he is so only as representative of the family. "Any member has the right to cultivate the land, but no individual member has the right to sell it. Such is practically never done, but if any land is sold it must be by consent of all the senior members of the family."[5] The Kabyle joint-family is highly developed and exhibits a strict union of property and work; "in no nation do we find a combination which is nearer to equality and farther from communism."[6]

In Coorg (India) "previous to Tipu's invasion, divisions of property and separation of families were rare; large house-communions existed, and it was not uncommon to find thirty-five or forty grown-up male relations and many

1 Krieger, *Neu-Guinea*, 191, 326-327.
2 Guise, in JAI, XXVIII, 212.
3 Bromilow, in AAAS, 1909, 473-474.
4 Lugard, *Brit. Trop. Afr.*, 284-285.

5 Dundas, C., in JAI, LI, 272, 274; Torday and Joyce, in JAI, XXXVI, 44.
6 Hanoteau et Letourneux, *Kabylie*, II, 468.

families consisting of upwards of one hundred or even one hundred and twenty members living under the same roof." Periodic reallotment was to be found in many parts of India. In Peshawa and in the Delhi district, "the redistribution took place after the lapse of five, fifteen, or even twenty or thirty years."[7] "The Indian joint-family rests upon the community of dwelling, meals, religion, and property. The common preparation of food and the eating together is . . . the most visible external mark of belonging together, and the members of the family are therefore designated in downright manner as 'those who cook together.' "[8]

Among the wild Veddahs of Ceylon each family has a portion of the jungle allotted to it;[9] while in the Malay Peninsula individual property does not exist, its place being taken by family property. "So, too, cultivation is carried on in common, and the plantation is cultivated by all the members of the family under the direction of the father, extra work being imposed in default. The produce is shared between all the members of the family."[10] In the East Indies all the land and in some instances the sago-bushes, tend to become family-property. The district remains the virtual owner of the land and can prevent the holder from selling to strangers; the holders have merely the usufruct, though they can sell or mortgage to fellow-members of the district. If strangers want to own land, they must become district-members. In the Javanese village-community (dessa), as there is too much land to make a correct division annually, one party often remains for years in possession of the same piece. The author quoted[11] thinks that the communal possession of land in Java dates from a remote period, since it has formed itself in so natural a way; in some places where there is no communism, the settlement is thin, and all have a large choice; there is a superfluity of land for the men. In Polynesia, but especially in Samoa, "the land belonging to each family is well known, and the person who, for the time being, holds the title of the family head, has the right to dispose of it. It is the same with the chiefs. . . . Although the power of selling land, and doing other things of importance affecting all the members of the family, is vested in the titled head of the family, yet the said responsible party dare not do anything without formally consulting all concerned. Were he to persist in attempting to do otherwise, they would take his title from him, and give it to another. The members of a family can thus take the title from their head, and heads of families can unite and take the title from their chief, and give it to his brother, or uncle, or some other member of the chief family, who, they think, will act more in accordance with their wishes."[12]

It is noteworthy that a Greek peasant-holding was called a klēros (lot).[13] According to Cæsar, confirmed by Tacitus,[14] the Germans had no private property in land, but it was divided and allotted, year by year, to kin-groups; and among the Suevi no one held the same fields for more than a year. In ancient Ireland the case was similar: " 'By the Irish custom of Gavelkind, the inferior tenanties were partible among all the males of the Sept (small kin-

---

7 Baden-Powell, Land Sys., III, 471; II, 637.

8 Jolly, in Grund. d. Indo-Ar. Philol., II, 76.

9 Stevens, in JASB, I, 136.

10 Skeat and Blagden, Malay Penin., I, 503-504.

11 Wilken, Vkde., 429 ff.; and in VG, I, 42-44.

12 Turner, Samoa, 176-177; Williamson, Cent. Polyn., III, 262; Letourneau, Prop., 69.

13 Beloch, Griech. Gchte., I, 88.

14 Bell. Gall., VI, 22; IV, 1; Germania, ch. XXVI.

ship group), both Bastards and Legitimate; and, after partition made, if any one of the Sept had died, his portion was not divided among his sonnes, but the Chief of the Sept made a new partition of all the lands belonging to that Sept, and gave every one his part according to his antiquity."[15]

Communal land with allotments is a modern phenomenon in Russia. Much has been made of it. The oldest Russian law book indicates the existence of strictly private property in land.[16] In a Russian village, "after the expiration of a given, but not in all cases of the same, period, separate ownerships are extinguished, the land of the village is thrown into a mass, and then it is re-distributed among the families composing the community, according to their number. This repartition having been effected, the rights of families and of individuals are again allowed to branch out into various lines, which they continue to follow till another period of division comes round."[17] The Slavic village community (mir) is not, apparently, a "natural" development, in the sense of preceding examples, but one due to special conditions, largely political. It is relatively modern and is a case of involuntary social cohesion under great pressure. "Its significance rested exclusively upon the levy of taxes. In this lay the unity of the community, and through this did it attain the character of such—in other respects the individuals who composed it had nothing in common with one another. . . . The Russian community has not developed itself by a natural growth, is not a society that has come into existence through free union, but has been organized by the government."[18]

Quite different appears to be the house-community of the South Slavs, known as the zadruga; a Croatian law of 1870 defines it as follows: "Several families or persons who, under the leadership of a head, dwell in the same house and manage the household, work together an undivided property, and enjoy the in-come communally, form a union which is called a Zadruga."[19] Unlike the Rus-sian village-community, in which there is redistribution, the house-societies of the South Slavs were invariable, that is, a certain family held a certain estate. The individual could lay claim to certain rights only in so far as he was a member of a family and lived in inseparable relations with the family. Prop-erty was not the share of a single person but belonged to the entire family as something common. Many writers think the zadruga a primitive form of do-mestic life, a natural development out of special conditions; when the condi-tions change—as they have in recent years with the coming in of a money economy and the impossibility of free occupation with the soil—this form of adjustment declines.[20]

15 Maine, Early Hist. Institutions, 186.

16 Simkhovitsch, Feldgemeinschaft, 353 (See Sumner, review of this book, in Yale Review, VIII, 95 ff.); Wallace, Russia, 133.

17 Maine, Anc. Law, 259.

18 Von Keussler, Gemeindebesitz, 11, 14-16, 18, 36, 65, 68, 69, 71, 72, 77, 84; Hildebrand, Recht, I, 108, 184, 187, 189.

19 Simkhovitsch, Feldgemeinschaft, 355.

20 Kaindl, in Globus, XCI, 81; Utiešenović, Haus-Kommunionen, 10, 13, 15, 18, 44, 59;

Simkhovitsch, Feldgemeinschaft, 357. For a discussion of the village community, see Vinogradoff, Villainage, 37, 220, 236, 354-362, 397-409; Letourneau, Prop., 115-122, 299, 369; Maitland, Domesday Book, 142, 150, 340-356; Gomme, Folklore, 101, 148, 149; Gedge, Vil-lage Community; Volz, in Globus, XCV, 7; Probyn, Land Tenure, 222, 224; Pollock, Land Laws; Jenks, Law and Politics, 160-161; Kowalewsky, Ökon. Entwick., I, 91-92.

§120. Ownership by the Chief.

An excellent case illustrating the transition from communal property in land or from family-holdings to private property *via* ownership by the chief is that of the Yoruba tribes of West Africa, for Ellis[1] states: "The notion that land, and not merely its usufruct, may be the property of the individual, instead of the community, is beginning to appear, for a chief can sell or give away land. No one but a chief can sell land; it is one of the prerogatives of chieftainship; but the land sold or given away must be unoccupied waste-land, the usufruct of which has not been yielded to any member of the community." The West African law regards property as attached to the "Stool" or the "Cap" of the king; "but he is trustee, not owner of the Stool property, and his family don't come in for the property on his death, for every profit made by the working of Stool property is like this itself the property of the Stool, and during the king's life he cannot legally alienate it for his own personal advantage, but can only administer it for the benefit of the Stool."[2] More definite is the ownership of the chief among the cattle-raising Bahima and more numerous are his duties: he has "to see that all the cattle in his district are cared for, that their pasturage is good, herding thorough, and that sick animals are tended; he must prevent the various guardians from killing too many for his own use, or selling them. Any one selling cattle or killing too many is deprived of all, and condemned as being unsuited for the office of herdsman, and injurious to the king's interests. . . . Even cattle taken in war, directly they reach the country, belong to the king."[3] The Wachaga chief owns all the spears, an important item of property among them in their struggle with the Masai; no spears may be made without his consent.[4] How important the connection of property and the chieftainship is may be gathered from the statement made with reference to the Ba-Mbala, that "land is owned by the chiefs, or rather, a man who owns land becomes a chief;"[5] or from the Loango Coast custom that, whereas after the death of a common person his hut is abandoned, when a prince dies, the whole village is moved.[6] Among the Kikuyu, "no sale or donation of land is considered valid unless it receives the formal consent of the chief. Even if, however, a landowner sells his land with the chief's consent, the chief appears to still exercise manorial rights over the land, for it is said that he can dispossess the new-comer if he seriously offends the tribal law. Every clan has its grazing lands which are common to all the members, and adjacent clans often graze their stock on each other's common land. The chief is however considered to be within his rights if he disposes of part of the common for agricultural purposes."[7] In Madagascar "all lands whether cultivated or not belong to the sovereign," who can evict a holder without warning or compensation and can prevent any use of land by the holder, since for its use the king's permission is required.[8]

The Bantu king "cares in many ways for his people. They do work for their lord and receive for it something from his possessions which they use as theirs. This condition of affairs is at present on the wane, since war has become less frequent and many have won private property for themselves by

1 *Yoruba*, 189.
2 Kingsley, *W. Afr. Studies*, 428.
3 Roscoe, in JAI, XXXVII, 98.
4 Meyer, *Kilimandjaro*, 210.

5 Torday and Joyce, in JAI, XXXV, 411.
6 Bastian, *Deut. Exped.*, I, 164.
7 Hobley, *A-Kamba*, 137-138.
8 Parker, in JAI, XII, 277.

working for the whites."[9] Such cases evolve at length into the right, real or fictitious, of a ruler of advanced nations compounded of several peoples. Under the Emperor of China "is the whole body of the people, a great family bound implicitly to obey his will as being that of heaven, and possessing no right or property *per se;* in fact, having nothing but what has been derived from or may at any time be reclaimed by him."[10] Baden-Powell[11] states that, as time went on, the local princes in India came to claim not only the waste but a right of ownership in all land whatever, and that they adopted the plan of granting to court-favorites, to ministers of state, and to military officers, the right to collect the revenue of a certain area of country and to take the amount collected, either to support their state and dignity, or—in the case of military chiefs—to equip a body of troops, to be available for the royal service. The right of seigneur in central Java in former times extended to the taking of each unmarried maid as concubine.[12]

In Samoa the land was owned alike by the chiefs and heads of families. The land belonging to each family was well known, and the person who for the time being held the title of the head of the family had the right to dispose of it. It was the same with the chiefs. In one of the Hervey Islands the soil was the sole property of the high chiefs and the under-chiefs, and these distributed the land in accordance with their own wishes.[13]

The American Indian chiefs had, naturally enough, no great connection with cultivated land, except as they stood for their tribes; as, for example, when the land about Guilford, Connecticut, was bought of a sachem squaw who appears alone as vendor.[14] Ancient Peru is widely regarded as having been a sort of communal state; but "it is a complete inversion of the facts to assert that all land in Peru belonged to the Incas and was let out to the common people, graciously, so to speak, as a sort of fief."[15] Here, again, we are in the presence of a complicated political development.

§121. Personal Property.

PROPERTY-MARKS are probably more common in Australia than present records show; a number has been noted on wild bee-hives as well as on arms, tools, and the like.[1] Very curious often are the personal belongings of the Melanesians and the methods adopted to keep possession of them exclusive. Among the Koita "a man's most valued possessions in these days are his pig and dog, his ornaments and dancing plumes, and in the days before the white man's coming, his weapons, adze and canoe were doubtless almost equally valuable. . . . With the advent of the store, one article has attained immense popularity. This is a camphor wood box, with the lock so arranged as to ring a bell when the key is turned. It is the ambition of every man to possess one of these, its key is often worn round the neck as a pendant, and it is certain that old keys may be worn for 'swagger' by youths who have never owned a box, and by men who have traded or gambled away the box they once possessed."[2] Pigs

9 Haarhoff, *Bantu-Stämme*, 63.
10 Williams, *Middle Kingdom*, I, 411.
11 *Land Sys.*, I, 189, 230; Hildebrand, *Recht u. Sitte*, 148-149.
12 Van den Berg, in *Bijd.*, XLI, 465.
13 Turner, *Samoa*, 176 ff.; Williamson, *Cent. Polyn.*, III, 229, 230, 232.

14 Atwater, *Hist. New Haven Col.*, 164.
15 Cunow, *Verf. Inkareichs*, 96; Seeck, *Antik. Welt*, 340.
1 Chamberlain, in AA, IX, 420.
2 Seligmann, *Melanesians*, 88.

and dogs, canoes, fishing nets, ornaments, and other native wealth in south-east Papua belong to the individual or the family; "all things too large for individual ownership are owned by the family."[3] In some of the Solomons, birds, called *malau,* which have not yet been domesticated, have become private property.[4] In British New Guinea there exists a sort of patent right, which makes exclusive to the originator a special make of pipe, a new variation in the mode of building a house, or, in fact, anything so long as it is something visible, such as a design.[5] Throughout Melanesia the badges of societies serve to protect the property and especially the gardens of members. A special feature of the Banks Islands property-mark is that it protects property only from persons other than the members of the society of which it is the badge; there is no inducement therefore for a man to join a large society, for his property will be better protected if he belongs to a small one. If, however, he belongs to a great many societies he may by combining their badges be able to protect his property against the whole of the rest of the population. A man who takes property protected by the badge of a society to which he does not belong, and is found out, has to give a pig to the members of the society that he has disregarded. "The use of the badges of the societies as protective signs plays a large part in disputes connected with gardens. If two men have a dispute about a garden, one may keep the other away by putting up the badge of a society to which the other does not belong and the latter may retort in a similar manner and keep his opponent away by the use of the badge of another society."[6]

The African Bushman who finds a bee's nest breaks off a stick and sets it up in the ground near by, being sure that his claim will be respected.[7] Some of the African Pygmies "stick an arrow into a bunch of bananas which is still hanging on the stalk, and announce thereby their claim to the fruit when ripe;" and bananas thus marked are not touched. Though the sanction here would seem to be not so much fear of the supernatural as of the vengeance of the dwarf-people themselves, yet the latter are held in considerable superstitious awe.[8] Besides their stock marks,[9] Africans use stronger devices. A magic powder may furnish the taboo; the highest ears in the corn-field are smeared with it; and "a touch of this magical substance on the part of the thief would bring about his immediate death."[10] "On either side of the path," says Miss Kingsley,[11] "we continually passed pieces of rubber vine cut into lengths of some two feet or so, and on the top one or two leaves plaited together, or a piece of bush rope tied into a knot, which indicated whose property the pile was." The *jujus,* or fetishes, safe-guard property; anyone who removes an article protected by them will surely die.[12]

Among the Ostiaks the property-mark is hereditary in the family. The Votyaks have one for each family; if there is more than one son, the mark is split up and each takes a part of it. The Ainos mark household chattels with the owner's device; and trees which have been cut down in the forest are

3 Bromilow, in AAAS, 1909, 474.
4 Codrington, *Melanesians,* 17.
5 Williamson, in JAI, XLIII, 272.
6 Rivers, *Melan. Soc.,* I, 92-95.
7 Hahn, in *Globus,* XVIII, 120.
8 Junker, *Afrika,* III, 92.

9 Ratzel, *Vkde.,* I, 235. See also "Kunst und Witz der Neger," in *Ausland,* 1884, 12, where specimens of these marks are given.
10 Holub, *S.-Afr.,* II, 21.
11 *Travels,* 290.
12 Granville and Roth, in JAI, XXVIII, 111.

also so marked.[13] In New Zealand, "an inferior kind of tapu exists which any one may use; a person who finds a piece of drift timber secures it for himself by tying something around it, or giving it a chop with his axe; in a similar way he can appropriate to his own use whatever is naturally common to all. A person may thus stop up a road through his ground, and often leaves his property in exposed places, with merely this simple tohu or sign, to show it is private, and it is allowed to remain untouched, however many may pass that way; so with a simple bit of flax a man secured the door of his house, containing all his valuables, or his food store, they were thus rendered inviolable and no one would meddle with them."[14]

Among the items of personal property of the American Indians are listed songs and rites pertaining to the use of healing herbs, whose owner could teach them to another on receiving the prescribed payment. "The right to say or sing rituals and ritual songs had to be purchased from their owner or keeper. Occasionally a spectator with quick memory might catch a ritual or a song, but he would not dare to repeat what he remembered until he had properly paid for it." The right to practise tattooing also belonged to certain men in the tribe.[15] Among the Dakota "the tipi might belong to either parent and was obtained by that parent through some ancestor who had had its character revealed in a dream or who had captured it in war."[16] An Indian hunter established his claim to an animal by his personal mark upon the arrow which inflicted the fatal wound.[17] The Nez Percés and many other tribes lean a pole across the door to indicate the absence of the family, and no one molests the dwelling.[18]

In ancient Chaldæa landed property was put under the guarantee of the gods. It was transferred by ceremonies partly religious, partly magical. The grantor pronounced execrations against anyone who should dispute or attack their authenticity. These execrations were written on oval stones and fastened up at the corner of the field; on them were carved the divinities who watched over the sacredness of the contract.[19] Petrie[20] says that marks to denote property were common as early as 6000 B.C. and that they seem to be the origin of signs which later developed into an alphabet.

§122. Property in Trees.

FRUIT-TREES, among the Papuans, belong to those who planted them, even if on someone else's land. "In a village every tree has its owner, though a young heir has the right to climb any tree."[1] In British New Guinea, "the woods are common property, but the land on which the trees stand, when cleared, goes over into the possession of the cultivator. Though the fruit-trees generally belong to the owner of the ground in which they stand, yet if they were planted before the ground was owned the land-holder has no right to tree or fruit, but only the right of compensation, chiefly from a part of the fruit. . . . In certain localities the custom is that after the death of a village-member, his coconut trees are inviolable, or even that, in his honor, a coconut tree

---

13 Andree, *Eth. Parallen*, 81, 82, 85, and plates.
14 Taylor, *Te Ika*, 171, 167.
15 Fletcher, in HAI, II, 309.
16 HAI, I, 378.
17 Fletcher, in HAI, II, 309.

18 Fletcher and Matthews, in HAI, I, 442.
19 Maspero, *Hist. Anc.*, I, 762.
20 In PSM, LVI, 627.
1 Bromilow, in AAAS, 1909, 474.

that belonged to him is cut down."[2] In the Torres Straits Islands every coco-palm is owned, and most of the inhabitants of an island appear to know the owner of every tree.[3] In this part of the world one "whole island was planted with cocoanut trees, each bearing the different marks of its owners, and it is astonishing that though some may belong to a man who perhaps lives many miles away, and in another country, and who only comes once or twice a year to collect the nuts, there is not a being on the island who could be persuaded to steal one."[4] "Fruit trees planted, with the consent and acquiescence of the owner, upon another man's land, remain the property of the planter and of his heirs. In a true sale, the minute and accurate knowledge of property in land and trees is remarkably displayed."[5] An unusual case of inheritance arises in connection with the ownership of trees on the land of others, which is a fre-quent occurrence in the Banks Islands; in this case, the son of the owner of the tree inherits it, but he has to pay money at the time to the owner of the land; even when inheritance was in general matrilineal, trees on the land of others were an exception to the rule.[6]

In Africa, Bastian[7] found that "whoever first prepares a palm-tree to yield palm-wine is its owner." On the Upper Congo the palm-trees wherever found are never without owners. "The proprietary rights in these trees are by in-heritance, or by planting them, and the rights in them are handed on from father to son in the proper line of heirship."[8] It is the custom in the Fezzan that everybody may pluck the dates or pick them up, as long as they are not ripe enough to be cut. They may eat on the spot as many as they like, but may not carry any home.[9] In all the oases of the Sahara, trees may be owned by others than the owners of the land, and can be inherited, given away, or sold. Disputes arise concerning irrigation: "here perhaps the owner of the land, in order to ripen his wheat and tomatoes, has the fields watered oftener than the palm-tree owner regards as endurable; while there the owner of the date-palms wants to garner his dates—a thing which the owner of the ground tries to hinder, because, in his opinion, his crops will be trampled in the process." Considerable complication arises.[10]

Recognition of separate ownership of cultivated trees was common in Poly-nesia, and in the Society Islands not only had every portion of land its respec-tive owner, but even the distinct trees on the land sometimes had different pro-prietors, and a tree and the land on which it grew might have different owners. Formerly every breadfruit and coconut tree had its proprietors, and a single tree sometimes had two. Subsequently, however, extensive clusters or groves of trees were to be met with, that had no other owner than the chief of the district in which they grew. "It was formerly their practice to gather the fruit of these, in its season, without asking the consent of any one. The proprietor of the land could appropriate to his own use any number of trees by affixing such marks [taboo signs] as were indications that they were prohibited; but later, as the population increased, the people became more careful of their trees, and the practice of gathering promiscuously the fruit from those trees not enclosed, appeared generally undesirable."[11]

2 Krieger, *Neu-Guinea*, 328, 187.
3 Haddon, in JAI, XIX, 308.
4 Cayley-Webster, *New Guinea*, 182, 183.
5 Codrington, in JAI, XVIII, 312.
6 Rivers, *Melan. Soc.*, II, 98.
7 *Deut. Exped.*, I, 208-209.

8 Weeks, in JAI, XXXIX, 425.
9 Nachtigal, *Sahara*, I, 269.
10 Rohlfs, *Kufra*, 125, 126, 127.
11 Williamson, *Cent. Polyn.*, III, 279-280, 317.

§123. Personal Holdings in Land.

THE following typical cases of private property in land should be scanned
with the population-land ratio in mind. In East Africa, the Wakarra distinguish themselves in custom from other Bantus: "They are a people living on
an island, every acre of which is cultivated, and the land therefore has a high
value, consequently individual tenure has been evolved and is very pronounced.
Every piece of land is privately owned and inherited. The owner may sell his
land, but when doing so will consult his relatives in order that they may purchase it if they so wish."[1] The rest of the neighboring Bantu, it should be
noted, have developed only up to family-holdings in land; the greater density
of population on the island-restricted territory of the Wakarra has forced
the latter to the most highly evolved system of land-tenure to be found in
this section, with only a vestige of the idea of family claim to land.

In the Naga Hills of India "private rights of property in land are the rule
amongst all the tribes in this district except . . . the migratory tribes. That
private rights of property in land are not recognized amongst these tribes is
due to the fact that they are in no way pressed for land, the villages being
small and uncut jungles extensive. When, however, we come to tribes . . .
who live in permanent and large villages, and amongst whom land is none too
plentiful, we find that the rights of individuals to property in land are well
known and well recognized, and the rules as to inheritance and partition of such
property settled by strict customary law."[2] "Land is freely bought and sold
by the Angámis of this district, especially permanent terraced cultivation,"
that is, land in which the investment is important.[3] "As civilization advanced,
and the advance of the commerce therewith gave an impetus to men to follow
various kinds of industry to derive wealth, the wealth so derived from separate
acquisitions brought into existence self-acquired [private] property."[4] In Oudh
"no historical evidence takes us back to any other state of things than that
where each villager held his own fields;" in the northwest provinces, "the village
group of Manu's time—each man claiming his own holding—was the original
condition of things."[5]

In the country of the Hill Dyaks, "where beasts of burden do not assist the
farmer in bringing home the produce of his lands, it is a great advantage to
the cultivator to have his field as near to the village as possible, and among
the tribes living at a distance from the river-banks, or where the brooks are
too small to admit of the use of the canoe, the property in the vicinity of the
houses is divided into plots, which are the acknowledged property of certain
individuals."[6] In northern Sumatra, "the prior possessor of a piece of land,
or his lawful heir, can at all times, even if the land has already for years
been turned into waste, make good his rights to it."[7] Here is a case of peculiarly persistent rights to private property; for in general land that has reverted
to waste comes under private ownership again only by re-clearing and cultivation, and is then the property of the one who redeems it. The Polynesians hold
the fishing places as private property.[8] Among the Maori, "land was held by

1 Dundas, C., in JAI, LI, 271.
2 Godden, in JAI, XXVI, 183, 30.
3 Assam, *Census Report* for 1891, 250.
4 Nathubhai, in JASB, III, 408.

5 Baden-Powell, *Land Sys.*, II, 224, 109.
6 Roth, *Sarawak*, I, 419.
7 Jacobs, *Groot-Atjeh*, II, 110.
8 Ratzel, *Vkde.*, II, 212.

tribal right, but within this each free warrior of the tribe had particular rights over some portion."9

Among the Indians of the Mississippi Valley, "there were no fences to divide the fields, but every man knew his own. . . . The work was done in common, though the fields were divided by proper marks, and the harvest was gathered by each family separately."10 "The waters are usually regarded by the Navaho as the common property of the tribe, but the cultivable lands in the vicinity are held by the individuals and families as exclusively their own."11 Among the Chinooks who gained their livelihood primarily by fishing, "definitely located fishing stations were a well-recognized form of personal property; the capture of the first salmon of the season was accompanied with a ceremony intended to give that particular fishing station a good season's catch."12 It is reported of the New England Indians: "I have knowne them make bargaine and sale amongst themselves for a small piece or quantity of Ground."13

Says Barton14 of ancient Babylonia: "individual property in land must have existed here several thousand years ago. . . . An unpublished archaic tablet in New York, which probably dates about 6,000 B.C., presents a plot of ground to a temple and so proves that individual ownership of land even then existed." In Deuteronomy we read: "Cursed be he that removeth his neighbor's landmark."15 "The usual picture which confronts us in the Old Testament is this, that land ownership was private ownership,"16 but, even in the later periods, the communal form existed alongside the private. In Homer the gods and kings held a *temenos* (piece cut off) and seem to be the first holders of private property in land. A *temenos* was also a public gift, for protection, and the givers commended their lives and property to its owner; it conveyed royalty with it or was a symbol of the bestowal of royal power. The Homeric system was on its way toward private holdings.17

Among the Teutons and Slavs private property in land started with the farm-yard, "which we may picture to ourselves even in primitive times as surrounded by a fence of twisted thorns and reeds."18 Land fit for agriculture, needing only cultivation, was present in superfluity in the Germany of Tacitus; but its superfluity left it without value and it was not an object of the property-interest. Agriculture was almost as primitive in the time of Tacitus as in that of Cæsar.19 "In North Russia individual property in land was by prior occupation. . . . In districts where game rights were valuable, the forests appropriated by individuals were heritable, salable, and mortgageable. Some such hunting appropriations were several miles square and were marked off by cutting trees on the boundaries with the individual's property-mark."20 Maine21 believes that in the Russian village community "the related families no longer hold their land as an indistinguishable common fund—they have portioned it out, at most they redistribute it periodically; sometimes even that

9 Tregear, in JAI, XIX, 106.
10 Carr, in *Smithson. Rep.*, 1891, 523 ff.
11 Mindeleff, in BAE, XVII, pt. II, 485.
12 Sapir, in HAI, II, 917.
13 William's *Key*, in *Coll. R.I. Hist. Soc.*, I, 89.
14 *Semitic Origins*, 158-159.
15 Deut., XXVII, 17; Gen., XXIII, 13.

16 Buhl, *Israeliten*, 55, 56.
17 Keller, *Hom. Soc.*, 192 ff. Full references to the text are here given.
18 Schrader, *Aryan*, 291.
19 Hildebrand, *Recht*, I, 122, 139.
20 Von Keussler, *Gemeindebesitz*, I, 75.
21 *Early Law*, 240; Wallace, *Russia*, 133.

stage has been passed. They are on the high road to modern landed proprietorship."

Property in the Waste. The rest of this section will be devoted to the redemption of waste-land and to similar usages in which individual initiative is recognized, all of which forecasts the development of land-ownership in severalty. A Melanesian custom which indicates foresight is that of planting land for an unborn child, in which case the father does the task with a dried coconut under his left arm or fixed on his left shoulder to represent the child, a coconut being the customary representative of an absent person; land so cultivated is no longer common but is the property of the individual to whom it has been thus assigned by his father.[22] While the Malays act much on the coöperative system of cultivating family plots in common, the Papuan, on the other hand, jealously guards his individual plot or garden and, however small or large it may be, surrounds it with a fence.[23]

In East Africa, while there is no recognition of property in land in our sense of the word, there is an approach toward that concept through the redemption of waste land, for "anyone almost may clear a piece of forest land and claim it as his own, as long as he wishes to cultivate it. When he dies it becomes, as a matter of course, the property (if indeed it can be called property, where purchase of land is unknown) of his nearest relative."[24] In Ukamba most of the land is unowned, "but where a man cultivates he acquires a right to the land which never lapses whether he make use of it or not." Such plots are inherited by all sons, of whom the eldest alone has any right to sell.[25] Among the Ba-Mbala of East Central Africa anybody can own land, but he has no right to the crops if raised by the labor of others, though he can, in the first instance, prevent the latter from establishing themselves there. There are no landmarks, but the owner of a piece of land buries a fetish in it; ownership exists as far as ponds and lakes are concerned, but running water has no proprietor.[26] Private ownership of land has to some extent made its appearance among the Kavirondo, for although the family in practice share the produce, theoretically the crop from each plot belongs to the member who tilled it.[27] With the Akamba every man owns his own *shamba* or cultivated field. "A man can pre-empt an area of unoccupied waste land as long as he marks the boundaries by felling a tree here and there along the proposed boundary line, and by cultivating a small patch within the pre-empted area. This done, his title to the land is recognized by the tribe and he can if he desires sell a portion of a piece of the land so pre-empted to a neighbour."[28] On the Upper Congo "men, women and children could own land that they had cleared for farms;"[29] while in Nigeria a man is free to mark out a farm on any unoccupied land; "he must consult the spirits, but no permission is necessary from the chief. If he has begun to till the land he establishes a claim to it so long as he keeps it under cultivation, but if he abandons the farm another can then take it."[30] In West Africa "a man may take up any unoccupied piece of land in the tract allotted to the community to which he belongs, free of charge, and cultivate it; but if he has access to his plot of ground through a plot be-

22 Rivers, *Melan. Soc.*, I, 56-57.
23 Ella, in AAAS, 1887, 488.
24 Cole, in JAI, XXXII, 314-315.
25 Dundas, C., in JAI, LI, 273.
26 Torday and Joyce, in JAI, XXXV, 411.

27 Northcote, in JAI, XXXVII, 60.
28 Hobley, *A-Kamba*, 82-83.
29 Weeks, in JAI, XXXIX, 424.
30 Tremearne, in JAI, XLII, 189-190;
Oliveira Martins, *Quadro*, 102-103.

longing to another man, he must pay the latter a small sum for his right of way."[31] The plots are evidently personal property. On the Zanzibar coast anyone may cultivate new land and so get title to it; in this case property is not derived from the chief but comes from appropriation and use.[32] According to the Musulman code everything vacant becomes the property of the first occupant; and the Koran assimilates to this category the booty taken from the enemy and the territory conquered from the infidel.[33]

The survival-value of such incentive to individual initiative as the above cases and those to follow show, is well depicted by Lugard:[34] "The labourer who works on land which is not his own, whether as the serf, or even as the paid servant of an estate owner, or as a unit in a communal estate, has little interest in its improvement during, and none beyond, his own lifetime. And so we find in Africa, 'the oldest of the continents,' no permanent irrigation works, such as those which terrace every hillside in Afghanistan, India, and China. The African plants few trees, and is careless of the productivity of the soil. Individual proprietorship is no doubt inimical to the supply of wage labour for large estates, but it makes for individual progress, thrift, and character. It is the strongest inducement to good farming, and politically an asset to the Government, to which the peasant owes the security of his holding. The French verdict is the same: 'The system of individual ownership is incontestably the one which is most favourable to production.'"

Among the Yakuts the sib (kin-group) allows the land to be appropriated by the improver so long as he does not claim too much and uses all he claims. If he rents any, the sib puts in its claim. The question is whether the improver has got back his capital and pay for his labor.[35] "Amongst the settled people of Central Asia the matter of artificial supply of water is as important for prosperity as cattle amongst the nomads. For a farmer to have control of a canal for irrigation means that he is rich. In consequence of this, the ownership of land in this district [chiefly that of the Kirghiz] is based upon the right of 'enlivening'; according to the local law, the fundamental right to the disposition of the land goes solely to him who has watered it; that is, enlivened it."[36] The laws of Manu grant the right of private property for clearing.[37]

Maine[38] has shown the difference between ancestral and self-acquired property in India, that is, wealth accumulated by trade and other personal exertion as distinguished from inherited wealth. The Tuareg divide at the death of a man all he has acquired by industry equally among his children, male and female, while things got by force, and regarded as a distinction of nobility— a sort of ancestral possession—go to the oldest son of the oldest sister. The latter are not alienable, but are used to maintain family prestige.[39] Evidently land obtained by breaking the waste is assimilated with goods obtained by finding, gift, raiding, buying, earning, or other forms of acquisition by personal initiative. A somewhat similar distinction between inalienable property or heirlooms and transferable estate is made in the D'Entrecasteaux Islands.[40]

31 Ellis, *Tshi*, 299.
32 Stuhlmann, *Mit Emin*, 35.
33 Hanoteau et Letourneux, *Kabylie*, II, 264, 265.
34 *Brit. Trop. Afr.*, 295.
35 Sieroshevski-Sumner, in JAI, XXXI, 74-75.
36 *Russian Ethnog.* (Russ.), II, 168.
37 Letourneau, *Prop.*, 223.
38 *Anc. Law*, 245; Nathubhai, in JASB, III, 408; Jolly, in *Grundr. d. Indo-Ar. Phil.*, 76.
39 Duveyrier, *Touâreg*, 397.
40 Jenness and Ballentyne, *D'Entrecasteaux*, 70-71.

To return to India, of peculiar interest among early Indo-Aryan theories of property is "the occupation of a *res nullius* as the foundation of property." The felling of trees gave the property-right. It was like hitting the game first; "whoever hit it afterward, dispatched his arrow in vain. Even through the cultivation of a piece of ground that was lying fallow only temporarily, one gained certain rights to it."[41]

In the Indian Archipelago, while in general ownership of all the land belongs to the different *fennas* or districts, an individual has a right to the waste and to all he cultivates, which may be sold, leased, or mortgaged to fellow-members of the *fenna*, or handed down to heirs. In this way has private property in land here developed out of communal. The individual loses his right if he leaves the land uncultivated until it looks again like waste. Only such ground can be mortgaged to which cultivation has lent value, as, especially, irrigated rice-fields. The local idea of mortgage is very different from the European: it can produce no transfer of possession; the only way for the owner actually to lose his land is to pass it over to the mortgagor in return for a share of the harvest or a rental. The mortgage-taker enters into all the rights of the owner but is obliged to return the land as soon as the owner or his heirs can pay up. The duration of the mortgage contract is not fixed and no interest is charged. As a rule the lifting of the mortgage is delayed, sometimes until after two or three generations; this, together with the fact that mortgages are contracted only by vocal agreement, is one of the causes for the land-disputes in the Malay lands, the witnesses being usually dead and the heirs not knowing enough to make the circumstances clear; so they commonly cut the knot by splitting half and half.[42] As regards the tenure by which land is held by the Sea Dyaks of Borneo, "it has been the immemorial custom that when a person fells the virgin forest, he acquires by that act a perpetual title to the land. It is his from thenceforth to do with as he pleases; he may sell it, or lend it, or let it. . . . The tenure has been modified within late years in view of the increasing demand for accommodation, and it is now generally understood that when the proprietor chooses to leave the district and remove into a distant country, he forfeits, by so doing, all title to the ground, and can no longer exact rent."[43]

In Polynesia there is some tendency toward private property in land from allotment or from appropriation from the waste,[44] while the Zuñi Indians appear to be in the transitional stage. Among them, if a man takes up a field of unappropriated land, it belongs strictly to him, but is spoken of as the property of his clan and on his death it may be cultivated by any member of that clan, though preferably by near relatives.[45] Among the Six Nations, while no individual could obtain an absolute title, "he could reduce unoccupied lands to cultivation to any extent he pleased; and so long as he continued to use them, his right to their enjoyment was protected and secured. He could also sell his improvements or bequeath them to his wife and children."[46] The household head among the Omahas "had a right to cultivate unoccupied land, and add it to his own."[47]

41 Jolly, *Recht u. Sitte*, II, 90.
42 Wilken, in VG, I, 39-41; II, 412-413, 416-417, 421, 422, 428-429; Van Eck, in *Ind. Gids*, 1883, I, 923.
43 Roth, *Sarawak*, I, 420.

44 Williamson, *Cent. Polyn.*, III, 245, 254, 255.
45 Fletcher, in HAI, I, 756.
46 Morgan, *League of Iroq.*, 326.
47 Dorsey, in BAE, III, 366.

In the ancient Akkadian laws it is provided that a married woman shall possess all she encloses.[48] Among the Arabs and in the Talmud, what the husbandman irrigates is his, while what is naturally watered belongs to the god who is *baal* or owner of the spot.[49] "Quod enim nullius est, id ratione naturali occupanti conceditur."[50] Mediæval economic history is full of provisions about the waste: "the more the population grows, the more agriculture extends, the more the amount of still uncleared land decreases. Thereby this too gradually wins a value, and so arises the property in land or a right even to till uncleared land, or a right to the land as such, quite independently of the work put in on it or the actual possession or cultivation."[51]

Modern cases in backward European districts follow the primitive ones: in north Russia individual property in land has existed from ancient times; the first occupant had as much as he could use; it was his while he used it. The meadows which a man cleared were his to the next revision, in forty years.[52] "Clearing new ground has always been regarded as the most tedious and scarching task of the Virginia laborer;"[53] it demanded some sort of special inducement. Oliveira Martins[54] says that between Andalusia and La Mancha the system may still be seen in action. The village possesses a waste where the villagers may pasture pigs, but one who chooses a piece out of it, and, by way of improvement, encloses it with stones collected from it, becomes proprietor of it. According to the customary law of mediæval Portugal he who cleared the land of thicket appropriated it but might not alienate it.

§137. Group-Hostility.

BEFORE Cook came to Australia, one hundred and fifty years ago, it was "a continent of innumerable tribal islands, each island carrying its own scanty population, each semi-isolated from its neighbour, each the possible cradle of a new physical type." There is said to be not a single record of the fusion of two or more tribes,[1] for they were continually at feud, always alert and suspicious: "The track of every one of a tribe's own people was known. A stranger crossing their country would be tracked down and killed as a matter of course, so they had recourse to boots made of hair rope and emu feathers; these effectually disguised the tracks made by their wearer. The fear of the uncanny kept a hostile tribe from attempting to track an unknown man, who might be a moora [ancestor], so that the wearer got a certain amount of liberty."[2] Although the Australians were not especially warlike, "it is quite true that, if a member of an unknown tribe made his appearance, except of course he come accredited as a sacred messenger, he would most probably be promptly speared. Anything strange is uncanny to the native, who has a peculiar dread of evil magic from a distance. Our two 'boys,' who went with us right through the continent, were particularly careful to keep close to camp, unless well armed, when they got amongst absolutely strange tribes." It seems that contiguous tribes are friendly enough; but "the members of one tribe will tell you that a distant tribe, with which they rarely or perhaps never come into

48 *Records of the Past*, III, 23.
49 Smith, *Relig. Sem.*, 97.
50 Gaius, *De Acq. re. dom.*, I, 111.
51 Hildebrand, *Recht*, I, 140.
52 Von Keussler, *Gemeindebesitz*, 73, 75.

53 Bruce, *Va.*, I, 196.
54 *Quadro*, 99.
1 Keith, in JAI, XLVI, 22, 23.
2 Horne and Aiston, *Cent. Aust.*, 138.

contact, is very fierce and bloodthirsty and given to making raids. The same tribe will be living upon most friendly terms with its immediate neighbours, and some of the latter will be doing precisely the same thing with the tribe of which your informants are afraid and suspicious." As for the traditional view that the various tribes are regularly hostile to one another, "nothing could be further from the truth;" but it appears that each tribe is surrounded by concentric circles of increasing fear and suspicion, and that the less they know the more apprehensive they are. The exercise of magic by the "giving of a bone," or the abduction of a woman, may lead to enmity and a fight, and someone may be killed, but harmony is restored by compensation. "In the case of a savage it must be remembered that when once compensation in any form has been made by an offending party, the matter is supposed to be ended, and no ill feelings are cherished. Of course there are exceptions to this, but, on the whole, it is strikingly true of the Australian savage."[3]

In Melanesia, "a stranger as such was generally throughout the islands an enemy to be killed. Thus a stranger who had escaped from a wreck on to an islet was killed when seen, and spoken of as a cocoa-nut that had floated ashore."[4] Again, they "hate all strangers and regard them as enemies. . . . The killing of a man not belonging to the tribe is not looked upon as murder, but is reckoned as a deserving act, whereby the number of enemies—and everyone not belonging to the tribe is an enemy—is diminished."[5] "This feeling might be justified if extended toward the intruding white man, but it is difficult to understand when entertained towards nearly all individuals of the same race, provided the distance which separates their respective villages exceeds that which can be accomplished in an easy ramble."[6] In New Guinea there have long been standing enmities between village communities.[7]

In northern Angola, "every stranger is an enemy, and whoever is not powerful enough to enslave the villagers must himself serve them as such. . . . The farther I led my negroes into regions unknown to them, the more were they under my hand, for, left to themselves, they would all have been immediately enslaved by the first kinglet they encountered."[8] In Togo, the heart of the native is "full of suspicion, not only against the white stranger, but also, and just as much, against his own countryman and tribal comrade." Not long ago six of these groups, comprising twenty towns and villages were at swords'-points.[9] On the Loango coast there is no sympathy for those outside the blood-bond.[10] The atomism and general attitude of fear and suspicion exhibited by the Teda are described in a previous connection.[11] The Galla, despite tribal rivalry and envy, live pretty peacefully among themselves; but any stranger "who has not parents or relatives in the country or has not been accepted in guestfriendship somewhere, is mercilessly persecuted."[12] Robbing and killing the stragglers from caravans is common.[13]

In India, among certain frontier-tribes, the kin-groups, or *khels*, "stand so far apart in hostile feeling that no effort would be made by one to check the massacre, within the village walls, of another. . . . Between the *khels* in the same village great rivalry exists, which in old days used to lead to blood feuds

3 Spencer and Gillen, *North Tr. Cent. Aust.*, 31-32; Havitt, in JAI, XX, 75.
4 Codrington, *Melanesians*, 345.
5 Von Pfeil, *Südsee*, 47, 76.
6 Von Pfeil, in JAI, XXVII, 181.
7 Keith, in JAI, XLVI, 28.

8 Bastian, *Afr. Reisen*, 62, 63.
9 Fies, in *Globus*, LXXX, 379.
10 Pechuël-Lösche, *Loango*, 10.
11 §9, above.
12 Paulitschke, *Nordost-Afr.*, I, 247.
13 Stuhlmann, *Mit Emin*. 51.

and frequent fighting, indeed, the inter-*khel* feuds were and are far more
bitter than inter-village feuds. . . . One marked peculiarity in their intestine
feuds is that we so often find a village divided against itself, one clan being
at deadly feud with another, whilst a third lives between them in a state of
neutrality, and at perfect peace with both."[14] In Madras, "relations are always
entertained and given food, but strangers never. One of another village and a
stranger would never ask anything; he would not get it if he did. People
of the same village would help one another, but never strangers."[15] The
term Lepchas, given to a people in the Himalayas by the usurping Tibetans,
means "ill-speakers," just as the term Welsh means, in Saxon, jabberers.[16]

The Scythians were very savage against outsiders, but just and kind
toward one another.[17] In Korea, every spring, permission is granted to the
people to fight with stones, and the men and boys go to the open spaces where
stones are plenty, form sides, usually town against country, and have regular
pitched battles. Many are killed and wounded.[18] In the Chinese communities
in Borneo, and even in China, the village-heads smooth out most of the quarrels; "but this does not prevent hatred and vengefulness from characterizing
the relation between neighboring villages, and from degenerating into blood-
vengeance when once it has come to fighting and some have fallen." If a villager
falls into the hands of his enemies he can look for severe treatment; "isolated
dwellings and vehicles are plundered and burned, graves desecrated and
grave-marks destroyed"—and then comes a bloody retaliation.[19] In Borneo,
each village is "instinctively conscious that it is a unit of a scattered people."[20]

In East Greenland "the people of one settlement form, as it were, a society
by themselves, which often is at enmity with the folk of another settlement" and
a people on one side of a fjord will volunteer the information that those on
the other side are bad men. "When we learned to know the natives better it
appeared that it was very common for the one to disparage the other at the
same time that he sought to place himself in the best light."[21] Among the
Central Eskimo, "every family is allowed to settle wherever it likes, visiting a
strange tribe being the only exception. In such cases the newcomer has to
undergo a ceremony which consists chiefly in a duel between a native of the
place and himself. If he is defeated he runs the risk of being killed by those
among whom he has come."[22] By the Eskimo at Bering Straits, "stealing from
people of the same village or tribe is regarded as wrong. . . . To steal from a
stranger or from people of another tribe is not considered wrong so long as it
does not bring trouble on the community."[23] This attitude, as we shall see,
is abundantly paralleled throughout the world. "In general the Eskimo are
extremely honest among themselves; but all consider it not only allowable, but
even very praiseworthy to rob strangers. A clever robber of foreigners is an
object of admiration, provided he does not let himself be caught."[24]

The ethnocentrism of the American Indians is manifested in the tribal names,
most of which, as applied by the tribes to themselves, mean "people" or "real
people," and, as applied to outsiders, mean "earth-eaters" or something simi-

14 Godden, in JAI, XXVI, 167, and
XXVII, 23.
15 Fawcett, *Saoras*, in JASB, I, 219.
16 Waddell, *Himalayas*, 92-93.
17 Lippert, *Kgchte.*, II, 10.
18 Saunderson, in JAI, XXIV, 314.

19 De Groot, *Kongsiwezen*, 103, 105.
20 Keith, in JAI, XLVI, 27.
21 Holm, *Ethnol. Skizze*, 45, 125.
22 Boas, in BAE, VI, 581, 609.
23 Nelson, in BAE, XVIII, pt. I, 293.
24 Letourneau, *Prop.*, 53-54.

larly derogatory.[25] "Among the North-west Indians there has existed up to the most recent times a steady condition of war among the minor tribes."[26] "As soon as a Pawnee meets another Indian, a fight begins between them without further ceremony."[27] The Pimas captured Apache children and sold them to Mexicans and Spaniards. "These captives were well treated, but their origin was never forgotten and the fear and suspicion of the tribe found expression at times in the decrees of the medicine-men that certain misfortunes were caused by the presence of the aliens."[28] Among the Mohave, "not only sexual connection but ordinary intercourse with other races were regarded with disfavor, as being a specific cause of sickness."[29] For racial aloofness of this order the Seri Indians, a very primitive type, are noteworthy: "The strongest tribal characteristic is implacable animosity toward aliens, whether Indian or Caucasian; certainly for three and a half centuries, and probably for many more, the Seri have been almost constantly on the warpath against one alien group or another, and have successfully stayed Spanish, Mexican, and American invasion. In their estimation the brightest virtue is the shedding of alien blood, while the blackest crime in their calendar is alien conjugal union."[30]

Among the Guiana Indians there is always some form of salutation, for the stranger is an enemy.[31] The Brazilian Indians believe that all misfortunes come from outside, not least of which are sickness and death caused by foreign magicians. [32] The Fuegians "dare not go where they have no friends, and where they are unknown, as they would most likely be soon killed. I have inquired of the natives if they think the Indians with whom we have not come in contact, would massacre a shipwrecked party; they unhesitatingly answer they would, on account of the following reasons:—1st—They would be afraid to let strangers live among them, they would distrust them; they would think the strangers whose language they could not understand had evil designs against them. 2nd—They would kill them in order to take undisputed possession of all they might have. 3rd—They know sufficiently well strangers to be jealous, and fearful of them; for they have heard of ships visiting their shores to steal their skins, ravish their wives, and do other deeds of violence. There are persons now living whose parents experienced such treatment, and there are several individuals over there, the descendants of these marriages. Thus through ignorance, covetousness, revenge, and distrust, they would certainly murder all foreigners indiscriminately."[33]

The ancient civilized peoples were very clannish and drew a close distinction between themselves and outsiders, between the citizen and the stranger. Their patriotism was based on ethnic unity: exterminate enemies, help clansmen. Generations probably lived and died in the same corner of land, which was to them the best in the world. With their ethnocentrism went hatred of aliens.[34]

25 HAI, I, 147, 246, 270, 520, 524, 556, 739, 805, 921; II, 104, 211, 214, 251, 326, 415, 712, 723, 764, 873, 920, 963, 1007.
26 Rink, Esk. Herkomst, 279.
27 Bernhöft, Verwandsftsnamen, 29.
28 Russell, in BAE, XXVI, 197.
29 Kroeber, in AA, IV, 279.
30 McGee, in BAE, XVII, pt. I, 11.

31 Roth, in BAE, XXXVIII, §803.
32 Von den Steinen, Zent. Bras., 332-333.
33 Bridges, in Voice for S. Amer., XIII, 201.
34 Maurer, Vkde., I, 165-166; Sumner, Folkways, §§16 ff.; Letourneau, Morale, 240; Zangwill, Ghetto, 143-145.

§138. Causes of War.

WAR for plunder is the order of the day in Africa. In some parts, as in Central Africa where one of the chief motives for inter-village war is cannibalism, the booty may consist of human beings, a practice not uncommon in Melanesia also. More generally the objects of war are slaves and cattle. In East Africa the slave-trader is always waiting about the courts of the principal chiefs.[1] The chief causes of the inter-tribal conflicts of the Bageshu are theft or infringing upon the land of another clan.[2] The Bahima are a peaceable people and seldom make war upon other tribes, their chief object in life being to live quietly with their cattle; "nevertheless, they have ever to be on the defensive, for other tribes have always looked upon their vast herds of cattle with jealous eyes, and whenever the chance has presented itself they have pounced down upon, and tried to carry off one of the herds."[3] As regards plunder, which is the main object of war among the Ba-Mbala, everyone takes what he can; there is no such thing as effective conquest, since they desire no territory.[4] In Uganda, "after a successful raid the elders of the clan divide the spoil (which is, of course, cattle, sheep, and goats), and the warriors so far respect the old men that they allow them to take what they require from out of the loot, while at least seven of the captured cattle are sent to the medicine man. When this has been done, the rest of the loot in live-stock is left to be snatched at by the warriors. This proceeding results in a general *mêlée*, in which men sometimes get killed by spear or club wounds."[5] Again, there are two types of war as distinguished by the natives. One is more like the European type, and is termed "call-out," for there is a declaration of war. One campaign generally completes the fighting, for the defeated rarely rally. Booty and slaves are taken, and the old and weak, as well as the chiefs, are killed. A second variety is mere plundering and stealing, arising out of ancestral feuds, with no definite cause. It is marked by treachery and surprise, and is carried on in great secrecy. Defenseless towns are attacked by night, and the result is slavery and great devastation. This type of war is common, especially at the beginning of the dry season, when the harvests are in and food is plenty."[6] In Dahomi, "the chief end of the annual expedition is plunder, not conquest. Dahomi may be likened to a vast association of banditti, who at fixed periods . . . make raids upon their eastern neighbors, and return on the approach of the rains, laden with spoil." These raids supplied slaves, in the days of the European slave-trade.[7] The wars of the Togo tribes "aim naturally, as in the case of almost all warlike negro tribes, only at the plundering of slaves, cattle, and other property from their neighbors."[8]

Among the Chukchi, "murder or infringement upon rights and property is punished by vendetta, but if the wrong is done within the limits of the family, outsiders have no right to interfere. Thus crimes against near kinsmen, which are by no means rare among the Chukchi, remain unavenged."[9] The causes of war in the Sema country are said to be three in number—two being economic, while the third is evidently war for glory: "First, shortage of land necessitating

---

1 Abbott, in USNM, 1891, 388.
2 Roscoe, in JAI, XXXIX, 190.
3 Roscoe, in JAI, XXXVII, 108.
4 Torday and Joyce, in JAI, XXXV, 416.
5 Johnston, *Uganda*, II, 879.

6 Oberländer, *Deut. Afr.*, 16-17.
7 Ellis, *Ewe*, 197.
8 Klose, *Togo*, 502.
9 Bogoras, in AA, III, 107.

forcible encroachment on that of neighbouring villages; secondly, the protection of trading interests, as an attempt on the part of one village to trade directly with another at some distance has often caused war with an intervening village through which the trade used to pass (much to the profit of that intervening village) and which retaliates for its loss by making war on the interlopers, cutting up their trading parties, destroying the intercommunication between the offending villages, and compelling their trade to return to its old channel. . . . The third cause is found in the fits of restlessness that from time to time afflict most Naga villages, the desire of the young men as yet untried to prove their manhood and gain the right of wearing the warrior's gauntlets and boar's tusk collar, all culminating in an overwhelming desire to get somebody's head, which not infrequently outweighs all riper considerations of policy and prudence."[10] Schwaner[11] mentions a war in Borneo, which had cost the lives of not less than one hundred and sixty men, and which arose over the abduction of a woman. It lasted on in the form of head-hunting for revenge a long time without the rest of the tribal-members seeming to feel that peace should be made. In New Zealand, "in later times the eating of the human flesh became the ruling desire and the chief incentive to war; this unnatural food was supposed to impart additional courage and ferocity to those who partook of it, and likewise to make their triumph over their enemies complete; nor must the love of plundering their foes, and despoiling them of their most valued property, their wives, highly-prized green stone . . ., jade ornaments, beautifully-wrought mats, carved weapons, stores of food, and women, be overlooked. All these circumstances combined to make war a delight, render the chief great, and destroy all feelings of compunction, if they ever had any."[12]

The Mohawk Indians, in the seventeenth century, descended annually upon the Algonquins near Manhattan to plunder or levy tribute.[13] "In former days the Wabanaki (Eastern Algonkins) nation, the Indians called Meg'wek, or Mohawks, and other members of the Iroquoian Six Nations, were wont to wage bloody and unceasing war with one another. . . . The cause of the strife was an hereditary dispute about hunting grounds." And the Wabanaki tribes had feuds among themselves.[14] The Apaches were spurred on to constantly renewed attacks upon the Pima "for the sake of the plunder that they might secure. Thus the feral pauper preyed upon the sedentary toiler, but paid dearly in blood for his occasional prize of grain or live stock."[15] "The Hopi Indians, as their name indicates, are preëminently people of peace. . . . For many years, unaided, they waged an almost constant warfare with the predatory Utes, Apaches, and Navahos, who devastated their farms and approached even to the foothills of the mesas on which their villages stand. During the seventeenth, eighteenth, and the first half of the nineteenth centuries these hostilities were almost continuous."[16] Here is a case of offensive warfare on the one side evoking necessary defensive operations on the part of a reluctant people—operations as indispensable to self-maintenance as the industry whose products tempted aggression.

"A pretty example of the rise of wars among nature-peoples" is as follows. "A whale was cast upon the coast of California, to the joy of the Indians who

10 Hutton, *Sema Nagas*, 167.
11 *Borneo*, II, 134.
12 Taylor, *Te Ika*, 353.
13 Tuckerman, *Peter Stuyvesant*, 41.

14 Leland and Prince, *Kulóskap*, 24.
15 Russell, in BAE, XXVI, 203.
16 Fewkes, in AA, IV, 482.

set themselves eagerly to cutting it up with their stone axes. When they were in the midst of this labor a hostile neighboring tribe appeared with the purpose of taking forcible possession of the whale." The latter withdrew when they saw that the Spaniards were going to take the part of the original finders.[17] The directors of the Dutch West India Company reported that "the aforesaid company could not exist except by war."[18] War among Brazilian natives is of a certain personal character when it is motived in blood-vengeance. "But aside from that it is at present most often undertaken to get as booty slaves who are sold to other tribes or to settlers of Portuguese origin, or to free prisoners, or, more seldom, to drive the enemy out of hunting and fishing grounds."[19] The chief motive of the reciprocal wars of the Orinoco Indians had for object the capturing of women and boys. "The original object of the capture was to insure, through the possession of captives, greater authority, a larger retinue, more laborers in their fields, and servants to wait on them"[20]— a combination, it seems, of self-maintenance and self-gratification. The religious motive enforces the economic in a South American case where the deity orders a tribe to live by making war on all others, slaying men and taking goods and women.[21]

It is hardly necessary to cite the devotion of the ancient nations to plundering raids and piracy. Assyria was devoted to raiding, though commerce was beginning.[22] In Homer cattle-raiding and piracy were reputable and even noble employments; Agamemnon wished he had been killed upon a cattle-raid rather than in the humiliating manner recorded.[23] The Ptolemies, having no ship-timber, warred on the Seleucidae for the cedars of Lebanon.[24] Carthage was "dives opum studiisque asperrima belli."[25] "Even in the writings of the most enlightened philosophers of Greece, war with barbarians is represented as a form of chase, and the simple desire of obtaining the barbarians as slaves was considered a sufficient reason for invading them."[26] In Arabia, "feuds are continual, but at little cost of life; the main object of a raid is booty, not slaughter; and the Bedouin, though a terrible braggart, has at heart little inclination for killing or being killed."[27] The Viking-raids of the Scandinavians were for booty and even for revenue; the Swedish king's men paid him a commutation if he stayed at home, and they kept all the rest of the loot.[28]

War for woman-stealing, which is closely allied to self-maintenance, for glory, or for some religious reason, will be illustrated in the following instances. In Victoria, "all arrangements connected with marriage cause trouble in the tribes."[29] The general cause for war, in Australia, is "the death in the tribe of some man, from sickness or accident, which is invariably set down to the sorcery of some hostile or little known tribe. In such cases, a party will set out after the burial, mad for bloodshed; march by night in the most stealthy manner, perhaps fifty or a hundred and fifty miles, into a country inhabited by tribes the very names of which they may be ignorant of. On discovering a party of such people, they will hide themselves, and then creep up to their camp

17 Friederici, in *Globus*, XC, 301.
18 Brodhead, *N.Y. Col. Docs.*, I, 61.
19 Von Martius, *Beiträge*, I, 131.
20 Roth, in BAE, XXXVIII, 579.
21 Tylor, *Anth.*, 225.
22 Rogers, *Babylonia*, I, 308-309.
23 Keller, *Hom. Soc.*, 92-93; Homer, *Odyssey*, XI, 398 ff.
24 Lindsay, *Merchant Ship.*, I, 57.
25 Vergil, *Æneid*, I, 14.
26 Lecky, *Europ. Morals*, II, 256-257.
27 Palgrave, *Arabia*, 23.
28 Lippert, *Kgchte.*, II, 536.
29 Smyth, *Vict.*, I, xxiv.

during the night, when the inmates are asleep, butcher the men and the children as they lie, and the women after further atrocities. If the party discovered be too large to slaughter wholesale, one or two will be disposed of by sudden onslaught, or likewise, and the invading party will quickly retire, to be followed in due course by warriors seeking their revenge. In *mêlées* of this sort it sometimes happens that a man or woman belonging to a tribe associated with the one whose members made the onslaught is killed in the darkness and confusion unrecognized, the result of which is further complications and bloodshed."[30] "Now and then they have inter-tribal quarrels and fights, but there is no such thing as the acquisition of fresh territory. No idea of this or of its advisability or otherwise ever enters the head of the Central Australian native. Very probably this is to be associated with the fundamental belief that his . . . ancestors occupied precisely the same country which he does now. The spirit parts of these ancestors are still there, and he has a vague kind of idea not only that the country is indubitably his by right of inheritance, but that it would be of no use to any one else, nor would any other people's country be good for him."[31]

Among some of the Melanesians, insults, wounded vanity, and jealousy were causes of war. "Boasting of success in love affairs, of which apparently a good deal went on among the young men at gatherings for feasts, and the jealousy thus aroused was another recognized source of minor warfare. . . . A brawl between members of a community arising over women or pigs might lead to wounding or killing." In other instances, long-standing feuds gave rise to warfare; "each hamlet-group appears to have had a traditional enemy with whom the greater part of its fighting was done, always in theory at least, to avenge the losses caused by its hostile neighbour." Cannibalism sometimes accompanied war.[32] Twenty-seven causes of war are mentioned by a writer on the natives of southeastern Papua, which are classifiable under the four elemental motives of hunger, love, vanity, and ghost-fear. Women appear to be an especially common source of difficulty here.[33]

The negroes of Gaboon war to get meat, but most often about women. Female chastity has a real money-value, but virtue is fragile. An adulterer flees to another village which cannot in honor give him up. Hence reclamations, discussions, palavers, and often war. In this country one village often gets the idea of destroying another. It has a member of a third village assassinated and lays it to the selected village-victim, offers alliance to the third, and the two carry out the program of destruction. A passion for thieving assists in keeping hostilities alive.[34] It is strongly characteristic of negroes, says Stuhlmann,[35] to determine on war from one day to the next, capriciously. The spread of Islam has heightened the destructiveness of tropical African war. While fetishists, the negroes have no idea of proselyting; they pillage but do not conquer, and their wars are like fires that die out. Once converted, proselytism just suits them, as the Koran gives so much booty into their hands.[36] Religion is conducive to warlike prowess among the Nigerian head-hunters, for the

30 Curr, *Aust. Race.*, I, 85-86.
31 Spencer and Gillen, *North. Tr. Cent. Aust.*, 13.
32 Seligmann, *Melanesians*, 541, 542, 543-544.

33 Bromilow, in AAAS, 1909, 476-478.
34 Letourneau, *Guerre*, 65, 66, 70.
35 *Mit Emin*, 231.
36 Letourneau, *Guerre*, 63.

strongest on earth will be the strongest in the next world, and the spirit of a slaughtered enemy will attend the slayer.[37]

The Kabyles have many pretexts for war, "but the real cause is always the same. The spirit of conquest not existing, and general interests not providing matter for discussion, the Kabyles fight among themselves only over questions of *amour propre*": real or pretended violations of public pledges or guarantees, abduction of women, private quarrels, and the like. "Every one fears to yield to his adversaries concessions interpretable in an unfavorable sense; they are obstinate, heads heat up, and war breaks out. The great majority of the combatants therefore have no really direct interest in the quarrels, and fight without hatred, through a spirit of solidarity and to satisfy a point of honor." The women upset their associative arrangements by awakening jealousies and by complaints to their husbands.[38]

In the East Indies wars arise over the most trivial circumstances. The debt of one member of a tribe is demanded of his tribe; and if it is not paid, war results. A notice in the form of a warning is given, and if it is not heeded, war begins at once.[39] Head-hunting expeditions are motived in religion as well as in the desire for trophies. "A further religious goad to war is the irksome mourning taboo after the death of a near relative or a chief, which cannot be lifted until a fresh head is obtained. The removal of the taboo by bringing home a head, described in song as a precious moment, and compared to a lump of gold, a lump of silver, and various favorite jungle fruits, is the occasion for one of their greatest festivals."[40] Veth[41] says that an inflammatory literary production, such as Havelaar's *Multatuli*,[42] could not have stirred up the Javanese, for they could not take it in; that the testimony of the past shows that every great exhibition of strength in the East Indies has always had cult-fanaticism at the bottom, as a lever. Once "the Sultan of Joló went to visit the Sultan of Mindanao, being escorted, for greater ostentation, by a squadron composed of sixty-seven craft. Seeing such a following, the Sultan of Mindanao . . . feared that it did not indicate peaceful intentions, and had the mouth of the river closed. At this the Sultan of Joló, being offended, challenged the Sultan of Mindanao to a personal combat. The challenge was accepted and the two sultans fought, 'body to body,' and with such rage that each killed his antagonist. Immediately war was kindled between the two peoples."[43]

Vanity was an important cause of war in Polynesia. The natives of Samoa were ambitious to signalize themselves by the number of heads they could lay before the chiefs. "No hero at the Grecian games rejoiced more over his chaplet than did the Samoan glory in the distinction of having cut off a man's head." The *summum bonum* of a New Caledonian was to be praised as a great warrior.[44] The Polynesians also engaged in constant conflicts about trifles. An insulting word from one to another did not lead to a personal combat but a tribal one. Jealousy of a tribe prospering by peaceful labor was a frequent cause for war; and they fought a good deal over women.[45] But it was only at the outset

37 Tremearne, in JAI, XLII, 183-185.
38 Hanoteau et Letourneux, *Kabylie*, II, 76, 473; Letourneau, *Guerre*, 260-261, 266, 272, 315.
39 Wilken, *Vkde.*, 389-392.
40 Morris, in *Jour. Am. Or. Soc.*, Sec. Hist. Relig., VII, 33.

41 Veth, in *De Gids*, 1860, II, 250.
42 Day, *Dutch in Java*, 330; Keller, *Colon.*, 484.
43 Montero y Vidal, *Filipinas*, I, 391.
44 Turner, *Samoa*, 192, 345.
45 Ratzel, *Vkde.*, II, 205.

of the nineteenth century that the conquest-motive appeared, and Tamehameha, the "Hawaiian Napoleon," dominated the whole archipelago. A cause for war in New Zealand was the eating of a whale stranded on the shore of one chief's territory by members of a neighboring tribe.[46] "We fought for slaves and women," said a Maori chief once; "we did not want the land."[47]

Among the Hurons and Iroquois, it was not the love of theft that led to war, but rather the desire for trophies. Murderers were pursued at once without ceremony. The violations of territory were a prime cause of hostilities. An Iroquois chief is reported to have asked a neighboring ruler to allow their young men to have a little war, in order to keep in practice. On the second chief's refusal, for he feared the consequences, he was asked with whom, then, "his children could play."[48] War-parties among the Omaha were of two classes—those organized for the purpose of securing spoils and those which had for their object the avenging of injuries. "The latter were held in higher esteem than the former, and the men who took part in them were regarded with more respect by the tribe."[49] Mason[50] reports that the Omaha wars were caused "by the stealing of horses, the elopement of women, and infringement on hunting grounds. . . . In aboriginal times war was occasioned by encroachments upon the standing order of things." The Passamaquoddy and Micmac tribes fought as a consequence of the quarrel of two lads, one the son of the Micmac chief, who was killed. The father would hear of nothing except vengeance, though the Passamaquoddy chief "even offered the life of his own son who had been guilty of the murder, but all to no purpose. In consequence of this unfortunate occurrence, the celebrated 'great war' was then declared, which lasted many years. . . . So great was the hostile spirit that the two tribes fought whenever they met, paying no heed to the time of year."[51] The motive of revenge accounts for many Indian wars and their traditional cruelties.[52] "The wars among the Indian tribes nearly always arise from individual murders. The killing of a tribesman by the members of another community concerns his whole people. If satisfaction is not promptly made, war follows, as a matter of course. When a neighboring people would neither join the confederacy nor enter into a treaty of alliance with it, the almost inevitable result would be a deadly war. Among the nomadic or unsettled Indian tribes, especially the Algonkins and Sioux, the young men are expected to display their bravery by taking scalps; and a race of farmers, hunters, and fishermen, like the Iroquois, would be tempting victims."[53] Among the Pima, any man of acknowledged courage might, with the approval of his fellows, organize a war-party. He received a title which lapsed, together with his authority, at the end of the campaign.[54]

Between the different tribes in the regions inhabited by the Jibaros of Ecuador there exists almost perpetual enmity and destructive wars are often carried out, especially between neighboring tribes. Not seldom the feuds arise for the sake of the women. The Jibaros live in polygamy and hold their wives in high estimation. The men are very jealous of their wives and adultery is severely punished; the relatives of the woman frequently take her part and try to inflict revenge upon the husband. A much more important cause of war

46 Letourneau, *Guerre*, 131, 119.
47 Cowan, *Maoris*, 3.
48 Lafitau, *Mœurs*, III, 159.
49 Fletcher and LaFlesche, in BAE, XXVII, 408-409.

50 *Invention*, 368.
51 Leland and Prince, *Kulóskap*, 24-27.
52 Lippert, *Kgchte.*, II, 75.
53 Hale, *Iroq. Rites*, 68, 92.
54 Russell, in BAE, XXVI, 196.

is the belief in witchcraft, as when the sorcerer belongs to another tribe, and this superstition is the reason why they never aim at territorial conquests. The Jibaros "fear and detest the country of their enemies, where secret supernatural dangers may threaten them even after they have conquered their natural enemies. The sorcerers of the hostile tribe may have left their witching arrows everywhere, on the road, in the forest, in the houses, with the result that the invading enemies may be hit by them when they least expect it. The land of the enemy is therefore abandoned as soon as possible. Besides, the Jibaros, who inhabit endless virgin forests, where they can make new settlements almost anywhere, have no need of conquering the territory of other tribes."[55]

The Aztecs warred to get captives as vicarious sacrifices for themselves and their children. What could give a greater sense of national power? They also had the motive of extending the boundaries of the empire.[56] "The wars of the Incas had an essentially religious character, and may be compared with those of the Mussulmans, at the time when Islamism, propagated by the sword, spread with such rapidity over whole regions." But the Incas also had conquest in mind. They are said to have warred without hatred or anger, to civilize the conquered; to have declared of one subjugated tribe that it was "not fit to be ruled by us," and to have withdrawn and abandoned it.[57] But these cases of conquest belong to a considerably developed civilization; "an expedition of conquest in and for itself witnesses already to a preceding high stage of development in the conquering people . . . a preceding amalgamation of many tribes into one well-ordered whole."[58] Wars to extend the cult or for conquest were common enough in the ancient monarchies of Assyria and Egypt.[59]

Stealing of women led to war among the ancient Hebrews, and they were eager for pillage of all kinds.[60] The doctrine that the Hebrew god was the only deity was a prolific cause of conflict. The Arabs before Mahomet were given over to feuds which they could not solve and end.[61] The Trojan War and the rape of the Sabine women are traditions of the woman-cause in wars; but Livy[62] cites other causes of Sabine-Roman hostility. Letourneau[63] lists numbers of classical, Scandinavian, and mediæval points of dispute. The Germans of the time of Arminius were at continual war "propter raptas virgines aut arripiendas" (on account of maidens stolen or to be stolen).[64]

§139. Warlikeness.

The habitudes of the Australians afford one of the most characteristic pictures of a petty strife which hardly deserve the name of war. In their formal conflicts the casualties are very light, and they do not possess enough to tempt robbery. "Between tribes actually engaged in barter, peace, of course, prevails for the time; but it is no guarantee against sorcery, nor, as soon as business is concluded, against those murderous night attacks by which native warfare

55 Karsten, Jibaro, BAE, Bull. LXXIX, 16, 10, 14-15, 19.
56 Letourneau, Guerre, 165.
57 Nadaillac, Preh. Amer., 437; Prescott, Peru, I, 160; De la Vega, Yncas, I, 332.
58 Gumplowicz, Rassenk., 293.
59 Rogers, Babylonia, I, 350; Records of Past, I, 78; Letourneau, Guerre, 288 ff.

60 Gen., XXXIV, 8; Judges, XII, XV; I Chron., XX, 4; Josh., XI, 12 ff.
61 Proksch, Blutrache, 51.
62 Hist., I, 30.
63 Guerre, 412, 490, 504, 506, 525-526.
64 Wilutzky, Mann u. Weib., 145.

is carried on." Tribes which are pretty well acquainted with one another may come into collision over some injury, such as murder, the refusal to give over a girl promised in marriage, abduction of a woman, or encroachment on hunting-grounds. "On such occasions the angered tribes meet to fight. The parties are drawn up in single file and open order, thirty or forty yards apart. The combat is principally with spears, which every man, his shield on his left arm, hurls straight, sharply, and horizontally, at the man opposite him. Spears which describe a curve in their flight are easily avoided. . . . I have witnessed combats of this sort more than once, and was struck by the novel effect produced by the straight, light, noiseless missiles passing in continuous, opposite, and horizontal streams. I wondered that so few persons could keep so many under way at once. It seemed to sleet spears. When the fight is in progress, there is very little noise. Very great agility is displayed in avoiding the spears and boomerangs, and the combatants have a very accurate perception of the flight of those weapons. For instance, I have seen a man lift his foot in the coolest manner to avoid a spear, which in effect plunged into the very spot on which his foot had rested. When one warrior has fallen, or several been obliged to retire disabled, hoarse shouts begin to be heard, and probably some pairs close with club and shield. Shortly a cry arises on both sides to part them; men, and perhaps women, interpose, and the combatants separate to look after the wounded. When one has been killed, both parties usually retire at once, and another battle may take place later. If nothing worse has happened than severe wounds, peace is made, and for a few nights the tribes corroboree in turn, one tribe being the performers and the other the spectators of the evening. . . . I should not think that a battle ever lasts more than half an hour. . . . No idea of conquest exists nor properly speaking of battle, for their fights do not lead to slaughter or spoils and are devoid of the ordinary consequences which follow battles and victories in civilized countries."[1]

"Sometimes a fight takes the form of a tournament or friendly trial of skill in the use of the boomerang and shield. Ten or twelve warriors . . . are met by an equal number at a distance of about twenty paces. Each individual has a right to throw his boomerang at anyone on the other side, and steps out of the rank into the intervening space to do so. The opposite party take their turn, and so on alternately, until someone is hit, or all are satisfied. . . . Quarrels between tribes are sometimes settled by single combat between the chiefs, and the result is accepted as final . . . but real fighting seldom takes place, unless the women rouse the anger of the men and urge them to come to blows. Even then it rarely results in a general fight, but comes to single combats between warriors of each side. . . . The first wound ends the combat. This is often followed by an encounter between the women, who begin by scolding, and rouse each other to fury, tearing each other's hair, and striking one another with their yam-sticks."[2]

One of the reasons for the unwarlikeness of the Australians is that they have little worth fighting over. "It is property which principally makes men dependent on each other, being the main source of power, the main means of suppression; and it is the lack of it in the Australian race which renders its tribes so free and autonomic. There is nothing which might tempt them to suppress a strange tribe, nor do they possess anything to incite the conquering tendency in others. Thus we hear nowhere of fights for superiority. The seizure of women, a

1 Curr, *Aust. Race*, I, 78, 84-85, 86.   2 Dawson, *Aust. Aborig.*, 77.

murder here and there, very rarely a quarrel about some boundary, give rise to fights of a mostly harmless nature."[3] There is no political organization within the tribe, but all are pretty much equal.

"A sudden death is often the cause of fighting amongst men of the bereaved tribe. They will exhibit their grief by spearing each other; and men have been killed at such times." A case is mentioned where a man died of heart disease and there was a quarrel over his grave. "The cause of the quarrel was not ascertained, but the results were fatal. One young man was killed, and he was buried in the very grave around which all had assembled for the purpose of paying respect to their dead relative. . . . Those who have lived amongst the blacks cannot fail to have observed that they are always expecting a fight. Distant tribes send messages to them relating to various matters, and other messages are returned, which are not always of a satisfactory character— anger and ill-will, at last, lead to an outbreak. . . . As a rule, fights are brought about by the misconduct of the women, the unauthorized killing of game, the sickness of some member of a tribe, the death of a prominent man, the quarrels of children of different families, or, not seldom, by trivial differences arising out of imaginary grievances. . . . But the combats between the fighting-men are not usually attended by very serious consequences. . . . Mr. Thomas states that of all the fights he has seen he has never known but one death to arise from their frays. He has seen desperate wounds inflicted very often, but none but one was mortal."[4]

Those who are inclined to see in these Australian customs an absence of war should not forget the bloody night-raids upon unsuspecting tribes that are motived in fear of sorcery.

Of the Papuans in northeastern New Guinea it is reported that even the boys quarrel little and never come to blows, but that this is due to cowardice, and that cruelty to the weaker, especially to women, is a consistent trait, and one regarded as manly. A state of war exists between the tribes but emerges in no definite wars. They fall upon an enemy's country and lay it waste, but their courage does not extend to a real battle. No leaders can get obedience or persuade men to go on the warpath. The leaders are the rich, and they send out raiders for shell-money, who loot and burn villages. Peace can be got by payments of money. "It is seen that such wars afford profit only to chiefs lustful for *dewarra* [shell-money] and are therefore only chances for specula-tion for them."[5] "Warfare, as we know it, is something incomprehensible to him. Here and there a man may distinguish himself by personal courage, in openly attacking his enemy and exposing himself to the risk of being speared; but it is not the Papuan method of fighting. He is an assassin, seldom a warrior. . . . This is in line with the cowardly methods the Papuan adopts in his war-fare. He has no armies. He never ranges a force of men in front of a force of his enemy, and openly fights. I say never: I should rather say that when he does, there is remarkably small death-roll at the end of the battle."[6]

In another region in New Guinea war plays "no great rôle." Hagen[7] could discover no big feuds or tribal wars. "Every village, every community knows its own strictly limited rights and duties, no one goes beyond his range, ambi-

---

3 Semon, *Aust. Bush*, 225.
4 Smyth, *Vict.*, I, xxix, 154, 156, 160; Letourneau, *Guerre*, 32-33; Letourneau, *Mo-rale*, 103 ff.
5 Von Pfeil, *Südsee*, 23, 125.
6 Abel, *New Guinea*, 130-131.
7 *Papua's*, 250.

tion and strenuosity are wholly lacking. . . . To this happy, easily satisfied people—whence should come war and feud? But yes, there is one cause, that great and universal one—woman, this enigmatic, sweet, terrible creature!" Krieger[8] knows of a locality where weapons of attack are altogether lacking, and of several others where the people live in peace and content, untroubled by annoying neighbors and without cares for the future.

Some of the Melanesians divided warfare into two classes: neighborly warfare and warfare between enemies. In the first kind there was no cannibalism, the dead were buried either by their own people, or by those who killed them. "Fighting between enemies was a sterner affair, the dead would be eaten, and women could not save the wounded by throwing a grass petticoat over them as in fights between 'friends.'" There are also instances of ceremonial fighting as an accompaniment to marriage. Some writers maintain that some of these islanders became savage and repellent only after they had been habitually injured by Europeans.[9]

The Todas of India do not at the present time use any weapons, but they retain in their ceremonies weapons which were, no doubt, formerly in use, such as the club and the bow and arrow.[10] Skeat and Blagden[11] give numerous instances of tribes in the Malay Peninsula which have little or no war. It is reported of one of these groups, the Sakai, that "thanks to their honesty, they can do without police"; they are a most peaceful race, kind and simple-hearted, "and now at all events never make war on each other or go in for any sort of inter-tribal fighting."

Among the Central Eskimo, duels are common between a stranger and a man of the tribe, sometimes resulting in the death of the former. Boas[12] thinks that real wars or fights between settlements have never happened, but that contests have been confined to single families. The last instance of a feud of which he knows had taken place seventy years before, that is, about 1815. "One tradition only refers to a real fight between the tribes." Around Bering Strait the Eskimo live in small groups and have no fighting weapons. They seem not to have understood what war means. The widely separated groups are so dispersed as to have no reason for conflict.[13]

Reclus[14] attributes to their hard struggle with nature the disposition of the Aleuts to avoid all quarreling. If they cannot rest under wrong, they arrange for a public contest in abusive singing and acting directed at one another. Their children do not fight, but wrangle in words; this is less satisfactory, as the language is weak in vituperative possibilities. The people do not understand what war is. Father de la Rosa[15] reports on certain aborigines of Colombia as follows. They are by nature peaceable, not using any arms, defensive or offensive. "Their fights and quarrels cause one to laugh, because their mode of avenging grievances one with the other is to go out to a place agreed upon, where there is a rock or great tree, each one carrying his cane (a black stick made of the heart of an elastic, lustrous wood), and then they strike ardently at the tree or rock, uttering a multitude of insulting words until one cracks or breaks his stick. To this one is accredited the victory, his enemy recognizing

8 *Neu-Guinea*, 205; *cf.* 323.
9 Seligmann, *Melanesians*, 546; Rivers, *Melan. Soc.*, I, 329-330; Im Thurn, in JAI, LI, 23-24.
10 Rivers, *Todas*, 586.

11 *Malay Penin.*, I, chs. V, VI; 527, 528.
12 In BAE, VI, 465.
13 Letourneau, *Guerre*, 193, 194.
14 *Prim. Folk*, 86, 108.
15 *Santa Marta*, trans. in AA, III, 612.

him as the braver; and, embracing, they return to their homes, renewing friendship and drinking." The Tupis do not quarrel even when drunk.[16]

Of the aborigines of the Canary Islanders, it is reported that they "were fond of fighting above all things, with the single exception of the natives of Hierro, who knew no war, and had no weapons unless their long leaping-poles were used as such when occasion demanded."[17]

Warlikeness is a much more common trait than unwarlikeness. It is said of the Hottentots and other South African tribes that at the time of discovery "the natives were then by no means in a state of childlike innocence, and one could well understand, from the mighty scars and wounds, with which the bodies of most of them were covered, that they must have undergone frequent wars and raids."[18] To the evidence given in the text of continual and serious hostility among both eastern and western blacks may be added instances of other peoples. Certain Tibetans are always at war, tribe against tribe, generally upon the most trivial pretexts. Two men may quarrel over a knife, and the aggrieved party returns and reports the case to his chief. "His right to the article in question is never considered; it is enough that he should have quarreled over it. War is immediately declared on the tribe of his rival;" it is carried on with ferocity and perhaps for years. In northeastern India, "the condition of some of the tribes may be seen in the facts that the Angami villages were practically strongly posted hill stockades; and that in the villages of North Kachar, during the night a watch was kept and the streets were regularly patrolled; and that among the Eastern Nagas in 1873 every village was constantly prepared against surprise, parties of men keeping continual watch and ward over the village gate-ways."[19]

The dominant and aggressive Sea Dyak is "a ruthless destroyer of tribes, which, owing to an inherent and fatal weakness, are already tottering to the verge of extinction."[20] The Aru Islanders "are rarely without fighting somewhere. Individual quarrels are taken up by villages and tribes, and the non-payment of the stipulated price for a wife is one of the most frequent causes of bitterness and bloodshed."[21] In Timorlaut there are incessant intertribal fights and no one dares go beyond the palisades without spear and bow.[22] "All of Nauru is a scene of war," even boys carrying weapons. Feuds arising out of trade are common.[23] When Turner[24] first visited the Loyalty Islands, in 1845, "a chronic state of war prevailed, and each island was divided into two parties. . . . Kidnapping from one another was common. These and others who fell in battle were dressed for the oven. They were inveterate cannibals." The Tannese lived in a state of perpetual war. They were fighting during five out of the seven months that Turner lived among them. "There is ample proof there," he states, "that war is the enemy of civilisation and the element of savage life. We were never able to extend our journeys above four miles from our dwelling at Port Resolution. At such distances we came to boundaries which were never passed, and beyond which the people spoke a different dialect. At one of these boundaries actual war would be going on; at another,

---

16 Southey, *Brazil*, I, 249.
17 Cook, in AA, II, 475, 489.
18 Fritsch, *Eingeb. S.-Afr.*, 450.
19 Reid, in *Cosmopolitan*, XXVIII, 448; Godden, in JAI, XXVII, 12.

20 Hose and Shelford, in JAI, XXXVI, 60.
21 Wallace, *Malay Archip.*, 471.
22 Forbes, in JAI, XIII, 21.
23 Bastian, *Mikron. Colonien*, 5-6.
24 *Samoa*, 337, 312-313, 343-344.

kidnapping and cooking each other; and at another, all might be peace; but, by mutual consent, they had no dealings with each other." The natives of New Caledonia thought they were more numerous now than formerly. "They accounted for it by there being less war now than formerly. Still, it was war, war, war, incessant war! They said that formerly they did not stop a fight until one party was killed right out to the verge of extinction, but that now they are more merciful." Raid and foray, massacre and pillage, were the order of the day in New Zealand and did not cease until the whites came. Many a Maori took to Christianity when the missionaries read to them an account of "a rattling good hip-and-thigh combat, in which the Israelites slew their thousands."[25]

The Pima Indians "kept themselves constantly in fit condition by their campaigns, and even engaged in sham battles for the practice. . . . Their daily duties were ordered with reference to the possibility of attack. Their arts were modified by the perpetual menace. Their myths were developed and their religion tinged by the same stress. In short, the Pimas were building up a war cult that in time might have led them from the lethargic state in which the natural environment tended to fix them." That many of the American tribes ordered their lives with warfare constantly in view is too well known to need much illustration. The injunctions given to the Pima boy might have been impressed upon any Indian youth. "If you are wounded in battle," said the father, "don't make a great outcry about it like a child. Pull out the arrow and slip away; or, if hard stricken, die with a silent throat. Go on the war trail with a small blanket. It is light and protection enough for one aided by the magicians. Inure yourself to the cold while yet a boy. Fight not at all with your comrades; preserve your strength for the combat with the Apaches. Then, if brave, will come to you high honor. Be unselfish or you will not be welcome at the fire of the friendly. The selfish man is lonely and his untended fire dies. Keep your peace when a foolish man addresses the people. Join not in his imprudent councilings. Above all, talk not foolishly yourself. Bathe in the cold water of the early morning, that you may be prepared for the purification ceremony after killing an enemy."[26]

One South American tribe believes that their deity has bidden them live by making war on others, taking their property and wives and killing their men.[27] A certain Brazilian tribe regards it as a natural duty to kill the members of a neighboring weak people, preserving the victims' heads as trophies. Almost every tribe has its open tribal enemy. There are tacit alliances for defense and offense. Another tribe, that specializes in plundering and killing, uses even its women in war; and the attack of the warriors is seconded, "with indescribable fury," by their large and strong dogs. The Indian "lives and thinks under the impression: bellum omnium contra omnes."[28] The Botocudos are in constant war with neighboring peoples.[29] In Paraguay there are "bloody fist-fights between men, women, and children" to let off their surplus pugnacity.[30] Darwin[31] wrote of the Fuegians: "The different tribes have no government or chief, yet each is surrounded by other hostile tribes, speaking

25 Cowan, Maoris, 3, 4, 5, 244 (quoted).
26 Russell, in BAE, XXVI, 204, 190.
27 Tylor, Anth., 225.
28 Von Martius, Beiträge, I, 56, 57, 260, 667.
29 Wied, Brasilien, II, 44.
30 Koch, in Globus, LXXXI, 45.
31 Voy. of Beagle, entries of Dec. 25, 1832, and Jan. 22, 1833.

different dialects, and separated from each other only by a deserted border or neutral territory;" and again, "I do not know anything which shows more clearly the hostile state of the different tribes than these wide borders or neutral tracts. Although Jemmy Button [a native the voyagers had with them] well knew the force of our party, he was at first unwilling to land amidst the hostile tribe nearest to his own." Among the Araucanians armed raids were constantly made on the neighboring villages, and thus a continual state of warfare was kept up. Latcham[32] thinks that to the abundance of comestibles is to be ascribed the warlike tendencies of these Indians, "who not having to give much heed to their food supply, the fertile soil producing it spontaneously almost everywhere, could indulge freely in the luxury of continual warfare. This also gave them an enormous advantage over the Spaniards in their long campaigns, as the latter were almost entirely dependent on their baggage trains or provision supplies, while the surrounding country catered to the wants of their indomitable foes."

This state of constant war is found also where a former political aggregation has broken up. It is a sort of reversion to primitive chaos. Junker[33] calls the splitting up of tribes "the real deadly enemy of all negroes. . . . The feeling of solidarity includes only the members of a branch-tribe or sub-tribe; but they get into feuds over some trivial cause such as a runaway cow or the like, and must in the end come into subjection to a common foe whom, if united, they could successfully withstand—especially if that enemy . . . knows how to stir up one tribe against another and to cause the negroes themselves to take care of the work of annihilation." The disintegration of the Niam-Niam people into little principalities had continuous hostilities and wars as a consequence. "No prince left his land any more by reason of eternal suspicion of the rulers of neighboring districts." Similar dissolutions of empires on higher stages of civilization have resulted in similar periods of violence.

§140. War-Usages.

In a savage society there was at least this advantage, that the whole male strength of the community—and sometimes the female as well—could take the field when necessary, fully equipped at short notice for defense and offense. There was no calling for volunteers, no hasty drilling of recruits, no trouble with slackers. This, thinks Cowan[1] was the natural outcome of the communal system, the gradual evolution of the family into the tribe, which was really only the family on a larger scale. The organization of the war-party was naturally rudimentary and the usual tactics were ambush and surprise. A number of the cases in the immediately preceding sections illustrate the present topic.

The customary method of fighting among the Melanesians was the night-attack. "In this, a village was, as nearly as possible, surrounded quietly during the hours of darkness, and the attack made at dawn; if all went well for the attacking party, they killed the majority of the inhabitants regardless of age and sex, and looted and perhaps burnt the village."[2] Some of the Papuan tribes were taught to paddle their war-canoes in one way only—bows on, the bow of a canoe being dedicated to war and the stern to peace. "They were

32 In JAI, XXXIX, 341, 354.　　　　1 Maoris, 223.
33 Afrika, I, 337; II, 189.　　　　2 Seligmann, Melanesians, 121.

thus taught not to jump up and turn round to paddle away from the enemy, but to steer straight for the opposing canoes. Canoes of any size were never brought on to our beach bows first, as it would have meant war." The boys among these people were encouraged to use small spears against any person, even their mothers, on the slightest provocation.[3] The aid of the supernatural is often sought by the Melanesians; the following case illustrates admirably how, among the Fijians, a religious theory may be criticism-proof. For days before a fight the warriors would steadily prepare themselves by songs and chants in honor of their war-god, the deity being held to enter into a selected stone taken from the larger water-worn pebbles of a running stream. "At length one man would exclaim that the demon had entered into him, and that he was now invulnerable; no weapon formed against him should prosper, the battle-axe would bound back from his toughened skin, the musket bullet would flatten against his body, and the spear-point glance harmlessly aside." Webb[4] continues: "I pointed out a young man with a gunshot wound through the neck, who, a few days before, had been in the invulnerable condition, and asked how they accounted for his hurt. 'He had broken the *tapu*, and eaten bananas,' was the reply. Another warrior limped past, with a hole in his thigh. 'He had connection with a woman just before the fight,' they explained, 'and that destroyed the charm.' These people are full of explanations as to failures."

The manner of fighting among some East African tribes was never very desperate; "they were women in war, but very dangerous in thick bush; but among themselves warfare seems to have consisted largely of much rushing about and shouting until one side or the other was terrified and ran away. This also is told by a missionary who witnessed such warfare in former times. Natives have told me that certain people had medicine which they smeared between their thumb and forefinger, the merit of which was that it made it impossible for them to err in their aim, and that such people were often not allowed to go to war because of the destruction that they did. This somewhat comic view of warfare shows that the object of the fighting was not so much the destruction of the enemy, but when, despite this, it is certain that numbers were killed, this is only to be explained by the fact that the fighting went on continuously."[5] A fight among the Ba-Yaka is usually prefaced by mutual objurgation, but ambushes and night-attacks on villages are common, and indeed, form an essential part of native tactics; consequently in war-time sentries are posted in the grass around a village.[6] The Akamba custom is to attack at night; "they would march under cover of darkness to within striking distance of the place of attack and there rest until between four and five a.m. so that after the attack was delivered it would be about sunrise and they could see to collect the captured live-stock."[7] One can hardly dignify the quarrels and fights among some of the Congo tribes with the name of war; there was no army and no organization, but all the men and lads took part in the fight that affected their family or their town. The fighting was simply an affray, a *mêlée*, in which there was no order and no words of command.[8] Much more developed was the war-organization of the Baganda, where, at the drum-call, all rush to

3 Bromilow, in AAAS, 1909, 475, 479.   7 Hobley, *A-Kamba*, 43.
4 In AAAS, 1890, 622-623.   8 Weeks, in JAI, XL, 412-413; Volkens,
5 Dundas, C., in JAI, XLIII, 505.   *Kilimandscharo*, 194, 195.
6 Torday and Joyce, in JAI, XXXVI, 49.

their immediate superiors—chiefs or earls—and these to the higher chiefs, and then to the king, considerable speed being shown in mobilizing. There is no commissariat, the soldiers being dependent on each day's loot for their food. All weapons are "medicined" before war, to make them more effective.[9]

This religious element in primitive war-preparation is seen in other African examples also. Before the Bahima king consents to the commencement of hostilities, he sends to consult his ancestors as to the advisability of undertaking the war and the prospects of its success; "a special messenger goes to the forest with a suitable present of cattle; the priest receives the messenger and, after offering some of the cattle to the sacred lions, he proceeds to consult the ghosts, giving special heed to the ghost of the king's father. If the answer is satisfactory the king chooses a general who collects his army by sending messengers to the leading chiefs in the country. The army consists, in almost all cases, of volunteers, each man brings his own weapons, and is responsible for his own food."[10] The Lumbwa raiders set forth amidst a complexity of omens and prohibitions: no sexual connection may take place on a raid; to meet soldier-ants when marching at night betokens a retreat at once.[11] Before a war is decided upon, among the Nigerian head-hunters, the elders and priests repair to the sacred grove and ask the opinion of the spirits. This is usually favorable, and then a leader is appointed who is chosen for his skill in arms. Among these people there is a very close connection between the hunting-and the war-parties; "a chase may easily be turned into a battle, even amongst the hunters themselves, when the arms for both are the same, and the search for beasts may become a hunt for men."[12]

The Chinese have had many bloody wars concerning the result of which on population the term "decimation" in its root-meaning is all too feeble. One case shows seven-ninths of the population destroyed by war.[13] Sudden raids, surprises, ambushes, and hurried evasion are among the Sema Nagas' methods of warfare and head-hunting; the pitched battle does not often occur. If the raiders find their prospective victims prepared, they come home rather ignominiously.[14] The Samoans in action never stood up in orderly ranks to rush at each other; according to their notions that would be the height of folly. "Their favourite tactics were rather of the surprise and bush-skirmishing order." Prayers over, arms ready, and equipped with their relic charms, the New Caledonians went off to battle.[15] From his early years every Maori was trained in the use of the spear, and later the gun of the white man; he learned, too, the various charms and spells and invocations that gave *mana* to his weapon and "more power to his elbow." On the war-path his commissariat did not trouble him overmuch; "he needed no waggon-loads of 'bully-beef' and hard biscuit; was not his enemy's own body to provide the rations?"[16]

War was at one time the chief occupation of the Tlinkits, and treachery was regarded as a lawful means by which to entrap enemies: "surprise, cunning, treachery and ambush entered more into their warfare than open valour."[17] The acquisition of the horse and of the firearms of the whites greatly changed the Indian methods of warfare, and among the Plains Tribes the introduction

9 Roscoe, in JAI, XXXII, 58, 59.
10 Roscoe, in JAI, XXXVII, 108.
11 Barton, in JAI, LIII, 46-47.
12 Tremearne, in JAI, XLII, 183-184.
13 Harvey, *Chinese Animism*, appendix.

14 Hutton, *Sema Nagas*, 171.
15 Turner, *Samoa*, 192, 345.
16 Cowan, *Maoris*, 223.
17 Jones, *Thlingets*, 112, 113.

of the horse furnished a strong motive for war—to capture something of great value. There were many ceremonies before setting out on the warpath, and failure to observe some law or custom would force the party to turn back.[18] Dreams sometimes influenced the acts of a war-party, and instances have been known where, because of a dream, the entire party has disbanded and returned home.[19] Some tribes wore arm-bands to which were attached metal jinglers, the sound of which was thought to be efficacious to lull the slumbering enemy.[20] Aggressive warfare was pretty generally under the control of rites, and the war leader who failed to get the sanction of the spirits was punished.[21]

When the Jibaro warrior of Ecuador prepares for an attack against an enemy he wears around his neck a necklace of jaguar's teeth and around his waist the usual cincture of human hair. Old warriors, however, for an attack prefer to gird themselves with a broad belt of skin of the great boa. The object of these paraphernalia is to impart strength and valor to the warrior. "The teeth of the jaguar and the belt of the boa skin naturally give the wearer something of the demoniac strength of these animals. Again, the power which the Jibaros attribute to the cincture made of human hair depends on the supernatural properties ascribed to the hair, which is regarded as the seat of the soul or the vital energy." After the preparations are made and the party sets out, there is to be seen the disciplinary effect of war. "The warriors march from the house of the chief in a single row, going one after the other, and strictly observing silence. The chief goes out last and shuts the door. During the whole journey to the scene of the war, a journey that takes several days, sometimes even weeks, the warriors are allowed to speak only when necessary, and even then not in a loud voice but in a whisper. Only the chief has the right to speak in a loud voice when at the camping places he gives his men the necessary instructions."[22] At the time of the Spanish invasion it was the Araucanian custom to march in disorderly bodies without any attempt at formation; later, "experience taught them to organise their methods better, and a stricter discipline was established and bodies of scouts thrown out in advance. But no discipline was of avail when some superstitious incident occurred upon the march, if such were considered inauspicious. The army immediately broke up and returned to camp. All discipline was lost, too, at the moment that booty presented itself. Then it became each one for himself."[23]

The Military Services of Women. In English New Guinea, the women "sometimes take part even in the councils of the men; and I saw girls armed with clubs in a fight, and active among the first ranks of the fighters." In one district there was even a female leader.[24] In another district, "women always follow to the fight, and they kill outright with their sticks any who may be severely wounded. The women also do the looting. The men say they are a great encouragement to them, as they urge them on; and they also create a feeling that they must be protected. The women themselves like it."[25] The women of the Marshall Islands "take part in sea-voyages as well as in war."[26] It is

18 Grinnell, *Cheyenne*, II, 1, 2, 6, 8, 10, 13.
19 Fletcher, in HAI, II, 915.
20 Skinner, in AA, XIII, 309.
21 Fletcher and LaFlesche, in BAE, XXVII, 403-404.
22 Karsten, "Jibaro," in BAE, Bull. LXXIX, 24, 25-26.
23 Latcham, in JAI, XXXIX, 362-363.
24 Finsch, *Ethnol. Erfahr.*, II, 298.
25 Chalmers, in JAI, XXXIII, 122-123.
26 Finsch, *Ethnol. Erfahr.*, III, 130.

reported of the African Pygmies that "the women are on an equality with the men and go hunting with them, and accompany them to the wars, taking their part in the combat." The result of this is that these tribes "are looked down upon by all the other tribes, and not being regarded as a warlike people, are hunted by the surrounding cannibals, to be cooked and eaten. They are a lower type than the others, and both men and women are shorter and differ also in color from the rest."[27] The women as well as the men, among another Pygmy group, in Angola, carry bows and arrows.[28] Among the Ba-Huana, the chief instigators of war are the women; "if the men are peaceably inclined and rather disposed to pocket an insult, the women make fun of them: 'You are afraid, you are not men, we will have no more intercourse with you!'" Then out go the men and fight.[29]

All authorities of the thirteenth century agree that Mongol women went into war with men, were fine archers, and fought as well as the men.[30] Says Schwaner[31] of a Bornean tribe: "They concede large freedom and rights to their women, who not seldom rule in the house and over whole tribes with the power of men, encourage to war-expeditions and in the war itself lead the combatant men." In Celebes "all full-grown persons, women as well as men, must practice the use of weapons."[32] Some of the Malay tribes have a tradition of a race of gigantic women or Amazons, who remain unmarried.[33]

In Samoa the young women took part in war; they had the task of decapitating the fallen enemy.[34] In Ponapé, when required, the women accompany their husbands and relations fearlessly into the battle.[35] In the fights of the Gilbert Islanders, the women not seldom take an active part; a missionary, in 1858, found the corpses of six women on one of their battle-fields.[36] The Maori women often accompanied their lords to war; they could fight as well as the men if need be. "The Maori *wahine* could be a horribly savage Amazon when on the war-path in ancient days."[37]

Of the American Indians it is said: "In defensive warfare the warriors sprang to the alarm and aimed to engage the enemy beyond the limits of the village, while the women hastily threw up breastworks or dug pits in which to thrust the children out of reach of flying arrows. Women fought only at close range, using their knives or any available object as weapons; but in rare cases women went to war and fought on equal terms with the men of the party."[38] The chief of one Brazilian tribe, which exhibits a well developed military organization, is surrounded by a number of women who with dexterity seek to parry the weapons thrown at him.[39] In Brazil there exist a number of tales of tribes of female warriors.[40] If one side has to retire, in a battle among the Guiana Indians, "they seek their dead before anything else to prevent them falling into the hands of the enemy, a business which the women have to see to, they following the men like pack animals."[41]

Von Götzen[42] mentions a "highly original body-guard," consisting of ten

27 Burrows, *Pigmies*, 128, 131.
28 Flower, in JAI, XVIII, 85.
29 Torday and Joyce, in JAI, XXXVI, 289.
30 Rubruck, *Eastern Parts*, 75 (Rockhill's note).
31 *Borneo*, I, 161.
32 Riedel, in *Bijd.*, XXXV, 79.
33 Stevens, in *Ztsft. f. Eth.*, XXVIII, 167.
34 Reinecke, in *Globus*, LXXVI, 8.

35 Christian, *Caroline Isl.*, 73.
36 Finsch, *Ethnol. Erfahr.*, III, 36.
37 Cowan, *Maoris*, 233, 234.
38 Fletcher, in HAI, II, 915; Grinnell, *Cheyenne*, II, 44 ff.
39 Von Martius, *Beiträge*, I, 69.
40 Spix and Martius, *Travels in Brazil*, III, 1092; Von Martius, *Beiträge*, 729-730.
41 Roth, in BAE, XXXVIII, 583.
42 *Durch Afr.*, 278, 311.

well-built girls, each carrying a gun of a different construction, mostly breech-loaders in a useless condition. The author states that the army which a certain chief brought over to help the Belgians, in their war with the Arabs on the Upper Congo in 1892, consisted of nine thousand, of whom three thousand five hundred were women; whether they all were combatants is not stated, but three hundred females, some of whom were armed with guns, formed a bodyguard for the leader. The Sultan of Atjeh, in the early part of the sixteenth century, had extirpated all the ancient nobility and murdered all the princes of the blood; he then feared assassination and surrounded himself with a bodyguard of women.[43] The familiar legend of the Amazons does not need to be rehearsed here. Certain tribes of the Don region are reputed by ancient authorities to have been in subjection to their women, who were just as warlike as the men. They are connected by Pliny[44] with the mythical Amazons. Eden's "First Three English Books"[45] contains references to Amazonian peoples. In an abridgment of the mediæval legend of Prester John, the story goes that there are three Amazon queens, who, when they go to war, have each three hundred thousand women, beside other women to carry food. These women are manlike in fighting, and very hardy. No men may come into this land except nine days in the year, during which period "the women have conversation with them, and no more in the year." This account about Amazons goes on to relate how Columbus, on his second voyage, came to an island which his captives told him was inhabited only by women, to whom the cannibals had access at certain times of the year. The male children were sent to their fathers, but the girls were retained. These women lived in caves or dens in the ground, and defended themselves with bows and arrows against any men who invaded the island. Some rationalization of the legend is attempted, namely, that the women are wives of very warlike cannibals and that when the men go away to hunt human prey, they defend the island against invasion. In Scandinavian graves are found female skeletons with bronze daggers. These women, probably battle-companions of their husbands, might have been the originals of the Valkyrs.[46]

Other services which women perform in war—notably the carrying of provisions, stimulating the men to action, and acting as intermediaries, their persons being then inviolable—are indicated in the following cases.

"In peace, even amongst the bitterest enemies, nobody attempts the life of a Somal woman; nor is the woman an object of blood-vengeance. Only in war do enemies seek out pregnant women," in order to destroy the unborn.[47] Among the Kabyles, "the women do not remain inactive during war. They cast bullets, make cartridges, and prepare provisions. Often they appear on the battle-field . . . their cries mingling with the noise of explosions and their warlike songs exciting the ardor of the combatants to a delirium." They are commonly under safe conduct and can circulate freely from village to village; and their presence confers immunity to fugitives. "If they discover, in the morning, an ambuscade about the village, the enemy retires, and their withdrawal must not be disturbed. In the midst of this society, which is rude to the limit of ferocity, woman carries, in the folds of her garments, pity and sympathy."[48]

43 Jacobs, *Groot-Atjeh*, I, 231-232.
44 *Hist. Nat.*, VI, 19.
45 Pp. xxxiii, 69, 177, 189.
46 Schweiger-Lerchenfeld, *Kgchte.*, I, 462.

47 Paulitschke, *Nordost-Afr.*, I, 244.
48 Hanoteau et Letourneux, *Kabylie*, II, 75, 76; III, 80-81.

Among one of the tribes of India, "if a virgin enterprise is to be inaugurated, it is *sine qua non* among them that no woman should know a word about the matter." On the contrary, when open hostilities have commenced with some other clan, the women accompany the warriors an hour's journey, carrying their provisions, and leaving them with a blessing and wish for success."[49] Among certain Indians the women were wont to run between the fighters and by continued cries urge them to stand fast.[50]

"The Arabs of former times, when they believed that victory could not be won without extreme effort, used to set the most beautiful girl of the tribe . . . upon a richly caparisoned camel and lead her into the battle." Before the beginning of the fight, such a woman, where possible one of the noblest rank, dressed as a bride, unveiled, and with loosened hair, and bare neck, rode up to the first ranks to solicit the promise of the élite of the army, the youth of the tribe, to win or to die. Then the girl moved on against the enemy and the battle began. To her capture and defense were directed the strenuous efforts of both parties. "Not seldom did the whole young manhood of the tribe perish."[51]

Just because the Arab house afforded protection against blood-vengeance, did the wife play in it a special rôle. She was herself sacrosanct in the blood-feud, and as the house-mistress she was the recourse of those who sought asylum.[52] It was not so far from this position to that of arbitrator of strifes. The Scandinavians had the "woman-peace," both in war and in family feuds; according to German laws, women were inviolate both as to person and to property. When peace was made, noble virgins were given as hostages. Injury to a woman was punished with double or triple penalty.[53]

§141. Rules of War.

Declaration of War. An important instance of the mitigation of war, and one which arose quite early, is the declaration of hostilities. The effect of this is, obviously, to give the enemy a chance, and it represents a sort of chivalrous action in contrast with the more usual primitive method of ambush and sur-prise. Letourneau[1] cites a number of cases of the declaration of war. In clan-wars the Masai allow no surprises or sudden attacks. The place of conflict is appointed and the whole population camps out there while the battle is fought by champions. The victors get an unquestioned claim to the cattle involved. This is quite different from the procedure in wars with aliens. The Kabyles declare war; no one may commence without warning, otherwise every death is regarded as an assassination demanding retaliation—a blood-debt; but they seize cattle and occupy the best positions beforehand. The wounded and prisoners are killed only under exasperation. Mohammedanism confirmed the habitude of declaration. The Hurons and Iroquois declared war by delivering a tomahawk whose handle was painted black and red. The Iroquois, however, waited a year after "digging up the hatchet" so that it might not be known when the blow was to fall. In Florida war was declared by planting in enemy

49 Lewin, *S.E. India*, 266.
50 Koch, in *Globus*, LXXXI, 73.
51 Junker, *Afrika*, I, 146, 149.
52 Proksch, *Blutrache*, 48.

53 Tacitus, *Germ.*, VIII; Weinhold. *Deut. Frauen*, I, 219; Stammler, *Stellung d. Frauen*, 9-10.
1 *Guerre*, 92, 268 ff., 152 ff., 359; §139, of the *Case-Book*.

territory arrows with a small piece of cotton or wool attached. Few tribes are like the Tenae of India who declare war, attack openly, and respect non-combatants.

To Letourneau's collection, of which the above are samples, a few may be added. In New Guinea, the declaration is sometimes the sending of a broken spear. Heralds or messengers are used elsewhere.[2] Declaration in West Africa, after the killing, accidental or not, of a villager, is by washing the hands in a brook. Then comes the "palaver."[3] A sort of warning occurred where there were, "close on the path, and in full view of every passenger, three objects suspended from the branch of a tree, viz., an ear of maize, the feather of a fowl, and an arrow. The guides explained these as meaning that whoever touched an ear of maize or laid his grasp upon a single fowl would assuredly be a victim of the arrow."[4] Again, war is declared by sending hatchets or picks, and peace by recalling them. Women are sent to get them, being employed, here as elsewhere in equatorial Africa, as go-betweens to do the parleying.[5] The Maoris sometimes launch a light spear at the enemy as a challenge to war;[6] while among the Guiana Indians the throwing of an arrow served the twofold purpose of a call to arms and a declaration of war.[7] Though the Ecuador Indians usually carried out the plan of attack in greatest secrecy, the victim was sometimes threatened beforehand.[8]

Less formal warnings of hostility are to be met with. Of some tribes in New Guinea it is the custom "that if the loin-cloth which a man wears, made of the bark of trees, be wound tightly around him, all is well and you may safely approach him; but should it be hanging down from behind, then beware, for he is in fighting trim and is on the war-path and sharpening his cannibal teeth preparatory to a feast."[9] Again, where wild ginger is chewed, "to give a piece to another person signifies 'war' against him: and for this reason it was some time before the writer could induce the natives to eat any gingerbread biscuits."[10] Amongst the Slave Coast negroes it is a sign of enmity and rancor to refuse a gift.[11]

Sometimes the destructiveness of war is limited by inability rather than unwillingness to destroy. In Melanesia the natives cut down each other's trees, but since their axes, often of shell, are poor, not much damage is done.[12] There is, as in Homer, a sentiment that the proper thing is to fight with the spear rather than, at longer distance, with the bow.[13] "Sometimes one tribe will challenge another, and a place of meeting is arranged. The hostile tribes arrange themselves in two lines facing one another, with an interval of about a hundred yards between. . . . The contest is of short duration, as a man or two wounded on one side is considered sufficient excuse for that side to run away."[14] Again, the warfare may be one of words or even gestures rather than of bloodshed. An odd case is that of the Rengmahs, who "wear a peculiar tail. It is of wood, about a foot and a half long, curved upwards,

---

2 Hagen, *Papua's*, 251; Von Pfeil, *Südsee*, 125.
3 Schmidt, *Deut. Kol.*, II, 28.
4 Schweinfurth, *Heart of Afr.*, II, 23.
5 Stuhlmann, *Mit Emin*, 391.
6 Cowan, *Maoris*, 282, 325.
7 Roth, in BAE, XXXVIII, 582.
8 Karsten, "Jibaro," in BAE, Bull. LXXIX, 17.

9 Cayley-Webster, *New Guinea*, 214, 215.
10 Somerville, in JAI, XXVI, 381, note.
11 Ellis, in PSM, XLV, 774.
12 Von Pfeil, *Südsee*, 125-126.
13 Codrington, *Melanesians*, 304, 305; Keller, *Hom. Soc.*, 59-60.
14 Guise, in JAI, XXVIII, 213.

broad at the base and tapering to the tip. Rows of white seeds are fastened longitudinally on it, and from it hang long tufts of scarlet and black hair. The broad part is fitted to the small of the back, and is suspended from the shoulders by a prettily embroidered belt (red, white, and black); a small cloth tied around the waist secures the tail. This tail is used in a fight to signify defiance. They turn it toward the enemy and by hopping around rapidly on each leg impart a defiant wag. 'Turning tail' with them means the opposite of what it does with us."[15] Where this sort of device is worn the fighting cannot be very serious. In the less fierce quarrels "the hostile parties confine themselves by mutual agreement to certain fixed bounds within which they might kill each other; in these milder quarrels the women and children are not injured. . . . It is noticeable that in these intestine wars the women of the contending parties visit each other at their different villages without fear of molestation. But when at war with other tribes, their attacks are treacherous, and they spare neither sex nor age."[16]

The Siouans had no standing armies and no general who held office for life or for a given term. There was no militia. "Military service was voluntary in all cases, from the private to the commanders, and the war party was disbanded as soon as home was reached. They had no wars of long duration, in fact, wars between one Indian tribe and another seldom occurred, but there were occasional battles. This was for want of transport and compact food."[17] "Battles would often go on for the greater part of a day without the loss of more than one or two men on each side. At last one party, becoming discouraged, would break and run."[18] The Fuegians "fight with clubs, spears, stones and slings; of course many are wounded, but seldom any are killed."[19]

The use of champions to decide the conflict operates further to check the destructiveness of war. There are instances of single combat running from the Eskimo and Melanesians to the ancient Hebrews.[20] Another check on war is the regulated combat, in which all the teeth, so to speak, are taken out of the struggle.[21] One instance, reported from the Caroline Islands, may be cited in full, in which there are firmly fixed formalities connected with the prosecution of war. "If the inhabitants of the West Islands have been injured by their easterly neighbors, or think they have been, they communicate with their adversaries through a properly accredited messenger to the effect that in five days from that time (they always choose the five-day interval) at such and such a time, in such and such a place, such and such a number of warriors, armed and fitted out in a certain manner, in a certain number of canoes, will land in order to join negotiations at the above place concerning the explanations due and the satisfaction demanded. Landing, conference, and negotiation all take place. If the affair is settled in a friendly way, it ends with a feast and both parties hold themselves to be satisfied. But if they cannot come to agreement, they take recourse to weapons. A number of warriors equal to the number of those presenting the complaint measure themselves with these, and the right of the stronger decides. For a half hour they fight like mad tigers and deal out wounds and death without mercy; then they

15 Woodthorpe, in JAI, XI, 197.
16 Godden, in JAI, XXVII, 12 and note.
17 Mason, Invention, 397, 398.
18 Grinnell, Folk Tales, 316.
19 Bridges, in Voice for S. Amer., XIII, 201.

20 Swanton, in HAI, II, 145; Ray, in JAI, XLVII, 293-294; I Sam., XVII, 4.
21 Torday and Joyce, in JAI, XXXV, 415-416; Landtmann, in JAI, XLVI, 322.

separate as if upon prearrangement and rest the remainder of the day. Both parties remain in the neighborhood of the battle-ground to bury their dead and take care of their wounded. On the next day, as soon as both parties have declared that they are ready, the battle begins with renewed violence and again lasts as long as it did the day before, unless one party retreats and declares itself beaten. Otherwise they separate again after an hour of embittered strife, lay aside their weapons and help each other, on both sides, to bury the dead and bind up the wounded. On the third day the conflict is decided. It begins in the morning and is continued until one party succumbs. If this happens to the aggressors, they turn over their canoes and weapons to the victors, who give the vanquished a feast and must convey them in safety to their islands, where the peace is sealed by a new two-day feast. Both sides then mourn fourteen days in honor of their friends who have been killed in the battle. Then friendly relations are again renewed and the members of both tribes come and go to each other as before. If, on the other hand, the aggressors are the victors, then the others grant their demands and make as favorable a pact as circumstances allow. It is always solemnized by a two-day feast. Prisoners captured during the fight belong to those who have seized them, if their party wins the victory; otherwise they are given back to the victors. The men of the defeated party are never regarded as captives, but honorably treated and convoyed back to their home."[22]

Poisoned Weapons. The practice of poisoning weapons was at one time widespread. It survives now only in the sub-tropic zones, as witness the following cases in illustration. The suppression of the use of poison was probably brought about by social influences sanctioned by the cult.[23] The most common primitive weapons to be poisoned are the arrow used with the bow and the dart of the blow-gun.[24]

The Australians have no plant-poison, and employ the products of putrefaction.[25] It is stated that the arrow and spear are not poisoned anywhere in New Guinea; but that such means are employed in several places in Melanesia and perhaps about Torres Straits.[26] The African Bushmen have an arrow whose poisoned point comes off in the game, and they have carried the weapon over into war; the Hottentots, though more civilized, use poison.[27] Other South African tribes do the same, and there is a good deal of this sort of thing farther north, generally among the more backward tribes.[28] To an East

22 Kubary, *Pelauer*, 8, 9.

23 Lippert, *Kgchte.*, I, 310-312.

24 On the manufacture of the blow-gun and the special poisons, see Wilken, *Vkde.*, 87 ff.; Schwaner, *Borneo*, I, 227-228; Perelaer, *Dajaks*, 66, 70 ff.; Nieuwenhuis, *Borneo*, I, 131 ff.; Roth, *Sarawak*, II, 185; Bock, *Borneo*, 83; Stevens, in *Königliche Museen zu Berlin*, 1892, 114; Skeat and Blagden, *Malay Penin.*, I, 254 ff., 261 ff.; 311 ff.; Wray, in JAI, XXI, 477, 479, 480; Furness, *Head-Hunters*, 177; Waddell, *Himalayas*, 99; Hale, in JAI, XV, 289; Ratzel, *Vkde.*, II, 503; Johnston, *Uganda*, II, 873; AA, X, No. 9, 298; Wake, in JAI, XI, 29; Kubary, *Karolinen-arch.*, 122; Peschel, *Races*, 186; Mason, *Invention*, 278, 280, note; Schomburgk, *Brit.-Guiana*, I, 425 ff., 445 ff.; Von Martius, *Beiträge*, I,

660; Spix u. Martius, *Bras.*, 1155, 1156, 1209, 1237, note; Roth, in BAE, XXXVIII, par. 117-124; Hitchcock, in USNM, 1890, 469, 470; White, in JAI, XIII, 251; Ehrenreich, in *Königl. Mus. Vkde.*, II, 56.

25 Ratzel, *Vkde.*, II, 55, 80; Letourneau, *Guerre*, 35.

26 Finsch, *Samoafahrten*, 78; Codrington, in JAI, XIX, 215; Codrington, *Melanesians*, 307, note; Haddon, in JAI, XIX, 331.

27 Ratzel, *Vkde.*, I, 65, 94; Letourneau, *Guerre*, 55-57; Fritsch, *Eingeb. S.-Afr.*, 431; Schmidt, *Deut. Kol.*, II, 255.

28 Letourneau, *Guerre*, 67, 81, 94; Letourneau, *Commerce*, 63; Klose, in *Globus*, LXXXIII, 311; Meinecke, *Deut. Kol.*, 14; Foureau, *Tchad*, 561-562; Junker, *Afr.*, I, 338, 520; Stuhlmann, *Mit Emin*, 36, 87, 108,

African "it is best to be cunning and deceitful; his weapons, the bow and poisoned arrow, are typical of such a character." The poison used in this section is extremely virulent; when fresh it is said to kill a man almost instantaneously.[29] Stuhlmann[30] says the Pygmies use poisoned arrows, but this is stated by Burrows[31] to be a "gross libel" upon that people.

Poisoned arrows are reported in ancient India,[32] Kamtchatka,[33] and Malacca; in the latter case, the poison is partly animal matter, from poisonous insects, reptiles, and fish.[34] The use of poisoned darts in blow-guns is common to a number of Malays, as is also the practice of placing poisoned splints in a path or in the shallow bed of a stream.[35] The Indians of the West used on an enemy an arrow, "generally poisoned, and with long flukes or barbs, which are designed to hang the blade in the wound after the shaft is withdrawn, in which they are but slightly glued," while the hunting-arrow is firmly fixed in the staff and the flukes inverted so as to be drawn out readily.[36] Some of the Apache poisoned their arrows "by dipping them in decomposed liver, to which had been added crushed tarantulas, scorpions, and often the venom of rattlesnakes. . . . The Menomini admit that their ancestors poisoned their arrows by besmearing the points with rattlesnake venom." Several other North American tribes are reported to have poisoned their arrows.[37] South Americans poison arrows other than those used in the blow-gun.[38] A certain Colombia tribe fears to put the poison on the arrow-point, lest its strength cause the metal to lose its temper, or lest it be weakened by the metal, and so they smear it in the binding. The only danger is contact with the thread used to fasten on the tip. "Arrows that are tipped with a shark's tooth, or hardwood worked into a point, are the worst because these they make without fear of loss, and saturate them with poison."[39] An Amazonian tribe, which "delights in war," uses an unfeathered arrow with poisoned head, notched and half cut through, so as to break off in the body.[40] The Araucanians poisoned their arrows, carrying the venom in small stone or earthenware jars and smearing it on the arrow-tips immediately before use. The Spaniards applied salt to the wound as an antidote.[41]

"Metal arrow-heads, especially those of bronze, like the bone missiles and sling weapons of the palæolithic age, frequently display arrangements for the reception of poison."[42] Hercules is figured as shooting Nessus with a poisoned arrow.[43] Poisoned swords are mentioned in the epics of the North.[44] The

409, 548; Stigand, in JAI, XXXIX, 41; Keane, Africa, 512; Schmidt, Deut. Kol., I, 32.

29 Dundas, C., in JAI, XLIII, 488 (quoted), 504; Johnstone, in JAI, XXXII, 270; Hobley, A-Kamba, 44; Tate, in JAI, XXXIV, 136.

30 Mit Emin, 452.

31 In JAI, XXVIII, 38.

32 Schrader, Aryans, 222.

33 Letourneau, Guerre, 194.

34 Stevens, in Königliche Museen zu Berlin, II (1892), 106; Danvers, Portuguese in India, I, 228.

35 Knocker, in JAI, XXXVII, 295; Skeat and Blagden, Malay Penin., I, 501, note; Hutton, Sema Nagas, 171-172; Roth, in JAI, XXII, 59; Mason, Invention, 402-403.

36 Donaldson, in Smithson. Rep., 1885, pt. II, 391.

37 Hoffman, in BAE, XIV, 284, 285.

38 Ehrenreich, in Königl. Mus. Vkde., II (1891), 64; Keane, in JAI, XIII, 205; Roth, in BAE, XXXVIII, 583; Von Martius, Beiträge, I, 447, 653; Letourneau, Guerre, 135.

39 De La Rosa, Santa Marta, trans. in AA, III, 620-621.

40 Markham, in JAI, XL, 101.

41 Latcham, in JAI, XXXIX, 362-363.

42 Schrader, Aryans, 223, note.

43 Ovid, Metam., IX, 101 ff.; Strabo, Geog., X, ch. II, §5; Sophocles, Trachiniae, 569 ff., 674 ff., 759 ff.

44 Corp. Poet. Bor., 161, 309.

Bretons are said to have used poisoned weapons in Druid times,[45] and the
ancient Slavs are aligned with them.[46] European peoples could be found using
poisoned arrows up to the seventeenth century.[47]

Treatment of Prisoners and Noncombatants. Under the least regulated
conditions prisoners are not taken, "no quarter" being the rule. This is
true in the case of some Melanesians, while among the Papuans "neither age
nor sex is spared in the wars; the enemy's property is destroyed excepting
what is carried away; his domestic animals are shot and coconut trees cut
down."[48] Until very recently "the chiefs of the Bawenda settled their political
differences quite independently by war, by invasions with murderous surprises
of the enemy during the night or in the early morning, by incendiarism, pillaging or waylaying. Many a single enemy has been surprised and assassinated
or deceitfully poisoned in order to get rid of him. The victory was celebrated
by a dance of the victors over the dead bodies of the enemy, and parts of their
flesh were mixed with beef and eaten by the heroes of the day."[49] In Maori
history we frequently find instances of the destruction of unsuspecting parties
of enemies by burning them to death in their large meeting-houses.[50] The aim
of Indian warfare was to destroy, and "as every person, old or young, was a
part of the present or future strength of the enemy, neither age nor sex was
spared and no non-combatants were recognized."[51] The wars between the different tribes in South America were often in principle wars of extermination.
In these, as among the Jibaro, "there is no question about weighing life against
life; the aim is to completely annihilate the inimical tribe, all members of
which form one organic whole and are animated by the same feelings and mode
of thought. The victorious party is all the more anxious to leave no single
person of the enemy's people, not even small children, alive, as it is feared
lest these should later appear as avengers against the victors."[52] Cruelty,
violence, and massacre have been common enough among historical peoples.[53]

Probably the first mitigation of these conditions occurred when women and
children were spared. We read, for instance, in the case of an African tribe:
"No prisoners are made and no quarter granted, except to women, who are
kept in captivity until the end of the war."[54] In Samoa, "prisoners, if men, were
generally killed; if women, distributed among the conquerors."[55] In Southern
Formosa "women and children are never molested in war; the former are
therefore very convenient as interpreters for traveling from one tribe to the
other."[56] Apache men were never taken captive by the Pima, but "women,
girls, and young boys of that tribe were sometimes made prisoners, while on
other occasions all the inhabitants of a besieged Apache camp were killed."[57]
While the wars of the Jibaros, mentioned above, are usually to the death,
younger women may be spared and carried off as prisoners of war, their fate
being later to add to the number of their victors', and especially the chief's,

45 Von Pflugk-Harttung, in *Trans. Roy.
Hist. Soc.* (N.S.), VII, 72.
46 Schrader, *Aryans,* 233, 234.
47 Letourneau, *Guerre,* 534.
48 Landtmann, in JAI, XLVI, 329; Seligmann, *Melanesians,* 668-669.
49 Gottschling, in JAI, XXXV, 371.
50 Cowan, *Maoris,* 232-233.
51 Fletcher, in HAI, II, 914.
52 Karsten, "Jibaro," in BAE, Bull.
LXXIX, 16; Frič and Radin, in JAI,
XXXVI, 383.
53 Schulz, *Deut. Leben,* 389, 390; Peschel,
Races, 190; Holtzmann, *Indische Sagen,* I,
170.
54 Torday and Joyce, in JAI, XXXVI,
289.
55 Turner, *Samoa,* 192.
56 Wirth, in AA, X, 367.
57 Hodge, in HAI, II, 252.

wives. "There are also numerous instances of small children being spared to be brought up as members of the victorious tribe."[58]

When, later, men were spared by being taken prisoner, further mitigation ensued, but it was not of much consequence until tribes became agricultural and therefore slave-holding. Amongst other tribes prisoners were commonly tortured and killed, though there are a few exceptional cases where they may be adopted into the tribe of the conqueror. Slavery, in its time and place, constituted one of the greatest means of mitigating the cruelties of war. Slavery resulting from war has been treated elsewhere;[59] here will be mentioned a few instances that are somewhat transitional.

In the Congo region, "prisoners taken are held to ransom, and if not ransomed they are retained and sold or killed according to the whim of the captor."[60] In one East Central African tribe "prisoners are sold as slaves, and, if wounded, are healed first;"[61] while in another, "if in a fight a man was overpowered and he seized the breast of his captor with his mouth his life was spared, and he lived in the village of his captor and worked herding cattle, but he could not be sold."[62] Among the Dyaks adoption is a sort of emancipation from slavery. "Other tribes keep their slaves in a condition of perpetual servitude, but the Dyaks allow their friends to ransom them, and if they still remain on their hands, they adopt them into the tribe and enfranchise them. This ceremony is usually performed at a great feast, the owner announcing that he has freed so and so and adopted him as a brother, and he is presented by the chief with a spear which he is told to use in slaying the man who shall afterwards dare to call him a slave."[63] The Pimas also treated their captives well, and many of the prisoners have been known to have married into the tribe.[64] The Tlinkit case seems to be clearly transitional: "Prisoners of war were either killed or held as slaves."[65] The Guiana Indians, among whom there is no settled slavery, tortured their prisoners of war.[66]

Letourneau[67] has made a collection along this line, ranging from the sparing of no one to that of nearly all the vanquished. Cortez's allies inflicted tortures on their captives to the extent of scandalizing even him, though he was not oversensitive to others' sufferings. Some make their captives work while awaiting the day of death, which is the beginning of slavery; some kill all who resist but treat those who surrender well; some are careful not to destroy property; often all the men are slain and the women and children preserved; sometimes there were asylums; and ransoms come into play as the property-motive strengthens. The Peruvians did not exterminate their enemies; they were spared, for "soon they will be ours with all that they own." Utilitarian considerations put the curb on cruelty. The Chinese prohibited useless destruction: overturning walls, destroying works of art, kindling fires, and attacking defenseless people.

The inviolability of emissaries is recognized by some savage groups. The bearer of a message in Australia is "never molested by any of the tribes through whose country he may have occasion to travel while engaged on this

58 Karsten, "Jibaro," in BAE, Bull. LXXIX, 28.

59 §104 of text.

60 Weeks, in JAI, XL, 414.

61 Torday and Joyce, in JAI, XXXVI, 49-50.

62 Hobley, A-Kamba, 48.

63 Roth, in JAI, XXII, 60.

64 Hodge, in HAI, II, 252.

65 Jones, Thlingets, 113.

66 Roth, in BAE, XXXVIII, §771.

67 Guerre, 85, 98, 102, 134 ff., 165, 176, 183 ff., 195 ff., 207 ff., 231, 316, 322, 333 ff., 435 ff., 476, 489, 490, 505, 514, 523.

duty, even although the people through whom he may pass are not on friendly terms with his tribe."[68] "When there is a misunderstanding between two tribes, the women of one are sent to the other as ambassadors to arrange the dispute, which they invariably succeed in doing, when women from the other return the visit to testify their approval of the treaty arrived at. The reason women are appointed in this capacity is that they are free from danger, while, should the men go, their lives would be in peril." There might, however, be one or two men in each tribe, called messengers or postmen, whose persons were sacred. "They could travel amongst other tribes with freedom. They carried news, and conducted all negotiations connected with barter."[69] In more developed tribes traders are similarly immune; and Tylor[70] regards such an arrangement, where traders are allowed to pass through tribes at war, as one of the first germs of international law.

In some parts of Africa the chief is employed as an ambassador, and his person is respected by the enemy.[71] Among the Kabyles exists a custom known as *anaia,* which is a promise of protection made to one or more persons either by an individual or a village or tribe. It is a sort of safe-conduct. It also permits a native to take refuge even in the house of an enemy, and prisoners on the field of battle may claim it. Under this chivalrous custom women are given special consideration.[72] During the Crusades the Franks preferred Syrian, Jewish, or Moslem doctors, the last of whom were especially noted for skill and were called in for bad cases which the Christian doctors could do nothing with. "Passing in this way from one party to the other, the doctors furnished a ready means of communication between the two, and were often employed in confidential missions, sometimes even as diplomatic agents. In addition, Franks and Arabs willingly exchanged medical prescriptions, and each one increased his own medical and surgical knowledge from the experience of the other. It is needless to add that the Franks were the great gainers by this interchange of ideas."[73] Sir Walter Scott has employed this situation in *The Talisman.*

There are, finally, a number of war-practices which introduce at least the germs of chivalry. Some Australians show a desire to equalize conflicts, and they have been known to provide unarmed Europeans with a set of (Australian) weapons before attacking. The Lushais consider it unsporting to ambush cultivators, for as a chief once said, "How can people live if cultivation is impossible?"[74] Cases have occurred, while the bellicose Maoris were at war, of their filling canoes with food for their hungry enemies.[75] In the Canary Islands, not only are women, old people, and children protected in war, but pillage is forbidden and places of worship are not molested.[76] Letourneau[77] has a list of similar cases of war-habitudes which mitigate the destructiveness and cruelty of the conflict.

The Greek rule was the slaughter of all men from youth up, and the sale of women and children into slavery; but there were modifications and the Amphictyonic League went to considerable lengths in regulation. The ideal was

68 Mathews, "Message Sticks," in AA, X, 290.
69 Smyth, *Vict.,* I, 165, 181.
70 *Anth.,* 282.
71 Torday and Joyce, in JAI, XXXVI, 289.
72 Hanoteau et Letourneux, *Kabylie,* III, 80, 82, 190-191.

73 Munro, in *Intern. Mo.,* IV, 702.
74 Shakespear, in JAI, XXXIX, 375.
75 Cowan, *Maoris,* 293.
76 Cook, in AA, II, 477.
77 *Guerre,* 31, 33, 37, 84, 90, 123, 146, 155, 156, 226, 256, 261, 270, 311, 407, 439, 496, 515 ff.

that Greeks should have milder rules of war with Greeks than with barbarians.[78] In the *Herakleidæ* of Euripides, which is a play designed to set the cultured mores of Athens in contrast with those of Argos, Alkmene, representing the latter, intends to slay Eurystheus, a prisoner of war. The chorus voices the Athenian view.

"Chorus: It is not allowable for you to kill this man.
Servant: Did we take him captive for nothing?
Alkmene: What law, pray, prevents this man from dying?
Chorus: To this country's leaders it is not agreeable.
Alkmene: What is this? They think it not proper to kill an enemy?
Chorus: Not one, at any rate, whom they take alive in battle."

After describing the woes of the Trojan War, Cassandra is made to say: "War, then, the man of sense should shun; but if it comes to that, to perish nobly is no mean glory to the city."[79] The laws of Manu include war-regulation of a detailed order: one must not strike with weapons concealed in wood or barbed or poisoned or blazing with fire, nor smite one who flees, nor a eunuch, nor a suppliant, nor one who submits, nor one who sleeps, has lost his coat of mail, or is naked or disarmed, nor a non-combatant, nor one who is fighting another foe, nor one whose weapons are broken, nor one in sorrow, or wounded, or in fear.[80] In the earliest epoch of the Mohammedan war-usages it was the rule not to kill or mistreat women and children of the enemy even if they were not Mohammedans, unless they took part in the battle.[81] During the Middle Ages chivalry was full of more or less empty sentiment, including horror of lies and perfidy, obligation to fight loyally and to defend the weak; but all sorts of excesses were tolerated when it came to the treatment of the unarmed masses. The sentiment and ideals were restricted in this field of application; their essentially grotesque character is burlesqued in Don Quixote. Lecky[82] finds that "the changes Christianity effected in the rights of war were very important," and lists the suppression of the gladiatorial shows which saved thousands of victims; the discouragement of the practice of enslaving prisoners; the ransoming of immense multitudes with charitable contributions, until "it became a recognised principle of international law, that no Christian prisoners should be reduced to slavery"; and the "creation of a new warlike ideal."

§142. The Drift toward Peace.

A FORMAL peace-making was customary among some of the Melanesians when it was felt that a respite was necessary from such severe inter-community feuds as were likely to be perpetual. "Probably such peace-makings did not often occur until the blood accounts between the two communities were tolerably even, and in these formal peace-makings, even when the number which had been killed on either side was the same, each side paid rigorously for those it had killed."[1] If a fighting tribe of Papuans desires to make peace, "they

78 Keller, *Hom. Soc.*, 293 ff.; Burckhardt, *Griech. Kgchte.*, I, 153-154, 173, 294; Curtius, *Greece*, I, 115; Mahaffy, *Greece*, 254; Plato, *Republic*, 479; Strabo, *Geog.*, X, 12.
79 Euripides, *Trojan Women*, 400-402; *Herakleidæ*, 961-966.

80 Bühler, *Manu*, VII, 90-93; VII, *passim*.
81 Von Kremer, *Kgchte.*, II, 103-104.
82 *European Morals*, II, 259.
1 Seligmann, *Melanesians*, 544-545.

let their wish be known by blocking the way to the enemy's village with a branch which they put across the path, and choose for this purpose some parting of the road which the enemy are sure to pass. In the case of the enemy agreeing to the proposition, they place another branch over the first one, but if they want to go on fighting they turn the branch so that it points in the direction of their antagonists, and place on it a bundle of small tally-sticks, which indicate the number of people they intend to kill before they are willing to make peace." The usual way of making friends is through the medium of the women. "A couple of men with their wives go to the hostile village, and the women are sent a few steps in front. It is a recognized rule in the district that the presence of women in such a case means peace. Such a proposition to cease hostilities is generally accepted—at all events temporarily—and the visitors are well received. The men mutually break each other's beheading-knives in token of peace, and sometimes exchange their arm-guards. In the night the men in the village have connection with the women of their guests, and that is the real object of the visit. This custom is called *era adogo* ('putting out the fire'). After a few days the visit is returned under exactly the same circumstances, and the visitors give up their women to the men in the other village."[2] There are a number of local peace-symbols: betel-chewing, eating of bits of coconut or other food, sacrifice of a dog, smoking of cigars[3]— all of which are well understood and must have been long and frequently in practice. In some parts of Southeastern Papua the peace sign is made by touching first the nose and then the navel. The signs at Dobu are somewhat different, each breast being touched in turn, to indicate that you are of one family.[4] War is ended in the Solomons by one party sending a certain amount of the local money and the same amount being sent in return.[5]

To the fighting Herero and Hottentots the missionaries were "sacro-sanct"; but they had great trouble in keeping the Herero from killing Hottentot peace-emissaries, for the former saw in the latter their former oppressors and the torturers and murderers of their relatives.[6] When two contending clans among the Bageshu wish to make peace, "the chiefs come together to some place and sit down, a dog is brought and one takes hold of its head and the other of its hind legs, whilst a third man severs it in two with a large knife. The dog is thrown away and the clans are free to intermingle without any fear."[7] Among the Ba-Yaka alliances are frequently contracted between chiefs, and peace is made in the following manner: "The chiefs of the two tribes meet and eat a cake made of flour in which have been put some of their nail-parings; a fowl is then killed, wrapped in leaves and buried. It is believed that he who breaks the truce will die."[8] Among the neighboring Ba-Mbala an alliance between two chiefs is contracted by making incisions in the breast of each and rubbing the blood of the other in the wounds. In this case death is the penalty for killing a man belonging to the village of the other. Similar ceremonies of blood-brotherhood will be considered later.[9] Among the same people there is one form of compact which deserves mention, the pact against bloodshed. The richest chief of the neighborhood will invite the rest of the chiefs in his vicinity to

2 Landtmann, in JAI, XLVI, 332-333; Gason, in JAI, XXIV, 173.
3 Hagen, *Papua's*, 251; Finsch, *Ethnol. Erfahr.*, II, 47.
4 Bromilow, in AAAS, 1909, 471.
5 Fox and Drew, in JAI, XLV, 213.
6 Büttner, *Walfischbai*, 70.
7 Roscoe, in JAI, XXXIX, 195.
8 Torday and Joyce, in JAI, XXXVI, 50.
9 §150 of text.

a meeting held on his territory in order to make such a pact. A slave is fattened for the occasion and killed by the host and the invited chiefs and their followers partake of the flesh. Supposing that a chief, after attending an assembly of this kind, kills a slave, every village which took part in the bond has the right to claim compensation, and the murderer is sure to be completely ruined.[10] Among the Nigerians, "when one side is tired of war, women of the other tribe married to men of the former tribe are sent to their relatives with offers of peace. They are naturally sacred, for they have friends on both sides." If peace is agreed upon, representatives of both tribes meet and swear friendship.[11] The Kabyles set stones upright to conclude peace-agreements, "and each of them represents the agreement or signature of a tribe to a concluded pact. They knock them down if the agreement is subsequently broken."[12]

The Nagas of India have an elaborate ceremony of peace-making between two villages.[13] In Borneo, "after past wrongs, peace and good-fellowship cannot be gained by simple asseverations; there must always be a palpable exchange of beads, highly prized jars, brass gongs, etc., as an indemnity. The perpetrator of the wrong, or one of his descendants, must be present with his adherents to join in the sham fight, known as the 'Jawa.'" And there is another ceremony signifying the obliteration of a feud, called "Usut." "The interchange of Usut is obligatory between descendants of enemies whenever they first enter each other's houses; they may have met many times on most friendly terms in the jungle or in the houses of neighbors, but they must not take shelter under one another's roof until they have appeased the wrongs done by and against their ancestors. The simple rite of giving Usut for ancestral wrongs is expanded into the performance of Jawa when, in addition, the descendants have been themselves wrongdoers." First a roughly made iron spear-head is flung into the center of the circle, and on its flat surface a young chicken is decapitated, then torn to pieces and its warm blood smeared over the point. Beads and trinkets are formally exchanged and blood from the spear-head rubbed on the chest or arms of everyone present. The two formerly hostile clans then hail each other as friends.[14] In Samoa there are practices which operate to prevent hostilities from taking place. If two families in a village quarrelled, and wished to fight, the other heads of families and the chief stepped in and forbade; and it was at the peril of either party to carry on the strife contrary to the decided voice of public opinion. In the same way strife may be prevented between any two villages of the district. Hostilities are often prevented by such acts as giving up the culprit, paying a heavy fine, or by bowing down in abject submission, carrying firewood and small stones used in baking a pig, or, perhaps, a few bamboos. "The firewood, stones, and leaves were equivalent to their saying, 'Here we are, your pigs, to be cooked if you please; and here are the materials with which to do it.' Taking bamboos in the hand was as if they said, 'We have come, and here are the knives to cut us up.' A piece of split bamboo was, of old, the usual knife in Samoa."[15] In one New Zealand case, the natives said they were equal and satisfied, "there being exactly the same number killed and wounded on both sides during the war, which was about half-a-dozen; since that time good feeling has existed."[16]

10 Torday and Joyce, in JAI, XXXV, 409.
11 Tremearne, in JAI, XLII, 185.
12 Hanoteau et Letourneux, Kabylie, II, 190, 238, 294, 297, 303.

13 Hutton, Sema Nagas, 179 ff.
14 Furness, Head-Hunters, 98, 112-113.
15 Turner, Samoa, 189, 180-181.
16 Taylor, Te Ika, 559.

Certain American Indian towns were consecrated to peace-ceremonies and were known as "white towns," while others set apart for war-ceremonials were designated as "red towns."[17] Among some tribes there was also a particular village or clan that had the right to shelter or protect a fugitive; among others the chief's tent afforded asylum, or if food was offered and taken the captive was spared.[18] Should the Osage, for instance, be warring against another tribe, and one of the foe slip into camp and beg for protection from the chief, the latter must help him. As soon as possible food was cooked and given the fugitive, and when he had eaten a mouthful he was safe. "He could then go through the camp with impunity. This condition of affairs lasted as long as he remained with the tribe, but it terminated when he returned to his home."[19] This right of asylum was a sort of peace-taboo, similar examples of which will be presented later. A fetishistic device used by the American Indians for many purposes, including peace-ceremonies and alliances, is the calumet. It was "employed by ambassadors and travelers as a passport; it was used in ceremonies designed to conciliate foreign and hostile nations and to conclude lasting peace; to ratify the alliance of friendly tribes; to secure favorable weather for journeys; to bring needed rain; and to attest contracts and treaties which could not be violated without incurring the wrath of the gods. The use of the calumet was inculcated by religious precept and example." When the calumet is designed to be employed in a treaty of alliance against a third tribe, a serpent may be painted on the shaft, and perhaps some other device indicating the motive of the alliance. "By smoking together in the calumet the contracting parties intend to invoke the sun and the other gods as witnesses to the mutual obligations assumed by the parties, and as a guaranty the one to the other that they shall be fulfilled."[20]

One or two incomplete accounts have been handed down as to the procedure by which peace has been concluded by the Guiana Indians. Thus, on the Orinoco, as soon as the preliminaries were arranged, the parties confirmed it, after their barbarous fashion, by interchanging as many blows with a cudgel as amounted to complete satisfaction. The method of attaining complete satisfaction is this: each member of tribe A, for example, receives a blow for each member of tribe B that he has killed, and *vice versa,* no canceling allowed. In another section the method of concluding a truce is as follows. The interested party, usually the captain, goes into the enemy's country with the chief men and all the youths, who march in battle-array, well equipped with weapons. When at one or two days' journey from the meeting-house they depute some of their number to go and inform the enemy that they wish to be friends and live henceforth on good terms with them. If the offer be well received, they tell those who have halted to come along. The two nations then range themselves in order of battle, just as if they wanted to fight. They fling abuses and reproaches at each other for all the outrages committed. "You stole our women," says one; "you killed and ate my father, cousin, brother," complains another. "Finally, after all these animated speeches, they suddenly throw their arms to the ground with loud manifestations of joy and then proceed to the karbet [meeting-house], where they drink for three or four days."[21]

Where primitive groups live in a state of continual hostility, intercourse is

17 HAI, pt. I, 364.
18 Fletcher, in HAI, II, 915.
19 Dorsey, in BAE, XV, 237.

20 Hewitt, in HAI, I, 192, 194.
21 Roth, in BAE, XXXVIII, §777.

naturally precluded and the phenomenon is presented of isolated, antagonistic groups speaking different dialects. Any device, therefore, which tends to permit intercourse and the treating of strangers as friends instead of enemies is a step toward peace. One such device is for the visiting party to make its presence known and to observe some ceremony instead of walking straight into a camp. In Australia, whether for friendly intercourse or for war, the tribe which seeks a meeting must give notice of its coming in due form. Another custom highly developed among the Australians is the use of ambassadors or messengers. The messenger has to carry a token, by virtue of which he passes safely through the lands of the several tribes. The token is a piece of wood on which are inscribed hieroglyphics that, being read and interpreted, suffice to notify all persons of the nature of the mission. If the mission is a friendly one, the token-stick is streaked with red ocher; if unfriendly, with white ocher. "However unpleasant the tidings may be, the persons of the messengers are held sacred, and they are always patiently heard and hospitably treated. If the message is of such a kind as to require an answer, the answer is given, and the bearer is conducted safely to the boundaries of the district he has invaded."[22] Another means of communication and intercourse found all over Australia is the smoke-signal, which is read with keen watchful eyes over considerable distances. According to the nature of the column of smoke the natives know whether a friendly tribe is coming, whether war threatens, where hunting is good, etc., while other signals mean an invitation to an initiation or a corrobboree.[23]

Blood-relationship and intermarriage operate in many places to prevent hostilities or to provide a means of reconciliation. The effect of the social bond upon war in Polynesia is found in the custom under which "any member of a group nearly related by blood or marriage to persons of another, might, not only during peace, but also in time of war, pass with impunity from the territories of the one to those of the other, and be regarded as a friend in both; and such persons were employed to bear proposals for peace. It is found in the fact also that in acts of violence and death in war persons and families allied by marriage were always spared." The Samoans regarded fighting between blood-relations with horror; one case is mentioned in which close relationship between two chiefs prevented war, even though the quarrel between them was that one of them had carried off the other's wife.[24] An instance is cited in the Solomon Islands of a man who had relations in all the islands and so, even in time of war, could go back and forth without fear.[25] In Brazil tribal marks serve as peace-guarantees.[26] From such situations as the above there developed in the course of time treaties of *connubium* which were peace-pacts of an enduring kind, linking the groups together and bringing them into permanent political relations.

Economic factors also have made for peace, as among the Araucanians where the harvest of the fruit of the pine was of such supreme importance that all inter-tribal quarrels and warfares were suspended by mutual accord during this period.[27] Access to deposits of stone, flint, salt, and other desirables implies either war with the people who hold the territory where they are, or a

---

22 Smyth, *Vict.*, I, 133 (quoted), 135; Dorsey, in BAE, 1881, 276.
23 Magarey, in AAAS, 1893, 498-513.
24 Williamson, *Cent. Polyn.*, II, 332, 333, 338, 350 (quoted).

25 Fox and Drew, in JAI, XLV, 210.
26 Spix u. Martius, *Bras.*, 1279, note; Von Martius, *Beiträge*, I, 377-378, 502-503.
27 Latcham, in JAI, XXXIX, 341.

treaty with them for peaceful access. Cases of peaceful access have already been considered;[28] here may be re-emphasized their tendency toward peace, as where, among the American Indians, the pipe-stone quarries constituted peace-centers; hostile tribesmen met there under a strongly sanctioned interdiction of violence.[29] The red pipe-stone of Minnesota was sought and carried away peacefully in the midst of war. The treaty of peaceful access was a breach in the relations of war between two groups and was the germ of international law.

Further evidence of the antagonism of trade and war, and of the pacific tendency of the former, is observed in the peace of the market. How hostility interferes with trading is to be seen in the marketing-customs of some Melanesians. One or other party would send a message that in two or three days' time they would come to a certain place prepared to trade. "Spears were always taken and carried at the market, where trouble often ensued and it was not uncommon for a man to be killed. In such circumstances the aggrieved tribe would seek revenge either immediately, or at a subsequent market." Under these conditions the market was necessarily held at irregular intervals.[30] Among the Papuans, "at the markets themselves and during the time of the circumcision-month festival the peace of God rules."[31] These festivals, with attendant suspension of hostilities, break in upon the tendency toward self-isolation and prevent utter lapse of the feeling of tribal unity.[32] Among the northern African tribes it took some public safe-conduct or peace-pact to overcome the mutual suspicions of peoples who had been killing one another, before they dared come together in a market.[33] Peace at market-places is one of the conquests of trade over war, which begin with silent barter;[34] and provisions are quite common which limit hostilities in time as well as in space, for they must not take place on holy days (holidays) or rest days.[35] The story of Herodotus[36] about the Argippeans of eastern Scythia, who are holy, just, peaceable, unarmed people, carrying on trade and the conciliation of strife in the midst of wild nomads, is repeated over and over again in the case of a sanctuary-grave of a hero or saint, or a relic-deposit, in charge of a reputedly sacred family which sells things required in sacrifices, adjudicates quarrels, protects fugitives, and in whose vicinity a market has developed.[37]

Religion has been an influential factor in the development of peace. Some evidence of this influence has already been given. The Australians never allowed any display of arms anywhere near the storehouses where the sacred stones, whirr-sticks, and amulets were kept.[38] A similar religious taboo on strife prevailed among the Cheyenne Indians during the ceremony of renewing the arrows: "While the arrows were being renewed, a guard of soldiers was stationed about the camp. No noise was permitted; no one was allowed to do anything that was bad. No one might be cross, speak angrily, or dispute with anyone; all must be good-natured and friendly."[39] The religious festival has operated to bring together sub-groups which by migrating over a great territory have become strange and perhaps hostile to each other, but at the time and

28 §77 of text.
29 Donaldson, in *Smithson. Rep.*, 1885, pt. II, 102.
30 Seligmann, *Melanesians*, 94-95.
31 Hagen, *Papua's*, 253.
32 Von Pfeil, *Südsee*, 164-165.
33 Foureau, *Tchad*, 564.
34 §§76, 77, of text.

35 Paulitschke, *Nordost-Afr.*, I, 247; for the general case, see Webster, *Rest Days*.
36 *Hist.*, IV, 23; 49, 100, 102, 103, 125.
37 Lippert, *Kgchte.*, I, 459; II, 170.
38 Spencer and Gillen, *Nat. Tr. Cent. Aust.*, 135.
39 Grinnell, *Cheyenne*, II, 53.

place of the meeting peace is imposed. A peace-covenant and peace-group may be formed under religious sanction which, even though temporary, is by no means trivial. There was a peace of the gods at the time of the great festivals among the Greeks, and sometimes a feud was brought to an end at such a time. "The god-peace of Olympia and the holy neutrality of all Elis have their own history. But real wars were not hindered by the festivals and scarcely momentarily interrupted."[40] There was a two months' peace of God for visitors to the festival mysteries of Eleusis.[41] The pre-Mohammed Arabs had certain asylums, but there were not many holy places recognized universally—in fact, Mecca was about the only one. There, before Mohammed's time, no blood except that of sacrificed animals might be spilled; there no weapons might be used, no trees felled, no wild animals killed. At first the tabooed area included only the temple and city, but was later much extended. There, where trade flourished, was an inviolable peace-area, called *harem*. For local communities the graves of the ancestors and the homes were asylums. The Mohammedans had also four holy months during which fighting was forbidden, a custom taken out of the heathen time. Not only war, but the chief cause of war, blood-vengeance, was interdicted during these months.[42]

A development of the Middle Ages was the so-called "house-peace." The Teutonic freeman, in his homestead, was in all aspects autocratic, though outside of it he was but a commoner of the mass.[43] "If you commit an act of violence in a man's house, whatever you may have to pay to the person whom you strike and to the king, you will also have to make amends to the owner of the house, even though he be but a ceorl or a boor, for you have broken his peace."[44] The notion that "every man's house is his castle" was the first effort of the law, thinks Lacroix,[45] to protect a man whom it could not protect in his person. Now that the law protects a man always and everywhere, this old principle is unimportant. The "house-peace" later extended to cover fields and roads, it played a considerable rôle in German law, and along with it went the church-peace, market-peace, and peace of God.[46] The "woman-peace," assuring her immunity of body and goods at all times, was early established in Northern and German law.[47] In Scandinavia there was a peace-interval for trade at religious festivals; in general, trade went with peace, but was readily replaced, on occasion, by robbery and war.[48] A common share in the sacrifices was a sign of obligation to peace; but the Upsala king was charged, as chief, with the sacrifices at that sanctuary of the race. Such a holy spot was tabooed for peace even to the gods. It is a case of a cult-group which is a peace-group, and led to the development of a trading-center and also of an assembly, or *thing*. Disputes were settled there and law developed. The great annual sacrifices collected and united the people. Where they were held was peace, and participation meant peace between the separate tribes. Under that peace-taboo were held feasts, conferences, judgments, sales, and contracts, so that *thing* meant not only assembly but also sacrifice, hospitality, parliament-day in court, and fair.[49] Church influence caused weapons to be left out of *thing* first in Ice-

40 Burckhardt, *Griech. Kgchte.*, I, 311.
41 Beloch, *Griech. Gchte.*, II, 2, note.
42 Von Kremer, *Kgchte. d. Orients*, II, 14, 103; Procksch, *Blutrache*, 42, 43, 44, 46.
43 Garnier, *Brit. Peasantry*, I, 88.
44 Maitland, *Domesday Book*, 99.

45 *Middle Ages*, 350.
46 Osenbrüggen, *Hausfrieden*, 5 *et passim*.
47 Weinhold, *Deut. Frauen*, I, 219.
48 Lippert, *Kgchte.*, II, 537.
49 Geijer, *Svensk. Hist.*, 38, 112; Brodeur, *Snorri Sturlason's Prose Edda*, 72.

land, then in Denmark and later in Norway.[50] "The dwelling-places of Northern kings seem, like sanctuaries, to have been regarded as possessing a sacred peace. The term 'field of peace' is found applied to the Swedish king's dwelling as early as Beowulf."[51]

The church-peace and king's peace are common phenomena of the Middle Ages;[52] the latter was bought by outlaws, Jews, and merchants.[53] Quarrels in a church were forbidden and if any occurred offenders were fined; fighting was interdicted during festivals or fasts and on holy days; and in other ways peace and order were enjoined under the truce of God.[54] To the Peace of God succeeded the Peace of the King and a rapid development occurred in the list of offenses which came within its orbit. At first the king's peace was purely personal; when he died there was no royal peace until his successor proclaimed his own; but later, following the death of Henry III in England, perpetual peace was proclaimed. Hitherto it had been the peace of the king, now it became the peace of the kingdom.[55] A most important step had been taken toward securing law and order within the group.

§149. Clan, Gens, Etc.

IN the dual organization characteristic of Melanesian society, the population consists of two exogamous groups which Rivers[1] calls moieties, a man of one moiety having to marry a woman of the other. In every case where this form of social organization is known to exist, descent is in the female line so that a man belongs to the moiety of his mother. By contrast, the word "tribe" is applied to a group of a simple kind, always in Melanesia settled in a definite locality, which speaks a common language and is capable of uniting for common action, as in warfare. In some instances the grouping seems to be by hamlets, the inhabitants of each hamlet being all more or less closely related either by birth, marriage, or adoption, so that besides constituting the functional social unit of public life the hamlet, in the majority of cases, is co-extensive with a family group.[2]

In all the villages of San Cristoval, Solomon Islands, exogamous clans with mother-descent prevail and form the most outstanding feature of the social organization of the people. "Just as the village is divided among the clans, so all property on the island is likewise divided; garden land, coco-nuts, and so on: each clan has its own. When a party of men from Santa Anna go on a canoe voyage up the coast to Haununu, the Haununu people remark on the fact that members of different clans will not even then, among strangers, eat food cooked in a common pot, but it must be cooked in a separate vessel for each clan. The members of the clans believe they are the descendants of the animals after which the clans are named; stories are told of the original animal ancestor of the clan: no member may eat of the animal from which his clan

50 Jørgensen, in *Annaler*, 1876, 176.
51 Chadwick, in *Folk-Lore*, XI, 285; *Beowulf*, line 2960.
52 Van Duyl, *Beschavingsgeschied.*, 110-111; Maitland, *Domesday*, 184 ff.; Vinogradoff, *Manor*, 123.
53 Lippert, *Kgchte.*, II, 123, 394.
54 Jenks, *Law and Politics*, 194 ff.; Lacroix, *Middle Ages*, 49, 350; Schulz, *Höf. Leben*, II,

127; Henderson, *Documents*, 208; Kluckhohn, *Der Gottesfriede*.
55 Jenks, *Law and Politics*, 87, 115 ff.; 239 ff.; Geijer, *Svenska Hist.*, 170; Henderson, *Documents*, 211; Barthold, *Gesch. der Hansa*, I, 127, 185; Pollock, "King's Peace," in *Law Quart. Rev.*, I, 37.
1 *Melan. Soc.*, I, 15, 17-18; II, 504-505; Kroeber and Holt, in JAI, L, 452-460.
2 Seligmann, *Melanesians*, 444, 479.

takes its name, and sacrifices and prayers are regularly offered by the members of clans to their animal ancestors. This seems to present a case of pure totemism, in which all the elements necessary to constitute totemism are present."[3]

Among the Nama Hottentots of Southwest Africa a tribe is composed of a number of patrilineal sibs or clans, that is, of groups of people claiming to be related in the male line; one of these sibs claims seniority, and the chieftainship is hereditary in this senior sib in the male line. Through the whole course of Nama history the sib was the strongest social unit. Time and again a strong sib would go off on its own, asserting its independence of the others, and sib loyalty was always stronger than tribal loyalty. "It is no wonder, then, that the chief among the Hottentots was little more than *primus inter pares*. He was acknowledged to be the head of the senior sib and, if a person of fine character, was accorded a great deal of respect, but the heads of the other sibs acted as his council and he could not do much without their coöperation." Membership in a sib guaranteed to a person a very strong measure of protection, for he could always count on the support of his fellow sib-members.[4] The Akamba population of East Africa is divided into clans and these into families. The ties between clan-members are extremely close; "so close is the relationship that members of the clan may not marry although they have not met for generations." A village among these people is really the abode of a family numbering as many huts as there are married women.[5] Up to comparatively recent times, the clan among the Kikuyu was a unit and each clan inhabited its own location.[6] The Bahima are divided up into fourteen clans, each having its own particular sacred object or totem. "The members of a clan are all closely related, the same term is used in speaking of a brother or sister or cousin; the clansmen must be cared for in sickness, helped in distress, righted when wronged, and avenged in death by the clan."[7] A Ba-Yaka child belongs to the village of his maternal uncle; no others save blood relations are admitted as members of the village community.[8] On the Upper Congo, as elsewhere, geographical nearness does not produce a feeling of kinship, but blood relations, no matter how far apart they live, feel the affinity strongly. The terms used here to designate the various social organizations are quite significant: *Muu* is the word used for family, and it also means hearth, fire-place, seeming to indicate those who sat around the same fire. *Mboko* signifies branch of family having the same male ancestors; *Ekanga* means tribe, clan, from *Kanga*, to tie together, probably showing that they were tied together by bonds of blood.[9] The importance of blood-relationship is seen in the custom among the Fan that when two natives who are members of the same tribe or of allied tribes meet, they recite their respective lists of ancestors, even up to twenty generations or more, to see if they are related. The ethnographer[10] who reports this states that when he used to arrive in a strange village he found it good policy to recite his own list of ancestors, taking care to make them correspond to the ancestors of the chief; for good measure he would add some more ancestors to indicate that he came from a family more closely related than the chief's to the primitive

3 Fox, in JAI, XLIX, 150-151; Fox and Drew, in JAI, XLV, 131-133.
4 Hoernlé, in AA, XXVII, 8-9, 11, 15, 16.
5 Dundas, C., in JAI, XLIII, 539, 492-493.
6 Hobley, *A-Kamba*, 138.

7 Roscoe, in JAI, XXXVII, 98-99.
8 Torday and Joyce, in JAI, XXXVI, 45.
9 Weeks, in JAI, XXXIX, 436-437.
10 Trilles, *Fân*, 5, 6, 122-123.

stock, and then, drawing on his memory of the Biblical genealogies, would finally arrive at Adam, the son of God, where he must of necessity stop. Upon this recital the astonished chief would recognize in him an ally and relative and treat him accordingly. "If fear is the beginning of wisdom, as the Scriptures say, it was often, in deference to me, the sentiment of my black friends."

Among certain West African tribes, the "family consists solely of persons who are connected by uterine ties. . . . The father is never related by blood to his children, and is not considered as belonging to the family. . . . The clan name is the test of blood-relationship, and as property follows the laws of blood-descent, it ensues that property never goes out of the clan; for, with descent in the female line, a family is only a small circle of persons, all of whom bear the same clan-name, within the larger circle of the clan itself." But this condition cannot hold when the blood-tie between father and child has been recognized; "the result of this recognition has been the inevitable downfall of the clan-system, which is only possible so long as descent is traced solely on one side of the house. . . . Since two persons of the same clan-name may, under the clan-system, never marry, it follows that husband and wife must be of different clans. Let us say that one is a Dog and the other a Leopard. The clan-name is extended to all who are of the same blood; therefore, directly the blood-relationship between father and child comes to be acknowledged, the children of such a pair as we have supposed, instead of being, as heretofore, simply Leopards, would be Dog-Leopards, and would belong to two clans. They in their turn might marry with persons similarly belonging to two clans, say Cat-Snakes, and the offspring of these unions would belong to four clans. The clan-system thus becomes altogether unworkable, because, as the number of clans is limited and cannot be added to, if the clan name still remained the test of blood-relationship and a bar to marriage, the result in a few generations would be that no marriages would be possible. Consequently the clan-name ceases to be the test of consanguinity, kinship is traced in some other way, and the clan-system disappears." Marriage within the known circle of consanguinity remains forbidden.[11]

Dundas[12] has described the social organization in East Africa, where ordinarily a village comprises simply the huts of the wives of one man. "The head of such a village is then the senior member of the family. The villages are generally built in groups, which at times are so close together that they form almost one continuous village; in other cases they are more scattered, but rarely completely isolated. Such groups form what is called a *thome*. . . . In practice the head of each village is alone recognised, because he is the head of the family, but since he is vaguely subordinate to the senior elder of the *thome*, the senior elder of the group is invested with a certain authority. The *thome* is almost the most extensive combination natural to the tribes, and the authority of its elder is the greatest individual authority comprehended." From the above he concludes that the state is simply the family, and for certain purposes it extends to groups of families. "It was between these groups that internal fighting broke out, but not infrequently also within the *thome* there were dissensions and hostilities. On the other hand, there are common objects, if not common rule, which form ties extending beyond the *thome*, and whereby at any rate a loosely connected community is made possible. Most important

11 Ellis, *Yoruba*, 174, 175, 176; Keane,   12 In JAI, XLV, 239-240.
Ethnology, 6, 7.

in this respect are the common places of sacrifice. . . . Thus a religious union is formed which centres around the sacred places, and combines the village groups through the common interest that their elders have in them. Apart from religion there is a great deal in ordinary custom which tends to create ties between certain groups. Thus a peculiar manner of performing a dance will draw together the members of certain families, even from youth."

Among the Gilyak of Siberia, "the father-in-law of one clansman is the father-in-law of the whole clan; and the son-in-law of a clansman is the son-in-law of the whole clan. The men form the permanent element in the clan; the women either leave the clan or come to it from another. So the clan forms a society or union, cemented by common rights and marital duties of men related through their fathers, taking their wives from another similar group, and giving their women in marriage to a third clan, all clans being thus exogamic and patriarchal in organization. In spite of the dominant patriarchal principle, Gilyak are related also through their mothers, for they have a common 'father-in-law' clan; and all women coming into a clan are to each other in the relationship of sister, aunt, or niece. . . . The principle that a man must take his wife from his mother's clan, that the wife must be a blood-relative of her husband, is a religious principle, connected with the cult of ancestors, especially with mother-cult. No clansman need fear that at his death he will leave his family without support, for even while he lives his wife and children are nominally, often even actually, the wife and children of his brother; and at his death one of his brothers, chosen by the clansmen, is bound to undertake the rights and duties of father and husband towards his widow."[13]

Yakut social divisions formerly depended upon the herds of horses, and these upon pasture. The mother-clan, called *rod,* was a group owning and using together, in some locality, herds, game, and houses, and "the feeling of blood-bond was at first very vague." At first only older and younger, brothers and sisters, mothers and children, were distinguished; later the family took form, and uncles, aunts, nephews, grandfathers, and grandchildren were recognized."[14] When the Yakuts began to herd cattle, this involved a division of the tribe into smaller social groups, so that the memory of the old large herds of horses and large groups of people was preserved only in the ancient poems. Thus, in the new economic conditions, the family came to be the most important social unit, more stable than the old clans of the horse-breeders. "Antagonism between family and clan shows itself nowadays in disputes which arise over questions of inheritance. Failing a male heir, claim to property lapses to the clan, and even a married sister of the deceased receives nothing." The whole clan to which a murderer belonged was held responsible for the crime, and must make compensation either in blood or by payment of damages. The clan-organization is relatively strong among the Tungus proper; the members of a clan may not marry each other; the clan is governed by an elder whose office is hereditary. This organization has been preserved most pure among those Tungus who have remained in isolated districts, mixing with alien elements only on their borders; that is, it has remained in its purest state among the nomadic and wandering tribes, especially the latter. "Christianity and a sedentary mode of life have been unfavourable to the preservation of their social structure no less than to that of their religious cults." The only well-defined

---

13 Czaplicka, *Aborig. Siberia,* 43-44.   14 Sieroshevski, *Yakuts* (Russ.), 436, 507; *Yakuts* (Pol.), 304.

and stable social unit among the Koryak is the family, though there are indications of a tendency for families related by marriage to draw together in larger groups, united by certain moral and material obligations—"a tendency that might have led to the establishment of a real clan organization, but for the destructive influence of the Russians." The transition from the kinship to the territorial basis of social organization may be seen in the case of the Finnic tribes of Siberia. Among them the clan has been in the past the most important social unit, being united by its descent from a common founder-protector and by a common cult, and comprising from ten to thirty villages. "At the present day, however, the group of villages is becoming more and more a territorial unit, known as *mer,* and less of a clan in the strict sense." On the other hand, these people have never exhibited a tendency to unite into anything resembling a nation or even an organized tribe; "they have always been grouped in clans independent of each other, each clan having its own chief, and there was seldom even anything like an alliance of clans. The chief (prince) was the real ruler, but on certain important occasions there was an assembly, in which only the oldest members of the clans were allowed to take part in the discussions."[15]

Among the hill tribes of Central India exists a situation closely analogous to that mentioned above in the case of certain West Africans: "the clan rule has to be replaced by some other formula, as, for instance, by prohibiting the marriage of any descendants of a common pair or tabooing the intercourse of cousins, which is actually what has happened among the more advanced Dravidians, while the Gonds marry cousins by preference."[16] The unit of Angami society is not the village but the *khel,* composed of supposed descendants from a common ancestor, whose name the *khel* bears. "These *khels* are exogamous, no man being allowed to marry a woman of his own *khel. . . .* Children belong to the *khel* of the father."[17] The unit of Sema society is not the exogamous clan, as among the Angamis; clan feeling exists, as does tribal feeling, but it has no organs. "The basis of Sema society is the village, or part of a village, which is under the control of a chief. . . . In most of such groups there are to be found men of many, or at least of several, different clans. The predominant position, however, of the chief, and of his relatives on the male side, leads to the rough classification of the whole group as of their clan. The real pivot of Sema society is the chief. This is not to suggest, however, that the clan is unimportant. It pervades the life of the ordinary Sema from his birth upwards, determining, or at any rate influencing, his choice of food, of wives, of friends, and sometimes of enemies."[18] Furness[19] has likened the village *khels* of the Nagas to the molecules of a tribe. "Let me borrow still further from the molecular theory," he continues, "and designate as atoms, of which the tribal molecules are composed, the *jhats* or clans which enter into the constitution of a *khel. . . .* Each *khel* in a village may be made up of one or several *jhats* living amicably together and intermarrying one with the other but never marrying within the *jhat . . .* that those who lived in *khels* composed of but one *jhat* declared that marriage within their own *khel* was prohibited, while those living in *khels* composed of several *jhats* declared emphatically that they did not have to go outside of their *khel* to seek a husband or wife. . . . This interdiction of marriage in the *jhat* was undoubtedly designed to prevent inbreeding,

15 Czaplicka, *Aborig. Siberia,* 57, 51-53, 32, 67-69, 36.
16 Crooke, in JAI, XXVIII, 235.

17 Godden, in JAI, XXVII, 23.
18 Hutton, *Sema Nagas,* 121-122, 124.
19 In JAI, XXXII, 447-448.

but, since the mother's *jhat* is ignored, it is but a half measure, and the marriage of first cousins on the mother's side of the family and also of uncle and niece are unrestricted." The fundamental feature of the social organization of the Todas is the division of the community into two perfectly distinct groups, which are endogamous. This is the so-called dual organization, again, into two divisions or moieties. Each of these primary divisions is subdivided into a number of secondary divisions, which are exogamous, and may be termed clans. The members of a clan have many common rights and privileges which bind them together, so that the clan-tie has a very real meaning. Property, however, is largely centered in the family or the individual, and "the Todas are in a state of social evolution in which the common bond constituted by membership of the clan has been largely replaced by the bond constituted by the family."[20]

The division of the Chinese into clans "has had a depressing effect upon their good government. It resembles in general the arrangement of the Scottish clans, as do the evils arising from their dissensions and feuds those which history records as excited among the Highlanders by the rivalry between Campbells and Macgregors. . . . There are only about four hundred clans in the whole of China, but inasmuch as all of the same surname do not live in the same place, the separation of a clan answers the same purpose as multiplying it."[21] "Originally developing by coalescence of villages lying near one another, the cities of the Middle Kingdom have preserved the clan-system in considerable purity. The hamlets and quarters into which they are divided have each one a patriarch at the head whose influence and ascendancy over the inhabitants does not fall much below that of the village-authorities." But they have lost most of their judiciary powers to the mandarins.[22] "Altogether there were in ancient Japan, after the beginning of the historic era, 1182 clans, great and small; and these appear to have established the same number of cults. . . . It was only with the breaking-up of the clan-system in Japan that the possibilities of starvation for the worker first came into existence. And as, in antique Europe, the enfranchised client-class and plebeian-class developed, under like conditions, into a democracy clamouring for suffrage and all political rights, so in Japan have the common people developed the political instinct, in self-protection."[23]

Among the Malays of Sumatra the tribe is built up out of families and kin-groups, whose heads form the actual government. Generally descent is to a brother born of the same mother or to a sister's son. These heads of kin-groups are the judges and receive tribute of rice and other gifts, and their subjects bear the cost of weddings and funerals for them. Among the Malays in general the foundation of the regulative system lies in the family bond.[24] In Sumatra the division within which a native may not marry is responsible for him, and must pay his fines if he cannot. Out of some of these bodies a member may be expelled, but the Batak never loses his membership. The bigger the *blah* the greater the influence of its headman.[25] The Alfurs of Buru are divided into various groups called *fennas,* each of which consists of a number of families. Each family is under the oversight of the oldest male blood-member and forms a more or less independent part of the fenna. "Though this union, in families,

20 Rivers, *Todas*, 540-541, 34.
21 Williams, *Middle Kingdom*, I, 482, 484;
Letourneau, *Polit.*, 167.
22 De Groot, *Kongsiwezen*, 17.

23 Hearn, *Japan*, 95, 490.
24 Ratzel, *Vkde.*, II, 438, 439.
25 Volz, in *Globus*, XCV, 4.

of the individuals who belong to the same fenna has acquired in a certain sense a political character, one must keep well in mind that the members of these families are still bound to each other by pure bonds of blood-kinship, in contrast with the fennas where the ties of kinship which originally bound the members to each other have, in the course of time, evolved into pure political bonds." The fennas may be united into federations when the heads are related or have long lived in good harmony.[26] The clan-system is found also in Polynesia, and always connects the political division with the religion. In general children belong to the mother's family and the children of a man's sister are his nearest relatives in the younger generation. A man must always marry a woman of another family. Each family is divided into four branches, each of which has numerous subdivisions which are sharply separated from one another. Each subdivision has its distinguishing symbol, generally an animal, which is protected from harm because the life of the group is closely connected with it. This clan-system has deeper influence than any other social institution.[27]

Morgan[28] has much to say of the clans, which he calls gentes, and other divisions in North America. The clan-system is not universal, but very widespread. The chief was only the first of the consanguineous group and called those under his jurisdiction "nephews." Each village was composed of several clans or parts of clans, and the head-assembly of clan-heads was the tribal council.[29]

Besides their geographical divisions, the Tlinkit had the dual organization; they "were separated socially into two sides or phratries, each strictly exogamic with descent through the mother. . . . One small group was outside of both the phratries and its members could marry into either. Each phratry was subdivided into clans or consanguineal bonds, the members of which were more closely related to one another than to other members of the phratry; and each of these bonds usually derived its origin from some town or camp it had once occupied. They were, therefore, in a way local groups, but they differed from the geographical groups . . . in being social divisions instead of comprising the accidental occupants of one locality. Thus every geographical division contained members of both phratries and usually of several clans of each phratry, while on the other hand a clan was often distributed among two or more geographical groups. Finally the clans were subdivided into house groups, the members of which might occupy one or several houses." One of the common errors of writers on the natives is to confound subdivisions with main ones. Another is to use the terms tribe and clan interchangeably. "A tribe may be divided into clans, but not a clan into tribes. A tribe may be composed of several sub-totems but of the same great phratry; a clan, on the other hand, is composed of people of the same totem. Every native has his sub-totem which, in turn, determines the main division to which he belongs."[30] Among the Kwakiutl, "each clan derives its origin from a mythical ancestor, who built his house at a certain place and whose descendants lived at that place;" so that the clan appears in the form of a village community.[31] The tribes of this region

26 Wilken, in VG, I, 29, 30 (quoted), 31, 32, 33, 305.

27 Ratzel, *Vkde.*, II, 279; Williamson, *Cent. Polyn.*, I, 258.

28 *Anc. Soc.*, chs. II, VI, and in *Contrib. N. Am. Ethnol.*, IV; Mooney, in BAE, XVII,

pt. I, 227; Fletcher, in *Proc. Am. Assoc. Adv. Sci.*, Minneapolis, 1883.

29 Lafitau, *Mœurs*, II, 172 ff.; Grosse, *Familie*, 152.

30 Swanton, in BAE, XXVI, 398; Jones, *Thlingets*, 53, 56, 170.

31 Boas, in USNM, 1895, 333.

vary between maternal and paternal descent, and the tribes of the Oregon coast show no sign of any totemic clan system.[32] Of the Seminoles it is written that their gens (clan) is a consanguineous group tracing lineage sometimes through the mother and again through the father. "The gens is the grand unit of social organization, and for many purposes is the basis of governmental organization."[33] In various villages, certain clans enjoyed a sort of hegemony.[34] Selecting the Iroquois tribes as typical of those in which the clan-organization had reached its highest development, it is found that "in such a tribe citizenship consisted in being by birth or adoption a member of a clan, and membership by birth in a clan was traced only through the mother and her female ancestors; hence it was solely through the mother that the clan was preserved and kept distinct from every other. But although the child acquired his birth-rights only through his mother, singularly enough it was through the father that his or her kinship was extended beyond his own into that of his father's clan, which owed to the offspring of its sons certain important obligations, which bound these two clans together not only by marriage but by the stronger tie of a recognized kinship. By this process the clans of the tribe were bound together into a tribal unity."[35]

McGee[36] enters quite minutely into the discussion of the clan, distinguishing it from the gens as a mother-descent group from one with father-descent. "The simplest demotic unit found among the aborigines is the clan or mother-descent group, in which the normal conjugal relation is essentially monogamous, in which marriage is more or less strictly regulated by a system of prohibitions, and in which the chief conjugal regulation is commonly that of exogamy with respect to the clan; in higher groups, more deeply affected by contact with neighboring peoples, the simple clan organization is sometimes found to be modified, (1) by the adoption and subsequent conjugation of captive men and boys, and, doubtless more profoundly, (2) by the adoption and polygamous marriage of female captives; and in still more highly organized groups the mother-descent is lost and polygamy is regular and limited only by the capacity of the husband as a provider. The second and third stages are commonly characterized, like the first, by established prohibitions and by clan exogamy; though with the advance in organization amicable relations with certain other groups are usually established, whereby the germ of tribal organization is implanted and a system of interclan marriage, or tribal endogamy, is developed. With further advance the mother-descent group is transformed into a father-descent group, when the clan is replaced by the gens; and polygamy is a common feature of the gentile organization. In all of these stages the conjugal and consanguineal regulations are affected by the militant habits characteristic of primitive groups; more warriors than women are slain in battle, and there are more female captives than male; and thus the polygamy is mainly or wholly polygny. In many cases civil conditions combine with or partially replace the militant conditions, yet the tendency of conjugal development is not changed. Among the Seri Indians, probably the most primitive tribe in North America, in which the demotic unit is the clan, there is a rigorous marriage custom under which the would-be groom is required to enter the family of the girl and

32 Farrand, in AA, III, 244.
33 MacCauley, in BAE, V, 508.
34 Speck, in AA, IX, 289.
35 HAI, I, 522; II, 816, 959-960; Dorsey,

in *Jr. Am. Folklore*, 1890, III, 227; Morgan, in *Smithson. Contr. to Knowledge*, XVII, 140, note.
36 In BAE, XV, 201 ff.

demonstrate (1) his capacity as a provider and (2) his strength or character
as a man, by a year's probation, before he is finally accepted—the conjugal
theory of the tribe being monogamy, though the practice, at least during
recent years, has, by reason of conditions, passed into polygyny. Among several
other tribes of more provident and less exclusive habit, the first of the two
conditions recognized by the Seri is met by rich presents (representing accumulated property) from the groom to the girl's family, the second condition
being usually ignored, the clan organization remaining in force; among still
other tribes the first condition is more or less vaguely recognized, though the
voluntary present is commuted into, or replaced by, a negotiated value exacted
by the girl's family, when the mother's descent is commonly vestigial; and in
the next stage, which is abundantly exemplified, wife-purchase prevails, and
the clan is replaced by the gens. In this succession the development of wife-
purchase and the decadence of mother-descent may be traced, and it is significant that there is a tendency first toward partial enslavement of the wife
and later toward the multiplication of wives to the limit of the husband's
means, and toward transforming all, or all but one, of the wives into menials.
Thus the lines of development under militant and civil conditions are essentially
parallel."

"Starting from the tribe or state as a whole, we find among the Omahas two
half-tribes. . . . Next to the half-tribes are the gentes, of which the Omahas
have ten. Each gens in turn is divided into sub-gentes," and these into groups
of a lower order.[37] The gens, which term is used by Fletcher and La Flesche
to indicate that the kinship-group traced descent in the paternal rather than
the maternal line, was called in the Omaha tongue by a word meaning "village."
"The same term was applied to the village in which all the tribe dwelt. When
the Omaha visited the towns and cities of the white people, they applied to these
settlements the same designation." While the idea of relationship is not directly
stated, the word which they added to the term for "village" is understood to
indicate a village of people who are kindred, of one kind, between whom marriage is prohibited. A subdivision differed from a sub-gens in not having a
distinctive rite, although it had a particular office in the rite belonging to the
gens. The common bond between the sub-gentes of a gens was that of kinship,
traced solely through the father. Marriage between the members of the sub-
gentes or subdivisions of a gens was forbidden. "It is apparent that the Omaha
gens was not a political organization. It differed from the Latin gens in that
the people composing it did not claim to be descended from a common ancestor from whom the group took its name and crest. There was, however, one
point of resemblance, and because of this one point of resemblance the name
gens is applied to the Omaha group; namely, the practice of a common rite
the title to share in which descended solely through the father. Beyond this
one point all resemblance ends. The rights and duties of the Omaha father in
no way corresponded to those devolving on the head of a Roman family. Nor
was the Omaha group a clan, for the bond between the people was not because of a common ancestor whose name and crest were the clan designation
and from whom were descended the hereditary rulers of the clan. The Omaha
gens was a group of exogamous kindred who practised a particular rite, the
child's birthright to which descended solely through the father; and the symbol
characteristic of that rite became the symbol, crest, or 'totem,' of the gens.

37 Dorsey, in BAE, III, 215.

There was no political or governing chief of an Omaha gens or subgens, but there were persons to whom belonged the hereditary right to be keepers, or 'priests,' in the ceremonies that were in charge of the gens. The Omaha gens, the two grand divisions composing the tribe, and the tribe as a whole, were each and all expressive and representative of certain fundamental religious ideas and beliefs that were dramatized in rites. Later, when the tribe was re-organized into its present form, the political government of the people was vested in certain chiefs, but these did not derive their position from their gentes as representatives of political organizations."[38]

The Arapaho recognize among themselves five original divisions, each having a different dialect, but these do not imply a clan or gentile system. "With the eastern tribes and those who have removed from the east or timbered country . . . the gentile system is so much a part of their daily life that it is one of the first things to attract the attention of the observer." The Comanches do not know that system, though they have five recognized divisions, and used to have thirteen or more. "The Kiowa do not have the gentile system, and there is no restriction as to intermarriage among the divisions. They have six tribal divisions, including the Apache associated with them, who form a component part of the Kiowa camping circle." The Caddo, originally along the lower Red River, had ten gentes, with animal names; and the members of a gens would not kill the animal from which it takes its name.[39]

It is to be noted that groups can get names from the place where they live, especially from a river, mountain, or other natural feature; from some bodily peculiarity, of which skin-color is only one; from peculiarity of language or pronunciation, or of customs; from a selected plant or animal, or even from diet; or from some ancestral hero or living chief.[40]

Letourneau[41] finds the Roman political origins similar to the Greek in some important respects. Gentes united to form larger aggregations, such as phra-tries or *curiae,* and gradually developed into cities, the larger political units. Of "gens" it is stated: "The etymology of the word is transparent: it is based on the nature of procreation, and that in the legal sense which gives the father authority over the son. Hence the two ideas of the family and of the sib [kin-group]: the former consists of the free persons under the authority of a living ascendant, the latter of those free persons who would have been under such authority, had no death taken place." The mark of the sib is the *nomen gentile,* or gens name, which is added to the name of the individual; Quintus Fabius means Quintus of the Fabian gens. "The members of the sib are called *gentiles,* also *patres,* 'house-fathers,' and *patricii.*"[42] The clan-relations in the North, covering the right of revenge, clan unity and possessions, duty of mutual support, and so forth, were essentially similar to those already sketched.[43] Abandonment of one's clan, under the Salic Law, demanded a special symbolic ceremony.[44]

Schrader[45] states that the Slavonic *bratstvo* is formed when the blood-brothers of a house-community separate, but still continue to form a political (territorial) and religious (common tutelary hero) organization, possessing a

38 In BAE, XXVII, 135-137, 195-196 (quoted), 199-200.
39 Mooney, in BAE, XIV, 954 ff.; 1044, 1079, 1092, 1093.
40 Von Martius, *Beiträge,* I, 54.
41 *Polit.,* 357 ff.

42 Schrader, *Aryans,* 398; De Marchi, *Culto Priv.,* II, 7, 27, 49, 58.
43 Finsen, in *Annaler,* 1850, 154, 178-179, 203-204, 254-256, 309-311.
44 Oliveira Martins, *Quadro,* 59.
45 *Aryans,* 397, 398.

common landed estate. Every *bratstvo* has its family legend in honor of the common ancestor. In the public assemblies, only the houschold heads have a seat and vote, the rest simply the right of acclamation. "The *bratstvo* in old days consisted of cousins to the n*th* degree, but in the nature of things it became necessary in time to subdivide large *bratstvos* in intermarriageable groups. At the present day in Montenegro the *bratstvo* does not go beyond third cousins who may marry. . . . The *bratstvo* held together very strongly. In case of the murder of one member the whole *bratstvo* flew to arms."[46] The Latin gens corresponds to this South Slav form and the Greek *phrētrē* is aligned with them.

Vinogradoff[47] draws three main conclusions from the survey of Aryan kinship organization: "(1) The kindred, as a variety of the clan system, was formed by the alliance between agnatic households for purposes of defence and mutual help. It involved a subsidiary recognition of relationship through women. (2) The arrangement of agriculture on the open-field system, based on the solidarity of the groups of neighbour cultivators, was originally conditioned by kinship. (3) The transition from tribal to village communities was brought about by a standardization of holdings which aimed at establishing a fair proportion between the rights and the duties of the peasants."

Starcke,[48] who theorizes much and tenuously over the clan, states that while the family is "the group which includes different generations, taking into account their more or less remote kinship, . . . the group in which the different degrees of kinship are not taken into account belongs to the category of the *Clan*. . . . Families are founded and again dissolved while the clan persists unchanged. . . . The clan consists of a group allied by blood, endowed with important juridical rights." He here defines the clan by unity of blood; elsewhere he has much to say about a tie resulting from social contact. "The tattoo marks make it possible to discover the remote connection between clans, and this token has such a powerful influence on the mind that there is no feud between tribes which are tattooed in the same way." He thinks social life begins with the family, ruled by the father, and that clans are subsequently formed. "The clan differed from the tribe as a part from the whole. The tribe was the unit with respect to other and hostile tribes but the clan could only be opposed to other clans." Yet the author thinks the family did not develop into the clan, but was swallowed up in it, rather; the forces that form the family cease to work when their spheres of operation become too great. The clan exists for the struggle for existence, but on a larger scale, and consists not of families, but of individuals, its organization being like that of the tribe rather than of the family. The blood-tie remains, however, even if in less definite form. The clan was consanguineous, even if artificially so through adoption.[49]

§150. Blood-Brotherhood and Guest-Friendship.

BLOOD-BROTHERHOOD is an important custom in many parts of Africa, where its effect in producing friendship between the contracting parties, in forming alliances, and in stopping feuds is well marked. When two persons of different

---

46 Durham, in JAI, XXXIX, 88-89.
47 *Hist. Jurispr.*, I, 342.
48 *Prim. Fam.*, 12 (quoted), 14 (quoted), 15,

25, 42 (quoted), 50, 53, 59, 108, 276 (quoted), 277 (quoted), 281.
49 Letourneau, *Morale*, 184; Letourneau, *Polit.*, 80, 257.

clans or tribes, among the Baganda, wish to make an indissoluble bond with one another, they perform the *mukago* or blood-brotherhood ceremony. "They each make a slight cut in the stomach below the navel, with the knife, holding the flesh with the left hand; the coffee bean pod is broken and each man takes a bean from it, smears it with his blood, and places it in the palm of his right hand; each takes the bean from the other's hand with his lips, and each holds his hand over the other's mouth until the bean is swallowed; when the berry is swallowed they tell each other their totem, and commit their children to each other's care. The witnesses are relatives or close friends; all partake of the feast which immediately follows. This is the most solemn and binding oath, and cannot be broken without bodily injury coming upon the person who breaks it; the consequence is often prolonged sickness and death." If a slave makes *mukago* with a member of his master's family he takes its totem and becomes a free man and one of the clan. The Bahima method of making blood-brotherhood is somewhat similar; it is done by pouring a little milk into the palm of the hand and dropping into it one or two drops of blood taken from the pit of the stomach. "Each promises to be true and faithful to the other, and to be a father to the other's family in case of need. Sometimes coffee berries are used for this ceremony," as in the instance above.[1] As an introduction to blood-brotherhood in the East African Protectorate, friendship is usually made by the exchange of honey-beer and a goat. "Later the two meet, bringing honey beer in a bowl from which each takes a mouthful and spits it out into the bowl again, after which each drinks half of the beer. After a few days the two meet again, and each cuts the other with a knife very slightly on the back of the right hand and licks the blood off. The brotherhood thus established is most binding and if broken by either party will result in his death. The blood brotherhood passes on to their children after their deaths, but a fresh ceremony between the children is not required. In consequence of this the children of blood-brothers may never marry." On account of the prohibition against children of blood-brothers marrying—having become by the covenant "blood-relations"—the Theraka say that they never make blood-brotherhood with members of other clans; since, then, it is an almost senseless undertaking between members of one clan it is rarely made with anyone but a foreigner.[2]

In British East Africa, when forming blood-brotherhood the contracting parties sit down opposite each other and each man will make two cuts on the breast-bone of the other with a knife so that blood flows. In the meantime a man who has killed a goat has taken out its liver and is roasting it at the fire. "When the meat is slightly cooked he cuts off two pieces from it and hands one to each of the contracting parties, who take it and rub it in the blood on their own chest. Each of these will now hand his piece of meat to the other, promising to help him in everything and in future to look upon him as his brother. Each eats the meat smeared with the blood of the other, and the ceremony is finished."[3] Again, the ceremony consists in inflicting a small wound on both of the parties and applying a few drops of blood from the wound of one to that of the other; after this their property is treated as being held in common.[4] How blood-brotherhood may put an end to hostility is clearly ob-

1 Roscoe, in JAI, XXXII, 68, and in JAI, XXXVII, 117.
2 Dundas, C., in JAI, XLIII, 526 (quoted), 547.
3 Barrett, in JAI, XLI, 35.
4 Johnstone, in JAI, XXXII, 268.

served among the Congo people, where, as in the case of the Bangala, a constantly recurring quarrel between families and towns of equal strength is settled by the important persons on each side entering into such a covenant. A go-between is appointed who arranges for a meeting at some neutral place; a stick called *ndeko* is procured and carefully scraped, and these scrapings are mixed with salt. "The contracting parties clasp each other's right hand with the *ndeko* between the palms; then some incisions are made on the arms and the mixture of *ndeko*-scrapings and salt is rubbed on the cuts; each then puts his mouth to the incisions on the other's arm and sucks for a few moments, after which one of the contracting parties takes the *ndeko* stick and strikes the wrists and knees of the other, saying: 'If ever I break this covenant may I be cursed by having my nose rot off.' Then the other takes the *ndeko* stick, and performing the same ceremony calls down the same curse on himself should he ever break the covenant." A palm-frond is then taken and split, and one part is placed across the path between the two towns that have entered into the above contract of friendship. "This is not only a sign that all past palavers are finished, but is also a fetish to punish anyone who breaks the treaty. It is firmly believed that the side that renews the quarrel will get the worst of it by wounds and death."[5] The effect of this rite of blood-brotherhood on the Upper Congo has been to stop all feuds and to cause the parties to it to act in all respects as blood-relations. "I have again and again seen a disturbed district," comments Weeks,[6] "where during several weeks there had been much fighting and many killed, quiet down directly the headmen had made blood-brotherhood. All the important men of the district had many cicatrices on their arms indicative of the frequency with which they had performed the ceremony."

Such mixing of blood is practised by most negro-peoples. Three light dagger-wounds are made on the lower arm, and the blood, drunk along with palm-wine, makes the participators blood-related—they have, as a West African negro chief expressed it, "two bellies but only one head."[7] Again, the two prospective blood-brothers sit on a hide with legs interlocked and a third party brandishes a saber over their heads anathematizing the one who should break the bond. They kill a sheep and the new brothers, after sprinkling it with blood from cuts in the pit of their stomachs, eat it. Or they may mix blood with oil or butter and rub it into each other's cuts. It is an amelioration of primitive savagery.[8] In the Gaboon region there is a friendship-sanction between two men called fetish-giving. "The whole body of inhabitants collects for it, and in the presence of all a kola-nut is divided among the friends, whereupon a fetish-man makes an incision in the arm of each of the two. Into the spurting blood are dipped the halves of the nut of which each eats one, after he has uttered an imprecation, laying a curse on all who might do harm to the friend or his family. . . . Then the almond chewed by the friend is laid on the arm of his friend, the wound of the one rubbed against that of the other, and a feast seals their intimate brotherhood, which is like that of blood-friends in Montenegro."[9]

Brunache[10] exchanged blood with a native, to find later that it was proposed with the idea of getting more presents. Junker[11] and an African chief

5 Weeks, in JAI, XL, 360.
6 In JAI, XXXIX, 444.
7 Schmidt, *Deut. Kol.*, II, 34.
8 Letourneau, *Guerre*, 72-73.

9 Bastian, *Afr. Reisen*, 296.
10 *Cent. Afr.*, 85.
11 *Afrika*, II, 499, 500.

established blood-brotherhood by each having a drop of blood drawn from the pit of the stomach, then wiping each other's blood off on the end of a piece of sugar-cane, chewing the cane, and spitting the fibers upon the pit of each other's stomach and necks. Hereupon each stated the essential reasons for the establishment of the relation, which must be adhered to as under oath. Each of these points was emphasized by adding: "And if thou dost not so, may my blood kill thee," and by having a third person hammer with a stone upon some convenient object at each repetition. There is something of the ordeal-element in this case. To accomplish a certain plan satisfactorily it has often been necessary to contract a treaty, offensive and defensive, with the natives, and nothing would suffice for this but a mutual interchange of blood—a "barbarous, but truly African custom."[12] Only by such means could a basis for mutual confidence be attained. Even when a blood-brother had committed a crime, his life must be preserved at all costs, or the magic would take effect and produce a painful death for the delinquent friend.[13] The motive of utility of course dominates: by establishing blood-brotherhood, one assures himself of support in need, and also secures an avenger of blood.[14]

Roth[15] quotes a full and variously significant description of the ceremony as presented by a man who went through it: "Selgie requested I would make *sobat* with him; on my gladly consenting, he went in person and stuck a spear into the ground above his father's grave. This being the signal for a general assembly, each of the chiefs sent a person to know the Rajah's pleasure; it was that every warrior should assemble around the grave by twelve o'clock the next day. Some thousands were present; a platform of bamboo was raised about twelve feet above the grave, and on this Selgie and I mounted, accompanied by an Agi, his high priest. After some previous ceremony, the Agi produced a small silver cup, which might hold about two wine glasses, and then with a piece of bamboo made very sharp, drew blood from the Rajah's right arm; the blood ran into the cup until it was nearly full; he then produced another cup, of a similar size, and made an incision in my arm, a little above the elbow, and filled it with blood. The two cups were then held up to the view of the surrounding people, who greeted them with loud cheers. The Agi now presented me with the cup of Selgie's blood, giving him the other one with mine; upon a signal we drank off the contents amidst the deafening noise of the warriors and others. The Agi then half-filled one of the cups again from Selgie's arm, and with my blood made it a bumper; this was stirred up with a piece of bamboo and given to Selgie, who drank about half; he then presented the cup to me, when I finished it. The noise was tremendous; thus the great Rajah Selgie and I became brothers. After this ceremony I was perfectly safe, and from that moment felt myself so during my stay amongst his people. Drinking the blood, however, made me ill for two days as I could not throw it off my stomach. The Rajah took his share with great gusto, as this is considered one of the greatest ceremonies, particularly on this occasion, between the great Rajah and the first European who had been seen in his country. Great festivities followed and abundance of heads were brought in, for nothing can be done without them. Three days and nights all ranks of people danced round these heads, after being, as usual, smoked and the brains taken out, drinking a kind of toddy

---

12 Schweinfurth, *Heart of Afr.*, I, 532.   14 Paulitschke, *Nordost-Afr.*, II, 143; I, 249.
13 Hutter, "Blutsfreundsft.," in *Globus*,   15 *Sarawak*, II, 205 ff.
LXXV, 2, 3.

which soon intoxicates them; they are then taken care of by the women who do not drink, at least I never observed them."

The same author relates the experience of another traveller as follows: "The following was observed on my initiation into the brotherhood with Lasa Kulan, the chief of Balaga on the Rejang, and of Tubow on the Bintulu river. Two days previous to that on which the bloody affair came off, the great hall of the chief was garnished with the weapons and gaudy skin war dresses of the men, and dashed with a fair sprinkling of the finery of the women kept more for show than use. On the day appointed, a number of the neighboring chiefs having arrived, several of them commenced proceedings by haranguing on the greatness and power of their own selves, and of all the wonders they had heard of the white people, and of their satisfaction in being visited by one of them, of whom their fathers had heard so much but had never seen. Next a large pig, provided for the occasion, was killed, the throat cutting part of the business being performed by one of the fair sex, seemingly with great satisfaction to the attendant crowd of men. Next were brought three jars full of arrack of three sorts, severally made from rice, sugar-cane, and the fruit tampui. In pieces of bambu it was dealt out in profusion to all present, the ladies excepted. On the chief taking a bambu filled with arrack, we repaired to the balcony in front of the house, and stood side by side, with our faces towards the river. The chief then announced his intention of becoming the friend or brother of a son of the white man, on which one of the attending chiefs gave me a small sharp-pointed piece of bambu, with which I made a slight incision in the fore-arm of the chief, and the blood drawn out was put on a leaf. The chief then, with a similar instrument, drew blood from my left fore-arm, which was put on the same leaf and mingled with the other. The blood was then mixed with tobacco and made up into a large cigar which we puffed alternately until it was finished, when my new friend delivered himself of a long and eloquent speech, invoking their god Tanangan, the sun, moon, and stars, and rivers, the woods and mountains to witness his sincerity. Three times during this declamation he sprinkled the arrack on the ground towards the river. My speech being delivered, several of the principal chiefs present held forth both long and loud enough. We afterwards returned to the hall, and the cheering beverage went around more merrily than before, calling forth their good nature and social disposition. Although no toasts were given, still each successive bumper was accompanied by a merry and noisy chorus. The feast came afterwards, and the whole affair was wound up by music and dancing which lasted until about midnight." In the case of the smoking, Hose[16] comments, "the smoke is inhaled into the lungs in some cases, to show the sincerity of the bond." Roth[17] cites several other cases of the brotherhood-ceremony in Borneo, exhibiting attendant religious performances which, though partially illustrated in preceding cases, belong under oath-sacrifices.[18] In Formosa, "I, of course, was made to pledge friendship in the orthodox savage fashion, by putting our arms round each other's necks, and mutually drinking, at the same moment, out of one basin."[19]

The Scythians, Lydians, and Armenians drank blood or mixed it with wine, as did the knights of the Middle Ages. The Vikings and Germans formed

16 In JAI, XXIII, 166.
17 Sarawak, II, 207, 208.
18 §277 of text.

19 Pickering, Formosa, 164; Wirth, in AA, X, 363.

such friendships; in the latter case the blood was mixed with beer, later fingers were put in the beer instead, and finally it survived only in the expression, *Brüderschaft trinken*.[20] Sworn brotherhood was till recently very frequent among the South Slavs. In Montenegro it has not carried blood-relationship, so far as intermarriage is concerned, nor has the bond been ratified by exchange of blood; in North Albania, however, it still carries full blood-relationship, and blood is exchanged when taking the vow.[21]

Guest-Friendship. A custom probably related to guest-friendship is the selection by the Loyalty Islanders of special friends from amongst strangers with whom they are connected by mutual good offices. "These are called *enehmus*. The *enehmu* feels bound to provide food and lodging for his friend when he visits him, and will assist him in any way he can, when he needs it, and in return expects the same good treatment when occasion offers."[22] The Melanesian custom of guest-friendship, however, is best seen in connection with trade. In some places the merchant would not dare to land unless he had at the place a guest-friend, to whose house he goes. Here he sits on a mat and is given a piece of betel, part of which he gives back, the motive being the same as drinking together to avoid being poisoned. At night the trader does not stay in the house of his guest-friend but goes to the shore to sleep. Some townsmen come to keep him company as evidence of goodwill. The host protects the guest from the plots of enemies.[23] Conditions of hostility and suspicion toward strangers are thereby modified so as to permit some intercourse and trade. Among the Papuans the peace of the market together with guest-friendship make trade possible. In the trade between villages each family has its special business-friends with whom it is in touch and whose right of hospitality it enjoys during the market time. The market is said to be the most important factor in the social life of the Papuans and to be conducted under rules and agreements which recall the modern commercial treaties of European nations[24] In Southwest Africa trade is possible only through the practice of guest-friendship.[25]

Guest-friendship is a recognized custom among the Bedouins,[26] while in India the ceremonial friendship established especially between women taken in marriage from different villages is regarded as a matter of tribal necessity.[27] To the Hebrews it was enjoined: "The stranger that sojourneth with you shall be unto you as the homeborn among you."[28] Among the Phœnicians, "before the departure of the guest they take a potsherd and break it into two pieces. The one half is taken by the stranger, the other kept by the host. If he wishes in future to recommend anyone to the care of his former protege, the former takes from him on the journey the half he has retained as a mark of identification. At presentation they try whether the fractured edges of the two pieces fit together, and the conveyor is accredited."[29]

"A series of words [for instance, those connected with *hostis* and *hostia*], which in milder times have assumed the meaning of 'guest,' 'guest-friend' undoubtedly in primeval ages had a more sinister and threatening meaning. It

20 Lippert, *Kgchte.*, II, 334-335, 337-338.
21 Durham, in JAI, XXXIX, 92; Anon., in *Globus*, LXXII, 163.
22 Ray, in JAI, XLVII, 276.
23 Von Pfeil, *Südsee*, 124-125.
24 Hagen, *Papua's*, 219, 220.

25 Büttner, *Walfischbai*, 29.
26 R.T.K., in *Globus*, LXXV, 190.
27 Roy, in JAI, XLIV, 327-328.
28 Lev., XIX, 34.
29 Pietschmann, *Phön.*, 286.

was at an early age the conviction that the stranger did continue to be exlex [outside the law], 'but that the divine ordinance (*fas*) made it a duty—more and more recognized as a human law (*jus*)—to protect the life and property of the stranger, and to receive him as a guest at the sacred fire of the hearth.' The institution of guest-friendship is by no means confined to Europe, but is found all over the globe, and in the most widely separated stages of culture . . . and is nearly always bound up with the exchange of gifts between host and guest." It was a device to make commerce practicable and safe in the absence of public protection, and probably the Phœnicians found the early Greeks "at least partially accessible to strangers with whom it was their interest to trade."[30] This quotation would seem to intimate that the custom took its origin in religion. That it was supported by the gods even before it became a recognized human "law" is entirely probable. Here is only a case of religion sanctioning the mores;[31] the custom was already there, for obvious reasons of expediency. Some of these reasons will appear in the following final and extraordinarily complete example of the practice.[32]

The Homeric Greeks were moving toward a more humane type of warfare and also to guarantees outside the bounds of the circumscribed tribal group. "Toward this end one of the chief contributors is a body of traditions and usages connected with strangers, suppliants, guests, and guest-friends. Since the stranger became at once a guest, and since a guest was forever afterward a guest-friend, this body of ideas and practices is appropriately called guest-friendship. Where syngenetic feeling is strong, 'stranger' means 'enemy'; it had no such signification to the genuine Greek of Homer's time. The stranger, at his arrival, was at once addressed as *xeinos*, and welcomed with fine courtesy; only the deepest domestic troubles led to neglect of strangers. No questions were asked until the newcomer had partaken of food and drink, and thus identified himself with the host and his interests; for when men had taken food and drink together, their 'brotherhood' was symbolically established. Strangers were welcome to feasts and sacrifices, were made participants of them, and were given the places of honour—all this before their identity was known. Menelaus is represented as feeling great irritation at the idea of sending strangers on to some other host; he felt and expressed his sense of reciprocal obligation for the hospitality extended to himself during his own wanderings. During his stay (and his departure must neither be hastened nor delayed against his will), the stranger must suffer no harm—that would be a shame to his host; while he remained, it was not in accordance with *dikē* that the guest should suffer lack of anything his host could provide, and at his departure he was presented with valuable *xeinia* in remembrance. In short, every liberty and privilege was granted to the stranger within the gates; he was cherished as a brother by the right-minded man.

These guests were not always persons of noble birth; any one who 'came' was welcome, though of course ancestral friends were most heartily received. Beggars were classed directly with *xeinoi;* the disguised beggar Odysseus was honoured with the best food, and reverence was paid to his age and misfortunes; when he spoke of departing so as to relieve his host of the burden, the

30 Schrader, *Aryan*, 350, 351; Haberland, in *Ausland*, LI, 281 ff.
31 Sumner, "Religion and the Mores," in *Coll. Ess.*, I, ch. V.

32 Keller, *Hom. Soc.*, 299-312 (where full references to text are given).

host, a poor swine-herd, was incensed at the thought and bade him stay on. Guests were often suppliants; this type of man was generally a fugitive, fleeing from the relatives of some tribesman whom he had slain, intentionally or otherwise. The suppliant sought the protection of the hearth's sanctity, was regularly received as an unfortunate, treated with the utmost kindness, and, if brave and of good birth, often became a *hetairos* [companion] to his host's son. The terms suppliant and guest are used together frequently; in a certain sense every guest was a suppliant to his host, in those days. The suppliant, however, was generally in some plight that required considerable aid; he was a special sort of guest.

"Such extended hospitality, such unguarded trust in a perfect stranger, is remarkable in any age of the world; a host virtually placed himself and all his at the will and mercy of his guest. He must have felt great faith in some strong guarantee which safeguarded the integrity of this relation. Such a guarantee was afforded in all needed strength by the heavy religious sanctions which rested upon all the relations of host and guest. The proper conduct of the host, as well as his duty of receiving the guest, was strongly emphasised by the gods; they might go about in disguise, observing the actions of mortals to see if they treated their guests rightly. Though the majority of divine injunctions had to do, naturally enough, with the reception and respect to be accorded to strangers, still the guest's conduct also was prescribed. No right-minded man would consent to surpass his host even in athletic contests, much less to steal his property. An oath by the host's table or hearth was a sacred one. It is not hard, therefore, to understand how a violation of this host-guest relation could bring on a Trojan war. Menelaus prayed to Zeus, as he took part in the ordeal-trial, for victory, in order that the rights of hosts might be upheld; in another place he speaks with contempt and wrath of those who rob the man who is entertaining them. The host had, then, strong religious sanctions to warrant his unguardedness. Doubtless his mind was satisfied in the belief that the gods would render his risks secure, and it never occurred to him to ask for a more rational explanation of his own hospitality. Any evidence as to the origins of this guest-friendship must be given by Homer unconsciously, if at all. The presence of the religious sanctions in such number and strength indicates that the birth of the host-guest relation took place in the more or less remote past; this is witnessed to also by the completeness of the relation's development. Apparently the origins of guest-friendship lay in the reachings forth of a developing people toward an advance and toward a further and larger acquaintance with a world of greater material wealth and luxury than their own; that is, the hospitality and love of guests so characteristic of the Homeric Greek were another product of the contact with the higher Eastern civilisation.

"The tribes of the Iliad and Odyssey, and their immediate ancestors, lived in a prosperous and populous culture-stage of combined cattle-raising and agriculture; conditions of life were such as to leave the lords of the people, if not the people themselves, free from the most grinding needs and from the enervating alternation of satiety and want. Settling in a land little suited to a continuance of nomadic life, and brought under the direct influence of the high civilisations of the East, attention was turning to other ideas and pursuits than those to which the earlier tribesmen had been attached—to the sea and to commerce, that is, to the outside world. The people were eager to learn, and men were their only books; a stranger, who, if he were not himself a Phœnician, could yet describe the wonders of those magical foreign lands, was a rare treasure to an isolated community. People came to be very fond of entertaining, and gladly accommodated another man's guest in his absence. One man is mentioned who had a house on the public road and entertained every one who came; a man was the more respected for entertaining freely. In time the real practical value of the relation became more and more apparent, and Zeus became the guardian of strangers, who were the heralds of the time's advance. Eagerness for news, for tales of the exterior world, its people and doings, is marked; it is characteristic of an energetic, isolated community. Whether guest-friendship is to be regarded as an institution of more than local importance or not, its origin seems to have been taken from a period several centuries earlier than the Homeric age, and to have been due chiefly to the quickening contact with an older and more polished civilisation. The Greeks identified the customs of guest-friendship with civilisation and culture. Examples of dishonour of guests are connected with the cannibalistic Cyclopes, the Læstrygonians, and other such crude beings and monsters; it is only lawless and violent men who carry on such practices. The Suitors turned strangers away by their treatment of them and suggested their sale into slavery. As for the Cyclopes, it is noticeable that they were especially godless, violent, and syngenetic; against their deeds appeal was made to Zeus Xeinios. As the Cyclops Polyphemus devoured the companions of Odysseus, he and his men held up their hands to Zeus; and by the aid of Zeus the monster was blinded. Besides these lawless tribes, the Trojan Paris, and the Suitors, some of the *ancient* heroes were guilty of breaches of the host-guest relation, notably Heracles; for he slew one to whom he had offered the hospitality of his table,—a terrible crime. The best evidence to show that the kindly relation, between host and guest was the gauge of a people's civilisation is given by the shipwrecked unfortunate; the first question of such an one as to the people among whom he is thus thrown, is: Are they just? Are they godfearing? Do they respect strangers? These qualities are contrasted with rudeness and injustice.

"From the reception of the stranger and the hospitality accorded to him arose an enduring relation, guest-friendship proper. After eating and drinking together, the two parties stood in a close mutual relation, which was strong enough to endure for generations; the reciprocal duties and rights of the parties were made permanent. A strong sense of mutual good-will was engendered, the gifts at the guest's departure standing as a symbol of the bond and not suffering its memory to fade; the importance of these gifts as symbols is shown by a case where gifts alone established the host-guest relation, although the parties were never to enjoy each other's hospitality. The once established relation afforded to each of the parties and to his children a special sponsor in a strange land, a land where otherwise he could claim no acquaintance; the obligations descended upon the houses of the respective parties, in the death or absence of the original guest-friends. Such an ancestral relation was particularly holy and strong, and treasured in the traditions of the family. Mutual visits preserved the bond, and consequent diffusion of knowledge, tending toward amalgamation of ethnic elements, was among the results.

"A further form of this bond is not unparalleled in ethnography; for it resembles closely the system of 'brotherhoods' common elsewhere. It has been stated that eating and drinking together established a sort of brotherhood; in time of war such brothers were expected to perform certain services for each other. A guest-friend was bound to make all effort to rescue the dead body of his *xeinos* for burial, and sometimes a prisoner was ransomed from slavery and set free, with gifts, by a guest-friend. Ancestral guest-friends would not contend in battle. On the plain of Troy, Glaucus of Lycia and Diomed of Argos met for combat; before they fought, Diomed asked his opponent his name and ancestry. Glaucus, with the usual race-pride, gave his genealogy in detail. Hearing this Diomed exclaimed: 'But you are an ancestral guest-friend of mine; we cannot fight. Let us avoid each other in combat, and exchange armour as a symbol of our relation.' This they did, with mutual pledges. The instance witnesses for many features of guest-friendship: the care with which its traditions were preserved in the family, the detailed knowledge of a guest-friend's ancestry, the symbolism of gifts, the mutual sponsorship.

"The many advantages of this relation of guest-friendship need scarcely to be indicated; one of its greatest services was of course to the traveller. Without this free hospitality, travel would hardly have been possible; the wayfarer could not take a band of retainers to defend him and forage for him, nor could he take with him cattle or treasure, with which to pay his bills. The host acted as defender, food-provider, banker, sponsor, escort; *all* the needs of the traveller were his host's to supply, from bath and bed to conveyance on sea or land, and all these duties were willingly discharged for the sake of the reciprocal claim upon the guest. Diomed witnesses to this in the passage to which attention has been called: 'So now I am your dear host in the midst of Argos, and you mine in Lycia, when I visit that people.' Within range of this custom, therefore, travel became possible and not very hazardous, and so arose diffusion of culture and mutual knowledge; the barrier of tribal narrowness was falling, for the stranger was a *friend*. And when we find that some such relation was recognised in Phœnicia and Egypt, its far-reaching importance in the education of Greece becomes still more apparent.

"The stern safeguarding of the integrity of this relation would follow almost instinctively upon a realisation of its value. Public and private, and probably local and national, interests, would here unite. It has been shown that desire for vengeance upon a perfidious guest was the prime motive of the Trojan war; whether the allies of the injured Menelaus were led to fight the Trojans for his (and Agamemnon's) sake alone, or whether, as appears more probable, a personal interest in the integrity of the violated relation roused their resentment,— at any rate, without guest-friendship and its anti-syngenetic power, such a united movement would have been impossible. Agamemnon and Menelaus enlisted their guest-friends by the story of the latter's wrongs, and in the wideness of the circle of their well-wishers and acquaintances lay the success of their undertaking. Such a united movement as the Trojan expedition, for which more than 29 peoples, 1100 ships, and (according to the ancients) about 100,000 men, mustered at Aulis, is a veritable wonder under a non-despotic government, even if large discounts be made from these estimates. Genghis Khan or Tamerlane might have been proud of it, and yet the expedition was a union of politically independent peoples. The mutual need of acquaintance, of security in travel and business, of external, stimulating communication, projecting itself upon the body of *mores* in the form of guest-friendship, was the most powerful factor in this great result. Such an aggregation of allies was hardly held together for so extended a period by allegiance to one or two kings, however rich and powerful. The element of personal service is not infrequently brought out, both by the chiefs and by Menelaus; still it seems that the allies were, in general attitude, less eager to aid the *king* (Menelaus or Agamemnon) than to aid an injured host to vengeance upon a treacherous guest and his whole tribe. The feeling of the allies had more than allegiance in it, and from the *ensemble* of the Iliad it appears that the evident thirst for vengeance (and for booty, of course) considerably out-weighs any expressed desires of serving the sons of Atreus. The whole force of public opinion supported the expedition in a manner which indicates a collective aim to avenge an attack upon a collective possession; the integrity of guest-friendship was certainly a far more vital matter to all Greece than intertribal alliances were to the separate tribes, though the latter are found to have been of high local importance.

"There remain several cases of guest-friendship which exhibit peculiarities valuable as throwing light upon the system, though they were not necessarily regular phases of it. Among the Phæacians, Odysseus, though the guest of Alcinous, was, by the latter's command, the recipient of gifts from each of the sub-kings. The donation seems to have been a state-function, for the people finally paid for all the hospitality of these princes. The host of Odysseus in Crete also had recourse to taxing the people to pay for his generosity; from them he collected the grain which he gave to his guest. Further, in Phæacia, the king and assembly provided Odysseus with conveyance to his native land, jointly; elsewhere the guest was a purely personal burden or acquisition. The presents received by the guest were an important feature; tours were sometimes a means of collecting wealth. Odysseus waited for the Cyclops's return to his cave in order to get a gift, and asked for it in a matter-of-fact way; thus he seems to have done elsewhere. He delayed a long time among the Phæacians in order to collect property, and was regarded as clever for so doing. Menelaus offered to take Telemachus the round of the Achaean cities, assuring him that no one would deny them presents; a guest was urged to stay and get a valuable present at departure. Guest-friends were also valuable in a business way; we are told that Ithaca was too stony and mountainous for the raising of horses and cattle, and elsewhere we find that the horses and cattle of the Ithacans were pastured in Elis and on the mainland. There *xeinoi* of Odysseus and his own herdsmen cared for them; evidently arrangements of this kind were common between *xeinoi,* which led to mutual advantages and benefits. Guest-friendship thus reaches out into all the phases of social life; whether it was an institution or not, it was a tangible, vigorous, social factor, and its importance at that stage of civilisation is scarcely to be over-estimated."

§153. Embryonic Government.

IN Australia each clan was autonomous and managed its own affairs by means of a camp-council. In every clan there was some one man who was regarded as the leader or head-man; his position was not hereditary, but was filled by a sort of informal election.[1] "There is no one to whom the term 'chief,' or even head of the tribe, can be properly applied; but, on the other hand, there are certain of the elder men, the heads of local groups, who, at any great ceremonial gathering . . . take the lead and superintend matters. They form, as it were, an inner council or cabinet and completely control everything. . . . The old

1 Brown, in JAI, XLVIII, 231.

men take absolutely no notice of the younger men, preserving their own counsels in the most quiet and dignified way possible."[2] "It is found that in most respects there reigns a communism, the liberty of the individual being limited by severe laws and customs which have developed through ages, and which every one without difference is obliged to obey. They accord some privileges to the older people, which are equally open to anyone who has attained a certain age."[3] "One man is as good as another. Great respect is shown to old men, and whatever authority is acknowledged is centered in the aged, because of their years. All matters connected with social affairs are settled in open council at night, when each man speaks from his camp in turn, and is listened to uninterruptedly. Young men and boys do not join in the talk."[4] "Only in cases of major offences, murder, incest, physical violence, etc., is there an application of any code, and that in the form of the Mosaic one. The old men and elders act the part of 'bosses,' 'kings,' 'judges,' etc., in influencing aboriginal public opinion in these matters of enforcing domestic policy; a ripe old age constitutes the highest social status in the camp, and the one calling for the greatest respect. There is no single individual chief to direct affairs."[5]

While there is no tribal chief, a family has a head "whose duty it is to keep order and settle any differences that may arise between the members of the household" or with those of any neighboring group. The head-man investigates jealousies and ensuing fights, acting "judicially and executively. He determines who is at fault, and he chastises him." The rest keep out of any such affair, for it is the head-man's business to control disputes and "whatever he does is right."[6] "The oldest man is head of the totem, and has authority in it as such, but this authority does not extend to any other totem besides his own. Though he is the oldest man, he does not necessarily have the greatest influence and authority in his totem; in other words, he is head of his totem because of his seniority, but not necessarily head man unless he shows some superior qualities fitting him especially for that position."[7]

In spite of the absence of any definite organization there exists among such primitive peoples the not inconsiderable control of custom, as evidenced in the following two instances.

Among the Australians, "under no circumstances is fighting of any description whatsoever allowed in camp at night, and the whole crowd collectively will see that no infringement of this rule ever takes place: if people want to fight, they must go outside, and, when necessary, kindle fires to see by." After a fight the victor must show to the elders that he had a grievance or he has to submit to the same mutilations by the vanquished as the latter received. When the women fight, it must be according to rule; each has to submit to a blow on the head from the other—and they use heavy sticks four feet long—without defending herself, alternately, till one gives in.[8] It is a fundamental rule in the Congo region that people shall appear at the palavers without weapons.[9] The Teda must bear no weapons in the village.[10] "Despite their sanguine temperament and great activity, the Tungus yet live for the most part in harmony and peace amongst themselves; one hears vituperation and cursing ex-

2 Spencer and Gillen, *North. Tr. Cent. Aust.*, 20, 21.
3 Semon, *Aust. Bush*, 225, 226.
4 Palmer, in JAI, XIII, 282.
5 Roth, *N.W. Cent. Queensland*, 141.

6 Smyth, *Vict.*, I, 129.
7 Howitt, in JAI, XX, 64.
8 Roth, *N.W. Cent. Queensland*, 141.
9 Henning, in *Globus*, LXXII, 102.
10 Nachtigal, *Sahara*, I, 439.

tremely seldom. Injuries and strifes commonly have as a consequence a knightly duel which is fought out after due preliminary challenge according to all the rules of the art."[11]

Wallace[12] tells of a community of about five hundred people of various races, all met in a remote corner of the East "to look for their fortune," as they express it. They are most of them people of the very worst reputation for honesty as well as for every other form of morality—Chinese, Bugis, Ceramese, half-caste Javanese, with a sprinkling of half-wild Papuans—yet all goes on very quietly. "This motley, ignorant, bloodthirsty, thievish population live here without the shadow of a government, with no police, no courts, and no lawyers; yet they do not cut each other's throats, do not plunder each other day and night, do not fall into the anarchy that such a state of things might be supposed to lead to. . . . Here may be seen in its simplest form the genius of Commerce at the work of Civilization. Trade is the magic that keeps all at peace, and unites these discordant elements into a well-behaved community. All are traders, and all know that peace and order are essential to successful trade, and thus a public opinion is created which puts down all lawlessness." If this case can be credited, and it is certainly upon high authority, it is one where naked public opinion is seen operating without intermediary agencies, under the stress of a clearly visualized interest.

The regulative system of many of the Melanesians is rudimentary. In British New Guinea the politico-social unit is the small community, in the majority of cases too small and of too little permanence to be called a tribe. In some districts true villages are found where there are hereditary chiefs possessing real authority, "which differs greatly both in quality and extent from the comparatively slight influence possessed by old or important men throughout the greater part of the area under consideration."[13] Among the Mekeo clans there was a feeling of affectionate consideration for their "chiefs" and a "ready recognition of the pre-eminence of the families to which these chiefs belonged." This fostered a sense of dignity, importance and responsibility on the part of the chiefs which is quite uncommon among Papuasians. "There are no big chiefs either at Milne Bay or Tubetube, nor are there even clan chiefs or heads of clans in any definite or executive sense. There were not even war chiefs, but merely leaders of individual war parties. . . . Certain men were, however, recognized as 'big' or important. In every case these were oldish men and their importance had not, as it appeared, come to them from their maternal uncles, their high repute being largely due to the prominent part they took in feasts. The fact that such men would readily be credited with some knowledge of magic, would increase their reputation and cause their opinions to carry weight in the councils of the old men. Further they were usually rich men, who had in their time bought many canoes and traded, i.e., travelled, extensively, or were known as specially successful fishermen." Although there is no chieftainship at Wagawaga there is "an elaborate system of distribution and division of food, which ensures that much of the best food obtained by members of the community falls to the share of the old men." There is no dominant or paramount chief of the Koita, or of any group larger than a section. Each clan has its head-man, called *iduhu rohi,* who enjoys little real authority. "The *iduhu rohi* is in charge of and is responsible for sharing out

11 Hiekisch, *Tungusen,* 68.   13 Seligmann, in JAI, XXXIX, 268-269.
12 *Malay Archip.,* 439-440.

the food at the feasts. He takes an important part in determining when these shall be held. . . . Though they may, and often do, exert considerable influence in their *iduhu* [clan], they have no power to enforce their desires against the general sense of the older men of the *iduhu* who represent public opinion. . . . The *iduhu rohi* also exert their authority to keep the peace in the village, and to mitigate friction between the clans. Captain Barton ascertained, that if a man beat or otherwise maltreated his wife, the case would be referred to the *iduhu rohi* who would reason with the man. 'In the event of the man declining to listen to advice, the *iduhu rohi* washes his hands of the matter, and the result in the old days was a general row and fight between the woman's relatives and the man's—other people also joining in.' Further, questions concerning land are formally brought before the *iduhu rohi* even when there is no quarrel or disagreement between the parties concerned. . . . *Iduhu rohi* have certain rights to game killed by all the men of their section, as well as rights in all large fish caught, though the latter rights are less well defined or perhaps more often ignored."[14] In the Loyalty Islands "there is no distinct division of the people into tribes. People related to one another generally preferred to live together in the same locality under the rule and direction of one of the older members, who was called the *Joxu* or chief." Sometimes this person was called by another term, meaning "father," the other members of the family styling themselves "children."[15] In D'Entrecasteaux there is "no all-powerful chief to sit in judgment. The *kauvea* or head man of a hamlet has only the influence which a man of years and experience is sure to command everywhere, but of actual recognized authority over his people he has none. It is not he who decides the disputes and quarrels but the rival parties themselves, aided at times by mediating friends; and only the fear of social ostracism compels compliance with the general will. Usually, therefore, the owner is forced to take the law into his own hands and inflict a summary vengeance on the thief."[16]

A considerable range of governmental development may be found in Africa, varying from the more primitive tribes to the kingdoms of Uganda, Dahomi, Ashanti, and Benin. The latter will be considered later. The primitive tribes vary in social status from those who recognize no chief and are still in the patriarchal stage, lacking any but the most rudimentary communal organization, up to those with well-defined tribal institutions, till they merge into the second class of more advanced communities. Among the most primitive the family is the unit and even the village-head has but little authority.[17] It is with such groups that we are concerned at this point. Among the Akamba "it is only rarely that individual chiefs have any great power and with the exception of presents of beer their people pay them no tribute. The real power is vested in the council of elders and they generally get their way."[18] In East Africa "the elders within one district would meet pretty regularly and try the cases of their locality. How far they could extend their authority beyond a very limited district is doubtful now; if there was hostility between the districts of accuser and accused legal proceedings would be useless, and on the other hand, doubtless many of the former feuds arose just where one party refused to acknowledge all legal authority; in either case redress would be

14 Seligmann, *Melanesians*, 342-343, 453, 454, 455, 456, 52-55.
15 Ray, in JAI, XLVII, 289.
16 Jenness and Ballentyne, *D'Entrecasteaux*, 76, 131, 132.
17 Lugard, *Brit. Trop. Africa*, 75-76.
18 Hobley, *A-Kamba*, 49-50.

sought by force of arms."[19] Among the Atheraka the elders form a judicial council identical with that of the Akamba; these elders perform priestly functions at sacrifices. Chiefs, as we understand the term, are non-existent.[20] Among the Mombasa "in each hamlet the elder is practically supreme, though almost powerless beyond its stockade. The community is governed by a council of all its notables, in which the will of the majority is sovereign."[21] The system of government found among the Ba-Mbala is extremely elementary; it has been described as "communism with a strong flavouring of anarchy." The unit is the village community, at the head of which is a "chief" who holds that position by reason of his wealth in slaves and wives. Upon his death the power devolves upon the individual who comes next in riches; there is no form of election. No tribute is paid to him, but he has several privileges, including the right to receive: (a) the ribs of every man killed for food, and (b) a hind leg of each beast slain during the common hunts. "His principal duty is to lend money to his 'subjects' when they have incurred fines which they are unable to pay, and, consequently, are in danger of becoming slaves."[22] Among the Bangala, who lacked paramount chiefs, the word of the head of the family was law to that group and to his own section of the town. These headmen met together to talk over town affairs. "Some were heads of larger families than others, and were richer than others. Such men necessarily had more influence, and their words carried greater weight than the words of poorer and smaller men. Sometimes a man with a loud voice and dominating will would get weaker men to follow him."[23] The Dinkas are a mere congeries of independent tribes; they have never been welded into a nation. "Every village governs itself by means of the village elders, and the chief is merely the leader in petty raids or in the equally petty and desultory wars resulting from blood-feuds. He presides, it is true, at the deliberations of the 'old men,' and appears to be the principal executive officer of the village or division of the tribe, but the real power is vested in the general body of the 'old men.'" The tribal system of self-administration is by "courts" of the "old people" of each village or clan. "These 'old people' are not elected, but are held to be qualified merely by the fact of old age, as having the best knowledge of tribal traditions and customs and the way to direct matters and settle disputes. It is the 'old people' of two quarrelling sections who arrange for peace and settle the terms. The sheikh is not the judge or lawgiver of his section. He is the leader of the warriors and acts as president and spokesman of his court of advisers, 'the old people.' "[24]

The principle of seniority holds sway among the aborigines of Siberia, not only in the family but in the settlement. In the latter, as long as no stronger man appeared, the founder was considered the elder, seniority implying superiority not only in age but also in physical strength. An eighteenth-century traveller says of the Chukchi people that they "have no chiefs or authorities. Each community has a man who is richer than the others, or who has a larger family; but he also is little obeyed and has no right to punish anybody." The important factors in the development of the regulative system among the Yukaghir were the "old man," the shaman, the "strong man" with

19 Dundas, C., in JAI, XLIII, 510, 537-538.
20 Dundas, C., in JAI, XLV, 243; Champion, in JAI, XLII, 87.
21 Johnstone, in JAI, XXXII, 269; Barton, in JAI, LIII, 49.

22 Torday and Joyce, in JAI, XXXV, 408-409.
23 Weeks, in JAI, XXXIX, 429-430, 435.
24 O'Sullivan, in JAI, XL, 171, 177.

his warriors, and the first hunter with his group of inferior hunters. "As a rule the oldest man of the clan was the 'old man,' but in some cases the ablest elder was chosen. In all important matters, the 'old man' of the clan consulted the oldest representatives of the separate families . . . who constituted a council, and by whose advice the 'old man' was not infrequently guided. His wife held a similar position among the women, although the powers of government were in the hands of the 'old man,' whom both men and women must obey. She superintended the division of the spoils of the chase. The shaman's position was of almost as great importance as that of the 'old man.' . . . The duty of the 'strong man,' with his warriors, was to defend the clan; neither he nor the hunter was necessarily of the same blood with the consanguineous part of the group." Through these factors the inner and outer groups in the clan were assimilated. In the natural Gilyak social organization there is no trace of a despotic authority. The "old men" of the clan decide questions of cult and clanship, for they are the repositories of the clan customs, traditions, and genealogies; apart from this they have no great influence or real authority. All the clans have some men who, either through wealth, physical prowess, or some accomplishment such as oratory, have an important though unofficial standing in the clan. In time of need such men may be called upon to assume the responsibility of upholding the customary law; but the clan as a whole has supreme authority over them.[25] Among the Soyots, reindeer-nomads of the upper Yenesei, each tribe has a head, chosen for a term and removable by a united public sentiment. His rule seems to be rather despotic, but the only luxury he has is to "drink himself full nearly every day."[26]

Though it is doubtful whether the Todas of southern India have as a whole any true chief, it is clear that the clan and its divisions often have definite leaders. Each clan has a headman and also an informal council of the chief members who settle matters arising within the clan. Over the affairs of the Todas in general is another and more formal council. In addition to its functions in disputes between individuals, which arise chiefly out of the custom of transferring wives from one man to another, the council had wide functions in connection with Toda ceremonial.[27] In British India, in general, there are communities grouped together in a village, generally owning land in common and dealing with other villages as units; but in Malabar individual property is universal and the village-organization comes in only for specific purposes such as the management of the temple-affairs and, in olden days, for military training and mobilization. Among these people custom and public opinion exert an enormous influence and are the real factors of regulative control.[28] In many groups in Assam the head-man is almost entirely without direct authority in secular matters; he is rather the religious head and many taboos surround him.[29] The petty chief of each Sakai village has every right but the capital one over the members of his settlement. "His authority is enforced (like that of the father of a European family) by means of the influence derived from his age and position in the tribe, rather than by that of any legal sanction. The tribe, in fact, merely forms (as it were) a rather larger family circle." The political and administrative organization of the Negritos is, like that of the Sakai, exceedingly simple; in each village there is a functionary invested with

25 Czaplicka, *Aborig. Siberia*, 34, 28 note, 37-38, 49-50.
26 Olsen, *Primitivt Folk*, 49, 50.
27 Rivers, *Todas*, 550-556.
28 Panikkar, in JAI, XLVIII, 257-258, 260.
29 Hodson, in JAI, XXXVI, 95, 98.

full powers, who is called by the Malays "Penghulu." "These Penghulus are all of equal standing, and own no superior. . . . Complete equality exists as between individuals, and caste is unknown. Even the chief is on an equal footing with his men, except when in discharge of his official duties. To the foregoing it should be added that all their property is in common."[30]

Among many of the Polynesians the form of government is found to be similar to the Australian system: "a democracy, or rather an oligarchy of old and influential men, who meet in council, and decide on all measures of importance, to the practical exclusion of the younger men. Their deliberative assembly answers to the senate of later times." The Marquesas Islanders cannot be said to have lived under any form of government other than a patriarchal one. "The oldest man of a tribe, if he possessed the most land, and was the owner of the most bread-fruit and coconut trees, was the most influential among them. Wealth . . . gave power. They also had rank which was hereditary, and took much pride in tracing ancestry. . . . The class of chiefs was in Polynesia the wealthy class, even though a chief of high rank and great possessions might sometimes, owing to misfortunes, become quite poor. Perhaps writers on the Marquesas have imagined that men could become chiefs because they were rich, whereas really they were rich because they were chiefs." In Easter Island "there was hardly a distinction observable between the magistrate and the subjects. They (that is, the magistrates) had the name and the dignity, and some attendance, and were, on the arrival of strangers, better dressed; but their authority was more like that of a benevolent parent than the. imperious dictates of a king."[31] The authority of a Tanna chief "did not seem to extend a gunshot from his own dwelling." In a settlement or village is a population of eighty to a hundred and one or two principal men among them who are called chiefs. "The affairs of this little community are regulated by the chiefs and the heads of families."[32] This primitive governmental system was later upset in many parts of Polynesia through war, which divided the population of some of the islands into victors and subjects, nobles and commoners, and chiefs and kings arose who exercised dominating power.[33] The social organization of the Maori tribe of New Zealand was "as wellnigh perfect a commune as can be imagined. It was communism almost pure and undefiled; a commonwealth in which practically all had equal rights—except the slaves, who were not of the tribe, but had been taken from other tribes in war. . . . The autocracy of the chiefs was really a nominal one. The Maori commoner considered himself as good as his lord or *Ariki* in most points. If a chief lost the respect of his people, his place as leader in emergency, such as war, could be filled by others. What he could not lose was his sacred *Ariki*-ship, which was vested in him by heredity. The real ruler of the people was the institution of *tapu*."[34]

Among the Point Barrow Eskimo, "there is no established form of government and there are no chiefs, but the people appear to be ruled by strong public opinion combined with respect for the opinions of older people, both men and women, and by traditional observances such as those concerning whale fishery. . . . In the ordinary relations of life a person avoids doing

30 Skeat and Blagden, *Malay Penin.*, I, 503-504, 499.

31 Williamson, *Cent. Polyn.*, I, 316, 324, 374, 386, 393-396. 402.

32 Turner, *Samoa*, 315.

33 Williamson, *Cent. Polyn.*, I, 370, 425; III, 396-400.

34 Cowan, *Maoris*, 142, 143.

anything to another which he would not care to have done to himself, and the affairs of the community in general are settled by a majority, after an informal discussion. The majority apparently has no means, short of individual violence, of enforcing its decision, but the matter seems to be left to the good sense of the parties concerned."[35]

We are told of the Aleuts that they have no government, but that the old men are deferred to. Whalers and medicine-men have some influence.[36] One of the Yukon tribes has "no chiefs, guides, or masters . . . every one commands and all obey if they see fit." Public opinion is the dominating and direct control. An injured person—their three crimes being murder, theft, and adultery—is authorized to punish.[37] Farther south, "in the sense in which the term is ordinarily used, there is no absolute chiefship. The family is the sociological unit. The head of that household in the village, which, through inheritance, wealth, numbers, and influence, predominates over the others, is nominally chief of the village. His authority is shadowy, and his power is largely due, aside from wealth, good birth, and family influence, to his prowess in war, or to personal and masterful qualities."[38] Among the Salish of British Columbia "each local community had its own headman and looked after its own affairs. In the earlier history of the Stock this local authority and direction of affairs would seem to have been shared by all the eldermen of the village or commune in common; or perhaps it would be more correct to say that the elderman of each family directed the affairs of his own household independently of all others; for the original social unit of Salish society was the family not the village commune. A primitive Salish community was a congeries of independent family groups, each ruled and directed by its own elderman."[39]

There was, in Oregon, "a marked tendency to local segregation of groups related by blood in every village. These consanguineous divisions often attained considerable size."[40] "The social organization of the Takelma was almost the simplest conceivable. Each village . . . and the villages were generally very insignificant, was entirely independent or practically so. Any one who was comparatively wealthy could be called a 'chief,' . . . there does not seem to have been a recognized head chief, though in time of war some one man probably was so considered. . . . It seems then that the local village community is the only purely sociological grouping to be recognized among these Indians, excluding the nearly self-evident ones of rich and poor, freemen and slaves . . . and the family."[41] Powers[42] calls the tribes of northern California "democratic," meaning that they had no political organization. The tribal organization of the Pawnee was based on village-communities, each village having its hereditary chief and its council composed of leading men.[43] Among the Eastern Dakota each gens had its own group of twenty councillors, and in the tribal camp each councillor's tent was pitched in front of the place occupied by his gens. On all occasions except when in tribal council the chief had no authority over the councillors. This rather advanced political organization was due, some of the older Dakota believe, to French suggestion.[44]

Of the Botocudos it is reported that there is no connection between their

35 Murdoch, in BAE, IX, 427.
36 Reclus, *Prim. Folk*, 114.
37 Jetté, "Ten'a," in *Cong. Intern. d'Amer.*, 1906, I, 395 ff.
38 Niblack, in USNM, 1888, 250.
39 Hill-Tout, in JAI, XXXV, 131.

40 Farrand, in AA, III, 243.
41 Sapir, in AA, IX, 267-268.
42 In *Contr. N. Amer. Ethnol.*, III.
43 Fletcher, in HAI, II, 215.
44 Skinner, in AA, XXI, 173.

clans. Ten or twenty families form a cluster.[45] "The Lengua natives rule their lives almost entirely by public opinion;" the chiefs are rather "fathers of the family" than political functionaries.[46] Among the Jibaros of Ecuador "each family father is theoretically absolute ruler over his house people, and in times of peace there is no recognized common chief even within the tribe, and still less any exercising authority over several tribes. . . . It is only in times of war that a chieftainship exists; . . . such a temporary chief of war is generally only called *unta,* 'the old one,' because the chiefs are nearly always old, experienced men who have killed many enemies and captured many heads. . . . As soon as a war has been carried to a successful end the power of the chief ceases, and he has, in spite of the great repute he always enjoys, no more authority or right to decide over the doings of his tribesmen than any other family father among the Jibaros."[47] There was no political organization, as we understand the term, among the Araucanians, and save only in times of great national peril, and then only in a military sense, did they recognize any supreme chief. "The danger over, they returned to their former customs, the functions of the chief ceasing from the moment the army was disbanded. The basis of their social and political life is the family, which develops into a clan, and afterwards a tribe, absolutely independent one from the other." The clan was governed by the head of the family; the authority of these family-heads was little more than nominal, and was confined almost exclusively to the direction of their feasts and ceremonies, and in a lesser degree to the political economy of the group. All important matters were treated in common council by the adult males, the chief presiding at the meeting. "No tribute is paid him, neither is he exempt from sharing the daily tasks of the clan, although in a general way he assumes the management."[48] Among the lowly Fuegians, on account of their wandering life, scarcely any political organization seems necessary. Generally they move in groups of about twelve—three men, five women, and four children, probably related. Their sorcerers have been mistaken for chiefs.[49]

To these contemporary instances there might be added historical cases, a number of which are covered by the statement that "the most ancient forms of government amongst Indo-European peoples are based on the organization of the family."[50]

§155. The Chieftainship.

WAR has been a powerful factor in the development of chieftainship, and some evidence of its influence in this respect should be given before considering the functions and powers of the primitive chief. In Australia and New Guinea the rudimentary chieftainships are founded more upon intelligence, strength, and wealth, and exist in fact rather than in law. "In the Bismarck Archipelago we see brave people with powerful personality move forward . . . to leadership in war and they appear also in peace as judges of quarrels."[1] On the Solomon Islands, wherever a warlike state of things prevailed, the chiefs won power and importance.[2] In New Ireland, "there are chiefs of important reputation

---

45 Keane, in JAI, XIII, 207.
46 Hawtrey, in JAI, XXXI, 280 ff.
47 Karsten, "Jibaro," in BAE, Bull. LXXIX, 7-8.
48 Latcham, in JAI, XXXIX, 355.

49 Ratzel, *Vkde.,* II, 677.
50 Schrader, *Aryan,* 393.
1 Hagen, *Papua's,* 226.
2 Ratzel, *Vkde.,* II, 280.

and greater power than in New Britain, and just for this reason, that the New Irelanders are much more warlike than the New Britons and need leaders for their incessant feuds."[3] A chief may further his son's claims to succession by teaching him his own special knowledge, often magical, by buying him a high position in the secret society, and by leaving him property; but after all the test is competence. "If a man has no son competent he may take his nephew; sometimes, the son perhaps being too young, a chief's brother will succeed him; sometimes a man will set himself up when no successor is acknowledged, or the people will choose some one to lead them."[4]

The Zulus have a remarkable military organization and a highly centralized government. Their great chiefs sacrificed the family to the state, forcing their warriors to put off marriage until their military service was discharged. The father is lord of his family and owner of his wives, and the king is father of his people. The king has a monopoly of all trade. Even here, however, the chief has two advisers (*indunas*) and the government is sometimes called a triumvirate.[5] Among the Guinea negroes there is "a regular military organization, with a regular War Lord, not one and the same with the Peace Lord."[6] A West African king "may be blamed if a war he has declared ends disastrously";[7] that is, the non-discharge of his war-function in so far imperils his position. Junker's[8] account of the largely disintegrated nations of the Sudan, compared with the Zulus, for instance, goes to show that the authority of the political chief is weak in the former cases, but rises to extremest despotism at home when a military ruler makes conquests and establishes an even rudimentary state.

The Pygmies own no territory, but settle on the land of some chief, "a tacit bargain being usual that they shall remain there unmolested on condition that they give their military assistance to him when he may be engaged in warfare. . . . As all these people are in a perpetual state of internecine warfare, the aid of the Pygmies is no small factor in the army of the chief under whom they live, nor are they a negligible factor in his domestic diplomacy."[9] Among the Berbers, the only exception to organization in "little republics" is where there has been need of defense either against the outsider or in the presence of a subjected element whose aspirations for independence had to be suppressed. Then a monarchical form has developed.[10] The state of warfare thus enables the chief to consolidate his power. Where every man is a soldier and there is a standing army of police, these are also body-guards for the king.[11]

"The more unstable peace is, the more stable and the greater is the power of these [Western Asiatic] tribal chiefs. Among the predatory and warlike Karakirghiz they appear even in peace as almost unlimited despots."[12] In Siberia "the 'strong man' in modern times is simply a man of great physical strength, daring temper, and adventurous disposition; but when the Chukchee were frequently at war with the Koryak, Eskimo, and Cossacks, the 'strong man' was the hero, as we see in the extant primitive Chukchee war epic."[13] Among the Bhils of India we see a very rudimentary form of government. "Let us draw in rough outline a history of the *Social Contract*, more truthful

3 Finsch, *Ethnol. Erfahr.*, I, 125.
4 Codrington, *Melanesians*, 56, 57.
5 Ratzel, *Vkde.*, I, 243, 254, 259.
6 Kingsley, *W. Afr. Studies*, 423.
7 Nassau, *Fetichism*, 16.
8 *Afrika*, II, 4 ff.

9 Burrows, in JAI, XXVIII, 38.
10 Hanoteau et Letourneux, *Kabylie*, II, 3.
11 Ratzel, *Vkde.*, I, 461.
12 Grosse, *Familie*, 125-126.
13 Czaplicka, *Aborig. Siberia*, 26.

than Rousseau's; let us reproduce in broad lines the establishment of political and civil administration. A roistering blade, a fellow with a clear head and a heavy hand, espies a rock commanding a defile between two fertile valleys; there he takes up his position and fortifies it. This man in possession falls upon the passers by, assassinates some, pillages and despoils the greater number. Having the power, he has the right. . . . The institution of robbery, which is not at all what a vain folk have imagined, gives birth to property and the police. Political authority, which was quite recently given out to be an emanation of Divine Right, and a good gift of Providence, was constructed little by little by the care of licensed highwaymen, by the systematic efforts of brigands who were men of influence. The police were formed and educated by ruffians who prowled about the outskirts of the forest, armed with a knotted cudgel, and shouted to the trader, 'Your money or your life!' Taxes were the subscription, the premium paid by the robbed to the robbers. Joyous and grateful, the plundered placed themselves behind the knights of the highway, and proclaimed them the supporters of order, of religion, of the family, of property, of morals; consecrated them a legitimate government. It was a touching contract."[14] In the Siamese language "to govern" is the same word as "to steal."[15]

Among some of the Central Polynesians "the man who rendered himself most formidable by warlike deeds" was the man of greatest consideration. In ancient times the ruling power of Niue was held by the fighting men, and the party that happened to be in the ascendant elected a king to be their mouthpiece. "It was a dignity that cost its holder dearly, for the object of the opposition party was invariably to kill the king, and a violent death had come to be so often an appanage of royalty that for eighty years before the introduction of Christianity, and the consequent cessation of warfare, no one could be found willing to undertake the office." Conquest in a number of places divided the population into the two groups of conquerors and conquered and enhanced the power of the chief.[16]

Some tribes of American Indians had a war chief whose duties pertained exclusively to war;[17] while among the Jibaros it was only in times of war that a chieftainship existed.[18] As in other tribes of Guiana, every settlement among the Makusi had its headman; in times of peace "he never gives his orders in a dictatorial sense, but in such a manner as, 'Would it not perhaps be better for this or that to be done?' In battle, however, he is absolute commander."[19]

Among the Arabs the sheikh possesses no great power over the members of his tribe but can make his personality felt. His commands may be treated with contempt, but his advice is generally followed. If war rises an "aegyd" is put at the head of the troops, but his function ends when the raiders get home. He possesses as little coercive power as the sheikh. But "if the aegyd is a man of extraordinary bravery and keenness he retains, even in peace-time, a great influence over the affairs of his tribe."[20] The Hebrews at first did as they chose, though they had in the Levites a theocratic class. Then judges tried to establish a hereditary rule, and finally kings—Saul and David—came out of war.[21]

14 Reclus, *Prim. Folk*, 272, 273.
15 Letourneau, *Polit.*, 104.
16 Williamson, *Cent. Polyn.*, I, 337, 354, 357-359; III, 133-135.
17 HAI, II, 706, 915.

18 Karsten, "Jibaro," in BAE, Bull. LXXIX, 7-8, 20.
19 Roth, in BAE, XXXVIII, 576.
20 Burckhardt, *Bedouin*, I, 116, 296-298.
21 Judges, XXI, 25; Levit., XXV, 32-33; I Samuel, VIII, ff.

Cæsar[22] says the Gauls had no common magistrate in time of peace, but in wartime authorities, with power of life and death, appeared. In Poland there was a governor or judge, who was old and selected for wisdom. Beside him there appeared a warrior-chief, or Voevoda, named for the time.[23] The system is like that of the sachem and war-chief of the Indians. The assembly of kinsmen of the South Slavs meets and debates; it is mainly the old men who talk. "It should always be remembered that if the association were habitually militant, both the old men and the youths would probably fall into the background, and the authority in council would belong to the mature warrior who is foremost in arms."[24]

The extent to which chieftainship is developed, among various groups of primitive peoples, the functions and authority of the chief, tests of the chief, and other customs related to chieftainship are indicated in the following ethnographical survey. It is highly desirable to mass evidence of all description upon the nature of the chieftainship—to view it from all sides—because it and its incumbent stand in a sort of focus not only of political life, but of societal evolution in general.

In central Australia "there is no such thing as a chief of the tribe, nor is there any individual to whom the term chief can be applied." But there is a head-man with somewhat vague prerogatives; and if he has the personal ability, he can "wield considerable power not only over the members of his own group, but over those of neighboring groups whose head men are inferior in personal ability to himself." This position is hereditary in the male line rather than elective; and the main function of its holder is as custodian of the store of sacred objects belonging to the group.[25] Smyth[26] lists the men of position as the doctors or sorcerers, who sometimes get supreme power; the warriors who in time of trouble are absolute masters; the dreamers, "who direct and control the movements of the tribe until their divinations are fulfilled or forgotten"; the old men, or councillors, whose advice weighs even with the warriors; and the old women, "who noisily intimate their designs." Some man from some one of these classes becomes the principal figure of the tribe and the young men, undistinguished elders, women, and children accept his leadership which is exercised "only in such manner as the old men and the sorcerers and the dreamers have agreed to approve." In West Victoria, "every tribe has its chief, who is looked upon in the light of a father, and whose authority is supreme. He consults with the best men of the tribe, but when he announces his decision, they dare not contradict or disobey him. . . . Great respect is paid to the chiefs and their wives and families. They can command the services of everyone belonging to their tribe . . . Should they fancy any article of dress, opossum rug, or weapon, it must be given without a murmur."[27] From such accounts, even though the agreement of authorities is not always perfect,[28] it is plain enough that the chieftainship has not become a settled institution in this part of the continent.

The power of the chief in the Solomon Islands depends on birth, wealth, and magic; if the chief orders the people to work, they will do it or not do it; if

22 *Bell. Gall.*, VI, 23; Chadwick, "Teut. Priesthood," in *Folk-Lore*, Sept., 1900, 276.
23 Spencer, *Prin. Soc.*, II, §§492, 473.
24 Maine, *Early Law*, 246.

25 Spencer and Gillen, *Nat. Tr. Cent. Aust.*, 10, 11, 15.
26 *Vict.*, I, 126 ff.
27 Dawson, *Aust. Aborig.*, 5.
28 Curr, *Aust. Race*, I, 55.

they refuse, he can say nothing. "The activities of the chiefs had mostly ceased with head-hunting."[29] In the Loyalty Islands, on the other hand, "a chief's orders would be implicitly obeyed." He directed the disposal of property and controlled marriage; some foods were especially reserved for him, and in early times he could order the killing of his subjects for his own food. "Persons were careful not to crack a coconut so as to startle or disturb a chief. Special words were used when speaking to him, or about him.[30] Among other Melanesians we find war-chiefs, chiefs who are expert in battle-magic, and clan-chiefs who settle minor quarrels and otherwise regulate the affairs of the local group.[31]

One South African chief attached young men to himself by distributing wives among those who could not afford them; they became strong and faithful vassals. Other chiefs by this system established an enormous economic system based on the harem.[32] But alongside such concentration of power there appeared also in South Africa very loose bonds between ruler and subjects.[33] The chief, even in Africa, may be criticized by his people; one orator said of his chief that he was getting too fat, which proved that the public interest did not worry him. And the speaker invited the assembly to look upon the person of the chief and see if it were not so.[34] The tribe, in one case, selected the chief wife of the ruler and presented her to him. Her son would be heir to the chieftainship to the exclusion of the children of his purchased wives. "This marriage is usually recommended and seen to by the tribe when the chief is getting on towards middle life."[35] Among some South African tribes the chief is credited with the power of rain-making and has other priestly functions.[36] There are certain well-recognized rights of the Bechuana chief: he alone has the right to order the great tribal ceremonies; he has the power of taxation and of administering justice; he alone can summon the civil assemblies and the armed assemblies, and declare war. "He alone has the power that pertains to a 'doctor,' and all who act as medicine men in his country do so by his permission and exercise the power which he has delegated to them." Moreover, there are two things which are peculiarly his prerogative: the felling of a special kind of tree for building a cattle-kraal, and the castrating of calves. "These two prerogatives strike one as being unworthy of the chief; but they are connected with cattle, and if the chief has inherited them from a time when the cattle were the totem of the tribe, and his ancestors priests of the totem-god, then there is nothing paltry about them."[37]

In the Congo region, "the chief is, as a rule, the head fetish-man." The great chief is assisted by a council consisting of all the fighting men; he may retire behind a confidential adviser, who is often a slave of great importance and impersonates the chief before strangers.[38] In East Africa, "everywhere the political sovereign was the supreme judge, whether that dignity was represented by an individual or a council. And for this reason the native will always regard the European judge or magistrate as his immediate ruler, wherefore a distinction between judicial and political officials dealing directly with the people of Africa is never to be recommended. The effectiveness and supremacy of the law depend mainly on the stability of the tribal organization: it is most

29 Hocart, in JAI, LII, 79.
30 Ray, in JAI, XLVII, 290, 291.
31 Seligmann, *Melanesians*, 216-220.
32 Ratzel, *Vkde.*, I, 305.
33 Holub, *Capstadt*, II, 254.
34 Letourneau, *Polit.*, 158.

35 Bent, *Mashonaland*, 271-272.
36 Grant, in JAI, XXXV, 267; Sheane, in JAI, XXXVI, 154.
37 Willoughby, in JAI, XXV, 308-309.
38 Torday and Joyce, in JAI, XXXVII, 139.

lax among the disorganized tribes, and most telling among those who are united under individual and powerful rulers. Therefore, it is necessary to consider jointly the political organization and the judicial system of each tribe. . . . In general it may be said that where chiefship was not known or hardly existed, it has developed under European rule, and where it was most firm and absolute it has declined."[39]

There is a Dinka legend about a powerful chief who seems to have had considerable intellectual curiosity along with his masterful disposition. He wondered where the sun went at night, having heard that it descended into the water and yet seeing no water toward the west. He sent some men to journey westwards and find out the truth of the matter. After he had been gathered to his fathers a few aged and battered members of the expedition returned to report that the sun did actually descend into the ocean. When asked why they had not returned before, they replied that they did not dare come back unsuccessful in their quest to face the anger of the chief "and the laughter of their sisters."[40] There was another enlightened chief in East Africa, named Nedia: "When Nedia saw that his people would die of starvation, he said: 'Let me go out and be killed [by the besieging enemy], that my people may live'; and he and eight of his elders came out and were slain. Nedia ran some 400 yards before being killed. He fell at the foot of some rocks, where his descendants to this day sacrifice annually to his spirit. . . . The following is one of the best-known stories told of him; . . . Nedia had a rooted objection to witchcraft, and to all who practised it, and to convince his elders of the absurdity of their belief in them, he one day hid his copper bracelets in the grass, and then accused them of having stolen them." These bracelets were the symbols of royalty. "They denied the theft and Nedia therefore sent for a witch doctor, who administered the potion given at trials by ordeal. The elders drank it, and one and all fell down insensible from the effects of the drug. The following day Nedia took the witch doctor and the accused men to the spot where he had hidden the bracelets, and showing them to the witch doctor ordered him out of the country, saying that he would not countenance such practices any longer."[41]

The West African king is sometimes subjected to a test of flogging prior to his elevation. "If he should cry out during the punishment, or show any signs of pain, he is at once rejected as unworthy, and the council makes a new choice; but if he bear himself bravely, without flinching, he is forthwith crowned. This ordeal appears to be designed to test the candidate's capacity for endurance, and his power of self-restraint and concealment of thought." In Sierra Leone they "scoff at and beat the new king while dragging him from his own house to the residence of his predecessor; where, if he has withstood the ordeal, the royal ornaments are put on him."[42] In Dahomi "the king is absolute, his will being law, and he is subject to no control whatever." When the king dies all law and order cease; anarchy prevails and there is no more safety for person or property. The laws die with the king, so closely identified are they with him. The despotism of the West African rulers, and at the same time the political cohesion of the tribes, are weakened in proportion as individuals get rich through trade. Any man becomes independent who can acquire a gun and powder. There comes about a state of affairs where nobody will accept the

39 Dundas, C., in JAI, LI, 218.
40 O'Sullivan, in JAI, XL, 176.
41 Dundas, K. R., in JAI, XLIII, 23-24.
42 Ellis, *Yoruba*, 165.

kingly dignity because he will not submit to the ceremonies. The last Congo kings lie unburied and the government is still carried on in their name.[43]

A strange procedure in West Africa is where chiefs are not properly buried, but kept "hanging about outside life, but not inside death; the reason for this seemingly unprincipled conduct in not properly burying the chief, so that he may be reincarnated to a complete human form, lies in the fact that he would be a political nuisance to his successor if he came back promptly; therefore he is kept waiting." But the new chief goes to the house of the dead one and tells him the political news. The so-called House-system of the Gold Coast allows the poorest boy who paddles an oil-canoe a chance to become king. Though the kings of Benin are little more than puppets in the hands of their chief officers, yet they could designate their successors from among their sons. "Now begins trouble for the non-successful claimants; the king's throne must be secure, so they and their sons must be suppressed. It was not allowed to shed royal blood; hence they were quietly suffocated by having their noses, mouths, and ears stuffed with cloth."[44] It is rather exceptional for the village king or chief to have great power; he seems to act mainly as a judge and mediator in quarrels.[45]

Klose[46] plainly sets forth the close relations of the chiefs, or "kings" and the fetish-men; the former often depend upon the latter. And the chiefs maintain a close connection with their dead predecessors; the chief's dead father has always a house in which gin, tobacco, clothes, and other property are kept for his use.[47] In the Congo region political organization is but feebly developed; "he is chief who has the most wives, children, slaves, pirogues, and particularly who has boldness to carry on transactions with the whites in the best interest of the tribe."[48] The natives, however, have great respect for force and totally despise gentleness.

That the king is a fetish-man admits of no debate; we seek to complete his picture here, even though we partially anticipate a later topic.[49] In Loango no king is legitimately installed until he has visited a certain sacred region. Again, a king may never quit his house or even his chair, but must sleep sitting; if he were to lie down no wind would rise and navigation would cease. A king is crowned amongst the corpses of his predecessors, and is so surrounded with taboos and inhibitions that he must be forced to submit to coronation. One prince, whose rule was characterized by unrelatable atrocities, always went armed lest he be overpowered and made king. "After a family council has determined in secret who the next king is to be, the latter is suddenly seized and thrown bound into the fetish-house, to be held there as a prisoner till he acquiesces." In other places, the king has to buy his position by presents and must endure preliminary humiliations. The priestly kingship is in force in all of Africa, and the chief is reputed to be lord of rain and weather. "In Loango the king is accused of having a bad heart . . . if they cannot fish because the

---

43 Ellis, *Ewe*, 162; Waitz, *Anthrop.*, II, 147; Ratzel, *Vkde.*, I, 603.
44 Kingsley, *W. Afr. Studies*, 147, 450, 451, 452.
45 Elliot, cited in JAI, XXIII, 81; Cummins, in JAI, XXXIV, 156; Parkinson, in JAI, XXXVI, 315.

46 *Togo, passim.*
47 Granville and Roth, in JAI, XXVIII, 112.
48 Clozel, in PSM, XLIX, 675; Weeks, in JAI, XXXIX, 132-133.
49 §§257, 259, 310, of the text.

surf is too heavy, and they depose him because he has no love for his subjects."50

The chief is almost always under some check and surveillance; he cannot bid
defiance to public opinion by systematically crossing the interests of his subjects. Even so low a people as the Teda of the Sahara seek to protect themselves against royal oppression. In one of their sub-tribes are two royal families,
the oldest male representatives of which succeed one another in turn. The one
succeeding must give up his property lest he be able to buy many slaves and
oppress the people through them. The chief has no power of life and death and
raises no taxes; he is only judge and military leader.51 In the Sudan the legitimate chief "is often enough set in the shadow by the intelligence and efficiency
of a superior tribesman who then is willingly recognized as actual chief. . . .
Further the chiefs can assert themselves only in council or in war-raids. . . .
No head-man has the power to judge alone, and the more disruption results
in separated groups without connection in the country, the more does each man
seem to steal, calumniate, and do wrong, so far as he can bear the consequences,
and the more is the injured party thrown back upon getting justice for himself."52 The Kikuyu chief always had his people absolutely under his thumb,
supplied all the arrow-heads used in hunting, and received all the tusks gathered.
He also had a sugar-cane press out of which he derived considerable profit. In
this region the biggest chief lives in a mud hut like anybody else.53

The king of Uganda had seven thousand so called wives. His popularity and
power depended on providing his great men with wives, and these probably
represented his stock. Elsewhere too wives are not bought but a man gets the
king or some magnate to give him one.54 A chief must, in some cases, inspect
the grain and decide upon the time of harvesting.55 In some cases the chief is
hidden away and his place taken by an impersonator.56 In Somal and Galla
tribes there is no central authority, but the chiefs, who are also the only merchants, rule petty divisions for a time, generally eight years.57

As among all Bantu peoples, all through the Batetela country land is vested
in the chief for the benefit of the tribe. The great chief, assisted by elders,
governs through a prime minister; in all sections the chief administers justice,
and a great part of his revenue is derived from the fines which he inflicts.58 The
Bahima chief has representatives or head-men from each clan to assist him in
government; clan matters are decided by the respective head-men, while the
chief attends to cases involving clan against clan.59 Certain kings of East
Africa are not allowed to die a natural death; should they become too old to
rule, or should they fall sick beyond recovery, they are strangled. The funeral
celebrations of the dead king are very similar to those of the common people,
but the manner of his interment is quite different. "The corpse is wrapped in
the hide of a newly slaughtered bull and buried in a sitting position in the
chief wife's hut, with the head above ground. A tube for sucking up beer leading
from an empty beer pot is stuck in the mouth, and an inverted bowl is placed

50 Bastian, *Deut. Exped.*, I, 69, 287 ff.,
353 ff.; II, 10, 11, 14, 230.

51 Rohlfs, Reise, in *Mitth. J. Perthes'
Geog. Anstalt, Ergänzband.* V, 26; Ratzel,
Vkde., III, 170.

52 Nachtigal, *Sahara*, II, 145, 146, 147.

53 Stigand, *Elephant*, 248, 249, 251; Hobley, *A-Kamba*, 137.

54 Ratzel, *Vkde.*, I, 476, 534.

55 Fabry, in *Globus*, XCI, 201.

56 Kandt, in *Globus*, LXXXVI, 214.

57 Ratzel, *Vkde.*, I, 430.

58 Torday, in JAI, LI, 373; Torday and
Joyce, in JAI, XXXVI, 284.

59 Roscoe, in JAI, XXXVII, 98.

over the head." Later the bones are deposited in the burial-place of the kings. The king is a semi-divine personage; he is first and foremost a priest or medicine-man; one of his chief functions in olden times was to make the war medicine. Among other East Africans the privileges of the chief consist in free labor and a contribution of foodstuffs. More nearly paramount was the position of the king in Ungoni. "He exercised powers of life and death and to a certain extent had a right to his subjects' wives, in that he could dissolve any marriage and appropriate the woman thus divorced. Yet he was distinguished only by the greeting accorded to him; his only source of wealth was the booty brought to him by his warlike people. . . . Judgment is delivered by the chief with the acclamation of his councillors. The decision is rarely enforced, but if the losing party defied the chief he was formally killed or enslaved. Under all circumstances, however, the claimant had full right to seize what he laid claim to of the defendant's property."[60] Priest-kings are common to the Turkana, Masai, Nandi, Wagogo, and are found in a number of cases in the Sudan.[61]

The East Central African chief is in a sense divine; his first duty is hospitality and he must never turn a wayfarer away. He must be generous to men in high rank who visit him. Yet he must not be too exacting in demanding presents from the people to replenish an exhausted exchequer. Just how he is to reconcile these duties is not stated. His first official act is to appoint a chief magician who is to be the confidential minister of state.[62] The Somal and neighboring tribes obey the commands of their chiefs, but with many an evasion upon plausible pretext. They do not respect them very much, nor do the chiefs conduct themselves with much dignity toward their subjects, though they display authority with impressiveness in dealing with strangers. There is a sort of double-chieftainship where two weaker tribes unite.[63] The Madagascar chief has the right to turn out a tenant at his pleasure, without warning and without compensation for improvements; to refuse permission for a tenant to give up, exchange, or shift his holding; to have his permission asked before doing anything with the land beyond building or planting.[64]

Among the Mongols worship at the tomb of his predecessors took the place of the chief's coronation. They believed that anyone who refused to recognize the still-existing authority of the sainted Genghis Khan would speedily be punished by him.[65] The Dnieper Cossack tribes lived each in a "saitch" or fortified camp, as pictured in Gogol's *Taras Bulba* and Sienkiewicz's *Fire and Sword*. Each clan had a common dwelling in which lived five hundred or more persons. Any member might become clan-chief and any clan-chief might be the tribal chief, or *Atamán,* for a year. "Bear patiently, Cossack; you will one day be *Atamán!*" After his term of office the chief became again a simple Cossack.[66] The Karakirghiz and Kalmuks endure, by exception among the Asiatic nomads, a despotic chief, who controls their property and is an unlimited judge. But generally "the economic need of the herders holds, with its centrifugal tendency, the preponderance over the centripetal tendency of their warlike disposition."[67]

---

60 Dundas, K. R., in JAI, XLIII, 26, 28-29, 57; Dundas, C., in JAI, LI, 222, 223, 224.
61 Cole, in JAI, XXXII, 319, 338; Barton, in JAI, LI, 89-90; Seligmann, in JAI, XLIII, 664 ff.
62 Macdonald, in JAI, XXII, 120.

63 Paulitschke, *Nordost-Afr.*, I, 242; II, 248.
64 Parker, in JAI, XII, 277.
65 Shchukin, *Shamanism* (Russ.), 37.
66 Wallace, *Russia*, 207.
67 Grosse, *Familie*, 103-104.

Chiefs in India have to submit to burdens and taboos like those reported of the kings of Egypt, "to whom only two kinds of flesh and a limited quantity of wine were permitted. The government is "distinctly democratic"; chiefs are "without much individual power and their rule is based on the general approval of the clan." There is no settled form of government. Nominally the tribesmen are "under the orders of the headmen of their different villages, who are chosen for wealth, bravery, skill in diplomacy, etc. Virtually every man does that which he considers right and is a law unto himself. The orders of the headman are obeyed in so far as they accord with the wishes of the community, but the minority will not hold themselves bound to act by the wishes of the majority. The Naga headman is simply *primus inter pares,* and that only for a time." Theoretically every man is his own master and avenges his own quarrel.[68] Among the Sema Nagas the chief is father and protector of his subjects, who are termed "orphans"—frequently being broken men, debtors, etc., who have attached themselves to the chief. The relation is partly patriarchal and partly quasi-feudal. The chief distributes his land among his villagers and gets in return a certain number of days' work. To abolish this system would necessitate provision for a large number of paupers.[69]

In the country of the Lhoosai, "the author one day standing in the path in a village, saw a drunken man stumbling along. The writer and a chief were talking together, but as they were somewhat in the way of the drunken man, he seized the chief by the neck and asked him why he stopped the road. The explanation given by the chief concerning this disrespect was that on the war-path or in the council he was chief, and there such behavior would be punished by death, but that there in the village the men were equals."[70] "When the village consists of a number of loosely aggregated cultivating occupants, it is very natural that they should choose or recognize some one of their number to be their headman"; but in the landlord village "the proprietary families were too jealous of their equal rights to allow of any great degree of authority residing in one head"; they managed village affairs by a council of family-heads.[71] The Nairs provided against having a senile chief by limiting the term to twelve years. The chief then presented his successor and stabbed himself. This provision occurs elsewhere, for instance, in Africa.[72]

In the Semang tribes of the Malay Peninsula the office of chief medicine-man appears to be generally combined with that of chief, but among the Sakai and Jakun these offices are sometimes separated.[73] "The dual kingship, as in Siam, on the Pelew Islands, and elsewhere, is to be regarded as a sort of transition from the priest-kingship to the complete separation of secular and spiritual power, while elsewhere the displacement comes through the commander-in-chief under the crown."[74] The manangs or medicine-men of the Sea Dyaks rank next in importance to the village-chiefs, and it is not unusual for the medicine-man himself to be the chief of the village in which he resides. In the interior where the Dutch resident's appointing power is not in evidence, "cunning, wealth, valour, honesty, knowledge of the ancestral regulations, integrity, and impartiality are qualities by which a man may command claims to the dignity of chieftainship. . . . The government of the Dyaks seems to be administered more

68 Godden, in JAI, XXVI, 169; Carey and Tuck, *Chin Hills,* I, 3; Woodthorpe, in JAI, XI, 68.
69 Hutton, *Sema Nagas,* 385-390.
70 Lewin, *S.E. India,* 250.

71 Baden-Powell, *Land-Syst.,* I, 152, 153.
72 Reclus, *Prim. Folk,* 148.
73 Skeat and Blagden, *Malay Penin.,* II, 196-197.
74 Bastian, *Deut. Exped.,* II, 14.

by general consent than from any authority lodged in the chief. His power, indeed, is one of persuasion, and depends upon his personal ability, nor can he in any way coerce his people to obedience."[75] He settles all disputes among the inmates of the long village-house, and decides the amount of the fine the guilty party has to pay. Great deference is paid him and the people generally abide by his decisions.[76] The Chinese settlements in Borneo had the system of a village-patriarchate, which revealed the sentiment of the village-dwellers that they were all of one kin. "The patriarch is the central point, the core about which the whole village is built, the heart out of which all the arteries branch, the knot into which all the bonds that tie together the villagers, run together." Respect for parents and the aged unites them all.[77]

In Sumatra the government is monarchical only in name. The ruler is chosen by a council and is only president of it. Princes care for nothing but the fines which they levy arbitrarily upon the rich and noble, who recoup themselves by plundering the people.[78] Yet Sumatra has had her heroic ruler, one who combined tact and firmness and brought Atjeh from a low condition to one of great prosperity. He was "cruel and of a very irritable character that tolerated no opposition and above all no injustice."[79] The Philippine chiefs attained their offices by valor or inheritance and held territory in proportion to their valor.[80] The Moro *datto* Pedro Cuevas was an escaped convict of high courage who attained chieftainship by his valor and by killing his predecessor. His despotism was absolute, and he had the fierce Moros in complete subjection. Any objection to orders was met with: "Cut off his head!"[81]

The government of Núkuóro resembles that once existent in the Tonga Islands, in that there are two heads, a secular and a religious. The former office descends from father to children regardless of sex, and the chief selects his successor. The other chief heads the priesthood and has to do with religion only, but to all appearance he is the object of more respect than the secular chief. Succession is rapid, being in favor of the oldest man among the people, even though he is not a priest and must first be initiated. The secular head—in the case reported, a woman—has the same rights as anyone else and moves without distinction among the people; no one needs to bow to her or render gifts, and she has to earn her living along with her family like all the rest. But as soon as a secular chief begins to function as such, he has absolute power, which he wields in connection with certain religious ceremonies. He has the taboo at his disposal, but must use it according to custom. "He may not impose or raise the taboo capriciously, and the exercise of it has either a religious, that is, less understandable, sense, or aims at an obvious utility for the society. For instance, no breadfruit trees may be felled for canoe-building without asking permission of the chief, who must be paid for every tree which he assigns." The chief also initiates the religious festivities that usher in the harvest; and he has a monopoly of all turtles.[82]

On the island of Yap, "the chief of the village has no right to punish, but only the over-chief"; but even so only in certain cases and on appeal; "so he does not mix himself *ex officio* in the affairs of his subjects, neither in the matter of property-law nor of criminal law. There is therefore no general gov-

75 Roth, *Sarawak*, I, 265; II, clxvii, 225; Nieuwenhuis, *Borneo*, II, 127.
76 Gomes, *Sea Dyaks*, 88.
77 DeGroot, *Kongsiwezen*, 83-86.
78 Ratzel, *Vkde.*, II, 444.
79 Jacobs, *Groot-Atjeh*, I, 231.
80 Montero y Vidal, *Filipinas*, I, 49.
81 Worcester, *Philippine Isl.*, 144 ff.
82 Kubary, *Núkuóro*, 9, 16-18.

ernmental criminal court, but the proposition stands: Where there is no plaintiff there is no judge. It is each Yap-native's own affair to get justice for himself and to gather the evidence for it."[83] On Chatham Island "they had no hereditary rule. The best fisherman or bird-catcher or one who distinguished himself over others by several superiorities was regarded as leader."[84] On Tahiti the people used to hide their possessions when the king and queen were to come by.[85] The chief in the Marquesas did not have much respect paid to him; the people were equal among themselves; they had not reached the Tahitian degree of civilization, and difference of rank did not take place among them. No particular honor was paid to the king, whose preëminence appeared only in his dress. In the Tongan Islands, the Hervey Islands, and elsewhere, there were both sacred kings and secular ones; while in Samoa certain great orator-chiefs were regarded as semi-divine, as they were the preservers of the traditions and genealogies and were consulted as diviners with reference to all important decisions. In Tahiti the highest civil and sacerdotal offices were united in one person; the king was generally chief priest of the national temple, and on many occasions of worship he was the representative of the god. Priestly duties were as commonly performed by the chiefs in different parts of Polynesia as were economic and general administrative affairs.[86]

The following facts are culled from the lengthy and painfully detailed work of Williamson[87] on the social and political systems of Central Polynesia. In the Hervey Islands there were three great offices: those of the secular head chiefs, of the "rulers of food," and of the sacred or praying chiefs. The first were warrior-rulers, whose selection and succession depended upon victories; the rulers of food attended to the economic needs; the sacred chiefs warded off, by means of rhythmical prayers of great antiquity, evil-minded spirits which might injure the island. The secular chief had to obey the sacred one; even in case of war, the latter had to offer human sacrifices beforehand and terminate hostilities by beating the drum of peace. "It sometimes happened that the temporal lord was at enmity with the king of his day. In that case the king would refuse to complete the ceremonies for his formal investiture; life would remain unsafe; the soil could not be cultivated, and famine soon followed. This state of misery might endure for years, until the obnoxious chief had in his turn been despatched." If the religious chief would not beat the drum of peace, the shedding of blood would continue indefinitely; "after the beating of the drum of peace, on the other hand, it was unlawful for any one even to carry a weapon, or even to cut down ironwood, which might be used for making weapons. . . . In Tonga the office of the sacred king . . . was distinct from that of the secular king, . . . though the legends suggest that at one time the two had been united." The former was hereditary, the latter subject to the vicissitudes of war. The author cites many cases where there was no separation or an indication of former union. "The Polynesian chiefs as a class, claimed and were accorded an inherent element of sanctity, the more important of them being in some islands credited with actual divinity or something closely approaching it." The author has a chapter (XXX) on the connection between the sacred and secular offices, showing all degrees of connection.

83 Senfft, in *Globus*, XCI, 171.
84 Weiss, *Chatham Isl.*, 19.
85 Letourneau, *Prop.*, 64.
86 Williamson, *Cent. Polyn.*, I, 82, 84, 131-132, 169, 430; II, 111, 356-357, 359-361, 396, 398; III, 34-35, 39, 41, 103, 105, 323, 362-363; Turner, *Samoa*, 172-175.
87 I, 252, 254, 256-257, 418-421; III, 32-33, 45-46, 53-54, 55, 87-88, 97-99, 189-192, 207, 210, 211, 212, 213, 396-400.

"I think the evidence is sufficient to justify us in believing that the head of a social group, large or small, the holder of its title or name, was recognized widely as its natural priest." It is recorded that "in Tonga the priests knew that the existence of their order depended upon the union of church and state, and that their oracular utterances . . . were always directed to upholding the privileges of the chiefs. Between the two orders there was a thorough understanding. The chief saw that the regular offerings to the spirits were not stinted; the priest, possessed by his god, retained sufficient self-command to gasp prophecies in remarkable accordance with the chief's interest. . . . The king stood at the head of all the chiefs on the one hand, and of all the priests on the other; consequently these two bodies supported their common head, while he protected and aggrandized each in return, to secure his own ascendancy." This last case refers to the Society Islands, where the secular and religious functions were united; similarly in the Marquesas Islands, "the political authority blended with the sacerdotal, and the government became perfectly theocratic. . . . Any marked division between the political authority of the chiefs and the religious authority of the priest was rarely seen. . . . In the island of Niue . . . a perfect understanding existed between priests and petty chiefs, to their mutual advantage, for the chiefs could not afford to ignore the political influence of the priests, and the latter, knowing that a chief could invoke a god without their aid, realized that they were not indispensable."

Williamson takes up somewhat the character of the chief. "Just as in Melanesia a man . . . became a chief by virtue of the belief that he was possessed of *mana* derived from a spirit; so in Polynesia, with its theism, his holding of his high office may well have been based upon a belief as to his supernatural powers derived from the gods, and his power of approaching the gods, learning their wishes and intentions, and assuaging their anger and securing their help by sacrifice and prayer." The author concludes that such a chief had first both secular and religious functions, but later handed over the former to others, or lost them for some reason, and devoted themselves to the gods. It is recorded of a king of Hao Island that he possessed very great virtue or power (*mana*). He had a large body and could hold four men's heads in his hands. He knew what passed everywhere, for his evil spirits told him. Thus a powerful frame was interpreted as a spiritual gift. "The French missionaries say that the chief of the island carried their catechist Murphy on his back from the shore to his house; and their explanation is that the people believed from his [Murphy's] greater bulk, as compared with that of the other missionaries, that he was a chief." They probably suffered some disillusionment when Murphy turned out to be an underling.

"The subject of the powers of the chiefs has to be considered from more points of view than one. There was their political power in connection with the general administration and control of the internal affairs of the areas or peoples over whom they ruled, and their power relating to external matters, including such questions as those of peace and war. . . . Much would depend upon the character, ability, personality and conduct (good or bad) of a chief, as displayed both in dealing with his own subjects, in external political enterprises and intrigues, and in war; and upon the corresponding qualities of those who might oppose him. . . . Their position as the heads of social groups over which they ruled would in itself give them the power possessed in a greater or less degree by the heads of all groups, great or small. . . . The amount of control over his subjects that rested with a man who could himself, or through the mouth of a priest, announce to them the wishes and intentions of the gods must have been great. There was also the supporting power of cursing" and that "of controlling food supply and of imposing a taboo, which also had a supernatural foundation. This power was in some cases used by chiefs for the benefit of the community, . . . but it was also used by them as a means of enforcing their authority, . . . of punishing those who had offended them, and in other ways for their own personal benefit. . . . On the other hand, the subjects of the chief had, . . . at all events in some of the islands, a means of defence in their power of deposing a chief who was guilty of misrule, or of excessive oppression of his people." The author gives a number of examples of deposition, in some cases involving a death-sentence; one instance represents a chief as being deposed because he showed himself "too authoritative, exacting, greedy and cruel"; again, because of a practice "of waylaying children and taking their fish." In one case, after a deposition, a tribe is said to have lived afterwards without a chief.

Among the Maoris there was "no proper form of government. A republic with leading men, or an oligarchy with a very large aristocratic class, partly describes the system. It was not a republic because the rights of heredity and of primogeniture were enforced; it was not an oligarchy because every free man was a member of the council. There was no king; the chief was head of his tribe, and when several tribes united for war, the best fighting man was made leader. The Ariki was the first-born of the elder branch, the head of the clan, priest as well as chief. To him descended the high ancestral knowledge, the command of the most potent charms and spells, the right of precedence everywhere. If the first-born was a female, she received the title of Ariki. . . . She was very powerful in the tribe, though being a woman she had not all the privileges, could not lead in war, lift the blood-*tapu*, etc. . . . The power of an ordinary chief in peace time was not great; and, however influential, he could not *compel* the men to do anything—he really had little authority except over his own family and slaves. The Ariki who could *tapu* the whole place or fleet was a power, and any chief could *tapu* a thing by naming it after himself, his head, etc., but if a stranger or greater man came along he could break the *tapu* of the lesser with impunity."[88]

The shaman was at one time the most highly revered person among the Tlinkits; next to him in station came the chief. "The chief is not only respected by all classes in his community, but throughout the entire country, no one daring to give him umbrage except one of his own class or rank. . . . None of a lower rank is allowed to build so large a house as his, or give a greater potlatch." The chief has the ruling voice in the adjudication of all affairs involving the tribe.[89] The Tsimshian chief seems to have been able to wield almost autocratic power, provided his personality was strong enough. "The chief has to carry out the decisions of the council; more particularly, he has to declare peace and war. His opinion must be asked by the tribe in all important events. He decides when the winter village is to be left, when the fishing begins, etc. The first fish, the first berries, etc., are given to him. It is his duty to begin all dances. He must be invited to all festivities; and when the first whistles are blown in winter, indicating the beginning of the dancing-season, he receives a certain tribute. People of low rank must not step up directly to the chief,

---

88 Tregear, in JAI, XIX, 112, 113.   89 Jones, *Thlingets*, 61, 62, 201-202.

whose seat is in the rear of the house, but must approach him going along the walls of the house."[90] There were but two classes or social divisions among the Salish: the chiefs and the people. The principal duties of the chief consisted in maintaining order in the village, deciding disputes and looking after the poor and aged. His privileges lay mainly in the honor of his position.[91] The first duty of the Cheyenne chief was to take care of widows and orphans; the second, to act as peacemaker.[92] Among the Pawnees, though the chieftainship was hereditary, "authority could be gained only by acknowledged personal accomplishments." There were four chiefs of different grades, "but often some warrior who held no office, and bore no title might wield more power and influence than any of these."[93] The Omaha chiefs were "respected not only because of their authority, but as having been favored by the unseen powers, who had granted them help and had strengthened their ability to be steadfast in purpose during the years wherein they struggled to perform the acts required to enter the rank of chief." Like other of the Indian chiefs they had sacerdotal functions. Despotism was very rare among the Indians.[94]

The Aztecs had a theocratic, monarchical system. "Of the monarch it was believed that like the modest sorcerer of a primitive tribe he could make rain or good weather, and at his coronation he had to swear to keep the sun regularly on its course, cause the clouds to pour down rain, the rivers to flow, and the grain to ripen."[95]

The Guiana chief sets the days for festivals and dances, gives the commands to set food before the guests, and calls to council at need. "He never gives his orders in imperious wise, but suggests them, as it were, for the free choice of his subjects. But he is an unlimited ruler in war-time. He gets part of every hunter's and fisherman's catch." Among the Caribs only courage and bravery receive acclaim; the wilder the former and the more striking the latter, the more does the hero's name resound in the war-songs. The candidate for chief has to go through the most cruel and difficult tests of his courage, endurance, and steadfastness; for instance, after a most severe and protracted fast, he must drink a large calabash of strong capsicum mixture without making any faces about it. Then he is laid in a hammock full of big ants, wrapped up in it, and subjected for hours to the attacks of the infuriated insects; and he must not move or sigh under the torture. "If he withstood all these tests with fresh courage, he was recognized as chief with cries of joy; his will was henceforth that of the whole society."[96] Among the Shingu Indians there were in all the larger villages several chiefs, only one of whom, however, represented the community. He was a sort of house-father on a grand scale, but had to be generous in order to keep the esteem of the others. The hereditary Bororo chief commands in war and ordains the hunt in peace; but the medicine-man is really more important.[97] The Shingu chief has no special privileges. He keeps order, directs cultivation, represents his village to visitors, and settles quarrels; but he may not punish.[98]

90 Boas, in BAE, XXXI, 499.
91 Hill-Tout, in JAI, XXXIV, 317-318.
92 Grinnell, *Cheyenne*, I, 336 ff.
93 Grinnell, *Folk-Tales*, 260.
94 Fletcher and LaFlesche, in BAE, XXVII, 201-202, 206-207, 601-602; HAI, II, 461, 819; Parsons, in AA, XX, 172-173.

95 Bancroft, *Nat. Races*, II, 143, 147; III, 295.
96 Schomburgk, *Brit.-Guiana*, II, 321, 430-431; Roth, in BAE, XXXVIII, 568-570, 576.
97 Von den Steinen, *Zent. Bras.*, 330, 500; Frič and Radin, in JAI, XXXVI, 388.
98 Koch, in *Mitth. Anthrop. Gsllsft. Wien*, XXXIII, 21.

The Botocudo chief exercises little power. His office is not hereditary, and his influence does not always suffice to smooth out the quarrels of even his own community—quarrels whose occasion is mostly provided by the women. A successful champion in a dispute often becomes chief.[99] In general in Brazil, only personal characteristics raise one to be leader—bodily strength, courage, wisdom, and ambition. Among the rudest tribes the chief stands forth but slightly from the mass. "Cannibals, who scarcely speak the native language, neither know nor tolerate any conception of leadership, in their dull pride wishing only to rule themselves. They have unconsciously become subjects out of laziness, vanity, and selfishness. For it is solely the relations with the whites which the chief knows how to manage for them all, that seem to have given him the ascendancy that he maintains among his fellows. From being a trading-commissioner he has become ruler of the horde."[100]

Even the Inca of Peru was restrained from action contrary to his tribesmen's interest and to custom; and there was alongside the tribal chief an influential spiritual chief. The two bore something the relation to each other that the Japanese Mikado and Shogun reveal; but the actual rule was fully in the secular chief's hands and the other was more and more restricted to purely priestly functions.[101] In the central Chaco the chiefs own the hunting-grounds and the standing of each depends upon the quantity of game he controls, which brings followers to him. In Paraguay, "the power of the chief is very limited and consists only in the ordering of the internal relations of the tribe"[102]—this despite the warlikeness of the tribes. Though the South American nomads of the plains are warlike, their political organization is loose. A rich chief may be able to gather followers at command, but in most cases the popular assembly is the deciding power.[103] Among the Araucanians "a chief's importance, socially and politically, depended directly on the number of male relations he could muster and on the number of unmarried daughters (basis of future alliances and riches) that he possessed."[104]

"Until shortly before the conquest, Teneriffe was one consolidated monarchy governed by two kings—one living, one dead. The latter remained until his successor died, when his body was removed to the common resting-place of kings, or, according to one authority, was thrown into a pit." When a new ruler came to the throne—a stone covered with skins—he was presented with the royal humerus, which served as a scepter and was carefully preserved in a leather case. Some say that he received the skull of a predecessor. The oath of office ran: "I swear by the bone of him who has borne the crown, to follow his example and to seek the happiness of my subjects." The under-chiefs swore allegiance upon this bone.[105]

A function of the chief which, although already alluded to, deserves special consideration is the regulation of industry. We have here probably the prototype of state aid to and regulation of agriculture, commerce, and other branches of industry. The chief in the Loyalty Islands fixes the time for the gathering of the harvest, and receives its first-fruits.[106] One South African chief fixes

99 Von Martius, *Beiträge*, I, 325; Keane, in JAI, XIII, 207.
100 Von Martius, *Beiträge*, I, 59, 60; Spix and Martius, *Bras.*, 1241, 1242.
101 Cunow, *Verf. d. Inkareichs*, 65, 66, 67.

102 Frič, in *Globus*, LXXXIX, 232; Koch, in *Globus*, LXXXI, 44.
103 Ratzel, *Vkde.*, II, 666.
104 Latcham, in JAI, XXXIX, 356-357.
105 Cook, in AA, II, 484-485.
106 Ray, in JAI, XLVII, 290.

the price of goats; no one dare ask more.[107] Amongst the Zulus the king sets the time for planting,[108] while in Togo no one may sow or harvest his yams and other plants without the permission of the priest.[109] The Somal chief is the only merchant; no subject may deal directly with strangers.[110] Among the Hovas, the government has free disposition of all subjects, and service to the state is demanded of all. "There is no payment for services rendered to the state, which is a most significant fact, on account of the extension of governmental power, and especially because the ministers of state are the chief merchants of the country. Not the least of the useful services which the Europeans have rendered to the social and economic welfare of the Hovas consists in the introduction of the wages system."[111]

Sikhim, in the Himalayas, has a sort of feudal or still more primitive government, which forces the people, other than the priests or lamas, to work for it whenever and wherever called on, without remuneration. On one occasion an uproar was made by the peasantry and serfs as a protest against a demand for forced labor, which they deemed unusually excessive and grievous.[112] The regular officials of a Sema village are five: the chief, the priest, the first reaper, the burier, and the divider of meat. It is the priest's business to initiate the sowing and to announce all the taboos for crops. From the point of view of religious ceremonial, he is the most important person in the village.[113] In Burma the chief superintends the gathering of the crops,[114] while in British North Borneo the chiefs decide on the farming-grounds for the year, a decision which is founded on information supposed to be vouchsafed by the birds of omen.[115]

In the Polynesian Islands commerce was carried on by or for the chiefs, which was favorable to its development because only they were capable of managing large expeditions, having both authority and knowledge. As especially good merchants are mentioned the Tongans, who carried on the trade between Fiji and Samoa.[116] Net-making for salmon in Polynesia was an affair of state; "the salmon net is seldom possessed by any but the principal chiefs."[117] In Tongatabu there was an important administrator "who controlled the food supply, inspecting, with the help of his deputies, all the produce of the island, giving directions as to cultivation, seeing that every man cultivated his quota, presiding over the food taboo, ordering what should and should not be eaten, and interdicting consumption of any form or forms of food of which a shortage seemed likely, not merely on account of drought, but in consequence of lavish consumption involved in the entertainment of visitors or the holding of a great festival, or arising from war."[118]

The chief of the Sitka Indians has always the entire management of all the trade belonging to his people, and takes infinite pains to dispose of their furs advantageously. "The moment a chief has concluded a bargain he repeats the word *Coo coo* twice, with quickness, and is immediately answered by all the people in his canoe with the word *Whoah,* pronounced in a tone of exclamation, but with greater or less energy, in proportion as the bargain he had made is approved."[119] Among the Pawnees, buffalo-hunts were tribal, and in conducting

107 Bent, *Mashonaland,* 23.
108 Ratzel, *Vkde.,* I, 250.
109 Fies, in *Globus,* LXXX, 382.
110 Ratzel, *Vkde.,* I, 431.
111 Ratzel, *Vkde.,* II, 513.
112 Waddell, *Himalayas,* 104.
113 Hutton, *Sema Nagas,* 216.

114 Oliveira Martins, *Raças,* II, 113.
115 Roth, *Sarawak,* I, 397.
116 Ratzel, *Vkde.,* II, 350.
117 Mason, *Invention,* 249.
118 Williamson, *Cent. Polyn.,* III, 324-326.
119 Niblack, in USNM, 1888, 338.

them officers were appointed to maintain order so as to permit each family to procure its share of the game.[120] In New Mexico the chief each day announced the tasks of the different families making up the inhabitants of the pueblo.[121] Among the Shingu Indians the chief superintended the planting, and saw to it that the necessary store of meal was laid up. At feasts, and when strangers came, he caused the cakes to be baked and the drink to be prepared. Among the Bororo the chief ordained the hunting-expeditions.[122] Supervision of agriculture was detailed by the Incas to the village-director, who each night gathered the adults together and arranged for their tasks the next day.[123]

The Arabian chief's duties were many and heavy: assistance of his own people in peril; revenge of outrages by aliens; the rendering of justice. Day and night he must be guarding the interests of his people, and in particular must make the rounds of the encampment at night. He must not be overbearing but hospitable and kind.[124]

Homer[125] is very clear upon the advantages of concentration of power and responsibility: "Not good is the rule of many; let *one* be ruler, *one* be king, to whom the son of Kronos has given it." The Homeric king was preëminently a war-chief; and the possession of physical and mental power was indispensable. He must secure victory without and peace and discipline within. He was the preserver of the *themistes*, or mores, "the guardian of those social customs and guarantees which the experience of preceding generations had evolved as rules of proper living. . . . In war and peace the king was the guardian of the social bond and order. Also from the patriarchal organization of the family he took over into the state the function of head-sacrificer. . . . The position was one of power and also of duties and responsibilities; besides the care of the people and their interests, he supervised public works, entertained publicly, and, if he was a good king, took a fatherly interest in his subjects. The position was, of course, one of great honour and emolument, and to be king was great fortune; 'speedily one's house grows rich and himself more highly honoured.' . . . The value of the king to the people was the value of strength and discipline in times of violence."[126]

In ancient Greece, as in old Germany, there were gentes with patriarchal "kings" over them—many of them in one district. If confederated for war or otherwise a chosen leader was set over them all. This was rational and expedient, not natural and necessary according to the blood-tradition. Odysseus was such a leader of gentes in Ithaca, and there was an intrigue to succeed him by marrying his supposed widow. On the larger scale Agamemnon was the chosen chief of the confederated kinglets warring on Troy.[127] But in considering the Homeric king at this time we are already advancing beyond the subject of mere tribal chieftainship.

§156. Succession and Distinction.

WHILE generally in Australia patriarchal dignity alone is recognized, there are hereditary chiefs to be found.[1] "There is an impression among the aborigines that the second son of a chief is generally superior to his elder brother;

120 HAI, II, 215.
121 Nadaillac, *Preh. Amer.*, 240.
122 Von Steinen, *Zent. Bras.*, 330, 500.
123 Cunow, *Inkareich*, 78.
124 Letourneau, *Polit.*, 228.

125 *Iliad*, II, 203-205.
126 Keller, *Hom. Soc.*, 251 ff. (where full references are given).
127 Lippert, *Kgchte.*, II, 524.
1 Bastian, *Deut. Exped.*, II, 13.

and, if proved to be so in fight, the latter gives up his claim as a matter of custom, and the tribe accepts the conqueror as its head."[2] In the New Hebrides and elsewhere in Melanesia, "there are no men distinguished by higher or sacred blood, none who have an official and political position which they inherit and transmit to their posterity"; but in some "Polynesian speaking communities, there are hereditary chiefs, who as children can succeed their fathers, and who alone possess the power of the *tapu*."[3] In one region of New Guinea, "in the succession to chieftainship, an uncle acts for the child chief, though obliged to give all orders in his name."[4] The Fiji institution of "Vasu" seems to have arisen "out of the natural reverence with which the subjects regarded the king's sister's son when he visited his uncle." Vasus [nephews] get gifts wherever they go; they bring them back and share them with the king, so that "the Vasu-right becomes an instrument in the king's hand for ruthlessly plundering the land."[5] In this case, with relationship reckoned in the female line, the nephew is heir-apparent and is endowed with the fetish-quality. In San Cristoval, Solomons, descent is usually reckoned from the mother, but in the clan of the chiefs descent may be reckoned either from father or mother. All men of this clan are called by a term meaning literally "great man," while all men of other clans are "people of no importance."[6] In southern Melanesia the person who succeeds is not the son but the sister's son.[7]

Among the Zulus, "the oldest son of the chief wife is the presumptive heir to the throne; if she has left no male issue the next brother of the dead chief, from the same ruling house, or the male issue of his chief wife succeed. Only in case there are no heirs at all from the original great house does the succession go over to the smaller houses."[8] In Mashonaland the status-wife, whose son is to succeed to the exclusion of all other wives' children, is designated by special insignia which she transfers to the child when it is born.[9] Among the Ovambo the succession goes to the son, or if there is none, to the daughter of the first wife.[10] The king of Uganda, who is an absolute monarch, is chosen from the princes by the prime minister and chief guardian of the princes; he must be of the blood royal. The royal family traces its pedigree through the maternal clan, but the nation through the paternal.[11]

When a king in Uganda dies, the three greatest dignitaries choose his successor from amongst his children, or if they cannot agree, they fight. A boy is always chosen, and his mother is regent, together with the three dignitaries, during his education. The king's brothers are imprisoned during his minority and at its end all but two or three of them are burned. The ones left continue the line.[12] The reigning sovereign of the Bahima, before death, announces who is to succeed him, but, should the chiefs have any special reason for disregarding the late king's wishes, another person is elected from among the princes. "The chief reason for setting aside the former king's selection is, dissolute life or evil temper; the choice of a successor is decided by his qualifications, and not by his seniority; when the chiefs differ about the selection, each party places its candidate at the head of a force, a battle ensues, and the war continues until one or other of the claimants is killed, when the conqueror takes

2 Dawson, *Aust. Aborig.*, 6.
3 Codrington, in JAI, X, 290.
4 Guise, in JAI, XXVIII, 212.
5 §417, of the text; Starcke, *Prim. Fam.*, 92, 286.
6 Fox, in JAI, XLIX, 105.

7 Rivers, *Melan. Soc.*, II, 510.
8 Fritsch, *Eingeb. S.-Afr.*, 92.
9 Bent, *Mashonaland*, 311.
10 Ratzel, *Vkde.*, I, 357.
11 Roscoe, in JAI, XXXII, 62.
12 Ratzel, *Vkde.*, I, 476.

the throne."[13] On the death of the Kavirondo chief his power descends upon the eldest son of his first wife, even though his second or third wife may have borne him a son before the son by the first wife was born.[14] Among some East African tribes chieftainship is hereditary to children; failing them, to brothers; among other tribes, the nephew of the chief succeeds; if none, the chief's sister succeeds.[15] In West Africa, the successor is appointed from among the king's sons. The eldest son is considered the next heir, but state-officers have the power of rejecting him and selecting one of the other children. There are here cases where succession is traced through females, "the heirs to the throne being the king's brothers in order of seniority, or failing these, a sister's son."[16] A king's son expects to succeed, but there is no invariable rule; he may not take the position by force. "He must be chosen; but the choice is limited to the members of one family, in which it is hereditary."[17]

"Despite the enormous distance from Guinea to the Great Lakes of the Upper Nile, the political system is identical, and it is about the same as that of all the countries between"—namely, small, despotic, hereditary monarchies.[18] The chieftainship of the Teda is hereditary, but not to the son. It goes to the oldest surviving member of the family.[19] In one African case, the chief's eldest son, his first wife, and the principal personages must commit suicide on his elevation. This custom "prevents the consequences, often very baneful, of an hereditary monarchy. . . . The king is always elected and his son can never succeed him."[20] The Ainu show no traces of allegiance to a single ruler; each village has its own hereditary chief.[21]

In a number of the Polynesian groups the title passed automatically from a father to his eldest child, whether the child was a boy or a girl. This no doubt means that the succession went to the first-born by the chief's official wife, and not to the first child of any of his wives. In some places the first-born was regarded as especially sacred. In Samoa the rule of primogeniture was not strictly followed, though the authority and title always remained in the same family. The qualifications for succession were: personal characteristics, presence of a claim through descent or adoption, nomination through the testator's will or by the family, and public recognition. There were three families on Bowditch Island from which the king was selected, and they always chose an aged man, holding that a young man was a bad ruler and that mature age was essential to the office. On Easter Island it was the custom for the king, as soon as his eldest son married, to abdicate in the latter's favor, and become an ordinary individual, and as a consequence of this practice they often prevented the royal children from marrying before they had reached an advanced age.[22]

Among the Tsimshian "when a chief dies, the chieftaincy devolves upon his younger brother, then upon his eldest nephew, and, if there is none, upon his niece. The chief's four counselors become the counselors of his successor. When a woman becomes a chief's successor, she also takes his name."[23] The office of head-man or tribal chief among the Salish bands was theoretically elective but practically hereditary. "It was this hereditary character of the chieftaincy

13 Roscoe, in JAI, XXXVII, 97.
14 Northcote, in JAI, XXXVII, 61.
15 Cole, in JAI, XXXII, 321.
16 Ellis, Ewe, 163-164, 177.
17 Nassau, Fetichism, 16.
18 Letourneau, Polit., 89.
19 Ratzel, Vkde., III, 170.

20 Letourneau, Soc., 213.
21 Hitchcock, in USNM, 1890, 432.
22 Turner, Samoa, 268; Williamson, Cent.
Polyn., III, 200, 203, 204, 206, 365, 367, 371, 372, 374, 380, 381, 383.
23 Boas, in BAE, XXXI, 499.

which gave rise to that threefold social division of chiefs, nobles, and base folk, which prevailed among the lower Salish tribes."[24] Among the American Indians generally, the chieftainship was usually hereditary in certain families of the community, although in some communities any person by virtue of the acquisition of wealth could proclaim himself a chief. Descent of blood, property, and official titles were generally traced through the mother.[25] Morgan[26] has explained the rules of succession especially among the eastern tribes: "When the Indian system of consanguinity is considered, it will be found that all the male members of a gens were either brothers to each other, own or collateral, uncles or nephews, own or collateral, or collateral grandfathers and grandsons. This will explain the succession of the office of sachem which passed from brother to brother, or from uncle to nephew, and very rarely from grandfather to grandson. The choice, which was by free suffrage of both males and females of adult age, usually fell upon a brother of the deceased sachem or upon one of the sons of a sister; an own brother, or the son of an own sister being most likely to be preferred. As between several brothers, own and collateral, on the one hand, and the sons of several sisters, own and collateral, on the other, there was no priority of right, for the reason that all the male members of the gens were equally eligible. To make a choice between them was the function of the elective principle."

Where ancient kings tried to consolidate their power by attaching able men to the throne, they still had to take account of the kinship bond by creating relationships and by adoption. To adopt even an adult, the breast was offered. So deeply does the kin-idea cut.[27] In Persia the project of making a noble king was given up, for "although the hero is favored by fortune and has an enlightened spirit, still the choice must fall upon a man of royal blood, who is in possession of memory of the past. With the army it is as with a ship, and the throne of the king is wind and sail for it. Every prince without consciousness of his position is unworthy of the chair of power; we must have a king whose star is victorious, upon whom the grace of God rests, and whose words radiate wisdom."[28] In Arabia the only accord in choosing a khalif was found in the case of an insignificant man. The six captains of Omar were to choose a khalif without delay. Their choice fell upon the eighty-year-old Othman, a feeble character, but of the Prophet's tribe and family. The khalifate passed speedily into an absolute, hereditary monarchy.[29] In a later day "Hungary appears, according to the strength of the parties, as an hereditary or an elective state; but the electors held, with a single exception, to the house of Arpad.[30] The old kin-criterion died a difficult death.

The custom of "tanistry," a system "under which the grown men of the tribe elect their own chief, generally choosing a successor before the ruling chief dies, and almost invariably electing his brother or nearest mature male relative," was preserved for a time in Europe because of the example of the Ottoman sultanate. In that office brother succeeded brother and all traces of election by the people, if it ever existed, were lost. "As followed by the Turks, the system of course excludes females, but it would probably have excluded them at all times, as its main object is to secure a military leader in the maturity

24 Hill-Tout, in JAI, XXXV, 130.
25 Hewitt, in HAI, I, 264, 499; Mooney, in HAI, I, 787; II, 301.
26 Anc. Soc., 72.

27 Maspero, Hist. Anc., II, 487.
28 Justi, Persien, 41.
29 Letourneau, Polit., 232-233.
30 Mayer, Oesterreich, I, 263.

of life." In the house-community, an institution of South Slavonia and neighboring regions, the most important member is the house-chief. He is elected by the collective brotherhood, who choose "a member of the family connected with the common ancestor through descents of primogeniture. Its inclination would be to choose the eldest son of the last chief, but its veneration for age, and its sense of the value of experience as a means of success in the struggle for existence, lead it constantly to elect the next brother of the last administrator."[31]

Distinction. The lower class of the people in some of the South Sea Islands is under complete subjection to the different chiefs, particularly to the king. "If one of them should chance to meet him, he passes him in a bending posture, at the same time repeating a few words, which manifest his obedience"; he nevertheless would go half a mile out of the way to avoid the encounter. The king's wife has respect shown to her by other women.[32] This deference to the ruler may be attributed in part to the belief that he is divine or that he is closely related to the gods. The sacred king in Fiji, for instance, seems to have been connected by office with the gods. "He was bound to uphold religion, and to maintain the custom of cannibalism. His person was peculiarly sacred. He never personally engaged in war. He alone could wear a turban during the drinking of kava. It was taboo to strangle his widow, though some of the widows of other men were always thus destroyed. It was taboo to cry or make lamentation on the occasion of his death. At his death alone was the conch-shell blown, this being a repetition of the ceremony annually practised on the supposed departure from earth of the Fijian Ceres."[33] In the Western Solomons the word which means chief in some places, in others means god. "A ceremony which in Rotuma was celebrated at the tombs of deceased sacred chiefs was in Eddystone of the Solomons performed at the shrines of the gods. The inference is that the Eddystone gods are chiefs and that the institution of divine kingship did once exist in those parts."[34] The etiquette to be observed when encountering the ruler is very strict. In one section, when the great chief comes from his house "no one dare walk about the village in an upright position. Everyone either walks in an abject, stooping position, or in some cases actually crawls on hands and knees, and no one speaks above a whisper when he is talking."[35] If the chief on another one of the islands is in his house, "a visitor who enters will kneel at the door and will move towards his superior on his hands and knees till he reaches him, when the pair touch noses in the customary manner. He then withdraws a pace or two and sits down crosslegged, no other position being allowed in the presence of a chief. The chief would then call out to his wife for food and the pair would talk while eating. When the talk is finished the visitor will ask permission to go and will leave on his hands and knees as he came without turning his back to his superior. If the chief is out of doors when he is visited the man who approaches him will kneel down at a few paces' distance and move towards him on hands and knees to salute him. . . . The sanctity of a chief seems too to be shown by the fact that no woman may go in his canoe which is known as a *tapu* canoe."[36]

Grant[37] was once talking to a Mavenda chief in South Africa when the latter

31 Maine, *Early Law*, 146, 248.
32 Im Thurn, in JAI, LI, 22.
33 Williamson, *Cent. Polyn.*, I, 345-346.
34 Hocart, in JAI, XLIX, 49.
35 Brown, in AAAS, 1898, 795.
36 Rivers, *Melan. Soc.*, I, 305-306.
37 In JAI, XXXV, 266.

had a severe cold; "his breathing was far from easy, and at short intervals he coughed and expectorated freely. Among the Zulu such discharge is invariably removed with a small broom made of grass, but on this occasion the hand of an attendant did duty for the broom, and two *incekus* (attendants) appeared to vie with each other as to who should first render the willing service of rubbing into the ground. During the act of coughing, every man present reverently bowed his head, noiselessly clapped his hands, and in a low tone of voice repeatedly uttered the expression, *Entowoo tobela,* meaning the *lion has done it.*" In court the king of Uganda sits in state upon a stool placed on a leopard-skin over which is spread a lion-skin; no one may step on the royal mat on pain of death. The second officer in the country is the keeper of the royal placenta; each new moon, in the evening, he has to carry this in state, wrapped in bark cloths, to the king. "On the birth of a prince the placenta is dried and preserved, placed in a pot which is made for its reception and sealed up." When a king dies the prime minister becomes the bearer of the jaw-bone which is called the "king" and which is placed with the placenta in the tomb. Directly the new king is elected he is placed upon a large stone on a high hill amid general rejoicing and feasting and is said to have "eaten Buganda." The king never walks anywhere outside his enclosure; he is carried on the shoulders of strong men who go at a quick trot with him.[38] The Ba-Yaka are ruled by one great chief who considers them all his slaves; on entering his presence all prostrate themselves and beat their breasts.[39] The insignia of office of the Wawanga chief of East Africa are the sacred spears, the leopard-skin cloak, and the copper bracelet. "Great importance is attached to this copper bracelet; by virtue of its possession alone does the king hold office." All sorts of superstitions have been woven round the king's copper bracelet by the common people, who regard it with the very greatest awe and reverence. One of these is to the effect that if the king wishes to cause the death of anyone, he can do so by striking together, at dead of night, this bracelet with another one he wears on the other wrist, pronouncing at the same time the person's name. The sacred spears are of a very great age, and several of them are of peculiar pattern and workmanship. The king has a prerogative to the tusks and tails of dead elephants, to all skins of leopards and lions, to the monopoly of sleeping on a lion-skin or wearing a leopard-skin cloak and of wearing certain stones and beads, to the skin and certain meat of the hippopotamus, and to all buffalo-skins, which last he gives to warriors to make shields. No one may sit on a stool or chair in his presence.[40]

The cruelty of despots always seems to engender politeness. The freest nations are generally the rudest in manners. An Indian official once remarked to Sir Harry Johnston that the excessive, deep-seated, elaborate politeness of the natives of India was due to the two thousand years' "whacking" they had received from dynasty after dynasty of cruel despots. "So it has been in Uganda. The chiefs and people became fastidiously prudish on the subject of clothing, and regarded a nude man as an object of horror. They preferred in their language not to call a spade a spade, but to substitute for any plain noun dealing with sex or sexual intercourse the politest and vaguest of paraphrases. Yet the nation was profoundly immoral, and the dances in vogue even at the present day can be exceedingly indecent. But the race became, and remains, the politest

38 Roscoe, in JAI, XXXII, 43-45, 62-63, 65.   40 Dundas, C., in JAI, XLIII, 21, 24, 25,
39 Torday and Joyce, in JAI, XXXVI, 44.   26-28.

in Africa."[41] In the Central African Lake region the mode of salutation is most elaborate. "An inferior in saluting a superior takes a piece of dried mud in his right hand; he first rubs his left arm above the elbow and his left side; then throwing the mud into his left hand, he in like manner rubs the right arm and side, all the time muttering away inquiries about their health. In making speeches the speaker always commences with the same salutation, and each time the chief's name is mentioned every one begins rubbing his breast with mud."[42]

On the Congo, shooting-stars and comets are supposed to signify the death of a great chief.[43] A chief in the Niger Protectorate never allows a native below him in rank to have an umbrella open before him, so an inferior closes his umbrella on approaching a chief, while the chief keeps his umbrella open.[44] On the Loango Coast the king has six titles connecting him with six divisions of sacred symbols; and an iron bell is the emblem of royal dignity.[45] In northeast Africa the symbol of power consists of several rods overlaid with metal-work, which the sultan sends by his soldiers to those places where he intends to extend his dominion.[46] The chiefs of the Dinka and the kings of the Shilluk are regarded as beings almost divine, upon whose correct conduct the preservation, or at least the welfare, of their people depends. "In fact, they belong to that class of ruler to whom Professor Frazer applies the name Divine Kings, believed to incarnate the divine spirit, and who were periodically killed lest that spirit should suffer from its retention in an ageing body. Every Dinka high chief is killed in his old age, this being done at his own request with all ceremony and reverence. The Shilluk king was also slain by his subjects, nor was his death postponed until, in his old age, he felt that he had done all that he could for his people, but he was killed while still in vigorous middle age directly his wives complained that his generative faculties were weakening."[47]

It is said that when a Genoese merchant in Tamerlane's camp declared that an act of Tamerlane was cruel, the latter was very angry, and asserted that he was not a man as other men, but sent by God for the destruction of the world.[48] The onerous life of semi-divine kings described by Frazer is led by several chiefs of northeast India.[49] In ancient India "every king is regarded as little short of a present god. In Manu's law-book a king is said to be created by drawing eternal particles from the essence of the eight guardian deities. . . . Again, he says, 'A king, even though a mere child, must not be treated with contempt, as if he were a mortal; he is a great divinity in human shape.' "[50] In general, we are confining our examples to primitive peoples, but we may bring them into relief by citing cases like the above and also the Chinese and Japanese theories. "In China the emperor is the second being of the whole universe; nobody is above him but the God of Heaven, the highest deity of the Pantheon, of whom he is the only son and vice-regent on earth. As over all human beings, he also bears sway over all divinities; and even these stand in rank and position below a mandarin in his quality of imperial proxy."[51] In Japan, "implicit obedience to the Mikado is required. It is admitted that he

---

41 Johnston, *Uganda*, II, 685.
42 Roth, in JAI, XIX, 176.
43 Weeks, in JAI, XL, 398.
44 Granville and Roth, in JAI, XXVIII, 123.
45 Bastian, *Deut. Exped.*, I, 54; Dennett, in JAI, XXXV, 48.

46 Paulitschke, *Nordost-Afr.*, II, 126.
47 Seligmann, in JAI, XLIII, 664.
48 Mexia, *Vida del Gran Tamorlan*.
49 Godden, in JAI, XXVI, 169.
50 Monier-Williams, *Brāhmanism*, 259; *Laws of Manu*, VII, 4, 8.
51 DeGroot, *Relig. Syst.*, I, 220.

may not always be good, but as his real character is that of a god, his authority is never to be disputed. It is a remarkable fact that never during the history of Japan have the people knowingly rebelled against or opposed the will of the Mikado. They have been misled at times by designing leaders, but in intent they have ever been faithful. The possession of the Mikado's person has always been a source of strength to either of the contending forces."[52]

In Sumatra the orders of the sultan of Atjeh are first communicated to a woman who stays at his feet. She tells them to a eunuch, who transmits them to an officer, who, finally, proclaims them before the assembly.[53] In Celebes the sign of respect for rank is to take a garment from the shoulders and wind it loosely around the hips.[54] In Java "it is respectful to cover the head, instead of uncover it; to sit instead of stand. It is the very highest degree of respect to turn one's back upon a superior, and often presumption to confront him. It is the custom to sit cross-legged and on the ground. When an inferior addresses a superior, his obeisance consists in raising his hands, with the palms joined before his face, until the thumbs touch the nose. This he repeats at the end of every sentence, and if very courtly, at the conclusion of each clause. When equals meet, their salutation is cold and distant, but in the ordinary intercourse of life, a relative superiority or inferiority of condition is usually confessed, and a demonstration of it constantly takes place. If a son has been long absent from his father, he throws himself at his feet and kisses them. A demonstration of affection, less profound, would extend the embrace only to the knee, but a very obsequious courtier will sometimes take his monarch's foot and place it on his head. . . . An inferior never stands upright before a superior. If he stands at all, the body is always bent; if he sit, it is the same thing, and his eyes are fixed to the ground. When he advances and retires, he moves as if on all-fours, and crawls or creeps rather than walks. There is one mode of demonstrating affection and respect, particularly nauseous and indelicate. It consists in the superior's offering to the inferior the chewed refuse of the betel and areca preparation as a mark of great affection, which the latter swallows with much satisfaction."[55] When the Rajah of Lombok, Malay Archipelago, appears, all the people squat down upon the ground in respect, and every man riding gets down off his horse and squats. The highest seat is literally the place of honor and the sign of rank. "So unbending are the rules in this respect, that when an English carriage which the Rajah of Lombok had sent for arrived, it was found impossible to use it because the driver's seat was the highest, and it had to be kept as a show in its coach-house."[56]

In Polynesia and Micronesia the presence of princes on earth is taken to be only an episode in the heavenly existence of god-born beings. A fate holds them here and they return only as souls. In Hawaii there was a peculiar court language, unknown to the people—or if it became known, the chiefs altered it. In Tahiti words which were holy, because they entered into the names of chiefs, must be replaced by others. There was no crime for the blood-royal. Flattery overpowered the infantile minds of the chiefs so that they came to believe all that was said of them.[57] The Samoans had two entrances to the spirit-world,

52 Hitchcock, in USNM, 1891, 504.
53 Marsden, *Sumatra*, 402.
54 Jäger, *Handwörterbuch, sub* Bugi.
55 Crawfurd, *Hist. Ind. Archip.*, 98-99.

56 Wallace, *Malay Archip.*, 219-220, 171, 180.
57 Ratzel, *Vkde.*, II, 199-200; Letourneau, *Morale*, 217.

one for chiefs and the other for common people. The dignity of chiefs was here too recognized by a court language, and their rank was distinguished by special words regarding their presence and speech. The people either squatted or stooped in the presence of chiefs.[58] The practice of killing the king once prevailed in Niue, and there resulted an unwillingness to take office. Turner[59] thinks the usage was due to the belief that the kings caused the fruit to grow; in times of scarcity the angry people killed them. On another island, the king was charged with the special duty of uttering prayers so as to keep away the evil spirits that might injure the land.[60] The Maori chief was looked upon as the counterpart of the gods. "He was the representative, the resting place, of the gods in this world. Also, he was extremely *tapu*, so much so that he could not keep himself clean. His head could not be washed, or his hair dressed, because of this intense state of *tapu*. Hence his hair became matted and dirt-laden."[61] The chief in Kushai, in the Caroline Islands, seemed to be an absolute ruler "and was treated by the people with a degree of subjection that I met nowhere else. In the presence of the exalted pair speech must be only low; the people approached with humble demeanor and crawled almost on their knees up the steps of the veranda where they set down baskets of food and other tribute. With exception of the chiefs and their kinsmen everybody must work for the ruler, who gives land only as a loan for which return in kind is given."[62] The chiefs let their beards grow for the sake of respect; their subjects heard their orders with lowered eyes and obeyed blindly.[63]

In Ponapé "so great respect is accorded the king that no one goes to his house except the two or three principal chiefs, and they sit down inside the house, but near the door and on the ground; the rest of the tribe come no nearer than its threshold, remaining outside. The women, when they pass before the king's house, do so bending over and if they are in the field when he goes by, they squat on one side or the other of the path he follows." At the great annual festivals the wives of the chiefs are not allowed to be present because it was forbidden the lower classes, under penalty of death, to see them.[64] The first chief of Núkuóro was raised to be a god and his soul is honored in the form of a stone on the public square.[65] The ruler of Tonga is a priest-king. He must marry the daughter of his brother, who is civil governor. When she has had one or two children she is taken away from him. Her son becomes the next chief and her daughter's dignity is very great. "Her rank is too high for her to marry any mortal, but she may have a family, and in case of the birth of a *daughter*, this child becomes the *Tomaha*, who rises higher than her mother in rank and is nearer the gods. Everyone approaches her with gifts and homage. Her grandfather will bring his offerings and sit down before her. Sick people come to her for cure."[66]

The omission of the American Indians, with the exception of the advanced groups of Maya, Aztecs, and Incas, from this account of subservience to the chief and belief in the divinity of kings, is noteworthy. In Homer the divine right of kings is recognized at times. The king not only is leader in war and the first in the council, but also represents his people before the gods. At the

58 Ella, in AAAS, 1892, 631, 642, and in AAAS, 1895, 598; Pratt, in AAAS, 1887, 448.
59 *Samoa*, 304 ff.
60 Gill, in AAAS, 1890, 634-635.
61 Best, in AAAS, 1909, 463.
62 Finsch, *Ethnol. Erfahr.*, III, 199.

63 Montero y Vidal, *Filipinas*, I, 470.
64 Pereiro, *Ponapé*, 111-112; Friederichsen, *Ruinen auf Ponapé*, 12.
65 Kubary, *Núkuóro*, 9.
66 March, in JAI, XXII, 318.

feast of the Achæan council before setting out for the first battle of the Iliad, Agamemnon offers the prayer for the sacrifice, as the head of the public family, and at the making of the truce for a single combat, he prays to the gods and cuts the throats of the lambs.[67] Among the ancient Hebrews the difference between judge and king was that between an elected official and a ruler appointed by God. While the right of the latter was divine, he felt himself to be the son of God, appointed to be first among men, and ruled under the divinity whose interpreter was the priest. The king united in himself the highest priestly dignity, while the judge had only two royal functions: that of chief officer in times of peace, and in war that of commander-in-chief. As the kingship became weaker, the influence of the priests on legislation and the administration of justice became greater until both were completely in their hands.[68] In ancient Sweden the King at Upsala is called by the bards "the keeper of the holy altar"; in fact, the sacrifices at Upsala were the foundation of the claim of that district to give a king to all Sweden.[69] With a genuine civilization equal in degree to that of their kindred in Britain and Scandinavia, the Germans of continental Europe found themselves called upon to live up to the elaborate civilization of the Roman Empire. They broke down under the strain. "Just as a party of savages will disport themselves in the garments of a shipwrecked crew, so the Merovingian and Karolingian kings and officials decked themselves with the titles, prerogatives, and documents of the Imperial State. No doubt the wisest of them, such as Charles the Great, had a deliberate policy in so doing. But the majority seem to have been swayed simply by vanity, or ambition, or admiration."[70]

Revenue. Taxation among the Bawenda of South Africa does not mean a contribution towards the good government of the country for the benefit of the people. It is rather a contribution toward the maintenance of the chief's household and position, either by way of a bribe or a fine, as the case may be. "The Mowenda dare not eat and he dare not drink unless he has first given his share to the chief. . . . The chief's subjects have to assist in building and repairing his houses, they have to work his gardens and to assist in harvesting. He receives part of the value recovered by one party from the other, and all the fines paid. The chief takes the greatest share of all confiscated property. . . . Any case laid before the chief has to be accompanied with a present, in order to find a hearing. This present is given *o wula khoro* (to open the gate). When the matter has been settled, the one who wins the case has to thank the chief again with a present, *o walela khoro* (to shut the gate)."[71] In South Africa, as elsewhere,[72] the chief owns the land and exacts tribute for its use. In many places he can demand work from his subjects.[73] The Marutse chief sends his men into the woods to seek honey; all belongs to him and death is the penalty for diverting any.[74] The taxes due to the supreme chief among the Ba-Yaka are collected by the great man in person, who goes the round of the villages.[75] The Baganda king, on the other hand, has tax-collectors whom he sends out into all parts of the country to gather in the annual revenues; "the office of collector

67 Seymour, *Hom. Age*, 81, 92-93.
68 Schrader, *Keilinschriften*, 214; Maurer, *Vkde.*, I, 148-149.
69 Geijer, *Svensk. Hist.*, 112.
70 Jenks, *Law and Politics*, 17-18.
71 Gottschling, in JAI, XXXV, 376-377.

72 §120, of the text.
73 Stuhlmann, *Mit Emin*, 91, 187, 189, 394; Connolly, in JAI, XXVI, 146.
74 *Illust. Afr.*, Feb., 1896, 7.
75 Torday and Joyce, in JAI, XXXVI, 44.

is highly prized, being a most lucrative one owing to the bribes the man receives; the king's favourites usually secure them." Another prerogative of this king is to get a percentage of the children born to the women he gives in marriage to his retainers. "A mother who does not wish her girl to be taken into the royal harem, makes a scar on her forehead or face, by burning her to disqualify her; because no woman with a scar can become the wife of a king."[76]

The right of a Polynesian chief or other head of a group to tribute in kind or first-fruits was generally enforced, even by raiding the subjects if necessary. In some instances there is evidence that what he receives is, in theory at least, an offering to the gods, handed to him as high priest. On the other hand, there is evidence of a widespread practice whereby chiefs are supplied in a more or less irregular and unsystematic way with food, and in some cases with other goods also. In the Marquesas the kings of districts had the right, in a fruitful season, to one-fourth of the produce of the lands of their subjects, and in other seasons a portion according to circumstances. In the island of Niue there were no taxes beyond the obligation to provide feasts for the councils and occasionally to carry food to the king or to the chiefs of villages. The subjects of a Society Island chief had to supply him with food and other things, while he had the power of confiscation over them. Pritchard says it was a maxim among the Samoans that a chief could not steal; he was merely regarded as taking anything he wanted from his people, and his own immediate followers would be rather flattered than otherwise to think that anything they possessed was coveted by him.[77]

Taxes in the modern sense were unknown to the Homeric Greeks. Though the king received gifts as tribute from his subjects, these gifts were not fixed and definite. Money payments could not be expected at a time when trade was barter; and no fixed ratio, as a tenth of the produce of flocks or fields, was determined for tribute; more than occasional presents, however, are implied in the words of Agamemnon, who offers to Achilles, if he will return to the work of battle, seven well-built cities in which dwell men who "will honor him as a god with gifts, and under his sceptre will pay delightful dues." The king could call upon his subjects for service in war; for the expedition against Troy each household was expected to furnish at least one warrior. If the king went on the foray in person he had a right to his ordinary share of the booty, as well as to his special gift of honor, which was set aside before the general division of the spoil. He had also an apparent right to an invitation to all feasts made by his subjects.[78] Herodotus[79] says that down to the time of Darius, the Persians paid no regular taxes, but brought gifts to the king; while we read that the children of Belial brought to Saul "no presents," that is, they did not recognize his authority.[80]

§157. Women as Rulers.

THE king of Uganda had a co-regent in his sister, and his mother was royal in a secondary degree. A female ruler south of Lake Albert, who had lost control of her chiefs and had very little authority, passed for a witch and might not

76 Roscoe, in JAI, XXXII, 65, 66.
77 Williamson, *Cent. Polyn.*, III, 343, 344, 345, 351-356, 358-360, 400.

78 Seymour, *Homeric Age*, 78-79, 83-85.
79 Herodotus, *Hist.*, III, 89.
80 I Sam., X, 27.

be seen, but received sitting behind a bark curtain. Her chief minister was an ugly old woman. Stuhlmann,[1] who reports these cases, doubts whether she exists and thinks a ventriloquist impersonates her. He tells also how the wife of a Latuka chief succeeds him if he dies childless. If she marries again, her second husband has no share in power nor do her children by him; the heir is her first husband's brother. In one of these equatorial states a unique dignitary is an unmarried woman who decides the selection of the new chief and has her own court and tributary territories. There are two states and two forms of government woven together. She has her man on whom she hangs all the decorations, and this "husband" is designated as a woman. Other tribes have the same tradition as these peoples, about how the kingdom was founded by a hunter who came from abroad and won the love of the ruling queen.[2] Nachtigal[3] found a female ruler in the Sudan. In Madagascar the Hova queen's husband is her prime minister. Three queens succeeded each other with only a short reign of one man between.[4] In the Maldive Islands a queen once ruled in place of her brother who had been deposed for misconduct. Her husband really governed, but entirely in her name.[5]

In one district of Borneo the most influential persons were two old women who had long had the power in their hands; they dressed in men's clothes, took sword and spear in hand, commanding the people in time of war, and working as hard as any of them. A female rajah occasionally appears in the Archipelago; in one case a "colossal woman" whose husband was relegated to insignificance.[6] There were four successive queens in the seventeenth century, in Atjeh, one of the most turbulent states in the Archipelago. "The spirit and the prudence of most of these queens, the policy with which they knew how to hold in equilibrium the parties of jealous and envious nobles, together with the influence of several powerful ministers, seem above all to have rendered that epoch of about sixty years the most peaceful in the annals of Atjeh." The Dutch found a similarly well-governed realm in the hands of a queen, on the east coast of the Malay Peninsula.[7] Celebes is "not the only country of the Archipelago in which women are raised to sovereign authority. There is hardly a country of it in which women have not at one period or another of their history sat on the throne; and it may be said that the practice is most frequent where the government is most turbulent."[8]

In Samoa "every larger community and every political unit possesses a 'taupon,' a maid, as representative, with special rights and duties. She always belongs to the highest family-group of the district or community and remains under strict oversight; her reputation is blameless and must be so so long as she remains in 'office and dignity,' . . . Almost more than in the male representatives of noble families there is incorporated in the taupons the dignity of position, of pride in ancestry with female descent. . . . In general the taupon represents a noble kin-group; she may therefore be ruler over a whole district. Under her then are many others of her kind, of less noble blood." In almost every village there rules a village maid, carefully supervised by older dames. The taupon "along with the first chiefs passes upon public affairs, and above

1 *Mit Emin*, 189, 252, 789; in *Globus*, LXXXVIII, 337, is an account of a visit to this person, who had become the tool of the stronger party in the state.

2 Ratzel, *Vkde.*, I, 563, 598.

3 *Sahara*, II, 675.

4 Ratzel, *Vkde.*, II, 511.

5 Yule, *Cathay*, II, 422.

6 Wilken, in VG, I, 382, 383.

7 Millies, *Récherches*, 88, 89, 91, 149.

8 Crawfurd, *Ind. Archip.*, 75.

all upon the female members of her district of authority."[9] In Micronesia there is a social division of the women parallel to that of the men, so that the women form a special state. In the Pelew group they have a queen of their own, with female chiefs about her. These maintain order among the women and judge them without interference from the men. The system seems to have arisen because the men were so strictly organized by themselves. The women have the right to claim particular taxes with which to celebrate feasts. The title of chief descends from one sister to the next younger. The wife of the king is therefore never the queen of the women, since marriages in the same family are forbidden. In order that the male and female rulers may never be combined or interfere in their spheres, the chief may not marry the daughter of a chief.[10]

"Women in the position of chief were not so rare, among the Indians, as has been thought. The first Spaniards on Haiti found such a phenomenon there, de Soto in Georgia, the Pilgrim fathers in New England, the French among the Natchez, and Juan Rodríguez among the Californians in the Monterey region. Later no more was heard of such female chiefs so that it seems almost as if in this matter too a change had come about after the entrance of the Europeans, as indeed in so many other customs, usages, and conceptions of the New World natives."[11] Newport[12] met a "queen" in Virginia with "rather more majesty" than Powhatan, to whom she was subordinate; she is presented as in full authority over her people. Drake[13] describes two squaw sachems, but without any explanations. One of the tribes of the Carolinas is said to have been ruled by two female chiefs, who held dignified court, with a retinue of young men and women.[14] Much has been made of the political influence of the Iroquois women, but they very seldom became actual chiefs. "Among Iroquois tribes the titles to the chiefships belonged to the women of certain clans in the tribe and not to the men, although men were chosen by the women to exercise the rights and privileges and to perform the duties pertaining to these chiefships." A number of women have filled federal chieftainships, and "these women chieftains have approximately the same rights, privileges, and immunities as the men chiefs, but exercise them fully only in emergencies; they, too, maintain the institutions of society and government among the women." In common with the other tribes of the Iroquoian linguistic stock, the Tuscarora traced the descent of blood through the line of the mother, and made the civil and official military chieftainships hereditary in certain clans over which the woman chiefs and the elder women presided.[15] In the early days of the Massachusetts colonies the widow of a certain Nipmuc chief assumed the chieftaincy and was known as the squaw-sachem of the Nipmuc.[16] Among the Siouans, "women are never acknowledged as chiefs, nor have they anything to say in the council."[17] Among the Haida, "one old dame, who could in appearance and ugliness have shamed Macbeth's witches, was greatly venerated . . . and was importuned at all times to enter their houses and make herself at home. When she condescended to enter their houses there was a special assembly. The children were quieted, and all was dignified. This woman had more authority than any chief. She was a chieftainess, and was descended

9 Reinecke, in *Globus*, LXXVI, 5, 6.
10 Ratzel, *Vkde.*, II, 186, 191.
11 Friederici, in *Globus*, XC, 305.
12 In *Amer. Antiq. Soc.*, IV, 51.
13 *Bk. of Indians*, III, 64.

14 HAI, II, 921.
15 Hewitt, in IIAI, II, 123 (quoted), 849.
16 Thomas, in HAI, II, 23.
17 Dorsey, in BAE, XV, 224.

from a long line of kings of the ages long gone past. She and her husband formerly ruled Queen Charlotte Islands."[18]

A case is mentioned of an old Makusi widow who ruled over an entire settlement, and another case, also in Guiana, where the chief's sister acted for him during his absence.[19] Among the Carib tribes the position of chief is open to women;[20] a female chief has been found in Brazil;[21] and a case where the chief judges the men and his wife the women.[22] In Peru, before the Incas, women held the chieftainship to the exclusion of men.[23] The inhabitants of Grand Canary were for a long time divided into ten tribes, but during the fourteenth century these were united under the control of one woman.[24]

§159. Checks on Monarchy.

AMONG the Bawenda of South Africa the power of the chief is limited by the unwritten law of old customs, and by the council and the witch-doctors. "No law can be made by the chief unless it has been sanctioned by the councillors above mentioned. However, all the honour of ruling is left strictly to the chief, even although the order or decision given may be altogether against his will."[1] A definite aristocratic class is not uncommon among African tribes. "In Upare the village headmen and the chiefs are always of this class. The position and powers of the chief are rather just what he can make them. . . . The real power of the land lies with the elders, who are consulted in all matters. His judicial power the chief shares with the elders and other men distinguished by their intelligence and eloquence. But the council thus formed is little respected by the more powerful individuals, and it is said that in former times it was frequently overawed by the number of armed followers brought by each party, and the proceedings often ended with a free fight in which the chief himself might not be spared."[2] The council of elders was more in the nature of a court of arbitration than of decision. The despotism of the king of Uganda is restricted by the right of asylum to the sacred hills, of which each district has one or more. "Earls and chiefs are frequently deposed or plundered by the king for petty offences, or for becoming too rich, or for making too great a display of wealth; if a chief gets any warning or an idea that he is going to be plundered he removes his cattle and property to one of the sacred hills in the district where they are safe even against the raids of the king; . . . if the person succeeds in reaching the place with his property before the party sent to loot arrives, his goods are secure; after a few days' residence on the hill, when the king's wrath has abated, he is able to return home. Sometimes people are seized by the king and put to death, the property confiscated, and all the family enslaved; if the latter are able to escape to one of the hills they are safe, and members of the clan then see to their future welfare."[3] The Kabyle village assembly attends to all that concerns the general interests of the community, even the most intimate matters of private life. Its often passionate action is counterpoised by its respect for usages consecrated by time. Age,

18 Harrison, C., *Family Life of the Haidas, Queen Charlotte Islands,* reviewed in JAI, XXI, 471.

19 Roth, in BAE, XXXVIII, 573.

20 Smith, *Araucanians,* 242, quoted in Starcke, *Prim. Fam.,* 46.

21 Von Martius, *Beiträge,* I, 267.

22 Ratzel, *Hist. Mankind,* II, 133.

23 Cunow, *Inkareich,* 31.

24 Cook, in AA, II, 487.

1 Gottschling, in JAI, XXXV, 376.

2 Dundas, C., in JAI, LI, 220-221.

3 Roscoe, in JAI, XXXII, 66-67.

position, birth, and personal valor are qualities fitting one to conduct public affairs.[4]

No people in the world are said to be so apathetic as those of Central Asia in the face of any fate whatever which befalls them. They have been trained to this by long submission to despotism and arbitrary abuse. This is why Russian rule was popular; it guaranteed them against any other tyranny.[5] Although the Kuki-Lushai clans are really democratic, they have in them the germs of a monarchical system; "a Lushai chief before our occupation was an autocrat, from whose orders there was no appeal, but if he exceeded the limits set by custom, or was uniformly cruel and unjust, his followers soon deserted him for more tactful rulers."[6] In Bengal the "long-houses have each its chief, but with a council of notables. All is discussed there and the decisions proclaimed outside by young men exactly as with the Redskins.[7] The East Indian chiefs do not stand alone. "Beside them there are always the elders of the families and with them the whole people whom the chiefs must consult in important cases. No arrangement may be made without the agreement of the elders and the consent of the whole people. In the essence of the matter the government is thus not of one head but of many; it is not monarchical but democratic. The chief, the rajah, is in the popular assembly only *primus inter pares*. . . . Every male inhabitant who is head of a kingroup has the right to speak and vote." Oratory is highly esteemed.[8]

Nowhere in Polynesia and Micronesia, however ferocious the despotism, is an intermediary between prince and people wanting; but the relation between ruler and intermediary often amounts to a secret union. In Polynesia the prince is the lord and priest of his people, but not always their military leader. Hence the government is not always simple, and we find a military leader with a nominal king behind him, as in Japan. The nobility also limit the king, while the greatest limitation comes from the council-meeting, in many parts called *fono*. There were several types of councils or assemblies, including a village, a district, or even a whole island. A village *fono* was composed of the chief, the orators, and the heads of families; all affairs of the village came before this body, and from its decision there was no appeal. Nothing was too great or too small for its attention, which would even be given to such matters as an alleged encroachment by a man on a widow's yam-patch or rudeness to a visitor. A great *fono*, that is the council meeting of a district or division or of the whole island, was a more ceremonious affair: it was held for the discussion of weighty matters affecting the whole area which it represented, dealing, among other things, with the appointment and installation of chiefs, and the declaring of war and making of peace. Either the *fono* or a council meeting of some sort was very common in Polynesia, and besides this great check on the powers of the chiefs and kings there was always the restraining influence of custom, while the personal character of the executive was also a factor to be considered. He would be a very bold chief who dared to act in direct opposition to the advice of the heads of families and other influential people.[9] In Micronesia the chief is half a despotic ruler and half president of an oligarchic republic,

4 Hanoteau et Letourneux, *Kabylie*, II, 8, 31-32.
5 *Russian Ethnog.* (Russ.), II, 625.
6 Shakespear, in JAI, XXXIX, 374.
7 Dalton, *Ethnol. Bengal*, 23.
8 Wilken, *Vkde.*, 337, 338, 339.

9 Williamson, *Cent. Polyn.*, I, 438; II, 441-482, 483-485, 489, 490, 492, 493, 494, 495-496; III, 100-101, 111-112, 114-115, 117, 119, 120, 121-122, 124, 125-126, 129-131, 132-133, 135-136.

and must be popular. The king treated commerce and the manufacture of money as monopolies, both of which he could abuse to his personal gain.[10] In the Carolines, the priest is the real leader of the council, for all decisions depend upon his revelations.[11]

As in many another social form, so in the matter of checks on monarchy, the evidence given unpremeditatedly in Homer is copious and typical. The king was the highest power in the government, but he cared for his popularity and did not obstinately oppose the will of the people. In fact, he would make a great personal sacrifice rather than incur the people's censure. "The popular assembly, as a means of taking the sense of public opinion, became a distinctive mark of civilisation. . . . The assembly was closely connected with, if not dependent upon, the kingship; its absence was a proof of anarchy, and in Ithaca coincided with the absence of the king; its renewal, as indicative of a reinstatement of law and order, was hailed with joy by the old and wise. The *agorē*, we find, was primarily a meeting for the discussion of questions affecting the *dēmos*, a gathering which apparently any one (probably of kingly rank) could summon; indeed sometimes the people called the king to assembly. The actual summoning was done by heralds. The ordinary assembly was composed of two parties, the people and the *gerontes*, and among the latter sat the king upon a special seat. It can hardly be said, in a modern sense, that the king presided over the assembly; speakers addressed him, or the people, or both, and the right to speak was conferred by the transfer of the royal sceptre, which was handed by a herald to the one desiring to speak. The assembly was held in a regular place which derived its name from that fact; the head-men sometimes sat upon 'polished stones,' and the place was evidently the most frequented part of the community, resembling the mediaeval *Roland* or *Mal.* The assemblies were regularly convened early in the morning.

"As has been said, matters of public interest were the general business of the assembly; the approving or discouraging of the king's projects. On the whole, the assembly seems to have had little or no power of initiative. Telemachus brought his own private need before an assembly, and urged the people to repress the Suitors; a discussion then ensued between the speaker and several of the Suitors concerning the re-marriage of the former's mother. All the people pitied Telemachus, and some were eager to coerce the lawless men, but the superior power and organization of the latter prevented such action. This assembly was evidently an irregular one. We read of another gathering called by the relatives of the dead Suitors to consider plans for taking vengeance, but it also was hurried and irregular. There is no adequate example of the assembly in time of peace, possibly because of the general state of disintegration of government in the Odyssey period, due to long absence of the rulers. War-assemblies, however, are quite numerous in the Iliad; and since they were not essentially unlike those of peace, a clearer idea of the latter can be gained by studying the councils of war. The conditions of war, it must be remembered, would tend, on the one hand, to draw the lines of discipline closer and to limit popular privilege, and, on the other hand, to make the head-king more dependent upon a small circle of advisors, the heads of the various contingents. That is, the centre of gravity of the system lay distinctly in the *boulē*, or council of chiefs, an organisation which does not appear to have been clearly

---

10 Ratzel, *Vkde.*, II, 196, 197.   11 Kubary, *Karolinen-Arch.*, 94.

differentiated in time of peace, and which does not occur among the Trojans in any developed form.

"The king's council was convoked in times of great need, and before it the ruler laid his perplexities and asked advice. The deliberations were usually accompanied by a feast, and the calling of such a council might be suggested by a sub-chief. The proceedings of the council were devoid of ceremony, except that the speaker stood while addressing the company. It was the king's duty to listen to good advice, though he was not compelled to take it; the *ruling* was the king's affair. Speech in the council was very free; the chieftains often severely blamed the king, who took the reproaches with humility when he had made costly mistakes. The council was not convened on all occasions, but was very much respected by the king, and always summoned when he was in distress. In general it preceded the popular assembly, and prepared the matter which was to come before it, the king depending upon the co-operation of the counsellors, men of maturity and experience, in order to influence the people as he wished. There is, however, no evidence to show that the council was more than advisory in its function.

"The popular assembly or *agorē* was a frequent gathering, perhaps a periodical one. As in the town, so in the camp, the general assembly was held in a fixed place—by the ships of the head-king, though separate nations had their assembling-places and public altars by their own ships. The assembly was convoked early in the morning by the king or by some chief, generally through the agency of 'clear-voiced' heralds, who summoned the people by shouting. Sometimes the chief himself did this summoning; in times of danger, the heralds and king went about quietly, summoning the men by name. The people gathered with tremendous outcry, and were restrained by heralds into a proper silence. The person who had convened the assembly then arose and explained the matter in hand, after which the question was open for discussion. Permission to speak was symbolised by the holding of a sceptre, probably that of the house of Atreus, and the speeches were very frank. In general, only the chiefs spoke, differing often from the king, and sometimes reproaching him severely before the whole people; it was *themis* to differ with the king in assembly, and he must not be angry. Only occasionally did the king restrict speech or flatly disregard advice; in general he felt bound to respect the wish of the people. Oratory was greatly admired in the assembly, and the effective style was that where words came 'thick and fast.' The counsel of the experienced and aged was most respected; a young man would sometimes urge his nobility of birth as an excuse for his speaking, in council as well as in assembly. The assembly was dismissed by the rising of the king or convoker, though sometimes the people rushed off under impulse.

"The relation of the king and the assembly as governing powers has been indicated in general lines; the assembly was a means of gauging popular feeling, to which a sensible king was prone to conform his action. The sentiment of the assembly was indicated by the silence of disapproval or the acclamations of approval. The popular attitude was the attitude of the '*Tis*' who, in an unofficial manner, communicated his views to his neighbour; the popular mind was awake and prone to express its feelings, and the consensus of many unofficial expressions of opinion constituted the approval or disapproval referred to. The common man might speak in assembly, but the one example of such a practice tends to prove it an exception, and brands it with a certain disapprobation.

The people might split into factions, however, and follow diverse plans and leaders; in general they were, in the assembly, subjected to a discipline and education whose value was well known to themselves. The assembly was an 'ennobler of men,' and though the humblest of the Greeks (*e.g.,* pilots) did not often come to the assembly, they took an interest in the society's vital doings; they were not mere slaves. Before them the king was sometimes forced to humble himself, and upon the people's expression of approval or disapproval regarding a course of action submitted to them, the king was glad to set his stamp of executive assent. Appeals were addressed not only to the king and sub-chiefs, but also to the people; the people had a share in the decision of the larger questions, for the king could not utterly disregard their evident wishes; the smaller questions were confided to the king alone.

"There are two fairly complete descriptions of assemblies and their action in Homer; though they are taken from war-times, the condition of peace can easily be deduced by slight modifications. Both should be studied in detail to gain a clear view of the relations of king and people. Here is no space for even a summary of what is so readily accessible in full, but certain general considerations emerge which may be mentioned. The power of the Trojan assembly convoked in Iliad VII (345-379) appears to have been very limited; proceedings were irregular and undignified and arrived at no result; no assent or disapproval were shown, and the people merely obeyed. There appears to have been no discipline, for one man could defy the will of all those who were day by day suffering and dying in expiation of his evil actions. This instance tends to prove the weaker organisation of the Trojans, and, as far as it goes, supports the theory that Paris was the oldest son and presumptive heir to the Trojan throne. In the Trojan assembly the same question of restitution had often appeared before, and Paris had maintained his position by bribes; such unjust and irregular acts were those which Zeus severely punished.

"The finest example of the relation of king, nobles, and people lies in the complication of plot which forms the introduction to the Iliad. The whole of this story is exceedingly instructive to the social scientist; a few among many points may be selected for special mention. The king, it seems, was not forcibly restrained by the assembly, nobles, or people from courses of action sure to bring calamity; his sin was expiated, without complaint, by the community. Discipline was such that private feelings and ends were subordinated to collective ends, except in the case of the blackest injustice. The king, however, was jealous of great and powerful sub-chiefs and disposed to prove his superiority by an abuse of power entrusted to him. The sub-chief, on the other hand, was jealous of the ascendancy of a man inferior in strength and bravery to himself, envious of his riches and prerogatives; the king could not, however, force this sub-chief to serve in war if he wished to retire. He was quite willing to dispense with a personality greater in the people's eyes than his own, with little thought of the consequences. By the sequel, *i.e.,* the ruling of the gods, the king's actions were judged, but not by the assembly or council; the king was *the* power, even in a confederation apparently of peers. But there were limits beyond which he could not go and still preserve the sacredness and inviolability of his person. In this episode the superiority of the king over his inferiors is set forth in the case of Calchas; in times of violence a common man was not safe unless he was under the protection of some one who possessed power to defend him. Dependence was better than freedom. If the power of the chief of a confederation was so strong over his sub-chiefs and people, it must be supposed that a like relation obtained upon a smaller scale. The rule of the king was a matter of force, and its perpetuation a matter of the maintenance of real power; tyranny can be supported if the tyrant can enforce order. Council and assembly were means of assuring such predominance."[12]

The Homeric case is typical of many, though it is more highly developed than that of most savage tribes and less differentiated in its organization than that of the real state. It is a fair parallel to that of the ancient Germans, where likewise the warrior-body and the assembly were one.[13] Standing midway between the undeveloped and the highly developed forms, it becomes, by reason of the relatively full evidence concerning it, justly representative of the relations between barbaric kings and their peoples. Particularly does it exhibit the various agencies for controlling the one-man power, from the unorganized checks existing in the mores and in tradition up to real institutional forms such as the council and assembly.

§161. Secret Societies.

THE more distinctly religious types of secret societies will be considered first. These societies are very common in West Africa, and in northern Cameroons are said to spring up "like mushrooms after a spring rain. Unfortunately they also disappear again just as fast, without being rescued to science." Strangely enough, they do not occur on the Gold Coast. Frobenius,[1] whose work teems with cases, thinks they belong to the West African culture-area and are relics of an older "Malayo-Negrito" system.

A number of authors furnish details concerning the African societies. "Every West African tribe has a secret society—two, in fact, one for men, and one for women. Every free man has to pass through the secret society of his tribe." But there are no mixed societies. "Those that I have mentioned . . . are all male, and women are utterly forbidden to participate in the rites or become acquainted with their secrets, for one of the chief duties of these societies is to keep the women in order. . . . A man who attempts to penetrate the female mysteries would be as surely killed as a woman who might attempt to investigate the male mysteries." Other societies "are practically murder societies, and their practices usually include cannibalism. . . . In the Calabar district I was informed by natives that there was a society of which the last entered member has to provide, for the entertainment of the other members, the body of a relative of his own, and sacrificial cannibalism is always breaking out, or perhaps I should say being discovered, by the white authorities in the Niger Delta." There existed a terrorizing society called the "Human Leopards, because when seizing their victims for sacrifice they covered themselves with leopard skins, and imitating the roars of the leopard, they sprang upon their victim, plunging at the same time two three-pronged forks into each side of the throat. . . . Sometimes, instead of the three-pronged forks, there are fixed in the paws of the leopard-skin sharp-pointed cutting knives, the skin being made into a sort of glove into which the hand of the human leopard fits. In

---

12 Keller, *Hom. Soc.*, 259-268 (where copious references to the text are cited).

13 Stammler, *Frauen*, 12; Jørgensen, in *Annaler*, 1876, 162.
1 *Masken*, 75 (quoted), 95, 243.

one skin I saw . . . this was most ingeniously done. The knives were shaped like the leopard's claws, curved, sharp-pointed, and with cutting edges underneath. . . . In the districts I know where human leopardism occurs . . . the victims are killed to provide human flesh for certain secret societies who eat it as one of their rites.[2] Lots are drawn to determine upon the member who "has to provide a victim who can be taken without fear of discovery. So important is this part of it, that they often fix on wife or child as involving the least possible risk. The murderers are then told off, and, dressed in leopard skins, they hide themselves in the thick bush, from which they leap out on the unsuspecting woman or child, digging into their necks a horrible little instrument with three pointed blades, specially made so that the wound they inflict should exactly resemble the claws of a leopard."[3]

The members of the Jevhe society are under taboo with respect to certain foods, actions, and usages; also with respect to rain-water from roofs and, at times, brandy.[4] Secret societies are general among the Yorubas and exist, under the same names, among negroes of Yoruba descent in the Bahamas. The members of one of them "meet every fifth market-day and pay their subscriptions, each member in turn taking the whole sum contributed at a meeting." Their method of reckoning market-days results in a sort of seventeen-day cycle. "These clubs or societies are so common that the seventeen-day period has become a kind of auxiliary measure of time."[5] It is reported that if a member of one of the secret societies "feels his death approaching, the rest are in the pleasant situation of having to kill and eat him, so that he may, so to speak, live on in his fraternity brothers."[6] On the lower Congo the initiation includes circumcision. The members of the society form a sort of free-masonry possessing certain pass-words or signs. The ceremonies last for six months and are repeated as the novice attains higher grades. They do not bathe during the six months. They are taught a new language by the medicine-man, which seems to be quite different from the ordinary tongue and is not taught to females. During the initiation-period they are sustained at the expense of the community. When the society is on the road its coming is announced by a sort of drumming noise, and all those who have not been initiated must clear out of the road.[7]

Secret societies occur in China; otherwise they are not so numerous in Asia.[8] The religion on the island of Ponapé was in charge of chiefs who formed an hereditary society to which other selected persons were admitted upon qualifications—knowledge of the peculiar language of the society, of its customs, ceremonies, and prayers. The outward sign of membership was long hair which was never cut but only singed off. This was done to all members except the two chief ones when any member died. There was an annual festival, a consecration of all new canoes, and a visit to a big sea-serpent alleged to be on a certain island.[9]

There is great variety in the nature and purpose of American societies. Some are military in character, others appear to be merely convivial. Many are connected with health, possessing certain therapeutic knowledge which is obtained

2 Kingsley, *W. Afr. Studies*, 214, 562; Kingsley, *Travels W. Afr.*, 526, 536.
3 Cator, *Head-Hunters*, 168-169.
4 Seidel, in *Globus*, LXXIII, 357.
5 Ellis, *Yoruba*, 150.
6 Esser, cited in *Globus*, LXXII, 355.

7 Johnston, in JAI, XIII, 472.
8 Cordier, "Les Sociétés secrètes chinoises," in *Revue d'Ethnog.*, VII, 52-72; DeGroot, *Relig. Syst.*, index.
9 Friederichsen, *Ruinen auf Ponapé*, 10.

only by initiation. There were two classes of societies among the Omaha: social and secret. "Membership in the social class was open to those able to perform the acts required for eligibility. To this class belong the warrior societies as well as those for social purposes only. The secret societies dealt with mysteries and membership was generally attained by virtue of a dream or vision. Some of these secret societies had knowledge of medicines, roots, and plants used in healing; others were noted for their occult and shamanistic proceedings and furnish the only examples of such practices in the tribe. There were no societies composed exclusively of women."[10] The right to a position in some of the secret organizations might be acquired for one's self "by killing a person of some foreign tribe and taking his paraphernalia, or for one's son by marrying the daughter of him who possessed it." Cannibalism sometimes plays a part; among the Tsimshian there existed a Cannibal Society. Initiation, accompanied by ordeals, was usual. "At the time of initiation the novice was supposed to be carried away for a season by the spirit which came to him, and after his return he usually went through the different houses in the town accompanied by other members of the society who had been initiated previously. In case his spirit were a violent one, he might break up boxes, canoes, etc., which the giver of the feast had to replace." Among the Zuñi, one of the ordeals to which an initiate into the Priesthood of the Bow was subjected was to sit naked for hours on a large ant-hill, his flesh exposed to the torment of myriads of ants. When introduced into one of the Omaha societies, one was shot in the Adam's apple by something said to be taken from the head of an otter. A person initiated into the Chippewa and Menominee society was "shot" with a medicine bag and immediately fell on his face. On the northwest coast, the secret society spirit or the guardian spirit of the shaman also made himself felt by causing a candidate to fall on his face. During the ceremony among the Hidatsa, devotees ran arrows through the muscles of different parts of their bodies, while the special ordeal of a Cheyenne society was to walk with bare feet on hot coals. Those initiated into the mysteries of the sacred trumpet in Guiana were subjected to flagellations, fastings, and other painful exercises.[11]

In some parts of America the clans are secret unions with initiation by the medicine-man for both men and women. The medicine which each clan uses is its bond and is a secret from all others.[12] This is really a secret, religiously bound kin-group. "The tendency of the Iroquois to superstitious beliefs is especially exemplified in their notion of the existence of a race of supernatural beings, whom they call False-faces. . . . The False faces are believed to be evil spirits or demons without bodies, arms or limbs, simply faces and those of the most hideous description . . . and possessed of a look so frightful and demoniacal as to paralyze all who behold them. They are supposed to have power to send plagues and pestilence among men, as well as to devour their bodies when found, for which reasons they were held in the highest terror. . . . Upon this belief was founded a regular secret organization, called the False-face band, members of which can now be found in every Iroquois village . . . where the old modes of life are still preserved. This society has a species of initiation, and regular forms, ceremonies, and dances. . . . If any one dreamed he was a False-face . . . it was only necessary to signify his dream to the

10 Fletcher and LaFlesche, in BAE, XXVII, 133, 459 (quoted).

11 Boas, in BAE, XXXI, 546-547; Swanton,

in HAI, II, 146, 496 (quoted), 497; Roth, in BAE, XXX, 137.

12 Schoolcraft, *Hist. Ind.*, II, 171.

proper person, and give a feast, to be at once initiated; and so any one dreaming that he had ceased to be a False-face, had but to make known his dream and give a similar entertainment to effect his exodus. In no other way could a membership be acquired or surrendered." Members wore hideous masks when appearing in character. They were all males save one, who was the mistress of the band and called the "Keeper of the False-faces"; she "not only had charge of the regalia of the band, but was the only organ of communication with the members, for their names continued unknown. The prime motive in the establishment of this organization was to propitiate those demons called False-faces, and among other good results to arrest pestilence and disease."[13] Thus public service was one of the objects of even so strictly religious an organization. There were two secret societies among the Lenape: one, called the Witches, was composed of twelve malevolent conjurors, all holders of the "bad medicine," while the other, comprising twelve benevolent shamans, was known as the Masks, and was quite similar to the False-face company of the Iroquois. Both had stated meetings and rites.[14]

The Dakotas had "medicine-lodges" and religious unions with secret rites which Schoolcraft called "clans."[15] On occasion "a council is held by the head-men of the order, who appoint to act as soldiers ten members of the order, who . . . erect a three-foot barricade . . . preserve order, wait upon the dancers, prevent spectators from leaning upon the barricade, and attend to a large cauldron of meat and wild turnips cooking over a fire." A novice is given secret instructions, stripped and painted black from head to foot, except for a small red spot between the shoulders. He is exhorted to remain good so that his medicine shall be strong and to give a feast once a year, and receives the holy claw or stone. The medicine-man transfers to him the spirit from his medicine-bag, at which the candidate falls upon the ground. The priest resuscitates him, he gets a medicine-bag, and is a recognized member of the order. "Dead Indians, men and women, are initiated into this order, through the same performance over a lock of hair of the deceased. . . . They say the spirit by this initiation is set on the right road, straight to his or her destination." The living candidate has to participate in a dance, "and as these dances are given, even in mid-winter, many degrees below zero, one can readily imagine the agony the candidates must undergo, clothed only in a coat of paint. It is generally supposed that the members of the order have secrets and signs, but the penalty is so sure and swift that no exposures have ever been made. Well-known instances have occurred where indiscretions of members have been punished by their mysterious disappearance, attributed to the medicine-men."[16] The Osages have secret societies which keep their myths secret.[17]

"Since the advent of the Paiute messiah, 'Jack Wilson,' a new society has been organized, designated as the 'Dreamers' society' "; it is a remote imitation of the ghost-dance, a craze of which many discontented and belligerent young men of various tribes took advantage to further their own designs. When a child who has been set apart to be dedicated to the Ojibwa Ghost Society dies before reaching the proper age of initiation, there is a feast at the mourner's wigwam, with dishes set apart for the dead, and the chief mourner is initiated

13 Dall, in BAE, III, 144 (quoting a report of Morgan on the Iroquois, presented in 1851)

14 Harrington, in AA, XV, 217

15 Cunow, Australneger, 177.

16 Beckwith, in Smithson. Rep., 1886, pt. I. 246.

17 Dorsey, in BAE, VI, 377, 396.

as a substitute for the deceased. The Ojibwa have a society of medicine-men of four classes. "Frequently the collecting of skins, peltries, and other goods that have to be purchased involves a candidate hopelessly in debt. So great is the desire, however, on the part of some Indians to become acknowledged medicine men that they will assume obligations which may take years of hunting or work to liquidate. If they should finally fail in this, their relatives are expected to assume the responsibility." The Menomini Grand Medicine Society consists of men, women, and a few boys and girls. Initiation may be accomplished through adoption by a member to fill a vacancy caused by death, or by submitting proofs of eligibility and paying the necessary presents and fees. Before initiation the candidate "is taught the mysteries of the remedies known to his instructor. Each remedy must be paid for separately, since no two preparations, roots, or other substances are classed together as one. Furthermore, the knowledge relating to different remedies is possessed by different medicine men, each of whom will dispose of the properties and uses thereof for a consideration only." At a service for the benefit of a shade of a dead member who had been allowed to return and be present at the meeting, a spirit is quoted as saying: "Whenever you are in trouble, place some tobacco aside for me, and when the odor of your smoke ascends I shall help you." One of the ways to show regret for unmindfulness of the injunctions and precepts taught through the ritual is to give a ball game. Such a game is given sometimes when a member of the family is sick; "this offering being equivalent to giving to the poor." A feast must go with it, like the bread with the circus in Rome.[18]

Boas[19] goes into considerable technical detail concerning the secret societies of the Kwakiutl Indians, remarking on "the wide distribution of secret societies and the general similarity of the underlying principle all over North America. . . . I believe the source of the ritual, as well as of the legends which are connected with it, must be looked for in the advantages and the prerogatives which the membership of secret societies gives." Men were led by desire for these to acquire membership in existing societies or, where these were not sufficient, to create new ones. "Of course I do not mean to say that the Indian invented traditions consciously and intentionally, but that the desire excited his fancy and his whole state of mind, and that in this manner, after appropriate fasting, the opportunity was given for hallucinations, the material for which was necessarily taken from the existing ideas, or from the ideas of neighboring tribes. . . . It is easily understood how the exciting aspect of the ceremonial of the cannibal society caused a young man who had gone fasting to believe that he saw in his hallucinations the same spirit under new conditions, and to tell of his experience after his return. As the notion had become established that the spirit, after having been seen, had a tendency to reappear to the descendants, an opportunity was given for the formation of a new place in the secret society." Boas thinks "the origin of the secret societies has a close connection with warfare."

The Zuñi child, becoming a member of the society at a tender age, is led to believe the impersonators of the gods are the gods themselves. Initiation is accompanied by whipping. The priest lectures the boys, imparting some of the secrets of the order; and the boys are told that betrayal will be punished by decapitation with a stone knife. Initiates get masks which are their personal

---

18 Hoffman, in BAE, VII, 164; Hoffman, in BAE, XIV, 63, 67, 68, 69, 77, 78, 127.

19 In USNM, 1895, 660 ff.

property and are buried with their owners so as to accompany them to the other world. "When a man dons a mask his body becomes the abiding-place of the spirit of the god and he is worshiped as such."[20]

The Pueblo *kivas,* or ceremonial chambers, with altars and fetishes displayed in them, were built in good part "by religious societies, which still hold their stated observances in them, and in Oraibi several still bear the names of the societies using them. A society always celebrates in a particular kiva, but none of these kivas are now preserved exclusively for religious purposes; they are all places of social resort for the men, especially during the winter, when they occupy themselves with the arts common among them. The same kiva thus serves as a temple during a sacred feast, at other times as a council house for the discussion of public affairs. It is also used as a workshop by the industrious and as a lounging place by the idle. . . . The kiva is usually spoken of as being the home of the organization which maintains it. Different kivas are not used in common by all the inhabitants. Every man has a membership in some particular one, and he frequents that one only. . . . In each kiva there is a . . . kiva chief, and he controls to a great extent all matters pertaining to the kiva and its membership. This office or trust is hereditary and passes from uncle to nephew through the female line—that is, on the death of a kiva chief the eldest son of his eldest sister succeeds him. . . . But the kiva chief is not necessarily chief of the society; in fact usually he is but an ordinary member. . . . A kiva may belong either to a society, a group of gentes, or an individual."[21] The Moki have a secret society, but they would not tell what it was for.[22]

A discussion of Melanesian secret societies, adapted in the main from Rivers,[23] may serve to introduce the topic of the regulative functions of such organizations. There is a close resemblance between the Duk-Duk society of the Bismarck Archipelago and the Tamate societies of the Banks Islands. "Both are societies consisting of initiated men meeting secretly in the bush and wearing masks, especially when their members come into relation with the uninitiated. The belief that the members represent the ghosts of the dead is almost certainly common to both, and both possess the power of protecting private property by means of taboo." Closely connected with the belief that the members of the societies are ghosts is the frequent occurrence, in the ritual of initiation, of features which point to this process as being symbolic of death and re-birth. "Thus, in Melanesia, a candidate, who leaves his family in order to be initiated, is mourned for as if he were dead, and there are frequent features of the ritual which point to its being in a large measure a symbolization of death." In addition to the features which bring these associations definitely into the category of religious groupings, there are other features of a political kind. Thus, "wherever these organizations are found in Melanesia, there is nothing which can properly be called chieftainship, the place of the chiefs being taken by men of high rank in the organization. Or, these men of high rank may be regarded as chiefs, in which case the rank of chief is not hereditary, but is attained by a process of successive initiations. Since men only attain this rank by a lengthy process, the rulers are necessarily old men, thus producing the mode of government which has been called a gerontocracy. In

20 Stevenson, in BAE, V, 553; Stevenson, in AA, (O.S.) XI, 39, 40.
21 Mindeleff, in BAE, VIII, 130, 133.
22 Bourke, *Snake Dance,* 182.
23 *Soc. Org.,* 121-136; *Melan. Soc.,* I, 64-65, 67, 68, 88-91; II, 513 (quoted), 515.

Melanesia, at any rate, there is a close association between this form of government and the existence of graded organizations entered by initiation." The economic significance of these organizations is evidenced by the fact that almost the only function of shell-money and money of other kinds is in connection with these societies, in the payments which accompany initiation and the attainment of higher ranks. Another economic function of the organizations, at least in the Banks Islands, is that they form the means by which the right to individual property is acquired; in opposition to the general communistic practices, each society has a badge by means of which property is protected from all except other members of the same group. Webster[24] has endeavored to show that secret societies in Melanesia and elsewhere have arisen through a special development of totemic clans. To this hypothesis Rivers makes an addition designed to explain the fundamental feature of the societies, viz., their secrecy: that Melanesian secret societies embody the religious cults of immigrants who, coming in small numbers among an alien people, practised their religion in secret, and only gradually admitted the indigenous people to participation in their rites. Secrecy, then, is due to the need felt by the immigrants for the practice of their totemic rites away from the alien population among which they found themselves. The extreme development of secret societies, as in the southern islands of the Melanesian Archipelago, seems to be connected with the decline of totemism as a social institution: the formation of bodies which enroll their members from all parts of the tribe, irrespective of clan-ties, must contribute to the disintegration of the clan-structure.

There is hardly a feature of the associations of Melanesia which is not reproduced in one or other of the societies of Africa, while there are certain African features which do not occur, or are exceptional, in Melanesia. Thus among the Ibo, there is in some cases a connection with occupation, the societies resembling gilds. It is noteworthy, in relation to the position of smiths elsewhere in Africa, that the highest grade among the Ibo is named after the blacksmiths.[25] Frobenius[26] adverts to the Melanesian societies in connection with the African. We shall follow his cases to begin with. In relation to the Melanesian societies he cites the fasting-period, which extends to a hundred days, and the renunciation of bathing which accompanies it. The candidate is thus spiritualized and re-born, getting a new name. Grades of spiritualization are attainable, the highest receiving honor as to the gods; but rising in the scale costs heavily. The more strictly regulative features of the African organizations, though bound up with religious notions, are indicated in the following examples.

In Loango the secret society attends to the matter of rain and also serves the king as a force to execute his will. It is particularly efficient in collecting debts or wreaking destruction on the property of the debtor. Sometimes the king is president of the local society; and regularly the societies terrify women and children and keep them in order. "The land remains, as it were, in a permanent state of siege, which is necessary by reason of the preponderant number of slaves and women." The recurrent "Egbo-days" are days of martial law, on which the traditional life is suspended in favor of general repression. "As soon as an Egbo-day is announced, slaves, women, and children flee in all directions,"

24 In JAI, XLI, 507-508; Rivers, *Melan. Soc.*, II, 222.
25 Rivers, *Soc. Org.*, 126 ff.
26 *Masken*, 251 ff.; 57, 60, 85 ff., 93 ff.; 103 ff., 114 ff., 133, 135, 138 ff., 145, 227, 232.

seeking to avoid the whip which the emissary of the society plies with little scruple. The Order of the Free Egbos started in certain market-places, it is reported, as a sort of House for the mutual guarantee of merchants' interests, "and later won the political significance of a Vehm, by drawing into its power the whole police-function of Calabar and the Cameroons." But "the Egbo laws aim only at the weal of its own members, in comparison with which the general well-being is not considered. The Egbo-tribunal must be well paid for rectifying injuries; sometimes people prefer to sell themselves in slavery to some powerful chief. "Like all exclusive societies, the Egbo will not willingly sacrifice the preferential rights of its members in favor of humbler people. What they have they hold tightly to. . . . Women, if they have not powerful fathers and brothers, must put up with the most humiliating treatment from their husbands. The only law which the society ever promulgated for the protection of slaves was given at the instance of foreigners."

Among the Yorubas the "Egungun" is regarded "as a sort of supernatural inquisitor who appears from time to time to investigate the general domestic régime of the people, especially that of the women, and to requite punishable actions. Although it is generally known that Egungun is only a selected man, yet it is believed among the people that to touch him is to invite death." Thus is the matter of private order attended to by an alleged daimon connected with the dead ancestors. The Ogboni society sends out a masked "Oro," who "is the public police-force, if one may so express it." His approach is heralded by the hum of the whirr-stick, at the sound of which all women must retire to their apartments. No one of them may see the bull-roarer itself. "The whole of Yoruba-land is ruled by this society or this authority organized in society form. Criminals condemned to death are given over . . . to the Oro." It is thought that Oro, "who is now only the guardian of the public order, as Egungun is of the private, was originally the spirit that directed the education of the boys"; he seems to be the spirit of the ancestors.

The Jevhe is another of the West African societies. It has a sort of cloister, and its fetishes, kept in a brandy-chest, are so-called "lightning-stones"; there is also an altar, blood-besprinkled and decorated with white chicken-feathers. Sacred implements, preserved in the dark interior of this holy place are two drums and an iron called "gongo." Members can lead an unrestrained life within the temple; and all the rights of the outside world are extinguished as regards one who treads the holy ground. "The believer may demand back no debt, the man no wife, the parents no child. While they lose all their rights in favor of the members of the Jevhe-association, there accrue to them, on the other hand, a mass of the most extensive duties, which they must fulfill, not alone to the members of their families residing in the cloister, but also to the rest of the Jevhe-members." Men deep in debt may be brought by their relatives to the capital and, at the chief's command, be struck dead or buried alive. Such debtors flee, if they can, into the Jevhe-sanctuary, and the priest announces that Jevhe has taken them. If the creditors dare then to press their demands, the debt having been, so to speak, outlawed by the god, they are likely to have to pay to the society the exact amount of the indebtedness. Men also enter voluntarily in the hope of getting a wife. The novice eats with the priest and a common member, called an "older dog," a brew of white chicken's blood and meal, and then enters into all the secrets. Girls can be entered by appeal to the priest. A female candidate is spirited away to the cloister; she goes through an initiation, including the shaving of the whole body, and gets a new name. She may not leave to get water or wood until the priest is sure that she has lost all feelings of affection for family and friends; but "after the completion of her education she may leave the cloister and go back to her people." So may the married woman return to her husband; but she remains more closely attached to the Jevhe institution than to anything outside. She must often return and attend to the duties of cleaning and getting wood and water for the cloister. If this results in strife with her husband, the latter is fined about a hundred marks [about twenty-five dollars], the sum being doubled and tripled if he does not pay up at once.

These Jevhe-associates, along with other duties, practice espionage. Priests and chief are hand in glove; the chief helps out the society and is well paid for it, and the priests can go their own way undisturbed by him. Creditors too can make use of the offices of the society. If they cannot collect, after repeated efforts, they take whiskey to the priests and ask aid. If the gifts of intoxicant are large enough, the brother of the debtor—not the man himself—is seized. Then the debtor is under obligation to buy his brother off, at a total cost represented by the amount of the debt, the cost of the whiskey, and the compensation of the abductors of the brother. It is to be noted that the society is ready to espouse either side of a debt-controversy that redounds to its profit; but the net result is some kind of a definitive settlement of extreme and long-drawn-out controversies.

In Senegambia, to continue with the lists of Frobenius, the chief of the secret society, who prescribes laws, lives in the forest and is always unknown to those who do not know his mysteries. In case of debts or thefts, complaint is made to him by offerings to a wooden fetish and the discharge of a flintlock at its feet. In Sierra Leone there are five districts each of which has its own authority and special government, but all are under a common secret society, with typical initiation, masks, tattoo-marks, and ceremonies. The chapters of this fraternity are the local tribunals and the chief chapter the general one. The former keep peace between the strongest families, compose local quarrels, and may also end wars between the districts. The general tribunal ends wars and punishes by death the spilling of a drop of blood after its proclamation is rendered. The guilty district is sentenced to a four-days' pillage, half of the product of which goes to the plaintiff-district and half to the general tribunal, which shares its part with the pillagers. If any family becomes too powerful the great tribunal sentences it to a nocturnal pillage by masked warriors. If the heads of the family resist, they are killed or spirited away, to be judged in the forest-depths, and almost always to disappear forever.

There is, in parts of West Africa, a special attempt at the safeguarding of husbands' rights, which seems not uncalled for in these regions of much intercommunication and trade. Women are stripped and severely chastised, at the instance of a monster called "Mumbo-Jumbo," for quarreling and other unseemly conduct. Masked men keep guard of the public order. Circumcision of novices is widely practised. Most of the African masked societies have also the function of joke-making and trick-playing. "Not only to become satisfactory husbands, but also good citizens, do the youths visit the solitude of the forest. The group of those thus educated together then readily takes on the character and significance of politically organized bodies. The uninitiated are "unclean, unholy, know-nothings, unintelligent, have nothing to say in any assemblies, and must take shame to be present at any councils."

"Thus there sound forth in the several melodies of the African secret societies all the motives of social life. In Egbo the despotism and hierarchy of the merchant is suppressed. The Purrah sets itself against the little-state system. The Mumbo-Jumbo drives coquettish women before him. The Belli educates good husbands, citizens, and soldiers. . . . In Jevhe is presented a memorial of the hateful transitional form which comes out where the Christian and European philosophy forces the savage to deceit, because he can not renounce his fathers' customs and views and yet can no longer attach value to his own ways. Of no one of these currents can it be said that it gave life to the secret societies. Only the direction of the orders, already in full, powerful development, was influenced. . . . That rude, primeval force, the spirit-world, was bridled and trained until, as a driving factor in the state-machine, it attained a field of activity rich in effectiveness and widely-branching."

So much for Frobenius. We turn now to other African examples and to cases from other parts of the world. Among the Fan the secret society gradually became legal and by force of circumstances one of the most vital organizations of the tribe.[27] The principal elders of the Akamba tribes, who form in fact the government of the country, are mostly old men who have attained to the higher degrees.[28] In Loango masked persons appear as executioners of the arbitrary and violent orders of the chief; but there is a secret, hereditary vigilance-organization which enforces the payment of debts, sending its agents to seize property on complaint of a creditor.[29] Unpopular persons are fallen upon and flogged with the sacred whip.[30] In Togo there is a society, of which Klose[31] gives a long account, which practises oppression, extortion, licentiousness, and terrorism. The Nigerian Idem is "a body of men formed for the purpose of governing the clan, household, or family to which they belong." The head of the house is always president. Its evil character is largely exaggerated.[32] Andree[33] collects other African examples.

In China, "the many secret associations existing among the people are mostly of a political character, but have creeds like religious sects. . . . They are traceable to the system of clans, which, giving the people at once the habit and spirit for associations, are easily made use of by clever men, for their own purposes of opposition to government." The people naturally connect some religious rites with their opposition and cabals in order to more securely bind their members together.[34] An illustration is given by the so-called "Boxers," who taught that proper initiation into mysteries would render its members invulnerable. They pretended to prove this by experiment: "several intelligent Chinese have told me that they had themselves seen advanced members of the society strike different parts of their bodies with sharp knives and swords with no more effect upon the skin than is produced by the wind." Death is easily explicable; in one case it was discovered that several Boxers who were killed "had broken the rules of the society by eating certain proscribed articles of food. In this way their death but strengthened the faith of those remaining. It was proposed at first to use no fire-arms in the extermination of foreigners,

27 Trilles, *Fân*, 51, 434-435.
28 Dundas, C., in JAI, XLIII, 539-541.
29 Bastian, *Deut. Exped.*, I, 80, 222.
30 Ratzel, *Vkde.*, I, 616.
31 *Togo*, 197-211.

32 Cobham, in *Jr. Afr. Soc.*, V, 40-42.
33 *Eth. Parallelen*, 135, 136.
34 Williams, *Middle Kgdm.*, I, 394 (Edit. 1848).

but to trust to the sword alone. Great reliance was placed on certain calisthenic exercises and posturings which were expected to hypnotize or terrify the enemy."[35]

The *kongsi,* or Chinese republic, which formerly existed in the western part of Borneo, was closely related to the secret societies. The Chinese went to that distant, unknown land knowing that they would be received with open arms and helped on. They migrated in groups, chiefly of family-members and village mates. The term *kongsi* is applied to great corporations and commercial houses, but as the term for a political body means "union for the object of managing the *res publica.*"[36] Among the Alfurs of Ceram there is a union having the alleged purpose of warding off foreign control, but it has become an institution whose most important purpose is to smooth over quarrels without the intervention of the government. Every member has a cross tattooed on his breast.[37]

The order of the Arreoi, on Tahiti, Raratonga, Nukuhiva, Hawaii, and the Ladrones, was in part religious, but also social. In the end it was only a means of living in vice and luxury, but originally it carried purity of color to the extreme. It was advantageous to the ruling class, and consisted of a voluntary union of warriors of the superior race, who agreed to let no children of theirs live; only the offspring of the highest group in it survived in order to perpetuate the race in its highest purity. As they lived on the subjugated race, whose surplus was limited, this holding down of numbers maintained their power. In Hawaii, the practice of infanticide had reduced the number of females in the society to one-third that of the males; hence the men were forced to take women of the lower race, and, as their children were killed, polyandry ensued. The society was dissolved about 1800 by the king, Pomare II. On the Society Islands this union was attributed to divine foundation. There were seven grades of tattooing, but all were united in close comradeship and their hospitality to one another had no limit. They did not labor; their land was cultivated by slaves, and their souls taken by the gods to paradise.[38]

Among the Dakotas, "the circling crow dance, also called the straw or grass dance, is controlled by three men, the most influential of the tribe, who wear a peculiar insignia, a tunic of crow and eagle feathers attached to a belt ornamented with beads and quills; over the small of the back project two sticks several inches long; at the ends are jingling bells, every motion of the wearer causing the sticks to vibrate and the bells to jingle. These tunics are held sacred, and no profane hand allowed to touch them. . . . Stewards are appointed to collect provisions, which are rarely refused. When sufficient is collected to last several days, the three leading men are notified, who, calling the lodge, make arrangements for the dance. The crier then goes through the camp announcing when and where the dance will be held. . . . Seating themselves upon the ground, wrapped in their blankets up to the eyes, the drummers open the ball, the dancers throw their blankets aside, and springing to their feet brandish their tomahawks or knives with violent gestures and an occasional whoop, chant and dance for a few moments, resume their blankets and their seats, leaving one in the ring, who, fiercely gesturing, and wildly waving

---

35 Davies, in *Nat. Geog. Mag.,* XI, 282.
36 DeGroot, *Kongsiwezen,* v, 113, 117-118, 138.
37 Ratzel, *Vkde.,* II, 454.

38 Webster, *Secret Soc.,* 164 ff.; Lippert, *Kgchte.,* I, 212, 214; Ratzel, *Vkde.,* II, 195; Cook, First Voy., in *Pinkerton, Coll.,* XI, 520.

a tomahawk or knife, will brag unmercifully over some exploit in war or chase; again all jump up, dance and yell. A repetition of the same performances is gone through with again and again for several days or until the provisions are consumed. They will imitate animals, taking raw meat or a fish, snarl, growl, and snap over it, tearing it with their teeth like the wild beast they are so well imitating. . . . A question of importance once decided, the head chief of the band will be called in, whether a member of the lodge or not, and he must perform the mission they have intrusted him with, and as their influence is largely kept up through these orders the chiefs are glad of these commissions. There are no signs or passwords, and with the exception of the skunk-skin garter, elaborately ornamented with beads, there is nothing to designate the members from the outside world. Though this order is of late date, it is the most powerful among the Indians. . . . There are no ceremonies of initiation; they generally give a horse, starting him off with a whip, for any one who chooses to catch him. The order is a charitable one. An old woman called on the order, stated her poverty; immediately the crier was sent around the camp, and in a few hours the members were all present, as they will drop any work or pleasure when called. The leader stated the cause of the meeting; the result was flour and pork, thirteen blankets, calico, fine cloth, and skins. Another instance: An Indian, wishing to build a house, invited the order to a feast; as he was not a member one stated his wants. After the feast the building was soon completed. Though a charitable and social society, it is one very much feared; and there exist lodges among all the different tribes and bands throughout the great northwest."[39]

Boas[40] describes the so-called winter ceremonial of the Kwakiutl Indians. All the officers of the ceremonial and their names "derive their origin from a myth telling how the animals held their first winter ceremonial." At the time of marriage, a bride's father "has promised to transfer his membership in one of the secret societies to one of his son-in-law's children. When a son of the latter has reached the age of 10 or 12 years, or even earlier, he is initiated in one of the lower secret societies," through which he must pass to become a member of the higher ones. The celebration of this initiation is exceedingly expensive and the three principal chiefs of the tribe investigate the debts and property of the man and his father-in-law beforehand, to be sure the expenses can be met. Permission is given if the result is promising, and there is a meeting of all the chiefs to ratify. "At this meeting, the man who gives the dance notifies his father-in-law that he desires to have the blankets which he paid for his wife returned, and that he wants to have the box containing his father-in-law's dance." Notification is made to the tribe to prepare for the ceremony; "in particular, they are asked to clean themselves and to refrain from intercourse with women." The ceremony itself is a presentation of the amount of property to be transferred.

In California a secret society existed in one of the tribes, the membership of which, "in conversation with their white acquaintances, make no secret of the fact that it is designed simply to keep the women in due subjection." One of their number impersonates the devil, being painted in alternate stripes of red and black, spirally. He is so masked by a hanging chaplet that he is not recognizable, and rushes out with pranks and capers and dreadful whoops while the

---

39 Beckwith, in *Smithson. Rep.*, 1886, pt. I,   40 Kwakiutl, USNM, 1895, 500-502.
248, 249.

assembly hall he has just left resounds with diabolical yells. He carries in his hand a sprig of poison-oak, with which, dipping it in water, he sprinkles the faces of the squaws as he pirouettes about them; "whereat they scream with terror, fall prostrate upon the earth, and hide their faces." Other "devil-dances" are practised by these Indian tribes to the same end of terrorizing the women; and an old chief in the end preaches to them on feminine obedience, industry, and chastity. They kill the women of their conquered enemies because thus they think to kill out the other tribes.[41]

Military and age-societies were frequent among the Indians. There were the progressive age-societies of the Plains and the permanent warrior-system of the Forest, by which latter a man, a woman, or a child performing a brave deed, automatically became a warrior for life. "The soldiers' lodge was erected in every band or tribal camp, and there the qualified braves resided with the chief."[42] The organizations of the Crows were, apart from their military character, essentially social associations similar to the four bodies of the present day, which join in the performance of the Grass Dance on certain occasions and otherwise have the functions of clubs and mutual-benefit brotherhoods.[43] Among the Cheyennes the soldier-bands included a large number, but not all, of the able-bodied and ambitious men of the tribe, from youth to old age. "They were the organized military force of the camp, and acted as its police force. To them was intrusted the enforcement of the orders of the chiefs. Since, in the Indian camp, public opinion was the ruling force, and since the soldiers constituted a majority of the bravest and most influential men in the tribe, the soldier bands were often consulted by the chiefs on important matters relating to peace or war. Sometimes one or more of these societies, acting unitedly, might force the tribe to adopt some certain course of action that it was not generally desired to take, or might even oblige some priest or important man to perform an act that he felt to be wrong or to threaten harm to the tribe."[44]

§162. Clubs.

THE secret society and the club are institutions of the same general type, though each has a number of special features which warrant separate treatment. "Where membership of the group is limited to male persons, it is natural to find that the associations are closely connected with the institution of the men's house, that is, a house common to men, in which the men of the community, or the initiated men, dwell, eat and sleep. . . . In some cases all the men sleep in the common-house, while more frequently only the bachelors sleep there, the married men sleeping in their own houses with their wives and families."[1] The men's house is a common feature in Melanesia. In every village of the Banks Islands there is a building called the *gamal,* which is used by men only, "and it is in this building only that men sleep and take their food." Each man sleeps and eats either in the compartment of his own rank or in one belonging to a rank lower than his own. The *gamal* is also the general meeting-place in the village.[2] Among a number of other Melanesian peoples such club-houses are common, serving as meeting-places for the men of the

---

41 Powers, in *Contrib. N. Amer. Ethnol.,* III, 141, 158.
42 Skinner, in AA, XVI, 317.
43 Lowie, in AA, XIV, 67.

44 Grinnell, *Cheyenne,* II, 48-51.
1 Rivers, *Soc. Org.,* 121 ff.
2 Rivers, *Melan. Soc.,* I, 60, 61-63.

local group, as halls to receive and entertain chiefs and strangers on official business, and in general as club-houses in the fullest sense of the term. They are always tabooed to women.[3]

"In all Melanesian groups it is the rule that there is in every village a building of public character, where the men eat and spend their time, the young men sleep, strangers are entertained; where as in the Solomon Islands the canoes are kept; where images are seen, and from which women are generally excluded. . . . But these are not club-houses, as are the *gamal* houses of the *Suqe,* which serve indeed to a considerable extent for public purposes, because almost every man is a member of the club, but are in fact the homes of a society in which every one has his place according to his rank in the society. . . . Nothing is known of the origin of the club. It is not connected with the secret societies of the ghosts, and is not a secret society of the same kind. The club-house is in the open, and every one, except when new members are admitted, can see what is going on, though women are most strictly excluded. It is a social, not at all a religious institution. The giving of feasts advanced the rank of the society-member, and he gave prizes and otherwise exhibited his liberality. "It was a great thing for a man to have a large assemblage at his feast, and a great satisfaction to his enemy to prevent it; each would therefore use charms to further his purpose." A place in the society was in old times valued for the advantages it carried with it after death. According to a native, "the reason for *Suqe* is this, that hereafter when a man comes to die, his soul may remain in happiness in that place Panoi; but if any one should die who has not killed a pig, his soul will just stay on a tree, for ever on it like a flying fox. . . . Consequently, on the birth of a son a man's first care was to give a pig in his name to make a beginning of *Suqe* for him. . . . Among children even, one whose father had not given a pig for his admission would be despised; and when a man had killed his pigs properly afterwards on his own account his position in society was secured." He could adorn himself with their tusks, which were like the insignia of degrees taken in modern secret societies. "Age has nothing to do with entrance into the society, or with rising in the ranks; it is merely a matter of giving pigs and mats, which serve for money. . . . The higher ranks of the *Suqe* give much power and authority, because those who have reached them can always keep back those who wish to rise, and the goodwill of each one of them has to be secured." Discipline is severe; anyone who should intrude into a division above his own would be clubbed or shot. To get the pigs and mats which advance one in the social scale he must have *mana,* or inherent virtue; and the chief, being at the top, is an almost godlike repository of that supernatural quality.[4]

The Nanga of Fiji is thought to be allied to the general Melanesian type of men's club; only here a young man may marry prior to initiation. The men, married and unmarried, assemble in their house in the evenings and sing.[5] The *fel* of the Mortlock people "is a hotel, a work-shop, a place for keeping the big canoes, a play-ground for the children, a place for the holding of all assemblies. . . . All state-business is transacted in this house, all visits received here; chiefly, however, it serves as a sleeping-place for those young

---

3 Seligmann, *Melanesians,* 60-62, 223, 226, 227, 330, 334, 335, 463-466.
4 Codrington, *Melanesians,* 102, 103, 110 ff., 299.

5 Fison, in JAI, XIV, 30; Crawley, in JAI, XXIV, 231; Weld, in PSM, XLVIII, 231.

male members who are not yet married or are separated temporarily from their wives. In consequence of the small population, as well as of the custom that the men marry away from home, the number of sleepers in the 'fel' is only a limited one."[6] The council-hall of the Maori was also a guest-house and village sleeping-house.[7]

The Point Barrow Eskimo have a house that will accommodate sixty, which is used in summer as a general lounging-place or club-room by the men. "Those who have carpentering and similar work to do bring it there and others come simply to lounge and gossip and hear the latest news, as the hunters when they come in generally repair to the club-room as soon as they have put away their equipments."[8] Around Bering Strait the *kashim* is the center of religious and social life for men. The unmarried sleep there always and so do the married except occasionally. Men work there, and the entertainment of guests, the shaman's exercises, the old men's tales, and dances find their place there. Women are excluded at times. Men are naked in the *kashim* and also bathe there.[9] The *kashim* of Alaska corresponds in some respects to the *estufa* of the southwestern Indians. "In villages untouched by white men the males, when not at work, all congregate in the *kashim* to sleep and while away the time, leaving the native houses in the possession of the women, who carry food to their lords and masters in the *kashim*, but enter at no other times except for certain dances." The location and identity of the *kashim* is not readily revealed, and the entrance is subterranean and somewhat tortuous.[10]

The California Indians have the men's house, which "is club-room, council-house, dormitory, sudatory, and medical examination room all in one, and is devoted exclusively to masculine occupation. . . . No squaw may enter on penalty of death except when undergoing her examination for the degree of M.D." There are always enough of these assembly-chambers in each village to furnish sleeping-room for all the adult males. Elsewhere women may enter only on festival days.[11] In Colombia the men spend their free time in such club-rooms.[12] The Shingu Indians had their flute-house which no woman might enter and which was used only for feasts, not work; other tribes did all the regular labor in making weapons and utensils, in the men's house. The central point of the existence of the Bororo is the house of the men. Here a noisy, uproarious life is carried on night and day, so that the family huts appear to be only the residence of the women and children. The men, as a united body, with especial reference to the hunting, are called Aroe. In the house of the men there is almost constant singing about topics which excite either joy or sorrow. When they are going on a hunt, instead of sleeping and resting they sing all night. "This tribe makes the impression upon us of a great male chorus of hunters, the members of which bind themselves not to marry before they are forty years old, but to live together in their club houses." The older ones, who have families, possess offices and dignities, and can therefore spend but little time in their houses. In the house of the men, where they were spinning, two would suddenly rise and have a wrestling match. There were always some who were idling, and although women were not generally present, there would be one or two pairs of lovers, to whom the others paid no attention.[13]

6 Finsch, *Ethnol. Erfahr.*, III, 327.
7 Cowan, *Maoris*, 163 ff.
8 Murdoch, in BAE, IX, 79 ff.
9 Nelson, in BAE, XVIII, 285.
10 Fulcomer, in AA, XI, 56, 57.

11 Powers, in *Contrib. Am. Ethnol.*, III, 24, 284.
12 Sievers, in *Globus*, LXXIII, 384.
13 Von den Steinen, *Zent. Bras.*, 480, 481, 489.

The bachelors' house is a conspicuous building where it occurs, and in it live all the young men of the village from the age of puberty until marriage; on a platform before it the young men sit and smoke.[14] In some cases only the small boys sleep in the bachelors' quarters, the older unmarried youths having apparently broken away from them. "The Zawlbuk is a large hall, with a huge hearth in the centre and a sleeping platform at the far end. The front wall stops about three feet short of the ground, and to enter the building you have to stoop under this, and then climb over a barrier of equal height placed a few feet further in. This building is the sleeping place of the young men of the village, and of any strangers who stop there the night. It is also a sort of general meeting house. The boys of the village have to keep up a sufficient supply of firewood for the Zawlbuk fire."[15] The barriers to entrance strikingly resemble those of the Eskimo *kashim*. One tribe requires the young men to sleep apart until a year after marriage. The bachelors' hall is similar to that of the Melanesians and the Malays, having the double purpose of guard-house and dormitory for the young men; in front "is a raised platform as a look-out, commanding an extensive view of all approaches, where a Naga is always kept on duty as a sentry," and there is a large hollowed tree-trunk for sounding the alarm or for use on grand occasions. Trophies are kept here, and it is used as a council-hall.[16]

The Malay bachelors' barracks generally stand on piles and have the usual purposes above mentioned.[17] The Sea Dyaks ornament their private houses with heads and other trophies, but the Land Dyaks display them in the bachelors' quarters. These buildings are entered by a trap-door in the floor. The head-house is "a circular building attached to most Dyak villages, and serving as a lodging for strangers, the place for trade, the sleeping room of the unmarried youths, and the general council chamber."[18] In Sumatra, from initiation to marriage, "the youths may not any longer sleep in the parental house, except in times of severe illness, but must spend the nights from sunset to sunrise in the village temple. . . . Into this village temple thus there come together every evening all the circumcized but unmarried males out of the village, while there also free lodging is offered to persons who are passing through." If the barracks are not big enough, a part of the bachelors are quartered in a sort of council-house near by. These places are tabooed to females. Where the village government is lax the men's house is the scene of cock-fights and vice.[19] In Ceram a youth puts on at puberty the bark-girdle, is given a place in the joint-house of the bachelors, and must take a head as soon as possible.[20]

In Formosa the bachelors' house is a sort of temple, ornamented with skulls of enemies and the pig-tails of the Chinese whom they have slain.[21] In the Loyalty Islands the bachelors' house is occupied by those not betrothed in infancy, or whose wives-to-be have died or been taken from them. They lead a club-life in common, and under polygyny are doomed to celibacy.[22] There is a men's assembly-house in Micronesia much on the plan of those described above; they "have nothing to do with religious purposes, for which the mis-

14 Woodthorpe, in JAI, XI, 199, 202; Shakespear, in JAI, XXXIX, 374.
15 Risley, *Ethnog. Ind.*, I, 212, 224.
16 Godden, in JAI, XXVII, 29; XXVI, 179 ff.; see plate XVII, in JAI, XI.
17 Ratzel, *Vkde.*, II, 415.
18 Roth, *Sarawak*, II, 156.

19 Jacobs, *Groot-Atjeh*, I, 199-200; Snouck-Hurgronje, *Atjèhers*, I, 64, 66.
20 Ratzel, *Vkde.*, II, 438.
21 Pickering, *Formosa*, 126, 148; Wirth, in AA, X, 364.
22 Ella, in AAAS, 1892, 625.

sionaries would have been so glad to use them, but serve only for public affairs and festivities and for the reception and sleeping-accommodation of strangers and bachelors."[23]

The unmarried men among the Atharaka, and those whose children are not yet circumcized, cannot sleep in the villages unless they are sick. In each settlement, therefore, the young men build for themselves one hut, generally hidden in a thicket close to the settlement. "Standing in the middle it gives one the impression of a circular saloon with berths all round. These huts are never occupied during the day, and I have never found any signs of habitation, except a fire. . . . The uncircumcized boys also build similar huts. These, however, are smaller and generally much closer to the settlement. The occupants sleep on the ground, there being no bedstead or similar contrivance."[24]

As among the Zulus, so with the Masai, the warrior is not allowed by the elders to marry until he is about thirty years old, has accumulated some property, or so distinguished himself as to merit an early retirement. He arranges by gifts for girls too young to conceive, whom he takes off to the warriors' village or settlement. "If by chance a girl remains with a warrior and conceives by him, no undue fuss is made, though he may probably have to support his child, and may make up his mind eventually to marry the girl. . . . The young girls who live in the warriors' settlements have as agreeable a time of it as can be provided in Masai society. They are supplied with food; the mothers of the young men do all the cooking, and the girls themselves spend their time in dancing, singing, adorning themselves, and making love. . . . After a woman is married—that is to say, is regularly bought by her husband—she is supposed to remain faithful to him."[25] A similar situation is found in Brazil, where a girl is forcibly taken to the men's house, that is, the large festival-house in the center of the village, and painted ornately. She is not married afterwards to any one husband, but all the men of the community occupy the place of father to her children. The whole institution arises from the predominance of the elders, who also receive the gifts that have been given to the girl.[26]

Not infrequently these houses are found to serve a distinctly educational purpose. In Liberia the girls in such houses learn to sing and dance, to tell tales, cook, attend to all kinds of domestic tasks, and knit nets. The author[27] calls the institution an "education-station." Among the Masai "the boys and girls up to a certain age live with their parents. . . . At the age of twelve the girls, and from twelve to fourteen the boys, are sent from the married men's kraal to one in which there are only young unmarried men and women." Peal[28] cites this case as a parallel to the *morong* of India; into the latter, as has been noted in another connection, when it is composed of girls only, no married woman may enter. Whether or not the young men and women are segregated in different *morongs*, "there is complete and *recognized* sexual liberty." The author knows of a single village where there was one girls' *morong*, and none for the young men. The institution of the maidens' sleeping-hall prevails among some Dravidians; "probably too much has been made of the custom in relation to sexual intercourse." In the larger villages of the Gilbert Islands there are men's houses, and "I learned besides of several assembly-houses for women . . . in which the females and the children were occupied, chiefly with weaving

23 Finsch, *Ethnol. Erfahr.*, III, 62, 63.
24 Champion, in JAI, XLII, 74.
25 Johnston, *Uganda*, II, 822, 824-825.

26 Von den Steinen, *Zent. Bras.*, 477, 502.
27 Frobenius, *Masken*, 121, 122.
28 In JAI, XXII, 248, 255, 260.

mats; and on the Marshall Islands the young women were shut up nights. In the central Carolines there are special women's houses, especially for females who are in their periods but also for women and children in general.[29] Among the Bororo Indians, "as soon as the children have been weaned, which generally does not take place before the fifth or even seventh year, they enter the *Bahito* (men's house) and only occasionally visit their parents. This *Bahito* is a public school where the children are taught spinning, weaving, the manufacture of weapons, and above all singing, upon perfection in which is centred the ambition of all those who wish to become chieftains."[30]

§163. Initiation-Ceremonies.

HOWITT[1] refers in a number of places to the Australian initiation-ceremonies. A knowledge of a great spirit, the sanctioner of social traditions, is given the boys at initiation; no women or children know of him, and his awful name is held secret. "The old men, referring to offenses against propriety and morality, say: 'If you do anything like that when you go back, you will be killed,'—that is, either by magic or direct violence. The things thus forbidden include disrespect towards old men, interference with unprotected women or the wives of other men, 'and those offenses for which, it is said, the Cities of the Plain were destroyed by celestial fire.'" Among the Kurnai the novices, with their blankets drawn closely over their heads, knelt in a row. Then sixteen men emerged, one after the other from the scrub some distance off, each whirling a bull-roarer. When the noise stopped, the novices were required to stand looking upward and the blankets were pulled off. Their gaze was directed from the sky to the performers on the bull-roarer. "Two old men now ran from one novice to the other saying earnestly, 'You must never tell this. You must not tell your mother, nor your sister, nor any one who is not Jeraeil.' The old head man then impressively revealed to the novices the ancestral beliefs." The Kurnai rules of conduct are as follows: "1. To listen to and obey the old men. 2. To share everything they have with their friends. 3. To live peaceably with their friends. 4. Not to interfere with girls or married women. 5. To obey the food restrictions until they are released from them by the old men." Among the Dieri, "in giving notice of the intention to 'make some young men,' the messenger takes a handful of charcoal and places a piece in the mouth of each person present without saying a word. This is fully understood to mean the 'making of young men.'" "In one part of Queensland the sound of the bull-roarer is said to be the noise made by the wizards in swallowing the boys and bringing them up again as young men."

"The community is divided into two exogamic sections, neither of which can by itself initiate its youths. At the age of puberty the boy is taken from his mother and the assembled women by the initiated men—that is, by the local organization. He undergoes certain ceremonies which are partly personal to himself, as circumcision, or the extraction of a tooth, and partly instructive, as by his being taught the ancestral laws which govern the relations of the sexes and the general morality of the tribe. . . . Some parts of the ceremonies are symbolical, as when the youth is invested with the 'belt of manhood,' or where his mother does some act signifying the termination of her maternal

---

29 Finsch, *Ethnol. Erfahr.*, III, 63, 338.   1 In JAI, XIII, 192, 450; XIV, 312, 316;
30 Frič and Radin, in JAI, XXXVI, 388.   XVI, 47; XX, 71.

control over him." The taboo on eating covers certain animals that are more nutritious than those permitted, and some that are more plentiful. Thus for a period up to a year he is placed on a sort of fast and thrown on his own resources. When the elders are satisfied with his fitness to rank with the men, he is recalled, and after a further probation is permitted to acquire a wife after the mode approved by the tribe. If he does that before getting the sanction of the local organization, he is put to death. He can now attend the general assembly of men, but may not yet speak during council.[2]

In another tribe, the young men having suffered the deep horizontal cuts above referred to, "a spray of blood is injected from the arms of several chiefs, on to the man's body, until his whole frame is covered with blood. This blood must not be rubbed off, but must wear off, and he cannot appear, nor can he be seen by women, children, or uncircumcized boys."[3] Among the Narrinyeri when the youths' beards have grown a sufficient length they are initiated. They are seized by night and carried off, the women resisting, or pretending to, by pulling at the captives and hurling firebrands. Then the men comb or tear out their matted hair with the point of a spear and pluck out a great part of their moustaches and beards by the roots. For three days and nights the initiates may not eat or sleep, are subjected to many discomforts, and for six months must go naked or nearly so. This condition lasts until their beards have been pulled out three times and each time have grown again to the length of about two inches. Everything they own becomes tabooed to woman's touch. They may not marry until the initiation is over, and any violation of the customs is punished by the old men with death. Again, there is a ceremonial of death and resurrection. The boy is laid on the ground and entirely covered with dust; then, in an almost stifled condition, is raised up by the ears. Later he receives the name which he inherits from father and mother and also a secret name, and is introduced to the rude mysteries. The Australian, while he is a boy, "lives under strict control; his food is regulated by the men, not as to quantity but as to quality. There are various kinds of meat which he must not eat; he cannot enter into any argument in camp; his opinion on any question is never asked, and he never thinks of giving it; he is not expected to engage in fights; and he is not supposed to fall in love with any of the young women. He is, in fact, a nonentity; but when he has gone through the initiatory process of being made a young man, he takes his proper place amongst the members of the tribe. He carries his war implements about with him, and has his share in aboriginal politics. He may now look upon a woman with eyes of love, and, if he be brave enough, seek a wife for himself."[4]

Mathews[5] somewhat emphasizes the disgusting and obscene phases of Australian initiations, which are, however, not fairly representative of initiations in general and are not reproduced here. The instructions given to the youths "are repeated every evening while the initiation lasts, and really form the principal part of it. The youth is to consider himself responsible for the good of the tribe, its ancient traditions, and its elders."[6] "There are four social stages for each individual, male or female, to be initiated into, and it may be years before all these ceremonials and corresponding grades are reached and

2 Howitt and Fison, in JAI, XIV, 154, 256.
3 Gason, cited in JAI, XVIII, 95.
4 Smyth, Vict., I, 65-66, 75, 82-83.

5 In JAI, XXVI, 278, 281; Mathews, in JAI, XXIV, 411; Mathews, in Zeitsft. f. Ethnol., XXXVII, 872 ff.
6 Palmer, in JAI, XIII, 296.

passed. . . . Before any individual can reach the next higher social stage than that of which he is a member, he must himself pass through all the duties of assisting in the initiating of others into the same rank as himself, until, by reason of his age, he comes to be the leader, chief director, or master of the ceremonies appertaining to his own degree: this coveted distinction having been once attained, he may be admitted into the next rank or degree at the first opportunity which presents itself. Sometimes there will be as many as three or four men accepted into the accorded rank all at the same time. It may be years, even up to old age, before all the social stages are reached."[7]

Of initiation in New South Wales we are told that "among all the tribes of this colony and most of those of others, the knocking out of one or two upper teeth is the sign that it has been performed. When the tooth is knocked out, a loud humming noise is heard. This is made by an instrument of flat wood with serrated edges, having a hole at one end, to which a string is attached." This is the whirr-stick or bull-roarer.[8] It is stated that the throwing of a boy into the air and catching him is supposed to be beneficial to his growth.[9] With few exceptions, circumcision is one of the attendant mutilations during the Australian initiation.[10] In Tasmania, the boys were given over to the old women, "who cut them on the thighs, shoulders, and muscles of the breast with stone-cutting implements, and thus raised cicatrices."[11]

The Australian case is quite complete, and there is a great deal of the same sort of practice in Melanesia. In New Guinea there is a circumcision-festival every ten years; the boys are secluded in the forest for five months, there is a sacred whistle which, like the bull-roarer, is tabooed to the women, and the boys are wakened as if to a resurrection. They are interned in the so-called "Asa-house" and fast for the next month, neither drinking water nor bathing; they must not be seen by a woman's eye. Circumcision was formerly accomplished with an obsidian knife, but later with a splinter of glass. A tremendous feast, for which much food is saved up by all, winds up the ceremony. The boys appear then, wearing each his new girdle of bark and other ornamentation proper to his new condition, and gaily painted. There is a procession, headed and brought up in the rear by drummers.[12] "In England more or less the same thing happens when a girl 'comes out.' She is then supposed to be on a footing with 'grown-ups' and this is practically what happens to the youth of British New Guinea. From the day of his 'coming-out' he occupies his hours in pleasure-seeking and has a good time generally; this goes on for a certain period and then he sallies forth alone into the bush to make his drum. This drum-making is the most serious part of his "coming-out,' and is conducted with a deal of formality and ceremony which is quaintly mixed with superstition. . . . The making of this musical instrument is an arduous task; it is hewn out from a solid block of wood by means of the crudest instruments, the hollow centre is made by burning it out with cinders of red-hot wood. . . . Many . . . curious superstitions relating to the eating of certain foods are attached to this operation; for instance, . . . if he drinks fresh water it will quench the fire with which he is trying to hollow out his drum, and other things too numerous to mention will happen if equally trifling details are not adhered to; but pro-

7 Roth, *N.W. Cent. Queensland*, 169.
8 Cameron, in JAI, XIV, 357; Collins, *N.S. Wales*, 364.
9 "Miscellany," in JAI, XXVII, 132.

10 Basedow, in JAI, XLIII, 296.
11 Barnard, in AAAS, 1890, 601.
12 Von Pfeil, *Südsee*, 315; Hagen, *Papua's*, 235 ff.

vided he comes through this important time without any calamities, and completes his drum to his own satisfaction, he steps forth from his seclusion to conquer the heart of a maiden."[13]

Up to ten or twelve years of age, the boys wear no covering of any sort. Then, on an appointed day, a boy is washed, smeared with coconut-oil, endowed with a loin-band, and decorated with all the family jewelry, such as boars' tusks and shells. He may eat no boiled food for ten days, but may stave off starvation by roasting a single banana now and then, eating only the center of it, and throwing away the extremities.[14] At fourteen to sixteen, again, a boy gets bow and arrow, but before getting them he must remain eight to ten days in deep silence. He and an old man, who is his preceptor, if they go abroad, walk with heads down and looking neither to right nor left. Women must get out of their way.[15] Schmidt[16] gives a detailed account, on information derived from a native youth at a Catholic mission, of the secret ceremonies practised at initiation by the Karesau Islanders of the then German New Guinea.

The broad features of initiation in New Guinea appear to be: a complete rupture from the old asexual life of childhood, a clan-rite of integration with the mountain-god, an intermediate stage, the explanation of the bull-roarer, 'the tribal warrior-festival, and a clan or tribal introduction to the god of the sea. The whole ceremony, which is regarded with absolute terror by the uninitiated, is a sort of schooling as well as a means of attaining social status, for it is on the faithful following-out of the instruction received by initiates that the social and moral welfare of the tribe depends.[17] "Instruction is given to the lads, both of a moral nature and relating to the ordinary occupations of life. The moral code runs something after this fashion:—It is wrong to steal. It is wrong to commit adultery, for if you do you will die quickly. It is wrong to beat your wife; if you do, other people will say you are like a dog. . . . In addition to these instructions given to the boys in the initiation house, the lads were told, 'Now you have seen the Spirit and you are fully a man. To prove yourself you must kill a man,' thus making a murder a social requirement."[18] Among the natives of the Papuan Gulf the boys receive "such information as is calculated to equip them for all the duties and obligations of citizens and worthy members of their tribe. From their guardian they receive all kinds of advice respecting their duty to their tribe; this must always take the first place in all their actions; the enemies of the tribe must be the enemy of the individual initiate; it will be to the best interests of the tribe that it should be so. In selecting a wife, the first thing to be considered is the interests of the tribe, whether she is likely to bear healthy children . . . Whatever serves the highest interests of the tribe is justifiable. . . . Their conception of right and wrong is governed by what public opinion requires in order that the tribe may maintain its position among other tribes."[19]

Codrington[20] says that "there is not known in these Islands of Melanesia any initiation or 'making of young men': there is only the entrance into the

13 Hardy and Elkington, *So. Seas*, 38-40.

14 Guise, in JAI, XXVIII, 207.

15 Schliermacher, in *Globus*, LXXVIII, 4-5.

16 Karesau-Ins., in *Anthropos*, II, 1029 ff.

17 Haddon, in JAI, L, 263, 264, 268-269.

18 Chinnery and Beaver, in JAI, XLV, 72 ff., 76 (quoted), 77-78.

19 Holmes, in JAI, XXXII, 420, 422 (quoted), 424.

20 *Melanesians*, 233; Somerville, in JAI, XXVI, 407.

various societies;" but Seligmann[21] mentions a case among the Roro-speaking tribes and another among the southern Massim, while in Fiji there is a ceremony which amounts to the reception of boys at puberty into the assembly of the men. Fison[22] describes it in some detail. "Every full-born male is by birth a member of the community, but he is not a *man* until he has been received into the Nanga, and even then he does not attain full membership until he has attended two of its celebrations, one of which is that at which he was initiated." The effect of this regulation is to keep him on probation for two years at least. "There are always a number of youths who are growing to the proper age, and the length of the interval depends upon the decision of the elders." The Nanga is a sacred place where any initiated man may find ancestral spirits for worship, offerings, prayer, or appeals. "Strictly speaking, the Nanga is the Stone Enclosure, but the word seems to be used for the ceremony of initiation also. . . . The heads of the novices are clean shaved and present a curious appearance, owing to the remarkable shapes, the heads being narrowed by lateral pressure during infancy." The climax for the novices is where, "following their leader, the old Vere with the graven staff, their eyes on the ground that they may tread exactly in his footsteps, they go to the Great Nanga as on the former occasions. When they arrive at the Great Nanga they find it deserted. The procession stops, and there is dead silence. Suddenly from the forest a harsh scream of many parrots breaks forth, and then there is a mysterious booming sound. The old Vere now moves slowly forward and leads the young men for the first time into the Nanga tambutambu. Near the outer entrance, his back to the Temple, sits the chief priest regarding them with a fixed stare, and between him and them lie a row of dead men, covered with blood, their bodies apparently cut open and their entrails protruding. The Vere steps over them, one by one, and the youths follow until they stand in a row before the high priest, their 'souls drying up' under his glare. Suddenly he blurts out a great yell, the dead men start to their feet, and run down to the river to cleanse themselves from the blood, etc., with which they are besmeared. These are the Vere with some of the Vunilolo matua, who represent the departed ancestors on the occasion, the blood and entrails being those of many pigs. The parrot screams and other hideous sounds were made by hidden performers, the roaring sound having been made by blowing into a bamboo trumpet, the mouth of which is partly immersed in water." This trumpet is the equivalent of the Australian bull-roarer; to sound it for sport would be impious. The next day the women, with hair dyed a reddish color, and strangely decorated, are allowed to crawl on hands and knees through the Great Nanga into the Nanga tambutambu (tabootaboo). "The chief priest dips his hands in the Sacred Bowl (filled with water) and offers a prayer for the mothers and their children. This is called the *vuluvulu* (hand-washing) of the women, the priest's action being vicarious on their behalf. When the prayer is over, the women return the way they came, crawling over certain earth mounds in the Nanga, which have been prepared for the occasion. As the women retire, they chant a song called the *Ruerue*. When they emerge from the Nanga, the men, hitherto concealed, rush upon them with a yell and an indescribable scene ensues. Accounts differ as to what takes place, but all informants agree that the men and women address each other in the vilest language, using expressions

21 *Melanesians*, 258, 260-261, 495-497.
22 In JAI, XIV, 15, 19, 20, 21 ff., 26; Fro-

benius, *Masken*, 251; Andree, *Eth. Parallelen*, 198.

which would be violently resented on ordinary occasions, and that from the time of the women's coming to the Nanga to the close of the ceremonies very great license prevails."

Circumcision is regarded in Fiji as cleansing and purifying, and "no man can expect to be respected unless he undergoes the operation;"[23] in New Caledonia it came "when the youth's whiskers reached the hair of his head."[24] In the New Britain group, "when a number of young men have arrived at the age of 15 or 16 years, a great feast is prepared, to which their relatives are invited. . . . The ceremony over, the young man must go into the bush and hide from his female relatives for from three to six months." If by accident he meets a female relative he gives her something that he happens to have in his possession, and which must then be redeemed by his friends. "This seems to be a sort of compensation of his having met her, it being regarded as an act to his shame . . . and he is supposed to be in disgrace until it is accomplished."[25]

In the Torres Straits Islands the lads, on arrival at manhood, were taken to the sacred meeting-place for men, located in the bush, and painted all over. They were washed daily and fresh color put on. Each wore a sort of mat-tent over him which completely hid him when sitting, and exposed only the legs when walking. "For a month the boys were kept in their peripatetic prisons, spending all day in silent darkness"; no female may see them and even their fathers might not visit them. Death was the penalty for infringing such regulations. During this period of retirement they were instructed in the customs, morals, and lore of the tribe: "You no steal" was one of the injunctions. The boy must not first propose marriage, but must wait for the lady to ask him. Two mates must not marry each other's sisters, lest they be ashamed by-and-by. "Look after mother and father, never mind if you and your wife have to go without." At the end of the probation the boys were thoroughly cleaned up, oiled all over, decorated, and anointed with "girl medicine," a sort of love-charm. For three months more the boy stayed with his uncle or brother-in-law, not his father. "It seems that the character of various girls was made known to the boys during their initiation, that they might be forewarned."[26]

The Kaffirs "render an especial attention to the boys at the time of puberty: when this period approaches, neighboring communities join and give over their boys of the same age to an older man who is chosen specially for the office, and they withdraw under his supervision into the wilderness." This mentor circumcises the boys and teaches them the usages, instruction which Fritsch[27] calls "academic studies." They stay in seclusion for over six months, then burn their huts, are newly washed and clothed, and return. Those who are initiated together form a kind of brotherhood and in fighting constitute a section of the army under the command of the chief's son who went through the ceremony with them. The boys are schooled in men's duties and are formally whipped, generally by their nearest relations, while kneeling.[28] Part of the ceremony is the use of white clay to daub the boys' bodies; they must steal all the meat they get and are punished for clumsiness; there is much violent dancing and running; and the initiates are kept sleepless. Many die under the ordeal. In the end they get the skin cloak, red paint, and arms, and are preached at; they

23 Brewster, in JAI, XLIX, 315.
24 Turner, *Samoa*, 341.
25 Danks, in JAI, XVIII, 286.

26 Haddon, in JAI, XIX, 409.
27 *Eingeb. S.-Afr.*, 109, 206.
28 Holub, *S.-Afr.*, I, 483-484.

are told to obey the chief and use their weapons at his command against even their mothers. Much sexual license is permitted.[29]

The maintenance of circumcision-lodges prevails in many parts of South Africa: in Cape Colony, the Transvaal, Rhodesia, and Bechuanaland. It existed at one time among the Zulus, but was prohibited by Chaka, against the advice of his councillors, at the time he successfully amalgamated the scattered Zulu tribes. These lodges, more commonly called schools, a term probably adopted since the advent among them of missionaries, are convened in some secluded spot where the cold at night is intense. "The cold is calculated, with other hardships, such as whipping and privations, to harden the physique of the young fellows attending, and to make them manly." Native public opinion drives many to submit to the rites. "They are jeered at if they refuse, and are treated to ridicule, such as the following expressions: 'You are a woman,' 'Your eyes are unopened,' and perhaps the still greater taunt, 'You will not please the women, who prefer circumcised men'; and it is generally said at the conclusion of the lodges, that the newly circumcised are greatly favoured by the women." When deaths take place under seclusion, the dead are quietly buried with no mourning; the deceased is looked upon as having simply disappeared; often the mother is not told until the period of seclusion is over.[30] While undergoing the rites considerable time is spent in instilling into the youthful mind sound principles for future guidance, the oldest of the chief's councillors usually acting as instructors. The boys are warned against certain wrongs and vicious habits, and encouraged to be faithful and loyal subjects to their chief, and good husbands and fathers. They are shown all the sacred things, or fetishes, of the tribe and made acquainted with their meaning and use, which, however, they are forbidden under heavy penalty to disclose to any outsiders; they are also drilled in the full range of etiquette of intercourse with their superiors and chiefs. "They are taught to be brave in war, cunning in stealing, and true to their special form of heathenism, i.e., to their ancestors. They are taught to bear pain without showing it, and are thus practised in self-restraint." A good part of the instruction given is in the form of proverbs, that is, of long-tested folk-wisdom. "The chief subject used in the proverbs is mankind itself in all its stages. . . . The lessons given are: to be prudent, to be diligent and careful, to avoid evil-doing, to help the needful, to cry with the one who is crying, to honour the last will of the deceased, and so on. Much use is made of proverbs in daily life, and if a stranger cites one or other, the Mowenda gets quite excited and finishes it as soon as he has heard only the beginning."[31]

Brown[32] disputes the claim that the circumcision-ceremonies are schools of self-restraint, morality, reverence for elders, and obedience to law. The "initiated man is the prey of the woman, as the woman of the man. This surely disposes of the claim to the teaching of self-restraint. Obedience to law is not taught to the initiated, nor do the songs contain much, if anything, to encourage law-keeping." They announce that "the law has an ending, or comes to an end, if it doesn't it can be left behind. Persistent refusal to abide by the law conquers eventually, and constant breakings of it will wear it out. . . . There

29 Macdonald, in JAI, XIX, 268; Frobenius, *Masken*, 31, 32.
30 Wheelwright, in JAI, XXXV, 251, 252-254, 255.

31 Gottschling, in JAI, XXXV, 372, 383-384; Grant, in JAI, XXXV, 268.
32 In JAI, LI, 426-427.

is no teaching of law, none of the righteousness of people, nor any teaching of veneration. There are many teachings that praise wickedness, the honouring of concubinage, and one's uncle and strangers. There is much teaching regarding the cattle, and to steal, but none that holds up law as that by which communities live and prosper. In its place is reverence for antiquity, aversion to change, conformity to traditional custom, and the completeness of Bechuana manhood and womanhood as embodied in the circumcision rites. But there must be no change. As things were in the days of long ago, so they are to-day, so they must remain." This author seems to lack understanding, as well as a command of his own tongue, and to condemn savage ways from some lofty coign of superiority.

The steps toward the gate of manhood are many and difficult among the Bantu. Perhaps the most prominent feature of the initiation-ceremonies after the act of circumcision is the application of the switch. The Bechuana novice is made to lie down with face to the ground and body stretched out, and is then well thrashed, being reminded the while of the faults of his childhood; some who have greatly misbehaved are so severely punished that they die under the chastisement. The ordeal is "to teach them, to develop them, to ensure that there shall be no rebelling against the ancient ways, or walking in strange paths. In short, it is to bring them to the full heritage of their birthright."[33] The headman of the village tells the Bageshu boys about their customs, history, marriage-usages, and impresses upon them the necessity of being brave to fight the battles for the tribe. In some cases, "youths shrink from the operation [of circumcision] and go on from year to year postponing it. They may find some women who agree to become their wives and they may have families, but they can never claim to be full members of the clan, nor may they wear the dress peculiar to those who are full members."[34]

Circumcision is a regular ceremony among most of the tribes of Central and East Africa, and in some cases is the only one of importance; no reason, however, is assigned for the custom and its origin is unknown. With hardly an exception, no uncircumcized man or woman might marry. There are certain natural grades, if they may be so termed, through which a native can expect to pass during his life; these compose a system of graduated initiation commencing when a child is circumcized; after the stages of the circumcision-rites are finished he becomes a full-fledged warrior; a little later a young married man; and when he has circumcized children he enters upon the various grades of the council. The initiation-ceremonies may well be regarded as the opening chapter in the tribal life of the individual, a life every event of which is marked by the performance of some rite. At the present time, among some of these tribes, there is a tendency for the rites to be performed at an earlier and earlier age so that the youths may benefit by the instruction given at the ceremonies before they come under missionary influence and lose the ties of tribal custom. One of the chief features of the initiation-ceremonies is the teaching of morals, of what in the native's mind constitutes right and wrong; bravery, justice, keeping one's wife in subjection, respect for riches, and good manners in the presence of superiors are some of the matters emphasized. One authority on these tribes, having in mind the rites symbolical of the entrance upon a

---

33 Brown, in JAI, LI, 421, 422, 423 (quoted), 424; Roscoe, in JAI, XXXVII, 107; Willoughby, in JAI, XXXIX, 235-236.

34 Roscoe, in JAI, XXXIX, 185, 191 (quoted).

new era in the life of the candidates, thinks that "the confirmation ceremony of the Christian church is in all probability an adopted relic of the initiation ceremonies handed down from ancient times."[35]

The stages of development to full manhood, among the Nigerian head-hunters, seem to be (a) circumcision, (b) initiation, (c) scarification, (d) the taking of a head if possible, (e) marriage, and (f) the shaving of the head.[36] In West Africa, "the boy, if he belongs to a tribe that goes in for tattooing, is tattooed, and is handed over to instructors in the societies' secrets and formulae. He lives, with the other boys of his tribe undergoing initiation, usually under the rule of several instructors, and for the space of one year. He lives always in the forest, and is naked and smeared with clay. The boys are exercised so as to become inured to hardship; in some districts they make raids so as to perfect themselves in this useful accomplishment. They always take a new name, and are supposed by the initiation process to become new beings in the magic wood, and on their return to their village at the end of their course, they pretend to have entirely forgotten their life before they entered the wood; but this pretence is not kept up beyond the period of festivities given to welcome them home. They all learn, to a certain extent, a new language, a secret language only understood by the initiated."[37] In West Africa a boy must die to the mother-clan and be born again to the father-tribe; the rite at puberty symbolizes this.[38] Frobenius[39] refers to initiation, chiefly in connection with the secret societies; only a limited number go through it, he says, at least through all grades. The medicine-man takes them into the forest and gives them a dose that robs them of consciousness. Circumcision takes place at this time. "They allow the young men 'for the alleviation of their pains' during this time to rob a hen-house or to steal an ox from a poor Fulbe herder, in order to keep themselves in spirits. The laws would at another occasion strictly take notice of this deed." But no murdering may be done. It is a great crime to have sex-relations before circumcision. The injunctions given to the initiates are enforced with heavy whips plied by men in fearful masks. In Senegambia much plundering and other violence is done under cover of the masks, which indicate membership among the politically mature men.[40] In other places young men test each other's endurance by duels with hippopotamus-hide whips, suffering severely, but with no whimpering.[41] Sacrifices and markings with blood and fat, together with feasts, are Northeast African puberty-ceremonies accompanying the circumcision.[42] In the course of numerous travels, Trilles[43] never saw a Fan who was not circumcised, and asserts that circumcision has been observed over the whole world, in the most diverse races, generally being part of the ceremonies of initiation, "which unite most intimately the young man to his tribe, to his god or gods." He agrees with those authors who regard the practice as, in origin, never hygienic but essentially religious. After mentioning cases of circumcision in the Sudan, Seligmann[44] cites from Strabo, who

35 Hobley, *A-Kamba*, 68, 70-72, 74 (quoted); in JAI, XLI, 414, 416; Dundas, C., in JAI, XLIII, 522-523, 547; Dundas, K. R., in JAI, XLIII, 61, 62, 64, 69; Barrett, in JAI, XLI, 22; Torday and Joyce, in JAI, XXXVI, 46; Tate, in JAI, XXXIV, 265; Barton, in JAI, LI, 90-91, 94; Stannus and Davey, in JAI, XLIII, 119-123; Stannus, in JAI, XL, 296, 299.

36 Tremearne, in JAI, XLII, 161-163.

37 Kingsley, *Travels W. Afr.*, 531; Weeks, in JAI, XL, 401.

38 Lippert, *Kgchte.*, II, 342.

39 *Masken*, 44, 145, 147, 148, 216.

40 Karutz, in *Globus*, LXXXIX, 368.

41 Junker, *Afrika*, I, 63, 64; III, 465.

42 Paulitschke, *Nordost-Afr.*, I, 194, 195.

43 *Fân*, 516, 520, 521.

44 In JAI, XLIII, 642, 644, 646, 647.

wrote two thousand years ago, certain historical evidence as to its antiquity. He says the practice is widespread among the Arabs and in Syria, is absent in North Africa among the Berbers, though the Tuaregs are said to circumcise, and is found in the French Sudan, in Sierra Leone, Benin, Akra, Old Calabar, and Loango. It was not originally Mohammedan or Arabic.

In ancient India there was a beard-ceremony for a youth of sixteen to eighteen, shortly before his marriage. In later times the ten- or twelve-year-old boy is simply invested with a garland of shells.[45] Among certain Tibetans the boy of fifteen is initiated by torture under the eyes of the chiefs and lamas. If he shows pain he is abused and scorned until he commits suicide; if not, he is subjected to the hunger-ordeal. Those who come through are given weapons and must prove their prowess as hunters and warriors.[46] The Chinese youth was "capped," that is, ceremoniously presented with three caps, when he was twenty.[47]

In Borneo, "the women often prove the courage and endurance of the youngsters by placing a lighted ball of tinder on the arm, and letting it burn into the skin. The marks thus produced run along the forearm from the wrist in a straight line, and are much valued by the young men as so many proofs of their power of endurance."[48] Among the Alfurs of Buru circumcision is performed on boys and girls of eight to ten years, but Wilken[49] says it has no religious character and is accompanied by no usages. Tattoo in the Society Islands was probably a mark of puberty,[50] while in Samoa until a young man was tattooed he was considered in his minority; "he could not think of marriage, and he was constantly exposed to taunts and ridicule, as being poor and of low birth, and as having no right to speak in the society of men. But as soon as he was tattooed he passed into his majority, and considered himself entitled to the respect and privileges of mature years. When a youth, therefore, reached the age of sixteen, he and his friends were all anxiety that he should be tattooed."[51] In the Gilbert Islands, "from the moment of weaning, a boy was regarded as a potential warrior, and from first to last the ceremonies which he underwent were performed with that idea predominating." At five he was taken by his father and, after being washed with fresh water in a bowl of wood as a sign that his infancy was done, he was set apart from his mother and sisters, forbidden the fellowship of all girls of his age, and obliged to sleep thereafter only beside boys and men. At eight his diet began to be strictly regulated, and when about twenty or twenty-five he was put through a series of trying ordeals, all of which had to be borne without a murmur.[52] In the initiation of the eldest son of the Maori head-chief, "the young chief is urged to sleep, and the priest watches for omens. . . . If an arm or a leg jerk inwards it indicates luck, but if it jerk outwards, the lad cannot be taught." But there are no special puberty-ceremonies except in the case of this one youth, who has to know the secrets of priestcraft and witchcraft.[53]

There are comparatively few cases of thoroughgoing initiation, thus far, outside of the black races; but when we come to America we find another classic

45 Zimmer, *Altind. Leben*, 322; Joshi, in JASB, I, 376 ff.
46 Reid, in *Cosmopolitan Mag.*, XXVIII, 450.
47 Müller, *Sacred Books* (Legge, *Sacred Books of China*), XXVII, 79, 478; XXVIII, 426.

48 Roth, *Sarawak*, II, 81; Nieuwenhuis, *Borneo*, I, 69.
49 In VG, I, 51.
50 Roth, in JAI, XXXV, 292.
51 Turner, *Samoa*, 88 (quoted), 89.
52 Grimble, in JAI, LI, 37, 38-41.
53 Tregear, in JAI, XIX, 99.

ground for the custom. Even in Greenland there are exchanges of blows to test endurance; "one beat the other with all his might unceasingly on the back, whereby the loser was he who first got tired either of giving or receiving the blows."[54] "Husquenawing" was "an ordeal to which certain promising young Virginia Indians were submitted, upon reaching the age of virility, as an initiation into a new state of life, that of manhood, and for the purpose of rendering them oblivious to every event of the preceding state of adolescence, and of preparing their mind for the reception of new impressions." They went into the woods under a custodian and were dosed with medicines that made them delirious; thereafter they were supposed to forget that they had ever been boys. "Huskanawed" is a local expression used of a person who looks as if he had been subjected to the action of an emetic. The initiates were supposed to have a "new body."[55]

According to Donaldson's[56] account, the Mandan initiation was held at the rallying-point of the whole nation, a religious center called the "big canoe," at a time indicated by the full expansion of the willow leaves. Then appears from the distance the "first or only man," impressively painted with white clay and carrying a large pipe, and enters the medicine-lodge. "During the first night of this strange character in the village, no one could tell where he slept; and every person, both old and young, and dogs, and all living things, were kept within doors, and dead silence reigned everywhere." The next day about fifty young men appeared as candidates. They were addressed in the medicine-lodge by the "first man" and an old medicine-man was appointed master of ceremonies; then the former marched away, after promising to return the next year. Thereafter for four days and nights the young men were watched by the medicine-man, who lay by the fire, with the medicine-pipe, crying to the Great Spirit, and were not allowed to eat, drink, or sleep. Catlin was allowed to enter the lodge because he had painted a full-length of the medicine-man which had so astonished him that he credited the artist with high skill in magic and mysteries. Various articles of extreme sanctity whose nature and use "could not be told" appeared in the lodge; liberal offers to buy them were firmly refused. Among them were four sacks of water which "had been contained therein ever since the settling down of the waters!"

Outside there occurred during these four days the buffalo-dance, or bull-dance, which was necessary in order that they might have bison-meat during the season. Then the evil spirit, personated by a man painted coal-black came rushing in from the distance and was held still and immovable by being confronted with the medicine pipe—a fetish competent to check and disarm him. It is noticeable that this spirit had turned his attention chiefly to the women, who had fled in terror before him. All applauded his defeat at the hand of the medicine-man, "and all eyes gazed upon him; of chiefs and of warriors, matrons, and even of their tender-aged and timid daughters, whose education had taught them to receive the moral of these scenes without the shock of impropriety that would have startled a more fastidious and consequently sensual-thinking people." Finally the evil spirit was teased and tantalized by the women, and was at length driven from the village with sticks and stones, to the deep satisfaction of all. He had come to disturb their worship. Since he had been ejected, they could turn to the chief task of the time: the initiation.

---

54 Fries, *Grönland*, 116, note.
55 Gerard, in AA, IX, 93-94.

56 In *Smithson. Rep.*, 1885, pt. II, 352 ff.;
Matthews, in USNM, 1890, 606 ff.

The inside of the medicine-lodge came now to present a sort of shambles, for the "cutting scene" was next staged. It is described, after Catlin's sketch and in awkward English, as follows. "Around the sides of the lodge are seen, still reclining, . . . a part of the group, whilst others of them have passed the ordeal of self-tortures, and have been removed out of the lodge; and others still are seen in the very act of submitting to them, which were inflicted in the following manner: After having removed the *sanctissimus sanctorum*, or little scaffold, of which I before spoke, and having removed also the buffalo and human skulls from the floor, and attached them to the posts of the lodge, and two men having taken their positions near the middle of the lodge, for the purpose of inflicting the tortures, the one with the scalping-knife, and the other with the bunch of splits [splints] . . . in his hand, one at a time of the young fellows, already emaciated with fasting and thirsting and waking for nearly four days and nights, advanced from the side of the lodge and placed himself on his hands and feet, or otherwise, as best suited for the performance of the operation, where he submitted to the cruelties in the following manner: An inch or more of the flesh on each shoulder or each breast was taken up between the thumb and finger by the man who held the knife in his right hand, and the knife, which had been ground sharp on both edges, and then hacked and notched with the blade of another, to make it produce as much pain as possible, was forced through the flesh below the fingers, and being withdrawn, was followed with a splint or skewer from the other, who held a bunch of such in his left hand, and was ready to force them through the wound.

"There were then two cords lowered down from the top of the lodge (by men who were placed on the lodge outside for the purpose), which were fastened to these splints or skewers, and they instantly began to haul him up; he was thus raised until his body was suspended from the ground, where he rested until the knife and a splint were passed through the flesh or integuments in a similar manner on each arm below the shoulder (over the *brachialis externus*), below the elbow (over the *extensor carpi radialis*), on the thighs (over the *vastus externus*), and below the knees (over the *peroneus*)

"In some instances they remained in a reclining position on the ground until this painful operation is finished, which was performed in all instances exactly on the same parts of the body and limbs, and which in its progress occupied some five or six minutes.

"Each one was then instantly raised with the cords until the weight of his body was suspended by them, and then, while the blood was streaming down their limbs, the bystanders hung upon the splints each man's appropriate shield, bow and quiver, &c.; and in many instances the skull of a buffalo, with the horns on it, was attached to each lower arm and each lower leg, for the purpose probably of preventing by their great weight the struggling which might otherwise have taken place to their disadvantage whilst they were hung up.

"When these things were all adjusted each one was raised higher by the cords, until those weights all swung clear from the ground, leaving his feet, in most cases, some 6 or 8 feet above the ground. In this plight they at once became appalling and frightful to look at—the flesh to support the weight of their bodies, with the additional weights which were attached to them, was raised 7 or 8 inches by the skewers, and their heads sunk forward on the breasts, or thrown backwards, in a much more frightful condition, according to the way in which they were hung up.

"The unflinching fortitude with which every one of them bore this part of the torture surpassed credulity; each one, as the knife was passed through his flesh, sustained an unchangeable countenance; and several of them, seeing me making sketches, beckoned me to look at their faces, which I watched all through this horrid operation without being able to detect anything but the pleasantest smiles as they looked me in the eye, while I could hear the knife rip through the flesh and feel enough of it myself to start involuntary and uncontrollable tears over my cheeks.

"When raised to the condition above described, and completely suspended by the cords, the sanguinary hands through which he had just passed turned back to perform a similar operation on another who was ready, and each one in his turn passed into the charge of others, who instantly introduced him to a new and improved stage of their refinements in cruelty.

"Surrounded by imps and demons as they appear—a dozen or more—who seem to be concerting and devising means for his exquisite agony, gather around him, when one of the number advances toward him in a sneering manner and commences turning him around with a pole which he brings in his hand for the purpose. This is done in a gentle manner at first, but gradually increased, when the brave fellow, whose proud spirit can control its agony no longer, burst out in the most lamentable and heartrending cries that the human voice is capable of producing, crying forth a prayer to the Great Spirit to support and protect him in this dreadful trial, and continually repeating his confidence in his protection. In this condition he is continued to be turned faster and faster, and there is no hope of escape from it, nor chance for the slightest relief, until by fainting his voice falters and his struggling ceases, and he hangs apparently a still and lifeless corpse. When he is by turning gradually brought to this condition, which is generally done within ten or fifteen minutes, there is a close scrutiny passed upon him among his tormentors, who are checking and holding each other back as long as the least struggling or tremor can be discovered, lest he should be removed before he is (as they term it) 'entirely dead.'

"When brought to this alarming and most frightful condition, and the turning has gradually ceased, as his voice and his strength have given out, leaving him to hang entirely still and apparently lifeless, when his tongue is distended from his mouth, and his medicine-bag, which he has affectionately and superstitiously clung to with his left hand, has dropped to the ground, the signal is given to the men on top of the lodge by gently striking the cord with the pole below, when they very gradually and carefully lower him to the ground.

"In this helpless condition he lies like a loathsome corpse to look at, though in the keeping (as they call it) of the Great Spirit, whom he trusts will protect him and enable him to get up and walk away. As soon as he is lowered to the ground thus, one of the bystanders advances and pulls out the two splints or pins from the breasts and shoulders, thereby disengaging him from the cords by which he has been hung up, but leaving all the others with their weights, &c., hanging to his flesh.

"In this condition he lies for six or eight minutes, until he gets strength to rise and move himself, for no one is allowed to assist or offer him aid, as he is here enjoying the most valued privilege which a Mandan can boast of, that of 'trusting his life to the keeping of the Great Spirit' in this time of extreme peril.

"As soon as he is seen to get strength enough to rise on his hands and feet and drag his body around the lodge, he crawls, with the weights still hanging to his body, to another part of the lodge, where there is another Indian sitting with a hatchet in his hand and a dried buffalo skull before him; and here, in the most earnest and humble manner, by holding up the little finger of his left hand to the Great Spirit, he expresses to him in a speech of a few words his willingness to give it as a sacrifice, when he lays it on the dried buffalo skull, when the other chops it off near the hand with a blow of the hatchet.

"Nearly all of the young men whom I saw passing this horrid ordeal gave, in the above manner, the little finger of the left hand; and I saw also several who immediately afterwards (and apparently with very little concern or emotion), with a similar speech, extended in the same way the forefinger of the same hand, and that, too, was struck off, leaving on the hand only the two middle fingers and the thumb, all which they deem absolutely essential for holding the bow, the only weapon for the left hand.

"One would think that this mutilation had thus been carried quite far enough; but I have since examined several of the head chiefs and dignitaries of the tribe, who have also given, in this manner, the little finger of the right hand, which is considered by them to be a much greater sacrifice than both of the others; and I have found also a number of their most famous men, who furnish me incontestable proof, by five or six corresponding scars on each arm, and each breast, and each leg, that they had so many times in their lives submitted to this almost incredible operation, which seems to be optional with them; and the oftener they volunteer to go through it the more famous they become in the estimation of their tribe.

"No bandages are applied to the fingers which have been amputated; no arteries taken up; nor is any attention whatever paid to them or the other wounds; but they are left (as they say) 'for the Great Spirit to cure, who will surely take good care of them.' It is a remarkable fact, which I learned from a close inspection of their wounds from day to day, that the bleeding is but very slight and soon ceases, probably from the fact of their extreme exhaustion and debility, caused by want of sustenance and sleep, which checks the natural circulation, and admirably at the same time prepares them to meet the severity of these tortures without the same degree of sensibility and pain which, under other circumstances, might result in inflammation and death.

"During the whole of the time of this cruel part of these most extraordinary inflictions the chiefs and dignitaries of the tribe are looking on, to decide who are the hardiest and stoutest hearted—who can hang the longest by his flesh before he faints, and who will be soonest up, after he has been down—that they may know whom to appoint to lead a war party, or place at the most honorable and desperate post. The four old men are incessantly beating upon the sacks of water and singing the whole time, with their voices strained to the highest key, vaunting forth, for the encouragement of the young men, the power and efficacy of the medicine-pipe, which has disarmed the monster O-kee-hee-de (or Evil Spirit), and driven him from the village, and will be sure to protect them and watch over them through their present severe trial.

"As soon as six or eight had passed the ordeal as above described, they were led out of the lodge, with their weights hanging to their flesh, and dragging on the ground, to undergo another and a still more appalling mode of suffering, in the center of the village, and in presence of the whole nation, in the manner as follows:

"The signal for the commencement of this part of the cruelties was given by the old master of ceremonies, who again ran out as in the buffalo-dance, and leaning against the big canoe with his medicine-pipe in his hand began to cry. This was done several times in the afternoon, as often as there were six or eight who had passed the ordeal just described within the lodge, who were then taken out in the open area, in the presence of the whole village, with the buffalo skulls and other weights attached to their flesh and dragging on the ground. There were then in readiness and prepared for the purpose about twenty young men, selected of equal height and equal age, with their bodies chiefly naked, with beautiful (and similar) head-dresses of war eagles' quills on their heads, and a wreath made of willow boughs held in the hands between them, connecting them in a chain or circle, in which they ran around the big canoe with all possible speed, raising their voices in screams and yelps to the highest pitch that was possible, and keeping the curb or big canoe in the center as their nucleus. . . .

"Then were led forward the young men who were further to suffer, and being placed at equal distances apart and outside of the ring just described, each one was taken in charge by two athletic young men, fresh and strong, who stepped up to him, one on each side, and by wrapping a broad leather around his wrists without tying it, grasped it firm underneath the hand and stood prepared for what they call Eh-ke-nah-ka-nah-pick, the last race.

"This the spectator looking on would suppose was most correctly named, for he would think it was the last race they could possibly run in this world. In this condition they stand pale and ghastly from abstinence and loss of blood, until all are prepared and the word is given, when all start and run around outside of the other ring, and each poor fellow, with his weights dragging on the ground, and his furious conductors by his side, who hurry him forward by the wrists, struggles in the desperate emulation to run longer without 'dying' (as they call it) than his comrades, who are fainting around him and sinking down, like himself, where their bodies are dragged with all possible speed, and often with their faces in the dirt. In the commencement of this dance or race they all start at a moderate pace, and their speed being gradually increased, the pain becomes so excruciating that their languid and exhausted frames give out, and they are dragged by their wrists until they are disengaged from the weights that were attached to their flesh, and this must be done by such violent force as to tear the flesh out with the splint, which (as they say) can never be pulled out endwise without greatly offending the Great Spirit and defeating the object for which they have thus far suffered. The splints or skewers which are put through the breast and the shoulders, take up a part of the pectoral or trapezius muscle, which is necessary for the support of the great weight of their bodies, and which, as I have before mentioned, are withdrawn as soon as he is lowered down; but all the others, on the legs and arms, seem to be very ingeniously passed through the flesh and integuments without taking up the muscle, and even these, to be broken out, require so strong and so violent a force that most of the poor fellows fainted under the operation, and when they were freed from the last of the buffalo skulls and other weights (which was often done by some of the bystanders throwing the weight of their bodies on to them as they were dragging on the ground) they were in every instance dropped by the persons who dragged them, and their bodies were left, appearing like nothing but a mangled and a loathsome corpse. At this strange and frightful juncture the two men who had dragged them fled through the crowd and away upon the prairie, as if they were guilty of some enormous crime and were fleeing from summary vengeance.

"Each poor fellow having thus patiently and manfully endured the privations and tortures devised for him, and (in this last struggle with the most appalling effort) torn himself loose from them and his tormentors, he lies the second time in the 'keeping (as he terms it) of the Great Spirit,' to whom he issues his repeated prayers and intrusts his life, and in whom he reposes the most implicit confidence for his preservation and recovery. As an evidence of this, and of the high value which these youths set upon this privilege, there is no person, not a relation or a chief of the tribe, who is allowed, or who would dare to step forward to offer an aiding hand, even to save his life; for not only the rigid customs of the nation, and the pride of the individual who has intrusted his life to the keeping of the Great Spirit, would sternly reject such a tender; but their superstition, which is the strongest of all arguments in an Indian community, would alone hold all the tribe in fear and dread of interfering, when they consider they have so good a reason to believe that the Great Spirit has undertaken the special care and protection of his devoted worshipers.

"In this 'last race,' which was the struggle that finally closed their sufferings, each one was dragged until he fainted, and was thus left, looking more like the dead than the living; and thus each one laid, until, by the aid of the Great Spirit, he was in a few minutes seen gradually rising, and at last reeling and staggering like a drunken man through the crowd (which made way for him) to his wigwam, where his friends and relatives stood ready to take him into hand and restore him.

"In this frightful scene, as in the buffalo-dance, the whole nation was assembled as spectators, and all raised the most piercing and violent yells and screams they could possibly produce to drown the cries of the suffering ones, that no heart could even be touched with sympathy for them. I have mentioned before that six or eight of the young men were brought from the medicine-lodge at a time, and when they were thus passed through this shocking ordeal, the medicine-men and the chiefs returned to the interior, where as many more were soon prepared and underwent a similar treatment, and after that another batch and another, and so on until the whole number, some forty-five or fifty, had run in this sickening circle, and, by leaving their weights, had opened the flesh for honorable scars. I said 'all,' but there was one poor fellow though (and I shudder to tell it), who was dragged around and around the circle with the skull of an elk hanging to the flesh of one of his legs; several had jumped upon it, but to no effect, for the splint was under the sinew, which could not be broken. The dragging became every instant more and more furious, and the apprehensions for the poor fellow's life apparent by the piteous howl which was set up for him by the multitude around, and at last the medicine-man ran, with his medicine-pipe in his hand, and held them in check, when the body was dropped and left upon the ground with the skull yet hanging to it. The boy, who was an extremely interesting and fine-looking youth, soon recovered his senses and his strength, looking deliberately at his torn and bleeding limbs, and also with the most pleasant smile of defiance upon the misfortune which had now fallen to his peculiar lot, crawled through the crowd (instead of walking, which they are never again at liberty to do until the flesh is torn out and the article left) to the prairie, and over which, for the distance of half a mile, to a sequestered spot, without any attendant, where he laid three days and three nights, yet longer, without food, and praying to the Great Spirit, until suppuration took place in the wound, and by the decaying of the flesh the weight was dropped, and the splint also, which he dare not extricate in another way. At the end of this he crawled back to the village on his hands and knees, being too much emaciated to walk, and begged for something to eat, which was at once given him, and he was soon restored to health.

"These extreme and difficult cases often occur, and I learn that in such instances the youth has it at his option to get rid of the weight that is left upon him in such way as he may choose, and some of those modes are far more extraordinary than the one which I have just named. Several of the traders, who have been for a number of years in the habit of seeing this part of the ceremony, have told me that two years since, when they were looking on, there was one whose flesh on the arms was so strong that the weights could not be left, and he dragged them with his body to the river by the side of the village, where he set a stake fast in the ground on the top of the bank, and fastening cords to it, he let himself half-way down a perpendicular wall of rock of twenty-five or thirty feet, where the weight of his body was suspended by the two cords attached to the flesh of his arms. In this awful condition he hung for several days, equidistant from the top of the rock and the deep water below, into which he at last dropped and saved himself by swimming ashore!"

Other initiation ceremonies, even among the Indians, seem to pale into comparative child's-play beside the foregoing. It must be understood that such thoroughgoing torture represents an extreme, and the vividness of this case should not be allowed unduly to color the impression of initiation-ceremonies as they occur about the world. Among other of the Siouans there is purification by fasting and the steam-bath, and finally armor is presented to the candidate. At that time the youth is told of some animal which must remain tabooed to him until he has slain numerous enemies, or for life.[57] At the age of seventeen or eighteen the young Comanche makes his first weapons, the shield from the hide of an old bison-bull killed with arrows, never with a gun.[58] The making of the labret perhaps took its rise "in the early custom of submitting the boy at puberty to a trial of his resolution and manly endurance, previous to his admission as a member of the community. . . . Tattooing is primarily a test of fortitude, besides, by its fashion, indelibly indicating the individual's particular commune in which his rights might be exercised."[59] In southern Alaska, when the nose and ears are pierced, there is a potlatch and a new name is given; similarly when the young are tattooed.[60] Throughout the eastern and central region of the United States the boy, when about fifteen years of age, made solitary fast and vigil to obtain communication with the medicine-spirit which was to be his protector through life; then, after the initiatory ordeal to which, in some tribes, he was subjected, the youth was competent to take his place as a man among the warriors.[61] Among the Zuñi "every male child must receive involuntary initiation at the age of four or five years and voluntary initiation at ten or twelve years into the society of the Kok-ko, in order to be admitted after death into the Great Dance-house."

---

57 Dorsey, in BAE, XI, 445.
58 Letourneau, *Guerre*, 141.
59 Dall, in BAE, III, 79, 80.
60 Niblack, in USNM, 1888, 369.

61 Mooney, Swanton, and Hewitt, in HAI, I, 266, II, 145, and II, 178 respectively; Fletcher and La Flesche, in BAE, XXVII, 131-132.

One of their non-kinship relations, described in terms of father and child, is that between the initiate and him who initiates.[62]

Among the tribes of northern South America the boys must bear wounds on breast and arms without betraying their pain before they can join the ranks of the men. If they cannot do so, they receive tests later on.[63] Elsewhere both boys and girls are subjected by the medicine-man to the bites of infuriated ants; if they cry out they are not admitted to the feasts of the elders. Scourging each other to show heroism and as an act of love is practised by both sexes. Circumcision of boys at the age of nine, followed by a month of solitude in the forest, is found; they get a new plant or animal name on the occasion, and a boy's mother becomes a stranger to him after initiation. He must also show that he can draw the bow, and then he may marry.[64] When the Jibaro boy reaches the age of puberty and is to be received among the full-grown men, he is obliged among other things to take a narcotic drink which has the power of awakening within him peculiar visions and hallucinations; these are ascribed to certain spirits, "the old ones." Only the youth who has seen these spirits in the dream and has been spoken to by them can expect to become a valiant and successful warrior, to kill many enemies, and to secure long life.[65]

In Peru, there was "a festival intended to signalize the arrival of young men at manhood, in which there was a sort of communion consisting of bread kneaded by the young virgins of the sun with the blood of victims. The same communion was noted at another festival occurring during September of each year."[66] The sons of the Incas were not confirmed as such until tested and their ears bored. Ear-rings were the sign of the Inca tie.[67] Among the Fuegians, "when boys and girls come to the years of virility they undergo a kind of discipline and teaching, which generally begins in the spring. This is done to make them quiet and good. The discipline of the girl is easy and brief, conducted in the common wigwam by her parents. She has to abstain from certain kinds of food, and has to behave herself very quietly, and to listen very attentively to the injunctions of her parents. After this she is shortly given in marriage. . . . The lads of about thirteen years of age are considered fit for this discipline. They are taken by their fathers away from their mothers and sisters, to a wigwam set apart for superstitious practices, which is out of sight of the dwelling wigwams. It is called Ceena. Here the lads are made to work hard in gathering fuel, they are kept on short allowance, when they go out to do anything some one is sent to watch them. They are dealt with very strictly, and this is done to make them obedient and docile. They are also here initiated into the superstitions of their sires, which they are strictly charged not to divulge to any female. They here see the cheats imposed on the young children and women . . . and they have to make themselves bloody with their own blood. They are also taught by their fathers not to steal, not to be quick to take offence, not to be too much given to jealousy, to marry not young women who would desert them, and cannot take good care of their canoes, and supply them well with fish, etc., but to marry oldish women, who will be steady

---

62 Stevenson, in AA, XI, 39 (quoted); Parsons, in AA, XIX, 1-7.

63 Schomburgk, Brit.-Guiana, I, 168; Waterman, in AA, XII, 332-333.

64 Von Martius, Beiträge, I, 403-404, 410, 482, 580, 631, 644; Spix u. Martius, Brasil.,

1074-1075, 1217, 1320; Appun, in Globus, XVIII, 301.

65 Karsten, "Jibaro," in BAE, Bull. LXXIX, 2-3.

66 Bourke, in BAE, IX, 527 (from Balboa's Hist. of Peru).

67 De la Vega, Yncas, II, 175.

and are well accustomed to all their duties. The lads often become very thin during this discipline, which lasts for several years, after which they are allowed to marry, and are then considered men. During the time the father and son is at Ceena, which is from a few days to about two weeks, neither father nor son sees any female; food is sent them by the women, through some man or other, daily. The ceremonies here conducted are to impose upon the women, to effect which the men make large conical masks of bark which completely cover the head; they also paint their bodies peculiarly, and when all is ready they rush out of the Ceena, and dance and jump about as nimbly as they can in view of the women, who look upon them as beings from another world. But sometimes when they are dancing the mask falls off through their tumbling down, and then the women laugh tremendously in derision."[68]

There are a number of cases of initiation-ceremonies, usually at puberty, for girls. Where circumcision is a regular tribal practice it is not uncommon for the girls as well as the boys to be subjected to it. In South Africa the girls, before being taken into the tribe as marriageable, must "undergo a strict instruction in their future duties which is conducted just as secretly as that of the boys and lasts several weeks." They too are toughened by being deprived of sleep.[69] The time of the ceremony is one of license for women and of considerable irregularity in the mores.[70] The girls are not sent to the circumcision-lodge or school, but receive their schooling from some old woman of rank on the banks of a river. "They are driven into deep water and kept there during the pleasure of the instructress, however cold it may be, till everything is done according to their particular rites."[71] In West Africa, along with the initiation of the boys, "the same removal from home and instruction from initiated members is also observed with the girls. However, in their case, it is not always a forest grove they are secluded in, sometimes it is done in huts." Again, "the girls go into a magic wood until they are married. Should they have to leave the wood for any temporary reason, they must smear themselves with white clay. A similar custom holds good in Okyon, Calabar district, where, should a girl have to leave the fattening-house, she must be covered with white clay. I believe this fattening-house custom in Calabar is not only for fattening up the women to improve their appearance, but an initiatory custom as well, although the main intention is now, undoubtedly, fattening, and the girl is constantly fed with fat-producing foods."[72] The Togo girl, arriving at maturity, has her head covered and is baptized thrice upon the head, as a sign that all uncleanness has left her. She goes about later in a condition of highly decorated undress, visiting all the people and thanking them.[73]

Among the Nairs "social puberty differs considerably in point of time from physiological puberty. It is a matter of great importance that the former should precede the latter. Any family in which a girl attains her physiological puberty . . . before she had attained her social puberty, is socially outside the pale."[74] In the Shan states a girl is not allowed to don the skirt without going through certain ceremonies, consisting in part of submitting to being

68 Bridges, Firelanders, in *Voice for S. Amer.*, XIII, 201.
69 Fritsch, *Eingeb. S.-Afr.*, 206; Holub, *S.-Afrika*, I, 484-485.
70 Haarhoff, *Bantu*, 27, 30-33.

71 Gottschling, in JAI, XXV, 372.
72 Kingsley, *Travels W. Afr.*, 531.
73 Fies, in *Globus*, LXXX, 382.
74 Panikkar, in JAI, XLVIII, 267, note.

pinched.[75] In Samoa there are prayers for the girl's health and happiness at the time of puberty.[76]

Numerous ceremonies must be observed when girls among the Tsimshian and Kwakiutl reach maturity. "When about thirteen or fourteen years old, they begin to practice fasting, eating in the afternoon only, as a very severe fasting is prescribed at the time when they reach maturity. It is believed that if they have any food in their stomachs at this time, they will have bad luck in all the future. They must remain alone and unseen in their room or in a hut for ten days, and abstain from food and drink." If a girl desires a certain number of sons when married, the same number of men chew her food for her; if she desires daughters, that office is performed by women. At the end of the fast she is covered with mats and held over a fire in order that her children may be healthy.[77] Among the Salish tribes the period of the seclusion of a girl upon reaching the age of puberty was a month and a half. She was under certain taboos or restrictions in the matter of food. "These restrictions had a two-fold purpose. First, to prevent her from becoming a greedy and sensual woman, and second, because of the 'bad medicine' or the malign influence she was supposed to exercise at this time upon animals by reason of her condition. A menstruating woman was a thing of abhorrence in the eyes of the Indian, and imparted misfortune and ill-luck to the opposite sex in many ways." The occasion of seclusion was taken advantage of by the elders to instruct girls in the several duties and responsibilities of womanhood. To teach them industrious habits, the girls were employed in plucking the needles from a fir branch one at a time, in picking yarn, and in spinning.[78] A Cheyenne girl was forced to sit up for long periods to prevent her from becoming lazy, and among the Haida she had to sleep on a flat rock with a bag of gravel or something similar for a pillow. If she ate too much, it was thought that she would be greedy in later life; if she talked too much, that she would become garrulous; if she laughed, that she would become too much inclined to hilarity. A Shuswap girl would climb trees and break off their tips in order to become strong, and play with gambling sticks that her future husband might be a successful gamester; a Hupa girl must not tell a lie during this time or she would become forever untruthful; elsewhere, she was laid upon green herbs caused to steam by means of a fire underneath, thereafter covered with blankets and left for four days and nights, while dancing and feasting went on about her to drive away the evil spirits. While this "roasting of the girls" ceremony is being performed, symbolic acts take place, such as throwing seeds over them that they might be prolific, and scattering property among the onlookers that they might be generous.[79] One of the Apache communities had a custom, when a girl arrived at puberty, of having the other young girls lightly tread on her back as she lay face downward, the ceremony being followed by a dance, while in another tribe the girl goes about a mile from home, where she lives in isolation for a year under the care of a relative of her betrothed; during this period fresh meat is tabooed, for otherwise game would become scarce during the ensuing year.[80]

In one California tribe "the puberty dance is celebrated as follows: For nine

75 Milne, *Eastern Clan*, 67.
76 Ella, *Samoa*, in AAAS, 1892, 623.
77 Boas, in BAE, XXXI, 531 (quoted); and in BAE, XXXV, pt. I, 699 ff.
78 Hill-Tout, in JAI, XXXIV, 32, 319, 320 (quoted).
79 Swanton, in HAI, II, 314, 315; Waterman, in AA, XII, 330-331.
80 HAI, I, 284; II, 884.

days the male relatives of the girl dance all night, but her female relatives do not join in the dancing, only in the singing. The girl eats no meat, and remains apart and blindfolded all this time. During the tenth night she is in the house, but keeps close in a corner. The finishing stroke of the ceremony is participated in by two old women and two young men, her relatives, the young men having around their heads leather bands thickly set with sea-lion's teeth—a ferocious looking head-dress consecrated especially to this ceremony. These five persons are in a row, the girl in the center, the two young men standing on either side of her and the two old women squatting on the outside. The girl goes forward a few steps and then backward. She does this ten times, chanting and throwing her hands up to her shoulders. The last time she runs forward and gives a leap; then the ceremony is ended." A second ceremony is thus described: "First, as a preparation for this festivity, the maiden is compelled to abstain rigidly from animal food for three days, and to allowance herself on acorn porridge. During this time she is banished from camp, living alone in a distant booth, and it is death to any person to touch or even to approach her. At the expiration of the three days she partakes of a sacred broth or porridge, called *khlup,* prepared as follows from buckeyes: the buckeyes are roasted underground a considerable time to extract the poison, then boiled to a pulp in small sand-pools with hot stones. The eating of this prepares her for subsequent participation in the dance, and consecrates her to the duties of womanhood. . . . In conclusion, the chief takes the maiden by the hand and together they dance down the line, the company singing songs improvised for the occasion. . . . Sometimes the songs are grossly obscene. Every Indian utters such sentiments as he chooses in his song, though strange to say, they keep perfect time. The women utter nothing impure on these occasions."[81]

Such ceremonies are rather mild; but the South American tribes used to put the girls through ordeals fit to compare with those endured by the boys. To try the fortitude of their maidens, one Amazonian tribe hangs them up in a net to the roof of a hut, exposed to continual smoke, where they fast as long as they can possibly bear it.[82] Among the Caribs, first the girl's hair was burned off, then she was gashed by the medicine-man with an animal's tooth on the back and pepper rubbed into the wounds. She must not betray any feeling during the operation. There followed three days without food or drink or any speaking, and then a month in a hammock without other sustenance than uncooked roots, cassava-bread, and water. At the end of the month these operations were repeated and only after the third month was the ordeal over.[83]

§164. Social Distinctions.

THE Teda of the Sahara are divided into nobles and people, with princes at the head. Several chiefs have had extended authority; "but this was always based more upon the personal characteristics of the head-chief than in his official position, which is in itself neither very influential nor remunerative." The princes preside over the assembly of the nobles where questions of public policy are ventilated and decided. "The common people has no rights, but also no duties. Taxes are unknown to them; but their lot, by reason of the poverty of the country, is despite this no enviable one." Except in favored

81 Powers, in *Contrib. N. Am. Ethnol.,* III, 85, 235-236.
82 Markham, in JAI, XL, 130.
83 Schomburgk, *Brit.-Guiana,* II, 431.

spots they are almost wholly given over to the mercy of the nobility which is as numerous as it is poor and covetous. "In the western part of the country, where almost no agriculture can succeed, every third man is a noble—really a nobleman in rags and devoured by hunger, but on that account no less proud of his high origin, and not less arrogant and exacting."[1] "Unlike the other races of the Welle, aristocracy of family is recognized among the Mang-bettou. Between the chief and the people are a race of freed men, who do not engage in manual labor of any kind. From the term freed men it must not be inferred that the people below them are slaves; they are equally free, but are without the hereditary rank of the so-called freed men, who are generally relations of the chief or in some way connected with him. Thus, a chief may receive an application for porters, and may have sixty or seventy men around him, not one of whom he can lend. 'These men do not work,' is his answer, implying that they would not so demean themselves. The distinction of caste is carried out in war; the so-called free men carry spear and shield, while the lower orders are armed with bow and arrow only."[2]

The pure-blooded Bahima are a sort of aristocracy or ruling caste in several parts of Uganda, and even furnish dynasties of kings. There are four classes, including slaves, peasants, and two ranks of dignitaries. The peasants are by far the most numerous and constitute the army. The second rank of dignitaries is not hereditary, and peasants rise into it, their sons becoming peasants again; these second-class dignitaries are rulers of provinces under the first class. Elsewhere are found two classes, the free, noble, lighter-colored and the subjects.[3] The Wasove people of East Africa are divided into five classes of which the first two are the issue of male and female members of the chief's family respectively; the third are the head-men; the last two are the peasants and strangers.[4]

Among the warrior-tribes of the Somali and Galla the entire people is divided into warriors and non-warriors. The former do not marry. The Masai have a middle class, who marry and go to war only occasionally. The warriors have four sub-classes and the non-warriors three. There are also the possessors and the possessionless, though in lesser number than elsewhere on the continent. The chief gathers the exceptional persons about him and gives them land, and from among them he selects his dignitaries.[5] Madagascar shows three classes: nobles, citizens, and slaves. They may not, with few exceptions, intermarry, nor may the clans into which they are subdivided.[6] Among the Tuareg the serfs tend the flocks, cultivate the oases, and fight under their masters; they are attached to the soil and may not be sold separately. Between the nobles and serfs is a superior class, the caste of smiths; they are charged with the making and repairing of weapons and enjoy much consideration. Professions are hereditary from father to son.[7] Slaves among the Oromo are not circumcised, the practice being a mark of distinction between free and unfree,[8] and recalling the similar significance of tattoo, as when Herodotus[9] states of the Thracians that "to be punctured they thought a mark of nobility, to have no punctures, that of being basely born."

1 Nachtigal, *Sahara*, I, 440, 441 ff.
2 Burrows, in JAI, XXVIII, 45.
3 Johnston, *Uganda*, II, 610; Ratzel, *Vkde.*, I, 471, 537.
4 Dundas, C., in JAI, LI, 223.

5 Ratzel, *Vkde.*, I, 432, 433; Paulitschke, *Nordost-Afr.*, I, 240, 323; II, 126.
6 Ratzel, *Vkde.*, II, 512.
7 Letourneau, *Polit.*, 205, 210.
8 Vannutelli e Citerni, *L'Omo*, 447.
9 *Hist.*, V, ch. 6.

"All the Ostiaks are equal among themselves; even the so-called Ostiak princes are not distinguished from the rest. The rich enjoy, as everywhere, a special respect on account of their possessions. The laborers of the rich, however, stand upon an equality with them. They sleep, eat, and dwell all together."[10] The Kirghiz have two classes, called the white bone and the black bone; the former are chiefs of families and magistrates, and are supposed to be the descendants of Genghis Khan. The black bone includes the rest who have no clear proofs of such descent.[11] Of the Cherkes it is reported that "the chiefs and nobles have no other business than war, robbery, and hunting. . . . The subjects or peasants, who render blind obedience to the chiefs and nobles, inherit their station; but they are not sold."[12] Tibet shows three classes: the priestly rulers, the warriors, and the peasants—the last pillaged by the first and second but pious to excess. India is the land of caste; the development of which it affords a classic extreme is reserved for a later connection. In China appears the nobility of letters; scholars, trained mainly in mnemonic exercises, and tested by competitive examination, held office, were too proud to work, and tended, at least in the upper strata, to become parasitic.[13] The civil authorities regularly outranked the military. The military mandarin was actually debarred from the performance of religious ritual, while that privilege was accorded as of right to civil officials. This literary nobility is an odd twist in the mores. "One of the curses of Korea is the privileged class of *yang-bans* or nobles, who must not work for their living, though it is no disgrace to be supported by their relations, and who often live on the clandestine industry of their wives in sewing and laundry work. A *yang-ban* carries nothing for himself, not even his pipe. *Yang-ban* students do not even carry their books from their studies to the classroom. Custom insists that when a member of this class travels he takes as many attendants with him as he can muster. He is supported on his led horse, and supreme helplessness is the conventional requirement. His servants browbeat and bully the people and take their fowls and eggs without payment."[14]

In the Indian Archipelago there is no absence of rank and position, and "almost nowhere is found the idyllic equality of which some dream." Not only is there the difference between free and slave but there exists a sort of nobility or aristocracy composed of those stocks favored by fortune and position, among whom the chiefs and other officials and their families take first place.[15] Although nothing is mentioned as to scales of rank below that of chiefs in Easter Island, except a reference to slaves, class-distinctions were pronounced among others of the Polynesian group, the most common social divisions being chiefs, middle classes, and common people, not to mention some who might be called slaves. In Samoa, next after the ruling class came the heads of families, who were the chiefs' councillors, then the body of citizens, while the lower classes were "men of the land," that is, workers without political rights and war-captives whose condition was little if any better than that of slaves. In Tonga there existed a group of honorable attendants on chiefs, their companions and councillors; the bulk of the people were peasants, and below them were persons who had forfeited their liberty by crime or had been taken cap-

10 Kondratowitsch, in *Globus*, LXXIV, 289.
11 *Russ. Ethnog.* (Russ.), II, 158.
12 Pallas, *Travels*, I, 401-402.
13 Letourneau, *Polit.*, 133, 174 ff.

14 Bishop, *Korea*, 101.
15 Wilken, in VG, I, 460 (quoted); Metcalf, in AA, XIV, 163.

tive in war. The class next after the king, in the Hervey Islands, was that of governors of districts; after these came the landholders and finally the tenants. There was not such inequality of rank as in Tahiti; caste did not exist as a system, yet each grade had its distinct position in society.[16]

On the island of Yap there is a class that is treated by the rest of the natives as a people under the yoke and fundamentally diverse of origin. A woman might lose all honors and rights of membership in her social rank or group by marrying a man of a lower rank.[17] In the Marshall Islands there were four classes: chiefs; sons of chiefs, generally very rich and influential; people with property; those without property and enfeoffed only with land.[18] In Ponapé the three classes are nobility, chiefs, and people, the last paying great respect to their superiors.[19] In the Pelew group, the nobles' wives receive especial respect; "woe to the native who unsummoned and otherwise than in the most humble, bent posture should approach such a woman," though she may at that very moment be arranging by signs an assignation with him.[20] In New Zealand "a curious point was that the son was greater than his father, because he was the result of two great people coming together, while his father was only one great person." The child held rank both by father and mother; "from his birth the Ariki was the greatest person in his little world, till his own son was born." Class-distinctions were made at the ritual feasts when food for different ranks was prepared in different ovens.[21]

The rank-system of the Northwest Indians is very remarkable; in connection with it especially "are found well defined, narrow bounds within which the sense for the acquisition of property can act, since property can be amassed only to be distributed at certain festivals or even to be deliberately destroyed for the purpose of gaining repute and rank."[22] Self-destitution for the sake of public recognition has been noted in the case of the potlatch.[23] Among the Tinneh of Alaska, "the social organization seems to be divided into the following classes: Tyones, skillies (near relatives of a Tyone), shamans, or medicine men, and vassals of varying degrees of servitude. In all assemblies seats are rigidly assigned according to rank." Vassals are found at the beck and call of masters. A member of the master-class, fourteen or fifteen years of age, sitting within a few feet of the river, orders a six-foot vassal to bring him water. These menials are used for all kinds of work, and are under all possible control of their masters, but corporal punishment is not observable. The threat of deprivation of food or shelter, in their poverty-stricken position, would doubtless command obedience.[24] Among the Tsimshian "class prejudice was very strong," and all marriages had to take place among members of the same social rank.[25]

Among the Arapaho there was an organization called "warriors," of eight degrees or orders, including nearly all the men above the age of about seventeen. "Those who were not enrolled in some one of the . . . orders were held in but little respect, and were not allowed to take part in public ceremonies

16 Williamson, *Cent. Polyn.*, II, 366, 369-371, 380-382, 393-394, 403; III, 138, 141.

17 Kubary, *Karolinen-arch.*, 27; Kubary, in *Mitth. Königl. Museen zu Berlin*, 1885, 84.

18 Finsch, *Ethnol. Erfahr.*, III, 128; Steinbach, cited in PSM, XLIX, 792, note.

19 Pereiro, *Ponapé*, 111, 112.

20 Semper, *Palau-Ins.*, 75.

21 Tregear, in JAI, XIX, 113; Best, in AAAS, 1909, 462.

22 Rink, *Eskimoernes Herkomst*, 292.

23 §113, above.

24 Allen, in *Smithson. Rep.*, 1886, pt. I, 266; Swanton in HAI, II, 609.

25 Boas, in BAE, XXXI, 498.

or to accompany war expeditions. Each of the first six orders had its own peculiar dance, and the members of the principal warrior orders had also their peculiar staff or badge of rank." Seven priests constituted the highest order of the military and social organization among the Blackfeet, Sioux, Cheyenne, Kiowa, and probably all the prairie tribes except the Comanche. "The warrior organization of the Kiowa . . . consisted of six orders, each with its own dance, songs, and ceremonial dress."[26] This instance reveals the relation between the men's organizations and the general class-stratification.

§165. Caste.

THERE is little evidence of a real caste-system among undeveloped peoples; a few cases approaching that condition will be cited before approaching the classic example of India. In San Cristoval, Solomon Islands, there are two clans, called Atawa and Amwea, which alone of the clans have no totem; they have traditions of hostility to one another. No Atawa can be enslaved; this is the difference in status which strikes the native most, and about which all agree. Amwea men and women may be bound, sold, beaten, or subjected to indignities, but Atawa men and women never. Amwea members who commit crimes are severely punished where an Atawa who offends may only be scolded. There seems to be some race-distinction here, the invading Atawa being fairer than the dark Amwea people whom they found in possession.[1] For a man in Malekula, New Hebrides, caste is a very important thing. "Both religious life and social position are inextricably bound up with it; and as a man's caste depends upon the number of large tusk-pigs he has killed at the sacred ceremonies, tusk-pigs come to play a prominent part in each man's life." A child is born without caste and rises in rank as each large tusk-pig is killed by his father at one of the sacred ceremonies. The castes are six in number; very few people reach the fifth rank, which is that of the chiefs. "The men of each caste eat together. A woman may cook the food for men of rank, but she may not take it off the fire, nor must she touch it after it is cooked; neither can she eat of it, not even of the scraps which the men have left. Each caste has its own fire, and Mr. Paton relates that one evening he saw a woman who had cooked three meals for her husband and two sons of different rank lean back and declare that she was too tired to prepare anything for herself: she would eat nothing till the next day. If a man of lower caste eats of the food belonging to the caste above, all men belonging to the higher caste must kill a pig. A man of rank must not be touched on the head; if a man of lower rank touches one of higher caste on the head, trouble will ensue." As social position and finally chieftainship depend on caste, and caste depends on the number of pigs killed, this grading seems to become a strong incentive to thrift. "A chief's son, being the son of a man with many tusk-pigs, will probably rise in rank much more quickly than a poor man's son, but any man can acquire tusk-pigs through thrift and care."[2]

The Loucheux of Alaska are reported to have been divided into three castes, designated by names which seem to signify "fair," "partly swarthy," and "swarthy." Those of the first caste lived principally on fish, and those of the last by hunting. They occupied different districts, and marriage between

---

26 Mooney, in BAE, XIV, 986, 989.   2 Sebbelov, in AA, XV, 273 ff.
1 Fox, in JAI, XLIX, 121-124, 129.

two individuals of the same caste was almost prohibited.[3] "Rank and caste play an important part in every Thlinget community. . . . The high-caste family strenuously opposes the marriage of one of its number to one of a lower class." At feasts the people are given positions and goods according to rank and caste, and in public councils "it would be considered a shame for those of high-caste connections to listen to talk from those of a lower class."[4]

Coming now to India, we find the suggestions included in the foregoing cases, that a caste-system implies ethnic differentiation, further developed. Rivers[5] thinks the existence of two divisions of the Toda people suggests some form of the institution of caste. Each division is endogamous, as is the caste, and each is divided into a number of exogamous septs resembling the gotras of a caste. There is, however, little restriction on social intercourse between the two divisions; they can eat together, and a member of one division can receive food from any member of another. He inclines to the view that the present organization of the Todas is due to the coalescence of two tribes or castes which came to the hills at different times.

The first trace of modern caste is found in Manu's Code; but even there one fails to see the present rigid caste-rules as to food, connubium, and intercourse. It may therefore be safely concluded that the primitive division of Indian people into Brahmins, Kshatriyas, Vaisyas, and Sudras was based upon their occupations, but at present does not denote definite ethnological groups. "Thus, founded originally on occupation, their later divisions and subdivisions have been according to the habitations, languages, manners, or migratory habits of the people, and sometimes even self-interest or vanity. But when the social position of a person was determined by merit and not by birth, when the son of a Brahmin was not a Brahmin, and each of the four primitive divisions of society was continually refreshed by the best blood of those who had the greatest aptitude for the work of the class he entered, qualified by a long apprenticeship or previous training, there was no isolation of one caste from another." There were mixed classes, "represented as having arisen from the mutual connubium of the higher castes with the lower."[6]

In India and Ceylon the oldest political form of society was the village-community; "in it a part of the members took over this sort of work, another that, useful for the persistence of the community, and so there were formed inside of it small groups in which the occupation of the father descended to the son. Therewith was developed within the groups a special esprit de corps under the pressure of which the lines of distinction between the several crafts became ever deeper. . . . A group of neighboring villages was served, for example, by its own smith, and it fell to no other smith to do any work for this region. . . . Within a community a certain moderate number of castes sufficed for all the needs of the whole; but when in the course of time an absolute monarchy united all the separate communities under one single rule, then the demands of the king and court, and later also those of Buddhism, which had attained great power, gave impulse to the formation of new social divisions. If new tasks were laid upon a caste, then the caste-spirit split off new groups that soon lost connection with their mother-caste." Thus the weaver-class took over the getting of cinnamon-bark and the palanquin-bearers became executioners.

---

3 HAI, I, 776,
4 Jones, *Thlingets*, 59-60.
5 *Todas*, 679-680, 691.

6 Nathubhai, in JASB, V, 78, 89; III, 393, 421.

"The several sub-divisions of artisans feel themselves to be separate castes, and neither intermarry nor participate in a common meal. . . . Every contact with a member of another class is avoided as far as possible; on two points above all are the caste-taboos inflexible: on the intermarriage and on the eating together of members of different castes. In both cases unmerciful expulsion from the caste would follow, and the person so punished would be a lost man. Even the shadow of a low-born person falling upon food makes it useless for the man of a higher order. Where the caste-prescriptions still persist almost unlimited in their old strictness, . . . even the breath or the remote presence of a man of lower caste renders unclean, and the segregation that the members of higher and lower castes observe toward each other must be maintained to the most painful degree; for the higher-born, detailed ceremonies of purification must ensue upon such proximity."[7]

The Nairs, who have been famous as a military aristocracy ever since Marco Polo travelled in Asia, come next to the Brahmins and Kshatriyas and have precedence over all other castes.[8] It is said that they are not a caste or even a tribe but are rather a community including various elements: an aristocratic group, a group of Sudras or menials, including drummers, musicians, potters, funeral priests, and so on. "The Tarakans, a class of brokers, have become Nāyars within living memory, and there is another section only partially assimilated, the members of which are refused admittance into the tribal sanctuaries."[9]

"The very strongest, and perhaps also ugliest, of all possible roots of caste is sense of race, the caste of blood." Protection from fusion is almost an instinct. "Here we have the secret of rigid caste, for the only rigid caste is hereditary, and of hereditary caste the essential characteristic is the refusal of intermarriage." Heavy fines are necessary to buy back a position lost by infringement of rules, say, on a European trip; and the unscrupulous make use of these fines to ruin those who resist their power.[10] As for the connection of caste with race, we may see "the evolution of a caste out of a tribe, one portion being still to a great measure in a primitive state, while the other section has been admitted within the circle of Hinduism." In cases cited by Risley[11] such tribes had been aboriginal habitants and rulers of their district. He thinks that the position an Indian caste holds in the orthodox scale of purity and rank is correlative with the nasal index; "it is scarcely a paradox to lay down as a law of the caste-organization in Eastern India, that a man's social status varies in inverse ratio to the width of his nose."[12] Sub-castes are always differentiating; in southern India there are the right-hand and the left-hand castes, of long standing. "The right hand castes, for instance, claim the prerogative of riding on horseback in processions, and of appearing with standards bearing certain devices, and of erecting twelve pillars to sustain their marriage booths, while the left hand castes may not have more than eleven pillars, nor use the standards and ensigns belonging to the right hand fraternity."[13]

Ridgeway[14] believes that distinctions of race and class went together in Rome and that "the dissensions between Patricians and Plebeians were far

7 Schmidt, Ceylon, 263 ff., 267, 268, 270.
8 Panikkar, in JAI, XLVIII, 255-256, 286.
9 Crooke, in JAI, XLIV, 277-278.
10 Nivedita, Indian Life, 133, 143-145, 197.
11 Ethnog. Ind., I, 165, 177, 181, 182-183, 185.
12 Risley, Bengal, cited in JAI, XXI, 340.
13 Thurston, S. India, 47-48.
14 In JAI, XXXIX, 23.

more deeply rooted than in a mere struggle between capital and labour. The excavations of Boni in the Roman Forum have since shown two different kinds of graves, the one, cremation, and the other inhumation burials. This most important archaeological fact taken in conjunction with the different kinds of marriage, the one Patrician, the other Plebeian, the different armature of the original First Classes, consisting wholly of Patricians, as compared with that of the other Classes, into which Plebeians were enrolled, as well as the fact that the three chief Flamines who must be Patricians ministered to Sabine deities, all combine to show that the Patricians were Sabines, the Plebeians the aboriginal population."

§166. Plutocracy.

MANY uncivilized people think that the common man after death is annihilated or goes to a region of gloom while men of noble blood descended from kings go to a realm of delights.[1] Allied with this is the notion that the wealthy fare better than the poor. Dyaks think the spirits pay far more heed to a rich man than to a poor vagabond.[2] In the New Hebrides it is believed that spirits rank in the other world according to the number of pigs they bring with them, that is, the number killed at their funerals.[3] In Eskimo life, good food-winners are the greatest heroes and these are the ones who get to the abode of the blessed, although they must also avoid evil.[4] It was believed in the Scandinavian mythology that souls ranked in Valhalla according to the wealth they brought with them. In the Eddas the leaders have gold and are generous with it, and the desire for it ranks as a motive with love of fighting. Gold is represented as the cause of good and evil; this had been learned from experience but observed evil effects had not led to any renunciation of wealth. These are typical examples of the projection of plutocratic ideas to the other world. Illustrations of the influence of wealth in society follow.

A man made himself king of the Basutos in 1815 by exchanging his cattle for women whom he gave to his adherents for wives. All their daughters were his for further operations.[5] Such practice has been alluded to before and will appear again. In equatorial Africa, riches consist in having a great number of wives and slaves, whom the owners can compel to work as they please.[6] We note once again that "ivory is everywhere an evil thing before which the quest for gold sinks into a parlor game."[7] Among the Ba-Mbala drunkenness is a sign of wealth and is much respected.[8] Property is uncommonly evenly divided among the Galla, but with neighboring peoples "only the greater or less wealth in cattle decides as to who may approach the prince and who may stay permanently near him. The chiefs of the several families . . . have a position in no way preferred in so far as they do not stand out through their wealth in herds." The Somal chief keeps in his intimate presence "men of his tribe who are noteworthy for intelligence, courage, experience, family connections, and, in consequence of this, also, for the most part, dis-

---

1 Tylor, *Prim. Cult.*, II, 78.
2 Perelaer, *Dayaks*, 57.
3 AAAS, 1892, 701.
4 Fries, *Grönland*, 142.

5 Fritsch, *Eingeb. S.-Afr.*, 483; §§155, 156, 365, of the text and *Case-Book*.
6 Du Chaillu, *Voy. dans l'Afr.*, 294, 372.
7 Kingsley, *Travels W. Afr.*, 325.
8 Torday and Joyce, in JAI, XXXV, 405.

tinguished for wealth, counsels with them over important business, and listens to their advice before making weighty decisions."[9]

Yakut plutocrats give out horses to the poor for an annual rental; also the rich pay in wares which the employee must often sell at a loss, compelling the latter also to hire to the same employer for a year before receiving any payment. The rich are powerful in Yakut society and surpass the Russians in the exploitation of their fellows. It is a violation of etiquette at an entertainment to give a big piece of meat to a poor man and a little piece to a rich one. The contrary is the rule.[10] While the Gilyaks have no aristocracy, the wealthy enjoy great prestige.[11] In Kafiristan "rich men give great feasts, qualifying themselves in this way for high social and religious rank in the tribe."[12] If Hindu descendants do not keep up sacrifices, the ancestral ghost may decline to a stage where he must go through life again. A man now poor is so because of faults in a former existence; he cannot pay for rites now by which to get a high place beyond. Hence he may stay base forever.[13] Of Indian tribesmen it is reported that "there is nothing they will not do for money"; everything is accomplished by the rupee, which plays a greater rôle in India than the ruble in Russia.[14]

Wergeld is a plutocratic device. Malay misdemeanors are atoned for by payments and if they are not forthcoming, the culprit is enslaved. Debt-slavery, so flourishing in the Archipelago, is a prominent factor in forming class-strata.[15] "On the Pelew Islands, just as in all the Malay states, money can atone for every punishment for every political, social, and religious transgression. Since no taxes exist the fines form the income of chiefs; they are their 'fountain.' . . . In social life everyone is forced by custom to take on expenses exactly corresponding to his position in the community. Everyone is responsible for his cousins, his children, and his clientage and must pay for them. . . . Family life can be founded . . . only upon the basis of money. . . . In illnesses finally the anger of the gods can be assuaged only by frequent payments to priests, seers, magicians, exorcists, and their ilk. Even the dead may not be buried unless first the sum set by usage is paid. The marvel is that with the existing limited supply of money the inhabitants are able to discharge these numerous payments, and it is therefore understandable that the demand for money and the eagerness to get it is inevitably very great. In order to meet this need of acquisition of money, Pelew Island custom has tried its own solution of the 'labor and capital' question, and since 'money' was presented as a 'conditio sine qua non' of societal existence, there has been an effort to regulate its circulation in the society. To this end belongs the idea of preventing an injurious centralization of money in the chiefs' possession by placing them upon a full equality with the people in the matter of penalization, and further in the most exact determination of the customary services owed by them to the people and the other chiefs, whereby the great expenditures saddled upon them bring the money down among the people. On the other hand, an exclusive accumulation of money . . . is made impossible by the provision that no one may live independently or produce exclusively for himself.

9 Paulitschke, Nordost-Afr., I, 197, 241.
10 Kohn, Yakuts (Russ.), 3; Sieroshevski, Yakuts (Russ.), 440; Sieroshevski-Sumner, in JAI, XXXI, 66.
11 Miroliubov, Sakhalin (Russ.), 158.
12 Robertson, in JAI, XXVII, 77.

13 Lippert, Kgchte., II, 416.
14 Carey and Tuck, Chin Hills, I, 168; Gehring, Süd-Indien, 144.
15 Marsden, Sumatra, 247; Wilken, Vkde., 422; §§105, 106, of text.

He may not use things which he himself has made, but must sell them; on the other hand, he must buy and pay for that which is for his own use. Here again, in order to control exploitation and exceptional opportunity, the prices and payments are stable, that is, determined beforehand, unchangeable, and known to everyone. There appears, then, as the fundamental principle of the above indicated social laws, the greatest possible decentralization of society through a mathematically exact and detailed regimentation."[16]

This exceptional system is enlightening as representing a determined effort to withstand the power of unequally distributed wealth. It is more usual to find "dishonorable plutocrats" to whom wealth is virtue and poverty vice, and a situation where "the highest chief exploits the poorest man as much as he can." There is an "unexampled struggle, which stops at nothing, to get rich." An old chief, with one foot in the grave, sought magic to attain wealth; the ancient glass and stone money was boiled and the water poured over children's heads, or given them to drink, to make them get rich. Bribery cannot be withstood. A man tries to get a wife from a rich family so that for every fault of the wife he can collect from her parents; and a father wishes to marry his daughter to the son of a wealthy house, for then he can foster differences between her and her husband and collect fines from the latter's father, who goes security, as it were, for his son's actions. "The power of money appears, with this little people, much more unadorned than in our country; for the greater simplicity of all social relations and the necessity of maintaining the laws of the land through tradition in the highest possible degree of immutability cause the driving forces to stand forth much more sharply here."[17]

The Eskimo of Labrador think that the owl annoys by its hooting only those people who are too poor to have extra garments; when they hear it they hasten to hang out some unworn piece of clothing.[18] Feasts are sometimes given by the Tlinkits to whitewash a disreputable character. "If a man has disgraced himself in the eyes of his people, he may give a generous feast, and no one after that is allowed to mention or talk about his dishonourable conduct. Giving a feast wipes out the stain, and the sinner may hold his head as high as ever."[19] Standing in the Haida tribe depended more on the possession of property than on ability in war, "so that considerable interchange of goods took place and the people became sharp traders."[20] Wealth consisted principally of implements, wives, and slaves. As to the totem-poles of the northwest coast, "none but the wealthy can afford to erect these carved columns and the owner of one is thereby invested with so much the more respect and authority that he becomes as the head of the household a petty chief in the village."[21] Among a people in Oregon, "no marriage is legal or binding unless preceded by the payment of money and that family is most aristocratic in which most money was paid for a wife. . . . So far is this shell-money aristocracy carried that the children of a woman for whom no money was paid are accounted no better than bastards."[22] Of the Brazilian tribes it is stated: "It is astounding what differences there are amongst these wild people between rich and poor," that is, not between rich individuals and poor individuals, but between tribes that are comparatively well off and those that are in hard circumstances. The chief of one

---

16 Kubary, *Karolinen-arch.*, 21, 22, 23.
17 Senfft, in *Globus*, XC, 282; Senfft, cited in *Globus*, LXXXIX, 371; Semper, *Palau-Ins.*, 167, 181, 182.
18 BAE, XI, 273.

19 Jones, *Thlingets*, 139.
20 Swanton, in HAI, I, 521.
21 Niblack, in USNM, 1888, 324.
22 Stearns, in *Smithson. Rep.*, 1887, pt. II, 333.

of the poorest of the villages on the Shingu, speaking of other tribes, said that they were rich because they had stone axes.[23] Chinese ancestor-worship is said to owe its great strength to the fact that it is a system by which the living man expects to make the grave of his ancestor a fountain of material blessings, long life, property, and rank, to himself.[24] The Zoroastrian religion was in practice a grand system of operating on the good and evil elements (spirits) by the individual to further his own luck in material goods, wealth, and power. The sanctions of the Jewish religion were material: longevity, wealth, power. The Greek religion hinged in the large on the aleatory element in life. Democracy and plutocracy were the reigning forces, plutocracy being the power of those who had, democracy of those who had not. At Rome "property and honor, property and full citizen-rights, property and social prestige were identical. Property was the criterion by which the worth of an individual in the state was measured. Property was won by pains and diligence and so it was the touchstone of the community. The related peoples held the same view."[25] Mediæval religion, though theoretically it looked to the other world, was a system of ritual the strength of which lay in the guarantee of good fortune here. All the historical religions have fostered indiscriminate giving; Confucianism, Buddhism, Mohammedanism inculcate charity—as a duty for the benefit of the giver, however, not of the receiver. The mediæval church taught the same view. It was well to have riches to give, but it was also well to be poor. In fact, if a poor man had been lifted out of poverty, which in the ecclesiastical view was a higher state than wealth, he would have undergone religious harm. The result was that the care of the poor was both wasteful and inefficient.[26]

§177. Retaliation.

Suicide. The Chuvash in Russia hang themselves at the gate or under the eaves of one on whom they wish to take vengeance. The Votyaks hang themselves on the premises of an enemy. This notion prevails widely in India and is explained by the belief that after death the ghost of the suicide can plague the one who drove him to this act. A modern Hindu threatens to commit suicide on the doorstep of a great man who has oppressed him and has refused to heed remonstrance. If he is not heeded, he executes the threat. Both believe that the ghost of the suicide will be an enemy of a very different caliber from the oppressed mortal being. Lasch,[1] from whom these cases are taken, suggests that this kind of suicide is a form of blood-revenge, in that the suicide causes blood-guilt to fall on his tormentor without incurring it for his family. The Hindus think that "one who rejects a suppliant and compels him to kill himself goes to hell." Hence a beggar coerces a giver by besieging his door and threatening to commit suicide there.[2] It is quite logical for those who think that ghosts have great power, to wish to become ghosts in order to attain ability to wreak vengeance. Among the Tlinkit "a man committed suicide simply to make trouble for one who offended him. According to native custom, if a person commits suicide because some one has offended him, or opposed a wish

23 Von den Steinen, *Zent. Bras.*, 112, 114.
24 DeGroot, *Relig. Syst. China*, I, pt. I; VII, 57, 220, 682.
25 Rossbach, *Röm. Ehe*, 91.
26 Eicken, *Mitt. Weltanschaung*, 508;

Aquinas, *Summa*, II, 2; Lea, *Inquisition*, II, 366-367.
1 In *Globus*, LXXIV, 37 ff.; and in *Globus*, LXXV, 72 ff.
2 Hopkins, in *Jour. Am. Or. Soc.*, XXI, 146.

of his, heavy damages or a life must be given to the tribe of the suicide by the tribe of the one giving the offence. So suicide is sometimes resorted to in order to harass and burden others. The threat of suicide is sometimes used as a bluff to get one's way."[3] Slaves in Brazil commit suicide in order to do pecuniary harm to their owners by way of revenge.[4] The hunger-strike is a modern parallel.

§178. Blood-Vengeance.

WHEN a death occurs in Melanesia the natives usually insist upon "taking payment," which applies not only in cases of murder but even under other circumstances, as when vengeance was sought on a man by his wife's relatives because she hung herself after quarrelling with her mother-in-law. Murder commonly leads to inter-tribal war, though hostilities may be averted if the murderer is given up. Vengeance is satisfied if one, anyone, of the offender's group is killed in battle, but as more were frequently killed, "battles such as these, instead of terminating a blood feud often started new ones, and in time might lead to a chronic state of enmity, punctuated by new murders and reprisals." In such warfare, not only was it meritorious to kill, but if possible prisoners taken were carried off to be tortured before they were eaten. "Such vengeance was looked upon as a duty, and to this feeling must be attributed the greater number of the murders of white traders that took place some fifteen to twenty years ago among the archipelagoes of the south-eastern extremity. Natives had been taken from many islands for the labour trade, and when they failed to return and no compensation was paid for their assumed deaths, these were avenged by the killing of the first stranger who gave himself into their keeping." Commonly prisoners would be tortured and killed only in such numbers that their deaths made the score even between their community and that of their captors.[1]

The principle of like for like is literally applied by the Bageshu. "If a man kills one of another clan, the members of the clan seek out either the murderer, or, failing him, some one of his clan about the same age as the person killed, and put him to death. If they are able they get a son of the murderer and they will sometimes wait a number of years until a child grows up in order to kill him when he reaches the age of the man who was murdered."[2] Among the Bahima, "it is the positive duty of each member of the clan of a murdered man to seek out and bring to justice the guilty person; if ordinary means fail to trace the murderer they seek out a clever diviner, who, by his magical arts, is supposed not only to discover the perpetrator of the murder, but also his motives for the deed. Should the person accused be found, he is put upon his trial, and if he denies the deed he must go through various ordeals to prove his innocence; it is next to impossible to escape death, because the reputation of the diviner is at stake, and he cannot allow that he has made a mistake, unless the relatives of the accused make it worth his while to find some other scapegoat. Should a murderer escape, one of the clan is seized and put to death, unless the clan rises and rescues him; if the clan rises the case goes before the king for trial; the king invariably settles the matter by imposing a fine.

3 Jones, *Thlingets*, 218.
4 Tschudi, *Reisen in S. Am.*, II, 77.
1 Seligmann, *Melanesians* (1910), 128-129 (quoted), 271-272, 566, note, 569 (quoted), 570;

Rivers, *Melan. Soc.*, I, 172; Murray, in AAAS, 1921, 179.
2 Roscoe, in JAI, XXXIX, 194-195.

But more frequently the murderer or the person seized in his stead is put to death before the members of the clan have time to rise. In some cases of murder, the clan of the murdered man may refuse to accept the fine ordered by the king; they wait on in the hope of finding the murderer, or until they are powerful enough to fight the clan of the murderer and kill some one of it. Directly a case is settled either by fine or by a substitute being killed in his stead, the murderer can return, his clan will receive him, he may go home; even the relatives of the deceased will bear no ill will toward him."[3] The old blood-feuds are still recognized by the Kavirondo, and a man may not eat with a person with whom his branch of the family has a blood-feud, or, it is believed, he will surely die within twenty-four hours. Group-responsibility among the Akamba is evidenced in the matter of compensation: all relatives of the murderer contribute their share and each member of the family to which the murdered man belongs receives a share of the compensation. The same people have a way of getting rid of an obnoxious person, one who kills people by witchcraft or poison, for example, and at the same time of avoiding compensation. If a number of persons have fallen victim to the machinations of the accused, the principal elder announces: "If one man kills the accused it means compensation, so we will do it all together and then no one will be able to say that any one man killed him." Then the people rush in a body at the accused and put him to death.[4]

Blood-revenge is known in the Congo, and often causes inter-village warfare; hostilities do not cease until a slave belonging to the village of the murderer is handed over to be eaten.[5] The Dinkas accept compensation in cattle for homicide resulting from accident or sudden anger; if, however, the deceased has been waylaid and killed, compensation is not accepted and "the only remedy in this case is to wait until one of each family is killed; then the 'old people' can meet with better chance of arranging a 'peace sacrifice' and peace-making." After killing, the offender generally hides or goes to another tribe for shelter and his family try, if possible, to arrange a "peace." If, at the meeting, the family of the offender refuses the decision given by the "seniors" of the people, a blood-feud is instituted and killing by stealth goes on until peace is finally effected.[6] Sir Charles Dundas[7] explains in a significant statement why blood-revenge rather than compensation prevailed among the East Africans before its check by the British: "When questioned as to the penalty provided by their law for the taking of human life, natives invariably speak of compensation to be paid to the deceased's relatives. But we can imagine how ineffectual such a penalty would be among men who, even if not bloodthirsty, always have little control of their passions, and who have scant if any chance at all of finding redress other than by personal retaliation. Moreover, the amount of compensation is usually not so exorbitant that the average well-to-do man cannot easily pay it, and since it is mostly paid by the family or even the whole clan, it is in effect hardly a penalty at all on the evildoer himself. It may be said here that whenever we find native law seemingly lax or ineffectual to excess, it is to be suspected that we have either not got to the root of it or that there are underlying aspects of the law which are not apparent to us.

3 Roscoe, in JAI, XXXVII, 112.
4 Hobley, in JAI, XXXIII, 357; and in JAI, XLI. 425; Hobley, A-Kamba, 95, 96, 122, 123.

5 Torday and Joyce, in JAI, XXXVII, 140.
6 O'Sullivan, in JAI, XL, 189-190.
7 In JAI, LI, 236 (quoted), 237-238, 242.

So it is with the law of homicide, for the truth is that compensation or blood-money was formerly not the normal penalty for homicide, but rather it was a composition voluntarily accepted in lieu of blood revenge, which is now suppressed by us, and therefore not often spoken of by natives." In former days the rules prevailing here for inflicting vengeance varied considerably: in some cases, if the murderer could not be found, any member of his clan or locality could be killed; in others, near relatives only, or a brother only, or the murderer's wife, or his sister; again, the rule required only a male for a male, only a woman for a woman.

In northeastern Africa, one "may not rest until he has taken blood-vengeance, and in his fury he not seldom kills people who are known to be harmless, provided only they belong to the hostile tribe." Yet blood-guilt can be atoned for by blood-money paid to the relatives of the murdered person. Among the Somal "the family of the murderer may either pay blood-money, or deliver up the murderer, or do battle." What they do is determined by the circumstances of the deed or by the eminence of the man; and the amount of blood-money is likewise adjusted to the circumstances of victim and murderer. If the murderer cannot pay at once, he is delivered to and held captive by the relatives of the murdered, till his family can raise the sum. "Blood-money falls upon the nearest family-relations and never upon the tribe." The penalty is generally put very high, but there ensues dickering, and it is seldom paid in full. If there is a fight in which a number are killed, and then the blood-money is not paid within a proper time or is refused, the tribe demanding redress kills as many members of the one refusing it as the former lost in the fight. Out of this, inasmuch as excuses for delay generally follow, grow new rights to compensation. "That blood-revenge . . . is not dissolved by a money-penalty, without doubt has its basis in the dense population of the Galla region."[8]

Among the Kabyles the blood-debt is contracted by the family of one who has committed homicide in time of peace. It is satisfied only by the death of the designated victim; wounds, however severe, are not sufficient. It is a head for a head. It is of little importance that the victim perished by an act of imprudence, or in a conflagration, or at the moment of perpetrating a crime. A minor child or an idiot is not exempted from vengeance; nor is the owner of a vicious animal. The latter is regarded as the direct author of the death of anyone killed by the animal.[9] In Egypt "the homicide, or any person descended from him, or from his great-grandfather's father, is killed by any of such relations of the person whom he has slain. In many instances, the blood-revenge is taken a century or more after the commission of the act which has occasioned it; when the feud for that time has lain dormant, and perhaps is remembered by scarcely more than one individual."[10]

Vengeance by blood was considered by the Koryak to be the duty of all blood-relatives, and not of single individuals. "A consanguineous group consisting of one or several families was also jointly responsible for a murder committed by one of its members, and in so far must be regarded as one juridical personality. We know that the old men often attempted to check the spread of blood-revenge. For this purpose ransom was resorted to." Com-

8 Paulitschke, *Nordost-Afr.*, I, 262, 263; II, 151, 156; §§2, 24, of text.

9 Hanoteau et Letourneux, *Kabylie*, III, 60, 62-64.

10 Lane, *Mod. Egypt*, I, 295-296.

pensation in money is a secondary and a modern consideration, and among the Gilyak cannot always, even nowadays, replace the ancient duty of exacting blood-revenge for manslaughter. Vengeance is demanded, even against animals: "if a man is killed by a bear, he must be avenged by the death of the animal in question, or of another bear in its place." Religion reinforces the custom, for "the soul of an unavenged victim cannot go to the land of the dead, but must remain near the living, incarnated as a bird-avenger, . . . and finally crumbles into dust. . . . As the soul of a murdered man, like that of any other Gilyak, continues to exist only for three generations, so the obligation to take vengeance for his blood binds his fellow clansmen only till the third generation if the act of vengeance is not performed by a contemporary. Vengeance is never executed upon a woman, or upon the private property of the guilty person."[11] Among the Ossetes, "my cousin in the hundredth degree, who bears my name, is my near relative, and I am, under proper circumstances, under obligation to take or to demand blood-vengeance for him; but my mother's brother is not my relative, and if he is killed I cannot demand expiation for him." This community of blood "alone guarantees political protection and assures the independence of the individual." Mere wounds may be compensated by money, according to a scale set by an elected tribunal. The society takes over the less serious cases of infringement of rights, that is, while the most serious is still left to the primordial method of settlement. A more developed form is where a tribunal decides and all parties are under curse if they do not carry out its decisions. They know no laws, but only customary rights.[12] Blood-revenge is practised among a number of other tribes in Russia. Whether the manslaughter was intentional or not, one who has committed a homicide is bound to send to the family of the slain every month for three years a sheep for each person. In the fourth year he makes a bargain to discharge the obligation.[13]

In certain parts of India observers find "the chief social restraint in the system of blood feud, a system which seems to have penetrated the whole social structure." These communities are thoroughly imbued and actuated by the idea of kinship. "When any difference occurs between two men of the same village, which is rarely the case, each individual has his party who cling to him and take up his quarrel, not by any means from a sense of justice, but from relationship—and a civil war ensues. The result of this system Stewart found to be a reluctance to enter into quarrels which entailed consequences so disastrous, and hence a society 'living in general peace and honesty.' He compares the action of the law or revenge as an efficient deterrent among the clans of the Scotch Highlands some 150 years before the date of writing. The restraint of life governed by inexorable blood feuds was mitigated among these North Kachar Nagas by a quaint custom. At stated times, once or twice a year, the whole village adjourned to some convenient place, and a general mêlée took place, everyone fighting for his own band. No weapons were used, but severe bruises and scratches resulted, yet these never gave ground for a quarrel, 'whereas at other times the lifting of a hand would lead to a blood feud.' This excellent system afforded vent for private grudges."[14] Again, "individual blood feuds were kept alive . . . by a custom by which men might be hired to carry on a quarrel, 'when the males of a family were wanting or unable to do so.' . . .

11 Czaplicka, *Aborig. Siberia*, 33-34, 46-48.
12 Von Haxthausen, *Transkaukasia*, II, 26, 29.
13 *Russian Ethnog.* (Russ.), II, 208, 326.
14 Godden, in JAI, XXVI, 174.

Murder admitted of no expiation, and instant death might be inflicted by the relatives of the murdered person, without reference to the council of elders, or even ten years after the deed the murderer might be surprised and killed; revenge for the death of a relative was considered 'a sacred duty never to be neglected or forgotten.' "[15] "The blood feud of the Naga, as with the Corsican 'vendetta,' is a thing to be handed down from generation to generation, an everlasting and baneful heirloom involving in its relentless course the brutal murders of helpless old men and women, innocent young girls and children, until, as often happens, mere family quarrels, generally about land or water, being taken up by their respective clansmen, break out into bitter civil wars which devastate whole villages."[16] "It is difficult to determine the cause or causes which involve participation in blood-feud. It may be said, however, that blood-feud involves the rendering of assistance by others, and it commences, therefore, with the group to which an individual belongs. It is only through such assistance that the compensation, whether in blood, cash, women or kind, which must inevitably be demanded for wrong done, can be obtained. It follows that, where a quarrel ending in murder takes place between members of one family, a blood-feud does not necessarily arise, for no one will assist the murderer. . . . But ordinarily, if an individual of one group is killed by an individual of another group, it is at once incumbent on the group to which the murdered man belongs to take blood for blood. Thus, if the antagonists belong to different groups within the tribe, we have two internal groups engaged in blood-feud, . . . and . . . each is likely to be joined by other groups, until the whole tribe is engaged in a fratricidal struggle. Or, if the murdered man is of a different tribe to the murderer, the feud may be taken up by the whole of two tribes, each of which may again be joined by other tribes, so that a small spark soon sets a large conflagration ablaze. Nor is the feud composed until a reckoning of death for death has been made and compensation paid to the group in which the largest number has taken place."[17]

In old Japan, blood-revenge was recognized under cognizance of the authorities and with certain restrictions. The great warrior-statesman "Iyéyasu himself maintained it—exacting only that preliminary notice of an intended vendetta should be given in writing to the district criminal court. The text of his article on the subject is interesting:— . . . A person harbouring such vengeance shall give notice in writing to the criminal court; and although no check or hindrance may be offered to the carrying out of his design within the period allowed for that purpose, it is forbidden that the chastisement of an enemy be attended with riot. . . . Why the duty of vengeance was not confined to the circle of natural kinship is explicable, of course, by the peculiar organization of society. We have seen that the patriarchal family was a religious corporation; and that the family-bond was not the bond of natural affection, but the bond of the cult. . . . To strike one's natural parent was a crime punishable by death: to strike one's teacher was, before the law, an equal offence. This notion of the teacher's claim to filial reverence was of Chinese importation: an extension of the duty of filial piety to 'the father of the mind.' . . . A peculiar interest attaches to the Japanese vendetta in view of the fact that it conserved its religious character unchanged down to the present era. The *kataki-uchi* was essentially an act of propitiation, as is proved by the

15 Godden, in JAI, XXVII, 24, 25.   17 Risley, *Ethnol. Ind.*, I, 71.
16 Woodthorpe, in JAI, XI, 67.

rite with which it terminated,—the placing of the enemy's head upon the tomb of the person avenged, as an offering of atonement."[18]

The head-hunters keep a sort of reckoning in heads which amounts to a chronicle of blood-vengeance. Dyak wars arise out of quarrels dating from the days of their forefathers, and the reasons they give are connected with the adjustment of the account in heads. Some tribes keep the strictest accounts, and always know just how many heads are owing between them.[19] The Aëtas of the Philippines, when sallying out for vengeance, warn their friends off their line of march; for they mean to kill the first living thing they encounter to expiate for a death, even where there is no murder in question.[20] On the island of Yap, if a person is killed while doing something that is forbidden, there can be no blood-vengeance; if, for example, anyone is killed while creeping into a strange house or going through the village at night without a fire-brand.[21]

Private quarrels gave birth to public quarrels in Polynesia, "for the collective body of natives was affected by an offence against an individual." Revenge on account of a murdered father or friend, if not obtained during the lifetime of the injured, was handed to posterity. In Samoa sticks were planted in the ground and renewed as they rotted until the wrong was avenged. Punishment might fall either upon the offender himself or upon some other member of his family. In Tahiti a woman bathed herself in the blood of her murdered sons on swearing revenge, while a blood-feud was sometimes indicated by a person causing his own blood to flow.[22] The following case from New Zealand will recall primitive ideas of property in their connection with the subject under review. "The shedding of blood was always considered a most serious thing, although but a drop were shed. A gentleman entering the writer's house knocked his head against a beam and cut his eyebrow so that blood flowed; the natives deplored the accident and said that according to their law the house would have been forfeited to him, and as they were of his party, it would have been their duty to have seen it given up to him, as every one present was affected by his blood being shed. In the same way, if a canoe should be dashed on shore in a storm, and the owner's life endangered he thereby acquires a title to the spot on which he is thrown. When blood is shed, it is the duty of every one related to the person who has suffered to seek for revenge. It does not matter whether it be the individual who drew it or any one else belonging to his tribe; but blood must be shed as an atonement for blood. This was one of the most fertile causes of war in former times. There were no cities of refuge to which a manslayer might flee, and his act endangered the lives of every one in his tribe."[23]

Among the Eskimo near Hudson Bay, "in the case of a premeditated murder, it is the duty of the next of kin to avenge the deed, though years may pass, while the murderer pursues his usual occupations undisturbed, before an opportunity occurs to the relative for taking him by surprise. Sometimes the victim is not overcome and turns upon the assailant and kills him. The man, now guilty of two murders, is suffered to live only at the pleasure of the people, who soon decree his death. Murder is not approved, either by the individual or the community."[24] Here we see a distinction upon the basis of premeditation,

18 Hearn, *Japan*, 321, 322, 323.
19 Veth, *Borneo*, II, 283.
20 Mason, *Invention*, 369.
21 Senfft, in *Globus*, XCI, 152.

22 Turner, *Samoa*, 326-327; Von *Bülow*, in *Globus*, LXIX, 192; Williamson, *Cent. Polyn.*, II, 346 ff.; 352 ff.; III, 4.
23 Taylor, *Te Ika*, 555-556, note.
24 Turner, in BAE, XI, 186.

and also the entrance, in an extreme case, of the community as the avenger. Among the Central Eskimo there is no way of punishing transgressors except by the blood-vengeance. It is not rare that when a man offends another, the latter kills the former. It is then the duty of the nearest relative of the victim to kill the murderer. "Their method of carrying on such a feud is quite foreign to our feelings. Strange as it may seem, a murderer will come to visit the relatives of his victim (though he knows that they are allowed to kill him in revenge) and will settle with them. He is kindly welcomed and sometimes lives quietly for weeks and months. Then he is suddenly challenged to a wrestling match, and if defeated is killed, or if victorious he may kill one of the opposite party, or when hunting he is suddenly attacked by his companions and slain."[25] "Blood revenge is considered a sacred duty among all the Eskimo, and it is a common thing to find men who dare not visit certain villages because of a blood feud existing, owing to their having killed some one whose near relatives live in the place."[26]

Blood-revenge was common among the American Indians. Many cases of massacre of war-captives are to be explained by the fact that the war was one for blood-vengeance.[27] Revenge was a duty not to be forgotten. It is said, for instance, that on the spot where the relative was killed in a fight a piece of cloth was dipped in blood and kept as a remembrance until his death was avenged by killing the slayer or one of the males of his family.[28] The Indians feared especially the unappeased ghosts of the murdered; flight from or composition with the avenger of blood was common.[29] One of the reforms of Hiawatha is said to have been "the regulation to abolish the wasting evils of intratribal blood-feud by fixing a more or less arbitrary price—10 strings of wampum, a cubit in length—as the value of a human life. It was decreed that the murderer or his kin or family must offer to pay the bereaved family not only for the dead person, but also for the life of the murderer who by his sinister act had forfeited his life to them, and that therefore 20 strings of wampum should be the legal tender to the bereaved family of the settlement of the homicide of a co-tribesman."[30] But the governmental system had not yet taken retaliation out of the hands of its constituent kin-groups. "The European settlers in the colonies of Pennsylvania and New York could not understand why, when in time of peace an Indian murdered a white man, they could obtain no redress from the tribal government with whom they had treaty relations. They regarded such indolence as breach of faith and proof of evil intention. It was nothing of the kind. A crime of blood was something which concerned the consanguine gens only; it was a family matter with which the tribal council had no concern and about which it could take no action; it was in no sense a crime against the commonwealth. This view of the case was something wholly incomprehensible to the Europeans, who belonged to States where a felony or a breach of the peace is something quite different when the nation appears on the stage of history from what it is in the tribal condition."[31] Among certain California tribes, if wergeld is paid without higgling, the slayer and the avenger are at once reconciled. If not, the latter must have the former's blood, and the system of retaliation thus initiated might go on endlessly were it not

25 Boas, in BAE, VI, 582.
26 Nelson, in BAE, XVIII, pt. I, 292.
27 Ratzel, *Vkde.*, II, 634.
28 Hodge, in HAI, I, 348.

29 Lippert, *Kgchte.*, II, 326, 595; Mooney, in HAI, pt. I, 253.
30 Hewitt, in HAI, I, 546.
31 Brinton, in *Smithson. Rep.*, 1893, 595 and ff.

that it may be arrested at any stage by money-payment.[32] The mode of settling troubles is to kill enemies at the first favorable opportunity, and then, if the murderer wishes to avoid a like fate, he settles with the relatives of the deceased, paying, according to the rank and station of the dead man, in Indian money—perhaps in white deer skins or woodpeckers' heads. All are thereafter supposed to be friendly. The wergeld is worth a hundred dollars for a man and fifty for a woman. "A man's life is valued . . . at six canoes, each one occupying in its manufacture three months' time of two Indians, or the labor of one man for three years."[33]

Of the Indians of the northwest coast we read: "In their disregard for the lives and feelings of slaves, and in their practices of compounding murder and other crimes by the payment of indemnity to the relatives of the injured, we see simply the operations of custom, which with them has the force of law. Murder, seduction, wounds, accidental killing, loss of articles belonging to another, refusal to marry a widow according to law, casus belli in general, any wrong may be righted by payment of an indemnity in the currency of the region. . . . Wars are frequently avoided by an indemnity arrangement, and they go so far in this system of compensation that they demand payment for losses from parties who have been in no way instrumental in causing them. For instance, an Indian at Sitka broke into the room of two miners in their absence, emptied a demijohn of liquor, and died in consequence, and the relatives of the robber demanded and received payment from the unfortunate Caucasians. If a man be attacked by a savage dog and kills him in self-defense, he must pay for the dog to the Tlingit owner. A small trading schooner, while running before a furious gale, rescued two Tlingit from a sinking canoe, which had been carried to sea. The canoe was nearly as long as the schooner and could not be carried or towed, seeing which, the natives themselves cut the worthless craft adrift. When the humane captain landed the rescued men at their village he was astonished by a peremptory demand for payment for the canoe, backed by threats of retaliation or vengeance."[34]

Thirst for revenge characterizes the Indians of British Guiana, a craving which is not satisfied until the offender himself and indeed his whole family is exterminated. "Blood-revenge is followed out by the Arawaks into its extreme consequences."[35] "Since the conception of blood-vengeance is very dominant and powerful among the Brazilian savages, it is taken for granted in the common council that it must be carried out; but whether, through the individuals concerned, merely upon the malefactor, or upon the tribe itself—that is the subject of the deliberation." Avengers paint black spots on their bodies, or cut off the hair. Again, "blood-revenge is practised still by the tribe with the energy and craftiness of the nature-man. It has its ground chiefly in jealousy and injury to marital rights."[36] Among the Jibaro blood-revenge is not strictly individualized in the sense that it always directs itself exclusively against the slayer: "The Jibaro certainly first of all wants to take revenge on the person who committed the crime, but if he can not be caught it may instead be directed against some one of his relatives—his brother, his father, even his mother or sister."[37] The Fuegians "are not very particular when seeking to revenge

32 Powers, in *Contrib. N. Amer. Ethnol.*, III, 21.
33 Mason, in *Smithson. Rep.*, 1886, pt. I, 233.
34 Niblack, in USNM, 1888, 241.

35 Schomburgk, *Brit.-Guiana*, I, 322; II, 460 (quoted).
36 Von Martius, *Beiträge*, I, 127-128, 693.
37 Karsten, "Jibaro," in BAE, Bull. LXXIX, 11.

bloodshed on whom they revenge it, so long as the victim is one of the same clan, whether man or woman. Sometimes the murderer is suffered to live, but he is much beaten and hurt, and has to make many presents to the relatives of the dead."38 The law of retaliation was the only one understood by the Araucanians, "although the keen commercial spirit of the Araucano led him to forego personal vengeance for its accruing profit. Thus every injury had its price, which varied with the importance of the offended. . . . Parricide, infanticide, wife-murder, intentional abortion, and similar acts committed within the first rank of blood relations were not considered as crimes, it being held that these relations were of the same blood, and that it was allowable for anyone to shed his own blood."39

Among the Arabs, "blood-revenge could be abrogated only by punishment. But this presupposes law and authority, not the moral ideal. Once the tribe may well have exercised real authority over all its members so that within its range the prevalence of blood-revenge was impossible. But we do not know these times. . . . For no public law of state had been developed which could have called a halt to the monstrous demands of family-sentiment and to the private right of feud. Thus are explained too the conflicts between little kin-groups shortly before Islam, which threatened to dissolve everything into a wild chaos. But how full of blessing here was Islam, in that it gave the split-up people a new idea and a new principle of law. . . . Upon the natural foundation of the family, the close blood-kinship, was based a solidarity which was scarcely capable of dissolution." Blood revenge was regarded as a family affair, as war was a tribal; every case of blood-spilling within was reckoned a murder. "Therewith the slayer came out into a quite new light; he was a criminal and was personally responsible for his guilt." Closely connected with the kinsman was the guest-friend, for his relations were with the separate families rather than the community. The guest-friend was not exposed to the vengeance which his entertainers might be under obligation to take on the tribe from which he came. If he was a fugitive or outlaw from his tribe, he must be protected against it. It is the greatest disgrace to have killed one's guest-friend. Medina was one of the most unfortunate pre-Islamic cities, for the two chief tribes occupied the region and the bloodshed was copious. Various attempts were made to avert it. The simplest was to surrender the murderer to the avenging tribe, and it was tried. But the practical means was found in the wergeld. Though nobody could be legally forced to accept it, the custom took root and became widespread. But it is an error to think that the arrangement of wergeld looked to the complete abrogation of blood-vengeance. The two disparate expedients stood side by side, and it cannot be said that one was capable of merging into the other. "The one was the utilitarian, which accommodated itself to the acceptance of money-reparation, the other that of Arabian family honor, which held any such acceptance to be a disgrace. In it religious motives were plainly embodied. . . . The maxim of the genuine noble Beduins went: 'The bird of the dead cried until he had had to drink.' This way of looking at things has never been overcome; it still lives on today despite Islam. We are told of a proverb of a Beduin tribe of the nineteenth century, which runs: 'Even if it means suffering hell-fire, we do not let go blood-vengeance.' Thus the principle was not to be overcome, though it could be cut across, by the ar-

38 Bridges, "Firelanders," in *Voice for S. Amer.*, XIII, 201.   39 Latcham, in JAI, XXXIX, 356.

rangement of blood-money; the practical advantages which were here presented were too great to win no elbow-room. . . . But since a full harmony between the disputing parties was scarcely to be attained without mediators—commonly the guilty party was inclined to the payment of wergeld, while the injured called for blood—in burning cases judges were appointed. For that they took persons of high reputation"—generally members of the tribe's princely family, for the function seems to have lost its religious significance.[40]

Blood-revenge has long been a custom among the South Slavs and occasionally occurs today. It is forbidden within the *bratstvo* or kin-group, and one method of reconciling a blood-feud and preventing further fighting between *bratstvos* is for the men in one to become godfathers to children in the other, for this relationship is regarded as equivalent to actual kinship.[41] Mohammedan law suppressed blood-revenge between believers.[42] A transition from the private to the public system occurred among the early Scandinavians: a manslayer must pay, besides wergeld to the heir and kin, a fine to the king and hundred; this was to atone for breach of the public peace. The former was gradually left out and was abolished about 1335; then the fine went to the king, hundred, and avenger and, finally, to the state alone.[43]

§182. Crime.

THE sense of responsibility and of effort, among the Melanesians, is communal and not individual; the system of morals, for instance, of the Koita of New Guinea, "does not teach or express individual effort and individual salvation, but on the contrary teaches the due subordination of the individual and his efforts in the sum of the tribal activities, which, broadly speaking, allow no room for individual initiative. Hence homicide and theft are not considered reprehensible in themselves, but only become so when directed against members of the community or tribe, or against outsiders strong enough to avenge themselves on the tribe." Because of their "non-individual system of morality," the author believes, this people has been but little influenced by the habits and beliefs of Europeans. "The moral disposition and system of the Koita not only suited their environment fifty years ago, but have been strong enough to bar the approach of some of the worst evils consequent on bringing civilisation to the natives of the Pacific." Where the southern Massim have come but little under white influence, "there still is nothing reprehensible about the sexual act so long as it did not entail adultery or take place between individuals who should keep apart on grounds of consanguinity or social custom; in fact, so long as these limitations were not infringed, a girl before she was married might dispose of her person as she pleased." This diminishes the category of sex-crimes and, as might be expected under these conditions, "rape or attempted rape is and always has been very rare. When it did occur the attempt whether successful or not, if made by an unmarried man on an unmarried woman, was not punished." In case of married people, the situation was quite different—undoubtedly on account of the element of property, that is,

40 Proksch, *Blutrache*, 18, 30 ff., 51 ff.   42 Müller, *Islam*, I, 127.
41 Durham, in JAI, XXXIX, 86, 88-89, 91,   43 Geijer, *Svensk. Hist.*, 303.
92.

of monopoly, in marriage—but "there is every reason to believe that the great majority of married women were, and are, faithful wives."[1]

In South Africa, "murder, theft, adultery, and incest are crimes against the Masarwa moral code, and are punished either by fines, expulsion from the tribe, or, in the case of the last two, by death, usually by retaliation on the part of the injured party."[2] All sections of the Akikuyu seem to follow much the same rules in respect to sexual offenses, and "it is curious that whereas no difference is made between illicit intercourse with a married woman or a girl, there is a very much more severe penalty for causing a girl to become pregnant than in the case of a married woman. . . . Rape appears to be regarded as the same whether committed upon an unmarried girl or a wife, but the elders seem to require extremely little proof in the former case, for the fact that a girl complains is quite sufficient." Primitive people do not often make a distinction between torts and crimes; in fact, crimes cannot be said to exist where the state has not taken over the punishment of what may be called public wrongs. The author quoted[3] cites an illustration among the East Africans. "A woman while going to fetch some honey beer for a man fell down and hurt herself; the man was fined two goats as compensation by a large council of elders. Thus, where we should see no offence committed, the Mkamba often holds a man responsible for results which were in no way intended by him. The real explanation of this is, I think, that the native law does not regard offences so much from a point of view of the intentions of the offender as from results to the other party. The essence of all offences under our laws is the intention, but by civil law we can claim damages irrespective of this, and if therefore we regard all native law as civil, which in fact it is, we find that the difference is not so great. The distinction, however, which we make between criminal and civil law often confuses them and clashes with their ideas."

Drunkenness and madness were no excuse for committing crimes in the region of the upper Congo. No one had the right to pardon except the injured person or family. "There was no distinction between premeditated and accidental homicide. Life had been taken, and it must be dealt with as murder. The family avenged all cases of assault on any of its members, no matter whether it was physical assault, abduction, rape, adultery, theft, or anything else. Retaliation in kind, when possible, was the essence of justice among the natives— an eye for an eye, a cut for a cut, a bump for a bump, and a life for a life. When retaliation was impossible, compensation by fines was enforced." When a case was heard, deliberate effort was made to prejudice the court. "Before the proceedings began the plaintiff and defendant would each take their party of followers on one side, but in different parts of the town, and state tersely their case to them, and then distribute from 200 to 600 brass rods among them according to the importance of the case. It was their duty to clap their hands, and applaud every point made by the one who hired them, and to laugh ironically at the arguments of the other side. . . . There was a fiction that they were genuinely interested supporters of the side they took, but," says Weeks,[4] who reports the above, "I have often seen the rods distributed among them, and know for a fact that the majority did not care which side won. They always made sure of their rods before they shouted and clapped."

1 Seligmann, *Melanesians*, 131 (quoted), 132-133, 566-568 (quoted). See review of Malinowski's *Crime and Custom in Savage Society*, §18, above.

2 Dornan, in JAI, XLVII, 56.
3 Dundas, C., in JAI, XLV, 273-274, and in JAI, XLIII, 516.
4 In JAI, XXXIX, 433.

Criminal intent is something unknown to the natives of the Chin Hills: "Might quashes right and avarice smothers justice and custom among the Chins, whose quaint reasoning has decided that drunkenness is a valid excuse for murder and adultery, but that the action of a sober man committed by inadvertence and pure accident must be punished in the same manner as a crime committed with deliberate intent."[5] It is characteristic of the hill-tribes of India to believe in the general honesty of mankind; "most of them are not civilized enough to be thieves."[6] What in our law amounts only to indications and suppositions is regarded in the Malay law as proof positive. Marsden[7] says: "If the stolen goods be found in the possession of a person who is not able to account satisfactorily how he came by them, he shall be deemed the guilty person. If a person attempting to seize a man in the act of thieving, shall get hold of any part of his clothes which are known, or his kris, this shall be deemed a sufficient token of the theft. If two witnesses can be found who saw the stolen goods in possession of a third person, such person shall be deemed guilty, unless he can account satisfactorily how he became possessed of the goods." Wilken[8] adds that when a buffalo is stolen and the owner, following its trail, finds that it stops near an inhabited house, the owner of the house is required to get the buffalo back or to make good its value.

In the East Indies, as wrongs are generally regarded as committed against individuals rather than communities, justice has a prevailingly private character. But there are regular punishments: stoning for adultery, maiming for theft. The talion has yielded, however, to composition in money and goods. In adultery and theft if persons are caught in the act, they may be killed; if not, there is a process and a fine. In general, retaliation is allowed within a certain period: a day, three days, a month, or, oftener, at once. If the evil-doer escapes to the prince, composition supersedes direct retaliation. Originally it was left to the injured to take life or atonement for life; but the limit indicated was later imposed. A fine is regarded as an indemnification rather than as a punishment. The fact that the crime is against the individual appears in the fact that if no plaintiff appears the case is dismissed. The law-books provide for no punishment if there is no charge. In cases of theft, one finds first if the thief is rich and then if he will repay; if he will, there is no process. A man's family may be held accountable for him. No account is taken of motive. For every killing wergeld is demanded, and it varies according to the sex, rank, and wealth of the parties. The payments for a slave, a female, a free man, a free woman, and a noble are in the proportion twenty, thirty, thirty, forty, and eighty. There is also a tariff on different parts of the body. For murder as well as theft the tribe is held accountable; if it does not pay, the offender is killed. The relatives of the victim can decide as to how the non-paying murderer shall die and may kill him themselves, with the same or another weapon. A murderer infrequently becomes a slave if he cannot pay. The thief or adulterer must reimburse, return the goods, or serve as a slave; in some tribes the adulterer must marry the woman and pay back her original purchase-price. Crimes against a chief, such as falsification of his commands, are punished by death.[9]

The chiefs do not appear to have had any magisterial jurisdiction in the Marquesas, nor does there seem to have been any other judicial tribunal. "Any

5 Carey and Tuck, *Chin Hills*, 205.
6 Risley, *Ethnog. Ind.*, I, 219.
7 *Sumatra*, 148.

8 "Strafrecht," in VG, II, 493-494.
9 Wilken, *Vkde.*, 448-464, *passim*.

man receiving an injury from another, instead of making complaint to the chief, at once resorted to the prowess of his own arm and took a lawless retribution." Travellers who have commented on the absence of any legal provisions for the well-being and conservation of society, have added that nevertheless everything went on with the greatest smoothness, the people seeming to be governed by a sort of tacit common-sense. The power of the mores is here in evidence. According to the writer,[10] in case of theft the injured man had the right to go to the house of the thief, if the latter were known, and to take back the article stolen, or, if it had disappeared, something amounting to two or three times its value, this being done without a word; but in case of theft from a chief, the chief might kill the thief. In Easter Island disputes were settled by the king or chief "without regard to law or justice; there was no code, and people avenged their own injuries." So, too, in other sections, there were no regular tribunals or systems of justice, the reason alleged being the power which the superiors had over the persons and property of their inferiors. "The right was always with the strongest, so tribunals were useless. If people of the same rank had differences, they arranged them amicably or fought; if they were chiefs, it meant war. It was not in the interest of the common people to quarrel, for they knew that the first chief who happened to come along would settle matters by appropriating to himself the object of litigation." Distinction was drawn between wrongs committed against group-members and those against outsiders: "In Niue, though the slaying of a potential enemy was a virtue, murder of a member of the tribe was punished by death. . . . Theft from a member of the tribe (but not from one of another tribe) was also regarded as a vice." How religion reinforces the mores is seen in a statement about a Micronesian group, that a man caught violating custom pays at once, but not so much from a sense of justice as from fear due to superstition, because anyone can avenge himself by his own gods or by purchased sorcery.[11]

Theft is little known among the Tlinkits. "Before the fine art of thieving was introduced by the white man, no man's house was ever robbed, nor his wood stolen though cut and banked in the forest; his garden was not plundered, though miles from his home, nor his blankets thrown over his canoe to protect it from the sun disturbed, nor any of his belongings appropriated by another. Valuable articles are deposited in deadhouses and on and around graves, articles that natives covet, yet these were never stolen. . . . The percentage of thieving by natives is much lower than that of the white races. For more than twenty years we have lived among them. Our doors have been left unlocked for them to walk in and out; frequently we were out and they had the house all to themselves, yet in all these years we have never had anything stolen by one of them."[12] Nor was thieving common among the Omaha, where restitution was the only punishment. "Assaults were not frequent. When they occurred they were settled privately between the parties and their relatives. In all offenses the relatives stood as one. Each could be held responsible for the acts of another—a custom that sometimes worked injustice, but on the whole was conducive to social order."[13] During the worst period of their demoralization the Pima Indians stole wheat from each other and sold it to buy whisky, but

---

10 Williamson, *Cent. Polyn.*, III, 13, 25-26, 27 (quoted), 28 (quoted), 29.
11 Kubary, *Pelauer*, 73.

12 Jones, *Thlingets*, 217-218.
13 Fletcher and LaFlesche, in BAE, XXVII, 213-214.

"it is to be remembered that by far the greater part of the tribe disapproved of such deeds, and the few that engaged in such enterprises had not the support of public opinion, which even in an Indian village is an autocratic power."[14] Incest, attempted suicide, and libel are no crimes among the Araucanians, "while robbery is part of the daily life of the Indian;" yet the latter applies only to the inter-group relation, for no stealing is allowed within the clan.[15]

Even murder was not yet a public crime among the Homeric Greeks; it was a private wrong against the murdered man and his family. The murderer withdrew from his country in order to escape vengeance, not legal prosecution or punishment in the strict sense. "The presence of a murderer then constituted no such pollution to the people of the land as it did in later times in Greece, and thus the act of killing in itself was no offense against either state or gods; just as, even to-day, among the Mainotes in southern Sparta, homicide is said to be regarded simply as a matter between man and man." Circumstances might, however, make homicide a dread offense against the gods, especially if the tie of kinship or guest-friendship existed between the slayer and the slain, that is, if it were in-group murder. "The Erinyes, or Furies, avenge wrongs to kindred, though they do not punish ordinary homicide. . . . The only court-scene which is depicted by the Homeric poet is between two men after a murder: one declares and the other denies that the 'ransom' or fine has been paid. No question arises as to the execution of the murderer, for which, indeed, the state had no provision." If homicide was a private offense, still more were all minor personal assaults matters of which the state as such took no cognizance. "Theft as well as murder was a purely personal cause, and each man had to protect the rights of himself and his family, although as in rude societies of the present day the neighbors of the injured party might be willing on their own account to aid in the punishment of one who might steal from them next."[16]

As among primitive peoples there are no binding precepts of conduct except those that rest on the principle of kinship, so among the Arabs the rule held good without substantial modification down to the time of Mohammed. "No life and no obligation was sacred unless it was brought within the charmed circle of the kindred blood."[17] The Vendidad, which is the code of the religious, civil, and criminal laws of the ancient Iranians, is apparently the joint work of the high priests during the period of several centuries. They started with old sayings and laws (Avesta) and interpreted them in various, often contradictory, ways, until in the course of time these interpretations, the so-called Zend, became as authoritative as the original text. In the development of these rules of conduct, religion played an essential part.[18] Further evidence of the nature of antisocial conduct will be given in the paragraph on the kinds of punishment meted out to offenders. It may be noted, as a general principle, that the category of crime is a variable; what constitutes wrongful behavior depends on time, place, and degree of economic and societal development.

Animals as Criminals. Says Train,[19] in his chapter on animals in court: "The idea that animals should not be held responsible for their acts would have been

---

14 Russell, in BAE, XXVI, 199.
15 Latcham, in JAI, XXXIX, 354.
16 Seymour, *Hom. Age*, 88, 89, 90.
17 Smith, *Relig. Sem.*, 287.
18 Haug, *Parsis*, 225-226.

19 *On the Trail of the Bad Men and Other Essays*, 125, 127-128, 131-132, 145; N. Y. *Times*, Dec. 1, 1926; Jan. 30, 1927; §§214, 256, of the text.

greeted with derision in ancient and mediæval times. Indeed by the law of England animals which caused the death of human beings were 'deodand,' forfeited to the crown, and either killed or sold for the benefit of the poor, as late as during the reign of Queen Victoria; while on the Continent animals were tried for their crimes, condemned and punished by mutilation, by hanging, or by being buried and burned alive until less than 200 years ago. The report of Berriat-Saint-Prix to the Royal Society gives a list of nearly 200 instances of the prosecution of animals between the beginning of the twelfth to the middle of the eighteenth centuries. Since he only cites the convictions, and as court archives of the Middle Ages are in large part lost or destroyed, and the cases imperfectly recorded at best, his list is probably a fragmentary one. The most interesting feature of this amazing docket is that no bug, bird, or beast was too small to be accused of crime and placed on trial for its offense; and the defendants include caterpillars, flies, locusts, leeches, snails, slugs, worms, weevils, rats, mice, moles, turtle-doves, pigs, bulls, cows, cocks, dogs, asses, mules, mares, and goats." Pigs appeared more frequently than any other animals at the bar of justice, probably because in mediæval times they ran wild and, in France, were so numerous and so dangerous that any one was free under the law in many places to kill them on sight. "The religious enthusiasts of the Middle Ages were ready to prosecute pigs and sows, not only on account of their habits and numbers but because they were always suspected of being possessed with devils. Many contemporary references exist to the Gadarene swine of the New Testament, which rushed down and cast themselves into the sea after having been so possessed. Indeed it was widely held and even taught by Thomas Aquinas, the greatest theological authority of mediæval times, that all beasts were but the embodiment of evil spirits. And more recently Père Bougeant, a French Jesuit, has sought to demonstrate the same theory in a philosophic thesis."

"Nowadays when animals are guilty of mischief, theft or violence we look not to them but to their owners for the purpose of fixing criminal responsibility, and if the owner can be shown to have used the animals as his instrument or agent, we visit upon him the retribution which a few centuries ago would have been inflicted upon the animal. Thus attacks by vicious dogs are sometimes made the basis for criminal indictments charging their owners with criminal assault." Yet survivals of the old notions remain, e.g., the reported trial and conviction of a chimpanzee a few years ago before a police judge for the crime of publicly smoking a cigarette in violation of the laws of Indiana; and, more recently, the trial and conviction by a jury of a foxhound for killing sheep at Winchester, Kentucky; the execution of a dog in Winnipeg, in 1926, for biting a woman who was pulling his mistress's hair during a fight; and the sentencing of a hawk to death for murdering a pigeon in Chicago in 1927.

§183. Detection of Crime: The Ordeal.

THE detection of theft is an elaborate affair in New Britain. All the suspected persons may be got together and, after an incantation has been muttered by the priest-detective, they are each in turn made suddenly to strike out with the fist or suddenly to straighten out the arm, and he whose elbow joint gives out a cracking sound is the thief. "No protest can save him from the consequences or clear his character." Another method is for all the town or village to gather in an open space and for the dealer in spirits to pass in front of them, his finger-tips to his lips and his elbow at right angles to his body and pointing to the people. Passing along the line, he mumbles his incantations, and suddenly his arm involuntarily, so it is said, straightens out in front of someone. That person is the thief. All believe the sign infallible; and the sooner the victim makes peace the better for himself. Should the detective pass all and no indication ensue, there is yet another plan. The priest enters the house from which the goods were stolen. "Standing in front of the place where the goods were usually kept, finger tips to mouth, elbow at right angles to body, muttering incantations, suddenly the arm straightens, and the direction in which the arm straightened is the direction in which the thief went."[1]

The poison-ordeal, which is an institution characteristic of West African culture, is found among the Ba-Yaka. "Though death otherwise than by violence is recognised as 'natural' by the natives, certain cases, invariably where a chief is concerned, are referred to the malign influence of the evil spirit *Moloki,* acting through the agency of some old man or woman whom he is supposed to have possessed. The individual suspected is forthwith subjected to the poison ordeal. . . . If it causes vomiting on the part of the accused, he is considered innocent of the charge, but if the dose proves fatal, or if it has no effect, his guilt is regarded as established. In the last case a grave of a peculiar pattern is dug for him; he then sits down hard by and eats and drinks as much as he wishes, after which he enters the grave, usually of his own accord, and is buried alive."[2] Such is the power of religious belief. Poison-ordeals are practised by the Dualla,[3] while on the Ivory Coast the ordeal, employed ostensibly to discover whether a death is natural or not, often issues in a mere exaction of fines.[4] Farther toward the south, if a sorcerer charges anyone with causing a death the latter may call in a physician who mixes a poisonous dose of which the accused and the nearest relative of the deceased drink. He who is rendered delirious in the higher degree is condemned. If this is the accused, he pays or dies; if the relative, he pays an indemnity to the accused.[5] Among the Loango Coast tribes when a wife has been accused of causing her husband's sickness by magic, and has been proved innocent by the poison-ordeal, she celebrates "a high festal day." This is natural enough, for it is reported that for every natural death an average of three or four persons die under ordeal. A prince whose wife died submitted to the ordeal, hoping to survive it and receive as indemnity all the property of his wealthy father-in-law; but he succumbed and his own possessions went to his accuser. Since the shaman may fix upon the amount of poison to be administered, and since he alone determines whether the brew is made from the poisonous or non-poisonous parts of the tree, men's fates lie largely in his hands. Ordeals are applied chiefly within the family, where envy and greed for property flourish, and where questions of inheritance periodically stir up trouble. When a person takes the draught, the bystanders are ready with uplifted weapons to cut him to pieces in case he does not vomit; but if one has successfully emerged from one ordeal he may not be accused of witchcraft again. It is to be noted that the ordeal is prepared for by fasting and purification; it is really a religious ceremony.[6]

---

1 Danks, in AAAS, 1909, 456.
2 Torday and Joyce, in JAI, XXXVI, 48-49.
3 Schmidt, *Deut. Kol.,* II, 22.

4 Anon., "Elfenbeinküste," in *Globus,* LXXXVII, 392.
5 Serpa Pinto, *Africa,* 111, 112.
6 Bastian, *Deut. Exped.,* I, 46, 61, 195, 206-207.

In the Congo region "for petty thief-catching, a form of ordeal by fire is in great repute";[7] but in more serious cases the poison-draught is administered.[8] In some cases there is a sort of court which may condemn a man to punishment; but the condemned can have recourse to the poison-ordeal. He can be helped through this by friends if they will pay for the privilege of setting him a warm bath and exerting pressure on his stomach to force the dose up. This method is applicable to all sorts of crimes.[9] If an article is stolen among the Bangala of the Upper Congo, "the owner walks through the town calling out a description of the thing stolen, and invoking on the thief all the fetish curses that come to his mind. These curses are so frightful as to intimidate the thief, and frequently the stolen article is secretly replaced. . . . If something valuable, such as a piece of cloth, or a large knife or axe is lost, and the owner has a suspicion that a certain man is the thief, he can accuse that man, and if the man denies the theft, his accuser can demand that he should drink the ordeal and so settle the matter definitely. To refuse to drink the ordeal is an admission of guilt. Should the test go against the accused, he will have to replace the stolen article, pay a fine, and all the expenses of the ordeal drinking. But should the test establish his innocence, the accuser will have to compensate the accused and himself pay the fees of those who gave the ordeal." Weeks,[10] who reports this, gives an interesting account of the administering of an ordeal which he once witnessed: "At last it was decided that the parties should take the *nka* [ordeal-drug]. Each was so confident of the righteousness of his claims that he was willing and eager to eat a portion of the poisonous drug to support it. . . . Two *nyangas* prepared equal portions of the *nka*. There was about a dessert-spoonful in each portion. The accused had first choice, after which each doctor with the portion of *nka* in the palm of his hand took up his position by the side of his client, and at a given signal the portions of *nka* were simultaneously held to the mouth of the two opponents, and at the same moment they began to chew the drug. After chewing for a few moments each washed it down with gulps of sugar-cane wine. After taking the ordeal, the men are allowed neither to sit down nor to lean against anything, nor even to touch anything with their hands. The *nka* given in the above quantity blurs the vision, distorting and enlarging all objects, makes the legs tremble, the head giddy; and gives a choking sensation in the throat and chest. In fact it gives all the symptoms of intoxication and a few more besides. The one who first becomes intoxicated and falls down is the loser, and the one who resists the effects of the drug and controls himself the longest is the winner. . . . Forty minutes after taking the *nka* the climax came. The 'doctor' threw the stalk to the defendant (the accused), who caught it in his hands and carried it to the centre, where firmly fixing his feet on the ground, he stooped forward and placed the stalk with both his hands in a straight line, then raising himself he went back to his place. The plaintiff then went to pick it up, but no sooner did he lean forward than a spasm of pain seized him, and he would have fallen had not a man, who for the last twenty minutes had followed him closely, caught him in his arms and quickly carried him to his house. . . . The next day both accused and accuser were walking about the town, and seemed none the worse for drinking so powerful and dangerous a narcotic. They apparently

7 Phillips, in JAI, XVII, 222.
8 Ward, in JAI, XXIV, 287; Burrows, in JAI, XXVIII, 43.

9 Frobenius, *Masken*, 135, 136.
10 In JAI, XXXIX, 432; and in JAI, XL, 362-365.

had no enmity towards each other, but chatted freely and laughingly over the events of the previous day. . . . By frequently drinking the *nka* one becomes immune from its effects, and I have noticed that old people, who had taken it many times, never fell intoxicated by it, but young people fell quickly, from its effects on their system. I have no doubt that the administrators of the various ordeals were open to bribery and other influences, and could and would dilute the ordeal for one in whom they were interested."

The Bongo utilized a sort of psychological system of detection. "Formerly, when anyone discovered that either his friend, or perhaps his brother or wife, had been killed and the criminal could not be detected, it was no unknown device to prepare beforehand an image carefully representing the murdered person, and very often the likeness would be singularly perfect. He would then invite all the men to a feast, at which the spirituous 'legyee' would be freely circulated; and then, when excitement was highest, in the very midst of the singing and dancing, he would unexpectedly introduce the figure that had been prepared. The apparition would be sure to work its effect; the culprit would not fail to be betrayed, as he cowed and exhibited his wish to slink away. Having thus detected the offender, the injured party could deal with him as he pleased."[11] The wizard has many forms of divination of the general type described under that topic,[12] and presides over the boiling water and emetic ordeals. A hot iron is sometimes applied to the heel of the suspected thief, or is clasped by the woman suspected of adultery.[13] If the Bageshu are not satisfied with the chief's decision, they appeal to the fire test. "They take a fowl to the medicine man who hears the case, he then heats an iron hoe and applies it to the leg of first one and then the other; the one who is burned is the guilty person. Should they both be burned, they are both considered equally guilty."[14] In East Central Africa "an accused thief may, if the evidence be overwhelming, plead guilty, or he may demand the poison ordeal. If guilty, he trusts to his demand being resisted by the prosecutor; if innocent, he believes that he will unfailingly vomit the poison."[15] In Uganda there is a clever form of detection that rests upon the physiological effects of fear. "Dry flour is given to the suspected person. If innocent, he can swallow it; if he is unable to moisten the flour with his saliva and swallow it, he is shown to be guilty."[16] A religious theory is always infallible, for the spirits cannot fail; when the Nyassaland tribes are confronted with the dilemma that the lot has apparently fallen on an innocent man, they nevertheless say that he must have stolen the goods, for the lot could not lie.[17]

In the case of the poison-ordeal, the shaman always gets two goats and an iron digger; and for this reason the women and the poor cannot afford it. The cheaper way is to get the shaman to stick a needle or a pointed wire through one corner of the mouth of the accused. If blood flows thereafter in spitting, he is guilty.[18] Again the sorcerer brings a magical twig and lays it before a suspected thief. If he can lift it to his shoulder, he is innocent. The belief is firm that no guilty man can lift it. "In consequence of this idea it probably comes about that the delinquent, caught under autosuggestion, cannot lift the twig, lets it lie, and confesses his guilt."[19] In northeastern Africa the ordeal is

11 Schweinfurth, *Heart of Afr.*, I, 286, 287.
12 §313 of the text.
13 Stuhlmann, *Mit Emin*, 39, 93, 188, 654, 780.
14 Roscoe, in JAI, XXXIX, 194.

15 Macdonald, in JAI, XXII, 109.
16 Johnston, *Uganda*, II, 792.
17 Moggridge, in JAI, XXXII, 471.
18 Volkens, *Kilimandscharo*, 249, 250.
19 Fabry, in *Globus*, XCI, 220-221.

employed only in very severe cases; "only persons who under all the circumstances are given up as lost are subjected to the heavier ordeals." Ordeal by fire can be evaded by anyone through payment.[20] In Madagascar the ordeal consists in taking a stone out of boiling water without harm, or swimming a river full of crocodiles, or having water poured in the nose.[21] In the last case, if the accused sneezes he is guilty; and in the first, if his hand is blistered. The water-test is called "the Creator's ordeal," and the swimming-test the "ordeal by crocodile." In the latter, if the accused survives unhurt, the accusers are fined four oxen, of which the swimmer gets two, the king one, and the councillors one. There is also a poison-ordeal along with which the accused swallows three small square-shaped pieces of fowl's skin. "Tepid water was after a few minutes administered to cause vomiting, and the proof of innocence was the rejection of these three pieces uninjured."[22]

That able authority, Sir Charles Dundas,[23] has written so discerningly on this subject as applied to the Bantu tribes of East Africa, that he should be quoted at length. In this section discovery of the "truth" by ordeal, test, divining, witchcraft, and cursing is always the business of a medicine-man. Two examples of tests of veracity witnessed in Kikuyu may be cited: "1. Two men were strongly suspected of a theft of cattle. A medicine man was called in, and his performance was as follows: A common lizard was produced, and after being encircled by the doctor's gourds, was held to the nose of one of the men, who was asked if he was the thief. The man denied it and nothing occurred, but when the second man likewise denied his guilt, the lizard immediately bit him in the nostril. The medicine man pronounced the first man innocent and the second an accessory to the theft but not a principal. The same test was applied to two other men, and this time so soon as they denied their guilt the lizard bit the man's nostril and hung on. These were pronounced to be the actual thieves. I endeavoured, by close observation and experiment with several persons, to discover how the trick was done, but could find nothing to explain it; the medicine man would hold the lizard on his open palm, so that there was no possibility of squeezing or otherwise provoking it to bite. 2. Two men disputed for the possession of a wife. The one was required to go on all-fours on the ground. A small gourd was then placed on his back, and inside this a leaf, and on it two small bottles sewn in skin. The whole was covered with the man's blanket for a few moments, and on being uncovered the gourd was found about a quarter full of blood—said to be his own and proof of his false statement. Here also I could not find out, despite several repetitions, how the blood was conveyed into the gourd, where the medicine man had a supply of blood about his person, or how he had kept it from coagulating." The Wachaga use a liquid concoction called Kimangano which seems to have an intoxicating effect upon the accused, who is believed to confess his guilt under its influence. "As a matter of fact, I have ascertained that the person subjected to Kimangano does not speak entirely of his own accord, but the most leading questions are put to him and in his muddled state he is as likely as not to reply in the affirmative, which is taken to be clear proof of guilt. The custom has spread over the whole of Upare from Kilimanjaro." The commonest test or ordeal is perhaps the licking of hot iron. "I have seen this per-

20 Paulitschke, Nordost-Afr., II, 150.
21 Ratzel, Vkde., II, 517.
22 Sibree, Great Afr. Isl., 282, 283, 284.

23 In JAI, LI, 228-229, 230, 231 (quoted);
and in JAI, XLV, 255-256, 257 (quoted), 511
(quoted).

formed on more than one occasion, but I have never seen more than a slight
scorching of the tongue result. I do not know how it is done in the other tribes,
but in Ukamba it was performed as follows: A knife was thoroughly heated in
a fire, but previously the medicine man dabbed and streaked a white powder on
it. The same medicine was streaked on the man's forehead, nose, on the palms
of his hands and on his tongue. The heated knife was then copiously licked
with the tongue on both sides. I am told that the powder used was probably
diatomite, and that diatomite is an excellent heat-insulator. Without some
such protection a man could not possibly touch the knife without severely
scorching his tongue, but I have seen it done without any visible results at all.
The same powder is used by medicine men for many purposes; whether they
know its true virtue in these cases I cannot say, but it is obvious that the
medicine man can direct the issue of the ordeal by the quantity or evenness of
smearing the powder on the knife and tongue as he pleases or accidentally
applies it." Similar ordeals to this are the licking of hot coals and picking an
axe-head out of boiling water. It is curious to note that in Sumbwa such
ordeals have become converted into formal oaths: for instance, the accused
will say, 'May I suffer the pain of boiling water if I did so and so,' but it is
never put to the test and remains a mere formula."

The same author discusses oath-taking, saying that such oaths differ from
ordeals in that they are not intended merely to betray the guilt of a man who
will thereafter be dealt with; they signify, rather, that the matter is thenceforth beyond the sphere of human justice and that the guilt as well as its
penalty is left to divine judgment. "The Kithito is an article endowed with
mysterious powers whereby if a man swear falsely he will die in a given time.
It varies very much in composition and effect; it may be a concoction of all
sorts of odds and ends in which hyaena dung is very frequently found, or
it may be simply an empty horn; it may kill the one who offends against it in
a year, in a month, or in a few days; so also it may bring death to the offender
alone or to his whole family; I am told that there are Kithitos which affect
even the whole clan." Facing the Kithito, the person says what he maintains
to be the truth; as he speaks he taps it with a twig and finally, tapping three
times, he says, "Listen well, if I tell a lie let the Kithito eat me." "Upon this
oath being taken nothing is decided in the case, for if the man dies the decision
is thereby arrived at; if not, then nothing can be proved against him. Thus in
the majority of cases the elders need give no decision excepting that the ordeal
shall be undergone, or if one party refuse to do so he thereby admits himself
to be in the wrong, and the case is decided." Oath by witnesses is rare; if administered, it is mostly a mere formula, such as stepping over a stick; or
the witness submits to an ordeal. In all these ceremonies the person taking the
oath should be naked. Among certain tribes the ordeal may be proved by proxy,
either dogs or fowls or another person, preferably a slave, being subjected to
ordeal on behalf of the accused.

Dundas believes the ordeals are more than mere trickery, for a medicine-man
could not maintain a reputation for long on so flimsy a foundation. "The most
successful method will always be that which works automatically, as, for instance, something which will make a man betray himself." All of these tests
must be administered in the presence of the elders, and those which have been
described as oaths and not ordeals are administered by the elders themselves.
"These in particular bear the appearance of being religious practices, and
they are said to be 'bad,' which always signifies that they are connected with

the spirits." A vast number of cases are disposed of by these methods among the more primitive tribes. "In fact, it is generally so when an accusation or claim is entirely disputed, for the judicial authority will not undertake to decide on evidence; indeed, it is more their duty to arbitrate than to decide, and therefore they are prone to leave decision to divine judgment." With all their crudity, these oaths and ordeals represent an effective adjustment to local conditions. As evidence of their adaptability a comparison may be made between their influence on native conduct and that of the European courts now established in the district. "The native is far too inclined to make claims of the most fanciful nature without any foundation. There being no necessity for caution in appealing to the European courts, the native takes advantage of this and regards them, I fear, very much as a convenient institution whereby he may obtain advantages which he could not get from his own tribunals. I have, in fact, heard natives make the most definite statements before magistrates such as they would not even repeat in the presence of the elders." So much for the evidence of Dundas.

The negroes carried their ordeals with them to the New World. In Surinam cases of death were always investigated with the idea of discovering the agent involved. The prepared draught was employed. "If the accused becomes sick, for instance, develops an eruption, hurts himself, gets a swelling, or talks in his sleep, it is regarded as the effect of the drink, and it is adjudged that the accusation is well founded. The consciousness of this danger in which the accused finds himself is for him of itself quite enough to undermine his health; always spied upon by his enemies, the smallest doubtful omission becomes fatal for him, and it is therefore not at all seldom that these accused negroes have shortened by voluntary death a life that had for them no further value."[24]

In Tibet a feud is sometimes settled, when everyone is tired of it, by setting before two representatives, one from each of the warring tribes, two bowls of food, one of which is poisoned. "The tribe whose representative is killed is looked upon as the aggressor and is obliged to pay a heavy fine of cattle and other articles of value to the tribe whose claims have been sustained by the process of ordeal." Here the ordeal appears as a substitute for intertribal blood-vengeance; but the same expedient is employed within a group. "Should two women engage in a quarrel, an unnamable code requires that their respective husbands should take upon themselves the burden of dispute, the frequency of such sanguinary encounters giving just cause for wonderment as to why these continued decimations do not have the effect of soon depopulating the country."[25] India shows an ordeal to test chastity which consists of plucking cakes out of boiling oil and then husking a small quantity of rice.[26] Finger-mutilation was another test of chastity. The cut fingers of the chaste became quite well fifteen or twenty days after the operation, and were ever afterward a sign of chastity; for if their owner became unchaste, nails would grow on the stumps of the fingers. Those who were unchaste would surely suffer bodily ailment for attempting what only the chaste could do.[27] In the first "tradition-law" of Manu the ordeals are by fire, water, and the oath. If misfortune happen within a certain time to the one who has sworn, he is guilty. "This oath-test is also employed in the case of witnesses at court, perjury

24 Hostmann, *Beschaving*, I, 273.
25 Reid, in *Cosmopolitan Mag.*, XXVIII, 449.
26 Thurston, *S. India*, 423.
27 Fawcett, in JASB, I, 463.

being indicated by the subsequent misfortune." Then there were the balance-test and the floating-test. In the former "the man stands in one scale and is placed in equilibrium with a weight of stone in the other scale; he then gets out and prays, and gets in again. If the balance sinks, he is guilty; if it rises he is innocent." In the latter, "the accused is put into a sack and a stone is put into another sack. The two sacks are connected by a cord and flung into deep water. If the sack with the man sinks and the sack with the stone floats, the accused is declared to be innocent."[28] Water in which a holy person has washed is utilized in India to get the judgment of God.[29]

"China supplies us with a curious form which is a combination of water ordeal and chance. If an injured husband surprises his wife, *flagrante delicto*, he is at liberty to slay the adulterous pair on the spot; but he must then cut off their heads and carry them to the nearest Magistrate before whom it is incumbent on him to prove his innocence and demonstrate the truth of his story. As external evidence is not often to be had in such cases, the usual mode of trial is to place the heads in a large tub of water, which is violently stirred. The heads, in revolving, naturally come together in the centre, when if they meet back to back, the victims are pronounced guiltless, and the husband is punished as a murderer; but if they meet face to face, the truth of his statement is accepted as demonstrated; he is gently bastinadoed to teach him that wives should be more closely watched, and is presented with a small sum of money wherewith to purchase another spouse."[30] The Ainos of Japan use the stone in hot water and also hot iron.[31]

Taking oath in the Indian Archipelago means that the person swearing utters a curse upon himself and represents it by one or another action. The Bataks cut off the head of a frog, the people of Nias that of a pig, and the Dyaks that of a black chicken, as a symbol of the lot one calls down upon himself if he is speaking falsely. The oath is generally laid upon the accused and is a sort of purification-device, a means of proving innocence. Before the court every dispute is viewed as a personal affair between the man who claims to have been injured in his rights and the alleged offender, and the affair must be fought out between the two of them. In this fight the oath is a weapon, with the accused having the first right to use it. "To the accused belongs the first chance to give evidence just as to-day in a duel the first blow or shot is the right of the challenged. Therefore it says in the law: componat aut, si negaverit, juret (let him settle, or, if he denies, let him swear)." This is the general rule among the Malays. They have also the usual varieties of the water- and the fire-ordeals, as well as the duel and various other forms.[32] If court-procedure fails, the Alfurs of Buru resort to the ordeal: they wind the hand of the accused with a cloth and pour melted lead on it; if the lead injures the hand through the cloth, the accused is guilty.[33] Other ways of seeking the judgment of heaven are, in Borneo, by resting the case upon the outcome of a head-hunting expedition or a cock-fight; and in some cases the accuser and accused each provides a pig, the heads of the two animals being severed at a single blow, and the verdict going to him whose pig shows signs of life after that of his adversary has ceased to do so.[34] In Sumatra, besides variations on the water-

28 Hopkins, *Relig. India*, 277, 278, 279.
29 Bastian, *Afr. Reisen*, 203.
30 Nathubhoy, in JASB, VI, 130-131.
31 Hitchcock, in USNM, 1890, 467.

32 Grimm, *Deut. Rechtsalterth.*, 859; Wilken, "Strafrecht," in VG, II, 494-495, 497, 504-510.
33 Wilken, in VG, I, 38.
34 Veth, *Borneo*, II, 316, 317.

and fire-ordeals, there occurs that of rice or flour; the accused was required to swallow a mouthful of uncooked rice or raw flour. "If he choked or coughed over it, then he was guilty."[35] In the Philippines the red-hot iron and the pebble in boiling water offered a stock type of ordeal, and the rice-chewing variation was also found; in the latter case the party whose rice was most moist was the guilty one.[36]

One Polynesian method of detecting a thief was to send for a sacred object from the temple—a coconut-shell drinking-cup, or conch-shell, or two stones— and each of the suspected parties, laying his hand upon the object, would pray that the god would look upon him and send swift destruction, if he had taken that which had been stolen. "Under this ordeal the truth was rarely concealed, as they firmly believed that it would be death to touch the sacred object and tell a lie; indeed any one who became ill soon after he had taken an oath, was regarded with suspicion." Cases are cited. The power of superstitious fear is further shown in the fact that, so implicitly did the people believe in the divine punishment or magical disaster that would befall a man who swore falsely on a sacred object, the oath of an alleged thief was considered evidence of guilt or innocence. In Tahiti, people who had been robbed and wished to discover the thief placed the matter in the hands of a priest, who, after praying to his god, caused a hole to be dug in the floor of the house and filled with water. "He then, holding a young plantain in his hand, stood over the hole, and again prayed to the god, who, if propitious, conducted the spirit of the thief to the house, and placed it over the water. The image of the spirit, supposed to resemble that of its owner, was thus reflected in the water, and identified by the priest, and the thief was discovered. Sometimes the priest failed in his first attempt, and postponed the operation until the next day; and as this adjournment became known by the people and came to the ears of the thief, the latter, in alarm at the prospect, usually returned the stolen property during the night, and so avoided further enquiry."[37] The fetish-preparation used as a means of securing the judgment of heaven, in the Tongan Islands, was the water in which the chief had washed his hands. The practice of swearing innocence prevailed here also. A man guilty of theft or any other crime was regarded as having broken the taboo and as being, in consequence, specially liable to be bitten by sharks; so a suspected person was required to go into water infested by sharks, and if bitten, was believed to have been guilty.[38] Aside from these cases, the ordeal was not very common in the Pacific; its existence in the island of Yap, as well as that of the duel and oath-taking, is denied.[39]

Among the Wyandot Indians, "in procedure against crime, failure in formality is not considered a violation of the rights of the accused, but proof of his innocence. It is considered supernatural evidence that the charges are false."[40] The Dakotas have a chastity-test. "If a derogatory report is circulated in camp, the girl immediately gets up a 'Virgins' Lodge.' An old man is selected whose duty it is to arrange the tipi or lodge, in which the feast is to occur, by smoothing the ground two or three yards in diameter in the center of the lodge. A round stone is placed in the middle of the cleared space, and near it is

35 Jacobs, *Groot-Atjeh*, I, 226.
36 Worcester, *Philippine Isl.*, 412-413, 491-492; Montero y Vidal, *Filipinas*, I, 54.
37 Ellis, *Polyn. Researches*, I, 379; Williamson, *Cent. Polyn.*, III, 5-7, 18-19.

38 Bastian, *Afr. Reisen*, 203; Williamson, *Cent. Polyn.*, III, 13-15.
39 Senfft, in *Globus*, XCI, 172.
40 Powell, in BAE, I, 67.

planted a knife, blade up. The crier goes through the camp, specifying the time and place of the feast. When all have assembled, the girl enters, places her hand on the point of the knife blade, typical of the god of war, that he may pierce her with this sharp blade if she be not pure; then on the stone, typical of the god of mountains, that he may crush her; then placing her head on the earth, typical of the god of the earth, that he may open the earth and ingulf her if she be not truthful; she then takes her seat, her accuser is brought forward and goes through the same ceremony, and then openly accuses her; if his accusation is not substantiated, he is led from the lodge amid jeers and laughter from the spectators. After the trial comes the feast, and the girl goes forth with unblemished character. This feast excites a beneficial effect morally upon Indian women, and serves to make an extremely immoral nation very circumspect."[41] In ancient Mexico, a man who had had property stolen assembled all the neighbors whom he suspected. "All must sit down on the ground and then comes the 'doctor,' as he is called here also, and takes the cover off a vessel in which he has a snake. It crawls out. If the thief is not among those present, it crawls back again into the vessel. But if it recognizes the thief, it creeps to him . . . and he is then seized and bound and confesses his guilt. It may be in this case that the consciousness of guilt caused the thief to move so that it gave the snake direction, or caused the sorcerer to direct the snake toward him."[42] Among the Indians of Colombia, "the woman accused of adultery had to swallow a certain quantity of red pepper; if she confessed her fault she was pitilessly put to death; but if she could stand the ordeal, her husband had to make public apologies to her."[43] In Peru, if the accused denied guilt, he was tortured to obtain confession; but if he withstood they proceeded to the ordeal—though the accused had no part in it. It was left to the diviners who used all sorts of hocuspocus to get at the truth. "The result which they announced was regarded as unconditionally trustworthy."[44]

Islam knows no civil law, says Ratzel;[45] the priest is in effect a judge and the mosque an asylum. Some traditional ante-Mohammedan methods prevail: a murderer is detected by putting red hot iron on the tongue, but there are said to be only two men in South Arabia competent to apply it. The ordeal of earth seems peculiar to the ancient Scandinavians: seated under a suspended festoon of grass, the accused took oath; if the grass parted, perjury stood proved.[46] The extensive use of the ordeal during the Middle Ages, culminating in the horrors of the Inquisition, is a matter of common knowledge.

§184. Punishments.

In Queensland, "the camp as a body, as a camp council, will take upon itself to mete out punishment in crimes of murder, incest, or the promiscuous use of fighting-implements within the precincts of the camping-ground: death, and probably the digging of his own grave, awaits the delinquent in the former case, while 'crippling,' generally with knives, constitutes the penalty for a violation of the latter. . . . In the case of a man killing his own gin [wife], he has to deliver up one of his own sisters for the late wife's friends to put to

41 Beckwith, in *Smithson. Rep.*, 1886, pt. I, 251.
42 Seler, in *Globus*, LXXVIII, 90.
43 Nadaillac, *Preh. Amer.*, 463.

44 Cunow, *Verf. d. Inkareichs*, 116.
45 *Vkde.*, III, 126.
46 Oliveira Martins, *Quadro*, 157.

death, he personally escaping punishment; but supposing an individual takes the life of another's gin, his own will be forfeited. On the other hand, a wife has always her 'brothers' to look after her interests. If two women fight, and one is killed, the survivor, unless, of course, proper cause be shown, would pay the death-penalty."[1]

Among the Melanesians, "if a murder comes to pass within the tribe, according to strict regulations there must follow a fight of the relations of both parties—only they prefer to set the occasion goodnaturedly aside and compose it with dewarra [shell-money]. . . . About a hundred strings are regarded as sufficient compensation for a slain man, and fifty for a woman." This process of composition may lead to more bloodshed. In the case of theft, "if the man who is robbed is not strong or influential enough to punish the evil-doer, he destroys some part of the property of a man to whom he attributes influence and power enough to help him to his rights. The latter then seeks compensation, not from the destroyer of his property, but from the one who has injured the destroyer. If his power is sufficient, it is understandable that he does not content himself solely with a demand for the replacement of his own loss and that of the man who has appeared in so peculiar a way as plaintiff; on the contrary he will generally, along with it, do a good stroke of business in addition. In most cases the thief must work out his debt, together with rich interest, in the gardens of the one who accomplishes his punishment."[2] Theft does not seem to have been common formerly, and it is said among the southern Massim that stealing from the gardens is now much more frequent than in the old days when the practice prevailed of waiting for a thief in the garden and, if he were a stranger, killing him there and then. "If a man killed another man's pig the owner of the dead pig would generally kill the man whom he now regarded as his enemy. Generally the matter seems to have been discussed and settled without bloodshed, for in theory there was a certain license to kill another man's pig if it was destroying his crops. Thefts of nets, pots, and other moderately bulky portable property appear to be, and to have always been, rare, and when discovered the property stolen was returned or paid for in kind."[3] A peculiar punishment in New Guinea is where, if a first-born son dies in childhood, "the event is looked upon as a fault of the father, who is then under obligation to give presents to the mother's brothers."[4] In the D'Entrecasteaux Islands the usual penalty for an offense is the payment of a heavy fine. Club law is resorted to only when the evil-doers refuse to compound and the aggrieved party considers itself the stronger. "A man who carries off another's wife may be allowed to retain her peaceably if the husband is not strong enough to take vengeance. Shame would probably induce the abductor to pay some compensation, and his kinsmen would certainly feel disgraced if he did not"; so the right of the stronger is limited by public opinion. Even non-human things which have been accessory to a death are often punished: "In Mitaita a man was badly injured through falling out of a coco-nut palm, and the natives were waiting to see whether he would die or not before chopping down the tree. Near Wagifa, too, there was a palm in which deep notches had been scored because a man had once fallen from it and sustained serious injury; had he died the tree would have been cut down altogether."[5]

1 Roth, *N.W. Cent. Queensland*, 139, 141.
2 Von Pfeil, *Südsee*, 76, 77.
3 Seligmann, *Melanesians*, 572, 573.
4 Krieger, *Neu-Guinea*, 164.
5 Jenness and Ballentyne, *D'Entrecasteaux*, 81-82.

Burning alive is found but rarely in Melanesia—that is, as a civil punishment. In war-time a captured enemy who had roused great anger might be executed by fire; but "when peace had been made, and the chiefs had ordered all to behave well that the country might settle down in quiet, if any one committed such a crime as would break up the peace, such as adultery, they would tie him to a tree, heap firewood round him, and burn him alive, a proof to the opposite party of their detestation of his wickedness. This was not done coolly as a matter of course in the execution of a law, but as a horrible thing to do, and done for the horror of it."[6] In the New Hebrides, offenses were judged by the head men of the villages and the chief. Violators of tribal law were punished by having their hands tied behind them and being left to the public gaze for hours,[7] a sort of pillory.

In South Africa the Marutse do not treat theft with severity, while the Damara punish cattle-stealing by death. Among the former, conspirators against the king were executed through the agency of the poisoned cup.[8] In the upper Zambesi country testimony was heard on the side of plaintiff and defendant and, theft having been proved, "the accuser asked that they deliver to him the robber's wife, being indemnified for the loss of several strings of beads, the object of the robbery, by the possession of the woman."[9] In West Africa "as a rule, murder, arson, and treason are punished with death. A first offence of theft is punished by flogging and a fine, a second by mutilation, and a third by death. When, however, cattle or sheep-stealing becomes prevalent, a detected thief is put to death, as a warning to others. In such a case, the criminal, instead of being executed by the Ogboni in secret, is decapitated on Ogun's stool, by the sword-bearers of the chiefs, in some public place. Criminals who cannot pay their fines are flogged with . . . a formidable whip made of hippopotamus-hide, which draws blood at each stroke."[10] It will be noted that the severity of punishment increases here with the prevalence of crime. The penalty for violation of law is generally an eye for an eye and a tooth for a tooth; in some cases, if the penalties heaped up against a man are more than he can pay, he is condemned to death; but that ends the matter and his family is free.[11] Certain mitigations are known: a criminal among the Ewe-speaking peoples, if he addresses the king, must be spared. Often, therefore, criminals are gagged. If an Ashanti criminal swears on the king's life he must be spared because his oath would involve danger to the king. In Dahomi, it is criminal to attempt suicide since every man, as well as all property, belongs to the king. A person whose house takes fire, even by accident, is put to death.[12]

One of the African penalties for theft, and also for abduction or infidelity, is the cutting off of parts of the body. Nose, ears, and even lips are mutilated, but the fingers suffer most. "Men generally pay for it with the three sections of all the fingers, while the woman in question often gets off with the loss of the finger-tips."[13] In a few cases intentional homicide is distinguished from accidental, the former calling for the death-penalty, the latter for a fine in cattle. The cattle are eaten at a big feast, the murderer being smeared with their blood but getting none of the meat.[14] "As a rule, along the Coast the death penalty for murder or adultery is commuted to a fine, or you can send a substi-

6 Codrington, *Melanesians*, 347.
7 Lawrie, in AAAS, 1892, 710.
8 Ratzel, *Vkde.*, I, 342, 375; Holub, in *Illust. Afr.* for April, 1896.
9 Serpa Pinto, *Africa*, II, 24.

10 Ellis, *Yoruba*, 191.
11 Ratzel, *Vkde.*, I, 604.
12 Ellis, *Ewe*, 224.
13 Junker, *Afrika*, II, 396, 397.
14 Schmidt, *Deut. Kol.*, II, 231.

tute to be killed for you if you are rich. This is frequently done, because it is cheaper, if one has a seedy slave, to give him to be killed than to pay the fine, which is often enormous."[15]

On the lower Congo, "in any dealings with the natives, if a European suffer aggression, and can clearly prove that such is the case, he is certainly adjudged to be in the right, and the offender condemned to a penalty which is assessed by the natives and the European: and further, if a chief promise that such and such a fine shall be paid, his word is in all cases sufficient. I have never known an instance where this statement fails, and the fact is the more remarkable as the chiefs present are not one whit better than the culprit, nor are the other natives who join in condemning him."[16] On the upper Congo, its own punishment or fine was attached to each crime. Adultery was fined from one hundred to three hundred brass rods, equal to from three to nine months' ordinary wages.[17] Among the Ba-Huana, "all crimes against the person, even of chiefs, and fetishes are punished by fines; adultery and rape are considered personal injuries to the husband or father, and compensation is assessed by the chief; murder, which may be compensated, is not considered disgraceful; on the other hand, a murderer is respected as a clever and brave man; this idea is carried to such lengths that a man who has murdered his brother, to whom he is heir, is not fined at all."[18] In British Central Africa, punishments for all offenses amounted practically to payment; in case of homicide, after compensation was paid, the murderer and his people were invited to drink and the affair was closed, no enmity being harbored.[19] In Uganda theft is severely punished: "The thief is fined a large number of sheep and goats, and if he cannot pay he is beaten to death with clubs. If he is able to pay the fine, however, he must still receive a severe whipping; and this often leaves him mortally injured. Among the Kamasia not only a murderer, but all his relations, suffer confiscation of their entire stock of cattle, sheep, and goats." By some tribes, murder is considered a capital offense and the culprit is immediately executed with spears by the warriors of the tribe; by others it may be atoned for by a heavy fine.[20] The convicted murderer among the Baganda is speared or clubbed to death and the body is burned at the crossing of two roads; the property of the murderer is always confiscated and goes to the relatives of the deceased and to his clan.[21] According to Dinka laws all bodily injuries are compensated by cattle; refusal to pay is likely to result in deliberate damage to the offender or his family in retaliation. Theft is very rare; when it occurs, the stolen article or a similar one, at least as good, must be returned.[22] The murder of a free Galla by a Galla can be atoned for by a thousand cattle—in the case of a woman by fifty; but this figure is generally reduced in practice. Though the Somals generally have but two penalties, death or money-payment, here and there are to be encountered both mutilation and outlawry. The ears may be notched as a sign of crime, and some persons show three notches.[23]

On this topic of punishments, as on many others, available information from East Africa is so pertinent as to deserve considerable space. With the exception of acts of blood-revenge and similar forms of homicide, an actual death-

15 Kingsley, *Travels W. Afr.*, 497.
16 Phillips, in JAI, XVII, 220.
17 Weeks, in JAI, XXXIX, 433.
18 Torday and Joyce, in JAI, XXXVI, 288.
19 Stannus, in JAI, XL, 290, 291.

20 Johnston, *Uganda*, II, 882.
21 Roscoe, in JAI, XXXII, 50.
22 O'Sullivan, in JAI, XL, 189.
23 Paulitschke, *Nordost-Afr.*, I, 263, 264; II, 152.

penalty is rarely inflicted among the Bantu, occurring almost solely in tribes with despotic chiefs. Among the Wapare, for instance, robbers were put to death at times and in districts in which there happened to be powerful chiefs who appreciated the advantages of ordered conditions. Another crime which frequently involved capital punishment was treason, the traitor being equivalent to an enemy and therefore without rights. "These examples of death penalties," comments Sir Charles Dundas,[24] "are the exception to the prevailing rule among the Bantu that a man's life could not be forfeited by his acts; they are not general among the tribes, and I doubt if they are commonly applied in any tribe. But there was one crime which invariably was punished with death, namely, witchcraft. Curiously enough, among tribes which I know personally I have always found that no other penalty than death is known for this crime: it is not compensated as murder, and if the detected wizard is not actually killed he is at least required to take an oath or submit to an ordeal which is believed to cause his or her death in the end. But I do not know of a tribe with whom witchcraft is not punishable by death."

The writer, who was a colonial administrator, shrewdly urges that the native customs, as representing tested adjustments, be disturbed as little as possible. "It is often argued that we must strive to impress upon the native a higher value for human life; but on the one hand he evidently esteems it most highly, and on the other hand our methods may often tend to cheapen life, either by killing the culprit, where such was not justifiable under native law, or by allowing him to be at large when his life was forfeited under the same law, as well as by disregarding and superseding the religious aspects of the crime. It is not easy to say exactly what changes are to be recommended in our present system, but briefly, our main object should be to give the utmost consideration to the native view of each particular case." The native is, in fact, not often guilty of murder, as we commonly understand the term; "of premeditated murder I have only known two cases, but ninety per cent. of the cases of people being killed may be said to be due to drunken brawls, and invariably these arise between persons whose youth would, under the old custom, have prevented them from drinking intoxicating liquors." Native law, we are told, has two apparently weak points which, however, before conditions changed, constituted no weakness but an expedient adjustment. "The first is that it is too lenient. For instance, the punishment for murder is inadequate, because either a man is rich and will not feel the loss of fifteen head of cattle, or if he is poor he will beg the stock from his clan. Of course the law is as it was required to be. The Mkamba is neither grasping, cruel, nor hot tempered, thefts are pretty rare, and murders are nearly all committed in drunken broils. Again, in former times when people lived more isolated, they had not much chance of offending against each other, or if they did, litigation would mostly be a useless means to redress. Thus the law did not need to be harsher than it is. The second weak point is that the law lacked authority, where it failed would be when a man refused to submit to all authority; and then no one could enforce it excepting by *kingolle* [any form of punishment by competent authority], and then indeed it became a very powerful authority that he had defied. . . . It was only on persons who repeatedly offended that *kingolle* was inflicted, and

24 In JAI, XLIII, 518 (quoted); in JAI, XLV, 258, 263 (quoted), 267, 268, note, 271-272, 273 (quoted), 274, 275-276 (quoted); in JAI, LI, 232-233 (quoted), 241-242, 244 (quoted), 247; Dundas, K. R., in JAI, XLIII, 52-53; Hobley, *A-Kamba*, 78.

when it amounted to a sentence of death this implied that the offender had become so incorrigible that he was regarded as a danger to the public."

A good example is the habitual thief. Here again is evidence of the fact that native customs, no matter how strange they may seem to us, are common-sense procedures under the conditions to which they are adjusted. "The offence of theft would formerly be most commonly restricted to the taking of stock, and this is the only form of provocation known to me which is admitted. Both in Ukamba and Kikuyu a man was entitled to kill a thief caught in the act of taking stock, without being liable for compensation. . . . A man who frequently stole stock would in the end be put to death by public consent, and the same fate awaited the one who stole honey or hives. Hives being placed in trees in uninhabited country, often several days' journey from the owner's village, it is natural that very severe penalties were required to protect the owners. . . . The penalty for stealing stock in Kikuyu was otherwise ten times the value of whatever was taken, besides three sheep for the elders, and this penalty was imposed on every person taking part in the theft. . . . Thefts from members of one tribe or section of a tribe are uncommon, and the offence is, comparatively speaking, severely dealt with. Above all it is recognised as provocation which may be a justification for causing death. It should be noted here that theft is the only offence in which we may speak of a fine being imposed, for, although the offence is amended by restoration of the property, over and above there is a payment due which far exceeds the value of that taken. Nevertheless this payment is made to the aggrieved party, and not to the public authority, so that the advancement of this crime to a matter of punishment, and not mere compensation, has still left it in the light of a private matter. It is a wrong done to the individual and not to the community. The name of thief carries a peculiar stigma with it, and while almost every other offence is attributed to circumstances rather than to character, that of theft signifies to the natives an unpardonable nature. Indeed, whereas they consider that in general we deal too harshly with crime, I have often heard them regret that we are too lenient with thieves: the following uncomplimentary observation was overheard on one occasion, 'The Government has come to help thieves and wizards.' "

The author goes on to consider the subject of compensation or blood-money. From the schedules which he gives it appears that this is not reckoned haphazard, but on a definite basis. "Some elders, being asked once what compensation a man should pay for causing the loss of both legs to another, replied that they had never heard of such a case, but since a man who had lost both legs would not be regarded as a man at all, full blood-money should be paid. Blood-money is perhaps the basis of all compensations for bodily injuries, but how other offences were determined at their present amounts we cannot say; they are, however, all representative of the degree of gravity attached to them, and incidentally also of the general wealth of the tribe." From the lists of compensation for hurts it appears that the loss of a leg, for instance, is reckoned at about one-third of full blood-money, and if a man has received such compensation it is deducted from the blood-money due should he be subsequently killed. The underlying idea here seems to be that not more than the value of a man's life may ever be paid for his person. No deduction is made if the individual killed has been crippled or deformed from birth. "The Akamba are good surgeons and skilfully sew up wounds with thorns. The amount of compensation for wounds not otherwise provided for is then reckoned by the number of thorns required to sew up the wound; each thorn is reckoned as one goat, to which is added another goat for slaughtering, and a third for the suffering in the event of many 'stitches' being required." A man who kills his own wife is not required to pay compensation in Ukamba, Kikuyu, and Theraka, but he is still liable for any balance of dowry unpaid at the time; in Unyamwesi, however, the husband who kills his wife may be put to death by her relatives or compelled to pay full blood-money. Compensation for the death of a woman is much less than that for the murder of a man. A transitional case toward fine in the legal sense, a penalty accruing solely to the state, is seen where, when a fine of several head of cattle is inflicted, the bull as a general rule goes to the chief; when the fine consists of a bull only, the hump or ribs, as the case may be, is claimed by him.

In ancient times the Yakuts practised torture upon the guilty.[25] In Kamtchatka the murderer is demanded and exactly the same treatment accorded him as to his victim.[26] As wood is extremely scarce and expensive in Dagistan, one of the most terrible punishments for crime is to tear down some rooms in a man's house; it will take him years to save enough to replace the floors, ceilings, and other parts destroyed.[27] The responsibility for payment of blood-money among the Gilyak rests with the clan as a whole; delivery is accompanied by a complicated ritual which includes an imitation of blood-vengeance: two champions, one from each clan, advance between the two parties to the dispute, bearing shields. They engage in a combat, which is usually merely a feigned one, though it sometimes develops into a real fight.[28] Among the Nagas of India the means for the prevention of crime "fall into two divisions, those offences liable to immediate punishment by the hand of the aggrieved persons; and those adjudged by a council of elders. Murder comes within the first category; 'the relations of the murdered person instantly, if possible, spear the murderer without reference to the council of elders.' In case of infringement of the marriage law, the injured husband speared the offender 'on the first opportunity,' it may be inferred without reference to any council. Thefts and other petty offences on the other hand were disposed of by the elders, who imposed a fine and restoration of the property or its equivalent."[29] In southern India, "if a difference arose between two people a meeting of the principal men of the thirty thousand was convened, and they sometimes decreed that the plantain trees, betel vines, betel-nut and cocoanut trees in the garden of the guilty person should be cut down, other plants destroyed with a sword, and his house unroofed."[30] Fines varied according to the caste of the thief, increasing, in Manu's time, in proportion to the dignity of the culprit.[31] In China the law inflicts a sort of civil death, forbidding certain offenders to offer sacrifices to their ancestors, and, under a penalty of flogging, to mourn for their dead relatives.[32] The Ainos club wrong-doers. "Their punishments are severe, but they do not take life, even for the crime of murder. The murderer is bound to a cross for a week, and, after his release, receives some good advice from the judge, when he again takes his place as an honorable citizen. The clubs are used for punishing thefts and other crimes." A murderer once had his nose and ears cut off, or the tendons of his feet severed. "These cruel

25 Sieroshevski-Sumner, in JAI, XXXI, 72.
26 Letourneau, *Guerre*, 194.
27 *Russian Ethnog.* (Russ.), II, 393.
28 Czaplicka, *Aborig. Siberia*, 46-48.

29 Godden, in JAI, XXVI, 173.
30 Thurston, *S. India*, 431, 432.
31 Buehler, *Manu*, VIII, 336-338.
32 Letourneau, *Soc.*, 291.

punishments are undoubtedly old practices no longer in vogue."[33] An anomalous case among these people is where a thief discovered by oracle is not tried, but the person robbed waits patiently for him to bring back the stolen property and ask forgiveness. In Japan banishment was a severe penalty. "We can scarcely imagine to-day the conditions of such banishment: to find a Western parallel we must go back to ancient Greek and Roman times long preceding the Empire. Banishment then signified religious excommunication, and practically expulsion from all civilized society. . . . Common folk were punished by cruel whippings for the most trifling offences. For serious offences, death by torture was an ordinary penalty; and there were extraordinary penalties as savage, or almost as savage, as those established during our own medieval period,—burnings and crucifixions and quarterings and boiling alive in oil."[34]

Among Malay groups on a low stage of civilization, offenses other than theft very seldom occur, and when they do, the injured party himself determines, if the guilty one is discovered, the amount of compensation. Only in those instances where the payment is refused in part or as a whole, does the case come before the chief.[35] In Sumatra, "if a man surprises his wife in the act of adultery, he may put both man and woman to death upon the spot. . . . If the husband spares the offender, or has only information of the fact from other persons, he may not afterwards kill him, but has his remedy at law, the fine for adultery being fifty dollars."[36] In the Philippines the relations themselves generally punished the offender, composition was allowed except in case of murder, to which the law of talion applied. The whole people might attack the district of the murderer, with bloodshed and enslavement as a result.[37]

In some of the Polynesian islands there seems to have been little or no organized system of justice, especially as regards offenses committed against persons not belonging to the aristocracy, the general bulk of the people being left to fight out their own quarrels. "Acts of oppression or cruelty by the head of a family, or haughty conduct of a chief, could not be punished; the only remedy for the oppressed person was to go away and live with another branch of the family. On the other hand, offences against other villages were often visited with very severe punishment, because they might lead to war. There is an example of a youth who stole a canoe belonging to a man of another village, and who was found out. The heads of families of his village therefore bound him in the usual way, like a pig intended for killing and eating, carried him to the other village, and deposited him as a symbolic sacrifice in the *malae* [council-house] there; and by this act of deep humiliation they appeased the anger which had been caused." While in Samoa punishment for an offense was to a large extent left to the injured person or persons, there existed also judicial punishment, in that the head of the family had some jurisdiction within his own kin-group and was in a way its official magistrate. As the various heads of families composed, with the chiefs, the assembly or *fono,* they also adjudged punishment to public offenders. The methods of punishment were divided into two classes, namely *o le sala,* destruction of houses, live stock and plantations, with, at times, the seizure of personal property and banishment, and *o le tua,* or personal punishment. The first type was usually inflicted by the whole available force of the district awarding it, that is, by the

33 Hitchcock, in USNM, 1890, 467.
34 Hearn, *Japan*, 111, 194-195.
35 Wilken, in VG, II, 459-460.
36 Marsden, *Sumatra*, 229.
37 Montero y Vidal, *Filipinas*, I, 53.

fono. It was, at times, imposed by one family upon another, if the injured group was strong enough to do so; on occasion it was the penalty for insulting a chief. The infliction of the death-penalty seems to have followed especially upon murder and grave political crimes. Minor offenses such as theft, insulting travelling parties, preparing pitfalls, and taking the comb out of a married woman's head were also the subjects of punishments, inflicted by the *fono,* and carried out, immediately after sentence had been pronounced, in the presence of the whole assembly. These different forms of punishment have become mostly obsolete, and fines of pigs and other property have taken their places. Various types of punishment are found in the Polynesian group. In Bow Island murderers were killed and eaten; in Niue the natives often got rid of a thief by sending him adrift in a small canoe, so that he perished at sea; in Fakaofu punishments were generally milder, the offender being set to make a certain length of rope or a number of fish-hooks for the king, though death by strangling was sometimes inflicted for stealing food in time of scarcity. On Easter Island thieves caught in the act might be beaten and knocked about, and were allowed to offer no resistance. The injured party, "in the event of the full value not being recovered, . . . could destroy the property of the offender to equalize the amount. Retaliation for theft could thus be enforced by the weak against the strong, and any resistance would call the entire community to the aid of the former."[38]

In consonance with their peaceable disposition, the Greenlanders have a mild way of settling disputes. The judicial procedure consists in pitting the litigants against one another in the midst of a circle of onlookers; each beats a drum and sings satirical songs about the other, telling his misdeeds and making him ridiculous. The one who succeeds best at this wins his case. This may seem very trivial to us, but the Eskimo has an extreme dread of being made ridiculous. The missionaries have put down this custom, which was called the drum-dance, saying that it leads to immorality; no form of justice now exists.[39] In the accepted sense of the term, there is no such thing as government among the Tlinkits of Alaska. "They have no courts, no jails, police nor statutory laws; in short, nothing corresponding to civilized government. They have no such thing as trials. All grievances, offences and injuries are settled according to tribal demand. The tribe or clan takes up its member's cause, and settlements are made according to the nature of the offence, or injury, and the standing of the injured. The tribe of the injured party determines the amount necessary to settlement." Any crime may be paid for on a money basis, but while they usually demand life for life, it is not necessarily the life of the murderer. "If a high-caste native kills one of a lower caste, it is not the one who did the killing that is taken, but one equal in station to the one killed. The same holds good if one of a lower caste kills one of a higher. If one higher than the one killed is taken, then the killing has to go on until it is considered equal. If a woman kills a man, not the woman, but some man of her tribe must be taken, as a woman is not considered the equal of a man. If a man kills a woman, not the murderer, but some woman of his tribe is taken. If a white man kills a native, the murdered man's friends are not particular as to what white man they kill in turn, so they get one whom they deem of equal station. . . . Accidental in-

---

38 Williamson, *Cent. Polyn.,* III, 1-3, 5 (quoted), 8-13, 25-26, 27, 28, 29 (quoted).

39 Nansen, *Esk. Life,* 186.

juries, or killing in self defence, must be atoned for precisely the same as if premeditated."[40]

Among the Indians, theft inside the tribe was rare and, when committed, the tribal authorities demanded restitution. The loss of the property taken, flogging, and a degree of social ostracism constituted the punishment of the thief. Instances could be multiplied to show the security of personal effects in a tribe.[41] As in the case of the Eskimo and others, slighter delinquencies may be left to family authority for punishment, while flagrant and repeated crimes are taken cognizance of by the council. "Treason consists in revealing the secrets of the medicine preparations or giving other information or assistance to enemies of the tribe and is punished by death. The trial is before the council of the tribe."[42] The Sioux have a sort of police force: "punishments by law, administered by the 'soldier-band,' are only for serious offenses against the regulations of the camp. He who simply violates social customs in the tribe often subjects himself to no worse punishment than an occasional sneer or taunting remark; but for grave transgressions he may lose the regard of his friends."[43] Here are grades of punishment, severe in proportion as they threaten the interests of the group. Among the Omahas, "when the life of a murderer was spared, he was obliged to submit to punishment from two to four years. He must walk barefoot. He could eat no warm food; he could not raise his voice; nor could he look around. He was compelled to put his robe around him, and to have it tied at the neck, even in warm weather; he could not let it hang loosely or fly open. He could not move his hands about, but was obliged to keep them close to his body. He could not comb his hair; and it must not be blown about by the wind. He was obliged to pitch his tent about a quarter of a mile from the rest of the tribe when they were going on the hunt, lest the ghost of his victim should raise a high wind, which might cause damage. No one wished to eat with him, for they said, 'If we eat with him whom Wakanda hates, for his crime, Wakanda will hate us.' Sometimes he wandered at night, crying and lamenting his offense. At the end of the designated period, the kindred of the murdered man heard his crying and said, 'It is enough. Begone and walk among the crowd. Put on moccasins and wear a good robe.' "[44] Running off with a man's wife or committing adultery was treated with severity. "In this class of offenses the husband or his near relatives administered punishment. The woman might be whipped, but the heavy punishment fell on the guilty man. Generally his property was taken from him, and if the man offered resistance he was either slashed with a knife or beaten with a bludgeon."[45] Among the Cree, "if a man murdered his wife through jealousy, as sometimes happened, he had to pay eight horses to his wife's relatives, or, if he could not afford this, he might flee alone on the warpath, kill one of the foe, and return to paint the faces of his parents-in-law with charcoal. They might then spare him. Eight horses, or an enemy's scalp, constituted the usual blood-money demanded by the parents of any murdered person."[46] Among the Hopi there seems to be no punishment for crime except sorcery, to which, under Hopi law, all transgressions may be reduced.[47] The delinquent among the Gulf tribes is assessed more or less, according to his neglect of his duties, by the proper

40 Jones, *Thlingets*, 193-195.
41 Ratzel, *Vkde.*, II, 634; Fletcher and Matthews, in HAI, I, 441-442.
42 Powell, in BAE, I, 66, 67.
43 Dorsey, in BAE, XV, 242, 243.

44 Dorsey, in BAE, III, 369.
45 Fletcher and LaFlesche, in BAE, XXVII, 213-215.
46 Skinner, in AA, XVI, 72.
47 Fewkes, in HAI, I, 565.

officers—a duty which the latter "strictly fulfill without the least interruption or exemption of any able person."[48]

There has been some change in the mores along the northwest coast. "When first visited by the early voyagers these Indians, like all others on the coast, were bold, arrant thieves. With them it was not dishonorable to steal, and, if caught, restitution settled the matter. On the other hand, they discriminated, and seldom or never stole from a guest, and never robbed one of their own totem. With them, to-day, an unwatched camp or an unlocked house is sacredly respected, and the most valuable property cached in the woods, as is the Indian custom, is as safe from other Indians as if guarded night and day."[49] Farther south, "murder is generally compounded for by the payment of shell money . . . no crime is known for which the malefactor cannot atone with money."[50] Among the tribes of Mexico, the restitution of a stolen object atoned for the theft; failing this, the thief became a slave for life. "Old men of more than seventy were alone allowed to get drunk; a drunkard younger than this had his head shaved, and if he held any office he was publicly degraded. . . . Corporal punishment was rare. It was considered shameful even for a slave to be chastised."[51] A young noble might be strangled for drunkenness, while an older lost rank and goods.[52] The San Domingo Indians impaled a thief.[53] In northern Nicaragua most crimes can be atoned for by money and no ill feeling remain; but "murder must be expiated by the suicide of the murderer, and if he wants to run away he is killed by a relative of the slain."[54] A thief was sometimes suspended by the hands from a branch and vituperated by the women; in one case the victim was pale and seemed to be near losing his senses. It was said that he had stolen some animals and would hang there till he told where they were. The Incas, Caribs, Araucanians, and others punished theft inside the tribe with death.[55]

In the ancient world execution by burning was applied only when some religious abomination was included in the crime or when it was politically outrageous. In the laws of Hammurabi an hierodule who opened a dramshop or entered one to get a drink was to be burned. A man who committed incest with his mother was to meet the same punishment, also one who married a mother and her daughter at the same time. Other typical punishments for different offenses were enslavement and the loss of hands.[56] Among the ancient Hebrews, if a man marries both a mother and her daughter, all are to be burned, and the daughter of a priest, if she becomes a harlot, is to be similarly punished.[57] In the old Norse laws, honorlessness meant civil death, the term being applied to such cowardly or despised acts as killing in a place under a peace-taboo; slaying a sleeping or a defenseless man, or one's house-master, or him with whom one shares meat and drink, or a woman; or fighting against one's fatherland.[58] Under the theory that severe penalties intimidate and deter, capital punishment accompanied by torture and accomplished in numerous excruciating ways was the penalty inflicted for many offenses during the

48 Carr, in *Smithson. Rep.*, 1891, 527, note.
49 Niblack, in USNM, 1888, 240.
50 Stearns, in *Smithson. Rep.*, 1887, pt. II, 332.
51 Nadaillac, *Preh. Amer.*, 314.
52 Biart, *Aztèques*, 249 *et passim*.

53 Letourneau, *Morale*, 161.
54 Sapper, in *Globus*, LXXVIII, 274.
55 Ratzel, *Vkde.*, II, 634.
56 Winckler, *Hammurabi*, 19, 26, 33, 34.
57 Lev., XX, 14; XXI, 9.
58 Geijer, *Svensk. Hist.*, 382.

Middle Ages and early modern times.[59] In recent days it has come to be suspected that the element of deterrence inheres less, perhaps, in the severity of the penalty than in the certainty and promptness of its imposition.

§199. Primitive Accuracies and Fallacies.

THE savage usually shows considerable adaptability in the practical affairs of the struggle for existence. Semon[1] finds the intellect and senses of the Australian brilliantly developed in all directions bearing on the hunt; he displays an excessively sharp power of observation, topographic sense and memory, and a particular faculty of drawing conclusions from the smallest signs and traces as to the whereabouts and the actual state of the game. All this, combined with great dexterity in the use of weapons, makes Australian game the helpless prey of these perfect huntsmen. Therefore he thinks it is a great error to represent the Australians as a half-starved miserable race struggling for life under the hardest conditions. The aptitude of the natives is further shown in their successful search for water in the arid regions and during the dry seasons. A curious discovery of the blacks, and one which shows how minute have been their food researches, is that some sorts of trees which grow in the most arid wastes contain water in their lateral roots, which lie just below the surface of the ground. "These, when pressed for water in such country, they partly grub and partly tear up, cut into pieces eight inches long, and stand upright in their wooden calabashes, into which the water slowly drains from them. By this means an experienced man may soon obtain a pint or two of pure, cool and tasteless water."[2] Another method of getting water from trees is seen in the case of a certain variety which, when the trunk attains a diameter of about six inches, becomes pipe-like, thus forming a natural reservoir in which the rains of the wet season are collected; the branches of the tree, which join at the top of the stem, act as conducting-pipes. "The narrow aperture prevents much evaporation, and the natives know how to obtain water here, where an inexperienced traveller would never dream of searching for it. To procure this water, the native ties a bunch of grass to the end of his spear, and then climbing the tree, dips his primitive piston-rod—if I may so call it—into this singular well. Drawing it up again, he squeezes the water from the grass into his bark dish, and thus proceeds until he obtains sufficient for his present requirements." The bottle tree of northern Australia also furnishes a refreshing beverage. The natives cut holes in the soft trunk, where the water lodges and rots the trunk to its center. "These trunks are so many artificial reservoirs of water. When a tree has been cut, its resources are not exhausted. The tired hunter, when he sees a tree that has been tapped, cuts a hole somewhat lower than the old cuts, and obtains an abundant supply of the sweet mucilaginous substance afforded by this plant." The natives are also acquainted with the fact that the bladder of the frog acts as a reservoir for water and occasionally they kill these reptiles for water as well as for food.[3]

In their battle with nature the African Bushmen are extraordinarily sharp and keen, as they need to be, for their habitat is one of the poorest on the

59 Lacroix, *Middle Ages*, 427; Judd, *Hist. of Hadley*, 269; Sumner, *Folkways*, §§233 ff.; *Wines, Punishment and Reformation*, *passim*.
1 *Aust. Bush*, 217.

2 Curr, *Aust. Race*, I, 83.
3 Smyth, *Vict.*, I, 220, 221 (quoted), 222 (quoted).

globe.[4] The Bawenda of South Africa "are more at home on the surface of the earth than in the heavens and in the air. There is not a single geographical fact of their country but they have given it a name of their own. Even geological features have not evaded their notice, for they have specific names for every kind of soil and also for every sort of stone and rock. Botany is the great field of the medicine doctor, for he knows all the poisonous plants, but besides that there is not a tree, shrub or plant that has not a name in their language. They distinguish even every kind of grass by a different name. The Bawenda have names of their own for any living creature found in their country."[5] This first-hand acquaintance with nature is acquired early in the school of experience. On the Upper Congo, "lads accompany their fathers and elders on their fishing and hunting expeditions, and learn by imitation, by listening to the talk around the camp fire, and by instruction. Most lads of fourteen to sixteen know the names of the fish in their river and creeks (and there are quite three hundred kinds of fish), their habits, and the best mode of catching them. They also know the names and habitat of most bush animals either by experience or repute; the names of birds, insects, trees, plants, etc., are all well known to them and easily distinguished. Boys and girls of a tender age will know all about sexual intercourse, pregnancy, and child-birth. In these matters they are very precocious."[6] In general, where the African native shines is in his home, the bush. "He can generally beat the white man in bushcraft, endurance under the trying conditions of a tropical climate, and at going through thick country he is often wonderful. To show himself at his best, however, he must be in his own locality; if he is transplanted, even a short distance, he deteriorates. The white man, who is a keen hunter, is generally much more in touch with the native and in sympathy with him than the one who does not care for sport. It is easy to see why this should be so. The latter meets the native over matters of discipline, taxes, labour, and many other things which are of the white man's invention and making, and so difficult for the native to understand. The hunter meets the savage on common grounds and on matters with which the latter is, in a primitive way, more conversant than he himself is."[7]

"Native experience of wild animals and their ways is far more extensive and thorough than ours, and, as a rule, they behave, in an emergency brought about by an encounter with wild animals, in a perfectly rational manner, based on a knowledge of that particular animal's habits. They will run away from a rhino and jump aside, well aware that its impetus will carry it past. But they know better than to run away from elephants. I have seen natives, under a charge of these, lie down and remain motionless on the ground, knowing that the short-sighted giants would mistake them for logs and step over them. . . . Besides their facility in learning new languages, negroes also have a remarkable gift for communicating with each other by signs. I have often been astounded to notice how all the inhabitants of a village, including the children, were able to converse fluently with a deaf-mute. A few signs with the lips and the fingers were sufficient to convey the meaning of a long sentence, and the mute did not seem to be in the least inconvenienced by his inability to enunciate words."[8]

In everything that pertains to daily life, trade, agriculture, and other prac-

4 Ratzel, *Vkde.*, I, 64.
5 Gottschling, in JAI, XXXV, 383.
6 Weeks, in JAI, XXXIX, 130.

7 Stigand, *Elephant*, 209.
8 Coudenhove, in *Atl. Mo.*, CXXVIII, 163, 168-169.

tical affairs the Dyaks often show keen judgment.[9] A Philippine Islander once boasted to Worcester[10] that, given a machete and a clump of bamboo, he could provide a good dinner. When the writer laughed at him, he walked to the nearest clump of bamboo, split a dry joint and kindled a fire, put water on to boil in a green joint, stewed some fresh young bamboo shoots in it, and then fashioned a platter to hold the "greens" and a knife and fork with which to eat them. The Shingu Indians display great powers of adaptation in matters of self-maintenance. Although living upon the product of the ground, they were obliged to continue hunting because of the raw material for implements which they got from the fish and animals. "They used the jaw with the teeth of a fish called the piranya, as a cutting instrument, especially for cutting all cords and fibers. The arm and leg bones of apes are used as arrow points. The tail spike of a skate was employed in the same way. The two front claws of the armadillo were used for digging the ground, as the animal himself uses them. The shell of a river mussel formed a plane, to scrape down wooden tool-handles or oars. For this purpose, however, they did not take the edge, but broke a hole in the shell and used its edges. These people were hunters without dogs, fishers without hooks, and tillers without plow or spade. They show of how much development life was capable in the pre-metal period."[11] The most valuable qualities of the Guiana Indians are their "agility, dexterity, and the intuitive tact of tracking, or discovering footsteps in the bush. Their acuteness in discovering the trail of an animal and its species is also surprising. They not only hear sounds in the woods which are imperceptible to others, but judge with surprising accuracy of the distance and direction from whence they proceed. Bates reports having noticed in Indian boys a sense of locality almost as keen as that possessed by a sand wasp. He gives an example of his little companion, about ten years of age, who had been playing all the way with bow and arrow while they had been hunting, and yet, almost unconsciously, had noted the course taken."[12]

In these everyday matters of the struggle for existence the native is accurate, capable, and resourceful; but when brought face to face with something not within his range of experience, especially with anything abstract, he has difficulty in understanding it, and if he thinks at all about it he does it in a simple, logical, but usually fallacious way. His mental and emotional makeup often seem paradoxical. The Australian aborigines are at one time impulsive, at another phlegmatic; "they can exert themselves vigorously when hunting or fishing or fighting or dancing, or at any time when there is a prospect of an immediate reward; but prolonged labor with the object of securing ultimate gain is distasteful to them. They are industrious and painstaking in fashioning things that they know are of value to them and to the use of which they have been accustomed; but they are slow in adopting the mechanical contrivances of the whites. They love ease even more than pleasure. The natives hunt in order to procure food, not for the delights of the chase. Without being quarrelsome, they are always ready to fight—and, perhaps without premeditation, they are often cruel to the stricken foe.'[13] So too the African: "The native can love, and he can hate, but he is neither a good lover, nor a strong hater.

9 Veth, *Borneo's Wester-Afdeeling*, II, 251.
10 *Philippine Isl.*, 504.
11 Von den Steinen, *Zent. Bras.*, 205.
12 Roth, in BAE, XXXVIII, 607.
13 Smyth, *Vict.*, I, 29-30.

His affections are neither steady or permanent. He will, however, remember a wrong committed against him much longer than a good deed done to help him. If you are powerful he will effusively smile on you a week after you have unmercifully thrashed him, but if you are a nobody he will scarcely greet you the day after you have saved his life. He is moved more by fear of pain, by loss of material profit, and by public opinion than swayed by principles and arguments. He will float with the stream rather than continually struggle against it, but at the same time he can obstinately and doggedly follow a course that will result in physical pain, material loss and ridicule if he is once persuaded that his ultimate interests lie in that direction."[14]

The word *walu,* eight, in the Solomon Islands expresses the range of the native's abstract mental process. It implies a large number, or at least as large as he cares to worry about. *Walu malan* (many islands) means the world; *walu ola inau* is accurate enough for "all my belongings."[15] The Kanaka does not think about abstract things nor does he give a thought to the conditions of existence.[16] The Kaffir does not willingly bother himself with thinking about everyday affairs until they are forced upon his attention so that he cannot escape them. Much less has he ever thought out earnestly and consequently any transcendental matters.[17] Holub,[18] referring to the same South Africans, says "only their needs educate savages and drive them forwards in culture;" while Livingstone[19] attributes much of native opposition to Christianity to the fact that they are forced to think about matters that have never before bothered them. "It is usually hard to make a native understand anything which is out of the way of his own simple life," writes Stigand[20] of the Bantu. "If one is well acquainted with his methods of thought, or rather his lack of method in this respect, and tries to turn the corner instead of going straight ahead, one may often convey a definite idea to him which it would be impossible to do otherwise. Or if one descends to his line of argument, one may prove to his complete satisfaction a point by absolutely worthless logic. A parallel occurs with us, where a smart repartee, having no logical value whatever and completely outside the point, will often discomfit an opponent and leave the maker with all the honours of war." The native comes in for much abuse owing to his vagueness about time and distance. "It is very annoying to the traveller, but it cannot be helped. He has never had a watch, he has no words for times of the day except morning, evening, and sometimes noon; and evening is the only time really very material to him. He generally knows if there is time to reach a certain place or village before it gets dark. As to distance, it really does not concern him much if he takes a few days more or less to reach a place. Time is no object to him. The same applied to season. He would probably remember if a certain event happened during the rains or during the harvest season, but practically never how many years ago it was. He would be equally vague about the number of months that have elapsed since an event. He generally errs on the lesser side; he will say it was two months, when it was ten, but never say ten, when it was really two. . . . The chief difficulty I laboured under was that there was no word for 'straight' in their language. When I came to think it out, those natives had never in their lives seen a straight line or anything straight. Their huts are round, their trees crooked, they lived in a

---

14 Weeks, in JAI, XXXIX, 133.
15 Fox and Drew, in JAI, XLV, 215, note.
16 Von Pfeil, *Südsee,* 137.
17 Fritsch, *Eingeb. S.-Afr.,* 57.

18 *Capstadt,* II, 78.
19 *Mission. Travels,* 255.
20 *Elephant,* 280, 211, 205.

state of nature, and there is nothing that I know of in nature that is straight except the horizon at sea. The same thing applies to balance, level, and almost everything that we have to do with in our life." The natives of the Niger Protectorate have difficulty in adapting themselves to something strange like stairs: "Many Jekris can now walk up and down stairs, but the Sobos and Ijos are still clumsy at it. In going up, they will take perhaps one step, while trying to take two; then when they have gone up two or three they look around to see how it is that they are so high up; then they take or miss a step or two, bark their shins, and look around again. Coming down is much worse, and but for the rails many would come to grief, as they cannot judge the distance from one step to the next lower. They put one foot forward but not downward, neither do they bend the standing leg, hence they paw the air and swing around towards the rail in the most awkward manner."[21]

Speaking of the logic of the savage, Trilles[22] says that if the native appears to us in any case to be ridiculous, foolish, or senseless it is most often because we have missed the true explanation, which is that his thoughts simply and rigorously follow the same channel, from what precedes to what follows. When viewed in the light of primitive logic, the beliefs and religious and social customs of savages form a body of doctrine which is compact and important when all the members are closely united. The tendency of the primitive mind to reason *post hoc, ergo propter hoc,* is universal. Many natives of the Congo now believe that European salt causes sleeping-sickness so they will not touch it but use native-made salt in its place.[23] In 1842 dysentery raged fearfully in one of the New Hebrides; the natives traced it to some hatchets taken on shore from a sandal-wooding vessel, and threw them all away.[24] Several centuries ago, certain Chinese, urged on by a reform governor, gave up their practice of sexual hospitality. "Poor harvests and general misfortune ensued, because, said the people, they had foregone a custom cherished by the gods."[25] When the Merkedes, an Arab tribe, became Wahabys, they had to give up the same custom; a drought followed and, considering it a punishment, they got permission from the Wahaby chief to return to the good old practice of their forefathers.[26] When the Arctic explorer, MacMillan, returned in 1924, he reported that his expedition had found coal in Ellesmere Land, but that the Eskimos had never used it. They did not know it would burn. "When we showed them a coal fire one family went to the coal deposits, but they were asphyxiated by the fumes [their igloos lacked modern ventilation] and some were killed. Now they will not touch it."[27] Numerous illustrations of this characteristic of the primitive mind will be found throughout the section on religion.

"Natives are as inquisitive as they are incapable of keeping a secret. The latter is a fortunate evil. Were negroes able to hold their tongues, there would not be a white man alive in Africa to-day. . . . It is extremely difficult to find, in native statements, the line of demarcation between deliberate falsehood, lapse of memory, and a congenital inability to distinguish accurately between the real and the unreal. They all lie, all, without a single exception, though in

21 Granville and Roth, in JAI, XXVIII, 108-109.
22 *Fân*, 6-8, 28.
23 Weeks, in JAI, XXXIX, 457.
24 Turner, *Samoa*, 328-329.

25 Parsons, in AA, XVII, 56, note.
26 Burckhardt, *Bedouins*, 102.
27 N. Y. *Times*, Sept. 24, 1924; Nelson, in BAE, XVIII, 294.

various degrees, and they themselves know and sometimes admit it; and I have met one, at least, who expressed to me, with apparently genuine feeling, his regret for this hereditary defect. The average native does not appear to see any fundamental difference between reality and imagination—a point of view for which, if they only knew it, they could find a measure of justification in the writings of more than one philosopher. . . . I then soundly rated Mohammad for telling such lies, when my head-boy interfered by saying in a conciliatory tone, 'He did not lie, master. He said it only to make conversation.' "28

§203. Death Not Inevitable.

THE Solomon Islanders have a legend which explains, to their satisfaction, how death came into the world. Agunua created men. He created a woman, who, when she became old, went one day to change her skin in the stream, for that was then the custom. She had a daughter whom she left in the village. When the old woman had changed her skin and came back, looking young and lovely once more, her daughter said, "This is not my mother, this is a strange woman," and would have nothing to do with her. So the old woman went back to the stream, but the water had carried away the old skin, and she wandered some way down the stream before she found it, where an eddy had carried it against a bough overhanging the water. She put on the old skin and returned to her daughter. "Now I know you," said her daughter; "you are my mother." And so death came into the world because the child cried and did not know her mother. Otherwise men would always have changed their skins when they grew old. The same story is told in the Banks Islands of *Iroul,* the grandmother of Qat; and in Florida of *Koevasi,* who is said to be superhuman. The stories are exactly alike, even in details.1

The explanation of death, in Lifu, Loyalty Islands, is of a quite different nature. The natives have no idea of the origin of the first man: they only know that his name was Walelimemë, that he had a wife and sons, and that he lived in peace and plenty. At that time there was not any sickness or death, and it was not necessary to work in plantations, because the food grew spontaneously and in abundance. This Garden of Eden did not last. "On one occasion the eldest son, in the form of a rat, went on an exploring expedition, boring his way through the earth until he came to the residence of an old man, the chief of the lower regions. This old chief lived upon yams, of which there were not any at that time on Lifu. . . . The old chief was angry with them, and told them that as they had taken his yams, he would henceforth live upon human flesh. Death should reign on Lifu in order to supply him with food." It was then that people began to die, as the Lifuans suppose, to supply the old chief with human flesh in exchange for his yams; and to this day some of the old men believe that there are more deaths when there is a good yam-harvest, the old chief requiring the bodies of men in proportion to the quantity of yams that they obtain. The traditions of these people have had their weight in leading them to embrace Christianity. When the missionaries arrived, the natives listened to the story of the Fall and said, "Yes, this is no doubt true, it is very much like what our fathers told us. They ate the forbidden yam, and

28 Coudenhove, in *Atl. Mo.,* CXXVIII, 169.   1 Fox and Drew, in JAI, XLV, 138.

death came among us, and we had all to work to provide food." Noah's Ark was Noi's canoe; and the Tower of Babel was the ancient *ija* or scaffolding. The account of the Creation was simply the act of their venerable fisherman who drew the islands from the sea; and they saw in the beloved Joseph the petted "Ulauleti" who could not be destroyed. In their unaffected state, "death, like sickness, was usually ascribed to ill will on the part of an enemy. The death of a chief, although he had lived to be a hundred years, was always attributed to sorcery, and when dead they would stuff his eyes, ears, nostrils and mouth full of leaves from a certain tree, that the person who they declared had caused his death might die. There was, and indeed is still, a remarkable indifference about death. They speak of it and bid each other good-bye as if going on a short journey."[2]

The natives of Trobriand Islands admit that there may be illness from natural causes, and they distinguish it from bewitchment by evil magic. According to the prevalent view, the latter only can be fatal. "Thus the third road to Tuma [spirit world] includes all the cases of 'natural death,' in our sense of the word, of death not due to an obvious accident. To the native mind such deaths are, as a rule, due to sorcery."[3] When a man dies in D'Entrecasteaux, his death is nearly always attributed to sorcery. At Afufuya a native died two days before the authors[4] visited the hamlet. "The symptoms, as far as we could learn, indicated dysentery, which was rather prevalent at the time throughout this region. But the Afufuya people believed that two men from the neighbouring district of Dududu had cut a cross in the track with the point of a knife and chanted a magic song over it. The deceased had trodden on this place, and fallen sick and died. It constituted a legitimate ground for hostilities, and two weeks later the two districts were at war."

To the mind of the African Baganda there is no such thing as death from natural causes. "Both disease and death are the direct outcome of the influence of some ghost. The reason why ghosts cause sickness or death may be due to some evil-disposed person who has invoked the ghost's aid against the person whom he owes a grudge, or it may be the sick person himself has transgressed some custom and incurred the wrath of the ghost."[5] In spite of all the illness, and they have a good deal of it, nobody dies a natural death, according to the belief of the Bawenda; while the Ba-Mbala employ the ordeal to discover "the malign influence which is supposed to be responsible for every natural death."[6] No deaths among the Nigerian head-hunters are due to natural causes, whatever the age of the deceased; a person is killed by magic.[7] Among one tribe in East Africa sleep is called a "little death;"[8] while another tribe believes that people did not die until one day when a lizard said to them: "All of you know that the moon dies and rises again, but human beings will die and rise no more."[9] It is said that the Ethiopians possessed a marvellous fountain the water of which kept them in perpetual youth.[10]

Indifference to life is witnessed by the often frivolous causes for suicide;

2 Ray, in JAI, XLVII, 277-278, 280, 287 (quoted).

3 Malinowski, in JAI, XLVI, 360.

4 Jenness and Ballentyne, *D'Entrecasteaux*, 80-81.

5 Roscoe, in JAI, XXXII, 40.

6 Gottschling, in JAI, XXXV, 375; Torday and Joyce, in JAI, XXXV, 400.

7 Tremearne, in JAI, XLII, 161, 163.

8 Cole, in JAI, XXXII, 327.

9 Barrett, in JAI, XLI, 37.

10 Herodotus, *Hist.*, III, xxiii; Maspero, *Hist. Anc.*, I, 666-667.

there is often in self-destruction a strong element of retaliation.[11] In parts of Africa, suicide "is resorted to quite as a matter of course, on the least provocation, even by children when they have been scolded by their parents."[12]

Among the Chukchi of Siberia "voluntary death"—suicide in the case of young people and, in the case of the old, being killed by some near relative at their own request—is considered preferable to a natural decease, which latter, indeed, is held to be the work of the *kelet,* or evil spirits. "To die by one's own volition is equivalent to freeing oneself from the malevolence of the *kelet,* and is at the same time a sacrifice to the *kelet,* since a breach of the formally expressed determination to die is punished by them. A voluntary death is not only better than a natural one, but it is even considered praiseworthy, since people who die this kind of death have the best abode in the future life."[13] It is well known to the Sema Nagas that death is caused by the soul leaving the body, more or less, it would seem, at the former's own desire. "Thus when a man is even unconscious from any cause or when he is seen to be dying, he is held up in a sitting posture, and two persons, by preference those with the strongest lungs, bawl into the dying man's ears. . . . Meanwhile all present are crying and howling, and as long as there is life in him are reasoning with the dying man, telling him it is better to live, and asking why he behaves in this untoward way. It seems clear from this procedure that the soul can perhaps be induced to remain in the body if convinced of its folly in leaving it. On one occasion the writer saw the eyes of the corpse carefully closed and the lips compressed and held together for a long time, as though to prevent the dead man's soul from escaping."[14]

The Alfurs of Buru believe that every man possesses a *moeli* and every woman a *kesan,* both terms signifying evil spirit, which can be used to inflict illness or similar misfortune on others. The religion of the Alfurs forbids using either. At every death there must be an investigation as to whether the deceased died a natural death or whether the death was the result of the action of a *moeli* or *kesan.*[15]

The general theory regarding death prevailing among the Quileute Indians is that it was originated by Raven, and the story told of its origin differs very little from similar tales among other Indians of this region. "The Quileute make no distinction between natural and unnatural causes of death; by this I mean between death caused, for example, by the infliction of a wound and between death caused by the occult powers of some malicious shaman. A person simply dies, because his soul has left him, the causes which brought about this departure being immaterial."[16]

The Omahas are said to have looked on death as one of the inevitable things in life. "The old men have said: 'We see death everywhere. Plants, trees, animals die, and man dies. No one can escape death and no one should fear death, since it can not be avoided.' While this view tended to remove from the thought of death any supernatural terrors, it did not foster the wish to hasten its approach. Length of days was desired by all."[17] This view seems extraordinarily sophisticated for an uncivilized people. More typical is the notion of the Araucanians that no one dies a natural death. "Death is due to sorcery, or poisoning,

11 §177, of the text.
12 Coudenhove, in *Atl. Mo.,* CXXVIII, 167.
13 Czaplicka, *Aborig. Siberia,* 317-318.
14 Hutton, *Sema Nagas,* 209.

15 Wilken, in VG, I, 61-62.
16 Frachtenberg, in AA, XXII, 337.
17 Fletcher and LaFlesche, in BAE, XXVII, 588.

frequently committed by some enemy in his *pilli* form, or some malign spirit, who assumed any shape at will, as that of a snake, lizard, fly, ant, etc., and thus operated with little fear of discovery, or became invisible, although his corporeal body none the less existed." When the head chief of one section died suddenly, probably of apoplexy, during a feast in a neighboring village, this manner of death, so uncommon among the Indians, was immediately set down to witchcraft, there being no visible cause to explain it.[18]

§210. Animistic Beliefs.

The Evidence from Sleep and Dreams. A relative of a murdered Australian in New South Wales goes to sleep with his head on the corpse, expecting that the deceased will reveal the murderer in a dream.[1] By the natives of the Papuan Gulf, dreams are associated with spirits and are said to be the communications of spirits who have wandered from the body whilst it was asleep and have had conversation with other spirits. "Great importance is attached to dreams, and sometimes trouble ensues in consequence."[2] In the excitement of a fight the soul of a man may "jump out of his body." The natives say, "That time you kill man, you lose sense altogether, no think about woman, pickaninny, house." The soul generally comes back during the sleep after a fight, and on the return of a war-party there is an observance calculated to restore the soul to its normal state.[3] The Bina of Papua believe the soul dwells in the stomach of a man and that it vacates the body during sleep and sickness, leaving by way of the mouth. The reason for leaving the body during sleep is in order to take counsel with the spirits. "A dream reflects the actions of the Niro-iopu (soul) when it leaves the body during sleep. Great importance is therefore attached to dreams. What induces it to vacate the stomach during sickness is not clear; but a Bina tribesman will never attempt to awaken suddenly a sleeping person, neither will he talk in a loud voice or permit noise in the vicinity of a sick person, for he believes that if the Niro-iopu was temporarily away from the body of the sleeper or the sick person it might be afraid to return, in which case the person would die. Further, he believes that prolonged absence of the Niro-iopu from the body is the real cause of sickness."[4] Among the southern Massim the souls of dead people might be seen in dreams, when they might talk to the dreamers;[5] while the natives of San Cristoval believe the soul goes out in dreams and in unconsciousness. "Death affects the body but not the soul. *Mae,* death, is the going out of the soul from the body, so that a person who is unconscious is said to be *mae,* dead. A person may be very ill, there may be obviously no hope of his recovery, but he is not *mae* till he becomes unconscious."[6]

Partly through dreams and partly through the condition during sleep, trances, and states of syncope, the Tshi-speaking negro has arrived at these conclusions: (a) that he has a second individuality, an indwelling spirit residing in his body, which he calls a *kra;* (b) that he himself will, after death, continue his present existence in a ghostly shape; that he will become, in short, the ghost of himself, which he calls a *srahman.* The Ewe term corresponding to the

18 Latcham, in JAI, XXXIX, 346 (quoted), 365.
1 Cameron, in JAI, XIV, 362.
2 Holmes, in JAI, XXXII, 429.

3 Landtmann, in JAI, XLVI, 330.
4 Lyons, in JAI, LI, 430.
5 Seligmann, *Melanesians,* 657.
6 Fox and Drew, in JAI, XLV, 161.

Tshi *kra* is *luwo;* both existed before the birth of a man, probably as the soul of a long series of men, and after his death it will equally continue its independent career, either by entering a new-born human body or that of an animal, or by wandering about the world without a tenement. Any involuntary convulsion, such as a sneeze, which is believed to indicate that the *kra* is leaving the body, is always followed by wishes of good health. "When a negro awakes feeling stiff and unrefreshed, or with limbs aching from muscular rheumatism, he invariably attributes these symptoms to the fact of his *kra* having been engaged in some struggle with another."[7] The Bangala of the Congo believe that if a person faints or becomes unconscious it is because his embodied spirit has left; on the patient reviving it is thought that the soul has returned. The soul of a dying man escapes through the nostrils and mouth; hence these are plugged and tied immediately on death to keep the spirit in the body.[8] The Ba-Mbala say nightmare is caused by ghosts returning and seizing people by the throat.[9] According to Ba-Huana notions, three elements enter into the composition of a man: body; soul, called *bun;* and double, called *doshi.* "The *bun* of a dead man who has had no fetishes can appear to other men; such an apparition occurs at night only, and the *bun* is seen in human form and appears to be composed of a white misty substance. It portends approaching death. The *doshi* is a shadowy second self, corresponding to the *kra* of the Tshi-speaking tribes of the Gold Coast, and the *ka* of the Ancient Egyptians. It leaves the body in sleep and visits other people in dreams; the *doshi* of the dead appear to the living in the same manner. All people have *doshi,* but only the adult have *bun.* . . . Animals have *doshi* but not *bun.* At death the *bun* disappears, no one knows whither, but the *doshi* lingers about in the air, visits its friends and haunts its enemies; it will persecute the relations if the body has not received proper burial; there are no means of exorcising it."[10] Among the tribes in British Central Africa, "the *mzimu* [soul or spirit] is not tangible, and has no substance, but has the form of the man, and when set free from the body can talk and can do practically anything. The *mzimu* may leave the body of a man asleep and appear as a dream to some other man, just as the spirit of a dead man may appear in a dream; spirits are not visible under other conditions. The spirit is said to leave the body of a dying man before death at the time when he becomes unconscious or comatose. His shadow, which is part of the *mzimu,* leaves the body at the same time. The *mzimu* may appear to men at some distance away at the time of death of a man. The inanimate objects appearing in a dream are seen by the dreamer's *mzimu,* who is abroad among the objects seen."[11] The Wachaga believe the images of dead persons seen in dreams to have actual existence, and regard dreams as due to the direct influence of spirits who let them foresee the good or evil in store, in order to prepare for it.[12]

In India it is believed that "whereas the soul of an ordinary human being leaves the body automatically in sleep, trance, or death, and wanders about like the wind, not as he chooses but as other forces determine, the soul of the wizard or witch can assume a material form, leave the body at will, and go wherever it chooses."[13] When a person sleeps, think certain natives of Farther

7 Ellis, *Ewe,* 15, 20 (quoted), 102, 105.
8 Weeks, in JAI, XL, 371.
9 Torday and Joyce, in JAI, XXXV, 418.
10 Torday and Joyce, in JAI, XXXVI, 290-291.

11 Stannus, in JAI, XL, 299-300.
12 Gutmann, in *Globus,* XCII, 166.
13 Roy, in JAI, XLIV, 338.

India, some parts of his *kar-bu* [spirit] leave his body. "The explanation of our having only a confused remembrance of dreams is that only part of the spirit has been abroad in sleep and has only a vague impression of what it has seen. A person, expecially one who is ill, should never be roused from sleep; in illness some of the parts of the *kar-bu* are in any case out of the body, and in sleep still more parts may have gone out. When these latter return, the person wakens naturally. Should he be rudely awakened he might die. Should he leave his bed when aroused, the wandering parts of the spirit, on their return, might fail to find him."[14] The religious observances of the Lolos of West China are mainly an attempt to propitiate the evil spirits and ghosts, who bring disease and other disasters to men. "The Lolos consider that man has a soul. When a live person is seen in a dream, it is his soul that comes; when a dead man is seen in a dream, it is equally his soul that is visible, and next morning there must be prayer and sacrifices to appease the wandering soul of the deceased. When death occurs, the soul leaves the body with the last breath, and it is considered of vital importance that this event should be witnessed by some person, otherwise the death is impure, and the ghost of the deceased (*i.e.*, the released soul) will cause trouble and sickness to his relatives. . . . The soul is supposed to leave the body in cases of chronic illness. A complicated ritual is then read, a kind of litany, in which the soul is called by name and besought to return. . . . After the ceremony is over, a red cord is tied round the arm of the sick man, to retain the soul, and this cord is worn till it drops of itself from decay."[15] The Dyaks place implicit confidence in dreams. "Their theory is that during sleep the soul can hear, see, and understand, and so what is dreamt is really what the soul sees. When anyone dreams of a distant land, they believe that his soul has paid a flying visit to that land. They interpret their dreams literally. The appearance of deceased relatives in dreams is to the Dyaks a proof that the souls live in *Sabayan*, and as in the dreams they seem to wear the same dress and to be engaged in the same occupations as when they lived in this world, it is difficult to persuade the Dyaks that the life in the other world can be different from that in this."[16]

Great importance was attached by the American Indians to dreams, whether they be common night-dreams or the dream fasting of youths during initiation-ceremonies; they often carry out instructions believed to have been imparted to them in a dream by superior powers.[17] There can be no doubt about the reality of the dream to the Guiana Indians, as evidenced in the following account by Roth:[18] "One morning when it was important for me to get away . . . I found that one of the invalids, a young Macusi, though better in health, was so enraged against me that he refused to stir, for he declared that, with great want of consideration for his weak health, I had taken him out during the night and had made him haul the canoe up a series of difficult cataracts. Nothing could persuade him that this was but a dream, and it was some time before he was so far pacified as to throw himself sulkily into the bottom of the canoe. . . . More than once, the men declared in the morning that some absent man, whom they named, had come during the night, and had beaten or otherwise maltreated them; and they insisted upon much rubbing of the bruised parts of their bodies." The dream-origin of the doctrine of the soul is common

14 Milne, *Eastern Clan*, 336.
15 Henry, in JAI, XXXIII, 102-103.
16 Gomes, *Sea Dyaks*, 161.

17 De Josselin de Jong, in AA, XVIII, 123; Mooney, in HAI, I, 544.
18 In BAE, XXX, 165.

to many South American tribes.[19] The Araucanians are convinced that their dreams are the nightly wanderings of their other selves or spirits, to which, however, they assign a material though invisible form. They are not invisible to the *pilli* or spirits of other Indians, and so when they dream of other persons they really believe their *pilli* have met. Thus also when they are attacked by nightmare or delirium tremens, the horrible forms their imaginations conjure up are considered to be real beings. "This belief that dreams are nothing but the wanderings of their bodies in invisible form, and that those persons dreamt about are really met, is the basis of their ideas of a future state, as they have thus an overwhelming proof that the dead frequently revisit this earth in the form of *pilli* or spirits. In the same manner the material forms given to their good and evil spirits are to be explained. If we duly remember that dreams and their events are very real facts in their theosophy, then we have the key by which many obscure and unexplained conceptions may be unravelled. It is common to hear one of these Indians relate in the most convinced and matter of fact way his having encountered one or other of these good or evil spirits, and give elaborate details of the meeting and its result."[20]

Breath, Shadow, and Likenesses. Very important is the shadow in folklore: the shadow as soul, the underworld of shadows, the shadowlessness of spirits and elves, the shadow as essential part of man, the fear of loss of the shadow under the equator, the correlation of power and strength with shadow, the shadow as a protective "demon," the loss of the shadow, magic connected with the shadow, proverbs and sayings about the shadow, and so forth.[21] Closely related to the widespread idea that man's shadow is his soul, is the belief that the soul is the breath, the reflection, or likeness.

At Eddystone, Solomons, "the soul is called *galagala,* which also means a shadow, a reflection; it is caught in a camera. A Shortlands man says 'it stop all over a man': by taking a looking-glass you can see it. When a man dies, his soul comes out at the mouth . . . it is just like a man and big or small according as it belongs to an adult or a child. A certain shadowiness seems associated with departing spirits, for one man asked us whether a vague figure in an advertisement of Odol was a ghost. Souls of natives are brown, that is, lighter than the living."[22] Significant of our interpretation of *mana* is the inference that the word *mana,* or *mena* in San Cristoval, originally meant breath, power being a secondary meaning, owing to the fact that it is the breathing upon an object which imparts power.[23] The name given to the spirit, shade, or soul of a dead man by the Southern Massim is *arugo.* "*Arugo* is also the name for a man's shadow and for his reflection in a glass or in water, and though trees and animals have no active living 'spirit,' their reflection bears the name of *arugo.* At death the *arugo* leaves the body and goes to the other world." To the Koita, *sua* is something which at death leaves a man to lead an independent existence. "In this sense *sua* means ghost or shade, and it is thus that the Koita usually employ the term. . . . *Sua* may leave the body during sleep; if a man wake before his *sua* has returned, he will probably sicken. Sneezing is a sign that the *sua* has returned, and if a man does not sneeze for

---

19 Koch-Grünberg, "Zum Animismus der Südamerikanischen Indianer," in supplement to Band XII of *Intern. Archiv. f. Ethnog.*
20 Latcham, in JAI, XXXIX, 345.
21 Pradel, *Der Schatten im Volksglauben,*

reviewed by Chamberlain, in AA, VIII, 587; Wilken, "Animisme," in VG, III.
22 Hocart, in JAI, LII, 81.
23 §§182, 303, of the text; Fox and Drew, in JAI, XLV, 153.

many weeks together it is a bad sign, his *sua* 'go long way away somewhere.' "[24] In D'Entrecasteaux "the soul is inside the body, a separate entity the presence of which is revealed in sneezing. For a sneeze is due to the soul's recollection of some dead kinsman or friend."[25] That a spirit may reside in a likeness is seen in the instance which occurred at Geelvink Bay. A missionary noticed a figure of a boy branded on the back of a man, and upon asking its meaning was told, "That represents my dead son, whom I now always carry with me."[26]

A word used by the Bangala of the Upper Congo River as an equivalent for spirit means literally shadow of person or thing, shade of tree or house, reflection in water or in a looking-glass, and, more recently, a photograph. The natives say a dead person casts no shadow, so to say that a person has no shadow is equivalent to pronouncing him dead. If for some reason a man did not see his shadow reflected when he looked into some water he thought someone had taken his spirit away and that he would soon die. Weeks,[27] who reports this significant case, states also that the natives believe their ancestors reappear and are "recognizable by similarity of features to those whose appearances the spirits took. When the white men arrived this belief seemed to be confirmed by the fact that they often thought they saw a likeness in the features, walk, or gestures of some white men to dead men whom they knew. I have often myself been amused when a motion, a glance, or some little peculiarity among these folk has called vividly to mind some person I knew at home. When we came here in 1890 my colleague was thought to resemble a chief who had died some time before, and I was thought to be like another who had died." A Bahima child is never allowed to see its own shadow cast upon the wall by firelight; "the shadow will become a ghost if looked upon by the child, and will catch and kill it."[28] The foundation of the Yao (Central Africa) religion is in the *lisoka,* the soul, shade or spirit which every human being possesses, and which is the inspiring agent in his life. "It is allied with the shadow, and would seem to bear to the body the relation which a picture has to the reality. Their word for a shadow is *chiwilili,* which is also the term that they use to denote a picture, and pictures they associate with the shades or shadows of the dead. I have known natives refuse to enter a room where pictures were hung on the walls 'because of the *masoka,* souls, which were in them.' The photographic camera was at first an object of dread, and when it was turned upon a group of natives they scattered in all directions with shrieks of terror. 'The European,' they said, 'was about to take away their shadows and they would die.' In their mind the *lisoka* was allied to the *chiwilili* or picture, and the removal of it to the photographic plate would mean the disease or death of the shadeless body." The author, with much difficulty, once persuaded a Yao chief to allow himself to be photographed, which permission was given only on condition that the picture was to be shown to none of his subjects but to be sent out of the country as soon as possible. He feared lest some ill-wisher might use it as a means toward his bewitchment. When, some months later, he became seriously ill, his illness was attributed to some accident having befallen the photographic plate, which was then in England. The

---

24 Seligmann, *Melanesians,* 189 (quoted), 655 (quoted), 657, 658, 734.

25 Jenness and Ballentyne, *D'Entrecasteaux,* 109.

26 Krieger, *Neu-Guinea,* 395.

27 In JAI, XL, 371, 398 (quoted).

28 Roscoe, in JAI, XXXVII, 116.

divining oracle, however, after consulting the lots, gave assurance that the picture was intact and that the disease must be ascribed to some other cause.[29]

To the Mkamba of East Africa the world abounds in spirits. "What a spirit is he does not pretend to know; they say 'We see a man's shadow, and we say perhaps that is his spirit,' and for this reason the camera is still feared, because it robs men of their shadows. Yet no Mkamba knows positively that his shadow is his spirit, for even stones cast shadows, and whether they have spirits he would not like to say for certain. But every man has a spirit which lives on after the body is dead, though the nature of after-life is very vague."[30] Among other East Africans the soul is likened to the shadow;[31] while the shades and manes of the Fan resemble those of the ancient Egyptians.[32] The shadows (Vu-Vu) of things and people are regarded by the Dinkas as important. "At death, the shadow departs to the place of God. The word 'Vu-Vu' is used in the sense of soul, when speaking of the departed. The Golo theory of dreams is that the shadows of things and people enter the dreamer's mind during sleep. From this it would appear that the connection between the shadow and the substance is believed to be severed during sleep. . . . The fact that this is believed to be efficacious shows that the Golo does not allow experience to shatter illusions."[33]

The Buryat of Siberia believe that man is composed of three parts: material body, lower soul or breath, and soul belonging to man only. The second is connected with decease; when it leaves the body, death occurs. The third has a similar connection with sleep, leaving the body when one is sleeping. The second part of the soul does not leave the earth, but continues to dwell on it in a manner exactly similar to that which the man formerly followed, while the third part of the soul is born again in the form of a human being. Among the Koryak a person is declared dead when breathing ceases; this is considered to signify that the chief soul has deserted the body. There is, however, another soul called "breath," and still another called "shadow." They draw no very sharp line of demarkation between life and death. A corpse is not "deprived of the ability to move. The deceased may arise, if he is not watched. . . . The soul of a deceased person does not leave the earth at once, but hovers high above the corpse. It is like a flame. During illness it is outside the body, hovering low over it if the illness is slight, higher if it is severe. . . . When the soul of a deceased rises to the Supreme Being, the deceased himself and his other soul, or his shadow, descend underground to dwell with the Peninelau—'the ancient people, people of former times.' " The word *tyn* signifies to the Altaians vitality, *i.e.,* a soul common to plants, animals, and man, and is synonymous with breath. "The Altaians say that one can hear a sound as of the snapping of a string when the *tyn* is departing. One must not approach too near to a dying man, for the belief is that in such a case the *tyn* of a living person can pass into the latter."[34]

In India the soul or spirit of a man is sometimes identified with his shadow; a man of strong individuality is said to have a powerful shadow, a weak or nervous person to have a light shadow. "The shadow of a man of the former type falling even on a venomous snake is believed to be able to hold the snake

29 Hetherwick, in JAI, XXXII, 89-90.
30 Dundas, C., in JAI, XLIII, 535.
31 Cole, in JAI, XXXII, 328; Hobley, in JAI, XXXIII, 327-328.

32 Trilles, *Fân*, 4, note.
33 Cummins, in JAI, XXXIV, 164.
34 Czaplicka, *Aborig. Siberia*, 149, 269 (quoted), 282 (quoted), 287.

spell-bound at the spot and make it unable to budge an inch."[35] A word which primarily means shadow is used normally in Sema eschatology for the soul of a dead person. The same word also means reflection and is used to denote any likeness or image. The daughter of a Sema chief was in much trepidation when the author[36] tried to photograph her, and was with difficulty reassured that he had not deprived her of her soul when he took her picture. She was only really satisfied when it was given back to her to keep in the form of a print. Palaung children are taught that they must not step upon the shadow of a monk, a chief, or any old person. "They do not now consider that the person on whose shadow a foot has stepped will be harmed in any way, but to step on the shadow of any important person is disrespectful. It will harm, not the person whose shadow has been treated with disrespect, but the person who does the disrespectful act."[37] A case related to burial-preparations is mentioned from the Malay Peninsula in which "there was some hesitation on the part of those present as to whether it was not actually noon, in which case they said the burial would have to be postponed till the afternoon, since the shortness of their shadows at noon would (sympathetically) shorten their own lives."[38] It is hard to get photographs of the Moros: "They were unduly influenced by the remarks in the Koran concerning the making of pictures of living things, and furthermore many of them believed that if they were photographed they were sure to die within a year."[39]

According to ancient Maori tradition as concerned with the first woman, the Earth-formed Maid, "when the spirit or soul, and the breath of life, were implanted in the figure of earth, behold it sneezed, breathed, and opened its eyes,—a thing endowed with human life, a person, a woman."[40] To questions about the nature of the soul the natives of the Trobriand Islands reply that the *baloma* is like a reflection in water or a mirror, and that the *kosi* is like a shadow. "When forced against a metaphysical wall by such questions, 'How can a *baloma* call out, and eat, and make love if it is like a *saribu* (reflection)? How can a *kosi* hammer against a house, or throw stones, or strike a man if it is like a shadow?' the more intelligent replied more or less to the effect: 'Well, the *baloma* and the *kosi* are like the reflection and like the shadow, but they are also like men, and they behave all the same as men do.' And it was difficult to argue with them." To judge leniently such inconsistencies of native belief, it is sufficient, as the author[41] notes, to remember that we meet the same difficulties in our own ideas about ghosts and spirits. No one who believes in them ever doubts that they can speak, and even act; they can rap on tables, lift objects, and make other material manifestations.

The Kwakiutl Indians believe the soul is like smoke or a shadow,[42] while those of British Columbia hold that the breath of a person is the manifestation of the spirit within him. "A person's breath conveys both good and evil influences. For example, a man seeking mystery power should never permit the breath of a woman to pass upon him or enter his lungs; it would nullify all his efforts, and effectually prevent the acquisition of the powers he sought if he did so. The verb 'to revive' . . . shows how closely and intimately the breath

35 Roy, in JAI, XLIV, 340.
36 Hutton, *Sema Nagas*, 199-200; and in JAI, L, 46, note.
37 Milne, *Eastern Clan*, 51.
38 Skeat and Blagden, *Malay Penin.*, II, 109-110.

39 Worcester, *Philippine Isl.*, 192.
40 Best, in JAI, XLIV, 145.
41 Malinowski, in JAI, XLVI, 367 (quoted), 369.
42 Boas, in BAE, XXXV, pt. I, 727-728.

and life or spirit of a person was connected in their eyes." The term means in English "to sigh or breathe *in* the spirit, and open the eyes."[43] Many Indians to-day view picture-taking devices with superstitious awe, and if they allow themselves to be photographed they often keep their eyes on the ground while they pose.[44]

The soul as a shadow was a concept familiar to the people of classical antiquity:

> Bis duo sunt homini, manes, caro, spiritus, umbra:
> Quatuor haec loci bis duo suscipiunt.
> Terra tegit carnem, tumulum circumvolat umbra,
> Manes Orcus habet, spiritus astra petit.

Miscellaneous Beliefs. Of a tropical Australian tribe it is said that they accept the existence of the soul before birth. The name given to the soul in this stage is Rai. "The Rai are supposed to be sitting in trees, like birds, and to enter the body of a woman independently of sexual intercourse."[45] The natives of both New Caledonia and New Hebrides thought white men were the spirits of the dead; in the former case, they believed these white spirits brought sickness and gave this as the reason why they wished to kill white men; in the latter, they thought the whites were made by the great spirit, *Nobu,* and to this day they call foreigners, whether white or black, by the name of *Nobu.*[46] In New Britain there is a realistic belief that the spirit of man may leave his body for a time and enter into animals, birds, or fish. But should the creature into which the spirit of a man has entered be killed while he is in it, then the man's body dies. "On one occasion in my town," reports Danks,[47] "a man was wounded by a spear thrust in the shoulder during the night. Next morning he was questioned about it, and declared that he had entered into a fish, and happening to come near the reef on which were some men with a torch and fishing spears, the fish was wounded close to the fore fin, and so his body received the wound."

The Buryat of Siberia think the soul is material and visible to human beings, and usually takes the form of a bee. In one of their legends a man saw how a bee came out of the nose of his sleeping comrade, flew and crept about the hut, crawled upon the edge of a water-receptacle, fell in, emerged with difficulty, and finally returned into the nose of the sleeper. From subsequent conversation it appeared that the dreams of the latter corresponded completely with the actions and adventures of the insect. The Buryats never kill a bee that flies into the hut lest damage be done to someone's soul. Again, two Votyaks went into the woods to work; and while they rested, one smoked and the other slept. The soul of the sleeper emerged from his mouth with a sudden sound, flew to a pine tree, entered a hole, returned, and entered the sleeper's mouth. He woke and reported a vision: that he had found, in a hole in a pine tree, some money in two hollow sticks. The two went home, but the smoker returned later and, on examining the hole which the soul entered, found the money.[48] The idea that the soul and body can be separated without death ensuing at once is common to many tribes of the Naga Hills. "Among the Aimol, the priest, after a child's birth, summons the soul to take possession of its

---

43 Hill-Tout, in JAI, XXXV, 147.
44 New Haven *Register*, October 21, 1919.
45 Klaatsch, *Tropical Aust.*, 580.
46 Turner, *Samoa*, 329-330, 342-343.

47 In AAAS, 1909. 454-455.
48 Michailovski, *Shamanism* (Russ.), 10, 25; Czaplicka, *Aborig. Siberia*, 158.

new dwelling, the child's body. Among the Lushais the father and mother keep quiet for seven days after a child's birth, for fear of injuring the little one's soul, which is thought to hover and perch like a bird on their bodies and clothes."[49] The Palaungs do not consider the soul to be one and indivisible but to be composed of many separable parts, some of which may detach themselves from the rest. "For instance when a man starting on a journey begs his father and mother to protect him on the way, he actually expects that part of their spirits will go with him. . . . No one would live in the house formerly occupied by a man known to have been bad, or wear his clothes, or use his household goods." If the powerful spirits are pleased, they show the way to a spirit that is looking for a mother; if they are angry, they may prevent any spirit that might become the soul of a future child from coming near. "A child may be born and may live without having a spirit in it. It is then an imbecile, but it must be kindly treated and cared for, as its spirit may yet find its way to the body that it should have entered before the child was born." By tying white threads round the wrist, the spirit may be kept from fleeing away.[50]

The Alfurs, believing that the soul of a newly born child is only lightly attached to the delicate body, close the door at childbirth, in order to prevent the spirit from gliding away; the Bulgarians, on the other hand, believe that the animation or "besouling" of the child takes place at the moment of birth and so they open the door to the entering spirit.[51] The idea of comparing the soul to a bird, or of identifying it in some way with a bird, of worldwide distribution, is well known to the Malays, who call the soul the *pingai* bird and in their magical invocations address it with a word used in calling chickens. "The Semang woman is said to carry about with her a bamboo receptacle, in which she keeps the soul-bird of her expected progeny; this bird is really the vehicle of her child's soul, and she is expected to eat it to enable the soul of her child to be developed." As soon as the child is born, the afterbirth is buried under the birth-tree or name-tree of the child. "The bird, in which the child's soul is conveyed, always inhabits a tree of the species to which the birth-tree belongs; it flies from one tree (of the species) to another, following the as yet unborn body. The souls of first-born children are always young birds newly hatched, the offspring of the bird which contained the soul of the mother." The Eastern Semang think that each man possesses a soul which is shaped like himself, but is "red like blood" and "no bigger than a grain of maize." It is passed on by the mother to the child, in a way they cannot explain.[52] The Sakai say the souls of the dead become white butterflies and that, for this reason, it is forbidden to kill such insects.[53] According to Maori belief, the soul of a child is implanted in the foetus before birth, at the time when the eyes assume form; they are believed to be the first parts so to gain form.[54]

The Greenland Eskimo think that man consists of three parts: body, soul, and name. The soul is small, not bigger than a finger or hand; if it gets sick or dies, so does the man; if bewitched out of the body, the shaman can get it back.[55] When fishing, the Tlinkits talk to their halibut-lines, hooks, and floats, calling them "brother-in-law," "father-in-law." It is believed that if they did

49 Hutton, in JAI, L, 51.

50 Milne, *Eastern Clan*, 277 (quoted), 335-336 (quoted), 307.

51 Von Negelein, in *Ztft. f. Vkde.*, XI, 267-268.

52 Skeat and Blagden, *Malay Penin.*, II, 1-2 (quoted), 3, 4 (quoted), 5, 194, 195.

53 Evans, in JAI, XLVIII, 195-196.

54 Best, in JAI, XLIV, 132.

55 Holm, *Ethnol. Skizze*, 70; Cranz, *Grönland*, II, 57.

not do so they would not have any good luck.[56] When Boas[57] asked the shaman among the Kwakiutl about the soul, the latter replied, "Did you not see the soul last night, which came and sat on my hand? It is the size of our thumb, when it shrinks and becomes small; then I put the soul on top of our head, and it grows so that it is of the same size as our body, for the body is the house of the soul." The souls fly about at night and in the morning when it is nearly daylight they come home to the owners of the souls and tell where they have been and what they have seen. Sometimes the soul comes back the wrong way, when it returns to the owner, and is hurt; this is especially the case when it returns quickly and goes in crosswise or upside down. The man then becomes sick and goes to the shaman, who tells him that his soul is in the wrong way. After an elaborate shamanistic treatment the soul is set right. Like the Eskimo, the Nutka and Hurons believe in the soul of a person in the form of a tiny man.[58]

Though the souls, in Homer, are as unsubstantial as dreams, yet they not only have the human form but also may feel anger or joy, or may weep; they partake eagerly of the blood and wine and honey which are provided.[59] In the Zend-Avesta it is stated that the soul is added to the fœtus after four months and ten days.[60] In ancient European mythology it was held that in sleep the soul might leave the body as a snake;[61] or that the soul-voice was like a bat;[62] while a few years ago in New Jersey a woman claimed she saw the soul of a dying man pass from his lips and take the form of a butterfly.[63]

§211. Transmigration and Reincarnation.

WHEN an Australian dies it is supposed that his soul leaves his body, by way of the mouth, and enters the body of a white man, also passing in through the mouth. "The whitefellow who thus becomes the domicile of the dying black man's soul is supposed to be born at the time of death of the blackfellow."[1] This belief in white reincarnation, found also in Tasmania, is thought by some to come from anthropophagy, the color of Tasmanian flesh when roasted and skinned being whitish.[2] According to a belief in New Britain, "every man dies six times, each time passing down to a lower stage, till he reaches Matika, and finally disappears."[3] Natives of San Cristoval firmly believe in the continued existence of the soul after death. "Death is merely a migration. The soul may pass into an animal, or may be born again in a descendant, or may merely exist without any incarnation."[4] The naming of a boy after the father's father and of a girl after the mother's mother may be due to a belief in reincarnation, combined with the idea that the reincarnate spirit must enter the body of one of his or her own moiety or clan. A case is cited where a boy was named as usual but was very sickly when but a few days old; at this time a man died and his spirit returned into the sickly baby, when it was given his name, and the boy recovered and grew strong. When a child cries, names of the dead are called till he stops crying, to show which he desires, that is, what

56 Jones, *Thlingets*, 167.
57 In BAE, XXXV, pt. I, 724.
58 Boas, "Soul," in HAI, II, 617.
59 Seymour, *Hom. Age*, 462, 464, 465.
60 Müller, *Sacred Books*, IV, pt. I, 173, note.
61 Grimm, *Deut. Myth.*, 1036.

62 Pyle, *King Arthur*, 129.
63 N. Y. *Tribune*, May 2, 1913.
1 Wells, in AAAS, 1893, 519.
2 Letourneau, *Soc.*, 237.
3 Macdonald, in AAAS, 1898, 765.
4 Fox and Drew, in JAI, XLV, 161.

ghost has been reborn. "I have, myself, seen this done," writes Fox,[5] "in the case of the baby of a man named Mamake; this baby refused many names till, finally, in despair, Mamake said perhaps it was a Christian spirit, and tried the name Mary, at which the baby stopped crying, and Mamake immediately called her by this name, and suggested she should be baptised."

A South African chief in a speech once boasted of his wisdom, attributing its possession to the fact that he had been several times dead and had come to life again.[6] A certain benevolent god of the Hottentots is a sort of grandfather of the whole people; his origin is accounted for as follows. A virgin, impregnated by sucking the juice of a certain grass-stalk, bore a son who grew rapidly to manhood, and who, the people believed, had been born several times before. He was recognized this time as their grandfather who had returned to his children.[7] Every family among the Congo Bangala has a place called *liboma*—it may be in the bush or forest, on an island, a creek, or a tree—which is a sort of preserve for the unborn children of the family. "The disembodied spirits of the deceased members of the family perform the duty of supplying these preserves with children to keep their families strong and numerous. They have misty ideas as to how these *liboma* are supplied with children, but I have a suspicion that underlying the *liboma* is some idea of reincarnation. . . . Only the family to which the *liboma* belongs can give birth to the unborn spirits there."[8] The Ba-Huana assert that in the case of a man who has been the possessor of many fetishes, the soul enters the body of some large animal—elephant, hippopotamus, buffalo, or leopard. Animals so possessed are recognized by their ferocity.[9] The belief in the werewolf, under different disguises, is very common the world over, both among civilized and savage peoples. The Somal believes in a being who is a man-leopard; by day it is a man and by night a leopard. It seizes people by night, the intimate knowledge of a kraal and its habitants being gained in the guise of a man by day. The Somals also believe that people can turn themselves into hyænas at night. "A man alleged to be in possession of such a gift was brought for enlistment in the Somali irregulars in 1900. He explained that the gift was not a common one, and, as his services would be most valuable to the force in scouting at night, he required rather more than the ordinary pay; in fact he estimated his services at thirty rupees [about fifteen dollars] a month." Nothing could prevail on the man to give a proof of his powers.[10]

The Koryak of Siberia hold that the soul of some ancestor is sent by the Supreme Being into the child in the mother's womb. "These souls are hanging on the cross-beams of the house of the Supreme Being. . . . The father of the child enumerates the names of the deceased relatives on his and his wife's side. When the name of the relative whose soul has entered the child is mentioned, the divining-stone begins to swing more quickly. Another way of determining the identity of the soul is by observation of the behaviour of the child itself. A number of names are mentioned. If the child cries when a name is pronounced it shows that it is not the name of the soul reborn in the child. When the proper name is pronounced the child stops crying, or begins to smile."[11] When the Peking child is one year old, the mother passes a knife

5 In JAI, XLIX, 143.
6 Holub, *Capstadt*, II, 180.
7 Quatrefages, *Pygmies* (N.Y., 1905), quoted by Dowd, *Negro Races*, I, 57-58.

8 Weeks, in JAI, XL, 419.
9 Torday and Joyce, in JAI, XXXVI, 291.
10 Stigand, *Elephant*, 293-294.
11 Czaplicka, *Aborig. Siberia*, 136.

along the floor between the child's feet, whereby the bond with which, in an earlier life, his legs were tied together following death, is symbolically severed.[12] A Jain believes that all souls are capable of being perfected by a series of lives of good actions, at length reaching a state of final liberation somewhat like the Buddhist Nirvana.[13]

The Nagas of India are firm believers in lycanthropy. "The theory and symptoms are clear and recognizable, and differ perhaps from most lycanthropists in other parts of the world. The Sema undergoes no physical transformation whatever. The 'possession,' if we may term it so, is not ordinarily induced by any external aid, but comes on at the bidding of spirits which may not be gainsaid, and under whose influence the man possessed entirely loses his own volition in the matter. . . . The soul usually enters into the leopard during sleep and returns to the human body with daylight, but it may remain in the leopard for several days at a time, in which case the human body, though conscious, is lethargic. . . . The possession is accompanied by very severe pains and swellings in the knees, elbows and small of the back in the human body, both during and consequent on the possession. These pains are said to be such as would result from far and continuous marching or from remaining long periods in an unaccustomed position. During sleep at the time of possession the limbs move convulsively, as the legs of a dog move when it is dreaming. A were-leopard of the Tizu Valley, in a paroxysm at such a time, bit one of his wife's breasts off. When the leopard is being hunted by men, the human body behaves like a lunatic, leaping and throwing itself about in its efforts to escape. . . . It is generally held, and doubtless not without some substratum of truth, that a man under the influence of the possession can be quieted by feeding him with chicken dung. Probably this produces nausea." A local chief once showed the author a wound in his back which he said was the result of someone having shot at him when he was in leopard form a few days before.[14]

Many Shan and Palaung children are born with curious patches of blue color on the skin, which generally disappear after a few months. At birth a child is carefully examined to see if it has any such markings. "If a man dies from the kick of a horse, and a child is afterwards born to his widow, with a blue mark in a similar position to that of the father's injury, it would not be considered by Palaungs to be the result of a maternal impression, but to indicate that the dead man's spirit has entered into the body of his child." The soul generally hopes to be reborn into the home that it still remembers, but it may happen that there is no woman there of an age to have another child, so the poor kar-bu wanders away seeking a new home and a new mother. For this task it is allowed only seven days. As the only place where the kar-bu can rest during the seven days of its search is in the body that it has so recently occupied, it often returns to rest there. The kar-bu and the two guardian spirits, all as small as the smallest insect, finally alight on the fruit or rice that its future mother is eating, and are swallowed by her along with the food. A Palaung story tells of children who after being poisoned and buried grew out of the ground as bushes. "When a flower was picked from one of these, the bush cried out, saying, 'Do not pick me, it hurts!' It is interesting to compare Dante's account

12 Grube, in Berl. Mus., VII, 7.
13 Deshmukh, in JASB, I, 77.
14 Hutton, in JAI, L, 43-44 (quoted), 45, 50 note. A bibliography on the subject of

lycanthropy will be found at the end of McLennan's article in the ninth edition of the Encyclopædia Britannica; it relates almost entirely to the European races.

of the Dolorous Wood in the *Inferno,* where self-murderers are found to have been turned into trees. Dante plucks a twig from a great tree, and the bleeding trunk cries out, 'Why dost thou tear me?' The idea was probably suggested to Dante by the passage in Virgil. . . . In both these instances from European classics, as well as in the Palaung story, the human beings transformed into trees and bushes, had died a violent death, and in all three cases they still retained their human sensitiveness to injury and the power to cry out when hurt."[15]

The idea of metempsychosis is not unknown to the Sea Dyaks of Borneo. Gomes[16] once met a native who treated a snake with the greatest kindness because he said it had been revealed to him in a dream that the spirit of his grandfather dwelt in that snake. "Some Dyaks speak of a series of spirit worlds through which their souls must pass before they become finally extinct. Some Dyaks say they have to die three times; others say seven times; but all seem to agree in the idea that after these successive dyings they practically cease to exist, and are absorbed into air and fog. They do not believe in an endless life, because perhaps they lack the mental capacity to conceive of such a thing." A notion of self-transformation into tigers is held by some of the tribes of the Malay Peninsula,[17] while Wilken,[18] writing of ideas of transmigration in the East Indies, under Hindu influence, says the conception is easy to primitive man because he feels no deep distinction between himself and the animals. In Samoa, if a body is lost beyond recovery, as at sea, the near relatives seek some insect or animal, whichever comes first upon a cloth spread for the purpose, into which they believe the spirit of the deceased has entered; that object is then carefully wrapped up and buried with ceremony and lamentation.[19] "In one of the Tongan islands they would not kill flies. In Tahiti it was an insect that gave warning of death. In Ra'iatea it was believed that the spirits of the dead became cockroaches. In Tahiti the souls of children killed at birth appeared as grasshoppers. In Mangaia the voices of warriors slain in battle were recognized in the chirping of a species of cricket, and the souls of the dead buried in the great Aureka chasm were associated in some way with a species of red fly. In Rarotonga the grasshopper was an omen of death. In the Marquesas the souls of the dead were often recognized in crickets, and those of priests were supposed to ascend to the sky in the form of moths, developing afterwards into birds. In the Paumotu the souls of the dead were believed to enter into birds. In Niue they were seen in insects, lizards, etc.; and in Fotuna in an insect or reptile, or perhaps a bird. In Ongtong Java the soul could revisit the island in the form of a bird."[20]

Among the beliefs of the Haida Indians reincarnation held a prominent place.[21] A notion is current in another tribe that when a person dies his spirit returns to a woman and is reborn.[22] Others figuratively resurrected the dead, especially great chieftains and persons noted for valor and wisdom, by the substitution of some person who they thought was like the deceased in person, age, and character. "The selection was made in council, by the clan of the deceased person; then all the people except the one chosen arose, and the master of ceremonies, gently lowering his hand to the earth, feigned to raise the

15 Milne, *Eastern Clan,* 28 (quoted, 337-338, 339, 344 (quoted).
16 *Sea Dyaks,* 143-144.
17 Skeat and Blagden, *Malay Penin.,* II, 191 ff.

18 "Animisme," in VG, III, 64-84.
19 Ella, in AAAS, 1887, 490.
20 Williamson, *Cent. Polyn.,* II, 315-316.
21 Swanton, in HAI, I, 522.
22 HAI, II, 884.

illustrious dead from the tomb and to give life to him in the person of the chosen one, on whom he then imposed the name and dignity of the dead chieftain, and the newly made chieftain then arose amid the ceremonial acclaim of the people."[23] One South American tribe thinks that all plants and animals are men transformed for bad conduct.[24] To the Guiana Indians the fact of the human actor having an animal form, or the animal an anthropomorphic one, is explained as being due to punishment or pure devilment at the instigation of the spirit of some person departed. "It is also a firm article of faith that the medicine-man, to whom nothing is impossible, can effect transformation of himself or others, similar to those produced by the Spirits. In addition, there is a widespread Indian belief that at every eclipse of the moon animals are metamorphosed—a tapir may change into a snake, a man into a beast, and vice versa."[25]

Initiatory rites often have in them the idea of rebirth.[26] "Such rites become intelligible if we suppose that their substance consists in extracting the youth's soul in order to transfer it to his totem." This would cause a semblance of death or real death—"an exchange of life or souls between man and his totem." Frazer[27] gives a number of examples to prove this view.

Herodotus says that the Egyptians were the first to assert that the soul of man was immortal, born and reborn in various incarnations, and this doctrine he adds was borrowed from the Egyptians by the Greeks. To Plato it was already "an ancient doctrine that the souls of men that come Here are from There and that they go There again and come to birth from the dead." "A people who saw in a chance snake the soul of a hero would have no difficulty in formulating a doctrine of metempsychosis. They need not have borrowed it from Egypt, and yet it is probable that the influence of Egypt, the home of animal worship, helped out the doctrine by emphasizing the sanctity of animal life."[28] The scarab is said to be a symbol of rebirth.[29] The doctrine of resurrection is definitely stated in the Avesta, while such a belief, which is one of the chief dogmas of Christianity and of the Jewish and Mohammedan religions, was also a genuine Zoroastrian doctrine.[30]

§212. The Name.

"DORIAN GRAY? Is that his name?" asked Lord Henry, walking across the studio toward Basil Hallward.

"Yes, that is his name. I didn't intend to tell it to you."

"But why not?"

"Oh, I can't explain. When I like people immensely I never tell their names to any one. It is like surrendering a part of them."

This excerpt from a modern author[1] embodies an idea familiar to many primitive peoples, that there is some connection between the name and soul

---

23 Hewitt, *Neutrals*, in HAI, II, 61-62.
24 Andree, *Eth. Parallelen*, 157.
25 Roth, in BAE, XXX, 199.
26 §163 of the text.
27 *Golden Bough*, II, 342, 343.
28 Herodotus, *Hist.*, III, 62; Harrison, *Greek Relig.*, 589-590.

29 Tiele-Gehrich, *Relig. im Altertum*, I, 74.
30 Haug, *Parsis*, 311-313; Justi, *Persien*, 91; Spiegel, *Eran. Alterthumskunde*, II, 158, 159; Kautzsch, "Relig. Israel," in Hastings's *Bible Dict.*, 715; Bousset, *Relig. des Judentums*, 261.
1 Wilde, *The Picture of Dorian Gray*, 4-5.

or that the name and the individual are closely identified. The same reluctance to tell one's name is common.

Hardy and Elkington,[2] writing of their experiences in the South Seas, remark: "You can implore a native to tell you his name, but it has no effect. He
will tell you some name, if you press him hard enough, but it won't be his, as
you will discover if you try to find him again." As an instance of this practice, Hardy, particularly struck by a canoe he saw lying on the sand in the main
street of Elevera, and seeing a native standing by, asked him if the canoe
belonged to him, as he would like to buy it. The native smiled blandly and
shook his head.

" 'Don't you know whose it is?' asked Mr. Hardy.

" 'Don't know; man over there, p'r'aps,' said the native.

" 'What's his name?' Mr. Hardy pursued.

" 'No name.' The native shook his bushy head.

" 'Well, show me which is the hut he lives in.'

At this question the man began to fidget, and then, glancing carelessly at
the row of huts, all as like each other as peas, he swept his hand past the
whole lot and said: 'That one.' And that was all the information concerning
the name and possessor of the canoe that Mr. Hardy obtained. Subsequently he
learned that the owner of it was the very man he had been questioning." The
same authors comment upon other attitudes toward the name: "If a native is
rich, the first way he shows it is by changing his name, and, as in England,
money has to be spent for this privilege; in the New Hebrides it means a
feast, and a big one at that. On announcing his desire for a new name to the
chief, and proving that he has the means of paying for it, the native goes away
by himself for a few weeks, during which time he is considered 'duli' and is
not allowed to see a woman, and only permitted to eat certain things, as in
the case of the New Guinea natives when they become *ibito*. After his seclusion
he is known by his new name, and attends the big religious feast which he
himself has provided. Other ways are found for changing names, and certain
natives are rewarded for their bravery and good deeds by being given a new
one, in much the same way as a man is knighted in England."

"Fifteen years ago the Port Moresby native was very unwilling to tell you
his name," reports an ethnographer,[3] from New Guinea. "He always got a
friend to tell you his name. Possibly there was some magical idea at the back
of this." The Papuans regard it as bad manners to ask anyone his name. "Lifuans
were reluctant to mention their own names."[4] Young men in Kenya Colony,
East Africa, refuse to state their first name, "from a desire not to impart anything of what is an essentially personal part of their being; the same idea
being found in their horror of anyone, however friendly, obtaining their hair.
Women refuse to mention the *kainet,* or first name, of their fathers or husbands; such is indeed a formula in the rare instances of divorce amongst the
tribe, the reason being given that it is unseemly to call a man by the name
used by his mother; there would seem to be a sexual idea underlying the prohibition. Men do not use their wives' names, but call them *kaita,* wife, or else
a nickname, for the same reason."[5] The fact of the matter is that the name is
intimately associated with the soul or the personality; it is an essential part
of a person. When an event of significance occurs in a person's life, this may

2 S. *Seas*, 26, 27, 166.
3 Strong, in JAI, XLIX, 297.
4 Ray, in JAI, XLVII, 296.
5 Barton, in JAI, LIII, 51.

be marked by a change in name, as when the Tubu takes a new name after killing an enemy.[6] By way of contrast, it is said of the lowly Bushmen that no one has a name peculiar to himself,[7] while the undeveloped Veddahs also appear to be without name.[8]

In India, the Sema has the same disinclination to mention his own name that most Nagas have; "it may have some connection with the notion that a man's soul answers to the name as well as his body." The Sema never gives to the child the name of a living relation, though the names of dead ancestors are popular among those with a child to name. "The explanation given is that, if the name of a living senior be given, the elder will die, as a substitute for him in this world has been provided."[9] In Assam, "each individual has a private name which may not be revealed. If anyone should allow his private name to be known, the whole village is genna [tabu] for two days and a feast is provided by the offender."[10] One day when Evans[11] was questioning a native as to how the Dusuns chose names for their children, the latter said, "You know, Tuan, my name used to be Logus, but it was a very dirty name, so I changed it to Gumpus." Wondering what he meant, and thinking that Logus had perhaps an indecent meaning, Evans asked him why he said Logus was a dirty name. "Oh," he replied, "while I used that name I was always ill and could not get down to the river to bathe, so I changed my name to Gumpus, and then I got well." In the East Indies no one wants to tell his name. The Dutch authorities had much trouble over this. The man asked would give a questioning look to a comrade or say, "Ask him." This is stated to be the situation in all Indonesia without exception.[12] In the Malay Peninsula the magician exercised great power over the tribe through the fact that he could deprive a recalcitrant member of the tribe of his or her name. "In such a case the magician went in full state to the house of the offender, and there solemnly burned the headband of the person concerned, who by this means was completely excluded from the clan."[13] The natives of Borneo believe that without a name there would be no existence. How could a nameless thing be admitted to the next life? "The receiving of a name is really the starting-point of life; and the bestowal of a name by the parents is probably the most serious of parental duties, and to be performed with ceremonies proportioned to their rank. So essential is the ceremony of naming that in the enumeration of a family an unnamed child is not counted; and should a child die before the ceremony of naming, a Kayan or Kenyah mother would mourn for it no more deeply than had it been stillborn. This is true even when an unnamed child lives to be nearly a year old."[14]

The naming of the Maori child indicates a belief in transmigration: the priest repeats a long list of names of ancestors, and when the child sneezes that which was then being uttered is the one selected.[15] When a Polynesian chief acquired the title a certain sanctity passed to him, water or oil being used in some islands as a medium by which the passage was effected. "It was on his succession that the god entered into him, having, perhaps, selected him as a successor, and influenced the will of the deceased chief, or the elective

6 Nachtigal, *Sahara*, I, 350.
7 Lichtenstein, *S. Afr.*, II, 49.
8 Davy, *Interior of Ceylon*, 117.
9 Hutton, *Sema Nagas*, 237.
10 Hodson, in JAI, XXXVI, 97.
11 In JAI, XLVII, 157.

12 Wilken, *Vkde.*, 221.
13 Skeat and Blagden, *Malay Penin.*, II, 12.
14 Furness, *Head-hunters*, 18; Nieuwenhuis, *Borneo*, I, 65.
15 §211; Taylor, *Te Ika*, 184.

body, that formed the human machinery for giving effect to the divine choice."
The sanctity may be thought to have been in the man because he had become
the duly appointed head of the group, yet there is some evidence which points
to a conception of sanctity as inherent in the title itself. There would be
nothing surprising in this, for the idea that a man's name is an actual part of
himself is widely spread among savage races; "the man would be identified
with the name, and the name with him, and the sanctity would be attributed
to both." The idea of identity between a man and his name is seen in the
consequences which followed an exchange of names. Further, the Tahitian
warrior, by securing the body of a dead enemy-chief and taking his name,
acquired a claim to his land, and a somewhat similar usage prevailed in the
Marquesas. There should be noted also the ability of a doomed victim to escape
by claiming the name of a taboo-chief, the use of another person's name for
placing a taboo on an object, and the employment of a man's own name or
that of some other person for the purpose of bewitching the property of a
suspected thief.[16]

The East Greenlanders, besides their notion that the name is one of the
souls, regard it as one of the components of a man. "The name is as large as
the man himself and enters into the child after its birth, on its mouth being
damped with water, while at the same time the 'names' of the dead are spoken."
The first child born after the death of a member of a family is almost always
called after him to procure peace for him in his grave. The name remains with
the body or migrates through different animals until a child is called by it.
If, therefore, this is neglected evil consequences may follow for the child who
should have had that name. There is a similar notion in Norway that the dead
seek after names. If, before her child is born, a woman dreams of a deceased
relative, she must name her child after him or the child will suffer. The Lapps
have the same superstition. The Koloshes in northwestern America think that
the mother sees in a dream the departed relative whose soul gives the child
its likeness. Among the Indians also the naming of children is made to depend
on a dream.[17]

The name was of great interest and significance in North America. Names
could be loaned, pawned, or even given or thrown away outright. On the other
hand, they might be adopted without the consent of the owner out of revenge.
The possession of a name was everywhere jealously guarded, and "it was considered discourteous or even insulting to address one directly by it." Personal
names were given and changed at the critical epochs of life, such as birth,
puberty, the first war-expedition, some notable feat, or elevation to chieftainship; and retirement from active life was marked by the adoption of the
name of one's son.[18] This and several subsequent cases illustrate the usage of
teknonymy.[19] Among the Iroquois, if captives succeeded in running the gantlet
they were adopted into the tribe with a new name which was proclaimed at
the next festival.[20] The child might be named soon after birth or not for a
year or more later—this child-name, like the milk teeth, being discarded as the
boy or girl grew up for another of more important significance.[21] Names were
sometimes the property of clans. Those bestowed on the individual members

16 Williamson, *Cent. Polyn.*, III, 155, 227-228 (quoted).
17 Nansen, *Esk. Life*, 228; Liebrecht, *Vkde.*, 311; Klemm, *Culturgchte.*, III, 77; Tylor, *Prim. Culture*, II, 4.
18 Swanton, "Name," in HAI, II, 16, 17.
19 The naming of parents after their children. §§406, 409, of the text and *Case-Book*.
20 Morgan, *League of Iroq.*, 342.
21 Mooney, in HAI, I, 265.

and, as on the Northwest Coast, those given to canoes and to houses, were owned by families.[22] The Indian, it should be noted, "regards his name, not as a mere label, but as a distinct part of his personality, just as much as are his eyes or his teeth, and believes that injury will result as surely from the malicious handling of his name as from a wound inflicted on any part of his physical organism. This belief was found among the various tribes from the Atlantic to the Pacific, and has occasioned a number of curious regulations in regard to the concealment and change of names. It may be on this account that both Powhatan and Pocahontas are known in history under assumed appellations, their true names having been concealed from the whites until the pseudonyms were too firmly established to be supplanted."[23]

On the Northwest Coast a man adopted one of the sacred potlatch-names of his predecessor when he gave the mortuary feast and erected the grave-post. At every subsequent potlatch he was at liberty to adopt an additional title, either one used by his predecessor or a new one commemorative of an encounter with a supernatural being or of some success in war or feast-giving.[24] Among the Tsimshians each person acquired new names as his social position advanced in the course of his life; they were bestowed at a potlatch amidst much ceremony and feasting.[25] When the Kwakiutl first begin to perform the winter ceremonial, both men and women change their names. "Thus it is also with the guests of a chief who gives a feast with oil, a great oil feast. As soon as all the guests go into the house in which the oil feast is to be given, the speaker of the chief rises, and speaks, and calls the chiefs by their feast-names, those who have given an oil feast; but he does not call the names of those, even if they are head chiefs, who have not a feast-name. Then the chiefs are ashamed because their names have not been called. . . . When the feast is at an end, all the men go out, and then they have no longer their feast-names, but they are called by their potlatch-names after this, which are the true family names."[26] Names and all the privileges connected with them may be obtained by killing the owner of the name, either in war or by murder; the slayer has then the right to put his own successor in the place of his killed enemy. In this manner names and customs have often spread from tribe to tribe. Furthermore, among the Kwakiutl, if a man's credit is poor, he may pawn his name for a year, during which time he may not use it. He has to pay about twenty-five per cent for a three months' loan to redeem his name.[27] Mystic and secret names are common among the Indians of British Columbia. The young men of the Salish will not reveal their Indian names; "they seem, however, to have no such scruples about their baptismal names or those casually bestowed upon them by the whites, evidently regarding these as something quite different from their own."[28] Among the interior Salish, where there are no clans, names are usually inherited in both the male and female lines for several generations, though new names, taken from dreams or noteworthy events, are continually introduced. A father, among some of the northern Athapascan tribes, lost his name as soon as a male child was born and was henceforth called after the name of his son; in one case a man changed his name after the birth of each successive child, while an unmarried man was

22 Fletcher, in HAI, II, 309.
23 Mooney, in BAE, VII, 343.
24 Swanton, in HAI, II, 17.
25 Boas, in BAE, XXXI, 510-512.

26 Boas, in BAE, XXXV, pt. I, 786-787.
27 Boas, in USNM, 1895, 335, 341.
28 Hill-Tout, in JAI, XXXIV, 322 (quoted); in JAI, XXXV, 126.

known as the child of his favorite dog. A Mohave child born out of wedlock received some ancient name, not commonly employed in the tribe.[29] In the case of the Indians of the Oregon coast, when a child was born he was given a nickname. This he retained until puberty, when he received his regular name, which was ordinarily that of one of his ancestors on either side. He might take the name of a living man, although in that case the giver must assume another; the same name was never used by two living people.[30]

Among the Attacapa, teknonymy is common: "a man ceases to bear his own name as soon as his wife bears a child to him, after which he is called the father of such and such a child, but . . . if the child dies the father again assumes his own name."[31] The naming feast of the Winnebago tribe is described as follows: "The clan name was generally bestowed on a child at a special feast held for the purpose or at any feast that happened to be given within a reasonable time after its birth. The bestowal of the clan name was not infrequently delayed by a father's inability to gather the requisite amount of food to be presented to the old man who was to select the name. Occasionally it even happened that a father under such conditions permitted the relatives of his wife to bestow a name on a child, which of course was a name from its mother's clan. The author has personal knowledge of a case in which the first child of a man had a name belonging to his mother's clan while the other children had names belonging to their father's clan. When questioned, the man said that at the time of the birth of his eldest child he was too poor to pay for the honor of having his child receive a name and that he had allowed his wife's relatives to give it a name. When his other children were born, however, as he was in better condition financially he had been able to name them in the usual way. Although a child, irrespective of his individual name, always belonged to his father's clan, there seemed to exist a feeling that a person having a name not taken from his own clan was more or less incomplete. A person possessing no clan name was regarded as having low social standing."[32]

Among the Cree, when a child is sickly, the doctor, upon investigation, may dream that it was wrongly named and prescribe a change. "If the diagnosis was correct, the child would recover in from a day to four days, and all was well." When a child is still young it is customary for the parents to call upon four old men and ask them to give it a name. "The parents gather a quantity of clothing and other presents, and a lot of food; then four old men, whom the parents have selected because of their fame for powerful dreams and for their war exploits, are invited by a runner who bears them tobacco and a pipe. Each tries to dream from then on, and when the appointed day arrives, the four men appear at the spot designated, where the parents have prepared a feast and where other guests are assembled. When all is in readiness, a pipe is filled and given to the spokesman of the elders, who rises and addresses the people. He tells them of whom or what he has been dreaming, and gives the infant a name that has some reference to his visions or to one of his adventures in war. He then turns to his three assistants and afterward to the people in general, asking each to repeat the name aloud and to call upon the namer's dream guardian to bless the child." In former times it was taboo to ask a man directly for his name, although it is now done very freely. The only time a man ever mentioned his own name was when he had done a brave

29 Swanton, in HAI, II, 16.
30 Farrand, in AA, III, 243.
31 Hewitt, in HAI, I, 114.
32 Radin, in BAE, XXXVII, 128.

deed; on such an occasion he might repeat the story of his exploit to his friends, crying, for instance, "I am Kiwistaihau, and that is the way I am accustomed to do!"[33] In the scalp-dance of the eastern Dakota a man might throw away his name and take that of a dead warrior relative, giving presents to the poor at the same time. Children were named by their grandfathers for some deed done in war or after a famous ancestor. Guests were invited to a feast, after which the old person named the child, and a crier was sent out to announce it.[34] Sometimes the Menomini child receives its name from the parents, but if there is evidence of its being under the special protection of the powers above (a boy is under that of the "thunderers," a girl under that of the "sky-sisters"), it is considered already to have a name which has to be found out, often by the help of an old seer who understands the language of babies. "Such children lie under certain obligations towards their supernatural protectors; so, for instance, they have to play, at least once a year, a sacred game (lacrosse for the thunderers and shinney or dice game for the sky-sisters); and on the other hand, they have to be treated with special consideration lest they should get tired of their earthly existence. Besides their real name they have a so-called 'lucky name,' which is used only in the family circle, but which sometimes supplants the other."[35]

Among the Guiana Indians there would appear to be an intimate relationship between an individual and his personal name of such nature that the very mention of it in his presence would be fraught with serious consequences. "The name is deemed to be part and parcel of the individual, and the mention of it under those circumstances would put him in the power, as it were, of the person mentioning it. It is kept strictly secret and is known only to the family relatives and friends and to the piaiman. Even among family relatives, according to age and sex, one will address another as brother, sister, father, mother, son, or daughter, etc., or will speak of him or her as the father or mother, etc., of such an one. . . . One can never discover an Indian's real personal name; he never divulges it, nor is he ever called by it. He is also known by some nickname or name of distinction for his prowess in war, hunting, or fishing. Thus, the greatest demonstration of trust that an Indian can show a white man or Negro is to tell him his name."[36]

What's in a name? The name, which we are accustomed to regard as something incidental, was in the view of the ancients an essential part of living creatures and inanimate objects through which their innermost essence was characterized and revealed. According to the Oriental idea, a thing had no existence until it was named.[37] The name of the deity was fetishistic: "The name of the God of Jacob defend thee"; "The name of the Lord is a strong tower; the righteous runneth into it, and is safe."[38] The Holy Scriptures etymologize with special predilection the names of persons and places and find an inner connection between the name and the bearer thereof. The Scriptures, moreover, pay homage to the tradition, which finds expression in a legion of popular etymologies, that *nomen est omen.* "As his name is, so is he."[39] Clay[40] compiled a list of more than ten thousand proper names occurring in the cuneiform literature of Babylonia and Assyria, especially during the period

33 Skinner, in AA, XVI, 68-69.
34 Skinner, in AA, XXI, 170.
35 De Josselin de Jong, in AA, XVIII, 123.
36 Roth, in BAE, XXXVIII, 676.
37 Maspero, *Hist. Anc.,* I, 537.

38 Psalms, XX, 1; Prov., XVIII, 10.
39 Blau, *Zauberwesen,* 117; I Sam., XXV, 25 (quoted); Ruth, I, 20.
40 *Personal Names from Cuneiform Inscriptions of the Cassite Period.*

1750-1173 B.C. He made a thorough study of these names, taken chiefly from business and legal documents, and found that a name at that time, as throughout early antiquity, was much more than a convenient appellation. It belonged to an individual as a part of his equipment and in many cases was regarded as too sacred to be used on all occasions, so that in addition to his real name an individual generally had some less solemn sobriquet by which he was known, often chosen to emphasize some physical peculiarity or distinction and invariably briefer than the real name used on official occasions. In most cases it formed a complete sentence with subject, object, and verb. An invariable element in the case of a person's full designation was the name of some deity, by the introduction of which the name became a prayer, or an expression of some hope, or praise of some deity. It obviously had fetishistic quality. "There are people living now, Celts for the most part, who shrink from the personal attack of a proper name, and call their friends, in true primitive fashion, the Old One, the Kind One, the Blackest One, and the like."[41] In Brandenberg and elsewhere the name is cut out of the garment of a dying person so that he may depart this life more easily.[42]

What may be regarded as a survival of the *nomen-omen* idea is reported in the newspapers of a few years ago. One Rex Glenwood of Cincinnati rescued a man named Edward Strietback from drowning. The latter was suffused with gratitude for his rescuer and wanted to do what he could for him. Whereupon Glenwood asked that he take his name. The name, it appeared, was hoodooed; but the bad luck was attached to the name only and not the individual. So Strietback manfully lived up to his promise, changed his name to Rex Glenwood, and apparently endured several years of hardship and misfortune. Eventually the hoodoo wore itself out. The real Glenwood is now convinced that the bad luck is over, so he wants his name back; and the substitute Glenwood apparently is glad to get rid of it.[43] Mary Antin[44] cites a similar superstition among the Jews of Russia: "My mother nearly died of cholera once, but she was given a new name, a lucky one, which saved her; and that was when she was a small girl."

§§213, 214. Location of the Soul.

ONE of the many places primitive people have hit upon as the seat of the soul is the heart. When, in 1823, Sir Charles M'Carthy was captured by the Ashantis and beheaded, his heart was made a feast of by the chiefs then present at the capital.[1] They devoured the heart of the lion-hearted as they did the heart of the lion. Such beliefs about the heart are widespread and traditional. "Captain Wells fought so bravely that after his death the Indians cut out his heart and ate it, which was the greatest compliment they could pay him."[2]

The Chukchi believe the soul resides in the heart or the liver. It may be in both, for these people believe in multiple souls. Various parts of the body have souls; there is a limb-soul and a nose-soul; and when a man's nose is easily frost-bitten they say he is "short of souls."[3] The Caribs, who also believed in several souls, located one of them in the heart, another in the head,

---

41 Harrison, *Greek Relig.*, 214.
42 Heilborn, in *Globus*, LXXVIII, 385.
43 N. Y. *Times*, July 9, 1922.
44 *The Promised Land*, 175.
1 Freeman, *Visit to Ashanti, Dahomi*, etc.,

London, 1844, quoted by Dowd, *Negro Races*, I, 187-188.
2 Bowen, "When Chicago Was Very Young," in *Atl. Mo.*, CXXXVII, 196.
3 Czaplicka, *Aborig. Siberia*, 260.

and other souls at all the places where an artery is felt pulsating.⁴ Allied to
the notion of the soul in the heart is that which places it in the blood, an
idea found in a number of instances.⁵

The soul is also located in other vital organs. The South Australians "feel
from their liver, not from their heart as we do;"⁶ and the Greeks felt anger
in that organ and also identified it with personality.⁷ The Eskimo regard the
bladder as the seat of life, though it is not the sole receptacle of the spirit.
They often gave little boys the kidneys of bears to eat in order that they
may become stout and courageous bear-hunters.⁸ Certain Africans locate the
seat of feeling in the belly,⁹ as is true also of the Bina in Papua, who will express grief by saying that his belly is sore. Similarly, he will "think along
his belly."¹⁰ The Tahitians, holding similar views, use the word bowels as we
use heart.¹¹ Other Polynesians regard the belly or womb as the seat of life
and feeling, the word they use acquiring a secondary sense signifying "the interior man," "the breath," or spirit. They have a symbol consisting of abdominal protuberance, with the hands usually resting upon the abdomen; "this
represents the soul and stands for the immortality or rather the longevity of
the gods and of the early ancestors of man."¹² In the South Sea Islands thoughts
are called "words in the belly" in the translation of the natives.¹³ It is to be
noted that we still speak of "bowels of mercy," and refer to one who "has no
bowels;" indeed, the shorter and uglier term is current.

A not less important seat of life, according to Semitic ideas, lay in the
viscera, especially in the kidneys and liver, which in the Semitic dialects are continually named as the seats of emotions, or more broadly in the fat of the
omentum (intestinal membrane) and the organs that lie in or near it. "Now it
is precisely this part of the victim, the fat of the omentum with the kidneys
and the lobe of the liver, which the Hebrews were forbidden to eat, and, in
the case of sacrifice, burned on the altar. . . . From this complex of fat
parts the fat of the kidneys is particularly selected by the Arabs, and by most
savages, as the special seat of life. One says, 'I found him with his kidney fat,'
meaning I found him brisk and all alive."¹⁴ The Australians are at one with
the Semites in this belief that the soul is in the fat and soft parts of the body,¹⁵
and Smith explains that the various kinds of fat, especially human fat, are
used as charms all over the world, the reason being "that the fat, as a special
seat of life, is a vehicle of the living virtue of the being from which it is
taken." Most gods are found to rejoice in "the smell of burning grease."

The ancient Greeks made much of the diaphragm as the seat of feeling and
mentality.¹⁶ "They have shut up their midriff"¹⁷ means that they are insensible
to pity. The region of the diaphragm or midriff (pit of the stomach, solar
plexus) is a spot where a blow produces characteristic effects; it "knocks the
breath" out of the victim, or "puts him to sleep." Even among the Chinese the

4 Frazer, Golden Bough, II, 339; copious examples follow.
5 Ellis, Ewe, 79; Taylor, New Zealand, ch. XXI; Letourneau, Prop., 71; Lippert, Kgchte., I, 53-54, 481-483; Wilken, "Animisme," in VG, III, 30 ff.
6 Gason, in JAI, XVII, 186.
7 Liddell and Scott, Greek-Eng. Lexicon, under hēpar; Iliad, XXIV, 212-213.
8 Reclus, Prim. Folk, 19; Nansen, Esk. Life, 208.
9 Paulitschke, Nordost-Afr., I, 153.
10 Lyons, in JAI, LI, 431.
11 Ratzel, Vkde., II, 132.
12 March, in JAI, XXII, 308.
13 Bastian, Afr. Reisen, 36, note.
14 Smith, Relig. Sem., 379-380, 383.
15 Smyth, Vict., I, 245.
16 Keller, Hom. Soc., 129 and references; Rohde, Psyche, I, 44-45.
17 Smith, Relig. Sem., 380; Psalms, XVII, 10; LXXVII, 9.

value of different parts of the human body, as reservoirs of diverse qualities and strengths, was recognized.[18] Some American Indians located the soul in the bones, as well as in the blood, the shadow, and the nape of the neck; the words for bones and soul are sometimes found to be cognate. At times the natives paint the bones and think they may put on flesh again.[19] In some cases they burn the bones of the dead and drink the ashes, mixed with intoxicating liquors, in order "that the dead may live again in them."[20] A later section on cannibalism[21] will reveal further beliefs concerning the location of the soul.

Another common location of the soul is in the head. Among the Melanesians "it is disrespectful at all times for a young man to take anything from above an elder man's head, for there is something naturally sacred, *rongo,* about the head, and no one will take the liberty of stepping over the legs of any but a brother or intimate friend."[22] In the Indian Archipelago the seat of the soul is thought to be in the head, and when a body is buried a coconut is used instead of the head, the natives saying, "We have given you a new head," meaning "Go along now and cease complaining."[23] Among the Yakuts *kut* is a physical conception of the soul, while *sür,* although in some degree a material conception, has more of a psychical character. *Sür* is connected with the head, and has no shadow; *kut* with the abdomen, and has three shadows. The word *sür* is also used to denote unusual psychic powers, such as are possessed by shamans; and, indeed, according to the legend, shamans receive their heads (the seat of *sür*) from heaven.[24]

If the soul is not located in the head generally, it may be in some part of it. Thus, although cannibalism is not practised by the Dyaks, a man who has taken a head sometimes eats a small piece from the cheek, in the hope of acquiring the bravery and virtues of the man killed.[25] In North Queensland, the seat of intelligence and life is located in the ear, and at death they escape through this exit; "hence, by shouting into the deceased's ears his friends are trying to restore these essentials to their proper place."[26] More commonly is the soul in the eye. While some tribes in Dutch New Guinea locate it in the blood and others in the abdomen, there are some who place it in the eye; all believe that after death the soul as spirit causes all good and evil, mostly the latter.[27] The Maori also thought the soul was in the eye, especially the left eye, and cases occurred where a chief drank the blood and ate the eye of his vanquished rival "that he might incorporate the qualities wherewith the vanquished man was endowed, and by assimilating his shadow, duplicate his own soul."[28] The Arawak believe in a soul which they explain flies away at the time of death, for then they can no longer see the reflection of a person in the pupil of the eye.[29] Other cases of this sort are to be found, while the evil-eye conception is evidence of the same belief.[30]

The idea that the soul or vital power of a person is concentrated in his head, and particularly in his hair, seems to be common to all lower people in the whole world and gives the explanation not only of a number of peculiar

18 Behrens, in *Globus,* LXXXI, 96.
19 Brinton, *Myths,* 255-257; Boas, in HAI, II, 367.
20 Von Martius, *Beiträge,* 485.
21 §§290, 292, 300, of the text.
22 Codrington, *Melanesians,* 43.
23 Wilken, "Animisme," in VG, III, 63.
24 Czaplicka, *Aborig. Siberia,* 279-280.

25 Gomes, *Sea Dyaks,* 83.
26 Roth, in BAE, XXX, 156, note.
27 Krieger, *Neu-Guinea,* 401.
28 Taylor, *New Zealand,* ch. XXI; Letourneau, *Prop.,* 71.
29 De Booy, in AA, XIV, 86.
30 §265, of the text; Letourneau, *Soc.,* 197; Seligmann, *Böse Blick,* II, 440 ff.

hair-customs but first of all of the practice, existing among some savage tribes, of taking the scalps of slain enemies or preparing their heads as trophies. The use which the Jibaros, like other Indians, make of the heads of their enemies and the ceremonies which they perform with them are throughout founded upon this idea. "The power which the Jibaros attribute to the cincture made of human hair depends on the supernatural properties ascribed to the hair, which is regarded as the seat of the soul or the vital energy."[31] "Years ago, when I was living in Taveta, in British East Africa, Malikanoi, one of the two paramount chiefs of the Wataveta, wore a shock of unusually long, unkempt hair. He was supposed to be a magician, and his subjects believed that his occult powers, like those of Samson as an athlete, lay in his hair. As he dressed, besides, in nondescript old discolored European garments, his appearance could not be called either prepossessing or dignified. As the time came near when his son—a splendid lad, who, at the age of sixteen, had killed a lion single-handed with his spear—was to come of age, Malikanoi announced that, in honor of the occasion, he would shave off his hair."[32] The Baganda child's hair must not be cut until it has been named, and "should any of it be rubbed or plucked off accidentally, it is refastened to the child's head either by tying it with string or knotting it to the other hair."[33] Wilken[34] has much to say about the hair-sacrifice and other practices which point to the notion that the soul is in the hair or has some vital connection with the hair, especially that of the head. In part he thinks it is connected with the custom of cutting the body in order to let the soul loose. The Kalmuk priest before burial cuts open the skin of the corpse so as to facilitate the exit of the soul. Monier-Williams[35] reports a similar practice from India: "When the body is half-burnt the skull ought to be cracked with a blow from a piece of sacred wood. The idea is that the soul may not have been able to escape through the aperture at the top of the head, and that the cracking of the skull may open a crevice and facilitate its exit. In the case of the death of a holy man whose body is buried and not burnt, the necessary blow is given with a cocoa-nut or with a sacred conchshell. A story was told me with great seriousness of a sorcerer at Lahore who made it the business of his life to make a collection of the skulls of dead men which had not been properly cracked in this manner at death and so retained the spirits of the deceased inside. The peasantry in the neighbourhood fully believed that he was able to make use of these spirits for magical purposes, and that he could force them to execute his behests." Wilken (as above) cites parallel cases from the Indian Archipelago and elsewhere and shows that in some places the same result is thought to follow by cutting off the hair of the deceased. The sacrifice of the hair he regards as a redemption-form of human sacrifice. He cites many legends and beliefs of savages and peoples of early civilization to the effect that the hair is closely connected with life, the loss of one meaning the loss of the other, or at least the loss of strength. And Samson said, "If I be shaven, then my strength will go from me, and I shall become weak, and be like any other man."[36] In some folk-tales spirits become defenseless when seized by the hair or beard. Some

31 Karsten, "Jibaro," in BAE, Bull. LXXIX, 26 (quoted), 87; Beckwith, in *Smithson. Rep.*, 1886, pt. I, 248.

32 Coudenhove, in *Atl. Mo.*, CXXVIII, 160.

33 Roscoe, in JAI, XXXII, 30.

34 Simsonsage, in VG, III, 556-579; "Haaropfer," in VG, III, 474-475, 478-480, 481, 483-485, 486, note.

35 *Brâhmanism*, 291, 297, 299-300.

36 Judges, XVI, 17.

groups believe that if a criminal is apprehended and tortured, he can endure all pain so long as he remains in possession of his hair; if that should be cut off, with it would go his secret strength. The mythologies of classical peoples relate tales of persons who are invincible and immortal owing to their hair.

Plurality of Souls. Instances of belief in several souls have already appeared. To the Siberian cases may be added that of the Gilyak who believe that an ordinary man has one soul, a rich man two, while a shaman may have as many as four. "Besides these principal souls, every one has a lesser soul, which they imagine as being like an egg, residing in the head of the principal soul. All that a man sees in dreams is the work of this lesser soul."[37] Many Malays believe a person has seven souls.[38] Belief in the plurality of souls is common in the Indian Archipelago and is one reason for wounding or cutting the body in many places, to free the various souls from the body of the deceased.[39]

Among some Eskimo the name is considered as one of the souls of man, another soul belongs to the body, and a third one is independent of the body. The central Eskimo suppose two spirits to reside in a man's body, one of which stays with it when it dies and may temporarily enter the body of some child, who is then named after the departed, while the other goes to one of several lands of the souls.[40] The Hidatsa and the Fraser River tribes of British Columbia believe in several souls, "the loss of one of which causes partial loss of life, i.e., sickness, while the loss of all, or of the principal one, entails death."[41] The Northwest Coast Indians hold that an individual comprises a body inhabited by two souls and a ghost. "In a slight illness the outer soul becomes separated from the body, in a serious illness the inner soul wanders to the country of souls but may be recalled by the shaman."[42] The Quileutes assert that each human being, animal, and inanimate object possesses a plurality of souls which, upon the termination of the visible existence of their owners, go to the Country of the Souls. These souls or shadows look exactly like the living being and may be taken off or put on in exactly the same manner as a snake sheds its skin. "The outside shadow leaves a person, as soon as he becomes sick, the inner soul departs a day or two before his death; and the ghost leaves the body at the very moment when death sets in. Death can occur only after the departure of either the inner soul or of the ghost; the loss of the outer soul does not necessarily involve death. In other words, the Quileute Indian regards sickness as a result of the departure of a person's outside soul; while death is caused by the loss of the inner soul or of the ghost."[43] The Cree say there are two kinds of souls: one which stays behind with the corpse in the grave, and another which goes to the hereafter. "The first, when seen, resembles blue fire; it is the sort that haunts folks. The second can sometimes be heard to cry out; it whistles like a gopher (a small burrowing rodent of the prairie that has a shrill call). When the northern lights are seen the Cree think them the spirits dancing in the hereafter."[44]

All Things Have Souls (§214). Not only has man at least one soul, but animals and plants and other objects have souls as well. Taro, sweet potatoes, and ba-

37 Czaplicka, *Aborig. Siberia*, 272-273.
38 Skeat and Blagden, *Malay Penin.*, II, 195.
39 Wilken, in VG, III, 126-128.
40 Henshaw and Swanton, in HAI, I, 435;

Boas, in HAI, II, 367; Holm, *Ethnol. Skizze*, 70.
41 Boas, in HAI, II, 617.
42 Frachtenberg, in AA, XIX, 319.
43 Frachtenberg, in AA, XXII, 334-335.
44 Skinner, in AA, XVI, 76.

nanas have each a separate soul answering to the human soul, though apart from these, trees and inanimate objects are not considered to possess a life like the life of men and birds. "Should a tree fall unexpectedly near some native, it is a spirit or a sorcerer who is trying to kill him; if a canoe breaks up and a man is drowned, the cause is probably the incantation of some enemy."[45] In the Trobriand Islands all of a man's valuables, but especially his ceremonial axe-blades, are put on his body when buried. "The spirit is supposed to carry these away with him to Tuma—in their 'spiritual' aspect, of course. As the natives explain simply and exactly: 'As the man's *baloma* goes away and his body remains, so the *baloma* of the jewels and axe-blades go away to Tuma, though the objects remain.' "[46] The Tshi-speaking negro does not confine the possession of a ghost, or soul, to man, but extends it to all objects, inanimate as well as animate; and, "acting logically upon this belief, he releases these ghosts, or souls, from their material parts, for the use of ghost-men in Dead-land. At the death of the chief he buries with the corpse, weapons, utensils, food, gold-dust, and cloth, for the use of the ghost-chief; just as he cuts the throats of the chief's wives and slaves in order that their ghosts or souls may be released from their bodies, and enabled to continue their attendance upon their lord in Dead-land." Not only in Dead-land does the ghost-man live in a ghost-house and use the ghosts of such implements as have been placed at his disposal; but "Dead-land itself, its mountains, forests, and rivers are, the Tshi-speaking negro holds, the ghosts of similar natural features which formerly existed in the world. The trees, as they die in the earthly forest, go and join the ranks of the shadowy forest in Dead-land."[47]

In the view of the Koryak of Siberia "there is still a living, anthropomorphic essence concealed under the visible inanimate appearance of objects. Household utensils, implements, parts of the house, the chamber-vessel, and even excrement, have an existence of their own. All the household effects act as guardians of the family to which they belong. They may warn their masters of danger, and attack their enemies. Even such things as the voice of an animal, sounds of the drum, and human speech, have an existence independent of the objects that produce them."[48] "The Japanese firmly believe that the pearl oyster has a soul. . . . One of the largest pearl firms in Japan has constructed a miniature pagoda in the Grand Imperial Shrine of Isé, using more than 10,000 pearls. This monument to oyster souls will be dedicated this month [Sept., 1926] with a public Buddhist mass." In Kobe, in a recent campaign against hydrophobia, about 5,800 wild dogs were put to death. "After the extermination of the unclaimed and unlicensed animals a special mass was held in their honor at the temple . . . which was attended by thirty Buddhist priests and numerous other officials." The Lolos of West China believe that the growing crops and the cattle of the farm are endowed with souls. When the rice is poor in growth, the soul of the crops is entreated by a ritual, a sort of litany, to return.[49] Similarly believe the Dusuns, for a native took Evans[50] on several occasions into his rice-store, "where were hanging up the rice-souls of former crops; for, contrary to the custom of many peoples who take the rice-soul, it appears that the Dusuns do not mix it with the seed for the next sowing." The

45 Jenness and Ballentyne, *D'Entrecasteaux*, 152.
46 Malinowski, in JAI, XLVI, 359.
47 Ellis, *Ewe*, 17-18.
48 Czaplicka, *Aborig. Siberia*, 268.
49 N. Y. *Times*, Sept. 12, 1926; Nov. 7, 1926; Henry, in JAI, XXXIII, 103.
50 In JAI, XLVII, 153.

same author reports that even manufactured articles may have souls, "for a Sakai . . . told me that blow-pipes and other articles, which are placed on graves, are purposely broken. This is evidently done with the object of setting free the souls of the offerings for the use of the spirits of the dead; indeed the Sakai himself, when questioned as to the reason for this custom, replied that a blow-pipe which was intact would appear to the spirit to be broken, while if it were broken it would seem to be intact."[51] A Palaung child is taught to be polite to any pot or dish in which food is cooked or served; "if such a utensil be accidently broken, the person who has broken it, while carefully picking up the broken pieces, says: 'I am sorry that I broke thee. It was an accident; I did not intend to break thee.' The broken pieces must be carried out of the house—not thrown out or swept out—and placed gently upon the ground. The first time that a pot is used, it is polite to say to it, 'Please be a pot of gold or silver for me.' "[52] From the Malay point of view, tin-ore is endued with vitality and the power of growth. Its spirit can assume the form of a buffalo and move underground from place to place. Certain words, such as elephant, buffalo, cat, snake, tin, the use of which would offend the spirit, are tabooed. As the spirits dislike noise, all eating-vessels should be of coconut-shell or of wood. No animal must be killed in a mine. The miner must wear trousers; yet it is forbidden to wear shoes or to carry an umbrella or to wear a sarong (Malay skirt) in a mine.[53] It is also believed that trees have souls, which belief is in evidence when the native, tapping for palm-wine, tries to stimulate their sex-passion by imitative magic.[54]

The Hudson Bay Eskimo believe that everything in the world has its attendant spirit. The spirits of the lower animals are like those of men, but of an inferior order. "As these spirits of course cannot be destroyed by killing the animals, the Eskimo believe that no amount of slaughter can really decrease the numbers of the game."[55] The principal element in the Bororo religion is the same as that found among the other South American Indians—fear of evil spirits, the spirits of the dead. "Only men, horses, parrots, and dogs possess immortal souls, the other animals and plants having souls that are freed through use and afterwards become mortal."[56] That trees are animate, and have perceptions, passions, and a reasonable soul, was argued even by the early Greek philosophers on such evidence as their movements in the wind and the elasticity of their branches.[57]

§217. The Ghost-Status.

THE natives of Victoria think that the soul lingers three days around the corpse, and then goes into a beautiful country full of kangaroo and other game.[1] The Solomon Islanders invoked and sacrificed to the souls of their dead ancestors, that is, to ghosts in the sense of disembodied spirits. "The people clearly distinguish in their minds between a spirit [a being that has never been a man] and a ghost, but they have no words to express the two conceptions, their language in this respect being no better than English."[2] Among the Koita the word *sua* means ghost or shade, and when a man dies his *sua* goes to

51 In JAI, XLVIII, 181.
52 Milne, *Eastern Clan*, 51-52.
53 Skeat, in *Folk-Lore*, Sept., 1900, 305-306.
54 Wilken, "Animisme," in VG, III, 46.
55 Turner, in BAE, XI, 200.

56 Frič and Radin, in JAI, XXXVI, 391.
57 Smith, *Relig. Sem.*, 132.
1 Dawson, *Aust. Aborig.*, 51.
2 Fox and Drew, in JAI, XLV, 133-134.

Idu, where it lives for an unknown period, longer than the life of man, but at length it weakens and ceases to exist. Perhaps the period of their existence is the time during which their memory or the memory of their names is retained on earth, for some Gaile men discussing this subject suggested that when their names were lost, they also must have vanished. The habits and amusements of the *sua* on Idu are those of mankind." Among the Roro-speaking tribes the term for the spirit or ghost of a dead man is *tsirama* which is used precisely as the Koita use the term *sua*. "*Tsirama* are considered to frequent the villages of their people; if they deserted the village, the inhabitants would have no luck in anything, and it was stated that if the *tsirama* are suspected of having left a village, measures are taken to bring them back." It was principally fear of *tsirama* that prevented any native leaving the village after dark unless accompanied by a companion, even if he desired to go only a few yards. An "evil spirit like fire" was said to intercept the *tsirama* on its way to the other world, to ask if its ears and nose had been pierced during life.[3] On its journey to the land of spirits, so believe the natives of Moresby Strait, the ghost has the form, now of a fish, now of a butterfly, for it changes from one to the other as often as it grows tired. "In the daytime it resembles wood, but at night it wanders about, casting no shadow."[4] A remarkable thing happens to the spirit immediately after its exodus from the body, according to notions held in the Trobriand Islands. "Broadly speaking, it may be described as a kind of splitting up. In fact, there are two beliefs, which, being obviously incompatible, yet exist side by side. One of them is, that the *baloma* (which is the main form of the dead man's spirit) goes 'to Tuma, a small island lying some ten miles to the north-west of the Trobriands.' . . . The other belief affirms that the spirit leads a short and precarious existence after death near the village, and about the usual haunts of the dead man, such as his garden, or the sea-beach, or the waterhole. In this form, the spirit is called *kosi.*" The connection between *kosi* and the *baloma* is not very clear, and the natives do not trouble to reconcile any inconsistencies with regard to this matter. The two beliefs exist side by side in dogmatic strength; "they are known to be true, and they influence the actions of men and regulate their behaviour; thus the people are genuinely, though not very deeply, frightened of the *kosi*, and some of the actions observed in mourning, and the disposal of the dead, imply belief in the spirit's journey to Tuma, with some of its details." In the minds of these natives "there is not the slightest doubt that a *baloma* retains the semblance of the man he represents, so that if you see the *baloma,* you recognize the man that was. The *baloma* live the life of man; they get older; they eat, sleep, love, both whilst in Tuma and on visits which they pay to their villages." The only almost general tenet concerning the *baloma* and *kosi* is that the former are like reflections, the latter like shadows. "It is noteworthy that this double simile corresponds respectively to the open, defined, permanent nature of the *baloma* and to the vague, precarious, nocturnal character of the *kosi.*"[5] The interval of sojourn of the ghost, in the Gilbert Islands, is either three or nine days; the body was kept for one or the other period, being buried on the fourth or tenth day, as the case might be. "Those who kept it for the shorter period were of the opinion that, as the soul had finally been driven from its neigh-

3 Seligmann, *Melanesians,* 189-190, 309-310.   5 Malinowski, in JAI, XLVI, 354-355, 368.
4 Jenness and Ballentyne, *D'Entrecasteaux,*
145-146 (quoted), 148, 149.

bourhood on the third repetition of the *bo-maki* ceremony, it might safely be laid to rest on the fourth day. But many families . . . believed that the soul might reinhabit the body at any time during the nine days after death."[6]

In several places on the west coast of Africa the soul of the dead is believed to require nine days to come to the place of rest.[7] What becomes of the soul at the moment of death? This question was answered by a Fan priest as follows: "I believe the soul continues to reside, alive, in the corpse, with the possibility of disengaging itself from it, not freely and in the open, but associated with something indeterminate, impalpable, a sort of phantom or specter, which has the exact appearance of the deceased body but none of its reality. It is in this death-form, which is in short the body incorporeal, that the soul will live henceforth in the region of the dead. For us Blacks, the soul is an essence distinct from the body and endowed with a more subtle nature but unable to subsist alone, independently of any phantom. This phantom does not always have the exact form of a human body: those unfortunates whose flesh has served for cannibal feasts (and they are numerous) will have the appearance of desiccated skeletons; those whose bodies have been reduced to ashes will forever have the form of a little smoke mingled with some ashes."[8] How such African beliefs lead to eidolism is explained by Frobenius[9] who says, "The questions in which the negroes are especially interested all culminate in inquiry concerning the influence and activity of the dead, whose intervention in daily life they observe in every unusual occurrence and in all striking peculiarities." The Baganda believe that every one has a soul which at death leaves the body and is then called the *muzimu*, ghost. "In this state it continues to exist and is capable of doing good or harm to the living; it is supposed to be capable of suffering cold, hunger, and pain." When the ghost leaves a man it goes to the place of the departed, to give an account to the deity of death; it then takes up its abode in the hut built by the relatives for its reception, either near the grave in the family burial-ground or near the enclosure of the relatives. "The ghost cannot be seen—it is like the wind; in fact, the gentle rustling of the plantain leaves is said to be caused by the ghosts, and a whirlwind which carries up dust, leaves, and straws is said to be the ghosts at play, so that whilst the ghost is invisible, the effect and influence of its presence are seen upon human beings and vegetable life. Ghosts can be captured and put to death either by fire or drowning."[10]

The Samoyeds of Siberia have a custom which requires the wife of a dead man to make a figure which represents her husband, from portions of the boat, skis, and branches. "This figure, which is dressed and adorned like the deceased, and whose features even are sometimes made by a careful widow to resemble him, is treated as the husband for six months after the death; it is placed in the most important seat, is fed by and sleeps beside the wife." The Buryats believe that the soul of a dead man acquires new qualities: "It is visible to the living, but leaves no tracks on the ashes of the hearth and passes noiselessly over dead leaves; it can be killed, and it then takes the form of a pelvis, but it has the power to become a soul again after three days unless prevented by a slight burning of the pelvis."[11] Another tribe celebrates a memorial for the

---

6 Grimble, in *JAI*, LI, 45.
7 Ratzel, *Vkde.*, I, 175, 610.
8 Trilles, *Fân*, 367.

9 *Masken*, 161.
10 Roscoe, in *JAI*, XXXII, 73.
11 Czaplicka, *Aborig. Siberia*, 163-165, 159.

dead on the fortieth day after the funeral.[12] Among the Palaungs one soul alone can hardly make any sound, "but when a number meet together, as when there is an epidemic, and many people die at the same time, their ghosts meeting together and talking make a faint humming sound high up in the air."[13]

The Eskimo believe that the souls of the deceased stay with the body three days.[14] The ghost of a person, the Quileute Indians affirm, is a trifle longer than the rest of the body, extending somewhat beyond the toes and above the head; it "leaves the body simultaneously with the setting in of death and goes directly to the underworld where it joins the two souls. . . . The ghosts sometimes come up from the underworld causing sickness among the living relatives so that these may die and join them. Occasionally they merely visit their former habitations. On all of these trips they are usually accompanied by the two souls. Ghosts travel at night only and may be heard whistling, which is their form of singing. For that reason the Quileute are forbidden to whistle at night, because it is feared this might attract a ghost to a whistling person. Ghosts never like to come up close to the village, for the smell of living beings is repugnant to them. . . . The ghost has the form of a human being and is provided with hands, feet, eyes, nose, etc. His body is covered all over with moss, including the face, mouth, hair, and hands. His nose is long and hangs down as far as the chin; his eyes are large, round, and of a yellow color; he walks crooked, crossing and recrossing his legs at each step and can run very fast. He eats and drinks just like a human being. One of my informants claims to have seen a ghost during a trip to the underworld. He could not come close to him, however, for the ghost disappeared as soon as he became aware of the intruder."[15] Ghosts are greatly feared by the Cheyenne Indians. "As a rule these do not seem to work much actual harm, but they come about and whistle and frighten people. . . . People who are walking through the timber at night are likely to sing loudly, or to utter loud calls, to frighten away the ghosts; and generally when the ghosts show that they are near at hand, anyone who possesses spiritual power will sing a medicine song to drive them away. . . . The ghost of a person is called *si'yŭhk*, which appears to mean rather the skeleton of a person. A pile of human bones would be called siyuhk. Some people declare that it is the siyuhk that taps on the lodge-skins, whistles down the smoke-hole, and makes queer noises near the lodge."[16] Among the Omahas too, "the restless ghosts were supposed to whistle and for this reason children were easily frightened by whistling."[17] Among the Araucanians the *Am* or ghosts of the dead, who appeared to the living, were distinguished from the *Pilli*, the souls of the living. "They also believe that their chiefs returned to visit the haunts of their relatives in the form of humble-bees. All their trials and adversities, even the most trivial, were set down to the malignity of evil spirits."[18]

Among the ancient Egyptians the *ka* of the dead, his double or second self, a kind of ethereal body which nevertheless needs food and drink in order to live, lingers in the grave or dwells with Osiris in the fields, where it must work hard; or it travels through the regions of the dead in struggle with monsters and demons, conquering through the magic power of the word, then to emerge

---

12 *Russian Ethnog.* (Russ.), II, 126.
13 Milne, *Eastern Clan*, 341.
14 Boas, in PSM, LVII, 629.
15 Frachtenberg, in AA, XXII, 336-337.

16 Grinnell, *Cheyenne*, II, 99-100.
17 Fletcher and LaFlesche, in BAE, XXVII, 590.
18 Latcham, in JAI, XXXIX, 348.

with the sun as a celestial being; or it goes about as a phantom, or becomes a soul represented as a bird with human head, at the death of which it passes away to become united with the body. All these contradictory views were firmly held side by side.[19] In old Roman religion all notions of death and lower world unite in the vague idea of *di manes* or, as they are euphemistically called, good gods, which does not mean definite divine persons but *di inferi*, the mass of divinities which work in the realms of the dead, indeterminate in number and character. They appear whenever death festivals occur and the infernals are invoked. The *lemures* in historical times were *larvæ*, nightly wandering souls of dead relatives. To keep them from the house, at the Lemuria, in May, the house-father nine times scatters beans as a sacrifice to them. The notion of *di manes* as the souls of the dead raised to be gods and as confined to particular families and persons is foreign to old Roman religion; it begins in imperial times and finds expression in grave-inscriptions.[20]

§218. Mortuary Practices.

THE possessions of the deceased, among some Australians, are placed on the grave, while the arrangement of the grave may indicate something concerning the deceased; water-vessels on it may denote that a woman is there buried and the perforations of the vessels that she has been speared.[1] Among the Tasmanians "during the whole of the first night after the death of one of their tribe they will sit round the body, using rapidly a low, continuous wail or recitation to prevent the evil spirit from taking it away."[2] In the treatment of corpses in the Pacific Islands, the prevailing idea is that of consecrating the corpse, which is taboo, by means of the nearness of the soul. "The desired union with the soul, which had been accepted amongst the gods, was found most easily in the neighborhood of the corpse."[3] In one part of British New Guinea "the corpse was formerly placed on a platform over a smoking fire, incisions were made to aid the escape of fluid, which, as it fell, was, in some cases, rubbed into the bodies of the mourners. Later the smoke-dried corpse was wrapped in bark-cloth and kept on a platform until certain rites were performed, when it was buried in the village within a small fenced enclosure under a roof of palm leaves;" in another section, "the body was allowed to dry in the sun and mourners stood beneath and anointed themselves with the fat which dropped from it. The skulls were afterwards kept in the houses, and on feasting occasions, painted and decorated as in life, were held by dancers during the ceremonies."[4] Both practices indicate that the soul is in close connection with the corpse.

In West Africa, burial-customs have undergone considerable change in recent years; in former times it was the practice to sacrifice one or more slaves at the funeral-ceremonies of a man who had attained a certain status. The rites of burial vary according to the age, sex, and importance of the deceased; more sacrifices are necessary for a man who is married and has children than for a young man who has not taken a wife. A woman who dies in pregnancy is not buried in the ordinary way; at Nibo, after a post-mortem Cæsarian operation has been performed, the woman is buried but not the child.

19 Tiele, *Relig. im Altertum*, I, 44.
20 Wissowa, *Relig. Römer*, 189, 192.
1 Klaatsch, *Trop. Aust.*, 586, 587.

2 Barnard, in AAAS, 1890, 606.
3 Ratzel, *Vkde.*, II, 334.
4 Chinnery, in JAI, XLIX, 282.

There are also certain diseases which render patients incapable of being buried in the ordinary way, for there is an idea that the disembodied spirit partakes of the nature of the body. "A man suffering from elephantiasis is not allowed to die in the house, but is removed to the farm, and sometimes simply exposed after death; in some cases a surgical operation is performed after death to remove the enlarged part, and then he may be brought home and buried in the ordinary way. Smallpox, dropsy, syphilis, leprosy, and a sort of cholera known as itolo, disqualify the sufferers from dying in the house and being buried in the ordinary way; at most they will be covered with leaves in a shallow grave. Second burial may, however, in many cases, be performed."[5] Burial is not the common manner of disposing of corpses in East Africa. Important elders and their senior wives, and also medicine-men, are buried; corpses of other persons are thrown out into the bush.[6] When a man or woman is mortally sick among the Suk of Kenya, the relatives collect a number of elders to perform what is to all intents a litany. An elder stands up while all the others cower; he declaims ahead of the congregation, "He will not die," "He shall live," "He will eat to-day." In case of death, adults are buried; the bodies of small children are thrown into the bush, while the father shaves the forelock and the mother the sides of the head.[7]

The tribes of the Altai Mountains, Central Asia, think that the soul cannot at once understand that it has left the body, and learns this only after three days, when it observes that its feet no longer leave impressions in the ashes. The Buryats have a similar notion.[8] De Groot[9] cites illustrations from Chinese literature of the belief that the grave is inhabited by the soul of the dead man who lies therein. Among the Nagas, "when the corpse has been placed in the burying ground it is the duty of the eldest brother or the nearest relative to remain near by and repeatedly shout the name of the deceased; when he is exhausted, the next nearest relative takes up the task."[10] The Kubus of Sumatra believe that the souls of their relatives hover as ghosts about the place where their bones rest.[11]

When a Winnebago dies, some person is invited to talk to him before he is buried. The person addressing the dead man or woman tells the deceased how to go to the spirit-land and what to do on the way there. For four nights a burning ember is placed on the grave, which "is supposed to be taken by the spirit of the dead man on his journey."[12] The custom of lighting fires on the grave for four nights after burial was common to most Algonquian tribes; the reason for the practice elsewhere is described as follows: "A fire is kept burning for four days, during which time the spirit is on its journey eastward to the land of the dead up above where the Sun is. There are four souls, but only one passes on to the future life, having as a finale to pass an obstacle at the entrance to the sky. If this point is passed in safety the journey is over, otherwise it returns to earth a menace to the happiness of the living."[13] Burial was a common practice among the Indians and objects of value were often strewn over the grave; it was a general belief among some tribes that the spirit often returns to visit the grave, so long as the body is not reduced to dust.[14]

5 Thomas, in JAI, XLVII, 181.
6 Hobley, in JAI, XLI, 147-418; Dundas, C., in JAI, XLV, 241, note.
7 Barton, in JAI, LI, 98-99.
8 Michailovski, *Shamanism*, 13.
9 *Relig. Sys. China*, II, 381.

10 Furness, in JAI, XXXII, 462.
11 Anon., in *Globus*, XXVI, 46.
12 Radin, in BAE, XXXVII, 140, 142.
13 Mooney and Thomas, in HAI, I, 42; Speck, in HAI, II, 1006.
14 HAI, I, 279; II, 31, 674.

Among the Zuñi and other tribes, "while a person is dying food is cast for him on the fire and food is put into his mouth—because it is the last meal.' The corpse is straightway placed with the head to the east," the idea being that thus the deceased faces the spirit-world, the journey to which takes four days. "Zuñi will not go to sleep, we may note, thus orientated. A child falling asleep careless of this rule will be asked 'Why do you wish to sleep like a dead person?' " The dead are fed elaborately on All Souls' Day, but it is a daily practice to drop or crumble a bit of bread at each meal or to put it on the fire.[15] In Cayenne, on a death, "the men, women, friends, and children assemble and weep, or rather sing; the singing is done mostly by the nearest female relatives who, sitting on their heels, slowly pass both hands over the corpse from head to foot, while reproaching him for having let himself die. 'Is it because you were not happy with us?' say some. 'What have we done for you to leave us like this?' say others. They add: 'You were such a good hunter, too! You caught fish and crabs so well! You knew how to make a proper provision-field.' "[16] The Jíbaro believe that the soul of an Indian killed with the lance flees in terror far away from the mutilated body and for some time does not remain in the neighborhood, as is believed to be the case at ordinary death.[17]

It was held by the ancient Greeks that the disembodied spirit still clung to the body which it formerly inhabited, and on the third and ninth day after the funeral they placed a meal on the grave.[18] Among the Bulgarians messages and requests are given to a corpse for the dead whom he will meet in the Beyond. The deceased is addressed as if he were alive.[19] Among the Montenegrins an elder calls aloud on the deceased by name; he hails him loudly and pauses for a reply. "Then, after a long silence, the whole lot shout together, 'Goodbye, brother,' and turn away from the grave."[20]

§219. Disposition of the Ghost.

DAWSON[1] holds that "before the minds of the aborigines were poisoned by the superstitions of the white people, they had not the slightest dread of the dead body of a friend, nor had they any repugnance to remain beside it." If this is true, it is highly exceptional. Curr[2] states that a man's ghost is accredited with all sorts of powers which the person himself did not possess whilst alive, but only the ghosts of men lately dead are feared. In the Solomons, "men who fall from trees and women who die in childbirth are 'evil spirits.' Their names may not be mentioned and if we came to one in the pedigrees he or she is described as 'an evil spirit.' " The former type cause the living to fall from trees when they are gathering nuts; the latter cause other women to die in the same way.[3] The rôle of the Trobriand ghosts is said to be purely passive, these people lacking a determinate ghost-cult; but out of this passivity they can be roused by being put into bad humor, "when they begin to show their existence in a negative manner, so to speak."[4] The Koita hold that the *sua* or ghosts of recently dead folk would punish any neglect or infringement of their funeral rites; that they especially frequent the neighborhood of their homes is the

15 Parsons, in AA, XVIII, 251-252; and in AA, XX, 180-181.
16 Roth, in BAE, XXX, 156.
17 Karsten, "Jibaro," in BAE, Bull. LXXIX, 28.
18 Rohde, *Psyche*, I, 227, 232, 233.

19 Strauss, *Bulgaren*, 427.
20 Durham, in JAI, XXXIX, 94.
1 *Aust. Aborig.*, 64.
2 *Aust. Race*, I, 44.
3 Hocart, in JAI, LII, 261.
4 Malinowski, in JAI, XLVI, 402.

chief reason for the ceremonial desertion of houses in which a death had occurred. "A dead man's *sua,* it was admitted, would not hurt a relative unless
something was done to annoy it, but even a son who did not show proper zeal
for his father's funeral rites would be punished, while any infringement of
tribal custom might determine the *sua* to smite the offender with sickness, or
bring bad luck in hunting or fishing. . . . Certain *sua* are, however, quite
harmless and no notice is taken of them. They appear to be the *sua* of the forgotten dead who are thought to haunt the bush, and cause only the slightest
annoyance to the living. . . . They are absolutely harmless, nevertheless the
living feel afraid when they see them."[5]

The South Africans believe that ghosts cause unaccountable illness and
especially mental troubles; they seem unable to do good.[6] One of Livingstone's
men "on experiencing a headache, said, with a sad and thoughtful countenance,
'My father is scolding me because I do not give him any of the food I eat.' "[7]
The spirits of the dead are adjured at a Madagascar burial: "This is what
you get, but you must not follow after his progeny, his grandchildren, his
brothers; this is the one you have got."[8] In West Africa, while the ghosts may
be well disposed, yet their touch is dangerous; "if the children are ill, the
illness is ascribed to the spirit of the deceased mother having embraced them."
Such "touching," it is explained, "comes not from malevolence, but from
loneliness and the desire to have their company." It is customary for the living
to send the dead out ahead of an army, to bear the brunt in the first attack.[9]
Ghosts of Togo murderers, poisoners, and sorcerers, having had no death-
feast, wander as malignant spirits,[10] while on the Loango Coast if the soul is
cheated of any of the cloth used to wrap up the corpse, it will return out of
the grave and do mischief.[11] If a Bakoko had many enemies during his life, who
did him much harm, after death he would change himself into a specter and
take revenge on them, cudgeling and tormenting them and playing all sorts
of mean tricks.[12]

In East Africa "the spirits are mostly malignant, and either out of revenge
or cupidity they plague people, particularly those of their own family. They
constantly require appeasing, and they also require attention in order that
their wrath should not be incurred. Attending to all these demands of theirs
is the religious cult of the Mkamba and his religion is thus a spirit religion."[13]
Among the Baganda, "the ghost of a father or grandfather is a guardian
spirit, and the ghost of an aunt generally an evilly disposed one; the ghost
of an aunt frequently kills children and brings various sicknesses upon wives.
When an evil ghost takes possession of a person, which sometimes happens, it
causes abdominal pains and swellings; to drive it out herbs are burned by
the medicine man and the patient inhales .the smoke, which is offensive to the
ghost, and causes it to release its victim."[14] The Nigerians think the spirits are
always hungry and thirsty, and unless looked after will soon punish their
relatives left alive on earth. It is lucky when the ghost is born again in the
body of some descendant, as observed through the likeness of a child to his
parents or grandparents, "for the ghost has returned, and has no longer any

5 Seligmann, *Melanesians,* 192-193.
6 Fritsch, *Eingeb. S.-Afr.,* 197.
7 Livingstone, *Mission. Travels.* 357.
8 Sibree, *Great Afr. Island,* 237.
9 Kingsley, *W. Afr. Studies,* 133, 134.

10 Seidel, in *Globus,* LXXII, 23.
11 Bastian, *Deut. Exped.,* I, 165.
12 Schkopp, in *Globus,* LXXXIII, 332.
13 Dundas, C., in JAI, XLIII, 537.
14 Roscoe, in JAI, XXXII, 73-74.

power to frighten the relatives until the new body dies, and it is free again."15 The Niam-Niam "spoke with high respect of their dead fathers, but this came in part from an indefinite fear of harm that the dissatisfied or angry ghost could do them."16 The son "cannot cut his nails or his hair without his father's eye being upon him, and if he should fail to bury such clippings, he may expect to be reminded of it in a most unpleasant manner.17

According to some Siberian traditions, *ada* are souls of wicked persons or of women who have died childless. "No sacrifices are made to them and they are represented as one-eyed, evil, malicious spirits, who always remain in the same *ulus* or house. . . . They are afraid of being seen, of angry men, of fire, of metals, of weapons, and of the smell of heath. Though easily frightened, they are not easily banished from a house, and they are especially harmful to young children under the age of seven." Some souls never leave the earth and are never quiet; such souls among the Yakuts are called *yor*. "The souls of those who have died young or suffered death by violence, or who were buried without ceremonies, as well as of the shamans and great people, become *yor*."18 The ghost of a Chinese alderman, in jealousy of his successor, might give him the disease of which he himself had died.19 Awe for the dead, who though dead are regarded as still present, is given as the origin of the religious ideas of the Saoras of Madras. The Saoras know a ghost has returned by its cry; there is here a striking resemblance to the Irish belief in the wail of the banshee. The Khonds attribute fevers to the ghostly visits. Ghosts are feared and propitiated by sacrifice, but never worshipped.20 Among the Nayars a *Prētam* is the spirit of a dead man. "The ghosts of men who died in the ordinary course of events are not really *Prētams,* because they do not wander about to overpower people and drink their blood. It is generally the ghosts of men who died as a result of foul play, or by accidents such as drowning, or by terrible diseases such as smallpox and cholera that wander about at nights. . . . The *Prētam* is supposed to hover round its burial place or the place of its accident. Everyone is warned off such a place at night time. The hours during which these *Prētams* appear are between 9 in the evening and 3 in the morning. It must be noticed here that the *Prētam* of a 'black-magician,' as distinct from a social magician . . . has more power to do mischief: it has more *orenda,* so to say. The man who practises black magic invariably dies a violent death, and his *Prētam* hovers round the scene of his former activities. . . . Only epidemics are put down to the wrath of offended gods. Other diseases as well as misfortunes are put down to the influence of *Prētams,* bribed into action by jealous or covetous relatives."21 The Palaungs think that the spirits of many people, especially if their death has been a violent one, do not go along the road of the dead, to eat of the fruit of forgetfulness. Such spirits are never called *kar-bu;* they become *kar-nam*—good or bad spirits inhabiting trees, water, air, earth, or stones, and able to leave their habitation at will. "A *kar-nam,* however, that has once been the *kar-bu* of a human being is much feared, especially if it has been the *kar-bu* of a bad man. Such a *kar-nam* is even more dangerous to a human being than is a bad man, because, being invisible, it can attack the unwary in unexpected ways." As illustrating the mode of at-

15 Tremearne, in JAI, XLII, 159.
16 Junker, *Afrika,* III, 292.
17 Macdonald, in JAI, XXII, 116.
18 Czaplicka, *Aborig. Siberia,* 161, 288.

19 Smith, *Chinese Char.,* 256.
20 Fawcett, in JASB, I, 245, 256; and in JASB, II, 249.
21 Panikkar, in JAI, XLVIII, 279-280.

tack, a native one evening was passing a place when he felt something spring on his back. "He felt it and yet he did not feel it. It threw its arms round his neck, holding him tightly, almost choking him, and yet when he put up his hands to loosen its arms he could get hold of nothing. Its legs seemed to hang loosely, swinging against his body, as he ran, and yet there was nothing that he could take hold of." Anyone dying a violent or a mysterious death is believed to become, for a time, a powerful spirit, remaining near the body in the grave. "If under or in a house any one is killed or suddenly drops down dead, the house is sometimes deserted and the dead person is buried under it. It is feared that the spirit of such a dead person may become an evil and malignant ghost haunting the house." When a woman dies with her child unborn, she is rolled in a mat and buried as quickly as possible. "It would be in a lonely place, far from the graves of others, for it is believed that people who have died a violent death, or on whom great misfortunes have fallen, must have committed some terrible crime in their last existence to come to such a horrible end."[22]

The Veddah, being quite callous about his dead, "even when closely related, the survivor would composedly re-open the grave, inspect the body or skeleton, when exposed, and not only carry the remains for several miles, but sleep with them suspended out of the way of jackals or iguanas immediately over him."[23] This, like the Australian case with which we began this set of illustrations, does not necessarily mean that there is no ghost-fear. The Land Dyaks have "very little respect for the bodies of the departed, though they have an intense fear of their ghosts."[24] A cutaneous tumor to which the Borneans are subject is called the "ghost's-clutch."[25] "Captain Cook was taken by the Hawaiians to be the embodiment of their old king Lono and was received with joy, but was later murdered when they thought they must conclude from his behavior that he intended to take vengeance for injuries he had suffered in his former life."[26] Among the Maori "the souls of children still-born were supposed to be of a particularly malevolent character, and, in revenge for loss of life on earth, they remained there and became plagues of blight, pains, accidents, misery, disease, and death."[27] Every death that takes place within the family of the slayer, among the Jibaros, in the period following the killing of an enemy, is set down to the secret operation of the revengeful spirit.[28]

The ancient Israelites reckoned ghosts as among evil influences.[29] The Egyptian ghost came forth at night to seek food: garbage, offal, and other offensive things. It was not shadowy, but had a firm body and emitted a pale light. It used all means to compel its surviving relatives to care for it, penetrating their houses and bodies, terrifying them by appearing when they were sleeping or waking at night, striking them with maladies or madness, or sucking their blood. The way to satisfy the ghost was to bring to the tomb sufficient offerings.[30] The Greek Erinyes were primarily human ghosts, "but all human ghosts are not Erinyes, only those ghosts that are angry, and that for a special reason, usually because they have been murdered." They are the outraged

22 Milne, *Eastern Clan*, 219, 183-184 (quoted), 265, 342-343 (quoted), 357-358 (quoted).

23 Stevens, in JASB, I, 138; Sarasin, *Weddas*, 494.

24 Roth, *Sarawak*, I, 137; Perelaer, *Dajaks*, 221.

25 Furness, *Head-Hunters*, 54.

26 Bastian, *Afr. Reisen*, 105.

27 White, in AAAS, 1891, 362.

28 Karsten, "Jibaro," in BAE, Bull. LXXIX, 41, note.

29 Duhm, *Geister*, 21.

30 Maspero, *Hist. Anc.*, I, 113.

souls of dead men crying for vengeance.[31] "Souls of those that had not received burial and funeral-rites or who were torn out of life untimely found no rest after death; such souls swept about in the wind with Hecate and her demonic hounds."[32] The malevolent ghost of the woman who has died in childbirth, will be noted, as a special case, in another connection.[33]

§220. Life in the Other World.

THE funeral rites of Oceania, though numerous and diversified, can be carried back to a few main principles which allow of inference as to the nature of the other world. First, it is a widespread feature of these rites that the bodies of the dead are placed in canoes or in representations of canoes. The canoe forms a feature of the ritual, both when the body is interred and when it is preserved on platforms or in the house. There can be no doubt, comments Rivers,[1] that the function of the canoe is to convey the dead to their future home, either on the earth or to some place from which there is access to the underworld. Another funeral-practice of Oceania may also be connected with the belief in a spirit-world accessible by crossing the sea, namely, the custom of throwing the dead into the sea. Rivers believes that both practices are to be explained on the basis of migration—that immigrants into Oceania believe in a return after death to the country from which they had come.

According to native beliefs in the Trobriand Islands the spirit leaves the body immediately after death has occurred and goes to Tuma, the land of the dead. "The route taken and the mode of transit are essentially the same as those which a living person would take in order to go from his village to Tuma. Tuma is an island; one must therefore sail in a canoe." The spirit leads a positive, well-defined existence in Tuma; it returns from time to time to the village; it has been visited and seen in Tuma by men awake and men asleep, and by those who were almost dead yet returned to life again; it plays a notable part in native magic and receives offerings; and finally, it asserts its reality in the most radical manner by returning to the place of life, by reincarnation, and thus leads a continuous existence. The after life is very real.[2] To get to the spirit-land souls must cross from the west end of Florida Island in a canoe. As they land, they realize for the first time that they are dead.[3] The natives of New Hebrides supposed that the spirit at death left the body, went to the west end of the island, plunged into the sea, and swam away to a place of spirits, where, it was said, there were two divisions, one for the good and another for the bad. Plenty of good food in the next life constituted the reward of the good, and the contrary the punishment for the thief, the liar, or the murderer. In accordance with their belief the natives cast their dead into the sea.[4] The Efatese think heaven is very near the earth; one may climb up to it. The aged are here buried alive, with accompanying sacrifice of pigs which are supposed to go with the deceased to the world of spirits; "the greater the chief the more numerous the pigs, and the more numerous the pigs the better the reception in their hades of heathenism."[5]

31 Harrison, *Greek Relig.*, 214-215.
32 Rohde, *Psyche*, II, 83.
33 §408, of the text.
1 *Melan. Soc.*, II, 269-271.
2 Malinowski, in JAI, XLVI, 357-358.

3 Codrington, in JAI, X, 304.
4 Turner, *Samoa*, 326.
5 Macdonald, in AAAS, 1898, 767; Turner, *Samoa*, 335-336.

The nature of the way to the spirit-world, as conceived by some natives of New Guinea, is as follows. The spirits of the dead descend into a huge cave on a rocky cape, at the bottom of which is the passage from the earth to the world beyond. At the bottom of the cave there lies a great serpent, its slimy body stretching away beneath the sea and its head resting on the shore. As the way is long and perilous, ample preparations must be made by the friends of the deceased. If their grief is great, and the food they bring to the feast is plentiful, the spirit will walk with ease along the slimy back of the great serpent; if they neglect their friend, he will be weak and his feet will slip. Should he fall into the sea he will be transformed into a fish. If the passage is successfully made, the spirit will be received by Sauga, who will light a fire under a frame of split cane and place him upon it. As the heat of the fire rises, the body will gradually come to life again, and his friends who are there will identify him and make a great feast in honor of his safe arrival.[6] In the Laughlan Islands, too, the spirit has to cross a big snake on the way to the realm of the dead, with the constant danger of falling into the sea.[7]

Life in the other world, among all the Melanesians, is a replica of life in this, with some idealization. In the Hades of the Southern Massim there is plenty to eat and no sickness or evil assails the spirits. The wealthy here are wealthy there. "Each community has its own place. The spirits can go out fighting as they did here, and it seemed that anyone then killed was destroyed for ever, indeed all could die again and that would be the end. They would know their own friends and, on the whole, life in the other world is a repetition of life here."[8] The Bina conception of heaven is that it is a land similar to this earth, though much fairer, where the spirits lead the same sort of life and eat the same food as they do in the land of the living.[9] The spirit-world is a reality to the natives of the Papuan Gulf; "each tribe has its own locality for it—it may be away in the west, toward the region of the setting sun, or it may be far back in the mountains of the Gulf Hinterland—but however uncertain they may be as to the precise locality of the abode of the spirits of their deceased relatives, of this one thing they are confident, that the latter still exist and can visit the living who are still in the flesh."[10]

Some distinction may be made in the land of spirits between the "good" and the "bad." There may be a record of what the soul has done and what it has left undone. When it appears in the next world the spirit may make its character known: "I am pure! I am pure!"[11] According to certain Papuans, "the reception of the spirit depends upon the condition of the life spent. The spirits of the rich, the brave, the well-formed, the healthy and wholesome, are welcomed with dancing, and led over the bridge across the chasm into everlasting life with the blest. The spirits of the poor, the emaciated through long sickness, of those who have suffered from scrofulous sores, are led by the dancers on to the bridge, which then turns into a snake, and by its wriggling precipitates the so-called bad spirits into a deep gulch, where they remain for ever and ever. The question of character or conduct does not determine the abode of the spirits, only that sorcerers who have so much power over life and death on the earth are requested to live in a special community of their own."[12] The Solomon

6 Abel, *New Guinea*, 97-98.
7 Thilenius, in *Globus*, LXXXI, 47.
8 Seligmann, *Melanesians*, 657; Rivers, *Melan. Soc.*, I, 321.

9 Lyons, in JAI, LI, 431.
10 Holmes, in JAI, XXXII, 428.
11 Tylor, *Anth.*, 102 ff.
12 Bromilow, in AAAS, 1911, 415-416.

Islanders nearly all believe that when a man or woman dies he goes to live with a good spirit in a far-off but pleasant land, where his companions will be as good as he is, or nearly so. The bad man, so judged by his companions, goes to a place of fire, the abode of the Evil One, where he has anything but a happy time. "During his existence there he does his best to make things unpleasant for the friends he has left behind him, by becoming one of the many evil spirits who are supposed to do harm to the living."[13] At Eddystone, the abode of the ghosts is a big cave, where they sleep in the daytime and go about at night; for day is like night to the ghosts. Sometimes the spirit of a father or mother turns into a butterfly and comes to settle upon the head of his child. "Oh! a spirit is on your head," the people say.[14] The spirits do not dwell in the next world for ever; eternity is a concept beyond the grasp of natives who often have no numeral beyond three.[15]

Among the Ewe-speaking peoples of West Africa, every man is believed to occupy the same position and to have the same powers, avocations, and tastes in Dead-land that he had in this world. So real is the other world that ambassadors were sent by the king of Dahomi to spirits there; one case is mentioned where a native was taken out to sea in a canoe and then thrown overboard, so as "to join the two porters of the sea-gate, to open it for his [the king's] father to enter in and wash himself."[16] Belief in the existence of another world also explains the readiness with which the negroes will commit suicide.[17] Among the Nigerian head-hunters, if it be time for the sick person to die, the soul crosses the bridge to the spirit-land, and then can never return to that particular body, which must die. "The *mobwoi* lead lives of ordinary men. Spirits of enemies will continue fighting until stopped by the Supreme God. The ghosts ride, eat, and hunt as in life, and are always ready for beer."[18] In East Africa the spirits are supposed to live as they did on earth, with cattle as their riches; some are rich, others poor.[19] The natives of British Central Africa do not conceive of an underworld, though a "bad man" is thought not to go to quite the same place as others; there is no idea of punishment or hell-fire, however. "The spirits in the spirit world are supposed to sit about doing nothing; they talk and see everything going on on the earth below. . . . They do not appear to speculate about going to the spirit world, and as they do not think of any retribution to be dealt out it makes no difference to their conduct on this earth."[20] More definite are the notions of the Bagobo, who hold that each individual has two souls, the one of the left side which is evil and which becomes a *buso* or demon, and the one of the right side which goes to the one Great Country beneath the earth where it lives forever. "At the entrance to the Great Country is the Black River in which the spirit bathes his joints and thus becomes naturalized to the world of spirits. In his eternal home he continues his life as on earth during the hours of darkness, but at the rising of the sun all is changed. Each spirit plucks a broad leaf, twists it into a vessel and seats himself on it, and there sits, waiting, until the hot rays of the sun cause him to dissolve, leaving the vessel full of water. When night returns, he resumes his personality and takes up his work or dance as if no break had occurred."[21]

---

13 Hardy and Elkington, *S. Seas*, 125.
14 Hocart, in JAI, LII, 95.
15 Hocart, in JAI, XLII, 448-449, note;
Strong, in JAI, XLIX, 306.
16 Ellis, *Ewe*, 64-65, 107.

17 Anon., in *Globus*, XCI, 163.
18 Tremearne, in JAI, XLII, 158-159.
19 Dundas, C., in JAI, XLIII, 535.
20 Stannus, in JAI, XL, 300.
21 Cole, in AA, XX, 217-219.

The Gilyak, like the Ainu, believe that the next world is a counterpart of the physical world; there the dead live in the same way as they did on earth—fishing, hunting, marrying, and having children—except that the poor man becomes rich there and the rich man poor. They have sickness and death, after which the soul goes to the third world. There is no real belief in immortality among the tribes of Siberia. Among the Samoyed, the dead, with whom many of his belongings are buried, is supposed still to exist for a short while, and during that time food is brought to the grave and the sacrifice of reindeer is repeated several times, but when the body has once turned to dust there is nothing beyond. Only the shaman attains to the privilege of a future life. The shadow has a difficult journey to make, climbing high mountains and crossing streams of fire. "To assist it in this, one must burn the portions of hair and nails which were cut and preserved during his lifetime, together with a few feathers of spring birds. The implements placed in the grave, and the food which is taken thither from time to time, are also destined to assist it on this terrible journey." A man, according to the belief of the Finnic tribes of Siberia, is composed of three parts: body, shadow, and soul. At death the soul passes to an infant of the same clan, while the shadow goes to a cold underworld, situated in the icy seas beyond the mouth of the Obi. "Here it lives for as long as the term of the dead man's former life on earth, and follows the same pursuits—reindeer-breeding, fishing, etc. Then the shadow begins to grow smaller and smaller, until it is no larger than a blackbeetle, (according to some it actually does turn into a blackbeetle), and finally disappears altogether."[22]

One account of the Sema Nagas says vaguely that the good souls go to the east toward the rising of the sun, while the bad ones go westward to its setting; another that souls go into butterflies or other insects, a common Naga belief; but the commonest and best-known theory, the holding of which, however, does not apparently preclude belief in one or both of the others, is that the souls go to the Hills of the Dead, to pass thence into another world. "With them they take those of their worldly possessions (or the 'souls' of them) that have been buried with them or placed on their graves, and all the mithans [buffalo] they have sacrificed or killed during life accompany them." The writer[23] has known a chief nearing his end to ask for a new Government red cloth, which is issued as a badge of office, in order that when he reached the world beyond the grave he might be recognized at once as a servant of the Government and treated with becoming respect. Once in the future home, the Sema dead live just as they did in this world. "He that is poor shall be poor still, and he that has been rich shall remain so. But though this belief holds but cold comfort for those who are poor and in misery, the Sema has it at least to his credit that he has not, with the detestable self-sufficiency of the purblind West, fatuously arrogated to man alone of animals the possession of a soul and the power of reasoning. It probably remains for the Christian missionaries to teach him that." The Angamis give a definite description of the abode of departed souls. "When a person dies, they believe that the spirit goes to a heaven under the ground where everything is exactly the same as in this life; parents are re-united with their children, and husband and wife live over again the happy days spent in the upper air. The land is rich in trees, flowers and animals

22 Czaplicka, *Aborig. Siberia*, 152-153, 162-163, 165 (quoted), 275, 290 (quoted).

23 Hutton, *Sema Nagas*, 211, 212-213.

of all sorts; the sun shines by day and the moon by night. When they die a second time, the souls pass to another heaven below the first, unlit by sun, moon or stars, where the souls live and die again; but when they die for a third time the souls come back to this earth as butterflies or small house flies, and in this shape perish for ever. When these small flies light on their wine cups, they will not kill them for fear of destroying someone of their ancestors."[24]

When the Todas of southern India die, their souls come to a ravine and river across which is a thread-bridge. Here those who have been bad during life fall into the river and are bitten by leeches, while the good cross the thread successfully and go straight to Amnodr. Those who fall into the river are helped out by the people who live on the farther bank, who may keep the offending Todas in their country for some time; the greater their offenses, the longer they are kept, but all, however bad, reach Amnodr sooner or later. Those who fall into the river are the selfish, jealous, and grudging people, and those who have committed any offenses against the dairy, which is a sacred industry among the Todas. The danger of falling into the river does not seem to have much influence on the people. "It has been spoken of as the Toda Hell, but it is rather a mild variety of Purgatory, and only involves some discomfort and delay on the journey to the next world." The buffaloes killed at the funeral are supposed to go to Amnodr with the dead person. "Sacred buffaloes are only killed at the funerals of men, for they would be useless to women, who, in the next world as in this, have nothing to do with dairies at which the sacred buffaloes must be tended."[25]

Among the more advanced people in India, as would be expected, there is a more definite notion of rewards and punishments for good and evil in the next world. There is a belief that when a bad man dies his spirit takes a downward course through the intestines and emerges in the same manner as the excreta; whereas the spirit of a good man finds its way through the tenth aperture of the body, which is a suture at the top of the skull, called "Brahma's crevice." No sooner has death occurred and cremation of the terrestrial body taken place, than Yama's two messengers, who are waiting near at hand, make themselves visible to the released spirit. Their aspect is terrific and, as if their appearance were not sufficiently alarming, they proceed to terrify their victim by terrible visions of the torments in store for him. The bound spirit is finally led along the road to Yama's abode. Standing before his judgment-seat it is confronted by the Registrar or Recorder, which officer stands by Yama's side with an open book before him. It is his business to note down all the good and evil deeds of every human being committed during his life, with the resulting merit and demerit, and to produce a debit and credit account made up and balanced on the day of death. According to the balance on the side of merit or demerit is judgment pronounced. The ceremonies performed on behalf of the dead by his relations have power, if properly carried out, to turn the scale and perhaps place a considerable balance to his credit. Finally, on the thirteenth day after death the spirit is conducted either to heaven or to one of the hells.[26]

The natives of Borneo believe implicitly in another world, some tribes having even a sort of courier-system to it. They buy a slave, tie him up, and one after

24 Furness, in JAI, XXXII, 463.
25 Rivers, Todas, 399, 401-403.
26 Monier-Williams, Brāhmanism, 291, 292-294.

another sticks a spear an inch or so into his body, all of them pronouncing messages to deceased friends as they do so. It was even harder to get them to leave off this custom than to abandon head-hunting.[27] While life is thought to go on as before, with the same class-distinctions and the like, there is some notion, though confused, that after death the spirits of good men travel toward the west to be absorbed into the effulgence of the setting sun, while the souls of the bad are devoured by specters which approach the graves for that purpose on the seventh day after interment. On that day fires are kindled to drive them away.[28] The natives of southern Borneo believe that the soul, in its journey to the next world, comes at length to the Rayah River—the river Styx of all the Bornean tribes—over which is placed a log that has this peculiarity: it is not quite long enough to span the stream from bank to bank. As the soul and its conductor reach the bank, the log glides up to them, when the soul of the deserving one steps on it and is ferried across in safety to the opposite shore; if, however, the soul of a wicked person approaches, the discerning log suddenly slips away as he steps upon it, thus precipitating him into the waters where dwell the fiends, typified by a huge fish. When it devours him, he dies a second and final death from which there is no resurrection. Hiller,[29] who reports this, once asked a man what constituted a crime so heinous as to cause a soul to be cast to the devouring fish. The reply was prompt: "Any man who refused to get married"; nor could the author get him to cite any other fault so wicked. In Sarawak paddling motions indicate travel to the next world.[30] Among the tribes of the Malay Peninsula the souls of ordinary people are variously represented as being compelled to cross a boiling lake by means of a tree-bridge, from which the wicked slip off into the lake below them, and as being sent to a different and a far less inviting paradise. In some cases, the soul after death is repeatedly washed in a cauldron of boiling water by "Granny Longbreasts," in order to purify it from its stains. Thereafter it is made to walk along the flat side of a monstrous chopper with which she bridges the cauldron, the bad souls falling in and the good escaping to the land of paradise. If the soul needs more purification, it is thrown in twice or three times; if still black, it is cast under the earth as a demon, of the kind most appropriate to the sin it had committed. The idea of a better spirit-world occurs several times, a future world in which all live in harmony together, a great island full of trees and pleasant fruits. "There, too, the souls marry and have children, as in the present world, but pain, disease, and death are unknown." Men who have died a bloody death do not go there but to a desolate and barren place.[31] According to the ideas of some Filipinos, when the new arrival in the next world is asked concerning his life, a louse on his body is the witness and answers for him. When Worcester[32] asked a native what would happen should the man not chance to possess any of these interesting arthropoda, he was informed that such an occurrence was unprecedented! "Every one was well off in this happy underground abode, but those who had been wealthy on earth were less comfortable than those who had been poor." Sickness and death come again, however; persons die seven times, each time with

27 Roth, *Sarawak*, I, 158.
28 Wilken, in VG, III, 51-52, 55, 60.
29 In *Bull. Geog. Soc. of Phila.*, III, 62; §342, of the text.
30 Lawrence and Hewitt, in JAI, XXXVIII, 391.

31 Skeat and Blagden, *Malay Penin.*, II, 194, 195, 239, 240-241, 321; Evans, in JAI, XLVIII, 180.
32 *Philippine Isl.*, 110, 111, 198.

an improvement of condition if the preliminary examination has been successfully passed. The author asserts that the Moros believe the soul lives forever.

Some Polynesians believe that the soul, having fallen into a dark realm
under ground, is eaten by the gods, parts of it being cut off with shells. This
operation is performed by the relatives of the deceased who died earlier.[33] The
Hawaiians believed in a subterranean world of the dead divided into two
regions, to the upper part of which went the good, while those who had not been
sufficiently religious had to go to the lower, where they had lizards and butterflies for food. Traditional points from which the soul took its leap into the
underworld are to be found at various locations in the islands.[34] In Samoan
mythology, the eighth heaven, like the third heaven of the Hebrews, was the
residence of the gods; in ancient times there was much intercourse between the
inhabitants of heaven and earth—probably before the occasion when, according to their tradition, the skies were raised from low down near to the
face of the earth into their present position. In those days the heavens were
thought so near that they could be reached by climbing into a tree.[35] In Bowditch Island, at death one would say to his friends, "I'm going to the moon—
think of me as being there." Another would say, "I'm going to be a star," and
mention the particular part of the heavens where they were to look for him.
Another might say, "I shan't go away, I shall remain in the grave, and be
here with you." Thus they seemed to think they had only to choose where their
disembodied spirits were to go after death.[36]

When a Maori died, his spirit was supposed to leave the body and fare forth
to the Spirits' Leaping Place, situated at the northwest extremity of the
North Island of New Zealand, where it plunged into the ocean and descended
to the underworld. "This abode of the dead much resembled that of the ancient Hebrews. It was a realm wherein the spirits of the dead seemed to live
much the same sort of life as they did in the upper world." There were also
future existences for the spirits of dogs, rats, and other animals, and one
for fish. In the old Maori belief, there was no suffering or unhappiness in the
spirit-world, and absolutely no punishment for the soul after death, no matter
what the character or acts of a person in this world may have been;[37] such
ideas came through missionary influence. At the southern gate of the spirit-
world, thought the natives of the Gilbert Islands, sat the guardian Nakaa, awaiting the souls that came from the land of the living. "And as he sat he was for
ever making nets, with his back turned to the path that led to the entrance
of his dwelling-place, but well he knew when a soul crept up behind him. So,
when it was near by his right hand, he reached forth and enmeshed it in the
strand of his netting-needle; he laid it across his knees; he searched its heart
for evil. And if he found incest therein, or thievishness, or cowardice, he
straightway cast the soul out of his sight into a place of everlasting nightmare . . . or he impaled it upon the terrible stakes . . . or he flung it into
the midst of a company who writhed together in eternal entanglement. . . .
If the paradise of an island folk is up in the heavens," comments the author,[38]
"it generally means that the people have been for so long resident on their
morsel of land that they have forgotten the direction from which their fore-

33 Ellis, *Polyn. Researches*, I, 396.
34 Beckwith, in BAE, XXXIII, 299.
35 Pratt, in AAAS, 1890, 447, 449, 655.
36 Turner, *Samoa*, 273.

37 Best, in AAAS, 1909, 464 (quoted); in
JAI, XLIV, 158; White, in AAAS, 1891, 361-
362, 364.
38 Grimble, in JAI, LI, 50-51, 52.

fathers came; they can no longer direct their dead back along the old migration-track to the ancient fatherland."

The Eskimo think that the dead go to a lovely land under the earth; they have no hell. But the journey is not easy: the dead must slide down a high, sharp rock on their backs. It takes five or more days to slide down this rock, which becomes covered with blood. This they call the second death, after which nothing is left of them; they fear it very much and surviving relatives and friends must observe certain precautions to protect them from it. The Indians also think of a mountain-ridge, sharp as the sharpest knife, along which souls must pass to their dwelling-place.[39] Boas[40] says that a young Eskimo girl once sent for him a few hours before her death and asked for some tobacco and bread to give her mother, who had died a few weeks before. The Tlinkits of Alaska call the place where the souls of the departed dwell the ghost's or the spirit's home, the word for ghost being the same as that for spirit. When the fire crackles, spirits are hungry and calling for food. The living put food in the fire, food and clothing in the tomb of the dead, and canoes beside the dead-houses of their deceased shamans.[41] The Salish Indians say that the seasons and also the times of the day in the land of the dead are exactly the opposite of what they are in this world. "When it is midwinter here, it is midsummer there, and when it is night here, it is daytime there. Therefore the most advantageous time to visit the land of the dead is during a night in midwinter, because then it will be a fine, bright summer day in the other world. In fact this is the only time of the year when the trail to the ghost-land is at all passable."[42] In the belief of the Northwest Coast Indians the country of souls contains two divisions, one inhabited by recently arrived souls and the other by souls which have been there for a longer time. "On their journey to this land the souls pass a rest-house, then a lake and a berry-ground. Their way is barred by a spring-pole, and they must cross a rotten log, the final barrier being a wide river."[43]

The beliefs of the Quileute Indians of this section have been well and fully described. All souls, whether they belong to male or female beings, to good or bad people, go to the same place and traverse the same trail, excepting the souls of infants. These have a country of their own, which will be described later on. "The dwelling place of the souls is called the Country of the Ghosts and is situated way under ground. The place and the trail leading to it have often been described by shamans who, accompanied by their guardian-spirits, used to go down there in order to bring back the souls of some of their patients. . . . The underworld or Country of the Souls is situated very far from the surface of the earth. A shaman traveling there with the aid of his guardian-spirit requires two days and two nights for that trip and, be it remembered, these guardians travel with lightning rapidity. The road is good and broad, and the underworld itself is a large valley with neither hills nor mountains. Through the center of the underworld runs a river, about a quarter of a mile wide, and the souls dwell on both banks of this river, occupying houses exactly like those of the living Quileute. The river divides the underworld into two equal parts. On one side live those souls who have died long ago, while on the nearer bank dwell the souls of recently departed Indians.

39 Nansen, *Esk. Life*, 238.   42 Haeberlin, in AA, XX, 252.
40 In BAE. VI, 613.   43 Frachtenberg, in AA, XIX, 319.
41 Jones, *Thlingets*, 234, 235, 236.

The river is crossed by means of a canoe, and for that reason the Quileute Indians bury their dead in canoes. The soul of a poor Indian whose relatives cannot afford a canoe-burial, crosses the river by walking on the fishtrap owned in common by all the inhabitants of the underworld." At a place situated about a third of the way from the upper world there stands a house called "mat-house" in which the traveling souls stay over night, resting and acquiring new strength for a continuation of their journey. In the morning they resume their travel and soon reach a lake called "sticky water" which is so situated that each soul must wade through it in order to continue the trip. "The water of this lake, when partaken of by a soul, causes the actual death of its owner. Hence, a shaman going in quest of a lost soul, will always refrain from tasting this water. Beyond this lake there are berry-grounds where the souls pick salmon-berries and strawberries. These berries, too, may be eaten by the souls only. A shaman, who even touches them, drops dead. Farther down the road there is a pole stuck into the ground and continually springing over the trail. The souls have no trouble in passing this pole. But the shaman, in order to pass by it safely, must have a special magic . . . which causes the pole to stop its swinging motion while the shaman goes by." Beyond this pole there is another obstruction in the form of a rotten log lying clear across the road in such a way that each person must step over it; "since this log keeps on shrinking and expanding just like a rubber, only a soul or a shaman having the 'ghost magic' can go over it. From here on the trail becomes fine and unobstructed, ending at the very river."

The souls of recently departed people cannot cross at once to the other side; if they do so, they are driven back. "They must stay on the nearer side until they have lost all scent of 'recent death.' The 'older' souls have a sentinel on each side of the river . . . whose duty it is to see to it that no 'new' soul comes across until the proper time has arrived. As soon as the 'new' soul has completed its apprenticeship and become 'ripe' for dwelling in the 'older community,' it is instructed by one of these sentinels how to act and what to do in the real Country of the Souls. New arrivals are usually met and welcomed by the souls of those relatives and friends who had preceded them into the underworld." The Country of the Souls differs in no respect from the upper world. "It is abundantly supplied with all necessities of life. Each soul pursues the same occupation as in the world above. Sickness prevails among the souls to the same degree as among the living Indians, and the soul-shamans are kept constantly busy. Good and bad weather, day and night, changes of the season prevail also in the underworld. Women bear children in the usual way, and wars are not infrequently waged among the souls. The souls have an ocean of their own, thereby giving them the opportunity to follow the whale-hunting profession. All souls stay in the underworld forever. Animals, birds, fish, etc., dwell in special underworlds of their own. These are visited by the dead hunters and fishermen who thus obtain their necessary supplies of fresh game and fish. No one knows the exact locations of these places, nor has any living person been able to find out how to reach them."

Attention has been called to the fact that, according to Quileute belief, infants and children live in a separate underworld. This is situated south of the country of grown-up souls, and has a trail of its own, which is covered with nice, green grass and is much shorter than the other road. "It is not dotted with obstructions and leads right into the habitations of the souls. . . . Swings made of poles are found everywhere and are used by the children constantly. The houses are located right behind the playgrounds. A beautiful lake is situated in the middle of this underworld, and the children bathe in it frequently. It is not known whether and what the souls of infants eat. All children are under the perpetual care of some old women . . . who stay with them all the time. No one has ever been able to find out how many of these keepers there are and how they came to live in this underworld. The children are never visited by the other souls, as there are no means of communication between the two underworlds."[44]

The Omaha assert that under certain conditions the realm of the dead is accessible to the living. For instance, "a person in a swoon was thought to have died for the time and to have entered the region of death. It was said of one who had fainted and recovered that 'he died [fainted] and went to his departed kindred, but no one would speak to him, so he was obliged to return to life' [recovered consciousness]. It was further explained: 'If his relatives had spoken to him he would never have come back but would have had to stay with the dead.' It seems probable that the stories told by certain persons who had swooned as to what they saw in visions have had much to do in forming the Omaha imagery of the other world. It will be recalled that the sign of the tabu was put on the dead in order that they might be recognized by their relatives. . . . These and like customs confirm the general statement that life and its environment beyond the grave were thought to be conditioned much as on the earth, except that the future state was generally regarded as being happier and freer from sickness and want. It was said that there are seven spirit worlds, each higher than the one next preceding, and that after people have lived for a time in one world they die to that world and pass on to the one next above. . . . There does not seem to have been any conception among the Omaha of supernatural rewards or punishments after death. The same conditions which make for good conduct here were believed to exist in the realm of the dead."[45] The place of the dead, in Cheyenne belief, is above. Brave and cowardly, good and bad alike, go there; all who have died are equal. "There the dead live as they lived on earth—they chase buffalo, hunt other game, and go to war."[46] In Hopi mythology the human race was not created but generated from the earth, from which man emerged through an opening now typified by the Grand Canyon of the Colorado; the dead are supposed to return to the underworld.[47] The Chippewa imagined that the shade, after the death of the body, followed a wide beaten path, leading toward the west, finally arriving in a country abounding in everything the Indian desires.[48] Life after death was very real to the Dakota Indians, among whom a dead man may be initiated into the esoteric medicine-club by ceremonies over a lock of hair.[49] Among the Sia of New Mexico, "the spirits of all animals go to the lower world; domestic animals serving the masters there as they did here."[50] The Zuñi conceive that the dead dwell in a region below the Sacred Lake, which is sixty-five miles to the southwest of the town of Zuñi; there life is just the same as at Zuñi, families and households being reunited.[51]

The journey to the next world is often beset with obstacles. A famous Kicka-

44 Frachtenberg, in AA, XXII, 337-340.
45 Fletcher and LaFlesche, in BAE, XXVII, 589-590.
46 Grinnell, Cheyenne, II, 91.
47 Fewkes, in HAI, I, 566.
48 Mooney and Thomas, in HAI, I, 279.
49 Beckwith, in Smithson. Rep., 1886, pt. I, 248.
50 Stevenson, in BAE, XI, 146.
51 Parsons, in AA, XVIII, 250.

poo prophet once displayed a chart of the path, leading through fire and water, which the virtuous must pursue to reach the "happy hunting grounds," and furnished his followers with prayer-sticks graven with religious symbols.[52] The Menomini believe in a four-day journey to the hereafter; before reaching the goal the soul is tested and must cross a log-bridge guarded by a dog.[53] "Like the Iroquois and Huron sages, the Algonquian philosophers taught that the disembodied souls of the dead, on their journey to the great meadow in which is situated the village of their deceased ancestors, must cross a swift stream precariously bridged by a tree trunk, which was in continual motion. Over this the manes of the justified pass in safety, while the shades of the vicious, overcome by the magic power of adverse fate, fail at this ordeal, and, falling into the abyss below, are lost."[54] According to Winnebago beliefs, the soul may be helped to overcome the hazards of the journey; warriors are invited to the wake because it is believed that the souls of the enemies they have killed become their slaves in the spirit-land and they can order them to take charge of the soul of the recently departed individual and clear his path of the obstacles that beset him on his journey from the land of the living to that of the spirits. "Especially difficult to the passage of the soul is an enormous girdle of fire which it must be carried over to reach the spirit home of its clan. The warrior relates his war experiences, but in so doing he is strongly admonished to be very careful and not tell them in a boastful way or to exaggerate in any detail, for if he does so the soul of the departed would fall into the abyss of fire. In this connection it may perhaps be suggestive to note, that it is not any transgression of the deceased that prevents him from reaching his goal, but a transgression of the warrior relating his war experience."[55] A belief similar to that of the Menomini, one found also among the Seneca of New York, is the Seminole notion of the other world: "The Seminole believe that the souls of the worthy dead go to an abode where existence is ideal, where social dances, feasts, and ball games are held uninterruptedly; but those whose earthly existence has not been above reproach are doomed to destruction. The souls must pass over a long trail from the world to the sky country. This journey requires four days, and a number of tests, consisting of tempting food placed at intervals beside the path, are encountered. If the ghost partakes of any of this food, some un known misfortune will overwhelm it. At length the wanderer arrives at a river, over which a slippery log gives access to the village of the blessed. The bridge is guarded by a dog, and if the wayfarer has led an evil life, the animal shakes the log and hurls the unfortunate being into the stream, where it is devoured by an alligator or a great fish." In accordance with this belief, a fire is kept beside the cairn for four nights after the burial, in order to provide light and warmth for the spirit of the deceased on its sky journey.[56]

When calamity threatened, the Mayas of Yucatan flung virgins down an abyss, after explaining to them what they were to ask of the gods before whom they were to appear.[57] The Guiana Indian's vengeance is carried beyond the grave: when the death of any member of the Akawai tribe is supposed to have been brought about by unfair means, the knife of the deceased is buried with him, that he may have the means of avenging himself in the world of spirits;

52 HAI, I, 650.
53 Skinner, in AA, XIII, 560.
54 Hewitt, in IIAI, II, 21.
55 Lamere and Radin, in AA, XIII, 437; see an account given by Henry Roe Cloud, a

member of the tribe: "The Land of the Setting Sun," in Kit-Kat, II, 17-21.
56 Skinner, in AA, XV, 73.
57 Nadaillac, Preh. Amer., 267.

the Warraus, in similar circumstances, place a bow and arrows by the side of the dead man, that he may by means of those weapons keep off malignant spirits in his passage to the other world; while at the burial of a male Makusi, not only the dead man's knife but several thongs are buried with him, the latter enabling him to tie to a tree the spirit who had caused his death. According to the views of the Caribs, the spirits of the good and bad rise after death toward the skies; "the former travel high, very high, above the clouds where they find pretty women; they dance every night; they drink cassiri, and do not work in the clearings (provision-fields). The wicked remain below the clouds where they are always roaming without any hope of getting higher. If the body is burned immediately after death, this is done in order that the spirit may ascend with the smoke." There are interesting records left us concerning the Island Caribs: "(a) Some hold that the most valiant of their nation are carried after death to the Fortunate Isles, where they have everything they can wish for, and that the Arawaks are their slaves; that they swim without being tired, in the wide and large rivers; and live delightfully and pass the time happily in dances, games, and feasts, in a country which produces all kinds of good fruits without being cultivated. (b) On the contrary, those who have been cowardly and timid in going to war against their enemies, have, after death, to serve the Arawaks, who inhabit desert and sterile countries which are beyond the mountains. (c) But others, the most brutal, do not trouble about what takes place after death: they neither dream nor talk about it."[58] The Araucanians believed in a future state but not in hell. "After death they went in an invisible, but corporeal, form to the other world, where the evil spirits had no entry, where there was always abundance, and where they passed their time feasting and drinking and dancing, waited on by their wives, who had either preceded them or would follow after. The same castes were preserved there as on earth, but the poor people and the public women went to another land where it was always cold. . . . To arrive at their future resting place it was necessary to cross the sea. For this reason the dead are buried facing the west. Before arriving at this happy land they had a long journey to make. So that they should want nothing on this journey, a good supply of provisions, blankets, skins, etc., were buried with the corpse, and a horse was either buried also or slaughtered over the grave. The island of Mocha was formerly believed to be the starting place for this long trip. Spirits of the dead had to follow a narrow path, guarded by a witch, who collected tribute from all passers. Even now the Araucanos bury some few coins or other objects with the dead to discharge this obligation. The coast tribes believed that certain witches transformed themselves into whales to ferry them from the mainland to the island, while the inland tribes supposed that they changed into canoes."[59]

In the earliest period of Egyptian history the picture which was drawn of the future life was gloomy. The rich, whose bodies were well cared for and secure in durable graves, could hope for continued existence, but the poor had nothing much to expect. When, later, a more blissful state was conceived, it belonged at first solely to the king and was only gradually extended to include wider and wider circles till at length all looked forward to ultimate felicity. This change was accompanied by new conceptions of moral values and with the introduction of the future judgment to which all were subject; only such as

58 Roth, in BAE, XXX, 156, 157, 160   59 Latcham, in JAI, XXXIX, 348.
(quoted), 161 (quoted).

could successfully withstand this judgment might hope. The goddess of truth led the soul to the throne of Osiris, where his heart was weighed on a scale, being balanced against the image of the goddess of truth. If found too light, the soul was annihilated. The good man addressed prayers to his heart not to speak out against him. The Book of the Dead prepared the souls with rituals and other magic means to assure their journey to the eternal dwelling-place. The Egyptians did not hold to what we mean by the phrase "the immortality of the soul"; rather was it a belief in revivification, a doctrine probably somewhat more developed than among the Babylonians and other Semites.[60] The earliest Hebrews held that at a man's death a kind of image or outline of his whole personality detached itself from the corpse and descended to Sheol. Their abode of the dead was thought of as a subterranean space, for one "goes down" to it, while it had two other constant features: a prevailing thick darkness and an impossibility of return. The concept of Sheol, which later became the hell-fire of the Christians, was probably Arabian-Syrian in origin. At a later time a favorable place was reserved in Sheol for the good, a kind of heavenly oasis, which developed into the Christian heaven. The idea of immortality is quite weak in the Old Testament, while in the pre-exilic prophecy there is not a trace of any expectation of a continued life after death or of resurrection.[61] The pre-Mohammedan Arabs knew no immortality; the souls merely lived on, in the memory of the living, in much the same way as on earth. As Abel's blood cried out to Jahweh, so did the murdered Arab call for revenge.[62] Belief in the life to come is one of the chief dogmas of the Zend-Avesta, and closely connected with it was a belief in heaven and hell.[63] In the Vedas the doctrine of the immortality of the soul is not very prominent; the great desire of men in that age was worldly prosperity, the "powers of the world to come" did not exert any great influence upon the community.[64] Belief in another life prevailed in ancient Rome and tablets have been found in graves there and elsewhere, which contain instruction to the dead for their conduct in the world below, exhortations to the soul, formularies to be repeated, confessions of faith and of ritual performed, and like matters.[65] Celebration of the birthdays of the dead was common in antiquity; "we see clearly that between life and death lies no impossible chasm; it is as if life were not interrupted by death."[66] The ancient Gauls were said to have been accustomed to lend money on the condition of its being repaid to the lender in the next life.[67] Among gypsies today, beads, combs, and jewels are placed in the coffin; in one instance, at the burial of a gypsy queen, two hats were also deposited in the casket, to enable the corpse to have comfort while going across the Styx.[68]

In Scandinavian mythology the shades take rank in Valhalla according to the wealth they bring with them. The Swedes thought that Odin at his death went back to the place, by tradition northeast of the Black Sea, whence their ancestors had come.[69] In the *Sampo,* a collection of Finnish legends, there is

60 Tiele, *Relig. im Altertum,* I, 44, 73-74, 17-18, 213; Lehmann, *Overtro,* II, 38-40.
61 Kautzsch, *Relig. Israel,* in Hastings's *Dict. Bible,* 668, 669, 689.
62 Procksch, *Blutrache,* 41-42.
63 Haug, *Parsis,* 311.
64 Wilkins, *Hinduism,* 472.
65 De Marchi, *Culto Priv.,* rev. in *Année*

Soc., I, 183; Harrison, *Greek Relig.,* 573; Theinert, in *Umschau,* VI, 623; Rohde, *Psyche,* I, 293; II, 3, 34-35.
66 Rohde, *Psyche,* I, 235.
67 Lecky, *Europ. Morals,* II, 215.
68 New Haven *Journal-Courier,* Apr. 29, 1915.
69 Geijer, *Svensk. Hist.,* 24.

a river to be crossed by boat in order to reach the realm of the departed.[70] Among the Mordvins, "on the eve of the day for commemorating the deceased, forty or forty-nine days after death, the nearest relative who most resembles the defunct is asked to personify him." He dresses in the clothes in which the dead man died and sits on his death-bed. Presents of food are brought him. "At night a very noisy feast is held, during which the personator tells of the life beyond the grave, and about the crops there. To the visitors that inquire after their dead relatives he gives the most circumstantial news. 'Your relative keeps good horses, and drives about the forest in a carriage;' 'Yours has ruined himself;' 'Yours keeps bees;' 'Yours is given to drink;' 'Yours has married a beautiful wife.' About midnight all gather round to listen to the wishes of the dead man. His personifier then advises them to live peacefully, to look after their cattle, not to thieve, and hopes they will have abundance of beer and brandy." The impersonator is then carried on a bed to the grave and set upon it. He is begged to eat for the last time and to return at the harvest, when they will reap his share for him. If ancestors are neglected and left to starve, they send warnings in dreams and the survivors are quick to take the hint. They make a feast, the greater part of which they eat themselves, and leave the remains of it near the cemetery.[71]

§222. Avoidance.

WHEN a native of Central Australia is dying, all the members of the tribe sit in a circle and sing a death-dirge, the body of the dying person being kept warm by being covered, all except the head, with hot sand taken from underneath a fire. After death, five small circular holes about two feet in depth are excavated by means of a boomerang round the hut of the deceased, and the hut is then burnt.[1] The Tasmanians, when feeling very ill and near death, objected to the presence of a white man; "they also disliked under these circumstances to be on a bedstead and always endeavoured to get down on the floor and lie in front of the fire."[2] The Melanesians very generally hold that it is necessary for all people not of the dead man's clan to disassociate themselves from him and all that belonged to him in every possible way. The house in which he died is usually deserted or destroyed, not so much as a sign of sorrow as through fear of the ghost of the deceased and the conviction that if this were not done evil spirits would come back again and other members of the family would be affected. Some groups carry out complete avoidance, as among the Roro-speaking tribes where, "on the day after a man's death many of his effects, but not his jewellery, are broken or damaged and hung beneath the eaves of his house, which usually is not again inhabited and is allowed to decay. It was said that when the vegetables planted by the dead man became ripe they were also hung to the eaves of the house and allowed to rot."[3] In the New Hebrides the natives sometimes did not wait until the sick person was dead, so anxious were they for his demise: "If a person in sickness showed signs of delirium, his grave was dug, and he was buried forthwith, to prevent the disease spreading to other members of the family. I was told of a young man in the prime of life who was thus buried. He burst up the grave and escaped.

70 Baldwin, Sampo, 127.
71 Abercromby, Finns, I, 177.
1 Wells, in AAAS, 1893, 516, 517.

2 Agnew, in AAAS, 1887, 480.
3 Seligmann, Melanesians, 13, 274 (quoted), 525, 631, 632.

He was caught, and forced into the grave again. A second time he struggled to the surface; and then they led him to the bush, lashed him fast to a tree, and left him there to die."[4] In D'Entrccasteaux the mourners sometimes pull down the dead man's house, though more often they leave it to rot with whatever food may be inside it; in one or two instances, however, a brother occupied it afterwards. "If the deceased be other than the father of the family, the house is almost certain to be pulled down, though it is rebuilt later on the same posts; a father who acted otherwise might be thought lacking in affection for his child."[5] In one of the Solomon Islands, a taboo lasting for six months is placed upon all coconuts that belonged to the deceased, no one being allowed to go near them, touch them, or trade with them.[6]

Throughout Melanesia people are afraid of meeting a ghost. When death occurs in a Trobriand village, "there is an enormous increase of superstitious fear," and "the immediate neighbourhood of the grave is absolutely deserted when night approaches."[7] In the Loyalty Islands, through fear of meeting a ghost when walking, the center of the company is preferred as being safer than the outside.[8] On the night of a death, among the Southern Massim, no one in the neighborhood will leave his house, and "in a modified form the custom is kept up till the next new moon, inasmuch as people will not walk about casually at night, nor use the path near where a death has taken place." The killer or captor of the victim who is eaten at the cannibal feasts of these people secludes himself for a month and observes various taboos, in order to avoid the evil influence of the dead man, of whose ghost he is in mortal terror.[9] Among the natives of the Papuan Gulf, the spirits of individuals who have met a violent death from the hands of a murderer, or from a crocodile, are supposed to roam about constantly and are frequently seen near their former abode, which consequently is avoided. The latter type, which often resides in the crocodile that ate the body, is especially malicious, but the natives have devised a method of avoiding it. "When a spirit becomes a nuisance, the people whom he troubles wait for his return, and then take a canoe and paddle away up the river or creek, the spirit following. They leave the canoe and get into the bush, where he gets bewildered, as his crocodile-affinity cannot find its way about the bush; the crocodile spirit being now lost in the bush, the party who came out to lay it ultimately return to the village and are not troubled by it again."[10]

Some tribes of South Africa never remain in a place where death has once visited them.[11] On the Loango Coast after a death the hut of the deceased is abandoned, and if a prince dies the whole village is removed.[12] Such is the dread of death among the Sakalava of Madagascar that when it occurs in one of their villages they break up their settlement and remove to a distance before rebuilding their houses. "They seem to believe that the spirit of the deceased will haunt the spot, and do some harm to those who stayed where it had lived in the flesh. This perpetual fleeing before death, of course, prevents the population from becoming settled in its habits, and produces a most unsubstantial style of house-building." The same notion is found among other tribes on the island, some of whom call such deserted dwellings "broken houses." The idea prevails generally here that it is improper to use anything belonging to the

4 Turner, *Samoa*, 336-337.
5 Jenness and Ballentyne, *D'Entrecasteaux*, 114, 46-47.
6 Rooney, in AAAS, 1911, 444.
7 Malinowski, in JAI, XLVI, 356-357.

8 Ray, in JAI, XLVII, 289.
9 Seligmann, *Melanesians*, 618, 557-559.
10 Holmes, in JAI, XXXII, 428-429.
11 Livingstone, *Mission. Travels*, II, 523.
12 Bastian, *Deut. Exped.*, I, 164.

dead, which leads also to the burial of royal property among the Hovas.[13]
Again, to avoid the return of the ghost no more food is cooked after the
funeral-ceremonies are finished, because "it made the dead man hungry."[14] It
was the usual custom in the Upper Congo to bury the owner in his house, and
"it, together with any other houses he might own in the row, would be deserted,
neglected and soon fall to ruin."[15] Among the Batetela "all huts belonging to
the deceased or his wives are burnt," or "the doorway of the house in which the
deceased lived is closed with strings and the building is allowed to fall into
ruins."[16] The hut of the deceased, among the Atharaka, "must be vacated and
allowed to rot away."[17] Any misfortune will signify to the Mkamba of East
Africa that the place he lives in is unlucky, and he will then move his village;
the Mkikuyu must move his village on the death of his father or uncle, generally to a distance of some six or eight miles. "If a stranger comes to a village
and dies in a hut there, the hut is completely abandoned if the owner belongs
to the Kikuyu guild; a big hole is broken away in the side of the hut by taking
out several of the wall slabs or planks; the corpse is left inside and the hyænas
come and carry it off. The hut is then left to fall into ruin, and nothing is removed from it, such as cooking pots, beer, jars, etc. The men who break the hole
in the wall are even considered unclean, the same as if they had handled the
corpse, and after performing the duty go straight off into the bush and stay
there until they have bathed and been anointed with *tatha* [the stomach-contents
of a sheep]; finally a very old woman comes and shaves their heads, they are
then ceremonially clean and can return to their families. A medicine man has,
however, to come and purify the whole village in the usual way." Both groups
also avoid the weapon with which a murder has been committed; "the idea
apparently is that it contains a harmful essence which it is impossible to remove, and it is believed that the evil will be passed on to whoever picks it up."[18]
Among the Wawanga, a man returning from a raid, on which he has killed
one of the enemy, may not enter his hut until he has taken cow-dung and rubbed
it on the cheeks of the women and children of the village and purified himself
by the sacrifice of a goat, a strip of skin from the forehead of which he wears
round the right wrist during the following four days. Abandonment of the village, especially following the death of a father of twins or of the village-head,
is common among these natives, the removal to another site taking place within
three or four months after the death.[19] In Nyassaland the roof is lifted bodily
off the hut of the deceased and put on the ground, the walls are taken down and
piled round the roof and the family live there till the mourning is finished. Then
a pot of beer is broken over the roof of the hut as it lies on the ground. In
some cases the hut is burned.[20] Among the Mombasa, "should a relative sicken
he is promptly deserted, unless he be an elder, when he is carefully tended."
An epidemic causes panic among these people so that they desert even babies.[21]

Some Nigerian tribes reoccupy a house on the death of the owner, although
he may be buried in the porch itself. The Hausa advise never to enter a house
in the dark, but always to get a light and hold it in front of you; so long as

13 Sibree, *Great Afr. Isl.*, 236, 290-291
(quoted).
14 Thomas, in JAI, L, 384.
15 Weeks, in JAI, XXXIX, 109.
16 Torday, in JAI, LI, 377.
17 Champion, in JAI, XLII, 84.
18 Dundas, C., in JAI, XLV, 241; JAI,

XLIII, 522; Hobley, in JAI, XLI, 408-409
(quoted), 426-427 (quoted); *A-Kamba*, 66-67.
19 Dundas, C., in JAI, XLIII, 38, 47, 61-
62, 68, 69.
20 Stigand, in JAI, XXXVII, 121.
21 Johnstone, in JAI, XXXII, 269.

you get past the threshold, you will be safe, even if the light goes out. Also, do not get up in the night and grope about in the dark, but strike a light before rising. By these precautions you will avoid encounter with a ghost. "On the night of the death, if the corpse is in the house, all the family and friends sit round it and talk all night, for anyone going to sleep would die. A knife is placed upon the breast of the corpse so as to keep the *kuruwa* [soul] from leaving it, and this, or another knife, will be kept by a wife during her three months odd of *takabba* [mourning] as a protection. A wife can hear it crying *chi-chi-chi*, and she is naturally frightened, so she tells some of her friends, and they abuse it until it has stopped, but she herself must not abuse it, else she would die. So sensitive of abuse is the *kuruwa* in Algiers, that no knife need be placed upon the corpse, the number of people present being sufficient protection for the widows. Animals are not allowed in the room, for they would make the *kuruwa* angry. Candles are kept alight for three nights, and the clothes of the deceased are washed at the end of three days."[22]

The Yakuts say that "in ancient times, when any one died, the inhabitants fled from the house, leaving in it the corpse with all the goods which belonged to the person when he was alive. . . . In some districts the people who are a little well-to-do, in the case of a death, at once abandon the house, if not forever, at least for a time."[23] One Yakut theory is that the dead are eaten up by devils who lurk about the place where they found their victim.[24] Among the Kamchadales, "the house in which a person died was always deserted, and its inhabitants at once removed to another dwelling at a certain distance. With the corpse, his clothes were also thrown away, and any one who should wear these afterwards was believed to be in danger of an early death."[25] The Soyots of the Yenesei pay no attention to the sick until they see that they are likely to die; then they leave them to their fate. The corpse, with his clothes and other belongings, is abandoned in the forest; fear of the dead man's ghost keeps the people away, the burial-places being seldom visited. If the corpse is not disturbed by the wild beasts, the people conclude that the dead man was very bad, while they hold that good peoples' bodies speedily disappear.[26] "In ancient historic China, it was an established mourning custom to give up to the defunct even the dwelling in which he had lived and breathed his last, with all its belongings, the children removing elsewhere, to miserable huts of clay, destitute of all bedding and furniture;"[27] while in ancient Japan men fled from the neighborhood of death; "it was long the custom to abandon, either temporarily, or permanently, the house in which a death occurred."[28]

Among the Nairs of India for fourteen days after a funeral all the members of the family are under pollution; they are untouchable, and any Nair who touches them must purify himself by a bath. "On the fourteenth day is the purificatory ceremony. The *Mārān* comes in the morning and gives everyone some oil. After smearing the body with this everyone goes and bathes, and comes back clad in white. The *Mārān* then sprinkles holy water, and a Brahmin priest purifies the house. There is generally a big feast for two days."[29] Since the Sema Nagas believe that the soul of the dead waits about in the house for some time after death, they postpone for a time the division of the deceased's

22 Tremearne, in JAI, XLII, 157; and in JAI, XLV, 30, 38 (quoted).
23 Sieroshevski-Sumner, in JAI, XXXI, 100.
24 *Russian Ethnog.* (Russ.), II, 531.
25 Czaplicka, *Aborig. Siberia*, 145.
26 Olsen, *Primitivt Folk*, 145.
27 DeGroot, *Relig. Syst.*, II, 479.
28 Hearn, *Japan*, 42.
29 Panikkar, in JAI, XLVIII, 276.

property, "to let the dead man's spirit go peaceably away first."[30] It used to be a common custom of the Todas to burn the house of a dead person.[31] If a Palaung woman who has a small child wishes to take it into a house where someone lies dead, she gets soot from the bottom of the rice-pot and makes a black mark between the eyebrows of her child. A mother may not be satisfied with a small dab of soot, but may blacken the whole face of the child if she goes into a house where someone has died, either on the day of the death or on any of the seven days thereafter. "As the spirit of the dead person probably returns to the home where its body is lying, or has so recently lain, it is feared that the spirit of the baby, being weaker than the spirit of the dead person, may be driven out by it." If a sick child is apparently dying, the mother will attempt to call back the departing spirit: "Do not wander, do not fly from us into the dark night. The spirits may hurt thee, the fireflies may burn thee. Come back to me, O my child! Fall into this water, alight on this food. Here it is dark and cold, in our home the fire burns brightly on the hearth. I do not set thee free, I will not let thee go. I take and keep thy shadow, I take and hold thy spirit. Come back, come back, my darling child! come to me quickly." When people in the neighboring houses hear that cry, "they shut their doors, so that the wandering spirit may not mistake its own home and enter theirs."[32]

The Malays very commonly abandoned or burnt the house in which a person died and sometimes even deserted the village.[33] In Borneo, "when a person dies the floor of the room in which he died is changed."[34] The Sakai desert a settlement if a member of it dies. "They said they did not bury a corpse, but left it in the abandoned house, for if they put a body into a grave, the spirit would not be able to make its escape upwards."[35] In Malacca, "invariably the house in which a person dies is burnt down and the place entirely forsaken, even at the possible loss of a coming crop of tapioca or sugar-cane."[36] The Kubus of Sumatra, in their wild state, "leave their dead unburied in the spot where they died, giving the place ever after a wide berth."[37] The Veddahs of Ceylon seek another cave, leaving that in which death has occurred to the spirit of the deceased.[38] In Car Nicobar the dying are removed to a mortuary hut in the graveyard in order to prevent defilement of the dwelling by death. After a native death, the author[39] took a walk into the village to see what the people were doing. "I found a fire in front of each house, the doors closed, and the people afraid even to talk to each other. Only a few old men had joined together, in a lonely house, to eat the mourning supper. When they saw me going about alone they were surprised, and asked me if I was not afraid of the ghost of the deceased man." The natives of Mindoro abandon a sick man when his condition becomes serious; after a time they steal back and, if the patient is recovering, aid him; if, as is more frequently the case, the man is dead, they flee, leaving everything in the house undisturbed and closing all paths to it with brush. The relatives then hide in the jungle, changing their names "to bring better luck."[40] In Samoa the house is abandoned to

30 Hutton, *Sema Nagas*, 159.
31 Rivers, *Todas*, 403.
32 Milne, *Eastern Clan*, 3, 287.
33 Wilken, in VG, III, 402; Skeat and Blagden, *Malay Penin.*, II, 89, 96, 100, 111, 106, 116.
34 Roth, in JAI, XXII, 32.
35 Evans, in JAI, XLVIII, 196.

36 Hale, in JAI, XV, 291.
37 Forbes, in JAI, XIV, 125.
38 Bailey, in *Trans. Ethnol. Soc. London*, II, 296.
39 Solomon, in JAI, XXXII, 217 (quoted), 238.
40 Worcester, *Philippine Isl.*, 427, 496.

the dead and to one or two relatives. All food is eaten outside; those who touched the corpse may not feed themselves but eat from mats or are fed by others.[41] At the death of a person of importance the Maoris sped the departing spirit: flax cords were tied with a slip-knot to a tassel of the mat in which the body was enshrouded, one cord was placed in the hand of each of the boys and girls who were relatives of the deceased, and as the last word of the chant was uttered by the priest, "each child pulled the flax cord with a jerk, to disconnect the soul from the body, lest it should remain and afflict the relatives."[42]

Among the Central Eskimo, if there is danger that a disease will prove fatal, a small snow hut is built, into which the patient is carried through an opening at the back. The opening is closed and subsequently a door is cut out. A small quantity of food is placed in the hut and the patient is left without attendants. If there is no fear of sudden death, the relatives and friends may come to visit him, but when death seems near the house is shut and he is left to die alone. If it happens that a person dies in a hut among its inmates, everything belonging to the hut is thrown away, even to the tools. The tent-poles may be used after a year has passed. This custom explains the isolation of the sick. If a child dies in a hut and the mother immediately rushes out with it, the contents of the hut may be saved.[43] The Tlinkits think it is terrible if the dying are not dressed for the tomb before life leaves the body. "This is to avoid touching the dead, of which they have a superstitious fear. We have seen men with their burial clothes on two or three days before death."[44]

Among the North American Indians pretty generally, the dwelling of the deceased was deserted or, more commonly, burned, and the camp was often removed.[45] One reason why the Navaho built such crude houses was that religious custom constrained them to destroy or desert a dwelling in which death had occurred. Such a place was called by a term meaning "devil-house." "Those who now occupy good stone houses carry out the dying and let them expire outside, thus saving their dwellings, and indeed the same custom is sometimes practised in connection with the hogan [hut]. No people have greater dread of ghosts and mortuary remains."[46] The layers of burned clay so frequently found in southern mounds are, in part at least, the plastering of houses which have been destroyed by fire. "The numerous instances of this kind which have now been brought to light, and the presence of skeletons under the ashes and clay, render it probable that the houses were abandoned at the death of a member or members of the family, burned over them after they had been buried or covered with earth (for the bones are very rarely charred), and that immediately a mound was thrown over the ruins."[47]

Not only did the American Indians desert or burn the house of the deceased, but they also gave away his clothing and weapons and other possessions or else destroyed them.[48] Furthermore, they regarded all persons who came into contact with the deceased to be unclean. Among the Zuñi, emetics are taken by the corpse-bearers on their return from the cemetery and baths or hairwashes by the other survivors. "If those who have handled the corpse subsequently, i.e., within a day or so, feel unwell they inhale the smoke of piñon gum. If in dying the deceased has 'frightened' anyone, a lock of his hair may

41 Ella, in AAAS, 1892, 640.
42 White, in AAAS, 1891, 362-363.
43 Boas, in BAE, VI, 612.
44 Jones, Thlingets, 149.
45 HAI, I, 284; II, 193, 499, 619-620.

46 Matthews, in HAI, II, 44.
47 Thomas, in BAE, XII, 664-665.
48 HAI, I, 42; II, 499; Skinner, in AA, XVI, 76.

be cut off and burned for the frightened one to inhale. Again if the deceased is thought of much by a survivor or dreamed of, the smoking piñon gum is inhaled. The name of the dead is taboo." During the four days it takes the deceased to journey to the spirit-land the mourners, that is, all the household-members, do not buy or sell, the house-door is left ajar, and the bowl used to wash the corpse and the tools used to bury it are left on the roof. At Acoma the possessions of the deceased are buried with him. The burial-company is made up of men, who afterwards wash their hair. For four days after death the spirit of the deceased lingers about home, but the house-door is not left open, as at Zuñi, nor is trade tabooed. After four days the medicine-man brings to the house of the deceased the prayer feather-sticks he has made, places them where the deceased had lain, prays and bids the deceased begone. Meanwhile the household drinks a cedar-brew and vomits, and the father's kindred come in and wash their heads. The heads of a widower and of his children are washed by the women of his mother's household. The widower's head is washed after the burial also.[49]

A great loss falls upon any family of Brazilian Indians which loses a member by death, for the hut is cleared out and all the things burned or packed in the basket with the bones, so that the spirit of the deceased may have no reason to come back.[50] The Guiana Indians abandon the village at a death; the body is buried in the house and all the possessions burned.[51] The relatives of a deceased Jibaro Indian, especially of one killed by a lance, stand in such horror of the dead body that they hurriedly bury it on the same spot where they find it, thereafter speedily leaving the place.[52] A survival is seen in the East Prussian custom of carefully cleaning the house, after a death, and carrying away the dust—all of which is supposed to accomplish the withdrawal of the deceased.[53]

§223. Precautions against Return.

PRECAUTIONS against return have often, as will be seen, an exorcistic aspect. This topic, therefore, is closely related to that of exorcism.[1] In D'Entrecasteaux, one of the Melanesian groups, "if a man be properly buried his hamlet will never be haunted by his soul. This can only happen if no food be put in with him, or if he be laid upon his left side instead of upon his right. Not long ago the father of our old friend Yanavolewa was buried upon his left side, and his soul, instead of going off on its long journey, stayed behind to haunt his relatives. The sister watched one night and threw hot water in its eyes, after which it never appeared again. Sometimes a haunting soul is driven away with spears and clubs and the noise of drums and conch-shells, but it will inevitably return again if the natives afterwards fail to throw these objects into the sea." This use of water, noise, and weapons is a common method of expulsion. It is to be noted that precautions against the return of the ghost are taken at the time of death or burial or shortly thereafter, that is, before the ghost has gone to the other world, for "under ordinary circumstances the souls of the dead can never return once they have departed to their long home." Another common

49 Parsons, in AA, XVIII, 251-252, 254 (quoted); and in AA, XX, 176-177, 180-181.
50 Von den Steinen, Zent. Bras., 502.
51 Roth, in BAE, XXXVIII, §§853 ff.

52 Karsten, "Jibaro," in BAE, Bull. LXXIX, 28.
53 Von Negelein, in Ztft. d. V. f. Vkde., XI, 264.
1 §§226, 227, below.

exorcistic element, fire, when employed at the time of burial, falls under the topic of precautions against return. "At the foot of the grave they make a fire to keep it warm and prevent the soul from walking. Sometimes they make another at the head, and a third on one side, but these are often omitted, while the fire at the foot is always lit. The grave-diggers keep them burning till the funeral feast is over, three or four days later."[2] In many cases in the Loyalty Islands, "burial took place in a grave dug in the ground, and the body was then usually bent with the knees up to the chest, as this was thought to prevent the deceased person from coming out of the grave and wandering about."[3] When a dead body was laid in the grave, in the New Hebrides, a pig was taken to the place and its head chopped off and thrown into the grave to be buried with the body. "This was supposed to prevent disease spreading to other members of the family. With the dead were buried cups, pillows, and other things used by the deceased, and even the sticks with which the grave was dug. On the top of the grave they kindled a fire to enable the soul of the departed to rise to the sun." The natives did not eat anything which grew within about 100 yards of a place where their own dead were buried, but strangers from another district would pluck coconuts, and eat freely of such things as grew there.[4] At Eddystone, Solomon Islands, whereas the general practice is scaffold-burial, "a man who died of a fall is buried and big stones placed on the top that he may not look back; a woman who dies in childbirth is also buried; lepers are buried or thrown into the sea."[5] The precautions against return which are taken at San Cristoval consist in placing the corpse in a canoe with two men who paddle out to sea, another canoe with two men following; the dead man is then committed to the sea in the sitting position and the canoe in which he was brought is broken up, the four men returning in the remaining canoe.[6] What chance now has the ghost of returning?

Among the Bageshu, a Bantu tribe, only people who have died from smallpox, together with suicides and thieves who have been killed in the act of entering a house by night, are buried; this is done because "they say they wish to suppress the disease, and in the other cases they are afraid of the ghosts." Among the Baganda, "bones of human beings are feared and avoided, and never disturbed unless it is absolutely necessary to move them. Sometimes a woman comes upon them when cultivating and must remove them; she either gathers them together with her hoe, to one side of her garden, and covers them with grass, or burns them. The ghost is always attached to them and fire is the safest and surest method of destroying it." A suicide is not buried, but burned at the crossroads, as the ghosts of those who take their own lives are especially to be feared. Among the cattle-raising Bahima, "the ghosts of the common people have no special abode, but wander about near the kraals. . . . The burial place of a commoner is always the dung heap in the kraal; the widow and relations guard the grave for three or four months to keep wild animals from disturbing the body; the kraal is then left, and a new one built some distance away."[7] One may conclude that by that time there is no fear of the ghost's returning. The Akamba of East Africa drag into the bush the bodies of peasants and women, leaving them there for the hyænas to devour, while

2 Jenness and Ballentyne, *D'Entrecasteaux*, 112, 120.

3 Ray, in *JAI*, XLVII, 288.

4 Turner, *Samoa*, 329, 335 (quoted).

5 Hocart, in *JAI*, LII, 102.

6 Fox, in *JAI*, XLIX, 179.

7 Roscoe, in *JAI*, XXXIX, 181; and in *JAI*, XXXII, 50; and in *JAI*, XXXVII, 102.

chiefs, whose ghosts are much more to be feared, are buried in a deep grave in the village, the corpse being covered with earth and two or three big stones placed over the spot. The natives never cultivate on the site of a grave and the plants that spring up on it are never cut.[8] It is common in this district to require a purification-ceremony in every case where a man kills another, while in some parts on every death the whole village is purified; the ceremony usually lasts but a few days, and may be regarded as a protective device against the return and malevolence of the ghosts of the slain. In deaths from an infectious disease in Kitui the corpse is dragged out by a cord round the neck. "For this work the elders are given a goat, and if the deceased's relatives are too poor or refuse to pay the fee the corpse cannot be disposed of at all, but will be left lying in the hut while the other members of the village will have to move elsewhere."[9] This seemingly sanitary device is prompted solely by ghost-fear, for the natives think all disease is caused by evil spirits. Among the Wawanga, the dead man's chief wife remains in the hut where the body is buried during the following two months for the purpose of tending the fire. After this the hut is broken down and stones and thorny branches are placed upon the grave, all of which may be regarded as precautions against return. Since it is naturally difficult to escape out of a swamp, persons killed by lightning and dead children who are monstrosities are buried in swamps, with the idea of preventing the ghosts from returning to the village. Suicides and people who have come by a violent death are not buried in the hut but in the kraal. In one of these districts, while all married men and women who are very old are buried, other women and children are thrown to the hyænas; the ghosts of the latter, being much less powerful, do not call for careful treatment.[10]

The negro slaves brought over to the New World many superstitions concerning ghosts, some of which relate to methods of thwarting or misleading these disembodied spirits. The following are examples. To feel a hot breath of air strike you at twilight signifies the presence of a ghost near at hand. Should you wish to avoid him, stop and turn your coat and trousers and hat wrong-side-out and the spirit cannot encounter you. If, however, he is a pugnacious sprite and approaches in spite of the change, turn and address him thus: "In the name of the Lord, what do you want?" Whereupon he will tell you his business upon earth, then depart and never trouble you again. If, on the other hand, it is a prowling ghost which crawls under the house, bumps against the floor, makes strange sounds, and whispers in the midnight hours, you have only to put in a new floor and he will do so no more. Some ghosts are obtrusive and will not only prowl about the house, but creep in through the cat-hole or under the crack of the door during the small hours of the night, and, once inside, expand to vast proportions. To spare yourself any disturbance of this sort, sow mustard-seed all about the doorstep before going to bed, or place a sieve there. Before entering, the spirit will have to count all the holes in the sieve or all the mustard seeds, and by this time daylight will have come and he will have to go. As the counting on one night will not do for another, you are always safe.[11]

---

8 Hobley, *A-Kamba*, 66, 102, 103.
9 Dundas, C., in JAI, XLIII, 521, 522; Barton, in JAI, LIII, 46-47.
10 Dundas, K. R., in JAI, XLIII, 34, 37, 59.

11 *Southern Workman*, quoted in New Haven *Journal-Courier*, May 31, 1912; cases in Puckett, *Folk Beliefs of the Southern Negro*.

The reindeer Koryak in Siberia had a method of misleading the ghost which consisted in a relative of the deceased walking round the pyre, first from right to left and then from left to right, "in order to confuse his tracks so that the dead might not follow him." He then took a few steps in the direction of the house, drew a line on the ground, jumped over it and shook himself, the rest of the burial-party doing likewise; "this was supposed to have the effect of forming a large river between the village and the funeral pyre." It is known, of course, that ghosts cannot cross water. The pastoral people of the Baikal province bury their dead in the ground and, as they return from the funeral ceremony, "the relatives try to obliterate the tracks they have made in the snow, or else cut down trees so that they fall across the way, in order to prevent the return of the dead." The Buryat either slaughter a horse near the grave or set one free; in the latter case, "should it return home it is driven away, because they fear it." For three days after the death they do no work, but remain at home; during this time the soul of the deceased wanders round his former habitation. On the third day the relatives hold a feast for their friends. This custom becomes perfectly intelligible when it is remembered that the Buryat, like the Yakut and other aborigines of Siberia, needs a horse in order that his soul may make the journey to the abode of the departed. If the horse is slaughtered, well enough, but if it is merely set free there is danger that it may return home rather than wander at large upon the steppes, and bring the ghost with it. Such an animal is always taboo. Further precautions taken by these peoples are, on the death of a child, to place its cradle on the grave and its toys on the nearest tree, rather than to keep these things in the house, While at the burial of an adult "a great wind is held to be favourable, as it will smooth out the tracks on the way to the place of the funeral, otherwise many of the living will follow the dead."[12]

In the Punjab province of India, "if a woman die within thirteen days of her delivery it is believed that she will return in the guise of a malignant spirit to torment her husband and family. To avert this a *shânti* is performed at her funeral, a piece of red cloth and the grass image of her child being placed on the bier. Some people also drive nails through her head and eyes, while others also fasten nails on either side of the door of their house."[13] Should a Sema Naga mother die in childbirth, "she is taken out by the back door and buried behind the house. The husband in such a case is genna [taboo] for eleven days." All the dead woman's beads, ornaments, and clothes are thrown away, and her husband's personal property is not touched by anyone "for a year," that is, until after the next harvest. "Even then all utensils, etc., are got rid of as soon as they can be replaced, and no one will touch them except the aged."[14] If a Palaung woman dies in childbirth, "her body is hurriedly washed and dressed in new clothes, the coins are tied to the wrists, and the usual food and other things are placed beside her in a new mat, which is wrapped round her body. She is then lowered through a hole which has been cut in the flooring-boards of the room where she died. As the desire of every one is to remove her body from the house and the village as quickly as possible for burial, a coffin is not made. . . . As soon as the body has been lowered, the floor is washed and the hole is closed with new boards. This, they hope, will prevent

12 Czaplicka, *Aborig. Siberia*, 150-151, 155-156, 158, 160-161, 306; Michailovski, *Shamanism*, 16.

13 Rose, in JAI, XXXVII, 225-226.

14 Hutton, *Sema Nagas*, 234.

the return of the spirits of the unfortunate mother and child, to Palaungs the most terrifying of unhappy spirits. . . . If a pregnant woman dies, no woman still capable of child-bearing and no girl should go into the house of the dead woman until the body has been removed. When the funeral has taken place, the mourners in the house may be visited by girls and young unmarried women, who should accept no food there until seven days have passed. They fear that if they eat in the house before the spirit of the dead woman has gone to eat of the fruit of forgetfulness, a similar fate may befall them should they marry." The author[15] who describes this case with much insight goes on to explain other precautions against the return of the ghost. Sometimes the coffin of the deceased is carried round the house before starting for the graveyard. "A man walks in front of the coffin carrying a lighted torch, even if the sun is shining brightly. After the grave has been filled with earth, the torch is laid on the top and there burns itself out. . . . Some say that the way in which a dead person is carried makes no difference to his spirit, but that if his feet point towards the village there will be many deaths there; others think that the ghost might return to his home and remain there if the body had not been carried in the right way." After the interment is completed, some clans place a stick in the path a short way from the graveyard and conjure the spirit of the departed not to pass it.[16]

Among the Dusuns of North Borneo, the ghosts of the dead, whose home is supposed to be at the top of Mount Kinabalu, are thought to be capable of loitering on their way thither and causing trouble, for when a death has recently occurred the old women will weep and call to the spirit: "Do not stop here, for your way lies to the left," that is, to Kinabalu; and natives always avoid graveyards as much as possible. "The bier on which the body has been carried is, in some cases, cut to pieces at the grave-side, probably in order to prevent the return of the ghost, and in others, the men on returning from a funeral slash with their *parangs* or chopping knives at the steps of the house and at the door of the room in which a death has occurred; the object here, again, being to prevent the soul from lingering near the house and bringing evil upon its inhabitants." The Sakai believe that evil spirits collect about the graves where food is placed and feast for a period of six days; the spirits of the dead are very much feared, and children are not allowed to go out after dark during the whole of that time.[17] "Those of the mourners who leave the grave last plant sharpened stakes in the ground, so that the spirit of the dead man may not follow them back to the Dyak house, the stakes planted in the ground being supposed to prevent his return."[18] Like the Finns, the Dyaks also close the grave with a fence too high for the ghost to "take" it, especially without a run.[19] The Sea Dyaks of Sarawak greatly fear that the dead, having become the victims of the most terrible of all powers, may harbor envious feelings, and possibly follow the burial-party back to their homes with evil intent. In order to prevent this, some of them will make a notched-stick ladder, and fix it upside down in the path near the cemetery to stop any departed spirit who may be starting on questionable wanderings; others plant bits of stick to imitate bamboo caltrops to lame their feet should they venture in pursuit.

15 Milne, *Eastern Clan*, 304-305, 295-296.
16 Shakespear, in JAI, XXXIX, 382.
17 Evans, in JAI, XLII, 380; and in JAI, XLVIII, 195.
18 Gomes, *Sea Dyaks*, 138.
19 Frazer, in JAI, XV, 66.

Another method of making it difficult for the spirit to find its way back home is to throw ashes after the corpse as it is being borne from the house. In some instances, ashes are strewn in front of each house before which the funeral procession passes. Some natives of the Indian Archipelago take the body to the grave in the dead of night and then, to make it still more difficult for the ghost to find the way home, they carefully obliterate their footprints. The crouching position of the corpse when buried is regarded by Wilken,[20] who has reported these cases, as an attempt to hinder the dead man from getting out of the grave; since it is usually bound into this position, the practice may be added to the other precautions against return. In northern Sumatra, for safety's sake, the corpse must be buried the day of the death and well before sundown.[21] In Formosa, at leaving the grave each man flings a handful of earth at the wooden slab they have erected and spits upon it, with a warning in formula not to think of returning. "If, in spite of this warning he persists in returning, he must understand that the spitting and stoning just performed is a sample of what his reception will be then."[22] In Samoa it was supposed that if the possessions of the deceased were left and handled by others, further disease and death would be the consequence.[23] The Hawaiians thought a spirit much stronger than a human being—hence the custom of covering the grave with a great heap of stone or modern masonry to keep down the ghost.[24]

In the belief of the Lenape Indians of Canada, a new-born child did not obtain a firm hold on this world for some time after its arrival, its little spirit being easily coaxed away by the ever-present ghosts of the dead. "For this reason it was wrapped as soon as possible in adult's clothing, by way of disguise, so that the ghosts would not notice it was new-born. Similarly deerskin strings or strips of corn-husk were tied on the wrists of children so that the ghosts would think they were tied fast to earth; and holes were cut in their little moccasins so that they could not follow the spirit trail. If the child's mother died shortly after its birth, these precautions were redoubled."[25] It was believed by the Omaha that "the spirit of a murdered man was inclined to come back to his village to punish the people. To prevent a murdered man from haunting his village he was turned face downward, and to impede his steps the soles of his feet were slit lengthwise. . . . Such a haunting spirit was supposed to bring famine. To avert this disaster, when a murdered man was buried, besides the precautions already mentioned, a piece of fat was put in his right hand, so that if he should come to the village he would bring plenty rather than famine, fat being the symbol of plenty. Even the relatives of the murdered man would treat the body of their kinsman in the manner described."[26] Precautions against return, on the Orinoco, consist in rooting up the fields which the deceased has planted; they say they do it to destroy all memory of the deceased. The Island Caribs put two weights on the eyes of the deceased, "so that he may not see his parents and thus make them ill."[27] The notion that if the eyes of the dead be not closed his ghost will return to fetch away another of the household, still exists in Bohemia, Germany, and England.[28]

20 In VG, 99 ff., 105, 408, 409.
21 Jacobs, Groot-Atjeh, I, 336-337.
22 Wirth, in AA, X, 366.
23 Turner, Samoa, 147.
24 Beckwith, in BAE, XXXIII, 301.
25 Harrington, in AA, XV, 212.
26 Fletcher and LaFlesche, in BAE, XXVII, 215.
27 Roth, in BAE, XXX, 159, 160.
28 Frazer, in JAI, XV, 71.

"Doors of the Dead." A custom resting on the belief that a corpse must not pass through any of the regular doors but must be carried out of the house by some other exit appears among the Ashantis, Zulus, Haussas, and a number of tribes of west central Africa.[29] After the South Africans have taken the trouble to break out a special door for the dead, the hut is nevertheless usually abandoned.[30]

The Hyperboreans regularly take the corpse out through a hole made for the purpose.[31] The Koryak do not carry out their dead through the usual door, but under the edge of the tent-cover, which is lifted up. Other tribes of this section remove the corpse through a window or through a specially-made hole.[32] When a Samoyed dies, "various precautions are taken to prevent the spirit of the dead returning to visit the living. For example, the dead body is not carried out of the room through the usual opening, but under the skin or bark wall nearest to the spot where the body lay at the moment of death."[33] Anuchin[34] confirms this information, and adds: "According to the folk-tales, wizards always die with great difficulty; in order to lessen their sufferings a beam in the ceiling is raised, and the bodies of such persons are taken out, not through the door, but through the window. . . . Even at the present day when a person lies long in the agonies of death, it is customary to raise a beam in the ceiling in order to help his soul to leave the body; hence the proverb, 'the beam cracks, somebody will die.'" This case represents the close connection between speeding the soul's departure and preventing its return. Among the Lolos of West China, "after death a hole is made with a pole in the roof of the house to enable the breath or soul to escape;"[35] while it is a general practice in China that "if the dead died in the flower of life or in full manhood, one of the first things for the family to do is to open one of the skylights, in order to allow the disastrous influences, which have caused the death and might attack others also, to escape from the house. . . . Many Chinese hold that the window is simply unclosed for the convenience of the soul, which ought to be allowed to wander freely in and out."[36] In the Naga Hills of India, there are small dead-houses, with windows left at the side for the escape of the ghosts. Fires burn in front of these resting-places.[37] In the Chittagong Hills, "on returning from the funeral pyre, all parties bathe themselves. If the master of the house has died, the ladder leading up to the house is thrown down, and they must make an entrance by cutting a hole in the back wall and so creeping up."[38] The idea here seems to be that the ghost, not being able to utilize the ladder, cannot enter.

"The Siamese, not content with carrying the dead man out by a special opening, endeavour to make assurance doubly sure by hurrying him three times round the house at full speed—a proceeding well calculated to bewilder the poor soul in the coffin."[39] The same custom prevails among the Alfurs, while some of the natives of southeast Borneo will rush with the corpse to the grave, hastily bury it, and then hurry away as fast as possible. Doors of the dead are quite common among the Malayo-Polynesians and have persisted longest

29 Ellis, *Tshi*, 239-240.
30 Bent, *Ethiopians*, 10; MacDonald, in JAI, XIX, 275.
31 Ratzel, *Vkde.*, II, 780.
32 Czaplicka, *Aborig. Siberia*, 150, 163.
33 Montefiore, in JAI, XXIV, 406.

34 Summary of memoir, in JAI, XXI, 322, 323.
35 Henry, in JAI, XXXIII, 103.
36 DeGroot, *Relig. Syst.*, I, 12.
37 Woodthorpe, in JAI, XI, 205.
38 Lewin, *S.E. India*, 133.
39 Frazer, in JAI, XV, 71.

in connection with suicides and criminals, whose ghosts are feared above all others. In those regions, as in the Minahasa, where the houses stand on piles, an opening is made in the floor for the purpose of removing the dead; while among other tribes there is in the dwelling a sort of window which reaches down to the floor, constructed in such a way that it can be used as a door for the dead.[40] Again, several boards may be removed and an opening made upon the veranda.[41]

"Doors of the dead" are not to be confused with mere exits from the grave, which are common enough. For instance, the Easter Islanders, who bury the illustrious in stone structures, always take precaution to leave two holes free through which the soul can eventually find exit.[42]

Corpses are taken out of the Eskimo house through a window, out of a tent by cutting a hole in the back of it. In Norway an opening is made in the wall. When the body is carried out a woman sets fire to a piece of wood and waves it about, saying, "There is nothing more to be had here." This is to show the soul that there is no property which it may come back for.[43] In the Hudson Bay Territory, "the nearest relatives on approach of death remove the invalid to the outside of the house, for if he should die within he must not be carried out through the door but through a hole cut in the side wall, which must then be carefully closed to prevent the spirit of the person from returning."[44] The Bering Strait Eskimo, after tying the corpse with strong cords, draw it up through the smoke-hole in the roof. Among the Tlinkits of Alaska, in the days of cremation and even later, "dead bodies were never taken through the door, but through a hole made in the side of the house and then closed up so that the spirit of the deceased could not find its way back into the house. Or the body was taken through the aperture in the roof and a dog taken along with it. If the dog were not taken they believed that some one of the family would surely die, but if the spirit of the deceased entered the dog it would not return to the injury of any member of the household."[45] The Dakotas always make a new opening for removal of the corpse.[46] Among the Kwakiutl, after a child has died, the body is taken out through a hole made in the side of the house by pulling out some planks. The mother of the dead gives all the best food and clothes to other women to burn behind the village, while she herself throws food into the fire of her house for four days. If a child belonging to the nobility dies, the roof-boards of his father's house are all pulled down, which custom is called "craziness strikes . . . on account of the beloved one who died."[47]

Among the Old Norse the dead could not be removed through the door through which the living went in and out. The people tore down a piece of the wall behind the head of the corpse and dragged it out backwards, or they dug a hole under the bottom of the south wall, through which the body was taken. This was also a common German custom. We find it observed in both North and South Germany in the case of malefactors and suicides who were dragged out, not through the door but under the threshold or through the wall. In this case the practice is an indignity, for these bodies are regarded as unclean,

40 Wilken, in VG, III, 406-408.
41 Furness, *Head-Hunters*, 52.
42 Geiseler, *Oster-Insel*, 31.
43 Nansen, *Esk. Life*, 245; Fries, *Grönland*, 121.
44 Turner, in BAE, XI, 191.
45 Jones, *Thlingets*, 151.
46 Beckwith, in *Smithson. Rep.*, 1886, pt. I, 253.
47 Boas, in BAE, XXXV, pt. I, 709.

whereas in heathen days, when every dead man was regarded as something gruesome and dangerous, it was done to all.[48]

Taboo on the Name of the Dead. The Tasmanians had great fear of pronouncing the name by which a deceased friend was known, as if his shade might thus be offended. "To introduce, for any purpose whatever, the name of any one of their deceased relatives, called up at once a frown of horror and indignation, from a fear that it would be followed by some dire calamity."[49] In D'Entrecasteaux, "the names of the dead must not be mentioned, at least not before their memory has begun to fade," which would indicate a fear of summoning the ghost. The authors[50] one day asked some youths the name of an insect which lay on the path in front of them. "A small boy told us without any hesitation, but an older lad immediately reproved him, saying, 'Hush, you must not say that name; you know the man is dead.' For a time the natives had to call it simply *manuga* (bird or insect). Any adult or child in that district whose name might be the same was obliged to drop it at once and take another." Such a name was unlucky or unclean, as it was connected with the dead; it was taboo.

The same practice is quite common among the Papuo-Melanesians, and the word *polola* among the southern Massim was used to designate the custom by which any word resembling the name of a deceased person is replaced by another word. "If the name of the dead is inadvertently repeated by a child or a stranger, someone says, 'Hush, that is *polola*,' and if a word with a similar sound is pronounced the speaker is told what the new word is; thus a man named Binama (his totem by-the-bye was *binama*, the hornbill) died and all the people of Taupota, whether of his own or other clans, adopted the new name *ambadina* (literally 'the plasterer') for the bird." In a number of places, as no man's name is mentioned after his death, and since people are commonly named after their elder clansmen, a large amount of name-changing takes place. Children are always re-named after the death of their name-sakes, usually maternal aunts and uncles. So flagrant an insult is it to mention the name of the deceased that a man would fight if the name of his dead father or other relative were uttered in his presence. Though among some of these groups the names of the dead are not so stringently avoided, yet "a certain delicacy exists about speaking them," the names of near relatives are not used for some time after a death, while a widow or widower is always spoken of by a special term until he or she marries again or removes the black mourning-pigment with which the body is covered.[51]

Among the Kaffirs, after the death of a chief, his name and all words like it are dropped from the language.[52] In the Upper Congo "the names of the dead are seldom mentioned, and always avoided if possible." A fisherman will take the utmost care to conceal his name while fishing, lest a ghostly enemy should hear it and divert all the fish from his traps and nets.[53] Among the Wagogo of East Africa the name of the dead is not mentioned without a prefix which means: absent, deceased, invisible;[54] while among the Lumbwa "the name of

48 Wilken, in VG, III, 405; Weinhold, *Alt-nord. Leben*, 476; Grimm, *Deut. Rechtsalterth.*, 726-728; Von Negelein, in *Ztft. d. V. f. Vkde.*, XI, 260-270.

49 Barnard, in AAAS, 1890, 605.

50 Jenness and Ballentyne, *D'Entrecasteaux*, 91-92.

51 Seligmann, *Melanesians*, 14, 441, 488, 630-631, 720.

52 Mauthner, *Sprache*, II, 177.

53 Weeks, in JAI, XXXIX, 438; JAI, XL, 370.

54 Cole, in JAI, XXXII, 335.

the deceased is not mentioned after death until a child is born to his family group when, should it cry when his name is called, it receives his name; the deceased is referred to as *kimaitet*, the dead one."[55] In Nigeria, "it is forbidden ever to talk of ghosts."[56]

In China if a child is born after several have died, the father "makes out after a name," that is, he goes out on the street and names the child from the first object he happens to see or the first word he hears. The deaths of the former children have been due to unlucky names; if the name is left to chance, one may be hit upon one which will not attract spiritual attention.[57] The Todas of India are by no means free from the idea that danger attends disrespect connected with the utterance of names. There are several conditions which lead Todas to change their names. If two men have the same name, and one of them should die, the other man would change his name, "since the taboo on the name of the dead would prevent people from uttering the name of the living." This change may be effected even when there is no more than a similarity between two names. Another reason for change is illness or other misfortune. "A man may not utter the names of his mother's brother, his grandfather and grandmother, his wife's mother, and of the man from whom he has received his wife, who is usually the wife's father. The names of the above are tabooed in life, while after death the restrictions are still wider, and it is forbidden to utter the name of any dead elder relative, while the names of the dead are in any case only said reluctantly." In addition to the definite taboos, there is often much reluctance in uttering personal names. "The Todas dislike uttering their own names, and a Toda, when asked for his name, would often request another man to give it."[58] This latter practice has appeared above;[59] it re-emphasizes the force of the taboo on the names of the dead. "Some of the most powerful *kar-nam* [spirits or ghosts] have special names, but the Palaungs are unwilling to utter them, considering it irreverent."[60] These Palaungs consider that if they mention the name of their chief it should be whispered. In Núkuóro, it is forbidden to mention the name of a native after death, and the taboo applies also to the name of the living chief.[61] The Tahitians drop from their language all words and syllables which resemble the names of the deceased kings and their relatives.[62]

The Greenlanders are much afraid of mentioning the names of the dead. Some think that the old names reappear when the deceased is forgotten, others that the word comes into use again when a child has been named after the deceased.[63] Holm[64] tells of a man who, "after having recounted his mother's death and burial, wanted to be paid for it, so that, as he said, the dead should not be angry." There is an account of how King Philip came to Nantucket to kill a man who had spoken the name of one of the Indian's dead relatives.[65] Mourning, among the Dakotas, "is kept up one year, amidst dirt and ragged garments; they then wash themselves, put on clean clothes, and never mention the name or allude to the dead person, and it is considered a deadly insult that the name of the departed should be mentioned in their presence." When

55 Barton, in JAI, LIII, 76.
56 Tremearne, in JAI, XLII, 163.
57 Grube, in K. Museum f. Vkde., VII, 7.
58 Rivers, Todas, 622, 625-627.
59 §212, of the text.
60 Milne, Eastern Clan, 349.
61 Kubary, Núkuóro, 17-18.

62 Mauthner, Sprache, II, 178.
63 Nansen, Esk. Life, 230; Fries, Grönland, 122.
64 Ethnol. Skizze, 129.
65 Macy, in Mass. Hist. Soc., 1st Series, III, 159.

a child is sick the father will take the child's name, believing it will cause others of the family to die if the name should die.[66] Dorsey[67] mentions four Siouan tribes which were exceptional in not holding to the name-taboo; when their relatives died, they did not cease to refer to them by name, "nor did their deaths involve the change of name for a single object or phenomenon. It was a very common occurrence for the name of the deceased to be assumed by a surviving kinsman." The Navaho give the impression of having forgotten the deceased, as his name is never spoken.[68] The Karok of California regard the mere mention of a dead relative's name as a deadly insult, to be atoned for "only by the same amount of blood-money paid for willful murder."[69] Like many other Indians, the Apache would never utter their own names nor on any account speak of a dead member of the tribe.[70] In Paraguay all the members of a family, at the death even of one of the slaves, changed their names, "in naïve precaution, that the ghost might not find them if he returned."[71] Among the Fuegians, "the mourning lasts long, sometimes for two years, but it gradually becomes less, till the memory of the dead passes from the mind. The name of the dead is not mentioned to the mourners, as it is considered very offensive, and would endanger a person's life. On this account it is impossible to trace back by name the ancestors of these people more than three generations."[72]

The African term "hlonipa" has been used to describe the general taboo on names, whether they be those of the dead or of tabooed relationships. Connected with it is the custom not to speak ill of the dead or to take the name of the deity in vain. Since personal names are often the same as the names of objects, this name-taboo has an impoverishing effect on language.[73]

§224. Disguise and other Forms of "Mourning."

THERE is said to be very little sentiment concerning death among the natives of Central Australia; they laugh at the contortions of anyone dying. "But immediately a death occurs all the camp unites in a dirgeful crying, which is kept up every night for a week." If a man dies his widow makes a mourning-cap of burnt gypsum, which is placed on her head in a plastic condition, weighing often up to eleven pounds. The cap fits right over the top of the skull down to a line with the eyes in front, and is about three-quarters of an inch thick; it is worn for a week, a month, or longer. In one place they hit the relatives on the head, during the burial, "to make 'em sorry."[1] In North Central Australia if a woman neglects to cut herself as a mark of sorrow on the death of a daughter, blood or tribal, another woman will go in search of her and, failing the chance of killing her, will strike one of the offending woman's brothers.[2] Among the tribes of West Australia, "when a man or woman is near to death the relatives often throw themselves on the body of the sick person and weep loudly. After

66 Beckwith, in *Smithson. Rep.*, 1886, pt. I, 253 (quoted), 257.
67 In BAE, XI, 371.
68 Yarrow, in BAE, I, 123.
69 Powers, in *Contrib. N. Amer. Ethnol.*, III, 33.
70 HAI, I, 283.
71 Koch, in *Globus*, LXXXI, 45-46.
72 Bridges, in *A Voice for S. Amer.*, XIII, 201.

73 Kropf, *Kaffir-Engl. Dict.*, 154; Mauthner, *Sprache*, II, 177; Letourneau, *Soc.*, 208; Lippert, *Kgchte.*, I, 115, 158; Bousset, *Relig. Judentums*, 302-303; Baring-Gould, *Relig. Belief*, ch. V.
1 Horne and Aiston, *Cent. Aust.*, 153-155; Freeman, in AAAS, 1902, 539.
2 Spencer and Gillen, *Nat. Tr. Cent. Aust.*, 486, 488, 489.

the death the relatives, both male and female, wail and cut their scalps until the blood trickles from their heads. The hair of the deceased is cut off and preserved, being worn by the relatives in the form of string. . . . The relatives of a dead man or woman are required during the period of mourning to abstain from eating the flesh of kangaroo. This was in former times the principal meat food of the natives."[3]

Self-mutilation, smearing the face or body with pigment, special treatment of the hair, and fasting are common forms of mourning in Melanesia. In San Cristoval, Solomon Islands, a widow shaves her head completely for a month, and then allows horizontal bands of hair to grow one at a time till her head is again completely covered. This is done by a widower also, while either may go about covered with a sort of cowl.[4] The period of mourning in another island of the same group generally lasts from eighty to two hundred days, during which time the widow may not leave the village. "She will not allow a drop of water to touch her body, nor a comb or knife to touch her head. Her hair grows long, and in a few months she is a most miserable and pitiable object to behold. Thus she lives to express her sorrow."[5] Neglect of personal cleanliness, a rather common method of showing bereavement, prevails on the Loyalty Islands, accompanied by mutilation, the perforated lobe of the ear being torn open and the mourners sometimes cutting their bodies.[6] In D'Entrecasteaux a widow usually goes to her parents' hamlet before the funeral is over, where she fasts for two days, then blackens her body and face with charcoal. "In the hamlet of the deceased, about day-break on the morning after the funeral, the kinsfolk also blacken their bodies, shave their heads, and put on white cane armlets; then, if their grief should overwhelm them, they break the dead man's pots and his canoe, perhaps even cut down his yam vines and banana trees and such of his coco-nut palms as chance to be in bearing." The mourners never mutilate themselves, "save when some woman works herself into a frenzy and hacks her body with a shell." All who have taken part in the burial must purify themselves as soon as they return to the hamlet. A near relative of the deceased sets a pot of water on the fire.[7] Black is the sign of mourning in New Hebrides, and is obtained by mixing oil and pounded charcoal, some of the natives making their faces glisten like the work of a bootblack. There is great wailing at death, and the mourners scratch their faces till they stream with blood.[8] Blackening the body, cutting the hair and gashing the scalp are mourning-practices among other Melanesians,[9] while abstention is stressed in some cases, as in British New Guinea, for instance, where the relatives must abstain not only from noisy amusements but also from the use of red paint on their bodies, and the male relatives must wear nothing that is painted any color; after the funeral the nearest relative of the deceased must disappear entirely from sight; "enveloped in a rude bark cloth covering, he must spend the days hidden from sight, and pass the nights weeping on the grave."[10] In Tikopia Island the period of mourning is long; all the relatives drink only water and eat only mammy apples for four or five months and they often abstain from coconuts, taro, yams and fish for as long as a year. In addition

3 Brown, in JAI, XLIII, 169.
4 Fox, in JAI, XLIX, 118.
5 Rooney, in AAAS, 1911, 444.
6 Ray, in JAI, XLVII, 287.
7 Jenness and Ballentyne, D'Entrecasteaux, 112, 113.

8 Turner, Samoa, 308, 335.
9 Seligmann, Melanesians, 273, 618-620, 715-717.
10 Williamson, in JAI, XLIII, 287-289.

to fasting, a widow shows her loss by making a number of burns on her face with a brand from the fire. She cuts off her husband's hair and wears it round her head till her death; she breaks the lobes of her ears and always keeps her hair short.[11] In Santa Cruz and Reef Island on the day of his death a man's wife and those in the house begin to fast: they renounce cooked food, some for about a week, some for a very long time; and every day they smear their bodies and faces with charcoal. The widow puts on her head a torn and dirty cloth and does not go about but lives like a prisoner. She remains always at the place where her husband is to be buried; and they bury him on the very spot where he died.

The widow, as has been seen in the above cases and as will be observed in those to follow, is the most important of the mourners. Among the Papuans it is held that the husband's spirit, thought to be most malignant immediately after the death of the body, close to which it hovers for about two or three months, pitches upon the widow as the particular object of its malignity. It is for this reason that "she will wear a piece of hair taken from her dead husband, suspended by a piece of bark or cord from her neck, and also other signs of mourning, in order to placate his Oboro [evil spirit]. His blood relatives, too, adopt mourning for the same purpose," but in their case the requirements are not so strict.[12] Here as elsewhere in primitive society the man is much more important when living and so, when dead, must be more elaborately mourned. He usually gets a better burial. Power, respect, awe, ghost-fear are commingled factors.

Disguise is very clearly the object of the mourning-customs of some negroes of the Gold Coast, for the men go to the grave with the funeral-procession dressed as women and the women dressed as men.[13] Disguise from the evil spirits is implicit at least in the mourning-customs of the Bangala of the Upper Congo. When mourning the body is smeared over with white clay or chalk and the sackcloth-and-ashes usage is followed. The widow either goes absolutely naked or dresses in a few leaves, and rubs dirt on the body. "For six weeks or two months they walk only in the bush, and if they hear anyone coming they hide, and during this time they may not walk about the town; then for another three or four months they wear long untidy-looking grass clothes." A man while mourning for a relative or a wife wears rags or an old string fish net, and allows his body to go unrubbed with oil and camwood powder. "Utter disregard of one's personal appearance was a sign of great grief. Men also at times wore a woman's dress instead of a man's in token of sorrow, and would shave half the hair off, or do it up in little bunches or knots, and shave the hair off the spaces between them. Some would rub their bodies with clay." In the majority of cases, the author[14] thinks, there is more noise and show than grief. Their word for sorrow is *nkele,* which really means anger, indignation, and "the idea is that they are 'angry' that their relative has been done to death by the *Moloki* [witch]. There is no other word for grief at the death of anyone than this *nkele.*" Among another tribe of the Congo basin the relatives take off all adornment, and "men and women wear as a sign of mourning their hair as Nature gave it to them."[15] Both Bahima and Baganda wear bark cloths as mourning-clothes; in the latter case the hair is unkempt, the nails grow to

11 Rivers, *Melan. Soc.,* I, 313-314.
12 Lyons, in JAI, LI, 432-433.
13 Vortisch, in *Globus,* LXXXIX, 281.

14 Weeks, in JAI, XXXIX, 101, 445, 449-450, 453.
15 Clozel, in PSM, XLIX, 677.

talons, and on the chest a white patch is made with water and ashes. A woman's funeral is the same as a peasant's, while in the case of children no two bodies would be put in the same grave lest the ghosts quarrel over the "right of ownership."16 In East Central Africa women lament for several days over the dead, and guns are fired to keep off the evil spirits.17 Among the Wawanga of East Africa, if the deceased be a male, the mourning-ceremony is as follows: on the first day, the corpse is buried, everybody bathes, a fowl is killed in the evening, and there are great lamentations; on the second, there are lamentations only; on the third, there are lamentations and the mourners shave their heads; on the fourth, they kill a bullock or other animal, and sweep up. If the departed be a woman, the mourning lasts but three days and is the same as in the case of a male, with the exception that the lamentations are omitted.18 With the Kavirondo, "the wailing is kept up in the case of a chief for six days, and performed twice a day, at sunrise and sunset, but after the day of the dance each village mourns by itself; for a common person three days is the limit."19 In Kenya Colony, the widows discard all ornaments, the eldest son wears his garments inside out, as does the youngest daughter on the death of her mother, while members of the family may not have sexual intercourse until the shaven hair of the head begins to grow again; marriage and other ceremonies are postponed.20 Among the Hausa "the ordinary work of the house is suspended when a death takes place, this being to show that the women are too sad to work: if they went about their ordinary duties, people would think that they did not care. Men should not work on the day of the actual death or of the funeral, but may do so directly after the last rites, when these take place in the morning, i.e., on the day following the death."21

In excess of grief, orphaned daughters among the Mordva scratch their cheeks with their finger-nails.22 Among a number of Dyak tribes the death-chamber is taboo for seven days and nights following a death, else the ghost will haunt the house. Music, noisy mirth, ornaments and gay clothing are tabooed during the family-mourning, which lasts forty days. White is the mourning-color; and every male must shave his head.23 In the East Indies the time preceding the feast to the dead is a dangerous period; people disguise themselves and abstain from customary occupations. Among the Alfurs of Minahasa the widower must keep to his room for five, seven, nine, or eleven days; in some cases the seclusion lasts a month. The painting of the face or body, which is such a general mourning-practice, is here very specifically done for the purpose of disguise, to protect the living from the dead. Black is the common mourning-color, usually obtained from powdered charcoal and oil. Another method of disguise found throughout the Indian Archipelago is a complete change of clothes. One must wear clothing quite different from the ordinary: dark for light, and especially old and ragged garments. Women must cover the head, which is usually bare, with a mourning-cap, which corresponds to the veil with us; these caps are sometimes three feet in diameter and afford considerable seclusion. All ornaments that cannot be laid aside must be covered. In Celebes the men too must wear large caps, while among the Buginese and some of the Dyaks they wear no trousers during the time of mourning

16 Roscoe, in JAI, XXXVII, 115; in JAI, XXXII, 46-49.
17 Torday and Joyce, in JAI, XXXV, 417-418.
18 Dundas, in JAI, XLIII, 36.

19 Northcote, in JAI, XXXVII, 62-63.
20 Barton, in JAI, LIII, 77.
21 Tremearne, in JAI, XLV, 38.
22 Russian Ethnog. (Russ.), I, 273.
23 Roth, Sarawak, I, 154-156.

but a cloth around the loins, or they tear their sarongs and go about with either the upper or lower part of the body naked. A third general method of disguise is to cut or otherwise alter the hair. The change this makes upon the appearance is remarkable, especially with the women. The shearing of the hair is regarded by Frazer and other authorities as a means of disguise, but Wilken[24] who has reported these practices from the Indian Archipelago, is of the opinion that this custom was originally a sacrificial act and that only later did it become a sign of mourning. Among some of the tribes of the Malay Peninsula the mourners hit their heads on the wall and the women tie cloths round their necks "as if to strangle themselves." The men interfere before any harm is done.[25] Formerly, it is said, the women put an end to their lives by strangling; if this is so, the practice cited is survivalistic.

The Samoans exhibited the most frantic expressions of grief, such as rending the garments, tearing the hair, thumping the face and eyes, burning the body with small piercing firebrands, beating the head with stones till the blood ran. This they called an "offering of blood" for the dead. "While a dead body was in the house no food was eaten under the same roof; the family had their meals outside, or in another house. Those who attended the deceased were most careful not to handle food, and for days were fed by others as if they were helpless infants." In Samoa, "the fifth day was a day of 'purification.' They bathed the face and hands with hot water, and then they were 'clean,' and resumed the usual time and mode of eating." Among the Savage Islanders the women, on the death of their husbands, singed off the hair of their heads, as a token of mourning. For fourteen nights after a burial, in the Tonga Islands, "the men would approach the mount, and pay their devotions to the goddess Cloacina, after which they retired to their homes. At daybreak next morning, all the women of the first rank, the wives and daughters of the greatest chiefs, would assemble, and with expressions of profoundest humility, would make the place perfectly clean."[26] This ceremony, which is probably an exorcistic device, the author thinks has no parallel in the burial-rites of the world. In the Caroline Islands the nearest mourners cut off the hair and beard, throwing them on the corpse; they fast rigorously all the day, leaving food at the tomb for the soul to eat, and then on the following night they feast.[27]

The Aleuts had a practice of putting a mask over the face of a dead person when the body was laid in some rock-shelter. "The departed one was supposed to be gone on his journey to the land of spirits, and he was masked to protect him against their glances."[28] The Tlinkit widow wears a coarse blanket as token of bereavement. Most of the time she lies hunched up on the floor beside the body and as silent as the corpse itself. Her hair is shorn and her face painted black all over.[29] The Indian mourners, in the Northwest, had "their faces painted black, their hair cut short, and sometimes their heads covered with eagle's down."[30] Four days after a Kwakiutl child has died, some non-relative is called in to cut the hair of the mother, father, and the child's brothers; "it is bad if relatives cut the hair. When they cut the hair, it is just as though they were cutting the throats of the relatives."[31] Both widows and widowers, among the Indians of British Columbia, had to undergo continuous

24 In VG, III, 413, 414, 416-422, 459, 463-465; *Vkde.*, 311-313.
25 Skeat and Blagden, *Malay Penin.*, II, 113.
26 "Anthrop. Miscell.," in JAI, X, 460.

27 Montero y Vidal, *Filipinas*, I, 468.
28 Dall, in BAE, III, 139.
29 Jones, *Thlingets*, 147-148.
30 Niblack, in USNM, 1888, 358.
31 Boas, in BAE, XXXV, pt. I, 709-710.

ceremonial washings or cleansings. The body of the deceased also was washed, the hair combed and tied back, the face painted, and the head sprinkled with the down of bull-rushes, "which was potent in checking the evil influences attending corpses." The mourners observed the usual custom of cutting the hair, the manner in which it was done indicating the depth of the mourners' sorrow. "A shorn head, therefore, among them had much the same significance as deep crape garments among ourselves."[32] The Dakotas mourned unkempt, besmeared with earth, in dirt and rags, for a year, and the women gashed themselves with knives.[33] Mourners among the Omaha seem to have found relief from sorrow by inflicting physical pain—slashing their arms and legs; to cut locks of hair and throw them on the body was a customary expression of grief, as was wailing. "Abandonment of all that otherwise would be prized seems to have been characteristic of the Omaha expression of grief . . . it might happen while the tribe was on the annual hunt that a woman who had left the camp to gather wild potatoes would suddenly remember the fondness of a lost child for these roots; on her return she would take the store she had gathered to the center of the tribal circle and there throw down the product of her digging and return empty-handed to her tent. Her act was recognized by all the people as that of a person in sorrow whose thought was fixed on the dead and whose grief made her careless of present physical wants."[34] Mourners among both Neutrals and Apache blackened their faces, and in the former instance they also blackened the face of the dead.[35] On the death of any member of a Kiowa family, all the rest take new names; similarly among other tribes and in Virginia three hundred years ago.[36] Among the Navahos, relatives at a funeral "protected themselves from the evil influence by smearing their naked bodies with tar from the piñon tree;" the forehead and the face under the eyes were thus discolored and the tar remained till it wore off.[37] The mourning mother, among the Diggers, singed her hair off, mixed the ashes with charcoal and pitch, and streaked her chin, cheeks, and forehead;[38] the Yokaia widow's procedure was not dissimilar, except that the ashes used were those of her husband.[39] A mourning-custom common to all parts of the country is that of putting clay on the head and sometimes on the joints of the arms and legs.[40]

Certain Brazilian tribes let the hair grow and color the face black to indicate mourning;[41] in Paraguay the hair is cut close and the face blackened, the mourning lasting until the hair has grown again.[42] If the Indians of the Chaco are forced to a night-march, the next day they all change their names, as also if one of their kin dies or they dream of one of the departed; this is with the object of leading the ghost astray and preventing another visit from him.[43] There was a more or less prevalent custom among Guiana Indians of bewailing the dead the first thing in the morning, as a matter of daily routine. Such daily lamentation of the dead is not unknown in other parts of South

32 Hill-Tout, in JAI, XXXV, 137-139; and in JAI, XXXIV, 320-321 (quoted).
33 Beckwith, in Smithson. Rep., 1886, pt. I, 253.
34 Fletcher and LaFlesche, in BAE, XXVII, 591-592.
35 HAI, I, 284; II, 61.
36 Mooney, in BAE, XVII, pt. I, 231; Thomas, in HAI, I, 947.

37 Yarrow, in BAE, I, 123.
38 Miller, in Globus, LXXII, 112.
39 Powers, in Contrib. N. A. Ethnol., III, 166.
40 Fletcher, "Mourning," in HAI, I, 951.
41 Von Martius, Beiträge, I, 95.
42 Koch, in Globus, LXXVIII, 220.
43 Frič, in Globus, LXXXIX, 233.

America. In other cases, lamentation was limited to the period intervening between death and final mortuary festivities, the varying expressions of sorrow depending upon the kinship and friendly relationship of the survivors. One of the most characteristic of the signs of mourning, in this region as elsewhere, is the renunciation of all ornaments and the cutting of the hair. When death removes any of their blood-relations, the Arawak women drop their knick-knacks and for a short while go about quite naked. The coloration of the body in varying degrees according to the kinship of the mourner was customary among certain of the tribes, red being employed for the purpose by some, blue or black by others.[44]

To "cut the hair and shed tears" were the ordinary tokens of mourning among the Homeric Greeks.[45] The prophets of Israel opposed the more violent expressions of mourning, but in vain; the shrieking of the professional mourners, the destruction of the whole domestic establishment, the tearing of clothes, blackening of walls, destruction of house-utensils, and also the blackening of the faces and the cutting of beards, went on.[46] In old Arabia the widow withdrew into the tent, put on her worst clothing, and touched no perfume for a year.[47] The ancient Arabians are said also to have cut off the hair, not so much as a sign of mourning as in homage to the deceased. When in many Greek states, through the influence of Alexander the Great, it began to be customary to shave the beard, the men took care, as they still do today, to let the beard grow long during the time of mourning. Plutarch says that whenever any misfortune occurred, whereas the Greek women cut their hair, the men let theirs grow; the former were accustomed to wear the hair long, the latter to cut it.[48] In former days when the Montenegrins shaved their heads and wore a long crown-lock only, it was customary to cut off this lock and throw it into the grave. "Women also cut off their hair. I have seen a long tress of a woman's hair fastened to the wooden cross on a grave in the Herzegovina." Self-mutilation has been and still is a mourning-custom with these people. "Face-tearing is now prohibited by law in Montenegro at funerals, but is still done in out-of-the-way places. I have seen a case." In default of a body to mourn over, a dummy is made. "Coat, waistcoat, knickerbockers, white gaiters and leathern sandals are laid out on the table in the semblance of a man and girded with the sash and weapons. A cap is laid where the head should be. I have seen this more than once. The forlorn emptiness of the man's actual clothes give an almost more poignant idea of loss than the actual corpse. . . . The tears streamed from them. They threw themselves on the dummy body, almost fighting to kiss it. Behind the table were the aged mother supported by her two married daughters. The younger, a most beautiful woman, had ripped her face down with her nails and, sodden with blood and tears, was, with her mother and sister, singing the praises of the dead boy. . . . The three women behind the table sang incessantly in a kind of awful possession, apparently unconscious of all that went on." There is here a certain pose and something of the nature of professional mourning: "The odd part of this is the mechanical way in which tears are caused" to flow. At a certain young man's funeral, the men "mostly did not know the poor boy's name and had to be coached in the details before beginning to wail, but within a minute or two of beginning they were sobbing

44 Roth, in BAE, XXXVIII, 638-639.   47 Wellhausen, *Arabern*, 454-455.
45 Seymour, *Hom. Age*, 175.   48 Wilken, "Haaropfer," in VG, III, 464-
46 Von Kremer, *Kgchte.*, II, 250-251.   465, 468.

bitterly. Coming home people compared notes as to who had cried best."[49] In Albania the neighbors as well as the kinswomen take part in singing the funeral dirge. "These dirges are fixed by usage, but it sometimes happens that one of the mourners is inspired by her grief to utter a lament of her own."[50] To a desire to deceive the dead man, Frazer[51] refers "the curious custom among the Bohemians of putting on masks and behaving in a strange way as they returned from a burial. They hoped, in fact, so to disguise themselves that the dead man might not know and therefore might not follow them." The king of France never wore black for mourning, not even for his father, but scarlet or violet. The queen wore white, and did not leave her apartments for a whole year. Hence we often hear of a tower of the white queen, in buildings of the Middle Ages which have been inhabited by the queens in mourning. In deep mourning for a husband or father, a lady wore neither gloves, jewels, nor silk; her head was covered with a low black head-dress, with trailing streamers.[52]

§226. Resistance.

OUR cases of resisting the ghost fall into the twofold classification of (a) maltreating the corpse, and (b) of completely destroying it. In his excellent article on "Burial Customs," Frazer[1] has said that a simple but effectual plan of resisting the ghostly peril is to nail the dead man to the coffin, or to tie his feet or his hands together, or his neck to his legs. "The Wallachians drive a long nail through the skull and lay the thorny stem of a wild rose bush on the shroud. The Californians and Damaras clinched matters by breaking his spine. The corpses of suicides and vampires had stakes run through them. Sometimes the heads of vampires are cut off, or their hearts torn out and hacked in pieces, and their bodies burned, or boiling water and vinegar are poured on their graves." These and additional practices will be illustrated in the following survey.

In Kurdistan if the rain is delayed the Kurds go to the Jewish cemetery, exhume the recently dead, cut their heads off, and throw them into the river.[2] The ancient Chinese way of burying the dead was "in the house, under brambles and wood over which came a layer of clay;" DeGroot[3] thinks this may explain why, "as the ancient tradition asserts, coffins or vaults of earthenware came into vogue even before coffins and vaults of wood were generally used." Among various peoples the corpse is placed in the grave in the sitting position; there are different reasons for this practice; among the polar people it may simply be that the living are accustomed to this posture.[4] Among the Maoris, common people were tied tightly in a rough mat and placed in a sitting posture;[5] here the idea of resistance seems to be implied.

The Hudson Bay Eskimo lash the limbs of the corpse to the body;[6] those of Bering Strait pour out for the ghost a drink the evil taste of which will drive him away.[7] The Kwakiutl mother will kick her dead child four times; "and when she first kicks him, she says, 'Don't turn your head back to me.' Then she turns around, and again she kicks him. And as she kicks him, she says, 'Don't

49 Durham, in JAI, XXXIX, 92-93.
50 Von Hahn, Alban. Studien, I, 151.
51 In JAI, XV, 73.
52 Lacroix, Middle Ages, 501.
1 In JAI, XV, 66.
2 Reinach, in L'Anthropologie, XVII, 633.

3 Relig. Syst., II, 376-377.
4 Nilsson, Scand., 139.
5 White, in AAAS, 1891, 364.
6 Turner, in BAE, XI, 178.
7 Nelson, in BAE, XVIII, pt. I, 313-314.

come back again.' Then she turns around again. She kicks him; and she says as she kicks him, 'Just go straight ahead.' And then she kicks him again, and says, 'Only protect me and your father from sickness.' "[8] The Sioux sometimes strapped the body to a stake in a sitting position and then carefully covered it with clay.[9] In the Dakota district "very often the skeletons were 'bundled,' that is to say, the bones were dislocated and formed into a bundle, the skull being placed on the top or at the end. Sometimes they were folded as completely as possible by drawing up the knees to the chin."[10] After torturing a captive, the Indians "leave him on the frame, and in the evening run from cabin to cabin, and strike with small twigs their furniture, the walls and roofs of their cabins, to prevent his spirit from remaining there to take vengeance for the evils committed on his body."[11] The tomahawk was used to drive off the evil spirit.[12] Tearing out the eyes was found among the Kokopas.[13] The Macusi shaman spat upon the face of the dead and stuffed hair into ears and mouth.[14] Other South American Indians sealed up the eyes, nose, and mouth of the dead, that his spirit might not cause anybody's death.[15] In contrast with the cases of maltreatment of the body, some Guiana Indians bury their dead in a standing position, assigning as a reason that although the deceased is in appearance dead, his soul is still alive. "Therefore, to maintain by an outward sign this belief in immortality, some of them bury their dead erect, which they say represents life, whereas lying down represents death. Others bury their dead in a sitting posture, assigning the same reason."[16]

Assurbanipal is said to have mutilated the corpse of a defeated enemy in order to do him harm in the other world.[17] Similar instances occurred among the ancient Greeks, though one Spartan king indignantly refused to repay on the corpse of his enemy the insults perpetrated by Xerxes on the corpse of Leonidas at Thermopylæ.[18] "In West Prussia a method of preventing a dead member of a family from inflicting disease on the living is to open the coffin and cut off the head. It is further a well-known prehistoric burial-custom."[19] In the *Saga of Grettir the Strong*[20] a revenant is decapitated, the notion being that a ghost can be laid by cutting off the head of the deceased and putting it by his thigh. Among the early people of England and Scotland there was a practice of burying a murderer or the doer of some dreadful deed by some lonely roadside and, above all, of driving a stake through his breast. This was done because their spirits were supposed to wander unless prevented; and as they needed the shadow of their bodies for that purpose, it was intended that the bodies should be so fastened as not to escape. Other means were employed for the same purpose; for instance, the head was sometimes severed from the body and placed between the legs or between the arm and side.[21] A survival is reported in which a person is alleged to have tampered with the grave of a relative with the intention of severing the head from the body and placing it at the foot of the coffin, in order by such action to put an end to a long

---

8 Boas, in BAE, XXXV, pt. I, 708-709.
9 Thomas, in HAI, II, 335.
10 Thomas, in BAE, XII, 539.
11 Rogers, *America*, 235.
12 Yarrow, in BAE, I, 96.
13 Nadaillac, *Preh. Amer.*, 119.
14 Schomburgk, *Brit. Guiana*, I, 421.
15 Michailovski, *Shamanism* (Russ.), 17.

16 Roth, in BAE, XXX, 154.
17 Maspero, *Hist. Anc.*, III, 436-439.
18 Homer, *Iliad*, XI, 147; XIII, 102; *Odyssey*, XXII, 412; Herodotus, *Hist.*, IX, 78.
19 Thomas, in *Folk-Lore*, XI, 249, note 2.
20 Magnússon and Morris, *Grettir the Strong*, 48.
21 Gomme, *Ethnol. in Folklore*, 123.

series of deaths in the family supposed to have been caused by the spirit of the deceased.[22]

Complete destruction of the body, which is the most effective way of resisting the ghost, though it may be performed for other motives, is usually accomplished by cremation or by throwing the corpse to dogs or vultures. The Tasmanian method of treating the dead, according to one account, probably falls under this head. "When a death occurs in a tribe, they place the body upright in a hollow tree, and (having no fixed habitations) pursue their avocations. When some time has passed, say a year or upwards, they return to the place and burn the body, with the exception of the skull; this they carry with them, until they chance (for I do not think they lose much time in seeking it) to fall in with a cemetery, in which a number of skulls are heaped together, when they add the one with them to the number, and cover them up with bark, leaves, etc. They do not bury them in the ground." This practice is not propitiatory, for the writer has never been able to ascertain that they put either weapons or food in the tree with the dead.[23]

In former times, among the Tati Bushmen, when death came to an encampment, the corpses of both men and women were dragged into the neighboring bush and there left to be devoured by the hyænas and vultures. "Sometimes they were placed in the clefts of rocks and the aperture closed up with stones and branches, or put in a hole in the ground," but "this was the case if the deceased had been a person of some importance."[24] The only way to put a stop to the malevolent actions of an evil spirit, think the Bakoko of the Cameroons, is to dig up the corpse and burn it.[25] A similar method of laying the ghost is to be found among the Wawanga of East Africa, where "if a man fall sick, and in delirium call out the name of a departed relative, the sickness is usually attributed to his spirit, and the medicine-man will tell them to dig up the corpse, that the sick man may be cured. Accordingly the bones are dug up and burnt in an open place over a red ants' nest. The ashes are then swept up into a basket and thrown into a big river." Sometimes, instead of disposing of the corpse in this manner, a stake is driven into the head of the grave and into the hole thus formed boiling water is poured.[26] To put a stop to the sleep-disturbing visits of deceased relatives, some tribes will open up the grave, take out the corpse and burn it, and then carefully reinter the ashes. "This procedure lays the ghost." Among another group in this section, "if a man comes to steal cattle by night and is killed during the attempt, next day they build a pile of firewood and cremate the corpse. Otherwise, his ghost or spirit will trouble the village and bring sickness to it." Again, "if a child dies and the mother does not bear again, the bones of the infant are dug up, wrapped in banana leaves, and thrown into the bush; it would appear that the spirit of the child is believed to be exercising a baneful influence on the mother and the digging up of the bones is thought to extinguish the spirit. Probably it is considered that, in the case of a child, such a drastic measure as cremation is not necessary."[27]

It occurs commonly in Mongolia that the dead are thrown out for the dogs to eat. Some natives think that the more eagerly the dogs devour the corpse the more righteous was the deceased. The animals are so used to the practice

22 New York *Times*, Jan. 7, 1922.
23 Roth, *Tasmania*, 132.
24 Dornan, in JAI, XLVII, 51.

25 Von Schkopp, in *Globus*, LXXXIII, 332.
26 Dundas, in JAI, XLIII, 38.
27 Hobley, in JAI, XXXIII, 339-340.

that they take their places in readiness when the time comes.[28] Andrews,[29] leader of the third Asiatic expedition of the American Museum of Natural History, who witnessed this method of disposing of human remains, states that the Mongol dogs are the fiercest of brutes: "When persons are about to die, the Mongols believe that evil spirits enter the body. Once death has occurred, the bodies are placed on carts and driven over the roughest possible ground. During the journey the body is thrown off, to be devoured by the following wild dogs. I have seen a pack of dogs completely devour a dead body within eight minutes." In Tibet the bodies are cut to pieces by a corpse-cutter and fed to the dogs, this being called the "terrestrial burial"; then the bones are crushed in a mortar, mixed with barley, made into balls, and fed to dogs and vultures, this being the "celestial burial." Both methods are considered highly desirable. The poor are thrown into streams.[30] Sometimes the crushed bones are scattered to all quarters, "so that every morsel is carried away, and nothing remains in the open plains."[31] The practice is explained by Cunningham[32] as due to lack of fuel to burn the bodies. In one tribe of the Indian Hills the richer cremate, the poorer bury or fling into the water; in another, they cremate, bury, or scorch the corpse and throw it into the water; in a third, they cremate, bury, fling into the water, or expose in the jungle. "Even among orthodox Hindus, the three methods are adopted; babies they bury; from babyhood till marriage or initiation they use water burial; adults they cremate."[33] The so-called "Towers of Silence" of the Parsees in India represent an elaborate apparatus of exposure. They are heavy stone cylinders twelve to fourteen feet high and at least forty in diameter with seventy-two compartments radiating like spokes from a central well. Around the top is a living coping of vultures, perched side by side, heads pointing inward. "The vultures do their work much more effectually than millions of insects would do, if the bodies were left in the ground; and by their rapid destruction putrefaction is entirely prevented." The dry bones are swept down the central well.[34] Similar exposure is practised by the Buddhistic Siamese.[35] If a Palaung chief should die at a great age, his body is burned instead of being buried; the ceremony is the same as that of the burning of a Buddhist monk in Burma; Palaung monks are cremated in the same way. Destruction of the body for the purpose of laying a malicious ghost occurs here. A story in illustration is told of an old woman who died of fever. "After her death one person after another died in rapid succession. The tenth dying person was asked, 'Who art thou?' and the answer was 'I am X,' naming the old woman who had died. The kar-bu [spirit or ghost] of the old woman had made its home in her body in the grave, and coming out at night it drove the kar-bu out of one person after another, really killing them. . . . Her body looked as if she were sleeping. They carried it to the jungle and cut it into small pieces, burying the pieces here and there."[36]

In Borneo, cremation seems to be confined to the Land Dyaks; "the body, being surrounded and covered with wood, is altogether consumed by the flames;" it is ominous of further deaths if the smoke rise at a slant.[37] On

28 Ivanovski, *Mongolei*, 15; Prjevalski, *Forskningsresor*, 6.
29 Interviewed in N. Y. *Times*, Nov. 15, 1923.
30 Rockhill, in USNM, 1893, 728.
31 Wellby, *Tibet*, 244, 245.
32 *Ladak*, 310.

33 Crooke, in JAI, XXVIII, 247.
34 Patell, in JASB, II, 57; Yarrow, in BAE, I, 104-106.
35 Wilken, *Vkde.*, 299.
36 Milne, *Eastern Clan*, 311, 341 (quoted).
37 Roth, *Sarawak*, I, 135, 137.

Easter Island, "slain warriors of high rank who fell into the enemy's hands in war, they dishonored by burning their skulls, as if to burn the soul along with them, and thus create the most evil condition the native can imagine."[38]

The Central Eskimo bury their dead, but "they do not heed the opening of the graves by dogs or wolves and the devouring of the bodies, and do not attempt to recover them when the graves are invaded by animals."[39] The American customs of handling corpses, including cremation, have the object of freeing the soul to find peace in the after-life.[40] The Tsimshian burned the bodies of all except the shamans. "Before the burning occurs, the heart is taken out and buried. It is believed that if it were burned, all relatives of the deceased would die."[41] The same custom was observed by the Tlinkit and Haida; of the former it is stated, with reference to the usage of never cremating the shamans, that "their bodies have never been burnt for the reason that it is a common superstition that fire will not touch them." Shamans, furthermore, were never buried in family grave-houses, like others who were not cremated, and were not coffined like others; "they were put, without coffin, in small grave houses, alone, situated in isolation at some lonely headland or such, which spot was often chosen by themselves before death." Cremation used to be a universal practice among the Carriers, without which one might not enter the spirit-world. "The spirits guarding the entrance there reject a ghost from earth because 'He does not smell of smoke.'"[42] The name Carriers is derived from a custom of this Athapascan group which requires the widow to remain upon the funeral-pyre of her husband till the flames reach her own body, when she must collect the ashes of the dead, place them in a basket, and carry them with her during three years of servitude in the family of her deceased husband; at the end of that time a feast is held, after which she is released from thralldom and permitted to remarry if she desires.[43] It is proved beyond a doubt by numerous instances that cremation was practised in certain cases by the Mound Builders.[44] In Georgia human remains, sometimes cremated and sometimes not, were laid on the sand with vessels of earthenware inverted above them.[45] Cremation was practised in some cases where persons died of unknown diseases. In the case of a Kutchin chief, the body was burned by men employed for the purpose, and the burned bones and ashes put in a wooden receptacle and hung in a tree. "The men who burned the body ate no fresh meat for a year, else, it was believed, they too would die."[46] Like the tribes of the northwest coast, the Indians of Guiana cremated the bodies of all except the medicine-men.[47]

Cremation is said to have been a regular practice during the later Bronze Age.[48] The old Norse graves which remain were probably those of the better class. So many skeletons, piled up in graves from floor to capping-stone, have been found that all the flesh must have been removed by action of air or otherwise before interment; here may be a case of "second burial."[49] Odin is said to have ordered that the dead should be burned.[50]

38 Geiseler, *Oster-Ins.*, 31.
39 Boas, in BAE, VI, 613.
40 Müller, *Oldtid*, 330.
41 Boas, in BAE, XXXI, 534.
42 Macleod, in AA, XXVII, 127, 129, 130, 133.
43 HAI, II, 675.
44 Nadaillac, *Preh. Amer.*, 117.

45 Moore, in HAI, II, 873.
46 HAI, II, 192, 884 (quoted).
47 Roth, in BAE, XXXVIII, §865.
48 Müller, *Oldtid*, 325, 332.
49 Worsaae, *Nordens Forhist.*, 39; Müller, *Oldtid*, 94.
50 Geijer, *Svensk. Hist.*, 23.

§227. Expulsion.

AMONG the means to which recourse is taken against the lingering ghost are fire, water, noise, and a show of force. In British New Guinea, where ghosts are known to walk about, even the police at times want to fire off their rifles to frighten them away.[1] When some Europeans made an excursion to a cave of the dead in Eddystone, Solomon Islands, the native guide threw stones ahead of him to frighten away the spirits, else the members of the party would fall ill, and on coming out they were given dark leaves to prevent sickness and were instructed not to look back. A Fijian will use an axe on any object which he thinks harbors a ghost.[2] In the Trobriands, after two or four weeks the return of the ghosts to the other world is compulsory, being induced by the ceremonial hunting-away of the spirits. The drums intone a peculiar beat which the spirits know; when they hear it they prepare for their return-journey.[3] To frighten away the spirits which attend every feast in D'Entrecasteaux, an old man comes forth and brandishes his spear toward every point of the compass; then the men seize their spears and the women sticks and stones, and hammer on all the houses. "A native dreads being overtaken in the woods by darkness lest he should encounter a spirit, and his fire is often as much for protection against them as for warmth. No attempt is made to propitiate them; they are enemies of the human race, and cannot be conceived of as ever doing good." The power of these ghosts or spirits is as unlimited as the people's imagination.[4]

During the funeral-rites in Mashonaland the natives chew and spit out a poisonous root, which is probably an exorcistic practice.[5] Among the Edo-speaking peoples, water is thrown on the roof as the child is carried in, and it must drip upon the child—water being a protective device against ghostly influence; while at an Ibo burial the husband sits in a special part of the house and mourns, with a fly whisk and a matchet near him, and "when his dead wife comes to kill him she sees the matchet and goes away."[6] Weeks[7] mentions an incident from the Upper Congo which recalls Tam O'Shanter: "There had been a death in the family, and the relatives had just performed all the necessary rites and ceremonies, and were returning to their homes. A small trench some twenty feet long was dug with a hoe. The relatives took up their position on the side of the trench nearest to the grave, the *nganga* [shaman] stood on the other side, and his assistant was placed at the end of the trench with a large calabash of water. At a signal the water was poured into the trench, and while it was running the *nganga* took each person by the hand, and mumbling an incantation, pulled him or her over the running water. When all had been pulled over one by one the water was allowed to run until the calabash was empty. I asked the reason of the ceremony, and they told me it was to keep the spirit of their buried relative from following them." An exceptional interpretation is given by this author to the funeral-practice of firing guns, shouting, wailing, and beating drums: "Such noises are heard in *longa* [other world] and give warning of the approach of another soul. The

---

1 Strong, in JAI, XLIX, 298.
2 Hocart, in JAI, LII, 100; and in JAI, XLII, 440.
3 Malinowski, in JAI, XLVI, 380.
4 Jenness and Ballentyne, *D'Entrecasteaux*, 151, 152.

5 Bent, *Mashonaland*, 77.
6 Thomas, in JAI, LII, 251; and in JAI, XLVII, 205.
7 In JAI, XXXIX, 454, 372.

louder the noise the greater is the anticipation of those in *longa* of seeing a great man arrive." The common object for making noise on such an occasion is to drive away the spirit, and it may well be that we have here a case of naïve rationalization.

In Madagascar during a heavy rain, the people beat the walls of their houses violently, to drive out the ghosts who may have tried to escape the rain.[8] Evil-disposed ghosts must be expelled because they cause sickness and other calamities; if they cannot be appeased, among the Baganda, a shaman is called who catches the ghost by thrusting into the roof a stick tipped with a horn. He then lowers the horn, covers it with bark, and plunges it into a pot of water, finally throwing it into a river or upon unreclaimed land.[9] Rumbling noises and abdominal pains are regarded by the Bahima as signs of possession by spirits. There are times when these evil spirits are especially likely to possess one and at such times means must be used to drive them away; for instance, when women are obliged to expose the body, "they take a small gourd with a longish neck in which is a mixture of tobacco and water, the water is then poured through a small hole in the gourd's neck over the parts to prevent evil spirits from entering the person whilst thus exposed."[10] After the East African burial all present proceed to the river to bathe; until they have done so they may not enter any hut but that of the deceased. "On their return a fire is lit on the grave over the feet. This fire is kept burning for one whole month. Should it go out, it must be re-lit from the fire in the hut; should this also be extinct, it must be lit again by means of a fire drill."[11] Such a fire, maintained by the most ancient methods, is especially effective in keeping away the spirit of the deceased. To dream of dead people in the estimation of the Kikuyu is highly undesirable; "the dreamer takes live charcoal in his hands next day and rubs it between his palms saying, 'I shall not dream of that dead man again.'"[12] After a dream the Hausa spit first to the front, then to the right, left, and back; "this averts evil in all directions."[13]

In Siberia the ghost is given forty days' "law"; after which, if he still hangs about, the shaman hunts him out and drums him down to hell. To prevent any possible mistake, he personally conducts the lost soul to the lower regions and treats the devils all around to brandy.[14] It is necessary to be protected against evil influence on an occasion such as marriage: among the Yukaghir, "some relative in the wedding party fires a gun to protect the bride from the attacks of evil spirits; this is called 'shooting into the eyes of the evil spirits.'"[15] The inhabitants of the Altai Mountains think they can drive the ghost into the underworld most effectively by the use of water.[16] In South India the dying man is given a bath and drinks holy water in which the priest's feet have been washed.[17] The Saoras pour water on the body while it is in the house.[18] People who die a violent death or perish by accident or of poison, cholera, smallpox, or leprosy are thrown into water and after some months cremated in effigy.[19] The holy water of the Ganges is used for death-purification.[20] Among the Parsees water is used along with cow's urine in funeral-

8 Frazer, in JAI, XV, 66.
9 Roscoe, in JAI, XXXII, 43.
10 Roscoe, in JAI, XXXVII, 116.
11 Dundas, in JAI, XLIII, 35-36.
12 Tate, in JAI, XXXIV, 261.
13 Tremearne, in JAI, XLV, 41.
14 Frazer, in JAI, XV, 66.

15 Czaplicka, *Aborig. Siberia*, 95.
16 Radloff, *Schamanenthum*, 52-53.
17 Thurston, *S. India*, 138.
18 Fawcett, in JASB, I, 248.
19 Crooke, in JAI, XXVIII, 246, 247.
20 Nathubhai, in JASB, III, 485.

purification. On the dawn after the third night, the soul goes to the other world, passing by way of a bridge.[21] During the process of cremation among the Nairs there is a ceremony called literally "to walk round a pot," which consists, as its name implies, in walking round the pyre with a pitcher, the bottom of which is pierced. One of the family fills this pitcher with water and carries it three times round the burning corpse, dashing it on the ground at the end.[22] Elsewhere in India, ten days after a death the potter makes small images of flour and water and places them in flowing water.[23] Among the Nagas the evil attaching to the manner of death and the prohibitions entailed can be avoided if before he expires the unfortunate can be caused to consume food or drink. It is enough to pour a little water into the mouth of the dying or even to spit into it.[24] At the funeral of a male Toda occurs a ceremony similar to that of the Nairs. A man of the same clan as the deceased goes round the burial-place three times ringing a bell, while another accompanies him, holding him by the waist. "The man who rings the bell then takes a new pot, ordinarily used for carrying water, and, raising it over his head, brings it down and breaks it on the stone covering the ashes. He bows down and touches the stone with his forehead, gets up, and goes away to the funeral hut without looking back."[25] Force also may be used, for "immediately a Rangte has breathed his last all present seize weapons and slash the walls, floor, and roof of the house shouting, 'You have killed him, whoever you may be we will cut you in pieces.'"[26]

An instance of imitative repulsion is the following: when the mischievous ghost of a person killed by a tiger is supposed to haunt its old home, a man belonging to a different family is made to assume the shape of a tiger, being provided with a tail and painted to resemble the striped appearance of the beast. Thus disguised, he is caused to walk on all fours like a quadruped, and is led by two men with strings tied to his hands and legs. The priest recites his *mantrams,* or spells, and makes a show of chasing away this sham tiger; meanwhile the evil spirit of the person killed is believed to take its flight. In general, water and fire are, like sacrificial blood, beneficent elements by the aid of which the mischievous influences of many an evil power may be neutralized. We have already seen that people who have touched a corpse may get rid of the evil influences of such contact by bathing; and the same may be accomplished by fire-lustration or fumigation. Sometimes an entire village is purified in a ceremony in which the head of the whole body of villagers traverses the village from one end to the other, ceremonially sprinkling water from a pumpkin-gourd on every suspicious-looking nook and corner and every bend and turn on his way. Water-lustration is employed by some natives on other occasions than death; purification by ablutions in cold water is required in the case of women who have attended a delivery, in the case of a priest or other person who has to offer sacrifices or make other offerings to a deity or spirit, and in the case of a bride and a bridegroom just before the wedding-ceremony. "Such ablutions are believed to remove all supernatural evil influences. Even the ceremonies of washing the feet of guests . . . and of members of the family on their return home from a distant place, though these may appear to us as only delightful exhibitions of Oraon and Munda hospitality and domestic

21 Modi, in JASB, II, 419, 437.
22 Panikkar, in JAI, XLVIII, 276.
23 Modi, in JASB, III, 477.

24 Hutton, *Sema Nagas,* 262.
25 Rivers, *Todas,* 382-383.
26 Shakespear, in JAI, XXXIX, 382.

affection, may not improbably have originated in the supposed efficacy of water in removing all possible supernatural evil influences of the strange places and strange roads."[27]

In China, "the doctrine that a dying person must give up the ghost on a water-bed is, now-a-days, far from obtaining as a peremptory customary law."[28] In the south of China one of the soul's trials in the nether world is the crossing of the yellow river. For this the priest makes a little ship of bamboo-leaves which he floats in a cup of water. With constantly intensified prayers, interrupted only by the tinkling of bells and the beating of drums, the priests run around the cup. At last they announce that by the power of their prayers the soul has successfully crossed the river.[29] The Chinese are also said to knock on the floor with a hammer, to chase away the lingering ghost, while the Northern Burmese dance the ghost out of the house, accelerating his departure by a liberal application of the stick. Among the Battas in Sumatra the priest, aided by female mourners, acts as ghost-sweeper.[30] Among the Palaungs, "when the labour pains begin, the woman sends for the friends who have arranged to be with her. They bring with them water, over which incantations have been recited, and sprinkle it in and round the house in order to keep evil spirits at a distance. They then go to the inner room where a good fire has been made."[31] From the Malay States is reported an instance in which a group, thinking that a ghost had stricken down two or three of their kinsmen in rapid succession, moved their settlement to the other side of the river, in the expectation that the ghost would not be able to follow them across the water.[32] Among a number of tribes in the Malay Peninsula, the children immediately after birth are carried to the nearest rivulet, washed, and brought back to the house; then a fire is kindled, incense thrown upon it, and the child passed over it several times. "We know from history that the practice of passing children over fire was in all times much practised among heathen nations; and that it is still practised in China and other places."[33]

In the Indian Archipelago, to take a bath or wash the hands and feet had a significance almost wholly lost to us. The original import of these acts must have been to place a physical barrier between the living and the dead. The first barrier so conceived was probably a river, which the dead must cross to get to the other world. To the Borneans the way to the spirit-world is over big trees as bridges and over paths as sharp as swords. If the soul falls off the bridge the fish eat and thus annihilate it.[34] Elsewhere the soul "has to go past burning water-falls, to cross a great many rivers and lakes, go through the abode of the criminals and climb over high bridges before it reaches the banks of the river "on which are the golden dwellings of its deceased ancestors."[35] The Timor-laut spirit-world is a certain island upon which no one dares land and by which they sail with fear and great vigilance.[36] Later, thinks Wilken,[37] out of this crossing of water arose the custom of prophylactic bathing, while still later the whole was reduced to the washing of hands or the sprinkling of water. Given such views, it is quite rational that as one deliberately steps through water on the way back from a burial, so, in the

---

27 Roy, in JAI, XLIV, 335 (quoted), 346.
28 DeGroot, *Relig. Syst.*, I, 8.
29 Rehatsek, in JASB, I, 320 ff.
30 Frazer, in JAI, XV, 66.
31 Milne, *Eastern Clan*, 280.
32 Knocker, in JAI, XXXIX, 144.

33 Skeat and Blagden, *Malay Penin.*, II, 17-18, 20.
34 Nieuwenhuis, *Borneo*, I, 149.
35 Roth, *Sarawak*, II, clxxiv.
36 Forbes, in JAI, XIII, 13.
37 In VG, III, 424-425, 427-428, 449.

opposite case, on going to a burial, one is careful to avoid water, as otherwise the soul might remain back in the village. This is actually the case with the Macassars and Buginese who, on the occasion of a burial, go out of their way so as to avoid as far as possible the passing of streams. Water-purification after touching the dead is common in the Archipelago, and in southeast Borneo is performed in a curious way: the entire family of the deceased get on board a small craft which is taken out into the middle of a river where it is capsized by a priestess, so that all fall into the water; "this ceremony is repeated three times and secures purification from contact with everything that belonged to the dead." The use of water in a less direct way is practised by the Sea Dyaks who break a jug of water on the floor the moment the corpse is carried out of the dwelling. Among the Mohammedans of the Indian Archipelago the custom prevails of sprinkling the grave immediately after the burial with water brought from the death-house. Washing the hands after a funeral is general. The Nuforese, surrounding the grave, take a blade of grass or leaf which they form in the shape of a spoon and bring several times into contact with the head as if pouring something out; in other words, they imitate the action of bathing while they murmur, "The ghost comes." Thereby they adjure the deceased not to come "spooking" around the relatives. Another device for expelling the ghosts mentioned by Wilken is the burning of salt in the house of the deceased, with the thought that the crackling so produced operates to keep the ghosts at a safe and proper distance. The practice protects not only against each ghostly visitation, but also keeps the souls of the deceased from entering the dwelling. There are still other methods of scaring away the ghosts: the spirit of a woman who has missed the joy of motherhood by dying during pregnancy is supposed to be especially averse to nudity; hence the widower, wholly naked or wearing a mere apron, climbs to the roof of his house, fully armed, and supported by armed friends round about and under the pile-supported house. "All begin to hack and stab in the air with mad rage, and thereby, according to their belief, the ghost is frightened and withdraws."[38] In Central Borneo it is thought that nudity scares the evil spirits and "that display of the private parts, or even an image of them, is especially effective."[39] Hurling lances at the coffin is another method,[40] while the Dusuns have a ceremony called "brushing," which they perform in order to rid the house of the spirits of disease; the men brush down all the walls of the house with bunches of flowers and bamboo-leaves, thereby, at least figuratively, brushing away the evil sprites.[41]

It was taught among the Maoris of old that "water is the life of all things; without water nothing could flourish." There are a number of ceremonies in which water is an essential element, but the most elaborate appears to be the baptism of the child. Two priests prepare for their part in the performance, which consists for the most part in taking off all their garments and donning a scanty apron. The chief priest takes his stand in the water, which is the "cleanest" to be found, immersed in which, in Maori eyes, he stands the least chance of being affected by polluting influences. He is, as it were, spiritually insulated for the time being. As he concludes a certain ritual, he dips a little water up in his right hand and sprinkles it over the parents as they stand at the edge of the water. The secondary priest hands him the infant's umbilical cord

38 Wilken, in VG, III, 320.
39 Nieuwenhuis, *Borneo*, I, 146-147.
40 Bock, *Borneo*, 99.
41 Evans, in JAI, XLVII, 153.

which he slips into the water. The child is then submerged up to his neck and the priest sprinkles some water on his head. This is but a skeleton of the ceremony. When the Maori first saw the European method of baptizing children, they did not approve of it; the general remark was that it was not correctly done, for it did not follow ancient custom; that nature's own font was the only proper place to perform such a ceremony; that as performed by white folks it was much less *tapu*.[42] The Maoris also have their river Styx. They are known to thrash the corpse in order to hasten the soul's departure.[43] In the Gilbert Islands, on the three nights following a death, the ceremony of *bo-maki* was performed. "All the people, irrespective of their kinship to the deceased, gathered together in the darkness, with sticks of pandanus wood and the butt ends of coco-nut leaves in their hands, at the southern extremity of the village, and, forming a line abreast from east to west, slowly advanced northwards, beating the ground and trees before them with their staves. Not a word was uttered. When the line had swept through the settlement from south to north it stopped, and the participants disbanded in silence. All pedestrians who happened upon the party while it was at work would seize a staff without a word, join in, and when it was finished pass on their way. The object of the ceremony was to encourage the soul of the dead to leave the neighbourhood of the body and also to drive away any evil spirit that might wish to possess it."[44]

In Alaska, "from the moment of death until the body is disposed of, some one must remain with the corpse day and night and a light must burn every night. This is to guard against the intrusion of spirits. The Greek church custom of burning candles about the dead appeals strongly to this phase of their superstition and conforms to their practice."[45] At night, when the common people of the Quilcute Indians of the Northwest Coast begin to feel creepy, in the belief that ghosts may be coming, "they shoot off their guns and make other noises, in the conviction that this will keep the ghosts away from their households."[46] Among the Omaha, a fire was kept burning on the grave for four nights, the reason given being "that its light might cheer the dead as he traveled; after that time he was supposed to have reached his journey's end." Many tales are told concerning ghosts, with advice as to how to escape them. "Ghosts bent on mischief, as tampering with food after it was prepared for eating, could be thwarted by placing a knife across the open vessel containing the food. A ghost would not meddle with a knife. Nor would ghosts ever cross a stream; so, if a person was followed or chased by a ghost, he would make for a stream, wade it, or even jump across it. No matter how small the stream, it made an impassable barrier between himself and his ghostly pursuer."[47] The Algonquins beat the walls of the death-chamber with sticks, while in ancient Mexico professional men were employed to search the house until they found the lurking ghost of the late proprietor, which they summarily ejected.[48] The Aztec priest sprinkled water on the dead man's head.[49] The mourners at the Makusi burial jump over the fire.[50]

The great mystery-feast of the Jibaro Indians is that celebrated by a

42 Best, in JAI, XLIV, 146-151, 153-154, 160.
43 Tregear, in JAI, XIX, 118; Frazer, in JAI, XV, 66.
44 Grimble, in JAI, LI, 44-45.
45 Jones, *Thlingets*, 151.
46 Frachtenberg, in AA, XXII, 336-337.

47 Fletcher and LaFlesche, in BAE, XXVII, 591, 593.
48 Frazer, in JAI, XV, 66.
49 Nadaillac, *Preh. Amer.*, 299.
50 Roth, in BAE, XXXVIII, 641.

warrior who has captured a head. Its aim is to purify the slayer from the blood attached to him after the killing of an enemy and to protect him against the spirit of the latter, who is thirsting for revenge. Both water and blood act as purifying agents. A little water is put upon the head of the slayer and then upon his wife and daughter who, by touching the still blood-stained hands and clothes of the slayer, have likewise been polluted with the blood of the murdered enemy and consequently are exposed to danger from the revengeful spirit. All three are subsequently sent down to the river to bathe. Purification is effected also by applying blood, which must of necessity be that of a chicken, to the legs of the slayer. The lance with which the enemy has been killed is looked upon with superstitious fear and the warrior is therefore anxious to exchange it as soon as possible. Tobacco-juice is given through the nose by the priest to the victor, and to his wife and daughter through the mouth. After the feast the Jibaro warrior retires to the forest, where he stays alone, taking tobacco-water, bathing every day in the waterfall, and sleeping at night in a small "dreaming hut." As soon as the black paint he has put on his body has disappeared he returns home, where he finally drinks some narcotic in order to see whether there are still enemies threatening him and whether everything will turn out happily for him in the future. This case is especially significant in that it clearly brings out the need of purification of the slayer; his case is like that of those who come into contact with a corpse. There is also in evidence here a number of expulsion-devices, many of them childish and naïve, by which the Indians fancy that they can keep the feared spirit at bay. In general they are the same as those resorted to for repelling a living human enemy. At one stage of the ceremony, for instance, three warriors rush into the house brandishing their weapons and shooting, thus trying to keep off the invisible enemy and inspire him with terror, for "the lance and the shield, and still more shots from firearms, are feared even by the spirits." Furthermore, "the measure to keep the trophy [head] tied to the murderous weapon, the 'demoniacal' chonta lance, the rattling with the shields at the most important ceremonies, the attempts to inspire the spirit with fear by making noise, by threatening movements and dancing, and to 'wash off' its malignity and desire for revenge by washing the head in a magical solution, all illustrate, in different ways, the primitive conception that the Jibaros have about the supernatural beings and the possibility of influencing them."[51]

The water-barrier between the living and the dead often dwindled into a mere stunted survival, especially among more advanced peoples. Thus, after a Roman funeral it was enough to carry water three times round the persons engaged and to sprinkle them. Modern Jews, as they leave the graveyard, wash their hands in a can of water placed at the gate; before they have done so they may not touch anything nor may they return to their houses. In modern Greece, Cappadocia, and Crete, persons returning from a funeral wash their hands.[52] Another Jewish practice is mentioned where a relative of the deceased goes to the toilet-table and turns the looking-glass to the wall, being afraid of seeing the ghost in the glass, and opens the window to empty the jug of water upon the sunlit grass.[53] At the Roman feast of the larvæ and

51 Karsten, "Jibaro," in BAE, Bull. LXXIX, 29, 37, 39, 42, 65, 76, 85, 87-88 (quoted).

52 Frazer, in JAI, XV, 78-80; Wilken, in VG, III, 424-425.

53 Zangwill, Ghetto, 259; Frazer, Golden Bough, I, 146.

lemures all intercourse ceased, the temple was closed, the hearth-fire and the sacrificial blaze were extinguished, the hands were washed repeatedly, black beans were strewn for expiation, and bronze cymbals were beaten together, all for the purpose of banishing the ghosts.[54] In Babylonian literature may be found means of exorcism which are directed explicitly against the wandering ghost of the dead as the cause of sickness.[55] The Germans waved towels about or swept the ghost out with a besom, after the Roman custom by which an heir swept out the ghost of his predecessor with a special broom. In Scotland and Germany, when the coffin was lifted up the chairs on which it had rested were carefully turned upside-down, lest the ghost should be sitting on them. In modern Greece when the corpse is once out of doors, the whole house is scoured.[56] These are a few survivals of the many practices for driving away evil spirits or laying ghosts.[57]

§229. Human Sacrifice.

In the cases which follow, human sacrifice is practised chiefly for the purpose of providing the deceased with a grave-escort, this being especially the case where wives and slaves are the victims. In some of the instances the cannibalistic motive is present. Common to all is the literal conception of life in the other world as a replica of life on earth.

Custom prescribes in the South Sea Islands that, should their husbands die before them, wives must submit to be strangled and put into the same grave; "this they do with the greatest alacrity, and should the man have ten wives at his death, all must suffer and be buried with him."[1] Occasionally among the Upper Congo natives male slaves are killed and sent with messages to the deceased head of the family. "Such a slave generally requested that the headman should remove his anger from his family and allow them to enjoy health and prosperity. It was after much sickness and many misfortunes in a family that such a messenger was sent. Only wealthy families could afford such a luxury as this, and the whole affair would be talked about all over the district and the family be greatly respected for this proof of their wealth." Failing in fisherman's luck was one of the unfortunate occasions requiring a sacrifice; "it was no uncommon thing, when a village was unsuccessful in its fishing, for the inhabitants to join their brass rods [local currency] together to buy an old man or old woman—old by preference, because cheap, and throw him (or her) into the river to appease these water spirits." In the old days it was also customary at a funeral to kill two slaves, putting one under the head of the dead as a pillow and the other under the feet. In every family of importance there was a slave wife, who went by a name which indicated that she was to be buried alive with her dead husband. "The number of wives buried in the grave was in proportion to the man's wealth and importance, but he always made certain of one." Further assurance of attendance was obtained by putting the skulls of enemies at the base of palm-trees and using them as foot-stools, the desire being to insult the fallen foe by these indignities and to have some hold on the spirits of those slain in war, that they might attend their conqueror

54 Rossbach, *Röm. Ehe*, 267.
55 Schrader, *Keilinschriften*, 460.
56 Frazer, in JAI, XV, 64, 66.

57 For collections of striking instances, see Frazer, in JAI, XV, and his *Golden Bough*, II, 158 ff.
1 Im Thurn, in JAI, LI, 22.

in the spirit-land.[2] In East Central Africa the Ba-Mbala sacrifice a goat, half of which is buried with the corpse and the rest eaten; in former times it seems probable that the victim was a slave.[3] Again, as soon as a king had breathed his last, two of his wives were instantly sacrificed. "On the burial day, when the body of the chief, now reduced to a skeleton, was laid to rest wrapped in a bull's hide, all his servants, councillors, and his wives were paraded before the tomb, and smitten between the eyes with a club. They were then left for dead at the tomb, and if by chance anyone managed to survive, he was not seized again, as the *Basing'anga* [medicine-men] who preside at these functions say that he is not acceptable to the dead chief's spirit." When a Wabisa chief died, instead of sacrificing all his attendants, his people only killed his head-wife, and this when the chief had lain for a long time in state and only his bones were left. "Her body was split in twain, and the bones of the chief were put inside, and buried in this ghastly winding sheet."[4] Formerly, among the Nigerian head-hunters, "if the deceased had been an important person, people were killed on the day of the funeral so that their ghosts might accompany his, and their skulls were left on the grave until the flesh was gone, and then added to the other trophies of the family." Today, if the deceased has been an important person or a parent, a goat is killed; if unimportant, a fowl; if a baby, nothing. The flesh of the goat or fowl is then divided amongst all the relatives present, who are always summoned; to forget them would be a deadly insult. "Meat is a message which must not be ignored."[5]

When the Ostyak were at war with the Samoyed, and afterwards with the Tartars and Russians, not only did they vie with the Samoyed in the custom of scalping a slain enemy, but some of their songs tell also of heroes eating the hearts of the foes they had killed.[6] On the day of the return from the war-path of the head-hunting Sema Nagas, the successful raiders must celebrate a certain ceremony, for until it is done they are unclean, taboo, holy, and a village that is sowing and tilling may not entertain them. Some of the eastern Semas skewer wads of meat to the mouth and eyes of the dead enemy, that the ghost, eating and being filled, may call his friends to come and be killed; then all sorts of indignities both in word and deed are showered on the trophy by the women and children of the village. On the day of a burial, cattle and pigs are killed and the skulls put up on a sort of fence or rack erected for that purpose, along with the skulls of those slaughtered by the dead man during his lifetime; the souls of these victims he either takes with him to the village of the dead or finds already awaiting him there. The practice of boring the lobe of the ear, which must be done some time by all, is probably a survival of human sacrifice and an identifying tribal mark; "if a man die with the concha of his ear unbored his forebears in the next world disown him."[7]

The practice of head-hunting, which is common enough in the Indian Archipelago and among many Papuans, is clearly in the nature of a human sacrifice when accomplished on the occasion of a burial; the possession of a head is necessary, among some of these tribes, to enable them to leave off mourning. So long as one has not found opportunity to get possession of a head, "the spirit of the departed continues to haunt the house and make its presence known

---

2 Weeks, in JAI, XXXIX, 452 (quoted), 455; JAI, XL, 370 (quoted), 372 (quoted).
3 Torday and Joyce, in JAI, XXXV, 417-418.
4 Sheane, in JAI, XXXVI, 157.

5 Tremearne, in JAI, XLII, 167.
6 Czaplicka, *Aborig. Siberia*, 68-69.
7 Hutton, *Sema Nagas*, 175-176, 235, 236, 245.

by certain ghostly rappings." The Dyaks think then to mollify its anger by having the nearest relative throw a packet of rice under the house every day, for its benefit, until it is laid to rest by their being able to celebrate a head-feast; "then the Dyaks forget their dead and the ghosts forget them."[8] Wilken[9] thinks that the practice of shearing the head at the time of a death was originally a sacrificial act, which seems likely in these cases cited by him, for the shorn hair is deposited in the grave with the dead. In the Indian Archipelago slaves are killed in order that they may follow the deceased and attend upon him. "Before they are killed the relatives who surround them enjoin them to take great care of their master when they join him, to watch and shampoo him when he is indisposed, to be always near him, and to obey all his behests. The female relatives of the deceased then take a spear and slightly wound the victims, after which the males spear them to death." In the Philippines also, when a noble died a number of slaves were sacrificed, so that he could have the proper social setting in the spirit-world.[10] In some of the more remote traditions of the Samoans reference is made to human sacrifice.[11]

Among the Chinook and a few other tribes of American Indians slaves were buried alive that they might accompany a chief to the next world; one writer, who speaks from hearsay only, mentions the killing of women of a hostile tribe by a chief in order that their spirits might serve his dying son in the other world.[12] In addition to the usual manifestations of grief at the death of a relative or friend, some Indians cut off their hair and burned it on the grave,[13] while in the scalp-dance there was probably some survival of former sacrificial practice.[14] Self-mutilation at funerals was a regular performance among the Guiana Indians[15] and in Brazil the natives cut off their fingers for the dead, a joint for each relative; some old men had only the thumb left.[16]

At the funeral of Patroclus, among other sacrifices, twelve young Trojans taken captive on the last day of battle were slain, their bodies laid on the outer part of the pyre, and fire applied. Shorn locks of hair were strewn on the corpse of Patroclus. In Euripides one reads of the drinking by the dead of the blood of human sacrifice, for instance, at the sacrifice of Polyxena at Achilles's tomb.[17] Among the ancient Arabs the cutting of the hair partook of the nature of a sacrifice.[18] There were relics of human sacrifice among the ancient Jews and Babylonians.[19] Head-hunting flourished in Europe well into the middle of the nineteenth century and was not yet extinct, a few years ago, in the Balkans, where it has long been common to Christian and Moslem alike. Sacrifice of hair also prevails, and till quite recent times the pigtail was sacrificed in South Slav lands. "The rest of the head was shaven and the long lock plaited. Many of the portraits of Serbian heroes of the beginning of the nineteenth century show it, and in many parts of Bosnia it is still worn by the Roman Catholic peasants. It is usually coiled up and hidden under the head wrap, but in church, when the head is uncovered, you may see long pigtails hanging down, and giving a Chinese

8 Wilken, in VG, III, 437, 438; Haddon, Austen, Riley, in *Man*, XXIII, 33-39.
9 In VG, III, 465-467; 92.
10 Montero y Vidal, *Filipinas*, I, 57.
11 Turner, *Samoa*, 201.
12 HAI, II, 598, 918, 921.
13 Mooney and Thomas, in HAI, I, 787.
14 Grinnell, *Cheyenne*, II, 40-41.
15 Roth, in BAE, XXXVIII, §§840, 842, 844.

16 Oliveira Martins, *Raças*, II, 86.
17 Seymour, *Hom. Age*, 477; Homer, *Iliad*, XXIII, 134 ff.; Euripides, *Hecabe*, 536-537.
18 Wilken, in VG, III, 465-467.
19 Schrader, *Alte Test.*, 506; Levit., XVIII, 21; Deut., XVIII, 10; Ex., XXII, 9; XXXIV, 20; Jer., XXXII, 35; Ezek., XX, 26, 31.

appearance to the congregation. At funerals, until about 1850, it was customary for the near male relatives of a deceased man to cut off their pigtails and throw them into his grave. One great use of the pigtail, I have been told, was to carry home heads by. The South Slavs, and especially the Montenegrins, had a passion for head-taking, excelled by head-hunters in no part of the world. We have record of the taking of huge numbers, in the poems by Veliki Voyvoda Mirko, the father of the present King of Montenegro. He published a number on the wars of 1850-60. They are devoid of any literary merit, but detail exactly the methods of the head-hunters of Europe. . . . Head-cutting was not practised in the last war, but nose-cutting was substituted, noses being more portable. This disgusting practice consists in cutting off the nose right through the nasal bone, and shearing away the whole upper lip with it. The trophy is then carried by the moustache." A certain ecclesiastic in South Macedonia "brought head-taking quite up to date in 1903 by having the head photographed afterwards, and sending copies to his friends as Christmas or Easter cards—I forget which."[20]

Modern Japan has furnished a number of illustrations of sacrifice before and after the death of the ruler, including cases that may be designated as voluntary human sacrifice. Before Emperor Mutsuhito died, in 1912, shrines over the countryside were thronged with worshippers praying for his recovery. At one shrine a young girl cut off her hair and offered it as a sacrifice; at another five men offered to the gods a prayer written on a scroll in their own blood. Devotion reached its climax in the suicide of General Nogi, following the Emperor's death. Similar scenes marked the passing of Emperor Yoshihito in December, 1926. The police were directed to exercise special precaution to keep Japanese from following General Nogi's example. All owners of firearms registered with the police were visited and requested to take care of their guns and not to lend them. That the fear was not ungrounded is evidenced by the suicide shortly afterwards of an aged man who died facing his ruler's portrait: Baron Ikeda shot himself, leaving a letter saying that he wished to follow the spirit of Emperor Yoshihito.[21]

§230. Food-Offerings.

In British New Guinea it is thought that the dead man hovers near the grave, sees the food placed upon it, is pleased, and then goes away.[1] "A small platform is made over the grave, or sticks are stuck along the sides, and on these are placed sago, yams, bananas, coconuts, cooked crabs and fish: all for the spirit to eat. A fire is also lighted by the side of the grave, and friends keep it alive so that the spirit may not be cold at night."[2] Substantial tokens of affection, in the form of direct offerings of food, are supposed by the natives in the Trobriands to please the departed spirits; indeed, the offerings are prompted as much by fear, for the spirits "get angry whenever there is little display of food."[3] Although the food put on graves in the New Hebrides is eaten by animals, it is thought to be pleasing to the spirits.[4] These people worshipped the ghosts of their ancestors; "they prayed to them, over the kava-

20 Durham, in JAI, XXXIX, 94 (quoted); and in JAI, XLVII, 445-446 (quoted); and in Man, Feb., 1923, 19-21.
21 N. Y. Times, Dec. 26 and 28, 1926; Jan. 2, 1927.

1 Strong, in JAI, XLIX, 297.
2 Chalmers, in JAI, XXXII, 119-120.
3 Malinowski, in JAI, XLVI, 377.
4 Ella, in AAAS, 1892, 644.

bowl, for health and prosperity; reminding us, again, of the origin of 'healths,' 'toasts,' etc."[5] The living, as is evident, expect something in return, even though it be but the negative withholding of calamity. Not long ago there was a big hurricane at Tikopia, in which so many coconut trees were blown down or damaged that there was a great scarcity of food. This disaster was of course caused by the spirits: "The people thought that the *atua* had sent the storm, being angry because they had not been giving enough kava, and in their turn the people were angry with the *atua*. To make matters worse there followed a drought; the sun shone continuously and dried up the earth and starvation was staring the people in the face. Offerings of kava were made daily to bring rain but without result. At last the brother of the chief of the Taumako asked John if he could do anything and John prayed for rain which fell three days later so that the taro and yams grew again. The apparent success of John led to a division among the people, some believing that the rain was due to his intervention while others believed that it had been sent by the *atua* to whom at last the long continued offerings of kava had become acceptable."[6]

A short time after a burial in Cameroons a goat is slaughtered over the grave and the blood allowed to flow down a tube which extends to the head of the corpse. Then the liver of the animal is chopped up fine, mixed with palm-oil, and dropped down the tube. Afterwards yams, dried fish, salt, and palm-wine are put down the tube and around its mouth. For these the people ask something in return: "as this was being done, the ghost of the head-chief was asked to use all his influence to make the crops produce plentifully and the women to bear children."[7] The grave among the Batetela is marked by a small mound, on which is erected a miniature hut, where food must be deposited daily by a relative who, should he neglect this duty, will be haunted by the dead man in his dreams. "If he does not mend his ways his wife and cattle will become sterile and his crops will fail."[8] Zulu graves are said to be decorated in a new way owing to contact with civilization: the Zulus have hit upon the device of placing on the graves of the departed the bottles of medicine prescribed by the doctor.[9] Among the Wawanga of East Africa the expectation of a *quid pro quo* is evident: "A pot of beer is brought, and one of the dead man's brothers pours a little over the grave saying: 'Drink this beer we have brewed for you,' and the kinsmen then consume the rest of the beer. . . . A bullock is then slaughtered and its blood poured over the grave. The ears, nose, windpipe, tongue, lungs, stomach, liver, the right hoof and the meat under the backbone are put in a pot, boiled and cut into small fragments; these are then tied all around the grave . . . and the souls of the departed ancestors are thus addressed: 'You are our eyes, accept this food, and keep us in good health.' 'See, brother, we have brought you this food, eat and be not angry with us and send us good health.' "[10]

The Todas of southern India hold a feast for the dead which in the old days was a great occasion, the proceedings lasting for two whole days and many buffaloes being slaughtered; the Government now allows but two buffaloes to be killed for each person, though if two or more funerals are held simultane-

5 Turner, *Samoa*, 334.

6 Rivers, *Melan. Soc.*, I, 317. John was a converted native of Wallis Island who gave the author much information.

7 Malcolm, in JAI, LIII, 396-397.

8 Torday, in JAI, LI, 376.

9 New York *Times*, Dec. 1, 1901.

10 Dundas, in JAI, XLIII, 37.

ously there is an appearance of the olden times.[11] The eating of meat was once universal in India; cows were sacrificed and the flesh eaten, especially at feasts in memory and honor of the dead, where the aroma of beef was thought to be an excellent aliment for the departed. The ancient law allows all sorts of animal food to be eaten, provided that small portions are first offered to the gods and to the spirits of departed ancestors. Of all the ceremonies connected with the Hindu religion the feast of the dead is the most important, and in some cases quite equal in expense to a marriage. It takes place on the thirtieth day after the death of the person on whose behalf it is celebrated. Its main features are the feeding of large numbers of Brahmans and Hindus of other castes and the presentation of offerings of food and sweetmeats to the spirit of the person recently deceased and to his or her ancestors.[12] The Feast of the Departed in Japan lasts for seventy-two hours, from July 15 to July 17, according to the lunar calendar. The dead come back from the spirit-world to live with their families for these days, and there is great rejoicing. The home is garnished and swept, food is placed in the alcove where the altar to the dead is erected, and the entire family behaves during the three days as if all their ancestors were in the home with them. On the last day signal-fires blaze before the doors of the homes of all Japan, lanterns twinkle in the graveyards, and there is general merrymaking, for on this day the dead join with the living in feasting. When one of the emperors of Japan was buried, chests containing rice and other food were deposited in the tomb.[13]

Wilken,[14] writing of conditions in the Indian Archipelago, says that the flesh of slaughtered animals, although in a few cases placed in the grave with the corpse, is for the most part eaten, and that out of this practice arise the feasts of the dead, which are nothing but sacrifices offered to the manes. In some cases the dead are thought to appear on earth to carry on a system of secret depredations upon the eatables and drinkables of the living, in other words, to come for their share. With the feast these "foraging expeditions" come to an end: the dead then are said to relinquish all claims upon the living, and to go henceforward on their way, depending upon their own resources. The feast of the dead ends the period of mourning, because then the souls, without further claims on the living, leave the earth and go to the spirit-world. The case of the Sea Dyaks is reported more fully. Among them mourning is observed until the feast in honor of the dead is held. On the third day an observance called *Pana* is made: a plate containing rice and other eatables, as well as a Dyak chopper, an axe, and a cup, is taken by several of the neighbors to the room of the dead person. "They go to tell the mourners to weep no more, and to give the dead man food. They enter the room, and one of them—generally an old man of some standing—pushes open the window with the chopper, and the offering of food is thrown out for the benefit of the dead man and his spirit companions. Up to this time the near relatives of the dead man live in strict seclusion in their room, but after it they may come out to the public part of the house and return to their usual occupations. Until this *Pana* is made, the Dyaks say the soul of the dead man is unsettled. It has not quite left this world, and Hades will not receive it or give it food and drink. But thereafter it is re-

11 Rivers, *Todas*, 372-373.
12 Bühler, *Manu*, V, 32; Monier-Williams, *Brāhmanism*, 195-196; Wilkins, *Hinduism*, 459.
13 Hearn, *Japan*, 42 ff.; New York *Times*, Nov. 18, 1923; Feb. 8, 1927.
14 In VG, III, 433-437, 439.

ceived and welcomed as a regular denizen of the spirit world."[15] The Sakai place food on the grave and light a fire there for six days after burial; then the ghost departs.[16] The Jakun fix a bamboo in the grave in communication with the mouth of the corpse for the purpose of feeding it.[17] Among the Filipinos food and other articles are placed in reach of the dead and on the fourth day, when the funeral-honors are celebrated, a place is left vacant for the deceased, the people believing that he really occupies it. Usually food is given to the dead to keep them from doing harm.[18]

Some time after the death and burial of a young man or woman, the Omaha parents gave a feast, inviting to it the companions of the deceased. Other similar acts of offering food, all of which partook of the character of remembrance, were practised, "none of which were done because of a belief that the dead needed or partook of the food."[19] Among the Arawaks all of a man's crop of cassava was used at his death for the feasts in his honor.[20] The final burial-festivities, which close the period of mourning, take place among the Guiana Indians upon the anniversary of the death; song, dance, drunkenness, and venery run riot.[21]

The idea underlying the death-festivals of the Romans was that the ghosts of the dead return at times to the upper world and must be conciliated by gifts, lest they harm the living; more than half the year was given over to holidays, until Marcus Aurelius ordered that there be not over one hundred and thirty-five festival days in the year. Among them were three which were sacred to the spirits of the lower world, nine on which the graves of relatives were decorated and the ancestral ghosts were offered sacrifices, and another on which all the relatives met for a feast.[22] Among the Zoroastrians, during the last ten days of the year the souls of the dead came in festive throngs to their surviving relatives; flowers, food, and wine were offered to them.[23] It has long been a Jewish custom to offer food to the dead.[24] According to the Aryan view, which has been preserved in all Indo-European nations, deceased persons still exist after their death as ghosts or "shades"; therefore they take with them into the grave, or upon the funeral-pyre, the things to which they were most attached; and they also need food and drink.[25] Most interesting in the folk-lore of the Bretons is the Feast of the Dead; as midnight approaches the watchers draw away from the fire, to make room for the spirits: " 'Come!' sighed a peasant, 'we have used the fire long enough. Now let us make way for our ancestors. You know the saying, "Death is cold! and the Dead are cold!" ' "[26]

§231. Sacrifice of Property.

SINCE the other world is conceived of in terms of this, the dead have need of property of various sorts, and so their possessions are placed on the grave, usually being broken or destroyed beforehand for the purpose of releasing their

15 Gomes, *Sea Dyaks*, 139-141.
16 Evans, in JAI, XLVIII, 195.
17 Skeat and Blagden, *Malay Penin.*, II, 90.
18 Montero y Vidal, *Filipinas*, I, 57.
19 Fletcher and LaFlesche, in BAE, XXVII, 592.
20 Schomburgk, *Brit. Guiana*, 458.

21 Roth, in BAE, XXXVIII, 642.
22 Wissowa, *Relig. Römer*, 187, 189; De Marchi, *Culto Priv.*, rev. in *Année Soc.*, I, 157; Pater, *Marius*, 187.
23 Justi, *Persien*, 79.
24 Zangwill, *Ghetto*, 224.
25 Ihering, *Aryan*, 38.
26 Le Braz, *The Night of Fires*.

souls and thus making them utilizable by the ghosts. In a normal burial in the Solomon Islands the things belonging to the deceased are broken without any ceremony. Some say they do this because the deceased is cross and does "something no good" to the man who keeps them; others that they are broken to prevent anyone from stealing them, though here as elsewhere the taboo on the possessions of the dead is very strong. The most likely explanation given by the natives is that by breaking the articles their shadows go to the spirit-world. "They also break the shield and spears, and cut down the betel vines of the deceased and take some of it with areca to the burial place."[1] Among other Melanesians, with certain exceptions, "the dead man's chief possessions, all carefully broken, are arranged by the side of the bisa; the centre of the bundle thus formed consists of broken spears thrust into the ground around which the other articles of property are wrapped and tied. . . . All these were so thoroughly broken as to be quite useless, but the dead man's bible—a mission has been established in Poreporena for 25 years—which entered into the composition of the tobi had not been torn up."[2]

In former times, among the Ewe-speaking tribes of West Africa, as soon as the king expired the women of the palace commenced breaking up the furniture, ornaments, and utensils, and then proceeded to destroy themselves; "the reason of course was that they might at once join their lord, and he be surrounded by familiar and useful articles."[3] Among the natives of the Upper Congo "the cloths and clothes of dead men were buried with them, or if the article was out of the common it was first broken (killed) or torn, and then placed on the grave."[4] When a Ba-Yaka dies all his pots are broken and left on the grave.[5] In Nyassaland the relatives put the dead man's cooking-pots near his grave, "having first made holes in the bottom of them which render them useless to the living."[6] When an Atharaka child dies the body is stripped of all clothing and ornaments; these are placed in a little heap by the side of the body in the bush. The spear and shield of a man are also left alongside his body. The author was informed that "theft of these things was quite impossible," and that "any man who did so would at once be suspected of having compassed the death of the owner and would be cast out by his people."[7] A chief or person of importance among the Asabs of the Niger is not buried until the goods, necessary to represent his wealth and station adequately, can be brought together, to be placed in the grave with the body. Until that is done, his spirit is considered as existing in a betwixt-and-between state, neither of this world nor of the next. "This does not apply to a common man, whose friends on his decease contribute a few goods, and whose spirit passes directly to the next world." In northeast Africa, "trophies of the hunt and of war, captured spears, shields, genitals of slain enemies, pieces of elephant hide, beer receptacles, wooden staves which are to show how many cows the deceased possessed, sun shades, and tufts of women's hair are preserved on the mounds as a grave-decoration."[8]

In Siberia, when the corpse is brought to the spot chosen for the funeral, it is put on the top of a symmetrical pyre with its face toward the west. "Four men, one at each corner, stand with poles stirring the fire, and many objects

1 Hocart, in JAI, LII, 81.
2 Seligmann, Melanesians, 160.
3 Ellis, Ewe, 128.
4 Weeks, in JAI, XXXIX, 98.
5 Torday and Joyce, in JAI, XXXVI, 43.

6 Moggridge, in JAI, XXXII, 470.
7 Champion, in JAI, XLII, 85.
8 Parkinson, in JAI, XXXVI, 314; Paulitschke, Nordost-Afr., I, 207.

such as weapons, sledges, and pans, are broken up and, with the sacrificial dogs, are cast upon the pyre."9 The ornaments and implements hung on the Naga grave are consecrated and "anyone stealing them would surely die a speedy and miserable death."10 A clearer case of projectivism than that of the property-sacrifice at a Palaung burial would be hard to find: "A comb for the hair and a looking-glass are laid in the coffin beside a dead girl; a flute beside the body of a young man; a favourite toy, such as a top, or the large beans which are used in games, beside a child. Betel-nut and tobacco with matches are placed in all coffins, also cooked rice and curry. . . . No instrument for work is ever placed in a coffin [the other world is somewhat idealized]; but if a policeman dies, a small wooden sword and gun are taken to the grave and left there. When a baby dies, a few drops of milk from the mother's breast are put into a tiny joint of bamboo and placed in the grave." The nature of the other world is further seen in the practice of laying a small silver coin on the tongue of the deceased. "Both Palaungs and Pales follow this custom, but they have not all the same beliefs as to the use of the coins. They all believe that the money is given to be used in some way by the spirit as toll-money; some think it is to be given to the spirits haunting the graveyard; others that the ghost carries it, in ghostly form, to a closed gate on the path which all spirits must tread, and gives it to the guardian so that the gate may be opened; others again believe that it is offered to the old man and woman who guard the tree on which the fruit of forgetfulness grows. In one Palaung family only, I found that they believed that the ghostly path lay across a river, and that the coins were to be given in return for permission to cross a bridge. They all agree that if no toll-money is buried with the dead, the spirit cannot go to its appointed place, but must wander miserably, returning again and again to the house where it was happy in its last life."11

When bodies were cremated by the Tlinkits, the ashes were carefully gathered and placed in a dead-house. "Deposited with the box of ashes were many possessions of the deceased, such as clothing, blankets, tools, food, water and other things. These were for his use in the spirit-land." A shaman was never cremated; his body was embalmed, and "things that he owned and prized in life were deposited with him. No matter how costly, they were never in any danger of being stolen, for the tomb of a shaman was regarded as especially sacred. No tomb, however, was ever in danger of being rifled by a native."12 The Indians of Oregon practised surface-burial in small huts, canoes and goods of all kinds being placed with the corpse. "The explanation given of this custom was that the bodies were animated and moved about at night if they so willed, so easy exit from the graves was afforded and the things deposited were for their use under such circumstances."13 The most notable feature of the religious beliefs and ceremonies of the Pujunan family was the autumnal "burning"—the sacrifice of property to the dead, in which large offerings of all sorts of property were made by friends and relatives.14 Among the Cree, "the grave is made small and lined with blankets. The body is placed in it, upright, with legs drawn up, and with it are placed all personal property, a fact which accounts for the extreme rarity of antique articles among these Cree. A pipe and tobacco are always included, so that when the soul of the

9 Czaplicka, *Aborig. Siberia*, 152.
10 Furness, in JAI, XXXII, 462.
11 Milne, *Eastern Clan*, 293, 294-295.

12 Jones, *Thlingets*, 119, 159.
13 Farrand, in AA, III, 241.
14 Dixon, in HAI, II, 327.

deceased reaches the other land it can give the ruler a smoke, saying, 'my friends that I have left behind are forlorn; I pray you give them good fortune.' "[15] The Cheyenne dead were buried in their finest clothing. "If the dead man owned horses, his best horse was saddled and bridled, and shot near the grave. Sometimes several horses were so killed. If the body was put in a tree or on a scaffold, the horses were shot under it."[16] In Guiana the property of the deceased was either buried or destroyed by fire. Such property might include his hammock, his weapons and domestic goods, his dog, even his wife or slaves. In many cases he was supplied with food also.[17]

Among the Araucanians, "the presents brought by the mourners are buried with the corpse, together with supplies of food, clothing and arms, to provide for his long journey. A sheep is sacrificed over the grave, and sometimes a horse, or the latter is buried with the corpse if the distance to the coast is considerable."[18] The last detail is significant of the location of the spirit-world, as well as of the ideas concerning the souls of animals and of projectivism in general.

It was thought by the Old Norse that the more property burned with the corpse the more the ghost brought with him to Valhalla.[19] In a barrow in Denmark there has been found an open coffin in which was a warrior of the Bronze Age in full dress and armor. The body had entirely disappeared, but the dress had been preserved by the acid from the oak wood. The whole contents were enclosed in a skin, probably of an ox. By the side of the corpse lay a bronze sword in a wooden scabbard lined with skin; at the feet was a large round box of wood, inside of it another smaller one, and in the last was a second woolen cap, with a horn comb and a razor of bronze. In a barrow in Jutland, in a coffin made of a hollowed oak tree, was found a woman's dress, also from the Bronze Age and again enclosed in cow-hide. In addition to some articles of clothing there were a bronze dagger, ornaments, and jewelry.[20] That there might have been some recognition of the waste incident to the burial of property with the dead is indicated in one of the Sagas, in which Thorfinn says: "I know that what wealth soever is hid in earth or borne into barrow is wrongly placed."[21] In 1904 there was found in southern Norway a grave-ship of such dimensions and with such interior equipment as to surpass anything of the kind ever discovered before. The find had been the ship-grave of a queen of the province in which the present capital of Norway is situated. Its date is the middle of the ninth century, as shown by the language of an inscription found and by the style of the wood-carvings. With the queen had been interred a slave-woman, and also a complete outfit of personal and household effects, such as had been found nowhere else in the Scandinavian North. There was, for instance, a four-wheeled wagon, three sleighs of unusual workmanship, three beds, a chair, two chests, a large loom and other apparatus for weaving, a mass of cloths, all needed kitchen and household utensils—in short, nothing that could be required for the needs or the comfort of a woman of such station in the world beyond seemed lacking. Oxen and dogs for her journey had been buried with her and the bones of a span of horses were found. The ship was preserved in a specially constructed building and the objects in the Historical

15 Skinner, in AA, XVI, 74-75.
16 Grinnell, *Cheyenne*, II, 160.
17 Roth, in BAE, XXXVIII, 640.
18 Latcham, in JAI, XXXIX, 365.

19 Geijer, *Svensk. Hist.*, 23.
20 Ratzel, *Vkde.*, II, 554, 555.
21 Magnússon and Morris, *Grettir the Strong*, 49.

Museum in Christiania.[22] Among the Letts the custom still prevails of deliberately breaking receptacles at a burial so that the dead may not lack drinking-vessels in the other world.[23]

§232. Treatment of the Body.

THE kind of burial given to the deceased and various other treatment of the body, notably the care taken to preserve it, are evidence of a belief that the spirit of the departed is still associated with it and may be propitiated by such means. Though the tribes of West Australia usually bury the body in the ground, occasionally they place it in a tree or in a hole in the rocks. "It would seem that this is a more honourable form of burial, reserved for those who are particularly esteemed as magicians or hunters."[1] In the Solomon Islands special attention is paid to the head of the deceased which, after the flesh is removed, is scrubbed clean with sand and salt water and bleached in the sun until it is white. It is then fastened on top of a stout post, on a sort of perch, and covered with thatching. Two small triangular holes are cut in this thatch, opposite the eye-sockets of the enclosed skull, and near by are deposited pipes, tobacco, rings, and food. At the conclusion of a hundred days the skull is removed and stored with those of the former chiefs or household lords. For the rest, when the flesh is completely gone from the bones, they are gathered together, cleaned, and buried either in the ground or, sometimes, in a cairn of stones like an altar, about which various old "properties" are placed.[2] In southeast Papua the dead of high rank were not buried, but the body was fastened on the top of a tree, with a well-thatched roof over it. When the bones dropped they were buried at the foot of the tree. "The person of low rank would be buried in the death-chair in a circular grave, and be put out of the way as soon as possible—even before the breath was out of the body. Those of middle rank were buried in the death-chair, but with much ceremony, and not until death had really taken place."[3] Cases of mummification are reported from Torres Straits. "The body was placed on a platform with a fire beside it, partly for the comfort of the spirit and partly to aid in dispelling the noxious fumes arising during the process of desiccation. The corpse was then removed to the sea and cleaned, the interior being filled with pieces of dried sago palm. It was hung up to dry, and adorned by the insertion of pieces of nautilus shell for eyes; the body was smeared with ochre and oil, and various ornaments were attached to it. When dried, it was fixed to the central pole of the hut, and after some years the head was given to the widow, and the mummified corpse was taken to one of the gardens of the deceased and allowed to decay, or in some cases it was buried inside the hut."[4]

In West Africa, the declaration to a criminal that after his execution no funeral-rites will be held over his body, is to him more terrifying than death itself; for the latter merely transmits him to another sphere where he continues his ordinary avocations, while the former opens up to his imagination all kinds of ill-defined terrors.[5] In Kenya Colony, East Africa, the kind of burial depends on the importance of the person: an old man who has grand-

---

22 New York *Nation*, CIII, 17.
23 Winter, in *Globus*, LXXXII, 371.
1 Brown, in JAI, XLIII, 169.
2 Somerville, in JAI, XXVI, 403.

3 Bromilow, in AAAS, 1909, 483.
4 Hamlyn-Harris, in AA, XV, 148.
5 Ellis, *Ewe*, 159.

children is buried to the right of the doorway, the place of honor; if the deceased has children, he is buried some distance from the hut, while if childless, his body is thrown into the bush for the hyænas and jackals.[6] All the different peoples inhabiting Madagascar expend a large amount of time, trouble, and money upon their tombs and burial observances; "this care arises in great part from their religious notions, for they believe that their departed friends become divine, in a certain sense, and are able to benefit their descendants."[7]

Platform-burial is found not only among the Melanesians but among various Malay groups as well.[8] The Jakun display scrupulous solicitude for the deceased's spirit, which is provided with a furnished hut to live in, provisions to feed upon, and even a trench full of water on which to paddle its canoe.[9] Embalming was known and practised with surprising skill in one particular family of chiefs in Samoa; "they assigned no particular reason for this embalming, further than that it was the expression of their affection to keep the bodies of the departed still with them as if they were alive."[10]

The American Indians employed a great variety of methods for disposing of human remains, with the idea in each case, it seems, of doing homage to the dead. Among the Tlinkits of Alaska, orientation in burials was regarded as of importance, for it was believed that if the dead were not placed with their heads to the east they could not be re-born.[11] It was most essential among the Winnebagoes that a red mark be painted across the forehead of the corpse, then a black one immediately below this, and finally that the entire chin be daubed with red, "in order that he may be recognized by his relatives in spiritland."[12] Mummification obtained in the historic period among the Aleuts and the Alaskan Eskimo; it was never used in the treatment of any corpses save of those of the rich and noble. The Aleuts mummified the bodies of both males and females of all the wealthy families. Among the Eskimo, however, only those males who did the whaling of the tribe were mummified, and even they were not equipped with all the paraphernalia of masks and effigies characteristic of Aleut mummies.[13] The Tsimshian followed the custom in olden times, in the case of a prince or chief or rich man or somebody dear to them, of taking out and burning immediately the bowels, stomach, heart, liver, and lungs of the deceased; when the body was empty, it was filled with red-cedar bark and kept for a long time.[14]

The only locality in the United States where stone vessels are known to have been used for burial-purposes is southern California, where non-cremated human remains were buried in vessels of stone, covered in various ways. In Utah such remains have been found covered with baskets.[15] Some of the extreme western tribes frequently practised burial on trees or scaffolds. The bodies of the chiefs of the Powhatan Confederacy were stripped of the flesh and the skeletons were placed on scaffolds in a charnel-house. For their ordinary burials they dug deep holes in the earth with sharp stakes and, wrapping the corpse in the skins, laid it upon sticks in the ground and covered it with earth. The Ottawa usually exposed the body for a short time previous to burial on a

6 Barton, in JAI, LIII, 74; §250, of text and Case-Book.
7 Sibree, Great Afr. Isl., 227.
8 Peal, in JAI, XXII, pl. 14.
9 Skeat and Blagden, Malay Penin., II, 89-90.
10 Turner, Samoa, 148, 149.

11 Fletcher, in HAI, II, 148.
12 Lamere and Radin, in AA, XIII, 437, 438.
13 Macleod, in AA, XXVII, 143-145.
14 Boas, in BAE, XXXI, 442.
15 Moore, "Urn-Burial," in HAI, II, 873.

scaffold near the grave. The Shawnee, and possibly one or more of the southern Illinois tribes, were accustomed to bury their dead in box-shaped sepulchers made of undressed stone slabs. The Nanticoke and some of the western tribes, after temporary burial in the ground or exposure on scaffolds, removed the flesh and reinterred the skeletons. Among the Athapascans the bodies of the dead were laid on the ground, covered with bark, and surrounded by palings, except in the case of noted men, whose bodies were placed in boxes on the branches of trees. The Santee buried their distinguished dead on the tops of mounds, built low or high according to the rank of the deceased, with ridge-roofs supported by poles over the graves to shelter them from the weather. On these poles were hung rattles, feathers, and other offerings from the relatives of the deceased. The corpse of an ordinary person was carefully dressed, wrapped in bark, and exposed on a platform for several days. "As soon as the flesh had softened it was stripped from the bones and burned, and the bones themselves were cleaned, the skull being wrapped separately in a cloth woven of opossum hair. The bones were then put into a box, from which they were taken out annually to be again cleaned and oiled. In this way some families had in their possession the bones of their ancestors for several generations."[16]

Three forms of burial were utilized by a division of the Miami: (a) the ordinary ground-burial in a shallow grave prepared to receive the body in a recumbent position; (b) surface-burial in a hollow log—sometimes a tree was split and the halves hollowed out to receive the body, when it was either closed with withes or fastened to the ground with crossed stakes; again a hollow tree was used, the ends being closed; (c) surface-burial wherein the body was covered with a small pen of logs, laid as in a log cabin, the courses meeting at the top in a single log. The Sauk, an Algonquian tribe, practised four different methods of burial: (a) the corpse was laid away in the branches of a tree or upon a scaffold; (b) it was placed in a sitting posture, with the back supported, out on the open ground; (c) it was seated in a shallow grave, with all but the face buried, and a shelter was placed over the grave; (d) there was complete burial in the ground. Some of the Carolina tribes first put the corpse in a cane hurdle and deposited it in an outhouse for a day; then it was taken out and wrapped in rush or cane matting, placed in a reed coffin, and buried in a grave. The Montagnals, who buried their dead in the earth, usually laid the corpse on its side, though sometimes the sitting position was chosen. "Above the grave is built a little birch-bark hut and through a window the relatives thrust bits of tobacco, venison, and other morsels." The bodies of the dead among the Hopi were sewed in blankets and deposited with food-offerings among the rocks of the mesas.[17] The Cheyennes let wild animals "bury" their dead; "men thought it well that the wolves, coyotes, eagles, buzzards, and other animals should eat their flesh, and scatter their bodies far and wide over the prairie."[18]

Sometimes the bones alone were buried, for it appears to have been a custom in the Northwest as well as in the East and Southeast to remove the flesh by previous burial or otherwise, and then to bundle the bones and bury them, sometimes in communal pits. Among the Choctaw, the work of cleaning the bones of

16 Mooney and Thomas; Mooney; Goddard and Swanton, in HAI, I, 42-43, 599; II, 301, 461; I, 110, respectively.

17 Mooney and Thomas; Hewitt; Thomas; Fewkes, in HAI, I, 853, 933; II, 479; I, 945; I, 565, respectively.
18 Grinnell, Cheyenne, II, 163.

the dead before depositing them in boxes or baskets in the bone-houses was performed by "certain old gentlemen with very long nails," who allowed these attachments to grow with this purpose in view. The people of this tribe followed the custom of setting up poles around the new graves, on which they hung hoops and wreaths, to aid the spirit in its ascent.[19] The custom of removing the flesh before final burial prevailed extensively among the mound-builders of the northern districts and was not uncommon among those of the south; cremation also was practised by them to a limited extent. In Kansas stones were heaped over the body to form a cairn, while a custom once prevailed among certain tribes in Wisconsin, on the burial of a chief of distinction, to consider his grave as entitled to the tribute of a portion of earth from each passer-by; hence the first grave formed a nucleus around which, in the accumulation of the accustomed tributes of respect thus paid, a mound was soon formed.[20]

Certain Arawaks are said by Schomburgk[21] to be the only tribe in British Guiana that burn their dead and bury the ashes. Another tribe of the same stock disinter the corpse about a month after the funeral, put it in a great pan or oven over the fire until it is only a black carbonaceous mass, which is pounded into a fine powder and mixed in several large vats of a certain liquid, to be drunk by the assembled company. In the lands back of Cayenne there are tribes that imbibe the ashes of the dead which they mix with their drink, "believing that by this means they are giving the defunct a more honorable burial than by leaving them a prey to worms and corruption." Among the Caribs, at the expiration of the year, the decomposed body is dug up and the bones distributed to all the friends and acquaintances. "The bones, having been cleaned by the fish, are packed according to size in a basket already provided, worked with glass beads of various colors; care is taken that the skull of the deceased forms the lid of the basket. The basket is then hung up to the roof of their houses . . . along with the many other baskets containing the bones of their forefathers. The women . . . who prepare the bones are considered unclean for several months."[22]

The Egyptian cult of the dead was highly elaborated. To be able to share in the happy fate of future life, one must leave nothing undone. Hence the great care bestowed on the corpse, the embalming, the deposit of the intestines in the four vases consecrated to the genii of death, the dedication of each member to a divinity, the well-sealed graves, the rich sacrifices for maintenance which were offered either directly to the deceased or to the gods with the request that the dead be given his share, and the many magical ceremonies in which precise magic texts must be recited in the right tone in order to restore to him the use one after the other of his limbs and support him in his struggle—not to mention all the objects which were given to him to take along on the great journey. All these were, however, only a part of what one must observe in order to face the dark future with confidence. Even the righteous man was not safe if one detail had been neglected. Wherefore there were gathered together a species of canonical books with all the prayers that were to be spoken. Here belonged the ritual of mummification and of sacrifice to the dead. At

19 Swanton; Thomas; Gatschet, in HAI, I, 288; I, 945; I, 286, respectively.
20 Nadaillac, *Preh. Amer.*, 111; Thomas, in BAE, XII, 17, 18, 658, 659.

21 *Brit.-Guiana,* II, 388; Roth, in BAE, XXXVIII, 650-651.
22 Roth, in BAE, XXX, 158, 159.

this sacrifice, certain ceremonious actions were performed partly on the mummy and partly on the image of the deceased—the first being the mystical opening of the mouth and eyes to restore to the deceased both speech and sight. Then, through the laying-on of hands, the blood of the gods was brought into the dead; through magical means color was restored to the lips and cheeks and flexibility to the jaws; and finally the dead, even as the gods, were presented with clothes, perfumes, fetishes, and amulets.[23] It was the old belief of the Hamitic peoples, shared also by the Iranians, that the deceased continued to live a shadow-like existence and that his resurrection, or at least his arrival in a blissful other world, was dependent on the preservation of his mortal remains.[24] In ancient Rome the first duty of the heir was to perform the obsequies; the Earth yielded her fruits to one who conveyed to her the corpse due her.[25] Odin is said to have ordered that tumuli should be built over the bodies of distinguished men and that stones should be set up over all who showed manliness.[26]

§233. Miscellaneous Forms of Propitiation.

THE East and South Australians provided a semblance of a duel, somewhat like the Roman gladiator-fights at a funeral, with light effusion of blood.[1] It was a universal custom in the Fiji Islands to invoke the ghosts of fathers and remoter ancestors: houses were sometimes built on graves as peace-offerings on behalf of a sick child; feasts and other sacrifices were made to the souls of men, and in offering them the votaries mentioned the father's name in the prayer. "This cult of the dead goes on at the present day in secret."[2] When a Koita dies, all his relations come in mourning-costume to his village and "immediately on arrival proceed to the dead man's house, where they 'kiss' his face, i.e., they touch his face with their noses, but do not inspire as they do when 'kissing' the living."[3]

There is a certain compulsion to perform the obsequies correctly and fully. The South Africans believe that many strokes of ill luck are due to the grudge or anger of a deceased chief who is not satisfied with the ceremonies performed at his grave.[4] Among the Edo-speaking peoples, non-performance or irregularity in attending to burial-customs entails penalties both on the deceased and on the living. The dead man takes with him to the other world the yams and other things offered at his funeral; but his family there assembled, after taking possession of them, may decline to recognize him as one of themselves so that he becomes a sort of spiritual outlaw. He must be in receipt, as it were, of an income from earthly sources. "He is, however, in a position to wreak his vengeance on the defaulters by making them ill, by preventing their wives from bearing children, and by causing them to lose their property. The remedy is for the son to kill a goat and beg his father to relent;" how far this affects the lot of the deceased the author did not ascertain.[5] A death in a family among the Ewe-speaking peoples is announced by an outbreak of shrieks and lamenta-

23 Tiele, *Relig. Altertum*, I, 45, 74-75.
24 Justi, *Persien*, 90.
25 De Marchi, *Culto Priv.*, rev. in *Année Soc.*, I, 188, 189.
26 Geijer, *Svensk. Hist.*, 23; Boye, in *Annaler*, 1862, 336-355; Allen, *Haandbog i Fadrelandets Historie*, 1 ff., 45 ff.

1 Letourneau, *Morale*, 172, 338.
2 Hocart, in JAI, XLII, 441.
3 Seligmann, *Melanesians*, 159.
4 Holub, *S.-Afr.*, II, 338.
5 Thomas, in JAI, L, 381.

tions on the part of the women, who throw themselves on the ground, strike their heads against the walls, and commit a variety of extravagances, meanwhile calling upon the deceased not to desert them and endeavoring, by all kinds of supplications, to induce the soul to return and reanimate the body.[6] No doubt some at least of this ostentatious mourning is conventional and ritualistic, for the ghost is thought to be pleased by much and loud lamentation. Glave[7] says that "there is no sympathy for another's pains in the soul of an African;" that the tears for a chief are only part of the funeral ceremony, though a mother may show real grief at the loss of a child.

The Yaos of Central Africa regard the soul or shade, after a person's death, as an object of worship and reverence, the controller of the affairs of this life, the active agent in the fortunes of the human race—which is an extension of the ghost-theory toward daimonism. Shrines are erected over the graves and many objects offered there. At the head of the mound a native pot is fixed in the ground for the reception of the offering of beer which is an almost invariable accompaniment of any act of worship paid to the shades of the dead. Should a long-continued drought endanger the prospects of the grain-crop, the departed chief must be solicited to send the lacking rain.[8] Each person among the Baganda keeps a small hut near his house where the spirits of deceased relatives reside; the latter are propitiated to obtain benefits. "If the suppliant had been sent to the *sabo* (hut) of one of his relatives he would kneel by the door and address the ghost inside; he would first recount all his troubles, and then make a promise of some present to the ghost according to his rank, and then beg its assistance or challenge it to overcome the other spirits. . . . The animal or fowl dedicated to a deity is turned loose by the hut (*sabo*) and always kept there as the property of the ghost, and replaced in case of death; if it is only a skin or feather it is tied to the doorpost, but the bark cloth is placed inside the huts; it is, however, removed to clothe the sick person for a time, who thus derives the ghost's assistance to throw off the illness." These huts of the ghosts are kept in good repair; they vary in size according to the honor of the ghost, some being small huts only a couple of feet high, whilst those of kings and other important personages are sixty feet high and afford accommodation for the priests to live in. "Offerings of animals, slaves, food, clothing, firewood, and beer, are frequently made at these shrines; the offerings are made to obtain some benefit, such as recovery from illness, to avert some calamity, sickness, or war, or again in fulfilment of a vow."[9]

Each caste in India had its fetish which brought quality into the rites for the soul—rites which must be kept up by descendants, else the soul lost rank and slipped down to a stage where it must go through the world again. Some souls hang head-downwards over an abyss of hell because they have no descendant to sacrifice for them.[10] In China, descendants expect that the great work of interment will secure them wealth, glory, and prosperity for all future ages; the things of good omen which are placed in the tomb are thought to cause the benefits they express or symbolize to become real blessings to the offspring of the deceased. "It is by no means merely a desire to ensure a happy fate to the dead which prompts children to place a hair-pin . . . on the deceased:

6 Ellis, *Ewe*, 157.
7 In *Century Mag.*, IX, 196.
8 Hetherwick, in JAI, XXXII, 91-95.
9 Roscoe, in JAI, XXXII, 41-42, 76.

10 Lippert, *Kgchte.*, II, 416; Holtzmann, *Ind. Sagen*, II, 159; Nathubhai, in JASB, III, 487.

the hope that it may serve with all its appendices like seeds sown, and ripen into real happiness and old age for the offspring, plays by far the greatest part in it. This also explains why the Chinese are so partial to dressing their deceased mothers in bridal attire:—this being in reality the uniform dress of mandarins' wives and, moreover, covered all over with symbols of felicity, wealth, joy and longevity, it will undoubtedly endow each woman, who wears it in the tomb, with the faculty of procreating happy, wealthy and long-lived descendants holding high functions in the empire—the greatest bliss and honor imaginable for every true son of China."[11]

Hired mourners were common among the Tlinkits and many other services connected with burial were paid for.[12] The following custom was observed among the Omaha and cognate tribes: "On the death of a man or a woman who was respected in the community, the young men, friends of the deceased, met at a short distance from the lodge of the dead and made two incisions in their left arms so as to leave a loop of skin. Through this loop was passed a small willow twig, with leaves left on one end; then, with their blood dripping upon the willow leaves, holding a willow stem in each hand, they walked in single file to the lodge, and, standing abreast in a long line, they sang there the tribal song to the dead, beating the willow stems together to the rhythm of the song. At the sound of the music, a near relative came forth from the lodge and, beginning at one end of the line, pulled out the blood-stained twigs from the left arm of each singer, and laid a hand on his head in token of thanks for the sympathy shown. The song continued until the last twig was thrown to the ground. The music of the song was in strange contrast to the bloody spectacle. It was a blithe major melody with no words, but only breathing vocables to float the voice." According to the Indian explanation, the song is for the spirit of the dead; it is to cheer him as he goes from his dear ones left behind on the earth; "so, as he hears the voices of his friends, their glad tones help him to go forward on his inevitable journey." The song is therefore addressed directly to the spirit of the dead. Of the ceremonial it is further explained that the shedding of the blood is for the mourners; they see in it an expression of sorrow and sympathy for the loss that has come to them.[13] The main ceremony of the Paiutes is an annual mourning-ritual or "cry," which generally lasts for five days in June or July; essential elements are the singing of numerous mourning-songs and the offering of valuables, such as baskets, articles of clothing, and horses, in memory of the dead. "At various stages during the singing, which forms the major part of the ceremony, ceremonial 'cries' take place which are conducted by a cry leader. On the last night of the mourning ceremony, during which it is forbidden to sleep, the articles which have been set aside as offerings to the dead are burned on a funeral pile; horses are shot, and valuable articles which have been exposed as offerings may be taken by others and replaced by objects of less value. It is evident that the Paiute mourning ceremony bears considerable resemblance to mourning ceremonies of various Californian tribes."[14] It is also evident that much of it is conventionalized. The Ahome are said to have uttered cries and lamentations for their dead during one entire year, for an hour at sunrise and another

11 DeGroot, *Relig. Sys.*, I, 57-58, 220.
12 Jones, *Thlingets*, 147-149.

13 Fletcher, in **HAI**, I, 952-953; Fletcher and LaFlesche, in **BAE**, XXVII, 593.
14 Sapir, in **AA**, XIV, 168-169.

at sunset.[15] Among the Mariposan family there was an elaborate annual mourning-ceremony for the dead of the year, which took place about a large fire in which much property was consumed. This ceremony, described as the Dance of the Dead, was followed by dancing of a festive character.[16] It was customary for the Otomacs to bewail their dead as a matter of daily routine; thus, "as soon as the cocks crow, about 3 o'clock in the morning, the air is rent with a sad and confused sound of cries and lamentations, mixed with tears and other appearances of grief. They mourn not by way of ceremony, but in very truth. When day breaks, the wailing ceases and joy reigns."[17] In antiquity the fear of the horrors of the realm of the dead were so powerful that people established funds or made contracts to assure for themselves in perpetuity a light in the temple, food for their maintenance in the burial chapel, and the service of their own priests. Among the Semites the great solicitude for the corpse, the inviolability of graves, the rich presents which were given to the dead for his sustenance and well-being, the loud lamentations, the sacrifice of hair, the wounds which were self-inflicted at the burial and in which one may see a substitute for earlier human sacrifice—all these witness to a fervent desire to gratify the soul and to a fear that it might otherwise take revenge for being neglected. The grave was the eternal home from out of which the dead went to rest in Sheol with the shades; if they were unburied or their graves desecrated, then their shades would have to wander dismally about and haunt places without finding rest.[18] In the Gilgamesh Epic, the ghost of Eadni tells Gilgamesh that those only are happy in Hades who died in battle and that the ghosts of those whom their relatives have forgotten suffer hunger and thirst.[19]

There is to be found in Homer but slight indication of apotheosis, of worship of the dead, or of sacrifices at their tombs, although the graves at Mycenæ, with openings to convey the offerings as directly as possible to the corpse, bear witness to the existence of such worship there long before Homer's day, and similar customs continued through the classical period. "The Homeric dead had no power to harm or to help, and no reason existed for propitiating them or for striving to please them in any way. Only slight indications are found in the poems of any sort of sacrifices, or offerings to the dead, but not only were these honors to the dead paid in Plato's time, when to secure them was a prime motive for marriage, and in the age of St. Chrysostom, who was scandalized by them, but the belief in their importance is very real in Greece to-day. In this matter the poet seems, indeed, as a very high authority has said, centuries in advance of his age."[20] One way of propitiating the deceased, according to the notions of the old Romans, was to take vengeance on the enemy of one's dead father: Cato said the libations which the manes of our ancestors crave are the tears of their condemned enemies.[21]

§234. Antagonism of Dead and Living.

WE speak, says Lippert,[1] of "sacrifice" to the dead; a share in all that the living like, need, and get is given to them. Sacrifice is really a toll; hence the fear that

15 Hodge, in HAI, I, 29.
16 HAI, I, 808.
17 Roth, in BAE, XXX, 254.
18 Tiele, *Relig. Altertum*, I, 64, 282-283.

19 Maspero, *Hist. Anc.*, I, 589.
20 Seymour, *Hom. Age*, 40-41 (quoted), 394.
21 Grupp, *Kgchte.*, I, 31-32.
1 *Kgchte.*, II, 246, 249.

it may not be great enough or that the "envy" of the spirits or gods will be provoked. It involves destruction, surrender, or loss made or incurred for the sake of some benefit expected in return. The sacrifice of property is sometimes so great that there is economic pressure against the practice; some primitive peoples are aware of the conflict of interests involved. The economic cost of mortuary practices was very considerable in the Savage Islands where "all the plantations, cocoa-nut trees, and other fruit trees of a person who died, were destroyed and thrown into the sea that they might go with him to the world of spirits."[2] In New Georgia the property of the dead man remained untouched for a hundred days.[3] In New Britain there was a scramble for the different articles thrown upon the sacrificial fire; "the dead man's soul was welcome to the shadow or spirit of these things, but it would be a pity to have the things themselves wasted."[4] By exception, the Murray Islanders supplied no food for the spirits' journey.[5]

In South Africa, trees, garden, and huts may be abandoned after a death; this practice, says Livingstone,[6] renders any permanent village impossible. There are some attempts, however, to avoid giving up all the dead man's property, for among the Kaffirs an old woman would hold up the weapons and other articles at the grave and say, "Behold all that is thine," and then would carefully take them away again.[7] In West Africa the "destruction of his property is intended to signify to the soul that he must now depart, since there is no longer anything belonging to him. In former times the destruction of property was carried much farther than at present."[8] "Ghosts have the same passions, appetites, needs, and necessities as living men; therefore, in the grave with the corpse are placed food and drink, tobacco, pipes, gold-dust, trinkets, and cloths, according to the wealth and position of the deceased." The entire body may be powdered with gold-dust. The value of such articles, in the case of persons of distinction, not infrequently amounts to some two or three hundred pounds sterling. "These sacrifices are repeated a second and third time. It is a point of honour amongst all but the most abjectly poor, to make a great display at funeral ceremonies; and families endeavor to outvie each other in extravagance. This is a common cause of debt and slavery, and poor people frequently pawn or enslave themselves in order to obtain the means of making a respectable funeral."[9] "As wealth in the Delta consists of women and slaves," writes Miss Kingsley,[10] "I do not believe the under-world gods of the Niger would understand the status of a chief who arrived before them, let us say, with ten puncheons of palm oil, and four hundred yards of crimson figured velvet." One king of Atta became very rich in cowries and other valuables which were all buried with him. His son and successor, poor and unhonored as a consequence, opened the grave to get the property and cut off the head of the corpse to punish his father for selfishness. The people were so shocked at this breach of custom and act of impiety that they rose in rebellion against the offender.[11] Burial-costs piled up so high in Togo that the negroes "hit on the practical thought of celebrating common funerary festivals for several of the dead."[12] The Guinea Coast grave-hut "contains everything which a living per-

2 Turner, *Samoa*, 306.
3 Somerville, in JAI, XXVI, 403.
4 Danks, in JAI, XXI, 354.
5 Hunt, in JAI, XXVIII, 8.
6 *Mission. Travels*, I, 338.
7 Letourneau, *Prop.*, 87.

8 Ellis, *Yoruba*, 159-160.
9 Ellis, *Tshi*, 157-159, 240-241.
10 *Travels W. Afr.*, 491.
11 Landers, *Niger*, II, 170.
12 Seidel, in *Globus*, LXXII, 41.

son needs."[13] Certain Baghirmi chiefs, "when they feel death approaching, have their movable possessions cast into the river."[14] Among the Unyamwesi the oxen of the deceased chief are often all killed and eaten, though no offerings are made on the grave.[15]

The relatives of a deceased Osetin dispose of his possessions without consent of his heirs, buy drink with the proceeds, and eat and drink up the property as they please.[16] Though the boats and nets of certain northern Asiatics are their most valuable and indispensable possessions, they sacrifice both at a death.[17] There is some tendency here to avoid funeral-waste, for the Chukchi who have customarily sacrificed reindeers and dogs, their most valuable property, sometimes offer substitute sacrifices—reindeer made of willow-leaves or even of snow.[18] In A.D. 992 the Tungus of Mongolia were forbidden by their ruler to sacrifice horses at funerals or to place harness, helmet, or gold and silver utensils in the grave; and in 1042 another ruler interdicted under penalty of punishment the sacrifice of reindeer, horses, and other valuables. These commands were undoubtedly prompted by economic motives.[19] In western China, when the coffin is being carried out for burial, a paper effigy is placed upon it, which represents clothes for the soul of the dead man.[20] In southern China they burn, close to the grave, small paper houses, paper clothing, tiny painted models of chariots harnessed with mules, palanquins, and other objects. Providing the dead with these paper models and also with tinfoil taels— "ghost money"—is a large industry, the yearly production of the latter amounting to fifteen million dollars.[21] Main[22] cites a number of cases of models being sacrificed instead of the real things, in an attempt to escape the burden of funeral-waste; he thinks that the widow's services to the grave and to her deified husband are of this nature—a substitute for former human sacrifice. In Korea food is offered monthly and on anniversaries, "all the descendants assembling, and these observances extend backwards to the ancestors of five generations. Thus it is a very costly thing to have many near relations and a number of ancestors, the expense falling on the eldest son and his heirs. A Korean gentleman said that his nephew, upon whom the duty fell, spent more upon it than upon his household expenses."[23]

The main object of a Hindu funeral is very different from that of European obsequies. "It is nothing less than the investiture of the departed spirit with a kind of intermediate body—a peculiar frame interposed, as it were parenthetically, between the terrestrial gross body which has just been destroyed by fire, and the new terrestrial body which it is compelled ultimately to assume." Were it not for this intermediate frame—believed to be created by the offerings made during the funeral ceremonies—the spirit would remain with its subtle body in the condition of an impure and unquiet ghost wandering about on the earth or in the air among demons and evil spirits, and itself condemned to become an evil spirit. Its reception of the intervenient body converts it from a ghost into an ancestor. But this does not satisfy all its needs: "the new body it has received, though not so gross as that of earth, must be

13 Frobenius, *Masken*, 169; Vortisch, in *Globus*, LXXXIX, 281.
14 Nachtigal, *Sahara*, II, 687.
15 Stuhlmann, *Mit Emin*, 91.
16 *Russian Ethnog.* (Russ.), II, 362.
17 *Prjevalski's Forskningsresor*, 140; Ratzel, *Vkde.*, III, 116.

18 Czaplicka, *Aborig. Siberia*, 291.
19 Hiekisch, *Tungusen*, 97-98.
20 Henry, in JAI, XXXIII, 103.
21 Letourneau, *Prop.*, 320; N. Y. *Times*, Nov. 7, 1926.
22 *Relig. Chastity*, 49-52, 52-58, ch. VI.
23 Bishop, *Korea*, 290.

developed and supported. It must, if possible, be rescued from the fire of purgatory. It must be assisted onwards in its course from lower to higher worlds and back again to earth. And these results can only be accomplished by the ceremonies called Srāddha—ceremonies which may in some respects be compared to the Roman Catholic masses for the dead." The first Srāddha is performed very soon after the funeral-rites and is always a costly affair. The funeral-ceremonies of the older members of a family occupy ten days, and with the succeeding Srāddha rites, carried on with the help of Brahmans and including the feasting of numberless guests and the distribution of presents, may involve an enormous expenditure. "It is well known that the expenditure incurred on such occasions by rich Bengal Rājās and Zamindārs of high family has often impoverished them for the remainder of their lives. Instances are on record of a single funeral and Srāddha costing a sum equivalent to £120,000, the greater part of that amount being squandered on worthless Brāhmans, indolent Pandits, hypocritical devotees, and vagabond religious mendicants." This funeral sacrifice is described as "an evil which has gradually grown till it has become a veritable curse to the country, and one of the principal bars to any advance in its social condition."[24] The spirit of a deceased Brahman is "the most difficult of all to propitiate. A timber merchant at Calicut some time ago spent more than a thousand rupees [$320] for this purpose."[25] Sometimes the funeral-expenses include gifts to charity to commemorate the name of the deceased: "during the five years, 1884 to 1889, the Parsee community of India has given about forty lacs of rupees [a lac, or 100,000, of rupees is about $32,000] in public charity. Of this sum more than half was announced at these funeral gatherings of the third day after death."[26]

Fawcett[27] was told that all a Saora's money was buried with him, but he is doubtful about it; he believes a little money may be destroyed. Even the Todas are trying to avoid the funeral waste. In their obsequies the body is swung three times over the fire and then replaced on the ground before it is finally lifted upon the pyre; then, before the last act, nearly all the objects of value are removed from the bier or from the pocket of the cloak. In one case Rivers[28] observed that the bangles were taken from the arms and all the rings except one from the fingers, and the coins were removed and redistributed to those who had given them. The people told him that when the body was swung over the fire, the dead person went to Amnodr with all the ornaments and objects then on the bier and that the removal of the things afterwards would not deprive the dead person of their use in the next world—an expedient rationalization. "It would seem as if this ceremony of swinging the body over the fire was directly connected with the removal of the objects of value. The swinging over the fire would be symbolic of its destruction by fire, and this symbolic burning has the great advantage that the objects of value are not consumed and are available for use another time." The funeral-ceremonies have undergone some modification in recent times owing to the intervention of the Government. The former custom of slaughtering many buffaloes at every funeral impoverished the people and was prohibited by the Government about forty years ago; since that time the number of buffaloes killed at each ceremony has been limited to two for each person.

24 Monier-Williams, *Brāhmanism*, 276-279.   27 In JASB, I, 249.
25 Thurston, *S. India*, 329.   28 *Todas*, 362-363, 338.
26 Modi, in JASB, II, 434.

In the Malay Archipelago it is thought that if a dead man reaches the spirit-world without proper equipment he not only suffers want but the other ghosts dishonor him. The richer the soul, the higher the honor and rank that await him in the next world. Funerals are often postponed for years until wealth can be accumulated, to be burned, broken on the grave, or buried.[29] A new rajah may be reduced to poverty through the provision made for his predecessor[30] just as a father, unfortunate in his family, may be ruined by the death of his children to whom he must furnish capital with which to begin life in the new existence. When a man of property dies in Sarawak, "sago trees are cut down with the belief that they will be found ready-grown for the owner's use in the other world."[31] "The articles of clothing and weapons deposited with the dead are of the highest value, no broken or damaged article being deemed worthy of a place in the grave." This is the case with the Sea Dyaks; elsewhere valuables are spared and there are sacrificed "merely a few old things, that even sacrilegious strangers would scarcely think worth plundering."[32] In the Mentawei Islands the trees of the dead man are regularly cut down.[33] Delay of the funeral until sufficient property can be collected for destruction is common in Timor.[34] Among some of the natives of the Philippines, where dishes, earthen pots and other articles are broken on the grave, there is some attempt to avoid complete impoverishment of the survivors; "all the belongings of the deceased, except such bare necessaries as may be needed by his immediate relatives, are left at the head of the grave."[35]

The East Greenlanders throw away or bury all the dead man's possessions except knives and things similarly precious.[36] The Bering Strait Eskimo "fear to die unless they have someone to make offerings to their memory, and childless persons generally adopt a child so that their shades may not be forgotten at the festivals, as people who have no one to make offerings for them are supposed to suffer great destitution in the other world." The souls appear at the feast of the dead to take back with them the spiritual essence of new garments; then these are solemnly put on by their namesakes.[37] A feast must be held whenever a Tlinkit dies, whether man, woman, or child; it cannot be omitted, as it would be regarded as a woeful lack of respect to the dead and would bring deep reproach on the family. Feasts are given for many purposes, such as to honor the dead, to benefit them, or in commemoration. There is nothing the Tlinkit likes better than to hold a feast. "Where the sick have been expected to die and then have recovered, natives have been known to be greatly disappointed and to regret the recovery, as the feast they anticipated in case of death did not come off. For this reason some are not urgent in employing a doctor when relatives are sick." While the feasting is in progress, food is thrown into the fire and the name of the dead in whose honor the feast is held is called out. The fire-spirit in some way conveys the food to him in the spirit-land. "If the feast were omitted, or a poor feast given, the spirit of the dead would feel badly about it and reproach relatives so remiss in their duty." At this feast all obligations incurred in the cremation or burial of the dead are met and extravagantly paid for. "The natives are not satisfied unless much

29 Wilken, *Vkde.*, 320-321.
30 Ratzel, *Vkde.*, II, 459.
31 Roth, *Sarawak*, I, 141, 144, 145, 155, 204.
32 Hose, in JAI, XXIII, 166; Roth, *Sarawak*, I, 145.
33 Pleyte, in *Globus*, LXXIX, 27.

34 Forbes, in JAI, XIII, 418.
35 Worcester, *Philippine Isl.*, 109, 495 (quoted).
36 Holm, *Ethnol. Skizze*, 65.
37 Nelson, in BAE, XVIII, pt. I, 364, 376-377.

money is spent." Everything done for the dead is by those of another totem than that of the deceased; the guests must be those of a different totem from that of the feast-givers. A feast is usually held immediately after the death of a person, but not always. "Death may occur when it is inconvenient for the friends of the deceased to give one at once. They may be too poor, or it may be in the summer time when the people are scattered. But as soon as the relatives of the dead can accumulate the means and the people are back in the village, then the celebration in honour of the memory of the dead must be given." With the Tlinkits no other event is so costly or involves so much as death. Articles of clothing and bedding, playthings for a child, and always a vessel of water are buried beside the coffin. "Sewing-machines, clocks, guns, and various other articles such as were used and prized in life are often deposited on the grave." Large sums are exacted for services rendered. "The most trifling service, such as putting gloves on the hands of the dead, or socks on his feet, or mourning, must be well paid for. Four young men acted as pallbearers for a little child. The mother gave them ten dollars each for this slight service. To build a coffin, dig a grave, erect a grave fence or tombstone commands a large compensation. This is largely due to the fact that the natives are not satisfied unless they spend large amounts on the dead." By the time the various claims and the other expenses have been met, two or three hundred dollars have been swallowed up, which is a very considerable amount among these primitive Alaskans; but every penny of this is cheerfully paid, as it would be a deep disgrace to refuse any of these claims. Indeed, there is an element of vanity here, as is seen in the feasts given for other purposes and in the potlatch, and the Tlinkits are actually fond of giving feasts for the dead. "They will even exhume bodies and bones to bury them in some other spot in order to have an excuse for such feasting."[38]

When a Cheyenne died, "all his property not placed with him—and often that of his father and even of his brothers—was given away, and to people who were not his relations. . . . Then the lodge was torn down and given to someone, and soon everything was gone, and the widow perhaps retained only a single blanket with which to cover herself." Death often meant the break-up of the family, for if a man died leaving a widow and, say, two or three growing children, they would have nothing after this funeral-waste, and the children would have to go to their grandfather or uncles and live with them for a year or two. "In the course of this time, however, some one of her relatives was very likely to have given a lodge to the widow, and she camped near a brother, who supplied her with meat; and after a time she began to get her children back, one by one, until at last all were living with her again. If she had growing boys, they learned to hunt, and assisted in supporting her and the sisters. Such a family always got along somehow."[39] The practice of abandoning not only the property and hut of the deceased but even the village where the death occurred, naturally meant great loss.

Mindeleff[40] has effectively described the hardships incurred through the practice of avoidance. "The occurrence of several years of drought in succession would be construed as a mark of disfavor of the gods, and would be followed by a movement of the people from the village. Even a series of bad dreams which might be inflicted on some prominent medicine-man by over-

38 Jones, *Thlingets*, 135-136, 137, 147-149, 150, 200.
39 Grinnell, *Cheyenne*, II, 162-163.
40 In BAE, XIX, pt. II, 646.

indulgence in certain articles of food would be regarded as omens indicating a necessity for a change of location. Such instances are not unknown. Toothache also is dreaded for mystic reasons, and is construed as a sign of disfavor of the gods; so that many a village has been abandoned simply because some prominent medicine-man was in need of the services of a dentist. Many other reasons might be stated, but these will suffice to show upon what slight and often trivial grounds great villages of stone houses, the result of much labor and the picture of permanence, are sometimes abandoned in a day." Among the Guiana Indians, who desert the hut and even the village visited by death, it may happen that the fields are all prepared for the crops or even that the seed has been planted. Yet the fear cannot be overcome that tarrying longer is perilous because displeasing to the spirits. Sometimes a bit of thrift creeps in, however, for one of the tribesmen may be deputed to watch the crops.[41]

Cases of avoidance where the dying are taken outside, so that death may not pollute the dwelling and necessitate its abandonment or destruction, are to be interpreted as an attempt to squirm out from under the economic burden of death. The clash of interests between living and dead continues for some time, for the welfare of the ghost in the other world is dependent on the sacrifices of the survivors. In Mexico it was held that ghosts, if neglected, would become animals. "If the dead person has been a particularly bad man, the medicine men have a hard time in rescuing him from the animal kingdom. It may take hours of prayers and dances to get his head through and then hours more of other dances and incantations with herbs and hikori to rescue the rest of his body." If people cannot pay the medicine-man, their ghosts may wander indefinitely as animals.[42] On such a basis is built the concept of purgatory; moreover, it is especially to be noted that the living have their part to play, and pay, in the process of expiation.

§239. Ancestor-Worship.

The Central Australians, who are said to have no idea whatever of the existence of any supreme being, are firmly convinced that their ancestors were endowed with powers such as no living man now possesses. They could travel underground or mount into the sky; could make creeks and water-courses, mountain-ranges, sand-hills, and plains. "In very many cases the actual names of these natives are preserved in their traditions, but, so far as we have been able to discover," comment Spencer and Gillen,[1] "there is no instance of any one of them being regarded in the light of a 'deity.'" So in the Loyalty Islands, "the natives had no idea of any God or devil, heaven or hell. Their religion or superstitious feelings were in connection with the departed spirits of their fathers."[2] Among the Elema tribes of British New Guinea the name for ancestors, *ualare,* is that by which all sacred objects are designated. The ancestor-cult here is involved with the totemic system, for certain animals are *ualare,* and as these were never injured or eaten by the ancestors, so their descendants hold them sacred; even natural objects or phenomena may be *ualare.* Certain generalities may be drawn from this complicated situation: (a) All tribal *ualare* are regarded as deities who in the long ago temporarily assumed human form when they became the ancestors of the respective tribes, and at the same time

41 Roth, in BAE, XXXVIII, 639.   1 *North. Tr. Cent. Aust.*, 490.
42 Lumholtz, in *Scribner's Mag.*, XVI, 444.   2 Ray, in JAI, XLVII, 295.

appropriated certain areas for their posterity, which they furnished with vegetable food. Some of the immediate descendants of the several original ancestors are credited with his supernatural attributes. (b) Clan *ualare*-deities are ancestors who acquired their powers from the father or from the mother (where descent is matrilineal), who created himself or herself from a natural object or is a nature-deity. (c) Individual *ualare,* unlike the others, are not inherited. A personal *ualare* may be that of either parent or of the person, living or dead, after whom the person is named, or adopted as the result of a dream. Every man has two *ualare,* such as a dog, a pig, a wallaby, a bird, a fish, or a tree, which he may not injure or eat.[3]

More unified is the system of ancestor-worship of the Fijians, who had an evolved set of ancestral gods, the Kalou-Vu. A deceased ancestor was a god; he had his temple, his priests, who themselves must become hereditary, and there was a strong motive of self-interest in keeping his memory green. "Being a god he conferred on the chief, his direct descendant, a portion of his godhead, and set him within the pale of the *tabu,* so that the chief's will might not be disobeyed nor his body touched without evoking the wrath of the unseen." Often the chief was metamorphosed into the tribal deity, and two tribes which had the same ancestor-god, that is, "were sprung from the same root," always refrained from fighting one another. "Members of that tribe may enter their village, slaughter their animals, and ravage their plantations, but they will sit complacently by; they are brothers and worship the same god."[4] One case is mentioned among the Fijians where the ancestral gods were light-colored, straight-haired men, probably Polynesians, who, owing to their prowess and personal appearance, were adopted by the Melanesian inhabitants of that period. "Time and ancestor worship have accorded divine honours to these illustrious strangers, and they were worshipped as the founders of the tribes they joined."[5] In the Trobriands, names of ancestral spirits are recited in the magical spells; in fact, "these invocations are perhaps the most prominent and persistent feature of the magical spells."[6] The Savage Islanders and the natives of New Caledonia worshipped the spirits of their ancestors, whose relics they preserved and idolized. At one place the latter people had wooden idols before the chiefs' houses. The office of priest was hereditary and almost every family had its priest. To make sure of favors and prosperity they prayed not only to their own ancestor-gods, but also, in a precautionary way, to the gods of other lands.[7] Until recently the Andaman Islanders had no knowledge of the outside world; the few voyagers who ventured near their shores were regarded as deceased ancestors who had been allowed to revisit the earth.[8]

It is well to keep on the good side of ancestors, for they bestow or withhold favors according as they are pleased or offended. Should anyone of the African Kaffirs dream about his ancestors who are dead, it was taken as an indication that they were displeased at some neglect and demanded a propitiatory sacrifice. Should there be illness either of man or beast, and a doctor declare: "I see, your ancestors are displeased because you have not rendered them their due," it was understood that a sacrifice was demanded. And should there be no rain, the people would go to the chief and ask: "Why do you allow it to be thus? Why don't you invoke your ancestors?" Whereupon he would offer

3 Haddon, in JAI, L, 262-263.
4 Thomson, in JAI, XXIV, 342.
5 Brewster, in JAI, XLIX, 309.

6 Malinowski, in JAI, XLVI, 371.
7 Turner, *Samoa,* 306, 345.
8 Man, in JAI, XII, 101.

a sacrifice.[9] In West Africa the word "spirit" is a conception from which often the signification of "deceased ancestor" has been lost.[10] In the matter of belief in ancestral spirits, there appears to be very little difference between Central Africa and Europe; "for they seem to be merely the souls of the departed which received such marked attention in Europe even up to present times, as for example the Feast of All Souls and St. John's Eve." The reality and imminence of the influence of the ancestral spirits upon the daily life of the natives cannot readily be realized. An evil-disposed ancestral spirit, for instance, will sometimes enter cattle to kill them; "the people know when a beast is so possessed by the animal shaking its head and by tears streaming from its eyes." The ancestral spirits may live underground or inhabit certain sacred fig-trees. The latter belief is found along the east coast of Africa and is prevalent all over India; "it is stated that in Burmah to this day the Government pays to the headman of certain forest tracts a fee called *murung* for appeasing the *manes* of their ancestors lodged in old *sal* trees."[11]

In East Africa ancestral spirits are thought to be able to cure disease. The method of treatment is as follows. After both legs and wings of a bird have been broken and a string passed through the under-beak, it is suspended round the patient's neck, whilst the ancestral spirits are thus addressed: "This is the custom, that we follow with this bird; if this person be cured to-day, we will give it to you to eat;" or "Grandfather, great uncle (or grandmother, great aunt, as the case may be), I give you this bird, cure now therefore this patient."[12] As with all Bantu faiths, so with the Awemba religion, ancestor-worship is the mainspring of their theology. Other Bantu tribes have no genuine nature-spirits, but appeal in all things, for rain and everything else, to the spirits of their ancestors. It is safe to conjecture that the spirits of very ancient chiefs have been exalted to the state of ancestral gods by the natives to whom their names, shrouded in the mists of antiquity, have become as mythical and meaningless as the prehistoric Dorus and Ionus were to the ancient Greeks. The general run of ancestral spirits may be divided into two classes: the spirit of the chief, who is worshipped by all his subjects, and the spirit of the head of each family, "who may be compared with the Roman Lar Familaris, since he is worshipped inside the hut at the hearth." In most cases the ancestral spirits of chiefs inhabit the thicket where their bodies were laid to rest; worship is paid to them at the burying-ground. The only way in which the spirit of an ancestor can communicate and warn his worshippers is in dreams or by meeting some person, inspiring him, and making him rave. Sometimes they become permanently reincarnated in the bodies of possessed women. "They demand food and beer as their due from the villagers, asking it in the name of the chief they represent, and curiously enough using archaic forms of speech, when asking for tobacco and beer." When, without any special warning, an ancestral spirit appears to a man in a dream, it is a sign that he has been neglected. The burial-sacrifices held in his honor must be renewed; if the dreamer neglects the warning, he is sure to fall ill.[13] Though the Nigerian head-hunters do not worship the ancestor, nevertheless his ghost is much feared.[14]

9 Kropf, *Kaffir-Eng. Dict.*, 53, 76.
10 Frobenius, *Masken*, 162; Bastian, *Deut. Exped.*, II, 200.
11 Hobley, in JAI, XLI, 432-433.

12 Dundas, in JAI, XLIII, 44, 45.
13 Sheane, in JAI, XXXVI, 150-152.
14 Tremearne, in JAI, XLII, 159.

Among the Buryat of Siberia only distinguished persons are venerated after death.[15] It is to China and Japan that one looks for a highly developed system of ancestor-worship. The Chinese type has been described by a well-known authority[16] as a calculated process for getting wealth, work, power, and all worldly success through the help of the ghost of the deceased. So ingrained is the custom that the bones of Chinese who die in America are disinterred, to be shipped back to China as their final resting place; then a new ancestral tablet will be added to the sanctuary of the house, before which the family members will worship.[17] Ancestor-worship of the Chinese type is unknown among the Palaungs, but sometimes prayers are said to the spirits of dead parents to invoke their spiritual aid.[18] Japanese Shintoism, or the belief in the "Way of the Gods," is the worship of the gods from whom the emperors claim descent— the worship of the "imperial ancestors." The Imperial House, even of the present time, is supposed to include the direct descendants of the ancient goddess, the first deity recognized in Japanese religion. To pay homage to the gods or to the departed ancestors of the Imperial family is the most important precept of Shintoism, though ancestor-worship on a lesser scale is practised by all families, in the hope of being protected from any evil or misfortune and of attaining health and prosperity. With ancestor-worship goes the desire for offspring and, in default of such, the custom of adoption. The principal object of the latter is to prevent the extinction of families and the consequent neglect of the spirits of the departed. An interesting case occurred when the famous general, Count Nogi, took his own life at the moment of national grief at the Mikado's death, for his two sons had been killed in war and he himself did not believe in adoption, even going so far as to provide by will that his distinguished family should become extinct for lack of an heir. This blow to ancestor-worship was later rectified by the Imperial appointment of a man to the countship, so as to revive the famous warrior's family. It is asserted that the future of Japan must depend upon the maintenance of a new religion of loyalty evolved, through an older type, from the ancient cult of the dead. Certain it is that the conception of ancestor-worship cannot keep its compactness against changing conditions in modern Japan. There are many forces working against it: "the fact that modern civilization is driving people away from the birthplaces of their own ancestors is certainly weakening the conception of ancestor-worship in that it deprives them of opportunities for observing the religious rites towards departed spirits. Again, the atmosphere of a city, exciting and unpoetically scientific, does not tend to cherish the somewhat ghostly and shadowy sense of ancestor-worship." Those who move to a foreign country, for instance to America, are especially inclined to forget past ages and departed spirits. "Furthermore, the main families in the old patriarchal system are already dying out in present Japan, and a branch family cannot be expected to be so devotional to the thought of the ancestors." The modern tendency of individualism does not encourage the idea of reverence for the ancients, and when, in this materialistic age, the ancestral spirits cannot reveal their worldly action in the lives of the people, bestowing on them physical prosperity and peace, modern minds—more or less touched by science and the evolutionary theory— will recognize them only through a sense of emotional feeling, which emotional

15 Czaplicka, *Aborig. Siberia*, 159.
16 DeGroot, *Relig. Syst.*, I, 57.

17 N. Y. *Times*, Nov. 22, 1908.
18 Milne, *Eastern Clan*, 356.

and imaginative faculty is not possessed by all.[19] To the extent to which these modifications of ancestor-worship are actual, we have an illustration of one of our major contentions: that the maintenance-mores are basic and that as the conditions of life change, the other groups of mores must also change, to be brought again into adaptation.

The doctrine which has the strongest influence on the minds of the Sumatrans is that which leads them to venerate, almost to the point of worshipping, the tombs and manes of their deceased ancestors. They are attached to them as to life itself, and to oblige them to remove from the neighborhood of their ancestral tombs is like tearing up a tree by the roots; they call upon their ancestors when taking solemn oath and apostrophize them in times of sudden calamity.[20] On the island of Nias the cult of ancestors develops whenever a man dies leaving one or more sons, for through the manipulation of the priest the spirit of the deceased is induced to enter an idol which henceforth remains in the house of the sons, bringing them blessings, and to it they sacrifice.[21] Ancestors' spirits, think the Filipinos, care for their good as a sort of intercessor-class with the great god. To these, their real Lares and Penates, they consecrate great feasts. They believe their ancestral spirits live in such places as large trees, isolated rocks, or in anything distinguished from the ordinary, and never pass such features of the landscape without asking permission, inclining, and joining the hands.[22] Among some Maori tribes, a woman's father, grandfather, or a priest would attend her during the period of parturition, playing upon a flute made from a bone of an ancestor of the woman or her husband until the child was born. "Such a flute was looked upon as a connecting link, or medium, between the living on the one hand, and their defunct elders and ancestors, as also the gods, on the other. As most gods of the Maori are ancestral deities, deified ancestors and spirit gods that care for, cherish, warn, admonish, and also punish, their living descendants in this world, the mediumistic idea and its advantages are fairly clear."[23]

Although the Egyptians did not make much of family and descent, ancestor-worship was not unknown to them.[24] Originally the Fravashis, or guardian-angels, in the religion of the Parsees represented only the departed souls of ancestors, comparable to the Pitaras, "fathers," of the Brahmans and the Manes of the Romans.[25] In all Græco-Roman societies, the state, the clan, and the family found their ideal and firmest bond in reverence for divine or heroic ancestors, a reverent piety toward the spirits who had passed into the unseen world.[26] "The worship of dead ancestors was certainly one of the earliest forms of the domestic rites, because the most spontaneous and simple, and it was favored also by modes of sepulture in the lowest civilization."[27] In Rome the sacrifice to the dead, in the shape of the *sacra,* adopted the form of a moral law under the protection of the Pontifices. The obligation could be enforced by the chief authority, and with the death of the one bound to fulfil it, it fell to the heir as a burden on the inheritance. *Nulla hereditas sine sacris* is a well-known maxim in the *jus pontificium.*[28] The *lares* were the deified souls of the

19 Noguchi, in N.Y. *Nation,* CII, no. 2654, 512-513.

20 Marsden, *Sumatra,* 291-292; Wilken, in VG, II, 248.

21 Raap, in *Globus,* LXXXIII, 151.

22 Montero y Vidal, *Filipinas,* I, 56.

23 Best, in JAI, XLIV, 160.

24 Erman, *Ægypten,* 226-227.

25 Haug, *Parsis,* 206-207.

26 Dill, *Nero,* 263; Schrader, *Aryan,* 424; Wobbermin, *Mysterienwesen,* 10.

27 De Marchi, *Culto Priv.,* rev. in *Année Soc.,* I, 37.

28 Ihering, *Aryan,* 42-43.

dead, the apotheosized spirits of ancestors conceived of as remaining in the house and worshipped by rites performed by the descendants. Wherever there was a domestic hearth or center of life which formed a family, in palace or hovel, *lares* were present as sanctifying spirits, as beneficent *genii* of the house. They identified themselves with the family where they lived, shared its joys and sorrows, its prosperity and misfortune. At the hearth of every house was the *lar familiaris,* associated with Vesta and the *di penates.* The latter were conceived of as many divinities under one point of view; any god, that is to say, could be among the *di penates* in any house. *Penates* were all divinities like Silvanus or Fortuna which were called in inscriptions "domestic," conservative of the house and property, distinguished by the name of the family (Fortuna Flavia), or retained as special protectors of the believer. They guarded stores and watched over the material prosperity of the household. They were abstract *genii* tutelary of the house as the public *penates* were *genii* tutelary of the state. *Penates* were arbiters of luck: they sent misfortune or punishment; they received thanks for escape from accident or for success in some enterprise. In time the *lares* and *penates* became equal and were associated. The *genius* of the head of the house (the term at first signified the generative principle and when applied to women was denominated *Juno;* later it was thought of as the divine personality of mortal men) was worshipped with the *penates* and the *lar familiaris.* The gods, ancestral or otherwise, were always brought into public and private life. In everyday affairs there was constant reference to the gods: at every meal the *lar familiaris* was in evidence; at all departures and returns there were salutations to the house-divinities, who were also present at all stages of house- and field-labors. They were invoked at every meeting, advised of all acts of administration and war; every incident called for prayer or thanksgiving, while on public tables were recorded all state religious acts and their occasions.[29]

§240. Hero-Worship.

THERE are numerous instances both past and present of the deification of the great man, who is often a culture-hero. In many mythologies the first man created all things; he is elevated to the status of a god, and chiefs and kings often descend from him.[1] As in the Bantu cult of ancestors one member is especially favored, so the great hero of the Hottentots is none other than the spirit of an earlier chieftain endowed with special power.[2] A hero in the making is to be seen in a Kaffir ruler in South Africa who, a Christian advised by missionaries, became a benevolent despot. He conducted church-services twice every Sunday, insisting upon observance of the Sabbath; decreed and actually enforced prohibition of the manufacture and use of alcoholic beverages; put an end to witch-doctors; ate the forbidden totem-animal. He was consequently highly revered, being regarded as a sort of father.[3] The Siberians and Mongolians have had their hero-gods besides Genghis Khan, some of them being of supposed supernatural birth; indeed, extraordinary persons have regularly been sent to earth upon special occasions to serve the human race.[4]

29 Wissowa, *Relig. Römer,* 145, 148, 153, 154, 323, 326; De Marchi, *Culto Priv.,* rev. in *Année Soc.,* I, 31, 39, 42, 44, 61, 64, 70, 71.
1 Lippert, *Kgchte.,* II, 255-257.

2 Fritsch, *Eingeb. S.-Afr.,* 338.
3 Bent, *Mashonaland,* 23 ff.
4 Michailovski, *Shamanism* (Russ.), 29.

The Chinese god of war is nothing but a canonized hero, identified clearly enough with an historical character.[5] A local divinity at the mouth of the Ganges, one whose name is a spell against tigers, represents the deification of some noted tiger-killer of several generations ago.[6] Mortals deified as heroes and not as ancestors have played some part in the evolution of the Toda religion.[7] Some of the degraded classes of India comfort themselves in their present depressed condition by expecting Kalki to appear as their future deliverer and as the restorer of their social position. "Indeed it is a remarkable fact that a belief in a coming Redeemer seems to exist in all religions, not excepting Buddhism and Muhammadanism."[8]

The founder of the republican settlement of Chinese in Borneo was called "big uncle Lo" or "old uncle Lo." The people were fully persuaded that their welfare and luck depended wholly on Lo, that their prosperity waited upon his support and protection. "Anger his spirit," they reasoned, "and it is all up with your luck; act, on the contrary, always in his spirit and follow in the footsteps he traced, and never will he withdraw from you his protection."[9] Different types of hero appear in the Hawaiian romance of Laieikawai: (a) the hero may be a human being of high rank and of unusual power either of strength, skill, wit, or craft; (b) he may be a demigod of supernatural power, half human, half divine; (c) he may be born in the shape of a beast, bird, fish, or other object, with or without the power to take human form or monstrous size; (d) he may bear some relation to the sun, moon, or stars, a form rare in Hawaii, but which, when it does occur, is treated objectively rather than allegorically; (e) he may be a god, without human kinship, either one of the "departmental gods" who rule over the forces of nature, or of the hostile spirits who inhabited the islands before they were occupied by the present race; (f) he may be a mere ordinary man who by means of one of these supernatural helpers has achieved success.[10] There is a remarkable modern instance among the Maoris of this tendency to exalt tribal and national heroes to the rank of gods. Te Kooti, the famous warrior who led his wild Hauhaus from 1868 to 1871, continually chased by the Government forces but never captured, is regarded as little short of a god by the Urewera people. "For three years he fought your Government troops," they will tell you, "and yet you never got him. He was a wonderful man, and he had *mana-tapu* and influence with the gods. Indeed he was a god himself."[11]

The nearest approach that the Tlinkits of Alaska ever made to worshipping any object was their reverence for their dead shaman. "They prayed to him for long life and success in their enterprises. In the morning they would take a mouthful of water, spit it out and pray. When in danger of drowning they would pray to him for deliverance. Not only would they thus pray to him, but to things that once belonged to him."[12] The brother of the culture-hero of the Sauk is held to be master of the ghost-world situated in the west beyond the setting sun, while the culture-hero himself is said to be at the north, in the region of snow and ice. "The Sauk are looking for his return, when they believe the world will come to an end, and they and the culture-hero will go to join his brother."[13] The chief god-hero of the Algonquian family was usually

5 "Kl. Nachrichten," in *Globus*, LXXVIII, 116; Harvey, *Chinese Animism*.
6 JASB, III, 104.
7 Rivers, *Todas*, 446.
8 Monier-Williams, *Brāhmanism*, 114.

9 DeGroot, *Kongsiwezen*, 121.
10 Beckwith, in BAE, XXXIII, 330.
11 Cowan, *Maoris*, 110.
12 Jones, *Thlingets*, 231-233.
13 Hewitt, in HAI, II, 479.

identified as a fabulous great rabbit bearing some relation to the sun. "He it was who created the world by magic power, peopled it with game and the other animals, taught his favorite people the arts of the chase, and gave them corn and beans. But this deity was distinguished more for his magical powers and his ability to overcome opposition by trickery, deception, and falsehood than for benevolent qualities."[14] The culture-hero and demigod Kulóskap the Master, the "Lord of Beasts and Men," taught hunting and fishing, the uses of animals, the names and tales of the stars, and other important things; he is called the deceiver, not because he befools or injures man, but because he is clever enough to lead his enemies astray, the highest possible virtue to the early American mind.

> Kulóskap got his name
> Which means the Liar, or,
> As Indians mean the word:
> A wise and crafty man.[15]

The individual who came into the village to open the torture-ceremonies of the Mandans is interpreted by observers as representing the Mandan Adam.[16] The Cheyennes had many culture-heroes and also a story of creation, which latter, however, appears to show Christian influence. It is to the effect that the Creator made man from a rib from his own right side; "and then from the left side of the man he took a rib, from which he created the woman."[17] The Pawnee hero-stories of Grinnell[18] are well known. Mooney[19] says that among the roving tribes of the north the hero-god is hardly more than an expert magician, frequently degraded to the level of a common trickster who, after ridding the world of giants and monsters and teaching his people a few simple arts, retires to the upper world to rest and smoke until some urgent necessity again requires his presence below. "In the south the myth takes more poetic form and the hero becomes a person of dignified presence, a father and teacher of his children, a very Christ, worthy of all love and reverence, who gathers together the wandering nomads and leads them to their destined country, where he instructs them in agriculture, house-building, and the art of government, regulates authorities, and inculcates peaceful modes of life. Such was Quetzalcoatl of the Aztecs, and such in all essential respects was the culture-god of the more southern semi-civilized races. Curiously enough, this god, at once a Moses and a Messiah, is usually described as a white man with a flowing beard. . . . The belief in the coming of a Messiah who should restore them to their original happy condition was well-nigh universal among the American tribes." So remarkable was the reign of Quetzalcoatl that myths grew about him and as the "Plumed Serpent" he was made into a god. He disappeared into legend until the archæologists of today traced his origin to its source. His virtues had been so extraordinary as to merit for him in popular estimation a second life on earth. There is some ground for the contention that when the natives saw Cortez land from strange ships, very close to the spot where, according to an embellished myth, Quetzalcoatl had launched his fabulous serpent-raft, they regarded him as the reincarnation of the "Plumed Serpent." Thus was his

---

14 Mooney and Thomas, in HAI, I, 40.
15 Leland and Prince, *Kulóskap*, 34, 45-46, 62.
16 Matthews, in USNM, 1890, 608.

17 Grinnell, *Cheyenne*, II, 337 ff.
18 *Pawnee Hero Stories*, 26, 46.
19 In BAE, XIV, 658.

conquest made easy.[20] The Yucatecs ascribed their progress to Zamna who, like Thoth of the Egyptians, was regarded as the inventor of hieroglyphics and the first to teach the people to give names to men and to things.[21]

In antiquity "the awe-inspiring kinsman or tyrant, the birth shrouded in secrecy, the rearing in a lower class and the wonderful elevation, are common features, whether the hero be . . . Romulus or Siegfried, Sargon or Cyrus."[22] An ancient culture-hero of the Persians taught the people to make garments of skins and to domesticate animals; he led in hunting by the aid of leopards and falcons, and made the subjugated devils teach his people writing. A prophet of the tribe of Zoroaster was held to have been supernaturally born of a virgin; it was believed that he would arise and help bring about the resurrection.[23] Zoroaster was to return at the end of time.[24] In the period of Greek art to which we owe most of the grave-reliefs found at Athens, hero-worship was submerged; it was an era of rationalism and the funeral-monuments of that time tended to represent this life rather than the next. Nowhere in Attic grave-reliefs of the fifth century are the dead so exalted, but once the age of reason was past, hero-worship re-emerged, apparently, in greater force than before.[25] The serpent was often not merely the symbol but even the representative of the deceased; it "appears everywhere as the symbol of the heroes, as well as of the chthonian cult-beings in general, and frequently enough the latter make their appearance directly in the serpent form." The serpent along with the torch is the chief symbol of the mysterious; this is true of the Eleusinian, the Dionysian, and other secret cults.[26] Another species of apotheosis, the deification of a living person, though contrary to common sense and to sound Roman tradition, was in the end almost universally adopted. "The sullen resistance of public opinion was overcome when the religions of Asia vanquished the masses of the population. These religions propagated in Italy dogmas which tended to raise the monarchs above the level of mankind, and if they won the favor of the Cæsars, and particularly of those who aspired to absolute power, it is because they supplied a dogmatic justification of their despotism. In place of the old principle of popular sovereignty was substituted a reasoned faith in supernatural influence."[27] In the North, Odin was at once god, hero, bard, lawgiver, and shaman. He took possession of land, building a temple and beginning the offerings; the people gave him tribute that he might defend the land from their enemies and sacrifice for a good crop. Property-rights and agriculture thus proceeded from the gods. Odin ordered three sacrifices annually, for productive soil and for victory. According to tradition he became ill of a fatal disease and caused himself to be pierced with a spear; thereafter to "mark one's self for Odin" meant not to die a natural death but to be smitten with a spear and win a soldier's end. The Swedes thought he had gone back to Asgard, the original home of the nation, north of the Black Sea. Often when at war they fancied that he appeared, giving some victory and calling others home to him in Valhalla.[28] The relation between the Valkyrs and the heroes was a romantic one: "The hero is speedily seized by love of his protectress; she, on her side, although she sees that only by retaining

20 Spinden, "A Great American Emperor Revealed," in N. Y. Times, May 10, 1925.
21 Nadaillac, Preh. Amer., 348.
22 Tiele, Gchte. Relig., I, 163.
23 Justi, Persien, 30, 91.
24 Tiele, Gchte. Relig., II, 105.
25 Harrison, Greek Relig., 353.
26 Wobbermin, Mysterienwesen, 86-87.
27 Cumont, Mithra, 91; Otto, Aegypten, I, 11.
28 Geijer, Svensk. Hist., 23, 112.

her maidenhood may she be worthy to be the All-Father's messenger, sacri
fices all for her love" and is reduced to a weak earthly woman.[29]

§241. Types of Daimon.

THE principle of local worship—the deification or spiritualization of rivers,
mountain-tops, crags and weird places, vegetation, and the forces of nature—
has been very widely held. Though the animistic basis is generally to be inferred, pure abstractions are encountered. Says Gomme:[1] "Earth deities, claiming their sacrifice of human blood; tree deities, claiming the life of their
priest; corn deities, whose death forms part of their own cult; rain deities,
claiming victims for their service, form no part of any recognizable tribal cult,
but are essentially the fixed heritage of the places where they originated and
fructified."

By the side of ancestor-worship and belief in ghosts there exist throughout
New Guinea undeniable traces of nature-worship. Natural forces are venerated: some tribes regard fire as a kind of divinity, others so revere thunder,
lightning, wind, and rain. According to certain Papuans, lightning is caused
by evil spirits which dwell in the air, and the storm follows as a consequence
of struggle between these aërial spirits. Thunder they dislike and close their
ears in order not to hear it. Volcanoes, mountains, and the sea are regarded
as abodes of invisible spirits.[2] When a person dies, think the Akamba, his
spirit goes to live in a wild fig tree.[3]

The daimons of Chukchee belief fall into three classes which are characterized by a good deal of anthropomorphism: (a) invisible spirits, bringing
disease and death; (b) bloodthirsty cannibal spirits, the particular enemies of
Chukchee warriors; (c) spirits which assist the shaman during his performances. As all these have an especial fondness for the human liver, "this belief
is the origin of the Chukchee custom of opening a corpse to discover from the
liver which spirit has killed the deceased." The third class, the shamanistic
spirits, sometimes called "separate voices," take the forms of animals, plants,
or icebergs, and can change their form very quickly—also their temper; "on
account of this last peculiarity the shaman must be very punctilious in keeping
his compact with them."[4] According to tradition, when the Oraon of India
settled in their present habitat, the land was cleared and occupied by groups
of brothers or cousins. "Ceremonies were held by these groups to propitiate
the disturbed spirits, and each sept today thus holds its land and has its own
group of spirits, to which, at annual gatherings of the members, offerings are
made. Part of the forest-land was set aside for the general spirits, the ritual
for whom is in the hands of the village priest. The Oraon have a well-developed
ceremonial life, some of the rites relating to agriculture, others to the tribal
hunts, etc."[5] In one of the Hindu myths it is related: "I did not fall to earth,
for eight elementary spirits encompassed me and with their arms caught me
in the air."[6] One class of divinities or spirits in the Rig Veda includes abstractions, such as Infinity, Piety, Abundance.[7] More elemental are the beliefs
in China where the human soul is the original form of all beings of a higher

---

29 Wisen, *Qvinnan*, 7.

1 *Ethnol. in Folklore*, 70; Frazer, *Golden
Bough*, II, 40-68.

2 Krieger, *Neu-Guinea*, 309, 405.

3 Hobley, *A-Kamba*, 85.

4 Czaplicka, *Aborig. Siberia*, 258-259.

5 Dixon, reviewing Roy, *The Oraons of
Chota Nagpur*, in AA, XVIII, 286.

6 Holtzmann, *Ind. Sagen*, I, 231.

7 Hopkins, *Relig. India*, 135-136.

order; "its worship is therefore the basis of all religion in that country."8
It would seem that the daimons, like human beings, do not like rivals: some
years ago the Christian mission at Tien Tsin was forced to move because
it was believed to interfere with the good luck of the place, so that none of
the students worshipping at the Confucian temple next door had been able
to take degrees.9 The religion of the Ainos of Yezo is a primitive nature-worship. "The gods are invisible, formless conceptions, known as *kamui,* such as
the house god, the god of fire, and the deities of mountain, forest, sea, and
river. The sun and moon occupy a subordinate position among them. There are
no priests nor temples, but within every house there is one corner sacred to
the house-god. The god of fire, who is esteemed highest of all, is worshiped at
the fire-place in the middle of the room."10

Before drinking of the waters in a new country, the Kayans of Borneo take
a knife in their teeth, immerse themselves in the stream, and mutter their petitions to the spirits. Hiller11 once witnessed such a scene, which he describes as
follows: "The Bukit went down into the first tiny brook, divested himself of
all clothing, took an ear-ring from his ear, threw it into the water and then
offered the following prayer to the water-nymphs: 'O spirit of the waters, I
make you this offering to show you that your children do not forget you;
protect me, I pray you, keep me from harm in the country I am about to
traverse, keep me from sickness, from poison and death in the land of your
waters; bring me back in safety to my own country!' He had wound a chaplet
of sweet-scented leaves about his brow; he was naked, and as he stooped there
in the running waters of the stream, lifting the first handful of water to his
lips, it was hard to realize that it was only Laioh, the Bukit, and not some
faun." Many nature-spirits are recognized by the Malays,12 while the natives
of Ceylon have personified all misfortunes and troubles, of which they have
their full share: sickness, hunger, danger from fire and water, and all other
evils which hang over mankind.13 In the Caroline Islands, every village, every
valley, hill, or stream has its *genius loci,* every family its household-god, every
clan its presiding spirit, every tribe its tutelary deity. "Thunder, lightning,
rain, storm, wind, fishing, planting, war, festival, harvest, famine, birth, disease, death, all these events and phenomena have their supernatural patron
or Master-spirit. The gloomy fancy of the Ponapean peoples the swamp, the
reef, the mountain, and the hanging woods of the inland wilderness with hosts
of spirits, some beneficent, the greater part malignant. All these Ani [deified
ancestors] are honoured under the guise of some special bird, fish, or tree in
which they are supposed to reside, and with which they are identified."14

The Tlinkit give ample proof in their actions of a belief in nature-spirits.
In earlier times they used to grasp at shadows cast by the sun and would
ask, after blowing on their hands, "Let me have luck." The wind was talked
to for the purpose of inducing it to moderate or cease; sometimes a piece of
fish was thrown to it. When in the neighborhood of a glacier or big iceberg
the Tlinkit always talked to it, saying, "My son's daughter, be very careful.
You might come down on us."15 The Cheyenne Indians believed in a being
known as Hoimaha, who brought the winter. "When Hoimaha came in winter,

---

8 DeGroot, *Relig. Sys.,* I, 1.
9 *Illust. Christian World,* July, 1897.
10 Hitchcock, in USNM, 1890, 472.
11 In *Bull. Geog. Soc. of Phila.,* III, 54.

12 Skeat and Blagden, *Malay Penin.,* II,
173 ff.
13 Schmidt, *Ceylon,* 291.
14 Christian, *Caroline Isl.,* 75.
15 Jones, *Thlingets,* 237.

and it snowed, and it was thought that too much snow was likely to fall, the people used to be called together and to have a feast. Then they filled the pipe, offered it to Hoimaha, calling him 'Father,' and 'Grandfather above,' and prayed to him, asking him to stop the snow from falling." When the thunder began in spring, they used to fill the pipe, offer a smoke to the thunder, and ask him to take pity on them. A certain species of butterfly was called the thunder-parasite; the belief seemed to be that when the Thunderbird shakes himself in anger, his parasites fall from him.[16] The morning-star is the principal god and protecting genius of the Cora, being characterized as a brother, a youth armed with bow and arrow who once shot the powerful sun at noontime on account of his intense heat. "The moon is also a god—both man and woman—and there are many others, as everything is believed to be animate and powerful."[17] The Conoy worshipped corn and fire.[18] In the Tusayan ritual ancestor-worship has developed into an elaborate system of minor supernaturals called *katcinas* that are most powerful to bring blessings; the term in their vocabulary also signifies rain. The names of these beings are legion, their ceremonials complicated.[19]

Certain South American Indians, who go to the rivers to seek gold only when they want to purchase some special thing not procurable except with money, if they extract more gold than they actually want, throw the surplus back into the river. "Nothing will persuade them to sell or barter it, for they say that if they borrow more than they really need, the river-god will not lend them any more."[20] The Indians of Guiana believe in a number of distinctly anthropomorphic nature-spirits. In this class are the spirits of the forest which can be recognized, even when invisible, by the whistling sound they make; it is like the sound made by a human being, beginning in a high key and dying slowly and gradually away in a low one. Sometimes, however, instead of a whistle they may indicate their presence by a noise somewhat like the neighing of a horse—this in places where horses are known not to exist. Such spirits, like human beings, can be fooled, at least some of the time: "If an Indian loses his way in the forest, the Spirit is the cause. The Caribs, however, know how to circumvent the latter, by making a string puzzle, which is left on the pathway: the object of this puzzle consists in removing, without cutting or breaking, an endless string from off two sticks upon which it has been placed. The Spirit coming along sees the puzzle, starts examining it, and tries to get the string off: indeed, so engrossed with it does he become, that he forgets all about the wanderer, who is now free to find the road again." The Spirits of the Forest are "blessed, or cursed, with strong patriarchal tendencies, are very fond of women, and of human flesh generally. They have an unconquerable attraction toward suckling babes and pregnant women, a statement which appears to be confirmed in the accompanying legends." Like the spirits of the forest, the water-spirits have strong sexual predilections. "Every night, in their anthropomorphic form, both males and females may come after Indians of the opposite sex, respectively, and no disastrous result follows the intimacy. But the Indians who happen to have such dealings must keep the fact absolutely secret: if divulged, either they will not live long, or they will never be visited again by their Spirit friends." These Indians have their special explanation for a lunar eclipse. Island Caribs attribute eclipses to the devil, who tries to

16 Grinnell, *Cheyenne Ind.*, II, 94-96.
17 Hodge, in HAI, I, 348.
18 Mooney and Thomas, in HAI, I, 340.

19 Fewkes, in *Smithson. Rep.*, 1895, 692.
20 White, in JAI, XIII, 245.

kill Sun and Moon; "they say that this wicked seducer cuts their hair by surprise, and makes them drink the blood of a child, and that, when they are totally eclipsed, it is because the Stars, being no longer warmed by the Sun's rays and light, are very ill." Some Orinoco tribes held that at an eclipse the moon was about to die; others that it was angry with them and would give them no more light; still others held to the death-theory and were under the conviction that if the moon were indeed to die, all exposed fires would be extinguished. "Their women, crying and yelling—an outburst in which the men joined—accordingly would each seize a glowing ember and hide it, either in the sand or underground. Moved by their tears and entreaties, the Moon however recovers, and the hidden fires are extinguished: but were he indeed to die, the concealed embers would remain alight." The Rio Negro Indians, believing at an eclipse that the moon is being killed, make all the noise they can to frighten the evil slayer away.[21] The moon, known as the wife of the sun, was the only beneficent deity of the Araucanians. She protected and advised them of any disaster, showing them their enemies, and frightening away the evil spirits. "This is easily understood when one remembers that night attacks are seldom undertaken on moonlight nights, and that most savages have a great fear of the dark when alone. It also accounts for the faith placed in the signs of the moon, whose phases were always consulted in their principal undertakings. A red moon was considered to be a sign of the death of some important personage. What is curious, especially if we consider their contact with the Incas, is that the sun has no place in their religious beliefs."[22]

When an Athenian was about to be married he is said to have prayed and sacrificed to the Tritopatores, that is, fathers in the third degree, forefathers, ancestors, ghosts, and, according to some, winds. To the winds were offered such expiatory sacrifices as were due to the spirits of the underworld. "The idea that the Tritopatores were winds as well as ghosts was never lost." They were sometimes called "lords of the winds" and "gate-keepers and guardians of the winds." It was held that the winds gave life not only to plants but to all things. "It was natural enough that the winds should be divided into demons beneficent and maleficent, as it depends where you live whether a wind from a particular quarter will do you good or ill."[23] Among the Romans there were no signs of the worship of nature or of personified natural phenomena. There was no worship of stars, sun, moon, or storm, and in the early ages there were no abstractions, though later talents, traits, and other qualities were personified and made into gods.[24] To primitive Semites the action of the wind in fructifying date-palms seemed divine work; indeed, the winds are cherubim.[25] In the Book of Enoch of the Apocryphal period, the sea, hoar frost, snow, mist, dew, and rain each has its special spirit. This idea is still further developed in the Book of Jubilees; the different elements are represented as each containing a spirit which, in turn, has its angel, so that it becomes possible to speak of the angels of the fire-spirit or the wind-spirit. Later, abstract conceptions had their angels bound up with them, as the angel of death, the angel of peace.[26] Originally the belief in angels was everywhere tied up with the notion of elementary spirits; those which, according to ancient folk-belief,

21 Roth, in BAE, XXX, 176, 180-181, 187, 246-247, 255, 257, 258-259; §266, of the text and Case-Book.
22 Latcham, in JAI, XXXIX, 347.
23 Harrison, Greek Relig., 279-280.

24 Wissowa, Relig. Römer, 20, 74, 271.
25 Barton, Sem. Orig., 94.
26 Fairweather, in Hastings's Dict. Bible, 287.

were active in the phenomena of the heavens, in storm and wind, thunder, light-ning, and hail, in field and wood, in fountains and trees, in plants and animals—in short, everywhere, but especially where something extraordinary and in-explicable occurred—these spirits became angels to the Jewish people.[27] There is plenty of evidence that the Old Testament notion of angels was borrowed largely from Babylonia. The seven archangels go back in the last analysis to the seven Babylonian planetary gods, the twelve angels of the zodiac to the twelve zodiac gods of Babylonia, and the twenty-four presbyters of the Apocalypse of John to the twenty-four divine judges of the Babylonians.[28] There is no uniform conception of angels, whose number is legion: some are angels over natural phenomena, as winds, fire, and waters; they form God's court, his ministers and reporters of what goes on on earth. Angels have inter-course with the daughters of men; they eat, bear weapons, and ride horses; an angel brought food and drink to Elijah, while another slew 185,000 As-syrians. They are media of God's will and execute his dispensations; when the mission is not punitive, they are beneficial to man.[29]

Finnish mythology invented unlimited classes of wicked spirits and demons for all kinds of misfortunes and trouble, finding in them an explanation of the aleatory element. "In epic poetry we find that a more human form is given to the influences dispersed throughout the world, where they opposed and strove to destroy the work of the gods and propitious genii. In this case, the wicked principle was personified by the giant Hiisi, who had a wife and children, horses, dogs, cats, and servants, all hideous and wicked like himself; in one word, the complete household of the chief of a tribe." Hiisi, scouring the plains on his horse, while his bird precedes him in the air, seems to have been originally a personification of the icy and fatal north wind. "The Finns con-sidered him as one of the most terrible demons, just as the Accadians feared the personification of the west wind, which produced by its excessive heat in their country quite as fatal effects."[30]

§243. Fear of the Daimons.

Though the Melanesians have not attained to the advanced conception of a devil, they nevertheless have a firm belief in evil spirits[1] and, as in the New Hebrides, ascribe all calamity to the fact that the spirits have not been satis-fied.[2] Nothing comes easier than death to the Papuan, when once his mind is fixed upon it; especially is this the case when he conceives that an evil spirit is interfering with his affairs. "The Papuan collapses before this illusion as quietly and certainly as we should sleep under the influence of a strong nar-cotic."[3] Although there is no cult of a superior intelligence nor any attempt to enter into personal relation with spirits, there is a sturdy belief among the Southern Massim in the existence of a large number of mythical beings. "Most of these unite malevolent qualities with a bodily form or mental attitude

27 Bousset, *Relig. Judentums*, 317.
28 Schrader, *Keilinschriften*, 458.
29 Job, XXV, 3; Matt., XXVI, 53; Rev., VII, 1, 2; XIV, 18; XVI, 5; Zech., VI, 7; Gen., VI, 2, 4; XVIII, 8; Ps., LXXVIII, 25; Num., XXII, 23; Josh., V, 13; Ezek., IX, 2; Zech., I, 8; I Kings, XIX, 5; II Kings, XIX, 35; Ps., CIII, 20; II Sam., XIV, 17, 20; XIX, 28; Matt., XVIII, 10;

Blau, in *Jewish Encyc.*, I, 583, 584, 589; Duhm, *Geister*, 52; Smith, *Relig. Sem.*, 446; Fairweather, in *Hastings's Dict. Bible*, 290; Kautzsch, in *Hastings's Dict. Bible*, 679; Charles, *Enoch*, LXI, 1; LXXXIX, 59.
30 Lenormant, *Chaldean Magic*, 257.
1 Codrington, *Melanesians*, 117, note.
2 Lawrie, in AAAS, 1892, 713.
3 Abel, *New Guinea*, 100.

which approach those of man sufficiently closely to permit of these creatures being characterised as ogres. The folk tales abound in examples of such ogres." The Koita believe also in a number of mythical beings with various external characteristics, all more or less malicious. "The most important of these, called *tabu,* inhabit definite areas, and in some instances at least have spheres of influence to which their power is limited. The places they inhabit are discovered by the occurrence of sickness or death after camping, eating, sitting, or urinating in these areas. The bites of insects, and accidental wounds received in such localities, are thought to produce especially severe and intractable sores."[4]

The African Bagobo is less concerned with good than with evil spirits, so far as the routine of daily life is involved. Countless pains and miseries come to him through the direct manipulation of evil spirits called *buso,* who, in all events, must be propitiated with offerings, tricked by subterfuges, or banished by magical rites. "These evil beings, some anthropomorphic, some zoomorphic, dominate the Bagobo's attitude toward life and death, and keep him constantly on the watch lest he be out-manœuvred, and thus become a prey to bodily suffering. Disease may also be caused by magical means, or because of the transgression of some custom or taboo, and to forestall such evil the behavior of the Bagobo is checked or redirected by rigid prohibitions at many points."[5] Among both West Africans and Bantu, though the firmament is the great indifferent and neglected god, he has great power if he would exert it. It is the lesser spirits or daimons which take up most of one's thought, but when things go very badly with him the African will rise up and call upon this great god in terror maddened by despair, that he may hear and restrain the evil workings of these lesser devils.[6] In the Congo region it is held that evil spirits or *mingoli* dwell everywhere, and are ever ready to pounce on any living person, and either carry their captive away, fasten a disease upon him, or kill him; "their life is one long drawn out fear of what the *mingoli* may next do to them, and their religion is a series of ceremonies, by *nganga* [shamans] and charm, to control, circumvent, and perhaps conquer the *mingoli.* Fortunately, these *mingoli* are limited in the area of their operations, and can be deceived. The *nganga* can cork them up in their calabashes, can cover them with saucepans, and when necessary, if the fee is large enough, can kill them, or rather, destroy them."[7] The Akamba call *Aiimu* the evil spirits which are supposed to be the disembodied relics of people who have killed their neighbors by the help of black magic; they have been banished by the Supreme Being to the woods, where they wander about without anybody to sacrifice to them. "They are a vindictive crew and enter into people who are working in distant fields and cause them to become seized with a kind of madness; persons so affected return to their villages, moan, groan, and roll about and the *Aiimu* speak through the mouth of the possessed person and perhaps say they want a *Ngoma,* a drumming feast, performed in their honour. The people of the village then collect in a hut, the possessed one sits in the center, the people make a drumming close by the patient for some hours and they kill a goat in the hut, if it is considered a serious case they may even kill a bullock close outside the door of the hut. Pieces of meat from each of the legs of the sacrifice are then placed close to the patient and after a little the *Aiimu* leave the person and

4 Seligmann, *Melanesians,* 646, 183.   6 Kingsley, *Travels W. Afr.,* 508.
5 Cole, in AA, XX, 217-219.   7 Weeks, in JAI, XL, 370.

he or she recovers."[8] Although the Nandi love their cattle more than anything else on earth, yet there are cases when their dread of the malignant supernatural overpowers this affection; for instance, "if one of their cattle is noticed to protrude its tongue to an excessive distance, or if a cow, as it is driven along, gets its tail twisted round a sapling by the road side, they are killed, for both of these instances are believed to be portents of great impending evil which can only be averted by the death of the animal."[9] In the relations of the black to his totem or divinity there rules a single bond, that of fear; if he does not obey orders, he will be punished. "This is true, so much so that if perchance, as sometimes happens, a negro changes tribes—is, for example, surrendered to another tribe as ransom for a murder—his first totem will become a thing of complete indifference to him. He will trouble himself about it in no way and without scruple will yield to the white man, who wants to buy it, the image representative of his former totem, to which he was but so lately so attached. It has become for him a thing without value, while the totem of his new tribe has become his all. There is therefore between the black and his totem no 'respect' [as Frazer says], but simply 'cult,' and a cult founded on fear."[10]

Monier-Williams[11] has asserted that the great majority of the inhabitants of India are, from the cradle to the burning-ground, victims of a form of disease which is best expressed by the term demonophobia. This dread of evil spirits haunts Hindus of all ranks and stations, from the highest to the lowest, with the exception of those fortunate persons whom a European education has delivered from the dominion of such ideas. "In fact, a belief in every kind of demoniacal influence has always been from the earliest times an essential ingredient in Hindu religious thought. The idea probably had its origin in the supposed peopling of the air by spiritual beings—the personifications or companions of storm and tempest. Certainly no one who has ever been brought into close contact with the Hindus in their own country can doubt the fact that the worship of at least ninety per cent of the people of India in the present day is a worship of fear. Not that the existence of good deities, presided over by one Supreme Being, is doubted; but that these deities are believed to be too absolutely good to need propitiation, . . . The simple truth is that evil of all kinds, difficulties, dangers, and disasters, famines, diseases, pestilences, and death, are thought by an ordinary Hindu to proceed from demons, or, more properly speaking, from devils, and from devils alone. These malignant beings are held, as we have seen, to possess varying degrees of rank, power, and malevolence. Some aim at destroying the entire world, and threaten the sovereignty of the gods themselves. Some delight in killing men, women, and children, out of a mere thirst for human blood. Some take a mere mischievous pleasure in tormenting, or revel in the infliction of sickness, injury, and misfortune. All make it their business to mar or impede the progress of good works and useful undertakings." It is probable that in surrounding the god Rudra-Çiva with armies of demons and impish attendants and making his sons lead and control them, Hindu mythologists merely gave expression to an idea inveterate in the Indian mind, that all disease, destruction, and dissolution are the result of demoniacal agency. People are often possessed by evil spirits, called seizers; these are Skanda's demons, and are both male and

---

8 Hobley, *A-Kamba*, 89.
9 Hobley, in JAI, XXXIII, 342.

10 Trilles, *Fân*, 28.
11 *Brāhmanism*, 79, 210, 230, 231.

female. "Until one reaches the age of 16, he is liable to be possessed by one group of 'seizers,' who must be worshipped in proper form that their wrath may be averted. Others menace mortals from the age of 16 to 70. After that only the fever-demon is to be feared. Imps of this sort are of three kinds. One kind indulge only in mischievous sport; another kind lead one to gluttony; the third kind are devoted to lust. . . . When they seize a person, he goes mad. They are to be kept at bay by self-restraint and moderation."[12]

Many gods and spirits, each with power to give prosperity and success or to inflict sickness and calamity, dwelt in the Angami hills; to these the people sacrificed cows, domesticated and wild, dogs, cocks, and liquor.[13] Sometimes fear of spirits takes the place of prudence and knowledge, as among the hill tribes of India where fear of the wood-spirits has prevented reckless waste of forests, for the natives believe that it offends the spirits of the woods to cut down trees unnecessarily.[14] Palaungs, Shans, and Burmans describe in their folk-tales a race of ogres with supernatural powers—a tall, dark-complexioned, curly-haired race, voracious in eating animal flesh in a half-cooked or raw condition, and preferring human flesh when obtainable. "It is by many supposed that these tales arose out of reminiscences of a Negrito race of cannibals, who inhabited the more northerly parts of the country and fought against the incoming tribes."[15] In Funchow, China, there were five idols called the Five Emperors who were the agents of the "Big White Devil" and the "Little Black Devil"; when cholera broke out there in 1858, processions were arranged for these images.[16]

The rampant demonolatry of the Tibetans seems to have developed the doctrine of tutelary deities far beyond what is found even in the latest phase of Indian Buddhism. "Even the purest of the Lamaist sects—the Ge-lug-pa—are thorough-paced devil-worshippers, and value Buddhism chiefly because it gives them the whip-hand over the devils which everywhere vex humanity with disease and disaster, and whose ferocity weighs heavily upon all. The purest Ge-lug-pa Lama on awaking every morning, and before venturing outside his room, fortifies himself against assault by the demons first of all by assuming the spiritual guise of his fearful tutelary, the king of the demons. . . . The Lama, by uttering certain *mantras* culled from the legendary sayings of Buddha in the Mahayana Tantras, coerces this demon-king into investing the Lama's person with his own awful aspect. Thus when the Lama emerges from his room in the morning, and wherever he travels during the day, he presents spiritually the appearance of the demon-king, and the smaller malignant demons, his would-be assailants, ever on the outlook to harm humanity, being deluded into the belief that the Lama is indeed their own vindictive king, they flee from his presence, leaving the Lama unharmed."[17]

A book could be filled with particulars of demonolatry as accepted by the natives of the Maldives. "Every accident, every illness, every misfortune is ascribed to the devil. No one goes out after dark if he can help it, for fear of meeting the devil in the streets."[18] "Any unusual noise or motion in the jungle, anything which suggests to the Dyak mind an invisible operation, is thought to be the presence of an antu, unseen by human eyes, but full of mighty power. He is mostly invisible, but often vouchsafes a manifestation of himself, and

12 Hopkins, *Relig. India*, 415-416.
13 Godden, in JAI, XXVI, 187.
14 Gomme, *Village Life*, 149.
15 Milne, *Eastern Clan*, 14.

16 Doolittle, *China*, I, 157, 284, in Andree, *Eth. Parallelen*, 111.
17 Waddell, *Tibet*, 152-153.
18 Rosset, in JAI, XVI, 172.

when he does so, he is neither a graceful fairy, nor a grinning Satyr, but a good honest ghost of flesh and blood, a monster human being about three times the size of a man, with rough shaggy hair, glaring eyes as big as saucers, and huge glittering teeth." Bad and angry spirits are far more numerous in Dyak belief than good ones, and are regarded with dire dread.[19] When pestilence threatens in Sumatra, sickness-idols are carved out of blocks of wood and erected in the village.[20] "In expiation of certain sins," think the aborigines of Formosa, "the spirits are doomed to roam through the air, being thereby peculiarly irritated and inclining to malignity; wherefore it behooves all to propitiate and avoid them."[21] In New Zealand even the fairies—white-skinned, golden-haired, pretty creatures—were dreaded, as sometimes they would carry mortals off.[22]

Each Eskimo is supposed to be attended by a special guardian "who is malignant in character, ever ready to seize upon the least occasion to work harm upon the individual whom it accompanies. As this is an evil spirit, its good offices and assistance can be obtained by propitiation only." The spirit is often materialized in the shape of a doll. "If the spirit prove stubborn and reluctant to grant the needed assistance, the person sometimes becomes angry with it and inflicts a serious chastisement upon it, deprives it of food, or strips it of its garments, until after a time it proves less refractory and yields obedience to its master." It is possible to pass such a spirit over to another person if the latter does not perceive what is being done. All the objects of nature, too, have guardian spirits which are malignant. They are all under a great spirit who "is nothing more or less than death, which ever seeks to torment and harass the lives of people that their spirits may go to dwell with him."[23] In the Arctic fall, when there are heavy storms and the air is full of noise from the crashing ice, the spirits are abroad, including one the sight of which kills the dogs with convulsions. All the spirits of evil are roused to bring death and destruction. Sedna, goddess of hell, rises from the ground, to seize the spirits of the dead.[24] Similar beliefs appear among the Labrador Indians who are "terribly superstitious, and everything not understood is attributed to the working of one of the numerous spirits. . . . The rule seems to be that all spirits are by nature bad, and must be propitiated to secure their favor."[25] The preposterous stories illustrative of belief in medicine-men's tales show in what sort of an intellectual atmosphere the Ten'a of central Alaska live. To them spirits have a sort of aërial body, something intermediate between body and soul, and are called by terms meaning "evil things," "swifts," or "quick-movers." They "are essentially malignant, and their sole purpose is to do harm." Even when they assist men, it is by doing harm to the enemies of the helped. Strictly speaking, they do not even help, for men have power to command them.[26]

The Iroquois believed in a variety of demons known as False Faces—simply heads, made terrific with large eyes and long hair—that brought pestilence.[27] The full ceremonies of the Midē' lodges, which the more southern Ojibwa translate as "grand medicine," were performed twice a year, in the fall and in the spring. "Those in the spring were of a rejoicing character, to welcome

19 Roth, *Sarawak*, I, 183, 185; II, clxx.
20 Raap, in *Globus*, LXXXIII, 153.
21 Wirth, in AA, X, 366.
22 Tregear, in JAI, XIX, 121.
23 Turner, in BAE, XI, 193.

24 Boas, in BAE, VI, 603.
25 Turner, in BAE, XI, 272.
26 Jetté, in JAI, XXXVII, 161.
27 Smith, in BAE, II, 53, 59; Andree, *Eth. Parallelen*, 161.

the return of the good spirits; those in the fall were in lamentation for the departure of the beneficent and the arrival of the maleficent spirits."[28] In connection with many ceremonials the *ko'yemshi* "gods" of the Zuñi visit from house to house to collect food. "Were they refused, 'something would happen,' something 'bad' even if you refused them merely 'in your mind.' A house was pointed out to me," writes Parsons,[29] "which they had on one occasion approached only to be locked out. The woman had nothing at hand, but her refusal was particularly flagrant because she was one the *ko'yemshi* had called *an tsita,* 'the mother,' having worked for her and her household during the year. In less time than the *ko'yemshi* needed to return to the pueblo,—the house in question was a little outlying,—a child in the house was burned, burned so badly that next day it died. In one of the most distinguished families in Zuñi there are two men blind of one eye. The middle-aged of the two . . . lost his eye as a result of smallpox; the elderly man, a medicine-man in the *ne'wekwe* fraternity, lost his in an accident from a horse. But both are supposed to have suffered for criticisms made by them against the *ko'yemshi.*"

While the Tarahumari Indians have very slight beards and pull out any hair that appears, their devil has a full beard.[30] In the daimonism of the Indians of British Guiana a special rôle is played by Kanaima, who appears not only as an evil, invisible, demoniacal being but also in many cases as an individual personality—the personification of human vindictiveness, the author and originator of all evil, the revenger of known or unknown offenses.[31] These Indians know also of various beings consisting of spirits residing in fabulous animal bodies. "Perhaps the nature of these beings is best made clear by saying that they correspond very closely to the dragons, unicorns, and griffins, and to the horned, hoofed, and tailed devils of our own folk-lore." Of this kind is the "ornar," a being with a body said sometimes to be like that of a gigantic fish, sometimes like that of a huge crab, at other times to be of various other forms, which lives under water, especially in rapids and cataracts.[32] The Caribs say their water-spirit is like a camudi snake, but much bigger; it lives in underground water; in habitat it corresponds closely to the variety of water-spirit of the Warraus. "In cases of snake-bite among certain tribes, in addition to any other treatment the bitten person must neither drink water, bathe, nor come into the neighborhood of water, during the period immediately following the accident. The same prohibition, for a similar period, is incumbent on his children, his parents, and his brothers and sisters so long as they reside in the same settlement. His wife alone is free from the taboo. The freedom of the woman from such an inconvenience is interesting when regarded in conjunction with the belief in human milk as an efficacious antidote for snake-poison." Each tribe seems to exhibit variations in the ideas held as to the form, shape, and peculiarities assumed by its respective bush-spirits. "Having no bows and arrows, these Spirits are accustomed to fight only with their limbs, so that when an Indian has been attacked and returns home, where he is sure to die shortly after, no marks will be found on his body." Sometimes the spirits will not even allow a victim to return alive, but will eat him, causing him to disappear totally. The old-time Arawak people used to call them by a term which literally means "bows-broken," and when returning home from some hunting or trading expedition, would sing out that name before reaching

28 Mallery, in BAE. X. 508.
29 In AA, XVIII, 247-248.
30 Lumholtz, in *Scribner's Mag.,* XVI, 296.

31 Schomburgk, *Brit.-Guiana,* I, 322.
32 Im Thurn, in JAI, XI, 371.

their houses, with the view to preventing them from making an entry. "Special words, or paraphrases, have to be used under particular circumstances; thus, in traveling over water—river or sea—the use of certain names otherwise employed in ordinary every-day conversation, is absolutely forbidden." To point the finger at a spirit must necessarily be a serious matter; many natives believe that if an individual points at certain rocks a heavy storm will immediately overtake him for his audacity. When an explorer once questioned some Indians about certain rocks that had a curious, vitrified appearance, he was at once silenced by the assertion that any allusion to their appearance would vex these rocks and cause them to send misfortune.[33] According to the Tucana Indians, discovered in the Amazon basin a few years ago, the Devil-Devil was an evil spirit who lived in the jungle, in swampy pools and thunderstorms. This evil spirit, called Jurupary, manifested himself in the failure of crops, tropical storms, and other violent workings of nature. If a crop failed the people said, "The Jurupary is after us."[34]

The world of spirits was to the ancients just as little organized as the peoples themselves. "All the spirits, even the highest, are but mighty magicians, mighty through their magic, sometimes beneficent according to their fancy or caprice, but always feared."[35] The conception of evil spirits often represented them as taking the form of some strange and fearful animal, like the leopard with wings and a human head of the Egyptians and Phœnicians, the snake in Persia and Assyria, or the jinns of the northern Semites—hairy beings, nocturnal monsters, haunting desolate places with jackals and other animals which shun the abode of man.[36] Harmful daimons are almost unrepresented in Homer.[37] In Chaldæan and Babylonian mythology evil spirits played a remarkable rôle.[38] Demonology was highly developed among the ancient Hebrews, with a host of divine adversaries under the command of Satan, one of the sons of God. The evil spirits are enemies of mankind; they are everywhere present: in every case of misfortune, of sickness and death, of human sin and wickedness are they active. They lie in wait for man during his entire life and for his soul after death.[39] Especially in the Apocryphal period was there an elaborate doctrine of demons, usually spoken of as the disembodied spirits of the giants, who were the progeny of the fallen angels and the daughters of men, and were to carry on their work of moral ruin upon the earth unpunished till the final judgment. In the Septuagint the heathen gods are uniformly depicted as demons.[40] "There is no use to try to disguise the fact that in the mind of Jesus, as revealed in the Synoptic Gospels, Satan and his legions occupied just as important a place and played as prominent a rôle as in the mental outlook of other Jews of that age, and of believers in every age precedent to our own."[41] All the names of strange gods became names of

---

33 Roth, in BAE, XXX, 171, 239-240, 243, 307.

34 Stark, in N. Y. Times, Sept. 3, 1922.

35 Tiele, Elem. Relig., pt. I, 79 (quoted); Friedmann, Wahnideen, 203.

36 Tiele, Gchte. Relig., I, 263; Pietschmann, Phönizier, 178-179; Justi, Persien, 84; Smith, Relig. Sem., 120; Leith, in JASB, I, 19.

37 Odyssey, V, 395; Keller, Hom. Soc., 109-110; Euripides, Electra, 990-1; Lehmann, Overtro, I, 68.

38 Lenormant, Chaldean Magic, 38; Schrader, Keilinschriften, 458.

39 Bousset, Relig. Judentums, 335-336; Duhm, Geister 19-20, 58, 60-61, 218-219; Schrader, Keilinschriften, 463; Blau, Altjüd. Zauberwesen, 61-62; Jewish Encyc., I, 592; XII, 249.

40 Fairweather, in Hastings's Dict. Bible, 275, 288-289, 290; Charles, Enoch, 52, 56; ch. VI, 1-6; ch. VIII, 2 ff.; ch. XIX, 1-2; Charles, Jubilees, III, 21 ff.; V, 1; XI, 2-4; XVII, 16; XLVIII, 2.

41 Conybeare, in Internat. Mo., V, 303.

demons to the Jews, and the Christians followed them in this view. In the early Christian era it was held that "the efforts of demons and unclean spirits are to lay waste God's kingdom and harm men. In this purpose they have by apparent miracles and oracles infused in people the fancy that they are gods and have thus created heathendom with its mythology and cult. They are the origin of magic, necromancy, haruspices, the science of augury and astrology. Besides they do harm in every possible manner. Yet the Christian need not fear their attack because the devil and his demons must live rather in continual fear of the Christian. For the Christian can not only drive them out everywhere, but can also force them to tell their names and to acknowledge that they are not gods, though they are worshipped [as heathen gods] in temples."[42] There arose a doctrine of a satanic empire in rivalry with the celestial, a doctrine that daily met with wider acceptance. The evil spirits may be the weaker side and suffer defeat, but they go about enlisting wicked men and seek thereby to replenish their host; compacts are made with the devil, who aids his confederates even during their earthly life, a notion quite prevalent during the Middle Ages.[43]

To some people, despite the advance of rationalism, the devil is still very real. In a competition among Russian children for the best short story, the Moscow Soviet Commissariat for Education specified that the tales must be devoid of all elements of superstition, and must contain no mention of angels, fairies, or evil geniuses.[44] Yet survivals are frequently enough reported in the daily press, as in the case where a child died from the effects of malnutrition yet was believed by his parents to have been the victim of a spell, for they claimed that they had been troubled with an evil spirit haunting the house; or in the story of a panic that occurred in one of the public schools in consequence of a statement made by a little girl that she had seen the devil coming into the building.[45] Along with other superstitions, belief in the devil is hard to down.

§244. The Familiar Spirit and Dualism.

THE personification of the aleatory element in its favorable aspect, among the Queensland aborigines, is Mulkari, the supernatural power which makes everything the natives cannot otherwise account for: he is a good, beneficent person and never kills anyone.[1] A personal familiar spirit in Australia is the animal by which each sorcerer works.[2] When an African Bageshu child is old enough to sit up unsupported, it is named after one of its father's ancestors; "the ghost of the person whose name has been adopted is supposed to take charge of the child." Should the child be illegitimate, the ghost will kill it. "In cases where a woman has been unfaithful, she gives the child another name secretly, and asks the ghost of the ancestor of the real father to protect it from the other ghost of her husband's ancestor. If a child is sickly after being named, the parents consult the medicine man, who tells them the reason and prescribes for it. If he ascribes the illness to the guardian ghost, they change the child's

42 Lehmann, *Overtro*, I, 89-91 (quoting Lactantius).
43 Stallybrass, *Grimm's Teut. Myth.*, III, 984, 985; Lecky, *Rationalism*, I, 68; Sayce, *Anc. Empires*, 155; Crane, in N.Y. *Nation*, XCII, 142.

44 N. Y. *Times*, June 18, 1921.
45 N. H. *Journal-Courier*, Feb. 25, 1915; PSM, editorial, Aug., 1896; Chamberlain, in AA, VIII, 171.
1 Roth, *N.W. Cent. Queensland*, 153.
2 Ratzel, *Vkde.*, II, 96.

name and call upon the new guardian ghost to protect the child."[3] The natives of the Cameroons believe in both good and bad spirits and in a primitive sort of dualism. "The dualistic schism which permeates the whole physical and moral world—light and darkness, day and night, birth and death, love and hate, truth and falsehood, right and wrong—extends through the consciousness of these people. Among more advanced groups it has developed into the concepts of god and the devil with their different qualities and attributes, heaven and hell, blessedness and perdition; with these childlike people it signifies simply: good spirits and bad spirits."[4]

As the sun and moon are deities to the Tungus, so are the stars alive and have, indeed, an astrological significance. "Each man has his star as a guardian spirit which influences his fate. Through the different positions of the stars it is known at birth what fate the gods have predestined for man, and in general the belief is held that the destiny of men is under the sway of heaven. This power, however, is no free agency, but is as immutable as the course of the stars themselves."[5] In the Manchu calendar the place in the house where the spirit of luck abides is specified for each day in the year.[6] Guardian spirits of industry form a part of Japanese belief: "Whatever his occupation might be, some god presided over it; whatever tools he might use, they had to be used in such manner as tradition prescribed for all admitted to the craft-cult. It was necessary that the carpenter should so perform his work as to honour the deity of carpenters,—that the smith should fulfil his daily task so as to honour the god of the bellows,—that the farmer should never fail in respect to the earth-god, and the food-god, and the scare-crow god, and the spirits of the trees about his habitation."[7] In the war of the gods and demons, as pictured in Hindu myths, we have the eternal struggle between good and evil. The demons had been gaining on the gods when Brahma told the latter how to make a drink which would render them immortal. A truce was made with the demons, who were to help and also share in the product. It was to be made by churning up all things in the sea, the churn-dasher being a mountain and the king of snakes lending himself as a rope to turn it, the gods pulling one end and the demons the other. When the process was complete the goddess of good luck, Sri, came out of the mountain with a cup of this drink, but the gods took it all. This angered the demons who recommenced the war but were now beaten and had to flee into the ocean.[8] At the funeral-rites of some of the wild tribes of southeast India there is a crude dramatization of this struggle: "The corpse is placed on a car to which ropes are attached in front and rear, and the persons attending the ceremony are divided into two equal bodies, who set to work to pull the car in opposite directions. The front party of men represent the good spirits, those in the rear are the evil powers. The contest is so arranged that the former becomes victorious."[9] Among the Nagas the aghau is a personal familiar, potentially possessed by all persons though its existence is not always apparent. The idea of fate or destiny is very often attached to aghau, but one also hears of it as a spirit inclined to be malignant, and in some aspects it appears almost as a soul; the aghau is also a house-spirit. "When a man migrates he scatters bits of meat on the ground behind him to induce his aghau to go with him, telling it that no one else will cherish it and

3 Roscoe, in JAI, XXXIX, 184.
4 Hutter, in Globus, LXXXVII, 237-238.
5 Hiekisch, Tungusen, 110.
6 Grube, in Berl. Mus., VII, 24.

7 Hearn, Japan, 169.
8 Holtzmann, Ind. Sagen, II, 132.
9 Basu, in JASB, II, 562.

feed it. A friend of the writer's has a dozen *aghau,* though he rarely sees them. Six are like apes and six like human beings. They belong to the family and attach themselves to the richest member of it,"[10] the one most favored by luck. A certain Sakai, who had inherited his familiar spirit from his father, a Malay-speaking Selangor aboriginal, proceeded to call upon it in Malay,[11] which was logical enough, though not imputing much linguistic ability to a supernatural being. The significance of the tutelary gods in the daily life of the natives of Núkuóro is very great, as almost every single act of life requires their influence, which must be sought through the medium of the priest. "Upon the occasion of building a house or a canoe, at marriage and confinement, in sickness and at death must the gods be called upon, and in most of these cases those in need turn to their special protecting deities."[12]

The Hawaiians have a very vivid belief in animal-helpers, half divine, half human; they utter their counsels through the lips of mediums who become for the moment possessed with their spirits. Such gods are called *aumakua.* "They are bound by obedience to their devotee, who becomes their keeper, and their worship, and consequent service, extends to his family and is handed down from generation to generation." This notion is illustrative of many aspects of the topic under review. Any creature, plant, or object may become an *aumakua.* The shark, cowrie-shell, limpet, squid, and eel are famous sea-*aumakua.* The mud-hen, plover, chicken, wild-goose, frigate-bird, and some song birds are important *aumakua,* while among insects the spider, among reptiles the lizard, and of quadrupeds the pig, dog, and rat are worshipped. "Rocks, too, are often set up as *aumakua* and worshiped as transformed deities. Certain trees, sweet-scented flowers and phenomena of nature and the elements, the volcano, for example, are powerful *aumakua.*" On the coast, sharks are the particular object selected for veneration, and each several locality along the coast has its special patron-shark whose name, history, place of abode, and appearance are well known to all. Each of these sharks has its keeper who is responsible for its care and worship. "The office of *Kahu* was hereditary in a particular family and was handed down from parent to child for many generations, or until the family became extinct." The shark-gods are invoked with particular prayers and have temples erected for their worship. "Their special function is to aid in the food supply of the household—generally by giving the fisherman good luck at sea—and to protect him from drowning. They are, in fact, regarded as spirits of half-human beings which, rendered strong by prayer and sacrifice, take up their abode in some shark body and act as supernatural counselors to their kin, who accordingly honor them as household divinities." In most cases these animal-helpers have the power to take either human or animal shape. Some are friendly spirits, others evil: those which, like the shark and limpet, calm the waves or provide food for their patron, are beneficent; others, like the dreaded worm and the lizard, are much to be feared. "The dog is beneficent, but a great thief. The pig is a mischief-maker, symbol of lechery and filth. The rat is, like the owl, beneficent, from the classic tale of the rat-god who, when *Makalii* (Little Eyes—the Pleiades) tied up all the food of mankind in a net and hung it in the heavens, gnawed the ropes and let it tumble back again to earth." Sorcerers can use their spirit-helpers to transmit disease to others. When the *aumakua* comes into

10 Hutton, *Sema Nagas,* 193.
11 Evans, in JAI, XLVIII, 187.
12 Kubary, *Núkuóro,* 27-28.

a home where illness or other trouble is present, it enters the body of some member of the family—by the head if friendly, by the feet if ill-disposed. The person falls asleep, the *aumakua* taking the place of the spirit thus ejected. If a friendly spirit, it offers advice as to how to escape the illness or other troubles—what prayers to offer, fish to catch, herbs to gather. To test the *aumakua*, a member of the family throws a wreath of some special plant about the neck of the person possessed. "If it is a friendly spirit, he will take it, if an evil spirit, he will spit, glare, tear his clothing, or even plunge naked into the bushes. Such insanity is relieved by a drink made from a coarse kind of grass. To keep out these evil spirits, house and yard are sprinkled with water to which salt and a bit of root similar to the ginger are added. This ceremony is also used in case of death." The presence of a spirit, as has been stated, is indicated by a divine possession in which the person possessed speaks not as he is accustomed but in the character and with the words of the spirit whose medium he is. "In order that the *aumakua* may be strong enough to act his part as helper, he must receive offerings of prayer, and of sacrifice in the shape of food and drink called 'feeding the spirit.' For example, a woman living near *Kealakekua* was seen each night to carry a pail from her house to the cliff and empty it over into the sea. It was found that the pail contained *awa* drink [the intoxicant of the Hawaiians] which was being fed to the household *aumakua*." The idea of the *aumakua* in the Hawaiian theogony seems to be that of enforced helpfulness within a kinship-group as a means to ensure superhuman coöperation in individual affairs. Although worshipped like a god, the *aumakua* belong to a group of lesser deities, a sort of servant class, because bound to obey those whom they serve. They may be compared with the Arabian jinns whose supernatural assistance is forced through the possession of some special talisman. In the Hawaiian case the talisman seems to be the social fact of kinship, the act of invocation perhaps serving as a charm to enforce service. Various phases of the notion of fetishism are also present here, and a species of personification of the aleatory element.[13]

"Like most other religions that of the Eskimo recognized two principles, a good and a bad, as ruling the world." The evil spirit is female, the maternal grandmother, mother, or wife of the good spirit. There is also the world's creator: "from him one could, through the angakok, seek help and advice in bad luck and danger." If one has been a good man, *i.e.*, diligent in working, one can go to him after death and be happy.[14] Some of the American Indians believed in *oyaron* or tutelaries. "The person whose life was regarded as being under the protection of some being embodied in a material thing, in this occult manner, had less reason for apprehension than he whose life was so protected by some particular animal, for should the animal die, it was a foregone conclusion that he himself incurred the risk of a like fate. This belief was so strong that many seemingly proved its truth by dying soon after the known death of the tutelary animal." In addition to the tutelaries belonging to every person, there were *oyaron* common to the family, the gens, the clan, and probably the tribe, which were located in the lodge, where sacrifices and offerings were made to them.[15] Among the gods or demi-gods of the Aboaki are those who particularly preside over the making of petroglyphs. "They lived in caves by the shore and were never seen, but manifested their existence by in-

13 Beckwith, in AA, XIX, 503-504, 505 note, 506, 507, 508, 514-516.

14 Fries, *Grönland*, 142, 144.
15 Hewitt, in HAI, II, 179.

scriptions on the rocks."[16] The Algonquian tribes had some notion of dualism, later reinforced by Christianity, while the Warraus of British Guiana held to a belief in one good spirit and many evil ones. The former was the author of creation, the source of all good fortune; the evil spirits were the enemies of mankind, the causes of sickness and every privation, who gloated over people's misfortunes and found joy in the sufferings of mortals.[17]

Nagualism, a belief of the Indians of Mexico and Central America, connects the life and welfare of man with animals and birds. We abstract an extended treatment of this creed.[18] The term "nagual" comes from the stem "to know" or "to recognize" (one's fate or destiny). A description of the rites as they existed in 1530, in Honduras, runs as follows: "The devil appeared to the natives in the form of some animal, to which they apply the name *Naguales,* meaning guardian or companion. 'When such an animal dies, so does the Indian to whom it was assigned.' For the formation of such an alliance, the Indian retired to some quiet spot, and there appealing to Nature, implored for himself the favors conferred on his ancestors. He sacrificed a dog or fowl, drew blood from his own body, and then slept. When dreaming and half awake an animal would appear to him, saying: 'On such a day go hunting and the first animal or bird you see will be my form, and I shall remain your companion and *Nagual* for all time.' Without a *Nagual* the natives believe no one can be rich and powerful. . . . The Aztecs had a belief in the protecting power of a personal guardian spirit or tutelary genius, and held that it was connected with the day on which each person was born. This was called the *tonalli* of a person, meaning that which is peculiar to him,—that which makes his individuality, his self. . . . The real purpose of the conjuring and incantations practiced by the native doctors when visiting the sick was to force or persuade the guardian spirit or *tonal* to return. The ceremony bore the name 'the restitution of the *tonal,*' and was deeply connected with superstitions of Nagualism. . . . In Mexico today, at New Year or at corn-planting the head of a family will go to the parish church and among the various saints there displayed will select one as his guardian for the year. This is in addition to his special personal guardian. . . . Every person at birth has a good or bad genius assigned to him. 'The good genius is known by the Nahuatl term *tonale,* and it is represented in the first bird or animal of any kind which is seen in or near the house immediately after the birth of the infant.'" The sorcerer having invoked the demon in behalf of a young child, "the *nagual* of the child would appear under the form of an animal or object set opposite its birthday in the calendar, a serpent were it born on the second of January, a flower were it on the thirteenth, fire were it on the twenty-fourth, and so on. The sorcerer then addressed certain prayers to the *nagual* to protect the little one, and told the mother to take it daily to the same spot, where its *nagual* would appear to it, and would finally accompany it through all its life."

Nagualism had its recognized centers of association, its secret councils, and its imposing ceremonies. It had high priests, teachers, practitioners, and brotherhoods—the latter dedicated to Iscariot or Pilate, to the Devil or the Antichrist, in derision and hatred of the Christian priests and teaching. Women often held high posts in the system which became after the conquest a potent factor in political and social development. "Expert Nagualists claimed power

16 Mallery, in BAE, X, 32.
17 Tylor, in JAI, XXI, 285; Schomburgk, *Brit.-Guiana,* 170.

18 Brinton, *Nagualism,* 5, 11 ff., 23, 28, 30, 40, 46 ff., 55, note, 60; Brinton, *Americanist,* 171, 172.

to transform themselves into a globe or ball of fire, and to handle fire or blow it from the mouth was common with them." Fire was the most important Nagual symbol, the primal element and the immediate source of life. The Tree, another symbol of the ancient cult, is still venerated among the present population. "When the change from the individual into his or her *nagual* was about to take place, it was required that the person be absolutely naked." The change could be prevented by throwing salt on the person. "The fury of many naked Nagualists, meeting at night in caves and dancing before their idols was a scene that greatly roused the Spanish missionaries. . . . Missionaries in Mexico saw a horrible caricature of this holy rite [selection of a patron saint] in the selection by the Indian priest of the *nagual* of a child. Their consternation was even greater when they saw that the pagan priest also performed a kind of baptismal sacrament with water and that the *tonal* by which the individual demon was denoted was the sign of the cross." Here is a whole cult built about the idea of the familiar spirit. There exist elsewhere in the world many cases of a similar though less organized relation between men and animals or even plants.[19]

The notions of the familiar spirit and of dualism were well known to the ancients. In the religion of Zoroaster, the Fravishis—literally, they who cherish, foster, or nourish—were the simple essences of all things, the celestial creatures corresponding with the terrestrial of which they were the immortal types. "Stars, animals, men, angels themselves, in one word every created being, had his Fravishi, who was invoked in prayers and sacrifices, and was the invisible protector who watched untiringly over the being to whom he was attached."[20] This notion led naturally to that of dualism wherein these protecting genii, created by Ormuzd, struggle against evil with an energy which is the more efficacious as their associates have displayed more virtue and purity during earthly existence. On a larger scale, whatever good thing Ormuzd—the principle of good, the guardian of mankind—creates, Ahriman corrupts and ruins. "Moral and physical evils are alike at his disposal. He blasts the earth with barrenness, or makes it produce thorns, thistles, and poisonous plants; his are the earthquake, the storm, the plague of hail, the thunderbolt; he causes disease and death, sweeps off a nation's flocks and herds by murrain, or depopulates a continent by pestilence; ferocious wild beasts, serpents, toads, mice, hornets, mosquitoes, are his creation; he invented and introduced into the world the sins of witchcraft, murder, unbelief, cannibalism, sodomy; he excites wars and tumults, stirs up the bad against the good, and labours by every possible expedient to make vice triumph over virtue."[21] The irreconcilable struggle between the powers of good and evil is the old myth of the struggle between light and darkness, fertility and barrenness, life and death, in a more ethical form. This dualistic view of life develops easily into a belief in a heaven and a hell, with punishment meted out in the latter place to the evil, inclusive of the unbelievers.[22] In the same way that every man, according to the Avesta, had his Fravishi, so also, according to the Accadian magical tablets, every one from the hour of his birth had a special god attached to him, who lived in him as his protector and his spiritual type. The god attending upon each man

19 Wilken, "Betrekking tusschen Menschen-Dieren- en Plantenleven," in VG, III, 299-300; §§256, 260, of the text.
20 Lenormant, *Chaldean Magic*, 199; Maspero, *Hist. Anc.*, III, 573.

21 Rawlinson, *Seventh Monarchy*, 624-625.
22 Tiele, *Gchte. Relig.*, II, 88, 160-162; Maspero, *Hist. Anc.*, III, 582.

was of peculiar character, partaking of human nature, its imperfections and its foibles. Like the man to whom he was united, he could be conquered by demons or by spells and become their servant. When Namtar, the plague personified as a goddess, seized upon an individual, his god as well as his body was at the mercy of the spirit of the disease.[23] The familiar spirit in Babylonia and Assyria was in a measure identified with one's better self.[24] Images were brought into the house as protecting gods against evil spirits, while the exorcism of sickness often ended with the wish: "May the evil demon go out and get off to one side; may the good demon, the merciful guardian spirit, remain fast in his (the sick person's) body."[25]

Familiar spirits are common enough in the Old Testament.[26] The Jews believed that each and every man had a protecting angel, which notion, says Bousset,[27] was affected by the old belief in ghosts. "The guardian angel of each man was originally nothing other than that part of man which remained over after death, as a ghost, and as such—a wondrous, often malicious, kind of being—was surrounded with religious reverence. Out of this notion grew the remarkable idea of a celestial double, a second higher self, which is not man himself and yet is indissolubly united with him." The belief in guardian angels of all individuals was expanded into the idea of guardian angels for whole groups. Among the Greeks, the Demeter of Eleusis remained the particular deity of the Eumolpidæ and the Athene of the Acropolis belonged to the family of the Butadæ; so also, the Politii of Rome had a Hercules, the Nautii a Minerva, the Julii a Venus. "When the deity of a family had acquired considerable reputation and, from the prosperity of his worshippers, was judged to be both benevolent and powerful, then it often happened that a whole city wished to adopt it and by diligent service win its favor."[28] Belief in fate-determining powers was well established among all Slavs before the introduction of Christianity. The poetical-religious issue of their belief in fate is *sreća*, from the standpoint of theology the most remarkable form of South Slavic folk-belief. *Sreća* is no mythical creature inherited from primitive times; rather is it, as formerly with the Roman Fortuna, a composite creation. This familiar spirit is closely allied with the luck element.[29] The Valkyrs were the personal attendants of heroes. If one of these maidens of Odin abandoned a man, since she had had charge of his luck, his luck and life came to an end.[30]

§245. Deities.

THE mores of a people are reflected in the character and actions of their gods, as among the Dobuans of Papua, one of whose deities is called the god of the thief, "whom he watches only, but does not protect, as anyone caught stealing food or property from one who is not a stranger or enemy may be killed by the owner of the food or property without fear of revenge being taken."[1] The gods have the same passions as men and must submit to similar social regulation, as witness the reason given for the drought in 1918 by the Africans of Lango. "To the north-east of the Lango is the river Moroto, and in March of

23 Lenormant, *Chaldean Magic*, 199-200.
24 Tiele, *Gchte. Relig.*, I, 215.
25 Schrader, *Keilinschriften*, 455.
26 Levit., XX, 6, 27; I Sam., XXVIII, 7; I Chron., X, 13; II Chron., XXXIII, 6; II Kings, XXIII, 24; Isaiah, XIX, 3.

27 *Relig. Judentums*, 317-318.
28 Bastian, *Deut. Exped.*, II, 225, note.
29 Krauss, *Südslaven*, 20, 29; and *Sreća*, 37, 77.
30 Wisen, *Qvinnan*, 7.
1 Bromilow, in AAAS, 1911, 415.

this year a man fell from the sky near this river, bringing with him a bag of money, a leg of a cow and four soldiers. He is black, and speaks Lango without any foreign accent, and states that though he comes from a place where there are cattle innumerable and wealth unspendable he will consent to live on the earth. Orweny of Batta, a powerful wizard, asked him about the drought, as he would be sure to have the latest information, and the heavenly visitant informed him that it was due to the fact that a certain *jok* (god) had committed adultery with the wife of another *jok* and refused to pay compensation, and that, therefore, in his wrath, the latter had stopped the rain. Orweny by his enchantments secured the arrest of the former and the payment of compensation towards the end of May. Hence the June rains."[2] If the gods were not involved in sexual difficulties with other deities, they were likely to get into similar complications with mortals, for they were an amorous lot, indeed rather promiscuous. Where relations of the sexes are institutionalized, the gods often display a looser morality than men. "Brought within the circle of proprietary ideas, a god must not encroach upon the property of others. His priest's property is of course his. His priest is in fact only his trustee. He has therefore an easily admitted claim on his priest's wife. Marriage with the priest is tantamount to marriage with the god. And yet, in many cases of this quasi-polyandry, it is difficult to tell to what extent the priest is the god's proxy, or which, priest or god, is the paramount husband." So also in ritualistic defloration and impregnation, and in the very general submission of women to sacred men, the god works through proxies. "Practically just as secular prostitution is somewhat of a guarantee against adultery, so the religious prostitute or the priestess-wife precluded undesired encroachments of deity upon other women."[3]

Primitive peoples are interested in those gods only who are concerned with the everyday affairs of men; exalted, remote deities are of no importance to them. The gods of the Bagobo may be grouped in two classes: (a) gods of exalted rank who live in the nine heavens above. "They are felt to be remote from human affairs and neither help nor harm is expected from them, hence no devotions are addressed to them. These spirits occupy an important place in the mythical songs and romances which the people delight to tell, but the interest is purely of a literary sort, and it is probable that these divinities are of foreign origin." (b) In intimate relation to the daily life are many unseen beings who have charge of the physical world; who act as divine protectors and helpers of man; who direct industries; who stimulate men to fight; and who, in their several departments, receive the prayers and gifts of the people.[4] Some of the West Africans believe in a great god—a creator, a god who has made all things, and who now no longer takes any interest in the things he has created. Their name for him is a compound of "spirit" and "good." He leases the government of affairs to a viceroy or minister, called Mbuiri, who "has never been, nor can he ever become, a man, *i.e.*, be born as a man, but he can transfuse with his own personality that of human beings, and also the souls of all those things we white men regard as inanimate. . . . The M'pongwe know that his residence is in the sea, and some of them have seen him as an old white man, not flesh-color white, but chalk white. Mbuiri's appearance in bodily form denotes ill luck, not death to the seer, but severe and diffused misfor-

2 Driberg, in JAI, XLIX, 70.
3 Main, *Relig. Chastity*, 123, 271, ch. X, appendix notes XII, XIII, XIV.

4 Cole, in AA, XX, 217-219.

tune. The ruin of a trading enterprise, the destruction of a village or family, are put down to Mbuiri's action. Yet he is not regarded as a malevolent god, or devil, but as an avenger, or punisher of sin; and the M'pongwe look on him as the Being to whom they primarily owe the good things and fortunes of this life, and as the Being who alone has power to govern the host of truly malevolent spirits that exist in nature. The different instruments with which he works in the shaping of human destiny bear his name when in his employ. When acting by means of water, he is Mbuiri Aningo; when in the weather, Mbuiri Ngali; when in the forests, Mbuiri Ibaka; when in the form of a dwarf, Mbuiri Akkoa. . . . This is the great difference between Mbuiri and the lesser spirits: the lesser spirits cannot incarnate themselves except through extraneous things; Mbuiri can, he can become visible without anything beyond his own will to do so. The other spirits must be in something to become visible. This is an extremely delicate piece of fetish." The authoress[5] says that apparitions are not always of human soul-origin. Tando, the Hater, chief god of the Northern Tschwis and Ashantees, is terribly malicious, human in shape, and though not quite white, decidedly lighter in complexion than the chief god of the Southern Tschwis. His messengers are the awful driver ants which it is not orthodox to molest in Tando's territories. He uses for weapons lightning, tempest, and disease, the last being the favorite. No trick is too mean or venomous for Tando. Among the Bantu there is a great female god who is more important, in so far as mundane affairs go, than their male god; whereas among the peoples who are called true negroes, the great gods are male. Weeks[6] speaks of a Congo term which "is the nearest equivalent we can get to God," that conception being "four persons all seemingly equal, and each supreme in his own department."

Of the Baganda it is reported that "the most influential of their gods was *Mukasa,* who seems to have been originally an ancestral spirit, and whose place of origin and principal temple was on the biggest of the Sese Islands. Mukasa became in time the Neptune of Uganda, the god of the lake, who was to be propitiated every time a long voyage was undertaken. In former times— in fact, down to the conversion of Mwanga to Christianity—Mukasa and some of the other gods were provided with earthly wives. Virgins were set apart to occupy this honourable position, and lived under the same disabilities as the Vestal Virgins, though it is to be feared that their infraction of the rule of chastity was more frequent."[7] The tribes at the head-waters of the Nile believe in a supreme being who made the world and man, and is too great to care for men. Hence they do not worship him.[8]

That the Koryak conception of one supreme being is not indigenous, or at least not very old, may be judged from the very vague account of his nature and qualities and from the fact that he takes no active part in shaping the affairs of men. "He is, of course, a benevolent anthropomorphic being, an old man with a wife and children, dwelling in the sky. He can send famine or abundance, but seldom uses his power to do either good or evil to men." The abstract names given to him are hardly consistent with the conception—distinctly material, as far as it goes—which the Koryak seem to have of his nature. Ainu tradition informs us that "the gods gather themselves together and consult with one another as to ways and means before they act, the Creator, of

5 Kingsley, *Travels W. Afr.*, 228, 229, 521; Kingsley, *W. Afr. Studies*, 423; Henning, in *Globus*, LXXII, 102; §210, above.

6 In *Folk-Lore*, XV, 326 ff.
7 Johnston, *Uganda*, II, 677.
8 Ratzel, *Vkde.*, I, 468.

course, acting as president, just in the same way as the Ainu chiefs used to meet together for consultation before they acted."[9] The Mongols are said to have no word for god. They conceive of the blue vault of the sky as solid and attribute omnipotence to it, together with all the qualities which we assign to godhead. All the spirits are subject to it and it is the source of existence for all. They adore sun, moon, stars, mountains, rivers, and all unusual things. It is thought that such ideas may have been borrowed from Buddhism, and that of Fate, also cherished by them, from Lamaism.[10] There is some evidence of sun-worship and of the belief that planets rule fate in India, while it is still a Brahman's daily prayer to say: "Let us meditate on that excellent glory of the Divine Vivifying Sun; may he enlighten our understandings."[11] The dawn of the twentieth century was commemorated in Tibet by the introduction of a new god, who makes the five-hundredth so-called god created since the arrival of Confucianism in the land of the Lamas. This new deity is held to be a direct representative of Buddha and is endowed with the power to silence the spells of all other divinities in the Tibetan calendar. The form chosen for him is that of a man with the head of a horned bull. The ox has long been a sacred animal in the Orient and this is considered to be the highest expression of incarnated deity.[12] The Kuki-Lushai clans have promoted some demons into local divinities. The Thados have two spirits unknown to other clans: a female ghost, the sight of which is followed by awful misfortunes unless averted by the immediate sacrifice of a dog, and a spirit which lives underground. Besides these spirits the Lushais believe in the *Lashi,* peculiar beings residing in precipices and controlling wild animals.[13]

There are many hill-deities known in certain localities about Madras, which "are little removed from the spirits of the deceased Saoras." They have no notion of any deity of whom they will ask anything in expectation of the request being answered through love.[14] "A female divinity is invariably found to be the patroness of the Indian robbers and thieves." This was true of the Thugs, "who had raised the profession of robbery by throttling and strangulation, into a semi-religious cult." Many tribes worship the female principle almost exclusively.[15] The typical Toda god is a being of a distinctly anthropomorphic type; in the legends he lives much the same kind of life as the mortal Toda, having his dairies and his buffaloes. "The sacred dairies and the sacred buffaloes of the Todas are still regarded as being in some measure the property of the gods, and the dairymen are looked upon as their priests. The gods hold council and consult with one another just as do the Todas, and they are believed to be swayed by the same motives and to think in the same way as the Todas themselves."[16] The Mahabharata describes the gods as casting no shadow, which recalls Dante's conception, and "without sweat or dust, with fresh chaplets and without blinking," floating in the air. The gods are by no means almighty. They fight and are beaten. Brahmans can conquer them; and they are dependent on sacrifices.[17] A still more remarkable characteristic of a god is that of being half-male, half-female; "it symbolizes both the duality and unity

9 Czaplicka, *Aborig. Siberia,* 261, 275.

10 Shchukin, *Shamanism,* 28, 29.

11 Monier-Williams, *Brāhmanism,* 19; Lippert, *Kgchte.,* II, 436.

12 Harvey, in New Haven *Register,* Jan. 21, 1901.

13 Shakespear, in JAI, XXXIX, 375.

14 Fawcett, in JASB, I, 245, 248.

15 Mitra, in JASB, III, 454; Hopkins, *Relig. Ind.,* 537.

16 Rivers, *Todas,* 182.

17 Holtzmann, *Ind. Sagen,* II, 17, 83; I, 288-289.

of the generative act and the production of the universe from the union of two eternal principles."[18]

In China, "the sovereigns of the empire stand above the gods even after their death."[19] China has shown her understanding of the close relation between new religious and political development by requiring all the incarnate gods in the Chinese Empire to register in the Colonial Office at Peking. "The Chinese Government, with a paternal solicitude for the welfare of its subjects, forbids the gods on the register to be reborn anywhere but in Tibet. They fear lest the birth of a god in Mongolia should have serious political consequences by stirring the dormant patriotism and warlike spirit of the Mongols, who might rally round an ambitious native deity of royal lineage and seek to win for him, at the point of the sword, a temporal as well as a spiritual kingdom."[20] In Japan, "all the dead become gods. . . . It is to be remembered, of course, that the Japanese word for gods, *Kami*, does not imply, any more than did the old Latin term *dii-manes*, ideas like those which have become associated with the modern notion of divinity. The Japanese term might be more closely rendered by some such expression as 'the Superiors,' 'the Higher Ones;' and it was formerly applied to living rulers as well as to deities and ghosts."[21]

Perelaer[22] says that "the Dyak is a monotheist. He believes in a single Superior Being who . . . is master of everything and is omnipresent." Though he has a very vague conception of this Being, however, not knowing whether it is male or female, he is sure it had no beginning and will have no end. Some Dyaks have a number of gods among whom the deity of the rice-harvest occupies first place. Again, while priests and chiefs recognize a "high father" as chief god, the ordinary Kayan attends only to his ghosts.[23] On the Island of Nias the cult is restricted to the most indispensable manifestations in that the gods are called upon only when one needs them.[24] In Núkuóro two kinds of gods are distinguished: those who arose of themselves and the souls of the dead, the former being in the majority. "The spirits of dead relatives and chiefs of the present generations do not come at all into account and never enjoy divine honor. The few gods of this category are derived out of the migration-periods." In Ponapé, on the other hand, the worship of deified ancestors, coupled with a sort of zoölatry or totemism, is the backbone of the faith.[25]

The Samoans had many gods, a number of them devoted to war and very often represented as eels.[26] On Easter Island the highest god was represented by the eggs of sea-birds, the chief and favorite native food, and received sacrifices of the first fruits of the earth.[27] These people had a god of thieving and thought it no harm if not detected; detection indicated that the god disapproved and the thief then must return the goods and submit without resistance to punishment by the owner.[28] In Mangaia all the gods are called the children of Vatea, and of these Tane is one. "His name indicates the generative principle in nature, and the word is used to designate a husband, and even a man who is betrothed." He is especially the drum-god and the axe-god; he presides

18 Monier-Williams, *Brāhmanism*, 85.
19 DeGroot, *Relig. Syst.*, I, 223, note.
20 Wallis, in AA, XVII, 654-655.
21 Hearn, *Japan*, 33, 64.
22 *Dajaks*, 5, 6.
23 Veth, *Borneo*, II, 307; Nieuwenhuis, *Borneo*, I, 139.
24 Raap, in *Globus*, LXXXIII, 151.
25 Kubary, *Núkuóro*, 22, 23, 24; Christian, *Caroline Isl.*, 75.
26 Turner, *Samoa*, ch. IV.
27 Geiseler, *Oster-insel*, 17, 31.
28 Thomson, in USNM, 1889, 465.

over the erotic dance as well as over the war-dance.[29] The annals of the Sandwich Islands and of the Society and Hervey groups give many a dark record of human sacrifice to propitiate their hideous idols or to appease their wrath. "These gods were generally represented as implacable and vengeful, and the authors of all calamities. The native mind seems never to have entertained the idea of a beneficent and compassionate Being in any of their deities."[30] Almost every valley, mountain, stream, or place on Chatham Island is under the influence of one god or another; the natives have little images of these deities. Among the important gods are Tametera, the sun-god, who is the father, and Papa, the earth or mother; from the father comes all that the mother has and she gives it to her children. Another deity is called Whale-flesh; still others are vermin-gods which plague mortals. Ko Matarangi (shadow) comes upon men unexpectedly, to injure them in the dark; Pukuhoni is an unclean spirit which does harm behind the back; Ko Puanga is the Pleiades.[31] Among the Maoris the cult of Io was very ancient; he was regarded as the origin of all gods. "Only priests of high rank were taught the cult of Io and its rites. No home was sacred enough in which to perform such rites, or even to mention the name of Io, hence all such ceremonial performances took place out in the open and in some isolated spot. In fact, it looks as if Io was looked upon as a creator and supreme being." Yet the Maoris have given up their old cult, for, like primitive peoples generally, they expect service from their gods and are not averse to renunciation of them in favor of others more promising. Best[32] has often asked old natives the reason why their fathers gave up the practice of their ancient religion and accepted Christianity. Their answers were prompt and plain: "It was because of the superior powers of the white man's God. A deity whose subjects could acquire written languages, make guns and numberless other wondrous things, must be one worth cultivating; the ignorant Maori people might gain much from him."

The tribes of the New World very generally chose the sun as the object of their adoration; it was sometimes one of the gods, sometimes a symbol or form of the gods, and sometimes the highest god. "The United States Indians regarded the sun as the symbol of light, life, power, and intelligence, and deemed it the impersonation of the Great Spirit. They sang hymns to the sun and made genuflections to it."[33] The Blackfeet Indians in Canada "know and observe the Pleiades, regulating their most important feasts by those stars. They have a sacred feast about the first and last days of the occultation of the Pleiades. The mode of observance is national, the whole tribe turning out for the celebration of its rites; these include two sacred vigils, the solemn blessing and planting of the seed. This opens the agricultural season. The rites are somewhat similar to the Hebrew Passover, and some of the mysteries held by the Ancients in honor of Ceres."[34] The Flatheads believed the sun to be the Supreme Being and that after death the good, brave, and generous went to the sun, while the bad remained near the earth and troubled the living; others supposed that the worthless ceased to exist at death.[35] Although the sun as a divinity is not represented by them as a malignant being, the worship accorded him is the most dreadful which the Dakotas practise. Aside from the sun-

29 March, in JAI, XXII, 324.
30 Ella, in AAAS, 1887, 492-493.
31 Weiss, *Chatham Isl.*, 16-17.
32 In AAAS, 1909, 460, 464.

33 Schoolcraft, *Ind. Tribes*, V, 407; Carr, in *Smithson. Rep.*, 1891, 536, note; Ratzel, *Vkde.*, II, 680.
34 L'Heureux, in JAI, XV, 301.
35 Bastian, *Deut. Exped.*, II, 48, note.

dance, there is another proof of the divine character ascribed to the sun in the oath taken by some of the Dakotas: "As the sun hears me, this is so."[36] With the Arapaho, as with many other tribes, the moon is masculine, and the sun is feminine.[37] The New England Indians worshipped the sun as a god and had a festival at harvest time. Lafitau[38] states that the name of the war-god of the Hurons and Iroquois was but another name for the sun, "who was their Divinity, as he was that of all the Americans." While the Zuñi have a plurality of gods, many of whom are the spirits of their ancestors, these are but mediums through which to reach their one great father of all—the sun.[39] The Chichimecs of northern Mexico adored the sun as the supreme god and also worshipped lightning, while both Moki and the ancient Mexicans held sun-festivals.[40]

Other deities of the native Americans may be cited to show their anthropomorphic character. The chief god of the Algonquins was depicted as a liar and a cheat;[41] again the ranking divinity was the one who cooked the food dearest to the tribe—deer-meat and mescal hearts.[42] How the aleatory element has influenced the idea of deity is well brought out in the following comment by Hewitt:[43] "While Teharonhiawagon is regarded as the Master of Life, it must not be inferred that he is also the god or ruler of all other things; and it must not be overlooked that all gods as such were themselves subject to the inexorable decrees of Fate, of Destiny. In primitive thought the concept or idea of Fate or Destiny is clearly developed out of the countless failures of the gods to bring about results contrary to the established course of nature; every failure of a god to accomplish a certain expected result was at once attributed to one of two things: either to the conjectured inability of the god to change the decree of Fate, *i.e.*, the established order of things, or to an abortive attempt of the people to perform a rite or ceremony in accordance with a prescribed ritual. These considerations exempted Teharonhiawagon and other gods from censure for the nonperformance of the impossible, and they also show that sometimes the gods stood in need of human aid, either directly or ceremonially." The Menomini divided the universe into two main sections, the upper and lower worlds; these in turn were divided into four parts or tiers each, separated by the earth. Each world had its presiding deity. The upper world, peopled by the beneficent powers, was ruled by the chief god, who had many mythical birds as servants. Since the latter came into actual contact with mankind, while their master remained aloof, they received more homage than the chief god, who really appeared only as a figurehead.[44]

The Mexicans had many gods and goddesses: deities of war, of fire, of the harvest.[45] In the temple of the war-god was a cage to receive statues of foreign divinities, that they might not be able to help their worshippers.[46] The chief Mexican god was white and bearded, and came from the east; and others of their gods were of similar appearance: "white, blue-eyed, heavily bearded."[47] This does not harmonize very well with the following explanation of the black Christ. "Of course, I saw black Christs in Mexico, but there one could trace

36 Dorsey, in BAE, XI, 450; §§163, 282, of text and *Case-Book.*
37 Mooney, in BAE, XIV, 1006.
38 *Mœurs* (Dutch ed.), I, 130; Carr, in *Smithson. Rep.*, 1891, 547, 550.
39 Stevenson, in BAE, V, 546.
40 Nadaillac, *Preh. Amer.*, 280; Chamberlain, in AA, IX, 428.

41 Brinton, in *Am. Antiq.*, VII, 137-140.
42 HAI, II, 712.
43 In HAI, II, 939-940.
44 Skinner, in AA, XIII, 559.
45 Preuss, in *Globus*, LXXXVI, 117, 118; LXXXVII, 381.
46 Nadaillac, *Preh. Amer.*, 360.
47 Quiroga, *Cruz*, 22.

their sable origin. When Cortez introduced Christianity into the land of the Aztecs, that swarthy heathen people could not be induced to worship anything white, and consequently the Christus was always represented as dark. Even now in remote places the figure remains of sombre hue, and in two of the chief churches of Mexico City there are still life-sized black Christs. In Europe Sicily is not alone the home of black Christs. Above the high altar in the marble cathedral of Florence at Easter, 1904, hung an enormous black Christ on a crucifix." Several others are mentioned, with their exact locations. "Probably these black Christs date from Arab times, a sort of compromise between the white and the dark-skinned people, as in the case of Mexico."[48] The people of Hierro, Canary Islands, prayed only when in trouble; the men had one god, the women another. On conversion to the Catholic faith the islanders gave the names of these two deities to Jesus and Mary respectively.[49]

In Egyptian mythology the soul or double of the gods did not differ at all in nature from the double of men. "The gods were only more refined and powerful men; better prepared to command, enjoy, and suffer than men. They had the same physical constitution, suffered hunger and thirst, had our passions, troubles, joys, and infirmities. A mysterious fluid called *sa* circulated in their members, giving them health and vital vigor. They differed in power according to the quantity of this which they had. They could transmit it to each other and to man. This operation was carried on in the temples; the person to be impregnated knelt before the statue of the god, with his back to it; the hand of the idol was placed on the back of his neck and the fluid passed into him temporarily, and had to be renewed. It was exhausted in the gods by use and they replenished it at a mysterious pool in the southern sky. This fluid caused the bodies of the gods to be preserved far beyond the time of men. Old age hardened their bodies into precious metals; the bones into silver, the flesh into gold, the hair into lapis lazuli. The later alchemists believed in the transmutation of metals as a hastening of this process. Still the Egyptian gods were liable to decrepitude; the sun having become old, his chin wobbled, and the saliva trickled from his mouth. The gods were represented in mummies and their tombs were shown." Death meant for the gods exactly what it meant for men among the Egyptians; the body decayed and the soul faded, unless the same means of preservation were used. They had no joys after death; their souls regretted the light and suffered hunger, and they became ferocious monsters toward men unless propitiated by the necessary offerings to relieve their wants.[50] The Babylonian god had much the same relation to his people that the deity of the Hebrews exhibits in the Old Testament: he became angry at them and afflicted them, directed their warlike operations, and all the rest.[51] "I think," states Lenormant,[52] "amongst no people do we find the idea that the gods obtained material sustenance and new strength from the offerings made to them, expressed in more set terms than in the Accadian magical documents." The graves of Babylonian gods were shown.[53] In Persia there was a sort of reverse process in god-building: "there is a period where, through the efforts of the theologists, the conception of godhood appears very much purified, where the survivals of the older polytheism are set aside by the transformation of the gods into heroes or into attributes of the single god. When this peak is reached, gradually the abstract characteristics and ac-

48 Alec-Tweedie, *Sunny Sicily*, 178.
49 Cook, in AA, II, 493.
50 Maspero, *Hist. Anc.*, I, 109-110, 116.

51 Tiele, *Gchte. Relig.*, I, 276-277.
52 *Chaldean Magic*, 49.
53 Henning, in *Globus*, LXXXIV, 152.

tivities of the god are incorporated again in saints, angels, gods, and again do the forms of mythology people the heaven which until then was filled, in its exalted emptiness, solely by the breath of the All-powerful."[51]

It can hardly be said that the Phœnicians borrowed their dwarf-gods from the Egyptians, for such deities are to be found in many ancient religions as the personification of cosmic forces, as earth-gods possessing great skill and working in hidden places. A special Phœnician touch is the image of a dwarf-god embellished on the cabin of each ship as the divine artist and architect.[55] Androgynous deities were common to Babylonians, Greeks, and other ancients, while traces of such a notion are in evidence in the Old Testament.[56] Baal was the god of the land, regarded as the bestower of its fruits, and was entitled to thanks accordingly.[57] Jahweh, the "Most High," had many anthropomorphic qualities: he interceded for his people; he "thundered with a great thunder" and helped them gain victory; he was a warrior in charge of a host and the destroyer of all things.[58]

In Homer the gods need sleep and food as much as any mortal. The Olympian household is full of strife, jealousy, and old grudges. The women in it act like women in French novels: they are clever at female artifices; they cajole and wheedle; they get into scrapes and lie out of them; they carry on intrigues of love and ambition on behalf of their protégés, Greek or Trojan. The men make large allowances for the women, pet them, are angry with them for disobedience and self-will, but have to remember that they are females and make the best of it. Both the allowances and the petting are derogatory to the women; they avail themselves of their privileges and manœuvre to get their own way without penalty. The picture is just about what a group of frivolous French nobles, men and women, living isolated in a château in the middle of the eighteenth century would have presented, including the meanness which such a group would show if their selfishness and vanity were at stake. "In a passage which more nearly resembles a burlesque than any other in the poems, —the conflict of the gods on the plain of Troy,—Athena hits Ares in the neck with a large stone, and overthrows him; Aphrodite then leads him from the battle, but Athena follows the two and with a blow of her 'thick hand' casts both upon the ground. A few verses later, Hera boxes the ears of Artemis, and sends her in tears from the field of battle. In the same episode, Poseidon reminds Apollo that they two were sent down by Zeus to serve Priam's father Laomedon for a year,—that the one built a wall for the city and the other tended flocks, but that at the expiration of their term of service, Laomedon had dismissed them without the pay which had been stipulated, and with the threat to bind them hand and foot, and send them to distant lands to be sold as slaves, or he would lop off their ears for them." Homer knows no divine providence, in the sense of a definite purpose and guidance for the life of a man or for the development of a city or nation. The gods discuss a plan just as men would—by no means seeing the end from the beginning. "In the chariot-race held in honor of the dead Patroclus, Apollo knocks the whip from the hand of Diomed that the advantage may be given to his chief competitor Eumelus, whose horses Apollo himself had tended during his year of service

54 Justi, *Persien*, 91.
55 Tiele, *Gchte. Relig.*, I, 265, 273-274.
56 Barton, in *Amer. Or. Soc.*, III, 71; Tiele, *Gchte. Relig.*, I, 245; Chamberlain, in AA, VIII, 723-724.
57 Kautzsch, in *Hastings's Dict. Bible*, 645.
58 Gen., XIV, 22; Ex., III, 14; I Sam., VII, 10; Jos., V, 13 ff.; Maurer, Vkde., I, 62-63.

to Admetus; but Athena sees the trick, restores the whip to Diomed, and breaks the yoke to the chariot of Eumelus,—thus causing him to lose the race. To such pettiness do these great gods descend." The gulf between mortals and immortals, though distinct, is not impassable. Four sharp distinctions are made between men and the higher gods: (a) these are mortal, while those are immortal and ever young; (b) these toil and labor, while the gods "live at ease;" (c) these eat bread and drink wine, while those feast on ambrosia and nectar; and lastly (d) these dwell on earth, while the gods inhabit heaven and Olympus. Of course the power and wisdom of the gods are far greater than those of men but, after all, they are of the same kind, differing chiefly in degree, while in their needs, appetites, and passions the divine is not far removed from the human.[59]

The Greek gods were not always and everywhere the same; Artemis was not always the patroness of virginity and chastity, for there were lascivious rites in her honor.[60] "The difference between the gods of the old religious ideas and of the newer or Hellenic thought tended to crystallize in the distinction between Chthonian and Olympian gods, though this distinction never became absolute and universal, and there is hardly any deity who belonged everywhere and at all times to the one class and never to the other. But the worship of the dead, i.e., of the heroes, and of the Chthonian gods, was marked off by broad lines from that of the Olympian gods, and most of what was really deep and heartfelt religion in Greece belongs to the former, while most of what is artistic and a permanent possession for the civilized world belongs to the latter. The even numbers and the left hand belonged to the Chthonian deities, the odd numbers and the right hand to the gods of heaven. White was the appropriate colour of the Olympian gods, the East their abode, and the direction to which their temples looked and their worshippers turned when sacrificing to them. The forenoon was the time suitable for their worship. The Chthonian gods preferred blood-red or black; the West was the direction to which their worshippers faced, the afternoon their chosen time. Offerings to the Olympian gods were shared in by men; offerings to the Chthonian gods were burnt whole. Men had community in the sacrifice with the former, with the latter they had none."[61] When it came to a belief that the cosmos was an orderly arrangement, like the state, then the scope of ghost beliefs, as distinguished from that in a hierarchy of gods, could no longer flourish.[62]

Worship of the sun and other heavenly bodies was very widespread in antiquity. Lippert[63] has made much of it, stating in part that the younger gods, those of the conquerors, are Uranian, while those of the conquered are earthy, ugly, female, and black; there is a resulting antagonism of light and darkness, white and black. The ghosts of men are separated into two groups: the heroes go to heaven or the sun, while the others go to Hades. In Egypt all petty divinities tended to merge into forms of the sun, the one essence.[64] In Persia, Mithra was the god of light, the defender of truth, and the enemy of the powers of darkness. Like Helios, who sees and hears everything, Mithra was the genius of oaths and agreements, the supervisor and ruler of the world. At first as god of light standing near the sun, Mithra later became identified

---

59 Seymour, *Hom. Age*, 400 (quoted), 401, 405, 406-407 (quoted), 414.
60 Farnell, *Cults*, chs. XIII, XVI.
61 Ramsay, "Relig. Greece," in *Hastings's Dict. Bible*, extra vol., 143.

62 Rohde, *Psyche*, I, 43.
63 *Kgchte.*, II, 425, 430.
64 Maspero, *Hist. Anc.*, II, 543.

with the sun himself. The ancient Persians also had a star-cult, and in the Avesta the starry sky is likened unto the garment with which Ahuramazda was adorned. The noblest star was Sirius, the Dog Star, who was benevolent in that he conquered the demon of barrenness and brought copious rain over the land so that the specter of hunger and of crop-failure had no power.[65] The sun-cult was very ancient in Babylonia, where Marduk, the chief deity of the Babylonian pantheon, was originally a local sun-deity. He was called the compassionate one, the lord of life. In the Hebrew notion of Jahweh much was borrowed from the sun-cults of other lands, chiefly Egypt and Babylonia. The Old Testament transfers Marduk's heroic deeds to Jahweh, who crushed the heads of the sea-monsters and under whom the helpers of the dragons collapsed.[66] The sun's horses and chariots and the worship of sun, moon, and stars were borrowed from the Babylonian-Assyrian sun-cult.[67]

A symbol of the sun-god which has continued for many centuries, from heathen times to our own day and in the Christian church, is the wheel. The shining orb of the sun was conceived of as a wheel revolving in heaven, and it was thus that classical and Norse writers spoke of it; this developed into a sun-chariot drawn by horses, lighting up the earth and bringing fruitfulness to both men and fields. Aryan as well as Semitic peoples had this notion in ancient times, and even among the American Indians the wheel was the symbol of the sun. Originally the wheel appeared with four spokes, later with several more, as upon Assyrian monuments. In Scandinavia the symbolic wheel with four spokes appeared in the earlier Stone Age, in the tombs of Denmark and Sweden; the Bronze Age, both in Scandinavia and Germany, as well as in Asia Minor and elsewhere, was rich in objects with four or more spoked wheels. The old Syrian churches, first destroyed by the Mohammedans in the seventh century, had the four-spoked wheel on columns and capitals. It was found also on the old Christian grave-stones in Germany. It is from this symbol that there developed the cross of the Norse; it came to be used as the representation of the Father and Son, even of the dove (the emblem of the Holy Ghost), over whose head the sun-wheel was placed as an aureole.[68]

In the last struggles of paganism with the Christian church, the cult which exercised the most powerful attraction was that of Mithra. Though at first a sun-worship of Persian origin, its early character was greatly altered by syncretism, that is by accretions from other cults, especially Phrygian, and by natural development, to meet the needs of the times. "The worship of the Sun was the central force in Julian's attempt to remedy the dogmatic and moral weakness of paganism. In the fourth century the ancient god of light has become the supreme Power, who is all-seeing, all-pervading, who is the lord and giver of life, the cleanser from sin, the protector of the miserable, the conqueror of evil dæmons and death, who assures to his faithful worshipers the hope of immortality. The monuments of Mithra have been found all over the Roman world, in all the regions of Italy, in Spain, Africa, and all the provinces bordering on the Danube and the Rhine, in Gaul, and in Britain. . . . His worship was conducted in underground grottoes, brilliantly lighted and adorned with symbolic figures. The symbolism of his ritual has exercised and

65 Justi, *Persien*, 79, 92.
66 Ps., LXXIV, 13; LXXXIX, 11; Job, IX, 13; XXVI, 12; Is., LVII, 9; Delitsch, *Babel u. Bibel*, I, 33.
67 II Kings, XXIII, 11; Deut., XVII, 3; Jer., VIII, 2; Schrader, *Keilinschriften*, 360, 367, 369-370, 371, 373, 387.
68 "Kl. Nachrichten," in *Globus*, LXXXVIII, 115.

puzzled the ingenuity of modern archæologists. Probably it conveyed many meanings to the devotee; but the central idea in the end seems to have been that of a Power who conquers the spirits of darkness, leads souls from the underworld, and gives peace by purification. The ritual was complicated and impressive. There was a kind of baptism of neophytes, confirmation, consecration of bread and water, cleansing of the tongue with honey, and other ablutions. The great festival of the god was celebrated on the 25th of December. His mysteries created a powerful bond of union, and in this respect satisfied one of the most urgent needs of society under the later Empire."[69] There was a revival of sun-worship at a later time; about 1610 the Duke of Alba, while hunting in the mountains near Salamanca, found in a remote valley an unknown people who adored the sun.[70]

§248. Types of Fetishes.

PRACTICALLY any object is thought by the Melanesians to be capable of harboring a spirit, and the objects so possessed have consequently special efficacy through spiritual agency. The effectiveness of the rites of the Banks Islands are held to depend upon the use of certain stones or other objects which possess *mana* or power for some special end, and "this *mana* is definitely associated with a belief in the presence of a *vui* or spirit."[1] In the Mekeo district of British New Guinea some stones are believed to possess a dangerous magical property. Strong[2] has known a Solomon Islands police sergeant scatter a whole crowd of Mekeo natives by picking up such a stone and chasing them with it. "On another occasion I was told protests were made against taking such a stone into a boat, on the ground that the boat would surely sink. Why these stones should have this evil property," he adds, "I do not know. They are simply plain ordinary rounded stones." So they may be in appearance, but they are not ordinary stones, not just plain stones, but stones possessing a mysterious power because of an indwelling spirit. In fact, in British New Guinea there are many kinds of stones which have special powers that certainly no ordinary rocks can possibly possess—"stones in and near the houses that had an influence on the life and health and prosperity of the people, sling-stones which had been kept for generations and which gave to others in the bag the power of direction so that they would certainly hit the victim aimed at. At Wedau there is a stone which gives strength and courage for war. From far and near people came to drink water in which chips of it had been boiled. In all the villages there are stones which are reverenced, and which may not be moved. In the Boianai villages many of them have signs on them, rude circles, chipped concentrically; their presence in the village ensures success to all garden work, a plentiful supply of food, and happiness to the people."[3]

Stones are not the only things that may be possessed or that exhibit spiritual agency or direct influence on human affairs. In British New Guinea, at the special feasts, the guests bring pigs, which are killed slowly "so that there may be much squealing, which pleases the mango tree, for otherwise crops would fail, and pigs and women be barren."[4] *Ficus* and other large trees are generally respected by the Bina tribesmen: "They will not cut them down, for

69 Dill, *Nero*, 78.
70 Burckhardt, *Renaissance*, 484; Wadsworth, *Spain*, 6, note.
1 Rivers, *Melan. Soc.*, II, 406.

2 In JAI, XLIX, 296.
3 Chinnery, in JAI, XLIX, 277-278.
4 Haddon, in JAI, L, 248.

they may be the haunt of some Oboro or other evil spirit. They do not believe that the trees themselves contain evil spirits, but that they are merely the resting-places of those of human beings."[5] Similar notions were held by the Solomon Islanders who thought that every spot where a man felt awe, such as a deep gorge, a waterfall, a dark pool, or a wide-spreading tree, was a sacred place inhabited by a *figona* or spirit. Thus, there is a large tree not far from Fagani, San Cristoval, where a *figona* lives, past which travellers go silently or speak in whispers. There is a deep river-gorge near the village Raumae, also inhabited by a spirit; if a man ventures into the gorge, his soul may be taken captive by the *figona,* whereupon the man on his return sickens and dies. Near the source of the Wango river is a deep and dark pool, the abode of a *figona;* as the native passes he throws in a bit of areca-nut. The people think that falling stars are wandering spirits and are much afraid.[6] Man himself, as we shall shortly see, may become possessed: "If a person meets a hostile *tamate* it may enter into him, and if several *tamate* enter in this way the man becomes raving mad, of enormous strength and of incredible swiftness of foot. He is caught with difficulty, mastered and held down by a number of men. A fire is lighted and bunches of a scented shrub called *sav* are heated over the flames to increase their smell and then laid over the sick man's nose. This treatment is applied again and again and the sick man calls out the names of the *tamate* within him, being violently convulsed as he utters them. At last he becomes calm and limp, and after a few hours in this condition, he revives and becomes well."[7]

In West Africa, says Ellis,[8] "the snake itself is not worshipped, but rather its indwelling spirit." Serpents are the representatives of the spirits among most of the Kaffir tribes; crocodiles, being regarded as such, are never killed.[9] Very often animals become fetishes through being possessed of the souls of the dead. "The Zulu believe that the spirits of their kings after death inhabit the deadly Mamba, and that the *ihloze, i.e.,* spirits of their ancestors, inhabit snakes of a more innocent type. The appearance of a medium-sized green snake among the wattles of a kraal fence is always welcomed, and considered to be a visit from, or by, the spirits of their forefathers. The reptile receives the kindest treatment, and is in no way disturbed."[10] The natives of Madagascar call the owl by a name which means "spirit-bird"; it is popularly supposed to be an embodiment of the departed spirit of an evil man.[11] Some Bechuana tribes protect the crocodile, thinking that these reptiles keep wolves away from the herds in the neighborhood of rivers.[12] Some Africans distinguish between two kinds of crocodiles: those which man eats and those which eat man.[13] Certainly where crocodiles eat human beings they become fetishes readily enough, being possessed of their victims' souls. Other tribesmen believe that the souls of the drowned migrate into the bodies of crocodiles; a crocodile that tries to seize a woman going for water is to them "a bad man"; they can even hear him calling for beer and food at night and complaining of the cold.[14] Hyænas are sacred animals among the Bageshu, because "they eat the dead

5 Lyons, in JAI, LI, 433.

6 Fox and Drew, in JAI, XLV, 135-136, 163, 182, 200, 202.

7 Rivers, *Melan. Soc.*, I, 164-165; §§257, 258, of text and *Case-Book.*

8 *Ewe*, 54.

9 Tyler, in *Ill. Afr.*, Dec., 1895.

10 Grant, in JAI, XXXV, 270.

11 Sibree, *Great Afr. Isl.*, 274.

12 Ratzel, *Anthropogeog.*, I, 380.

13 Reclus, quoted in Dowd, *Negro Races*, I, 73.

14 Sheane, in JAI, XXXVI, 154.

and are thus supposed to be related to the people."[15] The hyæna is almost uni
versally regarded as a sacred animal in equatorial East Africa. "Among the
Wa-Kamba the dead, with the exception of an elder, are thrown into the bush
to be devoured by that animal." The hyæna also has magical powers; it cannot, for instance, be shot. The use of hyæna-dung in magic is common.[16] The
connection between fetish-animals and the dead is most clearly seen in the case
of the Bahima. When the king dies, his body is wrapped in a large cow-skin
and taken to Ensanzi, the burial-place of the kings. "Ensanzi is a forest which
is inhabited by lions, which are said to be possessed by the spirits of former
kings of Ankole; in the forest is a temple and attached to it are a number of
priests whose duties are to feed and care for the lions, and to hold communications with the former kings when necessary." When the royal body arrives at
Ensanzi it is removed from the skin by the priest, who washes it with milk;
"it then lies in state for several days until it swells, and the stomach bursts.
During this time the priest is busy daily feeding and feasting the lions with
cattle which have been brought as offerings to the departed kings. He also has
to find a young cub to present to the people, because the swelling and collapse
of the corpse represent pregnancy and birth of the lion king. Directly the
collapse takes place a lion cub is produced, and the priest announces that the
king has brought forth a lion. He presents the cub to the people, and proceeds
to feed it with milk. For some days the people remain until the cub has
gained strength and begins to eat meat; all the interest and anxiety now
centre in the cub, the corpse receives an ordinary burial and is forgotten; the
king lives in the cub." The lions in this forest are sacred; no one may kill them;
they are said to be so tame that the priests can move amongst them without
fear. The corpse of a queen is treated the same way, but her spirit is supposed
to become a leopard. "The priest of the leopard forest takes the body out
of the hide and washes it daily with milk whilst it swells; this as in the case of
the king's body, is said to be pregnancy, and when it collapses he presents a
leopard cub which he says the queen has brought forth." The spirits of dead
princes and princesses enter snakes; another belt of the same forest is sacred
to snakes; in it is a temple with priests who feed and guard them.[17]

The sacred animals of the Hamites of Abyssinia include hyæna, snake,
crocodile, and owl. The Galla have a well-defined tree-cult, with sacrifice of
milk and black sheep.[18] According to the Hausa certain trees are bound up
with the lives of certain persons, while there is an enormous tree of life in
Allah's garden; every human being is represented by a distinct leaf and when
that leaf falls, the person has only forty days more to live. Nearly every compound has a tree in the center to which offerings are made.[19] In Kikuyu and
Kamba belief, fig-trees are sacred, being inhabited by spirits. At the foot of
each tree of this kind there is a small clearing, a shrine In fact, where offerings
of food are made; though they are known to be eaten by birds and rats, it is
believed that the spirits profit by them. If fig-trees are not found in any part
of the country, the spirits haunt a prominent rock or rocky hill. There is a
sacred rock in the Kitui district where people go regularly to pray to the
attendant spirit for increase of worldly goods such as cattle and goats, after
pouring a libation of mead at the foot of the rock and sacrificing a male goat.
In every Ketosh village, on a spot in front of the hut of the owner of the vil-

15 Roscoe, in JAI, XXXIX, 188.
16 Johnstone, in JAI, XXXII, 265.
17 Roscoe, in JAI, XXXVII, 101-102.

18 Seligmann, in JAI, XLIII, 653-654.
19 Tremearne, in JAI, XLV, 51-52.

lage there are four stones planted in the form of a square, in the center of which is a small fig-tree. "This constitutes a kind of village altar, and if any animal is slaughtered in the village, a little of the blood is sprinkled on the stones. . . . When a village is moved, the head of the village moves his altar stones to the new site, and plants a fresh tree amongst them; and in the many deserted villages the position of the chief's house can generally be identified by the wild fig tree. . . . As an example of the importance which they attach to their possession, it is said that it sometimes happens that a Mu-Wanga has stolen a cow from a native of Marama or Kisa, and if the owner could not induce the chief of the Awa-wanga to make the thief return the cow, he would go by night and carry off one of the *Muzimo* stones from the chief's village and hide it away; great excitement would then ensue and stupendous efforts would be made to recover the cow, which rarely failed to be returned to the owner before nightfall in order to redeem the sacred stone."[20] Among the Bageshu most large rocks are supposed to be animated. "At various times, when the elder of the village orders it, offerings are made of goats, fowls, and beer, whilst the children take plantains and small offerings of food." The rock-spirit generally speaks through an elder of a village by means of dreams.[21] A special fetish among the Akamba is a horn of an ox, antelope, or wart-hog, the hollow end of which is filled with samples of various foods and a piece of skin cut from the nose of a hyæna. These horns, called *Kithito,* are very old, having been handed down from generation to generation; "they are looked upon with great awe and mystery, being hidden away in the woods, and they must on no account be kept in houses or their presence would probably prove fatal to the inmates. A *Kithito* must never be handled with the bare hand but can only be safely picked up with a piece of sheep's fat in each hand." Such objects are used in oath-ceremonies; when making peace, the representatives of the belligerent parties will strike the *Kithito* three times with a stick and swear on behalf of their respective people: "If I fight again, may the *Kithito* kill me."[22] The idea of possession may be further illustrated by a Congo practice which transfers a spirit to a spear: "When a man is under the sway of the *mingoli* (disembodied souls) he gets his spear, and tying some dried plantain leaves to it he holds it before him with his left hand, and as he trembles with the excitement of the spirits in him, the spear shakes and rustles the leaves until the *mingoli* go out of him into the spear and that spear then becomes . . . a fetish spear, and his luck is bound up in it."[23]

The aborigines of Siberia believe that visible objects in general are merely masks or coverings for various anthropomorphic spirits which reside in them; this is especially the case with objects such as stones or roots which have an outward resemblance to the human form. "Animals, though outwardly differing in form from man, are in reality human beings, with human feelings and souls, and human institutions, such as the clan. Some of them, indeed, are superior to man, with higher qualities of mind and body." Such is the bear. It is not the animal, however, which is the object of their cult, but only its "owner," called *ys* by the Gilyak and *ichchi* by the Yakut. "The 'owners' of the *tayga,* of the mountain, of the sea, and of the fire, are, of course, the most important for men from the economic point of view. The gods of the sky are regarded as

20 Hobley, *A-Kamba,* 166, 167; and in JAI, XLI, 421, 422; and in JAI, XXXIII, 342-343 (quoted); Dundas, in JAI, XLIII, 31; Hetherwick, in JAI, XXXII, 91.

21 Roscoe, in JAI, XXXIX, 188.
22 Hobley, *A-Kamba,* 47, 48, 168.
23 Weeks, in JAI, XL, 380.

less important, for men do not come into direct contact with them." Nearly all sacrifices are offered to the "owners" of mountains, sea, and fire. Among the Yakuts "every river, lake, stone, and sometimes even parts of these, has its own *ichchi,* who controls it. Movable objects and those which can produce sounds also have their *ichchi* . . . accidents may often happen to a cart or some part of its equipment. Such misfortunes are attributed to the local *ichchi,* who must therefore be placated by sacrifices."[24] Pervading the Rig-Veda is a kind of theism which assumes that everything or anything—usually that which is useful to the worshipper, as the plough or the furrow—has a separate divinity; hymns are addressed to weapons and to the war-car, as to divine beings.[25] Of the various objects of reverence among the Todas the most important are hills and rivers; villages, dairies, their thresholds and contents; bells; the buffalo and its milk; trees and plants; the sun, fire, and light; and stones. "Any place connected with the gods is reverenced by the Todas, and this is especially the case with the hills where they dwell." It seems probable that the general idea underlying the dairy ritual is that the dairyman is dealing with a sacred substance, the milk of the buffaloes. The dairy is a sacred place, and "whenever a devout Toda visits a strange village, he goes to the dairy, and prostrating himself at its threshold, utters a prayer." As the contents of the dairy are regarded as sacred, definite means are taken to prevent these objects from contamination by the gaze or touch of ordinary mortals. Of the objects kept in the dairy the bells are undoubtedly the most sacred.[26] Fetish-animals are common in Asia, such as certain dogs and tigers in China, the fox in Japan, and snakes and tigers in India. The cobra is an object of veneration and superstitious awe to the Hindus, in whose mythology it takes a prominent place. Many natives refuse to destroy a cobra, even if they find it in their houses; and when one has taken up its abode in a hole in the wall, it is fed, protected, and conciliated, as though to provoke or injure the reptile would invoke misfortune on both house and family. The British have taken extensive steps to exterminate the poisonous snakes in India, but the natives secretly oppose their destruction. Such fetishistic notions cost dearly, for every year thousands of natives are killed by tigers or from the bite of poisonous snakes.[27]

If a dead cobra is found on a farm in Borneo after it has been burnt, it makes the farm *mali,* that is, the crops may not be consumed by the owner's family without a death occurring within a year.[28] The natives believe that good spirits can warn men against ill luck through animals that are holy—various birds and snakes.[29] Trees also come in for a share of reverence. When the Dusuns clear the jungle for planting they always leave a single tree in the middle of the clearing, "lest the birds, having no perching place left to them, should curse the crop." The sap of a certain kind of tree is used for medicine, "but when this is to be collected the proper name of the tree must not be mentioned."[30] It is believed by the Singhalese that the king of the devils uses a rod of rattan for punishing his refractory subjects; hence they have a great dread of that plant. "A proof of their dread is that rattan is especially efficacious in

24 Czaplicka, *Aborig. Siberia,* 271-272, 278-279.
25 Hopkins, *Relig. India,* 135.
26 Rivers, *Todas,* 231, 338, 339, 417, 419, 422, 423, 424.
27 Lippert, *Kgchte.,* II, 393, 404; Bourdeau, *Monde animal,* 106, 115, 120; Fitz-Gerald, in *Technical World Mag.,* May, 1907, 311-318.
28 Roth, in JAI, XXI, 111.
29 Nieuwenhuis, *Borneo,* I, 143.
30 Evans, in JAI, XLVII, 152, 154.

curing madness (possession) by whipping, the mere sight of it sometimes quieting the patient."[31] The Palaungs "do not worship trees or stones, but make offerings to the spirits that inhabit them."[32] A spirit is supposed by the Malays to inhabit iron, for that metal must not be used for cutting hair or finger-nails.[33]

All through the Pacific, stones are regarded as the abode of gods or spirits. In Samoa, besides stone idols, a special fetish is an old smooth staff kept in the family of one of the "disease-making craft" and considered to be the representative of the god. This was regularly carried by the priest when he was summoned to visit a case of sickness. "The eyes of the poor patient brightened up at the sight of the stick. All that the priest did was merely to sit before the sick man, and leaning on this sacred staff, to speechify a little, and tell him there was no further fear, and that he might expect soon to recover."[34] Gold in Timor-laut is a fetish, a gift of the gods, and when the natives go to wash the sands of the river for gold they set out en masse with religious ceremonies and sacrifices.[35] In former times when natives crossed Cook Straits they covered their eyes, "lest the people looked upon the thrice *tapu* rock known as Nga Whatu. Should any person look upon it, then assuredly would disaster overtake that vessel, paddle the crew never so bravely." A more refined notion of spiritual agency among the Maori is that the power of the mother to bear children is a sacred power, bestowed on woman by the great god Io.[36] Another ancient Maori belief, still prevalent, is that which pertains to the *tapu* of newly carved houses. "This *tapu* or baleful enchantment has its origin in the fact that the sacred children of Tane the Forest Father have been felled by human hands, and have been carved into the semblance of gods and ancestors. The *tapu* must be disposed of, or its dangerous powers averted, before the house can be safely occupied." Besides his carved house, the chief had two other fetishes: a sharp-edged club of greenstone and a dog-skin cloak.[37] When the king at Ponapé was drowned in a river the natives thought that the pitying gods changed him into a blue river-fish, a species which the people to this day refuse to eat.[38] Throughout Polynesia birds, beasts, and fish are regularly regarded as fetishes. "A very large number of the Polynesian gods were believed to be incarnate in or to have a practice of entering into creatures of the animal kingdom, and to be immanent in or enter into trees, plants and inanimate objects." It was held also that after a man's death his spirit sometimes either adopted an animal-form or some other or entered into an animal or object. There are examples of women giving birth to animals and of the latter having had a human origin in other ways; there are numerous instances of a man's unwillingness to eat, or even to kill, his sacred object, though other persons, to whom it was not sacred, would not hesitate to do so; there are many illustrations of the friendly and often helpful attitude of an object toward the people to whom it was sacred; and finally there is evidence of its acting as a forewarner of death. Prominent among the fetish-objects were eels, snakes, lizards, and sharks. Worship of these, and it would seem especially of sharks, was common; in one place in the island of Tutuila

31 Hildburgh, in JAI, XXXVIII, 200-201.

32 Milne, *Eastern Clan*, 355-356.

33 Skeat and Blagden, *Malay Penin.*, II, 251.

34 Turner, *Samoa*, ch. IV, 327-328.

35 Forbes, in JAI, XIII, 428.

36 Best, in JAI, XLIV, 131, 141.

37 Cowan, *Maoris*, 163 ff., 172, 173.

38 Christian, *Caroline Isl.*, 84.

there were two sharks which came in when called upon "in the name of an old famous chief."[39]

It was firmly held by the Tlinkits of Alaska that the evil spirits could not be conjured with any other objects than the drum and the rattle.[40] Among the tribes of British Columbia copper was held in great esteem; copper plates were named and even clothed, and were fed regularly.[41] There is much evidence among other tribes that implements, ornaments, and other objects of copper were regarded as having exceptional virtues and magical powers, while certain early writers aver that some of the tribes of the Great Lakes held all copper as sacred, making no practical use of it whatever.[42] Another fetishistic substance was red pipestone, regarded by some Indians as the flesh of their ancestors; "as this red stone was a part of their flesh," it would be sacrilegious for white men to touch or take it away—"a hole would be made in their flesh, and the blood could never be made to stop running."[43] Among the Cheyennes, the war-bonnet, the pipe, and stone arrowheads tied in the hair were fetishes. "They wear these stone arrowpoints in order that they may have long life. This is a part of the general belief as to the endurance, permanence, and perhaps even immortality of stone."[44] While the Apache will not let snakes be killed within the limits of the camp by one of their own people, they not only allow a stranger to kill them, but request him to do so. The fetish-snake is a central point in an important dance of the Mokis of Arizona.[45] Snakes appear in the arms of the city of Mexico; here birds are fetishes because they can conquer snakes.[46] In ancient Mexico precious stones were thought to possess mysterious power; there were persons who knew where precious stones grew because, wherever the latter were, they exhaled, at dawn, a vapor like delicate smoke. This cool and moist exhalation made the grass above them always green, which was another sign of their location.[47] The great boa is the most formidable of all demons who people the spiritual world of the Jibaros. "He is the original father of witchcraft; it is from his body that the sorcerers receive the poison with which their organism is impregnated and the invisible arrow, which they discharge against their victims. After death the souls of the medicine men are also believed to enter into the boa. The Jibaros, like all Indians, therefore particularly fear this monster, and when they kill a boa they think that they kill a powerful sorcerer."[40]

The snake was a notable fetish in antiquity. Its characteristics of living in holes, gliding noiselessly like a ghost, its association with the dead, and its subtlety and other peculiar qualities led easily enough to the notion that it was possessed by a spirit, often an evil one. "Of wild animals snakes had a peculiarly great meaning for the Chaldæans as for most savages of our days. Snakes were symbols of a supernatural wisdom—they were attributes of Ea, the godlike wisdom. Probably snakes were kept in some Babylonian temples and there used as oracles."[40] Snakes and dragons have been common as

39 Williamson, *Cent. Polyn.*, II, chs. XX, XXI, XXII, 217, 229, 231, 239, 242, 304, 308-309; Turner, *Samoa*, ch. V.
40 Jones, *Thlingets*, 156.
41 Boas, in USNM, XI, 204 ff.
42 Holmes, in HAI, I, 346.
43 Donaldson, in *Smithson. Rep.*, 1885, pt. II, 245; Perkins, in PSM, XLIV, 244.
44 Grinnell, *Cheyenne*, II, 10-11, 18, 117-118, 120-121.

45 Bourke, in BAE, IX, 470; Bourke, *Snake-Dance*.
46 Lippert, *Kgchte.*, II, 404.
47 Nuttall, in AA, III, 228.
48 Karsten, "Jibaro," in BAE, Bull. LXXIX, 61.
49 Lehmann, *Overtro*, I, 62; Lippert, *Kgchte.*, II, 403.

treasure-wardens; a familiar motif in mythology is the destruction of dragons by heroes.[50] The serpent has been worshipped in India, Phœnicia, Persia, Greece, Italy, Lithuania, and elsewhere,[51] and in China the dragon has been since time immemorial the principal divinity of rains and water.[52] Like the American Indians, the Arabs have their snake-dance.[53] The snake as an evil daimon, as tempter, and as a creature associated with wisdom has been clearly depicted in the Old Testament.[54] Snake-worship was well known in Greece, while in Rome snakes were regarded as house-genii and grave-spirits.[55] In the mysteries several characterizations of the serpent were manifest: as a good, protecting divinity; as an avenging cult-creature hostile to mankind; and as the cosmogonic principle. To serpents were also ascribed generative power.[56] Superstitions regarding snakes still exist. "Near Leeds they say that when a snake crosses the path rain is near; and in West Sussex to kill the first snake you see in the year gives you power over your enemies for a twelvemonth, or its skin hung up in the house brings good luck to the tenant. In Shropshire, the dragonfly is the supposed harbinger of the adder, and is consequently called the Ether's Nild or Needle, and the Ether's Mon (man) in various parts of the county. In the Isle of Wight they give the insect the name snakestanger for a like reason. A sickly-looking person with a ravenous appetite is said to have a 'nanny-wiper' in his or her stomach, and the only way to lure it forth, say the Sussex people, is to fill a saucer with milk and lie near it with the mouth open, feigning sleep. The nanny-wiper will shortly creep forth to drink the liquor, and may then be killed. In the North Country it is believed that if a native of Ireland draw a ring around a toad or adder, the creature cannot get out, and will die there, but in the West Country one should make the sign of the cross within the ring, and repeat the first two verses of the Sixty-eighth Psalm."[57]

In the old days gems were among the most important media for the transmission of supernatural powers. It is not surprising that the attention of people on the lookout for mystery and supernaturalism should have been arrested by precious stones, which seem to the dazzled observer to give out their rays as from a vital principle within themselves rather than to owe their glitter and gleam to reflected light; and it is easy to understand how they came to be regarded as the abode of occult powers. Most of the stories of the secret virtues of precious stones are derived from the East. "The diamond among the ancients was the symbol of severe and unswerving justice; the judges in Hades had hearts of adamant. It was believed to preserve its owner from illness—a property proved, it was considered, in the time of the plague, when the disease spread rapidly among the poor, and the rich who wore diamonds escaped. The stone gave victory if the cause espoused were just; it acted as a talisman against witchcraft, but lost its power if its owner sinned. It calmed anger, bestowed fortitude, and strengthened wedded love. It was a favorite superstition, frequently repeated in the old books on the subject—through the want, one would imagine, of any experimental ardor—that the diamond could be wrought upon by goat's blood. 'The diamonde which neither iron nor fier will daunt, the blood of the gote softeneth to the breaking.' Pliny adds that,

---

50 Lippert, *Kgchte.*, II, 407.
51 Lubbock, *Orig. Civil.*, 283; Letourneau, *Soc.*, 293.
52 DeGroot, *Relig. Syst.*, I, 53.
53 N. Y. *Post*, Feb. 16, 1897.

54 Duhm, *Geister*, 12.
55 Harrison, *Greek Relig.*, 165; Wissowa, *Relig. Römer*, 24; Lippert, *Kgchte.*, II, 405.
56 Wobbermin, *Mysterienwesen*, 89-90.
57 N. Y. *Times*, July 16, 1894.

since mortal ingenuity could not have discovered the fact, it must have been revealed to man from Heaven. The gem was held to be able to reproduce itself. De Boot, in his treatise, relates a story of a lady who had two hereditary diamonds which produced a numerous progeny; and Sir John Mandeville, who accepts the theory of reproduction, declares further that by personal experiment he convinced himself that diamonds grew in size. Most precious stones were used medicinally in a pounded state, but the diamond was held to be a deadly poison. It is enumerated among the poisons administered to Sir Thomas Overbury in the Tower, and Benvenuto Cellini, in his fascinating autobiography, relates how his life was spared through the dishonesty of an apothecary, who, engaged to poison him by pulverizing a diamond and putting it into his salad, substituted a beryl for the more costly stone. Many of the most potent gems were obtained from animals. Best known, perhaps, of these is the toad-stone, to which Shakespeare alludes: 'The toad, ugly and venomous, wears yet a precious jewel in its head.' This stone warned of poison by its change of color, and might be used to allay the pain of an envenomed bite; it was a preventive of the burning of houses and the sinking of ships. To test the genuineness of the gem, Lupton instructs the owner to 'holde the stone before a tode so that he may see it, and if it be a right and true stone the tode will leape towarde it and make as though he would snatch it. He envieth so much that none should have that stone.' " Serpents were supposed to possess precious stones of inestimable value. In the *Travels of Two English Travellers,* published in 1611, there is an account of a jewel taken from a serpent's head and used in conjuring. Alexander was said to have seen serpents in the Vale of Jordan with collars of huge emeralds. "A stone found in the head of the vulture bestowed health and success. The eagle stone, to be sought for in the nests of eagles, rendered its possessor amiable, rich, and sober. It might further be of service in the detection of theft. Two stones were possessed by the swallow, a red one for curing insanity, and a black one which brought good luck, and which, tied about the neck, prevented fevers and cured the jaundice. The swallow was further able to find a stone on the seashore which restored sight to the blind. The tears of the crocodile had their value for the ancients, since they crystallized into gems." The opal at the present day is considered unlucky, but in the Middle Ages it was highly prized, as it was held to unite the special virtues of every stone whose copy it simulated. "The emerald strengthened the eyesight. Nero, who was extremely shortsighted, was accustomed to view the combats of the gladiators in the arena through an emerald. The supposition is that it formed a concave lens, but the help it afforded him was considered due to the virtue of the gem. Worn in a ring, the stone was a preventive of epilepsy. A ruby, by its darkening of color, warned the owner of disaster. According to other authorities it conferred the power of seeing in the dark. If the four corners of a house were touched with it, it preserved from lightning and tempest. The strength of the topaz was said to wax and wane with the moon. It had the peculiarity of at once cooling boiling water, if thrown into it. The crystal dissolved all spells of witchcraft, while the onyx was a dangerous ornament, since it exposed the wearer to the assaults of demons and gave him bad dreams." The faith in the efficacy of certain stones to cure disease continued to a later period. The sapphire was generally believed in the seventeenth and earlier centuries to give help in all diseases and troubles of the eye. This idea was probably derived from Greek and Latin tradition as to the *sapphirus,* a name referring not to our sapphire but to lapis-lazuli, to the power of which a certain remedial effect might be conceded. As far back as the Ebers Papyrus, or about 1600 B.C., lapis-lazuli is noted as an ingredient in eye-washes. "In old St. Paul's was a sapphire given by Richard de Preston, citizen and grocer of London, for the cure of all infirmities of the eye. And, even in our own day, we must remember the widespread faith among nurses in coral and amber necklaces, as preventives of convulsions and other infantile disorders. Royalties naturally have always had more than their fair share of gems, magical or otherwise. The late Shah of Persia possessed a casket which was held under certain conditions to have the power of rendering the royal wearer invisible. A diamond set in a scimitar and a dagger made him invincible, while a talismanic star in his possession forced conspirators to confess their crimes. Our own King John, as a believer in their occult qualities, was an ardent collector of precious stones. Holinshed mentions that he suspected some pears to be poisoned, since the jewels he wore became covered with a dewy film. Both Charles V. and Queen Elizabeth possessed Bezoar stones. These were obtained from the kidneys of a wild animal of Arabia, where it was supposed they had been formed from the poison of serpents, and were a potent charm against plague and poison. One explanation of Elizabeth's power of healing the king's evil was that it was by virtue of some precious stone in the possession of the crown of England."[58]

Allied to the precious stones was jade. In ancient Britain it was an object of superstition, employed as an ornament or amulet and not for practical use.[59]

§249. The Exuvial Fetish.

An object that becomes a fetish merely through intimate association with a person falls in the class of personality-symbols. Such is the Australian *churinga*. Many of these objects originally belonged to the ancestors, though in some cases they are the *churinga* of men now alive who are regarded as the reincarnations of ancestors or of men who have lived within the recollection of those who are now handling the *churinga*. Reverential care is bestowed upon these objects and "no quarrelling of any kind is allowed anywhere near to where the *churinga* are stored, those spots being regarded as especially sacred."[1] In some cases the *churinga* representing certain animals are supposed to be endowed with special magic power. "If our native is desirous when a young man of promoting the growth of his beard, then he persuades an older man, who belongs to a rat totem, to rub his chin with a Churinga, which represents the rat. The sacred object is painted with long lines of black and red, which indicate the long whiskers of the animal, and the rubbing results in some whisker-growing virtue passing from the Churinga into the chin."[2] Personality-symbols often have a definite bearing on the institutions of marriage and government; in some places, for instance, "in order not to be troubled in the use of his rights, it sufficed the husband on duty to hang on the door of the house and on the wife's door his shield and his sword or knife"[3]—a practice developed under polyandry. In the Sahara, when a husband goes away for a long time he takes the precaution of leaving one of his shirts on the nuptial

58 N. Y. *Evening Post*, June 17, 1897 (from the *London Standard*); *Superstitions of Science* (a review of Garboe, A., *Kulturhistoriske Studier over Ædelstene*), in N. Y. *Nation*, CI, 415.

59 Dawkins, *Early Man in Britain*, 280.
1 Spencer, in AAAS, 1904, 402.
2 Gillen, in AAAS, 1901, 121-122.
3 Letourneau, *Marr.*, 81.

couch. "Henceforth his wife is protected, his honor is safe. If he finds on return an increase in his family . . . this posterity will be his. The little ones will be his . . . not merely by name, but of his flesh and blood. The son born two years after his departure was conceived by his acts! Nobody falters or smiles when he affirms this. The shirt has simply wrought a new miracle, or rather Allah has done it for he has caused the infant to sleep during this time in the womb of his mother. . . . Praised be He, the Powerful, the Mild, the Compassionate!"[4]

Insignia of office fall into the fetish-class, for they are personality-symbols of rulers. The Kaffir sign of royalty is a necklace of large reddish beads, which is put on at the king's inauguration. Royal women wear various ornaments which common mortals may not wear, even though they have them, or the first chief who came along would take them away as of right.[5] The umbrella, the stool (a solid block of wood corresponding in height to the importance of the chief), and the pipe and leather tobacco-pouch are insignia of state in West Africa; and there is the stick of office, usually silver-headed. "The same honors and respect are paid to the stick as to the person to whom it belongs. It has an almost sacred character, and it is an unheard-of crime for an ambassador, furnished with this emblem, to be molested."[6] In the Sudan the carrying of an umbrella is the exclusive right of the sultan, and the custom is paralleled in India.[7] So too the shoe is a personality-symbol, both in India and among the Hebrews.[8] Ear-plugs and labrets in Mexico, and forehead-bandages among the kin of the Inca—he himself alone having the right to wear a red one and a red aigrette—are American symbols.[9] Among the Norsemen the sword was used in oath-taking—at first that of the leader and later a special sword of ceremony.[10]

A more extensive group of personal fetishes are the exuviæ, parts of the body, whether of the living or of the deceased, in which the soul inheres. An excellent example of a part of the body which is not only dispensable but which must be severed, is the umbilical cord, and with it the placenta. The treatment accorded such exuviæ shows clearly enough their fetishistic nature. No sooner is a child born in Central Australia than it becomes the object of magic arts: the navel-string is dried, swathed in fur, and tied round the child's neck. "The necklace not only facilitates growth, keeps it quiet and contented, but it also has the admirable faculty of deadening to the child the noise made by the camp dogs."[11] Great importance is attached to the placenta in the Ibo country of Africa; it seems to be in some way a counterpart of the child, while the burial of the placenta is held to be a necessary rite if the mother is to bear any more children.[12] Among the Nigerians the part of the cord left on the child is washed continually until it atrophies and comes off, the time being variously given as between three and fourteen days. It is then either burnt, when the ashes are put into a pot of grease and rubbed on the child's head to make it hard, or ground and eaten with yam, or planted at the roots of yams, to ensure a good harvest the following year.[13] Seligmann[14] cites

4 Pommerol, *Sahariennes*, 167-168.
5 Kropf, *Kaffir-Engl. Dict.*, 146; Holub, *Capstadt*, II, 81.
6 Ellis, *Ewe*, 166-167, 178.
7 Rohlfs, in *Mitth. J. Perthes' Geog. Anst.*, Ergänzheft. 25, 15.
8 Holtzmann, *Ind. Sagen*, II, 344; Ruth, IV, 7.

9 Nadaillac, *Preh. Amer.*, 308, 419, note.
10 Jørgensen, in *Annaler*, 1876, 170.
11 Gillen, in AAAS, 1901, 111.
12 Thomas, in JAI, LII, 258.
13 Tremearne, in JAI, XLII, 173.
14 In JAI, XLIII, 658-660.

many cases to show that the placenta is regarded in Egypt as the double, physical or spiritual, of the infant. But the most striking example of the importance ascribed to the placenta is to be found among the Baganda, a Bantu people, with kings of predominantly Hamitic blood. Even among the commoners the after-birth was called the second child and was believed to have a spirit which at once became a ghost and attached itself to the stump of the umbilical cord. For this reason the umbilical cord of a prince was treated with the greatest reverence. "The placenta of a prince is always preserved; it is called the *mulongo*. It has power to kill the offspring of royalty if not respected and treated with honour. Kings therefore always keep their placenta and have it decorated and treated as a person; it is confided to the care of the second greatest earl. After death it is placed in the tomb with the *Lwanga*" (jaw bone). Each new moon, in the evening, it is carried in state, wrapped in bark cloths, to the king, and the earl in charge, on his return, smears the decorated cord with butter and leaves it in the moonlight during the night. The two ghosts, the one of the placenta attached to the *mulongo* and the other of the dead king attached to the *Lwanga,* are brought together in the tomb or shrine and form a perfect god to whom offerings are made.[15]

The Hindus treat the umbilical cord in the following manner: the cord is cut with a knife at a distance of two inches from the navel. This piece is buried, with turmeric and salt, in a corner of the accouchement-room. The piece that remains is smeared at the end with a little musk and tied with cotton thread; the latter is wound loosely around the neck of the child and remains thus until it gets dry and separates from the navel. It takes from four to seven days for the cord to fall off. The navel is then filled with a native preparation of dentifrice, and a copper piece is put on top and tied with a piece of cloth around the belly.[16] Among the Palaungs, "when the navel cord that is attached to the child drops off, it is kept with great care, as it is believed to be a remedy for toothache, if rubbed on an aching tooth. The string that had been tied round it is buried."[17] Among the Maoris, who had the curious belief that the unborn child receives nourishment through the fontanelles, which they called "food-holes," the umbilical cord of a chief's son was often placed under a stone or on a tree at the boundary of the tribal lands to maintain and strengthen the tribal influence over such boundary. At Te Ariki is a tree in which the cord of a priest's child was hidden, and the hole closed with a piece of precious greenstone; this latter addition was thought to enhance the *mana* of the umbilical cord.[18]

As the umbilical cord was considered by certain Indians of Canada to be closely connected with the child's disposition, care was taken to bury it in the woods to make a boy fond of hunting, near the lodge or in the garden to make a girl fond of domestic duties. If an animal found and devoured the cord, the child was likely to resemble that animal in disposition.[19] There was a sort of imitative magic in the treatment of the umbilical cord by the Kwakiutl. When the cord dropped off, the father, if he wished the child to become rich, tied it up and put it in a box in which he kept his expensive copper. "Therefore the child will be able to obtain coppers easily when he becomes really a man." When it is desired that the owner of an after-birth should understand the cries of the raven—which is an important thing to know, for the raven warns

15 Roscoe, in JAI, XXXII, 33.
16 Sukthankar, in JASB, I, 403.
17 Milne, *Eastern Clan*, 284.

18 Best, in AAAS, 1898, 773; in JAI, XLIV, 133.
19 Harrington, in AA, XV, 212-213.

of the advancing enemy—the after-birth is left on the beach where the ravens peck at it. If the parents desire the boy to become a seal-hunter, they give his navel-string to a successful hunter who puts it between the prongs of his harpoon-shaft; if they wish him to be a canoe-maker, they slip it under the deerskin lashing of the adze of a canoe-builder; if a song-leader, it is inserted in a hole in the end of a baton; if a salmon-fisherman, they put it into the neck-ring of a man who catches many fish; indeed, "all the expert workmen wear the navel-strings of boys, and wear them around their necks." The same thing is done with the navel-strings of girls: they are worn around the wrist by women basket-makers or around the neck by women who know how to dry halibut or how to cut salmon, or by those who know how to dig clams, so that the girl when she grows up will be successful in these occupations. "When they wish a girl or a boy to be a good dancer when he or she grows up, they put the navel-string of the girl around the legs of a woman who is a good dancer; and when she knows well how to tremble with her hands, they put it around the wrist of her right hand. They do this, that the girl may know well how to tremble with her hands when she dances. And they do the same with the navel-string of the boy; it is put around the wrist of an expert cannibal-dancer, that he may become a good dancer when he grows up."[20] A charm common to Sioux, Cheyennes, and Arapahoes consists of a small piece of the navel-string of new-born children, which is enclosed in a case made of buckskin, decorated with porcupine-quills and beads, and hung about the necks of women or tied to the clothing of children up to the age of six or seven years.[21]

The hair, often thought to be the seat of the soul, forms another type of exuvial fetish.[22] In Central Australia hair is associated with what we may call helpful magic. When a man dies his hair is cut off and made up into a girdle called by a native term which means "grave-flesh." "This, which descends to a son, is one of the most sacred possessions of a native, and when worn during a fight endows the possessor with all the warlike attributes of the dead warrior, and ensures to him accuracy of aim, and at the same time destroys that of his adversary. How sacred it is may be judged from the fact that as yet only one has passed into the possession of white men."[23] Among the Euallayi tribe a lock of hair is a token of hate rather than of love.[24] In Punjab the hair of a child, when cut off, is put into a silver amulet and carried about with one. It is deemed sacred. If one have it, no evil influence can prevail over him.[25] Among the Cree a little hair is sometimes cut off from the head or body of an old person and saved. That it is a fetish is evidenced by the fact that "it is asked from time to time to give the survivors a blessing." A mourning-custom of the Dakota shows the connection between the hair and a spirit: "A lock of hair of the deceased is taken and kept in a bundle which is placed in the rear of the lodge in the sacred place. After a time a feast is given, and a person of the same age and sex of the departed takes the clothes making up the bundle and eats the food. The lock of hair is then buried and the spirit remaining in the hair is thought to leave." The death-bundle, containing a lock of the deceased person's hair and supposed to harbor one of his spirits, was kept by the central Algonquins.[26] The Papuans of the Loyalty Islands set up the skulls of the dead as household gods and appealed to them for aid in diffi-

---

20 Boas, in BAE, XXXV, pt. I, 606, 607,
655 (quoted), 697, 698 (quoted), 699 (quoted).
21 Grinnell, *Cheyenne*, II, 110-111.
22 §213, of the text.

23 Gillen, in AAAS, 1901, 115-116.
24 Parker, *Euahlayi Tribe*, 32.
25 Rose, in JAI, XXXVII, 258.
26 Skinner, in AA, XVI, 74; XXI, 169.

culty.[27] The New Caledonians, in cases of sickness and other calamities, presented offerings of food to the skulls of the departed. "The bodies of the common people as well as those of the chiefs were treated thus. The teeth of old women were taken to the yam plantation as a charm for a good crop, and their skulls were also erected there on poles for the same purpose."[28] A fetish among the Fan, which the headman carries to war, is a tin canister containing portions of the skull of a male albino and of a chimpanzee, red powder, and a variety of native medicine.[29] The Filipinos preserved the hair and sometimes the skulls of the deceased as sacred relics.[30] The Maoris sometimes kept skull-fetishes and in one instance they cut off the head of an Englishman, believing that it had the gift of prophecy and that through its aid they would be rendered bullet-proof and gain victory.[31]

In South America too the skull of the deceased is a common exuvial fetish; especially is this true of the Indians of Ecuador who have an elaborate ceremony connected with the *tsantsa* or shrunken head. Their practices appear to rest on certain fundamental ideas: that in the trophy is seated the spirit or soul of the killed enemy; that the spirit, attached to the head, is thirsting for revenge and is trying to harm the slayer in every possible way; that in case this danger is neutralized through the different rites of the feast, the trophy is changed into a fetish, a thing charged with supernatural power which the victor may make use of in different ways and in various departments of life. If all rites are properly performed, the tsantsa becomes a source of blessing to the slayer himself and his whole family. "The power which the trophy is supposed to possess, of course, is due to the spirit attached to it, just as the natural magical power of the living human body depends upon the soul or vitality inherent in it. The souls or spirits of dead men are endowed with an especial energy and potency, and among the Jibaros, as among other South American Indians, all gods, spirits, and demons seem to be nothing but departed human souls." The ceremonies at the feast have as object to protect the victor against the spirit of his enemy and also to increase by artificial means the natural power of the trophy, in much the same way that a battery is charged with electric force.[32]

In all ages miscellaneous relics of the dead have been preserved as fetishes, any part of the body serving for the purpose. The Loyalty Islanders preserved finger-nails, teeth, and tufts of hair. "These seemed to be their principal idols. The priests, when they prayed, tied on to their foreheads, or to their arms above the elbow, a small bag containing such relics of their forefathers."[33] In each house in San Cristoval, "relics of the dead are preserved, the skull, or jawbone, a tooth, or hair. These are placed in a coconut leaf basket, and hung up at the top of the main post of the house. Sacrifices are burnt below and the smoke and savour of the burnt sacrifices ascends and is pleasing to the ghost."[34] The most striking feature of the funeral-customs of other Melanesians is that the skull and certain bones are taken from the body, the skull being kept and the bones worn, while certain limb-bones are made into spatulæ, with which relatives feign to take lime. The jawbone of the dead man is worn by his widow, and his vertebræ and phalanges by his wife's brothers

27 Peschel, *Races*, 345.
28 Turner, *Samoa*, 342-343.
29 Trilles, *Fâñ*, 349, 359.
30 Montero y Vidal, *Filipinas*, I, 57.
31 Friedmann, *Wahnideen*, 238-239.

32 Karsten, "Jibaro," in BAE, Bull. LXXIX, 22-78, 87, 88 (quoted); Roth, in BAE, XXXVIII, 589.
33 Turner, *Samoa*, 338.
34 Fox and Drew, in JAI, XLV, 166.

and his own children of both sexes. The dead woman's lower jaw is worn by her husband, while her cervical vertebræ are worn by her mother-in-law and her husband's sisters, the former also wearing a number of her phalanges. In some cases the dead man's jaw is worn as a bracelet by one of his children.[35] What immediately strikes the eye of the traveller in British New Guinea is the habit of wearing round the neck a dried human hand with the flesh and nails adhering and complete. To touch, the hand was quite pliable; it had evidently been smoke-dried. The writer[36] concluded that the hands were those of enemies. He also noticed "many men wearing necklaces of human bones and jaws," which he took to be those of relatives. He goes on to say that the upper Koko people, when making signs of hostility, instead of following the orthodox practice of drawing the hand across the throat, did the same to the wrist.

Relics take a noteworthy part in charms throughout India. "Not only are things brought from Lhāsa credited with occult virtue because of their association with that holy city, but dust from temples, scrapings from sacred rocks, leaves of sacred trees, the coverings of idols, bits of robes of re-incarnated Lāmas and other holy men, and even the nail parings and bodily refuse of the Grand Lāma, are similarly honoured."[37] Among some tribes a fragment of the charred remains of the funeral-pyre on which a man dying on a Sunday or a Tuesday has been cremated on the very day of his death, is valued as a powerful charm against many diseases. "Such a piece of charcoal is hung on the neck of a sick man with fresh thread which has never come in contact with water or other liquid. But such charm, to be efficacious, must have been brought from the burning-place the very night following the cremation, and the person bringing it must have gone to the cremation place stark naked. . . . Similarly, a mushroom growing on the remnant of a log of wood used in burning a corpse is believed to be a powerful remedy for hysteria. . . . A sword with which human blood has been shed and death caused, is believed to acquire a most powerful energy through contact with blood and death. In fact, the Orāons and the Mūndās say that a powerful spirit 'rides' on such a sword. Thenceforth the sword becomes an object of religious awe. It is carefully suspended against the inner wall of the owner's house, and at every festival a few drops of liquor are offered to the sword."[38] A few years ago, according to the newspapers, some Hindus in California tried to get the nails from the little fingers and the second toes, four teeth from the mouth, and a small disk of skull from the body of a Hindu who had been murdered.[39] Wilkins[40] states that except in the case of Krishna's bones being preserved in the image of Jagannātha at Puri and the parts of Parvati being preserved in these temples, there is no regard for relics shown by the Hindus. Enshrined in Kandy, a mountain town on the island of Ceylon, is an alleged tooth of Buddha. This "holy tooth" is to the Buddhists what the Holy Sepulcher at Jerusalem is to the Christians, and what the birthplace at Mecca of the greatest of Arabian prophets is to the Mohammedans. It is believed by the pilgrims to its shrine to have come from the sacred mouth of Gautama Buddha, the founder of their faith. As a matter of fact, this profoundly venerated object looks suspiciously like the tooth of a wild boar or a monkey. "If Buddha ever carried this tooth in his head and the rest of his teeth were of proportionate size his mouth must

35 Seligmann, *Melanesians*, 718-719, 721, 722.
36 Chinnery, in JAI, XLIX, 281-282.
37 Hildburgh, in JAI, XXXIX, 389.
38 Roy, in JAI, XLIV, 334.
39 N. Y. *Sun*, Mar. 1, 1916.
40 *Mod. Hinduism*, 253.

have been as large and ferocious as that of a gorilla."[41] Lip-amulets are common in the Indian Archipelago; if made from the mouth of a still-born child, they will whisper warnings. The skin of an unborn child is also used to foresee the future, while other exuviæ of a child are used as amulets.[42]

The Guiana Indians, believing that familiar spirits often ensconce themselves inside bones taken from a grave, wrap these up with cotton into grotesque figures, and expect them to give oracles: "they say it is the Spirit of the Dead that talks. They sometimes put the hairs, or some bones, of their deceased parents into a calabash. They keep these in their huts, and use them for some sorcery. They say that the spirit of the dead one speaks through these, and forewarns them of the designs of their enemies. More than this, bones prepared with cotton, as above mentioned, are used for bewitching their enemies, and for this purpose the sorcerers wrap them up with something that belongs to their enemy." Some of the tribes exhumed bones or bodies, burned them, and drank the ashes mixed with liquor.[43] Again, dice are fashioned from the thigh-bone of some celebrated player, much as horses' bridles are ornamented with the tail of some celebrated racer[44]—a logical method, once granted the major premise, of improving luck.

"And it came to pass, as they were burying a man, that, behold, they spied a band of men; and they cast the man into the sepulchre of Elisha: and when the man was let down, and touched the bones of Elisha, he revived, and stood up on his feet."[45] This is one of the early examples of the miraculous power of relics. "The adoration of relics among the Sunnites and Shiites has assumed just as repulsive a form as in Buddhism or in the Christian church."[46]

The press of today recurrently reports miracles connected with relics, and often goes into historic detail concerning the latter. We cite representative cases. A few years ago thousands of pilgrims from all parts of the Orient flocked to Goa, a Portuguese possession on the east coast of India, to view the exposure for the first time in twelve years of the incorruptible body of St. Francis Xavier, the first Jesuit missionary to India and the Apostle of the Orient, who in 1542 carried Christianity to the Far East. Thousands of Christians and Hindus were allowed to view the body and to kiss the feet of the saint. A Delhi correspondent, who was present, wrote in part as follows: "The right arm is missing, having been removed by order of the Pope in 1614 and divided into four parts, the largest of which is enshrined in . . . Rome. The fourth and fifth toes of the right foot are also missing, one having been bitten off in 1554 by a Portuguese lady . . . in a frenzy of religious zeal. Indeed, it was the vandalism of relic hunters that led to the abandoning of the annual exposition of the body."[47] A famous saint whose relics are highly revered in this country, and more especially in Canada, is Ste. Anne. Her first shrine on this continent was established on the banks of the St. Lawrence river above Montreal, at a little village which subsequently became known as Ste. Anne de Beaupré. It has been visited by thousands of people and many miraculous cures have been ascribed to the relics. The crypt of Ste. Anne is supposed to have been discovered by Charlemagne, toward the close of the eighth century; then the chief cities of Gaul begged a portion of the body, and fragments

41 N. Y. *Tribune*, Illus. Suppl., Mar. 5, 1905.
42 Wilken, in VG, IV, 76.
43 Roth, in BAE, XXX, 168 (quoted); and in XXXVIII, 642.

44 Latcham, in JAI, XXXIX, 350.
45 II Kings, XIII, 21.
46 Pischon, *Islam*, 50; Lea, *Inquisition*, I, 48.
47 N. Y. *Times*, May 26, 1923.

found their way to privileged destinations through the favor of princes or powerful prelates. The arm is said to have been put under the care of the monastery of St. Paul-Outside-the-Walls at Rome. From one of the hands, deposited in the Cathedral of Carcassonne, a finger-joint was in 1669 bestowed on Francis de Montmorency-Laval, first bishop of Quebec; and from the same source, we are told, came the relic of Ste. Anne, which Mgr. Marquis obtained in Rome in behalf of Quebec. It is this last relic which now reposes at the church of Ste. Anne de Beaupré. There are said to be two churches in Connecticut where there are relics of this saint: at St. Louis's in New Haven and at a French church in Bristol. Many cures have been reported in both places. Yearly the devout throng to make a special *novena,* and on July 26, Ste. Anne's Day, visit the church and touch the relic to attain cures.[48] It is stated that an exuvial fetish of another sort was discovered in 1924 in the National Library of Paris; it was the embalmed heart of Voltaire, in a small casket beside a plaster bust of the famous man.[49]

§250. The House-Fetish.

THE Melanesian Koita formerly buried their dead in front of their houses; this was done because "man no like pig and dog, take him [*i.e.,* pig or dog] long way from village, must bury him in street."[1] The natives of British New Guinea have an intense desire to keep the remains of dead relatives near them. "The old custom on the coast, both on the south and on the north coast, was for a dead body to be buried in or under the house or in the village. The government have forcibly compelled the natives to give up this custom. At Maiva, on the south coast, it once became the custom for the natives to openly bury the body in the appointed cemetery, and for them to secretly exhume it afterwards and to bury it in or under the house. In Mekeo it became the custom for the natives to go and live for two or three weeks in the cemetery after a relative had been buried."[2] Such is the tenacity of religious customs.

On the Upper Congo most bodies were buried in or near one or other of the houses belonging to the deceased.[3] The Wawanga of East Africa bury all their dead—males lying on their right side, females on their left; "married men are interred in the chief wife's hut, between the centre pole and right wall, looking towards the door; that is to say, feet at centre pole, heads towards wall. Women, children, and unmarried males are buried under the verandah of the hut—males to the right, females to the left of doorway; in both cases the feet towards the door."[4] The fetishistic nature of the threshold is clearly seen among the Hausa, where "the threshold is a dangerous spot, and children, who do not understand this, are always coming to grief there, their falls being due entirely to the presence of the spirits." Before the owner has completed a new building he must offer up a sacrifice at the threshold.[5]

With the exception of two tribes, all the Nagas bury their dead in the ground either close by the village or in the village-streets in front of the houses, or, in the case of a young child that dies or one that is born dead, inside the house, under the earthen floor. Furness[6] was told by a Sema Naga, who pointed

48 N. Y. *Times,* Jan. 1, 1924; N. H. *Journal-Courier,* July 18, 1917; July 27, 1918.
49 N. Y. *Times,* Feb. 17, 1924.
1 Seligmann, *Melanesians,* 161.
2 Strong, in JAI, XLIX, 297.

3 Weeks, in JAI, XXXIX, 452.
4 Dundas, in JAI, XLIII, 33.
5 Tremearne, in JAI, XLV, 28, 61.
6 In JAI, XXXII, 462; Hutton, *Sema Nagas,* 243-244.

out to him on the floor of his house the newly made grave of his little girl, that he had buried her there because she would be so frightened to be left out in front of the house with nothing but the sky above her at night. In Assam the graves are in front of the houses in the village.[7] The Samoans dug graves close by the house, while the natives of the Mitchell Group buried the dead inside the house.[8] The Tahitians often buried their dead in the *marae* or social center; a chief's grave, a temple, and a sacred enclosure were all one. "The presence of pyramids on the green is only natural since kings' and chiefs' tombs were often pyramidal, so it was at least in Tonga, and it is possible that the circular guest house in Samoa is derived from a pyramid."[9]

The Creeks usually buried their dead in a square pit under the bed where the deceased lay in his house.[10] The custom of burying the dead in the house was common in Brazil, and, according to von Martius,[11] injurious to health. Among the Guiana Indians the site for the burial of the dead was either the deceased's own house or its neighborhood, though special localities or cemeteries were not unknown. Among certain tribes some of the large houses have more than a hundred graves in them, but when the houses are small and very full the graves are made outside.[12]

§251. Hearth- and Altar-Fetishes.

In Melanesia and Polynesia that which localized the sacred ceremonies was the worship of spirits or departed souls at graves. Hence these became a place of worship at which was later added the service of other spirits and gods.[1] The *marae* or village-centers of the Polynesians, in which chiefs and kings were buried, were sacred enclosures containing pyramidal structures; they were places of sacrifice and worship. Many religious emblems were there, and there also were performed the religious ceremonies.[2] Among both peoples "certain weird spots in the bush, or on the mountains or seashore are tremblingly passed or avoided, as the dwelling-places of demons and spirits of the dead."[3] Among the Fijians and other Melanesians the *nanga* or sacred enclosure was the earthly dwelling-place of the ancestral spirits. The first fruits of the yam-harvest were always piled in the *nanga* and allowed to rot there; warriors before entering on an expedition always repaired to the *nanga* to be made invulnerable.[4]

In West Africa two different forms of shrines or temples have arisen from the method of burial. In one case, the corpse is buried in an underground cave, with a narrow passageway leading to the interior; dirt is prevented from falling in by walling the sides; upon the grave is erected a mound of stones. The two main characteristics of this form of burial give us the pyramid: a passage under the earth and a stone mound. The second type of temple also comes from the method of burial. When anyone on the Loango coast dies, a little hut is erected over his coffin and foodstuffs deposited there. On the north Guinea coast a little hut is built over the grave, containing everything the person used when living. In other places the bones of the deceased are preserved, dried, and enclosed in a wooden box, which is then deposited in an especially erected little house. Similar to these fetish-huts of the West Afri-

7 Hodson, in JAI, XXXVI, 96.
8 Turner, *Samoa*, 147, 281.
9 Hocart, in AA, XX, 458.
10 HAI, I, 364.
11 *Beiträge*, 598.

12 Roth, in BAE, XXXVIII, 639.
1 Ratzel, *Vkde.*, II, 327.
2 Hocart, in AA, XX, 456.
3 Ella, in AAAS, 1887, 493.
4 Webster, in JAI, XLI, 506.

cans are those, often only two feet high, which Livingstone found in the villages of the Mangaja—huts erected at the death of a relative in which a share of the best food and drink was left, so that the souls might be refreshed.[5] In Abyssinia, Bent[6] noticed the pyramidal type of tomb. As in the case of the Melanesians and Polynesians, the grave of a hero, chief, or king, with a mound or stone erected over it, becomes a temple, meeting-place, and center of tribal life. It often becomes a sanctuary as well. Throughout the Elgon district of East Africa there are certain places where a fugitive from justice may take refuge: "such spots are usually the burial places of great chiefs and are regarded as sacred; for instance, the cemetery of the Wawanga kings. If a man take refuge in a sanctuary, the owners of the same are bound to protect him and prevent others following him, even by the force of arms. As soon, however, as the fugitive leaves the sanctuary, he may be apprehended."[7]

At the highest point of a pass in Central Asia is a Buddhist shrine to which natives from all about bring rude gifts, such as horse-hair and camel-hair; they even leave empty bottles.[8] The Todas of the Nilgiris have a temple-hut,[9] while in Hindustan is a shrine which imitates in stone an old mound over a grave with an altar on top.[10] The Mongols regard the threshold of the tent as a fetish-place which visitors must not touch; nor may one handle the tent-ropes, "for they are held to represent the threshold of the door." The author's[11] companion unwittingly touched the threshold when backing out of the tent; he was arrested but got off with a reprimand. On Mindanao, in the Philippines, "in every house, even the poorest, is the *tambara*, the little bowl containing the usual offerings, the simplest form of house-altar. The greatest of their altars, the *patanon*, or war-altar, is also a house-altar. The erection of this altar is allowed to only a very few high datos, and is connected with their most important festival, which occurs sometime during rice planting." The Bagobos have other altars for different places and different occasions; "altars for the planting of their corn or rice; for the cutting of their crops; and very often they place an altar with their offerings near a great tree or a beautiful spring or running water, especially if the water is to be used for any ceremony of purification."[12]

The graves of shamans among the Tlinkits are located at some little distance from the village on a small island, conspicuous point, or high promontory, sometimes selected by themselves before death. The sepulcher itself consists of a small pen or enclosure of logs, usually elevated above the ground on four short posts. These are fetish-places, and "whenever an Indian passes one of them in his canoe he drops an offering of some value (usually a piece of tobacco) into the water to propitiate the *yake* of the deceased and bring fair winds and good luck to the superstitious donor." The Haida commonly put the ashes of the dead in a box within a mortuary column, while if the body was buried rather than cremated they erected commemorative columns in front of the house of the deceased, the body being deposited at some distance from it.[13] The American Indians commonly placed altar-shrines near springs, rivers, caves, rocks, or trees on mountains and near spots which certain deities were supposed to inhabit, "in the belief that the roads of these deities

5 Frobenius, *Masken*, 169-172.
6 *Ethiopians*, 77.
7 Dundas, in JAI, XLIII, 51, 52.
8 Prjevalski, *Forskningsresor*, 211.
9 Modi, in JASB, VII, 77.

10 Lippert, *Kgchte.*, II, 211.
11 Rubruck, *Eastern Parts*, 123, 184, 188, 192.
12 Metcalf, in AA, XIV, 163.
13 Niblack, in USNM, 1888, 353, 355, 356.

extend from these localities."[14] All springs of water are places of prayers
and offerings, and each has a shrine either near by or remote. Some shrines are
known by the character of their offerings; thus, as a warrior's shrine contains
netted shields, bows, and arrows, an eagle-shrine is furnished with painted
wooden imitations of eagle-eggs. Shrines sometimes mark places where mythological events are said to have happened; thus, "the shrine of the so-called
Heart-Contained-Here, in the foothills east of Walpi, is supposed to contain
the heart of a god who won a mythic foot-race. Those who aspire to speed in
these races worship at this shrine." A Hopi shrine is said to differ from an
altar in being a place in which the offerings remain permanently or until
they or their essence are supposed to have been removed by the gods.[15] The
Zuñi employ caverns as shrines and as depositories for images of their gods
and the painted bones of animals, and caves have an important place in the
genesis-myths of many tribes. "Burial in caves was common, and chambers
of various depths from the surface were used. Pits and crevices in the rocks
were also repositories for the dead."[16] One burial cave is called by a term
meaning "where the dead are dancing."[17] Whenever a permanent village of
earth lodges was established by the Osage and Kansa, there was a regular consecration of a certain number of fire-places before the ordinary hearths could
be made by the common people. "The consecrated fireplaces were made in
two parallel rows, beginning at the west and ending at the east. Four sticks
were placed in the fireplace, one pointing to each corner of the compass."[18]
The Indians of Virginia bestowed the greatest labor upon their temples; "these
buildings were about 20 by 100 feet, with the door to the east so as to catch
the first sunlight. There was a chancel at the western end, approached by a
labyrinthine passage, and here were placed many black images with their faces
turned to the east. The principal temple was situated at Uttamussack, on the
modern Pamunkey, and on either side of it stood buildings 60 feet long, containing effigies of kings and devils, and the royal mummies. The treasure-
house of Powhatan at Orepaks was doubtless a still more imposing structure;
it was 50 or 60 yards long, and upon each of its four corners was placed a
figure of a strange and grotesque aspect, one having the shape of a dragon,
another the head and form of a bear, a third that of a leopard, and the fourth
a gigantic man."[19]

Not far from old Babylon lie the graves of Ali and his son, which are fetish-
places to which pilgrims travel year in and year out from all Persia. A burial
in the neighborhood of these holy ones wipes out all sins, wherefore many Persians have themselves buried there.[20] Like the Aztecs, the Israelites took their
portable temple on their wanderings, and one may conclude that they once
carried the bodies of their tribal heroes. For the Israelites this is not easily
demonstrable, yet they took the body of Joseph out of Egypt with them and
buried it after the entrance into Canaan. Presumably the tabernacle was
originally a fetish-hut of the dead. The ark was a receptacle for fetishes; the
tablets of the law were placed in it. It was the palladium first of the family,
then of the tribe, and later of the people. Not only was it the Ark of the
Covenant but also a war-altar and a religious shrine.[21] According to one

14 Hough, in HAI, I, 46.
15 Fewkes, "Shrines," in HAI, II, 558, 559.
16 Holmes, "Caves," in HAI, I, 222.
17 HAI, II, 28.
18 Dorsey, in BAE, XI, 381.

19 Bruce, *Va.*, I, 148.
20 Hauri, *Islam*, 111.
21 Ex., XXV, 16; XL, 40; Maurer, *Vkde.*,
I, 66-67, 68-69; Kautsch, in *Hastings's Dict.
Bible*, Suppl. Vol., 628-629.

writer,[22] the Greek temples had their prototype in the house (for human beings and cattle together) of the Roumanian Alp-land. In Rome the first domestic altar was the hearth; as the local center and symbol of domestic intercourse, it was at the same time the altar upon which sacrifices were made to the household gods. What the hearth was to the individual family the hearth of Vesta was to the collective nation.[23]

§252. The "Word."

THERE is magic in words, written or spoken, for fetishes are not limited to material things.[1] When Nieuwenhuis[2] was travelling in Borneo he was once asked to drive out of some children the evil spirit which possessed them and made them obstinate, by reading out of a book. The Yaos of Central Africa have in recent years come under the influence of Mohammedan tenets which they merely graft on to their still cherished belief in the old faiths of their fathers. The Koran, or a few of its texts, are added to the many other charms they have already hung about their necks.[3] Fetishism is certainly implied in the notion that a holy book is the sum and source of all revelation. "Every prophet has uniformly drawn therefrom; indeed they become prophets through the holy book being made accessible to them or, as the technical expression puts it, being sent down to them. From it each of them gets insight from time to time, according as it is required, and draws out piecemeal the particular revelations which are in keeping with the time and people. This notion is highly developed in the Koran, and it significantly appears in the oldest suras."[4]

Among the Chaldæans the conjurations did not always work; the most powerful daimons were not frightened at them. But there was a power before which all on earth, both good and bad spirits, bowed and that was the authoritative god-name, "the highest name," the name of the god.[5] How powerful was the word of a god may be seen in the ancient versions of creation. "Through the word, that is, through the magic power of his formula and the correct tone in which he spoke, created he the world."[6] "Ahuramazda made the universe, not by the work of his hands but by the magic of his word."[7] His living word was before all things, good or evil. "It is the will of Ormuzd"—spoken several times—vanquished Ahriman. The Parsees say that Zoroaster's living word gave back new life to the world consumed by demons. The Avesta scatters demons; like the Koran and the Bible it is a fetish.[8] In the Middle Ages the eucharist, as ritual, was a fetish, and so was the Lord's prayer.[9] The word "Word" became too great for common use, as it meant the Word of God, so the Romance languages adopted "parabola," or derivatives from it like the French *parole*, for "word."[10] A common element of all religions is the Law; with the notion of the Word of God in Law fetishism becomes mysticism.[11]

22 Chamberlain, in AA, IX, 753.
23 De Marchi, *Culto Priv.*, rev. in *Année Soc.*, I, 125; Ihering, *Aryan*, 45.
1 §301, of the text.
2 *Borneo*, I, 120.
3 Hetherwick, in JAI, XXXII, 89.
4 Wellhausen, *Skizzen*, III, 210-211.
5 Lehmann, *Overtro*, I, 49-50.

6 Tiele-Gehrich, *Gchte. Relig.*, I, 42.
7 Maspero, *Hist. Anc.*, III, 583.
8 Lippert, *Kgchte.*, II, 459.
9 Lea, *Inquisition*, I, 49; Lippert, *Kgchte.*, II, 617.
10 Mauthner, *Sprache*, II, 184.
11 Lippert, *Kgchte.*, I, 100; II, 458.

§253. The Image.

IMAGES carved in a rude likeness of a man are common in Melanesia. Codrington[1] mentions some in San Cristoval which represent a man climbing up to shoot an opossum, the animal looking down upon him from the top of the pole. "This would hardly be taken for an idol, but is as much an idol as many figures which have found their way into museums as such. The canoe-houses, common halls, public-houses, called in those parts *oha*, were full of carvings in the constructive as well as decorative parts. Some of these, the posts for example which support the ridge-poles and purlins, are often figures of men, who would be loosely called ancestors by the principal people of the village, and these would be treated with respect; sometimes food and betel-nuts would be seen laid before them. But these had no sacred character, further than that they were memorials of deceased great men, whose ghosts visiting their accustomed abodes would be pleased at marks of memory and affection, and irritated by disrespect." In the New Hebrides images of the dead whose death-feasts are to be celebrated are very elaborately prepared, not with any attempt at representing the figure of the particular deceased but in conventional form; in the same islands "drums are set up for funeral feasts with fantastic faces cut upon them, and these remain as in a manner images of the deceased, taken by visitors for idols or devil-drums." On the same islands an image of split bamboo is made to resemble the deceased warrior or chief as much as possible. "It is hollow and plastered with clay, carved wood being used to represent arms, legs, etc. The head is smeared with clay, and modelled and painted so as to be a fair likeness of the dead. It is put on the model and the whole is set up in the god's house or temple, with the weapons and small personal effects of the deceased. Probably these images are worshipped."[2] Whether worshipped or not, they are distinctly fetishes, as is seen by the treatment accorded them. The Savage Islanders say that a long time ago, in the time of a great epidemic, they paid religious homage to an image which had legs like a man; then, thinking the sickness was caused by the idol, they broke it in pieces and threw it away.[3] Images consisting of carved posts are to be found at graves in Bathurst Island,[4] while the large wooden figures in Papua are certainly images of ancestors.[5]

In the northern part of the Congo, when one dear to them dies, the natives make a wooden statuette to which they give the name of the deceased and which they preserve in their huts.[6] Schweinfurth[7] says the true object of certain wooden figures found over the graves of the Bongo and other tribes is simply to constitute a memorial of some one who has departed this life; this is proved by the term, meaning "the figure of the wife," which is applied to an image raised by a surviving husband to the memory of his deceased wife and set up in the hut as a species of Penates. Stuhlmann[8] says there are scarcely any idols as embodiments of gods in all East Africa. West of Lake Albert he found in the grass a wooden female image which he calls a doll in memory of a deceased person. At a drought in Nigeria some liquor is thrown three times, after three incantations, on each corner of a special stone about two feet high, which is set up for the occasion in the grove and is supposed to be inhabited

1 *Melanesians*, 173, 174, 175.
2 Flower, in JAI, XI, 76.
3 Turner, *Samoa*, 306.
4 Basedow, in JAI, XLIII, 314 ff.

5 Hagen, *Papua's*, 275.
6 Henning, in *Globus*, LXXII, 104.
7 *Heart of Africa*, I, 285, 383.
8 *Mit Emin*, 189, 478.

for the time by the supreme god.[9] An African image and magical instrument is the war-drum of the Marutse: it is made of wood, painted with dark red ocher, the head being the tightly-drawn hide of a cow, with strips, still covered with hair, going around the instrument. The hairless drum-head is spotted with blood from the wounds of a boy whose fingers and toes have been cut off, as a sort of "foundation-sacrifice."[10]

In central Asia are big dark caves with colossal painted figures of gods, presenting an uncanny appearance.[11] A Korean expiatory offering consists of a bundle of straw tied with hoops of straw into the outline of the head and trunk of a man; arms and legs are fastened to the body.[12] The lamas in Tibet mix some of the ashes from a cremation with clay, making oval or circular molds, which they stamp with the image of Buddha; these are preserved in the shrines by the wayside or in the houses of the relatives. If made from the ashes of holy men, they are retained in the monasteries, where they can be purchased by the devout.[13] Among the Palaungs, until an image of the Buddha has been dedicated, it may be treated with scant ceremony, simply as a block of stone, valuable on account of the price that has been paid for it but in no way sacred; after it has been consecrated, it must not touch the ground and no woman should lay her hand on it. "Candles are set in a row in front, then, when all is ready, the monks come from the monastery and the chief monk blesses the image, which is thenceforth considered sacred. This is called the 'life-giving' ceremony." When a person sees a snake he is sometimes terrified, and the fright makes him ill; "in such a case it is good to make a picture of a snake and then make an offering to the picture."[14] Carved wooden effigies of the dead are placed above graves by the Naga and other frontier tribes of northeast India.[15] In epic Hinduism "all the weapons of the heroes are inspired with and impelled by *mantras*," or charms.[16] In Kafiristan female effigies are erected to the memory of the deceased one year after the funeral-ceremonies.[17]

Any one who visits northern India must desire to know the meaning of the little black stones under every conspicuous tree, which are so evidently set up for worship. They are said by Europeans to be of phallic origin; but if so, Hindus are no more conscious of the fact than we of the similar origin of the May-pole. Wherever one goes he finds them—by the roadsides in cities and villages, on the river-banks, or inside the entrance to a garden—wherever there is a tree that stands alone. The small stone pillar, called the *lingam*—the word meaning, literally, "symbol"—may have been taken from the bed of a stream, in which case it is likely to be of a long egg-shape. If it has been cut by the hand of man, it is short and slightly tapering, with a thimble-like top. Sometimes, in all good faith, the features of a human face have been more or less crudely marked on it, with white paint. In any case, it is only a question of time till some woman, passing by on her way from bathing, stops to pour a little water or sprinkle a few grains of rice tenderly over the head of the stone.[18] Some assert that there is nothing erotic about it.[19] In front of a village on the Rejang river in Borneo "there are four huge effigies, with the genital

9 Tremearne, in JAI, XLII, 163.

10 §294, of the text; Holub, in *Illust. Christian World*, Sept., 1896.

11 Prjevalski, *Forskningsresor*, 177, 178.

12 USNM, 1891.

13 Bishop, *Tibetans*, 107.

14 Milne, *Eastern Clan*, 257, 333-334.

15 Godden, in JAI, XXVII, 36.

16 Hopkins, *Relig. India*, 375.

17 Robertson, in JAI, XXVII, 89.

18 Nivedita, *Indian Life*, 212.

19 Monier-Williams, *Brāhmanism*, 83, 224.

organs as usual fully developed; no indecency is intended, [these] being merely relics of primitive worship."[20] In Indonesia, "under the symbol of the *lingam*—a representation, as is well known, of the sex-organs in the act of copulation—Çiva is earnestly prayed to by young maidens for a speedy marriage."[21]

The drum was a fetish in Polynesia; it was not only associated with a Tane-cult in the erotic dance, but was regarded as Tane's embodiment; "when the drum was beaten, it was Tane that was struck, and from the *kaara's* fissure it was Tane's voice that issued."[22] In Samoa, Finsch[23] discovered a big figure, carved out of a stump in the ground, of a man with a crocodile on his back; this was the image of a chief ancestor. The process of consecration among the Maoris is described as follows: "Some object was selected, often a stone, and over it certain incantations were recited by a priest. This ceremony had the effect of imbuing such object with the sacred life principle of the person, persons, land, hamlet, or forest, that it represented. This object was termed a *mauri*. It was carefully concealed, its hiding place being known to very few persons. So long as the *tapu* of this object was preserved, no arts or spells of black magic could affect the persons, land, or whatever it represented. It preserved, or protected the *Hau* of such persons or lands, that is to say, the sacred life principle, the physical, intellectual, and spiritual vigour and well-being." By this process a spirit is inducted into the object, making it a fetish. Care must be taken lest the indwelling spirit desert the object, leaving it null and void: "If the concealed *mauri* of a village community were found by an enemy, he would at once pollute its sacredness, destroy its *tapu,* whereupon it would no longer possess any power to protect the folk of the hamlet, and they would be open to the attacks of the magic arts of such enemy."[24]

Among the Eskimo the belief prevailed that "in early days all animated beings had a dual existence, becoming at will either like man or the animal form they now wear; if an animal wished to assume its human form the forearm, wing, or other limb was raised and pushed up the muzzle or beak as if it were a mask, and the creature became manlike in form and features. This idea is still held, and it is believed that many animals now possess this power. The manlike form thus appearing is called the *inua,* and is supposed to represent the thinking part of the creature, and at death becomes its shade." The induction of a spirit into an Aleut image was accomplished through certain religious dances and festivals. "During these, images or idols, temporarily prepared, were carried from island to island, and strange ceremonies, of which we have only dim traditions, were performed in the night. There were mysteries sacred to the males, and others to the females. . . . An idea prevailed that while these mystic rites were going on a spirit or power descended into the idol. To look at or see him was death or misfortune, hence they wore large masks carved from drift-wood, with holes cut so that nothing before them or above them could be seen, but only the ground near their feet."[25] Masks as sacred images had an important place in the religious notions of the Indians; paint rubbed from a sacred mask was regarded as efficacious in prayer; and men sometimes invoked their masks, thanking them for services rendered. By some tribes altars were formed by masks set in a row, and

20 Roth, in JAI, XXII, 32.
21 Wilken, in VG, I, 162.
22 March, in JAI, XXII, 328.
23 *Samoafahrten,* 175.

24 Best, in AAAS, 1909, 459.
25 Dall, in BAE, III, 139; Reclus, *Prim. Folk,* 94.

sacred meal was sprinkled upon them. When a man among the Zuñi dons a mask, his body becomes the abiding-place of the spirit of the god and he is worshipped as such; hence he is expected, when chosen to personate a god, so to conduct himself that he will be worthy to fill the sacred office. With the sacred masks there were prescribed methods for consecration and handling; for instance, among the Hopi they were put on or off only with the left hand; certain masks must never be touched by pregnant women. This tribe also observed rites of bodily purification before painting the masks. In the Southwest and the extreme North, little figures were made for ceremonies in which mythic ancestors or dead relatives were recalled. Among the Hopi they are of soft cottonwood, so carved and painted as to indicate in miniature the elaborate head-dress, decorated face, body, and clothing of those who represent *kachinas* or impersonations of ancestral "breath-bodies" or spirits of men. "These dolls are not worshipped, but are made by the priests in their kivas during the great spring ceremonies as presents for the little girls, to whom they are presented on the morning of the last day of the festival by men personating kachinas. In this way the young become familiar with the complicated and symbolic masks, ornaments, and garments worn during tribal and religious ceremonies."[26]

Images in form of animals or birds also were common. The Tuscarora at certain rites raised "three wolf's hides, figuring as many protectors or gods," to which offerings, consisting of their jewels, were made by the women. "In the middle of the circle, the chief shaman performed all manner of contortions, conjurations, and imprecations against the enemies of his country, while the populace danced in a circle around the wolf-hides." A chief of the Mohawks in 1634 showed a European his idol: "it was a head, with the teeth sticking out; it was dressed in red cloth. Others have a snake, a turtle, a swan, a crane, pigeon, or the like for their idols, to tell the fortune; they think they will always have luck in doing so." When the traveller, Van Curler, visited the town of Oneida, he saw a chief's grave at the entrance of which was a "big wooden bird, and all around were painted dogs, and deer, and snakes, and other beasts." Over the gates in the ramparts of the village were three wooden images, like men and adorned with scalps.[27] A human figure or idol has been found in the mounds of the Mississippi valley.[28] A special fetish of the Dakotas was made by using a grooved stone hammer as the head, with a withe tied about the middle of the hammer and the handle wrapped with buckskin or raw hide. "Feathers attached bear mnemonic marks or designs, indicating marks of distinction, perhaps fetichistic devices not understood. These objects are believed to possess the peculiar charm of warding off an enemy's missiles when held upright before the body. . . . Properties are attributed to this instrument similar to those of the small bags prepared by the Shaman, which are carried suspended from the neck by means of string or buckskin cords."[29]

One tribe in Mexico copied Cortez's horse in stone and added it to their idols.[30] Catholics in name, the Mayas of Yucatan in fact prefer to render homage to any stone figure that once ornamented the temples of their forefathers. "We have seen one, kept in a cavern underground, that served as a personification of Balam, for it represented a man with a long beard, and to it they make offerings of corn. . . . This statue is now black, owing to the

26 Fletcher, "Masks," "Dolls," in HAI, I, 814, 815, 395-396; Stevenson, in AA, XI, 40.
27 Hewitt, in HAI, II, 126, 128, 850.
28 Carr, in *Smithson. Rep.*, 1891, 545.
29 Mallery, in BAE, IV, 202.
30 Nadaillac, *Preh. Amer.*, 269.

incense and candles with which its devotees smoke it. Previous to sowing grain they place before it a basin of cool beverage made of corn, also lighted wax candles and sweet-smelling copal, imploring the god to grant them an abundant harvest. When the crops ripen the finest ears are carried to the smoke-begrimed divinity by men, women, and children, who within the cavern dance and pray all day long, some of their quaint instruments serving as accompaniment to the Christian litanies which they chant without having the vaguest idea of their meaning."[31] The idols in Guatemala and San Salvador are fungiform: the figures consist usually of three different parts; a base, a nearly cylindrical middle body upon which are incised the face and parts of the body of a man, and a hat-shaped nearly round upper segment.[32] The Indians who accompanied Von Martius[33] on his travels in Brazil once encountered upon a granite rock five figures with human heads, which they approached with awe, while they cried out "Tupána" (god). Schomburgk had the same experience with some Guiana Indians. The tribes of the Amazon "all worship Idols which they make with their own hands; to one of them they ascribe the authority of governing the waters, and put a fish in his hand in token of his power; they choose others to preside over their seed time, and others to inspire them with courage in their battles; they say these gods came down from Heaven on purpose to dwell with them and to show them kindness. They do not signify their Adoration of these Idols by any outward ceremonies, but on the contrary seem to have forgotten them as soon as they have made them, and putting them in a case let them lie, without taking any notice of them so long as they imagine they have no occasion for their Help; but when they are ready to march out to war, they set up the Idol in which they have placed the hopes of their Victories, at the Prow of their Canoes: so, when they go a fishing, they take that Idol with them to which they attribute the government of the waters."[34]

The ancients held that a spirit could be induced to enter the statue of a king or god, which would then speak as an oracle. According to Chaldæan theological doctrine, the statues in the temple were transubstantiated by consecration into the body of the divinity. The sovereign who dedicated them adjured them to speak in the days to come. "When they were interrogated according to the rite established for each one of them, the portion of the celestial spirit which had been drawn into them by virtue of prayers, and which was there kept captive, could not help but reply." Some of them perhaps were articulated, like those of Egypt, and movable by cords drawn by the prophet. A statue cut in stone could not have enjoyed sacrifices of food, but at its consecration its mouth was opened by a ceremony like that which was called opening the mouth of a mummy or statue of the dead. After that it could enjoy food and drink. The Chaldæan theory of animated and prophetic statues was the same as the Egyptian. A god could distribute his divine spirit among any number of men, beasts, statues, or natural objects. This is the sense of the apparent animal-worship. Without losing any of its religious significance, the statue later became an object of art in the sense that one admired it not only for its mystic utility but also for the way in which the sculptor interpreted his model.[35]

31 Le Plongeon, in PSM, XLIV.
32 Sapper, in Globus, LXXIII, 327.
33 Beiträge, I, 574-575; Schomburgk, Brit.-Guiana, I, 329; II, 225.

34 Roth, in BAE, XXX, 139.
35 Maspero, Hist. Anc., I, 504, 641, 679, 680.

The Old Testament, despite the fact that the representation of Jahweh by any figure is strictly forbidden, is rich in idolatry—and even though a curse is pronounced on the making of a graven or molten image by the hands of a craftsman.[36] Here, as in the Decalogue, the reference is to every species of divine image, including that of Jahweh. Presenting one's self at the sanctuary is spoken of as "beholding the face of Jahweh," which expression certainly referred originally to looking upon the image of the deity. As images of God we must reckon not only the very ancient *pesel* or carved image and the bull-figures (prohibited in Judah), but also the *ephod* and the *teraphim*. There are many passages in which *pesel* means an image of Jahweh, and such a carved image appears to have been for long regarded as unobjectionable, whereas the molten image (probably with allusion to Israel's bull-worship) is already prohibited. "Even if the prohibition of the *pesel* in the Decalogue[37] . . . extends to images of Jahweh, this would be simply proof that the Decalogue (or at least the prohibition of images) originated later than J—a conclusion which is favoured by the circumstance that there were also other species of images of Jahweh which, till far into the monarchical period, continued to be reverenced without opposition, or at least to be employed as a means of obtaining Divine oracles." The *ephod* and, at least from the monarchical period, the *teraphim* as well, were images of Jahweh, and were regarded as quite unobjectionable in the pre-Prophetic period, nay, even as late as Hosea,[38] but at last they were involved in the same condemnation as images of idols proper. The golden bulls set up by Jeroboam at Bethel and Dan were intended as images of Jahweh, and not as heathen images. "It might appear otherwise from the language of the Chronicler,[39] . . . but the truth was still quite evident to the Deuteronomic redactor of the Books of Kings.[40] . . . In like manner the narrative of Exodus,[41] . . . which belongs to the older sources of the Pentateuch, is quite aware that Aaron meant to represent Jahweh by the golden calf which had brought Israel out of Egypt, for he makes him . . . proclaim a feast to Jahweh. But even here the giving of this form to Jahweh is looked upon as a grievous offence on the part of Aaron."[42]

What kind of object was the *ashera*, which is translated in the King James version as "grove"? From one passage[43] it appears to have been either a living tree or a tree-like post; every altar had its *ashera*, even such altars as in the popular, pre-prophetic forms of Hebrew religion were dedicated to Jehovah. It is a thing made by man's hands, an image, a "grisly object."[44] "These expressions may imply that the sacred pole was sometimes carved into a kind of image. That the sacred tree should degenerate first into a mere Maypole, and then into a rude wooden idol, is in accordance with analogies found elsewhere, e.g., in Greece; but it seems quite as likely that the *ashera* is described as a kind of idol simply because it was used in idolatrous cultus." It would seem that later the *ashera* is taken as a symbol of the goddess Astarte, the Asherim being regarded as the female partners of the Baalim: "And the children of Israel did evil in the sight of the Lord, and forgot the Lord their God, and served Baalim and the groves." The pentateuchal law looks on the

36 Deut., IV, 15 ff.; XXVII, 15.
37 Exod., XX, 4 ff.; XXXIV, 17; Deut., V, 8.
38 III, 4.
39 II Chron., XIII, 8, *et al.*
40 I Kings, XII, 28 ff.
41 XXXII, 1 ff.
42 Kautzsch, in *Hastings's Dict. Bible*, 635, 641-642, 643, 680.
43 Deut., XVI, 21.
44 Is., XVII, 8; I Kings, XV, 13; XVI, 33; II Kings, XXI, 7.

use of sacred pillars as idolatrous.[45] "This is the best evidence that such pillars had an important place among the appurtenances of Canaanite temples, and as Hosea[46] speaks of the *masseba* as an indispensable feature in the sanctuaries of northern Israel in his time, we may be sure that by the mass of the Hebrews the pillars of Shechem, Bethel, Gilgal and other shrines were looked upon not as mere memorials of historical events, but as necessary parts of the ritual apparatus of a place of worship." It seems clear that the altar is a differentiated form of the primitive rude stone pillar, the *nosb* or *masseba;* but the sacred stone is more than an altar, for "in Hebrew and Canaanite sanctuaries the altar, in its developed form as a table or hearth, does not supersede the pillar; the two are found side by side at the same sanctuary, the altar as a piece of sacrificial apparatus, and the pillar as a visible symbol or embodiment of the presence of the deity, which in process of time comes to be fashioned and carved in various ways, till ultimately it becomes a statue or anthropomorphic idol of stone, just as the sacred tree or post was ultimately developed into an image of wood." At the time when the oldest of the pentateuchal narratives were written, the Canaanites and the great mass of the Hebrews certainly treated the *masseba* as a sort of idol or embodiment of the divine presence. "Moreover Jacob's pillar is more than a mere landmark, for it is anointed, just as idols were in antiquity, and the pillar itself, not the spot on which it stood, is called 'the house of God,'[47] as if the deity were conceived actually to dwell in the stone, or manifest himself therein to his worshippers." Melcarth was worshipped at Tyre in the form of two pillars; twin pillars stood also before the temples of Paphos and Hierapolis, and Solomon set up two brazen pillars before his temple at Jerusalem.[48] As he named them "The stablisher" and "In him is strength," they were doubtless symbols of Jehovah.[49]

Says Barton:[50] "These objects, whether called *nosbs* or *massebas,* or by whatever name, were in general in the form of rude phalli, and were no doubt chosen as the symbol of Semitic deity because of their resemblance to the organ of the god of life." Such objects have been found in many places and among many peoples. It seems certain that the phallic pictures on vases, statuettes, and the like were not made to gratify obscene propensities; either they were not regarded as obscene and were not noticed any more than we notice exhibitions of face or feet (the face is obscene in Mohammedan countries, and the foot in China) or from ancient usage the exhibition was covered by the convention which justifies the archaic, religious, or theatrical.[51] In the Norse sagas are mentioned figures of gods carved out of the posts of the house-father's seat of honor;[52] while a survival of the image-fetish is to be seen in the agricultural districts of England and Scotland where, during the harvest rejoicings, they use an image called the kern-baby, crowned with wheat-ears and dressed up in finery, with colored ribbons. In the north of

45 Judges, III, 7; Exod., XXXIV, 13; Deut., XII, 3.
46 III, 4.
47 Gen., XXVIII, 22.
48 Herodotus, *Hist.*, II, 44; I Kings, VII, 15, 21.
49 Smith, *Relig. Sem.*, 187-188, 188 (quoted), 189, 191-192, 196, 203 (quoted), 204 (quoted), 208 note, 210; Ward, in *Amer. Jr. Semitic Lang.*, XIX, 33, quoted in *Globus*, LXXXVI, 228.
50 *Sem. Origins*, 137.
51 Smith, *Relig. Sem.*, 457; Rossbach, *Röm. Ehe*, 344-345; Wilson, in USNM, 1894; Reich, *Mimus*, I, 503.
52 Geijer, *Svensk. Hist.*, 113.

England, at harvest time, these figures are made of oats; they are elaborately decorated and set on top of the dresser.[53]

§254. The Extraordinary.

The Extraordinary in General. We begin with a miscellaneous list of oddities, natural and artificial, but always inexplicable except by reference to an indwelling spiritual presence. There is a good deal of difference between throwing a spear by hand and throwing it by means of a throwing-stick, like the Australian *murriwun.* "The blackfellow perceives that the *murriwun* gives the spear a surprising impetus, and not being able to explain its mechanical action, he considers that it is magical. This is a good instance of the manner in which the aboriginal mind works."[1] It is customary to refer the strange and unusual to the ancestral ghosts. The reverence paid by the Australians to their *mooras* or ancestors is largely the reverence of fear, and "anything strange or unusual is set down to them. The Aurora Australis in this way creates great alarm, and to appease the *moora* indiscriminate intercourse is practised." Stones often appear to commemorate the death or disappearance of a *moora;* "trees sometimes spring and seem to have grown up where the *moora* first came or last went." So-called *mooras'* toe-nails were given to the author.[2] To him they were implements of various sorts, of semi-transparent chalcedony not found within 200 miles of these particular people, by whom, as unfamiliar, they were ascribed to the *moora.* There is a large body of magic among the Melanesians which is essentially popular in character; standing as it does in relation to the daily recurring wants of the people, it is practised to a greater or less extent by every adult. "The magical element consists in the employment of certain natural objects, immanent in which is a virtue communicable under appropriate circumstances to certain objects with which the first series of objects are brought into mediate or immediate contact." The qualities which lead to a natural body being recognized as a suitable charm, that is, as capable of exercising a beneficial effect on a particular class of objects, are generally (a) similarity in contour, or in other qualities, to the object to be influenced, or (b) rarity, or (c) unusual shape in not very uncommon objects.[3] Anything may fall into the category of *imunu* or religious objects: hunting-charms, old relics, grotesque carvings, freaks of nature. But such a list does not by any means exhaust the *imunu* class. "It appears that an exceptionally large tree might be thought to be the home of an *imunu.* Similarly the vast rivers of the Delta are in some way frequented by many *imunu.* But I cannot say that I have ever heard of an *imunu* as wholly immaterial: there has always been some material object with which it is identified."[4]

Nearly all the natives of Borneo make use of charms, and many will not go on a journey without taking some with them as a protection against any perils which they may encounter. "Any object of unusual shape, or one which is at all uncommon, is regarded as a charm. Among those which I have seen in use," writes Evans,[5] "are quartz crystals, shiny black river pebbles, curiously shaped pieces of wood, rhinoceros teeth, fossil shells, and ancient stone implements. Belts of cloth or string network are frequently made to contain

53 Gomme, *Village Life*, 145.
1 Howitt, in JAI, XVI, 28, note.
2 Horne and Aiston, *Cent. Aust.*, 126, 127.

3 Seligmann, *Melanesians*, 171, 173.
4 Williams, in JAI, LIII, 361, 362.
5 In JAI, XLII, 395.

such charms as the owner may wish to wear on his person, and each of these is sewn or netted into a small compartment separate from the others. Stone implements are, among the Dusuns, chiefly used as charms to keep their padi in good condition." Among Samoan household-gods were twins of the Siamese type. "Everything *double*—such as a double yam, two bananas adhering, etc.— was sacred, and not to be used under penalty of death."[6] Many moderns seem to share the primitive notion that there is something fetishistic about oddities found in nature. At the American Museum of Natural History there is a "fairy cross" of pyrite, the "cross" being formed by crystallization and, according to the superstitious, making of the mineral a good-luck charm. "There are probably very few people who know that nature has conferred upon one of her minerals a fairy cross that is sought after by collectors of minerals with all the zeal that actuated the 'forty-niner' in his quest for gold," says an announcement from the museum. "The mineral known as pyrite, or iron pyrites, which is a sulphide of iron, under certain conditions actuated by the mysterious force of crystallization, produces double crystals that are so placed with respect to each other that their prominent edges form a veritable cross. . . . But iron pyrites is not the only mineral that makes its crystals in the form of crosses. In some parts of Virginia and Georgia one hears much of the 'fairy stones' which are plowed up in the fields or found on the surface of the ground after a rainstorm. They are esteemed to bring more luck to any one who wears them than the proverbial rabbit's foot, and numbered among the converts to this particular form of mascot was the late President Roosevelt, who wore one on his watch chain. These odd shaped stones are in reality crystals of the mineral staurolite, a somewhat uncommon silicate, present in rocks in a number of places, of which Patrick County, Va., and Fannin County, Ga., are two. Like the iron crosses of iron pyrites, they are twinned crystals formed by the intersection of two, occasionally three, simple crystals. Sometimes these cross at right angles, making a very symmetrical cross, or again they may intersect at a steep angle, forming a St. Andrew's cross."[7]

These general illustrations may serve as typical of the great variety of fetish-objects that fall under a classification of the extraordinary, and to them must be added such objects as have demonstrated connection with spiritual powers because they have brought luck. They can control the aleatory element.

To weapons that have been successfully used, as well as to unusual devices like the boomerang, is often attributed fetishistic quality. The Australian boomerang is a remarkable construction, serving not only as a weapon but as a poker and shovel and as a general implement; some, especially old ones, are tied up with a person's luck.[8] The Bushmen despise an arrow that has once failed of its mark, and, on the contrary, consider one that has hit as of double value. "They will, therefore, rather make new arrows how much time and trouble soever it may cost them, than collect those that have missed and use them again." Similarly other tribes attach a special value to a hook that has caught a big fish.[9] On the Loango coast the thief makes a fetish for success in stealing: if he succeeds, that proves it a good one; if caught, that it was a failure.[10] The arrow-dance of the Veddahs of Ceylon was regarded as a

6 Turner, *Samoa*, 56.
7 N. Y. *Times*, Mar. 27, 1924.
8 Horne and Aiston, *Cent. Aust.*, 69-78.

9 Lichtenstein, *Travels*, II, 271; Leuba, in AA, XIV, 352.
10 Bastian, *Loango-Küste*, II, 180.

mechanical means of getting luck in hunting and protection against wild animals; the arrow was venerated as a fetish.[11] To the warrior of the American Plains the shield constituted a most sacred possession from the time when it was made for him, or given to him soon after his first encounter with the enemy, until it was laid under his head in the grave, unless before that time bestowed on some worthy younger warrior or left as a precious sacrifice at the grave of wife or child. "Every shield originated from a dream, in which the dreamer was told by the spirit how many shields he might make, how they must be painted and decorated, how the owner must paint and otherwise decorate himself and his pony, and what taboos and other sacred obligations he must observe through life in order to obtain the protection of the shield spirit, which might be a bird, a quadruped, a being of the tribal pantheon, or one of the personified powers of nature. The owner rarely made his own shield, but received it from the dreamer, usually an old warrior or recognized medicine-man, who made it on request as he had been instructed, for a definite compensation in horses, blankets, or other property."[12] In no country has the sword been an object of such honor as in Japan, where it was "a divine symbol, a knightly weapon, and a certificate of noble birth."[13] As among some Germanic tribes, so among the Scythians, the god was set up in the form of a sword. "The sword received sacrifices of horses and sheep, as of prisoners of war whose blood was caught in a vessel and sprinkled on the sword."[14] A Bosnian song relates how a woman tells a man not to go back for his gun which he has left; she has gold and will have a gold gun made for him; to which he replies: "I know that thou hast gold and canst have a better gun made, but not with the luck of my own gun." The hero's gun is alive: he complains to it of his troubles, he adjures and curses it; when aiming he calls on it not to fail him, being sure of his eye but not of it.[15] In the west of Ireland, flint arrow-heads are regarded with great superstition; "They are supposed to be fairy darts or arrows, which have been thrown by fairies, either in fights among themselves or at a mortal man or beast." At Bantam, the western province of Java, there is a cannon, a relic of the Portuguese occupation in the sixteenth century, which is supposed by the natives to possess those medicinal virtues identified in advertisements with certain German spas. In Batavia there is another cannon thought to be of the same origin. "The Javanese belief is that when these two cannon meet the Dutch rule will vanish. It is said to be due to the watchfulness of the Dutch Secret Service that a few days before the revolt broke out [late in 1926] the cannon were strongly guarded in order to prevent their removal. This precaution is also believed to have taken the heart out of the [communist] movement at its inception."[16]

The Whirr-stick and other Sacred Objects. A special type of fetish which is illustrative of the extraordinary is the bull-roarer or rhombus, the whirring or humming stick. In ancient Greece, modern Australia, North America, and Africa the instrument is one of sacred purpose. Only in certain civilized countries has it degenerated into a boy's plaything. The word itself is good English, signifying the flat strip of wood fastened to the end of a string—an instrument which has had a high mystic import in the barbaric and ancient

11 Sarasin, *Weddas*, 517.
12 Mooney, in HAI, II, 547.
13 Hubbard, in *Smithson. Rep.*, 1895, 671.
14 Justi, *Persien*, 97.

15 Krauss, *Sreća*, 17.
16 Gomme, *Ethnol. in Folklore*, 54; N. Y. *Times*, Dec. 26, 1926.

world. The Australian bull-roarers are generally made of a thin piece of wood, but sometimes of bark, and are of different sizes, varying in width from less than an inch to as much as four or five inches, and differing in length from four inches to two feet or longer. Both sides of the instrument are generally convex, with a small hole at one end, through which is fastened a string made either of the bark of trees, native flax, the fur of animals, or human hair, and sometimes as much as a dozen feet long. When whirled, it makes a loud humming noise.[17] This instrument is used with dread mysterious effect in the initiation-ceremonies. Until a boy is initiated he must not see one, and it is usually taboo to women. It is thought by the Dieri that if a woman were to see a bull-roarer which had been used at the ceremonies, and know the secret of it, the tribe would lack such food as snakes and lizards.[18] According to the Kurnai the sacred humming instrument, invented first by the Great Head Spirit, has kept its place among the magical apparatus of the wizard and is regarded as the means by which he, as also the dead, reaches ghostland.[19]

As the bull-roarer is too well known in the Banks Islands to be used in mysteries, a different apparatus productive of the same effect is employed. This is a flat, smooth stone, on which the butt-end of the stalk of a fan of palm is rubbed. "The vibration of the fan produces an extraordinary sound, which can be modulated in strength and tone at the will of the performer, and which proceeding in the stillness of daybreak from the mysterious recesses of the *salagoro* [secret society clubhouse], may well have carried with it the assurance of a supernatural presence and power."[20] Among the Papuans the bull-roarer is a taboo-instrument of religious significance at the initiation-ceremonies. In the district around the Gulf of Papua it may be seen only by men after manhood, and then pigs and much food have to be provided. "When the day comes for the feast and the introduction, the roaring bull may be heard from two in the morning and on until sunset. The day before, all females and young people have left the village lest they should hear it and die."[21] Extreme care is taken during the initiation-ceremonies to see that the instrument is not broken. "Should one break and a chip strike anyone, that person when next he goes hunting or fighting will be wounded by a boar's tusk or spear, as the case may be, in the place where he was struck by the bullroarer. There is absolute belief in this, and one or two men have marks to show where they have been struck by a bullroarer and afterwards gored by pigs. . . . The underlying idea about the bullroarer is that it is a spirit that makes the noise, and this belief is strongly impressed by every device upon uninitiated women, children, and those who have not passed through the ceremony. This belief will usually be found wherever the bullroarer is used in Papua."[22]

A Torres Straits sorcerer who wanted to raise a wind would cut out a piece of wood shaped like a bull-roarer, but made very thin. "This he attached to a piece of string and whirled around. The vibrations and revolutions were so rapid that the instrument was invisible. If more wind was desirable, he climbed to a tree-top and performed."[23] This recalls the Kaffir superstition that playing

17 Mathews, in JAI, XXVII, 52.
18 Howitt, in JAI, XX, 83; Bonney, in JAI, XIII, 127; Palmer, in JAI, XIII, 295; Starcke, *Prim. Fam.*, 122; Eyre, *Aust.*, 320; Mathews, in JAI, XXVII, 134.
19 Howitt, in JAI, XIII, 196.

20 Codrington, *Melanesians*, 80.
21 Chalmers, in JAI, XXVII, 329; Hagen, *Papua's*, 188, 189.
22 Chinnery, in JAI, XLV, 71.
23 Haddon, in JAI, XIX, 435.

with the rhombus invites a gale of wind. "Men will, on this account, often prevent boys from using it when they desire calm weather for any purpose." The superstition is identical with that which prevents many sailors from whistling at sea.[24] The natives on the Loango coast hear in the sounds produced by the whirring stick the voices of departed spirits, while among the Yoruba the supposed "voice of Oro" proceeds from a small piece of wood, actually worshipped as a god.[25]

The "whizzing-stick" was often used in the religious ceremonies of the Point Barrow Eskimo.[26] The bull-roarer was a very common instrument among the Indians, especially in the West, and while in some tribes it was merely a child's toy, usually it was regarded as a sacred implement, associated with rain, wind, and lightning, and among the Kwakiutl with ghosts.[27] Bourke[28] first saw the rhombus at the snake-dance of the Tusayan in Arizona: "The medicine-man twirled it rapidly, and with a uniform motion, about the head from front to rear, and succeeded in faithfully imitating the sound of a gust of rain-laden wind. As explained by one of the medicine-men, by making this sound they compelled the wind and rain to come to the aid of the crops." Later he found it in use among the Apache, and for the same purpose. "The Apache explained that the lines on the front side of the rhombus were the entrails and those on the rear side the hair of their wind god. The hair is of several colors, and represents lightning." He was led to believe that the bull-roarer of these people was made by the medicine-men from the wood of a pine or fir that had been struck by lightning on the mountain-tops. Apache, Hopi, and Zuñi bull-roarers bear lightning-symbols, and "while in the semi-arid region the implement is used to invoke clouds, lightning, and rain, and to warn the initiated that rites are being performed, in the humid area it is used to implore the wind to bring fair weather." The Hopi, who regard the bull-roarer as a prayer-stick of the thunder and its whizzing noise as representing the wind that accompanies thunderstorms, make the tablet portion from a piece of lightning-riven wood and measure the length of the string from the heart to the tips of the fingers of the outstretched right hand. The Navaho make the bull-roarer of the same material but regard it as representing the voice of the thunder-bird, whose figure they often paint upon it, the eyes being indicated by inset pieces of turquoise.[29] It is called by them "groaning stick" and they say that "the sacred groaning stick may only be made of the wood of a pine tree which has been struck by lightning."[30] The bull-roarer was used in religious mysteries, as among the Moqui, where in front of the procession of dancers, each with a live rattlesnake or two in his mouth, the priest walked whirling this instrument.[31] It was known, further, to tribes in Mexico and Central America, while in Brazil it seems to have been connected with funeral-rites and the notion was held that women and children must not see it lest they die.[32] A favorite fetish-instrument of the Guiana Indians was the sacred trumpet, which was sounded under the palm-trees that they might bear abundance of fruit.[33] In the mysteries of the Greeks the rhombus was whirled as in

24 Theal, *Kaffir Folklore*, 209-210; Bourke, in BAE, IX, 479.

25 Bastian, *Deut. Exped.*, I, 113; Batty, in JAI, XIX, 162; Frobenius, *Masken*, 165.

26 Murdoch, in BAE, IX, 378.

27 Hough, "Bullroarer," in HAI, I, 171; Mooney, in BAE, XIV, 975.

28 In BAE, IX, 476, 477.

29 Hough, "Bullroarer," in HAI, I, 170-171.

30 Matthews, in BAE, V, 436.

31 Howitt, in JAI, XV, 422.

32 Lumholtz, in *Scribner's Mag.*, XVI, 442; Sapper, in *Globus*, LXXVI, 352; Von den Steinen, *Zent. Bras.*, 327, 497, 498.

33 Roth, in BAE, XXX, 137.

the barbaric religious ceremonies; like the drum or tympanum, this instrument of the cult served to inflame the ministers and worshippers to the highest pitch of enthusiasm.[34]

A host of other extraordinary objects were regarded as fetishes by the aborigines of the New World. Among the Tlinkits charms are worn to ward off evil, and certain things are kept to bring good luck. "A woman has kept for years a lot of halibut bones taken from a halibut that was mysteriously caught by a native. The old woman would not part with these bones for anything."[35] The Micmac accorded supernatural powers to certain of their bowls, and thought that water standing over night in gaming bowls would reveal by its appearance past, present, and future events. Some bowls were supposed to have mysterious powers which would affect the person eating or drinking from them. Among the Pueblo tribes the pottery bowl, like the basket-bowl drum of the Navaho and others, is frequently a cult-vessel employed in religious ceremonies, the medicine-bowl with its nature symbols and the sacred meal-bowl furnishing familiar examples. Such vessels are sacrificed to springs or are deposited in shrines and caves.[36] This is paralleled to some degree by the D'Entrecasteaux belief that the greatest ruler of the winds and rain and sunshine was an ancient pot, which was kept in a special hut and once a year carried by its owner in a religious procession; a train of natives followed after, "crouching low towards the ground. In fear and trembling they brought it food, still crouching low, and hurriedly retired again."[37] The Cherokee sacred box was a rectangular affair, about three feet long, covered with a dressed deerskin and resting upon blocks to keep it from the earth. "It was watched by a sentinel with bow and arrows, who drew an arrow to the head and warned the stranger away when he attempted a closer inspection." The "flat pipe" of the Arapaho was kept by a priest, together with an ear of corn and a stone turtle, all of which, according to their tradition, they have had from the beginning of the world. "Around these centers the tribal genesis tradition, which is recited when the package is opened, as may be done on special occasions. . . . The box in which the sacred objects were kept was never allowed to touch the ground, and when on the march the priest in charge, even though mounted, was not allowed to rest it upon his horse, but must carry it upon his own back." The sacred metal plates of the Creeks were kept by priests in a depository on one side of the public square; at times they were said to give out a miraculous ringing sound without being touched. "Once a year, at the annual Green Corn dance, they were exhibited to the people from a distance, after which they were washed in the stream, rubbed and cleaned, and put away for another year." As usual with such objects, the people claimed to have received them from a supernatural being at the beginning of their existence as a people.[38]

Similar to the above was the sacred hat of the Cheyenne, made of a buffalo-cow's head and kept by special guardians whose office was hereditary. "The man who held the office was never killed or even wounded in war; nor was he ever sick, but lived to full age, dying at last nearly a hundred years old. His lodge had a sacred character, and in the old formal days certain rules were observed in it. . . . A person was not permitted to stand up in the hat lodge;

34 Showerman, *Mother of the Gods*, 237, 238-239; Batty, in JAI, XIX, 163; Lang, *Custom and Myth*, 29; Finsch, *Ethnol. Erfahr.*, I, 111.

35 Jones, *Thlingets*, 163.
36 HAI, I, 164.
37 Jenness and Ballentyne, 129, 130.
38 Mooney, in HAI, II, 194.

he who entered must walk to his place and sit down without delay. No one must speak in a loud voice. Low tones must always be used. A child brought into this lodge for the first time must be prayed over and warned to speak in a low voice. . . . If by a mischance anyone should throw against the lodge a little stick or stone he must be taken into the lodge and prayed over, and hands that had been placed on the earth should be passed over his body on both sides. An enemy who entered this lodge might not be harmed. He was safe—as safe as if in his own home. In this lodge certain things were forbidden. No moisture might fall on the floor. No one might throw water on the floor nor spit on it, nor blow his nose with his finger there. Any of these things would cause a heavy rain-storm." Many other taboos are mentioned, the infraction of which involved various evil consequences. The hat was shown only on the occasion of a great sickness, or when the medicine-arrows were renewed, or when it was taken out to be worn in war. In the first case it was exhibited in the lodge, which was thrown open, the people entering from the south side, passing around and out at the north. "As the people passed by the hat, they made their prayers and passed their hands over it, and then over their children." In olden times, when the camp was moving, the wife of the keeper of the hat walked carrying it on her back, for the hat might neither be carried on a horse nor hauled on a travois. "When the lodge in which the hat was kept had once been pitched, it was not permitted to move it. If it was found necessary to move this lodge, then all the lodges must be taken down and the whole camp must pack up and move, even if the new location were not more than a few hundred yards away."[39] Another special fetish, though not of the same magnitude as the Cheyenne hat, was "the sacred string of beads with which Tecumseh's brother, the Shawnee prophet, traveled among the Indian tribes, inciting them to war. Every young warrior who agreed to go upon the warpath touched this 'sacred string of beads' in token of his solemn pledge."[40]

The most profoundly sacred object of the Indians was the calumet. From its uses it would seem that it had a ceremonially symbolic history independent of that of the pipe, and that when the pipe became an altar by its employment for burning sacrificial tobacco to the gods, convenience and convention united the already highly symbolic calumet-shafts and the sacrificial tobacco-altar, the pipe-bowl. "As the colors and the other adornments on the shaft represent symbolically various dominant gods of the Indian polytheon, it follows that the symbolism of the calumet and pipe represented a veritable executive council of the gods."[41] Marquette[42] said of the calumet: "It is the most mysterious thing in the World. The Scepters of our Kings are not so much respected; for the Savages have such a Deference for this Pipe, that one may call it The God of Peace and War, and the Arbiter of Life and Death."

A fetish that plays an important rôle in Tibetan life is the khata or scarf of felicitation. This is a piece of silk nearly as fine as gauze, of bluish white color and about three times as long as wide. "There are khatas of every size and price; for it is an object that the poor as well as the rich cannot do without. No one ever goes anywhere without carrying a small supply of them with him. When one pays a formal visit, when one has a service to ask of some one, or to thank a person, the first thing to do is to unroll a khata; it is

39 Grinnell, in AA, XII, 562-567.
40 Bourke, in BAE, IX, 555.
41 Hewitt, "Calumet," in HAI, I, 192.
42 Quoted by Hoffman, in BAE, VII, 153.

taken in both hands and offered to the person one wishes to honor. If two friends, not having met for some time, suddenly run across each other, the first thing they do is to offer each other a *khata*. It is done with as much *empressement* and as promptly as one shakes hands in Europe. It is also customary when one writes a letter to fold up in it a little *khata*. It is incredible what importance the Tibetans, Si-Fan, Hung-Mao-Eul, and all the people living to the west of the Blue Sea attach to the *khata* ceremony." Besides these everyday uses, the *khata* is the most ordinary form of offering to the gods. "Hundreds and thousands of them are suspended on the statues of the gods in every temple or shrine in Tibet and Mongolia." Ceremonial scarfs appear at one time to have been in use among the Chinese, while a similar custom existed in India in olden times, for we read in early Buddhist works of a piece of light stuff being put over the shoulders or around the neck of an honored person.[43] The Parsees wear the girdle as an indispensable symbol of their religion; it is formed of seventy-two fine woollen threads twisted together.[44] In the *Iliad*, Aphrodite gave Hera her belt (*cestus*) containing her blandishments; from this fetish came the power of love, desire, and seductive speech.[45]

The Extraordinary in Inanimate Nature. Stones of one sort or another are fetishes, as we have seen, throughout the entire world. This applies especially to those which are out of the common. The notions regarding stones and the uses to which they are put make interesting reading. The Australians who attribute anything out of the ordinary to magic are always on the lookout, while hunting or travelling, for any stones of unusual shape. "If any were found that were small enough to carry home, they were taken and shown to the assembled old men. These invariably identified the stones as something to do with the moora [ancestors], and usually invented a use for them. If the stones were too big to shift they were also accounted sacred, and in the course of time legends sprang up about them." The authors[46] mention a case where an obsidian that had been picked up was called emu's eyes; it was supposed to have magical effect on that bird, making it go blind. As soon as possible after a tree has been struck by lightning some blackfellow will dig around the roots to get what he calls the lightning-stone. Any find of an unusual shape is carefully treasured and is thought to bring good luck. Here is illustrated one of the inconsistencies of the blacks: "They are horribly afraid of lightning and will on no account use the wood of a tree that has been struck. But they value the stone that is to them the visible sign of the lightning."

Sacrificial stones are quite common in Melanesia: one on Tikopia Island, to which the people pray, is thought to be of very great virtue; it is male, be it noted; there is also a female stone.[47] Inside a sacred enclosure on San Cristoval, is a smooth, round, highly polished black stone, compared by the natives with a cannonball. Like the Kaaba at Mecca it is an object of worship. In another place on the Solomon Islands the sacrificial stone is a large block of red jasper. "The priest was said to be able to make this stone float in the water, and it certainly was very sacred, for if the man's shadow fell upon it, he would waste away."[48] When Jenness and Ballentyne[49] were watching

43 Rockhill, in *Smithson. Rep.*, 1893, 723.
44 Haug, *Parsis*, 244.
45 Homer, *Iliad*, XIV, 214.
46 Horne and Aiston, *Cent. Aust.*, 60, 132, 136.
47 Rivers, *Melan. Soc.*, I, 339.
48 Fox and Drew, in JAI, XLV, 164; Fox, in JAI, XLIX, 177.
49 *D'Entrecasteaux*, 160-161.

a meteor fall, a native with them made the remark: "The *badibadi*, they fly about, they settle here and there, they wander about in the sky." When they asked him why they fly about, they received the tantalizing reply: *kaiiwa*, "I wonder." The more or less active volcano, Mt. Victory, on the northeast coast of New Guinea, is by surrounding natives reputed to be the abode of *dirava*, ghosts; "it is said that the steam rising from its top is the smoke of the *dirava* village."[50]

On a mountain in Nyassaland is a sacred stone; the natives leave old hoes there with the idea that rain may follow.[51] From being merely commemorative of some particular act or occurrence, many stones in Madagascar have become sacred objects and instruments of a cult which is practised even at the present time, especially by women desiring children or an easy delivery during child-birth, and who, having rubbed the stone with grease, rub themselves against it. "When either men or women desire the curing of an illness, or success in some undertaking, they throw fine gravel at the greasy part of the stone, and, if it sticks there, hope for success, or they try to throw a stone so that it lodges on the narrow top of the menhir; if after this their wishes are gratified they bestow another coat of grease on the stone."[52] The Niam-Niam worshipped stone hatchets or wedges.[53] Among the Fan, anything hit by lightning becomes a powerful fetish and may enter into the war-fetish to turn aside bullets and arrows.[54] In West Africa, as elsewhere, the fact that siliceous stones actually produce a flash when struck, gives a key to the widespread belief that flint implements are thunderbolts.[55]

In India, celts—called by the natives "toad-axes"—are believed to be thunderbolts fallen in a flash of lightning. The real essence returns to heaven, the mere husk remaining on earth. "The possession of celts is not, as a rule, so highly prized by Semas as by Angamis. The Sema who finds a celt, however, does not (like the Lhota) refuse to touch it. He always keeps it and believes that it causes fertility to his beans and possibly to his other crops of minor importance." Stones among these tribes are the subjects of some beliefs which are, from the civilized point of view, decidedly radical: their idea is that stones can breed, begetting and conceiving offspring. "A black stone about 18 inches long, picked up in the fields at Natsimi somewhere about the year 1906, had (in 1912) acquired a regular cult. It has an interpreter who communicates with it in dreams, in which it appears as a human being, the stone itself being said to walk about in human form by night. . . . The number of pice collected from its devotees by this stone is considerable, and, though he stoutly denies it, the stone's 'dobashi' no doubt disposes of them, while he gives out that the stone itself removes them by night."[56] The Todas have many stones which may be held to have some degree of sanctity; certainly many hold their place in the religious ceremonial. "All these stones have names, either general or individual, but two stones with the same name need not necessarily have the same function."[57] Some serpents of a very poisonous kind, think the Singhalese, contain luminous stones which they vomit up at night to give them light. Since it is impossible for them to live without these jewels, their

50 Strong, in JAI, XLIX, 299.
51 Moggridge, in JAI, XXXII, 469.
52 Lewis, in JAI, XLVII, 448.
53 Nadaillac, in *Bull. Institut Egyptien*, 1886, 16.
54 Trilles, *Fân*, 338.

55 Tylor, *Prim. Cult.*, II, 262; Ellis, *Ewe*, 38.
56 Hutton, *Sema Nagas*, 253-257, 174 ff.; Godden, in JAI, XXVII, 19.
57 Rivers, *Todas*, 438.

possessors never go far away from them. A luminous stone is borne by certain lizards, which may be recognized by their possession of two tails.[58] All these beliefs are natural enough among peoples who are ready to explain all kinds of occurrences not understood by them by reference to the influences of some spirit or saint. It is thus that the spirals of sand, known as dust-devils in the Punjab, are supposed to contain within them a sprite known as Bhai Pheru, or Brother Twirler.[59]

Two oblong smooth stones stood on a raised platform in one of the Samoan villages: "They were supposed to be the parents of Saato, a god who controlled the rain. When the chiefs and people were ready to go off for weeks to certain places in the bush for the sport of pigeon-catching, offerings of cooked taro and fish were laid on the stones, accompanied by prayers for fine weather and no rain."[60] A sacred stone of the Maoris is gifted with the power of locomotion, for if any person shifts it away it will return itself to its former position. A bold ridge which stretches out toward Lake Rotorua is a lightning-mountain of great *mana*. "It is regarded by the Arawa as a place of omen, and it is moreover *tapu* because of the fact that in the rocky caves and recesses on its face lie the bones of many generations of the people." When two flashes of lightning are seen above the bluff in quick succession, like the opening and closing of one's hand, then a young chief of the tribe will quickly die. Should three or more bright flashes be seen in quick succession, an aged man is called for by the gods and will presently pass to the spirit-land. In the Wairau district is a fetish-lake which was formerly a famous place for bird-snaring, but a thoughtless act led to its being lost forever to the Maoris. Being a *tipua,* or goblin, naturally it was necessary to treat it with great respect, and a famed chief of old told his wife to be very careful and not pass before him or near the lake with cooked food. "But that foolish woman did one day so pass before him carrying some cooked food, with the result that the demon lake concealed itself, and no man has ever since been able to find that pond or its prized bird-snaring trees. Now you can see what trouble a woman can cause."[61]

Among the Eskimo a very necessary article of trade, soapstone, is manufactured into lamps and pots. This is "bought" from the rock; that is, having dug out a piece, the natives feel they must give the rock something in return, for example, ivory carvings, beads, or food.[62] This is similar to the practice of the Indian medicine-man in putting a bead in each hole made by pulling up by the roots some medicinal herb, "as compensation to the earth for the plant."[63] Plummet-shaped implements to which mysterious properties were assigned were common to the Indians of the Pacific Coast, and were thought to possess magical power over fish and game. They were used by being suspended by cords from the ends of poles, the butts of which were planted in the bank in such a manner as to leave the stones suspended over the water where the Indians intended to fish. At other places they were hung in the mountains at points favorable to hunting. The Napa Indians said that they were sometimes laid upon ledges of rocks on high peaks, with the belief that, owing to their peculiar form and some occult power which they possessed, they

58 Hildburgh, in JAI, XXXVIII, 199-200.
59 O'Brien, in JAI, XLI, 513.
60 Turner, *Samoa,* 24-25.
61 Best, in AAAS, 1904, 448, 449; Cowan, *Maoris,* 210-211.

62 Mason, *Invention,* 354; Boas, in BAE, VI, 596.
63 Mooney, in BAE, VII, 339.

travelled in the night through the water to drive the fish up the creeks to favorite fishing-places, or through the air to herd the game up toward certain peaks and chosen hunting-grounds. The peculiar pear-shape was given them in order that they might cleave through the air or water the more easily. They were used also as war-charms or were supposed to travel about at night to worry the enemies of the tribe. Among others of the American Indians bird-stones, banner-stones, and boat-stones had uses in religious ceremony or magic; when worn by women, the bird-stones symbolized the brooding bird.

The Pueblo tribes had for war and hunting numerous fetishes of stone, small figurines cut to resemble various predatory animals, with eyes of inlaid turquoise; one or more arrow-heads were bound at the back or side and smeared with frequent oblations of blood from the slain game. A Cherokee hunting and divining fetish consisted of a transparent crystal which its owner kept wrapped up in buckskin in a sacred cave and occasionally fed by rubbing over it the blood of a deer. In some cases knives of obsidian were not properly knives, but jewelry for sacred purposes, passing current also as money.[64] Along the Mexican border loadstone is called "living stone"; in order that its action shall be efficacious, the natives believe it must be put into water every Friday, and then supplied with steel-filings. If hidden in the tresses of a girl one loves, the loadstone will draw one to her.[65] The rites of different Mexican divinities were conducted in caverns, which became fetish-places. To the native Mexican the earth was the common father of all, and to this day when he would take a solemn oath, he stoops to the earth, touches it with his hand, and repeats the formula: "Does not our Great God see me?"[66] Mt. Rainier, called by the Indians Tacoma, was to them God.[67] Fire-clay is a fetish in British Guiana,[68] while some tribes in other parts of South America regard meteors as rapacious animals which hurl themselves upon their prey.[69] The connection between stone-fetishism and the dead is clear in the case of the Guiana tribes who regard certain blocks of granite as local warriors who, after death, have been changed into stone.[70]

Stone-fetishism was widespread among the peoples of antiquity. The ordinary artificial mark of a Semitic sanctuary was the sacrificial pillar, cairn, or rude altar. Stones were used also in lots, being shaken in an urn until one "came out."[71] Jahweh as the old nature-deity differed little from the gods found throughout western Asia; as master of storm and thunder he dwelt on the heights. The places of worship were high places, and in the time of Elijah, the seat of Jahweh was at "Horeb, the mount of God."[72] Holy stones were reverenced by the Greeks, being regarded as symbols of divinity and anointed with oil. The fetishistic nature of such practice is not far removed from the reverence paid today to images in churches.[73] In the year 205 B.C., the decemvirs at Rome, consulting the Sibylline Books on account of the frequent showers of stones that year, came upon a *carmen* which said that whenever an enemy

64 Yates, in *Smithson. Rep.*, 1886, pt. I, 300; Holmes, in HAI, I, 148-149; II, 102, 268; Hewitt, in HAI, I, 458.
65 N. Y. *Times*, Nov. 18, 1894.
66 Brinton, *Nagualism*, 38.
67 Williams, *The Mountain That Was "God."*
68 Schomburgk, *Brit.-Guiana*, I, 261.
69 Weygold, in *Globus*, LXXXIII, 5.
70 Roth, in BAE, XXX, 145-146, 152.

71 Tiele-Gehrich, *Gchte. Relig.*, I, 281-282; Kautzsch, "Relig. Israel," in *Hastings's Dict. Bible*, 662-663; Fletcher. in AA, X, 212, note; Allen, in *Fortnightly Rev.*, Jan., 1890; Lang, in *Contemp. Rev.*, Mar., 1890.
72 Tiele-Gehrich, *Gchte. Relig.*, I, 300-301; Kautzsch, in *Hastings's Dict. Bible*, 661, 646; Strabo, *Geog.*, I, 456-457, 466; Seymour, *Hom. Age*, 418.
73 Beloch, *Griech. Gchte.*, I, 113.

from an alien land should wage war on Italy he could be expelled thence and conquered if the Idæan Mother should be brought to Rome from Pessinus. She was associated with a sacred stone called by the natives of that place the "Mother of the Gods."[74] But the most famous fetish-stone of antiquity was the black stone at Mecca. Before the time of Mohammed, Mecca was sacred territory and the black stone an object of veneration. As no one knew what it was, it long enjoyed immense reverence. It was housed in a building called Kaaba, which was the chief sanctuary and destination of pilgrimage for the Mohammedan world.[75]

During the modern period in Europe there have persisted many superstitions about stone celts, said to be useful in medicine,[76] while there is much evidence of the worship of stones through a long period of time in France. Sometimes the people, of their own volition, transformed the effigies from the graves of the nobility and gentry into statues of saints. That of a chevalier which was in the church of Vigeau received the name of St. Eutrope; the relatives of a sick person would scrape with a knife that part of the figure which corresponded to the seat of pain and give the scrapings to the sufferer in an infusion, while in the case of children the dust was put into their stockings or shoes. In order to christianize the practice to some extent, it appears that certain stones from which individuals came to demand cures were removed into churches. Marvellous impressions in stones were also objects of worship; Gregory of Tours cites several that were signalized by public veneration, among them one in the Basilica of Tours on which a saint had sat. New-born children who have a certain blue vein visible under the eyebrows, which they call "mal de St. Divy," are taken to Dirinon to the stone where Ste. Nonne, mother of St. Divy, left the impression of her knees, in order that the saint may preserve them from the premature death which the sign portends. "Every year on August 6th, from time immemorial the lame, the paralytic, the sick of every kind, come to the chapel consecrated to St. Estapin on the top of a mountain at a short distance from Dourgues (Aude). They make the tour nine times and then go to the platform on which rocks full of holes slightly project from the earth. Then each one finds a remedy for his misery, for all that is necessary is for him to insert the afflicted part into the hole in the stone to which it corresponds. The holes are of different caliber, corresponding to the head, the thighs, or the arms. This ceremony once performed, all attending are cured." The efficacy of visits to impressions depended also on the time of the day or night when they were made—an indication of the antiquity of the practice. Further, water remaining in basins or depressions was thought effective in case of illness; that in the depressions of the worn side of the "Pierre St. Benoit," or of the "Pierre qui Pleure," at St. James (Manche), always returns again into the cavities, no matter what is done to keep it out! People afflicted with skin-diseases came to bathe in a cradle-shaped rock in the neighborhood of St. Arnoux. The water in the grooves of the "Pierre qui Pleure" cures fevers, several sicknesses of infancy, and trouble with the eyes; that of a basin hollowed in a block of granite near the village of Termes also cures sore eyes, as did that which oozes into a little natural cup in the gorge

74 Showerman, *Mother of the Gods*, 225-226.

75 Müller, *Islam*, I, 197, 201; von Kremer, *Kgchte.*, II, 5, 6, 7, 9-10, 13, 14; Wellhausen, *Skizzen*, III, 69-71, 165; Tiele-Gehrich, *Gchte. Relig.*, I, 230; Snouck-Hurgronje, *Mekka*, I, 4, 5-6; Lippert, *Kgchte.*, II, 374.

76 Andree, *Eth. Parallelen*, 31; Worsaae, in *Aarbøger*, 1879, 308-309.

of Tarn, near the hermitage of St. Hilaire. After washing, the visitors generally threw into it a pin stuck into a piece of the clothes of the sick person.[77]

The practice of throwing stones upon a heap by the wayside is a custom found in many places and appears, in some cases at least, to have a religious significance. The natives of the Banks' and Solomon Islands throw stones, sticks, or leaves upon a heap at a place of steep descent, or where a difficult path begins, believing that they thereby "throw away their fatigue."[78] Stone-heaps are commonly met with in Africa, especially among the Bantu tribes who, however, have no explanation to offer for the practice.[79] Heaps of stones are to be seen on the summit of every pass in Tibet and frequently at the mouths of the valleys leading up to them; no traveller fails to throw a stone on the heap as an offering to the gods, at the same time uttering a short prayer which ends with: "Gods, give me a hundred years."[80] Sacrificial piles, consisting for the most part of rude heaps of sticks, antlers, and bones, are common in Siberia, especially among the Samoyeds and Yakuts; "although these piles are often surrounded by driftwood, no Samoyad will venture to take a single piece, however much he may need firewood."[81] Stones or sticks adorned with little rags are found among the Soyots, near the source of the Yenesei, on the banks of rivers or at the top of a difficult pass. These are "god-sticks" and are an offering to the demon of the place to avert the dangers of crossing. Whenever a Soyot acted as mountain guide or forded a river he expressed his gratitude for safety by adding a quota to the "god-stick" or at least by adding to the cairn one stone for each of the party saved.[82] Stone-heaps similar in shape and built for purposes similar to the above are found in the Navaho and Moki countries in Arizona. Speaking of the Moki, Fewkes[83] says: "Ma-sau-wuh shrines are simply heaps of sticks or piles of stones, and it is customary for an Indian toiling up the trail with a heavy bundle of wood on the back to throw a small fragment from the load upon these shrines or to cast a stone upon them as he goes to his farm. These are offerings to Ma-sau-wuh, the fire god, or deity of the surface of the earth." Explorers frequently find in the Americas piles of stone, which probably served as burial-places for the early Americans, formed in a manner similar to the Indian cairns of the present time. In this way the Ozark hills of Arkansas and Missouri have been covered with piles of stones.[84] Mention is made of an agreement between Indians and white settlers in New Hampshire which was sworn to at two heaps of stone called "Two Brothers."[85] In New Mexico there is a stone of large size which it is the duty of every visitor to the locality to push forward a space; what necessitates this performance is not known.[86] The custom of making offerings on mountain-tops is common in South America, and stone-heaps are especially frequent in the Andes; the ancient Peruvians and others cast stones as an offering for a safe passage.[87]

A peculiar use of stone-heaps among historic peoples is the practice known

77 Sébillot, in AA, IV, 94-96, 98-99, 101.
78 Codrington, *Melanesians*, 185 ff.
79 Fritsch, *Eingeb. S.-Afr.*, 200.
80 Rockhill, in USNM, 1893, 734; Anon., in *Globus*, LXXII, 173; Peschel, *Races*, 24.
81 Montefiore, in JAI, XXIV, 399; Shchukin, *Shamanism* (Russ.), 39; Sieroshevski, *Yakuts* (Russ.), 262.
82 *Pall Mall Gaz.*, quoted in N. H. *Register*, Nov. 28, 1897.

83 In *Jour. Amer. Ethnol. and Arch.*, IV, 41 (quoted by Rockhill, in USNM, 1893, 735).
84 Nadaillac, *Preh. Amer.*, 84; HAI, II, 277.
85 Belknap, *New Hampshire*, 330.
86 Fletcher, in AA, X, 213.
87 Rockhill, in USNM, 1893, 735; Mosbach, in *Globus*, LXXII, 5.

as "scopelism." It is a sort of reflection of the herder-tiller incompatibility,[88] and consists in setting stones in a heap as a threat to one who should till a field which is still wild, or in scattering stones on tillable ground to spoil it, or more commonly as a threat of harm of some agrarian kind to terrorize a population. The most definite purpose seems to be to forbid the conversion of pastoral into arable land, under penalty of death, the threat being signified by the ominous pile of stones which gives rise to the name. This practice was once common in Arabia, being classified as a crime, for the stones were placed as a warning that if any one should cultivate that field he would die a violent death by the arts of those who placed the stones, "which thing produced so much fear that no one dared to go to that field, fearing the cruelty of those who had made the scopelism. The authorities are accustomed to follow this matter up severely, even to inflicting the penalty of death, for the thing itself implies a threat of murder." A somewhat analogous offense existed in Germany under the name of *Landzwang,* which, in the penal code of Charles the Fifth, is defined as a threat on the part of dangerous outlaws to commit a crime, that crime having relation to agriculture and the rights of owners.[89]

The Extraordinary in Animate Nature. Animate objects often fall under the classification of the extraordinary and become fetishes. Such, for example, are the sacred trees. In San Cristoval the story runs that when the ghost-shark was killed by the people the sacred tree broke in two of its own accord.[90] No ordinary tree, evidently. The Buryats and Mongols worship trees, feeling special reverence for those which are crooked, with the tops curved over toward the ground. The Ostyaks regard with reverence the cedar standing alone in a pine wood, and attribute a sacred significance to places where seven larches grow in a row. The Samoyeds revere stones and trees; the Cheremis give sacrifices to the largest tree in the wood; the Votyaks think that very old trees have souls, to which they pay reverence. When a Votyak founds a household, he chooses as his protector a birch tree; tufts of its twigs are hung up in the house and renewed every year.[91] The original sacred tree in Tibet is thought to have sprung from the hair of Tsong K'aba, the restorer and purifier of the Buddhist religion; on its leaves a true believer can distinctly trace the figure of Sakya Muni or his name in Tibetan characters.[92] It is part of Hindu beliefs that to plant a pipal tree is a virtue, because on its every branch or leaf a god is supposed constantly to dwell. To cut it down or uproot it is a sin not easily forgotten by the gods; the man who trespasses against the pipal dies without male issue and thus without the hope of getting water in the next world. A man without issue worships the pipal tree daily with water in the hope of getting a son.[93] A Bengal folk-tale tells of a certain banyan tree haunted by spirits who had a habit of wringing the necks of all who ventured to approach at night. Another extraordinary tree is that which grew beside a Brahman's house and was inhabited by a female spirit of white complexion who one day seized the Brahman's wife and thrust her into a hole in the tree.[94] Furness[95] cites many examples of sacred trees among the Nagas and states that sacred rubber trees grow near the "morongs" (club-houses).

88 §31, of the text.
89 Fletcher, "Scopelism," in AA, X, 201, 209, 210.
90 Fox and Drew, in JAI, XLV, 164.
91 Michailovski, *Shamanism* (Russ.), 38;

Czaplicka, *Aborig. Siberia,* 188; Hitchcock, in USNM, 1890, 472, 473.
92 Wellby, *Tibet,* 287 ff.
93 Chowbe, in JASB, V, 227, 314.
94 Danks, in AAAS, 1909, 453.
95 In JAI, XXXII, 457, 458.

Before cutting down a large tree, Palaungs offer a prayer to propitiate the spirit that may have made its home in it; "this is only done if the tree is really large. Spirits that are strong take possession of the large trees, evicting any little spirits that may have made their homes there; these have to take up their abode in the smaller trees and bushes. The weaker spirits appear to be harmless and no one apologizes to them when their homes are cut down."[96] In Maori folk-lore occur a number of examples of goblin-trees: should a traveller when passing one such tree ask, "What place is this?" rain would set in. "So it behooves one to be careful when traveling in this region." Another goblin is a log which has the habit of chanting weird songs as it drifts along. A famous fetish-tree has the power of rendering barren women fruitful. "When a woman proves to be barren she proceeds to that tree, and by embracing it she may become fruitful. She is accompanied by a priest, who, during the performance, repeats the necessary invocations. One side of the tree, that towards the rising sun, is known as the male side, and that facing the setting sun is the female side. The sex of the child is determined by the side embraced by the would-be mother."[97]

Holy trees were common in Greece; travellers were accustomed to pray to them and to adorn them with ribbons and other sacrificial gifts. Each god had his sacred plant or tree, Zeus the oak, Apollo the laurel, Athena the olive, and Aphrodite the myrtle. Among the Semites, frankincense was the gum of a very holy species of tree, collected with religious precautions.[98] Pliny[99] states that the right even to see the trees was reserved to certain holy families, who, when engaged in harvesting the gum, had to abstain from all contact with women and from participation in funerals.

"Do you suppose," asked Cicero,[100] "that there is anyone so senseless as to worship as a god something which he eats?" Yet it is not at all uncommon in ethnography to encounter cases where plants and intoxicating drinks made from them are thought to be possessed of a spirit. The use of kava in Melanesia is associated with all the important events of a man's life: at the time of child-birth the husband will drink kava while he prays to some departed ancestor to aid his wife, and in throwing away the dregs the cry of "Tut" will indicate an appeal that harm may be averted from her; at a funeral and also at the feast of the dead the men who are present drink kava, which is supposed to have spiritualistic influence.[101] In East Africa, herbs which are thought to effect miraculous cures and many native poisons are fetishes, while in the west a new cult has grown up around a fetishistic drink which is supposed to protect against evil influences, to bring good health and prosperity, and to kill witches and those who deal in black magic.[102]

Besides being used as food, maize was employed by Indian priests and conjurors in their mystical ceremonies.[103] When an Indian takes up a ginseng plant he first asks its permission to take a little of its flesh, then "he drops into the hole a bead and covers it over, leaving it there by way of payment to the plant spirit."[104] Among the Seri, doubly consumed food is credited with intensified powers and virtues, and held to be especially potent in the relief

96 Milne, *Eastern Clan*, 177.
97 Best, in AAAS, 1904, 448; and in AAAS, 1898, 773-774 (quoted).
98 Beloch, *Griech. Gchte.*, I, 112-113; Smith, *Relig. Sem.*, 427.
99 *Nat. Hist.*, XII, 54.

100 *De Natura Deorum*, III, 16.
101 Rivers, *Melan. Soc.*, I, 118.
102 N. Y. *Times*, Oct. 4, 1908; Nov. 21, 1920.
103 Bruce, *Va.*, 159.
104 Mooney, in BAE, XIX, 425.

of hunger and in giving endurance for the hard warpath or prolonged chase.[105] Far-reaching examples of plant-fetishism are found among the Zuñi, who regard plants as sentient beings; the initiated can talk to them and the plants can talk back. "Plants also are sacred, for some of them were dropped to earth by the Star People; some originally were human beings, others are the property of the gods, and all are the offspring of the Earth Mother."[106] Among the many instances of the ceremonial use of plants among the Zuñi are the following: the blossoms of a certain plant ground to a fine meal and sprinkled into a bowl of suds used for bathing a new-born infant are said to make the hair grow on the head and to give strength to the body; another plant is made into a tea which is drunk by women desiring children; a very strong tea made of the root of a certain plant will cause a woman to become pregnant—"if the medicine fails it is because the wife's heart is not good"; if warriors chew the blossoms of another plant this will prevent the enemy from seeing how to aim their arrows truly; prayer-plumes attached to twigs of a certain plant will make rabbits appear in large numbers when sought by the hunter. Other uses of special plants are to cure timidity and to detect thieves.[107] The Indian of Mexico is inordinately fond of a kind of beer made from maize which he needs also for his ceremonies. It is given as medicine to the nursing infant; is set apart for the dead, as they cannot get rest without it; and is the great remedy in the medicine-man's hands. They never think of using it without first sacrificing a part of it to their god.[108]

Plants and intoxicants were fetishes to the ancients. An excellent example is *soma*, a kind of creeper with a succulent leafless stem, which, indigenous in the ancient home of the Aryans as well as in the soil of India and Persia, supplied an invigorating beverage supposed to confer health and immortality and regarded as the vital sap which vivified the world. Eventually the great esteem in which the *soma* plant was held led to its being itself personified and deified. The god Soma was once the Bacchus of India; the whole ninth Book of the Rig-Veda is devoted to his praise.[109] The inspiring effect of intoxication seemed to be due to the inherent divinity of the plant that produced it; and the preparation of the draught was looked upon as a sacred ceremony. "Indra, intoxicated by *soma*, does his great deeds, and indeed all the gods depend on *soma* for immortality."[110] Among the Persians and all Arabian peoples, a similar drink is regarded as the symbol of life and is made and drunk with religious ceremonies. The word *homa*, which is identical with the Vedic word *soma*, was used in two senses in the Zend-Avesta: first, it meant the twigs of a particular tree, the juice of which was extracted and drunk before the fire; second, they understood by it a spirit who had poured his life and vigor into that particular plant. There were many stories current in ancient times about the miraculous effects of the drinking of the *homa* juice—a panacea for all diseases—which led to the belief that the performance of this ceremony must prove highly beneficial to body and soul.[111] When Christianity was adopted by certain pagan peoples, the rite of communion was interpreted

105 McGee, in BAE, XVII, 209-212.
106 Hodge, in BAE, XXX, 25.
107 Stevenson, in BAE, XXX, 84-85, 88, 89, 92, 94, 98, 99.
108 Lumholtz, in *Int. Cong. Anthrop.*, 1893, 108.

109 Monier-Williams, *Brāhmanism*, 12; Phillips, *Vedas*, 49.
110 Hopkins, *Relig. India*, 113, 127.
111 Tiele-Gehrich, *Gchte. Relig.*, II, 92; Haug, *Parsis*, 152-153, 176, 282; Justi, *Persien*, 81-82; Geiger, *Ostiran. Kultur*, 230, 231; Jackson, *Zoroaster*, 67.

according to ancient views: "The draught from the mystic cup, originally the juice of Homa, was supposed to have supernatural effects. It imparted not only health and prosperity and wisdom, but also the power to conquer the spirits of evil and darkness, and a secret virtue which might elude the grasp of death."[112] The religious significance of intoxicants is seen perhaps in its most developed form among the Greeks, among whom the main distinguishing factor of the religion of Dionysus was the cult of an intoxicant.[113] In Rome the flower of the burning laurel furnished means for divination.[114]

§255. The Lucky and Unlucky.

In the East African Protectorate it is held to be unlucky to count cattle or any other living creatures, while it is particularly unlucky to count girls. "All odd numbers are unlucky, but more than any seven is a bad number. A man will never herd cattle six days and rest the seventh; he must go on to the eighth day. This is called 'Ndethia,' and were a man to cease herding on the seventh day all the cattle would die."[1] In Uganda nine is the sacred number.[2] In the dairy ceremonial of the Todas certain numbers recur with great frequency and may be regarded as having a special sanctity on this account. Such numbers are chiefly three, seven, and nine.[3] Among the Dyaks, even numbers are always an evil omen.[4] Chinese philosophy identifies even numbers with the Yin (female) part of nature, that is, with cold, darkness, and evil, while odd numbers represent the opposite male element (Yang),[5] Among the Chinese, as among the Hindus, sacred symbols are of great importance.[6] In Cambodia, years of even numbers are unlucky, so the tuft of hair on the head of children is cut off at eleven for girls and thirteen for boys, or at thirteen and fifteen.[7] Among the Indians of British Columbia to sneeze three times is lucky; it is also a good sign to sneeze through the right nostril.[8] With the Diegueno Indians the ceremonial number is three or four.[9] The modern notion that thirteen is unlucky is seen, among other exhibitions, in the desire of automobilists to avoid having it on their number-plates; some, indeed, go so far as to balk at any combination that includes the figure 13; a few even add up the numerals on the plate and if the total is thirteen insist on some other registration-number.[10]

McGee[11] mentions many survivals of the notion of mystical numbers. The vestigial uses of the binary-ternary system are innumerable. "Two persists as the basis of the semi-mystical Aristotelian classification, which still exerts strong influence on Aryan thought; two is the basis, also, of the largely mystical Chinese philosophy in which the complementary cosmologic elements, Yang and Yin, are developed into the Book of Changes; and it finds expression, either alone or in its normal union, in most Aryan cults. The mystical three pervades nine-tenths of modern literature and all modern folklore; it finds classic expression in the Graces and the Fates; it is particularly strong in Germanic and Celtic literature, cropping out in the conventional Three Wishes

112 Dill, *Nero*, 613.
113 Harrison, *Greek Relig.*, 413.
114 De Marchi, *Culto Priv.*, rev. in *Année Soc.*, I, 238.
1 Dundas, in JAI, XLIII, 526.
2 Roscoe, in JAI, XXXII, 40.
3 Rivers, *Todas*, 412.
4 Perelaer, *Dajaks*, 19.
5 DeGroot, *Relig. Sys.*, I, 65.

6 Hamy, in JAI, XVI, 243; Monier-Williams, *Brāhmanism*, 103-104.
7 Leclère, in PSM, XLIV, 776, 777.
8 Hill-Tout, in JAI, XXXV, 155-156.
9 Waterman, in AA, XII, 334.
10 N. Y. *Times*, Nov. 10, 1924.
11 "Primitive Numbers," in BAE, XIX, 847-848, 849.

and Three Tests (a survival of the ordeal), and also as a customary charm-number; and in these or related ways it persists in half the families and most of the child-groups even of this country and of today. The concept survives, also, in all manner of trigrams—triangles, triskelions, hearts, etc.—of mystic or symbolic character.

"The quaternary-quinary system survives conspicuously in the form of graphic devices, especially the world-wide cruciform symbol, which has taken on meanings of constantly increasing nobility and refinement with the growth of intelligence. Hardly less conspicuous are the classic and later literary survivals in the Four Elements—air, earth, fire, water—of alchemistic philosophy, the Four Winds of astrology and medieval cartography, the Four Iddhis of Buddha, and the Four Beasts of Revelation, with their reflections in the ecclesiastic writing of two milleniums; while the survivals in lighter lore are innumerable. The system persists significantly also in its augmentals, especially 9, 13, 25, 49 and 61. The numerical vestiges are naturally for the most part quaternary, since the quinary aspect is merged and largely lost in algorithm.

"The senary-septenary system survives as the bridge connecting almacabala and mathematics. In the graphic form it became Pythagoras's hexagram of two superposed triangles, the equally mystical hexagram of Brianchon, with which Paracelsus wrought his marvels, and the subrational hexagram of Pascal, while the current hexagram of the Chinese is apparently a composite of this and the binary as well as algorithmic systems. In the numerical form, 6 and more especially 7 play large rôles in lore and in the classic and sacred literature revived during the Elizabethan period; even so recently as the middle of the century the hold of the astrologic 7 was so strong as to retard general acceptance of the double discovery of the eighth planet, Neptune; and equally strong is the hold on the average mind of certain senary-septenary augmentals, particularly those coinciding with the augmentals of the lower system. In idealized form, the number 7 has exerted marvellous influence on thought and conduct, especially in the medial stages of human development; according to Addis, 'The common Hebrew word for 'swear' meant originally 'to come under the influence of the number 7''; and this is but a typical example of reverence for the magical number among various peoples.

"The almacabalic double of 13 (which is at the same time an augmental of 5) has largely lost its mystical meaning in Europe and America, apparently through friction with practical arithmetic; but it retains no little hold on the oriental mind, and finds expression in twenty-five-fold collectives in India and China, and in a rather frequent organization of Tibetan tribes into 25 septs or formal social units."

Fetish-directions are rather common among primitive peoples; the author[12] from whom we are quoting them refers them to life-experiences. In the conduct of both men and animals there is displayed a vague yet persistent placement of the two ever-present sides with respect to Self, a realization of a two-side universe—the danger-side in van, the safety-side in rear, with self the all-important center. "The evil side is outward, the good side at the place or domicile of the individual and especially of the group, as is shown by the homing instinct of the wounded carnivore, by the haste of the fire-crazed horse to meet the flames

---

12 In AA, I, 665-666, 667-668; in BAE, XIX, 844 (quoted), 846 (quoted).

in his familiar stall, by human and equine nostalgia, and by the barbarian longing for burial in native soil. Moreover, both animals and men reveal indications of instinctive placement of the sides in the individual organism; and the indications consistently point to persistent intuition of face and back as the essential factors of self. Yet there is a significant diversity in the assignment of the sides of the organism to the sides of the good-bad cosmos; in general it appears that among the lower and the more timid the back stands for or toward the evil, the face toward the good, and that among the higher and more aggressive the face is set toward the danger." It is stated also that right-handedness, apparently initiated by slight physiologic difference and unquestionably intensified by demotic selection, became even more predominant among primitive men than among their less superstitious descendants: "the dexter and dextrous hand came to be exalted in scores of languages as 'The One That Knows How' or 'The Wise One,' while the sinister hand was degraded by linguistic opprobrium into a symbol of evil and outer darkness. Naturally and necessarily the bilaterally symmetric division of the Ego into Right and Left fell into superposition with the antecedent Face-Back concept, and produced a quatern notion such as that expressed in the Cult of the Quarters. Happily this transition is crystallized in the language of the Pitta-Pitta of Queensland, which possesses directional inflections indicating Front and Back reckoned from the Ego; and it is especially significant that the inflection for Front applies also to Side."

A Hindu mode of worship requires the right side to be kept toward the object.[13] The left of the host is the place of honor in China, the right in Mongolia and Tibet.[14] When a war party including both of the great tribal divisions of the Osage was being organized, the people pulled down their wigwams and reset them in a ceremonial order, which was in two squares with a dividing avenue running east and west.[15] In all the ceremonies of the Parsees the north side is generally avoided. The children in the initiation-ceremony, the marrying couple at the time of the marriage-blessing ceremony, and the priests in all their religious ceremonies never sit with their faces turned toward the north. The old Iranians had a natural hatred for the north side, from which proceeded all kinds of dangers and evils, whether climatic, physical, or mental. On the other hand, the south was considered auspicious. The winds from the south were healthy and invigorating; coming in from the southern seas, they brought rain and plenty.[16]

Lucky and unlucky days or other periods of time have always had their devotees. In northeast Africa no marriages take place during three of the months, for they are held to be unlucky.[17] The influence of the aleatory element is even more striking in Madagascar; in one clan of the Sakalava all children born on Tuesday are put to death, while almost every family has a day similarly ill-omened to their newly-born offspring.[18] Nearly every Toda ceremony has its appointed day or days, the choice of these often being dependent upon another local institution, the sacred day of the village or of the dairy. "Every clan has certain days of the week on which people are restricted from following many of their ordinary occupations, although they are not the occasions of any special ceremonies." In addition to the village-day and the

13 Monier-Williams, *Brāhmanism*, 145.
14 Rubruck, *Eastern Parts*, 11.
15 LaFlesche, in AA, XVIII, 146.
16 Modi, in JASB, II, 410 note.

17 Paulitschke, *Ethnog. Nordost-Afr.*, I, 196.
18 Sibree, *Great Afr. Isl.*, 281.

dairy-day, another sacred day is that one in the week on which one's father died.[19] Among the Javanese, Sunday, Monday, Thursday, and Friday are good days; they marry preferably on Monday or Friday evening.[20] Among the Palaungs "it is considered very lucky for the child if it is born at or near the time of full moon. To be born during an eclipse of either the sun or the moon, or during the time when the old moon has disappeared and the new moon has not yet been seen, is most unlucky. If the first child of a family is born on a Saturday, it is considered unlucky not only for the baby but for the father and mother as well. In such a case the parents may die early; they may quarrel and divorce each other; or they may become ill or very poor. In order to prevent such misfortunes, offerings should be made in the image-house. Sometimes the relatives steal an unlucky baby as soon as it is born, bringing it back to the mother on the following day, telling her and the father that it was certainly born on Sunday."[21] In the Aztec year of eighteen months of twenty days each plus five supplementary days, the latter were unlucky; on them nothing was done.[22]

Although, with one exception, Homer has nothing to say of holy days,[23] they were common among other peoples of antiquity. In Babylon each day was consecrated to one or another god,[24] while Friday is still considered by the Persians to be an especially lucky day.[25] During the Middle Ages the aleatory element was prominent in folk-beliefs.[26] Among the South Slavs, days are fetishistic, some being lucky, others unfortunate.[27] In one of the Mediterranean islands, Tuesday is regarded as unlucky, and no work is ever begun on that day.[28] In East Prussia many days in the year are held to be unlucky: a child born on any one of these days, if it lives, will be sickly and will lead a precarious existence; no marriage concluded on one of these days will be successful, but will be marked by strife and poverty; purchase and sale will bring misfortune and misery; in short, no undertaking on such days will succeed. Five of them are especially unlucky and it is strongly advised not to do anything on those days. Especially unlucky days are April 1, when Judas was born, August 1, when the devil was thrown out of heaven, December 1, when Sodom and Gomorrah were submerged; persons born on these days are always unlucky. In Vienna the photographic studios have involuntary holidays on Wednesdays and Fridays, for people even of the more intelligent classes avoid being photographed then because it brings no luck.[29] Friday is widely regarded as an unlucky day, especially Friday the thirteenth. A newspaper has listed a number of famous happenings on Friday: the marriage of Washington and of Queen Victoria, the birth of Napoleon Bonaparte and of Shakespeare, the battles of Bunker Hill, Waterloo, and New Orleans; also the burning of Moscow, the discovery of America, the landing of the Mayflower's passengers, the execution of Joan of Arc, the destruction of the Bastille, the signing of the Declaration of Independence, the assassination of Julius Cæsar and of Lincoln. Such catalogues are significant of popular interest in the fetish-day.

19 Rivers, *Todas*, 405.
20 Wilken, *Vkde.*, 284.
21 Milne, *Eastern Clan*, 26.
22 Nadaillac, *Preh. Amer.*, 306.
23 Seymour, *Hom. Age*, 41.
24 Tiele-Gehrich, *Gchte. Relig.*, I, 210.

25 DeCunha, in JASB, I, 151.
26 Lacroix, *Middle Ages*, 100.
27 Krauss, *Sreća*, 89-90, 137.
28 Vuillier, *Forgotten Isles*, 133.
29 Frischbier, in *Am Ur-Quell*, I, 66, 157; Tamura, *Warum Hieraten Wir?* 37, 38.

§256. The Animal-Fetish.

BEFORE citing cases of animal fetishism, we list examples of the attitude taken by primitive peoples toward animals. That they do not hesitate to trace descent from beasts is a fact already familiar.[1]

The word for ancestors, among the natives of the Papuan Gulf, is practically the term by which all objects are designated that are held sacred. "A certain animal was regarded as sacred by the original ancestor; he never injured or killed it, never ate it as food when killed by anyone else, and because it was held sacred by him, his posterity for all time must also regard it as sacred. If a man accidentally kills a member of the family of his *ualare,* he sets aside a period for mourning, during which period he fasts from the principal kind of food, eating only enough to keep himself from absolute starvation; he also observes many of the customs of mourning as if he had lost a relative. If on the other hand he kills a member of his *ualare* family in a fit of anger or for any other reason that is not justifiable, as soon as he recognizes what he has done he gives himself over to violent grief, abstains from all kinds of food, isolates himself from his relatives, and ultimately dies of starvation."[2]

In the mythology of the Koryak the intimate association of men and animals is strikingly portrayed. At the time of Big-Raven, that is, during the mythological age, all objects on earth could turn into men, and *vice versa.* There were no real men then; Big-Raven lived with animals, and apparently with inanimate objects and phenomena of nature, as though they were men. "He was able to transform himself into a raven by putting on a raven coat, and to resume the shape of man at will. His children married or were given in marriage to animals, such as seals, dogs, wolves, mice; or phenomena of nature, as the wind, a cloud (or Wind-man, Cloud-man); or luminaries, like the Moon-man, Star-man;" or even to such lowly mates as special stones, trees, sticks, or plants. "Men were born from these unions. When Big-Raven was no more, the transformation of objects from one form to another ceased to take place, and a clear line . . . distinguishing men from other beings was established."[3] India teems with animal-life, and beasts of every description appear to live on terms of the greatest confidence with human beings. Everywhere they dispute possession of the earth with man. Metempsychosis leads the Hindus to think that a beast may at any moment develop human faculties; a noxious insect may contain a sage's soul; to them, stories of talking animals are not fables but incidents which contain no absurdity. The characteristics of animals and their relation to men also lead the natives to reverence them. "A Hindu," comments Monier-Williams,[4] "worships a cow because he is profoundly sensible of the services it renders him; he worships a serpent because he dreads its power of destroying him by the slightest puncture; and he worships a monkey because he stands in awe of the marvellous instinct it displays." Among the Nagas, men and tigers are still regarded as brothers; if an Angami kills a tiger, he says, "The gods have killed a tiger in the jungle" and never, "I have killed a tiger," while the priest of the village proclaims a day of abstention

1 D'Alviella, *Concep. God,* 49; Lippert, *Kgchte.,* I, 498; see JASB, III, 302, for list of cases of animal-descent.
2 Holmes, in JAI, XXXII, 426.

3 Jochelson, in AA, VI, 416-417.
4 *Brāhmanism,* 315, 316-317; Fawcett, in JASB, II, 271.

from work "on account of the death of an elder brother."[5] Wilken[6] cites many
fables, chiefly from the East Indies, of magicians whose lives were dependent
on the lives of animals so that they could be killed by killing the latter; also of
female jealousy exerted by getting control of a fish on whose life that of a
rival female depended; and he goes on to mention cases of a familiar beast or
bird with which one's welfare is thought to be connected. No one in Borneo
will intentionally kill a cobra, nor one particular species of the lizard, nor
owls, nor any of the birds of omen. There are certain animals and birds which
many families abstain from injuring, sometimes because of a dream, again
by reason of a tradition. Among some tribes a civet may not be killed, nor an
orang, nor a crocodile. It is believed by one tribe that an orang once helped
it on a critical occasion.[7] It may be recalled that the gibbon was similarly an
ally of the Bornean.[8]

Since the Samoan gods were supposed to have some visible incarnation, the
particular thing in which his god was in the habit of appearing was to the
Samoan an object of veneration. One, for instance, saw his god in the eel, others
in the shark, the turtle, the dog, or the owl. "A man would eat freely of what
was regarded as the incarnation of the god of another man, but the incarnation
of his own particular god he would consider it death to injure or to eat. The
god was supposed to avenge the insult by taking up his abode in that person's
body, and causing to generate there the very thing which he had eaten, until
it produced death." These cases approach totemism.[9]

There is some evidence among the Eskimo of a belief that bears, foxes, and
other animals had been at one time human beings.[10] The natives say that the
bear "talks sealish" to fascinate seals.[11] Nansen[12] reports a case where, a bear
having come near the house, the women untied their topknots that he might
think they were men and keep away—in the belief that bears had human
understanding. The mother of the boy who had first seen the bear slipped her
trousers down to her knees and shuffled about the room plaiting some straws,
which they said was to weaken the bear so as to make it easier to get the better
of him. There is evidence of a belief in imitative magic, for they all drank of
bear's blood in order to prove to the whole race of bears how they thirsted after
them. If they saw the track of a bear in the snow, they ate a little of it in
order to assure themselves of killing the bear if it should happen to come
back the same way. Little boys were given the kidneys of bears to eat in order
that they might be strong and courageous in bear-hunting.

"Among the Salish tribes it is uniformly believed that in the early days,
before the time of the tribal heroes or great transformers, the beings who
then inhabited the world partook of the character of both men and animals,
assuming the form of either at will."[13] The Indians of the Northwest Coast
ascribe to animals intelligence and the ability to understand human speech.
They believe that they themselves come from animals and so use animal-masks.[14]
A number of tribal names mean "those who became human beings by the
aid of the buffalo," or crane, or other animal, while the eagle, coyote, and

---

5 Hutton, in JAI, L, 41; *Sema Nagas*, 258 ff.

6 "De Betrekking, tusschen menschen-, dieren-, en planten-leven naar het volksgeloof," in VG, III.

7 Roth, in JAI, XXI, 111.

8 Furness, *Head-Hunters*, 55-56.

9 Turner, *Samoa*, 17-18, 69-70, 72; §260, below.

10 Hanbury, *Canada*, 68.

11 Reclus, *Prim. Folk*, 18.

12 *Esk. Life*, 204.

13 Haddon, quoting Hill-Tout, in *Brit. Assn. Adv. Sci.*, 1902, 741.

14 Andree, *Eth. Parallelen*, 159.

beaver are regarded as the original inhabitants of the world.[15] The Kootenay hold that there are spirits in all things, inanimate and animate; at death the human spirit enters into such things.[16] The Sioux, when they surrounded a herd of buffalo, demanded through their public criers that the souls of these animals should depart.[17] The turtle might be one's uncle, the mink an adopted son, the woodchuck a grandmother.

> All in the olden time,
> Or in the first of all,
> Of all things here on earth,
> Men were as animals
> And animals as men.
> But how this mystery was,
> No one can understand,
> Though some explain it thus:
> As Man was made the first,
> All creatures first were men,
> But as they gave themselves
> To this or that desire
> Like that of animals,
> And all their souls to it,
> So were they changed to brutes.[18]

"Although the belief in the powers of inanimate objects is common," comments Boas,[19] "we find in America that, on the whole, animals, particularly the larger ones, are most frequently considered as possessed of such magic power." In the folk-tales collected by Grinnell[20] there are many instances of animals helping men, even restoring the dead to life. In these stories animals talk: "Sometimes the buffalo-bulls talked to them, and sometimes the elk and the bear. It was always a male that talked. Not everyone could understand their language. Only now and then a person understood. . . . On the other hand, if favorably inclined, the mule-deer may help a person in many ways. As elsewhere pointed out, the white-tail deer is a powerful helper in love affairs. . . . It is said that in very old times beavers were not often killed, and that no Cheyenne woman would dress or even handle a beaver-skin. . . . The skunk possesses power. Doctors used its hide to hold their medicine. Men tied its tail to their horses' tails in war. It is engraved in ornament on the seeds employed by women in gambling, and is painted on robes and lodges. . . . In ancient times no one killed wolves or coyotes, and women would not handle their skins. . . . A man who could understand the speech of the wolves would turn back if a wolf or a coyote were killed by any member of a war-party with which he was journeying. These animals were seldom killed by the Cheyennes in old times, possibly because the medicine arrows were always wrapped up in the skin of a coyote."[21] Considering how important to self-maintenance were the various animals, notably the buffalo, it is not surprising that supernatural powers were attributed to them. From the buffalo the Indians had food, fuel, dress, shelter, and domestic furniture, shields for defense, points for arrows, and

15 HAI, I, 351, 531, 667, 859; II, 236, 717, 894.
16 Anon., "Northwestern Indians," in PSM, XLIII, 825.
17 Dorsey, in BAE, III, 288.
18 Leland and Prince, *Kulóskap*, 116, 162-163.
19 In HAI, II, 366.
20 *Folk Tales*, 87, 121, 155, 182, 195.
21 Grinnell, *Cheyenne*, II, 104-106.

strings for bows. According to the old Spanish chronicles of Coronado: "They make so many things of them as they have need of, or as many as suffice them in the use of this life." "The buffalo was the sign of the Creator on earth as the sun was his glorious manifestations in the heavens."[22]

"For the Indians nothing is dead, all things are alive, they are either gods or Indians. Animals, for instance, are not animals; they only look that way; but they are Indians just like the rest."[23] To understand the way of thinking of the Indians, comments Von den Steinen,[24] we must throw aside entirely our notions of the division between man and other animals. A medicine-man understands all the languages of beasts, birds, and fishes. The Indian does not say, "I am a man, and I think of the animals as acting like men." On the contrary, men are thought of as animals, both in the good and bad sense. The tribes identify themselves and each other with animals. Some animals are also thought of as being the lords of particular plants, such as tobacco, cotton, mandioca; others as lords of sleep, or of the hammock, or of the jars filled with water. The Indian is indebted to the animals for what he can do; they form the basis of his living. Why should he not attribute to them the other things whose origin he does not know?

In Costa Rica the deer is tabooed because the souls of the deceased, when they are not roaming alone in the darkness of the forest, seek out the body of the deer as an abiding-place.[25] Evil-workers among the Araucanians are thought to be malignant spirits who have taken the form of a beast, bird, reptile, or insect, and whose identity is revealed to the medicine-man in a trance. Frequently these agents are distinguished by some peculiarity or unusual color.[26] "Whereas the medicine-man among the Bakairi only temporarily, during narcosis, is transformed into beasts, and goes to heaven after death in human form, death among the Bororo is nothing else than a transformation into beasts, a dream the reality of which has become evident to everybody." The red parrots are Bororo, and the Bororo call themselves parrots; they never eat these birds and never kill tame ones, but lament when one of them dies. The dead of other tribes become other birds. The soul is thought of as a bird, on account of its flights in sleep.[27]

Animal forms in which the gods of the ancients were clothed have not an allegorical character; they indicate an animal-worship which reappears in more than one ancient and modern religion. "The ambiguous forms themselves, half-man, half-beast, simply prove the ignorance and credulity of the ancients in the matter of natural history.[28] The chief symbol of their gods might be a hewn image—Jahweh was often reverenced in the form of a steer—but was preferably a living animal, distinguished from all others by special marks, as a pledge of the nearness and eternity of God.[29] We also find the titles of Bear, Ox, Colt, and other similar names borne by the initiates of the different mysteries in Greece and Asia Minor; they go back to that period where the divinities themselves were represented under the forms of animals, and when the worshipper, in taking the name and semblance of his gods, believed that he identified himself with them.[30] When worshippers ate such animals, they

22 Mooney, in BAE, XIV, pt. II, 980.
23 Lumholtz, in *Scribner's Mag.*, XVI, 444;
"Aus allen Erdteilen," in *Globus*, LXXII, 19.
24 *Zent. Bras.*, 351; Preuss, in *Globus*, LXXXVI, 117.
25 Sapper, in *Globus*, LXXVI, 352.
26 Latcham, in JAI, XXXIX, 364.

27 Von den Steinen, *Zent. Bras.*, 511.
28 Maspero, in *Rev. de l'Hist. des Relig.*, I, 121, quoted in D'Alviella, *Concep. God*, 118.
29 Tiele-Gehrich, *Gchte. Relig.*, I, 310, 325-326; Tiele, *Sci. of Relig.*, 186.
30 Cumont, *Mithra*, 153.

thought they were eating the body of the god. "On the analogy of these instances we might conjecture that wherever a god is described as the eater of a particular animal, the animal in question was originally nothing but the god himself."[31] Owing to the capricious character of fetish-selection, one finds direct contradictions and usages exactly reversed. In Egypt, for instance, they worshipped their goats and ate their sheep; in one place the crocodile is venerated, while not far off it is exterminated.[32] The power of belief is seen in the statement by Diodorus[33] that in the time of famine the Egyptians ate each other rather than any animal which they considered sacred and that on one occasion a mob tore in pieces a Roman soldier who had killed a cat.

Islam admits to Paradise, and to a life hereafter, a long list of animals, beginning with the ass of the Prophet Mohammed, the camel of the Prophet Saleh, the calf of Abraham, the ram of Ishmael, the ox of Moses, the ant of King Solomon, the mule of the Queen of Sheba, the whale of Jonah, the dog of the Seven Sleepers, and last, but not least, the spider which spun its web across the entrance of the cavern in which Mohammed had sought refuge in his flight from Mecca; thus were his pursuers convinced that their human quarry could not be within.[34]

Fetish-Animals (*wild*). Turning now to specific fetish-animals, we find the serpent to be quite commonly in evidence and in some places to be the object of a cult. There are many instances in the Solomon Islands of the snake-fetish or snake-spirit.[35] One tribe in East Africa believes it is descended from the python; "these reptiles are looked upon as sacred and annual sacrifices are made upon a hill in Kadimu to the common ancestor. . . . Certain snakes, however, are looked upon as sacred animals among some of the Unyamwezi clans and it is highly probable that, as among the Kadimu, this is due to the belief that the snake was their common ancestor. Many Wanyamwezi consider it a deadly sin to kill a snake, and one occasionally meets an individual belonging to one of these clans who is said to be immune from the effects of snake poison."[36] There are also in Africa a number of cases of snake-cult and of belief in snake-incarnation.[37] In India the serpent is feared and revered, while it is thought that the name Nagar or serpent-men was given to a serpent-worshipping people by their neighbors. Every Nair family still holds the serpent sacred; it will not cut down a serpent-grove, as it is the place where the family serpents reside. A number of tribes have a serpent-totem: "the members will call themselves serpents, claim descent from a serpent, abstain from killing serpents." Not only do the Nairs still show traces of having done all this, but they continue to utter prayers and songs to the sacred serpents. "When anything goes wrong the astrologer generally finds something done to offend the sacred serpents."[38]

Wilken,[39] writing mainly of conditions in the East Indies, states that the python and the cobra are the animals generally selected by the spirits for their habitation—"not all the members of either class, but only individuals which become known as spirit-possessed through dreams or inference from other signs. Should one of these reptiles be in the habit of frequenting the vicinity

31 Frazer, *Golden Bough*, I, 325 ff.
32 Herodotus, *Hist.*, II, 42; Strabo, *Geog.*, XVII; Letourneau, *Soc.*, 272.
33 Quoted in Hutchinson, *Living Races*, 211.
34 Veteran Diplomat, in N. Y. *Times*, Feb. 14, 1915.

35 Fox and Drew, in JAI, XLV, 135 ff.
36 Hobley, in JAI, XXXIII, 348.
37 Main, *Relig. Chastity*, 301-302.
38 Panikkar, in JAI, XLVIII, 290.
39 In VG, III, 240-241.

of a village house, it is always regarded as the good genius of some one or other of the principal men in it." The snake must not be killed but handled with reverence. Among the many cases mentioned is one where a small cobra came under a house and crawled about, not heeding those who were watching its movements. "I found it was a constant visitor, and was said to be a 'spirit-helper' of a man of the place, who, no doubt, would have fined any one who dared to lay violent hands upon it. In another case, a large python went up into a house, and the inmates interpreted the visit as that of one of the beneficent powers." The great boa is the most formidable of all demons who people the spiritual world of the Jibaro Indians. "He is the original father of witchcraft; it is from his body that the sorcerers receive the poison with which their organism is impregnated and the invisible arrow, which they discharge against their victims. After death the souls of the medicine men are also believed to enter into the boa. The Jibaros, like all Indians, therefore particularly fear this monster, and when they kill a boa they think that they kill a powerful sorcerer."[40] The snake was revered by the ancients and sacred snakes were to be found in the temples.[41]

The turtle is regarded as a fetish in the Pacific Islands. "Turtle fishing is not gone in for much, as the natives are superstitious about the turtle, and civilisation has not yet been able to dispel their fears. One of the chief ones is that the eggs are sacred and may not be eaten. But one by one," comment Hardy and Elkington,[42] "their superstitions are going, for they see how the white man prospers in spite of scorning all their sacred ideas, and that now and then makes them courageous enough to break through the barrier, and when once a superstition has been found untrue, they are not slow in testing another, if by challenging it they can see any gain for themselves." This element of rational selection in their mores, it should be noted, is restricted to the economic interests, a field in which it is possible to get tests and verification.[43] In South Africa "the crocodile is held in respect by every Becwana tribe, even by those who do not venerate it as a totem. It is commonly believed that if a man wounds a crocodile, the man will be ill as long as the crocodile is ill of its wound; and that if the crocodile dies, the man dies too."[44] In the Upper Congo region, the crocodile is associated with witchcraft: in cases of accidental death such as the swamping of a canoe in a storm or through over-loading, the natives say god or providence caused the accident; but other accidents in which they observe what they consider exceptional circumstances, as the upsetting of a canoe by a crocodile, they put to the account of witchcraft, as no crocodile would have done it unless it had been instructed to do so by a witch or unless the witch had gone into the animal and made it commit the outrage.[45] Wilken[46] treats of the lizard as a fetish and as a motif in ornament; he finds it revered not only in the East Indies but all over Polynesia as well, though not so widely honored as the crocodile. In the legends of some of the American Indians the turtle appears as a perfect Falstaff, a worthless old scamp who is nevertheless liked by everybody and greatly privileged.[47]

Rapacious animals are often worshipped or revered, either being greatly

---

40 Karsten, "Jibaro," in BAE, Bull. LXXIX, 61.

41 Beloch, Griech. Gesch., I, 112; Main, Relig. Chastity, 302-304.

42 S. Seas, 181-182.

43 Keller, Soc. Evol., ch. V.

44 Willoughby, in JAI, XXXV, 300.

45 Weeks, in JAI, XXXIX, 449-450.

46 "Hagedis," in VG, IV, 131 ff., 142, 147 ff., 153-155.

47 Leland and Prince, Kulóskap, 124.

feared or admired on account of their powers. The first seems to be the case among the West Africans,[48] while in the Papuan Gulf region "the wild boar's tusk, the acquisition of which is greatly desired as a mark of bravery, is not so much coveted as a personal adornment, as for the courage, ferocity, and daring which it is supposed to contain and to be capable of imparting to anyone who secures it."[49] The mammoth plays an important part in Chukchi beliefs; "if the tusks are seen above ground, this is a bad omen, and unless an incantation is uttered something untoward will happen." Because of various beliefs, the search for mammoth-ivory was tabooed in former times, and "even now, a man who finds a mammoth-tusk has to pay for it to the 'spirit' of the place by various sacrifices. The search for such tusks is considered a poor pursuit for a man, notwithstanding the high price which the ivory brings." Another reason for the reverence accorded animals of prey is the belief that they may harbor the spirit of a deceased man; this is clearly seen in the attitude of the Gilyak toward the bear. "It is the common duty of clansmen to feed the bear, and to take part in the bear-festival, when the bear, either tame or wild, is killed. This festival has both a religious and a social significance. In the former case, it is a religious duty to venerate the slain bear, for he may belong to the fraternity of the 'owners of the mountain,' or be the incarnation of some remote fellow clansman's spirit, which has been received into that fraternity. Again, the bear is regarded as the intermediary between mortals and the 'owner of the mountain.' " The bear-festival serves to protect the people from the wrath of the slain animal and its relatives.[50]

Although the bear-festival is common to all the Palæo-Siberians and is celebrated also by some of the Neo Siberians, it has reached its highest development among the Ainos, who honor the animal as a god. They have good reason to respect the bear: it is most valuable to them, affording them food and clothing and a medicine, the bear-gall, which is greatly prized. On the other hand, it can do them great injury, as when it enters their dwellings or kills their domestic animals. Therefore it seems natural that they should seek to propitiate the bear, to confer upon it a title of great honor, and that they should consider an atonement necessary for putting it to death. At the end of winter a young bear is caught, confined in a wooden cage, and fed by the wife of the captor. The bear-festival usually takes place in September or October, by which time the captive has grown so large and strong as to threaten to break the cage. It is then killed with great ceremony. The man who gives the feast assumes all expenses and invites his friends and relatives. Such a festival is very expensive, for enormous quantities of saké are consumed; hence it is considered a great honor to give a bear-feast, though at the present time such celebrations are becoming less and less frequent. After some ceremonies in the house, offerings are made before the bear-cage by the host and others. Some saké is given to the bear in a special cup. The woman who has reared it weeps to show her sorrow at its approaching fate. A rope is thrown around its neck and it is led out of the cage and taken to the sacred hedge where it is killed. After it is skinned and disemboweled, the legs and trunk are separated from the head, which remains in the skin. The blood is caught in cups and greedily drunk; the liver is cut in small pieces and eaten raw; and the flesh and entrails are preserved in the house, to be divided among the participants in the feast on the following day. The head is placed on the sacred

---

48 Ellis, *Ewe*, 23.
49 Holmes, in JAI, XXXII, 427.

50 Czaplicka, *Aborig. Siberia*, 259-260, 45-46, 296.

hedge, found on the east side of every house, where it is held sacred and honored as a representative of the gods.[51]

Foxes play a conspicuous part in the legendary lore of Japan as retainers of Inari San, the god of rice, and Kitsune-mochi or "fox-possession" is a common belief. "So important have these followers become, that they almost obscure their lord, and have usurped his worship and his temples. All over Japan one sees their images, of all sizes and ages, funny and grotesque, but often menacing. In the popular fancy the fox is endowed with great powers. He can be invisible at will, or can assume human form, though his imperfect speech will often betray him in spite of his disguise. He brings good fortune, but is so punctilious in his etiquette that he is easily offended—and then woe unto him who offends! He will suffer endless misery, for the fox never forgives. Moreover, the beasts are rapacious and need a deal of feeding; and as all fox families are seventy-five in number, it is nothing short of ruinous to have them attach themselves to a human household, which is their uncomfortable habit. Consequently, a man said to possess foxes is shunned. His friends hesitate to visit his house for fear of incurring the enmity of the invisible animals. Even the land loses its value and cannot be sold, however rich it may be, for where once the fox has been foxes will go; and whoever occupies the place must feed the hungry seventy-five. So deep-rooted is this belief that intermarriage among the possessed families is almost compulsory, for the unafflicted would think not once but many times before allying themselves to the mysterious Kitsune. Besides, he is mean enough to enter the form of his human benefactor, and cause him to yelp and bark, frothing at the mouth, and fill him with a most undesirable form of madness."[52]

In India, as in other Asiatic countries, the elephant, on account of its nature as well as because of the Buddhist conceptions associated with it, supplies several sorts of amulet. Its ivory is considered to be protective against the effect of the jealous or envious eye, bad dreams, and the like, a virtue extended sometimes to bone which, possibly through ignorance, is taken as ivory.[53] Belief in transmigration accounts for some of the notions concerning leopard-men in the Naga hills. "Both the Angami and Sema agree in holding that there is no actual transformation of the body of the lycanthropist into a leopard. What he seems to do is to project his soul into a particular animal with which his human body also thus becomes very intimately associated." A leopard which is thus the recipient of a human soul may be recognized by having five claws on each foot, and is called by the Angami a term meaning "real man."[54] Tigers are honored in many places.[55] In Sumatra "they speak of the tigers with a degree of awe, and hesitate to call them by their common name, terming them respectfully *nenek* (ancestors), as really believing them such. No consideration will prevail on a countryman to catch or to wound one, but in self-defence, or immediately after the act of destroying a friend or relation. When an European procures traps to be set, by the means of persons less superstitious, the inhabitants of the neighbourhood have been known to go at night to the place, and practise some forms, in order to persuade the animal, when caught, or when he shall perceive the bait, that it was not laid by them, or with their consent."[56] The Jibaro Indians regard a jaguar which

51 Hitchcock, in USNM, 1890, 474 ff.; Czaplicka, *Aborig. Siberia*, 296-297.
52 Mumford, in *Cosmopolitan Mag.*, XXVI, 577.

53 Hildburgh, in JAI, XXXVIII, 197.
54 Hutton, in JAI, L, 42-43.
55 Wilken, in VG, III, 83.
56 Marsden, *Sumatra*, 292.

attacks and kills people as the incarnation of the soul of an evil sorcerer which has entered that wild beast with a view to harming or killing his enemies. Some years ago an Indian woman was killed by a jaguar in the neighborhood of Rio Zamora; the natives consequently resolved to take revenge, arranged a hunting of the animal, and succeeded in killing it. They thereafter made a trophy of its head and a victory-feast was celebrated in the ordinary way.[57]

Special qualities have given some wild animals a peculiar place in native beliefs. On account of its cunning, the jackal plays an important part in Hindu folk-tales, as the hare does in the folklore of the Bushmen of South Africa, the rabbit among the American negroes, Reynard the Fox in European folk-lore, and the badger in the folk-beliefs of the Japanese.[58] There are hundreds of tales in South Africa concerning the adventures of the hare, tales with which every Mocwana mother is familiar; and they all go to show that he is the "slimmest" [most rascally] of all the animals. Occasionally one sees a Mocwana wearing a hare's foot as a charm.[59] In northeast Africa the hare brings good or bad luck—good luck if he runs in the direction of the pedestrian, bad if in the opposite direction or if he crosses the path.[60] When the supply of hares becomes exhausted, as it frequently does, an Athapascan tribe believes that they have mounted to the sky by means of the trees and that they will return in the same way when they reappear.[61]

Fish, Birds, etc. The sea has furnished a number of fetishes. Fish, eels, and sharks are common fetishes in Melanesia.[62] In the Solomons all sharks are not sacred, but a great many are thought to be possessed by ghosts. At Ulawa there were two familiar sharks who were widely known and respected; "these ghost sharks did not harm their worshippers, but were often sent by them to kill men at a distance." One such shark was given some of the earth on which the victim's spittle had fallen or some of the earth from his footprints in the sand, so as to be able to trace the victim.[63] Toads among the Zuñi were regarded as sacred and were kept under pots in order to obtain rain and fine weather. "By some of the tribes frogs were regarded as the gods of the waters, and, like the toads, were beaten when rain did not fall."[64] Among the offerings which some South German women of today sacrifice at the time of child-birth or during women's diseases is the frog made of iron or wax or, less commonly, of silver.[65]

"The fish, as the inhabitant of the mysterious, indestructible never-resting water, early impressed man deeply, and was considered by him as the genius and representative of the life-producing element. Traces of the veneration of the fish, sometimes revealed in taboos, are found everywhere in ancient times and still exist in various parts of the world." A center of ichthyolatry in antiquity was Syria, where a fish-goddess was worshipped as a phase of the great Semitic mother goddess Astarte, being regarded as a personification of the fructifying power of the water. Reminiscences of this cult still survive in the cherishing of sacred inviolate fishes in some places near mosques. Certain species of fish were sacred and forbidden food to all the Syrians, who believed that if they ate the sacred fish they would be visited by ulcers. Yet fish were daily cooked and presented on the table of the goddess, being afterwards consumed by

57 Karsten, "Jibaro," in BAE, LXXIX, 33-34.
58 Mitra, in JASB, VI, 139.
59 Willoughby, in JAI, XXXV, 300.
60 Paulitschke, *Nordost-Afr.*, II, 26.

61 HAI, I, 667.
62 Rivers, *Melan. Soc.*, I, 336 ff.
63 Fox and Drew, in JAI, XLV, 163.
64 Hodge, in BAE, XXX, 26.
65 Thilenius, in *Globus*, LXXXVII, 105.

the priests; and Assyrian cylinders display the fish laid on the altar or presented before it, while, in one example, a figure which stands by in an attitude of adoration is clothed, or rather disguised, in a gigantic fish-skin. Such disguise implies that the worshipper presents himself as a fish, as a being kindred to his sacrifice and doubtless also to the deity to which it is consecrated. "Tales of the fish as a medium of transformation and incarnation of spirits and ghosts are met with among various nations, and in later times the fish seems to have been, next to the bird, a symbol of the departed human soul. The fish as carrier of man across the water was illustrated by the story of Arion and the dolphin as told by Herodotus, and by the Biblical narrative contained in the book of Jonah. Parallel narratives of a man being swallowed by a sea monster were quoted from Greek, Polynesian and Cherokee lore." The belief in the magical healing properties of the fish is also widespread. "The fish was generally considered as a being of good omen, benevolent and beneficent to man, and by reason of its own great fertility it was a symbol of increase and abundance. Various regions had their favorite species of fish which were endowed with supernatural qualities. Thus among the classical nations the dolphin was termed the 'saviour fish' (piscis salvator). In the Far East (China and Japan) the carp was the fish of good omen, while among the ancient Irish the salmon was the 'fish of wisdom,' the mere sight of which brought healing."[66]

Among the ancients, flies, vermin, and mice were thought to possess supernatural and daimonic qualities.[67] Like the dog, the cock is a defender by night, and also like the dog is the protecting fetish of nomads. Lippert[68] believes that the cultus of the cock led to his domestication. The cock was sacred to Buddha, and in Tibet was kept on the roofs of monasteries, never being killed nor, in some places, ever eaten. Our practice of having the cock on weathervanes (weather-cock) is a survival of the time when the bird was believed to keep watch against spirits; it figures in such a capacity in Teutonic mythology.[69] The Nagas use a red cock to get omens, while a white chicken is used in promoting harvests and good luck.[70] In the case of one Russian tribe a cock or hen is carried before the coffin and cast across the grave to some poor person, with a wish for an easy flight for the deceased to heaven.[71] In the South Seas the frigate-bird, being more or less sacred, is not eaten and seldom harmed.[72] In West Borneo the hawk is regarded as the first ancestor, which lived and had many offspring and then turned into a bird; it will come to aid one if he scatters rice.[73] In New Zealand two special varieties of owl are sure signs of a plentiful season.[74] In China, the bat is an emblem of happiness, from the similarity of the sound of its name and the word for felicity.[75] According to beliefs, here as in India, ghosts may appear in the form of birds of prey.[76] In 1921 a riot occurred in Bombay when two European boys killed some sacred pigeons in the streets of that city.[77]

Birds were common fetishes in the New World. One member of the Tlinkit tribe has had a red-bird in his possession for a number of years; he attributes

---

66 Casanowicz, in AA, XIX, 314-315; Smith, Relig. Sem., 292-293.
67 Justi, Persien, 88; Smith, Relig. Sem., 293.
68 Kgchte., I, 496-497, 556-562; II, 393; Müller, Sacred Books, IV, 193 ff.
69 Stallybrass, Grimm's Mythology, III, 1025-1026.
70 Furness, in JAI, XXXII, 460, 461.

71 Russian Ethnog. (Russ.), I, 444.
72 Hardy and Elkington, S. Seas, 131.
73 Veth, Borneo's Wester-afdeeling, II, 310-311.
74 Best, in AAAS, 1904, 449.
75 DeGroot, Relig. Syst., I, 53.
76 Goldziher, in Globus, LXXXIII, 301.
77 N. Y. Times, Jan. 26, 1921.

every piece of good fortune to his possession of this bird.[78] The Kwakiutl prayed to the lark for avoidance of sickness and misfortune.[79] The eagle was the greatest fetish-bird of the Indians; among the Haida, passes made with eagle fans were thought to be effectual in conjuring, a belief which reappears in many tribes. The wing-bones were often employed as sucking-tubes with which medicine-men attempted to cure disease; they were also fashioned into whistles to be carried by warriors or used in ceremonies; and the talons formed powerful amulets, having secondary value as ornaments, while the feathers were of even greater importance. "The eaglets, when required for feathers, have their heads washed; they are killed by pressure on the thorax, and buried with appropriate rites in special cemeteries, in which offerings of small wooden images and bows and arrows are yearly deposited." Some tribes had property in eagles.[80] The Caddo in old times would never kill an eagle, unless for its feathers by a hunter regularly initiated and consecrated for that purpose.[81] The Pimas have a legend of an eagle which would occasionally assume the shape of an old woman, visit the pueblos, and steal women and children, carrying them to his abode on an inaccessible cliff; on one occasion the eagle seized a girl with the intention of making her his wife.[82] The Jibaros look upon a certain mysterious night-bird with superstitious dread, believing that the soul of the murdered enemy may take the shape of that bird to send them sickness and death.[83] The Guiana Indians regard some birds as spirits bent on inflicting punishment; these may be killed; on the other hand, there are certain birds—owls, goat-suckers, and others—which must not be killed under any circumstance whatever. Such birds do not wish to injure the Indians but to give them a warning or token. "They are receptacles for departed souls, who come back again to earth, unable to rest for crimes done in their days of nature; or they are expressly sent by Jumbo to haunt cruel and hard-hearted masters, and retaliate injuries received from them. . . . If it be heard close to the negro's or Indian's hut, from that night misfortune sits brooding over it; and they await the event in terrible suspense." The natives have the greatest superstition with regard to the goat-sucker and would not kill it at any price. "They say it keeps communication with the dead, and brings messages to their conjurers. Even the common people on the coast return in a great measure this superstition, and hold the bird in great awe. Its nocturnal habits, the swiftness and peculiarity of its flight, and its note, which breaks the silence of the night, have no doubt contributed to the fear which Indians and Creoles entertain for the Wacarai or Sumpy Bird."[84]

Fetish-Animals (domesticated). Respect and reverence is paid to domestic animals among many pastoral peoples in various parts of the globe. They are regarded on the one hand as the friends and kinsmen of men, and on the other as sacred beings of a nature akin to the gods; their slaughter is permitted only under exceptional circumstances, and in such cases are never used to provide a private meal, but necessarily form the basis of a public feast if not of a public sacrifice. One of the clearest cases is that of a nomadic tribe in East Africa which "gave the name of parent to no human being but only to the ox and cow, the ram and ewe, from whom they had their nourishment."[85]

78 Jones, *Thlingets*, 163.
79 Boas, in BAE, XXXV, pt. II, 1328-1329.
80 Hough, "Eagle," in HAI, I, 409-410.
81 Mooney, in BAE, XIV, 1093.
82 Fewkes, in BAE, XXVIII, 45.

83 Karsten, "Jibaro," in BAE, Bull. LXXIX, 53.
84 Roth, in BAE, XXX, 175, 274.
85 Pinkerton's Collection: *Africa*, I, 8; Smith, *Relig. Sem.*, 296.

Cow-fetishism is indicated by many customs and taboos: by national custom no Yoruba may milk a cow, and in consequence cows are always tended by foreign-born slaves[86]—an exception to the prevailing custom of cattle-raisers.[87] Cases of Hindu reverence for the cow might cover much space: "the water it ejects ought to be preserved as the best of all holy waters—a sin-destroying liquid which sanctifies everything it touches, while nothing purifies like cow-dung."[88] In the Code of Manu[89] one of the blackest of crimes is to kill a cow. Among the Greeks of Homer's time there was evidently a taboo on the milk of cows, as on the flesh of fish;[90] and the late Professor Seymour once remarked, while commenting upon the non-use of cow's milk in Homer, that in Crete it is still believed that if a man milks a cow he will die before the year is out.[91] As with certain negro populations in the valley of the Upper Nile, the Egyptians used only bulls for food; to kill a cow, or even eat her flesh, was more than a crime, it was anathematized as a sacrilege. "Neither will any man or woman amongst them kiss a [cow-eating] Greek upon the mouth, nor use a Greek knife for the spit or cooking-pot."[92] The Apis at Memphis, a black animal with certain white markings, was regarded as a special incarnation of the highest deity; it was born in a miraculous way, was revered all over Egypt as a god, and after death was buried with the greatest ceremony.[93] The ass also figures in the cult of the ancients; so do goats and swine.[94] Male swine were the exclusive sacrificial animals of the Manchu and were fattened in the temple-court.[95] Cats also have a place in the cult, while many superstitions surround them today.[96] They enjoy special consideration in some European districts; whoever kills one is bound to die in the course of the year.[97] But more significant in primitive religion is the attitude toward the horse.

The horse has come in for much reverence and has been supposed to have special knowledge and powers indicating possession by a daimon. In Homer,[98] Hera inspires the horse of Achilles to prophesy. "Next to speed, the property of the horse most spoken of in the Avesta is that of sight. The horse was thought to possess the power to see on the darkest and most cloudy night a hair lying on the ground, and to distinguish whether it was a hair of the tail or mane of a horse." One horse saw, "from the distance of two forsangs, an ant on a black saddle cloth." The king's stable was deemed by more modern Persians one of the most sacred of sanctuaries; a noble who aspired to the throne took refuge there and remained unmolested till he was pardoned.[99] Oracles were taken by the ancient Germans and Slavs from the neighing or special movements of white horses.[100] Tacitus's[101] account of the observation of the sacred horses states that the priest and king regarded themselves as the servants of the gods but the horses as their confidants. The Greek Pegasus and Centaur have appeared in literature for ages. "The American Indian had a groundless fear of the horses he had never before seen; many victories have

86 Ellis, *Yoruba*, 119.
87 §102, of the text.
88 Monier-Williams, *Brāhmanism*, 318.
89 Bühler, *Manu*, XI, 59, 108-116.
90 Keller, *Hom. Soc.*, 33, 47-48, 169.
91 Seymour, *Hom. Age*, 218-219.
92 Herodotus, *Hist.*, II, 18, 41; Letourneau, *Prop.*, 147; Schweinfurth, *Heart of Afr.*, II.
93 Tiele-Gehrich, *Gchte. Relig.*, I, 94.
94 Lehmann, *Overtro*, I, 62; Deut., XXII, 10; Lippert, *Kgchte.*, I, 503-506, 543-553.

95 Grube, in *Berlin Mus.*, VII, 46.
96 Lippert, *Kgchte.*, I, 554-556.
97 Vuillier, *Forgotten Isles*, 133.
98 *Iliad*, XIX, 404 ff.
99 Modi, in JASB, IV, 8, 13; II Kings, XXIII, 11.
100 Schrader, *Aryan*, 263; Hehn, *Haus-thiere*, 20 ff.; Lippert, *Kgchte.*, I, 530-531.
101 *Germ.*, 10; Chadwick, in *Folk-Lore*, XI, 273.

been won solely through them." The Spanish estimated the military value of a horse as equal to that of six Spanish soldiers, and, to keep up the natives' fear, forbade any one of them to ride. Similarly with the dog. "The help of the dogs in the conquest of America is likewise not to be underestimated. The natives had a fearful terror of these big bloodthirsty beasts which represented a cross in which the mastiff-type predominated. Accustomed to dumb or at least only howling dogs, they could not even listen to baying without falling into the greatest fright."[102] It is said that the Indians regarded a dismounting horseman with terror, believing that a single being was separating itself into two parts before their eyes.[103] The same impression was made on the Herero, as one of their chiefs told Büttner;[104] while the natives were uncertain whether to flee or to defend themselves, the strange two-headed being separated into two parts, "an unknown quadruped and a man whose wide-floating mantle they had taken to be bird-wings." The horse was a marvel to the Indians and came to be regarded as sacred. For a long time it was worshipped by the Aztec and by most of the tribes was considered to have a mysterious or sacred character. "Its origin was explained by a number of myths representing horses to have come out of the earth through lakes and springs or from the sun. When Antonio de Espejo visited the Hopi of Arizona in 1583, the Indians spread cotton scarfs or kilts on the ground for the horses to walk on, believing the latter to be sacred. This sacred character is sometimes shown in the names given to the horse, as the Dakota *súnka wákan*, 'mysterious dog.' "[105] The Yakuts reverenced the horse, but for another reason: it was the basis of their self-maintenance.[106] The horse is a devil, according to a Roumanian folk-tale; its origin is as follows. Until the first human beings transgressed the law of God there was no horse; it appeared after the fall, when Adam and Eve were forced to work the land in the sweat of their brow. Adam started to work without asking God's blessing and help, and as fast as he ploughed the grass grew again. In despair he fell on his knees and cried: "Dear God, help me!" God heard his supplication and gave him the following advice: "Adam, take these two devils which I give to you; put them to the plough and work."[107]

That horses have souls and a life hereafter is the belief of some historical peoples. At the close of their war with China, the Japanese consecrated with much religious ceremony a magnificent monument, at Tokio, to the memory of their horses lost in the campaign, while in 1905 grand funeral-services were held at Miyagi for the horses killed in the war with Russia. "In the presence of the Governor of the province, of Princes of the imperial family, and of all the leading military, civil, and religious officials of the nation prayers were recited by the clergy of the Buddhist and Shinto rites for the welfare and repose of the spirits of the horses that had given their lives in the service of their country during the conflict. Offerings of wheat and oats were placed on a large altar, and then the ranking General present delivered a memorial address while the troops stood at attention. . . . He solemnly thanked their spirits—that is to say, their souls—in the name of the Emperor, of the army, and of the nation for the assistance which they had afforded to their human comrades . . . and assured them that their names would be held in affec-

102 See §99 of this *Case-Book;* Friederici, in *Globus*, XC, 304.
103 Haebler, *Amerika*, 370-371.
104 *Walfischbai*, 33.

105 Grinnell, "Horses," in HAI, I, 569.
106 Sieroshevski, *Yakuts* (Russ.), 262.
107 Kaindl, in *Globus*, XCII, 288.

tionate and honored remembrance." It would seem that Alexander the Great entertained the belief in the hereafter of horses for, not content with entombing his favorite charger, Bucephalus, killed under him in battle, in a splendid mausoleum, he founded and built as a lasting memorial to him the city of Bucephala. Frederick the Great erected one of the most beautiful Lutheran churches in Prussian Poland as a memorial to his favorite charger. There are instances of animals being interred within Christian churches, including a favorite dog, a pet monkey, and a famous horse. The Duke of Wellington erected at his country seat a stately tomb for Copenhagen, the charger which he had ridden throughout the battle of Waterloo, when he remained no less than seventeen hours in the saddle without dismounting. The horse was buried with full military honors.[108]

White Animals. A special cult-animal is one with a peculiarity or pronounced characteristic, like an albino or one of white color.[109] The Kavirondo in Africa use the feather from a white chicken to keep off hail and kill a white fowl to ward off disaster consequent upon killing a python.[110] White fowls are fetishistic in West Africa also.[111] Some Malay tribes trace their descent to two white apes, and believe that the soul of the chief goes into them.[112] The Uncpapas gave a festival to the man who killed a white buffalo.[113] The albino buffalo was sacred among all the close cognates of the Omaha and also among the Dakota tribes. Catlin mentions that the Mandan gave the Blackfeet the value of eight horses for a white buffalo-skin, which they deposited with great ceremony in their medicine-lodge. Personal names referring to the white buffalo occur in all the cognates.[114] A white or black deerskin possessed a wonderful charm for the Hupa Indians of California. A chief whom the writer saw had three which had been handed down so long as family heirlooms that he did not know when they were acquired. "The possession of them had exalted him to such a pitch that no one crossing the river with him in a canoe could possibly be drowned, and one or more added to the store would make him 'all the same as God.' "[115] White animals figure prominently in the religious ceremonies of the Tarahumari.[116]

For an oblation to Surya, the sun, the fee in Brahmanism was a white horse or a white bull, either of them representing the proper form of the sun.[117] At Kubla Khan's hunting-castle is said to have been kept a herd of ten thousand snow-white horses whose milk only descendants of Genghis Khan and another favored class might drink. A yearly offering of milk from this herd was made by the emperor to secure the favor of the various spirits. Some tribes west of the Yenesei show especial veneration for white horses, never riding or driving them but offering them to their gods; they sacrifice dark horses to the evil spirits. In Siam the white elephant appears as a symbol of purity and light and plays a great rôle in worship; great rewards are offered for catching one, and his entry into Bangkok is made a national festival. Such a case occurred in 1926. The white elephant is really an albino. The God Indra rode on one.[118]

108 N. Y. *Times*, Feb. 14, 1915.
109 Lippert, *Kgchte.*, I, 498, 531.
110 Hobley, in JAI, XXXIII, 343, 344.
111 Kingsley, *W. Afr. Studies*, 488.
112 Skeat and Blagden, *Malay Penin.*, II, 189, 190, 192.
113 Fletcher, in *Peabody Mus.*, III, 260 ff.

114 Fletcher and LaFlesche, in BAE, XXVII, 283, 284.
115 Powers, in *Contrib. N. Am. Ethnol.*, III, 78.
116 Lumholtz, in *Scribner's Mag.*, XVI, 440.
117 Hopkins, *Relig. India*, 192, note.
118 Ritter, *Asien*, I, 144, 476; N. Y. *Times*, Dec. 12, 1926.

Mithra drove a high-wheeled chariot which was drawn by beautiful white horses.[119] Sacred white horses were known to the Greeks and Romans, while such animals, used for purposes of divination, were pastured by the ancient Germans at public expense in sacred woods and groves.[120]

§257. The Man-Fetish.

PROMINENT among physical peculiarities that have conferred fetish-character is albinism. The albino is usually regarded as something strange and inexplicable, to be respected and avoided. Albinos are not rare in D'Entrecasteaux, though they are seldom able to marry; no one wants them. This is especially the case with the males; the girls avoid them. "Their colour, or rather their want of it, is regarded as a physical deformity, and a legend of a great flood tells how it was stayed by an albino being cast into the water."[1] In the Congo region, albinos are rare and are regarded with respect; "although they may marry, there are many women who, through fear, refuse to have them. The skin is a dirty white with a tint of pink in it. The hair is curly and very light, and the eyes are red and intolerant of the light. They are repulsive looking, and one is glad to turn the eyes quickly in another direction."[2] Yet another writer[3] on Africa says: "It used to make me homesick, in our little African clearing, to see the albino woman. . . . Homesick people are always longing for a visit, and that albino woman was so white!" Albinos are said to be treated no differently from the normal natives among the Ba-Mbala, yet this does not apply to other abnormalities, for the case is mentioned of a certain boy, who, though black, had red hair and brown eyes; "he was accused of being possessed by *Moloki* [evil spirits] and killed."[4] On the island of Nias all albinos are regarded as children of evil spirits. If the mother gives it out that she was ravished by a spirit, she and her child are spared; but if the child appears like a normal child, it is regarded as no albino, the man whom it resembles is declared to be the father, and he and the mother are both executed.[5] In Dutch Guiana albinos enjoy great honor.[6] According to the Department of Anthropology of the American Museum of Natural History, the so called "White Indians" of Panama are merely albino Indians. The albino population is despised and ostracized by the rest of the Indians.[7]

Any bodily peculiarity, atavistic or otherwise, may lead to the individual being regarded as possessed by a spirit. Six-fingered children are said to be more common among the negroes of the Gold Coast than in Europe, and because they were supposed to bring ill luck they were formerly exposed as a regular practice. Today they are made away with clandestinely.[8] The birth of a child among the Bondei people of Africa is attended by many perils, for if a single condition regarded as unfavorable occurs, the infant is strangled at once. "Its life is in danger again at the time of teething, for it may be so incautious as to let its upper teeth protrude first, and if this is the case it is held unlucky, and will almost certainly be killed. Even if it is allowed to live it will be in perpetual danger, and any disaster that happens to its parents

---

119 Modi, in JASB, IV, 6.
120 Herodotus, *Hist.*, I, 189; VII, 40; Livy, *Hist.*, V, 23; Tacitus, *Germ.*, 10.
1 Jenness and Ballentyne, *D'Entrecasteaux*, 49.
2 Weeks, in JAI, XL, 420.

3 Mackenzie, in *Atl. Mo.*, CXIX, 22.
4 Torday and Joyce, in JAI, XXXV, 420.
5 Wilken, in VG, I, 591-592.
6 Martin, in *Bijd.*, XXXV, 36.
7 N. Y. *Times*, July 12, 1924.
8 Vortisch, in *Globus*, LXXXIX, 281.

will be attributed to it."[9] According to newspaper accounts, Yuan Ke Huan was proclaimed by the people of China to be their next ruler because of the fact that he had three extra teeth.[10] Foreigners, being strange and differing often considerably from the natives, have been regarded as of fetishistic character. The first non-negro from the outer world to penetrate into Uganda was a Baluch soldier from Zanzibar, who arrived at the court of the king about 1850. "His handsome face and abundant hair and beard won him royal favour." Known as "The Hairy One," he became a power in Uganda, and possessed a harem of three hundred women.[11] The whites on the Ivory Coast were feared not only on account of their intelligence and their superior weapons, but for the following reason as well: it was believed that the Europeans lived under the water, where they could not have any women; the natives therefore feared lest their own women would be taken away from them.[12]

Strange people, especially aborigines, have been pretty generally regarded as possessed. Strong[13] was once about to cross the main range of mountains which form the backbone of New Guinea, when a native, trying to persuade him not to go, said: "On the other side of the range they are not men, but ghosts who, like birds, live on the tops of rocks and hills." The people proved to be ordinary natives, living on the peaks and ridges of stony mountains. The Chinese, who are the conquering race in Yunnan, look upon the natives with some dread and credit them with powers of witchcraft, partly because of the fact that they are pygmies. "It struck me that in Yunnan one can now observe a similar state of things to what may have existed in Britain and Ireland when a primitive pigmy population, driven into the mountain wilds and woods by their conquerors, and displaying similar characteristics of elusiveness and uncanniness, may have given rise to the fairy legends."[14] There are a number of similar examples in the Malay Peninsula. If the Jakun hates and fears the Malays, the Malays in return both despise and fear the Jakun. "The Malays consider the Jakun as infidels, and therefore despicable, and as being in a rank only a little higher than animals; but on the other hand the Malays themselves are superstitious in the extreme. For Malays, everything they do not understand is a mystery; everything not common must be endowed with extraordinary virtue; and consequently, to a Malay, a Jakun is a supernatural being, endowed with supernatural power, and with an unlimited knowledge of the secrets of nature. He must therefore be skilled in the arts of divination, sorcery, and fascination, and able to do either good or evil according to his pleasure; his blessing will be followed by the most extraordinary success, and his curse by the most dreadful of disasters. . . . Moreover, to a Malay the Jakun is a man who, by his nature, must necessarily know all the properties of every plant, and consequently must be a clever physician, a belief which explains the eagerness of Malays who are sick to obtain their assistance, or at least to obtain some medicinal plants from them. . . . Such are the effects of Malay superstition; and this is the reason why though they despise the Jakun they at the same time fear them, and will in many circumstances refrain from ill-treating them." All branches of the Sakai tribes, as is usually the case with autochthonous races, are credited by the immigrating Malays with the knowledge of charms of the most marvellous potency. By means of "sendings," or rather "pointings," they are believed to be able to slay their

9 Anon., in PSM, L, 100.
10 Cleveland News-Leader, July 2, 1922.
11 Johnston, Uganda, II, 216.

12 Anon., in Globus, LXXXVII, 391.
13 In JAI, XLIX, 298.
14 Henry, in JAI, XXXIII, 98.

enemies at a distance, and "many a Sakai has paid the penalty for sickness and trouble falsely ascribed to his malevolence by excited and not overscrupulous Malays." The authors[15] are of the opinion that the very circumstance of these tribes remaining unconverted is probably a principal cause of the belief crediting them with the possession of unhallowed powers. "In no country where new creeds are received is there a total immediate abandonment of the ancient ones. So long as the existence of the old gods and demons of the land is believed in there will always be multitudes ready either to ask their aid or deprecate their wrath, in spite of the fact that they believe it sinful to do so. To this day neither Hinduism, Islamism, nor Christianity itself have totally extinguished the ancient superstitions of the countries where they prevail. And this same unreasoning fear of the aborigines has doubtless in numberless cases operated more powerfully in their defence than the best of laws could have done."

Among the early Greeks, to the imagination of the conqueror the conquered are at once barbarians and magicians, monstrous and magical, hated and feared, craftsmen and medicine-men, demons, beings endowed like the spirits they worship. "The conquerors respect the conquered as wizards, familiar with the spirits of the land, and employ them for sorcery, even sometimes when relations are peaceable employ them as foster-fathers for their sons, yet they impute to them every evil and bestial characteristic and believe them to take the form of wild beasts. The conquered for their part take refuge in mountain fastnesses and make reprisals in the characteristic fashion of Satyrs and Centaurs by carrying off the women of their conquerors."[16] The same situation prevailed among the early Scandinavians. As late as the eleventh century the less civilized tribes in the mountains of Sweden and in the farthest north of Norway were called by the bards by such terms as giants, mountain-wolves, sons of the cliffs, cave-people. They were thought to be strong in witchcraft and necromancy and to know what was going on in any place in the world, to be able to bring whales ashore, and to do all the sorcery described in books.[17] It is a modern superstition that objects made by blind people bring good luck.[18]

Any mental disease or disorder marks a person as exceptional and to the savage is evidence of possession by a demon. Mental diseases are by no means confined to civilized people. Crawley[19] finds hysteria common among the Votyaks, Hottentots, Javanese, Brazilians, Mexicans, Peruvians; Bastian[20] states that hysteria and neurotic diseases are frequent among savages; while Brinton[21] mentions cases of such among the Iroquois and Hurons, the natives of New Zealand and Madagascar, and the Kaffirs, Abyssinians, and West Africans. Additional evidence of the prevalence of mental and nervous disorders among primitive peoples is given in the following examples, selected chiefly to illustrate the attitude taken toward such possessed persons.

"A savage in a temper," writes Abel[22] with special reference to the natives of New Guinea, "is one of the most distressing sights it is possible to witness. As a rule, however, the fury expends itself in violent abusive speech. I have seen both men and women possessed by devils. There could be no other way

15 Skeat and Blagden, *Malay Penin.*, I, 539, 563-564; II, 198, 199.
16 Harrison, *Greek Relig.*, 172, 385.
17 Geijer, *Svensk. Hist.*, 33, 79, 110.
18 Krauss, *Sreća*, 157.

19 In JAI, XXIV, 223, note.
20 *Loango-Küste*, II, 205.
21 In *Science*, Dec., 1892.
22 *New Guinea*, 58-59.

of describing the raging emotion which governed them, until it subsided from sheer exhaustion. As a relief to pent-up passion, a man will sometimes attack his house. Snatching up his axe, between the diabolical yells in which he flings his vituperative imprecations at his wife, he hacks away at his house, tearing up the floor, and hurling it in his frenzy as far as he can scatter it in all directions." In the Upper Congo, when a man is "on the drink" he sticks a leaf in his hair to show it, and then no notice is taken of any stupid or insulting remarks he may make.[23] He is possessed by spirits and so is not accountable for his actions. According to native West African beliefs, apoplectic and epileptic fits, hysteria, delirium, and mania are phenomena connected with the absence of the indwelling spirit of man; "but they do not directly result from its departure, and are caused by a spirit without a bodily tenement entering the body during the absence of the proper tenant, by the struggle between the two when the latter returns and finds his place usurped, or by the former trying to force a way in and displace the latter—they are in fact cases of 'possession.' "[24] Stuhlmann[25] found a number of huts in which women were treated for hysterical convulsions, the means of therapy consisting of cooking meat and beating a drum to drive out the devil spirit. Among the Nigerian head-hunters, "if a child be an idiot or unable to move about, it may be thrown into the water, 'but not killed.' This usually happens when the child is between the ages of one and four, but in some cases he may be given a much longer time in hope that he will recover. 'It is evidently a snake and not a human being. If after you have thrown him (or her) into the water you go away and then come back silently and hide yourself, you will see the child lengthen out into a snake.' "[26]

Mental disorders are common among the Siberians and the Hyperboreans generally, and appear to be more so the farther north one goes. The various phenomena of possession are evident and there are cases of whole tribes being affected by contagion and suggestion.[27] Miss Czaplicka[28] has made a careful investigation into this matter; excerpts from her study follow. "Unintentional visual suggestion shows itself in cases in which, when some of the younger people begin to dance, all the villagers, even the oldest, follow their example. Jochelson reports an instance of an old woman quite unable to stand alone, who on such an occasion stood up and began to dance without assistance until she fell exhausted. . . . Sometimes people who suffer from arctic hysteria are peculiarly susceptible to hypnotic suggestion, which, however, they receive while awake. Not only auditory, as in the case of the ordinary hypnotic trance, but also visual impressions are received by the patient as suggestions." It is affirmed that many Samoyeds, Laplanders, Tungus, inhabitants of Kamtchatka, and in a less degree the Tartars about the Yenisei, are occasionally "panic-struck"; an unexpected touch, a sudden call, whistling, or a fearful and sudden appearance will throw these people into a state of fury. "The Samoyed and the Yakut, who seem more to be affected in this way, carry the matter so far that, forgetting what they are about, they will take the first knife, axe, or other offensive weapon that lies in their way, and would wound or kill the object of their terror if not prevented by force and the weapon taken from them; and if interrupted will beat themselves about the hands and feet, scream

23 Weeks, in JAI, XXXIX, 120.
24 Ellis, Ewe, 106-107.
25 Mit Emin, 619.
26 Tremearne, in JAI, XLII, 146.

27 Mickewicz, in Globus, LXXXV, 262.
28 Aborig. Siberia, 308-309, 310-316, 318-319, 320-321, 323-324.

out, roll upon the ground and rave. The Samoyed and the Ostyak have an infallible remedy to bring such persons to themselves; which is, to set fire to a reindeer-skin, or a sack of reindeer hair, and let it smoke under the patient's nose; this occasions a faintness and a quiet slumber, often for the space of twenty-four hours." Fits of *menerik*—the Yakut term for a type of mental disease—are usually brought on by a shock or sudden pain, though sometimes the malady is periodical and comes on without any apparent immediate cause. "The patient is afflicted with spasms, or falls into a trance, howls or dances, and sometimes this ends in an epileptoid seizure. The natives ascribe this disease to the influence of evil spirits and it is curious to note that this influence is in most cases of foreign origin. A Yakut patient will sing in Tungus and a Yukaghir in Yakut, even if they do not speak these languages. The fits are often followed by a prolonged sleep lasting for several days." These hysterical seizures have been observed chiefly among young girls and some young men, especially those under training for shamanship. There is said to be scarcely any Yakut woman who is not more or less liable to hysteria. Another common disease is called *ämürakh* in Yakut and by other terms among other tribes. As the linguistic evidence shows, the first symptom of this disease is the marked impressionableness of the patient, his feeling of fright and timidity. He usually shouts the most obscene words or rushes at the cause of his terror; there is also an inclination to repeat all visual and auditory impressions. *Menerik* and *ämürakh* are met with most often among the peoples who have more recently come into the Arctic region, the Yakut, the Tungus, and some of the Russian settlers; while among the peoples longer domiciled the other nervous ailments such as melancholia or inclination to suicide are apparently more frequent. "In all cases the nomadic or reindeer peoples have less liability to this form of disease; but this may be due not only to their mode of life, but also to the fact that the reindeer-breeding peoples are better situated materially, and, except as the result of some occasional catastrophe, do not suffer so much hardship. Thus we know that during a famine sometimes half the inhabitants of a village become insane, temporarily or permanently." The term "arctic hysteria" has been given by travellers partly to religio-magical phenomena and partly to the nervous ailments which are considered by the natives to be a disease. A review of the various symptoms brings Miss Czaplicka to the opinion that nearly all cases described can be regarded as instances of hysteria. "But most of the symptoms enumerated are met with in Europe, and therefore the majority of these cases cannot properly be described as *arctic* hysteria. There is no question that the economic and geographical conditions of the arctic region lead to the development of nervous diseases, but since such ailments are met with in other geographical areas, it is clearly incorrect to class them as distinctly 'arctic.' Yet not all of the symptoms described are familiar to Europeans. Quite unknown among us is *ämürakh*, the imitative mania with its characteristic symptom of imitating unconsciously all gestures and sounds. . . . This peculiar form of the malady probably suggested to travellers the name of 'arctic hysteria,' and convinced them that all hysteria in the Arctic region differs from that prevalent in Europe and is, in fact, peculiarly 'arctic.' The use of the term 'arctic' seems appropriate enough at first sight, as nearly all travellers ascribe these hysterical maladies to arctic conditions, namely, dark winter days, light summer nights, severe cold, the silence, the general monotony of the landscape, scarcity of food, etc. The observed fact that these nervous diseases are especially fre-

quent in the dark season, or in the time of transition from one season to another, points to the same conclusion. But unfortunately for this hypothesis
we find the same symptoms which are held to be characteristic of Arctic
lands among the peoples of the Equatorial regions." The author cites a number of cases of similar nature, chiefly from among the Malays, and comes to
the conclusion that it is not so much the Arctic climate as extremes of climate
which account for this peculiar type of hysteria, and suggests that the title
"arctic hysteria" be discarded in favor of "hysteria of climatic extremes."
The racial factor is also of importance. The general conclusion of this study
is that the whole of northern and part of southern Siberia is a region where
the people suffer from nervous diseases more than in any other of the known
regions of the world. "Thus only in this region is such an institution as that of
'voluntary death' looked upon as praiseworthy and there only do such heredi-
tarily hysterical individuals as the best shamans certainly are enjoy the highest
consideration."

Among certain clans of India, spirits were thought to speak through a certain girl, who was often ill and who used to go into trances.[29] There is a Malay
game of turning into a civet cat, in which a boy is actually hypnotized and
caused to behave like that animal, becoming, as the Naga were-leopard does,
much exhausted when the trance is over. Skeat[30] records the inverse of the
Naga case, in the process by which a possession of the human body by a tiger-
spirit is invoked in order to cast out another and less powerful possessing
spirit, and also the induction of a monkey-spirit into a girl who, while thus
possessed, is capable of the most remarkable climbing feats. "In some cases
lycanthropy among Nagas seems to be hereditary, or perhaps rather one
should say that a tendency towards it may be inherited, as in the case of many
diseases; and indeed Mr. Baring-Gould described lycanthropy as a disease,
associating it in this respect with the mania for cattle-maiming and with a
morbid desire to devour human corpses. Cases of both of these I have met with
in the Naga Hills, the latter, however, being regarded by the Nagas themselves as symptomatic of extreme insanity; whereas the former is, like lycanthropy, merely a vice which is liable to be very troublesome to the neighbours
of those that practise it."[31]

Imbeciles among the Zuñi are regarded as being in intimacy with good
spirits; hence their words and actions are regarded as signs of divinity and
their doings and sayings are oracular.[32] This concept, including under it mental
disease as well as mental defect, was well known to the ancients; in Biblical
times mental aberrations were interpreted as being caused by possession, the
treatment being the casting out of the evil spirit.[33] Most religions have been
founded by epileptic, eccentric, or insane men and women, while a number of
religious communistic societies have been established, especially in the United
States, under the leadership of abnormal persons, many of whom have regarded themselves as reincarnations of Christ, in his second advent.[34]

There are other examples of the fetish-man, leading up to the god-man,
usually priest or king, who is divine. Among the Ba-Mbala of East Central

29 Shakespear, in JAI, XXXIX, 377.
30 *Malay Magic*, 436, 455.
31 Hutton, in JAI, L, 49-50.
32 Hodge, in BAE, XXX, 27.
33 Otto, *Aegypten*, I, 123; Mark, IX, 17 ff.

34 Mooney, in BAE, XIV, 931; Stoddart,
Mind and Its Disorders, 351; Love, *Care of
the Insane*, Ohio Bd. of Admin., pub. no. 3,
3; Noyes, *Amer. Socialisms*, ch. XIII; Hinds,
Amer. Communities, 21-25, 287, 300, 308, 309,
355 ff., 361 ff., 383 ff.

Africa is a class of men called *Muri,* whose existence can be explained only through fetishism. They may not eat human flesh nor the flesh of fowls, though the tribe is cannibalistic; they are distinguished by a fine iron bracelet and a head-covering of cloth. Great importance is attached to both these ornaments; to remove or appropriate either is punishable by death.[35] It is not admitted by the Fan that a man's being struck by lightning is a case of accident; it is someone's vengeance working through spirits. The deceased is deprived of all funeral-rites.[36] In the Congo a person may unknowingly be "full of witchcraft" and cause sickness and death to others; of course it is the evil spirit within him that does the damage. Chiefs, headmen, and freemen are more shabbily dressed than slaves for the reason that they are not anxious to display their wealth for fear of being charged with witchcraft.[37] Twins are regarded by the Hausa as possessing powers out of the ordinary. "If a twin licks his finger and rubs it over the bite of a scorpion, the pain ceases immediately. If a twin is angry with you and stares into your eyes, you will lose your eyesight until you have appeased him. Do not curse a twin, for if you do, the evil will recoil upon yourself. In fact everything will go wrong with you. . . . There seems to be no doubt that the fear of twins is due to their rarity, a double birth being regarded as strange, and even terrible."[38] The only explanation to the natives is spiritual agency.

"The divine person," comments Frazer,[39] "is a source of danger as well as of blessing; he must not only be guarded, he must also be guarded against. His sacred organism, so delicate that a touch may disorder it, is also electrically charged with a powerful spiritual force which may discharge itself with fatal effect on whatever comes in contact with it. Hence the isolation of the man-god is quite as necessary for the safety of others as for his own." An extreme case of sanctity is that of the chief of a Russian tribe who was so holy that he was not allowed to walk.[40] In India "the priest has long been regarded as a god, but in the epic he is god of gods, although one can here trace a growth in adulation." The king has also been identified with the gods; in the epic he is to his people an absolute divinity.[41] Mina Fu-yeh is regarded as the reincarnation of Buddha, and is now in his twenty-second lifetime. "This is, of course, only since he became an incarnate saint; there are no records of his previous lives. Sakya Muni had altogether 551 lives, 510 of which were prior to his becoming a saint."[42] "His Sublimity," the Dalai Lama of Tibet, was not raised to the throne by the usual ballot method: while an infant he was brought to Lhasa with two other babes, all of whom were regarded as incarnations of the Dalai Lama. Subsequently the Regent Lama and the ministers of state of that time had reason to consider that two of the infants were devils incarnate and that the third was the only genuine incarnation of the Dalai Lama.[43]

The Sumatrans are firmly persuaded that various particular persons are sacred and invulnerable.[44] Captain Cook was first treated by the Hawaiians as a god, and then was killed in a fight following the breaking of a native taboo. "His body was taken to a small heiau on the cliffs above Kaawaloa Bay and there the flesh was stripped from the bones which were deified and tied

35 Torday and Joyce, in JAI, XXXV, 409.
36 Trilles, *Fân,* 338-340.
37 Weeks, in JAI, XL, 396; XXXIX, 98.
38 Tremearne, in JAI, XLV, 34.
39 *Golden Bough,* I, 167.

40 Chadwick, in *Folk-Lore,* XI, 285 note.
41 Hopkins, *Relig. India,* 370.
42 Wellby, *Tibet,* 279.
43 Kawaguchi, in *Century Mag.,* XLV, 388.
44 Marsden, *Sumatra,* 293.

up with red feathers and subsequently hidden."[45] A cartoon of President Cleveland in *Judge,* representing him as a friar with a halo, was obtained by a native Filipino who framed it and offered evening petitions to it.[46]

The Chaldæan king on his accession was invested in the temple, according to the rites of his god. After that his time was consumed in minute devotions, being the homage which he paid to his lord. He was comparable to a steward, rendering accounts to his lord day by day.[47] The people had the highest interest in this because any defect or error in the performance of duties by the king would bring calamity on the nation.[48] Among Mohammedans the Iman or prince unites in his person supreme spiritual and temporal power; he is infallible and sinless, the incarnation of Logos, the divine Word.[49] Notions similar to the above two cases were held during the Middle Ages.[50] Man as the "image of God" is a fetish. The human body as a temple for the dwelling of good and bad spirits is a concept found in the New Testament.[51] All kings ruling by divine right, ecclesiastics claiming to be God's vicegerents on earth, and other "Men of God" are outgrowths of the man-fetish idea.[52]

§258. Ecstasy and Inspiration.

Fox and Drew[1] once witnessed a case of possession, that of a Banks Islands boy about eighteen years old, who complained of headache, went to sleep, and after about three hours became "possessed" and inspired. "He was extraordinarily strong, about eight men, most of whom were powerful fellows, endeavouring vainly to hold him. In the intervals of these violent paroxysms he spoke, certainly in a voice quite unlike his own. A compatriot, staring into his eyes, said to him, 'What is your name?' 'We are many,' replied the possessed boy. 'Is it so and so in you?' to which the possessed replied 'Yes' or 'No' till it was ascertained who were in him (various dead natives, some of whom were known to the writers). He was then asked for news of friends in other islands. Some inquiries he answered (his answers proved to be wrong in some cases). . . . Other inquiries he did not answer, saying, 'None of us have been there lately.' All this time he was exceedingly strong, and sometimes violent, and apparently insensible to pain. In about an hour he suddenly appeared to come to himself, staring wildly round, asking where he was and what we were round him for. After a long sleep of some 12 hours he appeared to be normal again." When the *atua* or ghosts of their ancestors are invoked by the Tikopians, it is not known who of those present will be inspired and all wait patiently for this to happen. "When the selected person begins to shake, betel is presented and questions are put to find out whether the sick man will recover, etc. . . . If the sick man becomes worse and the ghost is again invoked, the possessed man will on this occasion say definitely whether the patient will die or recover and will never come more than twice. If a favourable verdict is given, the man recovers and makes a large present of food to the man whom the ghost has entered."[2] Similar phenomena of posses-

45 N. Y. *Times,* June 29, 1924.
46 Worcester, *Philippine Isl.,* I, 490-491.
47 Maspero, *Hist. Anc.,* I, 705.
48 §279, of text.
49 Von Kremer, *Kgchte.,* I, 395.
50 Henderson, *Doc. of Middle Ages,* 20.

51 Matt. XII, 44; I Cor., III, 16, 17; II Cor., VI, 16; Eph., II, 22.
52 Lippert, *Kgchte.,* II, 462, 465, 495, 619, 622.
1 In JAI, XLV, 169-170.
2 Rivers, *Melan. Soc.,* I, 323.

sion have been observed in Papua.[3] There is evidence in all this of the close connection between the religious and the abnormal.

Among the Yaos of Central Africa, madness, idiocy, and the ravings of delirium or disease are accounted for by the agency of spirits, *masoka.* "The sufferers are *wa masoka,* they of the spirits, and a sudden fit of epilepsy or insanity is described as *gakamwile masoka,* the spirits have seized him. Such persons are usually regarded with awe, as living in close contact with the unseen. . . . Idiots and the insane are allowed to wander at will about the village, and only when violent symptoms show themselves as a danger to the community is any physical restraint put upon them. The *masoka* are also recognized as the inspiring agencies in the ravings of the witch detective."[4] The most common manifestation of the spirits in East Africa is madness, temporary and permanent. "The former is most usually seen during dances performed by women, and takes the form of a kind of trance but accompanied by convulsive movements of the body; women in such a state often utter gruesome cries and shed copious tears. . . . The possession is supposed to abate by the application of ghee to the head and shoulders. . . . It is very rare that a man is possessed by spirits; I have, in fact, only seen two cases of this, and it is said that a man so afflicted is always a medicine man or will become one."[5] How possession may be induced, and how the possessed person acts, are seen also in the case reported concerning the Hausa: "Ayesha sat upon a cushion in front of a pot of incense, and began to inhale it, meanwhile rubbing her right hand to and fro on the floor (the palm up) in order to salute the bori [spirits] in the ground, and also to show when they had taken possession of her, *i.e.,* when she had lost her senses. . . . Soon Haja Gogo began belching (because the bori were passing her by, leaving her at once), and Ayesha belching and yawning (some passing by, some entering). . . . Ayesha's yawns grew in number and intensity, and the movement of her hands more and more erratic. . . . Immediately Ayesha (or, rather, the bori in her) began roaring and wandering about on her knees, cursing and laughing foolishly."[6]

An important example of the inspired person or medium is that reported by Weeks[7] of the Bangala in the Congo; it emphasizes the importance of religion as a disciplinary factor, even when the person in question is a fakir or tries to utilize religious practices and beliefs to his own aggrandizement. "Bololi, the headman of his family, died and was buried in the usual way. Some time after his younger brother, Mangumbe, became subject to frenzies, during which his brother Bololi spoke his oracles through him. Mangumbe admired and coveted the wives of a certain man in his town, and he tried to buy them, and failing that to exchange others for them, but their husband refused all offers. One day Mangumbe worked himself into a frenzy, and when he was supposed to be under the sway of his brother's *mongoli,* he said: That a certain man (giving the name of the man whose wives he coveted) must get rid of his wives or they would encompass his death by a serious and fatal illness. Then Mangumbe went to a friend and told him to treat with the husband for the wives, and the husband, thoroughly afraid now of his wives, was quite willing to sell them at a cheaper price than Mangumbe had previously offered for them." Such was possible because "the people firmly believed that Man-

3 Williams, in JAI, LIII, 379, 381.
4 Hetherwick, in JAI, XXXII, 90.
5 Dundas, in JAI, XLIII, 535-536; Hobley, *A-Kamba,* 53.

6 Tremearne, in JAI, XLV, 57-58.
7 In JAI, XL, 369-370.

gumbe held counsel with his brother's *mongoli*, and when he acted as a medium they were quite willing to believe all he said. Ordinarily he was little respected by the people; he was of mean appearance, and of petty, shabby ways, and had no command over even his own people, and yet when acting as a medium in a *séance*, he was feared, obeyed, and his word accepted without the slightest demur."

Examples of "inspiration" which take the form of a call to preach have been numerous among the American negroes. Booker T. Washington[8] has described the process as follows: "In the earlier days of freedom almost every coloured man who learned to read would receive 'a call to preach' within a few days after he began reading. At my home in West Virginia the process of being called to the ministry was a very interesting one. Usually the 'call' came when the individual was sitting in church. Without warning the one called would fall upon the floor as if struck by a bullet, and would lie there for hours, speechless and motionless. Then the news would spread all through the neighbourhood that this individual had received a 'call.' If he were inclined to resist the summons, he would fall or be made to fall a second or third time. In the end he always yielded to the call." The recounter suspected, however, that the call often came because of a desire to avoid work, the chief ambition of many negroes being to get an education so that they would not have to work any longer with their hands. "This is illustrated by a story told of a coloured man in Alabama, who, one hot day in July, while he was at work in a cotton-field, suddenly stopped, and, looking toward the skies, said: 'O Lawd, de cotton am so grassy, de work am so hard, and de sun am so hot dat I b'lieve dis darky am called to preach!'"

Frenzy, hysteria, and other abnormal psychological manifestations are features accompanying "possession" in India and among the Malays. A definite way in which the gods of the Todas are believed to intervene in human affairs is in divination. "During the frenzy into which the diviners fall they are believed to be inspired by the gods."[9] When a girl among the Nairs is thought to be possessed of the devil, masked magicians come before her and execute frightful dances to the accompaniment of terrifying music. "Dancer succeeds dancer, each more terrible looking than his predecessor, and the poor girl loses control of herself and falls into a sort of hysteria, in which the devil in her confesses where it came from and who prompted it." The whole scheme of the dance—the music, the masks, the lighting—seems to be arranged with the sole purpose of rendering the subject liable to suggestion.[10] The effect of the dance in inducing possession is seen in a case reported from Manipur: "While the last portion of this dance was proceeding, one of the attendants began to dance wildly, and after going through most extraordinary contortions, reeling about as if drunk, he fell down and was dragged to the front of the shrine and placed there kneeling with his head on the ground, and remained there for some time shaking with emotion. Khumlangba had entered into him. . . . On the next day the second Maibi became possessed. She danced wildly, staggered about shaking her head, for the Lai is supposed to sit on the head of his devotee, then she knelt before the shrine, and trembling all over, shaking her head, began a long series of babblings, which were said to be prophecies."[11] Somewhat similar ceremonies leading to physical and mental collapse occur

---

8 *Up From Slavery*, 82, 128.
9 Rivers, *Todas*, 450.

10 Panikkar, in JAI, XLVIII, 281.
11 Shakespear, in JAI, XL, 356.

among the Singhalese.[12] Wilken[13] describes as follows the inspiration of the seers in Buru: the ghost seers light a little incense before them while they sit in a squatting posture on the ground; after a while their feet and hands and later their whole bodies are thrown into a violent, nervous, twitching movement, while they begin to mumble in a singing fashion words that cannot be understood. This is a token of the approach of the spirits. Then they begin to jump and dance to the measure of the music, an indication that a spirit has now possessed its medium. "It is a frightful sight to see the seer then, with loose-hanging hair and twisted features, leaping about until he falls senseless to the ground." When he comes to again, the questions to be answered by the spirits can be put to him. Evans[14] once had a Dusun woman ascertain for him by divination whether he would have a successful journey; he jotted down the following notes at the time, while observing the performance: "She starts singing in a quavery voice, then begins to quiver and shake as if convulsed with fever—pants—sings loudly—makes hysterical noises—moves her feet—jumps about with both feet together, first backwards, then forwards—stamps about—sings—talks in an hysterical voice—pants—calls, 'Adohi! Adohi!'—runs round and round—goes on all fours—sits—pants—sings—stands up—trembles—sings—jumps about with both feet together and does a few dance steps." In Nicobar *fai* means inspired, quaked, or felt; a person who, in the first stage of recovery from a severe illness or from a delirious attack, informs his people that he has been inspired or has quaked, becomes a Mâfai. Friends and relatives come with presents to the inspired man. "From this time forward, and until he thoroughly recovers, the people of the village and other friends and relatives contribute his meals and other necessities by turn. . . . The people venerate him much and take him at midnight to all sick quarters that he might heal them by his touch or shampooing, and he pretends to remove gravel or stones from the body of the invalid whom he shampoos." This is done until the Mâfai think that he is strong enough to work for his food, when he resigns his Mâfai-ship with a ceremony which literally means "undressing the Mâfai."[15] Throughout the Malay Peninsula may be observed cases of mental derangement similar to "arctic hysteria," more commonly among women than men. Sir Hugh Clifford,[16] who has given a full description of such occurrence, termed *lâtah*, thinks that every adult Malay is to a certain extent affected. One of the chief characteristics of *lâtah* is that the sufferer apes all the actions and gestures of the person he is observing.

Among the peoples of classical antiquity priests and priestesses brought themselves to ecstasy before giving their oracles.[17] The worshippers of Dionysus believed that they were possessed by the god. It was but a step farther to pass to the conviction that they were actually identified with him, actually became him. "This was a conviction shared by all orgiastic religions, and one doubtless that had its rise in the physical sensations of intoxication. . . . The savage doctrine of divine possession, induced by intoxication and in part by mimetic ritual, was it would seem almost bound to develop a higher, more spiritual meaning. We have already seen that the madness of Dionysos included the madness of the Muses and Aphrodite, but, to make any real spiritual

12 Seligmann, in JAI, XXXVIII, 368 ff.
13 In VG. I, 60-61.
14 In JAI, XLVII, 158.
15 Solomon, in JAI, XXXII, 224-225.

16 *Studies in Brown Humanity*, 186-201, quoted by Czaplicka, *Aborig. Siberia*, 321-324.
17 Lehmann, *Overtro*, I, 74-76.

advance, there was needed it would seem a man of spiritual insight and saintly temperament, there was needed an Orpheus. The great step that Orpheus took was that, while he kept the old Bacchic faith that man might become a god, he altered the conception of what a god was, and he sought to obtain that godhead by wholly different means. The grace he sought was not physical intoxication but spiritual ecstasy, the means he adopted not drunkenness but abstinence and rites of purification."[18] The scenes of initiation into the mysteries of Mithra were calculated to produce a profound impression on the neophyte: "The sacred emotion with which he was seized lent to images which were really puerile a most formidable appearance; the vain allurements with which he was confronted appeared to him serious dangers over which his courage triumphed. The fermented beverage which he imbibed excited his senses and disturbed his reason to the utmost pitch; he murmured his mystic formulas, and they evoked before his distracted imagination divine apparitions."[19] Instances of trance and vision are described in the Avesta.[20] Among the ancient Jews, seers and prophets of Jahweh were fitted for the exercise of their office by such inward working of his spirit that they were thrown into an ecstatic condition. It was not in man's power of his own initiative to effect the call to be a prophet or to complete it by his own determination; and, on the other hand, he had no power to evade it. Conditions of ecstasy are mentioned which rise to rapture and holy frenzy. Scriptural descriptions,[21] taken with the etymology of the word, show that we have to do with bands of enthusiasts, upon whom the spirit of God has laid hold with overpowering force and who, stimulated by loud music to greater frenzy, readily carry along others to participate in their conduct. "It reflects truly the character of such phenomena, as does also the statement that Saul stripped off his clothes, and lay naked for a day and a night in holy frenzy."[22]

§260. Totemism (Religious Aspects).

TOTEMISM is reported from the whole of Australia, from nearly the whole of North America, from many regions of Africa, and from several isolated locations in India and elsewhere. Alleged survivals of the system have been identified, to their own satisfaction, by authors who have written concerning this or that savage tribe or ancient people.[1] We are here interested in the characteristics of the system rather than in its distribution; the latter can be made out, however, from the series of cases cited here and in the text.

Australia. "In every tribe without exception there exists a firm belief in the reincarnation of ancestors"; whether the system of descent is maternal or paternal does not affect this situation. The general idea is that in the Alcheringa, or earliest traditional time, or "dream time," "there existed at first a comparatively small number of individuals who were half-human, half-animal or plant. How they arose no one knows. . . . These semi-human creatures were endowed with far greater powers than any living men or women possess. They could walk about either on the earth or beneath it, or could fly through the air.

18 Harrison, *Greek Relig.*, 445-446, 475 (quoted), 476-477 (quoted), 488; Showerman, *Mother of the Gods*, 236.
19 Cumont, *Mithra*, 162, 164.
20 Jackson, *Zoroaster*, 50, 51.
21 I Sam., X, 5 ff.

22 Kautzsch, Relig. Israel, in *Hastings's Dict. Bible*, 651, 653 (quoted), 660, 672, 673; Is. VIII, 11; Ezek., III, 14; I, 3; III, 22; XXXVII, 1; XL, 1; Jer., XV, 17.
1 Murray, in *Sat. Rev.*, CX, 75.

They were the ancestors of the different totemic groups." These ancestors are reincarnated over and over again. When a man dies, his spirit "goes back to the place at which it was left by the ancestor in the Alcheringa. . . . Here it remains for some time, but sooner or later it is reincarnated," by entering the body of some woman. As will be seen in a later connection, it must enter a woman of the proper totem.[2]

Typical of the usages connected with the totem are the following, practised by the Arunta tribe: "(1) That, except on one particular occasion, the members of the totem eat only very sparingly of their totemic animal. A very strict man will not even eat sparingly. (2) That the men of the totem perform a very definite ceremony, the sole object of which is that of securing the increase of the totemic animal or plant. (3) That the Alatunja especially, who presides over and conducts the ceremony, *must* eat a little or else he would be unable to perform the ceremony with success. (4) That after the men of the totem have eaten a little they hand on the rest to the other men who do not belong to the totem, giving them permission to eat it freely. (5) That only men of the totem and right moiety of the tribe are allowed to take any share in the actual ceremony, except in very rare cases." Certain tribes "believe that the members of each totemic group are responsible for providing other individuals with a supply of their totemic animal or plant. . . . If a water totem man be quite alone, then there is no objection to his drinking water with which he provides himself, but, so long as he is in the company of other men belonging to other totems, he must not obtain it for himself, but receives it from some individual who belongs to the moiety of the tribe of which he, the water man, is not a member. As a general rule, a man of the water totem receives this, when in camp, from . . . a man who belongs to the same class as his wife does." The complications of this matter may be judged from the following. "There is a fundamental difference between the relationship supposed to exist in the case of a man's own totem and that of the totems associated with his own moiety and, on the other hand, the totem of his mother. The latter he will eat *if it be given to him by a member of the moiety with which it is associated.* If it be his own, or his father's or father's father's, then he will not eat it at all; but if this restriction does not apply, then a man will only eat a particular animal or plant which is associated with a totemic group belonging to his own moiety of the tribe *if it be given to him by a man belonging to the other moiety of the tribe.*"[3]

Among the beliefs about the entrance of a soul into a woman,[4] the following are found: "The ancestor of the black-snake totem, for example, arose in a water hole on the Tennant creek; he wandered over the country performing ceremonies, making creeks and hills, and leaving all along his tracks plenty of black-snake children who are now resident in the rocks around the water-holes and in the gum-trees which border the creek. No woman of the present day will venture to strike one of these trees with a tomahawk, as she is firmly convinced that this would have the effect of releasing one of these spirit children, who would immediately enter her body. . . . Certain trees and stones . . . are supposed to be full of bee and goshawk spirits. The snake totem belongs to one moiety of the tribe and the bee and goshawk to the other, and the natives told us that the snake-man's wife could not possibly conceive a bee or goshawk

2 Spencer and Gillen, *North. Tr. Cent. Aust.*, 145, 148, 149, 153, 157, 576.
3 Spencer and Gillen, *North. Tr. Cent. Aust.*, 291, 167, note.
4 §334, below.

child there, because no such spirit would think of going inside the wife of a snake man. If she were to conceive a child at that spot it would simply mean that a snake spirit had followed the father up from his own place and had gone inside the woman . . . the natives are very clear upon the point that the spirit children know which are the right lubras [unmated women] for them . . . to enter, and each one deliberately chooses his or her own mother." It is to be noted that there are objects of stone or wood, called *churingas,* which may be covered with devices representing the totem and which are kept in a sort of sacred deposit. "It is certainly a rather curious thing that, with the exception of . . . two rather vague and unsatisfactory ones, the natives have not, so far as we could find out, any myth which pretends to explain what is after all one of the most striking features in connection with the totems, and that is the restrictions which apply to eating it at the present day. There is no attempt made to bridge over the wide gulf intervening between the Alcheringa times, when their ancestors are supposed to have eaten it freely, and the present when, excepting just at the time of Intichiuma [a ceremonial], each totem is practically tabooed to the members of the group to which it gives its name." A man "will not hesitate, under certain conditions, to kill his totem animal, but he hands it over to men who do not belong to the same totemic group, and will not think of eating it himself. The fundamental idea, common to all of the tribes, is that men of any totemic group are responsible for the maintenance of the supply of the animal or plant which gives its name to the group, and that the one object of increasing the number of the totemic animal or plant is simply that of increasing the general food supply."[5]

The authors quoted[6] find much the same conditions in other districts. "In some tribes there is a sex totem, in others there is no such thing; and in isolated cases we meet with an individual totem distinct from the totem common to a group of men and women. . . . In many Australian tribes it seems to be a general custom that a man must not eat or injure his totem, whereas amongst the Arunta there are special occasions on which the totem is eaten, and there is no rule absolutely forbidding the eating of the totem at other times, though it is clearly understood that it must only be partaken of very sparingly." In the Alcheringa there lived ancestors who, in the native mind, are so intimately associated with the animals or plants the name of which they bear that an Alcheringa man of, say, the kangaroo totem, may sometimes be spoken of either as a man-kangaroo or as a kangaroo-man. The identity of the human individual is often sunk in that of the animal or plant from which he is supposed to have originated. The totemic system of the Central Australian tribes "is based upon the idea of the reincarnation of Alcheringa ancestors, who were the actual transformations of animals and plants, or of such inanimate objects as clouds or water, fire, wind, sun, moon, and stars. To the Australian native there is no difficulty in the assumption that an animal or a plant could be transformed directly into a human being, or that the spirit part which he supposes it to possess, just as he does in his own case, could remain, on the death of the animal, associated with such an object as a Churinga, and at some future time arise in the form of a human being."

In connection with totemic religious rites there is a sort of sacrament. "The

5 §249, above; Spencer and Gillen, *North.*   6 *Nat. Tr. Cent. Aust.,* 35, 36, 73, 119,
Tr. Cent. Aust., 159, 160, 162, 169, 174, 276,   124, 125, 127.
278, 323, 327.

name *Intichiuma* is applied to certain sacred ceremonies associated with the totems, the object of which is to secure the increase of the animal or plant which gives its name to the totem. . . . We find amongst these tribes no restriction according to which a man is forbidden to eat his totem, as is stated to be the case amongst certain other Australian tribes. On the contrary, though he may only under ordinary circumstances eat very sparingly of it, there are certain special occasions on which he is, we may say, obliged by custom to eat a small portion of it or otherwise the supply would fail. These occasions are those on which the *Intichiuma* ceremonies . . . are performed." Herein lies the idea of the sacrament or communion. In the ceremony it is sometimes the chief performer who must eat a portion of the totem to prevent failure. "There is however one notable exception to the restrictions upon eating, and this is concerned with the Achilpa or wild cat totem. Only a very little of this is allowed to be eaten, and that only by the old people; but in this case the restriction is not confined to the members of the totem, but is of universal application, applying to every member of the tribe. . . . In the first place, it is supposed that any one, save an old man or woman, eating Achilpa would be afflicted with a special disease called *Erkincha;* and in the second, it is believed that if any man who had killed another at any time of his life were to eat this particular animal, then his spirit part or *Yenka* would leave his body, and he would soon be killed by some enemy, so that to a man who has ever killed another—and there are very few men who do not lay claim to this distinction—the Achilpa is tabu or forbidden for life, no matter what be his age." Returning to the *Intichiuma,* and "taking the tribe as a whole, the object of these ceremonies is that of increasing the total food supply."

Characteristic of the *Intichiuma* is copious blood-letting by the medicine-man and his sons, or others; in one case, where the central fetish was a stone in a pit, "before the ceremony commences, the pit is carefully swept clean by an old Unjiamba man, who then strokes the stone all over with his hands. When this has been done, the men sit around the stone and a considerable time is spent in singing chants, the burden of which is a reiterated invitation to the Unjiamba tree to flower much, and to the blossoms to be full of honey. The old leader then asks one of the young men to open a vein in his arm, which done the blood is allowed to freely sprinkle over the stone, while the other men continue the singing. The blood flows until the stone is completely covered, the flowing of blood being supposed to represent the preparation of Abmoara, that is, the drink made by steeping the flower in water, this being a favorite beverage with the natives. The ceremony is complete when the stone is covered with blood. . . . The totem of any man is regarded, just as it is elsewhere, as the same thing as himself; as a native once said when we were discussing the matter with him, 'that one,' pointing to his photograph which we had taken, 'is just the same as me; so is a kangaroo' (his totem). . . . We may, in fact say, that each totemic group is supposed to have a direct control over the numbers of the animal or plant the name of which it bears, and further that, in theory at least, they have the first right to the animal or plant. . . . It will be seen . . . that at the present day the totemic animal or plant, as the case may be, is almost but not quite tabu . . . to the members of the totem. . . . The purpose of the Intichiuma ceremony at the present time, so say the natives, is by means of pouring out the blood of kangaroo men upon the rock, to drive out in all directions the spirits of the kangaroo animals and so increase the number of the animals."[7]

Frazer[8] accredits to Spencer and Gillen the first demonstration of the totem-sacrament, of which he makes considerable use. "He could not be a Kangaroo man and make kangaroos unless he had in his own body the flesh and blood of a kangaroo; he could not be a Grass-seed man and make grass-seeds unless his corporeal substance were at least in part composed of grass-seeds; and so with the members of the other totem group. Here, it is plain, we have at last the long-sought totem sacrament which Robertson Smith with the intuition of genius divined, and which it has been reserved for Messrs. Spencer and Gillen to discover as an actually existing institution among true totem tribes."

Concerning the taboo on killing or eating the totem, "a certain mysterious connection exists between a family and its *kobong*, so that a member of the family will never kill an animal of the species to which his kobong belongs, should he find it asleep, indeed, he always kills it reluctantly, and never without affording it a chance to escape. This arises from the family belief that some one individual of the species is their nearest friend, to kill whom would be a great crime and carefully to be avoided. . . . An old man of one particular totem group, say the kangaroo, will not eat kangaroo at all under ordinary circumstances, but he will make and charm a *churinga* bearing a design characteristic of his group, and will give it to a man of another totem group so as to assist him to catch kangaroos." In the Warramunga tribe, "a man is absolutely forbidden to eat either his own or his father's totem. He may, if, for example, he be a kangaroo man, kill the animal and hand it over to men of the other moiety, and there is no objection to his assisting men who do not belong to his totem group to capture and kill his totem." Mention is made of some men who started out as wild-cat men and changed into plum-tree men and went on eating plums. According to another tradition we have the description of the "wanderings of a hakea-tree woman who set out with a bandicoot woman. The latter painted the hakea woman with down used during a sacred ceremony of the bandicoot totem group, and thereby changed the hakea into a bandicoot woman, who after that went on eating bandicoots." A man of a lizard group in the Arunta tribe, on being questioned, said at first that he was both lizard and grass-seed; on further questioning, that he was really lizard but very nearly grass-seed. The explanation given is as follows: "In the Alcheringa he was a lizard man or man-animal, but some grass-seed men came near to where he was camped and performed sacred ceremonies of their group in the hope of transforming him into a grass-seed man. They were not successful, and he remained a lizard man; but owing to this Alcheringa incident he regards himself and is regarded as very closely associated with the grass-seed people. He does not eat the grass-seed when it is fresh and young."[9]

Brown[10] writes of some tribes of Western Australia that "each of these clans forms a single totemic group, possessing a number of totems. All the totems of the clan are equally the totems of every member of the clan. For each totem belonging to the clan there is within the territory of the clan a cere-

7 Spencer and Gillen, *Nat. Tr. Cent. Aust.*, 167, 168, 169, 179, 184, 185, 201, 202, 203, 206; Spencer and Gillen, in JAI, XXVIII, 278; "Miscellany," in JAI, XXVII, 134.

8 In JAI, XXVIII, 284; Frazer, *Golden Bough*, II, 365 (edit. 1900).

9 Spencer, "Totemism," in AAAS, 1904, 405, 412, 413, 414.

10 In JAI, XLIII, 160.

monial ground or totemic centre for which the name is *talu*. . . . The purpose of the ceremonies is said to be to increase the supply of the animal, plant, or other object with which it is connected." "The totem center determines the totem of the child when first alive in the womb; . . . these centers are definitely localized and do not shift; . . . though sex and class change with each successive reincarnation, the spirit always returns to its proper totem center and . . . thus the totemic identity is never lost."[11]

Howitt[12] makes something of the sex-totem. One is given to the youth at initiation; again there is a totem which is "the brother of all the men" and one which is "the sister of all the women." "They are not true totems in the sense that these represent sub-divisions of the primary classes; yet they are true totems in so far that they are regarded as being the 'brothers' and 'sisters' of the human beings who bear their names. . . . The sex totems, when first seen, presented a novel but a perplexing problem, because they merely divide the tribe into two moieties, one including all the males and the other all the females. The true character of the sex totem is shown by the Wotjobaluk expression, 'The life of a bat is the life of a man,' meaning that to injure a bat is to injure some man, while to kill one is to cause some man to die. The same saying applies to the Owlet-nightjar with respect to women. A man who was lax as to his totem was not thought well of, and was never allowed to take any important part in the ceremonies." In one of the tribes, a man "would not harm his totem if he could avoid it, but at a pinch he would eat it in default of other food. In order to injure another person he would, however, kill that person's totem. To dream about his own totem means that some one has done something to it for the purpose of harming the sleeper or one of his totemites. But if he dreams it again, it means himself, and if he thereupon falls ill, he will certainly see the wraith of the person who is trying to 'catch' him."

Parker[13] found that "our blacks may and do eat their hereditary totems, if so desirous, with no ill effects to themselves, either real or imaginary"; but while he may eat of his family-totem, inherited from his mother, he must never eat of his own individual, familiar totem. None of the same totem as the dead person may dig his grave. "Every individual, as soon as he or she arrives at the necessary age, is forbidden to eat not necessarily to kill—certain animals, each paedo-matronymic group having its own particular group of things that are 'tabooed.' Notwithstanding very careful search, I can find no plants, trees, shrubs, or grasses, as prohibited. Upon this point these aboriginals appear to be extremely particular, and should one of them wilfully partake of that which is 'tabooed,' he is firmly convinced that sickness, probably of a fatal character, will overtake him, and that certainly it would never satisfy his hunger. Should such a delinquent be caught red-handed by his fellow-men, he would in all probability be put to death."[14] Gason[15] finds that the sons follow their fathers' totems and the daughters those of their mothers. Fathers at a funeral do not eat of their offspring, but female relatives must, in order to have the dead in their liver, the seat of feeling. Mathews[16] says that when the Central Australian woman first feels premonitions of maternity she reports a dream—that she has heard infants laughing in the leaves of a tree. When the child is born, it is given the totem of those who haunt that place, not the totem of either parent. The relation of the person and his *churinga* may

11 Wallis, in AA, XV, 115.
12 *S.E. Aust.*, 144 ff., and in JAI, XV, 416.
13 *Euahlayi*, 20, 29, 86.

14 Roth, *N.W. Cent. Queensland*, 57.
15 In JAI, XVII, 186.
16 In AA, X, 98.

be brought out in clearer detail by the following: "When one of these 'dream-time' ancestors died, he was turned into a spirit-child, and as such dwells near one of the camping grounds, always carrying in his hand one of the *churinyas.* Conception is believed to take place by the entry of one of these spirit-children into the mother, the spirit-child dropping his *churinya* on the ground at the time. On the birth of the child the place is searched for the lost *churinya,* and by the kindly offices of one of the old men the search is usually successful. If it be not, a wooden one is made of hard-wood. . . . The stone *churinyas* are the more ancient form, and do not appear to be made at the present day. This then fixes the totem for the individual, and explains why in the Arunta tribe the child is not of the same totem as one of the parents, as is the case in some of the neighboring tribes of Central Australia."[17]

Von Leonhardi,[18] upon evidence furnished by certain correspondents in Australia, imparts the following. Certain ancestral spirits that live in sub-terranean caves may come out in the evening and station themselves by a rock or tree. If a woman goes by, such a spirit may be seen by her suddenly to dis-appear, and this is attended by symptoms of pain which convince her that he has entered her body. So too if a woman experiences the first indications of pregnancy just after she has seen a kangaroo, which has run away and sud-denly disappeared, she will later bear a kangaroo-child. Further, if she ex-periences pregnancy after eating copiously of a certain fruit, the child will receive the plant in question as a totem. "Every individual stands in relation to two totems; to the one he belongs by birth or, more correctly, by con-ception . . . ; the other totem belongs to him, or is bound to him—has com-munity . . . with him. . . . In consequence of the view that a human germ of the most diverse totems can enter any woman whatever, there can be no heritable totems. The child may belong to another totem . . . than the father or mother. . . . Of course, generally . . . a germ from the totem of the husband enters any particular woman, so that the totem of the father and the children is the same."

America. "From one end of America to the other the native was reported to have eaten all living creatures—man not excepted—barring the fact, however, that one dare not eat the flesh of the animal selected as his guardian or which was the totem of his clan, lest its shade should resent the action. In certain sections, however, one was allowed to consume even his totem animal, pro-vided certain prayers and invocations were addressed to the shades of the dead animal, to which explanation was made of the necessity under which the in-dividual labored through hunger."[19] One of the native American doctrines is "that persons and organizations of persons are one and all under the protecting and fostering tutelage of some imaginary being or spirit. These tutelary or patron beings may be grouped, by the mode and the motive of their acquire-ment and their functions, into two fairly well defined groups or classes: (1) those which protect individuals only, and (2) those which protect organiza-tions of persons. . . . The exact method of acquiring the clan or gentile group patrons or tutelaries is still an unsolved problem." It would seem, then, that we have, in the American type of totemism something different from the Australian. Morgan[20] evidently regards the animal-designations, of which he cites a number, as merely distinctive class- and group-marks. "In the Ojibwa

17 Anon., in JAI, XXVII, 133. 19 McGuire, in AA, III, 263.
18 In *Globus*, XCI, 288. 20 *Anc. Soc.*, 165.

dialect the word *totem,* quite as often pronounced *dodaim,* signifies the symbol or device of a gens; thus the figure of a wolf was the totem of the Wolf gens. From this Mr. Schoolcraft used the words 'totemic system' to express the gentile organization, which would be perfectly acceptable were it not that we have both in the Latin and the Greek a terminology for every quality and character of the system which is already historical."

How the young Indian, having attained through fasting and torture to the state of trance, out of his visions derives some object which amounts to a tutelary spirit, has been alluded to elsewhere.[21] The object was generally an animal. The totems of the kinship groups, which traced descent through the father and practised exogamy, were the special manifestations of the supernatural which had appeared to the founders of the clans in their ancient visions, and which their descendants held sacred under the taboo. The religious societies laid hold of this situation, for they are a grouping together of men who have had similar visions. Under the totem the members of the gentes or tribe learned the duties of kindred and to maintain the unity of the tribe. The gentile totem gave no immediate hold upon the supernatural, as did the individual totem in the case of its possessor.[22]

Morgan[23] lists the gentes (clans) of many tribes, but one example will serve for all. The Seneca Iroquois gentes were those of the Wolf, Bear, Turtle, Beaver, Deer, Snipe, Heron, and Hawk; others of the Confederacy recognized alternatives, such as the Eel for the Heron, or recognized the Great Turtle and the Little Turtle.

But if the Indian type of theory and practice does thus differ from the Australian, there are many points common to the two. Among the Iowas no member of any clan can eat the flesh of the eponymic animal.[24] "The first fast is the first important event in an Ojibwa's life. For this he leaves his home and goes to a secluded spot in the forest, where he fasts for an indefinite time; when reduced by lack of food he enters a hysterical or ecstatic state, in which he may have visions and hallucinations. The spirits he most desires to see in this condition are those of mammals and birds, though any object, animate or inanimate, is a good omen. The object which first appears is adopted as the guardian spirit, and is never mentioned by the entranced without first making a sacrifice. A small effigy of this manido is made, or its outline drawn, which is carried suspended by a string around his neck, or, if he be a Midé [member of a medicine-society], he carries it in his 'medicine bag.' . . . Until recently it was the custom for each Indian youth to pass through a certain process of 'fasting and dreaming,' whereby he might receive a manifestation from the Great Unknown as to what particular animate form he might adopt as his tutelary daimon, or guardian mystery. . . . Among some of the Algonquin tribes the animal or bird forms thus adopted by an Indian are sometimes the same as the totem of which he is a member. Under such circumstances the animal representing the totem, and the 'familiar' or manido, is seldom hunted or shot; but if he should be allowed to hunt such an animal, the hunter first addresses the animal and asks forgiveness for killing him, telling him that certain portions, which are tabu, shall be set up in the place of honor. . . . For instance, if an Indian of the Bear totem, or one whose adopted guardian is represented by the bear, desires to hunt and meets that animal, he would

21 §§163, 244, of the text.
22 Fletcher, in JAI, XXVII, 438; Fletcher, report in PSM, LII, 284.

23 *Anc. Soc.,* 70; also ch. VI.
24 Dorsey, in BAE, XI, 426.

apologize to the bear before killing it. The carcass would be dressed and served, but no member of the Bear totem could eat the meat, though members of all other totems could do so freely. The hunter could, however, eat of the paws and head, the bones of the latter being subsequently placed upon .a shelf, probably over the door, or in some other conspicuous place. Due reverence is paid such a relic of the totem, and the custom is so strictly observed that no greater insult could be offered to the host than for anyone to take down such bones and cast them carelessly aside.[25] A portrait of a warrior, say Buffalo Bull, shows his medicine or totem, in this case the head of a bull-buffalo, painted on his face and breast.[26]

Among the Northeastern Algonquins the hunter is visited by a guardian-spirit in the shape of a beaver who instructs him where and under what conditions he will find game. Since this animal forms so important an element in the diet of the tribes of this region, the natives believe that the beaver-spirit in dreams directs them generally to where beaver may be found. The game so obtained must be cooked and eaten in a prescribed way. "Observing in this region the attitude toward the totem where relationship is maintained by killing the totemic animal and eating it, and by using its fur, the association with the creature is not so unlike the more common practice of reverence for the totem by not killing, eating or using it as may seem. In the whole northern region the various animals are treated with respect by their slayers who prepare the bones and other remains of the game and dispose of them in a manner thought to be satisfactory to the animals' souls, so to speak. Thus in the religious thought of the north a hunter is satisfying an animal's spirit about as much when he kills the animal and disposes properly of its remains as when he refuses to molest it at all. While the above procedure is quite contrary in practice to the procedure of African, Australian, and a number of American totemites, it is not so contradictory in principle, its objective in reality being the maintenance of the game."[27]

It is noteworthy and significant that two races so widely separated and so dissimilar as the natives of Australia and those of North America should have so many points in common in their system of naming. Both have hereditary "secret" or "mystery" names, which always refer to some event in the lives of the ancestors of the groups or families, or to the supposed origin of the founders of these. These family or hereditary names among all the tribes, but especially among the Delta and Coastal divisions, were regarded as among the most sacred possession of the kin-group and were most jealously guarded. It is the opinion of Hill-Tout,[28] who has made a special study of the Indians of British Columbia, that among the Salish, at least, the personal name and totem gave rise to the group- or kin-name and totem. According to the belief of these natives the *snam* or personal totem may be transmitted to another; this is usually accomplished by uttering some mystic words and by blowing or breathing upon the symbol of the *snam*. "A brother does not call his brother or his sister by a *snam* or hereditary or even by a *staz* [nick] name, but always by a term expressive of their relative ages; and when speaking of them to others he uses terms with similar meanings. A man's 'proper' names seem only to have been used among the Salish on ceremonial occasions, or when one

---

25 Hoffman, in BAE, VII, 163; and in BAE, XIV, 64, 65, 44.

26 Donaldson, in *Smithson. Rep.*, 1885, pt. II, plate 31.

27 Speck, in AA, XIX, 10, note (quoted), 16-17.

28 In JAI, XXXV, 146-147, 148-149, 151-152, 153, 154-155.

wished specially to gratify or honour a person. . . . On occasions of public ceremony, such as the potlatch or other feasts, or at the winter dancing, men were always formally addressed by their hereditary, mystery or *snam* names." Further evidence that the kin-name was originally the personal mystery-name or *snam* name of one of the ancestors of the kin may be found in the study of the crests. "Every individual had a *snam* mark or picture, in other words a personal 'crest,' the symbol of his nagual. This he customarily placed upon his personal belongings to mark or distinguish them from those of his fellows. But when we descend the river and meet the Delta and Coastal tribes, we find the personal 'crest,' like the personal totem, giving place to the kin-group 'crest,' which among these tribes is possessed by every family of standing, and is its peculiar distinguishing visual mark." Among the Salish a *súlia* or personal totem, whose material form was that of an edible object, enabled the owner of it to be eminently successful in his quest for that object. "It seems to suggest that the life of the owner of such a *súlia* was bound up, or intimately connected, with the well-being or existence of those objects under which his *súlia* manifested itself. . . . Not everybody acquired a *súlia;* only those who excelled in their special lines, such as great hunters, fishers, warriors, runners and the like"; women as a rule never acquired *súlia* unless they were witches. All the animals in the old time were not just common animals and nothing else; they were people as well, and could take the human or the animal form at will by putting on or taking off the skin of the animal. "This shape-shifting or transformation was invariably effected in this region by donning or casting off the skin of the animal whose character is assumed. . . . Shamans only inherited their *súlia* from their fathers; other men had ordinarily to acquire their own. But this applied only to the dream or vision totem or protective 'spirit.' In the case of the acquisition of a totem or protective 'spirit' by other means . . . a man could and did transmit the protective influence he had acquired." However we may view the "dream" *súlia,* there can be no doubt that "tutelary spirits" were transmitted and handed down from one generation to another; by which it becomes clear that "group"-totemism existed among the Salish. "We have, therefore, in this country," Hill-Tout[29] concludes, "three different kinds of 'group' totemism (not counting those of secret societies, or brotherhoods), *viz.,* that under matriarchal institutions, which American students, following Powell, now generally denominate 'clan totemism'; that under patriarchal rule distinguished from the former by the term 'gentile totemism'; and that which we find in social groups like the Salish, where a union of the two earlier states has taken place, and where the social unit is the 'family,' which comprises the relatives on both sides of the house, which I may denominate 'kin totemism' for lack of a better term. In all these groups there is the same transmission of the *common* 'protecting genius,' from one generation to another. Under matriarchy, this is effected by the 'conventional fathers' of the group on the female side of the house, that is, by the maternal uncles. Under patriarchy by the 'ostensible or real fathers' of the group on the male side; and under that social structure which results from a combination of the other two, like that among the Salish, by the 'fathers' on both sides of the house."

Boas[30] says that the Tlinkit, Haida, and other Indians of the northwest coast "have animal totems. . . . The clans of the northern tribes bear the names

29 In JAI, XXXIV, 324-326, 327-328.   30 In USNM for 1895, 323, 336-337, 393-394; and in *Proc. Nat. Mus.,* 1888, 202.

of their respective totems and are exogamous. It must be clearly understood, however, that the natives do not consider themselves descendants of the totem. All my endeavors to obtain information regarding the supposed origin of the relation between man and animal have invariably led to the telling of a myth, in which it is stated how a certain ancestor of the clan in question obtained his totem. . . . It is evident that legends of this character correspond almost exactly to the tales of the acquisition of manitous among the Eastern Indians, and they are evidence that the totem of this group of tribes is, in the main, the hereditary manitow of a family. This analogy becomes still clearer when we consider that each man among these tribes acquires a guardian spirit, but that he can acquire only such as belong to his clan. Thus, a person may have the general crest of his clan and, besides, use as his personal crest such guardian spirits as he has acquired. This accounts partly for the great multiplicity of combinations of crests which we observe on the carvings of these people. . . . There exists, however, another class of traditions, according to which the crests or emblems of the clan are not acquired in this manner, but brought down by the ancestor of the clan from heaven or from the underworld or out of the ocean, wherever he may have derived his origin." Then there is a variant connected with membership in the secret societies. "Many ancestors, when obtaining their manitous, were given the right to perform certain dances, or they were given secret songs, or the power to eat human flesh. These rights have also become hereditary, but they differ from the crest in so far as the character of the initiating spirit (the manitou) has been more clearly preserved. Each individual, who by descent or marriage is entitled to membership in one of the secret societies, must nevertheless, be initiated by its presiding spirit before joining the society." There is still "another class of legends which relate entirely to spirits that are still in constant contact with the Indians, whom they endow with supernatural powers. In order to gain their help, the youth must prepare himself by fasting and washing, because only the pure find favor with them, while they kill the impure. Every young man endeavors to find a protector of this kind. It is clear that this idea corresponds exactly to the manitou of the Algonquin Indians, and that we have to deal here with the elementary idea of the acquisition of a guardian spirit, which has attained its strongest development in America. Its specific character on the North Pacific Coast lies in the fact that the guardian spirit has become hereditary. This is the case among the northern tribes of British Columbia. It is also the case among the Kwakiutl and among the Chinook. When the youth prepares to meet a guardian spirit, he does not expect to find any but those of his clan. This is probably the reason for the relatively small number of such spirits—for among the Indians of the plains, among whom each man has his individual spirit, their number is unlimited—and it has also given occasion for the development of a more elaborate mythology relating to these spirits." The tribes of the northwest coast all claim to be autochthonous; the ancestor of each clan descended from heaven, in most cases in the shape of a bird, and the crest he adopted hints at his exploits. Tylor[31] thinks this set of beliefs to be "a special modification of the totem theory, made to fit with the belief in family descent by means of transmigration of ancestral souls."

The development of the totem-ceremonials and especially of the totem-pole is popularly connected with the northwest coast. "The Tlingit of southeastern

31 In JAI, XXVIII, 134.

Alaska, living under most favorable conditions of climate and food supply, with abundant leisure to cultivate an innate sense of art, evolved in time a rich ceremonial that had for its purpose the glorification of the family in the display of the totem, or the practice of shamanistic rites which constituted his nearest approach to any form of religion or worship."[32] The totem-poles of the natives of Alaska, while bearing images of creatures, were never erected to represent any imaginary deity or god. "Nor were they ever worshipped. They are highly revered because they carry the tribal emblem. What the coat-of-arms, or crest, is to families of the English aristocracy, so are totemic marks to native families. The Englishman reveres the family crest, but does not worship it; so does the native with his totemic emblem." Their names refer to this crest or totem, and as soon as one hears the name of another he knows exactly where to place him.[33] The Columbian tribes have a *tamanuus,* or medicine, which they reverence as their protecting spirit. Early in life each man chooses such a *tamanuus,* and it is usually an animal.[34]

Kroeber[35] says that the California tribes, so far as known, all lack any gentile or totemic system, while among the tribes of the southwest totemism is a marked feature of the social organization. But Merriam[36] finds that the ethnologists have overlooked the evidence. "This may be due to the less conspicuous part it plays in the lives of the people compared with its high development in some other regions, notably Alaska and British Columbia. Nevertheless totemism not only exists in California, but is rather widely prevalent; it is present in many tribes—tribes distributed among widely different stocks; and, when one comes to understand something of the inner life of the people, it is found to be as deeply rooted, and in some cases as important, as in other regions. . . . In California the totem is always an object in nature—usually an animal, but sometimes a tree or a rock. . . . Certain animals are never totems. Conspicuous among these are the Coyote and Fox. The only tree totem is the Black Oak. . . . In the Middle and Southern Mewuk the totem is hereditary and passes from father to child; the mother's totem is not carried down. If the father is a Deer, all the children—boys and girls alike —are Deer. In the Northern Mewuk on the other hand the totem is individual, not hereditary. The father may be a Bear, the son a Gray Tree-squirrel, the grandson a Lizard, the aunt a Yellowjacket Wasp."

"The psychic element of religion in the Snake dance is totemic ancestor worship which is fundamental in the whole Hopi ritual. The reptile is a society totem, the lineal survivor of a clan totem, and the totem ancestor, called the Snake maid, is, generally, like totemic ideas, an anthropo-zoömorphic conception. Members of the society claim immunity from the bite of the snake because it is their totem, and the idea of possession of the shade or 'breath-body' of the dead by the snake totem is in accord with universal totemic conceptions. The Snake dance is simply a form of clan totemism having special modifications, due to environment, to fit the needs of the Hopi. It is a highly modified form of ancestor worship in which the Sun and the Earth, as parents of all, are worshipped, but in which the cultus hero and the ancestors of the clan are the special divinized personages represented in secret rites."[37]

The *zemi* of Porto Rico primarily "corresponds with the totem of the North American, and zemiism is practically another name for totemism, a form of

32 Emmons, "Petroglyphs," in AA, X, 221.
33 Jones, *Thlingets,* 37, 169 (quoted).
34 Wilkes, *Narrative,* V, 118.

35 In AA, IV, 278.
36 "Totemism in Cal.," in AA, X, 558, 559.
37 Fewkes, in BAE, XIX, pt. II, 1009.

ancestor worship."[38] It is stated that some of the natives of South America
are totemists,[39] but the evidence is very scanty. We learn that the young Paraguay Indian, leaving his own family to go to his wife, takes along his family-
crest or totem with great ceremony and plants it before the bed. This is vague;
the author[40] cites similarly inconclusive evidence from Im Thurn and Ehrenreich. The Araucanians believe they originally descended from the animals
whose names they bear, but have no clear idea as to whether this descent was
on the mother's or on the father's side, although most of them incline to the
former. "The corporeal forms which they assign to their divinities also indicate
that there has been formerly an animal worship, which was possibly only a
transition from totemism, and may have originated in some form of ancestor
worship. . . . No prohibition attaches to the killing or eating of special animals, although there are a few such superstitions among the elders."[41]

Other Parts of the World. The Tasmanians showed no traces of the totemism
that was so widespread in the neighboring continent.[42] In New Guinea, in the
assembly-houses, the cross-beams are carved with lizards, turtles, fish, and
birds, "without doubt in honor of ancestors that have gone over to such forms
or have descended from these beasts . . . and so too is totemism current among
them, that is, the idea of once having had an animal in the kin-group and of
honoring it for this reason. Many an one derives his origin from a pig and therefore refrains from eating pork; by others again the crocodile is spared because
their tribal mother gave life, along with their ancestors and at the same time,
to a crocodile. Whoever has such ties through his mother is, according to the
notion of several tribes, turned into the related animal after death. It is noteworthy that, in case others kill such an animal, to which one thinks himself
kin, he has to undertake a fight, though only a counterfeit one, with them, and
must give a mourning feast in honor of the deceased related crocodile,
kangaroo, or whatever it was." Then too the form which the ancestor had is
incised upon amulets and even branded on the forehead, breast, and arms in
the form of the proper animal; "they consecrate themselves to the spirit of
their ancestors by portraying the original bodies of their ancestors upon their
bodies."[43] No man may carry or eat any kangaroo that he has killed. He generally exchanges it with another man similarly situated.[44]

In one of the tribes of the Papuan Gulf, a native's explanation why a certain
mammal, bird, or fish is regarded by him as his particular *ualare* is that it was
held to be sacred by his original ancestor. "For the present we have to be content with the statement that a certain animal was regarded as sacred by the
original ancestor; he never injured or killed it, never ate it as food when killed
by anyone else, and because it was held sacred by him, his posterity for all
time must also regard it as sacred. If a man accidently kills a member of
the family of his *ualare,* he sets aside a period for mourning, during which
period he fasts from the principal kind of food, eating only enough to keep
himself from absolute starvation; he also observes many of the customs of
mourning as if he had lost a relative. If on the other hand he kills a member
of his *ualare* family in a fit of anger or for any other reason that is not justifiable, as soon as he recognizes what he has done he gives himself over to

38 Fewkes, in *Science*, XVI, 94 ff.
39 Wilutsky, *Mann u. Weib*, 74.
40 Koch, in *Globus*, LXXXI, 45.
41 Latcham, in JAI, XXXIX, 360-361.

42 Roth, *Tasmania*, 75.
43 Krieger, *Neu-Guinea*, 183, 404.
44 Guise, in JAI, XXVIII, 217.

violent grief, abstains from all kinds of food, isolates himself from his relatives, and ultimately dies of starvation."[45] The natives of British New Guinea
believe that at death the spirit enters into wild animals, more especially crocodiles, pigs, and cassowaries. "It is said that certain persons have on occasions
recognised the features of their relations in crocodiles and pigs, and thereupon
not only refrained from killing them (which was done instead by some bystander), but also refrained from eating the flesh of these crocodiles and
pigs."[46] Again, in the same region, "if the *iauafangai* is an animal, a man will
not now, as a rule, be unwilling to kill it, but he will not himself eat it, though
he will give it to someone else to eat." The old unwillingness even to kill it
still survives with certain clans, and indeed among them, "if the *iauafangai*
animal is caught in a snare or trap, they will shed tears at the wrong committed, and release the animal."[47]

The most characteristic cultural feature of the Melanesian Massim is the
existence of a peculiar form of totemism with matrilineal descent. In spite of local variations, it is certain that special importance is attributed to the bird-
totem over the greater part of the Massim area. This is perhaps best shown in
one of the first questions commonly put to a stranger: "What is your bird?" So
too, if a man be asked his totem, he will commonly give his bird-totem only.
"There are no totem shrines, and people are not believed to have particular
influence over the birds or other animals which are their totems. There does
not seem ever to have been any ceremony which had for its purpose the increasing of the totem, nor was there any tendency for a man to tame and
keep his totem birds as pets." In spite of legendary close associations of men
and totem-animals, there does not appear to be any generally recognized
physical or psychical resemblance between men and their totems, nor are the
latter regarded as omen-giving. A man should not eat his totem-bird, the
penalty for transgressing this rule being a swollen stomach and perhaps death.
A man would go round his totem-snake on the road to avoid touching it.
Inquiry failed to elicit the purpose of the totems in the native mind.[48] In Mota
there are many persons, perhaps as many as half the population, who are not
permitted by custom to eat the flesh of certain animals, to eat certain fruits,
or to touch certain trees. "The ground for the prohibition in most cases is that
the person is believed to be the animal or fruit in question, his mother having received an influence from an animal or plant of the kind before his birth. . . . The
belief underlying the prohibition of the animal as food is that the person would
be eating himself. It seemed that the act would be regarded as a kind of cannibalism. It was evident that there is a belief in the most intimate relation between
the person and all individuals of the species with which he is identified." The
prohibition is a purely individual matter. Rivers[49] cites an instance of the
evil effects believed to follow non-observance of the restrictions in Fiji: "A
man whose people had always eaten snakes married a woman to whom these
animals were *tambu*. He did not give snakes to his children but their food
was cooked in pots which had been used to cook snakes and the constant
illness of his children was ascribed to this cause and, in order to escape from
continual trouble, he left his wife and took another woman."

In the Island of Aurora there are families within the two great exogamous
divisions of the people; one of these is named from the octopus. "If anyone

45 Holmes, in JAI, XXXII, 426.
46 Seligmann, in JAI, XXXIX, 266.
47 Williamson, in JAI, XLIII, 271-272.

48 Seligmann, *Melanesians*, 9-11, 450-451,
680, 682.
49 Rivers, *Melan. Soc.*, I, 151-153, 273.

of another family wished to get octopus for food he would ask one of this family to go to the part of the beach to which the family was said to have originally belonged, and standing there, to cry out, 'So-and-so wants octopus.' Then plenty would be got." In the Banks' Islands, the people identify themselves with certain animals or fruits, believe that they partake of their qualities and character, and refuse to eat them on the ground that in so doing they would practically be eating themselves.[50] One of the clans of San Cristoval, Solomon Islands, worships a man of former times who is now incarnate in a shark or other fish or the leaf of a tree. The group will not kill any of his several incarnations. It may be that we have here a group which might easily in the course of time develop into a totem-clan; probably it would be called the shark-clan and would have the shark and other associated totems. A Tawatana man once told the author[51] that he would not kill either the totem of his father (eagle) or that of his mother (crab), especially not the latter; he said that if one of the crab-clan were murdered, he, with all other crab-people along the coast, would feel bound to punish the murderer; but if an eagle-man were killed he would only be "a little angry."

Totemism, if such a term is applicable in the D'Entrecasteaux Islands, is an institution altogether apart. "The totems are inherited taboos of a certain kind which affect all the kin, causing them to abstain from eating certain articles of food. The children inherit them from the father, in a few cases from the mother as well; but generally the mother's totem is disregarded by her children. Since most if not all of the inhabitants of a hamlet are connected by kinship, and have in consequence inherited the same totems, one may speak of a hamlet as having a certain totem or totems of its own. . . . One man conjectured that their spirits passed at death into their totems, and hence the totem has received the name of 'grandparent'; but others emphatically denied this doctrine. . . . Whatever be the mystic bond which unites the native with his totem, there are, or were, very material penalties for any infringement of it. Eyes and cheeks will swell, the hair will drop out, ulcerous sores will cover the body of the man who dares to kill or eat it. Death will follow quickly unless for three days, morning, noon, and night, he washes in the sea, and three times during the hours of darkness inside his hut. Kinsmen dare not go near him, but friends whose totems are different must take care of him; thus only is there any hope of his recovery. Even if, wandering in the woods, a man should set his foot on his dead totem, his foot will be covered with ulcers; or should it be cooked and eaten in his village by another native, he will die, and the native who cooked it must pay the blood-price to his relatives."[52]

Codrington[53] finds the tribes in the Solomon Islands which have totem-groups also tracing descent in the female line, and a number of tribes with father-descent and no totem-groups. There are six mother-kin groups on Florida Island, called *kema*. "It adds very much to the distinction between these *kema* that each has some one or more *buto* from which its members must keep clear, abstain from eating, approaching, or beholding it. One of the very first lessons learnt by a Florida child is what is its *buto*, its abomination, to eat or touch or see which would be a dreadful thing. In one case, and in one case only, this *buto* is the living creature from which the *kema* takes its name; the

---

50 Codrington, in AAAS, 1890, 612-613; Brown, in AAAS, 1911, 409.

51 Fox, in JAI, XLIX, 103, 157-158.

52 Jenness and Ballentyne, *D'Entrecasteaux*, 66-69.

53 In JAI, XVIII, 310; Codrington, *Melanesians*, 31 ff.

Kakau kin may not eat the *Kakau* crab. The Nggaombata may not eat the giant clam; the Lahi may not eat of a white pig; the Manukama may not eat the pigeon; the Kakau, besides their eponymous crab, may not eat the parrot Trichoglossus Massena. The Manukama are at liberty to eat the bird from which they take their name. If the question be put to any member of these *kema,* he will probably answer that his *buto* is his ancestor; a Manukama will say that the pigeon he does not eat is his ancestor; but an intelligent native, describing this native custom, writes:—'This is the explanation of the *buto.* We believe these *tindalo* to have been once living men, and something that was with them, or with which they had to do, has become a thing forbidden, *tambu,* and abominable, *buto,* to those to whom the *tindalo* belongs.' He gives the example of the clam of the Nggaombata. The ghost, *tindalo,* of a famous ancient member of that *kema,* named Polika, haunted a beach opposite Mage, and a large snake, *poli,* was believed to represent him there. The Nggaombata could not approach that beach, Polika was their *buto.* On another beach where they catch fish wherewith to sacrifice to Polika is a *gima,* a clam, which they call Polika, and used to believe to be in some way Polika; hence the *gima* is their *buto.* . . . There will occur at once the question whether in this we do not find totems. But it must be asked where are the totems? in the living creatures after which two of the divisions are named, or in those creatures which the members of the several divisions may not eat? It is true that the Kakau kindred may not eat the crab *kakau;* but the Manukama may eat the bird *manukama.* If there be a totem then it must be found in the *buto;* in the pigeon of the Manukama and the giant clam of the Nggaombata, which are said to be ancestors. But it must be observed that the thing which it is abominable to eat is never believed to be the ancestor, certainly never the eponymous ancestor, of the clan; it is said to represent some famous former member of the clan, one of a generation beyond that of the fathers of the present members of it, a *kukau.* The thing so far represents him that disrespect to it is disrespect to him. The most probable explanation of these *buto* may indeed throw light upon the origin of totems elsewhere, but can hardly give totems a home in the Solomon Islands. The *buto* of each *kema* is probably comparatively recent in Florida; it has been introduced at Bugotu within the memory of living men. It is in all probability a form of the custom which prevails in Ulawa, another of the Solomon Islands. It was observed with surprise when a Mission school was established in that island, that the people of the place would not eat bananas, and had ceased to plant the tree. It was found that the origin of this restraint was recent and well remembered; a man of much influence had at his death not long ago prohibited the eating of bananas after his decease, saying that he would be in the banana. The elder natives would still give his name and say, 'We cannot eat So-and-So.' When a few years had passed, if the restriction had held its ground, they would have said, 'We must not eat our ancestor.' This represents what is not uncommon also in Malaita near Ulawa, where, as in Florida also, a man will often declare that after death he will be seen as a shark."

Tylor[54] quotes a letter which was sent to Codrington, as follows: "When a father is about to die, surrounded by members of his family, he might say what animal he will be, say a butterfly or some kind of a bird. That creature would be sacred to his family, who would not injure it or kill it; on seeing or

54 In JAI, XXVIII, 147.

falling in with such an object the person would say, 'That is *kaka* (papa),' and would, if possible, offer him a young cocoanut. But they did not adopt thus the name of a tribe."

In the westernmost Torres Straits Islands, "the transition from totemism to hero-worship was in process of evolution till it was arrested by the coming of the white man." Perhaps the change was correlative with a known change from the matriarchal to the patriarchal system. The author[55] thinks that Parkinson and Danks have proved true totemism for the northern Solomon Islands, New Britain, Duke of York Island, and New Ireland. The "close relations between man and totem were put to the service of the community. The Ongong-people were called upon when it was a question of alluring Ongongs to the coast. Then the Ongong-man, painted and ornamented, ascended . . . a peculiarly sacred place and here carried out magic operations in which a carved Ongong-figure was used. At the end of the ceremony the turtle-people received the image to take with them on the hunt."[56] The Fijians have both principal totems, which are animal and vegetable and are not to be destroyed or eaten, and secondary ones, which can be eaten with certain ceremonial. But many tribal names have no analogy with the names of their principal totems. These latter were deeply respected and consulted on all important occasions. An expectant mother was visited by the totem-animal. The tree-totem is connected by legend with the origin of the people.[57] Melanesians and Polynesians have a system of worship of animals, like the totem in America and the kobong in Australia.[58]

"Totemism on the one hand and a mass of differing and inconsistent myths on the other are demonstrated for Africa." There is totemism and tribal division on the basis of "animalistic" notions; the totem-animal is the incorporation or incarnation of the ancestors, and so there is a taboo on eating and, under certain circumstances, on killing. Persons of the same totem, even of different tribes, may not marry, for it would be equivalent to incest. Totemism is most marked among the Bechuanas and on the Gold Coast but along the whole western border of the continent there are survivals in the form of food-taboos and marriage-taboos.[59] "The different Bechuana tribes are named after certain animals, showing probably that in former times they were addicted to animal-worship like the ancient Egyptians. The term Bakatla means 'They of the monkey;' Bakuena, 'they of the alligator;' Batlápi, 'they of the fish': each tribe having a superstitious dread of the animal after which it is called. . . . A tribe never eats the animal which is its namesake, using the term 'ila,' hate or dread, in reference to killing it. We find traces of many ancient tribes in the country in individual members of those now extinct, as the Batáu, 'they of the lion'; the Banóga, 'they of the serpent'; though no such tribes now exist."[60] Another writer[61] reports that "tribal names are rarely the names of plants or animals, and totems are unknown." We are told that all good men of a certain tribe turn into lions when they die, and reappear to fight for the tribe.[62] In the old days there is no doubt that the totem was regarded by the Bechuana as the supernatural friend and ally of the tribe, that it was respected and protected, and that men swore by it as by a sacred thing. One would not eat

55 Haddon, in *Brit. Assoc. Adv. Sci.*, 1902, 744 ff.
56 Thilenius, in *Globus*, LXXXI, 330.
57 De Marzan, in *Anthropos*, 1907, II, 400 ff.
58 Ratzel, *Vkde.*, II. 292.

59 Frobenius, *Masken*, 192-193.
60 Livingstone, *Mission. Travels*, 15.
61 Macdonald, in JAI, XIX, 266.
62 Bent, *Mashonaland*, 288.

or even touch an animal of his totem. Chance might determine an individual totem, as in the case of a native who, in his extremity, hid in a thicket. "His pursuers had seen him but a little while before, and as he was now nowhere to be seen, they surmised that he must be in hiding; and they approached the very thicket, intending to examine it. Just as they approached, however, a duyker sprang out and bounded away. Upon this one of them remarked that a man and a duyker could not hide in the same thicket, and the party went on. Henceforth, says the story, the chief took the duyker for his totem." Some of the tribes regarded the hoe as a totem. When asked how these people cultivated their gardens if they refused to touch the hoe, they replied that it was strictly correct to use the hoe for gardening, but that it was profanation to use it for any inferior work, and that it would be a very serious thing to strike a dog with it.[63] The Herero have divisions that call themselves the relatives of the sun, or the rain, or the tree, and each regards a special plant as holy and as the symbol of the division. Such connections are inherited from the mother. "The prescriptions which forbid eating this or that animal, to behave thus and so in connection with certain natural phenomena, to pay reverence to certain cattle that are somehow marked out, and so on, are to be regarded as a sort of 'family custom' and seem to serve to sustain the memory of fellowship, since the members, even when they are lined up with different tribes, yet evince a certain spirit of community."[64] Frazer[65] thinks that "the totemism of the Bantu tribes of South Africa resolves itself into a particular species of the worship of the dead,—the totem animals are revered as incarnations of the souls of dead ancestors."

No person of a clan among the Baganda is allowed either to kill or eat his own totem, though any one of another clan may do so with impunity. Any infringement of this custom will be followed by sickness, sores all over the body, or even death. No one mentions his totem, but asks some other person present to give the information when it is necessary to make the totem known. A woman must not eat green locusts; she may, however, catch them for her husband who, immediately after eating, must have intercourse with her "in order to cause the locusts to increase and avert any ill consequences to her children, which might otherwise arise from her catching her totem."[66]

In West Africa, "to each clan its totem animal is sacred, and they will not eat of its flesh. In some parts this sanctity is regarded as so great that actual prayer and sacrifice are made to it. But in most of the Bantu tribes this totem idea does not exist as a worship. Indeed, the animal (or part of an animal) is not sacred to an entire clan, but only to individuals, for whom it is chosen on some special occasion; and its use is prohibited only to that individual. Only in the sense that it may not be used for common purposes is it 'sacred' or 'holy' to him."[67] "The Ewe-Speaking tribes, like the people of the Gold Coast, are totemistic, and the different communities are heterogeneous; that is, members of several, in some cases of all, of the clans are found in each community. . . . The usual reverence is paid by the members of a clan to the animal or plant from which the clan takes its name. It may not be used as food, or molested in any way; but must always be treated with veneration and respect. The general notion is that the members of the clan are directly descended

---

63 Willoughby, in JAI, XXXV, 297-298, 299, 300 (quoted).
64 Fritsch, Eingeb. S.-Afr., 230.
65 "S. Afr. Totemism," in Man, I, 135 ff.;

Wilutsky, Mann u. Weib, 80; Stow, in Folk-Lore, XV, 203 ff.
66 Roscoe, in JAI, XXXII, 29, 53 (quoted).
67 Nassau, Fetichism, 210.

from the animal, or plant, eponymous."[68] On the Gold Coast there are indications of totemism in the facts that when a man sees a dead leopard he anoints its muzzle with palm oil, and if he kills one by accident, he says, "I have killed my brother," and puts palm oil on the wounds. There are stories of adoption of a totem by a town and by a household; in both cases the animal had pulled them out of trouble, by showing them a ford in a river, for example, or by saving life. Thereafter the totem-animal must not be killed or eaten; if caught in a trap, it is let go. There is also some notion of the dead migrating into the totem and omens from its appearance. Food and prayers may be offered to it. The belief also is held that the fate of an individual is bound up with his individual totem.[69]

Trilles[70] has written extensively on totemism among the Fan. Originally, he believes, the totem was personal, applying only to a single individual, the father of the race; but by the very nature of things this totem became familial; then, in consequence of the extension of the family, it came, in the course of centuries, to apply to the clan, and finally to the tribe. Each secret society, and even each grade of each secret society, has its animal-protector, with its consecration, rites, cult, and particular prohibitions. The totem is generally an animal, but may also be a plant, a spirit, or even a natural phenomenon. The tribal totem is the most important. A clan, to be totemic, need not bear the name of the totem. Totemism, both as an object and as a body of doctrine, differs from, though it is allied to, fetishism, the taboo, nagualism, and other beliefs. The clans of the Fan do not consider the eponymous animal to be an ancestor, made of the same substance as themselves: they are kin because the same spirit animates them. In totemism the cult is directed toward the eponymic ancestor of the tribe, called guardian; in manism, or the ancestral cult, it is directed toward the true ancestor or father of the tribe. The former worships the effective materialization of the totem, also the living descendants of the eponymic ancestor; the latter worships the first ancestor, the very personification of the race. The whole race is issued from his loins; each individual's life is an episode or fragment of that of the race, as the fruit of the tree. There are many totemic rites, some of which concern the continuation and preservation of the race. One of these is the exchange of the blood of the totem; and in some cases there is a communion, which brings the stranger into the tribe and enlarges the range of the family or reunites two tribes in a common alliance by means of the chiefs who personify them.

"The Banyoro are divided into many clans, which would appear to have *totems,* as sacred symbols or ancestral emblems like the similar clans in Uganda. . . . It is unlawful by custom for a Munyoro to kill or eat the totem of his clan. . . . I have never been able to ascertain either from Banyoro or Baganda that their forefathers at any time believed the clan to be actually descended from the object chosen as a totem. The matter remains very obscure. It may be remotely connected with ancestor-worship, which is certainly the foundation of such religious beliefs as are held by the Banyoro, as by most other Negro races. . . . The paternal grandfather gives a name to the child. This naming is a very peculiar function. A great deal depends on the name given, and there are certain foods forbidden to families bearing certain names. For

68 Ellis, *Ewe,* 100; Ellis, in PSM, XLV, 780; Frobenius, *Masken,* 193, 194; Harper and Van Hien, both in JAI, XXXVI, 178 ff. and 185 ff. resp.

69 Harper, in JAI, XXXVI, 180-181, 185, 186, 187, 188.
70 *Fân,* 8-9, 15, 21-22, 23-24, 24-25, 162, 163, 249, 363-364, 500-501, 505-506.

instance, if a child is called *Luanga,* it must never eat the flesh of an otter; a
man named *Mayanja* cannot eat the flesh of a sheep; nor can one who is called
Katenda eat the *Protopterus* (lung-fish). The prohibition extends to the man's
descendants for all time, but it does not include his wife or wives. They may
have a prohibition of their own inherited from their father, but the sons or
daughters are only involved in the prohibition of their father: the prohibition
(if any) which applies to their mother does not affect them. These restrictions
regarding diet are no doubt connected with the totem or sacred symbol of the
clan ('kika') to which any person belongs."[71] In Madagascar a certain lemur
is believed "to be an embodiment of the spirits of their ancestors, and therefore they look with horror upon killing them."[72]

In East Africa a relationship akin to totemism exists, "but it is a playful
relationship, rigid only when choosing a wife, without the strict sanctions and
penalties attached to the cult elsewhere." In fact, one author[73] thinks that
totemism is a misnomer here; there is a need for another word. Totemic prohibitions seem to have been strict in the past, but are not binding today, save
in a few special instances. Among the Bantu people each clan appears to have
its own particular totem, and this may have given rise to their custom of
exogamy, but in Nandi each individual is said to have his own totem irrespective
of the clan. In all the groups in this region the totems appear to be animals; no
example of a vegetable totem has been discovered. The Bantu group use the
word *muziro* to denote the totem and, contrary to the usual belief, the eating
of a totem-animal is not believed to be followed by death, but only by a severe
skin-eruption; and if, by any mischance, the meat of the totem is eaten, the
evil consequences can be averted by making a medicine extracted from certain
herbs; this extract is mixed with the fat of a black ox and rubbed all over
the body of the patient. Among the Nilotic Ja-Luo there is a long list of totem
animals which are forbidden as food to both men and women. Curiously enough,
the animals on this *index expurgatorius* are considered malignant in their
influence and it is thought praiseworthy to kill them. There is hardly any trace
of totemism among the Masai.[74] Some of the Hausa clans kill their totem each
year, others every second, while some let three years pass between the rites.
"Priests who were very full of medicine would catch the lion with their hands—
there were only three of these priests. The animals were killed so that they
should not become too numerous, and they had to submit because they obeyed
the incense." It is stated that totemism is really a treaty of peace between
man and animals, the latter promising to aid the former if worshipped in
the proper manner and provided with offerings.[75]

"Totemism as a survival may be suspected in the 'fish' and 'dog' people of
the Rig Veda."[76] Certain families "have *devaks* or sacred symbols, which appear to have been originally totems, and affect marriage to the extent that a
man cannot marry a woman whose *devak* reckoned on the male side is the
same as his own. They are totems, worshipped during marriage and other
important ceremonies. . . . Septs with different names, but whose object of
special worship is the same, cannot intermarry. . . . They all pay reverence to
their own totem, in the case of a tree by never cutting or injuring it, or as a

71 Johnston, *Uganda,* II, 587 ff.; 691 ff.
72 Sibree, *Great Afr. Isl.,* 270.
73 Barton, in JAI, LIII, 48; Barton, in
JAI, LI, 87, 88; Dundas, K., in JAI, XLIII,
61-65; Cole, in JAI, XXXII, 308.

74 Hobley, in JAI, XXXIII, 347; Hobley,
A-Kamba, 161.
75 Tremearne, in JAI, XLV, 25, 26.
76 Hopkins, *Relig. Ind.,* 537.

rule employing it in any way, while in case of other objects they avoid injuring them in any way. They make obeisance to the totem when passing and their women do *Ghungat, i.e.,* veil the face when passing. Women desirous of children make an offering called *Mānnat* to the totem. As a rule some spirit is supposed to live in the tree, or other object."[77] "It is generally admitted that for many of these tribes there is ample evidence that at one time they passed through what is called the totemistic stage," but some of the evidence is not very conclusive. "To give a single instance, when we find the totem belief in this stage of degeneration, it is open to anyone to say that the connection of the sept or section with the sacred beast or plant is merely a case of tree or animal worship, and need not necessarily imply that the worshippers of it were ever consciously in the totem stage. . . . Nowadays most of the leaders of the totem school are prepared to admit the weakness of the evidence for totemism within the so-called Aryan area. Here possibly tree and serpent or animal worship will be found to explain most of the facts without the necessity of calling in the aid of totemism. . . . Under Hindu influence there has been a tendency to replace the old totem or sacred beast by some eponymous ancestor drawn from the ranks of Hindu saints or worthies, and here often the familiar influence of folk etymology comes into play. Thus Rikhmun, the divine ancestor of the Bhuiyas and Musahars, who is called a deified Rishi or saint, is probably in reality Riksha, the bear: so Kachchapa, the tortoise, has become the saint Kasyapa, and Bharadvaja, the lark, turns into a third Hindu worthy."[78] In Assam, "they cannot marry into their own tribe. The totem seems to come in here, *i.e.,* a 'Bear' can marry an 'Iron,' but not a 'Bear'; a 'Palm' can marry a 'Tiger,' and so on."[79] The *devak,* or totem, is a creeping plant, banana-tree, lotus-flower, peacock-feather, stone, ant-heap, or other object; the family spares the tree or animal that is holy to it.[80]

Strict taboos are in force in India among the members of a clan of the Orāons in regard to the totem, and not only will an Orāon himself abstain from killing, eating, or using his totem, but he will try to prevent others from doing so in his presence. In the case of totems such as rice or salt, whose use is indispensable, only some special form or manner of eating it is forbidden. "There are also interesting cases of the transference of totem taboos to other objects which happen to have in fact or in name, a resemblance to the totem proper. Thus the Tiger clan must abstain not only from the tiger, but from the squirrel, whose stripes suggest the tiger; the Monkey clan extend their taboo to a tree which bears the same name as the monkey, and therefore may neither cut or burn it, nor sit under its shade."[81] In Chōtā-Nāgpūr totemism has long ceased to be a living institution, except in its relation to exogamy, but facts from this district would seem to indicate that when primitive man found by experience that certain animals, plants, minerals, and other objects proved particularly helpful or inconveniently powerful and hostile, he sought by ceremonial alliance with such animal, plant, mineral, or other object to become "of one blood" with it, and thereby to secure its help and protection, or disarm its ill-will and hostility. It may be noted that according to Orāon tradition, no tiger would in olden days harm a man of the tiger-sept as both the man and the tiger were "of one blood."[82] Some of the food-taboos may no doubt suggest the possibility of some form of totemism having obtained

77 Risley, *Ethnog. Ind.,* I, 99, 162.
78 Crooke, in JAI, XXVIII, 233 ff.
79 Peal, in JAI, XXII, 259.

80 Wilutsky, *Mann u. Weib,* 78.
81 Dixon, in AA, XVIII, 285.
82 Roy, in JAI, XLIV, 328.

among the Sema Nagas, but with one exception there is not a single clan which genuinely traces its descent from an animal or plant, and none has anything like a definite totem. "Generally speaking, it seems that one would be rather going out of one's way to attempt uncalled-for ethnological gymnastics if one set about demonstrating the former existence of totemism in Naga tribes. It may conceivably have existed once, but if it did it has left singularly few traces behind."[83]

"The great authority on the religions of China, DeGroot, says that he has found no trace in China of animals being worshipped in the capacity of tribal progenitors, and he entertains serious doubts whether any so-called totemism exists in Eastern Asia as a religious phenomenon. It is interesting then to know that Lolo surnames always signify the name of a tree or animal or both tree and animal, and that these are considered as the ancestors of the family bearing the name. This name is often archaic." The common way in this part of West China of asking a person what his surname is, is to inquire "What is it you don't touch?" and the person may reply, "We do not touch the citron." People may not eat or touch in any way the plant or animal, or both, which enters into their surname. "The plant or animal is not, however, worshipped in any way."[84] In the Malay Peninsula, usages do not seem to show much if any totemism, but may indicate its former presence.[85]

The Sea Dyaks or Iban have a *nyarong* which is allied to the *manitu* of North America. It is a spirit-helper. "The Iban believe that the spirit of some ancestor or dead relative may come to them in a dream, and this *nyarong* becomes the special protector of the individual. An Iban youth will often retire to some lonely spot or mountain-top and live for days on a very restricted diet in his anxiety to obtain a vision. This custom is called *nampok*. On the following day the dreamer searches for the outward and visible form of the *nyarong*, which may be anything from a curious natural object to some one animal. In such cases the *nyarong* hardly differs from a fetish. In other cases, as the man is unable to distinguish the particular animal which he believes to be animated by his *nyarong*, he extends his regard and gratitude to the whole species. In some instances all the members of a man's family and all his immediate descendants, and if he be a chief all the members of the community over which he rules, may come to share the benefits conferred by the *nyarong* and pay respect to the species of animal in one individual of which it is supposed to reside. 'In such cases, the species approaches very closely the clan totem in some of its varieties.' Here we have a parallel to the North American custom, but the later stages are not carried as far."[86]

The name of the totem which the Australians call *kobong* is, in Polynesia, *atua*. It is forbidden to eat the animal or plant which is the *atua* of the tribe.[87] The *kalids* of the Pelew Islands are, in the narrow sense, "wholly identical with the 'totems' of the Americans, the 'kubongs' of the Australians, and so on. *Kalid* means in the Pelew tongue: 'holy,' 'consecrated object,' 'priest.' Every inhabitant has his special *kalid*, perhaps an heritage from his ancestors; perhaps also it may be connected with their notions about the soul-life after death." A native song proclaims that: "We call everything *kalid* that lives in the sea and in sweet water; but also all animals of which we are

83 Hutton, *Sema Nagas*, 128-129.
84 Henry, in JAI, XXXIII, 105-106.
85 Skeat and Blagden, *Malay Penin.*, II, 258 ff.

86 Haddon, in *Brit. Assoc. Adv. Sci.*, 1902, 742-743; he quotes Hose and McDougall, in JAI, XXXI, 210.
87 Ratzel, *Vkde.*, II, 165.

afraid; we believe that our forefathers live in them. Therefore every one of us has a different *kalid*."[88] The interchangeability of the fetish and the totem comes out in the story of the Eskimo who thought he had secured good luck through the ham-bone of a dog, so that he adopted a mark for it in place of his totem-sign, as did his son after him.[89]

Smith[90] finds in the Semitic tribal names a testimony to original totemism; they are named after beasts which were held in veneration and from which they believed they were descended. Sayce[91] thinks the distinction between clean and unclean animals comes from totemism; the totem is sacred, to be partaken of only sacramentally. Wellhausen[92] does not think that Smith has made out his case, and Wilken[93] is very skeptical. Maurer[94] discovers "numerous examples of totemism in the Old Testament, chiefly in the form of animal names applied to groups of kindred."

§261. Totemism (Social Aspect, and Theories about Totemism).

SPENCER and Gillen[1] generalize somewhat on totemism, finding that in Central Australia the religious aspect of the custom is predominant, while among the coastal tribes the social aspect, relating to tribal divisions and marriage-customs, is its chief feature, the religious aspect being but slightly marked. Between the center and east coast, while the social aspect is strongly marked, the religious is also clearly indicated. "With the Arunta and other tribes it is very different, and it seems quite possible that the original aspect of the totem is simply religious or magical, and that the social aspect has been, as it were, tacked on at a later period. . . . The most important point to be noticed is the traditional existence of totems long before that of exogamic groups, and the fact that when the latter did arise, the totems were not affected by them; in short, totemism appears to be a primary and exogamy a secondary feature. . . . The hypothesis which is now suggested . . . is that in our Australian tribes the primary function of a totemic group is that of ensuring by magic means a supply of the object which gives its name to the totemic group, and that further the relation between totemism and exogamy is merely a secondary feature." "Exogamy can and does exist," says Tylor,[2] "without totemism, and for all we know was originally independent of it, but the frequency of their close connection over three-quarters of the earth points to the ancient and powerful action of the totems at once in consolidating clans and allying them together within the larger circle of the tribe. This may well have been among the most effective processes in the early social growth of the human race." "The problem of the origin of exogamy is one," according to Frazer,[3] "which has hitherto baffled anthropologists. Still, without probing the depths of this central mystery of social life, the writer thinks it can be seen how, when the principle of exogamy came into operation, it may have been applied to the already existing totem-groups. In Australia, Melanesia, and North America, there is almost indubitable evidence of the bisection of a community

88 Semper, *Palau-Ins.*, 87, note, 193.
89 Nelson, in BAE, XVIII, pt. I, 325.
90 *Relig. Sem.*, 17, 137, 142, 188 ff., 213, 217 ff., 288-289, 339.
91 *Anc. Emp.*, 201.
92 *Skizzen*, III, 176-177.
93 In VG, II, 187-188.

94 *Vkde.*, I, 124-125; Stade, *Israel*, I, 408 ff.; Zapletal, *Totemismus*, 13; Cook, "Israel and Totemism," in *Jewish Quart. Rev.*, XIV, 446.
1 In JAI, XXVIII, 275 ff.
2 In JAI, XXVIII, 148.
3 In JAI, XXVIII, 284-285; and in *Fortnightly Rev.*, LXXI, 654 ff.

into two exogamous classes, each of which in some tribes has been again bi-sected into two exogamous sub classes. If, when the bisection of the com-munity first took place, the existing totem groups were arranged, as they naturally would be, some in one of the two new classes and the rest in the other, the exogamy of the totem groups would follow *ipso facto.*" And this despite the fact that "the group of persons who are knit to any particular totem . . . commonly bear the name of the totem, believe themselves to be of one blood, and strictly refuse to sanction the marriage or cohabitation of members of the group with each other."

It would seem that the totemic groups were anterior to exogamy; they formed first and then came the custom of marrying out. They were there and ready to be used. Spencer and Gillen[4] find traditions bearing upon this matter which they summarize briefly as follows; the periods indicated by the traditions are: "(1) A time when men of one totem had marital relations normally with women of the same totem; (2) A time when men and women of what are now exogamic groups had marital relations; (3) A time when exogamic divisions were in force but different from those of the present day; (4) A time when the present exogamic divisions were introduced. It may also be noted in passing, that the introduction of changes is definitely ascribed to leading in-fluential men who were the heads of powerful local groups." If this is so, then the totemic groups must have been formed as such at a very early period. Among the Arunta the mode of determining the totem has all the appearance of extreme antiquity; for it ignores altogether the intercourse of the sexes as the cause of offspring and, further, it ignores the tie of blood on the ma-ternal as well as the paternal side, substituting for it a purely local bond, since the members of a totem stock are merely those who gave the first sign of life in the womb at one or other of certain definite spots. This form of totemism, which may be called conceptional or local to distinguish it from hereditary totemism, may with great probability be regarded as the most primitive known to exist at the present day, since it seems to date from a time when blood-relationship was not yet recognized and when the idea of paternity had not yet presented itself to the savage mind.[5]

It is plain from these quotations that the intra-tribal sections represented by the totems, as well as other such group-divisions, are general modifications of the societal system and cannot be referred to the system of marriage-re-strictions or prescriptions as an unique cause. The foregoing citations are authoritative but they may be amplified by several additional ones of a more miscellaneous order and suggestive further of the social bearings of totemism.

Any general survey of Australian social organization reveals the wide prevalence of the totem-groups;[6] but they are not invariably exogamic. "In some tribes totems govern marriage. In others they have nothing to do with the question. . . . Whether there ever was a time when, in the Arunta and neighboring tribes, marriage was regulated by totem, it is difficult to say. At the present day it is not, nor can we find any evidence in the full and nu-merous traditions relating to the doings of their supposed ancestors which affords indications of a time when . . . a man might only marry a woman

---

4 In JAI, XXVIII, 277.
5 Frazer, in *Fortnightly Rev.*, LXXVIII, 453-454; Lang's Introd. to Parker, *The Euah-layi Tribe*, xxiii

6 Howitt and Fison, in JAI, XII, espec. 43-44.

of a totem different from his own." The authors quoted[7] enter into minute detail concerning the descent of the totem. Where there are two phratries, each with four sub-divisions, "totems consisting of animals, plants, and inanimate objects are attached to certain pairs of sections, and these totems descend generally from a father to his sons and daughters, but this rule is subject to modifications. Certain totems are allotted to, or are inherited by, two sections in common, one of the sections belonging to phratry A, and the other to phratry B."[8] A horde is thought by Cunow[9] to develop into an exogamic kin-group and to adopt an animal or plant as a mark or symbol of itself—an association-designation. This represents "the first beginning of the organization into clans." Howitt[10] writes: "From what I know of the Australian savage I can see very clearly how such a social change might be brought about. They universally believe that their deceased ancestors and kindred visit them during sleep, and counsel or warn them against dangers, or communicate to them song-charms against magic. I have known many such cases, and I also know that the medicine-men see visions that are to them realities. Such a man if of great repute in his tribe might readily bring about a social change, by announcing to his fellow medicine-men a command received from some supernatural being. . . . If they received it favourably, the next step might be to announce it to the assembled headmen at one of the ceremonial gatherings as a supernatural command, and this would be accepted as true without question by the tribes-people. . . . That such an identical legendary explanation of the origin of the classes and totems existed in two tribes so far distant from each other may be accepted as indicating a widespread belief in the supernatural origin of a practice which is universal throughout Australia."

Concerning the Onondaga Indians it is stated that "the rise of the different clans or stocks, likewise also the names of the tribes themselves, seem . . . to lead back to the original economic activity. . . . The clan-mark or totem therefore functions here as a sign of social differentiation."[11] On the northwest coast "an individual distinguishes himself, becomes wealthy, and hence a leading man in the village. His totem, or indeed his individual crest or subtotem, may have been an obscure one. As he rises, its importance in the tribe rises with him. Under his successor, the totem widens its numbers and influence, and finally eclipses other clan totems, which eventually melt away or are incorporated with it. In the course of time, either by the accession of other totems or else by its splitting up into sub-totems, it came finally to be ranked as a phratry, then a sub-phratry. In this evolution we see the sub-totem grow into a clan-totem, then into a phratry or sub-phratry, when decay sets in. . . . In childhood a transfer can be made from one totem to another. Supposing a chief desires his son to succeed him and to belong to his own totem; the babe is transferred to his sister to suckle, and is figuratively adopted by her. In this way the son acquires the totemship of his father, and at an early age is taken back by his own mother to raise. Dawson cites these cases of transfer as often effected among the Haida to strengthen the totem of the father when its number has become reduced and there is danger not only of loss of prestige but of extinction. The ties of the totem or of the phratry are considered far stronger than those of blood-relationship. A man can not marry in his own

7 Spencer and Gillen, *Nat. Tr. Cent. Aust.*, 34, 116; Spencer and Gillen, *North. Tr. Cent. Aust.*, 144, 148, 152, 174.
8 Mathews, in AA, II, 495-496.

9 *Australneger*, 81, 132.
10 *S.E. Aust.*, 89, 90.
11 Henning, in *Globus*, LXXVI, 225.

totem whether within or without his own tribe, or his own phratry within his own tribe. There is nothing to prevent a man from marrying his first cousin, and much to prohibit his marriage to a most remote connection or an absolute stranger." The totem is likewise a symbol of brotherhood, involving special privilege and treatment. "An Indian on arriving at a strange village where he may apprehend hostility would look for a house indicated by its carved post as belonging to his totem and make for it. The master of the house, coming out, may, if he likes, make a dance in honor of his visitor, but in any case protects him from all injury. In the same way, should an Indian be captured as a slave by some warlike expedition and brought into the village of his captors, it behooves any one of his totem, either man or woman, to present themselves to the captors, and, singing a certain sacred song, offer to redeem the captive. Blankets and other property are given for this purpose. Should the slave be given up, the redeemer sends him back to his tribe and the relatives pay the redeemer for what he has expended. Should the captors refuse to give up the slave for the property offered, it is considered rather disgraceful to them." There are peoples amongst whom ancestry is vaguely or not at all recognized and such have totemism.[12] Among the North Americans the regular rule is that in marriage the totem must be crossed, which is equivalent certainly, in view of the basic meaning of the term—namely, "one's kinship"— to the taboo of consanguine or supposedly consanguine marriage.[13]

Ethnological research in North America has revealed the fact that the social aspects of totemism vary with the social organization of the different stocks. "If totemism," comments Hill-Tout,[14] "were primarily and essentially, as some students hold, a social phenomenon originating only in, and properly belonging to, the matrilineal stage of savage society, we ought to find it decaying and falling into desuetude as matriarchy passes into patriarchy and the village commune. But we do not, at least in this country, and apparently not elsewhere. . . . The 'religious' or 'magical' aspects of totemism there are just as strong and pervasive in those tribes that have patrilineal descent as in those having matrilineal descent."

The reader will have noticed that it is impossible to keep the religious and the social aspects of totemism strictly apart. Rivers[15] devotes considerable special attention to totemism in Melanesia and Polynesia, his interest being, on the whole, involved with the social rather than the religious aspect. We conclude with a somewhat lengthy synopsis of his findings. By totemism he means a form of social organization which has three main characters: (1) the connection of a species of animal or plant, or of an inanimate object or class of inanimate objects, with a definite social group of the community, and typically with an exogamous group or clan; (2) a belief in a relationship between the members of the social group and the animal, plant, or object, a belief in descent from the animal, plant, or object being a frequent form which this relationship takes; (3) respect shown to the animal, plant, or object, the typical way of showing this respect being that the animal or plant may not be eaten, while an inanimate object may not be used at all or only with certain restrictions. "The people inhabiting the mountainous districts in the

---

12 Niblack, in USNM, 1888, 246, 248, 250.
13 Hewitt, "Totem," in HAI, II, 787 ff.;
Lowie and Farrand, "Marriage," in HAI, I,
808 ff.; Bourke, *Snake Dance*, 230.

14 In JAI, XXXV, 141-142.
15 *Melan. Soc.*, II, 75; and in JAI,
XXXIX, 156 ff.

interior of Viti Levu [Fiji] form a number of small independent communities, each of which has a sacred animal which none of the community eat. Further, the smaller divisions of the community . . . have also in many cases sacred animals or plants peculiar to themselves which none of the division may eat, though free to the rest of the community. The institution of exogamy does not exist, so far as is known, in Fiji, marriage being regulated by kinship, and the social organisation of the people has departed so widely from one founded on exogamy that it is impossible to tell which of their social divisions corresponds to the exogamous clan or sept. We have here a case in which one characteristic of typical totemism is not present, but we still have the apparent totem associated with at least two kinds of social unit. The third character of totemism, the belief in descent from the totem-animal, comes out among these inland people in a more decided manner than in any other case of which I have had experience. Here, in collecting a genealogy, an informant went back from human to human ancestor till as a perfectly natural transition he would state that the father of the last mentioned was an eel or other animal. In the special case of eel-ancestry the transition from animal to man was given as having taken place eight generations ago, and Mr. Joske told me that in several cases he had found the animal-ancestor of the whole people, but there is also a belief in descent from the sacred animals of the smaller divisions of the community.

"I do not think there can be any doubt that in the case of these mountain tribes we have to do with true totemism. It is in fact typical totemism except in the absence of association with exogamy, but there remains a clear connection with other social divisions just as might be expected in a community in which exogamy has been replaced by a different method of regulating marriage. . . .

"The clearest evidence for the existence of totemism in Polynesia is derived from Tikopia. This is a tiny island about 120 miles south-east of the Santa Cruz group. . . . These people call a number of animals *atua,* a word which they also use for an ancestor. Some of these animal *atua* belong to the whole community and may be eaten by no one on the island; others belong to one or other of the four sections into which the people are divided, the Kavika, the Taumako, the Tafua, and the Fangalele.

"The Kavika have the *feke* or octopus, which they may not eat, but it is also forbidden as food to the whole people. The Taumako may not eat the *toke* or sea-eel, nor may they eat a bird called *rupe,* and these prohibitions are limited to this division. The Tafua may not eat the *tuna* or fresh-water eel, nor may they eat the flying fox (*peka*) or the turtle (*fonu*), these two latter animals being also prohibited as food to the whole community, though regarded as especially sacred to the Tafua. The Fangalele may not eat a small black bird called *moko,* nor may they eat a fish called *one.* The *fai* or stingray may not be eaten by anyone, and it did not seem to be sacred to any special division. A man of a division who may not eat a certain animal may also not kill it. If one of the Fangalele caught an *one* fish he usually threw it back, but he might give it to a man of another division. . . .

"In addition to these animals there are also plant *atua.* One of these is a plant with large leaves like the taro, called *kape,* which is sacred to the Kavika and may not be eaten by the people of that division while free to the rest of the community. This plant seems to belong to the same category as the animal *atua.* . . . Three of the divisions have also vegetable *atua* which seem to belong to a different category. These are the yam, the taro, and the coconut, belonging respectively to the Kavika, the Taumako, and the Tafua. These plants might, however, be eaten by all, but the Kavika do not like to see any-one cut the taro with a knife, and they scrape off the skin with the shell of a mussel. In this case it was said that it was the top of the yam which was espe-cially regarded as the *atua*. Similarly, the Taumako do not like to see the taro cut with a knife, and here again it was a special part, the eye of the taro, which was regarded as the *atua*. The Tafua also objected to a knife being used to open a coconut, and always used a stone. This restriction on the use of a knife is of course recent, and is an interesting example of the feeling that sacred objects should not be subjected to usages which have come from without into the ordinary life of a people.

"The special relation between each division of the people and their sacred plant is shown in the planting season, the first yams being planted by the chief of the Kavika, while the chief of the Taumako plants the first taro. The chiefs of the respective divisions are also the first to eat their sacred vegetables. . . .

"There can be very little doubt that in the case of the animal *atua* we have true totems. The condition is not one of typical totemism, for the institution is not associated with exogamy. The four divisions intermarry with one another, and marriage also takes place between members of the same divi-sion. . . . It is probable that in Fiji the gods or god-like beings have been developed, at any rate in many cases, from heroes and that the animal nature of the gods is merely an indication of the close relation universally believed by totemistic peoples to exist between a man and his totem. The evolution would not be simply from totem to god, but from hero and totem together to god. . . .

"At the present moment it cannot be said that the presence of totemism in Melanesia (excluding Fiji) has been definitely demonstrated. In the Solomon Islands, Codrington described the connection of animals with exogamous so-cial divisions, but did not regard this connection as an indication of totemism. In the Banks' Islands and the New Hebrides the same author has described a few cases of connection between men and animals which again may possibly indicate totemism, but only as the most fragmentary relics. Totemism, how-ever, begins to appear definitely in the north and Ribbe has recorded totemism in the Shortland Islands, and it is probably definitely present in the Bismarck Archipelago. . . .

"I visited the group of islands known as the Matema or Swallow group. . . . The case of these islands differs from those so far considered in that we have now to do with typical totemism. The animals forbidden as food belong to exogamous divisions of the community, though these divisions have names otherwise derived, while there is also a belief in descent from these animals. . . .

"Santa Cruz . . . We have in this island all the cardinal signs of totemism; exogamy, belief in descent and prohibition of the use of the eponymous object as food. . . .

"Vanikoro. . . . It is quite clear that in this district in the heart of Melanesia we have genuine totemism, but the case is very different when we turn to the islands south of Santa Cruz or to the Solomons which lie north-west of it.

"The Solomon Islands. These islands are far from having a uniform culture and in some regions there is no totemism or only its faint relics, while in others it is present. . . .

"The evidence, taken as a whole, points strongly to the condition being one of genuine totemism, but in a relatively late stage, in which the totems and other sacred objects, including human ancestors, are all classed together as *tindalo,* while, so far as the social aspect is concerned, it is possible that there has been a considerable departure from the original condition. . . .

"Though developed totemism thus appears to be absent, there was found in the Banks' Islands a group of beliefs which are of the greatest interest in connection with the possible origin of totemism. In these islands devoid of the developed institution there exist beliefs which would seem to furnish the most natural starting point for totemism, beliefs which Dr. Frazer has been led by the Australian evidence to regard as the origin of the institution. . . .

"The course of events is usually as follows: a woman sitting down in her garden or in the bush or on the shore finds an animal or fruit in her loincloth. She takes it up and carries it to the village, where she asks the meaning of the appearance. The people say that she will give birth to a child who will have the characters of this animal or even, it appeared, would be himself or herself the animal. The woman then takes the creature back to the place where she had found it and places it in its proper home; if it is a land animal on the land; if a water animal in the pool or stream from which it had probably come. She builds up a wall round it and goes to visit and feed it every day. After a time the animal will disappear, and it is believed that that is because the animal has at the time of its disappearance entered into the woman. . . .

"I inquired into the idea at the bottom of the prohibition of the animal as food, and it appeared to be that the person would be eating himself. It seemed that the act would be regarded as a kind of cannibalism. It was evident that there is a belief in the most intimate relation between the person and all individuals of the species with which he is identified. . . .

"In the island of Motlav not far from Mota they have the same belief that if a mother has found an animal in her dress, the child will be identified with that animal and will not be allowed to eat it. Here again the child is believed to have the characters of the animal, and two instances given were that a child identified with a yellow crab will have a good disposition and be of a light colour, while if a hermit crab has been found, the child will be angry and disagreeable. In this island a woman who desires her child to have certain characters will frequent a place where she will be likely to encounter the animal which causes the appearance of these characters. Thus, if she wants to have a light coloured child, she will go to a place where there are light coloured crabs. . . .

"In 1905 Dr. J. G. Frazer[16] advanced a hypothesis to account for the origin of totemism which was based on the belief of certain central Australian tribes which assign to a child the totem belonging to the place where the mother first becomes aware of the new life within her. In his 'conceptional' theory Dr. Frazer assumed that the belief that a child had an animal or plant nature, or one derived from any other object, was due to something which had impressed itself on the mind of the woman at the time of quickening. . . . Dr. Frazer has assumed a series of situations very closely resembling that which I have actually found to exist in the Banks' Islands, and there is definitely established the existence of the belief which forms the basis of his conceptional theory. . . .

---

16 In *Fortnightly Review,* 1905, vol. 78, 455.

"It is improbable that totemism has had everywhere the same origin, or rather, one of exactly the same kind, and in some parts at least of North America the absence of belief in descent from the totem and the nature of the myths make it probable that there the institution has had its origin in the guardian animal. It is interesting that a belief in a guardian animal should also exist in the Banks' Islands, and it is significant that in this case again the mysterious connection between man and animal is accompanied by a taboo on the flesh of the latter."

Theories about Totemism. Totemism, according to Thomas[17] seems not to go with sacrifice or with domestication of animals. "In the two great totem-areas of Australia and North America sacrifice is either unknown or unimportant. Australia has no domestic animals; America had only the dog, and the dog was the only animal commonly sacrificed." In particular, as it seems to us, is totemism allied to fetishism;[18] the ghost of the ancestor lives on in the fetish-animal or other object. It is not mere reincarnation, for a whole species of animals bear the totemic character. So that totemism seems to be no more than a peculiar set of religious beliefs, related back and forth with other sets, except for the rôle it plays in social differentiation and in connection with the sex-taboo and marriage. This rôle is really what has given occasion for all the special theorizing concerning it. By itself it would have fallen in well enough, as a whole, under the topic of religion, along with such related matters as have been mentioned.

Taking totemism to be all it may mean in its most characteristic and complete exhibition, "true" totemism may be distinguished from allied notions which by some are thrown together under the convenient category. "It is a pity," says Tylor,[19] "that the word 'totem' came over to Europe from the Ojibwas through an English interpreter who was so ignorant as to confuse it with the Indian hunter's patron genius, his *manitou,* or 'medicine.' The one is no more like the other than a coat of arms is like a saint's picture. Those who knew the Algonkin tribes better made it clear that totems were the animal signs, or, as it were, crests, distinguishing exogamous clans; that is, clans bound to marry out of, not into, their own clan. But the original sin of the mistake of Long the interpreter has held on ever since, bringing the intelligible institution of the totem clan into such confusion that it has become possible to write about 'sex totems' and 'individual totems,' each of which terms is a self-contradiction. . . . Totems are the signs of intermarrying clans. . . . Totemism, as Dr. Frazer and I understand it, in its fully developed condition implies the division of a people into several totem kins (or, as they are usually termed, totem clans), each of which has one, or sometimes more than one, totem. The totem is usually a species of animal, sometimes a species of plant, occasionally a natural object or phenomenon, very rarely a manufactured object. Totemism also involves the rule of exogamy, forbidding marriage within the kin, and necessitating intermarriage between the kins. It is essentially connected with the matriarchal stage of culture (mother-right), though it passes over into the patriarchal stage (father-right). The totems are regarded as kinsfolk and protectors or benefactors of the kinsmen, who respect them and abstain from killing and eating them. There is thus a recognition of mutual rights and

17 In *Folk-Lore,* XI, 247.
18 Lippert, *Kgchte.,* II, 419; Zapletal,
Totemismus, 6.

19 In *Man,* II, 2; Tylor, in JAI, XXVIII, 138.

obligations between the members of the kin and their totem. The totem is the crest, or symbol of the kin."[20] It is evident from these citations how thoroughly the social aspect of this practice must enter into any final judgment of it, as a whole. A number of writers have, in their interpretations, stressed various aspects of the subject; and a survey of their views is enlightening.

Several of them emphasize the relation of the totemic ceremonies to the food-supply. They see in the ceremonies an indication "that each totem group was charged with the superintendence of some department of nature, from which it took its name. The control was by magical means to procure for the members of the community, on the one hand, a plentiful supply of all the commodities of which they stood in need; and, on the other hand, an immunity from all the perils and dangers to which man is exposed in his struggle with nature. . . . This hypothesis takes us back far into the time when the function of each totem group was to secure the multiplication of the particular object the name of which it bore."[21]

"A totem," writes Frazer,[22] "is a class of natural phenomena or material objects, most commonly a species of plants or animals, between which and himself the savage believes that a certain intimate relation exists." Again, in his work on Totemism,[23] he writes: "A totem is a class of material objects which a savage regards with superstitious respect, believing that there exists between him and every member of the class an intimate and altogether special relation. . . . The connection between a man and his totem is mutually beneficent; the totem protects the man, and the man shows his respect for the totem in various ways, by not killing it if it be an animal, and not cutting or gathering it if it be a plant. . . . Considered in relation to men, totems are of at least three kinds: (1) The clan totem, common to a whole clan, and passing by inheritance from generation to generation. (2) The sex totem. . . . (3) The individual totem, belonging to a single individual and not passing to his descendants. . . . The clan totem is reverenced by a body of men and women who call themselves by the name of the totem, believe themselves to be of one blood, descendants of a common ancestor, and are bound together by common obligations to each other, and by a common faith in the totem. Totemism is thus both a religious and a social system. In its religious aspect it consists of the relations of mutual respect and protection between a man and his totem; in its social aspect it consists of the relations of the clansmen to each other and to men of other clans. In the later history of totemism these two sides, the religious and the social, tend to part company. . . . On the whole, the evidence points strongly to the conclusion that the two sides were originally inseparable; that, in other words, the further we go back the more we should find that the clansman regards himself and his totem as beings of the same species, and the less he distinguishes between conduct towards his totem and towards his fellow-clansmen."

To continue with Frazer: "In general is it true that elsewhere than in Australia, members of a totem clan are credited with the power of exercising special control over a totem? The answer to this question is that it is true. For example, in one of the Torres Straits Islands, members of the Dog clan were believed to understand the habits of dogs and to be able to exercise special

20 Haddon, in *Brit. Assoc. Adv. Sci.*, 1902, 739-740.
21 Howitt, *S.E. Aust.*, 152, 153.
22 In *Fortnightly Rev.*, LXXI, 654 ff.
23 *Totemism*, 1-3.

control over them. On a cloudy morning the Sun clan of the Bechuanas were accustomed to perform a ceremony to make the sun shine out through the clouds; the chief kindled a new fire in his dwelling, and every one of his subjects carried a light from it to his own hut. The intention of the ceremony clearly was by means of sympathetic magic to blow up into a brighter blaze the smouldering fire of the sun. In the Murray Islands, Torres Straits, it is the duty of the Sun clan to imitate the rising and setting of the sun, probably to ensure the punctual performance of these offices. Among the Omahas of North America the Small Bird clan performs a magic ceremony to keep small birds away from the crop; the Reptile clan performs a similar ceremony to protect the crops from worms; and the Wind clan think they can start a breeze by flapping their blankets. The same Wind clan practises a magic ceremony to stop a blizzard. They paint one of their boys red and he rolls over and over in the snow, reddening it for some distance all around him. This stops the blizzard, the notion apparently being that the white snow will not fall when it knows that it will be thus reddened and defiled. In another North American tribe the power of causing the snow to stop falling would seem to have been claimed and exercised by men of the Snow totem. Some of these examples explain the attitude of the totem clan towards their totem, when the totem is of a noxious and maleficent nature. In such cases it is the function of the clan, not of course to multiply the numbers of the totem or increase its virulence, but on the contrary to disarm, counteract and keep within due bounds its dangerous influence. Hence, members of the Serpent clan in Senegambia profess to treat, by their touch, persons who have been bitten by serpents; and the same professions were made by Serpent clans in classical antiquity. Similarly in Central Australia members of the Fly totem claim to cure, by a touch of a magic implement, eyes swollen by fly-bites. And by analogy it may be concluded that certain Arab families who believed their blood to be a remedy for hydrophobia were descended from the Dog totem. . . . As to the prohibition to kill and eat the totem, it may be conjectured that this taboo originated in an attempt to carry out more consistently that principle of the identification of the man with the totem which seems to be of the essence of totemism. As a rule, animals do not live upon their own kind; hence, o.g., if an emu man regularly kills and eats emus, which he professes to regard as practically identical with himself, the other emus will distrust and avoid him; they will see that he is only a sham emu after all; he will no longer possess their confidence; and his power over them will be gone."[24]

The eminent Dutch ethnologist, Wilken,[25] is always deserving of attention. He comes out strongly for the close connection of totemism with the ghost-cult, through the link of transmigration and reincarnation. "It is seen that the dogma of transmigration has universally led, among the peoples of the Indian Archipelago, to the notion of the relationship of man with, and his descent from, certain animals, which animals are thus raised to the station of ancestors and are reverenced like other ancestors. In a certain sense we have here what is wont to be called, in the science of religion, *totemism*. This word is . . . original with the North American Indians. Each tribe here has, under the term *totem*, some animal or other which is revered as a fetish, and from it the tribe is named and its members derive their descent. . . . What

24 Frazer, in JAI, XXVIII, 285-286, 283.   *Golden Bough*, I, 9-62 (edit. 1900); §211, of the
25 In VG, III, 78 ff., 85-86; IV, 110-111, 185;   text.
Tylor, in JAI, XXVIII, 145, 146, 147; Frazer,

we have encountered among the peoples of the Indian Archipelago corresponds fully to this. Only they have not come to the point of naming themselves after animals that they honor as their tribal forebears. . . . According to our view, the totemism of the North American Indians, or wherever else it is found, must have developed in the same way out of transmigration of the soul as it did among the peoples of the Indian Archipelago; the animal in which the souls of the dead were thought by preference to be incarnated becomes a relative, a forefather, and is as such revered. Therefore it is not, as Spencer would have it, a 'misinterpretation of nicknames,' but soul-transmigration that is the connecting bond between totemism, on the one side, and the cult of the dead, on the other—a connection which, though it has fallen away among many peoples, is still, for the most part, obvious in the Archipelago." Wilken quotes from Schultze,[26] who writes concerning the relations of men and animals, as follows: "The nature man scarcely distinguishes himself at all from the animals, and upon more developed stages very little. The interests of both are the same. . . . But if man is not yet distinct from these animals, then he cannot yet conceive himself as something quite different from them; his own conduct and actions and those of the animals harmonize; there are the same efforts and the same motives in both. Nature-man finds himself over again in the animal; therefore he regards it necessarily as his like, as in every respect his equal in birth." To which Wilken adds: "That with such a way of looking at it, the dogma of transmigration must lead of itself to the conception of relationship between man and beast, is self-evident." This doctrine of transmigation has just been worked out by the author, and he makes totemism a development from it and from ancestor-worship. "The animals, now, thus raised to the rank of forefathers, are honored like other ancestors are honored. This is totemism." Wilken's editors note that Tylor took this theory over from him.

To Haddon[27] it is doubtful whether the Wilken-Tylor totemism deserves the name. He thinks the animals must be the residences of the ancestral spirits of a clan, not a tribe; and that exogamic provisions must exist in connection with the totems; otherwise there is nothing more than "theriomorphic ancestor worship." He thus insists upon the presence of the social function along with the religious aspect. But he acknowledges the difficulty of precise definition of such evolutionary forms: "The more one looks into the evidence the more difficult is it to find cases of typical totemism; almost everywhere considerable modification has taken place, often so much so that the communities cannot logically be called totemistic." This difficulty has been expected by evolutionists ever since the species-question was settled. Haddon's own theory is that "in favourable areas each group would have a tendency to occupy a restricted range owing to the disagreeable results which arose from encroaching on the territory over which another group wandered. Thus it would inevitably come about that a certain animal or plant, or group of animals or plants, would be more abundant in the territory of one group than in that of another." This does not seem to us to add much to the case.

Hill-Tout[28] sees the connection of British Columbian totemism with several allied forms: "There is little room for doubt that our clan totems are a development of the personal or individual totem or tutelar spirit, as this is in

26 *Fetischismus*, 196.
27 In *Brit. Assoc. Adv. Sci.*, 1902, 745.

28 Hill-Tout, in JAI, XXXIV, 328; XXXV, 141; XLI, 137; Haddon, in *Brit. Assoc. Adv. Sci.*, 1902, 741.

turn a development of an earlier fetishism." He believes that totemism *per se* had nothing originally to do with "clan"-structure or social divisions and was not dependent upon this social state for its existence, as some writers hold; he gives a reason for this view: "the fact that it survived such a radical social change as that which took place in the transition from the matriarchal to the patriarchial state; for it is equally, in this country, a feature of the latter as of the former condition of things, and that it still further survived the much greater social changes which resulted in the evolution of the 'family' from a union or modification of the two earlier groups or states." Taking the American evidence on totemism as a whole, it is to him impossible to doubt that totemism is as much a feature of patriarchy and the village commune, as of matriarchy. "It must be understood that I speak of totemism in the 'American' sense of the term. I am unable to regard it any longer in any other sense. Totemism to me is primarily and essentially a 'religious' phenomenon, the direct result and outcome of the savage's mental attitude towards nature. The social aspects of totemism I regard as something very secondary and incidental, which attained such importance as they possess in savage organisation only on account of their obvious convenience in classifying and distinguishing one kin group from another." He says, further, that a comparative study of the Salish as a whole "makes it clear beyond question or doubt that the group-totems found among them have sprung from, and are a development of, their individual totems, and that the same may be said of all other American stocks." He states that one investigator[29] discovered totemism in its three "most characteristic forms, viz., the non-hereditary *individual totem*, the hereditary *patriarchal totem*, and the hereditary *matriarchal clan totem*, among the tribes of California where totemism was not known to exist." Writing on the Tlinkits of Alaska, Jones[30] states that "after years of study of the subject and close observation of the working of the system, we are of the firm opinion that totemism had its origin in the belief of an animal ancestry, and that the distinguishing of clans, the effort to prevent war, and the knitting of tribes more closely together followed as a consequence from its adoption, rather than suggesting it."

Perhaps the statement that "totemism pure and simple has its home among races like the Australians and North American Indians, and seems always to lose ground after the introduction of pastoral life,"[31] has in it a practical suggestion—the suggestion, at any rate, that totemism belongs, in its completeness, to tribes who exhibit a relatively low civilization, and that it fades away into survivals and symbols with the advance of culture. Thomas[32] lists the survivals of totemism in Europe that may be found in the animal-superstitions; his list must not be accepted uncritically. "1. Descent from the totem. 2. Taboos (a) of killing the animal; (b) of eating, touching, or using it; (c) of seeing it; (d) of using the ordinary name. 3. Petting the totem-animal. 4. Burying the totem-animal. 5. Respect paid to the totem-animal. 6. (a) Lucky animals, (b) unlucky animals. 7. Adoption of (a) totem-marks, (b) totem-names, (c) totem-dress. 8. (a) Birth, (b) marriage, (c) death-customs. 9. Magical powers derived from the totem." The author adds the use of animals in magic, medicine, and divination, and the annual ceremonies of sacrifice and of communion with the sacred animal. Manifestly the totem-idea, as we have

---

29 Merriam, in AA, X.
30 *Thlingets*, 172-173.

31 Smith, *Relig. Sem.*, 355-356.
32 In *Folk-Lore*, XI, 229-230.

remarked, can be brought into connection with a variety of phases in religious evolution.

Lang[33] is led to very positive opinions. He thinks the totem-names were imposed upon a group from without, in the form of animal-sobriquets. IIc reviews many of the theories and juggles them one against the other. Other views of totemism regard it as having "no mystic religious character," as "more magical than religious," as due to a misunderstanding or forgetfulness of the savage, whereby he transformed an ancestor with an animal-name into an animal-ancestor, and so on.[34] Jevons[35] goes to an extreme in his deductions from totemism, making it, for example, account for all domestication. Durkheim[36] believes that "at the beginning the religion of the totem is certainly the center and altar of family life. One cannot understand the one without the other." He has been finally led to incorporate the concept of *mana* into totemism as an essential part of it; *mana,* in fact, is interpreted as the totemic force—as the principle or "god" of which the totem is the symbol. But the totem is not only the symbol of this mysterious force; it is the symbol of the social group as well. "It is its flag; it is the sign by which each clan distinguishes itself from the others, the visible mark of its personality, a mark borne by everything which is a part of the clan under any title whatsoever, men, beasts, or things. So, if it is at once the symbol of the god and of the society, is that not because the god and the society are only one? . . . The god of the clan, the totemic principle, can therefore be nothing else than the clan itself, personified and represented to the imagination under the visible form of the animal or vegetable which serves as the totem."[37]

Trilles[38] has some comments to make concerning totemism, as a result of his study of the Fan of West Africa. He regards totemism as one of the aspects of fetishism; like the latter it includes an ensemble of religious phenomena. "Just as totemism enters into fetishism and constitutes one of its aspects, though still profoundly differing from it, so does the totem form one of the aspects of the fetish, blending and mingling with it but otherwise profoundly distinct by its cult and the object of the cult." He mentions five conditions alleged to be necessary to the existence of totemism: (1) the clan has a totem; (2) the clan or tribe ordinarily takes the name of the totem; (3) the clan admits the parentage of the totem if it is an animate object; if not, of an animate object connected with the totem; (4) there is a taboo on marriage between clan-members or those with the same totem; (5) there is a taboo upon practices with relation to the totem, chiefly eating it, except on certain well-defined occasions. He agrees with the first condition and states with reference to the second that it is sometimes so and sometimes not, by virtue of special rules. There is no doubt, he says, about the third, while the fourth exists not as a consequence but as a concomitant of totemism, at least among the Fan. Taboos exist, not only in relation to foods, but also to practices and customs; with relation to the totem these taboos are the *éki.* He elaborates further: the totem is always a living or tutelary being; it materializes itself in an object in order to manifest its protection; the tutelary being is ordinarily an animal, more rarely a plant, still more rarely a mineral to which a special life is

33 *Social Origins; Custom and Myth,* 262.
34 Dodge, *Indians,* 225; Zapletal, *Totemismus,* 12-13; Spencer, *Prin. Soc.,* I, §172; Ellis. *Tshi,* 205; D'Alviella, *Concep. God,* 136-137.
35 *Relig.,* 114 ff.
36 Rev. of Kohler, in *Année Soc.,* I, 313; Durkheim, in *Année Soc.,* I, 24, 52, 53.
37 Durkheim, *Relig. Life,* 206, chs. VI, VII.
38 *Fân,* 25 ff., 38, 39, 74-75, 633, 635 (quoted).

attributed; when the totem is a spirit, it materializes itself in a natural phenomenon like thunder or in some manifestation which shall symbolize it; the phenomena (lightning, rainbow) materialize in their turn into objects having immediate relation to themselves (*e.g.*, mica for thunder or "heaven-stones" for lightning), or in some object determined by the "féticheur" (certain stones marked or spotted in a definite manner). We must here distinguish between the real totem and its materialization, and between the materialization of the living being and that of the spirit which is, so to speak, double.

According to Hopkins,[39] the essential feature in totemism is the belief in some association between the clan and an animal or a plant, whereas such other features, commonly associated with totemism, as descent, worship, exogamy, and the name of the clan, are features dependent upon special sociological conditions, by no means uniform even among peoples occupying the same primitive stage of culture.

§265. Avoidance: The Evil Eye.

THERE are numbers of instances drawn from tribes throughout the world where persons meeting with accidents are avoided as having incurred the wrath of the daimons. "In the Solomon Islands, if a man falling into a river succeeds in eluding the grasp of a shark with which he comes in contact, he is not allowed to escape, but his fellow-tribesmen throw him back to his fate, believing that he must be sacrificed to the river god."[1] Another type of avoidance refers to the use of the name of the deity. "The divine injunctions of Sinai, adopted in the Christian religion concerning God, as to the reverence and regard due to Him and His name, are quite intelligible to the tribes of Elema," on the Papuan Gulf.[2] A similar case is reported from New Zealand: "The name of Io was held in awe and respect to an extent that cannot be grasped by us, and the Maori of the early days of European settlement heard with amazement and contempt our name for the Supreme Being used in execration, and even in tones of pleasantry."[3] In Samoa it was forbidden members of a family to sit back to back, lest it should be considered mockery and insult to the gods.[4]

There are many cases in Africa where victims of accident, especially those who have been struck by lightning, are avoided. Among the Akamba, "if anyone is killed by lightning no one will touch or move the body, the people say the person is killed by God, if anyone does touch a person who has been killed by lightning he or she will also be struck. If a cow or other animal is killed by lightning it is eaten."[5] According to the Kikuyu belief, "if a tree falls on a hut it is considered extremely unlucky, the hut will not be abandoned, but it is necessary for the head of the village to kill a ram; it is led round the village before being killed. If this was not done, the owner of the village, or at any rate the woman who lived in the hut, would become the victim of a *thahu* or curse."[6] If lightning strikes a Wawanga hut or kills a person or beast a medicine-man is called in. "He asks for a black sheep and having killed it removes all skin and flesh from the skull, into which he puts medicine. The medicine is roasted in a pot, and everybody in the village is given a little to

39 "Totemism," in Amer. Or. Soc., session reported in the *Nation*, CVI, no. 2757.
1 Gomme, *Ethnol. in Folklore*, 74.
2 Holmes, in JAI, XXXII, 430.

3 Best, in JAI, XLIV, 128.
4 Turner, *Samoa*, 56.
5 Hobley, *A-Kamba*, 54-55.
6 Hobley, in JAI, XLI, 408.

lick up in the palm of his hand. Some is also put into a reed and hidden in the grass of the roof of every hut in the village. The remainder is poured into the skull, which is then buried by the medicine-man, where the lightning struck, he himself digging the hole. With it is also buried a stick from the hut or, in the case of a person or a beast, some grass or earth from the spot where the lightning fell. For his services the medicine-man is given a hoe and the whole of the sheep excepting one shoulder. A lily called the 'Ikakha' is often stuck on the roof of huts to keep off lightning; this is a very common sight in Kavirondo."[7] Among many tribes in East Africa the weapon used to inflict death upon anyone is in some way purified. "The performance of such acts originates in the idea that the weapon carries with it misfortune or fatality."[8]

Among the Ewe-speaking peoples of West Africa, although a person killed by lightning may not be buried, it is usual for the priests to allow the body of a free man to be ransomed. When houses are set on fire by lightning the conflagration may not be extinguished, "for the reason that to do so would be to act counter to the wishes or decrees of the god; and might consequently bring down his anger upon the entire community." Under any circumstances, such an accident is likely to prove disastrous to the owner. "If a house be struck by lightning and not set on fire, such an accident itself carries with it very serious consequences to the inmates; for it is at once invaded by a mob of priests and worshippers of the lightning-god; who, while pretending to search for the holy *so-kpe,* the thunderbolt, strip the house of everything portable, and secure their plunder in the large wallets always worn by followers of Khebioso. In addition, fines and compensation are demanded; for the fact of the house having been struck is proof that the inmates must have been guilty of some act or omission which has angered the god. If the fine imposed cannot be paid—the priests are usually very extravagant in their demands—imprisonment or slavery follows, and it is not at all uncommon for a whole household to be enslaved in consequence of such an accident."[9] To avoid ill luck the Hausa has to take many precautions, especially when on a journey to a far country. "When leaving home the Hausa should get his wife to pour water in front of his horse, and behind it near the threshold, for the water exerts a good influence. No one who has been fortunate in his own town should leave it without having taken a pinch of its earth, otherwise he may lose the town's *albaraka* [luck]. . . . Before entering a strange town, or when landing from a ship, the Hausa eats a little of the earth and drinks some of the water as soon as possible, for this puts the *mallams* of the new country on his side."[10]

Among some Siberians, if a death is due to lightning, the corpse is treated in a special way, while the flesh of an animal struck by lightning is never eaten. Many precautions are taken to avoid contracting disease by contagion from lepers, and leprosy is so dreaded by the Gilyak that they never mention it by name. The shamans, even, are unwilling to undertake to treat the sufferers.[11] This is similar to the Chinese practice of tabooing the name of smallpox, it being a crime to speak of or to allude to it. Inversion of language to avoid terms of ill luck is not uncommon.[12] The Sema Nagas regard death by

7 Dundas, K. R., in JAI, XLIII, 49.
8 Dundas, C., in JAI, XLIII, 526-527.
9 Ellis, *Ewe*, 38, 39, 40.
10 Tremearne, in JAI, XLV, 53-54.

11 Czaplicka, *Aborig. Siberia*, 162, 308.
12 Bordier, *Géog. Méd.*, 495; DeGroot, *Relig. Syst.*, I, 65.

lightning, fire, water, wild animals, the fall of or from a tree, or by suicide as in some way accursed and contagious. "The body must not be buried in front of the house, but at the back instead or in broken ground near by where men do not walk about." Animals killed by carnivora are regarded in a similar light: and their flesh may not be eaten by women.[13] Among the Palaungs of Farther India, no attempt is made to revive a person struck by lightning. Exuviæ of such persons play a part in magic, as well as the place where such a person is buried.[14]

By the Hudson Bay Eskimo "unlucky or disliked women are often driven from the camp, and such must journey until they find relief or perish by the wayside."[15] Among the Araucanians all deaths save those by combat were supposed to be the effects of supernatural causes or sorcery. If a person died from the results of a violent accident it was supposed that the evil spirits had occasioned it, by frightening the horse so as to make it throw its rider, by loosening a stone so that it might fall and crush the unwary, by temporarily blinding a person so that he might fall over a precipice, or by some other expedient equally fatal. In the case of disease, it was supposed that witchcraft had been practised and the victim poisoned.[16] There are many instances scattered throughout the literature where the Indians of Guiana have taken to their heels upon the development in their midst of diseases new to them, introduced by Europeans and negroes. They have so great a fear of fever and influenza that they will not touch with their hands a piece of money offered them by the whites before washing it with a stick. "These examples must not be taken as indicative of the Indians having any appreciation of the contagiousness of disease . . . but rather as indicative of their conception that disease can be sent them by their enemies or the medicine men."[17]

We now turn to the more specific case of avoidance as seen in the belief in the evil eye. The natives of the South Seas often put down the death of a chief to an evil eye having been cast on him. "This sometimes results in an unfortunate creature being picked out and killed through suspicion having fallen on him or her. At other times, when the supposed culprit has not been found, a terrible panic has taken place and the whole village has been deserted and a new one built. The old village then becomes 'hope,' and no amount of persuasion will induce the tribe to go back and settle in it, unless, as in one or two cases, the 'hope' is removed by some great chief or medicine man." The fear of evil wishing is very strong among the Solomon Islanders; when they are in mourning and so have to shave their heads, they bury the hair in order to prevent enemies getting hold of it.[18]

The Akamba are averse to telling any one outside the family the number of their children. The idea is held that boastfulness will induce jealousy on the part of others less favored and cause some envious person to use magic on the boaster's family so that the latter will die out.[19] When a person has received a slight injury, he attributes his hurt to someone with the power of the evil eye. If one audibly admires a beast belonging to a neighbor, and the animal shortly after becomes sick, he is thought to possess the power of the evil eye; this indicates that the idea is based on an envious thought rather

13 Hutton, *Sema Nagas*, 262.
14 Milne, *Eastern Clan*, 252, 264, 266-267, 306.
15 Turner, in BAE, XI, 187.

16 Latcham, in JAI, XXIX, 39, 364.
17 Roth, in BAE, XXVIII, 703.
18 Hardy and Elkington, *S. Seas*, 138, 139.
19 Hobley, *A-Kamba*, 165.

than an evil glance. "If a cattle owner hears that a man who has this power (or one ought, perhaps, to term it 'this infliction') has been admiring one of his cows, he will send for him and insist on him removing the evil; this is done by the man wetting his finger with saliva, and touching the beast on the mouth, and on various parts of the body with his wetted finger; this is believed to neutralize the enchantment." It is to be noted that the word *kita* means saliva as well as evil eye. "Even a medicine man cannot remove a curse imposed by a person possessing the evil eye; only the individual who imposed it can remove it, and he can do it only in the morning before he touches food. . . . No one who is not born with the power can acquire it, and it appears to be looked upon as an unavoidable misfortune, for they say it is the gift of God. . . . In time the people get to know who possesses the power, and if such a person enters a village he is asked in a friendly way to spit ceremonially on all the children to prevent anything untoward occurring to them owing to his visit. If a father possesses this power he can render his children proof against its action either from himself or any other person by shutting his eyes and then ceremonially spitting into each of their mouths. The power is said to be hereditary, but all the children are not born with the gift." Among the Masai also, spitting is supposed to remove the spell of the evil eye.[20]

Elsewhere in East Africa, the evil does not seem to be seated merely in the eye, but in the tongue also. "If a person of this peculiarity (called Kjeni) sees an article or living creature and says, 'this is good,' or words to that effect, the object is doomed to perish; even a stone is said to split asunder from the evil power of the person. If a man with the evil eye and tongue expresses his admiration for a woman who is pregnant at the time, she is sure to die in child-birth. The person possessed of this power can, however, also effect a cure for the evil by spitting on the object or person affected. There is a whole clan, the Mba Mwanziu, of which every member, no matter where he was born, has the evil eye and tongue, and curiously enough, they are often sought for the curing of small hurts, such as burns and bruises, which they do by spitting on the hurt."[21] The Kavirondo claim that the evil eye can make a sound man sick and kill a man who is ill or an unborn child.[22] The evil eye is dreaded throughout East Africa where there are all sorts of charms against it.[23] One native who remembered Henry M. Stanley well, remarked in awe-stricken words: "He could kill a man with a glance of his eye."[24] In the Upper Congo there is no distinct word for evil eye, but one person is supposed to bewitch the farm of another so that the produce will not grow. "To remove the effect of the evil eye the owner of the farm calls a nganga (shaman) who knocks a stake into the farm, and, if a person is bewitching the farm the stake is supposed to enter that person, and he or she will soon die unless they desist from their bewitchment." To call fishermen by their proper names is to destroy their luck; any person who does this is liable to a heavy fine or is compelled to sell the fish of the injured man at a good price so as to restore the luck again.[25] In Central Africa only the initiated may watch the smelting of copper, the cause of this limitation being fear of the evil eye.[26]

In Bornu, "the better horses, which through sale or gift changed hands, were

20 Hobley, in JAI, XLI, 433-434.
21 Dundas, C., in JAI, XLIII, 534.
22 Northcote, in JAI, XXXVII, 64.
23 Johnstone, in JAI, XXXII, 265; Torday and Joyce, in JAI, XXXV, 416-417.

24 N. Y. *Times*, May 18, 1914.
25 Weeks, in JAI, XXXIX, 128.
26 Basseur, in *Globus*, LXXII, 164, note.

preferably transported at night, to insure them against the 'evil eye' of men."[27] In the Sudan it is common to cover food carefully with conical straw covers, against the evil eye or envious glance of hungry people who admire and long for it.[28] In Kabylie, "the husband, left alone with his wife, . . . strikes her lightly three times on the shoulders with the back of a sabre or a dagger, to conjure off the effect of the evil eye."[29] In some sections one of the bridesmaids impersonates the bride; she attracts all attention, according to local belief, because if people were to say that the real bride was pretty or the reverse, she would be injured. The evil eye and the evil mouth are occult powers to conjure up an evil spirit residing in an evil-wisher, according to the Hausa. We all know what harm could be done "if a look could kill." A man who had an evil eye saw a stone while out walking, and remarked, "What an enormous stone," and immediately the stone broke into three pieces. This, say the natives, was a clear case of evil mouth, for the words did the mischief, though the evil eye could have acted by itself. Another case is mentioned where a man asked another to sell him one of the bulls he was driving to market. The owner refused. "The other said, 'Very well, but I shall eat of its flesh today nevertheless.' Soon afterwards the bull fell, and as it was apparently dying, the owner cut its throat, and had to beg his fellow-travellers to buy the meat. The other then came up and bought a portion for about one-tenth of what it would have cost him in the market."[30] In northeast Africa people may be sold into slavery on account of the evil eye.[31]

"An Arab never asks even his best friend how his wife is; at most he says: 'How is your house getting on?'"[32] "Beneath all Mohammedan fatalism lives the primæval fear of daimonic influences. At the forefront of all cares stands the fear of the evil glance; they protect themselves from it by stroking with the hand over the face—the people often did that when they noticed that they were 'snapped'—and by using the hand, the *fatma* or lucky hand, in every form on the house, furniture, tools, clothing, and bodily ornament and by choosing it as a tattoo-pattern."[33] A lucky egg is also used: a common hen's egg with three little horseshoes of lead fastened on it very cleverly so as not to break or crack it.[34]

The Todas of India believe that various misfortunes may befall a man if anyone says that he is looking very well or is well dressed. "It is also unlucky that anyone should look at a man when he is eating. Similarly it is unlucky for anyone to say that a buffalo is giving much milk; she will probably kick her calf, or will suffer in some other way soon after." This kind of misfortune is called by a term meaning literally "if looking anxiously," or evil eye. One of the commonest effects is indigestion.[35] In Nair life is an evil-working power called *Koti*. "The word literally means desire, but as an evil force it works only when a hungry person sees a rich and healthy fellow eating a good meal. If a poor man sees you eat, and his mouth waters at the delicacies before you, you are sure to suffer from his *Koti*, you will get stomach-ache and even dysentery. It is the particular look of the hungry man that has the evil effect.

27 Nachtigal, *Sahara*, I, 607.
28 Junker, *Afrika*, I, 69, 179, note.
29 Hanoteau et Letourneux, *Kabylie*, II, 219.
30 Tremearne, in JAI, XLV, 37, 48-49.
31 Paulitschke, *Ethnog. Nordost-Afr.*, II, 140.

32 Bruun, *Huleboerne*, 152.
33 Karutz, in *Globus*, XCII, 137.
34 Anon., "Glücksei," in *Globus*, LXXV, 19.
35 Rivers, *Todas*, 263.

When once a man begins to suffer from another's *Koti* the only way to get over it is to eat some salt over which some *mantrams,* or magical formulae, have been repeated."[36] Beneficent contagious magic is used by the Oraon and Munda of India to ward off the influence of the evil eye; they wear rings and armlets made of iron previously exposed to the influence of an eclipse of the sun, so that the wearer may offer to the evil eye of witches and the evil attention of ghosts and spirits a resistance as strong as that of iron so hardened. The idea of pollution by contact with the leavings of other people's food, now widely prevalent all over India, is thought to have its roots deep down in primitive fear of contact with evil powers and to have been borrowed by the so-called Aryan Hindu from the animistic aboriginal. Although subsequently the conceptions of physical cleanliness, hygienic necessity, and even internal purity have been super-added so as to transform the original idea beyond recognition, yet among some tribes we meet with the touch-taboo in its original naked simplicity. "The evil touch is not more effective than the evil eye. The evil eye of witches who are particularly averse to the sight of the gaudy dress or ornaments of others, make the well-dressed Oraon beau or belle dancing at the village *akhra,* or dancing ground, sometimes fall down in fainting fits. At times more serious consequences flow from the evil eye of a witch. . . . Food, like dress, is a favourite target for the evil eye. Oraon women are particularly anxious about the rice-flour they prepare on some festive occasions to make bread with. If the rice-flour happens to attract the evil eye of a witch, or the 'shadow' (*chhain*) of a ghost, the bread prepared out of it will either be imperfectly baked, or emit a foul smell, or cause diarrhoea or other sickness to those who partake of such bread. Similarly the evil eye of a witch or sorcerer directed against food or drink is believed to poison it. It is, however, not witches and sorcerers, alone, that possess the 'evil eye.' Anyone may possess it by nature." A method of avoiding evil powers is to divert their attention. Thus, "to divert the 'evil eye' of spirits or sorcerers and witches, and of malicious persons, the Oraon cultivator plants in the middle of his standing upland crops a wooden pole, over which is placed upside down an earthen vessel with its upturned bottom painted black and white. The magic of the colour diverts the 'evil eye' from the crops." Another method is to make a mimicry of driving the evil influences away, not so much by physical terrorism as by the cumulative spiritual force of a body of persons acting ceremonially. Thus may an evil spirit be driven out to another village, which, in its turn, performs the same ceremony and transfers the spirit to the next village, and so on. As an instance of avoidance in the form of threat may be mentioned the custom by which the father of an Oraon bride puts a small iron spear into the hands of his daughter before she starts for her husband's house. "She carries the spear in her hands during the journey to protect herself from evil spirits on the way. On reaching her husband's house, she inserts the spear into the roof of the house as a threat to such spirits of her father's village as may have shadowed her."[37]

In India, again, "the evil eye may be found among the upper classes if it be induced in them by exciting their jealousy, envy, or hatred; but usually the lower the class and the blacker the person, the more intense the potency of his evil eye."[38] This looks like the ascription of evil powers to the aborigi-

36 Panikkar, in JAI, XLVIII, 283.

37 Roy, in JAI, XLIV, 332, 340, 340-341, 344-345, 347.

38 De Cunha, in JASB, I, 128.

nal type.[39] Certain of the taboos imposed upon the parents during pregnancy are explicable as provisions against the evil eye. It can be averted by means of iron and "it is not unusual to find a small knife or a nail or a scissor attached to the cradle of a child."[40] A mother, on hearing someone speak of the healthfulness or plumpness of her child, says to the speaker, "Look at your feet." This is to avert the speaker's eye from the child. If a fruit-tree is loaded with good fruit, it is not good to point at it with the finger, for thus it will catch the evil eye of the person and the fruit will become rotten or the tree will cease to bear. One must point at the fruit, not with the forefinger, but with the middle part of the thumb.[41]

In the East Indies the evil eye is thought to be cast in anger, as in a quarrel, and the sign of the phallus is thought to be a safeguard.[42] In Sarawak if a native is seen while drawing a peculiar tattoo, he immediately covers it up. The reason why such a native would not allow the mark to be sketched "was that his wife was expecting a child, and he was afraid of my eye affecting her."[43] In Sumatra, simply to look at a child with admiring eyes is enough to harm it. The idea is that any look conveying admiration would evoke the envy and disfavor of evil spirits.[44] In the Malay Peninsula "the birth-name was sometimes superseded (as being unlucky) before marriage, when misfortunes happened to the child."[45] In the Caroline Islands when a ship arrived, they used to tie strips of leaf about the children's necks to keep off the evil glance. "For this reason they feared at first the missionary Snow because he wore spectacles." In canoe-building the work was protected from rain and the evil eye of the envious by a leaf-covering. No stranger may look on the work; and if a laborer hurts himself with an ax, he asks at once who lifted up the covering and looked. If he learns the name, he draws a human figure and cuts it in two with his ax, as punishment for the intruder.[46]

The Chaldæans believed not only in the evil eye but also in the malevolent mouth, that is, an unlucky word pronounced unintentionally.[47] There is much evidence in Norse tradition concerning the evil eye, which may be possessed without the knowledge and against the will of a person. One of its uses was to make blunt the sword of an opponent; to look backwards through one's legs was also a magic rite.[48] It was the custom among the ancient Greeks to put figures before bronze foundries; their object was the aversion of ill will, charms against the evil eye, and "if we may trust the scholiast on Aristophanes they formed part of the furniture of most people's chimney corners at Athens." It is held that the Gorgon mask was one of these. "What the beast was and how the story arose cannot be decided, but it is clear that the Gorgon was regarded as a sort of incarnate Evil Eye. The monster was tricked out with cruel tusks and snakes, but it slew by the eye, it *fascinated*. The Evil Eye itself is not frequent on monuments; the Gorgoncion as a more complete and more elaborately decorative horror attained a wider popularity. But the prophylactic Eye, the eye set to stare back the Evil Eye, is common on vases, on shields and on the prows of ships."[49] Hornell[50] has a convincing article on survivals

39 §257, of the text.
40 Modi, in JASB, II, 170.
41 Modi, in JASB, II, 169.
42 Wilken, in VG, III, 319.
43 Roth, *Sarawak*, II, 92.
44 Jacobs, *Groot-Atjeh*, I, 163.
45 Skeat and Blagden, *Malay Penin.*, II, 16-17.

46 Finsch, *Ethnol. Erfahr.*, III, 201; Kubary, *Karolinen-arch.*, 292.
47 Lenormant, *Chaldean Magic*, 38.
48 Feilberg, in *Ztschr. d. Ver. f. Vkde.*, XI, 305.
49 Harrison, *Greek Relig.*, 191, 196.
50 In JAI, LIII, 289-321.

of the use of *oculi* on modern boats. In modern Greece, "when they express liking or affection for a child that is plump, well formed, and healthy, after doing so, they spit on the ground to avert the influence of their evil eye drawn to the child by its beauty. . . . At Constantinople the writer saw the house of a Greek bearing an old flag on a pole; some houses bear an old shoe. This is to avoid the evil eye of passers by." The author draws parallels from Hindu life.[51] Plutarch[52] says: "And therefore people imagine that those amulets that are preservative against witchcraft are likewise good and efficacious against envy; the sight by the strangeness of the spectacle being diverted, so that it cannot make so strong an impression upon the patient."

To the investigator of Greek folklore no other superstition is more in evidence than the all-prevailing belief in the evil eye. "Greeks, both men and women, readily admit its existence and their own fear of it, for it is abundantly warranted by scripture, in particular by Solomon, notorious as an authority on magic. The investigator can therefore arrive in a village and at once, without danger of being baffled by shyness, suspicion, or stupidity, ask who suffers from overlooking. A little adroit playing on the belief that the more attractive a person is, the more he must fear the evil eye, will work wonders in the way of establishing sympathy between the investigator and the villagers." While beauty is a great danger to its owner, it is not the only thing that attracts the evil eye, for anyone, young or old, ugly or fair, may be attacked. "Only those born on a Saturday are exempt, but on Saturday afternoon, be it understood; for it was on Saturday afternoon that Christ was born, and it is from Christ that the Saturday-born derive their exemption. New-made mothers have much to fear from it until their purification, forty days after the birth of their child. Beasts and inanimate objects suffer no less than men; young children suffer most of all, although infants are safe until they are baptized or their mother celebrates her purification. . . . Any illness which is obviously not due to organic disease, a breakage, or a chill, is set down to the evil eye. The ordinary symptoms are discomfort, headache, whining, sleeplessness, and peevishness." Prevention is thought better than cure, so amulets are generally worn to keep the evil eye at bay; among such are rings and silver buckles which divert the visitor's attention to themselves, silver having in itself an additional power over evil magic, as in our own silver bullet. "Shops have a horseshoe or a clove of garlic suspended over the door. A Shatista man has particular confidence in a French horseshoe he picked up during the war; it is, of course, twice the size of an ordinary Macedonian shoe. Calves wear necklaces of bright wool tassels, as does even a young donkey of my acquaintance—adult donkeys, as is known, are unworthy even of being overlooked. . . . The spoken word may also effectively ward off the dreaded evil. As is well known, the pale skins of North Europeans are much admired by the dark-complexioned children of the South. As a result, on my removing my glove one day in Shatista, a woman screamed 'Garlic!' and kissed my hand, exclaiming, 'It is as white as a saint's.'" Any device is effective which serves to divert the attention of a possible overlooker. "Thus, a Kastoria small boy, who was frequently overlooked, was never allowed by his mother to leave the house until she had daubed some coffee grounds on his cheek, in order that the first remark made on him by passers-by might be a comment on his dirty face, *i.e.*, on something extraneous to his personality. . . . Another

51 Modi, in JASB, II, 169.   52 *Symposiacs*, V, q. 7.

small boy of Kastoria habitually wore stockings that were not a pair, or, if they matched, one was outside in. . . . The amulets, in short, are a species of lightning conductor, just as the power of overlooking is thought popularly to be a kind of electricity which resides in the eye. . . . Mothers make a point of buying some hair from the bear to store against future need." It is not difficult to learn the religious remedies for overlooking, but spells are more difficult to obtain. "Fortunately, the words must be *spoken* either to act or to break the spell, so that women who can write can usually be persuaded into writing down the words. . . . After banishing all her relatives from the room, she produced a well-thumbed piece of paper on which she had written down the words as dictated by the old woman who had taught her the exorcism. She wrote them down in my notebook from this piece of paper, but pulled me up short when I inadvertently repeated aloud one of the sentences." The authoress[53] has made a collection of charms, nearly all witnessing to the use of water, salt, and sometimes spittle in exorcising the evil eye. "Smoking" the child and the use of heat (live coals) are common practices, while sacred numbers, especially three and forty, are exorcistic.

In modern Egypt children are rendered dirty and shabby, particularly when taken out in public. This is "from fear of the evil eye, which is excessively dreaded, and especially in the case of children, since they are generally esteemed the greatest of blessings, and therefore most likely to be coveted." Boys are long kept in the harem and often dressed as girls. Alum is used, in a somewhat complicated ceremony, to counteract the effects of the evil eye. On being laid on burning coals, it assumes the form of the person who is envious or malicious. It is then pounded, put in some food, and fed to a black dog. At a wedding handsome chandeliers are hung before the bridegroom's house; but if a crowd gathers to see them, "it is a common practice to divert the attention of the spectators by throwing down and breaking a large jar, or by some other artifice, lest an envious eye should cause the chandelier to fall." A complaint reads as follows: "It is quite shocking to see fine sheep hung up in the streets, quite whole, tail and all, before the public eye; so that every beggar who passes by envies them; and one might, therefore, as well eat poison as such meat."[54]

In modern Persia, "the evil eye may be invited by beauty, by an exceptional run of luck, or by anything that is valuable or attractive."[55] The Imeritian Christians still fear the evil eye, especially when a child is praised or admired.[56] In Hungary to be "struck with the eyes" brings on the "eye-evil." Most children's diseases "come from the eyes." People whose eyebrows grow together are most to be feared. The belief is general and is parallel to the "mal occhio" of the Italians. Various unsavory practices are employed as safeguards.[57] In Anatolia, and among the Christians, this belief persists. Amulets are fastened to the necks of children and to the manes and tails of animals; generally these are metal triangles with a passage of the Koran upon them. Mohammedan boys draw the fez over the eyes, and girls cover the forehead with both hands, at meeting a missionary. Skulls of cows, horses, and camels protect gardens from the evil eye.[58] The veiling of Mohammedan women began

53 Hardie (Mrs. Hasluck), in JAI, LIII, 160, 161, 162-164, 165, 166 ff., 170-172.
54 Lane, *Mod. Egypt.*, 77, 381-382, 384-385.
55 De Cunha, in JASB, I, 150.
56 Hahn, in *Globus*, LXXX, 305.

57 Temesváry, *Geburtshilfe*, 75, 76.
58 De Jerphanion, Anatolien, in *Die Katholischen Missionen*, Jan., 1907 (abstract in *Globus*, XCI, 116).

with the beautiful ones to save them from the evil eye; it was thus an outcome of daimonism.[59]

Among the South Russian Jews "strangers may not praise children much, or caress them or look at them sharply." If that happens the mother bids the child to make a certain gesture, unseen by the stranger, whereby the evil glance is averted. Sickness comes from the evil eye, called euphemistically "a git Oig." To avoid it, the health of children is never praised. "In conversation with people of whom it is known that they have an evil eye, illnesses are even invented in order to lead them astray."[60] Mary Antin[61] writes of the Jews in Russia: "Pepper and salt tied in a corner of the pocket was effective in warding off the evil eye." In one of the Scottish islands there is a sort of nut which is used as an amulet against witchcraft or the evil eye. If a child wearing one of these about the neck is threatened with evil, the nut, which is white, changes, they say, into a black color.[62] It is a quite general belief that children should not be admired, and among some peoples custom prescribes that if one looks at a child for a while in admiration, the child should then be spat upon three times.[63] In Dundalk, Ireland, the superstition was recently dragged into court when one woman charged another with having cast the evil eye upon her child and doomed it to a life of ill luck. A witness testified that a third woman cut the fringe from the defendant's shawl and burned it under the child's nose in the belief that the spell cast upon the infant would disappear with the smoke. The magistrate refused to take the case seriously.[64]

§266. Disparagement; Deception.

Disparagement was part of the naming-ceremony in Fiji, where, on the day of circumcision, the initiates changed their names and everybody, including the women, "used the most filthy language possible to the aspirant."[1] If the first children die, the Altaians try to give the next a name implying worthlessness or humility, e.g., It-koden, the haunch of a dog. Under similar circumstances the Buryat and other Siberians practise deception: "When the first children die young, the newly born is hidden under the cooking cauldron, on the top of which is placed . . . a figure representing the child, made from barley-meal. Then the kam (shaman) is called, and begins to shamanize over this figure. . . . Then its body is cut into three parts and buried far away from the house. This ceremony will protect the child from death." The Diurbiut have a similar ceremony, in which soon after birth the child is stolen by some relatives and hidden under a cauldron, where it remains for three days, well fed and tended. "At the same time these relatives make an image of grass and throw it into the tent of the parents, who, when they find it, pretend to see in it their own dead child and bewail and bury it with much ceremony. This is to persuade the evil spirit who wished to harm the child that the latter is dead and buried." The Yakuts apply deception in the case of implements or other valuable objects by giving to them certain nicknames instead of names proper to them, in order that the spirits may not know that the objects in question are referred to, for if they did, they would destroy or

59 Snouck-Hurgronje, in Bijd., XXXV, 366.
60 Weissenberg, in Globus, LXXXIII, 316; and in Globus, XCI, 357.
61 Promised Land, 36.

62 Martin, "Scotland," in Pinkerton Voy., III, 587.
63 Temesváry, Geburtshilfe, 75.
64 N. Y. Times, Aug. 28, 1926.
1 Brewster, in JAI, XLIX, 311-312.

harm them. For the same reason the Yakuts often employ Russian names for things they value, being certain that the spirits will not understand these.[2]

Equivalent to giving an opprobrious name to a child is a birth-observance in the Punjab; half of the head is shaved and the other half left, "in order that the Angel of Death may pass them by as too ugly."[3] The ethnographers have in India a fertile region. Thurston[4] reports a number of examples from the southern districts. It is, for instance, a good thing to frighten anyone who expresses admiration of one's belongings. If a friend praises your son's eyes, say to him: "Look out. There is a snake at your feet." If he is frightened, the ill is averted. "The custom of calling a newly-born child, after the parent has lost a first born or more in succession, by an opprobrious name, is common amongst many castes in Southern India, including even Mohammedans. Kuppuswami (Sir dungheap) is one of the commonest names for such children, and they have the distinguishing mark of a pierced nostril and ear (on the right side) with a knob of gold in it." Again, children are called "gunda (rock), kalla (stone), hucha (lunatic), tippa (dung-hill). The last name is given after some rubbish from a dung-hill has been brought in a sieve, and the child placed in it. . . . Another device is to give a Hindu child a Mohammedan or English name, such as Bade Sahib or Rapsan (corruption of Robertson)." This is a case of deception as to the child's identity. In certain forms of address, the speaker must refer to himself as a foot-servant. "If he mentions his rice, he must call it gritty rice. Rupees must be called his copper coins. He must call his house his dung-pit, and so on." Thus he and his possessions appear to be less than they are. Again, "men cause their names to be cut on rocks by the wayside, or on the stones with which the path leading to the temple is paved, in the belief that good luck will result if their name is trodden on."

Abuse at the time of marriage brings good luck and wipes away sin:[5] "people who accompany the marriage procession to the bride's house are often vilely abused by the women-folk of the bride's family in the belief that it will lead on to the good fortune of the newly married couple." Again, at certain periods, "brothers are abused by sisters to their heart's content and this is done under the impression that it will prolong the lives of the brothers and bring good luck to them."[6] At a wedding the women of both parties, bride's and groom's, sing coarse songs, "abusing each other and charging each other's families with poverty and bad conduct. This abuse, which is called *phatana,* is considered lucky, partly because it is coarse and coarseness is lucky, partly because it makes out the abused to be poor and untrustworthy, and therefore untempting lodgings for house-seeking spirits. Praise is risky; abuse and blame are safe."[7] That coarseness pleases the daimons will appear in other connections.[8]

In China, "though endearing or fanciful names are often conferred, it is quite as common to vilify very young children by calling them *dog, hog, puppy, flea,* etc., under the idea that such epithets will ward off the evil eye."[9] Thus the notion of the evil eye may underlie disparagement; the two ideas belong to the same species. In Sumatra there is the same fear of admiration: "one could bring an Atjeh mother to despair by praising her child in her presence.

2 Czaplicka, *Aborig. Siberia,* 141, 140, 278-279.

3 Rose, in JAI, XXXVII, 257.

4 *S. India,* 257, 368, 369, 534-535, 542; Risley, *Ethnog. Ind.,* I, 111.

5 §373, of the text.

6 Mitra, in JASB, II, 598 ff.; Mitra, in JASB, IV, 393.

7 Campbell, in JASB, IV, 63.

8 §§277, 324, of the text and *Case-Book.*

9 Williams, *Middle Kingdom,* I, 797.

Even the parents refrain anxiously from mentioning and extolling among themselves one or another good characteristic of their child." Praising a good trait would lead to its speedy decline; they all know this and strictly refrain.[10]

In Homeric times "there was one very living danger from the gods that must be avoided as far as possible, the gods would not brook exceeding prosperity. Their natures were jealous, and they would allow to man but a moderate share of good fortune. Because Achilles' lot was so noble, his life was short and bitter; while Odysseus, having endured many sufferings, was to end a long life in peace and happiness. . . . After great prosperity, Bellerophon went mad. Worst of all, however was undue boasting and a desire to minimize divine power. Ajax boasted that he had escaped drowning in spite of the gods; Poseidon, angry at these words, split the rock 'upon which Ajax was sitting when he became greatly infatuated' and Ajax was drowned in the sea. 'Short-lived are those who fight with the immortal gods.' Therefore men were ever on their guard to avoid transgression in this respect and to turn aside all 'envy.' One should receive the gift of the gods in silence; compliments were turned off with some deprecatory remark; gradually there arose a sort of doctrine of excess, and, later, the conception of 'nemesis' "— which means only "censure" or "anger" in Homer.[11] Self-disparagement has become a sort of pose. The Chaldæan gods were jealous of men and would not let them share the prerogatives of gods.[12]

Herodotus[13] reports the coarse actions of the Egyptian women while floating in boats past a town; among other things they loaded the townspeople with abuse. All this was done, apparently, to scare off evil influences from the town. Coarse abuse and jokes occurred at Athenian festivals, especially in those held by the women in honor of Demeter. Songs with the coarsest ribaldry against the commander were sung at his triumph by the Roman soldiers.[14] The rude and lewd fescennine songs, at a marriage or a triumph, were supposed to avert the envy of the gods, or the evil eye, on great occasions of good fortune.[15]

Salutations. There is undoubtedly a multiple explanation of the methods of greeting employed by primitive peoples. In some instances they appear to be simply expressions of affection[16] or of respect,[17] while in others there is a suggestion of avoiding or deceiving the spirits. Though a few of the following cases may belong more properly under other topics, we have thought it best to include them all here.

Weeping often occurs as a form of salutation.[18] Among the Queensland aborigines a not uncommon form of greeting, say, after some years' interval, between mother and daughter, is for the elder woman to take any heavy stick, such as a fighting-pole, and, digging into the top of her head, rub it there until the blood comes, crying and sobbing as much as she can; the daughter from behind is all this time putting her arms round the old woman's waist, and when she thinks that her mother has given way sufficiently to her feelings, she will forcibly take the stick away.[19] Kissing seems to be indigenous in the Torres Straits; "this salutation, combined with embracing the head, would

10 Jacobs, *Groot-Atjeh*, I, 163.
11 Keller, *Hom. Soc.*, 114 (where references to the text are given).
12 Maspero, *Hist. Anc.*, I, 587.
13 *Hist.*, II, 60.
14 Smith, *Dict. Gk. and Rom. Antiq.*, II, 831, 897.

15 Munro, *Catullus*, 76.
16 §427, of the text and *Case-Book.*
17 §156, of the text and *Case-Book.*
18 Andree, *Eth. Parallelen*, 223.
19 Roth, *Queensland Aborig.*, 134.

only be performed after a long separation, especially if the man had been supposed to be dead; in the case of relatives this might perhaps be accompanied with shouting and weeping."[20] The Andaman Islanders, on meeting, remain gazing into each other's eyes for what would seem to us an absurdly long time. "Relatives testify their joy at meeting after a few months' separation by throwing their arms round each other's necks, and sobbing as if their hearts would break." There is little or no difference between the demonstrations of joy and sorrow.[21]

Wilken[22] mentions some cases of greeting with tears; his editor takes this to be a method of warding off evil influences. "Bengali women never weep, like their Behari sisters, on such joyous occasions as meeting after long separation."[23] When Polynesian friends meet, they "consider a sorrowful mien, the outpouring of tears, and contact of noses the correct behaviour. The contact of noses is usually termed 'rubbing noses' by European writers. It is, however, nothing of the kind; there is no friction applied to the process. The salutation is sometimes performed by the two parties standing, but more generally by one sitting and the other standing. Hosts receive their guests sitting. . . . Sitting down to receive guests is a mark of respect. . . . Both men and women use the same form of nose-pressure, but only on meeting, never at parting."[24] In New Zealand, on the arrival of a person of any consequence, or one much beloved, "they used to add to it [nose-pressing] by what they call the *tangi,* which was cutting the face, breast, and arms with a piece of lava or mussel shell, and giving utterance to a series of the most lamentable howls, whilst forced tears rolled down their bloody cheeks."[25]

Friederici[26] has treated, with numerous references to the literature of the subject and lists of the tribes where it is found, the custom of greeting guests and strangers by weeping and sighing. His cases include tribes in North, Central, and South America; he thinks it once existed over the entire continent. Some typical instances may be cited. When a Spanish ship was wrecked on the coast of Texas, "the coast Indians came down, sat—full of sympathy, as the Spaniards thought, over their shipwreck—beside them and began so to weep that it could be heard far off. This lasted over half an hour." In one case an Indian brought a gift of hides to De Soto; "he wept bitterly and threw himself at the governor's feet as soon as he reached him. Soto lifted him up and the man made an address, but no one could understand him." A later case of weeping was interpreted as a sign of obedience and remorse on account of a previous misdemeanor. The custom of greeting with tears was so general and took so striking a form among the Sioux in what is now Minnesota, that an early European traveller referred to them as "the weepers." Among the Lenguas, "when anyone returns after long absence, then both greeting Indians shed some tears before they speak a single word. To act otherwise would be an insult or at least a sign that the visit is not viewed with pleasure." Among the Tupi and others the greeting of guests and strangers with protracted weeping and sobbing was done mostly by the women. "When a stranger and even a tribal member came to a hut as a guest, he was given a place in the hammock, and the naked women squatted around him, put both the hands before the face and raised a protracted weeping and moaning, consoling with

20 Haddon, in JAI, XIX, 336.
21 Man, in JAI, XII, 147, 175; Roth, in JAI, XIX, 178.
22 In VG, I, 173.
23 Mitra, in JASB, III, 366.
24 Smith, *Polynesians,* 454-455.
25 Roth, in JAI, XIX, 179.
26 In *Globus,* LXXXIX, 30-33.

the guest for the trials and dangers of the journey he had endured and paying him all kinds of compliments. Custom demanded that the one so greeted should also weep or, if he as a European did not always have tears on tap, at least should act that way." The practice fell off after the end of the seventeenth century, largely through contact with Europeans, but it was still found in the latter half of the eighteenth century. The author considers this form of greeting nothing more than a senselessly exaggerated and degenerate form of courtesy.

§267. Anticipation and Interrogation.

Sneezing. The custom of saying "God bless you," or some equivalent expression, when a person sneezes, is ancient and very widely extended. "In fact, it is doubtful if there is a country in the world where traces of it cannot be found. Consequently the very general belief that the custom took its rise in one of the symptoms of the plague in Italy in the days of Gregory the Great cannot be credited." Its origin, of course, dates back to the religious ideas of primitive men, among whom "the sneeze was sometimes considered as an auspicious sign, sometimes as a most unlucky omen; but that it was due to the presence of spirits, either good or evil, was the belief of all."[1] In D'Entrecasteaux it is believed that the soul is inside the body, a separate entity the presence of which is revealed in sneezing. "For a sneeze is due to the soul's recollection of some dead kinsman or friend. The native will therefore say when he sneezes *tamanake* (*i.e., tamana keke,* 'his father is not'), or *inanake* ('his mother is not'), or whoever the relative may be the man has lost. He refers to his soul in the third person, for he is interpreting the meaning of its sneeze. If he has no deceased relatives he simply says *vaioma,* a word that implies some reference to fighting, the sneeze being then a reminder of some friend who has fallen in battle."[2] Among the Southern Massim "a man may sneeze when he becomes angry, otherwise sneezing is considered a sign of approaching illness."[3]

When the Mkamba in the East African Protectorate sneezes he always makes some remark; "it seems that as a rule such exclamations have reference to the sneezer's father or grandfather."[4] Elsewhere in East Africa if a child sneezes, the father or mother kisses it and prays that all evil may depart from it. In the case of an adult, he prays in a similar vein for himself.[5] Among the Awa-Wanga sneezing is supposed to be a bad omen, and if a man sneezes when about to start on a journey, he gives it up for that day. "If a person plans to visit a friend who is said to be sick unto death, and if a sneezing fit comes on before he starts, then he knows that his friend will certainly recover from his illness." The prejudice against sneezing went so far in the old days that if a warrior who sneezed en route, on a foray for cattle, were not speared, he was looked upon as a kind of Jonah who would bring ill luck to the raid.[6] Sneezing is supposed by the Hausa to expel the evil spirit.[7]

It is especially dangerous, think the Buryat of Siberia, to sneeze during sleep, for then the soul springs momentarily from the body, and the evil

1 Usher, in *Pop. Sci. News*, XXII, 161.
2 Jenness and Ballentyne, *D'Entrecasteaux*, 109.
3 Seligmann, *Melanesians*, 658.

4 Dundas, in JAI, XLIII, 526.
5 Cole, in JAI, XXXII, 335.
6 Hobley, in JAI, XXXIII, 341-342.
7 Tremearne, in JAI, XLV, 30.

spirits who are on the watch seize it before it can hide.[8] Among the Palaungs of Farther India, "to sneeze when setting out on a journey is unlucky and the journey had better be deferred. Sneezing is, at other times, not considered unlucky, except during a marriage-ceremony. If either bride or bridegroom sneeze, bad luck will follow them unless many offerings are presented in the image-house."[9] Among the Araucanian Indians sneezing violently while gambling was thought to bring bad luck.[10] A traveller who had been well received by the Guiana Indians, upon happening to sneeze, saw the circle around him broken; "the most timid betook themselves to a distance, the bravest closing their noses with the thumb and forefinger."[11]

The Norwegian peasants still hold that if a sick person sneezes, he will not die and their custom when a child sneezes is to say "Grow: it is a sign of health." They believe also that anything a person is thinking of when he sneezes will be sure to come true. The Highlanders believe that when a person sneezes, he is liable to be stolen by fairies, unless protected by some one invoking the name of the Deity. The Moslem, when he sneezes, is saluted by his friends with the formula, "Praise to Allah!"—a custom, it is said, that is conveyed from race to race wherever Islam extends. In France, an indication of the survival of this usage is seen by the following quotation from a *Book on Rules and Civilities* of the year 1685: "If his lordship chance to sneeze, you are not to brawl out, 'God bless you,' but, pulling off your hat, bow to him handsomely, and make the obsecration to yourself." The custom among the Jews, when a person sneezes, is to ejaculate, "A long life to you!" In Italy the exclamation is "Happiness!" and in Germany "Gesundheit!"[12]

Other Omens. The sneeze has been illustrated rather fully. There are countless other omens. If the Papuans want to decide whether to hunt on one river or another, they look to the canoes for answer: "for a negative answer there is no movement; for an affirmative the canoes will all fall into an uncontrollable rocking."[13] Comets are bad omens to the Akamba, being portents of the death of people and cattle and also of impending famine.[14] To most Congo natives it is a bad sign if a man kicks his foot against anything in the road. "Sometimes the strong-minded ones would laugh away the fears of those who were inclined to turn back if the omen were against them; but it more frequently happened that they turned *en masse*, glad of an excuse to postpone a fight."[15] In a village in West Africa, Garner[16] once saw the people screaming and clapping their hands at the moon, over which was passing a small, fleecy cloud. They regarded it as a bad omen for their town, and were trying to drive it away. "When the new moon's face was again free from the cloud the people rejoiced, and told me it was good for them, and that the moon would like them and give them light because they had driven away *m'buiri.*" The blacks of Trinidad refuse to engage in any sort of enterprise unless the aspect of the moon is propitious.[17]

In several districts of India, omens are drawn from the chirping of the lizard to the east, southeast, west, and other quarters. The lizard is taken to be a totem-animal.[18] "One of the worst omens possible is to see two snakes

8 Czaplicka, *Aborig. Siberia*, 158.
9 Milne, *Eastern Clan*, 221.
10 Latcham, in JAI, XXXIX, 350.
11 Roth, in BAE, XXXVIII, 703.
12 Usher, in *Pop. Sci. News*, XXII, 161-162.
13 Williams, in JAI, LIII, 373.

14 Hobley, *A-Kamba*, 55.
15 Weeks, in JAI, XL, 376.
16 In AAAS, 1895, 593.
17 N. Y. *Times*, Aug. 25, 1924.
18 Mitra, in JASB, VI, 33, 37; Strange, *Hindu Law*, I, 38.

copulating, and a man who sees this is not supposed to return to his house or speak to any one until the next sun has risen."[19] "If a deer crossed the path of an expedition when starting, an immediate return home was made, and the undertaking was postponed."[20] The mewing of a cat at night is ominous; she is an ancestress, and the mew betokens death.[21] The Tamil marriage go-between "will always still turn back when halfway to the parents of the bride and put off his errand till a better time if somewhere on the way there passes across his road a pig, a cat, a snake, or above all a widow."[22] The Parsees find fish a good omen, or the passing of a serpent at one's right, or over one's body when asleep. A serpent on the left is bad, as is also the crossing of one's path by a cat.[23] Among the Palaungs, a comet is always a sign of war or of danger to a king. "It is a royal star, and it only has power over royal people."[24]

In Borneo a single evil omen is quite enough to halt a well-laid plan or to cause it to be given up altogether.[25] There are a number of omen-animals.[26] Dyaks, like so many other tribes around the earth, take auguries from the flight of birds; and the cry of certain animals near the house of the newly-married causes their separation, for they believe the death of one of them would otherwise ensue. As for the birds, if they are "heard on the wrong side, if in the wrong order, if the note or call be of the wrong kind, the matter in hand must be postponed, or abandoned altogether; unless a conjunction of subsequent good omens occur, which, in the opinion of old experts, can over-bear the preceding ones. Hence, in practice, birding becomes a most involved matter, because the birds will not allow themselves to be heard in a straight-forward orthodox succession. After all it is only the balance of probabilities, it is seldom that Dyak patience can wait till the omens occur according to the standard theory. . . . The worst of all omens is a dead beast of any kind, especially those included in the omen list, found anywhere on the farm." The birds are the messengers of the all-knowing ghosts.[27]

Furness[28] and Gomes[29] enter very fully into the detail of Bornean omens and divination. The former portrays graphically the complexity of omen-ob-servation that attends the search for camphor. There are numbers of miscella-neous omens; for instance, if a house-post gives way the sign is one foreboding evil; the house is abandoned and a new one built. But the dominant type of omen described by these authors is derived from birds. "I have sometimes," writes Gomes, "argued with the Dyaks that if the warnings of the birds are to be trusted, then why make so much noise to prevent hearing them? The Dyaks reply to this was that as long as they did not hear the warning, the spirits would not be displeased at their not regarding it; so to spare themselves the trouble of choosing another site and building another house, they make so much noise as to drown the cries of any birds." Before a war expedition the head man goes apart to listen to the birds; if the first omens are unfavorable he waits till he hears some bird of good omen. "The system . . . is most elaborate and complicated, and the younger men have constantly to ask the older ones how to act in unexpected combinations of apparently contradictory

19 Carey and Tuck, *Chin Hills*, I, 199.
20 Godden, in JAI, XXVII, 38; *cf.* Mitra, in JASB, III, 454.
21 Chaube, in JASB, V, 72.
22 Gehring, *Süd-Indien*, 75.
23 Modi, in JASB, I, 290.
24 Milne, *Eastern Clan*, 366.
25 Schwaner, *Borneo*, I, 181.

26 Haddon, in PSM, LX, 80.
27 Bock, *Borneo*, 94; Roth, *Sarawak*, I, 127, 192, 194; Nieuwenhuis, *Borneo*, I, 180; II, 224.
28 *Head-Hunters*, 4, 138, 161, 164a, 167.
29 *Sea Dyaks*, 47, 48, 49, 79, 153-160. (48-49, 153, 155, 157-158, 159, quoted.)

omens. The law and observance of omens occupy a greater share of the thoughts of the Dyak than any other part of his religion." For a war expedition, birds heard on the right hand are best. "It is said that for farming, if a piece of gold be hidden in the ground, the hearing of the proper omen birds may be dispensed with. If a fowl be sacrificed, and the blood made to drop in a hole in the earth in which the fowl is afterwards buried, it is said the gods will be satisfied, and a good harvest ensue. And on the occasion of a war expedition, if an offering is made with beating of gongs and drums on starting from the house, it is said that no cries of birds need be obeyed afterwards. But none of these methods are ever used, the Dyaks preferring to submit to the tedious procedure of listening to the cries of the birds." They honor a good omen with respect to the crops by resting from work for three days. "So great is the Dyak belief in omens that a man will sometimes abandon a nearly finished boat simply because a bird of ill omen flies across its bows. The labour of weeks will thus be wasted. I have myself seen wooden beams and posts left half finished in the jungle, and have learned on inquiry that some bird of ill omen was heard while the man was at work on them, and so they had to be abandoned." No argument is of avail to shake the beliefs in vogue, though certain of the omen-animals are killed despite the taboo, sanctioned by sickness or death, which theoretically protects them. "It would seem that physical requirements are stronger than religious theory."

The Dyak system is very complete; and is approximated elsewhere in the Archipelago.[30] In Sumatra an eclipse is a strong portent of ill.[31] The day of the new moon is fortunate for an Indian child; it is believed that boys who begin to walk on that day will be fast runners.[32] Dreams are ominous to the Indian, as to most primitive folk. They are the natural and normal means of communication with the spirit-world. Dreaming of the dead is particularly unfortunate, for it means illness or death.[33] In the folklore of the Maoris, if a certain bird is seen hovering over a village it is known either that the tribe will soon lose a chief by death or that a defeat in battle is assured. It is an evil omen to eat of the food left by the first-born of a family. "The only cure for this dire affliction is for the unlucky person to seek out the first-born female of a family and get her to step over his body, which act breaks up the *pahunu,*" or evil omen.[34]

When an Iroquois prophet departed on a journey, he first assured his mother that, in the event of his death by violence or sorcery, the otter-skin, which he had hung head-downward in a corner of the lodge, would vomit blood.[35] Before foot-races or a war-expedition the Zuñi performed a certain religious ceremonial, after which each was asked what he had heard. "If he had heard the hoof beats of the Navajo horse or the roaring of the river or the hooting of an owl or the sound of lips smacking, all good signs, he would answer, 'It is well.' To hear nothing is a bad sign."[36] The following omens are accredited by the Indians of Guiana. Should the leaf of a certain plant which is suspended in the house when one of the inmates is ill, germinate, as under ordinary circumstances, the sick man will recover, but if it wither, that is an indication that he will die. The first night of the waxing moon is considered the proper occasion for obtaining clay for the manufacture of pots and other

30 Wilken, *Vkde.*, 584 ff.
31 Jacobs, *Groot-Atjeh*, I, 394.
32 Hrdlička, in BAE, Bull. XXXIV, 53.
33 Russell, in BAE, XXVI, 253-254.

34 Best, in AAAS, 1904, 447; and in AAAS, 1898, 775.
35 Hewitt, in HAI, I, 384.
36 Parsons, in AA, XVIII, 255.

utensils which will not speedily be broken. Owls are of evil portent and may indicate sickness, death, the presence of an as yet unborn babe, or a birth. When walking along the pathway one must not mind if a species of black ant bites his foot, because this means that he will obtain something very good and satisfying. It is considered a bad omen if either tree planted by parents when contracting for the marriage of their young children should happen to wither, as in that case the party represented by it is sure to die.[37] Among the Araucanians, "if vultures followed the route of a war party, many of the number would return home, considering slaughter and defeat as inevitable. A fox, crossing the path of a similar party, indicated, by the way it took, the fate of the undertaking. If it passed to the left, they returned home, assured of the uselessness of proceeding. If on the other hand it turned to the right they were convinced of their triumph."[38]

Interrogation. In New Guinea the wooden ancestor-figures are directly questioned; any movement of the figures conveys refusal. This is almost direct worship rather than specific divination.[39] Among the Amaxosa, "the common man carries his 'tollus' [charms] about with him in a leather pouch, and questions them with great care" as to where his comrades are, whither his cattle have run, or where the nearest water is to be found; sticks are thrown on the ground in divination.[40] In South Africa "bones are thrown" on a number of occasions, to see what the spirits say.[41] Divining tablets are common among the Bantu; each family has a set, and the use of dice is common.[42] In Togo there is an effort to find out what luck the coming year will bring; all the men stand about a special tree, and as the name of each is called out, a splinter is struck from the trunk. If it falls on the ground bark-side up, it is bad luck; if the other way, good. Similar divination takes place with cowrie-shells.[43] In the Niger region, *juju* is performed before beginning house-building, fishing, fighting, boat-building, or other undertaking, and before child-birth.[44] In Angola some tribes divine by the use of knotted strings; different combinations of the knots, as seven pieces of string are wound round the thumb, reveal coming events.[45] Again, a tree is planted at the settlement of a village; if it keeps green and buds, the place will be prosperous; if not, they leave hastily, to seek better prospects elsewhere.[46] In Unyoro fowls are kept in cages, not for food but for auguries.[47]

The Niam-Niam have several rather delicate devices for divination; they use, for instance, a smooth-topped stool, over which, when slightly wet, a smooth block is rubbed. "If the wood should glide easily along, the conclusion is that the undertaking will prosper; if the motion is obstructed and the surfaces adhere together, if according to the Niam-Niam expression a score of men cannot give free movement to the block, the warning is unmistakable that the adventure will prove a failure. . . . A way of trying fortune consists in seizing a cock and ducking its head repeatedly under water until the creature is stiff and senseless. Then it is left to itself. If it rallies, the omen is favorable;

37 Roth, in BAE, XXX, 233, 257, 274, 275, 277.
38 Latcham, in JAI, XXXIX, 350.
39 Krieger, *Neu-Guinea*, 402.
40 Fritsch, *S.-Afr.*, 105.
41 Garbutt, in JAI, XXXIX, 541 ff.
42 Bent, *Mashonaland*, 37; Bartels, "Würfel," in *Ztsft. f. Ethnol*, XXXV, 338 ff.
43 Klose, *Togo*, 302, 344.
44 Granville and Roth, in JAI, XXVIII, 110.
45 Bastian, *Deut. Exped.*, II, 38-39, note.
46 Frobenius, *Masken*, 165.
47 Stuhlmann, *Mit Emin*, 619.

but if it should succumb they look for adverse issue."[48] These people go through a rather elaborate ceremony of poisoning two fowls. "The man who is questioning the oracle makes an incantation somewhat to the following effect: 'Benge, tell me true! If this fowl die and this one live, the road is safe.' Then he addresses the fowls, 'You die!' he exhorts the one. 'You live!' he says to the other, and the result is watched with anxiety. Should the effect of the poison be different to that wished for, he will postpone his project or take another path."[49] If an Awemba child dies, the husband blames the wife, saying that the child has died because she has committed adultery. "If she denies this they resort to the hunting test. The husband goes out and fixes nets for game. If the game caught is a female it is the woman's fault, but if it is a male the husband is to blame."[50] In one African district two travellers were not allowed to see the chief till the signs had been consulted. "A goat was brought forward, both parties expectorated freely upon its head, and incantations were mumbled over it. A triangular piece of skin was cut from its forehead, much to the animal's distress; this was divided into strips and a slit cut in each. One of these strips was placed upon the middle finger of each of us by a prominent native, whom, in turn, we ornamented in a similar manner. After this the goat was killed and the entrails examined. The signs being pronounced favorable, we then proceeded to his majesty's presence."[51] In the Sahara region, a knot is tied in an elastic plant with the idea of testing a wife's faithfulness; if it remains tied she is faithful, if it is found untied, she is not.[52]

The Chukchi practise divination on the bodies of the dead; the head is lifted without effort if the answer to some question is affirmative.[53] In a Mongolian temple is the impression in sandstone of a human foot, which is examined, after a payment, to ascertain luck. If it is good, bright spots are supposed to appear on the surface of the stone in the footmark.[54] Cords, each representing several degrees of lucky and unlucky portents are used in Tibet; "the best out of three draws is held to decide the luck of the proposed undertaking, or the ultimate result of the sickness or the other question of fortune sought after."[55] The Nagas use the pancreas of a pig for auspices; it must be clear red, clean and smooth; if black, discolored, crinkled, or turned up at the edge, it foretells misfortune. Fowls also are used.[56] Auguries of good and bad luck are obtained in Madras from the speed with which the new rice comes to a boil.[57] An elaborate Hindu ceremonial determines whether a pregnant woman's first child will be a boy or a girl.[58] There is a Tamil treatise on house-building ceremonial. It descends to the most minute particulars as to the portents attending every step of the process, the lucky and unlucky time for every operation.[59] A bride selected one of eight balls of earth to find out what her wifely character is to be.[60] "Necromancy, or divination by communication with the spirits of the dead, is practiced in India today. A young boy is used as a medium, and is expected to see the future in a disc of lampblack. . . . The invoked spirit is then asked if he wants anything, and

---

48 Schweinfurth, *Heart of Afr.*, II, 32, 33; Junker, *Afr.*, II, 313-314, 472.
49 Burrows, in JAI, XXVIII, 43-44.
50 Sheane, in JAI, XXXVI, 156.
51 Abbott, in USNM, 1891, 395.
52 Pommerol, *Sahariennes*, 255, 259.
53 Bogoras, in AA, III, 95.
54 Rockhill, *Mongolia*, 69.

55 Waddell, *Tibet*, 465.
56 Furness, in JAI, XXXII, 464.
57 "Pongal, O Pongal" (anon.), in JASB, II, 305 ff.
58 Husain, in JASB, III, 143, 144.
59 Gomme, *Folklore*, 60.
60 Hopkins, *Relig. India*, 270.

any wants he may express are duly attended to. It is remarkable how closely this procedure resembles that described in the first book of Samuel."[61]

In Japan "there was divination by bones, by birds, by mice, by barley-gruel, by footprints, by rods planted in the ground, and by listening in public ways to the speech of people passing by." There were "strips of paper which pilgrims to Buddhist shrines chew into pellets, and then spit out at the Ni-o, or gigantic images of the guardian deities of the temples. If the pellet sticks, the pilgrim's prayer will be heard. If not, the prayer will not be heard."[62] The Ainos keep skulls to ward off evil and for consultation concerning lost and stolen property. The skull is offered drink, then held in both hands while a prayer is spoken. The under jaw is then placed on the head and the consulting party bows till it falls—toward the place where the property is. If it falls on its side or teeth down, there is no answer and the proceeding must be repeated.[63] In Korea twelve beans are enclosed in a bamboo and lowered into the well for the night. "Each bean represents a month. In the morning, when examined in rotation, they are variously enlarged, the enlargement indicating the proportion of rain in that special moon. If, on the other hand, one or more are wizened, it causes great alarm, as indicating complete or partial drought during one or more months."[64]

Divination from the bones of fowls is very popular among the primitive peoples of Farther India and even with the Chinese. As among the Greeks, the oracles are ambiguous and may be explained in more than one way; "as the circumstances of the case are generally known to the soothsayer, who, as doctor and wise man in the village, is generally a shrewd and far-seeing person, he probably translates the oracle to suit the requirements of the case."[65] The process of divination in the Malay Peninsula is accompanied by musical rhythm, incense-burning, and incantation. The spirit gives evidence of its presence by possessing someone, who falls down unconscious; while in this state of possession, questions are put to him.[66]

It was the common belief of the American Indians that dreams or visions must be sought through the observance of some rite involving more or less personal privation; an exception is found in the Mohave who believe that the dream seeks the individual, coming to him before birth or during infancy, as well as in mature life. "Forecasting the future was deemed possible by means of artificially induced visions. The skin of a freshly killed animal, or one that had been well soaked for the purpose, was wound around the neck of a man until the gentle pressure on the veins caused insensibility, then in a vision he saw the place toward which his party was going and all that was to take place was prefigured. In some tribes a skin kept for this special purpose was held sacred and was used for divining by means of an induced vision."[67] Among the Indians of Ecuador, "those preparing for the feud never omit to first consult the spirits, who will let them know whether in the planned attack they will be successful or not." This divination is carried out through drinking the narcotic maikoa. "The Indian for this purpose retires to the forest, where he remains for three days and three nights, fasting strictly and sleeping in a small 'dreaming ranch.'"[68]

---

61 Dymock, in JASB, I, 17.
62 Hearn, Japan, 167; Chamberlain, in JAI, XXII, 357.
63 Hitchcock, in USNM, 1890, 474.
64 Bishop, Korea, 266.
65 Milne, Eastern Clan, 270, 249.

66 Skeat and Blagden, Malay Penin., II, 307.
67 Fletcher, "Dreams," in HAI, I, 400.
68 Karsten, "Jibaro," in BAE, Bull. LXXIX, 17.

Questioning of the future took various forms among the Homeric Greeks. "Belief in the prophetic nature of dreams was very strong, though less implicit than in other methods of prophecy. The dream was a shadowy creature, sent by one or other of the gods, generally Zeus, which assumed the form of some well-known person; it stood at the head of the sleeper and spoke the will of the deity; or it prophesied or acted in such manner that an omen could easily be drawn." Birds were frequently employed in divination: "Be not a bird of ill omen to me."[69] Siegfried understands the birds when Fafnir's blood has fallen on his tongue. Many examples may be found among the ancient Scandinavians of divination by the shoulder-blade of an animal; it was warmed until it cracked and the direction of the fissures noted.[70] The pre-Mohammedan Arabs cast lots on important occasions.[71] Among the Montenegrins of today "a woman can tell if her child will be a boy or a girl by throwing a dried fish bladder on the fire. If it go off pop there will be a boy; if it only fizzles out, a girl." Needless to say, "there are great rejoicings when a boy is born and great disappointment over a girl."[72] Survivals of divination may be seen today in the reported attempts to locate a drowned person by means of bread thrown in the water—a method described in Mark Twain's *Huckleberry Finn*—and to find a lost child by placing a lock of his hair in a tube held in the searcher's mouth.[73]

§268. Religious Nature of the Taboo.

Notions of ritual uncleanness, which must be offset by ritual operations, have been a very important part of the mores. The conviction that women, at the periods, are unclean and dangerous is almost universal amongst nature people.[1] Child-birth also produces uncleanness of the mother. A third case is death. Corpses are unclean and make all those unclean who have anything to do with them. There are numerous and various other trifling causes of ritual uncleanness, all of which involve the taboo.

The Bechuana negroes, when they have touched a corpse, dug a grave, or are near relatives of a deceased person, purify themselves by prescribed ritual washings, put on new garments, and cut the hair, or purify themselves with the smoke of a fire in which magic-working materials have been cast. On returning from battle they ceremonially wash themselves and their weapons.[2] Without this process of purification, they would be unclean, unholy, taboo. In Madagascar no one who had been at a funeral might enter the palace or approach the sovereign for a month and no corpse might be buried in the capital city. The mourners wash their clothing, or dip a portion of it in running water, as a ritual cleansing.[3] The Tamils think that saliva renders ritually unclean whatever it touches; therefore, in drinking, they pour the liquid down the throat without touching the cup to the lips.[4] Pious Zoroastrians could not travel by sea without great inconvenience because they could not help defiling the natural element, water, a thing which they were forbidden to do. They were also forbidden to blow a fire with the breath, lest they should defile the element, fire,

---

69 Homer, *Iliad*, XXIV, 218-219; Keller, *Hom. Soc.*, 150, 152, 156 ff.
70 Olsen, *Primitivt Folk*, 142.
71 Procksch, *Blutrache*, 50.
72 Durham, in JAI, XXXIX, 94-95.

73 N. Y. *Times*, Sept. 15, 1926; N. Y. *World*, Feb. 23, 24, 1927.
1 §389, of the text.
2 Fritsch, *Eingeb. Süd-Afr.*, 201.
3 Sibree, *Great Afr. Isl.*, 290.
4 Gehring, *Süd-Indien*, 96.

and wore a cover over the mouth on approaching fire for any purpose. Parings of nails and cuttings of hair were unclean; they were weapons for demons unless protected by rites and spells.[5] The Greeks had the same conceptions of ritual uncleanness. Marriage was surrounded by rites of purification or precaution. Death and the dead produced uncleanness and purification by water, fire, or smoke was required.[6]

Letourneau[7] cites many cases to illustrate the survival-value of the taboo in developing restraint and discipline and in serving utilitarian ends, as the taboo on chickens and pigs when scarce and other "game laws." Instances of this nature will be mentioned below, as well as others which bring out the religious nature of the taboo.

Taboo-signs among the Koita indicate magical protection of the objects to which they apply; they are trustworthy safeguards, and "it is certainly to the fear of the results of infringing their magical properties, that their efficacy is primarily due."[8] Before the yam-feasts in New Guinea and New Britain, the principal chief, after certain ceremonies, ties a piece of prepared fiber round the posts of the yam-houses. "This makes them taboo, and no one can touch them"; they have become the property of the spirits.[9]

The sanctity of the taboo and its societal value are indicated in the following quotation regarding the natives of East Africa. "If space allowed of a closer study of native life we should see that the individual is constantly menaced by malignant spirits, the propitiation of which is not merely by sacrifices and charms; not only is the native called upon to perform certain acts and refrain from others, but the detail of many acts is of the highest importance. . . . Breaches of custom not directly connected with law often bring their own punishment, which is the anger of an offended spirit, and is manifested by a sore disease which breaks out all over the body. This is called *makwa*, the direct cause being a breach of custom. The elders . . . know best the cause, and they also know its cure. This they will effect by many curious performances, but it is clear that before they can do so they must question the sufferer about all that he has done, in order that they may diagnose the cause; thus an open confession is essential. This fact gives a great value to the belief in *makwa*, for however secretly a breach of custom may have been committed, it will not fail to require an open confession. The disease designated as *makwa* is invariably venereal, and is now often cured by medical treatment—particularly by certain missionaries, to whom even Akikuyu flock for treatment. The practical result of this may be good, but indirectly it is bad, because the public confession is evaded, and the moral restraint of the belief is in consequence destroyed."[10]

The expression *genna* (taboo) is loosely used to cover both the Sema words *chini* and *pini*. *Chini* means "is forbidden" and is used of any taboo. Thus a man may say that he is *chini,* meaning that for the time being he is unable to speak to strangers, or to anyone at all, or to be addressed by anyone. Again, some action may be *chini* or forbidden. In addition to the regular and recurring agricultural *gennas* there are a number of others observed by the whole village, which occur from time to time according to circumstances—

5 Müller, *Sacred Books*, IV, pt. I, XXXIV.
6 Rohde, *Psyche*, II, 72; Guhl und Koner, *Leben der Griechen*, 367.
7 *Morale*, 173 ff.

8 Seligmann, *Melanesians*, 136, 138.
9 Brown, in AAAS, 1898, 795.
10 Dundas, C., in JAI, XLV, 242-243.

gennas for making peace or war, for repairing the village defenses, or at the birth of some monstrosity. The situation is similar in Assam.[11]

A variety of religious prohibitions occur among the Nagas of India. It appears that a place or person under supernatural displeasure becomes taboo, "the spiritual infection extending even to the clothes of the household." We have seen that the victims of accident are regarded as sealed to the daimons; in India the taboo descends at large upon the family. "Should any member of a household be killed by a tiger, by drowning, by falling from a tree, or by being crushed by a falling tree, the surviving members of the household abandon the house, which is wrecked, and the whole of their property, down to the very clothes they are wearing, and leave the village naked, being supplied outside the village with just enough clothing to cover their nakedness by some old man amongst their relations. Thenceforth for a month they are condemned to wander in the jungle. At the expiration of this period, the wrath of the deity being supposed to be appeased, they are allowed to return to the village. Neither they nor anyone else can touch again any of the abandoned property, nor can a fresh house be built on the site of the old one that has been abandoned." Again, a household taboo occurs at the birth of a child, or if a domestic animal brings forth young; on such occasions no outsider may enter the house, and food and drink may not be given even to intimate friends. A British official was refused a drink at a house because the house-dog had pups. Of course a period of taboo on labor means a village holiday; an accidental death, or fire in the village, puts the whole community under taboo. "In like manner before commencing either to sow or to reap, an universal tabu has to be undergone, and is accompanied by propitiatory offerings to their several deities, and no man dare commence work before. If their crops have been suffering from the attacks of wild animals, a 'kennie' is the remedy—in fact there is no end to the reasons why a 'kennie' must or may be declared, and as it consists of a general holiday when no work is done, this Angami sabbath appears to be rather a popular institution."[12]

In Cochin China, before an expedition after aloe-wood the village head sacrifices to the ancestors and the guardian spirits of the aloe. He and all the rest must refrain from sex-relations and from eating a specified fish, and their relatives who remain must not quarrel or use cross words.[13]

Wilken[14] cites many cases to prove that "pamali" stands in close relation with religion; and that if it seems on the face of it not to do so, yet its origin will be found in ghost-fear. Taboos are of all places and times; of certain times and conditions; of certain places; for a whole people; or for one or more particular persons. The taboo on names, particularly on one's own, upon that of a father-in-law, parent, or chief, leads to prohibitions of words sounding like certain names; this leads to a multiplication of terms for the same thing, circumlocutions, and change in language. Flesh of animals which are the residence of departed souls is tabooed. Euphemisms form a method of reference to a feared beast, such as the tiger, which is called "the noble one" or "the kind one," much as the Greeks called the Furies the Eumenides. The East Indies show a full set of taboos at pregnancy, birth, sickness, and sacrifice;

---

11 Hutton, *Sema Nagas*, 220, 226; Hudson, in JAI, XXXVI, 96, 99

12 Godden, in JAI, XXVI, 191 ff.; and in XXVII, 33; Furness, in JAI, XXXII, 465-466.

13 Niemann, in *Bijd.*, XLV, 335.

14 *Vkde.*, 596 ff.; Lippert, *Kgchte.*, I, 118-121, 390.

there is a cessation of labor and of moving about. When certain places, rivers, or trees are *pamali,* it means that they are regarded as haunts of the ghosts of ancestors. No noise may be made near them and if one goes by he must beg pardon of the spirit domiciled in them. No hunting or fishing may be done there. If fish are scarce, the taboo is laid and coconut-milk is cast into the sea while calling on the spirits. A property-mark, being a taboo, is respected with fear. The religious nature of the taboo is also seen in the use by the Alfurs of the terms *poto* and *koin,* which are synonymous with prohibited and holy, consecrated, inviolable. *Poto* is stronger than *koin;* of it no transgression is thinkable. Against *koin* sin is often committed, sometimes intentionally, for a person can always make good by small sacrifices and thus escape punishment, which is mainly sickness. It is *poto* to speak the names of parents or parents-in-law. When the names are the same as or sound like the names of living or dead objects, then the Alfur must always use for the latter other explanatory words. To a younger brother it is *poto* to look at the mouth of the wife of his older brother while she is eating; if there are many young brothers of her husband in the house, the woman covers her face with a cloth when so engaged. To a woman it is *poto* to marry within forty days after the death of her husband; this time is called the "days of the dead." It is *poto* to sell of the newly harvested rice before the communal sacrificial meal has taken place.[15] It is significant that the sacred color, red, was used by the Maori to taboo an object. The house of death was thus colored; a red post was set up as a sign of a taboo's presence; and grave-marks were sure to be red.[16]

While the origin of some of the Eskimo taboos is obscure, their very seeming-whimsicality points to the irrational and daimonistic. "It is forbidden, after the death of a sea-mammal or after the death of a person, to scrape the frost from the window, to shake the beds, or disturb the shrubs under the bed, to remove oil-drippings from under the lamp, to scrape hair from skins, to cut snow for the purpose of melting it, to work on iron, wood, stone, or ivory. Women are forbidden to comb their hair, to wash their faces, and dry their boots and stockings."[17] In Pawnee lodges there hang sacred bundles of unknown contents, black with smoke and age, in the neighborhood of which it is forbidden to put a knife in the fire, or throw a knife, or enter the lodge with the face painted or with feathers in the hair. "On certain sacred occasions the bundles are opened, and their contents form part of the ceremonial of worship."[18] It is a rule among the Apache that for the first four times one of their young men goes on the war-path he must not scratch his head with his fingers or let water touch his lips. To keep this rule and at the same time avoid discomfort, he makes use of the scratch-stick and sucks water into his throat by means of a tiny tube called a drinking-reed. "A long leather cord attached both stick and reed to the warrior's belt and to each other."[19] Among the Guiana Indians children are discouraged from picking up certain feathers as these tend to weaken memory or may conduce to insanity. In the case of the Pomeroon Arawaks, "when an animal is killed with an arrow-trap or a gun-trap, its flesh has to be cooked in a pot without a cover, over a fire that it not too large, so as to avoid any water boiling over. Were either of these

15 Wilken, in VG, I, 55-60.
16 Taylor, *Te Ika,* 209.
17 Boas, in PSM, LVII, 628; Holm, *Eth. Skizze,* 63.
18 Grinnell, *Folk Tales,* 35.
19 Bourke, in BAE, IX, 490.

matters not attended to, there would be no further use either for the arrow or for the gun, as all the game of the same kind as that recently trapped would take its departure to another region." The power of the taboo in these sections is very great, death being the penalty for violation. On the upper Rio Negro the sacred trumpets are such a mystery that no woman may ever see them. "When the sound of them is heard approaching, every woman retires into the woods, or into some adjoining shed which they generally have near, and remains invisible till after the ceremony is over, when the instruments are taken away to their hiding-place, and the women come out of their concealment. Should any female be supposed to have seen them, either by accident or design, she is invariably executed, generally by poison, and a father will not hesitate to sacrifice his daughter, or a husband his wife, on such an occasion."[20]

There are many taboos mentioned in the Old Testament, the most famous being that laid upon the tree of knowledge. Uncleanness was the reason for a number of taboos, as applying chiefly to the dead, to sexual intercourse, menstruation, and leprosy. Everything which belonged to Jahweh or was used in his service was also taboo, while the priests, as Jahweh's servants, were rendered taboo through certain rites.[21] A member of the Jewish sect of the Essenes, who were all celibate men, always wore an apron, even when alone in the bath; for the genitals were impure and must not be uncovered to the eye of God.[22] Shoes could not well be washed, unless they were mere linen stockings; they were therefore put off before treading on holy ground.[23]

One author "ascribes in great part to the tabu system the loyalty, probity, and courtesy of the Japanese, and their close observance of the forms of natural objects and historic scenes evinced by their art and literature."[24]

§270. The Industrial Taboo.

In West Africa, different vocations have different days upon which no work may be done: thus, Tuesday is a rest day for fishermen and Friday for farmers.[1] In Togo, "two days in the week, Sunday and Wednesday, are sacred to the fetish. Nobody may go into the fields on these days and perform plantation labor. These days are also and at the same time market-days. All the people are at home; buying and selling are allowed to them, likewise domestic labors. On Monday and Tuesday as well, special areas of the farms are not worked, because the fetish consecrates these areas on those days. A transgression of these commands is sternly censured, and in addition the transgressor draws down on himself the curse of the gods: he is persecuted by scarcity of crops and ill luck of all sorts. Thursday, Friday, and Saturday are . . . really full labor-days, on which good work must be done."[2] The Galla, like the Abyssinians, keep two Sundays, Saturday and Sunday, the heathen Galla consecrating Sunday to their great god. The nomadic part of them, however, keep no special day, because herdsmen can keep any day.[3]

20 Roth, in BAE, XXX, 276, 295, 138.
21 Levit., XI-XV; Ex., XXIX, 37; XXX, 29; Maurer, in Globus, CX, 136-137, 138.
22 Lucius, Essenismus, 62.
23 Smith, Relig. Sem., 453; Ex., III, 5; Jos., V, 15.

24 Minakata, Tabu in Japan (review in JAI, XXVIII, 187); Kishimoto, in PSM, XLVI, 213.
1 Ellis, Tshi, 220.
2 Fies, in Globus, LXXX, 382.
3 Ratzel, Vkde., I, 439.

In Madagascar, prior to 1869, "every idol had a day sacred to it, on which day those who were especially its votaries abstained from work."[4]

The case of the Yakuts, among whom the household of the deceased is not permitted to do any work until after the next new moon,[5] recalls a prominent detail of the ghost-cult which is also classifiable under taboo. In February there occurs in India a festival in honor of the goddess of learning. "In case any writing has to be done on this day, it is done with chalk, not with the pens, 'which have a complete holiday.' "[6] In Assam, during the communal *gennas* (taboos) for the crops, all trade, fishing, hunting, and other activities are forbidden.[7]

In Borneo, a "lali" lasts ten days, during which feasting occurs and "no one is permitted to do a stroke of work that resembles the cultivation of rice; a parang or a billiong, or any tool used in felling the jungle, is a strictly lali article; should any restless creature express a desire for active work, he is scoffed at and scorned as a spoil-sport and kill-joy."[8] Evidently with the weakening of its sanction, the solemnity and strictness of the taboo are here on the wane. There is a "lali" for four days when ground for a plantation is selected; no stranger may enter the house and no dweller in it who has been absent one night. Members of the household do not carry out any extensive work, and do not use an axe. Then come three days of labor and four more of "lali"; then, after ten days, four more are tabooed, after which the work begins for good. In each moon there are several unfavorable days, during which "it is especially undesirable to build or repair houses or boats; for these would be possessed by an evil spirit which would cause the house to burn down or blow over and the boat to capsize, to break against the rocks, or to drift away from its rattan hawser."[9]

No stranger may enter the Borneo paddy-fields for several days; the public path frequently passes through them, but during the "pamali," a detour must be made. The existence of the taboo is made known by a bunch of dried palm leaves or other conventional sign, placed in a conspicuous position at all the entrances of the forbidden farm. The same practice is used when sickness is in the house, or for the preservation of fruit-trees or other property from interference by the general public. If a Dyak is asked to do anything contrary to custom, he invariably answers that it is "pamali."[10] If the basket in which paddy is put as it is cut during harvest be upset, that farm must rest for a day and a fowl must be killed, or all their paddy will be rotten.[11]

In northern Celebes, "when a man dies who has been accustomed to fish in any particular place, that place is often declared to be holy. It is given over to the dead, in order that his ghost may come and fish there as he did when alive. It is 'tabu,' as they say in the South Sea Islands, or 'pilah,' " according to the people here referred to. This taboo reflects typical ideas of projectivism and practices of the ghost-cult. It has also distinct social consequences, for "if any one is seen by the family of the deceased to go there in a canoe, or to fish there, he is at once brought before the rajah and becomes a slave of the family of the deceased."[12]

4 Sibree, *Great Afr. Isl.*, 281.
5 Sieroshevski, *Yakuts* (Russ.), 667.
6 Hopkins, *Relig. India*, 451.
7 Hodson, in JAI, XXXVI, 94, 101-102.
8 Furness, *Head-Hunters*, 165.

9 §255, of the text; Nieuwenhuis, *Borneo*, I, 178, II, 169.
10 Roth, in JAI, XXI, 136 (discussion by Low).
11 Roth, *Sarawak*, I, 401.
12 Hickson, in JAI, XVI, 142.

In New Zealand, "in former times, life in a great measure depended upon the produce of their cultivation, and it was therefore of the utmost importance that their kumara and taro should be planted at the proper season, and every other occupation be laid aside until that necessary work was accomplished; all, therefore, who were thus employed, were made tapu, so that they could not leave the place, or undertake any other work, until that was finished."[13] The author intends here to exhibit the essentially rational idea behind the taboo. Somewhat similar is the Tongan custom by which skilled handworkers become tabooed. But it is not reassuring for the case of rationality to find natives, as in Yap, allowed to raise bananas that they may not eat. In the Caroline Islands only those who have the proper training and designation may make the obscene figure set on the gable of the clubhouse; any other will die if he undertakes this task.[14] In the Bowditch Islands the death of the king was the occasion for the planting of coconuts; "if anyone planted them at other times he would die."[15]

A strict religious custom forbids the Eskimo to work on the deerskins which are obtained in summer before the ice has formed; they are only dried and tied up in large bundles. Among the Kwakiutl only old women are allowed to dig fern roots. Many taboos surround the canoe-builder. There are other taboos which forbid menstruating women, murderers, and mourners from performing certain kinds of work.[16] The Salish have a tradition that their ancestors used to observe a kind of Sabbath or seventh day ceremony long before they heard of the whites. "According to François and Mary Anne, the people used to come together every seventh day for dancing and praying" though it is "extremely improbable that the old-time Indians had any conception at all of a Supreme Being."[17] A sort of game law exists among the natives of Guiana. "If Indians hunt too many of one kind of game, the Bush Spirit of that particular animal may come and do them harm." The Indian must never himself bring into the house any game that he has caught, but leave it for his wife to carry in. "The reason given for this custom is that, were the food to be brought home direct by the man he would have bad luck in fishing or hunting on the next occasion."[18]

"The seventh day is the sabbath of the Lord thy God; in it thou shalt not do any work." The Hebrews borrowed the term and some of the ideas associated with it from the Assyrians and Babylonians. As a day of rest it was an adjustment characteristic of the agricultural stage, being unknown among any nomadic group. It was probably solely religious in origin.[19] In Rome anyone who did not cease labor on holy days was fined.[20]

§271. The Food-Taboo.

MANY food-taboos seem to be quite irrational. It is reported of the Tasmanians, for instance, that they "would rather starve than eat fish."[1] Some Australians will not eat pork.[2] The Australians eat worms, rotten eggs, and other things

13 Taylor, *Te Ika*, 165-166.
14 Ratzel, *Vkde.*, II, 196; Kubary, *Karolinen-arch.*, 244; Senfft, in *Globus*, XCI, 174.
15 Lister, in JAI, XXI, 54.
16 Boas, in BAE, VI, 578; and in BAE, XXXV, pt. I, 615-616; and in HAI, II, 368.
17 Hill-Tout, in JAI, XXXIV, 329.
18 Roth, in BAE, XXX, 292, 294-295.

19 Delitzsch, *Babel u. Bibel*, 22, 24; Maurer, *Vkde.*, I, 112, 113, 167, 170; Schrader, *Keilinschriften*, 592, 594; Grupp, *Kgchte.*, I, 439; Webster, *Rest Days*, 91, 235 ff.
20 De Marchi, *Culto Priv.*, rev. in *Année Soc.*, I, 18.
1 Roth, *Tasmanians*, 101.
2 Smyth, *Victoria*, I, 237.

of the sort and also plants which we reject because they taste badly or offer little nourishment; but on the other hand, they reject certain fish, molluscs, and fungi which we eat.[3] Totemic practices account for some food taboos. In Central Australia "the people of the emu totem very rarely eat the eggs unless very hungry and short of food, in which case they would eat, but not too abundantly." The same principle holds good through all totems.[4] Notions akin to imitative magic account for other food taboos: "No sooner does a boy begin to go about in the bush in search of food than he finds himself very considerably restricted as to what he may and may not eat. . . . Should he eat kangaroo tail or wild turkey, or its eggs, then he will become prematurely old; parrot or cocatoo flesh will cause the growth of a hollow on top of his head, and of a hole under his chin; large quail and its eggs cause the beard and whiskers not to grow; any part of the eaglehawk other than the sinewy legs will produce leanness, though the strong legs are admirable, as they improve the growth of the same limb; in fact, to strengthen the limb, boys are often hit on the calf by the leg bone of an eaglehawk, strength passing from the one into the other. Should the podargus, or night jar, be eaten then the boy's mouth will acquire a wide gape."[5]

Some Melanesians will not eat eels. There are ghosts in them.[6] In a book dealing with native life in Florida of the Solomon group "an old native is represented as horror-struck at the sight of dark blue trousers, because some part of the inside of the shark, of a dark-blue colour, was a forbidden thing to his family. . . . In the island of Aurora, in the New Hebrides, mothers sometimes have a fancy, before the birth of a child, that the infant is connected in its origin with a cocoanut or breadfruit, or some such object, a connection which the natives express by saying that the children are a kind of echo of such things. The child, therefore, is taught not to eat that in which it has had it origin, and is told, what the mothers entirely believe, that to eat it will bring disease."[7] Rivers[8] mentions a large number of animals which are not eaten, including the shark, the sea eel, and the octopus, but in every case a definite motive was given for the abstinence. "Thus, the shark is not eaten because it is believed that those who eat it would be caught by a shark when in the sea, and the eel is avoided because it is believed to be poisonous. Further, it seemed clear that the abstinence is observed by the whole population, and is in no way different for the members of the different social groups." In some sections a taboo is placed on coconuts. "A *tapu* is only imposed when the trees are not bearing well and is usually maintained till the nuts which have dropped from the trees have begun to sprout and are ready to be transplanted. The general *tapu* imposed by the chief of the Tafua on coconuts is but one example of a wide-spread practice among the Tikopians. Any chief may *tapu* a special place in order that the trees may grow to a proper size before the fruit is taken and anyone can initiate such a *tapu* which is later confirmed by a chief." Among the Roro-speaking tribes, there are special functionaries who alone have the power of pronouncing the most dreaded, and consequently the most rigorously observed, form of taboo on vegetable food. They are in fact taboo experts, and the office is hereditary. Among the Elema tribes the name for these men and the masks they wear is *harihu.* "The sign that a garden

---

3 Ratzel, *Vkde.,* II, 54.
4 Spencer and Gillen, *Nat. Tr. Cent. Aust.,* 202, note.
5 Gillen, in AAAS, 1901, 112.

6 Codrington, *Melanesians,* 177.
7 Codrington, in AAAS, 1890, 612, 613.
8 *Melan. Soc.,* I, 177, 318-319.

is tabooed is a small stone of a special shape placed at the entrance to the garden. It has on it certain 'private marks' of the *hurihu,* to tamper with which would render the offender liable to instant death."[9]

One tribe of African Bushmen will not eat goats, though they are the most numerous of the local domestic animals. The Hottentots share the general South African prejudice against fish to the extent of disdaining all those without scales. "As a rule . . . all the South African Bantu peoples abhor the eating of fish, which animals they call 'watersnakes' and avoid even touching them. Many eschew also the eating of pork but this does not occur so generally and not with the fanaticism shown in the rejection of fish," which are tabooed even by the tribes living near rivers.[10] Among the Zulus, bananas are reserved as a royal food.[11]

The following foods are prohibited to the cowmen of the Bahima: "any part of goat, sheep, or fowls; among vegetables, peas, beans and potatoes. To eat these and at the same time to drink milk would endanger the life of the cow from which the milk comes, and her calf."[12] Social distinctions account for some of the food-taboos of the Atharaka: "wild birds and fowls are not eaten except by uncircumcized children; eggs are not eaten by anyone. The reason that they give is that the circumcized people wish to make a distinction in the matter of diet between themselves and the uncircumcized. I suspect the existence of some other reason. Fish is not eaten by anyone; however, I am told that there is no prohibition, but that a man would be sick if he did so. Wild animals, cattle, sheep, and goats are all eaten by the Atharaka, but each person according to his sex, rank, relationship, and position in the village has his particular portion. The elder of the village eats the head, the heart, the front leg, and the spleen. The latter must not be boiled, but roasted, and eaten in company with other elders of the same standing as himself."[13] The Ba-Yaka of West Africa do not use milk as food.[14] In the Upper Congo, "milk was tabued by all and regarded with great abhorrence. Anyone drinking it was considered unclean for several days and was not allowed to eat with his family. They could touch milk, for they milked our goats and sheep, and carried it to us without suffering defilement, but it must not touch their lips. A boy of mine was known to have drunk some milky water out of a glass, and he was not permitted to eat with his family for five days. They could give no reason for this, but only stated it was their custom." Taboos among the Bangala in this region apply even to the manner of drinking; the author cites a number of examples. "All these various modes of drinking are rigidly followed out of regard to the strict injunctions of some *nganga* or medicine man, who has told them that in order to prevent the return of a sickness from which they have suffered or to escape some disease they must drink in such and such a manner or not at all." The only fish that all the natives refused to eat was the electric fish. "Nearly all fish were tabu to one person or another, and in very rare instances I have known persons not allowed to eat any kind of fish, they were all tabued." Food-taboos here have affected the methods of marketing, as is brought out in the significant quotation which follows: "If the

9 Seligmann, *Melanesians*, 299-301.
10 Ratzel, *Vkde.*, I, 73; Fritsch, *Eingeb. S. Afr.*, 325, 107; Conder, in JAI, XVI, 82; Macdonald, in JAI, XIX, 279 and XX, 138.
11 Tyler, in *Illust. Afr.*, for Nov., 1895.

12 Roscoe, in JAI, XXXVII, 111.
13 Champion, in JAI, XLII, 81.
14 Torday and Joyce, in JAI, XXXVI, 42.

owner of an animal wished to sell the flesh in open market the skin was not taken off, but the animal so cut up that a piece of skin was left on each portion. The buyer could then see the kind of animal flesh there was for sale, and would know for a certainty whether it was tabooed to him or not."[15]

On the lower Congo, when a famine threatens, it is forbidden to collect palm-fruit under penalty of death.[16] In Togo individual taboos arise out of vows in honor of a chosen fetish, at marriage, for instance, and are strictly observed through life; and there are general restrictions, especially on widows, who may not for the first six weeks of mourning eat beans, meat, or fish, or drink palm-wine or rum. If they do, the departed husband gets power over them and at once hales them away to the spirit-world. "During menstruation women may not drink milk, lest the cattle die." Members of a certain society may not drink the rain-water that flows from the roof. "The head of a household never quite finishes what he has on his plate, and the eldest son is the only one who can do it for him." Of these many taboos, a number "are laid solely with the object that they shall remain quite often unnoticed, in order thereby to give into the priest's hand a ready means of dragging light-minded sinners to punishment."[17]

The yam-customs of the Gold Coast represent both "a thanksgiving to the fetishes for allowing their people to live to see the new yams, and for the new yams, but they are also institutions to prevent the general public eating the new yam before it is ready. The idea is, no doubt rightly, that unripe yams are unwholesome, and the law is that no new yams must be eaten until the yam custom is made. The fetish-men settle when the yams are in a fit state to pass into circulation, and then make the custom." It is thought to be very perilous to eat of the new crop prior to that time. In Calabar the taboo on a certain food is called "ibet" and attaches to individuals; if one buys a slave he always inquires as to the slave's "ibet," for if he were given his "ibet" to eat he would fall ill. A person's "ibet" is discovered by magic shortly after his birth and he has to keep to it. In New Calabar the bull was at one time worshipped, but fresh beef was "ju-ju" until recently. The negroes of the French Congo "have a perfect horror of the idea of drinking milk, holding this custom to be a filthy habit, and saying so in unmitigated language. . . . Among Congo Français tribes certain rites are performed for children during infancy or youth, in which a prohibition is laid upon the child as regards the eating of some particular article of food, or the doing of certain acts. It is hard to get the exact object of the 'Orunda.' The prohibited article is not evil in itself, for others but the inhibited individual may eat or do with it as they please. Most of the natives blindly follow the custom without being able to give any reason, but from those best able to give a reason, you learn that the prohibited article is a sacrifice ordained for the child by its parents and the magic doctor as a gift to the governing spirit of its life. The thing prohibited becomes removed from the child's common use and is made sacred to the spirit." In one case a chief, "when given a glass of rum, had a piece of cloth held before his mouth that people might not see him drink. This was his Orunda."[18] One of these Africans said he did not dare eat of a fowl, as it was *orunda* to him;

15 Weeks, in JAI, XXXIX, 103, 115, 116-117, 119-120
16 Lippert, *Kgchte.*, I, 248.

17 Seidel, in *Globus*, LXXIII, 356-358; Ratzel, *Vkde.*, I, 614.
18 Kingsley, *W. Afr. Studies*, 174, 450, 451, 455, 456, 516.

another's *orunda* was that when on a journey by water his food should be eaten only over water.[19]

Thcre are numerous food-taboos among the natives of South Cameroons. If, for example, a person is healed through medicine which the priest has made from fowl, he may never eat fowl again. Leopards' flesh is interdicted because, according to tradition, a native woman once gave birth to leopards. Parents may forbid their children to eat certain foodstuffs, and these taboos hold as long as the former are alive.[20] On the Loango coast various foods are set before a child, and the one to which he shows aversion is, from that time on, his "xina" or "quixilles." Goat is not eaten lest the skin scale off; nor chickens, lest the hair fall out; nor birds, lest one's descendants be born with crooked feet. Not a few negroes eat nothing at all that has blood and life. Chiefs refrain, in some localities, from wild meat or pork.[21] The Banziri of the Congo basin eat dog-meat with great relish but it is "rigorously forbidden to the women, who have no part in preparing the dish. They believe, or affect to believe, that it would make women sick. So rigorously is the prohibition kept, that the Banziris wash themselves carefully after eating dog before touching a woman, if only with the tips of their fingers."[22]

In Borku, with circumcision "ceases the privilege of eating chickens and other fowls, fish, and eggs," foods regarded as improper for men.[23] Chickens are held in abomination by the Gallas and other tribes to the east. Wild meat is disdained and eaten only in need; this seems to be due to the prevalence of domesticated cattle and the lack of weapons with which the best wild animals could be brought down. Birds and fish are not eaten by the higher classes, though the rivers and lakes are full of fine fish. The Somal have a proverb: "Speak not with the mouth that has eaten fish." Where fish are eaten, only those with white flesh are allowed.[24] Poultry is abjured elsewhere in East Africa as unwholesome and unmanly; since neither poultry nor eggs are eaten it is hard to say why they keep fowls. Some of the tribes near the Zanzibar coast have learned to eat fish when visiting the shores.[25] The Madagascar "fadi" is laid chiefly against pigs, the chief abomination; other forbidden animals are dogs, fowls, crocodiles, and snakes. Some of the most nourishing vegetables, as manioc-root, are tabooed by certain individuals or families.[26]

The old rule in East Africa was that a man could not drink liquor until he had a circumcised child, but times have changed and at the present day youths of all ages drink.[27] In Equatorial East Africa cow's milk is not drunk, it being regarded as robbery of the calf—probably a rationalization.[28] Among the Kikuyu *thahu* is a sort of ill luck or curse following upon certain acts, many of which seem largely arbitrary. "If a woman is milking a cow and the calf climbs up on her shoulders while she is so occupied, the calf is not allowed to suckle the cow again and is forthwith slaughtered; this is a case for the elders. The people of the village must not eat any of the meat, half is taken by the woman to her father and the other half is eaten by the elders." *Thahu*

19 Nassau, *Fetichism*, 79.
20 Conradt, in *Globus*, LXXXI, 353.
21 Bastian, *Deut. Exped.*, I, 183, 185-186; *cf.* II, 39, note.
22 Clozel, in PSM, XLIX, 675; Brunache, *Cent. Afr.*, 69.
23 Nachtigal, *Sahara*, II, 178, 179.
24 Paulitschke, *Nordost-Afr.*, I, 151, 155; II, 27.

25 Johnston, in JAI, XV, 13; Volkens, *Kilimandscharo*, 244; Stuhlmann, *Mit Emin*, 36, 81.
26 Ratzel, *Vkde.*, I, 521; Sibree, *Gt. Afr. Isl.*, 278-279.
27 Dundas, C., in JAI, XLV, 272, note.
28 Johnstone, in JAI, XXXII, 265.

is also called *thabu,* thus bearing a strange similarity to *tabu,* and "in many ways there is very little difference between *tabus* and *thabus* or *thahus.*"[29] The pastoral Masai not only do not fish in any of the lakes and rivers, but they regard fish as a most unwholesome food. The agricultural Masai obtain fish by trapping and spearing, and eat it in much the same way as do their Bantu neighbours. The agricultural Masai also keep a few fowls, and eat them, together with their eggs; but fowls and eggs are absolutely eschewed by the pastoral Masai, who never keep this domestic bird. Among the Bantu Kavirondo, women do not eat fowls, sheep, or goats, and are not allowed to drink milk as a beverage, though they may use it in a kind of soup mixed with flour or meat. "In some instances chiefs do not eat sheep or fowls. People of both sexes may eat the flesh of the serval cat, and many of them will eat leopard meat. They devour most other birds and beasts, except the lion, vulture, crowned crane, and marabou stork. It is easy to understand their rejecting the last-named bird as an article of diet, because it is as filthy a scavenger as the vulture. Their respect for the *crowned crane,* however, actually seems to be due to admiration for its beauty, and the bird is found in large numbers in the Kavirondo country, where it is practically protected." All these people, except perhaps those of Mount Elgon, are like the Masai in their love of blood as an article of food. "They periodically bleed their cattle, and drink the blood hot, or else mix it with porridge. The women of all these tribes do not eat fowls, and neither men nor women eat eggs. As amongst most negro races, the men feed alone, and the women eat after the men have done."[30]

The Tuareg nobles taboo the flesh of the camel and sheep, and abominate fish, birds, and eggs. The heart and intestines of animals are eaten only by men, the liver and kidneys by women.[31] The Dinka are said to be more particular than other tribes in the choice of their animal food. There are many creeping things, not rejected by the Bongo and Niam-Niam, which they loathe with utmost disgust. Crocodiles, iguanas, frogs, crabs, and mice they never touch; they use turtles for making soup. The cannibalism of the Niam-Niam excites horror among them. Nothing is more repulsive to them than dog's flesh, which is enjoyed by the Mittoo. Dinka as well as Bongo have declared to the writer in the most decided manner that they would rather die than eat the flesh of a dog.[32] There are many "don'ts" connected with cooking among the Hausa, for not only the eating but also the preparation of food is dangerous. "It is not only the food which has to be considered. If your totem is a tree, do not eat food which has been cooked on a fire fed with its wood, for if you do you will become ill, and perhaps die. . . . Meal-times are always dangerous. . . . Do not eat anything against which you feel a repulsion, especially if your heart rises, your hair stands on end, or your flesh creeps, for your guardian-bori is setting you against it for your own good. From personal experience I can vouch for the fact that a European often experiences such sensations when near a Hausa dainty dish."[33]

"The Beja, the half-Hamites, and the Nilotes all have a large number of customs which have this in common, that they are connected with the chief product of their herds, *viz.,* milk, or with the grass upon which they feed. I am inclined to think that love and veneration are not too strong terms for the feelings towards their cattle which I believe form the basis of that special re-

29 Hobley, in JAI, XL, 430, 434.   31 Duveyrier, *Touâreg,* 401, 430.
30 Johnston, *Uganda,* II, 737-738, 812-813,   32 Schweinfurth, *Africa,* I, 158-159.
871-872.   33 Tremearne, in JAI, XLV, 28-30.

gard for milk and grass which occurs under varied forms among many of the tribes that have a strong infusion of Hamitic blood, or who have adopted elements of Hamitic culture. None of the Beja tribes with whom I am acquainted milk into a clay vessel or put milk into one of these, in spite of the fact that many of the Hadendoa make pots. Nor would it be permissible to milk into one of the modern tin bowls which Europeans have recently introduced into the country. Gourds and basket vessels, especially the latter, are considered the appropriate receptacles for milk, though skin vessels, *girba,* may be used. . . . There are also customs concerning the cooking of milk which vary from tribe to tribe; thus the Beni Amer and Bedawib commonly cook their milk by dropping into it hot stones as it stands in one of the widemouthed basketwork vessels called in Arabic *umra.* On the other hand, the majority of Hadendoa will not cook milk, and in this the Artega and Ashraf resemble them. Among the Artega, Ashraf, and Hasa only men may milk camels or sheep, and these tribes despise the Arab Zebediya, recent immigrants from Arabia, for allowing their women to milk their animals. . . . These facts all indicate that milk is not 'common' (using the word in its biblical sense) among the present day Beja; it might, indeed, almost be called sacred or sacrosanct. This is also the attitude of the southern Galla in British East Africa, for Miss Werner informs me that the only legitimate receptacle for milk, which may never be boiled, is a basket-work vessel called *gorfa.* . . . Among half-Hamites there are numerous ceremonial observances connected with milk. Gourds are the only vessels in which it may be received or stored. Milk may not be boiled."[34]

Mongols do not eat fish at all, or birds. "The Mongol abhors birds; every day I shot several partridges or bustards, and when I offered them to my Mongols, they turned away from me with signs of aversion."[35] The Chukchi use fish only in case of necessity, and have a distinct aversion to salt.[36] The Tungus will not eat reptiles and amphibians.[37] There is a general absence of food-taboos among the Saoras but the marriage of a girl into another class taboos beef for her. The Nagas abhor milk, though they will eat meat that has been three days buried. Milk is repulsive to the races bordering Assam. "It is a custom for no man in the North to eat the liver of any animal during his father's life-time, as it is deemed disrespectful to do so." It is significant that food otherwise tabooed may be eaten if offered in sacrifice; a discarded or tabooed food may be thus temporarily restored by the conservative cult. The almost omnivorous Veddahs will not eat cow or fowl. In southern Cochin China the children and grandchildren of a deceased person eat no meat.[38] In India the horse is a luck-bringing animal whose flesh is somewhat tabooed. "Eating horse flesh is supposed to bring on cramp, and when a sepoy at rifle practice misses the target, his comrades taunt him with having eaten unlucky meat."[39]

The Kayans eat lizards quite as little as do we; they are *lali* (taboo); "only to children and old men is it permitted to eat these animals."[40] The Dyaks eat

34 Seligmann, in JAI, XLIII, 1913, 654-656.

35 Prjevalski's *Forskningsresor,* 195, 319; Zichy, in *Globus,* LXXIV, 321; Rubruck, *Eastern Parts,* 75.

36 *Russian Ethnog.* (Russ.), II, 569.

37 Hiekisch, *Tungusen,* 83.

38 Fawcett, in JASB, I, 220, 223; Woodthorpe, in JAI, XI, 63; Peal, in JAI, XXII,

245; Collector of Sholapur, in JASB, V, 376, 378; Carey and Tuck, *Chin Hills,* I, 203; Wilkins, *Hinduism,* 168; Bailey, in *Trans. Eth. Soc. London,* II, 304, 305; Niemann, in *Bijd.* for 1895, 332.

39 Crooke, *N. India,* 318; Balfour, in JAI, XXVI, 342, note.

40 Nieuwenhuis, *Borneo,* II, 62.

snakes with gusto, but the swarming eels are held in aversion. Dyak taboos cover more or less strictly the flesh of cattle, buffalo, deer, she-goats, and hens, and also cows' milk and butter. The bull and cow are reverenced; and food prepared with butter is refused. One tribe will not kill a certain animal or eat it, while a neighboring tribe will. In southern Formosa, fish were tabooed.[41] Hose, one of the authors just quoted indicates a reason for these taboos: "when the soul separates from the body, it is supposed to take the form of an animal or bird, and, as an instance of this belief, should a deer be seen feeding near a man's grave, his relatives would probably conclude that his soul had taken the form of a deer, and the whole family would abstain from eating venison for fear of annoying the deceased." The deer would have become then a fetish-animal, to be tabooed. The Nicobarese entertain the same general aversion to the use of milk as an article of diet which is common to the various races of Indo-China and the Archipelago.[42] In the islands Luang and Sermatta, a sexual taboo is involved in the custom by which the husband gives a feast after a birth, at which only women may be present. "It is believed that any man tasting the food will be unlucky in all his undertakings."[43]

Significant again is the removal of the taboo upon solemn religious occasions. The Areoi, "a strange association of men and women, who prohibited the rearing of any offspring and practiced total infanticide, at the feast of admission to their society 'removed the tabu on females who partook with men of the pig and other sacred food.'" Polynesian women were formerly not allowed to eat eels, "and to this day they mostly turn away from this fish with the utmost disgust." In New Zealand, "women were allowed to eat what men ate, but human flesh was generally denied them."[44] Dogs and swine, where they have them, are kept for the nobles in Polynesia. They are very fond of fat, specially that of swine, and eat great quantities of it, even when rotten. Only common people eat rats; on Tahiti only women.[45] On Easter Island, as a sign of mourning, the taboo was laid upon the potato-fields or upon some other prized food-supply. Sea-birds' eggs, representing the chief god, were obtained from a certain island, which must not be visited for nine months in the year.[46]

The Micronesian taboo covers chickens and pigs. In the Marshall Islands the chief can taboo the coconuts. In the Carolines, the eel is held in the greatest horror, being called "the Dreadful One"; and the turtle, being sacred to the gods, is eaten only as a sacrifice in case of illness. In the Pelew Islands the chicken was once the symbol of bravery and tabooed; but contact with foreigners has led the younger generation and especially the women to break over the restriction. Participators in the catching of flying-fish must avoid association with women, the crossing of a brook, or the climbing of a mountain. They must not eat fish caught within the reefs.[47]

The Eskimo taboo certain foods to menstruating women. Greenlanders and

41 Perelaer, *Dajaks*, 27, note; Veth, *Borneo's Wester-Afdeeling*, II, 314; Roth, *Sarawak*, I, 388; II, 5, 6; Hose, in JAI, XXIII, 159, 165; Wirth, in AA, X, 364.
42 Man, in JAI, XVIII, 367.
43 Crawley, in JAI, XXIV, 433.
44 March, in JAI, XXII, 317; Ellis, *Polynesian Researches*, I, 233, 243; Tregear, in

JAI, XIX, 107; Taylor, 191; Best, in JAI, XLIV, 155-156.
45 Ratzel, *Vkde.*, II, 162, 165.
46 Geiseler, *Oster-Ins.*, 28, 30; Williamson, *Cent. Polyn.*, III, 340, 341.
47 Finsch, *Ethnol. Erfahr.*, III, 53, 130; Christian, *Caroline Isl.*, 73; Kubary, *Karolinen-arch.*, 168; Senfft, in *Globus*, XCI, 174.

Lapps will not eat the hare. For superstitious reasons the Indian of the American northwest coast will not eat whale blubber.[48] Among some tribes of British Columbia, "should a pubescent girl eat fresh meat, it was believed her father's luck as a hunter would be spoiled thereafter. The animals would not permit him to kill them; for it was held that no animal could be killed against its own wish or will. Indeed the Indian looked upon all his food, animal and vegetable, as gifts voluntarily bestowed upon him by the 'spirit' of the animal or vegetable, and regarded himself as absolutely dependent upon their goodwill for his daily sustenance. Hence his many curious customs and observances to propitiate the 'spirits' and secure their favour and regard. All his food taboos are conceived and carried out with this intention." Frequent deaths are taking place in Salish bands, and some of the old people do not hesitate to attribute this to the disregard of their old customs and practices. "Others attribute it to the white man's food, of the 'taboos' of which they are ignorant, and so suffer in consequence. For they imagine that we have food restrictions and taboos similar to their own, to disregard which means sickness or death."[49] Dorsey[50] lists a set of taboos on animals and parts of animals not touched or eaten by divisions of the Omahas and other Indians. Taboos rest upon the calf, especially if its hair is red. The system is too derived and detailed to be explicable, but is closely connected with totemism. The Navaho will not eat fish or pork, believing "with an earnestness that characterizes all his ideas, that if he should eat fish . . . his body would swell up to an enormous size and his skin break out in sores, while the fish-bones. whether he has eaten them or not, will come out through these sores." In Navaho mythology appears "that curious and widespread tabu with respect to eating in the underworld, or abode of the dead, known to classical readers as the myth of Persephone, but which, with slight modifications, appears in the lore of almost all races." The Mohave would not eat the lizards, turtles, beaver, and certain of the wild seeds utilized by their neighbors. Another tribe refused to eat fish. "This tendency led to specialization along certain lines of food-procuring instead of the utilization of all possible means of subsistence which the country scantily afforded."[51] Here we have the persistence of a taboo in the face of economic necessity or at least in the presence of opportunity for a higher grade of well-being. Although fish and bear were found in abundance in the country of the Apache, they were not eaten, being tabooed as food.[52] Pork is rarely eaten among the tribes in the Southwest of the United States and Northern Mexico, owing, perhaps, to Indian beliefs concerning swine, although the writer has been told a number of times by the natives that they dislike the taste of the meat. The Tlahuiltec, though living for centuries near the whites, still avoid milk, and no hogs are seen in their village. The Walapai eat no lizards or snakes, nor do they eat dogs or coyotes, but they like the flesh of the badger. They eat also the hawk but not the eagle. Field mice are "good." This tribe does not eat fish, saying that they smell bad, but there is, as with the Apache and some Pueblos, a mythical background for this peculiarity. The Navaho, besides tabooing fish, avoid eating bacon. The latter was given them during the captivity of a portion of the tribe at the

---

48 Turner, in BAE, XI, 208; Figuier, *Prim. Man*, 278; Niblack, in USNM, for 1888, 276.
49 Hill-Tout, in JAI, XXXIV, 315, and XXXV, 136.

50 In BAE, XI, 411-412, 426.
51 N. Y. *Post*, Dec. 31, 1896; Buckland, in JAI, XXII, 347; Kroeber, in AA, LV, 277.
52 HAI, I, 66.

Bosque Redondo, and as many died at that time the bacon was suspected of being the cause.[53]

The Guiana natives show a deep aversion to the eating of European swine. Some of them refrain from eating the big river-fish, though they use those found in brooks and ponds; and they will not eat game hunted with dogs or killed with guns. Certain tribes of Brazil abominate eggs, and reject milk, cheese, butter, beef, and the flesh of all their domestic animals, including fowl. The last they regard as members of the family. Again, the men alone eat venison.[54] All tribes of the Surinam Indians agree in refusing to eat the flesh of such animals as are not indigenous to their country but introduced from abroad, such as oxen, sheep, goats, and fowls. "It must, however, be added that, under great pressure of circumstances, such as utter want of other food, these meats are occasionally rendered eatable by the simple ceremony of getting a piaiman, or even occasionally an old woman [who may play the rôle of piai, or medicine-man], to blow a certain number of times on them; apparently on the principle that the spirit of the animal about to be eaten is thus expelled. . . . In Cayenne, they do not eat fowls (*poules*) and other birds though they be delicious; they imagine that out of spite these animals would cut their stomachs to pieces, gnaw their intestines, and cause frightful colic with the beak and spurs, although only the meat portion should be eaten." It would appear that in the olden times, it was strictly taboo for any one to take a meal after nightfall, though the true reasons for such a restriction are seemingly not now obtainable. "The certain punishment for infringement of this taboo was the transformation of the offender into some bird or beast."[55] Salt and bacon were despised by the Bororo. These Indians planted the mandioca and maize at some distance from the village so that the children could not eat the green and unripe husks of corn before they had been blessed by the priest. A similar ceremony is repeated whenever a large animal such as a tapir or wild pig, or some large fish is shot. "It is the firm belief of the Bororo that should anyone touch unconsecrated meat or maize before the ceremony has been completed, he and his entire tribe would perish."[56] The deer is the incarnation of a demon; "the Jibaros, therefore, never eat the flesh of the deer or even touch it with their hands." Food-taboos are prominent features of the ceremonies prescribed by Jibaro custom to protect the victor against the spirit of his slain enemy. "If one asks what ideas underlie the choice of the slayer's food—palm top, beans, mashed manioc, etc.—the Indians only give the explanation that he ought to eat such light kinds of food that remain in his stomach and which he does not run the risk of throwing up, which evidently would be regarded as dangerous for him. Their idea is, no doubt, that a very indigestible or irritating food could become a means through which the invisible, supernatural enemy of the slayer—the spirit of the killed enemy—could get an opportunity to harm him, perhaps cause his death. . . . That monkeys' flesh is forbidden to the slayer is due to the great likeness of these animals to man. The spirit of the dead enemy may hide in such an animal and cause the death of the slayer in case he tries to shoot it in the forest or eat of its flesh." It is recommended for the slayer to eat the flesh of the agouti.

53 Hrdlička, in BAE, Bull. XXXIV, 20, 23, 26.
54 Von Martius, *Beiträge*, I, 621, 403; Lippert, *Kgchte.*, I, 485; Von Koenigswald, in

Globus, XCIV, 223; Anon., in PSM, XLIX, 430.
55 Roth, in BAE, XXX, 184, 295-296.
56 Frič and Radin, in JAI, XXXVI, 392 (quoted); Von den Steinen, *Zent. Bras.*, 490.

"This small rodent is very shy and runs fast, being rather difficult to catch. By eating the animal the slayer will acquire the same quality, at present very useful to him. Similarly the fish *wámbi* is known as very shy and quick, great skill being required for catching it. The large fish *nápi* also cunningly hides in the depths of the great rivers and lagoons, thus easily escaping his persecutors. Even this fish, therefore, possesses qualities which are useful for the Jibaro warrior who is trying to evade his enemies."[57]

The fish-taboo is found among the aborigines of the Canaries,[58] and a strong aversion to fish as food persisted in Homeric and old Egyptian times. Egyptian priests who ate of it were considered unclean. The taboo is often noticed in the ritual.[59] In classical times cows' milk was not considered wholesome by many Greeks, and a generation ago only one cow was reported to be kept for milk in all Attica.[60] Plutarch, in consequence of a dream, abstained for a long time from eggs. One night, he tells us, when he was dining out, some of the guests noticed this, and got it into their heads that he was "infected by Orphic and Pythagorean notions, and was refusing eggs just as certain people refuse to eat the heart and brains, because he held an egg to be taboo as being the principle of life." As propitiatory offerings to the dead, eggs became "purifications" in general, and were tabooed as food.[61] "Among the Hindus the horse, the ox, the sheep, and the goat are mentioned as [sacrificial] victims; amongst the Greeks and Romans, oxen, sheep, goats, and pigs; though in ancient Italy it was regarded as sinful to kill and eat the plough-ox." The sacrifice of horses, and the eating of horse-flesh implied thereby, Schrader[62] regards as a custom which spread at a relatively late date through the northern peoples owing to Persian influence. The Phœnicians were forbidden to eat the flesh of both swine and cows.[63] In the Old Testament is listed what may and may not be eaten of beasts, fish, and fowls.[64] In the poetry of the old Norse the eating of carrion is spoken of as a sin.[65] The bones of horses found in ancient British caves indicate that these animals were an article of food. The Christian ecclesiastics forbade horse-flesh because the heathen ate it in honor of Odin. Modern prejudice against it is believed to be due to this fact.[66]

The Christian Church has aided in bringing food-taboos down to modern times. In 817 the Council of Aix la Chapelle forbade monks to eat poultry except during four days at Easter and four at Christmas, it being luxurious. But for a long time poultry and fish were regarded as identical in the eyes of the church. In the middle of the thirteenth century Aquinas ranked poultry amongst species of aquatic origin. When the church forbade poultry on fast days it excepted some kinds of aquatic birds and amphibious quadrupeds. For a long time the laws of the church about eating milk, butter, cheese, and eggs in Lent were unsettled. Eggs were eaten without scruple, since hens were thought to be aquatic. At first, especially amongst monks, dishes were prepared with oil instead of butter; but in northern countries animal fat had to be used. The discipline as to butter and milk varied very much. Papal dis-

57 Karsten, in BAE, Bull. LXXIX, 40, 41 note, 45.
58 Cook, in AA, II, 454.
59 Keller, *Hom. Soc.*, 48; Sayce, *Records of the Past*, II, 104.
60 Seymour, *Hom. Age*, 219.
61 Plutarch, *Quaest. Symp.*, II, 3. 1.; Harrison, *Greek Relig.*, 628, 630.

62 *Aryans*, 316.
63 Pietschmann, *Phön.*, 219.
64 Deut., XIV; Levit., XI; Maurer, in *Globus*, CX, 137.
65 *Corp. Poet. Bor.*, 348.
66 Dawkins, *Cave-hunting*, 132.

pensations to use butter were only obtained on onerous conditions. Anyone who ate meat on forbidden days was liable to fine or imprisonment, scourging or pillory. Clement Marot was imprisoned and nearly burned alive for eating pork in Lent. In 1534 the bishop of Paris granted dispensations to cease fasting to a lady eighty years old, only on condition that she should take her meals out of sight of every one and still fast on Fridays. Erasmus says: "He who has eaten pork instead of fish is taken to the torture like a parricide." In 1549 Henry II forbade the sale of meat in Lent to persons who had not a doctor's certificate. Charles IX forbade the sale of meat to the Huguenots. The butcher must take the address of every purchaser, even if he had a certificate. Later the certificate must be endorsed by the priest, specifying the quantity of meat. Even then pork, poultry, and game were forbidden.[67] Through the intervention of Boniface the Germans were forbidden to eat hare, beaver, jay, raven, and stork.[68] On the basis of taboos in the Old Testament and in the Talmud the Jews of today are forbidden to eat various kinds of food.[69]

§272. The Property and Civic Taboos.

THE following cases are illustrative mainly of the civic taboo and especially of sanctuary. In Central Australia may be found a tabooed location which is the germ of sanctuary, of a city or house of refuge. "Everything in its immediate vicinity is sacred, and must on no account be hurt; a man pursued by others would not be touched as long as he remained at this place."[1] In the neighborhood of Port Darwin is a neutral zone of some eight or ten miles, upon which no habitations are erected, where game remains unmolested, and where none trespass without good reason.[2] This is an example of the place-taboo.

There are various ways of denoting ownership in D'Entrecasteaux, some of which have a magical sanction attached to them. Stones are sometimes used in the banana-plantations, and woe betide the man who removes his neighbor's landmark. "Many other trees, especially the bread-fruit, and the coco-nut and betel-nut palms, are protected by taboos. You find a coco-nut palm leaf tied round the trunk or laid at the foot of the tree. . . . Emaciation is the penalty for the infringement of this taboo, and the whole hamlet will point the finger of reproach at the delinquent; his only cure is to bathe frequently in salt water. Sometimes a native will expectorate on his trees, making his saliva red by chewing betel-nut; then bloody pustules will form all over his body, and especially on the face and head, of any one who breaks the taboo." The authors[3] state that, despite all their taboos, the natives have never been inspired with a faith strong enough to make them keep the law and respect their neighbors' property, especially their fruit-trees and betel-nuts, but add that "no doubt the trees of a man famed for his skill and magic would be properly respected." Among the Marutse of South Africa is a city of refuge whose neutrality is sanctioned by the military power of a confederation.[4] In West Africa there is but one escape from the penalty and inconveniences of

67 Lacroix, *Middle Ages*, 126, 127, 134.
68 Weinhold, *Deut. Frauen*, II, 70.
69 Gen., XXXII, 32; Levit., XI, 9-12; Weissenberg, in *Globus*, LXXXIX, 27, 28; Stern, *Russland*, 96.

1 Spencer and Gillen, *Nat. Tr. Cent. Aust.*, 135.
2 Parkhouse, in AAAS, 1895, 638-639.
3 Jenness and Ballentyne, *D'Entrecasteaux*, 74-75, 76.
4 Holub, in *Illustr. Africa*, April, 1896.

accusations of witchcraft, and that is flight to a sanctuary. There are several sanctuaries in the French Congo, the great one in the Calabar district being at Omon; thither mothers of twins, widows, thieves, and slaves flee, and if they reach it, are safe.[5]

In the Pelew Islands if a festival is near and a shortage of necessary articles is feared, a taboo is laid upon them. Betel is passionately desired; there is little of it and it is difficult to raise; and it is most often the object of taboo. The chief may lay a taboo but custom controls him in so doing. It has a religious, mysterious sense, or is aimed at social expediency. No bread-fruit tree may be felled for a canoe without the chief's permission and payment to him. All turtles taken must be given to the chief. Several special taboos are cited: to go about on land with a fish-spear in hand; to own more than five such spears; to strive and come to blows with others; to cover the head and upper part of the body when in the town in the day-time.[6] In the Mortlock Islands the chief regulates by taboo but may not handle it capriciously. The taboo when laid is very strictly observed. Generally at the time of the bread-fruit harvest, for three or four months, coconuts are tabooed and must not be plucked, "in order that a sufficient store be made of old nuts, which the chief preserves." In this "political-economic provision for the tribe" the chief may also lay a "puanu" upon bread-fruit and sometimes even forbid fishing or allow it to certain persons only. This happens in order to restrain the people from frequenting the shore and the neighboring coco-groves, and so has, as everywhere, a practical basis, to prevent the need that often prevails upon these islands.[7]

On the island of Yap, limitations in the use of the soil are frequently met with; one writer thinks that "perhaps wise law-givers have by this means sought to prevent a too intensive use of the soil and overpopulation. This view receives a certain support in the circumstance that a long time ago the island was notoriously overpopulated, so that even infanticide is said to have existed. But since the great majority did not permit their actions to be determined by considerations for the general well-being, the shrewd law-giver took superstition to his aid, to reach by means of it his national-social aims."[8] We regard such an explanation as mythologizing in the same sense that the stories of Minos and other "law-givers" are myth-making about a core of reality, the core being the development of such preventive and preservative methods by the impersonal process of adjustment.[9] In ancient Hawaii land was tabooed so that no one could leave it until the taxes were fully paid. When they were, the priest and people chanted a prayer and the land was freed.[10] A "city of refuge" is reported from the Sandwich Islands for women, children, and even conquered warriors. Flags floating at the four corners of the sacred enclosure indicate its nature.[11]

A war-taboo, whereby the land was closed to aliens, is the "making of lines." Castañeda's account of the first meeting of Spanish soldiers and Hopi warriors mentions a Tusayan custom which has survived to the present day. "The Indian warriors drew a line [of meal] across the trail which led to their pueblo to symbolize that the way was closed to the intruders." In the same way they symbolically close the trails today with sacred meal.[12]

---

5 Kingsley, *Travels W. Afr.*, 466.
6 Kubary, *Pelauer*, 85; Kubary, *Núkuóro*, 18, 20.
7 Finsch, *Ethnol. Erfahr.*, III, 304, 305.
8 Senfft, in *Globus*, XCI, 174.

9 Keller, in *Yale Law Jr.*, XXVIII, 769 ff.
10 Culin, in AA, I, 204.
11 Letourneau, *Morale*, 111.
12 Winship, in BAE, XIV, pt. I, 428, 43; Fewkes, in AA, IX, 152.

The houses of the two hereditary chiefs of the Osages became sanctuaries not only for the people of the tribe, but also for members of other tribes, including enemies who were allowed to seek refuge there. "These two houses were made to represent the earth and all life contained therein. . . . Two doors were given to each of these sacred houses, one facing east and the other west, and an imaginary line running from door to door symbolized the path of the sun, which daily traverses the middle of the earth."[13] Williams[14] has written as follows of the Indian sanctuary of Paradise Valley near Mt. Rainier: "Here was the same bar to violence which religion has erected in many lands. The Hebrews had their 'Cities of Refuge.' The pagan ancients made every altar an asylum. Mediæval Christianity constituted all its churches sanctuaries. Thus, in lawless ages, the hand of vengeance was stayed, and the weak were protected. So, too, the Indian tradition ordained this home of rest and refuge. Indian custom was an eye for an eye, but on gaining this mountain haven the pursued was safe from his pursuer, the slayer might not be touched by his victim's kindred. When he crossed its border, the warrior laid down his arms. Criminals and cowards, too, were often sent here by the chiefs to do penance."

Holy places were common amongst the ancient Arabs.[15] "The god gave shelter to all fugitives without distinction, and even stray or stolen cattle that reached the holy ground could not be reclaimed by their owners. What was done with these cattle is not stated; possibly they enjoyed the same liberty as the consecrated camels which the Arabs, for various reasons, were accustomed to release from service and suffer to roam at large. These camels seem to be sometimes spoken of as the property of the deity, but they were not used for his service. Their consecration was simply a limitation of man's right to use them."[16] A number of references to cities of refuge occur in the Old Testament.[17]

§274. Sin.

NEARLY all calamities are explained by the South Sea Islanders as due to "some accident, or wrong action which they have done in their youth."[1] In New Caledonia "no whiskers was considered a sign of wickedness, a curse from the gods, and the mark of an outcast."[2] Though all the Gilyak have certain common religious and social laws which must not be broken, there are, besides, certain prohibitions, the forms of which are peculiar to a given clan. "The breach of these latter rules constitutes a 'sin' for that clan only. . . . Not only is the breaking of a taboo a sin, but also failure to perform religious duties. The sin of an individual acts in such a case to the detriment of the whole clan; just as, on the other hand, the observance of socio-religious duties is essential to the preservation of the clan as a whole."[3] There are few beggars in the Palaung hills, but people afflicted with blindness or some incurable disease sometimes come from a distance to Palaung festivals to beg for money. "They are received most kindly, not because the Palaungs are particularly sorry for their sufferings—holding the idea that they are suffering because of the sins that

13 LaFlesche, in BAE, XXXVI, 54.
14 The Mountain That Was "God," 31.
15 Procksch, Blutrache, 44.
16 Smith, Relig. Sem., 149.

17 Num., XXV, 6; Deut., IV, 41, Jos. XX, 9; Maurer, Vkde., I, 163.
1 Hardy and Elkington, Savage S. Seas, 61.
2 Turner, Samoa, 341.
3 Czaplicka, Aborig. Siberia, 49.

they have committed in a previous existence—but because it gives them an opportunity of acquiring merit by being charitable."[4] The latter statement recalls a common belief of mediæval times.

Tibetan Buddhism distinguishes six hells for different classes of sins: the first for suicides, murderers, ignorant physicians who kill their patients, fraudulent trustees, and tyrants; the second for those who have been disrespectful to parents, to Buddha, or the priests; the third for thieves, those indulging in hatred, envy, or passion, users of light weights and short measures, and those who cast refuse or dead animals upon the public roads; the fourth for obstruction of water-courses, grumblers at the weather ("clearly the English hell!" comments the author), and wasters of food. The fifth is the hell for heretics. In the sixth are punished those who roasted or baked animals for food.[5]

Among the sins of a dead woman were: poisoning food; misleading those who asked the way; refusing rice to the hungry; throwing thorns in the road; making a hole in a tank so that water escaped; spitting in a fountain and otherwise polluting fire or affronting the face of the sun; lying on a carpet when her father-in-law had nothing to sit upon; envying neighbors' harvests and cows; removing a landmark; and killing a snake, lizard, or cow.[6] "To pluck a branch—nay, a twig of the mango—wantonly or for making a toothbrush is a sin which no Hindu with a particle of sense will ever commit. A Hindu will rather die of hunger than sell a green mango tree to be felled."[7] Sweeping with a broom, splitting green branches, going to sleep after seeing an eclipse of the moon, polluting water or fire, reviling the soma; these are further sins. "By repeating sinful acts men are reborn in painful and base births, and are hurled about in hells; where are sword-leaved trees, etc., and where they are eaten, burned, spitted, and boiled; and they receive births in despicable wombs; rebirth to age, sorrow, and unquenchable death." Eight commandments interdict killing, stealing, telling lies, drinking intoxicating drinks, fornication or adultery, the eating of unseasonable food at night, the wearing of garlands or the use of perfumes, and sleeping except on a mat spread on the ground. Naturally the Buddhistic system is more sophisticated than that of a less developed religion.[8]

The Eskimo believe that the sea-mammals note the effects of sin upon a man, "who appears to them of a dark color, or surrounded by a vapor which is invisible to ordinary man. This means, of course, that the transgression also affects the soul of the evil-doer. It becomes attached to it and makes him sick. The shaman is able to see, by the help of his guardian spirit, these attachments, and is able to free the soul from them. If this is not done the person must die. In many cases the transgressions become attached also to persons who come in contact with the evil-doer. This is especially true of children, to whose souls the sins of their parents, and particularly of their mothers, become readily attached. Therefore when a child is sick the shaman, first of all, asks its mother if she has transgressed any taboos."[9]

Among the highly primitive Seri Indians the deepest sin is sex-relation with an alien.[10] Bad Haida Indians "are always quarreling and fighting. They

4 Milne, *Eastern Clan*, 318.
5 Waddell, *Buddhism*, 93 ff.
6 Reclus, *Prim. Folk*, 208.
7 Chowbe, in JASB, V, 226.
8 Thurston, *S. India*, 192-193; Phillips,

Vedas, 154; Hopkins, *Relig. Ind.*, 262, 267, 268, 269, 317, 491, note, 531; Holtzmann, *Ind. Sagen*, II, 40.
9 Boas, in PSM, LVII, 629.
10 McGee, in AA, IX, 375.

do not care to love their friends and they do wish to steal the property of the good Indians. All bad Indians hate the medicine man . . . which is the greatest sin; they despise his authority, and are consequently sent by him to a lower region." They will be handed over to a second evil spirit after the first has feasted on their bodies.[11]

In China it was a great sin to throw any impurity into the fire; and a parallel case of sin appears under the Zoroastrian system.[12] The terror of sin followed the Chaldæans all their lives and kept them in distress about their motives and intentions—for some of them had arrived at a stage where acts were not all. Maspero[13] quotes a penitential psalm which is as intense as any in the Bible. Sin did not affect the soul, but produced physical pain and death. Penitence cured sin, for a time, but death would at last gain the victory. "In any museum," says Tylor,[14] speaking of the Egyptian religion, "we may still see the scene of the weighing of the soul of the dead, and his trial by Osiris, the judge of the dead, and the forty-two assessors, while Thoth, the writing god, stands by to enter the dread record on his tablets. In the columns of hieroglyphics are set down the crimes of which the soul must clear itself, a curious mingling of what might be called ceremonial and moral sins, among them the following: 'I have not privily done evil against mankind. I have not told falsehoods in the tribunal of Truth. I have not done any wicked thing. I have not made the laboring man do more than his task daily. I have not calumniated the slave to his master. I have not murdered. I have not done fraud to men. I have not changed the measures of the country. I have not injured the images of the gods. I have not taken scraps of the bandages of the dead. I have not committed adultery. I have not withheld milk from the mouths of sucklings. I have not hunted wild animals in the pasturage. I have not netted sacred birds. I am pure, I am pure, I am pure!'"

Throughout the penitential psalms of Babylon breathes a deep sense of guilt. Words full of consolation are addressed to the last of the great monarchs of Ashur: "Thy sins, O Ashurbanipal! like the waves of the sea, shall be obliterated; like the vapours on the face of the earth, they shall melt away before thy feet!" The highest of the gods are neither created nor born, but have created themselves. Such was the doctrine taught on the banks of the Euphrates and the Tigris, and such on the banks of the Nile.[15] In the Vendidad, "it is safer to kill a man than to serve bad food to a shepherd's dog, for the manslayer gets off with ninety stripes, whereas the bad master is at once a Peshotanu, and will receive two hundred stripes. Two hundred stripes are awarded if one tills land in which a corpse has been buried within a year, if a woman just delivered of a child drinks water, if one suppresses the menses of a woman, if one performs a sacrifice in a house where a man has just died, if one neglects fastening the corpse of a dead man so that birds or dogs may not take dead matter to trees and rivers. Two hundred stripes if one throws on the ground a bone of a man's corpse, of a dog's carcase as big as two ribs, four hundred if one throws a bone as big as a breast bone, six hundred if one throws a skull, one thousand if the whole corpse. Four hundred stripes if one, being in a state of uncleanness, touches water or trees, four hundred if one covers with cloth a dead man's feet, six hundred if one covers his legs, eight

11 Harrison, in JAI, XXI, 18, 19.
12 Rehatsek, in JASB, I, 320.
13 *Hist. Anc.*, I, 682-683; *Records of the Past*, First Series, VII, 151.

14 *Anth.*, 370.
15 Tiele, *Sci. Relig.*, Part I, 117-118.

hundred if the whole body. Five hundred stripes for killing a whelp, six hundred for killing a stray dog, seven hundred for a house dog, eight hundred for a shepherd's dog, one thousand stripes for killing a Vanhapara dog, ten thousand stripes for killing a water dog. . . . There is hardly any prescription in the Vendidad, however odd and absurd it may seem, but has its counterpart or its explanation in other Aryan legislations: if we had a Latin or Greek Vendidad, I doubt whether it would look more rational."[16]

Among the greatest of sins is heresy. Tacitus[17] says that about 18 A.D. Egyptian and Jewish worshippers were expelled from Italy, being sent, if of military age, to Sardinia to suppress brigandage—"a cheap sacrifice if climate killed them." Others were to quit Italy within a day or to renounce their rites. In Japan "Christians who freely recanted were not punished, but only kept under surveillance: those who refused to recant, even after torture, were degraded to the condition of slaves, or else put to death. In some parts of the country, extraordinary cruelty was practised, and every form of torture used to compel recantation." People of nearly every rank, from prince to pauper, suffered for Christianity; "thousands endured tortures for its sake—tortures so frightful that even three of those Jesuits who sent multitudes to useless martyrdom were forced to deny their faith under the infliction;—and tender women, sentenced to the stake, carried their little ones with them into the fire, rather than utter the words that would have saved both mother and child."[18] The Spanish Inquisition is of course the classical example of "man's inhumanity to man" in this respect.[19] It is said by Lecky[20] that Philip II and Isabella the Catholic inflicted more suffering in obedience to their consciences than Nero and Domitian in obedience to their lusts.

§275. Remission.

IT will be noted from the cases that the topic of remission and that of exorcism, immediately following, cannot be sharply separated. Self-cleansing is exorcistic. The instances cited under Remission look, however, to forgiveness of sin rather than expulsion of evil influences.

In East Africa the weapon which has destroyed human life is looked upon with awe and dread. "Having once caused death it retains an evil propensity to carry death with it for ever. Among the Aklkuyu and Atheraka, therefore, it is blunted and buried by the elders. . . . These rites are intended for purification, and if omitted the direst consequences ensue, for the murderer will continue to slay friends and foes alike. . . . Purification is performed in all cases of homicide, no matter of whom and under what circumstances. There is one curious point about the custom in Theraka, namely that, if a man has killed a stranger, the purification is performed in public, but if he has killed a member of the tribe it is done secretly."[1]

Thahu is the word used by the Kikuyu for a condition into which a person is believed to fall if he or she accidentally becomes the victim of certain circumstances or intentionally performs certain acts which carry with them a kind of ill luck or curse. "A person who is thahu becomes emaciated and ill or breaks out into eruptions or boils, and if the thahu is not removed will

16 Müller, Sacred Books, IV, Pt. I, xcvii, xcviii.
17 Annales, II, §85.
18 Hearn, Japan, 353-354, 357-358.

19 Lea, Inquisition, passim; Wines, Punishment, 95-103.
20 Europ. Morals, I, 251.
1 Dundas, C., in JAI, XLV, 269-271.

probably die. In many cases this undoubtedly happens by the process of auto-suggestion, as it never occurs to the Kikuyu mind to be sceptical on a matter of this kind. It is said that the *thahu* condition is caused by the *ngoma* or spirits of departed ancestors, but the process does not seem to have been analysed any further. . . . The removal of the curse is effected by a process of lustration which, in the more serious cases, has to be done by the *mundu mugo* or medicine man, and in others by the members of the native council or *kiama;* the latter is an interesting case of the overlapping of judicial functions and those of a sacerdotal character. The lustration ceremony is almost always accompanied by the slaughter of a sheep and anointment with the contents of the stomach." The *thahu* is in nearly all cases removable by the elders and medicine-men for payment, and it may therefore be urged that the belief has not much value as a moral restraint. "This view cannot, however, be seriously maintained for the following reasons:—Take the case of a person who commits an act which he knows will bring *thahu;* it must be clearly understood that he never questions the liability of the principle, he goes about with the burden of the misdeed on his conscience, this worries him so much that he gradually gets thin and ill, and all this he puts down to the *thahu*. It therefore ends by his confessing to the elders and begging them to free him from the curse. It is in essence nothing more or less than the confession and absolution of the Christian Church. Then again we have to consider the publicity of *kraal* life, very little goes on which is not known to the neighbours; polygamy too increases this, a man confides in one wife, she tells another wife and so it goes through the village; if one person commits an act which inflicts *thahu* on himself or a neighbour, it will gradually leak out by some means or other, and public opinion will insist on measures being taken to remove it. No living person would ever dream that he could hope to evade the wrath of the *ngoma* or ancestral spirits. Of course occasions may arise when the commission of a prohibited act may involve a third party, and the person who committed it may preserve silence on the point, but the elders will in most cases be in possession of complete information as to the movements of every person in the neighbourhood, and moreover, the demeanor of the conscience-stricken culprit will invite suspicion, so in practice it is but rarely that the offender would not be detected." The Kikuyu people form the bulk of the labor supply of the upland colonists in British East Africa, and complaints of its capricious nature are often received from employers. "Upon investigation it was found that, apart from the natural ebb and flow of this supply, the charge of caprice was well founded, *i.e.,* there were many cases of desertion and often without any suspicion of ill-treatment, further, in some cases it was discovered that it was necessary to go away to get *dawa,* which is the general local synonym for medicine, whether of the nature of drugs or magical in character. The question then arose as to why such frequent calls occurred, and it was a long time before a definite clue could be obtained, but the principles gradually unfolded and became clear and were found to rest on the necessity of obtaining ceremonial purification to free the individual from either a *thahu* or the impurity left by a death in the family."[2]

Among the Bahima a man will divorce his wife if she becomes quarrelsome and abusive. "Abuse from a wife is a serious matter, the husband accuses her

2 Hobley, in JAI, XL, 428-429, 440, and XLI, 456-457.

to the head of the clan, who calls her to give account of her behaviour, and unless she can give an adequate excuse she is condemned to go to a lake near Karagwe for purification; a strong emetic, and a purgative, are administered; when these have done their work she is washed in the lake, and restored to her husband."3 Among the Asabs of Niger, "a woman confesses to the Diokpa [the head of the family, who is also a preparer of medicine] before parturition, naming all persons with whom she has had connection or familiarity. If this is not done, or any person is omitted, the danger of labour will be greatly increased and the woman may die."4

"To pray for ablution," ranks among the most sacred of the Buddhist rites, and is performed at every solemn assembly for the washing away of sins. Water is poured out from a vessel similar to a tea-pot over the vessel's well-cleaned cover, or a particular metallic mirror which is held so that it reflects the image, which stands on the altar.5 In the belief of the Hindus, when a woman dies unpurified within fifteen days after childbirth she becomes a demon, and is then always on the watch to attack other young mothers. "Whatever sins," says one of the sacred writings, "a man may have committed during life, if his bones are cast into the Ganges he must certainly go to heaven."6 For the purification-bath in India water of all seas and oceans is required; it is collected in small phials, each labelled to show from what particular body of water it came.7 Again, in the case of a woman found guilty of adultery, if her paramour is of low caste similar to herself, he has to marry her. But, in order to purify her for the ceremony, when a hut has been built and the woman put inside, it is set on fire, and the woman escapes as best she can. The same performance is gone through, until she has been burnt out seven times. She is then considered once more an honest woman, and fit to be married.8 "From the earliest period Shintō exacted scrupulous cleanliness— indeed, we might say that it regarded physical impurity as identical with moral impurity, and intolerable to the gods. It has always been, and still remains a religion of ablutions. The Japanese love of cleanliness—indicated by the universal practice of daily bathing, and by the irreproachable condition of their homes—has been maintained, and was probably initiated, by their religion. Spotless cleanliness being required by the rites of ancestor-worship,— in the temple, in the person of the officiant, and in the home,—this rule of purity was naturally extended by degrees to all the conditions of existence. And besides the great periodical ceremonies of purification, a multitude of minor lustrations were exacted by the cult."9 "Once each month a Shinto priest visits the homes of pious families having wells, and he repeats certain ancient prayers to the Well-God, and plants nobori, little paper flags, which are symbols, at the edge of the well. After the well has been cleaned, also, this is done. Then the first bucket of the new water must be drawn up by a man; for if a woman first draw water, the well will always thereafter remain muddy."10 A Korean expiatory offering consists of a bundle of straw tied with hoops of straw into the outline of the head and trunk of a man. Arms and legs are fastened to the body. Some bits of money are put in this figure, and it is thrown away under the impression that the influence of an evil star may be

3 Roscoe, in JAI, XXXVII, 106.
4 Parkinson, in JAI, XXXVI, 316.
5 Rockhill, in USNM, 1893, 741.
6 Monier-Williams, Brāhmanism, 229, 300-301.

7 Personally communicated.
8 Thurston, S.E. India, 427.
9 Hearn, Japan, 161-162.
10 Hearn, Out of the East, 126, 127.

overcome when the image is torn to pieces. The object apparently is to rid one's self of this as the Jews ejected the scapegoat.[11]

A rather forehanded case of remission is reported from Alaska, where "a noted woman of Sitka prayed openly in prayer-meeting that God forgive her for the sins she had in mind to commit the following week."[12] "The medicine arrows of the Cheyenne are 4 in number, of different colors, and were kept together in charge of a special priest from the earliest traditional period. . . . They . . . are exposed only on occasion of a solemn purification rite when a Cheyenne has been killed by one of his own tribe. They are still preserved among the Southern Cheyenne, by whom the rite of blood atonement was performed as late as 1904."[13] "Many or most solemn, mysterious or religious ceremonies are preceded by formal acts which appear to have the purpose of purification and suggest the same object that is attained by the burning of sweet grass or sweet pine, or the wiping off the body or a part of it by a wisp of white sage. The purpose of such acts is in part protective."[14] Blood-guilt, even from slaying of any enemy, must be cleansed; "there was no law among the Pimas observed with greater strictness than that which required purification and expiation for the deed that was at the same time the most lauded— the killing of an enemy." Sixteen days of isolation during which no one addresses the slayer; a day of abstention from food and drink, followed by a sparing diet not including meat or salt; observance of a number of other taboos; frequent river bathing; the covering of the head with a plaster of mud and mesquite—these are some of the details of self-clearance. If the man in question is married, his wife must not eat salt during his seclusion, else she will suffer from the owl disease and have stiff limbs. "The explanation offered for the observance of this law of lustration is that if it is not obeyed the warrior's limbs will become stiffened and paralyzed."[15]

This case may be compared with the practice in New Guinea, where, however, the object is to exorcise the ghost of the slain enemy, whose presence in the neighborhood of his slayer makes the latter unclean. "A man who has taken life is considered to be impure until he has cleansed himself and his weapon. He may eat only the center of toasted bananas. On the fifth day he walks solemnly down to the nearest water and bathes, while all the young untried warriors swim between his straddled legs in order to derive some of his courage and strength. "The following day, at early dawn, he dashes out of his house, fully armed, and calls aloud the name of his victim. Having satisfied himself that he has thoroughly scared the ghost of the dead man, he returns to his house. The beating of flooring boards and the lighting of fires is also a certain method of scaring the ghost. A day later his purification is finished."[16]

The post-Homeric Greeks have ceremonies of purification that "accompany human life through its whole course." The bearing woman and whoever has touched her are unclean; so is the new-born child; so are the dead and everything that comes near them. A series of purificatory acts surrounds marriage. Self-cleansing takes place after an evil vision, at the occurrence of prodigies, after recovery from illness. The purification of one who has spilled blood, even in lawful strife or unintentionally, is indispensable; if it has taken place,

11 USNM, 1891, plate XXXII.
12 Jones, *Thlingets*, 207.
13 Mooney, in HAI, II, 194.
14 Grinnell, in AA, XXI, 362-363.

15 Bourke, in BAE, IX, 475; Russell, in BAE, XXVI, 204-205.
16 Guise, in JAI, XXVIII, 213, 214.

even the calculating murderer is cleansed, though he has no intention of mend-
ing his ways. No sense of guilt demands it; it is a ritual matter. "Much more
was it superstitious fear of a spirit-world uncannily hovering about men . . .
that invoked the purifier and priests of conciliation for help and defense
against the terrifying figures of their own imagination."[17]

"All contact with holy things has a dangerous side; and so, before a man
ventures to approach the holiest sacraments, he prepares himself by ablutions
and other less potent cathartic applications. On this principle ancient religions
developed very complicated schemes of purificatory ceremonial, but in all
grave cases these culminated in piacular sacrifice; 'without shedding of blood
there is no remission of sin.'" The Arabian woman cut her nails or plucked
out part of her hair, parts in which the impure life might be supposed to be
concentrated; or rubbed herself against some animal presumably by way of
transferring her uncleanness. Handling holy things, as for instance the
Scriptures, entailed ceremonial washing.[18]

One of the ancient methods of purification was to spend a night in a crom-
lech or sacred stone cell. In Wales it was spent under the altar.[19] This recalls the Greek "temple-sleep," practised for cure of disease, and also the
ceremony of the bath, at entrance to knighthood.

In the Persian system are found minute and detailed precepts for the
treatment of the dead body, the construction of "towers of silence," and the
purification of men or things brought into contact with a corpse. The idea
pervading the whole is the utter impurity of a dead body, and the extreme
purity and sacredness of earth, fire, and water. No impure thing may, therefore, be thrown upon any one of these elements, because it would spoil the
good creation by increasing the power and influence of the demons, who take
possession of the body as soon as a man is dead. The corpse is, therefore, to
be carried on to the barren top of a mountain or hill, and to be placed on
stones (or iron plates), and exposed to dogs and vultures, so as to benefit in
this way the animals of the good creation. A man who touches a dead body,
the contagious impurity of which has not been previously checked by presenting
to the corpse a peculiar kind of dog, is said to be at once visited by a specter,
representing death itself. This is called "the destructive corruption." To
get rid of this annoyance he is sprinkled with water on the different parts
of his body, as described with the greatest minuteness.[20] In Egypt, "for the
preservation of health, purgation and vomiting were practised three days in
each month." The practice of temple harlotry in Chaldæa and elsewhere was
in part for expiation.[21] Hesiod[22] warns his hearers not to offer their morning
devotions with unwashed hands—the gods spit out such prayers. On the death
of Philip of Macedon, Demosthenes, though in deep mourning for the death
of his own daughter, donned a white robe and a garland, and offered sacrifice
of thanksgiving. Euripides[23] represents Alcestis as bathing and taking her
best array from her cedar chests before her prayer. Greek purification was
by means of cleansings and baths and aspersions, and "because of this a man

17 Rohde, *Psyche*, I, 219; II, 71, 72-74, 79-
80; Euripides, *Electra*, 655.
18 Smith, *Relig. of Semites*, 426, 427, 428;
Hebrews, IX, 22; Deut., XXI, 12; Num.,
XIX, 8, 10; Wobbermin, *Mysterienwesen*, 21.
19 Bent, in JAI, XX, 226 (Discussion by
R. Jones).

20 Haug, *Parsis*, 240-241; Justi, *Persien*, 88;
Spiegel, *Erân. Alterth.*, III, 695, 696, 698.
21 Maspero, *Hist. Anc.*, I, 215, 639; §343,
below.
22 *Works and Days*, 725, quoted by Seymour, *Hom. Age*, 506.
23 *Alcestis*, 159-160.

must keep himself from funerals and marriages and every kind of physical pollution, and abstain from all food that is dead or has been killed, and from mullet and from the fish melanurus, and from eggs, and from animals that lay eggs, and from beans, and from the other things that are forbidden by those who accomplish holy rites of initiation. . . . When Plutarch is describing the hapless plight of the man who thinks that affliction comes to him as a punishment for sin, 'It is useless to speak to him, to try and help him. He sits girt about with foul rags, and many a time he strips himself and rolls about naked in the mud; he accuses himself of sins of omission and commission, he has eaten something or drunk something or walked in some road the divinity forbade him.' This morbid habit of self-examination is a thoroughly Orphic trait."[24] The idea of Orphic mystery is that humanity is suffering and sinful and must be initiated to wash away its stains and redeem its sins. Initiation puts man in communication with the divinity.[25] In ancient Rome, if the offense to the deity was not involuntary the transgressor was *impius* and there was no expiation. Non-expiation applied only to a limited number of cases. There were expiatory rites for petty religious faults, as cutting wood in the sacred grove, neglecting inhumation of a corpse, or breaking the quiet of a holy day. There were many ceremonies of lustration.[26]

Mohammed declared that "each step taken while bearing a corpse shall be worth the remission of ten transgressions and the replacement of each of these sins by ten good acts."[27]

§276. Exorcism.

AMONG certain Africans "all sorts of charms and medicines are used to ward off the *rufiti,* which in the native's imagination dog his existence." All deaths are caused by their desire to eat the dead, and the corpses are carefully guarded against them. "While a body is lying unburied, people will not walk out at night except in bands, as the *rufiti* is supposed to be abroad."[1] In North Africa the exorciser drew a circle about the camp, praying the while; "and they believe that thereby not only robbers and wild animals, thieves and evil spirits are kept afar off, but the whole encampment is thought to become invisible for all of them."[2]

The Buryats have a belief in cannibal spirits who prey especially on the blood of new-born children. They allow no stranger to enter the dwelling where the new-born lies, lest the evil spirit press in with him. When the shaman imposes this taboo, the door remains constantly shut; "and outside before it they have a pot with a stick in it, and if a member of the family enters he must first knock on the pot with the stick; then the evil *ada* is frightened and flees." Koryak women wear grass-masks at the whale-festivals, while young men wear wooden ones in the fall of the year, to drive away evil spirits.[3] Here is an avoidance-device passing into an exorcistic one. "The Votyaks have a devil-driving day; the men from early morning get on horseback, and with

24 Harrison, *Greek Relig.*, 508-509, 517.
25 Roton, *Antiq. Grecque*, 220; Hatch, *Griechentum*, 213.
26 De Marchi, *Culto Priv.*, rev. in *Année Soc.*, I, 190, 246.

27 Pommerol, *Sahariennes*, 357.
1 Angus, in JAI, XXVII, 320-321.
2 Rohlfs, in *Mitth. Perthes' Geog. Anst.*, Ergänzheft. 25, p. 42.
3 Jochelson, in AA, VI, 421.

cudgels in their hands and with loud cries drive out the devil from their villages."[4]

In Ladak the lamas are always trying to get rid of the thronging evil spirits. When the hymn of exorcism fails, "one of them suddenly seizes a yak-tail lying near and lifts it on high. The red devils cannot stand that; they raise a whining howl and rush off."[5] "The intensity of the Ladakh's superstition may perhaps be connected with the impenetrability of his great mountains, fit homes for millions of demons, and to the suddenness of the disasters which overtake him." Here we have a more than usually direct inmixture of the aleatory element. "On a clear day, a storm may gather on one of the snowy passes and in an hour or two overwhelm a whole caravan. Under the influence of a mild drizzle or a bit of melting snow, the soil may be loosened so that avalanches of rock suddenly sweep down the steep mountain sides to block the roads, kill travelers, and bury villages. At other times . . . a flood of accumulated snow-water may burst out of an apparently dry valley, and destroy houses, fields, and villages. When he sees so many evidences of what he supposes to be the activity of demons, small wonder that the Ladakhi becomes nervous, and thinks it wise to save his crops from drought and frost by hiring a red lama to sit beside his field while it is being sown, and read all day from a leaf of the holy book. And it is equally wise to keep demons out of the house by smearing the lintels, doorposts, and corners with blood or red paint, a custom curiously suggestive of that of the ancient Israelites."[6]

The Sikhimese intensely dread all mining operations; for they believe that the ores and veins of metal are the stored treasure of the earth-spirits who are enraged at its removal and visit the robbery with all sorts of ill luck, plagues of sickness on men and cattle and failure of their scanty crops. The same author[7] reports that, coming inside a Lepcha house, he was about to put his hat on a clean-looking vacant spot, when the good-wife, with horror written on her face, snatched it up and placed it elsewhere, explaining that the devil of the house was at that time occupying that spot and that his fearful wrath would be incurred if anything were placed there. Some incantations were needed to undo the harm already done. Similarly in a Tibetan house. The Kirghiz represent mountain-sickness to themselves as a young lady; to get rid of it they utter "the most obscene and disgusting expressions, thinking thereby to shock the lady's modesty and drive her away."[8]

In a Shan funeral, the eldest son of the deceased goes first, "with a naked sword in his hand to clear the way, which is supposed to be barred by spirits."[9] The Naga believed in a disease-giving spirit which could be guarded against by shields and arms; and they practised as a funeral-rite a war-challenge to the power that had treacherously slain the dead man. Certain Hindus place a crowbar along the threshold of a confinement-chamber as a check against the crossing of any evil spirit; it is kept there for ten days. It is believed that spirits always avoid iron, and even nowadays pieces of horseshoe can be seen nailed to the sills or doors of native houses.[10] Unguarded openings are an invitation to entrance; "no Tamil will yawn without holding the hand before the mouth, or making protective signs with the fingers before the mouth,

4 *Russian Ethnog.* (Russ.), I, 292.
5 Francke, in *Globus*, LXXIII, 7.
6 Huntington, *Pulse of Asia*, 60.
7 Waddell, *Himalayas*, 97, 101; Waddell, *Buddhism*, 372-373.

8 Modi, in JASB, III, 342.
9 Woodthorpe, in JAI, XXVI, 23.
10 Godden, in JAI, XXVI, 192, and in XXVII, 34; Kirtikar, in JASB, I, 403 (Discussion by Sukthankar).

lest some evil spirit or other observe the opportunity and slip through the wide-open portal into the man." Similar practices have been alluded to under the topic of taboo on eating.[11] Again, a spirit is drawn away from a house and family by setting apart for it a piece of land, together with sacrifices; such a place is never cultivated, and people will not go near it at night.[12] In southern India, after other well-authenticated methods of exorcism have failed, the devil's retreat "may generally be hastened by the vigorous application of a slipper or broom to the shoulders of the possessed person, the operator taking care to assist the cure by reviling him in the most scurrilous language he can think of. After a time the demoniac loses his downcast look. He begins to get angry and writhe about under the slippering, and at length cries, 'I go, I go.' . . . When the demon consents to leave, the beating stops; often immediate preparations are made for sacrifice. The person now awakes as from sleep, and appears to have no knowledge of anything that has happened."[13] To be noted are the apparently hysterical or hypnotic state of the possessed person[14] and the fact that the possessing spirit is often a deceased relative.

Of the Nicobarese it is reported that "their whole belief is a childish spectre-fear; everywhere they fear and scent the *Iwi*, an evil, very intrusive, ravenous, prying, saucy spirit, and make an effort to scare him off with all sorts of roughly carved images. . . . Everything that worries, torments, oppresses, or pains is begotten by *Iwi* or is he himself. If it is a case of indigestion or a pain in the limbs, the conjurer, operating here as a physician, must come and drive the *Iwi* out of the sick person."[15]

In Korea, toward twilight on New Year's Day, the smell of burnt hair pervades Seoul; for on that day the carefully saved clippings and combings are burned in order to keep evil spirits out of the house during the year. Another New Year's ceremony is "walking the bridges": "Up to midnight, men, women, and children cross a bridge or bridges as many times as they are years old. This is believed to prevent pains in the feet and legs during the year." The authoress[16] quoted once encountered a small log with several holes like those of a mouse-trap in it, one of the holes being doubly plugged with wooden bungs. The ponies were led over the log and the men stepped over it. Into the bunged hole a sorceress had by her arts inveigled a sickness-bringing daimon and had corked him up. Such a log is buried at nightfall.

In Borneo certain tribesmen feared to remain on a mountain over night and "only confidence in the powerlessness of their evil spirits over against Europeans and the influence of reading in books" gave them the nerve to stay.[17] The apparatus of exorcism is always in evidence; at intervals of some fifty feet along the verandas are shallow boxes in which fires are lit at night for light and to keep off evil spirits. Barriers are constructed against the spirits: a circle of stakes cut on their sides into curled shavings, earthen jars of water, and cleft sticks with eggs in the clefts. Furness[18] took pictures of these things, despite the solemn warning that he would have bad dreams and be subject to the "ghost-clutch," which scars for life or, if at the throat, causes choking to death. In northern Sumatra it is better not to see a lunar eclipse directly, so it is viewed in a vessel of water. Meanwhile guns are fired in the direction of the moon, and people pound on rice-blocks and beat metal objects, with the

11 Schmidt, *Ceylon*, 291; §271, above.
12 Painter, in JASB, II, 152.
13 Caldwell, in JASB, I, 97 ff.
14 §§310, 311, of the text.

15 Svoboda, *Nicobaren*, 274.
16 Bishop, *Korea*, 265 ff., 335.
17 Nieuwenhuis, *Borneo*, II, 100, 119, 120.
18 *Head-Hunters*, 4, 99-100.

idea of frightening the sun into loosing his prey. Pregnant women must keep off the streets during an eclipse of sun or moon.[19] Of some of the Luzon natives it is reported that they frequently light great bonfires or burn the bush to exorcise the evil spirits.[20]

The Eskimo and Aleuts keep off evil spirits with fetid and malodorous substances, chiefly urine; the Cambodians use the urine of a white or fetish-horse against smallpox; and elsewhere over the earth parallelisms are not uncommon.[21] Again, fire is kept up at the Indian's grave and friends howl about it to protect the departing soul from spiritual assault.[22]

Fire, water, and noise are almost universally employed as exorcistic devices. One of the richest fields is China, where fire and noise are combined in the firecracker to scare away demons.[23] A case of exorcism by fire is reported of the Kwakiutl Indians as follows: as soon as the shells of the sea-eggs are all in, "the woman takes a large firebrand and puts it on top of the empty shells. Then she goes and pours them out outside the house. The reason why they put the firebrand there is that the spirits may not eat the refuse of the sea-eggs. If they do not put a firebrand on top of it, it is said that the spirits immediately go and eat it; and it is said that he who ate what was in the empty shells eaten by the spirits would be immediately sick."[24] Fire, together with noise, was a general method of curing sickness, as among the Apache, where, "when anybody fell sick several fires were built in the camp, and while the rest lay around on the ground with solemn visages, the young men, their faces covered with paint, seized firebrands and ran around and through the fires and about the lodge of the sick person, whooping continually and flourishing the brands to drive away the evil spirit."[25] The Indians of Guiana believe that the spirits of the forest shrink from exposure to sunlight or firelight, from hearing their names called or particulars of their origin talked about. Any of these eventualities will drive them away. Special precautions have to be taken, when any large animal has been slain, to protect the hunter from any harm that might be expected from the spirit of the animal he has just destroyed. "Thus, when a big snake or other large animal is killed, arrows are stuck into the ground in the middle of the pathway leading from the place of destruction toward the house, with a view to preventing the Spirit of the beast coming to do the slayer or his family any hurt." Some of these Indians practise a whip dance for the purpose of expelling the evil spirit, especially in the case of a re-marriage, when the widow and her future husband are severely chastised. Roth[26] thinks that the whipping of visitors as a salutation-ceremony among some of these tribes may similarly bear relation to the spirits which the host, in his welcoming speech, trusts that the visitors have not brought with them.

Eclipses and other natural phenomena call for exorcism, noise being regarded as especially efficacious under such circumstances. It is the belief of the natives of the D'Entrecasteaux Islands that "eclipses are due to a large black snake which tries to devour the moon, and is only prevented from succeeding by the natives frightening it away with the noise of drums and conch-

19 Jacobs, *Groot-Atjeh*, I, 394-395.
20 Scheidnagel, *Isl. Filip.*, 64.
21 Ratzel, *Vkde.*, I, 96; Reclus, *Prim. Folk*, 83; Blau, *Zauberwesen*, 162.
22 Yarrow, in BAE, I, 107; Von Martius, *Beiträge*, I, 327.

23 Harvey, *Chinese Animism*, ch. IV; Letourneau, *Soc.*, 289.
24 Boas, in BAE, XXXV, pt. I, 614.
25 HAI, I, 284.
26 In BAE, XXX, 193, 293, and XXXVIII, 643.

shells."[27] "Tonight," writes Solomon[28] from Nicobar, "there was an eclipse of the moon. The people here are under the same impression as some of my countrymen regarding this phenomenon. They think that the moon is actually being swallowed by a serpent. Throughout the night both the young and old refrained from sleep and occupied themselves in driving out the serpent in the following way. Having provided themselves with kerosene oil tins and planks they beat them and shouted 'Alas! alas! do not devour, let the moon alone and go away.' It was a comical sight." When a bad thunder-storm comes on, the Sakai climb down from the house to the ground, strike their working-knives into the earth, and leave them there. "Hot stones from the hearth, the supports for cooking pots, are also thrown out of the door of the house. Both these actions are thought to be helpful in dispersing the storm, and the hot stones, symbolically at any rate, dry up the rain."[29] In Cayenne, eclipses of the sun and moon upset the Indians a good deal: "they think some frightful monster has come to devour these heavenly bodies. If the eclipse is total or of short duration, they consider it a fatal thing for them: they make a terrible noise, and shoot a volley or arrows into the air to chase away the monster."[30] About four thousand years ago, Mitchell[31] tells us, two Chinese astronomers, Hsi and Ho by name, were drunk during an eclipse. They were thus unable to beat drums and gongs to scare away the dragon who was devouring the sun. The monster, it seems, was generous and disgorged his prey. The emperor, not so kind, had the unfortunate Hsi and Ho beheaded—a most salutary example for astronomers.

Chief among the birds used in exorcism, on account of the noise made by him, is the cock. The common practice of putting the figure of a cock on church steeples has long been popularly associated with the reproach that bird once conveyed to St. Peter. But there is still another significance to the old custom. In the early history of the world the figure of a cock was placed on the top of sacred trees and spun by the four winds in the popular belief that it would disperse evil spirits and ward off calamities. Its living prototype was supposed to accomplish the same results by crowing. The figure of the cock still decorates May poles in North Germany.[32] The Chaldæans represented the demons under forms so hideous that it was sufficient for them to be shown their own images, to cause them to flee away alarmed. In the museum of the Louvre is a curious bronze statuette of Assyrian workmanship. It is the figure of a horrible demon in an upright posture, with the body of a dog, the feet of an eagle, the claws of a lion, the tail of a scorpion, the head of a skeleton but half decayed and adorned with goats' horns, the eyes still remaining, and lastly four great expanded wings. The figure was originally suspended by a ring behind the head. On the back there is an Accadian inscription, which informs us that this is the demon of the south-west wind, and that by placing this image at the door or the window, its fatal influence might be averted. In Chaldæa, the south-west wind comes from the deserts of Arabia, and its burning breath which dries up everything, causes the same havoc as the *Khamsin* in Syria, and the *Simoon* in Africa. The winged bulls with human heads, flanking the entrance gates, were genii which kept real guard, and were held to their posts as long as their images dwelt there without being disturbed.[33] A

27 Jenness and Ballentyne, *D'Entrecasteaux*, 160-161.
28 In JAI, XXXII, 234.
29 Evans, in JAI, XLVIII, 188.

30 Roth, in BAE, XXX, 255.
31 *Eclipses of the Sun*, 1.
32 N. Y. *Times*, May 28, 1911.
33 Lenormant, *Chaldean Magic*, 50-52.

popular device in Scotland for frightening away witches and fairies was to hang bunches of garlic about the farms. "I have known," writes Barrie,[34] "a black-fishing expedition stopped because a 'yellow yite,' or yellow-hammer, hovered round the gang when they were setting out. Still more ominous was the 'péat' when it appeared with one or three companions. An old rhyme about this bird runs—'One is joy, two is grief, three's a bridal, four is death.' Such snatches of superstition are still to be heard amidst the gossip of a north-country smithy."

The use of water in exorcism, and the derived baptism by water or blood, may be illustrated by a few much-scattered cases. A sort of baptism by blood composed part of the initiation-ceremony of the Dieri in Central Australia.[35] Among the Tshi and Ewe tribes in West Africa, the mother and child are considered unclean. "The water which is always in the earthen vessels placed before the images of the gods, is brought to the house and thrown up on the thatched roof, and as it drips down from the eaves the mother and child pass three times through the falling drops. The babalawo next makes a water of purification with which he bathes the child's head, he repeats three times the name by which the infant is to be known, and then holds him in his arms so that his feet touch the ground. After these ceremonies have been duly performed the fire is extinguished and the embers carried away; the house is then carefully swept out, live coals are brought, and a fresh fire lighted. We thus appear to have a combination of a purification by water and a purification by fire. After the new fire has been kindled, another sacrifice of fowls is made to Ifa, and the proceedings are at an end."[36] In the Cameroons, after a man accused of witchcraft was sacrificed, the whole community went naked into the sea to wash away the magic.[37] In 1924 the members of a certain Filipino religious society engaged in a battle with the constabulary; hostilities arose when the latter destroyed a tank believed by the natives to hold sacred water. About three hundred members of the society were bathing in it, or drinking its waters, when the constabulary broke its walls and let the water out. The natives believed the waters possessed remarkable health-giving properties.[38] In Mexico there was a rite known as "baptism by fire," which "was celebrated on the fourth day after the birth of a child, during which time it was deemed essential to keep the fire burning in the house, but not to permit any of it to be carried out, as that would bring bad luck to the child."[39] Fuegian children were immersed in the sea immediately after birth.[40] In the Nibelungenlied there occurs, in the case of Siegfried, an instance of blood-baptism.[41] Snake and child to the primitive mind are not far asunder: the Greek peasant of today has his child quickly baptized, for till then he may at any moment disappear in the form of a snake. In the primitive Church the sacrament of baptism was immediately followed by communion. The custom is still preserved among the Copts.[42]

Spitting is an exorcistic device, though in some instances, especially in Africa, it appears to be merely a form of salutation. Even here, however, it may be exorcistic at bottom, and the same may be said of hand-clapping, an-

34 Auld Licht Idylls, 59.
35 Howitt, in JAI, XX, 82.
36 Ellis, Yoruba, 153.
37 Ratzel, Vkde., II, 353.
38 N. Y. Times, Jan. 12, 1924.

39 Brinton, Nagualism, 44.
40 Ratzel, Vkde., II, 677.
41 Lichtenberger, Nibelungen, 842 ff.
42 Harrison, Greek Relig., 133, 597.

other typical African mode of salutation.[43] The noise thereby produced and the "shooing off" effect would suggest exorcism as an original motive, though this theory should not be pushed too far. In the Papuan ceremony of fumigation, the spraying with spittle after chewing the "hot bark" or wild ginger, is meant to invigorate the fetish. "With the little hunting charm called *ke' upura,* it is the practice to chew some such bark, spit on to the palms, and then roll the charm between them; lastly, the intending hunter will rub the spittle over his own face and limbs."[44] Among the African Akamba "both father and mother spit on a new-born baby to bring it luck; a friend seeing the baby will do likewise. It is said that the custom of spitting at people for luck was general, but since the arrival of Europeans they spit on their hands instead, even this modified custom is not at all general."[45] The Wachagga regarded spitting as a mark of honor and in early days employed it even toward Europeans.[46] Among the Wagogo, by way of contrast, if one spits on his cousin, the offender will get warts; one who spits on another incurs a fine as purification.[47] Much more common is the practice of spitting on the person toward whom the spitter is well disposed.[48] With the Masai, spitting expresses the greatest goodwill and the best of wishes. "It takes the place of the compliments of the season, and you had better spit upon a damsel than kiss her."[49] Schweinfurth,[50] describing the Dyur, says: "Recently they have lost some of their ancient habits. For instance, the practice of mutual spitting, long the ordinary mode of salutation, has fallen into desuetude." Throughout his entire residence in Africa, the writer was never a witness of it more than three times: in all those cases the spitting betokened the most affectionate goodwill; it was a pledge of attachment, an oath of fidelity; it was to their mind the proper way of giving solemnity to a league of friendship. Miss Kingsley[51] describes how a West African once took leave of her: "The old lady's farewell of me was peculiar; she took my hand in her two, turned it palm upwards, and spat on it. I do not know whether this is a constant form of greeting among the Fan; I fancy not. Dr. Nassau, who explained it to me when I saw him again down at Baraka, said the spitting was merely an accidental by-product of the performance, which consisted in blowing a blessing; and as I happened on this custom twice afterwards, I feel sure from observation he is right." Among cabalistic words she thinks ought to be classed that peculiar form of friendly farewell or greeting which Dr. Nassau poetically calls a "blown blessing" and the natives, *ibata.* "The method consists in taking the right hand in both yours, turning it palm upwards, bending your head low over it, and saying with great energy and a violent propulsion of the breath, Ibata." Among the Dinkas, "if a chief is anxious to be very polite, his correct course is to spit in one's face."[52] When entering and when leaving a town, the Hausa spit upon a stone and throw it behind them in order to get rid of all evil influences which are in the rear.[53]

Sieroshevski[54] says that when two Yakuts engaged in a quarrel, stop and

43 Roth, "Salutations," in JAI, XIX, 172; Bent, *Mashonaland*, 66, 351; Müller, *Zambesi*, 131; Bastian, *Loango-Küste*, I, 65; II, 37, note; Paulitschke, *Nordost-Afr.*, I, 206.
44 Williams, in JAI, LIII, 379.
45 Hobley, *Akamba*, 61.
46 Volkens, *Kilimandscharo*, 253.
47 Cole, in JAI, XXXII, 335.

48 Vannutelli e Citerni, *L'Omo*, 233.
49 Roth, in JAI, XIX, 180.
50 *Heart of Africa*, I, 204-205.
51 *Travels W. Afr.*, 288, 453.
52 Cummins, in JAI, XXXIV, 153.
53 Tremearne, in JAI, XLV, 54.
54 *Yakuts* (Russ.), 570, note 2.

decide to make an alliance, they spit in each other's hands. Among the Sema
Nagas "a curse is effected by men naming the one to be cursed, flourishing
their daos and spitting in unison."[55] Spittle was a feature of the Tusayan
Indian snake ceremonies: "At a signal the Snake priests rushed to the reptiles, seized as many as they could, . . . departed hastily down the mesa trails
and distributed them to the cardinal points. As they left the plaza, a perfect
rain of spittle from the spectators on the surrounding house-tops followed
them."[56] If a Guiana Indian smells any decomposing matter, he spits. Spitting
is also done to show aversion to negroes, while it is in addition of exorcistic
value in burials. The medicine-man spits on the corpse.[57] Theocritus[58] mentions spitting as a means of warding off the evil eye.

Amulets. The Tasmanians were anxious to possess themselves of a bone from
the skull or the arms of their deceased relatives, "which, sewn up in a piece of
skin, they wore around their necks, confessedly as a charm against sickness or
premature death." As other charms, "thigh-bones were featured on the head
in a triangle."[59] In the Andaman Islands the bones of a child or of one long
dead discharge the same purpose; protection comes "through the intervention
of the disembodied spirit, who is supposed to be gratified by and aware of
the respect thus paid to his memory."[60] Certain Papuans esteem most highly
as a charm for good hunting or female sterility a stone found in the crop of a
pigeon. Such charms are worn about the neck or carried in a little bag.[61] In
the case of the New Caledonian, "if chance throws in his way stones whose
peculiar form gives his superstition something to think about, he ascribes to
them certain characteristics and a secret influence. . . . Since such stones are
rather rare, and their power therefore so much the more effective, they give
their possessor a big influence. . . . At the time of a doubtful or even successful draw of fish, the fetish-stone is held in the water ahead of the boat,
and its power is so great that it infallibly draws the fish into the nets." If
sunshine is wanted, there is set up in the fields a piece of quartz whose veins
spread radially from a ground-line; if rain, a stone is laid on the ground whose
natural striation is thought to indicate rain.[62] Here is a sort of imitative
magic.[63] On the Sierra Leone coast fetish-arrows serve as protective devices
against theft in the fields, as charms against sickness, and as talismans against
witchcraft.[64]

In North Tibet "some people wear on the left shoulder a piece of cloth,
decorated with turquoises and corals. This is one of the talismans consecrated
by a holy lama, which shall protect the bearer against all kinds of sickness and
ill luck."[65] Many of the printed charms in Burma have sympathetic relations
with their intended purposes: thus, for example, "a charm against ghosts may
bear a picture of a ghost in fetters; one against dog-bite may bear a chained
dog; or one to obtain greatness may have an elephant upon it. . . . As example of their use as instruments in magical ceremonies may be taken the

55 Hutton, *Sema Nagas*, 262.
56 Fewkes, in BAE, XVI, 285.
57 Schomburgk, *Brit. Guiana*, II, 194;
Roth, in BAE, XXX, 156 and XXXVIII,
§935.
58 *Idylls*, VI, 45; XX, 15.
59 Barnard, in AAAS, 1890, 605.
60 Tylor, in JAI, XXIII, 152; Man, in
JAI, XII, 86.

61 Guise, in JAI, XXVIII, 217; Finsch,
Ethnol. Erfahr., II, 337; Krieger, *Neu-
Guinea*, 403.
62 "Durands Besuch" (anon.), in *Globus*,
LXXX, 239.
63 §302, of the text.
64 Frobenius, *Masken*, 166.
65 Prjevalski, *Forskningsresor*, 215.

waving about in the air of a traveller's charm when the traveller is about to cross a river, and its exhibition to the devils of the vicinity; the showing of a charm to the devils in the four directions when a hailstorm occurs in order to cause the storm to depart; and the apparent transference of a disease to a charm placed with rice, the summoning of the devils to the food, with the subsequent throwing away or destruction of the charm." Parts of the elephant, as in other Buddhist countries where they are available, are highly valued as protections. As in Tibet and the neighbouring states and in Ceylon, so in Burma, the hairs from the elephant's tail are often used for the making of finger-rings. "Imitations of the elephant-hair rings, resembling their originals very closely, are made of palm-leaf, and are," writes Hildburgh,[66] "more common than the genuine rings. They are very much cheaper than the genuine rings, and although I have been told that they are worn merely as ornaments and not as 'medicine,' I think it reasonable to assume that in many, if not in most, cases their wearers rely upon their close resemblance to their originals to deceive the malignant spirits. . . . Elephant-nail is another material favoured, for the making of charms, by both Burmese and Shans. . . . Tigers supply, as in other Asiatic countries, various amulets and remedies. . . . It is worth noting, in view of the protective or curative virtues assigned to the colour red in many parts of the world, that, although the cords used for the suspension of a child's amulets or neck-ornaments in Burma are much more frequently red (or reddish) than any other colour, I was always told, in answer to my many inquiries concerning it, that no special protective virtue is assigned to red, and that it is favoured merely because of its decorative effect. Red coral is worn by Burmese children as a protection against sicknesses."

In India the possession of a rare or curious coin or medal is assurance of good luck; tiger's claws and bear's hair are set in gold and silver; glittering, swinging, fluttering things draw the evil eye to themselves and save the wearers. Mantrams, or sacred formulas, are very powerful; they are "combinations of the five initial letters of the five sacred elements, which produce sounds, but not words. These are believed to vibrate on the ether, and act on latent forces which are there." Cabalistic figures and mantrams on their metal plates are very effective. When a sick person talks of his illness, one who hears mutters defensive formulas, where in Italy he gently and imperceptibly taps from below on a table, or points his amulet at the talker, or, if he has no amulet, points with two spread fingers, to repel the illness.[67]

In China, a gourd shell, or a representation of a gourd painted on children's clothes, is a defense against smallpox; the children wear masks, on the last night of the year, to deceive this demon. A certain type of hair-pin, with small silver figures of animals attached, is widely effective. Cords bought of witches, often with leather cylinders attached, are charms against maladies; and in Burma "luck-pigs"—discs of gold, silver, lead, tortoise-shell, or horn, engraved with a pig and mystic symbols—are put under the skin of the breast or arm as amulets.[68] A special sort of family-amulet is the kite. "The Chinese

66 "Amulets," in JAI, XXXIX, 387, 398-400.

67 Da Cunha, in JASB, I, 391; Joshi, in JASB, I, 123; "Mantrams" (anon.), in JASB, II, 285; Thurston, S. India, 259, 260; Dubois, Moeurs, 190; Modi, in JASB, II, 169.

68 Doolittle, Chinese, II, 315-316; De Groot, Relig. Syst., I, 55; Leclère, in PSM, XLIV, 780; Roth, Note, no. 64, in JAI, XXX.

have a superstition that the bird kite and the dragon kite are a protection to the family against evil spirits; the first by frightening them away, and the last perhaps by abashing them by its harmonies, as those which infested Saul were influenced to depart from him at the sound of David's harp. Sometimes these kites—the cord being securely fastened—remain aloft for several days and nights; the family meanwhile enjoying an unusual sense of security." This "dragon-flying" is a religious custom in the Pelew Islands.[69]

Among the Malays any object becomes an amulet if it is found in a place where it was not expected. A huntsman prays to a stone for good luck, and if he gets it the stone becomes a fetish to him and his whole village. Any stone found in the entrails of a fish, bird, buffalo, or man, any lump of gum exuded from a tree in a peculiar form, any shell, root, or stone of striking form or color, any fruit which through disease has taken an extraordinary form, or any peculiar fruit-stone, will become an amulet. They keep a sharp lookout for such things. Amulets have a political significance; being owned by ruling families, they become state-jewels. They are kept in shrines, with priestesses assigned to them, and are the objects of cult. When a man dies without heirs his ricefields fall to the amulet; likewise the property of those who resist commands, and even their persons. A slave woman who resisted her master might dedicate herself to the amulet, whereupon the master lost all right to her. These amulets are only those of private persons, which have ceased to be private property and have been assumed by the state, that is, by the rulers. They come down from the time when there were many small independent states.[70] The above summary might well be cited under fetishism; it affords a good retrospect of the features of that subject as well as a clear indication of the connection of fetishes and amulets, the cult and the state.[71]

Talismans, including the phallic variety, are rife in the Indian Archipelago. The bezoar stone, a calculus formed in the stomachs of porcupines and monkeys, has especial virtue. Agate bracelets drive off all evil spirits. Holy jars are a protection and asset to their owners. Little wooden boats are protection against diseases which are supposed to put out to sea in them. The Tagals use shells, crocodile-teeth, and inscriptions consisting of senseless extracts from Latin prayerbooks, interspersed with Tagal words and phrases. Doubtless the reverence for skulls, which are prepared and preserved with the greatest art, is connected with their employment as talismans.[72]

"The heathen Greenlanders sought by amulets to protect themselves against magic and other evil, and still today among the Christians the same idea is found quite wide-spread and firmly rooted. For such amulets anything could be used—a bone, a bird's beak, an old shoe-sole, etc.—but in later times a certain tendency has been noticed to choose for this some object from a foreign country, such as a coffee-bean, a luck of hair from some prominent European, splinters from a ship's capstan, etc." A rare article like wood naturally lends itself to such use. They do not worship the evil spirits, "but to insure themselves against their doing damage all the people wear the most diverse things as amulets," which help against sickness and dangers, promote long life, and

69 Varney, "Kite-Flying," in PSM, LIII, 50; Finsch, *Ethnol. Erfahr.*, III, 310, note.
70 Ratzel, *Vkde.*, II, 463, 475.
71 §§254, 262, above.
72 Wilken, *Vkde.*, 52; Schwaner, *Borneo*,

I, 181; Roth, in JAI, XXII, 49; Perelaer, *Dajaks*, 42, 118; Hickson, in JAI, XVI, 141; Anon., "Zauberhemd," in *Globus*, LXXXI, 287; Ratzel, *Vkde.*, II, 334, 338; §§229, 249, above.

secure fulfilment of wishes.[73] Similarly with the Bering Strait Eskimo: "the images and fetishes used in hunting are supposed to watch for game and, by some clairvoyant power, to see it at a great distance; the hunter is then guided by the influence of the fetish to find it. They are also supposed to guide the spears so that they will be cast straight," and may even bring the game to the hunter. These amulets are things which have belonged to or been in contact with people of ancient times or fortunate hunters or supernatural beings, or "objects which merely by their appearance recalled the effect expected from the amulet," for instance, the "flint whale," hung around the neck for luck in whaling.[74]

The Indian amulets were "medicine," that is, "mystery." The warrior's protection in battle "was a feather, a tiny bag of some sacred powder, the claw of an animal, the head of a bird, or some other small object which could be readily twisted into his hair or hidden between the covers of his shield without attracting attention. Its virtue depended entirely on the ceremony of the consecration and not on size or texture. The war paint had the same magic power of protection." Mantles of invisibility, recalling the *Tarnkappe,* are met with, their fetishistic power depending largely upon the devices drawn on them. It was exceptional to find the medicine-bag and medicine-songs looked upon somewhat depreciatingly as witchcraft was in former days among the whites.[75]

The green so-called Amazon-stones were used widely in northern South America as amulets against fevers and snake-bite. They were in the form of fish and animals with figures cut on their surfaces. Certain lilies and other plants were cultivated as charms to make good hunters and fishermen. The use of amulets must always be painful; the nose-charm was a whip of fiber which was put up one of the nostrils and drawn through the back of the mouth. If the hunter fails, he must renew his strength, which he does by digging up a lily-root, slashing himself on breast and arms, and rubbing in the acrid juice; the more excruciating the torture the better the charm is working. "Next day he goes forth into the forest with renewed confidence, and is likely to be more successful on that account alone." In general, "when a warring tribesman slew an enemy, partly as a trophy, but chiefly as a mystical talisman and constant invocation to the powers, he appended the scalp to his spear or belt, or strung the teeth in a necklace, or converted the hand into a gorget. This stage and custom are well known among the primitive peoples of the earth."[76]

Among the Semites the gum of the acacia served as an amulet.[77] In Jewish antiquity, a special amulet called phylactery, consisted of a strip or strips of parchment inscribed with certain texts from the Old Testament, and inclosed with a small leather case, which was fastened with straps on the forehead just above and between the eyes, or on the left arm near the region of the heart. The four passages inscribed upon the phylactery were Exodus, xiii, 2-10, 11-17, and Deuteronomy, vi, 4-9, 13-22. The custom was founded on a literal interpretation of Exodus, xiii, 16, and Deuteronomy, vi, 8 and xi, 18.[78] "He which

73 Fries, *Grönland,* 160; Holm, *Ethnol. Skizze,* 21, 75.
74 Nelson, in BAE, XVIII, pt. I, 437; Murdoch, in BAE, IX, 434, 435.
75 Mooney, in BAE, XIV, 694; Mallery, in BAE, X, 503.

76 Schomburgk, *Brit.-Guiana,* II, 331; Rodway, in PSM, XLVI, 463; Muñiz and McGee, in BAE, XVI, 23.
77 Smith, *Relig. Sem.,* 132.
78 Ewald, *Gesch.,* IV, 479; Matt. XXIII. 5.

hath his Phylacteries on his head and armes, and his Knots on his garment, and his Schedule on his doore, is so fenced that he cannot easily sinne."[79] According to Deuteronomy there should be tassels or fringes on the borders of garments to remind of Jahweh's commands. Originally they were to keep off evil spirits.[80] In the desert and after the children of Israel had sinned, Jahweh commanded them to remove their ornaments that "I may know what to do with thee."[81] It would almost seem as if the dazzling character of the ornaments interfered somewhat with Jahweh's ability to plan and execute proper punishment.

The Oriental jinn are in such deadly terror of iron, that its very name is a charm against them; and so in European folklore iron drives away fairies and elves, and destroys their power.[82] Among the amber-ornaments deposited in the grave-vaults in Denmark are many shaped as axes or hammers. "On the basis of this form's general and wide extent in the north it is reasonable to suppose that the ax has here, as in the western and southern lands, a symbolic significance associated with ideas of a powerful thundering godhead, Thor, whose general and contemporary cult can also be demonstrated among Finnic and Celtic people, and that the ax-shaped amber-ornaments have been carried as protectors and weal-bringing amulets. In this connection it is not without significance that bigger and smaller stone axes have been bored in the same way and hung or worn as amulets both here and in other countries, e.g., in Greece and all through the Orient to China, where they were, somewhat later, provided with magic inscriptions. Indeed, they were almost universally called 'thunderstones' by the common people and were held to have fallen in thunderstorms or to stand in the closest connection with lightning and its effects."[83] In making a collection of Italian amulets, Miss Buell[84] attempted to bring together those in modern use and their ancient parallels. Six classes may be cited: 1. "Prophylactics against the evil eye, having in form some relation to a horn and representing phallicism, Diana worship, and defensive symbolism by means of the hand. Examples— a phallus, a tiger's claw, a boar's tusk, a crab's claw, coral and shell horns, lunar crescents, composite horned animals, hands making the sign of the *fico* and the sign of the horns. 2. Amulets that make the sound of metal, hateful to evil spirits. Examples— bells, clashing disks and pendants. 3. Grotesque and ocular guards against malevolence. Examples—masks, a humpback, compositions or stones resembling eyes. 4. Preventives and cures by suggestion. Examples—a fossilized trochus or 'eye of Santa Lucia,' for eye maladies; a limonite concretion with a loose inner particle, 'pietra gravida,' for miscarriage; fossilized corals, 'witch stone,' for witch spells; carnelian and jasper, 'blood stones,' for heart disease and hemorrhages; bronze and silver fish, for female sterility; a comb, for caked breasts (caused by the presence of a witch's hair); a dried sea horse, to increase milk in the breasts; a red woolen sack containing bread crumbs, salt, incense, and wheat from a field ripe but unspoiled by the harvester's iron, to guard against the evil eye and witchcraft. 5. Charms pertaining to animals. Examples—badger's hairs, for defense against witches; claw of a paradise bird and a monkey's paw, valid against the evil eye. 6. Roman Catholic amulets. (a) Authorized by the church. Examples—the Agnus Dei and medal of St. Benedict

79 Purchas, *Pilgrimage*, 186.
80 Wellhausen, *Prolegomena*, 449; Deut., XXII, 12; XXIV, 13; Num., XV, 38.
81 Exodus, XXXIII, 1-6.

82 Wilken, in VG, III, 378-379, note.
83 Worsaae, *Nordens Forhistorie*, 46.
84 "Amulets," in AA, XII, 84.

for divers bodily ills and storms. (b) Unauthorized, but popularly endowed with specific virtues. Examples—the medal of the Three Magi, 'witch money'; the medal of St. Anthony, Hermit, for animal protection; St. Joseph's carpenter's rule for child protection; the pig of St. Anthony for luck; the medal of St. Andrea Abellina for apoplexy; the coin and the key of the Holy Spirit for infantile convulsions."

The Cross. The cross as a religious symbol has been practically universal both as to time and place. It antedates Christianity by countless years, being found even on objects of the stone age.[85] Its invention, in one form or another, must have been rather easily accomplished. "The straight line, the circle, the cross, the triangle, are simple forms, easily made and might have been invented and reinvented in every age of primitive man and in every quarter of the globe, each time being an independent invention, meaning much or little, meaning different things among different peoples or at different times among the same people; or they may have had no settled or definite meaning." The principal forms of the cross, known as symbols or ornaments, can be reduced to a few classes, though when combined with heraldry its use extends to 385 varieties.[86] "The Latin cross, *Crux immissa,* is found on coins, medals, and ornaments anterior to the Christian era. It was on this cross that Christ is said to have been crucified, and thus it became accepted as the Christian cross. The Greek cross, with arms of equal length crossing at right angles, is found on Assyrian and Persian monuments and tablets, Greek coins and statues. The St. Andrew's cross, *Crux decussata,* is the same as the Greek cross, but turned to stand on two legs. . . . The *Crux ansata,* according to Egyptian mythology, was Ankh, the emblem of Ka, the spiritual double of man. It was also said to indicate a union of Osiris and Isis, and was regarded as a symbol of the generative principle of nature."[87] One writer considers it to be a picture of the lion girdle.[88] A most ancient type of cross is the swastika, which will be discussed later on. The three-armed cross of Odin is found in the bronze age, and also the four-armed cross of Freya. This is an equal-armed cross sometimes in a ring like the wheel-figures of the graves of the stone age, a religious symbol found in Europe, Asia, and America.[89]

The cross may be seen on prehistoric monuments in America, on objects of pottery found by Dr. Schliemann at Hissarlik and at Mycenæ, and, in more than one form, on pagan Roman altars still preserved in Germany and Britain. It appears frequently on tombs in Asia Minor. Missionaries discovered it in Africa, where it was employed as a mystic symbol by the priests long before Christianity was introduced. "A cross was used by the people of Erin as a symbol of some significance at a period long antecedent to the mission of St. Patrick or the introduction of Christianity to this island. It is found, not unfrequently, amongst the scribings picked or carved upon rock surfaces and associated with a class of archaic designs, to the meaning of which we possess no key." With the Chinese it was for untold ages a symbol of the earth. The Buddhists and Brahmins tell us that the figure of the cross, whether in a simple or complex form, symbolizes the traditional happy abode of their primæval

85 Figuier, *Prim. Man,* 283; Taubner, in *Gesellsch. f. Anthrop.,* 1888, 331-333; Krause, *Gesellsch. f. Anthrop.,* 1889, 419; Mortillet, *La Croix;* Cook, in *Amer. Antiquarian,* XIX, No. 4; Whittlesey, *Cross.*

86 Many illustrations are given in BAE, II.
87 Wilson, in USNM, 1894, 764, 765, 766.
88 March, in JAI, XXII, 314.
89 Worsaae, *Nordens Forhistorie,* 44, 99; Müller, *Oldtid,* 420.

ancestors. Travellers say that crosses are exhibited on the curtains of the monasteries of the Tibetan Buddhists to mean peace and quietness. "With the same conception the loop holes of the Japanese forts were in time of peace covered with curtains embroidered with crosses, which when war broke out were removed."[90] In Brittany a common amulet, but one of great power and regarded with great veneration, is the one called the *pierre du croix*, a mineral which crystallizes in the form of a cross, not always at right angles, but frequently so. This is regarded as a token from God in favor of the religion of the country, and is given to these his chosen people as a recognition of their piety and religious fervor. There are several quarries of these in Brittany. Gathered there, they are mounted by the jewelers and sold as amulets. There are others of the same nature, crystallized in star-shape, which are regarded in the same way. They are considered as talismans against shipwreck, drowning, and hydrophobia, and are a cure for sore eyes. When not mounted on a pin or a ring, they are worn in a small sachet or bag around the neck or in the pocket.[91]

Not to go into too much detail concerning the cross, we may center our attention upon its connection with the religion of the aborigines of America. Ingenious theories have been advanced to account for the presence of the cross among American symbols. Some believe that the great importance attached to the points of the compass—the four quarters of the heavens—by savage peoples has given rise to the sign of the cross. With others, it is a phallic symbol, derived by some obscure process of evolution, from the veneration accorded to the reciprocal principle in nature. It is also frequently associated with sun-worship, and is recognized as a symbol of the sun—the four arms being rays remaining after a gradual process of elimination. The cross has also represented the stars, dwellings, the dragon-fly, the Midé Society, human form, maidenhood, evil spirit, and divers others.[92] Among the Blackfeet Indians of Canada, "the 'T,' or tau-cross, is a sacred symbol used in the consecration of medicine men. It is painted in blue upon the breast of the newly initiated as a sign of power. It is connected with the gift of healing."[93] Another type of cross has arisen from the sign for the butterfly—a design roughly in the shape of a maltese cross. It is held that the butterfly brings sleep and dreams. "It is still a custom for the Blackfeet woman to embroider the sign of the butterfly in beads or quills on a small piece of buckskin, and to tie this in her baby's hair when she wishes it to go to sleep. At the same time she sings to the child a lullaby, in which the butterfly is asked to come flying about and to put the baby to sleep. . . . The use among the Dakota of the Latin cross to denote the dragonfly as a warner of the approach of danger, is interesting in this connection."[94] Among the Sioux the square or oblong, with the four lines standing out, is interpreted to mean the earth or land with the four winds standing toward it. "The cross, whether diagonal or upright, always symbolizes the four winds or four quarters."[95] With all the prairie tribes the morning-star is held in great reverence and is the subject of much mythological belief and ceremony. "It is universally represented in their

90 Mallery, in BAE, X, 731, 732; Hewitt, in *Westminster Review*, CL, 261-275; Carus, in *Open Court*, XVIII, 288; Johnston, *Uganda*, II, 678; Lacroix, *Middle Ages*, 387.
91 Wilson, in USNM, 1890, 677.

92 Holmes, in BAE, II, 270; Wilson, in USNM, 1894, 788.
93 L'Heureux, in JAI, XV, 303; Haliburton, in *Brit. Ass'n*, 1886.
94 Grinnell, in AA, I, 194, 195.
95 Dorsey, in BAE, XI, 451.

pictographs as a cross, usually of the Maltese pattern. In this form it is frequently pictured on the ghost shirts. The Arapaho name, *nagaq,* means literally 'a cross.' "96 Among the Tusayan, "the equal-armed cross in modern pictography is a symbol of the Star god or Heart-of-the-sky. How old this association is in Tusayan mythology is doubtful, but the cross is found on many decorated food bowls."97 A Maltese form of cross representing the four winds of heaven and repeated six times on an Apache cloak was held to make the wearer invisible. It was also painted by warriors upon their moccasins upon going into a strange district in the hope of keeping them from getting on a wrong trail.98 "The cross as portrayed by the Zuñi refers to the bright morning star, which symbolizes that one of the 'fire gods' who lights up the day." Sometimes the cross represents a conventionalized form of man; and among the Ojibwa, apart from symbolizing the four cardinal points as the abode of the wind-gods, it signifies the fourth degree of the cult society of the Midé, because, during the ritualistic ceremonies of the fourth degree, a cross is erected within the enclosure built for the purpose." This consists of two posts in the form of a cross. Marquette evidently did not know that the cross is the sacred post. The erroneous conclusion that it was erected as an evidence of the adoption of Christianity, and possibly as a compliment to the visitor, was natural on the part of the priest.99 A number of copper crosses have been unearthed in Tennessee, Ohio, and elsewhere, which cannot be accounted for by contact with Europeans. They probably were worn as ornaments; the form is an easy design to execute and one of natural conception.100 The Maltese cross of the ancient inhabitants of the Southwest is the emblem of a virgin, still so recognized by the Mokis. "It is a conventional development of a more common emblem of maidenhood, the form in which the maidens wear their hair arranged as a disk of three or four inches in diameter upon each side of the head. This discoidal arrangement of their hair is typical of the emblem of fructification, worn by the maiden in the Muinwa festival." This strongly marked form of Maltese cross appears frequently in the pottery and also in the petroglyphs of the Moki.101

The cross was generally used by the Mayas and Mexicans as a symbol of the cardinal points. Possessing four arms, it came readily enough to be regarded as indicating directions, and hence the four winds. As the winds brought rain, the cross became a symbol of rain or of the god of rain, and governed the Maya calendar.102 It occurs on one of the bas-reliefs of Palenque and on the monuments of Cuzco, in the very center of the worship of the sun, being similar to the Egyptian *tau.*103 One writer104 thinks that the crosses which were frequently used before the conquest by the aborigines of Mexico and Central America were merely ornaments and were not objects of worship, while the so-called crucifixes, like that on the "Palenque tablet," were only the symbol of the "new fire" or of the close of a period of fifty-two years. He believes

96 Mooney, in BAE, XIV, 1011; Plate XX, in BAE, II, 179.

97 Fewkes, in AA, IX, No. 5, 165.

98 Bourke, in BAE, IX, 479, 480; Mallery, in BAE, X, plate XXXIII.

99 Hoffman, in BAE, VII, 155; Hoffman, *Writing,* 162, 164; BAE, VII, plate XV; Powell, in BAE, X, ch. XX, 726.

100 Moorehead, *Prim. Man,* 55; Nadaillac, *Preh. America,* 129; Thruston, *Tennessee,* 299.

101 Mallery, in BAE, IV, 231.

102 Thomas, in BAE, III, 61; Quiroga, *Cruz,* xiv, 95, 115, 116-117, 121.

103 Nadaillac, *Preh. America,* 176.

104 Bandelier, *Arch. Inst. Amer.,* II, 184, quoted in Mallery, in BAE, X, 730; Lippert, *Kgchte.,* II, 377.

them to be merely representations of "fire-drills" more or less ornamented. On the other hand there is much evidence that the cross figured in the religion of various tribes of the peninsula of Yucatan and that it represented the god of rain, while Quetzalcoatl, the "Feathered Serpent," is represented with his robe marked with the sign of the cross to show that he was Lord of the Four Winds and of Life.[105] Trees were regarded as sacred by the Nagualists, and in Mexican mythology "the tree of life" is represented as having four branches, "each sacred to one of the four cardinal points and the divinities associated therewith." In the Mexican figurative paintings this tree resembles a cross. The ancient Mexican pictographic manuscripts abound in representations of trees, conventionalized in such a manner as to resemble crosses; these apparently take an important part in the scenes depicted. By a comparison of them with the cross in the Palenque tablet, Holmes[106] has been led to the belief that they must have a common significance and origin. "The analogies are indeed remarkable. The tree-cross in the paintings is often the central figure of a group in which priests offer sacrifice, or engage in some similar religious rite. The cross holds the same relation as the Palenque group. The branches of these cross-shaped trees terminate in clusters of symbolic fruit, and the arms of the cross are loaded down with symbols, which, although highly conventionalized, have not yet entirely lost their vegetable character. The most remarkable feature, however, is not that the crosses resemble each other in these respects, but that they perform like functions in giving support to a symbolic bird which is perched upon the summit. This bird appears to be the important feature of the group, and to it, or the deity which it represents, the homage or sacrifice is offered. These analogies go still farther; the bases of the cross in the tablet and of the crosses in the paintings are made to rest upon a highly conventionalized figure of some mythical creature. A consideration of these facts seems to me to lead to the conclusion that the myths represented in all of these groups are identical, and that the cross and cross-like trees have a common origin. Whether that origin is in the tree on the one hand or in a cross otherwise evolved on the other I shall not attempt to say." The sign of a cross, with arms of equal or unequal length, came to be the ideogram for life in the Mexican hieroglyphic writing. As such, varied in different ways, it was employed to signify the nagual, "the sign of nativity, the natal day, the personal spirit."[107] Among the cave-dwellers of the Sierra Madre, the medicine-man marks the forehead of the newly-born babe, if a boy, with three crosses, if a girl, with four. The Tarahumari, who inhabit this region, have a tradition involving the cross which is of significance in their religious rites. "Once when their god was intoxicated, the devil robbed him of his wife. 'I cannot remain here any longer,' said he, 'because the devil took my wife; but I will leave two crosses in the world.' He placed one cross where the sun sets and one where it rises. The cross in the east their god uses when he comes down to visit the Tarahumaris; that in the west is for the Tarahumari when he dies and goes to heaven. Between these two crosses lives the Tarahumari tribe. The Indians would like to go to the crosses and dance before them, one of their forms of worship, but they are prevented from doing so by large bodies of water, and they therefore have small crosses standing outside their own houses before which they hold

105 Brinton, *Nagualism*, 43; Preuss, in *Globus*, LXXIX, 262.

106 In BAE, II, 270.
107 Brinton, *Nagualism*, 48.

their nightly dances. They also sacrifice before these crosses, and here is where their god comes to eat. The Tarahumari invariably provides a smooth place near his house or cave upon which he erects his cross and where he holds his dances."[108]

On an isolated rock in a certain valley there is a round tower made by the Incas, of rough stones faced with stucco. "Above the door, and simulating windows, we meet again with the Egyptian *tau* that we have already seen at Palenque." The structure of this tower seems to indicate that it was a temple.[109] Among some tribes the cross was adopted as an amulet, as in the case of the Abipones who had crosses tattooed on the middle of the forehead.[110] In Surinam the cross is common and is in no way connected with Christian views.[111] That the cross in the Americas was an independent development antedating contact with the whites, there can be no doubt.[112]

The Swastika. An ancient form of the cross is the swastika. Its origin is unknown. The bars of the normal swastika are straight, of equal thickness throughout, and cross each other at right angles, making four arms of equal size, length, and style. Their peculiarity is that all the ends are bent at right angles and in the same direction, right or left. The swastika has been used as a symbol or as an ornament since prehistoric times from China to western Africa, throughout Europe, and in the two Americas. In the historic period it is found in Japan, Korea, China, Tibet, Armenia, Asia Minor, Greece and its islands, especially Cyprus and Rhodes, Italy, France, Germany, Scandinavia, Great Britain—perhaps only under Scandinavian influence—Ohio, Tennessee, Mississippi, Alaska, Mexico, and Brazil. Dr. Schliemann found many specimens of swastika in his excavations at the site of ancient Troy on the hill of Hissarlik. It is common on the prehistoric monuments of Western Europe; it occurs on Greek and Cilician coins and in catacombs, on bronze grave-plates and, in the Middle Ages, on priestly garments. It was adopted into heraldry as the cross cramponee.[113] In Scandinavia it used to be vulgarly called the hammer of Thor and Thor's hammer-mark; some authors, however, hold that it has no connection with the Thor hammer, which is reported to be the same as the Greek *tau,* having the form of the Roman and English capital T.[114]

The swastika is connected particularly with Buddhism, and its presence in Japan, China, and Tibet is thus explained. In Buddhism, the ends of the arms are always bent in the respectful attitude, *i.e.,* to the left; "for the Lamas, while regarding the symbol as one of good augury, also consider it to typify the continuous moving, or 'ceaseless becoming' which is commonly called Life." The Jains appropriated it for the seventh of their mythical saints; the heterodox Tibetans, the Bön, in adopting it have turned the ends in the reverse direction.[115] The swastika stands on the first page of Hindu ledgers and daybooks, and is a common stamp on East Indian coins. A saddle in the

108 Lumholtz, in *Scribner's Mag.*, XVI, 296; and in *Int. Cong. Anthrop.*, 1893, 110.

109 Nadaillac, *Preh. America*, 417.

110 Quiroga, *Cruz*, xv.

111 Martin, in *Bijd.*, XXXV, 52.

112 Quiroga, *Cruz*, 74, 82, 88-89, 93-95, 119-120; Charnay, *Nouveau Monde*, 65; Nadaillac, *Preh. America*, 327, note.

113 Wilson, "Swastika," in USNM, 1894, 767, 771, 777, 798, 809, 830; Andree, *Ethnog. Parallelen*, second series, 75; Truhelka, in *Globus*, LXXXI, 381; *Warren's Guide to Winchester*, 1902, 48.

114 Waring, *Ceramic Art in Remote Ages*, quoted in Wilson, "Swastika," USNM, 1894, 770; Worsaae, *Nordens Forhistorie*, 44, 98; Müller, *Oldtid*, 153.

115 Waddell, *Buddhism*, 389.

Chinese department at the Boston Art Museum bears a swastika in gold on the front of its pommel.[116]

It cannot be doubted that the swastika was known in the Western Hemisphere in prehistoric times. A specimen was taken by Dr. Edward Palmer in 1881 from an ancient mound opened by him on Fains Island, Tennessee. Excavations in the mounds in Ohio and among the ruined pueblos in southwestern Colorado have disclosed objects bearing the swastika.[117] The Pima use it for decorative purposes,[118] while it appears "alike engraved on Japanese bronzes and portrayed in the Navajo sand-pictures."[119] It occurs as a mystic symbol of the wind-powers on war-charts of the Kansa and Osage tribes.[120] The Spaniards found it in Yucatan when they first came there, while many examples have been collected from Brazil.[121] "If some learned traveller from the Orient chanced to stop overnight in an out-of-the-way corner of the United States, where patchwork quilts still sometimes take the place of woven counterpanes, and upon awakening in the morning should find his bedcover besprinkled at regular intervals with this mystic sign of the religion of his own land, surely, if he recalled Hans Christian Andersen's dramatic tale of 'The Tin Soldier,' and of his final reappearance in the very room from which he had been so lucklessly borne away, he too would exclaim . . . 'Nay, how wonderfully things can come to pass in the world!' "[122]

There are many theories concerning the symbolism of the swastika, its relation to ancient deities and its representation of certain qualities. There is nothing to prevent us from supposing that it was spontaneously conceived everywhere, like the equilateral crosses, circles, triangles, chevrons, and other geometrical ornaments so frequent in primitive decoration. It may have been merely decorative in its origin. There is good reason to believe, however, that it has been and is chiefly talismanic. "We see it, at least among the peoples of the Old Continent, invariably passing for talisman, appearing in the funeral scenes or on the tombstones of Greece, Scandinavia, Numidia, and Thibet, and adorning the breasts of divine personages—of Apollo and Buddha—without forgetting certain representations of the Good Shepherd in the Catacombs."[123] Some scholars say it is a solar symbol; others an earth or wind symbol. Says Wilson:[124] "Some writers have respectively considered it the emblem of Zeus, of Baal, of the sun, of the sun-god, of the sun-chariot of Agni the fire-god, of Indra the rain-god, of the sky, the sky-god, and finally the deity of all deities, the great God, the Maker and Ruler of the Universe. It has been held to symbolize light or the god of light, of the forked lightning, and of water. It is believed by some to have been the oldest Assyrian symbol. Others think it represents Brahma, Vishnu, and Siva, Creator, Preserver, Destroyer. It appears in the footprints of Buddha, engraved upon the solid rock on the mountains of India. It stood for the Jupiter Tonans and Pluvius of the Latins, and the Thor of the Scandinavians. In the latter case it has been erroneously thought to be a variety of the Thor hammer. At least one author thought it had an intimate relation to the Lotus sign of Egypt

116 Bergen, in *Scribner's*, XVI, 370.
117 Wilson, "Swastika," in USNM, 1894, 879, 897.
118 Russell, in BAE, XXVI, 121.
119 Buckland, in JAI, XXII, 353.
120 Dorsey, in *Amer. Naturalist*, July, 1885.

121 Wilson, "Swastika," in USNM, 1894, 904.
122 Bergen, in *Scribner's*, XVI, 370.
123 Mallery, in BAE, X, 732.
124 In USNM, 1894, 770, 771.

and Persia. Some have attributed a phallic meaning to it. Some have thought it represented the generative principle of mankind, making it the symbol of the female. Its appearance on the person of certain goddesses, Artemis, Hera, Demeter, Astarte, and the Chaldean Nana, the leading goddess from Hissarlik, has caused it to be claimed as a sign of fecundity." Various suggestions have been offered as to the derivation of its form. Some think it developed from the cross, the lotus-petal, or the circle; others regard it as the conventionalization of a flying bird.[125] Among the Buddhists, where it was especially associated with the divinity of Fire, it is thought that its origin was the cross-shaped part of the fire-drill.[126] It has been asserted by Max Müller[127] that the swastika was a mark of property which was put on the ear of a cow, from the time of the Vedas down; it was only one of many such marks. Prior to Christianity it was said to be a sign of submission like two bended knees.[128]

Definitions and derivation of the term "swastika" have been given, though the sign must have existed long before that name was applied to it. "It must have been in existence long before the Buddhist religion or the Sanskrit language." The word comes from the Sanskrit and its use can be traced back to about 400 b.c. The following analysis of the Sanskrit *swastika* has been given: "*Su,* radical, signifying good, well, excellent, or *suvidas,* prosperity. *Asti,* third person, singular, indicative present of the verb *as,* to be, which is *sum* in Latin. *Ka,* suffix forming the substantive."[129] It might be translated literally as "of good fortune." "What seems to have been at all times an attribute of the Swastika is its character as a charm or amulet, as a sign of benediction, blessing, long life, good fortune, good luck. This character has continued into modern times, and while the Swastika is recognized as a holy and sacred symbol by at least one Buddhistic religious sect, it is still used by the common people of India, China, and Japan as a sign of long life, good wishes, and good fortune."[130] It is a striking memorial of the universal significance of the aleatory element.

§277. Coercitives.

AMONG the Nairs of India there is an implicit distinction between practices to propitiate a god and those with which to bully a spirit. A ghost or spirit, though superior to man in power and intelligence, as well as in the will to do harm, can be rendered harmless and kept under control by magical practices.[1] This notion was fairly common among the ancients. It is expressed in writings composed under the Ptolemies upon the sacred science of the Egyptians. "They not only called the god by name, but if he refused to appear they threatened him." These formulæ of compulsion of the gods were named by the Greeks

125 Bobrinsky, in *Bull. de la Soc. d'Anthrop. de Paris,* 1901, 424-425; Anon., in *Globus,* LXXVIII, 180; Temple, in JASB, I, 182.

126 Waddell, *Buddhism,* 389; Ratzel, *Vkde.,* II, 435.

127 In Schliemann, *Ilios,* 390.

128 *Warren's Guide to Winchester,* 1902, 48.

129 Dumoutier, in *Revue d'Ethnog.,* IV, 329, quoted in Wilson, in USNM, 1894, 769.

130 Wilson, in USNM, 1894, 771, 952. For other sources on the swastika see Mortillet, *Signe de la Croix avant le Christianisme;* Müller, *Det Saakaldte Hagekors's Anvendelse i Oldtiden;* Zmingrodzki, "Suastika," in *Archiv f. Anthrop.,* XIX (a learned paper with a large number of illustrations); Hewitt, in *Westminster Review,* CL; Wake, in *Amer. Antiq.,* XVI, No. 1; Cushing, in AA, IX, 334; Prowe, in *Globus,* XC, 159.

1 Panikkar, in JAI, XLVIII, 278-279.

theōn anagkai.[2] In the religion of the Parsis one of the chief means of checking evil influences is the cultivation of the soil. In the *Avesta* it is written:

> When barley occurs, then the demons hiss;
> When thrashing occurs, then the demons whine;
> When grinding occurs, then the demons roar;
> When flour occurs, then the demons flee.[3]

In the imitative magic of the Athenian Thesmophoria, man attempts direct compulsion, he admits no mediator between himself and nature, and he thanks no god for what no god has done. "A thank-offering is later even than a prayer, and prayer as yet is not. To mark the transition from rites of compulsion to rites of supplication and consequent thanksgiving is to read the whole religious history of primitive man."[4]

Certain religious acts of self-denial can be interpreted here as coercitives. Continence is a preparation to come into the presence of God at Sinai.[5] Men abstain from their wives when on the warpath.[6]

Nudity, as has been shown in the text, is a typical coercitive. In southern India, on the third and fourth days of a festival held in honor of two divinities, a god and a goddess, women walk naked into the temple, but are covered with leaves and boughs of trees and surrounded by their female friends. The proceedings end with a procession around the boundaries of the village lands; here order and propriety cease, and the goddess is abused in the foulest language.[7] Crooke[8] cites many cases of nudity from Indian sources and from his own experience. Ritual nudity is common in religion and magic. In rain-magic, he says, the performers hope rain will fall and fertilize them, like thirsty vegetation. The religious orders practise it as symbolic of death to this world, renunciation of family and social ties. It is associated with fertility-rites, as when a woman walks naked one hundred and eight times around a certain tree to get offspring, or appears stark naked in various rites to get children, or when a naked man pounces on a lamb, tears its throat with his teeth, drinks some blood, and runs with the carcass to the village boundary "to expel evil and promote fertility." Nudity seems to be a necessary condition for magic and witchcraft. Cattle may be cured by a man walking around them naked, with a wisp of burning straw. Survivals may be seen in ancient priestly vestments composed of a few leaves.

The Aleuts had religious dances and festivals in December, during which images were carried from island to island and strange ceremonies, of which we have but dim traditions, were performed at night. There were mysteries sacred to males and to females. In some secret orgies both sexes joined without reproach. Hundreds of women wearing masks are said to have danced naked in the moonlight, men being rigidly excluded and liable to death if detected intruding. The men had analogous dances. An idea prevailed that while these mystic rites were going on a spirit or power descended into the idol.[9]

At Mecca, in the times of heathendom, the sacred circuit of the Kaaba was made by the Beduin, either naked or in clothes lent by a member of the religious community of the sacred city. The same custom appears in the wor-

---

2 Lenormant, *Chaldean Magic*, 101.
3 Müller, *Sacred Books*, IV, 32; Haug, *Relig. Parsis*, 151, 237.
4 Harrison, *Greek Relig.*, 124.
5 Exodus, XIX, 15.

6 §§140, 281, of the text.
7 Gomme, *Eth. in Folklore*, 23.
8 In JAI, XLIX, 237 ff.
9 Dall, in BAE, 1881-2, 139.

ship of the Tyrian Baal. It appears that sometimes a man did make the circuit at Mecca in his own clothes, but in that case he could neither wear them again nor sell them, but had to leave them at the gate of the sanctuary; they became taboo through contact with the holy place and function.[10]

Belief in the magic power of nakedness continued into modern times, as in the case of Charles II of Spain. This impotent king thought he was bewitched, a belief which was confirmed by his father confessor, a Dominican who had a vision that the royal pair were prevented from having children because of a charm. It was decided to break the spell by means of an exorcistic ceremony: the king and queen were to go out naked and the monk *in pontificalibus* was to tackle the charm. The king vigorously importuned the queen to accede to this, but that lady could not be persuaded to submit to the ignominy.[11] It is a modern superstition that single women desiring husbands should, the night before St. Andrew's day, call upon that saint naked, and they will see their sweethearts in their sleep. Also, "on Christmas-eve the girls sit up from 11 to 12. To find out if they shall get married the next year, they strip themselves naked, stick their heads into the copper, and watch the water hissing. If that does not answer, they take a broom and sweep the room backwards, and see the future lover sitting in a corner: if they hear the crack of a whip, he is a waggoner; if the sound of a pipe, a shepherd. Some rush out of doors naked, and call the lover; others go to a cross-road, and call out his name." The spiteful creature, who wants to do his neighbor a rascally mischief, "goes at midnight, stark naked, with a sickle tied to his foot, and repeating magic spells, through the middle of a field of corn just ripe. From that part of the field that he has passed his sickle through, all the grains fly into his barn, into his bin."[12]

Cursing. The invocation of injury or evil upon another, whereby, apparently, the spirits are forced to carry out the curse, is a coercitive of the first magnitude among primitive peoples. The Loyalty Islanders had "great faith in, and dread of, cursing. To be cursed by a parent or chief was regarded as the greatest calamity." Imprecation was a frequent method of causing sickness.[13]

The Bangala of the Congo calls down a curse on the thief; his formula witnesses to the local sex-division of labor. "Should the thief be a man he will henceforth have no luck in fishing, and should it be a woman she will have no more success in farming."[14] An interesting feature is the dying curse— the *kirume* of Kikuyu and *kiume* of Ukamba, "the general idea of this being that a dying person can put a curse upon property belonging to him, or can lay a curse upon another person, but only upon a person belonging to his own family; thus, for example, the head of a village, when dying, can lay a curse on a certain plot of land owned by him and will that it shall not pass out of the family, and if a descendant sells it, it is believed that the speedy death of the offender is the result." A case recently came to the author's knowledge where an elder was offered a very tempting sum for a particular piece of land, as well as equivalent land elsewhere, but it was refused by the owner because it had come down to him with a *kirume* on it. "This is a very interesting revelation, because when one comes to consider it, it is undoubtedly

---

10 Smith, *Relig. Sem.*, 451; Wilken, in VG, II, 17; II Kings, X, 22; II Sam., VI, 14.
11 Scherr, *Deut. Frauenwelt*, II, 95.

12 Stallybrass, *Grimm's Teut. Myth.*, II, 475; IV, 1781, 1797.
13 Ray, in JAI, XLVII, 297.
14 Weeks, in JAI, XL, 394.

the genesis of a last will or testament. Furthermore, it is the rude beginning of our principle of 'entail.' It moreover shows that these people have reached the stage of individual tenure in land." Examples may be found all over the country, where the curse is passed on from generation to generation, such is the strength of the belief. If a man does not receive his father's blessing he is believed to go through life attended by much misfortune. A daughter may be a trouble to her father; "she is, say, married to a husband who has paid over the required dowry to her father, she runs away, repeatedly misbehaves herself, and so forth, and the father will then be subject to continual worry, owing to the husband's demands for the return of the dowry. The father may eventually become so weary of all this worry that he will put a *kirume* on her and condemn her to perpetual barrenness." A man is, generally speaking, able to lay a *kirume* only upon a person belonging to his own clan, which really means that a curse will affect only one with a common blood tie. "If a person hears that, say, a brother intended to place a *kirume* on him, he would at once take a male goat or sheep to his village and kill it there, he would offer some of the fat, some milk and some beer to the dying man, who could not refuse to forgive the suppliant, and would ceremonially spit into his hands and rub a little saliva on his forehead, navel, and feet. The threatened person would then depart in peace free from any danger of a *kirume* from that person. . . . If a man hears that a near relative is very ill he makes a point of going to see him, and takes the precaution of getting him to ceremonially spit on his hand and rub his visitor on the navel. If a man goes to see his sick father or mother he takes a piece of mutton fat, and the sick parent ceremonially spits on it and the visitor rubs the saliva covered piece of fat on his navel." The effective power of the *kirume*, according to native belief, is derived from the spirit of the deceased person by whom it is imposed, assisted by the spirits of the ancestors of the family. Another type of curse, called *thahu*, is imposed by the elders; it is possible to have this curse removed. "To remove the curse the offender then goes to the elders and begs to be allowed to pay the amount of the judgment. This is done, and he brings in addition a sheep; the elders then say, 'Go back home, bring some beer, and the day after to-morrow we will come and spit on you.' . . . The elders then each take a little of the sheep's fat and rub it on their staves saying, 'We are glad that the man who defied our order has now obeyed it; we cursed him through our *mithegi* [staves], but we now smear our *mithegi* with fat, as a sign that we and our *mithegi* are glad, and there is now nothing to be feared, for we have come to cleanse you and your village from evil.' The elders then assemble in a circle with the man and his family in the middle, and one of the elders anoints the tongue of each individual of the family with a spot of *ira* or white earth, and the elders then ceremonially spit on the offender and each of his family and depart." The same belief occurs in Ukamba, where the council of elders can inflict upon a man, for disregard of its orders, a curse which, if he is still recalcitrant, is said to be so potent as to kill him and all the people of his village in a short time.[15] Among the tribes of British Central Africa, in some cases a man who is cursed will starve himself to death.[16]

In a Samoan case of stealing, fine mats or other gifts were taken by the injured party to pay the priest to curse the thief and make him ill. "The priest

15 Hobley, in JAI, XLI, 406, 416-417, 419,   16 Stannus, in JAI, XL, 302.
427-429.

would then sit down with some select members of the family around the bowl representative of the god, and pray for speedy vengeance on the guilty; then they waited the issue. These imprecations were dreaded. Conscience-stricken thieves, when taken ill, were carried off by their friends on a litter and laid down at the door of the priest, with taro, cocoa-nuts, or yams, in lieu of those confessed to have been stolen; and they would add fine mats and other presents, that the priest might pray again over the death-bowl, and have the sentence reversed."[17]

The formulæ of imprecation among the Chaldæans were really terrible. They called upon all the gods of heaven and of the abyss to display their power by overwhelming with misfortunes the person against whom they were directed.[18] Since the opening of the tomb of Tut-ankh-Amen a series of dramatic events has taken place, beginning with the death of Lord Carnarvon and being followed within two years by that of five others; this has led to a revival of theories about unseen powers protecting a tomb against desecration by profane hands.[19] One recalls the mortuary inscription on the sarcophagus of a Phœnician king of the sixth century, B.C., in which he cast his curse on the desecrator in no uncertain tone: "Let there be no resting place," the curse reads, "for the man, even if he be of royal lineage, who ventures to open this chamber of repose, or remove the sarcophagus in which I am at rest." The same sentiment is expressed by the lines cut on Shakespeare's gravestone: "Curst be he that moves my bones."

On its religious side the curse developed into the vow and the prayer, on its social side into the ordinance and ultimately into the regular law; hence the language of early legal formularies still maintains as necessary and integral the sanction of the curse. The formula is not "do this" or "do not do that," but "cursed be he who does this, or does not do that."[20]

The Oath. Allied to cursing in its religious aspect is the oath, a solemn affirmation made with an appeal to supernatural power to establish the truth of what it affirmed. The savage method of taking oath often makes evident the kind of punishment invoked in case the person is not speaking the truth.[21]

In affirming the truth the Papuans of Geelvink-Bay call upon heaven as witness, the Alfurs upon the sun, while the natives of Utanata River on such an occasion inflict a small wound on their bodies, mix the blood with salt water and drink it.[22]

The Koranna of South Africa confirm an oath by saying: "as truly as I have a mother."[23] The Makololo do not administer an oath, but occasionally when a statement is questioned, a man will say: "By my father," or "By the chief, it is so."[24] Generally among the Kaffirs an oath is affirmed by calling the name of a chief, usually of one who is dead, or by invoking a father or brother on the part of females, and a sister or mother, especially a mother-in-law, on the part of males.[25] To make an oath binding on the person who takes it, certain West Africans give him something to eat or drink which in some way appertains to a deity, who is then invoked to visit a breach of faith with punishment. The ordinary plan is to take something from the spot in which the deity resides. Thus, in the case of a marine god, a little seawater, or seaweed

17 Turner, *Samoa*, 30-31.
18 Lenormant, *Chaldean Magic*, 68.
19 N. Y. *Times*, April 7, 1923; Feb. 6, 1924; Mar. 28, 30, 1926.
20 Harrison, *Greek Relig.*, 142.

21 Frischbier, in *Am. Ur-Quell*, II, 58-59.
22 Krieger, *Neu-Guinea*, 405.
23 Holub, *Süd-Afr.*, I, 116.
24 Livingstone, *Mission. Travels*, I, 201.
25 Kropf, *Kaffir-Eng. Dict.*, 107.

from the rock or reef in which he dwells, is taken into the mouth and swallowed.[26] The Mandingo swear by Mumbo-Jumbo and regard such an oath as holy. In Liberia a woman accused of adultery must swear by the mark of the secret society so that the spirit of the club may kill her if she is guilty.[27] On the Loango Coast a most effective type of affirmation is that which involves driving a nail into a wooden image. He who drives in such a consecrated nail—in serious cases a red-hot one—is thought to be constantly reminded of his duty by the pain which he has caused, and only after fulfilment will the nail be drawn out and the wound (of the hole) healed. "As such a mighty demon, naturally filled with violent wrath against the author on account of the pain he has caused, strives to pursue him with full vengeance, the thief, when he hears that the victim has sent for the image of the fetish to have a nail driven in, tremblingly returns the stolen goods. The guilty party dares not drive in a nail and thus be counted among those suspected." These ceremonies are used in a preventive way also, as when a merchant, before sending out his slaves to bring in the goods he has purchased, will have the fetish brought and a nail driven in before the assembled house-servants, with maledictions against him who may be guilty of any peculation. Vows also are given a binding and coercing power through this means. If, for example, a master cannot cure his servant of drunkenness, he has a nail driven into the fetish before his eyes, and then the fear of sickness or death in case of transgression prevents the servant from violating his promise.[28]

In the ceremony of allegiance in Madagascar, a young calf is killed, the head and feet are reversed in position, spears are thrust into the carcass, and those who are about to be sworn hold spears in their hands while one of the judges repeats a form of oath, imprecating fearful penalties upon the heads of those who violate it, that they may in that case become like the mangled animal before them. To this they express assent by violently shaking their spears. This form of oath is employed chiefly for the more influential personages. For those of lower rank the following ceremony is considered sufficient: the parties stand round a small pond of water into which there has previously been thrown the dung of a bullock, the flower of a certain grass, a musket ball, the wadding of a musket, branches of a certain tree, a long grass, and a water flower. An oath of allegiance having been recited by one of the judges, assent is given by the persons to be sworn striking the water with boughs, a spear also being plunged into the pool and a musket fired over it. At the accession of one of the kings, another form of oath was devised: in this ceremony a quantity of red earth taken from the tomb of one of the kings was mixed with water and drunk by the common people, it being supposed that this would operate as a curse upon those who should violate the oath.[29] Oaths of fidelity are just as binding. "Among the Wakanda the emissaries of the two parties squat together in a circle round a pot as large as the fist, roughly moulded in clay and dried in the sun, containing water. The speakers take a stick in their hands and speak, tapping all the time on the pot, of the friendly disposition of their belongings, until one takes the pot in his hand, and with the speech, 'If we break the friendship which we have here promised, may we be broken like this pot,' dashes it to the ground. The Mussulman Swahelis, in place of an oath, dash down a cocoa-nut in the mosque.

26 Ellis, *Tshi*, 196.
27 Frobenius, *Masken*, 126-127, 150.
28 Lenz, *Westafrika*, 183.
29 Sibree, *Great Afr. Isl.*, 185-186.

The Wakikuyu strangle a lamb, wishing that they may undergo the same death if they break the oath."[30]

The Kilimanjaro native swears by his chief;[31] the northeast African by the repudiation of his wife; "If I don't speak the truth, may my wife be put away."[32] The oath of the Dinka tribe is taken on the sacred spear of the district. "Lying, after taking oath on the spear, is so much feared that I have seen cases of alleged injury withdrawn absolutely on the defendant taking the oath on the spear that he is innocent."[33] In some parts of the Sahara an oath taken on the foliage of certain trees is held to be just as holy as that of the Mohammedan upon the Koran.[34]

The oath among the Ostyak of Siberia consists in having the accused kiss the paw of a bear. "He who has kissed the paw is regarded as truthful; the Ostyak is of the firm belief that if one has lied he will be torn to pieces by a bear at the next encounter. This oath, however, has little by little lost importance; the young Ostyaks carry a bear's paw in fish-oil as an amulet and believe that they have thereby smeared, *i.e.*, appeased, the bear and that, in case they have actually sworn falsely, it will be lenient with them."[35] The form of oath, both in the Hindu Kush mountains and on the eastern frontier of Bengal, is licking salt.[36] A Naga case is cited where the natives erected a large stone on the occasion of taking an oath, and said, "As long as this stone stands on the earth no differences shall occur between us."[37] The commonest and most sacred form of oath is for the two parties to lay hold of a dog or fowl while the creature is cut in two, "emblematic of the perjurer's fate."[38] Another common method is to bite a tiger's tooth kept for the purpose, and then to eat some of the earth from a grave, saying at the same time, "The gods will see me, and if I am lying, they will send a tiger to eat me, or they will turn my head to earth like this grave." A form of oath used by the Angamis is: "May I be eaten by a tiger, and may my harvests be nothing but stalks; may my rice grow up and then may the beards of grain grow down into the earth again, if I am not speaking the truth." "They seem," writes Furness,[39] "to have absolute confidence in a man's statement, after taking oath in this manner. I once questioned the trustworthiness of such an oath, and an Angami Naga said: 'Possibly a white man might live after breaking his oath, but a Naga would surely die.' Their death rate must be large; the Angamis, above all others, are treacherous liars." It would be significant to know whether the last statement applies to their dealings amongst themselves or with the whites. The Chin take oaths when making agreements of every sort; the most common form is for both parties to kill an animal and paint each other with its blood. In some parts of the hills it is customary to eat earth when swearing, and in the south, earth is tendered to a witness in a criminal case to eat in court. "The eating of earth is considered a very binding oath, and, if there is any possibility of getting the truth out of a Chin at all, there is more chance of it after he has taken this form of oath."[40]

In the *Mahabharata*, vows of penance and fasting have power over the gods and they accumulate strength. One way of swearing is to touch one's head.[41]

30 Ratzel, *Hist. Mankind*, II, 380.
31 Volkens, *Kilimandscharo*, 249.
32 Paulitschke, *Nordost-Afr.*, II, 150.
33 O'Sullivan, in JAI, XL, 191.
34 Nachtigal, *Sahara*, II, 685.
35 Kondratowitsch, in *Globus*, LXXIV, 289.

36 Yule, *Cathay*, 555, note.
37 Godden, in JAI, XXVII, 38.
38 Woodthorpe, in JAI, XI, 71.
39 In JAI, XXXII, 464-465.
40 Carey and Tuck, *Chin Hills*, 194, 195.
41 Holtzmann, *Indische Sagen*, I, 216, 335-336.

Often the only binding oath is taken under a tree. When swearing the Hindu holds water or holy grass;[42] and if he does it with a mango leaf on his head, "none but a hardened sceptic will disbelieve him then."[43] When two villages in Assam are about to swear an oath of perpetual peace, "they place a cat inside a basket and the two headmen take hold of the basket at either end and then hack the cat in pieces. Both take care to make the first cut at the same moment for the efficacy of the oath depends on the guilt of the slaughter of the cat being shared equally until one or other commits a breach of the oath, when the whole of the guilt attaches itself to the offender. . . . The ceremony is intended, no doubt, to make the two villages one by means of the communion in the blood, or, since the blood is often regarded as the soul itself, by means of the communion in the soul of the cat which is a special animal—a god in fact."[44] The cutting off of a cock's head is the usual form of swearing among all Chinese, the intimation being that a like fate awaits the treacherous.[45]

In Sumatra the place of greatest solemnity for administering an oath is the burying ground of their ancestors. Their method of swearing is as follows: "The young shoots of the anau-tree were made into a kind of rope, with the leaves hanging, and this was attached to four stakes stuck in the ground, forming an area of five or six feet square, within which a mat was spread, where those about to take the oath seated themselves. A small branch of the prickly bamboo was planted in the area also, and benzoin was kept burning during the ceremony. The chiefs then laid their hands on the *koran,* held to them by a priest, and one of them repeated to the rest the substance of the oath, who, at the pauses he made, gave a nod of assent; after which they severally said, 'may the earth become barren, the air and water poisonous, and may dreadful calamities fall on us and our posterity, if we do not fulfil what we now agree to and promise."[46] The natives of Borneo in taking oath employ the teeth of tiger-cats; the person swearing holds the teeth in his hand and calls on them to harm him if he does not speak the truth.[47] Oath-ceremonies are performed in British North Borneo on occasions, such as the brotherhood-ceremonies and those of welcome. For the first type the jungle is cleared for about twenty yards and then a hole dug about a foot deep, in which is placed a large water-jar. The old men of the brotherhood commenced declaiming, "Oh, Kinarringan, hear us!" and then, for half-an-hour, went on declaring that by fire (represented by a burning stick), by water (brought in a bamboo and poured into the jar), and earth, that they would be true to all white men. "A sumpitan was then fetched, and an arrow shot into the air to summon Kinarringan. We now placed our four guns, which were all the arms my party of eight mustered, on the mouth of the jar, and each put a hand in and took a little clay out and put it away. Finally several volleys were shot over the place and the ceremony terminated." This is similar to the welcome-ceremony of the Dusuns described by Sir Charles Brooke: "First the chief cut two long sticks, and then sitting down, he had a space of ground cleared before him, and began a discourse. When he came to any special point in his discourse he thrust a stick into the ground and cut it off at a height of half-a-foot from the earth, leaving the piece sticking in. This went on until he had made two little armies of sticks, half-a-foot high, with a stick in the middle of each army

42 Hopkins, *Relig. India,* 277, 533.
43 Chowbe, in JASB, V, 226.
44 Hodson, in JAI, XXXVI, 99.
45 Williams, *Middle Kingdom,* II, 267.

46 Marsden, *Sumatra,* 242, 322.
47 Hose, in JAI, XXIII, 165; Schwaner, *Borneo,* I, 213-214.

much higher than the rest, and representing the two leaders. These two armies were himself and his followers, and myself and my men. Having called in a loud voice to his god, or Kinarringan, to be present, he and I took hold of the head and legs of the fowl, while a third person cut off its head with a knife. We then dropped our respective parts, and the movements of the dying fowl were watched. If it jumps towards the chief his heart is not true, if towards the person to be sworn in, his heart is not true; it must, to be satisfactory, go in some other direction. Luckily, in my case, the fowl hopped away into the jungle and died."[48] To swear, among the Alfurs, means to drink salt. They put salt water in a vessel, and add some wax, a bullet, a knife or other cutting tool. If the person lies, he will melt like the salt or wax, the knife will cut his throat, and the bullet will hit him even though aimed in a totally different direction. This is parallel to the case mentioned in the text as the most common way of taking oath in the Archipelago.[49]

An instance is mentioned in the early history of New Hampshire in which the Indians and whites swore to an agreement at two heaps of stones previously raised, called "Two Brothers."[50] In administering oaths to plaintiffs and defendants appearing before the three Indian judges of the Court of Indian Offenses of the Crow tribe, a tin arrow is used. "It is held in high and sacred esteem by all the older Crows, and it was claimed that no one can touch it and tell an untruth without meeting with a mishap such as bodily injury, the loss of a horse or other property, or even death. The pointed end of the arrow is painted red to resemble blood."[51]

Among the civilized people of antiquity it was not any singular regard for the truth, but a belief in the binding magic power of an oath, that gave the latter its awfulness.[52] The Scythians confirmed their oaths by drinking wine in which they had let drip some of their own blood and after they had immersed in the mixture a sword, arrow, axe, and spear.[53] Herodotus[54] tells a story of a mutual oath to give the best thing one has to the other on demand. As the Hindu today swears with some water of the Ganges in his hand, so among the ancient Hebrews "the priest shall have in his hand the bitter water that causeth the curse."[55] To raise the right hand as though in a challenge to heaven was so universal a custom among the Semitic nations that in some of their languages the right hand is used as equivalent to oath.[56] "When thou shalt vow a vow unto the Lord thy God, thou shalt not slack to pay it: for the Lord thy God will surely require it of thee; and it would be a sin in thee. But if thou shalt forbear to vow, it shall be no sin in thee." In another place we read that it was forbidden to swear, "The Lord liveth."[57]

Hera swore by the Styx, with one hand on land and one on the sea.[58] Roman soldiers swore by the genius of the emperor never to desert.[59] The ancient German oath of the women was upon "breast and hair."[60] The Norsemen had a ring-oath; the ring was kept in a temple, but at every gathering it was worn by the person presiding on his arm; every suitor and witness must

48 Roth, Sarawak, II, 207, 208.
49 Wilken, in VG, I, 39, 470.
50 Belknap, New Hampshire, 330.
51 Simms, in AA, V, 733.
52 Rohde, Psyche, I, 65.
53 Justi, Persien, 97.
54 Hist., VI, 61; Drumann, Griechenland, 138.

55 Num., V, 18; Maurer, Vkde., I, 162.
56 Gen., XIV, 22; Exod., VI, 8; Anon., in JASB, VI, 19.
57 Deut., XXIII, 21-22; Hosea, IV, 15.
58 Homer, Iliad, XIV, 275.
59 Apuleius, Golden Ass, 193, note.
60 Von Martius, Beiträge, I, 95, note.

first invoke the gods on it. Other oaths were by the ship's bulwark, the shield's rim, the horse's shoulder, and the sword's edge. On Christmas evening a boar was led into the hall before the king, and all men laid their hands on its bristles, taking the holiest oath and promise.[61] In 1247 a cardinal who went to crown a Norse king abolished the ordeal because, he said "it did not beseem Christian men to put God to an oath to bear witness in the affairs of men."[62] Under feudalism in England the oath of the freeman to his lord was as follows: "He shall hold his right hand on the book and shall say thus:—Hear you my lord that I shall be to you both faithful and true, and shall owe my faith to you for the land that I hold, and lawfully shall do such customs and services as my duty is to you, at the times assigned, so help me God and all his saints." Again, "the vilain, when he shall do fealty to his lord, shall hold his right hand over the book, and shall say:—Hear you my lord that I from this day forth unto you shall be true and faithful and shall owe you fealty for the land which I hold of you in villenage and that no evil or damage will I see concerning you but I will defend and warn you to my power, so help me God and all his saints."[63] The South Slavs of today swear, the mother or father by their children, the sister by the life and well-being of the brother, and so forth.[64]

Some of the official oaths in European courts at the end of the nineteenth century resembled those of ethnography. When appointed presiding judge at a special trial in the Isle of Man, Mr. Shee, Q.C., was required to swear that he would administer justice as impartially "as the herring's backbone doth lie in the middle of the fish." Before the Norwegian witness gives his testimony he raises the thumb, the forefinger, and the middle finger of his right hand. These signify the Trinity, while the larger of the uplifted fingers is supposed to represent the soul of the witness, and the smaller to indicate his body. "If I swear falsely," he exclaims, "may all I have and own be cursed; cursed be my land, field and meadow, so that I may never enjoy any fruit or yield from them; cursed be my cattle, my beasts, my sheep, so that after this day they may never thrive or benefit me; yea, cursed may I be and everything I possess." Even more conscientious, perhaps, was the first witness in the days of the Brehons, who took three separate oaths before he gave his testimony, the first standing, the second sitting, and the third lying, as these were the positions in which his life was spent.[65]

§279. Ritual.

According to Lippert,[1] it is the rites, not the shaman, who can draw forth divine power and coerce the gods; the shaman is merely one who understands the rites and has a familiar spirit. Ritual always has a pronounced fetishistic power.

In the Trobriand Islands, "a magical formula is an inviolable, integral item of tradition. It must be known thoroughly and repeated exactly as it was learnt. A spell or magical practice, if tampered with in any detail, would entirely lose its efficacy. Thus the enumeration of ancestral names cannot con-

61 Vigfusson and Powell, *Corp. Poet. Bor.*, 174, 403, 405; Jørgensen, in *Aarbøger*, 1876, 160; Wadenstjerna, in *Globus*, LXXII, 374.
62 Laing, *Icelandic Sagas*, IV, 261.
63 *Statutes of the Realm*, I, 227-228 (ed. of 1817).

64 Krauss, *Südslaven*, 42, note.
65 *London Law Journal*, quoted in N. Y. *Times*, Dec. 9, 1900.
1 *Kgchte.*, II, 446.

ceivably be omitted. Again, the direct question, 'Why do you mention those names?' is answered in the time-honoured manner . . . 'our old custom.' And in this matter I did not profit much from discussing matters with even the most intelligent natives."[2]

The Kabyle Mussulmans recite the first surah of the Koran in unison at the beginning and at the end of every important affair.[3] Their religion has fallen into the rut of ritualism, with details so numerous and standards of correctness so strict that a rite fails over and over again because of some error.[4] Islamic prayers are ejaculations of epithets of God and verses of the Koran, pure ritual. However meager and trivial, mechanical and arid the service is, yet there is in it intense devotion, fidelity, and punctiliousness.[5]

The present state of the Toda religion seems to be one in which ritual has persisted while the beliefs at the bottom of the ritual have largely disappeared.[6] Formalism marks more advanced religions. In Mongolia, no one seems to understand fully the meaning of the prayer of the lamas: *Om mani padme hum;* no one of the lamas could translate it, yet they say it is the quintessence of Buddhist wisdom and it is inscribed on all the temples.[7] According to the *Avesta,* the Almighty God has one hundred and one names, which signify all his virtues; these numerous names are recited in several ceremonies.[8] There are 1008 epithets of Siva, 1000 of Vishnu, 80 of Christ, 99 of God in Mohammedanism, and 100 of Zeus.[9] The day for the Brahman consists of a series of ritual acts, very minute and tedious.[10] The mourning-rites of a Hindu may serve as an example of the force of ritual. On the thirty-first day after a death, the son, accompanied by the officiating priest, goes to the river-side, bathes, and performs certain preliminary rites. A quantity of silver and brass utensils, besides shawls, cloth, and hard silver in cash are required for the ceremony and to serve as gifts for the Brahmans, Pandits, and other guests. The guests arrive early, and are asked to take their seats according to their caste. About ten o'clock the son begins the rite, the officiating priest reciting the formularies and the son repeating them. Meanwhile female singers of questionable character entertain the guests with their songs, while garlands and sandal-paste are distributed. On the following day an entertainment is given to the Brahmans; until this is done no Hindu can be released from the restrictions of mourning, nor regain his former purity. Every Hindu must have his guru or religious guide, for it is by him that he is initiated into the privileges of the Hindu religion. "The power of these men over their disciples is almost unparalleled in history." In the Laws of Manu, guru is referred to as a venerable one, he who performs the rites. The nature of the initiation through which the Hindu boy must go could scarcely be inferred from its name, which literally means "leading or bringing a boy to his Guru or spiritual preceptor." "But in real fact, until the boy was so brought, he could not be reckoned among the 'twice-born,' and until he was spiritually regenerated by the act of investiture he could not be permitted to use a single prayer, or repeat the Veda, or engage in any single religious service or sacrificial rite. Nor was any ceremonial observance effectual unless the thread was worn." This is a simple necklace made of a few strands of thread, but it is the mark

2 Malinowski, in JAI, XLVI, 401.
3 Hanoteau et Letourneux, *Kabylie*, II, 21.
4 Pischon, *Islam*, 37.
5 Müller, *Islam*, I, 197.

6 Rivers, *Todas*, 452.
7 Prjevalski, *Reisen*, 63, 506.
8 Modi, in JASB, II, 426, note.
9 Monier-Williams, *Brāhmanism*, 105.
10 Dubois, *Mœurs de l'Inde*, I, 336.

of the spiritual aristocracy of India; and in most cases an earl is not more proud of his coronet than is the Hindu of this thread which marks him as a special favorite of the gods. Of course, it is of no use unless blessed by Brahmans and consecrated by the recitation of Vedic texts. After the boy is given the thread he is now for the first time taught to repeat the Vedic prayer for illumination, translatable thus: "Let us meditate on that excellent glory of the divine Vivifier, may he illume our understanding." This is "the most ancient of all Aryan prayers, which was first uttered more than three thousand years ago, and which still rises day by day towards heaven, incessantly ejaculated by millions of our Indian fellow-subjects."[11]

In Manipur prayer and obeisance close the important ceremonies, of which every action and word is of importance. When asked for an explanation of their ritual, the natives replied: "It was the custom of our forefathers, how do we know its meaning?"[12] In Central Borneo there are long and minute ceremonies connected with planting, cultivating, and harvesting rice, all based on fear of the daimons.[13] An exceptional case regarding ritual is reported from the Malay Peninsula: "An error in the pattern does not, as a Pangan man said, take away the power of the comb. 'It is like a break or a hole in a bird-trap: the bird may slip through, instead of falling into the trap, but it is always a question whether it will see the hole.' . . . The error is no worse than, e.g., the writing of capital letters instead of small ones would be to a European."[14]

There were many superstitious observances in Samoa in preparation for fishing. "The person who attached the hook to the fly must first bathe his body, then put on a fisherman's apron of cloth, then seat himself on a mat and thus solemnly set to work. Only by a strict observance of the particulars could success be looked for in the subsequent use of the hook.[15] In New Zealand, no tree might be felled, nor bird taken by fowlers until certain rites were performed. If not, "then the forest would lose its 'health,' that is to say, its vitality and productiveness, hence birds would be scarce." Invocations were repeated in order to bring many birds to the forests. "If a traveller should see a lizard in the path before him, he would know that the creature did not come there of its own accord but had been sent by an enemy as an *aitua* (evil omen) for him and to cause his death. He, therefore, at once kills the reptile and gets a woman to step over it as it lies in the path. By this means the evil omen is averted. And he will also probably cast about in his mind to discover who the person or persons were who sent this dread object to bring misfortune to him. Then he will say, 'May so-and-so eat you.' Thus he will transfer the *aitua* to that person so named."[16]

The Indians of Vancouver Island celebrated a great ceremony which was repeated at one or more villages every winter: the first five days were devoted to secret rites and initiations. The first public performance was a procession on the fifth day of males and females, naked, or nearly so, with their limbs and bodies scarified and bleeding. Invited guests received presents. Every evening after the first secret days were over was devoted to masquerades, when

11 Monier-Williams, *Brāhmanism*, 307, 360-361; Wilkins, *Hinduism*, 26, 28; Bühler, *Manu*, II, 142.
12 Shakespear, in JAI, XL, 359.
13 Nieuwenhuis, *Borneo*, I, 180 ff.

14 Skeat and Blagden, *Malay Penin.*, I, 428
15 Pratt, in AAAS, 1887, 447.
16 Best, in AAAS, 1898, 771-772, 774; and in AAAS, 1909, 458.

each lodge was visited and a performance enacted.[17] This appears to have been somewhat similar to the mysteries of the ancients. The main object of the majority of Hopi ceremonials is the production of rain and the growth of corn. "There are three primal elements which permeate all Hopi ceremonies— the gods, the worshiper, and the needs of the latter, or what he wishes to obtain from the former. Ceremony is largely, if not wholly, made up of the methods adopted by the worshiper, man, to influence the gods to grant his wishes, and is directly the outgrowth of prayer, which is a reflection of desire or want, which in turn is the outgrowth of climatic influences. Agriculturists desire rain and crops, and they pray to the gods especially for these things."[18] Indian villages throughout almost the entire Southwest have kivas or sacred ceremonial chambers. As practically all the rites and dances take place after the harvest is gathered and before planting in the spring, they are performed in the home pueblos, as distinguished from the summer places, and such villages have kivas. The importance of the kiva and the part it played in the life of the aboriginal inhabitants cannot be overestimated. "Even to-day, after more than three centuries of white domination, during which period the region has been overrun and persistently Christianized, the dwindling remnant of the Pueblo Indians still clings tenaciously to its kiva mysteries. Every pueblo has at least one kiva, and sometimes several, as Taos in northern New Mexico. These are the rooms where preparations for the dances are made, where councils are held, and where the ceremonies of the pueblo take place—where, in short, the religious life of the group centers, and from which emanates the influence that regulates all the affairs of daily life as well as defines man's duties and obligations to his Makers."[19]

The religion of the Romans was austere and stiff; all emotional behavior was regarded with contempt; consequently their religious rites were pure ritual, and on their accuracy and correctness public and private fortune depended. The divinity had a right to be worshipped in the traditional way: every word and gesture must be correct or all was vain. No change was permitted in the language of prayer even if it had become unintelligible to the priests; otherwise the god would not recognize that he was being called upon. The cult acts were fixed by strict rules: the man states what he means, the god says nothing, while the priest does not answer the man but advises him how to approach the god, who is supposed to be bound if the act is correctly offered.[20]

In the centuries just preceding the Christian era there arose in the ancient world new rites and cults to which have been given the name "mysteries." In general, a mystery is a rite in which certain *sacra* are exhibited, which cannot be safely seen by the worshipper till he has undergone certain purifications.[21] He is under the obligation of secrecy. While the mysteries have much in common with the primitive religious secret societies,[22] they are treated here for their ritual and sacramental features. The most important of the mysteries were those of Mithra and the Greek mysteries such as the Eleusinian, Orphic, and Samothracian. They all appear to have had the purpose of imparting pre-

17 Dall, in BAE, III, 108-109.
18 Fewkes, in BAE, XIX, pt. II, 1009-1010.
19 Morley, in AA, X, 601-602, 609 (quoted); Mindeleff, in BAE, XIX, part II, 644; Nadaillac, *Preh. America*, 204, note.

20 Wissowa, *Relig. Römer*, 32, 330.
21 Harrison, *Greek Relig.*, 151; Jevons, *Religion*, 327 ff.
22 §§161, 163, of the text and *Case-Book*.

cepts and semi-magical formulæ supposed to ennoble this life and to impart a belief in a future life.

Mithra was a Persian god of the light of the middle zone, between heaven and hell, the defender of truth, and the chief helper of Ahura-Mazda in his struggle with the powers of darkness. The Mithra cult was attended with mysteries including sacraments closely resembling the Christian, celebrated in grottoes and underground chapels. To receive the sacred ablutions and the consecrated food, the participant was obliged to prepare for them by prolonged abstinence and numerous austerities; "he played the rôle of sufferer in certain dramatic expiations of strange character and of which we know neither the number nor the succession. . . . Sometimes, the terrified mystic took part, if not as an actor, at least as a spectator, in a simulated murder, which in its origin was undoubtedly real. In late periods, the officiants were contented with producing a sword dipped in the blood of a man who had met a violent death. The cruelty of these ceremonies, which among the warlike tribes of the Taurus must have been downright savage orgies, was softened by contact with western civilization. In any event, they had become more fear-inspiring than fearful, and it was the moral courage of the initiate that was tried rather than his physical endurance. The idea which was sought to be attained was the stoic 'apathy,' the absence of every sensitive emotion. The atrocious tortures, the impossible macerations, to which some too credulous or inventive authors have condemned the adepts of the Mysteries, must be relegated to the realm of fable, as must likewise the pretended human sacrifices which were said to have been perpetrated in the shades of the sacred crypts." The converts believed they found in the mystic ceremonies a stimulant and a consolation. "They believed themselves purified of their guilt by the ritual ablutions, and this baptism lightened their conscience of the weight of their heavy responsibility." The astonishing spread of Mithraism is due in large measure to these stupendous illusions, which would appear ludicrous were they not so profoundly and thoroughly human. "There can be scarcely any doubt that the practice of the taurobolium, with the ideas of purification and immortality appertaining to it, had passed under the Antonines from the temples of Anâhita into those of the *Mater Magna*. The barbarous custom of allowing the blood of a victim slaughtered on a latticed platform to fall down upon the mystic lying in a pit below, was probably practised in Asia from time immemorial."[23] The Mithra cult was introduced into Rome in the time of Trajan, and given powerful impulse by Commodus, who was an initiate. It was a prevailing religion among the Roman legionaries, by whom it was carried throughout the empire, and in the last days of paganism it was the most serious rival of Christianity.

Most of the oriental cults had become widespread in Athens by the time of the Peloponnesian War. They were all of an orgiastic character. At all times processions of the worshippers of Sabazios and the "Great Mother" went through the streets amidst deafening noise; at the Adonis festival the city resounded again with the lamentations of the women over the god who had died in the bloom of youth. Especially did the people flock to the consecrations with which the Phrygian-Thracian cults were associated. "The believers gathered at night, with intoxicating music of flutes, rolling of drums, and wild howling; soon all were whirling about in a mad dance, until ecstasy had mounted to the highest degree. Then they set the new candidates for admission naked upon the holy stool; there they were rubbed with earth and bran and then cleansed with water; therewith passages were read out of the ritual, full of scraps of Phrygian, which no one understood; at the conclusion the initiated person spoke the holy formula: 'I have escaped from sin, I have found salvation.' Then followed further exhibitions from the holy legends in which the shameless symbols of oriental superstition were presented to public view. As the dregs of the population, both sexes promiscuously, took part in these nocturnal celebrations, and as there was lacking any official supervision, the door was open to licentiousness of the worst sort. The great majority of the cultured people naturally looked on such actions with disgust."[24] The two outstanding characteristics of the Orphic Mystery were speculation on ultimate matters, on the being and becoming of gods and men, and the eager business of purification and consecration.[25] The rite of purification was common to all the mysteries. The ancients knew and felt that *mystery*, secrecy, was not the main gist of a "mystery": the essence of it all primarily was purification in order that one might safely eat and handle certain *sacra*. "It is significant of the whole attitude of Greek religion that the confession is not a confession of dogma or even faith, but an avowal of ritual acts performed. This is the measure of the gulf between ancient and modern. The Greeks in their greater wisdom saw that uniformity in ritual was desirable and possible; they left a man practically free in the only sphere where freedom is of real importance, *i.e.*, in the matter of thought. So long as you fasted, drank the *kykeon*, handled the *sacra*, no one asked what were your opinions or your sentiments in the performance of those acts; you were left to find in every sacrament the only thing you could find—what you brought."[26]

§280. Renunciation.

Then announced the Magnificent One
That she had made a vow
Three days and three nights long
To stand motionless, fasting.

THESE lines from the *Mahabharata*[1] express the notion of renunciation in general and of fasting in particular. The religious nature of fasting is also evident in the customs of the Palaungs of Farther India: as a perpetual offering to the image-house, they give up some kind of food that they particularly like, never in their lives touching it again. "There is no obligation on any one to fast, but a man or woman who never fasted would be looked down upon by the more religious."[2]

Fasting was a practice well known to the American Indians. "Simple garments or none were worn when fasting. Among some tribes clay was put upon the head, and tears were shed as the appeals were made to the unseen powers."[3] Among the Cora, fasting, which was sometimes conducted by shamans alone, was a ceremonial feature and was thought to be necessary to in-

24 Beloch, *Griech. Gesch.*, II, 7; Rohde, *Psyche*, II, 8 ff.; Eckert, *Myst. Gesellschaften*, 210, 217.
25 Wobbermin, *Mysterienwesen*, 44-45, 97, 145.
26 Harrison, *Greek Relig.*, 56 (quoted), 154 (quoted), 162, 251, 344, 621-622.
1 Holtzmann, *Ind. Sagen*, I, 257.
2 Milne, *Eastern Clan*, 316.
3 Fletcher, "Fasting," in HAI, I, 453.

sure good crops.[4] Among a number of tribes in the Southwest "the clan heads go into a retreat of continence and fasting for rain after the summer solstice."[5] An elaborate ceremony of many Indian tribes, but especially of those that formerly inhabited the Gulf States, and one which involved much renunciation, was the Busk, a rejoicing over the first fruits of the year. The term, which comes from the Creek *púskita,* literally means "a fast." It was an occasion of amnesty, forgiveness, and absolution of crime, injury, and hatred, a season of change of mind, symbolized in various ways. The new year begins with the busk, which is celebrated in August, or late in July. In connection with it the women broke to pieces all the household utensils of the previous year and replaced them with new ones; the men refitted all their property so as to look new. "When a town celebrates the busk, having previously provided themselves with new clothes, new pots, pans, and other household utensils and furniture, they collect all their worn-out clothes and other despicable things, sweep and cleanse their houses, squares, and the whole town, of their filth, which with all the remaining grain and other old provisions, they cast together into one common heap and consume it with fire. After having taken medicine, and fasted for three days, all the fire in the town is extinguished. During this fast they abstain from the gratification of every appetite and passion whatever. A general amnesty is proclaimed, all malefactors may return to their town, and they are absolved from their crimes, which are now forgotten, and they are restored to favor."[6]

Among the Jibaro Indians of Ecuador, abstinence is an essential part of the rites that must be observed by the avengers on return from a feud. "The diet is continued for two or three months. During the first month after having killed the sorcerer the Jibaro is likewise forbidden to sleep in his house, and passes his nights in a small ranch made on the bank of the river. After the lapse of the month he goes to a natural small waterfall and takes a cold bath, letting the water fall on his naked body. After this purification he returns to his home and may sleep in his house, not with his wife but in the foreroom or department of the men. This sexual abstinence is observed as long as the fasting, namely, for two, or, among some Jibaros, three months. If the rules mentioned are infringed by the slayer the soul of the killed enemy, who constantly follows him thirsting for revenge, will take his life."[7]

Fasting was a common practice of the Hebrews and Christians, as any concordance of the Bible amply demonstrates. Often something definite was expected in return, as when Ezra proclaimed a fast at the river of Ahava, "that we might afflict ourselves before our God, to seek of him a right way for us, and for our little ones, and for all our substance. . . . So we fasted and besought our God for this: and he was intreated of us."[8] An example of renunciation, so well known as not to call for extended comment, is furnished by the history of mendicancy in the Middle Ages. The notion that poverty was meritorious and a good in itself was widely entertained but unformulated at the beginning of the thirteenth century; it later gave rise to the mendicant orders. Renunciation of property was greatly admired and during the two following centuries high merit was attributed to beggary. "The social consequences were so great that this view of poverty and beggary is perhaps the

4 Hodge, in HAI, I, 348.
5 Parsons, in AA, XXII, 61.
6 Chamberlain, in HAI, I, 176, 177

(quoted), 178; Carr, in *Smithson. Rep.,* 1891, 543.
7 Karsten, in BAE, Bull. LXXIX, 18-19.
8 Ezra, VIII, 21, 23.

most important consequence in the history of the mores which go with the ascetic philosophy of life."9

§281. Continence.

AMONG the Melanesians, shortly before a trading-voyage starts the leaders must sleep apart from their wives, and during the absence of the expedition the latter do not wash themselves. Other similar "precautions" are taken to avoid ill luck and get good luck. Continence is also insisted upon when making a new garden; if a man so employed approach his wife his yams will grow but poorly.1

"To one who knows anything of the very low standard of sexual morality that prevails among the Becwana," states Willoughby,2 "it is not a little astonishing to discover the notion of a virgin priesthood. There is still some doubt in my mind as to the exact meaning of this virginity. I have been told again and again by men who would not willingly mislead me that of the officiating regiment only those are allowed to perform the duties of the *makgaye* who have never known women." Spiritual communications are said by the Kikuyu priests to be received only during dreams; "the only austerities they are called on to practise during the exercise of their spells are interdiction *a mensa et toro* as far as their wives are concerned."3 Among the Masai a man must abstain from having sexual intercourse with his wife as soon as she becomes pregnant, and he may not again have connection with her until the child cuts the two middle incisor teeth of its upper and lower jaws. "Should this rule be broken it is believed that the child will never be strong." Other occasions when continence is imposed are when poison is being made or honey wine is brewed. "During the time that a man is making poison (eight days) he is treated almost as an outcast. . . . When honey wine is to be brewed a man and a woman are selected for the purpose, neither of whom has had sexual intercourse for two days."4

The doctrine of religious celibacy prevails in India, Mongolia, and Tibet, but the usages of some districts admit of lamas having wives. "Eastern Mongol lamas like living here."5 "The Todas worship stone images, buffaloes, and even cow-bells, but they have a celibate priesthood!"6 The Sema Nagas believe it to be absolutely necessary that the taker of the omens should have remained chaste the preceding night. "The hunter who takes the head of the game killed must remain chaste that night, in addition to which he may eat no rice until the following day. Whoever kills a tiger must remain chaste for six days. He may eat no rice the first day, and for the whole six days may not eat any vegetables except chillies, nor any meat except pork, and he must sleep away from home, or at least away from his women-folk, on a bed of split bamboo to prevent sound sleep, during which the soul of the slain beast might attack and devour his own."7 The laws of Manu8 declare that "there is no sin in eating meat, in drinking spirituous liquor and in carnal intercourse, for that is the natural way of created beings, but abstention brings great re-

9 Sumner, *Folkways*, §§692 ff.
1 Seligmann, *Melanesians*, 84, 86, 100 ff., 112-113, 139-140; Turner, *Samoa*, 349.
2 In JAI, XXXIX, 232.
3 Tate, in JAI, XXXIV, 264.

4 §§407, 409, of the text; Hollis, in JAI, XL, 480-481.
5 Rockhill, *Tibet*, 135.
6 Hopkins, *Relig. India*, 537.
7 Hutton, *Sema Nagas*, 76-77.
8 Bühler, *Manu*, IV, 128; V, 56.

wards." A twice-born man aiming at the true life of a Brahman will abstain
from his wife on the day of the new moon, on the eighth lunar day of each
half-month, on the full moon, and on the fourteenth, though these are times
proper for intercourse. The practice of taking the sword-blade vow of chastity
existed, even down to recent times, in South Bihar. It was parallel to the German practice, to the effect that "when a man slept with a woman whom he did
not intend to touch, he placed a sword between himself and her." All the
ascetic sects of the Saivas are celibates; "it is, in fact, a much harsher and
more repulsive form of religious life than that followed by the Vaishnavas."[9]
It is one of the inconsistencies of the Hindu religion that "it enjoins the duty
of marriage upon all, yet honors celibacy as a condition of great sanctity and
a means of acquiring extraordinary religious merit and influence."[10]

The Zuñi Indians hold that failure to observe conjugal continence during
the four days before and after plume-planting would mean death. Does not
the planter of plumes promise when he or she plants them to be continent,
observing the decree of the Sun Father? "Of his deputy, the *pekwin*, the Sun
Father requires an even greater degree of continence. For one month after
the harvests the *pekwin* may have intercourse with his wife, if he wants it;
but the rest of the year he is to abstain. The position of *pekwin* is at present
vacant; four or five months ago, in April, 1915, the *pekwin* died, a victim, it
is said, to broken taboo. His relations to his wife were too intimate."[11] It
is said that there were virgins and youths in Mexico vowed to a life of chastity,
who cut off the hair and renounced all adornment.[12]

Certain Phœnician priests were bound to celibacy.[13] The Jewish tradition
was that at Sinai all the people were ordered to refrain from women for the
time, but that for Moses this injunction was unlimited.[14] In the rabbinical
period it was established doctrine that any one who desired to receive a revelation from God must refrain from women.[15] Other cases in the Old Testament
show that persons who were under a renunciation of this kind were in a state
of grace. The ritual of uncleanness was ascetic and it enforced ascetic views of
sex and marriage.[16] The religious scruples of the Talmudist permit him to
enjoy scarcely any of the pleasures of matrimony. Bound by the laws of marriage, he may not select his better half according to his own judgment, but as
prescribed, and for the most part a wife whom he hardly knows and whom he
has acquired from her father or other relatives. "If he then comes into possession of her property, he may not so much as have intercourse with her nor
enjoy her embraces as much as he would like, but must submit to certain
times and observances and regard them as a duty imposed."[17]

In the Egyptian system the religious ceremonies were veiled in mystery and
allegory. Chastity, abstinence from animal-food, ablutions, long and mysterious
ceremonies of preparation or initiation, were the most prominent features of
worship.[18] Among the Turks, the order of Calenders is bound to perpetual
virginity. As regards the pagan priesthoods, there can be little doubt that their
example had its influence in introducing the custom among the Christians.

9 Mitra, in JASB, VI, 116, 122; Wilkins, *Hinduism*, 90 (quoted).
10 Monier-Williams, *Brāhmanism*, 55; Nivedita, *Indian Life*, 31.
11 Parsons, in AA, XVIII, 246-247.
12 Westermarck, *Marriage*, I, 509, note 3.
13 Pietschmann, *Phönizier*, 223.
14 Exod., XIX, 15.
15 Kohler, in *Jewish Encyc.*, V, 226.
16 Levit., XV, 16, 18; Deut., XXIII, 11; Jer., XXXI, 15; Sumner, *Folkways*, §682.
17 Bergel, *Eheverhältn.*, 11.
18 Lecky, *Europ. Morals*, I, 325.

Absolute continence for ten days was a prerequisite to admission to the Eleusinian mysteries of Greece and to the Bacchic mysteries of Rome; while a declaration of virginity was exacted in the Dionysiac solemnities in Athens. It was not, however, until the end of the third century of the Christian era that the opposition against a married priesthood began to take form. The Spanish Council at Elvira (295 A.D.) enjoined celibacy on priests and deacons. Here was the beginning of the divergence on this question between the East and the West. Then came the Council of Ancyra in 314 A.D., forbidding a priest to contract a new marriage, if he had become a widower, under pain of deposition. The disputes between the Greek and Roman Sees began in the fifth century and culminated in "The Great Schism" in the ninth. The struggle to maintain a celibate priesthood was carried on by such determined prelates as Popes Leo IX and Gregory VII. The Fourth Council of the Lateran (A.D. 1215) gave a firm and clean pronouncement in favor of celibacy, which was later confirmed by the Council of Trent.[19] "Scarcely had the efforts of Nicholas and Gregory put an end to sacerdotal marriage in Rome when the morals of the Roman clergy became a disgrace to Christendom. . . . The pious Desiderius, Abbot of Monte Casino, better known as pope under the name of Victor III, declares that throughout Italy, under the pontificate of Benedict (1032-1045), all orders, from bishops down, without shame or concealment, were publicly married and lived with their wives as laymen, leaving their children fully provided for in their wills; and what rendered the disgrace more poignant was the fact that the scandal was greatest in Rome itself, whence the light of religion and discipline had formerly illumined the Christian world. Another contemporary writer asserts that this laxity prevailed throughout the whole of Latin Christendom, sacerdotal marriage being everywhere so common that it was no longer punished as unlawful, and scarcely even reprehended."[20] The priests of various Oriental churches took unto themselves wives before their ordination; and their right to retain their wives was formally recognized by a decree of St. Benedict.[21]

§282. Self-Discipline.

IF men torture themselves they can at least select their form of suffering. In this, as in the infliction of punishment on criminals, they have shown great ingenuity.[1] The passionless ascetics of Tibet are homeless mendicants, belonging to no sect in particular; they are now almost extinct, but all are regarded as saints who in their next birth must certainly attain Nirvana. "They carry thigh-bone trumpets, skull-drums, etc., and in the preparation of these instruments from human bones, they are required to eat a morsel of the bone or a shred of the corpse's skin."[2] In the *Mahabharata* it is averred that heaven may be won by standing on one leg and by eating little or nothing. Sacrifices, gifts, loyalty, and warlike deeds store up merit and win a place in heaven.[3]

If the Jain may kill himself, he may not kill or injure anything else. Not even food prepared over a fire is acceptable, lest he hurt the "fire-beings," for he

---

19 Thurston, in *Catholic Encyc.*, III, 485-486.

20 Lea, *Sacerd. Celibacy*, 66, 187-188 (quoted), 356 (quoted), 490.

21 Thurston, in *Catholic Encyc.*, III, 487-488; Harrington, in N. Y. *Times*, March 2, 1919.

1 Wines, *Punishment*, ch. V.

2 Waddell, *Buddhism*, 74.

3 Holtzmann, *Ind. Sagen*, II, 115-120.

believes in water-beings, fire-beings, and wind-beings. Every plant and seed is holy with the sacredness of life. He may not hurt or drive away the insects that torment his naked flesh. Lest animate things, even plants and animalculæ, be destroyed, he sweeps the ground before him as he goes, walks veiled lest he inhale a living organism, strains water, and rejects not only meat but even honey, together with various fruits that are supposed to contain worms; not because of his distaste for worms but because of his regard for life. Almost every city of western India where the Jains are found, has its beast-hospital, where animals are kept and fed. Five thousand rats were thus supported in a temple-hospital in Kutch, the town being taxed to pay for their food. "Patience is the highest good," and the rules for sitting and lying conclude with the statement that not to move at all, not to stir, is the best rule. To lie naked, bitten by vermin, and not to disturb them, is religion. Like a true Puritan, the Jain regards pleasure in itself as sinful. "What is discontent, and what is pleasure? One should live subject to neither. Giving up all gaiety, circumspect, restrained, one should live a religious life. Man! thou art thine own friend; why longest thou for a friend beyond thyself? . . . First troubles, then pleasures; first pleasures, then troubles. These are the cause of quarrels." The Fourth Vow reads: "I renounce all sexual pleasures, either with gods, or men, or animals. I shall not give way to sensuality. . . . The clauses here forbid the Niggantha to discuss topics relating to women, to contemplate the forms of women, to recall the pleasures and amusements he used to have with women, eat and drink too highly seasoned viands, to lie near women." In the Brahmanism of the Bharata, physical prowess is the one thing admirable. "To stand for years on one leg, to be eaten by ants, to be in every way an ascetic of the most stoical sort, is the truest religion." Such an ascetic has no ordinary rules of morality; to seduce young women is one of his commonest occupations. "The gods are nothing to him. They are puppets whom he makes shake and tremble at will." All the gods together are represented as weaker than a good hero, not to speak of a priestly ascetic. The greed and rapacity of these priests exceeds all imagination. "The royal priests are the king's constant advisors, his most unscrupulous upholders in wickedness, and there gave themselves up to quest of wealth and power. But one should err if he thus dismissed them all. . . . To offset rapaciousness there are tomes of morality of the purest sort. . . . There were doubtless good and bad priests, but the peculiarity of the epic priest, rapacious and lustful, is that he glories in his sins."[4]

As an offering to the deity, the Samoans, in terrible earnest, battered each other's scalps till the blood streamed down and over their faces and bodies. "Old and young, men, women, and children, all took part in this general mêlée and bloodletting, in the belief that Taisumalie would thereby be all the more pleased with their devotedness, and answer prayer for health, good crops, and success in battle."[5]

The American as well as the Asiatic Indians carry self-discipline to great lengths. The Dakota, prior to an important enterprise, purifies himself by the steam-bath and by fasting three days, during which he avoids women and society and tries to become pure enough to receive a revelation. Then comes the sacrifice. "Some, passing a knife through the breast and arms, attach thongs

4 Hopkins, *Relig. Ind.*, 288, 291, 294, 296, 352 ff.   5 Turner, *Samoa*, 57.

thereto, which are fastened at the other end at the top of a tall pole . . . ;
and thus they hang, suspended only by these thongs, for two, three, or even
four days, gazing upon vacancy, their minds being intently fixed upon the
object in which they desire to be assisted by the deity, and waiting for a vision.
Once a day an assistant is sent to look upon the person thus sacrificing himself. If the deities have given him a vision or revelation, he signifies it by
motions, and is at once released; if he be silent, he is left alone to his reverie."
Another method is to drag a buffalo-head, attached to a hook passing through
the large muscles in the small of the back, all over the camp. "A third class
pass knives through the flesh in various parts of the body, and wait in silence,
though with fixed mind, for a dream or revelation. A few will plant a pole upon
the steep bank of a stream, and attaching ropes to the muscles of the arm
and breast, will stand, but not hang, as in the first instance, gazing into space,
without food or drink for days." The essence of the matter is to get a vision,
which process is hastened by the fasting and suffering undergone. Some simply
concentrate for weeks, or even months, upon some deserved object, frequently
crying about the camp, mostly fasting, but intent upon a revelation.[6] Catlin
has a portrait of Four Bears, a Mandan, with scars on the breast, arms, and
legs that witness to several experiences in self-torture. Under the circumstances, the vision and revelation are pretty sure to come.[7] An Indian Agent
has reported the "medicine-dance" of the Cheyennes: A number of braves,
their bodies naked from the waist up, enter the "medicine lodge"; they gash
their arms and legs, and pierce holes in their chests, pass ropes through the
holes and suspend themselves from the center of the lodge until their struggling
tears the flesh loose. Each one has a whistle, and keeping their eyes on the
charm, they dance night and day without food or water until exhausted. These
"medicines" are a record of terrible suffering, endured with indomitable
heroism, which sometimes ends in death.[8]

At the time of the winter solstice the Hopi priests sat naked in a circle and
suffered gourds of ice-cold water to be dashed over them.[9] The following are
some of the episodes introduced in Tusayan ceremonials: "1. Inordinate eating
and begging, urine drinking, gluttony, and obscenity. 2. Flogging of one another, stripping off breechcloths, drenching with foul water, ribald remarks
to spectators, and comical episodes with donkeys and dogs. 3. Story telling
for pieces of corn under severe flogging by masked persons, races, smearing
one another with blood, urinating upon one another, tormenting with cactus
branches, etc."[10]

The Karoks of northern California have a grand dance of propitiation, to
prevent land-slides, forest fires, drought, and other calamities. First there is
selected a robust tribesman, called the "God-man" who fasts in the mountains
for ten days; "and their evident belief is that by the keen anguish he undergoes,
he propitiates the spirits vicariously in behalf of the whole tribe." He returns
at length and, with his last strength, seated upon a sacred stool, lights a
sacred fire. It is death for common people to behold him returning or to look
upon the sacred smoke. Somewhat the same ceremony occurs in the spring to
insure a good catch of salmon. The "God-man," on his return, again lights the
sacred fire after eating a portion of the first salmon of the catch.[11] In this

6 Dorsey, in BAE, XI, 436, 437.
7 §§160, 311, of text.
8 Donaldson, in *Smithson. Rep.*, 1885, pt.
II, 82, 93.

9 Swanton, in HAI, II, 146.
10 Fewkes, in BAE, XV, 294.
11 §240, of the text; Powers, in *Contrib. N.
Amer. Ethnol.*, III, 28.

case the self-discipline has extended to a community-discipline performed for all by one.

In a Brazilian dance the men flogged each other till the blood ran. The young men exhibited triumphantly long whip-scars on abdomen and upper thigh. This sort of dance is wide-spread over a good part of tropical South America, even among the so-called "Christian" Indians. Interrogated as to the occasion for it, an Indian answered: "I do not know. Our ancestors have been doing this already 'antigo de mundo,' and therefore today we do so still." Study of the matter reveals the procedure as a means of getting rich harvests, and therefore as propitiatory.[12] This seems to be the case among the Guiana Indians, where flagellation is part and parcel of the festival held to ensure abundance of fruit: they place young men in lines and a certain number of old men provide themselves with whips and rough thongs; "as soon as intimation is given that it is time to commence work, the whipping of these young men takes place, and notwithstanding the cuts and marks which their bodies receive, neither groan nor complaint escapes them." The flagellation is held to be a propritiation for favors already received or expected. Self-torture, through ant-biting, is imposed before hunting; regular frames, with ants fastened in them, are applied.[13]

The cult of the Great Mother of the Gods attained a notable development in Rome, probably because "there was something more genial and satisfactory to the soul in the religion itself than in the formal, stately, and passionless religion of the ancient gods of Rome. . . . Her devotees were brought nearer the divine and nearer each other than the worshipers of the classical divinities. . . . The priest of the Great Mother consecrated himself to her service with an act of self-sacrifice as great as that of any modern monk or priest. He knew what it was to fast, he was merciless to his flesh on the *Dies sanguinis,* and was no stranger to the pain of self-scourging." The final act of consecration, by which one became a minister of the cult, was castration. "Early in the first century B.C., in spite of the law forbidding it, a Roman citizen became a eunuch and devoted himself to the priesthood of the Mother. She begins to figure on coins about 83 B.C. . . . Cicero complains of the loss of the original purity of the worship, and speaks of the collection of money by priests as a serious drain on the finances of the people." Domitian, by his law against castration, opposed at least one feature of the worship, whether or not he directed the measure against the cult.[14]

§284. Nature of Sacrifice.

IF reported correctly, the case of the Bakoko of Cameroons is most exceptional. They are said to offer no sacrifices whatever to the god, who not only does not need such but, if he did, could procure food and drink himself.[1] The usual situation is that depicted by Ellis[2] with reference to the Tshi-speaking people, who, in addition to many offerings, make arrangements for the comfort of the imaginary beings, with a view to propitiation. For instance, "a country stool may be seen in some shadowy recess of the forest, or under a mass of rock, placed there for the use of the local god; or, raised from the earth on a light

12 Koch-Grünberg, in *Globus*, XC, 373-374, 261.
13 Roth, in BAE, XXX, 138; and in BAE, XXXVIII, §162.
14 Showerman, *Great Mother*, 256-257, 278, 300-302, 304.
1 Von Schkopp, in *Globus*, LXXXIII, 332.
2 *Tshi*, 73.

platform of sticks, to preserve the contents from animals, earthern saucers and pitchers, full of water for the god to drink, may be observed. As, exposed to the ardent rays of a tropical sun, the water gradually diminishes through evaporation, the natives have, to their minds, ocular demonstration of the existence of the gods, and of their need for drink, and hence for food." In the French Congo sheep and goats are kept for sacrifices and for the payments of heavy blood fines; they are rarely eaten for ordinary purposes.[3]

Among the Todas of the Nilgiris, at a short distance from the temple-hut is a small platform of earthwork, the place where they offer young calves of buffaloes as sacrifices. The offering in the temple itself consists mostly of milk.[4] According to the *Mahabharata*, "the acts by which one gains bliss hereafter are austerities, purity, truth, worship of parents, and the horse-sacrifice."[5] The various Vedic sacrifices are today either obsolete or obsolescent, and animals are now seldom killed in India, except as offerings to the bloody goddess Kālī.[6] When a high-caste Hindu dies, a pitcher full of water is hung from a branch of the pipal tree. This pitcher has a small hole in its bottom into which a twisted grass is put. "Water constantly drops from it during the ten days of the obsequies or funeral ceremonies of the dead. The man who burns the dead puts water in the pitcher afresh morning and evening during these ten days. . . . It is supposed that the ghost of the dead, who dwells for ten days on the pipal tree, drinks of the water-drops."[7]

The article most widely used in sacrifice by the American Indians was native tobacco. Next came articles of food, and then clothing and adornment, particularly the latter. The sacrifice of one tribe consisted of eels, of another fish-bones, while a third commonly sacrificed the offal of a buffalo. At a ceremony held by the Hurons in 1639, in answer to the direct order of an apparition, twenty-two presents were asked, among the items of which were six dogs of a certain form and color, fifty pieces of tobacco, and a large canoe.[8]

It was the belief of the ancient Persians that Ahura-Mazda desired only the soul of the immolated animal; the victim or parts of it were given back to the sacrificer.[9] The case is cited of some Arabs in the fourth century who fell upon a sacrificed camel and hacked out pieces which they ate raw. Later this crude practice was modified and pieces were distributed.[10] Only once does Homer refer to the offering of horses as a sacrifice to divinities. "On the last day of battle, Achilles, throwing the corpse of a son of Priam into the river Scamander, says that the Trojans shall not be saved even by the silver-eddying river to which they sacrifice many bulls, and into whose eddies they sink living horses. This sacrifice of horses is called un-Hellenic. Perhaps in this connexion, however, the slaughter of four horses at the burial of Patroclus should be noted, although these horses, like the two dogs who were then killed, were not a sacrifice in the ordinary sense." Reference is made to the sacrifice of a span of white horses by Mithridates before the war with the Romans and a similar sacrifice by Sextus Pompeius. Priests were not necessary among the Homeric Greeks, as they were among the Jews, for the proper performance of a sacrifice. Another man might do as well as they; and the king regularly performs the sacrifices for his people. "The only sacrifice con-

3 Kingsley, *Travels W. Afr.*, 451.
4 Modi, in JASB, VII, 78.
5 Hopkins, *Relig. Ind.*, 369, note.
6 Monier-Williams, *Brāhmanism*, 393.
7 Chowbe, in JASB, V, 227-228.

8 Swanton; Mooney and Thomas; Hewitt, in HAI, II, 403; I, 812; II, 940, respectively.
9 Maspero, *Hist. Anc.*, III, 593.
10 Smith, *Relig. Sem.*, 338.

ducted by a priest in the Homeric poems is one in which this priest is the chief person, apart from his priestly office, and which is on his own account. Evidently no complicated system of ritual was to be observed with precision, any more than by the Bedouins of to-day, and the ordinary rites were familiar to all men. In general, each master of a family was the priest of his household, *i.e.*, he was the representative of his family before the gods as well as before men. . . . In later times, as life became more complicated, the priests were supposed to have peculiar knowledge of what was pleasing to the gods; but the priestly families of classical times had for the most part inherited their rights to the sacrifices over which they presided, their shrine originally having been a family shrine, and they had inherited also special directions for worship." Feast, song, and dance were expected to propitiate the gods, better than fasting and prayer. "Men not only have no idea of inherited sin or natural sinfulness, but even when they have done a wrong, they have no vivid and painful sense of guilt, and their offering of sacrifice to the gods has no deep ethical meaning. The divinity at the moment, it is true, is vexed with them, but that may be due to his caprice rather than to their fault, and they are confident that the kindliness of his nature will finally prevail over his wrath. The fact that their victims for sacrifice were eaten proves that the sacrifice was not one of atonement."[11]

As part of the rite of cutting wood in a sacred grove the Romans offered a pig as an expiatory sacrifice, although they did not know to what deity the grove was sacred. Plutarch asks: "Why did the Romans not permit that the table should be ever entirely bare, but always left some food on it?" He gives many answers, among which is: because the table is sacred and they never left a sacred thing empty.[12] A rite of considerable importance was the *taurobolium*, the sacrifice of a bull, or its variation the *criobolium*, the sacrifice of a ram. The rise of this ceremony dates from the early part of the second century A.D., as the first evidence of its existence is an inscription of the reign of Hadrian, in the year 133, found at Naples. It spread rapidly throughout Italy and to all parts of the Empire, and was one of the most important rites of the cult up to the fall of Paganism.[13] During the days of feudalism in the North the peasants and landowners tried to make Hagen Adelsteen eat horseflesh at the sacrifices. This and similar events are cited to show that in the old Norse rule the king's power was limited.[14] They also indicate the persistence of old religious customs.

§285. Bargain Sacrifice: Prayer.

THE element of *quid pro quo* is evident in the prayer of the Bawenda of South Africa: "We pray Thee: give us food for us and for our children; give us cattle; give us happiness. Preserve us from illness, pestilence and war. In case of war give us victory over our enemies; give us always prosperity. See, here we bring from what we have harvested. Thou art our father, also our grandfather, grandfather's father and his grandfather," and so on as far as any ancestor is known. "After this or a similar prayer, every member of the family offers his sacrifice of the first-fruits and the first beer, and then all are at

11 Seymour, *Hom. Age*, 354-355, 497, 498.
12 De Marchi, *Culto Priv.*, rev. in *Année Soc.*, I, 116, 132.
13 Showerman, *Great Mother*, 280-283.
14 Rothe, *Nordens Staatsvrfssg.*, 58.

liberty to harvest and to enjoy the new food and the new beer."[1] Missionaries often find that savages take a practical view of religion. The people of Masonpa, South Africa, would not repair the church, saying that God could repair his own. One who had received a blanket for attending church, disappointed when the gift was not repeated, said: "No more blanket, no more hallelujah."[2] Prayer is offered by the Akikuyu only at the time of sacrifice, when it is a public ceremony. "In times of illness or epidemic among the herds prayers are offered to Ngai, but they are always accompanied by sacrifice. Only temporal benefits are asked for."[3] In the oasis of Fezzan, men pray not to let it rain at all. Their wells suffer and the rain destroys their houses made of salt-containing earth.[4]

Sacrifices among the Gilyak of Siberia are based on the principle of exchange, *i.e.*, one does not offer fish to the god of the sea. "Offerings of dogs are made chiefly at the beginning of the season for the trapping of sables and at the bear-festival. On these occasions the victims are killed by strangling, and as the dogs are dispatched they ask them to make intercession to the gods for them."[5] Buddhist pilgrims pass "with a step and a bow" over the boulevard which encircles the sacred city of Lhasa, Tibet. "Each clasps his hands in prayer above his head, lowers them to the mouth, to the breast, and prostrates himself face downward, with the clasped hands extended in advance. He marks the place where the hands rest, and rising, steps to that spot, prostrates himself, and rises again. In this way he measures in four days the distance he could walk in three hours, the most contrite pilgrims often marking each such step with coins or precious stones left in the roadway."[6] Buddhist prayer is not always associated with such austerity, for the famous prayer-wheel has both lightened the task and increased the merit thus gained. The same teachings which cause the northern Buddhists to believe in the efficacy of reiterated prayer-formulæ is responsible for the invention of this mechanical contrivance which, when turned from left to right, is as efficacious as if the person turning it recited all the prayers inclosed in it on printed slips of paper. Each complete revolution of the wheel counts as one repetition of all the prayers contained in the barrel. The prayer-wheel has been for five or six centuries a popular instrument in Tibet, Korea, and Japan. It is of two kinds: the first comprises hand wheels, those turned by the wind or by water, and small stationary wheels or barrels placed either in a house or in rows near a temple; the second class comprises much larger machines, found only in temples. They are sometimes thirty or forty feet high and fifteen or twenty in diameter. In them is placed a collection of the canonical books of lamaism, and by means of bars fixed in the lower extremity of the axis of the barrel it is put in motion. "The prayer-wheel consists of a cylinder of metal, or, in the larger wheels, of leather or even wood, through which runs an axle of wood or iron around which it pivots. In the interior are arranged, one on top of the other, sheets of paper or leaves of a book on which 'the *mani*' [a colloquial expression for the most universal prayer, the formula *om mani padme hum*] or some other spell is printed in very fine characters, the finer the better. The sheets are wound on the axle from right to left, and the wheel when set in motion must revolve in the opposite way, so that the writing passes in front

---

1 Gottschling, in JAI, XXXV, 380.
2 Bent, *Mashonaland*, 12.
3 Tate, in JAI, XXXIV, 264.

4 Rohlfs, in *Petermann's Mitth.*, Ergänz-heft. 25, p. 5.
5 Czaplicka, *Aborig. Siberia*, 272.
6 Kawaguchi, in *Century Mag.*, XLV, 390.

of the person turning the wheel in the way in which it is read, *i.e.,* from left to right."[7] Bits of cotton with prayers printed on them and tied to strings or to high poles placed over houses belong to the same class of objects as the prayer-wheels; each time these bits of stuff flutter in the breeze it is as if the prayer written on them had been recited, and the occupants of the house gain the merit of repeating this sentence. In Lesser Tibet "there are prayer-mills, sometimes 150 in a row, which revolve easily by being brushed by the hand of the passer-by, large prayer-cylinders which are turned by pulling ropes, and others larger still by water-power. The finest of the latter was a temple overarching a perennial torrent, and was said to contain 20,000 repetitions of the mystic phrase, the fee to the worshiper for each revolution of the cylinder being from 1d. to 1s. 4d., according to his means or urgency."[8]

The bargain-nature of sacrifice is expressed in the great epic of the Hindus, where complaint is made because misfortune—in this case the destruction of a caravan by elephants—occurred despite the cult. Why have we incurred this calamity? Was not the god worshipped by us? Didn't we bring sacrifices? Before the journey began, were not the flight of the birds and the position of the stars consulted? What is it, then, which brings this affliction upon us?[9] Of the "good man" in the *Rig Veda* are demanded piety toward gods and manes, liberality to priests, truthfulness and courage. In the Brahmanas the phrase "man's debts" is current. Whoever pays these debts, it is said, has discharged all his duties, and by him all is obtained. And what are these duties? To the gods he owes sacrifices; to the seers, study of the *Vedas;* to the manes, off spring; to man, hospitality.[10]

The Dyaks of West Borneo pray for long life, riches, plenty of good rice, and success in their undertakings, especially head-snatching. To a mountain-god supposed to be offended, they pray: Don't send skin disease, nor insects to destroy crops; don't let the pigs die.[11] Among all the tribes of the Malay Peninsula both prayer and invocations still remain in the stage in which material as distinct from moral advantages are sought. Among the Semang, however, "with the rarest exceptions, they appear to have scarcely reached the stage of fixed forms, the petitioner generally contenting himself with expressing his wish in a quasi-conversational phrase, addressed to the great spirits or deities of the tribe."[12]

A practice which seems peculiar to the American Indians is the use of sticks, to which feathers are attached, as ceremonial supplicatory offerings. The most familiar prayer-sticks are those made by the Pueblo Indians of New Mexico and Arizona, who use them extensively for a definite purpose, but analogous objects representing the same idea are employed in the ceremonies of nearly all American tribes. Such sticks are frequently found with the dead in ancient Pueblo cemeteries, and great deposits of them occur in ceremonial caves in southern Arizona. They are often consecrated by being moistened with medicine, sprinkled with sacred meal, and fumigated with tobacco, and by other rites; after prayers have been breathed into them they are sent out in the hands of messengers to be deposited in shrines, springs, or

7 Rockhill, in USNM, 1893, 671, 738 (quoted), 739; Rockhill, *Tibet,* 86.

8 Bishop, *Tibetans,* 42, 46 (quoted); Francke, in *Globus,* LXXVIII, 224; Potanin, in *Vestnik Evropi,* Feb., 1888, 781.

9 Holtzmann, *Ind. Sagen,* II, 39.

10 Hopkins, *Relig. Ind.,* 148, 202, 203, 204; Monier-Williams, *Brāhmanism,* 25.

11 Veth, *Borneo's Wester-Afdeeling,* II, 304, 305.

12 Skeat and Blagden, *Malay Penin.,* II, 198.

fields. "The sticks to which the plumes are attached indicate the gods to whom the prayers are offered, and the feathers convey to the gods the prayers which are breathed into the spiritual essence of the plumes. This conception is materialized in the 'breath feather,' generally the downy plume of the eagle. Prayers are also breathed into sacred meal, pollen, and other objects offered."[13] The Tusayan word for prayer is "scatter," that is, to scatter sacred meal. "When a Tusayan priest addresses a supernatural being of his mythology, he believes he must do so through the medium of some object as a prayer bearer; he breathes his wish on meal and throws this meal to the god. The prayer bearer is thought to have a spiritual double or breath body which carries his wishes. It is an old idea with him, reaching back to fetishism, for his breath with the talismanic words is the spell which brings the desired results. It must be mentioned, however, that oftentimes ethical ideas are associated with Tusayan prayers for rain, and I have frequently heard the priests at the close of their songs for rain exclaim, 'Whose heart is bad, whose thoughts are leaving the straight path,' and as they bewailed that the rains were delayed, sorrowfully resumed their songs and incantations." The simple act of breathing a prayer on a pinch of meal is all-sufficient in an individual's use of prayer-meal, but in the complicated rain-prayer this simple act is, in their belief, inadequate. "The prayer bearer intrusted with the prayers of a community of priests must be laid on the altar, smoked upon, prayed over, and consecrated by song before it is deemed efficacious. . . . The paho must be offered to the god addressed in a dignified manner worthy of its object and the care used in its consecration. A special courier carries it to a special shrine. He is commissioned to his task with formal words, and he places his burden in the shrine with prescribed prayers. It has thus been brought about that the manufacture, consecration, and final deposition of the elaborate paho or stick to bring the rain occupies several hours, and when repeated, as it is in all great ceremonies for several consecutive days, makes a complicated series of rites."[14]

The entire life of the East Iranians, according to the views set forth in the *Avesta,* consisted of a struggle against the powers of darkness. "In this fight against evil the gods rendered man assistance in various ways. They lent him a weapon through which he was able to ward off and nullify the pernicious influence of the daimons. This was the holy word which Mazda revealed to Zarathustra, the prayers which he taught him. . . . In the word dwelt a mysterious, one might almost say magic, power; the recital itself, if it is correct and flawless, brings this power into action. . . . As the daimons were always lying in wait to injure man, so the prescription was regular; it consisted in prayers, as a kind of preservative, to be recited at appointed hours of the day and at all constantly recurring functions and acts."[15] The Semites conquered the Sumerians in Babylonia but adopted their cuneiform writing and literature, which contained forms of worship, hymns of praise to gods, prayers for forgiveness of sin, and incantations for delivery from disease.[16] Ritual is here all-important. When praying, the Moslem is in duty bound to

13 Hough, "Prayer Sticks," in HAI, II, 304; Donaldson, in *Smithson. Rep.,* 1885, pt. II, 137; Buckland, in *Antiquary Lond.,* XXXIII, 299-305; Plate LXXXVI, in BAE, XIV, pt. II, 698; Plates LII, LIII, LXX, in *Smithson. Rep.,* 1895.

14 Fewkes, in *Smithson. Rep.,* 1895, 579, 689, 690 (quoted), 694.
15 Geiger, *Ostiran. Kultur,* 249 ff.
16 Rogers, *Babylonia,* I, 304.

perform all actions and utter all words in the prescribed manner that has been taught him, for any deviation makes the prayer invalid. Day after day he repeats the same passages, which are generally lacking in ideas. If he is unfamiliar with Arabic he may not know what he is saying, for even in non-Arabian lands the prayer must be said in that language.[17] According to one who seems to have been admitted to the divine confidence, prayer is the will of man moving the will of God. "It is ludicrous to think that by moving the will of God we alter His purpose, but if we mean not changing the Divine purpose but stirring it into action, then it is the essence of prayer. He is determined to give us all sorts of blessings, but His purpose in many instances is quiescent and inoperative simply because we fail to fulfill certain conditions."[18]

§286. Atonement.

THERE are so many creditors among the deities that it seems to be more than a life's work for a man to get out of debt. Incited by the declarations of the priests, shrine after shrine is visited by modern Hindus, and work after work is done; still in the minds of many there is a fear that some deity has been neglected who may at any moment demand his rights and punish them for neglecting him.[1] The idea lying at the basis of the Behari purificatory rites for absolving one's self from the pollution caused by the touch of a lizard seems to be akin to the custom of sin-eating. These rites consist mainly of bathing and of touching sesame, wheat, salt, or gold and giving away the touched articles to a Brahman. The latter, acting the part of sin-eater, takes upon himself the sins of the person who has offended the totem.[2] In Persia the cock is a sacred bird, and orthodox Zoroastrians do not eat of it, except in the case of very young ones that have not yet commenced to crow. When asked to eat a cock by the doctors, who at times prescribe it, they plant several fruit-bearing plants known as *sanjan*, as an act of atonement.[3] This expiates the breach of taboo.

The various aspects in which atoning rites presented themselves to ancient worshippers have supplied a variety of religious images which passed into Christianity, and still have currency. Redemption, substitution, purification, atoning blood, the garment of righteousness, are all terms which in some sense go back to antique ritual. The one point that comes out clear and strong, comments Robertson Smith,[4] is that the fundamental idea of ancient sacrifice is sacramental communion, and that all atoning rites are ultimately to be regarded as owing their efficacy to a communication of divine life to the worshippers, and to the establishment or confirmation of a living bond between them and their god. It was held by the Israelites that if an oracle is to be obtained, the applicant must be on good terms with the Deity. To one who is under the weight of guilt unatoned for, the oracle is silent. This happens even if it is not himself that has incurred the guilt, as when Saul obtains no response because of the offense of Jonathan, and where he consulted Jahweh, but "the Lord answered him not, neither by dreams, nor by Urim, nor by prophets."[5] The man to whom guilt attaches is unclean, and as such is *ipso facto* excluded from any approach to God and from handling objects conse-

17 Hauri, *Islam*, 80.
18 Oldham, in New Haven *Journal-Courier*, April 6, 1916.
1 Wilkins, *Hinduism*, 309.

2 Mitra, in JASB, VI, 40.
3 Modi, in JASB, V, 353.
4 *Relig. Sem.*, 439.
5 I Sam., XXVIII, 6; XIV, 37 ff.

crated to Him. The days of atonement "do not represent days of humiliation
on the part of the people, but contemplate an atonement for the sanctuary
by means of external ceremonies 'on account of those who may have offended
through error or ignorance.' The purifying of the temple building from Levitical defilement appears here as the main object to such a degree that the
cleansing of the heart, which to the pre-exilic prophets was by far the most
important matter, remains unmentioned."[6]

"Our whole modern conception of the scape-man," thinks Harrison,[7] "is apt to
be unduly influenced by the familiar instance of the Hebrew scape-goat. We
remember how . . .

> 'The scape-goat stood all skin and bone
> *While moral business, not his own,*
> *Was bound about his head.'*

And the pathos of the proceeding haunts our minds and prevents us from
realizing the actuality and the practicality of the more primitive physical taboo.
It is interesting to note that even in this moralized Hebrew conception, the
scape-goat was not a sacrifice proper; its sending away was *preceded by
sacrifice.* The priest 'made an atonement for the children of Israel for all
their sins once a year,' and when the sacrifice of bullock and goat and the
burning of incense, and the sprinkling of blood was over, then and not till
then the live goat was presented to the Lord. . . . The Hebrew scriptures emphasize the fact that the burden laid upon the goat is not merely physical
evil, not pestilence or famine, but rather the burden of moral guilt." The
Athenian festival of Thargelia was a rite of expulsion, of riddance, which incidentally involved loss of life to a human being. The event for which it was most
famous was the driving forth of two human scape-goats, indicating that a
chief function was the ceremonial purification of the city. It may be that many
of the so-called human sacrifices among the Greeks of mythological days and
a large number of cases so regarded by the tragedians were primarily not
sacrifices but ceremonies of riddance and purification. The ultimate fact that
lies behind such ceremonies is the use of a human pharmakos. "The pharmakos
is killed then, not because his death is a vicarious sacrifice, but because he
is so infected and tabooed that his life is a practical impossibility. The uneducated, among whom his lot would necessarily be cast, regard him as an infected
horror, an incarnate pollution; the educated who believe no such nonsense
know that the kindest thing is to put an end to a life that is worse than
death." When needing a scape-goat the Athenians utilized a man already condemned by the state, a device adopted by other peoples. "Why not combine
religious tradition with a supposed judicial necessity? Civilized Athens had its
barathron; why should civilized Athens shrink from annually utilizing two
vicious and already condemned criminals to 'purify the city'?" In the rituals
known as flight-ceremonies, common to both Egyptians and Greeks, the same
notion of transferring the pollution to a human victim is in evidence.

In the year 217 there was great excitement and fear in Rome; there were
many prodigies, and a heavy penalty seemed called for. The rite of *ver sacrum*

---

6 Kautzsch, in *Hastings's Bible Dict.*, 663,
705 (quoted).

7 *Greek Relig.*, 104 (quoted), 105 (quoted),
109, 110, 113-114. The authoress refers to
Herodotus, *Hist.*, II, 39.

—a special offering of the firstlings of spring—was renewed, but the old ritual offered few means of redeeming sin.[8]

§287. Insurance and Investment.

THE practice of offering first fruits is much in evidence in San Cristoval, Solomon Islands.[1] Among the African Bageshu, "at harvest time an offering of first fruits together with some of the last year's corn and a fowl are sent to the medicine man for the deity before anyone dare touch the new corn." These people are said to have no permanent temples nor appointed priests. "When occasion requires, the temple or hut is rebuilt and the offerings made, but directly the cause of anxiety passes, the temple is neglected and falls into ruin until required again, when a new one is built."[2] The lord of the thunder and lightning, among the Tshi-speaking people, was Bobowissi. At times he manifested his displeasure by killing persons by lightning, by storms and tornadoes, and especially by sending such torrents of rain that the mud dwellings of the natives fell in and crushed the occupants; and "after any great loss of life from this cause the people would offer sacrifice to Bobowissi, asking how they had offended him."[3] A Congo ceremony of insuring good fortune is as follows. "All the fetishes are spread out on a piece of cloth; the chief with two of his sons or slaves sits down opposite them. A cock is brought, and the chief cuts an artery at the side of the bird's neck and lets the blood trickle out through the mouth over the three first fetishes, scattering a few drops over the others. Then he chews kola, and, meanwhile, addresses the fetishes, alternately coaxing and threatening them, and making his petition, which is usually a request for fertility for his wives and slaves. After each sentence he spits on the three principal fetishes, and his sons or slaves spit on the others."[4] Among the Bangala of the Upper Congo, "the first-fruit of game and fish that a lad killed would be given to the lad's mother, or, if she were dead, to his mother's sister or the next to kin. The first-fruit of a farm was given in the same way by a girl to her mother, or her aunt."[5]

Before any crop can be eaten by the Akamba an offering of first fruits must be made to the *Aiimu,* or evil spirits. This occurs in a clearing called "the place of praying." "During the dance one of the women present is sure to be seized with a fit of shaking and cry out aloud—this sign is known to be the answer to the people's prayer to the *Aiimu.*"[6] The *mugomo* tree is regarded by the Kikuyu as sacred, and it is not ruthlessly cut down as is the case with all other trees which impede clearing operations during the making of fields. "Ngai is supposed to live up in its branches, but he descends in order to eat the meat of the sacrifice, which is offered below. . . . Those who worship merely cross their lips with a morsel of meat before sacrificing. . . . Generally speaking it seems to be their belief that constant sacrifices are necessary to propitiate even the good deities. The sudden death of a man, for instance by lightning, is ascribed to some evil act of his life being punished by Ngai."[7] In Kavirondo and Nandi the natives look upon the *sumba* or elves as rather malicious in their influence and are careful to propitiate them by offerings,

8 Wissowa, *Relig. Römer,* 54; §297, of the text.
1 Fox and Drew, in JAI, XLV, 142 ff.
2 Roscoe, in JAI, XXXIX, 188, 193.
3 Ellis, *Tshi,* 22-23.

4 Torday and Joyce, in JAI, XXXVII, 141.
5 Weeks, in JAI, XXXIX, 425.
6 Hobley, *A-Kamba,* 86-87.
7 Tate, in JAI, XXXIV, 263.

if any untoward circumstances happen. For instance, "when the fishing fails, the chiefs send a present of cattle to the island. And from time to time, the people take cooking pots and tobacco pipes, and leave them for their use. . . . The island being quite small, any cattle which have been brought as offertories to the *sumba* are transferred to the mainland and herded with the cattle of the tribesmen; but they are all known, and never sold or killed. Even if a neighbouring tribe made war, these cattle would never be carried off as booty, but would be regarded as sacred."[8] Sacrifice for a purpose is a daily ritual with the agricultural Kabyles. "At dawn they bury four hard eggs, four pomegranates, and four nuts for each pair of oxen. They leave them in the ground all day, and in the evening these titbits become the prize of the children of the village. Before leaving home, each laborer places some bread, fritters and cake on the horns and neck of his bullocks; then he rubs oil on them, in order to preserve himself and his beasts of burden from all malady during the year. Arrived at the place of work, he commences by scattering on the ground a handful of mixed seeds—wheat, barley, peas and beans; then he makes a new distribution of eatables to his assistants; finally all recite together the *fatha* [the first sura of the Koran], and the work begins."[9]

The original religions in Sikkim, India, and in Tibet have many points in common: in both systems temples and images are unknown, while propitiatory offerings occupy a prominent place; and neither recognizes a definite priestly order, while both encourage resort to shamans to ward off the malign influences which surround the human race.[10] All the iron deposits of Manipur are under the protection of the forest god, who has to be propitiated before the metal can be worked. When fresh ground has to be broken, a buffalo is sent by the Raja, and this animal is taken to the site of the proposed excavation, where in olden times it was slain; but since the introduction of Hinduism the animal is released and dedicated to the god, after a few hairs from each fetlock and the end of his tail, and a drop or two of blood from his ear, have been offered.[11] The modern features of this rite represent, in part at least, an attempt to avoid the burden of sacrifice. The same applies to a practice of the Borneans, who pour a poisonous mixture into streams to aid them in fishing. "But before any poison is cast in, a certain quantity must be set aside for the Spirits. One of the party, therefore, goes a little further up the stream to some insignificant pool which has been left on the pebbly bank, (wherein—alas! for poor human nature—any one could see with half an eye that there was no fish) and, pouring in the Tuba juice, he calls out: 'O Spirits of the Rocks! of the Wood! of the Smooth, Flat Stones! of the Karangans! of the Earth! and of the Leaves; here in this pool is your share of the numberless fish! Spoil not our sport by any interference!' "[12]

The Dyaks keep away from a cemetery, as an abode of spirits, except when they bury their dead; when they do that, they begin by scattering rice on the ground, as the price paid for the grave to the spirit owning the land. "Then a fowl is killed, and the blood sprinkled on the ground. These offerings are made to prevent the spirits from hurting any of those who take part in digging the grave."[13] Strewing rice, says Wilken,[14] was at first merely a means to keep a person's soul in his body or to bring it back; later it was used to allure spirits

---

8 Hobley, in JAI, XXXIII. 340-341.
9 Hanoteau et Letourneux, *Kabylie*, 478.
10 Risley, *Eth. India*, I, 203.
11 Shakespear, in JAI, XL, 349.

12 Furness, *Head-Hunters*, 188.
13 Gomes, *Sea Dyaks*, 136, 137.
14 In VG, I, 53-55, and notes on 569, 570, 571.

in general. Among the Dyaks the strewing of rice was not so much a sacrifice as a device to make the god called upon attentive to the fact that something out of the ordinary was going on and to indicate the place where divine help was needed. Among the Macassars of Celebes the usage is to have a chicken pecking at the kernels, especially during a pregnancy. A chicken is used in calling back the soul of a sick person; at the sacrificial feast a little rice is strewed while a chicken is swung about by the feet until it begins to squawk. The Alfurs of Buru, who have no priests, hold that ghosts and spirits can be called on by anybody and at any time and place, but most properly in little shrines built for them. If the Alfur has any project he always seeks to assure himself of the favor, help, and coöperation of the ancestral spirits. He also gives a thank-offering for the aid received and to assure future favors: "Thanks, ancestors, here is your food prepared from the first fruits of the rice." Such thank-offerings are not without their bearing upon future, as well as past, well-being.

Of fundamental importance in the religious attitude of the Bagobo, in the Philippines, are "the group assemblages at which sacrifices of human beings or fowls are presented to certain gods; sacred liquor is ceremonially drunk; formal lustrations in the river for the expulsion of disease take place; rites magically protective against ghosts and demons are manipulated; and material wealth in garments, ornaments, and weapons is offered up with the primary intention of obtaining an increase of riches. Yet it is noteworthy that the parents of every family, at their own home altar, are accustomed to perform devotions and to make offerings for the health and well-being of members of their household. Formal worship is carried on at fixed altars or at temporary shrines of recognized types, where fruits of the field and manufactured products are placed, or the slain victim is ceremonially offered up. But acceptable devotions may be performed by the wayside or in the forest, merely by laying on the ground an areca nut and a betel leaf with a word of prayer to some divinity."[15] The Maori "offered death sacrifices, sacred food for the dead, etc., rather with the idea of 'throwing a sop to Cerberus' in pacifying the evil deities, and also in paying honor to a chief, than from the faintest idea of adoration."[16]

In Greenland, gifts were offered to the spirits of certain rocks, capes, and ice-firths, principally when travelling and passing those places. Food, beads, and other desirables were cast into the water.[17] In the Yukon delta, at a celebration, "the inuas or shades of the various animals are invited and are supposed to be present and enjoy the songs and dances, with the food and drink offerings, given in their honor."[18] During the full moon of December the Eskimo held a feast to which the bladders of animals killed during the year were brought. These were supposed to contain the shades of the animals. We have seen elsewhere that the bladders were taken out to a hole made in the ice and thrust into the water. They were believed to swim far out to sea and there enter the bodies of unborn animals of their kind, thus becoming reincarnated and rendering game more plentiful.[19] Certain ceremonies among the Salish and other tribes were intended to placate the spirits of the fish, plant, or fruit, as the case might be, in order that a plentiful supply of the same might

15 Cole, in AA, XX, 217.
16 Tregear, in JAI, XIX, 120.
17 Rink, *Tales*, 56; Murdoch, in BAE, IX, 433; Nansen, *Esk. Life*, 292.

18 Nelson, in BAE, XVIII, pt. I, 359.
19 Fletcher; Swanton, in HAI, I, 454; II, 406, respectively.

be vouchsafed to them. "The ceremony was not so much a thanksgiving as a performance to ensure a plentiful supply of the particular object desired; for if these ceremonies were not properly and reverently carried out there was danger of giving offence to the 'spirits' of the objects and being deprived of them."[20] The Haida deposit certain offerings in the sea, and many tribes throw offerings into springs, lakes, and rivers.[21] The Canadian Indians hung a dog on a pole by his hind legs as a sacrifice.[22] Among the Kwakiutl, "when a beloved child is dying, the parents keep on praying to the spirit not to try to take away their child. 'I will pay you with these clothes of this my child, Sitting-on-Fire.' Thus they say, while they put on the fire the clothes of the one who is lying there sick."[23]

"Before eating, an Indian took a small piece of food from the dish and threw it into the fire as an offering to the evil spirit, also mumbling a short grace."[24] It was an Onondaga belief that "a magic feast at which all ate everything set before them without stint or escape as to amount might be necessary to save the giver's life, he eating nothing."[25] From the most remote period the Iroquois believed in the existence of a race of supernatural beings whom they called False-faces. They were evil spirits without bodies, arms, or limbs—merely faces, of the most hideous description, whose glance paralyzed the beholder. They could send plagues and pestilences among men, as well as devour their bodies. "Upon this belief was founded a regular secret organization, called the False-face band," very widespread in Iroquois villages, with initiation, forms, ceremonies, and dances. Membership was attained by dreaming that one was a False-face; and the only way to get out was by dreaming that he had ceased to be such. All the members but one, the "keeper of the False-faces," were men. "The prime motive in the establishment of this organization was to propitiate those demons called False-faces, and among other good results to arrest pestilence and disease."[26]

The Omahas have a sacred well or spring, located in western Kansas: "The miraculous quality of this pool, which chiefly astonishes the Indian mind, consists in a slow rising of the water whenever a large number of people stand around the brink. The water of the pool is perfectly limpid and considered to be bottomless; it harbors an aquatic monster which engulfs all the objects thrown into it, and never sends them up again. Indians offer to it beads, arrows, kerchiefs, earrings, even blankets, and all sink down immediately. Before putting clay or paint on their faces, the Indians impregnated these substances with the water of the well. . . . It was the custom of the tribe to offer the spearheads and other tokens to appease nature or their gods by depositing them in the spring, which they considered holy ground. This custom was observed whenever the tribe went on the war-path, to insure victory; when a child was born, to secure blessings for the child; and for any unusual undertaking, to make it successful. These deposits of tokens in the springs were also good-luck offerings. The spring was usually a shrine resorted to by the old-time Indians to commune with the unseen world. . . . The custom of making offerings at springs to the water deities is common to all primitive tribes, and among the Arapahos and Cheyennes I have myself seen shawls and strips of calico hung up as sacrifices upon the bushes about every little

20 Hill-Tout, in JAI, XXXIV, 330-331.
21 Hough, in HAI, I, 46.
22 Ratzel, Vkde., II, 698.
23 Boas, in BAE, XXXV, pt. I, 705.

24 Bruce, Va., I, 174.
25 Parkman, Old Régime, 37.
26 Dall, in BAE, III, 144.

watering-place in the vicinity of a regular camp. . . . The most notable examples of sacrifices of this general class are recorded by explorers of Central and South America, where offerings of gold and precious things of various kinds were cast into lakes, streams, springs, and the deep cenotes, or natural wells, to appease the gods believed to dwell therein."[27] Here is an excellent example of the extraordinary thing in nature being elevated to fetish-quality.

The offering of first-fruits among the Natchez was made by each father of a family, and on certain occasions when a live stag was sacrificed by the Iroquois it was the oldest man of the hut or village that gave the death-blow. "The Hupa offer dry incense root upon a rock, near which dwells a being supposed to have control of the weather, when they desire the rains to cease, but incense root mixed with water when they wish the frosts to melt and disappear."[28] Near the present Hopi villages there are shrines in which offerings of eagle eggs carved from wood are placed during the winter solstice for the increase of eagles.[29] Fewkes[30] says the prayer-objects employed by these people are not regarded as symbolic representations of sacrificial offerings, but as material representations of animals desired. "The sheep effigy of the modern Hopi is not a sacrifice to the god of growth, but a prayer symbol employed to secure increase of flocks. The painted eagle egg has a corresponding significance." As contrasted with their neighbors, the Pimas make little outward show of religion, though there is an occasional "rain dance" and other ceremonies for the cure of disease. Propitiation is directed chiefly to the sun: "When weary upon a journey, the Sun was appealed to, and the first whiff of cigarette smoke was puffed toward him." The sun-disk was regarded as the veritable person of the god, not his shield or head-dress.[31] Zuñi brides desirous of becoming mothers make an offering of *kunque* (meal) at a phallic shrine.[32]

In Mexico, "while the fishing is going on, a cross is set up near the river, upon which beads and girdles, head-bands, tunics, pouches, and arrows are hung. Should they omit this sacrifice to the spirit of the water, the fish will not die, 'for surely there is some great big man who is the master of the fish,' said an Indian to me; and he added, 'or it is perhaps only the oldest fish.' "[33] Much reverence was shown for an idol in a temple in Yucatan, and "when there was great mortality or a pestilence or other public calamities, all went to him, men and women alike, carrying a great number of presents to offer to him, and then, in sight of all, a fire descended at noon and consumed the sacrifice. Then the priest announced to them what would happen concerning the subject about which they desired information, such as diseases, famine or death, and, after that, they became acquainted with the good or evil fortune to come, although sometimes the event was contrary to what had been announced to them."[34] Von den Steinen's[35] Indian attendant, during his travels in Brazil, gave no encouragement to the idea that the April festival was one of thanksgiving for the crop; he said that they celebrated the feast at the time of the harvest because that was when they had the food and other things with which to celebrate it.

Twice in the Homeric poems, offerings are made which bear a close re-

27 Holmes, in AA, IV, 122, 123, 124, 126, 128.

28 Swanton, "Sacrifice," in HAI, II, 403, 406.

29 Hough, "Eagle," in HAI, I, 410.

30 In BAE, XXVIII, 135.

31 Russell, in BAE, XXVI, 250, 251.

32 Bourke, in BAE, IX, 509.

33 Lumholtz, in *Scribner's Mag.*, XVI, 450.

34 Hagar, in AA, XV, 18.

35 *Zent. Bras.*, 297.

semblance to sacrifices to the souls of the dead, although they may be distinguished from them: at the funeral-pyre of Patroclus, Achilles leans jars of honey and of oil against the bier on which the corpse lies; and when Odysseus goes to the realm of Hades to consult a seer, he digs a small pit in the ground and "pours about it a libation for all the dead, first mixed-honey [*i.e.*, milk and honey], then sweet wine, and thirdly water;" then after a prayer to the dead, including a vow that on his return to Ithaca he will sacrifice a farrow cow and burn a pyre full of treasures, and in particular that he will sacrifice a black ram to the seer, Odysseus cuts the throats of a ram and of a black ewe in such a manner that their blood flows into the pit. "When the Achaean army suffers from the plague, and Achilles calls an assembly to consider what shall be done, the question is not what drug can be found as a specific for the pestilence, but how the god is to be appeased; and not what sin has been committed, but whether some vow has been left unperformed or some sacrifice unoffered. The plague was sent . . . because Agamemnon had refused to give up for ransom the captive daughter of a priest of Apollo, in spite of the fact that this priest had presented reverence for his god, in addition to boundless gifts, as a motive for granting his request. The offense was a lack of respect,—not a moral crime. The god would not have been offended if Chryseïs had not happened to be the daughter of his priest." The importance which the divinities attach to the sacrifices offered by men is shown by the following incidents. Menelaus on leaving Egypt neglected to sacrifice to the gods, and he came no farther on his way than the island of Pharos before he was checked by lack of wind for his voyage, and there his supplies of provisions were exhausted before he learned from the sea-god Proteus the cause of his trouble. He returned to Egypt and offered the sacrifices which he had neglected, and then found no difficulty in sailing to his home.[36] In a later and more sophisticated age a Greek tragedian puts these words in the mouth of the Cyclops: "Wealth is the god for the wise; all else is bombast and fine words."[37] "That there are gods only for the rich," states Reclus,[38] "is a doctrine which, on careful investigation, seems ancient and universal." There is evidence in ancient Greece of economy in sacrifice, in that war-axes were so worked as to have no practical utility and fragments were made to look like complete axes so as to serve as offering or amulet. "Similar votive pieces, axes in which the shaft-hole is not bored through, but only indicated by a little depression, are known from later periods."[39]

On one of his expeditions, "Sennacherib went to the head of the column, and, standing on the prow of the flag-ship, he offered a sacrifice to the god of the Ocean, Ea. He poured the solemn libation, then cast into the water a model of a ship in gold, a fish of gold, an image of the god himself, also in gold."[40] Smith[41] sketches the typical Hebrew sacrifice. It was a public ceremony of a township or clan, private householders being accustomed to reserve their offerings for the annual feast and for the time being simply vowing. Victims appointed for the sacrifice were brought, and also a store of bread and wine for

---

36 Seymour, *Hom. Age*, 398-399 (quoted), 472-473, 504-505.
37 Euripides, *Cyclops*, 316-317.
38 *Primitive Folk*, 227.
39 Müller, *Oldtid*, 154.
40 Maspero, *Hist. Anc.*, III, 302.

41 *Relig. Sem.*, 254. His references are, in order: I Sam., IX, 12; XX, 6; I, 3, 21; Hos., II, 15; Isa., XXX, 29; I Sam., X, 3; IX, 13; II Sam., VI, 19; XV, 11; Neh., VIII, 10; Ezek., XXXIX, 17 ff.; Zeph., I, 7; Amos, IV, 5; I Sam., IX, 22; Judg., IX, 27; XVI, 23 ff.

the feast, whose law was openhanded hospitality; "no sacrifice was complete without guests, and portions were freely distributed to rich and poor within the circle of a man's acquaintance." The pious Jews of the time of Christ took on themselves enormous burdens of payments, ritual obligations and constraints in interests in order to comply with the Mosaic law.[42]

The Scandinavians brought tribute to Odin, that he should defend the land from enemies, and sacrificed for good crops.[43] Survivals of the ancient idea of sacrifice may be seen in the practice of German builders, who place a little tree on the gable of a new house. This custom has been explained as follows: "As a sacrifice was offered when the foundation of a house was laid, so was a sacrifice offered when the roof was completed. The roof was especially subject to assaults of the wind, and the wind was among the Northmen and Germans Odin, Woden, or Wuotan. Moreover in high buildings there was a liability of their being struck by lightning, and the thunder god Thorr had to be propitiated to stave off a fire. The farmhouses in the Black Forest to the present day are protected from lightning by poles with bunches of flowers and leaves on the top, that have been carried to church on Palm Sunday, and are then taken home and affixed to the gable, where they stand throughout the year. The bunch represents the old oblation offered annually to the God of Storm." The floreated points of metal or stone on the apex of the gable are a reminiscence of the bunch of grain originally offered to Woden's horse. "The sheaf of corn, which is fastened in Norway and Denmark to the gable of a house, is now supposed to be an offering to the birds: originally, it was a feed for the pale horse of the death-god Woden. And now we see the origin of the bush which is set up when a roof is completed, and also of the floral hipknobs of Gothic buildings. Both are relics of the oblation affixed to the gable made to the horse of Woden,—corn, or hay, or grass; and this is also the origin of the 'palms,' poles with bouquets at the top, erected in the Black Forest to keep off lightning."[44]

§290. Cannibalism.

THERE is little doubt but that the tribes of western Australia were originally cannibals, although at the present day it is impossible to obtain any reliable information on the subject. "It would seem, however, that in some cases they ate parts of their enemies slain in a fight, while in others they ate parts of their own relatives and friends."[1] Where cannibalism is of the corporeal type, one finds cases like the following. "The Nobo house, it appears, is always built at some little distance from the village, and is used as a trap for unwary strangers—in this particular instance, for Papia. Papia, the culprits told me afterwards, 'was a fat man with a light skin, and we wanted to eat him too much,' so, when the conversation had turned upon the recent dance and upon feathers, and plumes, and other ornaments, one of the Boboi casually remarked that there were some very fine feathers in the Nobo house, and that if Papia would walk over there he would show them to him. The unsuspecting village constable fell in with the suggestion, and entered the Nobo house, and

---

42 Bousset, *Relig. d. Judenthums*, 100, 102.
43 Geijer, *Svensk. Hist.*, 23.

44 Baring-Gould, *Strange Survivals*, 42, 51, 52.
1 Brown, in JAI, XLIII, 169.

was promptly killed, cooked, and eaten; the Nobo house was then burnt down, and a fresh one built in another place."[2]

The Edugaula tribe were the only natives in Southeast Papua who ate human flesh raw and drank human blood. "The other tribes were terrified at such doings."[3] Certain tribesmen of the Gulf of Papua "are not cannibals and never were, detesting it with a great detestation, so much so that some lads I took with me lately to . . . a cannibal district, would eat no food cooked by others lest it should have been cooked in a pot in which human flesh was cooked."[4] In the majority of cases among the southern Massim the eating of human flesh was part of the solemn act of revenge, "which it was the duty of each community to take on behalf of its own members killed and eaten by other communities with whom it was at enmity. . . . In a smaller number of cases human flesh was undoubtedly eaten for the pleasure it afforded, and complete strangers were commonly killed and eaten. . . . Human flesh is stated to resemble pig in flavour, but to make better food since, although they both taste much alike, the former has the more delicate flavour, as well as the further advantage (stated by everyone who talked freely on the subject), that it never produces any painful feeling of satiety or induces vomiting. It was pointed out that if too much pig flesh were eaten a man's stomach would swell up and he would be sick, but that human flesh might be eaten until a man found it impossible to swallow any more without producing these unpleasant symptoms; it was however admitted that it was very rare for any one to get as much of this food as he would have been pleased to eat."[5] In former times the people of Lifu, Loyalty Islands, ate the bodies of enemies slain in war. "They acknowledged that they positively like human flesh, and it was not merely eaten to express hatred, or to prove the completeness of a victory. . . . The natives were exceedingly fond of human flesh. The chiefs were despotic and ordered their subjects to be clubbed and cooked at their pleasure. I have heard the natives speak of a time of severe famine when those men who had the greatest number of wives and children were considered to have the most food . . . the dead were often exhumed to be cooked and eaten: and sometimes when a native was dying with plenty of flesh on his bones, some of those standing by would be rejoicing at the prospect of a feast, and arranging to steal the body."[6] In Tana, when the body of an enemy is taken, it is dressed for the oven, and served up with yams at the next meal. "They delight in human flesh, and distribute it in little bits far and near among their friends, as a delicious morsel. I recollect talking to a native one day about it," writes Turner,[7] "and trying to fill him with disgust at the custom, but the attempt was vain. He wound up all with a hearty laugh at what he no doubt considered my weakness, and added: 'Pig's flesh is very good for *you*, but this is the thing for us;' and, suiting the action to the word, he seized his arm with his teeth, and shook it as if he were going to take the bit out! It is different on some other islands, but at Tana cannibal *connoisseurs* prefer a black man to a white man. The latter, they say, tastes *salt!*" The natives of New Caledonia picked out the good bodies of the slain for the oven and threw the bad away; they tied up a captive to a tree, dug a hole, and kindled a hot stone oven for his body before his very eyes. "The women went to battle. They kept in the

2 Murray, in AAAS, 1921, 177.
3 Bromilow, in AAAS, 1909, 476.
4 Chalmers, in JAI, XXVII, 330.

5 Seligmann, *Melanesians*, 548, 550-553.
6 Ray, in JAI, XLVII, 261-262.
7 *Samoa*, 313, 344-345.

rear, and attended to the *commissariat!* Whenever they saw one of the enemy fall it was their business to rush forward, pull the body behind, and dress it for the oven. The hands were the choice bits, sacred to the priests. The priests went to battle, but sat in the distance, *fasting* and praying for victory. They fasted for days if they got no *hands.* If the body of a chief was cooked, every one must partake, down to the little child, and before a gourmandiser proceeded to *polish* the bones, he called out, 'Have *all* tasted?' If it was the body of a woman they ate only the arms and legs. On Mare they devoured all. Sometimes they cooked in joints, and sometimes the whole body was doubled up in a sitting posture, with the knees to the chin, put into the oven, and served up so, as they squatted around for their meal. Their appetite for human flesh was never satisfied. 'Do you mean to say that you will forbid us the *fish of the sea?* Why, these are our *fish!*' This is how they talked when you spoke against cannibalism."

In the New Hebrides cannibalism prevailed until recently. "A missionary on Efate said that there was not a single middle-aged man on the island who had not eaten human flesh, and that each village regarded the next as a larder for human meat." Elsewhere man-eating is practised "perhaps more as a religious ceremony than to allay hunger." A vendetta between two villages was closed, not as usual by the payment of pigs, but by the sending of a small boy as a sacrifice.[8] In New Britain human flesh is eaten and is sold in shops as we sell beef.[9] These natives boast of their cannibalism, and "people have told the writer how they have enjoyed their feast on the previous evening, which had been some portion of a human being."[10] They appear never to have eaten the bodies of slain Europeans. Some authors ascribe this to their fear of the magic powers which dwell even in dead white persons; others explain it as an aversion to unfamiliar food.[11] In New Ireland and the Admiralty group the natives are notorious cannibals; one tribe lives by fighting for hire, demanding no payment save the bodies of the slain.[12] In New Georgia cannibalism is still practised but in the utmost secrecy.[13] Elsewhere, "in returning boys to their homes the greatest care has to be exercised that they are landed at the villages whence they were recruited, as in the event of their being put ashore at a place only a few miles from where they belong, they would run serious risk of being instantly killed and eaten."[14] When the dreaded Nuya Malu warriors came as allies to Soloira, Fiji Islands, "an abundant feast was provided for them, in which figured several roast pigs; but the 'friends' murmured that that was not a feast for warriors, and asked why no human bodies were provided for them. Human flesh was then obtained for their sustenance, but as none of the enemy had been sufficiently accommodating to come within the power of the Soloira clubmen, the source from whence the stimulating banquet was furnished can be surmised. The mountain men were not fastidious where human meat was concerned; they have dug up bodies that have been buried for days, and eaten parts of them done up into puddings. On their war marches, when they have killed victims, they have been known to cut up the bodies and carry portions in their 'kit' for provender on

8 Somerville, in JAI, XXIII, 382.
9 Danks, in AAAS, 1892, 618.
10 Cayley-Webster, *New Guinea*, 75.
11 Kleintischen, in *Globus*, XCII, 17.

12 Ray, in JAI, XXI, 4.
13 Somerville, in JAI, XXVI, 382.
14 Woodford, *Head-Hunters*, 15.

the way, as with other kinds of food."[15] Johnson[16] makes the general statement that cannibalism is still (1922) practised in the South Seas.

In Africa, cannibalism is confined chiefly to the central interior, though some South Africans seem to have practised it in former ages.[17] "The Fang and other interior tribes eat any corpse, regardless of the cause of death. Families hesitate to eat their own dead, but they sell or exchange them for the dead of other families."[18] The Bonjo eat human flesh with relish and literally practise the breeding of human cattle. "In each village, as the missionaries know only too well, one will find men, children, and young girls thus destined to sale and the slaughter-house, and resigned to their fate."[19] In recent years European nations have had to take action against sporadic cases of cannibalism in Sierra Leone and the Cameroons.[20] A number of Bantu peoples are cannibals; in the Belgian Congo the custom has been very hard to uproot—charges have been made, indeed, that it was favored by the Belgian authorities. From this region has recently come an amazing account of a negro king who sued the hospital at Boma for the possession of his leg, which had been amputated as the result of a serious accident. The surgeons, well aware that the king was an open advocate of cannibalism, flatly refused his demand for the severed limb, knowing the use to which it would be put. The court, however, handed down a decision restoring the severed member to the king who, without further formality, took possession of his property and departed for his home.[21] The Mabode "are great cannibals, the presence of the white man having had little restraining influence over them. Their laws forbid them to eat a blood relation, even though he may have been killed in war. This, however, does not prevent them from cutting up and cooking the corpse, and selling the meat thus prepared to another person for food."[22] Actual paddocks, filled with "human cattle" that were being fattened for market, are reported.[23] In 1890 cannibalism was very general along the north bank of the Congo River from the mouth of the Mobangi River to the town of Likunungu. "It was the custom to eat those slain in battle, to buy slaves from the Lulanga River and other places on purpose to eat them, and to eat those also who by some criminal act had rendered themselves liable to the penalty of death. Slaves were dear, and bloody fights were infrequent, consequently the cannibal feast was one in which they could not often indulge. I could never obtain any other reason for eating human flesh than that 'it is very nice and better than any other meat.' " The Boloki folk of the Upper Congo also ate human flesh for the pleasure of it; "the palms of the hands were regarded as delicacies, although the whole hand was said to have much fat in it." Unlike other tribes in the Bangala district, only the men ate such flesh, which they cooked for themselves in saucepans reserved for that purpose. It was thought that human flesh had a beneficial effect upon those who ate it. "Dead bodies floating down the river were drawn to land and eaten by some, but not by all; some had no objection to eating relatives by marriage, and even their wives, but they never ate their blood relations. When fighting they would not eat one killed on their own

15 Webb, in AAAS, 1890, 626.
16 *Cannibal Land*, 189-191.
17 Macdonald, in JAI, XIX, 280.
18 Nassau, *Fetichism*, 11.
19 Trilles, *Fâñ*, 44.
20 New Haven *Journal-Courier*, June 3, 1913; N. Y. *Times*, June 14, 1923.

21 Keltie, *Africa*, 254 ff.; N. Y. *Times*, May 11, 1926.
22 Burrows, in JAI, XXVIII, 46; Stuhlmann, *Mit Emin*, 181, 391, 597, 598.
23 Keane, *Ethnol.*, 265; Henning, in *Globus*, LXXII, 103; Thonner, in *Globus*, LXXII, 120; Burrows, *Pigmies*, 151, 152.

side, but if they captured the body of an enemy they would eat it with gusto."[24] These facts are reported by a missionary who was an eye-witness to such scenes.

Among the Ba-Mbala of East Central Africa, cannibalism may be described as an everyday occurrence, and, according to the natives themselves, is based on a sincere liking for human flesh, which, when used for food, is called *Misuni*. "Enemies killed in war, people buried alive after the poison test or dying in consequence of it, relations (except father, mother, children, uncles, or aunts), and sometimes foreign slaves, are all eaten; in fact, any corpse which is not in the last stages of decomposition is considered a dainty. Victims killed for cannibalistic purposes are often buried for two days before being eaten, during which period a fire is kept burning on the grave; the body is then exhumed and cooked with manioc flour. . . . Vessels in which *Misuni* has been cooked are broken and the pieces thrown away. Cannibalism accompanies the ceremony by which a kind of alliance is established between chiefs of the same region." Cannibalism is general among the Ba-Huana, though practised by men only. "The habit cannot be ascribed to a craving for animal food, since game is plentiful in the Ba-Huana country. It is, in fact, due to a sincere liking for human flesh, of which the natives are in no way ashamed. The bodies of enemies are consumed, and expeditions are arranged for the purpose of recruiting the larder. No special ceremonies are observed in connection with cannibalism, and the flesh is prepared and boiled in the same fashion as any other meat. The blood is not touched, and the sexual parts are thrown away; the head is placed in water until the flesh rots away, and the skull is preserved as a trophy in a special hut."[25] The Bageshu, a Bantu people, are "a more primitive race and stand low indeed in the human scale; . . . they are, undoubtedly, cannibals, though each clan, when questioned, denied the fact and pointed out another which followed the practice of eating the dead secretly. Their land might be called a land without graves owing to the practice of throwing out the dead towards evening under the pretext of leaving them for the wild animals, whereas the old women visit the bodies and take what they consider the prime pieces and leave the refuse to the wild animals."[26] That there exists, principally in the region of the great lakes, a group or sect of people who habitually indulge in feeding on human flesh is an indisputable fact, to which several administrators and explorers have borne testimony. "One thing, however, is certain: natives, when brought in contact with corpses and putrefaction, do not feel the same horror that we do. A bright, intelligent young fellow once asked me, in a matter-of-fact way, if I had never tasted a corpse. To my indignant protest, 'The smell alone is sufficient to drive a man away,' he replied, 'No, the smell is very pleasant!' And on another occasion I was asked quite seriously if, among the many 'tinned stuffs' brought into the country by Europeans, there is not also tinned human meat."[27]

Of a tribe in the Malay Peninsula it is written: "It is undeniable that the Bataks as a race have a greater prevalence of social virtues than most European nations, and that truth, honesty, hospitality, benevolence, chastity, absence of private crimes, are here found actually to co-exist even with cannibalism."[28] During some of their wars, a body was occasionally cooked by the

---

24 Weeks, in JAI, XXXIX, 121, 457-458.
25 Torday and Joyce, in JAI, XXXV, 404; and in JAI, XXXVI, 279.
26 Roscoe, in JAI, XXXIX, 181.

27 Coudenhove, in *Atl. Mo.*, CXXVIII, 166, 167.
28 Skeat and Blagden, *Malay Penin.*, I, 556; II, 285.

Samoans; "but they affirm that, in such a case, it was always some one of the enemy who had been notorious for provocation or cruelty, and that eating a part of his body was considered the climax of hatred and revenge, and was not occasioned by the mere relish for human flesh. . . . It is the custom on the submission of one party to another to bow down before their conquerors each with a piece of firewood and a bundle of leaves, such as are used in dressing a pig for the oven; as much as to say, 'Kill us and cook us, if you please.' Criminals, too, are sometimes bound hand to hand and foot to foot; slung on a pole put through between the hands and feet, carried and laid down before the parties they have injured, like a pig about to be killed and cooked. . . . During a great scarcity occasioned by a gale cannibalism prevailed. When a light was wanted in the evening, two or three went to fetch it—it was not safe for one to go alone. If a child was seen out of doors, some one would entice it by holding up something white and calling the child to get a bit of cocoa-nut kernel, and so kidnap and cook."[29] Cannibalism is said to have been practised on Easter Island up to 1864. One old man boasted of the number of human beings he had eaten. "When asked how he liked 'long pig' he smacked his lips and expressed a regret that he could no longer enjoy the luxury."[30] Among the Maoris the eating of human flesh was usually a sequel of battle. A venerable warrior relates: "We cut off the heads of the slain, to be smoked and preserved as trophies of war, and we cooked and ate the bodies. That was indeed the warrior's food, the flesh of man. There was no other meat to equal it. In appearance it was like pork when cooked, and it tasted like pork, only sweeter. I ate it, and I also drank human blood. That was the custom of us all in those days. This was also a custom of our people: when a man had succeeded in killing a foe whom he particularly hated, he would drink the blood of the slain man and would cook the body and consume every portion of it—*kai katoa!*" In peace, slaves were frequently killed as a relish for the monotonous fare of taro or fern-root. "Sometimes a chief would become 'meat-hungry'; then a slave, preferably a girl, would be slaughtered and cooked to appease the aristocratic appetite." These epicurean eaters-of-man preferred their own countrymen to white sailors, saturated with tobacco and "salt-horse"; yet "in the Hauhau war with the white troops, cannibalism was revived, and as late as 1869 the flesh of colonial soldiers killed in bush fighting in Taranaki was frequently eaten by the Maoris."[31]

Cannibalism, writes Letourneau,[32] citing cases, "exists and has existed, in America, from the Arctic region down to the island of Tierra del Fuego;" but it was not an everyday affair. Together with human sacrifice, it rested upon religious motives, or revenge, or excessive savagery in war; there was about it something extraordinary and sacred, an air of exception and mystery, with some awe. The existence of prehistoric cannibalism is likely.[33] The term cannibal seems to have originated in a Spanish corruption of the word we know as "Carib";[34] but it is doubtful whether the Spanish accounts are trustworthy. In regard to the island Carib, "there are records preserved in Chanca's account of Columbus's second voyage in which he himself took part. 'These captive women [at Guadeloupe] told us,' says he, 'that the Carib men use them with such cruelty as would scarcely be believed, and that they eat the

29 Turner, *Samoa*, 108-109.
30 Cooke, in USNM, 1897, 712, 713.
31 Cowan, *Maoris*, 237-238, 239-240.
32 *Soc.*, 200; *Polit.*, 503.

33 Ratzel, *Vkde.*, II, 698; Somers, in PSM, XLVII, 203-207; Mooney, in HAI, I, 195.
34 Summerhayes, in JAI, XX, 112.

children which they bear to them, only bringing up those which they have by their native wives. Such of their male enemies as they can take away alive they bring here to their homes to make a feast of them, and those who are killed in battle they eat up after the fighting is over. They claim that the flesh of man is so good to eat that nothing like it can be compared to it in the world.' From the same authority it is learned that when the Carib take any boys as prisoners of war they remove their organs, fatten the boys until they grow to manhood, and then, when they wish to make a great feast, they kill and eat them, for they say the flesh of boys and women is not good to eat. Three boys thus mutilated came fleeing to us when we visited the houses." Roth,[35] who finds evidence of cannibalism both real and survivalistic among the Guiana Indians, goes on to say: "Were all historical evidence wanting for confirmation of the practice of cannibalism, there would still remain the middens, the bone and shell mounds, of the Pomeroon, Moruca, and Waini Rivers as silent but eloquent testimony of the prevalence of such a custom in earlier times throughout the neighborhood." There is not a little cannibalism in Brazil; there is plenty of food, but they fight and then eat the slain "as a kind of noble game." The Botocudos and others not only eat the slain who belong to another tribe, but "kill and eat even the old and sick of their own tribe, without sparing father or child, rather betimes, before the patient can become thin."[36] The Fuegians ate defeated enemies and, in time of famine, old women.[37] There are a number of anthropophagous tribes on the Amazon.[38] Even among historic peoples, a reversion to cannibalism has occurred during famines.[39]

§292. Animistic Cannibalism.

AUSTRALIAN cannibalism extends beyond the eating of children; it is often practised, not for the sake of food, but for strength and to prevent habitual sorrow. The fatty portions of the breast, arms, and legs are eaten raw just before burial and in very small quantities. "A black mark of charcoal and fat is made around the mouth of all who have partaken of the human flesh. The reason they assign for this barbarous custom is that should the relatives not eat they would be perpetually crying and become a nuisance to the camp." It would seem that the eating relieves them of the necessity of mourning by laying the ghost or pleasing it. "When they eat the fatty portions of an enemy, their reason is different; they think it will impart strength to them. When not the enemy, only near relatives partake of the dead."[1] In Victoria, where the fat of the corpse is eaten by the nearest relatives, the reason given is that they may thus forget the departed and not be continually weeping. "The Australian is not a man-eater as the New Zealander is. When severely pressed by hunger, he has been known to eat human flesh; and for the proper performance of certain ceremonials he is required by his laws to use the fat of

35 Roth, in BAE, XXXVIII, §§767, 768, 769, 773; 591 and 595 quoted; Von Martius, *Beiträge*, I, 571.

36 Andree, *Anthropophagie*, 79; Von Martius, *Beiträge*, I, 325, 430; Spix u. Martius, *Brasilien*, 1250, 1251; Bridges, "Firelanders," in *Voice for S. Amer.*, XIII, 201; Ehrenreich, in *Königl. Mus. Vkde.*, II, 59; Nadaillac, *Preh. America*, 53.

37 Fitzroy, *Adventure and Beagle*, 183, 189.
38 Markham, in JAI, XL, 101 ff.
39 §49 of the *Case-Book*; N. Y. *Times*, Jan. 4, 1921; Feb. 7, 1922; Feb. 28, 1922; New Haven *Journal-Courier*, Apr. 15, 1911; N. Y. *World*, Dec. 10, 1926.
1 Gason, in JAI, XXIV, 171; Howitt, in JAI, XX, 88.

the kidneys and other parts of the body for anointing himself, and he also swallows the fat and skin on some occasions; but he does not, like many of the South Sea Islanders, build a huge oven and cook a number of human bodies, in order that a whole tribe and its friends may enjoy a feast."[2] Cannibalism was not a general practice in Central Australia, but was more of a rite; cases are cited to show that it was a precaution against magic and probably also to ensure food[3] In the east central region, "if a strong black-fellow should die his body is suspended over a fire and the fat that exudes and drops is caught in a wooden vessel (koolaman); this fat is rubbed over their bodies. The sinews of the dead man are then eaten to make them strong. A corrobboree (dance) is held before the feast, and when all is over the koolaman is burnt."[4] "In the Gulf country the blacks killed in fight are eaten," but "the bodies of enemies killed are left where they fell, those of their own side only are eaten."[5] The fat around the heart and kidneys of slain enemies is eaten to appropriate their courage; in the north the head or the eyes are eaten with the same idea in mind. Sorcerers allege that they must eat human flesh to keep up their supernatural powers.[6]

Among the Melanesians cannibalism is becoming ceremonial, and turning into human sacrifice; "there was no sacrificial feast upon the flesh as when a pig was offered; only little bits were eaten by those who desired to get fighting *mana,* by young men, and by elders for a special purpose. Such sacrifices were thought more effectual than others, and advantage was taken of a crime, or imputed crime, to take a life and offer the man to some *tindalo.*"[7] Here is the ceremonial eating, or mere tasting, as part of ritual. On the Torres Straits islands, to make a boy brave he is given the eye and tongue of a slain enemy, cut up into small pieces and mixed with wine.[8] Cannibalism in the Solomon Islands, "as on the other islands of the South Sea seems not to have taken its origin from the absence of other animal food, but from the need of finding an expression for the highest humiliation that can be put upon an enemy. I certainly know cases where cannibalism had become a passion."[9] "Cannibalism is to a certain extent a religious ceremony to these natives. They do not kill and eat human beings for the sake of their taste, or because they are hungry, as some writers will insist on having us believe. The cause is farther back than this: in nearly every case when human beings are killed and eaten, it is on occasions when such a sacrifice is necessary, according to the natives' religious beliefs."[10] Some of the Melanesian practices in connection with appropriating the souls of the dead are too incredibly loathesome to reproduce.[11]

A rare form of cannibalism among the Southern Massim is that which consists in eating bodies exhumed for this purpose soon after they have been buried. "Although very little is known about this matter, the common opinion throughout the district that sorcerers commonly exhume and eat corpses seems to indicate that the object of the deed is the performance of an act of magic."[12] With reference to the natives of New Guinea it is stated that head-hunting and cannibalism are closely allied as to purpose, for both rest on the notion that

---

2 Smyth, *Victoria*, I, 120, 245-246.
3 Horne and Aiston, *Cent. Aust.*, 143.
4 Wells, in AAAS, 1893, 517-518.
5 Palmer, in JAI, XIII, 283; Murray, in AAAS, 1921, 177.
6 Ratzel, *Vkde.*, II, 55.
7 Codrington, *Melanesians*, 134, 135.

8 Haddon, in JAI, XX, 420.
9 Parkinson, in *Dresden K. Zöol. u. Anth.-Ethnog. Mus.*, Abhandl. VII, pt. VI, 14.
10 Hardy and Elkington, *S. Seas*, 95.
11 Cayley-Webster, *New Guinea*, 209.
12 Seligmann, *Melanesians*, 550 ff.

the soul-essence remains in the body at death. "Every man desires to increase his own soul 'strength, and so we have another inducement to homicide, for, by eating the body of an enemy, it is believed that a man adds to his own strength the quality of the portion eaten. So, in the belief that like produces like, the cannibal, when it is possible, eats that portion of the body of a victim which is weak in his own, that his deficiency may be reinforced."[13] On the Loyalty Islands, the victorious army carry off the bodies of their slain enemies and, on their arrival at home, prepare a feast and have them cooked and eaten. "The king eats the eyes, heart, and part of the breast. The women are not allowed to partake of it at the public feast, but I have been told they sometimes get a portion from their husbands in private."[14] In eating human flesh, and for that purpose alone, the Fijian chiefs used wooden forks.[15] Cannibalism has become a thing of the past in these islands, but memory of it is still vivid. When the district commissioner, a few years ago, was inspecting the mission schools, the native children sang for his benefit a dirge, the refrain of which ran thus:

> Oh! dead is Mr. Baker,
> They killed him on the road,
> And they ate him, boots and all.

This referred to the murder of the Rev. Thomas Baker, who, in July, 1867, had been killed and eaten by the hill tribes of Viti Levu as a form of reprisal for violation of a native taboo.[16] The cannibal feast in the D'Entrecasteaux Islands was always considered an act of revenge. "Sometimes the prisoner was dismembered and disembowelled on the stone platform while he was still alive, sometimes he was dispatched beforehand with a club. . . . Where only one prisoner had been taken, his head and hands were given to the wife or nearest kinsman of the man for whom the prisoner was the atonement. That night when the victim's soul returned to gather up its body and rebuild its earthly tenement it found each house-door closed and spears bristling through every wall to prevent its entering."[17]

Macdonald[18] gives, in two articles, evidence from South and East Central Africa, making some comparison of the two regions. "Among the mountain tribes of Natal, whenever an enemy who has acted bravely is killed, his liver, which is considered the seat of valor; his ears, which are considered the seat of intelligence; the skin of his forehead, which is the seat of perseverance; . . . and other members, each of which is supposed to contain some virtue, are cut from his body and baked to cinders. The ashes are carefully preserved in the horn of a bull, and being, when required, mixed with other ingredients, into a kind of paste, are administered to the youths by the tribal priest as a kind of bolus. . . . There is a close resemblance between the war usages of the South and those of Central Africa. There we find . . . the Basuto habit of cutting out an enemy's heart and liver and eating them on the spot. We also find the habit of mutilation for the purpose of reducing the parts to ashes to be stirred into a broth or gruel which must be lapped up with the hand and

---

13 Chinnery, in JAI, XLIX, 38.
14 Ray, in JAI, XLVII, 294.
15 Webb, in AAAS, 1890, 626.
16 Rev. of Brewster, "Hill Tribes of Fiji," in N. Y. Times, Dec. 10, 1922.

17 Jenness and Ballentyne, D'Entrecasteaux, 88.
18 In JAI, XX, 116; Macdonald, in JAI, XXII, 111.

thrown into the mouth, but not eaten as ordinary food is taken, to give the soldiers courage, perseverance, fortitude, strategy, patience, and wisdom."

In the Congo region, the traditional focus of cannibalism, "the motive for eating human flesh is mainly attributable to two sources: firstly, by eating prisoners of war, certain tribes consider they gain courage; and secondly, because human flesh is relished."[19] It is worth noting as an exception that "these Central African cannibals have not the belief which is held by others that to eat the heart of an enemy is to give them his courage, or that by eating his arms they receive his strength."[20]

Farther east, as in West Africa, witches are found practising cannibalism,[21] which consists in good part in getting portions of a human body for purposes of sorcery. Warriors do not eat human flesh, but they drink hot bullock blood before entering battle "and eat raw steaming meat hacked from live creatures. They also make incisions into their wrists, and suck their own blood to put heart into themselves."[22] In the Niam-niam country it is believed that drinking great quantities of human fat intoxicates.[23] In West Africa there are secret societies whose ritual includes a cannibalistic feast. Members of the fraternity are eaten instead of being buried, "in the belief that they will continue in the bodies of their friends." The skulls of slaves killed and eaten are preserved for vanity's sake; "several native chiefs apologized to us for the small number of skulls on their huts as man's importance was gauged thereby."[24] The communal cannibalistic meal of men joined to each other and to some daimon in a spiritual bond, is a common phenomenon in West Africa.[25] Extracts from testimony given in 1920 before a Naval Court of Inquiry reveal that in at least one case Haitian bandits, having killed a lieutenant of marines, removed and ate his heart and liver. It is asserted by marine officers that the natives believe "that eating the heart of a white man will give them wisdom, while eating a white man's liver will bring them courage, and smearing the sights of their rifles with the brains of a white man will bring accuracy in shooting."[26]

A survival of cannibalism is reported from Nigeria: corpses are smoke-dried, then pulverized and formed into small balls by the addition of water in which Indian corn has been boiled for hours; this mixture is allowed to dry and is then "put away for future use as an addition to the family stew."[27] "Schweinfurth maintains that dog-eating is an indication of cannibalism, but the Banziris strenuously deny every charge of this kind."[28] The Fan will eat prisoners of war in a ritual sacrifice, after the usual ceremonies; this is done through vengeance, to annihilate the body and hence the soul. Women and sometimes children are also eaten according to ritual ceremonies and solely by their relations.[29] Traces of cannibalism are still found among the Hausa. "Abu Bakar told me," writes Tremearne,[30] "that the Sarikin Kano, before fighting us in 1903, killed one of his officers, took his heart, eyes, and private parts, and, having had them cut up and cooked with the flesh of a ram, gave a small piece to each of his principal officers." In North Africa, as well as in

---

19 Ward, in JAI, XXIV, 298.
20 Burrows, Pigmies, 154.
21 Stuhlmann, Mit Emin, 351, 391; Johnston, Uganda, II, 587; Ratzel, Vkde., I, 555.
22 French-Sheldon, in JAI, XXI, 382.
23 Schweinfurth, in Petermann's Mitth., XVII, 139.
24 Chatelain, in Illustr. Afrika, July, 1897.

25 Frobenius, Masken, 178.
26 N. Y. Times, Jan. 4, 1921.
27 Kingsley, W. Afr. Studies, 566.
28 Clozel, in PSM, XLIX, 675; Brunache, Afr. Cent., 69.
29 Trilles, Fâñ, 44.
30 In JAI, XLV, 31.

Nigeria, the flesh of a young child is supposed to be the proper remedy for one of the stages of syphilis.

The notion that parts of the human body may cure disease is only a variation of the belief that one may get courage or other quality by eating the same. Cases are recorded, especially among the Chinese, in which persons out of self-sacrificing piety or compassion give some of their own flesh to the sick as a means of cure.[31] DeGroot[32] refers to "children who, in order to cure their parents or parents-in-law, gave them to eat, properly roasted, boiled, or otherwise prepared, a piece of their own flesh from the thigh, buttock, breast or arm, or a finger, or a dose of their blood. Such fanatic self-mutilation was publicly discountenanced in 1729 by an Emperor of the present dynasty. . . . Still it is not improbable that honorary gates are awarded now and then to pre-eminent models of perfection among the devotees of the great national virtue."

Partial and ceremonial cannibalism, similar to the foregoing cases, is to be found in lands where the actual practice is a thing of the past. Among the Buryat the black man-eating demons have their representatives in the "black shamans" who are believed to eat human flesh.[33] The Tibetans formerly ate their dead parents out of piety in order to give them no other sepulcher than their own bowels. This was given up before 1250 A.D., but cups made of the skulls of relatives were used as memorials. Tartars and some "bad Christians" killed their fathers when old, burned the corpses, and mixed the ashes with their daily food.[34] Funeral-cannibalism is also reported of the Birhors of Hindustan, who formerly used to kill and eat their aged parents, but "they repudiate the suggestion that they ate any but their own relations."[35] Reclus,[36] without citing authority, says that in this tribe "the parents beg that their corpses may find a refuge in the stomachs of their children, rather than be left on the road or in the forest."

In one tribe of India "it is customary for a young warrior to eat a piece of the liver of the first man he kills. This is said to strengthen the heart and give courage."[37] Further, sects of various description persist in or revert to anthropophagy.[38] Before a certain Hindu snake-doctor died—and by strange irony of fate he met his death by snake-bite he instructed the twenty-two disciples whom he had taken under his tuition, that on his death they should eat his flesh to acquire the powers he possessed in life. Accordingly, they cut his corpse to pieces, stewed the flesh and divided it amongst themselves in twenty-two leaf-cups. Each asked the other to begin eating. They were dissuaded. "One of the men placed his dona or leaf-cup on his head before consigning its contents to the fire, and a drop of meat-juice trickled down his cheeks and entered the corners of his mouth, and thus this man alone acquired a fraction of the powers that his late teacher had possessed. It is through this more fortunate disciple that the Nag-matis of our days have inherited what little knowledge of snake-charming and snake-bite cure they still possess. A similar story is related of the powers of the present race of witches and sorcerers."[39] Among Dyaks and others, "it is the practice still to cut up and consume the raw heart of 'a brave' killed in battle, under the

31 Kern, "Menschenfleisch als Arzenei," in *Intern. Archiv. f. Eth.*, Supplem., IX, 37 ff.
32 *Relig. Syst.*, II, bk. I, 793.
33 Melnikow, in *Globus*, LXXV, 133.
34 Rubruck, *Eastern Parts*, 81, 151.

35 Basu, in *JASB*, II, 571.
36 *Prim. Folk*, 249.
37 Lewin, *S.E. India*, 269.
38 Basu, in *JASB*, I, 492.
39 Roy, in *JAI*, XLIV, 332-333.

idea that the partakers will in time become braver." It seems that cannibalism has not long been obsolete in Borneo. In Cochin China, "the drinking of the gall of dead enemies, generally mixed with brandy, is looked upon as an important means of making anyone redoubtable in war."[40]

A case which may be a survival of cannibalism is reported from Hudson's Island, Polynesia: "The head of the parent was taken up on the third day after burial, and the skull cleaned by the *teeth* of the children. It was a disgrace and a byword if they refused to do so."[41] An old Maori warrior relates as one of the little incidents of his earlier years, that when the father died the sons divided the corpse amongst them, and cooked and ate it, both as a mark of respect and in order to acquire the inherent sacred virtues and *mana* of their parent. This devouring of parents, states Cowan,[42] appears to have been looked upon as a semi-religious act; but it could not have been a frequent practice, as the above case is the only one he heard of among them.

Cannibalism is an important part of the ceremonial of secret societies in the northwest of America, having been introduced among the Kwakiutl about sixty years ago and among the Tsimshian over seventy years ago. "Among the southern tribes the action of the cannibal was confined to his taking hold with his teeth of the heads of enemies, which were cut off in war." A slave might be killed by the owner, then torn and eaten; while pieces of flesh torn with the teeth from the arms and chests of prepared corpses were also consumed.[43] "The idea of eating any other human being than a brave enemy was to most Indians repulsive. One of the means of torture among the Indians of Canada and New York was the forcing of a prisoner to swallow pieces of his own flesh." Among the Iroquois, according to one of the Jesuit fathers, the eating of captives was considered a religious duty.[44] In a war with the Tuscarora, a mixed band of Indians "carried the day with such fury, that, after they had killed a great many, in order to stimulate themselves still more, they cooked the flesh of an Indian 'in good condition' and ate it."[45] The idea of feeding the gods is expressed by the Hopi prayer-stick to which a small packet of sacred meal is tied. Fewkes[46] regards the prayer-stick as a symbolic substitute for human sacrifice.

A number of Guiana tribes, about a month after the funeral, disinter the corpse and put it in a great pan or oven over the fire, till it is reduced to a black carbonaceous mass. This is pounded into a fine powder, mixed in large vats of caxiri and drunk by the assembled company. "They believe that thus the virtues of the deceased will be transmitted to the drinkers."[47] When the Jibaro is speaking of an enemy whom he particularly hates and wants to kill, he says of him: *"Yuotahei"*—"I will eat him." This expression may be a survival from a time when the Jibaros were cannibals, and as a matter of fact at the head-feast a ceremony formerly took place which may certainly be regarded as cannibalism.[48] The Tauaré burn their dead. The ashes are preserved in hollow reeds and at each meal some of them are consumed.[49] The Chavantes on the Uruguay eat their children to get back the souls of the latter; espe-

40 Roth, *Sarawak*, II, 217; Niemann, in *Bijd.*, XLV, 342.
41 Turner, *Samoa*, 289.
42 *Maoris*, 241.
43 Boas, in USNM, 1895, 664.
44 Hrdlička, "Cannibalism," in HAI, I, 201.

45 Hewitt, in HAI, II, 846.
46 In BAE, XVI, 297; Hough, in HAI, II, 304.
47 Roth, in BAE, XXX, 158.
48 Karsten, "Jibaro," in BAE, Bull. LXXIX, 48.
49 Stegelmann, in *Globus*, LXXXIII, 137.

cially young mothers do this, as they are thought to have given part of their own souls to their children too soon.[50] At the time of the Spanish invasion, the Araucanians were still cannibals, although it is now nearly a century since the last authenticated case was recorded. This cannibalism was not general, being practised only on prisoners of war. The occasion served as a national feast. The prisoner was made fast to the trunk of a tree, where he was subjected to a thousand torments, "till his captor rushed forward and hacked off a limb or piece of flesh. . . . This was the signal for the rest, who came one at a time, each one cutting off a portion of flesh, until the bones were stripped and life extinct. Men, women and children partook of the feast. The flesh was sometimes roasted, sometimes eaten raw. Before life was quite extinct they opened the breast and tore out the heart, which was passed from hand to hand among the chiefs and captains, each one biting it and sucking the blood and sprinkling it to the east. . . . The heads of the enemies slain in battle were cut off and carried in triumph to the villages, where they were afterwards used as drinking vessels in the feasts."[51]

Reversions to cannibalism out of hatred and revenge have probably been numerous. Dozy[52] mentions a case in which women cast themselves on the body of a chief who was responsible for the death of their relative, in 890 at Elvira, cut it in pieces and ate it. The same author reports that a woman made for herself a necklace and bracelets of the noses and ears of Musulmans and also cut open the body of an uncle of Mohammed, tore out the liver, and ate a piece of it. It is related of an Irish chief of the twelfth century that when his soldiers brought to him the head of a man whom he hated, "he tore the nostrils and lips with his teeth, in a most savage and inhuman manner."[53]

§294. Nature of the Offering.

THE usual sacrifice among African tribes, according to Gomme,[1] was "two human adults, one male and one female." The Kaffirs, just before a battle, send someone into the enemies' country "to steal a child, who is sacrificed to make the raid successful"; and, as among the Baganda, it is customary to flay a child and to lay its body in a path that the warriors may step over it on their way to battle. South African police recently saved an old woman from being sacrificed by a witch-doctor in a ceremony designed to give the natives strength in war.[2] In East Central Africa, in case of illness, the wizard is commonly put to death as a sacrifice, whereas in the South the culprit is executed as a criminal, after a tribal council has met and heard him "named" in the most formal manner. "In Central Africa the magician has the power of summary condemnation. . . . The custom of human sacrifice accounts for the difference, where on the whole, the customs are the same, and regulated by the same usages." Thus closely do religion and law align themselves. Again, "if the prophetess declares that a person must be offered as a sacrifice to a mountain deity, the victim is led by her and bound hand and foot to a tree. If during the first night he is killed by beasts of prey, the gods have accepted the sacrifice, and feast 'on his fat,' which is as the smell of spices in their nostrils. If he is not devoured, he is left to die of starvation or is thrown into

---

50 Andree, *Anthropophagie*, 50.
51 Latcham, in JAI, XXXIX, 361-362.
52 *Hist. des Musulmans d'Espagne*, I, 47.
53 Gomme, *Ethnol. in Folklore*, 149.

1 *Ethnol. in Folklore*, 73.
2 Tyler, in *Illust. Afr.*, Dec., 1895; N. Y. *Times*, Sept. 22, 1926.

a lake or river, with a sinker attached. He was considered unworthy. . . . The frequency of human sacrifices among certain tribes is appalling. When the gods are offended, men must die; when they are hungry, cattle and fowls serve their turn; and when they are only to be propitiated, as for a favor desired, flour or corn will answer."[3] A missionary who spent twenty-three years among a people of Central Africa says: "The streams of blood that flow at a king's death in the far interior of Africa are in a sad, sinister sense real red sunsets."[4]

On the Loango Coast, human beings are sacrificed at a burial and whenever a stroke of ill luck occurs, the latter being interpreted by the soothsayer as evidence that the ancestral spirits are angry and must be appeased.[5] On the wall of the king's palace in Benin was found a frame for crucifixion, with a woman on it sacrificed to the rain-god.[6] In Dahomi, besides the Grand Custom that is held after the death of a king, there is an Annual Custom which is designed principally for the purpose of supplying the dead kings periodically with fresh servitors. As a rule those sacrificed on the former occasion are the personal attendants of the king—his wives, the chief eunuch, and a suitable following of soldiers, Amazons, bards and drummers. The despatching of messages to the deceased kings causes a far greater loss of human life than do the Customs, it having been estimated that five hundred persons are slain in ordinary years for this purpose. The victims are said to resign themselves to their fate with the greatest apathy.[7]

In earlier days in East Africa, at a time of famine or visitation of cattle-disease, it was the custom to sacrifice at the shrine a small child and then bury it there. "The mother of the child was afterwards compensated for her loss."[8] In one Madagascar district human sacrifices were formerly offered every week, "Friday being the proper day, and those of high rank were considered the most appropriate offering; the victims were speared and left to be devoured by wild dogs and birds."[9] In northeast Africa, "the old custom of human sacrifice stands in connection with slavery"; the author[10] mentions the tribes who do and do not practise it. At the time of the Arab conquest a virgin in gay apparel was thrown into the river as a sacrifice to obtain a plentiful inundation. 'Amr, the conqueror of Egypt, prohibited this custom, but even in Lane's time a truncated pillar or cone of earth called *aruseh* (the bride) was raised some little distance in front of the dam shortly before the date of the great ceremony. The *aruseh* was washed away by the rising waters, generally a week or fortnight before the dam was cut.[11]

In India occur many instances of human sacrifice. One legend "speaks of the sacrifice as having been at first human, subsequently changing to beast sacrifice, eventually to a rice offering, the latter now representing the original sacrificial animal, man. . . . Human sacrifice must have been peculiarly horrible from the fact that the sacrificer not only had to kill the man but to eat him, as is attested by the formal statement of the liturgical works. . . . It cost 'one thousand cattle' to buy a man to be sacrificed. . . . Several of the modern Hindu sects have caused to be performed human sacrifices, even in this country. . . . Not long ago it was quite customary to fling children

3 Macdonald, in JAI, XXII, 104, 106, 113.
4 N. Y. *Times*, Mar. 3, 1912.
5 Bastian, *Deut. Exped.*, II, 60.
6 Carlsen, in *Globus*, LXXII, 309.
7 Ellis, *Ewe*, 121, 127, 137.

8 Hobley, *A-Kamba*, 57.
9 Sibree, *Great Afr. Isl.*, 303.
10 Paulitschke, *Nordost-Afr.*, I, 262.
11 Lane, *Mod. Egyptians*, 500 (1895);
Seligmann, in JAI, XLIII, 669.

also into the river."[12] "The goddess remains satisfied for a thousand years with a human being sacrificed according to prescribed rites and ceremonies, and with three human sacrifices for a hundred thousand years." Another divinity remains satisfied with human flesh for three thousand years. Human blood offered with mantras [spells] always becomes ambrosia. The wise offer a bloody human head and human flesh. In one drama, it is announced: "Human flesh is for sale—unwounded real flesh from the body of man. Take it, take it!"[13]

All the hill people of the eastern Ghats, except perhaps the Saoras, seem to have practised human sacrifice. The Khonds wished, in 1888, to renew the custom, and would have done so if allowed. In 1886, in Jeypore, all the preparations for such a ceremony were made but "at the last a black sheep was dressed up and adorned, its head shaved, etc., and it was beheaded instead of the man, who was given a present and released." During certain disturbances, in 1879-1880, the hill people made many human sacrifices.[14] This was evidently a case of reversion under calamity. "Three years ago [1887], an old man and his daughter were seized and their heads struck off,—a sacrifice to the goddess Meenachee—by another hill tribe in the neighborhood."[15] A report of 1854 shows that it was a very common practice with one tribe to cut off the heads, hands, and feet of anyone met with, "without any provocation or pre-existent enmity, merely to stick up in their field to ensure a good crop of grain." In the same region, on the death of one of the men immediately after the purchase of a captive boy, the latter was flayed alive, his flesh being cut off bit by bit till he died; "these superstitious savages then divided the whole body, giving a piece of the flesh to each man in the village to put into his . . . corn basket from which they suppose all evil will be averted, their good fortune will return and plentiful crops of grain will be ensured."[16] Kidnapping, followed by sacrifice, is done from private motives, to gain riches or win some coveted private revenge, and also for the benefit of the entire tribe.[17]

Slavery and human sacrifice are still going on in some of the mountain districts of Northern Burma, according to a recent report of the Commissioner of the Northeastern Frontier. In this territory, known as the Naga Hills, the number of human sacrifices is never less than from six to ten a year. The most common victims are Indian children captured from Assam, although any kind of available slaves may be included in the slaughter. In 1921 the inhabitants of a village in Rajputana burned an old woman alive "in order to call down the vengeance of heaven on the State," which had sent sepoys to assist in the collection of the usual revenue contributions.[18]

Thurston[19] reports at length upon the custom in southern India. Grown men are most esteemed as victims because they are more costly. Children are bought and reared for the altar; when old enough to realize their impending fate they are fettered and guarded. The victim is always purchased from parents or kidnappers; criminals or prisoners of war are not considered fitting subjects. In the ceremony the earth is addressed: "O God, we offer the

12 Hopkins, *Relig. Ind.*, 196, 198, 200, 363, note, 450.
13 Barrow, in JASB, III, 200.
14 Fawcett, in JASB, I, 258 ff.
15 Painter, in JASB, II, 153.
16 Godden, in JAI, XXVII, 9.

17 Risley, *Eth. Ind.*, I, 147.
18 N. Y. *Times*, June 21, 1923; June 14 and July 9, 1921.
19 *S. Ind.*, 511-512, 513, 515-516, 517-518; Reclus, *Prim. Folk*, 306.

sacrifice to you. Give us good crops, seasons, and health." And the victim is told: "We bought you with a price and did not seize you. Now we sacrifice you according to custom, and no sin rests with us." The victim is intoxicated and anointed with oil; then each participant touches the anointed part and wipes the oil on his own head. A hog is sacrificed and its blood allowed to run into a pit, into which the human victim's face is pressed until he is suffocated. Bits of the body are buried on the boundaries of the village. Or the victim has his flesh cut piecemeal from his bones, "till the living skeleton, dying from loss of blood, is relieved from torture, when its remains are burnt, and the ashes mixed with the new grain to preserve it from insects." Once more, in the sacrifice of three human beings, the live victim is hacked by the priest while he addresses the deity: "On account of this sacrifice you have given to kings, kingdoms, guns, and swords. The sacrifice we now offer you must eat, and we pray that our battle-axes may be converted into swords, our bows and arrows into gunpowder and balls; and if we have any quarrels with other tribes, give us the victory." To the victim he says: "That we may enjoy prosperity, we offer you a sacrifice to our God . . . who will immediately eat you, so be not grieved at our slaying you. Your parents were aware, when we purchased you from them for sixty rupees, that we did so with intent to sacrifice you. There is, therefore, no sin on our heads, but on your parents. After you are dead, we shall perform your obsequies." The last of these Khond sacrifices took place in 1852; a buffalo is now substituted for the human victim. It is hewn to pieces while alive, and pieces of its flesh buried in the soil to secure good crops. Sometimes as many as twenty or thirty human beings were thus sacrificed, the number being in proportion to the importance of the petition.

"Cannibal gods were hungry; they could pay; therefore purveyors made their appearance" to cater to the sacrificial needs. The custom was firmly rooted and has lasted down until recent days, as where a Goa fisherman killed his companion, "from no enmity against the deceased, but under a superstitious idea that the sacrifice would please the spirits of the river and bring him good fishing."[20] "Our own times have witnessed fishermen walking about with sacks on their shoulders near lonely habitations searching for little children, whose blood, when sprinkled on the sea, appeases it and facilitates fishing." But substitution is commoner: "they usually begin their fishing operations by the sacrifice of a cock or other animal instead of the human blood which they offered during their state of paganism in former times."[21] Two sacrifices common in India in the Middle Ages were the suttee[22] (sacrifice of a widow on her husband's pyre) and "the act of self-immolation by a votary before the image of a deity, with the object of compelling the deity to satisfy the votary's demands." This latter form is really one of coercion. Again, "the excavation of a well or the search for a supposed hidden treasure required the offer of a human victim. The lower classes of the Hindus still believe that whenever a difficulty is experienced in the sinking of a well, or in the construction of a bridge, or in the discovery of a supposed hidden treasure, the work can be facilitated by the offer of a human victim to the guardian spirit of the place."[23] Here we trench upon the next following topic of foundation-sacrifice.

20 Roth, in JAI, XXII, 225; Gomme, Village Life, 132; Schmidt, Ceylon, 293; "Anthrop. Scraps," in JASB, II, 177.
21 Rehatsek, in JASB, II, 28.

22 §394, below.
23 Joshi, in JASB, III, 276, 277, 285, 289, 290, 295 (quoted).

Human sacrifice plays an important part in the religious life of many tribes in the Philippines. Victims are needed as funeral companions, and when some great man is ill slaves are immolated in the belief that the evil spirit which caused the illness will be drawn off in the souls of the sacrificed men.[24] Through all Polynesian mythology runs the idea that the gods eat souls—an idea that almost by necessity involves human sacrifice.[25]

In the New World the custom is well represented, though it is asserted that the mounds offer no evidence of its presence.[26] In 1643 the Mohawks burned a young Algonquin with torture as a sacrifice to the war-god and then ate her flesh. This was contrary to the custom at other times.[27] It was a sort of common meal of men and the god. There is an account of a yearly sacrifice of children, celebrated about ten miles from Jamestown. "Fifteene of the properest young boyes, betweene ten and fifteene yeares of age," were put through a certain ceremony and finally "cast on a heape, in a valley as dead." The natives said that they were not all dead and that those whose blood had not been sucked by the evil spirit became priests and conjurors. If this sacrifice were to be omitted the evil spirit "would let them haue no Deere, Turkies, Corne, nor fish: and yet besides he would make a great slaughter amongst them."[28] Child sacrifice has appeared among the foregoing cases; and sometimes the victim must be a girl.[29] "Aharihon, an Onondaga chieftain of the seventeenth century, sacrificed forty men to the shade of his brother to show the great esteem in which he held him."[30]

In the far Northwest, slaves were regularly sacrificed, being despatched by means of ceremonial implements, called slave-killers, on occasions of building a house, or on the death of an important person.[31] The Pawnees show some revulsion from the practice; when they took captives, only one was sacrificed, the rest being adopted into the tribe. It seems that the death of the one captive assured good crops and plenty of everything; but the Indian who killed him fasted and mourned for four days, "for he knew that he had taken the life of a human being."[32] Among the Natchez, "at the death of the female chief in 1721, her husband, not belonging to the family of the Sun, was strangled by her son, according to custom."[33] This case might come under the ghost-cult except that the dead woman was really a goddess.

In 1700 the temple of the Taensa was struck by a thunderbolt and burned, upon which five women threw their infants into the flames as a sacrifice to the offended deity. On one occasion the Iroquois drove arrows into the body of a new-born babe, ground up its bones, and swallowed a little of the resultant powder before starting out to war.[34] As late as the first quarter of the nineteenth century the traditional ceremony of the Skidi was performed, in which a girl, typical of the evening star, was sacrificed to the masculine morning star, thus exemplifying their belief that the universe was dual—male and female—and that on the conjunction of these two forces depended the perpetuation of all forms of life.[35] At a festival held in honor of one of their

24 Montero y Vidal, *Filipinas*, 57; Worcester, *Philippine Isl.*, 245, 267; Cole, in AA, XX, 217-219.

25 Ratzel, *Vkde.*, II, 126.

26 Thomas, *Burial Mounds*, in BAE, V, 108.

27 Friederici, in *Globus*, LXXV, 260.

28 Tooker, in AA, VI, 674-675.

29 Bancroft, *Nat. Races*, II, 305, 308.

30 Hewitt, "Family," in HAI, I, 451.

31 Niblack, in USNM, 1888, 275.

32 Grinnell, *Folk Tales*, 363.

33 Letourneau, *Marriage*, 281.

34 Swanton, "Sacrifice," in HAI, II, 404.

35 Fletcher, in HAI, II, 590.

gods, the tribes of the Pacific States sacrificed thieves and prisoners of war. "At midnight the victims were taken from the chapel, where they had been compelled to watch, and brought before the sacred fire. Here the hair was shaven from the top of their heads. . . . Towards daybreak the prisoners were taken up to the great temple to be sacrificed," which was done by cutting open the breast and tearing out the heart.[36]

An author[37] from whom we have quoted in the text goes into detail that reveals the connection of such sacrifices with cannibalism. "Among the Aztecs, on the day consecrated to the god of fire, captives were sacrificed by burning. The most delicate morsels were reserved for the priests. Part of the body was given back to the person furnishing the victim. Sahagun tells us that this meat was cooked with hominy. This dish was called *Tlacatlaotli*, and the master of the slave sacrificed was not allowed to eat it, for the slave was looked upon as one of the family.'" Though the Maya gods were less sanguinary, prisoners of war were sacrificed and when these failed, parents offered up their children; also human sacrifices accompanied funeral ceremonies. But, whereas "the office of sacrificer was considered the greatest dignity to which a Mexican could aspire; among the Mayas, on the contrary, it was looked upon as impure and degrading." In Nicaragua, human sacrifices were offered on the first day of each of their eighteen months; "if the victim was a child offered or sold by its parents, the body was buried, custom not permitting the assistants to eat the flesh of one of their own people." These sacrifices lasted until the Spanish conquest and were attended by all sorts of revolting practices.

Some of the sacrifices of the Toltecs and Aztecs were to get rain, or in general to favor the new-sown crops; human sacrifice to that end has been very widespread, as the collections of Frazer[38] show. He cites the so-called "meeting of the stones," a ceremony attending the Mexican harvest-festival when the first-fruits were offered to the sun. "A criminal was placed between two immense stones, balanced opposite each other, and was crushed by them as they fell together." Preuss[39] thinks that "in the sacrificed human beings really daimons were killed, in order thus to renew them and to give them capacity for greater services to men." Men were sacrificed in the dress of the gods to whom they were offered; there was death and re-birth to avoid real death.

In South America the Chibchas, on rare occasions, offered human sacrifices to the sun. Under the Incas, as well as before their time, they were common, the Quito tribes sacrificing all the first-born. At the accession of the Inca, a thousand children are said to have been killed, and there was regular child-sacrifice at other times. When the Inca was sick, one of his sons was offered in his behalf.[40] In Brazil, at the sacrifice of a prisoner, "in order that nothing should be lacking to him during the time when he was awaiting death, rather, on the contrary, with the purpose of distracting him, they even gave him for a concubine the girl whom he chanced to choose, who, when the victim died,

36 Bancroft, *Nat. Races*, II, 306, 309, 329; III, 387, 392; Wilken, *Haaropfer*, in VG, III, 481-482.

37 Nadaillac, *Preh. Amer.*, 297, note, 295, 277, 266, 268.

38 *Golden Bough*, I, 381; Lippert, *Kgchte.*, II, 307.

39 In *Globus*, LXXXVI, 110, 118, 119, 321; Preuss, in *Archiv. f. Anthrop.*, XXIX, 140.

40 Nadaillac, *Preh. Amer.*, 461, 437, note; Lippert, *Kgchte.*, II, 307.

had, by way of ceremony, to shed a few tears. But, to her honor, she must immediately thereafter swallow (horror!) the first morsel of him."[41]

In Chaldœa of the most ancient periods there were human sacrifices; but later they became rare and animals were used instead. Juristic and exorcistic formulas mention the sacrifice of children and slaves.[42] "Among all Semitic peoples in the Near East, not excepting the Arabs . . . once prevailed the barbarous usage of sacrificing human beings, chiefly children, at particular times or on special occasions, to the highest gods. . . . The Aryans did not hold themselves free from it. But this custom appears among them only in the time of their barbarism or in out-of-the-way regions, where people held more obstinately to the old. . . . It is harder to understand why people who had reached such heights of a very refined culture, as the Ardmæans and the Phœnicians, had not long before abolished the bloody rite. . . . No colony was sent out, no campaign begun, without moving the gods by human sacrifice not to withhold their support. If they came home in triumph from the battle-field, they slaughtered the prisoners as a thank-offering to them. And every year they sought reconciliation for the sins of the people by burning a number of children, chiefly from the most noted families, on the altars of the king of heaven, while a hellish music drowned the shrieks of the victims and the lamentation of the mothers. This was true not only of the Phœnician religion of the metropolis but also of that of the colonies. So tenaciously did the Carthaginians cling to the barbaric institution that the Romans never succeeded, even when they had become complete masters of their old competitors, in getting rid of it. . . . Of the Ammonites and Moabites the same is known; and the Old Testament relates how Mesha, the king of Moab, when he was besieged by the kings of Judah and Israel, offered his own first-born son to Chemosh, in order to soften that god." The Egyptians "set the example of abolishing these sacrifices, but they were sturdily maintained none the less." The god Ra is reported to have replaced the sacrifice of men by that of beasts.[43]

The Phœnicians and their colonists have been infamous in history because of their persistent sacrifice of human beings and especially of children.[44] But sometimes the immolation bears a more heroic tinge. "Comparable to that Marcus Curtius, of whom the Roman legend related that he once . . . hero-ically cast himself into a chasm which had opened in the forum, is, it is said, the Punic field-marshal Hamilcar, son of Hormo. When, in the battle of Himera, 480 B.C., the defeat of the Carthaginian army seemed inevitable, he, to purchase the victory for his fatherland, himself leaped into the blazing flames of the sacrificial fire and found his death there." Again, after a Carthaginian victory the stateliest prisoners were cast into the flames of a mighty sacrificial fire—"a scene that recalls in lively manner the description . . . of the *noche triste,* that 'sad night' in which the Aztecs, in honor of their gods who were not less endued with a dark, insatiable thirst for blood, slaughtered the companions of Cortez who had fallen into captivity. . . . The duty of providing the sacrifice rested upon the most noble families of Carthage, as the representatives of the community. They undertook it according to a fixed order. Out of a number of children devoted to it the victim was chosen by lot. Secretly, therefore, and often, in these families, their own children were

41 Varnhagen, *Brazil,* I, 125.
42 Maspero, *Hist. Anc.,* I, 680; Schrader, *Keilinschriften,* 599.
43 Tiele-Gehrich, *Gchte. d. Relig.,* I, 240-

242; Tiele, *Sci. of Relig.,* pt. I, 176; Maspero, *Hist. Anc.,* I, 123.
44 Lippert, *Kachte.,* I, 441; Frazer, *Golden Bough,* I, 235 ff.

traded for those of other families, and the latter were adopted. At Carthage the victim is alleged to have been laid on the arms of a brazen figure of the god, hollow within, and thence rolled down through an opening into the interior, where a fire glowed. The parents, it is said, might not lament over the loss of the child; otherwise the sacrifice would have lost its virtue."[45]

In Homer, actual human sacrifice is represented by the one case where Achilles slew twelve Trojan youths at the pyre of Patroclus; this is really the provision of a grave-escort and Homer[46] calls it an "evil deed." The motif of human sacrifice originating in legend is carried over into Greek tragedy: Macaria sacrifices herself, on behalf of her brothers, to save the city of Athens; Alcestis buys off her husband by substituting for him; Iphigenia is sacrificed by her father; Polyxena is offered to the manes of Achilles.[47] In a number of legendary cases, however, the victim is not slain, but caught away; as the ram was the substitute for Isaac, so was the hind for Iphigenia; and Heracles wrests the victim of Death, Alcestis, from his very clutches.

In Rome human sacrifice "belonged to the essence of the old religion"; children were exposed and the old killed. "Of actual human sacrifices also there was no lack, on occasion, even at the time of the Republic. . . . According to Porphyry, human sacrifices were everywhere abolished under the Emperor Hadrian; but at the beginning of the fourth century the Romans still ordered, according to Lactantius, a bloody cult to the Jupiter of Latium by immolating to him a man every year."[48] "The gradual growth of the custom of selecting a criminal or a maimed person for sacrifice must be regarded as a modification of the original custom." The gladiatorial shows may well have grown out of human sacrifice, if, as in Mexico, the condemned captive was given a chance for his life.[49] It is typical of the mores of the age that Jews and Christians, on account of their secret rites, were charged with child-sacrifice.[50] Human sacrifice was consistent with the warlike mores of the ancient Scandinavians; ordinarily it was a penalty for misdeeds, but often the best and dearest was demanded.[51]

Foundation Sacrifice. In Melanesia, "in former days when a chief's dwelling-house or canoe-house was finished a man's head was taken for it as for a new canoe; a boy or woman was sometimes bought to be killed. It is a matter of tradition that men were crushed under the base of the great pillar of such a house, when it was set in its place."[52] In many of the tribes in the Gulf of Papua communal houses must not be occupied and canoes must not be launched until human blood has been sprinkled on them.[53]

"Several tribes of the Upper Congo . . . celebrate the occasion of a settlement of a political dispute between rival chieftains by the sacrifice of a slave as an indication of their seriousness. Upon such occasions the victim's arms and legs are first broken with sticks, after which torture he is buried to his neck at the junction of two paths, where he is allowed to die a lingering death."[54] Again, a form of oath among conspirators required the burning

45 Pietschmann, *Phönizier*, 108-109, 229-230; Freytag, in *Am. Ur-Quell*, I, 179.
46 *Iliad*, XXIII, 175-176.
47 Æschylus, *Agamemnon;* Euripides, *Heracleidæ, Alcestis, Iphigenia in Aulis, Iphigenia among the Taurians, Hecabe.*
48 Grupp, *Kgchte.*, I, 19, 20; Schmidt, *Soc.*

Civ., 135 (where full references to sources are given); Wissowa, *Relig. der Römer*, 31, 54.
49 Bancroft, *Nat. Races*, II, 305.
50 Lippert, *Kgchte.*, II, 310.
51 Geijer, *Svensk. Hist.*, I, 123.
52 Codrington, *Melanesians*, 301.
53 Chinnery, in JAI, XLIX, 38-39.
54 Ward, in JAI, XXIV, 290.

alive of a human being. In 1892, in such a case, a substitute was employed: the head was cut from a turtle and its blood, mixed with gin, was drunk by participants in a sworn enterprise.[55]

In India, among the Khonds, the "method of sacrificing a human victim is to put him into the cleft of a tree . . . or into a fire. . . . Victims offered either to the sun or to the war-god serve to mark boundary lines." The victims are captured young and treated with kindness. "At the appointed time they are slowly crushed to death or smothered in a mud bath, and bits of their flesh are then cut out and strewn along the boundary lines."[56] A southern tribe, in former times, "before setting out on a journey, used to procure a little child, and bury it in the ground up to its shoulders, and then drive their loaded bullocks over the unfortunate victim. In proportion to the bullocks thoroughly trampling the child to death, so their belief in a successful journey increased."[57] "On August 1, 1880, the Indian correspondent of the London Times wrote that the people had got the idea that the government was about to sacrifice a number of human beings to ensure the safety of the new harbor works. It is stated that seven or eight years earlier, when the bridge over the Ganges was built, the natives got an idea that Mother Ganges, indignant at being bridged, had at last consented to submit to the insult, on the condition that each pier of the structure should be founded on a layer of children's heads."[58] "But a few years ago, when the great railway bridge over the Ganges was begun, every mother in Benares trembled for her children."[59] These cases recall to mind the story of Kipling[60] called "The Bridge-Builders."

"There are found colossal burial-jars in Cochin and Travancore" which, the natives declare, contain the remains of sacrificed virgins. "All the petty Rajahs are said to have sacrificed virgins on the boundaries of their estates, to protect them from incursions and to ratify their engagements with neighboring chiefs." Again, "a young woman about to become a mother for the first time, was at certain times, chosen and brought before the shrine. She was beheaded with one blow, her head rolling before the image, on which her blood was then sprinkled. This was done until 1744. In the next year, a possession of the goddess came upon a bystander when the sacrifice was about to occur, directing that it should be discontinued. The descendants of the woman and child spared thus . . . live together in a small community of forty or fifty persons. They receive offerings made to the shrine and are exempt from government taxes. A public sacrifice of a sheep is now annually offered in place of and in the same way as the girls of old." When Mandalay was founded in 1858, "fifty-two persons of both sexes and various ages, mostly girls, were buried alive to feed and propitiate the demons; three being buried under each of the twelve gates, one under each gate-post, bearing the name of the entrance, and one at each of the four corners of the city."[61]

Among the Sema Nagas, "in the case of the renewal of the house of a chief there are particular rites to be observed. When the hole for the erection of the carved centre front post is dug, a chicken is killed in the hole and the post is erected on its body. If the hearth is moved from its old site even a little, a chicken must be killed and cooked on the new hearth and eaten by the owner and his family. In the evening of the first day of building, on which the centre

55 Frobenius, *Masken*, 76.
56 Hopkins, *Relig. Ind.*, 528, 529.
57 Thurston, *S. India*, 507.
58 Gomme, *Village Life*, p. 29.

59 Schrader, *Aryan*, 422.
60 In *The Day's Work*.
61 Walhouse, in **JAI**, XI, 416, 419.

front post has been stepped, any two old men . . . pick out the best red cock obtainable and kill it by knocking its head on the post."[62] This case appears to be survivalistic of a time when a human sacrifice was used. Among the Palaungs the wise man must be consulted as to the most fortunate day on which to make the hole for the chief post and to raise it into position. "This hole is dug deeper than the others, and rich men throw gold and silver, and sometimes gems, into it. A poor man throws in copper—a coin or two will do— and even lead. These offerings are for the spirits of the earth and the underworld. Sometimes a lump of iron is placed under each of the principal posts, and water in which raw rice has been washed is poured into the holes."[63] Wilken,[64] citing a number of examples of the use of horseshoes, concludes that it has some connection with foundation-sacrifice and that horse-sacrifice is a sign of it.

Among the Tlinkit it was customary to kill slaves and to bury their bodies beneath the corner-posts of the chiefs' houses at the time when they were erected. Other events which demanded the sacrifice of slaves were: the death of the owner or of any member of his household, an unusual feast, some occurrence to give shame to him, or the mere gratification of his vanity. The sacrifice at the erection of a house was made "to insure a good foundation."[65]

The Druids are said to have advised the British king, who was building a strong tower for his own safety, to seek out a youth whose father was unknown and let his blood bespatter the castle court, for thereby could it be built. When, in another legend, the walls fell down as fast as they were erected, the builder received supernatural information that they would not stand unless a human victim was buried alive. Again, in a district of Normandy, a newly built house must be purified by the slaughter of a cock, the blood of which is shed on its threshold, or the tenant would die in a year. In 1876, under an old church in Warwickshire, two skeletons were discovered, one under the north, the other under the south wall, about a foot below the original foundations, which appear to have been anterior to the church. Each skeleton was covered with an oak slab, which had been used as a bench. The skulls were said to be Danish. There is a Yorkshire superstition that the first child baptized in a new font is sure to die. A new church was built at Dalton. A blacksmith in the parish, after having seven daughters, had a son born. He asked the rector to baptize him in the old church. The rector asked him why he would not wait a few days and have him baptized in the new church. He said if it had been another girl he would not have minded, but as it was a lad he would be sorry that he should die. There is a Rumanian tale of a prince who tried to build a monastery but the walls fell down every night, as much as had been built in the day. At last the chief mason was warned in a dream that the work would be in vain unless he walled up, living, in the edifice the first woman who should come in the morning to bring them food. The first one who came was his own wife. Despite all sorts of miraculous portents which crossed her path, she came on, and was walled into the building. But when the house was done and the masons awaited the praise and reward of the prince, the latter caused a scaffolding to be broken down, and as the masons fell the husband heard the

62 Hutton, *Sema Nagas*, 44-45.
63 Milne, *Eastern Clan*, 178.
64 "Schedelvereering," in VG, IV, 78 ff.; Andree, *Eth. Parallelen*, 127 ff.

65 Jones, *Thlingets*, 117-118; Henshaw; Swanton, in HAI, II, 598, and I, 205, respectively.

cry of his wife through the wall.[66] A recent story illustrates similar ideas among the Bulgarians.[67]

Head-Hunting. From an old history of Dahomi is quoted a speech by a chief with reference to his collection of heads: "That makes me fearsome to my enemies and gives me this name in the bush. Besides, if I neglected this unescapable service, would my ancestors then permit me to live? Would they not plague me night and day and say that I sent nobody to look after them? That I was concerned only for my own name and forgot the ancestors? The white men are not acquainted with these circumstances; but I speak that you may at least hear and tell it again to your fellow-countrymen, that the festivals are fixed and shall remain in existence as long as the negroes shall hold their own land."[68]

"All the Nágá tribes of the Nágá Hills district are head-takers"; in other tribes no youth becomes a man and often may not marry until he has a head; he may not be tattooed until he has actively assisted in getting a head, hands, or feet of some enemy.[69]

Head-hunting finds its classic ground among the Malays. According to Wilken[70] its motive is three-fold: to serve the dead; to get glory; and to prepare for marriage.[71] All skulls are not of equal value: among the Dyaks, a man's is worth more than a woman's, a Malay's than a Dyak's, a Chinaman's than a Malay's, and a European's exceeds them all.[72] Head-hunting is the chief cause of war, and constant warfare prevents their advance; the boys of some districts practise decapitating straw men. The Dyaks, in so far as they are still head-hunters, do not name a new-born child until a head has been taken.[73] Heads must be secured for every great event in Dyak life: to win love, at the death of a rajah, at births. The son of a rajah may not don the war-garment until he has taken a head. Nothing can be done without heads: "all kinds of sickness, particularly the small-pox, are supposed to be under the influence of an evil spirit which nothing can so well propitiate as a head."[74] "To make their rice grow well, to cause the forest to abound with wild animals, to enable their dogs and snares to be successful in securing game, to have the streams swarm with fish, to give health and activity to the people themselves, and to ensure fertility to their women"—all these blessings "the possessing and feasting of a fresh head are supposed to be the most efficient means of securing. The very ground itself is believed to be benefited and rendered fertile."[75] "A nearer acquaintance with these usages will teach us that they are not based upon a natural thirst for blood, but upon superstition and deep-rooted prepossession."[76]

§295. Redemption and Covenant.

It is the custom in San Cristoval, Solomon Islands, to bury alive the first-born child.[1] In Rhodesia, in 1923, the chief and five members of a local tribe were

66 Gomme, *Village Life*, 32-33, 26, 35, 36, 53.
67 Tsanoff, in *Atl. Mo.*, CXIX, 85 ff.
68 Hostmann, *Beschaving*, II, 170-171.
69 Godden, in JAI, XXVII, 12, 15; Peal, in JAI, XXII, 247.
70 *Vkde.*, 393.
71 §365, below.

72 Perelaer, *Dajaks*, 168.
73 Ratzel, *Vkde.*, II, 406, 438, 447, 448.
74 Bock, *Borneo*, 91, 92, 93, 96, 97, 187; Roth, *Sarawak*, II, 142, note.
75 Roth, *Sarawak*, II, 143.
76 Veth, *Borneo's Wester-Afdeeling*, II, 253, 275; Perelaer, *Dajaks*, 165-166.
1 Fox, in JAI, XLIX, 100.

sentenced to death for burning alive the former's son in order to appease the rain-goddess and thus terminate a severe drought. Counsel for the defense commented on the high motives which led the chief to sacrifice his own son for rain so as to save his people from drought, and referred to parallel cases in Biblical history. It is noteworthy that the natives are firmly convinced of the efficacy of human sacrifice, for rain fell soon after the young man was killed.[2]

Where a person volunteers to serve as sacrifice, we have what might be called religious suicide. Such is the case among some primitive tribes in China where a voluntary human sacrifice is offered, in some cases annually, so as to preserve the group from disease, hunger, and distress. In one instance an ingenious device is used: a crescent-shaped instrument is placed with the sharp inner curve against the neck of the suicide-candidate, while he places his feet in chains which hang down from both ends of the instrument and are tied underneath into a kind of stirrup; with a violent jerk he cuts his head off almost as effectively as a guillotine could do it.[3]

On the fifth day after birth the Chukchi perform the ceremony of blood-painting, before which no person from outside may enter the house. "Even the father of the child has to subject himself to certain incantations before he can enter. This prohibition is repeated when the child is ill, or in the case of an infectious disease. . . . The blood-painting ceremony begins with the conveyance of the mother and child and the reindeer on the family sledge to the sacrificial place behind the tent. The reindeer is slaughtered, and with its blood the faces of the mother, child, and other members of the family are smeared."[4] Every clan of the Kuki-Lushai places offerings of food and drink over the grave, and kills some animal in honor of the deceased and as a ransom for his soul. Offerings of the first-fruits are made to their forefathers by almost every clan.[5] The following Hindu legend recalls the story of Abraham. A Brahman came to an old king and said he desired something to eat. "What shall I do?" said the king; "command me." The Brahman replied, "You must kill your son." This the king did, and when he told the most venerable one that the food was ready, the latter said, "Eat of it yourself." "Gladly," said the king, who as before was not disconcerted; but when he made ready to eat the Brahman seized his hand and said: "You have conquered anger. There is nothing you would not sacrifice for a Brahman." Whereupon he disappeared, and the king saw his son standing before him like a young god.[6] In India a short time ago a girl was sacrificed by her family who believed this was necessary to the recovery of her sick brother. As no improvement in the boy's condition was forthcoming, they deprived him of food and bound him, naked, near a holy place, where he died of exposure.[7]

The East Indians practise head-snatching on the occasions of marriage and birth; it is a sort of sacrifice of redemption, as well as an exhibition of courage. The evil spirits want a life; to offer such brings luck.[8] A Samoan once promised to give any offering the god required, if he would only preserve mother and child in safety. His prayer was thus expressed: "O Moso, be propitious; let this my daughter be preserved alive! Be compassionate to us; save my daughter, and we will do anything you wish as our redemption price." The

2 N. Y. *Times*, June 6, 1923.
3 Lasch, "Religiöser Selbstmord," in *Globus*, LXXV, 70, 72.
4 Czaplicka, *Aborig. Siberia*, 134.

5 Shakespear, in JAI, XXXIX, 382.
6 Sauer, in *Das Freie Wort*, II, 312.
7 N. Y. *Times*, Mar. 26, 1925.
8 Wilken, in VG, I, 574-576.

household god of the family of the father was generally prayed to first; but if the case was tedious or difficult, the god of the family of the mother was then invoked.[9] Here, it would seem, recourse was had to the older, matrilineal divinity as a last resort. The Maori used to offer human sacrifice at the baptism of the first-born child, the priests selecting the victim who was always a man. A survivalistic practice, known as "a forbidding of man slaying," is to place the child's head on a weapon.[10]

In Mexico, captive and slave were vicarious sacrifices for the citizens; the gods must have somebody. In terror of them, man's first thought was to offer his own children, especially the first-born, as a vicarious sacrifice for himself; that discharged the claim of the gods on the father. This was the most suitable sacrifice until one got slaves or captives. The state waged war for this purpose, while rich men bought substitutes. Later, with advance in the arts and more settled life, human sacrifice was raised to a great state-institution.[11]

Not only on pressing occasions, such as plague, drought, and misfortune in war, did the Phœnicians decide on human sacrifice and then, in order to enhance the value of the offering, spare not even the lives of their own children, but at annual festivals also they appear, at least in some places, to have followed the same practice. With the notion that no other kind of sacrifice would gladden and appease the gods more than this, there was joined the idea of redemption. Also, in expiation for wrong committed, one who was conscious of guilt sacrificed to the god, to whom he believed he had forfeited life and body, an animal as substitute for himself. In the same sense it was held requisite to promise or offer up similar sacrifices as soon as one found himself in any exigency. Even in the thank-offering there was something of the notion of substitution. But the higher gods were not always satisfied with animals and ordinary gifts; in their eyes such were only a paltry compensation for human sacrifice, in which a human soul as well as body fell prey to the gods. When from sure signs it seemed beyond doubt that a god had marked out a city as his victim and had determined to annihilate the inhabitants and destroy the land, then there was no delay in offering human victims so as to discharge the rage and curse upon the heads of some few and thus divert them from the whole. Similar vicarious sacrifices occurred when the first-born of the chief families were offered up for the community and when the first-born or, better yet, the only son of the king was sacrificed.[12] That this fancy as to the efficacy of child-sacrifice had not died out in Judah, is proved by the offering of his own sons by Ahaz during the stress of the Syro-Ephraimitic war.[13] We are told that the death of Christ was a sacrifice for all; it paid the cult obligation. All may share in this redemption by faith in him and by accepting his work and the life of the covenant. The old cult-works to assure future life were thus done away with; Paul repudiated them as a burden.[14]

From Madrid comes a story of a mother's sacrifice. When her only son was sent to Morocco to fight the Moors, she besought the Virgin del Carmel to protect him from all harm and made a vow to offer her own life on condition his was spared. When he returned, she prayed all night before the statue of the Virgin and then drowned herself in the river.[15] A recent newspaper report

9 Turner, *Samoa*, 78-79.
10 Best, in JAI, XLIV, 140-141, 151-152.
11 Lippert, *Kgchte.*, II, 295, 298.
12 Pietschmann, *Phönizier*, 167, 168.

13 II Chron., XXVIII, 3; Kautzsch, in *Hastings's Dict. Bible*, 699.
14 Lippert, *Kgchte.*, II, 616.
15 N. Y. *Times*, Dec. 25, 1924.

from the same place relates how a workman offered his daughter as a human sacrifice, "as a test of his faith, acting under divine command." He believed that he was required, as a final test, to make this sacrifice after the fashion of Abraham.[16] In Maine, some years ago, the police were just in time to prevent a child sacrifice "demanded by the Lord" at the hands of a frenzied religious sect.[17]

The communion and similar ceremonies throw further light on the notion of redemption. The Orāons and the Mūndās of India seek alliance with the good spirits or deities by periodical ceremonies, "of which the most salient feature is the worshippers eating together the liver of the animal or fowl sacrificed to the deity, and drinking together rice-beer, after a portion of both the liver and the rice-beer has been offered to the deity. The liver is considered by the Chōtā-Nāgpūr aboriginal to be the seat of the vital principle. . . . The blood, for which the rice-beer is apparently a substitute—for on certain important occasions such as a purificatory ceremony sacrificial blood is actually drunk— is identified by the Orāon and the Mūndā with the soul or spirit, as is indicated by their belief that an evil spirit sometimes attacks a person by appearing as a blood-spot on his clothes. And this sacramental eating and drinking with their deities may not improbably be a modification of an older practice of offering up a member of the tribe, and ceremonially eating with the gods the human meat and drinking the human blood by way of sealing a compact of alliance and friendship. . . . Whether this ceremonial eating of the sacrificial meat be a case of eating with the god, or, as is not unlikely, of 'eating the god,' the sacrifice being considered as partaking of something of the nature of the deity, and the consumption of the meat calculated to impart to the eaters something of the strength and other virtues of the god, such ceremonial compact or alliance with the deities through a sacramental meal is renewed at stated intervals by similar sacrifice and sacrificial meals. Delay in renewing the alliance may turn these supernatural allies into temporary enemies, and, in such a case, more than the ordinary sacrifices is required to convince them of your sincerity, and thereby placate their wrath and restore the old terms of friendship and alliance."[18]

The striking similarity between the Mexican ceremonies and the eucharistic service is thus described by Bancroft,[19] who quotes from the *Vatican Codex:* "The Mexicans celebrated in this month (December) the festival of their first captain Vichilopuchitl. They celebrated at this time the festival of the wafer or cake. They made a cake of the meal of bledos, which they called tzolli, and having made it they spoke over it in their manner and broke it in pieces. These the high priest put into certain very clean vessels, and with a thorn of maguey, which resembles a thick needle, he took up with the utmost reverence single morsels, and put them into the mouth of each individual, in the manner of the communion—and I am willing to believe that these poor people have had the knowledge of our mode of communion or of the preaching of the Gospel; or perhaps the devil, most envious of the honor of God, may have led them into this superstition in order that by this ceremony he might be adored and served as Christ our Lord." This is an author who never heard of parallelism.

Again, in Tibet have been found rites and other features which bear a close resemblance outwardly to those of the Church of Rome, viz., pompous services

16 N. Y. *Times*, Aug. 5, 1926.
17 N. Y. *Times*, Mar. 10, 1904.
18 Roy, in JAI, XLIV, 325-326.
19 *Nat. Races*, III, 323.

with celibate and tonsured monks and nuns, candles, bells, censers, rosaries, mitres, copes, pastoral crooks, worship of relics, confession, intercession of "the Mother of God," litanies and chants, holy water, triad divinity, and organized hierarchy. The Lamaist liturgy, on account of its dispensation of consecrated wine and bread, has been compared by many to the Christian eucharist, although in reality it is a ceremony for gratifying the rather un-Buddhistic craving after long earthly life.[20] Lamaists, such as the Buryat, will often enter a Russian church to sacrifice wax candles to St. Nicholas, in whom they recognize one of the higher lamas.[21]

The ancients showed special reverence to the queen of heaven: "Men, women, and children shared in this: the children gathered wood, the men kindled the fire, and the women, who played the chief rôle in this cult, kneaded the dough into cakes which must represent an image or symbol of the goddess. The meaning of this custom, which is found not only among the Semites but also generally among the Aryans—particularly with the ancient Germans—while traces of it still remain in our Christmas cakes, is that through the eating of the image one partakes of the deity."[22]

The festivities held in the month of the Egyptian god Thoth, in honor of Osiris and the dead, partook of the nature of mysteries. On one such occasion Herodotus[23] mingled with the crowd and was present at "the scenes of divine life which the priests represented on the lake in the light of their torches, episodes of the passion, mourning, and resurrection." Such terms as redemption, baptism, grace, faith, salvation, regeneration, were not invented by Christianity, but were household words of Talmudical Judaism.[24] The notion of animal sacrifices as a gift of food to the gods superseded the original notion of communion between men and their gods in the life of the sacrifice.[25] The cult was the center of the communal life of the Essenes, a Jewish sect remarkable for their strictness and abstinence. This was an entirely new kind of cult: in place of the sacrificial cult appeared the cult of the sacrament, with daily ablutions having the greatest sacramental significance. The bath brought forth a fundamental change in man; it made him an Essene. Only after a year was the novice granted the right to share in this purification-ceremony, which thereafter was consummated daily before the common meal. "If a member of the order touches another of a lower class, he must bathe. The water has a wonderful power, it obliterates all impurity, both external and internal. Associated with the bath is the holy common meal. Here is revived an ancient religious feeling from the time of Semitic tribal life. The conception of the sacrificial repast as the means of restoring a mystical spirit-body community of the members of the tribe with one another and with the deity, was to some extent come to life again. The common dining-room of the Essenes is in the temple into which one walks with timid awe, after having laid off his working-clothes and put on festive attire. Those who prepare the food and drink are the priests of the order. At the beginning and end of the meal the priest utters a prayer. The meal is eaten in solemn silence and reverential seriousness, so

20 Waddell, *Tibet*, 421-422, 444; Rockhill, in USNM, 1893, 741, note; Müller, *Essays*, IX, note 3.

21 Schimkjewitschs Reisen, in *Globus*, LXXIV, 253.

22 Tiele-Gehrich, *Gchte. Relig.*, I, 357.

23 *Hist.*, II, lxii, clxxi; Maspero, *Hist. Anc.*, III, 790-791.

24 Cook, *Fathers of Jesus*, II, 122.

25 Smith, *Relig. Sem.*, 385.

that the stillness within the house appears to those who go by outside as the celebration of an awe-inspiring mystery."[26]

The ancient mysteries had influence on Christianity. Up to a certain time we have no evidence that Christianity anywhere bore the character of secrecy; then a great change set in: what was once an open and easily accessible belief became a mystery and there were precepts which one did not mention before the ears of the unconsecrated. But the influence of the mysteries and of the religious cults analogous to them was not merely generally effective: the mysteries transformed in several important respects the Christian sacraments of baptism and the evening meal, that is, the custom of granting admission to the fellowship through a symbolic purification and of giving expression to the membership by eating together.[27]

There are various theories concerning the origin of communion as practised by the Christian churches. For some authors the ceremony is a survival from the cannibalism of remote ages, from anthropotheophagy.[28] If we heard that the Chinese or Mohammedans had a religious custom in which they used currently the figure of eating flesh and drinking the blood of a man or god, and if we had no such figure of speech in our own use, we should consider it very shocking.

§296. Sacrificial Prostitution.

INDIA shows a highly developed phase of sacral harlotry. "All the temples . . . maintain troops of dancing girls. . . . Furthermore, it is well-known that in ancient times women were dedicated to the service of the temples, like the Vestal virgins of Europe. They were held to be married to the god, and had no other duty but to dance before his shrine." They were once generally patterns of piety and propriety but are not so now. "No doubt they drive a profitable trade under the sanction of religion, and some courtesans have been known to amass enormous fortunes. Nor do they think it inconsistent with their method of making money to spend it in works of piety. Here and there Indian bridges and other useful public works owe their existence to the liberality of the frail sisterhood."[1] Prostitutes in the temples were at the will of any one who would pay; they were once exclusively for the Brahmans. No dishonor inhered in this devotion; in fact, wives entered, with the consent of husbands, in order to get a good confinement and barren women were promised fertility if they would yield to any comer. "It is generally admitted that the dedication of females to idols is a survival of human sacrifice." In antiquity females were obliged to purchase exemption from being sacrificed by prostitution, and the so-called Basivis in India, as well as other types in that country, represent later parallelisms.[2] Such prostitutes were originally for the priests and commerce with them was believed to cleanse sin.[3] A Portuguese traveller in Indo-China reported that he saw in a temple five thousand priestess-prostitutes: "all the women, virgin daughters of chiefs and lords

---

26 Bousset, *Relig. des Judentums*, 91, 182, 435-437 (quoted) ; Kohler, in *Jewish Encyc.*, V, 226 ff.

27 Hatch, *Griechentum*, 217-218 ; Heinrici, in *Ztsft. f. Wissnsft. Theol.*. XIX, 497.

28 Lejeune, "Communion," in *Bull. Soc.*

d'Anthr. de Paris, V, 404-411, rev. by Chamberlain, in AA, VII, 330.

1 Monier-Williams, *Brâhmanism*, 451 ; Wilkins, *Hinduism*, 242, 290 ; Dubois, *Mœurs*, II, 353, 370, 377.

2 Fawcett, in JASB, II, 345.

3 Dubois, *Mœurs*, I, 434.

of the kingdom and of all the other nobility, go there, in consequence of a vow they are made to take when little, to sacrifice their honor; for without this no eminent man wants to marry them."[4]

There is a special class of prostitutes among certain peoples of the Indian Archipelago. They get considerable honor among the Javanese, Sundanese, Macassars, and Buginese. This is partly due to the fact that they are priestesses of Terpsichore as well as of Aphrodite, have an art of their own, which is their chief interest, prostitution being a sort of avocation. In the looseness of these women we have a survival of sacrificial prostitution. Shamanesses are often singers and dancers by profession, there being no longer any exhibitions of ecstasy or other shamanistic characters; they are entertainers. They exercise a considerable influence over men by spurring them on to war and to trade-journeys which often have important results. They have a special art in influencing men. They are so respected that an injury done them is doubly punished. It is clear that the profession is regarded as favored by the gods and dedicated to them. Parents often make a vow to have one of their daughters become a dancer, so that even young girls not yet come to puberty are to be seen among them.[5]

Among the Phœnicians temple harlotry was common, being undertaken temporarily or for a lifetime, in consequence of a vow made voluntarily or by one's parents; the state of the girl was one of consecration to a god. "No more welcome gift could a woman bring to the deity than the payment she received for surrendering her body. In the service of female deities men gave themselves in the same way, as 'dogs,' so the expression signifies. To mark the denial of their sex they put on women's clothes."[6] In spite of the energetic protests of the prophets and the prohibitions of the law, such practices were widely prevalent in Israel. A number of passages indicate that it was nothing uncommon to bring the earnings of male and female hierodules as a votive offering into the temple of Jahweh.[7]

The case most commonly cited is doubtless that of the Aphrodite temple at Byblos, where the Adonis ceremonies were performed. These were funeral rites: dust was cast into the air and heads were shaved. Women who did not wish to be shaven might undergo prostitution for one day, with strangers only, the payment going as a sacrifice to Aphrodite. Elsewhere the giving of the hair was a substitute for prostitution—a species of exuvial sacrifice.[8] The worth of the sacrifice was enhanced by accepting a stranger, and no marriage might be contracted until it had been made.[9] Here was a species of redemption that has been interpreted as "expiation for marriage."[10] Women who did not get husbands lived in a sort of protected and hallowed prostitution in or near the temple, under the protection of an ancient goddess-mother.[11] "But seldom religious tradition refused to move forward with the progress of society; the goddess retained her old character as a mother who was not a wife bound to fidelity to her husband, and at her sanctuary she protected under the name of religion, the sexual license of savage society, or even demanded of the daughters of her worshippers a shameful sacrifice of their chastity, before

4 Oliveira Martins, *Raças*, II, 181.
5 Wilken, in VG, I, 602-603.
6 Pietschmann, *Phönizier*, 222-223.
7 Deut., XXIII, 17-18; I Kings, XIV, 24; XV, 12; XXII, 46; II Kings, XXIII, 7; Num., XXV, 1-15; Amos, II, 7; Hosea, IV,

13, 14; Kautzsch, in *Hastings's Dict. Bible*, 662.
8 Lucian, *De Syria Dea*, §6.
9 Pietschmann, *Phönizier*, 229.
10 §343, of the text and *Case-Book*.
11 Smith, *Relig. Sem.*, 59.

they were permitted to bind themselves for the rest of their lives to that conjugal fidelity which their goddess despised." The mores protected the practice; it was under convention.

"Prostitution is said to have entered into the religious rites of Babylon, Biblis, Cyprus, and Corinth, and these as well as Miletus, Tenedos, Lesbos, and Abydos became famous for their schools of vice, which grew up under the shadow of the temples."[12] The cases given by Herodotus[13] and Strabo,[14] as occurring in Babylonia, Egyptian Thebes, Lycia, Lydia, Armenia, and elsewhere, are mere variants of the above; often the dowry for marriage was thus collected, and there was no dishonor involved. Said Strabo: "The Armenians pay particular reverence to Anaïtis, and have built temples to her honour in several places, especially in Acilisene. They dedicate there to her service male and female slaves; in this there is nothing remarkable, but it is surprising that persons of the highest rank in the nation consecrate their virgin daughters to the goddess. It is customary for these women, after being prostituted a long period at the temple of Anaïtis, to be disposed of in marriage, no one disdaining a connexion with such persons. Herodotus mentions something similar respecting the Lydian women, all of whom prostituted themselves. But they treat their paramours with much kindness, they entertain them hospitably, and frequently make a return of more presents than they receive, being amply supplied with means derived from their wealthy connexions. They do not admit into their dwellings accidental strangers, but prefer those of a rank equal to their own." The cult of Ishtar, the Babylonian goddess of the reproductive forces of nature, was surrounded by a host of women who gave themselves to prostitution in her service. Male hierodules also were to be found.[15] "To live in Corinthian fashion" was a by-word for every kind of debauchery; "a journey to Corinth is not every man's business." The Aphrodite temple had a world-famous cult of unchastity, and its courtesans were reminded by vows that in case of success so and so many women would be dedicated. These temple-women had a festival of their own called Aphrodisia.[16] Even if the hierodules are not regarded as connected with sacral prostitution, the temples were yet in receipt of income from its practice.[17] "A genuine sacral prostitution in Scandinavia shortly before the introduction of Christianity" is reported.[18] The Corn-mother of the German field-cult bore the name of "Grosse Hure."[19]

§297. Survivals of Human Sacrifice.

CHIEF, perhaps, among the practices witnessing to the former prevalence of human sacrifice is the substitution, often with similar ceremonies, of an animal for a human victim.[1] When a sacrifice is required by the Papuans to consummate some rite, they use a bush pig; formerly they "caught a man just as they now catch a pig."[2] In olden times the Bawenda practised human sacrifice; today they offer only a black sheep, goat, or ox and all kinds of food, bits of

12 Lecky, *Europ. Morals*, II, 291.
13 *Hist.*, I, 93, 181-182, 199; Baruch, VI, 43; Maspero, *Hist. Anc.*, I, 577, 640.
14 *Geog.*, XI, ch. 14, §16; XIII, ch. 4, §7; Plautus, *Cistell.*, II, 3, 20.
15 Schrader, *Keilinschriften*, 422-423; Tiele-Gehrich, *Gchte. Relig.*, I, 160.

16 Dobschütz, *Christian Life*, 12; Athenæus, *Deipnosophists*, XIII, 32.
17 Otto, *Priester*, I, 316.
18 Hahn, in *Globus*, LXXV, 286.
19 Preuss, in *Globus*, LXXXVI, 360-361.
1 Wilken, in VG, III, 482.
2 Williams, in JAI, LIII, 385.

hide, and beer.[3] In Zululand "the women sometimes bury their children up to their neck in the ground, and then retire to some distance and keep up a dismal howl for a long time: the heavens are supposed to melt with tenderness at the sight. The women then dig the children out and feel sure that rain will follow."[4] Should a Bangala be successful in fishing or trading, without any particularly apparent cause, and shortly after this success should his wife fall ill and die, he may be accused of having passed over his wife to the spirits as an acknowledgment of his increased wealth. The ordeal is often taken to disprove such accusations, which amount, it would seem, to a charge of collusion.[5] When the medicine-man of the Baganda arrives to treat a sick man, the latter is carried out of the house into the open, where the former kills a cow or goat brought for the purpose, and catches all the blood in a vessel; "some of it he sprinkles on each doorpost, he also takes a stout stick three feet long, fastens a tuft of grass to each end, places it across the doorway, and sprinkles it with blood; the sick man is then anointed with blood on the forehead, on each shoulder, and on either leg. . . . Poor people who are unable to supply even a fowl for the blood are sprinkled with a mixture of water and ashes."[6]

Some of the Sema Nagas, on the day of burial, kill and cut up the dead man's dog, and distribute its flesh to all guests at the funeral who are not of the same clan as the deceased. On other occasions a dog or calf is killed, according to special rites; and "we shall perhaps not go far astray if we take the puppy-dog, with its spear and shield, and the bull-calf, whose liver is buried not eaten, and who is also vested by a spear and a cloth with sinister attributes of humanity, to be the unfortunate latter-day representatives of more terrible offerings of human life attending the erection of the monoliths at Dimapur."[7] On the occasion of the annual hunt of the Santals, the priest has to dip grains of rice into blood drawn out of his own body and offer such rice to the spirits believed to reside at different spots on the hill. "This rite . . . is probably a modified survival of the practice of offering human victims."[8] The Lushai believe that the only cure for a bewitched person is to eat the liver of the one who has bewitched him.[9] "The practice of sacrificing individual lives for the good of the community, which is so utterly opposed to Buddhist teaching, may be traced in Burma at the present day in all its stages, from the killing of a human victim to the mere offering of plantains at a shrine." In one place, a boy or girl is annually bought from a distant village and killed with much ceremony, the blood being sprinkled on the seed-paddy.[10] If a Palaung father and mother have lost many of their children, and another baby is born to them, "they may dedicate it to the monastery, in the hope of saving its life. By so doing, the evil spirits that have robbed them of so many children may not have the power to kill a baby thus dedicated. . . . When a baby is ill it is sometimes weighed, and, when its exact weight is known, the father takes uncooked rice, of the same weight as the child, and spreads it on a large flat board or tray. It is carried to the image-house and set before an image of Buddha. . . . The father and mother then shape the rice into a recumbent image to represent the child. They, and any friends who may have

---

3 Gottschling, in JAI, XXXV, 375.
4 Kidd, *Kaffir*, 117.
5 Weeks, in JAI, XL, 378.
6 Roscoe, in JAI, XXXII, 42-43.

7 Hutton, *Sema Nagas*, 246; Hutton, in JAI, LII, 69-70 (quoted).
8 Roy, in JAI, XLIV, 326, note.
9 Shakespear, in JAI, XXXIX, 384.
10 Brown, in JAI, XLV, 356.

accompanied them, pray for the health of the baby. They leave the candles and flowers beside the statue and return home. The rice, however, is not left, but is brought home, and on the same day is boiled or steamed. Four or five worthy old men, who have already been invited, are given this rice to eat, along with curry. They all pray for the health of the child, they eat the food, then they pray again and bless the baby. They are careful to eat every grain of the rice, none being thrown out to the birds. . . . The father then carries the little house containing the figure and the food—the mother assisting—to the highest point that can be reached in the monastery beside the image-house. There he rests his burden on a ledge overhanging the court-yard; he then turns round so that he cannot see the little house, but feeling for it with his hands behind his back he gives it a push and topples it over, saying: 'May this little house touch the planet of sickness, and may the sickness of our child disappear!' The planet to which offerings should be made when a child is ill depends on the age of the child. . . . Palaungs now believe that these effigies represent the child, but the custom may go back to pre-Buddhist times, when a living victim was perhaps offered."[11]

A common form of birth-ceremony among the Maori, and one which illustrates incidentally the division of labor by sex, consisted principally of "the dedication of a male child to the service of the god of war, and of a female child to the tutelary deity, or presiding genius, of the tasks of women."[12] In a story based upon the history of the League of the Iroquois they are represented as setting aside children at birth (Hidden Children) to be mated at maturity; this was an alternative, apparently, to their sacrifice. The Senecas debased this ceremony to one of bloody rites.[13] "The Hurons burned the viscera and a portion of the flesh of one who had been drowned or had died of a cold as a sacrifice to the Sky god, who was supposed to be angry."[14] The spirit of a dead Osage must be avenged; this was done by the sacrifice of the scalp of an enemy over the grave.[15]

Odin, dying of disease, caused himself to be transfixed with a spear. His worshippers later did the same in order to die, not of disease but like soldiers. This was called marking one's self for Odin. A death by violence pleased the gods. The aged sprang from a cliff, so as to attain Valhalla, or, if bed-ridden through age, were clubbed to death by relatives.[16] In Albania today, tradition prescribes that "when a child is born you should break an egg over its face to keep off the evil eye; and when a house is built you must kill a cock or a lamb and sprinkle the blood on the foundations. These two customs are still practised at Scutari, and the old fortress on the hill is one of the places, in the foundations of which a woman is said to have been built in the Middle Ages as an offering to the devils that destroyed it as fast as it was built." This is foundation-sacrifice.[17]

§298. Exuvial Sacrifice.

Mutilation. Cutting off the finger-joints, drawing one's own blood, boring the ears, and tattooing or marking the body are typical forms of exuvial sacrifice.

11 Milne, *Eastern Clan*, 32, 34-36.
12 Best, in JAI, XLIV, 128.
13 Chambers, *Hidden Children*.
14 Swanton, in HAI, II, 404.

15 Dorsey, in AA, IV, 404.
16 Geijer, *Svensk. Hist.*, I, 24; Stallybrass, *Grimm's Teutonic Myth.*, III, 1077.
17 §294; Durham, in JAI, XL, 464.

Wilken[1] demonstrates by copious examples the origin of self-mutilation as a form of redemption for human sacrifice, or at least as a survival of it. He cites a number of cases where human sacrifice is only simulated and others where the belief is held that the soul resides in the blood or hair, which is offered up in place of the victim.

A Mosaic law reads: "Ye shall not make any cuttings in your flesh for the dead, nor print any marks upon you."[2] This custom of flesh-wounding as a sign of mourning is very widespread, as Andree[3] has shown in his well-known work. It is especially common in the South Sea Islands. In Fiji, for example, at the death of a king or queen, every man or a member of a family, particularly children, cuts off a finger or toe joint, in some cases a whole finger, fastens it in a reed stalk and hangs it up in the house of the dead.[4] Some tribes in New Britain amputate a joint or two from the fingers of relatives when any of their friends are sick. A number of natives may be seen with one or more joints on several fingers gone; mere children are thus disfigured.[5] The San Cristoval Islanders believe that at the entrance to the spirit-world there stands a spirit who will admit only ghosts who have their ears and nose perforated and the proper marks under the right eye.[6] In New Hebrides the belief is that the shades of the dead are seized by a great spirit who cuts off their noses with a tomahawk if they lack certain tattoo-marks.[7]

The Bushmen cut off the joints of the finger of the left hand.[8] This practice is common among other South Africans who perform the operation especially on children, "so as to make them proof against evil influences of all kinds." There is said to be considerable difference in the way the amputation is done, so that the appearance of the stump serves as a family-mark.[9] The Bechuana bore the ears of their children when the latter are about twelve years old; and "sometimes if a woman has lost several children in infancy she will be afraid to wait so long, and will bore the baby's ears before taking it outside the house."[10] The Ba-Mbala perforate the ears, and wear no ornaments in them.[11] Again, "if a child dies who has not had the middle incisor in its lower jaw knocked out, this tooth is knocked out after death; this is considered very important, for if omitted someone is said to surely die in the village soon afterwards."[12] Wilken[12] thinks that the filing of teeth is a relic of breaking them out, though the religious significance has become lost.

In the southern provinces of India mothers will cut off their own fingers as sacrifices lest they lose their children.[14] In all Bengal there is said to be scarcely a respectable house, the mistress of which has not at one time or other shed her blood, under the notion of satisfying the goddess by the operation. At each sickness "a vow is made that on the recovery of the patient, the goddess would be regaled with human blood."[15] A number of sects bear on the forehead the cult-mark, modified as to color and line for the numerous subdivisions. Sometimes the "mark of Vishnu" represents one foot of the god, in other cases both feet. All followers of Vishnu have the vertical sign, those

1 "Haaropfer," in VG, III, 486 ff.
2 Levit., XIX, 28.
3 Eth. Parallelen, 147 ff.
4 Williams, Fiji, I, 198, quoted by Wilken, in VG, III, 468.
5 Brown, in AAAS, 1898, 794.
6 Fox and Drew, in JAI, XLV, 161.
7 Leggatt, in AAAS, 1892, 701.
8 Ratzel, Vkde., I, 74.

9 Fritsch, Eingeb. S.-Afr., 332.
10 Willoughby, in JAI, XXXV, 299-300.
11 Torday and Joyce, in JAI, XXXV, 402.
12 Hobley, A-Kamba, 67.
13 In VG, I, 579, 580.
14 Tylor, Prim. Culture, II, 401.
15 Mitra, quoted by Wilken, in VG, III, 472.

of Çiva a horizontal sign on the forehead.[16] The practice of tattoo is wide-spread in Borneo, and amongst Kayan women is universal. "They believe that the designs act as torches in the next world, and that without these to light them they would remain forever in total darkness."[17]

In parts of Polynesia everyone must carry on his body the mark of his protective spirit. In Tonga, during the illness of a person of importance, people vied with one another in cutting off a little finger so as to bring about his recovery. So general was this custom that all natives, with exception of the chief princes, lacked the little finger, even small boys submitting to the operation.[18]

As a sign of grateful acknowledgment to the spirits, an Indian woman went through the ordeal of the sun-dance and had her arms scarified from shoulder to elbow. This was done by a medicine-man, who also slit the ear of the babies born since the last sun-dance. "That the ghost may travel the ghost road in safety, each Lakota must during his life be tattooed either in the middle of the forehead or on the wrists. In this event the spirit will go directly to the 'Many Lodges.'"[19] In Central America part of the rite of naming the child consisted in conducting it to the temple and boring its ears.[20] In Mexico the people drew their own blood and cast it with their hands up to heaven.[21] On the seventh day after birth the ear of the Moslem child is bored.[22]

Hair-Sacrifice. Wilken[23] has written searchingly upon this form of exuvial sacrifice. It is connected with many events, such as birth, maturity, marriage, and sickness, and is performed on other occasions also to influence the super-natural powers. The immediately following cases are reproduced from Wilken. In Malabar it is the custom, at the exorcising of a sick person possessed of an evil spirit, to cut off his hair and consecrate it to the demon as a palliative. Among the ancient Greeks during sickness the hair was dedicated to the god of health, and at Sicyon the image of Hygeia was so covered with con-secrated hair that one could scarcely see it. Not only in sickness but also before starting on a journey, and especially before going to war, was it customary to cut off the hair and offer it to the gods or else to make a vow so to do upon safe return, as the author shows by many examples. After a war among the wild tribes of Central America, "he who had killed an enemy cut off his own hair." The ancient Mexicans used to shave the boy's head save for a lock in the back; "at the age of fifteen years the boy was sent to war in charge of veteran warriors, and if with their aid he took a prisoner, the tuft was cut off." When a Buginese prince must leave his land to seek the aid of the Dutch against an enemy, he climbs to the top of a mountain, ties a knot in a creeping plant as evidence of his inviolable vow, and says: "If I conquer Gowa and return home without injury, then will I have the long hair of myself and vassals cut off at this place and a huge sacrificial meal prepared, at which the rice shall be piled up as high as this mountain." Examples are here cited where the sacrifice of hair is made not by the person going on a journey or to war but by someone else for him.

16 Schmidt, *Ceylon*, 288-289; Hopkins, *Relig. India*, 501.
17 Hose and Shelford, in JAI, XXXVI, 67.
18 Waitz, *Anthrop.*, VI, 35-41, 397.
19 Dorsey, in BAE, XI, 464, 465, 486.
20 Brinton, *Nagualism*, 16.

21 Eden, *Three Books on Amer.*, 196.
22 Tornauw, *Moslimische Recht*, 85.
23 "Haaropfer," in VG, III, 490 ff.; Schoe-mann, *Griech. Alterthümer*, II, 206; Ban-croft, *Nat. Races*, I, 764; II, 401.

A sacrifice of this sort by a few persons may have the virtue of diverting a common danger. In 1799, for example, there occurred a volcanic eruption on a Pacific island, and in order to appease the angry gods, after a number of pigs had been offered up in vain, the king, surrounded by priests and chiefs, went to the troubled area and, "as the most valuable offering he could make, cut off part of his own hair, which was always considered sacred, and threw it into the torrent."[24]

The custom of cropping the hair of a child is very widespread, and is usually attended with religious rites. The Unyamwesi of Africa do this when the baby is only nine days old; the hair is preserved in a box.[25] The practice is general in the Indian Archipelago, being found among the Mohammedans as well as among the heathen. The Aru Islanders conceal the shorn hair in a plantain or banana tree, while the Amboinese bury it under a sago palm or put it in a silver box which is hung about the child's neck like an amulet against sickness. Elsewhere, when the child can crawl, its hair is shorn and the ceremony of name-giving takes place.[26] In Brazil, when the child is two months old, its hair is literally torn or pulled out to the accompaniment of music and dancing.[27] Cutting the hair in New Zealand was done with much ceremony and many spells. The operator was made taboo for his services, and the hair was placed on an altar in a holy grove.[28] On the seventh day after birth the hair of the Moslem child is cut off and alms in money equal to the weight of the hair are given.[29] The Buddhist novice in the first degree of monkhood must cut off his hair in token that he sacrifices his most prized decoration.[30] Ritual hair-cutting at marriage is common among the Malayo-Polynesian races.[31] On the wedding day the Greek bride and groom took a bath, and then went into the temple of some god to ask his blessing, at which occasion each sacrificed a lock of hair.[32]

Circumcision. The following survey discloses this practice in practically all parts of the world. It is a common rite in initiation-ceremonies, being performed on both sexes; it has much religious significance; it is related to the subject of self-perpetuation in that, among a number of peoples, it constitutes a prerequisite to marriage; it is associated likewise with vanity, being regarded as a mark of maturity and position [33]

A line drawn from the mouth of the Murray to the Gulf of Carpentaria roughly separates the area in Australia where circumcision is practised from that where it is not known. In the central section the ceremony is performed when a boy is nine or ten. The public proceedings are begun by a woman walking up to a youth and quietly slipping over his head a string of human hair to which is attached a mussel shell. There is immediately a row; the boy rushes out of camp and for several months after the circumcision no woman is supposed to see him. The night before the ceremony all the women see him for a few minutes only. As soon as the operation takes place, "the father stoops over the boy and believing himself inspired by Muramura, gives

---

24 Ellis, *Polynesian Res.*, IV, 60.
25 Stuhlmann, *Mit Emin*, 84.
26 Wilken, "Haaropfer," in VG, III, 500, 505.
27 Spix u. Martius, *Bras.*, 1188.
28 Gomme, *Village Life*, 173; Taylor, *New Zealand*, 91, note, 93-94, 206.
29 Tornauw, *Moslimische Recht*, 85.

30 Monier-Williams, *Buddhism*, 306, quoted by Westermarck, *Marriage*, I, 509, note 3.
31 Waitz, *Anthr.*, VI, 632; Wilken, in VG, I, 577-579.
32 Bergel, *Eheverhältnisse*, 18.
33 §§163, 229, 341, 445, of text and *Case-Book*.

him a new name." A stone knife is used.[34] In the different districts of Queensland the ceremonies are very elaborate.[35] Initiatory rites of circumcision and subincision are in vogue all over the northern territory except a part of the northwest; they are usually performed early in the morning, the whole tribe being gathered together.[36] Throughout the Carpentaria region no woman is allowed to marry until the operation of introcision has been performed, nor may a man marry until he has been circumcized.[37] Curr[38] thinks that circumcision is designed to prevent for a time the intrigues of the young males with the women. In Australia "uncircumcized" is as much a term of reproach as among the Hebrews.[39]

Circumcision is widely practised in Melanesia; in many districts, however, it seems to have no connection with initiation-ceremonies.[40] On the New Hebrides and other islands it is said to be necessary for marriage, for the purpose of making one fruitful, and for cleanliness and manliness.[41] On the island of Tikopia incision takes place when a boy is about twelve years of age and is done in the same fashion as in Tonga. "Before the operation the chief of the division will make an offering of kava to the dead and will pray that the boy may pass through the ordeal successfully. The relatives of the boy assemble in the house but the operation is performed by the maternal uncle of the boy just outside the house. While it is being done the relatives in the house cry, the male relatives on both father's and mother's sides cut themselves on the forehead so that blood flows over the face, and the female relatives tear their cheeks with their nails."[42] The blood-letting feature would seem to ally this case with the general practice of exuvial sacrifice. In Viti Levu, if a member of a Nanga union (the term is derived from the name of an enclosure in which they hold puberty-ceremonies for boys and girls) is sick, a friend of his or a boy not yet circumcized has this operation performed; it is a sacrifice for him.[43] Such notions prevailed throughout the Fiji Islands. "According to the native chronicler, sickness was the cause of circumcision. It was a sacrificial act made to appease and avert the wrath of the ancestral gods. When a man got infirm and old, and sickness got such a hold on him that he could not shake it off, he would say, 'I have sinned against the *Lawa Ruku* [canons and ordinances laid down by religion], therefore must I make a sacrifice.' Then he would get one of his younger relatives and one of his sons to go through the rite of circumcision as an act of atonement." One native told the writer that he had undergone the operation three times in order to propitiate his deity. Upon being reminded that that was scarcely possible, he explained that on the latter occasions he had only been bled in that particular spot, and added that the ancient gods continually required the spilling of blood. "He also told me that those who practised complete circumcision had a great contempt for those who only partially did it, and when they fought such people they advanced to the battle reviling them on their uncircumcised state, saying that they were unclean and stank. So when the Bible was

34 Howitt, in JAI, XX, 81, 85; Bastian, *Deut. Exped.*, II, 36; Spencer and Gillen, *Nat. Tr. Cent. Aust.*, 223, 224.
35 Roth, *Queensland*, 170 ff.
36 Bassett-Smith, in JAI, XXIII, 327; Chamberlain, in AA, IV, 555, 556.
37 Mathews, in AA, II, 500.
38 *Aust. Race*, I, 74.
39 Ratzel, *Vkde.*, II, 85.

40 Codrington, *Melanesians*, 234; Finsch, *Ethnol. Erfahr.*, II, sub. div. 2, 113; Ratzel, *Vkde.*, II, 234.
41 Ella; Gray; Creagh; Leggatt; Macdonald; in AAAS, 1892, 623, 646, 659, 680, 704, 722, respectively.
42 Rivers, *Melan. Soc.*, I, 312-313.
43 Andree, *Eth. Parallelen*, 2d ser., 198.

translated, the objurgations hurled by the Israelites at the uncircumcised Philistines were a familiar cry to them."[44] Missionaries have now and then had the way thus smoothed for their ministrations.

Many tribes in Africa practise circumcision or incision without having had contact with Mohammedans or Jews. Some isolated tribes have the custom although living among tribes that do not practise it.[45] The Herero and Damara perform the operation between the sixth and eighth year, celebrating the occasion with a feast.[46] Both boys and girls are circumcized among the Atharaka; it is believed that persons just circumcized are very susceptible to evil influences.[47] In West Africa the practice is universal among both sexes, with the exception of the Ewe, who do not perform it on girls. The operation upon the girls is done by old women, amidst much singing, dancing, and hideous noises of the other women present; after which the girls are publicly declared marriageable.[48] An uncircumcized native here is not considered to be a man in the full sense of the word—fit for fighting, working, marrying, and inheriting. He is regarded as nothing by both men and women, is slandered, abused, insulted, ostracized, and not allowed to marry.[49] On the Loango coast it is believed that circumcision helps in procreation, and should an uncircumcized man get married, he becomes the butt of a popular jest.[50] On the west coast and in the Congo basin circumcision is part of the initiatory rites of the secret societies; for the girls it is also an indication of their marriageability. In one case the boys are allowed to steal a fowl or an ox from another tribe "to alleviate their pain"; although at other times such action would be severely punished. The author[51] is impressed with Ellis's observation that in West Africa the diffusion of the phallic cult goes hand in hand with circumcision, while the latter is closely related also to the service of the sexblessing god. Circumcision among the Fan is said to rest on the notion of sacrifice; by the act alliance is renewed with the deity; it also partakes of the nature of the offering of first-fruits.[52] The Banziris of the Congo who do not practise circumcision are disposed to ridicule the men of the surrounding tribes who use this rite.[53] Circumcision is practised by all the males among the Bangala, the operation generally taking place between the ages of ten and fifteen. "Great shame is attached to being uncircumcised, and a person can be cut at any age. The only reason given is that women do not want them if they are uncircumcised."[54]

Among the Hovas of Madagascar, circumcision was attended by festivity second to no other occasion; it was also a time of licentiousness. Unlike the Semitic peoples, among whom the individual child was the object of attention, they circumcized at recurring periods, every few years, at times appointed by the sovereign. On these occasions children who had matured in the interval underwent the rite.[55] The Bantu peoples quite generally practise circumcision on both boys and girls. Among the Masai it differs in certain special features from the operation as performed elsewhere in Africa.[56] Among the

44 Brewster, in JAI, XLIX, 310.
45 Schweinfurth, *Heart of Africa*, 440; Andree, *Eth. Parallelen*, 174.
46 Ratzel, *Vkde.*, I, 340.
47 Champion, in JAI, XLII, 84.
48 Ellis, *Ewe*, 43; Müller, in *Globus*, LXXXI, 280; Griffith, in JAI, XVI, 308.
49 Nassau, *Fetichism*, 12.
50 Bastian, *Deut. Exped.*, I, 177.

51 Frobenius, *Masken*, 41, 118, 119, 120, 132, 145, 217.
52 Trilles, *Fán*, 529-530.
53 Clozel, in PSM, XLIX, 676; Brunache, *Cent. Afr.*, 68.
54 Weeks, in JAI, XL, 401-402.
55 Sibree, *Great Afr. Isl.*, 217-222, 273-274.
56 Johnston, *Uganda*, 556, 804; Ploss, *Knabenbeschneidung*, 17.

Wawanga it is quite the exception to find a family where every male member has undergone the operation.[57]

Female circumcision is common in Northeast Africa.[58] The Somali and other tribes that have been influenced by Islam circumcize boys, after the Mohammedan-Arabian rite, at the age of three.[59] In the Niger Protectorate all boys are circumcized, whether free or slave, the operation being performed at any age, on babies a few weeks old or on young fellows of fifteen or sixteen.[60] Among the Kabyles, when a boy reaches the age of four, his father fixes the day for the ceremony; in the case of girls, the operation is replaced by the pretense of making a cross-like incision, with the back of a knife, on the sexual parts of the newly-born child.[61]

Circumcision is not universal or obligatory in Borneo, and is performed only upon males. The patient must lie down and neither work nor bathe while the wound is healing.[62] In Central Celebes the operation is done by shamans.[63] In those parts of Sumatra where Mohammedanism prevails, boys are circumcized between the sixth and tenth year; the ceremony is called "casting away their shame."[64] In Java and in numerous places in the Indian Archipelago a corresponding ceremony is observed in the case of girls.[65] Circumcision is practised widely, but not universally, in Polynesia.[66] Dall[67] holds that the practice took its rise in the Pacific region as a test of fortitude.

The *Handbook of American Indians* contains no caption on circumcision; the practice is rare in America. Of an Athapascan tribe it is stated: "Many of the males are circumcised in infancy; those who are not are called dogs, not opprobriously, but rather affectionately."[68] It is to countries farther south, however, that one must turn to find more examples of this practice. Herrera[69] mentions it among a number of nations in Central America. Certain of the Guiana Indians have the custom, and perform it in such a brutal way that the children often die.[70] Certain tribes in Brazil and on the Amazon circumcize both sexes.[71] The Indians of the Urubamba River district make the girls drunk before performing the operation; circumcision is said to prepare them for marriage.[72]

Herodotus[73] states that the Colchians, Egyptians, and Ethiopians practised circumcision from time immemorial, and that the Syrians and Phœnicians borrowed it from them. Pietschmann[74] says that circumcision became a general tribal mark among the Phœnicians, while the custom was unknown to the Philistines. In Egypt only priests and warriors, not the common people, were circumcized.[75] The custom was in existence before the arrival of the

57 Dundas, K., in JAI, XLIII, 30.
58 King, in JASB, II, 3.
59 Paulitschke, *Nordost-Afr.*, I, 174; Junker, *Afrika*, II, 458.
60 Granville and Roth, in JAI, XXVIII, 117.
61 Hanoteau et Letourneux, *Kabylie*, II, 211, 212.
62 Roth, in JAI, XXII, 45; Perelaer, *Dajaks*, 46.
63 Riedel, in *Bijd.*, XXXV, 92.
64 Marsden, *Sumatra*, 287.
65 Wilken, "Besnijdenis," in VG, IV, 235, 236, 239; Crawfurd, *Ind. Arch.*, 94; Ploss, *Kind*, I, 377-385; II, 151-153, 220-234.

66 Ratzel, *Vkde.*, II, 139; Turner, *Samoa*, 81.
67 In BAE, III, 80.
68 HAI, I, 440.
69 *Hist. Gen.*, Decade IV, lib. 9, cap. 181.
70 Roth, in BAE, XXXVIII, 417-418.
71 Spix u. Martius, *Bras.*, 1188; Von Martius, *Beiträge*, I, 445, 582.
72 Von den Steinen, in *Globus*, LXXXIII, 134.
73 *Hist.*, II, 37, 104.
74 *Phönizier*, 228-229; Lippert, *Kgchte.*, I, 392.
75 Ploss, *Knabenbeschneidung*, 11.

Jews who adopted it.[76] Its universality among the Jews later incurred the derision of the civilized world.[77] Circumcision was in the nature of a ransom for human sacrifice—a part for the whole. Such seems to be the significance of the passage where Jahweh was in a killing mood before the son of Moses was circumcized: "Then Zipporah took a flint, and cut off the foreskin of her son, and cast it at his feet; and she said, Surely a bridegroom of blood art thou to me. So he let him alone. Then she said, A bridegroom of blood art thou, because of the circumcision."[78] The interpretation is that Moses himself was uncircumcized and for that reason Jahweh tried to kill him; but that his wife circumcized the son and smeared the blood upon Moses, so as to make it appear that the blood proceeded from an incision in him; then Jahweh was pleased. That a stone knife was used indicates the age of the custom. "Redemption through circumcision and through the Passover lamb belong to two different culture-periods. When in a later law circumcision is made a condition for sharing in the feast of the Passover, it follows that circumcision represents the older form of redemption. Ransom through the blood-sacrifice of a bodily incision and substitution through domestic animals are two practices which the Jews share with other peoples, the first with the African especially, the second with the Asiatic-European herdsmen; but a third form is common, so far as we know, only to the Jews and has contributed most to impress their ethical peculiarities: it is the offering to the deity of all blood as the price of redemption." The author[79] emphasizes the manifold significance of the custom. It was connected with the cult, a token of the covenant, and was ordered performed on every male child eight days old. It was further a form of ransom for human sacrifice. When Abraham circumcized the thirteen or fourteen year old Ishmael, it became at the same time a mark of puberty. The youth was declared a man, qualified for the cult and capable of bearing arms; he was permitted to marry. There is no mention of circumcision as an operation for hygienic reasons or as protecting against sickness. The strongest evidence of the Prophetical spiritualizing of the old ritual customs is the turn given to the ancient and strictly observed requirement of circumcision, where the circumcision of the heart is called for.[80] Such was the stress laid upon circumcision that in later times "circumcized" became a synonym for Israelite, and "uncircumcized" for a foreigner.[81] It also became a synonym for all the spiritual and ethical qualities for which the Jahweh-cult had then come to stand. Abraham, it was thought, would save from the pit all who bore the mark of circumcision. How deeply fixed this rite became is indicated by the struggle which Paul and others had in order to throw it off. The fixed and important character which it possessed at all periods indicates that from the beginning it must have been considered a vital part of the religion of Jahweh, and must have had its motive in a conception which identified the rite with some of Jahweh's most important functions.[82] The Zealots, who resorted to murder in attempting to expel the Romans from Palestine, would slay the uncircumcized unless they consented to the operation.[83] It is said that a certain governor had his mother,

76 Maurer, *Vkde.*, I, 41; "Aus allen Erd-teilen," in *Globus*, LXXII, 212.
77 Bousset, *Relig. Judentums*, 79.
78 Ex., IV, 25-26.
79 Maurer, *Vkde.*, I, 41-42, 241 (quoted); Maurer, in *Globus*, XCI, 111; Gen., XVII, 23, 25.

80 Kautzsch, in *Hastings's Dict. Bible*, 687.
81 I Sam., XXXI, 4; II Sam., I, 20; I Chr., X, 4; Rom., III, 30.
82 Rom., II, 28 ff.; Gen., XVII, 11; Barton, *Sem. Origins*, 280-281.
83 Cook, *Fathers of Jesus*, II, 36-37.

who was a Christian, circumcized so as not to be reviled with the epithet, "son of the uncircumcized." Greek women were chided for not having undergone mutilation.[84] The Mohammedan rule is to perform the ceremony between the twelfth and fourteenth year with the reading aloud of prayers of thanks and of intercession and with great festivity.[85]

§300. Exuvial Magic.

THROUGHOUT all of the tribes studied by Spencer and Gillen[1] in Central Australia the hair of the head is wholly or partly removed from the deceased immediately after death and used for magic purposes. In some cases the beard also is cut off; in each case the hair is made into some sacred object, which is taken out by the avenger of the dead man. "Such hair is always kept because it is supposed to be endowed with the attributes of the dead man, and therefore to give special power to its possessor." Generally such hair may be handled by men only; there is one case where the women carry about with them little locks of the beard of a maternal uncle. "It is this man who, when he is alive, has the power of betrothing them to other men . . . and the possession of a lock of his hair is supposed both to indicate the fact that they have been assigned to one particular man, and at the same time it magically protects them against the advances of other men." Among all the tribes the disposal of the hair of each individual, dead or alive, is regulated by strict rules. "As everybody presents his or her hair to some one else at stated times, it would be a comparatively easy matter for any evil-minded person to secure a clipping of the hair of any one else. He has only to ascertain, which he can do without the slightest difficulty, to whom the hair was given, and then nothing would be easier than to steal a little bit of string made from the hair of the person whom he desires to injure. The result is that no one is afraid of any one else possessing his or her hair, and there is never any attempt made to practise that form of magic so common amongst savage tribes, even in other parts of Australia, which consists in burning, or performing some kind of magic charm on the hair, with the idea that the person from whom it has been cut can be injured thereby."

Bones form another instrument of magic common in Central Australia. "All diseases are supposed to be caused by the bone of a dead blackfellow being pointed at the sick person. . . . The bones of the dead are never disturbed or touched, except for the purpose of obtaining an armbone to point at an enemy."[2] The method of using a bone varies slightly. "If one man has sufficient confidence in himself he will seize the bone in his left hand with the two fingers extended along it. He then takes up the hair string with his right hand and pulls it tight against his right hip, and kneeling down points towards his enemy's camp. . . . After he has finished the song the point of the bone is covered with *mindrie* pitch to keep in the poison that has been sung into it, and the man then waits until he hears that his enemy is ill. The bone in the meantime is buried in a hole in the sand and covered up with feathers. When the enemy becomes ill the bone-pointer digs up the bone and burns about half an inch off its point; he then covers up the burn with *mindrie* and again hides the

84 Wellhausen, *Skizzen*, III, 154-155.   1 *North. Tr. Cent. Aust.*, 477-478; Gillen,
85 Pischon, *Islam*, 21.   in AAAS, 1901, 116.
                                                   2 Wells, in AAAS, 1893, 516, 517.

bone. The sick man in the meantime, suspecting that he has been 'boned,' steadily gets worse. His friends travel in all directions searching for the man who has 'boned' him. If they find a partially burnt bone it is brought to the sick man, the *mindrie* is taken off the point and the whole bone is immersed in water. The sick man usually then gets better. . . . Usually some man who is a general nuisance to the camps is finally settled upon as the one that did the 'boneing,' and then, unless he can get into sanctuary, he is killed or at least badly knocked about. . . . The male children are taught the use of the bone almost as soon as they understand anything, the father sometimes getting the boy to assist him, but the boys very rarely use the bone until they are made men. Young girls very often 'bone' a man who has refused to have anything to do with them. In this case they usually boast of it, hoping that the young man will be frightened and come to them. . . . In the event of the bone not being found, every few days another half-inch is burnt off, and by about the tenth day the remainder of the bone, with the hair string and *mindrie,* is burnt. The sick man usually dies very soon after. . . . They distrust white man's medicine because it is not strong enough to cope with the poison of a bone."[3]

The Australians best illustrate the crude usages connected with fragments of the body. The Melanesians too are abject believers in exuvial magic. All the scraps from Papuan meals are burned or buried, "as they could be used in sorcery, to which all disease and calamity is ascribed."[4] The sorcerer gets hold of a bit of property of the person he wishes to charm, "for example, a lost hair, cuttings from fingernails, some tobacco, a bit of his food-leavings, a spear left standing. . . . This he puts into a fire, . . . observing all sorts of precautions, and as soon as the article is burnt up the life of the original possessor is thought also to come to an end. This process can be hurried or delayed. It is therefore comprehensible that the Papuan takes a ridiculous amount of pains not to let these things get into strange hands. . . . I think that this is the cause of the peculiar method of spitting of the Tamos . . . who wish thereby to prevent the spittle reaching the earth as a usable whole."[5] Thus, too, in the Ladrones, one must not spit near the house of an enemy, doubtless for fear of sorcery. Elsewhere there is a sacred pool into which scraps of the victim's food are cast; if the fish in the pool quickly devour them, the man will die. Friendly intervention is sometimes paid for by the intended victim, if he knows. "It is evident that no one who intends to bring mischief to a man by a fragment of his food will partake of that food himself, because by doing so he would bring the mischief also on himself. Hence a native offering even a single banana to a visitor will bite the end of it before he gives it, and a European giving medicine to a sick native gives confidence by taking a little first himself." Again, a person can acquire a vampire-like power by eating a morsel of a corpse; "the ghost then of the dead man would join in a close friendship with the person who had eaten, and would gratify him by afflicting anyone against whom his ghostly power might be directed." In the New Hebrides the bones of chiefs are used for arrow-tips and poisoned, a double combination of the fetish-motive.[6] The deadly quality of the poisoned arrows "was never thought by the natives to be due to poison in our use of the word,

---

3 Horne and Aiston, *Cent. Aust.*, 150-152.
4 Ella, in AAAS, 1892, 638; and in AAAS, 1887, 493.

5 Hagen, *Papuas*, 269; Safford, in AA, IV, 717.
6 Codrington, *Melanesians*, 178, 204, 221; Flower, in JAI, XI, 76.

though what was used might be, and was meant to be, injurious and active in inflaming the wound; it was the supernatural power that belonged to the human bone of which the head was made on which they chiefly relied, and with that the magical power of the incantations with which the head was fastened to the shaft."[7]

The essential part of one kind of magic in British New Guinea is that something which has been in intimate contact with a person is obtained by the magician, who places it in contact with some magical medicine, when it is believed that the person will get sick and may perhaps die. "Thus natives fear to leave fragments of their nails or hair about lest a hostile magician may get hold of them and cause sickness or death." The medicine in question is mainly some kind of vegetable product known only to the magician and thought capable of producing the desired evil effect. When Strong[8] once chewed some sugar-cane in an unfriendly village, he noticed that a loyal policeman from another district insisted on collecting and hiding the fibrous material he spat out. "He feared that the unfriendly village people, who had deserted their village on our approach, would be able to do me harm if they found such material. Another instance I know of occurred at Kerema in the Elema district on the south coast. A native came to me and quite seriously complained that another native had killed his wife by collecting some sand out of her foot prints, and had then placed the sand in a small bamboo with the requisite medicine." In some of the islands associations exist for mutual protection against magic. "If a member wishes to injure an enemy, he goes to the head man who commissions one of his followers to obtain something from the man to be injured, whether fragments of his food, his hair, nail-parings or excrement. It is usual to use food and the method employed if fragments cannot be otherwise obtained is the following: the man commissioned to obtain food roasts a yam and breaking it in half he gives one half to the man who is to be injured while he eats another piece of yam himself which the victim is led to believe is the other half of his own. As a matter of fact the piece of yam which is eaten has been substituted for the real other half of that eaten by the victim which is kept for the magical rite. Sometimes the device is discovered, when a terrible fight will ensue."[9] In New Britain "charms are made out of anything that has had connection or contact with a person, such as remains of food of which she or he has partaken, earth from a footprint, excrement, spittle, hair, or clothing. Any of these things may be buried with incantation ceremonies, and thus through the process afflict the people concerned in various ways." Against this kind of charm much precaution is taken. "Expectoration is in the form of infinitesimal spray. (Stooling is always in absolute secrecy, and with the greatest care.) When shaving or cutting the hair, every scrap of nair is carefully burnt, and the crumbs of one's food also burned."[10] The real gods in both Tana and New Caledonia may be said to be the disease-makers. "It is surprising how these men are dreaded, and how firm the belief is that they have in their hands the power of life and death. . . . It is believed that these men can create disease and death by burning what is called nahak. Nahak means rubbish, but principally refuse of food. Everything of the kind they bury or throw into the sea, lest the disease-makers should get hold of it. These fellows are always about, and consider it their special business to pick up and

7 Codrington, in JAI, XIX, 215.
8 In JAI, XLIX, 293.

9 Rivers, Melan. Soc., I, 161-162.
10 Danks, in AAAS, 1909, 455.

burn, with certain formalities, anything in the nahak line which comes in their way. . . . The people stare as they see him go along, and say to each other, 'He has got something; he will do for somebody by-and-by at night.' . . . When a person is taken ill he believes that it is occasioned by some one burning his rubbish. Instead of thinking about medicine, he calls some one to blow a shell . . . which can be heard three miles off. The meaning of it is to implore the person who is supposed to be burning the sick man's rubbish and causing all the pain to stop burning; and it is a promise as well that a present will be taken in the morning. The greater the pain the more they blow the shell, and when the pain abates they cease, supposing that the disease-maker has been kind enough to stop burning. Then the friends of the sick man arrange about a present to take in the morning. . . . We observed also, that the belief in the system of nahak burning was as firm in the craft as out of it. If a disease-maker was ill himself, he felt sure that some one must be burning *his* nahak. He, too, must have a shell blown, and presents sent to the party supposed to be causing the mischief. Some of our kind neighbours were surprised at our indifference on the matter, and felt so concerned for our safety that whenever they saw a banana skin lying at our back-door, or about the servants' houses, they would pick it up, take it away, and throw it into the sea lest the disease-makers should get hold of it."[11]

The Pygmies, when their hair is cut, keep the cuttings till the next morning and burn them in the ashes when they break camp.[12] In the French Congo, charms, which are made either to rouse good will toward the charmer or to work ill to an enemy, "must have in them some portion of the person to be dealt with—his hair, blood, nail-parings, etc.—or, failing that, his or her most intimate belonging, something that has his smell—a piece of his old waist-cloth." If another illustration of property being an attribution of personality is needed, we have it in this example. Blood from cuts or nose-bleed is most carefully covered up and stamped upon, if it falls on the earth; "if it falls on the side of a canoe, or a tree, the place is carefully cut out and the chip destroyed." Blood from a wound on a woman is held in high horror.[13] In Angola at the induction of a new chief the heads of an antelope and of a human being are magically used.[14]

Perhaps the most potent West African charm, stowed in the tusk of a young elephant, comprises hair from the head of a white man, a bit of human flesh, also said to be that of a white man, some large snake-teeth, the point of a leopard's claw, a fragment of the tooth of a crocodile, a few seeds of the plant from which poison for arrows is made, all mixed in a kind of paste. To this is added a little gunpowder and a few drops of snake-poison. "This gruesome compound is all held in the cavity of the tusk by a fragment of glass broken from the side of a gin bottle. The efficacy of this 'medicine' is largely enhanced by its being visible through the glass, and the sum of the matter is that the combined efforts of this fetish can subdue the terrors of the jungle; but the power of the charm resides in the things from which the parts are taken."[15] The Makoko think that human hair can bring rain; they wanted some from the missionaries and would have submitted to baptism to get it.[16] If a Bangala woman runs away, her husband gets out her nail-parings and hair-

11 Turner, *Samoa*, 320-322, 342. *Nahak* is equivalent to *narak* and *nuruk;* §§254, 302, 313, of the text and *Case-Book*.
12 Stuhlmann, *Mit Emin*, 451.

13 Kingsley, *Travels W. Afr.*, 447.
14 Serpa Pinto, *Africa*, I, 143.
15 Garner, in AAAS, 1895, 590.
16 Bastian, *Afr. Reisen*, 118.

cuttings which he has gathered for such an emergency, and takes them to a medicine-man, who puts them into a skin and returns them to him. The husband then utters the imprecation: "If my wife stops to eat at the place whence she has run away let her die quickly." The same is done to get back a runaway slave or to punish some one with whom the owner of such exuviæ has quarrelled. "For this reason nail parings and hair cuttings are always destroyed if possible."[17] Among the Bahima, "any portion of a person's clothing, a bit of hair, nail parings, spittle, a bit of grass which a person may have had in his mouth and thrown down, or earth where one has relieved nature, are eagerly sought for and carried off by those who wish to exercise an evil influence over the man or woman: any of these are taken to the priest to enable him to make the person ill or even to kill him."[18]

In East Africa, where married women only wear a special sort of loin-cloth, no such cloth has been known to have been sold, given, or bartered, with one exception in the possession of the authoress.[19] "The reason for this is that if the cloth should be given to any white man, or if he should obtain it in any way, the woman from whom it came would be under sexual obligation to him, and that he could bewitch her, at any time, wherever he might be, and however unwilling she might feel, and could take her away from her husband and people to the ends of the earth." The Wagogo, having cut out the private parts of slain enemies, cook and eat them with medicine, "in order to take away the *manlwoa* [not explained] from the enemy."[20] Dundas[21] once tried to purchase some of the tweezers used for pulling out the eyelashes from a party of young men who were dancing in his camp, and the result was an instant move to leave the place. On inquiry he found that the man whose tweezers he had purchased was supposed to be doomed to die by his hand. "It seems strange," he remarks, "that such a simple article, which is made by every boy and worn merely as an ornament, one would think, should be so vital to the owner's life, yet the belief is very strong and should be considered when natives appear unwilling to part with such articles." Among the medicines of these people are an extraordinary medley of articles such as crocodiles' teeth, lions' claws, berries of various sorts, and, as a much prized addition, a loaded cartridge. "The latter article gives one an idea of the meaning of these medicines: it is presumably the latent power of the cartridge which is valuable. The cartridge is lifeless yet full of strength, but so also there may be strength in the lion's claw and fruitfulness in berries." When a Kabyle herdsman returns home at noon to pass the period of heat, "he should not for one single instant let go the staff that serves him as a crook. The one who gets it at once makes all the milk of the flock pass into the udders of his cows."[22] Believing that negro hair is much more powerful in magic than that of other people, the Arabs of Algiers and elsewhere buy it to cure fever. They burn some and make the patient smell the smoke, putting the remainder away. "Finger nails may be used in a similar way, and are even more powerful. The negroes will sell their hair because they can avoid the results of the Arab charms by taking precautions, but they will not sell their nail-parings, as the spells produced are too strong to be overcome. If the hair was stolen, the owner might be injured, but even

17 Weeks, in JAI, XL, 392.
18 Roscoe, in JAI, XXXVII, 115.
19 French-Sheldon, in JAI, XXI, 364.
20 Cole, in JAI, XXXII, 319.

21 In JAI, XLIII, 528, 532.
22 Hanoteau et Letourneux, *Kabylie*, I, 497.

so, some people let their clippings blow about, and thus expose themselves to the risk. 'There are always some fools in the world,' according to Sambo, who is careful to spread a cloth in order to catch his own severed locks. . . . A person should not bite his nails in public, for he may not know where the bits go. All milk-teeth should be burnt. . . . When a person is ill, neither his hair nor his nails should be cut, lest too much of the vital force should be thus removed, and the patient rendered incapable of throwing off the malady. Indeed, even if he were not to become worse because of the original attack, some other bori [spirit] would probably take advantage of his state of weakness. A woman should not even plait her hair when ill. . . . A few say that a boy could certainly be killed by a magician who possessed the discarded foreskin."[23]

Certain tribes of India believe that some evil spirits are always on the look-out for a drop of the blood or urine of a pregnant woman, and that when such is found and licked up, the woman is sure to have difficult labor, which may end in death. "As for blood, not only a woman but also a man, promptly effaces with the feet or covers with dust any blood that may fall from any part of the body; for it is believed that if a witch licks up such blood or a spirit overshadows it, or ants or some particular species of birds lick it up, the person whose blood is licked up is sure to fall sick. Blood falling on the ground at midnight is particularly dangerous, as at that time evil spirits roam about in all directions. Sometimes a witch or sorcerer wishing to harm a man secures a little dust of his footprints and effects his mischievous purpose by uttering some magic spell over such dust."[24] The hair of grown-up people, when cut off, is placed by the Palaungs in the thatch of a roof or high up among the thick branches of a bush or tree, "the object being to prevent its being stepped upon or used as a charm. But that of a baby is nearly always hidden in the ground. No hair is ever burned." For a love-charm to be effective, the lover must secure some threads from the dress of the girl. He usually solicits the aid of some female friend. "The lover must be sure of the truthfulness of the girl whom he has asked to help, because if she gave him some of the threads from her own clothing, she might fall in love with him and he with her. It is therefore better to get a sister to help, if it is possible." To bewitch an enemy, his horse, or his ox, "a footprint of the man or beast should be carefully dug up, so that all the earth touched by the foot is secured, whether broken or in one mass. This should be wrapped in large leaves and roasted over a slow fire."[25] A Dusun once sold Evans[26] his long hair, but only after a fowl was given in addition to the purchase price; this was sacrificed in order to protect him should the white man try to make magic with his hair.

In the Gilbert Islands, "a girl's arrival at the age of puberty was a time of great anxiety to the parents, for then she was considered dangerously sensitive to enemy magic and especially to that sort which caused sterility. . . . Her urine was made into a coco-nut shell and most carefully destroyed, for fear of evil spells. The urine was, throughout the Group, considered one of the most powerful mediums through which magic might be directed against a man or woman. Therefore, a native will always, if possible, make water into the sea." Concern did not cease with marriage; "the mat was afterwards carefully burned in order that no enemy of the family might obtain it and, by using

23 Tremearne, in JAI, XLV, 26-27.   25 Milne, Eastern Clan, 31, 112-113, 263.
24 Roy, in JAI, XLIV, 339.   26 In JAI, XLII, 392.

evil magic upon the blood, curse the bride with barrenness."27 In the Hawaiian magical practice of "praying to death," if the victim be a chief or a person living at a distance, effort is made by the sorcerer to secure some tissue or secretion of the body, especially the saliva. "Unimpeachable, in truth, must be the character of the royal spittoon bearer, to this day an office of dignity in the farther isles of the Pacific. All the 'divinity that doth hedge a king' must prove of slight avail if speck or slightest trace of the kingly spittle fall into possession of any sorcerer ready for regicide. A nail-paring, a hair, or a tooth would also be favored (as in clairvoyance) by any business-like kahuna [sorcerer] who warrants a result. The kahuna seems to deify this material, which he then addresses as an idol or fetish, praying it to destroy the life of the patient."28 When travelling through the country of a hostile tribe, the natives of New Zealand hold that it is well to keep away from paths, and safer still to walk along the bed of a stream, so as to leave no footprint. "Because to every footprint you leave there clings a certain amount of *Manea,* which is the *Hau* [life-principle] of the human footprint. An enemy could, and would, take this subtle essence simply by scooping up some of the earth on which the foot-mark was imprinted. This would be taken to a warlock versed in black magic, who, by means of certain magic rites, would soon cause your death, the soil being employed as an agent to connect the spells with yourself, or your vitality. A shred of clothing, a lock of hair, or spittle can also be employed as such an agent." A Maori folktale relates how Rongo of the Ready Hand was once pursued by a monster; the world of death was already open to receive him when he bethought him of the means by which monsters and goblins are subdued. Hastily plucking a lock of hair from his head, he cast it into the troubled waters of the pond, repeating some magic words, whereupon the monster instantly retreated and the surging waters became calm.29

The Eskimo show a firm belief in magic, practising it with human bones, flesh of corpses, skulls, snakes, and spiders, as well as by special manufactured articles. Bits of bone, skin, and things that have belonged to the intended victim are tied up in a bag, and are by charms converted into a living thing which glides away in the water to do harm. If it fails it turns against the sender. The author30 thinks they borrowed this particular notion from Norway and Iceland. "The Indians along the Missouri River in Nebraska and Dacotah always used to allow their finger-nails to grow quite long and when necessary to cut them they placed the cuttings on a string, which they always kept at the belt or around the neck. Indians also have the belief that if an enemy gets hold of their pipes and smokes them, muttering an oath against them in the smoke, the smoke will carry up the oath to Heaven, and evil will come to them. I have a pipe which formerly belonged to Sitting Bull. He parted with it only on condition that it should never be smoked again, and it would require a pretty strong temptation to go against his wish."31 Sometimes a Winnebago woman would take a hair of her husband and stick it into some bad medicine. "In such case he would never leave her for he would become very much enamored of her. If ever she went away, he would miss her very much. However, he always had a headache. Finally he would get sick and lose his appe-

27 Grimble, in JAI, LI, 31, 41-42.
28 Nichols, in *Pop. Sci. News,* XXVII, 78.
29 Best, in AAAS, 1898, 771; in AAAS, 1904, 447; and in AAAS, 1909, 459-460 (quoted).

30 Nansen, *Esk. Life,* 285.
31 H. W. Mathews, communication to W. G. Sumner, Feb., 1896.

tite and then his eyesight. That is why it is forbidden to use this medicine, although some do it."[32] Some of the Plains tribes had "crazy medicine," consisting of a hair, a bit of nail paring, or even some small shreds of the victim's garment that had been secretly procured by a malignant sorcerer. "The medicine was suspended from the branch, and the more the wind blew the more the medicine danced and the crazier the victim became."[33] One mode of bewitching was similar to that employed in Europe and New England. "The wizard would possess himself of a lock of the victim's hair, parings from his nails, some of his saliva, a bit of the clothing he had worn, especially such as had absorbed his perspiration, a fragment left after he had eaten, some of his implements, or other personal belongings, and by treating them in certain ways would bring on him local or general sickness or some other misfortune. It was said that the wizard could affect any part if he obtained something taken from it. Thus sore throat might be brought about or a man made to 'spit himself to death' by means of a little saliva, and headache might be induced through a few hairs."[34] Certain Indians of South America use the bones of slain enemies to make points for arrows, because such are supposed to be more effective.[35] Fitzroy[36] cut a lock of hair off a Fuegian, whereupon the man snatched it, wrapped it up carefully, and handed it to a woman who stowed it in her bead-and-paint basket. Then the man very seriously asked the author to put away the scissors.

Belief that magic could be performed with exuviæ was common in antiquity, the Egyptians holding that bits of skin or hair from a corpse gave sorcerers power over the deceased.[37] Among the Jews it was explicitly ordained that natural functions should be performed in retirement and with precautions. The sanction was that God, when he walked through the camp, should see no uncleanness.[38] The Tyrolese spit on hair before throwing it away; otherwise witches could get hold of it and cause hail or storm.[39] In East Prussia, "if anyone wants to be truly loved by anyone else, he must give him secretly three drops of his blood in some food and drink."[40] For love-charms, in Germany of earlier days, magicians used sundry words, signs, wax images, nail-parings, a piece of the person's clothing or something else that had been in contact with him, which latter were buried under the threshold. Harlots and others of that ilk made use of sexual secretions, after-births, milk, perspiration, urine, spittle, hair, navel strings, and the brains of tadpoles or burbots. "A mixture of such ingredients or a concoction of one's own blood, testicles of a hare and liver of a dove. when taken by the coveted person, should awaken responsive love. Against these and other love-charms (love-apples, love-rings, Venus-talismans) there were remedies. In the *Mirror of Medicine* for 1532 it is stated: 'If you fear that a woman has given you a love-charm to eat, take a diapente of perlin, the same of iperikon, both powdered and drunk with melissa-water, and hang a lodestone on the neck.'"[41] In Russia, "they open the graves to remove a dead hand; if the dead hand is laid in the window where the thief breaks in, the victims will sleep so soundly that he can work in peace." This belief is connected chiefly with horse-stealing.[42] A Russian peasant "made the astonish-

32 Radin, in BAE, XXXVII, 263.
33 Skinner, in AA, XVI, 79.
34 Swanton, "Witchcraft," in HAI, II, 965.
35 Haseman, in AA, XIV, 345.
36 *Adventure and Beagle*, I, 53.
37 Maspero, *Hist. Anc.*, II, 510.

38 Deut., XXIII, 12.
39 Wilken, "Haaropfer," in VG, III, 550.
40 Frischbier, in *Am Ur-Quell*, I, 11.
41 Scherr, *Deut. Kgchte.*, 364.
42 Stern, *Russland*, 281.

ing statement that if you make a candle from human fat and light it you can see *all*."[43]

Upon earlier and later stages of civilization much magic has been performed by the use of excrement.[44] Retirement-taboos, alluded to above, as well as several other varieties of prohibition, are guaranteed by fear of magic.

§301. Other Instrumentalities.

"Medicine." Besides the use of exuviæ there is another kind of magic employed in New Guinea: that which is performed "by putting some 'medicine' in such a place that an enemy will touch it or perhaps that food will come into close contact with the 'medicine.' The following is a typical instance. A policeman at Port Moresby had a bad wrist. From his point of view it was caused by two Koiari natives being refused as police recruits. They then made the requisite 'medicine,' apparently not to be distinguished from ordinary sticks, placed it on the footpath, with the result that the policeman touched it and his hand became bad as a consequence."[1] The constituents of a sorcerer's kit are miscellaneous, but there are certain media, used to produce disease and death, which are universal, namely, snakes, certain magical stones, and the leaves and roots of a number of plants. "No layman would willingly touch or even look at the stones and other objects used by sorcerers, and any contact with them, even when not expected to produce death, would be avoided as unlucky." The greater number of cases of snake-bite, especially such as are fatal, are attributed to the machinations of the sorcerer. "Indeed, not only do sorcerers kill people by causing them to be bitten by snakes, but they are also able to obtain from the black snake a deadly stone which instantly kills any individual touched with it, even the sorcerer who uses it is said to take every precaution not to come into immediate contact with the stone. . . . To kill a man, it is sufficient to touch him with the snake stone, which is described as red and 'hot' and about the size of a filbert. A snake stone is rendered innocuous if it be dropped into a bowl of salt water which immediately hisses and bubbles as though boiling. When no more bubbles arise the stone is 'dead,' *i.e.*, harmless." The Southern Massim believe that the shoots of a certain tree, when chewed to the accompaniment of muttered spells, are capable of bringing about death. A sorcerer about to use this tree would by the aid of charms make himself invisible. "He would then spit the chewed shoots in the direction of his victim, who in two or three days would feel ill and lie down by the fire in his house, becoming gradually worse until he dies." Examples are cited to show that "only the sorcerer who had produced the illness could cure the stricken man, and the cure could only be effected by chewing another root and spitting it upon the victim while muttering spells."[2] It sometimes happens among the Melanesians that a man who has carried out a magical rite with the idea of killing his enemy repents when he sees that his purpose is about to be effected. "He may try to save the life of the man who is dying at his hands, and in order to do so he commissions his brother or some other man of his family to go to the house of the dying man and give him to drink a mixture of the milk of a coconut and the juice of certain leaves. The sick man will drink it and re-

43 Graham, *Way of Martha*, 69.
44 Bourke, *Scatalogic Rites;* Andree, *Eth. Parallelen*, 11.

1 Strong, in JAI, XLIX, 294-295.
2 Seligmann, *Melanesians*, 284, 287, 288, 281-283, 638-639.

cover but will at once know the cause of his illness and will seek to discover at whose hands he has suffered. The intermediary must never confess by whom he has been commissioned to bring the healing mixture and rather than do so, he will pretend that he has himself been the worker of the spell, even at the risk of the injury or even death which his pretence may bring on him. A man who undertakes this duty knows that he does so at the risk of his life. When the sick man has completely recovered, his relatives present a large sum of money to the intermediary."[3]

When a Pygmy has lost his wife through death or theft and wishes to obtain another, he drinks a kola-nut concoction night after night, in the belief that it will bring him good luck. The author says that many of the men succumb to the influence of this drink.[4] If a young man in South Africa loves a girl, but she is averse to his attentions, he secures a preparation containing the heart of a male rock-pigeon and applies this to her person or mixes it with her food. "In consequence she gets violent fits of hysteria, and it is supposed that she only recovers in the presence of her lover, to whom she will fly, if possible. While in this hysterical condition the girl emits a sound like the call of the rock pigeon—'vu, vu, vu, vu,'—which is often continued for hours. Whatever truth may be attached to the charm, the girl certainly becomes exceedingly excited, bites and scratches anyone who attempts to hold her, and is deaf to all reasoning."[5] Kaffir magicians manufacture fame-philtres, and "fools who wish to become renowned buy these philtres from them and have to slaughter an animal into the bargain."[6] The Mkamba has a "medicine" which he puts in a powder in the palm of his hand and blows in the direction of the intended victim; it is essential that the wind be blowing that way. "This medicine is so powerful that it will kill a person at a distance of a mile or two. A milder form of this kind of medicine is undoubtedly used by thieves who rob huts at night; they blow it in the direction of the inmates of the hut and they become stupified and the thief steals with impunity." A chief told the author that he had been recently robbed in this way; he and his wife saw the thief enter the hut but were unable to move or call out.[7] A form of witchcraft employed in East Africa is the secret deposit of the dead body of a domestic rat in the doorway of a hut; the occupants will then fall sick and may even die; pregnant women will abort. "If the body of a rat be discovered in this position and the owner of the hut has reason to suspect witchcraft, he consults a medicine man, who directs him to kill a red or white cock and to pour the blood on the spot, where the rat was found. Before killing it, the owner of the hut takes the fowl by the leg and brushes each member of the family with it on the chest. If this ceremony be performed unnecessarily, that is to say without consulting the witch-doctor, the people themselves will fall sick, and will not recover without his assistance."[8] One should not "doctor" himself, but should always consult a specialist. Other tribesmen too, when wishing to kill an enemy secretly, bury a dead rat or chicken at the victim's door. "If, when the latter comes out the next morning, he treads on the spot where the animal is buried, it is believed that he will die that day."[9] Burglary is rife in Hausaland, for all the hazards have been removed from the profession. "A charm made from

3 Rivers, *Melan. Soc.*, I, 159.
4 Lloyd, *Dwarf Land*, 349.
5 Garbutt, in JAI, XXXIX, 534.
6 Kropf, *Kaffir-Eng. Dict.*, 86.

7 Hobley, *A-Kamba*, 95.
8 Dundas, K., in JAI, XLIII, 44.
9 Northcote, in JAI, XXXVII, 63.

the ashes of a black cat will enable a burglar to open walls, render himself invisible, and paralyse anyone attempting to interfere with him." A medicine particularly valuable to warriors has the following ingredients: the flesh of an albino, the hearts of a lion, a leopard, and a ram which bleated when the men came to the flock, and as many flies as settled upon any of the meat during the preparation. "This mixture was given to war-horses also, and they would then smell out enemies, however well they were concealed, and would carry their masters to them. . . . The flesh of an albino would be available only for officers of the army, so the rank and file had to content themselves with something more easily obtainable." It is related of a native chief who was fighting against the French some years ago, that several bullets hit him, but rebounded and fell to the ground. "Only a silver bullet could have wounded him, for the Sariki had procured every medicine possible, including the head and skin of a lizard made into an amulet."[10]

Survivals of African beliefs and practices may be found among the negroes of the New World, especially in the activities of the "voodoo doctor" or "conjur' man." The physical sufferings of negroes who have been "conjured" are often, no doubt, real, as voodoo art includes skill in the preparation of poisons. "Arsenic mixed with the food of an intended victim accounts for the potency of many a charm, and the patch of weeds at every cabin door contains materials from which the experienced 'conjur' man' knows how to prepare poisons unfamiliar to the analytical chemist. Among the most dangerous articles sold by the voodoo man is the mixture of ground glass with water. This is known as 'obi water.' A vial of it put under a man's doorstep brings him the worst possible luck. A white cock's head found lying at your threshold with the beak pointing to the door is bad enough, but this is worse. It may be given a practical use. In small doses obi water produces a sort of dysentery, and if the doses are repeated a miserable death, after protracted suffering, is sure to follow. The jealous lover, or the man anxious to be rid of a neighborhood bully, does not, however, at present often obtain such effective charms. The vendor, not caring to get within the clutches of the law, lets his customer have instead a vial filled with live lizards, spiders, or tree frogs. A half-dollar more will buy a white cock's head, or an acorn hollowed out to inclose a bit of your enemy's hair and pierced in four places for the insertion of white chicken feathers. Add to this last device a bit of scarlet worsted, and no mortal but its possessor and his friends can come near it and live. The dealer in these noxious articles incurs very little risk, being secured from the danger of exposure by the prevailing belief among the negroes that to betray the voodoo, or hoodoo, man would cause one's fingers and toes to drop off."[11]

Among the Saoras of Madras, if a tiger or panther kills a person, the shaman is called, who on the following Sunday goes through a performance to prevent a similar fate overtaking others. Two pigs are killed outside the village and every man, woman and child is made to walk over the ground whereon was spilled the pig's blood. At the same time he gives to each individual some kind of "tiger medicine" as a charm against death by tigers.[12] How the extraordinary or inexplicable is related to magic through fetishism is seen in the Malay Peninsula in the case of a medicine made from a stump which was

10 Tremearne, in JAI, XLV, 48, 52, 171.   Times, Nov., 1894; Clark, in AA, XIV, 572-
11 "Old Southern Voodooism," in N. Y.   574; Puckett, Folk Beliefs, chs. III, IV.
                                     12 Fawcett, in JASB, I, 260.

"pinched in," that is, irregular, "a sure sign . . . of the late presence of the demon of which it had been the embodiment.[13]

Sometimes the Indian medicine-man draws animal-forms upon sandy earth or a bed of ashes. "For this purpose he uses a sharply pointed piece of wood, thrusts it into the region of the heart, and afterwards sprinkles upon this a small quantity of powder consisting of magic plants and vermilion." This is a part of the preparation of the hunters' "medicine" by a first-degree shaman.[14] "Many Winnebago are blind, because there is a medicine that causes blindness. If one person offends another who possesses such a medicine, the latter would cause the offender to become blind."[15] All of the sacred bundles of the Menomini contain the skins of the sacred birds of war and of snakes and weasels. In some, buffalo-tails may be found, for according to their traditions the bison was among the animals which agreed to help mankind. "Other invariable features are the reed whistles for signaling of the braves, deer-hoof rattles for accompanying the sacred songs, and paint given by the Thunderers to cure the wounded. The rest of the contents of the bundles varies in accordance with the instructions given in the dream of the owner. One may contain small medicine war-clubs, charms for the warriors to carry into battle; another a quill-worked bow, a scabbard, or some other valued trinket." The medicine-bundles are to be divided into four groups: those for war, for hunting, the witch-bundle, and that for good luck. They may also be classified into public and private medicines. The bundles of the Menomini differ from those of several other tribes in this, that in being transferred from one person to another, their full power is not preserved.[16] The Lenape warriors have "brave medicine," supposed to protect them from injury, if they follow the regulations.[17]

In Mexico, under the influence of "the divine remedy," an ointment made of insects burned in a basin and rubbed with other living insects, green tobacco leaves, and the powerful seeds of a local plant, "they conversed with the Devil and he with them, practicing his deceptions upon them."[18] Arawak, Warrau, Akawai, and Carib women all have their own binas or charms for managing the opposite sex. "The Arawak young woman plants her hiaro(girl)-bina usually in some secluded spot known only to herself; she will bathe with a leaf of it, or carry it about with her, and, provided the opportunity offers, without her being seen, may rub it over her lover's hammock, or she may rub her own hands with it, and then touch his. In any case, the man must be ignorant of what is going on, and, provided the procedure is strictly carried out as described, he will never have any desire to transfer his affections elsewhere. . . . The male Arawak has a corresponding belief as to the wajili(man)-bina, the leaf of which he generally carries about with the object of brushing over his girl's face or shoulders: he is very intent on going through this performance when he notices that she has a weakness for other men." Among these people, when the husband is very jealous and ill-tempered, his wife will cut off the head of a small lizard, burn it, and put the ashes into the water which she gives him to drink; "any man or woman can then make the husband do whatever he or she likes." When one woman wants another's husband, she will manage to

---

13 Skeat and Blagden, *Malay Penin.*, II, 230.
14 Hoffman, in BAE, VII, 222.
15 Radin, in BAE, XXXVII, 263.
16 Skinner, in AA, XIII, 304; de Josselin de Jong, in AA, XVIII, 125-126.
17 Harrington, in AA, XV, 216.
18 Brinton, *Nagualism*, 8.

put wasp-eggs into his drink, which will make him leave his wife and go off with her.[19]

Among the Semites, "the more notable unclean animals possess magical powers." The swine, for example, which the Saracens as well as the Hebrews and Syrians refused to eat, "supplies many charms and magical medicines."[20] The unclean or holy thing is dangerous to men because they are not on a plane with it. The magic powders and salves used in antiquity and later ages run all the way from Circe's herb, "moly," through the unguents of the Thessalian witches on down to the "philtres, charms, and ligatures for exciting desire or preventing its fruition, or for arousing hatred, which meet us at every step in modern sorcery."[21] The Telchines were the typical magicians of antiquity; it is said that one of their magic arts was to "besprinkle animals and plants with the water of Styx and sulphur mixed with it, with a view to destroy them."[22] Heathendom "seems to have practiced all sorts of magic by cutting off horses' heads and sticking them up"; Scandinavians, Germans, and Hollanders did this, and "a fox's head was nailed to the stable door, in some parts of Scotland, to bar the entrance of witches." In Scotland it was accounted unlucky to get possession of a clean house, for if a person wanted to harm his successor, he swept it clean on leaving. There were several pieces of magic which he could do in addition to bring discomfiture; but the suspicious newcomer could throw a cat into the house first, as a test; and if evil had been left behind the cat would sicken and die.[23] Among the southern Slavs, "in the burned-out coals, according to popular belief, there is still hidden a sure trace of the tree-soul, and therefore they can with profit use coals for various magical procedures, especially for healing and for divining the future."[24]

It was a German belief in the Middle Ages that a kiss was effective in winning love if one concealed a magic herb in his mouth.[25]

Miscellaneous Instruments. The pointing-stick is a common means of magic in Central Australia. "When a man wishes to use one of these he retires with it to a secluded spot in the bush, and, crouching down, mutters some such incantation over it as the following:—'May your heart be rent asunder, may your backbone be split open, may your ribs be torn asunder, and your head and throat be split open.' This is supposed to endow it with evil magic. The stick is then left for three or four days in the secret spot, and then brought near to the camp; finally, choosing his time, he steals out into the darkness beyond the area which is lighted by the camp fire, and turning his back upon his victim, jerks the stick in the direction of the latter, repeating each time the curses. This over, he conceals the instrument, and within a short time the man begins to sicken, and will surely die unless saved by the skill of a medicine man." In another form there are a number of small pointing-sticks attached to a strand of fur-string, at the opposite end of which are one or two eaglehawk-claws. After the usual pointing, jerking, and muttering of curses have been gone through, the man pinches up in front of him a little ridge of earth; "if this were not done, the victim would probably dream of the place

19 Roth, in BAE, XXX, 285, 288.
20 Smith, *Relig. Sem.*, 449; Preuss, in *Globus*, LXXXVI, 361.
21 *Odyssey*, X, 210 ff., 512 ff.; XI, 23 ff.; Keller, *Hom. Soc.*, 172-175; Lea, *Inquisition*, III, 391; White, *Sci. and Theol.*, I, 30.

22 Harrison, *Greek Relig.*, 171-172.
23 Gomme, *Ethnol. in Folklore*, 35; Gomme, *Village Life*, 66.
24 Krauss, *Südslaven*, 54.
25 Weinhold, *Deut. Frauen*, I, 237, note.

at which the operator's mother camped in the Alcheringa, and would then know at once who his enemy was. The eaglehawk-claws are supposed to grip the internal organs of the victim, and to cause great pain." Another instrument of magic is connected wth the legend of a man who, like Job, was afflicted with boils. "When he could bear them no longer he plucked them out, and threw them from him, each one turning into a stone, in evidence of which the stones may be seen at the present day by anyone who visits a sacred spot called Undiara." They are called the "stone boils." If a man desires to afflict anyone with boils, "he makes some small toy spears, and throws them at these stones, which part with some of their virtue to the spears, the latter in consequence becoming, as it were, charged with evil magic. The spears are then thrown one by one in the direction of the man whom it is desired to injure."[26]

The Papuans believe that eclipses of the sun and moon are caused by women with secret powers who throw spears made out of the small ribs of the coconut leaf through the interstices of the houses.[27] In New Britain there is a cheap and easy method of carrying on burglary: the offender provides himself with certain bones which he places on the chests of the inmates of a house when asleep; "they are supposed to keep them asleep while the thief takes possession of the household goods."[28] On special occasions the priest of the temple in Fiji would take a sacred axe and rub it with certain leaves to "make it kill."[29] Many taboos surround the South Sea Islander who undertakes to make a magic drum, which is used to conquer the heart of a maiden; unless they are strictly observed, the instrument will be ineffective.[30]

Some wizards in Africa use a wooden whistle.[31] On going out in the morning each man of a tribe in Mashonaland takes from one pile of stones a stone with which he scratches a line in the rock; he then throws it to another pile on the opposite side of the path. On his return at night he reverses the operation. They say that it is for luck.[32] There is magic connected with the fetish-image into which nails are driven, a West African practice. "As long as the nail remains in the figure, the man believes that breaking the law gives the fetish the power to kill him, and he therefore behaves himself on pain of death." This is an effective device in regulating the habits of the natives.[33] The negroes of the coast could not understand the European eagerness for ivory. Why build ships and go to all the trouble to get ivory for knife-handles, combs, and other things, when wood is equally useful? They were convinced that ivory was used in magic or other secret processes which were concealed from them lest the price should go way up.[34] Arab women think that the French government makes gold at will. It produces the gold, extracting it from nothing thanks to certain magic receipts, and then profusely distributes it among its officials, without counting.[35]

"Face-throwing" is a peculiar magical procedure observed in the region back of Sierra Leone, Liberia, and the Ivory Coast. Wishing to kill you without showing blood, an enemy throws his face on you. "You hardly know anything is wrong at first; by-and-by you notice that every scene that you look on, night and day, has got that face in it, not a filmy vision of a thing, but quite material in appearance, only it is in abnormal places for a face to be, and it

26 Gillen, in AAAS, 1901, 113, 114.
27 Bromilow, in AAAS, 1911, 419.
28 Danks, in AAAS, 1909, 456.
29 Webb, in AAAS, 1890, 624.
30 Hardy and Elkington, S. Seas, 39-40.

31 Stuhlmann, Mit Emin, 533.
32 Bent, Mashonaland, 83.
33 Phillips, in JAI, XVII, 228.
34 Mungo Park, Travels, 456-457.
35 Pommerol, Sahariennes, 399.

is a face only. . . . . This sort of thing tells on the toughest in time, and you get sick of life when it has always that face mixed up in it, so sick that you try the other thing—death. This is an ill-advised course, but you do not know in time that, when you kill yourself, you will find that on the other side, in the other thing, you will see nothing but that face, that unchanging silent face you are so sick of. The Kufong man who has thrown his face at you knows, and when he hears of your suicide he laughs."[36] Hearn,[37] in recounting an old Japanese story, cites a somewhat similar case. About two hundred twenty years ago while a lord had halted his train at a tea-house, the lord's attendant—Sekinai—found in the cup of tea he was drinking the face of a samurai. He filled another cup and the face re-appeared in that one. He ordered fresh tea only to find that the same face was present, but it now wore a mocking smile. Sekinai did not allow himself to be frightened. "Whoever you are," he muttered, "you shall delude me no further!"—then he swallowed the tea, face and all, and went his way, wondering whether he had swallowed a ghost. That same evening the samurai, whose face had been in the tea, appeared in person to Sekinai. He made a fierce thrust with his sword at the samurai's throat, but the latter noiselessly leaped sideward to the chamber-wall, and *through it!* The wall showed no trace of his exit.

The "pitar" or "tänk," in India, is connected with the dead. A piece of metal is put under the head of a dying person, and as soon as he dies is taken to a smith and stamped with a human figure. The pitars of the good, learned, or renowned can kill a man instantly. To kill with a pitar it is laid, face upwards, on the ground and struck three times with heel of a used shoe, and is ordered to kill such-and-such a person within so many days. The spirit becomes enraged at the beating it gets and carries out the order. "I will lay low your *pitar* in the dust" is a phrase reflecting the firm Hindu belief; it means that by counter-charms the soul of the relative represented by the pitar "will be imprisoned in the earth, and thus prevented from entering the abode of the blessed."[38] A metal amulet in use among the Palaungs may have a love-charm on one side and a charm to bewitch, for evil, on the other. "The lover must be careful to see that the love-charm lies uppermost; if the other side were uppermost, there might be disastrous consequences. In the same way, if any one wished to use a charm against an enemy, and the love-side of the charm remained uppermost by mistake, it might cause strange and unexpected complications."[39]

Sendings or "pointing" are common magical methods in the Malay Peninsula. A bamboo slip or sliver, laid on the right palm and commanded to go and kill the victim, is thought to fly through the air and pierce his heart. Wax, especially from an abandoned bees' nest, may be thrown in the same way by the magician.[40] A Filipino sorcerer, known as the "Pope," used wooden stamps in his "anting-anting." He was killed when the American troops destroyed a camp at which he was staying. His demise practically marked the end of pulahanism on Leyte, for a few days later the native leader and his followers surrendered. When questioned as to why he had come in, the Commandánte of Pulajanes replied that if the "Pope's" anting-anting would not protect the

---

36 Kingsley, *W. Afr. Studies*, 166.
37 Hearn, *Kottō*, 12-15.
38 Raghunathjee, in JASB, I, 353.

39 Milne, *Eastern Clan*, 109.
40 Skeat and Blagden, *Malay Penin.*, II, 233, 327.

"Pope" himself he was quite sure that they would not protect anyone else, so he thought it was about time he came in and surrendered.[41]

Two examples from the New World illustrate the tendency to ascribe to magic the inexplicable products and processes of civilization. To the Eskimo, MacMillan and his company, their ship and apparatus, were as much of a curiosity as the circus is to a small boy. "We showed them moving pictures on a screen and by means of the radio conjured voices and music from the air. To them it was pure magic, and the word went far and wide and they came with their dog sleds for a hundred miles and more, over the ice and snow, to see these strange and, to them, unbelievable wonders."[42] A member of an expedition to the Amazon basin gained the respect of the Indians by working magic. He put a pocket flashlight into his mouth, illuminating it suddenly; this was set down as a miracle. The Indians called it "cold magic" because the flashlight did not burn them when applied to their bodies. A small magnifying glass was another wonder-worker. With this he lit a pipe. When he focused the lens on a native's arm the latter would jump and howl. This was "hot magic."[43]

Magic and tokens have their votaries yet. According to a communication from Thuringia, one of the ways of baffling the binsenschneider (reaper) is as follows: on Trinity Sunday or St. John's day, when the sun is highest in the sky, go and sit on an elderbush with a looking-glass on your breast, and look round in every quarter; then no doubt you can detect the binsenschneider, but not without great risk, for if he spies you before you see him, you must die and the binsenschneider remain alive, unless he happen to catch sight of himself in the mirror on your breast, in which case he also loses his life that year. It is a modern superstition that he who looks in the mirror at night, sees the devil there.[44] During the World War there were found in possession of German prisoners numerous charms against "iron or steel, brass or lead, ore or wood"; but, evidently, not against being made prisoner of war. Many of these were ancient, havng been handed down for generations among the German peasantry.[45] The Little Russians are said to dislike kerosene, holding that when people were good that fluid did not come out on the earth; presently it will cover the whole world and judgment will ensue.[46] The following two cases are press-reports. An old woman was banished from a county in Virginia because she was believed to have killed the mules of her enemies with a magic wand. The "wand" was but a cane which she used to support her aged body, but to the negroes it was the staff of a sorceress.[47] Not long ago a woman went to the old cemetery in France, to tend her relatives' graves. She noticed that the statue of the Virgin on a mausoleum was covered with moss, which she cleaned away with her handkerchief. On returning home, according to the reports, she touched her little paralytic daughter with the handkerchief, and the girl was completely cured. Thereafter large numbers of pilgrims went every day to the tomb.[48]

Incantation. A Papuan must be very wise in counter-charming if he is to dare

41 Communicated by W. H. Taylor, Manila, P. I., April 14, 1907.
42 N. Y. *Times*, Sept. 24, 1924.
43 Stark, in N. Y. *Times*, Sept. 3, 1922.
44 Stallybrass, *Grimm's Teut. Myth.*, II, 476, 781.

45 Tremearne, citing press-report, in JAI, XLV, 42, note; §276, of text and *Case-Book*.
46 *Russ. Ethnog.* (Russ.), I, 52.
47 N. Y. *Times*, Mar. 6, 1924.
48 New Haven *Journal-Courier*, Jan. 20, 1913.

to walk alone. In fact, he must be able by incantations to do one of the following: charm his own body so that it becomes invisible; charm a tree so that it will split open and take him in until the wizard has passed; change himself into a bird, so that he may fly above the wizard's head, or into a snake, so that he may crawl through the bush.[49] The backbone of Kiriwinian magic is formed by its spells. "It is in the spell that the main virtue of all magic resides. The rite is there only to launch the spell, to serve as an appropriate mechanism of transmission. This is the universal view of all Kiriwinians, of the competent as well as of the profane, and a minute study of the magical ritual well confirms this view." In their formulas frequent mention is made of the ancestral names, which serve in a way as an invocation. "All such formulæ were hereditary in the female line."[50] Among some East African tribes only the males have magical powers. They can bewitch an enemy by blowing in a horn and saying: "I blow this horn and your heart will become like the wind I blow through this horn," meaning it will disappear and be lost. Another method is to place some eggs and leaves on a fire and say, "As these eggs burst and as these leaves shrivel up so shall this village be destroyed." Here we trench upon imitative magic. Certain men are believed to have the power of bewitching unknown thieves, and "it occasionally happens that a person who has had, say, some goats or some sugar cane stolen, will call in a Mweithaga and ask him to throw a spell on the thief."[51] Among the modern Egyptians the most approved mode of charming away sickness or disease is to write certain passages of the Koran on the inner surface of an earthenware cup or bowl, pour in some water, and stir until the writing is quite washed off. The water, with the sacred words thus infused in it, is to be drunk by the patient.[52] One sura in the Koran presents a special prayer against the "knot-blowers," that is, a kind of sorcerers who operate by tying a knot and then blowing it.[53]

No wonder the mystic formula in Lamaism, the *Om mani padme hum,* is so popular and constantly repeated by both Lamas and laity, for "its mere utterance is believed to stop the cycle of re-births and to convey the reciter directly to paradise."[54] The rosary, which is peculiar to the northern school of Buddhists, is "the outcome of the esoteric teachings of the Mahayana school, instilling belief in the potency of muttering mystic spells and other strange formulas."[55] Evidence is given in their formulas of the close relation between magic and religion among the Todas. "The formulæ of magic and of the dairy ritual are of the same nature, though the differentiation between the sorcerer and the priest who use them is even clearer than that between the sorcerer and the medicine-man."[56] By chanting formulas the Nairs believe that one becomes possessed of magical power. Persons who have devoted themselves to such practices are looked upon with great fear.[57] A typical example of the charms mentioned in an ancient Vedic collection may be seen in this one used in a woman's rite for obtaining a husband: "The creator (maker) sustains the earth, the sky, and the sun; may the maker make for (give to) this spinster a husband that is according to her wish." Or, in a charm for healing: "The berry and remedy, sufficient for life, the gods prepared." Again, against in-

---

49 Bromilow, in AAAS, 1911, 418.
50 Malinowski, in JAI, XLVI, 388-390.
51 Hobley, in JAI, XLI, 435-436.
52 Lane, *Mod. Egyptians,* I, 387.
53 Ratzel, *Vkde.,* III, 119.

54 Waddell, *Tibet,* 148-149.
55 Rockhill, in USNM, 1893, 736.
56 Rivers, *Todas,* 272, 273.
57 Panikkar, in JAI, XLVIII, 282.

sanity: "May all the gods give thee again, that thou mayest be uncrazed."[58]
Yantras are written charms among the Sinhalese, often astrological in character, which are used for protection, for curing, or for causing injury. They are usually engraved upon sheets of metal or upon ola leaves, although they are occasionally written upon paper. "Paper is, however, considered to be very unsuitable for the purpose, since if it becomes torn or otherwise injured, as may easily happen, the efficacy of the yantra may be changed or cancelled by the complete destruction or the changing of the form of some of its component characters. . . . Yantras are usually for the purpose of correcting unpropitious or harmful planetary influences causing misfortune or sickness."[59] Unlike the evil eye and the evil touch, the evil sound or *mantram* may be aimed at the intended victim from any distance in space and without the least chance of detection. "It is called the *bān* or arrow-shot of the witch and the sorcerer. The Orāons believe that with the help of a powerful *mantram,* a magician is even able to extract unperceived the liver of an intended victim, wherever the victim may be." The liver, be it noted, is regarded as the seat of the vital principle, so such extraction would be fatal; but this may be offset by the counter-spells of another magician who is called in to aid.[60] Throughout India the mantras or formulas are recited, chanted, or sung in a set fashion in order to obtain certain physical or psychical effects. By such means one exorcises, recovers weapons, causes it to rain or stop raining, cures or causes disease, makes flocks prosper, aids or prevents conception, or calls gods and demons. Often the sound alone is efficacious, all knowledge of the sense of the formula having long ago disappeared. "When misfortune or disease arrives it is invariably ascribed to the malignant action of a devil." In the *Mahabharata* the spell brings the god at once to the presence of the one exercising it; the magic is stronger than Indra.[61] Among the Palaungs, each time the incantation is repeated the wise man blows over the pots containing wax. This blowing is always done when any charm is said; during massage to ease pain, for instance, the masseuse constantly blows.[62] The soul, we know, is commonly associated with the breath.[63]

The Veddahs, getting lonely on the cliffs, sing in lively fashion songs which will soften the spirit of the rock and prevent him from casting the hunter off his ladder. It is with songs that they prepare themselves for their labors on the cliffs, so as to get into the state of excitement necessary to carry the task through.[64] This case looks at first like propitiation rather than coercion and it seems to be in part, like the war-dance, for the purpose of working up courage. All these forms and motives run one into the other and become intertwined.

By formulas "one gets power, not only over spirits but over persons; by them, in general, one gets all he wants. Batak formulas are composed of old or wholly senseless words—by which they get the greater power; they are effective against illness, to win a wife, to catch a runaway wife, to win in trade, to make a load light.[65] It is believed in all simplicity, by northern Sumatrans, that one person can be brought to love another "to his marrow

58 Whitney, *Atharva-Veda Samhita*, rev. in the *Nation*, LXXXII, 228.
59 Hildburgh, in JAI, XXXVIII, 203.
60 Roy, in JAI, XLIV, 341-342.
61 Hopkins, *Relig. Ind.*, 351-352, 374; Chamberlain, in AA, IV, 339.
62 Milne, *Eastern Clan*, 111.
63 §§210, 213, of text and *Case-Book*.
64 Sarasin, *Weddas*, 445.
65 Wilken, *Vkde.*, 581-583.

and kidneys," if the proper formulas are pronounced under the necessary precautions. If delivery in childbirth is delayed, they hurriedly consult a person
who has the name of making good incantations. He writes one out proper
for the occasion, washes what he has written with water and has the woman
in parturition drink the water; or he simply recites the formula, "with a loud
voice and much puffing, above a bowl of water, whereupon the woman, again,
must drink the water."[66]

On one of the Pacific Islands there is a house-incantation against mishap,
which is recited on entering one's house. It is a family secret; and the correct
recital of it by children has enabled their father, from whom they had been
separated, to recognize them.[67] The heathen Maori never undertook any work
or started on any journey without first uttering a spell for success or safety.
They "have spells suited for all circumstances—to conquer enemies, catch rats,
snare birds, and even to bind the obstinate will of woman, to find anything lost,
to discover a stray dog, a concealed enemy, in fact, for all their wants."[68]
Again, "a girl who did not respond to her lover's advances could be bewitched,
driven mad, and killed. The usual way of obtaining power over another was to
obtain (European fashion) some of the nail-parings, hair, etc., anything of a
personal nature, to act as a medium between the bewitched person and the
demon. Spells would be muttered over these relics, then they were buried, and
as they decayed the victim perished."[69]

One of the traditions of the Indians in Arizona is to the effect that So-and-so
came and witnessed the women dancing; he shook his rattle and sang a magic
song, which enticed them to follow him to another dance-place. A rival also
sang such a song, but found it powerless to prevent the departure of the
women; they were so bewitched by the first song that they could not or would
not obey him.[70]

The incantations of the civilized peoples of antiquity sought to mitigate
the influence of evil spirits in general. "All formulas are composed of a description of the bad spirit in question and a drastic sketch of his baseness;
thereafter follows last of all a calling on the high gods to display their help
against the daimons."[71] The sacred books of the magicians, which Assurbanipal
caused to be recopied in the seventh century B.C., for the instruction of his
priests, were written in the Accadian; a Semitic Assyrian version had been
added to them at a very early epoch, in order to render the incantations intelligible to those who had to recite them, but the Accadian was clearly the
only properly liturgical text, as is proved by the fact that some lines which are
repeated or are very easy to understand, have no translation attached to them.
Thus at the present day the Coptic priests always have an Arabic version
accompanying their missals, so that they may understand the words of the
ritual while they recite them in the Coptic tongue. The Accadian formulas
banished the demons which they had expelled from a man's body to the sandy
desert; the Finnish *runa* sends the plague away to Lapland. Such are the different forms we should expect the same idea to take with two nations placed
in such diverse geographical conditions.[72] The library of Assurbanipal consisted for the most part of treatises written by the most celebrated adepts of
the sciences for which Chaldæa was renowned—collections of celestial and

66 Jacobs, *Groot-Atjeh*, I, 31, 122.
67 Gill, in AAAS, 1892, 605, 607.
68 Taylor, *Te Ika*, 180, 181.
69 Tregear, in JAI, XIX, 116, 117.

70 Fewkes, in BAE, XXVIII, 45-46.
71 Lehmann, *Overtro*, I, 44, 84.
72 Lenormant, *Chaldean Magic*, 261, 264.

terrestrial omens, where the mystic sense of each phenomenon and its influence on human destiny were explained; conjurations to pronounce against demons, phantoms, and vampires, the causes of all malady; prayers and psalms which one should recite to wring from the gods pardon for one's sins; and chronicles of the gods and kings.[73] In Egypt from an early date there were engraved on the sarcophagus holy texts through whose magic power were secured mystical union with the deity and thereby victory over all the monsters of the other world. During later dynasties magical papyri abounded with all sorts of prescriptions for warding off evil and danger, rapacious animals and fantastic monsters, sickness and plague. As one of the surest preventatives were certain barbaric words, which were regarded as the more effective the more impossible it was to read any logical sense into them. Also hymns, which were not lacking in religious sublimity and had not been composed for such purpose, were used to exorcise evil spirits and other harmful creatures. Magic knew no boundaries, and views of nature and of man were purely daimonistic.[74] The most sacred formula of the Parsis, when recited without mistake, is equal to a hundred of the other principal stanzas; if with mistakes, to ten. Whoever shall recall one part of it, or "in the course of recalling shall mutter it, or in the course of muttering shall chant it, or in the course of chanting prays to it, his soul will I, who am Ahuramazda, carry all three times over the bridge to paradise." So clear-cut is the fetishistic concept of the word, that sacred verses or hymns were prayed to, as beings. Another effectual spell to guard against the influences of evil spirits is to utter the different names of the chief deity.[75] A Jewish soldier in the World War ascribed his immunity from wounds to bands on his head and hands inscribed with the Hebrew commandments.[76]

§302. Imitative Magic.

In most of the performances in Central Australia for the increase of the totemic plant or animal, decorated men imitate the actions of the animal whose totem they bear; the acting is described as wonderful. In one scene, a number of men, equipped with long tails made of grass, "put themselves in motion as a herd of kangaroos, now jumping along, then lying down and scratching themselves, as those animals do when basking in the sun. One man beat time to them with a club on a shield, while two others, armed, pretended to steal upon and spear them."[1]

In New Guinea the magical idea seems to be, at basis, that success may be obtained by imitating the desired result, e.g., "burying a stone to represent a potato when potatoes are desired; or by verbally in some way stating the desired result, as by proclaiming over a hunting area that it is the home or village of kangaroos, so that many kangaroos may be found when it is hunted over. Likewise giving a spear a 'thorny name' makes it pierce well, or coating it with red makes it draw red blood easily." Rain-makers exist both on the south and northeast coast; they are blamed when rain does not come. "In one such case a rain-maker was arrested and brought to me. His account was that after a long period of drought a cloud appeared which looked like rain. He stood forth on a hill, the centre of an admiring crowd, and did his best by

73 Maspero, *Hist. Anc.*, III, 462.
74 Tiele-Gehrich, *Gchte. Relig.*, I, 58, 93-94.
75 Haug, *Parsis*, 181, 185-186, 195.

76 Tremearne, quoting a press-notice, in JAI, XLV, 42, note.
1 Spencer and Gillen, *No. Tr. Cent. Aust.*, 224; Anon., in JAI, XXVII, 134.

making a fine spray of saliva come from his mouth on the usual principle of imitating an effect desired. However, his account was that he had done his best, but that the south-east wind proved too strong for him and blew the cloud away." A further illustration of their beliefs is furnished in the case of the native who was suffering from an obstinate ulcer on his arm. "Whenever the ulcer tended to get worse he would come and try to persuade me to arrest the suspected hostile magician. His view of the matter was that when the magician wanted to make the ulcer worse he hung the bamboo containing the article of intimate contact with the 'medicine' close to the household fire, and that the ulcer would only heal up if the magician was made to throw the mixture away into a stream of water. His idea clearly was that as the mixture became hot so would the ulcer become hot, inflamed, and get worse. I have noticed signs of a very similar belief on the south coast, including the inhibitory action of water."[2]

The Papuans attach great importance to preparing the young men before a fight, particularly if they have not killed anyone before, and for this purpose they are given various "medicines." The ingredients of one of these consisted of small bits of the eye, talons, beak, and tongue of a large hawk. "The eyes help the men to find the enemy, the pieces of the talons and beak to catch him, whereas the tongue of any animal, when it hangs out, represents the fury of fighting; therefore a piece of the tongue of a dog too is used for a medicine of war. Sometimes when an enemy is killed the natives cut off a piece of the skin above one eye and let the young men swallow a fragment of it, the explanation being that a man's brow is the foremost part of his body when he rushes at an enemy, and therefore in a way symbolizes fighting."[3] While the warriors were away the women would not sweep the villages and the children were not allowed to make a noise.[4] Before proceeding to battle in the Loyalty Islands, "a warrior placed water in the hollow part of a piece of coral, and drank from it, in order to make his heart hard like the rock. A woman whose husband or son was absent in war would place a piece of coral, to represent the warrior, on a mat before her, and move it about with her right hand to represent his movements in the fight. Then with her left hand she would brush away imaginary obstacles and evils. The warrior was thus thought to be protected by the charm performed at home."[5] At the birth of a male child in New Caledonia, a priest cut the umbilicus on a particular stone, "that the youth might be *stone-hearted* in battle. The priest, too, at the moment of the operation, had a vessel of water before him, dyed black as ink, that the boy, when he grew up, might be courageous to go anywhere to battle on a pitch-dark night, and thus, from his very birth, the little fellow was consecrated to war."[6]

The sympathy which the Baganda believe exists between themselves and the plantain offers an illustration of "contagion." Plantains used as vegetables are regarded as female, and those used for making beer as male. "When children go through the ceremony of being named, the piece of umbilical cord, which has been preserved for this occasion, is put on a male tree if the child is a boy, and on a female tree if the child is a girl. A married woman who does not bear children is driven away by her husband because she will ruin his garden, and cause the plantains to cease to yield fruit. Again a woman who gives

2 Strong, in JAI, XLIX, 293-294, 296.
3 Landtmann, in JAI, XLVI, 324.
4 Bromilow, in AAAS, 1909, 478.

5 Ray, in JAI, XLVII, 294.
6 Turner, *Samoa*, 340-341.

birth to twins is a source of blessing to the whole community."[7] The sex-act is often supposed to bring good luck, by stimulating nature to procreation, and seems to be a sort of coercitive.[8] The Kitui even hold it to be necessary for the husband and wife to have connection when their hut is completed; "failure to observe this is followed with the direst misfortune in the way of sickness and death."[9] The Lango people employ sacred rain-spears in the ceremony of rain-making, which goes on the principle that like produces like. The performer dips the blade of the spear into a bowl and with it flicks the water first east and then west, while chanting a prayer. Finally he sprinkles the water, scooping it up with his hands and throwing it high, first east and then west. "The owner of the spear also, having spat into the water and uttered a prayer for fruitfulness and good rains, sprinkles the water. The spear is stuck into the ground, blade down, near the porch, and is not moved into the house till the harvest is ripe. . . . When the dance is over, the old men, one after the other, asperse the water, using for the purpose a plant of the thistle order. . . . Fresh, cold water is drawn from a neighbouring spring at a traditional spot and each old man drinks a little, while other water in which medicines prepared from the roots of certain trees have been mixed is thrown up into the air (not aspersed over the people), and an old man climbs the tree, sprinkling the medicated water on its leaves, praying the while for good rains and harvest. . . . Water is thrown up from the well-into the air both with the hands and with the thistle called *ekwanga,* while the old men pray, 'May rain fall as this water falls: may it fall on our grain and fructify it exceedingly, bringing joy and increase to our wives and children.' "[10] In Algiers, to make rain fall, "Arabs and Hausas pour water over each other's heads and clothes, and promenade with a spoon dressed as a doll, throwing water over it and each other; bathe in the sea; and turn their cloaks from left to right over their shoulders in the mosques on a Friday." Another kind of imitative magic is performed in lieu of a fugitive slave law. If a slave ran away, "the master would trace a certain design upon the ground and stick a nail in the centre to which was tied a scarabaeus. The insect would walk round and round, thus shortening his radius, and as it approached the nail, so would the fugitive be forced to come nearer and nearer to the house. . . . Sambo says that if the slave had urinated upon his hands and feet, he would have counteracted the effect of the charm—such an act also enables one to swear falsely."[11]

A notable instance of imitative magic in India is the Oräon ceremony of rain-making. "On their arrival at the sacred tree, all the women simultaneously pour the water in their pitchers over the foot of the tree, saying, 'May rain fall on earth like this.' The wife of the village-priest now puts marks of vermilion, diluted in oil, on the trunk of the tree. After this the women depart, and the *Pähän* or village-priest proceeds to sacrifice a red cock to the god Bärändä at the spot. It is firmly believed by the Oräons that within a day or two after this rain-making ceremony, rain is bound to fall. And in olden times, it is said, a heavy shower of rain would even overtake the women on their way home from the sacred tree. In this case, apparently, direct alliance, by sacrifice and by anointing the tree with vermilion, have been superimposed on what was once, perhaps, purely a ceremony of imitative magic." Another

7 Roscoe, in JAI, XXXII, 80.
8 §277, of text.
9 Dundas, C., in JAI, XLIII, 525.

10 Driberg, in JAI, XLIX, 53-72.
11 Tremearne, in JAI, XLV, 51, 56.

instance of the same sort for securing plenty of rain and crops is the custom of all the families in a village heaping rice on the sacred winnowing-basket which the Pāhān carries in procession, while he drops rice as he proceeds and his assistant drops water from his pitcher, all along the route. By a similar process the yoke of a plough and three bundles of straw, on which the bride and bridegroom are seated at the wedding-ceremony, are calculated to bring to the married pair prosperity in agriculture. "Another instance of imitative magic in connection with an Orāon marriage is the practice of keeping apart at the harvest preceding the marriage a few of the best sheaves of paddy, carefully selected by a young bachelor who must be ceremonially clean during the process. These selected sheaves of paddy are used in the benedictory ritual of the marriage, and are calculated to bless the newly-wedded pair with agricultural prosperity—with abundant sheaves of paddy as full and fine as those." The principle of imitative magic appears to be further illustrated by the practice of omen-reading or divination. "If an intentional imitation of some desired result produces that result by something like spiritual attraction, an unintentional and accidental imitation, real or fancied, of something fortunate or calamitous—of some human event, or physical phenomenon—may, it is believed, attract such thing, event, or phenomenon by a similar spiritual sympathy. Thus, during the ceremonial ablutions at the village spring or tank where all the Orāon villagers assemble for the purpose on the occasion of the *Sarhūl* festival, if the Pāhān or his assistant, the Pūjār, happen to touch any part of his body with the hand, it is apprehended that fleas and mosquitoes will prove particularly troublesome to the villagers that year. The cawing of crows is an evil sound which bodes misfortune through sympathetic attraction. So is the sight of a jackal crossing the path of an Orāon or a Mūndā on a journey. Anything abnormal is an evil power which sympathetically attracts some evil or misfortune. Thus, the birth of a child with one or more teeth portends the death of either of the parents in a short time. Orāons, it is said, generally put such a baby to death by secretly making it swallow a large quantity of salt. An Orāon girl whose canine teeth grow out of the line, finds it difficult to get a husband, for the girl is fated to be a widow within a short time of her marriage. If a present event or phenomenon attracts a like event or phenomenon in the near future by sympathy, conversely does a future event or phenomenon sometimes cast its shadow before it in the shape of an analogous event or phenomenon."[12] In Assam "it was usual to kill a fish and scatter the bits about, at the same time informing the deities that the fish were all dying, and that rain was necessary. A similar method of attracting the attention of the rain power is common in Manipur, where a solemn procession of boats, headed by the great racing boat of the Raja, is formed. The boats are dragged along the mud of the moat and the Raja asks for rain."[13]

The wife of the Kwakiutl who has gone on the hunt enters her house and sits down on the floor, keeping quiet and eating a little food, but never enough to be satiated. It is said that the animals hunted by the husband do the same way as she does. If the man goes out for otters or seal, his wife always lies down in her bed covered with a new mat. "The reason why the hunter's wife does this is that the sea-otter and the fur-seal may be asleep when they are hunted by the husband. . . . The land-hunter and the sea-hunter get their game easily if their wives sit at home well." The hunter always pushes his

12 Roy, in JAI, XLIV, 330-331, 331-332.   13 Hodson, in JAI, XXXVI, 96.

paddle right over the fire, because he wishes it to become very black; and also that no young woman, or one who is menstruating, and no young man may step over it, for they never do right. When a canoe-builder has chopped deep into a tree he takes four chips, which he throws behind the tree, saying: "O, supernatural one! now follow your supernatural power!" Throwing another chip, he says: "O, friend! now you see your leader, who says that you shall turn your head and fall there also." Then a third, saying, "O, life-giver! now you have seen which way your supernatural power went. Now go the same way." Taking the last one, he utters: "O, friend! now you will go where your heart-wood goes. You will lie on your face at the same place." Then he answers himself and says: "Yes, I shall fall with my top there." He takes his ax and chops again; but "it does not take long until the cedar-tree falls backward." Among the Tsimshians, "if many members of one family die in quick succession, the survivors lay their fourth fingers on the edge of the box in which the corpse is deposited, and cut off the first joint, 'to cut off the deaths.' "[14] If it was believed that a man had died in consequence of being bewitched, they would take his heart out and put a red-hot stone against it, wishing at the same time that the enemy might die. If the heart burst, they thought that their wish would be fulfilled; if not, their suspicions were believed to be unfounded.[15] Among the Lenape the child was taught how to blacken with charcoal the inside of each milk tooth as it came out, then throw it away to the east before sunrise in the morning, repeating: " 'Come back quick, I want to eat sweetbeans!' This was said to insure a quick growth of strong new teeth."[16] There are similar examples of imitative magic among the Bellacoola and other Indians of Canada.[17]

Among the Great Plains tribes imitative magic took the form of dancing and acting. Before starting out on the hunt, the Sioux performed the bear-dance, in which they all joined in a song to the Bear Spirit, who must be consulted before success could be assured. For the dance one of the chief medicine-men clothed himself in the skin of a bear, put a war-eagle's quill on his head, and took the lead in the pantomime, looking through the skin which formed a mask over his face. Many others wore masks made of skin from the bear's head on their faces, and all, by the motions of their hands, closely imitated a bear's movements, some representing its motion when running, and others its peculiar attitude when watching for the approach of an enemy. The Mandans, Pawnees, Hopi, and others danced to make buffalo come when they were likely to starve for want of food. There was a song to the Great Spirit, imploring him to send them buffalo. According to Catlin's[18] account, "Every man in the Mandan village is obliged by a village regulation to keep the mask of the buffalo hanging on a post at the head of his bed, which he can use on his head whenever he is called upon by the chiefs to dance for the coming of buffaloes. The mask is put over the head, and generally has a strip of the skin hanging to it, of the whole length of the animal, with the tail attached to it, which, passing down over the back of the dancer, is dragged on the ground. When one becomes fatigued of the exercise, he signifies it by bending

14 Boas, in BAE, XXXV, pt. I, 608, 617-618, 638; and in BAE, XXXI, 535.
15 Swanton, in HAI, II, 144-145.
16 Harrington, in AA, XV, 214.
17 HAI, II, 211; Smith, in AA, XXVII, 116 ff.

18 Donaldson, in Smithson. Rep., 1885, pt. II, 308, 309, 311, 316, 358 ff.; Parsons, in Man, Feb., 1923, 21-26; Grinnell, Folk Tales, 273.

quite forward, and sinking his body towards the ground; when another draws a bow upon him and hits him with a blunt arrow, and he falls like a buffalo— is seized by the bystanders, who drag him out of the ring by the heels, brandishing their knives about him; and having gone through the motions of skinning and cutting him up, they let him off, and his place is at once supplied by another, who dances into the ring with his mask on; and by this taking of places, the scene is easily kept up night and day, until the desired effect has been produced, that of 'making buffalo come.'" We have here a fine example of play-acting.[19]

When the time came for battle, the Cheyennes performed a ritual which had for its purpose the confusing and alarming of the enemy. The keeper of the medicine-arrows took in his mouth a bit of the root which is always tied up with them, chewed it fine, and then blew it from his mouth, first toward the four directions and finally toward the enemy. "The blowing toward the enemy was believed to make them blind. After he had done this he took the arrows in his hand and danced, pointing them toward the enemy and thrusting them forward in time to the dancing. He stood with the left foot in front, and with this he stamped in time to the song and the motions. Drawn up in line behind the arrow keeper were all the men of the tribe, standing with the left foot forward as he stood, dancing as he danced, and making with their lances, arrows, hatchets, or whatever weapons they might hold, the same motions that he made with the arrows. At each motion made by the arrow keeper, all the men who stood behind him gave the shout commonly uttered as they charged down on the enemy. The first motion of the arrows by the arrow keeper is directed toward the (collective) enemy's foot, the second toward his leg from ankle to thigh, the third against his heart, and the fourth against his head. . . . After the arrow keeper had pointed the arrows four times in the direction of the enemy, he thrust them the fifth time toward the ground."[20] Charcoal, the product of fire, is regarded by the Hopi fire-priests as possessing most powerful magic in healing diseases, especially those of the skin in which there is a burning sensation.[21] The Zuñi give to persons who have been struck or shocked by lightning the rain-water of that same storm to drink—a sort of inoculative magic—plus black beetle and suet; otherwise they will surely die. "About three years ago a house on the south bank of the river was struck and the three women inmates failed to observe the proper measure of safety. The following summer two of them died and the third died this year. Properly doctored survivors are qualified by their experience to become medicinemen or women."[22]

As soon as the new moon is visible, all the men among the Makusi stand before the doors of their huts and draw their arms backward and forward in its direction at short intervals; "by this means they are strengthened for the chase." They also take certain leaves, roll them in the shape of a small funnel, and pass some drops of water through it into the eye, while looking at the new moon; "this is very good for the sight." To point the finger at a fellow creature, among the Arawaks, is to offer him as serious an affront as it would be to step over him when lying on the ground; "in the latter case, the recumbent person would rightly say, 'You can cross me when I am dead. I am not dead yet!'" If the occupants of a Carib settlement wish to assure victory for their

19 §442, of text.
20 Grinnell, in AA, XII, 571-572.
21 Fewkes, in BAE, XXVIII, 47.
22 Parsons, in AA, XVIII, 249.

warriors on the march and to assure themselves at the same time of the issue of the battle, perhaps already fought, they place two boys on a bench and whip them without mercy, especially over the shoulders. "If the boys bear the pain without shedding a tear or uttering a groan, victory is certain. One of the boys is then placed in a hammock, from which he has to shoot at a target fixed to one of the roofs: as many arrows as hit the target, so many of the enemy will be killed by the warriors."[23] Imitative magic is here evidently combined with interrogation. About one o'clock in the night, when the new day is supposed to begin, the Jibaro warriors assemble in the house of the chief to perform a magical ceremony by which they believe themselves able to conjure forth victory over the enemy. This, which they continue until the break of day, is repeated every night during one week. Besides the war-dance, the Jibaros try to secure the same end through a kind of war-song, which is sung by the warriors before starting for the expedition. While the men are absent on the warpath it is customary for the women to assemble every night and perform a special dance with rattles around the waist, while chanting conjurations. This is supposed to have the power of protecting their relatives against the lances and bullets of the enemy. Imitative magic is also employed to produce increase. "When the flesh of the animals killed is cooked early in the morning, at the first beginning of the new day, this will have as its consequence that henceforward there will be plenty of swine's flesh in the house of the slayer. . . . The slaughter takes place outside the house, but the animals are not all killed on the same spot, but one here and another there, close to the different walls of the house. In this way the impression is produced that the swine killed and eaten at the feast are very numerous, and the effect of this will be that they will really be numerous in the future." According to their notions all plants are animated by human spirits, some of male sex, some of female. "The manioc, like most other domestic plants, has a woman's soul. Hence—according to the principle 'like is best known by like'—the women have to cultivate this plant just as, in regard to the preparation of the manioc beer, they are believed to have a special power of promoting that mysterious and, to the Indian mind, unintelligible process of nature which is called fermentation."[24]

Effigy. A special type of imitative magic consists in making an image or other representation and treating it in a special manner, in the belief that the person or thing for whom it stands will be affected accordingly. This has been called *envoûtement*. To punish a woman, in Central Australia, "a rough diagram is drawn on the ground, which is supposed to represent her body, and by the side of this a piece of bark is placed, which again represents her spirit. All the time the men who are present keep singing exhortations to the evil magic, with which their singing is endowing the bark to go straight and eat up all the woman's fat. Then all of them stick miniature spears into the bark, which is finally thrown in the direction in which the woman has gone. Nothing further happens for, perhaps, some time, until one night they see a shooting star, and know that that is the woman's spirit, and that she is dead. If she should turn up at a later period the explanation is a very simple one—there was some counter magic stronger than theirs, and what they saw was the spirit of some other woman."[25] Like many other religious beliefs, this is an argu-

23 Roth, in BAE, XXX, 257, 271-272.   25 Gillen, in AAAS, 1901, 123.
24 Karsten, "Jibaro," in BAE, Bull. LXXIX, 22, 24, 60 (quoted), 81 (quoted).

ment-proof theory. Sometimes, among the Bangala of the Upper Congo, "a piece of wood or plantain stalk was roughly carved to represent the enemy, and wherever it was stuck or cut the enemy would feel intense pain, and to stick it in a vital part meant death."[26] Models of enemies, made of a candle in North Africa, of beeswax in Nigeria, are at night and in secret placed in cooking-pots over a fire. "Hunters used to practise this rite to secure success over beasts. A frog is useful in this connection, for if its tongue be slit in the shadow of an enemy, whatever happens to the frog happens to the enemy."[27]

The Buryat woman, desiring children, will carry a child's swaddling clothes or a specially made doll, and pretend to feed it at her breast. Those present ask her sympathetically, "How is your child? Is he quiet? Have you much trouble with him?" "Then the guests take turns in nursing it, and if the woman should leave the hut, they will call to her to return because the child is crying."[28] In accordance with their desire to escape some of the expense, the Chinese for *envoûtement* make paper figures instead of wax.[29] Nearly every Kuki-Lushai clan, while denying that its members have any knowledge of witchcraft, is firmly persuaded that its neighbors practise the black arts. "There are several ways of bewitching your enemy. Colonel Lewin has a tale in which the wizard takes up the impression of a person's foot in the mud and puts it to dry over the hearth, thereby causing the owner to waste away. Clay figures, into which bamboo spikes are thrust, also figure in all cases in which a person is accused of this offence. To cut off a piece of a person's hair and put it in a spring, is certain, unless the hair is speedily removed, to cause his death."[30] The Palaungs make small figures of men and women to represent an enemy, and subject them to the injury they would inflict on that person. "The figures are made of earth, and as that in the Palaung hills is not very plastic, it is moistened and modelled on a piece of board in the manner of a rough bas-relief. . . . Incantations are said over these figures, and splinters of bamboo are stuck into them, or a hand or foot is cut off."[31]

The Zuñi make small clay figures of sheep, horses, donkeys, cows, chickens, of chili and melons, of bracelets, and of gold and silver coins, over which they perform certain rites for the increase of all the objects represented. There is also a rite for the increase of children or the development of an unborn child. During a dance a woman who has had miscarriages may be given a *wiha* or doll, which, after certain ceremonies, she takes away with her secretly. The doll is usually kept as "the heart" of the child and "the family would not think of parting with what appears to be a kind of life token. Were they to sell the *wiha*, the child 'it brought would not live.' "[32] The Jibaro Indians will form of a piece of manioc a likeness of a human head, which is supposed to represent the enemy threatened. "This head is put on the top of a stick, and the stick is fixed in the ground in the neighborhood of the enemy's house. This procedure is supposed to have some power of promoting the plans of the avenger."[33] Among the Chaldæans wax figures were melted for sorcery.[34]

"In the primitive belief that, by means of certain human acts performed with a certain intention, the *life* of an individual or that of a divinity could be compelled to enter a certain medium, through which it might be subjected to

26 Weeks, in JAI, XL, 395.
27 Tremearne, in JAI, XLV, 51.
28 Czaplicka, *Aborig. Siberia*, 139.
29 Harvey, *Chinese Animism*, ch. IV.
30 Shakespear, in JAI, XXXIX, 383.

31 Milne, *Eastern Clan*, 263.
32 Parsons, in AA, XXI, 279-282.
33 Karsten, "Jibaro," in BAE, Bull. LXXIX, 17.
34 Lenormant, *Chaldean Magic*, 5.

human control, we have the explanation of a close relation which the practices and legends of the ancients imply as having existed in their minds between images and the personality of the being represented. By keeping this in view, a long series of legends, and of, to us, seemingly senseless folk-lore, receives a logical explanation: from the waxen serpent made in the image of the evil serpent Apap and inscribed with his name, which the Egyptians burned three times a day in order to avert the possibility of a storm, to the curious Arab legend . . . according to which Alexander the Great obtained control over the sea-monsters, who daily interfered with the building of Alexandria, by having their portraits taken, after which they disappeared and allowed the work to proceed—from the poetic legend of *Pygmalion* and *Galathea* to the part played in ancient mysteries by the dough images of the gods, which were carefully manufactured according to stated rules, and in which, no doubt, the real presence of the deity was thought to dwell. In the Osirian mysteries these dough images were used to represent the body of the dead god."[35]

As an illustration of the thesis expounded in the above quotation, it should be of interest to relate a story from the *Gesta Romanorum*,[36] a collection of short tales in Latin, much current in the late Middle Ages. "A certain man went to Rome, for to seek S. Peter and S. Paul; and when he was gone, his wife loved another, that was what men call a scholar-errant, and did covet her to wife. The woman saith, 'my good man is departed unto Rome; were he dead, or couldst thou take away his life, then would I have thee of all men.' He said, 'yea truly I can take his life;' and buyeth wax about six pound, and maketh an image thereof. Now when the good man was come to Rome into the city, there came one to him and spake: 'O thou son of death, what goest thou up and down? If none help thee, this day shall see thee alive and dead.' The man asked, 'how should that be?' And he said, 'come to my house, and I will shew it thee.' And having brought him home, he prepared for him a water-bath, and set him therein, and gave him a mirror, saying, 'look thou therein,' and sat beside him, reading in a book, and spake unto him, 'behold in the glass, what seest thou therein?' The man in the bath said, 'I see one in mine house, that *setteth up a waxen image on the wall*, and goeth and taketh his crossbow, and having bent it, *will shoot at the image.*' Then said the other, 'as thou lovest thy life, duck thee under the water when he shall shoot.' And the man did so. And again he read in the book, and spake 'behold, what seest thou?' The man said, 'I see that he hath missed, and is exceeding sorry, and my wife with him; the scholar-errant setteth to, and will shoot the second time, and goeth the half way toward.' 'Duck thee when he shall shoot.' And he ducked. Saith the other, 'look, what seest thou?' The man said, I see that he hath missed, and is sore troubled, and speaketh to the woman, If now I miss the third time, I am [a man] of death; and setteth to, and aimeth at the figure very near, that he may not miss.' Then spake he that read in the book, 'duck thee!' And the man ducked from the shot. And he said, 'look up, what seest thou?' 'I see that he hath missed, and *the arrow is gone into him,* and is dead, and my wife bestoweth him in the basement below.' Then said he, 'arise now, and go thy way.' "

35 Stevenson, in *Int. Cong. Anth.*, 1893, 308.

36 Quoted in Stallybrass, *Grimm's Teut. Myth.*, III, 1091, note 4.

Several other modern cases[37] may conclude this list. "A mountaineer in Tennessee heard his wife complain that no matter what she did, she could not make butter come that day. 'That thar's Nance Clay's doin's,' said the husband. 'I'll soon fix her.' He proceeded to draw the figure of a woman on a sheet of paper, and when it was finished he marked with an oval the place where her heart would be. He pinned the paper on the wall of his log cabin, melted a silver coin into the form of a bullet, took down his rifle, aimed at the drawing, and shot the bullet through the oval. He believed that a neighbor . . . had bewitched the milk, and that by shooting her through the heart in the drawing he could cause her to sicken and die. This is a very ancient notion found in one form or another among the red Indians, the negroes, the Asiatics, and many other old races."[38] Again there is the reported case of the Italian in London who "burned a pin-studded wax effigy of President McKinley on the doorstep of the United States Embassy last evening. He said he was a brother of Guido Mazar, who was lynched in Louisiana, and was avenging the death of his kinsman."[39] Magic is not yet defunct. Early in 1922, in a French village, there was found buried about ten inches below the surface of a grave-mound a young calf's heart stuck full of pins and enclosing a lock of hair. Investigation by a police-commissioner revealed it as a love-charm to bring back a faithless sweetheart.[40] In July, 1922, an Italian was sentenced to imprisonment and fine for telling fortunes and practising medicine in his home without a license. He had sold to one policewoman a charm to ward off the possibility of marrying a poor man and to another a mystic salve for the head, to prevent nervous collapse.[41]

§305. Applications of Magic.

In the immediately preceding paragraphs magic has been seen, incidentally, to have been employed for various purposes, such as to kill an enemy, commit theft, or win affection. Further applications of magic, as well as other features which shed light on this important part of religion, are mentioned below.

The Papuans use magic as a sort of universal expedient: "If the young folk become too fond of their distant relations and visit them too often, the near relations become jealous and secretly bewitch their food and drink, also their sleeping houses to keep them at home. . . . If visitors come repeatedly until their hosts are tired of seeing them, the latter will charm the rollers on which the visitors' canoe will be launched, so that they will not return for a long time. . . . If a young man becomes a hardworking gardener, much to the joy of his friends, the neighbouring families will become jealous and will secretly bewitch his gardening tools, so as to cause him to hate them and become lazy. . . . If a woman becomes the envy of other women because of her good gardening qualities, and the care she takes of her supplies of yams, thus earning the title of Arawata—the highest title a woman can possess—the jealous will try to get hold of her peeling shell, which they will bewitch so as to cause her to be reckless and careless over the food and to lose her title. . . . When making a garden knives and axes are charmed, and there are special incanta-

37 Other cases in recent times, in Sumner, *Coll. Ess.*, I, 124, 125.
38 Ralph, in *Harper's Mag.*, CVII, 38.
39 Assoc. Press Desp. for Dec. 14, 1900.
40 "A Weird Superstition," in N. Y. *Times* for Jan. 12, 1922.
41 N. Y. *Times*, July 14, 1922.

tions before burning off, before digging, before planting, while the crop is growing, when the harvest is reaped. . . . Every part of a canoe is charmed as it is being made right up to the launching. Fishing and hunting nets are charmed, spears and implements of warfare, houses and trees. . . . In order to make life at all bearable, and to counteract the evils strewn in their path, charming is resorted to. When preparing for a sea-voyage:—(1) The body is charmed to prevent the witches from knowing that anyone is coming. (2) The canoe is charmed to make it strong and so that it will not leak. (3) The steer-paddle is charmed so that the canoe will not broach to. (4) The wooden baler is charmed so that it will not sound against the canoe, which would attract the witches. (5) The mast is charmed that it may not snap. (6) The conch-shell is charmed so that when blown it will drive away the squalls. (7) The waves are charmed to keep the sea calm."[1]

In New Britain, "charms are a great power with the people and there are as many of them as there are clever or wealthy men. Every man may have (i.e.,—buy) his own *malira,* or charm. . . . It is dear or cheap, according to its reputation. They are used for any purpose the purchaser desires. Now a love charm, now to secure acquiescence to indecent proposals, now to inflict disease, now to prevent recovery, or any other purpose in view. They mostly consist of leaves, bark, or sap of trees, and are sometimes administered in the food of the person to be influenced and at other times are counted effective through the simple incantation of the wizard." A special charm, placed at the entrance of a fish-trap, is supposed to induce fish to enter.[2] "Magic plays an enormous part in the tribal life of the Kiriwinians (as it undoubtedly does with the majority of native peoples). All important economic activities are fringed with magic, especially such as imply pronounced elements of chance, venture, or danger. Gardening is completely wrapped up in magic; the little hunting that is done has its array of spells; fishing, especially when it is connected with risk and when the results depend upon luck and are not absolutely certain, is equipped with elaborate magical systems. Canoe building has a long list of spells, to be recited at various stages of the work, at the felling of the tree, at the scooping out of the dugout; and, towards the end, at painting, lashing together, and launching. But this magic is used only in the case of the larger sea-going canoes. The small canoes, used on the calm lagoon or near the shore, where there is no danger, are, quite ignored by the magician. Weather—rain, sun and wind—have to obey a great number of spells, and they are especially amenable to the call of some eminent experts, or, rather, families of experts, who practise the art in hereditary succession. In times of war—when fighting still existed, before the white man's rule—the Kiriwinians availed themselves of the art of certain families of professionals, who had inherited war magic from their ancestors. And, of course, the welfare of the body—health—can be destroyed or restored by the magical craft of sorcerers, who are always healers at the same time."[3]

Among the Kaffirs, the fruit of the wild chestnut is sometimes bound by hunters round their wrists for the purpose of charming the game.[4] Among Bantu beliefs, that in witchcraft "stands at the head and shows a shocking extension." No sickness or death would occur, they believe, if witches had not caused it. Drought and other forms of ill luck are referred to sorcery. They

1 Bromilow, in AAAS, 1911, 418, 419.   3 Malinowski, in JAI, XLVI, 384-385.
2 Danks, in AAAS, 1909, 455.   4 Kropf, *Kaffir-Eng. Dict.,* 15.

even believe in mass-bewitchment. They have a ceremony of the "smelling-out of a sorcerer by the shaman." "As soon as he is detected, even his best friends draw away from him, he is seized and they try by the most fearful torture to bring him to confess his guilt and to reveal the magical means which he has used. . . . Also his whole property is confiscated at the end of the process, and often the whole kraal of the unfortunate is devoured. Since in this manner the witch-process is at the same time an easy means of enrichment for the chief, it is the well-to-do who have drawn the hostility of the despot on themselves that are particularly menaced. Often it is known beforehand . . . just who is to be smelled out; sometimes those who are threatened save themselves by quick flight to a neighboring tribe, leaving their property behind."[5]

Others use the ordeal[6] to detect the suspect; "he had to dip his hand in boiling water; if he was scalded, they gave the guilty person poison and burned him while yet alive, amidst the curses of the onlookers." Elsewhere black ants whose sting is very painful, are spread over the bodies of those who are accused of witchcraft, after they have been sprinkled with water, to extort confession. The charge of sorcery is the Kaffir method of getting troublesome people out of the way; when anyone is once accused, he is hopelessly lost.[7]

In Cameroons, if someone is killed by a leopard or crocodile—the rivers are infested by the latter—it is believed that an enemy of the dead man has enchanted the beast. The shaman, by asking the crocodiles, is able to designate the culprit, who is made to drink poison. If he vomits at once, he is innocent; the crocodiles have lied and the doctor undertakes to punish them for it. Elsewhere the poison used in the ordeal acts "as an emetic, a purge, or a toxic, causing death by coma. The first of these effects indicates innocence, the others guilt." "Fetish-drinking" is found also in Togo. "Since the mixing of the fetish-drink is wholly the affair of the uncontrollable priests, it rests solely upon their good or ill will whether the condemned party is to get off alive or not. If he has wealth but is otherwise without influence or protection, he will do well to set his house in order and have done with life. He will certainly die of the poison and his property will go over into the hands of the sly witch-master." The priest secures this property for the moment by cutting off the dead man's fingernails and strewing them about the dwelling, "that everyone who removes anything out of it may also be carried off by the poison. After the burial the priest appears and demands the property of the deceased, and no one dares to oppose, for the people firmly believe in the infallibility and justice of the process."[8] There is no question about the hatred of magic by the West African priests, but it is equally abhorred where there is no organized priesthood.[9] It is an abominable thing to cause illness by tampering with what people drink; or even to cause the milk of a neighbor's cows to pass into the udders of one's own cows or the olives of his orchard to locate themselves in one's own jar of oil.[10] It is believed by everyone, however, that such things are being done all the time.

The ordinary Singhalese, with whom the European usually comes in con-

5 Fritsch, Eingeb. S.-Afr., 57, 99-100, 101.
6 §183, of text and Case-Book.
7 Bertrand, in Globus, LXXIV, 42; Kropf, Kaffir-Eng. Dict., 10; Ratzel, Vkde., I, 266; Macdonald, in JAI, XIX, 294.

8 Reichenow, Kamerun, 34-35; Phillips, in JAI, XVII, 222; Seidel, in Globus, LXXII, 40.
9 Kingsley, W. Afr. Studies, 158, 159, 160.
10 Junker, Afrika, I, 405; Hanoteau et Letourneux, Kabylie, III, 180.

tact, seems to know comparatively little about magical matters, although they have often no small part in the conduct of his life. "While in many cases his ignorance is of the same nature as that of Europeans where the practices of their own physicians are concerned, it is, doubtless, in others more or less feigned, prompted by the common disinclination to speak of magical matters to strangers of superior standing, and with different beliefs." Among them the science of charming is divided into eight parts: "the power of inducing swoons, illicit sexual intercourse, the expulsion of demons, compelling the attendance of demons, destruction by discord, causing death, the power of imprisoning, and the power of curing diseases, to each of which are assigned certain seasons, days, and hours for their successful performance."[11] The following graphic description has been given of the sway of magic among the natives of a district in Punjab. "A more utterly ignorant and superstitious people than the Bannuchis I never saw. . . . For him the whistle of the far-drawn bullet, or the nearer sheen of his enemy's sword, had no dangers; blood was simply a red fluid; and to remove a neighbour's head at the shoulder as easy as cutting cucumbers. But to be cursed in Arabic or anything that sounded like it, to be told that the blessed Prophet had put a black mark against his soul for not giving his best field to one of the Prophet's own posterity, to have the saliva of a disappointed saint left in anger on his doorstep, or behold a Haji who had gone three times to Mecca deliberately sit down and enchant his camels with the itch and his sheep with the rot—these were things that made the dagger drop out of the hand of the awe-stricken savage, his knees to knock together, his liver to turn to water, and his parched tongue to be scarce able to articulate a full and complete concession of the blasphemous demand."[12]

The Dyaks have an unshakable confidence in magic, and each individual has his own magic articles in the infallibility of which he thoroughly believes; magic power may be exercised promptly over miles of intervening space.[13] Praying to death, known as *pule-anaana,* has long been a practice in the Hawaiian Islands. Perhaps half of the people who die unattended by a regular physician are victims of the death-sorcery or incantation. The only scientific hypothesis offered as explaining this phenomenon is that it is a phase of hypnotic suggestion. A *kahuna-anaana* or sorcerer believed to be capable of exerting this power could have his services secured like a hired assassin by gifts of white fowls, brown hogs, or woolly dogs. "Death was almost certain to follow the machinations of a kahuna of approved power, unless his dupe could promptly secure the intervention of a kahuna of higher rank, that is, one of greater age." The processes of praying to death are as follows: "Any native whose goods were desired, or who might otherwise have given cause of offense, summoned by anaana instantly suspended his avocation and, hastening to the kahuna, crouched in abject submission to his will, until death took place, usually in a few hours, and apparently from exhaustion. Frequently a kahuna repairs in person to the abode of his victim and places himself in the presence of the man, thereupon muttering incantations and prayers. The kahuna's own favorite god is usually addressed and also such aumakuas [charms] and deities as are supposed to have been offended by the accused. The subject sits quietly before his antagonist, takes no food and but little drink,

11 Hildburgh, in JAI, XXXVIII, 150-151.

12 O'Brien, in JAI, XLI, 509-510.

13 Perelaer, *Dajaks,* 25; Roth, *Sarawak,* II, 208.

and dies in a few days." In some cases it is performed on the exuviæ of the victim. Dread of death and the expectation of it, which seize the natives when approached by anaana, chiefly explain its uncanny power. The native has no thought of resisting. "It is nearly impossible to induce a native, when sick, to submit to medical treatment. Here the power of the ordinary kahuna, one of the saving sort, is displayed. Black pigs are roasted for the invalid and his friends and the kahuna, while communications, well paid for, are held with the powers above and below. There is then no limit to the fortitude with which the patient will endure suffering unrelieved. Pretending to obey the foreign physician, he follows the directions of the kahuna, who, in his twofold function of doctor and priest, is preaching and practising behind the scenes and throwing away the mixtures of his foreign rival." The ready surrender to sickness is, in most cases, said to be "due to a definite belief in a demon whom the native feels working in his vitals, and whom it is hopeless to resist."[14]

Magic is a means, in America, of protection from the consequences of crime, or of discovering plots.[15] Among the Hudson Bay Eskimo, "an exchange of wives is frequent, either party often being glad to be released for a time, and returning without concern. There is so much intriguing and scandal-mongering among these people that a woman is often compelled by the sentiment of the community to relinquish her choice and join another who has bribed the conjurer to decide that until she comes to live with him a certain person will not be relieved from the evil spirit now tormenting him with disease. . . . Some wives are considered as very 'unlucky' and after trial are cast off to shift for themselves. A woman who has obtained the reputation of being unlucky for her husband is eschewed by all the men lest she work some charm on them."[16] A Haida shaman repeats the names of all persons in the village in the presence of a live mouse and determines the guilty party by watching its motions.[17] The Athapascans had "absolute faith in the necessity and efficacy of certain charms which they tied to their fishing hooks and nets."[18]

The magic connected with idol-worship was regarded by the old Hebrews as the worst of sins and the serpent as the author of it; in the New Testament magical books were burned, plainly because they prescribed heathen customs, formulas, and invocations by means of which the higher powers might be brought under control.[19] "The highest attainment in divine magic consists in the knowledge of the . . . 'most great name' of God, which is generally believed, by the learned, to be known to none but prophets and apostles of God."[20] Homer shows a number of isolated instances of magical performance through fetishes, and one complete case—that of Circe; but Homeric magic is connected almost wholly with divinities and foreigners.[21]

Out of later Greek religious beliefs, says Miss Harrison,[22] half-seriously, came a truth that it has taken science centuries to establish, namely the fact that disease is caused by germs—bacilli, we call them, where the Greeks used the word Kēres. "The Keres are physical actual things not impersonations. So when Æschylus puts into the mouth of his Danaid women the prayer

---

14 Nichols, in *Pop. Sci. News*, XXVII, 77-78.

15 Bandelier, in AA, VI, 444; Leland and Prince, *Kulóskap*, 187.

16 Turner, in BAE, XI, 189, 190.

17 Swanton, in HAI, II, 145.

18 Goddard ana Swanton, in HAI, I, 110.

19 Duhm, *Geister*, 13; Acts, XIX, 19; Blau, *Zauberwesen*, 28.

20 Lane, *Mod. Egypt*, I, 403.

21 Keller, *Hom. Soc.*, 172-175 (where full references to the text are given).

22 *Greek Relig.*, 167, 170; Æschylus, *Suppl.*, 684-685.

> 'Nor may disease, noisome swarm,
> Settle upon our heads, to harm
> Our citizens,'

the 'noisome swarm' is no mere 'poetical' figure but the reflection of a real primitive conviction of live pests." Much correction into science came from Chaldæan magic. Amongst the Accadian people there was no evil which the sorcerer could not work. "He ordered at will the fascination of the evil eye or of unlucky words; his rites and formulæ for enchantment subjected the demons to his orders; he let them loose upon the person he wished to injure, and made them torment him in every way; he sent ill-luck alike to countries or individuals, and caused demoniacal possession and other terrible diseases."[23] Yet out of such beliefs and fear came scientific investigation, especially in the field of astrology. The religious axiom was that the stars ruled all life, their mutual position being decisive of fate. "The astronomic studies gave means into the hand to prophecy all happenings if one once before had observed what happened on earth contemporaneously with a certain phenomenon in the heavens." Hence there were extended observations. From the belief that the gods were identified with stars came the notion that certain positions of the stars affected the possibilities of daimonic action; hence horoscopes. This led to the interpretation of a sequence of events from like earthly conditions previously observed; hence history. The accuracy of their observations, taken for ages and checked up by repetition, was surprisingly great. In alchemy, all was explained by some god's inworking; his aid was always needed. In the alchemic receipts there were formulæ, prayers, and, later on, astrology, each planet having its metal. Natural explanation dates from the Greek period, being at bottom the teaching of the Greek philosophers.[24] The orientation of the ancient megaliths in Britain is to the rising of the sun on definite days of the year—the festival days of the early Eastern Mediterranean nations, dates of common religious observance. Tombs are likewise laid out in one or other of these auspicious bearings, the cult of the dead thus being associated with the cult of the heavens. Such orientation argues considerable mental advance.[25]

Magicians were highly revered by the ancient Persians who believed also in mythical sorcerers, evil spirits which laid snares for men; against their black magic man called on the gods and heroes for help and protection. There came to be a deification of the elements: "indeed, this appears among lower people to have remained the chief form of religion. Especially were fire and water regarded as great gods. . . . First and foremost, however, was sorcery. . . . The Avesta frequently turns with great vigor against sorcery as an Ahrimanic evil."[26] The independent power attributed by Mazdaism to the principle of evil afforded justification for all manner of occult practices. "Necromancy, oneiromancy, belief in the evil eye and in talismans, in witchcraft and conjurations, in fine, all the puerile and sinister aberrations of ancient paganism, found their justification in the rôle assigned to demons who incessantly interfered in the affairs of men."[27]

The Arabs were all daimonists before Mohammed. The childbed was protected from jinns and the evil eye averted by a rag spotted with blood. A besieged city put a witch on the wall and compelled her to make a shameful

23 Lenormant, *Chaldean Magic*, 59-61.
24 Lehmann, * Übertro*, II, 45-70.
25 Somerville, in JAI, XLII, 51-52.

26 Justi, *Persien*, 70; Tiele-Gehrich, *Gchte. Relig.*, II, 73.
27 Cumont, *Mithra*, 125.

exposure, to scare the enemy and by magic to ward him off.[28] Still widespread is the belief in alchemy, astrology, and sorcery; "in the lands of Islam one finds soothsayers, dream interpreters, and magicians without number."[29] "Marcus Aurelius, in recounting the benefits he had received from different persons, acknowledges his debt of gratitude to the philosopher Diognetus for having taught him to give no credence to magicians, jugglers, and expellers of daemons. Lucian declares that every cunning juggler could make his fortune by going over to the Christians and preying upon their simplicity. Celsus described the Christians as jugglers performing their tricks among the young and the credulous."[30]

§308. The Black Art.

WITCHES are considered by the Papuans to have great power. "By occult influences a witch can deafen a person's ears, and so make him mad; or can cause his heart to burst, or drink his blood, or snap his veins, or break his bones. She can throttle a child at night by invisible fingers, can swamp or capsize canoes, climb to the top of mountains, cross from peak to peak on cords of fire which can be seen any dark night. She can descend into the earth and bring forth fruitful seasons, or epidemics of sickness, at her own sweet will." This by no means concludes the extent of such power. If a wizard, after fasting from food and drinking sea-water, performs special incantations in secret, then his touch will cause death; he can impale his victim with an imaginary stick or pierce the body with an imaginary spear; he can bewitch food left over after a meal, or a tuft of hair or portion of clothing, and so cause death; or bewitch food before it is cooked and make it poisonous; his hand placed secretly on the head of a child will cause its death; he can send poison into the mouth of a person as he is eating; can kill by spitting at a person; can cause a man to fall to his death when climbing; can bewitch a fireplace so that food cooked upon it becomes poisonous, and poison the drinking water by putting into it a leaf which he has charmed; and can bewitch a sharp-pointed stick and cause a man to walk with his bare feet on the spot where he has hidden it, so that it will pierce his victim's foot and kill him. "There are many other things he can do, but he must do them secretly; therefore no one must walk about alone. There must always be two or three together."[1] The Murray Islanders attribute disease, death, and trouble of all kinds to the evil influence of sorcerers; such influence can be averted only by liberal payments.[2] Except in the case of very old folk, death is not admitted by the Roro-speaking tribes to occur without some obvious cause such as a spear-thrust. "Therefore when vigorous and active members of the community die, it becomes necessary to explain their fate, and such deaths are firmly believed to be produced by sorcery. Indeed, as far as I have been able to ascertain, the Papuasian of this district regards the existence of sorcery, not as has been alleged, as a particularly terrifying and horrible affair, but as a necessary and inevitable condition of existence in the world as he knows it, so that the Roro-speaking tribes look on sorcery in the abstract with no more horror or fear than Europeans in their prime regard old age and death. . . . The attitude of the natives towards the in-

28 Smith, *Relig. Sem.*, 428; Wellhausen, *Skizzen*, III, 143.
29 Hauri, *Islam*, 87.
30 Lecky, *Europ. Morals*, I, 384.

1 Bromilow, in AAAS, 1909, 473; and in AAAS, 1911, 417, 418.
2 Hunt, in JAI, XXVIII, 8.

dividuals they recognize as sorcerers is one of perfect good fellowship; indeed a sorcerer may have great influence in his own village, and not only may not be feared but may be regarded generally as a real protection. . . . I have no doubt that in many instances sorcerers actually believe in their own powers, and a well-known sorcerer explained to Captain Barton that he was scarcely a free agent in the matter, since his father had been a sorcerer before him, and it was but natural that the power should pass to him." There is a general belief that these sorcerers endeavor to obtain access to newly dead human bodies, portions of which they use as charms, and it is suggested that this may have contributed to the practice of burial under the house of the deceased or in the village street.[3]

In the New Hebrides wizards and witches are necromancers who have familiar spirits and use their power malevolently. If many people become ill suspicion falls on a "sacred man" as the cause; but the latter sets in motion a witch-finding ceremony and the person finally designated by the process has to pay a pig to the relatives of the dead and another to the witch-finders.[4] Sorcerers in the Trobriand Islands are "those who possess the power to kill people by magic."[5] Both white and black magic exist in D'Entrecasteaux. No man would be at pains to deny knowledge of the first kind; on the contrary he is proud of whatever little he may know; but no one will confess that he knows black magic; "yet, wherever you go, you hear of some one who has just been victimized and is lying at death's door." According to the natives, a person cannot die except for one of two reasons: first, because a spirit has taken his heart away, and secondly, because some one has practised sorcery on him. Black magic differs from the white variety, so far at least as these natives are concerned, in its anti-social nature. "The two, however, sometimes tend to coincide; that which is anti-social from one point of view may favour society from another. The same magic which has slain your brother you may use to slay his enemy, and all your relatives will approve your deed." Many different methods for bewitching a man are cited.[6]

"The curriculum vitæ of the heathen Mowenda is a long succession of fear, superstition, suppression and misery. From birth to death they are haunted by their gods, by the ghosts of their ancestors, by all sorts of hobgoblins, and tremble from fear of their witchdoctors and chiefs. . . . The Batlapin, in common with all other native tribes in South Africa, had a firm belief that all deaths except those occasioned by violence and old age were caused by enchantments and sorcery. . . . In Matabeleland the wizards or witches believed that they had the power to bewitch a person and thus cause his death. They go to the graves of the dead to pray for power to bewitch others, and believe that they get it, and that by means of medicines (roots, etc.) they can influence a person so that he dies. When a native wished to learn to bewitch he would pay a big price to an established wizard, who would go with him to a grave and dig up a freshly buried body, cut it open and roast the liver, and teach him witchcraft."[7] A witchcraft case a few years ago was brought up in the native court in Southern Rhodesia: a man accused his wife of invoking a spirit against him. The jurymen decided in the woman's favor, because they

3 Seligmann, *Melanesians*, 279, 289.
4 Leggatt, in AAAS, 1892, 700, 707.
5 Malinowski, in JAI, XLVI, 426.

6 Jenness and Ballentyne, *D'Entrecasteaux*, 133-136, 141.
7 Garbutt, in JAI, XXXIX, 530-531, 533.

said that, had she really called upon the Juju, the spirit would have seen to it that the man should not have been alive to accuse her.[8]

Bent[9] tells of a South African chief who was convinced that Mrs. Bent had been sent by Queen Victoria, from a country ruled by a woman, to bewitch him. A Gold Coast chief is complaining of the way the English government is preserving vermin in the shape of witches. He says that the witches there live almost entirely on the blood they suck from children at night. In old days they did this furtively, and do now where the native custom is unchecked; but in districts where the Government regards witchcraft as utter nonsense and the killing of its practitioners as utter murder, which will be dealt with accordingly, the witch flourishes exceedingly, and blackmails the mothers and fathers, threatening that if they are not bought off they will have their child's blood; if they are not paid the child gradually dies—poison again, most likely.[10] Some negroes of the Guinea coast believe that "the soul that lives its life in a body fully through is held happy; it is supposed to have learnt its full lesson from life, and to know the way down to the shadowland home and all sorts of things. . . . Now if this process of development is checked by witchcraft and the soul is prematurely driven from the body, it does not know all that it should, and its condition is therefore miserable. . . . I well remember gossiping with a black friend in a plantation in the Calabar district on witchcraft, and he took up a stick and struck a plant of green maize, breaking the stem of it, saying, 'There, like that is the soul of a man who is witched, it will not ripen now.' "[11] Both heathen and Christianized natives believe that witches can turn into animals and can damage with a glance. A teacher in one of the missions had to be dismissed, "because he was continually accusing the wife of a catechist of witchcraft and always hid his child from her."[12] In one locality all the old women are killed because they are believed to become servants of evil spirits.[13]

"Infinitely the larger proportion of death and sickness is held to arise from witchcraft, more particularly among the Bantu. Witchcraft acts in two ways: witching something out of a man or witching something into him. . . . Witches are continually setting traps to catch the soul that wanders from the body when a man sleeps; when they have caught this soul, they tie it up over a canoe fire and its owner sickens as the soul shrivels. This is a regular line of business, and not an affair of individual hate and revenge. The witch does not care whose dream-soul gets into the trap, and will restore it on payment. Also witch-doctors, men of unblemished professional reputation, will keep asylums for lost souls, *i.e.*, those that have been out wandering and found on their return to their body that their place has been filled by a Sisa, *i.e.*, a low class soul. These doctors keep souls and administer them to patients who are short of the article."[14] A drawing of a soul-trap, as used on the Harvey Islands, is given by Bartels;[15] in this region the trap is hung on a tree by which the victim must pass. When he sees it he thinks his soul is caught in it and is terrified into decline and death. In Senegal those suspected of witchcraft or relation with evil spirits are killed or terribly mutilated, and their corpses thrust into a hollow of a sacred tree. Often strangers who are travelling through the country—Arabs or Europeans—suffer this fate.[16]

8 N. Y. *Times*, May 10, 1914.
9 *Mashonaland*, 285; Mayr, in *Anthropos*, 1907, II, 392 ff.; 633 ff.
10 Kingsley, *Travels W. Afr.*, 489, 490.
11 Kingsley, *W. Afr. Studies*, 167, 168.

12 Vortisch, in *Globus*, LXXXIX, 279.
13 Seidel, in *Globus*, LXXIV, 7.
14 Kingsley, *Travels W. Afr.*, 461.
15 *Medicin*, 38.
16 Scherer, in *Globus*, XCI, 15.

In Central Africa "witchcraft reigns supreme. Should the suspicion of witch-craft fall upon any one, only trial by ordeal can free them."[17] Those who prac-tise the black art in Madagascar are "accustomed to go about naked, but this is, of course, done by night."[18] The word for witch or wizard in Nyasaland implies the possession of something like the evil eye; such a person is also supposed to add to his or her supernatural powers by corpse-eating.[19] "Sor-cerers in Ukamba and Theraka are almost exclusively women, but in Kikuyu they are mostly men; in the former country witch-doctors are constantly em-ployed at great expense, and I have known them to be summoned from the coast to exhaust the evil spirits, the treatment costing in one case fifty rupees for every one treated. In Kikuyu, sorcery may be practised by many methods, and certain people, such as hunters and smiths, may put witchcraft on others through the secrets of their professions."[20]

Certain Africans have but little religion but they take great stock in witch-doctors, "who are continually fussing about supposed cases of witchcraft." This "smelling-out" of witches was a pest to the country. Sir Harry Johnston had to remove a prominent chief into exile "because he was continually accus-ing harmless individuals of witchcraft practices and having them executed."[21] African cases include that of cutting open the body of a supposed witch—a woman on the verge of childbirth—while she yet lived in order to tear out and burn the gall-bladder in which the witch-power was supposed to reside.[22] The sorcerer's body is not accorded burial after his execution.[23] Kabyle village-annals "teem with examples of fines imposed on sorceresses" who have caused the milk of their neighbors' cows to enter the udders of their own animals.[24] It is a well-known fact that the so-called *voodoo* practices of the negroes in the southern part of the United States came from Africa, by way of Haiti, about 1809.[25] Two negroes, regarded as witches by their associates, were ar-rested in Havana in 1906, charged with the murder of a white baby for the purpose of procuring the heart, which they prescribed as a poultice for the cure of barrenness.[26]

Witchcraft-beliefs are strong in southern India. It is believed that, to re-venge herself on a man, a witch "climbs at night to the top of his house and, making a hole through the roof, drops a thread down till the end of it touches the body of the sleeping man. Then she sucks at the other end and draws up all the blood out of his body."[27] Again, "witches and sorcerers often harm through direct contact. Thus, they generally have with them small rag bundles in which they carry small thin knives and nail-parers, besides nails, bones, and legs of chickens and other birds and animals. . . . A magician, thus called in, stands face to face before the patient so that the mouth and navel of the sor-cerer respectively touch those of the patient; and in this posture he goes on reciting his mantrams or spells until the bone, leg, or nail-paring comes out of the mouth of the patient into his own mouth." It is thought that witches and *mātis* perform their magic feats with the help of some powerful spirits with which they have entered into compact and alliance. The control exercised is not that of the magician over the evil spirit harming a client but of one

17 N. Y. *Times*, June 23, 1912.
18 Sibree, *Madagascar*, 292.
19 Moggridge, in JAI, XXXII, 472.
20 Dundas, C., in JAI, XLV, 278. A rupee is about 48 cents.
21 Johnston, *Uganda*, II, 610, 632.

22 Junker, *Afrika*, III, 111.
23 Stuhlmann, *Mit Emin*, 781.
24 Hanoteau et Letourneux, *Kabylie*, 497.
25 Dana, in *Metrop. Mag.*, XXVII, 529 ff.
26 N. Y. *Times*, Jan. 5, 1906.
27 Thurston, *S. India*, 323, 324.

powerful spirit, the magician's familiar, over another. "As the witch and the *māti* exercise their art for their own benefit and for harming others, they are believed to die invariably a miserable death. The *māti's sādhak,* or familiar, is an evil spirit which he holds under control; as soon as this spirit gets out of hand it brings ruin on the *māti* himself. Whereas the *pāhan,* or village-priest, the director of beneficent public magic, is respected and looked up to as the natural leader of the village, the sorcerer and witch are shunned and looked down upon as enemies of humanity. Here we see the tribal conscience of even such backward tribes as the Mūndās and the Orāons of Chōtā-Nāgpūr, recognizing the immorality of anti-social private magic. And the brutal persecution of a suspected or declared witch, of which we now and again hear rueful stories in Chōtā-Nāgpūr, however much we may condemn it, is due not to any perversity of nature but to a lamentable ignorance of the causes of phenomena, and to a laudable desire to punish the anti-social mis-chief-maker."[28]

In the Indian Archipelago women are more often witches than men, yet the power may be inherited in the male line. The head being regarded as the chief seat of the soul, the belief is that witches' heads detach from the body and, along with the vital organs which hang from them, fly about as vampires. They must get back to the trunk of the body before daylight, or the body decays. People susceptible to witchcraft are known by their shy demeanor and rolling eye-balls; such peculiarities lead to their elimination, through fear.[29] Probably the persons thus killed are defective. In New Zealand, "sorcerers were said to have the power of striking people dead by a look, and withering up trees and shrubs." Certain trees were thought to be enchanted men and able at times to move about. A story is told how "a sorcerer possessed of a magical wooden head caused the death of all who came within a certain distance of it. A brave warrior renowned for skill in magic resolved to rid the country of the pest. To gain his object he enlisted by the agency of powerful charms and incanta-tions the services of thousands of spirits kindly disposed to mankind, to fight the malignant spirits who guarded the head. A battle ensued, the evil spirits were defeated, the fortress was taken, and the cruel sorcerer and owner of the magical head was put to death."[30]

It is said to be almost impossible to exaggerate the Tlinkit's terror of witches. "It is for this reason rather than for hardness of heart or delight in human sufferings, that they torture them. They deem nothing too cruel for them because they hold them responsible for all human sufferings and death itself." In one case a young girl was tied up and after severe torture was compelled to admit that she had made witch-medicine. "She was then compelled to dive down and bury the concoction in the bed of the river, the natives believing that if this is done the bewitched will get well. . . . Witch-medicine is com-posed of several ingredients, such as hair and finger parings of the dead, herbs, and the tongues of birds, frogs and mice."[31] When a man among the Kwakiutl thinks that he has been bewitched, he goes into the woods and prays to the supernatural spirits of certain trees to save him; he then goes to bed, without eating, that he may dream. "Men say that the dream comes from the spirits of the trees who give instruction to the bewitched man how to cure himself, and generally the man gets well after that." There is also a special

28 Roy, in JAI. XLIV, 337, 349-350.   30 Stack, in AAAS, 1891, 384.
29 Wilken, in VG, III, 30 ff.   31 Jones, *Thlingets,* 157-158.

set of persons whose business it is to undo the wizard's work. They go through the same ceremonies as the wizard himself, but end by putting everything into the fire. Witchcraft among the Tsimshians is practised by people called *haldáwit*. "They steal a portion of a corpse, which they place in a small, long, water-tight box. A stick is placed across the middle of the box, and thin threads are tied to this stick. The piece of corpse is placed at the bottom of the box, and part of the clothing or hair of the person whom the witch desires to bewitch is tied to these strings. If it is in immediate contact with the body, the person will die soon; if it is hung a little higher, he will be sick for a long time. If hair is put into the box he will die of headache; if part of a moccasin, his foot will rot; if saliva is used, he will die of consumption. If the person is to die at once, the *haldáwit* cuts the string from which the object is suspended, so that it drops right on the corpse. This box has a cover, and is kept closely tied up. It is kept buried under the house or in the woods. After the witch has killed his enemy, he must go around the house in which the dead one is lying, following the course of the sun. After his enemy has been buried, he must lie down on the grave and crawl around it, again following the course of the sun, and attired in the skin of some animal. If he does not do this, he must die. Therefore people watch if they see any one performing this cere-mony. Then they know that he is a witch, and he is killed." Weapons, tools, and other objects are bewitched by blowing water on them, though blowing water on the body serves as a protective device. Also, "a person may be bewitched by catching his breath in shredded cedar bark, which is put into the mouth of a frog."[32] The Tsimshian suspected of witchcraft is tied up and starved until he confesses, when he is driven into the sea in order to expel the evil spirit. If he refuses to confess, he is starved to death or exposed on the beach at low tide until the water rises over him.

Among the Haida, "witchcraft was supposed to be due to mice which had got inside of a person's body, and if these could be expelled he might be re-stored to his right mind. There were said to be as many as ten of these mice sometimes, one of which (the last to leave) was a white one." As an illustra-tion of the influence of witchcraft on religious rites, it may be stated that a special ceremony of the Hopi was undertaken to relieve the land from the bewitchment of winter. The charge of witchcraft was brought not only against individuals but entire towns and tribes, and in the Southwest the people of the Hopi pueblo of Awatobi were destroyed on this ground.[33] The belief is hard to down, and now and then the newspapers report that some Indian has been tortured to death as a wizard.[34]

"Witchcraft played a very great part in the whole of ancient Egyptian life."[35] In the Euphrates valley from the earliest times to which our knowl-edge reaches demonism was the real religion. Demons in inconceivable hordes surrounded men and malignantly vexed or tormented them; but men could by sorcery control the demons and use them to do ill to other men. The incubus and succubus demons are met with in the oldest documents of history so that we find here already the notion of sex-commerce between demons and human beings.[36] The same notion prevailed among the ancient Hebrews,[37] who made

32 Boas, in BAE, XXXV, pt. II, 1327-1328; and in BAE, XXXI, 477, 563-564; Swanton, in HAI, II, 966.
33 Swanton, "Witchcraft," in HAI, II, 966.
34 N. Y. *Times*, Mar. 12, 1911; and Sept. 24, 1924.
35 Steindorff, *Relig. Anc. Egypt*, 106.
36 Lenormant, *Chaldean Magic*, 5-40.
37 Gen., VI, 2.

many pronouncements against witchcraft and ordered that "a man also or woman that hath a familiar spirit, or that is a wizard, shall surely be put to death."[38] The Romans held such beliefs.[39] The Christian Church of the Middle Ages led mankind back to witchcraft, for in the seventh, eighth, and ninth centuries it had been rejected. Great numbers of people practised sorcery and witchcraft. They were taught by the church that magic and sorcery were wicked but that they were real ways in which objects of human desire could be obtained. Thousands of men and women were ready to perpetrate the sin to gain their wishes; they therefore performed the acts which they understood would be effective to enter into relations with Satan, to destroy enemies, to win love or wealth, and to attain to objects of ambition.[40] Witch-epidemics broke out in nearly every country, and in Germany it is estimated that in a period of about two hundred years over one hundred thousand were executed.[41]

Among the Germans, "miracle is wrought by honest means, magic by unlawful; the one is *geheuer* (blessed, wholesome . . .), the other *ungeheuer.* . . . It is so with all nations, and was so with our ancestors: by the side of divine worship, practices of dark sorcery, by way of exception, not of contrast. The ancient Germans knew magic and magicians; in this foundation first do all the later fancies rest." Even the earliest antiquities impute witchcraft preeminently to women. The author[42] from whom we are quoting concerning the ancient Germans looks to "all the circumstances external and internal" to explain this belief about women. "The various ways of naming magic have led us to the notions of doing, sacrificing, spying, soothsaying, singing, sign-making (secret writing), bewildering, dazzling, cooking, healing, casting lots. . . . To woman, not to man, was assigned the culling and concocting of powerful remedies, as well as the cooking of food. Her lithe soft hand could best prepare the salve, weave the lint and dress the wound; the art of writing and reading is in the Middle Ages ascribed chiefly to women. The restless lives of men were filled up with war, hunting, agriculture and handicrafts; to women experience and convenient leisure lent every qualification for secret sorcery. Woman's imagination is warmer and more susceptible, and at all times an inner sacred power of divination was revered in her. Women were priestesses, prophetesses, their names and fame are embalmed alike in Old-German and Norse tradition; and the faculty of somnambulism still shows itself most of all in women. Then again, looked at from one side, the art of magic must have been chiefly monopolized by *old women*, who, dead to love and labour, fixed all their thoughts and endeavours on hidden science. . . . On all this put together, on a mixture of natural, legendary, and imagined facts, rest the mediaeval notions about witchcraft. Fancy, tradition, knowledge of drugs, poverty and idleness turned women into witches, and the last three causes also shepherds into wizards. . . . Sorceresses have also at their command a bird's shape, a feather-garment, especially that of the goose, which stands for the more ancient swan, and they are like swan-wives, valkyrs, who traverse the breezes and troop to the battle."

38 Levit., XX, 27; Exod., XXII, 18; Deut., XVIII, 10; I Sam., XV, 23; XXVIII, 7; II Chron., XXIII, 6; Galatians, V, 20; II Kings, IX, 22; XVI, 3; XXI, 6; Micah, V, 12; Nahum, III, 4.

39 Vergil, *Ecl.*, VIII, 99; *Cod. Just.*, IX, 18, 4, 7.

40 Levi, *Hist. de la Magic*, 281.

41 Scherr, *Deut. Kgchte.*, 153, 156, 382; Sumner, *Coll. Essays*, I, 105-126.

42 Grimm, *Teut. Mythol.*, III, 986, 990, 994-995, 999, 1000, 1015, 1017-1018, 1031 (quoted), 1032, 1038-1039 (quoted), 1044, 1045 (quoted), 1049 (quoted), 1051 (quoted), 1055 (quoted), 1056, 1057, 1058, 1061, 1062, 1054-1055, 1068, 1069. (Stallybrass's version.)

It is noteworthy that "it is *precisely salt* that is *lacking* in the witches' kitchen and at devil's feasts, the Church having now taken upon herself the hallowing and dedication of salt. Infants unbaptized, and so exposed had *salt* placed beside them for safety. . . . The emigrants from Salzburg dipped a wetted finger in *salt*, and swore. Wizards and witches were charged with the *misuse of salt* in baptizing beasts. I think it worth mentioning here, that the magic-endowed giantesses in the Edda knew how to grind, not only *gold*, but *salt* . . .: the one brought peace and prosperity, the other a tempest and foul weather." Again, with respect to the resorts of witches: they "invariably resort to places where formerly justice was administered, or sacrifices were offered. Their meeting takes place on the *mead*, on the *oak-sward*, under the *lime*, under the *oak*, at the *peartree*. . . . Sometimes they dance at the *place of execution*, under the *gallows-tree*, in the *sand-pit*. But for the most part *mountains* are named as their trysting-places."

These references to woman's function in magic, to salt, and to the several fetish locations and objects illustrate beliefs treated elsewhere,[43] which, in turn, throw light upon the passages just cited, enabling the reader to distinguish, among other things, between the actual and the fanciful in the passage quoted concerning woman. "After the conversion, sorcery links itself with the discredited gods, both foreign and domestic; not yet at once with the Devil, the idea of whom had scarce begun to take root among the people. The witches are the *retinue of former goddesses*, who, hurled from their thrones, transformed from gracious adored beings into malign and dreaded ones, roam restlessly by night, and instead of their once stately progresses can only maintain stolen forbidden conferences with their adherents."

Belief in witchcraft is not yet dead, nor even dormant. Among the women in a Scots village community in the fifties and sixties was a "witch," who had the evil eye and was shunned by everyone. "In her youth she had been brought before the Kirk Session, charged with a lapse from virtue. The 'ruling elder,' a well-to-do farmer, admonished her more sharply than she relished, and she told him that one day he would suffer for his severity. Thereafter, every night, so the story went, she pronounced upon the head of this farmer one of the imprecatory psalms. Within a year and a half an epidemic of foot-and-mouth disease struck the district, the polled Angus herd of the farmer was stricken, and he was ruined. Everyone believed that the witch had brought her curse to bear upon him. Intelligent people were in many ways . . . yet in general they entertained some primitive superstitions. My aunts Elspeth and Mary, who were by no means wanting either in acuteness of mind or in education, have been known to have their churn carried across a running stream so that their butter might be freed from witchcraft. Such harmless gaucheries are by no means the last, and may well be considered as the least, of the evidences of superstition."[44] Current newspapers in this twentieth century afford evidence that belief in witchcraft still flourishes and that witch-doctors still do business.[45] Dr. Alice Hamilton[46] writes concerning the belief in witchcraft among the Italians in Chicago: "In my twenty-five years at Hull House I have heard many a weird and dramatic tale of this hidden side of life in the Italian colony." Uncommon sickness is sometimes laid to this cause; an Italian woman once said

---

43 §§58, 254, above and 437, below.
44 Mavor, *Street of the World*, 16-17.
45 *Philadelphia Public Ledger*, May 14, 1904; N. Y. *Times*, Sept. 10, 1911; Jan. 7,

1921; Mar. 20, 1921; July 22, 1923; Jan. 7 and 30, 1927; Feb. 13, 1927.
46 "Witchcraft in West Polk Street," in *Amer. Mercury*, X, 71-75.

to her: "If the doctor can cure you, it's a sickness. If he can't do nothing for you and the more medicine you take the worster you are, you're witched." Love-potions and charms are numerous; to make or remove a charm one may consult *il mago* or *la maga*—the witchman or witchwoman. As an illustration of love-magic, the case is cited of a girl who bewitched a man by putting into a glass of wine three drops of her own blood and giving it to him, to drink. "After that he was helpless. Her blood within him drew him to her and, fight as he would, he had to follow her." Again, "Vincenzo was to marry Carolina, but Concetta wanted him, and when she found she could not get him she took a doll and called it Vincenzo. She stuck a pin into it every day and each time she did so a stroke went through Vincenzo's heart. Then, when the doll was full of pins, she threw it into the Lake. At this point Vincenzo's mother consulted a famous *maga* who told her that the only way to save her son would be to find the doll and pull out all the pins. How could the poor woman find a doll in Lake Michigan? So of course Vincenzo died."

§310. The Fetish-Man.

A GIRL was once sick in a village in British New Guinea. It was alleged that a shaman from another district had visited her, yet it was acknowledged by all that he was at that time in his own village, some miles from where the girl was. It was obvious to Strong[1] that the magician could not be in two places at once; "it seemed equally obvious to the natives that he could. Moreover, it was alleged that a footprint under the house was proof positive, because it was large like the footprint of the magician. . . . It was alleged that a native had been driven into a state of maniacal excitement because a brother miles away at Ioma had come and thrown a stone at him. The stone was produced—apparently identical with hundreds of other small stones lying around. It was admitted by all that the brother was miles away at Ioma, but at the same time contended that he had come and thrown the stone." A person with such power must be extraordinary. In the Mekeo district, "the prevailing belief was that the only way of rendering an evil magician harmless was to kill him. If he went to gaol he was only temporarily harmless, presumably because he would not have facilities in gaol for performing magic." Among the Fijians, "as soon as the god was supposed to have entered the priest, the latter became violently agitated, and worked himself up to the highest pitch of apparent frenzy, the muscles of the limbs seemed convulsed, the body swelled, the countenance became terrific, the features distorted, and the eyes wild and strained. In this state he often rolled on the earth, foaming at the mouth, as if labouring under the influence of the divinity by whom he was possessed, and, in shrill cries, and violent and often indistinct sounds, revealed the will of the god. The priests, who were attending, and versed in the mysteries, received, and reported to the people, the declarations which had been thus received."[2]

In the Andaman Islands, "these quasi-seers are invariably of the male sex, and it sometimes even happens that a young boy is looked upon as a 'coming,' . . . their position being generally in the first instance attained by relating an extraordinary dream, the details of which are declared to have been borne out subsequently by some unforeseen event, as, for instance, a sudden death by

---

1 In JAI, XLIX, 295.   2 Ellis, *Polyn. Researches*, I, 373-374.

accident." The seer "is credited with the power of communicating in dreams with the invisible powers of good and evil, and also of seeing the spirits of the departed, or of those who are ill. On the occurrence of an epidemic in an encampment, he brandishes a burning log, and bids the evil spirit keep at a distance; sometimes, as a further precaution, he plants stakes a few feet high in front of each hut."[3]

A certain South African negro was accredited with the power of understanding the speech of birds. "His friends thought that he had been chosen by the ghosts to be a magician or doctor and ascribed the fact that he did not attain to this dignity to a strife between the ghosts of his own house and those of his maternal uncle's; of these the latter wanted to confer on him the capacity, but the former resisted. Thus he had become only a sage and a dream-interpreter."[4] The activity of the bone-thrower in South Africa is more or less confined to sickness among cattle or human beings and to lost property and food. "It may be practised by either male or female, but is generally handed down from father to son. The son, when young, is given certain medicines to drink. At night he dreams that he finds out wonderful things by means of the bones. The father continues to give him medicine, and in due time the son, after he has proved to his father his ability to discover the cause of, and cure for, the sicknesses of people and animals, is proclaimed a bone thrower. To test his capabilities a stick or stone is hidden in a hut or corn bin in the kraal, or in the fence surrounding it. The discovery of this stick or stone is another proof of the power of the bones to reveal the thoughts of men and women."[5] In West Africa, "One cannot see his own bush-soul unless he is an Ebumtup, or sort of second-sighter. Ebumtupism is rare, and if one does happen to possess the gift, it is discovered by the presiding elders during initiation to the secret society of the tribe. When it is discovered, the presiding elders strongly advise that its owner enter the medical profession and become a witch-doctor, as the profession is a paying one, although dreadfully expensive to one's parents, for it has to be carried on by the established witch-doctor."[6] Again, soothsayers are such by heredity; if the father was a soothsayer, the son might not be, but only the grandson, to whom his grandfather appeared in a dream, urging him not to let the profession lapse.[7] Among the Fan the fetish-man is the special minister of the religious life; beside him, and striving in the shadow against him, is the sorcerer, a man of the extra-legal or illegal cult.[8] Black art is practised in the Upper Congo but is condemned by the natives, and its votaries have to pursue it in secret, else the hatred of the whole countryside would fall upon them. The medicine-man's white art is of a quite different character; it is used to cure people. Such practitioners "sometimes receive instruction from other witch doctors, but their fame, and consequently their wealth, depend upon their own craftiness and power to gull the people. Half-daft persons, and those who had recovered from insanity, were treated with much fear, and often spoken of as *nganga* of much power."[9] Magicians vary in importance among the Ba-Mbala, and also their prices in direct ratio. One such, if called by his name, replies *Galo*, a word the meaning of which is a great secret and is known to no one. "When he laughs he hisses loudly between his teeth, a performance which greatly

3 Man, in JAI, XII, 96.
4 Haarhoff, *Bantu-Stämme*, 36-37.
5 Garbutt, in JAI, XXXIX, 537.
6 Kingsley, *Travels W. Afr.*, 460.

7 Gutmann, in *Globus*, XCII, 165.
8 Trilles, *Fân*, 497.
9 Weeks, in JAI, XXXIX, 130, 396-397.

impresses the natives." Fetishes are carved from wood, but receive their power from the *Kissi* applied by the magician; "this *Kissi* is composed of clay or earth which he has inherited from his predecessors." One magician claims to be the inspired servant of his *Kissi*, "and alleges that when divining he does not know what he says, the *Kissi* speaks through him." Among the Ba-Yaka, the chief is the principal magician, but any man who possesses many fetishes with the requisite *Kissi* can become one.[10] The greatest of the Baganda deities is Mukasa; no suppliant is ever allowed in his hut, one must wait in an outer room for Gugu, the chief priest, to go in and inform Mukasa of the request, and also for the god to possess the priest. "The priest loses his identity and the god incarnated speaks and answers questions put to him and advises the suppliant how to act; when the interview is over the priest goes to the back of the hut and the ghost of Mukasa leaves him and returns to the hut and the priest is free to leave the enclosure if he wishes. During the time the priest is possessed by the *Lubare* [deity] he does not leave the hut. The priest is not allowed to drink beer, but must smoke a pipe of tobacco which prepares him for the reception of the ghost. When possessed he is able to lick hot iron, rub it with his hands, or strike his body with it and receive no harm."[11] Among some East African tribes, "a man can only become a medicine man if he is in direct communication with the *aiimu*, or ancestral spirits." Such a person points at a person or an object with the fingers extended but with the first and second joint doubled, for "if he pointed at a person with his finger he would be liable to an accusation of designs on the life of the person pointed at."[12] Among the Berbers of Tunis and Algiers, an ascetic who leads a pious, secluded, abstemious life is regarded as holy and is termed a marabout. Even the grave of such an one would shortly be called by the same term.[13]

The Soyots of the upper Yenesei are nominally Lamaists and Buddhists, but "without doubt shamanism still has the greatest authority." The lamas, like the shamans, have drums, flutes, and trumpets. The oldest of the three lamas is peculiar in that, in contrast to most Soyots, he has a long, coal-black beard. The shaman's job is inherited by sons or daughters; many women function as such. Their chief job is to prophesy and to drive out evil spirits from the sick; they hold converse with the dead in so doing. Their garb has pieces of iron on it and they are permitted to put on new ribbons for every time they have been in connection with the spirits, so that one can tell from his dress how experienced a shaman is. The iron attachments jingle as the shaman circulates about. It is very hard for a stranger to get such an outfit; to part with such would be like selling one's soul and endangering the community. A shaman must not operate on days of even number; overcast days are not good for a shaman's passage through the air. The fees of these specialists are usually three or four kroner (a krone is $.268); but if one is only slightly ill, he may have a "half-shamanization."[14]

Amongst the Yakuts the function of shaman is not hereditary; man became devoted to the service of the spirits without willing it. The guardian spirit of a deceased shaman seeks to find a place in somebody who belongs to the kin of the deceased. He who is to be a shaman begins to show signs of possession;

10 Torday and Joyce, in JAI, XXXV, 419; and in JAI, XXXVI, 51.
11 Roscoe, in JAI, XXXII, 74.
12 Hobley, in JAI, XLI, 414; Hobley, *A-Kamba*, 10.
13 Junker, *Afrika*, I, 22, note.
14 Olsen, *Primitivt Folk*, 95-97, 99, 105-106, 116, 122 ff.

has fits of unconsciousness; runs about the woods; lives on the bark of trees; casts himself into fire and water; seizes weapons and wounds himself so that his relatives take notice of him and recognize by these signs that he will be a shaman. They name him after the old shaman.[15] It is reported that the tendency of certain Yakuts to mental disease is quite extraordinary. "The Yakut woman is *without exception* hysterical," and is highly suggestible. One form of hysteria (*menerik*) appears to be epidemic and is characterized by paroxysms; it is artificially induced by the shamans. Hysteria major is also to be seen.[16] Marco Polo describes hallucinations of sight and sound in deserts, which often mislead travellers; no wonder the thought of the desert-dwellers turns to sorcery.[17] Miss Czaplicka,[18] generalizing about shamanism among all the Siberian tribes, states that "everywhere the supernatural gift is a necessary qualification for becoming a shaman." Among the Chukchi such persons are called "those with spirit." Although hysteria lies at the bottom of the shaman's vocation, yet at the same time the shaman differs from an ordinary patient suffering from this illness in possessing unusual power of mastering himself in the periods between the actual fits, which occur during the ceremonies. "He must know how and when to have his fit of inspiration, which sometimes rises to frenzy, and also how to preserve his high 'tabooed' attitude in his daily life." Whether his calling be hereditary or not, "a shaman must be a capable—nay, an inspired person. Of course, this is practically the same thing as saying that he is nervous and excitable, often to the verge of insanity. So long as he practises his vocation, however, the shaman never passes this verge. It often happens that before entering the calling persons have had serious nervous affections. . . . To be called to become a shaman is generally equivalent to being afflicted with hysteria; then the accepting of the call means recovery." The following is a typical statement as to how a person became a shaman: "When I was twenty years old, I became very ill and began to 'see with my eyes, to hear with my ears' that which others did not see or hear; nine years I struggled with myself, and I did not tell any one what was happening to me, as I was afraid that people would not believe me and would make fun of me. At last I became so seriously ill that I was on the verge of death; but when I started to shamanize I grew better; and even now when I do not shamanize for a long time I am liable to be ill." Generally in the features of a shaman there is something peculiar which enables a stranger after short experience to distinguish them from the other folk. The Chukchi are well aware of the extreme nervousness of their shamans and express it by a term meaning, "he is bashful." "By this word they mean to convey the idea that the shaman is highly sensitive, even to the slightest change of the psychic atmosphere surrounding him during his exercises." Examples are cited to bear this out. "The Altaians believe that no one becomes a shaman of his own free will; rather it comes to him *nolens volens,* like a hereditary disease. They say that sometimes when a young man feels premonitory symptoms of the call, he avoids shamans and shamanistic ceremonies, and by an effort of will occasionally cures himself. The period when the shamanistic call comes to the descendant of a shamanistic family is known as *tes bazin-yat,* 'the ancestor (spirit) leaps upon, strangles him.' " A child

15 Michailovski. *Shamanism* (Russ.), 73.

16 Mickewitz, cited in *Pol.-Anth. Rev.*, III, 203-204.

17 Yule, *Marco Polo*, 46, 128.

18 *Aborig. Siberia*, 169, 170, 172-174, 178, 185-187, 190, 194-196, 197-198, 199, 200, 201-202, 243-245, 320.

chosen to be a shaman is recognized among the Buryat by the following signs: "He is often absorbed in meditation, likes to be alone, has mysterious dreams, and sometimes has fits during which he is unconscious." According to the native beliefs, the soul of the child is then in process of being trained. "Living in the dwelling of the gods, his soul, under the tutelage of deceased shamans, learns the various secrets of the shaman's vocation; the soul must remember the names of the gods, the places where they live, the means by which they may be propitiated, and the names of the spirits which are subordinate to the high gods. After a period of trial the soul of the child returns to the body, which for a time resumes its normal life. But on his reaching adolescence, peculiar symptoms show themselves in the person who has undergone these experiences. He becomes moody, is easily excited into a state of ecstasy, leads an irregular life, wandering from *ulus* to *ulus* to watch the shamanistic ceremonies. He gives himself up with great earnestness to exercises in the shamanistic arts, for which purpose he segregates himself, going to some high mountain or into the forest, where, before a great fire, he calls on the spirits, and afterwards falls into a swoon. . . . If the future shaman belongs to a poor family, the whole community helps to procure the sacrificial animals and other things which are indispensable for the ceremonies. . . . But very few shamans go through all these purifications; most only undergo two or three; some, none at all, for they dread the responsibilities which devolve upon consecrated shamans. To a fully consecrated shaman the gods are very severe, and punish his faults or mistakes with death." The means of education among the Samoyed has been described as follows: "Two *tadibey* (shamans) blindfolded him with a handkerchief, and then beat him, one on the back of the head and the other on the shoulders, till his eyes were dazzled as with too much light, and he saw demons dancing on his arms and feet. It must be remembered, of course, that he had been taught beforehand about the Samoyed world of spirits. In former times Lapland was a school of shamanism, and all neighbouring tribes sent youths thither to be trained as shamans."

The smith, the authoress continues, who made the ornaments for the shamans' garments acquired some shamanistic power. "He was in contact with iron, which was of magical importance, and power came to him through this contact. (The smiths were, like the shamans, 'black' and 'white,' but among the Yakut one hears more of 'black' smiths than of 'white.') Thus the similarity between the vocation of a shaman and that of a smith becomes close, especially when the calling of smith descends through many generations in the same family. Smiths come to be considered as the elder brothers of shamans, and then the differences between them finally disappear, the smith becoming a shaman." This has been characteristic of the smith in other places.[19] "The smith and the shaman are of one nest," says a proverb of the Kolyma district. "The smiths also can cure, advise, and foretell the future, but their knowledge does not possess a magical character; they are simply clever people, who know much, and who possess 'peculiar fingers.' The profession of smith is generally hereditary, especially in the north. It is in the ninth generation that a [hereditary] smith first acquires certain supernatural qualities, and the more ancient his ancestry, the more marked are these qualities. The spirits are generally afraid of iron hoops and of the noise made by the blowing of the smith's bellows. . . . If the smith who makes a shamanistic ornament has not a sufficient

19 §72 of the text and *Case-Book*.

number of ancestors, if the noise of hammering and the glare of the fire does not surround him on all sides, then birds with crooked claws and beaks will tear his heart to pieces."

Miss Czaplicka considers the essential meaning of the word shaman. "In Sanskrit *sram* = to be tired, to become weary; *sramana* = work, religious mendicant. In the Pali language the word *samana* has the same meaning. These two latter words have been adopted by the Buddhists as names for their priests. But, according to Banzaroff, the word *shaman* originated in northern Asia: *saman* is a Manchu word, meaning 'one who is excited, moved, raised'; *samman* (pronounced shaman) and *hamman* in Tungus have the same meaning. *Samdambi* is Manchu: 'I shamanize,' i.e., 'I call the spirits dancing before the charm.' From the above we see that the essential characteristic of a shaman is a liability to nervous ecstasy and trances." Women are more prone to emotional excitement than men and many become shamans. "The woman is by nature a shaman," declared a Chukchi shaman to Bogoras. She does not need to be specially prepared for the calling, and so her novitiate is much shorter and less trying. Nearly all writers on Siberia agree that the position of the female shaman in modern days is sometimes more important than that occupied by the male. Taking into account the present prominent position of female shamans among many Siberian tribes and their place in traditions, together with certain feminine attributes of the male shaman (such as dress, habits, and privileges, which will be discussed later) and certain linguistic similarities between the names for male and female shamans, many scientists have been led to express the opinion that in former days only female shamans existed, and that the male shaman is a later development which has to some extent supplanted them. "The gift of inspiration is thought to be bestowed more frequently upon women, though it is reputed to be of a rather inferior kind, the higher grades belonging rather to men. The reason given for this is that the bearing of children is generally adverse to shamanistic inspirations, so that a young woman with considerable shamanistic power may lose the greater part of it after the birth of her first child." Thus does motherhood interfere with a career. The position of women as shamans is in accordance with what we have noted in respect to sex-differences and sex-destiny.[20]

The Siberian case is extensive and conclusive, but further instances may be briefly cited to show how generally the shaman is a fetish-man. Certain Todas have the power of divination, others are sorcerers, and others again have the power of curing disease by means of spells and rites, while all three functions are quite separate from those of the priest or dairyman. Before a dairyman enters upon office he has to undergo certain initiatory rites, which may fitly be spoken of as ordination-ceremonies. During the divining process the prophet is "in a distinctly abnormal condition of frenzy."[21] Among the Sema Nagas the *thumomi* is a seer, an interpreter of omens, a dreamer, and a clairvoyant. "Second sight he no doubt often has in some degree or other, and since it is an intermittent gift, he must simulate it when absent, for the sake of his reputation, and descend to deception just as a European medium does. In general the *thumomi* is in some degree possessed and is sometimes subject to fits somewhat resembling epilepsy." He is usually skilled in legerdemain. "If a man is ill or lame he will often go and consult a *thumomi,* who will tell him that there is 'dirt' in his body and will, after rubbing the injured place or

---

20 §§58 ff., of the text.   21 Rivers, *Todas,* 144, 153, 249, 253.

sundry and divers parts of the patient's body, extract, either by mouth or by hand, bits of stone, scraps of bones, teeth, chewed leaves, brown juices, or any old thing from the patient's body, leaving no mark where it came out."[22] The Saora "Kudang" communicates with the unseen world by some power which the ordinary Saora is not supposed to understand in the least and which is hereditary. He is the medium of communication between the spirits of the deceased and the living. "The Kudangs think they are to the manner born, and will reply, 'I do not know; my father, and his father before him, was a Kudang. I have always been a Kudang,' or words to that effect, if asked how he learned his trade."[23] In Manipur fitness for the post of priest or priestess is demonstrated by the spirits taking possession of one, throwing him into a species of fit, during which he babbles incoherently.[24] Among certain groups in India, as soon as priests begin to read the Veda, they dance, violently twist the limbs, roll their eyes, and foam at the mouth, thus becoming "possessed" and under the weather-god's control.[25] Among the Palaungs, a man or woman who has the power of projecting his or her spirit into another person's body is called a *bre*. "People with this power are greatly dreaded, and for this very reason are treated with great politeness. They live apart by themselves in the village, generally at one end, and only marry among themselves; their power is said to be hereditary. If a *bre* comes to a house and says, 'Friends have come to my house, give me, please, some rice or vegetables,' the things required would be given at once, without payment. Money is generally offered by the *bre*, but invariably refused, as no one would take money from a *bre*, for fear lest an evil influence should be transmitted with it. . . . When the wise man thinks that a *bre* has entered into a person who is mad or who has delusions, he gives him medicine, sprinkling some of it on the patient's face, saying, 'I order thee to say who thou art.' The patient generally gives as an answer the name of some person, either that of a living *bre*, of a person who is not known as a *bre*, or of the spirit of some one who is dead. In the latter case offerings must be made on the grave of the dead person. . . . If, however, the patient gives the name of a *bre*, the wise man proceeds to question him, saying, 'What dost thou wish to have?' The patient may answer nothing, or may say that he wants money, or some other thing. This request is supposed to come from the *bre* speaking in the patient. In that case friends go to the house of the suspected *bre*, taking with them the money or object desired. . . . The *bre* enters the room of the patient, holding the money, or the thing demanded, and says, 'Let us go, we have what we wanted.' . . . The *bre*, when a part of his spirit is supposed to be in the body of another person, appears tired and sleepy. The spirit or life of a person is made up of many separable parts, some may go out while others remain; so with the spirit of the *bre*, some part may leave his body and for a time may remain away; but if too many parts of his spirit go out, he will die."[26]

That the people of the Indian Archipelago "preferably choose the impotent for shamans has its natural reasons. . . . They 'are usually delicate of form and have a pale, languishing appearance, weak eyes, and a hoarse voice'— persons thus who certainly are more than others susceptible of being artificially brought into ecstasy."[27] It is stated, however, that in central Borneo

22 Hutton, *Sema Nagas*, 213, 247-249.
23 Fawcett, in JASB, I, 247.
24 Shakespear, in JAI, XL, 354.
25 Main, *Relig. Chastity*, 162.

26 Milne, *Eastern Clan*, 259-262.
27 Wilken, "Shamanisme," in VG, III, 376.

there is no especial selection of neurotic subjects for the priesthood.[28] Some Bornean priestesses are "self-appointed, hysterical girls."[29] Among the Dusuns there are regular fixed fees for young women wishing to enter the ranks of the initiated, their instruction covering a period of three months.[30] The chief power of the Sakai magician in earlier days consisted in his universally recognized attribute of being able to assure the health of his *clientèle.* "No demon could injure a magician, and the latter's death (no matter from what cause) was regarded solely as the act of heaven. . . . In addition to his staff, the Sakai magician also occasionally employed a sprinkling-brush with which, in the performance of certain ceremonies, he sprinkled the demons."[31] Among some tribes in the Philippines the shamans are mostly women; demons utter their will through "diabolic women" priests, often demanding the lives of innocent beings.[32] In the Gilbert Islands the priest's person was sacred.[33]

Among the Samoans, hunchbacks, epileptics, and others having any malformation or peculiarity of temper are suited to the office of shaman; it is also hereditary in the families of some chiefs.[34] "The priests in some cases were the chiefs of the place; but in general some one in a particular family claimed the privilege, and professed to declare the will of the god. . . . He fixed the days for the annual feasts in honour of the deity, received the offerings, and thanked the people for them. He decided also whether or not the people might go to war." On Tracey Island, "when the priest became 'red,' by which they meant flushed and excited, it was a sign that the god had something to say."[35] In the Friendly Islands, high priests could marry only the daughters of the king; their sons were priests, their daughters analogous to vestal virgins, not being allowed to marry.[36] Evidently both the royal and the priestly heredity carried a large element of the spiritual. Throughout Central Polynesia, the great chiefs or kings laid claim to actual personal sanctity, and sometimes even divinity. "It was considered dangerous to approach them, because of the deadly influence supposed to radiate from their persons. . . . not only that they might not be touched, but that their food had to be thrown to them; no one might eat the food they had left, and no one might sit beside them, a vacant place being always left on each side of the seat of honour on which they sat. . . . It would be sacrilege to disobey, hurt, or even touch him. . . . There were in Tonga certain contact taboos which apparently applied only or specially to the *tuitonga"* (priestly king). If he entered the house of "a subject it would become taboo and could never be inhabited by its owner; so there were particular houses for his reception when travelling. . . . The persons of the Tahitian kings were regarded as scarcely less sacred than the personifications of their deities. . . . The ground upon which the king and queen trod, even accidentally, became sacred, and it was for this reason that, when travelling on land outside their own private estate, they had to be carried on the shoulders of bearers, never for a moment letting their feet touch the ground, which, had they done so, would at once have become sacred. . . . No one was allowed to touch the body of the king or queen; and any one who should stand over them, or pass a hand over their heads, would be liable to pay for the sacrilegious act with his life. . . . Chiefs were sometimes taboo

28 Nieuwenhuis, *Borneo,* II, 227.
29 Main, *Relig. Chastity,* 159.
30 Evans, in JAI, XLII, 381.
31 Skeat and Blagden, *Malay Penin.,* II, 249-251.
32 Montero y Vidal, *Filipinas,* I, 55, 56.
33 Newell, in AAAS, 1895, 606.
34 Ella, in AAAS, 1892, 638.
35 Turner, *Samoa,* 20, 283-284.
36 Thomson, in USNM, 1889, 542.

for several days, and even months, remaining in a state of absolute inactivity, not being allowed to use their hands to eat, but being fed by others." Numerous examples on these points are given. A special body of Society Island officials, known as *harepo,* were the depositories and preservers of the sacred traditions. "The memory of these men was astonishing, and they could go on for whole nights, reciting these ancient traditions, word for word. On solemn occasions they would walk slowly at night-time round the temples and other sacred places, reciting all the time; and it was from this practice that they derived their name of *harepo,* or walkers in the night. If at any time they made a single mistake, or hesitated for a moment, they at once stopped, and returned home; and if their promenade had had as its aim some enterprise in which they wished to interest the gods, that single mistake sufficed to make them abandon the project, and not return to it; for success was no longer deemed possible." This is similar to the situation in Samoa where, if the priest stuttered over a single word in his prayer to the god, prior to war, it was a bad omen. It was the belief that "no one could have the power unless he had inherited it from his father; for we are told that, when a *harepo* was dying, his last moments were carefully watched; and the instant he expired they put to his mouth the mouth of the child who was to succeed him, thus making the latter, as it were, inhale the powers of the dying at the moment when his soul was about to leave the body." The extraordinary proceedings, with contortions and foaming at the mouth, of persons who were under the inspiration of a god are reported from a number of islands.[37] In New Zealand, Cowan[38] heard of numerous instances of mesmerism or hypnotic suggestion or whatever it may be, and "it has not yet been quite lost to the race. Telepathic powers the Maori *tohunga* undoubtedly had, and the power of projection of the will, by which he was enabled to afflict his enemies fatally. Many of the singular stories told of the occult powers of the adepts in *tohunga*-ism are obviously exaggerations and fables, but there is sufficient of fact left to suggest that the Maori priest enjoyed certain faculties which were widely possessed in the early stages of human history, but which through disuse—and civilization—have been lost to common knowledge."

The religion of the Eskimo appears to be "a belief in a multitude of supernatural beings, who are to be exorcised or propitiated by various observances, especially by the performances of certain specially gifted people, who are something of the nature of wizards."[39] Among the Tlinkits "the office of shaman may be inherited, like the ancient priesthood, but not necessarily so. As a rule, one must be consecrated to the office from infancy, and no comb, scissors or water must ever touch his hair. The longer and more matted the hair the greater the power the doctor is supposed to possess. For this reason the hair of an *ikt* was jealously guarded. If shorn of it his power vanished, and he was no longer consulted as a doctor. . . . They spent long periods in the forest in absolute solitude, supposedly in communication with evil spirits. They also had periods of fasting, and their diet differed in many respects from that of others. They ate the bark of devilclub and portions of bodies of the dead. They also procured and held in the mouth the finger of a dead *ikt*."[40] Among the Ten'a, "a man or woman, who has at his or her command one of these familiar spirits, is a medicine-man or a medicine-woman, as the case

37 Williamson. *Cent. Polyn.,* II, 409, 419-420; III, 72-82.
38 *Maoris,* 120.
39 Murdoch, in BAE, IX, 430.
40 Jones, *Thlingets,* 155.

may be. . . . The Russians designated them by the word *shamán*, which, according to Ivan Petrof, is 'a Kamchatkan term for sorçerer or medicine-man, used by many tribes who once were subject to Russian influence.' " There are about five times as many men as women in this category. Such a person does not choose his own spirit, but *vice versa*. "Some, indeed, are naturally predisposed to the calling. A peculiar deformity, which singles a man out of the vulgar crowd, is a sign of vocation. Thus the cross-eyed, the cripple, the lame, the sterile women, are more apt than others to be called to the devil-craft." One of the most famous of these shamans had "a sort of an appendix, probably a superficially located cyst, about the size and the form of the thumb, hanging from his breast." The calling to the profession is by the finding of a *karunih*, a small round body like a bead, to which is attached a spirit which becomes the familiar spirit of the new medicine-man. "A shaman is always supposed to die in the same way as he makes other people die, *i.e.*, his soul is eaten up by a spirit. I could obtain no particulars as to how this eating is done, but it is always the first and the last saying which one hears about a dying or dead medicine-man: 'A spirit is eating up his soul,' they will say: or 'his soul was eaten by a spirit.' Such is the summary of their funeral orations." Two shamans who were held in great repute and who undoubtedly were intelligent men, died in 1900, a Catholic priest assisting them during their last illness. "They both owned to him that they had never believed in their magical power, that they had been anxious for a long time to get out of their awkward situation, but were morally constrained to persevere in it by the fear of incurring universal reproof, if they had given it up. People, they alleged, would have considered them as mean and stingy fellows who refused to help the sufferers when they had the means to do so."[41]

When treating a patient or otherwise performing, a Northwest Coast shaman was supposed to be possessed by a supernatural being whose name he bore and whose dress he imitated. In general among the Indians north of Mexico, "there were two sorts of shamans—the shaman proper, whose functions were mainly curative, and the 'dreamer,' who communicated with spirits and the ghosts of the dead. All shamans were also dreamers, but not the reverse. During the winter months the dreamers held meetings in darkened houses, where they spoke with the spirits much like modern spirit mediums."[42] Among the Omahas there are mystery designs and decorations, to be used only by members of one of the orders of shamans. "The right to use such designs on a buffalo robe, blanket, tent, etc., must originate with one who has had a vision or a dream in which the mystery objects are manifested."[43] Any young man can become a doctor among the Apaches. His friends must be convinced that "he has the gift," that is, he must show that he is a dreamer of dreams, given to long fasts and vigils, able to interpret omens satisfactorily, and do other things which will demonstrate the possession of an intense spirituality. Then he begins to withdraw temporarily from the society of his fellows and to devote himself to long absences, particularly by night, in the "high places" which were interdicted to the Israelites. An Indian will climb to apparently inaccessible heights on a mountain to make his medicine.[44] With the Cheyenne Indians "a man cannot become a doctor by himself; when he receives the

41 Jetté, in JAI, XXXVII, 162, 165-166, 176-177.
42 Swanton, "Shamans," in HAI, II, 522, 523.
43 Dorsey, in BAE, XI, 394.
44 Bourke, in BAE, IX, 452.

power, his wife—who afterward is his assistant—must also be taught and receive certain secrets. . . . If the wife of the man who is receiving the power does not wish to become a doctor, the man must find another woman to act with him. A man may become a doctor through a dream, thus receiving spiritual power directly from above, but even in this case he must have a woman to help him. Even though he receive his power through a dream, he must still go to another doctor to be taught certain things."[45] Among one of the southwestern tribes, the chief, who is also chief priest, is blind. "It is presumed that after having been chief many years, he put out his eyes, according to a custom of the Indians, in order to become chief priest among them."[46] Iroquois women are reported traditionally to have been magicians. Among the aborigines of the Mosquito coast in Central America women often serve in the same capacity, and are said to exercise great power.[47] Among the Araucanians "the witchdoctor, through his training, mode of life, and natural temperament, is generally a person of a highly strung nervous disposition, to whom the faculty of throwing himself into a cataleptic or hypnotic trance is a second nature. When called in to discover the secret enemy who has caused the death of a certain individual, by the aid of powerful drugs, intensely concentrated attention and severe bodily exercise, he works himself up to such a pitch of nervous excitement that he finally collapses into a state of coma or trance, which frequently lasts for several hours. During this trance, any person or being which passes before his mind's eye is considered to have been the offender and is speedily denounced, there being no appeal from these decisions. Naturally enough, this gives the *machi* an immense power, as it offers him an opportunity for wreaking vengeance on anyone who has fallen into his bad books. But these opportunities are seldom taken advantage of, as it creates a blood feud with the kindred of the accused."[48]

The Nazarite was "one separated," a Jew who bound himself by a vow to a life of purity and devotion to Jahweh. Samson is the oldest example. To "separate themselves unto the Lord," the Nazarites had to abstain from wine, let their hair grow, and come at no dead body. In the post-exilic period they were very numerous, even among women, and in the time of the Maccabees exhibited symptoms such as later characterized the mediæval crusades.[49] In Rome the priests of the Great Mother of the Gods were called sorcerers, dwellers in caves. They and the priestesses, who were just as common, "often dedicated to the goddess their locks, which they had tossed wildly in the frenzied dance."[50] Cybele's dark-robed priests and priestesses were familiar figures in the Augustan age, "gashing themselves like the Galli of Magna Mater, catching the blood in shields, and dashing it over their train of followers who believed in its powers of expiation."[51]

Sex-reversal. As shedding light upon the abnormal, or at least peculiar, character of the shaman, a number of cases of sex-reversal could be cited. This practice of men posing and living as women, and *vice versa,* is also related to religious sexual perversions. In northeast Siberia the shamans put on women's dress and wear the hair in long braids like women. It is believed

45 Grinnell, *Cheyenne Ind.*, II, 128-129.
46 Bolton, in HAI, II, 8.
47 Mathews, "Magic," in HAI, I, 785.
48 Latcham, in JAI, XXXIX, 346.

49 Maurer, *Vkde.*, I, 90-91, 92; Numbers, VI, 1-22.
50 Showerman, *Mother of the Gods*, 236-237.
51 Dill, *Nero*, 558-559.

that any distinguished shaman can bear children.[52] On the Yakut shaman's apron there are sewn two iron circles, representing breasts. Other feminine attributes of the male shaman are as follows: he dresses his hair like a woman, on the two sides of the head, and braids it; during a performance he lets the hair fall down; both women and shamans are forbidden to lie on the right side of a horse-skin; the man-shaman wears the shaman's costume only on very important occasions, in ordinary circumstances he wears a girl's dress made of the skin of a foal; during the first three days after a confinement, when the deity of fecundity is supposed to be near the woman who is lying-in, access to the house where she is confined is forbidden to men, but not to shamans.[53] In Manipur, "the Maibi [priestess] is looked on as superior to any man, by reason of her communion with the god; and therefore if a man is honoured in the same way he assumes the dress of the Maibi as an honour."[54] The custom of a man adopting the life of a woman prevailed among some of the western Indians of the United States; an informant had known of eight cases during her lifetime. "She knew of no ceremonial functions performed by them, but she had heard of physical relations between them and men."[55] More definite is the account of this custom among the Cheyennes: "Of these halfmen-half-women there were at that time five. They were men, but had taken up the ways of women; even their voices sounded between the voice of a man and that of a woman. They were very popular and especial favorites of young people, whether married or not, for they were noted matchmakers. They were fine love talkers. If a man wanted to get a girl to run away with him and could get one of these people to help him, he seldom failed. When a young man wanted to send gifts for a young woman, one of these halfmen-halfwomen was sent to the girl's relatives to do the talking in making the marriage. . . . These men had both men's names and women's names. The one among the Northern Cheyennes was named Pipe and his woman's name was Pipe Woman. . . . When a war-party was preparing to start out, one of these persons was often asked to accompany it, and, in fact, in old times large war-parties rarely started without one or two of them. They were good company and fine talkers. When they went with war-parties they were well treated. They watched all that was being done, and in the fighting cared for the wounded, in which they were skillful, for they were doctors or medicine men. After a battle the best scalps were given to them, and when they came in sight of the village on their return they carried these scalps on the ends of poles."[56] The sorcerers among the Araucanians "wore woman's dress and their hair long and un-combed."[57] In Rome, the priests of the Great Mother of the Gods "were eunuchs, were attired in female garb, and wore their hair, fragrant with oint-ment, wound in coils on the top of the head, letting it hang loose, however, while performing their orgies."[58] There are numerous other cases of the same sort.[59]

---

52 Sieroshevski-Sumner, in JAI, XXXI, 103-104.
53 Czaplicka, Aborig. Siberia, 199.
54 Shakespear, in JAI, XL, 354.
55 Parsons, in AA, XX, 181-182.
56 Grinnell, Cheyenne, II, 39-40.
57 Latcham, in JAI, XXXIX, 351.
58 Showerman, Mother of the Gods, 236-237.

59 Crawley, in JAI, XXIV, 443 ff.; Roth, Sarawak, I, 270; Schwaner, Borneo, 185 ff.; Powers, in Contrib. No. Amer. Ethnol., III, 132; Ratzel, Vkde., II, 631; Dorsey, in BAE, XI, 378; Winship, in BAE, XIV, pt. I, 413 ff.; Roth, in JAI, XXI, 119; Bogoras, in AA, III, 99; Donaldson, in Smithson. Rep., 1885, pt. II, 313; Carr, in Smithson. Rep., 1891, 476 ff.. 531.

§311. Induced Possession.

IF the shaman is not already "possessed," he knows how to produce that ecstatic condition so essential to proper communication with the gods. Witness the case of the Fijian priest, who takes a whale-tooth and stares at it: "In a few minutes he trembles; slight distortions are seen in his face, and twitching movements in his limbs. These increase to a violent muscular action, which spreads until the whole frame is strongly convulsed, and the man shivers as with a strong ague fit. In some instances this is accompanied with murmurs and sobs, the veins are greatly enlarged, and the circulation of the blood quickened. The priest is now possessed by his god, and all his words and actions are considered as no longer his own, but those of the deity who has entered into him. Shrill cries of 'It is I! It is I!' fill the air, and the god is supposed thus to notify his approach. While giving the answer, the priest's eyes stand out and roll as in a frenzy; his voice is unnatural, his face pale, his lips livid, his breathing depressed, and his entire appearance like that of a furious madman. The sweat runs from every pore, and tears start from his strained eyes; after which the symptoms gradually disappear. The priest looks round with a vacant stare, and, as the god says, 'I depart,' announces his actual departure by violently flinging himself down on the mat, or by suddenly striking the ground with a club, when those at a distance are informed by blasts on the conch, or the firing of a musket, that the deity has returned into the world of spirits."[1]

A South African girl must enter the profession of the *i-shumba* or doctors if she is possessed by one of this class of spirits. She is put under blankets and given a vapor bath. "She generally has to remain inhaling the vapour until she is almost choked, and the more she suffers the greater is the credit given to the doctoress who is performing the operation. Whilst the patient is under the blanket the *i-shumba* woman asks her what her name is and generally receives in reply some odd name, which is taken to be the title of the spirit who wishes to enter the girl. . . . After this is done all the *i-shumba* women meet and the girl goes through the final initiation ceremony. This consists of drinking a compound of raw goat's blood, tobacco juice, meat and herbs. Should this make her sick it is taken as a sign that the *shumba* spirit rejects her. On the other hand should she retain the mixture she is entitled to wear the special costume of the *i-shumba*."[2] The following is a description of the means employed in Madagascar to call a spirit into a girl. Two old skinny hags stood on either side of her, but they were dignified and grave. From time to time they passed under the girl's nose incense with a penetrating odor, and made passes with wands before her. She was agitated by violent internal emotion, her chest expanding and contracting vehemently, and her eyes imploring. A song was sung urging the spirit to enter her. Suddenly she jumped to her feet and said, "I have arrived." The crowd became delirious. "The features of the young girl were changed before my eye," states a missionary who was an eyewitness, and who scouts the idea of being under hallucination. She seemed to get bigger in stature and form; she became taller by a head at least than the two old women. The sick and others were brought to her as a medicine-woman and prophetess. She told them the useful remedies, speaking in a guttural

1 Williams, *Fiji*, quoted in Wilken, "Shamanisme," in VG, III, 339-340.   2 Garbutt, in JAI, XXXIX, 554.

voice, brief and jerky, giving commands rather than advice. She did not look at the patients, her eyes were fixed on a distance and immobile. Thereafter occurred more passes by the old women and she shrank back to her ordinary stature, her eyes finally recovered their normal expression, and she (that is, the spirit within her) said, "I am going away." The missionary subsequently saw the girl from time to time; she had a distraught air and haggard eyes.[3]

In modern Egypt a magician, wishing to detect a thief, poured a little ink into a boy's palm. "Into this ink, he desired the boy steadfastly to look. He then burned some incense, and several bits of paper inscribed with charms; and at the same time called for various objects to appear in the ink. The boy declared that he saw all these objects, and last of all, the image of the guilty person; he described his stature, countenance, and dress; said that he knew him; and directly ran down into the garden, and apprehended one of the labourers, who, when brought before the master immediately confessed that he was the thief."[4] This is a variant of crystal-gazing.

Lehmann[5] reproduces a vivid description of the Tungus shaman and his process of securing inspiration: "A bright fire was burning in the middle of the hut, and about it was spread a circle of wild sheep's skins. Upon these a shaman circulated with slow, measured step, mumbling his incantations. His long black hair hung down over and almost totally covered his red and swollen face; through it, as through a veil, shone a pair of glittering, bloodshot eyes. His long robe of deerskin was from top to bottom bedecked with thongs, amulets, chains, little bells, and pieces of copper and iron. In his right hand he held his magic drum to which likewise bells were attached, and in his left a bow. His appearance was downright horrible, and the whole company observed him with the most spellbound attention. Little by little the fire died down, the glowing coals emitting a mysterious half-light. The shaman now threw himself to the earth and lay immovable, sighing and groaning in such manner as to give the impression of several different voices. Then the fire was again brought to a clear blaze and the shaman sprang up; he rested his bow upon the ground, leaned his forehead against its upper end, which he held in his hand, and thus began, at first slowly, then faster and faster, to run around the bow. This was kept up so long that one became dizzy simply from looking on. Suddenly the shaman stopped and began to draw magic figures in the air; then seized his drum and struck up a kind of melody, at the same time leaping about and contorting his body in the most incomprehensible manner. Meanwhile he smoked, off and on, several pipes of strong tobacco, and took whiskey in the interval between pipes. This, in combination with his gyrations, finally made him dizzy, and he suddenly fell and lay rigid and unconscious. Two of the onlookers lifted him up; he was now fearful to behold. His eyes were fixed, and protruded from his head; his face was copper-red and he seemed totally unconscious; except for a slight twitching of his body, no sign of life was to be observed in him. Finally he appeared to come to his senses; he swung his magic drum rapidly, causing the bells to jingle loudly; then let it fall upon the earth. This was a sign that he was ready to be consulted. His answers to questions propounded were given without reflection, as if he himself had no inkling of what was going on. For the most part, the answers were given in an ambiguous, oracular style, so that the questioners could interpret

3 Account quoted in Trilles, *Fân*, 644-646.   5 *Overtro*, I, 31-32.
4 Lane, *Mod. Egypt.*, I, 409.

them as they chose. But the most interesting thing about the account is without question the conclusion, that here we see employed intoxication and hypnotism as means of inducing a mental state in which sorcerers, unwittingly to themselves, are able to answer questions to which, in a normal state, they could scarcely give an intelligent response."

"The individual who is predestined by the power of the ancestors to be a shaman feels suddenly a languor and relaxation in his limbs, which announces itself by a violent trembling. There comes over him a vehement, unnatural yawning, a powerful pressure weighs down upon his breast, forcing him suddenly to emit loud, inarticulate cries. A feverish chill shakes him, his eyes roll wildly, he suddenly leaps up and whirls in a circle as if possessed until he falls covered with sweat, and grovels on the ground with epileptic twitchings and spasms. His limbs are quite without sensation, he seizes what comes to hand and swallows purposelessly everything he has laid hand to—glowing iron, knives, needles, axes—without any harm coming to him through this engorgement. After a time he rejects what he has swallowed, dry and intact. (Naturally I have all this only from hearsay and indeed from very trustworthy persons—a matter which is, in affairs of superstition, certainly, of complete indifference. Who is here the dupe is hard to decide; probably self-deception and deliberate imposition go hand in hand.) All these sufferings become stronger and stronger until the individual who is so tortured at last seizes the shaman's drum and begins to shamanize. Then only does nature become quiet; the force of the ancestors has gone over into him and he cannot now do otherwise—he must shamanize. If the man destined to be a shaman opposes the will of the ancestors, if he refuses to shamanize, he exposes himself to frightful agonies which result either in the person in question losing all spiritual power whatever, and so becoming imbecile and inert, or in his falling into wild insanity and commonly doing himself some injury within a short time or dying in paroxysm."[6]

Michailovski[7] says of Gmelin, an early authority, that in his studies in Siberia he was not guided by an objective spirit of investigation, but showed all the time the prejudices of a Lutheran pastor. He saw in the proceedings of the shamans only efforts to deceive, which he tried to expose. The fact is that the short and violent gestures, the sound of the drum, the convulsive writhings, the inarticulate cries, and the wild glances amidst the half gloom, all taken together, exert terror on the half-wild people and act powerfully on the nerves.

The so-called demonolatry in southern India exhibits the same methods and makes a similar impression. The official priest is called a "devil-dancer," and he dons the devil's insignia to strike terror into the imagination of the beholders. When the devil-dance is about to commence, the music is first comparatively slow and the dancer seems impassive and sullen; he stands still or moves about in gloomy silence. Gradually, as the music becomes quicker and louder, his excitement rises. Sometimes he uses medicated drugs to help create a frenzy, and cuts and lacerates his flesh until the blood flows, lashes himself with a huge whip, presses a burning torch to his breast, drinks the blood which flows from his own wounds, or drinks the blood of the sacrifice, putting the throat of the decapitated goat to his mouth. Then, as if acquiring a new life, he brandishes his staff of bells and dances with a quick but wild step. Sud-

6 Radloff, *Schamanenthum*, 16, 17.   7 *Shamanism* (Russ.), 4, 55, 69; Shchukin, *Shamanism* (Russ.), pt. II, 24.

denly the afflatus descends. There is no mistaking that glare or those frantic leaps. He snorts, he stares, he gyrates. The demon has now taken bodily possession of him; and though he retains the power of utterance and motion, they are under the demon's control, and his separate consciousness is in abeyance. The bystanders proclaim the event by raising a long shout, attended with a peculiar vibratory noise, caused by the motion of the hand and tongue or of the tongue alone. The devil-dancer is now worshipped as a present deity and every bystander consults him respecting his disease, his wants, the welfare of his absent relatives, the offerings to be made for the accomplishment of his wishes, and, in short, respecting everything for which superhuman knowledge is supposed to be available. "As the devil-dancer acts to admiration the part of a maniac, it requires some experience to enable a person to interpret his dubious or unmeaning replies, his muttered voices and uncouth gestures; but the wishes of the parties who consult him, help them greatly to interpret his meaning."[8] This is a case of what we should call daimonology rather than demonolatry or devil-worship. It is to be noted how the people read their own interpretations into the oracular or meaningless words of the intoxicated dancer.

In India the process called "hazirat" is based upon the principle of the magic mirror. The same idea underlies various other forms of divination, e.g., lecanomancy, hydromancy, catoptromancy, crystallomancy, and pyromancy. "All of these date back to remote antiquity. By the first method, the seer is required to gaze into a metal cup or basin, filled with water, wine, or oil; by the second, into a sacred pool or fountain; by the third, into a metal or glass mirror; by the fourth, into a crystal; and by the last, into fire or flame."[9] Some holy men in India claimed that they were able to asphyxiate themselves by rolling the tongue back, remain dead for forty days, and then come to life again.[10] "The Lushais believe that certain persons, both males and females, but more generally females, have the power of putting themselves into a trance and are in a state of communication with Khuavang. . . . The belief in a species of demoniacal possession is very common."[11] In Bangalore there is held, in the first month of every Hindu year, a feast in honor of Swami. At eight the next morning, the people still fasting, a stage of the proceedings is reached when those women who have been previously possessed by evil spirits show signs of possession. They sit in a row in front of the Swami and are questioned in turn by the chief worshipper. Two rude pieces of cane, three feet long and rudely ornamented, are always kept near the Swami. "A man, having previously bathed and put on clean cloths, twists one of these wands in a patient's hair and holds it with a handful of her hair in one hand at arm's length; another man on the other side of the patient also holds a handful of her hair at arm's length; between them they drag her by her hair to some trees half a mile away; nail a lock of her hair to a tree, and let her go. She flings herself about in frenzy (sometimes trying to climb the tree), and throws herself on the ground, leaving the lock of her hair, torn out by the roots, fastened to the tree by the nail. After a while she gets up, mistress of her person, the spirits having gone up the tree. All patients are treated in the same way." When these women found themselves possessed, they had been starving for about thirty-six hours.[12]

---

8 Caldwell, in JASB, I, 100, 101, 102.
9 Leith, in JASB, I, 25-26.
10 Stoll, *Suggestion*, 76 ff.

11 Shakespear, in JAI, XXXIX, 384.
12 Fawcett, in JASB, I, 534 ff.

In the East Indies, ecstasy was inspired in young boys and girls by various means and shamans worked themselves up into that state in the presence of the sick, thus receiving the evil spirit that afflicted them. In their ceremonies they often used a strange tongue, words generally from the Malay or some antique speech. To interview the spirits concerning the fishing prospects, a woman has incense burned before her and her body strewn with white and browned rice. Presently her eyes begin to glitter as they are fixed upon one point; she is then possessed and in a position to direct propitiation. Swaying back and forth, she addresses the spirits in an unknown tongue. There are other cases where ghost-seers work themselves into ecstasy, showing first a trembling movement and then springing up and dancing until they sink unconscious to the earth. For the duration of the ecstasy the shaman can see through the mysteries of the present and future. Precipitation of this state occurs in a ceremonious way in the presence of a large gathering who chant certain melodies and beat a drum to help transport the shaman. In their midst he performs the wildest and oddest sort of dance, usually called the dance of the witches, by which means he contributes to the enchantment of the stimulation until finally he reaches the acme of ecstasy. This makes him clairvoyant and able to answer the questions propounded to him.[13] The Dyak shamans depend largely upon dreams, in which they receive advice from spirits concerning the properties of various fetish objects.[14] Another means of communicating with the supernatural is to sleep on the tops of mountains. Swings may be used to produce vertigo, a trance resulting.[15] Cures are generally effected in darkness, for it is difficult and dangerous to have dealings with the spirits in the daytime. The shaman gazes into his "stone of light" to diagnose the character of the ailment and to see where the soul is.[16] Some of them seem to know that they are impostors.[17]

Among the Polynesians there were, in addition to the priesthood, certain persons who were inspired permanently or periodically, and "could at almost any time obtain inspiration, and make oracular statements as mouthpieces of the god, whose name they often took. These people formed a kind of college or corporation in Tahiti, and had considerable power; and, although linked with the priests, they rather supplanted them in their functions as augurers in time of war. The influence of these inspired men over combatants was accentuated by the positive and vehement nature of their pronouncements, as compared with the vague and uncertain statements which followed the investigation by the priests of victims, their consultation of the heavens and their experiences of dreams."[18]

To become an *angakok* the Eskimo goes into the wilderness and engages in contemplation. His brain becomes unsettled and he is then competent to discharge shamanistic functions. In the novitiate the candidate must rub one stone on another for three days. He is supposed to die in frightful agonies, partly from fear and partly from overexertion, but to rise again later on. The process goes on for three years or more, during which the novice has learned a number of mystifying tricks.[19] Among the Central Eskimo "most of the angakut believe in their own performances, as by continued shouting and in-

13 Wilken, *Vkde.*, 566 ff.; "Shamanisme," in VG, III, 332-333.
14 Roth, *Sarawak*, I, 185, 291.
15 Lawrence and Hewitt, in JAI, XXXVIII, 391.
16 Gomes, *Sea Dyaks*, 165, 166.
17 Nieuwenhuis, *Borneo*, II, 228.
18 Williamson, *Cent. Polynesia*, II, 418-419.
19 Cranz, *Grönland*, I, 253; Holm, *Eth. Skizze*, 79, 87.

voking they fall into an ecstasy and really imagine that they accomplish the flights and see the spirits."[20] Doubtless the not uncommon "flying dream" plays its part in this persuasion. Training is often from babyhood, through vigils, pain, the control of desires, silence, and solitary communion with nature. The aim is to attain trance or ecstasy, union with the spirits, absorption into the universe. Contortions, paroxysms, exhaustion, and fits of homicide and suicide are attendant phenomena.[21]

The use for narcotic purposes of peyote, a species of cactus grown in Northern Mexico, has assumed alarming proportions among the Indians of the United States. From time immemorial peyote has been used by certain tribes in Mexico to produce intoxication at religious ceremonies. From there it spread to the Kiowas of the Rio Grande, the Zuñis of Arizona, and others. The use of four or five peyote balls "produces a peculiar cerebral excitement attended with an extraordinary visual disturbance. There is uncertainty of gait, like that caused by alcohol, wakefulness, and over-estimation of time; minutes become hours; distances become accentuated; there is a sense of dual existence. The drug also produces visual hallucinations and affects the hearing. The habitué enjoys a regular kaleidoscopic play of most wonderful colors and an incessant flow of visions of infinite beauty, grandeur and variety." It is not strange to find that a drug producing such extraordinary effects is eagerly sought and that to it is ascribed supernatural power. Today there is a new, semi-religious movement among thousands of Indians which exalts peyote into a fetish to be worshipped as something supernatural. Meetings are generally held every Saturday night and last all night long. By midnight many have become intoxicated, enjoying the incessant and wonderful visions and music. In some tribes it is spoken of as the Holy Spirit, the "Comforter" that Jesus sent. It is believed that it causes the users to see their sins and makes their hearts feel kind toward God and man.[22] "The members of the peyote societies customarily see God, Jesus, or Heaven with perhaps some scenes from their past misdeeds. The terrifying visions of the novices are interpreted as the result of an unrepentant spirit, acceptance of the peyote as holy being in the nature of a conversion (reorganization of attitudes toward it) which carries with it pleasant visions. Due to the vividness with which the peyote vision portrays things and the ease with which Christian and pagan elements can be combined in it, peyote is regarded as the means of interpreting the Bible. It has been identified with the Holy Ghost and thus becomes one of the Trinity and through it the Bible becomes clear to the Indian, that is, through the visions the Biblical teachings are applied to the Indians' individual problems. . . . It is highly significant that all the older members of the peyote speak of the diseases of which it cured them. Along this line lay unquestionably its appeal for the first converts."[23]

Similarly wine is considered as a spirit or as containing a spirit, because it intoxicates or inspires. Some Indians of Spanish America intoxicated themselves to commit with impunity certain crimes. "It appears that in the primitive view intoxication or the inspiration produced by wine is exactly parallel to the inspiration produced by drinking the blood of animals. The soul or life is in the blood, and wine is the blood of the vine. Hence whoever drinks the

20 Boas, in BAE, VI, 594.
21 Reclus, *Prim. Folk*, 71.

22 Lindquist, *Red Man*, 69 ff.; N. Y. *Times*, Jan. 8 and 14, 1923.
23 Shonle, in AA, XXVII, 72, 73.

blood of an animal is inspired with the soul of the animal or of the god who is often supposed to enter into the animal before it is slain; and whoever drinks wine drinks the blood, and so receives into himself the soul or spirit of the god of the wine."[24]

The shamans of Hispaniola delivered oracles in a state of rhapsody produced by drinking a "secret water," and performed the usual shamanistic contortions.[25] The activity of the shamans of British Guiana included the production in themselves of a wild ecstasy by the use of a narcotic powder and the art of ventriloquism. They are identifiable by their gloomy and black looks, their lonely, secluded manner of life, and their ascetic severity. The whole village is unreservedly subject to the shaman.[26] Among the Shingu Indians any one may become a medicine-man but it is difficult and there is much to be learned. For four months one must drink only their starch extract, eat no salt, flesh, fish, or fruit, not sleep, bathe often, and scratch the arm and breast till the blood runs. The chief element of the art is the use of poisons with which the shaman kills others and also himself, in order to transform himself into other forms. The method used is excitement of the imagination; the idea is to work one's self up to a pitch of excitement which enables him to contend with the evil forces. Hence it is that the medicine-man takes the medicine; it is a sort of "Dutch courage." It is believed that the shamans, when they have narcotized themselves with tobacco, are transformed into animals and can go anywhere while in that state. Tobacco smoke cures everything; the natives blew it into the author's ears in order that he might learn their language more rapidly.[27]

Again, the *pajé* must begin even in youth to seek solitude in inaccessible spots, and through years he must fast, keep silence, and abstain. He engages in wild, obscene dances to the point of exhaustion and by these exercises, and also by injecting tobacco-juice and other strong liquids into his eyes, he becomes competent to associate with snakes and other poisonous beasts, to practise the healing art, to counsel the elders, and to excite the youth by nocturnal rehearsals of war-stories and tribal tradition. Many legends support the power of these shamans over animals and men.[28]

In Homer we find a long description of how Odysseus acted in order to come into relation with the spirits. Lehmann[29] says he is probably the oldest "medium" concerning whom there is any exact information. The Homeric poems give scarcely an inkling of the overexcitement of religious feeling which the Greeks of a later time knew and revered as god-sent madness. This originated in the Dionysus cult and came into Greek life as something new and foreign.[30] The great law-givers, such as Manu, Moses, and Zoroaster, were fetish-men in that they received the laws from God through revelation. God will answer only when the rites are fully satisfied, and most distinctly he answers the faithful priest. Aaron was to be the mouth of Moses, and Moses the god of Aaron.[31] Laurel was chewed in southern Europe to secure religious exaltation, to drive out consciousness so that some other spirit might enter and inspire the prophet. Later it yielded to better means.[32]

24 Frazer, *Golden Bough*, I, 184-185.
25 Eden, *Three English Books*, 215.
26 Schomburgk, *Brit.-Guiana*, I, 423.
27 Von den Steinen, *Zent. Bras.*, 343, 344, 347.
28 Von Martius, *Beiträge*, I, 585.

29 *Overtro*, III, 5.
30 Rohde, *Psyche*, II, 5.
31 Exod., IV, 16.
32 Lippert, *Kgchte.*, I, 625; II, 456; Achelis, *Ekstase*, 7, 23, 151 ff., 169 ff.

§312. Reputed Powers of the Shaman.

AFTER various initiatory features, such as are mentioned in the text, the new Australian medicine-man mingles with members of the craft, learning their secrets, such as they are, practising sleight-of-hand tricks, and, not least in importance, accustoming himself to looking preternaturally solemn, as if he knew and were constantly dealing with things hidden from the knowledge of ordinary men. By means of certain fetish stones he is able to combat the evil magic which an enemy has planted in the body of his patient. "These stones he can, unseen by any ordinary being, project into the patient's body."[1] Abel[2] often asked the natives of New Guinea: "Do you really believe the sorcerer extracts stones and sticks from the body?" and the answer usually was, "No, but he says he does. The man is dying and we don't know what to do."

It is said that in spite of all his superstitions the Bakoko is not dependent on the medicine-man nor deceived by him; for the religion is the common property of all and the ceremonies take place in the open.[3] The Ju-Ju priests of West Africa were supposed to be able to cause the water used in ordeals to rise in the well, and when it was suggested that there was here an underground water-supply brought from a higher elevation, the idea was scouted as follows: "White man he no be fit savey all dem debly ting Ju-Ju priest fit to do; he fit to change man him face so him own mudder no fit savey him; he fit make dem tree he live for water side, bob him head down and drink water all same man; he fit make himself alsame bird and fly away; you fit to look him lib for one place and you keep you eye for him, he gone, you no fit see him when he go."[1] "A peculiar facility for making fire when and where he likes is a distinguishing characteristic of a wizard, and intelligent English-speaking Fantis have assured me that their own eyes beheld unmistakable proofs of this magic in action."[5] Where the dead are supposed to ascend on a string to the spirit-world, the shaman summons them by tying a string to the top of the temple and letting it rest on his back as he kneels. The dead thus descend and possess him.[6] An illustration of clumsy work in mystery-making is related by Johnston.[7] When a witch-doctor becomes the father of a son, he contrives to have the baby disappear on the third night after birth, "and every one affects to bewail its loss and to search for it ineffectually. At dawn it is found outside the door of its mother's house with the tail of an ox tied round its neck (by the father, of course). This is a sign that the child is intended to be a sorcerer when he grows up." And it is found as easy to believe the impossible as to shut the eyes to such an obvious performance. Among the Galla it is related of a certain woman that she descended naked into a pool, dove under water and managed to get to the surface of the water again with a burning torch in her hand; whereupon she was declared, on the basis of this piece of art, to be the local magician.[8] Among the Kabyles a wise, virtuous man, faithful in his duties to god and fellow-men, will be honored and revered as a marabout or saint, which title he may bequeath to his male posterity. The credulous crowd is always ready to accord to the marabouts supernatural powers; "this belief once established, their influence becomes truly considerable and can operate effectually, at a given moment, on the

1 Gillen, in AAAS, 1901, 118, 119.
2 New Guinea, 100.
3 Von Schkopp, in Globus, LXXXIII, 332.
4 Kingsley, W. Afr. Studies, 499.

5 Connolly, in JAI, XXVI, 150.
6 Frobenius, Masken, 198.
7 Uganda, II, 882.
8 Paulitschke, Nordost-Afr., II, 63.

people. In fact, how could a Kabyle help but respect and especially fear a man who, with a word, can change him into a woman, make hail fall on the crops, or inflict him with any disease?" In Kabylie, as in all Moslem countries, there exist religious orders the chiefs of which, without being always mara-bouts, exercise considerable power over the spirits. "One divines that it is a question of the associations surrounding them and of the mystery of the secret societies."[9]

The Buryats believe that the "black shamans" eat human flesh; "the shaman eats the soul of the man, and the latter dies, for man cannot live without a soul."[10] This people has a legend that the first shaman was born, at the desire of the Good Spirit, of an eagle and a Buryat woman. He had unlimited power and God, desiring to test him, took away the soul of a rich maiden, so that she became ill. The shaman flew on his drum through the heavenly paths and through Hades, seeking the soul, until finally he saw it in a bottle on the table of God. To keep the soul in the bottle the god had corked it with a finger of his right hand. The coming shaman turned himself into a yellow horse-fly and stung the god on the right cheek so that he put his right hand to his cheek and let the soul escape. The angry god limited the power of the shaman and from that time the shamans have become worse and worse. The Buryat shamans believe so firmly in their profession that when they themselves are sick they call in their fellow-shamans to treat them by the stock methods.[11] "The characteristic of shamanism which distinguishes this school of religion from others is the belief in the close union which exists between now living men and their long deceased ancestors. Belief in the power of this bond engenders an un-broken reverence for ancestors.[12]

A Tibetan proverb states that without a lama in front God is not ap-proachable.[13] In India "there are two kinds of gods; for the gods are gods, and priests that are learned in the Veda and teach it are human gods." So the fees paid to the priests are like sacrifices to the gods. The priest comes to be, indeed, more important than the god.[14] From India have come tales verging on the miraculous of the feats of fakirs and magicians, but American and Euro-pean prestidigitators who have made investigations there report the situation as highly exaggerated. None of them brought back any notable addition to his repertoire of illusions.[15] In China, "the exorcists were a certain class of priests and priestesses entirely possessed by spirits of the Yang [white, male, good] material, and, as such, were deemed especially fitted to perform chiefly three several functions: (1) to call upon the spirits of the dead in order to make them partake of offerings; (2) to foretell future events by interrogating the spirits and communicating their will to the living; (3) to expel diseases and evil in general, especially droughts, by neutralizing through the Yang power residing in their persons the influence of the element of darkness Yin and the evil spirits identified with it."[16]

In Borneo, "some men, by a peculiar magic influence, or by gift of the bird spirits, are credited with possessing in themselves, in their own hearts and bodies, some occult power which can overcome bad omens. These men are able, by eating something, however small, of the produce of the farm, to turn

9 Hanoteau et Letourneux, Kabylie, II, 83, 89, 95.
10 Melnikow, in Globus, LXXV, 133.
11 Michailovski, Shamanism (Russ.), 54, 97.
12 Radloff, Schamanenthum, 16.
13 Waddell, Tibet, 169.
14 Hopkins, Relig. Ind., 179, 180, 181.
15 Kelly, in N. Y. Even. Post, June 4, 1904.
16 De Groot, Relig. Syst., I, 40-41.

off the evil prognostication [say, of a swarm of bees lighting upon a farm, which is a dreadful matter]. . . . . Anything grown on it which can be eaten, a bit of Indian corn, a little mustard, or a few cucumber shoots, is taken to the wise man and he quietly eats it raw for a small consideration and thereby appropriates to himself the evil omen which in him becomes innocuous and thus delivers the other from the ban of the tabu."[17] The priests and priestesses are supposed to be possessed by the souls of the dead which, however, do not remain in them all the time but can be invoked to enter them and thus enable them to oppose evil spirits. If the son of a priest enters the profession the soul that inspires him is a descendant of the one that inspired his father.[18] When the priests dance, it is not really the priests but the spirits who do so; and dancing with the women is allowed to them, which is otherwise forbidden.[19] The chief priests hold the unlimited confidence of the Pelew Islanders, as representatives of the devil.[20]

In Tahiti, the general class of inspired persons and sorcerers was not organized regularly; sometimes there were many, at other times none. "The god was supposed to select his man, and enter into his body; he manifested this by some marvel. The rumour spread, and the body of the man became sacred as an idol. Not only could he enter the *marae* [central inclosure] and everywhere he pleased, but he even ascended the altar, and gave himself up to the diverse extravagances which the god who was in his body inspired him to commit. The sorcerer was not always in a state of inspiration. Sometimes the god abandoned him, and he became again in every way like an ordinary mortal. Sometimes the inspiration occurred through a caprice of the god, who seized his man unawares. At other times he himself invoked the god by means of certain formulae, which afterwards became forgotten or unintelligible. These inspired persons enjoyed high consideration and their rank of blood did not matter. Besides the permanent sorcerers who were devoted for life to the whims of their deities, there was a class of sorcerers who confined their industry to certain miracles or *tours de force,* the principal of which was that of *pimato* or rock climbers, whose methods of climbing perpendicular rocks with smooth and shining surfaces are described."[21]

It is an Eskimo belief that everything has its *inua* (owner) which may become the genius of a man, but three kinds of spirits become protectors (*tornaq*) of the shaman: those in the shape of men, of stones, or of bears. They enable the shaman to have intercourse with others that are considered malevolent to mankind and are kind to him though they would hurt strangers who might chance to see them. The bear seems to be the most powerful of these spirits; it is a huge animal without any hair except on the points of the ears and of the tail and at the mouth. "If a man wishes to obtain a bear for his tornaq, he must travel all alone to the edge of the land floe and summon the bears. Then a large herd will approach and frighten him almost to death. He falls down at once. Should he fall backward he would die at once. If he falls upon his face, however, one bear out of the herd steps forward and asks him if he wishes him to become his tornaq. He then recovers and takes the bear for his spirit and is accompanied by him on the return journey. On the way home they pass a seal hole and the bear captures the animal for his master. The Eskimo is now

17 Roth, *Sarawak*, I, 194.
18 Nieuwenhuis, *Borneo*, II, 227.
19 Pleyte, in *Globus*, LXXIX, 31.

20 Semper, *Palau-Ins.*, 198, note.
21 Williamson, *Cent. Polyn.*, II, 421, 422, 423, 425.

a great angakok and whenever he wants help he is sure to get it from his bear."[22] According to the Tsimshians, shamans may be initiated by various kinds of supernatural beings. "One shaman is initiated by the Squirrels, who take him to their home in a tree, where his skeleton is finally found hanging. The body is spread on a mat covered with another mat, which is painted red and covered with bird's down, sacrifices are brought, while the young man's parents leave the house. When the people sing over the body, the man revives and becomes a powerful shaman. . . . Another shaman is initiated by a supernatural being that lives in a deep cave called the Cave of Fear, which only shamans are able to enter. He is let down by means of a cedar-bark rope, and on his way down is stung by great swarms of insects. At the bottom he finds a hairy young man, who leads him through a door shining like the sun, into a cave where the supernatural being that gives him power is seated. From the east side of the house a supernatural being enters, accompanied by attendants. They take their supernatural powers out of their mouths, and put them into the mouth of the visitor. Finally the chief of the house lays his hands on the visitor and rubs his eyes."[23]

Among the Haida and Tlinkit, generally speaking, the shaman obtained his position from an uncle, inheriting his spiritual helpers just as he might his material wealth; but there were also shamans who became such owing to natural fitness. In either case the first intimation of his new power was given by the man falling senseless and remaining in that condition for a certain period. Elsewhere in North America, however, the sweat bath was an important assistant in bringing about the proper psychic state, and certain individuals became shamans after escaping from a stroke of lightning or the jaws of a wild beast. Great influence was exercised by the shamans, to whose malign power death was generally ascribed. "If the soul had wandered, he captured and restored it, and in case the patient had been bewitched he revealed the name of the offender and directed how he was to be handled." He was believed to have "obtained from the deities, usually through dreams, but sometimes before birth, powers of recognizing and removing the mysterious causes of disease."[24] Among the Winnebago, "if a man was a good hunter or if he was wise and good, these bad shamans would poison him. If an individual was a great medicine man and these bad shamans got jealous, they would poison him. Indeed, only if a person was poor and lowly would they like him. Such a man they would never poison for they had no reason for being jealous of him. A bad shaman is always treated with the greatest respect and honor, because he kills many people."[25] The high-priests of the Creeks would "foretell rain or drought and pretend to bring rain at pleasure, cure diseases, and exorcise witchcraft, invoke or expel evil spirits, and even assume the power of directing thunder and lightning."[26] The Algonquin medicineman might announce that he was going to kill a rival shaman who lived a hundred leagues away.[27] In general, the Indian shaman seeks to cover himself in case of the failure of his art; "in nearly every boast there is some sort of a saving clause to the effect that no witchcraft must be made or the spell will not work, no woman should be near in a delicate state from any cause, etc. . . . Though the medicine men are considered to have wonderful power, it

22 Boas, in BAE, VI, 591-592.
23 Boas, in BAE, XXXI, 473.
24 Swanton; Sapir; Hrdlička, in HAI, II, 522; II, 674; I, 838, resp.

25 Radin, in BAE, XXXVII, 263.
26 Swanton, "Shamans," in HAI, II, 523.
27 Parkman, *Jesuits*, 34, 35 (Edit. 1880).

is conceded that baleful influences may counteract and nullify them. Among these are the efforts of witches, the presence of women who are sometimes supposed to be so 'antimedicinal' that the mere stepping over a warrior's gun will destroy its value."[28]

If one sets up as a medicine-man, his medicine, so the people think, ought to possess efficacy in all cases. If he fails, he may lose his life. Such was the fate of the medicine-man of certain Indians of Arizona, who was impotent before the great influenza epidemic of 1919.[29] A few years earlier an Indian in California killed a medicine-man in revenge for the death of his two children who had been subjected to bleeding by him "to drive away the evil spirits."[30] So among the Jibaro Indians of Ecuador: "Since supposed sorcery is nearly always the nearest cause of murders within the tribe, it is clear that the professional sorcerers or medicine men are those members of Jibaro society which are most frequently exposed to the revengeful attacks of their enemies. As a matter of fact, in large Indian societies sorcerers are almost continually assassinated, or at least threatened with death, by their enemies. When a medicine man has undertaken to cure a sick person and the latter dies in spite of the treatment, the 'doctor' is also generally made responsible for the death, the relatives of the dead reasoning that the medicine man, instead of curing the patient, on the contrary used his art to kill him. The unsuccessful curer is therefore murdered unless he escapes by flight."[31]

The apprenticeship of the medicine-man among the Guiana Indians was far from being the proverbial bed of roses. Among other tests, "he had for many months to practise self-denial, and submit under a stinted diet to the prohibition of what were to him accustomed luxuries. He had to satisfy his teacher in his knowledge of the instincts and habits of animals, in the properties of plants, and the seasons for flowering and bearing, for the piai man was often consulted as to when and where game was to be found, and he was more than often correct in his surmises. He also had to know of the grouping of the stars into constellations, and the legends connected not only with them, but with his own tribe. He had likewise to be conversant with the media for the invocation of the Spirits, as chants and recitatives, and also to be able to imitate animal and human voices. He had to submit to a chance of death by drinking a decoction of tobacco in repeated and increasing doses, and to have his eyes washed with the infusion of hiari leaves; he slowly recovered, with a confused mind, believing that in his trance, the effect of narcotics and a distempered mind, he was admitted into the company of the Spirits, that he conversed with them, and was by themselves consecrated to the office of piai priest-doctor. Bancroft says that the novitiate 'is dosed with the juice of tobacco till it no longer operates as an emetic.' Sometimes . . . other things were mixed with the tobacco, for example, a plant called quinquiva, as well as certain of the drippings from an exposed dead body. For the same colony Fathers Grillet and Bechamel record that the medicine-men proffer neither physic nor divination 'till they have made divers experiments, one of which is so dangerous that it often makes them burst. They stamp the green leaves of tobacco and squeeze out the juice of it, of which they drink the quantity of a large glassful, etc.; so that none but those who are of a very robust constitution, who try this practice upon

---

28 Bourke, in BAE, IX, 458, 459.
29 Boston *Transcript*, May 3, 1919.
30 New Haven *Journal-Courier*, Mar. 16, 1915.

31 Karsten, "Jibaro," in BAE, Bull. LXXIX, 9.

themselves, escape with their lives.' . . . During his course of training, in addition to his other instruction, the apprentice was taught to suffer the pangs of hunger and thirst, and to experience the martyrdom of pain without complaint or murmur. To teach him the latter, he was either bitten with ants or cut on various portions of the body. Among the Islanders 'his body is scraped with acouri teeth.' The ants were fixed into the interstices of plaited diamond-shaped mats or girdles and these were held or tied on the neck, breast, stomach, or legs. In some cases, during their period of probationership, the prospective medicine-men must not come into contact with Europeans, as this would destroy forever their influence over the spirit world. West of the Orinoco, 'they submitted to a seclusion of two years in caverns, situated in the deepest recesses of the forests. During this period they ate no animal food; they saw no person, not even their parents. The old Piaches or doctors went and instructed them during the night.' Magic stones are alleged to be placed in the novitiate's head." The curriculum must have been impressive for there is abundant evidence that the medicine-men practised what they preached and had every confidence in the powers with which they had been intrusted: "They practise those incantations over their own sick children, and cause them to be practised over themselves when sick. . . . They act the farce on themselves when they are disordered: a practice which has not a little contributed to overthrow all doubts of the sincerity of their pretensions. . . . The piai himself believes in it: one will put himself in the hands of another when sick. . . . Schomburgk was 'convinced that the piai believes in the efficacy of his witchcraft as firmly as his protégés.' "[32]

There were three classes of theurgists among the Araucanians: sorcerer, diviner, and witch-doctor or exorcist. The sorcerers were formerly the sacerdotal class, inasmuch as whatever rites, ceremonies, sacrifices or other religious observances took place were performed by them. They dwelt in caves in remote mountainous regions and were supposed to be in communication with the spirits over which their arts gave them certain powers, compelling them to work their wills. Contrary to the practice of the other two classes, "their incantations and spells were secret and mystic, wrought in the darkness of their caves, and hidden from the eyes of ordinary mortals, although some of their charms were done visibly, such as seeing visions in a bowl of water, and blowing smoke from their mouths in the direction of the dwellings of their enemies." The diviners exercise a considerable influence in Indian society, "as they are consulted on all doubtful points of social or domestic intercourse, and every-day events. It is they who indicate the author of a robbery, the whereabouts of a missing animal or mislaid object, the probable result of a given enterprise, the perpetrator of any evil happening to the flocks and herds." They perform their divinations outside their huts, their familiar spirits answering them from within. "By far the most popular and most consulted of these personalities is the *machi,* who combines in his person the offices of medicine-man, seer, and exorcist . . . the learner graduating after a long apprenticeship to some well-established *machi.* The principal accomplishments are a profound knowledge of medicinal herbs, with which the forests and plains abound, a slight acquaintance with surgery, a considerable mastery of simple conjuring tricks, and the talent of ventriloquism. Many never attained to this last art and had recourse to darkness and a different modulation

32 Roth, in BAE, XXX, 327, 338-340.

of voice, which served the purpose equally well, although it was less dramatic."[33]

Among the Zoroastrians the seer seems to have produced a marked effect by being able through his prescience, as the story goes, openly to disclose the thoughts of the king and of others, with astonishing results.[34] With the Arabs, as with other peoples, what is not customarily seen or heard by everybody, but by one alone, has naturally, at least for himself, the greater surety of higher origin and more mysterious meaning.[35] Apollonius of Tyana, whom the pagans opposed to Christ, had raised the dead, healed the sick, cast out devils, freed a young man from a vampire with whom he was enamoured, prophesied, seen in one country events that were occurring in another, and filled the world with the fame of his miracles and of his sanctity. He was born at nearly the same time as Christ. The Fathers of the fourth century always spoke of him as a great magician.[36]

Fire-Walking.[37] In several remote countries of the world, notably Mauritius, India, Japan, Hawaii, Tahiti, the Malay Archipelago, and the Fiji Islands, men are reported, on trustworthy authority, to have walked barefoot across living coals or over white-hot stones, and to have come through the ordeal uninjured. Eyewitnesses have testified as to the heat, while physicians have failed, upon examination, to discover any sign of burns. Burke[38] gives as corroborating evidence a number of photographs which he made of the fire-walkers of Fiji. In this case it takes the participants from ten to fifteen seconds to complete the circuit of the pit of hot stones. Langley[39] has described the fire-walk ceremony performed by native shamans in Tahiti; he certifies as to the high temperature of the stones. The ceremony of fire-walking is reported to be annually performed in Japan by a certain sect of Shinto. Treading slowly across a bed of coals while wildly gesticulating priests chant magic incantations, several hundred members of the sect prove in a modern ordeal by fire their moral purity and their faith in the Shinto god, Kami-sama. A witness describes a recent celebration as follows· "The signal at last was given and a priest who stood at the edge of the fire stepped boldly in. Straight across he walked, and behind him came his associates and the common folk in an unbroken line. They were all ages—men, women and children—barefoot and with their kimono tucked up from the fire. Young boys walked between old men, and on the backs of many of the women were babies who slept soundly through the whole performance, worrying not a bit about their standing with Kami-sama. Those who suffered from the heat of the coals were judged unrighteous and warned to mend their ways; all who passed through the ordeal unscathed were good and faithful, saved from harm by the supernatural powers of the god and the prayers of the officiating priests. Either that, or they escaped unburned because they had used proper care in rubbing their feet in a pile of sacred salt which lay at the point where the march across the coals began."[40]

---

33 Latcham, in JAI, XXXIX, 351-352.
34 Jackson, *Zoroaster*, 62.
35 Wellhausen, *Skizzen*, III, 151.
36 Lecky, *Europ. Morals*, I, 372.
37 §163, of the text.

38 In *Frank Leslie's Monthly*, April, 1903, 588-594.
39 In *Smithson. Rep.*, 1901, 539.
40 Morris, in *Philadelphia Public Ledger*, May 14, 1922.

§313. Shamanistic Practice.

DIVINATION is a common practice of Melanesian shamans. In the Solomon Islands, when a thing is lost a wizard is engaged to find it in a dream. "In Lepers' Island in case of theft or of any hidden crime some wizard who understands how to do it drinks *kava,* and so throws himself into a magic sleep. When he wakes he declares that he has seen the culprit and gives his name. . . . In Motlav and the other Banks' Islands they divined by means of a bamboo into which a ghost had entered, and which pointed of itself to the thief or other culprit to be discovered. A common method of divination in the Banks' Islands is called *so ilo,* and is used to enquire where a lost person or thing is to be found, who is the thief, whether an absent friend is alive or dead. The hands are lifted over the head and rubbed together with a magic song calling on a ghost. The sign is given by the cracking of the joints; when the question is of life or death, if the thumbs or shoulders crack the man still lives, if the elbows crack he is dead. So if a man sneezes he will *so ilo* to know who it is that curses him; he revolves his fists one over the other and then throws out his arms; the revolving is the question, and the answer is given as he asks, 'Is it So-and-So?' and his elbows crack."[1] Prophets may be found even in low civilization; in New Guinea one foretold calamities so as to get the natives away from white influence.[2] Communication with the spirit-world is held to be possible in New Britain, and "there are no more faithful and ardent spiritualists in the world than the New Britain savages." So writes Danks[3] who was present at a native séance. "It was black unrelieved darkness. . . . In the space there were two companies of men, one company at each end of the open space. They were all dressed in white, the spirits being supposed to like that colour. At the sound of a whistle these two companies marched past each other across the open, and so changed ends, making a weird procession, amid a profound silence. I said something to my neighbour and was immediately warned to keep silent. In answer to the question put in the lowest of whispers, What are they doing? I was informed that *Ingal,* the spirit they sought, would presently be so pleased with their wooing in this way, that he would reveal himself to them. . . . I waited long, but he came not that night, and it was soon mentioned that I was the unbeliever who kept him away, and I was urged to leave, which after a while I did. I was told next day that after I left he came, a sure evidence that I was the hindrance, which added to my security, for if I was stronger than *Ingal,* I must indeed be strong. I was never again invited to a séance. This *Ingal* may enter into a man, and through him may be revealed the secrets of the *Malira,* or charm either for good or evil use, and he is therefore much sought after. *Ingal* is supposed to live at the top of very high trees, and may be induced to come down and converse with men."

In the New Hebrides, Uhgen is the power behind all things.[4] "A watch, a gunlock, even a wall that a missionary will build is a thing made by god. This Uhgen made natural features what they are, gave names to the district units of territory and population, gave customs to the forefathers, and conferred the sacred stones. But some man is said to make bread, fruit, fish, yams, rain, and wind by virtue of power given to the ancestors long ago." In short, Uhgen made the world and committed what we call Providence to certain men. On the

---

1 Codrington, *Melanesians,* 209, 211.
2 Abel, *New Guinea,* 107.
3 In AAAS, 1909, 454.
4 §258 of the text.

caprice of these their fellowmen must depend. It is these fellows that do all the mischief in human life; and their instrumentalities are the sacred stones, knowledge of the use of which is a revelation from Uhgen. His disclosures concern talismans to bring the enemy within range, to render the person invisible, and so on *ad infinitum;* and also the taboo, which preserves property from theft by fetishes. Through such vehicles spirits work ills as punishment on violators. Different varieties of stones are used as fetishes to make crops grow, to make rain or wind, or to bring game. The mightiest stone is called Nuruk (narak), and has the power of life and death. They are kept by a Nuruker, but to work them he must have something which has been used by or has been in contact with the person of his victim. Such a thing must not be carried over fresh water, and if it can be washed it is Nuruk-proof—another case of the exorcistic effect of water—but if it is rubbed on the Nuruk-stone and burned by a slow fire the victim wastes away with disease. Black-mail is common, whereby the Nuruk-process is threatened if some coveted thing is withheld. When a person is ill there is always a great effort to trace the Nuruk. Facts seem to support the belief. "Good intelligent Christians accept evidence of direct answers to prayer less satisfactory and conclusive than that presented in cases of Nuruk." Every Nuruker, who is evidently a shaman, is a chief by virtue of the possession of the stones. Natives shudder at the sight of them. Knowledge of their use is handed down from father to son.[5] Elsewhere in the New Hebrides if a man dies, the shaman says that though he went to Hades to try to bring back the ghost of the dying, the other shades seized it, drew it away into their cave, and shut the door.[6]

In Africa the priests have great influence and power; they make sacrifices and incantations, carry out the frequent ordeals, sprinkle babies with water, give them a name, practise circumcision, and lead in the festivals of reconciliation and harvest, the mask dances, and the funerals. The chief function of the Zulu shaman is to communicate with the souls of the dead who have much to do with the affairs of the living. From the cradle to the grave, the life of the Bechuana is entangled in the most complicated and time-wasting usages. Ceremonies of a special nature go on till death, so that one of them could not live without a shaman. A European could get on much better without a physician or clergyman. In 1857 a Kaffir maiden, not a Zulu, declared that she had a revelation from the spirits that the Kaffirs would drive the whites out of their land, provided that the natives, by sacrifices, would secure the assistance of the spirits. In the first place, they must kill and eat the best cattle. This they did, although it was contrary to all their laws and customs, the chiefs approving of it apparently with the idea of bringing the people to despair. The result was a terrible famine, and thousands died.[7] In West Africa the shaman brings news of the recently deceased, usually announcing his safe arrival in Deadland, and in return gets a sumptuous but private entertainment—for to see him eating is death. The family intrust him with messages to the deceased.[8] There is no denying that such speedy and natural resumption of relations is comforting to the bereaved. The shaman among the Fan sits on the ground and pretends to listen to mysterious voices which, in fact, can be heard coming from the soil. "This is very probably a simple effect of ven-

5 Gray, in AAAS, 1892, 650; §§254, 302, of the text.
6 Macdonald, in AAAS, 1892, 727.

7 Ratzel, *Vkde.*, I, 187, 267, 279.
8 Ellis, *Yoruba*, 109.

triloquism; certain shamans are past masters at it." Some of the shamans possess secrets transmitted from generation to generation. "These are sometimes beneficent remedies composed of medicinal plants, the medical effects of which are incontestable: in other cases they are philtres the power of which I have repeatedly been obliged to verify; there are also poisons, especially vegetable poisons, which paralyze or cause an incurable malady, or again kill without leaving a trace. And finally there are charlatans who ape the others without having the science: their mysterious airs and pretenses sometimes deceive the people more than a true power. It is here as elsewhere."[9] Certain of the Bangala shamans are said to scrape their eyes with the sharp edge of the sugar-cane grass, "which operation clears the vision and enables them to see the *moloki* or witch afar off and frustrate its evil designs." Another special class make a charm which is rubbed on the body or tied on the wrist or leg of the client who, when thus protected, "can walk right among his enemies, and if they catch him they find only his cloth, for the person in the cloth has vanished. This charm is used in times of war as the possessor can fight and kill without being seen by the enemy, and this charm is also in great favour with thieves."[10]

A means whereby a medicine-man may direct the path of life for a Mkamba is by making little cuts in his skin and rubbing in a particular medicine for various purposes. "This done to the tongue gives a man the power of great authority in his speech; the same treatment to the forehead and throat just above the breast bone ensures to a man the admiration of women, and applied to the chest or abdomen brings him great riches. Almost every Mkamba has one or more of these magic medicines about his body which serves him all through life, or if not, a reason for its failure is, of course, easily found."[11] A native claiming the gift of prophecy was interviewed and cross-examined by Hobley;[12] he stated that "at intervals, about twice a year, during the night he falls into a deeper sleep than usual, a trance in fact, and that while in this condition he is taken out of his bed and statements are made to him by a voice, but he cannot see who gives him the message. The trance always occurs at night, and he is generally taken outside his house while in this cataleptic condition, but says that he never remembers being able to distinguish the huts or any familiar objects in the village. The interior of the hut appears to him to be lighted up, and the message comes with a booming sound which he understands. . . . The day following one of his seizures he collects the elders and delivers to them his message. He states that after one of these seizures he is very exhausted, and for three days cannot rise from his bed. His father and paternal grandfather had this gift or power, and he says that his father told him that his paternal grandmother had three breasts, two on her bosom and one on her back, but whether he considered that this had any connection with the other phenomena he did not disclose." Other statements about his personal history indicate that he was a typical fetish-man. "He was seized before the great famine of 1900 and foretold its arrival. Later on he was told to inform the Kikuyu to sacrifice at the . . . sacred fig trees a white sheep, a red sheep and a black male goat, and that the chief Kinanjui was to sacrifice a *mori*, white heifer, at the head waters of the Mbagathi River. These orders were obeyed, and the famine and small-pox were lifted from the land. . . .

9 Trilles, *Fân*, 562, 642.
10 Weeks, in JAI, XL, 385 ff.

11 Dundas, C., in JAI, XLIII, 529.
12 In JAI, XLI, 437-439.

He says that sometimes when rain does not come he is accused of stopping it, but that such accusations are due to ignorance, that he is merely the unconscious and involuntary agent for utterances from a Supreme Power, and that all he can do in such cases is to take a sheep to a sacred fig tree, sacrifice it there, and pray for rain, just like any other elder who is qualified to do so." The Beja of the Sudan follow their priests in all things. "Each family has a priest who erects a tent of skins in which he practises his vocation. When consulted he strips himself and enters the tent backwards. He comes out behaving as a maniac or epilept and says: The spirit salutes you and advises you to give up a particular journey for such and such a tribe is about to attack you. . . . When they determine to move their encampment, the priest loads the tent of which I have spoken on the back of a camel which bears no other load. They allege that this animal rises and travels as if heavily laden, and that it sweats profusely although the tent is absolutely empty."[13]

Of the Siberian shamans it is believed that they can control rain and snow at will and bewitch men and beasts.[14] A local Yakut tradition narrates that a great shaman once seized death and, having shut it up in some iron boxes which were enclosed one within the other, buried it in a grave. People ceased to die; and they increased to such numbers, became so old, and grew so weary of life that they begged to have death set free.[15] The Buryats think the shamans find out secrets and can foretell the fate of each man. The priests decide all details of burial. They exploited the Buryats and hindered them from coming to terms with the Russians.[16] Yet the shaman-to-be is adjured: "When a poor man calls you, do not demand a great price from him for your labors but take what he gives. Always exert yourself for the poor; help them, and pray the gods for protection against evil spirits and their power. If a rich man calls thee, ride to him on an ox and do not demand much for thy labors. If a rich and a poor man call thee at the same time, go first to the poor man." This sounds a little like the Oath of Hippocrates but for the Siberian practitioner it is a rather hopeless counsel of perfection. The fact is that the consecration of a shaman costs heavily, and such sacrificial ceremonies are established for it that the impression exerted upon all those present remains long in the memory of the people and elevates the calling of the shaman in their eyes. It is strange to find that the shamans are not respected among the Chukchi, where their activities are restricted to healing and the performance of magical rites.[17] The Soyots believe that the soul of the shaman flies through the air on his drum while his body remains behind. When performing, he falls into a state of mind resulting often in unconsciousness. One case is cited where the shaman really died; he fell into the fire and was fatally burned. Things happen in the operations that Europeans cannot well explain; e.g., a shamaness who had bad legs and could not move or stand, began to "shamanize" seated; presently she got up and capered about; furthermore, the prophecies often come true. Before beginning, the shaman drinks ten cups of water, which represents blood-drinking; he smokes some, and then mumbles and sings formulas while lightly striking his drum; the movements get faster and more violent, the drumming harder; the voice seems to come from deep in the chest; he looks earnestly ahead; the "flight" is begun. He whirls about, falls over, and

13 Seligmann, in JAI, XLIII, 661.
14 Prjevalski's *Forskningsresor*, 236.
15 Sieroshevski, *Yakuts* (Russ.), I, 667, note.

16 *Russian Ethnog.* (Russ.), II, 501, 504.
17 Michailovski, *Shamanism* (Russ.), 75, 77, 90.

is seized and supported by someone; he then reports what happens on his "flight"—dialogues with people and devils that he feigns to meet. The practices are similar in the case of the ancient Lapps.[18] "It may be said that all over Siberia, where there is a shaman there is also a drum. The drum has the power of transporting the shaman to the superworld and of evoking spirits by its sounds." It is the most important of the many accessories of the profession. The novice must learn singing, dancing, various tricks, including ventriloquism, and how to beat the drum. "The beating of the drum, notwithstanding its seeming simplicity, requires some skill, and the novice must spend considerable time before he can acquire the desired degree of perfection. This has reference specially to the performer's power of endurance. The same may be said of the singing. . . . The amount of endurance required for all this, and the ability to pass quickly from the highest excitement to a state of normal quietude, can, of course, be acquired only by long practice." The ecstatic shaman communicates with spirits. "This includes all kinds of intercourse with 'spirits' which become apparent to the listeners; that is, the voices of 'spirits' talking through the medium of the shaman, ventriloquistic performances, and other tricks—generally speaking, the whole spectacular part of shamanism, which forms the main content of the shamanistic *séances*. . . . With increasing years some of the shamans discontinue most of these tricks. . . . The majority of shamans, however, combine in themselves the gifts of all these categories and in the name of 'spirits' perform various tricks, foretell the future, and pronounce incantations." The Altaian shaman purifies the host, his family, and relatives, by "embracing them in such a way that the tambourine with the spirits collected in it touches the breast and the drum-stick the back of each. This is done after he has scraped from the back of the host with the drum-stick all that is unclean, for the back is the seat of the soul."[19]

Among the Tibetans, "every act in trade, agriculture, and social life needs the sanction of sacerdotalism, whatever exists of wealth is in the *gonpos* [monasteries], which also have a monopoly of learning, and eleven thousand monks, linked with the people, yet ruling all the affairs of life and death and beyond death, are connected closely by education, tradition, and authority with Lhassa." At the beginning of every one of the harvest operations the presence of lamas is essential, to announce the auspicious moment and to conduct religious ceremonies. They receive fees and are regaled with the fat of the land.[20] The lama "performs sacerdotal functions on every possible occasion; and a large proportion of the order is almost entirely engaged in this work. And such services are in much demand; for the people are in hopeless bondage to the demons, and not altogether unwilling slaves to their exacting worship."[21] In India barren women go to the temple of Vishnu to spend the night. They are humbugged by a priest whom they take to be the god.[22] A Hindu epic states: "We see through the power of penitence what is future and what is past."[23] The medicine-men of the Sema Nagas frequently resort to tricks. "The sucking out of the extracted object is often accompanied by a shrewd nip, which the patient takes for the pain attending the object's emergence from his body. The writer has been operated on by one of these practitioners. The objects produced are bits of stone, quartz, iron, tin, old teeth, chewed leaves,

18 Olsen, *Primitivt Folk*, 99 ff.
19 Czaplicka, *Aborig. Siberia*, 178-180, 193, 194, 203 ff., 301.
20 Bishop, *Tibetans*, 48, 91.

21 Waddell, *Buddhism*, 153.
22 Dubois, *Mœurs*, II, 366.
23 Holtzmann, *Ind. Sagen*, II, 41.

mud, hairs, etc., the latter being invariably produced from a patient with a cough. . . . A really clever *thumoni* extracts not with the mouth, but with his bare hands, so that the object is probably not concealed in his mouth, but in such cases he usually does it in the inner darkness of a Sema house where little skill or sleight of hand is needed. For a consideration a *thumoni* will sometimes teach his trade, but no case of a pupil's having given away his teacher is known. Indeed they appear to have a belief in their own powers which assorts most ill with the impostures they practise. But to go out of one's way to convict the *thumoni* of fraud is to break a bluebottle upon the wheel. Sufficeth it that the *thumoni* believes in himself and is believed in by his patients and in very truth often cures them by faith alone. After all, he differs little from a 'Christian Science' practitioner, unless it be in that he uses a trifle more deception to induce the state of mind in which the patient recovers of his affliction."[24] Cases of hypnotism appear rare among the Palaungs or Palês, but from what Mrs. Milne[25] heard, they are not unknown. "I was told of a Palê at Kangwantok who was said to have strange powers over both men and women. The Palaungs who told me of him, said that he 'knew how to blow.' Blowing is used in all sorts of mysterious ways. A wise man blows into the air, or on a charm, while he is invoking the help of spirits; a wise woman, after massaging a limb, blows upon it. This Palê seems to have used his hypnotic power chiefly for making practical jokes." Among these people, "every monastery is also a school, taught by the monks, the scholars being all boys. There, besides learning the precepts of Buddhism, the children learn to read and write a certain amount of Burmese and Shan, enough to help them in later life."

The medicine-basket in Sarawak usually contains a "sight stone," that is, a quartz crystal with which the medicine-man is reputed to see the condition of a patient's soul; he goes into a trance and wakes with the soul in hand. Other items are a beetle whose movements indicate the outcome, resin, the fumes of which blind the evil spirits, bark, "waterworn" crystals, and, as charms against the evil eye, porcupine-quills, and bamboo-slips.[26] "If a Dyak dreams of falling into the water, he thinks that this accident has really befallen his spirit, and sends for a *manang,* who fishes for it and recovers it." It is the shadow spirit that falls into the water.[27] It is noteworthy that the man who has the reputation of being fortunate and has had large paddy-crops is selected to be the augur who shall undertake to obtain omens for a large area of land on which he and others intend to plant. He must hear the cries of birds in a complicated order and from the right directions.[28] The male and female shamans of the Mentawei Islands lead the festivals and, in case of storm or earth-quake, must drive off the evil spirits causing the disturbance.[29] The offices of the local shaman are indispensable to the young child, in Atjeh; "he lays it before him on the ground, utters a prayer, and whispers the usual prayer-formulas in its right ear, after which the child is restored to its mother."[30] The Semang of the Malay Peninsula have a most undeveloped religion, but the shamans are very necessary as intercessors between men and spirits.[31] In Núkuóro the intercessor gets no fees and the pressure of the priesthood on the people is due to immediate fear of the gods rather than to priestly domination.[32] Certain Filipino

24 Hutton, *Sema Nagas*, 231-232.
25 *Eastern Clan*, 262, 319.
26 Shelford, in JAI, XXXIII, 74 ff.
27 Roth, in JAI, XXI, 112.
28 Gomes, *Sea Dyaks*, 153, 154.

29 Pleyte, in *Globus*, LXXIX, 31.
30 Jacobs, *Groot-Atjeh*, I, 150.
31 A., "Heidenstämme," in *Globus*, XCI, 109.
32 Kubary, *Núkuóro*, 31.

priests prophesy over a slain pig, distributing all but the best parts among the crowd.[33]

In Polynesia there were graded classes of men who engaged in operations, some of which were obviously religious, whilst others were of the character of magic. Writers call some of these people "priests," and others "sorcerers," the latter being, generally speaking, an inferior class. "The evidence shows, however, that some of the priests, who in their observances were in the habit of appealing to the gods, engaged in operations which we should, from their character, include under the term magic; and it was in some cases through a god, who might or might not comply with the prayer of the priest, that the processes of magic were put into operation." The priesthood of the Marquesas was composed of several ranks: first were the *atua,* or gods; "they were men who had been actually deified in their lifetime, and performed their sacred offices, not by virtue of professed inspiration or possession by some other supernatural being, but with their own powers as gods. They were believed to be able to control the elements, impart fruitfulness to the productions of the earth, or smite them with blasting and sterility, and to cause illness and death." They lived lives of mysticism and seclusion. Next came the *tau'a,* a more numerous and tangible class than the *atua,* but allied to them in office and reputation, for "though they did not profess to be gods, they were supposed to possess an hereditary gift of inspiration and a power of causing a god to dwell within them, and sometimes usurped the dignity and name of *atua;* they seemed to be a combination of prophet and sorcerer. . . . They also cured ills of soul and body, supposed to be the effect of divine wrath. A sort of mystery surrounded them, and the power they had of disposing of the taboo and of demanding human victims rendered them very terrible." The *tahuna,* or priests, were next in order, a more numerous but less formidable class, and less presumptuous. "Their offices were various, consisting mainly in offering sacrifices and performing religious ceremonies; in singing sacred songs, beating the drums of the temple, celebrating funeral rites and performing surgical operations." The *u'u* were the assistants of the priests, helping them in the conduct of ceremonies, and especially in the more laborious parts of the performance of human sacrifice. "Admission to this office was only granted to men who had killed an enemy in battle with the short club or battle-axe—*u'u*—from which they derived their name; they had the privilege of feasting with the *tau'a* and *tahuna.*" There were female *tau'a,* but they never entered the temples; "some of them, claiming divine inspiration, had little altars in their own houses; whilst others, having no power actually to invoke the gods, were able to predict events."[34]

Holm[35] says that the East Greenland angakoks played no great rôle in social life; yet the natives feared to go hunting alone lest they should fall victim to some angakok's vengeance. And Fries[36] tells how the angakok united in himself the priest, judge, physician, and chief; he was the bearer of his nation's science, however insignificant, and upholder of the rules of living inherited from the fathers; in all extraordinary situations his advice was sought by those who needed help, within the little human society where he lived. By the aid of their guardian-spirits the angakoks of the Central Eskimo cure the

33 Montero y Vidal, *Filipinas,* I, 55.
34 Williamson, *Cent. Polyn.,* II, 405-406, 428-432.
35 *Ethnol. Skizze,* 44, 133.
36 *Grönland,* 141.

sick and make good weather; they discover transgressions of taboos and other causes of ill luck.[37] The person settled on by the Tlinkit shaman as a witch was "generally some unimportant member of the community, an uncanny-looking creature, a slave, or some one who had the ill will of the doctor or the relatives of the patient. This was a very effective way of ridding one of his enemy. No one, not even the victim himself, thought of disputing the shaman's judgment."[38] Among these people, as among the Haida and Tsimshian, the shaman proper and the sorcerer were quite distinct functionaries. Among the Kwakiutl, at least, those sorcerers who served chiefs to counteract the evil of other hired sorcerers were distinguished as a class from those who used sympathetic magic in the treatment of illness. "The ability of the shaman to see and control the souls of the living and the dead appears to have caused the assignment to shamans of the disagreeable and dangerous duty which ordinary persons are less well equipped to perform—the preparation and burial of the corpse. To the shaman for the same reason was given the collection of the bones of the dead and the dispatching of food and clothing to the deceased. . . . The specialization of functions peculiar to shamans was reflected in the specialization of duties for shamans in mortuary practices, and this resulted in the differentiation of several shamanistic mortuary castes. In this mortuary development the shaman becomes a priest, so far as his behavior goes, but his qualification for office and the basis or origin of his functions are shamanistic."[39] As a display of power, without any particular purpose, but always sure to be repaid by a shower of presents, the medicine-men of the Ten'a used to indulge occasionally in exhibitions of wonderful feats, such as any sleight-of-hand performer accomplishes to amuse an audience. A certain one, before falling into a trance, during which he held intercourse with the spirit-world, used to put aside his head. Jetté[40] ventures to suppose that the bystanders lost theirs, rather than he his. "Other shows could be commemorated here, but hardly deserve more than a passing mention. Shamans allowed themselves to be shot at with a rifle [which they themselves had loaded, or allowed another man to load], dropping down as dead and afterwards jumping to their feet, making an infuriated run, and finally coughing and spitting out the bullet. Others covered an empty dish-pan with a piece of drill, raised it toward heaven, and when they put it down it was found filled with powder or shot or gun caps. Another one took the stars from the sky and laid them on the floor of the cabin before his wondering admirers. He must have been very careful to put each back in its own place, unless, perhaps, he be the one who is answerable for the loss of one of the Pleiades. If there be any truth in these facts, they would prove that the medicine-men in the old times were skilful performers, a qualification which their actual successors lack conspicuously. . . . Their profession seems to exercise no special influence on their moral character. They are generally smart, somewhat crafty, but not to a degree that would greatly transcend the ordinary. Some are very wicked, but others, on the contrary, are benevolent and genial." They are losing their power, probably through white influence; and the old ability to predict a person's death is now discredited and hence remains without effect, though some natives fall sick from fright.

---

37 Boas, in PSM, LVII, 631.
38 Jones, *Thlingets*, 156, 160-162.
39 Macleod, in AA, XXVII, 134, 142.
40 In JAI, XXXVII, 168, 174-176.

Hewitt[41] says that Iroquois shamans are all jugglers and have annual meetings at which they show their skill. They believe that each trick comes from a "dangerous dream." Each juggler is obliged at these meetings to show a new trick or he forfeits his life, and a simple trick will answer the purpose if it deceives the other jugglers. These tricksters can swallow pebbles, knives, and the like, by the use of a tube inserted in the throat. They also cause "appearances" in the smoke after putting tobacco and perfumes upon the fire. A juggler who could not tell the meaning of a dream also forfeited his life. LaFlesche[41] related some tricks played by the Pawnee shamans. One feat, the swallowing of a deer's head, he could not explain. "Arrows" were swallowed which were made of a vine soaked and greased so as to render them pliable. Their performances were remarkable in that the shamans were nearly nude, remained in the midst of the audience, and did not use any of the aids employed by professional prestidigitators. Before the Cheyenne doctor treated a patient, he purified himself and the sick man, largely through the use of smoke. "The hands were frequently passed through the smoke, the palms held up to the sun, and then rubbed on the ground, and afterward placed on the patient, while prayers were made." All the medicine-men were also horse-doctors. "The very great usefulness of the horse in all aspects of Plains Indian life, but especially in war, gave an extraordinary importance to the work of curing injured horses or—by means of mysterious power—enduing them with an added measure of activity, speed, strength, and endurance. The doctor who possessed the power to heal men exercised this power as well on horses. When a doctor instructed a young man how to cure sickness, he usually taught him also the secrets of doctoring horses. . . . If the Cheyennes were going to race horses against another tribe, those who were backing the horse might take a pipe, and, generally, also some arrows, as a gift, to ask help from the horse doctor. To do this in ordinary tribal races was not admissible. The horse doctor then sought and found a track of the opponent's horse, and taking a handful of dirt from the track, he put this earth in a gopher's hole. This, it was believed, would cause the horse to step in a hole and fall or get hurt. . . . No horse doctor would eat horseflesh, and no horse doctor would shoot a horse, wild or tame."[42] In some cases the object of Indian sorcery was, by means of divination, to find out the plans of the enemy.[43] Some of the Californian medicine-men, through their incantations, pretended to be able to bring fish as well as to cure the sick.[44]

The Indians, like the Hebrews, had their prophets who urged the people to return to the ways of righteousness. Such an one was Tenskwatawa, the famous "Shawnee Prophet." "He declared that he had been taken up to the spirit world and had been permitted to lift the veil of the past and the future—had seen the misery of evil doers and learned the happiness that awaited those who followed the precepts of the Indian god. He then began an earnest exhortation, denouncing the witchcraft practices and medicine juggleries of the tribe, and solemnly warning his hearers that none who had part in such things would ever taste of the future happiness. The firewater of the whites was poison and accursed; and those who continued its use would be tormented after death with all the pains of fire, while flames would continually

41 Both in AA, XVII, 622.
42 Grinnell, *Cheyenne Ind.*, II, 130, 139, 140, 143.
43 Leland and Prince, *Kulóskap*, 187.
44 Anon., in HAI, I, 397.

issue from their mouths. This idea may have been derived from some white man's teaching or from the Indian practice of torture by fire. The young must cherish and respect the aged and infirm. All property must be in common, according to the ancient law of their ancestors. Indian women must cease to intermarry with white men; the two races were distinct and must remain so. The white man's dress, with his flint and steel, must be discarded for the old-time buckskin and the firestick. More than this, every tool and every custom derived from the whites must be put away, and the Indians must return to the methods the Master of Life had taught them. When they should do all this, he promised that they would again be taken into the divine favor, and find the happiness which their fathers had known before the coming of the whites. Finally, in proof of his divine mission, he announced that he had received power to cure all diseases and to arrest the hand of death in sickness or on the battle-field." The movement was therefore a conservative reaction against the break-down of old customs and modes of life due to contact with whites, but it had at first no military object. To establish his sacred character and to dispel the doubts of the unbelievers, the prophet continued to dream dreams and announce wonderful revelations from time to time. "A miracle which finally silenced all objections was the prediction of an eclipse of the sun which took place in the summer of 1806; this was followed by his enthusiastic acceptance as a true prophet and the messenger of the Master of Life."[45]

On four special occasions the Island Caribs needed the services of their medicine-men, with their incantations and tobacco smoke: (a) to be revenged on some one who had done them harm, by drawing punishment upon him; (b) to be cured of some illness and learn the results of it; (c) to consult the gods on the issues of their wars; and (d) to hunt away the Evil Spirit. "When the Boyé [medicine-man] has made his Familiar Spirit appear, the latter is heard to reply clearly to the questions put to him: he is heard to click his jaws as if eating and drinking the anacri, but next morning they find that he has not touched it. These temporal viands which have been soiled by these unfortunate spirits are deemed so sacred by the magician and the people whom they have abused that it is only the old men and the most illustrious among them who are free to partake of them, and even then they dare not taste them unless they have a certain cleanliness of person."[46] One of the head chiefs of the Arau-canians died suddenly of apoplexy. This manner of death, so uncommon among the Indians—there being no visible cause to explain it—was immediately set down to witchcraft. There was nothing to do but call in the medicine-man. He arrived, carrying in his right hand a wand about eighteen inches in length, covered with snake's skin and garnished with human teeth. "The *machi* took his stand in front of the fire, with arms extended, face upturned, and eyes un-blinking for more than half an hour, inhaling without flinching the clouds of suffocating smoke that enveloped him, and seemingly lost to everything around him. Suddenly he recovered consciousness, and rushed into the hut where the body was laid out on a bed of skins. What he did there, no one could tell, but after a short while he reappeared, showing signs of mental and bodily exhaus-tion." In a jar he placed exuviæ from the corpse and then started to dance. "By degrees, the dance became more and more furious, the contortions more com-plicated, and at length he broke out into a wild monotonous chant. This was kept up till human nature could stand no more, and he fell back in a fit, or

45 Mooney, in HAI, II, 729-730.   46 Roth, in BAE, XXX, 167-168.

state of coma, produced by utter exhaustion. . . . In a short time he announced that the chief had been slain by an enemy who had taken the form of
a black *caita* (wild bull), and that it was necessary to sacrifice such an animal,
when the evil-doer would immediately suffer for his act."[47]

Divination was a regular practice among the advanced peoples of antiquity.
The Hebrews "ask counsel at their stocks, and their staff declareth unto
them."[48] Prophetism exhibited a connection with various survivals of the most
ancient conceptions, even with magic.[49] Among the early Scandinavians the
future was foretold by a prophetess, who was queen of the goblins and was
long remembered in Sweden.[50] The greatest of the Grecians treated the Oracle
of Delphi with respect; Plato and Aristotle did not hesitate to express publicly
their belief in her prophecies, which were interpreted by a body of very learned
and experienced priests. Recent excavations have revealed something of the
inner history of this famous shrine. The investigation of the temple-founda-
tions shows that the *sanctum sanctorum* of the Oracle was no bigger than a
ship's cabin; "this Adyton was like a small box contained in a bigger one,
and was, like the rest of the temple, built of limestone, had a flat wooden
ceiling and four smooth walls, one of which was pierced by a door. The interior floor surface measured only fifteen square meters." The inquirers sat
on stone benches. A stairway led down to the vault, where the tripod stood and
under which issued the prophetic spring. This tripod was called "the common
hearth of Hellas." "Curiously enough, the priestess might not be a learned
or an experienced person in the ways of the world; she must have as far as
possible an utter simplicity. For a time the Pythia was a young girl, but the
priests for very good reasons decided that she must be of more mature age,
and yet she was always dressed as a youthful damsel and expected to assume
the airs of maidenhood. The priests of Apollo were her prophets. If the Pythia
shrieked and foamed at the mouth the priest interpreted her in vocal syllables
and made her articulate. In the beginning these interpretations were given in
hexameters, but later the answers were in prose. Dr. Poulsen believes that the
Pythia was ignorant and sincere and that her madness was genuine; he gives
the priests of Apollo credit for great shrewdness and knowledge of affairs,
but he does not venture an opinion as to whether they played tricks on the
credulity of their clients or not. There seems, however, to have been something
more than mere frenzy on the part of the Sibyl, and if the priests were tricksters they were extraordinarily wise and potent tricksters, for from the beginning of the seventh century B.C. the Oracle of Delphi became not only the
arbiter of the destinies of Greece, the directress of great men's minds, but
the guiding star of the founders of its colonies."[51]

Oracles like the Greek were unknown at Rome, but the custom of learning
the will of the gods by incubation was most ancient and Italian. Divination
was accomplished also by cards written, mixed, and extracted at sanctuaries;
other means were dreams and the flame of the burning laurel. At one time
nothing, whether ploughing or marrying off a daughter, was done, even in
private, without auspices.[52] Nearly all the successors of Augustus in the first
and second centuries were infected by the fatalist creed of astrology. Astrolo-

---

47 Latcham, in JAI, XXXIX, 365-368.
48 Hosea, IV, 12.
49 Kautzsch, in *Hastings's Dict. Bible*, 655.
50 Geijer, *Svensk. Hist.* I, 26.

51 Poulsen, *Delphi*, reviewed by Egan, in
N. Y. *Times*, Jan. 23, 1921.
52 De Marchi, *Culto Priv.*, rev. in *Année
Soc.*, I, 232, 238; Cicero, *De Div.*, I, 16, 28,
46, 104.

gers "were banished again and again in the first century, but persecution only increased their power, and they always returned to exercise greater influence than ever. Never was there a clearer proof of the impotence of government in the face of a deep-seated popular belief."[53] Astrology suddenly appeared in the foreground of Italian life in the thirteenth century. Rulers had a corps of such persons at court; in the universities from the fourteenth to the sixteenth centuries there were special professors of this pseudo-science. The popes openly espoused star-questioning, and Paul III held no consistory court without the star-gazers having decided the hour for him.[54] Among the portents of the Great Plague noted by Defoe was "running about to fortune tellers, cunning men, and astrologers." Sadly he reports that "this trade grew so open and so generally practiced that it became common to have signs and inscriptions set up at the doors: 'Here lives the Fortune Teller,' and the like." The same gentry are still with us; fully one thousand fortune tellers may be found plying their ancient trade in New York City alone. Under the name of psychic and occult there is carried on a profitable business which is supposed to have disappeared with the Middle Ages.[55]

§314. Rain-Making.

In Australia, the rain-maker may merely go to a pool "and, taking care that no women or strangers are in sight, bends down over and 'sings' the water; then he takes some up in his hands, drinks it, and spits it out in various directions. After that he throws water all over himself, and after scattering some all around, returns quietly to his camp, and rain is supposed to follow." Again, there is a rain-bird whose mate, a snake, lives in a water-hole. The performer first sings the bird, then secures one of the snakes and puts it alive into the water-hole. "After holding it under for a little time, he brings it out, kills it, and lays it down by the side of the creek." He then makes a grass imitation of the rain-bow. "All that he then does is to sing over the snake and the imitation rain-bow, and sooner or later rain falls." While only a special performer can make rain, "any black-fellow can stop it by simply taking a green stick, warming it in the fire, and then striking it against the wind."[1]

In southeast Australia, a log hut is built over a hole about twelve feet long, eight to ten feet wide, and two feet deep. Then two supposedly inspired men are lanced in the arm with a sharp flint, and while they bleed, down is thrown into the air—the blood symbolizing rain and the down the clouds. Two large stones also symbolize gathering clouds. The men who are bled carry away these stones and place them in the highest possible location in the tallest available tree, while others gather gypsum, pound it fine, and throw it into the water-hole. The hut is then thrown down by the old and young men who butt at it with their heads; "the piercing the hut with their heads symbolises the piercing of the clouds, and the fall of the hut symbolises that of the rain." Failure is referred to the adverse influence of some neighboring tribe upon the rain-giving powers.[2] In the East Central district the process is similar: "In order to make rain the old men cut themselves on the ears and both sides of the face. Rain is also made by the following ceremony: Twelve old men sit down

53 Dill, *Nero*, 447.
54 Burckhardt, *Renaissance*, 513-514.
55 N. Y. *Times*, Apr. 18, 1909; Dec. 12, 1909; Nov. 5, 1911; July 14, 1922.

1 Spencer and Gillen, *North. Tr. Cent. Aust.*, 314-315.
2 Howitt, *S. E. Aust.*, 394-396.

at a small waterhole and make a large copi [gypsum] ball about 10 lbs. in weight. The ball is put into the waterhole and the twelve men return to the camp. Then one by one they go and have a look at the ball to see if it is dissolved. When it has dissolved it is bound to rain."[3]

Among certain Melanesians, "if the rain expert is lazy, and stays much in his house wrapped in his blanket, rain is likely to come; on the other hand by getting up and walking about the village he is able to stop rain. He also has certain charm stones which are suspended by strings over vessels of water; when rain is required the stones are let down so as to touch the surface of the water; when enough rain has fallen, the stones are drawn up again. Bats are said to frequent the house of the rain expert, and should he build a new house these animals forsake the old house and fly to the new one of their own accord."[4] The rain-maker holds a very responsible position in New Guinea; failure on his part may bring disaster. On one occasion the natives accused him of trying to kill them, the charge specifically being that he was not making rain, as a result of which the native gardens would fail and the people starve and die.[5] In New Caledonia "there was a rain-making class of priests. They blackened themselves all over, exhumed a dead body, took the bones to a cave, jointed them, and suspended the skeleton over some taro leaves. Water was poured on the skeleton to run down on the leaves. They supposed that the soul of the departed took up the water, made rain of it, and showered it down again. They had to fast and remain in the cavern until it rained, and sometimes died in the experiment. They generally chose, however, the showery months of March and April for their rain-making. If there was too much rain, and they wanted fair weather, they went through a similar process, only they kindled a fire under the skeleton and burned it up."[6]

Every tribe in Mashonaland has its own Mondoro or protecting god, and there is always a medium through whom he speaks. "If rain does not come when it should, then all the women in, say, one kraal take small baskets full of grain to the hut of the oldest woman in the kraal, who must be of the same M'tupo 'totem' as the tribe of the Mondoro. She then takes the grain to a flat rock and finds a hollow place into which she pours all the grain, and takes a dipping calabash and walks round the grain and calls upon the Mondoro to send rain because his children are starving. They then wait a few days and if rain does not follow, the whole kraal proceed to the kraal of the medium of the Mondoro, and offerings of snuff are made to her and she is requested to call up the spirit of the Mondoro and ask him what the people have done wrong that no rain has fallen. The medium retires to her hut and the people remain outside all night waiting for the spirit to enter the medium. This usually happens in the early morning, when the medium comes rushing from her hut foaming at the mouth and shouting out to the people, who all follow her and ask questions as to what is to be done to get rain. The medium may tell them that they have offended the Mondoro in some way and must make an offering of a goat, head of cattle or a hoe, and if this is done then rain is sure to follow." In South Africa one also finds specialists—"rain doctors" and "callers for rain," as the native terms signify. Usually the king is the chief rain-maker, but the profession is not necessarily practised by males only; one of the most famous rain doctors was a chieftainess, said to have four breasts and credited

3 Wells, in AAAS, 1893, 518.
4 Seligmann, *Melanesians*, 295.
5 Strong, in JAI, XLIX, 307.
6 Turner, *Samoa*, 345-346.

with being the source of the locusts.[7] Obviously she was a fetish-woman. When rain is threatening on the Upper Congo a certain ceremony is performed in order to ascertain how long it will be before the rain will fall, "If the leaf breaks at the first whack the rain will begin to fall in twenty minutes, and so on. They will start a journey or remain at home according to the indications of this performance." On the shelves in most of the houses are sticks with "medicine" tied round them, which are taken down and plunged into water with some leaves so as to bring rain. "It is rarely that they resort to this as the rains fall with great regularity all the year round. Throwing salt on the fire will cause a superabundance of rain to fall."[8] Among the Bageshu are special men whose duties are to regulate the elements; they bring the rain when it is necessary and cause sunshine when it is required. "They have not always the most pleasant time, because their failure to produce the necessary rain is never attributed to inability, but to disinclination to accommodate the people. The people try persuasion, bring presents and offerings to them, begging them to act for them; if the rain does not come they lose patience and demand it; if the men persist in their obstinacy and if the rain does not come, they resort to strong measures and deeds of violence. They rob them of their cattle, and if the rain does not come then, they proceed to burn their houses down, and the rain-makers are fortunate if they escape a severe handling, or even death. The method commonly practised by the medicine-man is to take a couple of fowls which have been brought by the suppliant, and kill one of them by striking it on the head with a stick; he cuts it open by making an incision from the under side of the beak down the breast to the tail, then lays it open and examines the entrails for the markings upon them, and for any speck. . . . If the strong measures fail, the people are reduced to seeking out the man, and again try by flattery and presents to obtain his help. They rebuild his house and restore his cattle and make reparation for the ill he has suffered. The man may agree to go to the extreme measure of a visit to the deity on the mountain which he professes to fear doing."[9]

Among the Wagogo of East Africa the art of rain-making is kept secret, but the color black appears to be an essential. Offerings of black fowls, black sheep, and black cattle are made at the graves of ancestors, while during the rainy season the rain-maker wears black clothes.[10] Serpa Pinto[11] says the African rain-makers note the winds that bring rain and operate accordingly. Doubtless such weather-wisdom is a tradition of the profession. The Wawanga make the medicine-man a present of a bullock and request him to produce rain. "So long as the drought lasts the chief sends him the humps of all bullocks killed by him; and at harvest time, should the medicine-man have been successful in producing rain, he sends round to all the plantations for a contribution of grain. If, however, no rains come, the people argue that some other medicine-men are jealous of him and are working against him. They accordingly go by night to their own medicine-man and kill him. It is asserted that heavy rains invariably follow his death."[12] Although the wizard is held in abhorrence and dread by the Nilotic Kavirondo, the rain-maker is greatly esteemed. "His success probably depends upon a knowledge of the signs of the heavens, but his methods are as follows: His village is to be found as a

7 Garbutt, in JAI, XXXIX, 547-548, 550.   10 Cole, in JAI, XXXII, 325.
8 Weeks, in JAI, XL, 382-383.   11 Afrika, I, 112.
9 Roscoe, in JAI, XXXIX, 189.   12 Dundas, K., in JAI, XLIII, 48-49.

rule near a big tree, which he asserts is sacred; when rain is wanted he gathers some herbs and puts them in a large pot containing water, which he boils beneath the holy tree. Of the decoction thus prepared he draws off a little into a smaller pot, above which he squats on his haunches. Next a reed is produced, and through this the rain-maker draws up a little of the liquid and then squirts it forth into the air after blowing through the reed and causing the fluid in the pot to bubble; the whole process being punctuated by voluble mutterings and *abracadabra.*"[13] The principal function of the magician-chiefs of the Upper Nile is to make rain, for this is the one thing that matters to the people in those districts; if it does not come down at the right time, it means that their animals and crops, their only resources, are destroyed. "These chiefs, the rain-makers, have various ways of producing rain. One may have a collection of rain-stones such as rock crystals and amethysts. These he plunges into water and, taking a cane, beckons with it to the clouds, accompanying his gesture with an incantation."[14] The position of rain-maker in the Anglo-Egyptian Sudan is precarious; "he has great power as long as the rain behaves within bounds, as he can always get more goats slaughtered up to a certain amount and feast upon them. But there comes a time when the need is too great, and he is given a last chance. Then an ox, if they can afford it, is slaughtered and a great feast prepared, and some of the blood with some round pebbles is put in one of the hollowed stones used by the women for grinding corn. This is left on one side, I presume as an offering to some higher power. The feast is held with much drumming; at its conclusion, on a given signal, amid dead silence, all retire to their huts, and not a sound is made till morning. If no rain comes in three weeks from that day the rainmaker is killed."[15]

In Manu's time an oblation thrown on the fire reaches the sun, whence comes rain.[16] A native writer[17] goes into some detail concerning rain-producing ceremonies in India, exhibiting, among other expedients, the employment of coercive nudity. The women parade the streets at night, singing, for ten or twelve days; or they strip naked and draw a plow across the fields. In the latter case, if they should be seen by men, the spell would lose its effect. Hook-swinging for rain, where the victim has hooks fixed in his back and is drawn up forty feet into the air, is parallel to other forms of self-torture.[18] Abuse of the men by the women, whereby the former "are supposed to be offered as sacrifices to the offended rain-god in order to appease his wrath so that he may cause rain to fall," is another variant; and there are ceremonies by the women to cause the rain to cease. Abuse of the lame, halt, and blind, by pouring water on them and receiving their vituperations, is believed to be sure to bring rain in a dry time. If Brahman women, who never plow for themselves, engage in such undignified manual labor, it is thought that rain will pour down in torrents immediately after. If there is hesitation about subjection of such high-caste females to actual labor in broad daylight, they touch the plow early in the morning, before people are up, and the plowing is done later in the day by the men. Slaughter of animals was, in one case, forbidden, in consequence of a long period of drought; "but in two days the rains set in, and the prohibition was removed." In Bengal, in times of drought and threatened failure

13 Northcote, in JAI, XXXVII, 64.
14 N. Y. *Times*, Apr. 28, 1924.
15 Seligmann, in JAI, XLIII, 673.
16 Bühler, *Manu*, III, 76.

17 §277, above; Mitra, in JASB, IV, 387, 388, 392, 393, 394; Mitra, in JASB, III, 25, 32; Mitra, in JASB, V, 4.
18 §291, above.

of crops, all the outlets of a certain temple were closed and a hundred to one hundred and fifty Brahmans poured water on the idol till it was immersed to the chin; the people confidently believed that rain-clouds would at once gather and send down showers. Another writer[19] reports that the women assemble alone and dance, nude, around a mystic tree—a plantain stem or young bamboo stuck into the ground—singing old songs and charms. This rite is to get rain and a good harvest when they are suffering or likely to suffer from drought.

In the Japanese highlands, after a prolonged drought, five or six hardy hunters are sent as a deputation to the god supposed to dwell on the summit of Jonendake. Armed with guns and primed with rice-beer, they climb to the top of the mountain and make a fire. "By discharging their guns, rolling masses of rock down the cliffs and otherwise making a din, they endeavour to attract the attention of the spirit of the place to their prayers. By the noise and flames they intend a mimic representation of the storm they are seeking, and the practice may be classed with those commonly known to folk-lorists as 'sympathetic magic.'" The hunters declare that rain always comes within a few days after the ceremony.[20] The submerging of prehistoric stone axes in pots of water is a rain-producing device in north Celebes.[21] In the Gilbert Islands, writes Finsch,[22] "a woman promised to raise a 'good wind' on payment of several pieces of tobacco; when it did not come, and I jokingly demanded the tobacco back, she (and I) were derided by the natives." The Eskimo *angakok* is called in to get a good wind.[23]

Mandan medicine-men perform their rain-producing ceremonies inside the lodge and young men volunteer to stand upon the lodge from sunrise to sundown, in turn, commanding it to rain. "Each one has to hazard the disgrace which attaches . . . to a fruitless attempt; and he who succeeds acquires a lasting reputation as a *mystery* or *medicine-man*. They never fail to make it rain! as this ceremony continues from day to day until rain comes. . . . He who has once made it rain never attempts it again. . . . On future occasions of the kind he stands aloof who has once done it in presence of the whole village, giving an opportunity to other young men who are ambitious to signalize themselves in the same way."[24] The ceremonies of the Indians of the arid regions to secure rain are too protracted and complicated to reproduce in description; they include the well-known Snake-Dance, with its bands of priests and accessories of imitative magic.[25] An individual intrusts his prayer to sacred meal, over which he breathes his petition; but a society of priests uses a more powerful charm, called a prayer-stick whose manufacture, on account of all the symbolical accessories, takes time and complex rites. The snakes are intercessors between men and the rain gods, and there is "a compulsion of the rain and growth supernatural to perform their functions." Members of the medicine-society "claim immunity from the bite of the snake because it is their totem. . . . The main object of the majority of Hopi ceremonials is the production of rain and the growth of corn. . . . The modern Tusayan Indians believe that the dead have certain occult powers over rain deities. 'You have come to be a rain-god,' is the import of their prayer to a deceased friend or

---

19 Basu, in JASB, III, 103 ff.
20 Weston, in JAI, XXVI, 30; §286, above.
21 Wilken, *Vkde.*, 85.
22 *Ethnol. Erfahr.*, III, 48.

23 Holm, *Ethnol. Skizze*, 88.
24 Donaldson, in *Smithson. Rep.*, 1885, pt. II, 332, 335, 336.
25 §§256, 302, above, and 442, below.

relative."[26] From Arizona comes the report that immediately following the close, in 1926, of the annual snake-dance of the Hopi Indians such a heavy deluge fell that many of the automobiles of the returning sightseers were mired in the Painted Desert. Records show that the Indian priests have rarely failed to time the dance so as to coincide with the break in the dry season. "Generations of skill in desert weather lore have taught the priests of the Snake and Antelope clans of the Hopi Indians to foretell with almost uncanny correctness the exact day of the first rains. In fact, so wise are they that the snake dance ceremony is usually followed by a shower within an hour of its termination. Usually the first rain is light. This year it appears to have been a cloudburst."[27] Among the Zuñi, rain-making is properly the function of the rain-priests and of a certain esoteric society.[28] The Huichol Indians of Mexico have a yearly festival to bring rain. They abstain for a long period before the festival from sexual relations, salt, and bathing; and both sexes drink a decoction expressed from the cactus which is stimulating and quells hunger, thirst, and sex-feeling; it leaves a certain lassitude and headache behind but evokes colorful visions.[29] A skull on a pole, facing northwest, was supposed by certain South American Indians to secure dry weather.[30] In Teneriffe, "in time of drought, men and women cried aloud and danced around a pole in the ground, not eating until rain fell"; or, in case of disappointment, a holy man freed a sacred pig to roam till it rained. "This pig was thought to be the devil, who was greatly learned in the ways of nature and produced rain to blind the people and make them worship him."[31]

It is the belief of the Guiana Indians that rain can be produced as well as stopped by human, animal, or spirit agency; at the same time it appears to have an independent existence. "To make rain on the Pomeroon, one of the authorized methods consists in plunging into water a length of cassava stalk held at one extremity. Next the stalk must be tied up in the center of a bundle of other cassava stalks, and the whole left to soak in water: rain is sure to fall within twenty-four hours. Another method practised here is to wash in water the scrapings from one of an alligator's largest teeth. Arawaks as well as Warraus believe also in the piai [medicine-man] or any layman burning the carcass of a camudi as an inducement for the rain to fall. The Oyambis of Cayenne have the same belief in the efficacy of the killing of a snake. . . . In the Moruca River district, there is a half-submerged tree stump, known as Ibúma (lit. 'young woman,' in the Warrau language), believed to be the site where either an Indian murdered his wife or where she killed herself. In dry weather the tree is exposed, and as the Indians pass it in their corials, they call out, 'Ibúma!' and slash their cutlasses into it, with the avowed purpose of making the woman vexed, and so causing the rain to fall. Rain can also be made to fall in this district by cursing the black kurri-kurri bird. . . . On the upper Mazaruni it is a large eagle and a camudi that can cause the rain to fall; frogs are reputed to be able to do the same thing." The infringement of certain taboos can entail a downpour of rain, as for instance, "when traveling on the sea or any other large sheet of water, as a big river, the Indians

26 Fewkes, in *Smithson. Rep.*, 1895, 690, 696; Fewkes, in BAE, XV, 267; Fewkes, in BAE, XIX, pt. II, 1008, 1009, 1010; Fewkes, in *Smithson Rep.*, 1895, 581.
27 N. Y. *Times*, Aug. 25, 1926.
28 Swanton, in HAI, II, 495.

29 Lumholtz, in *Bull. Amer. Mus. Nat. Hist.*, X, 1 ff.
30 Von Nordenskiöld, in *Globus*, LXXXVII, 28.
31 Cook, in AA, II, 490, 493.

(Arawaks, Warraus, etc.) have to be very careful as to what they do with the pot-spoon. . . . After use they must wash it in the traveling boat or wait until they get on land, but never wash it in the river or sea: otherwise, big squalls and storms will arise. Near the Chichi Falls, upper Mazaruni, on giving the Indians rice to cook that evening, the men told them to wash it first by dipping the earthen pot into water, but to this they demurred, saying that if they placed their pot in the water the rain would fall more heavily. In the same way a Cayenne bush-negro, in order to stop the rain, advises his fellow-servant not to wash the inside of the pot." There are other methods of stopping rain. In a certain district "there was a hill close by on which, the Indian said, a 'Spirit at the approach of the end of the rainy season, made a noise like the report of a gun to stop the rain.' 'We passed an old man,' says Brett, 'fishing in a canoe on the Manawarin. The clouds threatened rain, and when he perceived it, he began to use extraordinary gesticulations, flourishing his arms, and shouting his incantations to drive it away. It soon cleared up, and the old sorcerer rejoiced at his success, as he deemed it.' So again, Dance on the Potaro: 'A cloud was gathering windward, and threatened rain. The Indian who had the front paddle in my woodskin commenced to blow away the threatening rain cloud. This he attempted to do by blowing into his fist and dashing his hand upward toward the cloud.' Schomburgk describes a similar manœuvre executed by a Warrau. On the Pomeroon, should rain fall at a time when it is particularly not desired, as when traveling in an exposed corial, one of the occupants will address the 'Boss' Spirit of the Rain somewhat as follows: 'Pass on. We don't want you here. Clear out to the head of the river where you are wanted,' at the same time pointing with his finger toward the direction he wishes it to take. Another of the occupants will as often as not then get up in the boat on all fours and, pointing his posterior in the direction of the Rain, will address it with an obscene remark."[32]

Civilized peoples and savages may not be so far apart, suggests a journalist, facetiously; the former merely operate in the field of politics. "In the region of the Upper Mississippi and its major tributaries, among such tribes as the Wisconsians, the Illinoisans, the Indianians and the Non-Partisan tribes of Minnesota and the Dakotas, the custom is to select every four years a chieftain, resident at the national kraal called Washington, whose chief function is to make rain, develop a high production of sunlight, ward off cyclones, and in every other way promote the growth of the crops and the hogs upon which these tribes depend for their subsistence. If climatic conditions have been unfavorable under a chieftain of one great clan, known as the Republicans, the tribesmen replace him with a chieftain from another clan, known as the Democrats, and vice versa. The Republicans have amassed a large collection of magic rain-stones, such as Home Markets, American Standards of Living, Foreign Pauper Labor, etc. When the kettle begins to boil, once every four years, they plunge these magic stones into the hot water and, taking up a magician's wand, known as the Tariff, they perform incantations with it, and immediately the rain begins to fall, the crops begin to burgeon and the hogs begin to fatten like anything."[33]

32 Roth, in BAE, XXX, 267, 268.   33 Editorial in N. Y. *Times*, Apr. 28, 1924.

§315. Theory of Disease.

THE Central Australians have a suggestive theory of the cause of pain: the spirits are supposed to use a special form of pointing-stick, which is hooked at one end. "This is projected into the body of the victim, and every now and then the spirit gives a malicious tug at the hair string which is attached to the hook, so as to increase the victim's pain."[1]

In British New Guinea there are people who suffer much from ulcers on feet and legs, which probably start with wounds from sharp coral. The natives have no medical skill in treating these wounds, merely lying by the fire and heating them or strewing them with ashes or resin.[2] They are exceptional in that they do not even use curative magic. In the New Hebrides, "in an ordinary case, when it is supposed that a ghost is the cause of the complaint, the friends of the sick man send for the professional dreamer and give him now tobacco, as formerly they gave mats, to find out what ghost has been offended, and to make it up with him. He sleeps, and in his dream goes to the place where the sick man has been working; there he meets some one, like an old man it is likely, of small size, who really is a ghost, and he learns from him what is his name. The ghost tells him that the sick man as he was working has encroached upon his ground, the place he haunts as his own, and that to punish him he has taken away his soul and impounded it in a magic fence in the garden. The dreamer begs for the return of the soul, and asks pardon on behalf of the sick man, who meant no disrespect; the ghost pulls up the fence in which the soul is enclosed, and lets it out; the man of course recovers." It is usually a case of recovering the soul. "In the Solomon Islands, if a child starts in its sleep it is believed that some ghost is snatching away what must be called in translation its shadow. A wizard doctor undertakes to go in sleep and bring it back; he dreams and goes; if those who have taken the 'shadow' let him take it back the child recovers, but if the child dies the dreamer reports that they would not let him come near them."[3]

"The bush-soul is always in the form of an animal of the forest. Sometimes when a man sickens it is because his bush-soul is angry at being neglected, and a witch-doctor is called in, who, having diagnosed this as being the cause of the trouble, advises the administration of some kind of offering to the offended one. . . . The witching of things into a man is the most frequent method among the Bantu, hence the prevalence among them of the post-mortem examination—a practice the writer has never found among the Negroes."[4] The Yorubas have a smallpox god, who is accompanied by an assistant ready to wring the necks of those attacked by the disease.[5] When Serpa Pinto[6] had a severe fever, near the headwaters of the Zambesi, the local chief visited him bringing his personal physician, an old man, small and thin, with white beard and hair. The latter began by solemnly pronouncing several magic words and went through a form of divination, concluding that Serpa Pinto's dead parents had taken possession of him and must have some gift if they were to leave. "I stood it all with the greatest patience, feigning to believe what he said to me, and gave him a little present of powder." In another case of illness, "the physicians, by the inspiration breathed into them by the daimon, had decided

1 Gillen, in AAAS, 1901, 113. 4 Kingsley, *Travels W. Afr.*, 459, 462.
2 Pöch, in *Globus*, XCII, 281-282. 5 Ellis, *Yoruba*, 73.
3 Codrington, *Melanesians*, 208, 209. 6 *Africa*, 13.

the night before that the sickness was caused by the fact that the man who fell ill had eaten a food forbidden by the quixilles [taboo] of his family, and so had offended the fetish who was now punishing him." One can bring a swollen stomach upon his enemy by driving nails into the fetish; therefore sick persons who fear that such a thing has been done, "if they are rich enough, send for him and his priest, so that the latter may find the nails in question and then, after going through proper ceremonies, pull them out again."[7] Some negroes feel the danger of even naming an evil disease; in their eyes the name and the thing itself are the same, and might one not, at the name of the sickness, be suddenly attacked by it? So they call it "bad beast." The negro thinks of the disease as corporeal, "as a specter that slinks from village to village— a view which, *mutatis mutandis*—has its justification."[8]

In all cases which are fatal, excepting death from actual visible injury, the natives of British Central Africa ascribe illness to the workings of some person—"he having compassed the death of his victim either by making medicine against him or actual administration of some noxious drug with the idea of eating the dead body, the evildoer being possessed."[9] The Bahima account for sickness in four ways: "1. It is thought to be caused by the departed king, who has been offended in some way; the Mandwa (chief priest to the king) is the only person who can assist in such a case; paralysis is attributed to this source. 2. It is set down to witchcraft (*kuloga*), which is practised by a person with the desire to kill another secretly; the illness may take any form of disease. 3. Fever is attributed to natural causes. 4. Illness is attributed to ghosts (*mizimu*), which take possession of people for various causes, and have to be exorcised." Witchcraft usually takes the form of chest complaints and skin diseases. The seemingly strange statement about fever is elucidated as follows: "Fever is brought on by local or climatic conditions of the country, no person is held responsible for it; it is a freak of nature." When a person becomes delirious, it is put down to possession by a malicious ghost, and the medicine-man has to come and smoke out the ghost. "A common complaint amongst these people is a deep-seated abscess; their cure for this is to transfer the disease to some other person by obtaining herbs from the medicine man, rubbing them over the place where the swelling is, and burying them in the road where people continually pass; the first person who steps over these buried herbs contracts the disease, and the original patient recovers."[10]

One of the commonest duties of the medicine-man in East Africa is the curing of sickness, "but of course he has first to discover its nature and causes, and this is very commonly found to be the anger or possession of a spirit. To a similar cause barrenness in women may frequently be attributed by the medicine man. His cure may be quite simple: it may be the construction of another doorway to the village, presumably because the existing one harbours a malignant spirit, or he may even recommend entire abandonment of the village. Frequently a sacrifice is offered and the names of many deceased members of the family are called until that of the particular spirit molesting the patient is mentioned, when the trouble will abate."[11] "The Akikuyu apparently do not believe that a demon enters into a man during illness, but they say if Ngai foreordains that he will live, he will do so, and *vice versa*. A medicine

7 Bastian, *Deut. Exped.*, I, 59, 78.
8 Struck, in *Globus*, XCII, 149.
9 Stannus, in JAI, XL, 293.

10 Roscoe, in JAI, XXXVII, 103.
11 Dundas, C., in JAI, XLIII, 529-530.

man, however, is generally called in if the illness does not leave the sick man for several days."[12] In Uganda it is thought that either the sick are bewitched or a snake has crept into them.[13] The Hausa theory of disease is implied in the manner of treatment: the illness, or part of it, is induced to enter a cock, then a hen; the medicine-man then places the fowls upon the ground and, treading upon them, opens the mouth of the cock, holds the tongue to the mandible, and cuts its throat. He throws it upon the ground at some little distance from him, treats the hen in the same way, and finally sticks his knife into the ground. "The reason for opening the beaks was to give the disease-bori [spirits] free exit."[14] In southern Tunis certain Mohammedan saints are worshipped in order to secure cures of illness or sterility.[15] Among the Arabs of the Sahara occurs the exceptional belief that disease is a blessing; for if a person is sick over three days his sins are remitted. "Allah says to the angel on the left: 'Cease writing his bad deeds.' And he says to the angel on the right: 'Write down his good deeds as better than they are.' "[16]

One tribe of India has a legend that God sleeps and that while he sleeps a snake causes diseases and carries men off in death. This is the serpent that interfered at the creation by devouring every night, while God slept, the man and woman whom he had made during the day. This went on until God made a dog, which frightened the snake. But the latter has grown bolder now and the barking of dogs when a man dies does not drive him off.[17] The Saoras, "believing all ills of the body to be the work of ancestral spirits, or little further removed deities, they will have nothing to do with medicine as an alleviative."[18] The Palaungs hold that "if sickness has been caused by a water-spirit, the patient, if he has not been far from his home, has probably offended a spirit living in a neighbouring spring, stream, or well. He therefore takes an offering of cooked rice, curry, and flowers, in separate bowls; these he places near but not in the water, saying, 'I have offended thee by accident, not intentionally, O spirit! In future I shall not do so. I did not intend to do so. O spirit of the water! please let my illness disappear.' "[19]

The Veddahs have no system of medicine. In cases of sickness they sprinkle water on the patient, invoking their deceased ancestors to heal them. Sometimes they simply utter the name of the spirits as they dance around the sick man; again they offer a garland of flowers to the spirit who has afflicted him. The whole affair is daimonistic. They believe in the so-called devil-dance but cannot perform it.[20] The Cingalese practise this dance to get rid of the spirit causing sickness. There are twenty-four types of devils and that costume and mask must be worn which will drive off the particular spirit in question. "The dance lasts often through two nights, until all the masks have been tried out and the right one found." The dancers work themselves up to great excitement and then ask for an object in which the spirit might have entered. Generally a friend or relative of the sick man provides a cock, which is variously munched by the teeth of the masks until it sinks down in a sort of stupor. This is a sign that the dance has worked, for the spirit is now in the bird. The latter is resuscitated by the use of water and tortured again; if it dies it is a sign that

12 Tate, in JAI, XXXIV, 262.
13 Stuhlmann, Mit Emin, 181.
14 Tremearne, in JAI, XLV, 62-63.
15 Bruun, Huleboerne, 238, 239.
16 Pommerol, Sahariennes, 405-406.

17 Lewin, S.E. India, 225.
18 Fawcett, in JASB, I, 218.
19 Milne, Eastern Clan, 247.
20 Bailey, in Trans. Eth. Soc. London (N.S.), II, 303.

the spirit has killed it and the sick man is free of possession.[21] It is a sort of redemption-sacrifice. In Kafiristan, a husband who tried to do everything he could to save his sick wife, sacrificed a cow, distributing its flesh, and lit a big fire in the dying woman's room where he invited a large company to dance to squeaking pipes, while slaves banged an accompaniment on drums.[22]

The Chinese believe that diseases and epidemics are simply the work of evil spirits.[23] The Annamites fear the ghosts of children who have died at birth or in tender years, for they are always eager to become incarnated and yet, when they have got into a body, are not capable of living.[24]

"The Dyak theory of sickness is that it is either caused by the presence of evil spirits in the patient's body, or that he has been struck by one of them, or that one of them has enticed his soul out of his body. To expel *Hantu* from the human body, and to be able to see a vagrant soul, and then rescue it from the greedy clutches of the malignant spirits—in these things consists the perfection of the healing art. . . . Dyaks believe that every individual has seven souls, and that when a person is sick one or more of these are in captivity, and must be reclaimed to effect a cure. . . . The Dyaks regard small-pox as an evil spirit, with the notion which induced our English peasantry to use the same caution in reference to fairies—they never venture to name the small-pox, but designate it politely by the titles *Rajah* and *Buah-Kagu.*" Here are examples of avoidance by silence and of deception and flattery.[25] "As the natives ascribe all men's illnesses to the influences of evil spirits, their whole medical art is confined to conciliating these spirits on behalf of the patient, or, when it is supposed that the spirits have entered the body, to driving them out again. Only a few roots and herbs are used as internal and external remedies." By food-offerings, drum beating, and singing the spirits responsible for the illness are summoned and the assistance of the superior good spirits is invoked. The patient is repeatedly touched by the sorceresses with a leaf, which is then withdrawn with a shrill cry, as if to remove the curse resting on the patient. Solemn vows conditional on recovery are made to the gods.[26] "The Sakai idea with regard to sickness appears to be that diseases are generally, if not invariably, caused by spirits." According to one native, illness is caused by a spirit lying in wait for a human being and striking his shadow with a club. "If a young child should suffer from any itching complaint, the navel-cord, which appears to be usually buried under the house, is dug up and inspected: if this has been attacked by ants, they are killed with hot water, and it is reburied in another spot. Similarly if a man is on a journey in the jungle and is troubled with a rash, or with itching sensations in his body, he will return to his last camping-place and dig up the ground on which he lay, to see if there is an ants' nest in the soil."[27]

A Cheyenne Indian, by name Sun's Road, having built a cabin on Muddy Creek, soon after moving into it became sick and for a long time was in bad health. Nothing seemed to help him, though the tribal medicine-men and the agency physician did what they could. At length, however, he discovered the cause of his illness. "In the hills on the north side of the Muddy, standing out a little from the higher bluffs, is a peculiar conical peak, odd in shape and

21 Th. S., "Teufelstänzer," in *Globus*, LXXIV, 9, 10.
22 Robertson, in JAI, XXVII, 77.
23 DeGroot, *Relig. Syst.*, I, 134.
24 Bartels, *Medicin*, 18.

25 §§223, 264, 266, above.
26 Roth, *Sarawak*, I, 260, 269, 291; II, clxxv.
27 Evans, in JAI, XLVIII, 184.

color, and on the south side of the stream is another odd-looking peak. Sun's Road's house was in the line between these two peaks, and thus was on the trail traveled by the spirits dwelling in them, when they went from one peak to the other to visit. . . . This obstruction in their trail annoyed them, and to punish Sun's Road for troubling them, they made him ill. When Sun's Road awoke to the situation, he at once moved his house out of the line between the hills, and also turned it half round so that if they wished, the spirits might pass through the house, instead of climbing over it, if it still stood in their way. He became better at once, and in a short time recovered his health. Sun's Road often expressed astonishment that he could have been so careless as to build his house in such a situation, and so to have subjected himself to danger." The older Cheyennes formerly had much to say about the new diseases introduced by white men, which were very fatal, the cholera epidemic of 1849, for instance, being said to have killed half the tribe. On that occasion, one Indian, "a very brave man, donned his war-dress, mounted his war-horse, and rode through the camp with a lance in his hand, shouting, 'If I could see this thing [the cholera], if I knew where it came from, I would go there and fight it!' As he was doing this he was seized with the cramps, fell from his horse, and died in his wife's arms. Again the people rushed away in terror, and all night fled through the sandhills to the Arkansas."[28] Two epidemics at Zuñi, one of smallpox in 1898-1899 and the other of measles in 1910-1911, were both ascribed to witchcraft. "The two men held responsible, both youngish men at the time they were accused, are still living in Zuñi—thanks probably to outside intervention. The story goes that in the smallpox case the American school teacher got in a detachment of American soldiers to protect the 'witch.' He was saved [he had actually been hung up by his thumbs, the Zuñi method of witch-execution], but at Pescado some of the soldiers and some of their horses died of poisoned water. The medicineman who poisoned the water is now dead. It was his disciple, consequently a legitimate medicineman I infer, who was accused of causing the measles epidemic. He was so pestered to 'confess' that finally his family begged him to 'say something' and he did finally say that he had 'done something' to cause the bloody diarrhœal discharge that had been characteristic of the disease. Fortunately for him, after his 'confession' he was smuggled out of Zuñi for a few weeks to a settlement where the same epidemic had not been so fatal—there were too many Americans living there, it was said, and witches have no influence over Americans. Americans are 'raw,' they are *kwa akna* (not cooked), *i.e.,* their mothers have not been confined on the heated sand bed Zuñi women lie in on."[29]

Disease is accredited by the Yuchi to the presence of a harmful spirit which has been placed in the system by some offended animal-spirit or malevolent conjurer. "Herbs, which have names corresponding in some way to the name of the animal causing the trouble, are brewed in a pot and administered internally. By this means of sympathetic healing and by the use of song formulas the disease spirit is driven out by the shaman."[30] One of the most important of the final labors on earth of Teharonhiawagon—an imaginary anthropic being of the cosmogonic philosophy of the Iroquoian and other American mythologies —was his great victory over "the hunchback Hadu''i', the unborn primal being, Disease and Death, whose forfeiture of life was redeemed by his promise to

28 Grinnell, *Cheyenne Ind.,* II, 126-127, 164-165.   29 Parsons, in AA, XVIII, 245-246.
30 Speck, in HAI, II, 1006.

aid man by curing, on certain conditions, diseases arising from the infection of the earth with the malign potency of the body of Hadu"'i' by hio having first wandered over it. To this event the important Masked-face Society of exorcists of disease owes its origin. At the New Year ceremony its members essay to exorcise and banish disease and death-causing agencies from the community."[31]

The Jibaros of Ecuador make a distinction between evil caused by witchcraft and by disease. "The illness of a patient is generally attributed to witchcraft when it consists in violent pains in some part of the body, especially when the pain is accompanied by swelling of that part. Thus, for instance, headache, rheumatic pains, and colic are ascribed to witchcraft. On the other hand, to the category 'disease' (súngura) the Jibaros set down especially such illnesses as have originally been brought to them by the whites and which are not particularly accompanied by pains, like dysentery, smallpox, and most other fever diseases." When one member of a family is sick the rest have to diet in the same way as the patient himself, "for if they eat unsuitable food it would be the same as if the patient ate that food, and his condition would grow worse."[32] Both sexes among the Pawumwa Indians wear a small short stick in the nasal septum, the ends protruding into the nostrils. "This peculiar custom is associated with a primitive idea of medicine. They claim that disease is something solid and travels in a straight line like an arrow, while air is like nothing and can bend corners. Hence, when they breathe the disease strikes the end of the stick and falls out of their nostrils, while the purified air passes into their lungs."[33]

The Chaldæans thought all diseases were due to demons and lived in constant superstitious terror of them. Both the ancient Accadians and the modern Finns believed diseases to be the daughters of an ancient dame of the gloomy abyss and of the dead. Pleurisy, gout, colic, consumption, leprosy, and the plague were regarded as so many distinct personages. It is to be noted that all these ancient and evil spirits are female.[34] Among the ancient Aryans diseases were "universally regarded as due to the influence of evil spirits. Physician, magician, and priest may have been identical in the most ancient epochs of culture."[35] The Jewish belief in the uncleanness of the sick rests upon ghost-fear; for often illnesses were interpreted as visits from the ghosts of the departed. "Therefore on this stage is to be found, not the medical art but magic, which lies in the hands of the priests. In the Old Testament there are only a few instances."[36] It was Satan who brought Job's illness upon him; then, again, it is the arrows of the Almighty that bring illness.[37] Disease is believed today by the Fellahin in the Holy Land to be daimonic in origin. In their view "the three principal causes of sickness are: (1) Spirits or demons who are everywhere, in fact they fill out the space between heaven and earth and are organized in several hierarchies with princes at their head; (2) the evil eye, which again lurks everywhere, as its baneful potency is due to a poisonous substance inherent in all men which emanates through the eye, working its mischief unwittingly and unconsciously, even animals not being immune from its destructive effects; (3) the evil soul, secretions of dangerous influences from one's soul which pass through the breath of evil-minded peo-

31 Hewitt, in HAI, II, 722.
32 Karsten, "Jibaro," in BAE, Bull. LXXIX, 9, 12.
33 Haseman, in AA, XIV, 342.
34 Lenormant, *Chald. Magic*, 30, 258; §417.

35 Schrader, *Aryan*, 420.
36 Maurer, *Vkde.*, I, 108; Blau, *Zauberwesen*, 23.
37 Job, II, 7; VI, 4; XXXIII, 19-20.

ple. Secondary causes are the four temperaments in conjunction with the four elements, the planets and the constellations of the zodiac. Then there are malformations, due to the ungratified appetites of the pregnant women, congenital defects, and the harmful supernatural potencies and influences of a woman during the monthly period and in childbirth."[38]

The story of the plague in the *Iliad* is a perfect exposition of the contemporary theory of disease: "no treatment was possible or thought of. The question was, 'How have we sinned against Apollo?' The real healers of the plague were the prophet who disclosed the sin and the appeased priest who prayed for its removal. The attack was due to arrows of the enraged god and the malady stopped short when that god had been propitiated."[39] Illnesses were either sent by the gods or were coincident with the appearance of certain stars.[40] It is a far cry from this to Hippocrates, who writes that "every disease has its natural cause and without natural cause nothing whatever happens."[41] The Roman folk-belief regarded all illnesses as due to daimons, especially all sudden, burning, irritant illnesses, like fever and convulsions; and in German antiquity the same persuasion held. So magical means of all sorts, such as amulets, expectoration, etc., were much in use; great virtue was assigned to human excreta of all sorts. The physicians started from this view and tried to get divine help.[42] Said Luther: "There is no doubt that pestilence and fever and other severe illnesses are nothing else than the Devil's work."[43] An English abbot could not be consecrated, in the thirteenth century, because he was a skilful leech; "the prejudice against the practice of physic as incompatible with the purity of an ecclesiastic was wide-spread and long-lived." Yet "in 998 Theodatus, a monk of Corvey, received the bishopric of Prague from Otho III. as a reward for curing Boleslas I., Duke of Bohemia, of paralysis, by means of a bath of wine, herbs, spices, and three living black puppies four weeks old."[44] A fresco of the sixteenth century shows God the Father shooting at men with a bow. The Mother of God protects them with her mantle against which the arrows crumple.[45] In Virginia, in 1610, there was a severe penalty against throwing soapsuds into the open street. "This was because at that time it was thought in London that 'not only soap-boilers and venders of it, but all the washer-women and all they whose business it was to use soap—nay, they who only wore shirts washed with soap—presently died of the Plague.'"[46]

The old views are still widely held by the ignorant. The Christian Imeritians of the Caucasus think disease is often a punishment for a broken vow; they make vows to the saints when ill.[47] The southern Slavs think the pest can be started by cursing,[48] and the Jews of southern Russia are similarly primitive in their body of beliefs about sickness and death.[49] Among the Mexican peasants "any disease whose origin is obscure or which refuses to yield to the usual remedies, is supposed to be the result of witchcraft"; an article[50] upon

38 Canaan, *Aberglaube und Volksmedizin im Lande der Bibel*, reviewed by Casanowicz, in AA, XVII, 352-353.
39 Keller, *Hom. Soc.*, 180; Homer, *Iliad*, I, 37 ff.
40 Homer, *Odyssey*, V, 395-396; IX, 411-412; XI, 200-201; Homer, *Iliad*, XXII, 26-31.
41 Beloch, *Griech. Gchte.*, I, 604-605.
42 Grupp, *Kgchte.*, I, 103.
43 Bartels, *Medicin.* 9.
44 Lea, *Sacerd. Celib.*, 238.
45 Bartels, *Medicin*, 27.
46 Brown, *First Repub. in Amer.*, 131 (italics removed).
47 Hahn, in *Globus*, LXXX, 304.
48 Krauss, *Südslaven*, 65.
49 Weissenberg, in *Globus*, XCI, 357 ff.
50 Lucier, "Mex. Superst.," in *Pop. Sci. News* for April, 1895, 59-60.

Mexican superstitions concerning sickness relates a number of heroic but successful treatments based upon that theory.

§316. Diagnosis and Treatment.

DIAGNOSIS and treatment are difficult to segregate. It is often only in the treatment that the diagnosis appears. We have not tried to separate them one from another, either in the text or here. The present section will be found to run together, to a considerable extent, with the two which follow. In general, §316 will cover practices that have not resulted in any direct utility; §317 will review therapeutic agencies that square better with modern practice, whether or not their adequacy is accidental; and §318 will deal chiefly with medicaments of various descriptions.

In the procedure of the Tikopians there is nothing which can be regarded as treatment unless the laying on of "the hand of the ghost" is to be regarded in this light. "It is rather a method of divination to discover whether the invalid will recover."[1] Coughs, influenza, dysentery, and some skin diseases, the Tannese attributed to their intercourse with white men, and called them "foreign things." "When a person was said to be ill, the next question was, 'What is the matter? Is it nahak or a foreign thing?' The opinion there was universal that they had tenfold more of disease and death since they had intercourse with ships than they had before. We thought at first it was prejudice and fault-finding, but the reply of the more honest and thoughtful of the natives invariably was: 'It is quite true. Formerly people here never died till they were old, but nowadays there is no end to this influenza, and coughing, and death.'"[2] In the D'Entrecasteaux Islands the remedies are numerous: bleeding for headaches, counterirritant for stomach-ache, sucking, magic songs, and sprinkling with sea-water. Sickness with no cause, such as pneumonia and dysentery, the natives set down to sorcery.[3]

Sickness is South Africa is diagnosed as caused by witchcraft, and the procedure is to smell out the witch. In the Congo the natives "recognise an evil spirit who causes sickness through the instrumentality of someone he has possessed." An individual accused of possession is forced to drink a poisonous decoction; "he then runs about the village followed by his friends and enemies, the former proclaiming his innocence, the latter his guilt. His innocence is proved by his vomiting the *whole* of the poison he has swallowed; if he fails to vomit, or vomits only a small quantity, he is killed."[4] The Bangala have many specialists among the medicine-men or *nganga* who diagnose and treat the various ailments. If the spirit causing the illness takes refuge in the house, "the *nganga* springs forward, enters the house, darts his spear in all directions, yelling loudly and screaming terrifically; then a frightful cry is heard, and in a few moments the *nganga* comes out with the blade of his spear well smeared with blood." Another group is composed exclusively of women who deal with a spirit that causes debility. "They dance, chant, and shake a rattle until the patient says he has the *bwete* spirit stirring in him, by the way he jerks and sways his body. . . . This *nganga* makes all the necessary medicine for a pregnant woman, attends her at confinement, helps at the delivery of

1 Rivers, *Melan. Soc.*, I, 323-324.
2 Turner, *Samoa*, 322-323.
3 Jenness and Ballentyne, *D'Entrecasteaux*, 137-141.

4 Torday and Joyce, in JAI, XXXVII, 151.

the child, and conducts the ear piercing on the fifth day after birth." A *nganga* whose fee is comparatively small operates with a saucepan of water; "placing it in a good position he then pours some sugar-cane wine by the side of it, as the *bilimo* [embodied spirits] are very fond of this. wine; then he calls the *bilimo* by putting a leaf on the closed fist of the left hand and striking it with the palm of the right hand; thereupon the *bilimo* show themselves in the saucepan, into which only the *nganga* is allowed to look. . . . By-and-by, a spirit appears that persistently refuses to show its face after being repeatedly ordered to do so by the *nganga,* and at last the *nganga* stabs the spirit with a splinter of bamboo, and the owner of that *elimo* who is the *moloki* [the witch] is supposed now to die very soon, and release the *nganga's* client from its malign influence." Another *nganga* "looks at the arteries in the stomach of a dead person to discover whether the person died by his or her own witchcraft or by the witchcraft of someone else." If there is smallpox in the district, the nervous go to a special medicine-man, "who makes some small cuts in his client's body and sucks out some blood which he spits on to a leaf, and examines carefully. If some small threads are seen in the blood, the *nganga* points them out to others, and says, that as he has sucked out the *likundu* the person will not die even though he may become infected with smallpox. . . . It is a very cute performance. The person's blood is sucked and the threads are shown, and if he does not have smallpox then the *nganga* has the credit of drawing the *likundu* out of him. If, however, he has smallpox then he has his own *likundu* in him and the only way to recover is to confess his guilt; this exonerates the *nganga*. If no threads are seen and the person has smallpox then his own *likundu* has given it, and he must confess, and here again the *nganga* is cleared. If a person has not been operated on by the *nganga,* and gets smallpox, he must confess to bewitching others, and should he recover, well, his confession cleared him, should he die then someone else bewitched him. If a person did not get smallpox then he was not bewitched by anyone and had no *likundu* himself." For sleeping sickness the patients go to a *nganga* who makes numerous small cuts on their bodies and then sprinkles them with hot water and rubs pepper paste in the cuts, and puts a drop or two of pepper juice in each eye. That ought to keep them awake. For madness a patient immerses his face in a saucepan of water in which some medicines have been mixed and then has some juices dropped into his eyes. In the practice of some medicine-men an offering of food is required; if the food partly disappears this is accepted as evidence that the spirits have partaken of the feast and the patient will get better. From a study of their diseases it will be seen that they fall into two classes: "(1) Those whose symptoms are observable and easily diagnosed, as gleet, dysentery, insanity; and (2) those whose symptoms, while apparent, are difficult to diagnose because their causes are hidden, as those named *lela* (great debility) and *luwa* (sleeping sickness)." The former are regarded as simple sicknesses, but the latter are put to the credit of spirits or to the evil influence of *moloki* or witch. In the first case, herbs are used, medicines are made, and taboos inflicted; when sickness is caused by evil spirits, stick-charms are erected before the patient's house and he is put under various taboos; and finally, in cases due to witchcraft, the first object is to discover the witch or, failing that, by powerful charms to counteract and overcome the malign influence. The *nganga's* verdict that the deceased died as the result of his own witchcraft has a marked effect on the people. "It exonerates the *nganga* from all blame, for while he may drive out *mēte* or spirits, and deal with other spirits by his powerful charms, and while he may overcome the witchcraft used by someone else against his patient, if he is innocent of witchcraft himself, yet how can it be expected of him to save a patient who himself is full of *likundu* or witchcraft? Thus, to 'save his own face,' the *nganga* after his post-mortem examination declares in ninety-nine cases out of a hundred that the deceased died by his own witchcraft. The result of the verdict is that the corpse is buried and no one is accused of being a witch, and consequently no one has to take the ordeal." It should be noted, finally, that the diseases diagnosed as originated by the spirits are believed to be due to the latter affecting "the life springs, that is the soul of the individual."[5]

Among the Bahima, "the origin of illness is determined by examining the entrails of fowls, sheep or goats, or by a pot of water into which powdered herbs are cast to make it froth, and four coffee beans are dropped. The positions of the berries in the water, or the specks on the entrails of the animals, enable the medicine man to decide who has used magic. Once the person is discovered by these tests, the relatives of the sick man go and accuse the person, his plea of innocence is useless, he must prove it; in most cases the accused acknowledges his fault, states his reason for committing it, and tells what drugs must be used to heal the sick man. Should a person continue to deny the charge brought against him, the case goes before the king, and, if he still persists in asserting his innocence after the king's verdict, he is put to the fire ordeal; if he comes out without hurt he is acknowledged to be innocent; but if he is burned he is heavily fined."[6] If the sick person among the Bageshu is a rich man, "a goat or cow is killed, a small hut is built near the sick man's house in honour of the ghost which is supposed to be troubling the man, some of the meat and the blood are put into the little hut, whilst a large piece of the meat is placed upon the spike upon the top of the house. When the people gather together for the ceremony the medicine-man climbs on to the house and cuts the meat up into small pieces and throws it amongst the people, who snatch it up and eat it. In this way the sickness is scattered over a large number of people and is harmless, and they suffer no ill effects from it, whilst the sick man recovers."[7] In the East African Protectorate there are charms to protect against returning disease besides many others which are used to relieve pain or to assist in the speedy healing of a sore. The ordinary spirits causing sickness are more or less bound to one locality; hence if the shaman's performances will not get rid of the troublesome spirit, the only remedy is for the whole family to move elsewhere.[8] The medicine-men of the Akamba carry round with them a miscellaneous assortment of powders, "which are usually of a herbal origin; some of these are magical and some only ordinary medicinal remedies, but there is no hard and fast line between magic and medicine in the minds of the natives of this country." If a person is bitten by a poisonous snake, a medicine-man with power to cure snake bite is called in; such a person has a cut in the end of his tongue into which certain medicines have been put. "If a medicine man or a person so inoculated spits on a person bitten by a snake the patient recovers forthwith."[9] In Kenya Colony, "illness is generally attributed to the shade or spirit, *oiindet,* of a deceased ancestor or relative, and the advice of a 'wise woman' is generally sought. . . . The

5 Weeks, in JAI, XL, 385-389, 423, 424, 425.

6 Roscoe, in JAI, XXXVII, 115.

7 Roscoe, in JAI, XXXIX, 187.

8 Dundas, C., in JAI, XLIII, 527, 537.

9 Hobley, A-Kamba, 93-94, 100.

patient should sneeze the following morning, and relatives and friends visit him to enquire whether he has sneezed; if he has, then his illness was a sickness, and not due to ancestral spirits."[10]

According to the Nigerian head-hunters all deaths are due to black magic, so when a person is sick it is necessary to discover who is responsible. "An ordinary individual cannot see these evil souls, but a witch-doctor (*tenshi*) can, and is invited to 'smell out' the owner. . . . The accused is then caught and shut in a house with a fire in it, into which pepper is thrown, and he is kept there until he agrees to remove his curse. If he 'really returns the bowels' the sick man recovers."[11] African-American "voodoo doctors" advertise that they can diagnose any disease and furnish medicine to cure every ailment. One of them, since prosecuted for using the mails to defraud, had his patients spit on a piece of white cloth and send it to him; several days later the patient would receive some "medicine" with directions. Here is a sample reply: "Dr. Sir Yos Receved Listen Emty contents in A Pint Bot fil it with clen water take a table Spoon 3 times A Day Before meals Shake the Bot till all ReSolve x x x x is the Cause Yo Being like yo ar to Cure you & make you luck & never go Brok & get all the Work yo can do & Bor All the Money Yo want to run eny bus yo Want will cost 21 Dols."[12]

In a certain district in India "a man was discovered sitting outside his house, while groans proceeded from within. He explained that he was ill, and his wife was swinging on nails with their points upwards to cure him."[13] Again, a hideous mud figure is moved three times up and down before a patient's face and three times around his head. It is then put into a basket along with scraps of food and flowers and removed after dark to a path or crossroad. The spirit afflicting the patient has taken up its abode in the mud figure but will not stay long. The basket is put down and a lamp lit and put into it. When anyone is seen or heard approaching, a fowl's throat is cut over the basket and the operator decamps. The newcomer, seeing the hideous figure and the blood, is supposed to start; the spirit has then taken up its abode in him. There is no compunction felt about passing on the unwelcome spirit.[14] In Hindustan, "chronic complaints are sometimes cured by a magician who draws cross lines in the middle of a road, and makes some worship; the first person who passes or crosses the figure carries away the complaint and the original sufferer is cured." Figures, with sacrifices, and recitations, and incense are effective in the house of the afflicted.[15] The Khonds provide a meal for the fever-spirit, to induce him to leave the sick man he has possessed; the meal was laid in a set of circles of saffron-powder, charcoal-powder, rice, and some sort of yellow powder, with an egg or a small chicken in the middle.[16] "A distorted part of the body is cured by passing over it the foot of an individual who had been born with his feet foremost."[17] In ancient India there were three ways of healing: surgical, medical, and by incantation or formula; the last was the purest and most effective.[18] "Where the Mūndā believes that a certain trouble is due to the wrath or malice of some spirit, the Orāon thinks the spirit is merely a tool in the hands of some magician by whom it has been put

10 Barton, in JAI, LIII, 73.
11 Tremearne, in JAI, XLII, 160.
12 N. Y. *Times*, Nov. 21, 1924.
13 Thurston, *S. India*, 304.
14 Fawcett, *Kodos*, in JASB, I, 469.

15 Anon., "Mantrams," in JASB, II, 283, 285.
16 Fawcett, "Notes," in JASB, II, 248.
17 Rehatsek, in JASB, II, 31.
18 Lippert, *Kgchte.*, II, 459; Holtzmann, *Ind. Sagen*, I, 155.

up to the mischief. So, if a Mūndā gets a sudden attack of headache or griping in the stomach, or pain in the legs, or falls down in a fit of epilepsy, he at once concludes he must have come in collision with some spirit, that he must have trodden some spirit under his feet, or jostled against it while walking or working on his fields or elsewhere. As a means of conciliation with the offended spirit, he scatters a little powdered turmeric around himself. The Orāon, who suspects magic or witchcraft where the Mūndā scents a spirit, always takes particular steps to ward off the evil eye of witches or the malicious intentions of sorcerers."[19] By means of a diagram, divided into twenty-one parts, the wise man among the Palaungs finds out the number of the part of the hand in which he has found the pulse to be the strongest. He then refers to the corresponding number in the table and finds the cause of the illness.[20]

In the East Indies, noise, fire, and light were used against disease. Amulets were common, and people who could get a little written exorcism, such as a verse from the Koran, were supposed to be well protected. It is clear that every one cannot know all the means of exorcism; hence the power and influence of the shaman.[21] Of the Dyaks it is reported that "there is nothing like assurance and utter deceit for making way among these people. Their medicine-men look wise, chew some leaves, colour them, spit on the people who are sick, rub them up and down, tie a piece of string round the neck, fasten a stone, bone, or piece of stick to it, finally ask a high price for the charm, and so get on, and are sent for from all parts. To be able to do this they must have a lot of dreams in which the antu [spirit] tells them of a drug or plant, or stone, bone, pig's, dog's, or deer's tooth, which is in a certain place and possesses certain properties. Having first caught their hare, they skin it. They get the tooth, etc., and narrate their dream, which is the best part of the charm."[22]

The *manang* manipulates the ailing part of the body and pretends to draw something out—a stone, for instance—which is exhibited as the cause of pain. He always has a medicine-box filled with scraps of wood, curiously twisted roots, pebbles, and quartz fragments. "These medicinal charms are either inherited, or have been revealed by the spirits in dreams." Treatment is in a darkened room, whence issue sounds of scuffling, clashings of weapons, and shouting. Then the door is opened and the disease-spirit is said to be dead. "He was cheated into coming to torment his prey, and instead of a weak and helpless victim he met the crafty and mighty *manangs*, who have done what ordinary mortals cannot do—attacked and killed him. As a proof of the reality of the deed lights are brought in, and the *manangs* point to spots of blood on the floor, and occasionally to the corpse itself in the shape of a dead monkey or snake, which they say was the form the spirit took for the occasion. The trick is a very simple one. . . . There is a good deal of deceit and humbug and a little clumsy sleight-of-hand on the part of the *manang*, and an unlimited amount of faith on the part of the patient. The *manang* must be conscious of his own deceit, but he believes that his incantations do good, and I have often known cases of *manangs* having these ceremonies for members of their own family who are ill. But as a rule a *manang* is not a truthful man at all. There can be no doubt that the average Dyak knows that there is a great deal of deceit connected with the *manang's* profession, but he also knows he must sub-

19 Roy, in JAI, XLIV, 329.   21 Wilken, *Vkde.*, 577-581.
20 Milne, *Eastern Clan.* 245.   22 Roth, *Sarawak*, I, 291.

mit to that deceit if he wishes to have his help, and he believes that in some
way the incantations and remarkable actions of the *manangs* help to scare
away the evil spirit which is the cause of the diseases."[23]

Nieuwenhuis[24] made use of native methods against a cholera epidemic,
securing a four days' taboo on unboiled water and green fruit, and a limitation on bathing. The disease-spirit was bound from the paths that led up from
the river by a rotten cord, nude figures carrying arms, and phallic representations. The native taboos are themselves often of hygienic effect. In Sarawak
the spirit of water is held responsible for dysentery, while a case of spontaneous blindness is ascribed to a spirit having hit one in the eye.[25] Goiter
is widespread throughout the East Indies; the natives lay it largely to
drinking-water and apply the steam of hot springs as a curative.[26] The
medicine-men in the Malay Peninsula have some knowledge of the secrets
of nature, but their actual acquisitions in that respect are not so great as is
ordinarily reputed, and in fact "they are very little more clever than the
others."[27] Polynesians had a religious mystery and a profane tradition of
healing.[28] "The Samoans in their heathenism seldom had recourse to any internal remedy except an emetic . . . on some occasions, mud, and even the
most unmentionable filth, was mixed up and taken as an emetic draught. . . .
Shampooing and anointing the affected part of the body with scented oil by the
native doctors was common. . . . As the Samoans supposed disease to be
occasioned by the wrath of some particular deity, their principal desire, in
any difficult case, was not for medicine, but to ascertain the cause of the
calamity."[29]

Among the Greenland Eskimo "none of the spirit-beings was the object
of worship, love, or fear. Only through the *angakok* could one set himself in
any relation with them, but a Tornarsuk's order, given through an *angakok*,
men felt obliged to obey. If all went well, no one asked about another world,
but if sickness or dangers entered, the *angakok* must take a so-called flight
to Tornarsuk to get advice and enlightenment."[30] "Together with sickness is
also reckoned a man's inability to catch seals or his wife's to have children."
To cure the latter the *angakok* makes a journey to the moon whence a child is
thrown down to the woman.[31] An Eskimo shaman, in endeavoring to dispel a
disease, parted several men from their wives, the latter being "compelled to
dwell with other men who were at the bottom of the conspiracy. Other couples
had to flee from that place to prevent being divorced, at least temporarily.
. . . A more plausible scamp does not dwell in these regions than this shaman. . . . His power over the spirit controlling the reindeer is widely believed
in and invoked by the other shamans, who feel incapable of turning the heads
of the deer and thus compelling them to wander in the desired direction."[32]

In the Northwest the word *tamanhous* means guardian-spirit, or familiar
spirit, and also a performance of magic for healing. It is used also as a verb
covering the hocus pocus of healing.[33] The Apaches "minister to the recovery
of fever patients by dancing, singing and beating drums the whole night

23 Gomes, *Sea Dyaks*, 165, 172, 173, 175.
24 *Borneo*, I, 116-117, 140.
25 Lawrence, in JAI, XXXVIII, 393.
26 Wilken, in VG, IV, 285 ff., 356 ff.
27 Skeat and Blagden, *Malay Penin.*, II, 362.

28 Ratzel, *Vkde.*, II, 130.
29 Turner, *Samoa*, 139-140.
30 Fries, *Grönland*, 144.
31 Holm, *Ethnol. Skizze*, 89.
32 Turner, in BAE, XI, 179, 180.
33 Mallery, in BAE, X, 500.

through."[34] Among the Omahas, when a man is threatened with death, the medicine-man goes into a lodge sweat-bath with him and sings, at the same time "pronouncing certain incantations and sprinkling the body of the client with the powder of the artemisia, supposed to be the food of the ghosts. . . . To say that a certain powder is the food of the ghosts of a tribe is to say indirectly that the same powder was once the food of the tribe's ancestors." This last comment will be clearer in the light of a succeeding paragraph.[35] The Apache shaman uses a "medicine cord": "If the circle attached to one of these cords is placed upon the head, it will at once relieve any ache, while the cross attached to another prevents the wearer from going astray, no matter where he may be."[36] The Mohave Indian medicine-men are nearly all specialists: the rattle-snake doctor, the fever doctor, and doctors for rheumatism, colds, dropsy, and wounds.[37] Among an Athapascan tribe, "a doctor when called in heats a stone in the fire, touches it with his finger, and with the same finger presses various parts of the patient's body in order to divine the seat and character of the malady."[38]

The medical practice of the Cheyennes is reported rather fully and in a pertinent manner. "When a person was sick, it was thought that the cause of the disease existed in a certain place in the body. Over this place the doctor shook the rattle, to drive out the evil influence, and then with the mouth strove to suck out the cause of the disease. . . . Different doctors had different methods. In addition to the rattle, some used the wing of a hawk or an eagle, to fan and cool the sick person . . . the afflicted part being sucked, or, as the Cheyennes call it, 'bitten.' Then a tea was administered—a warm drink suited to the disease. The doctor bit off a piece of the medicine root, chewed it, and spat it on various parts of the patient's body, which were now cooled by patting and fanning with an eagle's wing. Then the pipe was smoked again. . . . At the conclusion of the singing, the pipe was smoked before the doctoring was continued. The doctor now mixed medicine with deer fat and rubbed the mixture on his hands, and held them over the fire until they were warm, when the hands were placed on the part of the body where the pain was felt. . . . After the nine songs were sung, the doctor, grasping the pipe in his right hand, held it up to the south, west, north, and east, to the sky and to the ground. The pipe was then changed to the left hand, and they smoked. This ended the doctoring." Added to the spiritual side of healing—that is, exorcising or frightening away the spirits or evil influences which cause disease—was the practice of medicine by administering remedies. "For the greater part these remedies were herbs, many of which unquestionably were more or less efficacious, and in not a few cases the Indians appear to have some practical ideas of the medicinal properties of certain plants. . . . In some cases it was a part of the administration of the remedy to stir (before the patient drank it) the water in which the medicine had been mixed, with the claw of the animal, or with the beard of the turkey, or perhaps with the little stone arrowhead which was tied to the bundle. . . . Cheyenne doctors were skilful and successful in treating such injuries as broken bones, gunshot wounds, and arrow wounds. In the treatment of wounds—i.e., where blood had been shed—rattles made from gourds were thought to be especially useful. Broken legs were often set, and

34 Reclus, *Prim. Folk*, 132.
35 §324, below.
36 Bourke, in BAE, IX, 527, 550.
37 Hrdlička, in BAE, Bull. XXXIV, 228.
38 Dorsey and Goddard, in HAI, II, 467.

made excellent unions, so that no evidence of the injury remained." A case is described of the treatment for rattlesnake bite: "At last came a sister of Turkey Leg, who had some medicine which she moistened and wrapped on the wound. It ceased to be painful almost at once. The woman took hold of the patient's right great toe and shook it; then she took hold of the right little finger and shook it, and of the left little finger and of the left great toe in succession, and shook each; then she said to the young man, 'Now, you will see all sorts of snakes.' Arapaho Chief felt very sick, as if he were going to die, and he did see many snakes, more than he had supposed were in the whole world. The woman began to rub his leg from thigh to ankle, and soon the swelling commenced to subside. The pain left him, and before long he was able to stand on his feet."[39] Among some of the Southwestern tribes the *kaan* or medicine-man "will look into a bowl of water on the surface of which 'powder' is spread, in order to see into the machinations of the witches, senders, as always, of disease. The disease-causing things the witches have sent into the body the *kaan* take out with their eagle wing feathers—a familiar Pueblo Indian curing rite—and from the feathers are seen to drop into the *ollas* pebbles, bits of cloth, etc., and cactus points. This curing or exorcising motion is a motion of sweeping in, 'like catching a fly,' and then shaking down, shaking the things caught from the feathers to the *olla*."[40]

Among the Guiana Indians, "independently of the treatment of disease as practiced specially by the medicine men, *e.g.*, the incantation of certain spirits, and their exorcism, the blowing of tobacco smoke, and the extraction by suction of the offending cause of the complaint, . . . there is a sort of routine treatment followed by the lay and medical fraternity in general." When attacked by fever, many natives set themselves up to the neck in water, "not inquiring into the cause which occasions it, until the paroxysm of fever is over or sudden death prevents his coming out again." It is not necessary to be a medicine-man to suck out pains, and a case is cited where a native hung on to his comrade's shoulder for half an hour "sucking out the rheumatism."[41] Among the Araucanians, "the direct cause of illness is supposed to be either an invisible wound or some extraneous substance introduced into the body of the patient. This foreign element has to be extracted. For this purpose the *machi* [shaman] goes provided with a worm, grub, beetle, lizard, or other small creature that can easily be hidden, and made to appear as if taken from the sick person. If the patient dies, the *machi* saves his responsibility by declaring that he has been poisoned, and then proceeds to discover the poisoner. To avoid feuds and reprisals, the blame was generally cast on a *huecuvu* [evil spirit], who had taken the form of some living creature, revealed to the *machi* in a trance, but was sometimes imputed to some individual against whom the exorcist had a grudge, or else to a known enemy of the deceased or his family. . . . The *machis* have no hard and fast ritual for these ceremonies, but each one introduces the innovations he considers necessary."[42]

In antiquity, incantations, together with purificatory ceremonial, were in wide use, and fetishes, such as the twigs of a holy tree and holy water from the sea or from sacred streams, were regarded as highly effective.[43] In Persia, washings and spells drove off the sickness sent by Ahriman. "In fact, the

---

39 Grinnell, *Cheyenne Ind.*, II, 130-132, 134, 147.
40 Parsons, in AA, XXII, 62.
41 Roth, in BAE, XXXVIII, 705-707, 708.
42 Latcham, in JAI, XXXIX, 353.
43 Tiele-Gehrich, *Gchte. d. Relig.*, I, 155.

medicine of spells was considered the most powerful of all, and though it did not oust the medicine of the lancet and that of drugs, yet it was more highly esteemed and less mistrusted."[44] Wounds were washed and bound up by the Homeric Greeks, though in one case the bleeding was stopped by incantation.[45] In connection with the most ancient phase of the art of healing, it is important to note that the Indo-Europeans possessed a tolerably thorough knowledge of their own bodies and to this they may have been assisted by the practice of sacrificing animals.[46] Phylacteries were used amongst the Assyrians as talismans against disease; they bound texts of the sacred books upon their heads and doorposts.[47] In the book of Tobit,[48] the heart and liver of a fish, burned before a sick person, relieved him of the evil spirit of disease; while the gall was "good to anoint a man that hath white films in his eyes."

As early as B.C. 323 Greek physicians at Alexandria were dissecting the human body but later such practice was regarded as profanation. Though Galen dissected apes, he could not, of course, distinguish the various differences between men and apes.[49] While, however, the Christians were entering into a period of obscurantism, the Mohammedans did not lose what had been gained. The difference between the intellectual status of the Crusaders and the Saracens is brought out in an anecdote related by a Moslem physician, who was called in, as was customary in desperate cases. "They brought to me a knight with an abscess in his leg, and a woman troubled with fever. I applied to the knight a little cataplasm; his abscess opened and took a favorable turn. As for the woman, I forbade her to eat certain foods, and I lowered her temperature. I was there when a Frankish doctor arrived, who said, 'This man can't cure them!' Then, addressing the knight, he asked, 'Which do you prefer, to live with a single leg, or to die with both of your legs?' 'I prefer,' replied the knight, 'to live with a single leg.' 'Then bring,' said the doctor, 'a strong knight with a sharp axe.' The knight and axe were not slow in coming. I was present. The doctor stretched the leg of the patient on a block of wood, and then said to the knight, 'Cut off his leg with the axe, detach it with a single blow.' Under my eyes, the knight gave a violent blow, but it did not cut the leg off. He gave the unfortunate man a second blow, which caused the marrow to flow from the bone, and the knight died immediately. As for the woman the doctor examined her and said, 'She is a woman with a devil in her head, by which she is possessed. Shave her hair.' They did so, and she began to eat again, like her compatriots, garlic and mustard. Her fever grew worse. The doctor then said, 'The devil has gone into her head.' Seizing a razor he cut into her head in the form of a cross and excoriated the skin in the middle so deeply that the bones were uncovered. . . . Then he rubbed her head with salt. The woman, in her turn, expired immediately. After asking them if my services were still needed, and after receiving a negative answer, I returned, having learned from their medicine matters of which I had previously been ignorant."[50]

The Druids performed their healing by magic and incantations. As a safeguard against the poisonous weapons of the Bretons, a Druid recommended that the milk of twice seventy white hornless cows should be put in a trench on

44 Müller, *Sacred Books*, (Zendavesta) IV, xciii.

45 Homer, *Odyssey*, XIX, 457; Keller, *Hom. Soc.*, 179-180.

46 Schrader, *Aryan*, 421, note.

47 *Records of the Past*, III, 142; Deut., XI, 18.

48 VI, 2 ff.

49 Topinard, *Anthropologie*, 15-16; Payne, *Eng. Med.*, 58-59, 95-96, 102-104, 147.

50 Munro, in *Internat. Mo.*, IV, 703.

the battlefield. Wounded men who bathed in it would be healed.[51] Collections
of medical charms used in early England have been made by Cockayne.[52] The
"girdle of St. Bridget" was a sort of straw collar through which the sick were
passed by their friends.[53] The mediæval period was full of the use of relics
and magic quite as benighted as that of heathen times; in fact, the development
of scientific medicine was delayed well up toward the present.[54] In France
there is a great stone of Ymare which now forms a roughly squared table
with a cross engraved on one of its angles. It stands but eighty centimeters,
or less than thirty-two inches, from the ground; but in order to be cured of
rheumatism or even of madness the patient must not, in passing under, touch
it with his back nor must his knees touch the earth.[55]

Among the southern Slavs "one marries his fever to the willow, a favorite
resort of tree-souls. . . . The wedging and corking of a sickness into a tree is
known to south-Slav folk-belief as well as to the German." Creeping through
a tree or bush which is split by nature or purposely by human hand is practised by the south Slavs only in attacks of fever, while the Germans take recourse to it in cases of spinal curvature and similar maladies. A tree-spirit
may send disease by means of the insects and worms that haunt its bark, roots,
and leaves. Spirits are often identified with worms, grubs, millers, and crabs;
they creep into the body and cause pain. Diseases were also given human form,
such as the Pest-woman. The Bulgars conceive of diseases as red-haired women
who rove from village to village, shooting arrows at man and beast. All wood-
spirits have red hair. Cakes smeared with honey, and made every Saturday,
are left at cross-roads for the disease-spirits. It is even believed that boils
can be banned by exorcistic means.[56] In tree-plugging as done elsewhere,
something from the diseased body or which has been in close contact with it,
is wedged, as a sort of "scape-goat," into a hole in a tree—preferably one that
has been struck by lightning or a tree in a cemetery.[57]

Among the Jews of southern Russia, in case of lumbago (called Hexenschuss
or witch-shot), one lies face down on a door-sill and has the oldest child step
over his body and, having done so, spit several times. An exostosis (morbid
growth on the bone) is to be bitten every day by the eldest son; this is mentioned as a "really rational procedure." In stubborn cases this swelling is
stroked by the hand of a dead person, which helps in the case of many other
swellings and of rheumatism. The idea here is probably that a superfluous illness cannot harm the dead man and so can be shoved off on him; "the dead
takes sickness along" is the expression used. In consumption woman's milk is
not seldom used, and even pork. Eczema is helped by soot from a clay pot.[58]
They work on the principle of *similia similibus curantur:* thus against roaring
in the ears, shells (on account of the noise characteristic of them) are used;
against vertigo crystal-glasses (looking into which causes vertigo); and against
anæmia coral necklaces. For dropsy a spider, carried in a nut-shell about the
neck, helps, for the spider will suck up the superfluous water. The notion of

51 Von Pflugk-Harttung, "Druids," in
Trans. Roy. Hist. Soc. (N.S.), VII, 72.
52 Leechdoms, I, 374-395; III, 285-295.
53 Bourke, in BAE, IX, 557.
54 White, Sci. and Theol., ch. XIII; Molmenti, Venezia, I, 109; Prescott, Philip II,
518, 519.
55 Sébillot, in AA, IV, 90.
56 Krauss, Südslaven, 38, 39 ff., 54.
57 Hellwig, in Globus, XC, 245, 246.
58 Weissenberg, in Globus, XCI, 358, 359.

passing disease over to the dead is not confined to the Russian Jew. The inscription ABRACADABRA on a card is good for toothache and fever.[59]

"A correspondent of the *Lancet*, who seems well acquainted with the Highlands of Scotland, writes about the medical folk-lore there, and mentions among rational cures that for whooping-cough some recommend that the child should be taken across a ferry; others, that he should above all go to live in another property; others, that he should go to a house where master and mistress have possessed the same surname. All these procedures involve change of air, which has in such cases no doubt been found beneficial." The ferry-crossing looks like the stock water-exorcism, and doubtless the other cures are based upon ancient ideas wholly irrational to us. The quotation goes on to say that "colt's-foot is used in asthma, warts are washed in pig's blood, and a person with weak lungs takes with great advantage a preparation of twenty-four different herbs. . . . An infusion of adders' heads is used as a dressing in snake-bite, and, it is said, with excellent results. This is on the homeopathic principle."[60]

§317. Therapeutics.

Massage. Cases are cited among the Melanesians in which the singing of incantations to exorcise a malevolent spirit is combined with massage and suction, terminating with the extraction from the patient of a number of foreign bodies.[1] Incantations are also combined with massage in the D'Entrecasteaux Islands.[2] Among the African Bangala, "simple massage was a favourite operation, and much enjoyed by the patient, and its curative qualities were not placed to the credit of friction, warmth, magnetism, but to the fetish power of the rubber." The operation was also performed by some quasi-medicine-men—men and women who had recovered from some serious complaint would set up as quacks to cure that particular sickness; "they used massage with hot or cold water, and no water at all, and simple herbs, and there was no doubt that they effected a considerable amount of good."[3] A case is reported from East Africa in which "an old medicine woman treated a man for a pain in his side by rubbing on the affected part some fat, which she said was medicine, but it was perfectly obvious that what she was doing was simply massage, and she was doing it very well, too, with successful results." Dundas[4] is convinced that she herself thought that the whole secret of her art lay in the fat she was using. A remedy in Algeria for bruises and strains is as follows: "Wrap a piece of camel's fat in cotton material, warm it over a fire and then gently rub the part affected with the cotton containing the fat. I have tried this myself," comments the author,[5] "with beneficial results to my knee when bruised and twisted by a fall." Among the Palaungs, "if the wise man decides that an illness is due to the twisting or straining of the muscles of the stomach, a prayer is said over oil, and the abdomen and stomach are massaged with it."[6] Turner[7] states that "the advocates of *kinnesipathy* would be interested in finding, were they to visit the South Seas, that most of their friction, percussion, and other manipulations, were in vogue there ages ago, and are still

59 Carsten, in *Am Ur-Quell*, I, 11; Handelmann, in same, I, 169, 186.
60 Anon., in *Pop. Sci. News*, XXVII, 44.
1 Seligmann, *Melanesians*, 167-169.
2 Jenness and Ballentyne, *D'Entrecasteaux*, 141.

3 Weeks, in JAI, XL, 382, 424.
4 In JAI, XLIII, 533.
5 Hilton-Simpson, in JAI, XLIII, 713.
6 Milne, *Eastern Clan*, 250.
7 *Samoa*, 140.

practised." Among the Tlinkits old women are rubbers or masseuses.[8] These cases may be taken as typical of what is a widespread primitive practice.

Cupping. The sucking and biting of the afflicted part, together with the removal of some object secreted for the purpose by the shaman, is rather a stock procedure. In the Upper Congo cupping was often practised. "Sometimes it was simple bleeding, and at other times it was cupping proper with horn and suction. The part to be benefited was snicked with a knife, and a horn which had at the upper end a hole was put over the cuts. The operator put a pill of clay or soft wax into his mouth, sucked at the hole, and with his tongue put the wax over it. This he repeated until the air in the horn was exhausted and then the blood ran freely. The clyster was used for relieving pains in the stomach." The many cicatrices, like elliptical punch-marks, to be seen on the stomachs, chests, shoulders, thighs, backs, and arms of the natives were largely, if not entirely, due to the practice of cupping. "They were very fond of blood-letting as a cure for aches and pains in various parts of their bodies."[9] In British Central Africa sucking of wounds is a common practice, while dry cupping is performed with small gourds and horns.[10] With the Ba-Yaka, "cupping is practised by means of a portion of a gourd from which the air is exhausted by suction through a small hole, and the latter is closed with a plug of wax. The gourd is usually applied over small incisions made immediately in front of the ear, and is allowed to operate for half-an-hour at a time."[11] For ordinary diseases in Kenya Colony, "decoctions of bark, roots, and leaves are used, cupping and cauterizing are followed, likewise superficial surgery and bone-setting."[12] A Sudanese case of ophthalmia was treated by dancing and singing, anointing, breathing upon the patient, suction by mouth, and the alleged extraction of "worms."[13] In Uganda, "it is sometimes noticed that there is a circular bare patch on a man's head where the hair has been shaved, almost like a tonsure. The explanation of this is that the tonsured individual is subject to fever or has frequent headaches. He therefore keeps a portion of his head shaved, so that it may be readily scarified and cupped."[14]

A British Columbia doctor sucked at the chest of a consumptive until he had actually perforated the chest-wall. "The operation was varied by the endeavor to draw the 'evil one' from his patient by dancing and singing. . . . The doctor was so terribly in earnest that it seemed impossible to doubt that he was fighting some unseen adversary."[15] Sometimes the medicine-man has a sucking-bone which has all the qualities of a rude "cup." "Although witches and witchcraft did not exist among the Omaha, disease was sometimes supposed to have its origin in the magical introduction into the human body of a worm or other object, which could be removed only by means of magical formulas, by sucking, or by manipulation."[16] A very common trick among Indian charlatans was to pretend to suck foreign bodies out of the persons of their patients.[17] Among the Cheyennes, "when a person was sick, it was thought that the cause of the disease existed in a certain place in the body. Over this place the doctor shook the rattle, to drive out the evil influence, and then with

8 Jones, *Thlingets*, 228.
9 Weeks, in JAI, XL, 424; and in JAI, XXXIX, 101-102.
10 Stannus, in JAI, XL, 295.
11 Torday and Joyce, in JAI, XXXVI, 50.
12 Barton, in JAI, LIII, 74.

13 De Zeltner, in *Bull. Soc. d'Anthr. de Paris*, VIII, 348.
14 Johnston, *Uganda*, II, 647.
15 Allison, in JAI, XXI, 311.
16 Fletcher and LaFlesche, in BAE, XXVI, 585.
17 Matthews, in HAI, I, 784.

the mouth strove to suck out the cause of the disease. He appeared to draw out from the patient's body buffalo-hair, stones, and even lizards, which were thought to be the cause of the sickness. When the cause was removed, the patient would recover."[18] In the case of an Athapascan tribe, the medicine-man "sucks the affected place, pretending to draw out the disease and spit it from his mouth, the performance being accompanied with the beating of a drum and the shaking of a rattle."[19] In some cases among the Zuñi, "the theurgist makes no use of medicine, but, acting under the influence of the animal gods, with the mind's eye he penetrates the flesh, locates the cause of the disease which has been 'shot' into the body by means of sorcery, and ex-tracts it by sucking, or he may merely manipulate the spot with his hand and draw the malevolent substance from the body. This is so dexterously done that, although the writer has been seated beside the nude theurgist innumerable times, she was never able to observe that he had secreted any object in his mouth or hand until Nai'uchi, in an almost dying condition, treated a patient who imagined a sorcerer had injured his eyesight. It was then evident to the writer, who sat by the side of the old man, that the pebbles he was supposed to press from the patient's eyes were held in the most remarkable manner in the palm of his right hand, which apparently was held in a natural position. Such treatment is usually practiced on one who imagines that he has been face to face with a wizard or witch and so subjected to malign influences."[20] Formerly the Guiana Indians had professional chupadores or suckers, but today anyone may suck out pains. A snake bite is always cut and sucked. "As to the extraordinary variety of visible objects inserted into the body of the victim by the invisible Spirit and similar agencies, and subsequently extracted by massage and suction, the following will give some idea: Fangs of the much-dreaded *Lachesis mutus,* 'bushmaster' snake, grass-roots, gravel-stone, fish-bone, bird's claw, snake's tooth, or piece of wire, a worm, a miniature bow and arrow. The last-mentioned is very interesting in view of the Arawak Indians' belief that all pain is due to the Evil Spirit's arrow. The medicos of the Otomac nation suck with such force as to extract blood from the patient, and when this is spat out on a cleared space, minute stony particles are to be seen in it."[21] The Bororo shaman treats the sick in the usual way, at last sucking a bone out of the affected part. He operates at night only and never lets the bone out of his hand.[22]

Scarification; bleeding. In the Island of Tanna, "local bleeding was a common remedy for almost every complaint; they did not open a vein, but merely made a few incisions with a bamboo knife. When the case was considered dangerous, their last resort was to burn the foot. I have seen, for instance, a poor fellow dying from an arrow wound in the neck; and the sole of his foot just burned to a mass of raw flesh."[23] The natives of the D'Entrecasteaux Islands practise bleeding for headache.[24] Phlebotomy is extensively employed by the natives of Lifu, "often to such an extent as to cause blindness, or, if the patient was a child, very serious injury. Macfarlane says: 'For all pains and bruises they cut with a piece of a glass bottle. A man with a pain in his head would never

---

18 Grinnell, *Cheyenne,* II, 130.
19 Dorsey and Goddard, in HAI, II, 467.
20 Stevenson, in BAE, XXX, 40.
21 Roth, in BAE, XXXVIII, 352, 707-708, §928.

22 Von den Steinen, *Zent. Bras.,* 491.
23 Turner, *Samoa,* 323.
24 Jenness and Ballentyne, *D'Entrecas-teaux,* 137.

suppose that it arose from the state of his stomach. He must cut his head at the very place where he feels the pain. They lance for the most trivial things. About two years ago (1871) a native on the south side of Wide Bay had a pain in his neck, was applying the usual remedy, cut his throat, and died. If their children get the least knock they must be lanced. I have known a child to fall, or rather roll off, a board only raised three inches from the ground, on which account the parents felt that they must lance it.' "[25]

Bleeding is very common among the Tlinkits.[26] The only medical practises which Jetté[27] witnessed among the Ten'a are "puncturing, and the preparation of spruce-tea, and of a decoction of a bush resembling juniper. The puncturing, which consists in thrusting a small pointed blade through the skin previously seized and held up between the thumb and forefinger—just as whites do with the hypodermic syringe—is their method of blood-letting." In cases of rheumatism and congestion the American Indians draw blood and scarify the whole body in the most cruel manner.[28] Medicine-women of the Ojibwa chiefly treat women and children and also tattoo for the cure of headache and chronic neuralgia. "The mark consists of round spots of one-half to three-fourths of an inch in diameter immediately over the afflicted part, the intention being to drive out the demon. Such spots are usually found upon the temples, though an occasional one may be found on the forehead or over the nasal eminence."[29] Among the Omaha, "bleeding was commonly employed in treating ailments; for this purpose gashes between the eyebrows were made with a flint knife or cupping on the back was effected by the use of the tip of a horn."[30] The theory of disease accepted by certain California Indians "is that it all resides in the blood. To prove this, they cite the fact that the blood always collects under a bruise and makes it dark; also that drawn blood coagulates. Hence the favorite remedy was scarification with small flints. When they became acquainted with the process of cupping, they wearied the reservation surgeon with applications to have it performed for every little ailment."[31]

In Central America bleeding has been long in practice; it is done generally on the middle of the forehead and on the temples, or on the inner surface of the elbow.[32] In Guiana, next to the use of heat and of water comes bloodletting, which is used in almost all cases of illness and even for some insignificant discomfort. It is practised both as a preventive and as a cure. They open the vein nearest the seat of pain or make long perpendicular cuts in the skin, stopping the bleeding at length with an astringent and mordant juice.[33] As a therapeutic agent, blood is also employed for anointing another person, "but in these circumstances there would appear to be some intimate relationship existing between the giver and the receiver. . . . As to other therapeutic properties, I append the following extract: 'The only remedy is the voluntary submission of Aaron to have blood taken from his body and with it to wash the girl he has poisoned."[34] "I have seen no native," writes Ehrenreich,[35] "whether aged man, aged woman, boy, or girl, who did not carry on himself

25 Ray, in JAI, XLVII, 273.
26 Jones, Thlingets, 226.
27 In JAI, XXXVII, 177.
28 Ratzel, Vkde., II, 567.
29 Hoffman, in BAE, VII, 223.
30 Fletcher and LaFlesche, in BAE, XXVII, 582-583.
31 Powers, in Contrib. N. Amer. Ethnol., III, 378.

32 Anon., "Chirurgisches Instrument," in Globus, LXXIII, 68.
33 Schomburgk, Brit.-Guiana, II, 333-334.
34 Roth, in BAE, XXXVIII, 707.
35 In Veröffentl. aus d. Königl. Mus. Vkde., 1891, II, 33; Von den Steinen, Zent. Bras., 188.

the scars of such barbaric bleedings. Severe fasting accompanies the rest of the healing processes. Other South American tribes scratch the seat of pain till the blood runs; in fact, they do this to increase their strength when they are not sick at all. Boys have the face and upper arm scratched in order to give them a good eye and a strong arm for shooting. Scratching is a universal cure, and perhaps is in many cases effective as a counter-irritant to congestion or inflammation."

A peculiar case of scarification is reported by Hanbury.[36] An Eskimo woman had a white speck on her eyeball. Another woman caught a louse and tied it on a hair leaving its legs free; then dropped it on the eyeball and drew the lid over. It scratched the eye and the patient said it felt better.

Surgery. Primitive medicine-men often show skill in surgery and even attempt trepanning. "It is strange," write two authors[37] on the Central Australians, "but the latest treatment by the German Doctor Bier has its exact counterpart in our aborigines' surgical method. It is carried out amongst them with a piece of fur string. This is bound firmly round the inflamed or painful part and then tied off. First, however, if you are a blackfellow, you will get your string 'sung,' that is, you, or the local *koonki* [doctor or magician] will chant over it, exhorting it to cure. I have tried using the rubber bandage, but have never used fur string that has been sung. . . . Round wrists, arms, forehead, ankles, thighs, everywhere the little tie of twisted fur obtruded itself." Hagen[38] maintains that skull trephining or trepanation is done in Melanesia and the French doctors Malbot and Verneau[39] report that it is in practice in Algiers. In the New World also it was known. Says Ray[40] of the Loyalty Islanders: "The natives of Lifu had considerable skill in surgical operations. They have wonderfully trepanned, removing a portion of the skull and replacing it with a piece of coconut shell. Pressure on the brain is frequently relieved by scraping, and thus making thin a part of the skull." Turner[41] confirms this and says that at Uea "the cure for headache was to *let out* the pain at the crown of the head by the following horrid surgery: The scalp was slit up and folded over, and the cranial bone scraped with a fine edged shell till the dura-mater was reached. A very little blood was allowed to escape. In some cases the scraped aperture was covered over with a thin piece of cocoa nut shell, in other instances the incised scalp was simply replaced. The 'cure' was death to some, but most of the cases recovered. To such an extent was this remedy for headache carried on, that the sharp-pointed clubs . . . were specially made for the purpose of striking that weak part on the crown of the head, and causing instant death."

In Kenya Colony, East Africa, superficial surgery and bone-setting are commonly done by the medicine-men.[42] "An almost incredible piece of surgery, to which, nevertheless, a whole village bore witness," is reported from among the Ba-Yaka: "It was said that a certain man, who was pointed out to me, had had an artery severed by an arrow, and that an old man had tied it with fine copper wire."[43] Hilton-Simpson[44] has written convincingly of trepanning in Algeria, giving a careful description and showing plates of the tools used.

36 *Canada*, 171.
37 Horne and Aiston, *Cent. Aust.*, 85-86.
38 *Papua's*, 257.
39 In *L'Anthropologie*, VIII, 174 ff.
40 In JAI, XLVII, 273.

41 *Samoa*, 339-340.
42 Barton, in JAI, LIII, 74.
43 Torday and Joyce, in JAI, XXXVI, 50.
44 In JAI, XLIII, 715 ff.

It is a real surgical operation, he says, known "all over the desert." The cases he mentions are those where the skull had been fractured by accident and also where the idea was to get the "bad bone" out. No antisepsis is employed, the surgeon working with dirty hands and using dirty rags. An Arab is reported as saying that such an operation was "a little bit dangerous," but, states the author, "he certainly did not consider it a critical one."

Among the Palaungs, "to open a boil, a piece of a broken pot is perforated and placed on the swelling, so that the head of the boil comes under the hole; a nail, which has been sharpened and heated, is then driven through the hole. No anæsthetics are ever used to prevent pain during an operation; but opium is sometimes given to a lad while he is being tattooed." An operation on a goiter is described as follows: "He used as a surgical instrument a small piece of sharp glass, fixed near the end of a flat strip of green bamboo, and projecting about a eighth of an inch from the surface. The sharp point of the glass was laid against the goitre; the wise man, with one hand firmly holding down the lower end of the bamboo, with the other hand bent back the end with the glass, and then let it spring forward with such force that the glass pierced the goitre to the depth of about the eighth of an inch. This was done in fifteen or more places, according to the size of the goitre. As much blood as possible was then pressed out, and a paste was well rubbed in."[45] The Samoans "lanced ulcers with a shell or a shark's tooth, and, in a similar way, bled from the arm. For inflammatory swellings they sometimes tried local bleeding; but shampooing and rubbing with oil were the more common remedies in such cases."[46]

In Mexico a skull is reported, the opening of which "is almost filled with new bone, which indicates a long survival of the subject after the operation"; yet the tribe in question, the Tarahumari, apparently have no implement for such an operation.[47] In the Peruvian skulls "there are many indications that the operators were (1) inexpert in manipulation, (2) ignorant of physiology, (3) skilless [sic] in diagnosis and treatment, and (4) regardless of the gravity of the operations performed. . . . In short, there is nothing to indicate definite plan or deft execution in any of the operations. The extravagant incision and violent elevation characterizing many of the operations necessarily rendered the artificial lesions much more extensive and dangerous than necessary. . . . The only definite suggestion of post-mortem operation found in the collection arises in the reckless and inhuman slashing of integument, bone, and brain. . . . In short, Peruvian trephining . . . can only be regarded as crude in plan and bungling in procedure; and study of the procedure only occasions surprise that the results were not worse, and awakens admiration for the powerful vitality which enabled so large a proportion of the victims to survive." The authors[48] think "the treatment may have been for vertigo, headache, or other disease; for coma, produced by shocks or blows of such character as to leave no marks, or for trifling wounds; but it is safe to consider the trephining thaumaturgic and (albeit perchance beneficial) wholly independent of physiologic knowledge and etiologic skill."

Recent translation of a papyrus dating from the seventeenth century B.C. has uncovered much of Egypt's medical lore. Breasted,[49] the translator, has

---

45 Milne, *Eastern Clan*, 251, 258.
46 Turner, *Samoa*, 141.
47 Lumholtz and Hrdlička, in AA, X, 390 ff.

48 Muñiz and McGee, in BAE, XVI, 27, 55, 61 (quoted), 63 (quoted), 65 ff., 69, 70 (quoted).
49 In *N. Y. Historical Society*, Bull. VI, 15, 16, 20, 21, 22, 27-28.

the following to say concerning the parts of this treatise dealing with surgery: "The first group deals with wounds in the head, of which the first seven are knife or sword wounds penetrating to the bone. They vary in character according as the skull itself escapes injury or suffers contusion, a gash, a fracture, etc. In all these cases the surgeon is instructed in the examination: 'You should probe the wound.' If he finds only a contusion of the skull or no injury at all, the verdict is favorable; a gash in the skull, doubtful; a fracture in the skull (several kinds), unfavorable. Case 7, which occupies over two columns and is the longest case in the treatise, describes three different conditions of the injury to the skull under the knife wound, gives two verdicts (one doubtful, one unfavorable), and in the third condition says to the surgeon: 'You should have made for him a wooden brace padded with linen (and have) the head fastened to it. His treatment should be sitting, placed between two supports of brick, until you know whether he is making any progress.' These contrivances are evidently devices familiar enough to the Egyptian practitioner to need no further description. The first might be variously explained, but the second, built of sundried brick like the beds of the poor, is obviously intended to prevent the sufferer from lying down and disturbing a badly injured skull. It may be mentioned also that the examination in this case notes a feeble pulse and fever as among the symptoms. . . . Case 8 deals with a 'fracture of the skull under the skin.' When examination has demonstrated the presence of the fracture the surgeon is unconditionally charged to operate, to open at the point of contusion, and 'to elevate the depression outward.' It may be for the modern surgeon to decide whether this could be done without trephining; if trephining is involved, as would seem probable, we have here the earliest reference in literature to this famous operation. Although an operation known to have been practiced by peoples in a primitive state of culture, trephining has not yet been unmistakably identified on surviving ancient Egyptian skulls. In any case, the proposed operation was a desperate measure. The verdict was unfavorable, recovery doubtful and the patient was to be treated sitting up, as in Case 7." The treatise devotes twenty-seven cases to the head and then proceeds lower. The fourth group of cases (six in number) concerns the throat and neck. References are made to dislocation of the neck and other injuries. "Among the mechanics employed on the great buildings of Egypt, like the pyramids and temples, there must have been many such cases. A single excavation campaign, which exhumed between 5,000 and 6,000 bodies, disclosed one person with a fractured bone among every thirty-two people." Following the cases of trouble in the cervical vertebræ comes a group consisting of five cases devoted to the collarbone and shoulder. "The operations for a dislocated clavicle and scapula are both described. In both the patient is laid out on his back and to repair the shoulder the arms are spread out 'in order to stretch out the shoulder until the dislocation falls into place.' . . ." With the forty-eighth and last case the treatise passes to a seventh group, cases of the spine. "In these forty-eight cases . . . only one mentions or makes use of a magic charm, and it is evidently not an accident that this case, which resorts to a charm, is also the only one which lacks any verdict. The physician evidently excluded it from his list of cases to be treated by other than magical means. We have here, then, a group of the earliest recorded observations in natural science made by man. Here was a realm where the physician was confronted often enough, to be sure, by the unknown, but not by the demoniacal. Here was the physician's exclusive realm, to be dealt with by the physician's skill. He knew it and recognized it and applied to it the phrase 'art of the physician,' as he repeatedly calls it in contrast with the 'art of incantations,' applied to ailments arising from demoniacal causes."

In modern Montenegro "native surgeons have a great local reputation for dressing wounds and setting bones. The traditional way of dressing a wound is remarkably antiseptic. It was on no account to be washed with water, but cleaned out several times with strong wine. . . . The local surgeons had also a great reputation for trepanning. In such a rocky country plenty of people tumble over cliffs and dent their skulls in. I have not seen any of the instruments. When the piece of bone had been removed a lump of sheep's wool was used to swab out the hole."[50]

Obstetrics. In the Indian Archipelago the woman must not bear her child in a house; she goes into the bush and is assisted by a person who exercises strong pressure.[51] In one of the backward Borneo tribes the woman is smoked and the next day resumes her duties.[52] Again, kneading is the only means known of assisting; and hæmorrhages cannot be arrested.[53] Among the Sea Dyaks one doctor takes charge of the lying-in room and another enacts on the veranda an imitation of the process of forcing-down applied by the *manang* inside, utilizing a stone to represent the child.[54] Kneading may even go to the length of treading with the feet.[55] In Sumatra delivery scarcely halts the woman's activities, and the presence of a *sage femme* is often deemed superfluous; but there are midwives who have some real skill.[56] The shamaness is generally called in, in Celebes, when a woman bears her first child; later on, she attends to herself in the bush or by the river. After bathing, the mother goes about her usual duties.[57] In Malacca, the midwife has a house apart, tabooed to men, and differently constructed from ordinary dwellings. The assistance rendered is the usual pressure and manipulation. A half-hour after delivery the mother takes a bath in the sea.[58] The case is not much different in Luzon and the Pelew Islands.[59]

Jetté[60] reports the case of a young woman among the Ten'a who was in the pains of labor. "As these were unusually severe, she sent to Nulato for some medicine, which I gave to the messenger, instructing him how she should use it. She did so, but as the result was not instantaneous, accounted it null, and called in the medicine-man. He gave her a cup of water to drink in which he had blown, and immediately she was delivered. When she related to me the fact, I felt almost sorry that I had given her anything at all, but I could never persuade her that the first medicine had contributed more than the second to the desired result."

Among the Indians all sorts of taboos surround the women during pregnancy, the menstrual periods, and childbirth, owing to the belief in their "uncleanness."[61] Also fastings and food-taboos accompany childbirth, and the Mohave mother must diet for forty days, during which she must not wash or

50 Durham, in JAI, XXXIX, 95, 96.
51 Pleyte, in *Bijd.*, XLI, 597; §408, below.
52 Roth, *Sarawak*, II, cxcvii.
53 Nieuwenhuis, *Borneo*, I, 118.
54 Gomes, *Sea Dyaks*, 99, 100.
55 Grabowsky, in *Globus*, LXXII, 270.
56 Marsden, *Sumatra*, 284, 285; Jacobs, *Groot-Atjeh*, I, 115, 116, 117.

57 Riedel, in *Bijd.*, XXXV, 91, 92.
58 Stevens, in *Ztsft. f. Ethnol.*, XXVIII, 164-165, 188, 189, 197-198.
59 Blumentritt, *Igorroten*, 96; Kubary, *Pelauer*, I, 55.
60 In JAI, XXXVII, 169.
61 §388, below; Mooney, in BAE, VII, 330.

comb her hair.[62] The Pima mother bathed in the river immediately after delivery, during which she is attended by women friends.[63]

Water and Vapor. Sprinkling sea-water on a patient is one method of treatment in the D'Entrecasteaux Islands. A native expression for getting well is to say a man has bathed.[64] In South Africa a cap or any sort of clothing worn by a witchdoctor until it has become saturated with filth "is considered the most infallible cure for all kinds of diseases, poisonous bites, etc. On emergencies a corner of this treasure is washed, and the dirty water thus produced is given to the patient—beast or man—to drink."[65] Among the Palaungs, who always speak of the illness disappearing or being overcome and never of the patient recovering, the rule is: "To cure stomach-ache make stones very hot in the fire, then throw them into cold water to cool their surface, then lay them upon the painful place. . . . If a person is clawed or bitten by a tiger or by a leopard, dip a cat under water in a vessel—all but its head, for it must not drown. Stroke its fur under water, then use water to wash the wounds. If this is done, Palaungs believe that the poison will not take effect." Water poured over a magnet is believed to be good also for healing wounds. In order to drive away the spirits causing an epidemic, the people sprinkle sand, paddy, rice, and water on the floor of every house in the village and beat the walls of each room with sticks; sometimes they go through the streets firing guns.[66] The Alfurs of the East Indies bathe to remove disease and all ill. In bathing they say: "May the water remove sickness, weariness, and evil dreams and bestow them on those who are bad." They bathe *en masse* against epidemics, which are ascribed to evil ghosts. Water is a prime means of banishing ghosts and hence ghost-sent disease.[67] "Those who have had intercourse with Malays often try their remedies, after the attempts of their own priests have failed to cure. All remedies are external, either rubbing, washing, or sprinkling." The writer[68] has never known a Daya doctor to give a drug or any internal medicine or to interfere with the diet. "If one excepts, therefore, such few cases where rubbing or washing would rationally be of use, the whole medical treatment of the Dayas rests on their heathen system of superstition, in some cases approaching sympathetic cures professing to transplant sickness." A case is reported where the contents of three water-receptacles were poured over a woman suffering from eczema, an affection which should be kept quite dry.[69] On the island of Ponapé, "the fundamental principle of their medicine is hydrotherapy, for in almost all their maladies they use hot water, applying a moistened sponge, renewed frequently, over the location of the illness, whether the patient complains of pains or whether it is a question of ulcers or wounds, tumors or eruptions."[70] Incantations and prayers, cold-water bathing and sprinkling seem to be the principal stock-in-trade of present-day medicine-men in New Zealand.[71]

All the men among the Cheyenne Indians took a morning plunge. "This was for good health, to make them hardy, and also to wash away all sickness."[72] A cure for fits, among the Guiana Indians, is to drink water in which singed

62 Hrdlička, in BAE, Bull. XXXIV, 61, 62.

63 Russell, in BAE, XXVI, 185-186.

64 Jenness and Ballentyne, *D'Entrecasteaux*, 138.

65 Garbutt, in JAI, XXXIX, 535.

66 Milne, *Eastern Clan*, 250-251, 254, 256.

67 Wilken, *Vkde.*, 30; Lippert, *Kgchte.*, II, 241, 243.

68 Roth, *Sarawak*, I, 289.

69 Moszkowski, in *Globus*, XCIV, 313.

70 Pereiro, *Ponapé*, 134.

71 Cowan, *Maoris*, 117.

72 Grinnell, *Cheyenne*, I, 63.

tapir hoofs have been placed.[73] Water is used by "the wise women" in Montenegro today as a cure or rather charm for rupture. "The wise woman puts some water, which must be freshly drawn, into an *ibrik* [long-necked metal pot]. She puts it on the fire and crosses it three times. When it boils she says, 'Water, I call on you three times from Heaven to earth. If Mr. So and So of such an address is ruptured, let his bowel return like this water.' So saying, she turns the boiling water out into a metal dish, and holds the *ibrik* mouth down in it. As the hot metal pot cools some of the water rises again into the *ibrik*, the more the better. A fee of 2d. is asked, and the operation should be repeated till relief is obtained. It is usual also to give the operator some eggs or a cheese to induce her to begin."[74]

On August 15, most of the bathing beaches in this country and Europe are taxed to capacity, the reason being that on this date which is the feast of the Assumption and one of the most important holy days of obligation in the Roman Catholic Church calendar, the salt water is supposed to be possessed of peculiar curative qualities, not characteristic during the rest of the year, and he who bathes on that day believes that he will be free from bodily ills for another year at least.[75]

In some places steam or fumes are applied to the patient, while sweating is also employed. In South Africa, "should a boy fall sick, it is said that an *i-shumba* spirit has taken possession of him and finds his quarters uncongenial. He must, therefore, be transferred to a girl. This transference is carried out by killing a goat and putting some of the blood into a broken vessel. Herbs and leaves of certain trees, and heated stones or burning charcoal are placed in a vessel causing a dense steam. A blanket is placed over the rising steam, and the girl to whom the spirit is to be transferred is placed under the blanket with the possessed boy kneeling beside her. By inhaling this steam she is supposed to receive the spirit, and the boy to be dispossessed."[76] The tribes of British Central Africa use a medicated vapor bath for sick children.[77] The Nilotic Kavirondo in sickness use smoke, which probably has the quality of fumigating. "While the sick man is dying his relatives howl in chorus round his hut, while the doctors rattle stones in gourds and puff clouds of tobacco smoke around the invalid, their object, undoubtedly, being to drive away the evil spirits."[78] In Morocco and Algeria, where the chameleon is largely used for medicinal purposes, "privet or mallow leaves, fresh honey and chameleons split open alive are considered good for wounds and sores, while the fumes from the burning of the dried body of this animal are often inhaled."[79] Among the Arabs and Swahili, "as soon as the spine of the sick person becomes arched, a fire is lighted in the sick room. A mixture is then made from donkey's dung, dog's excreta, garlic, *mvuge*, (asafoetida), sulphur and *sunduna* (a black kind of seaweed). All this is made into a paste by the addition of castor-oil, and lumps of it are cast on to the fire, from which then emanates acrid smoke with an appalling smell. This is supposed to relieve the patient."[80]

In the East Indies the steam of hot springs is regarded as therapeutic in cases of goiter.[81] Sweating was employed by the Cheyenne Indians in the following manner. "Stones were heated in a fire outside the sweat-house, passed

73 Roth, in BAE, XXXVIII, §928.
74 Durham, in JAI, XXXIX, 95.
75 New Haven *Journal-Courier*, Aug. 16, 1913.
76 Garbutt, in JAI, XXXIX, 553.

77 Stannus, in JAI, XL, 294.
78 Northcote, in JAI, XXXVII, 62.
79 Hilton-Simpson, in JAI, XLIII, 710.
80 Skene, in JAI, XLVII, 433-434.
81 Wilken, in VG, IV, 359.

in by a woman, who handled them with two forked sticks, and placed in a shallow rectangular hole dug in the center of the lodge. Water was then sprinkled on them from the mouth or by means of a brush made of a buffalo-beard, creating dense steam and heat, which were confined by a covering of skins or canvas or blankets spread over the framework. While the sweat was being taken, the doctor prayed, sang, and used his rattle. After the sweat a plunge in the river followed."[82] Among the Omaha, "both men and women took sweat baths but not together; these were employed to relieve headache, rheumatism, weariness, snow-blindness, or any bodily ailment. . . . The Omaha used the sweat lodge not only for curative purposes but to avert disaster, as impending death, and also as a preparatory rite."[83] In general among the American Indians sweating was important in medical practice for the cure of disease. "The underlying idea was doubtless analogous to its religious and ceremonial use, since it was intended to influence disease spirits and was usually prescribed by the shaman, who sang outside and invoked the spirits while the patient was in the sweat-house. It was sometimes the friends and relatives of the sick person who, assembled in the sweat-house, sang and prayed for the patient's recovery. Among the Plains tribes all priests who perform ceremonies have usually to pass through the sweat-house to be purified, and the sweating is accompanied by special rituals. Whether the Indian's therapeutic theory was rational or irrational, sweating was an efficacious remedy in many diseases to which he was subject, though used with little discrimination." A third purpose for which sweating was practised may be designated as social and hygienic—"a number of individuals entered the sweat-house together, apparently actuated only by social instinct and appreciation of the luxury of a steam bath."[84] Among the Guiana Indians, "a steam or vapor bath is often resorted to in the case of fevers."[85]

As an illustration of medicine upon a considerably higher stage, and with at least a considerable element of the rational, and very little of the daimonistic, in it, stands the case of Père Ripa's description of the treatment he underwent in China after a severe fall. He was thrown from his horse and lay fainting in the street until he was carried into a house, where a native surgeon attended him. "He made me sit up in bed, placing near me a large basin filled with water, in which he put a thick piece of ice to reduce it to a freezing point. Then stripping me to the waist, he made me stretch my neck over the basin, while he continued for a good while to pour the water on my neck with a cup. The pain caused by this operation upon those nerves which take their rise from the pia mater was so great and insufferable that it seemed to me unequalled, but he said it would stanch the blood and restore me to my senses, which was actually the case, for in a short time my sight became clear and my mind resumed its powers. He next bound my head with a band drawn tight by two men who held the ends, while he struck the intermediate parts vigorously with a piece of wood, which shook my head violently, and gave me dreadful pain. This, he said, was to set the brain, which he supposed had been displaced, and it is true that after the second operation my head felt more free. A third operation was now performed, during which he made me, still stripped to the waist, walk in the open air supported by two persons; and

82 Grinnell, *Cheyenne*, II, 133.
83 Fletcher and LaFlesche, in BAE, XXVII, 587.
84 Henshaw, "Sweating," in HAI, II, 661-662.
85 Roth, in BAE, XXXVIII, 705-706.

while thus walking he unexpectedly threw a basin of freezing cold water over my breast. As this caused me to draw my breath with great vehemence, and as my chest had been injured by the fall, it may easily be imagined what were my sufferings under this infliction; but I was consoled by the information that if any rib had been dislocated, this sudden and hard breathing would restore it to its natural position. The next proceeding was not less painful and extravagant. The operator made me sit on the ground, and, assisted by two men, held a cloth upon my mouth and nose till I was almost suffocated. 'This,' said the Chinese Esculapius, 'by causing a violent heaving of the chest, will force back any rib that may have been dislocated.' The wound in my head not being deep, he healed it by stuffing it with burnt cotton. He then ordered that I should continue to walk much, supported by two persons; that I should not sit long, nor be allowed to sleep till ten o'clock at night, at which time I should eat a little thin rice soup. He assured me that these walks in the open air while fasting would prevent the blood from settling upon the chest, where it might corrupt. These remedies, though barbarous and excruciating, cured me so completely that in seven days I was able to resume my journey."[86]

Heat. Among certain Melanesians "the wound is bathed with hot water and leaves are then put on again and the wound is thus dressed daily till it is healed. For a pain in the back a hot stone is applied locally."[87] A case is reported from among the Hausa of a man who was quite helpless with rheumatism but was cured by means of a hot iron—after all, only our mustard plaster in a more severe form.[88] For water on the knee, the Algerian prescription is: "Make some oil very hot; wrap a little salt in a rag, dip it in the hot oil and gently 'dab' the swollen knee with it. The oil used is presumably that of the olive. Massage is also recommended for water on the knee. Both these forms of treatment were recommended to me when suffering from water on the knee at El Kantara, but I noted a far more drastic remedy some years ago in the Sahara. One of my camel men [a native of Morocco] had 'fired' his knee with a red-hot knife when fluid had formed on it during a long journey, and this treatment had been successful."[89] Marks are occasionally seen on the wrist and other parts of the body among the Todas; "in men these are always the result of treatment for pain or illness and are made . . . by means of a hot stick."[90] Among the Palaungs, "the giving of medicine is almost always accompanied by incantations, and a fire must be burning close at hand while these are being said. It is good to burn a light near a sick person. It is left to the wise man to decide where it should be placed."[91] In Guiana, "Indians will allow abscesses to develop and apply heat with fire until they burst."[92]

Branding around the navel is a cure for colic in India; one man showed a series of large and small branded discs on chest and abdomen for illness when he was a baby. A newly born child is branded with a hot needle in twenty vital parts. Children who have fits are branded with a heated twig or glass bangle and branding on the forehead is held to cure sore eyes. Branding is a regular dedicatory religious ceremony; it is sometimes merely a pretence when the child is very young, for sandalwood paste is interposed between the skin and the heated brass instrument. "In some cases, disciples, who are afraid of being

86 Williams, *Middle Kingdom*, II, 124-125.
87 Rivers, *Melan. Soc.*, I, 324.
88 Tremearne, in JAI, XLV, 50.
89 Hilton-Simpson, in JAI, XLIII, 713.

90 Rivers, *Todas*, 576.
91 Milne, *Eastern Clan*, 247.
92 Roth, in BAE, XXXVIII, §929.

hurt, bribe the person who heats the instruments; but, as a rule, the guru [priest] regulates the temperature so as to suit the individual." It is high for a strong man, cooler for a weakling, and in the case of babies the instrument is pressed against a wet rag before application.[93] In Algeria the branding is done on a goat, probably with the idea of imitative magic; this is the treatment for enlarged spleen. "Take the spleen of a goat and lay it upon the patient's left side over his spleen. Then take a 'minjel,' the small sickle hook with a serrated edge in use all over Algeria, and, having made it very hot in a fire, apply it as in branding to the goat's spleen lying against the patient's side. Repeat this seven times. . . . Hang the goat's spleen up in the house so that the patient cannot fail to see it directly he awakes in the morning. When he sees it he must say, 'It is my own spleen that grows smaller,' for as the goat's spleen dries and shrinks so does that of the patient decrease in size until it resumes its normal proportions."[94] A Guiana Indian who falls ill rests for several days in his hammock, with a small fire underneath.[95] The Shingu Indians cover the seat of pain with warm pitch in which feathers are thickly planted. Decoration with feathers was itself a remedy for disease, so that the line between remedy and ornament could not be drawn.[96]

Rhythm; faith-cure. Many of the performances of the medicine-man have a beneficial effect on the patient's mind; they, combined with the faith of the latter, often aid in his recovery. This is especially true in mental ailments. In South Africa women "dance around the person afflicted by the spirit, calling upon the spirit to come out of the woman and leave her in peace; they work themselves into a great state of excitement, and it is dangerous for the men to go near them when they are going through this dance."[97] Among the Bangala, the medicine-man "beats his drum near the patient, talks excitedly, chants various phrases, the sense of which neither he nor the people very often understand, but the lilt of the metre together with the rhythm of the drum make the patient sway to and fro and have a hypnotic effect on him." Confidence in the shaman aids in the cure. "Whether the *nganga* deceives himself— believes in himself—is a question difficult to decide. Undoubtedly through generations of inherited knowledge concerning herbs, etc., they have remedies that do good to their patients, and there are many faith cures, the result of an implicit belief in their *nganga* and the means used. The system is founded on quackery, but, like quackery in Europe, the remedy sometimes meets the disease, and such successes are remembered and talked about, and the failures are forgotten."[98] The Swahili cure for *pepo,* a word equivalent to the Arabic *jinn* or evil spirit, is principally drumming. "The natives of Africa are particularly sensitive to rhythm, pure and simple, even more so perhaps than Europeans. The rhythm of certain kinds of drumming has the effect of exciting the nerves to an ecstatic degree, while other rhythms appear to have the contrary effect upon the nervous system of Africans. It is the latter rhythms that are used as a cure for *pepo.* This physiological effect of rhythmic drumming is, however, unknown to the inhabitants of the coastal zone, and believing as they do, that the nervous disturbance known as *pepo* is caused by the presence of evil spirits in the body, they set about propitiating the *jin* and putting him in a good temper by giving a drumming entertainment in his honour, so as to

93 Thurston, *S. India,* 398-400, 405.
94 Hilton-Simpson, in JAI, XLIII, 708.
95 Schomburgk, *Brit.-Guiana,* II, 333.

96 Von den Steinen, *Zent. Bras.,* 476.
97 Garbutt, in JAI, XXXIX, 548-549.
98 Weeks, in JAI, XL, 396-397, 425.

induce him to depart from the body of the person possessed. . . . If, however, success is attained in making the *pepo* speak through the lips of the patient, which is very often the case owing to leading questions being asked by the *fundi,* and perhaps to a certain amount of mental ascendancy on his part, to which a hypnotic element may not be foreign, arrangements are then made to fulfil the desires of the *pepo,* which invariably take the form of an *ngoma* or dance repeated every day for seven days, with or without a *pepo* feast, and a male goat to be ridden by the *pepo* on the last day of the dance."[99]

Rhythm is used in therapy by natives of Sarawak. "When a person falls sick, the mode of procedure is as follows: a medicine man (orang bayoh) is called in to diagnose, and he decides which spirit (antu) must be considered to be responsible. Then he returns home, procures a log of sago palm, and the next day appears at the patient's house with a dakan representing the antu. Then, sitting down by the patient, he begins to beat a drum, not loudly, but in a peculiar way that cannot be mistaken, reciting a monotonous chant in a semi-obsolete language the while: thus calling on the spirit to enter his image and beseeching him to stop the sickness, he now spits on it with sireh, which marks the end of his incantation, and then he pours water over the dakan, letting it trickle from the image over the affected part of the patient." In treating the sickness, therefore, there is no need whatever to administer medicines, the treatment simply being the pacification of the spirit by sacrifices and by injunctions offered through the medium of pith images. "It will be seen, in fact, that their method of healing is but a form of the world-wide faith cure and that to the great healer, Dame Nature, the Milano patient owes his recovery after the ministrations of the witch doctor."[100] In New Zealand there are today medicine-men of a sort, but "those who so style themselves are chiefly really faith-healing 'bush-doctors,' who travel from place to place practising their particular brand of the Christian-Science doctrine amongst the natives. They use incantations or prayers of meaningless and unintelligible character, often composed by themselves, over their patients, . . . but they are very often successful, for the Maori imagination is strong, and the patient's faith works wonders."[101]

Strange as they may seem to us, the performances of the medicine-men of the Ten'a, in Central Alaska, inspire faith in the patient. The doctor sings while he dances with a blanket over his head and shoulders, he works himself up to a frenzy, sweats, his face becomes distorted, he gets hoarse from yelling, and saliva drips from his mouth. This may go on for from one to three hours. All the assistants get excited too, and the patient's imagination and credulity are stimulated. The medicine-man then squeezes the patient with his hand, pretending to extract something, which he generally introduces into himself or throws into the fire or out of the window. On one such occasion, "the sorcerer came to the window to despatch his captive spirit into the aerial spaces, when he unexpectedly beheld the missionary's head laughing at him through the window. He lost all self-control: 'The priest! the priest!' he exclaimed. An indescribable confusion followed. The lights were put out, and the audience skedaddled in all directions." If the patient fails to recover the medicine-man is expected to return the gifts he has received; they are given

99 Skene, in JAI, XLVII, 420-421, 424.   101 Cowan, *Maoris,* 117.
100 Lawrence   and   Hewitt,   in   JAI,
XXXVIII, 389.

not to attempt a cure but to effect it. "This practice is so constant, that the Ten'a, at first, expected that the white physicians would conform to it." The medicine-man generally imposes abstinence of some sort, temporary or for life. These orders are scrupulously observed. In this way he gets a stronger hold on the people's minds; they are trained to obey him.[102] Of course, if they do not, some coincidence will confirm him. Rhythm, dance, and faith play their parts in the performances of the Kwakiutl shaman, by which he undertakes to restore the soul. In one case a woman was about to be placed in her grave-box when the shaman made her sit up, whereupon "the great shaman swung his rattle, and all the time-beaters beat time. Then the shaman went towards her, opened his right hand; and as soon as he came to the sick woman, he gave his rattle to his friend the shaman, who was holding up the sick woman. And he made the soul sit on her head. For a long time he blew on the top of her head; and when he finished blowing on it, he pressed the top of the head of the sick woman. Then he finished. He arose and spoke. He said, 'Now let our sisters dance.' Thus he said to the four women who were to dance merrily, because he had recovered the soul of the one who had come back to life, the one who had been walking with the spirits. Thus he said. Then he sang with slow time-beating, and the time-beaters began to sing. Now the four women danced and the great shaman also danced. As soon as the song ended, they finished. Then they were paid by him with one hundred blankets, and one hundred blankets were given to the time-beaters of the shaman. Then the woman came back to life after this."[103] Among the coast Salish the cure is brought about by a dramatization of the restoration of the patient's guardian-spirit from the spirit-world, whither it has wandered. By an elaborate performance, including much fine acting, the shamans undertake the perilous journey to recover the lost soul. "If the sick person did not get up and dance, it meant that the shamans had not brought back the right guardian-spirit. In that case, the shamans had to return the payment which they had received at the beginning of the ceremony."[104] Among the Omaha, "as all medical aid was given with more or less ceremony and with songs accompanied by the beating of a small drum, these noises evidently exercised a psychical influence on the patient and did not injuriously affect the nervous system, as they would have done in the case of one to whom the sound was without meaning. The patient knew that the songs were sung to invoke supernatural aid and that on the efficacy of the appeal he must largely rely for relief."[105]

The dramatization mentioned above is not unlike the practice of the ancient Chaldæans who thought the gods fought with the evil spirits of illness and that the shamanistic operations performed according to receipts were the weapons of the gods in this fight. "The healing incantations describe the sickness, its nature and course, but they are much more interesting in their dramatic form, in that the gods themselves are introduced discussing and arranging what shall be done in the patient's case."[106]

Belief in mystic healing is still common, as judged by the many cases of faith cures reported in current newspapers. The scientific basis underlying such seems to be either that anything will cure the patient when actually nothing is the matter with him, or that many of the ills and complaints of

102 Jetté, in JAI, XXXVII, 170, 171.
103 Boas, in BAE, XXXV, pt. I, 723.
104 Haeberlin, in AA, XX, 249-251.

105 Fletcher and LaFlesche, in BAE, XXVII, 585.
106 Lehmann, Overtro, I, 45, 46.

mankind are fostered by the mental attitude of the sufferers and the symptoms complained of are aggravated by anxiety, in which case the remedy is the popular "cure" of the hour to which human-kind accords temporary faith and allegiance. In this way probably millions have been "cured" of their ills or at least restored to happiness through belief in their delusions.[107]

Miscellaneous. Here are grouped other primitive methods of treatment including counter-irritants, fasting, dieting, and some practices that are purely irrelevant. Sometimes the natives' physical condition is due to immunity to certain diseases or to high resistance. It is said that the resistance of the Central Australian to inflammatory trouble is marked, and "though the power of combating the germs of disease such as consumption, measles and smallpox is low, the opsonic index for strepto- and staphylococci is high; which means that the black's resistance to inflammation is great compared with that of the whites, although he more easily contracts other diseases."[108] As a counter-irritant for stomach-ache, the natives of the D'Entrecasteaux Islands rub on something like stinging nettles. Some of their remedies are really curative.[109] It is said in Central Angoniland that if the wind blow from the west for seven days then smallpox will come. "There seems to be something in this, for such a wind would come over Portuguese territory, where variola is endemic."[110] Emetics and purges are the most popular kinds of medicine among the Dinkas. "Counter-irritation is believed in for most local illness. A headache is treated by a tight cord round the head; and bronchitis, and other chest affections (to which the Dinkas are very prone), are similarly alleviated by a tight cord round the thorax. It is possible that this latter treatment may have gained a reputation by placing the chest-wall at rest, and thus relieving the pain of, say, pleuritis. 'Firing' with a hot iron, cutting with knives over the seat of pain, and 'cupping' with a cow's horn after first scarifying the surface, are all tried for local diseases. These methods are all, probably, copied from the Arabs, who believe in counter-irritation as the sovereign remedy for every disorder."[111] In East Africa, "where there are injuries due to mauling by lions or leopards, tobacco and water are given as an emetic."[112]

Among the Palaungs, "if a young unmarried boy or girl becomes ill, a wise man may find that the only remedy is marriage. Sometimes no girl can be found at a moment's notice who is willing to marry the boy, or no boy can be found ready to marry the sick girl, so a cock or a hen is made to play the part of bridegroom or bride. . . . If the sick child is married to another child of the opposite sex, they are not in any way bound to each other when they are of a marriageable age."[113] The Singhalese of Ceylon believe in demons, despite Buddhism which teaches that they exist but cannot hurt the virtuous; hence the shaman is called in at every turn. An altar is set up before the sick and an animal, often a cock, is sacrificed on it; meantime the sorcerers dance in masks representing the demons.[114] The natives of British North Borneo believe they can call into spears certain spirits which will attack the smallpox-spirits.[115] An unusual rite is reported from New Zealand: "A sick person would be

107 Walsh, *The Story of Cures that Fail,* reviewed in N. Y. *Times,* Aug. 19, 1923.
108 Horne and Aiston, *Cent. Aust.,* 17.
109 Jenness and Ballentyne, *D'Entrecasteaux,* 137.
110 Stannus, in JAI, XL, 294.

111 Cummins, in JAI, XXXIV, 156.
112 Barton, in JAI, LIII, 74.
113 Milne, *Eastern Clan,* 251-252.
114 Andree, *Eth. Parallelen,* 2d ser., 113.
115 Evans, in JAI, XLIII, 455-456.

taken to the village latrine, where, while the priest recited a charm, he would
be told to bite the horizontal beam of the latrine. This would cure him, at least
so sayeth the Maori. Likewise, a person about to start on a journey to distant
parts would go through a similar performance, in order that the evil spells of
enemies might be rendered harmless, or 'toothless,' as my informant put it."[116]
Fasting is often required of patients among the Tlinkits.[117] When a Tsimshian shaman believes that a disease is going to visit a village, "he will sing
his song at midnight to warn his or her people of the coming of the disease.
Thus they invite in all the people of the village; and when they are in the
house, the shaman opens his rattle-bag, takes out a small leather bag filled
with red ocher, and passes it around among all the people in the house to
paint their faces—men, women, and children. After all the people have painted
their faces, the shaman takes a dried sea-lion bag filled with eagle down,
and passes it about among the people to put the down on their heads."[118]
Among the Zuñi, during the period of treatment for rattlesnake bite, a male
patient must not look on the face of a woman who is nourishing an infant,
otherwise "his poisoned limb would swell and he would surely die within four
days."[119] A sort of routine treatment followed by the lay and medical fraternity in general, among the Guiana Indians, consists of "restrictions in diet,
emetics and purgatives, ablutions and vapor baths, bleeding, counterirritants,
and drugs, but as to how far and in what order one or all of these procedures
are carried out will depend upon circumstances—generally upon how long the
poor patient's condition is able to survive them. The restrictions of diet may
vary from the limitation of several foods to a cooked drink of cassava meal,
often an absolute fast. But the curious part of the affair is that similar taboos
may be, and are, simultaneously imposed upon the sick person's kinsfolk. The
majority of the medicine men on the Orinoco demand that no one belonging to
the household should eat anything hot, anything cooked, or peppers. Similar
restrictions are observed in cases of snake bite. Let the disorder be what it
may, an emetic is first administered, followed by a purgative. Both of these are
of such proportions that many die from sheer exhaustion." Certain biting ants
are used for counter-irritants. "For the cure of fever the patient [Carib]
picks up a yoku ant and causes it to bite him on the temple. For a headache
the ant is placed so as to bite the crown of the head, and it is applied to any part
of the body to relieve by its bite the particular part affected. . . . A still more
effective manner would seem to be that which I have known more than once
to happen, where the patient afflicted with fever has deliberately lain down
and rolled himself in an ant's nest." These natives believe, probably because
of the fetishistic power of the breath, that blowing on a person will cure him.
A number of travellers have reported the custom. "When on the point of leaving, a woman stepped forward to an old Indian in one of our canoes, and held
up her head. He tapped her forehead with his fingers, muttered a few words,
and then blew on her temple. This was done to charm away a pain in the head,
the old fellow being a peaiman, and capable of effecting such cures. On our
arrival at villages I have sometimes seen a woman carry her infant round to
one after another of the Indians of my party, each man as she passed stooping
down and blowing gently on the face of the child. . . . The Serekong women
brought us several of their sick children for us to breathe upon their faces,

116 Best, in AAAS, 1909, 463.
117 Jones, Thlingets, 228.
118 Boas, in BAE, XXXI, 560.
119 Stevenson, in BAE, XXX, 54.

and so restore them to health. . . . A pretty-looking Makusi mother insisted upon my blowing in the face of her sickly infant, which she believed would act as a charm, and restore her child to health. . . . With the same tribe, the piai will blow upon the girl after the menstruation ceremony with the object of disenchanting her."[120] The instruments of the healer among the Araucanians consist of the following items: a flint lancet, small stones which he pretends to pass through the body of the patient (if they come out bloody, there is no hope), a stone pipe, a wooden spitting bowl to receive what the doctor sucks from the sick body, a dish for preparation of remedies, a syringe consisting of a bladder and bone tube for clysters, and chief of all the drum; no doctor begins operations without a drum, to which, indeed, healing powers are attributed.[121]

With the Greeks as with other peoples of antiquity, medicine was practised by priests in temples. "In the *Iliad* it appears that the Greeks before Ilion had physicians, who in all cases of wounds went to work quite rationally, in that they washed the wounds and bound them with healing herbs." The patient in the temple must fast and diet; then he was shown the holy tables and images, the mementos of former miracles. Prayers and holy songs followed, which the sick one sang with the priest. Offerings were made to the gods. Both anointings and rubbing with hands were practised, and fumigation with various herbs; the patient then went to sleep and a dream announced to him the result, though not even then did he always recover.[122]

§318. Medicines.

IN Central Africa the medical treatment for babies and children consists in a perhaps excessive use of purging, by means of a clyster with an infusion of herbs and peanut-oil.[1] The native pharmacopœia in East Africa, though associated with irrelevant practices, is said to comprise efficacious remedies for all kinds of diseases; "and when the time comes for it to be investigated thoroughly and extensively, it will probably add some invaluable and quite unforeseen data to our own store of medical knowledge. Native doctors are notoriously reticent. For years, in German East Africa, Europeans have tried in vain to find out the cure of the Wahehe tribe against syphilis—a cure which, at least as far as all outward symptoms are concerned, is wonderfully effective. Doubtless there exist, among native tribes, secret medicine about which we know nothing at all."[2] Sir Charles Dundas[3] states of other East Africans that "many herbs and natural medicines are known to these people which are of real use."

In Uganda is found the custom of using cows' urine regularly for medicinal purposes; there are antidotes for snake-poison, remedies for diarrhœa, constipation, and ulcers, salves for wounds, and even drugs supposed to prevent miscarriage. Cows are bled and the blood greedily drunk; this is said to be "the only way in which the Masai warrior obtains the salt necessary to his well-being. Cows' blood is often thought to be (and no doubt is) a cure for dysentery."[4] Splinters of a tree struck by lightning are taken as medicine

120 Roth, in BAE, XXXVIII, 704, 707-708; and in BAE, XXX, 164.
121 Latcham, in JAI, XXXIX, 352.
122 Lehmann, *Overtro*, I, 73-74; Keller, *Hom. Soc.*, 179-181.

1 Brunache, *Cent. Afr.*, 135.
2 Coudenhove, in *Atl. Mo.*, CXXVIII, 163.
3 In JAI, XLIII, 533.
4 Johnston, *Uganda*, II, 787, 795, 818.

against headache.[5] The peoples of the eastern horn of Africa think all cures come from drinking liquids, and drink any chemical with simple faith. They eat the salves. Whatever has a drastic effect, however poisonous, pleases them; vitriol is a universal remedy through Galla-land, being sprinkled in powdered form upon wounds; and sulphur is much in evidence. Pepper stands beside the vitriol in high estimation, clearly because of its drastic effects. Woman's blood is used for wounds sustained from snakes and scorpions.[6] Thick vapors of resin are used by the Berber women to cure headache; the sufferer must dance thereafter; "in fact, however bizarre the thing may seem, the sick woman always recovers on the next day, by the triple force of the dance, the prayer, and the resin.[7] A drastic remedy of the natives of the Egyptian Sudan against the Guinea-worm and snake-bite is hyæna-dung taken internally.[8] The therapeutic action of drugs is not understood by the Asabs of the Niger: "any given medicine cures because of a spirit resident in it. Each medicine-pot around a house has its resident or attendant spirit."[9] As medication for a pain in the stomach "an Arab wrote a text from the Koran upon a piece of dried skin taken from a sheep that had been killed for the 'Sheep Feast,' and bound it over the boy's stomach so that the text lay over the seat of the pain. This put an end to the trouble." The hedgehog is known to possess a high immunity to a great many poisons; "it seems possible that this immunity may be known to the Shawia, who have, perhaps, observed the animal after having been bitten by a snake, and this may be the reason for their supposition that the burnt body of the hedgehog can be useful in medicine. Hedgehogs are systematically hunted . . . and are sold for medicinal purposes."[10]

The aborigines of Siberia often believe in the superiority of their own medicines over the European variety. When a Samoyed boy was once taken sick, as a Russian doctor happened to be staying in the village, the boy's father called him in. Medicine was prescribed, but was received with some reservations: "Only such a little drop of medicine in much water, and he so ill!" The father waited for a week, and still the child was no better. Then he lost patience. He solemnly collected all his ikons, and carrying them to the roof of the house, spread them out to the weather in ignominy, to show his contempt for the Russians and their beliefs. Then he returned to the gods of his own people. The boy recovered.[11]

In southern India the urine of a wild monkey is a remedy for rheumatic pains, if applied to the affected parts with a mixture of garlic; and for chronic fever its blood is sometimes taken. "The Burmese believe that, when the powers above quarrel, they throw celts at one another, and that, when one misses, it falls to the earth. They attach considerable importance to them for medicinal purposes, and powdered celt is said to be equally good for a pain in the stomach or an inflamed eye."[12] "There is but one medicine current among all the Toungtha; this is the dried gall bladder and the dung of the boa constrictor, which is supposed to be, and is used as, a remedy for everything."[13] "Epilepsy may be cured by drinking water out of the skull of a suicide, or by

5 Stuhlmann, *Mit Emin*, 489.
6 Paulitschke, *Nordost-Afr.*, I, 183; II, 284.
7 Pommerol, *Sahariennes*, 289-291.
8 Junker, *Afrika*, I, 161.
9 Parkinson, in JAI, XXXVI, 315.

10 Hilton-Simpson, in JAI, XLIII, 710-711, 712.
11 Haviland, *Yenesei*, quoted in N. Y. *Times*, Sept. 26, 1915.
12 Thurston, *S. India*, 271, 351.
13 Lewin, *S.E. India*, 196.

tasting the blood of a murderer"—a belief still surviving in Britain.[14] In northern India and adjacent countries lizard oil is a popular remedy for loss of virility. "The natives also extract from them an oil which is used for rheumatism and as an aphrodisiac."[15] The Orāons believe that water under certain circumstances acquires more than ordinary energy or soul-power. "Thus, rainwater collecting in the old hollow trees is a beneficent power which cures fever that has baffled the art of the medicine-man." A fever-patient "goes to such a tree with a handful of rice, a pinch of red-lead, a few yards of thread, and a small new earthen pitcher. . . . The red-lead mark is probably the reminiscence of a blood-covenant. . . . Any weed or other plant growing on such a cleft tree is used as a medicine for various diseases. The unusual appearance of the tree invests it with such power in the minds of these people."[16] Other Hindu medicinal substances include hair, bones, tiger's tongue, and stones.[17]

Many seemingly foolish practices may actually follow sensible laws of hygiene. In India "a pregnant woman will not touch papaya or papita if she wants her child to live. The Indians say that for a pregnant woman, papaya is 'unclean.' Conversely, many prostitutes, and even married women, especially of the very poor class, will eat papaya purposely in order to bring on abortion. They believe the abortions are brought on because they have eaten something 'unclean,' that is, religiously unclean. As a matter of fact, medical experts of India hold that there seems to be some agent in papaya which actually does cause abortion. For a non-pregnant woman, papaya is clean, and may be eaten with impunity. . . . A child is often seen with a small bag of asafoetida strung around its neck along with a lot of silver and brass charms. The people think it 'keeps away the evil eye.' Asafœtida, the doctors say, is a good germicide. Indian mothers oil their babies and put them in the sun for a little while. It is the religious duty of a Hindustani mother to do this. The mothers say it makes their babies nice and fat. The Indian sun is a powerful disinfectant. . . . Oiled and sunned babies were healthier than those not so treated. Children are often seen with great black daubs underneath the eyes. This, the Shastras declare, will keep away the evil eye, and the mothers not only believe that, but believe also that it very much enhances the beauty of their children. The blacking is lampblack made of the soot of sesamum oil, and it gives protection to the eyes by acting as a shade from the glare of the sun. One may accept a drink of water from one's own caste fellows or from a Brahmin. The water is always poured into one's own cupped hands, or into one's own drinking bowl. One never drinks out of another's drinking bowl. Here we have the precursor of the individual drinking cup."[18]

The following are a few of the most popular remedies among the Palaungs: "To cure rheumatism it is good to tie a cord of twisted cotton thread round the leg, or a young shoot of a rattan cane may be used. A finger-ring made of rhinoceros horn is good for warding off plague or cholera, also for curing diarrhœa. If a buffalo is killed by lightning, its horns—which may be sold for a considerable sum—are carved into dagger-like charms, and the water in which they are afterwards soaked is used as medicine. . . . Whiskers of tigers or of leopards are carried as a protection against the attacks of evil

14 Balfour, in JAI, XXVI, 351.
15 Mitra, in JASB, V, 64, 65.
16 Roy, in JAI, XLIV, 335-336.

17 Hildburgh, in JAI, XXXIX, 394, 395.
18 Pendleton, in Jour. Soc. Hyg., X, 361-362.

spirits, or they may be burnt and the ashes swallowed as a strengthening medicine. . . . A strengthening medicine for a woman who is pregnant, is made by pouring rice-water over a magnet; she then drinks the water, which should also be smeared on the body from the head downwards." A paste rubbed in the wound, after an operation for goiter, had the following ingredients: alum, vitriol, sulphur, arsenic, saltpetre, cuttle-bone, sulphate of copper, and borax. "Most of these ingredients are more or less medicinal, but to them a mixture of the ashes of the following things was added: a piece of an old cap that had been worn by a child; feathers from the tail of a peacock; part of the skin of a Barking deer; a piece of cotton; some hair; the excrement of man, pig, and dog. These were burnt, equal parts of the ashes of each were weighed and mixed together, and then added to the vitriol, alum, etc. All these were pounded together in a mortar, with a little petroleum and a very little of the water in which rice had been boiled. This mixture might be kept for future use, but when it was used it was to be made thinner with a few drops of the juice of a lime. The paste was to be well rubbed on the goitre twice a day, and, at the same time, as much of the paste as would stick to the point of a finger dipped into it, was to be swallowed."[19] The killing of a single rhinoceros is said to place the wealth of a Punan village almost beyond the dreams of avarice, for the flesh is coveted food, while the horn, nails, hair, skin, and even the contents of the stomach are traded at the highest rate of exchange to the Chinese, who use them all for medicinal purposes.[20] A report of the Third Asiatic Expedition refers to the use in China of fossil dust as drugs. "China is one country where fossil teeth and bones have a considerable value, quite aside from their scientific interest. Fossils have been used as fertilizer, it is true, . . . but in China they have quite another use, as medicine, and have been mined for centuries to supply the Chinese drug-shops with 'dragon's teeth' and 'dragon's bones,' a regular article of the Chinese pharmacopeia. There are, it appears, four ways of administering them. They may be ground to powder in a mortar and eaten raw. Or they may be ground and fried with oil in a skillet. Or the powder may be stirred up with sour wine and either drunk off fresh or the mixture left to settle, decanted and the clear liquid drunk. They are specific for certain nervous diseases, heart troubles and disorders of the liver. Without recommending the remedy for adoption in this country, it is perhaps permissible to point out that mixing with sour wine would result in a combination of bicarbonate and acid phosphate of lime that might really have some medicinal value, just what may be left to physicians to decide."[21]

The American Indian medicine of today is not very different from that of our forefathers a few hundred years ago; it is a mingling of charms and herbs. "If occasionally the administration of a plant remedy appears to be followed by good results, they try it again, and presently come to have faith in it. On the other hand, many of the plants are used less for their material than for their spiritual effect. . . . A variety of things, organic or inorganic, are thought to transfer to the individual possessing them the special attributes or powers that they possess. . . . In administering plant medicines, two methods are commonly used. Either an infusion is made, to be taken internally

19 Milne, *Eastern Clan*, 250, 254, 258.
20 Furness, *Head-Hunters*, 175-176.

21 Expedition conducted by the American Museum of Natural History; account quoted in N. Y. *Times*, Oct. 28, 1923.

or used as a lotion; or occasionally poultices of the pulverized plant wet with cold water are applied and renewed as frequently as may be." The author[22] lists ninety-four medicinal plants in use among the Cheyennes, with a statement as to what each is supposed to cure. A number of these remedies are efficient, while some, though possessing no medicinal properties known to science, appear to effect cures. Among the Omaha, "herbs were used not only in the treatment of disease but for the purpose of healing wounds. That success often attended the cure of wounds and other injuries is well known."[23] Such faith was placed in the Wyandot medicine for war and other purposes that it was treason, punishable by death, to divulge the medicine-preparations.[24]

The Cherokees have a myth which accounts for the appearance of diseases and for the existence of counteracting medicines. The animals, being crowded and slaughtered by men, and the insects, being crushed without mercy, resolved to consult upon measures for common safety. They devised and named various diseases, and had not their inventiveness fallen short, not one of the human race would have survived. But "when the plants, who were friendly to man, heard what had been done by the animals, they resolved to defeat their evil measures. Each tree, shrub, and herb, even to the grasses and mosses, resolved to furnish a balm for some one of the diseases and each said: 'I shall appear to help man when he calls upon me in his need.' Thus did medicine originate, and each plant furnishes an antidote for the evil wrought by the revengeful animals. 'When the doctor is in doubt what treatments to apply for the relief of a patient, the spirit of the plant suggests to him the proper remedy.'" Hence the shaman in search for medicinal plants recognizes this helpful attitude, and when he pulls a plant up by the roots he drops a bead into the hole and covers it up. It is unnecessary to comment upon the essentially daimonistic viewpoint here revealed. "In one of the formulas for hunting ginseng the hunter addresses the mountain as the 'Great Man' and assures it that he comes only to take a small piece of flesh (the ginseng) from its side, so that it seems probable that the bead is intended as a compensation to the earth for the plant thus torn from her bosom." There are, however, animal-medicines such as buzzard-flesh; for that bird is believed "to enjoy entire immunity from sickness, owing to its foul smell, which keeps the disease spirits at a distance."[25] The Indian proposed to appropriate some of this offensiveness.

The Navaho prepare a porridge from baked green corn and water which is eaten sacramentally and with prayers by the sick person and the others present. Certain fetishes, such as peculiarly shaped stones or wooden objects, lightning-riven wood, feathers, claws, hair, and figurines of mythic animals are supposed to embody a mysterious power capable of preventing disease or of counteracting its effects.[26] Medicines are said never to be used by the Mohave but singing, laying on of hands, and blowing, accompanied by a spray of saliva;[27] saliva itself, however, is a common curative as well as a fetish-substance used in magic.[28] The Karok root-doctor follows the barking diagnostician, "and with numerous potions, poultices, etc., seeks to medicate the part where the other has discovered that the ailment resides. No medicinal simples

22 Grinnell, *Cheyenne*, II, 166, 167, 169 ff.
23 Fletcher and LaFlesche, in BAE, XXVII, 583.
24 Powell, in BAE, I, 67.
25 Mooney, in BAE, VII, 319, 339, 334.

26 Mathews, in AA, IX, 53; Hrdlička, "Medicine," in HAI, I, 836.
27 Kroeber, in AA, IV, 279.
28 §§300, 301, above.

are of any avail, whatever their virtues, unless certain powwows and mummeries are performed over them. Another California tribe, for bowel diseases "boil up a mess of a large and very stinking ant, and give it internally."[29] Among the Mokis the mother of the Snake Priest was versed in spells and herbs above the rest, and she only knew the secrets of mixing the medicine used in ceremonies.[30]

Among the tribes farther north, "recent circumstances have developed the fact that poison is used by these Indian doctors to hasten the death of patients considered incurable. I have been told that a poison made from toadstools was formerly used."[31] The doctors, aside from their mysteries, have really some valuable medicines. People apparently in the last stages of consumption have been cured by them. For blood-spitting they use a decoction of the fibrous roots of the spruce; for rheumatism, the root of the soap berry (from which lebine is made), while the berry itself is used with success as a stomachic. A decoction of swamp poplar bark and spruce roots is used in syphilis. The wild-cherry bark and tansy root are much used by the women. . . . The wild cherry is used both as a tonic and expectorant, and is good for consumptives. There is a plant resembling the anemone, the root of which when bruised makes a powerful blister; and another resembling the geranium, the root of which will cure ring-worm and dry up an old sore. The inner bark of the pine is used early in spring when the sap is rising; the tree nettle is used as physic, also as a wash for the hair, which it renders thick, soft, and glossy. Wild strawberry acts as an astringent.[32]

Some of the tribes in the Southwest use the offal of animals as medicine.[33] Among the Zuñi "it is usual for the doctors to treat the patient with his personal or fraternity medicine for ordinary ailments; if the disease does not yield, he knows that his patient is not suffering from some minor enemy, such as ants (ants cause many cutaneous troubles because of their anger over the disregard shown for their houses. 'Ants shoot tiny pebbles into the flesh,' the Zuñi say), but has been bewitched by man. Then he acts in the capacity of theurgist, employing the medicines of the gods, whom he invokes for their spiritual presence and bestowal on him of power to heal the disease." When operating, these medicine-men use what appears to be a real anæsthetic, a species of the thorn-apple. A case is cited. "The late Nai'uchi, the most renowned medicine-man of his time among the Zuñi, gave this medicine before operating on a woman's breast. As soon as the patient became unconscious he cut deep into the breast with an agate lance, and, inserting his finger, removed all the pus; an antiseptic was then sprinkled over the wound, which was bandaged with a soiled cloth. . . . When the woman regained consciousness she declared that she had had a peaceful sleep and beautiful dreams. There was no evidence of any ill effect from the use of the drug."[34]

The Guiana Indians use some one-hundred and forty medicinal herbs; a list of diseases and treatments is given.[35] In Brazil an organ of a monkey is regarded as a remedy against fever and, indeed, against all sorts of illness. It might almost be said that woman is a medicine on the principle referred to in

---

29 Powers, in *Contrib. N. Amer. Ethnol.*, III, 26, 378.

30 Hough, in AA, XI, 138.

31 Willoughby, in *Smithson. Rep.* for 1886, pt. I, 275.

32 Allison, in JAI, XXI, 311.

33 Parsons, in AA, XX, 185.

34 Stevenson, in BAE, XXX, 40-41, 46.

35 Roth, in BAE, XXXVIII, §§927 ff.

a former connection of *"venenum veneno."*[36] The Bolivian Indians "have no anesthetics, properly so called, but the constant use (or I might say abuse) of *coca* creates insensibility. The plant is always applied by them to wounds, bruises, and contusions, and it certainly tends to deaden pain, if not to eliminate it. In this manner the Indians unconsciously employ an anesthetic, although they believe only in its healing qualities."[37] In the Gran Chaco, spittle is the medicine-man's chief reliance.[38]

Von Humboldt is quoted as referring in his travels in the tropics (1803) to the fact that native shepherds in the Mexican Cordilleras believed in the protection afforded by vaccinia against smallpox, and Brun is said to have made a similar statement in reference to the clan of Elihots in Baluchistan. Peasants in different parts of Europe, especially in Germany and England, were firmly convinced of the fact. "It was known to most Oriental peoples, from whom the idea was introduced into England by the communications of Tinsoni and Pilarini to the Royal Society in 1713."[39]

The Greeks probably owed much of their medical lore to the Egyptians. In addition to various therapeutic practices they used medicaments such as hemlock juice, oxide of iron, hellebore, squills, lime water, and drugs to allay pain.[40] Pliny is the chief source of information regarding Roman folk-medicine, but some can be picked from Cato, Livy, Tacitus and Lucian. There was a touch of magic in their mode of treatment which had drifted down from Chaldæan days, and is still to be found among ourselves. George Eliot termed it "the medicine given with a blessing." Folk-medicine of the Romans was probably as separate and distinct from the practice of the Greek physicians in Rome as the Negro remedies in the South are different from the usages of the medical practice of today. Among the notions connected with Roman folk-medicine we find the following. "The dung of goats was supposed to expel the stone, as was also the ashes of the hair; the roasted flesh was used for falling sickness, the roasted liver for dimness of sight, the eyes being held over the steam. Mixed with honey, the liver was given for dropsy, and with bran was used for dysentery. For gout in the left hand the tooth of a field mouse killed in a manner prescribed was taken and was stitched to the skin of a freshly slain lion; the skin was then bound around the left leg, when the pain was supposed to cease. A bronze statue in the garden was extolled for tertian ague, and a bronze statue of Hippocrates would cure as Hippocrates did in life. A charm with the mighty name of Solomon would drive off tertian fever. The liver of a hedgehog roasted and eaten, the grease rubbed on the eyes, followed by an application of asses' dung, was claimed to cure the night blindness. An application of crabs' eyes was used for swollen eyes. Augustus was said to have been cured of sciatica by a sound thrashing with a stick. A ring of myrtle wood that had never been touched by iron was said to be a specific for swelling of the groin. Onions and goose grease were recommended for deafness. Four seeds of heliotrophum were said to cure quartian fever, three to cure tertian. Dittander attached to the arm on the suffering side was used for toothache. Root of parsley was worn around the neck for affections of the uvula. Another cure for tertian fever was as follows: 'Take three grains of

---

36 Spix u. Martius, *Brasilien*, 1077, 1251, note.

37 Bandelier, in AA, VI, 445.

38 Hassler, in *Anthrop. Cong. Chicago*, 1893, 357.

39 *New International Encyc.*, XXII, *sub* "vaccination."

40 N. Y. *Times*, Jan. 11, 1914.

coriander or parthenium, hold in the left hand, mention who it is for and look not back.' Hoarhound and stale axle grease was claimed to cure the bite of a dog, and the juice of mallow taken daily was said to prevent all diseases. Eryngo boiled with a frog was used as an antidote for aconite and other poisons. Nettle leaves beaten with bear's grease were used as a cure for gout and nine grains of barley held in the left hand and traced three times around a boil and then thrown in the fire was said to give immediate relief. To cure scrofula, the following procedure was recommended: 'Trace a circle around a quince root, pull it with the left hand, state for what and for whom, pull and wear as a charm.' The calyx of blossom of a pomegranate plucked with the thumb and fourth finger, rubbed on the eyes and swallowed without touching the teeth was supposed to prevent maladies of the eyes for a year. Scrofulous sores were treated as follows: 'Bite off a knot from a fig tree without being seen by anyone, then wear it in a leather bag suspended by a string around your neck.' A sprig of myrtle, that had touched neither the ground nor iron, worn on the person, was said to prevent ulceration of the glands, while a sprig of poplar held in the hand was used to prevent chafing. Red pimples were treated by scourging with a bunch of elder. Tamarisk sprigs if not allowed to touch earth or iron were supposed to allay pain in the bowels. A smilax sprig of an even number of leaves was used for headache. Jaundice was treated with madder worn as an amulet and looked at now and then. Wild madder was supposed to prevent hydrophobia and the person bitten needed only to look at the plant and the flow of corruption from the wound would be staunched at once. Pliny discoursed on pennyroyal, anise, saffron, dog's tongue, wormwood, dill, fennel, cumin, rue, parsley, savin, myrrh, acacia, elecampane, melissa, catnip, lovage, althaea, symphetum, betony, chelidonium, asarum and galbanum. Mustard was recommended as a rubefacient and as a blister; linseed meal with figs was used to ripen abscesses; forests of pine and hemlock were known to be beneficial to patients suffering from phthisis; to breathe such air was more beneficial than a voyage to Egypt. Tar ointment cured itch, as did crude petroleum."[41]

In treating wounds, the Montenegrins, until recently at least, were content to follow the old-time Scriptural usage of oil and wine. All wounds are washed out several times with strong wine or *rakija*, a term really referring to the spirit of wine. Herein was displayed more science than they realized. "The traditional way of dressing a wound is remarkably antiseptic."[42] The discovery of salicylic acid for rheumatism is said to have been the result of an idea that, for every ailment prevailing in a locality, the deity had placed a corresponding cure in the same region. "In the eastern part of England, rheumatism had for centuries been a curse to the inhabitants. The idea that now sprung up caused the natives to search assiduously for the magic herb, root or extract which grew as a rheumatism panacea in the rheumatism country. Crushed grass, boiled clover, chopped dandelion and mashed thistle were applied to the aching limbs and swallowed with no results. Finally after a trial of almost all the native flora had proved unsuccessful, some one skinned off the bark of the willow tree, and making a crude extract from it, swallowed the draft. The stiffness in his joints disappeared. He reported his relief, and the cause of

41 *Druggists Circular*, quoted in Boston *Herald*. July 12, 1916.

42 Durham, in JAI, XXXIX, 95; Pycraft, "Curious Customs," in Boston *Transcript*, July 5, 1913.

it—the willow bark—in the form of salicylic acid capsules, has persisted as a legitimate ameliorative ever since."[43] In an article on executed criminals and folk-medicine are collected instances of belief in the medical effects of the touch of the body of an executed criminal.[44]

In a lecture on "Drugs, Old and New," recently delivered at the City of London School by the Gresham Professor of Physic, it was stated that castor oil was employed 5,000 years ago by the ancient Egyptians, that rhubarb was used in China long before the Christian era, that saffron was in vogue in remote ages, and that opium was well known as a potent drug by Greek and Roman writers. The use of animal-products as remedies dates back to very early days, as Egyptian, Greek, and Roman physicians prescribed them. But these agents became so revolting in character that the marvel is how patients could submit to such treatment. "Fox's lungs for a cough, pigeons cut in half while alive and applied to the feet warm, a dried toad put into the armpit or tied to the head for fever, hedgehogs, earthworms made into syrup, snails, vermin, cats, new-born puppies—all figured among old remedies, many up to comparatively recent times. One was advised to cut off a lock of one's hair and drink it with wine or beer to cure plague. A live spider rolled in butter to form a pill and then swallowed was recommended against jaundice. Vipers used to be held in the highest esteem, and the belief in their virtues as medicine has not entirely died out among some country folk in England. Broth of vipers, salt of vipers, vipers boiled, vipers stewed or pounded, all were believed in and swallowed with infinite faith. The belief in the virtues of unicorn's horn dated from very early times, and the value of these horns, which were possibly the horns or tusks of the narwhal, was immense. It was said that one brought to the King of France in 1553 was valued at £20,000. Most remarkable, however, was the belief which our ancestors had in man as a medicine: The skull, the blood, the hair—nothing came amiss or was too revolting. Most valued of all were the skulls of persons who had died violent deaths. The heads of criminals who had been hanged were, therefore, highly prized, and fetched as much as 8s. to 11s. apiece, if moss had grown on them. A sympathetic ointment was made of this moss in the seventeenth century—an infallible remedy against epilepsy. The skull itself was powdered. Charles II., when he suffered from a stroke of apoplexy, was ordered by his four physicians twenty-five drops of spirit from human skulls. In the seventeenth and eighteenth centuries there arose a profound belief in powdered mummies as internal remedies. But a few skeptical spirits denounced the use of this remedy because it led to much fraud, for far more mummies were prescribed than ever came out of Egypt. Judging by the herbals of the fifteenth, sixteenth, and seventeenth centuries ague and dysentery were among the most prevalent diseases. After these the most common allusions were to hair dyes, baldness, complexion improvers, and melancholy, which was considered a common affliction curable by drugs. The constant recommendation of drugs for 'blackenesse or bruisinge cominge of strypes' was striking. . . . Paracelsus was the first prominent advocate of the so-called 'doctrine of signatures.' According to him, medicinal herbs had distinct outward signs to proclaim their virtues. Thus the leaves of the cyclamen, which had some resemblance to the human ear, must be useful for aural diseases, and so forth. The doctrine of the connection between astrology and medicine dated from Babylon, where it first arose. The importance of herbals

---

43 N. Y. *Times*, Dec. 28, 1923.   44 Peacock, in *Folk-lore*, VII, 268 ff.

declined as a finer distinction came to be drawn between botany and medicine, and for the study of drugs the pharmacopoeias took their place, the first pharmacopœia published under authority being that of Nuremberg, which appeared in 1542." It is quite probable that some folk-medicine notions are connected today with the use of so-called "patent medicines." To the ignorant and credulous the term stands for secret medicine. "If the composition of most of these drugs were truthfully, patently declared, it would probably ruin their sale, for their success rests chiefly in the mystery which surrounds them."[45]

§320. Social Position of the Shaman.

TRILLES[1] has a queer idea concerning the position of the medicine-man among the Fan. He thinks that the chief, being absorbed in political and social matters, delegates religious authority to the medicine-man, who then tries to create a social unity of which he will be recognized chief. The association of young warriors, under his influence, gradually evolves an ensemble of secret practices. Here the chief is secondary to the medicine-man; admission into the secret societies, which are creatures of the latter, comes completely under his control; all must render absolute obedience to him. In East Africa, "among many tribes the medicine man is a person of importance second to none, or the chief medicine man may be practically the ruler of the tribe. Among the Akamba this is not so. . . . More particularly the medicine man's importance must suffer from the fact that many of what one would expect to be his most important duties are performed by the elders, such as the curing of Makwa and the offering of sacrifices."[2] With the Bahima the office of priesthood is hereditary, which tends to augment its importance; "the priest's children live with their father in the forest, and become acquainted with the duties of the office in their early days."[3] The priests among the Nigerian head-hunters get presents, but no regular salaries. The head priest is much more powerful than the chief.[4] When certain African natives are asked what would happen if they did not pay up after being cured, they declare that "the cured patient would immediately fall ill again, and, if he persisted in his refusal, die."[5] This belief both aids in the collection of fees for professional services rendered and otherwise strengthens the position of the practitioner.

The Siberian shamans occupy an exceptional position in society; because of their supernatural powers they are allowed to do things denied to other people. They really form a distinct class. Where they cannot keep on their own side of the boundary line between themselves and the other classes, they cease to be such; for instance, the shamaness during menstruation or childbirth belongs again to the community of women.[6]

Priests and other holy men form over half the male population of Mongolia.[7] They are the teachers of the young in Persia, Central Asia, and India.[8] In Tibet, half of the property of the deceased is given away in charities and half to the Lamas, "who are invited to read the sacred books to his intent and entertained while so doing." Relatives get none of the personal property. Among some pastoral tribes the sons may divide the flocks and herds of their

---

45 From the London *Morning Post*, quoted in the N. Y. *Times*, Oct. 12, 1913.
1 *Fân*, 143.
2 Dundas, C., in JAI, XLIII, 527.
3 Roscoe, in JAI, XXXVII, 109.

4 Tremearne, in JAI, XLII, 160.
5 Coudenhove, in *Atl. Mo.*, CXXVIII, 162.
6 Czaplicka, *Aborig. Siberia*, 254.
7 Ivanovski, *Mongolei*, 4.
8 Prjevalski's *Forskningsresor*, 139, note.

father only "after deducting a large proportion for presents to the clergy."[9]
Again, "all the property which a person had in actual personal use at the time
of his death, such as clothes, boots, saddles, horses . . . goes to the lama on
his demise."[10]

In India the king receives in the first place from a Brahman the divine
sacrament of initiation; he can take nothing from the priests. All that is in
the world is in some degree the Brahman's property and he is set in the
highest earthly rank.[11] "The spirit of a deceased Brahman (man and woman)
is the most difficult of all to propitiate. A timber merchant at Calicut some
time ago spent more than a thousand rupees (over three hundred dollars) for
this purpose. He had built a new house, and on the morning after the kutti₁
pūja (house-warming) ceremony his wife and children were coming to occupy
it. Just as they entered the grounds, a cow ran against one of the children, and
knocked it down. This augured evil, and, in a few days, the child was attacked
with small-pox. One child after another caught the disease, and at last the
man's wife also got it. They all recovered, but the wife was laid up with some
uterine disease. The astrologers said that the house was once a Brahman's,
whose spirit still haunted it. It had been disturbed, and must be propitiated.
Very expensive ceremonies were performed by Brahmans for a fortnight. The
house was sold to the Brahman priest for a nominal price. An image of the
deceased Brahman was made of gold, and, after the purification ceremonies,
taken to Rāmēsvaram where arrangements were made to have daily worship
performed to it. The house, in its purified state, was sold to the maternity
hospital. The astrologer had predicted that the displeasure of the spirit would
be exhibited on the way by the breaking of dishes and by furniture catching
fire—a very strange prediction, because the bed on which the woman was lying
in the train caught fire from the engine. After the spirit had been thus propitiated, there was peace in the house."[12] The sacred thread was the sign of
priesthood, signifying a rebirth. This thread was not spun but twisted in the
fingers, in the good old primitive style.[13]

The medicine-man among the Sema Nagas "is not as a rule a man of any
social standing or personal influence, and is almost invariably poor, so
markedly so that it is generally held that a *thumomi* is unable to acquire
riches, a belief which assists credulity in the *thumomi's* impostures as it meets
the most obvious criticism as to the *thumomi's* object in deceiving. No stigma
attaches to the activities of a *thumomi* or to his practice of magic."[14] The
Nairs "never accepted the superiority of the magician, and never accorded
him any privilege. The magico-medicine man is, on the other hand, considered
to be a sort of servant-in-attendance on a noble-man's family, something like
a family doctor."[15] At funerals in Southern China, Buddhist priests or Bonzes
generally officiate; "though in general this class of Wo-shongs or Bonzes is
despised, they are quite indispensable to the people when contact with the
world of spirits is required."[16] Veth[17] calls the shamans of Borneo "harpies."

According to one writer the habits of the priests of Tonga were precisely
the same as those of other persons of the same station; and when they were

9 Rockhill, in USNM, 1893, 683.
10 Rockhill, *Mongolia*, 134, note.
11 *Law of Manu*, I, 100; VII, 130-6; IX,
189; Letourneau, *Soc.*, 501.
12 Thurston, *S. India*, 329-330.

13 Gehring, *Süd-Indien*, 59; Hopkins,
Relig. India, 518.
14 Hutton, *Sema Nagas*, 232-233.
15 Panikkar, in JAI, XLVIII, 279.
16 Rehatsek, in JASB, I, 317.
17 *Borneo's Wester-Afdeeling*, II, 251.

not inspired, the respect that was paid to them was only that which was due to their own rank. Another writer asserts that "the office of the priests was hereditary, and that their power was second only to that of the chiefs, they exercising powerful influence even over warrior chiefs. They took their rank from their gods and chiefs, the worship of the former determining in a great measure the popularity of the latter. According to Mariner, the veneration offered to a priest depended upon the rank of the god that inspired him. He says that a priest, when inspired, commanded the reverence of the whole people; if the king happened to be present he retired to a respectful distance and showed his deference by sitting down among the body of the spectators." In the Society Islands, "all the priesthood, wearers of some sacred emblem or sign, always obtained more or less veneration and respect; and everyone, even chiefs, bowed down, and dared not speak, when a priest, wearing such an emblem, passed by announcing some taboo, feast or ceremony. The priests were regarded with fear and respect, as it was known that a word or sign that displeased them involved death, for not only did they announce the sacrifices exacted by the gods, but they were believed to be able to take away life at will, the gods avenging their offended ministers in this way. . . . They had the highest authority among the people . . . referring to a famous priest of the island of Borabora, they say that he enjoyed great wealth in land, pigs, etc., and exercised a corresponding influence by power and terror, even kings and chiefs being in awe of him." On the other hand, the priest might be "only an emanation of the power of the chief—simply a delegate—in what concerned the religious ceremonies; the king was a direct descendant of the god. . . . The power of the priests of Mangaia [Hervey Islands] is indicated by the statement that ordinary people were the slaves of their warrior chiefs, and the warrior chiefs the slaves of the priesthood. All people, except the priests, sucked the milk from a coconut through the natural aperture; but for a priest the opposite end had to be knocked off, so that he might quaff freely, thus symbolizing the doctrine that the power of life and death lay with him; this symbolism was based on the idea that the nut represented the human head, and was connected with the war oracle of splitting open the nuts of Rongo, all human life being at that god's disposal. It was an unpardonable offence to offer a nut to a priest without first splitting it open. The priests of Motoro, in particular, are said to have ruled the island from the time of Rangi downward." The chief priest of Paumotu is described as being "a great person and very holy, enjoying the highest privileges. He was exempt from ordinary work; the smoke from the cooking ovens was not to touch him or come near him; the only authority superior to him was that of the king, while at times his influence was as powerful even as that of the king. . . . Passing now to the general body of priests . . . there were a great many of these. . . . They saw to the carrying out of the sacred rites, and exercised the greatest influence over the people, and the king himself submitted to the yoke of their authority, and if he tried to shake it off, they threatened him with the anger of the gods. . . . The sorcerers were simply vile charlatans, belonging to the lowest class of society, prevented by the vulgarity of their birth from aspiring to the rank of true priests, but wishing to rise above the common people in order to enjoy honours and riches. . . . They gained the favour of the masses by flattering their credulity, and so secured complete independence, even as regarded the priests, who, not wishing to attract the anger of the people to themselves, were forced to tolerate these sorcerers, and even to treat them in public with high consideration, while, among themselves, they regarded them with the utmost contempt." In Rotuma, "the priests were doctors, and their knowledge, held by families, was a mystery handed down with the office from father to son." Apparently there were different priests for different gods. In the Ellice Islands, the priest had more influence than the king because of his supposed supernatural powers. "He was consulted about the weather, and as to the attitude, favourable or otherwise, of the spirits towards proposed camping out and fishing expeditions." Finally, it is said that in Easter Island "the priests were simply wizards and sorcerers, who professed to have influence with evil spirits, and to be able to secure by incantations their co-operation in the destruction of an enemy; also that they uttered the wishes of the gods oracularly, and declared the divine requirements of human sacrifice, and subsistence by which they themselves lived."[18]

Among the Ten'a of Central Alaska, the medicine-man "is influential, feared, respected to a certain extent, receives abundant gifts from his fellow natives, but he is not loved, nay, he is strongly disliked. He may win the gratitude of patients who believe they have been cured by him; but he is always considered a dangerous person, who may at any time turn against his best friends and cause their death, either willingly and by witchcraft, or even unwillingly by the inadequate protection of his spirit. He is aware of this feeling, too, and though he generally disregards it, it weighs at times heavily upon him. He then wishes that he had never become a sorcerer. But it is too late; to renounce his profession, he would need courage enough to withstand the general discontent of the people, who, though they dislike the sorcerer, firmly believe that they are in need of his services. To them he is a necessary evil. To abdicate would be to incur the popular disgrace, and there are few Ten'a who have the strength to do so. . . . Although a medicine-man, as such, is considered to be above the common people, his ordinary life and his daily occupations in no wise differ from those of his fellow tribesmen." His gains come to him as gifts, and he always has plenty, even playing upon the credulity of the people to get what he wants; for instance, if he notices that someone has a desirable article such as a fine blanket, a valuable gun, or a new cooking-stove, he will go to the owner and confidentially warn him that "he has had sad intelligence communicated to him, concerning the said person, and this he discloses, as it were, reluctantly; the unfortunate man is doomed to die within a certain space of time, say, for instance, before the next spring." By thus scaring the person into seeking his aid, he secures the article as a gift. "Even now there are few Ten'a who will start on a long hunt, or set to work during the salmon run, without giving a bribe to the medicine-man, or at least promising him a tithe or commission on the catch. The sorcerer has not to perform any extraordinary conjuration, but just directs his spirit to give help, and if the catch is good, obtains a goodly addition to what he may get himself by his own exertions, thanks to the spirit." This trickster used to drop through a hole in the ice every year on a pretended embassy to the powers of the fish kingdom to induce them to provide for the annual catch. "Nowadays, however, the shaman no longer goes to call the salmon, and still these well-meaning fish continue to swim up the rivers every year, as well as if they responded to the yearly in-

---

18 Williamson, *Cent. Polyn.*, II, 411, 413-414, 420, 426, 436-437, 438, 439.

vitation. We should draw an inference of no small moment from this fact; a Ten'a won't."[19]

Not one of the Kwakiutl shamans names the price to be paid for a cure; a common man generally gives two pairs of blankets to the shaman, while a chief gives "as much as is proper for the greatness of his position."[20] Nor did the Cheyenne doctors set a price for their services. "When they first entered the lodge they were told what would be given them—it might be a horse or a blanket—and they doctored the patient, taking what was offered."[21] Among the Creeks, the high priests were persons of consequence and exercised great influence in the state, particularly in military affairs.[22] The Pima have always given a special burial to the priests.[23] The high priest of a confederacy of East Texas was fed and clothed, we are told, by community gifts, to insure which he sometimes preyed upon the superstition of his people. "At the house of each *caddi*, or civil chief, and of each of the other dignitaries, a special seat of honor and a bed were scrupulously reserved for the use of the *xinesi* during his visits."[24] The influence of the shamans among the Araucanians is not political, and they take no active part in the government of the tribe, save in times of tribal or national peril. They officiate as priests in the religious ceremonies of the people.[25]

Among some of the civilized peoples of antiquity, while the king ruled and commanded, he had the clergy to thank for his scepter, and woe betide him if he forgot it. In Assyria, at least, as the power of the priesthood increased, that of the king declined.[26] About the temples in Hellenistic Egypt grew up much industrial activity: trade, agriculture, cattle-breeding; and finally money-transactions were represented there.[27] The Hebrew priest was the "knowing" one, who fathomed the will of god and inclined it through sacrifice. The sacrifices and presents which he at first received as recompense for his services later became necessary to the exorcism of disease-producing daimons. In time the sacrifice for the convalescent became a duty and a tax for the deity and his priests. Because the deity revealed himself through his priests, they were in position to decide between right and wrong; for where customary law did not reach, the god decided through an oracle. In this manner the priests won influence on the administration of justice. When, later, jurisdiction was claimed by the rising kingship, they appeared, along with the prophets, as advocates of moral rights.[28] Among the sins of King Ahaz was the diverting of the brazen altar to his own offerings; King Uzziah, waxing proud, invaded the priest's office, and was smitten with leprosy.[29] In case of defilement of serious or unusual nature, the Zoroastrian could not himself undertake the ceremonies but must refer the matter to a priest. The religious observances of the priestly caste were innumerable and minute, but the virtues which they imposed upon themselves won for them unlimited influence over the minds of the people.[30]

In Greece, where the priests have any real and abiding power, they obtain it only by participating to the utmost of their ability in the spiritual prog-

19 Jetté, in JAI, XXXVII, 164-165, 167, 172-174.
20 Boas, in BAE, XXXV, pt. I, 731.
21 Grinnell, *Cheyenne*, II, 143.
22 Swanton, in HAI, II, 523.
23 Fewkes, in BAE, XXVIII, 109.
24 Bolton, in HAI, II, 981.
25 Latcham, in JAI, XXXIX, 361.

26 Tiele-Gehrich, *Gchte. Relig.*, I, 190-191.
27 Otto, *Priester*, I, 323.
28 Maurer, *Vkde.*, I, 60-61.
29 II Kings, XVI, 10-16; II Chron., XXVI, 16-21.
30 Geiger, *Ostiran. Kultur*, 261; Maspero, *Hist. Anc.*, III, 590-591, 594-595.

ress of their age, and by appropriating its results. "This is the religion of humanity in its noblest sense."[31] In the early days of Rome there was no priestly caste;[32] it came in with the oriental religions of the imperial period. The initiated were associated for mutual support in sacred gilds. The priesthood of Isis formed an aggressive and powerful caste. "The sacerdotal colleges of the Latin religion were never, except in the case of the Vestals, separated from ordinary life. The highest pontificate was held by busy laymen, by consuls or emperors or great soldiers. After the performance of his part in some great rite, the Roman priest returned to his civic place and duties." Later all this was changed. The abstinence, which was required of ordinary votaries as a preparation for communion, became a lifelong obligation on the priest. "The use of woollen garments, of wine, pork, fish, and certain vegetables, was absolutely forbidden to them. Chastity was essential in the celebrant of the holy mysteries, and even Tertullian holds up the priests of Isis as a reproachful example of continence to professing followers of Christ. The priesthood is no longer a secondary concern; it absorbs a man's whole life, sets him apart within the sanctuary as the dispenser of sacred privileges, with the awful power of revealing the mystery of eternity, and preparing souls to meet the great ordeal."[33]

Several facts show that in northern Europe the chiefs bore a more or less sacred character. In the prehistoric age they were, according to the legends, liable to be sacrificed in times of misfortune. Such was the fate of two Swedish kings, who were believed to have been responsible for famines occurring during their reigns—calamities which showed that the god was not satisfied with his representatives. Again, popular chiefs were sometimes worshipped after death. From the Norwegian evidence it is clear that from the king or earl down to the village chieftain, priestly duties were everywhere combined with temporal power. There is but one distinct reference to the existence of priestly officials at the Upsala sanctuary: "Assigned to all their gods they have priests to present the sacrifices of the people." Though these priests may have been identical with the councillors, the position of high-priest seems to have belonged properly to the king. Priestly duties are everywhere combined with temporal power; the temporal chief is both judge and sacrificial priest.[34]

Among the Tartars, silver spoons were regarded as evidence of luxury, wherefore out of respect to the clergy they might not be used in the latter's presence.[35] It is said that the Pope's collectors were the first Christian professional money-lenders.[36] The sale of indulgences, thinks Lea,[37] illustrates effectively the sacerdotalism which formed the distinguishing feature of mediæval religion. "The believer did not deal directly with his Creator— scarce even with the Virgin or hosts of intercessory saints. The supernatural powers claimed for the priest interposed him as the mediator between God and man; his bestowal or withholding of the sacraments decided the fate of immortal souls; his performance of the mass diminished or shortened the pains of purgatory; his decision in the confessional determined the very nature of sin itself." A vast hierarchy was built up, from God through saints down to demons; the priests formed a caste within it.

31 Tiele, *Sci. Relig.*, pt. I, 198.
32 Wissowa, *Relig. d. Römer*, 30, 410.
33 Dill, *Nero*, 580-583.
34 Chadwick, in *Folk-Lore*, XI, 277, 279, 280, 281, 283-284, 285.

35 Von Stenin, in *Aus allen Weltteilen*, XXIX, 64, note.
36 Ehrenberg, *Zeitalter der Fugger*, I, 44.
37 *Inquisition*, I, 47.

§322. Alleged Absence of Religion.

"The Australian aborigines do not recognize any divinity, good or evil, nor do they offer any kind of sacrifice, so far as my knowledge goes."[1] According to the observations of people who have lived a long time among the tribes of New South Wales and Queensland, it is perfectly certain that with the most of them there is no vestige of a belief in any higher superhuman being. There does exist a general belief in ghosts, in the spirits of the deceased who have not received the right order of burial or who have been bewitched by sorcerers. This the author[2] has experienced among the blacks he has known. Their fear of ghosts showed itself particularly in their unwillingness to leave the surroundings of the fireplace at night and in the fact that they strictly refrain from nocturnal hunting. Some of the more developed tribes have risen to a somewhat higher level of religious ideas. They believe in several good and bad spirits who have separate names and also separate qualities and attributes. Combined with these they possess some very simple cosmogonic ideas. A certain spirit is considered as founder of the tribe and at the same time as creator of the entire world. Probably he was originally a celebrated warrior and patriot whose ghost was soon regarded not only as a spirit or demon but as a god—a passage onward from daimonism, such as may be observed in the development of many races. "Apparently there were no idols or signs of religion, but the people believe in a Devil Devil, who comes out of the water, and goes about at night, and they are therefore afraid to do so themselves."[3] Certain of the natives, "as far as is known, have no religious belief or ceremonies. . . . They are not fond of entering upon abstruse subjects, and when they are induced to do it, it is more than possible, from our imperfect acquaintance with the language, and total ignorance of the character and bent of their thoughts upon such points, that we are very likely to misunderstand and misrepresent their real opinions. It appears to the writer that different tribes give a different account of their belief, but all generally so absurd, so vague, unsatisfactory, and contradictory, that it is impossible at present to say with any certainty what they really believe, or whether they have any independent belief at all."[4] The fact is that the Australians exhibit a crude variety of ancestor-worship.[5]

The Papuans are said to be without a conception of a god or creator and in this respect to fall in with other Melanesians.[6] The Papuan "has no idols, he has no form of worship, he offers no prayers to any god or spirit, and he has no temples. . . . To begin with, we find he believes in a spirit-world. He believes in ghosts, and his ghosts are the spirits of the dead, who return sometimes and haunt the places which were familiar to them when they lived on earth. He believes in a future life. He buries his dead in some faint hope of meeting them again. He has his charms; he practises his sorcery; he puts himself in touch with the unseen and what we call 'supernatural' powers, when sickness threatens his life and when he starts upon an expedition to attack his enemy. There is little more than this in his life which can be dignified by the name of religion."[7] He has no "real religious conception"; but he fears and

---

1 Howitt, *S. E. Aust.*, 756.
2 Semon, *Aust. Bush*, 222, 223.
3 Bassett-Smith, in JAI, XXIII, 327.
4 Eyre, *Cent. Aust.*, II, 355-356.

5 Spencer and Gillen, *North. Tr.' Cent. Aust.*, 490.
6 Hagen, *Papua's*, 264.
7 Abel, *New Guinea*, 87-88.

tries to placate the ghosts of the dead.[8] "There is no belief in a good spirit, though there are any quantity of evil ones. All dead ancestors are on the watch to deal out sickness or death to anyone who may displease them, and natives are very particular to do nothing to raise their ire."[9] Of other tribes in New Guinea it is reported that they worship nothing and make offerings only to the sorcerer. "The people are very superstitious on nearly everything, but are wonderfully free of fear, going about at night without lights or even clubs or any other weapon. . . . Their only guardian spirits are those of father and mother and to these they appeal in distress or want by land or sea."[10] Of another tribe it is said that "religion is lacking"; yet they fear, like the New Britain islanders, an evil spirit that prowls at night, and "there is no lack of all sorts of superstitions."[11] "The religious conceptions of the Papuans are crude, and their sole cult is a sort of worship of ancestors, to whose images, carved in wood, special reverence is paid."[12] In New Britain, "unless one wants to regard the . . . festivals for the dead as religion, there can be no talk of it among the contemporary natives. They possess neither idols, temples, or priests, but fear ghosts, which . . . may be in part the dead or even shooting stars. . . . There are no genuine ghost-exorcisers, but there are rain-makers, and people who exorcise illnesses."[13] Of the Andamanese, Man[14] reports: "Though no forms of worship or religious rites are to be found among them, yet there are certain beliefs regarding powers of good and evil, the Creation, and of a world beyond the grave." It is impossible to believe that the natives did not repeat to this author the things they had learned from him or others about theology. After citing certain notions that appear to be reflections of those of more developed minds, Man adds: "For all this, their belief in and dread of evil spirits is much greater; almost all sickness and death is attributed to them."

Ratzel[15] says that "the Bushmen have religious notions, but no religion in the higher sense." They all carry amulets to ward off evil spirits and get luck in their undertakings, and cast lots to find out the will of the spirits. He generalizes vaguely as to the negro, to the effect that whether or not he believes in God, he feels the need of bringing into connection with one highest being a group of notions which pertain to the supernatural. Coming to more specific evidence, we find that "the early travellers could discover no traces of religion among the Hottentots. They were believers in witchcraft and had a superstitious reverence for some insects and animals, for the moon and other heavenly bodies, for the spirits of their ancestors. Their notions of a Supreme Being were extremely vague and contradictory, and there was no belief in a future existence."[16] "The fact that their tongue possesses terms for God, spirits, and even for the Evil One, seems to show that they were not utterly ignorant in these matters, although there is nothing else available in the expressions of the language or in ceremonial usages and superstitions, that could afford proof of anything more than a rude idea of a spirit-world. . . . They have much more confidence in magical powers than in religion." Similarly with the Bushmen, who cling to superstition and magicians.[17] The Bushmen are reported as not believing in a god, but having only "great fear of the

8 Krieger, *Neu-Guinea*, 306.
9 Guise, in JAI, XXVIII, 216.
10 Chalmers, in JAI, XXVIII, 329, 334.
11 Finsch, *Ethnol. Erfahr.*, II, 337.
12 Evans, in PSM, LII, 36.

13 Finsch, *Ethnol. Erfahr.*, I, 115.
14 In JAI, XII, 156; Man, in JAI, XI, 288.
15 *Vkde.*, I, 73, 173.
16 Frere, in JAI, XI, 323.
17 Fritsch, *Eingeb. S.-Afr.*, 353, 443.

ghosts of their deceased grandparents, into the exorcism of which their whole cult ran out."[18] In reply to the question, "Do you believe in the existence of a God?" the Mavenda of South Africa answered: "Undobona linyi," "Who has seen him?" The author comments: "Although the conclusion, or belief, is not reached by any process of mental or moral reasoning, they undoubtedly are materialists, for they assert that the *monya, i.e.,* 'breath,' or 'spirit,' goes into the grave with the body, and that constitutes the end of everything. Whether the Mavenda sacrifice to appease the spirits in case of illness or domestic calamity, as is the invariable case with Zulu, I did not ascertain; but, singularly enough, in the early spring of every year some twenty or thirty head of cattle are slain under the directions of the chief, when they pray for 'peace, prosperity and plenty;' and so we find even among a people absolutely devoid of any idea of a hereafter, some vague and misty notions which connect with a spirit world."[19]

Holub[20] noticed no signs of religion among certain South African peoples, but found in one case esteem for a certain snake, in another "a kind of freemasonry," and in a third a belief in fetishes. "Previous to the introduction of Christianity, the Bechuana appear to have had only very vague religious ideas, and their attention was chiefly occupied by the detection of wizards and witches. The word Morimo for God (also used in the plural to signify the Manes of the dead) appears to have meant a great and angry personage living in 'the great hole in the north.'" They have no word for God, though they have a term for the spirit of the departed.[21] The Bantu of the southwest coast is vague on religious subjects as compared with the West African; he gives to one accustomed to the latter "the impression that he once had the same set of ideas, but has forgotten half of them, and those that he possesses have not got the hold on him that the corresponding or super-imposed Christian ideas have over the true Negro."[22]

In Angola, one people "has not the least idea of any religion whatsoever. They live with their fetishes and give no thought to the existence of a Supreme Being who directs all things." Another people have no idea of religion, "do not adore sun, moon, or idol, and live with their fetishes and divinations." They believe the soul will be troubled in the other world if due vengeance is not taken for death.[23] A belief in witchcraft may prevail, or there may seem to be "no trace of religion at all, beyond a wavering fancy that the spirits of the dead return after death."[24] In some cases hunting fetishes are employed; "otherwise there is not much to notice among them in the way of religious usages."[25] "We could not learn whether the Banziris have any elements of religion. They wear no amulets and have no visible fetishes. We observed only one sign of superstition among them. Before starting a-fishing they planted some twigs in the ground, put in the midst of them a handful of cowries, and sprinkled them with fat. The ceremony was supposed to secure an abundance of fish to the one who performed it, but I never learned to whom the sacrifice was offered."[26]

In Uganda, "the Bahima have no very clear idea of an over-ruling God, and but little definite belief in a future life on the part of any individual man or

18 Gentz, in *Globus*, LXXXIV, 159.
19 Grant, in JAI, XXXV, 270.
20 In JAI, X, 5, 7, 10.
21 Conder, in JAI, XVI, 82; Ratzel, *Vkde.*, I, 300.

22 Kingsley, *Travels W. Afr.*, 442.
23 Serpa Pinto, *Africa*, I, 108, 141.
24 Johnston, in JAI, XIII, 468.
25 Thonner, *Afr. Urwald*, 35-36.
26 Clozel, in PSM, XLIX, 675.

woman; though it is to be assumed that they believe in the spiritual continuance of chiefs and prominent personages, since they worship them as spirits. They have, however, a name for God, though, when questioned, they can only associate the overruling Power with the sky, the rain, and the thunderstorm." The Wanyoro appear not to believe in a future state.[27] The Azande have no religion but divination.[28] "The only conception which the Shillook entertain of a higher existence is limited to their reverence for a certain hero, who is called the Father of their race, and who is supposed to have conducted them to the land which they at present occupy. In case of famine, or in order that they may have rain, or reap a good harvest, they call upon him by name. They imagine of the dead that they are lingering amongst the living and still attend them. . . . The Bongo have not the remotest conception of immortality. They have no more idea of the transmigration of souls, or any doctrine of the kind, than they have of the existence of an ocean. . . . All religion in our sense of the word is quite unknown . . . and, beyond the term 'loma,' which denotes equally luck and ill-luck, they have nothing in their language to signify any deity or spiritual being. 'Loma' is likewise the term that they use for the Supreme Being, whom they hear invoked as 'Allah' by their oppressors." Evidently these people go back with singular directness to the aleatory element. The author,[29] though he is disposed to see little or no religion here, goes on to say: "Quite amazing is the fear existing among the Bongo about ghosts, whose abode is said to be in the shadowy darkness of the woods." A chief is reported to have said: "Can a dead man come out of his grave unless he is dug up?" There was here no belief in ghosts.[30] "The Jaluo religion is extremely slight. They worship the sun, and to a less extent the moon. They regard the sun as a deity seldom beneficent, more often malignant, and usually apathetic; as one of them said to the writer, 'It does not matter how much you pray, you fall sick and die just the same.' The offerings made at all important occasions in their daily life they make more with the idea of appeasing him than of obtaining positive benefits."[31] "The Suk may be said to believe in an Unknown God; that there is a belief seems certain, but it baffles description not only to the European but amongst themselves. . . . *Tororut* (the heavens) and *Ilat* (thunder and lightning) are in some fashion associated with supplication and with fear. . . . There is no ascertainable belief in a future life."[32] All negroes, according to Stuhlmann,[33] have more or less notion of a supreme being but they have no abstract conceptions, so that they never credit him with interference until they need him to explain some phenomenon for which their notions do not suffice, such as a fire in the village or a sudden death. He is the scapegoat upon whom they lay blame. They do not worship him but sacrifice in his honor after the harvest. In Ruanda religion is a superstitious fear of a higher being; amulets are worn to keep off disease and sorceresses supported to exorcise evil spirits.[34] The Abyssinians fear night and its shadows, while the Somali and others show no such fear.[35]

Among Siberian tribes "fear is the beginning of religion,"[36] and it does not get far beyond that beginning. It is reported of the Tibetan that "as to reli-

27 Johnston, *Uganda*, II, 631; Wilson and Felkin, *Uganda*, II, 47.
28 Burrows, in JAI, XXVIII, 44-45.
29 Schweinfurth, *Heart of Afr.*, I, 91, 304-305.
30 Peschel, *Races*, 259.

31 Northcote, in JAI, XXXVII, 63.
32 Barton, in JAI, LI, 88-89.
33 *Mit Emin*, 528.
34 Von Götzen, *Afr.*, 192.
35 Paulitschke, *Nordost-Afr.*, I, 246.
36 Melnikov, in *Globus*, LXXV, 133.

gious convictions, he has absolutely none, a result of the profound ignorance in which the lamas leave the people, either on account of their incapacity to teach them, or perhaps so as to keep the business of worship in their own hands, as it insures them a large revenue. The religious acts of the people are only performed through routine; they do not understand them or care to understand them; hence ignorance in the lower classes, scepticism and indifference in the others, principally among the mandarins and lamas."[37] Waddell[38] speaks of "the earlier animistic and fairy worship of the Lepchas, which can scarcely be called a religion." "On the subject of religion and a future state the Angámi appears to have no definite ideas."[39] The tribe of Bhils "is almost devoid of native religion, but is particularly noted for truth, honesty, and fidelity."[40] "The Chin is often described as a devil-worshipper. This is not correct, for he worships neither god nor devil. The northerners believe that there is no Supreme Being and although the southern Chins admit that there is a Supreme God or 'Kozin' to whom they sacrifice, they do not worship him and never look to him for any grace or mercy, except that of withholding the plagues and misfortunes which he is capable of invoking on any in this world who offend him."[41] The Angamis are said to have "practically no religion," though they recognize a supreme creator for whom they have two terms. "They also believe in the existence of evil spirits which reside in rocks, trees, and pools of water. These are usually propitiated in cases of illness by offerings of fowls, pigs, or cattle. Customs similar to these are common to the whole of the Naga and Kuki tribes within this district. Of a future state after death, their ideas are extremely vague. They certainly believe that the soul does not die with the body, but what becomes of it they cannot say, resembling in this respect more civilised nations."[42]

As is so often the case, alleged absence of religion turns out to be merely undeveloped religion, and following the principle of consistency of the mores, is associated with a general state of rudimentary development. Such is clearly the case of the Sungei Ujong in the Malay States, an isolated, unwarlike, very primitive group. A number of correlations may be discerned in the following quotation. "They possess no idea of warfare or racial strife, and freely admit their preference for a life of seclusion and peace. The Orang Bukit is born, arrives at man's estate, is married, and eventually dies, without the performance of any ceremony or rite to mark any one of the events. Marriage is merely a mutual compact entered into by the two parties concerned, and co-habitation is sufficient to acknowledge a man and woman as husband and wife. Death is treated in much the same casual way. The corpse is laid to rest on its back in a hole a few feet deep, the relatives mourning the loss for three days; but the 'mourning' consists merely of voluntary confinement to the camp. In the event of two or three deaths occurring in the same camp at short intervals, the place is deserted and a fresh camping ground is selected. They have no belief in a spiritual existence in any form after death; and, in one instance, when first questioned on the subject, it seemed to strike them as rather humorous, evoking much laughter. Of ghosts, phantoms, good and evil spirits, supernatural signs or warnings, they apparently know nothing; and I have known

37 Rockhill, in USNM, 1893, 677.
38 Tibet, 52.
39 Godden, in JAI, XXVII, 37, note.

40 Hopkins, Relig. India, 533, note 2.
41 Carey and Tuck, Chin Hills, I, 195.
42 Risley, Ethnog. India, I, 210.

many instances when, without the slightest hesitation, they have felled jungle, denounced by Malay and Chinese wood-cutters as haunted."[43] The Burmese "utterly deny, in theory at least, an intelligent and Eternal Creator, yet they distinctly recognize and apprehend future punishment for sin, or rather the violation of the Buddha's commandments."[44] The non-Buddhistic Karens of Burma totally lack "higher religious conceptions." If asked about the life after death, they say: "Concerning that we know nothing and do not think about it either." Though they know no kind of worship they fear magic above all things. Yet "need teaches prayer, for if ill-luck comes, then they remember two daimons who strike them with these woes and thereby give notice that they want to be fed."[45] In Korea there are no temples or other signs of religion. Ancestor-worship and a propitiation of daimons, the result of a timid and superstitious dread of the forces of nature, take among the Koreans the place of religion. The author[46] regards both practices as the result of fear, the worship of ancestors being dictated far less by filial piety than by the dread that their spirits may do harm. "Multitudes of Chinese will testify that the only act of religious worship which they ever perform (aside from ancestral rites) is a prostration and an offering to heaven and earth on the first and fifteenth of each moon, or, in some cases, on the beginning of each newyear. No prayer is uttered, and after a time the offering is removed, and, as in other cases, eaten. . . . There are hundreds of square miles of populous territory in China, in which there is scarcely to be seen a single priest, either Taoist or Buddhist. In these regions the traveller will generally find no women in the temple, and the children are allowed to grow up without any instruction in the necessity of propitiating the gods. In other parts of China conditions are wholly different, and the external rites of idolatry are interwoven into the smallest details of every day life." . . . One observer states: "If religion is held to mean more than mere ethics, I deny that the Chinese have a religion. They have indeed a cult, or rather a mixture of cults, but no creed; innumerable varieties of puerile idolatry, at which they are ready enough to laugh, but which they dare not disregard."[47]

The Mangyans of Mindoro, Philippine Islands, emphatically denied any belief in a future life, and said, "When a Mangyan is dead, he is *dead!*" They are said to have no words for gods and to offer no evidence of idolatry, spirit-worship, or any kind of cult. The only clew to a belief in supernatural powers found among them is the theft-ordeal, in which the hands, holding a red-hot iron, are raised to heaven.[48] The Araucanians of South America are said to be in a similar state as respects religion; their "belief is not exactly the ghost-worship of many of the tribes of North America, animism having little place in their theories. Neither do they believe that all inert objects are endowed with a spirit; considering that such objects may become temporarily the abiding place of an invisible being, but always attributing to it a concrete form. The Araucanos recognise no supreme being with definite attributes. They have no temples, no idols, no established religious cult, and no priesthood in a religious sense, although they occasionally sacrifice to one or other of their divinities, but without a fixed ritual, and only as a conciliatory or expiatory act." Yet these Indians display all sorts of ghost-fear, as the author says else-

43 Knocker, in JAI, XXXVII, 293.
44 Yule, *Ava*, 23.
45 Von Hellwald, "Karen," in Reichenow's *Handwörterbuch*, IV, 412-413.

46 Bishop, *Korea*, 61.
47 Smith, *Chin. Char.*, 291, 299, 306.
48 Worcester, *Philippine Isl.*, 412.

where, and "besides the coarse pottery used for domestic purposes, the Arau-canos make a finer kind such as is frequently found in their burying places."[49]

Ratzel[50] discusses, in his usual diffuse manner, the question whether there is any people without religion and concludes that it is the more correct con-ception that elements of religion are to be recognized in everything which be-longs to the domain of unknown causes, when men extend their thoughts and feelings beyond the things of daily life; hence he thinks there is no people without religion. The opinion presented by Brinton[51] is an exceptionally clear and positive statement from a writer whose contentions are not ordinarily so well expressed. "All statements that tribes have been discovered without any kind of religion are erroneous. Not one of them has borne the test of close in-vestigation. The usual mistake has been to suppose that this or that belief, this or that moral observance, constitutes religion. In fact, there are plenty of immoral religions and some which are atheistic. The notion of a god or gods is not essential to religion. For that matter, some of the most advanced reli-gious teachers assert that such a notion is incompatible with the highest reli-gion. Religion is simply the recognition of the unknown as a controlling ele-ment in the destiny of man and the world about him. This we shall find in the cult of every nation and in the heart of every man." The Reverend James Carmichael,[52] combating Sir John Lubbock's assertions that many if not all of the most savage races are entirely without a religion or an idea of deity, finds the original meaning of the word religion to be "that of binding fast the human mind to a sense of the obligation which it owes to supernatural powers." He then goes on to say that "the most indefinite belief may—and indeed, as a rule, does—lead a savage to fashion his conduct in accordance with what he believes to be the will of higher powers; as far as personal actions are con-cerned, he stands on exactly the same platform as the most devoted believer in natural or revealed religion." Says Quatrefages:[53] "When the lowest savage admits the existence of a superior Being whom he regards as the agent of the good or ill which he experiences, when he addresses prayers and homage to that Being, when he conforms to certain rules which he thinks have been established by that Being, it is impossible for me not see in that *faith* and in those *acts* so many facts identical at bottom with those which, as we know, are produced among Christians. If then the latter have a religion, the savage also has one."

§324. Conservatism of Religion.

THE use of ancient instruments and methods, despite knowledge of more modern ones, the employment of archaic language and ceremonies, and the punishment of variants from established custom are the main forms of the conservatism of religion illustrated in the cases which follow.

In Central Australia a special stone knife is used "exclusively for surgical work, circumcision, subincision, for the making of the marks on the chest and back, or for opening veins."[1] Being old it is holy. In the Island of Tikopia, "when a yam is prepared for eating the skin is always removed with a shell. Similarly, the taro is sacred to the Taumako who regards the eye of the tuber as especially the *atua* [spirit], and they also have an objection to

49 Latcham, in JAI, XXXIX, 340, 345.
50 *Vkde.*, I, 31; Quatrefages, *Hist.*, 254.
51 *Races*, 67.

52 "Relig. of Savages," in PSM, XLVIII, 220, 221.
53 *Hist.*, 255.
1 Horne and Aiston, *Cent. Aust.*, 88.

the use of a knife in preparing the plant for food. The Tafua have the coconut as their *atua* and again will not have it opened with a knife but use a stone."2 In the D'Entrecasteaux Islands, "many songs are quite unintelligible even to their singers. They have been handed down from one generation to another, often incorporating words that have long gone out of use; or they have been brought from some other place and the clue to their meaning has not been transmitted with them. Often, too, they are changed and mutilated in the transfer, especially if the dialects are somewhat different. Topical allusions of course soon cease to carry any meaning."3

In South Africa, "the Masarwas practise circumcision according to the Bechuana mode of performing the rite, usually with a stone knife. They circumcise the boys when they are about twelve or fourteen years of age. I inquired if they had the practice independent of the Bechuanas, and the reply was in the affirmative."4 Among the Ba-Yaka, all food is cooked except in time of famine, when manioc is eaten raw.5 This is probably propitiatory. It is necessary for the investigator among the Fan to have a profound knowledge of their language, and not only the actual language but also the archaic, for the latter is almost always employed in their chants. "One finds there a number of words and expressions which have today fallen into desuetude; moreover, one must know the hieratic language, where a certain number of words are diverted from their usual meaning so as not to be understood by the non-initiated. When one does not combine these three conditions—a profound knowledge of the language, of the archaic words, and of the hieratic speech— it is easy to remain unaware of a number of cult facts and, consequently, sometimes to deny even their existence, through a regrettable misapprehension. Finally, the situation is complex for a third reason. The Fan does not like to talk about his religion, rites, or cult. If you are 'initiated,' your questions are idle. If you are not, what is the use?"6

Weeks7 points out in a significant statement how the religious beliefs of the Bangala put an effective check on the acquisition of new ideas; by way of contrast, in the field of self-maintenance they are rather alert to see the advantages of superior articles. "The natives are quick to imitate where imitation is possible. . . . No sooner did they perceive the advantages possessed by our larger houses over their huts, than they began to build houses of three rooms, and made tables, chairs, forms, cupboards and bedsteads. They saw the advantages of a hammock chair over their uncomfortable wooden stools, and imitated it. We exchanged tools, screws, nails, hinges, etc., for fowls." Now observe the other side of the picture. "Some twenty-five years ago I knew a blacksmith who made a very good imitation, from old hoop iron, of a trade knife, and when the king heard of it he thought he was too clever and threatened him with a charge of witchcraft if he made any more like it. If the man who made our locomotives had lived here, in Africa, and had given play to his inventive genius, he would not have been honoured, but killed as a witch. The native had a deep-rooted feeling that anything out of the ordinary was due to witchcraft and treated it as such. Some years ago I knew a native medicine woman who was successful in treating certain native diseases, and as she

2 Rivers, *Melan Soc.*, I, 317-318.
3 Jenness and Ballentyne, *D'Entrecas-teaux*, 166.
4 Dornan, in JAI, XLVII, 50.
5 Torday and Joyce, in JAI, XXXVI, 42.
6 Trilles, *Fân*, 80-81.
7 In JAI, XXXIX, 108, 135.

became wealthy, the natives accused her of giving the sickness by witchcraft in order to cure it and be paid for it; for they said, 'How can she cure it so easily unless she first gave it to them?' She had to abandon her practice or she would have been killed as a witch. . . . Through this fear of being charged with witchcraft, the natives would never of themselves have made any progress in art, science or civilisation. This fear was so real and so widespread that it stultified and killed every tendency to change and progress. . . . For generations it has been the custom to charge with witchcraft anyone who has commenced a new industry or discovered a new article of barter. The making of anything out of the ordinary has brought on the maker a charge of witchcraft that again and again has resulted in death by the ordeal. To know more than others, to be more skilful than others, energetic, more cute in business, more smart in dress has always caused a charge of witchcraft and death. Therefore the native, to save his life and live in peace, has smothered his inventive faculty and choked all initiative skill." Among Kikuyu and Kamba beliefs is that of purification of woman by a decoction composed of the fat and meat of a slain animal cooked in a pot "with some bitter herbs."[8]

Furness[9] once tried to persuade the old tattooer of a Naga village to accept some fine needles as substitutes for the thorns she used, but "she maintained that although they might be all right for white people, their use would surely make Nagas sick. Very probably she was right and spoke from experience; without proper care rust would soon collect on them, and then blood poisoning would inevitably follow." A custom which this writer found constant throughout Borneo and the Naga hills, on all ceremonious occasions when fire is necessary, is that of making new-fire by means of the fire-saw. "When a new house is built, it is by this method alone that the fire may be started, and when a family goes out of mourning for a dead relative the first food cooked must be prepared over a fire started by this method. It is probably the most primitive process for obtaining fire, and on this account looked upon as the invention of the demigods who were ancestors of all mankind, and therefore sacred. It is a striking instance of the tendency to return to the primeval in all ceremonials." Among the Palaungs, "It is very important that when the fire is lighted for the burning of the dry jungle, only flint and steel should be used. Were matches used, the Palaungs fear that they would not be able to control the fire, as it would spread so rapidly that jungle on ground not required for the paddy would also take fire."[10] Similar examples may be found in an earlier paragraph on fire and religion.[11] At a feast in Assam, "villagers do not use their bamboo cups or bowls to drink from but make cups from leaves."[12] "Nothing shows so much the extreme persistence of primitive culture, even in the face of higher civilising agencies, than the wide and almost universal acceptance of spirit-worship, and the almost entire absence of religious life among the Nāyars after at least twenty centuries of contact with Hinduism. . . . Yet, with all the great religions of the world to choose between during the last two thousand years, it is nothing short of marvellous to see the Nāyars, who have, it must be remembered, assimilated a very great deal of the material and intellectual culture of their neighbours, and, more than that, excelled them in literature and music, still maintain with undiminished vigour their

---

8 Hobley, in JAI, XLI, 425.
9 In JAI, XXXII, 456, 466.
10 Milne, *Eastern Clan*, 224

11 §92 of the text and *Case-Book*.
12 Hodson, in JAI, XXXVI, 98.

spirit-worship, black-magic, and demoniacal ceremonies, and are devoid of almost every element of true religious life."[13]

In common with other tribes, the Omaha conserved in his religious ceremonies those articles which had contributed to the betterment of the people in their long, slow struggle upward. "One of the earliest, if not the earliest, garment which served to protect the body from cold and storm seems to have been the unfashioned hide. This garment retained the semblance of the animal and the comfort the skin contributed to the body seems to have served to increase the native confidence in the close relation he conceived to exist between all other visible forms and himself. Although in later times his ordinary clothing ceased to exemplify this close relation, yet when the Omaha entered on sacred ceremonies with the desire of securing supernatural aid there was a return in his apparel to the primitive form. . . . Many of the mythic stories found among this group of cognate tribes are in some of their details obscene, a characteristic for which no adequate explanation is to be found in the daily life and customs of the people or in the rites as practised during recent centuries. Offensive as some of these stories are, they often exhibit a titanic audacity that gives to them a kind of grotesque dignity. Even mythic stories of this class may also be survivals, which have suffered not only from the wear and tear of ages but from accretions of minds not of the highest type. Natural functions have demanded explanation, and in the absence of teaching based on knowledge of physical laws, man's fancy here as in the world around has run riot. Among all peoples there is an undercurrent of indecent stories that show a strange kinship and that may have a common psychical origin. . . . An interesting example of the conservation, in ceremonies, of early types of useful articles is found in the requirement that one of the gifts essential in the rite of tattooing was a number of the strong, red-handled knives of the kind first known to the tribe. . . . The lock of hair taken from the head of the male child when he was consecrated to Thunder was cut by a flint knife; only a flint knife could be used when bleeding for curative purposes. . . . The stone implements connected with the daily needs of the people were the first to be displaced by iron ones."[14]

Persistence of old religious forms is seen in the rites of tribes that have been converted to Christianity: "The Iowa and Winnebago both use the Bible as a sacred object, placing it near the sacred peyote, and include in the service Bible reading, sermons, confessionals and prayers as well as songs with a Christian flavor. In fact, the Iowa ceremony . . . bears some resemblance to a revival meeting. After the initial eating of the peyote and a round of singing, while incense is burned on the fire, the leader reads the Bible and preaches and then calls upon the members to confess their sins and repent, in response to which the members rise and testify that they have given up such habits as drinking, smoking, or chewing. . . . The use of the Bible and the Christian interpretation of ancient symbols represents a second accretion, and usually entails no serious change in the ritual. The prayers once made to the Indian spirits are redirected to the Christian God. The Bible is added and Bible reading introduced. The talks become sermons. The songs are patterned after Christian hymns."[15] Among the Jibaro Indians, in one of their important reli-

13 Panikkar, in JAI, XLVIII, 277-278.   15 Shonle, in AA, XXVII, 67, 69-70.
14 Fletcher and LaFlesche, in BAE, XXVII, 357, 600-601, 613, 614.

gious ceremonies, "a number of short formulas are repeated, the exact meaning of which seems to be unknown even to the dancing Indians themselves. We are here dealing with an archaic or ceremonial language which, at the most, is understood by some of the oldest Indians."[16]

§325. Religion Is Evolutionary.

THERE is said to be much in the religion of Mahomet which appeals to the African and suits his conditions. "It sanctions polygamy, which is natural to the tropics. It not merely approves the institution of domestic slavery, but has done much harm by countenancing the ruthless raiding for slaves. It has the attraction of an indigenous religion spread by the people themselves, or by men of like race with similar social standards, and not depending on the supervision of alien teachers. Its great strength lies in the fact that it combines a social code with simple religious forms, and is thus interwoven with the daily life of its followers. Originating in the tropics, it is essentially a code and a religion of the tropics, which has never made headway in the temperate zones, just as Christianity has been the religion of the temperate climates. . . . Christianity, on the other hand, has not proved so powerful an influence for the creation of political and social organisations. . . . Christianity is, I think, sometimes apt to produce in its converts an attitude of intolerance, not intended by its teachers, towards native rulers, native customs, and even to native dress, especially when wholesale conversions have overtaxed the supervision of the European mission staff."[1] In a word, it is all a question of adaptation. A writer on East Africa warns us: "The fact must not be lost sight of that, in the vast majority of cases where an up-country native embraces Islam, his conversion begins and ends with the rite of circumcision."[2]

If Christianity is not tolerant, the religions of Asia are. "Among the yellow races . . . it was never considered necessary to kill your neighbour because he differed from you in his religious beliefs, unless these threatened the security of the State; and in Japan we have what is to most Europeans the puzzling phenomenon of two religions, which might be expected to be mutually exclusive, professed at the same time by the same individuals. Shintoism, the State religion, is a development of animism, which in Japan has never quite fallen to the disreputable position occupied by animism in Burma. It is now honoured by the State as the official wife, whereas in Burma animism is a mere concubine. But a concubine is often powerful, and the cult, with its thousands of years of life behind it, is so ingrained in the nature and instincts of the people that even their Buddhism, real and deep as it is, has never been able to kill it."[3]

There are a number of striking parallels between evolved and simple religions. In the natural religion and folk-lore of the natives of the Malay Peninsula occur "world-cataclysms" such as the Flood, and other parallelisms.[4] The Samoans have a Jonah: "One of their people, they say, fell into the sea, and was immediately swallowed by a *whale*. After a time the projecting pieces of wood, which he wore horizontally as earrings, pricked the inside of the whale

---

16 Karsten, "Jibaro," in BAE, Bull. LXXIX, 54.
1 Lugard, *Brit. Trop. Africa*, 77-78.
2 Dundas, K., in JAI, XLIII, 58.

3 Brown, in JAI, XLV, 355-356.
4 Skeat and Blagden, *Malay Penin.*, II, 186.

and made it vomit him forth again. He was still alive, but as he walked up from the beach he was thin and weak! . . . A story is told at Vate of a man who was standing on a projecting rock out at the reef, and amusing himself by whistling on his bamboo fife. A large fish came and swallowed him up, fife and all. He split up the bamboo flute, made a knife of it, and commenced cutting the inside of the monster. It died, floated ashore, and the man got out alive."[5]

Astonishment has been expressed by some writers at the resemblance between the institutions of the American Indians and those of ancient Rome and the modern Catholic Church. "The Spanish conquerors of America, good Catholics as they were and innocent of any knowledge of comparative religion, were nevertheless made curious by the likenesses between the Old and the New World religions. Unfortunately their embryonic studies in religious anthropology were curtailed by the pious conclusion that the Devil had been masquerading in the New World. This complacent theory quelled their wonder over the likeness, among others, between Peruvian Sun-bride, Roman Vestal, and Christian nun. Perhaps their naïveté is hardly to be criticized when three centuries later it is merely re-expressed by their nineteenth century compiler."[6]

It is a question to what extent primitive people may actually take on a more evolved religion; normally the old beliefs merely persist under a new form. Of the Araucanians it is reported that Christianity "has made little headway among them, probably because they cannot even conceive of, much less understand, the principal dogmas and tenets of a highly developed religion. The stories of numerous converts are inexplicable to one who has probed the Indian's mode of thought and state of intellect. At most they can be only nominally Christians, accepting certain moral ideas and outward forms, such as baptism, crosses in their burial grounds, etc., and all that appeals to the senses, but in the real bases of their ideas they are as pagan as they were three centuries ago. As a proof of this I have seen sacrifices made during a dry season to *Nguruvilu,* the god of rain, by nominal Christians at less than half a mile distance from the Quino mission. It is also shown by their adhering to their old burial customs. They would never consent to the Spanish mode of burial, alleging that to do so would be to leave their dead without resources for their journey to the other world. It seems to be a futile task to engraft an intensely spiritual religion on a mind that is entirely materialistic, as it only leads from one form of paganism to another. Not that missionary work should be discouraged, on the contrary it is of the highest benefit when properly undertaken, but the only immediate results are from material and moral teaching, and only after long generations can we hope to find practical results from a strictly religious point of view."[7]

§334. The Making of Marriage.

IN Central Australia, a native exhibiting an abnormal craving for sexual intercourse is held in much contempt.[1] Among the Papuans, the sex-function is regarded as not different from eating, sleeping, and other functions of the body. No secret is made of it and there is no sense of propriety in respect to

5 Turner, *Samoa,* 331, 337.
6 Prescott, *Conq. of Peru,* I, 114-115; Main, *Relig. Chastity,* 175.

7 Latcham, in JAI, XXXIX, 348-349.
1 Spencer and Gillen, *Nat. Tr. Cent. Aust.,* 471.

it. Yet the women are as chaste as European females, "wed in artificial prudery and hypocrisy."[2]

There is considerable uncertainty about the whole matter of impregnation and birth. "On the very rare occasions on which the child is born at a very premature stage as the result of an accident, nothing will persuade them that it is an undeveloped human being; they are perfectly convinced that it is the young of some other animal, such as the kangaroo, which has by some mistake got inside the woman."[3] Madame Pommerol[4] states that she was once taken to be a man, in spite of her female costume, because the native women were convinced that "the female species existed only among the Saharan races." The women eyed her fearfully, as if in the presence of an unknown animal.

As respects conception otherwise than by sex-union, several examples additional to those cited in the text may be given. In Australia, "when a woman conceives, her condition is said to be due to the action of some particular member of her tribe, who is spoken of as the *wororu* of the child after it is born. If a man of the right relationship gives a woman some food and after eating it she becomes pregnant, this man becomes the *wororu* of the woman's child. Sometimes the *wororu* does not give the woman food to eat, but when he is hunting and has speared a kangaroo or an emu, as he is killing it he speaks to the spirit of the kangaroo and tells it to go to a certain woman. The spirit of the kangaroo follows the man home to the camp and goes inside the woman indicated, who thereby becomes pregnant."[5] Fox[6] thinks the physical fact of fatherhood is probably recognized now in San Cristoval; "but there are certainly a number of facts on the other side; and the embryo . . . is said to be put into the womb of women by an *adaro*" or ghost. The African Pygmies believe that impregnation eventuates from the sucking of a certain grass-stalk.[7] Among the Hausa, "according to the folk-lore a woman can conceive by swallowing. Thus, a man who had transformed himself into an iguana so as to be eaten by a girl whom he desired, caused her to bring forth a son like him. In another tale a cow eats flowers, which are really children, and later on they are born and become children again. If a woman wishes to have a son like her husband, she will kneel over him while asleep and take seven sips from a cup of water while in that position, making her request each time either to Allah or to the bori [spirits], according as to whether a *mallam* (priest) or a *boka* (medicine-man) has directed the proceedings."[8] This last item is significant of the distinction between priest and shaman.

Wilken's[9] editor, Ossenbruggen, cites several sources, in particular Hartland's *Primitive Paternity*, upon the subject of ignorance of the causes of conception.

§342. Normality of Marriage.

In Tikopia Island, Melanesia, by exception, "many people never marry. Children call the unmarried sister of their mother . . . 'my mother unmarried' . . . and such a woman will help her married sister to look after her children and

2 Maclay, quoted by Wilken, in VG, I, 163.
3 Spencer and Gillen, *Nat. Tr. Cent. Aust.*, 52.
4 *Sahariennes*, 400-401.
5 Brown, in JAI, XLIII, 168.
6 In JAI, XLIX, 119.

7 Quatrefages, *Pygmies*, 213 (quoted in Dowd, *Negro Races*, I, 57).
8 Tremearne, in JAI, XLV, 32.
9 In VG, I, 228, and *Register*, sub "bevruchting"; Johnson, *Lucina sine concubitu* (a letter addressed to the Royal Society, 1750).

will take care of them when the mother goes out to work."[1] In East Africa there is a "large number of unmarried adults in many of the villages"; yet the females do not outnumber the males, as the author[2] had at first inferred. Much more normal are the following cases. In Nyasaland, "marriages between natives are essentially *mariages de convenance,* and sentiment rarely plays a part in them. But it is an ill wind that blows no one any good, and the great advantage connected with this materialistic attitude lies in the fact that enforced celibacy is practically nonexistent among natives."[3] Again, "celibacy is rare, in fact only the result of poverty or ugliness amounting to deformity."[4] In East Africa, "a widowed woman is very rarely, excepting in the case of the big wife, left unmated. . . . Spinsters are, so far as I know, non-existent, and bachelors are very rare; I have, in fact, hitherto only heard of one or two in the whole country."[5] Serpa Pinto[6] relates the custom of asking in marriage the daughter of a pregnant woman. If a girl is born, the suitor must provide clothing for mother and child up to the latter's puberty, that is, age of marriage. It is a usage of rich people. If the child is a boy, the suitor must clothe mother and son.

In ancient Indo-Aryan usage, it is conceived to be a sin if a marriageable maiden remains unmarried; such delay amounted, as it were, to contraception. Girls were betrothed early so as to pass to the husband at puberty.[7] This explains to some degree the custom of child-marriage. In China, by the "complete luck-blessing" is understood in the case of woman the possession of husband, sons, virtue, and long life; in the case of man, a wife, property, sons, and grandsons.[8] The conviction of the normality and even necessity of marriage leads to unions of the dead. "In the northern parts of the Realm it is customary, when an unmarried youth and an unmarried girl breathe their last, that the two families each charge a match-maker to demand the other party in marriage. Such go-betweens are called match-makers for disembodied souls. They acquaint the two families with each other's circumstances, and then cast lots for the marriage by order of the parents on both sides. If they augur that the union will be a happy one, (wedding) garments for the next world are cut out and the match-makers repair to the grave of the lad, there to set out wine and fruit for the consummation of the marriage. Two seats are placed side by side, and a small streamer is set up near each seat. If these streamers move a little after the libation has been performed, the souls are believed to approach each other; but if one of them does not move, the party represented thereby is considered to disapprove of the marriage. . . . Such go-betweens make a regular livelihood out of these proceedings. . . . Posthumous marriages are peculiarly interesting as showing that the almost unlimited power of parents in choosing wives or husbands for their children does not cease to exist even when the latter have been removed to the Realms of Death, so that in fact children are there subject to the will of their parents."[9] It was, in fact, ancestor-worship that led the Chinese to marry their children off when very young. This caused population to be excessive and kept the vast majority of the people on the verge of famine.[10] Early marriages caused the disability

1 Rivers, *Melan. Soc.*, I, 346.
2 Hobley, in JAI, XXXIII, 354.
3 Coudenhove, in *Atl. Mo.*, CXXXII, 188.
4 Torday and Joyce, in JAI, XXXV, 411.
5 Dundas, C., in JAI, XLIII, 521.
6 *Africa*, I, 116.

7 Jolly, in *Grundr. Indo-Ar. Phil.*, II, 55; and in *Sitzgsber. Münch. Akad. Philos. Philol.*, 425.
8 Grube, in *Berl. Mus.* VII, 17.
9 DeGroot, *Relig. Syst.*, II, 804-805, 806.
10 Smith, *Chinese Char.*, 188, 195.

to marriage known as "disparity of position on the family tree," which debarred a man from marrying a kinswoman or connection of any generation senior or junior to his own. "It is by no means an unusual thing for a woman to have a sister 30 or 40 years younger than herself, and supposing her to marry at 15, and her son at 16, the fact of her grandson being able to marry her sister becomes easy of credit."[11] In China, as in India, occurs the so-called "rearing-marriage" by which "the girl is made over to the family into which she is to be married, and is by that family brought up and married whenever their convenience dictates."[12] Formerly among the Osetins the boy married at eight if he could pay for a wife, but the Russian government forbade this, and the limit is now fourteen. As soon as the Cheremis boy is sixteen or seventeen betrothal and wedding are in order. The Crimean Tatar girls marry at fifteen or even thirteen. With these instances may be joined the statement that "in Russia the natural labor unit, if I may use such a term, comprises a man, a woman, and a horse. As soon therefore as a boy becomes an able-bodied labourer he ought to be provided with the two accessories necessary for the completion of the labor unit." Hence the early marriages.[13] Among the Trans-caucasion Armenians, betrothals of children at the breast or even unborn children are common, "in order to forge a firm bond between the two families."[14]

Wilken,[15] in an article on "Defloration in Child-marriages," cites a number of cases of such early unions. Girls are married to old men for the sake of protection against seizure by agents of the ruler. Puberty is said to appear before the age of ten, a number of cases in evidence being cited. In Sarawak, as the children grow up they are encouraged to associate with one another and presently "the parents no longer hesitate to allow them their own fire-place,"[16] that is, their domestic establishment.[17] Little girls are sometimes married to older men; Jacobs[18] knew a girl of about thirteen, and not nearly full-grown, who was already the repudiated wife of a third husband. This was not a rare case. The consequence is that a wife of twenty-five who has had two or three children is already an old woman.

An Eskimo marriage is stable only after there is a child, but children are delayed because they marry before they are full-grown.[19] Turner[20] knew of girls of thirteen and fourteen having children. Child-betrothals are found, and even ante-natal arrangements; the boy goes to the girl's family and when she reaches puberty, after a taboo of a month, he enjoys the rights of a family-head.[21] Among the Tlinkits "there are no old maids . . . nor do widows long remain such. It is considered a disgrace for a girl to remain many months without being married after she becomes a woman."[22] Among certain Indians there is a sort of "rearing-marriage."[23] In British Guiana the girl becomes a wife at ten, and at twenty loses all charm; the author[24] saw mothers of eleven or twelve with children a year or two old.

Says Seymour[25] of the Homeric period: "Of course the normal state of

11 Medhurst, in *Trans. China Br. Roy. Asiat. Soc.*, IV, 22.

12 *North Chinese Herald*, in JASB, II, 221; Nivedita, *Indian Life*, 35.

13 *Russ. Ethnog.* (Russ.), II, 356, 358, 90; Wallace, *Russia*, 85-86.

14 Von Seidlitz, in *Globus*, LXXVIII, 243.

15 In VG, I, 613 ff.

16 Roth, *Sarawak*, II, clxxix.

17 §90, of the text.

18 *Groot-Atjeh*, I, 27, 80, 87, 112; Nieuwenhuis, *Borneo*, II, 276-277.

19 Holm, *Ethnol. Skizze*, 52.

20 In BAE, XI, 188.

21 Nelson, in BAE, XVIII, pt. I, 291-292.

22 Jones, *Thlingets*, 126.

23 Wickham, quoted in JAI, XXIV, 205.

24 Schomburgk, *Brit. Guiana*, I, 122, 123, 164.

25 *Hom. Age*, 242.

woman in such a civilization is in the marriage relation. No arrangement is made for her except as part of a family, and on her marriage she becomes a member of her husband's family. She has no property of her own, because she needs none." The feeling of the later Greeks is expressed by Antigone in her lament concerning her unmarried state.[26] We are told that mere children were affianced in ancient Rome.[27] Roman citizens were exhorted by the censor to marry, although marriage is represented as a necessary evil.[28] Furnivall[29] has collected more modern cases of child-betrothal, and regards property-arrangements as the main cause, with the desire to evade the feudal law of the sovereign's guardianship—which amounts to a tax or fine. In Montenegro children are betrothed shortly after birth and married at thirteen or fourteen;[30] and a similar situation prevails among certain Jews of southern Algiers.[31]

Says Starcke:[32] "The unmarried whether man or woman are and must always remain the exception, and they must accept whatever is arranged for them. It would be impossible for their sakes to imperil all which the experience of a thousand years has shown to be the best means of promoting the development of those aspects of human life which are the most productive of happiness. The movement for the emancipation of women has not always been mindful of this general law."

§343. Rudimentary Regulation.

THE Dokos of Abyssinia are reported to lack, along with the use of fire, also marriage and the family.[1] Wolff[2] has the novel idea that peoples who were formerly free with their women, in the matter of lending them, as did several Siberian tribes, gave up the custom with the increasing menace of sex-disease. The Eastern Finns had loose forms of address which did not distinguish between boy and son, woman and wife, etc. "Professor Smirnov maintains that these facts can only be explained by assuming the existence of communal marriage or general hetairism as the basis of the family, and presupposes a state of society in which every adult woman of a group was the concubine or potential wife of every adult man in it; the children being children of the group, no distinction could be drawn between boy and son, girl and daughter, woman and wife."[3] Such inferences must be taken with reservation. The sharp concept of a child of a pair was a relatively late development among the Yakuts; such a conception has never yet got a name except through the use of the Russian words. Even now the kin-group claims authority over all children in certain respects and under certain contingencies.[4] Wilutzky[5] cites from India an ancient law-book according to which a bride is given over, not to an individual man but to his whole family.

A case of what may be taken as "expiation for marriage" is reported of the Todas. This people is divided into two strata or classes between which there are reciprocal duties. "Certain ceremonies are performed shortly before the girl

26 Sophocles, *Antigone*, 860 ff.
27 Gregorovius, *Lucretia Borgia*, 38; Gubernatis, *Usi Nuz.*, 50, note.
28 *Aulus Gellius*, I, 6, quoted by Jolly, *Seconds Mariages*, 38.
29 *Child Marriages*, 56, xxvii ff., xlii-xliii.
30 Simkhovitsch, *Russland*, 359.

31 Casanowicz, in AA, VII, 357-358.
32 *Prim. Fam.*, 272.
1 Wilken, in VG, I, 228.
2 In *Umschau*, V, 643.
3 Abercromby, *Finns*, I, 184.
4 Sieroshevski, *Yakuts* (Russ.), 559 ff.
5 *Mann u. Weib*, 79.

reaches the age of puberty. One is called . . . 'mantle over he puts,' in which a man belonging to the Tartharol if the girl is Teivali, or to the Teivaliol if she is Tarthar, comes in the day-time to the village of the girl and lying down beside her puts his mantle over her so that it covers both and remains there for a few minutes. Fourteen or fifteen days later a man of strong physique, who may belong to either division and to any clan, except that of the girl, comes and stays in the village for one night and has intercourse with the girl. This must take place before puberty, and it seemed that there were few things regarded as more disgraceful than that this ceremony should be delayed till after this period. It might be a subject of reproach and abuse for the remainder of the woman's life, and it was even said that men might refuse to marry her if this ceremony had not been performed at the proper time."[6] "Miklucho-Maclay heard from Malays and members of the Catholic Mission at Malacca that communal marriage existed among the Sakai. . . . Some days or weeks after marriage the girl was said to leave her husband with his consent and take up with the men of his family in turn. She then came back to her husband, but kept up these irregular liaisons, which were regulated by chance and her own wishes."[7] Wilken[8] lists a number of tribes in the Archipelago which, it was alleged, lived in a marriageless state; "the Semang women, like those of the ancient Massagetae, . . . are said to be in common like their other property."

Rivers[9] finds the traditional accounts of a condition approaching promiscuity, in Hawaii, to be rather doubtful; but he states that "side by side with the presence of individual marriage as a social institution there existed, especially among the chiefs, a state of very general laxity, while the claims of the chiefs on the women of the ordinary people (and of the women of chiefly rank on the men of the lower class) extended this laxity to the relations of the whole community. Part of this laxity was due to the existence of certain definite institutions. One was the claim which a chief had over the virgins of his district, a right allied to that of the *jus primæ noctis*, which appears to have existed in the Hawaiian Islands, but without the limitation which is implied in the title of that right. Another and more important institution is that of the *punulua*. There existed among the Hawaiians a definite system of cicisbeism in which the paramour had a recognised status. Of these paramours those who would seem to have had the most definite status were certain relatives, viz., the brothers of the husband and the sisters of the wife. These formed a group within which all the males had marital rights over all the females."

Among the Eskimo to the west of Hudson Bay free love is reported to have been universal, there being no marriage-rites and no divorce.[10] By others of the Eskimo "promiscuous intercourse between married or unmarried people, or even among children, appears to have been looked upon simply as a matter for amusement."[11] Among the Aleuts, "promiscuity and the most bestial practices obtain."[12] One writer[13] generalizes concerning the North American Indians, asserting that "the traces of communal marriage appear everywhere," while another[14] thinks that promiscuous sex-relations occur occasionally in a

6 Rivers, *Todas*, 503 ff.
7 Skeat and Blagden, *Malay Penin.*, II, 56.
8 In VG, I, 107, 415-416, 600.
9 *Melan. Soc.*, I, 386-387.
10 Hanbury, *Canada*, 69.

11 Murdoch, in BAE, IX, 419.
12 Niblack, in USNM, 1888, 240.
13 Bernhöft, *Verwandsftsnamen*, 62, 15-16.
14 Hrdlička, in BAE, Bull. XXXIV, 47.

few tribes. Of one Athapascan tribe it is reported that they "take and divorce their wives at pleasure, there being no marriage ceremony among them. Although the men outnumber the women, polygyny is common among them."[15]

Among the Apaches, at times there was outright promiscuity.[16] Certain California Indians "may be said to set up and dissolve the conjugal state about as easily as do the beasts";[17] the early Spanish missionaries found there no word for marriage, which fact seemed to correspond to the actuality of things.[18] In the Sia community there was an indiscriminate living-together of the sexes.[19] The Botocudos are said to have no regular alliances, though they "have advanced beyond the stage of promiscuous intercourse";[20] they show, says another writer,[21] "commercialism of wives or a changing concubinage." Von Martius[22] states categorically of one South American tribe that "the chief has *jus primæ noctis.*" Fitzroy[23] thought that parties of Fuegians "lived in a promiscuous manner—a few women being with many men."

The Chinese annals record that men once lived like beasts and women were in common; children never knew their fathers, but only their mothers. Then the Emperor instituted marriage.[24] In an argument against the Babylonian gods we read: "The women also with cords about them [to form lanes between them by which men passed to select] sit in the ways burning bran for incense, but if any of them, drawn by some man that passeth by lie with him, she reproacheth her fellow that she was not thought as worthy as herself."[25] The legend ran that in ancient Athens there was no regulated marriage, but that Cecrops introduced individual unions. Before that, connection had been random and wives held in common.[26] This condition was later ridiculed by the comedians.[27] The Ichthyophagi of the south Asian coast were believed to have women and children in common, like cattle; all notions of decency and shame were foreign to them.[28] Of the Massagetæ, it is reported that each man had a wife, but she was free to all. When a man wanted a woman he indicated it by a conventional act and had her without ceremony. The Agathyrsi, along the Carpathians, are reported to be all related to each other, and to have their women in common, while the Garamantes lived in "promiscuous concubinage with their women."[29] Strabo[30] reports communalism in women in Arabia. The Galaktophagi had women and property in common, and their terms for father, son, and brother are explained[31] as equivalent to older, younger, and contemporary. Tyrrhenian children were brought up in common, as the parents were unknown, and the ancient Etruscans had a similar communalism.[32]

Says Gomme,[33] concerning these cases of loose regulation, or even of absence of regulation: "Just as there is no excuse for calling this system of temporary

15 In HAI, II, 1009.
16 Reclus, *Prim. Folk*, 130.
17 Powers, in *Contrib. N. Amer. Ethnol.*, III, 317, 238.
18 Baegert, in *Smithson. Rept.*, 1863, 368.
19 Stevenson in BAE, XI, 75.
20 Keane, in JAI, XIII, 206.
21 Von Martius, *Beiträge*, I, 322.
22 *Beiträge*, I, 485.
23 *Adventure and Beagle*, II, 182.
24 Westermarck, *Marriage*, I, 105; Puini, *Civiltà*, 34.

25 *Baruch*, VI, 43; Maspero, *Hist. Anc.*, I, 639.
26 Athenæus, *Deipnosophists*, XIII, 1; Wilutsky, *Mann u. Weib*, 17.
27 Bruns, *Frauenemancipation in Athen*, 22.
28 Diodorus, *Hist. Libr.*, III, ch. I.
29 Herodotus, *Hist.*, I, 216; IV, 172, 104; Pliny, *Nat. Hist.*, V. 8.
30 *Geog.*, XVI, 4, 25.
31 By Nicholas of Damascus, quoted by Lippert, *Kgchte.*, II, 18.
32 Athenæus, *Deipnosophists*, XII, 14.
33 In JAI, XVII, 122.

monandry by such a historical term as family, so there is no excuse for using the term 'utter promiscuity.' There is no reason again to suppose that 'paternity' was uncertain and was, therefore, incapable of being recognized. Both paternity and maternity were certain, and they were fully recognized. . . . In short, the relationship between the sexes was a *natural* and not a *political* relationship. Because primordial men did not, throughout life, recognize a bond of affection for offspring, and did not use the potent fact of kinship to constitute a social unit, it does not follow that they did not know of the paternal and maternal instincts, were not influenced by sexual jealousy, and did not know of the connection between parent and child. All that can be said of them is that they did not use these several natural facts to produce artificial, or, as it is best to say, political combinations." This is a sample of reasoning about a situation without much attention to actual cases, but it conveys a warning against tenuous theorizing in any direction when materials are scanty and inconclusive. It is safe to conclude that in the most primitive cases regulation was minimal.

It is possible to interpret the instances collected by Lubbock[34] as exhibitions of pure licentiousness, but their ceremonial character does not accord with that view. They appear, rather, as formal reversions to previous practice. Other cases shade off into increasing uncertainty.

In Australia, youths were not allowed to marry during initiation or probation, but during the latter had full license as respects the unmarried, including those of their own clan and totem.[35] As indicated in a former case, it is not necessarily all the men who have the first or any right for the marrying woman, but certain individuals whom some think to be representative of the group-right.[36] In British Central Africa "a virgin on her marriage is 'broken' by a friend of the bridegroom before the latter cohabits with her. The friend is said 'to eat new things.' "[37] In East Africa, "at marriage, four friends of the bridegroom pursue the girl, who is soon captured with much show of resistance, and conveyed to the hut of the groom's mother, where she is kept a close prisoner for five days. Meanwhile the young people dance and carouse to excess. The girl is now accessible to these four friends, and afterwards the husband claims her."[38] Such capture-ceremonies are interpreted by those who wish to refute promiscuity[39] as a recognition of the share-claim of the participators in the results of the enterprise. Lippert[40] sees a deeper significance in them, and in the Serbian custom of assigning a special right to the groomsman prior to the groom, and in the modifications of that ancient custom whereby the groomsman avails himself of his right only ceremonially, or where a mere boy is chosen as groomsman. In North Luzon a six to eight years old boy lies between the pair the first night, and the couple may not address one another. Ceremonial priority of others' rights over those of the groom are found among the Slavs. The representatives of such rights are commonly brothers of

34 *Origin Civil.*, ch. III. Other cases and comment in Roth, *N.W. Cent. Queensland*, 69, 174; Howitt, in JAI, XX, 87; Cunow, *Verwdsftsorg.*, 116.

35 Howitt and Fison, in JAI, XII, 37, note.

36 Lippert, *Kgchte.*, II, 19.

37 Stannus, in JAI, XL, 309.

38 French-Sheldon, in JAI, XXI, 365-366; cf. also Johnston, *Kilima-Njaro*, 431; Johnston, in JAI, XV, 7-8; Thomson, *Masai Land*, 93; Mucke, *Horde*, 139-140.

39 Westermarck, *Marriage*, I, 166 ff.

40 Rajacsich, *Südslaven*, 180; Lippert, *Kgchte.*, II, 19, 12.

the bridegroom.[41] Lippert cites also the *Polterabend,* where every guest kneels before the bride on a pillow, kisses her, and leads her to the dance—the grooms-man demanding from each a piece of money, as another modification of an original communalism in women.[42] It is unsafe to dismiss the survivalistic interpretation of such ceremonial in favor of plain intuition and guess-work. Is it "symbolic" only? Then why this particular symbol?

In Fiji, when a man of note is dangerously ill, a circumcision takes place as a propitiatory measure, the exuvial parts being offered to the ancestral spirits, with prayer for recovery. "Then follows a great feast which ushers in a period of indescribable revelry. All distinctions of property are now for-gotten," including property in women. The nearest relationships form no bar. Said the local chief: "While it lasts, we are just like pigs." In a few days the ordinary restrictions recur: "rights of property are again respected, married couples are recognized in place of the abandoned revellers, and brothers and sisters may not so much as speak to one another. . . . This rite seems at least open to interpretation as a remarkable case of 'consanguine marriage' being kept up as a ceremonial institution," for it appears that tribal brothers and sisters are intentionally coupled.[43] It should be noted that the suspension of the taboo touches property when it touches marriage and is re-applied to the one when it is again enforced as respects the other.[44]

The Hottentots allow the most unbridled freedom at the festival of the pot-dance, making away with any children whose conception might go back to that time.[45] The latter practice prevents uncertainty as to legitimacy and in-heritance. A case is reported from Madagascar, where on the birth of a child in the royal family, complete sexual license was allowed. Death could not then be inflicted for any offense, as there was a general suspension of regulation. Here is an interrelation of marriage and governmental institutions: both were abrogated at once. The author quoting this case[46] aligns similar practice in India[47] and Peru and believes that these instances, together with the removal of restraint shown in the Tahitian Arreoi festivities, fall into the same category with "the licentiousness witnessed among the Australians on the occasions re-ferred to by Mr. Fison." A brief period of license is reported at a fertility-feast in Borneo.[48] Formerly, at the death of a Hawaiian chief, "houses were burnt, property plundered, even murder sometimes committed, and gratifica-tion of every base and savage feeling sought without restraint.[49] This is an-other of the cases aligned with Mr. Fison's; here there is a simultaneous re-laxation of property-rights, marriage-ties, law, and order, and primitive chaos and anarchy return.

At the festival of Sedna (female spirit of death), Eskimo men and women pair off as man and wife for a night and a day.[50] Of the Point Barrow Eskimo it is reported as follows. "I am informed by some of the whalemen who winter in the neighborhood of Repulse Bay, that at certain times there is a general exchange of wives throughout the village, each woman passing from man to man

---

41 Wilken, in VG, I, 502. Cases of the pro-husband also in Lewin, *S.E. India,* 127 (younger brother); Thurston, *S. India,* 3; Wilken, in VG, I, 501, 502; Kostomarov, *Gt. Russians,* 240; Rhamm, in *Globus,* LXXXII, 189.

42 Balch, *Slavic Fellow Citizens,* 146; Sin-clair, *Jungle,* 13, 14; Gubernatis, *Usi Nuz.,* 274.

43 Fison, in JAI, XIV, 27, 28.
44 §341, above.
45 Fritsch, *Eingeb. S.-Afr.,* 328.
46 Ellis, *Hist. Madagascar,* I, 150.
47 Fawcett, *Saoras,* in JASB, I, 231.
48 Roth, in JAI, XXI, 126.
49 Ellis, *Polyn. Researches,* IV, 177 (2d ed.).
50 Boas, in BAE, VI, 605.

till she has been through the hands of all, and finally returns to her husband. All these cases seem to me to indicate that the Eskimo have not wholly emerged from the state called communal marriage, in which each woman is considered as the wife of every man in the community."[51]

Relaxation of sex-regulations at the time of religious festivals has been common. In Mexico there appear to have been obscene practices in connection with the worship of the mother-goddess, which recall similar conditions among the people of antiquity. The Mother of the Gods, by her sex-activity to bring about growth, became goddess of lewdness and filth, as the German Cornmother became a harlot. The same was true in the case of another goddess, one by whose activity the earth bears flowers; she was honored at a festival at which nine and ten year old boys and girls became senselessly drunk and committed fornication.[52] The Arabian Lāt was worshipped by the Nabatæans as mother of the gods and must be identified, thinks Robertson Smith,[53] with the virgin-mother worshipped in South Syria. At Carthage the mother of the gods seems to be identical with Dido. "The foul type of worship corresponding to the conception of the goddess as polyandrous prevailed at Sicca Veneria, and Augustin speaks with indignation of the incredible obscenity of the songs that accompanied the worship of the Carthaginian mother-goddess; but perhaps this is not wholly to be set down as of Punic origin, for the general laxity on the point of female chastity in which such a type of worship originates has always been characteristic of North Africa." The cult of the Great Mother of the Gods attained a notable development in Rome, probably because "there was something more genial and satisfactory to the soul in the religion itself than in the formal, stately, and passionless religion of the ancient gods of Rome. . . . Her devotees were brought nearer the divine and nearer each other than the worshipers of the classical divinities."[54]

§344. License.

"In the part of the Solomons which I know best, Eddystone Island, sexual relations before marriage are very general and are the subject of social regulations which show that they are recognised as legitimate and even orthodox. After marriage, however, relations with any but the consort are strictly prohibited, and customs of avoidance between relatives by marriage which might indicate the possibility of wider relations are completely absent. Individual marriage in these islands seems to have reached an exceptionally high degree of development."[1] Seligmann[2] cites a number of cases of regular cohabitation prior to marriage; it is a phenomenon of courtship and winds up in proposal by the women. In one part of New Guinea, "girls are quite free sexually before marriage, and promiscuous intercourse between young people is the rule."[3] "General sexual morality can hardly be said to exist among the Mekeo people [of British New Guinea], though immoralities are not openly practised. Boys and girls, unmarried men and women, and husbands and wives all indulge in immorality, and the marriage tie is very loose. Girls are especially free when they are under the marriageable age at which childbirth could occur. There is

51 Murdoch, in BAE, IX, 413.
52 Preuss, in *Arch. f. Anthrop.*, XXIX, 150.
53 *Relig. Sem.*, 56.

54 Showerman, *Great Mother*, 256-257.
1 Rivers, *Melan. Soc.*, II, 140.
2 *Melanesians*, 708, 709, 711, 737, *et al.*
3 Liston-Blyth, in JAI, LIII, 468.

no punishment for immorality, but the parents of a girl whose indulgence in it is discovered will be very angry with her, if she has reached the marriageable age."[4] In the Trobriand Islands, "the *katuyausi* are expeditions of amorous adventure, in which the unmarried girls of a village go *en bloc* to another village and there sleep with the youths of that village. Any single male who fancies one of the girl-guests gives her (through an intermediary) some small present. . . . If accepted, the two belong to each other for the night. Such expeditions, though well established and sanctioned by custom, are strongly resented by the young men of the village from which the *katuyausi* starts, and they end as a rule in a sound thrashing administered by the male to the female youth of the village. . . . The sexual freedom of unmarried girls is complete. They begin intercourse with the other sex very early, at the age of six to eight years. They change their lovers as often as they please, until they feel inclined to marry. Then a girl settles down to a protracted and, more or less, exclusive intrigue with one man, who, after a time, usually becomes her husband. Illegitimate children are by no means rare."[5] A similar condition existed in the Loyalty Islands.[6]

In the Congo region, "from early age to puberty the boys and girls had free access to each other. After puberty, restrictions were placed on the girls, and the act was regarded as adultery." The author[7] saw only one prostitute in Monsembe, who was treated with little or no respect. Sir Charles Dundas[8] says of East Africa: "Professional prostitution within the tribe is practically unheard of among all these peoples, and if now thousands of prostitutes are found in our townships and centres they are detribalized women cut off from their own families. . . . Native women may leave their homes and live as prostitutes in the towns, or in concubinage with aliens, but prostitution among women within the tribe seems to be unknown." Unnatural offenses are equally rare. Among the Ba-Mbala, "virginity is not considered of the slightest importance, consequently unmarried women indulge freely from a very early age, even before they have reached maturity; one result of this is that solitary and unnatural vices and prostitution are unknown; but, on the other hand, sexual excess is having an evil effect upon the mental and physical characters of the race." The authors[9] quoted speak elsewhere of the Ba-Huana, among whom sexual morality "is conspicuous by its absence; the unmarried indulge as they please from a very early age, the girls even before puberty. Hence virginity in a bride is never expected and never found. Indulgence of this sort is not considered in the slightest degree shameful, and parents do nothing to check it. Marriage seems to make little difference, in spite of the fine with which adultery is punished when discovered, and it may be said that the only time during which a woman contents herself with her husband is during pregnancy, since it is believed that adultery at this period would prove fatal to the child. . . . One of my men asked my permission to marry a girl who was certainly under six years of age; when I was angry and wanted to punish him the girl's chief told me, 'It is a long time now since she knew the first man.'" "Prostitution is common among the Sungu, and meets with no disap-

---

4 Williamson, in JAI, XLIII, 278.
5 Malinowski, in JAI, XLVI, 362, note, 407, note.
6 Ray, in JAI, XLVII, 286.

7 Weeks, in JAI, XXXIX, 448.
8 In JAI, LI, 248; and in JAI, XLV, 275.
9 Torday and Joyce, in JAI, XXXV, 410; and in JAI, XXXVI, 288.

proval; the northern Batetela tolerate it though they regret it, while the Olemba frankly condemn it."[10]

Roscoe[11] reports that among the Bageshu, at the time of initiation, "there is the fullest license given to both sexes, men and women have promiscuous intercourse without any restraint." He records what is something of an exception in that the Bahima end restriction after marriage, whereas premarital license is often followed by strict chastity of the wife. "Once a woman is married all restrictions are ended, she may welcome to her bed any of her husband's friends or relations with impunity; the children resulting from such intercourse belong to the husband. When a friend visits a man he sleeps on the same bed with him and his wife; the rules of hospitality are such, the man must leave his wife to his friend in the early morning; when a man is away from home and a visitor arrives, the wife must entertain him, and if he desires it act as his wife. It is also customary to exchange wives; for instance, when a man and his wife visit a friend, they invariably exchange wives during the time of the visit." Elsewhere in East Africa, "free love is permitted amongst the unmarried men and girls, but on her marriage it is the duty of the girl to tell her husband the names of all those Ngoromo who have had connection with her, and they must each bring a goat to the husband's village."[12] Among the Suk of Kenia, "free love is usual amongst the youths and girls, but not approved by the elders; after marriage the women are usually very faithful to their husbands, and conjugal disputes on this head are rare; there is real affection between middle-aged and old couples." The author[13] just quoted goes into considerable detail concerning the peculiar arrangements of the Lumbwa. "In European morals the tribe would be deemed flagrantly immoral, in fact, they are non-moral. The incest prohibition is never broken, and the prohibited degrees of affinity are wider than those of the Prayer Book. There is, moreover, more than a mere regard for chastity and virginity, despite the fact that the youths and girls are prone to free-love. . . . The old people prefer a settled home, the warriors must go far afield to good grazing areas, they set up men's club-houses, and girls visit them to take back the milk to the parents, and are necessary for their dances; the rest naturally follows. . . . Each youth has a sweetheart in particular, with whom he sleeps from time to time away from her mother's hut; if she is a virgin, he respects her virginity for years while sleeping with her. . . . A number of youths and girls may sleep in one hut. There are no indecencies, indecency in the European sense is as yet unknown when living in the tribal state. . . . The striking thing about these youth-and-girl friendships is the real affection shown, most noticeably absent in married couples until they reach old age; unfortunately, the lover rarely marries his sweetheart, she is married to an older and richer man. A man may not have relations with his wife if she is a virgin; she is deflowered by her former lover with his tacit and uninquiring consent. . . . Every woman has a lover and every man a number; it is literally true that the common practice is for a wife to bring girls to her hut for her husband's gratification, and the more lovers he has amongst the unmarried girls the prouder woman she is."

Among the Akamba, "chastity is neither expected nor valued among women before marriage, and after all dances, in which young men and girls unite,

10 Torday, in JAI, LI, 375.
11 Roscoe, in JAI, XXXIX, 187; and in JAI, XXXVII, 105.

12 Champion, in JAI, XLII, 86.
13 Barton, in JAI, LI, 96; and in JAI, LIII, 68-69.

promiscuous connection is indulged in and connived at by the parents of the latter. In the same way all married women have lovers. . . . Although it sometimes happens that in the case of unmarried girls pregnancy results from their intercourse with their lovers, this condition of the girl is no bar to her marriage with another man, but rather a recommendation, since he is sure of at least one child from her."[14] Again, "an unmarried woman who has reached the age of puberty may have as many friends, as they call them, as she likes, provided that they come from another clan; after marriage she must confine her attentions to her husband."[15] Among the Nile tribes, "female chastity before puberty is not much regarded, though it is generally considered reprehensible if more than what might be termed 'philandering' takes place between the sexes. Adultery with a married woman is regarded as a serious crime."[16] The absolute immorality of the women of Nyasaland, strange to say, goes along with a modesty, both of word and gesture, in both sexes, which could not be excelled in the most respectable and *collet-monte* community of white people. Exceptions occur only when a woman gets drunk. . . . The Masai woman . . . is a model spouse; but the unwritten law of the nation imposes upon her husband the duty temporarily to surrender his house and its inhabitants to any one of the Elmorao (members of the warrior caste, who are bound to celibacy as long as they belong to it) who desires to take possession of them, and to keep away as long as he sees the latter's long spear sticking in the ground in front of the door. This husband was an Elmoran himself before his marriage."[17] The Tuareg father may, before marrying off his daughter, demand reimbursement from her for what she has cost the family. This is "collected upon her body," and the girl, "dishonored according to our ideas, redeemed according to local views," is the more sought in marriage the greater the success in trading on her charms.[18]

"In the Chukchee language there is no term for 'girl,' for virginity is not required or expected. . . . Still, many of the Chukchee girls are chaste until their marriage; and in comparison with the other tribes of this country, the Chukchee are considerably more decent." If a woman "has children before marriage they are treated in the same way as children born after marriage." Among the Yukaghir, "men of authority or of wealth can choose any woman, married or unmarried. Officials, Cossacks, merchants, and even missionaries introduce these habits into the villages and camps of non-Russian tribes." Recurring to the Chukchee, we find them celebrating a so-called "trading-dance," which "takes place between the members of a 'compound marriage,' beginning with a dance in which a male member of the group has one of the women for his partner. . . . After the dance, the man must give some present to the woman; and the following night they sleep together, leaving their respective mates to arrange matters between themselves. On the next day the husband of the woman and the wife of the man perform a similar dance, in which the man gives an equivalent of the present of the day before, and each newly-mated couple sleep together for another night. Such dances are arranged chiefly among cousins or other relatives, who, among the Chukchee, frequently assume the bond of compound marriage. Conversely, a new bond of compound

---

14 Tate, in JAI, XXXIV, 137.
15 Northcote, in JAI, XXXVII, 65.
16 Johnston, *Uganda*, II, 778.

17 Coudenhove, in *Atl. Mo.*, CXXXII, 194, 195.
18 Duveyrier, *Touâreg*, 340.

marriage may be concluded through a trading-dance."[19] In Mongolia, a girl need not keep her virginity until marriage; it is rather against her if she does.[20] Votyak women up to marriage are entirely free; but the wives are remarkable for strictness of morals.[21] The Ostiaks allow freedom but regard the birth of a child to an unmarried woman with disfavor; "hence infanticide is frequent."[22]

Among the Hill Tribes of India, "it may be said that any mode of connection between the sexes which does not contravene the rules of exogamy and is approved by the kinsfolk, ranks as a marriage with all its usual incidents and privileges. It is a later development of custom which draws any distinction between the children of a bride married as a virgin, a widow or other woman whose connection with a man is legal under their marriage code."[23] Several tribes that allow premarital freedom insist upon chastity after marriage.[24] "Among the hill tribes and many menial castes in the Plains prenuptial infidelity is recognized or tolerated. It is true that this refers only to members of the group, and an intrigue with an alien is sharply punished. Women, once married, are said to be generally chaste, but the relaxation of moral control in early life must inevitably suggest miscegenation."[25] "Among most of these tribes much freedom is accorded to unmarried girls, as success in the courts of Venus is a sure passport to the Lushai heaven."[26] The Nairs, as has been seen, show some possible relics of primordial communism in women; among them "a system of sexual relationship, the laxity of which made it in many cases indistinguishable from promiscuity, seems to have been prevalent . . . even as late as the eighteenth century. The literature of the time abounds in allusions as to how fickle ladies jilted their husbands and married others. A child was supposed to be legitimate as long as a man was willing to meet the expenses of child delivery, and that phrase still survives as a form of reproach against a father who does not treat his son well. . . . The *Talikettu* ceremony was, under these conditions, the actual and religious marriage. After that custom the girl was allowed to choose her own suitor, and when such a suitor, who was her husband, dies, she does not mourn his death, or become a widow, while, when the man who actually tied the *Tali* dies she undergoes certain formalities of mourning. Also the man who tied the *Tali*, though he never sees the girl again, is called 'little father' by all the members of the family. All these go to prove that the actual marriage ceremony was the *Talikettu*. It must be remembered that *Tali* (an ornament round the neck) is a symbol for marriage for all Hindus, and among Brahmins all over India the *Tali* round the neck is only broken when the husband dies. If this, then, was the real marriage, what was the actual position occupied by the priest or warrior who tied the *Tali*? The fact that he is conducted to the house after the ceremony seems to point to at least a latent conjugal right. . . . In this connection it is well to remember a like ceremony performed with great festivities among the *Deva-Dasis* or the 'Temple-girls' in other parts of India. They also have a form of marriage which lasts for four days. On each day the girls puts on the dress of the women of different communities, and sits in a big hall, where are

19 Czaplicka, *Aborig. Siberia*, 70, 91, 293-294.
20 Ivanovski, *Mongolei*, 14.
21 *Russian Ethnog.* (Russ.), I, 298; Kohler, *Urgchte. d. Ehe*, 26, 27.
22 Kondratowitsch, in *Globus*, LXXIV, 290; Prjevalski's *Forskningsresor*, 352.
23 Crooke, in JAI, XXVIII, 237.
24 Lewin, *S.E. India*, 121, 233, 254.
25 Crooke, in JAI, XLIV, 272.
26 Shakespear, in JAI, XXXIX, 375.

gathered together all the women of her local community. This ceremony, it seems, must precede before the girl devotes her life to 'temple service.' Since the . . . women, in olden days, do not seem to have had any settled form of marriage, and were free to cast off one husband and choose another, the religious rites of marriage had to be performed without any definite marital relationship with any particular man. This seems to be the explanation of *Talikettu Kalyanam.*"[27]

License prevailed rather widely in other parts of India.[28] In the East Indies, Wilken[29] finds much indifference to premarital chastity. Say the Bataks of Sumatra of a young woman who has had few premarital love-affairs: "It is no delicious cake upon which not even one fly settles." Young girls are wholly free and are habituated to wide license; but "the woman who, being betrothed, is unfaithful to her groom, or, married, commits adultery, pays for her transgression with her life." This is the case with many peoples of the Archipelago. Whether or not premarital chastity is insisted upon, wifely fidelity is demanded. The married woman is viewed differently from the young maid whom they regard more as common property; in the case of the former, the smallest freedom is a punishable offense. Love is regarded like hunger, as a natural appetite that needs satisfaction; it is as foolish to speak of prostitution among savages as among animals. Only within the institution of marriage is it delimited, and even there the husband often has the so-called right of prostitution over his wife. Where young girls are not held to chastity and where a married woman, by the will of her husband, may have relations with others, there is no place for prostitution as a trade, and for money, carried on by a special class of persons. In fact, the practice is not found in the Archipelago, except in the case of the public singers and dancers of the Javanese and Sundanese. These courtesans are not held in contempt at all but share in the favor of the people. There are many cases where dancers, after having led several years of loose life, make a good marriage, for example with a village head-man, and are regarded by village associates, female as well as male, as worthy members of society. Other authorities corroborate Wilken. In Sumatra, one tribe will inflict the death penalty upon an unchaste girl, while another will at most favor an attempt to conclude a legal match.[30] In Borneo, one very backward tribe admits license, while the Dyaks and Kayans generally attach disgrace to premarital pregnancy.[31] Among the Mentawei Islanders the birth of children to an unmarried woman hurts her standing in no way, but seems to advantage her; for "they are the unquestioned property of the mother, and the father, even when known, can raise no claims to these children."[32] In the Philippines morals were loose and virginity was an impediment rather than an advantage. There were professional violaters.[33]

In Polynesia, premarital relations were generally pretty free: in Tahiti, the Society Islands, Samoa, Easter Islands, the Pelew group, and New Zealand. In the last, "formerly every woman was *noa* or common, and could select as

---

27 Panikkar, in JAI, XLVIII, 269-270.
28 Carey and Tuck, *Chin Hills*, I, 188; Godden, in JAI, XXVI, 178; Risley, *Ethnog. Ind.*, I, 182, 225; Fawcett, in JASB, I, 235; some cases of non-toleration in Scott, in JASB, IV, 361.
29 In VG, I, 197, 511, 582-588, 595-596, 597, 601.

30 Jacobs, *Groot-Atjeh*, I, 224-225; Marsden, *Sumatra*, 298.
31 Roth, *Sarawak*, II, clxxxiii, cxcvii; I, 116; Nieuwenhuis, *Borneo*, I, 75, 78; Gomes, *Sea Dyaks*, 68.
32 Pleyte, in *Globus*, LXXIX, 25.
33 Montero y Vidal, *Filipinas*, I, 62.

many companions as she liked, without being thought guilty of any impropriety, until given away by her friends to some one as her future master; she then became tapu to him, and was liable to be put to death if found unfaithful."[34] "Young girls were allowed to do pretty well as they pleased, and they and the boys enjoyed full liberty in sexual matters, unless the girl was a *puhi*, like the *taupo* or village maid of Samoa, or was *tapui'd* or betrothed to some young chief. But when a girl became a wife all that was changed, and promiscuous love-making was interdicted, punishable by a *taua muru* [punitive plundering of village or family] or often the tomahawk."[35] License prevailed widely in the Caroline and Gilbert Islands.[36]

In East Greenland, "there is no shame in an unmarried girl having children but, on the contrary, blame attaches to a full-grown, married woman when she cannot have offspring."[37] The women prefer the commonest European to the best Eskimo hunter and on the west coast there is scarcely a pure-bred native to be found.[38] Among the Omahas, "prostitution, as practised in a white community, did not exist."[39] Along the northwest coast, promiscuous rights in unmarried women were obsolete when the whites first came.[40] Some of the Guiana Indian celebrations end with promiscuous mating; in fact, "this intermixing really occurred, as it still does, throughout the whole performance, so soon as the effects of the liquor are felt. Thus, Van Berkel says 'In the meantime I here . . . found the old tag to be true that a drunken woman is an open door. . . .' What Schomburgk has stated of the Makusi can be repeated with equal truth of all other Guiana Indians. Every girl, without in the slightest degree damaging her reputation, can enjoy the favors of many lovers, but as soon as she is married the most inviolable observance of her honor is demanded. . . . Speaking in general, the Indian girl, after her first menstruation, will take up with some young fellow for a month or so, then make a change and live for some years, perhaps, a life of pleasure. Finally, she will meet her life companion and become a true and hard-working wife. As a rule she will not bear a child during her years of freedom; if she does, she will probably settle down. . . . Free love is quite the ordinary thing among these people, and that there should be anything wrong in this so-called immoral life is absolutely unintelligible to them. . . . Once married, however, the Indian expects fidelity to his bed, and the older records would show that he seldom hesitated to take drastic steps to enforce and punish it." Numerous cases are cited.[41] The Chibchas of Colombia pay no attention to virginity but rather regard it as an indication of inability to inspire love.[42] Of other American peoples Bancroft[43] writes that, while jealous of their wives, "to their unmarried daughters, strange as it may seem, they allow every liberty without censure or shame. Latcham[44] attributes much of the Araucanians' sexual immorality to drunkenness; at their feasts "they give themselves up to a sexual promiscuity that respects no condition of relationship, each one taking forcible possession of any woman that strikes his fancy or happens to be nearest at

34 Ratzel, *Vkde.*, II, 123; Ella, in AAAS, 1892, 621; Geiseler, *Oster-Insel*, 29; Kubary, in *Mitth. Berl. Mus.*, 1885, 77; Tregear, in JAI, XIX, 101; Taylor, *Te Ika*, 167 (quoted).
35 Cowan, *Maoris*, 146-147.
36 Finsch, *Ethnol. Erfahr.*, III, 30, 302.
37 Holm, *Ethnol. Skizze*, 54.
38 Nansen, *Esk. Life*, 164.

39 Fletcher and LaFlesche, in BAE, XXVII, 325.
40 Dall, in BAE, III, 81.
41 Roth, in BAE, XXXVIII, 470, 471, 560, 561.
42 Spencer, *Prin. Soc.*, I, §280.
43 *Nat. Races*, I, 123; II, 676.
44 In JAI, XXXIX, 353-354, 356.

hand. . . . Absolutely no bonds of relationship [were] . . . recognised in their drunken amours, even incest being of the most frequent occurrence. . . . Chastity is not prized among unmarried girls, and few of them are virgins at the time of their marriage. Once married, however, they are generally modest, chaste and faithful."

Wilken[45] collects considerable evidence concerning the extreme license of Beduin manners; "dogs are better than we are," was a common expression of theirs. Their temporary unions were at best no more than trial-marriages; no idea of a durable tie existed.

§346. Group-marriage.

As is intimated in the text, there is considerable doubt concerning the applicability of the term; that there is a form of union which amounts to local absence of regulation within a circumscribed group admits of no denial. It has been called limited promiscuity. Several cases which might well have been ranged under §343 have been reserved for special illustration.

Among the Masai, "though individual marriage is recognised, sexual communism or something very like it prevails between all the men of one age-grade and the women of the corresponding age-grade, subject to the rules of exogamy and relationship, which forbid a man to marry or have sexual intercourse with a woman of his own clan or with a near relative. In other words the Masai may be said to live in a state of group marriage, based on the organisation of the whole community in age-grades, and restricted by the exogamy of the sub-clans and the rules regarding incest."[1] Miss Czaplicka[2] records the existence, among certain Siberians, of what she calls "supplementary unions." They have been called group-marriage. "The husbands belonging to such a group are called 'companions in wives.' . . . A man has a right to the wives of all his companions, and may exercise this right when visiting the camp of any one of them. . . . In former times this custom embraced only members of the same family, except brothers; but now friends, unrelated, may join such a group, after which they become like relations, helping and supporting each other. As in the case of individual marriage, a similar rite is performed, consisting also in anointing each other with blood, first in one camp and then in the other, and sometimes the man will even serve with the herd in order to be received into the group. . . . Sometimes such unions become polyandry, if a bachelor is accepted as a companion. Bogoras heard of certain cases in which each companion takes the wife of another and lives with her for several months, or even permanently. At the present time all Chukchee families take part in such organizations. . . . Such relations with the Eskimo have existed for a very long time, and are undoubtedly due to trade intercourse." The authoress notes that "the Chukchee form of supplementary union does not correspond by any means exactly to any of the types of group-marriage instanced by Prof. Westermarck in his *History of Human Marriage*." She quotes from several authorities to show the merging of the supplementary union into survivalistic forms.

Naturally, in the case of such an ancient and obsolescent usage, it is difficult to define such a term as group-marriage; but there is an unmistakable kinship

---

45 In VG, II, 7, 8, 16, 17, note, 26; Barton, *Sem. Orig.*, 61.

1 Hollis, in JAI, XL, 480.
2 *Aborig. Siberia*, 78-80, 100, note.

between the variants. Among the Todas, "wives are constantly transferred from one husband, or group of husbands, to another, the new husband or husbands paying a certain number of buffaloes to the old." There results a sort of consort-shifting within the group that is alignable with the group-marriage type, though representative of variation about it rather than identification with it. Rivers[3] continues: "The amount of the compensation or *ter* is settled by a council, and from this the transaction has received its name of *terersthi,* or 'compensation he tells (decides).' . . . It would be impossible that such a custom as that of *terersthi* should remain limited in scope, but there is no doubt that at the present day it has become the custom for any man who takes a fancy for the wife of another to endeavour to obtain her for himself, and I was told that he would give large bribes to the elders of the Todas to attain his object. It seems quite clear that, at the present time, it is not considered necessary to obtain the consent either of the wife or of the husband, and in some cases the wife has been taken from her husband by force."

The curious phenomena of concubitancy deserve further illustration here. "In the Gilbert Islands it was considered unworthy for a man to exercise his physical rights over the persons of all his potential concubitants, the relationship being esteemed as a means of guaranteeing him against childlessness primarily, and secondarily of providing for surplus female population. Nevertheless, all *Taua-ni-kai* were theoretically at the disposition of their houselord, and any infidelity on their part was an adultery against him. He might elect to give one of his wife's sisters intact to a friend, in which case, as a virgin, she would have the right to become the ceremonial bride of her husband. Hence a curious result, for as *Rao ni-kie* she would carry to her husband the right of *Taua-ni-kai* (a name applying equally to the relationship and to the persons subject thereto) over all her uterine sisters, one of whom was married, while she herself could never be free of the obligations of *Taua-ni-kai* to her sister's husband. Thus two men might share the same rights over a single group of women, the wife of each being the concubitant of the other, and upon this was established the system of *bita-ni-kie, changing of mats,* or *wife-exchange,* so common in the Group."[4]

§348. Consanguine Marriage.

MELANESIA shows cases of royal incest. "The highest kind of marriage was that between a brother and sister, children of the same father and mother of the highest rank. . . . Such chiefs were so sacred that all had to prostrate themselves in their presence and they were not allowed to take off their clothes in the presence of others." A lower grade of union was where the spouses were half-brother and half-sister. "The usual case was that a woman had two husbands; the first child would be regarded as the offspring of the first husband and the second child as belonging to the second husband and, if they were male and female and married one another, the marriage would be *naha,*" that is, of the type under review. "People had to sit in the presence of chiefs of this rank." Other types follow. "It was said that marriage between father and daughter might also occur. . . . It seems to be quite clear that these consanguineous marriages were carried out with the very definite aim of main-

---

3 *Todas,* 523, 525.   4 Grimble, in JAI, LI, 28.

taining the purity of the royal blood."[1] Such closeness of consanguinity in marriage was not confined to the higher classes. In New Caledonia, "no laws of consanguinity were observed in their marriages, the *nearest* relatives united."[2] In a number of African tribes "the marriage of brother and sister, or a man with his sister's child, is permitted to compensate for the law by which a man's property goes to the son of a stranger, but nothing of the kind is allowed among the Yaos. Indeed, they view any incestuous union with particular horror, and such must be very rare. I have heard of a case of a man committing incest with the idea that he would thereby become endued with supernatural power, but all he gained was ostracism; in the old days he would have been burned."[3] Among the Bahima, "no man may marry into his father's clan; all women of that clan are his near relations, and are called either mothers or sisters, etc. These restrictions do not apply to princes, they may marry their sisters, and have intercourse with their married sisters; only betrothed or unmarried princesses are forbidden them."[4] In Uganda, "the king's actual sisters are also his wives, for it is illegal for princesses to marry anyone but the reigning king or his gods"; if they do not marry the king-brother, they are forced into celibacy, if not chastity. Royalty follows the *muziro* or totem of the mother, where common people follow that of the father; it clings to the old and holy.[5] Among the Hovas, where also blood and rank follow the mother, unions between brothers and sisters are not rare.[6]

Among the Chukchi of Siberia, marriages between relatives, especially between cousins, is the most frequent form. Sexual relations between father and daughter have been reported, and there are "examples of Chukchee tales relating to marriage between brother and sister, which in actual life are considered incestuous." The authoress[7] cites one of them. "The Maritime people living in that country were exterminated by famine. Only two were left: a full grown girl and her infant brother. She fed him with pounded meat. When he grew up he asked him to marry her. 'Otherwise we shall remain childless,' said the sister. 'We shall have no descendants, and the earth will remain without people. It cannot be peopled otherwise. And who sees us? Who will say "shame"? Who will know about it in the world? We are all alone in the world.' The brother said, 'I do not know, I feel bad; it is forbidden.' . . . One child is born, then another. The family multiplies and becomes a people. From them are born all the people in the camps and villages." Other legendary matter is quoted with respect to the Yakuts: "Thy sister was thy wife; thy mother was thy wife; the wife of thy brother was also thy wife. . . . Of old when the youth could draw the bow he took to wife his sister and led her to a quiet place. . . . In ancient times when an older or younger sister was given in marriage into another clan, the brothers did not let her go before they had lain with her. . . . When strangers take to wife from her brothers a woman who is still a virgin, the brothers account it a shame for themselves."

The Yakuts laugh at the Russian horror of incest; among them occur unions of brother and sister, mother and son.[8] Fraternal incest existed among the Kamchadales.[9] The only limits recognized by the mediæval Mongols was

1 Rivers, *Melan. Soc.*, I, 380-382.
2 Turner, *Samoa*, 341.
3 Sanderson, in JAI, L, 375.
4 Roscoe, in JAI, XXXVII, 105.
5 Roscoe, in JAI, XXXII, 27; Main, *Relig. Chastity*, 144.

6 Letourneau, *Polit.*, 92.
7 Czaplicka, *Aborig. Siberia*, 71, 72, 111, 112.
8 Sieroshevski-Sumner, in JAI, XXI, 560, 561.
9 Mucke, *Horde*, 89 (where references are given).

as respects mothers, daughters, and sisters by the same mother.[10] Among the Veddahs the marriage of a man with his younger sister was once the one proper marriage· "To marry an elder sister or aunt would, in their judgment, be incestuous, a connection in every way as revolting to them as it would be to us—as much out of the question and inadmissible as the marriage with a younger sister was proper and natural." Among the Singhalese royal families, marriages of brothers and sisters were common.[11] Much has been made of these cases from Ceylon.[12]

The only taboo recognized by the Kukis is that prohibiting a mother to wed her son.[13] The Pulluvans, or medicine-men, of Malabar, are said to permit marriage between brother and sister. "Whatever the truth may be, it is probable that something of the kind was once the case, for, when a man is suspected of incest, they say 'He is like the Pulluvans.' "[14] In the *Rig-Veda,* Yama, the first man and king of the Dead, and Yami, his sister-wife, "indulge in a moral conversation on the propriety of wedlock between brother and sister.[15] Such unions were evidently once in the mores, though they became later an abomination. Where such a marriage was regarded as wrong, sex-intercourse could take place.[16] Incest is reported of the Annamites and Cambodians and out of the Chinese classics.[17] In old Japan occurred a curious exception to the taboo on fraternal incest. "The birth of twins of opposite sex is not of frequent occurrence, but it is not considered wise to separate them through life. These marriages rarely result in issue, it is said by native authorities."[18] With this treatment may be compared the strange Melanesian custom reported by Fison:[19] When twins are born they are allowed to live if they are of the same sex, but if they are of different sex they are both killed as violating the consanguinity law of exogamy.

The Alfurs, several decades back, practised incest between parents and children, brothers and sisters; the Kalangs of Java regarded a son's marriage with his mother as sure to bring luck and wealth; in Timorlaut there was no conception of incest; while among the Balinese there existed, again, the strange case of the twins—if of different sex, and especially among the highest castes, they were regarded as betrothed and were united when they had attained marriageable age.[20] In Sarawak, "members of the same family are allowed to contract marriage, nay, even the nearest relations, brothers and sisters, parents and children."[21] Dyaks of the Borneo coast strictly taboo close in-marriage, while those of the interior allow it in all grades.[22] By another tribe which practised fraternal incest, "that sort of union was preferred over all others as the most appropriate and most natural."[23] The Dyaks of the Barito region allow brothers and sisters, parents and children to marry, and the Kalang son lives with his mother as man and wife, as a means to secure luck. Wilken[24]

10 Rubruck, *Eastern Parts,* 77.
11 Bailey, in *Trans. Ethnol. Soc. London,* II, 294-295, 311; Sarasin, *Weddas,* 466, 467.
12 Westermarck, *Marriage,* II, 90; Starcke, *Prim. Fam.,* 224; Grosse, *Familie,* 57-58; Mucke, *Horde,* 87; Kohler, *Urgchte d. Ehe,* 12.
13 Lewin, *S.E. India,* 276.
14 Thurston, *S. India,* 58.
15 Hopkins, *Relig. India,* 131.
16 Zimmer, *Altind. Leben,* 323, 333.

17 Mantegazza, *Amori,* I, 272; Legge, *Chinese Classics,* IV, 53 (preface), 155.
18 Pfoundes, in JAI, XII, 224.
19 In AAAS, 1892, 693.
20 Wilken, in VG, I, 458-459.
21 Roth, *Sarawak,* II, clxxxi.
22 Wilken, *Vkde.,* 267, 268.
23 Mucke, *Horde,* 89.
24 In VG, I, 458 ff.; Schwaner, *Borneo,* I, 198.

cites a number of cases from the Malay Archipelago; they are both legendary and also observed.

Missionaries to the Sandwich Islands speak of a chief and his five young queens; "two of them are his half sisters, and one of them was formerly the wife of his father."[25] Again, in another part of Polynesia, where now fraternal incest is tabooed, among the gods and goddesses "the first thirty-six divine married couples were supposed all to have been brothers and sisters, whilst afterwards this kind of union had ceased."[26] Boas[27] quotes. as follows, in his article on the Kwakiutl Indians: "When the father [of a princess] dies, then her brother has her for his princess. Then he is no longer her brother, for she is now the princess of her brother who is now her father. Only the eldest one of the brothers has his youngest sister for his princess." Whatever formalism there may be in this arrangement, it falls in with the other cases of royal procedure. There are a number of cases reported from Guiana of the union of nearest kin. Thus a widow may take her son, or a widower his daughter, to replace a dead mate. Some Island Caribs marry their own daughters; in other regions, "incest between father and daughter, son with mother, brother with sister, is common. . . . If a Roucouyenne marries a woman (widow), she already having daughters, he becomes the spouse not only of the woman but also of her children."[28] This last case is, of course, non-incestuous, but it illustrates the matter-of-course quality of the disposition of females.

Details of royal incest in Egypt are rather well known. Thus Rameses II married his daughters by his sisters in order to annul their claims to the throne; the king, in fact, had to marry all women of the solar blood. The Ptolemies exhibit a complicated interrelation. Persian examples are likewise to be found, though the code of Hammurabi countenances nothing such.[29] Semitic literature reports close unions, together with reprehension of the same.[30]

"When, in the Song of Solomon, the bride is called 'sister,' this simply points to the fact that among the ancient Hebrews men were wont to woo their half-sisters—a thing which the actual cases likewise teach us."[31] Abraham says of Sarah:[32] "And moreover she is indeed my sister, the daughter of my father, but not the daughter of my mother; and she became my wife." Isaac says the same, falsely, of Rebecca.[33] It is noteworthy that Solon allowed marriage with a half-sister on the father's side, but forbade it with one on the mother's, an arrangement which the Lacedæmonian law reversed.[34] A union of this order was denounced by Ezekiel,[35] who cites incest as one sin of the Jews. The relation of Lot's daughters with their father is not represented in the primary narrative as noteworthy or abominable, considered as incest. The law about incest varies through the Old Testament; the success of the Deuteronomic

25 Ruggles, in *Atl. Mo.*, CXXXIV, 651.
26 Williamson, *Cent. Polyn.*, II, 203.
27 In BAE, XXXV, pt. I, 779.
28 Roth, in BAE, XXXVIII, 673.
29 Maspero, *Hist. Anc.*, II, 424; III, 588-589; Mahaffy, *Egypt*, 67; Spiegel, *Eran. Alterthkde.*, III, 678, 679; Justi, *Persien*, 50; Müller, *Sacred Bks.*, IV, xlv-xlvi, note; Harper, *Hammurabi*, 119; Winckler, *Hammurabi*, 26.
30 Gen., XX, 12; Levit., XVIII, 9; XX, 17; Ezek., XXII, 11; Wellhausen, "Ehe bei

d. Arabern," in *Gött. Gsellsft. d. Wissensften*, 1893, 441; Strabo, *Geog.*, XVI, 4, §25.
31 *Song of Songs*, IV, 9, 10, 11; V; Tietz, *Blutsverwandsft*, 10.
32 Gen., XX, 12; *cf.* II Sam., XIII, 11, 12; Lippert, *Kgchte.*, II, 44.
33 Gen., XXVI, 7.
34 Tietz, *Blutsverwandsft*, 10; Schroeder *Geschlechtl. Ordnung*, 80.
35 Ezek., XXII, 11.

prohibition seems to have been slight.[36] At a much later time, in the early Church, incest was represented as permissible.[37] The Phœnicians permitted fraternal incest, but it appeared only "when there was a legal claim hereditary in the female line which the male did not possess.[38]

In Homer unions appear between mother and son, brother and sister, nephew and aunt, uncle and niece.[39] No shame is attached to any of these except the first, the Œdipus case, of which more later on. Also it is to be noted that fraternal incest is a practice confined to the gods or demi-gods. Hermann[40] says there was in Greece no limit to consanguine marriage except in the ascending and descending scale; that, except in the old times, fraternal unions were disapproved; and that when fraternal incest was excused by showing that the incestuous parties did not have the same mother, that was only an excuse. In Greek tragedy incest is referred to as a practice of barbarians.[41] Wholesale incest was exhibited in the marriage of the children of Dionysius of Syracuse.[42] Cases of incest occurred in the Roman imperial family.[43] Strabo[44] cites with some reservations the custom of incest in the small islands about Britain; and among the heathen Germans there were all sorts of unions, barring only those between parents and children; "everywhere among the Germans there was ignorance of the doctrine of forbidden grades of kinship."[45]

Remoter Degrees of Consanguinity. Among a number of Australian tribes "the proper person for a man to marry is his second cousin, being his mother's mother's brother's daughter's daughter, or his father's father's sister's son's daughter, or some person who stands to him in the same relation and is denoted by the same term."[46] This may be contrasted with the Papuan usage, that "a man may not have connection with sister, half-sister, aunt, and first cousin, and it is considered hardly correct in the case of second cousins, though this is winked at. . . . The only reason given for this is 'shame,' and that it is 'dirty,' and the children would have bad skins."[47] "The young Fijian was from his birth regarded as the natural husband of the daughters of his father's sister and of his mother's brother. They were born his property if he desired to take them." In Tonga and Fiji, "the marriageable relationship between cross-cousins was extended so as to include rights to demand or order marriage and an obligation to comply."[48] "The Torres Islands, and especially Hiw, are noteworthy for the number of cases in which those related by blood may marry or are even expected to marry. In Hiw there appeared to be a definite connection between marriage with the father's sister and marriage with her daughter. It was said that if the father's sister was young enough a man would marry her, but if not, he would marry her daughter. The cross-cousin marriage was spoken of as a kind of substitute for marriage with the father's sister. If a man marries the daughter of his mother's brother he does not pay anything for her. A man desires especially to have his sister's son as a son-in-

36 Levit., XVIII, 6-21; XX, 11-21; Deut., XXVII, 20-23; Maurer, *Vkde.*, I, 149.
37 Dobschütz, *Christian Life*, 53.
38 Pietschmann, *Phönizier*, 237.
39 Keller, *Hom. Soc.*, 232 (where all references to text are given).
40 Becker-Hermann, *Charicles*, III, 288; Gubernatis, *Usi Nuz.*, 98.
41 Euripides, *Andromache*, 170 ff.

42 Burckhardt, *Griech. Kgchte.*, I, 197-198.
43 Gubernatis, *Usi Nuz.*, 98, 99.
44 *Geog.*, IV, 5, §4.
45 Weinhold, *Deut. Frauen*, I, 359-360.
46 Brown, in JAI, XLVIII, 239.
47 Liston-Blyth, in JAI, LIII, 468.
48 Williamson, *Cent. Polyn.*, II, 141-142 (citing Thomson, in JAI, XXIV, 373 ff.; Fison, in JAI, XXIV, 360 ff.).

law and will not look for payment. . . . In the island of Loh a man is not now allowed to marry his father's sister though there seems to be no doubt that this form of marriage was once practised." The author[49] quoted says that Melanesian marriage has apparently "undergone a progressive change from a condition in which it was orthodox and habitual to marry certain relatives to one in which marriage with relatives was wholly prohibited. At the same time, there seems to have come into being the custom of purchasing a wife which has gradually become more definite and habitual." Rivers connects the existence of this cross-cousin marriage with the dominance of the old men under the system of dual organization. "In Fiji, as in many other places, cousin-marriage was not merely permissible, but imperative. But the Fijians made a distinction among cousins. The children of two brothers were not allowed to marry. So, likewise, the children of two sisters were not allowed to marry. But the children of a brother and sisters were compelled to marry. And the progeny of such marriages was more numerous, and the physical conditions of it much superior, than in the case of the progeny of mixed or outbred marriages. The greatest vitality is found among the inbreds."[50]

"Practically all the old regulations with regard to marriage have broken down among the Hottentots. . . . All my older informants are agreed that the marriage of direct cousins was out of the question in the old days. With regard to the cross cousins there is some difference between the tribes. . . . The terminology for these relatives seems however to show that in the past marriage with both the mother's brother's daughter and the father's sister's daughter was allowed, and the behavior towards these relatives confirms this."[51]

"If a Gilyak woman has a son, she usually asks her brother to betroth the boy to his daughter. . . . The typical Gilyak marriage-right includes cousins (though it is exogamic)." Among the Ostiaks it is held "sinful and disgraceful to marry relations of the same name; yet they attend only to the male line. If a woman has married into another family, and has borne a daughter, the brother of the mother, or his children, may legally marry that daughter. In short, all marriages are legal, if only the fathers of the bride and bridegroom respectively are of different families."[52] The Ostiaks marry any relative on the female side but none on the male.[53]

Among the Chukchi, "marriages are usually restricted to their own kindred. Unions of couples closely related by blood are very common, and the bond is regarded as stronger than when the pair are not consanguineally related. In such cases no payment is made for the bride, but the family of the latter have a right to expect an equivalent from the groom's family should they need it later."[54] A number of Asiatic cases of similar tenor, where the restriction is a formal one, are given by Mucke.[55] Among the strictly patriarchal Ossestes, "a marriage with a mother's sister is held to be quite proper while one with a father's sister is punished as in the highest degree incestuous."[56]

In China, "children of brothers and sisters may marry at pleasure, while those of brothers cannot be united on pain of death."[57] "It is also permitted that a girl marry the son of a sister of her father, whereby the sister's son is,

49 Rivers, *Melan. Soc.*, I, 184-185; II, 121 ff.
50 Smith, in AAAS, 1913, 376.
51 Hoernle, in AA, XXVII, 21.
52 Czaplicka, *Aborig. Siberia*, 100, 126.
53 Pallas, *Voyages*, IV, 69.

54 Bogoras, in AA, III, 101-102.
55 *Horde*, 215-216, 219.
56 Von Haxthausen, *Transkaukasia*, II, 26; Westermarck, *Marriage*, II, 98.
57 Medhurst, in *Trans. Roy. Asiatic Soc.* (China Branch), IV, 24, note.

so to speak, restored to the ancestral house. . . . This is, however, the only case in which a marriage union between relatives in the male line is regarded as allowable; a man may never . . . marry the daughter of a sister of his father."[58]

In southern India a boy is married to his paternal aunt's or maternal uncle's daughter, however old she may be. Again, "the bridegroom's sister meets the newly-married couple as they approach the bride's home, and prevents them from entering till she has extracted a promise from them that their child shall marry her child." Elsewhere, "the most proper alliance is one between a man and the daughter of his father's sister; and, if an individual has such a cousin, he must marry her, whatever disparity there may be between their respective ages." Failing a cousin of this sort, a boy "must marry his aunt or his niece, or some near relative. If his father's brother has a daughter, and insists upon his marrying her, he cannot refuse; and this whatever may be the woman's age." The author quoted[59] cites many other cases. In one district the brother has a prior claim to demand two daughters from his sister for marriage with his sons.[60] "The Tamul system, which to Morgan represents the Asiatic folk-groups, rests upon the fact that marriage within the closest grade of relationship in the side line ('brothers' and 'sisters') is forbidden, but in the more distant grade ('cousins') is precisely the rule."[61] In one district of Baluchistan, marriages are contracted between persons as closely related as possible, so long as they are outside certain prohibited degrees; a man will, if possible, marry his first cousin.[62] Among the Veddahs, whole districts must inevitably have come to be blood-related; there seems to be little objection to consanguine unions. The normal marriage is with a cousin.[63] The Singhalese exhibit the formal distinction alluded to above and below: marriage between a sister's son and a brother's daughter is regarded as the most proper one, while marriage with a daughter of a father's brother is regarded as incestuous, for such parties are looked upon as brother and sister.[64] Among the Todas, Rivers[65] "failed to find a single case in which marriage has taken place between the children of two own sisters, or of marriage between the children of two women who would call each other 'sister' whose names occur in the same genealogical table. . . . While marriage with the daughter of a father's brother and a mother's sister is prohibited, the daughter of a father's sister or a mother's brother is the natural wife of a man. The orthodox marriage is marriage between *matchuni,* the children of brother and sister. Thus it is obviously not nearness of blood-kinship in itself which acts as a restriction on marriage, but nearness of blood-kinship of a certain kind." The Hindu law-giver imposes a heavy penance upon one who has approached the daughter of his father's sister, "who is almost equal to a sister" or of his mother's sister or full brother. Wise men will not wed any one of these three, for they are *sapinda* relatives; "he who marries one of them sinks low."[66]

The Nair "may not marry his mother's sister's daughter, who is to him as his own sister. All his sisters, own and collateral, together with ladies of a previous generation in his family, form a legal incestuous group. A man has, there-

58 Grube, in *Veröffentl. aus dem K. Museum f. Völkerkunde,* VII, 29.
59 Thurston, *S. India,* 16, 52-53.
60 Scott, in JASB, IV, 359.
61 Bernhöft, *Verwandsftsnamen,* 16.
62 Risley, *Ethnog. India,* I, 71.

63 Sarasin, *Weddas,* 466, 467, 477; Grosse, *Familie,* 57-58.
64 Bailey, in *Trans. Eth. Soc. London,* II, 294.
65 *Todas,* 510, 512.
66 Bühler, *Manu,* XI, 172.

fore, to marry either entirely out of the circle of his relations, or from among his *cross-cousins*. . . . Your maternal uncle's daughter . . . is your *a priori* wife, if such an expression could be used. She is spoken of as the *Mura Pennu* (*Mura* = customary, and *Pennu* = female or wife, meaning customary wife)."[67] "The common rule regulating marriages among Brahmans, and indeed people of almost every caste in Southern India, is that the proper husband for a girl is her mother's brother or his son." In some cases, while a girl may not marry her mother's brother, "the children of a brother and sister may marry, and should do so, if this can be arranged, as, though the brother and sister are of the same *khilai* [kin-group], their children are not, because the children of the brother belong perforce to that of their mother, who is of a different *khilai*. It very often happens that a man marries into his father's *khilai*, indeed, there seems to be some idea that he should do so if possible. The children of brothers may not marry with each other, although they are of different *khilais*, for two brothers may not marry into the same *khilai*."[68] In the Malay Peninsula too it is found that "the children of brothers might not intermarry, but those of sisters or of a brother and sister might do so."[69]

This same rule is in evidence in the Archipelago, in the Aru Islands and elsewhere. Among the Letinese, as among the Hovas of Madagascar, unions between brothers' children and between those of brother and sister are allowable, but not those between sisters' children. Again, while children of two brothers or two sisters may not marry, those of brothers and sisters may. The inconsistencies are due to the presence, in one place and another, of descent in the female or male line. Wilken,[70] who records these cases, goes on to say that in the Minahasa district of Celebes, though marriage between cousins is allowed, the feeling that it is not quite right has not wholly disappeared, so that parents on both sides feel that they must make a small sacrifice of atonement. A goat is killed and blood sprinkled on the steps of the houses of officials, while the flesh makes a meal for all the village head-men. It seems that unions between brothers' and sisters' children have always been permitted. In Amboina there are two terms for female cousin, according as she is the daughter of a mother's brother or a father's sister. These are, respectively, *anamakain* and *tauli*. With the former a male cousin may allow himself all sorts of liberty: laugh at her, jest, dally, without hindrance from his elders. Marriage with her is allowed and often takes place. Quite different is his conduct with his *tauli;* the two are closer, regard each other as brother and sister, and may not marry. The impropriety of union with a *tauli* is expressed by the expression that one thereby "returns to his own source." Here, evidently, relationship is closer in the male line, according to local ideas; from the standpoint of consanguinity as we understand it, however, *anamakain* and *tauli* are equidistant, and the distinction is arbitrary. Meerwaldt[71] supports such cases by evidence from the Batak system. This tribe forbids union between the children of two brothers or between a brother's son and a sister's daughter; but a marriage between a man's daughter and his sister's son is preferred and, though not prescribed, is expected. A man's sister marries outside and he regards her daughters as his daughters; he will not give them to his son, who would, in such case, become his son-in-law. He gives his actual daughters to his sister's sons in order to

67 Panikkar, in JAI, XLVIII, 264-265;
Ghurye, in JAI, LIII, 79.
    68 Fawcett, in JAI, XXXIII, 62.

69 Skeat and Blagden, *Malay Penin.*, II, 84.

70 In VG, I, 453-454, 455, 456.
71 In *Bijd.*, XLI, 203.

establish the relationship which he formed when his sister married out. Tradition says that formerly a man took the daughter of his father's sister to wife, but that to such eventuated calamities. The author believes that descent in the female line is due to Malay influence. By contrast, in parts of the Philippines incest is extended to include first cousins; it is "the most serious of all crimes and merits the severest punishment."[72]

In Samoa "they say that, of old, custom and the gods frowned upon the union of those in whom consanguinity could be closely traced. Few had the hardihood to run in the face of superstition; but if they did, and their children died at a premature age, it was sure to be traced to the anger of the household god on account of the forbidden marriage."[73] Yet in central Polynesia, "the union of the grandchildren (and occasionally even of the children) of a brother and sister was . . . regarded as a fit and proper custom for the superior chiefs, but not for the common people. . . . The approval of marriages between the children of the cross-cousins more generally than as between the cousins themselves would probably be based upon the fact that their kinship was not so close." Coming down to special localities, we find that "in the island of Niue . . . the children of two brothers, or of a brother and sister, might marry without shocking the sentiments of the country; but the marriage of the offspring of two sisters was absolutely forbidden, this prohibition dating from the time when a man who married a girl had the right to marry all her sisters, so that it was never certain that children of sisters had not the same father. . . . In Rotuma marriage within the *hoang* was forbidden. The *hoang,* the smallest unit, except that of the individual man, in the social system of the island, was . . . a consanguine family, occupying a number of houses, placed together and forming, if the family was large enough, a small village." In Easter Island, the restriction went down to and included second cousins; third cousins might marry. "There was no other restriction as to marriage within the clan nor with any outside its borders." The author[74] quoted cites Moerenhout to the effect that in the Society Islands "marriages between near relations were not common; they were repugnant to the natives, and only took place when political interest made them absolutely necessary. . . . One cannot conceive an idea of the horror with which marriage contracted between near relations inspired the people." The author has a chapter on exogamy, containing chiefly taboos on consanguinity.

The relatives of the Thlinkit girl "are very desirous, as a rule, to marry her to some one on the father's side of the family. It may be an uncle, a cousin, or a grandfather. . . . Such marriages are not only considered very proper among the natives, but they more heartily desire them than marriages of any other connection."[75] One traveller, noting that certain Indian chiefs married the daughters of their younger brothers, asked the reason for this usage. "The one whom I asked said to me that they do this because they do not want their privileges to go out of their family. They keep their privileges among themselves by doing so."[76] Among the Tsimshians, "the normal type of marriage, as described in the traditions, is that between a young man and his mother's brother's daughter."[77] "Both on the islands and on the mainland, certainly in Cayenne, . . . it was customary for the Carib to marry their cousins german

72 Lobingier, in AA, XII, 253.
73 Turner, *Samoa,* 92.
74 Williamson, *Cent. Polyn.,* II, 136, 137, 142-144, ch. XVII.
75 Jones, *Thlingets,* 128.
76 Boas, in BAE, XXXV, pt. I, 782.
77 Boas, in BAE, XXXI, 440.

as a matter of right. Thus, they have a privilege to take all their cousins german, and have no more to say than that they take them for their wives; for they are naturally reserved for them." It is said that the Surinam Indians also commonly marry their nearest relatives, cousins or nieces. Of the Arawak it is written that, "unlike our families, these all descend in the female line, and no individual of either sex is allowed to marry another of the same family name. . . . That this arrangement neither checks nor prevents consanguinity is easy to recognize, for according to it, a woman can cohabit with her father's brother, but not with her mother's brother, or she can live with her cousin on her father's side, but not with the cousin on her mother's. With the Makusi, where descent was likewise claimed through the mother, . . . almost the very opposite rules would seem to have been enforced. For here the uncle on the father's side cannot marry his niece, because she is regarded as a relation next in degree to his brothers and sisters; he is called 'father' also. On the other hand, he is permitted to bind himself to the daughter of his sister, the wife of his dead brother, or his stepmother when the father is dead." An Arekuna "can not live with his mother's sister's daughter, but he can with his mother's brother's daughter; also with his father's brother's and father's sister's daughter."[78] Among the Araucanians, "it is probable that formerly exogamous customs prevailed, but at present the only restrictions imposed are that a man may not marry his mother or sister."[79]

In antiquity consanguineous unions were practised to keep the blood of a small minority of nobility pure.[80] It was customary, among the ancient Arabs, to marry a paternal uncle's daughter; her designation was also a term for "lover." By survival of maternal descent, the paternal relationship was not regarded as consanguine. It was a regular right of the Beduin to marry his first cousin, and there were no ill results. Wilken,[81] who reports this, quotes from Burckhardt: "All Arabian Bedouins acknowledge the first cousin's prior right to a girl, whose father cannot refuse to bestow her on him in marriage, should he pay a reasonable price; and that price is always something less than would be demanded from a stranger." Burton also is cited: "Every Bedouin has a right to marry his father's brother's daughter before she is given to a stranger; hence cousin . . . in polite phrase signifies a wife."

In Homer, Arete is the niece-wife of Alcinous.[82] In the *Institutes of Gaius*,[83] it is lawful to marry a brother's daughter but not a sister's. Among the heathen Germans "only the marriage of brother and sister was already, as it appears, forbidden."[84] In later times, in Corsica, "the marriages between consanguines are frequent and are regarded as the most auspicious."[85] In Europe, first cousins may marry except in Spain, Austria, and Hungary, where the canonical prohibition persists, and in Russia, where no nearer unions than those of third cousins have been allowed.[86] In this country, first-cousin marriage is forbidden in about twenty states.[87]

78 Roth, in BAE, XXXVIII, §§874, 876.
79 Latcham, in JAI, XXXIX, 359.
80 Tiele-Gehrich, *Gchte. Relig.*, II, 165; Jackson, *Zoroaster*, 42-43.
81 In VG, II, 44 ff.
82 *Odyssey*, XII, 338; XIII, 57; Keller, *Hom. Soc.*, 205.

83 I, 62.
84 Rudeck, *Oeffentl. Sittl.*, 186, 187.
85 Gubernatis, *Usi Nuz.*, 273.
86 Westermarck, *Marriage*, II, 101, 149-150.
87 Snyder, *Geog. of Marriage*, 51.

§349. Taboos of Narrower and Wider Scope.

Tʜᴇ following sets of cases are arranged roughly in the order of declining consanguinity: first come the taboos upon known relationship, then those upon what may be called probable relationship through common clan-membership, and, finally, those upon artificial kinship, where there is in reality no consanguinity. It is to be noted throughout that horror at the breaking of the taboo is horror of incest, whatever that may be taken to be. Certain of the cases will be similar to those reviewed in the preceding section, but are viewed from a somewhat different standpoint.

In parts of Australia, a man may marry a woman who stands in a certain denominated relationship to him and no one else may become his wife. This may mean that he is constrained to marry his cousin: "indeed we may say that the proper person for a man to marry, if it be possible, is his own first cousin. In the genealogies collected by me I found that in nearly every case where such a marriage was possible it had taken place." The case is complicated by the custom, common in most Australian tribes, of exchanging sisters. Two men who bear a certain relationship to one another, marry each other's sisters. "As a result of this practice it often happens that a man's father's sister is at the same time the wife of his mother's brother. If these two have a daughter she will in the ordinary course of events become the man's wife." The woman to whom a man has the first right as a wife is preëminently the daughter of his own mother's brother, or, failing this, of his own father's sister. The author[1] quoted sums up the Australian usage as follows: "In all the Australian tribes about which we have detailed information marriage is regulated by relationship. In all tribes a man may only marry women who stand to him in a certain relationship of consanguinity." The taboo extends to all others, related or not in our sense. There are two types here distinguished, the first being the one cited above, where "a man marries the daughter of his mother's brother, or some woman who stands to him in an equivalent relation. Where the marriage law is of Type II, a man marries his mother's mother's brother's daughter's daughter, or some woman who stands to him in an equivalent relation." The second type is very much more widespread in Australia than the former. "Corresponding to each type of marriage rule there is a type of relationship system." But the marriage laws "are not in any way whatever affected by the existence in the tribe of two or four named divisions. . . . The fact that a tribe has two or four named divisions tells us nothing whatever about the marriage law of the tribe, which can only be ascertained by a careful study of the system of relationship." Furthermore, the prohibition of the marriage of first cousins is shown by observed facts not to be due to change from maternal to paternal descent of the totem.

In Southeast Papua "it is forbidden to marry blood relations on the mother's side. Susu includes all these relations. A village is made up of various Susu separated by clear boundaries. Marriage may be contracted in a village outside of the mother's Susu." Evidently the criterion of consanguinity is passing into one of a territorial order. "It is also forbidden to marry in the father's Susu, but only because by so doing rules concerning mourning feasts would be broken. Marriage does not admit into the Susu. Proper respect must always be

1 Brown, in JAI, XLIII, 155-156, 184-185, 188, 190-194.

paid to married relatives. There must never be too much familiarity with the spouse's Susu."[2] Among certain Melanesians, "ultimately, the regulation of marriage depends on the avoidance of marriage within the forbidden degrees, which extend to third cousins; . . . marriage within the *iduhu* [clan] is, and always has been, rare, in spite of there being no avowed objection to the practice. . . . A large proportion of marriages take place between individuals of the same or neighbouring villages. This fact, perhaps, gives a clue to the rarity of marriages within the *iduhu* in spite of the fact that there is no avowed objection to the practice. Since even third cousins are not allowed to marry, experience may have shown that it is generally impossible for men and women of the same *iduhu* to marry without infringing the law of consanguinity.[3] In Tikopia Island, "within each class marriage is regulated purely by kinship. . . . The social divisions have no significance in connection with marriage. Provided two persons are unrelated it is a matter of no importance whether they are of the same or a different division."[4] In Lifu, Loyalty Islands, "there was no division of the people for marriage purposes as in the islands of Melanesia northwards, and there were no restrictions as to whom a man might marry, except near kinship. Marriages between cousins (first and second) were prohibited."[5]

On the Upper Congo "a man cannot marry his mother, his sister, his aunt, his daughter, his grandmother, nor his granddaughter. Neither can he marry his nieces or cousins—they are his brothers, sisters or children. He can marry his father's wives but not that one who is his own mother."[6] In British Central Africa, "a man may not marry any member of his wife's family, nor of the same clan names, nor two sisters, nor a deceased wife's sister."[7] In East Africa, "marriage is prohibited between persons of one family, one clan, and between children of men who have entered into blood-brotherhood."[8] Among the Dinka, "by 'incest' is meant the offence of sexual intercourse between persons related by blood from either the father or mother of either of such persons. . . . This is carried back for many generations, and appears to be limited only by the accuracy with which family tradition can trace the genealogy of persons so offending. . . . Any children born from the offence belong to the father or guardian of the girl, but go with her when married, an increase of 'marriage payment' being required on this account."[9] Among the Masai, "first cousins and second cousins may not marry, but there is no objection to third cousins marrying if the relationship is no nearer than" certain grades established by local nomenclature. "Thus, a man's son's son's son may not marry the man's brother's son's son's daughter, nor may a man's son's son's son marry the sister's son's son's daughter, but there would be no objection to a man's son's son's son marrying the brother's daughter's daughter's daughter or the sister's daughter's daughter's daughter. Likewise though a man's son's son may not marry the man's maternal uncle's son's son's daughter, he may marry the maternal uncle's son's daughter's daughter. These unions are always contingent on the two parties not belonging to the same sub-clan. The rules of consanguinity and affinity which regulate marriage also apply to the sexual intercourse of warriors with immature girls before marriage and to the rights of hospitality after marriage. . . . Members of the various sub-clans are

2 Bromilow, in AAAS, 1909, 481.
3 Seligmann, *Melanesians*, 81-83.
4 Rivers, *Melan. Soc.*, I, 309.
5 Ray, in JAI, XLVII, 286.

6 Weeks, in JAI, XXXIX, 443.
7 Stannus, in JAI, XL, 309.
8 Dundas, C., in JAI, XLV, 286.
9 O'Sullivan, in JAI, XL, 187.

usually to be found in all the districts and sub-districts. Marriages are not affected by geographical considerations, and a man has the same lawful marital relations in all the sub-districts as he has in his own home sub-district. . . . The rules are quite simple if one remembers (i) that though the clans are not exogamous, the sub-clans into which the clans are divided are exogamous; and (ii) that no man may marry a nearer relation than a third cousin, and then only if the terms of address," the local designations, are as prescribed.[10]

In Samoa, "all the evidence points to the spreading of the family net, within which matrimonial alliances were prohibited, very widely. . . . The conception of the family or related group, within which marriages were not allowed, showed no clear distinction between relatives on the father's side and those on the side of the mother. . . . If we are told that persons of specific degrees of relationship might not marry, this is, I gather, a question of incest. But if the statement is that a man might not marry a woman loosely described as of his own family or social group or clan, it seems to become a question of what the evidence means. . . . Marriages between members of the same domestic family, or other relatively small social group, would generally come within laws against incest; but, as groups became larger, this probability would diminish. . . . It follows therefore that we cannot always say whether the evidence points to mere rules against incest, or whether it also indicates a system of group separation for matrimonial purposes the character of which went beyond what was necessary for the avoidance of incest. . . . The recognition of fictitious bonds of kinship would perhaps enlarge the conception of kinship even as regards questions of incest. . . . I may say that the evidence as to the practices connected with courtship and betrothal, and the ceremonies of marriage, and what occurred afterwards, points to a common custom for a man to seek a wife in another village or district, or whatever it may be called, than his own."[11] In the Gilbert Islands, "a native was forbidden to marry—(a) Lineal kin; (b) All descendants of a common ancestor, on male or female side, out of his or her own generation; (c) Descendants of a common ancestor in his or her own generation, to the second degree of cousinship. Adoptive relationships and those of half blood were counted the same as those of full blood. The native catchword concerning the marriage of kinsfolk was, and is, . . . the fourth generation goes free; thus if three generations separated each of the parties to a marriage from a common ancestor, no ban of consanguinity rested upon them. Several such unions have taken place within my own experience; . . . nevertheless, they were not regarded with any great favour by the old people of the respective families, who considered that, in the ideal state, collaterals should await the fifth generation before coming together."[12]

Among certain Indians of Oregon, it seems that "the exogamous tendency was local and extended to villages rather than to tribes. The expressly forbidden degrees extended to any recognized relationship."[13] In one British Columbia tribe, the only bar to marriage discoverable was "sameness or nearness of blood. It was not lawful for any of near blood to intermarry. The only reason they could give for this bar was that it was considered 'shameful' for those of the same blood to marry or have intercourse with one another. . . .

10 Hollis, in JAI, XL, 479.
11 Williamson, Cent. Polyn., II, 127, 130-132, 135.
12 Grimble, in JAI, LI, 26.
13 Farrand, in AA, III, 242.

The old people expressed astonishment that first cousins, who with them are regarded as 'brothers' and 'sisters,' should be permitted by us to intermarry."[14] Elsewhere there was an epithet "kiyuksa ('breakers,' so called because the members broke the marriage law by taking wives within prohibited degrees of kinship)."[15]

"A comparison between the forbidden degrees of Greeks and Romans clearly shows where we have to seek for the real cause of the prohibitions. Among the former, even very close relationship was no hindrance to intermarriage, whereas, among the latter, it was not allowed between rather distantly related persons. This difference . . . was due to the fact that the family feeling of the Greeks was much weaker than that of the Romans, among whom in early times, a son used to remain in his father's house even after marriage, so that cousins on the father's side were brought up as brothers and sisters. Later on, the several families separated from the common household and the prohibited degrees were considerably retrenched."[16] "The Talmudists, by reason of anxiety over the possible infringement of the Mosaic order, extended the scope of the prohibition to more distant grades of relationship"; this extension was indefinitely widened later on.[17]

The clan was an extension of the closer consanguine group; when, now, the prohibition rests upon inter-clan unions, it is passing into a phase where consanguinity is theoretic rather than demonstrable. Among certain Australians, a man "may not marry a woman of his own clan," nor of any other clan that has the same totem as his own. He may not take a wife from his mother's clan, or that of his father's mother, his mother's mother, his father's father's mother, or his mother's father's mother. "He may marry into any other clan, but he may not marry a woman who is related to him by any of the recognised blood-relationships." Sometimes marriage gets to be "difficult to arrange owing to the excessive limitations imposed by the system. In different parts of Australia we find attempts to get over this difficulty by modifying the system in some way or other. . . . There is a tendency, easily perceived in some Australian tribes, and probably present in all, to maintain the unity of the clan as a part of the system of relationship by means of a rule that if an individual stands in a close relation to one member of the clan, then that must determine his relation to all the members of the clan." Following this out, as the author[18] does, he finds it issuing in a very serious restriction on marriage which would not exist if there was a large number of smaller clans. He then describes certain curious so-called blood-divisions which operate to reduce restriction.

Among the Akamba, "if a man visits his friend belonging to the same *Mbaya* or clan he is given a temporary wife during his stay, the wife however must of course be of a different clan, *e.g.*, if a Mweombi man visits another Mweombi he will be given one of the wives of his host, who will, say, be of the Mutangwa clan. Sometimes a very intimate friend not belonging to the same clan may also receive this honour while on a visit, but it is a rare occurrence."[19] In East Africa, "excepting for the prohibition which forbids a man to marry a girl out of his own clan, there are no restrictions in the choice of a wife."[20] "If a

14 Hill-Tout, in JAI, XXXV, 133.
15 HAI, I, 711.
16 Rossbach, *Röm. Ehe*, 421-423, 429, 439 (translation by Westermarck).
17 Bergel, *Eheverhält. d. alten Juden*, 6.

18 Brown, in JAI, XLVIII, 238; and in JAI, LIII, 439, 443, 444.
19 Hobley, *A-Kamba*, 64.
20 Dundas, C., in JAI, XLIII, 521.

man find that he has married a woman of the same clan as himself, the following procedure is resorted to. The man and his wife climb on to the roof of the hut and after swallowing a blue bead both cry out: 'Now we have no longer any clan.' Descending they enter the hut and shut the door. An old man then comes to the door and calls to them: 'Come forth now, for you have no longer any clan'; and they leave the hut and sacrifice a white goat, from the belly of which a strip of skin is cut with which the man ties his right hand to the woman's left hand; this is then severed. After this they may live together as man and wife."[21] Each Bageshu clan "seeks wives outside itself from one of its neighbours. . . . Blood relationship is a bar to marriage, that is, a man may not marry any one of his father's clan and he also avoids his mother's clan; all the women of that clan are his mother's near relations, those who are her real sisters he calls his mothers. . . . The people are all polygamists and may marry sisters of the first wife if they wish; there are no restrictions as to the number of wives, nor how many they may take from one family."[22]

Rivers[23] writes, in connection with the Toda system: "In nearly every known community, whether savage, barbarous or civilised, there is found to exist a deeply rooted antipathy to sexual intercourse between brother and sister. In savage communities where kinship is of the classificatory kind, this antipathy extends not only to the children of one mother, but to all those who are regarded as brothers and sisters because they are members of the same clan or other social unit. In some communities, such as those of Torres Straits, this antipathy may extend to relatives as remote as those we call second and third cousins, so long as descent through the male line from a common ancestor and membership of the same clan lead people to regard one another as brother and sister. It is very doubtful whether this widespread, almost universal abhorrence is shared by the Todas. I was told that members of the same clan might have intercourse with one another." Yet they have definite restrictions on freedom of joining alliances. "One of the most important of these is that which prevents intermarriage between the Tartharol and the Teivaliol. These groups are endogamous divisions of the Toda people. . . . Each of these two divisions of the Toda community is divided into a number of septs or clans, and these are definite exogamous groups. No man or woman may marry a member of his or her own clan, but must marry into another clan. . . . In the whole of the genealogical record given in the tables at the end of the volume there is not a single case in which marriage has occurred between two members of the same clan. Among many races at or below the stage of culture of the Todas prohibition of marriage within the clan is usually accompanied by prohibition of sexual intercourse, and such intercourse is regarded as incest and often as the greatest of crimes. It is doubtful whether there is any such strict prohibition among the Todas. . . . The Todas have never married people outside their own community, and a strong prejudice against such marriages still exists." Inter-caste union is tabooed among the Nairs. "The men that a girl could possibly marry were strictly restricted by certain conditions. A . . . girl is not allowed to contract a marriage with men of a lower subcaste. She can marry either in her own subcaste or in castes above hers. She is not allowed to marry one who is not at least two years older than herself. She cannot marry anyone who shares pollution with her (that is descended from the same ancestress on the

21 Dundas, K. R., in JAI, XLIII, 30-31.   23 Todas, 530, 508.
22 Roscoe, in JAI, XXXIX, 182-183.

maternal side, however remote). There are cases when the common ancestress lived nearly four hundred years ago, but still her descendants are supposed to be so closely related in blood as to preclude matrimonial relationship of any sort."[24]

Wilken[25] is quite copious in illustration of the prohibition of intra-clan union. Among Malays, union with a clan-mate is considered by all exogamous peoples as incest, with some departures where a marriage outside the village is in question. The Bataks adhere strictly to the taboo; formerly those who broke it were killed and eaten. In South Sumatra, persons who trespass against the taboo are destroyed, along with their offspring, by the gods. Nor may children marry into the *sumbai* (kin-group) of their parents. With regard to grandchildren, these limitations do not exist, so that these may marry freely into the *sumbai* of a grandparent, provided that they themselves or their parents do not belong to it. Everything depends wholly upon whether the grandfather was married with the brideprice or not. In the former case, the grandchildren may not form a union in his *sumbai*, but only in that of the grandmother; in the latter, just the opposite. Sometimes in Sumatra the prohibition is relaxed, so that a man may marry a woman of his kin-group if she is not of his family. Thus the taboo has been shifted from the larger kin-group to its constituent families. Still, one may not marry within that larger group without first giving a feast and paying a sum of money in order, as it were, to make good the transgression. Where, among the Malays, "exogamy does not exist, or at any rate no longer exists, the punishments for incest are very definite. As a rule, the guilty are condemned to death and there is no composition through fine allowed."

In Albania, "a *fis* or tribe . . . consists of one or more *bariaks,* that is, groups of men that fight under one standard. . . . In some tribes all the *bariaks* trace descent from a common male ancestor, and the divisions have only been made for convenience when the tribe grew large. In other cases certain *bariaks* are of other blood, and have been adopted into the tribe. . . . The tribes are strictly exogamous. That is, they invariably take wives from outside the tribe, excepting when a *bariak* within it is of different blood. Male blood only counts. . . . The rule is so strict that even tribes who trace origin from several brothers will not intermarry. . . . All descendants of a common male ancestor rank as brothers and sisters, and their union is looked on as incestuous and in the highest degree horrible. . . . So deeply rooted is the feeling that in all my eight months of wandering I heard of only one instance in which the law was broken. A girl eloped with a distant cousin on her father's side. He was far enough removed for the Roman Church to marry them. But it was incest in the eyes of the outraged family. The luckless couple fled to another tribe for shelter, but were hunted down. The bridegroom was shot down within the year, as was also his brother, who had aided the elopement and the bride's life was only saved by the intervention of the Franciscans." That such strictness does not preclude actual inbreeding appears from the following. "As it has been the almost universal practice to take a wife from the tribe next door and to marry the resultant daughters back into it (unless of course the tribe be one that is consanguineous), it follows that certain tribes must be very closely inbred on the female side. So far as I could learn among

---

24 Panikkar, in JAI, XLVIII, 271.   25 In VG, I, 306-307; II, 223-226, 335, 347, 478.

the .Moslems, two tribes will go on exchanging daughters backwards and for-wards for generations (I ascribe to this practice the very marked type of the Moslem tribes); and it has only recently been checked among the Christians. But the people declare that such tribes are in no way related—have not one drop of the same blood. I said a child had some of its mother's blood, but they said, 'No, only the father's.' The people all know most exact lists of their relatives on the male side. The fact that I could not enumerate my paternal cousins beyond second cousins was reckoned as a proof of the barbarous state of English society. 'Just like dogs or cattle.' In fact, many of our habits, about which they perpetually questioned me, filled them with contempt or disgust, and they explained the superiority of their own."[26]

The cases that are to follow show, on the face of them, little or no element of consanguinity. They are, for the most part, wholly irrelevant to any con-tention that taboos on marriage arose from appreciation of the ill effects of in-breeding. Thus, in Melanesia, Rivers[27] thinks he has shown that several of the taboos upon unions where there can be no community of blood demonstrated are due to "a social system characterised by dominance of the old men." Selig-mann,[28] citing Hobley,[29] records that among the A-Kamba there is "a special curse used for a bad wife, the husband draws a little milk from her breast into his hand, and then licks it up, this is a curse which has no palliative, after it the husband can never again cohabit with the woman." Then Seligmann, hav-ing put this illiterate statement into italics, goes on to remark: "I venture to think there can be little doubt as to the significance of this ceremony, espe-cially when it is remembered that in the Hamitic area it is not infrequent for foster children to be looked upon as related to each other in the same degree as blood relations. Thus milk affords as valid a bond as blood, and the cere-mony just described can only mean that the husband purposely makes himself of one blood (milk) with the woman and thus cuts himself loose from her for ever." Among the Kabyles, "though custom does not prohibit it, the man of good family will never take a wife from a family whose members practise a profession reputed to be dishonorable, such as those of butcher, dancer, saddler, or cobbler."[30] This is almost a caste-taboo. Miss Czaplicka[31] records a series of taboos from Siberia: among blood-relations a man is forbidden to marry his mother, daughter, own sister, cousin, father's sister, mother's sister, brother's daughter, own sister's daughter. "Between all other blood-relations marriages are permitted." As for relatives by affinity, a man may not marry the following: "(1) stepmother; (2) sister of living wife (i.e. simultaneously two sisters); (3) cousin of living wife (i.e. simultaneously two cousins); (4) younger brother's widow; (5) deceased wife's elder sister; (6) nephew's widow; (7) sister of brother's wife (i.e. two brothers cannot marry two sisters); (8) cousin of brother's wife (i.e. two brothers cannot marry two cousins); (9) simultaneously an aunt and her niece; (10) two brothers can-not marry, one an aunt and the other her niece; (11) two male cousins cannot marry, one an aunt and the other her niece; (12) an uncle and nephew can-not marry two sisters, two cousins, or two women of whom one is an aunt and the other her niece; (13) a step-daughter." To a questioner concerning

26 Durham, in JAI, XL, 458, 459.
27 *Melan. Soc.*, II, 119; ch. XVII.
28 In JAI, XLIII, 657.
29 *A-Kamba*, 105.

30 Hanoteau and Letourneux, *Kabylie*, II, 165.
31 *Aborig. Siberia*, 81-82.

these taboos, a Koryak answered that "relatives of the categories mentioned would die soon if they should enter into cohabitation with one another."

In China, "the degrees of unlawful marriages are comprehensive, extending even to the prohibition of persons having the same *sing,* or family name, and to two brothers marrying sisters. The laws forbid the marriage of a brother's widow, of a father's or grandfather's wife, or a father's sister, under the penalty of death." There was a prohibition of intermarriages between Manchus and Chinese, as between conquerors and conquered. The honorable and the mean "cannot intermarry without the former forfeiting their privileges; the latter comprise, besides aliens and slaves, criminals, executioners, police-runners, actors, jugglers, beggars, and all other vagrant or vile persons, who are in general required to pursue for three generations some honorable and useful employment before they are eligible to enter the literary examinations."[32] Among other detailed proscriptions are marriage with the step-daughter and with female relations within the fourth degree of relationship, with the widow of a relative of the fourth degree, or with the sister of the widowed daughter-in-law. "Marriages with widows of relatives of a nearer degree are considered incestuous."[33] Legislation regarding marriage occupies a prominent place in the Penal Code of China. It strictly prohibits parties who labor under certain specific disabilities from entering into the state of matrimony, and renders its obligations fully as sacred and secure (taking into consideration the peculiar notions of the Chinese) as they can be with ourselves."[34]

The Land Dyaks do not allow union with a deceased wife's sister, while the Sea Dyaks almost universally permit it; it is often encouraged for the very good reason that the children will then be brought up as one family. In the Indian Archipelago, social position counts heavily in the contracting of alliances; "there is no absence of rank and position, and almost nowhere is to be found the idyllic equality of which some dream." There are distinctions between free people and slaves, including pawns, also a species of nobility or aristocracy composed of those stocks favored by fortune and treated with respect, among whom the chiefs and other officials and their families take first place. "As a general rule it can be stated that among the peoples of the Indian Archipelago difference in position is taken strictly into consideration in marriage, so much so that not alone are unions between free and unfree, but also those between the aristocracy or nobility and the common people, reprobated, here and there even forbidden." Position comes under consideration especially when the woman is of higher rank; there is less repugnance at a union of a nobleman with a woman of the people, because by payment of the bride-price the children, following the father, belong automatically to his rank.[35] In Samoa, "the widower may marry his deceased wife's sister; the widow her deceased husband's brother. Both cases often occur at the wish of the dying parent in order to secure loving treatment for the children. Such wishes do not constitute a command, although often complied with from superstitious reasons." The author quoted[36] cites a novel twist in the mores. "The effect of division in war of a tribe is specially interesting, for here the question of marriage restrictions depended not on degrees of relationship, but upon what Gill calls 'clan

32 Williams, *Middle Kingdom*, I, 792-793, 412, 412-413.
33 Von Mollendorff, *Fam. Law*, 16, 17.
34 Medhurst, in *China Br., Roy. Asiatic Soc.*, 1853-1854, pt. IV, 3.
35 Wilken, in VG, I, 312, 460-463.
36 Williamson, *Cent. Polyn.*, II, 125, 139-140.

law.' People who could not marry so long as the tribe was all one tribe could do so when it was regarded as having been divided into two; and the clan idea appears to have been so strong as to enable marriages to take place between people who under laws of incest would not be allowed to do so." It is a "curious fact that marriage in a group might be allowed if, as the result of internal war, the group was regarded as having been split up into two groups." Certainly such a case is strong evidence of the arbitrary nature of restrictions. On the island of Yap cousins might not marry and earlier it was regarded as a transgression against custom if a pair of brothers married a pair of sisters. It is allowed to marry the sisters of one's dead or separated wife, but the father may not marry his widowed or divorced daughter-in-law or a man his foster-child.[37]

In the code of Hammurabi, the following punishments were listed: for incest with a son's betrothed, a fine; with a son's wife, drowning; with a father's wife, disinheritance.[38] Among the Mohammedans of Spain the reprobation of marriage with two sisters is represented as law but not yet in the mores.[39] Marriage between believer and unbeliever was forbidden.[40] In the regular Moslem law the union of those related through the nurse (foster-relations) was not allowed, nor might two sisters be married together. Two living in vice may not marry until after confession and punishment. There must be no marriage with a relative of a woman with whom one has had illicit relations.[41] In Roman law marriage might not be concluded between persons who stood to each other in the relation of guardianship, as *tutor* and *pupilla* or between a *præses provinciæ* and a woman of his province.[42] A curiosity is the provision that at the feast of the Bona Dea and the astum Cereris, a purification-ceremony for women, the mere presence of a man counted as incest and even the representations of male animals were covered. On this day and the preceding the women refrained from all sex-relations.[43] An example of a rational taboo is given by Plutarch,[44] he says of Cato that "in the belief that his slaves were led into most mischief by their sexual passions, he stipulated that the males should consort with the females at a fixed price, but should never approach any other woman."

At times of famine in Iceland marriage was forbidden to those who had no property, and eighty-year-old persons or weak-minded might not marry without the consent of their relatives.[45]

The year 1907 saw the eventual passage of a bill by the British House of Lords permitting a man to marry his deceased wife's sister. The authority for that taboo lay in the Mosaic Law, as understood. But the abrogation did not carry with it the repeal of the law against a woman marrying her deceased husband's brother, which is distinctly commanded and prescribed by the Mosaic Law. As late as 1920, Mr. Lloyd George declined to introduce a bill in the House of Commons to legalize the latter union. It took half a century to pass the bill first mentioned, and the church has yielded only reluctantly. "That English Church Council, which at its recent session in London, condemned marriage with a deceased wife's sister by a vote of 224 to 14, has no

37 Senfft, in *Globus*, XCI, 141.
38 Harper, *Hammurabi*, 125.
39 Dozy, *Hist.*, I, 36-37.
40 Wellhausen, in *Gött. Gesellsft. Wissnsften*, 1893, 438.
41 Tornauw, *Moslim. Recht*, 64.

42 Von Mollendorff, *Family Law*, 18, 20, note.
43 Rossbach, *Röm. Ehe*, 266, 268.
44 *Cato*, §XXI.
45 Leo, *Island*, 476.

real authority," reads a communication of 1909. "Bishops and other ecclesiastical dignitaries were members, but it is a purely voluntary association, and we are surprised that it should undertake to vote on the subject, and to reprobate the use of the Prayer Book in solemnizing such unions. Parliament, the only authority which has any right to rule in the matter, has decided that such marriages are legal. There is no Bible against them, and if there were a Mosaic prohibition it would have no more validity than the command to sprinkle the ashes of a red heifer, or to raise up seed to a brother who has died childless. The action of the council is not simply impertinent; it prejudices the public against the meddlesome Church. Is it not plain that when the state has decided such marriages lawful, it is well that they should be solemnized with all religious weight by the Church? Of course, it will be declared that it is not the State but the Church, that rules in marriage; but the whole world knows better."[46]

§350. Causes of the Taboo.

It is evident from foregoing examples that primitive peoples are almost universally horrified at incest, whatever they may consider that to be. The following few cases may serve to complete the list cited in the text.

"Bula! is said to the circumcised boys, i.e. confess your incest; when they heal slowly, they are understood to have been guilty of impurity with relatives; bula! confess your incest, is said to a woman in child-bed and to her husband, when the child refuses to take the breast, which according to their superstition is caused by the man or woman having been unfaithful in heart at least."[1] If the harvest fails for the Macassars and Buginese, that is a sure sign that incest has been practised and that the ghosts are angered. In 1877 and 1878 the west monsoon failed utterly, the rice did not thrive as a result, and besides thousands of buffaloes perished from the cattle-pest. At that time there was in prison a condemned man who had earlier committed incest. A part of the people of the district where that person belonged sought his release, since it was the universal persuasion that there would be no end to the trouble so long as the guilty one had not undergone the proper punishment. All his powers of persuasion, says the controller, were necessary to persuade them to go back home again quietly, and when the condemned man shortly thereafter came to the end of his sentence, he was given the chance, at his own request, to escape in a boat, he not believing that he would be safe in his own country.[2] "Incest was punished on Tamana and Arorae by laying the offenders face down in a shallow pool of water and suffocating them; in the Northern Gilberts the culprits were lashed to a log of wood and set adrift in the ocean; the lightest punishment seems to have been to put the incestuous couple aboard a small canoe, with a few coco-nuts, a paddle but no sail, and thus abandon them to the elements. The belief was that the sun would hide his face from the place in which two such offenders were allowed to live unpunished."[3] Among the Salish Indians, "first and second cousins fell within the prohibited degrees, but beyond those limits there seem to have been no hard and fast

46 N. Y. *Tribune*, August 25, 1907; N. Y. *Times*, July 16, 1919; Nov. 9, 1920; Nov. 9, 1924; *The Independent*, LXVII, 381-382 (quoted). The Levitical law is stated in Levit., XVIII, 16.

1 Kropf, *Kaffir-Eng. Dict.*, 46.
2 Wilken, in VG, II, 335.
3 Grimble, in JAI, LI, 26.

rules. When questioned concerning the reason of these prohibitions they could give no other reply than that it was their 'custom,' and that it was considered 'big shame' for persons connected by blood to intermarry. This is in keeping with the general practice and belief of the Salish. . . . Whatever may have been the origin of these prohibitions among the Salish, it is certain that marriages between those nearly related were held in abhorrence long before there was any possibility of missionary influence making itself felt among them."[4]

The genesis of the view that in-breeding causes certain specific physical ills would form a protracted and engrossing study. "Gregory the Great placed the objection to the marriage of cousins wholly upon physical or sanitary grounds. Impressed with the popular belief which then prevailed, and which still prevails to some extent, he believed that such marriages were not fertile and declares: 'We have learned from experience that from such marriages offspring cannot grow.' "[5] Wilken[6] quotes a hardheaded writer of 1768 who combats the alleged "horror naturalis" of incest. "I hope it will be permitted also to ask whether we really have such a natural impulse or horror? And it is not enough merely to allege it: investigation is easy, for if there is some such natural impulse, everyone must perceive it clearly in his own case—yes, it must be found not merely in the case of one and another, but must be common to the human species. If this is not so, then it must be held to be, not a natural impulse but a consequence of education."

§352. Divisional and Tribal Endogamy.

MATHEWS[1] makes a sweeping denial of the presence of exogamy in New South Wales, Victoria, Queensland, and in northern and western Australia. This is consonant with the backward condition of the tribes in question. In Mombasa, East Africa, "marriages outside the tribe are discouraged, the elders requiring an assurance of the girl's consent before allowing her departure. This should act as a deterrent, for a girl of thirteen or fourteen is not often willing to change familiar for strange surroundings. In periods of famine however such unions are very frequent, owing to the wholesale migration of a starving tribe into the territory of its more fortunate neighbours."[2] A case of this order supplies hints as to special variations in the direction of exogamy which may well have supplemented general trends toward that form. "Marriage between persons of different tribes is of course hardly contemplated by tribal law, and in so far may be considered as no marriage. It is perhaps for this reason that among certain tribes smiths and hunters may not marry women of other classes, they being originally not members of the tribe, but aliens, such as the Derobbo and other aborigines."[3]

"All our earlier evidence concerning the Koryak seems to point to endogamic marriage. In the 'Description of people living near Yakutsk, Okhotsk, and in Kamchatka,' compiled by the local administration *circa* 1780, . . . we read that the Koryak 'do not take wives from another *ord,* and do not give their daughters for wives out of this *ord,* but marry among themselves.' Though the term *ord* is not defined, one may suppose that it corresponds to a clan or

---

4 Hill-Tout, in JAI, XXXIV, 319.
5 Snyder, *Geog. of Marr.*, 45; Bergel,
Eheverhält. d. alten Juden, 6.
6 In VG, II, 333.

1 In *Mitt. Anth. Ges. Wien*, XXXVI, Heft
5 ("Kl. Nachr.," in *Globus*, XC, 356).
2 Johnstone, in JAI, XXXII, 267.
3 Dundas, C., in JAI, I., 251.

local group. . . . 'They take their wives mostly from their own stock, first cousins, aunts, step-mothers; the only people whom they do not marry are sisters, mothers, step-daughters.' Jochelson himself asserts that in Koryak mythology only marriage with a sister or a mother is held to be a crime, but there are many instances of marriages between cousins. Thus we may suppose that most of the marriage prohibitions are of later introduction. . . . This most important regulation of Gilyak marriage is implied in their saying: 'Thence, whence you came forth—from the clan of your mother—you must take your wife.' " The Gilyak system, while it prescribes a certain type of exogamy as between the sub-divisions of the clan, is characteristically endogamous. "The Gilyak calls not only his own mother *ymk,* but also all her sisters and all the wives of his father's brothers, real and classificatory, as well as the sisters of these women. He calls not only his own father *ytk,* but also the husbands of his mother's sisters, and his father's brothers. . . . A Gilyak woman names by the term *pu* not only her husband, but his brothers and the husbands of his sisters. The Gilyak calls not only his wife *angey,* but also the wives of his elder brothers (real and classificatory), and these wives' sisters, and similarly all sisters of his wife. He used the same term for all daughters of his uncles (proper) and all daughters of the brothers of the women whom he calls *ymk.* These classes could only originate under a rule by which all men in one class, A, had to take wives from another class, B, so that the men of class A are destined from birth to marry the daughters of their mother's brothers." This is the important regulation alluded to above. The following schematic table showing the original marriage-regulations of three family-gentes, forming one clan, is given:

Gens A	*Gens B*	*Gens C*
Male A marries female B (sister of male B). Their sons marry daughters B; and their daughters marry sons C.	Male B marries female C (sister of male C). Their sons marry daughters C; and their daughters marry sons A.	Male C marries female A (sister of male A). Their sons marry daughters A; and their daughters marry sons B.

"Inside the clan there is an endogamic arrangement, while each gens is exogamic. . . . All people who are in the relation of *angey* and *pu* have really the right of sexual intercourse, not only before, but also after, the individual marriage. In the absence of her husband, a wife can have intercourse with any man who is *pu* to her."[4] Such usages appear to verge upon survivals of a much looser form of union, approaching group-associations. The terminology is characteristic of systems of address later to be considered.[5] The essentially endogamous nature of the regulations comes out clearly enough upon scrutiny; in fact, evidence for closeness of in-breeding appears in connection with any such loose systems or survivals.

Among the Kuki-Lushai of India, "marriage among nearly all the clans, . . . is endogamous, as regards the clan, but exogamous as regards the family. . . . A man may marry any woman, except his sisters, mother and grandmother; maternal first cousins marry freely, but there is a certain prejudice against paternal first cousins marrying."[6] "The Nilgala Veddahs,

4 Czaplicka, *Aborig. Siberia,* 82, 98-99.   6 Shakespear, in JAI, XXXIX, 381.
5 §423, of the text.

who still maintain an almost total isolation from other people, are rapidly disappearing. The Veddahs of Bintenne, who have abandoned the pernicious custom of marriage between a brother and younger sister, and still intermarry among themselves, are becoming extinct, though more gradually."[7] In Borneo, "though it is not forbidden to marry into a neighboring, non-related group, yet that comes about so seldom that Tamans and Kayans have lived a half-century and longer next to each other without mingling, the while they retain their own language and customs. Most aliens have come over from related groups and remain attached through marriage for a shorter or longer time."[8] The Alfurs of the Minahasa and the Dyaks have some tendency to and phenomena of endogamy.[9] "In the typical case of the Seri [Indians] interclan marriage is continued in order that tribal union may be maintained. Mating or even sporadic connection with aliens is strictly forbidden, that the integrity of the tribe may be preserved."[10] The Araucanians of Chile show little propensity to marry outside their own people; they never submitted to the yoke of Spain and preserved what might be called race-endogamy.[11] Here was a kind of political basis for in-marriage; and the religious basis has not been lacking in history. Mixed marriages were the horror of the old Persian priests who thought that the influence of the alien mothers, since the early years of the child were so predominantly under that influence, must lead to heterodoxy.[12] The feeling of the orthodox Hebrews toward union with the Gentiles is well-known; modern rabbis still emphasize the ill effects of mixed marriages. "We are opposed to intermarriage because we believe in our own religious mission and we feel that whatever tends to weaken that mission ought not to be encouraged. By intermarriage we understand the union of two persons of different faiths who after marriage still cling to their respective religions. The Jews never objected to that kind of intermarriage as the result of which the non-Jewish party became a convert to Judaism."[13]

§353. Divisional and Tribal Exogamy.

WHEN one approaches the subject of marriage-prohibitions, he finds the materials in evidence both copious and complicated. We are seeking here to illustrate rather than to explain; explanation, whether persuasive or not, is a highly technical matter.

Brown,[1] in treating of three tribes of West Australia, writes as follows: "The Kariera tribe is divided into four parts that I shall speak of as *classes*. The names of these are Banaka, Burung, Palyeri, and Karimera. . . . A man of any given class is restricted in his choice of a wife to one of the other classes. Thus a Banaka man may only marry a Burung woman and a Burung man may only marry a Banaka woman. The two classes, Banaka and Burung, thus form what will be spoken of as an *intermarrying pair* or simply a *pair*. This does not imply that a Banaka man may marry *any* Burung woman, but only that he may not marry a woman of any other class. . . . The rules of marriage and descent of the Kariera tribe are shown in the following table:—

7 Bailey, in *Trans. Ethnol. Soc. London*, II, 296.
8 Nieuwenhuis, *Borneo*, I, 77; index *sub* "huwelijk."
9 Wilken, in VG, I, 453.
10 McGee, in AA, IX, 378.

11 Latcham, in JAI, XXXIV, 170.
12 Spiegel, *Eran. Alterthskde.*, III, 679.
13 Krass, reported in N. Y. *Times*, March 3, 1924.
1 In JAI, XLIII, 147-148, 159

Father.	Mother.	Child.
Banaka.	Burung.	Palyeri.
Burung.	Banaka.	Karimera.
Palyeri.	Karimera.	Banaka.
Karimera.	Palyeri.	Burung.

This may be expressed more concisely by means of a diagram.

```
  ⟶BANAKA  ——— = ——— BURUNG ⟵
  ⟶KARIMERA——— = ——— PALYERI ⟵
```

The sign = connects the two classes of an intermarrying pair, and therefore shows the relation of husband and wife. The sign $\overset{\curvearrowright}{\curvearrowright}$ connects the class of a mother with the class of her child. I propose to speak of the classes so related as together forming a *cycle*. In the Karimera tribe Banaka and Karimera form one cycle and Burung and Palyeri the other. The children of a woman always belong to the same cycle as herself, but to the other class of the cycle. The sign ——— connects the class of a father with the class of his child. I propose to speak of the two classes so connected as together forming a *couple*. In the Kariera tribe Banaka and Palyeri form one couple and Karimera and Burung form the other. The children of a man always belong to the same couple as himself, but to the other class of the couple." Native terms express these several relationships. "It is obvious from the above account that a man can never marry a woman of his own local group, since such women are either *kandari, toa, turdu, mari, kundal,* or *maeli* to him. We therefore find in this tribe the condition often called 'local exogamy' by ethnologists. On analysis, however, we see that this local exogamy is simply the result of the regulation of marriage by relationship, together with the peculiar constitution of the local group."

It is evident enough that such complicated taboos go back to the local idea of what consanguinity is, and that the constant trend is to get away from what is considered to be in-breeding. And whatever the taboos may be, there is no question about their power; mating is controlled by an iron system, backed up by religious considerations of the most compelling sort.

Singular complications arise in the cases represented in Cunow's[2] schematic arrangement, based on a southeast Australian system which prevents marriage between individuals in the same life-status group, and so amounts to a new restriction under the one based upon age. Here, after the phratries are formed, each consisting of a collection of totem-groups, four marriage-classes are distinguished, which consist of males and females and run through the totem-groups, including parts of each. The divisions are as follows:

	Phratry A		*Phratry B*	
	Male	*Female*	*Male*	*Female*
1. Parents of married:	Kumbo	Buta	Murri	Mata
2. Adult married:	Ippai	Ippata	Kubbi	Kubbotha
3. Not marriageable:	Kumbo	Buta	Murri	Mata

2 *Australneger*, 2, 5, 14; Mathew, *Eaglehawk and Crow*.

There are thus two marriage-classes in each phratry and each comprises males and females, whose names alternate in the life-status strata. A man in the third stratum who comes to marry is, for example, in some totem of phratry A and is, being a male, a Kumbo. He must marry in the other phratry and in the same life-status stratum. His wife is a Mata; if he were a Murri of phratry B, she would be a Buta. For the same reason any Ippai of the older generation must, when he married, have taken a Kubbotha, and any Kubbi an Ippata. Also the oldest stratum must have combined like the youngest; but, owing to the age-taboo, no Kumbo of that stratum could marry a Mata of the youngest. If the family is under father-descent, the children of Kumbo are Ippai if male and Ippata if female; of Murri, Kubbi and Kubbotha; of Kubbi, Murri and Mata; of Ippai, Kumbo and Buta, respectively. If it is a family under mother-descent, the children of Buta must be Ippai and Ippata; of Mata, Kubbi and Kubbotha; of Ippata, Kumbo and Buta; of Kubbotha, Murri and Mata, respectively. Curr[3] has constructed a table in which he endeavors to illustrate, with English names, this type of restrictions to marriage.

First Generation.	Second Generation.	Third Generation.
Male Smiths marry female Jones. Their children are	Male Kellys, who marry female Robbins. Children	M. Smiths / F. Smiths
	Female Kellys, who marry male Robbins. Children	M. Jones / F. Jones
Male Jones marry female Smiths. Their children are	Male Robbins, who marry female Kellys. Children	M. Jones / F. Jones
	Female Robbins, who marry male Kellys. Children	M. Smiths / F. Smiths
Male Kellys marry female Robbins. Their children are	Male Smiths, who marry female Jones. Children	M. Kellys / F. Kellys
	Female Smiths, who marry male Jones. Children	M. Robbins / F. Robbins
Male Robbins marry female Kellys. Their children are	Male Jones, who marry female Smiths. Children	M. Robbins / F. Robbins
	Female Jones, who marry male Smiths. Children	M. Kellys / F. Kellys

In New Guinea, "Mekeo marriages are governed by a rule of exogamy which makes it improper for a man to marry a girl of his own clan, or even of his own *ngopu* group, of whatever village she may be, though he may marry a girl of his own village who is not of his clan or *ngopu* group. . . . Marriage between the children of two sisters (first cousins) is not allowed, and even marriage between the children of those children (second cousins) is not strictly regular, though as regards the latter they constantly shut their eyes to the irregularity and permit it."[4] Seligmann[5] speaks of these same people: "In

3 *Aust. Race*, I, 113.
4 Williamson, in JAI, XLIII, 275.
5 *Melanesians*, 365, 366, 486.

spite of the statement that no one marries within the *pangua,* Father Egidi's genealogies show that to a limited extent the members of large clans . . . have contracted endogamous marriages. The figures given in the table indicate that such marriages were never frequent and the genealogies show that no cases have occurred recently." Specifically, *"ongoi,* the breadfruit tree, and a palm called *imöu,* were in each tribe assigned to one of its *pangua* which stood in the reciprocal relation of *ufuapie* to the other *pangua* of the tribe. Since in both tribes marriage is not, and never was, allowed within the *pangua,* the original *ufuapie* groups were intermarrying groups, but this does not seem to have been due to any conscious desire to avoid marriage between individuals having the same *iauafangai,* for in the past as at the present day the only bar to marriage was identity of *pangua* or near blood relationship." A curious case is reported by the author quoted, as he writes of the Southern Massim: "Formerly, children approaching puberty captured in war were sometimes adopted into the clan. In these cases whatever the sex of the prisoners, they assumed the totems of the man adopting them, so that it became impossible for a man to marry a female prisoner adopted by himself or, in the old days, to have prolonged intercourse with her. It was repeatedly stated that these rules were formerly most stringently adhered to, and a female prisoner adopted into the clan was in fact looked upon as the sister of the man adopting her." It is evident, again, that the taboos had little to do with actual inbreeding.

Haddon[6] has "more than once called attention to the fact that among some Papuans marriage restrictions are territorial and not totemic. Dr. Rivers has shown that in Murray Island [in the region of Torres Straits] marriages are regulated by the places to which the natives belong. A man cannot marry a woman of his own village or of certain other villages. The totemic system which probably at one time existed in this island appears to have been replaced by what may be called a territorial system. A similar custom occurs in the Mekeo district of British New Guinea, and it is probably still more widely distributed. I was informed by a member of the Yaraikanna tribe of Cape York, North Queensland, that children must take the 'land' or 'country' of their mother; all who belong to the same place are brothers and sisters, a wife must be taken from another 'country': thus it appears that marriage restrictions are territorial and not totemic. The same is found amongst the Kurnai and the Coast Murring tribe in New South Wales."

In general the East African tribes are exogamous. "Marriage with sisters is unknown and strict endogamy is nowhere the rule. . . . Marriage within the clan is unlawful among the Wakamba, Wakikuyu, Watheraka, Wachagga, Wasove, and Bagwe. . . . With several tribes marriage between children of blood brothers is unlawful by reason of the spiritual relationship between their parents."[7] There is in East Africa a peculiar usage of reckoning by generations which has its effect in the marriage-taboos. Each generation, like each circumcision-group, has its own name; and, strangely enough, "there is in every age one generation which is the ruling one, or, as the natives say, 'the generation which owns the country.' . . . This retiring of one generation, and the assumption of their place by another, takes place at a great ceremony . . . at which

---

6 "Totemism," in *Brit. Assoc. Adv. Sci.,* 1902, 14. His reference to Rivers is JAI, XXX, 78.   7 Dundas, C., in JAI, LI, 261.

the succeeding generation is said to 'buy' the country. . . . We are accustomed to think of one generation as comprising persons of a certain age, although this is not its real meaning. If we would compare the genealogy of any two Europeans we might find that although their ages might be equal, the order of their respective generations might be vastly different. In polygamous societies there is of course a much greater range of age between the sons of one father, and in fact there is often a surprising difference of age between members of one generation in Kikuyu; illegitimate children are reckoned to the generation of their legitimate brothers and thus it is possible for a man to beget a son who belongs to a generation senior to his own."[8] Among the Masai such generations are connected with circumcision and are restricted to the male sex. "Women do not have *poror* [generations], that is to say they are not circumcised or operated on in groups but at odd times when they are considered old enough." These generations, irrelevant as they are to any considerations of consanguinity, constitute a basis for marriage-taboos. "A man cannot marry the daughter of a man of his own age—he must marry the daughter of a man of a previous age to his own. Like many other races it is the custom among the Masai for a man to be provided with a temporary wife when he sleeps at a kraal" encountered in the course of a journey. "He can however only cohabit with the wife of a man of his own *poror* or age; these relations are looked upon as quite lawful."[9] In the Kenya colony these age-grades "partake of the nature of a social division; it is impossible, for instance, for a man to marry a woman whose male compeers are of a senior grade to his own and a nominal respect is paid to the senior grades." A number of cases follow. Age-grades may occur every five years.[10]

"Sexual intercourse between persons of the same exogamous group is not approved by the custom or sentiment of the Semas, nor indeed by that of the neighbouring Naga tribes."[11] Thus the rule does not confine itself solely to marriage. Again, the rule may prescribe in-marriage and yet be constantly infringed: the Chinese law "forbids intermarriage with some of the savages, but this is not carried out in practice. In Formosa the Chinese constantly intermarry with the savages."[12] Another arbitrary rule concerning unions is where a younger sister may not marry ahead of an older, unless the latter is deformed or otherwise incapable; again this can be done only upon payment of a small sum to the older sister or mother. In some cases there is a fictitious marriage of an elder brother to some inanimate object to clear the way for a younger brother's union.[13]

Among certain Indians of Oregon, "there was no well-defined rule against marriage within the village, but as it must very often have happened that practically all the residents of a village were related, it was customary to look beyond the village for a mate, and in many cases even to marry into some neighboring tribe of alien speech."[14] Among the Tlinkit, "to marry one of the same great totemic phratry, though no blood relation, is a matter of deep disgrace, and in earlier times one who violated this custom was punished with death. Any who offend in this matter now are deeply execrated."[15]

Among the Arabs, "one shall not seek a bride outside of his circle, his village.

---

8 Dundas, C., in JAI, XLV, 244-247.
9 Hobley, *A-Kamba*, 122.
10 Barton, in JAI, LIII, 59, 61.
11 Hutton, *Sema Nagas*, 133.
12 Von Mollendorff, *Fam. Law*, 22.

13 Wilken, in VG, I, 451, 452, note; Gen., XXIX, 26.
14 Sapir, in AA, IX, 268.
15 Jones, *Thlingets*, 213.

Yet endogamy is not alone legitimate." Exogamous unions appear "very frequent and show how extended, despite all feuds, peaceful relations must have been between the tribes."[16] "The old Serb custom of exogamy is illustrated in almost all the ballads of the weddings of Serb heroes. Nearly every one begins: 'When So-and-so wedded he sought a wife from afar.' We see, too, how the wife is usually chosen in order to make a strong alliance with her family."[17]

§355. The Ascendancy of Exogamy.

IT is said of some Melanesians that "avoidance of marriage within the clans holds out, but even this begins to weaken. I know of one case in which a man is married to a woman of his own totem. He is jeered at by the others who say: 'This man has married his sister.' Cases of sexual connection between people of the same totem are not infrequent, but great secrecy is maintained, and there is a feeling of shame about admitting it."[1]

Among the Asaba people of the Niger, "a man marrying into a neighbouring village derived a certain advantage in regard to intercourse with that village, as he could, in the troublous times existing some twenty years ago, pass freely without danger of murder or robbery from his own to his wife's town."[2] How exogamy may strengthen a tribe for war is indicated in a case from New Zealand. "If a well-born member of one tribe marries into another, he or she will act as a 'cord' to draw that tribe to our assistance in war. The two tribes will call upon each other for assistance at such times."[3]

"It has been noticed by good observers in India that the comparative liberty of intermarriage permitted by Mohammedanism is part of the secret of its success as a proselytising religion. It offers a bribe to the convert in relieving him from the undoubtedly vexatious restraints of the Brahmanical law of marriage."[4]

Roth[5] notes that it seems very possible that the spread of agriculture was due to the system of wife-capture. "In North America there are all the elements for such conclusion; exogamy was almost universal among the Indians, and among them also agricultural and hunting tribes dwelt side by side, while agriculture was in every stage of development."

We do not attach enough importance to the various theories about the origin of exogamy to attempt any survey or critique of them. Perhaps the classic explanation is that of Lubbock,[6] which emphasizes the favored position of the man who possesses a stolen woman. As she has no defenders and therefore no rights, her owner can do what he pleases with her. This renders him enviable and also an object of imitation. This theory seems plausible on the face of it and is as good as any other; it has been adopted by eminent writers;[7] but we find it no very valuable key to the cases.

For the several theories, together with a rather elaborate discussion, the reader may refer to Lang, *Social Origins*. An illustration of this author's

16 Wellhausen, in *Gött. Gesellsft. d. Wissensften*, 1893, 437.
17 Durham, in JAI, XLVII, 447.
1 Seligmann, *Melanesians*, 683-684.
2 Parkinson, in JAI, XXXVI, 316 (written in 1906).
3 Best, in JAI, XLIV, 159.
4 Maine, *Early Law*, 235.

5 In JAI, XVI, 127.
6 *Origin Civ.*, 86, 98, 103, 104-143.
7 Lippert, *Kgchte.*, II, 84 ff.; Spencer, *Prin. Soc.*, I, 631 ff.; Müller, *Sex. Leben*, 42 ff. Oddities in Thomas, *Sex and Society*, 192 ff.; Durkheim, "Prohibition de l'Inceste," in *Année Soc.*, I, 31 ff.

manner follows; discussing the views of Westermarck,[8] who sees in propinquity
—the feeling toward those with whom one lives—the factor deterrent of in-
marriage, he writes: "As to exogamy, Dr. Westermarck explains it by 'an instinct' against marriage of near kin. Our ancestors who married near kin would
die out, he thinks, and they who avoided such unions would survive, 'and thus
an instinct would be developed' by 'Natural Selection.' But why did any of
our ancestors avoid such marriages at all? From 'an aversion to those with
whom they lived.' And why had they this aversion? Because they had an instinct against such unions. Then why had they an instinct? We are engaged in
a vicious circle."[9] This criticism may seem to be a mere piece of dialectics; the
fact is that Westermarck is not clear as to the distinction between evolution
as it appears in two of its main phases, the organic and the societal.

What is in some respects the most interesting of all the theories is that of
Atkinson,[10] a man "far from books" and who developed his ideas around a
few remarks of Darwin in *The Descent of Man*. Darwin believed that jealousy
led early man to guard his mate or mates against other men; that the older
and more powerful male drove off the younger one who, "being thus expelled
and wandering about, would, when at last successful in finding a partner,
prevent too close interbreeding within the limits of the same family." Atkinson
starts with this suggestion thrown out by his prophet and goes on concerning
extra-family marriage: "If I am correct, we shall find that it was connected
with the sexual relations of primitive man, *whilst in the animal stage*, and
especially with the mutual marital rights of the males within a group. Such
idea in travail, hastened and sharpened by needs of environment, created issues
which necessarily gave birth to a 'Primal Law' prohibitory of marriage between
certain members of a family or local group, and thus, in natural sequence, led
to *forced* connubial union *beyond* its circle, the family or local group—that is,
led to Exogamy."

Reflection upon theories as to the origin of exogamy reveals them as more or
less ingenious speculations, analogous in differing degrees to those of the
philosophers. They will sustain little weight of superstructure. As we have
nothing better to suggest, we have ignored the question of origins,[11] assumed
the existence of variations toward exogamy, and compared the merits of the
two systems of in- and out-marriage.

§358. "Capture-Marriage."

AMONG some Australian tribes who practised wife-stealing, if the offending
party was caught by the pursuing tribe when travelling in company with the
kidnapped gin, the guilty pair were brought back to the place of departure
and the man made to undergo the ordeal of spear-throwing. "This consisted
in having 100 spears cast at him, when stationary, by five men, as fast as
possible. The dexterity displayed by the culprit in avoiding them is said to
have been wonderful. If he escaped without fatal injury, the matter was considered settled; honor was satisfied, and the woman was allowed to remain
with him as his wife. If, on the other hand, the runaways should be found
cohabiting at the place of refuge, dire vengeance was immediately administered,

---

8 *Human Marriage* (original single volume
edition), ch. XV *et passim*.
9 Lang, *Soc. Orig.*, 33; Fison, in JAI,
XXIV, 370-371.

10 *Primal Law* (212-213 quoted).
11 §454 of the text.

the man killed, and his body disposed of."[1] Sometimes the Solomon Islander steals a woman from a neighboring tribe, "and takes her to wife, if the tribal mark allows of it—if not, then he sells the stolen woman to a native whose mark allows him to enter a matrimonial union with her"; but wife-purchase is by far the commoner procedure.[2] Though in some parts of British New Guinea capture now occurs, it leads to quarrels and is rare; subsequent payment is required to give satisfaction.[3]

The Fan used to attack neighboring tribes, kill and eat the men without further formality, and capture the women as wives. This led to a constant contribution of new blood to the tribe, which explains, the author[4] thinks, both the profound vitality of the race and the traces of successive crossings. The militant Zulus stole their wives freely.[5] In Mashonaland the revenge for woman-capture was the seizure of the thieves' cattle.[6] Again, the woman was held inviolate for ransom. An African chief said he had not taken a certain captured virgin to wife because he ought not; for her father had given notice of his intention to redeem her and she was to be restored as she was obtained.[7] Among the Dinkas a wife is obtained by purchase or by capture from hostile clans or tribes. "The wives obtained in the latter way are inferior in position to the purchased wives; but their children are the equals of those of the superior wives."[8] Capture-marriage of the female barley spirit is ceremonial in Morocco.[9]

All the evidence goes to show that Yakut wives were originally war-captives. If a man while hunting saw a handsome woman, he and his friends watched their chance, killed her husband, and took her like a war-captive. In the Yakut epic tales one of the great motives is to steal women; in all war stories maidens are won by the victors. They are given to conciliate and to avert threatened war, and as amercement for men killed or cattle stolen; thus they are property and booty and the wedding might be a ceremony connected with peace negotiations and settlement. At a wedding the attitude of the two parties is one of hostility or suspicion, of watchfulness and of readiness to fight or flee.[10] Among some peoples of Russia, wife-stealing exists; the abduction of a woman from her parents' home is considered by others as a great piece of boldness for which the perpetrator often pays very dearly. Among the Cherkes a woman who has been promised to a man is regarded as his even while in the house of her parents, and if she is stolen, it is an insult to him which demands exemplary revenge, and has led repeatedly to bloody scenes. If the parents have connived in the enterprise they have to repay the bride-price and the prospective groom often seeks vengeance on them; the abducted girl remains the wife of the robber.[11]

"A young Badaga of the Nilghiri hills, who cannot obtain the girl of his choice, makes known that he will have her or kill himself. Understanding which, some friends place him at their head, go, if need be, to seek reinforcements among the Todas, and return with a band of sturdy fellows. Generally the abduction is successful."[12] While Sema marriage is still practically a matter

---

1 "Miscellanea," in JAI, XXI, 82.
2 Parkinson, in *Dresden K. Zoöl. u. Anth.-Ethnog. Mus.*, Abhandl. VII, pt. VI, 7.
3 Krieger, *Neu-Guinea*, 300.
4 Trilles, *Fân*, 405.
5 Ratzel, *Vkde.*, I, 264.
6 Bent, *Mashonaland*, 277.

7 Serpa Pinto, *Africa*, I, 81.
8 Cummins, in JAI, XXXIV, 150.
9 Harris, in JAI, XXVII, 68.
10 Sieroshevski-Sumner, in JAI, XXXI, 552, 553.
11 *Russ. Ethnog.* (Russ.), II, 254, 440, 223.
12 Thurston, *S. India*, 21.

of purchase, capture is not and would seem never to have been a basis for marriage. "The women of a Sema's enemies are regarded as the possessors of heads to be taken and of long hair to be made into ornaments, not as possible wives or slaves."[13] "The Hindus had a special name for marriage by abduction: the *rakshasa* form, which was confined to the *Kschatriya* or warrior class;" and cases of abduction are celebrated in the *Mahabharata* epic.[14]

In the Dutch East Indies it sometimes happens that young men abduct girls of their choice. This is a rather dangerous proceeding, for if the man is caught he can be killed unless he belongs to a higher rank than the girl. If the abducted girl was already betrothed to another, the abductor must pay indemnity.[15] In this case, abduction is almost elopement. In northern Sumatra, Jacobs[16] found a combination of usages connected with marriage, dating from various periods, which prove that in ancient times and before the matriarchate was here introduced, marriage took place through violent abduction of the woman. If two communities in the Malay Peninsula were at feud and the young people had no opportunity of making a choice, matches were effected by capture and both the women and their dowry taken by force. This was done through organized attacks.[17]

Speaking of the peoples on the western border of China, Ratzel[18] says there are no pure races at all; slavery and wife-stealing have been long at work to mix them. In the *Shiking,* or Chinese Book of Odes, are found traces of marriage by capture.[19]

By the side of marriage by purchase, wife-capture existed among the Indo-Germanic peoples in antiquity.[20] Clytemnæstra recounts how Agamemnon slew her former husband Tantalus and, tearing her babe from her arms, dashed it on the ground and then married her by force; yet she boasts what a good wife she has been to him after she was reconciled to him on this footing.[21] Traces of wife-capture may be found both in the Bible and in the Talmud.[22] Up to the time of Mohammed, woman-stealing was in vogue in Arabia.[23]

Survivals. In British New Guinea a man arranges with the girl of his choice, and at night goes stealthily and carries her to his father's house, where they sleep together. "The girl is supposed to be stolen by the young man and his friends. In the morning, the girl is missed, and her father or uncle and his friends arm, and, amidst great appearance of wrath and loud shouting, make for the house of the young folks and surround it, demanding their girl. The young man's party issue out sometimes, and arrows are fired, and many hard and angry things are said. The girl's father is supposed to be very heart-sore at the loss of his girl, and he returns with his party again and again for several days, to the great delight of the girl, who feels she is a much loved daughter, and thinks how much she will be valued by her husband's family."[24] In the island of Tikopia the relatives decide on a day to sally out and seize the woman who has been chosen, the bridegroom remaining in the house. "The

13 Hutton, *Sema Nagas,* 134.
14 Schrader, *Aryan,* 383; Holtzmann, *Ind. Sagen,* I, 212-213.
15 Van Eck, in *De Indische Gids,* II, 841.
16 *Groot-Atjeh,* I, 72.
17 Skeat and Blagden, *Malay Penin.,* II, 86; Stevens, in *Ztsft. f. Eth.,* XXVIII, 174.
18 *Vkde.,* III, 48.
19 Von Mollendorff, *Family Law,* 4.

20 Schrader, *Aryan,* 382.
21 Euripides, *Iph. in Aulis,* 1148 ff.
22 Klugmann, *Frau im Talmud,* 22, note.
23 Wellhausen, in *Gött. Gesellsft. d. Wissensften,* 1893, 435; further cases in Letourneau, *Marriage,* ch. VI; Lippert, *Kgchte.,* II, 95.
24 Chalmers, in JAI, XXXIII, 124.

seizure of the woman is resisted, and a fight takes place with clubs and bows and arrows in which no one is ever killed though some are often badly wounded. At the end of the fight the father and maternal uncle of the woman are given presents of mats and cloth, and the woman is taken to the house of her future husband. . . . On the fifth day the wife goes to her father's house and helps to prepare food which she takes back to her new home, and after this the marriage is consummated."

The procedure in Pentecost, New Hebrides, is as follows: "Some man is chosen to go into the house, pretending that he has come to fetch fire, and he goes quietly to the girl and, seizing her by the wrists, says 'Marry.' The girl is very much astonished and begins to cry and before she knows what is happening she is wrapped up in the new mat brought the day before by the future husband. This is done by his sister who has come into the house. . . . The man who has told the girl to marry then seizes a stick which he knows will be wanted and goes out of the house to encounter a man belonging to the moiety of the father of the girl. This man has a club with thick thorns on it with which he strikes at the man who comes out, it may be so severe a blow as to break his arm. . . . As soon as the blow is struck all the men of the village produce sticks prepared the night before and begin to fight with the party which has come to fetch the girl. . . . The girl is then taken to her future home, the people of her own village standing in the way and resisting her removal, and anyone who offers much resistance is appeased with a present." Rivers,[25] from whom these cases are taken, suggests that the simulated capture came into existence as the result of the social condition which he has called a gerontocracy; the marriage of a girl while still an infant, he is convinced, was the result of an attempt to escape from the dominance of the old men and from their monopoly of the younger women of the community. "In the early stages of the breaking down of the dominance of the elders, the younger men could only obtain wives by the gift of their maternal uncles during the lives of the latter or by marrying the widows of their uncles. This being insufficient to satisfy their needs, the younger men were driven either to elope with, or carry off by force, the young girls of the other moiety, either marrying them at once or putting them in the charge of their mothers till the girls were old enough to marry. . . . To the older view of McLennan and others that such a custom as that of Pentecost is a survival of capture from a hostile tribe, the fact that the capture is so obviously a sham, so evidently carried out with the connivance of the relatives of the captured woman, has long been a difficulty, to many an insuperable difficulty. This connivance, which seems so difficult to understand as a survival of capture from a hostile tribe, becomes perfectly natural if the so-called capture was merely intended to keep the women from the clutches of the old men of their own community. The sham nature of the whole proceeding is clearly intelligible if the belief in the magical powers of the old men, which I have taken to be the original source of their dominance, still persisted sufficiently to make it desirable to disguise from the old men the understanding which existed between the relatives of captive and capturer. If I am right, just as the ceremonial capture is the survival of a real capture, so is the ceremonial connivance the survival of a real connivance."

Especially in East Africa are there numerous examples of mock-capture and of survivals in the wedding-ceremony. Among the Bahima, "the bride-

25 *Melan. Soc.*, I, 309-310, 207-208, 105, 108.

groom enters, takes the bride by the right wrist, and leads her out of the house; she is still closely veiled in a finely dressed cow hide, so that nothing of her face or form is visible. Directly the bride is brought out her relations produce a strong rope, one end of which they tie to her leg, and the relatives of the bride and bridegroom take sides and have a tug of war for her, the bride's party struggling to retain her, while the opposite party try to drag her off. During this tug of war the bridegroom retains his hold of the bride's wrist and she stands weeping and sobbing at being carried off from her father's house. This contest always ends favourably to the bridegroom's party. The bridegroom hurries his bride along a few yards to a spot where a few of his friends stand ready, with a large cow hide spread on the ground; the bride is placed upon this, and the young men hoist her up, and rush off with her in triumph to the bridegroom's father's house. . . . On the third day the marriage is consummated."[26] Again, "marriage is by capture, the young couple coming beforehand to an understanding with regard to its time and place."[27] A survival of capture is seen in the Wagogo ceremony where a friend of the bridegroom takes the bride on his shoulders and runs away with her in triumph to her new home. The bride is veiled.[28] A kind of marriage by capture, with or without the consent of the girl, is found among the Wangonde. The bridegroom, assisted by friends, lies in wait by the water-supply, seizes and carries her home. The relatives are in honor bound to rescue her if the groom is "so maladroit as to make it impossible for them to affect ignorance of the abduction." A present to the girl is necessary before consummation.[29]

After preliminary payments, among the Wawanga, "the bridegroom proceeds with at least four of his kinsmen to the bride's village and there seizes her by force. The girl at once commences screaming for help, and in answer to her cries the women of the village come running up. The bridegroom beats and drives them off with a stick. The girl is then carried away to the village. In the evening the bride's girl friends and relatives proceed to the bridegroom's hut, where they are witnesses to the consummation of the marriage and the bride's virginity."[30] In the case of the Akamba, "in former days on the day of the marriage the bridegroom went with five or six brothers and friends and seized his prospective bride in the fields near the village, the girl would call out and her brothers would assemble and attack the bridegroom's party; they would fight with sticks and even swords and if the girl's brothers won they would take their sister back to their village."[31] "When a man has paid dowry, or as much of it as was stipulated, and the time has come for him to take the bride to his village, the relations are very fond of protracting this event in order to extort presents from him by vain promises that such and such shall be the last gift demanded. But when he has given as much as he considers reasonable he will go and steal away the bride at night. In any case this is done in Ukamba, the parents affecting not to be aware of the intention, and if the bridegroom be a young man his friends will act a sham robbery. At other times there is less fiction about this, and the girl is carried off by stealth because she cannot be got by other means."[32]

Among the Somali the girls willingly let themselves be carried off while tending sheep, "and precisely this sort of woman-stealing is said very often to wipe

---

26 Roscoe, in JAI, XXXVII, 104-105.
27 Johnstone, in JAI, XXXII, 271.
28 Cole, in JAI, XXXII, 311.
29 Sanderson, in JAI, LIII, 453.

30 Dundas, K. R., in JAI, XLIII, 38.
31 Hobley, A-Kamba, 62.
32 Dundas, C., in JAI, XLV, 287. "Dowry," with this author, means "bride-price."

out existing blood-feuds, because in this way restitution is made to the tribe robbed of labor-forces, and so complaints and feud-conditions can have an end." Among the Galla there are several forms of bride-abduction: in one, "several young men take to horse, in order to carry off the girl at some one of her ordinary occupations. The one who gets hold of the bride and with her on his horse seeks the open country is called brother and protector of the girl. . . . He brings the bride to a place of safety, kills an ox, streaks the abducted girl's neck with the animal's blood, and at the same time gives her some of the blood of the sacrificed animal to drink, out of his hand. The relatives of the girl soon learn of her location and hurry with weapons and with insults to her abductor. The bridegroom calls together the village elders . . . and these determine the sum which the bride-stealer must pay the girl's father so that she may become his wife."[33] Among the Dinkas, the bridegroom's party arrives and demands the bride. "The women reply that without gifts she cannot be given up. Bargaining then commences; the young men saying 'for what will you give her?' and the women replying 'for so much.' Or sometimes the young men pretend to try to force their way in and carry the lady off; and while this mock strife is going on, one of the party cuts a hole in the grass wall of the hut, from behind, and carries the bride off to her husband's quarters."[34]

In southern Tunis the groom keeps hidden with his friends for eight days before the wedding.[35] Berber ceremonial exhibits survivals that are becoming less obvious. After the wedding-feast, when the bride is to go to the groom's tent, the latter "mounts the bride and himself upon a mare and gallops amongst the tents of the village, the girl screaming out the while, and striking each tent three times with a stick, as if to call attention to the fact that she is being abducted by force. None of the writer's informants could give any idea of the origin of the ceremony, beyond stating that 'formerly' brides *were* abducted. A like custom exists to-day in the neighborhood of Tangier. When the women congregate in the fields to weed the green barley or reap the crops, a straw figure, dressed like a woman, is taken with them. This figure is placed standing in the field amongst the corn. Suddenly men appear from a neighboring village, mounted on horses, and galloping into the field, the figure is lifted to a horse and stolen, amidst the screams and cries of the women. A fresh body of horsemen then appear upon the scene and the straw lady is rescued, and handed from one to the other and fought for, until, generally in a very dishevelled condition, it is returned to the women again." The day and hour for this ceremony are made public previous to the event. "Each village formerly practised this mimic struggle for the possession of the imitation lady, but now-a-days it has dropped largely out of practice and is seldom seen."[36]

Among the Yakuts, "whether the stealing of women was the cause of . . . hostilities, or the relatives gave the woman voluntarily in compensation for a man who had been killed, or for stolen cattle, is immaterial. In any case she was regarded as *booty,* and the wedding resembled a *peace negotiation and conclusion.* To this day both the parties who come into relations with each other at a wedding behave to each other during the feast with respect, yet still with a certain concealed distrust and jealousy. They are constantly on the look-out lest the others get the better of them in the gifts, or cheat them." The

33 Paulitschke, *Nordost-Afr.*, II, 286; I, 198.
34 Cummins, in JAI, XXXIV, 150.
35 Bruun, *Huleboerne*, 46, 47.
36 Harris, in JAI, XXVII, 68.

horses of the groom's party are saddled, as are also those of the bride's relatives who have come to the wedding. "A Yakut who was asked why he did not unsaddle his horse at a wedding answered, 'Differences are apt to arise at a wedding.' "[37] Here is a typical transition toward composition of differences and peace, such as can be observed in the case of any other sort of booty-raiding[38] as it evolves distrustingly toward a more developed system.

Among the Koryak, "the marriage ceremony itself, which gives husband full right to his wife, is the act of 'seizing' his wife, described by all our authorities with only slight variations. Most of them agree . . . that the bride must not surrender to the bridegroom without a struggle, nor will the bridegroom take her without encountering the usual difficulties. . . . The girl herself resists, and tries to run away, and besides this, her girl friends attack and try to beat the bridegroom back; and if the girl does not care for the man she tries to hide among the neighbours." On the marriage-day the friends and relatives are invited; and, "to the accompaniment of the drum and songs, the bride runs round the *yurta* [tent]. The groom pursues her, and at each corner is attacked by the women, who try to stop him with their feet, and beat him unmercifully with branches of the alder-tree. Finally the bride slackens her speed, or she would not be caught at all. . . . When the bride approaches the house of her bridegroom's parents, the latter come out with firebrands taken from the hearth to meet her." Although a Kamchadale has obtained permission to take his bride, he is still obliged to capture her, "because now all the women of the village protect her from him. She is dressed in several heavy gowns and closely wrapped up so that she looks like a stuffed figure. . . . There is a case on record of a man who for ten years had been trying to obtain his wife, and his head and body were much disfigured by his struggles, which were nevertheless quite in vain." According to the customs of the northern Altaians, "the bridegroom is supposed to capture the bride. As a matter of fact, the girl has been apprised beforehand of his intention, the matter is settled with her, and she gives to the young man's envoy a kerchief from her head as an earnest of the fulfilment of her part of the compact. Then the bridegroom comes with one or two friends on good horses, and carries her off at night." Among the exogamous Buryat, a symbolical representation of the capture of the wife is the essential feature of the wedding ceremony. "The bride hides herself within a ring which her girl friends form around her, holding hands, and strengthening the chain with their kerchiefs. When men try to break through the ring, the girls do their best to prevent them, weeping and shouting aloud. . . . After the feast the bride goes into the bridegroom's *yurta,* and then at last the veil is removed from her head." The Samoyed bride is forcibly placed on a sledge by the women and tied on. When an Ostyak bridegroom visits his bride before the purchase-price is fully paid, he must observe a certain custom of avoidance with regard to his father-in-law: "Should he meet him by accident the bridegroom must turn his back or cover his face; and he must make his way as quickly as possible to his bride, and as quickly return from her."[39]

The first day's ceremony in a Mongolian wedding is the "attack" on the bride's camp, delivered peacefully enough nowadays, however. "At various times during the day women of the bride's people and men of the groom's

37 Sieroshevski-Sumner, in JAI, XXXI, 86.   39 Czaplicka, *Aborig. Siberia,* 83-84, 84-85,
38 §77, of the text.   87-88, 116, 118, 119, 123-124, 126-127.

have mock disputes. In one of these, one of the women takes a bottle from one of the men. A heavy argument ensues, and finally she draws out the cork, breaks the string with which it is attached to the bottle and hands back the latter, signifying that the relationships of the bride-to-be with her family are broken."[40]

In Assam "the chief's marriage ceremony includes a mimic fight and mock capture of the bride, as she is *en route* to her new home."[41] In southern India the groom carries his bride off on his back, being surrounded by twenty or thirty young fellows who protect him from the desperate assaults of a party of young women who seek to regain possession of their comrade. Again the bride is handcuffed until the third day with brass bracelets weighing from twenty to thirty pounds, to prevent her from escaping to her old home. The bride is supposed in other cases to weep loudly and deplore her fate. Otherwise she is considered an "ill woman"; "when she can no longer produce genuine tears, she must proceed to bawl out. If she does not do this, the bridegroom will not marry her."[42] In the mock-conflict the groom's party always wins.[43] If a Saora man wants a girl but cannot afford the liquor and other presents for her people, he carries her off. If she likes him she stays; if not, she runs away to her home. He will carry her off thrice; if she runs away the third time, he leaves her. The Saoras say that formerly everyone took his wife by force.[44] Again, "a Bengali bridegroom is often likened to a thief, because he has to put up patiently with all sorts of liberties which the female members of the bride's family take with him on the day of his marriage, just as a thief, when caught, patiently suffers the maltreatment which he receives at the hands of his captors."[45] "Sometimes the bridegrooms mark their foreheads with blood, which seems, indeed, to be the origin of the singular and nearly universal custom in India . . . of marking the forehead of the bride with vermilion. The vermilion has apparently replaced the blood, and the blood may, and doubtless does, symbolise a violent rape."[46] Among the Palaungs, "the bridegroom must still be careful to cover his face with his blanket if he goes out of doors, as he must not be seen by any of the relatives of the girl. Should they meet and recognize him, custom demands that they should greet him with insulting remarks."[47]

In Cochin-China, "if a young fellow is much in love with a maid and her parents repulse his proposal, then it may happen that, during the twilight when the house door stands open, he suddenly enters her dwelling, embraces his loved one, and entwines about her and himself a scarf or girdle. Then he only has to bear patiently the insults and blows of her family, who may mishandle him so long as they do not severely wound him; and in that case the girl belongs to him," on condition, however, that he gives her parents money as indemnification for the disgrace he has brought upon them.[48] Laos parents hide the bride, at the time of the wedding-feast, in the woods, and the groom must find her; marriages are therefore not celebrated in the rainy season.[49]

Sham fights occur in some districts of Tibet, Sikkim, Bhutan,[50] and in Korea, where the fight is "often more than a make-believe one, for serious blows are

40 Communicated by a correspondent.
41 Peal, in JAI, XXII, 254.
42 Thurston, *S. India*, 10-11, 13, 48-49.
43 Risley, *Ethnog. Ind.*, I, 182.
44 Fawcett, in JASB, I, 235.
45 Mitra, in JASB, III, 454.

46 Letourneau, *Marriage*, 98.
47 Milne, *Eastern Clan*, 143.
48 Niemann, *Tjams*, 340-341.
49 Anon., "Reise d. Prinzen Heinrich," in *Globus*, LXXII, 157.
50 Rockhill, in USNM, 1893, 725.

exchanged and on both sides some are hurt. Death has occasionally ensued."
The worsting of the groom's or bride's party forecasts ill luck for him or for
her respectively.[51]

Wilken[52] writes extensively of such customs in the Indian Archipelago, where
abduction *de facto* appears as a regular form of marriage. He regards it as a
transition from the matriarchate to the patriarchate, the whole affair being
finally reduced to ceremony. Among the Amboinese every marriage is preceded
by an abduction, and among the Alfurs of Buru it is not uncommon. He
stresses the fact that "the abduction itself represents the marriage without
the parents of the girl having the right to utter a veto on it." In many cases
abduction is pretended in order to bring about marriage in the traditional
form. The Javanese and Sundanese word for getting a wife means "to seize
the bride before the house door with both arms about the hips and so carry
into the house—a custom at a wedding." It is usual for the Alfur boy to seize
the girl away from her parents, although he has paid the bride-price, she
ostensibly resisting; this usage is called "to be taken away." In the northern
peninsula of Celebes the groom must feign to get his wife from her relatives
by violence. If the marriage is in Mohammedan fashion, the bride need not
be present, but may be represented. Connected with marriage there are always
many formalities which cost not only time and trouble but money. This is the
reason why, among the Balinese, recourse is taken to elopement or abduction in
about nine-tenths of the marriages. The battle is sometimes a sort of tournament, together with a cock-fight, in front of the public assembly-hall, care
being taken that the girl's relatives are defeated; there are also armed parties
that strut about threateningly. The same applies to the Macassars, while among
other tribes marriage amounts to little unless there is a feigned abduction of
the bride either in secret or openly. Further survivals, thinks Wilken, are to
be seen in the throwing of sand and rice and in splashing the bridal pair with
mud—like shoe-throwing among other peoples. Further examples are the
fencing-in or hindering the pair, which degenerate into stretching a beam or
rope across the path, the throwing of a broom before the groom's door to
keep the bride from entering, the presence of a man with a sword, and other
methods of obstructing the way to the chamber.

Among some of the tribes in the Malay Peninsula occurred a dance, in the
midst of which the bride elect darted off into the forest, followed by the
bridegroom. "A chase ensued, during which, should the youth fall down, or
return unsuccessful, he was met with the jeers and merriment of the whole
party, and the match was declared off. Elsewhere during the banquet a large
fire was kindled, all the congregation standing as witnesses; the bride then
commenced to run round the fire; the bridegroom, who was obliged to run
in the same direction, following her; if he succeeded in catching her the marriage was valid, if he could not, it was declared off."[53] In New Zealand, "the
ancient and most general way of obtaining a wife was for the gentleman to
summon his friends, and make a regular *taua,* or fight, to carry off the lady
by force, and often times with great violence." If the girl had eloped with
someone she liked, her father and brothers would refuse consent; in any case

51 Bishop, *Korea,* 116.
52 In VG, I, 475-476, 477, 478, 480-481, 485-
486, 490, 492, notes 37 and 38, 494, 498; 155 ff.,
150-152, 155 ff., 165, 167-168; 47-48.

53 Skeat and Blagden, *Malay Penin.,* II,
82-83.

there would be a fight to regain possession of her, during which the girl would suffer considerably. If the weaker party saw itself losing, some member of it was likely to kill her to prevent her from becoming the property of another. "Even when all were agreeable, it was still customary for the bridegroom to go with a party, and appear to take her away by force, her friends yielding her up after a feigned struggle; a few days afterwards, the parents of the lady, with all her relatives, came upon the bridegroom for his pretended abduction; after much speaking and apparent anger, it ended with his making a handsome present of fine mats, etc., and giving an abundant feast." Intertribal raids were frequent. "Nothing could be done without the semblance of war." When the war-party was expected, "food and various garments were placed in order as presents, so when the rush took place, they were taken as plunder, and all terminated amicably."[54]

Among certain Indians in Guiana, "there is no particular ceremony at marriage, except that of always carrying away the girl by force or making a show of doing so, even when she and her parents are quite willing."[55] What seems to indicate that exogamy was an ancient practice among the Araucanians is the fact that "all marriage ceremonies begin with the pretended rape, or carrying off of the bride, which of late years has given way to a simple elopement, unless the bride be unwilling, when the older custom is resorted to. The marriage ceremony consists of two parts: the rape. . . . and the payment. . . . Having arranged the price with the father or eldest brother of the girl, the bridegroom arranges the details of the rape. He calls together his male relations, and while one of them goes to the bride's house on some pretext or other, the rest make a sudden attack on the dwelling. This is energetically resisted by all the womenfolk, the men of the household remaining passive spectators. One of the raiders seizes the struggling girl, and none too gently drags her to where the bridegroom is waiting on horseback. . . . This custom of carrying off the bride is only practised in the case of the first wife."[56]

The Arabian bride was like a war-captive. "After the women had brought the bride into the house, the groom took possession of her, by clutching her front hair while she knelt; then he prayed with her and performed the rites to avert evil omens or influences."[57] Among the Spartans, after the elders on both sides had come to an agreement, the bridegroom brought his bride to a female relative who cut off her hair and led her into the bridal chambers, where the young groom could visit her only surreptitiously.[58] The Dorians kept capture as a symbol; the Roman bride, having fled to the lap of her mother, was torn away and forcibly brought into the house of the bridegroom.[59]

§359. Elopement.

It is stated of certain Australians that what looks to the observer like capture "is in reality an elopement, in which the woman is an aiding and abetting party."[1] Howitt and Fison[2] think that the monopoly of the women by the

54 Taylor, *Te Ika*, 336-337; 354-355.
55 Roth, in BAE, XXXVIII, 670.
56 Latcham, in JAI, XXXIX, 359.
57 Wellhausen, in *Gött. Gesellsft. d. Wissensften*, 1893, 443.
58 Bergel, *Eheverhältn. d. alten Juden*, 18.

59 Dionysus of Halicarnassus, *Antiq. roman.*, II, 30; Letourneau, *Marriage*, ch. VI; Rossbach, *Röm. Ehe*, 214, 215, 216.
1 Spencer and Gillen, *North. Tr. Cent. Aust.*, 32.
2 In JAI, XII, 36, 39.

older men, which is found in many tribes, has been a great stimulus to elopement, though perhaps not so effective in reality as it appears at first sight likely to be, for "the monopoly is an assertion of the old men of property in the women, not of exclusive marital rights over them. It claims the right of regulating their intercourse with the younger men who are their 'husbands' by hereditary status." Among the Yuin, where marriage was arranged by the fathers of the parties, "elopement of the girl with a preferred suitor was also severely punished—the man having to stand up in an arranged fight with clubs, until either he had been knocked down four times, when he was free, but lost the girl, or until he had knocked down all 'her men' when he kept her." It is stated further that the *jus primæ noctis* was exercised only in the rare cases of elopement where the parents' consent could not be obtained.

Elopements often occur in British New Guinea. "The girl will probably steal some of her parents' property, and the pair go off together to another village, or into the bush, and remain there until the anger of the girl's parents has been appeased, which may be in two or three days or not for months. The propitiation of the girl's parents is secured by the relatives of the boy by offering a marriage price of articles and pigs; but in the case of an elopement the price is not so great as it is in that of a regular marriage, as there is a certain amount of shame in the girl's family."[3] Of the Roro-speaking tribes it is written that "elopements, which seem always to have occurred, are common at the present time, and may be expected to become even more frequent, since the members of the Sacred Heart Mission having found that such love matches commonly turn out well, exert themselves to conciliate the offended parents. The chief cause of elopements seems to be unwillingness on the part of the girl's father to accept what is generally considered to be a fair price for his daughter. The young folk will then take to the bush for a couple of days, after which the bridegroom leaves the bride in charge of his clan and bestirs himself to make his peace with the girl's relatives, the gift of a pig being an early and generally successful step in this direction, after which a price agreeable to both local groups is arranged."[4]

In East Central Africa, "the bridegroom elopes with the girl, the mother conniving. The father then has to dun his son in law for a considerable time for the bride-price, which he extorts only in small instalments. The son-in-law appoints a friend to deal with him, and this friend is remunerated according to his success in whittling the price down."[5] Sometimes among the Akamba a young man and girl agree to elope; "if the father does not approve the girl has to return to her father."[6] "Among the Waseguha, Wachagga, Sumbwa, and Wanyamwesi abduction of girls is commonly done with their consent, when the suitor is unable to pay dowry or the parents are unwilling to let her go after dowry has been paid. In Ukamba parents often withhold the bride in order to exact further gifts from the suitor, and in such cases she will arrange with him to come at night and steal her away. Where such practices are in vogue it will be found that the abduction is accepted in place of the ordinary marriage ceremony, and though the parents may deny the husband's right to the girl unless dowry is paid at once, a lawful marriage is considered to have been contracted. . . . The girl's consent is a necessary condition, but notwith-

3 Williamson, in JAI, XLIII, 277.
4 Seligmann, *Melanesians*, 271.
5 Torday, in JAI, LI, 374-375.
6 Hobley, *A-Kamba*, 64.

standing this it is regarded as a point of decency that she should protest and scream loudly."[7]

That the Hindu girl had some choice in determining her destiny is indicated in the laws of Manu, which permitted a damsel to wait three years and then choose for herself a husband of equal caste; but in this case she was not allowed to take any ornaments with her.[8] Among the Alfurs of Buru, as elsewhere in the Indian Archipelago, the groom, when sure of a girl's liking for him, abducts her, with the foreknowledge of her parents, and hides in the bush with her, during which time the parents and clan of the girl are talked to about the bride-price.[9]

The elopement, which is part of the wedding-ceremony in many of the Palaung clans, though not in all, generally takes place at night. "The time has been chosen by the soothsayer of the village, with due regard to the days of the week on which the lovers were born. This being settled, the young man invites a number of his friends, young men and maidens about the same age as himself, to help him in the elopement. Sometimes he sends a friend to the mothers of the girls, to get their permission for their daughters to be out at night; sometimes he invites the girls himself, and they tell their mothers. . . . The lover chooses friends with persuasive tongues, who can help him to talk to the girl, to give her courage to run away should she grow timid at the last moment. The girls are generally the special friends of the eloping damsel. Sometimes there are six, eight, or ten girls and young men, an equal number of each sex. . . . If the bride happens to be alone, matters may be arranged very quickly; but it sometimes happens that other young men, who have no idea that an elopement is pending, may be already there in possession, talking to the girl. . . . When no men remain but the bridegroom and his friends, they urge her to set out. She, however, with real or pretended shyness, refuses to go. She throws more wood on the fire, and, pushing tobacco or betel-nut near them for their refreshment, continues to sit by the hearth, as if she expected to be there all night. . . . When it is past midnight the bridegroom grows impatient; he whispers to the girl, 'It is surely time to go!' She answers, 'Why hurry? Outside it is cold, here the fire is warm.' Another hour may pass and she finds it difficult to keep the conversation going. Each time it flags her lover urges her to set out. He says, 'Surely now is a good time to start! It will soon be rice-pounding time, when thy mother will rise and call thee.' The girl says, 'Why art thou in such a hurry? Who pounds rice in the middle of the night? Perhaps I shall not go at all!' Her lover answers, 'Do not say so, little sister, why should we not set out?' As she shows no signs of rising from her place on the floor, the young men try to persuade her. . . . Not every girl, however, requires so much persuasion. At last she rises and takes a few steps towards the entrance-door; then she stops, and turning again towards the hearth, with her hands palm to palm, she makes a deep reverence towards the place by the fire where her father is accustomed to sit. . . . The eloping couple generally go to the house of some elderly relative of the bridegroom, who has a wife or a sister living with him, and who receives from the bridegroom a small present of money, to be spent on tobacco and food for the runaway pair and their friends. Sometimes, however, the bridegroom takes the bride, with her escort, to his own home if his father is dead. His mother may be living with him, and if

7 Dundas, C., in JAI, LI, 253. Dowry = bride-price.

8 Bühler, Manu, IX, 90.
9 Wilken, in VG, I, 48.

not, there is sure to be some elderly woman who is willing to act as chaperon.
. . . If the young people are both poor, the bride's parents give their consent
in a few days—if they approve of their new son-in-law—so that their stay at
the house of the relative is not long; but, as in European countries, when the
parents are rich, there may be much more ceremony connected with a wedding,
and more money spent on it than when the people are poor; the father of the
bride, if a rich man, may not give his consent for ten days or more." When
the mother understands that her daughter has run away, she generally sits down
and cries. "This rouses her husband, who anxiously asks what is wrong. When
the husband knows that his daughter has eloped, he is, or pretends to be,
very angry, saying that the girl is far too young to think of marriage, and
that he requires her to help with the work in the house and tea garden. He
works himself up into a rage, scolds his wife because she has not prevented
the elopement—though he has to admit that he himself ran away with his
wife when she was as young as his runaway daughter—and finally sits down
beside the fire." Except the actual elopement, the bridegroom does not take
an active part in the proceedings and is practically ignored by the relatives
of the bride during all the preliminary arrangements. "The girl, although she
protests that she does not wish to return, generally obeys and accompanies
the three women back to her home. When she enters the house nothing is said—
if the parents are satisfied with the young man—and the day passes as if she
had never run away at all. Sometimes a girl, after she has been brought back
for the first time, discovers that she is not really so much in love with the
young man as she thought: in such a case a marriage is sometimes broken off,
after the first elopement. This elopement would be no obstacle to her engagement, later on, to another man, and would not in any way compromise
her. Indeed it would rather enhance her value in the eyes of other young men,
if they knew that a man was so desirous of making her his wife that he was
willing to run away with her." To resume, the girl spends the day after the
first elopement in doing her usual work in the house, though she would not
be seen out of doors. In the evening, when the bridegroom and the young men
come for her, she is quite ready to go with them. Three women go to her father
and say that she will not return. He replies, "Go again and bring her back.
Her mother and I do not consent. Tell her that she must wait till next year."
The matter is then taken up by the father of the young man, but the girl's
father still refuses. A Pa-jau or professional go-between is called in. "The
Pa-jaus have nothing to do with the lovers during their courtship, they are
only called in to help when the elopement is a *fait accompli*. The Pa-jau is
usually an elderly man who has studied his profession by assisting other
Pa-jaus and has learned to repeat the long speeches which must be said, and
who knows well all the ceremonious etiquette connected with marrying and
giving in marriage." After the Pa-jau has spoken the father replies. "If the
father really meant that he would insist on the return of his daughter, the
Pa-jau would understand this from the tone of his voice. This time the voice
of the father expresses no indignation, so the Pa-jau knows that all is well
and that the words of the father really mean nothing." When it is known that
the parents of a girl really object to a young man who is paying court to her,
and the man has a bad character, it is not easy to find an escort for her when
she elopes. "When the father knows that his daughter has gone off with a man
whom he dislikes, he sends his wife to his female relatives to ask them to
bring back the runaway girl as quickly as possible. . . . The Pa-jau is sent

to her father, but is received badly, the father saying angrily, 'Take away thy tobacco! I do not like the young man. Bring back my daughter. When she comes back I shall tether her to the house.' If a father is really very angry, he may go himself to bring back his daughter, but this is considered a most undignified proceeding. If he goes, he does not enter the house where the girl is staying, but stands at the foot of the housesteps and calls her to come to him." What is more like real elopement occurs where the father has definitely refused to give his consent. "When a girl is determined to marry a man against the wishes of her father, she elopes several times, following the usual customs; but after she realizes that the consent of her father will not be given, the young man comes to fetch her, on an evening previously arranged, bringing only one friend—a man—to be her escort. When he reaches her home, he gives some signal—by coughing or whistling—to let the girl know that he is waiting. She then tiptoes through the entrance-room as softly as possible, in order not to wake her parents, and hurries down the steps to her lover, while the friend gently closes the door. Tobacco and rice are not left in such a case. Sometimes a girl cannot easily escape from the house, as she is well watched by her family, but unless they tie her to one of the house-posts—this is occasionally done by an angry father—she generally manages to escape. They go at once to a tea garden at a distance from the village, and live together there, unchaperoned, as husband and wife, in one of the huts built for the tea-pickers. The father of the young man, or some one else favourable to the marriage, calls the Pa-jau to make another attempt to gain the consent of the girl's father." The girl's mother and the relatives may also plead for the girl. If the father is obdurate, he says: "I am too angry to give her in marriage, let her uncle arrange." Arrangements for the wedding then go on, the uncle acting precisely as if he were the father. "The young man's father gives the usual amount of money, and the Elders are invited and feasts are held at the houses of the young man's father and of the girl's uncle. There is little ceremony and no gongs or drums are beaten. The parents of the girl are not present and often they refuse to receive their daughter and her husband until after the birth of a child, when the young couple are generally forgiven. Such a runaway marriage and the forgiveness of the parents form the subject of many Palaung songs."[10]

Among the Samoans, "if there was a probability that the parents would not consent, from disparity of rank or other causes, an elopement took place; and, if the young man was a chief of any importance, a number of his associates mustered in the evening, and walked through the settlement, singing his praises and shouting out the name of the person with whom he had eloped. This was sometimes the first intimation the parents had of it, and, however mortified they might be, it was too late. After a time, if the couple continued to live together, their friends acknowledged the union by festivities and an exchange of property."[11]

With the Omaha, "marriage was usually by elopement. The claims on a girl by men holding a potential right to marry her almost necessitated her escaping secretly if she would exercise her free choice in the matter of a husband. When a young couple during their courtship determined on taking the final step of marriage, they agreed to meet some evening. The youth generally rode to a

---

10 Milne, *Eastern Clan*, 128-131, 133, 135-136, 136-138, 141, 170, 171-174.   11 Turner, *Samoa*, 95-96.

place near the lodge of the girl and gave the proper signal; she stepped out and they galloped off to one of his relations. . . . In the course of a few months the father of the bride generally presented his daughter with return gifts about equal in value to those he had received and the young husband was expected to work for a year or two for his father-in-law. This latter claim was frequently rigidly exacted and the father-in-law was sometimes a tyrant over his son-in-law's affairs."[12] Among the American Indians in general, elopement was more or less necessitated by the marriage-customs, as Powell[13] points out: "A group of men may greatly increase in number, while the group of women from whom they are obliged to accept their wives diminishes. At the same time another group of women may be large in proportion to the group of men to whom they are destined. Under these circumstances, certain men have a right to many wives, while others have a right to but few. It is very natural that young men and women should sometimes rebel against the law, and elope with each other. Now, a fundamental principle of early law is that controversy must end; and such termination is secured by a curious provision found among many, perhaps all, tribes. A day is established, sometimes once a moon, but usually once a year, at which certain classes of offenses are forgiven. If, then, a runaway couple can escape to the forest, and live by themselves until the day of forgiveness, they may return to the tribe and live in peace. Marriage by this form exists in many North American tribes."

According to an edict, in 497 A.D., of Theodoric the Ostrogoth, "the abductor of a free woman or virgin, with his accessories or agents, when the facts are proved according to law, we command shall be put to death and if the abducted woman shall have consented to her abduction, let her likewise be put to death." If the parents or guardian of the woman do not prosecute, but make terms with the abductor, they are to be exiled. A slave who knows that an abduction is being compounded and who gives evidence, shall get his liberty. After five years no accusation for abduction shall hold, especially if children have resulted from the marriage.[14]

Among Italian immigrants in the United States may be found survivals which partake partly of the nature of elopement and partly of abduction. With reference to the Sicilian colony in Chicago it is stated: "Sometimes a girl is coveted by a man considered undesirable by her parents, or by one who did not know her before she was engaged. In such a case the man may try to force his attentions on her in the hope of attracting her in spite of her parents or her promise. If she does not respond and will not elope voluntarily, it is not unusual for him to try to take her by force, either carrying her off himself or getting his friends to kidnap her and bring her to some secret place. When a girl becomes engaged her family is on the lookout for just such occurrences, and if they have any suspicion that she is being pursued she is kept a prisoner until she is safely married. If the man is known he is dealt with in no uncertain way—told to stop or take the consequences. If a girl permits herself to be kidnaped the affair is usually ended with the blessings of all concerned, though the jilted one sometimes makes it necessary for the couple to move to another part of town, at least until he consoles himself with another wife. If a girl is carried away entirely against her will there may be bloodshed as a result. Not

---

12 Fletcher and LaFlesche, in BAE, XXVII, 324.
13 In BAE, III, lx.

14 Haimensfeld, *Collectio Const. Imperialium*, III, 18.

all kidnapings occur in this way; often impatient men, tiring of the long and ceremonious period of betrothal and failing to persuade the fiancée to elope, try to carry her away. A well-bred girl will put up a good fight to escape, and if she succeeds the engagement is broken; but if she is forced to submit the family accept the situation and all is forgiven. There are, of course, many voluntary elopements by young people who are attracted by one another and who, because of family differences, could never get the consent of their parents."[15]

§361. Wife-Purchase.

In some Australian tribes, a man can only obtain a wife by giving a woman in exchange; "in rare cases a woman might be married without having been paid for by another given in exchange, but this was looked upon as a disgrace for the woman herself and for the clan into which she married."[1] Among the Narrinyeri and other tribes, "women were bartered as wives by their male relatives for goods, such as skin rugs, weapons, etc., and a perpetual reproach lay against a woman if she went to her husband for nothing."[2]

Among the Mekeo of New Guinea, "a girl must always be solemnly bought; otherwise her family would be dishonoured." The procedure of collecting the purchase-price and related ceremonies are described as follows. "The girl's family, having accepted the offer, take possession of the things actually handed to them, and immediately, or within a day or two afterwards, make an armed raid upon the boy's clan in his village for the pigs, and perhaps dogs. They go to the houses of the boy's relatives, and carry off everything they find there, and they make a general raid upon the pigs, dogs and coconuts of the entire clan in the village. The raid, however, has been anticipated and prepared for by removal and concealment, and the raiders, so far, at all events, as pigs and dogs are concerned, do not get more than had been promised them. . . . There may be reluctance on the part of one or both of the couple to consent to the marriage, and the girl will probably feign reluctance, even if she does not feel it. Family persuasion may, therefore, be requisite, and during its continuance the couple remain seated back to back on the verandah. Then, the boy being willing, and the girl having overcome her genuine or feigned hesitation, the girl passes behind her back to the boy a piece of betel, or perhaps a pipe, into which she has inserted a cigarette, which she has lighted and smoked, so as to fill the pipe with smoke, in the usual way; and his acceptance and chewing of the betel or smoking of the pipe is the signal for one or other of those present to call out the names of the boy and girl and announce the marriage in a loud voice, whereupon all the others applaud, and the ceremony is completed."[3] Throughout British New Guinea the usual essential feature of a marriage contract is that the woman shall be paid for. "The word for 'wife' (or 'husband'), a-dava-na, pretty clearly contains the root -dava, 'paid for' or 'payer,' combined with a suffix -na, indicating a substantive, and a prefix a, probably indicating a person. Thus adavana would equally denote the payer (the husband) and the paid for (the wife). Curiously, in one small district . . . there is no payment, and the only requisite for a native marriage

15 Park and Miller, *Old World Traits Transplanted*, 156-157.
1 Brown, in JAI, XLVIII, 238-239.

2 Howitt and Fison, in JAI, XII, 36.
3 Williamson, in JAI, XLIII, 275-276.

would seem to have been that the woman should make the man's leglets and shall cohabit with him. . . . On the north-east coast a similar exogamous marriage by payment is very common. But occasionally a man will marry inside his clan, when no payment is made."[4] When a youth of the Roro-speaking tribes is of an age to be married, his father asks the members of his local group to help him to collect the bride-price for his son. "The head of the girl's family, usually her father, will say that the bridegroom's folk have not offered enough. The latter dissent, but add further valuables, until the girl's people are satisfied. . . . If all goes well the girl's father piles the bride-price into a heap, and, taking an areca nut from the bunch brought by the bridegroom's father, tears off the husk with his teeth, and biting it in half gives one piece to the bridegroom's father." The author[5] comments significantly on the stabilizing effect of property—conspicuous by its absence among some of the southern Massim, with the result that marriages last only a short time, being dissolved by mutual agreement and without any strong opposition. "Where no considerable wedding price is paid by either party, and where the wedding celebrations consist rather of reciprocal presents of equivalent value and often of identical nature, one strong element tending to the permanence of marriage is obviously absent." In Santa Cruz, "when a man is betrothed to a woman he gives at first to her father a sum of money; this sum makes the woman *tapu*, lest anyone else might buy her."[6]

The system of payment of a certain number of cattle by a bridegroom for his bride, which is a universal custom among South African tribes, obtains also among the Mavenda. "The number is determined by the father of the girl and the son-in-law elect, and varies according to the position of the contracting parties. In the event of marriage being sanctioned without the prior payment of cattle, then, in accordance with native law, the issue of the marriage becomes the property of the bride's father, until the number of cattle agreed upon have all been delivered."[7] What may be regarded as a perversion of the property-interest exists in British Tropical Africa, where the custom of elderly women procuring young girls, whom they call "wives" and with whom they go through a marriage-ceremony, prevails. "The purchase money is misnamed 'dowry,' and the woman-husband becomes absolute owner of the girls. The same thing is sometimes done for an identical purpose by very old and decrepit men. In some few cases it may be that the purchaser wishes to assure herself of a 'wife' who will tend her in her old age, but the more usual reason is in order to claim fees for adultery, and to gain possession of the children of such intercourse, who by native custom are the property of the 'husband' who has paid the dowry. In such cases, no doubt, the woman, who is in fact the keeper of a brothel, would be prosecuted on a criminal charge, and awarded no compensation for the loss of her 'wives' and their dowries." One such woman was found to have nineteen "wives."[8] Marriage among the Bageshu is said to be "purely a financial transaction between the elders or parents of the couple, though a man seeks to find a woman who is strong and able to work to be his partner."[9] Among the Ibo, "the sons-in-law at the present day bring powder, cowries, and one goat if the bride price is finished; in former days they had also to bring a slave. If any of them have not completed

4 Strong, in JAI, XLIX, 300-301.　　　7 Grant, in JAI, XXXV, 270.
5 Seligmann, *Melanesians*, 267, 268, 510.　　8 Lugard, *Brit. Trop. Africa*, 387.
6 O'Ferrall, in JAI, XXXIV, 223.　　　9 Roscoe, in JAI, XXXIX, 182-183.

payment of bride price they are reminded that it is necessary for them to do so."[10]

On the Niger, payment in cloth, gin, coral, or other commodities is made to the parents or to the brothers, sisters, or guardians of the girl.[11] An indication as to what is being paid for in wife-purchase, as well as to the relation between parents and children, may be seen in the case of the Nigerian head-hunters. "When a woman conceives, or within a certain time after the birth (three years is the outside limit), the husband, if he wants the child, must make a present of three goats to his father-in-law. . . . A child always belongs to the woman's father unless the husband has paid the proper fee within the proper time, and never to the woman herself."[12] Ownership of the woman extends then to her offspring, as was noted also among the South Africans. In West Africa the payment exacted varies with the rank of the girl. "The amount to be paid is fixed by the family of the girl, and the marriage is arranged without, as a rule, any reference being made to her wishes, though she cannot be forced into a union that is absolutely repugnant to her. The payment of 'head-money,' as the sum paid for a wife is termed, constitutes a marriage; and the head-money may be paid in actual coin or cowries, or, as is more commonly the case, in merchandise and rum. Amongst the poorest people the sum paid may be merely nominal; but something, even if it be only a bottle of rum, must be paid as head-money, in order to give a union the dignity of marriage."[13] This connection between marriage and property[14] appears regularly elsewhere, "the poorest always pay a small sum for their wives, so as to give the unions the title of a marriage, and distinguish it from concubinage." But the bride-price is often stated to be "compensation to her parents for the loss of her services in the household, and the transaction is not in any sense the purchase of a chattel."[15] The bride's family remains responsible for the payment made, in case she runs away, and must replace it also if she should die.[16]

In West Africa the virgin ranks first in price, then the divorced woman, and last of all the widow. The payment is by instalments and is supposed to be completed in one or two years after marriage. Other relatives beside the girl's father, such as her brothers, sisters, and cousins, may make demands upon the would-be husband, this illustrating the complexity of interests surrounding marriage. In fact, there is always a more than individual interest present, for no young man saves up enough to buy a wife; he squanders what he gets and his family must contribute to get him one. They have a claim on her for various services and work, though he owns her; and neither he nor she could refuse these claims. On the death of a wife, a part of the money received for her is returned to the widower as compensation for loss on his investment, though if she dies childless there is no repayment. Though sometimes a woman is actually "paid" over as a fine, this does not alter the marriage custom; those who paid her over in lieu of penalty may come and ask a portion of goods for her as a wife. A father, thus discharging his obligation, has no claim on her as a daughter; he will get the goods, however, for the common belief is that if they are refused the children of the marriage will die early.[17] Reimburse-

10 Thomas, in JAI, XLVII, 186.
11 Granville and Roth, in JAI, XXVIII, 107.
12 Tremearne, in JAI, XLII, 189.
13 Ellis, *Ewe*, 199.
14 §341, of the text.
15 Ellis, *Yoruba*, 182.
16 Bastian, *Deut. Exped.*, I, 166-167.
17 Nassau, *Fetichism*, 7, 21, 157.

ment of parents for the rearing of a daughter is often delayed so that the husband may remain a debtor all his life; and since obligations of this sort are incumbent upon the family, they may be handed on for a long time.[18]

It is not easy for an African without means to marry. If he negotiates for himself he must satisfy the demands of the chief, who can exercise an absolute authority in these matters, and then he may succeed in obtaining a wife without previously paying down any sum by way of compensation.[19]

Purchase is the common form of marriage through Uganda; Johnston's[20] account is rather complete. Goats and iron hoes are the stock articles given for a wife. Beer-drinking at the groom's expense commonly accompanies marriage-negotiations. The chief's consent is needful, and he sometimes provides the purchase-price. A girl may be betrothed at the age of six or seven, and the intending husband then makes repeated small presents to her father, paying up in full at the time of marriage. If the girl does not prove to be a virgin at the public consummation, she is restored with contumely and all the goods paid in instalments must be restored, plus an amount equal to the whole purchase-price, as an acknowledgment of the disgrace entailed by the girl's real or supposed misconduct. Again, while the cattle of the marriage gift become the property of the wife's father, their offspring go to the son-in-law or his heirs. The total of the marriage payment may amount to six cows or their equivalent. In the case of instalments, if the man stops paying, his wife will return to her home till he resumes. If the wife does not bear a child within a year of marriage, the husband may stop paying, though he has no claim for restoration of what has been paid so long as his wife remains with him. If she dies childless, her purchase-price is returned unless the husband agrees to accept one of her sisters, for whom only a small complimentary present is given. A woman may refuse to stay with her husband; but if she goes to another man, whatever the latter gives for her is paid over to the first husband. If a woman who has a child is ill treated, though she may leave her husband, the child must remain with him. If a woman finds herself unmarried after a long period, it is customary for her to go to a chief or rich man and state that she has come to stay and cook for him. In such case she is usually taken to wife, with a small complimentary payment. Chiefs may have from ten to forty wives. This device disposes of the old-maid question and almost forces polygyny upon the rich.[21]

By far the most common disputes in the East African Protectorate are those regarding the bride-price when a father takes back his daughter or she runs away. "In such cases a man can take two courses: either he can claim back all dowry paid, with its increase, and also all presents made at the time of purchase, or he can drop his claim to this and retain the children, in which case he can also claim all children the woman may have by a later husband. In such a case it seems pretty clear that the woman is not regarded as legally married, or belonging to the man she has gone to, for if she dies at the latter's village, or if any of the children die there, the man has to pay full blood money to the first husband. The fact is, that so long as a woman is not properly bought she is not married, and thus it is that the husband, by refusing to accept payment for her, can prohibit her ever marrying again." The price of

18 §§83, 105, above; Gutmann, in *Globus*, XCII, 31.
19 Schweinfurth, *Heart of Afr.*, II, 213; §365, of the text.
20 *Uganda*, II, 553, 578, 609, 632, 687, 688, 747, 748, 790, 791, 878.
21 §§398, 399, of the text.

a Mkamba wife varies from two to five cows, besides one bull. There is much haggling over what the groom shall pay. "In any case, however, he will be required to make many presents of blankets, knives, and honey beer to the father and other relations, who are, therefore, always bent on prolonging the negotiations as long as possible, always putting him off with hints that another present is desired, until finally he may steal her away at night. Later on the girl's family may regret their greed, for if ever she leaves the husband he will claim every present given, besides the price paid for her: every item has been carefully recorded by a little stick which is added to a bundle treasured up in the hut." The death of a woman does not usually entitle her husband to make any demands on her family, but in Ukamba and Kikuyu, as also in Ubena, it is customary as an act of goodwill to refund a portion of the bride-price; in Ukamba, if no child is born, one cow is refunded, in certain sections of Kikuyu two-thirds of the purchase-price if no children are born, or one-third if only one or two children. Such returns cannot, however, be demanded as of right.[22]

If the man cannot pay the bride-price, he must work it out. In Ukamba, "chiefs like to marry their daughters to poor men for if their sons-in-law are poor they can call upon them to work for them. If a son-in-law of a chief refused to work for his father-in-law the latter would call his daughter back to his village, and the husband being a poor man, with probably only one wife, would then have no one to work for him and would soon go and make terms with his father-in-law. The marriage price is paid by instalments and the girl is married before the payments are complete."[23] So among the Turkana, "should the bridegroom not be in a position to pay the full amount, he may, provided of course the parents agree, pay instalments, in which case he moves to his father-in-law's village, and his wife, and any children she may have, then live at the expense of her parents, until the final payment is completed."[24] Again, "on the wedding-day the bride is led by her paternal grandmother or, failing her, by the aunt whose name she bears, to her future husband's hut. One of the most essential points in the conclusion of the matrimonial arrangements is that her conductor must see with her own eyes what has been paid of the bride-money before performing her part of the function, otherwise the marriage is null and void."[25] In Kenia, "it being settled that the clans of the contracting parties have intermarried before, elders of the groom's clan, his mother's clan, the bride's clan and her mother's clan meet to discuss the bride-price; this varies from a few goats with the Hill Suk to up to eighty head of cattle with the Pastoral Suk. . . . The bride demands a present before leaving her mother's hut, demands a present when she crosses a stream, demands a present before entering the village of the groom, a present before she sits down, a present before she eats, and on every possible contingency. The groom mentions certain cattle in his holding which he will place to her credit, and these particular cattle may not be used for the purpose of other subsequent wives and ultimately descend to the bride's youngest male offspring."[26]

Though the wife is bought as chattels are, this does not mean that she can be sold by her husband as a chattel can be. The Galla husband sometimes exercises such a right, but not often. Among both the Somali and others the bride-show, with the girl magnificently attired and heavily perfumed, is held with

---

22 Dundas, C., in JAI, XLIII, 517, 519-520; and in JAI, LI, 258.
23 Hobley, A-Kamba, 62.

24 Dundas, K., in JAI, XL, 67-68.
25 Johnstone, in JAI, XXXII, 266-267.
26 Barton, in JAI, LI, 95-96.

intent to excite the bridegroom and thus extort a higher purchase price from him.[27] In one section of Africa goats are the stock means of exchange for wives; "for woman and goat are there almost equivalent conceptions."[28] In Fantiland the payment varies from three pounds, twelve shillings to seven pounds, four shillings (that is, one or two ounces of gold); but ten or twelve pounds are paid for an educated girl and even twenty for a mulatto.[29] Elsewhere the price varies from ten to one hundred and fifty milch camels, ten to fifteen horses, two hundred to five hundred sheep, or, in the case of poor people, from ten to twenty goats. Where the Maria Theresa dollar is current, prices range, for the rich, from one hundred and fifty to a thousand, while the poor pay from eight to thirty dollars.[30]

Among the Dinka laws are the following. "If, after taking possession of the girl, the man fails to pay the remainder of the 'marriage payment' as arranged by the council, the father of the girl can apply to a Dinka court, and if the man does not satisfy him, he can take his daughter back and any children she has borne, returning to her husband all the cattle already paid for her and all their young." From this it will be seen how inappropriate the term divorce is to the tribal "breaking of marriage." Again, "a 'marriage payment' not completed is binding on the heirs of the man should he die, and is due not only to the father or guardian of the wife, but to the heirs of the creditor. Example.— A marries B's daughter. He still owes two cows. A and B die. B leaves no heirs, but his daughter buys a 'wife widow' in his name and the girl gives birth to a son Z. Z claims from A's heirs two cows. They must be paid him."[31] The list of presents given by a Hausa at marriage include: asking-money, that is, the first present to the girl's parents; binding marriage-money, when the wedding has been arranged; "glory-box," or presents sent to the bride by the groom and displayed at the marriage; presents to the bride both to unveil and to speak to the groom; and finally, the rest of the dower, due at marriage, "but seldom given before divorce."[32] Among the Kabyles a girl is sold in marriage and the laws of humanity and modesty are not respected in the bargain;[33] but a Saharan Arab father is ashamed to sell his daughter, although the form of marriage is by purchase. He gives as much as he gets, and the groom pays only half the petty price agreed upon.[34] Here is the germ of dowry.[35] It is said that Sudanese profiteers now ask eight spearheads for a wife. "In the Sudan before the war, a wife could be got for four spearheads. Now the price has doubled. In the cattle country it used to be four cows; now the price is seven cows."[36]

Among the aborigines of Siberia occur many instances where the man performs services to get a wife, instead of purchasing her, and also where a marriage-negotiator or go-between is employed. The following is typical. "When a Kamchadal wishes to marry, he looks for a woman in the next village, very seldom in his own. Having chosen one, he asks her parents to allow him to serve them for a certain period: this permission is easily obtained, and during the time of service he endeavours to win their favour. When the period is at an end, he asks to be allowed to take the woman, and if he has found favour in

27 Paulitschke, *Nordost-Afr.*, I, 199; II, 142.
28 Junker, *Afrika*, III, 124.
29 Connolly, in JAI, XXVI, 144.
30 Paulitschke, *Nordost-Afr.*, I, 196-197.
31 O'Sullivan, in JAI, XL, 181, 182.

32 Tremearne, in JAI, XLV, 36.
33 Hanoteau et Letourneux, *Kabylie*, II, 149.
34 Pommerol, *Sahariennes*, 250.
35 §364, of the text.
36 N. Y. *Times*, Feb. 19, 1922.

the eyes of her, her parents, and her relatives, he marries her; if not, they recompense him for his services." Among the Gilyak, "the custom of payment for a wife exists, but this is either merely a formality, or what is received is divided among relatives. . . . The higher the price of a wife, the greater is the respect paid to her in her husband's family." With the Altaians, "a rich son-in-law pays his *kalym* at once, a poor one in instalments covering several years. . . . To enable the bridegroom to pay the *kalym,* his bachelor friends help him by making each a small offering from his store. But the larger the *kalym,* the worse is the position of a woman in her widowhood. Her father-in-law treats her as property bought for much money, and if she wishes to marry again, he demands from the suitor as large a *kalym* as the deceased husband formerly paid for her. Sometimes the widow marries her brother-in-law."[37]

Among the Cherkes of the Caucasus, who live as joint-families in big houses, wives are bought or captured in common. Darinsky[38] thinks that this arrangement has been threatened by allowing those who so desired to buy separate wives. Polygyny is permissible but is not practised because the bride-price is too great an expense. It is related that some Cherkes women, on their way to Constantinople, were taken by a band of Russians and offered the choice of marrying them and returning home or of going on, which meant to be sold. All without hesitation chose the latter. There was no shame in being sold; it was in the mores; that was the way in which one became a wife.[39] It is said that in the dominion of the Great Khan of Tartary the poor who could not afford to give their daughters a dowry brought them into the market place with the sound of war-trumpets; there the girls exposed first their backs to the shoulders and then their front parts and were married to such as liked them best.[40] The Tartars of Kasan have a tradition concerning the origin of a similar bride-show, which relates that a rich Tartar who had many daughters gave a feast and invited all the young people to it, in order to find husbands for them. The festival, kept up ever since, offers an occasion for acquaintance between men and women and for marriages of inclination.[41] Whereas the Mongolians used to capture their wives, nowadays they purchase them, the price being five or six head of cattle and ten sheep.[42] According to an Associated Press dispatch, the Turkestan Government in 1926 issued a decree prohibiting polygyny, the exploitation of women, and the sale of infant girls in marriage. The professional marriage-brokers, who thrived on the sale of women, were suppressed; it will no longer be necessary for a man to pay a price for a wife, and those forced to do so may later recover in court. In a trial preceding this decree it was revealed that young girls were often sold into marriage without their consent, frequently becoming third or fourth wives of old men they had never seen before. It was also disclosed that parents who sold their immature daughters into marriage encouraged divorce so that the girls could be sold a second time. Some girls were resold five times.[43]

Just outside of Hsuan-hua is a poplar grove where in the fifth moon is celebrated the bride-show, known as "airing-the-feet-festival;" the women walk up and down, dressed in their best, and the men admire, criticize, or condemn the shape, as well as the size, of each one's feet. The author[44] has never heard

37 Czaplicka, *Aborig. Siberia,* 39 ff., 87-88, 100, 117.
38 *Ztsft. f. vergl. Rechts-Wissnsft.,* XIV, 180.
39 Von Haxthausen, *Transkaukasia,* 6.
40 Eden, *First Three Books,* 24.
41 *Russ. Ethnog.* (Russ.), II, 24.
42 Communicated by a correspondent.
43 N. Y. *Times,* Oct. 9, 1926.
44 Rockhill, *Mongolia,* 5.

of this feast being celebrated elsewhere in China. Only in case of dire necessity do the Sifan Tibetans make a foraying expedition for wives; the method more generally employed consists of wife-purchase with much bargaining. When a man desires a wife, he waits upon the father of the girl who has attracted his eye and makes an offer of marriage. "The father, after weighing the matter carefully, for a refusal is likely to provoke a long and disastrous feud, in turn waits upon the priests and acquaints them with the nature of the offer, at the same time paying to them a munificent bribe in order to secure the answer of the deities as to whether the marriage should be entered into. The young man, should he be diplomatic enough, meantime has carried a larger bribe to the lamas, who 'bleed' both father and suitor to limits of safety, when a decision is given invariably favoring the claims of the latter. This, however, is but the commencement of the ordeal through which the lovelorn suitor must pass. During an entire month he must keep the family of his favored one supplied with meat and other luxuries, and must also be constantly on his guard against rival suitors, who are bound to enter similar offers. At the end of a month the chosen one is invited to a grand feast provided by the father of the girl, where the betrothal is sealed by each cutting a small incision in the arm and mingling the blood flowing from the wounds. . . . The girl is then brought forward in all her native charms, smeared with grease and variously colored pigments, adorned in all her finery, and with a rope tied round her neck as a badge of subservience. Then ensues a scene of the shrewdest bargaining, the father dilating on the good points of the girl much in the manner that a connoisseur of blooded stock would expound the good points of an animal, while the suitor, having calculated how many cattle he is willing to give, strives to secure her at the lowest possible price. The wishes or inclinations of the woman are never consulted, but the bargaining goes on for days and even weeks until a final settlement has been arrived at. The requisite price having been paid, she is led to the house of her husband, where she is subjected to a severe beating, in order to humble her spirit properly, and made to run round the village loudly proclaiming the merits and valor of her husband, and touching those objects that are supposed to have a potent influence over her future welfare, such as the teats of the cattle or the little stone idols placed in front of each dwelling. By her sale, however, the father does not relinquish his claims upon her, but may sell her time and time again to suitors who may come after, until she may have half a dozen husbands."[45]

Woman's purchase-price seems, in the case of a certain tribe of India, to be independent of the law of supply and demand; "it is strange that the bride price should be so high amongst the Lusheis, as the women of this tribe largely exceed the men in numbers."[46] In this tribe, "if a man is willing at once to marry a girl whom he has seduced he is not expected to pay more than the usual marriage price." Again, a woman may discharge debt to a man by marrying him; but after she has borne a child or two all talk about her indebtedness, in case of divorce, is out of order.[47] Not only the nearest male relative of the bride, but also her aunt, her elder sister, her maternal uncle, and a special chosen male and female guardian, all have to be paid certain sums, and traces of this custom are found among many other clans.[48] In some

45 Reid, in *Cosmopolitan Mag.*, XXVIII, 451.

46 Risley, *Ethnog. Ind.*, I, 224, note, 225.

47 Van den Berg, in *Bijd.*, XLIII, 280.

48 Shakespear, in JAI, XXXIX, 381.

communities the custom of exchange is definitely connected with the bride-price, which may be so large as almost to compel a man to give his sister in exchange for the wife he takes from another clan, but among the Todas "the bride-price is so inconsiderable that it is unlikely that it would form a motive for exchange."[49] Betrothal by exchange is common in the Punjab, and in case of disparity of age the party giving the older girl must be paid something extra.[50] Among the Sema Nagas marriage is never made against the girl's will, though it may often happen that she does no more than passively acquiesce in the arrangements made by her parents or guardian. "The prices paid for wives vary very considerably indeed according to their station in life, ranging in value from Rs. 20/— or even less to as much as Rs. 400/— or Rs. 500/—," the rupee being valued at 32 cents. "Besides the girl's birth, her capabilities are also taken into account, a girl who is thrifty, can weave, or is a hard and good worker in the fields commanding a higher price accordingly. Personal appearance has little bearing on the marriage price."[51] Similar conditions prevail in the Chin Hills, where parents practically sell their daughters to be wives, demanding a certain price for them. "The facts are that the girl cultivates her parents' fields and performs the household duties, and if any man wants her to do the same for him, he must compensate the parents for the loss of an able-bodied servant." In the Southern Hills the eldest brother is the guardian of his sisters, and if a man aspires to the hand of a woman he must address himself to the brother and not to the parents. The price of the bride is divided among her relations, the eldest brother taking the largest share and the re-mainder being divided among the parents, sisters, brothers, cousins, uncles, aunts, and the chiefs of the tribe. Even the slaves of the house expect presents. "It is not rare to find men quarrelling over the still unpaid portion of the mar-riage price of their grandmothers and other female ancestors. More feuds have their origin in the payment for wives than in the killing of men."[52]

One of the laws of Manu reads: "If after one damsel be shown another be given to the bridegroom he may marry them both for the same price." This seems astonishing after reading another section where the sale of daughters is forbidden; it shows in fact that wives were purchased. The section last referred to reads: "No man who knows the law may take even the smallest gratuity for his daughter; for he who through avarice takes a gratuity is a seller of his offspring." One may also discern the custom of wife-purchase in the law which states that if a man who has a wife weds a second, having begged the money to pay the expenses, he gains only sensual enjoyment, while the issue of the second marriage belongs to the creditor.[53] As a matter of fact, as Jolly[54] points out, despite the ideal conceptions of the nature of marriage, it is founded on purchase, robbery, or deception. Though the law-givers protested against wife-purchase, the custom still prevails in many parts of India, while in the south it is today almost the only form of con-tracting marriage. The opposition of the Brahmans to wife-purchase has had little effect. "While it is found in Bengal prevailing only among the lower castes and wild tribes, on the other hand it is widespread in the presidency of Bombay even in the case of the higher castes. In Guzerat the sale of girls

49 Rivers, *Todas*, 522.
50 Rose, in JAI, XXXVIII, 414.
51 Hutton, *Sema Nagas*, 184.
52 Cary and Tuck, *Chin Hills*, 189, 190, 191.

53 Bühler, *Manu*, III, 51; VIII, 204; IX, 98; XI, 5.
54 *Stellung der Frauen bei den alten In-dern*, 435; and *Recht und Sitte*, II, 49, 52 (quoted); Wilkins, *Hinduism*, 178.

is said still to occur frequently and secretly, even among such castes as openly condemn it, and in the city of Bombay an earnest is commonly given by a deposit of valuables. With the Samvedis, an esteemed and strictly religious caste of Brahmans in Thana, from two hundred to a thousand rupees are received as the purchase price. Also in the presidency of Madras is the payment of a bride-price customary with different castes, just as in the Punjab. In Assam marriages are concluded almost solely through wife-purchase, this prevailing even among the Brahmans. To be sure, in Bengal and elsewhere there often appears a bridegroom's price alongside the bride-price, as the custom of child-marriage has greatly increased the demand for men in the marriage-market."

Among the Palaungs, one of the tasks of the Pa-jau or go-between is to arrange for a certain sum of money to be given by the young man's father to the father of the girl. "The money is given to the father of the bride, to be spent by him in food for the wedding-feast at his house. Sometimes, if the bridegroom is very poor and his father is dead, the girl's father asks for a merely nominal sum; indeed, if the young man bears a good character, and the father of the bride likes him although he is poor, he is privately supplied with money by his future wife, given to her by her father, and they all pretend that the young man has given it. . . . The father leaves this pretended bargaining to his kinsfolk; he sits quietly by the fire, smoking, seemingly unconcerned. When they name the sum that the father of the young man is prepared to give, and the bride's father to accept—a usual amount is forty rupees and two large baskets full of rice—the relatives say, 'If thou art not able to give this amount, then we shall take back our daughter.' The Pa-jau again makes three bows and sits up, no longer looking so humble, while a satisfied expression comes over his face as he says, 'Now it is good. If this amount satisfies you, we too are satisfied.' "[55] Among the poor in China "the expenses of a wedding are much lessened by purchasing a young girl, whom the parents bring up as a daughter until she is marriageable, and in this way secure her services in the household. A girl already affianced is for a like reason sometimes sent to the boy's parents, that they may support her."[56]

The Malay term for bride-money goes back to a stem meaning purchase-price. The case of the Timorese is very clearly one of purchase, the size of the bride-price varying chiefly with the social position of the parties. In many cases early marriages are held up by the institution: the mores allow marriage without bride-price, but in that case the man is forced into a sort of debt-slavery, being obliged to live with the woman's parents and perform certain services; this is sufficient to deter many from taking the step. Among the Alfurs, if the man dies before he has paid the whole bride-price, the wife and children remain in her fenna (clan) until the fenna of the deceased pays up in full. Numerous cases are cited of the exact amounts of the bride-price.[57] Among the Mohammedan Buginese and Macassars the bride-price takes the chief place in the marriage contract; priestly sanction is of little or no value so long as it is not paid. If not, then the union is illegal and the children belong to the mother.[58] As illustrating the power of taboo in relation to wife-purchase, Wallace[59] relates how a Balinese woman, who lived with an English

55 Milne, *Eastern Clan*, 143-147.
56 Williams, *Middle Kingdom*, I, 789.
57 Wilken, in VG, I, 344-346, 439; 448-449; 47-48.

58 Van Eck, in *Indische Gids*, II, 842.
59 *Malay Archip.*, 174.

trader in a relation which the natives recognized as honorable, once accepted a
trifle from another man during a festival, this being against the *adat* (mores)
for women in such condition. The rajah tried to seize and execute her despite
the remonstrances of the trader, who refused to give her up. He desisted for
a time but later sent a man who stabbed her at the door of her house. Among
some of the more powerful and rich Malay tribes, the rights derived from the
purchase of a wife caused many quarrels, so that a century ago this was mentioned as the most fruitful source of misunderstanding.[60] Among some of the
tribes in the Philippines, if the suitor offers the price set by a father on his
daughter, and the father is unwilling to accept, the latter must pay a fine to
the injured man.[61]

Among the East Greenlanders, "a young man may sometimes pay the
father with a harpoon or the like, to wed his pretty daughter, just as, *vice
versa,* good hunters are paid by fathers to take their daughters to wife. Girls
are obliged to marry as the father wills. They often act as if they are forced
although they have nothing against it, and are therefore glad to be taken by
force."[62] Exchange of property stabilizes marriage among the Tlinkits, where
"the presents are given not in the sense of a purchase of the girl, but as the
binding feature of the contract. This is to make the union solid, and generally
is very effective, especially on the girl's side; for if she proves unfaithful or
should run away from her husband, her people must pay back to his people what
they gave as a dowry [bride-price], or its equivalent. This inclines them to
encourage and advise the girl to be faithful and to stand by her husband."[63]
"Marriage among the Kwakiutl must be considered a purchase, which is conducted on the same principles as the purchase of a copper. But the object
bought is not only the woman, but also the right of membership in her clan for
the future children of the couple. . . . Many privileges of the clan descend
only through marriage upon the son-in-law of the possessor, who, however,
does not use them himself, but acquires them for the use of his successor. These
privileges are, of course, not given as a present to the son-in-law, but he becomes entitled to them by paying a certain amount of property for his wife.
The wife is given to him as a first installment of the return payment. The crest
of the clan, its privileges, and a considerable amount of other property
besides, are given later on, when the couple have children, and the rate of interest is the higher the greater the number of children. For one child, 200 per
cent of interest is paid; for two or more children, 300 per cent. After this
payment the marriage is annulled, because the wife's father has redeemed his
daughter. If she continues to stay with her husband, she does so of her own
free will (wulē'l, staying in the house for nothing). In order to avoid this
state of affairs, the husband often makes a new payment to his father-in-law
in order to have a claim to his wife."[64] Marriage among the Hidatsa is usually
made formal by the distribution of gifts on the part of the man to the woman's
kindred. "Afterwards presents of equal value are commonly returned by the
wife's relations, if they have the means of so doing and are satisfied with the
conduct of the husband. Some travelers have represented that the 'marriage
by purchase' among the Indians is a mere sale of the woman to the highest
bidder, whose slave she becomes. Matthews regards this a misrepresentation

60 Ratzel, *Vkde.,* II, 430, 431.
61 Worcester, *Philippine Is.,* 108.
62 Holm, *Ethnol. Skizze,* 54.

63 Jones, *Thlingets,* 127.
64 Boas, in USNM, 1895, 359.

so far as it concerns the Hidatsa, the wedding gift being a pledge to the parents for the proper treatment of their daughter, as well as an evidence of the wealth of the suitor and his kindred. Matthews has known many cases where large marriage presents were refused from one person, and gifts of much less value accepted from another, simply because the girl showed a preference for the poorer lover."[65] Among the Indians of the Oregon coast, marriage was by purchase, the family of the man assisting him in procuring the purchase-money for the bride. The money thus paid was later refunded by the bride's family, apparently chiefly in the form of gifts and feasts, though the exact method is not clear. In certain ways the potlatch system of Vancouver Island is suggested, for there was an apparent effort on the side of each family party to contract to keep the other family in debt to it.[66] In the case of certain California Indians, "a wife is seldom bought for less than half a string, and if she belongs to an aristocratic family, is pretty, and skillful in making acorn-bread and weaving baskets, she sometimes costs as high as two strings—say $80 or $100. . . . No marriage is legal or binding unless preceded by the payment of money, and that family is most aristocratic in which the most money is paid for the wife. For this reason, a young man does well to accumulate shell-money and not to be a niggard in bargaining with his father-in-law. So far is this shell aristocracy carried, that the children of a woman for whom no money was paid are accounted no better than bastards, and the whole family is held in contempt."[67]

Among the Warraus of British Guiana the parents of a girl choose a bridegroom for her when she is very young and later give her over to him without further ceremony. "Beginning with the day on which the girl is destined to him, the bridegroom must serve her parents until he attains manhood. In the meantime he pays his youthful bride every attention, adorns her with pearls and brings her the best that he can capture in the hunt."[68] Among some of the Guiana tribes, good connections replace the bride-price. "Girls may be offered to a man by their father, mother, or by themselves. Among the Arawak of the Moruca, if a father wants some celebrated person as husband for his daughter, he lets her place food before him during the course of a visit. If he eats of it, the marriage is concluded; if not, the father knows that their wishes do not correspond. But with the Island Carib there were occasionally circumstances when the young man dared not refuse the girl so offered him. . . . He who had killed most enemies had much ado that day to escape with one wife, so many would there be proffered to him; but cowards and persons of no worth were wanted by none, for, to be married among them there was a necessity of being courageous. . . . Happy did the father think himself . . . who could first approach and seize about the body some one of those valorous sons-in-law whom the captain had commended."[69] Among certain tribes in Brazil the bride-price consists of game and fruit, which, thinks Von Martius,[70] serve more as a symbol that the man can support the woman than as an exchange present for her. With the more developed tribes the bride-price includes weapons, adornment, European goods, especially iron implements, horses, or slaves, which are given now and then before the marriage. If an Araucanian bridegroom cannot pay at once the whole of the price agreed

65 Dorsey, in BAE, XV, 242.
66 Farrand, in AA, III, 242-243.
67 Powers, in *Contrib. N. Am. Ethnol.*, III, 22.

68 Schomburgk, *Brit.-Guiana*, I, 164.
69 Roth, in BAE, XXXVIII, 670-671.
70 *Beiträge*, I, 109, 110.

upon, he lives with his father-in-law till the debt is cancelled. "Generally he puts the whole of his relations under contribution, and, as this debt is considered one of honour, it is usually paid in a very short time."[71] The Fuegian works for his wife's parents both before and after marriage, until she bears her firstborn, when the husband is exempted from further duty, save occasional gifts of fish, blubber, canoes, and spears, and a willingness to help his father-in-law in difficulties.[72] Among other South American Indians, where wife-purchase obtained, prices were often so high that marriage was delayed.[73] In one case, "the husband was obliged to subtract one-tenth of the game he killed for the relatives of his wife and he was not exonerated until a girl was born to him who became the property and sometimes later the wife of her maternal uncle."[74]

Wife-purchase was generally in vogue among the ancient Babylonians. "The bridegroom was obliged to give a present to the girl's father, which consisted of gold or slaves and naturally varied according to the position of the contracting parties: the sum fluctuated between a shekel and a mina"—a mina consisted of sixty shekels, and was in value about eighteen dollars. "As compensation therefor the young woman brought a marriage-portion to her husband, which usually consisted of household utensils."[75] The Jews at first purchased their wives by goods or services, prices varying up to fifty shekels of silver. Saul desired no bride-price for his daughter Michal but "an hundred foreskins of the Philistines."[76] This recalls the Galla practice of taking the foreskins of slain enemies as a necessary preliminary to marriage.[77] At one time in Egypt no marriage was legitimate unless sanctioned by a transfer of property from the man to the woman or *vice versa*. Under a system of free contract a woman could rent herself, in which case she was lower than if she sold herself permanently or gave herself away.[78] Marriage arrangements among the East Iranians took on the character of a purely business affair, in which the sentiments of the persons most concerned were not considered.[79] Wilken[80] says that the bride-price among the ancient Arabs was not a purchase, for it was given to the bride herself. He mentions four kinds of marriage as prevailing among them, in none of which did purchase occur. Among the southern Arabs, Ratzel[81] finds both purchase of wives and exchange of maidens. Formerly in Mecca occurred a bride-show, when daughters and slave-girls, upon coming of age, were dressed in their best and taken to the mosque and once around the Kaaba unveiled, that they might be seen and call out offers of marriage. Later this was given up.[82]

Schrader[83] makes the categorical statement that "Indo-European marriage was based on the purchase of the bride. This fact appears clearly and plainly enough amongst Indo-European peoples, and amongst some continued in its effects up to the threshold of the present." In the Homeric age concubines had values set upon them, were given as prizes and bought like cattle; they were mere slaves and treated as such. "A wife, on the other hand, was regularly

---

71 Latcham, in JAI, XXXIX, 359.
72 Bridges, "Firelanders," in *Voice for S. Amer.*, XIII, 201.
73 Ratzel, *Vkde.*, II, 618.
74 Letourneau, *Soc.*, 325.
75 Meissner, *Altbabylon. Privatrecht*, 13-14.
76 §365, below; I Sam., XVIII, 25; II Sam., III, 14; Exod., XXII, 16-17; Deut., XXII, 28-29; Freisen, *Canon. Eherechts*, 94.

77 Waitz, *Anthrop.*, II, 515.
78 Paturet, *Anc. Egypte*, 18, 20.
79 Geiger, *Ostiran. Kultur*, 241, 242.
80 Wilken, in VG, II, 20-26, 48.
81 *Vkde.*, III, 152.
82 Snouck-Hurgronje, in *Bijd.*, XXXV, 368.
83 *Aryans*, 381.

sought with gifts, that is, was bought in a more formal and distinctive way. Gifts in the case of the (supposed) widow Penelope were presented to the woman herself before she made any decision; they were apparently turned over later to the possession of her husband's house. A wife was called *polydōros,* and maidens were 'those who bring cattle.' These 'gifts' to the bride's father and family were usually cattle, and the woman went to the highest bidder. A preliminary meeting of the managing parties, for the sake of bargaining and settling terms, is indicated. Payment was sometimes made in part and promised in part, and in one case where the bride's father retained a child, some idea of payment may have been in question."[84] The stages through which wife-purchase went at Rome have been set forth by Rossbach[85] as follows: "First step. *Manus* [marriage with bride-price] originated in the remote antiquity of the Italian people and was the result of their common development. The bases of contracting marriage, namely, purchase and religious wedding-usages, were both equally requisite. All marriages were *cum manu,* there was yet no difference between *manus* and marriage, nor between the marriage contracts of different ranks. Second step. The mores came to disdain actual purchase of a wife. The patricians completely did away with purchase, at least in so far as their marriages qualified them for duties of the priesthood. Their marriage therefore consisted merely in the *consensus* and in the religious wedding-feast, which was directed by priests (*confarreatio*). The old unity of purchase and wedding-feast was preserved indeed for the patricians as for the clients and plebeians, but the purchase was symbolic, the religious customs were not conducted by priests and they declined in significance (*coemtio*). All marriages were still contracted *cum manu.* Third step. The endeavor to avoid the *manus* made its influence felt . . .; marriages *cum manu* remained in existence and for a long time were still the more usual. But the concepts of *manus* and marriage were separated; there could be marriage *sine manu.* Fourth step. Free marriage won an independent form. Thus four forms existed together. Fifth step. Free marriage prevailed and supplanted the restricted, . . . the *confarreatio* no longer entailed *manus,* and only two marriage forms stood opposed—free marriage and *coemtio.* Sixth step. Even *coemtio* fell into disuse after the third Christian century, and free marriage became the only form; it was severed completely from the old family situation and was regenerated by Christianity."

The custom of bride-purchase prevailed throughout Teutonic antiquity. It was in vogue among the Thracians and Lithuanians and also ruled among the southern Slavs, where girls became so high in price that at the beginning of the nineteenth century the price to be paid for one girl was limited to one ducat, or about $2.32.[86] The bride-price among the Norse did not allow possession of the bride's person, but bought for the man and his kin the guardianship over the bride; "it was thus a purchase of a right, not that of a human being."[87] The son of a woman not obtained by purchase was disinherited.[88] In the fourteenth century in Germany *kaufen* was the term used to signify taking a wife or a husband. The author[89] suggests that the word for marriage (Heirat) may be derived from *heuern,* to hire. He quotes a law of Ethelbert in England (560-616), to wit, "if a free man lies with a free man's wife, he

84 Keller, *Hom. Soc.,* 212-213.
85 *Römische Ehe,* 246, 248, 251-252 (quoted).
86 Krauss, *Südslaven,* 272 ff.; Schrader, *Aryans,* 381.
87 Wisen, *Nordens Forntid,* 17.
88 Finsen, in *Annaler,* 1849, 206-207.
89 Stammler, *Stellung der Frauen,* 19, 20.

shall purchase her with her wergild and acquire another wife out of his own property and bring her home to him." A subsequent English law deals with the case of a person who buys a wife and does not pay the purchase-price. Lippert[90] states that in some German districts the custom still remains of having a bride-show on the evening of the wedding-day, when every respectable guest may claim a dance with her, giving a piece of money, which, however, goes to pay the musicians. In Lapland a bride remains for eight days before the wedding in the house of the groom, veiled; anyone who wishes may see her by giving a few kopecks.

§363. The "Ambil-Anak" and Allied Forms.

THE modes of marriage according to the original institutions of the Sumatrans are by *jujur*, by *ambil-anak*, or by *semando*. The first is a certain sum of money given by one man to another, as a consideration for the person of his daughter, whose situation, in this case, differs not much from that of a slave to the man she marries, and to his family. It is marriage *cum manu*. His absolute property in her depends, however, upon some nice circumstances. The other forms are variations from it. In a marriage *cum manu*, the wife, in one *sine manu*, the husband, is the one who leaves his family and suffers loss of the power of inheriting from agnates, including first of all the parents. Among the Rejangs, besides the *batang jujur* or main sum, there are certain appendages or branches, one of which, the *tali kulo*, of five dollars, is usually, from motives of delicacy or friendship, left unpaid, and so long as that is the case, a relationship is understood to subsist between the two families, and the parents of the woman have a right to interfere on occasions of ill treatment; the husband is liable to be fined for wounding her, and there are other limitations of absolute right. When that sum is finally paid, which seldom happens except in cases of violent quarrel, the *tali kulo* (tie of relationship) is said to be *putus* (broken), and the woman becomes to all intents the slave of her lord. Among the Lampongs the father of the girl never admits of the tie of relationship being broken, or the whole sum being paid, and thereby withholds from the husband, in any case, the right of selling his wife, who, in the event of divorce, returns to her relations. Where such is the case, the husband has property in her little differing from that in a slave.[1] On the island of Serang a youth belongs to the family of the girl, living according to her customs and religion, until the bride-price is paid. He then takes both wife and children to his tribe. "In case he is very poor, he never pays the price and remains perpetually in his wife's tribe."[2]

Throughout Sumatra the man married in *ambil-anak* must work for his wife, aid her in cultivating her land, and be helpful to her family in all their enterprises; in case of divorce he has no claim. The oldest daughter is regarded as the preserver of the line and when she marries she stays in her parents' house while the man must come to live with her. If there are no daughters, then the oldest son is head of the family. If he dies, his widow takes his place. "Through the daughters, therefore, the line is carried on and it is only in default of daughters that the sons come into consideration." The daughter thus fills a rôle which in other tribes generally falls to the son, while the son functions as a daughter. More complete in South Sumatra than elsewhere is the cognate

90 *Kgchte.*, II, 21.
1 Marsden, *Sumatra*, 257-258, 300.
2 Thomas, in *Am. Jr. Soc.*, III, 771.

or parental inheritance. What a man and his wife gain together remains common to them, while a distinction is strictly drawn between what each brings into marriage. The last type of property falls to sons and daughters; if there are no children, it goes back to its original source. Some of these parental forms look like the old unions *cum* and *sine manu*, for now the man follows the wife, now *vice versa*. The system of relationship based upon a like division of the children between the parents is found only in three places in the Indian Archipelago, among the Rajat-Laut, Macassars, and Buginese. The first child belongs to the mother, the second to the father, and so on in alternation. As to the origin of the *ambil-anak*, one writer would have it that a certain Rajah in Sumatra abrogated the *jujur* system because he did not like to see daughters sold. Wilken,[3] from whom these facts are derived, points out that such humanitarianism is not characteristic of the Malays, while such a change could not be made on the initiative of a few people. Another view is that the *ambil-anak* was introduced by the Mohammedans for propaganda-purposes: their daughters, well raised in the Mohammedan faith, must remain heads of families and not be lost by marrying unbelievers. This view, says Wilken, is not improbable; but the first enthusiasts for Islam did not have to bring in the *ambil-anak* as a new thing; more probably they met it along with the *jujur* and preferred it for the reason given.

Several other forms break away from purchase in the same general direction. Nor is *ambil-anak* confined strictly, except in name, to Sumatra.[4] Among the Bataks, where marriage by purchase is the rule, the so-called *angkap*-marriage, where no price is paid and the son-in-law goes to live with the father-in-law, is popular.[5] The people of Timor show matriarchal alongside of patriarchal marriage, without bride-price, where the man goes to live with the bride's parents, and has services to discharge. Children follow the mother-kin and the father has no rights over them. In one place there is an actual purchase of the groom. "According as the payment of the wedding gift thus goes out from the side of the bridegroom or from that of the bride, does the patriarchal or the matriarchal marriage take place, or does the latter go to live with the former or the former with the latter."[6] The Pelew type is thought to be of the primitive Malay variety which was once widespread over Oceania.[7] Mazzarella[8] thinks he proves the *ambil-anak* marriage to have been universal in one epoch and cites many peoples who practised it; but he uses the term in a very wide sense to cover all cases where the man goes to the woman's home. "The grade," he says, "of purity and diffusion of *ambil* institutions is always proportional to the multiplicity and importance of the survivals of mother-family."

A form like the *ambil-anak* is reported from East Africa: "In Upare a poor man may voluntarily become a slave by marrying a woman of a rich family without dowry [by which term the author means bride-price]. His children then belonged to the woman's family, but the slave owned property and could acquire freedom by payment of dowry. His sons were given wives by the master, who took the dowry for all daughters. Such a person is called *mzoro*, and is much in the position of a serf."[9] In certain rare cases, among the

---

3 Wilken, in **VG**, II, 197, 276-277, 289, 291, 297-298, 300-301, 305 (quoted), 306-307.
4 Gomes, *Sea Dyaks*, 122.
5 Volz, in *Globus*, XCV, 4-5.

6 Wilken, in **VG**, I, 244, 347 (quoted), 364, 437.
7 Kubary, *Pelauer*, 35, 37.
8 *Cond. Giurid. del Marito*, 136 ff., 89, 92.
9 Dundas, C., in JAI, LI, 264.

Siberian Koryak, "it is the son-in-law who comes to live with the bride's family. In such cases he is adopted into the family. The young wife coming to the house of her husband must join him in the cult of his ancestors. Nevertheless, to a certain extent, she is always under the protection of her blood-relatives." It is said that if a Chukchi wife bear only daughters her husband remarries until he obtains a son; but another investigator did not notice this as a rule, "because a daughter can replace a son very easily among reindeer-breeding people. He saw some families consisting only of daughters—also in this case sons-in-law may be adopted. Among the Maritime Chukchee, however, a girl cannot replace a boy."10

In India there is a marriage-form called *beena,* wherein the groom lives with the family of the bride. It prevails widely in the Hills, and is thought to be a survival of the adoption of the groom into the bride's kin.11 The bride has the right of inheritance in common with her brothers.12 Among the Sema Nagas, "the adopted son-in-law now becomes a son and an absolute member of his adoptive parent's clan and family and entitled to all the rights of a son, sharing with other and genuine sons in their father's property at his death on equal terms. . . . No formality seems to accompany this adoption except the casual present of a cow, but the results of its taking place are permanent, and involve an entire contradiction of the otherwise imperative custom of exogamy. It seems to be resorted to but rarely."13 In the Arab *mota* marriage, which Smith14 thinks the same as the *beena,* the man is a mere "sojourner" in her tribe, and the children stay with her and belong to her tribe. It was an exception to Arab patriarchal usage, practised by women of high rank, as it is, to some degree, by modern female rulers. Usage limits the *mota* form to very temporary unions; indeed, the term is often applied to relations which should not be designated as marriage.15

India shows a form resembling *ambil-anak* in several particulars. So-called "Basivis"16 are daughters "who have been dedicated to duties, who take a son's place in performance of funeral rites of parents and in inheritance of property. . . . They live in their father's house; they do not marry, yet they bear children, the father of whom they may choose at pleasure, who inherit the family name. . . . Failing male issue, one daughter must be dedicated as a Basivi; there is no alternative." She really bears sons for her father; "if she has only a daughter, she makes her a Basivi, and so it goes on until there is a male child, whose birth may put an end to such dedication."17 This form is evidently a variant of procedure calculated to get male heirs by renunciation of bride-price and insistence upon retention of the daughter. It starts like the *ambil-anak* and works out into a sort of sacral harlotry.

One reads in the laws of Manu: "He who has no male child may charge his daughter to give him a son, who shall become his and shall perform the funeral ceremony in his honor. To that end, the father must appear before the husband of his daughter and pronounce this formula: 'I give you, adorned with jewels, this girl who has no brother; the son who will be born of her shall be my son and shall celebrate my obsequies.' The usage was the same at Athens; the father could have his lineage continued through his daughter by giving

10 Czaplicka, *Aborig. Siberia,* 85, 77, note.
11 Crooke, in JAI, XXVIII, 241.
12 Starcke, *Prim. Fam.,* 78.
13 Hutton, *Sema Nagas,* 163.

14 *Kinship,* 64 ff., 71, 72, 74; Letourneau, *Marriage,* 85-86.
15 Grosse, *Familie,* 119.
16 §296 of the text.
17 Fawcett, in JASB, II, 322 ff.

her to a husband with this special condition. A son born from such a marriage was reputed the son of the wife's father. . . . In Hindu law this child inherited from his grandfather as if he had been his son; it was exactly the same at Athens. When a father had married his only daughter in the manner we have just described, his heir was neither his daughter nor his son-in-law, but the *son of his daughter.* . . . Under some Punjab usages, the daughter, when there are no sons, inherits a limited interest in her father's property; but she must resign it when she marries. It is usual, however, for the husband of such a daughter to be adopted by his father-in-law." The Basques, continues the author,[18] showed the female line of descent in some cases: the first-born inherited, irrespective of sex; if a daughter, she was in the position of exclusive heir, head of the house and of the possessions of the family. "She chose for herself a mate and he came to live with her; he lost his name, to take that of his wife, while the children too were named after her." A similar situation appears to prevail in Japan. "Should there be no son, but a daughter, the father will provide a suitable man for her, whom she then takes into her house instead of following him into his. He then takes her family name and occupies the place of the oldest son of the house. This procedure we call 'yoshi' (adoption). A young man does not like to let himself be adopted in order to marry the daughter, no matter how beautiful she may be, for in her house he can exercise no such authority as in his own. This is the only case in which the Japanese wife has some power over her husband."[19] There appears likewise to be only one Chinese situation in which a child takes its mother's name: when a man who has only a female child brings into his house a husband for her; then if more than one son is born to her, the second takes her family name.[20]

Under certain circumstances a form of marriage similar to the *ambil-anak* appears among some California Indians; the relative position of man and wife is determined in connection with the balance of interests. "The Yuroks of Northern California are monogamists, and marriage is illegal without the prepayment of money. When a young Indian becomes enamoured of a maid, and cannot wait to collect the amount of shell-money demanded by her father, he is sometimes allowed to pay half the sum and become what is called 'half married.' Instead of bringing her to his cabin and making her his slave, he goes to *her* cabin and becomes *her* slave. This only occurs in the case of soft, uxorious fellows." Or, "a bride often remains in her father's house and her husband comes to live with her, whereupon half the purchase money is returned to him."[21] Among the Winnebago, "a man generally lived with his parents-in-law during the first two years of his marriage. During these two years he was practically the servant of his father-in-law, hunting, fishing, and performing minor services for him. Many Winnebago interpreted these enforced services of a son-in-law as part of his marriage obligations toward his father-in-law."[22]

Certain Iranian forms appear wherein a first-born son was not regarded as a son of his father but was to inherit his maternal grandfather's or uncle's property in default of male heirs; "the woman obtained her son's share of

18 Wilken, in VG, I, 405-406 (quoted), 511, note 31; 246-247, note.
19 Tamura, *Warum Heiraten Wir?* 7-8; Hearn, *Japan,* 69, 74.
20 Morgan, in *Smithson. Contrib. Knowledge,* XVII, 424.
21 Powers, in *Contrib. N. Amer. Ethnol.,* III, 56, 221.
22 Radin, in BAE, XXXVII, 138.

her father's property, and she was remarried to her husband when her first-born son was fifteen years old."[23] Among the southern Slavic house-communities, in cases where men are few, a man is taken in as the husband of a girl and adopted.[24] The marriage of an heiress in old Israel was in a certain sense a marriage with mother-right, similar to the situation among the Hindus, Greeks, and South Slavs. "He who would marry into the family of the heiress must, in so far as we take it, renounce his father-right, since the child to be begotten bore the name, not of his father, but of his maternal grandfather." Take as example the case of Zelophehad, who had no sons, but daughters. "Why," demanded the daughters, "should the name of our father be done away from among his family, because he hath no son? Give unto us therefore a possession among the brethren of our father." And when Moses brought their cause before the Lord, the Lord spake unto Moses, saying: "The daughters of Zelophehad speak right: thou shalt surely give them a possession of an inheritance among their father's brethren; and thou shalt cause the inheritance of their father to pass unto them. And thou shalt speak unto the children of Israel, saying, If a man die, and have no son, then ye shall cause his inheritance to pass unto his daughter . . . and it shall be unto the children of Israel a statute of judgment, as the Lord commanded Moses."[25] To resume with Klugmann's[26] exposition: this customary right could not be maintained permanently. "Indeed, when in after-days the matriarchal views were completely overcome by the patriarchal, it must even have appeared undignified to marry a brotherless girl, for through such a marriage a man renounced his paternity as respects the children he might beget. Accordingly it is readily understandable that in one place in the Talmud it reads: 'He who would marry must take into consideration the brothers of the wife he is to choose'—even though it is here not so distinctly expressed as, for example, in the Hindu law-books: 'For fear (of giving up his paternity a man) should not marry a girl who has no brothers.' "

§364. Dowry.

In British Tropical Africa, "dowry is, properly speaking, given to a wife only. If a concubine has received presents from her master, they should be regarded as having been liquidated by his sexual relations with her, and if she asserts her freedom (as she has a perfect right to do when the legal status is abolished), he can neither claim their return, nor any rights over her on the grounds that she is in his debt, nor can he retain her children as being his slaves."[1] The East African bride always brings with her a few household utensils, but not infrequently she also brings a small amount of livestock which she may have acquired by gift from her parents or by her own industry. Thus among the Wachagga a girl is always given a little stock according to the wealth of her parents. "It is customary for a father to give his daughter at least one cow to provide her with milk, and wealthy men such as chiefs may give as many as ten cows. Actually the Chagga woman often brings to her husband's hut more than her husband pays in dowry [bride-price] for her, but most usually she leaves all but one cow with her parents until she has children, when she

23 Spiegel, *Eran. Alterthumskde.*, III, 678.
24 Utiešenović, *Hauskom.*, 18.
25 Num., XXVII, 4-11.
26 *Frau im Talmud*, 77-78.
1 Lugard, *Brit. Trop. Africa*, 377.

will make a gift of her livestock to these. . . . With two exceptions women are otherwise sole owners of all property which they bring at marriage or subsequently acquire, and though the husband has, of course, the benefit, he cannot lay claim to any such property."[2]

A number of Siberian tribes have the custom of dowry. If we take into consideration the fact that the reindeer and other presents exchanged during the marriage-ceremonies of the Yukaghir are fairly equal in value, we cannot regard any of them as the purchase-price of the bride. Among the Altaians, "sometimes the bride's parents give the whole *kalym* [bride-price] as a dowry to their daughter, and even make it larger by adding presents from themselves." So among the Buryat, "a father not only bestows on his daughter at her marriage a dowry consisting of cattle, household utensils, etc., but makes similar gifts to his son-in-law, so that the value of the dowry together with these other gifts offsets that of the *kalym.*" As soon as a Samoyed youth has paid the *kalym,* "the father-in-law loads him and his company with reindeer meat. . . . A father always gives with his daughter in marriage a certain quantity of clothes. . . . Some time after marriage the young wife pays a visit to her father, and stays with him a few weeks, during which time she has the liberty to receive her husband. At their taking leave, the father must make her a number of presents, and do the same at every visit; so that the young woman for a length of time shall have no occasion to apply to her husband for anything. In cases of divorce the *kalym* is returned." Among the Ostyak the bride-price is proportioned to the fortune the father gives with his daughter. "The woman's dowry is provided, strangely enough, from the *kalym* which has been paid for her."[3] In one of the Hindu epics is an episode which illustrates how the father may secure his daughter's position in marriage by imposing conditions at the time.[4] There is a suggestion of dowry in the Chinese custom whereby well-to-do fathers, at a daughter's marriage, add to the outfit wherewith she is sent to the house of the partner of her future joys and sorrows, a coffin of gilded silver, a few inches in size. "This is to signify the old man's willingness to provide his child not only with all the requisites of life in the form of a trousseau, but also with those of death, amongst which none is so important as the coffin."[5]

With some of the Filipinos, marriage centered about the dowry and was a species of trade. A man could renounce his wife at any time without justifying the divorce, but he had to pay back the dowry or its equivalent. If a woman contracted marriage for the first time, she kept the dowry carefully until she had children, when it became common to both spouses.[6] There is a Samoan legend concerning dowry, to the effect that Sun-beam (born from a union of the Sun with a mortal woman) "married a Fijian woman, the daughter of the king of Fiji. Then were brought two fine mats, the dowry of the wife of Sun-beam. . . . Then the man took a voyage to Fiji to bring the property to his father the Sun."[7]

The Kwakiutl ceremony of providing a marriage-gift for a chief's daughter is described briefly as follows. "Not long after she has been married to her husband, her father pays the marriage debt; and she has for her canoe mast an expensive copper. And he gives as a marriage-gift a name to the

2 Dundas, C., in JAI, LI, 257-258.
3 Czaplicka, *Aborig. Siberia,* 96, 117, 118, 123-125, 126-127.
4 Holtzmann, *Ind. Sagen,* II, 108.
5 DeGroot, *Relig. Syst. China,* I, 325.
6 Montero y Vidal, *Filipinas,* I, 54.
7 Pratt, in AAAS, 1887, 451.

husband of his princess and much food with it, and also canoes. This is what is called 'paying-the-marriage-debt, sitting-in-the-canoe-of-the-princess;' for generally there are twenty who sit in the canoes of the princess of a real chief, when they put down the copper bracelets and small coppers and many dishes and the anchor-line of many spoons."[8] Among the Salish there appears no longer to be any idea of barter or profit in the mind of the father in the disposal of his daughter in marriage, and he makes nothing out of the occasion. "Etiquette demands that he shall return to the bridegroom gifts of like value to those he himself received from him. Indeed the acceptance or rejection of a suitor is not left to him individually, but is the decision of the whole family in council assembled."[9] It is said of the Mayas that "it was no unusual thing for parents of the lower orders to send their daughters on a tour through the land, that they might earn their marriage portion by prostitution."[10]

In the Code of Hammurabi can be traced the beginning of dowry. A present to bind a betrothal is made to the bride's father, which is to be returned to her at marriage or held in trust for her by the father. If the groom breaks the engagement, he forfeits it; also, a like sum is forfeited by the girl's father if he break the contract. Should the husband divorce her without cause, he forfeits a duplicate sum; if the wife die childless, her father restores the betrothal present to the groom; if not restored, the groom deducts it from the dowry given by the father-in-law, which he must restore.[11] The word for bride-price is later used to mean dowry; there is also a word for "gift" from the father to the bride herself.[12] Wife-purchase was rare in Babylon; generally the wife brought a dower of money or outfit which remained hers. There were cases of marriage-contract in which the fathers on both sides specified what they would give to the young couple. Receipt of dower was acknowledged sometimes in the contract, while there also occurred cases of suit for unpaid dowry.[13] Often the dower was paid in instalments; it was a debt. The bridegroom got it, though in case of land it belonged to the woman, while the usufruct went to the man. A married woman bore the name of her father and the master of her family. In the marriage-contract the husband was put under penalty if he took another woman; in that case, his wife was free to go where she would.[14] In ancient Egypt, in the class of nobles, every woman brought to her husband some land as dower, but her daughters took it away again, so that the chances of a family in this respect were at the sport of fortune.[15] At a later date no marriage was recognized as legitimate unless sanctioned by dower or property-transfer from man to woman or woman to man. A woman not dowered was a concubine.[16] Among the ancient Arabs the marriage-portion belonged to the wife. It was also the rule that the bride-price was given, not to the father-in-law but to the bride herself, and thus became her private property.[17]

"There is absolutely no dower as such in Homer, nor more than the beginning of return-gifts to the bride,"[18] but in later times Greek women regularly brought dowries to their husbands. "The significant difference between

8 Boas, in BAE, XXXV, pt. I, 777.
9 Hill-Tout, in JAI, XXXIV, 318.
10 Bancroft, *Nat. Races*, I, 123; II, 676.
11 Harper, *Hammurabi*, 115.
12 Winckler, *Gesetze Hammurabis*, 23.
13 Kohler and Peiser, *Babylon. Rechtsleben*, I, 8; II, 10.

14 Marx, in *Beiträge zur Assyriologie*, IV, 2, 5, 24, 28, 30.
15 Maspero, *Hist. Anc.*, I, 300.
16 Paturet, *Anc. Egypte*, 18.
17 Wellhausen, *Ehe*, 445; Buhl, *Israeliten*, 33, note.
18 Keller, *Hom. Soc.*, 213.

Homeric and later times lies in the fact that in the first case the bridegroom buys his bride and accompanies his wooing with a tender of cattle, which ceases only when the girl's father offers her and gives her in addition something for herself; while at the other time she receives at most a part of the bride-price as her dowry, which in case of separation is returned to the father, just as, on the other hand, the purchase-money can be reclaimed if the wife is guilty of adultery. Only in a later period, . . . in any case before Solon, did it become the custom that the father or, in case he was not living, the other relatives to allow the girl a marriage-portion, occasionally with the obligation of doubling it if offspring were obtained."[19] The Spartan lawgiver Lycurgus forbade any marriage-portion on the side of the bride, but later on, with increasing wealth, the law was not seldom evaded.[20] According to Plutarch, Solon strove to check the practice of giving gifts to daughters, though this regulation may have been rather a sumptuary law to restrict the magnificence of the trousseau, and Euripides makes Medea complain of the lot of women in that they are obliged to "buy themselves masters."[21] In general, the dowry came in Greece to be thought almost necessary to make the distinction between a wife and a concubine; while the Romans thought it a great misfortune to be an unendowered woman.[22]

§365. Group-Consent and Test.

SINCE group-consent is given or withheld upon the basis of test, these two topics merge indistinguishably in a number of cases.

Group-Consent. In central Cameroons marriage is regulated by the head-chief. "When there is a likely girl or woman in the tribe, the head-chief is informed. Instructions are issued to one of his attendants to have her handed over to the head-chief's mother or one of his head-wives. If she is already betrothed the father is informed of the head-chief's instructions, from which there is no escape. . . . At certain times the head-chief decides to change his younger attendants, and he issues orders that they make preparations to be married. The selection of eligible girls is made by the head-chief himself, not only from the townspeople, but from his own relatives. . . . In the event of a man and woman disagreeing, the matter is referred to the head-chief for settlement. If the dispute cannot be settled, then the head-chief may transfer the woman to someone resident either in one of his own sub-towns or else to someone resident in an outside town."[1] The marriage arrangements of the Baganda are as follows. "After sunset two torch-light processions start, one from each place, and meet half way between the two houses; the bride wears a lovely bark cloth, brass, copper, and ivory armlets and anklets, and bead necklets, she is veiled and carried on the shoulders of a strong man; her brother escorts her with all their relatives. The other party is headed by the bridegroom's sister and his relatives. . . . When they reach the door of the bridegroom's house the bride is set down, but refuses to enter until the bridegroom comes out, welcomes her, and gives her two or three cowries. Again, when she enters the

19 Blümner, *Griech. Privatalterthümer*, 262-263.
20 Bergel, *Eheverhältnisse*, 16.
21 Plutarch, *Solon*, 20; Euripides, *Medea*, 233; quoted by Seymour, *Hom. Age*, 132-133.

22 Westermarck, *Marriage*, II, 428; Freisen, *Canon. Eherechts*, 90.
1 Malcolm, in JAI, LIII, 393, 394; §156, of the text.

house, she won't sit down until two or three more cowries are given her by her husband; later on when food is served she refuses to eat until he has again given her a few more cowries. These are tokens of his love, and should he refuse them or neglect to give them, the bride is free to return home and the marriage can be broken off. . . . For a month the bride is secluded, and only receives near relatives; she wears her veil all this time. . . . At the end of the month the bridegroom chooses four men called *Bazala* (they who give birth), who come to the house; the husband and wife give in their presence mutual promises to be faithful to each other, to respect each other, and the wife promises obedience to her husband. These men are not only witnesses of these promises but also act as judges and peace-makers in case of any disagreement or difference arising between the husband and wife. . . . When the *Bazala* come the marriage is disannulled if either contracting party wishes, but if they agree to continue together the husband may in the future appeal to the authorities for the restitution of his wife if she leaves him."[2] The group's interest in and regulation of marriage are especially to be noted.

Initiation-ceremonies may be construed as tests the passing of which confers group-consent. At the present day in British East Africa, and particularly in Taveta, "the people seem to assume that the initiation must be followed by marriage, and since they include the youngest boys in the celebrations the result is that absolute child marriages take place. The boys and girls so married do not, however, necessarily live together."[3] When a Niam Niam resolves upon matrimony, the ordinary rule would be for him to apply to the reigning prince or the sub-chieftain, who would at once endeavor to procure him a suitable wife. "In spite of the prosaic and matter of fact proceeding, and notwithstanding the unlimited polygamy which prevails throughout the land, the marriage-bond loses nothing of the sacredness of its liabilities, and unfaithfulness is generally punished with immediate death." Festivities observed on the occasion of a marriage are on a limited scale: "there is a simple procession of the bride, who is conducted to the home of her future lord by the chieftain, accompanied by musicians, minstrels, and jesters."[4]

In a Palaung marriage the securing of consent and the placing of responsibility are important matters. "When the father of a girl who has eloped is dead, and she has only small brothers, the proposals of the Pa-jau [go-between] would be made to her oldest uncle, on her father's side, or, failing an uncle, to a cousin. If she has a brother twenty years or more of age, the proposals would be made to him. He would not, however, give his consent without sending for all his kinsfolk—the men of his family—and asking for their consent also. . . . When the Pa-jau has finished speaking, and has again bowed, one of the old men says, 'O Pa-jau! do not be too hasty. What if this young man, who wishes to take this young girl, does not respect his father-in-law and the Elders? We fear that some day he may divorce his wife.' The Pa-jau again makes three bows and says, 'Do not be afraid, O Elders! I and his relatives, who are before you, will be responsible for him.' Some of the bridegroom's relatives, who are married men, now come forward, saying, 'We shall be responsible.' The Elders reply, 'If the young man does not keep his promises, we shall cause him to pay a fine.' The relatives answer, 'If the young man does not keep his promises, we shall see that the fine is paid.' The old men say, 'It is

2 Roscoe, in JAI, XXXII, 36-38.   4 Schweinfurth, *Heart of Africa*, II, 27-28.
3 Dundas, C., in JAI, LI, 252.

good,' and the Pa-jau again bows low to them. After this he lifts the bowl with the roll of velvet and the money and sets it before the mother of the bride, saying, 'This is for the mother's milk.' Sometimes he says, 'This is for the tears of the mother.' The offering is made in recognition of the mother's care and trouble when the bride was a little child."[5] The bride-price, it will be recalled, is often alleged to be recompense for rearing.[6]

When a boy, among the Indians of British Columbia, had arrived at marriageable age, "his parents would ask him if he looked with favour upon any girl of their acquaintance. Upon his replying in the affirmative, and on learning his choice, they would select one of the eldermen of the kin-group to act as intermediary. It was not etiquette for the youth or his parents themselves to make the first move. . . . Two eldermen of the bride's family now rise, go over to the bridegroom, take him ceremoniously by the arms, conduct him to their side of the house, and seat him next his bride. This constitutes the marriage. . . . These customs were those observed by the chiefs and notables of the tribes. The marriage ceremony among the base folk was less formal. . . . It is this formal inclusion in the family circle of the bride that constitutes the marriage."[7] The essential and fundamental characteristic of marriage among the Seri is said to be the collective motive under which marriage is prescribed for the welfare of the group, rather than inspired by individual appetite and selfish inclination.[8]

According to the opinions of the Roman philosophers and legislators, marriage was not a bond of souls, it was only a union formed in the interest of the state for its perpetuation. The censor Metellus told the people that marriage was only the sacrifice of a particular pleasure for a public duty; one recalls that soon the public duty was sacrificed to particular pleasure, and celibacy was preferred to a union for life with a tiresome mate.[9] In the Massachusetts Bay Colony, "none were allowed to marry except they entered into bonds with sureties to the governor, to be forfeited in case there should afterwards appear to have been any lawful impediment. Magistrates still continued to join people in matrimony. Other provision could not immediately be made. There was but one episcopal minister in the country. . . . Sir Edmund considered the congregational ministers as mere laymen. Randolph wrote to the bishop of London, 'I press for able and sober ministers, and we will contribute largely to their maintenance; but one thing will mainly help, when no marriages shall hereafter be lawful but such as are made by the ministers of the church of England."[10]

Marriage-Tests. In British New Guinea, "no young man could marry, as no woman would have him, without skulls. Often a family would leave, and go far away for a length of time, and then return with skulls—perhaps all of them were bought—so that it might be said they had skulls. Sometimes a young man would go to friends at a distance . . . and would remain there for many months, and on his return home would have several skulls, which he bought from or through his friends, but on reaching his village, he would put on a solemn and sacred air, and, although in confidence to his relatives only, it was soon known by all in the tribe he was a great brave, and the lady he loved

---

5 Milne, *Eastern Clan*, 148-149, 162.
6 §361, of the text.
7 Hill-Tout, in JAI, XXXV, 131-132.

8 McGee, in AA, IX, 378-379.
9 Schmidt, *Soc. Civ.*, 28, 38-39.
10 Hutchinson, *Mass. Bay*, 355.

would soon be his."[11] While quite young, a girl of the Roro-speaking tribes accompanies her mother to the garden, and "insensibly begins to pick up a knowledge of the work, and to be a help to her mother. . . . When the girl is considered to be of marriageable age the buttocks, legs, and last of all the face, are tattooed, a small feast being given before work on the buttocks is begun. . . . Decked in her finery, the girl parades ceremonially up and down the centre of the village for a short time, and for five days after this she should sit upon the verandah of her father's house for the greater part of each day, wearing all her ornaments."[12] This is presumably to let the world know that she has passed inspection and is nubile.

In earlier days, among the Akamba, "no warriors but those who had killed a Masai or helped to kill one were supposed to be able to marry. As however in practice this proved to be an impossible condition, a successful combatant would secretly meet his friends in the woods and would distribute among them portions of the outfit of the dead enemy [say a few ostrich feathers out of the dead man's headdress]; they would then go back and successfully pretend that they had assisted in the *mêlée* and this would be accepted as qualifying them for a bride."[13] This recalls the Galla practice of taking the foreskins of slain enemies as a necessary preliminary to marriage.[14]

It is said of a rude tribe under Russian rule that stealing is a badge of merit. A girl will often say to a youth, "You haven't yet succeeded in stealing even one horse or redeeming a single captive." A mother blessing her son prays God to help him get much booty.[15] Among a group in the Punjab, "when a girl is marriageable, an athletic competition is held, and the competitors jump, run, and so on. The winner has a right to marry the girl, but she has no choice."[16] As a rule among the Manchu, a day is appointed when the marriage go-between introduces the bridegroom to the parents of the bride in the presence of all the relatives. "This introduction is called 'making the acquaintance of the young man,' and is a veritable crux for the pitiable youth, who must submit to a formal examination without being told what is the matter in question. He is simply commanded to put on his gala-dress and in company with the match-maker pay a visit to the family concerned, whom he often does not know personally at all. If he guesses at the purpose of the visit, which is usually the case, he must nevertheless play innocent, which makes his already uncomfortable situation all the more painful."[17]

Furness[18] says that the fairest of bridal gifts, and one which no female Kayan heart could possibly resist, is "a lovely, fresh, human head." Wilken[19] supports this: "Among some peoples one may not marry until he has brought his beloved several heads." But Schwaner[20] insists: "The generally prevalent opinion that it is obligatory to present a severed head to the bride when contracting a marriage, belongs to the realm of fiction." From the Malay Peninsula is reported a case of canoe-race where love usually unnerves the girl.[21] It must not be overlooked that the initiation[22] was a group-test for marriage. "The age at which a male Gilbertese married lay somewhere between 25 and 28 years. The actual date of a young man's marriage depended upon the length

11 Chalmers, in JAI, XXXIII, 123.
12 Seligmann, *Melanesians*, 264, 265.
13 Hobley, *A-Kamba*, 45.
14 Waitz, *Anthrop.*, II, 515.
15 *Russ. Ethnog.* (Russ.), II, 239.
16 Vishwanath, in JAI, XLVII, 35.

17 Grube, in *Berl. Mus.*, VII, 11.
18 *Head-Hunters*, 74-75.
19 *Vkde.*, 393.
20 *Borneo*, I, 191.
21 Skeat and Blagden, *Malay Penin.*, II, 79.
22 §163, of text and *Case-Book*.

of time it took him to pass through his initiation into full manhood, while the inception of that initiation depended again on his physical development. A healthy, lusty boy might begin younger than a weakling, but as a rule it was not muscular development that was watched so much as the growth of axillary and pectoral hairs. When these were well in evidence, and not before, the lad was considered ripe enough to be *kaunaki, i.e., made into a warrior* (lit., *made angry*); this, among a people by no means given to great hairiness, would not normally be until he was 23 or 24 years old. Taking his age to be 23 at the beginning of the initiation period, we must allow a minimum of three years for the completion of the various rites he must undergo. . . . A girl would be given in marriage on her release from the *Ko* (*Bleaching-house*), wherein she was confined, as a rule, for about two years after the first menses appeared. Her age would thus normally be about 14 or 15 years at marriage."[23]

In America the test is common, even among the most backward tribes. The primary mating of the Seri is attended by observances so elaborate as to show that marriage is one "of the profoundest sacraments of the tribe, penetrating the innermost recesses of tribal thought, and interwoven with the essential fibers of tribal existence." The groom has to go through a two-fold probation, one material and one moral. He must for one round of the seasons provide for and protect the entire family of the bride, displaying "skill in turtle-fishing, strength in the chase, subtlety in warfare, and all other physical qualities of competent manhood." Then also, although sharing his future wife's sleeping-robe, he must maintain continence. "The would-be grooms who fail in their moral tests are ostracized and at least semi-outlawed, and range about like rogue elephants, approved targets for any arrow, until they perish through the multiplied risks of solitude, or until some brilliant opportunity for display of prowess or generosity brings reinstatement."[24] If he passes his ordeal satisfactorily, "he is formally installed in the family as a permanent consort guest, and his children are added to the clan of his mother-in-law."[25] Among the Diggers, the girl enacted the performance of Atalanta. If she "opposed her suitor, she might run a race with him. She was allowed a certain number of feet the start when the signal was given to run. If she won she was free, but if he caught her, she had to go without a murmur."[26] In Nicaragua "the bridegroom must first wrestle with a strong man of his tribe; if he is defeated he must, without twitching, let himself be flogged by his tribal fellows. And if he cries out during the whipping, he may not marry, but must go through the same test again later."[27]

In British Guiana the test is calculated to show ability to support a family rather than physical endurance. Before marrying, the youth must "within a defined time clear of all trees a piece of land measured off for him—which land later serves him as a means of support—or he must fell a big tree within a given time. . . . If he emerges victorious from the ordeal he possesses the qualities of a man, may appear in the men's council and take part in its deliberations. If he does not pass the test, he must subject himself to it again later."[28] Here, as often elsewhere, the maturity-test is also a marriageability test. Among certain tribes of Cayenne, an ordeal to be undergone by the male aspirants for marriage consists in the main of submitting without a

23 Grimble, in JAI, LI, 27.
24 McGee, in BAE, XVII, pt. I, 279-281, 283, 273.
25 McGee, in AA, IX, 375.
26 Miller, in PSM, L, 208.
27 Sapper, in *Globus*, LXXVIII, 274.
28 Schomburgk, *Brit.-Guiana*, II, 317.

murmur to the stinging of certain ants or wasps. "The victims invariably faint and are carried to their hammock in a shed, where they have to remain 15 days, eating only a little dry cassava and small fish roasted on ashes." Among the Caribs of this section the medicine-man applies ants to the chest and wasps to the forehead, the whole of the body being subsequently stung by these insects. In some instances, "with their backs turned, the candidates for marriage have to throw cassava pellets at a piece of board on which a circle has been traced, and those who fail to hit it three times running are subjected to another ant and wasp stinging." The natives believe that the ordeal renders young men skilful, clever, and industrious; and "certainly the obligation of publicly braving severe bodily suffering has an assured intrinsic value." Women may have corresponding proofs to show of their fitness for permanent sexual union, indicated first and foremost by the advent of puberty; "the first signs of which, by the Makusi and others, were met with a whipping. With the present-day Pomeroon, Arawak, Warrau, and sophisticated Carib, the general practice is for the parties not to 'marry' until the girl has given proof of her child-bearing capacity by becoming pregnant. An Indian requires his wife mainly for this purpose, being always able to satisfy his lust elsewhere." In some cases the young women are also subjected to the ant-ordeal. For example, "in order that the Arawak girl, now become a woman, may henceforth have strength and willingness to work, some old stranger whose character is known to be strong and good, and a willing worker, is chosen to place an ant-frame on the young woman's forehead, hands, and feet. The ants are attached at their middles in the interstices of the plaited strands forming the framework, the frame itself being applied on the side from which all the little heads are projecting." In olden times the Orinoco Indians, before marrying their daughters, subjected them to a forty days' fast. The reason for this semi-starvation was given by a chief as follows: "Our ancestors observed that wherever women, at their monthly periods, trod, everything withered, and if any man trod where they had placed their feet his legs swelled. Having studied the remedy, they ordered that we should starve our women so that their bodies might not contain poison." It was asserted for the Carib girls on the Islands, who were treated similarly, that the idea of the fasting was "to prevent them becoming sluggards, not likely to work when married."[29]

It is said of a half-vagabond tribe in Brazil that the women are mostly won through a fist-fight in which all the lovers of the girl join. In the case of another tribe the young man must work a long time for the bride promised to him when a child and must bear all the cares of the house-father before he is married to her. This might be interpreted as service in lieu of purchase, as well as a test of the man. Again, "only tested marksmen receive the desired bride, because they have demonstrated the capacity to take care of her."[30] Among the Bororo Indians "every young man who wishes to marry must have killed either five peccaries or one jaguar, thus giving proof that he can support a family."[31] In the Gran Chaco, the youth must kill a jaguar to prove his manliness.[32] In Paraguay the groom must, "in order to demonstrate his capacities as a future paterfamilias, undergo a test as hard as it is original. Dressed in

---

29 Roth, in BAE, XXX, 309-310, 314; and in BAE, XXXVIII, 679, 680.
30 Von Martius, *Beiträge*, I, 411-412, 600, 688.
31 Frič and Radin, in JAI, XXXVI, 390.
32 Hassler, in *Inter. Cong. Anthrop. Chicago*, 1893, 354.

festal array, he makes music for eight full days before a little hut into which the maiden has been brought for this purpose by her parents."[33]

It is said of the Essenes, a strict Jewish sect, that "they test their wives for a three years' space, and then, after they have given evidence by three purifications that they are fit to bear children, they marry them. They have no connubial intercourse with their wives when with child, showing that they do not marry for gratification, but for the sake of offspring."[34] Strabo[35] has a report of a tribal custom whereby "no one marries before he has cut off the head of an enemy and presented it to the king, who deposits the skull in the royal treasury." Ritual cannibalism accompanies the act. Among certain Mohammedans the groom must have put an end to war between two tribes.[36] A report to the Pope made by an archbishop from the Albanian mountains in 1702 states: "Among the execrable customs of the mountain people, the wretched parents are in the habit of buying young girls for a price for their sons who are of tender age, and of keeping them in their houses till of age to cohabit, and of omitting to contract matrimony unless a male child be born, even after fifteen years of sinful cohabitation."[37] This custom illustrates trial marriage as a test for women, to which we now turn.

Marriage of Trial or Term. As an accompaniment of trial marriage may occur a birth out of wedlock. Such a situation is no cause of reproach among the tribes of British Central Africa. The child belongs to the mother.[38] In Akkra temporary unions are contracted by the man giving the woman a skirt; when that garment is worn out she may return to her parents. In the Congo region there are marriages of test, while in Abyssinia marriages may be for the duration of the market.[39] Nothing is said to be simpler than the process by which, in Nyasaland, a man and a woman enter matrimony. The author[40] asked a native how he got his wife; "he said: 'I met her on the road and gave her tobacco. Shortly afterwards she came in to my hut and brought ugali (porridge). I asked: "For whom is this ugali?" She replied: "It is for you." I then asked her: "Why do you bring me ugali?" She replied: "Because I want you very much." I said: "But you have a husband already." She replied: "No! my husband left me a long time ago." I said: "This is surely a lie." She said: "It is not a lie: go and ask my brother." I then went and asked her brother, and he said: "She has told you the truth; her husband left her a long time ago." I then went to my own brother [his eldest brother] and asked him if he had any objection to my courting that woman. He said he had none and so she came to live with me.' In due time, when the two came to the conclusion that there existed no radical *incompatibilité d'humeur,* the preliminary arrangement became a permanent one." Of a tribe near Victoria Nyanza it is said that girls and young soldiers live in a kind of trial marriage with each other. When a girl becomes a mother she is restricted to a husband, not before.[41]

In the case of a Hindu king's daughter who was destined to carry on the royal line, the important thing was that she should have issue; her marriage was a matter of quite secondary concern. "This may explain the *swayamvara,* which allowed her not only to choose her husband, but possibly also any man,

33 Koch, in *Globus,* LXXXI, 106.
34 Cook, *Fathers of Jesus,* II, 36.
35 *Geog.,* XV, ch. II, §14.
36 Von Kremer, *Kgchte.,* II, 97.
37 Durham, in JAI, XL, 458-459.
38 Stannus, in JAI, XL, 312.

39 Waitz, *Anthrop.,* II, 114; Wilken, in VG, II, 17-18.
40 Coudenhove, in *Atl. Mo.,* CXXXII, 189-190.
41 Kaiser, in *Archiv. f. Rassen- u. Gesellsfts-Biol.,* III, 216.

to be the father of the heir to the throne. The only limitation on her choice of a husband seems to have been a rule that she must choose the winner in the tournament, if one was held."[42] This case resembles the *ambil-anak* form, with a test of the man superadded. The connection of trial marriage with illegitimacy comes out in the case of the Palaungs. "An unmarried woman very seldom has a child by a man who afterwards deserts her, but if this happens, she goes for advice to one of the village Elders. He in turn calls other Elders, and they discuss the matter; then they try to persuade the man to marry the girl. If he refuses, but owns that the child is his, they oblige him to pay to her a fine of about thirty rupees, and, if the mother is willing to give up her child, the man generally takes it to his home after it has been weaned. In such a case it will rank as a legitimate child in the household, and should the man at a future time marry some other woman, the step-mother is kind to it. I have never heard of a case where a step-mother was unkind to her husband's children, whether legitimate or illegitimate. In after-life no one will reproach the child for its unfortunate birth."[43] It is asserted that trial marriages are centuries old in Japan and are still practised. "The mother-in-law insisted that the girl selected for her son should live with him for three or four months, under close inspection, before a formal marriage occurred. Often the poor girl then was rejected."[44]

Of the Tlinkits it is written that "in former years men and women commonly took each other on trial. If, after having lived together for some weeks or months, they found that they liked each other and were satisfied to live together permanently, then, by a mutual understanding, they became husband and wife for good."[45] It is said that among the North American Indians unions for a time only and on trial were common. After the fixed term they were dissolved or, where mutual consent and marital affection were present, they might be protracted for the same period and then established for good. Among the Hurons marriages were concluded for not longer than a few days; among the Muskhogeans they were entered into for a year only, thereafter to be regularly renewed, especially if there were children. Again, in New England marriage was for a time; only in case the parties liked each other would it be established for good. In Virginia the chiefs, who had many wives, were married originally with the first one alone, and with the others only when they had lived together more than a year.[46]

In ancient Egypt it was permissible to have a year of trial in marriage, which was then dissoluble by payment.[47] Among the Semites, and in particular the Arabs, occurred the *mot'a* marriage, where the woman received her lovers for a time. The term seems to mean marriage of pleasure or convenience.[48] It was a temporary union, a sort of trial marriage, though it might be aligned with monandry.[49] Wilken[50] has written much about it, claiming that marriages where the woman was bound for good to a definite man were unknown to the ancient Arabians, who joined marriage for a time only. It is said that the Saracens hired their wives for money for a definite time following a contract, and in order that there might be an appearance of marriage, the wife offered

42 Vishwanath, in JAI, XLVII, 35.
43 Milne, *Eastern Clan*, 127.
44 Philadelphia *Public Ledger*, Aug. 20, 1926.
45 Jones, *Thlingets*, 132.
46 Waitz, *Anthrop.*, III, 105.

47 Erman, *Aegypten*, 221.
48 Barton, *Sem. Orig.*, 61.
49 §345, of the text.
50 "Matriarchaat bij de oude Arabieren," in VG, II, 8, 9, 13-18, 26-27.

to the man, under the name of marriage-gift, a spear and a tent, that she might after the fixed day leave him. The twenty-eighth verse of the fourth sura of the Koran reads: "It is allowed to you to take women for your money. . . . Give her her pay for what you have enjoyed from her." A later orthodox version says that this refers simply to common marriage and that the word pay means bride-gift. Some think this verse refers to the *mot'a* relation; one translates it: "Give her her pay for what you have enjoyed from her for the completed term." If so, it refers to a temporary marriage-bond. There is no other reference in the Koran but the traditions are fuller and agree that Mohammed allowed *mot'a* marriage to his followers. The Shiite chalifs tried to bring it in again. The *mot'a* was a marriage for a definite time, dissoluble of itself at the end of the period without any form of divorce. It had no formality, official, or witness. The man paid a certain compensation to the woman. In the earlier days of Islam such temporary unions were suited to special circumstances such as when the men were on war-expeditions and did not have their wives with them, and also when they were in foreign cities for a time. Wilken quotes a traveller's account of conditions in Mocha: "In all the streets there are brokers for wives, so that a stranger, who has not the conveniency of an house in the city to lodge in, may marry, and be made a free burgher for a small sum. When the man sees his spouse, and likes her, they agree on the price and term of weeks, months or years, and then appear before the cadjee or judge of the place, and enter their names and terms in his book, which costs but a shilling, or thereabout. And joining hands before him, the marriage is valid, for better for worse, till the expiration of the term agreed on. And if they have a mind to part, or renew the contract, they are at liberty to choose for themselves what they judge most proper; but if either wants to be separated during the term limited, there must be a commutation of money paid by the separating party to the other, according as they can agree; and so they become free to make a new marriage elsewhere." The trial marriage of the old Arabians was readily dissolved if the spouses had no pleasure in each other's company. It is related of one woman that she had in swift succession more than forty husbands belonging to twenty different tribes. Each who came to her said simply, "I ask you in marriage;" to which she replied, "I take you in marriage." "Hassanyeh Arab wives," we read, "enjoy at times a freedom from the ties and responsibilities of the marriage state, unknown, I believe, to any other race in the world. When the parents of the man and woman meet to settle the price of the woman, the price depends on how many days in the week the marriage tie is to be strictly observed. The woman's mother first of all proposes that, taking everything into consideration, with a due regard to the feelings of the family, she could not think of binding her daughter to a due observance of that chastity, which matrimony is expected to command, for more than two days in the week. After a great deal of apparently angry discussion, and the promise on the part of the relatives of the man to pay more, it is arranged that the marriage shall hold good, as is customary among the first families of the tribe, for four days in the week; and, in compliance with old established custom, the marriage rites during the three remaining days shall not be insisted on, during which days the bride shall be perfectly free to act as she may think proper, either by adhering to her husband and home, or by enjoying her freedom and independence from all observation of matrimonial obligations."

§366. Chastity.

AMONG the western tribe of Torres Straits, three cicatrices cut on a girl indicated marriageability. "If a girl was too free in her favors to the men, the other women cut a mark down her back to make her feel ashamed; she subsequently married without difficulty. A man in a corresponding delinquency would only have a charcoal mark painted on him, for it must be remembered that 'woman he steal man.' "[1] Of certain Papuans it is said: "The woman has invariably been deflowered before marriage, and in fact they prefer such a woman to a virgin."[2] "Illegitimate, or according to the Kiriwinian ideas, fatherless children, and their mothers are regarded with scant favour." Malinowski[3] cites several instances in which girls were pointed out to him as being undesirable, "no good," because they had children out of wedlock. "If you ask why such a case is bad, there is the stereotyped answer, 'Because there is no father, there is no man to take it in his arms.' . . . This by no means implies that a girl who has been a mother finds any serious difficulty in marrying afterwards." Both in an encampment and at home the Andamanese are careful to place the bachelors and spinsters at either end of the camp or building and the married couples in the space between.[4]

A writer on the negroes of the Gold Coast comments favorably on local conditions of morality, at least as regards the native attitude toward European women. Unmarried women teachers often go alone from station to station.[5] The native women of Central Africa are said to be extremely well behaved. "They flirt, it is true, but without affectation or false prudery; they have complete self-respect. They do not treat boys with preference but surround their girl children with tenderness and care, in which the brothers join. . . . After marriage they care for the house and observe a little more reserve with the men."[6] Boys and girls in British Central Africa play at being man and wife, building little houses in the bush and sleeping together. "Promiscuous sexual intercourse among girls before puberty is common."[7] Coudenhove[8] comments on the variation between tribes concerning the conduct which is expected from unmarried girls. "The Zulu of South Africa punishes girls who have disgraced themselves, by death through warrior ants. The Wataweta of the Kenia province allow their young a license as great as that of the Wayao. On the other hand, the Wapare of the Tanganyika province, near neighbors of the Wataweta, in order to keep their young girls out of harm's way, were, and perhaps still are, in the habit of shutting them up for periods sometimes extending to four years, often in solitary confinement, in lofts built into the roofs of their huts! . . . It is to be feared, however, that those tribes which are concerned about the proper behavior of their maidens before marriage, are not so from any appreciation, or even comprehension, of 'virtue' in the white man's sense of the word. Chastity merely increases the girl's value as a commercial asset. That this is the case follows from the fact that it is insisted upon chiefly in those tribes where the girl is bought from the parents by the bridegroom, without being herself consulted; while it is treated as a negligible quantity where the girl's consent is a condition of marriage."

Among the Bahima, "should a girl go wrong before marriage she is degraded

---

1 Haddon, in JAI, XIX, 368.
2 Liston-Blyth, in JAI, LIII, 469.
3 In JAI, XLVI, 408.
4 Man, in JAI, XII, 108.

5 Vortisch, in Globus, LXXXIX, 1279.
6 Brunache, Cent. Afr., 64.
7 Stannus, in JAI, XL, 309.
8 In Atl. Mo., CXXXII, 189.

and cast out by her clan; if she is with child she is sent out of the country until her child is born. . . . After the child is born the girl may return to the country, but no one of position will marry her, only a serf or some disgraced person who is unable to obtain another wife."[9] Among the Ba-Yaka virginity on the part of the woman is considered essential; in fact, "if she is found not to be a virgin she can be repudiated. . . . Sexual intercourse is forbidden to the unmarried; should it occur, the man must pay a fine to the father of the girl, the latter is not punished, but it must be remembered that great stress is laid upon the virginity of a bride."[10] So far as the information of Sir Charles Dundas[11] goes, free love is nowhere in East Africa recognized as the normal and approved custom for unmarried adults. "At the same time it is not punished, and the tendency has been in the direction of increased immorality of this sort during recent years. . . . Where a young couple consort sexually it is generally understood that they must subsequently marry. Such is the strict rule among the Wabunga. In practice such relations are in fact and invariably only a prelude to marriage, and the long period of betrothal customary among most of these tribes more or less ensures that the girl either remains pure or consorts only with her betrothed. . . . Europeans are, of course, often misled as to the actual nature of native practices. Thus I have found that it is popularly believed that the Wakikuyu permit free sexual intercourse between the unmarried girls and youths. Actual sexual connection is, however, not permitted nor indulged in excepting in rare cases, but the girls and warriors may and do indulge in any other extreme of intimacy." Among the Unyamwesi, if a man begets a bastard he is obliged to make a payment to the girl's father and to marry her, without paying any more.[12] Amongst themselves the Pygmies are said to be very moral; "their women, however, soon degenerate into immorality when they come into contact with Sudanese or Swahilis. But even then they observe outward decorum and assume an affectation of prudishness."[13] Among the ruling class of the Niam-Niam, if a man is disillusioned as to the virginity of the bride he has purchased, "he simply returns the girl to her father, upon whom the opprobrium falls, and gets back all his presents."[14]

In Baghirmi, the girls "were in maiden fashion retiring, and witnessed through their bearing the well known fact that modesty and chastity are not connected with clothing."[15] It is reported that morality among negroes varies inversely with the amount of clothing worn, the most fully clothed being the most immoral.[16] Galla and Somal girls are scrupulously guarded; "any young woman who . . . is not a *virgo intacta* . . . cannot, among the Galla, be legally married."[17] Again, the death-penalty falls upon seduced and seducer, prostitution scarcely appears, and chastity and nakedness are correlative.[18]

Mongol women are chaste and nothing is heard amongst them of lewdness; this was so in the thirteenth century and is reported to be true still.[19] The Yakuts use straps that go about the body and are tied in intricate knots to guarantee the fidelity of wives and the virginity of daughters; but they see no

9 Roscoe, in JAI, XXXVII, 105.
10 Torday and Joyce, in JAI, XXXVI, 45, 48.
11 In JAI, LI, 246-247.
12 Stuhlmann, *Mit Emin*, 93.
13 Johnston, *Uganda*, II, 543-544.
14 Junker, *Afrika*, III, 291.

15 Nachtigal, *Sahara*, II, 590.
16 Wilson and Felkin, *Uganda*, I, 223.
17 Paulitschke, *Nordost-Afr.*, I, 171, 194.
18 Volkens, *Kilimandscharo*, 252.
19 Rubruck, *Eastern Parts*, 79, and Rockhill's note.

immorality in illicit relations unless someone is materially injured, in the matter of property-rights, by it. The conduct of girls is restrained lest it injure their marriage-value.[20] If the bride-price has been partly or fully paid, the parents do not take any further interest in preserving the girl's chastity. In other words, "the real legal marriage precedes the actual official wedding ceremonies sometimes by several years; and, in fact, is accomplished when the suitor formally hands over to the father of his bride a certain portion of the kalym [bride-price]. During this time the husband has to visit his wife in the house of her family, and any children born in this period live with the mother." Contrary to the custom of all neighboring tribes, Koryak girls must have no sexual intercourse before marriage. "It is considered shameful for a girl to bear a child before marriage; she must go out into the wilderness to be delivered, and afterwards she kills and buries the child. . . . When taking the census of the Maritime and Reindeer Koryak families, Jochelson did not find a single illegitimate child, while among the Yukaghir, northern Tungus, northern Yakut, and Russian settlers in northern Siberia, it was almost impossible to find a family not including such children."[21] In Korea "daughters have been put to death by their fathers, wives by their husbands, and women have even committed suicide, according to Dallet, when strange men, whether by accident or design, have even touched their hands, and quite lately a serving woman gave as her reason for remissness in attempting to save her mistress, who perished in a fire, that in the confusion a man had touched the lady making her not worth the saving."[22] Cambodian maidens rarely go astray.[23] Certain Turkomans, by exception, exact chastity of the man till marriage.[24]

Among the Sema Nagas free intercourse with bachelors is not allowed to unmarried girls as in the Angami and Ao tribes. "This is not to say that the unmarried Sema girl is invariably chaste, but she is a good deal more so than the girl of any neighbouring tribe. The care which is taken of her is partly due to the desire not to damage her value in the marriage market, as a girl who is known to have had an intrigue commands a much lower marriage price as a rule. Accordingly the fine for an adultery with a girl of position is much higher than that for a similar affair with the daughter of a man of none, since the marriage price of the latter is in any case much lower than that of, say, a chief's daughter."[25] Among certain Borneans the punishment for sex-relations with a girl, who as a consequence has an illegitimate child, is eighty dollars, which goes to the injured parents or the nearest blood-kin.[26] Of the Rejangs of Sumatra it is said: "Chastity prevails more, perhaps, among these than any other people. It is so materially the interest of the parents to preserve the virtue of their daughters unsullied, as they constitute the chief of their substance, that they are particularly watchful in this respect." In the country prostitution for hire is unknown; it is confined to the more polite bazars. In the case of crimes against nature, neither the things nor terms for them are known in Sumatra.[27] Among the Sea Dyaks, "the women are so keenly sensitive to disgrace that they will not part with their virtue for fear of the consequences." Death is preferred above a life of shame and suicide is not infrequent for this cause. If a man prove false, which is unusual, and the woman commit suicide, he is

20 Sieroshevski, Yakuts (Pol.), 342; Sieroshevski-Sumner, in JAI, XXXI, 96.
21 Czaplicka, Aborig. Siberia, 80-81, 108.
22 Bishop, Korea, 341.
23 Leclère, in PSM, XLIV, 779.

24 Guse, in Aus Allen Welttheilen, XXIX, 319.
25 Hutton, Sema Nagas, 133, 183.
26 Schwaner, Borneo, II, 168.
27 Marsden, Sumatra, 261.

very heavily fined.[28] Young unmarried girls are secluded from danger.[29] Among the Sengirese who have a matriarchal system, morality is strict, while the Alfurs of the Minahasa are patriarchal and somewhat lax.[30] Over against the many peoples in the Indian Archipelago who hold virginal chastity in small honor, there stand others who strictly insist that even before marriage the woman must be chaste and who punish the least misstep with the severest penalties. "If even the rain fails for a while, then all the maids in the village are narrowly spied upon whether one of them may not be suffering from vomiting."[31] Examples are given.

If, on any island of the Gilbert Group, a girl was discovered at the marriage-ceremony to have failed in the test of virginity, the bridegroom's mother, on establishing the fact, would cry aloud, "An old woman! An old woman!" and proceed to drag the naked girl from the loft. "But as a rule the unhappy girl was disowned from the moment of detection; she was branded with the name of *nikira-n-roro* (lit., the *remnant-of-her-generation*) and earned her living by the favour of promiscuous suitors. . . . Wilkes mentions that women were offered in traffic to his sailors by the people of Tabiteuea and other islands, and deduces that the islanders had a low standard of morality. The fact was that the girls offered were *nikira-n-roro*, whose existence argues a high standard of virginity."[32] Insistence on virtue varies with class: on the Nauru islands, "before marriage a girl can do what she will, as no limitations are imposed; but in the families of chiefs there is more stress laid on purity. If a girl has a child it is looked upon as a shame" and the ignominy descends to the child. Abortion is frequent.[33] Heathen Malays of the Philippine mountains guard the virginity of daughters, who are sometimes educated apart by the old women.[34] In Samoa "chastity was ostensibly cultivated by both sexes; but it was more a name than a reality. From their childhood their ears were familiar with the most obscene conversation; and as a whole family, to some extent, herded together, immorality was the natural and prevalent consequence. There were exceptions, especially among the daughters of persons of rank; but they were the exceptions, not the rule."[35] By the old navigators the women of Easter Island "are said to have been the most bold and licentious in Polynesia, if the reports are correctly stated, but we found them modest and retiring and of higher moral character than any of the islanders."[36]

A waning custom among the Tlinkits is that of confining girls when approaching womanhood in some cramped, coop-like place. "In these little dungeons, not high enough for them to stand in nor long enough for them to stretch out in, girls are confined anywhere from four months to one year. When they come out they are fairly bleached, and the great wonder is that they ever live to come out at all. . . . In most cases she is spoken for before she leaves her solitary confinement, and she steps out of her little prison only to step into matrimony."[37] Pre-marital chastity was not considered a virtue among the Cree Indians, though infidelity of a wife was sometimes severely punished.[38] Among the Omaha, on the other hand, "young girls were carefully guarded; they never went to the spring or to visit friends unless accompanied by an older

28 Roth, in JAI, XXI, 130; Veth, *Borneo's Wester-Afdeeling*, II, 251.
29 Gomes, *Sea Dyaks*, 45.
30 Hickson, in JAI, XVI, 142.
31 Wilken, in VG, I, 587, 590-591.
32 Grimble, in JAI, LI, 32-33.

33 Brandeis, in *Globus*, XCI, 77.
34 Blumentritt, *Philippinen*, 12.
35 Turner, *Samoa*, 91.
36 Thomson, in USNM, 1889, 463.
37 Jones, *Thlingets*, 133, 134.
38 Mooney and Thomas, in HAI, I, 360.

woman—mother, aunt, or relative. Young married women seldom if ever went anywhere alone. Custom permitted only elderly women to go about unattended."[39] Among both Mandans and Yuroks the sexes bathed apart, the bathing-place of the women being guarded against the approach of men.[40]

In Homer the young of both sexes conversed freely, and the young woman of the house bathed and anointed the guests; yet the mores were strong and modesty was formal, not instinctive.[41] Letourneau[42] holds that life in society brought shame and modesty; it was not delicacy but the brutal egoism of the man that determined modesty and sexual morality. The woman was his personal property and chastised for unauthorized intercourse. Whatever other causes may have been at work to produce the demand for chastity in unmarried girls, Starcke[43] believes that "its chief source is to be found in early marriages and in the consequent habit of desiring and enforcing discreet behaviour in young girls." Westermarck[44] has collected a number of examples of chastity, as disproof of the theory of free cohabitation before marriage. The Serbs derided harshly the young wife who became a mother early in married life.[45]

§367. Courtship.

As respects courtship in Melanesia, "over a large area marriage does not normally take place except after more or less prolonged sexual connection which must be looked upon as the normal method of courtship, but it is equally clear that connection may occur under circumstances which do not lead to marriage and which are not expected to do so. . . . Certain houses are dedicated to the use of unmarried girls above the age of puberty who habitually pass the night in them. These, like the local man-houses, are called *potuma,* and are usually old houses, which, when their owners build new ones, are given over to the girls. The girls resort to these houses in the dusk, and after dark a number of young bachelors of the community will proceed to such a *potuma,* and with the exception of one of their number, squat down outside. This youth enters the house and asks the girls if any of them are willing to receive any of the boys whose names he repeats. . . . If after their first night together the girl asked the boy to return, he would do so, but not otherwise, and the proposition to spend a second night together never came from the male. . . . A more or less prolonged period of connection precedes marriage, and that this, in the ordinary way, constitutes courtship is shown by the method in which betrothal is brought about. After a time, said to extend from one to three months, during which a girl has constantly received the same boy, she may propose marriage." In certain sections a custom called *viagagavu* prevails as a preliminary to marriage: "A boy and girl pass the night together, sleeping in each other's arms, either in a rough shelter built in the bush, or in the house of the girl's parents. . . . In many, perhaps the majority of cases, connection does not take place; . . . a widow or widower about to marry would practise *viagagavu* with his or her future spouse."[1]

When a native of Choiseul Island makes a proposal for the hand of the girl

---

39 Fletcher and LaFlesche, in BAE, XXVII, 337.
40 Donaldson, in *Smithson. Rep.,* 1885, pt. II, 86; Powers, in *Contrib. N. Amer. Ethnol.,* III, 55.
41 Keller, *Hom. Soc.,* 208 ff.

42 *Morale,* 149-150.
43 *Prim. Fam.,* 212.
44 *Marriage,* I, 138-157.
45 Rhamm, in *Globus,* LXXXII, 190.
1 Seligmann, *Melanesians,* 499-501, 502, 503-504.

of his choice and is accepted, "he immediately informs his father, or should the father be deceased, the chief of the village, of his intention to marry. When the parent, guardian, or chief, is satisfied that all is well he hands over to the bride's father or guardian a portion of the purchase money. The balance is paid at the end of the probationary period (which lasts from a month to three or four months) provided that all is satisfactory and the parties are agreed that they can live happily together."[2] In the D'Entrecasteaux Islands there is said to be plenty of idle flirtation, both by day and by night. "A lad, for example, may find a girl alone in the woods or on the shore, and invite her to sit beside him and share his betel-nut or tobacco. Kissing is quite unknown." A girl's heart will glow with pride that so gay and fine a youth should come to woo her love, but she will not admit it for a single moment. "On the contrary she will deny it emphatically, even to her bosom friends, and roundly assert that she will never marry him. Nevertheless the youth's suit prospers." The typical method of courtship is as follows. "At night, when all is silent, the lad steals quietly beneath her hut and plays a soft tune on his jew's harp till she wakes. Her father may hear him and ask him what he wants, and the lad will answer that he has come to court his daughter. Possibly fathers are more indulgent in this land, or it may be they have greater self-control, for the girl will merely be told to go below and stir up the fire and do her courting there. More usually though the girl at this period will be sleeping in the maidens' hut. Then when her lover's serenade awakes her from her dreams—if, that is, she needs awakening—she rises, stirs the fire, and with her own jew's harp she plays an answering tune. The lad responds, and the girl then softly calls to him and bids him enter. There they sit beside the fire, conversing in low tones and chewing together the betel-nut which he has brought until it is time for him to retire again. . . . Most lads, however, are too shy to go alone to the maidens' hut, at least in the beginning of their courtship. They club together, share their betel-nut, and visit the hut in a body and play their jew's harps. The girls invite them in, and they separate off in pairs, the acceptance of the betel-nut which each lad offers as he enters being a token of consent; any poor unfortunate lad left over must go sadly home."[3]

Courtship with gallantry much after the European style is reported among the Banziri of the Congo basin.[4] With the Akamba, "if a young man sees a girl he fancies he will talk to her now and again, and eventually tell her he wants to marry her."[5] In Nyasaland the girls have absolute freedom of movement. "They will go to a young fellow 'on trial' without first informing their parents, until, perhaps, one day, the father asks casually: 'Where are you always going to, taking food-stuff with you?' The girl then replies: 'I go to a young fellow whom I like very much.' Then the swain, after having been informed by his fiancée that the father is beginning to manifest curiosity, will go to the latter and tell him that he wants his daughter; and then the father will say: 'Go and speak with her brother.' It is always the brother, or the uncle on the mother's side, who is consulted as the weightiest authority."[6]

A case of real wooing is reported among the Malays;[7] but among the Karens of Burma it is not respectable.[8] The Palaung suitor has the aid of religion, for

---

2 Rooney, in AAAS, 1911, 443.
3 Jenness and Ballentyne, *D'Entrecasteaux*, 96-97, 99, 100.
4 Clozel, in PSM, XLIX, 676.
5 Hobley, *A-Kamba*, 62.

6 Coudenhove, in *Atl. Mo.*, CXXXII, 190.
7 Ratzel, *Vkde.*, II, 433.
8 Von Hellwald, *sub* "Karen," in Reichenow, *Wörterbuch*, IV, 414.

it is their belief that the spirit, when in the body, does not pervade the whole of it, but moves through it, being sometimes in one part and sometimes in another. Thus, "on Sunday the spirit or life of a woman is in her left thigh; on Monday in the chin; on Tuesday in the nape of the neck; on Wednesday in the middle of the back; on Thursday in the left wrist; on Friday in the right thigh. This should be remembered by every lover, because it is the spirit and not the body that can feel love; therefore, if on a Tuesday he can put his hand—especially a charmed hand—on the back of the neck of a girl, or put his arm round her waist on Wednesday, or take her left hand and stroke her left wrist on Thursday, while he is saying nice things to her, she will be more inclined to listen than if he held her right hand on Thursday or stroked her cheek instead of the nape of her neck on Tuesday." But the way of the suitor is not always so smooth. "The first man who comes to the house where a young girl lives to whom he wishes to talk, finds out where she sleeps from his sister or from a girl-cousin. Then at night, when her father and mother are still talking in the entrance-room, he cuts with a sharp knife a hole near the place where he thinks her pillow should be. He then gently inserts his hand and feels round the hole for the girl. If he should touch her, he tries to wake her by pulling her blanket or a lock of her hair if it has escaped from under the bed-clothes. . . . It may happen that, as a joke, he has been deceived as to the place where she sleeps. In such a case, when he puts his hand through the hole that he has cut in order to wake the girl, he may catch hold of the hair or blanket of the father, who, if he is a nervous man—and has not realized that his daughter has begun to have sweethearts—probably cries out in fear, thinking that a ghost has seized him. The young man of course runs away and does not wait to explain. The first man to arrive in the evening may talk through the hole as long as he pleases, other men coming later must wait till the first man goes away, then the next-comer has the right to the hole till he retires, and so on. . . . The girls have distinctly the best of the game, as the young man is sometimes hanging in a precarious position outside in the cold night wind, which often blows fiercely among the Palaung hills, while the girl, cosily wrapped in her blankets, squats in the house."[9]

The Rejangs of Sumatra show little of courtship; their manners do not admit of it, for the young people are kept carefully apart and the girls seldom trusted from under the maternal wing.[10] A Macassar youth presses a coin upon the forehead of the girl he wishes; if it is not given back, he is accepted. He may also show his love by smashing a coconut so that the sweet juice besprinkles the girl. In one district, young men and women meet in the evening to pass the time; they exchange mutual compliments in singing tones, and "most of the love-affairs are brought to pass in connection with these circumstances." In Java, the rice-harvest, in which all take part, offers the finest chance for young people to court, and wedding-feasts are never more numerous than in the first weeks of harvest time. Also during other festivals, when the opportunities for the sexes to meet are generally pretty free, the young people have a good chance to make choices. In a number of cases proposal of marriage is made by the girl. Generally the young man declares himself and tries to find out how the girl feels; in this the use of betel is very common, as it also is later, in the exchange of love-tokens between engaged people. Among the Alfurs and others the word for wooing means to ask each other continually

9 Milne, *Eastern Clan*, 114-115, 121-122.   10 Marsden, *Sumatra*, 265.

for betel. After puberty the girl sleeps with a full betel-vessel near by, so as to be able to make use of it at will. Wilken,[11] from whom the above is taken, quotes from a tale as follows: "The crown-prince embraced his wife now long and heartily and begged her to give him her betel-chew. Mutually they offered them to each other." The offering of a chewed-out quid is a great proof of affection. To continue, "The prince took a chew of betel, embraced his wife, kissed her, and gave her a chewed quid." There are cited cases analogous to the evening wooing described above, though not so complicated. If the girl "blows up the fire," it is a sign of negation. There are also instances, especially among the Bataks, where the young couple spend the night together in chastity, the man leaving early in the morning. Among the Alfurs, however, there is some immorality. Again, there is the same flowery, symbolic talk as among the Palaungs. Wilken cites cases similar to "bundling" and aligns them with the placing of a naked sword between Siegfried and Brünhilde and the traces of this custom in Switzerland, Tyrol, some parts of Germany, Norway, Sweden, and Heligoland.

Among the Samoans a pig was sometimes used as a courting present.[12] In the island of Ruk, the lover uses a "recognition-staff," with shallow notches in the end. He sticks this through the house-wall, when he calls at night, at the place where his chosen sleeps. She knows whose staff it is by the shape of the end and by the notches and accepts or refuses the summons to a tender tryst. There is here an element of romance elsewhere most exceptional in the whole region.[13]

There is said to be no such thing as courtship among the Tlinkits, the girls not seeing the men who are designed to become their husbands until they are wedded to them.[14] Among the Salish tribes, "the common way in which a man sought to learn whether he was acceptable to the parents and relatives of the girl he desired for wife or not, was to take a large bundle of good firewood to her father's house or apartment and offer it to the family. This constituted a formal request for her hand, as it were. . . . The significance of the gift is fully understood by all, and a family council is immediately held. The youth awaits the decision of this council."[15] As Omaha custom did not permit the young men to visit young women in their homes, the opportunities for the young people openly to become acquainted were limited to gatherings for tribal ceremonies and during the confusion incident to breaking up or making camp when the tribe was on the annual hunt. "The stream and spring were at all times the favorite trysting places. Men sometimes composed their own love songs and by the song the girl not only identified her lover but became aware of his nearness. . . . It has been stated that a true love song, one that had for its purpose the honorable wooing of a maid, did not exist among peoples living in the stage of development represented by the native tribes of America. This statement does not hold good for the Omaha and their close cognates,"[16] as the authors demonstrate by a number of examples. Proposal of marriage among the Osage was accompanied by gifts of horses and blankets.[17] Of the Winnebago it is said that "if the young girls have any lovers they always come to the menstrual lodges at night. This is therefore the time for wooing. It

11 *Vkde.*, 283; and in VG, I, 503-504, 507, 508, 509, 510, 511-514, 517, note 31.
12 Pratt, in AAAS, 1887, 448.
13 Finsch, *Ethnol. Erfahr.*, III, 308.
14 Jones, *Thlingets*, 125-126.

15 Hill-Tout, in JAI, XXXIV, 318-319.
16 Fletcher and LaFlesche, in BAE, XXVII, 319.
17 LaFlesche, in AA, XIV, 129.

is said that the girls cohabit with their lovers in these menstrual lodges. Those girls who have parents are attended by watchers, so that no unworthy men may visit them. They are especially guarded against ugly men, who are very likely to have love medicines. However, generally it is of no avail to struggle against such men, for they are invincible."[18] With some of the Apaches, "a young warrior seeking a wife would first bargain with her parents and then take a horse to her dwelling. If she viewed his suit with favor she would feed and water the animal, and, seeing that, he would come and fetch his bride, and after going on a hunt for the honeymoon they would return to his people. When he took two horses to the camp of the bride and killed one of them it signified that her parents had given her over to him without regard to her consent."[19]

Among the Seminole Indians the girl's feelings are considered. A proposal is handled in the following way: "A warrior of twenty sees an Indian maiden of sixteen and wishes to marry her. He calls his immediate relatives in council and tells them his wish. If the girl is not a member of the lover's own gens, and if there is no impediment in the way of the alliance, some one from their own number is selected, who, at the proper time, goes to the maiden's kindred and tells them that they desire the maid to receive their kinsman as her husband. The girl's relatives then consider the question. If the decision is favorable, they ask the girl her wishes. If she is willing, news of this is conveyed through the relatives, on both sides, to the prospective husband, and there is excitement in both households. The young man's female relatives take to the girl's mother a blanket or large piece of cotton cloth and a bed canopy. There is returned to the young man thence a wedding garment—a newly made shirt."[20] Among the Guiana Indians "engagement and courtship are out of the question, while kissing and cuddling are said to be practically unknown. Among Arawak, as well as Carib, the beauty of a girl is judged by her feet, her face being of secondary importance. . . . Even at the present day, the comparatively civilized Surinam Carib regards kissing as a stupidity peculiar to the white race."[21]

On one of the Balearic Islands, Vuillier[22] was startled by several loud reports. On inquiry, the priest led him to the foot of a little hill, where he saw a girl slowly walking home from church. A youth with a musket was hurrying after her and as he reached her, he suddenly fired at her feet, raising a cloud of stones and dirt which almost hid her from view. But without so much as the quiver of an eye-lash the girl continued to walk serenely on and, the young peasant placing himself by her side, they both continued their road chatting amicably together. This, it appears, is the customary form of salutation between man and maid throughout the island, the girls making it a point of honor to betray no emotion at the firing, though always taken unawares. Here is a variety of courtship analogous to the "showing-off" of the small boy. But the firing is also more serious, for while a caller discharges his musket in the middle of the room at farewell, adding "Buenas noches," he may say goodbye first and fire afterward. That is a challenge to a rival suitor which is always accepted, the challenger waiting outside the door.

---

18 Radin, in BAE, XXXVIII, 137.
19 HAI, I, 283.
20 MacCauley, in BAE, V, 496.

21 Roth, in BAE, XXXVIII, 666, 667.
22 Forgotten Isles, 126-127.

§368. Betrothal.

AMONG the natives of Port Darwin, "infants are betrothed spouses, and in some cases the bestowal is made, sex being favorable, antecedent to birth."[1] With both the Koita and Motu, "betrothal results as soon as a boy and girl who have been enjoying a period of unwedded happiness consider it well to get married. The proposal in the first instance always comes from the girl, while they are together at night, and is never directly refused by the boy. . . . The young couple continue their nocturnal meetings during the whole time of betrothal," the bridegroom meanwhile setting about to collect the price he will have to pay for his bride.[2] Betrothal-ceremonies are elaborate in southeast Papua. "A man proposes to a woman by first getting the woman's consent to his sleeping with her in her usual sleeping place; then repeating his visits for several consecutive nights. The woman now speaks to her mother, who tells her husband. If the man is accepted, the woman informs him that her friends know, and that he may help them in their gardens. The woman's brother will take the man to the future mother-in-law's garden. The first day he works all day, and his relatives are informed of the fact. Then commence betrothal ceremonies and the Tabu, which apply also to the betrothal of children. *Tabu I.*— The betrothed pair must not eat in the presence of their respective relatives-in-law. *Tabu II.*—The betrothed boy or man is expected to sleep with his betrothed in her mother's house, but only as brother and sister. Should the man go further than the compact allows, and the woman become pregnant, her relatives will reproach him with having anticipated the proper course of betrothal, and angrily hand the woman over to him without further ceremonies— an act which will be a constant disgrace to the woman in the future. In quarrels with her sex she will often be brought to tears by their reminding her of her premature marriage. If the woman is of good rank the man has to pay much native wealth to appease the anger of the woman's relatives. From the commencement of the betrothal, feasts are exchanged between the relatives of each party. The man has to help the woman's relatives in gardening, house-building, etc., his family often joining with him. The woman helps the man in his private garden, and after a time there is exchange of help between the relatives of each party. The parents of the man or woman may call the betrothed parties son-in-law or daughter-in-law, but the couple cannot call the parents father or mother-in-law; nor can the betrothed call each other spouse. If a man and woman wish to be betrothed and the woman's relatives object the man withdraws generally. In some cases when the man's relatives object and he persists, they tell him to marry by himself, as they will not help him to give the food and presents necessary to complete the betrothal. Proper betrothal ceremonies cannot be carried on without both families are agreeable." The completion of the betrothal-ceremonies, terminating in marriage, includes such acts as the exchange of presents and the cooking of food for the relatives on both sides.[3] "The Andamanese look upon a girl betrothed by her parents as so far a wife that with her pre-marital unfaithfulness is accounted a crime."[4]

The Bushman generally employs his sister as intermediary, sending by her a present to the girl of his choice. If the present is not returned, he knows that

1 Parkhouse, in AAAS, 1895, 640.
2 Seligmann, *Melanesians*, 76-77.
3 Bromilow, in AAAS, 1909, 480-481.
4 Man, in JAI, XII, 136.

his proposal has found favor.[5] The engagement of the Bawenda is a very ceremonious affair, if not performed when the girl is yet a little child, as is often the
case. Sometimes the child is promised conditionally even before it is born. "The
uppermost question to be settled is that of the number of cattle to be handed
over to the girl's father by the bridegroom. With the payment of the first instal-
ment the engagement is considered complete. The girl's wishes are of no moment
in the matter. The two middlemen are the legal witnesses of the engagement
and of the subsequent marriage."[6] In West Africa, "betrothals are made by the
payment on account, by the intending husband, of a portion of the head-money
demanded for a girl; or, between children, by a present made by the parents
of the male child to those of the female child. In the first case the girl need
not be of a marriageable age; she may be a mere child, and sometimes even
she may not yet be born. . . . Betrothal seems to confer all the rights of marriage upon the male contracting party, except that of consummating the union
and of deriving benefit from the girl's services." If she dies, her family must
find a substitute.[7] Girls of the lower classes are not betrothed and may live
with great freedom, but those of the upper classes, who are almost always betrothed, must be chaste."[8] In Togo betrothal even precedes birth, with the
approval of the fetish and on condition of proper sex. "If now it is really a
girl, the youth works for his later wife and deposits the earnings with his
future parents-in-law."[9] The Galla have a sort of ring and chain ceremony;
in fact, proposal consists sometimes in the casting of the suitor's neck-chain
into the girl's lap, without a word being said. "If the chain is accepted, the
betrothal is concluded thereby."[10] The African children play father and mother
and the girls are often betrothed at ten years of age. This is a sort of temporary surety, but it makes the girl a calculating being, for she compares her
gifts with those of others and loses all idea of sentiment. The boys save in
order to give these gifts and also the big purchase-price; but the richest
presents may not hinder the girl, after four or five years, from accepting a
man she likes better.[11] In South Africa, a woman betrothed to a chief wore
on her neck a large white whorl of shell as an emblem. This was transferred to
the neck of her child. Men wore such whorls as love-charms and would not
part with them.[12] In Madagascar, a betrothed girl is called by a term meaning
"bespoken or engaged wife," and it is considered quite proper for her to become a wife in fact previous to actual marriage.[13]

The young people of the Cherkes are often married at sixteen or seventeen
without having seen each other before. In such cases, evidently, both courtship
and proposal are absent so far as the immediate parties are concerned. The
betrothal-ceremony culminates in putting out the fire and joining hands, the
parents not being present.[14] Until she marries, the Ainu girl is quite free in
her intercourse with men. "Some of the myths mention that some time after
a girl was married to a man, she married him again 'for good.' In this case
we must understand the first 'marriage' as in fact a betrothal, accompanied by
sexual intercourse; while the second marriage referred to was the real marriage, after which the woman was called *macipi*, 'the wife.' "[15] During the pre-

5 Fritsch, *Eingeb. Süd-Afr.*, 445.
6 Gottschling, in JAI, XXXV, 373.
7 Ellis, *Ewe*, 201.
8 Ellis, *Yoruba*, 182.
9 Klose, *Togo*, 251.
10 Paulitschke, *Nordost-Afr.*, I, 197.

11 Gutmann, in *Globus*, XCII, 1-2.
12 Bent, *Mashonaland*, 271-272.
13 Sibree, *Great Afr. Isl.*, 251-252.
14 *Russian Ethnog.* (Russ.), II, 223.
15 Czaplicka, *Aborig. Siberia*, 103.

liminaries of a Khond marriage, a knotted string is put into the hands of the so-called "searchers for the bride," and the girl's people retain a similar string. The reckoning of the date of the betrothal ceremony is kept by untying a knot every morning.[16] In the Punjab, when once the promise has passed the lips of the girl's father, it can be withdrawn for grave causes only. "Betrothal thus effected creates a kind of relationship, so that if one of the parties to it dies, the other is counted impure for three days. . . . Amongst the Hindus betrothal is a contract, and is, as a rule, an indispensable preliminary to the marriage of a girl, though a woman once married cannot again be betrothed according to the ceremonies of a first betrothal." Betrothals are of three kinds: one in which the girl is given by her parents as a quasi-religious offering to her future husband; another, called exchange, in which two or more families exchange brides; and a third, in parts of the southwest Punjab, where a bride-price is more or less openly paid. "Thus betrothal in the South-west Punjab is a solemn rite and the tie it creates is irrevocable, so much so that it can only be annulled owing to impotence or incurable disease, and even when the boy or girl is thought to be dying the tie between the pair is solemnly cancelled by the following rite:—the boy is called to the girl's death-bed and made to stand by her pillow and drink some water. The girl also drinks, and then the boy says, 'Thou art my sister.' This, of course, dissolves the betrothal, but it is understood that if the patient recover the tie will hold good. . . . Briefly, the essentials of a valid contract of betrothal are the public acceptance of the match, feasting and the exchange of gifts, the religious rites, if any are observed, being of secondary importance, even indeed if these are necessary to the validity of the contract. It may be said generally that a contract of betrothal is irrevocable, except for certain definite causes, or in cases when it has become impossible of fulfilment. Even when its literal fulfilment is impossible owing to the death of the boy, there is a widespread feeling that an implied contract subsists to marry the girl to another member of his family. . . . It would appear that the castes or tribes which allow widow re-marriage have a strong feeling that the betrothal duly effected gives the boy's family a claim on the girl's hand, so that, in the event of her original fiancé's death, she may be married to another boy of the family. . . . Thus the advantages of the contract are all on the boy's side, in having secured a valuable chattel, little is thought of the girl's claim on the boy, only very exceptional circumstances would make the boy's family refuse to find another match for her in the event of his death. . . . Speaking generally, the contract is considered much more binding on the girl's relatives than on those of the boy, so much so that among the Jats of Lahore this principle is pushed to an extreme, and it is alleged that the boy can break off his betrothal at pleasure, whereas a girl cannot." There is a tendency to defer betrothal among the higher castes to a somewhat later age than is usual among the middle castes: "in Lahore, Jats betroth from four to six, and Rajputs from twelve to fourteen; in Shahpur, Hindus betroth from eight to twelve, and in Jhelum, before ten. Generally speaking in the Western Punjab girls are betrothed at a very early age, much earlier than is customary among the Muhammadans, but boys are often not betrothed till puberty or later. The feeling that it is a disgrace to have a grown-up daughter

16 Thurston, S. India, 13.

unmarried is very strong among Hindus. Throughout the Punjab pre-natal betrothal is unusual, but not unknown."[17]

Betrothal affords one of the resources, it will be recalled, which a Batak girl can employ to get her own way in marriage. It generally takes place together with an exchange of love-guerdons, and formally, before the groom sends his relatives to arrange about the purchase-price. If the girl's relatives try to coerce her into marrying an old and rich suitor, she can fly to the giver of her guerdon, who is obliged to take her in, and then his relatives must arrange about the price. Regularly the proposal comes from the boy, though sometimes the opposite is the case. Wilken[18] thinks *a priori* that this would be so where the mother-family exists, the woman being the head of the group and the man following her into marriage. This view is supported by the facts; in the *ambil-anak* form the proposal comes from the father of the girl. If one party refuses, the other is limited to pecuniary damages. In Sumatra, if the union falls through by will of the groom, he must pay ten gulden [four dollars]; if the bride is responsible, she pays five. If an engagement is broken without lawful reason, the guilty one has to pay an amount equal to the bride-price agreed upon. Not seldom when an engagement is broken capriciously, the betrothal-pledge is forfeited; this is the case in Java also. Throughout the Indian Archipelago occur instances of child-betrothal. Among the Igorrotes of Luzon the engaged couple live together despite the rigid insistence upon chastity. Here is a type of trial-marriage. As soon as the betrothal is made "the girl's parents arrange for the youth to live in concubinage with their daughter, for the most important matter is to test her fecundity."

In China the father and elder brother of the young man send a go-between to the father and brother of the girl to inquire her name and the moment of her birth, that the horoscope of the two may be examined, in order to ascertain whether the proposed alliance will be a happy one. If the characters seem to augur well, the boy's friends send the go-between back to make an offer of marriage. If that be accepted, the second party is again requested to return an assent in writing. Presents are then sent to the girl's parents according to the means of the parties, and the go-between requests them to choose a lucky day for the wedding. The preliminaries are concluded by the bridegroom going or sending a party of friends with music to bring his bride to his own house. The match-makers contrive to multiply their visits and prolong the negotiations, when the parties are rich, so as to serve their own ends. From the time of engagement until marriage a young lady is required to maintain the strictest seclusion. "The office of match-maker is considered honorable, and both men and women are employed to conduct nuptial negotiations. Great confidence is reposed in their judgment and veracity, and as their employment depends somewhat upon their tact and character, they have every inducement to act with strict propriety in their intercourse with families. The father of the girl employs their services in collecting the sum agreed upon in the contract, which, in ordinary circumstances, varies from twenty-five to forty dollars, increasing to a hundred and over according to the condition of the bridegroom; until that is paid the marriage does not take place. The presents sent at betrothment are sometimes costly, consisting of silks, rice, cloths, fruits, etc.; the bride brings no dower, but both parents frequently go to expenses they can

---

17 Rose, in JAI, XXXVIII, 411-413, 416, 417.

18 Wilken, in VG, I, 467, 468, 473 ff., 516, 517, 521, 522, 527.

ill afford when celebrating the nuptials of their children, as the pride of family stimulates each party to make undue display."[19]

In the Gilbert Islands "children might be betrothed at a very early age, sometimes before birth. Two friends not yet married would sometimes make a compact that if they should ever beget children of opposite sex, they should marry one another. When the girl child whose fate had thus been arranged was born, she was taken by the parents of the prospective husband and brought up by them." On two of the islands there was usually no betrothal and no marriage-ceremony, "a wife being simply appropriated and carried off by her suitor;" this existed side by side with more formal institutions. On another island marriages were often made without preliminary betrothal, by a fictitious fishing-ceremony.[20]

Among the Eskimo, "frequently there are child betrothals, but these are not considered binding."[21] Among some of the Athapascans, "girls are often betrothed at 10 years of age and married at 14. After betrothal they must look no man in the face."[22] With certain Apaches "often girls were married when only 10 or 11 years of age." Again, "couples were often betrothed in marriage while children, the arrangement of course being made by their parents, although the engaged couple had a voice in the question of the final marriage. When between 10 and 15 years the boy went to live with the parents of the girl, but they were not married until the boy was able to support a wife."[23] "At 15 years the Cora reach the marriageable age. Marriages are arranged by the parents of the boy, who on five occasions, every eighth day, go to ask for the bride they have selected."[24] According to Osage marriage customs, the initiatory steps must come from the family of the young man; it is the duty of the parents or other near relatives to seek a suitable wife for him. When a suitable maiden has been found the parents summon four old men, each of whom has the title of Good-man, which belongs to a person who has been married according to the established customs of the tribe, has successfully raised and married off his own children, and lived to become a grandfather. They "are employed to conduct the negotiations between the family of the youth and that of the chosen maiden, and for their services they receive a fee. When the four men present the proposal of marriage, they extol the character of the family of the young man and also that of the young man himself."[25] Among some of the nations on the Orinoco it was customary, when a boy was born, "to have a look around and wait for the first little girl to appear and then to ask the parents for her, alleging that they ought to be helpmates, through having come into the world one in pursuit of the other. On that day the marriage would be settled, and as the youngster grew and began to use his bow and arrows, everything that came to his hands he took to the little girl, were it fish, birds, or fruits, a consideration (*tributo*) which he recognized and paid until the time arrived for her to be given him as wife. Makusi may be betrothed by their parents from their earliest youth, in which case the young man is bound to serve his girl's elders until she develops into womanhood. But this betrothal is in no sense binding, though while it lasts the man shows her

---

19 Williams, *Middle Kingdom*, I, 785, 786, 787.
20 Grimble, in JAI, LI, 29-30.
21 Lowrie and Farrand, in HAI, I, 809.

22 Dorsey and Goddard, in HAI, II, 467.
23 In HAI, I, 283; II, 884.
24 Hodge, in HAI, I, 348.
25 LaFlesche, in AA, XIV, 127-128.

every attention, brings her beads, and the best that he can get from the chase."26

According to the views of the North Germans, betrothal was not merely an act preliminary to marriage, but also a part of the contract of marriage itself. In the ancient Icelandic law it is stated that only he is legitimate whose mother was betrothed and wedded. The two acts of betrothal and wedding were necessary for legal marriage, and the assumption is that betrothal was the original requirement.27 The office of marriage-broker still prevails among modern peoples, especially the Jews. Recently a case was brought before an Arbitration Court in New York in which a match-maker sued for his commission of ten per cent of the dowry, citing as expenses incurred in bringing about the marriage, the money he spent on cigars and the time he devoted to playing pinochle—whether profitable or not was not disclosed—with the girl's father.28

§369. Reason for the Ceremony.

IN Melanesia "a binding marriage is constituted by the relatives of the girl and boy exchanging certain presents of food and by the young people living together publicly." In some cases, besides reciprocal presents of food, the boy's father takes an arm-shell and gives it to the girl's mother; the next day the girl's father makes a return present of a similar gift or one of equivalent value to the boy's mother.1

In central Cameroon "no special ceremonies are held if a slave woman is married."2 Along the Upper Congo, when the time arrives for the marriage, "the parents will take some plantain, cassava, fish, and various other kinds of food, and a calabash of sugar-cane wine, and together with the girl will go to the house of the husband, and hand over the girl by putting her hand in the man's hand in the presence of some witnesses. . . . The girl borrows all the finery she can of her female friends, decorates herself with oil and camwood powder, and for two or three weeks walks about the town with her husband— a sign to all that she is now his wife. If the man has already a few wives they will help to 'dress her' by the loan of their own trinkets and will lead her about the town, as a proof that she is now a fellow wife and belongs to their husband."3 The marriage which was regarded by the Baganda as most honorable and binding was the one by contract, when both parties agreed to come together as husband and wife. "The engagement is recognized by the relatives when the man sends the girl's parents two or three large gourds of plantain beer; each gourd contains about two gallons. The beer plays a most important part in the ceremony; it is the official sign of recognition by the parents on both sides, and relatives, of the engagement, and signifies the girl's consent has also been obtained. . . . The giving and receiving the beer is of greater importance than the dowry, it is the contract which proves the legality of the marriage if any dispute arises afterwards."4

There are eight forms of marriage among the Hindus, ranging from those with little or no formality to the higher type involving elaborate rites. Transfer of property is characteristic only of the latter.5 Cases exist among the East Indians of no special marriage-ceremony, but there is always some form of

26 Roth, in BAE, XXXVIII, 667.
27 Lehmann, *Verlobung*, 97-98.
28 N. Y. *Times*, Aug. 31, 1922.
1 Seligmann, *Melanesians*, 504, 505.

2 Malcolm, in JAI, LIII, 392.
3 Weeks, in JAI, XXXIX, 440.
4 Roscoe, in JAI, XXXII, 36.
5 Nathubhai, in JASB, III, 400 ff.

publicity, however slight. A number of tribes have the custom of a common meal like the Roman *confarreatio*. At a Dyak wedding there is smearing of blood, to summon the ghosts to bless the union with many children.[6] "Among all the wild tribes of the Peninsula, as indeed among the Malays, an important ingredient of the marriage rite is a form of ritual purchase, commonly followed by a repast which is shared between bride and bridegroom, with their relatives and the chief of the tribe as witnesses. Among the Negritos these two ingredients appear to constitute the entire ceremony, though even the act of purchase alone is said to be regarded as sufficiently binding, so long as it is performed before proper witnesses." After the meal gifts are presented to the bride's parents, and one of the minor chiefs of the tribe then inquires: "What about these children of ours? Are we to make them one?" To this the parents reply in the affirmative and the head of the tribe then gives both bride and bridegroom new names. Among the Sakai the form of marriage was extremely simple: the groom and bride, together with their relatives, went to the tribal chief's house where the chief investigated the prospects of the joint *ménage*, after which, if no obstacles were encountered, "he formally declared them married, and all was over." One author declares that there was no religious ceremony, but scrutiny of other evidence shows this an error. Sometimes the groom is catechized: "Have you built a hut?" "Do you know how to smoke cigarettes?" The details of the wedding show little or no ceremony, but the presence of publicity is clear enough.[7] The marriage-ceremonies of the common people in Samoa were performed in a house, with less display than in other cases. A prominent feature was the test of the bride's chastity.[8]

The groom among the Seminole Indians goes at sunset of the appointed day to the home of his mother-in-law, where his bride receives him. "From that time he is her husband. The next day husband and wife appear together in camp and are afterwards recognized as a wedded pair."[9] Among some of the Guiana tribes dancing and drunkenness constitute the whole ceremony of marriage. "The relations on both sides are invited on such occasions. The men bring along with them materials proper to build a hut for the young pair and the females present them with fish, fruit, bread, and drink. The former chant couplets to the bridegroom and the latter to the bride. As soon as it becomes dark the young wife is presented to her husband, which concludes the ceremony. . . . The same ceremonies prevail among all the tribes inhabiting the banks of the Orinoco." In some cases old hags who accompany the bride cry out, "Ah, my girl, if you only knew what troubles your husband will bring you, if you only knew what pains of travail are, you would not get married," and in this manner, "with the men dancing, the old women weeping, and the brides out of their wits, they make the round of the whole village." The formal offer and acceptance of food is a subject of common mention in the description of the marriage-ceremonies. "Besides the acceptance of food there are traces of certain customs connected with the hair as symbolic of consent or consummation of marriage. Thus, it is said of the Carib Islanders that some, without saying a word, go and lie down near the girl that pleases them best, and the mother acquaints her daughter that it is time to get married, though, often, she is only 12 years of age. The next morning she combs her master's hair before

6 Wilken, in VG, I, 529-532, 544, note, 551-553; Schwaner, *Borneo*, I, 197; Perelaer, *Dajaks*, 51-52.

7 Skeat and Blagden, *Malay Penin.*, II, 55, 61, note, 71, 74.
8 Turner, *Samoa*, 95.
9 MacCauley, in BAE, V, 496.

the others, and brings him cassava. Through this public act, their wedding is declared. In Cayenne, . . . when they want to marry, and everything is agreed upon, both parties throw one of their hairs into the air . . . and sling their hammock under a tree, where they proceed to consummate the marriage."[10]

In the laws of Hammurabi marriage consists of a contract made before witnesses.[11] Among the Mohammedans, too, there is an expression of consensus before two witnesses, with a statement of the morning-gift and other terms in the contract.[12] In the case of kings and nobles the custom of witnessing marriage and its consummation was longest retained, because for them legal technicalities were more important.

As was pointed out in the text, the chief reason for primitive marriage-ceremonies is to give publicity to the event. In the absence of any means of registration, such a device is necessary. Modern civilized peoples, realizing the importance of recording these events, aim at compulsory registration of marriages, births, and deaths. The value of such records both to the individual and to society may be illustrated by the use of birth-certificates. These are necessary in order that sanitarians and the government may have a complete record of vital statistics. They are also used as the basis for calculating infant mortality-rates, and for testing the results of child-hygiene. Birth-certificates often have a great value to those persons whose births are registered. The following are some of the personal uses to which birth-records are put: to provide evidence of age on entering school; to prove age and relationship in inheritance of property; to establish age of consent in court; to secure marriage-licenses—a birth-certificate being required in some European countries; to acquire passports—evidence of birth being required by the United States Government; to obtain working-papers, which in many states are not issued without evidence of age; for entrance into or exemption from the military or naval service of the United States.[13]

§370. Nature of the Ceremony.

IN western Australia, "when a girl is old enough to be claimed as a wife she is handed over by her father to the husband, who takes her away to his own camp. There does not seem to be any ceremony on such an occasion."[1] In Lifu, Loyalty Islands, "there is no marriage, all is decided by consent of the parties, who take up with or leave one another according to the caprice of the moment."[2] In New Britain, "after two or three days the bridegroom begins to pay a daily visit to the bride, she giving him a meal. Then he may go with her to her field work. After some weeks he builds a house and the first night the couple spends in it the marriage is considered to be finally contracted."[3] Less rudimentary are the ceremonies in New Hebrides. "At twelve the East Malekula girl is usually married. The marriage is arranged by her father, who offers her to the highest bidder and receives for her ten pigs at least. The evening before the wedding the bride calls together her childhood friends, and they play together on the beach. The marriage ceremony is held at the

10 Roth, in BAE, XXXVIII, 680-683.
11 Winckler, *Hammurabi*, 22.
12 Tornauw, *Moslim. Recht*, 64.
13 Overton and Denno, *Health Officer*, 102;
§341, of the text.

1 Brown, in JAI, XLIII, 158.
2 Ray, in JAI, XLVII, 292.
3 Parsons, in AA, XVIII, 45, note.

village of the bridegroom, and the bride's relatives and friends attend. The bride's face is painted bright red. She is seated on a log in an open square where everyone can see her. The relatives of the bridegroom first carry across the square beautiful *Dracæna* leaves and poisoned arrows, and hand them over to the relatives of the bride as a token of peace between the two villages. Then ceremonial mats are trailed across, and after each mat a tusk-pig is led by a rope tied to its leg. Each pig is tied to a post till the full price has been paid. A return present, consisting of one tusk-pig, is made to the bridegroom's friends, conch-shells are blown and the bridegroom goes over to claim his bride. He sticks a poisoned arrow into the mat she has about her shoulders. This action signifies that he has the power of life and death over her, and also that he must defend her with his life." At the death of a husband, his brother has first claim to the widow, who is paid for again with pigs, but there is no second marriage-ceremony.[4]

At a Sea Dyak wedding two iron staves are laid on the ground where the bride and groom take their places, probably as a sort of insulation from the spirits, while in the hands of each are placed a cigarette and a quid of betel. The priest then takes a pair of fowls and waves them above the young people, invoking blessing. Then he knocks the heads of the couple together thrice, whereupon the groom puts betel in the mouth of his bride and a cigarette between her lips, while she later does the same with him, thus recognizing him as a husband. Among the Alfurs in Celebes the groom takes a piece of betel and chews it with lime, gives it to a young man who further masticates it, and then to the bride for the same treatment. No one may spit out any of the juice.[5] All the information that could be obtained concerning the marriage-ceremonies of one of the Mindoro tribes was that "the old folks get together and talk."[6]

In accordance with the marriage-customs of the Kickapoo Indians, "the young man goes to the woman's lodge at evening and spends the night with her. This he does for two or three or more evenings and nights, leaving each time at morning. This marks the beginning of their career as man and wife. The next stage in the ceremony is a visit to the bride by a woman who stands in relation to the husband as a sister's daughter. She might be called his niece in English; she certainly would be if she was really the daughter of a sister. She takes to the bride a horse and all kinds of presents."[7] In another case, "if the presents of a young warrior were accepted by his mistress, she was considered as having agreed to become his wife, and, without further explanation to her family, went to his hut, which became her home, and the ceremony was ended."[8] In California, "people are said to have been married and parted without ceremony, mothers taking their children with them, and men often took whole families of sisters for their wives."[9] Again, "marriage among the Pima is entered into without ceremony and is never considered binding."[10]

Among more developed peoples we find a different situation. In the Chinese Li Ki or Ritual of Propriety it is stated that the extreme manifestation of reverence is illustrated in the great rite of marriage, when the bridegroom in his square-topped cap goes in person to meet the bride. "The duke said, 'I wish that I could say I agree with you, but for the bridegroom in his square-

4 Sebbelov, in AA, XV, 278-279.
5 Wilken, in VG, I, 545-546.
6 Worcester, *Philippine Isl.*, I, 413.
7 Jones, in AA, XV, 332-333.
8 Mooney, in HAI, II, 301.
9 In HAI, I, 397.
10 Hodge, in HAI, II, 252.

topped cap to go in person to meet the bride,—is it not making too much (of the ceremony)?' Confucius looked startled, changed countenance, and said, '(Such a marriage) is the union of (the representatives of) two different surnames in friendship and love, in order to continue the posterity of the former sages, and to furnish those who shall preside at the sacrifices to heaven and earth, at those in the ancestral temple, and at those at the altars to the spirits of the land and grain;—how can your lordship say that the ceremony is made too great?' "11 A Hindu marriage is a kind of drama in three acts. At the age of about nine or ten and before he is really marriageable, a Hindu boy is made to go through the second matrimonial act with a girl of about seven, his previous betrothal having constituted the first, and cohabitation at the age of fifteen or sixteen with his child-wife at the age of twelve constituting the third. "The second is the religious and legal ceremony, and is a most tedious process, involving large fees to the priests and festivities prolonged for many days, at a cost, in the case of the rich people, of perhaps 100,000 rupees [a rupee is valued at about thirty-two cents]. Often the savings of a whole lifetime are so spent. This is one of the greatest evils of Indian society. Every well-to-do parent is compelled to squander large sums on mere idlers and pleasure-seekers, instead of giving the money as a grant in aid to the newly-married pair on first starting in life. He knows, in fact, that if he were to allow the wedding to be conducted with an eye to economy he would sink irretrievably in the estimation of his friends and caste-fellows. He would never be able to hold up his head again in his own social circle. Nor must it be supposed that he spends his money unwillingly. On the contrary, the more lavishly he spends the more pride and satisfaction he afterwards feels in looking back on what he regards as the most meritorious act of his life."12 Thus does vanity reinforce the mores.

For marriage the Homeric Greeks had no formal ceremony of words: "the feast and the sacrifice which accompanied every feast were the only formalities of which we learn; very likely the hand of the bride was placed in that of her husband, but the poet has no occasion to mention this." The feast was the marriage, just as the funeral-feast was the funeral. "As a rule it was held at the home of the bride's father, and the bride was then conducted to her husband's home. Such a procession is represented on the Shield of Achilles."13 Among the Jews, formal betrothal was considered proper in rabbinical days and came to be the real wedding. There were three modes: (1) by gift of valuables or money, the smallest coin sufficing; later, a ring, which should not be considered as a pledge to marry at a future time but as a pledge of good faith in marriage to duty as construed then by the mores; (2) by a document; and (3) by copulation. Words and acts before two witnesses were required, with the formula: "Be consecrated to me" or, later, "Be consecrated to me according to the law of Moses and Israel." Each mode of wedding was of equal validity, but in the third century A.D. the third was forbidden. The three ways corresponded to appropriation of property. A feast was given in the house of the bride and then the husband and friends gave her presents. The bride remained some time, regularly a year, in the house of her father; if a widow, thirty days. Then came the real wedding, or delivery of the bride; the groom came for her and took her to his house. In the evening the bride

11 Legge, *Li Ki*, pt. IV, Bks. XI-XLVI, 264-265.

12 Monier-Williams, *Brāhmanism*, 379-380.
13 Seymour, *Hom. Age*, 146.

was led to the bridal chambers; later a tent into which the pair entered was ceremonially substituted, while still later the survival existed of using a scarf for the tent.[14]

Among the Romans, on the day before her marriage the girl laid aside the *toga prætexta* which she had worn up till then, dedicated it and her toys to the gods, and received the woman's attire, the *toga pura* and *tunica recta,* the *vittæ laneæ* and the veil which was called *flammeum.* At the same time her hair was cut and parted with a *hasta cælibaris.* This act was performed by the *pronubæ,* or women who as a good omen were present at the first marriage and at the wedding were busied about the bride. They led the trembling and reluctant bride to the man, encouraged her, managed the *dextrarum junctio,* accompanied her at the home-coming, had her lifted over the threshold, prepared the *lectus genialis* and put the bride to bed upon it. Each act of dressing had its analogy in the *tirocinium fori* (first public appearance) of the boy. It thus appears that the Roman maidens were married at their entrance into womanhood. Then for the first time were they regarded as grown-up; before this they were children. It was the duty of the father to give his nubile daughter in marriage as soon as possible, so that her youth might not be lost. The age which was regularly regarded as the time of puberty for the girl was the twelfth year, a reckoning which reaches back into antiquity and which was maintained until the latest imperial age.[15]

§371. Survivals and Symbols.

ON the wedding-day, among the Roro-speaking tribes, "a party of men belonging to the bridegroom's local group but not including the bridegroom, surround the house of the girl's parents and carry it by mimic assault, with great fury and shouting. The bride rushes out, and runs away as fast as she can, and although she is soon overtaken and caught, she defends herself to the best of her ability, with hands, feet and teeth. Meanwhile a sham fight rages between the adherents of the bride and bridegroom. In the midst of the commotion is the bride's mother armed with a wooden club or digging stick, striking at every inanimate object within reach and shouting curses on the ravishers of her daughter. Finding this useless, she collapses, weeping for the loss of her child. The other women of the village join in the weeping. The girl's mother should keep up the appearance of extravagant grief for three days, and she alone of the girl's relations does not accompany the bride to her father-in-law's house."[1] Further survivals of capture and hostility occur on the morning after the wedding, when "the bride's father takes up his stand outside the house of the bridegroom's father and, although he has already been paid-up, proceeds to indulge in abuse. He has to be pacified by the present of a dog. Three days later the bride's mother visits her to weep and groan until a pig is killed for her. Then her bewailment gives place to praise of the generosity of her son-in-law and his family."[2]

The most essential item of the ceremonial wedding-proceedings in East Africa is usually the conducting home of the bride, who is generally carried. "In some localities mock fights take place during the procession to the bridegroom's

14 Freisen, *Canon. Eherechts,* 92; Judges, XIV, 10; Ruth, III, 9.
15 Rossbach, *Röm. Ehe,* 274.

1 Seligmann, *Melanesians,* 268-270.
2 Parsons, in AA, XVIII, 48.

hut; among the Wabunga pretence is made of enticing the girl, small gifts being made at intervals on the way. These practices are reminiscent of wife robbery in former times, and in fact although forcible capture of wives is not actually recognized to-day, it does occur, and mock abduction as a form of marriage ceremony is not uncommon."[3] Among the Akamba the groom, when he gets to the gate of the girl's village, takes hold of her and leads her off. The following day the girls of the village and her clan go off to his village to wail. "They cry all day and sleep that night in the bridegroom's hut. They sleep there three days; on the fourth day they return and the bridegroom gives them each a present of beads; they will not leave him alone with his wife until he has paid them to go."[4] After the wedding-feast the Kabyle bride is dressed and a charm suspended about her neck to preserve her from all evil. She is veiled and lifted upon a mule by a negro, if one is to be found in the village.[5]

At a Yakut wedding the sister of the bride keeps her hair covered.[6] The marriage-rite among the Chukchi consists of sacrificing to the hearth and, generally, of anointing with red ochre instead of blood. The Samoyed couple sit side by side, and the bridegroom feeds the bride meat and wine. "This is held to be the essential symbol of the consummation of the marriage."[7]

"The remarkable peculiarity amongst the Lolos [of West China] is that invariably, some days after marriage, the bride escapes and runs home to her father's house. The husband sends presents to her father to induce her to return, but often she will not go back without much persuasion; and in the event of several requests for her return being unheeded, the husband is permitted to go for her, and beat her until she yields."[8] Good form demands, among the Manchu, that the mother and daughter break out into tears at the marriage festival, a custom which popular wit has characterized by the following adage: "A bride, upon leaving her parents' house, laughs inwardly when she weeps; a rejected candidate inwardly weeps when he laughs."[9] In the coiffure of a Chinese bride is put a silver hair-pin with a head of precious stone; "such an instrument has been considered from the highest antiquity an indispensable object for consummating a girl's marriage."[10] A peculiar custom is the so-called brawl-room: "During the first three nights the newly married couple are constantly disturbed by practical jokes executed by relations (in some provinces even by complete strangers), everybody trying to obtain clothes or other necessary or valuable objects from the bridal chamber, which the groom has to redeem the next day with wine, cake, etc."[11] According to the *Li Ki* the ceremonies of marriage are symbolic of the beginning of a line that shall last for ages, through bringing together parties of different surnames, and of the position of the woman in the new household. "The gentleman went in person to meet the bride, the man taking the initiative and not the woman,—according to the idea that regulates the relation between the strong and the weak (in all nature). . . . In passing out from the great gate (of her father's house), he precedes, and she follows, and with this the right relation between husband and wife commences. The woman follows (and obeys) the man;—

3 Dundas, C., in JAI, LI, 252-253.
4 Hobley, *A-Kamba*, 63.
5 Hanoteau et Letourneux, *Kabylie*, II, 217.
6 Sieroshevski, *Yakuts* (Russ.), 562.
7 Czaplicka, *Aborig. Siberia*, 80, 124-125.
8 Henry, in JAI, XXXIII, 106.

9 Grube, in *Berl. Mus.*, VII, 21.
10 DeGroot, *Relig. Syst. China*, I, 54.
11 Von Mollendorff, *Family Law of Chinese*, 28-29; Williams, *Middle Kingdom*, I, 789.

in her youth, she follows her father and elder brother; when married, she follows her husband; when her husband is dead, she follows her son. . . , Husband and wife ate together of the same victim,—thus declaring that they were of the same rank. Hence while the wife had (herself) no rank, she was held to be of the rank of her husband, and she took her seat according to the position belonging to him. . . . The father and mother-in-law then entered their apartment, where she set before them a single dressed pig,—thus showing the obedient duty of (their son's) wife. . . . Next day, the parents united in entertaining the young wife, and when the ceremonies of their severally pledging her in a single cup, and her pledging them in return, had been performed, they descended by the steps on the west, and she by those on the east,—thus showing that she would take the mother's place in the family. . . . Thus the ceremony establishing the young wife in her position; (followed by) that showing her obedient service (of her husband's parents); and both succeeded by that showing how she now occupied the position of continuing the family line;—all served to impress her with a sense of the deferential duty proper to her. . . . In this way when the deferential obedience of the wife was complete, the internal harmony was secured; and when the internal harmony was secured, the long continuance of the family could be calculated on. Therefore the ancient kings attached such importance (to the marriage ceremonies)."[12]

The arranging of a Palaung marriage is a piece of elaborate acting from beginning to end, and although the father and mother may be delighted with the choice that their daughter has made, they must pretend to be very much annoyed and disturbed; and the girl, though happy at the prospect, must give way to copious tears. "On the day of the blessing the bride weeps at intervals all through the day, both at the house of the bridegroom's father and in her father's home," and she weeps loudly when she reaches her new home, crying out, "A tiger has caught me, a tiger has caught me." As it was the custom some years ago in England to interpolate Latin phrases in an eloquent and studied speech, so here is it the custom of the Pa-jaus or go-betweens to use whole sentences in Shan—"indeed many of the wedding-speeches are almost entirely in that language—with many expressions from Burmese, and even from the ancient Pāli, the language of the Buddhist scriptures. One sentence may be in Palaung, followed by another, meaning exactly the same, in Shan; and the Burmese and Pāli words are sprinkled all through." The day of the blessing by the Elders, which is the final ceremony of the marriage, is chosen by a wise man, according to the days of the week on which the bride and bridegroom were born. "A chosen groom's relative will attend to the tea; he will go to the head-man of the village, to ask for the loan of the dishes, the cups, the plates, and the carpets, which belong to the village, and are either kept at the monastery or at the head-man's house. . . . On the day before the wedding, young girls, who from childhood have been the companions of the bride, go to the house where she is staying, in order to weep with her. In fact the bride and her friends sometimes spend together more than one day in tears. . . . Then they sob and cry, and often it is no pretence at all, and they are really much distressed when a favourite companion marries. It is in vain that the bride assures them that she will love them just the same, and that marriage will make no difference to her; but they all know that marriage will

---

12 Legge, *Li Ki*, 259, 428 ff., 439 ff.

make a very great deal of difference in their lives, for girls are always together, and the young married women keep by themselves, so that as soon as a girl is married she can no longer join her unmarried girl-companions. At this time it is considered the proper behaviour for the bride to show that she has no appetite. If she eats at all, she should do so very sparingly, and only when her friends insist that she must take the food that they have brought to her. . . . When the old men have smoked and have been given food, the Pa-jau comes forward, bearing in his hand the hood of the bride and the turban of the bridegroom. These must belong to the young couple, but it is not necessary to take those they are actually wearing. The Pa-jau, assisted by the mother of the bridegroom, folds the hood into an oblong shape, then winds the turban round it. As he is doing this he says, 'May these children live peacefully together! for they are now united as this turban and hood are bound together.' The combined hood and turban are then set on a layer of tobacco in a large lacquer bowl. . . . There is very little sleep for any one that night, and early next morning the young couple go to eat their first meal together in the house of the bride's father. . . . The newly married pair go into each house, while the other young people, who act as an escort, wait outside. When every house where there is an old man has been visited—and sometimes the blessing of a good old woman is asked for as well—the young people return to the house of the bridegroom's father. From this time the bride is treated as a daughter by her father- and mother-in-law. . . . The bridegroom generally spends the second night, after the bride has been brought to live in his house, with his bachelor friends, returning to his home and his bride before dawn. In the evening, and for several days afterwards, when he meets any girls they pretend to beat him, saying, 'O married man! run away home.' "[13]

"Among people," comments Wilken,[14] "who look at forcible abduction as a lawful way of attaining possession of a woman, the parents, in order to safeguard their daughters against it and to prevent their own plans concerning her from being upset by others, can do nothing else than take recourse to the means of child-marriage." Universal in the Indian Archipelago is the custom of feigned abduction, for however satisfactorily the preliminaries have been settled, the girl must be ostensibly abducted. On the island of Sumba the parents on both sides arrange the marriage and come to a settlement about the price; then the groom is told to be on guard at a certain place in the bush with several of his friends. The girl is sent thither to get water or the like, and is abducted. At the first news of the abduction the relatives of the girl arm themselves and follow the abductor, but they arrange it so that they never overtake him anywhere else than at his house. There the girl who has been ostensibly abducted is demanded back, is refused, and the previously arranged bride-price is paid. It appears that this public ceremony belongs to the marriage of the more prominent. In the Lampong district of Sumatra the young man abducts the girl, with the connivance of her parents, and hides her in his house. "In the space before the public assembly-house there takes place a sort of tournament between both parties, and a cock-fight is held in which they take care that the party of the father of the bride shall be conquered; following that, the amount of the bride-price is determined." Veiling accom-

13 Milne, *Eastern Clan*, 134, 141, 149, 151-152, 158, 168, 402, 418.

14 In VG, I, 153-154, 154-155, 553-557, 558, 559-562.

panies abduction, the girl being covered so as to be unrecognizable.[15] The
closing act of the marriage-ceremony in some places is the removal by the husband of all his wife's ornaments and jewels, which she never again resumes
unless she wishes to commit that supreme crime in the eyes of her husband,
of appearing to wish that she were a maiden again. Wilken mentions a number
of symbolic acts, such as stepping on the foot, taking the bride on the lap
or putting a child on her lap, bumping the heads of bride and groom together,
possibly so as to bring the souls together—the head being the seat of the soul—
and joining the right hands, which last is done much after the ancient Roman
method.

On certain of the Philippine Islands the groom's and bride's messengers
fight, the former always winning the bloodless duel.[16] In the Gilbert Islands,
"the bride's kinsfolk would have been much disappointed and ashamed had
she surrendered herself without demur to the embraces of the bridegroom,
for that would have denoted a lack of modesty unseemly in a well-born
maiden."[17] After the Tsimshian Indian's suit has been accepted, he takes a
number of armed slaves and embarks with them in a canoe to the bride's house.
"As soon as her clan relatives see them coming, they arm themselves with clubs
and stone hammers, and rush down to the landing-place. They break the canoe,
and try to drive off the companions of the young man." They fight seriously,
and sometimes one of the slaves is killed. "This foretells that the couple will
never part. After the fight is over, the bridegroom and his companions are
carried into the bride's house. Then her friends strew on the companions of the
bridegroom eagle down. . . . Her father puts on his headdress and dances,
while her friends sing. Then a feast is given, during which the young man
pays the remainder of the purchase money. . . . Her father and brothers give
the groom a new canoe in place of the one which was broken in the morning.
Then the bride is carried down to the canoe, and she departs with her husband to his village, where they live."[18]

"Jewish law emphasizes in the strongest manner the *copula carnalis;*" this
is the essential idea of marriage. Advance of the mores made this into mere
ceremonial use of a tent and then a scarf, as was mentioned in the preceding
section. A similar survival exists in Germany, in taking off a shoe or loosening
the girdle; now the pair retire to a special room and take a meal together.[19]
The Jews of today also have the symbolic "penny purchase," though in the
old Mosaic law there was no bride-price. This is aligned to the wedding-usage
in Little Russia, where as a prank the youngest brother of the bride sells her
nominally for a couple of ducats.[20] The marriage-ceremony of the East
Iranians consisted in the recitation of prayers and holy formulas while the
hands of the youth and his bride were joined together. "The joining of hands
made the union a legal contract."[21] Among the Beduins the groom cuts the
throat of a lamb before the tent of the bride's father; the marriage is complete when blood falls to the ground. Soon after sunset the groom shuts himself up in a special tent outside of the camp, the bride runs about it and is
caught by some women who make her enter it, the groom helping to force
her in. She cries out as a proof of maiden timidity. In some cases the bride-

15 Quoted from Riedel, De sluik- en
kroesharige rassen tusschen Selebes en Papua,
448.
16 Worcester, *Philippine Isl.*, 492 ff.
17 Grimble, in JAI, LI, 31.

18 Boas, in BAE, XXXI, 531-532.
19 Freisen, *Canon. Eherechts*, 96; Levit.,
XVIII, 10; Deut., XXII, 28.
20 Friedberg, *Eheschliessung*, 20, note.
21 Geiger, *Ostiran. Kultur*, 242.

groom rides up to the tent of his bride and swings his whip over a "bride-doll" which is offered to him. In a tribe near Nazareth the groom's father gives the bride's father a green leaf and calls on all present to witness. Some tribes regard it as scandalous for the girl's father to take a "daughter's price." At Mt. Sinai the lover wears for three days a sprig of green given him by her father; the girl must pass the first night with him but may leave the next day, whereupon she is captured.[22] In Moslem law a morning-gift is required for valid marriage; it may be a survival of purchase, though it is given by the man to his wife, the amount being set down in the contract.[23]

At Athens the bride fled to the hearth, was taken therefrom and carried to her husband's house, where her hair was cut off as a sign of servitude.[24] The ingredients, especially sesame, of Greek wedding-cakes were thought to have vital relation to the future fertility of marriage. This was unquestionably the case with quince, which Solon ordered the bride to eat before receiving the groom in the bridal chambers.[25] Also at a Greek marriage a child of free-born parents, crowned with acanthus and acorns, carried about a basket of bread. As he offered this he said: "I have fled from the bad; I have found the better," meaning the acorn food given up for bread.[26] At Rome the bride went to the house of the groom and was led to the hearth before the images of the lares and penates. After having sacrificed and uttered prayer-formulas, the young pair ate together a sacrificial cake (panis farreus, libum farreum) in the presence of the Flamen Dialis, the Pontifex Maximus, and ten witnesses. "It was especially the joint eating of the cake that made marriage. So in old Athens, as a seal of the marriage tie, bride and groom ate a sesame-cake, in India a common meal. Still to-day, here and there in Germany, in Thüringen and the Harz Mountains, the engaged pair, especially on the morning of the wedding, must eat out of the same dish, while the custom of the inevitable bridal cake, that always must be cut by the young woman, is in England a survival of the same usage. . . . In place of eating of the same food sometimes the drinking of the same drink appears. Up to the beginning of this century, in Sweden, especially in the northern provinces, the so-called 'brudköp dricka' belonged to the ceremonial of the wedding, and today in Serbia the bridal couple must three times drink a little red wine out of the same glass."[27] Macedonian marriage-custom prescribes that a loaf of bread be cut with a sword and then eaten by the couple.

Rossbach,[28] who reports the preceding case, says that the Roman libum farreum was employed not only at the confarreatio but frequently in the cult also. It was a sacrifice to the gods who presided over marriage, not a symbol of the table-companionship which took place in marriage. It was carried in front of the procession to the altar, then thrown into the sacrificial fire and burnt, but not eaten. As a symbol of fertility the bride was set upon the phallus of a Priapus or in the lap of a phallic god. The pronuba led the bride to the groom and joined their right hands; this, thinks the author, was not symbolic but a token of power. The bride spoke the formula, ubi tu Gajus, ibi ego Gaja, before the house of the bridegroom, rubbed the door with fat, and decorated it with woollen bands; then she was lifted over the threshold and "with fire and water taken into the community of the household." The employ-

22 Burckhardt, Bedouins, 61, 62, 149; Ratzel, Vkde., III, 152.
23 Tornauw, Moslim. Recht, 74.
24 Lippert, Kgchte., II, 99.

25 Blümner, Griech. Privatalterth., 276-277.
26 Foucart, Assoc. Rélig., 74, note.
27 Wilken, in VG, I, 533-535.
28 Röm. Ehe, 107, 115, 264, 308, 369, 370.

ment of fire and water was so common at weddings that *aqua et igni accipi* was used even in later times for marriage-celebration. Water and fire signified the community of hearth and house. "Servius says that even in his time torches were carried ahead, while on the other hand the old custom of washing with water the feet of the betrothed was discontinued, although water was still brought by a boy or girl from a spring." Similarly in Vedic India, the nuptial-fire which was never to be extinguished went before the pair, while fire and water were employed when the wife entered the house. "The children who, with the Bretons, are put in the nuptial bed of the spouses, recall the Vedic usage of putting a handsome child on the breast of the bride for the same augury of fecundity."[29]

Among the ancient Scandinavians, a ring of relatives and witnesses was formed around the couple, whereupon the representative put to both groom and bride the question whether they would marry one another, and then through some symbolic act, probably by passing over of sword or ring, consigned to the husband rights over the bride. The fiancé then placed a ring on the bride's finger; sometimes the two were tied together with a thread, as a sign that their destinies were inseparable. The bride received from the man also a shoe which she put on and was then regarded as under his power. It must be a right shoe; if the bride could fool the man into giving her a left shoe there would be woman rule, so-called slipper-rule. The couple drank a goblet together, first pledging Thor, the protector of marriage and the home, and then Odin and the other gods. The bride was led to the room where the groom waited. By touching her body with the sacred hammer the marriage was consecrated and the vows strengthened. Finally, after the couple had gotten into bed and were covered up before witnesses, the marriage was legally concluded.[30] From Martin Luther's "Table-Talk" Friedberg[31] takes a reported instance which supports the theory of the shoe as a symbol of authority. In old German marriage the bride had to conceal her hair which she had hitherto worn flowing as a sign of her freedom; with its concealment began the husband's rule over her.[32] According to old Portuguese law, a maid must leave her hair flowing, a married woman must gather it in a knot as a token of conjugal submission; a widow covered it with a cap.[33] When the Princess of the Asturias was married according to Spanish custom, a white satin ribbon, called a yoke, was tied about the necks of the couple, the knot being made between them signifying their union.[34] In the wedding-practices of Berry, a district in the heart of France, the bride is quite as unmistakably bribed as is the Fijian. Barred out, the bridegroom's party sing to her: "Open the door, open, Marie, my darling. I have some beautiful presents for you. Ah! my love, let us enter." And then the song goes on to specify all the charming things they have for her—ribbons and lace, a fine apron, a hundred pins, a cross of gold.[35]

In the rotogravure section of the New York *Times* for August 15, 1926, is a picture of a bride and groom jumping over a bench. The legend reads: "Jumping into Matrimony: The bride and bridegroom, after their marriage at the Parish Church at Alnmouth, England, follow the old village custom of leaping over a bench placed by fishermen outside the door of the church."

---

29 Gubernatis, *Usi Nuz.*, 175, 178-179.
30 Wisen, *Nordens Forntid*, 18; Weinhold, *Altnord. Leben*, 243, 247.
31 *Eheschliessung*, 28, note.
32 Stammler, *Stellung d. Frauen*, 32.

33 Lang, "Portuguese in New Engl.," in *Jour. Amer. Folk Lore*, V, 9-18.
34 N. Y. *Times*, Feb. 14, 1901.
35 Parsons, in AA, XVIII, 46-47, quoting George Sand, *La Mare au Diable*.

§372. Religious Aspects.

For good fortune, states a law of Manu, there should be recitation of benedictory texts and sacrifices at a marriage.[1] Should there be an eclipse when the
Palaung wedding-procession is setting out, "it would be considered so unlucky
that the proceedings for the day would be stopped: to see a barking deer, or
to hear one call, would also be considered unlucky; or to hear a dog howl. On
the other hand, to hear cats caterwauling, or to see a cat cross the road in front
of a wedding-procession, would be considered lucky."[2] According to ancient
Chinese tradition, the day and month of the marriage should be announced to
the spirits of ancestors with purification and fasting. "One must not marry a
wife of the same surname with himself. Hence, in buying a concubine, if he
do not know her surname, he must consult the tortoise-shell about it."[3]

The Chaldæans feared spirits at a wedding. The priest blessed the couple
and said: "All which is bad in this man do ye [gods] put far away and give
him strength. Do thou man give thy virility and let this woman be thy spouse
and do thou woman give that which makes thee woman and let this man be
thy husband." The next morning a ritual was performed to chase away the
evil spirits.[4] In a Hebrew marriage the rabbi joins the hands of the pair and
blesses a cup of wine from which they sip; the groom puts a ring on the
bride's finger and says, "Behold, thou art consecrated unto me with this ring,
according to the rites of Moses and Israel." The rabbi then reads the marriage-
contract and blesses another cup of wine with seven blessings, all about luck.[5]
In Homer the gods presided over marriage but no priest or sacrifice was
needed.[6] Euripides[7] has Orestes say that mortals are happy who marry wisely,
while misfortune betides those who do not, both in public and in private; to
which the chorus, giving the opinion of women on marriage, replies, "Women always cross the fortunes of men to their sorrow." Electra opines: "He who, looking at wealth or rank marries a wicked woman is a fool. A humble home-com-
panion is better than a proud one, if good." The chorus answers that chance
rules a woman's marriage; some turn out well, some ill. "There is unmistakable
evidence that a marriage ceremony of a religious nature existed, and that
this ceremony stood in close relation to a part of the ritual of the mysteries. In
fact, the marriage was, as it were, a reproduction by the bride and bridegroom
of a scene from the divine life, i.e., from the mystic drama. The formula: 'I
escaped evil; I found better,' was repeated by the celebrant who was initiated
in the Phrygian mysteries; and the same formula was pronounced as part of
the Athenian marriage ceremony. Another formula: 'I have drunk from the
kymbalon' was pronounced by the initiated, and drinking from the same cup has
been proved to have formed part of a ceremony performed in the temple by
the betrothed pair."[8] In Attica the wedding was a religious festival, a holy
consecration of marriage, at which the gods presided.

In Rome, "if purchase were omitted, there was lacking the consent of the
father or guardian; if the wedding customs were omitted, there was lacking
the consent of the gods." No marriage in olden times was concluded without

---

1 Bühler, *Manu*, V, 152.
2 Milne, *Eastern Clan*, 160-161.
3 Legge, *Li Ki*, I, 78.
4 Maspero, *Hist. Anc.*, I, 736.
5 Pick, "Marriage among the Hebrews," in
Schaff, *Relig. Encyc.*, 1416.

6 *Odyssey*, IV, 7; VI, 180; XV, 26.
7 *Orestes*, 602 ff.; *Electra*, 1097 ff.
8 Ramsay, in *Hastings's Dict. Bible*, 129-
130.

sacrifices. A marriage based on *confarreatio* was a true sacrament. The formalities of marriage were clung to even to the point of utter superstition. "The *tunica recta* was white in color and woven in the ancient manner. So superstitious were they that the way of weaving the wedding-clothes could not be changed." What occurred without the gods had no power and no fortunate consequences, what happened against their will was a transgression and brought evil. "As in the old Roman state-affairs no important act was valid which had not received consecration by the gods, so in marriage it was essential to interrogate the gods, consult the auspices and offer sacrifice." Servius said that nothing was so unfavorable for marriage as thunder and earthquake. "There can scarcely be any doubt that sitting on a skin was united with the religious acts of the *confarreatio*. This is indicated by the veiling of the head, which was indispensable at every sacrifice, that distraction and evil omens might be avoided." It is said that since at one time the patricians at Rome had under their control the auspices and other religious functions necessary to marriage with *manus*, their marriages were in consequence of greater sanctity than the plebeian; this was one ground of rank-distinction. Auspices at marriage ceased in Cicero's time, though the form was kept up, it being formally stated that nothing unfavorable to the marriage had taken place. "Toward the end of the pagan imperial age Roman marriage had no longer any religious element; only the civil remained. Christianity restored the religious element, which at first had place only in the discretion of the individual, but later became more and more fixed and finally became necessary."[9]

§373. Defensive and Propitiatory Measures.

WITH all their priestcraft, the Brahmans never claimed power to marry.[1] One reads in the ancient Chinese *Ritual of Propriety:* "When a son had done everything (for his sacrifice) that he could do himself, he proceeded to seek assistance from abroad; and this came through the rites of marriage. Hence the language of a ruler, when about to marry a wife, was:—'I beg you, O ruler, to give me your elegant daughter, to share this small state with my poor self, to do service in the ancestral temple, and at the altars to (the spirits of) the land and grain.' This underlay his seeking for that assistance (from abroad). In sacrificing, husband and wife had their several duties which they personally attended to."[2] In Fuhkien, "when the lucky day for the wedding comes, the guests assemble in the bridegroom's house to celebrate it, where also sedans, a band of music, and porters are in readiness. The courier, who acts as guide to the chair-bearers, takes the lead, and in order to prevent the onset of malicious demons lurking by the road, a baked hog or large piece of pork is carried in front, that the procession may safely pass while these hungry souls are devouring the meat." When the bride takes her seat in the marriage sedan, she is completely concealed. "As she approaches the door the bridegroom conceals himself, but the go-between brings forward a young child to salute her, while going to seek the closeted bridegroom. He approaches with becoming gravity and opens the sedan to hand out his bride, she still retaining the hat and mantle; they approach the ancestral tablet, which they reverence with three

9 Rossbach, *Röm. Ehe*, 49, 56, 92, 113, 115, 119 ff., 223, 254-255, 255-257, 276; Cicero, *De Div.*, Bk. I, ch. XVI, 1-3; Moscatelli, *Condizione della donna*, 103.

1 Bühler, *Manu*, III, 20-35, 43, 44.
2 Legge, *Li Ki*, 238.

bows, and then seat themselves at a table upon which are two cups of spirits. The go-between serves them, though the bride can only make the motions of drinking, as the large hat completely covers her face. They soon retire into a chamber, where the husband takes the hat and mantle from his wife, and sees her, perhaps, for the first time in his life."[3] It is still customary in some provinces of Japan, on the occasion of the marriage of a very unpopular farmer, to make the bridegroom feast Jizō. "A band of sturdy young men force their way into the house, carrying with them a stone image of the divinity, borrowed from the highway or from some neighboring cemetery. A large crowd follows them. They deposit the image in the guest room, and they demand that ample offerings of food and of saké be made to it at once. This means, of course, a big feast for themselves, and it is more than dangerous to refuse. All the uninvited guests must be served till they can neither eat nor drink any more. The obligation to give such a feast is not only a public rebuke: it is also a lasting public disgrace."[4]

"The Jewish marriage," asserts Freisen,[5] "had no ecclesiastical character. The blessings pronounced at betrothal and delivery of the bride prove nothing to the contrary. They only gave character of publicity to the ceremony of marriage. They are not priestly blessings and are not essential to the validity of the marriage." Bergel[6] corroborates this and states that while a certain religious tinge was given to the ceremony, there were no priests present, everything being arranged and performed by the family without requiring any ecclesiastical consecration. In Greece, "marriages were generally, though not always contracted at the divine altars and confirmed by oaths, the assistance of a priest, however, not being requisite. Before the marriage was solemnized the gods were consulted and their assistance implored by prayers and sacrifices, which were usually offered to some of the deities that superintended the union of the sexes, by the parents or other relations of the persons to be married. . . . From the Homeric age we have no instances of marriages being contracted with sacrifices and religious rites, but we must not therefore take for granted that they were entirely wanting."[7] Later, marriage received its religious consecration chiefly through a great sacrifice, which occurred on the day of the wedding and was followed by a feast in the house of the bride's father.[8]

Rossbach[9] speaks of a nuptial sacrifice by which the Roman marriage was concluded in sight of the gods, and sums up the sense of a relief on a sarcophagus as follows: "The betrothed, with the assistance of Juno, goddess of marriage, solemnly make the covenant of their love, to which Venus and the Graces are favorable, by prayer and sacrifice, before the gods. By the aid of Juno love becomes a legitimate marriage." Before the sacrifice was made, the procession of participants walked around the altar from left to right, a boy carrying the wedding-water and torches, and perhaps also the spelt-cake. "Probably we are not amiss when we see in the *certa et solemnia verba* holy formulas which were directed to the gods for their blessing and consent to the marriage about to be performed. The gods to whom these applied could not have been other than the usual marriage-gods Juno, Ceres, Tellus, and Mars Picumnus. . . . These formulas were apparently once used at every mar-

---

3 Williams, *Middle Kingdom*, I, 787, 788.
4 Hearn, *Out of the East*, 259-260.
5 *Canon. Eherechts*, 95.
6 *Eheverhältnisse*, 19 ff.

7 Westermarck, *Marriage*, 426 (one vol. ed., quoted); II, 575 (three vol. ed.).
8 Blümner, *Griech. Privatalterth.*, 271 ff.
9 *Röm. Ehe*, 107, 109, 111, 112, 128, 268, 279.

riage, but later they were maintained only by the patricians in their ancient form (at the *confarreatio*). The significance of the *certa et solemnia verba* was that the betrothed were united in the presence of the gods and placed under their protection." The author notes that at a Hindu wedding certain holy words were spoken, consisting in part of prayers to the gods and in part of responses by the betrothed pair concerning the purpose of their marriage. In the early days there was no mention of priests being present at a marriage; each paterfamilias was priest in his own household and had the right to apply to the gods himself, and, without the intervention of a priest, to offer sacrifice and prayers. As the ancients feared sorcery most when they were happy and prosperous, marriage was an occasion for the employment of devices to ward off magic.

§374. The Continuance of Precaution.

In southwest Victoria the married pair are kept apart for two months, during which time they may not see one another; the bride keeps her head covered. They sleep on opposite sides of the same fire, but a man stays with him and a woman with her.[1] In Geelvink Bay, New Guinea, the newly married pass the first four nights sitting up back to back, awake; they sleep in the daytime, separating before light lest the wife see the husband's face.[2] No sexual intercourse is permitted the Papuan bride and groom till they have planted two gardens and fattened up a pig and sold it, that is to say, for one year after marriage. At the end of that time, "when a feast is given the girl has connection with a man not her husband and is then free to the husband."[3] In German Melanesia, when all the preliminaries to marriage have been made, the bridegroom goes into the bush for three months, where he lives on the fruits of the forest. During this time he may not be seen by any member of the family or village; whoever sees him is forced to give him a present. The girl is taken by her mother to the man's house, where he gives a big feast. For completion of the wedding the young husband must change his name and take a new one.[4] Among the Roro-speaking tribes, "although the young couple have been reconciled to each other, cohabitation is not supposed to begin for a few weeks, and the boy still sleeps in the *maroa* [men's house], while his wife sleeps in her father-in-law's house. It appeared, however, that in most cases intercourse takes place in or near the gardens soon after marriage. It was stated that formerly it was not customary for a woman to have children until her garden was bearing well, that is to say, until she had been married from one to two years."[5] In Pentecost, New Hebrides, "when she first goes to live in the house of her husband's mother, and if she is young it may be for several years afterwards, the girl will not speak to her husband, who does not live in the house but continues to spend all his time in the club-house. The man may sometimes come into the house to give food to his mother but even this would be exceptional. When the girl is old enough the husband will tempt his wife to speak to him and may offer her food but so long as she does not speak there are no sexual relations between them. This state of things may last for years and it was said that a wife would sometimes die without having spoken to her husband, in which

1 Cunow, *Australneger*, 98.
2 Wilken, in VG,. I, 501.
3 Liston-Blyth, in JAI, LIII, 469.

4 Von Pfeil, *Südsee*, 29, 30.
5 Seligmann, *Melanesians*, 270.

case marital relations between the pair would never have taken place. When she speaks, even if only a single word, the man will tell his mother that his wife has spoken and the pair will live together as man and wife."6 "For five days a New Britain bride stays alone in the bridegroom's house, while he hides away in the forest or in some place in the high grass known only to the men."7

The Samoyed bride sleeps by her husband, but undisturbed for the first month. "The bride does not go to her husband's home until some time has elapsed. When she arrives certain ceremonies are held which symbolize the capture of the bride."8 Brahmans may not shave for six months after marriage, for a year after the death of a parent, and till the birth of the child when their wives are pregnant.9 In some groups in Assam, "the young couple are forbidden to come together until they have slept under the same roof at least three nights without intercourse. This prohibition is relaxed in the case of the marriage of widows."10 For many months after a Palaung wedding "young husbands and wives are very shy about appearing in public. They rarely go out together, and, even in their own home, hardly exchange remarks if any one else is present to hear. After a child has been born to them, they no longer have any feeling about appearing together and talking together."11 In the Indian Archipelago, consummation is deferred for four days among the Sundanese, for seven in Atjeh. Cases are cited where an old woman, or a boy six to eight years old lies between the couple as they sleep.12 The Dyak bridal pair not only do not spend the first night together but do not sleep at all, for fear, says Perelaer,13 that spirits will make them sick or that they will have unlucky dreams. Schwaner14 confirms this interpretation. Probably an analogous case is where the ears are stopped the day before a wedding so as not to hear ill omens from the birds' cries.

An ecclesiastical law of 505 A.D. ordained: "When the bride and bridegroom are to be blessed by the priest, let them be offered by their parents or groomsmen; and when they have received the blessing, let them remain the same night in virginity, out of respect for the blessing." A marriage was regarded as clandestine unless such abstinence was practised for two or three days.15 It is asserted that "it was for a long time the practice of the French Roman Catholics not to touch their brides during the first three nights (Mme. de Sevigné mentions this when writing of the marriage of her son), and that the Armenians still observe a similar custom, because of their fear of the spirit displaced by the bridegroom."16

§376. Sex-Rights in Marriage.

A MODERN publicist1 holds forth rather testily upon the inequalities between the sexes in woman's favor; he is somewhat irritated by the accusations brought against man for his oppression of the weaker sex. Woman, he says, gets the vote but incurs no obligation for military and other services to society. In marriage man assumes the burdens, assuming the responsibility for woman's

6 Rivers, *Melan. Soc.*, I, 209.
7 Parsons, in AA, XVIII, 45.
8 Czaplicka, *Aborig. Siberia*, 125.
9 Thurston, *S. India*, 3.
10 Hodson, in JAI, XXXVI, 97.
11 Milne, *Eastern Clan*, 169-170.
12 Wilken, in VG, I, 500-503.

13 *Dajaks*, 53.
14 *Borneo*, I, 197.
15 Reichel, *Canon. Law*, I, 351, note.
16 Tremearne, in JAI, XLV, 37.
1 Saloman, "Downtrodden Sex," in N. Y. *Times*, Dec. 12, 1920.

financial obligations. He is answerable for the debts his wife contracts as well as for her support. There is no reciprocal obligation; she can keep her property and is not required to assist him. He must support her even if she has means, while she need not care for him, though he is ill and infirm. Woman's property is her own and she has an equity in her husband's; in a few states a husband has a dower right in his wife's property, but she always gets a definite proportion of his. In the matter of alimony, the husband is always liable for support, alimony being in some cases a preferred claim. Man has had to perform military service, as aforesaid, and must do jury duty and assist the police; and while he has been at the front woman has taken his place and will not let go. Society considers discriminatory legislation in favor of women as an added safeguard for itself.

Consider the relative positions of the jilted woman and the jilted man. Where does popular sympathy lie? Consider the suit for breach of promise. Can a man bring such suit and still retain a position of dignity? He is laughed at. There are all sorts of discrimination in the mores in favor of modern woman which it is convenient to overlook when making out a case for man's selfishness and brutality. So long as women admitted inequality men protected them. What is going to happen if they insist upon genuine competition with men? Will men still defer to them when that means deference to rivals and the surrender of advantages in the struggle for existence carried on by men for themselves and their families?

We have expanded slightly upon the text provided by the writer whose views are summarized in order to point the contrast between what women have had and what they now possess in the way of rights. There is, in his comments, together with somewhat of the exaggeration that goes with polemic mood, a very real core of truth. We are interested only in having such controversy carried on in the light of evolutionary perspective. When women object, on account of the discrimination involved, to laws prohibiting female labor under certain conditions of bodily health and strength, it seems to us that theory has quite run away with fact. One does not need to espouse either side of a theoretic controversy to the extent of ignoring plain physical facts; and he will always come out better in the end for a knowledge of how the race has grappled with the perennial condition of bi-sexuality. For many a notion of the present, hailed as novel, is not new at all, but has been tried out and has failed, sometimes over and over again, in the long course of societal evolution.

§379. Liberty-Rights.

Seclusion of the Wife. Niekrassoff,[1] in his poem, "For Whom is Life Happy in Russia?" introduces a woman who tells her own life-story of ill-treatment and misfortune, but also of kindness, and sums up the lesson of it in these words: "You were not clever when you sought the happy ones amongst women." She then quotes an aged pilgrim woman as follows: "God himself threw away and lost the keys of woman's happiness and liberty. Hermits, holy women, and learned men have sought them, but never found them. Probably some fish swallowed them. Warriors worn by cold and hunger traversed deserts and towns, and asked sorcerers, and tried to read the stars; but the keys were not to be found. They searched through all God's world, in mountains and subterranean

1 *Poems* (Russ.), II, 233.

caverns. At last heroes found priceless keys, but not those keys. All assembled and for God's chosen people there was a grand festival. They came to the prisoners and the prison doors were opened. Over the earth there came such a joyful sigh of relief—but yet the keys of our woman's freedom were not,— they were not! Great champions still to this day strive; but nowhere, nowhere are those keys to be found. Alas! they will hardly be found ever! Those forbidden keys have been swallowed by some fish, and in what sea that fish swims God has forgotten."

There are a number of ways of exercising control over women and restricting their freedom. In the Gulf of Papua masked men "run and dance through the village carrying a short stick of hard wood, and frighten women and children."[2] An Indian tribe on the lower Sacramento have a ceremony of raising the dead and another of raising the devil; but both are employed for sordid purposes. "The former was in early times used merely to keep the women in subjection, but now merely to extort from them the gains of the prostitution into which they are forced by their own husbands and brothers!"[3]

The chief method, however, of limiting woman's freedom lies in the custom of seclusion. Annexed to the temples in ancient Mexico were large buildings used as seminaries for girls.[4] The Hindu woman is partially veiled; she is not allowed by custom to converse with her husband. One should never address the women of a house nor ask for them. Poor people cannot seclude their wives, but would like to.[5] Owing to the extension of trade at Cawnpore many men have become wealthy and aim at a standard of social respectability much higher that that of their rural brethren, and "some have begun even to seclude their women, which every native does as soon as he commences to rise in the world."[6] The more prominent Hindus at least send their daughters to school if possible; a Mohammedan girl, on the other hand, never has this opportunity. Tamil women may on occasions appear on the streets; when they meet a man they draw only a tip of their dress over the face. On the other hand, one sees Mohammedan women only when some pressing occasion forces them to leave the house, and then they appear dressed in thick, tasteless clothes and barricaded behind shades and curtains.[7]

It was impossible for the Jesuit missionaries to penetrate into Chinese family life and especially to learn about the women, for, as the ancient book of moral catechism instructs, "men do not speak of such private matters." When a foreigner asks about the "honored ladies," the Chinese host assumes that their inquiries refer to his mother, not to his wife.[8] Up to the age of eight the boys and girls of the respectable classes in Korea are allowed to grow up together, "but after that age the girl retires into the women's quarters where she lives in utter seclusion until her marriage. Marriage for her means but the exchange of one person for another. She is taught that the most disgraceful thing a woman can do is to allow herself to be seen or spoken to by any man outside her own family circle. After the age of eight she is never allowed to enter the men's quarters of her own home. After her marriage, which takes place usually at the age of sixteen or seventeen, she is allowed to see no man but her husband. The boys in the same way are told that it is unbecoming and undig-

2 Chalmers, in JAI, XXVII, 329.
3 Powers, in *Contrib. N. Amer. Ethnol.*, III, 224.
4 Mason, *Woman's Share*, 208.

5 Wilkins, *Modern Hinduism*, 337; Dubois, *Mœurs*, 441.
6 Risley, *Ethnog. India*, I, 175.
7 Gehring, *Süd-Indien*, 82-83.
8 W. C. A., in *Globus*, LXXVIII, 263.

nified to enter the portion of the house set apart for the females. The men and women have their meals separately, the women waiting on their husbands. . . . In Seoul (the capital) they have a curious curfew called *pem-ya*. A large bell is tolled at about 8 p.m. and 3 a.m. daily, and between these hours only are women allowed to appear in the streets. In the old days men found in the streets during the hours allotted to women were severely punished, but the rule has been greatly relaxed of late years."[9] It is only with difficulty that an European gains an intimate view of Japanese family relations, for according to Japanese notions it is forbidden to speak of one's own family or to ask another about his family.[10]

In Chaldæa all women, even princesses, were cloistered in the harem, and were never found by the side of their husbands or brothers, as in Egypt.[11] The Jewish woman led a simple quiet life for her husband who treated her with consideration but showed her no special tenderness; to public life she remained foreign.[12] In Homer, the wife's place was at home, though she was not cloistered; a princess was veiled.[13] In a Greek play a woman apologizes for her boldness in coming out, for it is a woman's· greatest merit to be silent and discreet and stay at home.[14] In Periclean Athens the best woman was the one least spoken of, whether well or ill, amongst men. Women of the higher classes were locked up with Asiatic jealousy.[15] Mohammedan countries are the classic ground for female seclusion. It is against all propriety to greet the wife or grown daughter of the house or to ask concerning their health.[16] The wife is excluded from all social intercourse with the other sex and from all intellectual interests; she remains throughout life restricted to the narrow circle of the home, which makes it impossible for her to develop mentally.[17] "An impenetrable veil of ignorance and obscurity separates her from the world." There exists a wide gulf between an educated man and his wife.[18] In Arabia, women, young or old, never sit at table with the men of the family, rarely join in their pleasure-meetings, and above all may not in seemliness thrust themselves forward to welcome guests or strangers and converse with them. "Of course, in the dwellings of the poor women and men all live together, and little separation is or can be kept up; a narrow home going far to bring its tenants on a level. But in richer families and chieftains' houses the women are bound to occupy a separate quarter, whence, however, curiosity or business often draws them forth into the apartments of the other sex. Nor is the covering veil, though generally worn, nearly so strict an obligation as in Syria or Egypt. It is a matter of custom, not of creed, and readily dispensed with when occasion requires. Indeed, in some parts of Arabia . . . it is barely in use. Nor are Bedouin women apt to impose on their grimed and wizened faces a concealment that might on the whole be for their advantage. Among the rigid Wahhābees alone the veil and the harem acquire something like exactness, and there Arab liberty consents to inflict on itself something of the ceremoniousness of Islam."[19]

---

9 Saunderson, in JAI, XXIV, 304, 306.
10 Crasselt, in *Globus*, XCII, 58.
11 Maspero, *Hist. Anc.*. I, 707, 739.
12 Bergel, *Eheverhältnisse*, 11.
13 Keller, *Hom. Soc.*, 221.
14 Euripides, *Heracleidæ*, 470.

15 Mahaffy, *Greece*, 133; Bergel, *Eheverhältnisse*, 9.
16 Pischon, *Islam*, 17.
17 Hauri, *Islam*, 124.
18 Bey, in *Asiatic Quarterly Rev.*, 3d Series, VIII, 393.
19 Palgrave, *Arabia*, 155-156.

Self-Disposal in Marriage. Many cases illustrate the liberty of women in this respect, and in addition the reader is referred back to the section on elopement.[20] In the Upper Congo, a girl sometimes objects to being handed over in the usual fashion of wife-purchase, and, "if her protests are disregarded, she will run away to a neighbouring town and select her own husband, and her parents will have to make the best bargain they can in the way of marriage money. . . . If a free woman did not want to marry the man who was trying to arrange for her, she would tell him frankly that if he persisted in marrying her she would run away from him. If, in spite of this threat, he completed the arrangements, then one day she would escape to a neighbouring town, and put herself under the protection of the chief by tearing his cloth. The chief would give the husband notice of what had happened, and before he could get his wife back he would have to pay the chief 600 brass rods = 39s. If the man would not then permit her to marry the man she wanted, she would run away again, and again, and every time she ran it would cost her husband 600 brass rods. A sensible man would take warning by the first threat and would not marry her. If a free woman were badly treated by her husband, she would resort to the above method of making him pay for his ill-treatment of her, and would thus force him to use her more kindly. A slave wife he could kill for acting thus, but a free woman has a family not far away who would avenge her murder." There is an even more drastic way of punishing a husband for ill-treatment. "A woman has been very badly treated by her husband and in spite of her protests and warnings he continues to ill-use her, so one day she runs to the *nganga* [shaman] and smashes the *eboko* = the fetish saucepan of the 'medicine man,' and in so doing she commits a very great offence. The *nganga* therefore holds her as a hostage until her husband redeems her by the gift of a slave and the payment of a sum of money to replace the *eboko* and make fresh medicine. Having paid the money he will treat his wife better in future, or she will again break the *eboko.*"[21] Among the Ba-Yaka, "the consent of the woman is regarded as absolutely necessary."[22] With the Wa-Giriama, the girl is asked by her brother whether she wants to marry the suitor. "If she declines the honour the matter is finished." Even after negotiations have begun, she may change her maidenly mind, whereupon the gifts are returned and the affair ended.[23]

Coudenhove[24] has discovered feminism in Nyasaland. "When I tried to explain to a husband that it cannot, in fairness, be expected from the mother of a family to collect firewood in the forest, to bring water from the river, and to carry all the household goods on a journey, I was invariably met by that vacant stare which natives who cannot, or will not, understand know so well how to assume; and as to the women themselves, my discomfiture amounted to a fiasco! They had two attitudes in response to my veiled incitements to rebellion: the one was that of benevolent toleration, if not exactly approval, of my intentions rather than my words, the humoring, so to speak, of the harmless hobby of a good-natured eccentric; the other, more humiliating still, was that of boundless merriment, finding expression in peal after peal of laughter, to which the listeners gave way, and which kept on reaching me from the distance, growing fainter and fainter, as they moved away from my camp." Hard as

20 §359, of the text and *Case-Book.*
21 Weeks, in JAI, XXXIX, 440, 441-442.
22 Torday and Joyce, in JAI, XXXVI, 45.
23 Barrett, in JAI, XLI, 20, 21.
24 In *Atl. Mo.*, CXXXII, 186-188.

he might think their lot, the women knew better. "Undoubtedly, the relations of native men and women to one another are based, not on an idea of inferiority of the one sex to the other, but on division of labor. If, in some tribes, like, for instance, the Wayao, the woman throws in, by way of *pourboire*, an outward show of extreme humility and submission, she does so, as I will show later, on an entirely noncommittal understanding, merely, I am afraid, because the cunning creature is well aware of the weak spot in the cuirass of the lord of creation. When, in the last-named tribe's country, I saw a woman kneel in the dust when addressing her husband or handing him anything, I could not repress a feeling of indignation with the male, for what I considered to be the outcome of insufferable arrogance on his part; nor would I believe him when he replied to my outspoken comments with the words: 'Have *I* told her to kneel down? She is following her own heart.' I subsequently found out, however, that this excuse was quite correct. In most of the Nyasaland tribes, permanent connubial life is preceded by a term of probation, which can be broken off at will by either party. When the woman has finally made up her mind to stay, she punctuates her decision by kneeling when she addresses her husband. . . . By thus humbling herself, *she has taken possession of her husband*. . . . Barring a few concessions to traditional custom, native women in British Central Africa enjoy to-day a liberty greater than that of most European married women."

There are many cases in East Africa in which not only is the girl consulted as to her marriage, but it is she who, in fact, commences the negotiations and decides the question. "The fact is that at the dances, where it is the girl who chooses her partner, she has the opportunity of declaring her affections by always selecting the same young man, and if he can pay what the father asks for her the matter is practically settled." The author,[25] with his usual discernment, discourses further on the liberty a native girl has as to her choice. "The betrothals made in early childhood are but family arrangements which may or may not be fulfilled, and are in no way binding; in general, it may be said that no betrothal exists until the couple themselves have contracted to marry. The marriage ceremony always includes a formal signification of consent on the part of the girl, and everywhere it will be found that it is considered bad custom to coerce a girl into marriage. I do not say that girls will not marry to please their parents, or that the influence of the family may not decide for her, but those who know natives will appreciate the difficulty of forcing their women to do anything against their inclinations; and native custom was never so foolish as to permit coercion in these matters, for even if a girl does submit to a forced marriage, it is certain that she will not long abide by it. Parental persuasion has, of course, its weight in Africa as well as in Europe, but the native parent is extremely indulgent towards his children, and is no less anxious than is the average European father that his daughter should exercise her own choice in the matter." Instead of being improved by European example and rule, the marriage-customs of the native tribes have tended to degenerate, and with this decline follows a loss not only in morals but in the standing of native women. "The ideal native marriage presumes the free consent of the woman; as a wife she then becomes the mainstay of the village, the provider of comforts, and the idol of her children, for to the African a

25 Dundas, C., in JAI, XLIII, 519; and in JAI, LI, 257, 263.

mother is all in all. Unfortunately, our methods and mistaken conceptions of what marriage is to the native have loosened the ties of matrimony and given it a commercial character. We have freely granted divorces in favour of frivolous girls, and permitted them to run from one man to another, heedless of the bad example thereby set."

Among the Nigerians, "the girl has a right of veto though not exactly of choice, as the father's fee must be paid before she is supposed to know that she is being sought. A father will therefore, sometimes accept presents secretly from several suitors, and after he has spent the money, simply tell them that his daughter—or ward—will not marry them."[26] Shuli women have a voice in the choice of their husbands and their status is better than usual in Africa.[27] Parental refusal of a maiden's hand occurs but seldom and then the girl can create an uproar that leads the elders of the tribe to declare her marriage legal. Poor girls, unwelcome to the parents of the groom, may jump the hedge and remain in the house. "Rich Gallas, therefore, provide their houses, when their sons are marriageable, with high hedges, so that poor girls cannot intrude."[28] Berber women are independent, uncloistered, and unveiled; they eat with the family, even when guests are present, and are free to go out and buy in the market whatever they need; in short, they enjoy the same freedom as European women. This applies also in Kabylie, in the Sahara and with the Atlas tribes. The Kabyle girl enjoys premarital freedom, and will mount her camel alone and go to visit her lover who may be twenty or thirty hours away, without injuring her reputation at all or hindering her from finding a husband.[29]

In India the groom may even be abducted, though he modestly pretends to run away. Also the girl may get into his house and the effort to dislodge her may include the throwing of red pepper on the fire; "but if she endures this ordeal without leaving the house, she is held to have won her husband and the family is bound to recognize her."[30] Again, the woman's tribe is insulted if a man asks for her; or her consent may be indispensable. Princesses select husbands out of a review of suitors. In Sikkim a present of eggs to a young man is a proposal of marriage.[31] Even Manu, who put all periods of a woman's life under guardianship, allows her an independence in matters of marriage— in some cases a full independence by withdrawing her wholly from parental control. The latter is especially true in the *gandharva*-marriage.[32]

"A Palaung girl is free to marry whom she will, provided that the young man wishes to marry her. Parents do not often interfere, or object to men who visit their daughters. Indeed it is not very easy for them to know who the men are who come at night to their house. The father and mother retire to the inner room to sleep, about ten o'clock, and if they want anything from the outer room, where their daughter is sitting, they must on no account go to fetch it. . . . A young man, when he visits a girl in the evening, always wraps himself in a large grey blanket, which completely envelops the body and head, shading the face; a disguise that is not easy to penetrate when a man is

26 Tremearne, in JAI, XLII, 170.
27 Wilson and Felkin, *Uganda*, II, 61.
28 Paulitschke, *Nordost-Afr.*, I, 197, 198, 199.
29 De Goeje, in *De Gids*, XXXI, pt. II, 29-30; Wilken, in VG, I, 267-268; Hanoteau et Letourneux, *Kabylie*, 72.
30 Hopkins, *Relig. Ind.*, 534; Risley, *Ethnog. Ind.*, I, 146.

31 Tylor, in *Nineteenth Cent. Mag.*, XL; Godden, in JAI, XXVI, 175; Gubernatis, *Usi Nuz.*, 71; Holtzmann, *Ind. Sagen*, I, 15, 17, 98-100, 102-103, 133-134, 250; Waddell, *Himalayas*, 86, 87, 433.
32 Bühler, *Manu*, V, 148; IX, 3, 90.

sitting on the floor."[33] The Dyak girl inveigles the man she wants into her house, closes the door, hangs cloths and ornaments on the wall, serves food, and informs him of her wishes. If he declines he must pay the value of the hangings and ornaments. Parental consent is seldom refused, though it is possible to anticipate matters by not allowing the visits of the enamored swain.[34] Elsewhere, "in their marriages the will of the girl plays the chief rôle"; she proposes by presenting the chosen youth arms or a shield. In northern Sumatra a girl is consulted only when she has lost her virginity.[35] Parental permission is not indispensable in certain Pacific islands. In Samoa the girl's consent is asked, but she has to agree if her parents are in favor of the match. Maori girls have a cord ready, to hang themselves with in event of parental refusal.[36]

Eskimo women are ordinarily forced; still they have some small chance of postponement, which may discourage the suitor.[37] Tlinkit girls, acting in obedience to the dictates of their relatives and the rules of the people, seldom have any choice in their own marriage, but "occasionally headstrong youth defy all customs and marry as they will."[38] Among the Indians "often, though less directly than among whites, the girl exercises the right of acceptance and the married woman the privilege of separation."[39] Algonquian maidens "were allowed to signify their desire to enter matrimonial life, upon which a marriage would be formally arranged."[40] An Iroquois myth tells the story of a girl who ran away and tried to drown herself over Niagara because she was to be forced to marry a hideous old man. The Osage girl may present an ear of maize as a proposal to a great warrior. Among the Pueblos, "no girl is forced to marry against her will, however eligible her parents may consider the match." In fact, "the usual order of courtship is reversed; when a girl is disposed to marry she does not wait for a young man to propose to her, but selects one to her own liking and consults her father, who visits the parents of the youth and acquaints them with his daughter's wishes." The woman occupies a comparatively high place in Tarahumari family life and the girl does the courting. Her mother goes to the parents of her choice and praises her as an expert weaver and housekeeper; then the matter is referred to the young man. "Actual proposal consists in the girl throwing small pebbles at him; if he does not return these the match is off, but if he throws them back they are betrothed." Bears' entrails, smoked and seasoned, are a common gift of Indian girls to their lovers; "for, when cast around the neck as a necklace, it means 'I love you.'"[41] Consent of parents is not asked in certain Brazilian tribes, husbands being chosen by young women from the young men gathered at festivals. The girl almost always chooses the man, in one case by making a mark upon a tree. In one region, "the women make their stipulations before marriage—what they are to do in the household, whether the marriage is to be polygamous or polyandrous, and the like."[42] Among both the Bororo In-

33 Milne, *Eastern Clan*, 97.
34 Gomes, *Sea Dyaks*, 121, 122.
35 Schwaner, *Borneo*, I, 198, 230; Roth, *Sarawak*, II, clxxi, cxcvii; Wilken, *Vkde.*, 280; Jacobs, *Groot-Atjeh*, II, 39.
36 Kubary, *Núkuóro*, 34; Turner, *Samoa*, 92; Weiss, *Chatham Isl.*, 30.
37 Turner, in BAE, XI, 188.
38 Jones, *Thlingets*, 125.

39 Hrdlička, in BAE, Bull. XXXIV, 47.
40 Mooney and Thomas, in HAI, I, 787.
41 Smith, in BAE, II, 54; Bancroft, *Nat. Races*, I, 547, 549, note 206; Lumholtz, in *Scribner's Mag.*, XVI, 299; Leland and Prince, *Kulóskap*, 191-192.
42 Von Martius, *Beiträge*, I, 103, note; Von den Steinen, *Zent. Bras.*, 501; Frič, in *Globus*, LXXXIX, 218; Starcke, *Prim. Fam.*, 45.

dians and the Chaco tribes the proposal of marriage comes from the woman.[43] In the case of the Patagonians, "marriages are always those of inclination, and if the damsel does not like the suitor for her hand, her parents never force her to comply with their wishes, although the match may be an advantageous one."[44]

Von Kremer[45] says that the ancient Arabian women had the freest rein in the choice of their husbands and it even happened that the wife of a caliph, after his death, married another husband of her choice. She brought to him from the first marriage limitless possessions, but finally repudiated him because of her suspicion that he was having relations with a female slave. Wilken[46] cites a number of cases in substantiation, and states that in some of the islands off the west coast of France the young girls ask the young men in marriage.

§380. Woman as Property.

IN Australia woman is a domestic animal, a servant or slave who feeds after her master on the leavings.[1] To the Zulu a purchased wife represents an outlay of capital and he hopes through the work she does and the children she bears to derive interest on his investment. If this does not eventuate—if his wife becomes sick, weak, or is childless, so that he fails to recoup expenses, he sends her back to her father and seeks the return of the cattle he paid.[2] Among the Ba-Mbala a woman is merely "a variety of domestic animal."[3] While the Un-yamwesi man is away from home, his wife must eat no meat and she must save up for him the layer burned on to the bottom of the porridge-pot.[4] Among the Wagogo, men and women eat apart, the father and sons first, the mother and daughters later eating what is left.[5] Customs such as these show that the wife is mainly a servant.

If one of the problems of civilized man is how to live with a wife, the question that worries many Africans is how to get along with only one. To have many wives means to control many workers. "A Mkamba may have as many wives as he can afford to buy. A large number of them are a sign of wealth and consequently they bring their husband respect and position: not a few invest all their riches in wives, considering them more profitable than cattle, for they are first and foremost workers, but also they bear him children who, in the case of girls, are valuable assets, and sons are much desired to strengthen the family." The alignment of women with property is further illustrated by the fact that compensation for injury done to a female is appropriated by her father or husband, as the case may be. "In Ukamba, however, that which is paid or due ultimately belongs to the husband when the girl gets married. If it is already paid, the husband will claim it from the father; if the injury was caused at any time previous to the girl's marriage, but was not compensated at the time, the husband may claim it from the offender. The Atheraka have some curious and primitive rules in this respect. If a man severely injures a girl, he is obliged to take her in marriage, and to pay full dowry [bride-price] for her; if he injures a man's wife so as to impair her usefulness, he must pay

43 Frič and Radin, in JAI, XXXVI, 390.
44 Musters, *At home with the Patagonians*, 177, quoted by Wilken, in VG, I, 270.
45 *Kgchte. Orients*, II, 100.
46 In VG, I, 518; II, 49.

1 Letourneau, *Soc.*, 160; *Morale*, 126-135; Mucke, *Horde u. Familie*, 116.
2 Fritsch, *Eingeb. S.-Afr.*, 141.
3 Torday and Joyce, in JAI, XXXV, 410.
4 Stuhlmann, *Mit Emin*, 89.
5 Cole, in JAI, XXXII, 317.

the amount of dowry to enable the husband to buy another wife."[6] Among
the Dinkas, in case of seduction, the offended person is the father, owner, or
guardian of the girl or woman seduced. The guilty man is liable to a fine of
from one to five cattle. Should the girl give birth to a child, the child becomes
the property of her guardian, "who demands a larger 'marriage payment' for
her in consideration of passing the ownership of the child to her husband with
her."[7] "As a Kagoro woman very seldom sleeps away from her home her children are nearly always born there; the husband would very seldom allow his
wife to go to her father's house, for if he did the father-in-law would probably
keep the child and marry the woman to someone else when possible."[8] Women
are very cheap in Uganda, as they far exceed the men in number; a man may
sell his wife into slavery for any misdemeanor. "The purchase-price for the
woman is like a compensation to the labor-force of the family from which the
woman is withdrawn, and . . . may legally be demanded back in case of
divorce."[9]

To the Kruman a woman is an investment. He ships on a European vessel
and by strenuous labor earns a small sum, of which he is allowed to retain, in
the family division of spoils, only enough to buy a wife. "When the honeymoon
is over he goes to sea again, and anew does he subject himself for a year or
two to the severest renunciations in order to be able on his return to celebrate
a second wedding. In this manner he goes on until his harem numbers enough
members so that he may be comfortably supported by them and can enter
into carefree retirement."[10] Serpa Pinto[11] found that as a rule the African
women he saw were the most abject slaves of their husbands. It is thought
that the low status of woman in Africa is due to "overproduction of women"
and that it appears chiefly among warlike tribes.[12]

Among some of the aboriginal tribes of Siberia, the men get the best pieces
of food and the women receive what is left over. Thus among the Reindeer
Koryak, "only the men sit around the food which is served in the inner tent;
and, besides the children, only the mother or the eldest wife is present, who
distributes the food, or treats the guests. The other women and girls receive
the leavings, which they eat in the outer tent. Among the Maritime Koryak,
too, the women and girls eat separately, by the hearth, after the men have
eaten."[13] Women among the Kirghiz are valued as property along with
weapons, beasts, and slaves; the husband has absolute power over them and
their children.[14] Tungus women, on the other hand, though not much more
than slaves of the men, may not be injured with impunity.[15] The Yakut woman
has no rights in the family and no property; once she was a war-captive, now
a purchased slave.[16] In Tibet, woman, though a valuable commodity, is a
miserable slave.[17] Among the Turkomans she "is regarded as a very costly
ware, but only just as a ware," and the same is true among many of the wild
tribes of Russia. Young girls bring great buckets of water from the river, while
boys of the same age and older do nothing; the women become old early and

6 Dundas, C., in JAI, XLIII, 520-521; and
in JAI, XLV, 272-273.
7 O'Sullivan, in JAI, XL, 186.
8 Tremearne, in JAI, XLII, 172.
9 Johnston, *Uganda*, II, 779; Ratzel,
Vkde., I, 476; Paulitschke, *Nordost-Afr.*, II,
142.
10 Bastian, *Afr. Reisen*, 250.
11 *Africa*, I, 297.

12 Frobenius, *Masken*, 223; Spencer, *Prin.
Soc.*, I, ch. X.
13 Czaplicka, *Aborig. Siberia*, 34.
14 De Greef, *Soc.*, 141.
15 Hiekisch, *Tungusen*, 89.
16 Sieroshevski-Sumner, in JAI, XXXI, 94.
17 Reid, in *Cosmopolitan Mag.*, XXVIII,
449.

are misshapen. "The man considers it a shameful thing to help a woman in her work, even when she is sick. The death of a wife makes a mountaineer poor in the fullest sense of the word." Among the Usbeks, women do all the work and are treated like cattle; the men ride around and visit each other. The position of woman is, if anything, lower and more miserable among the western Russian tribes.[18]

In China "custom required mourners to divest themselves for a time of their wives and concubines, who constituted mere objects of wealth, as is nearly always the case among uncivilized and semi-barbarian peoples."[19] Jolly[20] states with reference to the position of woman among the ancient Hindus: "Rich in hostile expressions about the female sex, the Hindu law not only subordinates women wholly to men, but in general does not recognize them at all as independent, as possessors of rights." The Code of Manu states: "During her childhood a woman depends on her father; during her youth, on her husband; her husband being dead, on her sons; if she has no sons, on the near relatives of her husband; or in default of them, on those of her father; if she has no paternal relatives, on the sovereign. A woman ought never to have her own way." A child belongs to the master of a wife as a calf to the owner of a cow. "As the product comes to the owner of a field, who also may have sowed the seed, so is the child of him to whom the mother belongs, through whomsoever it is begotten." A woman must serve her husband as a god and do nothing to displease him, even if he is devoid of every virtue. The wife is referred to as "servant" and "slave," the husband as "master" and "lord." She should not call her husband by name nor eat with him.[21] According to Tamil principles the man is ruler, the wife a slave. He addresses her with the familiar "thou," while she must use the most honorary plural, which signifies "gracious lord." When she speaks of him, she must never mention his name but refer to him in the third person, as "my master." This usage is so much in the blood and flesh of the people that even Christian Tamil brides, who hold to the English form of the marriage vow, are moved only with great difficulty and pressure to speak out the name of the groom at the marriage-ceremony.[22] A modern Hindu lady is quoted as follows on the duties of a wife: "The husband is the wife's religion, the wife's sole business, the wife's all in all. . . . To a chaste wife her husband is her god."[23] If a married girl who is not yet nubile dies while still dwelling in her parents' home, her blood-relations must mourn for her a rather short time, while, under other circumstances, they do not mourn for a married daughter at all.[24] She resides and belongs elsewhere.

On the island of Nias, "in spite of the fact that the woman is so fully the property of the man that she goes over as a piece of heritage to his immediate family, her position is less bereft of rights than it is, for example, among the Bataks." In the latter case, a wife has neither property nor rights. "The Batak regards the female sex only as a useful domestic animal; he never concedes to women the same civil rights as men, and excludes them from all possession, from all his councils, pleasures, and amusements." Wives are regarded not as persons but as things. "A wife can really never possess anything;

18 Ratzel, Vkde., II, 767; Russ. Ethnog. (Russ.), II, 96, 267, 328, 379, 407, 497, 639; Abercromby, Finns, I, 181.
19 DeGroot, Relig. Syst. China, II, 609.
20 Stellung d. Frauen, 421.
21 Bühler, Manu, V, 147, 148, 154, 156; IX, 48-51; Hopkins, Relig. India, 370.
22 Gehring, Süd-Indien, 83, 84.
23 Wilkins, Hinduism, 358; Dubois, Mœurs, II, 1.
24 Jolly, Recht u. Sitte, II, 56.

she herself is rather always the possession of another—be it her father or brother, if she is still unmarried, or her husband, who has purchased her, or his heirs, whether brothers or sons, after his death." In South Sumatra, "as soon as the *jujur* is paid the wife is the inalienable property of the man." Her position is one wholly without rights. She is an article of possession, as well for the parent who sells her as for the man who buys her, or for his brother or other blood-relations to whom she passes as a heritage by virtue of the levirate marriage.[25] In northern Sumatra the girl has no right over her own hand; she is the property of her father or guardian, who can sell her when and to whom he likes. In marriage the woman merely changes masters.[26] Among a number of tribes in the Malay Peninsula the men always eat before the women, which may be a sign of the inferiority of the latter or, as some assert, may be merely because they have to look after the food.[27]

Among certain American Indians, woman held a servile position; "whether maiden or widow she was owned by her father or brother, to be sold, with her children, if any, at his pleasure. Marriage was a matter of bargain and sale."[28] It is reckoned indecent in the man, among the Guiana Indians, to caress or notice the women in public, and "our practice in this respect appears to them highly contemptible." The Surinam Carib woman "is the servant, or rather the slave, of her husband, although this is more imaginary than real. Nevertheless, she does the hardest work and carries the heaviest loads; and she often does this with a suckling on her back. Only in his presence or in that of his family folk may she speak to another man. Only when he has eaten may she venture to partake of something, so that when he is sick she sometimes hungers. All the money that she earns in making hammocks, pottery, etc., goes to the husband, who generally squanders it. . . . No wonder need be aroused at unhappy marriages and husbands ill-treating their wives, especially when they are drunk. But woe to the woman if she dare offer resistance or attempt to give her man a sound thrashing, because on his recovery she would receive double in return. And if a man allows himself to be led or ruled by his wife, he is regarded with the greatest contempt."[29] A Paraguay Indian "found it quite natural to rest in the hammock from fancied fatigues, while his poor little wife, hardly a dozen years old, lay upon the bare ground at a nearly freezing temperature, although she was in a delicate condition."[30] The Araucanian wife "is considered the absolute property of the husband, and he can dispose of her as he thinks fit, even to killing her, without anyone interfering any more than they would at the disposal of his other property."[31] Among the Fuegians, though the women win a large part of the nourishment, they get less of it than the men; at certain times they are allowed only fish.[32]

The laws of Hammurabi state: "When anyone becomes a prisoner of war and in his house there is enough to live on, but his wife leaves the house and domestic establishment and goes into another house; because that wife has not kept her home but has gone into another house, she shall be legally convicted and thrown into the water."[33] Among the Israelites the position of woman was characterized by the fact that she was always the property of her hus-

25 Wilken, in VG, I, 241-242, 244, 331, 332, 335-337.
26 Jacobs, *Groot-Atjeh*, I, 27.
27 Stevens, in *Ztsft. f. Eth.*, XXVIII, 167; Skeat and Blagden, *Malay Penin.*, II, 87.
28 Dixon and Hodge, in HAI, II, 192.

29 Roth, in BAE, XXXVIII, 684, 685.
30 Machon, in PSM, LII, 401.
31 Latcham, in JAI, XXXIX, 353.
32 Ratzel, *Vkde.*, II, 677.
33 Winckler, *Hammurabi*, 23.

band. "As long as she was unmarried, she belonged to the household of the father and had to do her share of the domestic work. If she became married, she was sold for a price to her husband and became his property. Her duties as housewife were first to bear him children and second to do all sorts of work in his house. For that she could claim from her husband clothing and food. . . . She was indeed merely his property and through marriage entered into no intimate relationship with him; wherefore even the priests mourned for their nearest blood-relations but not for their wives. . . . According to all these customs the wife was always dependent, which also finds expression in the fact that the vow of a woman is valid only when her father or husband confirms it."[34] In the commandment, "Thou shalt not covet thy neighbour's wife," the connotation is one of property.[35] According to Biblical-Talmudic law the father could sell his daughter. The Persian wife was in a similar position. Zarathustra said: "The wife must honor her husband as god." Later follows the precept: "In the morning the wife must stand before her husband, fold her hands and nine times repeat the words: 'What willst thou that I should do?'" Then she had to kiss his body, lay her hand three times from the forehead upon the earth and from the earth upon the forehead, and then set out to execute his commands.[36] Among the ancient Arabs the female sex was wholly excluded from inheritance. A wife could not inherit from her father, since by her marriage through purchase she left her family for good; nor could she inherit from her husband at his death; on the contrary, as a purchased thing, that is, as a part of his possessions, she herself belonged to the heritage.[37] The wife of the fellah belongs to his movable possessions which he can alienate at any time; her purpose is merely to satisfy his wishes and take care of his children. Should she prove sterile, he takes a second wife and separates from the first or she becomes the maid of her happy successor.[38] The *Koran* states that men are superior to women because of the qualities by which God has placed them above women and because men employ their wealth to endow women. The virtuous woman is obedient and submissive.[39] No tribesman in Albania eats with his wife; and "the odd custom still prevails of a married couple never addressing each other by name. To eat with a woman seems to be thought very degrading. The men eat first and the women eat up the bits left over afterwards at the other end of the room or, if Moslems, in their own quarters."[40]

§382. Types of Disposition over Women.

IT is still the general custom in Papua "to 'lend' wives to the guest for the night, and in this the wife has no say whatever, whether she likes the man or not." Also, "permanent exchange of wives is carried on, and the women have no say in the matter. They are 'thrown away' for bad temper, bad work, and continued unfaithfulness."[1] In both Nyasaland and Uganda it is a common practice for wives to be lent to friends and guests.[2] Among the Bantu tribes of

34 Buhl, *Israeliten*, 30, 31; Ex., XXI, 10; Gen., XXXI, 50; Levit., XXI, 1 ff.; Num., XXX, 4 ff.

35 Freisen, *Canon. Eherecht*, 94.

36 Klugmann, *Frau im Talmud*, 8, 56.

37 Wilken, in VG, II, 50.

38 R. T. K., in *Globus*, LXXIX, 106.

39 Letourneau, *Marriage*, 140; Hanoteau et Letourneux, *Kabylie*, II, 167; *Koran*, sura IV, verse 38.

40 Durham, in JAI, XL, 460.

1 Liston-Blyth, in JAI, LIII, 468, 469.

2 Stigand, in JAI, XXXVII, 122; Johnston, *Uganda*, II, 882.

East Africa, "it is customary for a man to offer a visitor the hut of one of his wives, and the *usus* of his wife, provided that the visitor is of about the same age as his host. Children born of such, or of unlawful unions, are in all cases taken possession of by the father or husband of the woman, as the case may be, but the child of an unmarried woman is taken by her husband when she marries."[3] Among both the Maritime Koryak and the Chukchi, "when friends exchange visits, or when guests come to the house, they sleep with the wife and daughters of the host, who leaves the house for the night, in some cases to spend it with the wife of the guest."[4] The Sea Dyaks and Kayans lend daughters to visitors as wives.[5] On the west coast of Borneo men often trade wives among themselves for a shorter or longer time and anybody coming into a kampong or village where he has a name-comrade has the right to go to him, and to expect that he will turn over not only his house but also his wife, in the literal sense of the word. Among certain peoples of Billiton it is reckoned as a duty of guest-friendship to loan wives to guests.[6] The leader of an expedition to the Arctic reports that it is a mark of friendship among the Eskimo for a man to trade his wife to another. "They trade mates for days, weeks, months, years and sometimes always. It seems to be mutually satisfactory. One man told me that he had a perfect wife except that she didn't like to be traded."[7] Exchange of wives and the offering of the wife to a guest are among the practices of the Athapascan tribes in Canada.[8] Among the nations of the Orinoco and to the westward of it, "the practice of making a temporary exchange of wives for a limited time was in vogue. At the expiration of the period agreed upon they are received back without the smallest objection being raised on either side. . . . By mutual contract they will exchange their wives for a definite number of months; and the day of settlement over, each woman returns to her husband's house."[9]

In addition to exchanging or lending wives, primitive men may sell them along with their other property. "The Mkamba wife is bought and sold, and may even be traded as a piece of goods."[10] Some Polynesian husbands sold their wives for a small payment.[11] The old Norseman could make over his wife in his last will and testament, give her away, or sell her with his house and furniture. "The hardest and most offensive was the sale. A Norse example shows how deeply the wife felt this injury. The Icelander Illugi the Red sold his domestic establishment with all movable property, including his wife . . . who, however, hanged herself because she could not endure this traffic in human beings. Among other German peoples the sale of wives is likewise demonstrated."[12]

Wives may also be inherited. As regards the inheritance of a father's wives in East Africa, "the Agricultural Hill Suk do not take their father's wives, old or young, but maintain them unless they re-marry; the Pastoral Suk have adopted the custom of the Turkana and Karamojo and take their father's wives, but not their own mothers. They discard the older women but maintain them. As regards the inheritance of brother's wives, these go to the next elder brother, and he may give permission to marry elsewhere if he wishes, or pass

3 Dundas, C., in JAI, XLV, 275.
4 Czaplicka, *Aborig. Siberia*, 86.
5 Veth, *Borneo's Wester-Afdeeling*, II, 251.
6 Wilken, in VG, I, 200-201.
7 N. Y. *Times*, Sept. 24, 1924.

8 Chamberlain, in AA, IX, 763.
9 Roth, in BAE, XXXVIII, 669.
10 Dundas, C., in JAI, XLIII, 519.
11 Ratzel, *Vkde.*, II, 187.
12 Weinhold, *Deut. Frauen*, II, 10, 12.

them on to a younger brother of the deceased. Failing sons and brothers, the women pass to the husband's clan as other property wanting heirs."[13] Among the Sungu, widows follow the property of their deceased husband but can free themselves entirely by restoring the bride-price; among the Olemba they can choose a husband among the brothers of the deceased; while the northern Batetela allow them no say whatever in the matter.[14] In the case of certain Russian tribes, if a man dies, his wife goes to his brother, and if that one dies, to the next brother, and so on—if they are unmarried, for a man can have only one wife at a time. If the brothers are already married, then the widow is free to marry anyone she likes.[15] Among the Bataks, a slave is more of a person than is a free woman; she, in consequence of the payment of bride-price, is a family-possession which, just like other goods, goes over by inheritance.[16] Among the Israelites the widow did not inherit from her husband; "rather, as the property of the husband, she originally went over to the possession of the heirs. Only what she had brought into the marriage—usually her slaves, and what the husband had given her—was her property. . . . If she did not re-marry, it was the duty of the heirs to care for her."[17] The widow among the ancient Arabs was inherited along with the rest of the property, by the brother, uncle, nephew, or stepson of the deceased.[18] With the ancient Germans, upon the death of the husband, the *mundium* or guardianship of the woman descended upon the nearest male relative, usually upon the son of an earlier or of the last marriage.[19]

A recent example of wife-inheritance is reported from Afghanistan. In 1926 a native of this country, who was married to a German woman, died, and when the widow applied to the courts for possession of her husband's property, she was informed that the clan to which her husband belonged still held to the old custom that the brother of the deceased gets all the property, including the wife, whom he is allowed to marry or sell. The brother in this case offered marriage, which was rejected, and he then used the clan prerogative of bringing the wife to the auction place. In order to save her from being sold as a slave the German Minister at Cabul was obliged to purchase her in the name of his Government.[20]

§383. Infidelity.

In Central Australia, an adulterer, when found guilty by the elders, may be killed.[1] In West Australia, if a woman who is promised or married to a given man runs away with another, and the two who thus elope are not *ñuba* to each other, they are separated by the tribe and punished, the woman being beaten by her female relatives and the man speared through the thigh. "If they are of the proper relation, that is, if they are *ñuba* to each other, it rests with the husband of the woman to get her back if he can. This often leads to a fight in which one or the other gets killed. Practically all the quarrels amongst the natives are about the women."[2]

In the New Hebrides men are said to be very jealous of their wives. Women

13 Barton, in JAI, LI, 99.
14 Torday, in JAI, LI, 374.
15 *Russian Ethnog.* (Russ.), II, 267.
16 Wilken, in VG, I, 332.
17 Buhl, *Israeliten*, 30.
18 Wilken, in VG, II, 50.

19 Stammler, *Stellung der Frauen*, 37.
20 N. Y. *Times*, Jan. 14, 1927.
1 Spencer and Gillen, *Nat. Tr. Cent. Aust.*, 15; Müller, *Sex. Leben*, 58.
2 Brown, in JAI, XLIII, 158.

dare not enter the premises of an unmarried trader or of a Romish priest.[3] The Lifu women are stated to have everything to fear on the part of an excessively jealous husband.[4] The original male ancestor of the Elema tribe is accredited with having decided that theft of property and immorality of the sexes were identical; "hence both evils became known by a common name, and the death penalty was recognized as the common punishment for both crimes." Adultery carries with it "unspeakable disgrace in the minds of the Ipi people, and is never referred to openly, except as an incitement to fight with bows and arrows on the occasion of a quarrel."[5] Severe punishment is sometimes inflicted upon the guilty pair in the New Britain group. "The woman is speared immediately and without mercy. The man may fall into an ambush formed by the husband and some friends. They pounce upon him, beat him fiercely with a stick, and then twist his neck as far as it is possible for them to do so. They then leave him in fearful agony in the path for any to help him who care to do so. He never speaks again. He lingers for a few days, the tongue swelling to a great size, and he dies a dreadful death."[6] If a wife in New Caledonia misbehaved, "the chief did not divorce her, but made her work all the harder."[7]

Grant[8] mentions a case among the Mavenda of South Africa in which one of the chief's most prominent indunas (sub-chiefs) had been guilty of a misdemeanor with the wife of an induna of equally prominent rank. "In the whole of my experience among Zulu," he comments, "a similar case had never once come under my notice, and had it occurred, the crime would have been expiated by death. In connection with the case in point, a fine only, of 14 head of cattle, was imposed, and the induna sent to Coventry for a month or so. His short term of banishment from the chief terminated only a few days prior to my arrival, and I found him in office discharging his accustomed duties." In West Africa, "adultery is often only the matter of laying one's hand, even in self-defense from a virago, on a woman—or brushing against her in the path. These accusations of adultery, next to witchcraft, are the great social danger to the West Coast native, and are often made merely from motives of extortion or spite, and without an atom of truth. To escape heavy punishment, a woman will accuse some man of having hustled against her, or sat on a bench beside her, etc., and the accused man has to pay up. If he does not, in the Calabar district, Egbo [the secret society] will come and 'eat the adultery,' and there will not be much of that man's earthly goods left. Sometimes the accusation is volunteered by the women, and frequently husband and wife conspire together and cook up a case against a man for the sake of getting damages. There is nothing that ensures a man an unblemished character in West Africa, except the possession of sufficient power to make it risky for people to cast slurs."[9] Among the Ewe, "it is an offence punishable by fine to praise the beauty of another man's wife, it being considered adultery by implication."[10] In Togo the husband has the right to kill the adulterer or to castrate him, according to the council's decision, "whereby the culprit has his sex parts crushed with stones."[11] With the Bangala of the Upper Congo, among whom it is said to be impossible to find a girl above the age of five years who is a virgin, "the only thing a man can do is to see that his wife does not commit adultery after

3 Leggatt, in AAAS, 1892, 706.
4 Ray, in JAI, XLVII, 254.
5 Holmes, in JAI, XXXIII, 127-128.
6 Danks, in JAI, XVIII, 293.
7 Turner, Samoa, 341.

8 In JAI, XXXV, 269.
9 Kingsley, Travels W. Afr., 497.
10 Ellis, Ewe, 92.
11 Klose, Togo, 505.

he has married, without his consent and receiving compensation for it. Should she do so the man is punished by a fine, but the woman goes unpunished. If she were punished she would not confess, and without her confession the husband could not enforce a fine on the man. The woman's word is always taken against a man." Weeks[12] has strong suspicion that this power is often abused, first, by the woman so as to pay off a grudge against someone who has slighted her and also so as to be regarded by the other women of the town as one after whom the men run; and, second, by the husband as a means of replenishing an empty purse—the fine being shared by husband and wife. "There are, undoubtedly, women who remain faithful to their husbands, but there are very few." In the Congo, "the name of a married woman may not be pronounced by any man except her husband or brother; she must be addressed as 'wife of so-and-so.' Neglect of the rule is a great insult and would be regarded as an excuse for manslaughter; it is punishable, at the least, by a heavy fine."[13] With the Baganda, "adultery was invariably punished by death, both the man and woman being put to horrible tortures to extract confession, and afterwards killed. If a peasant or slave looked at one of his master's wives he was liable to have his eyes gouged out. If a woman who is pregnant by her husband commits adultery she will be sure to suffer; either she will die with cross birth, or fall ill of *amakiro* (insanity in which she tries to kill and eat her child). If a woman dies in child-birth her relatives fine the husband because they say they did not marry her to two men, and he has allowed by negligence some one beside himself to have connection with her. He has to pay two women or two cows, two goats, two hoes, and two bark cloths. Cross birth is a sure sign of adultery, they affirm."[14]

No native woman in Nyasaland is said to be capable of even faintly suspecting that her white sister's attitude toward certain problems of life is either beautiful or reasonable. "A redeeming, although rather ludicrous feature of the question is, that Isolde is expected to make, without delay, full confession of her fault to her husband, who otherwise would die if he partook of food in company with Tristan. This is implicitly believed in by the natives of Nyasaland, and confessions of this kind are of very common occurrence. A somewhat similar idea is the universal belief that a woman whose husband has been unfaithful will grow ill and die of her next child; or that a child at the breast will die if its father is unfaithful to the mother. All the deaths of women with child, or of a child at the breast, are attributed to this cause. Nothing, however, appears to happen nowadays to the guilty father, except that he is excluded from the family mourning ceremonies."[15] In case of adultery among the Ayao the woman's husband demands a present from the culprit; if the present is not suitable, the case goes to the chief. Sometimes the co-respondent, instead of a present, lends his wife for the same number of nights as he slept with the other man's wife.[16] Although free love exists amongst the boys and girls of the Suk, who meet by assignation in the bushes, adultery is a very serious offense, and the offender is liable to forfeit the whole of his property to the clan of the injured party. "Usually, however, he is allowed to compound by slaughtering one or two bullocks and inviting the husband and his friends to a feast." With the Turkana, "the price of a wife being so high, it follows

12 In JAI, XXXIX, 442-443.
13 Torday and Joyce, in JAI, XXXVII, 140.
14 Roscoe, in JAI, XXXII, 39.
15 Coudenhove, in *Atl. Mo.*, CXXXII, 194.
16 Stigand, in JAI, XXXVII, 122.

that adultery is a most serious crime, and, if caught, the offender is condemned to death by the community and executed. If however he abscond, the whole of his property, or, if he be a poor man, his wives, or, if they be too old, his marriageable daughters, pass into the possession of the injured party. After the lapse of a few years the fugitive may return, but to the end of his days, whatever property he may become possessed of is claimed by the family of the man whose wife he seduced. As regards the woman, if she be old, no action is taken against her; if she be as yet childless, she is sent back to her father, and the marriage price is returned; but if she has already borne children, her husband divorces her, allowing her however, for the sake of her offspring, to remain in the village. As may be imagined cases of adultery are not of very frequent occurrence."[17] In Uganda, on the other hand, adultery entails little or no punishment. Among some tribes the woman is beaten and the man let off; among others the man is beaten and the woman let off, unless the co-respondent cannot be found and the woman refuses to give his name, in which case she is severely beaten.[18] At the present day, among the Bantu tribes of East Africa, adultery and other sexual offenses are dealt with according to the law of compensation, and the amount paid, though high in some districts, is moderate in others; but compensation was far from being the only means whereby crime was punished in former times. "While the husband may prosecute for adultery committed with his wife, the wife can never complain of adultery committed by her husband, but unfaithfulness on the part of the husband is very commonly the reason for her desertion. The guilt lies entirely with the man, and mostly the husband will not even reproach his wife for unfaithfulness. . . . A peculiar custom of the Wachagga suggests the view taken by the native: here a man who betrays the adultery of a woman to her husband must himself pay as much as the adulterer pays. It is argued that it is not his business to watch another man's wife, and that by so doing he usurps the rights of a husband, which in point of fact is the essence of the offence of adultery. The same idea, and also the total disregard of the woman's share in the blame, are reflected in the law regarding rape. Strange to say, the compensation demanded for this crime is in most cases the same, or practically the same, as in the case of adultery." The author[19] is convinced that the killing of an adulterer was not permitted under any circumstances; "in fact, it is often said, though not rigorously adhered to, that if a man had not been an eyewitness to the adultery of his wife he could claim nothing."

There is said to be practically no adultery among the Nigerians—"the change of husbands with the woman's father's consent being legal—but if a husband were to find a man with his wife he would beat him, and perhaps her also. . . . There are no prostitutes. Women are not allowed out of their houses at night for fear of ghosts, and this, no doubt, is a great check to immorality." In case of adultery, "the woman would not be killed, for she would be a loss, also no other woman would marry the slayer."[20] The Alur used to punish adultery by death; now the man is beaten until he buys off. If he cannot or will not, the chief makes him atone in some way.[21] Junker[22] found a number of cases in Africa where the man's fingers were cut off as a punishment for adultery. Among the Tuaregs adultery is punished by death.[23] Kabyle society not only

17 Dundas, K. R., in JAI, XL, 60, 68.
18 Johnston, Uganda, II, 882.
19 Dundas, C., in JAI, LI, 244-245, 274-275.
20 Tremearne, in JAI, XLII, 172, 190.

21 Stuhlmann, Mit Emin, 524.
22 Afrika, II, 458.
23 Ney, in Cosmopolitan Mag., XVIII, 151.

punishes by fine or sometimes with exile the person who brings dishonor into a family, but it demands that the husband, even the kinsman, try at least to take vengeance on the culprit.[24]

The Reindeer Koryak are reported as being very jealous, "so that a man will kill his wife merely through suspicion, and if he find her with a lover, will rip open with a knife the abdomens of both offenders. Owing to this, married women make themselves as repulsive-looking as possible, having uncombed hair, unwashed feet and hands, and worn-out clothing. On the contrary, among the Maritime Koryak, as among the Chukchee, when friends exchange visits, or when guests come to the house, they sleep with the wife and daughters of the host, who leaves the house for the night, in some cases to spend it with the wife of the guest; in consequence of this the women are very careful as to their appearance."[25] In ancient times the Chinese husband's adultery was punished by castration.[26] According to the Legacy of Iyéyasu, a ruler of sixteenth century Japan, the injured husband is confirmed in his ancient right to kill, but with this important provision, that should he kill but one of the guilty parties, he must himself be held as guilty as either of them. Should the offenders be brought up for trial, Iyéyasu advises that, in the case of common people, particular deliberation be given to the matter, suggesting that among the young and simple-minded some momentary impulse of passion may lead to folly, even when the parties are not naturally depraved. But in the next article he orders that no mercy whatever be shown to men and women of the upper classes when convicted of the same crime. "These," he declares, "are expected to know better than to occasion disturbance by violating existing regulations; and such persons, breaking the laws by lewd trifling or illicit intercourse, shall at once be punished without deliberation or consultation."[27] The same ruling has applied up to recent times, the husband being liable to imprisonment for ten years if he fails to get the adulterer.[28]

Half a century ago, in southern India, adulterers were seated on an ass, face toward the tail, and marched through the village. The public disgrace was enhanced by placing garlands of the despised *arka* leaves on their heads.[29] Should a wife among the Lushai be led astray, custom decrees that the various sums paid to her relatives as bride-price are to be returned to the husband, the co-respondent getting off scot free; among other clans the latter compensates the husband and takes the lady. "The former system is found in practice to be more conducive to morality, as under it a woman feels that her fault will bring shame and loss on her relatives and friends, whereas under the latter she becomes a mere chattel, and a husband is often a consenting party."[30] Among certain groups in the Dekkan, adultery is considered the gravest of caste-offenses. "This is not, however, because the women are so very moral, for they are just the opposite when away from their husbands for the purpose of selling milk and butter-milk in the towns. In former days, an unchaste woman, if detected, was tied to a tree and severely flogged with the twigs of the tamarind tree. This form of punishment has now been changed to that of excommunication, re-admittance to caste privileges being purchased by payment of fines. A male, found guilty of the same thing, is made to appear, dressed in female

24 Hanoteau et Letourneux, *Kabylie*, III, 74, 141, 187.
25 Czaplicka, *Aborig. Siberia*, 86.
26 Von Mollendorff, *Family Law of Chinese*, 30, note.

27 Hearn, *Japan*, 377-378.
28 Saint-Aubin, in *Umschau*, III, 462.
29 Thurston, *S. India*, 45.
30 Shakespear, in JAI, XXXIX, 381.

attire, before an assemblage of caste-men, and is subjected to further in-dignity. After being thus put to shame, he is made to pay a fine, varying ac-cording to his means, from Rs. 2 to Rs. 100,"[31]—a rupee being valued at about thirty-two cents. "Never," states a law of Manu, "must a prudent, well-trained man who knows the Vedas . . . and desires long life, cohabit with another's wife." Following the principle of property in women and hence in their off-spring, men who commit adultery benefit the owner of the woman, not them-selves, for the children, if such there be, go to the husband. For violating a guru's (wise man's) bed, the female part is branded on the forehead. Other penalties include the devouring of the unfaithful wife by dogs in the public place, roasting the guilty man on an iron bed, cutting off his genitals, and seizing all his property.[32]

Regarding the Palaungs, Milne[33] was told by a village-elder that in the time of one of the old chiefs a guilty wife and her lover, if caught, were shut together in a small room for three months, and were supplied day by day with just sufficient food to keep them alive. "He said that when at length they were set free they never wished to see each other again. Under another Chief the guilty pair were marched from the village where they were found, to the next village on the way to the frontier, and handed over to the head-man, to be passed on in a similar manner from village to village until the frontier was reached. They were then expelled from the State. The injured husband was allowed by public opinion to put to death the guilty pair, but this was not considered a wise proceeding on the part of the husband, as he would suffer for the act in his next existence." Adultery, again, frequently occurs among the Kubus of Sumatra, yet it gives no occasion for bloody revenge.[34] On the Mentawei Islands, free love comes to an end with marriage, and both parties guilty of adultery are put to death.[35]

Jealousy is said to be unknown amongst the Indians of south Alaska and northern British Columbia, and sanctioned prostitution a common evil; "the woman who can earn the greatest number of blankets or the largest sums of money wins the admiration of others for herself, and a high position for her husband by reason of her wealth."[36] Though their women are reputed to be extraordinarily beautiful, "you will seldom find a jealous husband, either among the Hurons or the Five Nations Indians."[37] Among the Apache, faith-less wives were punished by whipping and cutting off a portion of the nose, after which they were cast off.[38] Among the tribes of the Nahuatl race, death was the penalty for seducing a woman who had taken a vow of chastity or a married woman belonging to the same clan. The adulteress was quartered, her limbs being divided among all the men of the clan.[39] Religion acts as a check on adultery among the Warraus of the Orinoco. "On the death of a woman, the husband lies down in front of her. He remains there a few minutes, weeping and singing, and then makes way for each and all who have ever had connection with the deceased. As no Indian will willingly act contrary to the established usages of his tribe. . . . such a custom seems calculated to prove a check upon persons who are not desirous of having their actions exposed

31 Gunthorpe, in JASB, I, 47.
32 Bühler, *Manu*, VIII, 371, 374; IX, 41, 51, 237.
33 *Eastern Clan*, 418.
34 Anon., in *Globus*, XXVI, 45.

35 Pleyte, in *Globus*, LXXIX, 26.
36 Niblack, in USNM, 1888, 347.
37 Rogers, *America*, 239.
38 Fletcher and Mathews, in HAI, I, 442.
39 Nadaillac, *Preh. Amer.*, 314.

to public notoriety."[40] Among a tribe of the Rio Negro, the adulterer has a bath of Spanish pepper, while the woman is subjected to the bites of big ants.[41] If a Bororo suspects his wife of infidelity he puts her at the disposal of the young men in the *bahito* or men's house, and she becomes what is known as a tribal prostitute. She remains permanently there, and is prohibited from attending the more important religious festivities. "She receives many presents from the young men, is painted with *uruku,* and in general enjoys a fairly comfortable life." The authors[42] never met more than two such women in any village. Among the Araucanians, "adultery was not considered as an outrage to the honour of the husband, but a damage to the feminine property of the offended, and was punished by him at will, either by the death of the wife, or her sale, but most frequently by a heavy compensation by the co-respondent, except in the case of the culpable parties being caught *flagrante delicto* when the husband was within his right in slaying them both." In some cases, instead of selling her, the husband would return her to her father as damaged goods, insisting on the price paid for her being given back.[43]

The Code of Hammurabi makes several pronouncements on adultery. "If a man point the finger at a priestess or the wife of another and cannot justify it, they shall drag that man before the judges and they shall brand his forehead. . . . If the wife of a man be taken in lying with another man, they shall bind them and throw them into the water. If the husband of the woman would save his wife, or if the king would save his male servant (he may). . . . If a man force the (betrothed) wife of another who has not known a male and is living in her father's house, and he lie in her bosom and they take him, that man shall be put to death and that woman shall go free. . . . If a man accuse his wife and she has not been taken in lying with another man, she shall take an oath in the name of god and she shall return to her house. . . . If the finger have been pointed at the wife of a man because of another man, and she have not been taken in lying with another man, for her husband's sake she shall throw herself into the river."[44] Among the ancient Arabs adultery was punished by death, but "adultery occurred solely in association with a woman of another tribe."[45] Three instances of adultery are mentioned in the Homeric poems—Helen with Paris, Clytæmnestra with Ægisthus, and Aphrodite with Ares. The word itself does not occur, only "adultery-fines." Moral reprehension for the adultery itself, considered from the standpoint of what we regard as conjugal rectitude, was utterly lacking. In the famous case of Helen, the offense was that Paris violated guest-friendship and stole property. The affair of Ares with Aphrodite was regarded as a sensual jest.[46] With the poets of a later age adultery appears to have been both condoned and reprehended. In one of the plays of Euripides a nurse states: "How many sensible men when they see their wives unfaithful pretend not to see; how many fathers assist their sons in amours when they see that they are entangled. It is wise to conceal shame." In the same play, Phædra says. "May that wife perish in all ill who first did shame her couch for lovers other than her lord"—which would indicate that the marriage-vow was exclusive. Hecuba

40 Roth, in BAE, XXX, 160.
41 Von Martius, *Beiträge,* I, 632.
42 Frič and Radin, in JAI, XXXVI, 390-391.
43 Latcham, in JAI, XXXIX, 353-354, 356.

44 Harper, *Hammurabi,* 45, 47; Winckler, *Hammurabi,* 22.
45 Wilken, in VG, II, 7-8.
46 Seymour, *Hom. Age,* 403-404; Keller, *Hom. Soc.,* 214, 227 ff., 280, 287.

wanted Helen killed and a law to be established meting out death to every traitress to her husband. Herakles's wife knew not how to harbor indignation against him for his amours and took to her heart Iole whom he loved. "But who that is a woman could endure to dwell with her, both married to one man? . . . He will be called my husband but her mate, for she is younger. Yet no prudent wife would take this angrily." Clytæmnestra refers to her husband's escapades: "He is fallen who shamed me in dalliance with Chryseis and the rest before Ilion. And here is his captive [Cassandra], his prophet-mistress, that faithfully shared his bed and his bench in the ship. . . . She too now lies in death."[47] Greek law let the husband avenge himself on his wife's paramour, but she was never put to death. The guilty man might be dishonored and fined. At Kyme the woman was exposed on a stone in the market place and paraded around the city on an ass.[48] Human mores were in advance of those of the gods: Zeus rehearses his adulteries to the number of seven when wooing Hera to his side.[49]

In Rome, until Constantine's time, the law gave the woman's father the right to kill her if caught in adultery.[50] "Adultery was not only a violation of the most sacred bond, it was at the same time a crime against the Republic. Epictetus wanted to base marriage on reciprocal fidelity, on the chastity of each of the two spouses. The most beautiful ornaments of women are modesty and shyness; the stern and delicate conscience of the philosopher was indignant at the corruption of the Roman ladies of his time, who had forgotten those virtues and who, to justify their libertinism, cited Plato's advocacy of community of women."[51] In the *lex Julia* of the time of Augustus, the penalty for adultery was severe. Besides property-penalties attended by disgrace, the man was banished to a remote island and the woman to another. In Justinian's time deportation was dropped, and bodily punishment and imprisonment in a cloister were substituted.

According to Bohemian folk-justice, if the husband did not himself punish the guilty pair, their genitals were mangled in a public place. Among the Saxons the husband had the right to kill; if he did so in *flagrante delicto*, he was required to sit on the slain pair and send to court. The judge would then allow him to tie the pair together, take them under the gallows, and there bury them, "after he had driven a stake through their bodies, 'whether they were living or dead'" The Christian Church widened the scope of adultery and narrowed the penalty. Pope Alexander III. had adultery placed among the *crimina minora*. Clerical adultery was treated leniently though it was shameless. But the offended husband, or even the bridegroom, who caught the priest and killed him, was not excommunicated but could receive absolution.[52] German law of the twelfth century provided that the guilty man should be drawn through the city *per veretrum*. Adultery of a Jew with a Christian woman was punished by cutting off the genitals and putting out the eyes. Between the thirteenth and fifteenth centuries the law made no distinction between seduction and rape which were punished by the sword or by burying alive.[53]

The Bulgarians punished an adultress by placing her backwards on an ass, holding its tail in her hand, while her paramour led the beast through the

47 Euripides, *Hippolytus*, 462 ff.; 407 ff.; *Trojan Women*, 1030 ff.; Sophocles, *Trachiniæ*, 545 ff.; Æschylus, *Agamemnon*, 1438 ff.
48 Becker, *Charikles*, III, 321, 324, 325, 326.
49 *Iliad*, XIV, 250.

50 Rossbach, *Röm. Ehe*, 60.
51 Schmidt, *Soc. Civ.*, 397.
52 Schroeder, *Geschlechtl. Ordnung*, 112, 113, 116, 117, 119, 120.
53 Rudeck, *Oeffentl. Sittl.*, 168, 169, 178.

entire village amidst the laughter and spitting of the people.[54] Among the
North Albanian tribes, who still have local laws and courts, Miss Durham[55]
found that the woman in such cases was rarely if ever punished. "She was
regarded as not responsible and as the property of her family, who took vengeance for damaged goods. . . . Nose-cutting appears to have been a very old
Serb custom. In the laws made by the great Tsar Stefan Dushan in 1349 we
find that a married woman guilty of libertinage shall have her nose and ears
cut off. When I was first in Montenegro I was told that there was a woman
still living near Podgoritza whose nose had been cut off by her husband, who
suspected her of infidelity, and at the Serb village of Vraka, near the shore
of Lake Scutari, I have heard of more than one case. The French Consul,
Degrand, recorded one about 1890. In this case the husband continued living
with his wife. I expressed surprise to my guide, who was a quite uneducated
mountain tribesman, and he cheerfully said that now it would be all right;
she would be so hideous there was no fear of her finding any other man to
carry on with."

§384. Other Rights and Disqualifications.

Woman's Property. Papuan women are by no means slaves, but have a voice
in all the concerns of family and village. "In many duties the women have a
distinct sphere from the men, but in general matters they have an equal voice.
They have ownership in land, and frequently prevent the men from selling
native wealth."[1] Throughout New Guinea women do the trading and take care
of the most valuable property.[2] In the New Hebrides, "the women own
the plantations, and land is inherited through the mother. When a woman
marries into another tribe she loses her right in the old tribe, though a child
sometimes inherits land in the old tribe through the mother. The women, as well
as the men, own tusk-pigs and fowls, and they have a right to these even against
their own husbands. A man may have two wives, but each wife must have her
own hut. Some women attain high enough rank to have club houses or sacred
lodges of their own. To each hut belongs a storehouse built on piles, in which
the women keep their yams, vegetables, cocoanuts, and bananas."[3]
Despite the fact that among certain Africans the wife is regarded as the
property of her husband, her position is one of independence. She owns her
own hut, field, and poultry, and provides for her husband's necessities. Under
these circumstances, the man is of course unable to rule his wife. Where these
conditions exist, the female line of descent generally prevails.[4] A big chief
in West Africa will have three or more wives, each of them living in her own
house or, as in Calabar, in her own yard in his house, having her own farm
away in the country, where she goes at planting and harvest times. She possesses her own slaves and miscellaneous property, which is really that of
her family, just as most people's property is in West Africa.[5] Among the
Bangala, "every woman had her farm, which was her exclusive property, and
not even a fellow wife had any rights over it."[6] In East Africa, "women
cannot be said to have any rights to land or stock, but are often recognized as
trustees or guardians of property during the minority of their male children.

54 Strauss, *Bulgaren*, 302.
55 In JAI, XLVII, 440, 446.
1 Bromilow, in AAAS, 1909, 471.
2 Turner, *Samoa*, 347.

3 Sebbelov, in AA, XV, 279.
4 Starcke, *Prim. Fam.*, 67.
5 Kingsley, *W. Afr. Studies*, 438.
6 Weeks, in JAI, XXXIX, 129.

Should any such children die in infancy the estate reverts to the nearest male relation."[7] In one case three distinctive phases of ownership are represented in the same tribe: the Sungu woman may own practically anything, and at her death her property returns to her own family; the Olemba woman may own certain things, but at her death they revert to her husband; and, finally, the northern Batetela woman cannot own at all.[8] Among the Wawanga, "every wife receives from her husband a certain quantity of stock. The chief wife is given most, unless she prove incompetent. On the death of the husband this property is divided up amongst the woman's children. If one of the wives have a larger number of children than the others, their portion is increased from the common stock. Every woman has also her own banana plantation, which goes to her eldest son."[9] The Tuareg wife is mistress of her fortune. As among the Berbers and Abyssinians, the children belong to her and bear her name. She marries as she likes, eats with her husband, smokes, inherits, and controls most of the property.[10]

Among the ancient Hindus the husband's right to chastise, far from being a right of life and death as in early Roman law, was limited to relatively harmless blows, not on a "noble part." In the range of rights to property there gradually developed a not insignificant independence of women.[11] "In East Turkestan bazaars it is not only men who do selling, but not seldom also women."[12] In the East Indies the woman is often at the head of the family and the man an underling. Where this is not the case, the woman still has great influence in the house, is recognized in all important situations, and has in common with the man control and disposal of the goods of which she is often co-owner. If a traveller wants to buy anything of a man, the latter must speak to his wife first; yet, strangely enough, this is where the wife is regarded as the man's slave. In South Sumatra, as elsewhere, distinction is made between the possessions which a man has won by inheritance and those which he has got by his own diligence, the inherited goods and those self-won. The last are generally known under the name *harta-pentjarian;* this is of course individual property, and although it consists for the most part of movable goods it may also include land that one has got for himself. The inherited goods, called *harta-pusaka,* are mostly the communal possession of the family. To them all members of the family have equal rights, the head of the family being the controller and regulator. In general, with unions following the agnatic system, especially with those *cum manu* (with a bride-price), the marriage-goods are exclusively the property of the man, and the wife possesses none of them. The conception that the wife was bought must itself have excluded the idea that she, herself a piece of property, could have any property-right in what the man brought into marriage. Even the self-won goods, the *pentjarian,* in the winning of which she had participated with her work, she might not call her own; all belonged exclusively to the man, as a number of examples indicate. From this it appears that the woman who is in *manu mariti,* the wife of a *jujur* marriage, possesses nothing, so that when she dies she leaves nothing and nothing can be inherited from her. There are only a few exceptions to this rule in South Sumatra. Besides the *cum manu* marriage stands the *sine manu* type, without bride-price. Here the regulations touching the right of property

7 Hobley, *A-Kamba*, 137.
8 Torday, in JAI, LI, 374.
9 Dundas, K. R., in JAI, XLIII, 56.

10 Letourneau, *Prop.*, 183; *Marr.*, 175 ff.
11 Jolly, *Stellung d. Frauen*, 438, 439.
12 Prjevalski, *Forskningsresor*, 438.

are in general wholly different from the above. In such a marriage it is the woman alone who has any property-right, the man possessing nothing. Where, in default of sons, the daughter must carry on the line, she is the one who brings to marriage the property, especially the *pusaka;* the man comes empty-handed. Furthermore, there is in *sine manu* marriage also the other kind of property, things which the spouses have won by common labor. Of these the wife is sole owner and the man can make no kind of claim to them. All writers are unanimous on this point. Among the Macassars, Buginese, and others there is no community of goods in marriage; the possessions of each spouse are sharply distinguished, movables as well as immovables. If a man gets into debt, it is his property alone that can be attached, except where the debt is contracted with the knowledge of the wife, whose goods in that case can also be attached, as she appears as a guarantor.[13] Among the Mohammedan families in Java the same holds true, and the giving and selling of property between spouses are allowed as between strangers. The man pays the wedding-gift, which goes to the wife as her property, and to it she or her heirs have irrevocable claim after the consummation of the marriage or her death or that of her husband. The latter must support her and pay the cost of the domestic establishment; even if the wife is personally rich and the man poor, she need not contribute.[14]

Among the Tlinkits, "the husband's earnings are wholly turned over to his wife. She is, therefore, the banker of the household. If he desires to make a purchase he must appeal to her and get her consent."[15] Private ownership of property on the part of women was common in North America. Among the Eskimo the lamp belonged to the women; in many Indian tribes all raw materials, as meat, corn, and, before the advent of traders, pelts, were woman's property. Among the tribes of the plains the lodge or tipi was the woman's, but on the northwest coast the wooden structures belonged to the men of the family. In some cases individual houses were built and owned by the women. Like the houses, the small garden-patches were also the property of the women, who alone cultivated them. Cooking- and eating-utensils, the mortar and pestle for grinding corn, and the packs for storing food and clothing—all these things which pertained to the household were the property of the wife.[16] In California and on the northwest coast "wives are consulted in matters of trade, and in fact seem to be nearly on terms of equality with their husbands." In divorce, "a strict division of property and return of betrothal presents is expected, the woman being allowed not only the property she brought her husband, and articles manufactured by her in wedlock, but a certain proportion of the common wealth."[17] Wives have much to say concerning property in Brazil; a certain European was unable to purchase a canoe because the owner's wife refused.[18]

The free Accadian woman was not the creature of her spouse; she had her own rights and her own fortune. Even under the control of her husband she could possess personal property and take the necessary steps to acquire it. Her husband's creditors could not touch it. A rich wife managed her own property and used the revenues at her pleasure.[19] The ancient Egyptian wife

13 Wilken, in VG, I, 261, 264, 367; II, 272-273, 275-276, 292.
14 Van den Berg, in *Bijd.*, XLI, 471.
15 Jones, *Thlingets*, 51.
16 Chamberlain; Fletcher; Hodge, in HAI, I, 741; II, 308; and II, 323, 692, respectively;

Fletcher and LeFlesche, in BAE, XXVII, 362.
17 Bancroft, *Nat. Races*, I, 196-197; Spencer, *Prin. Soc.*, I, 753-754.
18 Koch-Grünberg, in *Globus*, XC, 261.
19 Lenormant, *Chaldean Magic*, 385; Maspero, *Hist. Anc.*, I, 737.

administered her own property; she was also absolute mistress of her dowry. If she contributed to the family support she did it of her free will and not by law or contract. In the marriage-contract the husband promised not to claim authority, to give her certain slaves and let her thereafter dispose of them without his interference, and to assign to her all debts due her. The woman joined her husband in property-deeds, while at Nineveh occurred a case where a married woman sold a share in some property wholly without her husband's coöperation. So high was the wife's position that Herodotus made fun of the Egyptian husband and said that the wife went to market while the husband stayed at home and wove.[20] The *Koran* provides that women shall inherit. The Prophet's wife, before her marriage to him, carried on large commercial transactions on her own account.[21] The veneration of the Teuton for woman is strikingly illustrated by the Anglo-Saxon marriage-laws. A bridegroom had to produce sureties and a pledge before the marriage-ceremony could be legally performed. His *morgengabe* corresponded to the modern settlement, and a wife who had brought forth children alive and survived her husband obtained half his property. It was only in very early ages that the morning-gift reverted to the donor if the wife was sterile. Women both inherited and disposed of property, and appear frequently in Domesday as tenants-in-chief. A widow was protected by legal penalties, varying in proportion to her rank, from any outrage or wrong.[22]

Public Functions and Influence.[23] What is said to be the only exception to the general oppression of women among the Australians is the custom of the West Australians to make an old woman grandmother of the tribe, which gives her a prominent position and qualifies her to reconcile strife, to separate fighters, and to summon to war.[24]

Although South African women are not supposed to enter the assembly-place, Livingstone[25] reports one exception. Among the Banyai the chief is elected, and they chose the son of the deceased chief's sister in preference to his own offspring. With the Manganya the chieftainship is hereditary in the direct line but in case of doubt the descendant of the king's sister is preferred. These people have been tormented by robber-bands and slave-hunters, but one of the least burdened of the tribes was one ruled by a woman.[26] Among the Basuto, besides prostitution, the career of prophet and the exercise of civil power, even as chief, are open to women.[27] In every town among the Yorubas is a local female magistrate to whom are regularly referred all disputes between women.[28] In Dahomi the women-soldiers are stronger and more skilful than the men; in Ashanti the sister of the king has a power over his female subjects which gives her an almost independent position.[29] Among the Baganda the new king elects a queen-mother or dowager-queen, who is his real mother if the latter is living. She has many privileges, an enclosure, and officers like the king. The queen-sister also has an establishment with lands and officers; she takes charge of the king's tomb at death.[30]

20 Paturet, *Anc. Égypte*, 39, 41, 72; Herodotus, *Hist.*, II, 35; Letourneau, *Marr.*, 175-182.

21 Wilken, in VG, II, 50-51, 52.

22 Garnier, *British Peasantry*, I, 98; Freisen, *Canon. Eherechts*, 183.

23 §157, of text and *Case-Book*.

24 Ratzel, *Vkde.*, II, 67.

25 *Mission. Travels*, I, 316.

26 Ratzel, *Vkde.*, I, 404.

27 Chamberlain, in AA, IV, 337.

28 Ellis, *Yoruba*, 167; Dowd, *Negro Races*, I, 209.

29 Ratzel, *Vkde.*, I, 81.

30 Roscoe, in JAI, XXXII, 167.

In the early philosophical period in India, "wise priests meet together to discuss theological and philosophical questions, often aided, and often brought to grief, by the wit of women disputants, who are freely admitted to hear and share in the discussion." The very fact that in the *Mahabharata* a woman is the disputant "gives an archaic effect to the narration, and reminds one of the scenes in the Upanishads, where learned women cope successfully with men in displays of theological acumen."[31] Perhaps nowhere in the Indian Archipelago does woman take so high a rank as among the Macassars and Buginese. "Among the nations of Celebes, the women appear in public without any scandal; they take an active concern in all the business of life; they are consulted by the men on all public affairs, and frequently raised to the throne, and that too when the monarchy is elective. Here the woman eats with her husband, nay, by a custom which points at the equality of the sexes, always from the very same dish, the only distinction left to the latter being that of eating from the right side. At public festivals, women appear among the men; and those invested with authority sit in their counsels when affairs of state are discussed, possessing, it is often alleged, even more than their due share in the deliberations."[32] Woman-rule among the Dyaks is not rare, but with the Macassars and Buginese its existence seems the more remarkable since we here have to do with Mohammedan people, and Islam sets itself against the rule of woman. That the woman comes out in the open and even urges troops to the fight, is not seldom reported. If she takes such a sure rank in public life, she must have no less power in the kin-group. Dyak women participated in the assembly. In 1847 the separated wife of the Sultan of Kutei ruled as princess over the Dyaks on River Kutei. After getting out of her marriage, she had a harem of men and punished infidelity with death. Armed and clad as a man, she led, in her youth, many a pillaging raid. A more remarkable case of woman-rule in the Archipelago was in the kingdom of Atjeh, north Sumatra; in the seventeenth century, over a period of fifty-eight years, this country was ruled by four successive sultanesses. Even among the Bataks, whose women are described as slaves, the female sex is not entirely excluded from public consultations. Often the women shriek their opinions and advice into the council houses; not only are they listened to but, especially when they are old sibyls, their words are taken to heart. In one place some old women passionately advised that a certain European be killed as a spy and eaten. Other Bataks allow women to have a voice in choosing chiefs. Again, in council they stand by the men, advising them, and even themselves speaking up. The women, further, take part in war by stirring the men to strife.[33]

In the Caroline Islands "the oldest women of the clan exercise the most decisive influence on the direction of its affairs and the headman does nothing without a previous thorough taking of counsel with them, which relates even to state and external political affairs."[34] In the Marianas Islands women held property and could speak in council;[35] while in the Friendly Islands discoverers found a woman above the king, honored by him as all others honored him, but without governing power.[36]

In many cases among the American Indians women held a place in the

31 Hopkins, *Relig. India*, 382.
32 Crawfurd, *Indian Arch.*, 74.
33 Wilken, in VG, I, 257-258, 259-260, 365-366; Bock, *Borneo*, 21.

34 Kubary, *Pelauer*, I, 39.
35 Waitz, *Anthrop.*, V, 107.
36 Lippert, *Kgchte.*, II, 217.

management of tribal affairs. They nominated and deposed chiefs and took part in the government which was democratic. Where they held no official position in the tribe they were nevertheless consulted on important matters.[37] Especially among the monogamous Iroquois did they have great political influence.[38]

A queen of the Arabians figures in the wars of Tiglath-Pileser III and Sargon. From 740 B.C. a college of priestesses at Thebes became the real governing authority in that city and district; its power later became concentrated in the chief priestess.[39] The women of the harem got up a conspiracy against Thothmes III of Egypt, drawing their male relatives into it; this was no slight affair.[40] Scythian women, according to Diodorus,[41] were equal to the men in warlike spirit and gave them their most renowned leaders. The king did not have as much honor as the queen. In Judah the mother of the ruling king had an influential position, and there is offered even an example of a ruling queen. The women in Israel took part in the great sacrificial meals.[42] Goddesses played a great part in Semitic religion, and not merely in the subordinate status of wives of the gods.[43] While the majority of the Oriental cults accorded to women a considerable rôle in their churches, and sometimes even a preponderating one, finding in them ardent supporters of the faith, "Mithra forbade their participation in his Mysteries and so deprived himself of the incalculable assistance of these propagandists."[44] Gide[45] says: "Nothing proves better the important part played by women in the primitive Church than the great number of tracts concerning them in the works of the Fathers. Saint Jerome, out of a hundred theological letters, addresses fifty to women; fifteen of his treatises out of twenty have the education of women as their subject." The same may be said of Saint Cyprianus and Saint Ambrose.

A modern example of woman-rule is reported from Russia. As the men of a certain village leave for work in Moscow and other large cities, the only representatives of the strong sex remaining are a few old men and some boys. These will not accept the responsibility of attending to certain current community-affairs which require immediate action, and so the men have arranged, during their absence, to transfer their votes to the women. Community-affairs have by no means suffered through this arrangement; on the contrary, the women are better acquainted with local needs than the men, who live for the greater part of the year in the large cities, and they take their tasks more seriously, do not let themselves be influenced in their decisions by wretched "Schnaps," and attend the councils with the greatest regularity.[46]

Respect for Women in the Home and Community. In southeast Papua, "the men seem generally content to let the women have their own way in domestic and general affairs, as long as they are themselves allowed to rule in war, and carry out trade expeditions. Occasionally a woman will be thrashed, but she has her remedy in divorce if the thrashing is too cruel or unjust. Occasionally,

37 Fletcher, in HAI, I, 301; Morgan, in *Contrib. N. Amer. Ethnol.*, IV, 66; Bolton, in HAI, II, 706; Mason, *Woman's Share*, 195; Fletcher and LaFlesche, in BAE, XXVII, 337.
38 Schoolcraft, *Indian Tribes*, III, 195; Morgan, *Anc. Soc.*, 455 (quoted); Starcke, *Prim. Fam.*, 282; Parkman, *Old Régime*, 30; Anon., in AA, 145.
39 Maspero, *Hist. Anc.*, III, 172, 188, 244.

40 Erman, *Aegypten*, I, 87.
41 *Hist.*, I, 27; III, 33; Wilutzky, *Mann u. Weib*, 26.
42 Buhl, *Israeliten*, 32.
43 Smith, *Relig. Sem.*, 52.
44 Cumont, *Mithra*, 173.
45 *Condition privée de Femme*, 201; Schmidt, *Soc. Civ.*, 202.
46 "Kl. Nachr.," in *Globus*, LXXXII, 393.

too, a witch will be drowned."[47] Among the Melanesians generally, "a man may address his wife by her personal name though the wife should not take this liberty, but should speak of her husband as *I gene* if he has no children, or as the father of his child *'Taman X'* if there have been children of the marriage. . . . I was told that there are no less than three women in the district of Veverau alone who address their husbands by name, thus showing that they do not respect them. There is little doubt that this is the result of external influence, and that in former times the usual signs of respect would have been enforced." There are five different ways of referring to a wife: by name, as *Ro gene* (of which no meaning is given), as the mother of her children, as the children themselves, or as the wife of her husband.[48]

Unlike Bantu wives, those of the Bushmen are life-companions, and each sex has its share of toil. "Sentimentality is certainly little to be found in the conjugal life of the Namaqua; rather does the wife employ off-hand the wonderful facility of her tongue and her equally marvellous wealth in most insulting epithets, even against her husband; the latter, by reason of the inequality of his verbal shafts, then sees himself obliged to employ 'striking' answers to her offensive songs. Right afterwards, however, they are again the best friends in the world and joke together like the tenderest lovers."[49] Domestic slavery and that of women do not exist among the Pygmies to the same extent as with the surrounding tribes. The women have a good position as compared with those of agricultural negroes. They seldom marry into other races, "because they do not know the work."[50] Among the Kimbundas, who believe death to be the result of magic, when a wife dies her relatives try to have the guilt fastened on her husband, because then he will be obliged to pay them damages. "With this in mind he pays her respect in proportion to the power of her kinsfolk."[51] A husband in the French Congo may whack his wife or wives with impunity as long as he does not draw blood; "if he does, be it ever so little, his wife is off to her relations, the present he has given for her is returned, the marriage is annulled, and she can re-marry as soon as she is able."[52] In the Upper Congo "men slaves were sold at 500 to 600 brass rods, worth about 6s. 6d. per hundred. Women slaves were worth from 2,000 to 2,500 brass rods on account of their farm work, and child-bearing capacity."[53] Such valuable property should be treated with care. Among the Akamba, women are not subjected to rough treatment as an African conceives of it.[54] A writer on Nyasaland pays his respects to the native women. "If the native woman's conduct as a spouse, looked at from the white man's point of view, leaves much to be desired, it must be proclaimed, on the other side, that no words of praise could even approximately do justice to her in her character as housewife and as mother. Her thrift, her patience, her endurance, her uncomplaining and quiet cheerfulness, are the incomparable qualities against which her husband has nothing to put into the balance except official representation and the prestige of masculine strength, which, as a protection, is becoming more and more superfluous. . . . When one asks the men what part of the work is left for them to do, as the women do practically everything, they invariably reply: 'Oh, but do not we get the money for the women to buy cloth with, by hiring ourselves out to Europeans? Where are the women to get money from, if we do not get it

47 Bromilow, in AAAS, 1909, 473.
48 Rivers, *Melan. Soc.*, I, 40-41.
49 Fritsch, *Eingeb. S.-Afr.*, 363, 444-445.
50 David, in *Globus*, LXXXVI, 196, 197.

51 Starcke, *Prim. Fam.*, 67.
52 Kingsley, *Travels W. Afr.*, 225.
53 Weeks, in JAI, XXXIX, 420.
54 Dundas, C., in JAI, XLIII, 490.

for them?' . . . The adaptability of native women to their surroundings, and their equanimity under all circumstances, are remarkable. They are very like gypsies in this respect."[55]

The Koryak husband will often advise with his wife about affairs, and a daughter's preference is frequently consulted with regard to her marriage. "Generally, the attitude towards a wife is one of kindly protectiveness." Though the uncivilized Ostyak considers his wife but as a necessary domestic animal, and scarcely favors her with a good word for all her hard labor, yet "he dares not strike her, even for the greatest crime, unless he has consent of her father; for, in such a case, the provoked wife would run to her parents and persuade her father to return the *kalym* [bride-price] to his son-in-law, and she would marry some other man."[56] "The position of women among the Semas is on the whole far from the degradation sometimes alleged of Nagas in general. . . . The women have to work very hard in the fields, but their husbands do the same, and both as daughters, wives, and mothers they are treated with real affection and respect by their parents, their husbands, and their children."[57] The Hindu epics venerate women: "The best medicine of the physician is for man not so good, in every pain, in every need, as a true and loving wife." Again: "Because you, oh slender of form, chose me, a man, before the gods, so know that I, your spouse, am always mindful of your word; so long as life's breath holds out in my breast, oh lovely one, so long do I not withdraw from you;—that I swear to you, sweet-laughing one!"[58] And in the Laws of Manu: "Women must be honored and adorned by their fathers, brothers, husbands, and brothers-in-law, who desire their own welfare. . . . Where women are honored there the gods are pleased, but where they are not honored no sacred rite yields reward. . . . In that family where the husband is pleased with his wife and the wife with her husband happiness will assuredly be lasting."[59] While many Hindus may despise women socially, they have a high esteem for motherhood and pay almost exclusive adoration to the female deities.[60]

Although women in the Indian Archipelago often work beyond their strength, field-labors are divided in quite definite manner between man and wife. "A Batak woman generally knows how to get her husband to do what she wants; often she employs, when other means do not help, the threat of suicide. To prepare a rope, and with it to make a motion as if to hang herself, is sufficient to bring the man to terms." Wilken[61] goes on to tell of a case where a village was in uproar because a woman was found busy hanging herself to a coffee-tree—"an innocent performance, for she could see over the tree. The reprobation of the man who through his obstinacy had brought his wife to any such pass, was universal." Among the Alfurs, the position of the wife as compared to that of the husband is indicated by the names given to her, *viz.*, cook, pounder (with pestle), and nurse. Man and wife call each other "fellow-eater," the term indicating equality of sexes, since they eat together. Although hard work is woman's portion on the island of Nias, "she does it with spirit, for she is not handled as a slave but as a housewife; if not honored, at least recognized; and as to this her lot is not harder than that of most women of the lower classes in Europe." In the Malay Peninsula, "should a Mantra woman

55 Coudenhove, in *Atl. Mo.*, CXXXII, 190-191.
56 Czaplicka, *Aborig. Siberia*, 34-35, 127.
57 Hutton, *Sema Nagas*, 187.

58 Holtzmann, *Ind. Sagen*, II, 18, 27.
59 Bühler, *Manu*, III, 55, 56, 60.
60 Wilkins, *Hinduism*, 92.
61 In VG, I, 263, 264 (quoted), 336 (quoted).

offend her husband, he might complain to her parents, who would themselves chastise her. The wife, on the other hand, had a reciprocal right to appeal for protection to the parents of her husband. Should the husband commit any serious offence against his wife, her relatives might complain to the Batin or chief of the tribe, who would authorise them to deal summarily with him. They would then repair to the offender's house and strip it of every article that it contained. The goods thus summarily appropriated were carried to the Batin, who would give one portion to the wife's relatives, and distribute the remainder between himself and his officers."[62]

Among the Tlinkits, "the husband chastises his wife, sometimes beating her unmercifully. The wife does not always tamely submit to this, but defends herself to the best of her ability. Often she is more than a match for her husband in brute strength and in the science of handling her fists." Her relation is not that of a slave to her master. "She is as independent as he, and she asserts her independence, too. In truth, the average husband stands more in fear of his wife than she does of him. . . . No person is more stubborn than the average Thlinget woman. You can neither coax nor drive her. She would sooner be beaten to a pulp than have to admit she was compelled to do a thing. If she did she would be sneered at as a slave, and that would be worse than death, for slaves are despised as the very lowest of creatures."[63] Women were respected by the Omaha, the value of their industry was recognized, and their influence was potent in all affairs pertaining to the home.[64] Among other Indians also the woman held a comparatively high place in family life, being consulted as to bargaining and other matters.[65] Gynæcocracy was not inconsistent with drudgery of women.[66] The Guanches of Teneriffe were chivalrous in the extreme. "If a man met a woman in a solitary place he stood aside to let her pass and could not even look at her nor speak unless she first addressed him. Transgression of this law was severely punished."[67]

The most striking feature of the condition of the free Accadian woman was the importance attached to the mother in relation to her children, which was superior even to that of the father.[68] In the Chaldæan marriage-contract the man could be called on to promise that he would not take a second wife, and an indemnity was provided for the woman in case he broke his word. Women of rank and property were protected by the marriage-contract so that they retained independent power in marriage for the control of their property, with competence to make contracts. This also made their husbands treat them well.[69] The spouses in ancient Egypt were on an equal footing; they could make contracts with themselves or with others.[70] Although polygyny was allowed by the East Iranians, the wife was not the slave, but the comrade and helpmeet, of her husband.[71] Among the Israelites the wife actually stood higher than one would expect from their customs; practice was much better than the law. Father and mother stood side by side in family authority.[72] Before Mohammed, the position of the Arabian wife was one of dignity and worth. There

62 Skeat and Blagden, *Malay Penin.*, II, 79.

63 Jones, *Thlingets*, 50-51.

64 Fletcher and LaFlesche, in BAE, XXVII, 337.

65 Hodge, in HAI, II, 692.

66 Morgan, in *Contrib. N. Amer. Ethnol.*, IV, 122.

67 Cook, in AA, II, 487.

68 Lenormant, *Chaldean Magic*, 385.

69 Maspero, *Hist. Anc.*, I, 735, 737.

70 Paturet, *Anc. Égypte*, 6, 42.

71 Geiger, *Ostiran. Kultur*, 337.

72 Buhl, *Israeliten*, 31 ff.; Gen., II, 18; Deut., XXI, 18-21; Maurer, *Vkde.*, I, 50-51.

is no lack of examples of love and fidelity between spouses, even among the Arabs of today. "The wife was mistress of the house, the unlimited ruler in the circle of the family." To wound or kill a woman was always regarded as the most offensive, the most dishonorable act. An old Arabian writer asserts: "The true Arab had only one love and did not give her up till death; the same was true of her." Among the rich city-dwellers, women freely associated in society; they adorned the meals at which guests were present and took part in the religious festivals; indeed, a knightly *Minnedienst* developed, as later occurred in the Occident. During this period poems glowing with love celebrated the beauty and nobility of women. Thus for a long time there remained in the circle of Arabian aristocracy a higher and freer position of woman than that granted to her by Islam.[73]

Among the Homeric Greeks, to bear children was woman's destiny and her honor. The women were far from being kept in semi-Oriental seclusion; they were freer and more influential than their daughters and successors of the historical period.[74] The status of women was probably higher in Sparta than elsewhere in Greece; Plutarch thought it was too high, for the husbands appear to have been ruled by their wives. In many marriages the wife dominated by force of character, by arrogance, or because of her property. If no other factor could assure her independence, she might resort to excess of tenderness or to female tyranny, as Aristotle warned. Socrates declared that by her nature woman was not inferior to man; she merely was lacking in reflection and force, which it was the duty of her husband to supply by instruction. Euripides would satisfy the modern feminists. Like any suffragette, Medea knew the answer to the argument that man's superiority before the law is founded upon the fact that he alone performs military service: "They say we lead an unimperilled life within the home, while they contend with the spear. An ill thought! Thrice to stand forth with shield would I choose, rather than once to give birth."[75]

At Rome the key to state subordination lay in the *patria potestas;* this almost monarchical principle preserved from disorder. *Patria potestas* was not a burden but a beneficent thing—a protection to non-weapon-bearing women. Women had care of the hearth, the holy center of the family; they took part in family religion, were married into religious relation with their husbands, and came under the special care of the gods. All this united to keep the marriage bond clear and strong; hence the high position of woman. "The farther we go back in antiquity the more dependent is the woman on her husband, but also the more dignified is her place in the family, the greater her influence on the form of societal relations. This principle may be set up as one generally effective for the whole Indo-germanic race." It was in the family that the Roman citizen learned to subordinate himself; this was a lesson in citizenship. The position of woman was characterized by the term *manus,* which, with the house-master's power, was as old as the oldest Indo-germanic family. "When

73 Smith, *Kinship,* 100-106, 171, 275; Von Kremer, *Kgchte. Orients,* II, 95, 100, 101, 102, 103; Wellhausen, *Ehe bei Arabern,* 451; Hauri, *Islam,* 128-129; Palgrave, *Arabia,* 155; Pischon, *Islam,* 61.

74 Keller, *Hom. Soc.,* 233 ff.; Seymour,

Hom. Age, 127, 128. Beloch, *Gr. Gchte.,* I, 471-472, thinks there was no decline in status.

75 Becker, *Charikles,* 319; Schoemann, *Griech. Alterth.,* I, 274; Drumann, *Arbeiter,* 136; Schmidt, *Soc. Civ.,* 121; Aristotle, *Ethics,* VIII, 14; *Econom.,* I, 4; Euripides, *Medea,* 248-251.

the people of our race were all together in inseparable unity, language, religious consciousness, and family-organization all formed themselves." The Romans brought all under one will, the expression of which was the state. All were alike before one law. Men lost their power over slaves and wives; *patria potestas* and *manus* declined.[76] Even in the worst reigns there were homes with an atmosphere of old Roman self-restraint and sobriety, where good women wielded a powerful influence over their husbands and sons, and where the examples of the old Republic were used, as Biblical characters with us, to fortify virtue. The position of woman was improved with the adoption of Christianity which imposed duties on the husband as well. "If, leaving aside for a moment the juridic formulas, we observe what woman was in their customs, in their social life—in a word, in reality—we see the scene, so to speak, suddenly change: she was no longer a powerless and oppressed slave; she was the matron, the mother of the family, revered by the slaves, clients, and children, respected by her husband, cherished by all, mistress in the house, and extending her influence outside to the midst of popular assemblies and the councils of the Senate. The Romans did not relegate woman to the solitude and silence of the gyneceum; they admitted her to their theatres, their festivals, their meals; everywhere a place of honor was reserved for her; everyone gave precedence to her, the consul and lictors cleared the way for her. Besides, one rarely met her in a public place or in popular gatherings: as sedentary by virtue as the Greek woman was by constraint, her habitual place was by the domestic hearth, in the atrium."[77]

An early Swedish law established "the housewife's right to her sphere of honor and activity as mistress of the home, to lock and key, to half the bed, and to a lawful third of the homestead." Women were equally under the law's protection with men, and favored as regards penalties. Some crimes involving the death penalty to men could be paid for by women; if condemned to death, that manner of execution was chosen which was regarded as easiest and least dishonorable.[78] A case from Iceland is cited where a woman, enraged because her husband had betrothed their daugher without her knowledge, decided not to raise any more children and had her next child exposed. "She explained to the despairing father, after the deed, that she would rear no more children to be given away against her will."[79] In spite of the harsh conditions of life, the ancient German wife had a high and dignified position. In the twelfth and thirteenth centuries homage was paid to womankind by the minnesingers, while throughout the Middle Ages the motto, "Honor to God and women!" resounded in the combats as in the festivals, among all peoples of the Germanic race.[80]

Today, among certain peoples in East Prussia, the husband is as a rule subject to his wife; separations seldom occur, for both parties would be thereby economically ruined. The author[81] who states this regards as empty talk the common statement that the South Slavic wife is more of a beast of burden and less esteemed by her husband than her Central European sister, and asserts that the Serbian folk-songs, from which the detractors get their weapons,

76 Rossbach, *Röm. Ehe*, 35 ff., 45.

77 Dill, *Nero*, 188; Moscatelli, *Condizione della donna*, 122; Schmidt, *Soc. Civ.*, 214-215, 218; Gide, *Condition privée de femme*, 108-109 (quoted); Bergel, *Eheverhältnisse*, 10.

78 Geijer, *Svensk. Hist.*, I, 159, 309; Wisen, *Nordens Forntid*. 15.

79 Weinhold, *Deut. Frauen*, I, 94.

80 Stammler, *Stellung d. Frauen*, 6, 39; Lichtenberger, *Nibelungen*, 375, 391; Gide, *Condition privée de femme*, 243-244.

81 Tetzner, in *Globus*, LXXV, 145; and in LXXXVI, 87.

demonstrate the opposite. The present Magyar standard of comfort and decency is attributed largely to the high position always held by their women, who are honest, self-respecting, and industrious. "Everyone—peasant, overseer, shepherd, cowherd, or swineherd—kisses the hands of the ladies of their master's house, and there is no servility, only graceful courtesy, in the act."[82] The Russian wife is said to enjoy a freedom much greater than that accorded to the German spouse. Besides, separation of the possessions of man and wife is the legal rule in Russia, and the wife, by administering and disposing of her fortune, has more independence than is the case in the rest of Europe. French law has thrown into relief the general idea that the married woman is subject to the authority of her husband, to whom she owes obedience. The theory is the same in the laws of Belgium, Holland, and Spain. The author quoted[83] thinks, however, that in fact if not in law there is no woman more independent than the French wife. He believes that in general the effect of Christianity has been to raise the status of women and to restore the dignity of marriage. Certain authors[84] hold approximately true the frequent statement that the position of woman is the surest gauge of a people's civilization. Fritsch[85] quotes with approval the following sentiment: "The one sex is just exactly as important, indispensable, as the other; the one is unthinkable without the other; neither is self-sufficient; they tend toward one another and each demands and takes from the other what it itself has not and what the other only can give." This relation, he says, holds true despite all modern strainings.

§388. The Sex-Factor in Status.

AMONG certain tribes in East Central Australia, "the left foot of a woman is considered unclean."[1] Among the Koita, "there is no special ceremony when the catamenia first appear, nor is a girl at this time specially avoided or considered especially dangerous."[2] The Tshi peoples of West Africa cause women to retire at the periods to huts prepared for the purpose in the bush, because they are offensive to the deities.[3] In Nyasaland, "a native woman is very little upset by the occurrence of menses, and works in the fields or carries loads just the same as usual, but a string or bit of grass is generally tied round the head, as for head ache."[1]

Woman is generally considered unclean by the Samoyed and she may not eat of bear's meat. At times her presence is considered a misfortune which can be condoned for only by fumigation with bear's fat.[5] Among the Todas "the seclusion-hut of a woman has attached to it the same ideas of impurity which attach to a corpse or its relics."[6] During menses the Igorrote woman wears a breech-cloth, but she will not remove her skirt. If at any time, even at the ford across the river, where both sexes uncover themselves as a matter of course, men should see women wearing only the breech-cloth, they would ridicule them; consequently women are sensitive about exposing themselves with it. The author

82 Colquhoun, *Whirlpool of Europe*, 121.

83 Roguin, *Mariage*, 17, 97-98, 181, 182, 186, 218; Du Camp, *Paris*, 159; Gide, *Condition privée de Femme*, 399, 401, 402; Burckhardt, *Renaissance*, 391-392.

84 Letourneau, *Marr.*, 148, 186; Westermarck, *Marriage* (one vol. ed.), 403.

85 In *Pol.-Anth. Rev.*, III, 514.

1 Wells, in AAAS, 1893, 516.

2 Seligmann, *Melanesians*, 140.

3 Ellis, *Tshi*, 94.

4 Stigand, in JAI, XXXVII, 122.

5 Montefiore, in JAI, XXIV, 406.

6 Rivers, *Todas*, 566.

has ascertained that the women on the west coast of Luzon avowedly wear this garment "to hide any possible evidence of menstruation."[7]

The Kwakiutl believe that a sick person at once becomes worse if a menstruating woman comes near him. "Also they do not allow young people who are just married to see the sick one, because they believe that they are always in bed together, and that is the same as menstruation. Their exhalation is bad for the sick one."[8] Among certain Athapascan tribes in Canada fear is inspired by menses.[9] Winnebago women "always take their blankets with them when they go to a menstrual lodge, for they never lie down but remain in a sitting posture, wrapped in their blankets. The women are always watched, so that when their menstrual flow comes everything is in readiness and lodge poles are placed around them and a lodge erected above their heads just about large enough to fit their body. They are not permitted to look upon the daylight nor upon any individual. If they were to look out during the day the weather would become very bad, and if they were to look at the blue sky it would become cloudy and rain. If they looked at anyone that person would become unfortunate. For four days they do not eat or drink anything; not even water do they drink. They fast all the time. Not even their own body do they touch with their hands. If they ever have any need of touching their bodies they use a stick. If they were to use their hands in touching their own body their bones would be attacked with fever. If they were to scratch their hands their heads would ache. After the fourth day they bathe in sight of their home. Then they return to their homes and eat. . . . If any women have to stay longer than four days they have to fast for that entire period. They always fast during this period and often some spirits bless them. When a woman who has stayed in the menstrual lodge for 10 days is ready to return to her lodge, she bathes herself and puts on an entirely new suit of clothes. Then her home is purified with red-cedar leaves and all the sacred bundles and medicines removed. Only then can she enter her parents' lodge. As soon as she returns to her parents' lodge after her first menstrual flow she is regarded as ready to be wooed and married."[10]

The Karoks of California think that if a menstruating woman approaches any medicine about to be given to a sick man, she will cause his death.[11] A peculiar feature of the customs among the Menomini is that "if a menstruating woman should, contrary to rule, enter a house in which there are sacred objects, this can do no harm."[12] A Cheyenne girl purifies herself by allowing smoke from sweet grass, cedar needles, and white sage to pass over her body inside of her blanket. Swanton,[13] from whom this case is taken, has written concerning the menstrual customs of the Indians in general. The dishes, spoons, and other articles belonging to a girl who had just entered womanhood were kept separate from all others and had to be washed thoroughly before they could be used again, or, as with the Iroquois, an entirely new set was provided for her, while salt especially was tabooed at this period. "Among many tribes it was believed that the supernatural beings were especially offended by menstrual blood. Therefore a Haida girl at this time must not go down to the beach at low tide, lest the tide come in and cover one of the chief sources of food supply.

---

7 Jenks, in AA, VI, 703; and in AA, VII, 173.
8 Boas, in BAE, XXXV, pt. I, 719.
9 Chamberlain, in AA, IX, 763.
10 Radin, in BAE, XXXVII, 137.

11 Powers, in *Contrib. N. Amer. Ethnol.*, III, 31.
12 De Josselin de Jong, in AA, XVIII, 123.
13 In HAI, II, 314, 315.

She must not step across a small stream, lest the old woman who resides at its head leave and take all the fish with her. When her people went to a salmon creek to dry fish she must get out of the canoe just before they reached it and approach the smokehouse from behind, for if she saw a salmon jump all the salmon might leave." Among other misfortunes caused by a woman in such a condition is the belief that "if a hunter's glance happened to fall upon a girl during her menstrual period, blood would be injected into his eye, preventing him from seeing game, and a crust of blood would surround his spear, making it unlucky." This recalls the Alaskan Eskimo belief that a girl was surrounded by a sort of film at this time which would attach itself to a hunter who came too near and enable every animal to see him. On the other hand, the imagined effect was not always deleterious, for "armed with the blood of a menstruant woman a man would attack and destroy hostile supernatural powers or put to flight any by which he was himself assailed;" and again, "if a menstruant girl scratched any place where one felt pain, the pain would stop."

The Makusi of British Guiana forbid women to bathe during the period and also to go into the forest, for they would risk bites from enamoured snakes.[14] On returning from her first bath after the first menstrual period, "the Makusi girl must during the night sit upon a stool or stone, to be whipped by her mother with thin rods without raising the slightest cry to wake the sleeping occupants of the hut, an occurrence which would prove dangerous for her future welfare. The whipping takes place also at the second menstrual period, but not subsequently." Among other tribes, "the 'Devil' who three days before has been making terrible music in the forest at last enters the house of the poor young girl, who tries to take to flight. A piai [shaman] at this moment runs up and, binding her eyes, leads her through the village while the Devil all by himself is making a frightful hubbub. Now is the time for the festival of the beating with the sticks, when the men strike the unfortunate girl, who dares not complain. At last a young man, admiring her courage, takes her place, and exposes himself to the blows of the company; if he bears the pain without murmuring she chooses him for her husband." We have here to do also with puberty-ceremonies and the marriage-test. "With the Warraus the girl must not speak or laugh or eat during the two or three days of the period. Were she to do so, she would lose all her teeth when she grew into a big woman. . . . The Pomeroon Carib girl who, for the space of three days had to do without food or water, was not allowed to utter a word. She was subsequently starved for a month on a diet of roots, cassava bread, and water. Girls may die under this treatment." A chief on the Orinoco has rationalized about such customs as follows: "Our ancestors observed that wherever the women, during their monthly periods, happened to tread, there everything dried up, and that if any man trod where they had placed their feet, his legs would swell: having studied the remedy, they ordered us to starve them, so that their bodies should be free from the poison."[15]

In the chapters of Leviticus on uncleanness in general is included that of both men and women in their issues. "If a woman have an issue, and her issue in her flesh be blood, she shall be put apart seven days: and whosoever toucheth her shall be unclean until the even. And every thing that she lieth upon in her separation shall be unclean: every thing also that she sitteth upon shall be unclean. . . . And on the eighth day she shall take unto her two turtles, or

---

14 Schomburgk, *Brit. Guiana,* II, 316.　　　15 Roth, in BAE, XXX, 308-309, 310-311.

two young pigeons, and bring them unto the priest, to the door of the tabernacle of the congregation. And the priest shall offer the one for a sin offering, and the other for a burnt offering; and the priest shall make an atonement for her before the Lord for the issue of her uncleanness."[16] Among the ancient Iranians a menstruating woman was taken to a special place where she could not come in contact with people, particularly men, and where she could see neither fire nor the sun. "The food offered her was given in metal vessels and indeed at best in such as were made of useless metals. After the cessation of menstruation the woman had to cleanse herself. . . . Association with a menstruating woman was regarded as a grave offence."[17] The Zoroastrians held that the menses of women were caused by the evil god, Ahriman. A woman, during the period, was "unclean and possessed by the demon. She must be kept confined and apart from the faithful whom her touch would defile, and from the fire which her very look would injure. She is not allowed to eat as much as she wishes, as the strength she might acquire would accrue to the fiends. Her food is not given to her from hand to hand, but passed to her from a distance in a long, leaden spoon."[18] At this day in the house of a Parsee there is a room for the monthly seclusion of women. It is bare of all comforts and from it neither sun, moon, stars, fire, water or sacred implements, nor any human being, can be seen.[19] Among the Greeks impurity in the temple was supposed to come from women, pork, and garlic; the last two were Asiatic, not Greek, and were so regarded in Cybele and Syrian Astarte worship.[20] The Romans held that nothing had more marvellous efficacy or more deadly qualities than the menstrual flow. The Arabs thought "a great variety of natural powers" attached themselves to a woman during the period. The gum of the acacia was thought to be a clot of menstrual blood, the tree itself a woman; therefore, the gum was regarded as an amulet.[21]

These few illustrations, considered together with those on the uncleanness of women in childbirth and on uncleanness in general,[22] may serve to show how far-reaching was the influence on the mores of such notions. All the above-mentioned ritual created a feeling that women were dangerous to men, different from men by virtue of their subjection to influences which did not reach men. Men were free and independent but subject to harm from women, as is further illustrated in the following section.

§389. Mistrust of Women.

A LEGEND of the Euahlayi tribe in Australia avers that at first the tribes were meant to live for ever, but woman spoiled this design. "The women were told never to go near a certain hollow tree. The bees made a nest in this tree; the women coveted the honey, but the men forbade them to go near it. But at last one woman determined to get that honey; chop went her tomahawk into that hollow trunk, and out flew a huge bat. This was the spirit of death which was now let free to roam the world, claiming all it could touch with its wings."[1] She was the Australian Eve or Pandora. Among the Southern Massim a woman

---

16 Levit., XV, 19-33.
17 Spiegel, *Eran. Alterthumskunde*, III, 699.
18 Müller, *Sacred Books*, IV; *Zend-Avesta*, I, xcii.
19 Geiger, *Ostiran. Kultur*, 236.

20 Foucart, *Assoc. Rélig.*, 123.
21 Smith, *Relig. Sem.*, 133, 448.
22 §§268, 408, of the text and *Case-Book*.
1 Parker, *Euahlayi*, 98.

can save the life of a man struck down in battle by throwing her petticoat over him, a custom explained by the statement: " 'The fear of witchcraft caused the man to be unmolested.' It seems probable that this custom may be connected with the power believed to reside in the body of the woman, and it is significant that it is the petticoat worn nearest the skin that confers protection." It is also the belief that *labuni* or "sending" is a magic power possessed by women, which, like a shadow, emerges from a woman who appears to be sleeping at the time and produces disease by means of a sliver of bone or fragment of stone which is inserted into the victim's body. "A woman might be bribed to send her *labuni* to injure an individual against whom she had no personal grudge."[2]

In South Africa women may not enter the cattle-kraal or the place where cattle are accustomed to rest upon returning from pasture; they are forced to follow special ways around these places.[3] On the Loango coast a married woman is forbidden to receive anything directly from any man's hand; the objects are laid down on the ground whence she picks them up.[4] In the Upper Congo "the lobe of the right ear of a male child, or the left ear of a female child is pierced—the left is always a sign of inferiority."[5] No sexual intercourse is permitted by the Katanga before going to war or when mining copper.[6] Among the Akamba a man must pay a fine if he unwittingly sits on a stool belonging to a woman. "The fine is really for the purification of the man who is considered to have become ceremonially unclean through sitting on a woman's stool."[7]

Among the Ainu, "the ghosts of deceased women are greatly feared, and that of an old woman especially is believed to have an extraordinary capacity for doing harm to the living. Even while alive on earth old women have great power over men, and children are much afraid of them. Formerly the hut in which the oldest woman of a family died was burnt after her death to prevent the spirit returning to work mischief to her offspring and to her sons- and daughters-in-law. The soul returning from the grave to exercise its spells upon the living was thus unable to find its former home, and wandered about for a time in a furious rage. During this period the grave was carefully avoided. . . . Some of the Ainu hold that women, who are considered inferior to men 'both spiritually and intellectually,' have 'no souls, and this is sometimes stated as a reason why women are never allowed to pray.' But Batchelor thinks that the real reason for this prohibition is that the Ainu are afraid that the women will appeal to the gods against their ill-treatment by the men."[8] In 1922 the Japanese press, bitter against President Wilson for not supporting a proposed amendment to the Covenant of the League of Nations, charged him with having "a female demon within him"—a term vividly denunciatory to the Oriental mind.[9] The teaching of a certain type of Buddhism is that woman is unclean and a scapegoat.[10]

There is no doubt that women have a subordinate position in the Toda community. "The ceremonial of the dairy has a predominant place in the lives and thoughts of the people, and the exclusion of women from any share in this

2 Seligmann, *Melanesians*, 640-643.
3 Fritsch, *Eingeb. S.-Afr.*, 115.
4 Bastian, *Loango-Küste*, I, 168.
5 Weeks, in JAI, XL, 379.
6 Anon., in *Globus*, LXXII, 164.

7 Hobley, *A-Kamba*, 38.
8 Czaplicka, *Aborig. Siberia*, 275-276.
9 N. Y. *Times*, Aug. 27, 1922.
10 Tamura, *Warum Heiraten Wir?*, 3.

ceremonial must have influenced the attitude of the community towards the sex. The laws regulating the relations of the dairymen with women also can hardly have contributed to raise the esteem in which they are held. . . . Not only are women excluded from any share in the work of the dairies connected with the sacred buffaloes, but they are also prohibited from any part in the milking of the ordinary buffaloes or in the churning of their milk, which is performed solely by males in a part of the hut with which women have nothing to do. . . . I am doubtful whether they are allowed to cook, at any rate to cook food in which milk forms one of the ingredients. With such occupations as divining and sorcery they have nothing to do."[11] In the conception of the Hindu lawgiver, women are a necessary evil, "in order to evolve one's self to the longed-for fruit of marriage." As an immediate consequence of the dependence of women appears the guardianship under which they remain their entire lives. It is expressly provided that they shall possess no property, bear no witness, undertake no legal business, especially sale, mortgage, and disposal by gift, and sign no contract.[12] In one of the epics we read: "Bad are the women in the world; to the husband who protects and nourishes them they no longer pay attention, as soon as misfortune casts him down. So is it characteristic of women that they no longer think of long-enjoyed fortune as soon as any misfortune, though quite trivial, hits them. It is hard to fetter their hearts; their feelings are extinguished in a moment. Not nobility, virtue, knowledge, nor gifts and affection can fetter woman's heart; for woman is of unstable heart."[13] Manu[14] declares that through their passion for men, their mutable temper and natural heartlessness, women become unfaithful however carefully they may be guarded. Since god made them so, man should guard them. In India of today, the women, being naturally impure and unholy in body, and bringing man to harm, may not eat offerings to ancestral spirits. If a man is thrashed with a woman's garment, "he is so much disgraced in the eyes of his fellowmen that he is not admitted into their society." A woman may worship village-deities only from afar; her personal offerings are never accepted by them. At the time of sacrifice women must veil their heads so as not to see. To rise in the scale of being, a woman must first be re-born a man. At marriage the bridegroom murmurs to himself prayers that the bride may not be fatal to brother, husband, or son. He adjures the fire-god to extirpate the substance dwelling in her that brings death to husband, children, the cattle, the home, and the husband's good name, pouring out water at every request. It is the waters drawn by the priests that avert death from the husband. Rites of purification abound, some of them highly ridiculous.[15] It is a common custom, as in New Zealand, that "all men on a war party were *tapu* to women—they could not go near their wives till the fighting was all done."[16] The same provision attended any other strenuous undertaking and doubtless contained a rational element.

Among the Eskimo the mammals are divided into two classes: the noble and the inferior beasts. "The skins of the former are used, though not exclusively, by the men, while the latter may be worn only by the women. No man would

11 Rivers, *Todas*, 566-568.
12 Jolly, *Stellung der Frauen*, 422, 423.
13 Holtzmann, *Ind. Sagen*, II, 266.
14 Bühler, *Manu*, IX, 10, 17.
15 Chaube, in JASB, V, 72; Thurston, *S. India*, 453; Modi, in JASB, III, 477;

Modi, in JASB, VII, 78; Schrader, *Aryans*, 387; Zimmer, *Altind. Leben*, 313; Oppert, in *Globus*, LXXXIV, 357-358; Peterson, in JASB, III, 318 ff.
16 Tregear, in JAI, XIX, 111.

debase himself by wearing a particle of the fur of the hare or of the white fox; the skins of these timid creatures are reserved for the women alone."[17] In America, the coast-tribes of the Northwest do not allow women to enter the houses that shelter their venerated copper plates. Dakota women must not play ball or touch the ball-stick. They must not enter the sacred underground shrines or touch the god-masks. "The Indians of California take especial pains to kill the women of their enemies when at war; they say that one woman destroyed is equivalent to five men, because they have such trouble with their own." This procedure was rational in the sense that to annihilate enemies the best way is to extirpate the potential mothers. A Yucatan "captain," during his three years of office might know no woman, nor might his food be served by women. A Miranha chief informed a traveller that association with a woman cured fever; all ill came from women, hence woman, on the principle of poison to poison, was the cure.[18]

Both ancient Accadians and Finns considered diseases as so many distinct personages, the daughters of "the lady of the gloomy abyss and of the dead."[19] In the popular poetry of Chaldæa occurs a slave's complaint that her master passed her by unnoticed; he feared her magic.[20] There are some pronouncements in the Old Testament disparaging women.[21] Smith[22] states that among the Arabs sexual intercourse was forbidden for pilgrims to Mecca. "The same rule obtained among the Minæans in connection with the sacred office of collecting frankincense. Among the Hebrews we find the restriction in connection with the theophany at Sinai and the use of consecrated bread . . . and Herodotus himself tells us that among the Babylonians and Arabs every conjugal act was immediately followed, not only by an ablution, but by a fumigation, as is still practised in the Sudan. This restriction is not directed against immorality, for it applies to spouses; nor does it spring from asceticism, for the temples of the Semitic deities were thronged with sacred prostitutes, who, however, were careful to retire with their partners outside the sacred precincts." Hartmann[23] comments: "It is well known how the Old Testament speaks of woman and that it is only the natural outflow of those ideas when the Jew in his daily prayers thanks God that he created him a man and not a woman. Similar crude notions are also to be found in the Koran, where women are characterized as those who grow up in ostentation and strive without reason. Man has to command, woman to obey, and if she is disobedient, she is flogged. . . . 'Men go before women because God gave the preference of grace to the one before the other.' " The Mohammedan woman is thought to be almost soul-less, and it is even forbidden her to enter the mosque at the public hours of prayer; "her moral consciousness is therefore shrunken and spoiled."[24]

The question of woman from time to time engages the attention of the Greek tragedians. Œdipus refers, as a sort of contrast to Greek mores, to the Egyptian custom, whereby the men keep house and weave, sitting within doors,

17 Boas, in USNM, 1888, 210; and in USNM, 1895, 421; Turner, in BAE, XI, 218 (quoted).

18 Hoffman, in BAE, XIV, 129; Mindeleff, in BAE, VIII, 134; Matthews, in AA, IX, 56; Bancroft, Nat. Races, II, 741; Powers, in Contrib. N. Amer. Ethnol., III, 160 (quoted); Thomas, in HAI, I, 200; Spix und Martius, Brasilien, 1251, note.

19 Lenormant, Chaldean Magic, 258.
20 Maspero, Hist. Anc., I, 738.
21 Prov., IX, 13; XII, 4; XIV, 1; XXI, 9, 19; XXV, 24; Eccles., VII, 28.
22 Relig. Sem., 454-455; Exod., XIX, 15; I Sam., XXI, 5; Herodotus, Hist., I, 198.
23 In Ztsft. d. V. f. Vkde., XI, 242-243.
24 R. T. K., in Globus, LXXIX, 106.

while their wives are abroad, providing with ceaseless toil the means of liveli-hood. In the *Trachiniæ* of Sophocles, Deianeira condones the love of Heracles for Iole, for whose sake he has sacked her father's town, subsequently sending her home to his own house: "No shame to either and no harm to me." Androma-che, telling how she behaved as the wife of Hector, pictures the ideal wife; she stayed at home, did not gossip, was silent and modest before her husband, knew when to rule him and when to yield. She says a woman must be content with her mate, even though he is worthless, and not make demands or try to impose her notions or the ways in which she was brought up upon him. She must adapt herself. A chorus in the *Medea* hails the dawn of respect for the female sex. The base tongue of slander will no longer attach to women; the ancient poets wrote ever of their faithlessness, but this is to cease. If Apollo had given to women the gift of versifying, they could have answered men; for history contains many reflections upon the male sex as well as on women.[25] There was much attention given, in dialectics, to women.[26] In the learned com-mentary attached to Becker-Hermann's *Charicles*,[27] we learn that the poets had a high ideal of woman and that some lofty female characters appear in history, but that there was no need felt or, apparently, any interest, in develop-ing the theme. The state had no use for woman except as a mother; she was let alone, in so far as she was good, and restrained when she did ill. Some citations may show "that the Greek perceived the correct idea, but not that he ever understood the proper means to realize it." Culture touched only half of the nation; hence stagnation was bound to ensue, at any rate for the women. Many citations are given. Athenæus[28] quotes many authors in vituperation of women and marriage. A Moorish sage of Cordova, writing in the twelfth century about women, remarks: "Our social state does not permit us to see how great re-sources women have. It seems that they are destined only to give birth to children and suckle them and that this state of servitude has destroyed in them the faculty for great things. That is why we see amongst us no woman endowed with moral virtues. Their lives pass like those of plants and they are burdens to their own husbands. Hence the misery which devours our cities, for the num-ber of women in them is more than double that of the men and they cannot by their labor earn the necessaries of life."[29] A German proverb states that when the Devil cannot go on an errand himself he sends an old woman.[30]

§392. Divorce.

AMONG certain tribes in East Central Australia, "the parents of the bride have a ball made of copi (gypsum) and the parents of the bridegroom have one made of red ochre. The red ochre ball is given to the bride and the gypsum ball to the bridegroom. If the bride cannot agree with her husband, she buries her ball in the sand, and vice versa; and if she wants to leave her husband altogether, she smashes the ball in pieces and throws the pieces into the air. The husband then gathers her belongings and burns them, and vice versa."[1]

---

25 Sophocles, *Œdipus at Kolonoi*, 337 ff.; *Trachiniæ*, 441 ff.; Euripides, *Trojan Women*, 643 ff.; *Andromache*, 208 ff.; *Medea*, 418 ff.

26 Xenophon, *Economist* (Dakyn's transl.), in *Works*, III, pt. I, 211, 226 ff.; Theophras-tus, quoted by Jerome, *Adv. Jovinianum*, I, 47.

27 III, 252 ff.
28 *Deipnosophists*, XIII, 8.
29 Renan, *Averroès*, 161.
30 Collier, *England*, 241.
1 Wells, in AAAS, 1893, 516.

Among the Southern Massim, "a man would divorce a woman for prolonged neglect of her garden or if she were constantly careless or unpunctual in the cooking of his food. Such carelessness is, however, very unusual unless a woman has a liking for, or an intrigue with, some other man and desires to be rid of her husband, in which case one method of bringing this result about is for the woman to neglect the garden and her husband's food to such an extent that the latter returns to his own hamlet-group, or if living in his own hamlet, tells his wife to go to hers. Most husbands, however, before proceeding to such extreme measures will try the effect of one or more severe thrashings. A man may also get rid of his wife, if the latter prove barren or suffers from a chronic disease severe enough to incapacitate her." On the other hand, "a woman may divorce her husband for confirmed laziness when he will not do his share of the hard work in the garden, or for acts of infidelity; if the woman is living in her husband's hamlet she simply takes her children, petticoats and cooking pots and goes with these to her mother's hamlet. In such a case a man has no remedy, he has no right to bring his wife back by force, even if he were able to do so, nor is he allowed by public opinion to take vengeance on the people of her hamlet. If man and wife are living in the latter's hamlet and the woman wishes to be rid of her husband, she tells him to go and it seemed that under these circumstances a man would leave his wife's hamlet without making any difficulty. There is no special form or ceremony of divorce."[2] Among the Dobuans of Papua, "a wealthy man is not divorced readily; neither is a woman who is possessor of much yam seed. . . . A divorced woman is not paid for by her next husband. The divorced man does not receive anything back after divorce, unless the divorce occurs soon after marriage, in which case the valuable articles are returned or their equivalents." Twenty-two causes of divorce are listed, those applying to the woman being: extravagance with yams, stealing from the man's relatives, not cooking food for his visitors, adultery, talking very loudly in the man's village when strangers are present, rattling the spatula loudly as she takes lime from the gourd when the man's elders are present, and not cooking food properly. On the man's side the causes are: not gardening properly, his relatives not giving the woman cooked food occasionally as a sign of good feeling, not fishing or not helping to provide other food for the children, being too lazy to join in trading-expeditions, using the canoe of his wife's relatives without permission, thrashing his wife in the sight of her relatives, or severely thrashing her in his village. Mutually operative causes include: breaking etiquette in each other's village, entering a house in the spouse's village when the owner of house is absent, climbing on the platform of the spouse's elder while the elder is seated on the ground, filthy language, calling by the name orphan or bastard and saying that either party has no food, saying "Ugly mouth," "Ulcerous mouth," calling each other old (it is an insult for either spouse to tell the other that he or she was born first), and saying "Your ears are thick and stuffed up. What did your mother ever teach you?"[3] Strictly speaking, there is no divorce in the D'Entrecasteaux Islands. "If the wife is guilty of misconduct her husband thrashes her; a man for the same offence is either speared or pays a heavy compensation. A woman who is tired of her husband goes off with another man, who makes an appropriate payment to the husband soon afterwards. For the husband the case is different; he may

---

2 Seligmann, *Melanesians*, 511-512.   3 Bromilow, in AAAS, 1909, 481-482.

have as many wives as he likes to keep. . . . However jealous the natives may be of their wives, they show singular indifference to losing them provided only that they receive an adequate payment."[4]

Among the Zulus the childless wife is sent home and the morning-gift is demanded back.[5] As long as the bridegroom in Nyasaland has incurred no expenses on behalf of his lady, and as long as the relations of both have not been formally and solemnly informed of the union, the separation is not treated as being of any importance, but "where all these conditions have been fulfilled, it is sure to be followed by litigation."[6] In Kenya Colony, "divorce is extremely rare, and a woman who has borne children cannot be divorced, whether her children are by her husband or by a man with whom she has lived for years; harlotry is no ground for divorce." The author[7] says there are some grounds for the statement that divorce occurs only where one of the parties has offended grievously against the family-group of the other, as in the case of a man killing his mother-in-law, or where he has relations with his wife's sister. Divorce is rare among the Suk; when it does occur, the reasons are sterility and "breach of the husband and wife food taboos." Among the Wayao, "owing to the abrogation of the drastic native laws regulating the sanctity of the marriage tie, marriages are becoming increasingly temporary in character. This is reflected in the system of relationship, as the relatives by marriage are becoming equally temporary."[8]

Sir Charles Dundas[9] has commented at length on the situation in East Africa: "Divorce may arise in two ways: either the husband may return his wife to her parents—'drive her away,' as they express it—or the wife deserts. The former is more rare than the latter. I observe that some writers lay down specific grounds for divorce, but I incline to regard such as the result of attempting to give a European cast to native law and am sceptical of any such fine or hard and fast rules on the subject. . . . In the long run, of course, even primitive men have no method whereby they can compel a woman to live with a man she refuses to remain with, so that if she deserts and faces all the consequences there is no remedy, and anyone who has experience of Africans will know that if the woman claims few rights and liberties, she holds most tenaciously to what she conceives to be her right, and is not near so easily intimidated as is the average native man. In so far, then, a woman can divorce herself, but not by recognized right, not without penalty, as we shall see. As to her husband, if he rejects his wife, he will be the loser in one way or another, unless he can come to terms with her family. In every divorce there will be two questions in issue, namely, the possession of the children and return of dowry [bride-price]. As to the first, one rule can be accepted, that the husband has the right to retain his children. . . . In the matter of divorce there are undoubtedly very strongly conflicting considerations at stake, for on the one hand payment of dowry gives an undisputed right to a woman's children, and clanship constitutes an inseparable bond between father and child, while on the other hand offspring is naturally attached to the mother; the adult child's affections will always lie more with the mother than with the father (among polygamous peoples), and for practical reasons the young children must remain

4 Jenness and Ballentyne, *D'Entrecasteaux*, 107-108.
5 Anon., in *Globus*, LXXV, 271.
6 Coudenhove, in *Atl. Mo.*, CXXXII, 190.

7 Barton, in JAI, LIII, 73; and in JAI, LI, 97.
8 Sanderson, in JAI, L, 376.
9 In JAI, LI, 261, 262-263.

with their mother. Corresponding to such opposite interests there appears very frequently much vagueness and uncertainty in suits of this sort, where one would look for very definite laws. . . . Now when a woman deserts from her husband it is almost always because she is enticed away by another man, or if she goes back to her father she will eventually want to marry another man; but after much enquiry, I found that in Ukamba the old custom made this practically impossible, for the reason that if the husband rejected return of dowry and the woman or any of her children begotten by her husband, or subsequently begotten by another man, died out of her husband's custody, full blood-money could be claimed from the seducer, and moreover the husband would claim every child born of his wife, no matter by whom. When this custom was revived, it was found that in the first place the wife would not leave her husband, being faced with the prospect of remaining childless, and the would-be husband declined to accept the possible burden of blood-money for an entire family. The result was that nothing came of the affair: the numerous cases of desertion by wives transpired to be due merely to the convenient corruption of recent times, which admitted of women leaving their husbands on the slightest or no provocation at all, without any disadvantage to themselves, and this affords a striking example of the evils of laxity in tribal customs. . . . Talking on the subject with the elders, I was told by them that formerly no woman ever left her husband after she had borne him children, and that if she did so, the husband would certainly seek to kill the seducer. I imagine that similar provision against divorces and desertions may be found in the original customs of most or all tribes. It must be considered how greatly native society is founded in the family, wherefore this foundation would be preserved by many strict rules or religious precepts. Certain it is that divorces were formerly far less frequent than they are now. Asked about this, elders have repeatedly mentioned two causes for the present-day state of affairs: one, the spread of laxity due to Swahili influence, and the other immunity from private revenge, and to this I would add the uncalled for interference in domestic affairs by European officials; to these, foolish and obstinate women run on the slightest pretext, and, unfortunately, too often receive a ready hearing of their garbled accounts of imaginary wrongs done to them."

In northeast Africa, in each case of dissolution of marriage a part of the purchase-price must be returned and the wife recompensed besides.[10] Among the Unyamwesi, if a man finds his wife lazy or sterile he may send her back and demand her sister.[11] Sometimes, in case of sterility, the wife is subjected to a test by the male relatives; and if she does not then become pregnant, is sold at auction.[12] "Divorce is almost unknown among Masai, and it is only barren women who may be divorced."[13] In Kabylie, "the right of repudiation pertains under all circumstances to the husband, without limit and without cause, without being counterbalanced by the right of the wife to get a divorce. It is the necessary consequence of the nature of marriage, by which she is not united to the man but bought by him." Still "to the right of oppression corresponds the right of flight," by which she can extricate herself.[14] "The idea of love between husband and wife was hardly thought of among the Hovas. Marriage indeed was compared to a knot so lightly tied, that it could be undone

10 Paulitschke, *Nordost-Afr.*, II, 142.
11 Stuhlmann, *Mit Emin*, 81.
12 Letourneau, *Marr.*, 232-233.

13 Hollis, in JAI, XL, 473.
14 Hanoteau et Letourneux, *Kabylie*, II, 176-177, 182.

with the slightest possible touch. . . . The marriage state was regarded chiefly as a matter of mutual convenience, each party carefully retaining separately his or her property." One of the tribes allowed any woman of noble birth who had married a commoner to divorce him, although he could not divorce her.[15] "By men and women, rich and poor, barrenness is still considered, in the East, a curse and a reproach; and it is regarded as disgraceful in a man to divorce, without some cogent reason, a wife who had borne him a child, especially while her child is living."[16] Among the Sahara tribes, "the woman is free in the matter of a second marriage; the father's authority is absolute only in the case of the first.[17] Among the Nigerians, "when the girl is once married she will seldom leave her husband of her own free will, except on account of cruelty or impotence. . . . If she be given to another, the former husband has no power over her, and is supposed to bear his supplanter no malice, but he may try to persuade her to run away and come back to him." Although the rival husbands are supposed to feel no animosity, there is a belief that if they meet during a raid or a hunting-expedition one of them, usually the supplanter, "will be hurt by an arrow and die. As every man has his special mark on his arrows, and the arrow which kills the rival is unmarked, the death is put down to magic."[18] In order to "break a marriage," as the process is called by the Dinkas, all that is necessary is that the cattle paid for the bride, with all their young, or an equivalent, be repaid to the husband. "She is then entitled to return to her own family, together with any children she may have borne. Various causes are enumerated for breaking the marriage; but the wife's unfaithfulness is not one of them, provided she be willing to remain in her husband's enclosure. . . . All the blame is laid upon the man, who is liable to pay full compensation to the aggrieved husband. Until recently, indeed, among the southern Dinkas he was liable to be killed. On the other hand, as among many of the negro peoples on the West Coast, the woman's character is unstained by an act of infidelity, and she is subject to no legal punishment." If a marriage be fully "broken" by the repayment of all the cattle, all children borne by the woman become with her the property of her father or guardian; but part of the cattle may be left with the wife's father, by arrangement, to permit one or more of the woman's children being left with her husband as his property. The husband may sue for breaking of marriage if the girl fails to give birth to a child within two years of marriage, if she runs away from him and refuses to return, or if there is quarrelling or ill-will between their families. In the first instance, before suing, the husband must have had recourse to the tribal custom of permitting one of his male relations to cohabit with the girl, to support the alleged inability to conceive.[19]

Among the Tungus "trivial causes are often sufficient to lead to a separation, for instance a birth-mark or a small bodily defect; for such things are regarded as brought about by evil spirits."[20] The Cherkes husband has power of life and death and may divorce his wife without subjecting her to any punishment. Divorce exists among the Kalmucks, but there must be important reasons. A woman can sue for divorce but a man need not submit to the demand of the court if, for instance, she is not a good housewife. It is reported

15 Sibree, *Great Afr. Isl.*, 250, 254.
16 Lane, *Mod. Egypt.*, I, 74.
17 Pommerol, *Sahariennes*, 265.

18 Tremearne, in JAI, XLII, 171.
19 O'Sullivan, in JAI, XL, 172, 182-183.
20 Hiekisch, *Tungusen*, 89.

of the Armenians who fall within Russian boundaries that they have absolutely no divorce.[21] Though divorcing a wife is easy among the Kurds, it is
often repented if done in passion. The wife may not come back again till she
has been re-married and divorced. But the Kurd is jealous, and if he wants his
wife back, gets her married to a sort of functionary known as "the ass of the
Kasi," who for a certain sum will go through the form of marrying and divorcing her. If this functionary is distrusted, she may be married to a clay pitcher,
which her former husband "murders," thus freeing its widow to re-marry
him.[22]

In Korea a husband may repudiate a wife for seven reasons: incurable disease, theft, childlessness, infidelity, jealousy, incompatibility with her parents-
in-law, and a quarrelsome disposition.[23] In China there are also seven causes
for divorce of a wife, differing little from the above list. "Probably the most
common cause is adultery, for the reason that this is the crime most fatal to
the existence of the family." Indeed, a husband is liable to punishment if he
retain a wife convicted of adultery. "If a wife merely elopes she can be sold by
her husband, but if she marry while absent she is to be strangled; if the husband be absent three years a woman must state her case to the magistrates
before presuming to remarry." There are three considerations that set aside
repudiation: "first, the wife having mourned for her husband's parents; second,
her having risen with him from poverty to wealth; and third, her having no
home to which she can return." She cannot go back to her parents because
there is no provision for her support, the land having been set aside for her
parents' and then her brothers' maintenance.[24] Divorce has been in the past
extraordinarily common in Japan; "for four marriages there is, on the average,
one separation."[25]

In some parts of India divorce is a very simple matter and is effected simply
by a public declaration and the gift to the woman of a few cowries or coins
which she throws away. A bad dinner is one of the trivial grounds for the frequent separations; and no stigma attaches to either party.[26] Among the Todas
a man divorces his wife for two reasons, and for two only, "the first reason
being that the wife is a fool and the second that she will not work." Barrenness is not generally regarded as a reason for divorce, though the author
quoted[27] was told of one case in which a man had sent away his wife on this
account; it was more usual in such a case to take a second wife. Among the
Lhoosai, "if a woman has a son by her husband, the marriage is indissoluble;
but if they do not agree, and have no son, the husband can cast off his wife
and take another."[28] A Saora woman may leave her husband whenever she
chooses and he cannot prevent her. Her next husband pays a buffalo and a
pig.[29] In the Chin Hills a husband can always divorce his wife for her indiscretions, but if he does so he loses the price which he paid for her when he
bought her. "He hence overlooks the matter as regards the woman, and he will,
if he can, make the seducer pay him compensation; but he seldom succeeds, as

21 *Russ. Ethnog.* (Russ.), II, 220, 463, 337.
22 Von Hahn, in *Globus*, LXXXVI, 32.
23 Bishop, *Korea*, 343.
24 Medhurst, in *Trans. China Br. Roy. Asiat. Soc.*, pt. IV, 25-26; "Chinese Girl." in N. China *Herald*, quoted in JASB, II, 221 ff.; Williams, *Middle Kingdom*, I, 794; Von Mollendorff. *Family Law of Chinese*, 33, 34.
25 Von Fircks, *Bevölkgslehre*, 243.
26 Risley, *Ethnog. Ind.*, I, 199.
27 Rivers, *Todas*, 525.
28 Lewin, *S.E. India*, 276.
29 Fawcett, in JASB, I, 230.

popular opinion is averse to the shedding of blood over the virtue of women."30
In the Naga Hills, "marriage and divorce are among the simplest of their
rights and often follow each other within the year without comment or surprise. Incompatibility of temper is here quite sufficient for either the man or
the woman to demand a divorce and take it. Although strictly monogamous,
both sexes may marry [, divorce,] and remarry as often as they please; such
offspring as require the maternal aid follow the mother, and are tended and
cared for by her until able to look after themselves, when they return to their
father."31 "Divorce by mutual consent was easily arranged, the woman taking
her property. A man might put away his wife with or without her consent."
At divorce there is an equal division of goods; a young man sometimes marries
and divorces a rich old widow, "receiving half her property, when he is in a
position to marry a nice young girl."32 In one district a wife may divorce her
husband for impotency.33 Among the Shans, "divorce can be readily obtained,
but except among young people of low rank, it is comparatively rare." The
applicant for divorce, or the one at fault, always loses considerably in the division of the property.34 Among the Palaungs, "if a husband and wife should
quarrel and separate, the money arranged by the Pa-jau [marriage go-be-
tween]—the 'helping money'—must be returned to the man's father, if it was
he who supplied it at the time of the marriage; but money given after the
wedding need not be returned unless the wife, after her return to her father's
house, has taken another husband. In this case the new husband is expected
to find enough money to pay for all the presents given by the father of her
first husband."35

In ancient India divorce could occur to a betrothed pair. The woman could
regain her freedom if the bridegroom had "a flaw"—if he were very sickly or
deformed, insane, impotent, expelled from his caste, entirely destitute, or was
in disagreement with his relations. "The bridegroom on his side was free from
obligation if a fault was disclosed in his bride which had been suppressed by
her father or other guardian, such as loss of virginity, deformity, or an organic affliction." Among the legal grounds for divorcing a wife were the following: adultery, sterility, giving birth only to girls, miscarriage, not loving her
husband, eating before him, being quarrelsome, given to drink, sickly, deceitful,
extravagant, dissolute, or an evil woman. One sees from this that the legal
grounds for divorce were rather vague; moreover the character of the separation varied with occasions, for Manu speaks of the separation for three months
from a wife who shows no respect to a dissolute, drunken, or sick husband.
"Even in the case of repudiating the wife for a lifetime, the husband, so it
seems, never entirely took his hands off her, but banished her to a neighboring
house, whereupon sexual intercourse and a share in the religious usages, but
not participation in the affairs of the household, came to an end."36 In the
Code of Manu, a wife can never be repudiated so that she can become the lawful wife of another. "Once is the partition of an inheritance made; once is a
maiden given in marriage; and once does a man say, I will give. Each of those
three acts is done once only." On the other hand, a wife who "drinks spirituous
liquors, is of bad conduct, rebellious, diseased, mischievous, or wasteful, may

30 Carey and Tuck, *Chin Hills*, I, 207.
31 Woodthorpe, in JAI, XI, 68.
32 Godden, in JAI, XXVII, 28, note, 177.
33 Anon., in JASB, V, 60.

34 Woodthorpe, in JAI, XXVI, 22.
35 Milne, *Eastern Clan*, 169.
36 Jolly, *Stellung d. Frauen*, 427-428, 443-444.

at any time be superseded." A barren woman may be superseded in the eighth year; she whose children all die, in the tenth; she who bears daughters only, in the eleventh; but she who is quarrelsome, without delay; while a sick wife who is kind to her husband and virtuous may be superseded only with her own consent and may never be disgraced.[37] In strong contrast to most primitive codes is that of the Veddahs. They have no divorce and are kind and considerate to their wives; few of their Kandyan neighbors could say, as the Veddah can: "Death alone separates husband and wife."[38]

Among the Sea Dyaks divorce is unusual after the birth of a child, though common before that event. "A divorce is not absolute until the property has been divided and a ring is given by the man to the woman in token of her freedom to marry elsewhere."[39] "The Dyak men view marriage as an arrangement for the mutual convenience of both parties in order to obtain children. . . . I have known many [childless] Dyak couples who have continued to live together, and have perhaps adopted a child; but they have done so in spite of all that has been said to them and in opposition to the wishes of their friends. I have often heard Dyaks say: 'When you plant a fruit-tree you expect it to bear fruit, and when you marry you expect your wife to bear children.' The Dyak women generally regard marriage as a means of obtaining a man to work for them. A woman will often separate from her husband simply because he is lazy, and will not do his fair share of the work."[40]

In Sumatra, the loosing of the marriage-bond, at least for the man, is as simple as the preliminaries to marriage are complicated. The woman has to go through considerable formality or buy her divorce from her husband, while the man needs the help of no third party to get rid of his wife. He has only to provide a sum sufficient to maintain her for three months and ten days. He never divorces her if she is pregnant and seldom when she is sickly or even insane. If he takes her back, and finally divorces her a third time, she must be married to another man and divorced from him before he can regain her. This may be only after the period of three months and ten days. A poor old man is selected and paid a small sum to marry the divorced wife and divorce her the next day.[41] It is easy for a woman to divorce a man who comes "like a child" into her family; he can take away only the clothes on his body.[42] In the Lampong district, "as soon as the *jujur* is paid the wife is the inalienable property of the man. Death alone can dissolve the marriage. As a consequence the *adat* [mores] does not allow divorce. I recall that a certain man was condemned to several years of hard labor in chains, and that nevertheless the effort of his wife to get a divorce was rejected on the ground that he had bought her." The closeness of the wife to the man appears also in the fact that a slave-family may not be separated when bought, not at all as a consequence of any right that the slave has, but simply because of the *adat* that the woman is the inalienable property of the man, so that there is no thought of separating a slave from his wife so long as they are bound in marriage. According to old custom among the Bataks, divorce is not allowed from either side; only in case of barrenness can the woman be returned to her parents, who are obliged to

37 Bühler, *Manu*, IX, 46 and note, 47, 78, 80, 81.
38 Bailey, in *Trans. Ethnol. Soc. London*, II, 293.
39 Roth, in JAI, XXI, 132.
40 Gomes, *Sea Dyaks*, 69, 128.
41 Jacobs, *Groot-Atjeh*, I, 86-87, 89, 91, 93.
42 §363, of the text; "Adat Lembaga," in *Bijd.*, 1891, pt. I, 281.

furnish another girl. The parents have the same duty in case the woman dies without presenting her husband with children. "Neither protracted abandonment, nor the severest maltreatment, nor adultery give either to the wife or the man the right to demand divorce. In one sole case may it take place, namely, by an attempt of one spouse on the life of the other." On the island of Nias, where the father-family exists, if a man gets sick of his wife he can divorce her by sending her back to her family. With his consent she may marry again, he getting the bride-price. Even the woman may withdraw from marriage if mishandled or wounded by the man or if he fails to provide for her. Originally there was no divorce on either side, and today there are certain Nias people who allow divorce on no account, death alone separating the couple. Where, as among the Alfurs of Buru and Ceram, the woman goes to the man's tribe and is subject at his death to the levirate, divorce is impossible. The only case in which it is permitted is that of adultery, the paramour being obliged to marry the woman and to repay the price originally given for her, part of which goes to the offended husband and part to the village. The children stay with the father. "Every divorce must take place with foreknowledge and consent of the *fenna* [clan]." Among the Buginese and Macassars of Celebes, by way of contrast, divorce is frequent and is granted to either party, often for trivial reasons. One cause of this situation is stated to be the arrangement of marriage by the parents on both sides without consulting the young people, who sometimes meet one another for the first time at the wedding.[43] In the Mentawei Islands the husband may cast off his wife for any cause, and she may not re-marry without his consent, "for he has bought her by the presents which he has given his father-in-law at the wedding."[44]

In earlier days, before there was much contact with the Malays, the peoples of Malacca did not regard divorce so lightly; quite the reverse, for it was unknown to some of the tribes and unpopular with all. A man did not cast off his wife, because he would thus lose the children and not easily get another mate; if, however, a clumsy, lazy, or disagreeable wife ran away and the husband made no effort to regain her, they were divorced and he kept the children.[45] In the Malay Peninsula, "the rule was that if the divorce was proposed by the husband, he lost the dowry he had given to the woman; but that if the woman asked to be divorced, she must return the dowry she had received at marriage. The children followed the father or the mother according to their own (the children's) wishes; if, however, they had not yet arrived at the age of reason, they followed the mother."[46] In southern Formosa, "divorces are frequent and infidelity is common, it not being considered a heinous sin."[47] In Samoa the dissolution of marriage is purely at the will of the man, and the wife cannot get away from an undesirable husband without his consent except in a case where the woman stands higher in rank than the man.[48] In the Gilbert Islands, divorce, unlike marriage, was effected without formalities. "It might lead to the surrender of land-forfeits on one side or the other, but there was no fixed custom by which bonds were dissolved or penalties assessed. For a man to put away his wife he had simply to eject her from his house; equally

---

43 Wilken, in VG, I, 49, 333, 336-337, 341-342, 370, 390-391; II, 241-242.
44 Pleyte, in *Globus*, LXXIX, 26.
45 Stevens, in *Ztsft. f. Eth.*, XXVIII, 179-180.
46 Skeat and Blagden, *Malay Penin.*, II, 83.
47 Wirth, in AA, X, 365.
48 Von Bülow, in *Globus*, LXXIII, 185.

well a woman might dissolve the partnership by returning to her parents, who, if there seemed good cause, would harbour her and take her part in any unpleasantness that might ensue. The right to decide in such a matter was thus accorded as freely to the wife as to the husband, and this is a fair indication of a woman's general status in the Group, where mother right and father right seem to have impinged upon one another and eventually come to a compromise. On every divorced woman was pronounced the charm . . . by which she was protected against the evil magic of her late husband's family, and at the same time absolved from her duty of concubitancy to him."[49]

Among the Eskimo, "divorce is as informal as marriage; either party may leave the other on the slightest pretext, and may remarry. The husband may discard a shrewish or miserly wife, and the wife may abandon her husband if he maltreats her or fails to provide enough food." Among certain Labrador Eskimo the conjurers often separate man and wife on the plea that their union causes ill luck. On the Northwest Coast, "if a husband expels his wife from caprice he must return her dowry; if she has been unfaithful he keeps the dowry and may demand his wedding gifts." Among a number of the Plains Indians "the men had absolute power over their wives, and separation and divorce were common." Among the Hidatsa, Kiowa, and Omaha the women had a higher social position, and wives could leave cruel husbands. Each consort could remarry and the children were left in the custody of their mother or their paternal grandmother. Separation was never accompanied by any ceremony. During the dance among the Dakota any participant could divorce one of his wives by rising and declaring that he repudiated her. Among the Pima, "husband and wife may separate at pleasure, and either party is at liberty to marry again." There are other instances of the same sort, while in one case "divorces are granted only on the ground of unfaithfulness." A Delaware husband could put away his wife, especially if she had no children, and a woman could leave her husband. To the Iroquois "divorce was discreditable, but could easily be effected. The children went with the mother." In general, the marriage-bond could be dissolved by the wife as well as by the husband, and little ceremony was involved.[50] The same applies to certain South American Indians, divorce being pretty free, especially by the husband, though sometimes not permissible if there were children.[51]

In the Code of Hammurabi, if a man without just cause divorces either his concubine or wife who has borne him children, the woman takes the dowry and children, gets a share in the estate so as to rear her children, and is permitted to remarry as she will; if the husband makes over property to the children, she receives a child's portion. If a childless wife is divorced, she receives her dowry and an amount equal to the betrothal gift; if the latter were lacking, then one mina of silver.[52] The frequent command in Semitic antiquity not to dissolve marriage indicates that divorce was common. "In such a case the man wrote a deed of separation, affixed his seal to it, and simply ejected the wife from the house." The only restraint on divorce was the requirement that the husband indemnify the woman.[53] Such statements as these may be read: "The man can

49 Grimble, in JAI, LI, 33.
50 Lowie and Farrand, in HAI, I, 809; Hodge, in HAI, II, 252; Henshaw, in HAI, I, 538; Dorsey and Goddard, in HAI, II, 467; Anon., in HAI, II, 647; Beckwith, in Smithson. Rep., 1886, pt. I, 249.

51 Roth, in BAE, XXXVIII, §898.
52 Harper, Hammurabi, 120; Winckler, Hammurabi, 23-24.
53 Meissner, Altbabylon. Privatrecht, 14.

be divorced from his wife if he has found a more beautiful one. . . . The woman can legally be forced by the man to agree to divorce if she has found fault with him. If she had known of this defect before marriage, then she could say: 'I thought I could tolerate it, but now I see that it is impossible.'" The following are grounds for divorce for the wife, as mentioned in the Talmud: if the husband either will not or cannot fulfil the marriage-duty, if he follows a loathsome trade, leads a disorderly, dissolute life, or, finally, if he mistreats his wife.[54] According to Moslem law, the husband can divorce without giving reason, but must give the woman her property and the morning-gift if he has not paid it. Among the Shiites the man gets the children, among other sects the woman, especially during their childhood. For formal divorce the formula must be pronounced before two witnesses. The woman too may apply for divorce, in which case she pays the husband an indemnity. She can demand divorce of the man if she says she intends to marry another who is better than he. A couple may divorce by mutual agreement. In Islam economic difficulties and sacrifices make divorce an unwelcome recourse for either party. A rich man or woman can do almost anything by paying the prescribed costs, but a woman with no property and no means of earning is slow to seek divorce entailing sacrifice of her dower.[55]

In ancient Greece divorce was regarded as shameful for a woman. Menelaus says that he thinks it a serious matter for a woman to lose her wifely status; "all else that a woman can suffer is relatively secondary; but for her to lose her husband is to lose her life."[56] Later, and especially at Athens, divorce was easy and of very frequent occurrence.[57] A ground of divorce in olden times in Iceland was the presence of too many poor relatives who had to be supported.[58] For divorce in the Massachusetts Bay Colony, "female adultery was never doubted to have been sufficient cause; but male adultery, after some debate and consultation with the elders, was judged not sufficient. Desertion a year or two, where there was evidence of a determined design not to return, was always good cause; so was cruel usage of the husband."[59] In 1923 the British House of Commons passed by a vote of nearly ten to one the bill providing that Englishwomen may hereafter, like Englishmen, obtain divorce for infidelity alone, instead of having to bring additional charges of cruelty or desertion against their husbands. Such action may aid the theory of the moral equality of the sexes.[60]

§394. Widowhood.

BEFORE considering cases illustrating the lot of the widow, we may cite, by way of contrast, the situation of the widower in East Africa. "In Unyamwesi, if a woman dies leaving only one child, the widower receives back half the dowry [bride-price], or one-third if there are two children; but in lieu of this he may demand another wife, and if he is given his wife's sister he will pay only five rupees [approximately two dollars and a half] in dowry for her. In Useguha the husband has an absolute right to marry his deceased wife's sister

54 Klugmann, *Frau im Talmud*, 45, 46, note.

55 Tornauw, *Moslim. Recht*, 168; Hartmann, in *Ztsft. f. Vkde.*, XI. 244.

56 Euripides, *Medea*, 236 ff.; *Andromache*, 370 ff.

57 Blümner, *Griech. Privatalterth.*, 264 and note.

58 Weinhold, *Deut. Frauen*, II. 44.

59 Hutchinson, *Mass. Bay*, 445.

60 N. Y. *Times*, June 11, 1923.

without payment of dowry; the same rule applies among the Wasove, excepting that the widower cannot claim a right to his sister-in-law. In Sumbwa, again, only a very small sum is paid if the widower marries his sister-in-law, and among the Bakumbi he may demand another wife if he had no children by his deceased wife. In the Bungu and Banjika tribes it is usual for a man to marry his deceased wife's sister, but here it cannot be demanded, and dowry must be paid. In Ukarra, again, it is so much the rule for a widower to marry his sister-in-law that if he does not do so his young children will always be taken over by their maternal grandparents."[1]

Among the natives of Port Darwin "a widow and orphans are kept alternately by her own and by her deceased husband's family, and in some instances," comments the author, "I know the time of relief is eagerly looked for." In Central Australia widows are sometimes not allowed to speak for twelve months; they use a gesture-language with considerable dexterity.[2] In British New Guinea, where as a rule a person is addressed by his own personal name or by his ceremonial double name, a widow or widower is denied this privilege and is referred to as "widow" or "widower," a practice which sometimes continues even after remarriage.[3] Among the Koita, the dead man's brother's wife blackens the widow from head to foot, and her head is shaved. "For six months the widow wears her mourning ornaments; during this time she may show herself but little in public, she should not speak much or loudly, neither may she walk along the main village street nor leave her house by the front verandah. There are no cooking or fire *taboos* on the widow, but she and all other relatives of the dead man must abstain from such articles of food as he specially cared for until after the feast, called *ita,* some six months later."[4] In Eddystone, Solomon Islands, widows sometimes follow their husbands to the grave. "Kera did not cry or she could not have died, for a widow who cries can not hang herself; she kept smoking and eating betel nut. . . . Widow Mali and Widow Pongo held up both ends of a pole, and Kera hung herself in the middle." The term *ungi,* meaning to follow, "is specially reserved for women who die to follow their husbands. . . . Men do not *ungi.*"[5]

On the African Gold Coast loud singing at a man's funeral is to warn off women who are not relations, and whose own husbands would die within a year if they should see the widow. "The uniform custom among Negroes and Bantus is that those escaping execution on the charge of having witched the husband to death, shall remain in a state of filth and abasement, not even removing vermin from themselves, until after soul-burial is complete—the soul of the dead man being regarded as hanging about them and liable to injury." For the same reason they are confined to their huts. "They maintain an attitude of abasement and grief, sitting on the ground, eating but little food, and that of a coarse kind. In Calabar their legal rights over property, such as slaves, are considerably in abeyance, and they are put to great expense while the spirit is awaiting burial. They have to keep watch, two at a time in the hut, when the body is buried, keeping their lights burning, and they have to pay out of their separate estate for the entertainment of all friends of the deceased, who come to pay him compliment."[6] The period of mourning may be

1 Dundas, C., in JAI, LI, 258.
2 Parkhouse, in AAAS, 1895, 640 (quoted); Spencer and Gillen, *Nat. Tr. Cent. Aust.,* 500.
3 Williamson, in JAI, XLIII, 271.
4 Seligmann, *Melanesians,* 162, 164.
5 Hocart, in JAI, LII, 86.
6 Kingsley, *Travels W. Afr.,* 516, 483.

forty days or even six months, at the end of which "the widows wash, shave the head, pare the nails, and put on clean clothes, the old clothes, the hair and the nail-parings being buried."[7] "The more eminent the husband was in life, the heavier are the duties that devolve on the widow after his death"; she is beaten by the dead man's relatives, on the burial-day, till she can reach the nearest water and bathe in it.[8] In the Batanga interior, most widows are still required to go perfectly naked, sometimes for a whole year.[9] Among the Ibo, "the widow takes off her neck ornaments and stays in the house during the day; at night she carries the ashes of her fire to the ajoifia ["bad bush"]. In twelve days the woman who removed the neck ornaments shaves her head and puts cotton on her neck; the hair is thrown in the ajoifia; they break down the wall at the back of her house for her to go out; she does not cook for anyone and no one cooks for her, except a small girl who has not yet put on neck ornaments; she may not touch any male person except a small boy who has not put on a loin cloth; only her son may go to her house at night; no one may go into the water where she is washing, nor step over her legs; after twenty-eight days they rebuild the wall, she uses the ordinary door and they go to market"; the final act is one of sacrifice.[10]

In Madagascar, in the case of the death of a man of position and wealth, his widow is dressed in her best and remains in the house until the family returns from the tomb. As soon as they enter the house, they begin to revile her in the most abusive language, telling her that it is her fault that her fate has been stronger than that of her husband and that she is virtually the cause of his death. "They then strip her of her clothes, tearing off with violence the ornaments from her ears and neck and arms; they give her a coarse cloth, a spoon with a broken handle, and a dish with the foot broken off, with which to eat." She remains under a coarse mat all day and may not speak to anyone who enters the house. She is not allowed to wash her face or hands. This lasts not less than eight months; "and even when that is over, her time of mourning is not ended for a considerable period; for she is not allowed to go home to her own relations until she has been first divorced by her husband's family."[11]

A proverb in Punjab runs as follows: "A Jāt, a Bhāt, a caterpillar, and a widow woman, these four are best hungry. If they eat their fill they may do harm."[12] Wilkins[13] quotes a Hindu widow's description of the treatment she receives. She is addressed as if she were to blame for her husband's death; her head is shaved; she is allowed only one meal a day; and must frequently fast. She says a suttee is better. The suttee[14] went on probably for two thousand years until the English interdicted it about 1830. A trustworthy verse of the *Atharvaveda* testifies to the death of the wife with the deceased husband as an extremely old custom.[15] The practice of wife-suicide has not entirely disappeared, and so long as the social stigma of widowhood exists sporadic cases are likely to occur. In 1923 a young Hindu wife is reported to have mounted her husband's funeral-pyre and to have been consumed in the flames.[16]

An old book refers to a similar practice in China: "Among the people of this countrey, one man hath manye wyues, whiche declare theyr loue to their

7 Ellis, *Ewe*, 160.
8 Bastian, *Deut. Exped.*, I, 167.
9 Nassau, *Fetichism*, 222.
10 Thomas, in JAI, XLVII, 175, 177.
11 Sibree, *Great Afr. Isl.*, 255.
12 Risley, *Ethnog. India*, I, 76. For the use

of "widow" as a term of insult, see Kipling, *Naulahka*, ch. XIX.
13 *Hinduism*, 365, 391.
14 §229, of the text.
15 Zimmer, *Altind. Leben*, 328, 331.
16 N. Y. *Times*, Feb. 24, 1923.

husbandes after this sort. When the husband is dead, euery one of his wiues pleade their cause before a iudge, to proue which of them was most louing to her husband and beste beloued of him: so yat she which by the sentence of the iudges is found to haue been most faythful and diligente, decketh her selfe moste gorgiously in all her sumptuous araye, and procedeth like a *Virago* stoutly and cherefully to the fire, where the corps of her husbande was burnte, castinge her selfe into the same fyre, embrasing and kissing the dead bodi of her husband, untyll she also be consumed by the fyre, whiche she reputeth for an honourable sepulture: whereas his other wyues are estemed to lyue in shame and infamie."[17] In China today, when a girl "spills the tea"—that is, loses her betrothed by death—"public opinion honors her if she refuse a second engagement; and instances are cited of young ladies committing suicide rather than contract a second marriage. They sometimes leave their father's house and live with the parents of their affianced husband as if they had been really widows."[18] They may even be formally united with the dead in marriage. After such a ceremony the widowed bride changes her costly bridal dress for the mourning-costume prescribed for widows, weeps and laments at the side of the coffin, and goes through all the mourning-ceremonies which are incumbent on a widow, pledging herself forever at the altar of her bridegroom's manes and waiting on his parents as if she were really their daughter-in-law.[19]

The general sign of widowhood among the Dakota Indians was loosening the hair and cutting it short in a line with the ears. "It was the wife's duty to light a fire for four nights on her husband's grave and watch that it did not die out before dawn."[20] Winnebago widows were supposed to continue single for four years. They were told to play or dance, or in fact do anything that would make them forget their sorrow, such admonition being usually given by the sisters or aunts of the deceased husbands.[21] Sometimes the Guiana Indian widow is whipped, sometimes immolated. She cuts her hair and takes off her ornaments.[22]

Among the ancient Germans the widow was free to choose whether to follow her deceased husband or not, but the general opinion was that a true wife would choose the former. This was especially the case in the north and among the Scandinavians.[23]

§395. The Lot of the Widow.[1]

Re-marriage. If the Australian widow has no near relatives, her re-marriage is arranged by the chief of her tribe. Her own inclinations are not consulted.[2] Of the aborigines of Tasmania it is affirmed that widows, unless given in marriage, were "the common property of the males of the tribes into which they had married."[3] Among the Koita "no levirate exists, in fact it is stated that marriage with a deceased husband's brother does not occur; on the other hand, the marriage of a widow, with a son of a brother or sister of her deceased husband's father, although not compulsory, is considered an especially suitable match." Concerning the Louisiades, "it was stated that a man had the right to

17 Eden, *First Three Books*, 24.
18 Williams, *Middle Kingdom*, I, 793-794.
19 DeGroot, *Relig. Syst. China*, II, 763 ff.
20 Fletcher, in HAI, I, 952.
21 Radin, in BAE, XXXVII, 153.
22 Roth, in BAE, XXXVIII, §897.

23 Von der March, *Germanen*, I, 290-291; Estrup, *Samlede Skrifter*, 260.
1 See Levirate in §406, below.
2 Dawson, *Aust. Aborig.*, 27-28.
3 Barnard, in AAAS, 1890, 601.

marry his brother's widow after the latter had completed her mourning, and that the widow would not refuse such a marriage; it was even said that her new husband would not pay for her. If another man wished to marry the widow he would have to pay the dead man's brother the price that the dead man had paid for the woman, even if he were a clansman of the deceased."4 On Tikopia Island "marriage with the brother of the deceased husband is *tapu* or forbidden. If such a marriage were to occur, it is believed that the ghost of the dead husband would injure the brother who has taken his place." At the present time it is the established custom on the Banks Islands that "a man shall marry the widow of his mother's brother if he is not already married, while in the old times when polygyny was still practised it is clear that he would take the wife or wives of his dead uncle even if he were already married." This marriage with the wife of the mother's brother, states Rivers,5 may be regarded as an exceptional form of the levirate, but this institution also exists in its more usual form. "It is right for a man to marry the widow of his deceased brother and it seemed that the widow might be taken either by the elder or younger brother of the late husband. A third orthodox form of marriage is that with the wife's sister. At the present time or till recently a man naturally married the sister of his deceased wife while still farther back it often happened that in case of polygyny the wives were sisters." In the New Hebrides, "the wife of a deceased husband was taken by the brother of the departed."6 Among the natives of Choiseul Island, "when a widow wishes to marry again she cuts off her hair—which has grown to a great length during the period of mourning—bedecks herself with all her ornaments and finery, moves about from village to village and lets it be known that the first good offer of marriage will not be rejected."7 In the D'Entrecasteaux Islands there is no marriage-ceremony for widows. "Never can they return to the maidens' hut, never be wooed again with the vibrant jew's harp. If a widow finds a man attractive she may ask him to visit her at night and cohabit; and the man will make her a present for her favours. The relatives are sure to see it and keep watch, and finally her late husband's brother one night will squat down before her door and call to the couple within. The woman will begin to weep, and the man hurriedly cry out that he has just arrived to take her away. . . . At daybreak a conch-shell is sounded in the hamlet, and proclamation is made that 'so-and-so' was found in the widow's hut. The man goes home, but presently her brother-in-law and the other kinsmen bring his new wife to him, and he makes them a payment as a peace-offering. This constitutes their legal marriage."8

In South Africa, "should a childless widow return to her own people, and the cattle be restored to her late husband's representatives, and she remarry, the restored cattle must again be handed over to her friends. In this case it is not she who failed as. a wife, as is evidenced by another man marrying her."9 In Ashanti, "if the husband disappears for three years, his wife may marry again, but should the first husband return all the children of the second marriage will belong to him."10 "Widows enjoy in general no good reputation in Bassari, since they frequently fall into prostitution in case they do not soon

4 Seligmann, *Melanesians*, 79, 738-739.
5 *Melan. Soc.*, I, 48-49, 346.
6 Turner, *Samoa*, 329.
7 Rooney, in AAAS, 1911, 443.

8 Jenness and Ballentyne, *D'Entrecasteaux*, 103-104.
9 Macdonald, in JAI, XIX, 273.
10 Letourneau, *Soc.*, 318.

marry again after their husbands' deaths."[11] When a widow among the Ibo wishes to remarry "she sits down, legs stretched out in the house of a bachelor, and her suitor steps over her legs; he takes the string from her neck and waist and she takes them to the ajoifia ["bad bush"] and washes; after second burial the widow can take her property to the house of the dead man. Before the marriage is finally completed an Nri man puts two cowries on a string round the waist of the husband saying, 'Oh, husband, take your hand from the woman, let the new husband come and take her.'" In another case the widows put black thread on their necks, which is worn for one year, after which "they shave and cut off the thread, rub cam-wood and mark the body with black stuff; the thread and the hair are thrown on the ash heap. After this they are free to marry."[12] There are no widows among the Boloki, for as soon as a husband dies, the woman becomes the wife of his heir.[13] Among the Bahima, "the father's brother takes the widows, unless he happens to have two wives already; under such circumstances the eldest son takes charge of them, though they are regarded as the property of the uncle, and he pays them marital visits from time to time; any children born to these widows are accounted the children of the deceased, not of the uncle."[14] In the case of the Ba-Mbala, widows can be claimed by the brother of the deceased.[15] In Kenya Colony "a widow may not re-marry. On the death of her husband she falls to his eldest brother. If there are more widows than one the brothers take in order of seniority; should there be no husband's brothers living, they go to the sons of their husband's paternal uncles—failing these to a near member of the husband's clan. This only applies to women capable of bearing children. A widow is not strictly a wife to the man who takes her, for any children she may bear, by whomsoever begotten, take her dead husband's name, and on attaining maturity take the stock and its increase which their 'father' left; if he had mature sons living at his death, these post-mortem children have a claim to a re-division."[16]

Among the Theraka of East Africa a man states before he dies which of his sons and wives shall be married to each other; "if this is not done they cannot be married until the elders . . . have consented to it, in which case the brother of the deceased must first cohabit with the big wife [the first wife]. If this is not observed Makwa [curse] will ensue. If on a man's death neither he nor his wife have any near relations left, the woman can marry whom she pleases, but she must first have connection with a stranger. For this purpose a Mkamba is usually chosen, and as my informant added, 'a Mkamba never refuses because he knows that he will get honey beer.'" Probably both connections are precautionary—one against infringement of the levirate, the other to pass possible evil over to a stranger.[17] The author[18] from whom the above has been taken discusses in general the East African customs applying to widows, including the question of their remarriage. "One of the main principles of marriage, which is rarely disregarded, is that a woman can never be married twice,

11 Klose, in *Globus*, LXXXIII, 314.
12 Thomas, in JAI, XLVII, 177; and in JAI, L, 402.
13 Weeks, in JAI, XXXIX, 445.
14 Roscoe, in JAI, XXXVII, 103-104.
15 Torday and Joyce, in JAI, XXXV, 411.

16 Barton, in JAI, LIII, 77. (Punctuation revised in the interests of intelligibility.)
17 §225, of the text.
18 Dundas, C., in JAI, XLIII, 546; in JAI, XLV, 287; and in JAI, LI, 258, 259, 260.

in the sense that she is paid for twice, excepting in the following cases: 1. If her husband dies before she has borne children. 2. In Ukamba a woman who cannot be remarried is lent as a mate to another man, but if she leaves him and goes to a third man, her brother-in-law or son, as the case may be, may consent to accept dowry [bride-price] for her from that one, and she is then lawfully married to him. A lawful marriage may be said to exist only when the man to whom the woman is given has full claim to all her children. Herein lies the distinction between a man who is a mere companion to the woman, and a husband who may have paid nothing at all in dowry. The first wife married by a man (styled the 'big wife') can never be remarried to anyone after her husband's death; as widows they live either with the brother of the deceased or quite alone. . . . . The idea that a single wife of a convert should remarry is repugnant to the pagan code of morality."

The writer goes on to state that it is at times difficult to distinguish the custom applying to widows and children from that of inheritance, but cautions us that it would be a mistake to regard widows in the same light as heritable property "merely because it is most usual for the widow to remain with her deceased husband's heir or other relative. Here, of course, it is of great consequence whether or not dowry [bride-price] has been paid in full, for whatever rights were accorded to the husband, the claims of his relatives will not be respected in like degree unless he had paid full dowry for his wife, nor will she consider herself bound to his family as she was to her husband unless the claims of her family were fully satisfied. Hence, in cases where men die without having paid full dowry, a dispute generally arises as to their widows and children. But provided full dowry has been paid, it seems that there is remarkably little variance in the customs of these various tribes in this respect, and I incline to think that original custom nowhere permitted a widow to marry outside her husband's clan or family. . . . The most common rule is that a widow is taken to wife by her deceased husband's brother, but it may be noted that, in Ukamba and perhaps elsewhere also, a man cannot marry the widow of his younger brother, because he stands in the relation of a father to the latter." The author states further that the reason why widows are not allowed to marry strangers is the desire to keep the children within their own clan. "For the maintenance of the clan and family strength is all important, wherefore it could never be held right that the offspring of one clan should go over to another clan. By consequence, provision has been made for the re-marriage of a widow to a member of her husband's family, lest she should lose her children, who must remain in the father's family. It is also the consideration of her children which will induce a widow to prefer marriage with her husband's relatives. Notwithstanding custom and common practice, at the present day, widows are very often permitted to marry strangers, but always against return of dowry and the loss of their children, which is not advantageous to the new husband either, for he will consider that he has less chance of rearing up a numerous progeny, which is the ideal of every African. For this reason it will be found that only rarely does a widow desire and find it possible to marry a stranger."

The Mongol widow does not re-marry, for she is to serve her husband in the next world. The youngest son inherits his father's wives and may take any of them but his own mother; for if they go back to his father in the next life he does not care.[19] Among some Siberian tribes, "after the death of one of several brothers, the next brother succeeds him, and acts as husband to the woman and father to the children, for whom he keeps the herd of the deceased. If the woman is too old, he does not exercise his right of levirate, which is here considered more as a duty than a right and only appertains to the younger brother, cousin, or even nephew, and never to the elder brother or uncle." The Koryak levirate rules are as follows: "1. The widow must be married to the younger brother, younger cousin, or nephew (son of sister or brother) of her deceased husband. 2. The widower must marry the younger sister, younger cousin, or niece (daughter of sister or brother) of his deceased wife. According to Jochelson, the Koryak levirate has for its object the maintenance of the union between two families." If this is so, then why, asks the authoress,[20] may not a widower marry his deceased wife's elder sister, and why may not a widow marry her deceased husband's elder brother? "To this question Jochelson suggests the following reply: That the elder brother and elder sister occupy the places of the mother or father in the family should either of the parents die, and so marriage of the widower with the elder sister of his former wife, and of the widow with the elder brother of her former husband, are held to be as incestuous as if these relations-in-law were actually the parents." Among the Gilyak, "after the death of a husband, his wife passes, without any *kalym* [bride-price], to one of his younger brothers, according to the decision of the clan."

In China it is considered censurable for widows to marry. "The widow is occasionally sold for a concubine by her father-in-law, and the grief and contumely of her degradation is enhanced by separation from her children, whom she can no longer retain. Such cases are, however, not common, for the impulses of maternal affection are too strong to be thus trifled with, and widows usually look to their friends for support, or to their own exertions if their children be still young. . . . It is a lasting stigma to a son to neglect the comfort and support of his widowed mother. A widower is not restrained by any laws, and weds one of his concubines or whomsoever he chooses; nor is he expected to defer the nuptials for any period of mourning for his first wife."[21] In the southeastern districts of Fuhkien, scarcely any marriage-maker is inclined to accept a widow for a young man in whose behalf he is seeking a wife. "Such a woman, it is believed, must bring bad luck to her second husband and his clan, because of the revengeful manes of her first husband, which, offended at the infringement upon his ownership, will hover over them all. Consequently a second husband is almost always either a widower or a man of middle age, no longer under control of others regarding the choice of a wife, and moreover a man of small means who cannot pay the large sum of betrothal money generally demanded for a virgin." It is hard to find any one who is willing to draw up the contract, for "perfectly aware that holy antiquity condemns second marriages of women by the word of the Li Ki, he feels sure that, should he presume to write such documents, the gods, and the spirit of the first husband in particular, would send down punishments upon him and frustrate all his future endeavors to obtain a degree at the examinations of the State. . . . Only some old or pettifogging student who has lost all hope of ever taking a degree and obtaining a place in the service of the State, attracted by the pecu-

19 Rubruck, *Eastern Parts*, 78.
20 Czaplicka, *Aborig. Siberia*, 79, 85, 101.
21 Williams, *Middle Kingdom*, I, 793-794.

niary reward, can be found to do such debasing work. He must draw up the contracts in the open field; for, were they written in a house, great misfortune might befall the inmates. And on the spot where the rest of the water with which he has rubbed the ink, is poured away, no blade of grass, or moss, or weed, will ever grow. Such is the curse that sticks to a widow's marriage contract."[22] In some parts of China a marriage between a widow and a widower, usually both of advanced age, is concluded with the understanding that the widow belongs spiritually to her former husband, that is, when she dies her body is claimed by his family and is buried with him.[23]

Among the Palaungs, instead of the usual rice and curries, lumps of rough unrefined sugar are given to guests at the marriage of a widow.[24] It would seem that the Hindu code does not contemplate the case of a man taking a widow as his only wife.[25] Westermarck[26] collects cases indicating the sense of degradation connected with the re-marriage of a widow in India. In instances where it is not prohibited, the higher families do not generally practise it. At such a marriage the ceremony is a maimed rite and there is no sacred fire. By the marriage of widows Rajput families lose their rank and precedence.[27] Marriage of widows and divorced women goes with the eating of mutton, pork, and fowls and the drinking of alcohol.[28] Widow-marriage may prevail among the lower castes and not among the higher.[29] Where divorced women and childless widows may re-marry at pleasure, "widows with children are not supposed to remarry, having to devote themselves to the bringing up of their children."[30] Again, where they may re-marry, widows with children refrain, "as a widowed mother is paramount in a son's house."[31] Widow re-marriage is allowed, once more, provided the groom promises one daughter to the widow's family or a money-equivalent for her. Till mid-day of the day following the marriage, the couple should not be seen by any one.[32] "Widows may marry, but never with the deceased husband's brother, nor with any member of the same sub-division to which the husband belonged. . . . In the case of re-marriage, the Brahmin or any experienced elderly man inverts the order of the prayer."[33] In Travancore, Hindu widows are incapable of re-marriage. A case is cited where there was given in marriage a young daughter who was only nominally a widow through the death of her betrothed. The Brahman father was excommunicated from the temple and from his caste, and the temple cleansed at great expense and with solemn ceremonies from the pollution caused by his entrance after the marriage.[34] In general, a man who marries a widow is boycotted and ostracized; he has to leave his home and take government employment at a distance.[35] This attitude is of long standing, for in the Code of Manu[36] a second husband is nowhere prescribed for a virtuous woman; indeed, a woman should "never even mention the name of another man after her husband has died." So strongly has the re-marriage of a widow been disapproved by Hindu mores that it had to be established by the English through a special law, in 1856.[37]

22 DeGroot, *Relig. Syst. China*, II, 761-762.
23 Von Mollendorff, *Family Law of Chinese*, 39.
24 Milne, *Eastern Clan*, 173, note.
25 Peterson, in JASB, II, 465.
26 *Marriage*, I, 322.
27 Risley, *Ethnog. India*, 125, 182, 74, 75
28 Thurston, *S. India*, 219.
29 Mitra, in JASB, VI, 119.

30 Godden, in JAI, XXVII, 28.
31 Lewin, *S.E. India*, 253.
32 Gunthorpe, in JASB, I, 413.
33 Modi, in JASB, III, 475 ff.
34 Mateer, in JAI, XII, 295.
35 Monier-Williams, *Brāhmanism*, 472.
36 Bühler, *Manu*, V, 154.
37 Jolly, *Stellung d. Frauen*, 451.

Today, however, enforced widowhood is losing its hold, especially in Upper India. This has been accomplished partly through the efforts of an organization which seeks to promote the re-marriage of widows. Particularly noticeable in its report is the large number of re-marriages taking place among Hindu widows of the highest castes. The society has had more success in the Punjab than elsewhere, and it is estimated that if the present rate of re-marriage continues unchanged, there will soon be not a single young widow unmarried unless by choice. This re-marriage society conducts a sort of matrimonial bureau and also a boarding-house for the accommodation of widows desiring to be married.[38]

In Sumatra, "on the death of a man married by *jujur* or purchase, any of his brothers, the eldest in preference, if he pleases, may succeed to his bed. If no brother chuses it, they may give the woman in marriage to any relation on the father's side."[39] Wilken[40] mentions cases where the betrothed of a dead man went over to his brother because the bride-price had been paid up as a whole and the father of the boy did not want to have made all the expenditures for nothing. Youth is no hindrance in this custom whereby the control of the widow belongs to the brother; children, even sucklings, are found for whom four, six, and sometimes more wives are waiting. It is simply a matter of inheritance that one gets his brother's widow. In the Rejang country this results in polygyny; one district-head is mentioned who had seven wives of whom five were widows of his deceased brothers. The children born of a levirate-marriage are nevertheless regarded as the dead man's offspring. Among the Alfurs the levirate-marriage does not prevail; "at death of one spouse, the survivor may never again unite with another. In that case he or she would be exposed to the hatred and vengeance of the family of the deceased."

In Samoa, "the brother of a deceased husband considered himself entitled to have his brother's wife, and to be regarded by the orphan children as their father. If he was already married, she would, nevertheless, live with him as a second wife. . . . The principal reason they alleged for the custom was a desire to prevent the woman and her children returning to her friends, and thereby diminishing the number and influence of their own family. And hence, failing a brother, some other relative would offer himself, and be received by the widow."[41]

Among the Tlinkits, "when a brother dies some one of his surviving brothers must take his widow to wife. If the deceased left no brother, then the next closest relative of his must make the widow his wife. On the other hand, if the wife dies, then a sister of the deceased, or a close relative, must be given to the surviving husband for a wife. . . . It will be seen that this form of marriage among the Thlingets corresponds precisely with that of the ancient Hebrews. It is also interesting to note that there is a correspondence in other respects between the marriage customs of the two peoples; for example, in the dowry, the choice of husband and wife by parents, etc. It is very common for the nephew of the deceased husband to take his widow to wife, the nephew being considered the nearest relation to a man next to his brother. Also for the niece of the deceased wife to marry the widower, as the niece is the nearest relative of a woman next to her sister. In levirate marriages no presents are passed from the man's people to the people of the woman he takes to wife, for

38 Anon., in *Jour. Soc. Hygiene*, X, 569.
39 Marsden, *Sumatra*, 228-229.
40 In VG, I, 341; II, 237-239; III, 532-540.
41 Turner, *Samoa*, 98.

this is only making good his loss. . . . If a brother should refuse to take to wife his deceased brother's widow he would be disgraced among his people."[42] This usage prevailed also among the Indians of British Columbia, a man's widow or widows going to his surviving brother. "It was also customary for a man to marry all his wife's sisters, who are always younger than herself, the eldest daughter being always the first to be disposed of in marriage among primitive people like the Salish. . . . A man might also wed a widow other than his brother's wife, and if she had daughters these also became his wives provided they were not akin by blood to him. A widow had the privilege of bestowing her own hand in a second marriage if she had no brother-in-law to claim her."[43] Among some Algonquians, "widows and widowers were left to their own inclinations."[44] The Omaha still observe the old rule of exogamy and "when a man dies, his widow feels that she honors her husband's memory by remaining in the family, a feeling shared by any unmarried brother of the deceased, who, even if much younger than the widow, promptly becomes her husband."[45] Among the Guiana Indians the husband's brother sometimes claims the widow; to be re-married she must be bought from him. In some tribes, on the occasion of the marriage of a widow, "after having covered her husband's remains with earth, they put her on the grave, and remove the rag which, for the time being covers her chest; she then holds her hands above her head: a man comes forward and strikes her breasts with a switch—this is her future husband: the other men hit her on the shoulders, and she receives the flagellation without a groan: her fiancé in his turn is struck with the switch, his hands joined above his head and without a murmur."[46]

In Arabian custom a widow before re-marriage makes a bird fly away with the uncleanness of her widowhood.[47] It is regarded as a disgrace, especially for her son, if a woman remarries.[48] Although in the Homeric poems a woman is expected to marry again on the death of her husband, yet no widower takes a second wife.[49] Theseus consoles the ghost of his wife by a declaration that he will not marry again, Admetus promises to take no other wife after Alcestis, and Andromache hates the woman who loves her new husband after her former husband's death.[50] Re-marriage of widows was manifestly disapproved of by the ancient Germans; among some stocks it was even forbidden.[51] The law provided that children born of a second marriage belonged to the first husband.[52] Today, "an Albanian tribesman, whether Christian or Moslem, has but one wife at a time, unless he choose to take as well his brother's widow. This by tribe law he may do one month after her husband's death. As all men of a tribe rank as brothers, it follows that a man may take his cousin's or uncle's widow, or both, should there be no nearer male relative than himself surviving. . . . When there is no child, and the husband has been shot very soon after marriage, there is no doubt that the idea is to beget a child that is to rank as his. Children so produced are still reckoned by many people as the actual

42 Jones, *Thlingets*, 129-130.
43 Hill-Tout, in JAI, XXXV, 133.
44 Mooney and Thomas, in HAI, I, 787.
45 Fletcher and LaFlesche, in BAE, XXVII, 641.
46 Roth, in BAE, XXX, 314; and in BAE, XXXVIII, §897.
47 Smith, *Relig. Sem.*, 422.

48 Wellhausen, *Ehe bei Arabern*, 433.
49 Seymour, *Hom. Age*, 151.
50 Euripides, *Hippolytus*, 860-861; *Alcestis*, 305 ff., 328 ff., 1087 ff.; *Trojan Women*, 667-668.
51 Von der March, *Germanen*, I, 290-291.
52 Schroeder, *Geschlechtl. Ordnung*, 115.

offspring of the dead man, in spite of the Franciscans, who study medical works, and gravely assure their flocks that the thing is impossible."[53]

§397. Polyandry.

In reviewing this topic and the following, which have to do with plurality of union, it is of course to be borne in mind that mere sexual relation does not constitute marriage of an institutional type. Plurality of sex-connection is often nothing but lack of all organization whatsoever. If, then, several men have access to the same woman, the case is really as logically alignable with prostitution as with polyandry; in matter of fact, it is neither, for there is no institution present either to receive the name of polyandry or to be abrogated by lawless procedure subversive of institutional arrangements. Nevertheless these very instances of unregulation, like those reviewed in a former connection,[1] cast light from an especial angle upon institutional development. They reveal a tendency in the direction of adjustment to the governing condition of bi-sexuality. Under circumstances of extreme unregulation, or poverty, or disproportion in the number of the sexes, human beings move into such-and-such relations which may, if the conditions persist, ultimately approach institutional form. There is therefore no apology for inserting instances of what is, strictly speaking, not yet polyandry (or polygyny) under the present and following topics.

In Australia this sort of looseness or lack of organization, permitting of plurality in both directions, is to be found: "every man has one or more . . . women who are especially attached to him and live with him in his own camp, but there is no such thing as one man having the exclusive right to one woman"; and while one man may have a preferential right to a woman, other men have a secondary right. In this region "individual marriage does not exist either in name or in practice."[2] Multiplicity of husbands occurs under peculiar circumstances in the Fiji Islands: "polyandry is to be seen under our eyes here in Fiji among the 'imported labourers'; . . . the women being very few in proportion to the men became something like communal wives to those of their island, or group, one of whom they could have married at home." It is evident that there was no real marriage here, though the tendency to plural mating under great disproportion of the sexes is manifest. Among the natives who are not expatriated, "anything properly called Polyandry is unknown, nor is it easy for natives to conceive of it as a possible marriage state."[3] In San Cristoval, Solomon Islands, there exists a custom which, if not true polyandry, is at least a variation of it. "A man gives money and goes and lives with a married couple. Often, it is said, he has no access to the woman, and lives with them merely to have someone to cook for him and help in the garden work; but if he wishes to have access to the woman, he may do so on payment, and will have children by her. In some villages there are three or even four men living thus with a woman, but never more; and all the children born are considered to be the children of the first husband."[4]

53 Durham, in JAI, XL, 461.
1 Ch. XLIII.
2 Spencer and Gillen, North. Tr. Cent. Aust., 72; Brown, in JAI, XLIII, 158.

3 Codrington, Melanesians, 246, note, 245.
4 Fox, in JAI, XLIX, 118-119.

Among the Ba-Mbala of East Central Africa polyandry does not exist, but "a childless man will secretly introduce his brother to his wife in order that he may have a child by her; such a proceeding is, of course, a *secret de polichinelle*"[5]—that is, no secret at all. Sometimes among the Bahima a man finds himself too poor to marry; he has insufficient cattle or cannot afford the bride-price; "in such a case he asks one or more of his brothers to join him, and together they raise the necessary number of animals; a woman will readily agree to this arrangement and become the wife of two or three brothers. They have the right of sharing her couch turn and turn about until she becomes pregnant, when the elder brother alone has the right of access to her: the children born under such circumstances belong to the elder brother. Such an agreement, however, does not deter the younger brothers from obtaining wives themselves later when they can afford them." The only other Bantu people known to the writer[6] to be polyandrists are the Baziba to the south of Uganda.

Scattered through India are several tribes which admit plurality of husbands.[7] "Such as haue wyues, do often tymes chaunge theyr wyues, one frende with an other for th[e] encrease of further frendship. . . . Among some of them, one woman is married to seuen husbandes. . . . And when she hath broughte forth a child, she sendeth it to whiche of her seuen husbandes she list, who maye in no case refuse it."[8] Of one tribe in the Nilgiris "it is said to be the custom for several brothers to take one wife in common."[9] In the Sholapore District, "polyandry is permitted on the death of the husband or on his relinquishing his sexual prerogative."[10] "There seem to be indications that fraternal polyandry may at some time have existed among the Santāls. Even now . . . a man's younger brother may share his wife with impunity; only they must not go about it very openly. Similarly a wife will call in her younger sister," who may be married as a second wife, to avoid scandal.[11] The fraternal polyandry reported of the Todas is now obsolete or nearly so. "This old custom of polyandry seems to have been the result of the custom of female infanticide once prevalent amongst them."[12] "It is probable that the latter custom still exists to some extent, though strenuously denied. There is reason to believe that women are now more plentiful than formerly, though they are still in a distinct minority. Any increase, however, in the number of women does not appear to have led to any great diminution of polyandrous marriages but polyandry is often combined with polygyny. Two or more brothers may have two or more wives in common. . . . It seems possible that the Todas are moving from polyandry to polygyny through an intermediate stage of combined polyandry and polygyny."[13] All accounts of the Todas agree in attributing to them the practice of female infanticide, while the records of the population in the past all show a considerable excess of men over women. Rivers,[14] writing in 1906, described their "completely organised and definite system of polyandry" as follows. "When a woman marries a man, it is understood that she becomes the wife of his brothers at the same time. . . . In the vast majority of polyandrous marriages at the present time, the husbands are own brothers. A

5 Torday and Joyce, in JAI, XXXV, 410.
6 Roscoe, in JAI, XXXVII, 105.
7 List in Jolly, in *Grundr. d. Indo-Ar. Philol.*, II, Heft 8, pp. 47-48.
8 Eden, *First Three Books*, 17-18.
9 Thurston, *S. India*, 113.
10 Scott, in JASB, IV, 361.
11 Risley, *Ethnog. Ind.*, I, 145.
12 Starcke, *Prim. Fam.*, 139; Reclus, *Prim. Folk*, 197; Modi, in JASB, VII, 80-81.
13 Thurston, *S. India*, 109-110.
14 *Todas*, 479, 515-520.

glance through the genealogies will show the great frequency of polyandry. . . . The arrangement of family life in the case of a polyandrous marriage differs according as the husbands are, or are not, own brothers. In the former case it seemed that there is never any difficulty, and that disputes never arise. The brothers live together, and my informants seemed to regard it as a ridiculous idea that there should ever be disputes or jealousies of the kind that might be expected in such a household. When the wife becomes pregnant, the eldest brother performs the ceremony of giving the bow and arrow, but the brothers are all equally regarded as the fathers of the child. . . . If a man is asked the name of his father, he usually gives the name of one man only, even when he is the offspring of a polyandrous marriage. I endeavoured to ascertain why the name of one father only should so often be given, and it seemed to me that there is no one reason for the preference. . . . When the husbands are not own brothers, the arrangements become more complicated. When the husbands live together as if they were own brothers there is rarely any difficulty. If, on the other hand, the husbands live at different villages, the usual rule is that the wife shall live with each husband in turn, usually for a month at a time, but there is very considerable elasticity in the arrangement. It is in respect of the 'fatherhood' of the children in these cases of non-fraternal polyandry that we meet with the most interesting feature of Toda social regulations. . . . Usually it is arranged that the first two or three children shall belong to the first husband, and that at a succeeding pregnancy (third or fourth), another husband shall give the bow and arrow, and, in consequence, become the father not only of that child, but of all succeeding children till some one else gives the bow and arrow. The fatherhood of the child depends entirely on the *pursütpimi* [bow and arrow] ceremony, so much so that a dead man is regarded as the father of a child if no other man has performed the essential ceremony. . . . There is no doubt whatever as to the close association of the polyandry of the Todas with female infanticide. As we have seen, the Todas now profess to have completely given up the practice of killing their female children, but it is highly probable that the practice is still in vogue to some extent. It has certainly, however, diminished in frequency, and the consequent increase in the proportion of women is leading to some modification in the associated polyandry. . . . It seems to me that the correct way of describing the present condition of Toda society is to say that polyandry is as prevalent as ever, but that, owing to the greater number of women, it is becoming associated with polygyny. When there are two brothers it does not seem that each takes a wife for himself, but rather that they take two wives in common. It is probable that this will lead in time to a state of society in which each brother will come to regard one wife as his own; and in a few cases it seemed to me that there was already a tendency in this direction. If this forecast should be fulfilled, the custom of monogamy among the Todas will have been developed out of polyandry through a stage of combined polyandry and polygyny."

Some license in flirtation is permitted with a husband's younger brother in Bihar and Bengal, and marriage with him is allowed in case of widowhood.[15] Polyandry is reported from Calicut.[16] A peculiar form is where a woman of sixteen to twenty years of age, married to a boy of five or six or younger, lives

15 Mitra, in JASB, VI, 119.　　　16 Eden, *First Three Books*, 18.

with his father, uncle, or some other relative of her husband on the mother's side. When her husband grows up she is already old and he takes the wife of some related boy.[17] Westermarck[18] says that this occurred among the Russian peasants prior to emancipation. Polyandry in Ceylon is said to be practised chiefly by the rich.[19] Indications of fraternal polyandry appear in the Hindu traditions; in one case a man who had won a girl in a contest for her hand gives her up as of right to his older brother.[20]

The question of polyandry among the Nairs is a much debated point. "This can be said with certainty: there has been no authenticated case of it at least for the last fifty years. All the evidence that we have of this custom among the Nāyars in the sixteenth, seventeenth, and eighteenth centuries, are from foreign travellers who, it must be remembered, were not allowed to come within sixty yards of a Nāyar house. Their evidence, therefore, is an extremely unsatisfactory ground for dogmatising on Nāyar customs. On the other hand, the extensive Malayalam literature of that period contains no single allusion to polyandry. . . . McLennan, in his well-known book, *Studies in Ancient History,* divides polyandry into two classes, and calls one the Nair type and the other the Tibetan type. 'It is in the nature of the cases,' says he, 'that all the possible forms of polyandry must lie between the Nair and Tibetan forms.' A good deal of what McLennan says about the Nāyar customs is vitiated by the unsatisfactory character of the information at his disposal. Buchanan, on whom he chiefly depends, made a journey through Malabar, and his account is wholly untrustworthy. The loose character of the sexual tie and the licentious habits of the richer Nampudiri landlords, as far as their immediate Nāyar tenants were concerned, were naturally enough interpreted as polyandry by foreign observers. As a matter of fact distinct polyandry of any type was very rare in Màlabar except among the Kāniyāns (or the astrological caste) and among them it is of the Tibetan type. . . . A wife, for example, is the only woman who is allowed to smear oil on a man's back; and when a woman does it to a man it is considered to be a sort of semi-marital function. A man can always ask his brother's wife to do it for him, and it is done very often, even in the presence of the brother. Such customs are, however, open to two interpretations. As we have seen elsewhere, the *Machuna* marriage (or the marriage of cross-cousin) is the orthodox form of marriage among the Nāyars. To all the brothers alike the girl stands in the same relation before the marriage. *She could have been, in fact, the wife of any of them,* provided she was not older than her cousins. Even after her marriage with one of them this potential relationship continues to exist, and therefore all the brothers treat her 'half as a sister and half as a wife.' . . . This does not seem to me to be true. Nāyar tradition gives no support to this view. We have no Nāyar stories that speak of one woman who was the commonwife of her cross-cousins. In fact we have no tradition of any polyandry at all. Nevertheless, we find McLennan giving the Nair name to a particular type of polyandry supposed by him to be practised universally among them."[21]

Polyandry in China proper is found exclusively in one city in the province

17 Thurston, *S. India,* 52-53.
18 *Marriage,* III, 131; Fawcett, in JASB, II, 337.
19 Westermarck, *Marriage,* III, 132; Starcke, *Prim. Fam.,* 136; Mucke, *Horde,* 134-135.

20 Holtzmann, *Ind. Sagen,* I, 11; II, 103; Phillips, *Vedas,* 150; Zimmer, *Altind. Leben,* 325-326.
21 Panikkar, in JAI, XLVIII, 271-272, 293.

of Fukien; it has been carried by emigrants to Formosa but is of local origin, being caused by the extreme poverty of the district, in which only the very poorest practise it. Brothers live with a common wife alternately for some defined period. In the same place infanticide, which seems also to spring from poverty, is of common occurrence.[22] In the Malay Archipelago, "no regulated polyandry appears." The writer[23] finds only one instance, among the Dyaks, reported; in this case a woman may have more than one husband without being the worse thought of. It is not done secretly and all the children belong to the first husband. In Borneo Schwaner[24] found something like polyandry without a marriage-ceremony, which is, of course, of little significance to us. One Macassar case is reported where, since two brothers had one wife between them, both could not be hired for an expedition—one had to stay home and look after her.[25]

An isolated case of polyandry with brothers is reported from the westernmost of the Caroline Islands.[26] In Nukahiva, one of the Marquesas Islands, a woman had a real and an auxiliary husband, the latter being generally poor and handsome.[27] This is merely a case of a lover with perhaps a more than incidental standing. Cranz[28] says that an Eskimo woman with two husbands has been observed. In cases where the men were much more numerous than the women two-husband polyandry "is not uncommon."[29] Aleut girls reserve the right to take a lover at marriage.[30] In some Iroquois tribes a woman could lawfully have two husbands.[31] The brother of the husband is regarded as a second husband by the Kolush Indians;[32] this practice is interpreted as a survival of group-marriage.[33] The customs and traditions of the Seri Indians are thought to suggest a former polyandry.[34] In those cases among the Guiana Indians where the number of women is extremely small, a kind of polyandry has developed.[35]

On the Canary Islands, many of the women "had three husbands, who held the position in turn by months, the one next to succeed to the honor serving until his time came to be lord."[36] It was the case in Sparta where "it is traditional law, and a matter of common custom, for three or four men to have one wife, or even more if they are brothers."[37] Roman epitaphs occur indicating that two men had a common wife.[38] The old Teutonic myths represent Odin's wife as married during his absence to his brothers.[39] Caesar[40] reports some tribes of Britain as polyandrous; but this passage and one from Herodotus[41] about the Agathyrsi are believed to be no more than inferences from joint-household life.[42]

The cases which run out into the mere maintenance of a woman by several

22 Von Mollendorff, *Family Law*, 38.
23 Wilken, *Vkde.*, 290.
24 *Borneo*, 168; Roth, *Sarawak*, II, cxcix.
25 Cayley-Webster, *New Guinea*, 165, 166.
26 Kubary, *Karolinen-arch.*, 93; Finsch, *Ethnol. Erfahr.*, III, 307, note.
27 Westermarck, *Marriage*, III, 147; Starcke, *Prim. Fam.*, 137.
28 *Grönland*, I, 193.
29 Anoh., "Amundsen's Polar Exped.," in *Globus*, XCI, 368.
30 Reclus, *Prim. Folk*, 66.
31 Lafitau, *Zeden*, 273.
32 Waitz, *Anthrop.*, III, 328; this is disputed; Müller, *Sex. Leben*, 31.

33 Wilutzky, *Mann u. Weib*, 72.
34 McGee, in BAE, XVII, pt. I, 11.
35 Roth, in BAE, XXXVIII, 686.
36 Cook, in AA, II, 480; Westermarck, *Marriage*, III, 151; Bethencourt, *Canarien*, 135; Müller, *Sex. Leben*, 30.
37 Polybius, *Hist.*, XII, §VI, 86; Starcke, *Prim. Fam.*, 137; Schoemann, *Griech. Alterth.*, I, 273; Drumann, *Arbeiter*, 137.
38 Pellison, *Roman Life in Pliny's Time*, 100.
39 Weinhold, *Altnord. Leben*, 249.
40 *Bello Gall.*, V, 14.
41 *Hist.*, IV, 103.
42 Schrader, *Aryan*, 394.

men, with no idea of marriage, belong under prostitution.[43] It is stated that
the Albanian, returning from work abroad, "shows in particular more attention to the wife of his eldest brother than to his own and will certainly never
bring anything special for the latter";[44] but to align such procedure with
polyandry would be a far cry.

§398. Polygyny.

POLYGYNY is practised by the tribes of western Australia, but in the genealogies Brown[1] did not find a case of a man having more than three wives alive
at the same time. "Where there are several sisters in a family they are all regarded as the wives of the man who marries the eldest of them. He may, if he
chooses, waive his right in favour of his younger brother, with the consent of
the father of the girls. . . . When a man dies his wives pass to his younger
brother or to the man who stands nearest to him in the relation of *margara*
[younger brother]. This man marries the widow and adopts the children."
In British New Guinea, "polygamy is practised among the Mekeo people,
but the number of wives rarely extends beyond three, and generally only
wealthy men can afford the luxury. The ceremony on a marriage with a second
wife is somewhat similar to that on marriage with the first; but on the second
wife coming to the man's house the first wife will often leave it, and he has, if
possible, to appease her and induce her to return. One factor which makes
for polygamy is the right of the eldest brother or nearest male relative (married or single) of a dead man to the latter's wife. . . . Her entry to her new
home, even if agreed to by the first wife, is not a peaceable one—at all events
in form. The husband has with him a number of his male friends, all. armed
with sticks, and the party on reaching the house find the first wife there, and
with her they find all her women friends, and possibly some of her male relatives, all armed with sticks. A fight, generally a sham one only, takes place
between the two parties, in which the first wife's party try to defend the house
against the entry of the second wife, and the husband's party, acting only on
the defensive, support her in her effort to get on to the verandah platform of
the house."[2] In Papua "a man may have as many wives as he likes, but polygamy is mainly confined to chiefs. This is a matter of being able to pay,
rather than anything else."[3] Each wife has her own house and garden, but all
must obey the first or chief wife.[4] Throughout the domain of the northern Massim polygyny is a privilege theoretically restricted to the families of chiefs.
This rule is not strictly kept since on the Trobriands wealthy commoners, especially if they have a reputation as sorcerers, not infrequently take more than
one wife, knowing that no one will dare to challenge their right to do so. "It
seemed that great consideration was shown to the senior wives even when they
became old and ugly, and there is no doubt that the senior wives directed and
exerted a good deal of influence over the younger wives."[5] On Lifu, Loyalty
Islands, "a common man might have several wives; a chief often had many, as
the number of wives was regarded as adding to a man's position and influence

43 Molmenti, *Venezia*, I, 386.
44 Rhamm, in *Globus*, LXXXII, 191.
1 In JAI, XLIII, 158.
2 Williamson, in JAI, XLIII, 277.

3 Liston-Blyth, in JAI, LIII, 469.
4 Bromilow, in AAAS, 1909, 481; Hagen,
Papua's, 200.
5 Seligmann, *Melanesians*, 712, 713.

among his people."6 In New Caledonia, "chiefs had ten, twenty, and thirty wives. The more wives the better plantations, and the more food. Common men had one or two."7 The reason given for the recent diminution of polygyny in the Fiji Islands is that the men greatly exceed the women in numbers, so that those men who had no wives objected to others having three or four, and in time the matter was equalized by forbidding any man to have more than one. Even under this rule there are said to be many bachelors who would marry if they could.8

Among the Tati Bushmen "a man will have as many as four wives or even more. Plurality of wives is largely a matter of wealth, and it gives a man distinction."9 Polygyny among the Zulus seems always to have been limited by the expense of wife-purchase; it is now waning owing to the increased cost of living. In former years a man could purchase a wife for eight oxen, but now the price has gone up to almost twice that number. Some parents have adopted the expedient of disposing of their nubile daughters on the instalment-plan, the terms generally being two oxen down and the remaining at fixed intervals. Only the very rich now have several wives.10 In West Africa there are men "who must remain bachelors because either they are not rich enough to buy a wife, or because wives are not to be had."11 In the Congo Basin "polygamy is general, but except with rich and influential persons, the Banziris rarely have more than one free wife. The other wives are slaves."12 Among some tribes the chiefs have so many wives, sometimes five hundred, that there are no young women left for the young men to marry.13 It is said to be the ambition of every Bangala woman to have a house of her own, and "it is the invariable practice for a man to build a house for every one of his wives, which she will regard as her own and in which she will live and bring up her family. A man of any pretence to importance will also have a house built exclusively for his own use. To this house he invites the wife he wants for the time being, or sometimes he simply goes to the wife's house for the night." When a man acquires a new wife the old ones exhibit no jealousy but regard her as an acquisition—"the new wife being one more to help keep the husband." A man can marry as many women as he can afford to pay marriage-money for; monogamy is the exception, being the result of poverty.14 Among the Ba-Mbala "polygamy is common, but all wives have equal rights." With the Ba-Yaka, "polygyny is the general rule, and the number of wives possessed by one individual is conditioned solely by the length of his purse; monogamy, still more celibacy, is merely the result of slender resources."15 While among the Batetela who have been under Arab influence polygyny is practised as a sign of rank and wealth —important chiefs have harems of hundreds of wives—"the more primitive Batetela contents himself with a few spouses, even important chiefs being satisfied with a dozen or so."16 In British Central Africa the number of wives per ordinary man is from one or two to six or ten; for a chief, from thirty to forty.17

---

6 Ray, in JAI, XLVII, 287.
7 Turner, Samoa, 341.
8 Brewster, Hill Tribes of Fiji, reviewed in N. Y. Times, Dec. 10, 1922.
9 Dornan, in JAI, XLVII, 47.
10 Ratzel, Vkde., I, 254; N. Y. Times, May 28, 1922; Aug. 31, 1924.
11 Lessner, in Globus, LXXXVI, 393.

12 Clozel, in PSM, XLIX, 676.
13 Burrows, in JAI, XXVIII, 46.
14 Weeks, in JAI, XXXIX, 435, 441.
15 Torday and Joyce, in JAI, XXXV. 410; and JAI, XXXVI, 45.
16 Torday, in JAI, LI, 375.
17 Stannus, in JAI, XL, 309.

In Uganda a great chief may have a hundred sons and be the probable progenitor of a thousand grandchildren. Kavirondo women are in excess of the men, but "it is highly improbable that any woman goes to her death unmarried; for if no suitor asks for her in the ordinary way, she will single out a man and offer herself to him at a 'reduced price.' The man would be hardly likely to refuse, since a woman in that country is a first-class agricultural labourer." The Kavirondo are reported to be much more moral than their neighbors, or were so before being corrupted by foreigners, including whites.[18] The daughter of a chief becomes, on marriage, the chief wife, women taken earlier sinking to a subordinate position.[19] Where losses of life in war result in a sex-proportion of five females to three males, as among the Kilimandscharo tribes, polygyny exists and every man has as many wives as he can get.[20] Few of the Mombasa of East Africa indulge in the luxury of more than one wife, though the number permissible seems to be limited only by the means of the parties.[21] "The Wa-Sania are polygamous, but are not permitted to marry more than three wives, as it is considered that no man is able to provide food, etc., for more than this number. Wives are obtained by purchase."[22] Some of the missionaries are of the opinion that in a generation or so polygyny will practically cease among the Akamba owing to the shortage of women, but Hobley[23] says this will really be due to the greater percentage of survivals of male lives. The births of the two sexes are now about equal in number. So far as Sir Charles Dundas[24] is aware, polygyny is the rule with all Bantu tribes of East Africa with but one exception, and even there it has recently been introduced by certain chiefs. "Polygamy is the normal estate. A single wife is the indication of poverty; many wives mean wealth. They bring strength to the family and by consequence the husband of many wives is respected and esteemed. Excepting among the Wakarra there is in no tribe any limit to the number of wives a man may have. It depends only on the wealth of each one. I have known natives who had twenty, forty, and even over a hundred wives; but if it is possible to generalize at all, I should say that five is a number exceeded only in exceptional cases."

In East Africa "the system of polygamy is based upon a very sound principle. No man has more wives than his live stock and plantations warrant, and the wife or wives installed in the 'boma' seem utterly devoid of jealousy. A new wife is hailed with delight, and the established household exert themselves to the utmost to do her honor."[25] The curse, "May you be married as a second wife," and the proverb, *"One* hand cannot remove the louse from the head," sufficiently indicate the status of the head-wife and co-wives and the comfort of the husband of many. Wives generally vie in the effort to please a husband; but if they quarrel, none of them cook for him but each refers him to another; hence the proverb, "If a man has two wives, there are two hyenas in his home." The competition leads to mutual injury, through magic, of the competitors themselves and even of their children. Wives may so behave as to justify the saying, "Though you possess ever so many things and marry a wife, then you lose all of them." What the woman loses by polygyny she mostly regains as a

18 Johnston, *Uganda*, II, 590, 720-721, 746;
Ratzel, *Vkde.*, I, 476.
19 Volkens, *Kilimandscharo*, 252.
20 Abbott, in USNM, 1891, 388.
21 Johnstone, in JAI, XXXII, 267.

22 Barrett, in JAI, XLI, 30.
23 *A-Kamba*, 12, 14.
24 In JAI, LI, 248-249.
25 French-Sheldon, in JAI, XXI, 360.

mother; her children cleave to her and sometimes a man fears to marry a
widow with sons lest they grow up to force him out of his property.[26] Again,
"because of polygyny, prostitution is excluded and actually does not appear."[27]
Here, as in a number of the preceding cases, it is found that the wives live
apart, each in her own house, unless the desire to evade the house-tax on the
separate establishments enforces one big dwelling, presided over by the head-
wife, for all. "Unfortunately nowadays the hut tax has played havoc with the
old custom and very often two or three women are found in one and the same
hut."[28] The nomadic tribes of the northeast hold strictly to the separate establishment; a man will have wives, up to four, located in different places.[29] This
custom is explained as preventive of quarreling.[30] In Madagascar, "so invariably has the taking of more wives than one shown itself to be a fruitful cause
of enmity and strife in a household, that this word . . . which means 'the
making an adversary,' is the term always applied to it," that is, to polygyny.
"The different wives are always trying to get an advantage over each other
and to wheedle their husband out of his property; constant quarrels and jealousy are the result, and polygamy becomes inevitably the causing of strife,
'the making an adversary.'" Here also is one "grande femme" along with the
"petites femmes"; and Christianity has had to compromise with the system.[31]

Among the Nigerians a man may have all the wives he can pay for, but six
is generally the greatest number found.[32] Polygyny is the rule among the
Dinkas, where "the number of wives is only limited by the ability of the husband to support them."[33] In Mohammedan Africa the first wife remains the
head-wife, at least in name, "even when the love of her lord has long belonged
to another."[34] The toleration of polygyny, to which tradition and custom have
familiarized the Africans, gives Mohammedanism an advantage over Christianity as a proselytizing religion.[35] In modern Egypt there is little polygyny
on account of the expense and discomfort incurred, except in cases of barrenness of the first or succeeding wives; yet "a poor man may indulge himself
with two or more wives, each of whom may be able, by some art or occupation,
nearly to provide her own subsistence." The women do not approve of polygyny.[36] Where, as among the Osmanli, the common people are monogamous,
the man changes his wife frequently.[37]

The custom whereby a father procures an adult wife for an infant son and
lives with her, is found in central Asia.[38] "A Gilyak will usually have two or
three individual wives; rich people have more."[39] Although the Palaung chief
has many wives, polygyny is not customary among the common people unless
there is lack of children. "The rate of mortality among Palaung children is
very high. Sometimes out of a family of five, seven, eight, or even ten children
but few live to grow up. I knew the head-man of a village near Namhsan whose
wife bore to him thirteen children. Twelve died young, some before they were
one year old, others lived to be two to seven years old. The wife, who loved
children, was greatly distressed. Her husband was a rich man who owned large

26 Gutmann, in *Globus*, XCII, 2, 3, 30.
27 Fabry, in *Globus*, XCI, 222.
28 Dundas, C., in JAI, XLIII, 520.
29 Paulitschke, *Nordost-Afr.*, I, 198.
30 Vannutelli e Citerni, *L'Omo*, 192.
31 Sibree, *Great Afr. Isl.*, 161; Letourneau,
Marriage, 129-130, 132, 164; Ratzel, *Vkde.*,
II, 510.

32 Tremearne, in JAI, XLII, 174.
33 Cummins, in JAI, XXXIV, 150, 163.
34 Nachtigal, *Sahara*, II, 177.
35 Ratzel, *Vkde.*, III, 114.
36 Lane, *Modern Egypt.*, I, 274-275.
37 Pischon, *Islam*, 13.
38 Abercromby, *Finns*, I, 192.
39 Czaplicka, *Aborig. Siberia*, 101.

tea gardens, and she feared that the only remaining son might die too, and that there would be no one to succeed to the property. She therefore begged her husband to take another wife. When he consented, she chose a girl whom she liked. There were five children of the second marriage, and although both wives loved and cared for the children, all died young except one." In another case, "their children being all dead, the old lady persuaded her husband to take another wife, and he agreed, stipulating that she should choose the young lady. This was done, and they appeared to be a happy family. The younger woman did all the housework."40 Williams41 thinks that polygyny in China finds its greatest support from the women themselves. "The wife seeks to increase her own position by getting more women into the house to relieve her own work and humor her fancies. The Chinese illustrate the relation by comparing the wife to the moon and the concubines to the stars, both of which in their appropriate spheres wait upon and revolve around the sun."41

In India the first wife is treated the best because she is more troublesome and expensive to get than the rest. Though separate establishments are common, the wives coöperate.42 Manu had ten wives. Only the great men practised polygyny and one wife outranked the others. The chief reason for plurality of wives was lack of children by the first wife. "In cases where seven years after marriage no son is born, the Law Books authorize a man to take a second wife, because the son is regarded as necessary to perform the funeral rites of his father"; still the percentage of men living under polygyny is never important; in Madras where that system is strongest, only four per cent of the men have two wives and in the Punjab those with more than one constitute less than one per cent.43 The Sema Nagas at present practise polygyny, though "it is usually only chiefs and other rich men who keep more than one wife, the ordinary villager being unable to afford it. . . . One of the wives is usually regarded as the head wife, but she does not necessarily take the lead in regulating her husband's household, and her position as the principal wife does not seem to be very definite." In the case of a chief's son she would normally be the one married first.44 The invasion of Bengal by the Mohammedans in 1203 had deep effect on the native matrimonial organization. The natural balance of the sexes had been disturbed, and keen competition for husbands set in among the three original groups. The demand was especially great for Kulin husbands, and a bridegroom-price supplanted the earlier bride-price. "In order to dispose of the surplus of women in the higher groups polygamy was introduced, and was resorted to on a very large scale. It was popular with the Kulins, because it enabled them to make a handsome income by the accident of their birth; and it was accepted by the parents of the girls concerned as offering the only means of complying with the requirements of the Hindu religion. . . . The honour of marrying a daughter to a Bhanga Kulin is said to have been so highly valued in Eastern Bengal that as soon as a boy was ten years old his friends began to discuss his matrimonial prospects, and before he was twenty he had become the husband of many wives of ages varying from five to fifty."45

In the Malay Archipelago many tribes are monogamous or, to avoid quar-

40 Milne, *Eastern Clan*, 38, 103.
41 *Middle Kingdom*, I, 792.
42 Fawcett, in JASB, I, 230.
43 Wilkins, *Hinduism*, 179; Jolly, in *Grundr. d. Indo-ar. Philol.*, II, Heft 8, pp. 64-

67; Zimmer, *Altind. Leben*, 323-325; Bühler, *Manu*, IX, 183.
44 Hutton, *Sema Nagas*, 135, 185.
45 Risley, *Ethnog. India*, I, 189-190.

rels, a man has only one wife in any one village.[46] The first wife must be appeased with presents if there is to be a second.[47] In South Sumatra the third wife is subject to the first and the fourth to the second, while the wives without status are subordinate to those who have it, the first wife standing above them all.[48] In Atjeh, while a man can seldom afford more than one wife at a time, divorce and re-mating are very easy. The fact that there are separate establishments to be maintained keeps the ordinary man from polygyny. Four lawful wives are the limit set by the Koran.[49] Among the Alfurs polygyny is confined to chiefs and the rich. Wilken[50] thinks the custom was adopted from the Mohammedans. There is very little polygyny in the Malay Peninsula, because of poverty rather than conviction.[51] On the island of Mindoro, although a woman can have but one husband, a man may have as many wives as he can support.[52] "On islands where the chiefly system prevailed, which is to say, on all the units of the Gilbert Group north of and including Abemama, only a chief might take more than one wife. Slaves were at the most monogamous."[53] Polygyny exists in a limited measure in the western Carolines; "no man may have more than four wives at a time, while in most cases monogamy prevails."[54] Polygyny of chiefs, and even concubinage where property is exchanged as in marriage, occur in Polynesia.[55] It has been noted that on Easter Island, where the women are scarce, they are treated with solicitude; and "polygamy, under these circumstances, does not, of course, exist."[56] Instances of polygyny for those who could afford it occur throughout Turner's book on Samoa and other islands. Among the Maoris, "a plurality of wives is in some quarters still considered the perquisite of a *rangatira*," or big man.[57]

Among the Hudson Bay Eskimo a designing woman will often cause a man to cast off his legal wife and come and live with her. In such instances the real wife seldom resents the intrusion, but occasionally gives the other a severe thrashing and an injunction to look to herself lest she be discarded also.[58] Polygyny was permitted by the Cheyenne Indians, as was usual with the prairie tribes.[59] It existed among the Omaha, although it was not the rule. "A man rarely had more than two wives and these were generally sisters or aunt and niece. These complex families were usually harmonious and sometimes there seemed to be little difference in the feeling of the children toward the two women who were wives to their father. No special privileges were accorded to the first wife over the others. Polygamy was practised more among the prominent men than among any other class. On the former devolved the public duty of entertaining guests from within and without the tribe. This duty brought a great deal of labor on the household. . . . The question of domestic labor had a good deal to do with the practice of polygamy. 'I must take another wife. My old wife is not strong enough now to do all her work alone.' This remark was made not as if offering an excuse for taking another wife but as stating a condition which must be met and remedied in the only way which

46 Ratzel, *Vkde.*, II, 430.
47 Schwaner, *Borneo*, I, 199; Roth, *Sarawak*, II, xlcci.
48 Wilken, in VG, II, 281-282.
49 Jacobs, *Groot-Atjeh*, I, 75-76.
50 In VG, I, 48-49.
51 Skeat and Blagden, *Malay Penin.*, II.
52 Worcester, *Philippine Isl.*, I, 413.
53 Grimble, in JAI, LI, 27.

54 Senfft, in *Globus*, XCI, 141.
55 Finsch, *Ethnol. Erfahr.*, III, 307; Kubary, *Pelauer*, I, 62; Gray, in AAAS, 1892, 626.
56 Cook, in USNM, 1897, I, 716.
57 Cowan, *Maoris*, 147.
58 Turner, in BAE, XI, 189, 190.
59 Mooney, in IIAI, I, 253.

custom permitted."[60] Polygyny, correlative with wealth, existed among a number of tribes, the wives in some cases being sisters.[61] In polygynous marriages among the Winnebago, "the second wife was usually a niece or a sister of the first wife. According to a reliable informant it was the wife herself who often induced her husband to marry her own niece. This she did if she noticed that he was getting tired of her or losing his interest in her."[62] Although both custom and tradition tell of former monogamy, with a suggestion of polyandry, polygyny has prevailed among the Seri, "professedly and evidently because of the preponderance of females due to the decimation of warriors in battle."[63] Morgan[64] says of the American Indians: "The females are usually more numerous than the males from the destruction of the latter in war. In some nations, as the Blackfoot and the Shiyann, they are said to be two to one." Plural marriages are no longer permitted and the number is declining, there being 588 in 1912 and but 187 in 1920.[65]

Roth[66] cites many examples to substantiate his statement that polygyny was practised throughout the length and breadth of the Guianas, including the islands. "But, generally speaking, there are few who have many wives, not because they do not want them, but because they can not get them; or, granted they can get them, because they have not the wherewithal to pay the parents for them or because they do not care to complete the necessary tasks. . . . The Orinoco chiefs were accustomed to have, more by way of pomp and vanity than anything else, as many as 10 or 12 wives, and at times more. . . . The larger number of wives held by the chiefs and medicos as compared with the common crowd is repeatedly noted elsewhere. The plurality of wives was also proportionately dependent upon the ability of the husband to support a larger or smaller household. . . . Among remaining factors that have to be taken into consideration is the economic one of the value of woman's work and the number of women available." It frequently occurs that the wives are sisters. "Coudreau goes so far as to state that among the majority of the tribes one finds Indians having two or three wives, generally sisters. 'The marriage of two sisters to the same husband,' says Rev. Charles Dance, 'has often been justified by the elder sister as a preventive to family jars and conjugal jealousies. "Better,"' she says, "take my sister, who loves and will obey me, than take a stranger who will hate me."'" An instance of a Makusi Indian who had three wives and a progeny of eight children, with prospect of more, is cited as a rare case of numerous children among natives who practise polygyny. The following picture is given of a polygynous household on the Orinoco. "As might be expected, quarrels are not wanting among the wives, although they do not live together in the one house, but each one has her separate habitation together with her children and her separate hearth. The fish which the husband gets is divided proportionately among all of them according to the children which each one has. When mealtime arrives they stretch the mat, which is his table, on the ground and each wife, after placing in front of him his plate of meat, his cassava cake, or caizu of maize, retires. Whether he eats or not, no one speaks

60 Fletcher and LaFlesche, in BAE, XXVII, 326; Dorsey and Thomas, in HAI, II, 120.

61 Henshaw; Mooney and Thomas; Huntington; and Sapir, in HAI, I, 538; I, 360; I, 30; II, 674, respectively; Anon., in HAI, I, 283.

62 Radin, in BAE, XXXVII, 138.

63 McGee, in BAE, XVII, pt. I, 11.

64 In *Smithson. Contrib. to Knowledge*, XVII, 477.

65 Rep. Commissioner of Ind. Affairs, 1920.

66 In BAE, XXXVIII, 685, 686-687, 688.

to him. After the lapse of a sufficient time, each wife brings a drink of beer (*chicha*), which she places in front of him, and, this done, then retires to her hut to eat and drink with her children; and so strife is avoided. In the field a similar separation is arranged for. The husband divides the land, which he and his friends have cut into as many portions as he has wives, each woman sowing, cultivating, and looking after her own portion without meddling with the other's. Nevertheless, it is true that squabbles are not entirely wanting; e.g., over one having a better or bigger plot than another, over one wife's children stealing fruit from another wife's piece of land, etc."

While monogamy is general among the Bororo Indians, an exception occurs in the case of the priest who is enabled to support two wives through the wealth he obtains from his profession.[67] "Polygamy is very generally practised among the Araucanos, the only limit to the number of wives a man may possess being his ability to provide the purchase price, and to maintain them and their families. Formerly it was common for a chief of importance to have as many as twenty, but now the number rarely passes four or five. . . . As a general rule there is little jealousy among the wives."[68] In every district among the Peruvians there was stationed a special officer whose exclusive duty it was to pick out the comeliest young girls and take them for the Inca's disposal. Part he sent to Cuzco for the numerous human sacrifices, part he had shut up in women's houses, called "houses of the chosen," where they were excluded from the outer-world and brought up by matrons. There were three kinds of such houses. In some were enclosed the girls who were designated for the service of the Sun; it was their duty to prepare the objects needed for the sacrifices. From others the Incas got their inferior wives and concubines; and finally from the third type were taken girls to be given over to the officers as wives and bedfellows. The number of the "chosen" was considerable. In the selection of girls no kind of consideration was given as to how many had already been taken from a village. The official simply took those who seemed to him suitable, and "the parents could under no circumstances refuse or redeem them." The surrender of their daughters was very deeply felt by the population, and it would have been still more hateful had not the belief been spread abroad among the Indians that the souls of the sacrificed girls enjoyed full peace in after-life.[69] Letourneau[70] quotes de la Vega to the effect that various Incas left several hundred children apiece; they were properly termed "fathers of their people." In Mexico the father of Montezuma left one hundred and fifty sons.[71]

In ancient Babylonia polygyny was known as early as 2000 B.C., it being related, for example, that a man married two sisters. Many men, whose means allowed, had several concubines who came mostly from the slave-status. The relation between the different women was regulated and strife forbidden.[72] The Code of Hammurabi permitted a man to take a concubine if his wife were barren or another wife if she were a chronic invalid. On the other hand, bigamy on the part of a woman, without the excuse of lack of support, was a capital offense.[73] Cases of a man having more than one wife occurred in every period among the early Egyptians. Frequently it was a case of a love-wife and a

---

67 Frič and Radin, in JAI, XXXVI, 390.
68 Latcham, in JAI, XXXIX, 358-359.
69 Cunow, *Verf. d. Inkareichs*, 110.
70 *Polit.*, 114.

71 Bancroft, *Native Races*, II, 182.
72 Meissner, *Althabylon. Privatrecht*, 14.
73 Harper, *Hammurabi*, 115, 116.

status-wife, while harems were kept by the rich.[74] The Talmudists stated that a man might marry as many women as he could support, and at the same time they imparted the well-meant advice not to marry more·than four, so as to do justice to the marriage-duty. It appears, however, that not much use was made of their precepts. In the Talmud mention is quite often made of the wife, but never of the wives, of one learned in Scripture. "Perhaps the monogamy which Zoroaster prescribed for the Persians was not wholly without influence on the practical life of the Jews."[75] Tradition states that Zoroaster was thrice married and had several sons and daughters, and that the three wives survived him. By the first or privileged wife the Prophet had one son and three daughters.[76] At the time of Herodotus the Persians had several wives, and concubines besides, while Strabo asserts that not only did the Medean kings have many wives but that the Medes living in the mountains could take no less than five wives. It appears that only the wealthy had a plurality of wives, the mass of the people having to be content with one apiece.[77]

Euripides,[78] in his handling of the Medea-tragedy, causes his characters to display a situation of a tangled order. Jason has taken an alien woman to wife, being under deep obligation to her, both as respects life and prosperity. He had given strong pledges with his right hand. Now he is going to marry the daughter of a king. It appears that a man may marry a second wife so far as public law is concerned. Says the chorus to Medea: "If thy lord prefers a fresh love, that is his affair; do not be angry. Zeus will judge between thee and him in the matter." Medea calls upon the gods that guarantee oaths. "He who was all to me, my husband, has turned out to be the worst of men," replies Medea. "Of all creatures that are alive and have reason we women are the most wretched race. First we have to buy a mate at a high price, and get a tyrant." It is a very great question whether we get a scoundrel or a good man. Divorce is discreditable. Coming into a new situation and new ways of life, one has to be a soothsayer, not having learned how to act at home, to know how best to deal with her spouse. If she does this with tact, she is happy; if not, she had better die. The chorus admonishes Jason bluntly that he has sinned in casting off his wife; and Medea asserts that if he had not been a villain he would have got her consent and then made the new marriage, and would not have done it clandestinely. When Ægeus hears what Jason has done, he calls it a dastardly deed. Jason says women are weak, given to tears, and that it is natural for them to rave against a husband who is planning another marriage; that she could endure his second marriage if she had self-control. He excuses himself on the ground that what he is doing will be for the welfare of the children. "Men ought to get children from somewhere else, and there ought to be no female sex." Medea, after reminding him of the services she has done him, goes on: "And having been thus served, oh worst of men, by me, thou hast betrayed me and got a new love—and that when we had children. For if thou wast still childless, to desire this new union would be pardonable."

"Polygamy," says Ratzel,[79] "is an old Arabic, or rather old Semitic, tradition. In ancient times economic facts restrained it. In the midst of the wealth

74 Erman, *Aegypten*, 217.
75 Bergel, *Eheverhältnisse*, 10.
76 Jackson, *Zoroaster*, 20-21.
77 Herodotus, *Hist.*, I, 135; Strabo, *Geog.*,

XV, 733; XI, 526; Spiegel, *Eran. Alterth.*, III, 677.
78 *Medea*, 16 ff., 155 ff., 161-163, 230 ff., 578, 586-587, 695, 908 ff., 1368 ff., 566 ff., 475 ff.
79 *Vkde.*, III, 152.

of the conquerors it became a worm gnawing at the vitals of every nation which accepted Mohammedan doctrine." Ali, the son-in-law of the Prophet, married more than two hundred women. Sometimes he included as many as four wives in one contract and divorced four at one time, taking four others in their stead. An Arab is mentioned who married eighty women in the course of his life, while a certain dyer of Bagdad who died at the age of eighty-five is said to have married in all more than nine hundred women. If he began his marital career at the age of fifteen, he must have had on the average nearly thirteen new wives a year through his whole life.[80] This liberty is exercised in Arabian countries still. "Palgrave relates that the Sultan of Qatar in eastern Arabia married a new wife every month or fortnight, on whom the brief honors of matrimony were bestowed for a like period, and who was then retired on a pension."[81] Burckhardt[82] says: "I have seen Arabs about forty-five years of age who were known to have had above fifty different wives. Whoever will be at the expense of a camel, may divorce and change his wives as often as he thinks fit." The caliph of Cordova begot one hundred sons; the number of his daughters is not mentioned.[83] Von Kremer[84] explains the persistence of polygyny in the Orient through the facts that it quickly increases the family-group and thus satisfies the need for descendants and that valuable kin-unions with other tribes and families are thereby instituted. He draws attention to its maladaptation, however, by describing conditions in a typical harem, where, besides innumerable daughters, thirty, forty or even a hundred sons of different mothers are growing up, raised in the mutual jealousy and rivalry of their mothers. "This glow of passion and hate is kindled by ambitious and jealous women in the youthful souls. . . . Each sees in his brother a burdensome, evil-minded, and illegitimate rival. If one from their midst finally ascends the throne, all the others unite in one thought—to upset him in order themselves to rule." Pischon[85] remarks about such conditions: "Where there are several women in the house, jealousy and intrigues play their evil rôle. The Mohammedan women fear more the intellectual superiority than the corporeal charm of their comrades; for they know that every somewhat gifted man can be attached more closely by the former than by the latter. . . . Affection between brothers and sisters who are derived from one mother is seldom observed; between those who have the same father but different mothers, almost never seen. How could it, where it arises at all, maintain itself against the jealousy with which the mothers watch every expression of paternal attachment to children who are not their own! . . . From sun-set to sun-rise the man belongs in the harem. If he neglects his duties here, the women can make his life very hard (in case he is no tyrant) and can even make legal complaint against him." On the other hand, the author points out that brothels, women of the street, and complaints and trials for adultery are seldom found in the capitals of Islam, at any rate more seldom than in the main cities of Christendom. "But the satisfaction of the sex-impulse is made by the Moslem in the home so much the chief thing in the whole matrimonial association, spiritual relations between man and wife are so little attended to, the bodily strength of the male sex is so used up through association with slave-concubines, that the Mohammedan population shows a decrease of numbers that in any case merits no mean con-

80 Lane, *Arabian Nights*, I, 318 ff.
81 Barton, *Sem. Orig.*, 47.
82 *Bedouins*, I, 110, 270.
83 Conde, *Arabes en España*, 158.
84 *Kgchte. d. Orients*, II, 113, 118-119.
85 *Islam*, 12, 14, 15-16, 18.

sideration." On the woman's side, there is no means of self-expression outside of the harem.[86]

While the Koran permits four wives, most Turks have long been monogamous, partly for economic reasons and partly, it is said, on principle. According to a recent news-item from Constantinople, a law has been passed which forbids marriage to more than one wife except in "unusual cases."[87] Polygyny is said to be fast disappearing in Turkestan because of disparity in the proportion of the sexes, the men outnumbering the women three to one. "Men who once had as many as nine wives are now having a hard time getting one." Owing to the shortage of women, the Moslem natives are marrying Russian and Christian women, who, unlike their Mohammedan sisters, demand no dowry or fee for themselves. Such marriages previously were unknown. By reason of the great demand for them as wives, the women of Turkestan are said to enjoy many privileges. "Their husbands do all the housework, cooking, washing, ironing and marketing and generally show their spouses the utmost deference."[88]

§400. Monogyny.

THE major portion of this section will be devoted to a consideration of the position of the chief wife, the wife of status as contrasted with the concubine and courtesan—a contrast that has already appeared in the cases—and of other factors exhibiting a tendency toward monogamy.

In Australia, "most tribes live in monogamy and this because the scantiness of the population and the complex character of the marriage laws render it difficult enough to find even one suitable wife."[1] Although there is no limit in central Cameroon to the number of wives a man may have, "in all cases the first wife is the legal one, and her eldest child is the husband's heir."[2] Among the Kaffirs, should the great wife fail to have male offspring, a woman is appointed to bear a son for her who shall afterwards become chief.[3] In Fantiland, "every wife of a polygamist was a free woman, became a member of her husband's family, had a protector during his life, and was provided for after his death. The case is a little different now. The second wife is little better than a slave kept as a concubine, for she has to do most of the drudgery, and to cook her husband's food, or even procure it for him. This is particularly true in the case where a negro has one wife, 'married in church,' and the other 'married in native fashion.' "[4] Sir Charles Dundas[5] generalizes about the situation in East Africa as follows. "Among the wives one is the senior or superior, generally called the 'big' wife, and so far as I am aware she is always the one first married. She supervises the other wives. . . . Actually she is mistress of the home to a far greater extent than the husband is the master, and contrary to the accepted theory it is a fact that the 'big' wife, at least in her own home, is very far from being the down-trodden slave of her husband. . . . Not that the senior wife will object to other wives, for apart from considerations already mentioned she will favour it because a single wife has always more work to do than one of several, and thus it comes that notwithstanding incessant

---

86 Vambéry, *Morgenlande*, 63.
87 N. Y. *Times*, Aug. 6, 1924.
88 N. Y. *Times*, Jan. 2, 1927.
1 Semon, *Austral. Bush*, 231.

2 Malcolm, in JAI, LIII, 392.
3 Kropf, *Kaffir-Eng. Dict.*, 328.
4 Connolly, in JAI, XXVI, 145.
5 In JAI, LI, 250-251.

jealousy and resulting quarrels between the wives, a man is more often than not urged by his first wife to marry a second or more wives. . . . In Ukamba, Kikuyu, and Theraka the senior wife may not marry again on the death of her husband, and this distinction between her status and that of other wives suggests one reason why the position as a junior wife is not objected to, despite a certain inferiority attaching thereto. It also indicates very strongly that the position of the senior wife is not merely a matter of formal rank. . . . One thing I am sure of, namely, that while second and subsequent marriages are mostly matters of convenience, that with the first wife is generally one of affection, and hence in spirit and in fact the whole relationship differs in the one case from the other. It does not follow that a younger wife may not become the husband's favourite, but his right-hand and most intimate companion is in almost all cases his first and senior wife." In Abyssinia courtesans are reported to be highly honored; "queens and princesses are desirous to see their courts graced by fair adventuresses."[6]

The Belunese in the Dutch East Indies "can enter a lawful marriage with only one wife."[7] Van den Berg[8] says of the Mohammedan peoples of Java and Madura: "Islam knows only one sort of marriage and only one sort of spouse. . . . In some regions occurs the usage that the oldest of one's wives or rather the woman with whom one has been longest married has, in a sense, a higher position than the others and exercises over them a certain moral rule." In the Gilbert Islands, "strictly speaking, a man had only one true wife in a life-time, who was distinguished from the rest of his harem by the title *Rao-ni-kie*, signifying *Companion of the sleeping mat.* With her alone he underwent the marriage ceremony. . . . None of his other womenfolk were ceremonially married to him; they were of two orders—*Nikira-n-roro* or Concubines, and *Taua-ni-kai,* which may be translated Concubitants. The *Nikira-n-roro* were chosen promiscuously, for mere beauty, at the lust of the houselord. They were only to be found in the households of the high chiefs, . . . their status in the harem was regulated by favour, not right of custom. The *Taua-ni-kai* accrued by customary right; they belonged to either one of two classes of women marked out as a man's potential, though not necessarily actual, concubitants. These were: (a) The widows of his deceased brother, who passed into his care by a custom akin to, if not quite identical with, the Hebrew Levirate. They might be more precisely termed *contingent concubitants,* as they would become *Taua-ni-kai* to a brother-in-law only if their own houselord died. (b) The uterine sisters of his wife, who became his potential concubitants as soon as he married their sister."[9] What is probably an exceptional case of concubinage is reported from Samoa. "When the newly-married woman took up her abode in the family of her husband she was attended by a daughter of her brother, who was, in fact, a concubine. Her brother considered that if he did not give up his daughter for this purpose, he should fail in duty and respect towards his sister, and incur the displeasure of their household god." Each such person took with her a dowry "which, perhaps, was the most important part of the business, for, after presenting her dowry, she might live with him or not, as she pleased. Often the addition of these concubines to the family was attended with all the display and ceremonies of a regular marriage."[10] Among the Guiana Indians

6 Letourneau, *Prop.*, 154.
7 Wilken, in VG, I, 346.
8 In *Bijd.*, XLI, 466-467.

9 Grimble, in JAI, LI, 27-28.
10 Turner, *Samoa*, 96.

"there is reason to believe that the first, generally the oldest, of the wives was specially intrusted with the performance of certain duties, the exercise of certain privileges and powers. On the upper Rio Negro she is never turned away, but remains the mistress of the house." Similarly among other tribes, "though the other wives may be young enough to be her daughters, and comparably far more attractive, the old hag will retain her position as head of the household."[11]

Among more advanced peoples the custom of monogyny is more highly developed. In the case of a Russian tribe a man may have besides his lawful wife a number of others. The children of the latter constitute a special class deprived of many rights and becoming through inheritance the property of the legitimate children of the father.[12] A system of concubinage exists among the Chinese very similar to that practised among the Hebrews or that permitted under the Roman law. The concubine may be procured without the ceremonies prescribed in case of the wife, the simple exchange of a written contract and a pecuniary consideration being the only needful conditions for intercourse. "Concubines are principally obtained by persons in affluent and easy circumstances, and are generally chosen from amongst the lower classes, the confidential or favorite handmaidens of the wife, who follow her from her father's roof, being often selected for the purpose. The relative positions of the wife and concubine are distinctly laid down, and the law strictly prohibits the degradation of the wife to the position of a concubine, or the elevation of any of the latter to the rank of the former during her lifetime." By the wife the man is recognized as husband, and she is on equal terms with him; but with the concubine the case is different: she recognizes her partner, if he may be so called, as "head of the family," "master," one who has power over her person to do whatever he will.[13] While only one wife is permitted, there is no limit set by law to the number of concubines. The wife is considered the mother of all the children born in the family.[14] Four classes of wives are reported from Siam: "the first is the wife of royal gift; the second, the legal wife; the third, the wife of affection; the fourth, the slave wife—that is, the handmaid who has borne children to her master, and in consequence is manumitted."[15]

In ancient India polygyny was hindered by financial considerations; still more discouraging to it was the custom of "always regarding one woman only as the really legitimate spouse, and with her completing the religious ceremonial." The tendency toward monogamy was also furthered by law. "As in the law of inheritance only the claims of the one legally married widow were recognized and she was designated as the surviving half of her husband, so also in the marriage-law man and wife were in duty bound to mutual fidelity, and in the religious law, e.g., at the sacrifices, man and wife likewise appeared usually as a duality." In the fifth century ß.c. the express principle was laid down that a man might marry no other woman if he had one wife who took part in his religious operations and had borne him sons.[16] In India today many men do not scruple to keep concubines, who, however, have a separate establishment; it is not uncommon for the children of these separate homes to meet together, fully aware of their common fatherhood. Only prostitutes used to

11 Roth, in BAE, XXXVIII, 687.
12 Russ. Ethnog. (Russ.), II, 356.
13 Medhurst, in Trans. Roy. Asiatic Soc., IV, 15.
14 Von Mollendorff, Family Law of Chinese, 11, 12, 32; Williams, Middle Kingdom, I, 792.
15 Mason, Woman's Share, 225.
16 Jolly, Stellung d. Frauen, 446-447; and Recht. u. Sitte, 65.

learn to read, but now English missions teach many.[17] An honest woman would be ashamed to possess such knowledge. Courtesans alone dance and sing; an honest woman may sing at work but never in public.[18]

According to the Code of Hammurabi, "if a man takes a wife but closes no agreement with her, then is this woman not a wife;" that is, a contract is necessary. "If a man takes a wife and she gives him a maid-servant and the latter bears children, if that man purposes taking an accessory wife, it shall not be permitted and he shall take no additional wife. . . . If anyone takes a wife and she presents him with no children and he purposes to take an additional wife, then if he takes the latter and brings her into his house, this accessory wife shall not stand on an equality with the wife of marriage. . . . If the father during his lifetime have not said to the children which the maid-servant bore him: 'My children,' then, after the father dies, the children of the maid-servant shall not share in the goods of the father's house with the children of the wife. The maid-servant and her children shall be given their freedom."[19] In Egypt the chief wife of Pharaoh was, if possible, his sister, as the only one who could be his equal in blood. She lived a free and equal life by his side, while his other wives were more or less cloistered.[20] Among the ancient Babylonians the wife had the right of disposal over her property, could independently conclude private contracts, and appear in her own interests to defend them. Later Babylonian marriage developed even more toward monogamy, in that the wife, as in Egypt, had the right to leave her husband if he married another woman, and to get a sum of money.[21] There were concubines in Israel from the time of Abraham. Tradition distinguished concubinage from marriage in that there was no ceremony connected with it and no marriage-gift. The concubine became *de facto* wife and enjoyed *affectus maritalis* by the side of the wife, but the children were those of the wife.[22] "Polygyny, as with all Oriental peoples, where it is still the rule, and with most peoples of the Occident—Romans, Slavs, and Germans—existed among the ancient Jews. But earlier there was a warning given against going too far, and besides there was a head-wife, who was bound to develop, as *prima inter pares, to prima par excellence.*" This, with changes in social and economic views, gradually backed polygyny off the stage.[23] Among the ancient Iranians, in contrast to jural wives, concubines were mostly slaves whom one got as booty, bought, or even received as presents. The chief distinction was that children of concubines could not inherit.[24] In early Arabia wives sometimes bound their husbands in the marriage-contract not to take other wives or concubines.[25] Von Kremer[26] says that the most ancient polygyny may not be in any way compared with the later Oriental harem-economy. "In the house or tent of the tribal chief several wives of equal rights did not rule at the same time: one was the mistress of the household, namely the nobly-born, the full-blood spouse; the others were accessory consorts who took a place midway between that of the first and of the rest of the house-mates." In 1924 Turkey passed a law establishing monogamy, with this exception, that if the first marriage proved childless, a man, through legal procedure, might take a second wife, provided he could

17 Wilkins, *Hinduism*, 180, 374.
18 Dubois, *Mœurs*, I, 476.
19 Winckler, *Hammurabi*, 22, 24-25; Harper, *Hammurabi*, 51, 53, 61.
20 Maspero, *Hist. Anc.*, I, 270.
21 Buhl, *Verhältn.*, 34, note.

22 Freisen, *Kanon. Eherechts*, 47.
23 Klugmann, *Frau im Talmud*, 37.
24 Spiegel, *Eran. Alterth.*, III, 679.
25 Wellhausen, *Ehe bei Arabern*, 466, 468.
26 *Kgchte. Orients*, II, 113, 114.

support her. "As the average Turk was finding it impossible to keep more than one wife, the new Act is supporting merely what has become a custom. Many persons who have studied social relationships in the East credit the change in laws more to economic conditions than to a general shift to monogamic ideals."[27]

Among the Homeric Greeks a sharp distinction existed between the chief wife and the others. "The prevalence of concubinage, together with one chief wife, marks the form of Homeric marriage as 'juridic monogamy,' [monogyny] in distinction from factual monogamy, which is, on the whole, quite rare, and as opposed to polygamy [polygyny], which is demonstrable only in the case of Priam among men. Yet even Priam had a chief wife; among the gods, as usual, the looser system was more pronounced. All such distinctions must rest upon the presence or absence of public ceremonies; whether the marriage was an 'open' one or not made all the difference in the world in Homer's time. Juridic monogamy allowed freely the gratification of affection, while the solidity and firmness of the house was assured by the offspring of the chief wife; this system was tempering polygamy toward monogamy in its modern sense." The ceremonially-bought wives were "recognised and sanctioned organs for the production of a line of descent and property-inheritance;" while the position of the concubine was one of far fewer rights. She was a piece of booty, won in war, kidnapped, or bought from some one who had acquired her in one of these ways.[28] "Concubinage had for the Greeks only this that was repellent, that its fruits lacked the civil or at least family-right advantages of legal offspring. . . . In the Homeric period it was not at all uncommon even for wives to raise the children of their rivals [concubines] along with their own." The author mentions betrothal as the essential precondition of a jural marriage; the offspring of a union without this essential were regarded as illegitimate.[29]

Sentiment favorable toward monogamy is exhibited in the plays of Euripides.[30] Admetus says, "Since I had thee in life, in death too shalt thou be called my only wife." Hermione asserts that it is a shame for a man to have two wives; "all men who care to live honorable lives are content to devote themselves to one lawful love." Says the Chorus: "Never shall I commend a double marriage. . . . Let a husband love one wife." Orestes affirms that it is "an evil state of things for a man to have two wives." Courtesans, however, were common and had a rather high position. Athenæus[31] quotes Demosthenes as saying: "We have courtesans for pleasure, concubines for daily companions, wives for mothers of legitimate children and for our housekeepers." He mentions a great number of courtesans and gives anecdotes about them and their relations with all the distinguished men of Athens. They were the emancipated women, the only ones who had education. Aspasia even instructed Pericles and Socrates; she tried to raise woman's position through education.[32] "It was due to the hetairæ above all that the Greek wife in the Hellenistic period again became the companion of equal birth with the husband. When that was attained, the dominant rôle of the hetairæ in society was played out."[33] In Rome even more than in Greece, the marriage portion became a mark of distinction for a legitimate wife. She had her father as her protector, while the concubine was defense-

27 Anon., in *Jour. Soc. Hygiene*, X, 564.
28 Keller, *Hom. Soc.*, 218, 219, 220.
29 Blümner, *Griech. Privatalterth.*, 253 ff., 261-262; Müller, *Attisch. Eherecht*, 857 ff.
30 *Alcestis*, 328-330; *Andromache*, 179-180, 465 ff., 911.
31 *Deipnosophists*, XIII, 31.
32 Bruns, *Frauenemancipation*, 19, 20.
33 Beloch, *Griech. Gchte.*, I, 473-474.

less against the husband.[34] Among the Icelanders only the children of the chief or legal wife inherited. "That man is not heritable whose mother was not bought with a *mund* of a mark or more money, or that had no bridal made for her, or that was not handfasted. . . . A bridal is lawful made if the lawful guardian handfast the woman and there be six men at the bridal at the least, and the bridegroom goeth with light in the same bed with the woman."[35]

§403. Restriction of Numbers.

A FEW scattered cases of what may be termed a "population-policy," especially as it relates to restriction of numbers, are here cited. At the Australian puberty-ceremonies, "the elder men have a right to their young women."[1] A similar practice is reported of the African Bushmen.[2] Sodomy is said to have been practised in New Guinea for the purpose of restraining population.[3] Papuan women will not have over two children, nor a second child till the first is three or four years old. If they conceive, they use abortion, so there are few mothers of three. The ways of inducing abortion are rude, cases being cited of lying a cord about the body and then treading on it with the feet.[4] On Lifu, Loyalty Islands, "children were often suckled for a period of two years or longer, chiefly in the hope of delaying pregnancy."[5] Among the tribes of British Central Africa the child is suckled for two or three years, "by mother, or grandmother if the former die," or by a maternal aunt. Suckling may be prolonged for four years in the belief that pregnancy is thus avoided.[6] Dundas[7] writes of the Bantu tribes of East Africa: "Intentional procuring of abortion cannot be common among people with whom offspring is so highly valued, but occurs with some tribes." Belgian oppression in the Congo Free State is reported to have caused a great fall in the native birthrate. Women refused to bear, saying, "It is difficult enough to save ourselves when the State soldiers arrive, and how could we save our children?"[8]

In many instances the harshness of primitive life tends automatically to restrict numbers, the deathrate of children being particularly high.[9] With reference to conditions among the Congo tribes it is said: "It is truly a survival of the strongest; and this undoubtedly accounts for the absence of cripples, delicate persons, and feeble-minded folk. It is a struggle for life from birth upwards, and only the fittest survive in the fight."[10] In Kenya Colony "infant mortality ranges as high as 45 per cent throughout the tribe, and is chiefly due to exposure to cold, and colic due to early part-feeding on half cooked meal."[11] "Before the introduction of Christianity probably not less than two-thirds of the Samoan race died in infancy and childhood. This mortality arose principally from carelessness and mismanagement in nursing; evils which still prevail to a great extent. Even now, perhaps, one-half of them die before they reach their second year. The poor little things are often carried about with their bare heads exposed to the scorching rays of a vertical sun. Exposure to

34 Westermarck, *Marriage*, III, 49.
35 Vigfusson and Powell, *Orig. Isl.*, I, 332; handfasting is a form of trial-marriage; §365, of the text.
1 Howitt, in JAI, XX, 87.
2 Hahn, in *Globus*, XVIII, 122.
3 Beardmore, in JAI, XIX, 464.
4 Wilken, in VG, III, 217, note.

5 Ray, in JAI, XLVII, 286.
6 Stannus, in JAI, XL, 311.
7 In JAI, LI, 247.
8 Weeks, in JAI, XL, 418.
9 Carr-Saunders, *Population Problem*, 159, 172, 183, 196.
10 Weeks, in JAI, XL, 418.
11 Barton, in JAI, LIII, 50.

the night-damps also, and above all stuffing them with improper food, are evils which often make us wonder that the mortality among them is not greater than it is."[12]

Among the Cheyenne Indians "it was long the custom that a woman should not have a second child until her first was about ten years of age." Then they publicly announced their intention and were commended for self-control.[13] "The red, barren clay from beneath a campfire is used by White Mountain Apache women to induce sterility."[14] Analogous to the Australian and South African cases mentioned above is that of the Shingu Indians, where the doctrine prevailed that the old men should have the young wives and the young men the old ones.[15] Among the Araucanians families are not large, even where there are several wives. One enumeration of 245 families showed an average of 2.77 children per family.[16]

War and other conditions may lead to a policy of increase of numbers. One-niote, a former Cayuga village, "became greatly reduced in the war with the Hurons in the middle of the 17th century, and resorted to a common Iroquois expedient in perpetuating its people by sending to the Mohawk, their neighbors, 'for some men to be married to the girls and women who had remained without husbands, in order that the nation should not perish. This is why the Iroquois (Mohawk) name this village their child.' "[17] It is written of the Egyptians of the century before Christ that every child which was born had to be brought up, because they were needed for the prosperity of the country. Strabo[18] thought it a peculiarity of the Egyptians that every child must be reared.

§404. Infanticide.

A MOTIVE ascribed to the practice of infanticide among the Australians is the belief that the second son is superior to the first.[1] Among the natives of British New Guinea abortion is induced by violent exercise, especially jumping, by having a woman stand on the patient's back while the latter lies on her stomach, and by applying hot stones to the abdomen.[2] The modes of infanticide among the Dobuans are: "1. Putting foot on the throat. 2. Choking with hands. 3. Burying alive with deceased mother. . . . 4. Leaving child on beach in the sun. 5. Refusing to suckle the child." Illegitimate children are sometimes killed by these people, and a case is cited where a woman was taunted about such a child, "whereupon she put him in the sun to die, and finally poured salt water into his mouth." When the author[3] asked her why she did this, she replied that she could not bear the taunting. Other occasions of infanticide are the death of the mother when the child is too young to run about; the birth of a child following a compulsory marriage, in which case the girl who has been forced to marry against her will kills her offspring in secret; when the mother's milk dries up and a wetnurse is not available; "when the husband turns out to be a rake"; and when the husband upon pregnancy deserts his wife for the time and marries a second wife. "A Tikopian family is usually limited to four children, any in excess of this number being killed by burying them alive in the

12 Turner, Samoa, 135.
13 Grinnell, Cheyenne, I, 149.
14 Hrdlička, in HAI, I, 837.
15 Von den Steinen, Zent. Bras., 331.
16 Latcham, in JAI, XXXIX, 171.

17 Beauchamp, in HAI, II, 128.
18 Geog., VIII, 24; Lippert, Kgchte., I, 215.
1 Cunow, Australneger, 98.
2 Seligmann, in JAI, XXXII, 302.
3 Bromilow, in AAAS, 1909, 482-483.

house or just outside it; occasionally five or six may be kept alive but never more. If the first four children are all girls, one or more of these may be killed in the hope that succeeding children may be boys, in which case the lives of the boys would be spared."[4] In the New Hebrides "infanticide was sadly prevalent. As the burden of plantation and other work devolved on the woman, she thought she could not attend to more than two or three children, and that the rest must be buried as soon as born. There were exceptions to this want of maternal affection. At times the husband urged the thing, contrary to the wishes of his wife. If he thought the infant would interfere with her work, he forcibly took the child and buried it, and she, poor woman, cried for months after."[5] In the D'Entrecasteaux Islands, if the mother dies in childbirth, the baby, whether alive or dead, is generally buried with her. "Everywhere there is a desire for male offspring in preference to female, and when food is scarce it is the girl child who suffers most. This is significant when we remember that in the census the males numbered 55 per cent of the total population, and that the proportion of the unmarried males to the unmarried females was as 100 to 82."[6] To the Andaman Islanders infanticide is unknown, but the children are killed with kindness.[7]

Abortion is looked upon by the Kaffirs of South Africa as a crime, for which payment must be made to the chief who has lost by this practice one of his subjects.[8] The Hottentots expose sickly infants and female twins.[9] In one part of West Africa it was customary until recently to bury alive the tenth child of the same mother.[10] Again, illegitimate children are killed and also those whose upper incisors appear first—for the latter will later kill their fathers. Other omens and portents have their victims.[11] In British Central Africa deformed infants are strangled by the women in attendance at childbirth.[12] Among the Ba-Mbala, monsters and cripples are buried alive.[13] The natives of the Congo Free State are said to have practised abortion and infanticide during the period of Belgian oppression. Other reasons for abortion are the desire to avoid trouble incurred by children and from hatred of the husband.[14] On the Zanzibar Coast weakly and deformed children were exposed to die; the Catholic missions having saved many of these, the people exposed more children, to get rid of them.[15] The Malagasy kill all children born on unlucky days. One method formerly in use was to place the child at the entrance of the cattle-fold of the village, to be trampled to death by oxen. Should the child escape death from their hoofs, its life was spared; it was believed that such children would become extremely rich.[16] Infanticide is common in Kenya Colony. "Invariably the child of an unmarried, that is uncircumcised, girl is smothered by placing a cow-dung pad over the mouth of the child; this is done by the girl's mother, the reason given is that the child could not live because the clitoris has not been excised from the mother, and no argument will convince the people otherwise." Infanticide also occurs when the child is delivered legs first and again when the child is born with teeth. Deformed children are

4 Rivers, *Melan. Soc.*, I, 313.
5 Turner, *Samoa*, 333.
6 Jenness and Ballentyne, *D'Entrecasteaux*, 51, 106.
7 Man, in JAI, XII, 329.
8 Kropf, *Kaffir-English Dict.*, 339.
9 Ratzel, *Vkde.*, I, 104.
10 Ellis, *Tshi*, 234.

11 Volkens, *Kilimandscharo*, 252.
12 Stannus, in JAI, XL, 311.
13 Torday and Joyce, in JAI, XXXV, 411.
14 Weeks, in JAI, XL, 418.
15 Stuhlmann, *Mit Emin*, 38.
16 Waitz, *Anth.*, II, 441; Sibree, *Great Afr. Isl.*, 284-285.

not made away with, nor is abortion practised.[17] Among a number of other East African tribes the child born feet foremost is killed, for it is believed that if it should be permitted to live the crops would wither, the cattle die, and other ills afflict the tribe.[18] In one case, if an infant cuts its lower before its upper teeth, it "dies," that is, they let it die, "since the suckling was painful to the mother"[19]—probably a rationalization. In Kabylie, children of incestuous or adulterous alliances are killed and have no right to a tomb; their mothers get rid of them to avoid punishment.[20]

The Asiatic Hyperboreans practise infanticide because of food-difficulties.[21] In India, female infanticide is ascribed to various beliefs rather than to tangible conditions: that it was divinely enjoined because one woman made the whole world suffer; that woman, as a mischief-maker, is better out of the world than in it; that it conduces to male issue. In addition there is the difficulty of providing marriage portions. It was a former Toda custom to kill children; the tribe was then very poor and could not support them. Only girls were killed and not the sickly or deformed, for that was regarded as a sin.[22] The Khonds killed girls "from a feeling that intermarriage in the same tribe is incest."[23] It is reported of one tribe that, since widows are allowed to re-marry, "the murder of female infants has, therefore, never prevailed."[24] Wilkins[25] says that six-sevenths of the population of India have for ages practised female infanticide. Legends contain the story of the exposure of the Sun-god's son in a basket of rushes set afloat on a river.[26] According to a newspaper account a few years ago, an infant was burned alive by some villagers who believed that it was a demon because it began to acquire teeth so early.[27]

The cases from India are mainly those of female infanticide, which, since they involve special motives based upon convictions as to woman's special qualities, are but slightly indicative of any population-policy. Female infanticide, by exposure and otherwise, was common in China and has been referred purely to need under conditions of overpopulation; but the Chinese took it over to Formosa with them and all classes practised it, to the horror of the aborigines, both civilized and savage.[28] There is no infanticide in Cambodia.[29] Female children, especially if illegitimate, were destroyed by native tribes of the Philippines. Among the poor the act of infanticide—casting into a river— was celebrated by a feast of all the relatives.[30]

Infanticide was, in ante-Christian Polynesia, one of the most firmly established institutions. In Tahiti two-thirds of the children were killed; three or four were considered a heavy burden. The girls suffered most, as being of no use in war, service of the god, fishing, and navigation. Thus there were often four or five men to one woman. The cause was not necessity but laziness.[31] There was no infanticide in Samoa and but little in New Zealand, where boys were wanted for war and girls for breeding and all children were idolized and

17 Barton, in JAI, LIII, 50.
18 Barrett, in JAI, XLI, 22, 32; Cole, in JAI, XXXII, 308.
19 Johnstone, in JAI, XXXII, 270.
20 Hanoteau et Letourneux, Kabylie, III, 220-221.
21 Ratzel, Vkde., II, 769.
22 Thurston, S. India, 505, 506, 507, 508.
23 Hopkins, Relig. Ind., 531.
24 Meade, in JASB, I, 283.

25 Mod. Hinduism, 431.
26 Holtzmann, Ind. Sagen, I, 110.
27 N. Y. Times, Dec. 27, 1914.
28 Pickering, Formosa, 61; Meinecke, Deut. Kol., 101.
29 Leclère, in PSM, XLIV, 779.
30 Montero y Vidal, Filipinas, I, 16.
31 Ratzel, Vkde., II, 126; Waitz, Anth., V, 139; Lippert, Kgchte., I, 209.

spoiled.[32] In Central Polynesia, "in cases of unequal marriages there was a custom to kill the children of the marriage one after another, by which the parent of inferior birth was progressively raised in rank, and so reached a point of equality with the other parent, after which their offspring were allowed to live. . . . Williams says that if a woman of rank was united to a man of inferior grade the destruction of two, four or six infants was required to raise him to an equality with her; and that when this had been effected, the succeeding children were spared; and he refers to a case of a chief woman married to a man of inferior rank, and in which, after one child had been killed, a second and third were put to death on the insistence of the mother and her relatives, in spite of the opposition of the father."[33] In Núkuóro the population has dwindled through the destruction of children before and after birth, a practice not due to misery, although the formal excuse is the inability of the mother to provide for them. "The children of young women, who are not yet tattooed, all fall under the same fate."[34] On Nukufetau, as elsewhere in the Gilbert Islands, "infanticide or foeticide was the law of the land. Only one—some say two—were allowed to live in each family; the rest were strangled. But it was possible for the parents to ransom their offspring by giving presents to the chiefs, of whom at one time there were said to be forty." This ransom consisted of seven large bowls of taro prepared with the juice of the coconut.[35] Of special note is the Arreoi society of the Society Islands and other groups, a religious association whose members swear the grand oath that they will kill all children born to them. Thus they attain special divine protection and paradise after death.[36] Rivers[37] comments in general: "The practice of infanticide was confined to the Areois of the Society Islands and seems to have been wholly absent in other groups such as the Marquesas. Even in Tahiti it was probably a late growth, a special development of the practice of infanticide as it existed widely throughout Polynesia. Similarly, the licentious dances and representations of the Areois were limited to the lowest rank of the societies and seem even among them to have been only a fair sample of the morals of the people as a whole."

The heathen Greenlanders killed deformed and sickly children and those whose mothers died in childbirth. The conditions of life were such that they could not care for them.[00] The Bering Strait Eskimo used to kill, at birth or later, the female children who could not help with the food-supply and depleted it.[39] Infanticide is said still to exist among the Hudson Bay Eskimo, being reported by Rasmussen,[40] to be due to the rigors of existence. "If the girl baby prior to birth is pledged in marriage, the mother preserves it. If not, the infant is smothered. Boy babies are more valuable and are rarely killed." "A male child has always been a welcome addition to the Thlinget household. But not so a female. In earlier times, when they came too fast, their little lives were strangled."[41] Among the Apache, Pima, Mohave, Navaho, Zuñi, and other western Indians deformed and monstrous children were killed, and some normal ones; but the latter were generally half-breeds or children of an unmar-

32 Ella, in AAAS, 1892, 621; Tregear, in JAI, XIX, 99.
33 Williamson, *Cent. Polyn.*, II, 115-116.
34 Kubary, *Núkuóro*, 9, 35-36.
35 Newell, in AAAS, 1895, 609.
36 Cook, *First Voy.*, abstract in Pinkerton's *Collections*, 520; §161 above.

37 In AA, XVII, 432.
38 Nansen, *Esk. Life*, 151; Reclus, *Prim. Folk*, 34.
39 Nelson, in BAE, XVIII, 289.
40 In N. Y. *Times*, April 1, 1925; N. Y. *Tribune*, Apr. 1, 1925.
41 Jones, *Thlingets*, 121.

ried girl ashamed of her condition.[42] The Pimas have a horror of abnormality; inquiries concerning albinos met with the reply that "there never were any"; and they even tried to kill a grown man who had six toes. A woman does not care to have many children lest she be saddled with their support in event of the death of her husband.[43] Some tribes are said to have destroyed their female infants to prevent them being taken by their enemies and thus becoming the means of increasing the latter's numbers.[44]

Among the Guiana Indians "infanticide would appear to have been more or less permissible under one or other of at least three circumstances, whether the child were one of twins, a cripple, etc., or a female. . . . Barrère, in writing on the Cayenne Indians, says that as soon as a child is born its fate is decided; if anything is wrong with it it is killed and buried without pity; hence, no dwarfs, hunchbacks, lame, and crippled are to be seen. . . . On the other hand, there is no less an authority than Schomburgk for the statement that the practice was not so general among the savages of Guiana as had been supposed. All the same it is very uncommon to see an Indian either lame or deformed."[45] On the upper Amazon, "when a mother dies, her young infant may be buried alive with her"; while not seldom sick children are killed.[46] Among the Araucanians, "owing to the continual warfare and the desire to bring up robust and warlike descendants, all misformed or delicate children were slain at birth." Twin children and children born feet foremost were considered unlucky and killed.[47]

Readers of history and literature are familiar with the classic cases of exposure of infants in antiquity. The rescued infant who came to a high position, as for instance Œdipus, was a sort of stock figure in tradition. Infanticide was almost universally admitted among the Greeks, and supported by the authority of law-givers and philosophers; yet Aristotle[48] bears witness to the fact that such mores can lead to race-suicide, and Polybius[49] attributes to its prevalence the depopulation of cities and districts. "The Roman policy was always to encourage, while the Greek policy was rather to restrain, population, and infanticide never appears to have been common in Rome till the corrupt and sensual days of the Empire." Children of the poor and of slaves were long exposed, however; exposure, in fact, was a sort of evasion of infanticide; "it was practised on a gigantic scale and with absolute impunity, noticed by writers with the most frigid indifference, and, at least in the case of destitute parents, considered a very venial offence."[50]

The early Arabs practised infanticide in the face of need, but one of Mohammed's commandments forbade killing children for fear of starvation.[51] The early practice applied mainly to girls, who were buried alive. "Men killed girls in part to avoid care of raising them, also, in the frequent wars between tribes, to save them from a later imprisonment and dishonor and thereby save them-

42 Hrdlička, in BAE, Bull. XXXIV, 165-166.
43 Russell, in BAE, XXVI, 185; Yarrow, in BAE, I, 99.
44 Fletcher, in HAI, I, 805; II, 997.
45 Roth, in BAE, XXXVIII, 558, 559.
46 Von Martius, Beiträge, I, 409; Roth, in BAE, XXX, 157 (quoted).
47 Latcham, in JAI, XXXIX, 354, 358.
48 Polit., VII, 14; II, 9; Lecky, Europ.

Morals, II, 25-26; Sutherland, Moral Instinct, I, 133-134.
49 Hist., XXXVII, ch. IV.
50 Lecky, Europ. Morals, II, 27, 28; Lippert, Kgchte., I, 221; Blair, Slavery amongst the Romans, 44 (full references); Sutherland, Moral Instinct, I, 136-137.
51 Smith, Kinship, 282; Wellhausen, in Gött. Gesell. d. Wiss., 1893, 458; Peschel, Races, 303.

selves from shame."[52] The Hebrews showed no tendency toward infanticide but were eager for posterity. "That which appealed so powerfully to the compassion of the early and mediæval Christians, in the fate of the murdered infants, was not that they died, but that they commonly died unbaptised; and the criminality of abortion was immeasurably aggravated when it was believed to involve, not only the extinction of a transient life, but also the damnation of an immortal soul." Despite strong denunciation, however, the destruction continued.[53]

The custom of allowing the father to lift up the child or not, thus conferring the right to life or refusing it, is familiar; if not taken up it was exposed.[54] In Iceland exposure might be ordered if dependency was likely to result or on account of an evil dream or of shame. Further, the ancient Germans, despite the assertion of Tacitus,[55] were accustomed to practise exposure; "all the Teutonic sagas are full of the exposure of children and there can be no doubt that in the early days of heathenism it was lawful."[56] A writer on Spain "has noticed the almost complete absence of infanticide in that country, and has ascribed it to the great leniency of public opinion toward female frailty." Abandonment took the place of the ruder custom, with the result of promoting vagabondage.[57]

Twins. In East Central Australia, "when twins are born, and one should happen to be a male child, he is killed. Half-caste children of either sex, when born, are always killed and occasionally eaten by the tribe."[58] Among some Melanesians it is regarded as a good thing to have twins if these are both of the same sex. "If they are boy and girl they are regarded as man and wife, but my informant could not tell me what was done on such an occasion. It is probable that in old days they were killed." Among the Tikopians, "in the case of twins, called *masanga,* one or both are usually killed, the decision as to what shall be done resting with the mother."[59] The birth of twins is an occasion of infanticide with the Dobuans of Papua. "One twin is killed because of the great trouble in nursing. Generally the female child is preserved because of descent, but if the mother has no male child to climb cocoanut trees for her she may ask for the female to be killed. A case was mentioned in which both female children were kept alive. Triplets are apparently not known. When we asked some old men if they knew of triplets they laughed boisterously over the very idea of such a thing happening."[60] In another part of Papua, twins are accounted for as follows: "If a woman has given the cold shoulder to a man who wants her, either before or after marriage, he wants revenge; he takes a snip from the string of her *rami,* makes it in a parcel, folding it V-shape; taking a small stick, he buries the two objects deep in the ground. This will have the effect of causing her to suffer heavy labour, and she cannot be delivered till the stick is unburied; she will also probably have twins. The father of twins always wants to find the man who did this, as they believe it the only way twins are caused; they are not thought abnormal in any way, only some one's revenge."[61] In the D'Entrecasteaux Islands twins are held to

---

52 Wilken, in VG, II, 41-42.
53 Lecky, *Europ. Morals,* II, 23 (quoted), 29; Sutherland, *Moral Instinct,* I, 138.
54 Wisen, *Quinnan,* 9; Leo, *Island,* 467.
55 *Germania,* XIX.
56 Weinhold, *Deut. Frauen,* I, 91, 93; Grimm, *Rechtsalt.,* 455 (quoted).

57 Lecky, *Europ. Morals,* II, 25, note; Chandler, *Romances of Roguery,* 30.
58 Wells, in AAAS, 1893, 515.
59 Rivers, *Melan. Soc.,* I, 145, 313.
60 Bromilow, in AAAS, 1909, 482.
61 Liston-Blyth, in JAI, LIII, 471.

be due to several causes; for instance, "if the mother had eaten two bananas which were joined along one side, or a man had tied together along some track two wisps of grass that grew on opposite sides, and the woman, not noticing perhaps, had caught her foot in it. A commoner method of causing twins is to lay side by side upon some track the two halves of a small green fruit called *bwaibu,* which the boys often use as sling-stones in their quarrels. Twins will result if the woman merely steps over them."[62] There is probably a suggestion of imitative magic here.[63] In the Solomon Islands one of the twins is killed, preferably the girl if there is one;[64] again, the first child born is preserved and the second destroyed.[65]

In Africa, there are a number of cases where twins are welcome, but in Mashonaland they are destroyed at birth, being considered "an unnatural freak on the part of a woman" and the phenomenon is supposed to indicate famine or some other calamity.[66] The Kaffirs put to death one of twins "through fear that if both are allowed to live, some calamity will overtake the father." But if twins are born to the Bunyoro king, the attendant celebration may last for months.[67] In Togo the belief is that an evil spirit has had a hand in a twin-birth and the children are killed. If a woman bears twins a second time, the infants are put in an ant-hill to prevent future recurrences. A woman who has borne twins is tabooed from field-work as dangerous to the crops; only after subsequently bearing a single child is she restored.[68] Where a twin-birth was once a scandal, the people believing that no woman could have two children by one man, it is now a cause for honor.[69] "Twins are killed among all the Niger Delta tribes, and in districts of English control the mother is killed too, except in Omon, where the sanctuary is. There twin mothers and their children are exiled to an island. . . . They have to remain on the island and if any man goes across and marries one of them he has to remain on the island too." Elsewhere the mother is secluded for a year and elaborate ceremonial precedes her return to ordinary life.[70] "All over Africa the birth of twins is a notable event, but noted for very different reasons in different parts of the country. In Calabar they are dreaded as an evil omen, and until recently were immediately put to death, and the mother driven from the village to live alone in the forest as a punishment for having brought this evil on her people."[71] The women who bear twins are as horrified as the rest and even Christianized natives cannot shake off the old belief. Interference in one case led to the chief's order to kill the twins and also two other persons as atonement.[72] Twins who are raised must have everything at the same time from their parents or both will die.[73] In Central Cameroons twin-birth is not usual, and is greatly desired. Very rarely triplets are born, and "on such occasions there are great rejoicings in the tribe. Twins and triplets are considered to be under the special protection of the head-chief."[74] Among the tribes of the Upper Congo, "twins were not frequent, but when they did come they had to be treated properly. . . . At this ceremony

62 Jenness and Ballentyne, *D'Entrecas-teaux,* 106-107.
63 §302, of the text and *Case-Book.*
64 Somerville, in JAI, XXVI, 393.
65 Hunt, in JAI, XXVIII, 11.
66 Bent, *Mashonaland,* 316.
67 Tyler, "Kaffirs," in *Illust. Afr.,* Dec., 1895.
68 Klose, *Togo,* 350, 510.

69 Ellis, *Ewe,* 52.
70 Kingsley, *Travels W. Afr.,* 472.
71 Nassau, *Fetichism,* 206; Kingsley, *W. Afr. Studies,* 460; Granville, in JAI, XXVIII, 107.
72 Seidel, in *Globus,* LXXIV, 6.
73 Bastian, *Deut. Exped.,* I, 174.
74 Malcolm, in JAI, LIII, 389.

the names are given which are the same for all twins, and these names are retained through life. Other folk can change their names according to fancy, but twins never."[75] The Congo mother is sometimes proud of twins, who are a good omen.[76]

Twin-births are said to be common in British Central Africa and to be liked, but the mortality of twins is high.[77] When twins are born the Bageshu beat drums with a special rhythm which conveys the information to the relatives. "The relations hurry together to the place and hastily collect building materials and build a hut into which both the parents and the children are put for three days. They leave a small aperture through which the food is handed to the parents inside. On the third day one of the relations comes and cuts a doorway into the hut." Then follow the usual bathing and purificatory ceremonies. Among the Bahima, when twins are born the father makes the fact known by mounting the house or by standing in the doorway of the kraal and shouting, "My wife has twins." They prefer twins to be of one sex; "it is unlucky to have them of opposite sexes. They are afraid to speak about them in a disparaging way lest a ghost should overhear them and be angry and cause illness in the clan." The Baganda make no announcement of the birth of twins, nor do they mention the word twins until the rejoicings are over, else the children will die. The father of twins is called by a special name and must go through certain elaborate ceremonies.[78]

In the Baringo District of East Africa it is not regarded as lucky to have twins. Certain propitiatory ceremonies must be performed, else the twins will die and the mother go into decline. "A cow giving birth to twins is immediately slaughtered together with its offending progeny." Among the Wawanga, who do not generally bury the dead, the father of twins is buried and then the village is abandoned. A woman giving birth to twins must undergo purification-ceremonies before leaving the hut; otherwise ill luck will follow her through life. Many taboos surround her: "A woman who has borne twins may not look at a cow in calf for fear the milk will dry up. . . . In a village, where a woman has borne twins, a warthog's tusk, a hartebeeste's hoof or a piece of buffalo horn is hung round the neck of a cow to avert any evil effects; this charm is removed once the calf is weaned. Similarly a mother of twins may not cut grain at harvest time or sow seed in the plantations without first taking special precautions to counteract evil effects. Again, if she pass by fermented grain, for making beer, spread out to dry, she must spit upon it and take some in her mouth and put it back; otherwise the beer will be spoilt. Such a woman, therefore, smears white clay on her temples and forehead whenever she goes on a visit to another village, and this is supposed to counteract the evil effects of her presence. She does the same when she goes to reap or sow the crops."[79] Although neighboring tribes kill twins, the Wagogo do not, but they kill children born feet foremost.[80] The Akamba consider such a manner of birth to be most unlucky, and "a boy so born cannot get a wife or a girl so born a husband." If twins are born two goats are killed. "The birth of twins is not now-a-days considered as being of either good or bad omen, but it is said that a long time ago, if a woman bore twins of opposite sexes the female

75 Weeks, in JAI, XL, 420.
76 Ward, in JAI, XXIV, 289.
77 Stannus, in JAI, XL, 311.
78 Roscoe, in JAI, XXXIX, 184-185; XXXVII, 107; and XXXII, 33.

79 Dundas, K. R., in JAI, XL, 60; and XLIII, 33, 37-38.
80 Cole, in JAI, XXXII, 308.

child was always buried."[81] Among the Suk the birth of twins is a serious matter. "The mother and father may not leave their huts for three or four days, when people who have begotten twins collect and dance a secret dance; a he-goat is eaten, and the tail of a sheep is bitten off and eaten by twins. The parents may not wear sandals for three or four days. . . . The birth of twins is disliked and possibly this is due to an idea that more than one child at a birth is an animal trait pronounced in sheep and goats."[82] Sir Charles Dundas[83] comments concerning the Bantu tribes of East Africa: "Excepting a few isolated examples of tribes with whom it is customary to kill human beings at the burial of a chief, the only other permissible taking of life is in the form of infanticide, and this is very common, particularly in respect to twins." Again, "twins are either not permitted to survive, or one is given to a family of another clan, and becomes the child of that family. . . . I recollect two Wapare who gave twin children to a Christian native because for one cause or another they were unlucky. To my arguments they had only to say that they themselves wanted to keep the children, but they knew well that so soon as any ill-fortune befell their neighbours they would at once be accused of having brought it, through these children. And if such a child years later is liable to be put to death as the bringer of disaster it must be admitted that the parents do it a doubtful kindness to allow it to survive. The originators and promoters of this evil belief are of course the medicine men."

The Asabs of the Niger look upon twins with disfavor and "formerly both were thrown away, a proceeding justified by saying that the birth of twins is purely animal in its nature."[84] This explanation recalls the one given in the case of the Suk mentioned above. Among the Nile tribes twins are considered to be lucky; but their birth is also "rather a tempting of Providence; and a woman who bears twins must live away from her husband's village for some months, and on no account go near the kraal where the cattle are kept."[85] On the Zanzibar Coast twins bring bad luck and are killed; in the Lake region they are a cause of rejoicing; again, they are unlucky, and the second born is killed or exposed, the father having to live retired for some months and to refrain from joining the hunt until another child is born to him.[86] Von Götzen[87] notes a peculiar case where, when one of a pair of twins dies, a puppet is made which is lengthened to conform to the size of the other, as it grows up. Twins are very seldom born in northwest Africa and are regarded as a remarkable freak of nature.[88]

Twins among the Semas are more frequent than among neighboring tribes. "They are on the whole held unfortunate, partly owing to the added trouble to the mother, partly owing to a belief that they are less strong than single children, and that if one die the other will not long survive. . . . Some appear to think that the birth of twins is followed by the early death of both parents. More than two children at a birth seems to be unheard of."[89] "Double bananas are not eaten by the women in the Ulu Kinta, as it is thought that a woman who eats one will give birth to twins, which are apparently not welcome, because, the Sakai said, one of them always dies."[90]

Among the things regarded by the Tlinkit as of evil omen is the birth of

81 Hobley, *A-Kamba*, 61.
82 Barton, in JAI, LI, 97.
83 In JAI, LI, 234, 235; and XLV, 301.
84 Parkinson, in JAI, XXXVI, 317.
85 Johnston, *Uganda*, II, 778, 878-879.
86 Stuhlmann, *Mit Emin*, 38, 83, 392, 796.
87 *Durch Afr.*, 83.
88 Paulitschke, *Nordost-Afr.*, I, 192.
89 Hutton, *Sema Nagas*, 262.
90 Evans, in JAI, XLVIII, 194.

twins. "In former years a man felt justified in leaving his wife if she presented him with twins, and she was looked upon by all as something uncanny. Twins were also put to death. In this age they are accepted as a matter of course."[91] Boas[92] gives attention to the peculiar place of twins among the Kwakiutl. Among them and the Tsimshian as well, twins are believed to control the weather. The parents of twins are fetish-persons;[93] "nobody ever succeeds in anything if the parents of twins wish ill to him." The father in such a case is not allowed by his tribe to do anything; "he is not even allowed to get fire-wood and water. His relatives always sit by his side in the house in order to get the fire-wood and the water and food for the couple. . . . As soon as the twins are four days old, when the navel-string comes off, the two cradles are put on the floor—one on each side of some woman who has already been the mother of twins. She cares for the twins, going through at the same time the most elaborate ceremonial practices." The parents "purify themselves every fourth day in water after the twins are four days old, and they do not forget to paint themselves with ochre after purifying themselves in water, the twins as well as the married couple. They continue to do this until the twins are ten months old." The requirement that the parents of twins do no work for four years after the birth may lead to infanticide if they have no relatives to do the work for them, for under such circumstances the mother asks the midwife to choke the twins "that they may go back home to where they came from; and the midwife is not allowed to disobey the wishes of the one of whom she is taking care. Then she at once strangles the twins. . . . She tries to do this before any-one else sees the woman who has given birth; and when the twins are dead, they ask the father of the twins to go and tell his relatives that his wife has given birth to two dead twins." Among some of the American Indians, "twins are usually regarded as uncanny, and are rather feared, as possessing occult power. With some Oregon and other coast tribes they were formerly regarded as abnormal and one or both were killed."[94] Among the Omaha, on the other hand, "the birth of twins was considered a sign that the mother was a kind woman."[95]

The birth of twins was one of the several occasions among the Guiana Indians when infanticide was permissible. "On the Orinoco twins were regarded as dishonorable. Indeed, as soon as word went round that so-and-so had been delivered of a double birth, the other women, without considering that they might fall into a similar predicament, as was occasionally the case, would rush up to the patient's quarters and crack their jokes, that she must be like a rat which gives birth to four at a time, etc. But the mischief did not end here, for the Saliva Indian, as soon as one child was born, and she felt another remaining, would immediately bury it so as to avoid the chaffing and the joking of her neighbors as well as the displeasure of her husband. For he, on his part, deeming that only one of these twins could possibly be his own, was fully convinced that the other must be proof of his wife's disloyalty."[96] By the Araucanians "twin children were considered unlucky, and either one was brought up in the family of some near relative as their child, or it was killed at once."[97]

91 Jones, *Thlingets*, 162-163.
92 In BAE, XXXI, 545; and BAE, XXXV, pt. I, 633-634, 635, 667, 673 ff., 685-687, 689.
93 §257, above.
94 Mooney, in HAI, I, 266; Dixon and Hodge, in HAI, II, 192.
95 Roth, in BAE, XXXVIII, 558.
96 Latcham, in JAI, XXXIX, 358.
97 Fletcher and LaFlesche, in BAE, XXVII, 327.

§406. Sterility and Fecundity.

It is said of certain Papuans: "On the whole, they are not desirous to have children, though this is due mainly to the women, who dislike the pains of childbirth and the attendant troubles of nursing. Boys are much preferred, and girls are looked on only as a necessary evil."[1] A more nearly typical situation is that depicted among the Bageshu, where "It is essential that every woman should have children; if she fails to do so, her chief value in the eyes of her husband has gone. She is given a reasonable time to test her, and her husband will do all he can to assist her; he will pay the medicine men their fees to make drugs and thus give her every chance to become a mother. Should his efforts fail, he returns her to her parents, and demands the dowry [bride-price] he paid for her." So far is the desire for fecundity carried that "a woman who has a child prior to marriage is not despised, nor does this in any wise detract from her chances of marriage; on the contrary it is a proof to the man who wishes to marry her that she can have children, and thus adds to her value."[2] Among the Ba-Yaka, "if the woman dies before giving birth to a girl, the marriage-price is repaid."[3] The fear of non-fecundity underlies a number of avoidance-usages among the Akamba.[4] In East Africa exists a custom whereby "a childless woman, perhaps one of several wives, 'marries' a girl, and performs all the male parts of the . . . ceremonies; the girl lives with her, and if one of the co-wives of the 'husband' has a grown son he cohabits with the 'wife,' if there is no such son another man is chosen, and any children he has by her are the childless woman's not the mother's; bride-price is paid by the woman for this girl, it is small, and generally consists of the stock she received as presents when she was a bride herself. In one instance, a woman had as many as three 'wives,' there is no admitted trace of a servile status in the 'wife,' and no coherent answer is given to the question why, if a woman is childless, should not her husband marry another woman himself."[5]

Among certain aborigines of Siberia, "sterility is a punishment and a sign of disfavour on the part of dead relatives. A barren woman may ask the help of a shaman, who descends to the world of the deceased and persuades the soul of a relative to enter the woman's body, but such a child very often dies."[6] Fecundity is a virtue among the Sema Nagas, and "a large number of children is a great source of strength to a trans-Tizu chief. His daughters bring him profit in marriage prices as well as alliances, and many sons are even as 'the arrows in the hand of the giant,' for they go out from his village founding buffer colonies in all directions and facilitating the taking of revenue from weaker neighbours, securing the parent village and one another from attack, and often creating a small league of villages, something after the manner of an ancient Greek city state and her colonies."[7]

A case is mentioned among the East Greenlanders where a mother wanted the Danes to lay hand on her married daughter's abdomen, probably with the idea of rendering her fecund; she was afraid that the husband would leave the daughter if she were to be childless; the daughter seconded the request but blushed vividly at so doing.[8] To produce conception in women apparently barren, the Kwakiutl used to tie a male and female lizard together, chest to

1 Liston-Blyth, in JAI, LIII, 470.
2 Roscoe, in JAI, XXXIX, 183.
3 Torday and Joyce, in JAI, XXXVI, 45.
4 Hobley, A-Kamba, 65-67.

5 Barton, in JAI, LIII, 73.
6 Czaplicka, Aborig. Siberia, 133.
7 Hutton, Sema Nagas, 46.
8 Holm, Ethnol. Skizze, 57.

chest, while they were still alive. These the husband was to tie on the right side of his waist and wear for four days. After removing them, he was immediately to cohabit with his wife, who would become pregnant.[9] On reaching puberty, Hopi girls "dress their hair in whorls at the sides of the head, in imitation of the squash blossom, the symbol of fertility."[10]

The first duty of the Chaldæan wife was fecundity.[11] Procreation was the sense of early Hebrew marriage. Every man was bound to marry and could be compelled to do so and to live in marriage until a son or daughter was born. Sterility of the woman was an obstacle to marriage. The Talmudists disputed over the number of children it was one's duty to have.[12] Lycurgus put a kind of public stigma upon confirmed bachelors. "They were excluded from the sight of the young men and maidens at their exercises, and in winter the magistrates ordered them to march round the market-place in their tunics only, and as they marched, they sang a certain song about themselves, and its burden was that they were justly punished for disobeying the laws. Besides this, they were deprived of the honour and gracious attentions which the young men habitually paid to their elders."[13] The ancient Aryan woman was expected to bring forth children, as many as possible and preferably of the male sex. A woman who bore only boys was highly esteemed; to bear more girls than boys, or only girls, was a misfortune to her; to bear no children at all, a curse. Childlessness was held to be her fault, and "even the legislature of later times was guided by this idea, in that it exempted the husband from the punishment of childlessness (*orbitas*) when one child was born to him; the wife was not exempt until she had given birth to more children (in Rome three, in Italy four, in the provinces five). This is based on the idea that it is the wife's fault if there are not any more children; she, out of dread of the pangs of child-birth and of the trouble of bringing up children, had circumvented nature; if she had wished it there would have been more children; her first confinement showed that she was not barren; the man was exempt from all blame."[14]

The despair and rage of the barren wife, who supposes herself to be in that condition because of evil magic, are strikingly portrayed in the *Andromache* of Euripides. Characteristically, the sorceress is a foreigner and barbarian, hence under suspicion. The sentiments of the sufferer's father and of the onlookers faithfully represent the mores.

Teknonymy.[15] Desire for offspring and a high regard for children are indicated in the practice whereby parents are named after their children. A man among the East African Akamba is generally called by the name of his first child, whether male or female. When a woman marries, "she is often referred to as the mother of 'so and so,' the name of her first child."[16] Among the Gilyak, "after the birth of the first child, the father ceases to be called by his own name, and is known as 'the father of So-and-so.'" With the Yukaghir "it is still customary for the parents, after the birth of the first child, to be known by its name—thus, 'the Father and Mother of So-and-So.'"[17] Among the East Indian Alfurs, "at the birth of the first child the parents, so to speak, give up their names and the name of the child is given to them, with the prefix of the

9 Boas, in BAE, XXXV, pt. I, 644-648.
10 Fewkes, in HAI, I, 564.
11 Maspero, *Hist. Anc.*, I, 740.
12 Freisen, *Kanon. Eherecht*, 23.
13 Plutarch, *Lycurgus*, §15.

14 Ihering, *Aryan*, 343-344.
15 §212, above.
16 Hobley, *A-Kamba*, 127.
17 Czaplicka, *Aborig. Siberia*, 101, 132.

word: 'si ama ni . . . ,' that is to say 'the father of . . . ,' and 'si ina ni . . . ,' that is to say, 'the mother of . . . .' "[18] Among some peoples of the Malay Peninsula, "the birth-name was sometimes superseded (as being unlucky) before marriage, when misfortunes happened to the child, and the second name of the parents frequently gave place to the name of the eldest child with the prefix Pa' (Father) or Ma' (Mother). The latter was considered a peculiarly pleasing mode of address." Among the Jakun, who follow this system, if the child is called Bijan, then the father becomes Pa' Bijan, and the mother Ma' Bijan.[19] The Palaungs have no surnames. "When a number of people in a village have the same name, they must be distinguished in some way from each other. After a son is born, the names by which his father and mother were known before his birth are seldom heard; if the name of the child is A-lön the parents become known as 'The father of A-lön' and 'The mother of A-lön.' "[20] Among the Malayan and Papuan races in Polynesia, "on the birth of a child, the mother loses her own name, and is now called the mother of so-and-so—whatever the child may be named."[21] Among the Tlinkits of Alaska, "the name of a man is changed when he becomes a father and he is called after his child with the word *ish* (father) appended."[22] Again, among the Indians of the Pacific coast, "when a child is named, the father drops his former name and substitutes that of the child, so that the father receives his name from the child, and not the child from the father."[23] Finally, it is said of the Patagonians that the parents "are frequently known by the name of a child, which usurps the place of their own."[24]

The Levirate and Allied Forms.[25] Livingstone[26] wrote of the Bechuanas that when an elder brother dies, the brother next in age takes his wives, as among the Jews, and the children that may be born of these women he calls his brother's also. "He thus raises up seed to his departed relative." In Kikuyu exists a practice whereby "if a man dies without male issue his widow may pay dowry [bride-price] out of his property for a girl who is then at liberty to co-habit with any male member of the deceased's clan; her male children subsequently inherit the deceased's property.[27] The Dinkas probably follow farther than any other semi-civilized people the practice of procuring artificially a son for the deceased. Many other African tribes regard the children born of a widow, at whatever distance of time from her husband's death, as his children, but O'Sullivan[28] is not aware of any others which "provide for the extreme case of a man's dying childless, or at least sonless, without near male relatives and leaving only widows beyond the age of child-bearing, by allowing the widow or daughter in whom his property may temporarily vest, to contract marriage in his name with a woman who is, by the act of marriage, to become his widow and bear his heir. It is absolutely certain that the son born of such a woman can have none of the blood of his 'father.' He is his son only by a legal fiction as ingenious as any ever propounded by lawyers of more civilised countries." It is a law among these people that "all children borne by a man's widow are his children and the property of his heirs, irrespective of who is

18 Wilken, in VG, I, 106 (quoted), 280 ff.
19 Skeat and Blagden, *Malay Penin.*, II, 16-17, 69.
20 Milne, *Eastern Clan*, 30.
21 Ella, in AAAS, 1887, 488.
22 Jones, *Thlingets*, 37.
23 Bancroft, *Native Races*, I, 132.

24 Musters, *Patagonians*, 177, cited by Wilken, in VG, I, 283.
25 §395, above.
26 *Mission. Travels*, I, 203.
27 Dundas, C., in JAI, LI, 267.
28 In JAI, XL, 173, 179-180, 184-186.

their natural father and of time elapsed since his death; and, if boys, are in name and rights of inheritance that man's sons." An example is cited. "A dies, leaving one widow and one daughter by another wife. He has no male relatives. The widow is beyond the age of childbirth. He leaves no cattle. The widow marries the daughter to a man for ten cows. With these cows she buys a girl as widow to her dead husband for 'eight cows, there being none of her husband's. She brings a man from her own people, if possible, and he lies with the girl. In the next few years the girl gives birth to two daughters and a son. The two remaining cows have meanwhile increased to five with their young. By the time the son has grown up the two daughters have been given in marriage, and the cows paid for them are held 'in trust' by A's widow who purchased his mother. The son inherits all the cattle, also his own mother, and her purchaser, A's widow. His own natural father has no claim of any kind on him, beyond such presents of cattle as A's widow paid him for his services. The son carries A's name." Under the term "widow" is included, in Dinka laws, not only the wives of a man who is dead but also any bought as wife (widow) in his name after his death by his daughter or his widow, in order to raise children in his name. "It is the duty of a widow to raise children to her dead husband's name. This she does by cohabiting with her husband's brother or other of his close male relations." If she is beyond the age of child-bearing, it is her duty to purchase a girl and arrange for some male relation to cohabit with her for that purpose. These people also have the custom whereby if a sheik is "too old to be sexually efficient, he nevertheless continues to take wives, but these cohabit with his sons. Children so begotten are regarded as the children of the Sheik, and as the brothers of their actual fathers."[29]

There are a number of cases of the levirate in India, especially in connection with the dead husband's younger brother.[30] The Saora widow is considered bound to marry her husband's brother or his brother's son if he has no younger brother.[31] They give the name *putra* to the "one who saves from put, a hell into which those who have not produced a son fall."[32] That the custom is ancient is indicated by the fact that the *Vedas* and the laws of Manu report marriage with a brother's widow and the *Mahabharata* mentions it.[33] Jolly[34] says that while Manu chiefly lays weight upon this, that the sexual relation between the widow and her brother-in-law cannot be begun without special empowerment from the guardian, and after the birth of a son must not be carried on any farther, he offers also much more exact regulations over the protraction and even over the form of this relation and the mood suitable to it, which should be free from all lust of the flesh and governed only by the desire to beget seed for the dead. "Almost all the other old lawgivers sanction levirate in case of inheritance and otherwise, so the prohibition of it and the attempt to confine it to widowed brides and their brothers-in-law is only a later interpolation."

Closely allied to the levirate is the *niyoga*—a sort of injunction to a widow to have by her husband's brother or some more distant kinsman a son who shall be regarded as the son of the deceased and, on coming of age, inherit from him. Under certain circumstances the practice may even be put into operation while the husband is alive: "Since it is the expressed purpose of this

29 Cummins, in JAI, XXXIV, 151.
30 Chatlopadhyay, in Man, XXII, 36-41.
31 Fawcett, in JASB, I, 231.
32 Thurston, S. India, 50.

33 Phillips, *Vedas*, 151; Jolly, *Sec. Marriages*, 12 (references given); Bühler, *Manu*, IX, 58 ff.; Holtzmann, *Ind. Sagen*, I, 37.
34 *Stellung d. Frauen*, 453-454.

levirate-marriage to care for the propagation of the line, in order thereby to prevent the cessation of sacrifice for the dead and the loss of heritage, it appears only reasonable that the still living husband too, who on account of impotence or sickness no longer hopes for progeny, may himself evoke the levirate" (*niyoga*). "At present there still commonly occur marriages with the deceased brother's widow, if not the *niyoga*," especially in the Punjab where so much that is old is preserved. These often bring it about that a man has two wives at once. It is a Tibetan custom that Buddhistic monks beget a son and heir for a dead brother.[35] The custom of *niyoga* is still reported from India for the purpose of obtaining progeny from the widowed princesses—"a practice permissible in emergency, though not accorded recognition as an ordinary course of social conduct. It consisted in inviting some great sage to become the father of children who, being born of a widowed queen, were to be considered the offspring of her dead husband."[36] Wilken[37] reports the same institution from the East Indies, according to which the widow has the right to have relations with the brother of her deceased husband who has died childless, in order to get for him an heir and successor. Such a relation is merely temporary and should not be aligned, he thinks, with the levirate. There is, however, a genetic connection between the two and an author is quoted who thinks that levirate is the principal and original form of the *niyoga*. The latter, it should be noted, can be put into operation during a man's lifetime; the childless husband may have his brother or some other person take his place, and regard the child begotten of his wife as his own. Only one such case is known to Wilken in Indonesia.

The levirate prevails in the East Indies among the Bataks and other tribes and in New Guinea. In one district, "cases are known in which the betrothed of a dead man went over to his brother because the *jujur* [bride-price] was already fully paid and the father of the boy did not wish to have paid all the expenses for nothing." Thus may a woman become the wife of a younger brother who is a mere child, and such a child may have several wives. Among the Bataks the widow always goes to the younger brother. The marriage of an older brother with a younger brother's widow is regarded as incest and as such is punished by death. Union in the first case may take place even before burial, but it is without ceremonies. The rule that the woman through marriage belongs inseparably to the kin-group of the man and thus may never marry out of it, is insisted upon strenuously. The same applies to South Sumatra.[38] In Malacca there was a ruling custom of monogamy "which was broken through only by the existence of the so-called levirate-marriage."[39] In Samoa a man married his brother's widow, even when he had a wife of his own, to keep the children and the property in the husband's family.[40] Von Mollendorff[41] comments that the levirate can never be of the same importance with the Chinese as with other people, *e.g.*, to retain the family-property, for posthumous adoption, which the Chinese substitute for it, fully meets the object.

The Greenlanders see no moral delinquency in a childless man's wife having

35 Jolly, in *Grundr. d. Indo-Ar. Philol.*, II, Heft 8, pp. 70, 71.
36 Vishwanath, in JAI, XLVII, 33.
37 In VG, II, 286, note.
38 Wilken, *Vkde.*, 326, 327; Wilken, in VG, I, 328-329; II, 237; Ratzel, *Vkde.*, II, 433.
39 Stevens, in *Ztsft. f. Ethnol.*, XXVIII, 177.
40 Ella, in AAAS, 1892, 642.
41 *Family Law of Chinese*, 17.

children by some other man; payment is offered to such a substitute.[42] Among
the Indians of southwestern Oregon, if a man died, his brother was compelled
to marry the widow, no matter how many wives he already had.[43] Of the
Chippeways it is reported: "Sometimes a brother of the deceased takes the
widow for his wife at the grave of her husband, which is done by a ceremony
of walking her over it. And this he has a right to do; and when this is done
she is not required to go into mourning; or, if she chooses, she has the right
to go to him, and he is *bound* to support her."[44] Among the Miwok, "the oldest
brother is entitled to his brother's widow, and he may even take her home with
him on the return from the funeral, if he wishes, though that would be thought
very scandalous."[45] The levirate is reported of a number of other tribes.[46]
Kohler[47] thinks the levirate-marriage is connected closely with polyandry:
"How closely this levirate-right is connected with the present polyandry is
shown in the life of the Tlinkit: here the wife has sexual relations, even during
the life of the husband, with his brother as a secondary husband (as he is
called) and then follows him when she becomes a widow."

In Mexico the levirate was lawful even when the husband's brother was already married.[48] The custom whereby the oldest brother or in his absence the
nearest male relative takes the widow, is prevalent among almost all Brazilian
savages. It is coupled with the provision that the widow's brother marries her
daughter, if she is marriageable and there is no other bridegroom available.[49]
When a Jibaro Indian dies, his brother must marry the widow. "The departed
husband, who is still jealous of the wife he left behind, does not cede her to
any other man than his brother, who with himself forms one personality and
represents him in the most real sense of the word."[50]

Should the brother among the Hebrews refuse to take the widow, "then
shall his brother's wife come unto him in the presence of the elders, and loose
his shoe from off his foot, and spit in his face, and shall answer and say,
So shall it be done unto that man that will not build up his brother's house."[51]
In the Talmud it is written: "The judges shall call the Levir and give him good
advice. If he is young and the widow old, or the reverse, let them say to him:
'Wherefore to you an old woman (or a young)? Take your own like and bring
no quarreling into the house!' If the brother-in-law is not suitable for the
widow and yet holds to his 'right' to marry her, he could be promised a certain sum of money for the dispensation. But the widow after the ceremony is
over need not redeem her promise; rather may she compromise with the declaration that she had 'held him a fool.' "[52] In Persian tradition, if a man over
fifteen dies unmarried, his relatives must dower a maid and marry her to
some man. She is to be the dead man's wife in the next world and half her
children are reckoned as his. This kind of wife is termed "adopted." If a childless widow marries again, half her children by the second marriage belong to
her first husband and she is his wife in the future life. She is called "serving."
The first child of an only child and daughter belongs to her parents and they

42 Nansen, *Esk. Life*, 172.
43 Sapir, in AA, IX, 268.
44 Yarrow, in BAE, I, 185.
45 Powers, in *Contrib. N. Amer. Ethnol.*, III, 356.
46 Lowie, in AA, XXI, 34; Hewitt, in HAI, II, 478; Sapir, in HAI, II, 674; Anon., in HAI, I, 655.

47 *Urgchte d. Ehe*, 139.
48 Letourneau, *Soc.*, 329.
49 Von Martius, *Beiträge*, I, 117, 393.
50 Karsten, "Jibaro," in BAE, Bull. LXXIX, 12.
51 Deut., XXV, 9.
52 Klugmann, *Frau im Talmud*, 26.

give her one-third of their property in compensation. She is called an "only child" wife.[53] On the death of Aristobulus (105 B.C.) his childless widow endowed his oldest brother with the rule and with her hand, by levirate-marriage.[54] To the Romans, marriages of brother and sister and those with brothers-in-law, as occurred among the Egyptians, seemed loose and immoral, correlative with an undeveloped idea of property which made theft almost allowable.[55] Among the Germans there existed customs aligned with the *niyoga*,[56] while among the Beduins of today, "if a young man leaves a widow, his brother generally offers to marry her; custom does not oblige either him or her to make this match, nor can he prevent her from marrying another man. It seldom happens that she refuses, for by such an union the family property is kept together."[57]

§407. Pregnancy and the Couvade.

AMONG some natives of British New Guinea pregnancy is thought to be due to frequent cohabitation and conception to take place in the breasts, which first show the condition. The child is then supposed to drop. There is no idea of a special intra-abdominal organ in which the child is lodged. During the suckling period the woman foregoes cohabitation and observes the same taboos as in pregnancy.[1]

From the fifth month of pregnancy the Edo woman of West Africa wears her hair in a special manner; "it must be dressed by a woman who has borne one son, and kola is offered to the comb and pin used in the operation."[2] Among the Ba-Yaka the kola-nut is considered an aphrodisiac. No means are taken to prevent conception, and abortion is unknown. "During pregnancy the husband must abstain from his wife, and also during the period for which the child is suckled (about a year)."[3] With the Bangala "a woman never had sexual relations with her husband from about three months before confinement until the child was weaned, *i.e.*, from twelve to eighteen months. It was believed that if this prohibition were not observed, the child would sicken and die."[4] Among the Baganda, "when a woman conceives, all sickly or delicate children are kept from her, and she is surrounded by strong healthy ones."[5] The natives of the Niger Protectorate think that a pregnant woman's milk will suffer, and hence also the unborn or born child, if she does not leave her husband as soon as she knows of her state. It has thus become customary for a woman to avoid cohabitation with her husband for nearly three years after pregnancy.[6]

Among certain Siberian tribes "a pregnant woman must be active and energetic so that the child also shall have these qualities and issue easily and quickly from the mother. She ought in walking to raise her feet high, and on finding stones or lumps of earth in her path she should kick them away, symbolizing the removal of obstructions at child-birth."[7] In India, "to be the blessed mother of a child is considered so much a blessing and a meritorious

53 Evans, in PSM, XLV, 89.
54 Ewald, *Gesch. Israel*, IV, 504, note 4.
55 Grupp, *Kgchte.*, I, 420.
56 Weinhold, *Deut. Frauen*, 308; Grimm, *Deut. Rechtsalterth.*, 433.
57 Burckhardt, *Bedouins*, I, 112-113.
1 Seligmann, in JAI, XXXII, 300, 302.

2 Thomas, in JAI, LII, 250.
3 Torday and Joyce, in JAI, XXXVI, 51
4 Weeks, in JAI, XL, 367.
5 Roscoe, in JAI, XXXII, 29.
6 Granville and Roth, in JAI, XXVIII, 106.
7 Czaplicka, *Aborig. Siberia*, 130-132.

deed in the East, and to remain barren is considered so great a curse, that from the very time of conception every possible care is taken as well for her health as for her being out of the way of drawing on evil eye on her blessed condition."[8] The pregnant woman is spared household labors; must not be out of doors after dark for fear of evil spirits; receives presents and decorations and various other little attentions.[9] In the Punjab it is thought that man and wife during pregnancy are particularly susceptible to the effects of an eclipse. It is safest for the woman to keep to her bed and not see it, though the man may. Both must refrain from locking and unlocking a lock lest the child's fingers be bent and powerless. To cut wood with an ax will make the child have hare-lip; to stamp or print during an eclipse is liable to leave an impress on the child's body.[10]

The same sort of prescriptions as to conduct recur in variant forms among most of the East Indians and are generally good examples of imitative magic.[11] Especially must there be no killing of animals or head-hunting; no blood must be spilt. In Celebes, the wife "may not stand under the supporting-beam of the house, as this effects miscarriage, and must split no wood."[12] "Oh, child," says the Javanese father, in sacrificing, "I kill this cow, but it shall be done dexterously; therefore thou must not come into the world untimely or misshapen."[13] The wife has to be "careful not to disparage any man or beast, or the qualities she dislikes will be reproduced in her child. And she must not sleep in the daytime, or her child will fall a prey to evil spirits."[14]

In Micronesia "the moon played a rôle, as well as certain incantations;" and taboo and renunciation of all labor, for both man and wife, occur.[15] In the Nauru Islands no nuts may be touched that fall within a hundred feet of the hut. The wife may eat nothing that the husband, father, or mother have touched. "From the fifth month on, no nail may be driven in the house and not the least noise may be made. Nothing may be taken from the wall till the child is born. Especially in the case of the first-born are these rules most painfully observed."[16] In the Gilbert Islands, "when a woman was known to be pregnant, the greatest care was taken to conceal her condition from all outsiders. . . . Remnants of her food, toilet materials, old clothes, and all other things closely connected with her person were burned as soon as might be, for through such things some foreign sorcerer might most easily bring evil upon her. . . . The fifth month of pregnancy was considered to be the most dangerous of all to mother and child. When it arrived she was taken to the eastern shore of the island, where a small clearing in the bush had been prepared, and as she sat there a girdle of the inner bark of the *kanawa* tree . . . was bound about her middle. This was called her *bunna,* or protection against enemy magic, but incidentally it played the part of an abdominal support that helped her to bear the increasing weight of her child." Two kinswomen "paid constant attention during the last two months of pregnancy to the position of the child in the uterus, and if it seemed at any time unsatisfactory it

8 Modi, in JASB, II, 170.

9 Kirtikar, in JASB, I, 394, 396, 397; Rose, in JAI, XXXV, 271 ff.; Reclus, *Prim. Folk,* 201.

10 Rose, in JAI, XXXV, 277, 278; Modi, in JASB, II, 170.

11 §302, of text.

12 Wilken, *Vkde.*, 203, 204; Roth, *Sarawak,*

I, 98; Bock, *Borneo,* 97; Nieuwenhuis, *Borneo,* I, 79; Grabowsky, in *Globus,* LXXII, 269; Riedel, in *Bijd.,* XXXV, 91.

13 Pleyte, in *Bijd.,* XLI, 587.

14 Skeat, in *Folk-Lore,* XI, 307.

15 Finsch, *Ethnol. Erfahr.,* III, 31; Kubary, *Núkuóro,* 36.

16 Brandeis, in *Globus,* XCI, 59.

was adjusted by extremely careful massage. I have heard a competent medical authority speak in praise of the methods of these old experts, whose art is not yet quite extinct in the less visited islands of the Group."[17] When a Maori woman of the high chieftain class was known to have conceived, she was not allowed to perform any laborious work; more especially was she forbidden to carry any food-products on her back—the common native way of bearing burdens—"inasmuch as such an act would have a most injurious effect upon the unborn child, for, be it known, such a child is *tapu* even before birth. The proximity of food-products has ever a desecrating or polluting effect upon *tapu* persons, objects, or places."[18]

Among the Tsimshian Indians "a woman who is with child is not allowed to eat tails of salmon, otherwise the confinement would be hard. She must rise early in the morning, and leave the house before any of the other occupants leave it. Before the child is born, the father must stay outside his house, and must wear ragged clothing. After the child is born, he must abstain from eating any fat food, particularly porcupine, seal, and whale. The mother is confined in a small house or in a separate room."[19] The Minsi Indians of Canada say that the husband of an expectant mother was often accompanied on his hunting-trips by the spirit of the unborn child, whose romping and playing about the bushes, invisible to mortal eye, would nevertheless frighten away the deer and send the hunter home empty-handed. "To prevent this a little bow and arrow were made and attached to the prospective father's garments, in the hope that the little spirit would play with them and stay quietly with his parent. Should this precaution fail, the child was thought to be a girl, and a little corn mortar and pestle were substituted for the miniature bow and arrow."[20] The Dakotas believe that "women with child are but torturing sports for the vengeful Anogite [two-faced monster]."[21] In all the tribes the pregnant woman must observe certain taboos. The Zuñi woman "must be guarded from the sight of moving water, fish, and water reptiles no less than from fierce and fearful things."[22] Were a man to kill a snake during his wife's pregnancy the child would be born spotted like a snake and would die. "Were a pregnant woman to look upon a corpse her child would be still-born, or, born alive, would soon pine away."[23] Among the Pima, "a pregnant woman was not allowed to eat anything that an animal had touched. For example, if a gopher had cut a vine upon which a melon was ripening, she might not eat the fruit; or, if the mice nibbled at a basket of wheat she might not eat of the tortillas made therefrom. She dared not go where Apaches had been killed, or the baby would die. If her husband killed a rattlesnake at that time, her child's stomach would swell and it would die soon after birth. She must not eat liver or her child would be disfigured by birthmarks."[24] Among the Pawnees "a woman must not look hard at any animal before her child is born, for the child may be like it."[25]

By many of the tribes of the Southwest beliefs of imitative magic are held in connection with conception, pregnancy, and growth; Parsons[26] has described a number as follows. "To conceive a male, a woman will wash a bow and arrow and drink the water; to conceive a female, she will wash the grinding stone, and

17 Grimble, in JAI, LI, 34-36.
18 Best, in JAI, XLIV, 129.
19 Boas, in BAE, XXXI, 530-531.
20 Harrington, in AA, XV, 212.
21 Dorsey, in BAE, XI, 473.

22 Hrdlička, in BAE, Bull. 34, 53, 54.
23 Parsons, in AA, XVIII, 248-249.
24 Russell, in BAE, XXVI, 185.
25 Grinnell, *Folk Tales*, 122.
26 In AA, XX, 176.

drink. A man or woman who eats corn whose grains grow in a double row or two chili growing together will beget or conceive twins. The remains of the lunch a hunter takes with him in the sacred rabbit hunts should not be eaten by a married woman or by the unmarried, otherwise they will have twins. A pregnant woman will not eat rabbit. The skin on the belly of a rabbit is thin and her child's belly would be over large. A pregnant woman should not stand looking out of a window, nor, once she has started to cross a threshold, should she return, for example, for anything forgotten. She should first cross the threshold and then return, otherwise the labor will be slow. To hasten labor, throughout her pregnancy a woman should rise quickly on awakening and put on her dress and belt, not dawdling about getting up. When it thunders a child will pull his hair to make it grow and stretch up his arms to grow tall. To make a backward or feeble child grow quickly and strong, a father will take it often out doors before the dawn."

In British Guiana neither parent must do any work, and the father may leave the hut only in the evening and for a moment. He must not bathe or handle his weapons. Thirst may be assuaged only with lukewarm water. It is forbidden to scratch the body or head with the finger-nails, a special implement being used. "The transgression of one of these prescriptions and prohibitions would bring about the death or lifelong sickness of the child."[27] Among certain Arawaks, "though the killing and eating of a snake during the woman's pregnancy is forbidden to both father and mother the husband is allowed to kill and eat any other animal. The cause assigned for the taboo of the snake is that the little infant might be similar, that is, able neither to talk nor to walk. Neither parent, however, when carrying a piece of cassava cake, may either turn it over in the hand, or curl it up at the sides; otherwise, the ears of the child, when born, will be found curled over. Any game hunted by dogs is strictly forbidden the pregnant woman of this tribe, just as it is at her menstruation; otherwise the dog would be spoiled for hunting purposes, permanently in the latter circumstances, temporarily in the former, the dog recovering its powers only when the baby was born." Cooking for a man is strictly prohibited to a pregnant woman; "she may however 'clean' the meat, but in cleaning any animal or fish she must not cut off the ears, nails, or fins." If a Carib fisherman's wife is with child, he must take special precautions lest he be unsuccessful.[28] Certain tribes of Brazil enforce fasting upon both spouses; they eat only ants and fungi, and drink water in which certain medicaments are dissolved; and they both cut themselves so as to lose considerable blood.[29]

Samson's mother when pregnant was to drink no wine and avoid unclean food.[30]

The Couvade and Allied Practices. By certain Melanesians "it is considered kind and respectful to call a man when he has a child the father of so and so; his station in society is advanced by his paternity, and it is recognized in this way." This teknonymy, indicating the pride of fatherhood, is in evidence in the couvade. The most conspicuous example of the couvade among Melanesians appears to have been in the region where descent follows on the father's side.[31] In San Cristoval, Solomon Islands, "for two or three weeks after the birth of

27 Schomburgk, *Brit.-Guiana*, II, 314.
28 Roth, in BAE, XXX, 319, 323.
29 Von Martius, *Beiträge*, I, 402-403; 643; Spix u. Martius, *Brasilien*, 1189.

30 Judges, XIII, 4-14.
31 Codrington, in JAI, XVIII, 309, 311; Ratzel, *Vkde.*, II, 273.

a child the father guards himself carefully from the sun and from the cold wind which comes up nightly from the river valleys, and from the rain. He is careful to do no heavy work, and especially not to carry anything heavy."[32] In New Guinea, "there is a distant reminiscence of the couvade in the usage whereby the father abstains for a time from tobacco and betel." If he goes upon the water, "the fish retire before him and the sea is stirred up;" if he eats crocodile-flesh or fish the child may have crooked legs.[33] Similar taboos obtain among the Andamanese.[34]

In West Africa "a carpenter whose wife is pregnant must not drive a nail. To do so would close the womb and cause a difficult labor. He may do all other work belonging to carpentering, but he must have an assistant to drive the nails."[35] Along the Upper Congo "the father during the pregnancy of his wife is prohibited certain foods, and may not hunt or fish during the pregnancy and confinement of his wife, unless she goes to a 'nganga' [medicine-man] and has certain ceremonies performed on and over her. The prohibitions varied considerably, and when a man was observing these tabus, he was said to be in a state of liboi, a noun derived from the verb bwa = to deliver of a child, to be confined. I have always regarded this as a remnant of 'la couvade.' They have no tradition of the man ever having taken the place of the confined woman by lying in bed during confinement."[36] Among the Bageshu, "the husband of the woman is not allowed to take violent exercise, nor may he climb a tree, or go on to a house roof, or climb rocks, lest he should slip or overexert himself, and thus bring on a miscarriage for his wife."[37] In East Africa the father who fears twins must stay a month in his hut and drink a special concoction; this is called "a species of male child-bed."[38] Among the Awa-Wanga, many believe that within five or six days of the birth of a child the parents must cohabit, or the child will die. "After the birth of twins, the parents are secluded for from twenty days to a month; at the end of the ordained period the brother of the man then formally opens the door of the hut and the couple can go about as usual. This seclusion of the male parent is probably an attenuated relic of the 'couvade' custom."[39]

The couvade exists, we are told, among both Land and Sea Dyaks. "If a Land Dyak's wife be with child, he must strike nothing, never tie things tight, nor do any household work with his parang (chopping-knife), or some deadly harm will happen to his unborn offspring. At a birth the husband is confined to his house for eight days, and obliged to stay his appetite with rice and salt only. For one month, moreover, he may not go out at night, unless he wishes his infant to cry continually during his absence."[40] The Sumatran must stay by his wife from the first appearance of pregnancy till the forty-fourth day after delivery, especially between sun-set and sun-rise, to ward off evil spirits. He must not kill animals lest their qualities go over into the child. He has a sort of "invisible contact" with the latter and by his conduct exercises a strong influence over its destiny.[41] In the Mentawei Islands the father shuts himself up for two months in the house, while his wife attends to the field-labors; and

32 Fox, in JAI, XLIX, 118.
33 Hagen, Papua's, 234, 229; Kreiger, Neu-Guinea, 164-165, 293.
34 Man, in JAI, XII, 354.
35 Nassau, Fetichism, 192.
36 Weeks, in JAI, XXXIX, 444.
37 Roscoe, in JAI, XXXIX, 183-184.
38 Anon., in Globus, XCII, 147.
39 Hobley, in JAI, XXXIII, 358.
40 Roth, Sarawak, I, 97 (quoted from Grant's Tour); Roth, in JAI, XXI, 133.
41 Jacobs, Groot-Atjeh, I, 106-107, 108, 109.

in Luzon he must refrain from certain foods.[42] So strict is the rule about husbands leaving their wives that Stevens[43] often had difficulty in securing carriers and guides. Wilken[44] gives a list of East Indian peoples among whom the couvade or like practices obtain, and cites regulations for both husband and wife. If these be omitted, the placenta may be retained, and the child be still-born or defective. The regulations of some Pacific Islanders form variants upon the foregoing,[45] while fasting by the husband is found in China.[46] Among the Malayan and Papuan races in Polynesia, "a few days after giving birth the poor woman has to go off to her daily toil as usual, and the father stays at home to nurse the child, and feed it with the expressed juice of cocoanut."[47]

In British Guiana the husband hangs his hammock near his wife's and is confined along with her. Among all the Indians practising the couvade a number of taboos surround husband and wife. The Makusi father during his time of couvade is forbidden his usual bath. "Strange to say, it is the bath which in most tribes constitutes the final purification of the mother, at the end of her lying-in period, whether such period be of a few hours' or several days' duration." In many of the tribes during the couvade, and often for long afterward, the husband is prohibited from engaging in certain of his ordinary occupations. "The Pomeroon Arawak must neither smoke, lift any heavy weight, use a fish-hook, nor have intimate relations with any woman. The Main-land Carib of Cayenne was not allowed to cut any big timber with an ax. The Makusi must not touch his weapons. Should these and similar prohibitions be not observed, some evil would be sure to befall the child. There is another interesting example recorded of a man during couvade lying in his hammock and twisting a new bow-string; baby began to scream, with the result that the father had to undo the whole line."[48]

In the old French story, *Aucassin and Nicolette,* is a striking case resembling the couvade.[49]

§408. Child-Birth.[1]

Among the aborigines of Victoria there exists a peculiar custom associated with the disposal of the navel-strand. "When a man has a child born to him, he preserves its umbilical cord, by tying it up in the middle of a bunch of feathers. This is called *kalduke.* He then gives this to the father of a child or children who belongs to another tribe, and those children are thenceforth *ngia-ngiampe* [under a sort of taboo] to the child from whom the *kalduke* was pro-cured, and that child is *ngia-ngiampe* to them. From that time none of the children to whom the *kalduke* was given may speak to their *ngia-ngiampe,* or even touch or go near him; neither must he speak to them. . . . When two indi-viduals who are in this position with regard to each other have arrived at adult age, they become the agents through which their respective tribes carry on barter." This estrangement is said to answer two purposes: "It gives se-curity to the tribes that there will be no collusion between their agents for their own private advantage, and also compels the two always to conduct the

42 Pleyte, in *Globus*, LXXIX, 24; Blu-mentritt, in *Globus*, XLIX, 125.

43 In *Ztsft. f. Ethnol.*, XXVIII, 185.

44 In VG, II, 149 ff.

45 Senfft, in *Globus*, XCI, 142; Brandeis, in *Globus*, XCI, 60.

46 Legge, *Li Ki*, I, 471.

47 Ella, in AAAS, 1887, 488.

48 Roth, in BAE, XXX, 323, 324.

49 Suchier, *Aucassin und Nicolette*, 32-35; see notes with parallels, 54-55.

1 §317, of the *Case-Book*.

business through third parties." The taboo of the woman during child-birth is found here; in South Australia, "when a woman is married, she is not allowed to speak at all until she has done breeding."[2]

Among the Melanesian Koita, "should labour be unduly prolonged, the child's father is sent for. He, after having opened any boxes there may be in the house—and in the Port Moresby villages there are few house-fathers who have not at least one camphor wood box—sits down near his wife and proceeds to untie the cord which confines his hair, and to remove the *gana* from his arms. If this does not improve matters her brother is sent for, and he in his turn removes hair band and *gana;* should this fail a 'medicine woman' is the last resource." The play of imitative magic is here in evidence. "While his wife is secluded in the house, the child's father must abstain from chewing betel, and observe the same food taboos as his wife, under penalty of his child becoming seriously ill. . . . Cohabitation should not be resumed until the child can toddle about; if it is resumed before then the child will weaken, sicken and perhaps die."[3] Among certain Solomon Islanders, "no married woman is allowed to sleep with a woman in her confinement, but it is quite permissible for unmarri d girls to sleep in the same house."[4] In New Georgia, "after the return of the mother with the twenty-five days' infant, she sleeps with the child, in a separate bed from her husband, until the baby's teeth have come, or until it is beginning to talk, when cohabitation again begins."[5] For a considerable time after the birth of a child the Loyalty Islands mother was regarded as taboo, and was required to live a secluded life. "During this period her husband did not cohabit with her."[6] Papuan women go to an outside hut to bear; this may be to force segregation of husband and wife at the time. Cases occur where women have to stay in the places of their delivery for months. These customs are said to explain in good measure the existence of polygyny and the difficulties of missionaries in trying to eradicate it.[7]

African tribes require seclusion for a month or so after confinement. The husband must take his weapons out of the house and stay out himself till eight days after the birth and may not live in the house till three or four weeks after he has first seen his child. Again, the woman may not leave the hut without peril of great ill luck to her and the child. "This custom seems to be solicitously observed." Throughout East Africa there must be no fire taken into or out of the house. The seclusion may be upon both "sanitary and æsthetic grounds."[8] In East Angola, it seems that the husband is held in some degree accountable for the fate of the wife: "when a woman dies in child-birth the husband is obliged to bury her by himself, carrying the corpse on his back to the grave and doing the work of interment alone. Then he has to pay for her life to her parents; and if he has not the wherewithal, he becomes their slave."[9] The Ewe-speaking people of West Africa consider a mother and child unclean for forty days after child-birth.[10] Among the Baganda, before confinement, the lower part of the woman's body is massaged with butter. A

2 §§76, 141, of the text and *Case-Book;* Smyth, *Vict.,* I, 181-182; Miscell., in JAI, XXIV, 181.
3 Seligmann, *Melanesians,* 84-86.
4 Rooney, in AAAS, 1911, 444.
5 Somerville, in JAI, XXVI, 407.
6 Ray, in JAI, XLVII, 285.
7 Wilken, in VG, III, 217, note.

8 Fritsch, *Eingeb. S.-Afr.,* 115; Holub, *S. Afr.,* II, 239-240; Pater, L., in *Globus,* LXXIX, 352; Stuhlmann, *Mit Emin,* 392; 504; Johnston, *Uganda,* II, 553; Fabry, in *Globus,* XCI, 223; Paulitschke, *Nordost-Afr.,* I, 192.
9 Serpa Pinto, *África,* I, 116.
10 Ellis, *Ewe,* 153.

child born feet-first is called by a term of reproach; a stillborn child or one who dies in infancy is buried at the cross-roads and thorns put on its grave. Passing women throw grass on the grave to prevent the ghost from entering them to be reborn. If a child is found by the father's relatives to have any symptoms of disease, the mother is accused of breaking the taboos.[11] If the child is a boy, the Bahima father brings the gate-posts from the kraal, and places them on the fire to keep the mother and son warm; "this fire is kept burning brightly for seven days, by day and night. The mother is given the cord, which her husband uses to tie the legs of restive cows during milking, to wear as a waist-band. But should the child be a girl the mother has to use a strip of her own clothing for a band, and also has only ordinary fire-wood for her fire."[12] With the Atharaka, "on the birth of a child the father must call together his relations and slaughter a goat. This ceremony takes place outside the village, for no one can enter the village for five days after the birth. Should the father himself be away at the time of the birth he cannot himself enter the village till the goat has been slaughtered. During this period of five days no property can leave the village."[13] In the Baringo District, the husband may not enter the hut for at least two months after delivery, and cohabitation must not be resumed until the child is weaned and the mother has gone through the purification-ceremony.[14] Among the tribes of British Central Africa, purification consists in washing the whole body and in placing a piece of burning wood between the mother's legs, where it smoulders for several hours.[15] In this region the mortality from obstructed labor is high, contrary to the usual experience of the natives. In Nyasaland the woman makes no fuss about child-birth, and works up to the last moment. "It is a common occurrence," says Stigand,[16] "for a child to be dropped while at work in the fields. The woman performs all the necessary offices, picks up the child, and walks home."

Northern Asia shows the special tent for child-birth. After two months the mother goes out, putting on new clothing and making the old into amulets. While in the child-bearing tent the woman may eat only meat killed by her husband or the first booty brought home by a child. If she goes out of this tent she must not go by the door but through an opening made for the purpose. The Kalmuk husband whose wife is confined stretches a net around the outside of the tent and beats the air with a club until the child is born, crying the while: "Be off, devil!" If the pregnant woman accidentally steps on a net, it is cut into and sewed together again at that point.[17] At the first attack of labor-pains, among the Yukaghir and Yakut, "the wife, the husband, and the midwife must loosen all the fastenings of their garments that the child may not be hampered in any way. . . . Then the midwife purifies the woman by means of smoke. Dry grass is kindled on the floor of the house, and the woman passes through the smoke, stopping a while and shaking her body." Miss Czaplicka[18] states that all the cases of child-birth observed among these people were very difficult, and "the barbarous practices attendant upon them produce nervous diseases and premature age in the mothers." The Tungus wife must bear her child alone in the forest, "just as is the case among many tribes of

11 Roscoe, in JAI, XXXII, 30, 31.
12 Roscoe, in JAI, XXXVII, 106.
13 Champion, in JAI, XLII, 83.
14 Dundas, K. R., in JAI, XL, 60.
15 Stannus, in JAI, XL, 310.

16 In JAI, XXXVII, 122.
17 Ratzel, Vkde., II, 769; Rubruck, Eastern Parts, 75; Kondratowitsch, in Globus, LXXIV, 290.
18 Aborig. Siberia, 130-132.

North America."[19] The Tibetan mother gets gifts a week after confinement, on the occasion of the birth-feast, but must remain home a month.[20]

Among the Naga tribes of India the mother was carefully secluded in her house, alone with the child, for five days, during which time she was fed only on fowls. "The meaning of this seems to be that the woman and all her surroundings are unclean. After the five days had elapsed all the woman's clothes were washed, and the clay pots used by her for cooking since her confinement were thrown away. She was then allowed to mix as before with the villagers, who made her small presents of food, drink, etc."[21] Again, "after the birth of a child, it is generally the custom that the mother must not leave the house for some days, and among the Lushais neither parent must work for seven days lest the soul of the child, which is supposed to be hovering around them should be hurt."[22] Among certain people of Malabar, "as soon as the pains of delivery come upon a pregnant woman, she is taken to an outlying shed, and left alone to live or die as the event may turn out. No help is given to her for twenty-eight days. Even medicines are thrown to her from a distance; and the assistance rendered is to place a jar of warm water close by her just before the child is born. Pollution from birth is held as worse than that from death. At the end of the twenty-eight days the hut in which she is confined is burnt down. The father, too, is polluted for fourteen days, and, at the end of that time, he is purified, not like other castes by the barber, but by holy water obtained from Brahmans at temples or elsewhere."[23] After the birth of a child, among the Nairs, "there is a mild pollution (as compared to the strong untouchable pollution caused by death) in the family. This pollution does not carry any disabilities except the prohibition to enter any sacred precincts."[24] Water appears to be a purifying substance *par excellence*. "When a male-child is born in a family, the father of the new-born child rushes headlong to the mother Ganges and jumps into it. He then begins to repeat the names of his ancestors and throw water upwards, apparently believing that his ancestors in heaven are receiving the oblations of water thus thrown up by him. . . . It is believed by an average Hindu that a male-child is the fruit of the propitiation of ancestors."[25]

Rose[26] has written extensively concerning Hindu birth-observances in the Punjab. To prevent mischief to the mother of the child, a number of precautions are taken. Fire must be kept in the room, as must also grain, close to the bed, as an emblem of good luck. Water must be kept there, as it is a purifier; and a weapon should be placed close by the mother. Under the bed should be kept the handle of a plough. There should be a lock on the bed, or else it should have a chain round it. On no account should a cat be allowed in the room, nor should the mother hear one call, or even mention the word "cat." It is most unlucky for her to dream of the animal, and if one is seen in the room, ashes should be thrown over it. An eighth-month birth is attributed to a cat having entered the mother's room in a former confinement. The house should not be swept with a broom, lest the luck be swept out of it. No small drain into the room should be left open, lest ill-luck enter by an aperture which must be unclean. A lamp must be kept burning all night and allowed to burn itself out

19 Hiekisch, *Tungusen*, 91.
20 Rockhill, in USNM, 1893, 725.
21 Godden, in JAI, XXVII, 34.
22 Shakespear, in JAI, XXXIX, 381-382.

23 Thurston, *S. India*, 548.
24 Panikkar, in JAI, XLVIII, 273.
25 Chaube, in JASB, V, 71-72.
26 In JAI, XXXVII, 220-235, 237-247.

in the morning; if the lamp were blown out, the son would be destroyed. Monday is an unlucky day for birth; the remedy consists in boring the child's nose or ear. An averting ceremony follows a birth under an eclipse, one of the details of which is that the parents, with the child in the mother's lap, are placed under a sieve through which water is poured. There are also practices which consist in deceiving the mother. For instance, she is generally told that she has given birth to a girl, for if she knew she had had a son, the after-birth would not come away. If she bears a girl, she is told she has borne a stone. In one place the after-birth is buried at the spot where the child was born "after the eldest matron of the family has made the mother worship it." There is a great deal of bathing all through these ceremonies and also the use of cow's urine to cleanse. The Mohammedans of the Punjab have similar birth-observances. To facilitate delivery, they place a leaf in a jar of water: as it opens out, so the birth takes place. The mother is told that she has given birth to a one-eyed girl; the heat engendered by this ill news forces the after-birth out quickly; joy would retard it if she knew a son was born. The navel cord is sometimes incased in silver and hung round the child's neck as a defense against stomach-ache. In other instances it is buried in a corner of the house. Neither parent should touch it. After the child is born, a knife, sword, or piece of iron is kept under the mother's head so as to ward off evil spirits. Again, no cat is allowed in the room; it is possessed of genii and might harm the cord. When the mother goes out later to see the stars, points of swords are placed together over her head so that jinns and other evil spirits may not pass over her; thereafter danger no longer shadows her. Sometimes the father shoots an arrow into the ceiling over the wife's bed.

Similar cases of uncleanness, segregation, and purification are reported from other districts of India.[27] China and Japan show analogous customs, among them the "parturition-house."[28] In Assam there are regular gennas or taboos at child-birth, name-giving, ear-piercing, and other ceremonies. "The genna at birth varies not only according to the sex of the child but in some groups according to the number of children, being always most extended for the first-born. Naturally the poor mother and the child are particularly exposed to the malice of the evil spirits at the hour of birth. The shedding of blood at birth is regarded as dangerous to all who are in the house, and in exogamous communities it must be remembered that the woman, whose blood is shed, is by birth a member of another sub-section."[29] There are no professional midwives among the Palaungs, "child-birth being looked upon as a perfectly natural event, and not as an illness. The presence of an elderly woman, however wise, would only delay the birth and make the delivery more difficult. . . . The husband of a woman in labour may be in the house and even in the same room as his wife if she desires his presence. Other men should not come near the house for eight days from the birth of the child. Their presence would not harm either the mother or the baby, but if they happened to be tattooed with any charms, the efficacy of those charms would pass away. A child is often stationed on the veranda to warn any man, who, not knowing that a child had been born, might enter the house. If by accident a man does enter, he should leave at

27 Risley, *Ethnog. Ind.*, I, 95, 112, 138; Gehring, *Süd-Indien*, 82; Kirtikar, in JASB, I, 401 ff.; Painter, in JASB, II, 149; Fawcett, in JASB, I, 536 ff.

28 Reid, in *Cosmopolitan*, XXVIII, 443; Westermarck, *Marriage*, III, 66, 67; Hearn, *Japan*, 162; Kishimoto, in PSM, XLVI, 212.

29 Hodson, in JAI, XXXVI, 97.

once, go home as quickly as possible, and wash himself all over; if he can immerse a silver charm in the water, so much the better."[30]

In the Malay Archipelago the less civilized natives are much exercised in mind over the perverted appetites of women who are bearing children; the women must not give birth in the house.[31] Among the Jakun, or aboriginal Malayans, is found the greatest development of the custom of "roasting" the new mother over a fire—"an Indo-Chinese practice which is general among the Malays, by whom it is called 'salei-an' "—as well as a system of birth-taboos which regulate the diet and the movements of both parents. "A considerable amount of noise is made by the Orang Laut as soon as a child is born to them. All present unite in shouting and in beating anything which will make a noise, the greater din that it makes the better. The hubbub lasts for about ten minutes at the shortest to half an hour at the longest, and is especially intended to scare away any evil spirits which might otherwise attack either mother or child. As soon, however, as the cord is cut, the demons are thought to have lost their opportunity."[32] To keep off the evil spirits that impede birth, the Filipino husband bars his door, starts a fire, strips himself, and lunges furiously in the air.[33]

The Nauru Islanders used to have parturition-houses.[34] In New Zealand "the mother is not secluded before birth; but she is *tapu* afterwards, until made *noa*, or 'common' by ceremonies."[35] Best[36] states: "On account of the *tapu* pertaining to both birth and death, but few persons were ever born or ever died in a dwelling-house in Maoriland." A special hut was constructed for a woman's occupation during and for some time after the period of parturition. "After all ceremonial performances following the birth of the child had been duly performed, and the party had returned to the village community, then the 'nest house' was destroyed. It was demolished and taken away piecemeal, together with any items, such as floor-mats, etc., used thereat, by a member of the priest class. Timbers, thatch, every item was conveyed by him to some place, probably the *turuma* or latrine, and there burned. The task of this man was to render the spot *noa*, common, or free from *tapu*, that is to take the *tapu* off it." Both mother and child remained in the "nest house" until the cord fell off, which occurred about the eighth day after birth, whereupon the child was taken to the water in order to undergo the ceremony of baptism. Both parents and child were sprinkled with water.

"The majority of Thlinget women suffer very little, and some not at all, when their children are born. They have been known to give birth while sleeping. In former years the universal practice was for the mother to lie outside of the house in a booth, or in the bushes. . . . In an incredibly short time after giving birth to a child, the mother is up and about."[37] Among the Kwakiutl, in the case of a twin-birth, "the afterbirth is well washed, and hung up until it is quite dry. When it is dry, it is folded up and put into the workbox of the mother of the twins. It is kept in the box as a medicine."[38] Such a mother is a fetish-woman. When the time for delivery came, it was the custom among the Winnebago for the woman to occupy a small lodge

---

30 Milne, *Eastern Clan*, 278-279.
31 Pleyte, in *Bijd.*, XLI, 589, 597; Jacobs, *Groot-Atjeh*, I, 117, 146; Crawley, in JAI, XXIV, 433; Nieuwenhuis, *Borneo*, I, 64.
32 Skeat and Blagden, *Malay Penin.*, II, 2, 26.

33 Montero y Vidal, *Filipinas*, I, 58.
34 Brandeis, in *Globus*, XCI, 58.
35 Tregear, in JAI, XIX, 97.
36 In JAI, XLIV, 133, 134, 146 ff.
37 Jones, Thlingets, 46.
38 Boas, in BAE, XXXV, pt. I, 694.

erected especially for her use. "None of her male relatives were permitted to be present and her husband was not even permitted to stay at home. He was supposed to travel continually until the child was born, in the belief that by his movements he would help his wife in her delivery. According to one informant the husband had to hunt game, the supposition being that this procedure on his part would cause his wife to have enough milk for the child. This traveling of the husband was called, therefore, 'Looking-for-milk.' "[39] The Apache woman in confinement went off to a hut by herself, attended by her female relatives.[40] At the birth of a Yuchi child, "its navel cord is ceremonially disposed of, and the father is henceforth prohibited from association with his friends, besides having restrictions for a month against the use of certain foods, manual labor, and hunting."[41]

Among the present-day Arawak and Warrau, "a woman is delivered either in a separate banab (utilized also at the menstrual period by other women) or in a portion of the house screened off." In former times the Surinam Carib woman, as soon as the time of her confinement grew near, retired into the forest. "By hiding in the forest she thus had an opportunity of killing the child or shuffling it away before her man or remaining women in the village noticed anything. . . . As soon as she had taken a little rest she returned with her baby to the house, where she immediately continued on with her work." Many instances are noted where an accouchement has apparently made no difference in the daily routine: "when on the march an Indian is taken with labor, she just steps aside, is delivered, wraps up the baby with the afterbirth and runs in haste after the others. At the first stream that presents itself she washes herself and infant. 'So again, the mother with her first born in her arms, had been in our hut,' says Schomburgk, 'only a few minutes before. Within half an hour she appeared with another baby that she had just given birth to in the bush without any assistance.' " As to the navel-strand, it is either bitten, cut, burned, or tied. "Arawak at the present day use a piece of sharpened arrow reed, but the women tell me that in the olden days a fire stick was employed. This is confirmed by a passage in Bancroft, that they divide the umbilic vessels with a brand of fire, which cauterizes their orifices and renders a ligature unnecessary. Arawak tell me that the mother keeps the cord until her child, as man or woman, dies, when it is buried with the body. . . . Delivery would seem to be followed, sooner or later, by the ablution of both mother and child."[42] Many examples are cited. It was a former custom among the Araucanians not to permit a woman to give birth to a child within the precincts of the village, as it was considered to cause infectious diseases. "She was driven out, on beginning to feel the labour pains, and retired to the banks of the nearest stream or lake. As soon as the child was born the mother stepped into the water and performed the necessary ablutions, returning afterwards to a small hut constructed for the purpose near the *ruca,* which constituted her home. Here she remained a week attended by some compassionate friend. At the end of this time she bathed again, and returned to her own home, where all her relations and friends were assembled to celebrate a feast in honour of the babe."[43]

The notion of uncleanness is familiar from the Old Testament. It applied also to the woman in child-birth, who was unclean seven days if she bore a

39 Radin, in BAE, XXXVII, 126.
40 In HAI, I, 283.
41 Speck, in HAI, II, 1006.

42 Roth, in BAE, XXXVIII, 693-694.
43 Latcham, in JAI, XXXIX, 359-360.

son and two weeks if a girl. Ceremonies accompanied by offerings were prescribed for her purification.[44] On account of her impurity the child-bearing
Greek woman was kept from the temple, and the house was purified.[45] Among
the Zoroastrians, the mother at child-birth was unclean in spite of the logic of
the religion, according to which she should be pure because she had increased
life. "The strength of old instincts overcame the drift of new principles;" that
is to say, the mores were too strong for the new faith. A woman who bears a
dead child is a grave and must be ritually purified as such. Only to save her
from death may she drink water, which she would defile, and if it is given to
her she must undergo a penalty. These views go back to the notion that she
has been near. death and has had the death-fiend in her. A great fire is lighted
to drive off the demons.[46] The Iranian woman who had given birth to a child
was regarded as unclean for forty-one days and was given food and drink in
the precautionary manner employed in the case of menstruating women. Later
she purified herself with cow's urine and water, put on a new dress, and was
then clean.[47]

§409. Solicitude for Posterity.

Observances after Birth. The Hottentots use fat and other substances to make
the child supple and strong; if it is a boy they sacrifice oxen and if a girl sheep
or nothing.[1] During the period of the Kaffir mother's seclusion, a lunar month,
"wise women sprinkle the child daily with a decoction of herbs, and repeat
certain rhymes, mostly utterly meaningless, which are supposed to insure natural development and physical health. Then there is a fire of aromatic tomboti
wood kindled at intervals on the floor, and the child is passed and re-passed
through the smoke. This insures mental vigor, wisdom, valor, strategy, and
eloquence of speech. The spirit of fire escapes the smoke as it ascends, and
this the child receives and retains, providing the smoking process is duly performed by qualified persons."[2] "When the little one is several months old, the
father first takes official notice of it by having a ceremony carried out by which
it is solemnly taken into the family." He plucks out of a cow's tail a bunch of
long hairs which the mother knots together in a secret manner and fastens
about the child's neck. The cow in question may not be sold but is given with
the girl-child when she is married. It does not become the property of the
bridegroom. This custom is believed to exorcise all future ills that may befall
the child.[3]

On the Gold Coast the infant is subjected to certain fetish-preparations to
fortify him against all kinds of evil.[4] In this region, as in a number of others,
the living child of a woman who dies in parturition is buried with her.[5] In
southern Cameroons it is customary to lay the child before the door of the
house and then to apply a medicine in streaks of red to the child, to the threshold and door-frame, and to the soles of those who have carried the child. The
procedure is repeated at all the doors of the village.[6] Anointing the child with

44 Levit., XII ; XV, 19-33.
45 Maurer, *Vkde.*, 28.
46 Müller, *Sacred Books* (Zend-Avesta), I,
xcii.
47 Spiegel, *Eran. Alterth.*, III, 699.
1 Ratzel, *Vkde.*, I, 104.

2 Macdonald, *S. Afr.*, in JAI, XIX, 266.
3 Fritsch, *Eingeb. S. Afr.*, 108.
4 Kingsley, *W. Afr. Studies*, 173, 174.
5 Ellis, *Tshi*, 234.
6 Conradt, in *Globus*, LXXXI, 337.

the blood of a sacrificed fowl is practiced in the Congo Basin.[7] As long as the Ba-Yaka child is "in arms" (about a year), both it and the father must abstain from washing.[8]

In Uganda the mother is subjected to the common roasting by the fire and then the priest presents the child to the ancestral spirits, asking for it long life, riches, and, above all, that it may be a faithful believer in the tribal and ancestral spirits. He accompanies each special request by spitting on the child's body and pinching it all over. For his services he gets one hundred and eight cowrie-shells, nine for each of the child's arms and ninety for the body. Birth of twins is lucky and "is celebrated by an obscene dance which, however, is only lewd in its stereotyped gestures," the latter being doubtless survivalistic. The dried navel-cord of princes is set with pearls and hung up on a post, with a man to watch it.[9] Near Lake Victoria the hair of a child nine days old is shaved off the body, to be preserved in a box. Despite the desire for children, if any of the numerous portents and omens that are watched for at the birth of a child are bad, it is strangled; also if its upper teeth come first.[10] Among the Hovas if a child is born out of due time, it is put in the opening of the cattle-pen and the cattle driven over it. If it escapes unharmed, it is allowed to live. The normal child is twice passed over the fire.[11] The Kabyles cause several drops of the blood of a sacrificial victim to fall on the child's face which "ought to repel evil influences and assure the child a prosperous future."[12]

The newly born among the Ostyaks are rubbed with snow or laid directly in it. Exposure to the sun's rays for several days, after licking by the mother, is practised in Tibet.[13] The Hindu child is received on a tray of bamboo-chips used for winnowing grain and a drop of honey is put into its mouth even before it receives its first bath. Its horoscope is cast and an evil spirit is propitiated which would otherwise be malicious.[14] Rose[15] says with reference to the ceremonies after birth in the Punjab, that "it is as difficult to distinguish between the religious and social observances as it is to say what usages are based on magic and what on the first glimmerings of medical skill. Nevertheless, under much that is barbarous and puerile there are traces of more rational ideas regarding cleanliness, and even a kind of primitive anticipation of antiseptic treatment. One important point to note is that the observances are far less elaborate in the case of a girl child, and this idea, that the birth of a girl is a misfortune, re-acts injuriously on the mother, less care being bestowed upon her, and every observance being hurried over and many stinted, if the child is not a boy. Thus in Râwalpindî the mother of a son is carefully tended for forty days, but if the child is a girl for only twenty-one."

In old Japan "the infant is not allowed the breast for nearly three days and is dosed often with the horrible decoction used for staining the teeth, composed of water that has become putrid in an old teapot in which were a quantity of old rusty nails."[16] Malay children born on an unlucky day are buried alive,[17] such practice being strong evidence of the fear of the aleatory element, for

7 Clozel, in PSM, XLIX, 676; Brunache, *Cent. Afr.*, 68.
8 Torday and Joyce, in JAI, XXXVI, 46.
9 Johnston, *Uganda*, II, 586-587, 748; Stuhlmann, *Mit Emin*, 184.
10 Dale, reported in PSM, L, 100.
11 Ratzel, *Vkde.*, II, 517; Gomme, *Village Life*, 108.

12 Hanoteau et Letourneux, *Kabylie*, II, 209, 210-211.
13 Kondratowitsch, in *Globus*, LXXIV, 290; Rockhill, in USNM, 1893, 724.
14 Kirtikar, in JASB, I, 398.
15 In JAI, XXXVII, 226.
16 Pfoundes, in JAI, XII, 223.
17 Ratzel, *Vkde.*, II, 455.

children are much desired. It is customary in parts of Borneo to cut the navel-cord with a sword that may never be sold; the ears are pierced as soon as the child is bathed.[18] The theory of the Sea Dyaks seems to accord more concern to the mother. If she died in consequence of delivery, "the child should pay the penalty (i) as being the cause of the mother's death, (ii) because no one remained to nurse and care for it." "No woman would dare to suckle such an orphan lest it should bring misfortune upon her own children."[19] To the Dyaks, ghosts are right at hand to plague the child, so that it cries a great deal. A cock is sacrificed to an evil female spirit that is particularly dangerous to young children.[20] The Macassars sprinkle colored rice upon the body of the woman and try to get a cock and a hen to pick it off, in order to remove all disasters and adversity. If they will not do that, there is doubt about the child living long.[21] The peoples of Malacca have hit upon the practice, rational in its results, of plugging the nostrils for a short time with cloth "to cause the child to cry."[22]

After the Maori child is baptised, "the priest casts the six pieces of grass or leaves into the stream, and the movements of these are carefully watched. Should they drift away without scattering or separating much, the fact is hailed with pleasure, it being a good omen for the child's future, he will be healthy, vigorous, clever, and will attain manhood. But should the pieces separate, and drift apart, the omen is a bad one for the child." Best[23] states that the main idea of the religious ceremonies after birth is "to endow the child with *mana atua,* supernatural power or attributes, such as the gods possess, the divine powers that emanated from Io, as also with intellectuality."

Among the Hopi Indians, "ashes or sacred meal are rubbed on the newborn babe."[24] "The Acoma mother lies in for four days. During this time an ear of corn is placed next to the child. On the fourth morning, according to one informant, the 'medicine-man' and his wife are sent for. They arrive with the 'medicine-water' some time before dawn. The 'medicine-man' prays and sings four or five songs. He then takes the child out the east side of the mesa to show it at sunrise to the sun. The child's mother goes along and during the ceremonial sprinkles meal. It is the 'medicine-man' who proposes a name for the child. If his suggestion is not acceptable, any relative may name the child."[25] Both Sia and Zuñi have the superstition that "should one suffering from a snake-bite look upon a woman furnishing nourishment for an infant, death would be the result."[26] Among the latter people, "if the cord of the new-born infant 'runs,' it is because, it is believed, some one who has been bitten by a snake has been in the room. That person must be found and must then proceed to wave some ashes four times around the heads of mother and child—otherwise the child will die."[27]

"Until her youngster is able to walk well, the Arawak mother on the Pomeroon must eat neither deer, turtle, nor iguana, animals which, for some days after birth, creep or crawl very slowly, in contradistinction, for instance, from the bush-hog, that will start to run directly it has littered. The idea is that by eating such flesh the mother will cause her infant to walk too slowly. On

18 Nieuwenhuis, *Borneo,* I, 61, 62.
19 Roth, *Sarawak,* I, 100; Gomes, *Sea Dyaks,* 100, 101.
20 Grabowsky, in *Globus,* LXXII, 270, 272.
21 Pleyte, in *Bijd.,* XLI, 579.
22 Stevens, in *Ztsft. f. Eth.,* XXVIII, 189.

23 In JAI, XLIV, 153-154, 157.
24 Mooney, in HAI, I, 265.
25 Parsons, in AA, XX, 174-175.
26 Stevenson, in BAE, XI, 87.
27 Parsons, in AA, XVIII, 248-249.

the islands, the Carib mother abstained from female crabs, which would give the child stomachache, while the father had to avoid certain animals for fear of the youngster participating in their natural faults. If a father ate turtle, the child would be heavy, and have no brains; if he ate a parrot, the child would have a parrot nose; if a crab, the consequence would be long legs."[28] In Eastern Ecuador "custom requires that after a child is born the parents shall fast and observe other rules of abstinence for a couple of years, or until the child is named. This is due to the idea that something of the souls or essence of the parents inheres in the child, so that all three in one way form a single organism, a single personality."[29]

Weaning.[30] "Long after our children are weaned," said Lubbock,[31] "milk remains an important and necessary part of their food. We supply this want with cow's milk; but among people who have no domesticated animals this cannot, of course, be done, and consequently the children are not weaned until they are two, three, or even four years old, during all which period the husband and wife generally remain apart." Ethnographical evidence on this point, as well as on infant-feeding, follows.

Among the Southern Massim "the child is usually suckled until a number of teeth have appeared, but before this he is given taro, yam or banana, which has been first masticated by his mother."[32] The Bushwomen of Africa nurse their children long, but begin from an early date to feed them with roots and meat which they chew for them. The children are taught to chew tobacco very young.[33] According to a missionary in northern Rhodesia babies are fed on an alcoholic drink similar to beer and are taught to smoke a pipe at the age of two; these practices are said to account in large part for the high rate of mortality.[34] The Baganda child is nursed for two years and then fed with cow's milk or bananas.[35] When the Bawenda child is five years old the medicine-man comes to wean it; he gives it some "medicine" to make it forget its mother's breast.[36] In British Central Africa the child is suckled for two or three years. Suckling may be prolonged for four years in the belief that pregnancy is thus avoided. Mortality is high because of improper feeding, big lumps of porridge being thrust in the infant's mouth when a few months old; diarrhœa and malaria are common.[37] There are no wet-nurses among the Dinkas; if the mother is unable to nurse her child, it is fed on goat's or cow's milk.[38] Among the Nigerian head-hunters, "if the child lives the mother will suckle it for two to three years [in some cases up to five years] and during this time she will not have connection with her husband for fear of injuring it. If, however, she did lapse and conceive again within this time she would at once wean her child. . . . There is apparently no artificial feeding, and as women continue lactation so long there is never any difficulty in finding a wet nurse."[39]

Among the Sema Nagas "children are suckled for from one to three years, and it is not unusual to see a Sema mother suckling two children who may have more than a year's difference between them in the matter of age."[40] Nivedita[41]

---

28 Roth, in BAE, XXX, 320.
29 Karsten, "Jibaro," in BAE, Bull. LXXIX, 12.
30 §30, of the text.
31 *Origin of Civ.*, 74-75.
32 Seligmann, *Melanesians*, 490.
33 Ratzel, *Vkde.*, I, 72.
34 Fell, in N. Y. *Times*, April 29, 1923.

35 Roscoe, in JAI, XXXII, 31.
36 Gottschling, in JAI, XXXV, 371.
37 Stannus, in JAI, XL, 311, 312.
38 Cummins, in JAI, XXXIV, 151.
39 Tremearne, in JAI, XLII, 174.
40 Hutton, *Sema Nagas*, 234.
41 *Indian Life*, 22.

thinks that the tenderness of parents and the veneration of children, which feelings are deep-rooted among the Hindus, are to be explained by the fact that every child is a nursling for its first two years of life. The food of the Benua children of the Malay Peninsula was eked out with hog's grease from about the third or fourth day of their existence. According to Skeat and Blagden,[42] "this might be owing to the habit of not weaning children till they were two, three, or even sometimes four years of age. It was no uncommon spectacle," the authors add, "to see an infant of a few weeks and a fat nursling of two years at the breast together." A Palaung mother nurses her child as long as she can possibly do so, but "many babies die because mothers cannot continue to suckle them, and it is difficult to get any cow's milk. As Palaungs neither drink milk nor know how to milk cows—cattle being kept solely as beasts of burden—the milk goes to the calves. . . . A Palaung baby is not brought up on its mother's milk alone. When it is a few days old, its mother takes a small quantity of well-cooked rice that has been steamed, not boiled—about half an ounce to begin with—which she chews thoroughly, until it has become a kind of smooth pap. This she puts direct from her mouth into that of the baby."[43] In Samoa, "for the first three days the infant was fed with the juice of the chewed kernel of the cocoanut, pressed through a piece of native cloth, and dropped into the mouth." The juice of the sugar-cane was also given to infants. "Many fell victims to this improper treatment. At a very early period the child was fed, and sometimes weaned altogether at four months. This was another fruitful source of mortality among children."[44]

Eskimo women suckle their children for three or four years and sporadically long thereafter; there is no soft food available and if the mother dies the child dies also. The child is offered blood at an early age.[45] The Indians do not wholly wean their infants till they are two, three, or even four years old. The reasons assigned for this protraction are that "it is good for the infant," or "it makes the child strong and healthy," or "it wants it," or "does not want to give up." The period is three years among the Apache; Chichimec women nursed up to six or seven years. In British Guiana the period is three or four years and two children of different ages may be nursing at the same time; the women even suckle certain domestic animals.[46] "The practice of keeping infants at the breast to a comparatively advanced age is universal. The Warrau mother will suckle her offspring up to 3 and 4 years of age. Sometimes she will have one at each breast. Both among the Arekuna and Makusi the child is also given the breast up to the third or fourth year, and if a new baby appears the previous one will be handed over to the grandmother, who carries out the mother's duties with it. This has been observed among the oldest of Indian women. It is also the old lady's business to bring up the young mammals found by the father or son. When Schomburgk expressed surprise at these occurrences, he was informed that the women practice a means whereby the milk is retained to extreme old age."[47] Among the Araucanians "a man does

42 *Malay Penin.*, II, 19.
43 Milne, *Eastern Clan*, 36.
44 Turner, *Samoa*, 80-81.
45 Cranz, *Grönland*, 196; Nansen, *Esk. Life*, 152; Reclus, *Prim. Folk*, 37; Holm, *Ethnol. Skizze*, 49-50; Murdoch, in BAE, IX, 415.

46 Hrdlička, in BAE, Bull. XXXIV, 76; Reclus, *Prim. Folk*, 131; Nadaillac, *Preh. Amer.*, 281; Schomburgk, *Brit.-Guiana*, I, 166-167; Spix u. Martius, *Brasilien*, 1225.
47 Roth, in BAE, XXXVIII, 697.

not cohabit with his wife after childbirth till the child is weaned, which does not take place till it has cut all its teeth."[48]

The Egyptian mother nursed her infant three years; under Mohammedan influence the period ran into the fourth year, though the Koran prescribes its continuance only into the second. Such prolongation was to protect against the influence of the summer-heat.[49] In Hungary and elsewhere nursing may be protracted for three to four years, though the rule for Hungarian and German women is ten to twelve months. Exceptional cases show six or seven years.[50]

Cases similar to that of the Guiana Indians, where the grandmother takes over the function of nurse, seeming quite able to do so, are not infrequent in ethnography; and Fritsch and Livingstone think there is evidence, belonging to abnormal physiology, that the husband has been known to exhibit this power.[51]

Desire for Children; Adoption. "The practice of adopting the children of others is very frequent in the Banks Islands and is accompanied by many interesting features. Of these features the most important is that a man who fulfils certain conditions [such as making the necessary payment to the midwife] may take the child of another in spite of the unwillingness of the parents to part with their offspring. The true parents may be unable to keep their own child if others want it and it is interesting in this connection that the word for adoption . . . seems to have primarily the meaning of 'snatch.' . . . It seemed clear that the real father could recover his child from the adopting parents by making certain payments, but the conditions were such that this was rarely possible. The father would have to repay all money which had been expended by the adopting father on behalf of the child with cent per cent interest. . . . The fact of his real parentage is carefully kept from the adopted child and any approach of the real father to his child is resented on account of the fear that the true parentage may be revealed. . . . The only other Banks island from which I obtained an account was Merlav. Here a man who wishes to adopt a child about to be born waits till he hears of the birth and then runs quickly to plant the leaf of a cycas tree in front of the door. The man who first plants a leaf is the father of the child. . . . Several motives were given for the practice of adoption. Childless persons have no honour and may be the object of ridicule because they have no one to call or command. . . . It was said also that adoption is designed to prevent property passing out of the family; the more children there are in the family the less is the risk of this."[52] Adoption is not uncommon among the Koita. "Girls are more commonly adopted than boys, because their fathers do not often care to part with the latter. Usually the adopter is a great friend of the father of the adopted child, and the latter asks the former to help him to feed one of his children. It seems that such a request is never refused; the adopted child assumes its adopter's *iduhu* [clan], calls him father, and if a girl, her adopted father receives her marriage-price."[53]

Rivers[54] says that the custom of adoption of children is not practised by the

48 Latcham, in JAI, XXXIX, 360.
49 Maspero, *Hist. Anc.*, II, 502; Erman, *Aegypten*, I, 224; Pischon, *Islam*, 17, 110.
50 Temesváry, *Geburtshilfe*, 113-114.
51 Jacobs, *Groot-Atjeh*, I, 159; Stannus, in JAI, XL, 311; Von den Steinen, *Zent. Bras.*, 501; Von Martius, *Beiträge*, I, 622, 623; Fritsch, *Eingeb. S.-Afr.*, 407; Livingstone, *Mission. Travels*, 140-141.
52 Rivers, *Melan. Soc.*, I, 50-55.
53 Seligmann, *Melanesians*, 70.
54 Todas, 549.

Todas. "They denied its existence emphatically, and I met with no instance which led me to suspect its presence in compiling the genealogies. If a child is left an orphan, it is looked after by the people of its clan, but it is always clearly recognised that the child retains the father's property." He adds a detail which would seem to be highly exceptional: "There is, so far as I could ascertain, no religious custom which makes it necessary that a man should have children. The duties of a child at the funeral ceremonies can quite well be performed by some other member of the clan."

The aim of marriage among the ancient Hindus was the perpetuation and increase of one's own stock; "this is possible only through male descendants. On sons rested the hope of the house; abundant male descendants gave power and reputation, and were an ornament. . . . Never do we find in the Vedic songs the wish for a daughter; her birth was publicly viewed with displeasure." The custom of exposing daughters was not very widespread, but there was a definite persuasion that "to have daughters is a woe."[55] It is stated that in China only children out of families who bear the same family-name may be adopted, as otherwise, according to the Chinese, the difference between families would soon cease to exist. The levirate, thinks Von Mollendorff[56] can never be of the same importance with the Chinese as with other people, that is, to keep the family-property together, as posthumous adoption, which the Chinese substitute for it, fully meets the object. "The Palaungs, like all Eastern races, are very anxious to have children. Girls as well as boys are welcome, and infanticide is unknown. Still, on the whole, boy-babies are preferred. When boys grow up they are stronger to help their parents in the work of the tea gardens or in the cutting down of jungle trees; also the son may continue to live at home after he marries, but the girls, when they marry, must go to a new home and must give their help first to the husband's father and mother. . . . After many incarnations a spirit that has acquired much merit may inhabit the body of a woman who will live to be very old, and who will lead such a good life that when her spirit is re-born again in a human body it may be in that of a baby-boy." Palaungs think that it is better to have a child who lives only a short time than to have no child. "The entrance of the kar-bu [spirit] into the foetus insures that the child will be born with a normal human spirit; otherwise it might be still-born (without a kar-bu), or be an idiot (having only a fragmentary kar-bu)."[57]

The object of a certain Spartan treatment which a married couple underwent in the Gilbert Islands was to encourage them to beget a child quickly. "When at last the girl became pregnant they were allowed to don clothes and to live in the communal dwelling of the husband's family." Adoption was also a practice here. "The object of the Gilbertese father in giving his son in adoption to an elder of his family was to provide for his aged relation a companionship and support which he, as a busy breadwinner, had no leisure to afford. It was a very sensible arrangement, calculated to promote high reverence in the young for the old and responsible for a great family solidarity."[58]

"Children are very much desired by Thlinget parents. A barren wife is not enviable. Parents who are so unfortunate as to have no children sometimes adopt them. . . . Boys are, on the whole, more desirable than girls, because

55 Zimmer, Altind. Leben, 318, 320.   57 Milne, Eastern Clan, 25-26, 338.
56 Family Law of Chinese, 17, 53-54.   58 Grimble, in JAI, LI, 32, 38.

a man is esteemed of more worth than a woman."[59] With the Winnebago Indians, "when a child dies, then the father mourns for many years, and if during that time he happens to meet a child that resembles his dead child he asks to be allowed to adopt him. The parents of the child can hardly object to such a request." The author is of the opinion that "quite a number of parents believe that such a person is really their reincarnated child."[60]

Adoption occurred among the ancient Babylonians and was effected by a formal transfer of the child by the parents.[61] The Egyptians had great desire for children and took much joy in them.[62] The aim of marriage among the Iranians was the begetting of progeny which was regarded as a possession, as a part of property. According to Strabo, the king rewarded those who had begotten the most sons. A much higher value was laid on boys than on girls, and on healthy children in contrast with defective; the latter were often exposed. "The crippled and sickly, who remained alive, were in Persia as in Armenia left to themselves and led a miserable existence; in Armenia it was a chief service of Christianity that it lightened the lot of these unfortunates."[63] Boys were much preferred in Arabia, and "it went so far with the Arabs that quite commonly the barbarous usage prevailed of getting rid of newly born daughters, whose rearing threatened to become inconvenient, by simply burying them alive."[64] The sentiment is expressed in the plays of Euripides[65] that children are the greatest bliss but cause their parents much worry.

Sale of Children. In 1792 the British government in India issued a proclamation against dealing in slaves, "but the proclamation was not to prevent the privileged superior castes from purchasing the children of famine-stricken parents, on condition that the parents might re-purchase their children on the advent of better times."[66] Among the Dyaks "every pawn-holder has the right to sell his pawns, while every free Dyak has the right to trade with his children."[67] About 200 B.C. the founder of the Han Dynasty in China allowed the poor to sell their children; to this Chinese historians trace the institution of slavery.[68] Though now prohibited by law, the sale of children still exists. Exception seems to be virtually allowed to families permanently distressed by famine or other causes, and many accordingly sell their children from mere stress of poverty; boys are seldom parted with, but slave-girls abound, there being scarcely a respectable family without one or more of them. "At Peking a healthy girl under twelve years brings from thirty to fifty taels, rising to two hundred and fifty or three hundred for one of seventeen to eighteen years old." Among the more opulent families, a number of girls are attached to each child as personal attendants and playmates, and these are often chosen by the future husbands of the young ladies as concubines. Boys once enslaved appear to continue in a state of bondage, their children becoming the property of their masters; girls become free upon marriage, as they follow the fortunes of their husbands, whosoever they be.[69] Somewhat aligned to the sale of children is the geisha-system in Japan, which is roughly as follows. "Parents of girls whom

59 Jones, *Thlingets*, 45.
60 Radin, in BAE, XXXVII, 139, and note.
61 Kohler and Peiser, *Babylon. Rechts-leben*, I, 9.
62 Erman, *Aegypten*, 221.
63 Spiegel, *Eran. Alterth.*, III, 681, 682; Strabo, *Geog.*, XV, 733.
64 Müller, *Islam*, I, 48.

65 *Ion*, 472 ff.; *Medea*, 1090 ff.
66 Thurston, *S. India*, 443.
67 Perelaer, *Dajaks*, 160.
68 Cognetti de Martiis, *Forme Prim.*, 273.
69 Medhurst, in *Trans. Roy. As. Soc.*, pt. IV, 17-18; Williams, *Middle Kingdom*, I, 413 (quoted). A tael is about ten-sevenths of a Mexican silver dollar.

they feel unable to maintain present them, when children of from 7 to 12, to the masters of geisha training houses. These masters select the comeliest and brightest and those having a natural musical talent and practically adopt them. The parents enter into contracts that the girls shall remain with their master and be subject to all his commands until such time as they shall, from their earnings as entertainers, have repaid all the cost of their education in music, dancing, flower arrangement, color matching, deportment, table etiquette, and conversation. . . . Until they have earned their way out, they are practically slaves." Such was the rule until 1922, when the higher court at Osaka rendered a decision that no girl might be bound by a contract made without her consent and knowledge and enforced against her will.[70]

With certain Indians, "the practice of selling children seemed to have been common."[71] Among the slaves of the Aztecs were children sold by their parents.[72] "Among the Makusi a man may sell his children, in spite of the bitterest tears of the mother, to a married couple who have none. The price is the same as that demanded for a dog, i.e., a gun, ax, or something similar, but the buyer has in addition to give some little things, e.g., beads, to the relatives, who report themselves in considerable number to the new father."[73] Botocudo fathers, "attracted by a good trade," have often sold their children to Brazilians.[74] Among the laws and ordinances mentioned in Exodus occurs the following: "And if a man sell his daughter to be a maidservant, she shall not go out as the menservants do. If she please not her master, who hath betrothed her to himself, then shall he let her be redeemed: to sell her unto a strange nation he shall have no power, seeing he hath dealt deceitfully with her."[75]

§410. Treatment of Children.

In South Australia "all afflicted, infirm, diseased, imbecile, blind, deaf, or otherwise afflicted, are *never* put away. On the contrary, the greatest sympathy is shown, while the greatest care and attention is paid the infirm and sick."[1] Among the Southern Massim, "both sexes make affectionate and indeed over-indulgent parents, while the children brought up under these conditions make as a rule excellent sons, daughters and even relations-in-law, and no old man or old woman—too old and worn to work—is neglected by his or her children or grandchildren, including in this term, as the native does, nephews and nieces on the maternal side." The author[2] reports the same for the Koita—"the men especially often seeming absurdly indulgent to their children who are never ill-treated nor even punished. In their turn the children grow up imbued with kindliness and consideration for their elders, and especially for the old men. Although the men make undemonstrative husbands, wives are usually well treated." On the D'Entrecasteaux Islands, "children do very little work before they are about twelve years of age. A girl as soon as she is big enough will carry water, and peel the yams and help to sweep the hamlet clean each day, but she lends no aid to her parents in the gardens. The lads do even less: they play and fish, and follow the men about, but no work is expected of them."[3]

In the Upper Congo, "the father has the right to kill his own child, and

70 *Social Hygiene Bull.*, IX, No. 11.
71 Henshaw and Hodge, in HAI, I, 330.
72 Cognetti de Martiis, *Forme Prim.*, 355.
73 Roth, in BAE, XXXVIII, 599.
74 Von Martius, *Beiträge*, I, 322, 643.

75 Exod., XXI, 7-8.
1 "Miscell.," in JAI, XXIV, 175.
2 Seligmann, *Melanesians*, 134, 566.
3 Jenness and Ballentyne, *D'Entrecasteaux*, 92.

although the act may be strongly condemned by neighbours, they have no power to punish him even though it may be a clear case of murder." Weeks,[4] who lived among them for many years, says: "I may say that I never heard of a father killing his child . . . but there were many cases of a father pawning his children for debt, and occasionally selling them." Among the Ba-Yaka, "the father may neither kill his child nor sell it as a slave, and, as a matter of fact, men seem to be very fond of their children, indeed, in most villages the care of the children seems to be undertaken by the men."[5] Child-birth out of wedlock is no cause of reproach among the tribes of British Central Africa; the child belongs to the mother.[6] When Coudenhove[7] once asked a Yao why black babies make so little noise compared with white ones, the latter replied: "The European father teaches his child to make plenty noise and to break everything it touches, because, if it does not, he thinks it is ill." The author comments: "The placidity and the contentment of native as compared with European babies is due, no doubt, to their close companionship with their mother, from whom they are as inseparable, *mutatis mutandis,* as little kangaroos from theirs. During the first years of their life, they spend nearly all their time snugly and comfortably berthed in the *kuveleka,* the pouch formed by the cloth slung over their mother's back. If they want to sleep, they sleep; when they are awake, there is always something interesting to see, or to hear, by peeping round the corner. The larder is always full, the table always laid, the perambulator always ready to start; they are kept warm by the best and most natural of warming-pans." It is stated of the Mkamba that "towards his children he is remarkably kind and tender." Throughout East Africa no difference is made between legitimate and illegitimate children, and "children of slave women married to the father have equal rights with freeborn children."[8]

"Children in the Maori commune are petted and given a great deal of liberty by their parents. A father may often be seen nursing his *potiki* or youngest child for hours, carrying it about with him on his back in his shawl or blanket. Young girls were allowed to do pretty well as they pleased, and they and the boys enjoyed full liberty in sexual matters, unless indeed a girl was a *puhi,* like the *taupo* or village maid of Samoa, or was *tapui'd* or betrothed to some young chief."[9] In Samoa, children born outside of marriage were those of a mother who, while living with her family got into sex-relations secretly with a man, without being led into his house as spouse. Such children could inherit only if taken by the father into his family—that is, recognized as his offspring. Then they would have rights equal to those of legitimate children.[10] "Love of family is a strong trait in their character," writes Thomson[11] of the Easter Islanders; "children are fondly cared for, and the desire for offspring is general." On the Island of Yap, "among the several members of the family there reigned deep affection, especially of parents toward children. The children in their early years were treated carefully and especially mildly; they were allowed the greatest freedom and were punished scarcely so as to give pain."[12]

4 In JAI, XXXIX, 444.
5 Torday and Joyce, in JAI, XXXVI, 45-46.
6 Stannus, in JAI, XL, 312.
7 In *Atl. Mo.,* CXXXII, 191-192.

8 Dundas, C., in JAI, XLIII, 490; and LI, 270.
9 Cowan, *Maoris,* 146.
10 Von Bülow, in *Globus,* LXXIII, 186.
11 In *Smithson. Rep.,* 1889, 466.
12 Senfft, in *Globus,* CXI, 142.

Jones[13] writes of the Tlinkits: "Children are so beloved by their parents that they are indulged to their detriment. They are rarely punished. When they are it is because the parent has been grievously aggravated by them, and then punishment is brutally administered. The wishes of children are usually gratified to the extent of the parental ability. They are usually allowed to have their own way, and little or no parental restraint is thrown about them. This is due not so much to laxness as to misdirected parental love. It is considered a mark of their love to let their children have what they demand and do as they please." On the other hand, "children born out of wedlock, especially illegitimate half-breeds, are more or less despised. In earlier times they were put to death immediately after birth." The child among the Cheyenne Indians was carefully trained, almost wholly by advice and counsel; no whipping occurred. As a sign of affection, the child's ears were pierced, actually or ceremonially (by proxy); wealthy people had images and pierced the child's ears on them even before birth, paying a fee to the one doing it.[14] "In the Omaha family the children bore an important part; they were greatly desired and loved. . . . Careful parents, particularly those who belonged to the better class, took great pains in the training of their children. They were taught to treat their elders with respect, to be particular in the use of the proper terms of relationship, to be peaceable with one another, and to obey their parents. Whipping was uncommon and yet there were almost no quarreling and little downright disobedience. Much attention was given to inculcating a grammatical use of the language and the proper pronunciation of the words. There was no 'baby talk.' Politeness was early instilled. No child would think of interrupting an elder who was speaking, of pestering anyone with questions, of taking anything belonging to an older person without permission, or of staring at anyone, particularly a stranger."[15] It is said in general of the Indians of the United States: "Both parents alike were entirely devoted to their children, and bestowed upon them the fullest expression of affection and solicitude. The relation of parent to child brings out all the highest traits of Indian character."[16]

The children of the Guiana Indians are almost never corrected, yet show considerable respect for their parents. Little regular attention is paid to their education; they learn from seeing and doing, the boys going with the men and the girls with the women.[17] "Punishments, like chastisings in general, the Indian did not know; for only the dog, not the Makusi, needs blows."[18] Of the same group it is said: "Up to the time when the child can trust himself to his own feet, his mother is seldom seen without him; he is up to then an integral part of her ego. Despite this tender love, she is not observed kissing him; no caressing words are heard." At puberty the boy becomes a stranger to his mother.[19] Visitors have mentioned love of children as the only noble feeling of which the Fuegians are capable, but it is said to disappear as the children grow older.[20]

---

13 *Thlingets*, 46-47, 45.
14 Grinnell, *Cheyenne*, I, 103, 104, 105, 106.
15 Fletcher and LaFlesche, in BAE, XXVII, 327-331.
16 Mooney, in HAI, I, 265.

17 Roth, in BAE, XXXVIII, §§912, 914, 915.
18 Schomburgk, *Brit.-Guiana*, II, 315.
19 Von Martius, *Beiträge*, I, 643.
20 Ratzel, *Vkde.*, II, 677.

§414. Primitive Family-Organization.

The Joint-Family. In British New Guinea a village is often comprised of one house several hundred feet in length. The longest that Chalmers[1] measured was 692 feet long. "These *darimo* (large houses) are divided into stalls say 12 feet long and 8 feet broad, and run down each side, leaving, in the centre, a fine broad path where feasting and dancing take place." In Papua, "all the villages are built on the same principle—a great house (that at Mida, or Kubu, is about 200 feet long and 40 feet wide) with a central hall, which runs the entire length of the house and is reserved for the use of the men; on either side are the walled-off private apartments. These consist of three storeys."[2] "The basis of the whole social structure on Goodenough [D'Entrecasteaux Islands] is the family, which consists, as with us, of a man, his wife, and their descendants. The son, as soon as he reaches manhood, seeks a wife in another hamlet and leads her away to his own; the daughter, with rare exceptions, removes to the hamlet of her husband. Each hamlet, therefore, consists of a number of families closely connected with one another by ties of kinship. One man, the recognized head of the related families, is likewise the head man, *kauvea,* of the hamlet. These families garden in the same place, hunt and fish together, participate in every rite and ceremony that affects one of their number, rejoice together in the common feast, and stand with united front against private and public foe . . . The bond which at bottom unites the hamlets of a district is largely one of common interest, though it is always vastly strengthened by intermarriage and by the possession of a common dialect."[3]

In the *thadoukeli boukhkham* or joint-house of the Kabyles, "the members of a family contribute to the society all their property (of which only the enjoyment is common), their work and their industry. The oldest man, if he is sufficiently intelligent, is charged with administration. It is he who buys and sells, leases the land, presides at the harvest or the gathering of the fruits, goes to market, pays and receives. However, his power is not limitless, and the family must be consulted every time when it is a question of an important transaction, notably the sale or purchase of real estate. It is the community which furnishes each of the members with the instruments of work, a musket, and the capital required for the trade he undertakes or for conducting the industry to which he wishes to devote himself. Each is bound to devote his work to the community and to turn into the hands of the chief of the family all his salary or profits. Should he divert a farthing of it he would be forced to make restitution and would be dishonored by his fellow-citizens and expelled by the family, if the case should appear very serious. The immovables which come to one of the associates by gift or bequest remain his particular property, but the enjoyment of them is acquired by the family. . . . In the case of movables the men have as their private property only their clothes. The women possess only their wearing-apparel and the jewels which they received the day of their marriage. Fancy clothes and ornaments purchased at the expense of all, and with which they adorn themselves on festive days, are common property. When the family is not very numerous, the food is prepared by each of the women in turn. This one gives to each his share of cous-cous [a favorite dish], and the head of the family apportions the meat. If the members of the associa-

1 In JAI, XXXIII, 118.   3 Jenness and Ballentyne, *D'Entrecasteaux*,
2 Haddon, in JAI, XLVI, 336.   63-64.

tion are too numerous for the repast to be taken in common, they divide each month the dry provisions and the oil needed for each fire. Meat is distributed, without being prepared, every time animals are slaughtered or when the head of the family buys meat in the market. The strictest equality must preside over these apportionments. Each of the members of the family has the right to a share; the infant at the breast counts as one. The direction of the household is confided to the oldest woman, if she is judged capable; if not, the family chooses another, or each of the women receives for one day the keys and the domestic management. The head of the family must show a rigorous impartiality. . . . Each of the [male] members has the right to correct the women and all the children. When the association breaks up, the property, movables and immovables, acquired during the existence of the community, is not divided equally, but in proportion to the hereditary rights and the contributions of each. The only exception is the yearly provisions: grain, oil, and commodities of all kinds. The death of one of the associates does not dissolve the community. If his heirs do not wish to remain with the family, just as in the case where one of the members wishes to retire, their share is calculated and delivered to them, and the community almost always continues. The duration of the *thadoukeli boukhkham* is never fixed in advance; in the large families the association exists for several generations, and this persistence in communal life is one of their best titles to the estimation of their fellow-citizens."[4] Wilken[5] cites a number of cases where Malays, Dyaks, and others have big houses for related stocks, containing two hundred and fifty to three hundred persons. Communal long-houses are also found among the Indians of British Columbia. "These houses do not appear to have been as long generally as among the Delta tribes, where continuous structures of from 100 to 200 yards were not uncommon fifty years ago. . . . Each family group was customarily divided off from the rest by permanent wooden partitions. . . . In the walls of this passage-way, at about the centre, was a doorway on each side which gave access to the compartments. Within each of these compartments there dwelt usually four fire-groups, one to each corner. These fire-groups made up the family, and were invariably of blood-kin to each other. They were sometimes made up of four generations of the same family, sometimes by a group of brothers with their wives and children, sometimes of a father and his married sons, and sometimes partly of one and partly of the other; but all were related to one another by blood ties, and no marriage was permitted between them." The author mentions one long-house that extended three hundred feet along a river bank; most of them are about twenty-four feet in width, and practically open from end to end. Privacy is not known and "apparently undesired."[6] The southern Caddoan tribes lived in agricultural hamlets or single households scattered around a main village. "A household consisted of several families living in a large conical grass lodge. The semi-communal households seem to have been organized on the basis of paternal right; but an elder woman served as the economic head."[7]

The old Slavic custom of joint-householding is kept up by the Bulgarians; the family, consisting sometimes of scores of individuals, constitutes one household and one society. The larger family-groups are the poorer ones; where in-

4 Hanoteau et Letourneux, *Kabylie*, II, 468-473.
5 In VG, I, 372-373.
6 Hill-Tout, in JAI, XXXIV, 331, 332; and in JAI, XXXV, 134.
7 Bolton, in HAI, II, 50.

dividual initiative has broken loose the community dissolves. In the Bulgarian case all are subject to the chief householder, called *dyado,* who oversees arrangements and keeps peace. He appoints the work for each one, pays the tribute, keeps the money earned by the family, and in general sees to the common interests. He holds a council with the older members, where a majority vote decides. At a meal the men sit on his right and the women on his left, always in order of age. They pay much attention to age-precedence, dividing the work by age and marrying by age, the oldest brother first, unless he waives the right. The younger brother must ask the permission of the older, without which he may not marry even though the parents should desire it. Thus, too, the girls marry in order of age. All the immovables belong to the community but each member can have his own property. When all the community-affairs are finished, each can go about his own business; he can work for wages and what he wins he can dispose of without the knowledge of the *dyado.* A leading woman, called the *baba,* presides over the household-work and keeps the keys. When the men go off to work, she takes the *dyado's* place. She presides over buying and selling, borrowing and paying debts, and all her contracts are sacred for the community. When the *dyado,* who is usually the *baba's* husband, returns, he carries out her contracts as if made by him. Though the women have to work hard, they are treated with great respect.[8]

To the question as to what broke up the house-community, the unexpected answer is: "The women." They "do not acquiesce in it and urge the men to family-division. Their position is, in many localities, unendurable, domineered over as they are by all. The chief fault of the house-community is the quarreling of its members; yet it is the fundamental institution of the South Slav country-population.[9] Similar forms are to be found in other parts of Europe: *participanze, parsonneries,* etc.[10]

Vinogradoff[11] writes of the joint-houses among the Celtic population of Great Britain, with special reference to Wales. "The house of the tribal king, and, in a smaller degree, that of the better tribesman, the 'uchelwr,' is not meant to be the dwelling-place of a small family household surrounded by a certain number of dependents. It is adapted for the joint occupation of a number of tribesmen living together. The great hall, opening between trees, the boughs of which met to form the roof of the house, was the common room and the dining hall of the whole household, and in the aisles on the right and left of it lay the beds or compartments of the families which constituted it. This mode of building answers well to the indications of the laws and extents as to the joint management of affairs by members of gwelys [agnatic grouping]. The more usual course was however to provide a young man when he married with a *tyddyn,* a separate dwelling of modest size and light construction. These *tyddyns* sometimes lay in proximity to each other, and were grouped into small hamlets or villages (*trevs*), in which the inhabitants clustered according to their distribution in kindreds and 'beds.' "

Says Schmoller[12] of the family in its relation to the development of economic life: "The family, associated with its dwelling, and carrying on an ordered domestic economy, became the first social organ which learned how and then

8 *Russ. Ethnog.* (Russ.), I, 478.
9 Krauss, *Südslaven,* 64 ff.; Simkhovitsch, *Russland,* 355 ff.; Kowalewsky, *Oek. Entw.,* I, 16-17; Utiešenović, *Haus-Kom.,* 10, 13, 15, 18, 44, 59, *et passim.*

10 Demoor and others, *L'Évol. Régr.,* 159.
11 *Manor,* 15-16.
12 "Die geschichtliche Entwickelung der Unternehmung," in *Jahrbuch f. Gesetzyeb.,* XIV, 769.

taught mankind to accumulate, hold together, and control possessions in herds, land, and capital; to transfer property from generation to generation and in connection with it to develop and render stable habitudes of labor and of division of labor." The family rested upon "an inexorable, stern principle of coercion, the mastery of the family-head, which only in millennia of evolution becomes mild, and unites itself, to form a whole, with the noblest and purest sentiments of sympathy characteristic of conjugal, filial, and parental love. . . . Groups of four to ten, even of twenty to forty and more persons, totally disappear in the conception and aims of the family. Egoism, which is suppressed within it, grows all the more stern toward what is outside. Until the individualism of later culture arises, there exists what is an economic family-egoism rather than a personal egoism. Mighty epochs of a rising economic culture rest predominantly upon this . . . basis; almost the whole of economic activity, for hundreds and thousands of years, was supported upon the life, discipline, and organization of the family; the ordering of rights and the mores characteristic of the family governed and set limits to all economic performance. But, conversely, economic life and the increasing self-centered desire for gain, on the part of the father of the family, introduced into the family-organization elements which were bound to become perilous to it, especially where growing hosts of slaves, acquired not from family-considerations but in the prospect of gain, expanded the family all too widely."

Schroeder[13] gives as the historical, natural evolution of the sexual organization: "I. The primitive family, an apparently unlimited blood-kin-family without any limitation in sexual relations except the exclusion of alien individuals not belonging to the family. II. The blood-kin-family with the limitation that sexual intercourse is allowed only between the family-members of the same generation. III. The group-family in narrower sense as the very most advanced form of the group-family, with the wider limitation that real and collateral brothers and sisters also are excluded from mutual sexual relations; Morgan calls this the Punalua-family. IV. The pairing-family with free individual marriage. V. The patriarchal family with the father-right and the supervision of the women (polygyny). VI. The monogamic family."

Lowie[14] compares the family with the sib: "The sib, like the family, is a kinship group. It is at once more and less inclusive than the rival unit. On the one hand, it excludes one half of the blood-kindred—the father's side of the family in matronymic, the mother's side in patronymic societies. On the other hand, it admits on equal terms all kindred of the favored side regardless of degree and even individuals considered blood-relatives merely through legal fiction, whence the rule of sib exogamy. The sib normally embraces not merely the descendants through females of an ancestress, or through males of an ancestor, but several distinct lines of descent, which are only theoretically conceived as a single line."

§415. Sex-Ascendancy.

AMONG the southern Massim, "it was optional whether a man first went to live in his wife's hamlet or not; very often he did, especially if their homes were not close together, but it was obligatory that the first garden made after his marriage should be on his wife's land. As soon as a good garden had been

---

13 *Geschlechtl. Ordnung*, 19, 20.   14 In AA, XXI, 28.

made there, he would usually make a garden in his own hamlet, where he would probably take his wife to stay for some time before he again visited her hamlet, and a semi-migratory existence between the hamlet groups of the husband and wife might sometimes be kept up for years. But whether or not a man lived often or long at his wife's hamlet, he almost invariably returned to his own when getting old. . . . Very much the same condition of things is found on Tubetube."[1] On Goodenough Island, "the son, as soon as he reaches manhood, seeks a wife in another hamlet and leads her away to his own; the daughter, with rare exceptions, removes to the hamlet of her husband. . . . Neither in the terms which denote relationship, nor in the inheritance of property, nor in the legends and folk tales handed down from past times, is there any trace of a matrilineal system such as prevails in the Trobriands."[2]

Among the African Wayao and those tribes into which their influence has penetrated, "woman rules supreme in the household and in the village. I have spoken," writes Coudenhove,[3] "with many men who, after some hesitation, ended by admitting it. In the villages it is the women who make or mar reputations, as they did in Europe before the advent of the suffragette, and in the house the men follow their advice in almost everything. It is they who decide whether a stranger shall be allowed to settle in the village and to remain there, and whether one of the community who, for some reason or other, is making himself obnoxious, shall be given, by the men, the *consilium abeundi*. When the wife of a native servant desires a change, she will prevail on her husband to leave his situation, however much he may like it personally. 'Boys' who have been scolded in the presence of their women invariably give notice; most thefts committed by men are due to direct or indirect instigation by their wives. Black men are extremely sensitive to ridicule, and what they fear more than anything else, is to appear ridiculous or weak before their women. The latter know this, and harp on that string with consummate virtuosity. What gives the women of the Wayao such a hold over the men is the unique custom that, after marriage, the man follows the woman to *her* village, not *vice versa;* and if, later, the man goes to reside in another place,—as, for instance, when he finds employment on a plantation,—it seems to be left to his wife's discretion entirely, whether she shall follow him or not. Frequently she refuses." Though wives among the Ba-Mbala follow their husbands, the man often takes up residence in his father-in-law's village.[4]

Miss Czaplicka[5] states that among the Yukaghir the son-in-law occupies a very subordinate position. "Only when he has his own children does he acquire the right to use some of the furs and other objects without permission. Only after the death of his father-in-law and other old men of the family, and when his wife's brothers go away to their fathers-in-law, does he become the head of the family. If the young man wants to leave his father-in-law, he can be prevented from taking his wife with him, unless he has his own children. . . . Although we see in the Yukaghir marriage some matrilocal arrangements, it does not follow that we have here an instance of matriarchy; for the children are called by the name of the father, they reckon their descent from their father's male ancestors, and the duty of blood-revenge is incumbent on paternal

1 Seligmann, *Melanesians*, 508-509.
2 Jenness and Ballentyne, *D'Entrecasteaux*, 63-64.
3 In *Atl. Mo.*, CXXXII, 192-193.

4 Torday and Joyce, in JAI, XXXV, 410.
5 *Aborig. Siberia*, 94, 97, 102, 103, 119-120, 127-128.

relatives. According to an old Yukaghir, there once existed the custom of reckoning the first son and daughter among the relatives of the mother and the rest
among those of the father; but, as Jochelson observes, this was probably in
order to keep the son-in-law in the house of his wife's parents." With the
Buryat, "after the wedding a wife remains with her husband for a month;
then he lets her go for six months to her parents, and during this time is not
allowed to visit her. . . . Then she spends one month with her husband, and
returns again to her parents, after which follows another visit to her new home.
The visits to her husband become more and more frequent, until at last she
settles down with him for life. . . . In former times the husband always went
to live in the home of his wife's parents." Among the Ostyak of the Yenesei, "the
young couple live with the husband's father-in-law for about a month after
the wedding, and only then does the husband take his wife home." Finally,
among the Ainu of Japan: " 'If the young woman herself or her parents have
been the main movers in the business'—proposals of marriage—'the bridegroom
is removed from his own family to take up his abode close to the hut of his
father-in-law; he is, in fact, adopted. But if the bridegroom did the wooing, or
his parents were the prime movers, the bride is adopted into his family. Or
if a woman of one village chooses a man of another, he, if agreeable, goes to
live with her; or if a man chooses a woman who resides at a distance, she, if
agreeable, goes to live with him.' . . . Batchelor says that if a girl courts a
young man, she 'may enslave herself to his parents as a price for their son.'
Pilsudski, however, states that though the custom of women trying to win
men did formerly exist, it is no longer observed."

By exception, when a Bornean removes to the house of his wife's parents,
she remains slavishly subject to his will and is obliged to do most of the work
both within the house and in the fields. It is but rarely that a Land Dyak does
not have to reside with and labor for the wife's father for a time before the
couple can set up for themselves; but the husband has complete control of the
wife. The demand for a high bride-price may delay a girl's marriage for some
time; and the issue may be settled in the end by the man coming to live with
her family.[6] Where it is customary, in Borneo, for the husband to reside with
the father-in-law until he can set up his own establishment, the "father-in-
law is treated with even greater respect and deference than one's own father.
The son-in-law may not venture to utter his name or contradict him when
speaking. He cannot lie on the same mat with him, eat off the same plate,
drink from the same cup, or walk in front of him.[7] In some parts of Java, "so
much deference is paid to the bride's wishes, that if she demands it, the husband,
if of a different village, must come and live in hers."[8] Among the Sea Dyaks,
"the bridegroom generally betakes himself to the apartment of his wife's
parents or relations, and becomes one of the family. Occasionally, as for
example when the bride has many brothers and sisters, or when the bridegroom
is the support of aged parents, or of younger brothers and sisters, the bride
enters and becomes one of the family of her husband." The birth of a daughter
is regarded as being more desirable than that of a son, for at marriage a son
may have to follow his wife, whereas a daughter obtains for her parents the

6 Schwaner, *Borneo*, I, 198-199; Roth, *Sarawak*, I, 108, 109, 124; II, ch. XXXI; Veth,
Borneo's Wester-Afdeeling, II, 269; Nieuwenhuis, *Borneo*, I, 55, 74.

7 Roth, in JAI, XXI, 134.
8 Crawford, *Ind. Arch.*, 90.

benefit of her husband's labour and assistance." The Bataks say: "The steer follows the cow, the man follows the woman." The woman is the basis of the family. A poor Batak goes to live with his wife. "This comes out clearly in the word *mandingding,* a word which properly signifies: to live in the same place with a creditor, being under obligation to assist him if he has pressing work. Indeed this is also the position of the man in marriage with respect to the family of his wife." Such a marriage has been called by a term which conveys the idea of being in pawn. If the bride-price is not paid, says Wilken,[9] who reports these cases, the "matriarchal marriage" takes place and the man goes to live with his wife's group. The children are divided between his and her families or, in some cases, remain with the mother's kin. Where a low bride-price is paid, it is a matter of indifference which party goes to the other, the children and property belong to both, and the pair may have their own house. In South Celebes "it is quite a matter of indifference at a marriage whether the man moves in with the woman or the woman with the man. All is regulated according to which of the two is the landholder." If he is, she goes; if not, he does; only if they live far apart may she go, even though the landholder. It is evident that financial considerations rather than others are likely to govern such cases.

Among the Sengirese the man goes to the woman's house and stays there; the children, when they are old enough, may choose which family they will belong to.[10] Again, the prospective father-in-law may allow a suitor to live with his daughter, more or less under his paternal control, until the aspirant can afford to marry.[11]

In Guiana, "when an Indian marries he takes up his quarters close to his father in-law, or may occupy the same house. He becomes part and parcel of his wife's family. According to the Indian rules of marriage, the young hus-band is bound to live in the same settlement with his wife's parents. The wife's father expects the bridegroom to work for him in clearing the forest and in other things, and the young people often remain with him until an increasing family renders a separate establishment necessary. This also was the rule on the islands among the Carib. The woman continues to live in her father's house after the wedding and she enjoys more privileges than her husband, because she can speak to everybody, but he can not speak to the wife's relations with-out great caution, or when he finds them in liquor. They always shun such meeting. Talking of the mainland, Brett says that the Carib woman is always in bondage to her male relations. . . . The old men regard their sons-in-law as servants to wait on them and from the time that their daughters are mar-ried have no more cause to work. The newly married Indian has to see to the plantation, the home, the hunting, and the fishing."[12]

When Samson took a wife from among the Philistines, his marriage was matrilocal, for he went to her.[13] Smith[14] says that the formula, "he went in unto her," was used to indicate the matrilocal arrangement. Barton,[15] disagree-ing somewhat, says this was a primitive Semitic matrilineal practice. The chil-dren remained with the mother.

9 In VG, I, 253, note, 254 (quoting St. John, *Life in the Forests of the Far East,* I, 162, 165); 334, 354-355, 356-357, 365, 391-392; Wilken, *Vkde.,* 332.
10 Hickson, in JAI, XVI, 138.

11 Pleyte, in *Globus,* LXXIX, 25, 26.
12 Roth, in BAE, XXXVIII, 683, 684.
13 Judges, XIV.
14 *Early Arabia,* 167, 168.
15 *Sem. Orig.,* 55.

§416. The Mother-Family.

Matrilineal Descent. In Australia some tribes count descent in the maternal line, others count it in the paternal; indeed, it is not as yet possible to say which of these methods is the more widely practised. Some writers think that maternal descent is the general rule. Where the maternal line exists, every child belongs to its mother's class and totem; "thus in every family the father belongs to one class and totem, while the mother and all the children belong to another."[1] "Descent is necessarily through the mothers" in Australian group-marriage; children are of the father's horde but of the mother's totem. Again, "the father has nothing to do with the disposal of his daughter, the reason given being that the daughter belongs to the class of her mother's brother, and not to that of her father. Notwithstanding this, they believe that the daughter is of the father solely, being only nurtured by her mother."[2] Evidently there is here a persistence of ancient practice alongside an altered theory. An Australian hunter gives little of his quarry to his wife, but in that case it is the rule for her brother, or someone else on her side, to give her of his hunting.[3] "The wedding presents are not given to the bride and bridegroom, but by the latter to his mother-in-law, to whom, however, he is never allowed to speak. Failing a mother-in-law, the presents are given to the nearest of kin to the wife."[4] Says Howitt[5] in a letter to Tylor: "When a man marries a woman from a distant locality, he goes to her tribelet and identifies himself with her people. This is a rule with very few exceptions. Of course I speak of them as they were in their wild state. He becomes a part of, and one of, the family. In the event of a war expedition, the daughter's husband acts as a blood-relation, and will fight and kill his own blood-relations, if blows are struck by his wife's relations. I have seen a father and son fighting under these circumstances, and the son would most certainly have killed the father if others had not interfered."

In one case of cannibalism it is reported that the nearest relatives did the eating in order to "forget the departed and not be continually crying." So far as the eating is concerned, almost any relation can eat any other except that "the father does not eat of his off-spring, or the off-spring of the sire."[6] The father-child relationship is not, then, a close one, as compared with the rest.

In New Guinea, the man goes back to his own kin in case of war. In some localities "the mother-line still rules everywhere in very marked degree, and therefore is the structure of the Melanesian state so extraordinarily loose. . . . The sons follow the maternal uncle and oppose in the field the father and his kin." In some localities, though the mother-line is dominant in the rules of inheritance, the father-line is on the gain and is really determinative. The wife follows the husband; only rarely does the husband remove into the wife's village. "Earlier, when blood-vengeance was still in full swing, the relatives on the mother's side, the *Gai's* . . . had the duty of avenging the dead, and that not alone on the murderer but on his family or the whole tribe, of which every single member, even the women and children, were held responsible and could

1 Spencer and Gillen, *Nat. Tr. Cent. Aust.*, 34, 113, 114, 115; Mathews, in AA, X, 98; Howitt, in JAI, XX, 37; Grosse, *Familie*, 59-60.

2 Howitt, *S.E. Aust.*, 195; Howitt and Fison, in JAI, XII, 35, and in JAI, XIV, 144.

3 Palmer, in JAI, XIII, 285.
4 Parker, *Euahlayi*, 58.
5 Quoted by Tylor, in *Nineteenth Cent.*, XL, 89.
6 Smyth, *Vict.*, I, 120.

be killed in expiation—a direct sequel and survival of the earlier group- or horde-marriage."[7] Among the Dobuans, "descent is through the mother, to whose family the children belong. On the death of a woman the surviving consort goes into severe mourning under the charge of his mother-in-law, from whom he is only released after a succession of ceremonies. The widower then goes to his own village, leaving his children and all but his own actual possessions to his late wife's family."[8] Among the Northern Massim, "children take the mother's totem, and although adoption is practised the adopted child retains its true totem. . . . Children are not infrequently named after a maternal uncle or aunt, and instances were found in which people were named after their maternal grandfather or grandmother; I could hear of no case in which a man was called after his father or father's relatives." It is the custom here for brothers to make a garden for their married sister and continue to help her as long as she and they live. On this account brotherless girls find it extremely difficult to find husbands; "a man hesitates to marry into such a family, saying to himself: 'Where are the brothers to make a garden for my wife, their sister?' " On the other hand, "one girl in a family of about five boys will have numerous suitors, and large quantities of property, perhaps reaching a trade value of as much as £20 or £30, may be presented to her father and other relatives as the bride-price."[9]

In the New Britain group, if one of two brothers (of the same totem) marries, his children follow the maternal line. Then one brother may marry the other's daughter, and no exception may be taken to it because the girl does not belong to his totem but to her mother's. But a man may not marry his sister's daughter because she is of his totem.[10] In the Fiji Islands, where the mother-family has been extraordinarily well preserved, the women are cruelly treated and sometimes commit suicide to escape their lot; "for the rule of the man over the woman is quite absolute and he can with impunity kill and eat her."[11] In the New Hebrides, "the first of the human race, they say, was a *woman*, then her son, and from them sprung the race of men."[12] Says Malinowski[13] of the ideas concerning the relationship between father and child, as it is conceived by the natives of the Trobriand Islands: "They have only one generic term for kinship, and this is *veiola*. Now this term means kinship in the maternal line, and does not embrace the relationship between a father and his children, nor between any agnatically related people. Very often, when inquiring into customs and their social basis, I received the answer, 'Oh, the father does not do it; because he is not *veiola* to the children.' The idea underlying maternal relationship is the community of body. In all social matters (legal, economic, ceremonial) the relationship between brothers is the very closest, 'because they are built up of the same body, the same woman gave birth to them.' Thus the line of demarcation between paternal or agnatic relationship (which as a generic conception and term does not exist for the natives), and maternal kinship, *veiola*, corresponds to the division between those people who are of the same body (strictly analogous, no doubt, to our consanguinity), and those who are not of the same body. But in spite of this, as far as all the minute details of daily life are concerned, and further, in various rights and privileges, the

7 Hagen, *Papua's*, 224, 225, 243, 253.
8 Bromilow, in AAAS, 1909, 471.
9 Seligmann, *Melanesians*, 705, 706.
10 Danks, in JAI, XVIII, 283.

11 Waitz-Gerland, *Anthrop.*, VI, 627, 628.
12 Turner, *Samoa*, 331.
13 In JAI, XLVI, 409-410.

father stands in an extremely close relation to the child. Thus the children enjoy membership of the father's village community, though their real village is that of their mother. Again, in questions of inheritance they have various privileges granted them by the father. The most important of these is connected with the inheritance of that most valuable of all goods, magic. Thus very often . . . when the father is able to do it legally, he leaves his magic to his son instead of to his brother or nephew. It is remarkable that the father is, sentimentally, always inclined to leave as much as possible to his children, and he does so whenever he can. Now, such inheritance of magic from father to son shows one peculiarity: it is given, and not sold. Magic has to be handed over during the man's lifetime, of course, as both the formulae and the practices have to be taught. . . . Thus, in the native mind, the intimate relationship between husband and wife, and not any idea, however slight or remote, of physical fatherhood, is the reason for all that the father does for his children. It must be clearly understood that social and psychological fatherhood (the sum of all the ties, emotional, legal, economic) is the result of the man's obligations towards his wife, and physiological fatherhood does not exist in the mind of the natives."

"If any argument concerning the social relations of parents and children is to be drawn from the customs of adoption of the Banks Islands, it is as much in favour of lack of recognition of physical motherhood as of physical fatherhood. There are, however, here and there customs which indicate that the close relation with the father did not at one time exist." The author[14] cites examples and makes the following generalization regarding the situation in Melanesia: "The first conclusion, then, to be drawn from the data is that the most ancient terms of relationship now found in Melanesia are those for the mother, child, mother's brother and the terms for the brother-sister relationship, i.e., those relationships which have the most important place in a condition of mother-right. . . . If the assumption that diversity indicates antiquity is correct, it is clear that the most ancient social condition of which the systems of relationship bear evidence was one of mother-right. Those who wish to show that the patrilineal descent of Melanesia is the older form will have to show that the diversity in the terms for mother and mother's brother have been the result of a later development."

Livingstone[15] sees in the state of vassalage into which a young man enters when he goes to live with his wife's mother "only a more stringent enforcement of the law from which emanates the practice which prevails so very extensively in Africa, known to Europeans as 'buying wives.' Such virtually it is, but it does not appear quite in that light to the actors. So many head of cattle or goats are given to the parents of the girl 'to give her up,' as it is termed . . . and allow an entire transference of her and her seed into another family. If nothing is given, the family from which she has come can claim the children as part of itself: the payment is made to sever this bond."

In Togo the prospective mother-in-law receives the bridegroom's embassies and presents and "mother and daughter remain most intimately bound together up to the last breath."[16] In West Africa, again, the Igalwa, one of the proudest and most noble tribes, accounts relationship only through the mother and in a perfected and elaborated form; "brothers and cousins on the mother's side

14 Rivers, *Melan. Soc.*, II, 151, 185.   16 Fies, in *Globus*, LXXXVII, 76.
15 *Mission. Travels*, 667-668.

being in one class of relationship, and called by one name. . . . The father's responsibility, as regards authority over his own children is very slight. The really responsible male relative is the mother's elder brother. From him must leave to marry be obtained for either girl or boy; to him and the mother must the present be taken which is exacted on the marriage of a girl; and should the mother die, on him and not on the father, lies the responsibility of rearing the children; they go to his house, and he treats and regards them as nearer and dearer to himself than his own children, and at his death, after his own brothers by the same mother, they become his heirs." The negro resents the effort of the whites to reverse what is to him the natural order of relationship and to saddle him with the support of his children; "moreover, white culture expects him to think more of his wife and children than he does of his mother and sisters, which to the uncultured African is absurd."[17]

Among the Ewe, the child belongs to the mother and not to the father, unless the mother is a slave, in which case the child of the slave belongs to the slave's owner. Kinship is traced through females. If a woman has to pay a fine, she often pledges her children to her husband; he, however, may refuse to assist, so that he can get full control over them.[18] "That the Yorubas formerly had the system of female descent is shown by an ancient proverb, which says, 'The *esuo* (gazelle), claiming relationship with the *ekulu* (a large antelope), says his mother was the daughter of an *ekulu.*' If the male system of descent had been in vogue when this proverb was invented, the *esuo* would have been made to say that his father was the son of an *ekulu.* Moreover, in spite of the legal succession from father to sons, children by different mothers, but the same father, are by many natives still scarcely considered true blood-relations. . . . In Dahomi, blood-descent is on both sides of the house, and succession in the male line. This change, has, however, only taken place in the royal family of Dahomi, and among what may be termed the aristocracy, who appear to have followed the lead of their sovereign. The lower orders still trace descent in the female line, and that the higher orders used also to do so is shown by the terms in use for expressing relationships. Brother and sister, for instance, can only be rendered by 'mother's son' and 'mother's daughter' respectively."[19] On the Loango Coast, "the father possesses no power over his son, whom he may not, like the uncle the nephew, sell, and if separation occurs the children follow the mother because they belong to her brother, as uncle. The children may then inherit from the mother while the property of the father goes over to his brother or nephew." Princes, regarding themselves as all brothers in one family, may not marry princesses but must take wives from the people, and their sons may not bear the title of prince. The sons of princesses, on the other hand, are full princes, even though their fathers are almost always common men. Princesses are mostly unmarried, as they may not marry princes and because common men avoid marrying them by reason of the disadvantageous position they come thus to occupy. Only when poor and insecure do men seek security in the rank of a princess-wife.[20] In British Central Africa "children take the clan-name of the mother, and members of the same clan are regarded as brothers and sisters; they are blood relations and may not intermarry." When

17 Kingsley, *Travels W. Afr.*, 224, 225; Kingsley, *W. Afr. Studies*, 377.
18 Ellis, *Ewe*, 205, 207, 221.
19 Ellis, *Yoruba*, 176, 298.
20 Bastian, *Deut. Exped.*, 166, 197-198.

about five years old, children go to live for a time with their maternal grand-mother.[21]

In Uganda, "the goodwill of the girl's mother must be won by the making of repeated presents, which may last over a period of two or three years."[22] The Alur suitor addresses the mother of the girl he wants to marry, with gifts; if she accepts him he goes two days later to the father. The maternal uncle also gets presents.[23] Folk-tales and sayings witness to the dignity of the mother; but few of the stories have to do with the helpfulness of husband to wife—"it is always the brothers of the woman who with bold spirit snatch her out of danger. It is therefore a threat for which every husband has respect when she says to him: 'Do not torment me as if I had no one at home.' The most insignificant quarrel . . . may cause her to return to her people, and she is sure always to find there protection and partisanship."[24] In Madagascar the root of the word for tribe or family is "mother," those who come from the same mother. A sharp distinction is made between the children of two brothers, who marry, and those of two sisters who may not marry down to the fifth generation. Children of a brother and those of his sister may marry with a special ceremony.[25]

Among the Tuareg, women are held in great respect. "If there had been only women among us, the Touâreg would have conquered the world. They would have possessed as far as Paris!" Women go alone wherever they like, are admitted to councils, and partake of the chieftainship of their husbands. "The son of a slave or serf father and a noble woman is noble; the son of a noble father and a serf woman is a serf; the son of a noble and a slave-woman is a slave."[26] Berber names are metronyms—as, for instance Massinissa, meaning son of Issa—and property and political position have long been inherited in the female line. This state of affairs is interpreted as a relic of the time when there was no marriage in North Africa and passages in classical writers appear to support the interpretation. An Arab traveller of the 14th century wrote: "The state of this people is marvelous, their customs are strange. As for the men, they know no jealousy. None of them gets his name from his father but everyone draws his source from the uncle on the mother's side. Only sisters' children inherit, to the exclusion of own children. Nowhere in the world have I seen anything of the sort elsewhere than among the heathen Hindus of Malabar."[27]

Seligmann[28] finds "indisputable traces of a former matriarchy" in the marriage-customs of the Hamitic peoples of the Sudan. The bridegroom goes to the bride's village to be married and stays there for from one to three years. Though he pays the price, the bride's relatives provide the tent, furniture, and other necessities. The groom accompanies the father-in-law as a son. The first child is likely to be born among the mother's people; sometimes this is so arranged. The author also refers to "a feature of the social organization of the ancient Egyptians and certain African peoples of mixed Hamitic and Negro

21 Stannus, in JAI, XL, 307, 327.
22 Johnston, Uganda, II, 778.
23 Stuhlman, Mit Emin, 501.
24 Gutmann, in Globus, XCII, 30, 31.
25 Letourneau, Polit., 92; Ratzel, Vkde., II, 511; Sibree, Great Afr. Isl., 248-249.
26 Pommerol, Sahariennes, 310, 312; Duvey-

rier, Touâreg, 269, 337; Ney, "Tr. of Sahara," in Cosmopolitan Mag., XVIII, 151.
27 De Goeje, in Gids, XXXI, II, 27, 28; Wilken, in VG, I, 233-236 (quoting Ibn Batuta, 235, note); Livy, XXIX, 23; XXX, 12.
28 In JAI, XLIII, 650, 651-652, 653; §348. of the text.

descent which there is every reason to believe is connected with matrilineal descent and which is probably a legacy of an old Hamitic practice, namely, the custom of brother sister marriage in the royal family. It is so well estab lished that this occurred in Egypt that it does not seem necessary to cite spe- cific instances. But it cannot be said that the fact that such unions occur among the powerful lacustrine tribes of Central Africa has received the attention that its importance warrants. . . . The Baganda also trace their descent in the male line, except in the case of the royal children, who take their mother's totem as well as certain totems claimed by every prince and princess. Clan exogamy was strictly observed except in the case of the ruling prince, who, on his becoming king, was ceremonially married to one of his half-sisters, who shared with him the coronation ceremonies and the official mourning of his predecessor. . . . We thus reach the conclusion that brother-sister marriage was a widely spread early Hamitic institution. Nor were consanguineous mar- riages limited to the royal family, or even to the aristocracy, for the practice occurs among commoners in certain Galla tribes at the present day and there is evidence that marriages between near relatives were by no means repugnant to the feelings of the Egyptian populace."

The Yakuts are vague in their terminology covering relationship on the father's side. The term for mother means "case," "matrix," "place of birth," while that for father means "an elderly man." "This vagueness in regard to the male blood tie, side by side with the definiteness of the female connection with the offspring, is very significant." All names of female ascendants are clearer than those of male; the word for family means mother-family, with a woman- origin. It is a current fact in the legends that the heroes do not know who their fathers were. The same Russian word is used for both *sib* and *kin*. The *familia,* in the Latin sense of the word, bears a name which means "mother- kin." From the facts about names "we may infer that when, amongst the an- cient Yakuts, a number of related persons were living together, the relations of 'mother' and 'wife' were the first ones which called for expression, 'mother' meaning a woman who had children. This inference would support the belief that the matriarchate once existed among the Yakuts,"[29] with a sort of group- marriage in the background.[30] The Lepchas of the Himalayas trace descent through their mothers and not through their fathers.[31] In Baluchistan, a man marries a kinswoman as nearly related as possible, so long as she is outside a certain few prohibited degrees. The belief is current and strong that heredity follows the mother. In another district of India, the woman is the head of the family. The man, married or not, who remains in his mother's house is earning for her family and at his death his property goes in the first instance to his mother, then to his grandmother, sisters, or sister's children, in order. All rela- tionship is reckoned through the woman and the child takes the clan of his mother.[32]

In the Chin Hills a brother controls the marriage of his sister; the woman is the guardian of the children and if divorced takes them with her, though the husband's claim is usually satisfied by compensation. "The children of a slave woman were born in slavery, and every child she bore, be the father chief or slave, was the slave of the mother's master, and therefore as generation after

---

29 Sieroshevski-Sumner, in JAI, XXXI, 92, 108, 109-110.
30 §346, above.
31 Waddell, *Himalayas,* 99.
32 Risley, *Ethnog. India,* I, 71, 199; Hop- kins, *Relig. Ind.,* 534, 535, 541.

generation passed the slave population increased and multiplied."[33] On the Malabar Coast, " 'a man's sister's son and a woman's own son as their respective nearest blood relations perform funeral rites,' as the rule. . . . Though everywhere succession is altogether through women, funeral rites are still performed by men."[34] If the matriarchate is found anywhere, says Letourneau[35] it is among the Nairs of Malabar; the man raises and rules the family of his sister and must show much more grief at their death than he would for his own children. It is said that no Nair knows his father. The patriarchal Brahmans could not change the Nair system. In another Malabar district the Kooch husband resides with his mother-in-law and does the coarse work; she rules, with her daughter second in command. He must meet any expenses he incurs without authorization. A woman's property goes to her daughters. Brothers obey their oldest sister and respect the younger.[36] Again, the eldest daughter of a Rajah "never marries, but takes now one, now another Brahman as her lover; her sons become Rajahs and her eldest daughter carries on the family."[37] Ghurye[38] thinks there is good reason to believe that there was in South India once "a wide prevalence of dual organization with matrilineal descent." The Khasi in Assam are said to "offer the best example of the matriarchate."[39]

Traces of the mother-family in Cambodia are found in the fact "that the price of the 'nursing milk,' as it is called, is paid to the mother; and also in the much more lasting and profound respect had by the son for his mother, and in the general and uncontested principle that the woman put away by her husband has the right to take her children with her. . . . It is the custom, always observed, for the father not to consent to a marriage which the mother opposes, and not to pledge a child without the consent of its mother; then there is the instinctive horror, much more marked than when the father is the victim, which Cambodians feel at the thought of a child beating its mother. One of the most conclusive proofs appears in the word for cousin-german, which when analyzed means brother-grandmother, or brother by the same grandmother, but never brother by the same grandfather. This affords an almost incontestable trace of an ancient social *régime* when relationship followed the female line."[40]

The most ancient Chinese traditions assert that in the earliest times men knew their mothers but not their fathers. The ideographic character for family is said to combine the signs for "woman" and "to be born." It came to be applied to the descendants of a male ancestor.[41] The groom's maternal uncle gives him instruction in conjugal duties; if there is no maternal uncle, the paternal uncle does it.[42]

The mother-family is the oldest form in the Malayo-Polynesian race and must once have been general. Though it is now considerably modified and has been superseded as a system by the patriarchal system, it has left many traces behind it.[43]

Among the Alfurs of Minahasa the word for family is the same as the root

33 Carey and Tuck, *Chin Hills*, I, 190, 204, 208, 209.
34 Fawcett, in JASB, II, 344.
35 *Marr.*, 81-82, 311; Thurston, *S. India*, 120, note.
36 Reclus, *Prim. Folk*, 158-159, 165; Starcke, *Prim. Fam.*, 285; Grosse, *Familie*, 143-144.
37 Starcke, *Prim. Fam.*, 85.
38 In JAI, LIII, 91.

39 Gurdon, *The Khasis*, rev. by Chamberlain, in AA, X, 689.
40 Leclère, in PSM, XLIV, 777.
41 Puini, *Civiltà*, 30, 176; Grosse, *Familie*, 192, 193-194.
42 Grube, in *Veröffentl. aus dem k. Museum f. Vkde.*, VII, 24.
43 Wilken, *Vkde.*, 265-266; Ratzel, *Vkde.*, II, 430.

of the word for milk, meaning those who are suckled by the same milk, a fact which Wilken[44] interprets as a survival of the mother-family. He cites several cases of female rulers in the Archipelago, even among the Mohammedan tribes. "Certainly this phenomenon, so much at strife as it is with the spirit of Islam, is to be conceived, here as elsewhere, as merely an echo, an after-effect out of the time of the matriarchate, when the woman stood on an equality with the man in public law and could be called to the discharge of public offices and services as well as he could." Such female rule was proscribed by Mohammedan influence in Sumatra. Indeed, it is probable that the mother-family in Atjeh was suppressed by Arabic influence at a relatively recent date.[45]

In Celebes the mother is paid at the time of loosing the zone of the bride.[46] In the northern part of the island the marriage-customs are purely matriarchal. The man always goes to his wife's house and becomes a member of her family. "The only persons who are free from the matriarchal system are the sons of the rajahs, who do as they please about following their wives."[47] Certain Malay examples are cited by Stevens[48] to show that the matriarchate is not a token of the preferential position of the female sex but, on the contrary, for its misprision. Children who belong to the mother are neglected. He once said to some of the Orang Laut: "The fact appears to be that you can be sure who the mother is, but not who the father may be." In reply, "they laughed and agreed" with him.

In the Mortlock Islands, "the members of a tribe regard themselves as blood-related brothers and sisters and therefore marriage between tribal members is completely ruled out; even an extra-marital sex-union would count as incest and be punished as such by death. A man can therefore have intimate relations, or marriage, only with a woman from another tribe; he must commonly go to her dwelling and there work the land that belongs to her. If in addition he owns land in her locality he must bring the products to the relatives of his wife. Among these the father-in-law is a mere accessory person, while the brothers-in-law and the chief of the tribe and village to which the woman belongs are of the greatest consequence. The wife is quite independent in the family and has at worst to suffer the tyranny of the sons, who let the unmarried sisters too feel their predominance. . . . Men of the same tribe may not fight against each other, while on the other hand brothers or even father and son must oppose one another insofar as they belong to different tribes. In strange contradiction to this stand the peculiar provisions which most strictly separate the tribal members according to sex—as men and women, brothers and sisters—if they do not, on the mother's side, come from different tribes. For it is the mother who passes on to the children the tribal connections, which consist of the duties of citizens in the natal village of the mother. . . . It is clear that brothers and sisters could not sleep under the same roof and that women could not enter the men's house of their own tribe, though this was not objected to in the case of women of other tribes. Less intelligible are the regulations of native etiquette, according to which the woman in the presence of her husband must not touch her brother or must go by him crouching."[49] Every village-community consists of a kin-group bound together by maternal

44 Especially in VG, I, 121 ff., 376; Jacobs, Groot-Atjeh, I, 98.
45 Jacobs, Groot-Atjeh, I, 15, 18.
46 Riedel, in Bijd., XXXV, 90, 91.
47 Hickson, in JAI, XVI, 138.

48 In Ztsft. f. Ethnol., XXVIII, 175-176; Skeat and Blagden, Malay Penin., II, 87.
49 Finsch, Ethnol. Erfahr., III, 304, 305, 306, 307.

blood and the feeling of blood-brotherhood shows itself stronger than political enmity; blood-brothers must not fight together. Therefore groups fight
each other only in the sense that their mutually alien tribal components fall
into hostilities.[50]

The tribal organization of the Carolines, where every tribe forms a state,
"is not suited for the establishment of a true family-life, for the children are
for the mother true children but for the father they are aliens not belonging
to his tribe. In case of a war between two tribes, father and son stand over
against each other in hostility."[51] "That the natives do not contribute in the
least to the increase of the . . . wild-growing native fruit-trees scarcely needs
to be noted: they are just children of the present or rather of the moment. For
whom should they plant? Their children do not become the heirs and the
nephews, who will sometimes enter upon the heritage, can then just look out
for themselves."[52] In Ponapé, "descent is traced through the mother—a custom
tolerably common amongst Oceanic races in general."[53] In the Pelew Islands,
the family includes only the descendants of the women; and "there is no doubt
that originally on all the islands of Oceania there existed this primitive tribal
organization which still prevails in very clear form only on the Carolines." If
a man's wife dies in her home while he is living there, his relation to her family
ceases and he goes home. His children remain, unless they are grown up and
fond of him, when he sometimes gets them for his lifetime; then they go back
to their maternal grandparents. If a wife lives at her husband's home, she is
well treated by his relatives. However, they watch all his gifts of money to her.
If he dies, his relatives extort all the money they can from her; and if she
yields they come to terms with her. After the mourning, she takes her children
and goes home. Hence a wife is trying, during her husband's life, to get all
she can from him. Envy, jealousy, and greed for money appear at every point.[54]
In the Nauru Islands, "at marriage the man moves into the woman's house. If
the eldest daughter marries, the parents surrender to her their house and
build themselves a new home near by."[55]

Among the Polynesians "are to be found more or less significant survivals of
a maternal system of relationship which fully justify the inference that this
system must once have been universal among them."[56] Polynesian mythology
tells of a chief who, in anger at his wife for not having cooked well, beat her
and asked: "Are the logs of firewood as sacred as the bones of your
brother?" And he threatened: "I will serve the flesh of your brother in the
same way; it shall frizzle on the red hot stones."[57] Some of the Polynesian
pedigree-sticks give evidence of descent through a female lineage, while survivals may be found in the marriage-ceremony, where "on some occasions the
female relatives cut their faces and brows with shark's teeth, receive the
flowing blood on a piece of *native cloth,* and deposit this, sprinkled with *the
mingled blood of the mothers* of the married pair, at the feet of the *bride.*"[58]
In New Zealand, "often the husband went to live with his wife's people,—not
of course, if he was a great chief, or had several wives. If he went to live with
his wife's people, he was considered as one of her tribe, and fought on their

50 Grosse, *Familie,* 147-148 (quoting Kubary).
51 Wilken, in VG, I, 398.
52 Kubary, *Karolinen-Arch.,* 165, 166.
53 Christian, *Caroline Isl.,* 74.
54 Kubary, *Pelauer,* 35, 37, 57.

55 Brandeis, in *Globus,* XCI, 57.
56 Wilken, in VG, I, 399.
57 Gomme, *Village Life,* 172.
58 March, in JAI, XXII, 320, 323; Ellis,
Polyn. Res., I, 272 (quoted).

side."[59] Williamson[60] cites many cases of matrilineal descent among the Central Polynesians.

The Iroquoian system, mentioned in the text, is unique in the completeness with which it has been worked out,[61] but the female line is represented in the less elaborated codes of many tribes.[62] Relationship-names are widely indicative of maternal descent.[63] One ethnologist[64] thinks it "safe to look for the original seat of the clan system with maternal descent on the northwest coast among the Tlingit, Haida, and Tsimshian"; with these tribes "the organization is based on mother-right; that is, birth-rights, such as rank, wealth, property, etc., are received from the mother." Father-right is found farther south.[65] Among the Columbian tribes, "it is said, that the husband almost invariably joins the tribes to which his wife belongs, under the idea that among her own family and friends she will be better able to provide for her husband's and children's wants. This also may proceed from the fact of the influence the women possess; for they always assume much authority in their tribe, and are held in high respect. They have charge of the lodge and the stores, and their consent is necessary for the use of them; for after coming into their possession, these articles are considered the women's own."[66] In one tribe "it was thought wicked for a man or woman to marry any of their mother's relations, but they might marry their father's relatives."[67] Again, "as the father is never of the same caste as the son, who receives caste from his mother, there can never be intertribal war without ranging fathers and sons against each other." This condition works out into avoidance of war.[68]

The mother-descent group is the simplest unit among the Slouans, but is passing. "There are traces of descent in the female line; for example, sisters have great privileges; all the horses that a young man steals or captures in war are brought by him to his sister. He can demand from his sister any object in her possession, even the clothing which she is wearing, and he receives it immediately."[69] Among the Ojibwa, who made great amounts of maple sugar, each woman who was head of a household had her own clump of trees and her sugar-hut to which she always went. These were inherited by mother-descent and totem.[70] Shawnee matrons had the right to name the children, that is, to determine whether they should enter the maternal or paternal clan. When a Shawnee sachem "expressed a desire that a son of one of his sisters might succeed him in the place of his own son," the young man's name had to be changed to comply with the request. This incident "tends to show that at no remote period descent among the Shawnees was in the female line. The author[71] cites a number of similar instances.

"Much is said of the inferior position of woman among the Indians. With all advanced tribes, as with the Zuñis, the woman not only controls the situation

59 Tregear, in JAI, XIX, 103.
60 Cent. Polynesia, II, 87 ff.
61 See also Powell, in BAE, I; Lippert, Kgchte, II, 32, 78; Starcke, Prim. Fam., 36, 282; Grosse, Familie, 161 ff., 174, 175, 176; Hewitt, in HAI, I, 617.
62 For cases among other tribes of North and South America, see Morgan, Anc. Soc., ch. VI.
63 Bernhöft, Verwdsftsnamen, 25-26.

64 Swanton, in AA, VI, 484 (quoted); Boas, in BAE, XXXI, 478.
65 Niblack, in USNM, 1888, 243.
66 Wilkes, Exped., IV, 447.
67 Allison, in JAI, XXI, 315.
68 Bancroft, Nat. Races, I, 109, 132 (quoted).
69 McGee, in BAE, XV, 201; Dorsey, in BAE, XV, 241; HAI, I, 655.
70 Hoffman, in BAE, XIV, pt. I, 288.
71 Morgan, Anc. Soc., 169, 170.

but her serfdom is customary, self-imposed, and willing absolutely. To her belong also all the children; and descent, including inheritance is on her side."[72] The Zuñi man "must work in the field of his prospective mother-in-law, that his strength and industry may be tested; he must collect fuel and deposit it near the maternal domicile, that his disposition as a provider may be made known; he must chase and slay the deer and make from an entire buckskin a pair of moccasins for the bride, and from other skins and textiles a complete feminine suit, to the end that his skill in hunting, skin-dressing, and weaving may be displayed; and finally he must fabricate or obtain for the maiden's use a necklace of seashell or of silver, in order that his capacity for long journeys or successful barter may be established; but if circumstances prevent him from performing these duties actually he may perform them symbolically, and such performance is usually acceptable to the elder people. After these preliminaries are completed, he is formally adopted by his wife's parents, yet remains merely a perpetual guest, subject to dislodgment at his wife's behest, though he cannot legally withdraw from the covenant; if dissatisfied, he can only so ill-treat wife or children as to compel his own expulsion."[73] The Zuñi are agricultural and pastoral; their gardens are cultivated exclusively by the women and inherited by the daughters. Zuñi women hold a high social and political status.[74]

So too under the Navaho system descent is in the female line; the children and practically all property except horses and cattle belong to the wife. Sheep and goats are exclusively hers and the head of the family may not sell a sheep without first obtaining her consent.[75] The pueblo was the result of the gradual growth of a group with maternal descent, for the daughters drew husbands from other groups and a joint-house system was evolved.[76] Hodge[77] is authority for the statements that "all the Pueblos are monogamists, and the status of women is much higher than among most tribes. Among the tribes in which descent is reckoned through the mother, at least, the home is the property of the woman, and on the marriage of her daughters the sons-in-law make it their home. Marriage is effected with little ceremony, and divorce is lightly regarded, the wife having it in her power to dismiss her husband on a slight pretext, the latter returning to his parents' home, sometimes for a trifling cause. . . . The children are spoken of as belonging to the mother; i.e., among most of the Pueblos they belong to the clan of the mother; and in this case, at least, if the father and the mother should separate, the children remain with the latter."

The Seri Indians "are the most primitive people in North America, and their disposition is so savage and treacherous that they remain nearly unknown to scientific students." Descent is reckoned exclusively in the female line and their simple property belongs to the housewives. A groom's claims "are presented chiefly by his older female relative, when, if the suit is favorably regarded by the maiden's mother and uncles, he is provisionally installed as a member of the family without ceremony, without any suggestion of purchase-price, and without presents." If he shows himself a good protector and provider and also endures a continence-test, he is formally installed in the family as a permanent consort-guest, and his children are added to the clan of his mother-in-law. The

72 Cushing, in *Century Mag.*, IV, 35.
73 McGee, in AA, (O.S.) IX, 374.
74 Stevenson, in BAE, XXIII, 290-291.
75 Mindeleff, in BAE, XVII, pt. II, 485;
Matthews, in HAI, II, 44.

76 Morley, in AA, X, 600.
77 In HAI, II, 323; Hewitt, in HAI, II, 970.

matrons own everything and their brothers are entitled to places in the house; "the husband has neither title nor fixed place, 'because he belongs to another house.' " The matrons discuss community-questions and they are settled "by the dictum of the eldest in the group." "Mortuary ceremonies attain their highest development in connection with females, the recognized blood-bearers and legis-lators of the tribe. The special signification of females in respect to funerary rites is without precise parallel among other American aborigines, so far as is known, but is not without analogues in the shape of (presumptive) vestiges of a former magnification of matrons in the mortuary customs of certain tribes. The vestiges are especially clear among the Iroquoian Indians."[78]

Among the Seminoles the man goes to the home of his mother-in-law. Later he builds a house for himself and his wife "either at the camp of the wife's mother or elsewhere, except among the husband's relatives." All the persons in a camp except the husbands are of one kin-group. A man may not marry a woman of his own clan; and his children belong to the mother and are of her clan.[79]

In British Guiana, "tribal relationship is never derived from the father but always only from the mother; the child of a Warrau-Indian and an Arawak is numbered with the Warraus. Inheritance too aligns itself with this right of tribal claims."[80] There are some traces of mother-right among the Shingu. Although they have the patriarchal family-organization, the mother's brother is equally with the father the protector of the children and takes the father's place if he dies. He, and not the mother, manages the property. The protector of the woman, in other tribes too, is always her brother.[81] In tropical South America the married man does not eat with his own family but with that of his married sister and he gets his share of booty, not in his own house but in that of his sister. In general where the mother-family prevails women are free, respected, and dominant, whereas under the patriarchal régime they are held in subjection and little respected.[82] Among the West Tupis, "not the fathers but the brothers give away the maidens." If the mother is a Macusi the children also are Macusis; yet the paternal uncle may not marry the niece, while it is allowable to marry a sister's daughter. Arawak descent is strictly through the mother; marriage is forbidden with members of the mother's tribe but not with those of the father's. The father's or mother's brother has a weighty voice in the family-council.[83] Humboldt[84] refers to a legend about a tribe of "women who live alone"—a case paralleled to the "woman-land" of southeast New Guinea, wherein men exist only to breed with the women.[85] Latcham[86] thinks that to the unbridled license which prevails during Araucanian feasts "may possibly be due the custom of reckoning parentage and descent from the mother's side, it being frequently impossible to determine with any certainty who is the father of a given child."

Traces of descent through women are found in ancient Egypt and Mesopo-

78 McGee, in AA, (O.S.) IX, 375; McGee, in BAE, XVII, pt. I, 270*, 287*.
79 MacCauley, in BAE, V, 496 507, 508; Skinner, in AA, XV, 77.
80 Schomburgk, Brit.-Guiana, I, 169; II, 314.
81 Von den Steinen, Zent. Bras., 331, 502.

82 Ehrenreich, in Königl. Mus. Vkde., II, 27, 28, 29.
83 Von Martius, Beiträge, I, 217, 643, 645, 690.
84 Reise, III, 399.
85 "Aus Allen Erdteilen," in Globus, XXXI, 334.
86 In JAI, XXXIX, 354.

tamia;[87] and the Israelites show some reminiscences. Abimelech says to his mother's brethren: "I am your bone and your flesh." He wants them to make him, not one of his father's sons, their king. Several details appear in connection with the marriage-arrangements of Rebecca and in the Talmud.[88] Wilken[89] has collected considerable material relating to the existence of the matriarchal family among the ancient Arabs, which leaves him in no doubt as to the matter. He cites several Old Testament cases indicative of the closeness of relationship through the mother and finds parallels among the Arabs of the older time and also among Arabized peoples of the Malay Archipelago. The customs of the princely houses of Arabia show undoubted traces of descent through women; the term "mother" itself signifies "folk," "tribe," "community"; and the terminology "is not purely fossil, for there still exists among the Arabs, in the present as in antiquity, the feeling that the mother determines the nature and the natural relationship, the character of the child. The mother is more sacred than the father, the mother's sister stands nearer to the child than the father's sister, and cousinship on the father's side involves by nature less kin-feeling than that on the mother's side. Ever and anon does the vein of the mother or the mother's brother crop out in the child. . . . On the political and legal range, at the time of Mohammed, relationship through the mother yielded to that through the father; the latter is the political relationship."[90] "The Arabs generally consider innate virtues as inherited through the mother rather than the father, and believe that a man commonly resembles, in his good and evil qualities, his maternal uncle." A complimentary form of address is: "Thou who hast a valiant maternal uncle!"[91]

The first proponents of the matriarchal theory[92] rested their case chiefly upon evidence from classical antiquity. Most modern scientists would doubtless agree with Starcke[93] that Bachofen's method of interpreting and applying mythical tales inspires little confidence, being "prompted by a poetic inspiration, which snatches at every kind of allegory." There is very slight reason to assert that Homer affords evidence for the mother-family.[94] Æschylus[95] has a line about "Amazons who feed on flesh and know not men." Amazon-legends have been interpreted as pointing back to a "matriarchate." The Orestes story, as worked over by Æschylus,[96] develops a peculiar opposition between the gods of the new dispensation and those ancient female avengers of matricide,[97] the Erinyes. Apollo asks the latter: "What of husband-slaying wives?" and receives the answer: "That blood bears not the blame of kindred violence." There is no blood-tie between man and wife but only a marriage-tie, a sort of master-servant relationship. Several passages bear upon the relative nearness of relationship with father and mother. Orestes said to his maternal grandfather:

87 Sayce, *Anc. Emp.*, 88; Kohler and Peiser, *Bab. Rechtsleben*, I, 7; Tiele-Gehrich, *Gchte. Relig.*, I, 169; Maspero, *Hist. Anc.*, I, 51; Paturet, *Cond. Jurid.*, 26; Erman, *Aegypten*, I, 224; Wilutsky, *Mann u. Weib*, 89.

88 Maurer, *Vkde.*, I, 147; Barton, *Sem. Orig.*, 53-54; Judges, VIII, 30; IX, 2; Gen., XXIV; Wilken, in VG, I, 238-239; Wellhausen, in *Gött. Gesellsft. d. Wissensch.*, 1893, 478, note; Klugmann, *Frau im Talmud*, 22; Buhl, *Israeliten*, 28, 29.

89 In VG, II, 1-55.

90 Smith, *Kinship*, 23, 95; Von Kremer, *Kgchte.*, II, 106; Welhausen, in *Gott. Gesellschaft d. Wissenschft.*, 1893, 474, 476 (quoted).

91 Lane, *Mod. Egypt*, II, 135.

92 Especially Bachofen, *Mutterrecht*.

93 *Prim. Fam.*, 246.

94 Keller, *Hom. Soc.*, 201-207; Lippert, *Kgchte.*, II, 76.

95 *Suppliants*, 287; §§140, above, and 418, below.

96 *Eumenides*, 605-608, 658 ff., 735 ff.

97 Æschylus, *Eumenides*, 728, 846.

"My father begot me, thy daughter bore me, a field receiving the seed from another; and without the father there could never be a child. I argued therefore that the prime leader of my being caused me to be, rather than the nurse who received me."[98] In the *Electra* of Euripides[99] there is a sort of protest against naming the child from the mother, even when she is of lofty family and the father is of low station. It is reported that the ancient Athenians were named after their mothers and that Solon allowed marriage with a half-sister on the father's side while forbidding union with such a relative on the mother's side.[100] "Ask a Lycian who he is, and he will answer by giving his own name, that of his mother, and so on in the female line. Moreover, if a free woman marry a man who is a slave, their children are free citizens; but if a free man marry a foreign woman, or cohabit with a concubine, even though he be the first person in the state, the children forfeit all rights of citizenship."[101] Much later it is reported that they "honor women more than men and call themselves after their mothers; they leave heritages to their daughters and not to their sons."[102]

Miss Harrison,[103] in presenting evidence for matriarchal conditions in early Greece, seems to support Lippert's[104] view, especially with respect to the greater antiquity of goddesses as compared with gods. "At Delphi in historical days Apollo held the oracle, but Apollo, the priestess . . . knows, was preceded by a succession of women goddesses:

> First in my prayer before all other gods
> I call on Earth, primæval prophetess.
> Next Themis on her mother's oracular seat
> Sat, so men say. Third by unforced consent
> Another Titan, daughter too of Earth,
> Phoebe. She gave it as a birthday gift
> To Phoebus, and giving called it by her name.

Gaia the Earth was first, and elsewhere Æschylus tells us that Themis was but another name of Gaia. Prometheus says the future was foretold him by his mother:

> Themis she
> And Gaia, one in form with many names.

In historical days in Greece, descent was for the most part traced through the father. These primitive goddesses reflect another condition of things, a relationship traced through the mother, the state of society known by the awkward term matriarchal, a state echoed in the lost *Catalogues of Women,* the *Eoiai* of Hesiod, and in the Bœotian heroines of the *Nekuia.* . . . Of the many survivals of matriarchal notions in Greek mythology one salient instance may be noted. St. Augustine, telling the story of the rivalry between Athene and Poseidon, says that the contest was decided by the vote of the citizens, both men and women, for it was the custom then for women to take part in public affairs.

98 Euripides, *Orestes*, 552-556.
99 Lines 932 ff.
100 Wilken, in VG, II, 32 (quoting Augustine, *De Civ. Dei.*, XVIII, 9); Howitt and Fison, in JAI, XIV, 163.
101 Herodotus, *Hist.*, I, 173 (Rawlinson's transl.).

102 *Nikolaus of Damascus*, 517, 518; in Stobæus, *Florilegium*, 41, 44.
103 *Greek Relig.*, 131, 260-261, 261-262, 316-317.
104 *Kgchte.*, II, 257.

The men voted for Poseidon, the women for Athene; the women exceeded the men by one and Athene prevailed. To appease the wrath of Poseidon the men inflicted on the women a triple punishment, 'they were to lose their vote, *their children were no longer to be called by their mother's name* and they themselves were no longer to be called after their goddess, Athenians.' The myth is ætiological, and it mirrors surely some shift in the social organization of Athens. The citizens were summoned by Cecrops, and it is noticeable that with his name universal tradition associates the introduction of the patriarchal form of marriage." The authoress quotes classic authority to the following effect: " 'Women give to each successive stage of their life the same name as a god, they call the unmarried *Maiden* (Korē), the woman given in marriage to a man *Bride* (Nymphē), her who has borne children *Mother* (Mētēr), and her who has borne children's children *Grandmother* (Maia).' Invert the statement and we have the whole matriarchal theology in a nutshell. The matriarchal goddesses reflect the life of women, not women the life of the goddesses." Again: "The Hera who in the ancient Argonautic legend is queen in Thessaly and patron of the hero Jason is of the old matriarchal type; it is she, Pelasgian Hera, not Zeus, who is really dominant; in fact Zeus is practically non-existent. In Olympia, where Zeus in historical days ruled if anywhere supreme, the ancient Heraion where Hera was worshipped alone long predates the temple of Zeus. At Argos the early votive terra-cottas are of a woman goddess, and the very name of the sanctuary, the Heraion, marks her supremacy. At Samos, at the curious festival of the *Tonea*, it is the image of a woman goddess that is carried out of the town and bound among the bushes, and Strabo tells us that in ancient days Samos was called Parthenia, the island of the Maiden. At Stymphalus, in remote Arcadia, Pausanias says that Hera had three sanctuaries and three surnames; while yet a girl she was called Child, married to Zeus she was called Complete or Full-Grown . . ., separated from Zeus and returned to Stymphalus she was called Chera (Widow). Long before her connection with Zeus, the matriarchal goddess may well have reflected the three stages of a woman's life; Teleia, full-grown, does not necessarily imply patriarchal marriage." One further survival: "A man when he married by thus obtaining exclusive rights over one woman violated the old matriarchal usages and may have had to make his peace with the community by paying the expenses of the Thesmophoria feast."

The Italian Locrians reckoned blood-relationship only in the female line.[105] From a study of data in classical literature, covering the position of women, Farnell[106] concludes that "the matriarchate has not left so clear an impress on classical religion as has been supposed," and that "many of the curious phenomena in the relation of the sexes to cult are not excessively distinctive indications of any special family organization."

"One of the latest discoveries . . . is that the Teutons, before they reached the stage of paternal right, passed through a stage of maternal right."[107] "Now it is not contended that the Germans, even when they first came within the ken of history, recognize no bond of blood between father and son. . . . The most that can be said by ardent champions of 'mother right' is that of 'mother right' there are distinct though evanescent traces in the German laws of a later day. On the other hand, we seem absolutely debarred from the supposition that

105 Polybius, *Hist.*, XII, §5.
106 In *Archiv f. Religionsw.*, VII, 70 ff.
107 Ihering, *Aryan*, 40; Wilken, in VG, I, 239; Weinhold, *Deut. Frauen*, I, 105, 107.

they disregarded the relationship between the child and its mother's brother."108 "According to the Law of Tanistry, even among the Picts and Scots, in a case of doubtful succession [to the chieftaincy] the choice fell upon the one nearest eligible in the female line."109 "Let no one think that the patriarchal rule of the woman is milder than that of the man; rather the reverse." A Ural mother who was head of a household had a son flogged to death because he tried to comfort his wife when she was being badly treated by the old woman. To no avail did the oldest members of the joint-family beseech the irritated house-mother.110

In a sprightly article on "Royal Marriages and Matrilineal Descent," Miss Murray111 expresses the opinion that royal power went by matrilineal descent and that the cases of consanguine marriage were with the idea of marrying the heiress—all possible heiresses. The case of Hamlet is cited. Where such consanguineous marriages occur, one must look for inheritance in the female line. Man lays claim to the throne by marriage and not by inheritance. In Egypt, "the queen is queen by right of birth, the king is king by right of marriage." The king could have any number of wives—all the heiresses, if he could get them; the queen could have only one husband at a time, he being the rightful ruler by reason of his marriage with her. Cæsar and Antony legitimized their position by marrying Cleopatra. The tables of the Ptolemies are given and from the house of Judah are cited cases of consanguine marriage. Maachah married her cousin and then her son.112 In the case of the Roman Emperors, the authoress asserts that the amazing alliances were not vicious, but political. Matrilineal descent and female inheritance were admitted for Roman kings. Again tables are given. The wife of Cæsar must be above suspicion! In the imperial family the son did not succeed the father. These views are mentioned because they are suggestive and may contain several grains of truth.

The Maternal Uncle, and Nephew-Right. Among certain tribes of West Australia, "the mother's brother of a girl occupies an important position. If there are several claimants for his sister's daughter it is often he who decides which shall be the favoured one. This man is the *talyu* of the girl's future husband. If a man wishes to obtain a girl in marriage he must therefore pay his attentions not only to the girl's father (his *yuji*), but also to her mother's brother (his *talyu*)."113 In the Baniara District of Papua, the maternal uncle is considered the child's nearest relative and guardian. When the baby's hair is to be cut for the first time, the parents give large presents of food to that uncle and the grandfather. "The maternal uncles decorate the children and they are given their dance ornaments."114 Again, "the man normally responsible for introducing the boy [to the body of mature men] is his maternal uncle, or *apono*. It may be explained that the *apono* has certain rights over his nephew, and may call upon him for small services. Furthermore, he officiates ceremonially for the boy, especially in the piercing of his nose and ears in babyhood, and later in his passage through seclusion and the *Pairama* ceremony. . . . In some cases it appeared that the child was introduced into the *ravi* [men's house], not by his *apono* but by his father. But it would seem usual

108 Pollock and Maitland, *Eng. Law*, II, 238.
109 Bastian, *Afr. Reisen*, 167.
110 Simkhowitsch, *Russland*, 364, note.

111 In JAI, XLV, 307 ff.; §348, of text and *Case-Book*.
112 I Kings, XV, 8, 10.
113 Brown, in JAI, XLIII, 185.
114 Liston-Blyth, in JAI, LIII, 470.

for the child to undergo his seclusion and initiation under the especial care of his *apono*—in general, of his mother's male relatives. In a certain percentage of cases a boy passes, by a sort of adoption, into the group of his *apono,* i.e., into the *larava* (or *ravi*-alcove) of his maternal uncle rather than that of his father, as is normally the case."[115] Among the Koita, "a boy usually receives his first perineal band (*sihi*) from his maternal uncle (*raimu*), and in return owes him certain services. . . . In a general way he performs the same services for his *mama,* whether father or paternal uncle, though a maternal uncle is supposed to exert more authority than any *mama.* . . . A man or boy might refuse to accompany his father or paternal uncle (*mama*), but would always go with his maternal uncle (*raimu*) without demur." In the case of the Roro-speaking tribes, "some time after a boy has had his ears pierced and while he is still a *miori,* his father kills a dog which he first hangs to the front of his house, and then takes to the house of the boy's maternal uncle to whom he gives it. . . . The boy is then sent to his uncle, who in his own house puts the *itaburi* on his nephew. The boy then returns to his father." With the Southern Massim, "it is a father's part to teach his son the various methods of fishing and garden-making, but in these duties he would be assisted by his wife's brothers who shared his responsibility. If a boy's father died his maternal uncle acted in his stead in every way. In the same way a child's maternal aunt replaces its mother, this being especially the case if the child be a girl. . . . A boy had to give a portion of the fish he caught or pig he speared to his maternal uncle. When travelling with his uncle he would do the hard work such as gathering firewood and cooking food, and in a çanoe journey he would be required to make himself generally useful to his uncle."[116]

In San Cristoval, Solomon Islands, "the *mau,* mother's brother, stands in a very close relationship to his sister's children. When he dies they share the property, though some of it goes to his brothers. A boy will marry his uncle's widow or her younger sister. He is expected to work in his uncle's garden, and may freely take of his uncle's possessions. If a boy wishes to go to school or to recruit on a plantation, the uncle's permission is asked. If he wishes to marry, he looks to his uncle to make the arrangements for the purchase of the woman he desires for his wife (from £8 to £10 is the price nowadays in Arosi). The uncle takes a part in the series of feasts made for small children, including that at which the name is given, and in the initiation of boys. When the actual brother of the mother dies, his nephew shaves a line across his head from ear to ear. . . . A boy and his mother's brother are on a relation of great freedom toward one another."[117] "The special relation of a sister's son to his uncle," says Rivers,[118] "has reached its highest known manifestation in the *vasu* institution of Fiji, while these islands also furnish a most pronounced example of the avoidance between brother and sister. . . . The special relation between a man and his sister's son still persists, though shorn of many of its most picturesque features. At the present time among the inland people the mother's brother still takes the chief part in the direction of his nephew's life. . . . In the old days the sister's son could take any of the possessions of his uncle and could, if he wished, kill any of his pigs. In this respect the old custom is no longer followed, and if the right were exerted, the nephew might be taken

115 Williams, in JAI, LIII, 368-369.
116 Seligmann, *Melanesians,* 67, 256, 257, 483.
117 Fox, in JAI, XLIX, 117-118, 144.
118 *Melan. Soc.,* I, 290-292.

to the court where his act would be treated as an ordinary case of larceny. On the coast it is well known that in the old days the *vasu* of a chief could go to the town of that chief and take any woman he desired and it seemed that this was once also true of the island tribes. . . . I inquired especially into a point which the many previous accounts of the *vasu* institution have left doubtful, viz., whether there is any difference between the duties and privileges of the own sister's son and of the many other persons who would be classed with him through the classificatory principle. It seemed quite clear that the rights would be exactly the same for the actual sister's son and for the son of a woman called by the same term of relationship as the sister, but in reality the father's brother's daughter. . . . It was also said that the husband of the father's sister, classed in nomenclature with the mother's brother, had the same duties and privileges and was liable to have any of his possessions taken by the son of his wife's brother." Hocart[119] suggests that the right of the sister's son to plunder his uncle is "an integral part of divine chieftainship, i.e., a natural consequence of the divinity of chiefs: if this can be definitely confirmed it cannot be a survival of a primitive mother-right as is commonly supposed." With respect to Fijian heralds, he says: "A man is sent to his mother's kinsmen because he is safe among them and because he is sure, in virtue of the sister's son's irresistible right (*vasu*), to obtain what he asks for. This usefulness of the sister's son may in turn have reacted upon his right and helped it to the extreme pitch to which it has attained in Fiji."

"The relationship between a man and his mother's brother is very close throughout the Banks Islands." In addition to the right to the property of an uncle after his death, "any of his goods may be taken by his sister's son during his lifetime, a right which is the source of many quarrels. . . . The difference in the status of the uncle and father is brought out very clearly in one way. If a man imposed on his sister's son a difficult task which resulted in his death or injury, no compensation could be demanded, but if a man put his own son to such a task compensation could be demanded by the mother's brother of the boy. If a man who is fighting is told to stop by his mother's brother he will do so at once, and it was said that if he had refused in the past he would have been killed by his uncle, but a man told by his father to stop would only do so if he felt inclined. A man treats his mother's brother with far greater respect than his father and may not put his hand above his head." Examples of this are cited, as well as of the following points. "The sister's son always goes in his uncle's canoe; it would not be necessary for a man to ask his nephew but the latter would take his place naturally, and if he refused to go he would be a despised man and if young he might be thrashed by his uncle." There are also special relations between a man and his father's sister, which are introduced for the sake of comparison with the foregoing. "The relation between a woman and her brother's child is one of the utmost importance in the Banks Islands. . . . It is in connection with marriage that the rôle of the father's sister becomes of the most importance. She arranges the marriage of her nephew in the ordinary course, and if the latter chooses for himself, she may forbid the match. A man would never marry against the will of his father's sister. . . . There is a certain amount of community of goods between a man and his father's sister. The latter could take her

---

119 Hocart, in JAI, XLIX, 51, 118. He has developed this further in his "Chieftainship in the Pacific," in AA, XVII, 634.

nephew's things but only those which he had received from his father. If a man wants any of the possessions of his father's sister, it is customary first to ask her son but they may be taken without his permission. This account applies to Mota." The husband of the father's sister also comes in for characteristic treatment. "The special feature about this relative, who is called *usur*, is that he is continually the subject of chaff from his wife's nephew."[120]

The maternal uncle plays an important rôle in the marriage-ceremonies in British Central Africa. "A man seeing a girl he would like to marry deputes his brother to go to the brother of the girl, who then calls the girl's maternal uncle, and he speaks to the mother on the subject. The mother consults the girl; if she refuse, nothing further is done. . . . After six months the mother of the girl prepares beer. The uncles of the young couple, mothers, fathers, sisters, and brothers are invited. The girl's maternal uncle then speaks, addressing himself to the maternal uncle of the husband, saying, 'We have called you here to drink beer and to see the house of your brother that you may return when you like. Should anything arise between these two newly married ones in the nature of a dispute, let them come to their respective uncles about the matter.' . . . The child is named usually after the maternal uncle's child-name which is given by the uncle."[121] In the case of child-marriage among the Ba-Mbala, who reckon kinship on the female side, "their children belong to the eldest maternal uncle." Among the Ba-Huana, "children are considered to belong to the family of the mother, and are sent to the village of the maternal uncle as soon as they arrive at puberty. . . . Great respect is paid to the eldest maternal uncle, and frequent presents must be made to him. . . . In the case of an orphan, the maternal uncle is the guardian." In the Congo region, "children appear to belong to the maternal uncles." The father leaves it to the maternal uncle to decide whether a son should accompany a visitor when the latter departs.[122]

In Nyasaland the maternal uncle of a girl is the first to be approached by the intending husband. He arranges with the parents. In some tribes the brother is first asked and the present is divided between father, mother, brother, and maternal uncle.[123] Among the Masai, "a maternal uncle (*ol-apu*) exercises great influence over his nephews, as it is believed that if he were to curse them they would die. He can at any time stop a fight in which one of his nephews is engaged by merely calling on his nephew to desist, as the nephew would be afraid of his right arm withering if he were to disobey. This power is to a certain extent reciprocal, and if a man were to start beating his wife he would have to stop if his maternal nephew ordered him to do so. . . . Besides the power of a maternal uncle to stop a fight, he has also the right to take anything which belongs to his nephew. If the uncle desires anything that is the property of his nephew's father, the nephew must buy it from his father, who will at once give it up when he knows for whom it is required. This power of taking property is reciprocal, and in fact applies to all persons who address one another as *ol-apu, ol-le-'ng-apu*, etc. A nephew, for instance, can go to his maternal uncle's kraal, and if his uncle is absent, he can slaughter a goat or drink his uncle's milk, and nothing would be said. He cannot, however, drive

120 Rivers, *Melan. Soc.*, I, 37-40.
121 Stannus, in JAI, XL, 308, 311.
122 Torday and Joyce, in JAI, XXXV,

410; in JAI, XXXVI, 284, 285, 286; and in JAI, XXXVII, 150.
123 Stigand, in JAI, XXXVII, 122.

off a cow without his uncle's sanction, but permission would not be refused. Other relatives have likewise some power of taking property."[124]

A custom among the Altaians, which is possibly a survival from an older family-system, is the presentation of *barky*, i.e., a gift, from the maternal uncle. "Until a boy is seven years old his hair is braided into two tresses worn in front of the ears. When he reaches his seventh birthday, his maternal uncle sends to him saying: 'Come; I will restore to you *barky*.' He goes, and his uncle cuts off the tresses, in return for which he is supposed to present the boy with a horse." Among the Ainu, "relationship through the mother is of more importance than that through the father, the maternal uncle being very often the most important member of the family."[125] In Tibet the maternal uncle has the deciding voice as to a girl's marriage.[126] In some districts, the Chinese groom's maternal uncle instructs him prior to his marriage.[127]

"It has been remarked that in the marriage of the widow by her son a trace of a former matrilineal system may perhaps be detected. It is possible to detect a more definite trace in the position of a mother's brother. Among the Semas, as among other Naga tribes, the greatest respect is enjoined on a man for his mother's brother. . . . In the case of a girl's relations to her mother's brother we find a definite obligation existing, which is inherited from the mother's brother by his son if it has not been discharged. When a man's sister's daughter is married, or when, after his father's death, his father's sister's daughter is married, he must give her a present."[128] Among the Kuki-Lushai clans "the name is usually chosen by the maternal uncle, but sometimes omens are consulted."[129] The Nairs of Malabar have a "song of the maternal uncle," wherein he invokes luck for the bridal pair.[130] Says Panikkar;[131] "It must be acknowledged that the Nāyar *Kārnavan* loves his sister's children more than his own. The explanation of this apparently unnatural feeling lies in two directions. First, the father is not necessarily of the same caste as the son. Secondly, there is always the possibility of a break in the union. Divorce is not a matter of any difficulty among the Nāyars, both the husband and wife having equal right to announce such a termination of their connection whenever either of the parties desires to do so. This instability of relationship is the principal reason why a man's affection for his own son is neither so intense nor so important as his affection for his sister's son. Also, in matrilineal communities family tradition descends only through the sister's progeny. As the Nāyars formed a fighting aristocracy before the British conquest, they had naturally acquired family tradition, mottoes and arms, which descend of right only in the female line. Hence also a man looks to the training of his sister's sons to keep up his family tradition. All these contribute to an extraordinary, and at first sight inexplicable, tenderness towards the children of one's sister."

The power of the maternal uncle among the Nairs is analogous to the *patria potestas* in groups living under the father-family.[132] "Authority in the family is wielded by the eldest member, who is called *Kārnavan*. He has full control of the common property, and manages the income very much as he pleases. He arranges marriages (*sambandhams*) for the boys as well as the girls of the family. He had till lately full power (at least in practice) of alienating

124 Hollis, in JAI, XL, 478-479.
125 Czaplicka, *Aborig. Siberia*, 54, 105.
126 Rockhill, in USNM, 1893, 725.
127 Grube, in *Veröffentl. aus dem k. Museum f. Vkde.*, VII, 24.

128 Hutton, *Sema Nagas*, 137.
129 Shakespear, in JAI, XXXIX, 382.
130 Risley, *Ethnog. Ind.*, I, 137.
131 In JAI, XLVIII, 262-263.
132 §419, of the text and *Case-Book*.

anything that belonged to them. His will was undisputed law. This is, perhaps, what is intended to be conveyed by the term *Matri-potestas* in communities of female descent. But it should be remembered that among the Nāyars the autocrat of the family is not the mother, but the mother's brother. The power of the *Kārnavan* over the family property has always been, in theory, limited, because the property was supposed to belong to every member of the family jointly. Till lately, however, it was practically impossible to limit the *Kārnavan's* power of mortgaging or even fully alienating it, because when it came to litigation the *Kārnavan* always pleaded that such action as he took was necessary for the welfare of the family, and justified himself by basing his arguments 'on the discretionary power' vested in him. However, the old theory has lately been asserted in law that a *Kārnavan* can sell or mortgage the property only with the consent of the other members of the family. All the moneys owing to the family can be paid only through him. He alone can give permission for the use of what belongs to the family. He can punish all the members of the family, either by depriving them temporarily of their allowance, or by prohibiting them to enter the house. In short, he is virtually the head of a tribe rather than the senior member of a family. '. . . . The wife of the *Kārnavan* has no standing in the family; yet as is but natural, she is supposed to be a dark and sinister force working against the interests of the *Tharawad*. Since she does not belong to the *Tharawad* of her husband she has no interest in its well-being, and it is generally supposed that the *Ammāvi* (the wife of the maternal uncle) is interested only in getting as much out of her husband's family for her own children as her influence over her husband allows. All the tales told to children have as the villain the *Ammāvi*, whose position is not only that of the wife of the maternal uncle, but also the mother-in-law of the brother. She is universally considered to be a sort of sinister step-mother."[133]

Williamson[134] quotes several authors with regard to the relationship between a child and his mother's brother in Tonga. "Pritchard says that the term *tamaha* referred to a sister's children, who could appropriate anything belonging to their maternal uncles and their offspring." Another writer reports that the *fahu* or sister's son had the right to take all he wished from his maternal uncle, and his descendants could do so from those of the uncle. "These statements indicate an extension of the rights of the children so as to be exercisable by their descendants, and against those of the uncle (as in Samoa), and thus take the matter beyond what is involved by the ordinary conception of the relationship." Rivers[135] gives more detailed information. "In Tonga the *tuasina* or mother's brother is 'the same as a servant for his sister's son. He has to listen to the boy all the time.' The sister's son is especially honoured by his uncle and can take anything he likes from his uncle's place; his pig, his canoe or anything he chooses, and no objection will be raised. Indeed, I was told that a man would be very glad to see his nephew take any of his goods. A man looks after his sister's son while he is young and, when the latter goes to his uncle's house, he can do as he chooses and is subject to no restrictions on his conduct such as we shall find affect him when he visits his father's sister. On the other hand, a boy has not to be especially obedient to his maternal uncle; if the boy's father tells him to do anything, he will do it, but, if told

---

133 Panikkar, in JAI, XLVIII, 262.
134 *Cent. Polyn.*, II, 182.

135 *Melan. Soc.*, I, 366-367.

by his uncle, he will do it or not as he pleases. . . . I could not discover that the *tuasina* would take any special part in ceremonial connected with his nephew either in connection with naming, incision or marriage. . . . A woman can also take anything from the house of her maternal uncle and has the same rights and privileges as her brother. . . . The aunt may take anything from her nephew. A man honours his father's sister more than any other relative, even more than his father or his father's elder brother, and it was believed in the old time that, if anyone offended his father's sister, he would die. . . . There are many restrictions on the intercourse of a man with his father's sister; he may talk to her and address her by name, but he may not eat in the same place with her nor may he eat anything which she has carried. He will not sit on her bed and if she comes into a house in which he is present, he will at once go out."

Among the Tlinkits, "when a man dies, leaving children, their maternal uncles and aunts assume their support and care."[136] The custom is found in some American tribes that a nephew must marry the widow of his uncle; this being a development of relationship through females.[137] Pontiac "often intimated to me that he could be content to reign in his country in subordination to the King of Great Britain, and was willing to pay him such annual acknowledgement as he was able in furs, and to call him his uncle."[138] The Omaha have been long on the father-family stage; yet mothers' brothers and own brothers "seem to have more authority than the father or mother in matters relating to a girl's welfare. They were consulted before she was bestowed in marriage, unless she eloped with her husband. . . . Girls can be more familiar with their mother's brother than with their own brothers. . . . Even boys are more familiar with their mother's brother than with their own father, and they often play tricks on the former."[139] "In the event of the death of the mother and father, provided the father had no brothers, the uncle (mother's brother) had full control of the children and no relative of the father could dispute the right of the uncle to the children. During the lifetime of the parents the uncle was as alert as their father to defend the children or to avenge a wrong done them. The children always regarded their uncle as their friend, ever ready to help them." In the spring, after the thunder sounded, the boys of the same tribe had a festivity called, literally, "striped face," the word referring to the mask worn at that time. "A dried bladder, with holes cut for the mouth and eyes, was pulled over the head; the bladder was striped lengthwise in black and white, to represent lightning. The boys carried clubs and scattered over the village. Each boy went to the tent of his uncle (his mother's brother) and beat with his club against the tent pole at the door, while he made a growling sound in imitation of thunder. The uncle called out, 'What does Striped Face want?' The boy disguised his voice, and said, 'I want leggings or moccasins or some other article.' Then the uncle called him in and made him a present. Should the uncle refuse to give anything the boy might punch a hole in the tent or do some other mischief. But generally the sport ended pleasantly and was greatly enjoyed by old and young."[140] "Among the Choctas . . . if a boy is to be placed at school his [maternal] uncle, instead of his father, takes him to the mission and makes the arrangements. An uncle,

136 Jones, *Thlingets*, 199.
137 Ratzel, *Vkde.*, II, 629.
138 Rogers, *America*, 242.

139 Dorsey, in BAE, III, 268, 270.
140 Fletcher and LaFlesche, in BAE, XXVII, 325, 370.

among the Winnebagoes, may require services of a nephew, or administer correction, which his own father would neither ask nor attempt. In like manner with the Iowas and Otoes, an uncle may appropriate to his own use his nephew's horse and gun, or other personal property, without being questioned, which his own father would have no recognized right to do. But over his nieces this same authority is more significant, from his participation in their marriage contracts."141 Among certain Colombia Indians, girls are sold in marriage under the full authority of their maternal uncles.142

In Damascus the close connection between nephew and maternal uncle is indicated in formulas of appreciation or of imprecation: "God bless his uncle!" and "God damn his uncle!" The following proverb refers to a case where a nephew even exceeds a bad uncle in baseness: "If a son goes to pieces morally, he belongs two-thirds to his maternal uncle;" that is to say, two-thirds of his baseness he has from his uncle and one-third is his own contribution. "The maternal uncle has more love for his nephews and nieces than has the paternal uncle, just as the love of mothers for their children is greater than that of fathers. An Arab proverb states: 'The vein of the maternal uncle sleeps not.' The Prophet, who wanted to recognize with gratitude the services of Saad, took him by the hand and said: 'This is my maternal uncle.' The cited examples set clearly into light the belief in a spiritual relation between anyone and his maternal uncle."143

Inheritance and Succession. In New Guinea, "even where the family is patriarchal, the chief heirs are, as is understandable in a matriarchal state, the relatives on the mother's side, the *Gai's.* In the second grade come the children, then the man's brothers, and last of all the widow. . . . The *Gai's* inherit the most valuable house-utensils . . . and weapons," but they do not get them all.144 Against the servile position of the woman is to be contrasted her determinative influence in matters of inheritance, "which goes so far that the uncle starts nearer to his sister's children than their father."145 Among the Dobuans, "when a man dies his private property is taken by his sister's children principally, then by his brothers, and even his own sons may have a small share. If his sister's children are too young, his brothers will take their share, and pay the children back when they have grown up. Should one of the nephews attend to his uncle with loving care during the illness preceding death, he will become the tobuio, or preferred heir, and receive the biggest share of the property. . . . When a woman dies her bodily ornaments belong to her sister's children, and her other property to her own children."146 In San Cristoval, "the nephew receives his uncle's property when the uncle dies, except some portions reserved for the brothers of the dead man; and during lifetime the uncle and nephew share things, and are quite free to take each other's possessions if they so wish."147 "The relationship between a man and his mother's brother is very close throughout the Banks Islands. In the old days there is no doubt that the sister's son would have been the heir of his uncle and would have taken all his property, including any objects of magical value, but at the present time this has been much modified." In Pentecost, which is the most archaic part

141 Morgan, in *Smithson. Contrib. to Knowledge,* XVII, 158; Westermarck, *Marriage,* II, 284-285.
142 Nicholas, in AA, III, 647.
143 Wilken, in VG, I, 402-403, note.

144 Hagen, *Papua's,* 261, 262.
145 Blum, *Neu-Guinea,* 28.
146 Bromilow, in AAAS, 1909, 474, 475.
147 Fox, in JAI, XLIX, 145.

of Melanesia included in the author's[148] survey, "it is clear that inheritance should properly be matrilineal, the land and personal possessions of a man passing at his death, not to his own children, but to members of his own moiety, and especially to the children of his sister. At the present time it is becoming the custom to transmit property, or, at any rate, property of certain kinds, to the children; but this is quite recent and has perhaps only come about as the result of European influence, not necessarily as the direct result of European teaching, but as the result of the increased intercourse between different parts of Melanesia which has followed the arrival of Europeans. I was told that inheritance by the children is quite modern, and this information receives strong support from the account of Dr. Codrington. At the time when it was written, only about thirty years ago, the son received nothing except what his father gave him during his life. . . . A clear indication of the priority of matrilineal inheritance is to be found in the case of land. Dr. Codrington[149] has pointed out the definite distinction between the modes of inheritance of ancient cultivated ground and land newly reclaimed from the bush. The former passes to the sister's children, while the latter is taken by the children of the man who cleared it."

In South Africa, where the patriarchate prevails, "the king's son remains the heir, but he must be the eldest son of the chief wife; and so much weight is given to the mother by this qualification, that in the long run the kingship is also subject to the female line of descent."[150] Among the Banyai the successor to the throne is chosen rather from the descendants of the last king through his sister than directly.[151] Among the Ewe-speaking peoples, who trace kinship through females, the order of inheritance is from elder to next younger brother or, if there are no brothers, from uncle to the eldest son of the eldest sister.[152] In most of the tribes of the Gold Coast the law of nephew-inheritance prevails; "at the death of the family-head, the heritage—rights as well as debts—goes over to the oldest son of the oldest sister of the man."[153] On the lower Congo, "if a man die, the bulk of his property goes to his sister's son, not to his son; the reason being that of the blood-relationship of the nephew there can be no doubt, but the descent of the son may be questioned. . . . A strange exception is made when a man marries a slave of his; the son then ranks first in this case, as the natives say that he is not only presumably the next-of-kin by birth, but also by purchase, as the mother belonged to the father."[154] In Nyasaland, "the sultan is succeeded, not by his own son, but by his eldest sister's eldest son"; if that son is "very stupid," his next younger brother succeeds, and so on down. The chief's subjects "kneel to him, as he himself kneels to his invalided old mother."[155] In East Central Africa, a man's heir is the son of his mother or, failing him, his sister's son; his own children are excluded. "The succession to the chieftainship is based on the same principles, which is curious, considering the terrible severity with which known cases of adultery, in the case of chiefs' wives, are punished."[156] A man's heir, among the Ba-Huana, is his eldest brother, then his eldest sister, then her eldest son. If there are no heirs, the goods are burnt and the slaves freed. The magician

148 Rivers, *Melan. Soc.*, I, 37; II, 96-97.
149 *Melanesians*, 64, 67.
150 Starcke, *Prim. Fam.*, 73.
151 Ratzel, *Vkde.*, I, 405.
152 Ellis, *Ewe*, 207.

153 Vortisch, in *Globus*, LXXXIX, 280.
154 Phillips, in JAI, XVII, 229.
155 Coudenhove, in *Atl. Mo.*, CXXXI, 60.
156 Macdonald, in JAI, XXII, 102.

is succeeded on his death by his sister's son.[157] The son never succeeds his father, among the Mombasa, the estate becoming the property of the nearest male relative in the female line, generally the grandson by the eldest daughter.[158] The Ilova mother gives blood and rank. Inheritance through women is much preferred.[159] With reference to succession among the Wayao it is said: "The common rule of discriminating between the children of a brother and sister and those of two brothers or of two sisters is present here, and is combined with the equally common one of succession to the sister's son. The rule of succession is, strictly speaking, to the eldest son of the eldest sister. If, however, a man and his advisers consider him to be unsuitable, or in event of his death, the succession passes to the following in order of precedence: younger son of the eldest sister, younger son of a younger sister, and son of own daughter. . . . An heir, on succeeding, may marry the wife or wives of his maternal uncle, but not if he has previously married one of his daughters."[160] The Tuareg count inheritance through the mother; one is the heir of his uncle, not of his father.[161] Among the Berbers, property and political position have long been inherited in the female line. The sister's son inherits or, if she has no children, the brother of the same mother. Own children can merely receive presents.[162]

In the Punjab, a bride "should be a virgin, beautiful, young and free from disease. She should also have a brother, for otherwise, according to the marriage contract, her first-born son would have to be given to her father, in order that he might become his maternal grandfather's heir."[163] On the Malabar Coast, "where succession through the female line is observed, a man's sister's son, and not his own, inherits."[164] "The Nāyar family consists of all the descendants from the same ancestress, counting relationship exclusively from the side of the mother. Theoretically it may contain all those who have a common ancestry of this kind, but, in practice, when families grow unwieldy, they divide the common property and live under different roofs. . . . The family owns property in common. What a private individual earns belongs to him exclusively, but when he dies it is joined to the rest of the family, according to the old Nāyar law which is still prevalent in some parts. When the family becomes unwieldy, or certain members show insubordination, the family property is partitioned equally among *each female line*. That is to say, if there are three sisters in the family, each having daughters and granddaughters, the partition is done in such a way that each of the ancestresses founds a separate family among whom the original property is equally divided. . . . There are many instances in which, though family partition took place at least a hundred and fifty years ago, the members continue to call each other brothers and sisters, as if they were the nearest blood relations."[165] In Travancore the royal line ran out because there were no sisters through whom nephew-heirs could be born.[166] "The laws which govern the succession to the State of Travancore are very peculiar. The descent, according to the usages of the Nairs of the Western Coast, is in the female line. Thus on the death of the Raja the sovereignty passes not to his sons, who can in no case inherit, but to his uterine

157 Torday and Joyce, in JAI, XXXVI, 284, 291.
158 Johnstone, in JAI, XXXII, 270.
159 Letourneau, *Polit.*, 92.
160 Sanderson, in JAI, L, 370-374.
161 Pommerol, *Sahariennes*, 310, 312.

162 De Goeje, in *Gids*, XXXI, II, 27, 28.
163 Rose, in JAI, XXXVIII, 410.
164 Fawcett, in JASB, II, 344.
165 Panikkar, in JAI, XLVIII, 260-261.
166 Mateer, in JAI, XII, 305.

brothers if he has any. Failing these, or on their demise, it passes to his sister's sons, or to his sister's daughter's sons, and so on. Hence it follows that the only adoptions which are performed by the Rajas of Travancore are not of males to supply the place of sons of their own body, but of females through whom the line must be continued. Any failure of the direct female descent requires the selection and adoption of two or more females from the immediate relatives of the family who reside at certain places in Travancore. The females so adopted are designated the Tumbrattees or Ranis of Attingah, and by the laws and usages of Travancore are assigned a distinguished rank as alone entitled to give heirs to the state, and enjoy many important privileges. Such an adoption occurred in 1788, when two sisters were selected and adopted as Ranis of Attingah. The younger sister died after giving birth to a female child which also died. From the elder sister the present family of Travancore are descended, the late Raja being the grandson (daughter's son), the present the great grandson (daughter's daughter's son). In 1857 the line of Travancore was again threatened with eventual extinction. The sister of the late Raja (granddaughter—daughter's daughter—of the elder of the two sisters adopted in 1788) left five children, four sons, the second of whom is the present chief, and one daughter. The daughter died suddenly, leaving two sons. The Tumbrattees of Attingah thus became extinct, and although the state after the death of the Raja would devolve successively on his four nephews and his two grandnephews, the line, unless recruited by the adoption of Tumbrattees as before, would have expired with them. Under these circumstances the late Raja intimated to the Resident that, in strict conformity with former usage and precedent, he proposed to bring in two, the most eligible female members from among his relations, as senior and junior Ranis. Two ladies were accordingly adopted with the sanction of the British Government."[167]

In South Celebes nobility reproduces itself more through the woman than through the man, for the latter is not in a position to raise wholly to his own rank a child begotten by him with a woman of lower birth, while the woman can, in a corresponding case, raise her child to her own status. This is regarded by Wilken[168] as an undoubted survival of an original matriarchate, for under it the woman has precedence in ennobling. "Rank is inherited from the mother, not from the father, corresponding to the Marshall Islands view that the mother of a child is always known but it is not always known who the father was." Examples are given. The same system prevails on Kushai, in the Carolines, and a case is mentioned where a man's oldest son, a boy of about fourteen years, stood higher than his father because his mother was the daughter of the deceased king, while a younger sister of this marriage had a still higher rank than her brother. It is the custom on Ponapé that "rank is inherited from the mother and not from the father."[169]

"As far as Polynesia is concerned, we find the maternal arrangement clearest in the Tonga Islands. Here inheritance of property still follows the female line and so too is nobility transmitted."[170] "In Tonga, according to Mariner, nobility depended upon relationship to the *tuitonga* or the *hau*, that was in effect upon relationship to one of the three great ruling families of Tongatabu. In every family nobility descended by the female line, children acquiring their

167 Murray, in JAI, XLV, 307-308, quoting from Sir Charles Aitchison's *Treaties*.
168 Wilken, in VG, I, 361.

169 Finsch, *Ethnol. Erfahr.*, III, 128, 199, 240.
170 Wilken, in VG, I, 399.

rank by inheritance from the mother's side, for where the mother was not noble, the children were not nobles, but all the children of a female noble were, without exception, nobles." Examples are given in profusion. "So far as definite statements are concerned, the evidence of a survival of a system of matrilineal descent in Tonga is fuller and stronger than in Samoa." In the latter case, "succession was in the main, though apparently not entirely, patrilineal; but I am going to refer to evidence which seems to point more or less clearly to ideas derived from a system of matrilineal descent which had prevailed in the past, and which, indeed, had not died out completely, and to customs which may have had their origin in matrilineal descent. . . . As regards my references to the passing of descents from mothers to daughters, I must point out that they would pass to sons also, as all the children of the same mother would, under a system of matrilineal descent, belong to her social group. The point of the matter is, however, that each son would be, so far as the line of descent was concerned, a *cul-de-sac;* it would come to an end on his death, and it would be *through* his sister that it would be continued to subsequent generations. . . . Why was it that a chief, on succeeding to the official title of his predecessor, has to make a valuable present to his sister? I suggest that the custom was based upon the effect upon a system of patrilineal succession of a still lingering recognition of the right of succession involved by matrilineal descent —that he was buying from his sister the possible claims that her children might through her have to the succession." The bulk of the information which the author[171] has with respect to the question of matrilineal descent in the Society Islands comes from Tahiti. "Moerenhout, who apparently applies the title *ari'i* to the great chiefs only, distinguishing the minor chiefs by the term *tavana,* says that if a daughter who was the only scion of a noble family married a man who was not the son of a principal chief, a son born of the marriage immediately took the title of *ari'i;* and that, when the father was only a subordinate chief, and the mother belonged to the high aristocracy, then she was regent. This is probably a case of succession at birth; but I think it involves the proposition that the mother's high nobility of family rank descended to the son, notwithstanding the inferior rank of the father. . . . On the other hand, if a prince made a *mésalliance,* the children born of that union had no right to the privileges or the position of their father, and only inherited a mixed position, in proportion, it is true, to the power of the father." Examples are cited. "A woman could pass her rank to her child notwithstanding the inferiority of its other parent, whilst a man could not do this. These statements suggest some recognition of a system of matrilineal descent." The Maori have the matriarchate, though the patriarchate is coming in; the wife lifts the man to her rank, not the man the wife.[172]

The Mexican emperor was chosen from the brothers of the dead ruler or, in default of these, from his nephews.[173] In Peru, heritage followed the lines characteristic of the mother-family.[174] In British Guiana, "the sons of the daughters of a chief have the right of succession to the dignity of their grandfather, not the sons of the chief, though they do not hold at all strictly to such a succession."[175] Among the Shingu the chieftaincy descends to a son or, if

171 Williamson, *Cent. Polyn.*, II, 88, 92-93, 97, 109, 110, 113, 114.
172 Wilken, in VG, I, 399.

173 Biart, *Aztèques*, 45 (edit. 1885).
174 De la Vega, *Yncas*, 334.
175 Schomburgk, *Brit.-Guiana*, I, 169.

there is none, to a sister's son.[176] "Among some [Araucanian] tribes the eldest brother of the deceased inherits at his death, as being more certainly of his blood. This peculiarity attracted the attention of the chroniclers at the time of the Spanish Conquest, throughout America."[177]

Survivals of these practices exist among the people of the Pyrenees. "When the daughter marries, her name is added to that of her husband, is borne by her children, often even registered by the civil state. . . . Usage still bestows upon the sons of heiresses the name of the house where they were born: if they have left the country, and return imbued with the ideas of our civilization, they are amazed sometimes at the silence to which the memory of their father has been relegated, and they seek, but in vain, to relieve themselves of the maternal name. . . . And, again, in the country, when it is a daughter who is the oldest, she becomes the actual head of the family and, in reality, the sole heiress. Then, again, she exercises power in the house, and the people of the country say that her husband is her chief domestic;—at most, her man of affairs. He has brought into the house with his person only his work and the hope of posterity. In the eyes of society, it is the woman who personifies the house and not her husband. In the relations of family to family she intervenes alone: hers to receive, to express the congratulations and condolences of private life."[178]

§418. Transitional Forms.

SPENCER and Gillen[1] have pointed out the difficulty, if not the impossibility, of stating definitely whether descent in an Australian tribe is through the men or through the women. "It is not easy to say with anything like certainty that one tribe is in any particular respect more 'primitive' than another. It is, for example, generally assumed that counting descent in the female is a more primitive method than counting descent in the male line, and that of two tribes, in one of which we have maternal descent and in the other paternal, the former is in this respect in a more primitive condition than the latter; but it may even be doubted whether in all cases the counting of descent in the female line has preceded the counting of it in the male line. The very fact that descent is counted at all, that is, that any given individual when born has some distinguishing name, because he or she is born of some particular woman, indicates the fact that men and women are divided into groups bearing such distinctive names, for it must be remembered that in these savage tribes the name which is transmitted to offspring, and by means of which descent is counted, is always a group name. When once we have any such system, whether it be totemic or otherwise, then we have arrived at a stage in which it is possible to imagine that the men of one particular group have marital relations only with women of another particular group. Supposing we take two of these exogamous groups, which we will designate A and B. Thus men of A have marital relations with women of B, and *vice versa*. When once these groups are established, then, there is, in reality, no difficulty whatever in counting descent in the male just as easily as in the female line. It is quite true that the individual father

176 Von den Steinen, *Zent. Bras.*, 331.
177 Latcham, in JAI, XXXIX, 354.

178 Cordier, *Droit de famille aux Pyrénées*, quoted by Wilken, in VG, I, 246.
1 *Nat. Tr. Cent. Aust.*, 36, note.

of any particular child may not be known, but this, so far as counting descent under the given conditions is concerned, is a matter of no importance. The only name which can be transmitted, and by means of which descent can be counted (as indeed it is amongst the Australian tribes of the present day), is the group name, and as women of group B can only have marital relations with men of group A, it follows that the father of any child of a woman of group B must belong to group A, and therefore, though the actual father may not be known, there appears to be no inevitable necessity for the child to pass into group B rather than into group A. On the other hand, if we suppose men of one group to have marital relations with women of more than one other group, then, unless each woman be restricted to one man, descent, if counted at all, must of necessity follow the female line." Referring to one particular tribe, Mathews[2] states: "I have been trying for some years to ascertain definitely how the totems descend—whether through the men or through the women; but I am not yet satisfied. . . . Some of them follow the father, some the mother, and some follow neither parent. Other individuals have two totems."

In Murray Island, Torres Strait, the wife retains her own totem, while the children may take that of their mother's sister or of their father.[3] "We shall not go astray in ascribing to the Papuans of German New Guinea a mean between the systems of father-right and mother-right, under which the mother's group as well as the father's lays claim to the child, and which leads to all thinkable compromises. For instance, guardianship is arranged regularly according to the maternal system while inheritance follows now the maternal line and now the paternal." In Melanesia, despite the system of mother-descent, "in practice, as in the devolution of property and in the handing on of religious and magic rites, a man always put as far as he could his son into his own place, and a rich and powerful man would secure a high place in the Suqe [society] for his son in very early years; thus the great man's son would succeed to his place, and become to some extent an hereditary chief. . . . The son does not inherit chieftainship, but he inherits, if his father can manage it, what gives him chieftainship, his father's *mana,* his charms, magic songs, stones and apparatus, his knowledge of the way to approach spiritual beings, as well as his property." Again, "a first-born son remains ten days in the house in which he was born, during which time the father's kinsmen take food to the mother." On the tenth day, "they, the kin of the father, and therefore not kin of the infant," perform a ceremony indicating that they will feed and keep the son. "There is clearly in this a movement towards the patriarchal system, a recognition of the tie of blood through the father and of duties that follow from it. Another sign of the same advance of the father's right is to be seen in the very different custom that prevails in the Banks' Islands on the birth of a first-born son; there is raised upon that event, a noisy and playful fight, . . . after which the father buys off the assailants with payment of money to the . . . kinsmen . . . of the child and his mother. It is hardly possible to be mistaken in taking this fight to be a ceremonial, if playful, assertion of the claim of the mother's kinsfolk to the child as one of themselves, and the father's payment to be the quieting of their claim and the securing of his own position as head of his own family."[4] These cases illustrate the "remarkable tendency throughout the is-

---

2 In AA, VII, 303, 304.
3 Hunt, in JAI, XXVIII, 10.

4 Codrington, *Melanesians,* 55, 56, 57, 230, 231.

lands of Melanesia towards the substitution of a man's own children for his sister's children and others of his kin in succession to his property; and this appears to begin where the property is the produce of the man's own industry."[5]

Among the Southern Massim a blood-price would be paid to the brother of the deceased. "If there were no brother, the mother or maternal uncle would take it, and it appeared that even the sister might be compensated, especially if the mother were not alive. When deaths on both sides occurred in a brawl, the survivors did not as a rule cry quits immediately even if the number killed were equal; but ceremonial atonement was made for each. It was pointed out that the blood price was a matter which concerned the family rather than the hamlet-group (though these two groups were often identical), and this was one of the instances where the relationship of a man to his father was practically acknowledged; it was distinctly the duty of a father to help find the blood price paid for his son's misdoings."[6]

Rivers[7] writes: "There is a wide difference between the modes of descent and inheritance in Melanesia. While descent is almost always matrilineal where it is proper to speak of descent at all, inheritance is largely patrilineal at the present time, even in the islands which possess the most archaic forms of social structure. The island in which matrilineal inheritance is most strict is Pentecost . . . and there is evidence that not long ago, the matrilineal mode of inheritance existed in this island in a pure form. In other islands the available evidence points to a process whereby the matrilineal is gradually passing over into the patrilineal mode, and it is clear that this is no recent innovation, but one which goes back to a time long before the advent of European influence." With reference to Pentecost Island, "it was said that formerly all property belonged to the verana, viz., the subdivision of the moiety the exact nature of which is uncertain, and it was said that even if property belonged to individual persons it was not inherited by individuals but by the verana as a whole. Canoes are in no case individual property even now, but always belong to the verana as a whole. At the present time it is clear that property in general is owned by individuals and should properly be transmitted to the sister's son, though a change is going on whereby the property of a man is being inherited more and more by his own children." By way of contrast the author cites the society of Amhrim, also in the New Hebrides, which is organized on the most definitely patrilineal basis. "An examination of the social structure of the island showed no signs of matrilineal institutions, nor of any dual system. The existence of local exogamy made the village a social unit of great importance, and this grouping was strictly patrilineal, while another social group, called the vantinbül, of especial importance in connection with the tenure and transmission of property, consisted mainly of persons related through patrilineal ties, though it also included the sister's son and certain other relatives through the mother. It was only on examining the ceremonial observances of the people that there came to light a number of facts pointing to earlier matrilineal institutions." There exists here an organization called the Mangge, in which men, and also to some extent women, gradually rise in rank. "There are about twenty stages, the ritual of which becomes more and more elaborate on pass-

---

5 Thomson, in JAI, XXIV, 381, note.
6 Seligmann, Melanesians, 571.

7 Melan. Soc., II, 99; I, 209; Rivers, in JAI, XLV, 230, 232, 233.

ing upwards in the hierarchy. The record of its ritual forms a large mass of data of the most varied kind, but I did not hear of a single feature which brought the participants in the rites into any sort of relation with the mother's relatives or the mother's village. On the other hand, there were observances which showed the existence of the closest ties with the father's relatives. The whole organisation is founded on a cult of dead ancestors. In most of the higher grades an image in human form is made, which becomes the abode of the ghost of the father's father of the man who is taking new rank, or if his father is dead, it may be the ghost of the father who inhabits this image. In either case it is the business of the ghostly resident to look after the welfare of his descendant, to shield him from injury by others and to further his material prosperity. . . . The social relations between a man and his mother's brother in a patrilineal community have long been regarded as an indication of a preëxisting condition of mother-right. The Ambrim condition differs from most previously recorded cases in that the social ties with the mother's brother show themselves only in ceremonial and not in the transactions of everyday life, but this only makes the case for regarding these social functions as survivals all the stronger, for even the most determined opponents of the doctrine of survival will acknowledge that if survival occurs at all, it is in ceremonial. An important feature of the Ambrim practices is that the social functions of the mother's brother clearly fall to his lot as a member of the social group formed by the mother's relatives. Feature after feature of the indigenous ceremonial of Ambrim shows that this ceremonial embodies an old order in which social relations of the most definite kind must have existed between a man and his mother's people. Last, and I think most instructive, of all these Ambrim customs is the persistence of the old social order in connection with death. The repetition of the rites of the *Mangge* as the leading feature of the funeral ceremonies shows definitely that the *Mangge* has permeated the whole ritual of death, but it has not been able to exclude the fulfilment of certain obligations towards the village of the dead man's mother. This persistence of the old order in connection with death is shown even more decisively in the duty of the mother's father to look after his descendant in the world of the dead while his father's father is responsible for his welfare during life. The evidence now brought forward comes only from one island of Melanesia. Standing alone it would not justify us in accepting the precedence of matrilineal institutions as a general feature of Melanesian society. There is, however, much evidence from other parts of Melanesia showing that an earlier matrilineal mode of transmission has changed in the patrilineal direction." Before presenting such evidence from another of the author's writings, we may note his conclusion with respect to this study: "While in Melanesia the general social condition of the matrilineal peoples supports the idea that they represent an earlier stage of social progress, elsewhere, and especially in North America, the matrilineal peoples have on the whole advanced in general culture beyond the level reached by those who practise father-right. It is possible that some mechanism has been in action here which has produced a change from father- to mother-right, or has led to the development of each from some state of society which cannot strictly be regarded as either patrilineal or matrilineal. Only when far more attention than hitherto has been paid to the social functions connected with relationship, both in ceremonial and secular life, can we expect to reach conclusions of any value concerning the relation to one another in time of mother- and father-right." The author is an adherent, though not a fanatical one, of acculturation as against parallelism.

In his *History of Melanesian Society,* Rivers[8] mentions other transitional cases and the difficulty of determining relationships and descent, especially when native words have a meaning for which there is no exact English equivalent. He cites many examples. To illustrate at length: "The *sogoi* of a Banks islander are those of his own *veve* or moiety; the Melanesian has learnt, quite wrongly, that the English equivalent of *sogoi* is 'related,' and as his father is not his *sogoi,* he believes that he is justified in saying that he and his father are not related to one another. When such a statement is made in a scientific publication, the writer is making the same kind of mistake as the Melanesian, a mistake due to an assumption which is at the present moment a most serious hindrance to progress in anthropology. This assumption is that European languages possess terms which are the exact equivalents of the terms of Melanesian or other families of language belonging to rude forms of culture. The word *sogoi* can only be translated by 'kin' or 'relative,' if these words are used in senses very different from those they ordinarily possess in the English language. It is quite possible that at one time the relations between father and child in Melanesia were of such a kind that it would have been correct to say that father and child were not kin in the usual English sense. The regulation that a man and his father may not eat together, the belief that father and son necessarily have different mental dispositions, and the fact that, if a man injure his own child, he is held to be responsible to its maternal uncle, suggest that, at one time, the father was so much a stranger to his offspring that it would perhaps have been correct to say that kinship with the father was not recognised. In the present condition of Melanesia, however, the relations between father and child are of such a kind that the superficial observer of Melanesian life would probably fail to notice anything which would differentiate the relationship from that of a civilised family. There is thus a considerable mass of evidence which shows that there exist in the matrilineal communities of Melanesia social relations with the father and with the father's relatives which differ in no obvious respect from those existing between related persons of the same social group, and there is evidence that this condition is not recent, but goes back far into the past. At the same time, it is probable that the relations with the father and the father's moiety were once different from those which now exist. . . . The available evidence, then, points to a great change having taken place in the freedom and intimacy of the social relations between members of different social groups. With this increased freedom there seems to have gone on a progressive increase in the degree of recognition of the relationship of a person with his father and his father's relatives, until the present condition has been reached in which the superficial observer would see nothing exceptional from the civilised point of view, in which it is necessary to look below the surface, to consult tradition and study social relations in detail, in order to find indications of widely different functions of the social grouping. . . . The result of this inquiry into the nature of descent in Melanesia is to show that, in the matrilineal communities of this area, a change has taken place in the social importance of the line of descent which shows itself especially clearly in the altered status of the father."

8 I, 384; II, 92, 95, 96, 102-103, 155-158, 573.

In the same work is considered the position of the maternal uncle, as indica-tive of the transition to the father-family. "The great interest in this relation-ship arises from the fact that its special functions in patrilineal communities have so often been regarded as survivals of mother-right. The records of this book allow us to compare the position of this relative in communities practising matrilineal descent with that which he occupies where descent follows the father. . . . When we turn to the patrilineal people of Fiji, we find the mother's brother still occupying a most important place. The rights of the sis-ter's son or *vasu* in Fiji are so well known that it is unnecessary to enter on the subject here; it need only be noted that the right of the *vasu* which stands out preëminently is that he may take any of his uncle's property, and we have seen that in the matrilineal Banks Islands also the sister's son may take any, even the most valued, possessions of his uncle. The Melanesian evidence is in ac-cord with the widely held opinion that when the special relation between a man and his mother's brother is found in a patrilineal community, it is a survival of mother-right. . . . Among a people with mother-right the position of the mother's brother as an elder of a person's own social division is clearly established; it is so much a commonplace and familiar matter that special regulations con-cerning the relationship need not exist. It is only as the rights of the father increase that those of the mother's brother gradually become more obvious. In every community in which the rights of the father are gradually growing in strength and importance there must be occasions of conflict between the mother's brother and the father, and it will only be slowly that the respective positions of the two will become defined. . . . I take as an example the special case of the compensation given to the mother's brother by a father who in-jures his own child. We can have little doubt that at one time this compensa-tion had to be given to the mother's brother by any man who injured a child, and that there was no thought of distinguishing the father from other men. At this stage no one would think of formulating a regulation concerning the case in which it was the father who had injured his child. As the rights of the father grew, there would sooner or later come a time when it would happen that a father caused the injury or death of his child. He might put forward the claim of exemption from the penalty, or more probably, this claim would not be definitely made, but the matter would be talked about, and thus a vague formulation of the special condition would arise. As succeeding cases occurred, this formulation would gradually grow more definite until there was reached such a regulation as that of which I was told in Mota. In fact, we have here simply a special instance of the growth of Law; in the different degrees of defi-niteness of the formulation of the functions of the mother's brother in Melane-sia, we have a simple example of the way in which this growth takes place."

With reference to succession, the author continues: "Among the chiefs it seems that royal succession was counted in both lines and, as we have seen, chieftainship of the highest rank depended on both parents having been of royal rank and in these cases it is certainly not correct to speak of succession as matrilineal. As we have seen also, the grade of the marriage and the rank of the children depends quite as much on the rank of the father as on that of the mother, and the only case in which it seems applicable to use the term matrilineal succession is when a child has only one parent of chief's rank. When it is the mother who has the rank of a chief it seems that the offspring belongs to the chiefs, though it is recognised that the chiefly rank is stained by the plebeian condition of the father. If, on the other hand, it is the father who is of higher rank in a mixed marriage, it seems that the offspring is not counted as a chief at all, and the Hawaiians seem themselves to recognise that this is due to the uncertainty of male parentage."

Certain conclusions follow: "The inquiry conducted in this chapter has led to the conclusion that matrilineal descent is a feature of Melanesian society which now possesses far less social significance than in the past. In some places it is perhaps only the last relic of a condition of mother-right which once governed the whole social life of the people; which regulated marriage, directed the transmission of property, and, where chieftainship existed at all, determined its mode of succession, while many other aspects of social life were altogether governed by the ideas of relationship arising out of this condition. The definite recognition of the relationship between father and child seems to have greatly affected these social functions. It would seem that a gradual process has been in action whereby the matrilineal organisations of Melanesia have been robbed of much of their social importance, until in some cases they have become little more than empty forms." Again, "the dual organisation with matrilineal descent which is now found only here and there in Melanesia once had a far wider distribution, and was accompanied by a condition of communism, together with a state of dominance of the old men so pronounced that they were able to monopolise all the young women of the community. The study of the varieties of social organisation and of marriage at present existing in Melanesia showed that the early dual system had developed into a number of complex forms, all of a kind which would be produced if the institution of individual marriage and the social recognition of the relation between father and child had arisen in this society."

The social system of the Ba-Yaka is "an interesting mixture, patriarchal in the main, but exhibiting peculiarities which may be survivals of an early matriarchal organisation." Thus, "the tie between a woman and her own village is by no means dissolved by marriage; on the birth of her child, her chief must make a present to her husband, and the child itself, as soon as it can walk, is sent to its mother's village to which it legally belongs and from which the father cannot even purchase it. . . . Nevertheless, a man's heir is his eldest brother, and not, as might be expected under the circumstances, his sister's son, who only becomes his heir in default of brothers. . . . Moreover, in connection with certain food tabus a mysterious connection appears to exist between a man and his son until the latter arrives at puberty. . . . A cock must be eaten by one man alone or illness results; he may however give some to his son if not yet circumcised. This fact is particularly interesting since it seems to show that a male child before circumcision is not supposed to possess an individuality apart from the father, although it is regarded as belonging to the village of the mother." The Ba-Yaka are a pushing, encroaching tribe, invading the Ba-Mbala. A comparison of the two, which looks like a good case of father-family as opposed to the mother-family in organization and effectiveness, is as follows:[9]

---

9 Torday and Joyce, in JAI, XXXVI, 39-40, 41, 42; §421, of the text and *Case-Book.*

Ba-Yaka	Ba-Mbala
Circumcision.	None.
Scars and tattooing exceptional.	Practically universal.
Burial contracted.	Extended.
Feudal chiefs.	Independent petty chiefs.
Eldest brother inherits.	Sister's son inherits.
No slave concubines.	Slave concubines.
Virginity of bride essential.	Not essential.
Cannibalism abhorred.	Daily occurrence.
Slaves treated cruelly.	Treated with kindness.
Drunkenness condemned.	Admired.
Cripples preserved, cared for.	Buried alive.
Wars of occupation.	No wars of occupation.

Among the Yakuts, "there are two names for a clan: *ye-usa*, 'mother-clan,' and *aga-usa*, 'father-clan.' Nowadays *ye-usa*, whatever its original signification, is a 'mother-clan' only in name, being really subordinate to the *aga-usa*. . . . In comparatively recent times, until the coming of the Russians, indeed, the Yakut had the custom of polygyny. The offspring of a man by all his wives formed the basis of an *aga-usa*; while the offspring of each separate wife would form that of a *ye-usa*." Again, "both Sternberg and Pilsudski agree that the Ainu are the only people of northeastern Asia among whom strong traces of mother-right are found. Pilsudski says that they are just at the stage of transition from mother-right to father-right. As traces of matriarchy he cites the superior position of women among the Ainu as compared with neighbouring tribes, e.g., the Gilyak. This is especially evident during pregnancy, when she is surrounded with every care, and even regarded with veneration. Marriage is never by purchase. If the husband does not go to live in the house of his wife's parents, the wife goes to him, but the first few years after marriage are usually spent with her parents, in whose house her first child is often born."[10]

"Descent among the Todas is always reckoned in the male line. . . . The Todas show few traces of mother-right. In some communities there is little reason to doubt that such acts as are performed by a Toda towards his sister's son are survivals of a condition of society in which the mother's brother was responsible, largely or altogether, for the welfare of the child. Among the Todas, however, the *mun* stands in two relations to a child. He is the mother's brother, and he is also the prospective or actual father-in-law, and we have no means of telling in which of these two *rôles* he performs his duties. If the duties of a man towards his sister's son among the Todas be a relic of mother-right, there can be little doubt that this condition must have been very remote."[11] Fawcett[12] has written in reference to the system of inheritance through females among the Nairs. "The girl on marriage joins the sept of her husband, but she retains her own sept name, and her children are of her sept, not of their father's. Marriage between persons of the same sept name is prohibited, and this is regulated solely through the mothers. The tribe is endogamous, but the septs within it are exogamous. Thus, a man or a girl cannot marry any one of the same sept having the same sept name (which is inherited

---

10 Czaplicka, *Aborig. Siberia*, 59, 104-105.   12 In JAI, XXXIII, 61.
11 Rivers, *Todas*, 546, 547.

through their mother), and *must* marry some one within the tribe, but of a different sept to his, or her, own—of his father's sept or any other. Though property devolves through the men, degrees between which marriage is prohibited are inherited through the women."

Wilken[13] remarks with reference to certain Malays that despite exclusive descent in the male line the free-born father has not the power to raise to his social level the child begotten by him in lawful union with a slave-woman, while the mother, a free woman, can raise a child of hers with a slave-man. This practice he regards as an unquestionable survival of the mother-family. The primitive arrangement among the Bataks was the mother-family; they now have a strong father-family, with the rules of exogamy and the patriarchate in full swing. "Over against the marriage with bride-price, *cum manu,* stands that without bride-price, *sine manu.* In this marriage the wife remains in the house of her parents, whither the man removes, while the children belong to the kin-group of the mother." So in South Sumatra. The most frequent unions "are those wherein the man leaves his *sumbai* [clan; exogamy being the system here], and comes to live with his wife, being taken in as a child, not so much by her parents as by her *sumbai.* . . . After the death of his wife, the man may, at his own choice, go back to his *sumbai,* and the children, if they are still small, he may take along with him without hindrance. When, later on, they no longer need the father's care, the *sumbai* of the mother may demand them. . . . Originally, then, in the transition from matriarchate to patriarchate, marriages *cum manu* and *sine manu* appeared side by side; and the idea existed that the stock could be carried on as well in the male as in the female line."

Van Ossenbruggen,[14] editor of Wilken's posthumously collected writings, comments upon the latter's ideas about father- and mother-family. He asserts that there is no single demonstrated case of the latter succeeding the former. In both types of family the child belongs to the tribe of the men who have power over the mother; in the father-family, these are strangers, in the mother-family, tribal associates of the mother. Wilken makes much of the social position attained by the woman under the mother-family; his editor thinks there is no correlation of the sort.

In northern Sumatra the children always remain with the mother and are regarded as hers. Daughters bring their husbands home, and sons belong to the maternal group, though they visit their wives from time to time. These customs are, however, really survivalistic, for when they speak of a family in the broad sense, or of a stock, they mean the descendants of one man in the male line, however far apart they live. And this conception is not a new one or referable to Islam, though strengthened by it; the patriarchal type is very old.[15] It is reasonable, according to Ratzel,[16] to assume that wherever exogamy is now found co-existing with inheritance through the father, this was formerly through the mother, and that the later system is the result of dislike of the inconveniences to the husband of his insecure and dependent position in the wife's family. A curious case is found in Celebes: "During the wedding the man

13 In VG, I, 327-328; II, 246-247 (quoted).

14 In Wilken, VG, I, 228, 255; I, 235-254. Here are many cases of the mother-family, both in the Archipelago and elsewhere, especially throughout Africa and America, and a number of Biblical references are cited. A list of native female rulers is given (260),

with a reference to Veth, *Vrouwenregeeringen in den Indischen Archipel,* in *Tijdschrift voor Nederlandsch Indië,* Jaargang 1870, deel II, 365.

15 Snouck-Hurgronje, *Atjèhers,* I, 46-47.

16 *Vkde.,* II, 433.

and woman declare to what tribe or family they want to belong, that of the father of the young woman or of the young man. The children follow their parents."[17]

In the Tonga Islands children of the common people belong to the mother's class but inherit from the father.[18] In the Mortlock Islands, while consent for a marriage is desired from the mother and her kin-group and the father has nothing to say, yet, along with the chief and the girl's brothers, he generally gets gifts from the bridegroom.[19] In New Zealand the husband generally went to the wife unless he were a great chief or had several wives.[20] Grosse[21] assembles several cases showing that a peculiarly prominent man did not give up his kin-group but forced his wife to give up hers.

Everywhere on the American continent, in primitive times, "the system of mother-right was interrupted by father-right, and the man took the wives to live in his lodge." The author quoted[22] believed the mother-family to have been antecedent and universal and to have been broken by the man taking the wife home.

Among the Tlinkits it is the great men who already give the paternal name to their children; the poorer people are still in a stage of uterine filiation. Certain tribes have quite recently adopted the system of paternal filiation. This is due to European influence.[23] Again, a child's totem can be changed by giving him to his father's sister to nurse. Though the man-family "is the sociological unit," property-inheritance is through women.[24] Kohler[25] finds in the legends of the Columbia tribes that the main totem came from the animal ancestress while the lesser ones were derived later by the men. And he finds among the patriarchal Omahas several reminiscences of transition: the brother and mother's brother, not the father, control the daughters; inheritance goes to sons, but in their absence to brothers, sisters, mother's brother, and sister's son; and prohibition of marriage is not limited to the agnatic or paternal line. "A child belongs to its father's gens, as 'father-right' has succeeded 'mother-right.' But children of white or black men are assigned to the gentes of their mothers, and they cannot marry any women of these gentes." Mother's brothers and brothers retain authority over girls.[26] "In the family the father was recognized as having the highest authority over all the members, although in most matters pertaining to the welfare of the children the mother exercised almost equal authority."[27]

"At the time of the discovery, most of the Siouan tribes had apparently passed into gentile organization, though vestiges of clan organization were found—e.g., among the best-known tribes the man was the head of the family, though the tipi usually belonged to the woman."[28] While most Indian tribes reckon descent in the maternal line, a number have the father-right; of some of these, like the Winnebagoes, it is known that they had the maternal system earlier. Carver[29] found traces of descent in the female line in 1787 among the Winnebagoes. "Some nations . . . when the dignity is hereditary, limit the succession to the female line. On the death of a chief his sister's son sometimes

17 Riedel, in *Bijd.*, XXXV, 83.
18 Starcke, *Prim. Fam.*, 89.
19 Finsch, *Ethnol. Erfahr.*, III, 306.
20 Tregear, in JAI, XIX, 103.
21 *Fam.*, 167.
22 Mason, *Woman's Share*, 224.
23 Letourneau, *Marr.*, 292.

24 Niblack, in USNM, 1888, 250.
25 *Urgchte. d. Ehe*, 53, 54, 63.
26 Dorsey, in BAE, III, 225-268.
27 Fletcher and LaFlesche, in BAE, XXVII, 325.
28 McGee, in BAE, XV, 177.
29 *Travels*, 132.

succeeds him in preference to his own son; and if he happens to have no sister the nearest female relation assumes the dignity. This accounts for a woman being at the head of the Winnebago nation, which, before I was acquainted with their laws, appeared strange to me." Among the pueblo tribes, "tribal custom requires the groom to make his home with his wife's family, the couple sleeping in the general living room with the remainder of the family; but with the more progressive pueblos, and with the Sia to a limited extent, the husband, if he be able, after a time provides a house for his family."[30] "The Zuñi are divided into a large number of clans. . . . A boy or a girl is regarded as belonging to the mother's clan, but is spoken of as a 'child' of the father's clan, and marriage into either of these is practically prohibited."[31]

With one possible exception, "each of the twenty-two camps into which the thirty-seven Seminole families are divided is a camp in which all the persons but the husbands are members of one gens. The camp at Miami is an apparent exception. There Little Tiger, a rather important personage, lives with a number of unmarried relatives. A Wolf has married one of Little Tiger's sisters and lives in the camp, as properly he should. Lately Tiger himself has married an Otter, but instead of leaving his relatives and going to the camp of his wife's kindred, his wife has taken up her home with his people."[32]

The question of priority as respects the mother-family and father-family in North America has been much discussed. "Among the village communities of Oregon, Washington, and southern Vancouver Island the child belongs to the father's village, where the married couple generally live, and it seems that among many of these tribes the villages are exogamic. Among the Kwakiutl the clans are also exogamic, and certain privileges are inherited in the paternal line, while a much larger number are obtained by marriage. The existence of the former class suggests that the organization must have been at one time a purely paternal one. Three causes seem to have disturbed the original organization—the development of the more complex organization mentioned above, the influence of the northern tribes which have a purely maternal organization, and the development of legends referring to the origin of the clans which are analogous to similar traditions of the northern groups of tribes. Taking up the last-named point first, we find that each clan claims a certain rank and certain privileges which are based upon the descent and adventures of its ancestor. These privileges, if originally belonging to a tribe which at one time has been on the paternal stage, would hardly have a tendency to deviate from the law governing this stage. If they have, however, originated under the influence of a people which is on a maternal stage, an abnormal development seems likely. In the north a woman's rank and privileges always descend upon her children. Practically the same result has been brought about among the Kwakiutl, but in a manner which suggests that a people with paternal institutions has adapted its social laws to these customs. Here the woman brings as a dower her father's position and privileges to her husband, who, however, is not allowed to use them himself, but acquires them for the use of his son. . . . I can not imagine that it is a transition of a maternal society to a paternal society, because there are no relics of the former stage beyond those which we find everywhere, and which do not prove that the transition has been recent at all. There is no trace left of an inheritance from the wife's brothers; the

30 Stevenson, in BAE, XI, 22.
31 Swanton, in HAI, II, 610.
32 MacCauley, in BAE, V, 507.

young couple do not live with the wife's parents. But the most important argument is that the customs can not have been prevalent in the village communities from which the present tribal system originated, as in these the tribe is always designated as the direct descendants of the mythical ancestor. If the village communities had been on the maternal stage, the tribes would have been designated as the descendants of the ancestor's sisters, as is always the case in the legends of the northern tribes." Elsewhere the same author[33] writes: "Totemism and maternal descent have existed in earlier times among many people where they have now disappeared, and a complete recurrence to these customs, after they have once been given up, is rare, and has never been observed in the history of the civilized world. From this it is inferred that totemism and maternal descent belong to an earlier period in the evolution of civilization, and have gradually been superseded by other forms of social organization and belief. While we may grant that this is the general course of events, the conclusion that totemism and maternal descent precede everywhere paternal descent and family organization does not seem to me necessary. The tendency to their disappearance may exist everywhere; but this does not prove that they are a necessary stage in human development."

Kroeber has argued that "the evidence as a whole indicates the very powerful probability that nearly every nation in North America has reached the matrilineal condition from the patrilineal, the unilateral reckoning from the bilateral, exogamy from a previous non-exogamic state; or at least that the apparent drift, so far as our mental eyes can at present follow it, has been predominantly in this direction. . . . Within the confines of exogamy, patrilineal reckoning prevails among the less advanced nations [of North America], and every important acme of civilization is situated among matrilineal peoples." Hartland replies: "Either matrilineal reckoning must have emerged out of patrilineal reckoning, or *vice versa*. Now the greater general advance of patrilineal peoples elsewhere than in North America is admitted, as I understand, by Dr. Kroeber and those whose views he shares. But it is claimed that in North America the case is different, and that, since there the peoples possessed of the higher degree of civilization are found to be generally, though not universally, matrilineal, therefore the patrilineal organization is the more primitive. This inference is, however, by no means inevitable. . . . There is one thing that cannot be left out of account in such correlation: the connection which seems to exist between matrilineal institutions and an agricultural civilization, based as it is upon female organization and labor, not only in North America, but elsewhere. This would lead to resistance of paternal, and a consequent prolongation in strength of maternal, institutions. On the other hand, the nomadic life of hunters would result in the enhanced importance to the family and authority of the husband and father, and tend to change the reckoning of descent, as it has done in Australia. If so, then matrilineal reckoning cannot be relied on as an essential constituent or a product of the advanced civilizations of North America, for it may be a survival of an earlier stage, and conversely patrilineal institutions may be a relatively modern development. In these circumstances it is important to enquire whether the institutions of patrilineal tribes contain any evidence of a previous matrilineal reckoning; for this would be crucial. Accordingly this is what I have done,

---

33 Boas, in USNM, 1895, 334-335; and in JAI, XL, 535-536.

and I submit with success. For such evidence has been found, embedded like fossil remains in geological strata, among the very tribes where it was summarily denied. The evidence may be challenged, or its effect may be attenuated, or conceivably even destroyed by explanation; but it cannot be merely ignored or pooh-poohed as 'special pleading.' "[34]

In Yucatan "the name of the child was formed by *combining* the names of the father and mother; the mothers name, however, had the precedence."[35] The Waimare, near the source of the Paraguay, say that their fathers were Waimare and their mothers Paressi. Hence their names were not derived from their mothers, although the man dwelt in the home of the woman.[36] In the South American tropics the father-family is not found in full development. In the different tribes the two systems are much mixed; though the child almost everywhere belongs to the clan of the mother, the clan is of little importance.[37]

Moses is reported as making a ruling on the complaint that daughters, marrying out of the tribe of Joseph, would carry away the land inherited by them. He ordered that they must marry within the tribe of their father, whomsoever they pleased. The daughters in question married their father's brother's sons.[38] The doctrine of two births, says Lippert,[39] reconciles the mother-right and father-right; when circumcision (the period of second birth) comes at birth, not at puberty, the latter has, as in the case of the Hebrews, prevailed.

According to Smith[40] religion follows the mores in that "in various parts of the Semitic field we find deities originally female changing their sex and becoming gods, as if with the change in the rule of human kinship. So long as kinship was traced through the mother alone, a male deity of common stock with his worshippers could only be their cousin, or, in the language of that stage of society, their brother. This in fact is the relationship between gods and men asserted by Pindar, when he ascribes to both alike a common mother Earth, and among the Semites a trace of the same point of view may be seen in the class of proper names which designate their bearers as 'brother' or 'sister' of a deity. . . . The Babylonian Ishtar in her oldest form is such a mother goddess, unmarried, or rather choosing her temporary partners at will, the queen head and first-born of all gods. . . . So far as religion kept pace with the new laws of social morality due to this development, the independent divine mother necessarily became the subordinate partner of a male deity, and so the old polyandrous Ishtar reappears in Canaan and elsewhere as Astarte, the wife of the supreme Baal. Or if the supremacy of the goddess was too well established to be thus undermined, she might change her sex, as in Southern Arabia, where Ishtar is transformed into the masculine 'Athtar.' " "It appears that the patriarchate has not always had the mastery in Arabia; there are indications at hand that it remained for a time in strife with the other system, and also that it did not win to victory without compromises and shadings."[41]

34 "Discussion and Correspondence," in AA, XX, 224-226.
35 Bancroft, *Native Races*, II, 680.
36 Von den Steinen, *Zent. Bras.*, 427.
37 Schmidt, in *Ztsft. f. vergl. Rechtswiss.*, XIII, 286, 297.

38 Num., ch. XXXVI.
39 *Kgchte.*, II, 344.
40 *Relig. Sem.*, 52, 56, 58-59.
41 Wellhausen, in *Gött. Gesellsft. d. Wissenschaft.*, 1893, 479.

§419. The Father-Family.

THE social organization of the African Ba-Yaka is in many points purely patriarchal. "Agricultural produce belongs to the head of the family. . . . The village chief is responsible for the payment of fines incurred by his subjects . . . and, when a woman is given in marriage, receives a goat from her father. The marriage price is paid to the father of the woman; and the death of a wife without having given birth to a daughter is considered so much to the detriment of the husband that the money he paid for her is refunded." These people appear to be "distinctly progressive. Situated to the south and southwest of the Ba-Mbala, they are gradually encroaching upon the territory of the latter, whose exceedingly loose system of social organisation, under a number of practically independent village chiefs, renders them incapable of anything like organised resistance."[1] It is a belief of the tribes in British Central Africa that the child is formed solely from that which man introduces into the woman;[2] while in the Upper Congo the child is thought to be kin to the father only.[3] "Kinship is derived by the Dinkas through males only. But to this there is one exception. The definition of incest extends it to sexual intercourse between persons connected by blood on either side, so far as the genealogies can be traced in tradition. For no other purpose . . . is kinship traced through both parents."[4]

" 'Paternal relationship is considered to be much stronger than maternal relationship. There is a Chukchee saying that has it that even a distant relative on the father's side is much nearer to the heart than a maternal cousin.' There is no word for 'family' in Chukchee; *rayirin* means 'houseful' or 'those in the house,' and *yaratomgit* signifies 'house-mates.' "[5] "The purely patriarchal nature of Sema society as it exists at present cannot be too emphatically stated. The female line is of no account, and relationship through the female, though recognised as existing, is barely recognised and nothing more. A Sema may not marry his wife's mother, but can marry practically any female relation of his own mother on her father's side. For although some Semas are said, like the ancient Athenians, to forbid marriages with a mother's sister by the same mother, even though the father be different, the vast majority hold that a man may marry his mother's sister by the same father and mother without any suggestion of impropriety, whereas he would be guilty of incest, and banished from the village, if he took to himself, say, a third cousin in patrilineal descent. He may also marry his father's sister's daughter, though such marriages are regarded as unfertile. . . . There is much to suggest that a matrilineal system survived till comparatively recently."[6] The Naga *khel* being a unit composed of descendants of the same ancestor, children take the *khel* of the father.[7] A Santal proverb says: "No one heeds a cow track or regards his mother's sept."[8] "In Bengal the house father exercises a despotic rule over his family; he controls the education, manner of life, and marriage of his sons and daughters, receives the incomes of all family members, and determines the expenditures." The wife rules the female members of the household, eats sparingly and "never in the

---

1 Torday and Joyce, in JAI, XXXVI, 39; see table of comparisons in preceding section.
2 Stannus, in JAI, XL, 309.
3 Weeks, in JAI, XXXIX, 443.
4 O'Sullivan, in JAI, XL, 173.

5 Czaplicka, *Aborig. Siberia*, 29.
6 Hutton, *Sema Nagas*, 130-132.
7 Godden, in JAI, XXVI, 168, and XXVII, 23.
8 Risley, *Ethnog. Ind.*, I, 144.

presence of her husband, chiefly the leavings of his meal, lives simply and thriftily, and is bigoted and superstitious."[9] Even the Nature-Veddahs have the father-right.[10]

When the missionaries came to the East Asiatics they taught that one must leave father and mother and cleave to his wife. "In China and Japan, where love for father and reverence for ancestors had reached the highest grade, such teachings raised a storm of anger, were regarded as simply immoral, and became a powerful weapon to the hand of the anti-Christian natives." The case is parallel to that of the children of the matriarchal Iroquois, who objected to the translation: "Thou shalt honor thy father and mother," and insisted earnestly upon the form: "Thou shalt honor thy mother and father."[11] The Chinese wife followed the husband even to her own grave; he walked in front of her coffin, not behind it.[12] "In China and among the other Mongolian races, as well as among the Finns," according to Starcke's[13] sweeping conclusion, "individuals are distributed into patriarchal families, and no direct traces of the female line of descent exist." "The *animus matrimonii,* the intention of the husband and wife to form a connection for life, can, with some exceptions, have no place in China. . . . Among the Chinese the heads of the families alone choose, and the inclination of the principal parties is never consulted. . . . The *patria potestas* over children, whether legitimate or adopted, is unlimited. The father (or after his death the mother) can do with them as he likes; he may not only chastise, but even sell, expose, or kill them." Here as in pre-Christian Rome, *mulier est finis familiæ.* "A woman alienates herself from her own kin on marriage, and becomes a part of the stock upon which she is grafted."[14] "The theory of Chinese government," says Williams,[15] "is undoubtedly the patriarchal. . . . This may, to be sure, be the theory of most governments, but nowhere has it been systematized so thoroughly, and acted upon so consistently and for so long a period, as in China."

In northern Sumatra, "the stock dies out with the woman, if she has no brothers; the man only carries the stock on. . . . The children born of the marriage belong to the father; they are regarded as of *his* blood and *not* of that of the mother. The wife is *his* property, which he has bought from her parents or next blood-kin, and therefore also, just as in the case of his field, his fruit-trees, his cattle, the fruit which she bears is his." While children of a free man and a slave are free, those of a slave and a free woman are the property of the slave's master"—contrary to the Mohammedan prescription. "And this goes even so far that the wife who is in danger of divorce or repudiation from the side of her husband has no right to abort the child with which she is pregnant, except with the pre-knowledge and full consent of the husband, to whom everywhere and always the unborn child belongs." The father has full right to marry off the daughter and the mother has nothing to do with it. Even if a man goes to live with his wife, he is to be buried in his own family-grave, for the children must be buried along with the father. It takes a family-council to allow of any exception. If the distance is too great to allow of transporting the body to the burial-place of the kin, a piece of clothing

9 Jolly, in *Grundr. d. Indo-Ar. Phil.,* II, Heft 8, p. 80.
10 Sarasin, *Weddas,* 490.
11 "Kl. Nachr." in *Globus,* XCI, 20.
12 DeGroot, *Relig. Syst.,* I, 195.
13 *Prim. Fam.,* 77.

14 Von Mollendorff, *Chinese,* 23, 41, 42; DeGroot, *Relig. Syst.,* II, 507; Medhurst, in *Trans. China Br. Roy. Asiatic Soc.,* pt. IV, 3-4.
15 *Middle Kingdom,* I, 296.

must be sent to the kin who keep it as a relic.[16] Thus does the patriarchate really reach beyond the grave.

With the Maori, "in regard to the functions of sex, it was taught of old that the seed of man is with the male, and the sheltering haven with the female; the male has the kernel provided by the Deity, while the female shelters the same, and nurtures it, hence the growth of all things."[17] In Samoa children remain in the father's family unless the woman is of a superior tribe, in which case one of her relatives adopts them and they take their position in her tribe in war and peace.[18] The family-organization of the island of Yap "is founded upon a well-marked father-right, in contrast to most of the islands of Micronesia, and in particular to the neighboring Pelew and central Carolines."[19]

Despite the striking examples of the maternal family in North America, the male line of descent is widely recognized.[20] Among the Greenlanders "the newly married pair remains with husband's parents, and his mother, as long as she lives, manages the domestic economy."[21] The Menomini Indians have moved from their older usage of counting descent in the female line to that of the father-right.[22] In British Guiana the father's brother may never marry the niece; he is too nearly related, and is, indeed, called "papa." But anyone may marry his sister's daughter.[23] "The Indian designates the grade of relationship with precision and especially sets the highest value upon the paternal blood. On this ground the father's brother plays a very weighty rôle in the family. He is the born counsellor and after the death of the father, according to the usage of many peoples, he enters in relation to the widow and the children upon the rights and duties of the deceased. . . . The son, coming to manhood, forms his own family by taking a wife who has either been determined for him in youth or whom he has won by several years of service in the house of his father-in-law."[24] Among the Tupis, "descent was regulated from the father, in opposition to what is found among the barbaric peoples of Africa. The mother was considered only, in the manner of the ancient Egyptians, as the guard or depository of the embryo until it came to the light; the son whom she suckled contracted no duties toward her."[25] "When a Tupinamba, who is married, dies, his eldest brother is under obligation to marry the widow, and if there is no elder brother at hand, the nearest male relative. The brother of the widow must marry her daughter, if she has one, and if there is no brother of the widow, this union devolves upon the nearest male relative on the mother's side. If this person does not want to take his relative as wife, he can keep her from any union in order to give her a husband of his own choice. The paternal uncle may take the niece, but must hold her in the status of a daughter, she calling him father. If this relative is lacking, instead of him the niece takes the nearest paternal relative. She calls all paternal relatives father and is called by all of them daughter, but belongs to the nearest only. In like manner, grandsons call the brother or cousin of their grandfather, grandfather, and

16 Jacobs, *Groot-Atjeh*, I, 11-12, 13, 37-38, 352-353; §108, of the text.

17 Best, in JAI, XLIV, 130.

18 Ella, in AAAS, 1892, 627.

19 Senfft, in *Globus*, XCI, 141.

20 Starcke, *Prim. Fam.*, 30; Bernhöft, *Verwdsftsnamen*, 59. Swanton ("Clan Syst.," in AA, VI, plate XV), offers a map showing

the distribution of mother-right, parental descent, and transitional forms.

21 Cranz, *Grönland*, I, 215.

22 Hoffman, in BAE, XIV, 43.

23 Schomburgk, *Brit.-Guiana*, II, 318.

24 Von Martius, *Beiträge*, I, 352, 393; Schmidt, in *Ztsft. f. vergl. Rechtswiss.*, XIII, 297.

25 Varnhagen, *Brazil*, I, 126.

are all called grandsons by him." Likewise, on the mother's side; "but the attachment is not so intimate as to the paternal relatives."[26]

Among the Semitic peoples, the ancient Hebrews show the agnatic relationship. The wife was bought from her parents, the widow was transferred to a brother or other relation of the deceased, while inheritance was exclusively to male agnates. Sons inherited exclusively from the father; only in default of sons did the daughter inherit, and then such an heiress was obliged to marry somebody from the stock of her father so that the heritage thus remained in the stock.[27] The passages in Greek tragedy which set in contrast to the reigning patriarchate the theory of maternal descent have been referred to in a preceding connection.[28]

Patria Potestas. In some Australian instances it is the grandfather who has the power to decide whether a child shall be kept alive or not. If not, it is eaten, the parents not partaking. "The father could not order the child to be killed; for if he did so, the grandparents would raise a party against him and he would have to fight them."[29]

In East Africa the Mtumia is "the father, elder and despot of the family, and the true Mkamba knows no authority beyond his. To him belong all the cattle and goats, none of his sons possess anything, even their wives are bought with his property, all the dowries [bride-prices] paid for daughters of the village, and blood moneys for members of the family who have been killed, go to increase the father's stock. Meanwhile the father is not expected to use the cattle as he likes, for he is essentially the head of the family, and as such he is the sole owner of its wealth. If a son leaves the village he will get what would be his portion of the stock, but so long as he stays with his father there is only one common ownership, represented by the father. . . . As marks of his position he carries the forked stick and three-legged stool. . . . Next to the Mtumia (pl. Atumia) comes the 'Nthele'; these are men who might be called middle-aged; as a rule reference is made to them as those who do not dance any longer."[30] Dinka society is patriarchal. "The father is the head of the family; but it would seem that he is far from being absolute ruler. Although Captain O'Sullivan describes his wives and unmarried children as his property, they can hardly be so in the same sense in which his slaves, cattle and so forth, are his property. He must have duties towards them, though such duties may be more vaguely recognised and more difficult of enforcement than his duties towards members of other families. This is clear from the rule that when a dispute arises within the family he does not settle it himself, but refers it to the 'old men.' If a woman be killed by her husband it is treated as an accident and a misfortune to the husband; but Captain O'Sullivan significantly remarks: 'He may have to pay a cow or more to propitiate the girl's family and stop talk.' If the wife were, in the full sense of the term, the property of her husband, there would be no payment of cattle to propitiate her family. The truth is that the payment of a bride-price has been very apt to mislead European inquirers as to the real status of the wife and children. . . . Speaking generally, its effect undoubtedly is to transfer to the husband large powers over the person of his wife. . . . But all this comes very far short of vesting their absolute ownership in him. They are not slaves, however servile their status

26 Von Martius, *Beiträge*, I, 353, note.
27 Wilken, in VG, I, 401-402.
28 §416, of *Case-Book*.

29 Howitt, *S.E. Aust.*, 749.
30 Dundas, C., in JAI, XLIII, 493-494.

may appear to superficial observation."[31] O'Sullivan[32] lists a man's property as follows: his wives, sons whilst unmarried, daughters whilst unmarried, children of unmarried daughters, daughters whose marriage has been "broken," children of such daughters, slaves, children of slaves, cattle, corn, and property earned by people who are his property. "No woman can possess property, she being herself property; but a woman can hold property 'in trust':—(a) If she is the widow of a man none of whose male relatives are living. (b) If she is the daughter of a man none of whose male relatives are living, and if her own mother is also dead."

In northeast Africa, the house-father or family-father "is at once the master and possessor of the whole property of the family and lord over the life and death of all the members thereof." Children "are the property of the father for whom they have to work . . . who may sell them, and from whom they must be bought off. The father has no duties toward them. . . . Their working power belongs to the father up to the moment when they leave the family and themselves become heads of families. . . . No other right save that of inheritance alone, which enters only after the father's death and is in favor of the eldest son, alters this relation. The wife stands in a still worse, fully unprivileged relation to the house-father, because she does not possess even the right of inheritance. She too remains, bought as she is with goods, a possession of the man. Under such circumstances it remains noteworthy that, along with the naturally developing estrangement of the children from the parents, the patriarchal prestige of fathers and tribal chiefs does not suffer at all, but, on the contrary, is very lively and in vigorous activity."[33]

In India, "marriage is solemnized when the bridegroom's father accepts or approves of the bride, and the son marries her thus approved."[34] "Although most of the educated young men of modern days have a desire to select spinsters, of their own accord, after the European system, the iron rod of custom prevents them from adopting such a procedure. It is only in very rare instances that the son overrules his father's decision in matrimonial matters."[35] "The constitution of the Hindu family is analogous to that of the Roman family, wherein it was only the *paterfamilias* who was *sui juris,* his children having no will independently of him."[36]

Wilken,[37] who mentions a number of cases of the patriarchate in the Indian Archipelago, says that the power of the father is best shown by the sale of children into slavery, as in the Lampong District of Sumatra. It is common for parents to sell their children, especially in time of famine, when children, mainly girls, are sold for a relatively small amount of rice and thus doomed to slavery. Thus the children form a part of the housefather's property. Again, the father has unlimited power over his daughter, "whom he always actually sells into marriage," although the will of the girl is taken into account. The author is of the opinion that despotism of the father is not so much a phenomenon of lower as of higher civilization, the less cultured peoples being more likely to be on the mother-family stage.

Among the Guiana Indians, "A father possesses such authority over his own children that they must give their hand where he pleases, the girls being entirely

31 Hartland, in JAI, XL, 171-172.
32 In JAI, XL, 178-179.
33 Paulitschke, *Nordost-Afr.*, I, 189.
34 Nathubhai, in JASB, III, 407.

35 Naidoo, in JASB, II, 385.
36 Athalye, in JASB, I, 69.
37 In VG, I, 186, 428 ff.; II, 246; §409, of the text and *Case-Book.*

under his control, even to a certain extent after marriage. Capt. Quio . . . had given his child to an Indian, but having had a quarrel with him, he ordered the child home. He next gave her to another, and a short time after, a drunken quarrel and fight ensuing, he deprived his pugnacious son-in-law of the girl. The third husband was abandoned because, as the captain affirmed, he was too lazy to work. . . . At last the father of the girl talks somewhat as follows: 'I cannot give you an answer until I hear from the girl and her mother; if the girl likes you, you will know for yourself, and I can not refuse you.' . . . After a few days the bridegroom may take his new wife on a visit to his mother's, but he soon returns to his father-in-law's place, where he takes up his permanent abode. . . . He removes all his property to his father-in-law's hut and devotes all his attention to him—hunts, fishes, and clears a field for him. If he complains of the exertion or does not appear energetic enough for his father-in-law, the latter will get rid of him with a word or two of thanks."[38]

Among the early Scandinavians, figures of gods were carved out of the pillars which surrounded the housefather's seat of honor. The father was called prince, and was priest, judge, and leader of his descendants and dependents.[39] Wilken[40] cites the following passage from *The Taming of the Shrew:*

> I will be master of what is mine own:
> She is my goods, my chattels; she is my house,
> My household stuff, my field, my barn,
> My horse, my ox, my ass, my any thing.

§421. The Mother-Family as an Adjustment.

TYLOR's[1] views do not fully accord with the position we have taken; but we are in entire sympathy with his chief purpose, which is "to make it clear that the matriarchal system is one framed for order, not disorder." He cites a number of cases of the most complete types of mother-family which have lasted on into modern times. "Although examples of the matriarchal family . . . are few in number in modern times, perhaps not exceeding twenty peoples, yet the important point has now been made out that they are to be found in all the great regions of the barbaric world. With and around them, moreover, are found twice or thrice as many imperfect systems, which appear from their fragments of maternal rules to belong to the period of transition into the new paternal stage."

Tylor's conclusions from his cases are, first, that there is no "matriarchate"; in communities where the maternal line exists, "women enjoy greater consideration than in barbaric patriarchal life, but the actual power is rather in the hands of their brothers and uncles on the mother's side." Next, he finds the cause of the maternal system to be "connected with the custom of the father's residence in the wife's family." Starcke[2] concurs with this view. Tylor adduces the *ambil-anak* marriage[3] of the Malays and similar forms in evidence; and makes much of the heiress-husband—the German *Erbtochtermann.* But this explanation is not sufficient "to account for the presence of the maternal system, complete or partial, among toward half the known peoples of the lower

---

38 Roth, in BAE, XXXVIII, 668, 669.
39 Geijer, *Svensk. Hist.*, I, 113.
40 In VG, I, 435; Shakespeare, *Taming of the Shrew*, Act III, Sc. II, 231-234.

1 In *Nineteenth Cent.*, XL, 83, 86-90.
2 *Prim. Fam.*, 35; Tylor, in JAI, XVIII, 245.
3 §363, above.

culture. We are led to look for some world-wide influence at work in periods early in time and civilization, though probably far removed from the primitive state of mankind."

Tylor finds the maternal system to be closely connected with exogamy. "While maternal peoples are exogamous, exogamous peoples are not necessarily maternal, but may be either maternal or paternal, clanship being reckoned on the mother's or father's side accordingly. . . . There is no proof that at any period the maternal system held exclusive possession of the human race, but the strength with which it kept its ground may be measured by its having encompassed the globe in space, and lasted on from remote antiquity in time." We can see in this correlation with exogamy nothing that might have favored the mother-family system over that of the father-family. Both are present in potentiality, for Tylor has just said that "there are two alternatives: either for the wife to remain in her own home, or to be taken by her husband to his home; according to which of these customs prevails, the family will be prone to become maternal or paternal." Either would have prospered in conjunction with exogamy.

Exogamy is a winning policy, and if any incipient institution can be favored by an exclusive relationship with it, there is every prospect of the wide extension of the attached system. We cannot see, however, that the maternal system is in the position of exclusive beneficiary or that Tylor's contention is innocent of conjecture; and we regard a number of his points as highly debatable. The same is true in a greater degree with respect to Starcke,[4] whose whole argument is that locality or proximity makes the mother-child tie, that the current notion that blood is important is untrue, and that the mother-family is not original but transitional. Westermarck[5] uses the term "metrocracy" for mother-right and gives a list of cases where it never existed, to refute the doctrine that all nations have passed through it. It is very rare in Asia, being restricted to parts of Ceylon, India and the Malay Archipelago, and is more common in Africa. Wilken[6] coincides fully with the position taken by us as respects the basis of the maternal system in notions about blood-kinship; but he believes that the "matriarchate" rises only with exogamy and that under that system "the criterion for the patriarchal or matriarchal marriage" consists of the payment or non-payment of the bride-price. Since in the *ambil-anak* marriage it is not paid, that form is matriarchal. Letourneau[7] cites a number of cases of the maternal family and concludes that "the maternal family and the matriarchate are very different things. The first is common; the second is very rare, if indeed it has ever existed." Kohler[8] thinks that "among tribes, to which nature has accorded a horde-wise association, the mother-right must be more stubbornly preserved than with tribes which have been speedily scattered by lack of food and resources." Brinton[9] contributes the opinion that the habit of reckoning ancestry in the female line was not on account of doubt of paternity but because parental affection is, among primitive peoples, largely confined to the mother. Hewitt and Swanton[10] solemnly challenge the antecedency of the maternal line, citing a quite unique consideration. "There has been prevalent hitherto among many ethnologists the opinion that the tracing of descent

4 *Prim. Fam.*, 25, 28, 37, 40, 54, 65, 77, 100.
5 *Marriage*, I, 275 ff.
6 In VG, I, 324-325, 372 ff., 391.
7 *Marriage*, ch. XIX and 282.

8 *Urgchte. d. Ehe*, 55 ff.
9 *Races and Peoples*, 55.
10 "Kinship," in HAI, I, 692.

through the paternal line is in most cases a development from the system of tracing descent exclusively through females, and that, therefore, the latter system is antecedent and more primitive than the former. But it is not at all clear that there has been adduced in support of this contention any conclusive evidence that it is a fact or that either system has been transformed from the other; but it is evident that such an improbable procedure would have caused the disregard and rupture of a vast body of tabus—of tabus among the most sacred known, namely, the tabus of incest." No explanation is offered by these authors, who are specialists on American ethnology, of the many facts cited by the writers they criticize.

§423. Terms of Address.

In many Australian tribes, "persons never address one another by name, but use instead the proper term of relationship." Brown[1] mentions a number of points regarding the practice of a group in West Australia. "(1) The relationship system of the Kariera tribe is not only a system of names or terms of address, but is preëminently a system of reciprocal rights and duties. A man owes the same duties (though not in the same degree) to all the persons to whom he applies the same term. Thus the relationship system regulates the whole social life of the people. (2) It is based on actual relations of consanguinity and affinity that can be traced by means of the genealogical knowledge preserved by the old men and women. (3) The recognition of relationships is so extended that everyone with whom an individual comes in contact in the ordinary course of social life is his relative. It is impossible for a man to have any social relations with anyone who is not his relative because there is no standard by which two persons in this position can regulate their conduct towards one another. I am compelled to treat a person differently according as he is my 'brother,' 'brother-in-law,' 'father,' or 'uncle.' If I do not know which of these he is, all intercourse is impossible. (4) Within the body of relatives of a given kind distinctions are made between nearer and more distant relatives, just as in English we distinguish between nearer and more distant 'cousins' though still calling them all by the same name. These distinctions are not of kind but of degree, if we may use the phrase. Thus though a man owes certain duties to all the men he calls 'father' he must observe them more particularly in regard to his own father or his father's brothers than in regard to a distant cousin of his father. The same is the case with every other relationship. (5) In Australia, much more than in civilized communities, a great deal of attention is paid to actual relationship by blood and marriage. Thus the Australian system is characterized, not by a less intense, but by a more intense recognition of actual relationships of consanguinity. (6) The classes of the Kariera tribe are groups of related persons. The rule that a man of one class may only marry a woman of one of the other classes is the result of the more fundamental rule that a man may only marry a woman bearing to him a certain relation of consanguinity, namely, the daughter of his mother's brother. Marriage is regulated by consanguinity and by consanguinity alone."

The Mekeo of British New Guinea "have no word representing the idea of a family. Their words for father and mother are *ama* and *ina;* but these words

---

1 In JAI, XLIII, 157-158; and in JAI, XLVIII, 240; Cunow, *Australneger*, 55.

are not confined to actual parents, nor are there any expressions so confined. All brothers and sisters of a man's father and mother are also his fathers and mothers. Similarly, the word *ufu,* which means a grandparent. . . . Every relation on the mother's side, other than true uncles and cousins, is, however, generally called *ekefaa,* which means friend."[2]

The dual grouping of the clans among the Southern Massim regulates the terms by which each person is addressed, while "it formerly decided who should take part in the cannibal feast held in revenge for a member of the hamlet-group killed by a hostile community. Further, until recently it determined a particular form of exogamy, but with the extinction of warfare and cannibal feasts within the last few years, the dual grouping has so fallen into decay as to be largely ignored in the regulation of marriage, although totem exogamy is still quite generally observed." A further word about these clan-groups is in order before discussing the terms of address. They "resemble phratries in that a man may not marry a member of his own clan-group, and may marry a member of the other clan-group of the community, if that clan-group be not barred to him by its being the clan-group to which his father belongs. I tend to regard the clan-groups as originally phratries, which, as the importance and avoidance of the father's totem became marked, ceased in a very large number of instances to be intermarrying groups although the old prohibition of marriage within the clan-group persisted. It is obvious that the Massim are generally in a condition of transition from matrilineal to patrilineal descent while at the extreme west of the Massim area the transition has actually taken place." Terms of address vary according to the clan-group of the individual addressed. "A native of Wagawaga of either sex in addressing an old man of his own clan-group, would call him *aü* (maternal uncle), and the speaker would be answered by the same term (meaning in this case sister's child). An old woman of the same clan-group as the speaker would be addressed as *hina* (mother), and in reply would use the term *natu* (child). A man will address an individual of his own sex, status, and clan-group, as *warihi* (brother or cousin), while he will address a woman of his own status and clan-group as *nowe* (sister or cousin). Both these terms, i.e., *warihi* and *nowe,* are reciprocal. A man or woman would address any man belonging to his or her father's generation and clan-group as *mahia* (paternal uncle), and would reciprocally be called *mahia* (brother's child)."[3]

Rivers,[4] writing of the Melanesians in general, says: "In peoples with patrilineal descent the community of designation for the father and father's brother, for their consorts and children, follows naturally if the system be founded on the clan-organisation. . . . The nomenclature for the father's brother and mother's sister, their consorts and children, points to the dual organisation having at one time been universal in Melanesia." Further, "it may be pointed out at the outset that the mother's brother and father's sister must always belong to different social groups wherever there is exogamy, and this must be so whether descent be patrilineal or matrilineal. Similarly, their children must always belong to different social groups. . . .

"In the great majority of the systems which have been recorded the mother's brother is denoted by a special term. . . . The relationship of mother's brother is one which brings out in the clearest manner the connection between the absence

2 Williamson, in JAI, XLIII, 269-270.   4 *Melan. Soc.,* I, 257; II, 16, 17-19, 56-57.
3 Seligmann, *Melanesians,* 435-436.

of a special term for a relative and absence of function. Throughout Polynesia, so far as we know, the mother's brother has no special duties or privileges except in places where he has a special designation." Copious illustration is presented. "Thus, wherever the mother's brother and sister's child have special functions, terms are used which distinguish them from other relatives. . . . As already indicated (I, 48), we have in the position of the wife of the mother's brother the clue to one of the peculiar features of Melanesian relationship, that according to which cross-cousins, the children of brother and sister, stand to one another in the relation of parent and child, the children of the father's sister being classed in nomenclature with the parents and the children of the mother's brother with the children." On the island of Pentecost, "there have been found certain correspondences, all of which receive a perfectly natural explanation as the survivals of an ancient institution in which a man married a woman having the same status as his daughter's daughter. Among the Dieri of Australia this form of marriage is still in existence (or was at the time Howitt's record was made); here also the children of a woman are considered as being the younger brothers and sisters of the woman's father, just as in Pentecost, while the mother's mother is sometimes called by a term including that for elder sister, again just as in Pentecost. In this case we have no doubt about the origin of the correspondences in an ancient form of marriage. Among the mountain tribes of Viti Levu and in the Buin district of Bougainville there have been found correspondences which again receive their most natural explanation in an ancient form of marriage between persons separated by two generations. In this case the marriage which will explain the correspondences is one in which a man marries a woman two generations above his own, viz., the wife of his father's father or a woman having the same status as this relative. The marriage of a man with a woman belonging to a generation two generations senior to his own may seem in the highest degree improbable, but this improbability becomes much less when we consider the nature of the classificatory system of relationship. Where this system exists, the difference of age between those who call one another by the same terms as grandparent and grandchild may be very slight. It may even be possible, though it probably rarely happens, that a man may be actually older than a woman two generations above him whom he classes with his own grandmother. Further, it may be pointed out that the marriage with the wife of the father's father does not stand alone. We have in Melanesia the clearest evidence for the existence, not only in the past but even at the present time, of marriage with the wife of the mother's brother. The definite existence of marriage with one of the immediately preceding generation certainly diminishes the improbability of marriage with a member of a still older generation."

That terms of relationship may be survivals of a form of marriage which has existed in the past seems to be true of the Solomon Islands also. Fox[5] has written at length concerning the practice in San Cristoval. "A child belongs to his mother's clan and necessarily marries a member of some other clan, and then all the members of these two clans are his relatives (though there is no word quite corresponding to the Mota. sogoi) either by birth or by marriage. But in a general sense so are the members of the other clans with which he is not directly connected. Roughly, the people are classed by the generation in

5 In JAI, XLIX, 108-110, 119-120, 141, 175; §409, of the text and Case-Book.

which they stand. Those of the father's generation are classed with the father, unless they are of the mother's clan; the father's sisters and mother's sisters are classed with the mother. So all the children of a man's own age are classed with his brothers and sisters, unless they are the children of those classed with his mother's brother. This classificatory system seems simple, yet it is hard for an Englishman to think in terms of it: he cannot resist using English words such as father, brother, sister, as equivalents for native words, which they are not, and he has a feeling that the word used for father is only loosely used when it is used for other men of the father's standing. . . . I discovered that about half the men and women who were married in Arosi had married either a generation above or a generation below their own, at any rate in the case of the first wife or husband, and that in some cases a man had married a woman two generations above him, a woman whom he classed with his father's mother, when using a native term for their relationship. With this key many puzzles were speedily unlocked, and these marriages were evidently the principal reason for my bewilderment. . . . But next to the marriages into another generation, the most prolific source of error or of difficulty is the native custom of adoption. Adoption is very common and puts a person into the actual place, as it were, of those born in these relationships: a boy adopted is considered the real son of the man who adopts him, just as much as one born to him by his wife. The woman who cuts the umbilical cord, and who shaves the head of the baby, is the baby's mother henceforth. Children bought become the 'real children' of the man who buys them—again a difficult point of view for an Englishman, who insists that these are not 'real children' at all; but when a man is giving a pedigree he makes no distinction between adopted children and those born to him. Yet in using relationship terms he may think of the relationship in which the boy stood before he was bought, and give that, or sometimes that and sometimes the new relationship. Moreover, people are not merely adopted as sons or daughters, but also as fathers, mothers, grandfathers, and grandmothers. A boy may be adopted to take the place of a man's father and keep his memory green; the father's name is given to him, and he takes *his* standing: he is classed as grandfather to boys of his own age or even older than himself. The unusual marriages, helped perhaps by this system of adoption, have made it now impossible to tell from a person's age in what generation he stands: one classed as your father may be of your own age, a brother may be as old as your father." Again, "if only one sort of marriage were taking place and it were taking place uniformly, the terms would be regularly and uniformly affected; but as this is not the case, the result on the terms used seems at first sight merely confusion, since they have not a fixed meaning, and vary from pedigree to pedigree. However, these marriages which seem strange are after all not the normal ones; in at any rate about half the marriages the man has married in his own generation a 'sister' of another clan, and the woman in her own generation a 'brother' of another clan, so that the proper value of the terms is easily obtained. Perhaps 'generation' is not quite the right word to use, for such marriages as those mentioned, like a fault in geology, have brought different strata on a level, so that children brought up together, and therefore of the same generation, are in terminology of different generations." The author gives some statistical evidence: out of sixty married men, twenty-nine married a woman of their own generation, and thirty-one a woman a generation above or below. Twenty-eight married a younger sister, nine a niece, thirteen a daughter, and nine a mother. "The general tendency now is for a man to marry a woman a generation below him (unless he marries, as at least half do, in his own generation); whereas the evidence points to a time when a man married a generation above him, and to a still earlier time when he married a woman two generations above his own."

"The kinship system of the Hottentots is a classificatory one with many similarities to the kinship systems found among the Bantu. The relative ages of the person speaking and of the person spoken of are very carefully recognised in these kinship terms. There is a special term for the mother's brother who stands in a very close relation to his sister's children, and there are special terms for cross cousins, corresponding to the special relation in which these people stand to one another."[6]

In West Africa neither of the words now used to express "father" has any relation to the act of begetting. They do not mean "he who begets" but "he who owns" and "he who maintains." Similarly with the words for "mother"; they mean "she who stays in the house" or "she who cooks." "*Baba* now means lord, master, great personage, or father. It appears to be derived from a root having the meanings of violence, strength, and power, and so, in the classificatory system, might well be applied to the grade of men who would be the hunters and warriors of the community."[7] Again, brothers and first, second, and third cousins are all called brothers; all uncles are called fathers. The mother and her sister are called mother.[8] Among the Bangala the same word stands for grandparent and grandchild.[9] In Madagascar names for brother and sister show distinctions which we do not possess; "and so much is the near kinship of brothers' and sisters' children recognized that, as with the words father and mother and child, it is difficult without close inquiry to find out what actual relationship there is between members of a family."[10]

In the following quotation from Sanderson[11] regarding the relationship-systems of certain Nyasaland tribes, the terms "brother" and "sister" are used in the full classificatory sense: all children of uncles and aunts are "brothers" and "sisters." "The wife of a 'brother,' whether older or younger, uterine or not, is called by the same term (*nkasi*) as a wife. I am informed that sexual intercourse, though not countenanced, is not uncommon, and such cases are apt to be treated leniently should they come to (native) court. This might be regarded as evidence of former 'group marriages,' but it should be noted that a man's first heir is his brother, who succeeds to the wives in common with the rest of the 'property.' . . . The 'sisters' of a wife are also called *nkasi*. The husband of the eldest of a family has a prior right to marry her uterine sisters, and a semi-right to her other 'sisters'; such marriages are very common." Other similar cases follow. All "grandmothers" are *nkasi*, probably, and so all "grandmothers" of the wife. A man has often to marry his "grandmothers" on the death of the "grandfather"; it is the rule to do so if they are destitute. Cross-cousins are classed as "brothers" and "sisters" and so first cousins are unmarriageable. Succession goes (1) to a younger brother by the same father and mother; (2) to a younger brother by the same father and a different mother; (3) to any younger "brother."

Among the Yakuts there are no special terms for son, daughter, or husband; and the wife is generally "my woman." "From all this we may infer that when,

6 Hoernlé, in AA, XXVII, 17-18.
7 Ellis, *Ewe*, 213, 215; Ellis, *Yoruba*, 181.
8 Bastian, *Deut. Exped.*, II, 216, note.

9 Weeks, in JAI, XXXIX, 438.
10 Sibree, *Great Afr. Isl.*, 247.
11 In JAI, LIII, 448-450, 451 (quoted), 452.

amongst the ancient Yakuts, a number of related persons were living together, the relations of 'mother' and 'wife' were the first ones which called for expression, 'mother' meaning a woman who had children. . . . The children belonged to the whole horde. Any one of the adult men might be the father of a certain child since the sex relations were undefined and perhaps unregulated. It is a curious circumstance that the heroes in the ancient folk tales often set out to find their *fathers*. We see, further, that the terms of relationship amongst the Yakuts express, first of all, the distinction between *younger* and *older* than the speaker. There is one word for older brother and another for younger brother; one word for older sister and another for younger sister, but there is no general term for brother or sister, since all were brothers and sisters within the compass of a *sib*. Hence nowadays *ubaj* means not only 'older brother' but also 'older male cousin,' 'older nephew,'—in short 'older member of the *sib*' than the speaker. *Ini* expresses not only 'younger brother,' but also 'younger male cousin,' 'younger nephew,' and in general 'younger member of the *sib*.' The case was the same as to female relations. In current speech, especially in personal address, the Yakuts use no other terms than these."[12]

"The Toda system of kinship is of the kind known as classificatory with several interesting special features. Perhaps the most important of these is the use of the same terms for mother's brother and father-in-law on the one hand, and for father's sister and mother-in-law on the other hand. This is a natural consequence of the regulation which ordains that the proper marriage for a man is one with the daughter either of his mother's brother or father's sister. . . . Thus the children of two brothers are brothers and sisters, and the children of two sisters are also brothers and sisters, while . . . the children of brother and sister receive another name. The children of two sisters belong to different clans except in those cases in which the sisters have married men of the same clan."[13] The classificatory system of relationship is prevalent among the Nairs also. "As a matter of fact, the distinction between own brothers and collateral brothers does not exist. All the persons of your own generation older than you are called brothers, and equal respect is shown to them. They are called by such terms as big brother, small brother, etc., *only when they are older than you*. Those who are younger are always called by their names. All women of your mother's generation are called mothers; those older than your mother are called *Peramma* or *Valiamma,* which means nominal mother or bigger mother, and those younger are called *Kochamma,* little mothers. But unlike among brothers, the distinction between one's mother and other females of the same generation is always maintained. Though respect is paid to all of them alike, own mother is always spoken of as mother, without qualification, and she alone has complete right to command you." The author[14] asserts that while the classificatory terminology to express relationship, when in use in a patrilineal community, may show the existence in some earlier time of group-marriages, "on the other hand, in a matrilineal community [such as that of the Nairs] such terms have nothing to do with the system of marriage, but only with relationship counted on the mother's side." He continues: "The mother-in-law has no special name. This is, of course, due to the universal prevalence

---

12 Sieroshevski-Sumner, in JAI, XXXI, 109; Czaplicka, *Aborig. Siberia,* 39 ff., gives consanguinity- and affinity-tables of relationship-terms.

13 Rivers, *Todas,* 483, 487.
14 Panikkar, in JAI, XLVIII, 263, note, 263-264.

of first cross-cousin marriage. The mother-in-law is generally addressed as *Ammavi Amma,* the first word being the same as the wife of the mother's brother, and the second an honorific addition to it. Dr. Rivers, in *Kinship and Social Organisation,* as well as in *Melanesian Society,* has conclusively shown that wherever first-cousin marriage prevails, there the mother-in-law has no special name. His explanation that this is due to the obvious fact that, in most cases, the mother's brother's wife is the same person as the mother-in-law, and that the former position was antecedent to the latter, is fully borne out by the terminology among the Nāyars." Says another writer[15] on India: "Dr. Rivers, whose loss we all deplore, drew our attention to the fact that some of the features of the classificatory system were such as could be derived only from dual organization of society. He pointed out that, first, one's mother's sister's children, father's brother's children and one's own brothers and sisters were grouped together under one term; secondly, mother's brother's children were classed together with those of father's sister. These features follow easily from a dual organization of society, and are hard to explain on the hypothesis of more classes than two."

In America, "the Coast Salish have a single term for paternal and maternal uncles, but distinguish children from all nephews and nieces. . . . Because primitive peoples attach an extraordinary importance to names the more remote cousin who is *called* cousin or sister may become more closely related in thought and marriage may be tabooed regardless of degree of propinquity. . . . Among the Nez Percé even third cousins were not allowed to marry and the union of second cousins roused ridicule in Thompson River communities."[16] There is no full gentile system among the Mohave, "but something closely akin to it, which may be called either an incipient or a decadent clan system. Certain men, and all their ancestors and descendants in the male line, have only one name for all their female relatives. Thus, if the female name hereditary in my family be Maha, my father's sister, my own sisters, my daughters (no matter how great their number), and my son's daughters, will all be called Maha."[17]

The fundamental principles of North American Indian tribal organization through kinship are formulated by Powell[18] as follows. "1. A body of kindred constituting a distinct body politic is divided into groups, the males into groups of brothers and the females into groups of sisters, on distinctions of generations, regardless of degrees of consanguinity; and the kinship terms used express relative age. In civilized society kinships are classified on distinctions of sex, distinctions of generations, and distinctions arising from different degrees of consanguinity. 2. When descent is in the female line, the brother-group consists of natal brothers, together with all the materterate male cousins [children of maternal aunt] of whatever degree. Thus mother's sisters' sons and mother's sisters' daughters' sons, etc., are included in a group with natal brothers. In like manner the sister-group is composed of natal sisters, together with all materterate female cousins of whatever degree. 3. When descent is in the male line, the brother-group is composed of natal brothers, together with all patruate male cousins [children of paternal uncle] of whatever degree, and the sister-group is composed of male sisters, together with all patruate female cousins

15 Ghurye, in JAI, LIII, 79.
16 Lowie, in AA, XXI, 29, 30-31.
17 Henshaw and Hodge, in HAI, I, 920.
18 In BAE, II, xliv-xlv; Letourneau, *Marr.,* 285-286.

of whatever degree. 4. The son of a member of a brother-group calls each one of the group father; the father of a member of a brother-group calls each one of the group son. Thus a father-group is coextensive with the brother-group to which the father belongs. A brother-group may also constitute a father-group and grandfather-group, a son-group and a grandson-group. It may also be a patruate-group and an avunculate[maternal uncle]-group. It may also be a patruate cousin-group and an avunculate cousin-group; and in general, every member of a brother-group has the same consanguineal relation to persons outside of the group as that of every other member."

"Among the Carib Islanders the uncles and aunts—as many as are of the collateral line—are called fathers and mothers by their nephews. . . . All the male cousins are also called brothers and all the female cousins sisters, but between male cousin and female cousin the former calls the latter youëilleri; that is to say properly, my female, for, naturally, among them the female cousins become wives to the male cousins."[19] Among the Shingu Indians older and younger brothers had different names and rank. The author[20] was called "older brother" or "grandfather," or "uncle," while his comrades were designated as his younger brothers. In Central Brazil there was a single term for father's brother and father and for mother's sister and mother. The mother's brother and father's sister are uncle and aunt. The paternal uncle and maternal aunt call their nephews and nieces, sons and daughters. Cousins whose fathers are brothers or whose mothers are sisters call each other brother and sister. [21] Among the Fuegians "a man and woman's brothers and sisters, nieces and nephews, call themselves respectively, the mothers and fathers, brothers and sisters in law, of his or her sons and daughters in law; and expect to be treated by these sons and daughters in law as such."[22] Among the Araucanians a son's son is called lacu, the same name as grandfather on the father's side. It "really means blood relative (male) once removed." In the same way mother's father and daughter's son are called chedchi.[23]

Among the Eastern Finns, finally, "as a rule no distinction is drawn between boy and son, girl and daughter, woman and wife, woman and mother; each doublet is usually expressed by a single word. As a rule, too, there is no word for brother or sister, only for elder brother, elder sister, and these are nearly always coupled with the connotations of uncle and aunt. Native words, too, for nephew, grandson, and first cousin are generally absent. . . . Traces of a classificatory system, founded on seniority, are still found among the Eastern Finns. . . . Exclusive of the father and mother, all blood-relations are divided, with regard to oneself or to a given person, into two categories of older and younger persons."[24]

§425. Relationship-Mores.

Avoidance of the Mother-in-law. In West Australia, says Brown,[1] "a man applies the name *toa* to his father's sister and to the wife of any *kaga,* that is to any woman who might be his mother-in-law. He may not speak to any of these women, nor have any social dealing whatever with them. If for any reason

19 Roth, in BAE, XXXVIII, 675.
20 Von den Steinen, *Zent. Bras.*, 331.
21 Ranke, in *Korresp. d. Deut. Anth. Gesellsft.*, 1898, 123.

22 Bridges, in *Voice for S. Amer.*, XIII, 201.
23 Latcham, in JAI, XXXIX, 357.
24 Abercromby, *Finns*, I, 183, 184, 185.
1 In JAI, XLIII, 156-157.

he is obliged to be near one of his *toa* he must take care that he does not look at her. He will, if possible, interpose a hut or bush between himself and her, or else he will sit with his back to her. This rule breaks down when a man gets on in years and has been long married with children of his own. He then ceases to speak of these women as *toa,* calling them *yumani* instead, and he is permitted to speak to them if he wishes, although the old habit still shows itself, and he has very little to do with them. I was not able to make out that the necessity of avoidance was more intense in respect to the actual mother-in-law. . . . There is no similar avoidance in the case of a woman, that is to say, she does not need to avoid her father-in-law or her mother-in-law, but only her son-in-law."

In Southeast Papua, "as mother-in-law woman is almost supreme. A man must always pay due respect to all his married relatives, but he must be especially considerate of his mother-in-law. On betrothal the young man must begin to make presents to his betrothed's mother, and continue the gifts to the end of the chapter. The best fish caught, the finest bunch of bananas grown, the most costly native wealth must go to the mother-in-law. Marriage is almost exclusively arranged by the women, and divorce is in nearly every case caused by the mothers-in-law."[2] Again, "no man will speak first to his father-in-law or mother-in-law, though if addressed he will answer. He will not walk straight up to them, and will not stand immediately in front of them. The same marks of respect are shown to chiefs."[3] Among the Southern Massim, "a man avoids his mother-in-law less rigidly than his wife's sisters, although if he meets her alone he treats her in the same way, and even in public does not usually enter her house unless he is living there. In his own house he may talk to her a little, and he may eat food she has cooked, but he does not take the pot containing food directly from her."[4] In Santa Cruz and Reef Islands, "when the woman is bought, the bridegroom must not see his mother-in-law's face as long as he lives; he must not speak her name; it does not matter if it be any article or thing of hers near, he must give it a different name."[5] In other islands, "if a man is sitting and his daughter's husband wishes to pass him, he will ask his father-in-law to get up, but if the latter does not wish to rise, he may meet the occasion by turning his face away as his son-in-law goes by. The behaviour towards the wife's mother is of the same kind. A man must not go near this relative nor say her name and he may only talk to her from a distance of five or six yards. If for any reason he has to pass her at a smaller distance than this he will do so in a crouching attitude and in no case will he pass her if she is sitting. If, on the other hand, the wife's mother has to pass her son-in-law even at a greater distance, she will go down on her hands and knees and will not pass him at all if he is sitting. It was said that formerly a man might marry the mother of his wife but that such an event would be the occasion of a fight." Again, "in the case of the wife's father there are, in addition to this name-avoidance, other signs of respect. . . . With the wife's mother, on the other hand, the avoidance is far more thorough. A man must not enter a house if his wife's mother is within and near the door; he will wait till she goes or moves away from the door, and in the latter case he may enter but must sit as far away from her as possible. If he meets her in the bush he will turn off the path and make a wide detour through the bush in order to pass her. If on

2 Bromilow, in AAAS, 1909, 472.
3 Liston-Blyth, in JAI, LIII, 471.
4 Seligmann, *Melanesians,* 486.
5 O'Ferrall, in JAI, XXXIV, 223.

the other hand he has climbed up a tree, his mother-in-law must turn out of her way to pass him. She may not drink the water from any bamboo that he has carried and if she wants him to help with any work she will speak first to her daughter who in her turn will speak to her husband. Any infringement of these rules can only be condoned by payments of money."[6]

Among the Nama Hottentots, a "wife's mother had always to be treated with the greatest deference by a husband. They were said to be 'shy' of one another, and the man might never look at her when speaking to her. There used in the past to be a special form of address between all relatives-in-law, the formal 'You' being applied both to the mother-in-law, to the brothers of a man's wife, and to her father, but it is not so used nowadays."[7] In Madagascar "there are proverbs in the language which warn people about the desirability of being on good terms with one's mother-in-law, speaking of it as being far more important than even agreeing with one's wife!"[8] An injunction of this character might, perhaps, be taken to indicate the former importance of the wife's mother as wielding authority under a matrilinear system—an authority recognized even by ensuing avoidance-customs.

In British Central Africa "a man used never to speak to his mother-in-law till after the birth of his first son. Neither a man nor his wife will eat in company of their mother or father-in-law until after birth of a child. If a man sees his mother-in-law eat he has insulted her and is expected to pay damages. If a man meets his mother-in-law coming along the road and does not recognise her, she will fall down on the ground as a sign, when he will run away. In the same way a father-in-law will signal to his daughter-in-law; the whole idea being that they are unworthy to be noticed till they have proved that they can beget children."[9] Among the Bangala of the Upper Congo "the mother-in-law is the only relative avoided. She and her son-in-law must not look on each other. Directly a man hears the word *bokilo* = mother-in-law, he runs and hides. They can sit at a little distance from each other, with their backs to one another, and talk. The only reason I have been able to ascertain for this avoidance," says Weeks,[10] "is: 'My wife came out of her womb.' *Bokilo* is from the verb *kila* = to forbid, prohibit, tabu. *Bokilo* in its wider use is also relation-in-law, e.g., daughter-in-law, brother-in-law, sister-in-law, sisters of mother-in-law, father-in-law, and it was regarded as incest to have sexual intercourse with anyone who was *bokilo*. I knew a case in which a man married his mother-in-law by marriage. The woman was not his wife's mother, but his wife's father's wife, and as such was his mother-in-law. I have seen him avoid her many times, and it was evident from this that all the wives of the wife's father are regarded as joint mothers of the children, and hence mothers-in-law. The man's wife's father died, and the man wanted to have one of the wives (i.e., one of his mothers-in-law) as his own wife, so he arranged with a friend to pay the marriage money and take her as his wife, then she by that marriage being no longer his mother-in-law, he was able to take her as his own wife. He paid the money for her and took her to his house." With the Baganda "no man may see his mother-in-law or speak to her. If he wishes to hold any communication with her it must be done through a third person or she may be in another room out of sight and speak to him through the wall or open door. A daughter-in-

6 Rivers, *Melan. Soc.*, I, 42, 182.
7 Hoernlé, in AA, XXVII, 23.
8 Sibree, *Great Afr. Isl.*, 250.
9 Stannus, in JAI, XL, 307.
10 In JAI, XXXIX, 438.

law may speak to her father-in-law, but may not hand him anything. Any breach of these customs will cause nervous debility with tremors in the hands and other parts of the body. The reason why a man may not see his mother-in-law is because he has seen her daughter's nakedness. A man must not touch his wife's uncle's daughters, that is, the man who secured his wife for him; this also will bring on tremor."[11] A different reason is given for the custom among the Ba-Huana: "A peculiar taboo, similar to the *Hlonipa* of the *Zulu-Xosa,* exists between a man and his parents-in-law; he may never enter their house, and if he meets them in a road he must turn aside into the bush to avoid them. . . . Repeated enquiries as to the reason of this avoidance on the part of a man of his parents-in-law, elicited the invariable reply 'that he was ashamed'; to a further enquiry of what he was ashamed, the answer would be 'of marrying their daughter.' No other reason could be obtained."[12]

In East Africa, "amongst the Wahehe the bridegroom has first to sleep with his mother-in-law, when he may cohabit with the daughter." A case is mentioned where the marriage was broken off because the man refused. On the other hand, a man may speak to his mother-in-law only at a distance, and may not look at her. The same restriction affects the woman in relation to her father-in-law.[13] Among the Mombasa, "no man may behold his mother-in-law. If he hears she is coming along his path he will make any detour to avoid meeting her."[14] In the case of the Lumbwa "there is a natural avoidance between the lover and his sweetheart's mother, as in the mother-in-law prohibition."[15] Dundas[16] remarks that "after marriage the relations between the husband and his parents-in-law are very curious, for although this relationship is very close, a Kikuyu, for instance, cannot sit together with his father-in-law, and a Mkamba may not meet or look at his mother-in-law; if he meets her on the path he will make a detour off the pathway." Hobley[17] gives further information concerning the latter group. "If a man meets his mother-in-law in the road they both hide their faces and pass by in the bush on opposite sides of the path. If a man did not observe this custom and at any time wanted to marry another wife it would prove a serious stigma and parents would have nothing to do with him. Moreover if a wife heard that her husband had stopped and spoken to her mother in the road she would leave him. If a man has business he wishes to discuss with his mother-in-law he goes to her hut at night and she will talk to him from behind the partition in the hut. A man can however take steps to remove this prohibition: he gives due notice of his intention and then on a certain day the people of the neighbourhood collect at the village where his mother-in-law lives and the man sends them an ox, a big goat, several pots of honey and a supply of beer, the assembled company then hold a great dance and feast, and the man formally presents a blanket to both his father-in-law and mother-in-law and after that he need take no special precautions in the matter." It is a rule of Masai relationship that "mothers-in-law and their sons-in-law . . . must avoid one another as much as possible, and if a son-in-law enters his mother-in-law's hut she must retire into the inner compartment and sit on the bed, whilst he remains in the outer compartment; they may then talk."[18] Among the Ababda in the eastern desert of Egypt, "a man avoids his

11 Roscoe, in JAI, XXXII, 39.
12 Torday and Joyce, in JAI, XXXVI, 285-286.
13 Cole, in JAI, XXXII, 312.
14 Johnstone, in JAI, XXXII, 270.

15 Barton, in JAI, LIII, 69.
16 In JAI, XLV, 287.
17 *A-Kamba,* 103-104.
18 Hollis, in JAI, XL, 481.

mother-in-law by not speaking to, touching, or eating in her presence. A very few avoid this prohibition by paying a fine of about 30 piastres [a coin worth about four and a half cents] to the mother-in-law. The mother-in-law's sister is not avoided in the same way. . . . A woman does not avoid her mother-in-law."[19]

Among the Ostyak, "no married woman can appear before her father-in-law whilst she lives; nor the bridegroom before his mother-in-law until he has children. They must avoid them as much as possible; and if they chance to meet them must turn their backs and cover their faces."[20] In one case in India the bride's mother "is, by a curious custom, not permitted to approach the bridegroom on the wedding day or after, lest she should cause ceremonial pollution."[21] Among the hill-tribes of Central India "the most common of the taboos is that which prevents a man from addressing, touching, or even looking at his mother-in-law. This has been explained by Sir John Lubbock as a survival of marriage by capture, the relatives of the bride being hostile to the man who has captured their woman; or, as by Mr. Keane, from the analogy of the Patagonian practice that on the death of any young person the head of the family was required to despatch some aged woman, and he naturally selected his mother-in-law as the appropriate victim. Hence, it is said that through fear of such a fate, women acquired the habit of avoiding their sons-in-law."[22]

In Celebes "after the marriage it is specifically forbidden to the son-in-law to speak with his mother-in-law."[23] Evans[24] was informed that among the Hill Sakai of Upper Perak "avoidance of the mother-in-law was strictly observed, and that it was not allowable to speak to her directly, to pass in front of her, or even to hand her anything." "If a man is in the least degree too familiar with his mother-in-law, thunderbolts, said the Semang to me, will assuredly fall. For this reason (if for no other!) the contingency never arises. But they also assured me that they of the jungle were far more distant and circumspect in their dealings with their mothers-in-law than was the case with their neighbours the Malays."[25] In New Zealand the bride's mother resisted and vociferated at her daughter's marriage, abusing the missionary, "but telling him at the same time in a low voice not to mind, for she was not serious."[26]

The Alaskan natives "consider it the proper thing for a brother to sit with his back to his sister or his mother-in-law; if he needs to communicate with them it must be through a third party, or in such a manner as if he were not addressing them."[27] Among the Omahas "as much as possible a woman avoids passing before the husband of her daughter. . . . A man addresses never a word to the mother or grandmother of his wife."[28] The Mandan mother-in-law "never speaks to her son-in-law, unless on his return from war he bring her the scalp and gun of a slain foe, in which event she is at liberty from that moment to converse with him. . . . While the Dakota, Omaha, and other tribes visited by the author have the custom of 'bashfulness,' which forbids the mother-in-law and son-in-law to speak to each other, no allowable relaxation of the prohibition has been recorded."[29] By the Menomini, "besides the mother-

19 Murray, in JAI, LIII, 420.
20 Czaplicka, *Aborig. Siberia*, 127.
21 Thurston, *S. India*, 21.
22 Crooke, in JAI, XXVIII, 238, quoting Lubbock, *Orig. Civ.*, 11 ff., 192, and Keane, *Ethnol.*, 218.
23 Riedel, in *Bijd.*, XXXV, 91.

24 In JAI, XLVIII, 195.
25 Skeat and Blagden, *Malay Penin.*, II, 204-205.
26 Letourneau, *Marr.*, 99.
27 Jones, *Thlingets*, 212.
28 Dorsey, in BAE, III, 262.
29 Dorsey, in BAE, XV, 241.

in-law taboo, the father-in-law taboo is observed to a certain extent, but for the latter there is no fixed rule."[30] In good Cheyenne families "indirect courtesies often passed between a wife's mother and her son-in-law. . . . Since a man was not permitted to speak nor ever to look at his mother-in-law, it was usual for her to ride up behind the lodge and step into it at a time when she knew he was abroad. . . . A woman might face her son-in-law if she chose formally to present him an ornamented robe." There were certain ceremonies attending upon such a presentation. "After an exchange of gifts such as described, the mother-in-law tabu ceased to be in force."[31] As among the Navaho, so with the Chiricahua, "a man never spoke to his mother-in-law, and treated his wife's father with distant respect."[32] Says Roth:[33] "As with the Carib, a Warrau does not talk to his mother-in-law; but I have noticed the latter doing so at a distance in a lowered tone of voice, and with head turned in a different direction. She turns her face away whenever he passes anywhere near. Arawak have told me that 'in the old days' their women used a large basket, under which, inverted, they would crouch and hide their heads on the approach of their son-in-law." The Araucanian mother resists the removal of her daughter, sulks, and will not speak to her son-in-law.[34]

Other Avoidance-Practices. Of special significance in the following cases are the brother-sister relation, avoidance of bride and father-in-law, and customs surrounding connections by marriage; equally noteworthy is the taboo on the names of certain relatives.[35] A few cases refer to the duties and privileges of relatives.

Among the Arunta and Urabunna tribes of South Australia, "the husband is, all his life, under certain obligations to supply food to the relatives of his wife. The portions of the chase go to (1) his father-in-law, (2) himself, wife, and children, (3) his wife's brothers' children, (4) his mother-in-law, (5) father of his mother-in-law, (6) sisters of his mother-in-law's father. Nor is he allowed to eat the flesh of an animal caught, killed, or touched by any of the above mentioned people."[36]

Among the Southern Massim, "every native avoided speaking the name of a large number of people who may be grouped as follows: (1) Living relatives. (2) Dead relatives. (3) Connections by marriage." A number of examples are cited. "The majority of connections by marriage who are of opposite sexes and between whom there is name avoidance also avoid coming into contact with each other. A man would most rigidly avoid talking to a sister of his wife whether he met her alone or in the company of others. If he met her alone he would avoid coming near her at all; if this were impossible, as when meeting on a jungle track, brother-in-law and sister-in-law would turn their backs to each other in passing and one, usually the woman, would step aside into the bush. . . . Father-in-law and daughter-in-law avoid each other very much as do mother-in-law and son-in-law. A man does not avoid his brothers' wives." In the Louislade Islands, "a wife's sister may take anything she likes belonging to her brother-in-law without any objection being raised; she may even borrow and damage a big canoe without incurring blame. This is all 'pay belong girl.' The bride's brothers have similar rights. . . . Toakina stated that

30 De Josselin de Jong, in AA, XVIII, 122.
31 Grinnell, *Cheyenne*, I, 146, 147, 148.
32 In HAI, I, 283.
33 In BAE, XXXVIII, 685.
34 Waitz, *Anthrop.*, III, 516.
35 §212, of the text and *Case-Book.*
36 Wallis, in AA, XV, 110.

he found it advisable to keep his more valuable jewellery constantly on his person in order to be sure of retaining it for himself. . . . A son-in-law avoids his mother-in-law, and a father-in-law avoids his daughter-in-law; a wife avoids her husband's brothers, and a husband avoids his wife's maternal and paternal aunts; he will also avoid his wife's sisters' daughters."[37] Rivers[38] remarks: "The custom of chaffing or mocking certain relatives seems to be so well established a custom of the Banks islanders as to be a regular social institution. . . . It is clear that there is an established custom of mocking certain relatives by marriage and the example which has been recorded suggests that the whole business has a deep-seated meaning to those who indulge in it." A similar case among the American Indians appears later on.

"On the south coast of Bauro, at Parigina and elsewhere, intercourse between brother and sister (actual brother and sister) is forbidden. A brother must never: (1) Name his sister. (2) Approach her. (3) Laugh or play in her presence. (4) Touch anything belonging to her or even lying near her. (5) Go into a house where she is. (6) Enter the same canoe. (7) Tread on her bed mat. (8) Meet her in the path (one turns into the bush). (9) Go into the garden she is in. (10) Speak to her. And these restrictions hold even when both are grown up and married, and until their death; to an Englishman accustomed to think of his sisters as his most intimate friends and counsellors, a truly strange state of affairs, but nevertheless one that holds also elsewhere in Bauro, though the regulations are not everywhere so strict, yet everywhere a man should avoid his sister and never name her or speak to her."[39] In the New Hebrides, father-in-law and son-in-law avoid one another almost as strictly as mother-in-law and son-in-law. If they touch each other they must kill a pig to cleanse the stain; otherwise the son-in-law will be poor or the eyes of both will be weak in battle.[40] In the Torres Straits Islands, the son-in-law may not utter the names of his wife's relations and may speak to his father-in-law only through his wife. These customs are regarded as "vestiges of a condition in which a man lives with and serves the family of his wife."[41] Among the Andamanese, "until a man attains a middle age he evinces great shyness in the presence of the wife of a younger brother or cousin, and the feeling is invariably reciprocated; it is, however, otherwise in the case of the elder brother's (or cousin's) wife, who, moreover, should she be many years his senior, receives from him much of the respect accorded to a mother. . . . When a man wishes to address a married woman older than himself, he cannot do it himself, but must find a third person to act as a medium."[42]

Among the Nama Hottentots, "the relation of a man to his sister's children was one of the greatest indulgence and good will. A boy could do almost anything at his maternal uncle's . . . home, without being blamed for it. He could take, without asking, any of the specially fine animals among his uncle's herds, and the uncle had no redress but to take misformed ugly animals from his nephew's herds. . . . A woman considered her husband's younger brothers as her husbands, and used in the old days to be inherited by one of them. In the early missionary records there are numerous instances of a younger brother taking over his elder brother's widow. . . . It will be seen from the account

37 Seligmann, *Melanesians*, 484-486, 738.
38 *Melan. Soc.*, I, 46-47.
39 Fox, in JAI, XLIX, 143-144.
40 Macdonald, in AAAS, 1892, 723.
41 Rivers, in *Man*, 1901, 172; Haddon, in JAI, XIX, 338.
42 Man, in JAI, XII, 136, 355.

given of the kinship system and the 'behavior patterns' accompanying kinship terms that the type of behavior which is expected of a person by another is directly indicated by the kinship term in use between them, so that a knowledge of these relationships is essential for an understanding of the whole moral regulation of the lives of the people." The author[43] writes also of the duties and privileges of relatives. "The chief consideration in the behavior of Nama to one another is the relative ages of the people concerned. Respect for age is inculcated in every possible way, and the whole social organization of the people is an illustration of the fact. In the family deference and respect must always be paid to elders. Thus, of a number of brothers the eldest always has the honored place and the first voice in any debate. . . . In the old days the behavior of a brother and a sister was very strictly regulated. As tiny children they ran about together, but once they were grown up, they had to avoid one another completely. A brother was not allowed to speak to a sister directly, he must never be alone with her in the hut, he must never speak of her except in the most respectful terms. A sister was a *tàras*, that is, a person to be respected, not to be spoken to or of lightly. In the old days an oath by a sister was one of the greatest oaths a man could take, and a sister could generally be relied on to stop any fight in which her brother was taking part."

Among the Ba-Huana a man must avoid his wife's parents, while a woman must show respect to her parents-in-law and visit them. She must not have anything to do with the maternal uncle of her husband.[44] Such is the power of conventionality in Nyasaland that "if the husband's brother, or his maternal uncle, come on a visit, the wife will at once leave the hut and sit by herself, alone and disconsolately, at some distance, until he has gone. And if one asks her why she acts in this way, she replies: '*Ninaona haya.*' (I feel shy.) The visitor, if the same question was put to him, would probably say, as an explanation needing no further comment: 'Is she not my daughter-in-law?' "[45] Among the Akamba, "if a girl of the age of puberty meets her father in the road she hides as he passes, nor can she ever go and sit near him in the village until the day comes when he tells her that it has been arranged for her to marry a certain man. After marriage she does not avoid her father in any way."[46] Own brothers-in-law and sisters-in-law among the Masai must avoid one another, though this rule does not apply to half-brothers-in-law and sisters-in-law. "This rule," thinks Hollis,[47] "is possibly due to the fact that when a man dies his own brother may not marry his widow, though there is no objection to his half-brother (paternal) or one of his paternal cousins taking her to wife. In fact, the only person who may marry a widow is one of the deceased husband's half-brothers or paternal cousins. It frequently happens, however, that widows never re-marry, but live with their children in the kraal of their eldest living brother of their late husband, who becomes the guardian of their children."

In the Sudan region the relatives of a man's wife "seem to have the feeling that they have entered into a highly delicate and difficult position with respect to him. For the parents-in-law and the brothers and sisters of his wife he becomes an individual whom they mention only by necessity by his own name and whom they avoid so far as possible. If he is sitting in a company of men

43 Hoernlé, in AA, XXVII, 21, 22, 22-24.
44 Torday and Joyce, in JAI, XXXVI, 274.
45 Coudenhove, in *Atl. Mo.*, CXXXII, 193.
46 Hobley, *A-Kamba*, 104.
47 In JAI, XL, 481.

and his father-in-law comes along, he rises very quickly and goes away; if his brother-in-law comes and sees him, he remains sitting, it is true, but the other goes by. On the other hand he does not sit down in a gathering in which his brother-in-law is but hitches his *litâm* [face-veil] over his face and strides by. If he has children and his name has to be mentioned, they use the circumlocution: 'father of such-and-such son' or 'father of such-and-such daughter.' "48 Among the Ababda "the father-in-law may be saluted by name by his son-in-law, but otherwise he is avoided, and though his daughter-in-law may speak to him, she does not eat in his presence. A woman does not avoid her mother-in-law. The following relatives may not be addressed by name by an Abadi: father's brother, father's sister, mother's brother, father's father, mother's father. Further, among the Ababda of the hills a wife may not address her husband, nor a husband his wife, by name."49

The Yakut bride "should avoid showing herself or her uncovered body to her father-in-law." She used to avoid her husband's male relatives and they tried not to meet her, saying, "The poor child will be ashamed." "If a meeting could not be avoided, the young woman put a mask on her face. Sometimes she died before her father-in-law had seen her face. Not until then was it proper for him to look at her so as to know whether she was pretty or what she was like. Nowadays the young wives only avoid showing to their male relatives-in-law the uncovered body. Amongst the rich, they avoid going about in the presence of these in the chemise alone."50 Evidently there is here a variation toward modesty, set afloat by the upper classes. This taboo is explained as prudential, against love. The prohibition which binds the Yakut woman is with regard especially to her father-in-law, but refers also to other older male relations. "It is known as *kinitti,* and according to this she (i) is not allowed to pass in front of the fire of the father-in-law and other older male relatives, but must pass behind it from the northwest; (ii) must not talk in a loud voice, nor use words with a double meaning; (iii) must not call her father-in-law by his name, and even if his name signifies an object in common use, she can only name this object by means of a periphrasis—e.g., if he is called 'Flint,' she must say 'fire-stone' when speaking of a flint; (iv) must not eat of the head of any animal, for the father-in-law is head of the house; (v) must, when addressing her father-in-law or mother-in-law, draw her cap down as far as possible over her eyes; (vi) must not show her hair to her father-in-law, or bare her feet or any part of her body before him. Sieroszewski says that the custom of *kinitti* was formerly much more strict. The bride was forbidden to show herself for seven years after her marriage to her father-in-law or brothers-in-law, or to any male relative of her husband." A similar situation exists among the Buryat, where "the bride has to observe the following restrictions: (i) she must never address her father-in-law or mother-in-law by name; (ii) all relatives of her husband older than he, and her father-in-law as well, she must call *khadam;* (iii) in the presence of a *khadam* she must never be without her cap and face-covering; (iv) she must not remove or change her dress in his presence; (v) her sleeping-place should be in a separate *yurta* [tent]; (vi) if she meets a *khadam,* she must not cross his path, but pass behind him; (vii) she must not ride in the same wagon with him, and generally not be close to him. He, on the other hand, must not dress or undress in her

48 Nachtigal, *Sahara,* I, 450.
49 Murray, in JAI, LIII, 420.
50 Sieroshevski-Sumner, in JAI, XXXI, 93.

presence, not sit or lie down on her sleeping-place. He must not utter any indecent language before her; and before entering the *yurta,* must make a signal to her of his approach, in order that she may have time to put her dress in order." The Kalmuk bride is also obliged to keep certain rules of behavior with regard to her father-in-law and the older male relatives of her husband. "She must not sit down while they remain in the *yurta.* She enters their *yurtas* only when invited; on going out she must cross the threshold with her face turned towards the interior of the *yurta.* . . . She must not address her husband's parents or other older relatives by their own name, but must invent names herself for them. This custom holds even with regard to the parents' dog. Tereshchenko writes that the bride throughout her life must not show her bare feet or head to her father-in-law or male relatives older than her husband." Among the Ostyak, "the custom of avoidance is binding upon the bride as well as her brothers-in-law. There are also certain restrictions governing the relations between a girl and her brothers. After she has reached the age of thirteen she may not eat with them or talk to them."[51]

Among the Nairs a young man or woman "is not supposed to talk to any relations of the opposite sex in the same family *if they are of almost the same age.* A younger brother can talk to a sister considerably older than himself; but under no conditions may he talk to a younger one, and in orthodox families this restriction is carried so far that if it is known that a brother is standing somewhere near, the sister scrupulously avoids him. . . . This involves considerable inconvenience, for, if the mother is dead and there is no one of *her generation* living, a man loses all touch with the family, because his sisters and women of that generation may not speak to him, and he may not go near them. In such cases, it is customary for young men to go and stay in their wives' houses and visit their own families for business arrangements."[52] Among Dravidians, one of the most important of marriage-taboos is that which prevents a man from coming in any way into contact with the wife of his younger brother. Most of these races protect her from her senior brother-in-law by a most stringent sanction which, in the case of the Dharkars, reaches the point that a man contracts a stain if even her shadow crosses his path. Second comes the taboo of the wife's elder sister. A man may marry two sisters, but he may not marry the elder if the younger be already his wife. She is said to be in the position of mother to her younger sister, but this is obviously a later development of the taboo. Third, there are taboos of more distant female relations—the maternal aunt, the first cousin on the mother's side, the relation of Samdhi, that is, of persons allied by the marriage of their children. Among the Pankas the father-in-law and mother-in-law of a married pair do not speak to each other. So there are taboos of the wives of the paternal uncle and nephew. Among the Majhwars a woman may not address her father-in-law by name. Last and most significant, the Korwas extend the taboo to their sisters. The author[53] suggests that the real explanation of this group of marriage-taboos is to be found in the fact that they include persons with whom, under the primitive rule of group-marriage, connection was permissible. They have persisted long after the social system which gave them birth has disappeared and have been replaced by a new series of exogamous rules and prohibited degrees.

51 Czaplicka, *Aborig. Siberia,* 110-111, 120, 122, 128.

52 Panikkar, in JAI, XLVIII, 261-262.
53 Crooke, in JAI, XXVIII, 238, 239.

"The prohibition with regard to mentioning the names of near relations, either by blood or marriage, so common in the Malayan region, is also found among some of the mixed Negrito-Sakai and Sakai-Jakun tribes, and also among the Sakai proper. A man of a Sakai-Jakun tribe, which was living close to Kuala Tembeling in Pahang, told me that they were forbidden to mention the names of fathers-in-law, mothers-in-law, brothers-in-law, or sisters-in-law; while a man from near Pertang in Jelebu, Negri Sembilan, said that his people did not dare to mention the names of their fathers, because they were afraid of being struck by the indwelling power (*daulat*) of that relation."[54] On Mortlock Island "brothers and sisters are strictly taboo and must not even speak to one another."[55] In Samoa "the remotest reference, even by way of joke, to anything which conveyed the slightest indelicacy in thought or gesture was prohibited when brothers and sisters were together. In the presence of his sister the wildest rake was always modest and moral; and in the presence of her brother the most accommodating coquette was chaste and reserved. Krämer says the relation between brother and sister was a sacred one, and this was so as between male and female cousins [who would under the classificatory system be brothers and sisters]. . . . A man's sister has some functional duties in connection with his burial."[56]

Among the Tlinkits "the absurd custom of brothers and sisters (as soon as the latter attain to womanhood), the mother-in-law and son-in-law, males and females of the same totem, refraining from speaking to each other, still finds favour with many." The author[57] has known "sisters who, on their return to Alaska, after being away to school in the States, could not get their uneducated brothers to speak to them. A nephew, who had been educated in one of our schools, made repeated efforts to get his aunt to speak to him while on a long journey, but failed. The untutored aunt would not condescend to speak to her nephew, as it was contrary to her notions of womanly modesty and ethics. It is considered improper for a brother and sister to sit in the same room if no others are there. A brother refused to enter the church until the arrival of others because his sister was the only one inside. A brother may not make a present to his married sister, but may to her husband. It is considered highly improper for a brother to give his married sister anything."

"The Cheyenne young man was not permitted to speak to his adult sister." This began when she was fifteen years old. If he wanted to speak, he addressed someone else in her presence, even a new-born child. The practice continued up to old age.[58] The name-taboo was strict among the Omahas and conversation between certain relatives was circuitous. "A man did not directly address his wife's father or mother, nor did any of his brothers do so. If the parents were visiting in the same tent with their son-in-law or any of his brothers, conversation could be carried on but it was generally done indirectly, not directly between these persons. A wife did not directly address her husband's father but this did not apply to his mother. This custom has been explained by old Omaha men to mean that respect was thus shown by the younger to the elder generation. . . . Etiquette demanded also that a person's name should not be mentioned in his presence. It may be recalled that a man's name referred to the rites in charge of his gens or to some personal experience—a

54 Evans, in JAI, XLVIII, 194.
55 Finsch, *Ehnol. Erfahr.*, III, 306, note.
56 Williamson, *Cent. Polyn.*, II, 159, 161.

57 Jones, *Thlingets*, 145-146.
58 Grinnell, *Cheyenne*, I, 155, 156.

dream or a valorous deed. The personal name sustained therefore so intimate a relation to the individual as to render it unsuitable for common use. . . . It is more likely that the benefits to be derived from the daily emphasis of kinship as a means to hold the people together in peaceable relations had to do with the establishment of the custom, which was strengthened by the sanctity attached to the personal name. . . . 'It sounds as though they do not love one another when they do not use terms of relationship.' "[59] Among the Chiricahua, a man's "brothers were never familiar with his wife nor he with her sisters and brothers."[60] In the Winnebago tribe, "a man was not permitted to take even the slightest liberties with any of his near relatives or with his mother-in-law or his father-in-law, but a curious exception to this rule was permitted for his father's sister's children, his mother's brother's children, his mother's brothers and his sisters-in-law and brothers-in-law. In the two cases last named not only was a man permitted to joke with those relatives, but he was supposed to do so whenever he had an opportunity. Under no circumstances were any of these individuals supposed to take offense. This relationship was of course reciprocal. If a person attempted liberties with people who did not belong in the category of the 'joking relationship' they would stop him immediately, saying, 'What joking relation am I to you?' "[61]

§426. Artificial Relationship.[1]

In southeastern Papua prisoners and all strangers were treated in one of two ways: "they were either killed and eaten, or adopted into the tribe with full rights. If it were decided that a prisoner should not be killed, he would be received without ceremony of a secret character by being presented with a block of land by the family adopting him. He would be called son, brother, nephew . . . and be treated in everything as a member of the tribe."[2]

There are five kinds of adoption known to Fox[3] which are regularly practised in certain of the Solomon Islands, all common and all vitally affecting the social life of the people: "(1) the *marahu* adoption; (2) adoption of children or adults taken in war or punished for offences by being sold to people at a distance; (3) adoption of children by buying them from a distance; (4) adoption of children at birth; (5) adoption to keep green the memory of the dead. (1) *The Marahu Adoption.* The meaning of the word *marahu* has already been given as (1) a namesake, (2) one with whom a man exchanges names, (3) one with whom he exchanges wives, (4) a friend. The third is seldom seen nowadays, the first and fourth are common enough, the second is the most interesting. Most natives, one is told, have a *marahu* in this sense. There is the famous case of Karani of Santa Anna who became 'Moto,' exchanging names with the Wango chief, who became 'Karani.' The practice is to emphasise friendship by the exchange of names, and this gives a man the status of his *marahu*. A small present is exchanged, and the man is considered to have a right to the property of his *marahu*, which will not be withheld from him; he may take his coco-nuts, his yams, or even tobacco from the bag of the *marahu*, and he has very much the close and intimate relationship to his *marahu*

59 Fletcher and LaFlesche, in BAE, XXVII, 334-335.
60 HAI, I, 283.
61 Radin, in BAE, XXXVII, 133-134.

1 §409, of the text and *Case-Book.*
2 Bromilow, in AAAS, 1909, 470.
3 In JAI, XLIX, 138-140.

that a boy has to his *mau* or mother's brother. I should know something of the custom, as I have a *marahu* both in Bauro and in Arosi, and have frequently been addressed by their names, both directly and in letters. When I became *marahu* to a Bauro man I was received into his place in the society of the village, called all the people in it by the terms used by him and was called by the terms they gave him. I was told how to address each, to call a young boy grandfather and another uncle; and it was explained to me that the names of certain of my new relatives must never be used, i.e., the native name—the baptismal might be; and how to get over the difficulty when I wished directly to address people whose names I must never use. Above all I must never use the name of one I called *wauwa* (in practice these were elder brothers), not only in direct address but in any conversation, and he might be addressed directly as *Warua* (i.e., the numeral two, with the masculine prefix). I found that not only was I now Amwea, but Amwea people everywhere gave me food as a matter of course, and if I wanted a native bag or limebox, they were made for me without any payment being expected or asked, and getting boys for odd jobs became a much easier matter; tobacco, no doubt, was expected by all Amwea people when they called, and other little gifts, but this was hardly a new fact due to the *marahu* adoption. A *marahu* is a close friend with whom one is on terms of great freedom: like a boy and his uncle, carrying much the same privileges as that relationship; and is a means of adoption for a foreigner.[4] (2) and (3) have already been mentioned; (3) is practised partly to get children without the trouble of rearing them, and to replenish the population dwindling through disease or from the practice of child murder; and also to strengthen alliances, thus making relatives at a distance and sometimes ending in this way a long period of hostility.[5] (4) Adoption at birth is very common. In Arosi the first woman to cut the umbilical cord and shave the child's head becomes the mother. Both (3) and (4) put the child exactly into the same position as if he or she had been born into it. (5) Adoption to keep green the memory of the dead. (Perhaps this might be called 'memorial adoption.') This is common and important, in that it alters relative terms used, and brings men and women of the same age into the status of those one or two generations removed from them, and so may be the cause of the anomalous marriages found in San Cristoval, or a contributory cause of the apparent confusion in the use of relationship terms. The commonest forms of adoption in Bauro are as follows: A man adopts a small boy to the name and status of his (1) father, (2) mother's brother, (3) grandfather, and a small girl to the name and status of his (1) mother, (2) grandmother. A woman adopts a child to the name and status of (1) her father, (2) herself. The reason given is to keep green the memory of the dead, and it is usually done when the relative dies." The author writes further regarding his own experience with the *marahu* adoption: "The father of my *marahu,* a man named Mono, wished to remember his own father Sutagera, who had lately died, and bought a boy from twenty miles away somewhat younger than or about the same age as my *marahu,* Waiau Gafuafaro. This boy was then called Sutagera and took his status, becoming Waiau's grandfather, though younger than Waiau. Mono's brother (and Mono himself) always called this young boy Mama (father). I, of course, called him grandfather. Later on he married a girl of about his own age whom he called daughter, and Waiau called mother. A boy of the

---

4 §§212, 416, of the text and *Case-Book*.   5 §142, of the text and *Case-Book*.

place may be adopted in this way and then all the terms he used before must be altered to suit his new standing. It is an interesting question whether such adoption might not have just the effect of bringing the different genealogical strata together which we find in San Cristoval, and so causing what we call anomalous marriages."

Among the Fan of West Africa "the ceremonies of adoption are the same as those of birth. The adopted child loses all his former totems to take those of the tribe which he enters. A single ceremony is added: the effusion of blood. . . . The adoptive father makes some slight scarifications on the left arm of the child, collects the blood which flows, and throws it on the skulls of the ancestors, then on the *akaméyôn* [objects connected with the totem]. He then takes a portion of a skull, some ashes of the totemic sacrifices and rubs them vigorously on the arm of the child. This is the distinctive sign of adoption."[6] In the Upper Congo, "there is no adoption, but there is both blood-brotherhood and milk-brotherhood, but these carry no right of inheritance, although to the latter a portion of the estate is sometimes given. There is also milk sisterhood, and when a woman is a milk sister it is not usual for her milk brother to marry her. It is permissible but is regarded as irregular. There is no blood-brotherhood between men and women."[7]

In South Sumatra any person may recognize another as his brother or father, with the exception that, by virtue of the rule that adoption must mimic nature, a person may not take as his son a person who is older or of about the same age as himself. Anyone may adopt an alien for his lawful father, brother, or son, and in such cases name him as his heir, even though he buys a slave for that purpose. This takes place by killing a buffalo or a goat and making a meal. The custom of accepting or recognizing children prevails chiefly in Minahasa. It is so common among the Alfurs that everyone seems to be recognizing or being recognized as a child. If one wants to take an old man as a father or an old woman as mother, he lets it be known, and if there is consent he takes it upon himself to be helpful to the old people; then, like a regular child, he inherits from them after their death. Similarly when an older person wants to bind to himself a younger. In this adoption there is not much ceremony, merely a feast or meal, though during heathendom a sacrifice was common. There are always witnesses; and in later times also a document of agreement. Seldom does the adopted child go to live with the older, adopted parent, but merely enters upon the rights and duties of a child; he must help from time to time, especially at rice-cultivation, lend assistance in case of need, and help pay the costs at death. The adopted child shares with the own children in the heritage. The same custom obtains among the Dyaks, where the ceremony consists in taking a little blood from each of the two parties, putting it on a betel-quid and giving it to both to eat.[8]

In Central Polynesia fictitious kinship exists alongside of real. "A child, and, indeed, an adult, belonging to one social group, might be adopted into another group, and thereupon become, speaking generally, an actual member of that group—just as much, or almost so, as he or she would have been if his or her claim to membership were based upon blood relationship. . . . As regards what is spoken of as *real* kinship, . . . whilst systems of matrilineal descent of blood, or traces of them and of exogamy are found in some of the islands, succession

6 Trilles, *Fân*, 572.
7 Weeks, in JAI, XXXIX, 444.
8 Wilken, in VG, I, 387-388; II, 288.

to the name or title of a social group was mainly patrilineal; and therefore the distinction between maternal and paternal relationship does not appear to have been nearly so closely recognized as it would be among people with more archaic social systems, and a true brother and sister relationship between the children of a father of one social group by wives of different social groups would commonly be recognized."[9]

Among the Menomini Indians "a person is in 'joking-relationship' with his uncles and aunts, nephews and nieces, sisters-in-law and brothers-in-law on either side. The joking-relationship also implies the lawfulness of sexual intercourse. Very near is the relationship with nephews, nieces, brothers-in-law and sisters-in-law."[10] Elsewhere "adoption by marriage or by residence of more than a year was common."[11] Hewitt[12] has written generally concerning adoption among the North American tribes. "From the view point of the primitive mind adoption serves to change, by a fiction of law, the personality as well as the political status of the adopted person. For example, there were captured two white persons (sisters) by the Seneca, and instead of both being adopted into one clan, one was adopted by the Deer and the other by the Heron clan, and thus the blood of the two sisters was changed by the rite of adoption in such wise that their children could intermarry. . . .From the political adoption of the Tuscarora by the Five Nations, about 1726, it is evident that tribes, families, clans, and groups of people could be adopted like persons. A fictitious age might be conferred upon the person adopted, since age largely governed the rights, duties, and position of persons in the community. In this wise, by the action of the constituted authorities, the age of an adopted group was fixed and its social and political importance thereby determined." Again, "the Iroquois, in order to recruit the great losses incurred in their many wars, put into systematic practice the adoption not only of individuals but also of entire clans and tribes. The Tutelo, the Saponi, the Nanticoke, and other tribes and portions of tribes were forced to incorporate with the several tribes of the Iroquois confederation by formal adoption."

§427. Family Life.

Domestic Segregation. In Fiji the family-life is characterized by constrained relations with relatives-in-law on the order of those above described. "What wonder that the domestic life of the Melanesians is full of distrust and suspicion and terror, in the face of the constraining customs which prevail!" Husbands are abroad a great deal. Hatred of a wife for a husband and in lesser degree of a husband for a wife is popularly regarded as a usual thing. There is a superficial friendliness in their intercourse but, except for the mothers, few have any deep feelings. Fathers teach their sons to beat their mothers lest, being controlled by women, they may become cowardly.[1] Husband and wife never trust one another; the slightest rumor of infidelity is believed on either side. "The man may punish the woman, but she can only retaliate for his offense by means of her tongue, which she often allows to do all it will."[2]

Affection between Bantu husband and wife, parent and child, as we know it, "is practically non-existent in many of the savage peoples, whilst the moth-

9 Williamson, *Cent. Polyn.*, II, 1-2.
10 De Josselin de Jong, in AA, XVIII, 122.
11 Chamberlain, in HAI, I, 741.

12 In HAI, I, 15, 16.
1 Ratzel, *Vkde.*, II, 277.
2 Danks, in JAI, XVIII, 293.

er's love for the child is much the same as that of an animal."3 "The family-sense is not very well developed; at least children were constantly being offered to my people for sale."4 It is common for several men to eat together, their wives serving them and eating later.5 Says Weeks6 of the natives of the Upper Congo: "All the food was cooked together and then divided by the woman-cook into two lots, one for the males of the family and the other for the females. They never ate together. If stress of weather forced them to seek the shelter of a house, the males took one end of the building and the females the other end. The boys and girls would eat with either party, but as soon as they knew the meaning of sex they no longer did so." In British Central Africa, "men and women never take their food together, a husband never sits and talks with his wife, the sexes congregate separately. A man taking his food in his hut is looked upon as greedy. Outside he invites anyone near to share with him."7 In private the Baganda eats with his wife and children; if there are guests, the wife and children keep out.8 In the southern Sahara husband and wife live in separate places, the former visiting the latter from time to time.9

Spencer10 cites the classic case of the Tatar woman who complained that her husband did not love her because he never beat her. She valued any atten-tion whatever from him over stark indifference. Among several tribes in Rus-sian territory, women never show affection to husbands or sons; children are generally taken away from their parents and given to strangers to be brought up; hence love for parents is unknown. A woman may not enter into conversa-tion with her husband unless he addresses her or sit down beside him when others are present. She receives direction from him only through a third per-son. She hurries to hold or take care of his horse. A man will take a girl from her parents as his wife without marrying her until he finds out whether she is a good worker; he can send his wife away when he likes and get another. If a sick woman cries out for her husband they think it a violation of propriety and the women will say, "What a sinner; although she is dying she thinks about her husband. What a scandal!" After marriage the bride covers her face except eyes and nose. Besides her husband, sister, and little children, she must not talk with any one. She answers her parents-in-law by signs and her husband ought not to call her by name.11

In ancient India, according to Manu, it is the "nature of woman to seduce man in this world . . . not only a fool but even a learned man, and to make him a slave of desire and anger. . . . One should not sit in a lonely place with one's mother, sister, or daughter, for the senses are powerful and master even a learned man." A woman is angry at her husband for showing affection for her before others, as if she were base; he should be severe and overbearing. While the man eats, the wife serves him. The wife "must live in the woman's apartments, keep her face veiled when her brothers-in-law are present, and never be seen speaking even to her husband in the daytime."12

In Korea, among the upper classes, the bridegroom, after passing three or four days with his wife, leaves her for some time to show his indifference. To

3 Stigand, *Elephant*, 208.
4 Von Götzen, *Durch Afr.*, 191.
5 Stuhlmann, *Mit Emin*, 81.
6 In JAI, XXXIX, 120.
7 Stannus, in JAI, XL, 292.
8 Roscoe, in JAI, XXXII, 52.
9 De Goeje, in *De Gids*, XXXI, pt. II, 29.

10 *Study of Soc.*, 134.
11 *Russ. Ethnog.* (Russ.), II, 241, 284, 340, 379.
12 Bühler, *Manu*, II, 213, 215; Dubois, *Mœurs*, I, 478; Wilkins, *Mod. Hinduism*, 18, 355.

act otherwise would be "bad form." Wives generally submit quietly to the exac-
tions of their mothers-in-law, but "those who are insubordinate and provoke
scenes of anger and scandal are reduced to order by a severe beating, when
they are women of the people. In the noble class custom forbids a man to strike
his wife, and as his only remedy is divorce and remarriage is difficult, he
usually resigns himself to his fate."[13]

Says Vámbéry, with special reference to Turkish society:[14] "The picture of
family life in the Occident, which is so confidential and charming, is in the
Orient veiled in mystery and fearfully cold." The duties of the housewife
among the Mohammedans devolve upon the head of the house. With sleepy,
peevish mien he goes through the accounts of the household-expenses and
grudgingly provides for their payment out of funds which he keeps by him
even at night. He pays with a heavy sigh, knowing that a half or third of the
bills are spurious and that peculation is going on all the time. The children
are presented to their father and must stand up, no matter how young. This
respect, the author asserts, crushes love. The busiest time of the day is up to
eleven in the morning, for the Oriental soon tires of the slightest labor and
only in the early morning has he energy enough to do anything. Exertion is
hateful to him and he avoids it just as he eschews superfluous bodily movement.
Contrary to our view, he regards physical and mental rest as the chief necessity for perfect health. Despite this torpidity, the appetite of these people is
gigantic. They are slow in everything else—in walking, talking, and the like—
but very swift in eating. From about 11.30 A.M. they retire and the house appears to be empty. Then the mice come out to play. Apparently the family
feels free only when the master is asleep. Often servants never see the family,
though they hold conversation with the female members of it. There is in the
Oriental family an unnatural feeling of embarrassment due to the mores regarding women, even in the most intimate relations of the family. "There can
be no talk of family-festivals and associations—in a word, of the family at all
—under such circumstances." The man and his wife are separated for the
greater part of the day; there is no mutual sympathy, joy or sorrow, and no
companionship in married life. Husband and wife are two parties in the house,
between whom religion and civil law have erected a high wall. This sharp separation takes shape in some cases at the beginning of marriage, in others several
months or years later, and the house-master, unless willing to overlook peculation and to put up a good front in face of intrigues and insulting talk, gets
so disgusted with the harem that he avoids it during the day and spends his
time in his own quarters.

Generally in Polynesia men and women may not eat together, nor may
women eat what men have prepared. There is nothing that might be called
domestic happiness. Man and wife may not play at the same fireside with their
children. The two sexes are separated from birth on; mother is alienated from
son, for he is called holy and she is called base. The joint-houses are unfavorable to family-life as we know it. It is regarded as shameful that a woman
should be in confidential relations with her husband. A man will never appear
on the street with his lawful wife, although his woman-friends always follow
him. When there is a stranger in the house, the wife retires from the presence
of the husband.[15] In the Pelew Islands wives are selected for their bodily

---

13 Bishop, *Korea*, 118.   15 Ratzel, *Vkde.*, II, 166, 183, 188.
14 *Sittenbilder*, 11 ff.

strength and efficiency in the taro-patch. Man and wife are fully aware of the purpose of their union and acquiesce. "The least external manifestation of tenderness, any caress whatsoever, is barred and interdicted out of the domestic life, and jealousy on the man's side is less the work of wounded feeling than of external propriety." A man spends his youth without domicile, being by day a guest in the house of the chief or of his parents and by night sleeping in the men's house. As a young husband he may not stay at night in his wife's parental home and when he gets a house of his own, he must devote most of his time to club-life.[16]

In the Mortlock Islands brothers and sisters live together and with their parents only in early childhood. At the age of seven or eight "the boys keep together or play only with tribally unrelated girls. Later they follow the father and sleep with him in the men's house, while the sisters stay with the mother in the special women's houses, so that the family is not united under one roof."[17] A Nauru woman never eats anything her eldest son has touched or carried. In chieftains' families this applies to the eldest daughter. They believe that it would weaken the child, harm the mother, and be shameful in the eyes of others.[18] In Yap "the woman occupies a house by herself and also eats alone. So long as the children are small they all live with the mother; of the older children the boys go to the father's house and the girls remain with the mother or have their own huts."[19]

In some North American Indian tribes "men and women used different forms of speech, and the distinction was carefully observed."[20] This situation was characteristic of certain South American groups. Schomburgk[21] wrote that a noteworthy peculiarity in the speech of the Arawaks was the fact that there were certain words which men only might use and others which were restricted to women. "The Island Caribs have two distinct vocabularies, one used by men and by women when speaking to each other, and by men when repeating in *oratio obliqua* some saying of the women. Their councils of war are held in a secret dialect of jargon, in which the women are never initiated."[22] Other Caribs show a diverse language of man and wife, which is accounted for by the tradition that they let only the women of conquered peoples live. Among a number of tribes in Brazil there are separate languages for men and women. In some instances only a few words are entirely different, the variation lying mainly in the inflexion.[23]

In Guiana, "among the Galibi, those that are married dine everyone apart, and those that are unmarried eat all together; and all the women, maids, and little children go to another side of the hut to eat. This would seem to be the rule almost everywhere, the two sexes having their backs turned to one another. No Indian wife eats with her husband."[24] In Central Brazil the man's house plays its part in the separation of husband and wife.[25] In one Colombia tribe, after marriage the pair "go home by different roads, the woman to her house and the man to his, and from that day never by any circumstance will they go into each other's houses, nor do they so much as speak together while at

16 Kubary, *Pelauer*, 59-60, 62; Semper, *Palau-Ins.*, 75.
17 Finsch, *Eth. Erfahr.*, III, 307.
18 Brandeis, in *Globus*, XCI, 59.
19 Senfft, in *Globus*, XCI, 141.
20 Fletcher, in HAI, I, 443.
21 *Brit.-Guiana*, I, 227.

22 Crawley, in JAI, XXIV, 234.
23 Bernhöft, *Verwdsftsnamen*, 61; Ehrenreich, in *Berl. Mus. Vkde.*, 1891, 9; Von Martius, *Beiträge*, I, 106-107, 704; Chamberlain, in AA, XIV, 578-580.
24 Roth, in BAE, XXXVIII, 236.
25 Von den Steinen, *Zent. Bras.*, 501.

home. When the wife prepares food for her husband, she places it on a stone between the two houses, where she leaves it; then the man comes and takes the food to his house. Having eaten, he returns to the stone the empty gourds in which the food was served, and goes away; then the wife comes and takes them again. They have only one place that is common ground to them, and that is their garden, where in some secluded spot they cultivate the soil together. At all other times they are strictly separated, and the reason for it all is, as stated by Father de la Rosa, their belief that a child conceived without the light of the sun will be born blind and have no light in its eyes."[26]

§428. Treatment of the Old.

AMONG the northern tribes of Central Australia "there is no such thing as allowing an old and infirm person to starve. It is the duty of every one to supply certain other older people with food, and this they do cheerfully and ungrudgingly. In this way and in accordance with the needs and conditions of the community, these savages have long ago settled the question of old-age pension, or rather they have rendered any such thing quite unnecessary."[1]

The aged African Bushman, on the other hand, is abandoned with a little food and water; similarly among the Hottentots the old man or woman is shut up in a little hut and left to die of hunger or be killed by wild beasts. Certain other South African tribes used to hurl the old or dependent relatives over lofty cliffs. Occasionally they were exposed to the vultures.[2] In Borku there is no respect for age; if a father is old and feeble and has a young wife, the son sometimes takes possession of her without ceremony. The northeast African tribes show no great respect for age; it often happens among the Somal that "they simply expel the old father and give him over to want and death by hunger."[3] "I fear it cannot be denied," says Cummins[4] of the Dinkas, "that the elderly people are usually thin and starved-looking to an extent not explicable by the flight of time; whereas the younger men and women, especially the more attractive of the latter, are always sleek and well-fed."

The Chukchi kill children who are weak or defective and old people who cannot work or endure the hardships. A case is given of an old man who at his own request was put to death by relatives who thought that they were performing a sacred obligation. "The custom of putting to death the aged and sick is due to the hard conditions of life in the arctic wilderness. It is also a part of the Chukchi system of ethics. The old and sick consider death a right, not a duty, and often claim this right notwithstanding the opposition of their kinsmen." The victim often takes a lively interest in the preparations for his own demise. "An old man, whose strangulation I witnessed, was as interested as anybody in the preparations for his own death. I was speaking to him on the shore about it a few days before the ceremony. He did not seem dejected, but merely remarked in English, 'Me die Monday.' He even set out the whisky barrels and prepared the walrus thong for his execution. He was rendered

26 Nicholas, in AA, III, 638-639.
1 Spencer and Gillen, *North. Tr. Cent. Aust.*, 32.
2 Hahn, in *Globus*, XVIII, 122; Kolben, *Beschreibung*, 195-196; Fritsch, *Eingeb. S.-Afr.*, 334, 335; Holub, *S. Afr.*, I, 409-410; Tyler, in *Illust. Afr.*, Dec., 1895.
3 Nachtigal, *Sahara*, II, 176; Paulitschke, *Nordost-Afr.*, I, 205.
4 In JAI, XXXIV, 155.

insensible with drink before being dispatched."5 Again, " 'volunteer death' is a regular custom among the Chukchee. It is accounted for as being the result of disease and helplessness, of deep sorrow at the death of some near relative, or of a quarrel at home, or sometimes simply of the feeling of *tædium vitæ*. Bogoras knew of various instances of 'voluntary death' due to each of these causes. . . . Mature or old people are killed by some near relative at their own request. Bogoras thinks that the custom of killing old people sometimes ascribed to the Chukchee does not exist as such, but that, as a matter of fact, old people are often killed because they prefer death to the hard conditions of life as invalids. . . . Jochelson says that the custom of killing old people existed until recently among the Koryak."6 In an old book it is related: "Whoever in Siberia is seventy years old is taken by his nearest relatives into the woods where they build him a hut, give him food for three days, and then take leave. When the old man has eaten the food, he dies of hunger." Later travellers support this; for instance, it is said that the Koryak, due to their nomadic life, kill the old and sick; killing them is "a measure dictated by wisdom and also sympathy."7

The Yakuts do not respect age; the younger plunder the older and scold and abuse the weak and decrepit. "A local tradition is met with that in ancient times, if an old person became extremely decrepit, or if anyone became ill beyond hope of recovery, such person generally begged his beloved children or relatives to bury him. Then the neighbours were called together, the best and fattest cattle were slaughtered, and they feasted for three days, during which time the one who was to die, dressed in his best travelling clothes, sat in the foremost place and received from all who were present marks of respect and the best pieces of food. On the third day the relative chosen by him led him into the wood and unexpectedly thrust him into a hole previously prepared. They then left him together with vessels, tools, and food, to die of hunger. Sometimes an old man and wife were buried together; sometimes an ox or horse was buried alive with them; and sometimes a saddled horse was tied up to a post set in the ground near by, and left there to die of hunger."8 The Tatars and some others killed their fathers when old; they burned the bodies and sprinkled the ashes on their food every day.9 Herodotus10 reports that the Massagetæ kill and eat the old and that this is esteemed a happy end. Those who die of disease and are buried are regarded as less fortunate.

In one district of India the eldest son, at marriage, turns his parents out of their home and claims two-thirds of all they possess. Young chiefs oust their fathers and small boys mock and spit at the old without shame or fear of reproof.11 It is different among the Palaungs, where "an old man is greatly revered, because the number of his years shows that he has been a really good man in many previous existences. The fact of his age is the proof of previous merit, and for this reason his blessing is asked by the young. . . . Old people have happy lives among the Palaungs. . . . Elders are heartily welcomed at

5 *Russ. Ethnog.* (Russ.), II, 578; Bogoras, in AA. III, 106; "De Windl's Residence among the Chukches," in N. Y. *Times*, May 10, 1897.
6 Czaplicka, *Aborig. Siberia*, 317, 318.
7 Stern, *Russland*, 476.

8 Sieroshevski-Sumner, in JAI, XXXI, 76, 100; Czaplicka, *Aborig. Siberia*, 161.
9 Rubruck, *Eastern Parts*, 81 (Rockhill's note).
10 *Hist.*, I, 216.
11 Watt, in JAI, XVI, 366; Carey and Tuck, *Chin Hills*, I, 203.

all feasts, and are offered the best seats and the best food."[12] The Easter Islanders have no respect for old age in either sex.[13]

When people get so old, in Greenland, that they cannot take care of themselves, especially women, they are often treated with little consideration. The Central Eskimo believe that all who die by violence go to the happy land; hence it is lawful to kill the old. Again, "old and infirm people are treated with severity, and when dependent upon others for their food they are summarily disposed of by strangulation or left to perish when the camp is moved. . . . Aged people who have no relatives on whom they may depend for subsistence are often quietly put to death. When an old woman, for instance, becomes a burden to the community it is usual for her to be neglected until so weak from want of food that she will be unable to keep up with the people who suddenly are seized with a desire to remove to a distant locality. If she regains their camp, well for her; otherwise, she struggles along until exhausted and soon perishes. Sometimes three or four of the males retrace their steps to recover a lost whip or forgotten ammunition bag. They rarely go farther than where they find the helpless person, and if their track be followed it will be found that the corpse has stones piled around it and is bound with thongs." An old woman at Fort Chimo had but one eye, and this was continually sore and very annoying to the people with whom she lived. "They proposed to strangle her to relieve her from her misery. The next morning the eye was much better and the proposed cure was postponed."[14] In the case of a tribe of Labrador Eskimo "the aged and the diseased are frequently deserted, sometimes quietly strangled. An unlucky woman is driven out into the wilderness. A bad man is not admitted into the houses, and if he commits murder the others stone him to death."[15] Among the Sekani, an Athapascan group, "when a member of the band was believed to be stricken with death they left with him what provisions they could spare and abandoned him to his fate when the camp broke up."[16]

Powers[17] cites the case of an old squaw who, having been abandoned by her children because she was blind, was wandering alone in the mountains. Nomadic habits among savages of low grade are little better than death to the aged and infirm, for they cannot readily follow and the few poor conveniences and comforts which they collect around themselves when stationary have to be abandoned. It would be hard for a tribe to find a better way of ridding themselves of those whom they account as burdensome. Farther north, "the aged people were formerly neglected, and their death hastened by starvation and abuse; but fear of punishment now restrains the Indians from this cruelty."[18] "Favored by the mildness of the climate, the lot of the aged among the Pimas was less unenviable than among most of the other Indian tribes. As they were a sedentary people, the custom of abandoning the aged on the march could not prevail. As a matter of fact, the old and helpless were not killed by the active members of the community, though they were sometimes neglected until they starved to death and sometimes they set fire to their houses to commit sui-

12 Milne, *Eastern Clan*, 314-315.
13 Geiseler, *Oster-Ins.*, 31.
14 Nansen, *Esk. Life*, 178; Boas, in BAE, VI, 615; Turner, in BAE, XI, 178, 186.
15 In HAI, II, 647.
16 In HAI, II, 499.
17 In *Contrib. N. Amer. Ethnol.*, III, 112, 319.
18 Willoughby, in *Smithson. Rep.*, 1886, pt. I, 274.

cide."[19] Old people were treated by some of the tribes "with contumely, both men and women."[20]

Many South American tribes "are wont to put their own relatives to death as soon as they have become helpless and burdensome to them, in the belief that without hunting, war, and drinking-bout nothing further of enjoyment can come to the old man. Among the old Tupis sometimes a sick person concerning whose recovery the shaman was doubtful, was on his advice killed and—eaten."[21] In some places, among the Guiana Indians, there is great respect for aged parents; other peoples regard them as nuisances and kill them, often with their own consent, for they realize their uselessness.[22] Among the Tobas, "older persons were not usually killed by blows of a club but were buried alive. Often the old people, irritated over their feebleness, themselves asked for the favor." The deed was done exclusively by the women, for they feared it might make the men cowardly.[23] The Fuegians were expected to support aged parents and generally did so, but sometimes killed them to get rid of the trouble of keeping them.[24]

"The custom of putting a violent end to the aged and infirm survived from the primeval period into heroic times not infrequently amongst the Indo-European peoples. . . . It can be authenticated in Vedic antiquity . . . amongst the Iranians . . . amongst the ancient Germans, Slavs, and Prussians." Deposition of the father with the marriage of the eldest son took place and "is very simply explained on the basis that dominion belongs to him who has the power to uphold it."[25] The Greeks pushed the old aside without scruple or sentimentality;[26] but the Roman father held the *potestas* to the end. However the expressions *Sexagenarii de ponte* and *depontani senes* are indicative of at least the sacrifice of the old; the latter expression is explained as "those who were cast, as sexagenarians, into the Tiber."[27]

§430. The Function of Idealization.

The following survey of the various elements entering into Christian marriage —elements which, if not representing idealization in the stricter sense, yet portray the play of the imaginative factor—is a portion of an unfinished manuscript found among the papers of the senior author of this book.

At the time of Christ the whole civilized Western world had reached the stage in which actual monogamy was, for economic reasons, the practice of all but the rich and great. This, however, was not pair-marriage, for polygyny was fully tolerated in the mores everywhere. By pair-marriage we refer to marriage which is exclusive on both sides and in which both religious disapproval and legal penalty fall on a man who has a second woman at his disposal. It is evident that there is a wide gulf between *de facto* monogamy and actual pair-marriage. The latter has been called sacramental monogamy. In modern poetry and romance pair-marriage is presented as love-marriage. The

19 Russell, in BAE, XXVI, 192.
20 Bancroft, *Nat. Races*, I, 390.
21 Von Martius, *Beiträge*, I, 126-127.
22 Roth, in BAE, XXVIII, §§911, 917.
23 Koch, in *Globus*, LXXXI, 108.
24 Bridges, in *Voice for S. Amer.*, XIII, 201.

25 Schrader, *Aryan*, 379; Ihering, *Evol. of Aryan*, 33, 34; Spiegel, *Eran. Alterthumskde.*, III, 682.
26 Mahaffy, *Soc. Life in Greece*, 229.
27 Grupp, *Kgchte.*, I, 19, note 2.

engrossment of the parties in each other results in exclusiveness as respects all others. The fatality of love-marriage has been that inasmuch as it demands a highly exalted state of emotion it has not lasted. Use and wont have been against it. To get the same tension there must be novelty and variety. The ancient people all knew the passion of love and needed Venus and Cupid to account for it. None of them believed in its durability and therefore none of them put any confidence in it as a basis of matrimony.

When the early Christians came to this subject they were controlled by the following facts. In the first place, they were all of the class in whose usage monogamy was and had long been the practice, although the epistles of St. Paul to the Greek churches show that laxness and uncertainty and vicious practices prevailed amongst them. When the Christians turned to the Old Testament in order to get support for their ideas about marriage they found no light at all. It is astonishing that so little information is yielded about the Jewish marriage-institution or the wedding-ceremony before the captivity. The system was purchase and there are cases of capture; a father probably consented to give his daughter and that was the end of the matter. It is also noteworthy that there is no picture of conjugal felicity in the Old Testament and no case of a woman who is a heroine of womanliness.

In the Anglican wedding-ceremony Isaac and Rebecca are set forth as models. The earlier mediæval rituals mentioned also Tobias. Isaac and Rebecca must have been chosen because they alone amongst the patriarchs, so far as the record shows, lived in pair-marriage. The reformers dropped Tobias because the book in which he appears was adjudged not to be in the canon of scripture; in any case, its significance was entirely misunderstood. The early Christian ecclesiastics were especially interested in the fact that Tobias refrained from his wife for three nights after what would seem, by analogy, to be his wedding. This detail is in the Vulgate which Luther followed in his translation but not in the Septuagint upon which the more recent English revisers based their translation. The custom of such abstention is well known to us from barbarian life, the motive of it being to defeat the evil spirits. Primitive marriage-customs are largely molded by the desire to secure good luck and avoid bad luck in matrimony; evil spirits are supposed to surround the marrying pair and to secure their opportunity, when the marriage commences, for interposing their evil machinations. The context of the Tobias story is full of Chaldæan daimonism and his abstention is to be explained by the view of daimonism which we find elsewhere. The daimons were defeated if the critical moment was undefined and therefore unknown to them. A woman-figure which has been selected from the Old Testament for veneration by Christians is Ruth; we now recognize in the Ruth story, however, only a question of usage in regard to the duty of a next-of-kin to which also ethnography gives us the explanation. And though the Jews made a heroine of Esther, she is a model of patriotism, not of womanliness.

The most useful fact in the Old Testament for the development of the Christian idea of matrimony was the conception of Adam and Eve in Paradise as a pair. The theologians made a distinction which is still presented in the Anglican service between matrimony as God instituted it in Paradise and the revised version of it after the Fall. This left the paradisaical form of it as a subject for speculation and idealization. The utmost point ever reached by this tendency is in Milton's *Paradise Lost*. It is strange that it took men so long to see that there are two myths combined in the Bible account of the creation of woman. In the first chapter of Genesis this incident of creation is covered by the incidental clause: "male and female created he them." The only additional facts are that they are told to "be fruitful and multiply" and that they are given dominion over the rest of creation. The ecclesiastics construed marriage into the command to be fruitful and multiply. The alternate myth in the second chapter does not simply narrate the fiats by which things were created; it enters into a description of the method. Man was made from dust and woman from a rib of man, to be a helpmeet for him.

God "brought her unto the man." Though this clause is as simple and matter-of-fact as language could offer it, laborious attempts have been made to construe it into a wedding-ceremony with delivery of the woman. The saying attributed to Adam: "Therefore shall a man leave his father and his mother, and shall cleave unto his wife: and they shall be one flesh" is very remarkable in its form. It is quoted three times in the Bible. The Israelitish society was on the father-family basis through all the time during which we know it, although survivals of the mother-family are to be found in the Bible. Why, then, should this text have put the case in that way? In general, the ecclesiastics passed over this point and were contented to find in the text a strong statement of the union of a pair in matrimony. Adam, in the context, bases the fleshly unity of man and woman in marriage on the fact that woman was made from a rib of man and so is "bone of my bone and flesh of my flesh." The ecclesiastics referred this to the sex-relation and indulged in analyses and deductions which were not very edifying. The fact that God blessed the pair is stated in the first myth and not in the second. The blessing of the married couple came to have such importance in the history of Christian marriage that much stress was laid upon the benediction mentioned in this text; but there is nothing at all in the textual connection which would be required for the deductions desired. There is plainly no wedding at all; the two are supposed to be alone, made for each other, placed in a position which affords no precedent for human society and is therefore not to be cited at all in discussions of human marriage. This story stands on the first page of a book through which polygyny appears as the common usage and without the slightest disapproval. This is so because in the mores of the Israelites during the period covered by the canon of the Old Testament there was no objection to polygyny. It was in the interval between the Old and New Testaments that monogamy seems to have entered into the mores of the Jews. Philosophically it may have been due to contact with the Persians; practically it was due to poverty.

In the New Testament there is little heed given to the marriage-institution. Much has been made of the fact that Christ attended a marriage at Cana. This argument proves only the poverty of that side of the case. He gave no law or institution about marriage. There was at the time a dispute amongst the Jews, some desiring to introduce more stringent usages of divorce, others desiring to continue the existing ones, which were those characteristic of the father-family. When this question was put to Christ, he took the stringent side and laid down a law which the Christian Church has never obeyed; some have gone beyond it; others have fallen short of it. In this connection he added to the citation from Genesis a more explicit enunciation of the union-of-the-flesh doctrine: "So that they are no more twain but one flesh. What therefore God hath joined together let not man put asunder." The best interpretation of this text is that inasmuch as God has made two sexes with a need of their union man ought not to try to prevent their union. He then added some utterances about eunuchs which are unintelligible as they have come down to us, although historically they have been very important in connection with what we have to notice in a moment about celibacy and virginity.

Before coming to that, let it be noticed that there is in the New Testament no ideal of marriage, no wedding-ceremony, no model woman. The Virgin Mary alone has been put forward as such by the Church but she, for obvious reasons, cannot be so regarded; nor can Mary Magdalen. Martha, who was a good housekeeper, is treated rather with disdain. It is also to be noticed that there is, in the New Testament, no injunction of monogamy or pair-marriage. It is assumed as in the mores but there is nothing which exhibits concubinage as outside of toleration. There is no explicit statement about it.

The ideal of the New Testament is celibacy, which is made one with chastity. In the seventh chapter of First Corinthians Paul treats the subject at length, and his view of marriage is that it is only a last resort. To desire marriage is to yield to a lust of the flesh and to incur trouble; if one can master one's self it is better to remain virgin; in case of marriage, each of the pair must fulfil the sexual duties of the relationship; it is not wrong to marry; it is not a shame to marry; it is, however, falling below the Christian ideal. This is the plain teaching of the text, although it is noteworthy that the Apostle marks off grades in his own conviction as to whether he is right on different points of it. When the Christian Church started off upon the line of exalting celibacy above marriage it was faithful to the Apostolic teaching.

The fifth chapter of the Epistle to the Ephesians also requires attention. The Christian Pharisees have found in this chapter materials for heavy burdens which they have bound and laid on men's shoulders. The Apostle exhorts men to love their wives and women to be submissive to their husbands and, in so doing, uses Christ's headship and leadership of the Church as a parallel for the relation of husband and wife. The parallel is not one which is calculated to have influence on the mind by its simplicity or aptness, though it is intelligible. If one has accepted the idea of Christ as living and reigning in heaven and watching over the Church, the relationship of leadership and headship is not mysterious. It may be that it is to this continued life and relation of Christ to the Church that the Apostle refers when he says: "This mystery is great, but I speak in regard of Christ and of the Church." Between the two things, then, the relation of matrimony and that between Christ and the Church, which is the known thing and which the unknown? Which explains the other? Each is a mystery. Do we so fully understand the mystery of matrimony that it illuminates the relation of Christ to the Church? It is impossible to answer yes. Though in ecclesiastical language, marriage has been used to set forth that relation, there is no force or sense in the usage. The parallel fails at every point. Does the relation of Christ to the Church throw any light on marriage? Obviously it does not, beyond the relation of leadership and headship. The argument of the theologians has run about as often from marriage to Christ's leadership of the Church as from the latter to the former. The most important point, however, is that a chance was offered for subtleties and quibbles, for the elucidation of parallels and contrasts, antitheses, and types, out of which arbitrary restrictions on human happiness were spun by schoolmen and monks and upon which priestcraft flourished luxuriantly.

Another circumstance contributed to the mischief. In the Vulgate version of the Bible the word here rendered as "mystery" is translated "sacramentum." But for this accident of language it is very doubtful whether marriage ever would have been put in the list of sacraments. A sacrament is a means of edification in religious life; the other six sacraments are all religious observances which enter into religious life and produce religious results in experience. Marriage, on the contrary, is no more a sacrament than trade or agriculture. It is a practical interest. Religion may be and perhaps ought to be interwoven with all interests; it has been interwoven with trade and agriculture; in this sense and no other is it interwoven with marriage. Consequently we find theologians of high standing denying that marriage is a sacrament.

It has, moreover, been a great puzzle to other theologians to say in which aspect or element of marriage the sacrament lies. I have collected the various statements which I have met with. It would take half an hour merely to enumerate and explain them. The practical importance of this point is that if, in any sense, marriage was a sacrament, ecclesiastics got control of it and through it controlled the family, the descent of property, questions of legitimacy and divorce, and family-alliances—matters which are inseparably connected with the control of marriage.

In the fourth and fifth centuries the interest of the Church turned with passion to the ideas of virginity, chastity, celibacy, and marriage. As we have seen, the Church started out with Apostolic teaching in which there were two standards of right and Christian virtue. The desire was to define and determine the relation of these two standards to each other. Two standards of right are irrational and immoral; we know that because we see and use two or more standards all the time. The ecclesiastics wanted to urge the highest standard, that is, virginity, as the only proper one, but at the same time they had to make allowance for the lower one, marriage, because of the Apostle's teaching. Tertullian was a rigorist and a fanatic on this point; he had a wife to whom he wrote a letter about marriage which amounted to saying that she and he were in a licentious and corrupt relationship. Jerome in his tract against Jovinian swings around and around the paradox of the two standards: you may but you had better not; if you were sanctified you would not want to; if you want to, you may; you had better seek higher holiness; if you will not do that, it is no sin for you to marry; if you do marry, be chaste; but it is only a lesser evil—and so on, over and over again. The Church could not go far on this line before finding itself enclosed in a contradiction. It was enjoined on married people to pay the conjugal debt to each other and yet the conjugal act was to be regarded as a base and shameful thing in its nature. Especially, however, the attention of the Church turned to the Holy Family, asking how all these paradoxes were to be understood with respect to its history. If it is a mystery that a virgin bore a son, so let it stand; but Augustine and his followers attempted to analyze this mystery. A virgin, who was married, bore a son, who had no father. She remained a virgin and a wife yet was neither a virgin nor a wife. In the Middle Ages there was a tradition that Christ took the Virgin from Joseph and gave her to St. John. These grotesque speculations were of great importance in the development of the Christian doctrine of marriage.

Although the Christian Church started with confused and heterogeneous traditions and dogmas, it actually developed between the sixth and eleventh centuries a wholly rational doctrine of marriage. The consensus of the parties followed by concubitus constituted a marriage recognized by the Church. It had no function except to recognize and to bless; blessing, however, was no essential part of the ceremony of wedding or of the institution of marriage but was external to it. If we believe that blessing has any efficacy we must believe the same of cursing; then we have come to the doctrine that men can invoke the power of God for and against each other. If we do not accept this doctrine, then blessing and cursing are only expressions of good-will or ill-will and are of no practical importance. Still it was always a conservative and beneficial influence which was exerted by the Church when it guided the mores as to marriage and it made a great difference whether people felt that they were acting with the approval or disapproval of the best opinion of the society in which they lived.

Religious people liked to get the benediction of the priest on a marriage or to connect it with religion in some way. This was entirely informal before the twelfth century. Christian society conceived of marriage directly, simply, and correctly: a man and a woman agreed to enter the conjugal state together, this consensus being the first thing. It did not contemplate fornication but matrimony, joint life, united interests, children, conjugal relations, as long as both should live. What was wanted was just what had been wanted from the days of barbarism, namely, a clear decision, determined and expressed in public, simply in order that the pair's acts might not be open to misconstruction. Then they proceeded to execute their agreement and the marriage was complete. Hence what was needed by way of ceremony was that some third person should, in the presence of witnesses, ask them if they had the intention or if they did then and there take each other. This third person appears in all ancient and mediæval marriages; he is the father, a person of social weight— even a goddess acting through some representative. In strictness all that was witnessed was a promise.

Through these usages there runs the true legal notion that a promise is not a performance; that a betrothal is not a marriage. For centuries there was an oscillation of attention and interest between these two acts. Although the canon law of the twelfth century is distinctly upon the plane of doctrine about marriage which has just been stated, the ecclesiastics were pushing earnestly from that time to the sixteenth century for more definite priestly control over marriage. Should the Church aim to consecrate the betrothal or the consummation? In the nature of the case, when a pair came to an agreement, some interval of time elapsed before they entered upon matrimony. Local usage shows much variation. Among the common people it became customary in many places that when a pair walked together at a certain time or in a certain place, for instance on Sunday afternoon or in Lover's Lane, that was taken as an announcement that they were to be married. The priest urged them at this time to come before the church door and there get the blessing of the Church on their engagement. The engagement thus became irrevocable and so the usage arose which now exists very widely that a betrothal is irrevocable. The priest now became the functionary who asked the question and elicited the consensus and thereupon consummation followed at any time. To this the Church objected or at least it urged that a blessing should be invoked on the matrimony which had begun. In the German poems of the thirteenth century, the betrothal of great people is made for the pair, who stand in a ring of witnesses, by an important third person. Concubitus follows the same night and the pair go to mass for a blessing the next morning. Very gradually the betrothal fell into neglect; the irrevocable promise was brought to the point of time just before consummation and the wedding was made all important. This arose from sound considerations of expediency and from the interest of the Church. The priest found other opportunities for intervention which were set aside by refinement of the mores.

Through all the ancient forms of marriage down to recent times the idea has prevailed that a man must give a property-pledge or gage in marriage in order to make the union good. The idea was that if he was led by sentiment alone his affection might wane. As he might change his mind or try to get out of it, a property-pledge was necessary to hold him. A woman who had no such pledge was a concubine, not a wife; hence the wedding-gifts given by the man, the marriage-contract of the Jews, the similar document of the Romans, and the marriage-gifts of the German husband. Our wedding-ring is a survival of this. A "wed" is a pledge and a wedding is a pledging. The revived engagement-ring is a renewal of the same idea in a secondary stage, such as we often see in the history of ceremonial. If a man gave any gift to a woman when he promised to marry her she could prove his promise later, if he repudiated it, by showing the gift; the man could then be asked to explain how it came into her possession if what she said was untrue. If he gave her a coin, it was unidentifiable; hence the usage of breaking a coin in two and giving a piece of it.

A subject of constant complaint was the clandestine marriage. Such an union defeated the will of parents and the authority of the Church. It was also open to doubt and therefore exposed the honor of women, the legitimacy of children, and the security of property. At the Council of Trent it was proposed to forbid clandestine marriages and the means adopted were in the interest of Church authority. There was great opposition in the Council to any change of the Church-rules about marriage as they then stood in the Canon Law and as they have been described above; but so long as the Church was obliged to recognize any union which had been contracted with a consensus of matrimony and consummation, it could scold and preach and set penance but it could not prevent clandestine marriages. The royal and noble families united with the ecclesiastics in favor of a law making marriages null and void if not solemnized before the parish-priest with at least three witnesses. Ever since 1563 that has been the law of the Roman Catholic Church, wherever the decrees of the Council of Trent have been promulgated. By this law marriage became an affair of ritual. It was incorporated in the mass and there was a requirement that the parties should confess a few days before marriage. The next step was easy. At first the priest merely pronounced, as in the Anglican ritual, that the parties by virtue of their own consent and pledge had become man and wife. Then, with his accession to greater power, he confirmed their act in the nave of the Church. At length it became his priestly fiat which made them man and wife. It was not their act, then, which married them, but his; he was the fetish-man who alone was endowed with the power to make them one flesh and he did that by a fetishistic fiat.

The doctrine that marriage is entirely indissoluble, that it is not to be contracted within the fourth degree of relationship, the injunction to keep the so-called Tobias nights, and the prohibition of marriage at certain seasons of the Church year are other details in the multiplication by ecclesiastical authority of arbitrary regulations which meant worry and pain unless ecclesiastical remission was to be obtained. No men ever have lived or ever can live under absolutely indissoluble marriage. The Church has prohibited unions between third cousins or nearer relatives and also between persons in the same degree of affinity by marriage and has interposed also other bars. It is doubtless expedient that marriages should be prohibited between persons who are blood-kin to each other within certain degrees; beyond this, however, there is no sense or reason in any of the sweeping traditional restrictions. The Church proscriptions are not scriptural; they have been invented by men who, if they were honest, were celibates and ignorant of what they legislated about or who, if they had knowledge, must have got it by what they themselves averred to be an abominable sin.

The English Puritans were driven by hostility to the excessively ecclesiastical doctrine of Trent into the opposite extreme. When they examined the Bible, they could find no evidence that marriage is a divine ordinance, for there is no such evidence. They therefore regarded it as in part a private arrangement like friendship, in part a civil institution. The ministers did not preside at marriages. This function, even in a sect which mixed religion with every life activity, fell to magistrates. In New England, at the end of the seventeenth century, the ministers began to solemnize marriages as a result of rational consideration of the advantages to be won from a connection of this important personal and societal interest with the sanction of religion.

No sooner had the ecclesiastical movement for the control of marriage won complete success as a law (although it is not yet realized as a fact, even in strictly Catholic countries) than the ecclesiastics began to lighten the load, provided they could get submission and obedience. The attitude of the Jesuits in the seventeenth century does not seem to be understood as it ought to be. They offered an epicurean life-philosophy of ease, pleasure, and indulgence, without worry about the other world, provided only that the laymen would submit to the Church and obey her implicitly. The mediæval Church had become a grand organization for winning societal power and the Jesuit way of confirming and securing this was to give comfort and wide indulgence with immunity to all who would submit to the ecclesiastical authority. They had ritual means for securing all that a man could want in the way of good things in the next world and of divine favor in this.

In the Form of Solemnization of Matrimony, in the Anglican prayer book, it is first stated to the parties that matrimony is not "to be taken in hand . . . to satisfy men's carnal lusts and appetites, like brute beasts that have no understanding," and then three purposes of matrimony are stated: (1) "for the procreation of children"; (2) "for a remedy against sin and to avoid fornication that such persons as have not the gift of continency might marry"; (3) "for the mutual society, help, and comfort that the one ought to have of the other, both in prosperity and adversity." Although the coarseness of some of these phrases is not widely resented because of conventionalization, refined people are revolted by them and insist upon their deletion.

§437. Sense-Gratification: Taste.

Salt. This much-desired condiment has influenced the customs and practices of a number of tribes. In the circumcision-ceremonies of the Bechuana "the chief song is the Song of the Salt. Just as salt was the great taboo in the days of the novitiate so this song in its praise, extolling its excellencies, is the great song of the *Bogwera*. . . . It is a song common to all the *Bogwera* camps."[1] When the men of the East Central African tribes are on the road, they must not use salt; if they did, and their wives were not behaving well in their absence, the salt would act as a virulent poison. Few Africans would risk this. Another superstition in this region is to the effect that if a woman morally guilty were to put salt in her husband's food, and he should eat of it, he would die; hence many women have a habit of always asking a little girl to put in the salt.[2] The Ba-Yaka drink salt water, deriving the native salt from the ashes of the water-plant.[3] In Nyasaland preparations of salt are made from grass as follows. "Certain kinds of tall grass are gathered, dried, and burnt. The ashes are collected and put in an earthenware vessel, with a small hole in the bottom. They are well pressed down and the pot placed on the top of another empty one. Water is put in the first pot and filters through to the second, dissolving the salt. This salt water is either boiled down to a thick fluid or used as it is to cook food in. Salt is made from the ashes of *gumbwa* (papyrus), dried and burnt, also from a grass called *chesa*."[4] The Nigerian head-hunters get salt from the Hausa traders; when unable to do so, they use ash from guinea-corn or millet.[5] In common with the other Nilotic tribes of British East Africa, the Kavirondo "draw blood from the living cattle and drink it. The custom, however, has its justification, for in many parts of Kavirondo this is the only method by which the natives can obtain salt."[6]

In India, to pass salt from hand to hand is believed to portend some quarrel. It is generally handed over in a plate. If passed from hand to hand, the giver, after giving the salt, pinches the hand of the receiver to avert the quarrel and end it in a pinch. A somewhat similar superstition prevails in Europe, while the custom of throwing over the shoulder a little of the salt that has been spilled is known to all readers. In India salt is also considered to be very auspicious on a joyous occasion. The author[7] began many a birthday of his boyhood by eating a few grains of salt the first thing in the morning. To do this on one's birthday, before eating, portends good, indicating that during the whole of the ensuing year the person so doing will be sure to get his salt and bread, or livelihood. In British North Borneo a feud is not actually settled until peace has been made by swearing an oath; in the ceremony undertaken by the chiefs of the two tribes an important rôle is played by salt. Following the oath there is "one more test, after which the two parties feel themselves perfectly secure against any renewal of hostilities from each other, and that is when they have eaten each other's salt."[8] In Formosa "to eat salt from the same dish is a mark of friendship."[9] Some peoples do not know salt. In Buru, for example, "the use of salt is far from universal and the tribes located in the inner districts have become insensible to the use of it."[10] A Samoan legend refers to the use of salt water in the preparation of food.[11]

Certain Indians of northern California did not use salt in food because they believed such use would cause sore eyes.[12] One tribe refrained from eating salt

1 Brown, in JAI, LI, 424.
2 Macdonald, in JAI, XXII, 104, 110.
3 Torday and Joyce, in JAI, XXXVI, 42.
4 Stigand, in JAI, XXXVII, 120.
5 Tremearne, in JAI, XLII, 176.
6 Northcote, in JAI, XXXVII, 65.
7 Modi, in JASB, II, 168.

8 Roth, *Sarawak*, II, 205; §142, of the text and *Case-Book*.
9 Wirth, in AA, X, 363.
10 Wilken, in VG, I, 68.
11 Pratt, in AAAS, 1887, 450.
12 Dixon, in AA, X, 212.

in the belief that it turned the hair white.[13] The Papagos regularly visited a salt lake which lay near the coast and just across the line of Sonora, from which they packed large quantities of salt to be sold at Tubac and Tucson. Strict ceremonies had to be observed, which would indicate that salt was regarded as a fetish. As they approached the shore of the lagoon in which the Great Spirit resided they ran at topmost speed and circled four times around the salt-deposits before those who understood the proper ritual began to collect the mineral. Even on the homeward journey there was magic power in the salt, and if a horse died the whole load was thrown away. As the salt-gatherers approached the home-village they were given a noisy welcome but were compelled to remain outside for four days, and for a long time thereafter they must abstain from certain acts that need not be detailed here. For four days those who remained at home sang for those who journeyed, and then all might eat the salt and were free to bring it to the Pimas. The latter sometimes made journeys to the lake for salt, being two days on the way to Quijotoa and two days on the trail beyond.[14] Among the Hopi salt was gathered with ceremony by making sacrifice to the Goddess of Salt and the God of War, whose shrines were located in the Grand Canyon of the Colorado. "The Pueblos have important salt deities, that of the Hopi being Hurúng Wuhti, 'The Woman of the Hard Substances.' . . . Pottery vessels of special form were used to contain salt, and mortuary vessels which contained food for the dead are frequently saturated with this substance, causing exfoliation of the surface of the ware." The Zuñi "Salt Mother" was Mawe, genius of the sacred salt lake. "At certain seasons war parties were sent to the lake for salt, and while there ceremonies were performed and offerings made."[15] "Naoudiche means 'salt,' and the village bearing this name was so called because of the salt supply near by."[16] The above salt-expeditions recall the custom of peaceful access and other transitional forms between war and trade.[17]

The use of salt is said to be unknown to the Cayuas.[18] Schomburgk[19] pays a tribute to the honesty of the Guiana Indians, especially noticeable because salt was involved. He writes: "The unconditional trust which we reposed in the honor of our friends had not been betrayed; we found our things untouched, although the hut in which our packs were had been again occupied by the family to which it belonged. Every child of the settlement knew that the boxes and chests held articles of barter, objects as bearers of which they had followed us, for which they undertook every burdensome effort and gladly gave to us their weapons and ornaments, on which they had spent months of work. By an oversight our receptacle for salt—the highest article of luxury known to the Indian, which he eats only a grain at a time—had been left open; but this too had been held so sacred that a film of dust lay upon it." The heir to the throne of Bogotá in Colombia had to undergo a severe training from the age of sixteen; one requirement was that he must not eat salt.[20]

The Romans regarded salt as a necessary and desired element of nutrition. It was a sacred thing, one of the first to be sacrificed to the gods. The salt-cellar consecrated the profane table and had a character of domestic religi-

13 West, in PSM, LII, 244.
14 Russell, in BAE, XXVI, 94; §248, of the text and Case-Book.
15 Hough, "Salt," in HAI, II, 419, 420.
16 Bolton, in HAI, II, 1.

17 §77, of the text and Case-Book.
18 Von Koenigswald, in Globus, XCIII, 379.
19 Brit.-Guiana, II, 291.
20 Waitz, Anthrop., IV, 359.

osity.[21] "The mountain people of North Carolina and West Virginia are said to put salt in their shoes in order to keep off the witches."[22]

§438. Intoxicants and Narcotics.

Intoxicants. Torday[1] mentions as a remarkable phenomenon the fact that "though the Batetela come from a country where the native drink is 'pombe' beer, and live now among people who freely indulge in palm wine, produced both from the elaïs and the raphia, yet they use no other beverage but water, and are ignorant of intoxicants." The Baganda have a plantain-drink which is slightly alcoholic; the natives manage to become intoxicated after a day of drinking.[2] All the quarrels among the Nigerian head-hunters are over women and drink.[3]

A black drink, made by boiling leaves of the *Ilex cassine* in water, "was employed by the tribes of the Gulf states and adjacent region as 'medicine' for ceremonial purification. It was a powerful agent for the production of the nervous state and disordered imagination necessary to 'spiritual' power. Hall says that among the Creeks the liquid was prepared and drunk before councils in order, as they believed, to invigorate the mind and body and prepare for thought and debate."[4] This case and some of the following recall the practices mentioned earlier in connection with ecstasy and inspiration.[5]

Roth[6] writes of the natives of Guiana: "It is true that Indians drink but little or nothing at their ordinary meals until they have finished eating, and then commonly drink one draft; but when they assemble together for a drinking party they keep up the revelry until they have drunk up all their liquor; and this may, on occasion, last for three or four days. As soon as an individual has drunk all he can he will vomit it up and drink more. This vomiting is to some extent part of the festivities, because he never once leaves his seat. . . . As to intoxication at a drinking feast, certain women, as well as certain men, whose business it is to keep sober especially for the purpose, hide away all weapons on the first signs of inebriety. The women will carry some of the disturbers of the peace to their hammocks and tie them up firm—a position from which no amount of exertion or raging can free them, and where, with continued swinging, they soon fall into a deep sleep. The same plan is followed on the Pomeroon at the present day, where it is usually the house master or mistress, perhaps both, who purposely keep sober to put an immediate stop to any rows and disputes arising. . . . Pinckard, speaking of the Arawak Indians on the Berbice, says: 'They are very fond of drinking rum and eagerly swallow it to intoxication. But they observe a kind of method in their drunkenness, for when they come to the towns in bodies of considerable number it is remarked that half the party will freely devote to Bacchus, while the other half carefully refrain, in order to watch the helpless; and these, when restored by sleep, are observed to take their turn of watching, and to guard their late protectors through similar visits to the deities of turbulence and repose. They have no pleasure in long sipping, but swallow large drafts of rum or drink quickly glassful after glassful till they are unable to move.' . . . A more drastic

21 De Marchi, "Culto Privato," rev. in *Année Soc.*, I, 121.
22 West, in PSM, LII, 244.
1 In JAI, LI, 379.
2 Roscoe, in JAI, XXXII, 53.

3 Tremearne, in JAI, XLII, 175.
4 Quoted by Hough, in HAI, I, 150.
5 §258, of the text and *Case-Book*.
6 In BAE, XXXVIII, 237, 238, 239.

remedy would seem to have been in vogue in Surinam, where plaited mats and girdles, with stinging ants attached, would be placed upon the backs of the helplessly intoxicated guests."

After drinking either *maikoa* or another narcotic drink, prepared from the stem of the vine *Banisteria caapi* and called *natéma*, "the Jibaro warrior generally receives the revelations of the spirits while sleeping alone in the virgin forest in a small ranch made of palm leaves, usually situated many miles away from the habitations of the Indians." A drum is beaten when the Jibaros drink the narcotics, the object being "to summon the spirits that inhabit these sacred drinks." Manioc-beer is prepared by the natives in a ceremonial way. "After the fruit has been boiled it has to be masticated, a work which it takes some two hours to perform. The masticating of the manioc for the feasts is a real ceremony and is called *nauma*. Generally only the women take part in it, since the preparation of the beer is a work particularly incumbent on the women. Of the fruit, however, only a part, or at the most a half, is masticated. The rest of it is only mashed. The manioc masticated is thoroughly mixed with saliva and then spat out in a number of large clay pots."[7] Caapi-drinking is practised also by the natives of southeastern Colombia, being done to cast out all fear and to impart "the valor of a warrior." The region where this prevails is called by a name which signifies in English "The Land of No Regrets."[8] Of the Araucanians it is said: "In regard to fermented liquors they are exceptionally well provided, a considerable number of wild fruits supplying them with materials." These people are an outstanding example of the disastrous effects following the introduction of "firewater" by Europeans. "The introduction of spirituous liquors did not, for a considerable time, make much headway. The relations between the whites and the Indians were so strained, and the stern, hard discipline of constant warfare so maintained, that the results of this traffic were not for a long time apparent. But after the declaration of the Republican Government, when there were longer lapses of peace, it became a lucrative business, and many large fortunes were made by distilling cheap 'firewater' in the frontier districts. To such a degree did this traffic attain that it is a common saying in the south that the distillers did in a few years what the Spaniards failed to accomplish in three centuries—reduced the tameless Araucano. This vice has taken such a hold of the Indian that in general it has completely changed his character and mode of life, and from being a fierce, untiring, vengeful patriot, he has become a drunken, cringing, soulless vagabond, who would sell land, stock, wife, daughters, or his soul itself to indulge in his craving desire for drink."[9] In this connection it may be mentioned that fourth in the list of the chief causes of decrease of the Indian population of North America, ranged in order of importance, are "whisky and attendant dissipation." They stand ahead of war in the category of destroyers.[10]

Tobacco and Drugs. Pitcheri is a Central Australian narcotic, the effect of which is to produce drowsiness. It has no long action and is not habit-forming. Expeditions are sent often afar to get it.[11] "If tobacco is really a recent importation into British New Guinea," writes Strong,[12] "the way it has spread over the country is very remarkable. I have always found it in profusion cultivated

7 Karsten, "Jibaro," in BAE, Bull. LXXIX, 3, 6, 58-59.
8 H. H. Rusby, quoted in N. Y. *Times,* Sept. 7, 1924.
9 Latcham, in JAI, XXXIX, 335, 343.
10 Mooney, in HAI, II, 286.
11 Horne and Aiston, *Cent. Aust.,* 64, 65.
12 In JAI, XLIX, 299-300.

far inland among the mountains both on the south and on the north-east coasts. And this, although I was practically the first European to visit some of the districts." Says Weeks[13] of the African Bangala: "Tobacco, called by the natives *makaiya*, was largely used by the men, but all the years I was there I never saw a woman smoking." Among the Nagas of India a crying baby is quieted by two or three puffs at its mother's pipe.[14]

MacMillan[15] says that in many ways the white man has been detrimental to the Eskimo. "He has brought coffee and tea and tobacco and the Eskimos have formed these habits, and when the white man goes they are unable to get the things they want. This has had a depressing effect." All sorts of ceremonial surrounded tobacco and pipes among the Cheyenne Indians, of which Grinnell[16] has written a great deal. "The word tobacco is of American origin, and has been adopted, with slight variation, into most foreign languages to designate the plant now smoked throughout the world, although there is evidence that the early Spanish settlers employed the word to designate the instrument in which the plant was smoked, rather than the plant itself. . . . To the Indian the tobacco plant had a sacred character; it was almost invariably used on solemn occasions, accompanied by suitable invocations to their deities. It was ceremonially used to aid in disease or distress, to ward off danger, to bring good fortune, to generally assist one in need, and to allay fear. The planting of medicine tobacco is one of the oldest ceremonies of the Crows, consisting, among other observances, of a solemn march, a foot race among the young men, the planting of seed, the building of a hedge of green branches around the seed bed, a visit to the sweat house, followed by a bath and a solemn smoke, all ending with a feast; when ripe, the plant was stored away, and seeds were put in a deerskin pouch and kept for another planting. . . . At times both priests and laymen smoked plants or compounds that were strongly narcotic, those using them becoming ecstatic and seeing visions."[17]

It is said that "the term tobacco does not appear to have been a commonly used original name for the plant. It has come to us from a peculiar instrument used for inhaling its smoke by the inhabitants of Hispaniola (Santo Domingo). The instrument described by Oviedo in his *Historia de las Indias Occidentales,* Salamanca, 1535, consisted of a small hollow wooden tube shaped like a Y, the two points of which, being inserted into the nose of the smoker, the other end was held into the smoke of burning tobacco, and thus the fumes were inhaled. This apparatus the natives called 'tabaco.' "[18] The Shingu Indians speak of tobacco as having come from the north, in the most ancient time, having been won for them by their culture-heroes. They use it in medicine.[19]

§442. Dancing and Acting.

"As with all primitive folk," says Basedow[1] of the natives of Bathurst Island, "song and dance constitute the ultimate stage of any social intercourse or festivity. The islanders are even more ready than their brothers on the mainland to resort to this means of entertainment. It thus happened that, wherever we came into contact with the blacks and presented them with divers small

13 In JAI, XXXIX, 122.
14 Furness, in JAI, XXXII, 456.
15 In N. Y. *Times*, Sept. 24, 1924.
16 *Cheyenne*, I, 74 ff.
17 McGuire, in HAI, II, 767, 768.

18 Roth, in BAE, XXXVIII, 240.
19 Von den Steinen, *Zent. Bras.*, 210.
1 In JAI, XLIII, 305 (quoted), 308-311.
Horne and Aiston, *Cent. Aust.*, 37 ff., describe a welcoming corrobboree.

articles, a corrobboree was immediately inaugurated; even though the encounter happened to occur in the middle of the day." He describes a corrobboree of a ship of war and of a fight, in which there was much imitation, really the beginnings of drama.

The mimetic dances of the natives of New Guinea show how the cassowary majestically stalks, how the herons and the doves feed their young and how a large bird chases a little one. "The women take part in the dances, and to make the exhibition more graphic put feathers on the backside of their bark aprons. The movements of the women are most graceful and the exhibition is truly fascinating. The men for their part show how a kangaroo is followed by dogs, how the dog goes after the bitch, and how the cock circles the hen. Quite masterfully they know how to portray animals in the dance and to represent in pantomime how they chase each other, quarrel, and fly, so that it is a pleasure to look on."[2] Among the Koita, "dancing takes place at almost all feasts, and most dances are accompanied by songs and the beating of drums or the thudding of dancing sticks and the shaking of rattles. . . . Dancing is not limited to ceremonial occasions, and the majority of the Koita dances are not obviously pantomimic and, according to their exponents, are not imitative or memorial in intention. . . . Both songs and dances are strictly copyright, and in the old days the unauthorized use of a song or dance might have led to war. The only legitimate manner for people to obtain the right to a dance or song not their own was to buy it."[3]

Dornan[4] says that the dances of the Tati Bushmen "do not strike one as at all graceful. They consist of little more than stamping and jumping in a circle, narrowing and enlarging, while the performers go through various stoopings and twistings of the body, intended to represent the various attitudes of the animal from which the dance is named. For instance, in the Eland Bull dance the leader represents the animal grazing, running, fighting, or licking itself. It requires some knowledge of the dance to be able to understand what animal is referred to, although some of the representations are not at all bad. I have heard it said that some of these dances are very indecent, but I cannot say that they struck me as being particularly so."

In New Zealand "the 'dancers' do not really dance, but stand in rows and twirl the light *poi*-balls (made of dry *raupo*-leaves) over their heads, from side to side, beating them at intervals on their heads, breasts, shoulders, and even their feet, all in perfect time to the rhythm of the song or the musical accompaniment. The *poi* is often an action song—some represent the work of planting food, some the action of paddling a canoe, some imitate the fluttering of the wild birds. The Taranaki Maoris are amongst the cleverest *poi*-dancers in New Zealand, but the *poi* had always been something of a religious ceremony in their district."[5]

Among the American Indians there are "personal, fraternal, clan or gentile, tribal, and inter-tribal dances; there are also social, erotic, comic, mimic, patriotic, military or warlike, invocative, offertory, and mourning dances, as well as those expressive of gratitude and thanksgiving. Morgan gives a list of 32 leading dances of the Seneca Iroquois, of which 6 are costume dances, 14 are for both men and women, 11 for men only, and 7 for women only. Three of the costume dances occur in those exclusively for men, and the other 3 in

2 Krieger, *Neu-Guinea*, 210.   4 In JAI, XLVII, 54.
3 Seligmann, *Melanesians*, 151.   5 Cowan, *Maoris*, 149.

those for both men and women. . . . Among some tribes, when the warriors were absent on a hunting or war expedition, the women performed appropriate dances to insure their safety and success."[6] When the scalp-dance was performed, the scalps were carried not by the men but by the women.[7] An Apache medicine-man once taught the tribe a new dance, claiming that it would bring dead warriors to life.[8] The Patwin had dances to celebrate a good harvest of acorns or a successful catch of fish.[9] Grinnell[10] mentions a constant spitting on the hands in the Cheyenne dances, and a regularly recurring use of the number four. There is also much story-telling among these people. Lowie[11] has stressed the element of propitiation in the Indian dances. "Among the Arapaho the seven ceremonies distinctive of the age-societies, as well as the Sun Dance, are performed only as the result of a pledge made to avert danger or death. The dances of the Kwakiutl, differing in other respects, resemble one another in the turns about the fireplace made by entering dancers; paraphernalia of essentially similar type (head-rings, neck-rings, masks, whistles) figure in Kwakiutl performances otherwise distinct; and the object of apparently every Kwakiutl society's winter ceremonial is 'to bring back the youth who is supposed to stay with the supernatural being who is the protector of his society, and then, when he has returned in a state of ecstasy, to exorcise the spirit which possesses him and to restore him from his holy madness.' Among the Hidatsa the right to each of a considerable number of esoteric rituals must be bought from one's father: in each case the requisite ritualistic articles were supplied by a clansman of the buyer's father; a 'singer' conducted the ceremonies; the purchaser received the ceremonial bundle, not directly, but through his wife; and so forth. All important bundle ceremonies of the Blackfeet require a sweat-lodge performance; in nearly all rituals the songs are sung by sevens; for almost every bundle some vegetable is burned on a special altar; and every ritual consists essentially of a narrative of its origin, one or more songs, the opening of the bundle, and dancing, praying, and singing over its contents." Dorsey[12] gives some details regarding the Sun-Dance. "On the completion of the altar the priests decorate the bodies, naked except for a loin cloth, of those who are to dance; these, together with the priests, have taken neither food nor drink since the preceding night. After the dancers have been painted, and decked with sage or willow wreaths about the head, neck, waist, wrists, and ankles, the dancers, forming in line, dance toward the center pole, representing the sun, blowing whistles made of the wing-bones of eagles to accompany Sun-dance songs, which are sung by musicians seated about a large drum at the southern side of the entrance. After an interval, which may be a day, the paint is removed and renewed, and the ceremony is resumed, and to the end the dancers thus alternately dance and rest. At the close of the performance the dancers in some tribes take an emetic, drink medicine-water, break their fast, and then enter the sweat-lodge. In all tribes, so far as known, the lodge with its accompanying altar is abandoned to the elements, for it is considered sacred and may not be disturbed. Among several taboos of the ceremony, one most frequent and almost universal is that forbidding the presence of menstruating women. . . . In the majority of tribes one of the most common rites of the public performance is that of voluntary self-laceration or torture. The two

6 Hewitt, "Dance," in HAI, I, 381, 382; Morgan, Iroquois, I, 278.
7 Mooney, in HAI, II, 483.
8 In HAI, II, 12.
9 In HAI, II, 211.
10 Cheyenne, I, 76 ff., 150; II, 211 ff., 285 ff
11 In AA, XVI, 618.
12 In HAI, II, 650, 651.

most common forms of torture were (1) to attach the free end of a reata that had been fastened to the center fork of the lodge, to a skewer inserted in the loose skin of the breast, and (2) to drag around inside the camp circle one or more buffalo-skulls by a reata the other end of which was attached to a skewer inserted in the back. In some tribes a small piece of flesh was cut from the arm or shoulder of the dancer and was offered with tobacco seeds at the foot of the center pole."

§446. Treatment of the Skin and Hair.

Tattooing. In British New Guinea "the tattooing of a girl is commenced when she is quite young, and is afterwards added to from time to time prior to her marriage; but no further tattooing is done after then. . . . Men do not usually tattoo, but they sometimes do so either before or after marriage, and tattooing on the breast used to be a sign that a man had taken human life."[1]

Among certain South Africans, girls could not be married until some four thousand stitches had been made on their breasts and stomachs, and a black fluid rubbed in. It caused great torture. "A Krooman can always be distinguished by a peculiar mark consisting of a broad blue-black line running from the forehead down to the end of the nose," the most extensive bit of real tattoo known in West Africa. In Liberia, only the initiated and tattooed boys may take part in palavers. In the Sudan, slave-women are marked by scarring and tattoo. Various patterns, which are often raised scars rather than true tattoo, are common in this region and the body rather than the face is the object of attention. In East Africa, though tattooing is chiefly for beautification, the patterns also distinguish tribes. Other marks confer luck in hunting. Curves and spirals are rather rare.[2]

The Tungus, Yakuts, and Ostyaks used to tattoo the face by means of sewing; Ostyak women decorate the hands with figures of birds and animals and with conventional designs; among the Koryaks only married women tattoo, in the hope of thus obscuring the effects of time. Mongolian tattooing is infrequently ornamental; it is a mark of criminality. Devotees in Lhasa often have the three mystic syllables, *Om, A, Hum,* tattooed on the crown of the head, on the forehead, and on the sternum respectively.[3]

In India, tattooing is practised in all quarters among the lower classes and has filtered in among the higher. "It is only an infinitesimal portion of the educated men of India who have been inducing their fair sex to give up the practice. The tribe, the caste, the religious sect, and the profession of the wearer of the mark can often be traced from the symbol selected. Many again are charms. Imitative magic likewise plays an important part in the selection of these drawings; for instance, the mark of a scorpion protects one from the bite of that vermin, and a snake from that of a cobra, and so forth. Among the Burmese, gunshots are tattooed to protect from fire-arms. A Shan thinks he acquires agility by tatuing a cat, or tiger, on his body. . . . Some charm, superstition, hope, myth, or something is connected with the devices, especially those

---

1 Williamson, in JAI, XLIII, 269.
2 Mauch, "Makalaka," in Petermann's *Mitth.*, Ergänzb., VIII, no. 37, p. 38; Griffith, in JAI, XVI, 304; Kingsley, *Travels W. Afr.*, 646; Frobenius, *Masken*, 118, 120; Junker, *Afr.*, I, 149, 337-338; II, 306; Seidel,

in *Globus*, LXXX, 290-291; Stuhlmann, *Mit Emin*, 240, 241, note.
3 Hiekisch, *Tungusen*, 72; Ratzel, *Vkde.*, II, 757; *Russ. Ethnog.* (Russ.), II, 482, 581; Rockhill, in USNM for 1893, 697; Rockhill, *Mongolia and Tibet*, 58, 67.

of women." The custom is waning with the refinement of the people. There are professional female tattooers in southern India and many people are profusely tattooed beneath their clothes. Worshippers of Vishnu are branded with his emblems. Some of the wild tribes tattoo after taking a first head. Tattoo "seems to have been the sign of full membership in the tribe; not till a man had shown his efficiency as a fighter might he wear the tribal badge or take the position of a married man." Again, the tattoo confers upon women immunity in a feud: "These women are much sought for by the southern men, because, however fierce may be their feuds, a tattooed woman always goes unscathed, fear of the dire vengeance which would be exacted by her northern relations were she injured giving her this immunity."[4] Among the Todas "tattooing is only practised by women. . . . The tattooing must not take place before puberty, but it may be done either before or after childbirth."[5]

"The practice of tatu is so widely spread throughout Borneo that it seems simpler to give a list of the tribes that do not tatu, than of those who do. . . . The Kayans are, with one or two exceptions, the most tatued race in Borneo, and perhaps the best tatued from an artistic point of view; the designs used in the tatu of the men have been widely imitated and much ceremonial is connected with the tatu of the women." The men tattoo chiefly for ornament. No special significance is attached to the majority of designs employed, nor is there any particular ceremonial or pattern connected with the process of tattooing the male sex. "Amongst the Sarawak Kayans, if a man has taken the head of an enemy he can have the backs of his hands and fingers covered with tatu. . . . Although a single figure of the dog is the most usual form of tatu, we have met with an example of a double figure. . . . A woman endeavours to have her tatu finished before she becomes pregnant, as it is considered immodest to be tatued after she has become a mother. . . . The operation of tatuing is performed by women, never by men, and it is always the women who are the experts on the significance and quality of tatu designs, though the men actually carve the designs on the tatu blocks. Nieuwenhuis states that the office of tatuer is to a certain extent hereditary and that the artists, like smiths and carvers, are under the protection of a tutelary spirit, who must be propitiated with sacrifices before each operation." As to the operation, "the tatuer or her assistant stretches with her feet the skin of the part to be tatued, and, dipping a pricker into the pigment, taps its handle with the striker as she works along a line, driving the needle points into the skin. The operation is painful, and the subject can rarely restrain her cries of anguish, but the artist is always quite unmoved by such demonstrations of woe, and proceeds methodically with her task. As no antiseptic precautions are ever taken, a newly tatued part often ulcerates, much to the detriment of the tatu, but taking all things into consideration it is wonderful how seldom one meets with a tatu pattern spoilt by scar tissue."[6]

Along with tremendous ear-rings that distorted the ears and were a sign of nobility, the Filipinos blackened the teeth and tattooed to such an extent that for a long time the Spanish term *pintados* was applied to them. Slaves might not tattoo.[7] All the Maoris tattooed, but not at puberty. A warrior's full tattoo

4 Sinclair, in AA, X, 376, 377; Leclère, in PSM, XLIV, 780; Basu, in JASB, II, 93; Thurston, S. India, 377-379; Fawcett, in JASB, II, 330; Woodthorpe, in JAI, XI, 206, 208, 209; Godden, in JAI, XXVI, 185; XXVII, 21; Peal, in JAI, XXII, 247; Mason, *Woman's Share*, 186.

5 Rivers, *Todas*, 578.

6 Hose and Shelford, in JAI, XXXVI, 63 ff.

7 Montero y Vidal, *Filipinas*, I, 15.

took place after he had distinguished himself in war. "The tattooing of a slave's face was only a vile practice, introduced lately for the sake of selling dried heads (fully tattooed) as European curios."[8] The drawers or knee-trousers pattern common in Samoa is represented also on Ponapé; it is closely connected with sex-considerations. In Micronesia tattooing has become almost exclusively ornamental. Núkuóro women have to live in a temple for three months before their tattooing; it is attended by long religious ceremonies, where in the case of men the whole matter is arbitrary. The patterns in these regions generally indicate rank. Representations of the dead were, in the Bowditch Islands, often tattooed upon the chests of near relatives. Easter Island patterns used to be limited only by the fancy and ability of the artist, whereas standard figures were the rule in most of the Pacific islands. Marriage-marks were tattooed upon the husband's neck just below the larynx, if he belonged to a chieftain's family. All tattooing has now been given up by these islanders.[9]

Sinclair[10] says: "The most elegant work is done in Japan and Burmah. Next come the Marquesas, Samoa, New Zealand, and other South Sea islands. That of the Haida Indians of Queen Charlotte islands is elaborate, and finely wrought, by far the best of any in the Americas."

Tattooing was probably once practised throughout the American continent. Sometimes it was no more than scarring, resulting from blood-letting for religious reasons. Painting the skin h⸗s largely superseded puncturing and cutting. Tattooing is common among Eskimo women, where among the men it is on the decline. It is thought to make the East Greenland women more effective in their work and men are sometimes marked "that they may be able to harpoon well." But the chief motive is adornment and pleasure. Central Eskimo women tattoo by "sewing" the skin—passing needle and thread covered with soot under the skin, or by puncture. At Point Barrow, "tattooing on a man is a mark of distinction. Those men who are, or have been captains of whaling oomiaks that have taken whales have marks to indicate this tattooed somewhere on their persons, sometimes forming a definite tally." These tally-marks are usually pricked upon the cheek, chest, or arms. Occasionally the wife of such a man had an extra mark put at the corner of her mouth. The tattooing of women is almost universal across the whole continent and in Siberia. It is done especially at the age of puberty. "When an Eskimo girl reached maturity a line was tattooed from the edge of the lower lip to the point of the chin; later two or more lines were added to mark her as a married woman." "Among the Kiowa the tribal mark was a circle on the forehead of the woman. With the Omaha and some of their cognates a small round spot on the forehead of a girl, and a four-pointed star on the back and breast, were marks of honor to signify the achievements of her father or near of kin. In other tribes certain lines on the face indicated the marriageable or married woman. . . . On the middle Atlantic coast geometric designs were tattooed on the person so as to have a decorative effect. The same type of design was incised on the pottery of that region. Tattooing was extensively practised among the tribes of the interior. The Wichita, because of their profuse use of this decoration, were known to the French as 'Pani Piqué. . . . As tattooing gave a permanent line, it served a different

8 Tregear, in JAI, XIX, 100.
9 Finsch, Ethnol. Erfahr., III, 173, 267, 268; Pereiro, Ponapé, 128; Kubary, Núkuóro, 10, 29-30; Ratzel, Vkde., II, 137; Gardiner, in JAI, XXVII, 414; Lister, in JAI, XXI, 55; Thomson, in USNM, 1889, 466; Geiseler, Oster-Ins., 25; Cook, in USNM, 1897, I, 718.
10 In AA, X, 381.

purpose from decoration by paint. Among men it marked personal achievement, some special office, symbolized a vision from the supernatural powers, or served some practical purpose, as among the Hupa, where the men have '10 lines tattooed across the inside of the left arm about half way between the wrist and the elbow' for the purpose of measuring strings of 'shell money.' . . . The Chippewa sometimes resorted to tattooing as a means of curing pain, as the toothache. The process of tattooing was always attended with more or less ceremony; chants or songs frequently accompanied the actual work, and many superstitions were attached to the manner in which the one operated upon bore the pain or made recovery. Most tribes had one or more persons expert in the art who received large fees for their services."[11]

Body-Painting. A few scattered cases may illustrate this widespread practice. In Bathurst Island "both male and female walk about in the nude state. The body is anointed with grease and besmeared, in one or more shades of colour, with ochre."[12] Red is the mourning-color among the African Ba-Yaka, and widows are painted this hue. To avoid the vengeance of the soul of a man killed in battle, the forehead is painted red and red tail-feathers of the parrot are worn in the hair.[13] In the Upper Congo, "it was the custom to wash the body well, anoint it with palm oil, and then dust it with cam-wood powder. . . . The skin thus treated kept healthy and soft and free from scabs, etc., and received much protection from rain, sunshine or cold."[14] Among some of the American Indians "the face of the dead was frequently painted in accordance with tribal or religious symbolism."[15] "The Araucano neither daubs his face with paint nor uses tattooing as a means of beautifying his personal appearance, although formerly their war parties painted their faces to strike terror into the hearts of their enemies. The elaborate designs and totem marks used by some of the northern races seem to have had no counterpart among them, and they seem to have had no special identification mark to distinguish them if slain in battle."[16] In Ecuador "body painting among the Indians nearly always serves magical ends, being regarded as a protection against disease and witchcraft, and this is especially the case with the black painting. According to the ideas of the Jibaros and the Canelos Indians there is a demon . . . in the black genipa paint."[17]

Treatment of the Hair. "All Batetela remove the body hair, women by plucking, men by shaving; the Olemba, moreover, shave the eyebrows and pull out the eyelashes."[18] The Polynesians pluck out all the facial and bodily hair; they have a proverb: "No wife for the hairy man." On Ponapé hairiness is viewed with horror and they pull out their hair with hinged shells.[19]

Of the Indians Catlin says: "Beards they generally have not, esteeming them great vulgarities, and using every possible means to eradicate them whenever they are so unfortunate as to be annoyed with them. . . . From the best information I could obtain amongst forty-eight tribes that I have visited . . .

11 Ratzel, *Vkde.*, II, 567, 737; Holm, *Ethnol. Skizze*, 17; Boas, in BAE, VI, 561; Murdoch, in BAE, IX, 139; Turner, in BAE, XI, 208; Fletcher, in HAI, II, 700.
12 Basedow, in JAI, XLIII, 296.
13 Torday and Joyce, in JAI, XXXVI, 50, 51.
14 Weeks, in JAI, XXXIX, 100.

15 Fletcher, in HAI, I, 16.
16 Latcham, in JAI, XXXIX, 337.
17 Karsten, "Jibaro," in BAE, Bull. LXXIX, 39.
18 Torday, in JAI, LI, 380.
19 Ratzel, *Vkde.*, II, 139; Kubary, *Núkuóro*, 10; Kubary, *Karolinen-Arch.*, 90; Pereiro, *Ponapé*, 127, 128.

at least the proportion of eighteen out of twenty by nature are entirely without the appearance of a beard; and of the very few who have them by nature, nineteen out of every twenty eradicate it by plucking it out several times in succession, precisely at the age of puberty, when its growth is successfully arrested; and occasionally one may be seen who has omitted to destroy it at that time, and subjects his chin to the repeated pains of its extractions, which he is performing with a pair of clam-shells or other tweezers nearly every day of his life." The Apache used to pluck out eye-lashes and often eyebrows but have given it up. The Choctaws are said to have plucked "all the hair off their bodies with a kind of tweezers, made formerly of clam shells." It is thought by some that depilation originated in the attempt to facilitate face- and body-painting; natives cease to pluck out their beards when they cease to paint. Sioux men, having almost no beards, commonly pulled out what little they had; both sexes plucked out hair on other parts of the body.[20] The Cheyenne pulled out hair with tweezers called "eyebrow pluckers." It may be inferred that eyebrows were first removed; the practice today is to remove the lashes and other hair as well.[21]

Depilation was not the only method of treating the hair among the North American Indians. "In some tribes the women dressed their hair differently before and after marriage, as with the Hopi, whose maidens arranged it in a whorl over each ear, symbolizing the flower of the squash, but after marriage wore it in simple braids." With some tribes, as the Omaha, the hair of children was cut in a pattern to indicate the gens or band of the parent, and in some, as the Kiowa, to indicate the particular protecting medicine of the father. "The first cutting of the hair was usually attended with religious rites. Among the Kiowa and other southern Plains tribes a lock from the first clipping of the child's hair was tied to the forelock. Among many tribes the hair was believed to be closely connected with a person's life. This was true in a religious sense of the scalp-lock. . . . Among the Dakota a bit of the captured scalp-lock was preserved for a year, during which period the spirit was supposed to linger near; then, when the great death feast was held, the lock was destroyed and the spirit was freed thereby from its earthly ties. . . . One can be bewitched and made subservient to the will of a person who becomes possessed of a bit of his hair; consequently combings are usually carefully burned."[22] The name Pawnee is probably derived from *pariki*, or horn, "a term used to designate the peculiar manner of dressing the scalp-lock, by which the hair was stiffened with paint and fat, and made to stand erect and curved like a horn."[23] Among the Tarahumari, "both men and women wear long, flowing, straight black hair, which in rare cases is wavy. It is held together with a woollen head-band made for the purpose, or with a narrow pleated band of palm-leaf. . . . Very often the men, for convenience, gather their hair at the neck, leaving off the band. . . . Beards are very rare, and if one appear, the Indian pulls it out with great care. Their devil is always represented with a beard, and they call the Mexicans the 'bearded ones.' My offer of some tobacco," says Lumholtz,[24] "was once refused by a man because he feared that it would cause a beard to grow on his face—because I was a bearded man. A medicine-man once astonished

20 Donaldson, in *Smithson. Rep.*, 1885, pt. II, 529; Bourke, in BAE, IX, 475; Holmes, in BAE, II, 212; Mallery, in BAE, X, 620; McGee, in BAE, XV, 185.
21 Grinnell, *Cheyenne*, I, 166.

22 Fletcher, in HAI, I, 525; Mooney, in HAI, I, 266; §§213, 300, of the text and *Case-Book*.
23 Fletcher, in HAI, II, 213.
24 In *Scribner's Mag.*, XVI, 296.

me by having his hair cut short. When I asked him why he had done so, he said it was not good because it was old; his head would get new and good thoughts with new hair. When the hair is cut off for this reason, the head is covered with a piece of cotton-cloth to keep the man's thoughts from escaping. When they cut hair from the head because it is too long, they place it under a stone or hang it from the branch of a tree."

"As soon as an Indian is captured in war he is deemed a slave, and one forthwith cuts his hair to make him understand that he is indeed so. In fact, hair is a sign of liberty, and only those who are free let it grow, and never cut it unless they are in mourning. From the Archivos de Indias . . . it is evident that the practice of cutting prisoners' hair as a mark of slavery was followed by Arawak as well as Carib." These Guiana Indians also depilate.[25] The Shingu pull out all the hair on the body. The beard is slight, and they seem to enjoy plucking it, being accustomed to it from youth up. Strangers who wear beards seem to them ugly. There might be rational ground, the author[26] thinks, for depilation— on account of parasites or special heat-irritation, or uncleanliness, or danger of entanglement in the bushes, or of the chance given an enemy in a fight; but it is more plausibly connected with the custom of painting the body, where the hair would be in the way, especially in case the painting is designed to kill insects. "In short, he who removes the hair is so much better off, and has lost nothing. This is sufficient to account for the custom." Von Martius[27] thinks that depilation is everywhere practised in America in proportion to the development of tribal pride. Again, "the pulling out of the sparse face-and body-hair ranks with them as a law of beauty and is always practised." In Brazil too the eye-brows and eye-lashes are sometimes removed.[28] Among the Araucanians "the men pull out the beard, and both men and women remove all the eyebrows except a narrow strip."[29]

Pincers for depilation are found in many prehistoric graves, for instance, in Scandinavia.[30]

An excellent observer[31] remarks: "To pluck out, to cut, or to shave is nothing but a question of thoroughness, or of the instruments at command, or of delicacy of feeling. The hair was cut or pulled out before it was combed."

§447. Ornament and Clothing.

In Bathurst Island, "the females carry folded sheets of paper bark or large food-carriers about with them, which, upon the approach of strangers, they hold in front of their person."[1] In British New Guinea "women usually wear their nose ornaments on special occasions, but men wear them more generally." The war-feast after a victorious raid upon an enemy is the occasion for the donning of a large disc of white shell or an ornamental design. "Formerly only a man who had killed an enemy was allowed to wear these, and they were therefore insignia of which the wearers were greatly proud."[2] "Men of Lifu wore no clothing, but for ornament wore round the body the vine of a kind of bind-weed. The name of the beautiful convolvulus-like flower of this plant—*wanaithihle*—

25 Roth, in BAE, XXXVIII, 600 (quoted), §508.
26 Von den Steinen, *Zent. Bras.*, 176, 193.
27 *Beiträge*, I, 642.
28 Von Koenigswald, in *Globus*, XCIII, 378; Koch, in *Globus*, LXXXI, 7.

29 La Fetra, "Araucanians," in *Illust. Christ. World*, Dec., 1896.
30 Müller, *Vor Oldtid*, 240.
31 Von den Steinen, *Zent. Bras.*, 176.
1 Basedow, in JAI, XLIII, 296.
2 Williamson, in JAI, XLIII, 269, 279.

after the introduction of Christianity and clothing, came to signify a heathen, and the adoption or rejection of Christianity was compared to the putting on or taking off of clothes."[3]

In southwest Africa iron is worth more than silver for it keeps its shine in the dry air and is used for ornament. The native women carry pounds of it and have to walk slowly and slouchily; this gait is regarded as aristocratic.[4] The Bangala "were fond of brass ornaments, especially the women, who often wore heavy solid brass collars weighing from 2 lbs. to 18 lbs. When they died their heads were cut off to remove the collars. . . . The anklets were various in shape and weight, sometimes heavy brass rings were put on one above the other, and here and there would be seen a woman with a spiral leg ornament reaching from the ankles to the knees."[5] Among the Atharaka "the only clothing originally worn by the men was a fringe of *mbuyu* threads (*ngigi*)." Small boys are unclothed, but after six or seven "wear the *ngigi,* to which is frequently added a piece of goatskin in order to more effectively conceal the fact that they are not yet circumcized. . . . Uncircumcized girls wear beads round the loins, to which is attached a fringe of *mbuyu* threads, so as to cover the genitals. . . . At an early age the lobe of the ear is pierced, and great care is taken in the gradual operation of its extension. A circular peg of wood is put in, and this varies in size and shape according to the owner's taste. . . . The women are literally weighed down with the weight of their beads and metal ornaments. . . . The unmarried girls do not wear the *matulutia,* but insert a small round piece of wood in the lobe of the ear (*ndingi*). They also wear goat's hair brushes stuck through the rim of the ear. These are called *ndiro,* and seem to serve no further object than decoration. The weight of these causes the rim of the ear to droop over, which I am informed is much to be desired. I was also informed that the *ndiro* flap about when the girls are dancing, which greatly fascinates the young men."[6] Among the Kavirondo, "the women do not wear iron wire to the same extent as their husbands and brothers. These may frequently be seen with from six to ten pieces wound round their arms and legs, which shine from constant rubbing and polishing with oil and fat. Happily there are signs that this wire is going out of fashion, whereby they will be spared the sores and ulcers which are its continual accompaniment."[7]

According to an Associated Press despatch, shoe-polish by the ton is coming into Calcutta from England, to meet the desire of Indian natives in cities and towns to "outshine" their neighbors in the matter of footwear. "Until a few years ago comparatively few Indians wore shoes. At first the natives never thought of shining their shoes, but now it has become a fetish. The more perfect the shoe shine, the native believes, the greater the envy of all his fellow-beings."[8] Formerly the wealth of the natives in Mindanao was in slaves, animals, *aguns,* and fine clothes. "The days of slavery are past; the *aguns,* or big gongs, they still possess. These are their most important musical instruments, and the magnificence of tone coloring of many large gongs played together is indescribable. The Bagobos have other instruments of percussion, wind, and strings, but these large gongs serve also as a medium of exchange, and a man's wealth is usually reckoned by the number of gongs he possesses."[9] In Polynesia, "to bring someone's comb into contact with food, or to lay it in an oven, was the grossest of

3 Ray, in JAI, XLVII, 255.
4 Büttner, *Walfischbai*, 28-29.
5 Weeks, in JAI, XXXIX, 99.
6 Champion, in JAI, XLII, 74-77.

7 Northcote, in JAI, XXXVII, 59.
8 N. Y. *World*, Feb. 25, 1927.
9 Metcalf, in AA, XIV, 162.

insults,—but to the owner of the comb. Food, to the Polynesian, is profane and defiling, while the comb, which is in contact with the head, is emblematic of personal dignity."[10]

The members of one of the Dakota tribes "wore looking-glasses suspended from their garments. Others had papers of pins, purchased from the traders, as ornaments. We observed one, who appeared to be a man of some note among them, had a live sparrow hawk on his head, by way of distinction; this man wore also a buffalo robe, on which 8 bear tracks were painted. . . . The squaws we saw had no ornament, nor did they seem to value themselves upon their personal appearance."[11]

§448. Clothing as Adjustment.

THE Australian case mentioned in the text is pretty complete, but not by any means extreme. Says a missionary[1] of wide knowledge: "My own experience, gained by ten years' residence in Polynesia and New Guinea, is that the advent of the white man is invariably followed by the gradual extinction of the native race. Unintentionally, perhaps, but none the less certainly, the white man carries with him, wherever he goes, causes which ultimately destroy the native population. Foreign foods, foreign clothing, intoxicating liquors, foreign modes of living, and the direct introduction of specific diseases all tend to the one result. And of these I consider that the introduction of foreign clothing is one of the most fatal. In this matter the missionaries have to bear a share in the responsibility. Invariably adopted from a love of display rather than from any other reason, the native generally wears his foreign clothing during the daytime. Then at night, when it can no longer be seen, he throws it off, and sits in the cool night air, wet or fine, without anything on. The natural result of this exposure is the introduction of pleurisy, pneumonia, and other chest and lung diseases which cause terrible havoc."

The same diseases reduced the Andaman Islanders, and it was decided "to supply them only with drawers, leaving the upper part of the body exposed. A marked improvement in the general health resulted from this change."[2] The same story is rehearsed by Sir. H. B. Frere[3] concerning South Africa, "where the natives have adopted such clothing without regard to European health customs." Another writer on South Africa says that the missionaries who teach tribes accustomed to nudity to wear clothes are responsible for three things: lung diseases; the spread of vermin; the disappearance of inherent and natural modesty.[4] Consistency in the mores is one of the texts of these last quotations. Others report the usual story of bad hygiene following upon the adoption of clothing,[5] though Livingstone[6] thinks that clothing helped against inflammatory diseases like rheumatism.

In South India, we are told, "one of the Government Agents some years ago insisted on a young woman being properly clothed. The result was she survived the change only three days."[7] Here, doubtless, was a case of death by fright on account of some transgressed taboo or religious scruple.[8] In the Caroline Is-

10 Kroeber, in AA, XII, 442.
11 In HAI, II, 892.
1 Hunt, in JAI, XXVIII, 18.
2 Man, in JAI, XII, 82.
3 In JAI, XI, 340.
4 Bent, *Mashonaland*, 27.

5 Mason, in *Geog. Jr.*, LII, 30-41; Kidd, *Kafir Socialism*, 210.
6 *Mission. Travels*, 143.
7 Thurston, *S. India*, 528.
8 §268, of the text and *Case-Book*.

lands, health has been much imperilled by the adoption of European clothes, the result being all manner of rheumatic and pulmonary ailments.[9] The Maori died in numbers because the missionaries made them wear clothes.[10]

On the east coast of Greenland everybody when in the house goes naked or very nearly so. This is very wholesome because the furs worn out-of-doors would impede transpiration. On the west coast, the missionaries have preached down the habit of indoor stripping. Nansen[11] cannot say whether this has improved morality, but doubts it, and unhesitatingly declares that it has not been conducive to sanitation.

Of certain low California tribes we learn that "though filthy, these people do not neglect the cold morning bath until they have learned to wear complete civilized suits . . . and never since the fatal hour when Adam and Eve tied about them the fig-leaves in Eden has clothing been a symbol so freighted with evil portent as to these miserable people. On excessively hot days they would lay off the miserable rags of civilization which hampered and galled their free-born limbs; and then would come colds, coughs, croups, quick consumption, which swept them off by thousands."[12]

Of the Guiana Indians it is written: "For decency's sake, as Gumilla tells us, the missionaries distributed clothing, especially among the women, but in vain. They fling it into the river or hide it, but do not cover themselves, and when remonstrated with, they reply 'We do not cover ourselves, because it gives us shame.' . . . They recognize shame and bashfulness, but the signification of the terms is changed. . . . They feel abashed at being clothed. . . . Among the nations bordering on the Amazon, the Indians are entirely nude. They regard almost as a certain sign that he who would cover what shame obliges us to hide would soon be unfortunate, or would die in the course of the year. . . . It is well to bear in mind what is already well known in connection with many other races, but so pertinently expressed by Kirke relative to the Guianese Indian: The climate of Guiana is exceedingly warm and moist; up the rivers scarcely a day passes without several showers of rain. The natives in consequence go about in a nude state, and the rain as it falls runs off their oiled backs like water off the proverbial duck. But when, by the efforts of some well-meaning but misdirected missionary, they don clothes they soon become victims of phthisis and pneumonia, their clothes getting wet through and drying on their bodies several times a day. It is not from want of knowledge of clothes that the Indian goes naked. As Coudreau pointed out, the Indians regard European clothes as ornaments, wearing them over their own bead or feathered decorations. He mentions how the Atorradis, etc., speak of clothes as the *cachourous,* i.e., beads, necklaces, of the whites."[13]

§449. Prestige.

Trophies. Somerville[1] notes in New Georgia "the custom of keeping the skulls of any animals eaten; these may usually be seen inside the houses, threaded on long sticks. They consist, for the most part, of opossum, turtle, and frigate bird skulls, and are kept either merely for ornament, or as a bragging record

9 Christian, *Caroline Isl.*, 73.
10 Hutchinson, *Races*, I, 42.
11 *Esk. Life*, 26.

12 Powers, in *Contrib. N. Amer. Ethnol.*, III, 55, 92, 403.
13 Roth, in BAE, XXXVIII, 441, 442.
1 In JAI, XXVI, 367.

of former feasts and good living. I think that perhaps the custom has also some 'religious' meaning." In Bougainville the beard is scalped and worn as a trophy.[2] In Mowat the victor wears as a charm the private parts of a great warrior slain in battle.[3]

With the Bangala, "when a man kills his opponent in a fight he cuts off the head and removes the lips, which he thoroughly dries in the sun, and then sticks in brass chair nails and wears them as an ornament with as much pride as the Victoria Cross is worn—it is the man's medal for bravery."[4] In Victoria Nyanza the hunter makes rings from one of the hind feet of the elephant and wears one for each animal killed. He has great pride in them; an old hunter has fifteen or twenty. The tuft on the end of the tail is also a trophy.[5] In northeast Africa, "the first business of the victor, who has killed a man, is, if time permits, to sever the private parts with a knife—a gruesome usage which is characteristic also of the Bantu, for instance, the Kaffirs."[6]

Among the frontier tribes of northeast India warriors of distinction, who have slain many people, wear the hair of their victims depending from the side-ornaments of the helmet. It accumulates into a kind of fringe around the face. Women's tresses are preferred as being longer.[7] The oldest brother in a Naga family, besides his own trophies, gets the skulls taken by his brothers, to decorate his portal. Skulls of enemies taken in battle are generally decorated with a pair of horns or with wooden imitations of them.[8] "The successful head-hunters of the Ao tribe wear, as badges of their prowess, collars composed of pairs of boar's tusks, which are tied point to point and base to base, so that they encircle the neck. . . . Each pair of tusks so worn indicates an enemy's head taken in battle."[9]

The skulls acquired by Malays in head-hunting are ornamented and set up in the houses; he who has the most of them is a great man. Among the Dyaks the shield is ornamented with human hair; whenever the warrior takes a head, he inserts a tuft of the hair in his shield.[10] In Borneo the most valuable ornament of the verandah is the bunch of human heads which hangs over the fireplace like a cluster of fruit; these are obtained on various warpaths by the members of the family, dead and living, and are handed down from father to son as precious heirlooms.[11] On the island of Nias only those natives may wear a ring around the neck who have been successful on a head-hunting foray.[12] The Samoans are said in vainglory to have piled up the heads of their enemies before the public assembly, the head of the most important chief being put on top.[13]

Mutilation of the dead was neither universal nor constant among the American Indians, but "the cutting off of the head or taking of the scalp was generally practised. The fundamental reason for scalping has not yet been fully explained, but there is evidence to indicate that it was connected with the rites observed when a boy was recognized as a member of the band and his life was dedicated to the God of War."[14] "The Menomini endeavored to take the entire scalp, including the skin over the forehead, but if there was not time enough

2 Letourneau, *Soc.*, 241.
3 Beardmore, in JAI, XIX, 462.
4 Weeks, in JAI, XL, 414.
5 Stuhlmann, *Mit Emin*, 87.
6 Paulitschke, *Nordost-Afr.*, I, 256.
7 Godden, in JAI, XXVII, 14.
8 Woodthorpe, in JAI, XI, 205.

9 Furness, in JAI, XXXII, 455.
10 Ratzel, *Vkde.*, II, 406, 448; Wilken, *Vkde.*, 393-395.
11 Roth, in JAI, XXII, 29.
12 Raap, in *Globus*, LXXXIII, 151-152.
13 Gomme, *Ethnol. in Folklore*, 156.
14 Fletcher, in HAI, II, 914.

for this, a small piece, including the place where the hair radiates from the crown, was sufficient. While the scalp was fresh the warrior licked the blood from it to symbolize the devouring of the enemy by the Sun." After the scalp-dance, "the sister of the warrior washed his hands with presents and took the scalp from him, so that in the end the trophies accrued to the women."[15] Some tribes took no scalps. The Pima, for instance, "considered their enemies, particularly the Apache, possessed of evil spirits and did not touch them after death." While the Patwin refrained from scalping, they are said "often to have decapitated the most beautiful maiden they captured."[16]

"During the battle the Mundrucû spares no enemy. As soon as he has stretched one on the ground by arrow or spear, he seizes him by the hair and with a reed-knife cuts through his neck-muscles and vertebræ with such dexterity that the head is speedily separated from the trunk. The head thus won becomes then the object of the greatest care on the part of the victor. As soon as he has rejoined his comrades many fires are kindled and the skull, relieved of the brain, muscles, eyes, and tongue, is dried on pegs, daily repeatedly washed with water and with oil . . . and exposed to the sun. When it has become quite hard, the skull is provided with an artificial brain of colored cotton and with eyes made of resin and teeth, and is ornamented with a feather cap. Thus outfitted, the gruesome trophy attends the victor, who carries it with him on a string and, when he sleeps in the common house, by day puts it in the sun or the smoke, by night right by his hammock, like a guard."[17] The Guaycuru cut off the heads of slain enemies as trophies, sometimes the hair or even little pieces of the body. "These trophies of victory they give over to their wives who have their jokes with them."[18] The Jibaro Indian does not make trophies solely of the heads of his human enemies but also of the heads of certain animals. There is one animal especially which in this respect plays a curious part in the superstitions of the Jibaros, namely, the sloth. Feasts with trophies made of the head of the sloth are among them as common as feasts with human head-trophies.[19] It is said that tourist curiosity has so stimulated traffic in human heads as souvenir trophies that whole tribes of South American Indians are threatened with extinction. Ecuador has declared war on the head-hunters and has asked Peru and Brazil to assist her. The Jibaro Indians are masters of the secret of how to reduce the human head to the size of a doll's without distorting the features. The heads which formerly were preserved as battle-trophies are now being smuggled into the cities to be sold to tourists, usually for fifty dollars apiece. A skilfully reduced specimen sells at Quito, Guayaquil and other South American ports for as much as three or four hundred dollars. "The tourist in buying them is innocently increasing the savagery of the head-hunters, with the result, it is claimed, that in a short time certain tribes will be extinct."[20]

The Scythians are said to have taken scalps as trophies, sometimes sewing a number together as a cloak. Those who possessed many scalps were highly honored.[21] There is an Irish legend that a warrior, having killed an enemy,

15 Skinner, in AA, XIII, 309, 310.
16 Hodge, in HAI, II, 252; Anon., in HAI, II, 211.
17 Von Martius, Beiträge, I, 392.
18 Koch, in Globus, LXXXI, 73.
19 Karsten, "Jibaro," in BAE, Bull. LXXIX, 32-33.
20 N. Y. Times, June 15, 1924; Mar. 19, 1925.
21 Herodotus, Hist., IV, 64; Justi, Persien, 97.

broke the skull and took out the brains, which he worked up into a ball, dried in the sun, and preserved as a trophy of valor and a presage of victory.[22] Bastian[23] mentions several historical cases of skulls being made into beakers, and states that the church adopted the custom of drinking out of saints' skulls.

---

22 Gomme, *Ethnol. in Folklore*, 147.   23 *Deut. Exped.*, II, 11, note.

BIBLIOGRAPHICAL NOTE

In the following list of books and articles consulted by the authors are included the titles of several studies, made by former candidates for the doctorate and not yet published, which are deposited in the Yale University Library. Occasionally two editions of the same author's work are cited; for instance, the original and the popular editions of Darwin's *Origin of Species,* or the German and the English versions of Ratzel and Lichtenstein. Anonymous articles in journals are listed under "Anonymous," in the alphabetical order of their key-words. The titles of books and articles, abbreviated in footnotes throughout the body of this book, are cited in full below.

Asterisks have been used to indicate exceptionally important sources, and daggers to designate publications that are readable, apart from their intrinsic scientific value. In some few cases, an asterisk appears before an author's name, thereby conveying a high estimate of his work in general. With almost no exceptions, and those readily identifiable, the publications in the following list have been personally consulted by one or other of the authors. Where reliable writers have quoted from sources not readily accessible to us, such excerpts have been accredited to the secondary source.

The authors wish to express their appreciation of the assistance rendered, in the making of this bibliography, by Miss E. L. Brown and Mr. T. C. Weiler.

AA. American Anthropologist (n.s. unless o.s. specified).
AAAS. Australasian Association for the Advancement of Science.
BAE. Bureau of American Ethnology.
Bijd. Bijdragen tot de Taal- Land- en Volkenkunde van Nederlandsch-Indië.
HAI. Handbook of American Indians.
JAI. Journal of the Anthropological Institute of Great Britain and Ireland.
JASB. Journal of the Anthropological Society of Bombay.
PSM. Popular Science Monthly.
USNM. United States National Museum.

A. Die Heidenstämme der Malaiischen Halbinsel. Globus, XCI.

A., W. C. Pekinger Familienleben. Globus, LXXVIII.

Aarbøger for Nordisk Oldkyndighed og Historie, udg. af det Kongelige nordiske Oldskrift-Selskab. Kjøbenhavn, 1866-1913. (Preceded by Annaler for Nordisk Oldkyndighed og Historie, 1836-63.)

Abbott, W. L. Ethnological collections in the U.S. National Museum from Kilima-Njaro, East Africa. USNM, 1891.

Abd-Allatif. Relation de l'Égypte, Paris, 1810.

Abel, C. W. †Savage life in New Guinea. London, 1902.

Abercromby, J. *The pre- and proto-historic Finns, Eastern and Western, with magic songs of the West Finns. 2 vols. London, 1898.

Abhandlungen und Berichte des Königlichen zoologischen und anthropologisch-ethnographischen Museums zu Dresden. I-XV. Berlin, 1886—.

Abulhasan Ali-Almasudi, *see* Masudi.

Achelis, A. Die Geschlechtsgenossenschaft und die Entwickelung der Ehe. Ztsft. f. Erdkunde, XXV.

Achelis, T. Die Ekstase in ihrer kulturellen Bedeutung. Berlin, 1902.

Acosta, J. de. Historia natural y moral de las Indias. Madrid, 1792.

Acworth, H. A. On the Marathi ballad written on the suttee of Ramabai, widow of Madhavrao Peshwa. JASB, II.

Adams, H. The education of Henry Adams. Boston, 1918.

——*Mont-Saint-Michel and Chartres. Boston and New York, 1913.

Adams, W. B. Domestic and quack remedies in the Levant. Bull. Amer. Acad. Med., X.

Æneas Sylvius. De vita et rebus gestis Frid. III., trans. as Die Geschichte Kaiser Friedrichs III, by Th. Ilgen. Leipzig, 1899.

Æschylus. Aeschyli Tragoediae. Recensit Arturus Sidgwick. Scriptorum Classicorum Bibliotheca Oxoniensis. MDCCCCII.

Agnew, J. W. The last of the Tasmanians. AAAS, 1887.

Aiston, G., see Horne, G.

Alec-Tweedie, Mrs. †Sunny Sicily. New York, no date.

Alexander, W. M. Demonic possession in the New Testament. Edinburgh, 1902.

Allen, C. F. Haandbog in faedrelandets historie med stadigt henblik paa folkets og statens indre udvikling. Kjøbenhavn, 1849.

Allen, G. Sacred stones. Fortnightly Review, XLVII (n.s.).

Allen, H. T. Atnatanas; natives of Copper River, Alaska. Smithson. Rep., 1886, pt. I.

Allison, Mrs. S. S. Account of the Similkameen Indians of British Columbia. JAI, XXI.

d'Alviella, see Goblet d'Alviella.

Am Ür-Quell. Monatschrift für Volkskunde. Neue Folge, Bd. I-VI. Lunden, 1890-6.

Ambrose, Saint. Opera.

Ambrosetti, J. B. Die Kaïngang in Argentinien. Globus, LXXIV.

America, A Catholic review of the week. I-XXXV. New York, 1909-26.

*American Anthropologist, I-XI, Washington, 1888-98 (o.s.); I-XXVIII. New York, 1899-1902. Lancaster (Pa.), 1902-21; Menasha (Wisc.), 1921-6 (n.s.).

American Antiquarian and Oriental Journal, The. I-XXV. Chicago, 1878-1913.

American Economic Review, The. I-XV. Princeton (N. J.), 1911-25.

American Historical Association, Papers of the. I-V. New York and London, 1886-91.

American Historical Review, The. I-XXXI. New York, 1895-1926.

American Historical Society. Section for the historical study of religions. IV-IX. New Haven, 1901-9.

American Journal of Sociology. I-XXXI. Chicago, 1895-1926.

American Medicine. I-XXXII. Philadelphia and York (Pa.), 1901-26.

American Mercury, The. A monthly review. I-IX. New York, 1924-6.

American Naturalist, The. A bimonthly journal devoted to the advancement of the biological sciences with special reference to the factors of evolution. I-LX. Salem (Mass.), 1867-1926.

American Oriental Society. Section for the historical study of religions, publications. IV-XI. (From Jour. Am. Or. Soc., XXII-XXIX). New Haven, 1901-9.

Ammon, O. Die Gesellschaftsordnung und ihre natürlichen Grundlagen. Jena, 1896.

Amundsen. Von Amundsens Polarexpedition. Anon., Globus, XCI.

Andree, R. Die Anthropophagie. Leipzig, 1887.

——*Ethnographische Parallelen und Vergleiche. Leipzig, 1st series, 1874. 2d series, 1889.

——St. Georg und die Parilien. Globus, XCIII.

——Das Weib in der Natur und Völkerkunde. Globus, XLVI.

Andrews, E. A. A new Latin dictionary. New York, 1907.

Andriessen, W. F. Münzen u. andere Tauschmittel in Afrika. Ausland, LXV.

Angerstein, W. Volkstänze im deutschen Mittelalter. Berlin, 1868.

Angus, H. C. A year in Azimba and Chipitaland: the customs and superstitions of the people. JAI, XXVIII.

Annaler for Nordisk Oldkyndighed og Historie udg. af det Kongelige nordiske Oldskrift-Selskab. Continued as Aarbøger. Kjöbenhavn, 1837-65.

L'Année sociologique. I-XII. Paris, 1896-1912.

Anonymous. Anthropological Miscellanea. JAI, XXVII.

——Aus allen Erdteilen. Globus, LXXII.

——Bantu totemism. Folk-Lore, XV.

——Ceremony of the Tasso. Illustr. Afr., March, 1896.

——Child Marriage. JASB, II.

——China and the Chinese. Sci. Amer., LXXXIII.

——Customs of the Australian aborigines. Anthropological Miscellanea. JAI, IX.

——Dolores. HAI, pt. I.

——Editorial. The devil in the public schools. PSM, XLIX.

——England lifts the ban on play by Shaw. Jr. Soc. Hygiene, X.

——Fragments of science. PSM, XLIX.

——Das Glücksei gegen den bösen Blick aus Tunis. Kleine Nachrichten. Globus, LXXV.

——Das Hahnornament bei den Amurvölkern. Globus, LXXVIII.

——Kleine Nachrichten. Globus, LXXV, LXXVIII, LXXIX, LXXXI, LXXXIV, LXXXV, LXXXVII, LXXXVIII, XC, XCI, XCII.

——Die Königin Njawingi von Mpororo. Globus, LXXXVIII.

——Mantrams, spells, amulets. Miscellaneous notes. JASB, II.

——A monster meeting of Bombay barbers. Anthropological scraps. JASB, II.

——The natural history of a Chinese girl. Résumé from the North Chinese Herald in JASB, II.

——Naturwissenschaft und Religion. Politisch-Anthropologische Revue, III.

——Note on the British Association. PSM, XLVIII.

——Notes. (July 6, 1916.) Nation, CIII.

——Notes on the Bondei. PSM, L.

——The old scepticism. Nation, XCIII.

——Die östliche Elfenbeinküste. Globus, LXXXVII.

——Parias und Schmarotzer unter den Völkern. Politisch-Anthropologische Revue, I.

——Die Pfahlbau von Dolnja Dolina. Globus, LXXXI.

——Pongal, O Pongal. JASB, II.

——Prähistorisches Feuer. Globus, XCIII.

——Precolombian metallurgy in Venezuela, S. A. Anthropological Miscellanea. JAI, XX.

——Rassefrage und Ehefreiheit in den Kolonien. Umschau, XI.

——The recent royal marriage at Kohlapore. A letter to the Times of India. JASB, II.

——Some characteristics of Northwestern Indians. PSM, XLIII.

——Some Highland cures. Pop. Sci. News, XXVII.

——*Das Volk der Orang Kubus auf Sumatra. Globus, XXVI.

——Turkey passes law establishing monogamy. Jr. Soc. Hyg., X.

——Völker und Politik. Politisch-Anthropologische Revue, III.

——Ein Zauberhemd der Filipinos. Globus, LXXXI.

Another Bachelor. Courtship after marriage. Atl. Mo., CXXVIII.

L'Anthropologie. I-XXXV. Paris, 1890-1925.

Anthropology of Poland, Collection of contributions to the. Edited by the

Anthropological section of the Academy of Sciences in Cracow (Polish). Cracow, 1877-95.

Anthropos. Ephemeris internationalis ethnologica et linguistica. International review of ethnology and linguistics. I-XX. Wien, 1906-25.

Antin, M. †The promised land. Boston and New York, 1912.

Antiquary, The. A magazine devoted to the study of the past. I-L. London, 1880-1914.

Anuchin, D. N. The use of sledges, boats, and horses at burials in Russia. Summarized from a "Memoir" by J. O. Wardrop, JAI, XXI.

Appun, F. Die Getränke der Indianer Guyanas. Globus, XVIII.

Apuleius. Golden ass.

Aquinas, Thomas, see Thomas Aquinas.

Arber, E. Editor. The first three English books on America. Birmingham, 1885. See Eden, R.

——Travels and works of Captain John Smith. In 2 vols. Edinburgh, 1910.

Arce, see Nuñez de Arce, G.

Archiv für Anthropologie; Zeitschrift für Naturgeschichte und Urgeschichte des Menschen. I-XLVII. Braunschweig, 1866-1923.

Archiv für Rassen- und Gesellschafts-Biologie, I-XVIII. Berlin, München, 1904-26.

Archiv für Religionswissenschaft. I-XXIII. Leipzig, 1898-1925.

Archivio per l'Antropologia e l'Etnologia. I-LI. Firenze, 1871-1921.

Aristotle. Works.

Asakawa, K. The early institutional life of Japan. Tokyo, 1903.

——The origin of the feudal land tenure in Japan. Reprinted from the Amer. Historical Review, XX, no. 1.

Ashton, J. Social life in the reign of Queen Anne. London, 1883.

Asiatic Quarterly Review, The. 1st ser., I-X, 1886-90. 2d ser., I-X, 1891-5. 3d ser., I-XXXIV, 1896-1912. London, 1886-91. Woking, 1891-1912.

Assam Census Report for 1891.

Athalye, Y. V. On betrothal among the Maháráshtra Bráhmanas. JASB, I.

Athenæus. Naucratitæ Deipnosophistarum.

Atkinson, J. J., see Lang, A.

Atlantic Monthly, The. A magazine of literature, science, art, and politics. I-CXXXVIII. Boston, 1857-1926.

Atwater, E. E. History of the colony of New Haven. New Haven, 1881.

Aucassin et Nicolette, see Suchier, H.

Aus Allen Weltteilen. Illustrirtes Familienblatt für Länder- und Völkerkunde. I-XXIX. Leipzig und Berlin, 1869-98.

Ausland, Das. I-LXVI. München, Stuttgart, 1828-93.

D'Aussy, see Le Grand d'Aussy.

Austen, L. Karigara customs. Man, XXIII.

*Australasian Association for the Advancement of Science (AAAS).

Autenrieth, G. A Homeric dictionary. Trans. from German by R. P. Keep. New York, 1889.

Avenel, G. d'. *Histoire économique de la propriété, des salaires, des denrées, et de tous les prix en général, depuis l'an 1200 jusque'en l'an 1800. Paris, 1894.

Bachofen, J. J. Das Mutterrecht. Eine Untersuchung über die Gynaikokratie der alten Welt nach ihrer religiösen und rechtlichen Natur. Stuttgart, 1861.

Bacon, A. M. Japanese girls and women. New York, 1902.

Bacon, F. Sylva Sylvarum: or, a natural history, in ten centuries. London, 1664.

*Baden-Powell, B. H. The land-systems of British India. Oxford, 1892.

Baegert, J. An account of the aboriginal inhabitants of the Californian peninsula. Smithson. Rep., 1863.

Bagehot, W. *Physics and politics, or thoughts on the application of the principles of natural selection and inheritance to political society. New York, 1873.

Bailey, J. An account of the wild tribes of the Veddahs of Ceylon: their habits, customs, and superstitions. Trans. of the Ethnol. Soc. of London, II.

Bailey, S. I. A new Peruvian route to the plain of the Amazon. Nat. Geog. Mag., XVII.

Baker, S. W. Ismailïa. New York, 1875.

——The Nile tributaries of Abyssinia, and the sword hunters of the Hamran Arabs. London, 1868.

Balch, E. G. Our Slavic fellow citizens. New York, 1910.

Baldwin, J. The Sampo. New York, 1912.

Balfour, H. Life history of the Aghori Fakir. JAI, XXVI.

Ballentyne, A., see Jenness, D.

Baltzly, A., see Woods, F. A.

Bälz, E. Bessessenheit und verwandte Zustände. Pol.-Anth. Rev., X.

Bancroft, H. H. *The native races of the Pacific states of North America. 5 vols. New York, 1875-6.

Bandelier, A. F. Aboriginal trephining in Bolivia. AA, VI.

Barclay. When people sneeze. N. Y. Times, July 27, 1902.

Baring-Gould, S. Origin and development of religious belief. London, 1869-70. New York, 1870.

——Strange survivals. London, 1892.

Barnard, J. Aborigines of Tasmania. AAAS, 1890.

Barnett, S. A. The poor of the world: India, Japan, and the United States. Fortnightly Rev. (n.s.), LIV.

Barrett, W. E. H. Notes on the customs and beliefs of the Wa-Giriama, etc., British East Africa. JAI, XLI.

Barrie, J. M. Auld licht idylls. New York, 1888.

Barrow, H. W. Aghoris and Aghorapanthis. JASB, III.

Bartels, M. *Die Medicin der Naturvölker. Ethnologische Beiträge zur Urgeschichte der Medicin. Leipzig, 1893.

——Der Würfelzauber Südafrikanischer Völker. Ztsft. f. Ethnol., XXXV. (50 figs.)

Barth, P. Die Philosophie der Geschichte als Sociologie. Leipzig, 1897.

Barthold, F. W. Die Geschichte der Hansa. Leipzig, 1862.

Barton, F. R. Children's games in British New Guinea. JAI, XXXVIII.

——Tattooing in South Eastern New Guinea. JAI, XLVIII.

Barton, G. A. An androgynous Babylonian divinity. American Oriental Society. Section for the historical study of religions, III.

——*A sketch of Semitic origins. New York, 1902.

Barton, J. Notes on the Kipsikis or Lumbwa Tribe of Kenya Colony. JAI, LIII.

——Notes on the Suk Tribe of Kenia Colony. JAI, LI.

Baruch, S. Why women lack great originality. N. Y. Times, Aug. 4, 1915.

Basedow, H. Notes on the natives of Bathurst Island, North Australia. JAI, XLIII.

Bassett-Smith, P. W. Aborigines of North-west Australia. JAI, XXIII.

Basseur, Kommandant. Die Gewinnung des Kupfers durch die Neger in Katanga. In "Le Mouvement géographique," 25 Juli 1897. Review in Globus, LXXII.

Bastian, A. *Afrikanische Reisen. Bremen, 1859.

——Die Culturländer des Alten Amerika. Berlin, 1878.

——*Die Deutsche Expedition an der Loango-Küste. Vol. II. Jena, 1874.

——Ethnologisches Bilderbuch mit erklärendem Text. Berlin, 1887.

——Ideale Welten. Nach uranographischen Provinzen in Wort und Bild. Berlin, 1892.

——Der Mensch in der Geschichte. Leipzig, 1860.

——Die mikronesischen Colonien aus ethnologischen Gesichtspunkten. Berlin, 1899.

Basu, K. Funeral rites and ceremonies. JASB, II.

——Note on some curious customs among the Kochs. JASB, III.

——On the minor Vaishnava sects of Bengal. JASB, I.

Batty, R. B. Notes on the Yoruba country. JAI, XIX.

Baudouin, M. L'influence du maria-chinage sur les formes de natalité. Bull. Soc. d'Anthr. de Paris, 1904.

Beardmore, E. The natives of Mowat, Daudai, New Guinea. JAI, XIX.

Beauchamp, W. M. Oneniote. HAI, pt. II.

Beaver, W. N., see Chinnery, E. W. P.

Bebel, A. Die Frau und der Sozialismus. Stuttgart, 1905.

Beck, L. *Die Geschichte des Eisens in technischer und kulturgeschichtlicher Beziehung. Braunschweig, 1881-1903.

Becke, L. Pacific tales. New York.

Becker, W. A. Charikles. Bilder altgriechischer Sitte, zur genaueren Kenntniss des griechischen Privatlebens. Neu bearbeitet von Hermann Göll. Berlin, 1877-78.

Becker, W. A. und Hermann, K. F. Charikles. 3 Bände. Leipzig, 1854.

Beckwith, M. W. Hawaiian romance of Laieikawai. BAE, XXXIII.

——Hawaiian shark Aumakua. AA, XIX.

Beckwith, P. Notes on customs of the Dakotahs. Smithson Rep. for 1886, pt. I.

Beer, T. The mauve decade. New York, 1926.

Behrens, Dr. Der Kannibalismus der Chinesen. Globus, LXXXI.

Beiträge zur Assyriologie und vergleichenden semitischen Sprachwissenschaft. I-X. Leipzig, 1890-1913.

Belknap, J. The history of New Hampshire. 3 vols. Boston, 1791-2.

Bell, A. An inquiry into the policy and justice of the prohibition of the use of grain in the distilleries. In Economical Tracts printed by Lord Overstone. Edited by J. R. MacCulloch. London, 1859.

Beloch, J. Griechische Geschichte. 4 Bände. Strassburg, 1904.

Bent, J. T. The ruined cities of Mashonaland. London, 1892.

——The sacred city of the Ethiopians. London, 1893.

Bent, T. The Ansairee of Asia Minor. Discussion by R. Jones. JAI, XX.

Beowulf.

Bergel, J. Die Eheverhältnisse der Alten Juden im Vergleiche mit den Griechischen und Römischen. Leipzig, 1881.

Bergen, F. D. The tapestry of the new world. Scribner's, XVI.

Bernhöft, F. *Verwandtschaftsnamen und Eheformen der nordamerikanischen Volksstämme. Rostock, 1888.

Bertrand. Bertrands Reise ins Land der Barotse. Anon. Globus, LXXIV.

Best, E. Ceremonial performances pertaining to birth, as performed by the Maori of New Zealand in past times. JAI, XLIV.

——Customs and superstitions of the Maori. AAAS, 1898.

——Maori folk-lore. AAAS, 1904.

——Maori religion. AAAS, 1909.

Bethencourt, J. de. Le Canarien. Rouen, 1874.

Bey, K. A. The emancipation of Egyptian women. Asiatic Quar. Rev., 3d ser., VIII.

Biart, L. Les Aztèques, histoire, mœurs, coutumes. Paris, 1885.

Bible, The Holy. (References are to book, chapter, verse. American Revised Version is used in most cases.)

*Bijdragen tot de taal-, land-, en volkenkunde van Nederlandsch-Indië. I-LXXXII. 'sGravenhage, 1853-1926 (Bijd.).

Binger, Capt. Du Niger au golfe de Guinée par le pays de Kong et le Mossi. Paris, 1892.

Biot, E. C. De l'abolition de l'esclavage ancien en occident. Paris, 1840.

Bishop, A. L., see Gregory, H. E.

Bishop, I. L. B. Among the Tibetans.
New York, 1894.

——Korea and her neighbors. New
York, 1898.

——The Mantzu of Western Sze-
Chuan. Anthro. Rev. in JAI, XVIII.

Bitterfeld, K. Hand und Schutzbrief.
Volksglauben. Am Ur-Quell, I.

Blackstone, W. Commentaries of the
laws of England. 1857.

Blagden, C. O., see Skeat, W. W.

Blair, W. Slavery amongst the Romans. Edinburgh, 1833.

Bland, R. H. Aborigines of Western
Australia in the early history of
that colony. JAI, XVI.

*Blau, L. Das Altjüdische Zauber-
wesen. Strassburg, 1898.

——Angelology. Jewish Encyclopedia,
I.

Blum, H. Neu-Guinea und der Bis-
marckarchipel. Berlin, 1900.

Blumentritt, F. Hochzeitsgebräuche
der Zambalen. Globus, XLIX.

——Die Igorroten von Pangasinan.
Nach den Mittheilungen des Mis-
sionäre P. Fr. Mariano Rodriguez.
Mitth. d. K.K. Geogr. Gesellschaft.
in Wien, 1900.

——Die Philippinen. Hamburg, 1900.

——Versuch einer ethnographie der
Philippinen. In Petermanns Mit-
theilungen. Ergänzungsband XV,
Ergänzungsheft 57.

Blümner, H. Lehrbuch der Griechi-
schen Privatalterthümer von Dr.
K. F. Hermann. Freiberg I.B. und
Tübingen, 1882.

Boas, F. Articles: Religion; Soul.
HAI.

——*The Central Eskimo. BAE, VI.

——The development of the culture
of north-west America. Science,
XII (o.s.).

——Ethnological problems in Canada.
JAI, XL.

——*Ethnology of the Kwakiutl.
BAE, XXXV, pt. II.

——Facial paintings of the Indians
of Northern British Columbia.
Memoirs of the American Museum
of Natural History, 11, 1. The Jesup
North Pacific Expedition, I. Ab-
stracts by C. L. Henning under
title, "Die Gesichtsbemalungen der
Indianer von Nord-British-Colum-
bia." Globus, LXXIV.

——The houses of the Kwakiutl Indians, British Columbia. Proceedings of the USNM, 1888.

——The mind of primitive man. New
York, 1911.

——The mythology of the Bella Coola
Indians. Memoirs of the Amer. Mus.
of Nat. Hist., II.

——Mythology of Bella Coola Indians.
A review by E. S. Hartland in
Folklore, XI.

——Religious beliefs of the Central
Eskimo. PSM, LVII.

——*The social organization and secret societies of the Kwakiutl Indians. USNM, 1895.

——Tsimshian mythology. BAE,
XXXI.

Bobrinskoy, A. Note de M. Th. Vol-
kow, relative aux trois volumes,
d'Archéologie et d'Anthropologie
russes, de M. le comte A. Bobrinskoy. Bull. et Mem. Soc. d'Anthr. de
Paris, V, ser. II.

Bock, C. *Reis in Oost- en Zuid-Bor-
neo. 'sGravenhage, 1887.

Boeck, R. India and the Hindus. Lecture reported in N. Y. Times, Feb.
28, 1898.

Boggiani, G. I Caduvei. Rome, 1895.

Bogoras, W. The Chukchi of Northeastern Asia. AA, III.

Bolton, H. C. The counting-out
rhymes of children; their antiquity,
origin, and wide distribution. A
study in folk-lore. London, 1888.

Bolton, H. E. Articles: Nacono tribe;
Neche, a Hasinai tribe; Tama;
Tawehash; Xinesi. HAI, pt. II.

Bonney, F. On some customs of the
aborigines of the River Darling.
New South Wales. JAI, XIII.

Bonwick, J. Daily life and origin of the Tasmanians. London, 1870.

Book of the dead. In "Egyptian literature." Introd. by E. Wilson. Revised ed. London and New York. 1901.

Bordier, A. La géographie médicale. Paris, 1884.

Borlase, W. Antiquities, historical and monumental of the county of Cornwall. London, 1769.

Borodine, N. The Ural Cossacks and their fisheries. PSM, XLIII.

Boshart, A. Zehn Jahre Afrikanischen Lebens. Leipzig, 1898.

Bosman, W. A new and accurate description of the coast of Guinea, divided into the Gold, the Slave, and the Ivory Coasts. (Trans. from Dutch.) London, 1721.

Boulger, D. C. Belgium: Geography and statistics. Encyclopedia Britannica, III. 11th Edition. Cambridge (Eng.), 1910-11.

Bourdeau, L. Conquête du monde animal. Paris, 1885.

——Les forces de l'industrie: progrès de la puissance humaine. Paris, 1884.

Bourke, J. G. Distillation by early American Indians. AA, VII (o.s.).

——*The Medicine-Men of the Apache. BAE, IX.

——Scatalogic rites of all nations. Cambridge, Mass., 1891.

——The Snake-Dance of the Moquis of Arizona. New York, 1884.

Bourne, H. R. F. Civilization in Congoland: a story of international wrong-doing. London, 1903.

Bousset, D. W. Die Religion des Judenthums im neutestamentlichen Zeitalter. Berlin, 1903.

Bowen, L. deK. When Chicago was very young. Atl. Mo., CXXXVII.

Boye, V. Udgravning af en Jaettestue ved Hammer. Annaler, 1862.

Brand, J. Popular antiquities of Great Britain. 3 vols. London, 1870. 2 vols. London and New York, 1905.

Brandeis, A. Ethnographische Beobachtungen über die Nauru-Insulaner. Globus, XCI.

Braut-Sero, J. O. Dekanawideh, the law-maker of the Caniengahakas, Man, 1901, 166-170. Reported in AA, IV.

Breasted, J. H. The Edwin Smith papyrus. New York Hist. Soc., Quarterly Bull., VI.

Brewster, A. B. Circumcision in Noikoro, Noemalu, and Mboumbudho, Fiji. JAI, XLIX.

——Hill tribes of Fiji. London, 1922. Reviewed in N. Y. Times, Dec. 10, 1922.

Bridges, T. *Manners and customs of the Firelanders. A Voice for South America, XIII.

Brinton, D. G. American hero-myths. Philadelphia, 1882.

——The conception of love in some American languages. Read before the Amer. Phil. Society, Nov. 5, 1886. Philadelphia, 1886. (Extract from this is in the author's Essays of an Americanist.)

——Essays of an Americanist. Philadelphia, 1891.

——The myths of the New World. Philadelphia, 1896.

——*Nagualism. Philadelphia, 1894.

——The "Nation" as an element in anthropology. Smithson. Rep., 1893.

——Nervous disease in low races and stages of culture. Science, XX.

——Races and peoples: lectures on the science of ethnography. New York, 1890.

——The religious sentiment, its source and aim. New York, 1876.

British Association for the Advancement of Science. Reports of the meetings, I-XCIV. London, 1832-1926.

Brodeur, A. G. The Prose Edda, by Snorri Sturlason. Trans. from Icelandic by Brodeur. New York, 1916.

Brodhead, J. R. Documents relative to the colonial history of the state of New York. Vol. I. Albany, 1856.

Bromilow, W. E. Dobuan (Papua) beliefs and folklore. AAAS, 1911.

——Some manners and customs of the

Dobuans of S. E. Papua. AAAS, 1909.

Brown, A. First republic in America; an account of the origin of this na tion. Boston and New York, 1898.

Brown, A. R. Notes on the social organization of Australian tribes. JAI, XLVIII, LIII.

——Three tribes of Western Australia. JAI, XLIII.

Brown, F. Writing from China. Ill. Christian World, July, 1897.

Brown, G. Origin of totemism. AAAS, 1911.

——Recent journey to New Guinea and New Britain. AAAS, 1898.

Brown, J. T. Circumcision rites of the Becwana tribes. JAI, LI.

Brown, R. G. The Taungbyón festival, Burma. JAI, XLV.

Browne, J. A history of the highlands. 4 vols. Glasgow, 1843.

Browne, J. C. Biology and Ethics. PSM, XLIV.

Bruce, P. A. Economic history of Virginia in the seventeenth century. 2 vols. New York and London, 1896.

Brunache, P. Le Centre de l'Afrique. Paris, 1894.

Bruns, I. Frauenemancipation in Athen, ein Beitrag zur Attischen Kulturgeschichte des Fünften und Vierten Jahrhunderts. Kiliae, 1900.

Bruun, D. Hulcboerne. I Syd Tunis. København, 1895.

Bücher, K. Arbeit und Rhythmus. Leipzig, 1896, 1899, 1902.

Buchner, M. Kunst und Witz der Neger. Ausland, 1884.

Buckland, A. W. Message-sticks and prayer-sticks. Antiq., XXXIII.

——Points of contact between old world myths and customs and the Navajo myth, entitled "The Mountain Chant." JAI, XXII.

——Surgery and superstition in Neolithic times. JAI, XI.

Buell, R. Amulets. AA, XII.

Buhl, F. P. W. *Die socialen Verhältnisse der Israeliten. Berlin, 1899.

Bühler, G. The laws of Manu. Trans.

by Bühler. In F. Max Müller's Sacred books of the east, vol. XXV. Oxford, 1886. See Müller.

Bulletin de l'Institut Egyptien, Cairo. Alexandrie, 1860-86. Le Caire, 1886-97.

Bulletin of the American Academy of Medicine. Later called the Journal of Sociologic Medicine. I-XX. Easton (Pa.), 1891-1919.

Bulletin of the American Museum of Natural History. I-LV. New York, 1881-1926.

Bulletin of the Geographical Society of Philadelphia. I-XXIII. Philadelphia, 1895-1925.

Bulletins et Mémoires de la Société d'Anthropologie de Paris. 1st ser., I-VI, 1859-65. 2d ser., I-XII, 1866-77. 3d ser., I-XII, 1878-89. 4th ser., I-X, 1890-9. 5th ser., I-X, 1900-09. 6th ser., I-VIII, 1910-17. Paris, 1859-1917.

Bülow, W. von. Die Ehegesetze der Samoaner. Globus, LXXIII.

——Kenntnisse und Fertigkeiten der Samoaner. Globus, LXXII.

——Samoanische Sagen. Globus, LXIX. Quoted in Williamson's "Central Polynesia."

——Samoanische Schöpfungssage und Urgeschichte. Globus, LXXI. Quoted in Williamson's "Cent. Polynesia."

——Der Stammbaum der Könige von Samoa. Globus, LXXI. Quoted in Williamson's "Cent. Polynesia."

——Das ungeschriebene Gesetz der Samoaner. Globus, LXIX. Quoted in Williamson's "Cent. Polynesia."

——Der vulkanische Ausbruch auf der Insel Savaii (Deutsch-Samoa). Globus, LXXXIII. Quoted in Williamson's "Cent. Polynesia."

Burckhardt, J. C. Griechische Kulturgeschichte. 3 Bände. 2te Aufl. Stuttgart, 1898.

——Die Kultur der Renaissance in Italien. Basel, 1860.

Burckhardt, J. L. Arabic Proverbs. London, 1830.

——Notes on the Bedouins and Wahabys. London, 1830.

——*Travels in Arabia. 2 vols. London, 1829.

Bureau of American Ethnology, *Annual Report of the United States. (BAE) I-XLVI. Washington, 1881-1925.

Bureau of American Ethnology, *Bulletin of the United States. (BAE Bull.) Nos. I-LXXXI. Washington, 1887-1923.

Burke, W. The Fire walkers of Fiji. Frank Leslie's Monthly, April, 1903.

Burnaby, A. Travels through the middle settlements of North America in 1750 and 1760. London, 1775.

Burnett, F. H. The head of the house of Coombe. New York, 1922.

Burns. In Wide World Mag., I.

Burr, G. L. The literature of witchcraft. Amer. Hist. Assoc. Papers IV. New York, 1890.

Burrows. G. *†The land of the Pigmies. London, 1898.

——On the natives of the Upper Welle District of the Belgian Congo. JAI, XXVIII.

Burton, I., see Burton, R. F.

Burton, R. F. Personal narrative of a pilgrimage to El-Medinah and Meccah. London, 1856.

Burton, R. F. and Burton, I. Lady Burton's edition of her husband's Arabian Nights; translated literally from the Arabic; prepared for household reading by J. H. McCarthy. 6 vols. London, 1886-7.

Buschan, G. Der Stand unserer Kenntnis über die Basken. Globus, LXXIX.

Butler, M. A history of the commonwealth of Kentucky. Louisville, 1834.

Büttner, C. G. *Das Hinterland von Walfischbai und Angra Pequena. (Bound in vol. with title "Kamerun.") Carl Winter, Heidelberg, 1884.

——Aus Natur- und Völkerleben Südwest-Afrikas. Ausland, 1882.

Byron, Lord G. G. N. Don Juan.

Cæsar. De Bello Gallico et civili Pompeiano.

Cæsar, von Heisterbach. Works.

Caine, T. H. H. The Christian. New York, 1908.

Caird, E. The evolution of religion. New York, 1894.

Cairnes, J. E. The slave power: its character, career, and probable designs. New York, 1862.

Calderon, Y. Bolivia—a country without a debt. National Geographic Magazine, XVIII.

Caldwell, R. On demonolatry in Southern India. JASB, I.

Callaway, H. *The religious systems of the Amazulu. Natal, 1868-70.

Cameron, A. L. P. Notes on some tribes of New South Wales. JAI, XIV.

Campbell, H. *Differences in the nervous organization of man and woman. London, 1891.

Campbell, J. M. The Bharwád Jang or Shepherds' Wedding. JASB, IV.

——Honey. In Indian Antiquary, Bombay, Sept., 1895. Quoted in AA, IX (o.s.).

Cantor, M. Das Gesetz im Zufall. Berlin, 1877.

Carey, B. S. and Tuck, H. N. The Chin hills. Rangoon, 1896.

Carlsen, F. Benin in Guinea und seine rätselhaften Bronzen. Globus, LXXII.

Carmichael, J. Sir John Lubbock and the religion of savages. PSM, XLVIII.

Carr, L. Mounds of the Mississippi valley. Smithson. Rep., 1891.

Carstens, H. Totengebräuche aus Dithmarschen. Am Urquell, I.

Carter, J. C. Law: its origin, growth and function. New York and London, 1907.

Carus, P. Pre-Christian crosses as symbols of Chthonic deities. Open Court, XVIII.

Carver, J. Three years travels through the interior parts of North America. Philadelphia, 1789.

Casanowicz, I. M. Book review of Aberglaube und Volksmedizin im Lande der Bibel by T. Canaan. AA, XVIII.

——"The fish in cult, myth, and symbol." Proceedings of the Anthropological Society of Washington. AA, XIX.

——The Jews of Mzab. A review of M. Huguet's account. AA, VII.

Castiglione, B. The book of the courtier (1528). Trans. by L. E. Opdyke. New York, 1903.

Castrén, M. A. Vorlesungen über die Finnische Mythologie. St. Petersburg, 1853.

Catlin, G. *†Letters and notes on the manners, customs, and condition of the North American Indians, written during eight years' travel amongst the wildest tribes of Indians in North America. 2 vols. Third edit. New York, 1844.

——Life amongst the Indians. London, 1861.

Cator, D. Everyday life among the head-hunters. New York, 1905.

Catullus. Poems.

Cayley-Webster, H. Through New Guinea and the cannibal countries. London, 1898.

Century Monthly Magazine, The. I-CXI. New York, 1870-1926.

Chadwick, H. M. The ancient Teutonic Priesthood. Folk-Lore, XI.

Chalmers, G. Political annals of the present united colonies from their settlement to the peace of 1763. 2 vols. London, 1780.

Chalmers, J. Notes on the natives of Kiwai Island, Fly River, British New Guinea. JAI, XXXIII.

——Toaripi. JAI, XXVII.

Chamberlain, A. F. Articles: Creeks-Busk; Kutenai. HAI.

——Women's languages. AA, XIV.

Chamberlain, B. II. Notes on some minor Japanese religious practices. JAI, XXII.

Chambers, R. W. The hidden children. New York, 1913.

Champion, A. M. The Atharaka. JAI, XLII.

Chandler, F. W. Romance of roguery. New York, 1899.

Chanler, W. A. Through jungle and desert. New York, 1896.

Charles, R. H. The book of Enoch. Society for Promoting Christian Knowledge. London, 1917.

——The book of Jubilees or the little Genesis. Trans. from the Ethiopic. London, 1902.

Charnay, D. Les anciennes villes du nouveau monde. Paris, 1885.

Chastellux, Marquis de. Travels in North-America, in the years 1780, 1781, and 1782. London, 1787.

Chatelain, H. In Illust. Africa. March, 1896.

Chatlopadhyay, K. P. Levirate and kinship in India. Man, XXII.

Chaube, R. G. Ancestors as messengers of death. JASB, V.

——Notes on ancestor-worship. JASB, V.

China Review, The. I-VI. New York, 1921-4.

Chinnery, E. W. P. The application of anthropological methods to tribal development in New Guinea. JAI, XLIX, 1919.

——Stone-work and gold fields in British New Guinea. JAI, XLIX.

Chinnery, E. W. P. and Beaver, W. N. Notes on the initiation ceremonies of the Koko, Papua. JAI, XLV.

Chowbe, Pandit Ram Gharib. On Hindu beliefs about trees. JASB, V.

Christian, F. W. *The Caroline Islands. London, 1899.

Christison, D. The Gauchos of San Jorge, Central Uruguay. JAI, XI.

Cicero. Works.

Cincinnati Lancet-Clinic, The. A weekly journal of medicine and surgery. LVII-XCI. Cincinnati, 1887-1904.

Citerni, C., see Vannutelli, L.

Ciszewski, S. Künstliche Verwandtschaft bei den Südslaven. Globus, LXXII. (Bücherschau.)

Clark, A. H. Ingenious method of causing death employed by the Obeah men of the West Indies. AA, XIV.

Clark, W., see Lewis, M.

Clarke, H. *The right of property in trees on the land of another, as an ancient institution. JAI, XIX.

Clavigo, see Gonçales de Clavigo.

Clay, A. T. Personal names from cuneiform inscriptions of the Cassite period. Yale Oriental Series. Vol. I. New Haven, 1913.

Clemens. S. L. Works.

Clement, E. Ethnographical notes on the Western-Australian aborigines. Internationales Archiv für Ethnographie, XVI.

Clement, K. J. Das Recht der Salischen Franken. Berlin, 1876.

Clifford, H. Studies in brown humanity. London, 1898.

Clodd, E. Animism, the seed of religion. London, 1905.

——Magic in names and in other things. New York, 1921.

Cloud, H. R. "The land of the setting sun." The Kit-Kat, II.

Clozel, M. F. J. The Banziris of the Congo basin. PSM, XLIX.

Cobham, H. The Idem secret society. Jour. of African Society, V.

Cockayne, T. O. Leechdoms, wortcunning and starcraft of early England. London, 1864-66.

Codex, in Corpus Iuris Civilis.

Codrington, R. The central Angoniland district of the British Central Africa protectorate. Geographical Journal, XI.

Codrington, R. H. *The Melanesians. Oxford, 1891.

——On poisoned arrows in Melanesia. JAI, XIX.

——*On social regulations in Melanesia. JAI, XVIII.

——*Religious beliefs and practices in Melanesia. JAI, X.

——Totems in Melanesia. AAAS, 1890.

Cognetti de Martiis, S. Le forme primitive nella evoluzione economica. Torino, 1881.

Cole, F. C. Book review of "A Study of Bagobo Ceremonial, Magic and Myth," by Laura Watson Benedict. AA, XX.

Cole, H. Notes on the Wagogo of German East Africa. JAI, XXXII.

Collections of the Massachusetts Historical Society. 1st-7th series, each, vols. I-X. Boston, 1792-1925.

Collector of the Khandesh district. JASB, V.

Collins, D. An account of the English colony in New South Wales, from its first settlement in Jan. 1788 to Aug. 1801. London, 1804.

Collins, W. The moonstone. New York, 1908.

Collier, P. England and the English. New York, 1910.

Colmeiro, M. *Historia de la Economia Política en España. 2 vols. Madrid, 1863.

Colquhoun, A. R. Whirlpool of Europe. Austria-Hungary and the Hapsburgs. New York, 1907.

Compton, R. H. String figures from New Caledonia and the Loyalty Islands. JAI, XLIX.

Conant, L. L. Primitive number systems. Smithson. Rep., 1892.

Conde, J. A. Historia de la Dominacion de los Arabes in España. Paris, 1840.

Conder, C. R. Hittite ethnology. JAI, XVII.

——The present condition of the native tribes in Bechuanaland. JAI, XVI.

Congrès International des Américanistes. I-XXIre session, 1875-1924.

Connolly, R. M. *Social life in Fanti-Land. JAI, XXVI.

Conradt, L. Die Ngúmba in Südkamerun. Globus, LXXXI.

Conrau, G. Leichenfeierlichkeiten bei den Banyang am oberen Calabar (Crossriver), Nordkamerun. Globus, LXXV.

Constant, A. L., see Levi, Eliphas.

Contemporary Review, The. I-CXXX. London, 1866-1926.

Contributions to North American Ethnology. I-IX. Washington, 1877-93.

Conway, W. M. Climbing and exploration in the Karakoram-Himalayas. London, 1894.

Conybeare, F. C. Decay of the belief in the devil. International Monthly, V.

Cook, A. C. The aborigines of the Canary Islands. AA, II.

Cook, J. A voyage to the Pacific Ocean. In 3 vols. Dublin, 1784.

Cook, K. R. The fathers of Jesus: a study of the lineage of the Christian doctrines and traditions. 2 vols. London, 1886.

Cook, Lady. The sign of the cross. American Antiquarian and Oriental Journal, XIX.

Cook, S. A. Israel and Totemism. Jewish Quarterly Review, XIV.

Cooke, G. H. Te Pito Te Henua, known as Itapa Nui; commonly called Easter Island, South Pacific Ocean. USNM, 1897, pt. I.

Cooper, H. S. Coral Lands. Strange funeral ceremony in the Tonga Islands, South Sea. Quoted from Cooper's "Coral Islands." Anthropological Miscellanea. JAI, X.

Cooper, T. T. T. T. Cooper beim Volke der Mischmis in Assam. Globus, XXVI.

Cope, E. D. The relation of the sexes to government. PSM, XXXIII.

Corbin, A. L. *The law and the judges. Yale Review, III.

——Rights and duties. Yale Law Jr., XXXIII.

Cordier, H. Les sociétés secrètes chinoises. Rev. d'Ethnog., VII, 52-72.

Corpus Iuris Civilis (the codification of Roman Law completed under the direction of Justinian I).

Corpus Poeticum Boreale, the Poetry of the old Northern Tongue, from the earliest times to the 13th Century. See G. Vigfusson and F. Y. Powell, Editors.

Cosmopolitan, The. I-LXIX. Rochester (N. Y.), 1886-1920.

Coto, Fr. T. Diccionario de la Lengua Cakchiquel (MS.) in the Library of the American Philosophical Society at Philadelphia.

Coudenhove, H. African folk. Atlantic Monthly, CXXVIII.

——Feminism in Nyasaland. Atlantic Monthly, CXXXII.

——Nyasaland Sketches. In the Chikala range. Atl. Mo., CXXXI.

Coulanges, F. de. La cité antique. Paris, 1874.

——The origin of property in land. Trans. by Margaret Ashley. London, 1891.

Cowan, J. †The Maoris of New Zealand. Christchurch, 1910.

Cox, K. Concerning painting. Considerations theoretical and historical. New York, 1918.

Crane, L. Indians of the Enchanted Desert. Atlantic Monthly, CXXXVI.

Crane, T. F. The legend of the soul dispossessed by a devil. Letter to The Nation, XCIII.

Cranz, D. Historie von Grönland bis 1779. 2 Bde. Leipzig, 1780.

Crasselt, F. Japanische Erziehungsgrundsätze in Schrift und Praxis. Globus, XCII.

Crauford, L. Victoria River Downs Station, Northern Territory, South Australia. JAI, XXIV.

Crawford, C. E. G. Notes from cases tried at Thana from May to Sept., 1890. JASB, II.

Crawfurd, J. *History of the Indian Archipelago. 2 vols. London, 1820.

Crawley, A. E. The mystic rose; a study of primitive marriage. London and New York, 1902.

——Sexual taboo: a study in the relations of the sexes. JAI, XXIV.

Crawley, E. S. Origin of number systems. PSM, LI.

Creagh, S. M. Notes on the Loyalty Islands. AAAS, 1892.

Creighton, M. Historical essays and reviews. New York, 1902.

Crichton-Browne, H. Dwarfs and dwarf worship. Nature, XLV.

Crooke, W. *The hill tribes of the Central Indian hills. JAI, XXVIII.

——Nudity in India in custom and ritual. JAI, XLIX.

——Review of his paper describing ethnographical research in Northern India. JAI, XXII.

——The stability of caste and tribal groups in India. JAI, XLIV.

Culin, S. Games. HAI, pt. I.

——Games of the North American Indians. BAE, XXIV.

——Hawaiian games. AA, I.

Cummins, S. L. Sub-tribes of the Bahr-el-Ghazal Dinkas. JAI, XXXIV.

Cumont, F. V. M. Les mystères de Mithra. Bruxelles, 1913. Trans. into English by F. J. McCormack. Chicago, 1903.

Cunha, J. G. da. An address on amulets and talismans. JASB, I.

——The nasal index in biological anthropology. JASB, II.

——Notes on the vernacular language of Konkan. JASB, II.

——Numismatic notes on the Fanam of South India. JASB, II.

——On the primitive and autonomous coinage of India. JASB, II.

——Professor Lombroso and criminal anthropology with reference to the population of Bombay. JASB, II.

Cunha, J. T. de. Note on the statistics of suicide. JASB, I.

——Omens among the Hindus. JASB, I.

——On the belief in the evil eye among the modern Persians. JASB, I.

——On the evil eye among the Bunnias. JASB, I.

Cunningham, A. Ladak. London, 1854.

Cunnington, W. A. String figures and tricks from Central Africa. JAI, XXXVI.

Cunow, H. Die soziale Verfassung des Inkareichs. Eine Untersuchung des altperuanischen Agrarkommunismus. Stuttgart, 1896.

——Verwandtschafts - Organizationen der Australneger. Stuttgart, 1894.

Curr, E. M. *The Australian race. 4 vols. Melbourne and Leipzig, 1887.

Curtin, R. G. Medical superstitions of precious stones, etc. Bull. Amer. Acad. Med., VII. Philadelphia, 1907.

Curtius, E. History of Greece. Trans. 5 vols. London, 1868-73.

Cushing, F. H. My adventures in Zuñi. Century Mag., IV.

——Observations relative to the origin of the Fylfot or Swastika. AA, IX.

——Outlines of Zuñi creation myths. BAE, XIII.

——Pueblo pottery and Zuñi culture-growth. BAE, IV.

——A study of Pueblo pottery. BAE, IV.

Cutler, J. E. Lynch-law, an investigation into the history of lynching in the United States. New York, 1905.

Czaplicka, M. A. *†Aboriginal Siberia. A study in social anthropology. Oxford, 1914.

Daily Consular Reports. U.S. Dept. of Commerce and Labor. Washington.

Dale, G. Note concerning the Bondei people of Africa. PSM, I.

——Some African war customs. Reported in PSM, XLIX.

Dall, W. H. On masks, labrets, and certain aboriginal customs, with an inquiry into the bearing of their geographical distribution. BAE, III.

Dallaway, J. Constantinople ancient and modern, with excursions to the shores and islands of the archipelago and to the Troad. London, 1797.

Dalton, E. T. *Descriptive ethnology of Bengal. Calcutta, 1872.

——The "Kols" of Chota-Nagpore. Trans. Ethnol. Soc., VI.

Dalton, O. M., *see* Read, C. H.

Dana, C. E. The color red. PSM, LVII.

Dana, M. Voodoo, its effects on the Negro race. Metrop. Mag., XXVII (1908).

Dana, R. H. Two years before the mast. London, 1841.

Danielevski, G. P. The fugitives from New Russia (Russ.). St. Petersburg, 1884.

Danks, B. Burial customs of New Britain. JAI, XXI.

——*Marriage customs of the New Britain group. JAI, XVIII.

——New Britain and its people. AAAS, 1892.

——Savage life in New Britain. AAAS, 1909.

——*Shell money of New Britain. JAI, XVII.

Dante Alighieri. Divina Commedia.

Danvers, F. C. The Portuguese in India. Being a history of the rise and decline of their Eastern Empire. 2 vols. London, 1894.

Darinsky, A. Die Familie bei den Kaukasischen Völkern. Ztsft. f. vergl. Rechtswissenschaft, XIV.

Darmesteter, J. The Zend-Avesta. In F. M. Müller's "Sacred books of the East," vols. IV, XXIII. *See* Müller.

Darwin, C. R. The descent of man and selection in relation to sex. 2d edit. New York, 1898.

——The same work. Home Library Ed. New York, no date.

——The effects of cross and self fertilization in the vegetable kingdom. New York, 1877.

——The origin of species by means of natural selection. Home Library Ed. New York, no date.

——The variation of animals and

plants under domestication. Judd and Co., New York, 1868.

——Voyage of a naturalist. Home Library Edition. New York, no date.

Darwin, F. Life and letters of Charles Darwin. 2 vols. New York, 1887, 1898-9.

Darwin, F. and Seward, C. C. More letters of Charles Darwin. 2 vols. New York, 1903.

Darwin, G. H. *Marriages between first cousins in England and their effects. Jour. of the Royal Statistical Soc., XXXVIII.

Dasent, G. W. The story of Burnt Njal or life in Iceland at the end of the tenth century. From the Icelandic of the Njals Saga. 2 vols. Edinburgh, 1861.

Dasent, G. W., *see* also Vigfússon, G.

Davey, J. B., *see* Stannus, H. S.

Davids, J. Uber die Pygmäen am oberen Ituri. Globus, LXXXV.

Davidson, A. A. The Murchison and Davenport ranges, Central Australia. Geographical Journal, XXIX.

Davie, M. R. *†The evolution of war. A study of its rôle in early societies, New Haven, 1929.

Davies, L. J. The Chinese "Boxers." Nat. Geog. Mag., XI.

Davis, J. J. The iron puddler. My life in the rolling mills and what came of it. New York, 1922.

Davy, J. An account of the interior of Ceylon and of its inhabitants; with travels in that island. London, 1821.

Dawkins, W. B. Cave-hunting, researches on the evidence of caves respecting the early inhabitants of Europe. London, 1874.

——Early man in Britain and his place in the tertiary period. London, 1880.

Dawson, J. Australian aborigines in

the Western district of Victoria. Melbourne, 1881.

Day, C. Policy and administration of the Dutch in Java. New York, 1904.

Day, C. S. The crow's nest. New York, 1922.

Debacq, G. Libéraux et démagogues au moyen âge. Paris, 1872.

DeBooy, T. Lucayan remains on the Caicos Islands. AA, XIV.

Decle, L. Funeral rites and ceremonies amongst the 'Tshinyai.' Reviewed in JAI, XXIII.

——On some Matabele customs. JAI, XXIII.

Delitzsch, F. Babel und Bibel. Leipzig, 1902.

Dellenbaugh, F. S. *†The North-Americans of yesterday. New York and London, 1902.

Demoor, J., Massart, J., Vandervelde, E. L'Evolution régressive en biologie et en sociologie. Paris, 1897.

Denecke, A. Beiträge zur Entwickelungsgeschichte des gesellschaftlichen Anstandsgefühls in Deutschland. Dresden, 1891.

Dennett, R. E. Notes on the philosophy of the Bavili [Luango]. JAI, XXXV.

Denno, W. J., see Overton, F.

Deschamps, E. Reise auf Cypern. Globus, LXXII.

Deshmukh, M. G. On the habits of a Jain ascetic. JASB, I.

Deshmukh, R. B. G. H. On Hindu sacrifices. JASB, I.

Dezobry, C. L. Rome au siècle d'Auguste. 4 tomes. Paris, 1875.

Diamond, H. M. The cult and early economic organization. Scientific Mo., XVIII.

——Religion, a factor in primitive economic adaptation. Doctor's thesis deposited in Yale Univ. library.

Dill, S. Roman society from Nero to Marcus Aurelius. London and New York, 1904.

Diodorus Siculus. Works.

Dionysius of Halicarnassus. Archæologia.

Dixon, R. B. Achomawi and Atsugewi Indians of Northern California. AA, X.

——Book review of "The Oraons of Chota Nagpur: their history, economic life and social organization," by Sarat Chandra Roy. AA, XVIII.

——Piejunan family. HAI, pt. II.

——Some aspects of the American shaman. Jour. of Amer. Folk-Lore, XXI.

Dixon, R. B. and Hodge, F. W. Palaihuihan. HAI, pt. II.

Dixon, W. A. The morbid proclivities and retrogressive tendencies in the offspring of mulattoes. Medical News, Philadelphia, LXI.

Dobschütz, E. von. Christian life in the primitive church. Trans. by G. Bremner. New York.

Dodge, R. I. Our wild Indians. Hartford, 1882.

——The plains of the Great West and their inhabitants. New York, 1877.

Donaldson, T. *The George Catlin Indian gallery. Smithson. Rep., 1885, pt. II.

Doolittle, J. Social life of the Chinese. 2 vols. New York, 1865.

Dornan, S. S. The Tati Bushmen (Masarwas) and their language. JAI, XLVII.

Dorsey, G. A. Articles: ceremony; sun dance. HAI.

——A cruise among Haida and Tlingit villages about Dixon's entrance. PSM, LIII.

——The Osage mourning-war ceremony. AA, IV.

Dorsey, J. O. Hopi Indians. PSM, LV.

——Kansa mourning and war customs. Amer. Naturalist, XIX.

——*Omaha sociology. BAE, III.

——*Siouan sociology. BAE, XV.

——*A study of Siouan cults. BAE, XI.

Dorsey, J. O. and Goddard, P. E. Sarsi. HAI, pt. II.

Dorsey, J. O. and Radin, P. Winnebago. HAI, pt. II.

Dorsey, J. O. and Thomas, C. Omaha. HAI, pt. II.

Doughty, C. M. *Travels in Arabia Deserta. Cambridge, 1888.

Dowd, J. The Negro races. A sociological study. 2 vols. New York, 1907, 1914.

Doyle, A. C. The White Company. New York, 1891.

Dozy, R. Histoire des Musulmans d'Espagne. Leyde, 1861.

Drake, S. G. The book of the Indians; or, biography and history of the Indians of North America from its first discovery to the year 1841. Boston, 1845.

Dresslar. Suggestions on the psychology of superstition. N. Y. Times, June 5, 1910.

Drew, F. H., see Fox, C. E.

Dreyer, W. The main features of the advance in the study of Danish archeology. AA, X.

Driberg, J. H. Rain-making among the Lango. JAI, XLIX.

Drumann, W. K. A. Die Arbeiter und Communisten in Griechenland und Rom. Königsberg, 1860.

Dublin, L. I. The fallacious propaganda for birth control. Atl. Mo., CXXXVII.

Dubois, J. A. Mœurs, institutions et ceremonies des peuples de l'Inde. 2 tomes. Paris, 1825.

Du Camp, M. Paris, ses organes, ses fonctions et sa vie. 6 vols. Paris, 1875.

Du Chaillu, P. B. A journey to Ashangoland. New York, 1867.

——Voyages et aventures dans l'Afrique équatoriale. Paris, 1863.

Dudgeon, J. H. The land question, with lessons to be drawn from peasant proprietorship in China. Glasgow, 1886.

Dudley, J. Memoir. In Collections, topographical, historical and biographical relating principally to New Hampshire. Edit. by J. Farmer and J. B. Moore. 3 vols. Concord, 1822.

Duhm, H. *Die bösen Geister im Alten Testament. Leipzig, 1904.

Dundas, C. *History of Kitui. JAI, XLIII.

——*Native laws of some Bantu tribes of East Africa. JAI, LI.

——*The organization and laws of some Bantu tribes in East Africa. JAI, XLV.

Dundas, K. R. *Notes on the tribes inhabiting the Baringo District, East Africa Protectorate. JAI, XL.

——*The Wawanga and other tribes of the Elgon District, British East Africa. JAI, XLIII.

Dunlop, W. Australian folklore stories. JAI, XXVIII.

Durand. Durands Besuch bei den Webias auf Neukaledonien. Anon. Globus, LXXX.

Duras, Duchesse de. Prison journals during the French Revolution.

Durham, M. E. Head-hunting in the Balkans. Man, XXIII.

——High Albania and its customs in 1908. JAI, XL.

——Some Montenegrin manners and customs. JAI, XXXIX.

——Some South Slav customs as shown in Serbian ballads and by Serbian authors. JAI, XLVII.

Durkheim, E. The elementary forms of the religious life. Translated from the French by J. W. Swain. New York, 1915.

——Prohibition de l'Inceste. Année Sociologique, I.

——Les règles de la méthode sociologique. Paris, 1895.

Duveyrier, H. *Exploration du Sahara: Les Touâreg du Nord. Paris, 1864.

Duyl, C. F. van. Beschavingsgeschiedenis van het Nederlandsche Volk. Groningen, 1895.

Dymock, W. India as a field for anthropological research. JASB, II.

——Note on Indian necromancy. JASB, I.

——Note on the same subject. [Basivis women.] JASB, II. *See* Fawcett, F.

——On the narcotics and spices of the east. JASB, II.

——On the use of Ganja and Bhang in the east as narcotics. JASB, II.

——On the use of turmeric in Hindoo ceremonial. JASB, II.

Earle, A. M. Curious punishments of bygone days. New York, 1907.

Eberman, O. Zur Aberglaubensliste in Vintlers Pluemen der Tugend. Ztft. d. Vereins f. Vkde., XXIII.

Eckart, E. E. Die Geheimen oder Mysterien-Gesellschaften der alten Heidenkirche. Treu dargestellt und erklärt. Schauffhausen. 1860.

Eckerman, J. P. Gespräche mit Goethe in den letzen Jahren seines Lebens. 3 vols. in one. Leipzig, 1884 or 1885.

Edda, *see* Brodeur.

Eden, R. The first three English books on America. Translations, compilations, etc., by Richard Eden from the writings, maps, etc., of Pietro Martire, Sebastian Münster and Sebastian Cabot. Edit. by Edward Arber. Birmingham, 1885.

Eels, M. The Twana Chemakum, and Klallam Indians of Washington Territory. Smith. Rep., 1887, pt. I.

Ehrenberg, R. Das Zeitalter der Fugger. Jena, 1896.

Ehrenreich, P. *Beiträge zur Völkerkunde Brasiliens. Veröffentlichungen aus dem Königlichen Museum für Völkerkunde, 1891.

——Über die Botocudos der brasilianischen Provinzen Espiritu Santo und Minas Geraes. Ztsft. f. Ethnol., XIX.

Eicken, H. von. Geschichte u. System der Mittelalterlichen Weltanschauung. Stuttgart, 1887.

Eitel, E. J. Slavery in China. China Review, vol. X.

Elenitski. The Strangers of Siberia (Russ.).

Eliot, George. Works.

Elkington, E. W., *see* Hardy, N. H.

Ella, S. The ancient Samoan government. AAAS, 1895.

——Comparative view of customs and social habits of the Malayan and Papuan races of Polynesia. AAAS, 1887.

——Samoa, etc. AAAS, 1892.

Elliot, G. F. S. Some notes on native West African customs. JAI, XXIII.

Ellis, A. B. *The Ewe-speaking peoples. London, 1890.

——*The Tshi-speaking peoples. London, 1887.

——West African folklore. PSM, XLV.

——*The Yoruba-speaking peoples of the slave coast of West Africa. London, 1894.

Ellis, H. The criminal. London, 1890.

——The evolution of modesty. Psychological Review, VI.

——*Man and woman: a study of human secondary sexual characters. London, 1894.

——The psychology of red. PSM, LVII.

Ellis, W. History of Madagascar. 2 vols. London, 1838.

——*Polynesian researches. 4 vols. London, 1831-2.

Elton, F. Natives of the Solomon Islands. JAI, XVII.

Emerson, E. R. The book of the dead and rain ceremonials. AA, VII.

Emerson, R. W. Essays. 2 vols. Boston, 1890.

Emmons, G. T. Petroglyphs in southeastern Alaska. AA, X.

Encyclopædia Britannica. A dictionary of arts, sciences, literature, and general information. 11th ed. 29 vols. New York, 1910-11.

d'Enjoy, P. Le Baiser en Europe et en Chine. Bull. et Mem. de la Soc. d'Anthrop. de Paris. Ser. 4, tome VIII.

Erman, A. Aegypten und Aegyptisches Leben im Altertum. Zwei Bände. Tübingen, 1887.

Ernst, L. Die abessynische Eisenbahn. Umschau, VIII.

Ersch, J. S. and Gruber, J. G. Allgemeine Encyclopädie der Wissen schaften und Künste. Leipzig, 1818-32.

Esser, M. An der Westküste Afrikas. Cited in Globus, LXXII.

d'Estournelles de Constant, P. Les sociétés secrètes chez les Arabes et la conquête de l'Afrique du Nord. Revue des Deux Mondes, 1886, LXXIV.

Estrup, H. F. J. Samlede Skrifter. Kjøbenhavn, 1842.

Euripides. Euripidis Fabulae. Recognovit. . . . Gilbertus Murray. Tomus I, II, III in one vol. Scriptorum Classicorum Bibliotheca Oxoniensis. MDCCCCI.

European Messenger, The (Russ.), see Vestnik Evropi.

Evans, E. P. Religious belief as a basis of moral obligation. PSM, XLV.

——Semon's scientific researches in Australia. PSM, LII.

——Superstition and crime. PSM, LIV.

Evans, I. H. N. Folk stories of the Tempassuk and Tuaran districts, British North Borneo. JAI, XLIII.

——Notes on some beliefs and customs of the "Orang Dusun" of British North Borneo. JAI, XLVII.

——Notes on the religious beliefs, superstitions, ceremonies and tabus of the Dusuns of the Tuaran and Tempassuk districts, British North Borneo. JAI, XLII.

——Some Sakai beliefs and customs. JAI, XLVIII.

Evarnitzky, D. I. The Zaparoge Cossacks (Russ.). 2 vols. St. Petersburg, 1888.

Ewald, H. Geschichte des Volkes Israel. 8 vols. Göttingen, 1864.

Eyre, E. J. *Journals of expeditions of discovery into Central Australia and overland from Adelaide to King George's Sound. London, 1845.

Fabié, A. Ensayo Histórico de la Legislación Española en sus Estados de Ultramar. Madrid, 1896.

Fabri, F. Fünf Jahre deutscher Kolonialpolitik. Gotha, 1889.

Fabry, H. Aus dem Leben der Wapogoro. Globus, XCI.

Fairchild, H. P. Greek immigration to the United States. New Haven, 1911.

Fairclough, T. L. Notes on the Basuto. Jr. Afr. Soc. London, IV.

Fairweather, W. Development of doctrine in the apocryphal period. Hastings's Dictionary of the Bible.

Falbe-Hansen, V. A., see Hansen, V. A. Falbe-.

Farnell, L. R. Greece and Babylon; a comparative sketch of Mesopotamian, Anatolian and Hellenic religions. Edinburgh, 1911.

——*Greek hero cults and ideas of immortality; the Gifford lectures delivered in the Univ. of St. Andrews in the year 1920. Oxford, 1921.

——Religion of Greece. Hastings's Dictionary of the Bible. Extra volume. New York, 1904.

——Sociological hypotheses concerning the position of women in ancient religion. Archiv für Religionswissenschaft, VII.

Farr, W. Vital statistics. London, 1885.

Farrand, L. Basis of American history. New York and London, 1904.

——Notes on the Alsea Indians of Oregon. AA, III.

Farrand, L., see also Lowie, R. H.

Fawcett, F. The Kondayam Kottai Maravars, a Dravidian tribe of Tinnevelly, Southern India. JAI, XXXIII.

——Miscellaneous notes. JASB, II.

——Note on the mouth-lock vow. JASB, II.

——On a mode of obsession. JASB, I.

——On Basivis: women who, through dedication to a deity, assume masculine privileges. JASB, II.

——On some festivals to village goddesses. JASB, II.

——On the Berulu Kodo, a sub-sect of the Moras Vokaligaru of the Mysore province. JASB, I.

——*On the Saoras (or Savaras), an aboriginal hill people of the Eastern Ghats of the Madras Presidency. JASB, I.

Fedorow, G. G. and Kondratowitsch, O. W. Eine Ob-expedition während des Sommers 1895. Zur Ethnographie der Ostjäken, von O. W. Kondratowitsch. Reviewed in Globus, LXXIV.

Feilberg, H. F. Der böse Blick in Nordischer Überlieferung. Ztsft. d. Vereins f. Volkskunde, XI.

Felkin, R. W., see Wilson, C. T.

Fell, J. R. Rhodesian babies are bred alcoholic. N.Y. Times, April 29, 1923.

Fenton, J. The right of preëmption in village communities. Antiq., IV.

Ferrero, G., see Lombroso, C.

Fewkes, J. W. Articles: Hopi; Shrines; Spruce-tree house. HAI.

——Casa Grande, Arizona. BAE, XXVIII.

——*The group of Tusayan ceremonies called Katcinas. BAE, XV.

——The lesser new-fire ceremony at Walpi. AA, III.

——Minor Hopi festivals. AA, IV.

——*Notes on Tusayan snake and flute ceremonies. BAE, XIX, pt. II.

——The Owakülti altar at Sichomovi pueblo. AA, III.

——Prehistoric culture of Cuba. AA, VI.

——The prehistoric culture of Tusayan. AA, IX.

——Prehistoric Porto Rico. Science, XVI.

——Preliminary account of an expedition to the cliff villages of the Red Rock country, and the Tusayan ruins of Sikyatki and Awotabi, Arizona, in 1895. Smithson. Rep., 1895.

——Property-right in eagles among the Hopi. AA, II.

——Tusayan Katcinas. BAE, XV.

Fies, K. Das Fetischdorf Avhegame und seine Bewohner auf dem Aguberge in Deutsch-Togo. Globus, LXXX.

——Der Hostamm in Deutsch-Togo. Globus, LXXXVII.

Figuier, L. Primitive man. London, 1870.

Finley, J. B. Life among the Indians. Cincinnati, 1857.

Finsch, O. *Ethnologische Erfahrungen und Belegstücke aus der Südsee. Wien, 1893.

——*Samoafahrten. Leipzig, 1888.

——Über die Bewohner von Ponapé. (östl. Carolinen) Ztsft. fur Eth., XII.

——Über die ethnologischen Sammlunger aus der Südsee. Original-Mittheilungen aus der ethnologischen Abtheilung der Königlichen Museum zu Berlin. Erster Jahrgang, Heft 2/3. 1886.

Finsen, V. Fremstilling af den Islandske Familieret. Efter Grágás. Annaler, 1849 and 1850.

Fircks, A. von. Bevölkerungslehre und Bevölkerungspolitik. Leipzig, 1898.

Fiske, J. The destiny of man viewed in the light of his origin. New York, 1912.

Fison, L. *The classificatory system of relationship. JAI, XXIV.

——Group marriage and relationship. AAAS, 1892.

——*Land tenure in Fiji. JAI, X.

——The Nair polyandry and the Dieri Pirauru. AAAS, 1892.

——*The Nanga, or sacred stone enclosure, of Wainimala, Fiji. JAI, XIV.

——*Notes on Fijian burial customs. JAI, X.

Fison, L., see also Howitt, A. W.

Fison, L. and Howitt, A. W. *Kamilaroi and Kurnai. Melbourne, 1880.

Fitz-Gerald, W. G. War against the silent death. The Technical World Magazine, 1907.

Fitzroy, R., Editor. Narrative of the

surveying voyages of His Majesty's ships Adventure and Beagle, between the years 1826 and 1836, describing their examination of the southern shores of South America, and the Beagle's circumnavigation of the globe. 3 vols. London, 1839.

Fletcher, A. C. Articles: adornment; Avavares; Caddo; Civilization; Dolls; Dreams and visions; Earth lodge; Etiquette; Fasting; Feasts; Hairdressing; Land tenure; Mariames; Masks; Mourning; Palaquesson; Pawnee; Property; Skidi; Tattooing; War; Yguases. HAI.

——*Häusliches Leben bei den Indianern. Globus, LXXIII.

——The significance of the scalp-lock. JAI, XXVII.

——Significance of the totem. Reported in PSM, LII.

——Some observations on the laws and privileges of the gens in Indian society. Proc. Am. Assoc. Adv. Sci. at Minneapolis, 1883.

—— Star cult of the Pawnees. AA, IV.

——The white buffalo festival of the Uncpapas. Reports of the Peabody Museum of Amer. Archeology and Ethnol. in Connection with Harvard University, III.

Fletcher, A. C. and LaFlesche, F. *The Omaha tribes. BAE, XXVII.

Fletcher, A. C. and Matthews, W. Ethics and morals. HAI, pt. I.

Flower, W. H. Discussion by Dr. Summerhayes on Flower's "Exhibition of two skulls from a cave in Jamaica." JAI, XX.

——On a collection of monumental heads and artificially deformed crania from the island of Mallicollo, in the New Hebrides. JAI, XI.

Foelsche, P. On the manners, customs, etc., of some tribes of the aborigines, in the neighborhood of Port Darwin and the West Coast of the Gulf of Carpentaria, North Australia. JAI, XXIV.

Folk-lore. A quarterly review of myth, tradition, institution, and custom.

Being the transactions of the Folklore Society and incorporating the Archeological Review and Folk-lore Journal. I-XXXV. London, 1890-1924.

Foote, J. A. Medicine fakes and fakers of all ages. Strange stories of nostrums and kingly quacks in every era and clime. Nat. Geog. Mag., XXXV.

Forbes, H. O. Ethnology of the Timor-Laut. JAI, XIII.

——On some of the tribes of the Island of Timor. JAI, XIII.

——*On the Kubus of Sumatra. JAI, XIV.

Fortnightly Review, The. I-VI, 1865-6 (o.s.). I-CXX, 1866-1926. London, 1865-1926 (n.s.).

Forum, The. I-LXXV. New York, 1886-1926.

Foucart, P. F. Les associations religieuses chez les Grecs. Paris, 1873.

Foureau, F. D'Alger au Congo par le Tchad. Paris, 1902.

Fox, C. E. *Social organization in San Cristoval, Solomon Islands. JAI, XLIX.

Fox, C. E. and Drew, F. H. Beliefs and tales of San Cristoval (Solomon Islands). JAI, XLV.

Frachtenberg, L. J. Eschatology of the Quileute Indians. AA, XXII.

——On "The religious ideas of the northwest coast Indians." Proceedings of the Anthropological Society of Washington. AA, XIX.

Francke, H. Ein Besuch im buddhistischen Kloster Hemis (Ladāk). Globus, LXXIII.

——Eine Besteigung des Karsongpasses. Globus, LXXVIII.

Frank Leslie's Popular Monthly. New York, 1876-1904.

Fraser, M. In Stevenson's Samoa. New York, 1895.

Frazer, J. G. Ancient stories of a great flood. JAI, XLVI.

——The beginnings of religion and totemism among the Australian

aborigines. Fortnightly Rev.,
LXXVIII (n.s.).
——Folklore in the Old Testament;
studies in comparative religion and
law. 3 vols. London, 1918.
——*†The golden bough. A study in
magic and religion. 2 vols. London
and New York, 1890.
——*†The same work enlarged. 12
vols. London, 1900-19.
——*†The same work. The twelve vol-
ume work condensed into one vol-
ume. New York, 1923.
——Observations on Central Aus-
tralian totemism. JAI, XXVIII.
——*On certain burial customs as il-
lustrative of the primitive theory of
the soul. JAI, XV.
——The origin of totemism. Fort-
nightly Rev., LXXI.
——Totemism. Edinburgh, 1887.
——Totemism and exogamy. London,
1910.
Freeman, E. A. Western Europe in
the fifth century. New York, 1904.
Freeman, W. Aboriginal burial rites.
AAAS, 1902.
Freie Wort, Das. Blätter für religiöse
Aufklärung. I-III. Basel, 1857-9.
Freiherr, O. Zwei Reisen durch
Ruanda 1902 bis 1903. Globus,
LXXXVI.
Freisen, J. Geschichte des kanonischen
Eherechts. Tübingen, 1888.
French-Sheldon, Mrs. Customs among
the Natives of East Africa, from
Teita to Kilimegalia. JAI, XXI.
Frere, H. B. *On systems of land
tenure among aboriginal tribes in
South Africa. JAI, XII.
——On the laws affecting the relations
between civilized and savage life, as
bearing on the dealings of colonists
with aborigines. JAI, XI.
Freytag, L. Riesen und Menschenop-
fer in unseren Sagen und Märchen.
Am Ur-Quell, I.
Frič, V. Eine Pilcomayo-Reise in den
Chaco Central. Globus, LXXXIX.
Frič, V. and Radin, P. Contributions

to the study of the Bororo Indians.
JAI, XXXVI.
Friedberg, E. Das Recht der
Eheschliessung. Leipzig, 1865.
Friederichsen, L. Die Ruinen von
Nanmatal auf der Insel Ponapé.
Hamburg, 1874.
Friederici, G. Die Behandlung weib-
licher Gefangener durch die In-
dianer von Nordamerika. Globus,
LXXV.
——*Die Ethnographie in den 'Docu-
mentos Inéditos del Archivo de
Indias.' Globus, XC.
——Der Indianerhund von Nord-
amerika. Globus, LXXVI.
——*Skalpieren und ähnliche Kriegs-
gebräuche in Amerika. Braun-
schweig, 1906.
——Tränengruss der Indianer. Glo-
bus, LXXXIX.
Friedmann, M. Über Wahnideen im
Völkerleben. Wiesbaden, 1901.
Fries, T. M. *Grönland dess Natur
och Innevånare. Upsala, 1872.
Frijs, J. A. Wanderungen in den drei
Lappländern. Aus dem Norweg-
ischen von Dr. Mähwald. Globus,
XXII.
Frischbier, H. Der Eid im Volksleben.
Am Ur-Quell, II.
——Ostpreussischer Volksglaube und
Brauch. Am Ur-Quell, I.
Fritsch, G. *Die Eingeborenen Süd-
Afrikas. Breslau, 1872.
——Frauentracht.　Politisch-Anthr.
Rev., III.
Frobenius, L. *Die Masken und Ge-
heimbünde Afrikas. Nova Acta
Acad. Caesareae Leopoldino-Caro-
linae Ger. Naturae Cur., LXXIV.
Frontinus, S. J. Fragmenta ex II libro
de controversiis agrorum collecta et
disposita a C. Lachmann. Prefixed
to Index Lectionum. Berlin, 1844-5.
Fulcomer, A. An Eskimo "Kashim."
AA (o.s.), XI.
Furness, W. H. The ethnography of
the Nagas of Eastern Assam. JAI,
XXXII, 1902.

——*†The home-life of Borneo head-hunters. Philadelphia, 1902.

Furnivall, F. J. Child-marriages, divorces, etc., 1561-1566. (Early Engl. Text Society, No. 108.) London, 1897.

Gaius. The commentaries of Gaius. Trans. by J. T. Abdy. Cambridge, 1870.

Galton, F. Essays in eugenics. London, 1909.

——*Hereditary genius. New York, 1870.

——*Human faculty. New York, 1883.

Garbutt, H. W. Native witchcraft and superstition in South Africa. JAI, XXXIX, 1909.

Gardiner, J. S. The natives of Rotuma. JAI, XXVII.

Garner, R. O. Superstitions of the West African tribes. AAAS, 1895.

Garnier, R. M. Annals of the British peasantry. London, 1895.

Garrett, T. R. H. The natives of the eastern portion of Borneo and of Java. JAI, XLII.

Gason, S. *The Dieyerie tribe of Australian aborigines. Adelaide, 1874.

——*The Dieyerie tribe, South Australia. JAI, XVIII.

——ᴿOf the tribes, Dieyerie, Auminie, Yandrawontha, Yarawuarka, Philladapa. (South Australia.) JAI, XXIV.

Gatschet, A. S. Chitimacha. HAI, pt. I.

Gautier, E. F. Nomad and sedentary folk of northern Africa. Geog. Journal, 1921.

Gautier, T. Jettatura. Boston, 1900. London, 1901.

Ga-wa-su-na-neh. Letter to New York Times, Jan. 21, 1913.

Geare, R. I. Healing by magic and mummery (or "medical magic and mummery"). Amer. Med., XXII.

Geddes, P. and Thompson, J. A. The evolution of sex. London, 1889.

Gedge, J. D. The history of a village community in the eastern counties. Norwich, 1893.

Gehring, H. *Süd-Indien. Gütersloh, 1899.

Geiger, L. Goethe und die Seinen; quellenmässige Darstellungen über Goethes Haus. Leipzig, 1908.

Geiger, W. Ostiranische Kultur. Erlangen, 1882.

Geijer, E. G. Svenska folkets historia. Stokholm, 1851.

——The same work translated by J. H. Turner as The history of the Swedes. London, 1845.

Geiseler, W. Die Oster-Inseln. Eine Stätte prähistorischer Kultur in der Südsee. Berlin, 1883.

Gentz, Leutnant. Einige Beiträge zur Kenntniss der südwestafrikanischen Völkerschaften. Globus, LXXXIV, LXXXV.

Geographical Journal, The. I-LXVIII. London, 1893-1926.

George, W. L. Notes on the intelligence of woman. Atl. Mo., CXVI.

Gerard, W. R. Virginia's Indian contributions to English. AA, IX.

Gerland, G., see Waitz, T.

Gessmann, G. W. Die Geheimsymbole der Chemie und Medicin des Mittelalters. München, 1900.

Ghurye, G. S. Dual organization in India. JAI, LIII.

Gibbons, A. St. H. Quotation in PSM, LI.

Giddings, F. H. The principles of sociology. New York, 1896.

Gide, P. Étude sur la condition privée de la Femme dans le droit ancien et moderne. Paris, 1867.

Gids, De. Jaarg. I-LXXXIX. Amsterdam, 1837-1925.

Giesebrecht, F. *Die Behandlung der Eingeborenen in den Deutschen Kolonieen. Berlin, 1897.

Giles, H. A. The travels of Fa-hsien. Cambridge, 1923.

GilFillan, S. C. In review of Bowman, "The new world." Sewanee Rev. Quart., XXXI.

Gill, W. W. Kings of Rarotonga and Mangaia. AAAS, 1890.

——Omens of pregnancy, Mangaia, Hervey Islands. AAAS, 1892.

——The story of Tu and Rei; a Manihikian myth. AAAS, 1892.

Gillen, F. J. Magic amongst the natives of central Australia. AAAS, 1901.

Gillen, F. J., *see* also Spencer, B.

Glaber, R. Chronique de Raoul Glaber. In Guizot, F. P. G.: Collection de mémoires relatifs à l'histoire de France, vol. VII.

Glave, E. J. Glave in the heart of Africa. Cent. Mag., XXX (n.s.).

Globus. *Illustrierte Zeitschrift für Länder- und Völkerkunde. I-XCVIII. Hildburghausen, 1861-1910.

Glotta. Zeitschrift für Griechische und Lateinische Sprache. I-XII. Göttingen, 1909-1923.

Gmelin, J. G. Reise durch Sibirien, von dem Jahr 1733 bis 1743. 4 Bände. Göttingen, 1751.

Goblet d'Alviella, E. F. A. Origin and growth of the conception of God (as illustrated by anthropology and history). Hibbert lectures for 1891. London and Edinburgh, 1892.

Goddard, P. E., *see* also Dorsey, J. O.

Goddard, P. E. and Swanton, J. R. Athapascan family. HAI, pt. I.

Godden, G. M. *Naga and other frontier tribes of North East India. JAI, XXVI.

Godwin-Austen, H. H. On the stone monuments of the Khasi Hill Tribes and on some of the peculiar rites and customs of the people. JAI, I.

Goeje, M. J. de. De Berbers. De Gids, XXXI, pt. II.

Goeken. Das religiöse Leben der Bella-Coola-Indianer. Original-Mittheilungen aus der Ethnologischen Abtheilung der Königlichen Museen zu Berlin, I. Berlin, 1885.

Goethe, J. W. von. Works.

Goitein, H. Primitive ordeal and modern law. London, 1923.

Goldstein, F. Die Frauen in Haussafulbien und in Adamaua. Globus, XCIV.

——Das Menschenopfer im Lichte der Politik und der Staatswissenschaften. Globus, LXXXIX.

——Politik, Staatswissenschaften und Ethnographie. Globus, XC.

——Die Saharastädte Rhat und Agades. Globus, XCII.

Goldziher, I. Alois Musils ethnologische Studien in Arabia Petraea. Globus, XCIII.

——Der Seelenvogel im islamischen Volksglauben. Globus, LXXXIII.

Gomes, E. H. *†Seventeen years among the Sea Dyaks of Borneo. London, 1911.

Gomme, G. L. *†Ethnology in folklore. London, 1892.

——*†Folk-lore relics of early village life. London, 1883.

——On the evidence for Mr. McLennan's theory of the primitive human horde. JAI, XVII.

Gonçales de Clavigo, R. Historia del Gran Tamorlan e itinerario y enarracion del viage y relacion de la Embaxaca que Ruy Gonçalez de Clavigo le hizo por mandado del Hen. III de Castilla. Y un breve discurso fecho por Gonçalo Argoté de Molina. Sevilla, 1582.

Gorton, M. J. The sun-dance of the Nez-Perces: initiating a brave. Pop. Sci. News, XXVII.

Gottschling, E. The Bawenda: a sketch of their history and customs. JAI, XXXV.

Götzen, G. A. von. *Durch Afrika von Ost nach West. Berlin, 1899.

Grabowsky, F. Ein Besuch auf Molokai, der Insel der Aussätzigen. Globus, LXXIX.

——Gebräuche der Dajaken Südost-Borneos bei der Geburt. Globus, LXXII.

Graham, S. The way of Martha, and the way of Mary. London, 1916.

Grandidier, M. G. Review of the scientific observations of Dr. Muraz in the Lake Tchad region, in the Paris *Illustration*, summarised in Literary Digest for June 16, 1923.

Grant, U. S. Personal memoirs of U. S. Grant. New York, 1885-86.

Grant, W. Magato and his tribe. JAI, XXXV.

Granville, R. K. and Roth, F. N. Notes on the Jekris, Sobos and Ijos of the Warri district of the Niger Coast Protectorate. Prepared by H. L. Roth. JAI, XXVIII.

Gray, W. Notes on the natives of Tanna. JAI, XXVIII.

——Some notes on the Tannese. AAAS, 1892.

Greef, G. J. de. Introduction à la sociologie. Paris, 1886-9.

Green, F. Eskimos are still living in the Stone Age. N. Y. Times Mag. Sec., Oct. 10, 1926.

Green, Mrs. J. R. Town life in the fifteenth century. New York and London, 1895.

Gregorius I, the Great, Saint, Pope. Opera.

Gregorovius, F. History of the city of Rome in the middle ages. Trans. from the German. London, 1894-1902.

——Lucrezia Borgia. (Trans. by J. L. Garner.) New York, 1903.

Gregory, Hilton (nom de plume), A note on priestcraft. Amer. Mercury, VII.

Gregory, H. E., Keller, A. G., Bishop, A. L. Physical and commercial geography. Boston, 1910.

Grettis Saga. The story of Grettir the strong. Translated from the Icelandic by Eiríkr Magnússon and William Morris. London, 1869.

Grey, G. *Journals of two expeditions of discovery in North-West and West Australia. London, 1841.

Grierson, P. J. H. *The silent trade, a contribution to the early history of human intercourse. Edinburgh, 1903.

Griffith, T. R. On the races inhabiting Sierra Leone. JAI, XVI.

Grimble, A. From birth to death in the Gilbert Islands. JAI, LI.

Grimm, J. L. K. Deutsche Mythologie. 2 vols. Göttingen, 1854.

——Deutsche Rechtsalterthümer. Göttingen, 1854.

——Deutsche Sagen. 2 vols. in 1. Berlin, 1891.

——*Teutonic mythology. Trans. from the fourth edit., with notes and appendix by J. S. Stallybrass. 4 vols. London, 1880-8.

Grinnell, G. B. A Buffalo sweatlodge. AA, XXI.

——*†The Cheyenne Indians. Their history and ways of life. 2 vols. New Haven, 1923.

——Cheyenne woman customs. AA, IV.

——Great mysteries of the Cheyenne. AA, XII.

——Horses. HAI, pt. I.

——*Pawnee hero stories and folktales, with notes on the origin, customs and character of the Pawnee people. New York, 1889.

——*Tenure of land among the Indians. AA, IX.

Gröndal, B. Folketro i Norden. Annaler f. Nord. Oldkynd., 1863.

Groos, K. The play of animals. Trans. by E. L. Baldwin. New York, 1908.

——The play of man. Trans. by E. L. Baldwin. New York, 1901.

Groot, J. J. M. de. Het Kongsiwezen van Borneo. Nijhoff, 1885.

——*†The religious systems of China. 6 vols. Leyden, 1892-1910.

Grosse, E. The beginnings of art. (Trans.) New York and London, 1914.

——Die Formen der Familie und die Formen der Wirthschaft. Freiburg und Leipzig, 1896.

Grote, G. A history of Greece. London, 1846.

Grotius, H. De jure belli et pacis libri tres.

Grube, W. *Zur Pekinger Volkskunde.

Veröffentlichungen aus dem Königlichen Museum für Völkerkunde, VII.

Gruber, J. G., *see* Ersch, J. S.

Gruber, M. Moral und Hygiene. (Quotations from Dr. M. Gruber.) Umschau, IV.

Grupp, G. Kulturgeschichte der Römischen Kaiserzeit. Münden, 1903.

Gubernatis, A. Usi Nuziali in Italia e presso gli altri Popoli Indo-Europei. Milano, 1878.

Guerard, B. E. C. Polyptique de l'abbé Irminon. Paris, 1844.

Guhl, E. K. und Koner, W. Das Leben der Griechen und Römer nach antiken Bildwerken. Berlin, 1860-61.

Guise, R. E. On the tribes inhabiting the mouth of the Wanigela River, New Guinea. JAI, XXVIII.

Guizot, F. P. G. Collection de mémoires relatifs à l'histoire de France. 30 tom. Paris, 1823-35.

Gumplowicz, L. *Grundriss der Sociologie, Wien, 1885.

——*Der Rassenkampf. Innsbruck, 1883.

——*Sociologie und Politik. Leipzig, 1892.

——*Die sociologische Staatsidee. Graz, 1892.

Gunkel, H. Zum religionsgeschichtlichen Verständnis des Neuen Testaments. Göttingen, 1903.

Gunthorpe, E. J. Note on the Bhonde Koomars. JASB, I.

——Sancholoos, a criminal wandering tribe. JASB, I.

Gunthorpe, Lieut.-Col. Ghosi or Gaddi Gaolis. JASB, I.

Guse, Premier-Leutnant. Die Tekke-Turkmenen. Aus allen Weltteilen, XXIX.

Gutmann, B. Fluchen und Segnen im Munde der Wadschagga. Globus, XCIII.

——*Die Frau bei den Wadschagga. Globus, XCII.

——Wahrsagen und Traumdeuten bei den Wadschagga. Globus, XCII.

Guyot, I. Les Indigènes de l'Afrique du Sud. Bulletins et Mémoires de la Société d'Anthropologie de Paris, 1901.

Haarhoff, B. T. Die Bantu-Stämme Süd-Afrikas. Leipzig, 1890.

Haberland, C. Die Gastfreundschaft auf niederen Culturstufen. Ausland, LI.

Haddon, A. C. *The ethnography of the western tribes of Torres Straits. JAI, XIX.

——Evolution in art: as illustrated by the life-histories of designs. London, 1895.

——†Head hunters, black, white, and brown. London, 1901.

——The Kabiri of Girara District, Fly River, Papua. JAI, XLVI.

——Migrations of cultures in British New Guinea. JAI, L.

——Notes on children's games in British New Guinea. JAI, XXXVIII.

——The omen animals of Sarawak. PSM, LX.

——String figures from South Africa. JAI, XXVI.

——Stuffed human heads from New Guinea. Man, XXIII.

——Totemism. President's address. Brit. Assoc. Adv. Sci., 1902.

Haddon, E. B. The dog-motive in Bornean art. JAI, XXV.

Haddon, K. Cat's cradles from many lands. New York, Bombay, etc., 1911.

Hadley, A. T. Economics, an account of the relations between private property and public welfare. New York, 1898.

Haeberlin, H. K. A shamanistic performance of the Coast Salish. AA, XX.

Haebler, K. *Amerika. In Helmolt's Weltgeschichte, vol. I. Leipzig und Wien, 1899.

Hagar, S. Izamal and its celestial plan. AA, XV.*

Hagedorn, C. B. Our friend the Sultan of Joló. Cent. Mag., LX.

Hagelstange, A. Über süddeutsches

Bauernleben im Mittelalter unter besonderer Berücksichtigung gleichzeitiger litterarischer Quellen. Erfurt, 1897.

Hagen, B. *Unter den Papua's. Wiesbaden, 1899.

Hager, S. Micmac customs and traditions. AA, VIII.

Haggard, H. R. Montezuma's daughter. New York and London, 1893.

Hahn, C. von. Die Milchverwandtschaft im Kaukasus. Globus, LXXII.

——Neues über die Kurden. Globus, LXXXVI.

——Sitten und Gebräuche in Imeritien. Globus, LXXX.

Hahn, E. Zur Theorie der Entstehung des Ackerbaues. Globus, LXXV.

Hahn, J. G. von. Albänische Studien. 2 Hfte. Jena, 1854.

Hahn, T. Die Buschmänner. Ein Beitrag zur südafrikanischen Völkerkunde. Globus, XVIII.

Haimensfeld, M. G., Editor. Collectio constitutionum imperialium. Frankfurt, 1615.

Hale, A. On the Sakais. JAI, XV.

Hale, H. Ethnography and Philology. Vol. VI of United States Exploring Expedition. Philadelphia, 1846.

——Four Huron wampum records. JAI, XXVI.

——*The Iroquois book of rites. Philadelphia, 1883.

——The Iroquois sacrifice of the white dog. Amer. Antiquarian and Oriental Journ., VII.

Haliburton, R. G. Tau cross on the badge of a medicine man. Brit. Assoc. Adv. Sci., LVI.

Hall, H. Society in the Elizabethan age. London, 1887.

Hall, T. F. Has the North Pole been discovered? Boston, 1917.

Hamilton, A. Witchcraft in West Polk Street. Amer. Merc., X.

Hamlyn-Harris, R. Mummification in Papua. Anthr. Misc. AA, XV.

Hammer-Purgstall, J. von. Die Geisterlehre der Moslimen. Wien, 1852.

Hamy, E. T. An interpretation of one of the Copan monuments (Honduras). JAI, XVI.

Hanbury, D. T. Sport and travel in the northland of Canada. New York, 1904.

*Handbook of American Indians North of Mexico. (HAI) Edited by F. W. Hodge. BAE, Bull. XXX. 2 vols. Washington, 1907.

Handelmann, H. Volksmedizin. Am Ur-Quell, I.

*Hanoteau, A., et Letourneux, A. La Kabylie, II. 3 tomes. Paris, 1893.

Hansen, J. Zauberwahn, Inquisition und Hexenprocess im Mittelalter. Leipzig, 1900.

Hansen, P. Bidrag til det danske Landbrugs Historie: Jordfællesskabet og Landvæsenskommissionen af 1757. København, 1889.

Hansen, V. A. Falbe-. Stavnbaandsløsningen og Landboreformerne, set fra national økonomiens Standpunkt. 2den Del. Tiden fra 1807 til Nutiden. Kjøbenhavn, 1888-9.

Hardie, M. M. (Hasluck, Mrs. F. W.). The evil eye in some Greek villages in the Upper Haliakmon Valley of West Macedonia. JAI, LIII.

Harbord, J. G. The army as a career. Atl. Mo., CXXXII.

Hardy, N. H. and Elkington, E. W. *†The savage South Seas. London, 1907.

Harley, G. Comparison between the recuperative bodily power of man in a rude and in a highly civilized state; illustrative of the probable recuperative capacity of men of the Stone-Age in Europe. JAI, XVII.

Harnack, A. Dogmengeschichte, 3 Bände. Leipzig, 1894.

Harper, C. H. and others. Notes on the totemism of the Gold Coast. Communicated by C. G. Seligmann and N. W. Thomas. JAI, XXXVI.

Harper, R. F. The code of Hammurabi. Chicago, 1904.

Harper's Monthly Magazine. I-CLIII. New York, 1850-1926.

Harrington, J. W. Priest's celibacy meets opposition. N. Y. Times, Mar. 2, 1919.

Harrington, M. R. A preliminary sketch of Lenápe culture. AA, XV.

——Some Seneca corn-foods and their preparation. AA, X.

——Vestiges of material culture among the Canadian Delawares. AA, X.

Harris, W. B. The Berbers of Morocco. JAI, XXVII.

Harrison, C. Family life of the Haidas, Queen Charlotte Islands. Notice in JAI, XXI.

——Religion and family among the Haidas. JAI, XXI.

Harrison, J. E. *Prolegomena to the study of Greek religion. Cambridge, 1903.

Hartland, E. S. Introductory note to "Dinka laws and customs," by H. O'Sullivan. JAI, XL.

——The matrilineate again. AA, XX.

——Presidential address. Folk-Lore, XII.

——Primitive paternity, the myth of supernatural birth in relation to the history of the family. 2 vols. London, 1909-10.

——The sin-eater. Folk-Lore, III.

Hartmann, M. Die Frau im Islam. Ztsft. d. V. f. Vkde., XI.

Hartmann, K. R. E. von. Phänomenologie des sittlichen Bewusstseins. Berlin, 1879.

Harvard, Law Review, The. I-XL. Cambridge (Mass.), 1887-1926.

Harvey, E. D. Chinese animism. A doctor's thesis of 1924, deposited in the Yale Univ. Library.

Haseman, J. D. Some notes on the Pawumwa Indians of South America. AA, XIV.

Hasluck, Mrs. F. W., see Hardie, M. M.

Hassler, E. Die Bewohner des Granchaco, Paraguay. Internat. Cong. Anthrop. Chicago, 1893.

Hastings, J. *A dictionary of the Bible; dealing with its language, literature and contents, including the Biblical theology. New York, 1898-1904.

——Encyclopaedia of religion and ethics. 12 vols. New York, 1908.

Hatch, E. Griechenthum und Christenthum. Freiburg, 1892.

Haug, M. Essays on the sacred language, writings, and religion of the Parsis. Boston, 1878.

Hauri, J. Der Islam in seinem Einfluss auf das Leben seiner Bekenner. Leyden, 1881.

Havemeyer, L. The drama of savage peoples. New Haven, 1916.

Hawes, C. H. Hawes' Wanderungen auf Sachalin. Globus, LXXXVIII.

Hawtrey, S. H. C. The Lengua Indians of the Paraguayan Chaco. JAI, XXXI.

Haxthausen, A. F. von. *Transkaukasia. 2 vols. Leipzig, 1856.

Haywood, J. The civil and political history of the state of Tennessee. Reprint from edit. of 1823. Nashville, 1891.

Hearn, L. *†Japan. An attempt at interpretation. New York, 1904.

——Kottō. New York and London, 1902.

——Out of the East. Boston and New York, 1895.

Hearne, S. A journey from Prince of Wales' fort in Hudson's Bay to the Northern ocean. London, 1795.

Hedin, S. A. †Through Asia. 2 vols. London, 1899.

Hegar, A. Der Geschlechtstrieb: eine social-medicinische Studie. Stuttgart, 1894.

Hehn, V. *Kulturpflanzen und Hausthiere. Berlin, 1902.

——Das Salz, eine kulturhistorische Studie. Berlin, 1873.

Heierli, J. Die ältesten Gräber in der Schweiz. Globus, LXXII.

Heilborn, A. Zur Volkskunde von Hiddensee. Globus, LXXVIII.

Heimskringla, see Laing, S.

Heinrici, G. Die Christengemeinde

Korinths. Ztsft. f. Wissenschaftliche Theol., XIX. Leipzig, 1876.

Hellwald, F. von. Battak. In Jäger's Handwörterbuch der Zoologie, Anthropologie und Ethnologie. Erster Band. Breslau, 1880.

——Gês. In A. Reichenow's Handwörterbuch der Zoologie, Anthropologie und Ethnologie. Dritter Band. Breslau, 1885.

——Karen. In A. Reichenow's Handwörterbuch der Zoologie, Anthropologie und Ethnologie. Vierter Band. Breslau, 1886.

Hellwig, A. Das Einpflöcken von Krankheiten. Globus, XC.

Henderson, E. F. Translation of select documents of the middle ages. London, 1892.

Henley, W. of. Walter of Henley's Husbandry. The manuscripts, translations, and glossary of E. Lamond. London, 1890.

Henne am Rhyn, O. Kulturgeschichtliche Skizzen. Berlin, 1889.

Henning, C. L. Die Ergebnisse der Ausgrabungen am Beltempel zu Nippur. Globus, LXXXIV.

——Die neuesten Forschungen über die Steinzeit und die Zeit der Metalle in Aegypten. Globus, LXXIV.

——Die Onandaga-Indianer des Staates New-York. Globus, LXXVI.

Henning, L. Die Kongoausstellung in Brüssel-Tervueren, 1897. Globus, LXXII.

Henry, A. The Lolos and other tribes of Western China. JAI, XXXIII.

Henshaw, H. W. Articles: Havasupai; Slavery; Sweating. HAI.

——Popular fallacies respecting the Indians. AA, VII.

Henshaw, H. W. and Hodge, F. W. Articles: Comeya; Mohave. HAI, pt. I.

Henshaw, H. W. and Swanton, J. R. Eskimo. HAI, pt. I.

Hermann, K. F., see Becker, W. A.

Herodotus. History.

Herrera, A. de. Historia general de los hechos de los Castellanos en las islas i tierra firme del mar oceano. Escrita por Antonio de Herrera Coronista mayor de Sv Md. de las Indias y sv coronista de Castilla. En quarto decadas desde el año de 1492 hasta el de 1531. Madrid, 1726-7.

Herrman, R. A. Die Bevölkerung der Insel Pitcairn. Petermann's Mitth., XLVII.

Herrmann, F. Eine Geisterbannung im Schlosse zu Darmstadt. Hessische Blätter für Volkskunde, IV. Leipzig, 1905.

Hessische Blätter für Volkskunde. Hrsg. im Auftrage der Hessischen Vereinigung für Volkskunde. I-XX. Leipzig, 1902-21.

Hetherwick, A. Some animistic beliefs among the Yaos of British Central Africa. JAI, XXXII.

L'Heureux, J. Ethnological notes on the astronomical customs and religious ideas of the Chokitapia or Blackfeet Indians, Canada. JAI, XV.

Heusler, A. Deutsches Privatrecht. 2 Bde. Leipzig, 1885.

Hewitt, J., see Lawrence, A. E.

Hewitt, J. F. History as told in the Arabian Nights. Westm. Rev., CXLIII.

——The history of the forms and migrations of the signs of the cross and the su-astika. Westm. Rev., CL.

*Hewitt, J. N. B. Articles: Adoption; Attacapa; Calumet; Chiefs; Confederation; Dance; Family; Fetish; Government; Iroquoian family; Iroquois; Mohawk; Mythology; Neutrals; Oneida; Onekagoncka; Oyaron or tutelaries; Reform of Hiawatha; Sauk; Teharonhiawagon; Totem; Tuscarora; Wampum; White dog sacrifice; Women. HAI.

——Era of the formation of the League of the Iroquois. AA, VII.

——Orenda and a definition of religion. AA, IV.

Hewitt, J. N. B. and Swanton, J. R. Kinship. HAI, pt. I.

Heyd, W. von. *Geschichte des Levantehandels im Mittelalter. 2 Bände. Stuttgart, 1879.

Heyer, F. Die Ausbildung der Priesterherrschaft und die Inquisition. Berlin, 1877.

Hickson, S. J. *Notes on the Sengirese. JAI, XVI.

Hiekisch, C. Die Tungusen. St. Petersburg, 1879.

Hieronymous, St., see Jerome.

Hildburgh, W. L. Notes on Sinhalese magic. JAI, XXXVIII.

——Notes on some Burmese amulets and magical objects. JAI, XXXIX.

——Notes on some Tibetan and Bhutia amulets and folk medicines, and a few Nepalese amulets. JAI, XXXIX.

Hildebrand, R. Recht und Sitte auf den verschiedenen wirtschaftlichen Kulturstufen. Jena, 1896.

Hildreth, R. The history of the United States of America. 3 vols. New York, 1849.

Hill, S. A. Life statistics of an Indian province. JAI, XVIII. (Extract from Nature for July 12, 1888.)

Hiller, H. M. Manners and customs of the people of Southern Borneo. Bull. Geog. Soc. of Phila., III.

Hills, F. L. Psychiatry—ancient, medieval and modern. PSM, LX.

Hill-Tout, C. British North America. I. The far west. The home of the Salish and Déné. Copp Clark Co., Toronto, 1907.

——*Curious and interesting marriage customs of some of the aboriginal tribes of British Columbia. Amer. Antiquarian, XXIV.

——*Ethnological report on the StsEé-lis and Sk·aúlits tribes of the Halkō-mélEm division of the Salish of British Columbia. JAI, XXXIV.

——*Report on the ethnology of the Okanák·ēn of British Columbia, an interior division of the Salish stock. JAI, XLI.

——*Report on the ethnology of the Síciatl of British Columbia, a coast division of the Salish stock. JAI, XXXIV.

——*Report on the ethnology of the StlatlumH of British Columbia. JAI, XXXV.

Hilton-Simpson, M. W. Some Arab and Shawia remedies and notes on the trepanning of the skull in Algeria. JAI, XLIII.

Hinds, W. A. American communities. Chicago, 1902.

Hippocrates. Hippocratis opera omnia. Vol. XXI of Medicorum graecorum opera omnia quae existant. Ed. C. G. Kühn. Lipsiae, 1825.

——The genuine works of Hippocrates. Trans. by F. Adams. London, 1849.

Historische Zeitschrift. I-CXXXIV. München, 1859-1926.

Hitchcock, R. *The Ainos of Yezo, Japan. USNM, 1890.

——The ancient burial mounds of Japan. USNM, 1891.

——Shinto, or the mythology of the Japanese. USNM, 1891.

Hobley, C. W. *†Bantu beliefs and magic. London, 1922.

——British East Africa. Anthropological studies in Kavirondo and Nandi.

——Ethnology of A-Kamba and other East African tribes. Cambridge, 1910.

——Further researches into Kikuyu and Kamba religious beliefs and customs. JAI, XLI.

——Kavirondo and Nandi. JAI, XXXIII.

——Kikuyu customs and beliefs. Thahu and its connection with circumcision rites. JAI, XL.

Hobson, J. A. The evolution of modern capitalism. A study of machine production. London and New York, 1895.

Hocart, A. M. The cult of the dead in Eddystone of the Solomons. JAI, LII.

——Early Fijians. JAI, XLIX.

——The Fijian custom of Tauvu. JAI, XLIII.

——Fijian heralds and envoys. JAI, XLIII.

——On the meaning of Kalou and the origin of Fijian temples. JAI, XLII.

——Polynesian tombs. (Discussion and correspondence.) AA, XX.

Hodge, F. W. Articles: Cora; Maricopa, an important Yuman tribe; Papago; Pima; Pueblos; Tarahumare. HAI.

——Note. BAE, XXX.

——Rites of the Pueblo Indians. N. Y. Times, Oct. 26, 1924.

Hodge, F. W., see also Dixon, R. B., also Henshaw, H. W.

Hodson, T. C. The "Genna" amongst the tribes of Assam. JAI, XXXVI.

Hoensbroech, Graf von. Das Papstthum in seiner sozial-kulturellen Wirksamkeit. (Erster Band.) Leipzig, 1901.

Hoernlé, A. W. The social organization of the Nama Hottentots of southwest Africa. AA, XXVII.

Hoffman, W. J. *†The beginnings of writing. New York, 1895.

——*The Menomini Indians. BAE, pt. I.

——*The Midē'wiwin or Grand Medicine Society of the Ojibwa. BAE, VII.

Hollis, A. C. A note on the Masai system of relationship and other matters connected therewith. JAI, XL.

Holm, G. *Ethnologisk Skizze af Angmagsalikerne. Kjøbenhavn, 1887.

Holmes, John Haynes. A new age of miracles. Bookman, XLIV.

Holmes, J. H. Initiation ceremonies of natives of the Papuan Gulf. JAI, XXXII.

——Introductory notes on the toys and games of Elema, Papuan Gulf. JAI, XXXVIII.

——Notes on the Elema tribes of the Papuan Gulf. JAI, XXXIII.

——Notes on the religious ideas of the Elema tribe of the Papuan Gulf. JAI, XXXII.

Holmes, O. W. Natural law. Harvard Law Rev., XXXII.

——Opinion, in Vegelahn vs. Gunter, 167 Mass.

Holmes, S. J. *†The trend of the race. A study of present tendencies in the biological development of civilized mankind. New York, 1921.

Holmes, W. H. Art in shell of the ancient Americans. BAE, II.

——Articles: Bird-stones; Caves and rock shelters; Copper; Obsidian; Ornament; Pearls; Plummets. HAI.

——Flint implements and fossil remains from a sulphur spring at Afton, Indian Territory. AA, IV.

Holt, T. B. Marriage laws and customs of the Cymri. JAI, XXVIII.

Holtzmann, A. *Indische Sagen. 2 Bände. Stuttgart, 1854.

Holtzmann, H. Sakramentliches im neuen Testamente. Archiv für Religionswissenschaft, VII.

Holub, E. *Central South African coast tribes. JAI, X.

——In Illustr. Africa, June, Sept., 1896.

——*Sieben Jahre in Süd-Afrika, 1872-1879. 2 Bände. Wien, 1881.

——*Von der Capstadt ins Land der Maschukulumbe. Wien, 1890.

Homer. Iliad. Odyssey.

Hopkins, E. W. The fountain of youth. Jour. Am. Orient. Soc., XXVI.

——On the Hindu custom of dying to redress a grievance. Jr. Am. Or. Soc., XXI.

——The religions of India. Boston, 1895.

——The sniff kiss in ancient India. Jr. Am. Or. Soc., XXVIII.

——Totemism. Paper read at the Amer. Oriental Society Meeting, New Haven, April 2-4, 1914. Reported in the Nation, CVI.

Horace. Works.

Hornaday, W. T. The extermination

of the American bison. Smithson.
Rep. 1887, pt. II.

Horne, G. and Aiston, G. Savage life
in Central Australia. London, 1924.

Hornell, J. Survivals of the use of
oculi in modern boats. JAI, LIII.

Horsley, V. Trephining in the Neolithic Period. JAI, XVII.

Hose, C. *The natives of Borneo. JAI,
XXIII.

Hose, C. and McDougall, W. The relations between men and animals in
Sarawak. JAI, XXXI.

Hose, C. and Shelford, R. Materials
for a study of tatu in Borneo. JAI,
XXXVI.

Hostmann, F. W. Over de beschaving
van negers in Amerika, door kolo-
nisatie met Europeanen, of be-
schouwingen omtrent de maatschap-
pelijke vereeniging der negers in
Afrika, den staat, waarin zij door
den zoogenaamden slavenhandel
komen, en later door abolitie en
emancipatie overgaan. Amsterdam,
1850.

Hough, W. Articles: Altar; Bull-
roarer; Clothing; Eagle; Fermentation; Foods; Mescal; Prayer sticks;
Salt. HAI.

——Environmental interrelations in
Arizona. AA, XI.

——*†Fire-making apparatus. USNM,
1888.

——The Hopi in relation to their
plant environment. AA, X.

——Methods of fire-making. USNM,
1890.

——The Pulque of Mexico. Proceedings, USNM, XXXIII.

Howard-Bury, C. K. The Mount
Everest expedition. Geographical
Jr., LIX.

*Howitt, A. W. The Dieri and other
kindred tribes of Central Australia.
JAI, XX.

——The Jeraeil, or initiation ceremonies of the Kurnai tribe. JAI,
XIV.

——Migrations of the Kurnai ancestors. JAI, XV.

——Native tribes of South Eastern
Australia. London, 1904.

——Notes on the Australian class systems. JAI, XII.

——Further notes on the Australian
class systems. JAI, XVIII.

——On Australian medicine men; or,
doctors and wizards of some Australian tribes. JAI, XVI.

——On some Australian beliefs. JAI,
XIII.

——On some Australian ceremonies
of initiation. JAI, XIII.

——Remarks on the class systems collected by Mr. Palmer. JAI, XIII.

*Howitt, A. W. and Fison, L. From
mother-right to father-right. JAI,
XII.

——On the deme and the horde. JAI,
XIV.

Howitt, A. W., see also Fison, L.

Hrdlička, A. Articles: Cannibalism;
Medicine and medicine men; Southern Ute. HAI.

——Notes on the Indians of Sonora,
Mexico. AA, VI.

——A painted skeleton from northern
Mexico, with notes on bone paint-
ing among the American aborigines.
AA, III.

——*Physiological and medical ob-
servations among the Indians of
Southwestern United States and
Northern Mexico. BAE, Bull.
XXXIV.

Hrdlička, A., see also Lumholtz, C.

Hubbard, W. A general history of
New England, from the discovery
to MDCLXXX. Cambridge, 1815.

Humbert, A. Japan and the Japanese.
New York, 1874.

Humboldt, A. *†Essai politique sur
le royaume de la Nouvelle-Espagne.
Voyage de Humboldt et Bonpland.
Paris, 1811.

Hunt, A. E. Ethnographical notes on
the Murray Islands, Torres Straits.
JAI, XXVIII.

Huntington, E. *†The pulse of Asia.
New York, 1907.

Huntington, F. Ahtena. HAI, pt. I.

Husain, M. S. Hindu ceremonies observed in the Madras presidency. JASB, III.

Hutchinson, H. N. Marriage customs in many lands. New York, 1897.

——Prehistoric man and beast. New York, 1897.

Hutchinson, P. The future of religion in China. Atl. Mo., CXXVII.

Hutchinson, T. The history of Massachusetts Bay. London, 1760-1828.

Huth, A. F. The marriage of near kin considered with respect to the laws of nations, the results of experience, and the teachings of biology. London, 1887.

Hutter, H. Der Abschluss von Blutsfreundschaft und Verträgen bei den Negern des Graslandes in Nordkamerun. Globus, LXXV.

——Politische und sociale Verhältnisse bei den Graslandstämmen Nordkameruns. Globus, LXXVI.

Hutton, J. H. Carved monoliths at Dimapur and an Angami Naga ceremony. JAI, LII.

——Leopard-men in the Naga Hills. JAI, L.

——*The Sema Nagas. London, 1921.

Huxley, L. Life and letters of Thomas Henry Huxley. 2 vols. New York, 1901.

Huxley, T. H. Evolution and ethics. PSM, XLIV.

Ibn Batuta, see Muhammed ibn Abd Allah.

Ibn Fozlan. Om Nordisk Begravelsesskikke (fra det Arabiske oversat og med Anmaerkninger oplyst af C. A. Holmboe), Vidensk.-Selsk. i Christiania. Forhandlinger for 1869. XX.

Ihering, H. von. Die künstliche Deformirung der Zähne. Ztsft. f. Ethnol., XIV.

Ihering, R. von. Vorgeschichte der Indo-europäer. Leipzig, 1894.

——The same work, translated as

"The evolution of the Aryan," by A. Drucker. London, 1897.

Illustrated Africa. Continued as Illustrated Christian World. Vineland (N.J.) and New York, 1894-6.

Illustrated American, The. I-XXV. New York, Chicago, 1890-99.

Illustrated Christian World. Continued from Illustrated Africa. Merged into Christian Herald. Vineland (N.J.) and New York, 1896-8.

Im Thurn, E. F. *Among the Indians of Guiana; being sketches chiefly anthropologic from the interior of British Guiana. London, 1883.

——*On the animism of the Indians of British Guiana. JAI, XI.

——On the thoughts of the South Sea Islanders. JAI, LI.

Indische Gids, De. Tevens nieuwe serie van het Tijdschrift voor Nederlandsch-Indië. I-XLVIII. Amsterdam, 1879-1926.

Inge, W. R. Address at Johns Hopkins. Rep. in N. Y. Times, May 2, 1925.

——The Catholic Church and the Anglo-Saxon mind. Atl. Mo., CXXXI.

Inglis. From China. Osage City Free Press, Dec. 22, 1898.

International Congress of Americanists, see Congrès International.

International Congress of Anthropology. Memoirs. Chicago, 1893.

International Monthly, The. A magazine of contemporary thought. IV. Continued as International Quarterly. Burlington (Vt.), 1900-02.

International Quarterly, The. Continuation of International Monthly. VI-XII. Burlington (Vt.), 1902-03. New York, 1904-06.

Internationales Archiv für Ethnographie. I-XXVI. Leiden, 1888-1925.

Institutes, in Corpus Iuris Civilis.

Ivanovski, A. Die Mongolei. Leipzig, 1895.

Iwanowski, N. P. Über Menschenopfer. Globus, LXXIV.

Jacobs, Julius. *Het Familie- en Kampongleven op Groot-Atjeh. II. Leiden, 1894.

Jackson, A. V. W. Notes on a journey to Persia, I. Jour. Amer. Oriental Soc., XXV. First Half.

——Zoroaster. London, 1899.

Jäger, G. Handwörterbuch der Zoologie, Anthropologie, und Ethnologie. 8 Bände. Breslau, 1880.

Jahrbuch für Gesetzgebung, Verwaltung und Volkswirtschaft im Deutschen Reich. Jahrg. I-XXXVI. Leipzig, 1877-1912.

James, M. R., see Ryle, H. E.

Janke, H. Die Uebervölkerung und ihre Abwehr. Leipzig, 1893.

Jastrow, M. Religion of Babylonia. Omens and oracles. Hastings's Dictionary of the Bible. Extra vol. New York, 1904.

Jefferson, C. E. The delusion of militarism. Atl. Mo., CIII.

Jefferson, T. The writings of Thomas Jefferson. Collected and edited by Paul L. Ford. 10 vols. New York, 1892.

Jenks, A. E. Bontoc Igorot clothing. AA, VI, VII.

——The wild rice gatherers of the Upper Lakes. BAE, XIX, pt. II.

Jenks, E. Law and politics of the Middle Ages. New York, 1898.

Jenness, D. Papuan cat's cradles. JAI, L.

Jenness, D. and Ballentyne, A. *The northern D'Entrecasteaux. Oxford, 1920.

Jerome, Saint. Works.

Jerphanion, P. W. de. Über abergläubische Vorstellungen und Gebräuche des Volkes in Anatolien. In Die katholischen Missionen. Jan., 1907. Review in Globus, XCI.

Jetté, J. *On the medicine-men of the Ten'a. JAI, XXXVII.

——L'organisation sociale des Ten'as. Cong. Intern. d. Amér. XVe. session, Québec, 1906, I.

Jevons, F. B. An introduction to the history of religion. London, 1896.

*Jewish Encyclopedia. New York, 1905.

Jewish Quarterly Review, The. I-XX. London, 1888-1908. I-XVI. Philadelphia, 1910-26 (n.s.).

Jhering, see Ihering.

Jochelson, W. The mythology of the Koryak. AA, VI.

Joest, W. *Tätowiren, Narbenzeichnen und Körperbemalen. Berlin, 1887.

Johnson, A. Lucina sine concubitu (a letter addressed· to the Royal Society showing that children can be got without commerce with man). London, 1750. Collectanea Adamantæa, VII, ed. by E. Goldsmid. Edinburgh, 1885.

Johnson, A. H. Europe in the sixteenth century. New York, 1897.

Johnson, M. Cannibal land. Boston, 1922.

Johnston, H. H. *The Kilima-Njaro expedition. London, 1886.

——The negro in the new world. New York, 1910.

——*On the races of the Congo and the Portuguese colonies in western Africa. JAI, XIII.

——*The people of eastern equatorial Africa. JAI, XV.

——*†The Uganda protectorate. 2 vols. New York, 1902.

——The Veneerings. New York, 1922.

Johnstone, H. B. Notes on the customs of the tribes occupying Mombasa sub-district, British East Africa. JAI, XXXII.

Jolly, Jules. Des Seconds Mariages. Paris, 1896.

Jolly, J. Recht und Sitte. In Grundriss der Indo-Arischen Philologie und Altertumskunde, Bd. II, Heft 8. Strassburg, 1896.

——Recht und Sitte der Indo-Aryer. Strassburg, 1896.

——Über die rechtliche Stellung der Frauen bei den alten Indern nach den Dharmaçāstra. Sitzungsberichte der Münchener Akad. Philos. Philol. Hist. Klasse, 1876.

Jones, C. J. The four hundred of the

plains. The Illustrated American, 1895.

Jones, L. F. A study of the Thlingets of Alaska. New York, 1914.

Jones, W. Kickapoo ethnological notes. AA, XV.

Jónsson, F. Hárbarpsljóp, in Aarbøger f. Nord. Oldkynd., 1889.

Jørgensen, A. D. Bidrag til Oplysning af Middelalderens Love og Samfundsforhold, in Aarbøger f. Nord. Oldkynd., 1872, 1876.

*Joshi, P. B. Gondhalis or Maratha bards. JASB, I.

——On the evil eye in the Konkan. JASB, I.

——On the household and village gods of the Maharashtra. JASB, II.

——On the rite of human sacrifice in ancient, mediaeval, and modern India and other countries. JASB, III.

Josselin de Jong, J. P. B. de. Book review of "Social life and ceremonial bundles of the Menomini Indians," by Alanson Skinner. AA, XVIII.

Journal and Proceedings of the Royal Society of New South Wales, Sydney, Australia. VI-LVIII. Sydney, 1872-1924.

Journal of American Folk-Lore. I-XXXVI. New York, 1888-1923.

Journal of Social Hygiene. I-XII. New York, 1914-26.

Journal of the African Society of London. I-XXV. London, 1901-26.

Journal of the American Oriental Society. I-XLV. Boston, 1842-9. New York, 1849-56. New Haven, 1856-1925.

*Journal of the Anthropological Society of Bombay (JASB). Bombay, 1886-1904.

*Journal of the Royal Anthropological Institute of Great Britain and Ireland (JAI). I-LV. London, 1871-1925.

Journal of the Royal Statistical Society, London. I-LXXXIX. London, 1838-1926.

Joyce, P. W. A social history of an-

cient Ireland. In 2 vols. London, 1903.

Joyce, T. A., see Torday, E.

Judd, S. History of Hadley, Massachusetts. Northampton (Mass.), 1863. Springfield (Mass.), 1905.

Julleville, L. Petit de, see Petit de Julleville.

Jung, J. Zur Würdigung der agrarischen Verhältnisse in der römischen Kaiserzeit. Historische Zeitschrift, XLII.

Jung, K. E. Der Weltteil Australien. Leipzig, 1882.

Junker, W. *Reisen in Afrika. 3 Bände. Wien, 1875-1886.

Justi, F. Geschichte des alten Persiens. Berlin, 1879.

Justinian I, see Corpus Iuris Civilis.

K., R. T. Unter den Beduinen der Aegyptischen Wüste. Globus, LXXV.

Kaindl, R. F. Aus der Volksüberlieferung der Bojken. Globus, LXXIX.

——Neuere Arbeiten zur Völkerkunde, Völkerbeschreibung und Volkskunde von Galizien, Russisch-Polen und der Ukraine. Globus, XCI.

——Reviewing ethnol. books on Galicia, etc. Globus, LXXXII.

——Ruthenische Hochzeitsgebräuche in der Bukowina. Zeitschrift des Vereins für Volkskunde, XI.

——Totenhochzeit. Globus, LXXXVIII.

——Zur Volkskunde der Rumänen in der Bukowina. Globus, XCII.

Kaiser, A. Rassenbiologische Betrachtungen über das Masai-Volk. Archiv f. Rassen- u. Gesellsfts-Biol., III.

Kålund, K. Familielivet på Island. In Aarbøger f. Nord. Oldkynd., 1870.

Kandt, R. Ein Marsch am Ostufer des Kiwu. Globus, LXXXVI.

Karasin. Story of Russian military and hunting life in Central Asia. (Russ.)

Karsten, R. Blood revenge, war, and

victory feasts among the Jibaro Indians of Eastern Ecuador. BAE, Bull. LXXIX, 1923.

Karutz, R. Eine schottische Rachepuppe. Globus, LXXIX.

——Nach den Höhlenstädten Südtunisiens. Globus, XCII.

——Zur westafrikanischen Maskenkunde. Globus, LXXIX.

Kate, H. ten. Die blauen Geburtsflecke. Globus, LXXXVII.

——Eine japanische Rachepuppe. Globus, LXXIX.

Kaumanns, F. Der Adlerstein als Hülfsmittel bei der Geburt. Hess. Bl. f. Volksk. Leipzig, 1906, V. Review by Chamberlain in AA, IX, 411.

Kautzsch, E. F. *Religion of Israel. Hastings's Bible Dictionary.

Kawaguchi, E. The latest news from Lhasa. Century Magazine, XLV.

Keane, A. H. Africa. London, 1878.

——Ethnology. Cambridge, 1901.

——On the Botocudos. JAI, XIII.

——The Lapps. JAI, XV.

Keith, A. On certain factors concerned in the evolution of human races. JAI, XLVI.

Keller, A. G. Birth control. Yale Review, VII.

——Colonization. (Boston, 1908.)

——Homeric society. New York, 1902.

——Law in evolution. Yale Law Jour., XXVIII.

——The luck element. Sci. Mo., Feb., 1917.

——The right to life. Unpopular Review, VII.

——Societal evolution, a study of the evolutionary basis of the science of society. New York, 1915.

——Societal Evolution, in Lull, R. S. and others, Evolution of Man.

——Sociology and Homer. Amer. Jour. of Soc., IX.

——Sociology and science. Nation, CII.

——Sociology and the epic. Am. Jr. Soc., IX.

——Starting-points in social science. Boston, 1923.

——Through war to peace. Revised ed. New York, 1921.

Keller, A. G., see also Gregory, H. E., Keltie, J. S.

Kelly, A. Feats of Hindu "Magic" compared with those of our sleight-of-hand men. N. Y. Evening Post, June 4, 1904.

Kelly, H. A. and Burrage, W. L. American medical biographies. Baltimore, 1920.

Keltie, J. S. Africa. Revised and edited by A. G. Keller, vol. XIX of "The History of Nations" edit. by H. C. Lodge. Philadelphia, 1906.

——The Partition of Africa. London, 1895.

Kern, H. Menschenfleisch als Arzenei. Internat. Arch. f. Ethnog. Leiden, 1896, IX, suppl.

Kerr, R. A general history and collection of voyages and travels, arranged in systematic order: forming a complete history of the origin and progress of navigation, discovery and commerce by sea and land, from the earliest ages to the present time. Edinburgh, 1811-24. 18 vols.

Keussler, J. von. Zur Geschichte und Kritik des bäuerlichen Gemeindebesitzes in Russland. Riga, Moskau, Odessa, 1876-87.

Kidd, B. Social evolution. New York and London, 1894.

Kidd, D. The essential Kaffir. London, 1904.

——Kaffir socialism and the dawn of individualism. London, 1908.

King, J. S. Female circumcision and infibulation in North East Africa. JASB, II.

Kingsley, M. H. Letter to the Spectator, Mar. 19, 1898. Spectator, LXXX.

——*†Travels in West Africa. New York, 1897.

——*West African conception of property. JAI, XXVIII.

——*†West African studies. New York, 1899.

Kipling, R. Works.

Kirby, W. W. A journey to the You can, Russian America. Smithson. Rep. 1864.

Kirtikar, K. R. On the ceremonies observed among Hindus during pregnancy and parturition. Discussion by S. V. Sukthankar. JASB, I.

Kishimoto, N. Shintō, the old religion of Japan. PSM, XLVI.

Kit-kat, The. I-IX. Columbus (Ohio), 1912-20.

Kitts, E. J. Common terms of native abuse. JASB, II.

Klaatsch, H. Scientific travel amongst the black population of tropical Australia. 1907.

Kleintischen, P. A. Die Küstenbewohner der Gazelle-halbinsel (Neupommern—deutsche Südsee), ihre Sitten und Gebräuche. Globüs, XCII.

Klemm, F. G. Allgemeine Culturgeschichte. Leipzig, 1843-52.

Klose, H. Das Bassarivolk. Globus, LXXXIII.

——Religiöse Anschauungen und Menschenopfer in Togo. Globus, LXXXI.

——*Togo. Berlin, 1899.

Kluckhohn, A. Geschichte des Gottesfriedens. Leipzig, 1857.

Klugmann, N. *Die Frau im Talmud. Wien, 1898.

Knight, M. M. The companionate and the family, the unobserved division of an historical institution. Jr. Soc. Hyg., X.

Knocker, F. W. The aborigines of Sungei Ujong [Malay States]. JAI, XXXVII.

——Notes on the wild tribes of the Ulu Plus, Perak. JAI, XXXIX.

Knoop, W. J. Indische Kriegsgeschiedenis. De Gids, 1860, II.

Koch, T. Eine Forschungsreise nach Südamerika. Ztsft. f. Eth., XXXVI.

——Die Guaikurú-Gruppe. Mittheil.

d. Anthropol. Gesell. in Wien, XXXIII.

——Die Guaikurústämme. Globus, LXXXI.

——Kreuz und quer durch Nordwestbrasilien. Globus, XC.

——Die Lenguas-Indianer in Paraguay. Globus, LXXVIII.

——Der Paradiesgarten als Schnitzmotiv der Payagun-Indianer. Globus, LXXXIII.

——Zum Animismus der Südamerikanischen Indianer. Supplement zu Band XIII von Internationales Archiv für Ethnographie.

Koenigswald, G. von. Die Carajá-Indianer. Globus, XCIV.

——Die Cayuás. Globus, XCIII.

——Die Corôados im südlichen Brasilien. Globus, XCIV.

Kohler, J. Blutrache bei den Albanesen. Pol.-Anthrop. Rev., I.

——Studien aus dem Strafrecht. Mannheim, 1890.

——Zur Urgeschichte der Ehe. Stuttgart, 1897.

Kohler, J. and Peiser, F. E. Aus dem babylonischen Rechtsleben. Leipzig, 1890.

Kohler, K. Essenes. In Jewish Encyclopedia, V.

Kohn, F. Physiological and biological material about the Yakuts (Russ.). Minusinsk, 1899.

Kolbens, P. Beschreibung des Vorgebürges der Guten Hoffnung und derer darauf wohnenden Hottentotten. Leipzig, 1745.

Kondratowitsch, O. W., see Fedorow, C. C.

Koner, W., see Guhl, E. K.

Kopplin, O. R. Fighting influenza among the Navajos. N. Y. Times, April 28, 1919.

Korrespondenz-Blatt der Deutschen Gesellschaft für Anthropologie, Ethnologie, und Urgeschichte. I-LI. (Bound with Archiv für Anthropologie.) Braunschweig, 1870-1920.

Kostomarov, N. I. *Domestic life and mores of the Great Russians in the sixteenth and seventeenth centuries. (Russ.) 3d ed. St. Petersburg, 1887.

Kowalewsky, M. Die Ökonomische Entwicklung Europas bis zum Beginne der kapitalistischen Wirtschaftsform. 2 vols. Aus dem Russischen von Leo Motzkin. Berlin, 1901.

Krämer, A. Samoa-Inseln. 2 Bde. Stuttgart, 1901. Quoted in Williamson's "Cent. Polynesia."

——Zur Nomenklatur der Pacifischen Inseln. Globus, LXXV. Quoted in Williamson's "Cent. Polynesia."

Krasinski, H. The Cossacks of the Ukraine. London, 1848.

Krass, N. Intermarriage, a sermon, rep. in N. Y. Times, March 3, 1924.

Krause, A. Bedeutung des Hakenkreuzes. Verhandl. d. Berl. Anthr. Gesellsch., 1889.

Krauss, F. S. Geheime Sprachweisen. Am Urquell, II.

——*Sreća. Glück und Schicksal im Volksglauben der Südslaven. Wien, 1886.

——Vilen als Heilkundige im Volksglauben der Südslaven. Memoirs of the Inter. Cong. of Anthrop. Chicago, 1893.

——*Volksglaube und religiöser Brauch der Südslaven. Münster, 1890.

Kremer, A. von. Kulturgeschichte des Orients unter den Chalifen. 2 Bände. Wien, 1875-77.

Krieger, M. *Neu-Guinea. Berlin, 1899.

Kroeber, A. L. Classificatory systems of relationship. JAI, XXXIX, 1909.

——Discussion of E. S. Hartland on "The Matrilineate Again." AA, XX.

——Morals of uncivilized people. AA, XII.

——Preliminary sketch of the Mohave Indians. AA, IV.

Kropf, A. A Kaffir-English dictionary. South Africa. Lovedale Mission press, 1899.

Kruijt, A. C. Het animisme in den Indischen Archipel. 's Gravenhage, 1906.

*Kubary, J. S. Beitrag zur Kenntniss der Núkuóro- oder Monteverde-Inseln. Hamburg, 1900.

——Ethnographische Beiträge zur Kenntniss des Karolinen-Archipels. Leyden, 1895.

——Ethnographische Beiträge zur Kenntniss der Karolinischen Inselgruppe u. Nachbarschaft. Heft I. Die Socialen Einrichtungen der Pelauer. Berlin, 1885.

——Mikronesien. Die Verbrechen und das Strafverfahren auf den Pelau-Inseln. Original-Mittheilungen aus der Ethnologischen Abtheilung der Königlichen Museen zu Berlin, 1885.

——Die Todten-Bestattung auf den Pelau-Inseln. Original-Mittheilungen aus der Ethnologischen Abtheilung der Königlichen Museen zu Berlin, 1885.

Kunz, G. F. The curious lore of precious stones. Philadelphia and London, 1913.

——The magic of jewels and charms. Philadelphia and London, 1915.

Kurnig. Das Sexualleben und der Pessimismus. Leipzig, 1897.

Lacroix, P. Manners, customs, and dress during the Middle Ages and during the Renaissance period. London, 1874.

La Fetra. Araucanians. Ill. Christian World, Nov., 1896.

Lafitau, J. F. Mœurs des sauvages amériquains, comparées aux mœurs des premiers temps. 2 vols. Paris, 1724.

——De zeden der wilden van Amerika. (Trans. from French.) Amsterdam, 1751.

LaFlesche, F. Osage marriage customs. AA, XIV.

——The Osage tribe. BAE, XXXVI.

——The right and left in Osage rites. AA, XVIII.

LaFlesche, F., see also Fletcher, A. C.

Lahontan, Baron L. A. de. Nouveaux

Voyages dans l'Amérique Septentrionale. 2 tomes. A la Haye, 1703; new edition by R. G. Thwaites, from the English edition of 1703. Chicago, 1905.

Laidlaw, G. E. Some ethnological observations in South Africa. Amer. Antiquarian and Oriental Jour., XXIV.

Laing, S. *The Heimskringla or Sagas of the Norse Kings, from the Icelandic of Snorre Sturlason. 2d ed. 4 vols. London, 1889. See Morris, W., also Vigfússon, G.

Lala, R. R. Pirates of the Philippines. Frank Leslie's Pop. Mo., May, 1900.

Lamere, O. and Radin, P. Description of a Winnebago funeral. AA, XIII. (n.s.)

Lamond, E., see Henley, W. of.

Lamprecht, K. G. Beiträge zur Geschichte des Französischen Wirthschaftslebens im elften Jahrhundert. Leipzig, 1878.

Lander, R. L. Journal of an expedition to explore the course and termination of the Niger. New York, 1841.

Landnamabok. Saga Library, XLIV. See also Laing, S., also Morris, W.

Landor, A. H. S. Corea, or Cho-sen, the land of the morning calm. London, 1895.

Landtmann, G. The magic of the Kiwai Papuans in warfare. JAI, XLVI.

Lane, E. W. *†An account of the manners and customs of the modern Egyptians. 2 vols. London, 1837.

——The thousand and one nights. London, 1841.

Lane, R. W. The peaks of Shala. Being a record of certain wanderings among the hill-tribes of Albania. London, 1922.

Lang, A. Custom and myth. London, 1885.

——Was Jehovah a fetish stone? Contemporary Review, LVII.

Lang, A. and Atkinson, J. J. *Social origins. Primal law. Longmans, Green, Co. New York, 1903.

Lang, H. R. The Portuguese element in New England. Jour. of Amer. Folk-Lore, V.

Langley, S. P. The fire walk ceremony in Tahiti. Smithson. Rep. for 1901.

Langsdorff, G. H. von. Voyages and travels in various parts of the world. 1803-07. Carlisle, 1817.

Lapouge, G. de. Grundfragen der historischen Anthropologie. Politisch-Anthropologische Revue, III.

Lasch, R. Einige besondere Arten der Verwendung der Eier in Volksglauben und Volksbrauch. Globus, LXXXIX.

——Rache als Selbstmordmotiv. Globus, LXXIV.

——Religiöser Selbstmord und seine Beziehung zum Menschenopfer. Globus, LXXV.

——Die Verbleibsorte der Seelen der im Wochenbette Gestorbenen. Globus, LXXX.

Latcham, R. E. Ethnology of the Araucanos. JAI, XXXIX.

——Notes on the physical characteristics of the Araucanos. JAI, XXXIV.

Laufer, B. Origin of the word shaman. AA, XIX.

Laveleye, É. De la propriété et de ses formes primitives. Paris, 1874.

——The same work trans. from French by G. R. L. Marriott, as "Primitive property." London, 1878.

Law Quarterly Review, The. I-XLI. London, 1885-1925.

Lawrence, A. E. and Hewitt, J. Some aspects of spirit worship amongst the Milano of Sarawak. JAI, XXXVIII, 1908.

Lawrence, D. H. Indians and entertainment. N. Y. Times, Oct. 26, 1924.

Lawrie, J. Aneityum, New Hebrides. AAAS, 1892.

Lawson, J. The history of Carolina. Raleigh, 1860.

Laxdæla Saga. Trans. by M. A. C. Press. London, 1899.

Lazăr, V. Die Hochzeit bei den Süd-rumänen (Kutzo-Wlachen, Zinza-ren) in der Türkei. Globus, XCIV.

Lea, H. C. *A history of the inquisi-tion of the Middle Ages. 3 vols. New York, 1888.

——*An historical sketch of sacer-dotal celibacy in the Christian church. Philadelphia, 1867.

Leaf, W. Companion to the Iliad. New York, 1892.

Le Braz, Anatole. The night of fires; and other Breton studies. Trans. from French by F. M. Gostling. New York, 1912.

Lecky, W. E. H. Democracy and lib-erty. New York, 1896.

——*†History of European morals from Augustus to Charlemagne. 3 ed. New York, 1877.

Leclère, A. Incidents of Cambodian life. PSM, XLIV.

Lee, F. E. The influence of the Jesuits on the social organization of the North American Indians. A doc-toral dissertation deposited in Yale University Library.

Lefèvre, A. Race and language. New York, 1894.

Leggatt, T. W. Malekula, New Heb-rides. AAAS, 1892.

Legge, J. The Chinese Classics. 7 vols. London, 1871.

——*The Lî Kî. In F. Max Müller's "Sacred Books of the East," vols. XXVII-XXVIII. Oxford, 1885. See Müller.

Legrand d'Aussy, P. J. Fabliaux ou Contes Fables et Romans du XIIme et du XIIIme Siècle. Paris, 1829.

Lehmann, A. *Overtro og Trolddom fra de aeldste Tider til vore Dage. Kjøbenhavn. 1893-96. 4 parts.

——The same work translated into German by Dr. Petersen as "Aber-glaube und Zauberei." Stuttgart, 1898.

Lehmann, K. Verlobung und Hoch-zeit. München, 1882.

Leith, E. T. On divination by Házirát

among the Indian Musulmáns. JASB, I.

Leitner, Dr. Address. JASB, I.

Lejeune, C. La Communion. Bull. Soc. d'Anthr. de Paris, 5th ser., V.

Leland, C. G. and Prince, J. D. Kulóskap the Master. New York, 1902.

Lenient, C. La satire en France au Moyen Age. Paris, 1883.

Lenormant, F. Die Anfänge der Kul-tur. Jena, 1875.

——Chaldean magic: its origin and development. London, 1877.

Lenz, O. Skizzen aus Westafrika. Ber-lin, 1878.

Leo, H. Einiges über das Leben und die Lebensbedingungen in Island in der Zeit des Heidenthumes. (From Historisches Taschenbuch, Jahr-gang 6. Leipzig, 1835.)

Leonardo da Vinci. See McCurdy, E.

Leonhardi, M. Freiherr Von. Über einige religiöse und totemistische Vorstellungen . . . in Zentral-australien. Globus, XCI.

Lepsius, R. Briefe aus Aegypten, Aethiopien und der Halbinsel des Sinai. Berlin, 1852.

Lessner, Oberleutnant. Die Baluë-oder Rumpiberge und ihre Bewohn-er. Globus, LXXXVI.

Letourneau, Ch. L'evolution de l'es-clavage dans les diverses races humaines. Paris, 1897.

——L'évolution du commerce dans les diverses races humaines. Paris, 1897.

——†The evolution of marriage and of the family. London, 1891.

——L'évolution de la morale. Paris, 1887.

——L'évolution politique dans les diverses races humaines. Paris, 1890.

——La guerre dans les diverses races humaines. Paris, 1895.

——†Property: its origin and develop-ment. New York.

——*†La Sociologie d'après l'ethnog-raphie. Bibliothèque des sciences contemp. Paris, 1880.

Letourneux, A., see Hanoteau, A.

Leuba, J. H. Varieties, classification and origin of magic. AA, XIV.

Levi, Eliphas (Pseudonym for Constant, A. L.) Histoire de la magie. Paris, 1860.

Levick, M. B. Pursuit of the elixir of life. N. Y. Times, Sept. 9, 1923.

Lévy-Bruhl, L. Les fonctions mentales dans les sociétés inférieures. Paris, 1910.

——La mentalité primitive. Paris, 1922.

Lewin, T. H. *Wild races of southeastern India. London, 1870.

Lewis, A. L. The Menhirs of Madagascar. JAI, XLVII.

——The nine stones. Man, III.

Lewis, F. The professional ministry. Atl. Mo., CXVI.

Lewis, M. and Clark, W. Travels. 3 vols. London, 1815.

Libby, W. The history of medicine in its salient features. New York, 1923.

Lichtenberger, H. Le Poème et la Légende des Nibelungen. Paris, 1891.

Lichtenstein, H. Reisen im südlichen Africa. Berlin, 1812.

——*Travels in Southern Africa. Trans. London, 1815.

Liddell, H. G. and Scott, R. A Greek-English lexicon. 7th edition. New York, 1879.

Liebrecht, F. Zur Volkskunde. Heilbronn, 1879.

Lindquist, G. E. E. The red man in the United States. New York, 1923.

Lindsay, W. S. History of merchant shipping and ancient commerce. 4 vols. London, 1874-6.

Lippert, J. *Kulturgeschichte der Menschheit in ihrem organischen Aufbau. 2 vols. Stuttgart, 1886. See Murdock, G. P.

Lister, J. J. Natives of Fakaofu (Bowditch Island.) JAI, XXI.

Liston-Blyth, A. Notes on native customs in the Baniara District, Papua. JAI, LIII, Miscellanea based on J. G. Frazer's "Questions."

Literary Digest, The. I-XCI. New York, 1890-1926.

Livingstone, D. The last journals. New York, 1875.

——*†Missionary travels and researches in South Africa. London, 1858. 2 vols. New York, 1858.

Livy. History.

Lloyd, A. B. In dwarf land and cannibal country. New York, 1899.

Lobingier, C. S. Primitive Malay marriage law. AA, XII.

Locke, W. J. Works.

Lockyer, J. N. Early temple and pyramid builders. Smithson. Rep., 1893.

Loeb, E. M. Human sacrifice. A doctoral dissertation deposited in Yale University Library.

Lombroso, C. and Ferrero, G. La donna delinquente, la prostituta e la donna normale. Torino, 1894.

London, J. Works.

Loskiel, G. H. Geschichte der Mission der evangelischen Brüder unter den Indianern in Nordamerika. Barby, 1789.

——Mission of the United Brethren among the Indians of North America. London, 1794.

Love, G. R. History of the institutional care of the insane. Ohio Board of Admin., Pub. no. 3. May, 1915.

Lowie, R. H. Ceremonialism in North America. AA, XVI.

——Ethnology of the Crow and Village Indians. AA, XIV.

——Family and Sib. AA, XXI.

Lowie, R. H. and Farrand, L. Marriage. HAI, pt. I.

Lubbock, J. The origin of civilisation and the primitive condition of man. New York, 1873.

——*Pre-historic times. London, 1872.

Lucian. Works.

Lucier, V. A. (Mrs.). Mexican superstitions concerning sickness. Pop. Sci. News, April, 1895.

Lucius, P. E. Der Essenismus in

seinem Verhältniss zum Judenthum. Strassburg, 1881.

Lugard, F. D. The dual mandate in British tropical Africa. Edinburgh and London, 1922.

Lull, R. S.; Ferris, H. B.; Parker, G. H.; Angell, J. R.; Keller, A. G.; Conklin, E. G. The evolution of man. New Haven, 1922.

Lumholtz, C. Cave dwellers of the Sierra Madre. Int. Cong. Anthr., 1893.

——The Huichol Indians of Mexico. Bull. Amer. Mus. Nat. Hist., X.

——Tarahumari dances and plant-worship. Scribner's, XVI.

——*†Tarahumari life and customs. Scribner's, XVI.

Lumholtz, C. and Hrdlička, A. Trephining in Mexico. AA, X.

Lund, T. Norges Historie. Kjøbenhavn, 1885.

Luquiens, F. B., Translator. Three lays of Marie de France. New York, 1911.

Lyons, A. P. Animistic and other spiritualistic beliefs of the Bina Tribe, western Papua. JAI, LI.

M., Dr. Physiologie und Soziologie des Inzestes zwischen Vater und Tochter unter den Indianern. Umschau, VIII.

McCabe, J. St. Augustine and his age. New York, 1903.

MacCauley, C. *Seminole Indians of Florida. BAE, V.

McCulloch, J. R., Ed. A select collection of ancient and valuable tracts printed by Lord Overstone. London, 1857-9. I. Volume on the national debt and sinking fund. II. Volume on paper currency and banking. III. Volume of miscellaneous tracts. IV. Volume on commerce. (Not published as vols. I-IV, but cited thus in the text.)

McCurdy, E. Leonardo da Vinci's note-books arranged and rendered into English with introductions. New York, 1923.

MacCurdy, G. G. The sixteenth international congress of Americanists. AA, X.

——Human origins, a manual of prehistory. 2 vols. New York, 1924.

Macdonald, D. Efate, New Hebrides. AAAS, 1892.

——Mythology of the Efatese. AAAS, 1898.

Macdonald, J. *East Central African customs. JAI, XXII.

——*Manners, customs, superstitions, and religions of South African tribes. JAI, XIX, XX.

MacDougall, W., see Hose, C.

McGee, W J. Anthropology at Detroit and Toronto. AA, X.

——The beginning of marriage. AA, IX.

——The beginning of mathematics. AA, I.

——Piratical acculturation. AA, XI.

——*Primitive numbers. BAE, XIX, pt. II.

——*The Seri Indians. BAE, XVII.

——*The Siouan Indians. BAE, XV.

McGee, W J, see also Muñiz, M. A.

MacGregor, J. K. Some notes on Nsibidi, a form of writing. JAI, XXXIX.

MacGregor, W. Fishing with kites. From Morning Post, Dec. 28, 1898. JAI, XXVIII.

McGuire, J. D. Articles: Pipes; Smoking; Tobacco. HAI, pt. II.

——Ethnology in the Jesuit relations. AA, III.

——Pipes and smoking customs of the American aborigines, based on material in the USNM. USNM, 1897, pt. I.

Machon, Dr. The Cainguá of Paraguay. PSM, LII.

MacKenzie, A. Voyages from Montreal. London, 1801.

Mackenzie, J. K. Appreciations. Atl. Mo., CXXXI.

——The black commandments. Atl. Mo., CXVIII.

——Exile and postman. Atl. Mo., CXIX.

Maclaren, Ian, *see* Watson, J.

McLennan, J. F. The levirate and polyandry. Fortnightly Rev., XXVII.

——The patriarchal theory. London, 1885.

——Primitive marriage. Edinburgh, 1865.

MacLeod, H. W. Native land transfer on the Gold Coast. JAI, XXI.

MacLeod, W. C. Certain mortuary aspects of Northwest Coast culture. AA, XXVII. Reprinted as "The incipient suttee."

——Debtor and chattel slavery in aboriginal North America. AA, XXVII.

——A primitive clearing house. Amer. Econ. Rev., XV.

——Some aspects of primitive chattel slavery. Social Forces, IV.

Maçoudi, *see* Masûdî.

Macy, Z. A short journal of the first settlement of the Island of Nantucket. Coll. of the Mass. Hist. Soc., 1st ser., III.

Maddox, J. L. *†The medicine man. A sociological study of the character and evolution of shamanism. Berlin, 1922. New York, 1923.

Magarey, A. T. Smoke signals of Australian aborigines. AAAS, 1893.

Magnin, Ch. Origines du théâtre moderne. Paris, 1838.

Magnus, Olaus, *see* Olaus Magnus.

Magnússon, E. and Morris, W. *The story of Grettir the strong. London, 1869.

Magnússon, E., *see* also Morris, W.

Mahaffy, J. P. A history of Egypt under the Ptolemaic dynasty. London, 1899.

——Social life in Greece from Homer to Menander. Oxford, 1874.

Main, J. Religious chastity. An ethnological study. New York, 1913.

Maine, H. S. *†Ancient law. New York, 1871.

——*†Early law and custom. New York, 1883.

——*†Lectures on the early history of institutions. London, 1875.

——Village communities in the East. London, 1895.

Maitland, F. W. Domesday Book and beyond. Cambridge, 1897.

——Select pleas in manorial and other seignorial courts. Selden society, II. London, 1889.

Majewski, E. La science de la civilisation, prolégomènes et bases pour la philosophie de l'histoire et la sociologie. Paris, 1908.

Malbot, H. et Verneau, R. Les Chaouïs et la trépanation du crane dans l'Aurès. L'Anthropologie, VIII.

Malcolm, L. W. G. Notes on birth, marriage, and death ceremonies of the Eyāp tribe, Central Cameroon. JAI, LIII.

Malinowski, B. *†Baloma: the spirits of the dead in the Trobriand Islands. JAI, XLVI.

——*†Crime and custom in savage society. New York, 1926.

Malkus, A. S. Those doomed Indian dances. N. Y. Times, April 8, 1923.

Mallery, G. Pictographs of the North American Indians. BAE, IV.

——*Picture-writing of the American Indians. BAE, X.

Maltzan, H. von. Sittenschilderungen aus Südarabien. Globus, XXI.

Man. A monthly record of anthropological science. II-XXVI. London, 1902-26.

Man, E. H. Marital relations of the Nicobar Islanders. Noticed in Miscellanea, in JAI, XXII.

——*The Nicobar Islanders. JAI, XVIII.

——*On the aboriginal inhabitants of the Andaman Islands. JAI, XII.

——On the Andamanese and Nicobarese objects presented to Maj.-Gen. Pitt Rivers. JAI, XI.

——On the use of narcotics by the Nicobar Islanders and certain deformations connected therewith. JAI, XXIII.

Mannhardt, W. *Die Korndämonen. Beitrag zur Germanischen Sittenkunde. Berlin, 1868.

Manning, C. A. Language and international affairs. Sewanee Review, XXXII.

Manning, H. E. (Cardinal Archbishop.) Distress in London. A note on outdoor relief. Fortnightly Rev., XLIII (n.s.).

Mantegazza, P. Gli Amori degli Uomini. Milano, 1886.

——Rio de la Plata e Tenerife: viaggi e studi. Milano, 1876.

March, H. C. The mythology of wise birds. JAI, XXVII.

——Polynesian ornament and mythography, or a symbolism of origin and descent. JAI, XXII.

March, see Stauf von der March.

Marchi, A. de. Il Culto Privato di Roma Antica. Reviewed in L'Année Sociologique, 1897.

Marcosson, I. F. An African adventure. London, 1921.

Marett, R. R. From spell to prayer. Folklore, XV.

Margry, P. Les navigations françaises. Paris, 1867.

Marindin, G. E., see Smith, W.

Mariner, W. An account of the natives of the Tonga Islands in the South Pacific Ocean. Compiled and arranged from the extensive communications of Mr. Wm. Mariner, several years resident in those islands, by J. Martin. 2 vols. Edinburgh and London, 1827.

Markham, C. R. A list of the tribes in the valley of the Amazons, including those on the banks of the main stream and of all its tributaries. JAI, XL.

Marquardsen, Hauptmann. Beobachtungen über die Heiden im nördlichen Adamaua. Globus, XCII.

Marsden, W. *The history of Sumatra. London, 1811.

Marshall, C. Extracts from the diary of Christopher Marshall kept in Philadelphia and Lancaster during the Amer. Revolution. Ed. by William Duane. Albany, 1877.

Martin, K. Bericht über eine Reise ins Gebiet des Oberen Surinam. Bijd., XXXV.

Martin, M. A description of the western islands of Scotland. In Pinkerton's "A general collection of the best and most interesting voyages and travels in all parts of the world." Vol. III. London, 1809.

Martins, see Oliveira Martins.

Martius, K. F. P. von. *Beiträge zur Ethnographie und Sprachenkunde Amerikas, zumal Brasiliens. 2 vols. Leipzig, 1867.

Martius, K. F. P. von, see also Spix, J. B.

Martrou, P. L. Les "Eki" des Fang. Anthropos, I.

Marx, V. Die Stellung der Frauen in Babylonien gemäss den Kontrakten aus der Zeit von Nebukadnezar bis Darius. Beitr. zur Assyr., IV.

Marzan, J. de. Le totémisme aux îles Fiji. Anthropos, 1907, II.

Mason, M. H. The Transkei. Geog. Jour., LII.

Mason, O. T. Aboriginal American zoötechny. AA, I.

——†The origin of invention. New York, 1895.

——†Primitive travel and transportation. USNM, 1894.

——The Ray collection from Hupa reservation. Smithson. Rep., 1886, pt. I.

——Summary of progress in anthropology. Smithson. Rep. for 1893.

——†Woman's share in primitive culture. New York, 1905.

Maspero, G. *Histoire ancienne des peuples de l'Orient Classique. 3 vols. Paris, 1895-9.

Massart, J., see Demoor, J.

Masûdî, Alî ibn el Husain el-. Les Prairies d'or. Texte et traduction par C. Barbier de Meynard et Pavet de Courteille. Paris, 1861-77.

Mateer, S. Nepotism in Travancore. JAI, XII.

——On social reforms amongst the Nayars of Malabar. JASB, II.

Mathew, J. *The origin of the Australian phratries and explanations of some of the phratry names. JAI, XL, 1910.

——*Eaglehawk and crow. A study of the Australian aborigines including an inquiry into their origin and a survey of Australian languages. London, 1899.

Mathews, M. C. On the manners, customs, religion, superstitions, etc., of the Australian native. JAI, XXIV.

Mathews, R. H. The Bora, or initiation ceremonies of the Kamilaroi tribe. JAI, XXIV.

——The Burbung of the Wiradthuri Tribes. JAI, XXVI.

——Marriage and descent in the Arranda tribe, Central Australia. AA, X.

——Message-sticks used by the aborigines of Australia. AA, X (o.s.).

——Sociology of the Chingalee tribe, northern Australia. AA, X.

——Some initiation ceremonies of the aborigines of Victoria. Zeitsft. f. Ethnologie, XXXVII.

——The Wombya organisation of the Australian aborigines. AA, II.

Matthews, W. Articles: Color symbolism; Magic; Navaho. HAI.

——The Catlin collection of Indian paintings. USNM, 1890.

——The Earth lodge in art. AA, IV.

——Some illustrations of the connection between myth and ceremony. Int. Cong. Anthr., 1893.

——A vigil of the Gods—a Navaho ceremony. AA, IX (o.s.).

Matthews, W., see also Fletcher, A. C.

Mauch, C. Die Makalaka. In the following.

——Reisen im Inneren von Süd-Afrika. Petermanns Mitt., VIII, Ergänzungsheft 37.

Maurer, F. Die Ablösungsformen im Alten und Neuen Testament. Globus, XCI.

——Das Tabu im Alten Testament. Globus, XC.

——*Völkerkunde, Bibel, und Christenthum. Leipzig, 1905.

——*Völkerkundliches aus dem Alten Testament. Naumburg, 1905.

Maurer, G. L. von. Geschichte der Fronhöfe, der Bauernhöfe, und der Hofverfassung in Deutschland. Erlangen, 1862-3.

Mauss, M. La religion et les origines du droit pénal. Revue de l'Histoire des Religions, 1897.

Mauthner, F. Kritik der Sprache. 3 Bände. Stuttgart, 1901-1902.

Mavor, J. My windows on the street of the world. London, 1923.

Mayer, F. Geschichte Oesterreichs mit besonderer Rücksicht auf Culturgeschichte. Wien, 1874.

Mayne, J. The City-Match. In A Select Collection of Old Plays. Vol. IX. London, 1825.

Mayr, F. The Zulu Kafirs of Natal. Anthropos, Salzburg, II, 392-9, 633-45, 12 pl. Review by Chamberlain, in AA, X.

Mazzarella, G. La Condizione Giuridica del Marito nella Famiglia Patriarcale. Cantania, 1899.

Meade, M. J. The Moghiáhs, a criminal tribe of Rajputana and Central India. JASB, I.

——On the Moghiáhs or Báoris of Rajputáná and Central India. JASB, I.

Meakin, J. E. B. The Morocco Berbers. JAI, XXIV.

Medhurst, W. H. *Marriage, affinity, and inheritance in China. Trans. of the China Branch of the Royal Asiatic Society. Part IV, 1853-4.

Medical News, The. A weekly medical journal. I-LXXXVII. New York and Philadelphia, 1843-1905.

Meerwaldt, J. H. Wijzen de tegenwoordige Zeden en Gewoonten der Bataks nog Sporen aan van een oorspronkelijk Matriarchaat? Bijd., XLI.

Meigen, W. Über essbare Erde in

Deutsch-Neuguinea. Ztsft. d. deut. geolog. Gesellsft. 57 Jahrg., 1905. Résumé in Globus, XC.

Meinecke, G. Die deutschen Kolonien in Wort und Bild. Leipzig, 1900.

Meissner, B. Beiträge zum Altbabylonischen Privatrecht. Leipzig, 1893.

——Neuarabische Geschichten aus dem Iraq. Leipzig, 1903.

Melnikow, N. Die ehemaligen Menschenopfer und der Schamanismus bei den Burjaten des Irkutskischen Gouvernements. Globus, LXXV.

Memoirs of the American Museum of Natural History. I-XIV. (n.s.) I-III. New York, 1892-1921.

Mencken, H. L. The Library. Amer. Merc., VI.

Merriam, C. H. Totemism in California. AA, X.

Metcalf, E. H. The people of Sandao-a (Philippines). AA, XIV.

Metropolitan Magazine, The. I-LI. New York, 1895-1920.

Mexia, P. El gran vida del Gran Tamorlan. In Gonçales de Clavigo's Historia.

——Vida del gran Tamorlan. In Colleccion de las cronicas . . . de los Reyes de Castilla. Tom. 3. 1779.

Meyer, C. Der Aberglaube des Mittelalters und der nächstfolgenden Jahrhunderte. Basel, 1884.

Meyer, E. Geschichte des alten Aegyptens. Berlin, 1887.

Meyer, E. H. Deutsche Volkskunde. Strassburg, 1898.

Meyer, H. Der Kilimandjaro. Berlin, 1900.

Meyerfeld, M., see Synge, J. M.

Michael, E. Geschichte des deutschen Volkes seit dem dreizehnten Jahrhundert bis zum Ausgang des Mittelalters. 6 vols. Freiburg i. B., 1897-1915.

Michailovski, V. M. Shamanism (Russ.). Moscow, 1892.

Mickewicz, C. Verbreitung der Geisteskrankheiten bei den Jakuten. Kleine Nachrichten. Globus, LXXXV.

Mickewitz, S. Die Hysterie im äussersten Nordosten Siberiens. 1903. (Cited by R. Weinberg in III Pol.-Anth. Rev., pp. 203-204.)

Middlebrook. Middlebrooks Photographieen aus dem Leben der Zulukaffern. By "S." Globus, LXXV.

Migeod, F. W. H. Some observations on the physical characters of the Mende nation. JAI, XLIX.

Miklucho-Maclay, N. von. Ethnologische Bemerkungen über die Papuas der Maclay-Küste in Neu-Guinea. In Natuurkundig Tijdschrift voor Nederl.-Indië, XXXVI.

——Über die Mika-Operation in Central-Australien. Zeitschrift für Ethnologie, XII.

Mill, J. S. Autobiography. New York, 1873.

Millard, T. F. Chinese Christians. N. Y. Times, Sept. 8, 1925.

Miller, H. A., see Park, R. E.

Miller, M. L. The so-called California "Diggers." PSM, L.

——Der Untergang der Maidu oder Digger-indianer in Kalifornien. Globus, LXXII.

Miller, N. The child's position in a simple society. Doctoral dissertation deposited in Yale Univ. Library.

Millies, H. C. Recherches sur les monnaies des indigènes de l'Archipel Indien et de la Péninsule Malaie. La Haye, 1871.

Milne, (Mrs.) L. The home of an eastern clan. A study of the Palaungs of the Shan states. Oxford, 1924.

Milton, J. Paradise Lost.

Minakata, K. On tabu in Japan in ancient, mediaeval and modern times. Review in JAI, XXVIII. .

Mindeleff, C. Localization of Tusayan clans. BAE, XIX, pt. II.

——Navaho houses. BAE, XVII.

Mindeleff, V. A study of Pueblo architecture in Tusayan and Cibola. BAE, VIII.

Mitchell, S. A. Eclipses of the sun. New York, 1923.

Miroliubov, I. P. Eight years in Sakhalin (Russ.). St. Petersburg, 1901.

*Mitra, S. C. Behari customs and practices. JASB, III.

——Behari omens from the chirping and falling of lizards. JASB, VI.

——Belief about the lizard. JASB, V.

——Note on sword-blade vow. JASB, VI.

——On North Indian folklore about thieves and robbers. JASB, III.

——On rain ceremony in the district of Murshidbad, Bengal. JASB, V.

——*On some ceremonies for producing rain. JASB, III.

——On the Harparowri or the Behari women's ceremony of producing rain. JASB, IV.

——On vestiges of moon-worship in Behar and Bengal. JASB, II.

——A short note on burial-customs among the Bhuinhar Brahmans, in the Saran district, Behar. JASB, III.

Mitteilungen der Anthropologischen Gesellschaft in Wien. I-LV. Wien, 1871-1925.

Mittheilungen der Kaiserlichen königlichen Geographischen Gesellschaft in Wien. I-LVI. Wien, 1857-1913.

Modi, J. J. Charms or amulets for some diseases of the eye. JASB, III.

——The cock as a sacred bird in ancient Irân. JASB, V.

——*The Dhangurs and the Dhavars of Mahableshwar. JASB, III.

——A few notes on the Todâs of the Nilgiris. JASB, VII.

——The horse in ancient Irân. JASB, IV.

——*†On a few superstitions common to Europe and India. JASB, II.

——*On the funeral ceremonies of the Parsees, their origin and explanation. JASB, II.

——Paper on a Persian coffin said to be 3000 years old, sent to the Museum of the Society, by Mr. Malcolm, of Bushire. JASB, I.

Moerenhout, J. A. Voyages aux îles du Grand Océan. 2 tom. Paris, 1837.

Moggridge, L. T. The Nyassaland tribes, their customs and their poison ordeal. JAI, XXXII.

Mollendorff, P. G. von. The family law of the Chinese. Shanghai, 1896.

Möller, J. Über das Salz in seiner culturgeschichtlichen und naturwissenschaftlichen Bedeutung. Berlin, 1874.

Molmenti, P. G. La storia di Venezia nella vita privata. Torino, 1885.

Monier-Williams, M. *Brāhmanism and Hinduism. New York, 1891.

Monseur, E. L'âme pupilline. Révue de l'Histoire de Religion. Paris, 1905, LI.

Montaigne, M. de. Œuvres complètes. Essais. (Ed. A. Armaingaud.) Paris, 1924.

Montefiore, A. Notes on the Samoyads of the Great Tundra. JAI, XXIV.

Montelius, O. Forntiden. (Being vol. I of Hildebrand, E.: Sveriges Historia.) Stokholm, 1903.

Montero y Vidal, José. Historia General de Filipinas, desde el descubrimiento de dichas islas hasta nuestras dias. 3 vols. Madrid, 1887, 1894, 1895.

——Historia de la piratería Malayo-Mahometana en Mindanao, Joló y Borneo. Madrid, 1888.

Mooney, J. Articles: Ball play; Calusa; Cheyenne; Child life; Coup; Heraldry; Labor; Peyote; Powhatan; Sautee; Scalping; Tenskwatawa. HAI.

——Calender history of the Kiowa Indians. BAE, XVII, pt. I.

——*The ghost-dance religion and the Sioux outbreak of 1880. BAE, XIV.

——*The sacred formulas of the Cherokees. BAE, VII.

Mooney, J. and Thomas, C. Articles: Algonquian family; Chippewa; Conoy; Cree; Illinois; Mascoutens;

Miami; Mohican, an Algonquian tribe; Montagnais. HAI.

Mooney, J., *see* also Swanton, J. R.

Moore, C. B. Urn-burial. HAI, pt. II.

Moore, F. Diary of the American Revolution. 2 vols. New York, 1860.

Morehead, Ex-Gov. J. T. Boonesborough address of May 25, 1840. Quoted in Collins, L., History of Kentucky. 2 vols. Covington, Ky., 1882.

Morel, E. D. The black man's burden. London, 1920.

Morgan, L. H. *†Ancient society. New York, 1877.

——Houses and house-life of the American aborigines. Contributions to N. Amer. Ethnology, IV.

——*League of the Ho-de'-no-san-nee, or Iroquois. Rochester, N. Y., 1851.

——*Systems of consanguinity and affinity of the human family. Smithsonian Contributions to Knowledge, XVII.

Morgulis, S. Fast and famine. In Scientific Monthly, XVI.

Morley, S. G. The excavation of the Cannonball ruins in southwestern Colorado. AA, X.

Mörner, Herr. Die Peruanischen Indianer. Ausland, XLIII.

Morris, J. R. Our Japanese letter. Philadelphia Public Ledger, May 14, 1922.

Morris, M. The influence of war and of agriculture upon the religion of Kayans and Sea Dyaks of Borneo. Jour. of Amer. Orien. Soc., XXV, Second half. New Haven, 1904. Also, Sect. f. the Hist. Study of Relig., VII.

Morris, W. and Magnússon, E. The saga library. 6 vols. London, 1891-1905. *See* Laing, S., also Vigfússon, G.

Morris, W., *see* also Magnússon, E.

Mortillet, G. de. Signe de la croix avant le Christianisme. Paris, 1866.

Mosbach, S. Streifzüge in den bolivischen Anden. Globus, LXXII.

Moscatelli, A. La condizione della donna nelle società primitive e nell' antico diritto Romano. Studiata nei suoi rapporti colla evoluzione storica della famiglia. Bologna, 1886.

Moszkowski, M. Die Inlandstämme Ostsumatras. Globus, XCIV.

——Mittelalterlicher Feudalismus in Inner-Sumatra. Globus, XCVI.

Movers, F. C. Die Phoenizier. 2 vols. Bonn, 1841, vol. 1. Berlin, 1849-50, vol. 2.

Mucke, J. R. Horde und Familie in ihrer urgeschichtlichen Entwickelung: Eine neue Theorie auf statisticher Grundlage. Stuttgart, 1895.

Muhammed ibn Abd Allah (Ibn Batuta). Travels. (Trans. from Arabic by S. Lee.) London, 1829.

Mühlhofer, F. Der mutmassliche Timavotalschluss. Globus, XCII.

Muirhead, J. F. English pamphlets on the war. The supernatural host in the retreat from Mons. Nation, CI.

Müller, A. Der Islam im Morgen- und Abendlande. 2 vols. Berlin, 1885-7.

Müller, D. H. Die Gesetze des Hammurabi. Wien, 1903.

Müller, F. H. Der Ugrische Volksstamm. Berlin, 1837-9.

Müller, F. M. Introduction to the science of religion. London, 1909.

——Essays. Aus dem Englischen ins Deutsche übertragen. Leipzig, 1869-79.

——Editor. *The sacred books of the East, translated by various Oriental scholars. Edited by F. Max Müller. 50 vols. Oxford, 1879-1910.

Muller, H. P. N. Land und Leute zwischen Zambesi und Limpopo. Giessen, 1894.

Müller, J. *Das Sexuelle Leben der Naturvölker. Leipzig, 1906.

Müller, Josef. Über Ursprung und Heimat des Urmenschen. Stuttgart, 1894.

Müller, J. G. Geschichte der Amerikanischen Urreligionen. Basel, 1855.

Müller, L. Det saakaldte hagekors's anvendelse og betydning i oldtiden. Kjøbenhavn, 1877.

Müller, O. Untersuchungen zur Geschichte des Attischen Bürger- und Eherechts. (From the 25th supplementary volume of the Jahrbuch für Classische Philologie.) Leipzig, 1899.

Mumford, E. W. Note on art. Cosmopolitan Mag., XXVI.

Muñiz, M. A. and McGee, W. J. *†Primitive trephining in Peru. BAE, XVI.

Munro, D. C. Christian and infidel in the Holy Land. International Monthly, IV.

Munson, W. L. Superstitions about health. Address rep. in N. Y. Times, June 24, 1925.

Muntz, E. E. Race contact: a study of the social and economic consequences of the contact between civilized and uncivilized races. Doctoral dissertation deposited in Yale Univ. Library.

Murdoch, J. *Ethnological results of the Point Barrow expedition. BAE, IX.

Murdock, G. P. Kulturgeschichte, by Julius Lippert: a translation and critical edition. Vol. I. Doctoral dissertation deposited in Yale Univ. Library.

Murray, G. Totems. Sat. Rev., CX.

Murray, G. W. The Ababda. JAI, LIII.

Murray, J. Address by the president. AAAS, 1921.

Murray, M. Royal marriages and matrilineal descent. JAI, XLV.

Murray, M. A. The witch-cult in western Europe: a study in anthropology. Oxford, 1921.

Myers, C. S. Ethnological study of music. Anthropological essays presented to E. B. Tylor; Oxford, 1907.

Nachrichten von der königlichen Gesellschaft der Wissenschaften und der Georg-Augustus-Universität zu Göttingen. Göttingen, 1864-93.

Nachtigal, G. *Sahârâ und Sûdân. 2 Bände. Berlin, 1879-81.

Nadaillac, J. F. A. du P. de. L'anthropophagie et les sacrifices humains. Revue des Deux Mondes, LXVI, 1884.

——*†Prehistoric America. trans. New York, 1884.

——Peuples Préhistoriques, in Bull. Institut Égyptien, 1886.

Nägelsbach, K. F. von. Homerische Theologie 2te Aufl., bearbeitet von G. Autenrieth. Nürnberg, 1861.

Naidoo, C. P. S. Hindu matrimonial rites in Madras. JASB, II.

Nansen, F. *†Eskimo life (trans.). London, 1893.

Nasmyth, G. W. Social progress and the Darwinian theory. New York and London, 1916.

Nassau, R. H. Fetichism in West Africa. New York, 1904.

Nathubhai, T. M. Certain social questions connected with marriage and inheritance among the Hindus. JASB, III.

——Hindu castes. JASB, V.

——On Hindu wills. JASB, V.

——On the death ceremonies among the Kapola Bania and others. JASB, III.

——On the origin and account of the Kapola Bania caste. JASB, III.

Nathubhoy, T. M. The Bombay census (1901) and Hindu castes. JASB, VI.

——Ordeal. JASB, VI.

Nation, The. A weekly journal devoted to politics, literature, science, drama, music, art, finance. I-CXXIII. New York, 1865-1919.

National Geographic Magazine, The. An illustrated monthly. I-XLIX. Washington, 1889-1926.

Nature. A weekly illustrated journal of science. I-CXVIII. London, 1869-1926.

Naturkundig Tijdschrift voor Nederlandsch-Indië, uitgegeven door de Kon. natuurkundige vereeniging in Nederlandsch-Indië. Deel I-LXXXI. Batavia (Java), 1851-1925.

Negelein, J. von. Die Reise der Seele

ins Jenseits. Ztsft. d. Vereins f. Volkskunde, XI.

——Seele als Vogel. Globus, LXXIX.

Nehring, A. Die Anbetung der Ringelnatter bei den alten Litauern, Samogiten und Preussen. Globus, LXXIII.

Nekrasov, N. A. Works.

Nelson, E. W. *The Eskimo about Bering Strait. BAE, XVIII.

New International Encyclopædia, The. 23 vols. New York, 1914-16.

New York Historical Society, Quarterly bulletin. I-X. New York, 1917-27.

Newell, J. E. Notes of Tokelau, Ellice, and Gilbert Islanders. AAAS, 1895.

Newell, W. W. Ritual regarded as dramatization of myth. Int. Cong. Anthrop., 1893.

Newport, C. Capt. Newport's discoveries, Virginia. Trans. and Coll. of the Am. Antiq. Soc., IV.

Ney, N. The tribes of the Sahara. Cosmopolitan Mag., XVIII.

Niblack, A. P. *†The coast Indians of Southern Alaska and Northern British Columbia. USNM, 1888.

Nicholas, F. C. The aborigines of the province of Santa Marta, Colombia. AA, III.

Nichols, C. F. Pule-anaana, or praying to death at the Hawaiian Islands. Pop. Sci. News, XXVII.

Nieboer, H. J. *Slavery as an industrial system. The Hague: Nijhoff, 1900.

Niehus, H. Zenana-Leben in Ostindien. Globus, LXXXIX.

Niemann, G. K. Ethnographische Mededeelingen omtrent de Tjams en eenige andere Volksstammen van Achter-Indie. Bijd., XLV.

Nieuwenhuis, A. W. *In Centraal Borneo. 2 tomes. Leiden, 1900.

Nilsson, S. Les habitants primitifs de la Scandinavie. Paris, 1868.

Nineteenth Century, The, and after. A monthly review. I-XCVIII. London, 1877-1925.

Nivedita, Sister (Margaret E. Noble). *†The web of Indian life. London, 1904.

Noble, M. E., see Nivedita.

Noguchi, Y. The future of Japanese Shintoism. Nation, CII.

Nogueira, A. F. A Raça negra sob o ponto de vista da civilisação de Africa. Lisboa, 1880.

Nolan, J. B. Germany revisited. Atl. Mo., CXXVII.

Nordenskiöld, N. A. E. Studier och Forskningar föranledda af mina resor i höga norden. Stockholm, 1883.

Nordenskiöld, E. von. Ueber die Sitte der heutigen Aymara und Quichua Indianer, den Toten Beigaben in die Gräber zu legen. Globus, LXXXVII.

Northcote, G. A. S. The Nilotic Kavirondo. JAI, XXXVII.

Notor, G., nom de plume of Roton, G. de.

Nova Acta Academiæ Cæsareæ Leopoldino-Carolinæ germanicæ naturæ curiosorum. Abhandlungen der Kaiserlichen Leopoldinisch-Carolinischen deutschen Akademie der Naturforscher. I-CVIII. Norimbergæ, 1757-1926.

Noyes, J. H. History of American socialisms. Philadelphia, 1870.

Nuñez Cabeça de Vaca, A. The narrative of Alvar Nuñez Cabeça de Vaca. Translated by B. Smith. Washington, 1851.

Núñez de Arce, G. El haz de leña. Ed. by R. Schwill. Boston, 1903.

Nutting, C. C. Antiquities from Ometepe, Nicaragua. Smithson. Rep., 1883.

Oberländer, R. Deutsch-Afrika, Land und Leute, Handel und Wandel in unseren Kolonien. Leipzig und Berlin, 1885.

O'Brien, A. The Mohammedan saints of the Western Punjab. JAI, XLI.

Oetker, K. Die Neger-seele und die Deutschen in Afrika, ein Kampf

gegen Missionen, Sittlichkeits-Fana-
tismus und Bürokratie vom Standpunkt moderner Psychologie. München, 1907.

O'Ferrall, W. Native stories from
Santa Cruz and Reef Islands. JAI,
XXXIV.

Ogburn, W. F. On population of N. Y.
City. N. Y. Times, May 13, 1923.

Ohio Board of Administration, Publications of the. Nos. 1-19. Mans-
field (O.) etc., 1915-21.

Olaus Magnus. A compendious history
of the Goths, Svvedes, and Vandals,
and other northern nations. London,
1658.

——Historia de Gentium Septentrion-
alium variis conditionibus. Basel,
1567.

Oldfield, A. On the aborigines of
Australia. Trans. Ethnol. Soc. of
London, III.

Oldham, G. A. Prayer and its answer.
A sermon in New Haven. Rep. in
New Haven Journal-Courier, April
6, 1916.

*Oliveira Martins, J. P. As Raças
humanas e a Civilisação Primitiva.
Lisboa, 1881.

——Civilisação Iberica. Lisboa, 1885.

——Historia de Portugal. 2 vols. Lisboa, 1901.

——Quadro das Instituições Primi-
tivas. Lisboa, 1883.

Olsen, O. El Primitivt Folk. De Mon-
golske Ren-nomader. Kristiania,
1915.

Open Court, The. A monthly magazine. I-XXXIX. Chicago, 1887-1925.

Oppert, G. Buddha und die Frauen
Globus, LXXXIV.

Original-Mittheilungen aus der ethno-
logischen Abteilung der Königlichen
Museen zu Berlin (Berlin Staatliche
Museen, Museum für Völkerkunde).
Berlin, 1885-8.

Orléans, H. von. Die Reise des Prinzen
Heinrich von Orléans von Tonking
nach Vorderindien. Anon. Globus,
LXXII.

Osenbrüggen, E. Der Hausfrieden.

Ein Beitrag zur deutschen Rechts-
geschichte. Erlangen, 1857.

Ostwald, W. *Energetische Grundlagen der Kulturwissenschaft. Leipzig, 1909.

——Grosse Männer. Leipzig, 1910.

O'Sullivan, H. Dinka laws and customs. JAI, XL.

Otto, W. Priester und Tempel im
hellenistischen Aegypten. Ein Beitrag zur Kulturgeschichte des Hel-
lenismus. Leipzig u. Berlin, 1905-08.

Overstone, Lord S. J. L., see McCulloch, J. R.

Overton, F. and Denno, W. J. The
health officer. Philadelphia and London, 1920.

Ovid. Works.

Outlook, The. I-LVII. New York,
1870-1926.

Paine, L. L. The ethnic trinities and
their relation to the Christian
trinity. A chapter in the comparative history of religions. Boston,
1901.

Painter, A. W. On the Hill Arrians
(of Travancore). JASB, II.

Palgrave, W. G. Personal narrative
of a year's journey through central
and eastern Arabia. (1862-63.) London, 1883.

Pallas, P. S. Travels through the
southern provinces of the Russian
empire. 2 vols. London, 1812.

—— Voyages de M. P. S. Pallas, en
différentes provinces de l'empire de
Russie, et dans l'Asie septentrionale.
Traduits de l'Allemand par M.
Gauthier. Cinq volumes. Paris, 1790.

Palmer, E. Notes on some Australian
tribes. JAI, XIII.

Pandects, in Corpus Iuris Civilis.

Panikkar, K. M. Some aspects of
Nāyar life. JAI, XLVIII.

Park, M. Travels. London, 1800.

Park, R. E. and Miller, H. A. Old
world traits transplanted. New
York, 1921.

Parker, A. C. The constitution of the
five nations. A reply. AA, XX.

Parker, G. W. Land tenure in Madagascar. JAI, XII.

Parker, K. L. The Euahlayi tribe. London, 1905.

Parkhouse, T. A. Native tribes of Port Darwin and its neighbourhood. AAAS, 1895.

Parkinson, J. Notes on the Asaba people (Ibos) of the Niger. JAI, XXXVI.

——Yoruba string figures. JAI, XXXVI.

Parkinson, R. Ein Beitrag zur Ethnographie der Neu-Guinea-Küste. Internationales Archiv für Ethnographie, XIII.

——*Dreissig Jahre in der Südsee. Stuttgart, 1907.

——Zur Ethnographie der nordwestlichen Salomo Inseln. Dresden K. Zöol. u. Anth.-Ethnog. Mus., Abhandl., VII, pt. VI.

Parkman, F. The Jesuits in North America in the seventeenth century. Boston, 1880.

——The old régime in Canada. Boston, 1885.

Parsons, A. B. Sex and genius. Yale Review, XIV.

Parsons, E. C. Ceremonial friendship at Zuñi. AA, XIX.

——A few Zuñi death beliefs and practices. AA, XVIII.

——Holding back in crisis ceremonialism. AA, XVIII.

——The Hopi Buffalo dance. Man, XXIII.

——Increase by magic: a Zuñi pattern. AA, XXI.

——Links between religion and morality in early culture. AA, XVII.

——Notes on Acoma and Laguna. AA, XX.

——Notes on Isleta, Santa Ana, and Acoma. AA, XXII.

Paske, E. Buddhism in the British provinces of Little Tibet. JAI, VIII.

Passarge, S. Die Mambukuschu. Globus, LXXXVII.

Patell, B. B. Notes on the towers of silence in India. JASB, II.

Pater L., in Klein-Popo. Namengebung und Hochzeitsbräuche bei den Togo-negern. Globus, LXXIX.

Pater, W. H. Marius the Epicurean. London, 1885.

Paturet, G. La Condition Juridique de la Femme dans l'ancienne Égypte. Paris, 1886.

Patursson, S. O. Siberien i vore Dage. Kjøbenhavn, 1901.

Paulitschke, P. *Ethnographie Nordost Afrikas. 2 Bände. Berlin, 1896.

Payne, E. J. History of the New World called America. 2 vols. Oxford, 1892-9.

Payne, J. F. English medicine in the Anglo-Saxon times. Oxford, 1904.

Peacock, M. Executed criminals and folk-medicine. Folk-Lore, VII.

Peal, S. E. *On the "Morong" as possibly a relic of pre-marriage communism. JAI, XXII.

Pearl, R. World overcrowding. N. Y. Times, Oct. 8, 1922.

Pearson, K. Ethic of free thought. London, 1888.

——Grammar of science. London, 1900.

Pechuël-Loesche, E. Volkskunde von Loango. Stuttgart, 1907.

Peel, C. V. A. Somaliland, being an account of two expeditions into the far interior. London, 1900.

Peet, S. D. Secret societies and sacred mysteries. Int. Cong. Anthrop., 1893.

Peiser, F. E., see Kohler, J.

Pellison, M. Roman life in Pliny's time. (Trans.) Meadville, Penn., 1897.

Pendleton, A. M. Superstitions arising from ancient laws of hygiene. Jour. of Soc. Hyg., X.

Pennant, T. A tour in Scotland, 1769. Chester, 1771.

Pennsylvania, Minutes of the Provincial Council of. I. Philadelphia, 1852.

Pereiro, A. C. Estudios sobre Carolinas; La Isla de Ponapé. Manila, 1895.

Perelaer, M. T. H. *Ethnographische Beschrijving der Dajaks. Zaltbommel, 1870.

Perkins, G. H. The Calumet in the Champlain Valley. PSM, XLIV.

Perry, W. J. The orientation of the dead in Indonesia. JAI, XLIV.

Peschel, O. The races of man. New York, 1894.

——Völkerkunde. Leipzig, 1885.

Peter Martyr (Pietro Martire d'Anghiera). The decades of the newe worlde. Written in the Latine tounge. In "The first three English books on America," by Eden, R.

Petermanns Mitteilungen aus Justus Perthes' geographischer Anstalt. I-LXXI. Gotha, 1855-1925. Also Ergänzungsbände, I-XL, Hefte 1-187. Gotha, 1861-1925.

Peters, S. A. The Rev. Samuel Peters' LL.D. general history of Connecticut, from its first settlement under George Fenwick to its latest period of amity with Great Britain prior to the Revolution. London, 1871.

Peterson, P. Retiring President's address. JASB, III.

——Vatsyayana on the duties of a Hindu wife. JASB, II.

Petit de Julleville, L. Histoire du théâtre en France. La comédie et les mœurs en France en Moyen âge Paris, 1886.

Petri, E. I. Anthropology (Russ.). St. Petersburg, 1890.

Petrie, W. M. F. Migrations. JAI, XXXVI.

——Race and civilization. Smithson. Rep., 1895.

——Recent years of Egyptian exploration. PSM, LVI.

Pfeil, J. von. *Duk Duk and other customs as forms of expression of the Melanesians' intellectual life. JAI, XXVII.

——*†Studien und Beobachtungen aus der Südsee. Braunschweig, 1899.

Pflugk-Harttung, J. von. The Druids

of Ireland. Transactions of the Royal Historical Society. (n.s.), vol. VII.

Pfoundes, C. On some rites and customs of Old Japan. JAI, XII.

Phillips, M. The teaching of the Vedas, what light does it throw on the origin and development of religion? London, and New York, 1895.

Phillips, R. C. The lower Congo: a sociological study. JAI, XVII.

Pick, B. Marriage among the Hebrews. In Schaff's Religious Encyclopedia, III.

Pickering, W. A. *Formosa. London, 1898.

Pierer, H. A. Universal-Lexikon der Vergangenheit und Gegenwart. 19 vols. Altenburg, 1857-65.

Pietschmann, R. Die Phönizier. Berlin, 1899.

Pigeonneau, H. Histoire de la commerce de la France. 2 vols. Paris, 1887.

Pinkerton, J. A general collection of the best and most interesting voyages and travels in all parts of the world. 2 vols. London, 1808.

Pinto, see Serpa Pinto.

Pischon, C. N. Der Einfluss des Islam auf das Leben seiner Bekenner. Leipzig, 1881.

Pitard, E. A propos de la polyandrie chez les Thibetains. In Bull. de la Soc. Neuchâteloise de Géographie, XII, 302 ff. Résumé in AA, III.

Pitré, J. Volksmedizin. Am Ur-Quell, I.

Plato. Works.

Pleyte, C. M. Die Mentawei-Inseln und ihre Bewohner. Globus, LXXIX.

——Plechtigheden en gebruiken uit den cyclus van het familie-leven der volken van den Indischen Archipel. Bijd., XLI.

Pliny. Natural History.

Plongeon, A. D. Le. Customs and superstitions of the Mayas. PSM, XLIV.

Ploss, H. H. Geschichtliches und Eth-

nologisches über Knabenbeschneid-
ung. Leipzig, 1885.
——Das Kind. Leipzig, 1884.
——*Das Weib in der Natur und
Völkerkunde. Ed. by M. Bartels.
Leipzig, 1885, 1905.
Plutarch. Works.
Pöch, R. Eine Reise an der Nordost-
küste von Britisch-Neuguinea. Glob-
us, XCII.
——Reisen an der Nordküste von Kai-
ser Wilhelmsland. Globus, XCIII.
Politis, N. G. On the breaking of
vessels as a funeral rite in modern
Greece. Translated by L. Dyer. JAI,
XXIII.
Politisch-anthropologische Revue. Mo-
natschrift für das soziale und geist-
ige Leben der Völker. I-XII. Leip-
zig, 1902-14.
Pollock, F. Essays in jurisprudence
and ethics. London, 1882.
——King's peace. Law Quarterly Re-
view, I, 37.
——The land laws. London, 1883.
Pollock, F. and Maitland, F. W. The
history of English law before the
time of Edward I. Cambridge, 1895.
Polo, M. The book of Ser Marco Polo
the Venetian, concerning the king-
doms and marvels of the East.
Trans. and edit. by Col. Henry
Yule. London, 1871.
Polybius. Historia. Edidit Ludovicus
Dindorfius. Lipsiae, 1867.
——The histories of Polybius. Trans.
by E. S. Shuckburgh. London, 1899.
Pommerol, J. *Une femme chez les
Sahariennes. Paris.
Ponder, E. The reputed medical prop-
erties of precious stones in ancient
and medieval times. N. Y. Times,
June 3, 1926.
Pöppig, E. F. Reise in Chile, Peru,
und auf dem Amazonenstrome
während der Jahre 1827-1832. Leip-
zig, 1835-36.
*Popular Science Monthly (PSM). I-
CIX. New York, 1872-1926.
Popular Science News. I-XXXVI.

Boston, 1866-1893. New York, 1894-
1902.
Post, A. H. Die Geschlechtsgenossenschaft der Urzeit und die Entstehung der Ehe. Oldenburg, 1875.
——Studien zur Entwicklungs-
geschichte des Familienrechts. Leipzig, 1889.
——Über die Sitte, nach welcher Ver-
lobte und Ehegatten ihre gegen-
seitigen Verwandten meiden. Globus, LXVII.
Potanin, G. Three nationalities in
Eastern Asia. (Russ.) Vestnik Ev-
ropi (The European Messenger),
Feb., 1888.
Poulsen, F. Delphi. London, 1920. Re-
viewed in the N. Y. Times, Jan. 23,
1921.
Powell, F. Y., see Vigfússon, G.
Powell, J. W. Esthetology, or the
science of activities designed to give
pleasure. BAE, XIX and AA, I.
——Indian linguistic families of
America, North of Mexico. BAE,
VII.
——Report of director. BAE, XVII,
pt. I.
——Third annual report of the direc-
tor of the BAE, BAE, III.
——*Wyandot government. BAE, I.
Powers, S. *California Indians. In
Contributions to North Amer. Eth-
nol., III.
Pradel, F. Der Schatten im Volks-
glauben. Mitt. d. Schles. Ges. f.
Volksk., Breslau, 1904, H. XII, 1-
36. Chamberlain, Periodical Litera-
ture, AA, VIII.
Pratt, A. E. Strange sights in far-
away Papua. National Geographic
Magazine, XVIII. Abstracted from
the following.
——Two years among New Guinea
cannibals. Philadelphia, 1906.
Pratt, G. Genealogy of kings and
princes of Samoa. AAAS, 1890.
——Genealogy of the sun—a Samoan
legend. AAAS, 1887.
Prescott, W. H. History of the con-

quest of Mexico. 3 vols. Philadelphia, 1871, 1876.

——History of the conquest of Peru. 2 vols. Philadelphia, 1874.

——History of the reign of Philip the Second, king of Spain. Philadelphia, 1868-71.

Prestage, P. The kraal family system among the Amandebele. Folk-Lore, XII.

Preuss, K. T. Phallische Fruchtbarkeits-Dämonen als Träger des altmexikanischen Dramas. Archiv für Anthropologie, I (n.s.).

——Phallische Fruchtbarkeits-dämonen als Träger des mexikanischen Dramas. Archiv für Anthropologie, XXIX.

——Der Ursprung der Menschenopfer in Mexiko. Globus, LXXXVI.

——Der Ursprung der Religion und Kunst. Globus, LXXXVII.

Price, C. Loneliest islanders in all the world. N. Y. Times, April 26, 1925.

Prince, J. D., see Leland, C. G.

Pritchard, W. T. Polynesian reminiscences; or, life in the South Pacific Islands. London, 1866.

Prjevalski, N. M. (Spelled also Przhevalskiï, Prschevalskij, Prschewalski, and Przwalsky.) *General Prschevalskij's Forskningsresor i Centralasien. Efter de ryska, tyska och franska original upplagorna af Sven Hedin. Stockholm, 1891.

——Reisen in der Mongolei, im Gebiet der Tanguten und den Wüsten Nordtibets in den Jahren 1870 bis 1873, von N. von Prschewalski. Aus dem Russischen und mit Anmerkungen versehen von A. Kohn. Jena, 1881.

——Third journey in Central Asia. (Russ.) St. Petersburg, 1883.

Probyn, J. W. Systems of land tenure in various countries. London.

Proceedings of the American Association for the Advancement of Science. I-LXXVII. 1848-1925.

Proceedings of the Royal Geographical Society of London. I-XXII. (n.s.) I-XIV. London, 1855-92.

Proceedings of the United States National Museum. I-LXV. Washington, 1879-1925.

Procksch, O. Über die Blutrache bei den vorislamischen Arabern und Mohammeds Stellung zu ihr. Leipzig, 1899.

Prowe, H. Das Wissen der Quiché-Indianer in mythischen Form. Globus, XC.

Psychological Review, The. I-XXXIII. New York, 1894-1926.

Puccioni, N. Delle deformazioni e mutilazioni artificiali ethniche più in uso. Archivio per Antropologia (Firenze) XXXIV.

Puckett, N. N. *†Folk-beliefs of the southern negro. Chapel Hill, N. C., 1926.

Pudor, H. Geschlechtsleben u. Nachkommenschaft. Politisch-Anth. Revue, V.

Puini, C. Le Origine della Civiltà. Firenze, 1891.

Puller, F. W. Marriage with a deceased wife's sister, forbidden by the laws of God and of the Church. New York, 1912.

Purchas, S. His pilgrimage or relations of the world. London, 1617.

Pycraft, W. P. Some curious customs. (Montenegrin surgery.) Ill. London News, quoted in the Boston Transcript, July 5, 1913.

Pyle, H. The story of King Arthur and his knights. New York, 1903.

Quatrefages, A. de. Histoire générale des races humaines. Paris, 1887.

——Hommes fossiles et hommes sauvages. Paris, 1884.

Quiroga, A. Calchaquí-Altertümer. Globus, LXII.

——La cruz en América. Imprenta "La Buenos Aires." Buenos Aires, 1901.

Raap, H. Reisen auf der Insel Nias bei Sumatra. Globus, LXXXIII.

Radin, P. The Winnebago tribe. BAE, XXXVII.

Radin, P., *see* also Dorsey, J. O., also Lamere, O.

Radiguet, M. R. Les derniers sauvages: souvenirs de l'occupation française aux îles Marquises, 1842-59. Paris, 1861.

Radloff, W. Das Schamanenthum. Leipzig, 1885.

Rae, J. Remarks on the natives of British North America. JAI, XVI.

Raghunathjee, K. Pitars or Tánks. JASB, I.

Rajacsich, Baron. Das Leben, die Sitten, und Gebräuche der in Kaiserthume Oesterreich lebenden Südslaven. Wien, 1873.

Ralph, J. Our Appalachian Americans. Harper's Magazine, CVII.

Ralston, W. R. S. Songs of the Russian people. London, 1872.

Ram, G. Sir Ganga Ram's widow remarriage society. Anon. Jour. of Soc. Hyg., X.

Ramsay, W. M. Religion of Greece and Asia Minor. In Hastings's Dictionary of the Bible. Extra volume.

Ranke, J. *Der Mensch. 2 vols. Leipzig, 1894.

Ranke, K. E. Beobachtungen über Bevölkerungsstand und Bevölkerungsbewegung bei den Indianern Central-Brasiliens. Korresp. d. Deut. Anth. Gesellsft., 1898.

Rathenau, F. Ein englisches Eheverbot. Ztsft. f. Vergl. Rechtswiss. XV.

Ratzel, F. *Anthropo-geographie. 2 Bde. Stuttgart, 1882-91.

—— *Völkerkunde. 3 Bde. Leipzig, 1885.

—— The same work, translated as The history of mankind. 3 vols. New York, 1896-98.

Ratzenhofer, G. Die sociologische Erkenntnis. Leipzig, 1898.

Rawlinson, G. The five great monarchies of the ancient eastern world, or the history, geography, and antiquities of Chaldæa, Assyria, Babylon, Media, and Persia. New York, 1871.

—— The seventh great oriental monarchy. London, 1876.

Ray, S. H. Note on the people and languages of New Ireland and Admiralty Islands. JAI, XXI.

—— The people and language of Lifu, Loyalty Islands. JAI, XLVII.

Read, C. No paternity. JAI, XLVIII.

—— The origin of man and of his superstitions. Cambridge, 1920.

Read, C. H. and Dalton, O. M. Works of art, Benin City. JAI, XXVII.

Reclus, E. †Primitive folk. New York, 1891.

Records of the Past: being English translations of the Assyrian and Egyptian monuments. Published under the sanction of the Society of Biblical Archaeology. 12 vols. Ed. by S. Birch. London, 1874-81.

—— The same. New series. 6 vols. Ed. by A. H. Sayce. London, 1889-93.

Rees, O. van. *Geschiedenis der Staathuishoudkunde. 2 vols. Utrecht, 1865.

Rehatsek, E. On a descriptive alphabetical list of twenty occult sciences of the Muslims. JASB, I.

—— On superstitions of the Goa people from Portuguese sources. JASB, II.

—— Veneration of the dead in (southern) China. JASB, I.

Reich, A. and Stegelmann, F. (Mit einem Begleitwort von Karl v.d. Steinen.) Bei den Indianern des Urubamba und des Envira. Globus, LXXXIII.

Reich, H. Der Mimus. Berlin, 1903.

Reichel, O. J. Canon law: I. Sacraments. London, 1896.

Reichenow, A. Die deutsche Kolonie Kamerun. Berlin, 1884.

—— Handwörterbuch der Zoologie, Anthropologie, und Ethnologie. Breslau, 1886.

Reid, W. J. Among the farthest people. Cosmopolitan Mag., XXVIII.

Reinach, S. Charme pour obtenir la pluie. L'Anthropologie, XVII.

Reinecke, Dr. Zur Kennzeichnung der

Verhältnisse auf den Samoa-Inseln. Globus, LXXVI.

*Relations des Jésuites. Burial ceremonies of the Hurons. Trans. by Miss Nora Thomas from Relations des Jésuites, 1636, pp. 128-139. BAE, V.

Renan, E. Averroès et l'Averroïsme. Paris, 1861.

Report of the commissioner of Indian affairs to the secretary of the Interior. U. S. office of Indian affairs. Washington, 1832-1926.

Report of the Peabody Museum of American Archæology and Ethnology in connection with Harvard University. I-LVIII. Cambridge (Mass.), 1876-1925.

Retzius, G. The so-called north European race of mankind. JAI, XXXIX.

Reumont, A. von. Geschichte der Stadt Rom. Vier Bänder. Berlin, 1868.

Reuter, E. B. Population problems. Philadelphia, 1923.

Révész, G. Das Trauerjahr der Witwe. Ztsft. f. Vergl. Rechtswiss. XV.

Revue d'Anthropologie. I-XVIII. Paris, 1872-89.

Revue d'Ethnographie. I-VIII. Paris, 1882-9.

Revue de l'Histoire des Religions. I-LXXXII. Paris, 1880-1920.

Revue des Deux Mondes. Paris, 1831-1926

Rhamm, K. Der Verkehr der Geschlechter unter den Slaven in seinen gegensätzlichen Erscheinungen. Globus, LXXXII.

Rhode Island Historical Society Collections. Providence, 1827.

Rhys-Davids, T. W. Buddhism and Christianity. The International Quarterly, VII.

Ridgeway, W. *†The early age of Greece. Cambridge (Eng.), 1901.

——*†Origin of metallic currency and weight standards. Cambridge, 1892.

——The relation of anthropology to classical studies. JAI, XXXIX.

Riedel, J. G. F. De Topantunuasu of oorspronkelijke Volksstammen van Centraal Selebes. Bijd., XXXV.

Riley, E. B. Dorro head-hunters. Man, XXIII.

Riley, I. W. †The founder of Mormonism. New York, 1902.

Rink, H. J. Om Eskimoernes herkomst. 2 vols. Kjøbenhavn, 1871-90.

——Tales and traditions of the Eskimo. Edinburgh and London, 1875.

Risley, H. H. *Census of India, 1910. Vol. I. Ethnographic appendices. Calcutta, 1903. (Text references are to "Ethnography of India.")

——The tribes and castes of Bengal. Book-review in JAI, XXI.

Ritter, C. Die Erdkunde im Verhältniss zur Natur und zur Geschichte des Menschen. Band I. Die Erdkunde von Asien. Berlin, 1832.

Rivers, W. H. R. Descent and ceremonial in Ambrim. JAI, XLV.

——*The history of Melanesian society. 2 vols. Cambridge, 1914.

——Medicine, magic, and religion. London, 1924.

——Mother-right. Hastings's Encycl. Relig. and Ethics, VIII.

——On the functions of the maternal uncle in Torres Strait. Man, I.

——On the functions of the son-in-law and brother-in-law in Torres Strait. Man, I.

——*†Social organization. (Ed. by W. J. Perry.) New York, 1924.

——Sun-cult and megaliths in Oceania. AA, XVII.

——*†The Todas. London, 1906.

——*Totemism in Polynesia and Melanesia. JAI, XXXIX.

——The unity of anthropology. JAI, LII.

Robertson, G. S. Káfiristan and its people. JAI, XXVII.

Robertson, W. The history of America. London, 1777.

Röck, F. Das Vorkommen des Pentagramms in der Alten und Neuen Welt. Globus, XCV.

Rockhill, W. W. *Diary of a journey

through Mongolia and Tibet in 1891 and 1892. Smithson. Inst. Washington, 1894.

——The land of the lamas. London, 1891.

——*Notes on the ethnology of Tibet. USNM, 1893.

——*Translation of William of Rubruck's Journey to the Eastern Parts of the World, 1253-1255. Hakluyt Society, 2d Series, No. 4, London, 1900.

Rodgers, W. C. A treatise on the law of domestic relations. Chicago, 1899.

Rodway, J. Nature's triumph. PSM, XLVI.

Rogers, R. A concise account of North America. London, 1765.

Rogers, R. W. A history of Babylonia and Assyria. 2 vols. New York, 1915.

Roguin, E. Traité de droit civil comparé. Vol. I, Le mariage. Paris, 1904.

Rohde, E. *Psyche. Freiburg, 1898.

Rohde, R. Süd-Amerika. Original-Mittheilungen aus der Ethnologischen Abtheilung der Königlichen Museen zu Berlin, 1885.

Rohlfs, G. Expedition zur Erforschung der Libyschen Wüste. Bd. I. Drei Monate in der Libyschen Wüste. Cassel, 1875.

——*Reise durch Nord-Afrika vom Mitteländischen Meere bis zum Busen von Guinea 1865 bis 1867. 1 Hälfte. Von Tripoli nach Kuka. In Dr. A. Petermann's Mittheilungen aus Justus Perthes' Geogr. Anstalt. Ergänzungsband V, Heft 25.

——*Reise durch Nord-Afrika von Tripoli nach Kuka. Gotha, 1868.

——*Reise von Tripolis nach der Oase Kufra. Leipzig, 1881.

Roman de la Rose.

Roman Law, see Corpus Iuris Civilis.

Rooney, S. R. Customs and beliefs of natives of Choiseul, Solomon's Group. AAAS, 1911.

Roosevelt, T. †African game trails. New York, 1910.

——Grover Cleveland and the coal strike. Outlook, LXXXIX.

Rosa, Father A. D. J. N. de la. Floresta de la Santa Iglesia Catedral de la Ciudad de Santa Marta. Portions translated in an article, "The aborigines of the province of Santa Marta, Colombia. AA, III.

Roscoe, J. The Bahima: a cow tribe of Enkale in the Uganda Protectorate. JAI, XXXVII.

——Further notes on the manners and customs of the Baganda. JAI, XXXII.

——Notes on the Bageshu. JAI, XXXII.

Rose, H. A. Hindu betrothal observances in the Punjab. JAI, XXXVIII.

——Hindu birth observances in the Punjab. JAI, XXXVII.

——Hindu pregnancy observances in the Punjab. JAI, XXXV.

——Muhammadan birth observances in the Punjab. JAI, XXXVII.

Rose, H. J. Celestial and terrestrial orientation of the dead. JAI, LII.

Rosenberg, S. B. H. von. *Reistochten naar de Geelvinkbaai op Nieuw Guinea, 1869-1870. 's Gravenhage, 1875.

Ross, B. R. The Eastern Tinneh. Smithson Rep., 1866.

Rossbach, G. A. W. *Die Römische Ehe. Stuttgart, 1853.

Rosset, C. W. The Maldive Islands. JAI, XVI.

Roth, F. N., see Granville, R. K.

Roth, H. L. *The aborigines of Tasmania. London, 1890.

——*The natives of Borneo. Edited from the papers of the late H. Brooke Low, Esq. Two parts, in JAI, XXI and XXII.

——*Natives of Sarawak and British North Borneo. New York, 1896.

——Note on a Hkoung beht set. Anthropological reviews and miscellanea no. 64. JAI, XXX.

——On the signification of couvade. JAI, XXII.

——Origin of agriculture. JAI, XVI.

——Tatu in the Society Islands. JAI, XXXV.

Roth, W. E. *Ethnological studies among the North-West Central Queensland Aborigines. Brisbane, 1897.

——*An inquiry into the animism and folklore of the Guiana Indians. BAE, XXX.

——An introductory study of the arts, crafts, and customs of the Guiana Indians. BAE, XXXVIII.

Rothe, T. J. Nordens Staatsverfassung vor der Lehnszeit. (Aus dem Dänischen.) 2 vols. Leipzig, 1784-9.

Roton, G. de (under nom de plume G. Notor). La femme dans l'antiquité grecque. Paris, 1901.

Rousseau, J. J. Discours sur l'origine et les fondements de l'inégalité parmi les hommes. In Œuvres Complètes, I. Deux-Ponts, 1792.

Roy, S. C. Magic and witchcraft on the Chota-Nagpur Plateau—a study in the philosophy of primitive life. JAI, XLIV.

Royal Commission on Marriage, 1868.

Rubruck, W. of. See Rockhill, W. W.

Rudeck, W. Geschichte der öffentlichen Sittlichkeit in Deutschland. Jena, 1897.

Ruggles, S. and N. From a missionary journal. Early days in the Sandwich Islands. Atl. Mo., CXXXIV.

Ruppin, A. Darwinismus und Socialwissenschaft. Jena, 1903.

——Inzuchtserscheinungen bei den Karaiten in Halicz. Politisch-Anthropologische Revue, II.

Russell, F. *The Pima Indians. BAE, XXVI.

Russian Ethnography (Russ.). Edited by the editors of the weekly "Priroda i liudi." Abridged from Pauli's Les peoples de la Russie, written by various authors. 2 vols. St. Petersburg, 1878-80.

Rütimeyer, L. Die Nilgalaweddas in Ceylon. Globus, LXXXIII.

——Über Masken und Maskenge-
bräuche im Lötschental. Globus, XCI.

Ryle, H. E. and James, M. R. Psalms of Solomon. Psalms of the Pharisees. Cambridge, 1891.

S., Th. Die Singhalesischen Teufelstänzer auf Ceylon. Globus, LXXIV.

Saad, L. Die neueren Ausgrabungen in Gezer. Globus, XCV.

Safford, W. E. Guam and its people. AA, IV.

Saga Library, see Morris, W.

Saga of Grettir the Strong; see Magnússon, E. and Morris, W.

Saint-Aubin, G. Leben und Treiben in Japan. Umschau, III.

Saint-Martin, V. Le Nord de l'Afrique dans l'antiquité Grecque et Romaine. Paris, 1863.

Sale, G. The Koran. Trans. London, 1844.

Saloman, S. The down-trodden sex. N. Y. Times, Dec. 12, 1920.

Salvado, R. Mémoires historiques sur l'Australie. Paris, 1854.

Samter, A. Gesellschaftliches und Privat-Eigenthum als Grundlage der Social-politik. Leipzig, 1877.

Sanderson, M. The relationship systems of the Wangonde and Wahenga tribes, Nyassaland. JAI, LIII, 1923.

——Relationships among the Wayao. JAI, L, 1920.

Sapir, E. Articles: Takelma; Wasco. HAI, pt. II.

——The mourning ceremony of the southern Paiutes. AA, XIV.

——Notes on the Takelma Indians of Southwestern Oregon. AA, IX.

Sapper, C. *Ein Besuch bei den Guatusos in Costarica. Globus, LXXVI.

——Ein chirurgisches Instrument der mittelamerikanischen Indianer. Globus, LXXIII.

Sapper, K. Ein Besuch bei den Chirripó und Talamanca-Indianern von Costarica. Globus, LXXVII.

——Der Charakter der Mittelameri-

kanischen Indianer. Globus,
LXXXVII.
——Reise auf dem Rio Coco (Nica-
ragua). Globus, LXXVIII.
Sarasin, P. und F. Über die Toála von
Süd-Celebes. Globus, LXXXIII.
——*Die Weddas von Ceylon und die
sie umgebenden Völkerschaften. 2
Bde. Weisbaden, 1893.
Sartori, P. Votive und Weihegaben
des katholischen Volkes in Süd-
deutschland. Globus, LXXXVII.
Saturday Review of politics, litera-
ture, science, and art, The. I-CXLI.
London, 1856-1926.
Sauer, W. Priesterübermut. Der in-
dische Abraham. Das Freie Wort,
II.
Saunderson, H. S. Notes on Corea and
its people. JAI, XXIV.
Saxo Grammaticus. The first nine
books of the Danish history of Saxo
Grammaticus. Trans. by Oliver
Elton. London, 1894.
Sayce, A. H. Ancient empires. New
York, 1885.
Sayce, A. H., see Records of the past.
Schaaffhausen, H. Die Menschenfres-
serei und das Menschenopfer. Archiv
für Anthr., IV.
Schaff, P., Editor. A religious ency-
clopedia or dictionary of biblical,
historical, doctrinal, and practical
theology. 4 vols. New York, 1894.
Schallmayer, W. *Vererbung und
Auslese im Lebenslauf der Völker.
Jena, 1903.
Scheidnagel, M. Las colonias Españ-
olas de Asia. Islas Filipinas. Mad-
rid, 1880.
Schell, O. Abwehrzauber am ber-
gischen Hause. Globus, XCI.
——Die Ostgrönländer. Globus,
XCIV.
Scheltema, J. *Volksgebruiken der
Nederlanders bij het Vrijen en
Trouwen. Utrecht, 1832.
Scheltema, J. F. Opium en Nog Wat.
De Indische Gids, XXXVI.
——The opium trade in the Dutch

East Indies. Reprinted from the
Amer. Jour. of Sociology, vol. XIII.
——Roostam, the game-cock. Re-
printed from The Journal of Ameri-
can Folk-Lore, Vol. XXXII.
Scherer, J. Eine Schädelstätte im
Boabab. Globus, XCI.
Scherr, J. Deutsche Frauenwelt. Leip-
zig, 1898.
——Deutsche Kultur- und Sitten-
geschichte. Leipzig, 1879.
Scherzer, K. von. Die Anfänge Mensch-
licher Industrie. Berlin, 1883.
Schiller, F. von. Works.
Schimkjewitsch. Schimkjewitschs Reis-
en bei den Amurvölkern. Anon.
Globus, LXXIV.
Schkopp, E. von. Religiöse Anschau-
ungen der Bakoko. Globus,
LXXXIII.
——Zwergvölker in Kamerun. Globus,
LXXXIII.
Schleiermacher, P. C. Religiöse An-
schauungen und Gebräuche der Be-
wohner von Berlinhafen (Deutsch-
Neuguinea). Globus, LXXVIII.
Schliemann, H. Ilios. With notes by
M. Müller et al. London, 1880. New
York, 1881.
Schmidt, C. La société civile dans le
monde Romain et sa transformation
par le Christianisme. Strassbourg,
1853.
Schmidt, E. *Ceylon. Berlin, 1897.
Schmidt, K. Jus Primae Noctis. Frei-
burg, 1881.
Schmidt, M. Aus den Ergebnissen
meiner Expedition in das Schingú-
quellgebiet. Globus, LXXXVI.
——Über das Recht der tropischen
Naturvölker. Zeitschrift für ver-
gleichende Rechtswissenschaft XIII.
Schmidt, R. *Deutschlands Kolonien.
2 vols. Berlin, 1895-96.
Schmidt, W. Die geheime Jünglings-
weihe der Karesau-Insulaner
Deutsch-Neuguinea. Anthropos, II.
Schmoller, G. Die geschichtliche Entwickelung der Unternehmung. Jahrbuch f. Gesetzgeb., XIV.

Schoemann, G. F. Griechische Alter-thümer. Berlin, 1897.

Schomburgk, R. *Britisch-Guiana in 1840 1844. Leipzig, 1847.

Schoolcraft, H. R. *Information respecting the history, condition and prospects of the Indian tribes of the United States. Philadelphia, 1855.

Schotel, G. D. J. Het Oud-Hollandsch Huisgezin der Zeventiende Eeuw. Haarlem, 1867.

Schrader, E. Die Keilinschriften und das Alte Testament. Berlin, 1903.

Schrader, O. Linguistisch-historische Forschungen zur Handelsgeschichte und Warenkunde. Jena, 1886.

——The prehistoric antiquities of the Aryan peoples. (Trans.) London, 1890.

——Totenhochzeit. Jena, 1904. Anonymous review in Globus, LXXXVII. Review by Kaindl-Czernowitz, R. F. in Globus, LXXXVIII.

Schroeder, E. A. Das Recht in der Geschlechtlichen Ordnung. Berlin, 1893.

Schuller, R. Discussion and Correspondence. AA, XVII.

Schultz, A. Deutsches Leben in XIV-ten und XVten Jahrhundert. Leipzig, 1892.

——Das Höfische Leben zur Zeit der Minnesinger. Leipzig, 1879-80.

Schultze, F. Fetichism, a contribution to anthropology and the history of religion. New York, 1889.

——Psychologie der Naturvölker. Leipzig, 1900.

Schurtz, H. *Altersklassen und Männerbünde. Eine Darstellung der Grundformen der Gesellschaft. Berlin, 1902.

Schurz, H. *Entstehungsgeschichte des Geldes. Deutsche Geographische Blätter, XX. Bremen, 1897.

——Werthvernichtung durch den Todtenkult. Ztsft. f. Soc. Wissnsft., I.

Schuster, H. M. Das Spiel, seine Entwickelung und Bedeutung im deutschen Recht. Wien, 1878.

Schwaner, C. A. L. M. *Borneo. Amsterdam, 1853.

Schwatka, F. The sun-dance of the Sioux. Century Mag., XVII.

Schweiger-Lerchenfeld, A. F. Kulturgeschichte, Werden und Vergehen im Völkerleben. Wien, 1907.

Schweinfurth, G. Aus der Region des Gazellenflusses in Afrika. Globus, XXI.

——*†The heart of Africa. (Trans.) New York, 1874.

——Reise nach den oberen Nil-Ländern. Petermann's Mittheilungen, XVII.

——Völkerskizzen aus dem Gebiete des Bachr el Ghasal. Globus, XXII, XXIII.

Science I-XXIII (o.s.). I-LXII (n.s.). Cambridge (Mass.), 1883-1925.

Scientific American, The. I-CXXXV. New York, 1859-1926.

Scientific Monthly, The. I-XXI. New York, 1915-25.

Scott, District Deputy Collector, Sholapore. Kaikadis of Malsiras in the Sholapore District. JASB, IV.

Scott, R., see Liddell, H. G.

Scribner's Magazine. I-LXXX. New York, 1887-1926.

Sebbelow, G. Social position of men and women among the natives of East Malekula, New Hebrides. AA, XV.

Sébillot, P. The worship of stones in France. AA, IV.

Sedgwick, A. D. (Mrs. B. de Sélincourt). The little French girl. Boston and New York, 1924.

Sedgwick, W. T. Feminist revolutionary principle is biological bosh. New York Times, Jan. 18, 1914.

Seebohm, F. The tribal system in Wales. London, 1895.

Seeck, O. Geschichte des Untergangs der Antiken Welt. Berlin, 1895.

Seidel, H. Aus der Fetischstadt Issele am unteren Niger. Globus, LXXIV.

——*Krankheit, Tod und Begräbnis bei den Togonegern. Globus, LXXII.

——*System der Fetischverbote in Togo. Globus, LXXIII.

Seidlitz, N. von. Hochzeitsgebräuche der Armenier Transkaukasiens. Globus, LXXVIII.

Seler, E. Zauberei im alten Mexico. Globus, LXXVIII.

Seligman, B. Z. A devil ceremony of the peasant Sinhalese. JAI, XXXVIII.

Seligmann, C. G. A classification of the natives of British New Guinea. JAI, XXXIX.

——The medicine, surgery, and mid-wifery of the Sinangolo. JAI, XXXII.

——*The Melanesians of British New Guinea. Univ. Press, Cambridge, 1910.

——Note on the preparation and use of the Kenyah dart-poison Ipoh. JAI, XXXII.

——The physical characters of the Nuba of Kordofan. JAI, XL.

——Some aspects of the Hamitic problem in the Anglo-Egyptian Sudan. JAI, XLIII.

Seligmann, S. *Der böse Blick und Verwandtes. 2 vols. Berlin, 1910.

Sellers, G. E. Observations on stone-chipping. Smithson. Rep., 1885, pt. I.

Sembrzycki, J. Volksmedizin. Am Ur-Quell, I.

Semon, R. Australier und Papua. Kor-respondenz-Blatt der Deut. Ge-sellsft. f. Anth., Ethnol. u. Ur-gschte., XXXIII.

——*In the Australian bush. (Trans.) London, 1899.

Semper, K. Die Palau Inseln. Leipzig, 1873.

Semple, E. C. *Influence of geographic environment, on the basis of Ratzel's system of anthropo-geography. New York, 1911.

Seneca. Works.

Senfft, A. Die Bewohner der West-karolinen. Globus, XC.

——Die Rechtssitten der Jap-Einge-borenen. Globus, XCI.

——Über die Bewohner der Karolinen-insel Yap. Deutsch-Kolonialbl. 1900, S. 416. A review of this article in Globus, LXXVIII.

——Über eine neue Rundreise im Bezirk der Westkarolinen. Cited in Globus, LXXXIX.

Senior, N. W. An introductory lecture on political economy, delivered be-fore the University of Oxford, on the 6th of December, 1826. London, 1827.

Serpa Pinto, A. A. da Rocha de. *Como eu atravassei Africa. 2 vols. London, 1881.

Severijn, P. Verslag van een onder-zoek der Poggi-Eilanden. Tijdschrift voor Indische Taal-, Land- en Volk-enkunde, III.

Sewanee Review Quarterly, The. I-XXXIV. Sewanee (Tenn.), 1892-1926.

Seward, A. C. (Ed.) †Darwin and modern science. Cambridge, 1909.

Seward, A. C., see also Darwin, F.

Seymour, T. D. Life in the Homeric age. New York, 1907.

Shakespear, J. The Kuki-Lushai clans. JAI, XXXIX.

——Notes on the iron workers of Manipur and the annual festival in honour of their special deity Khum-langba. JAI, XL.

Shakespeare, W. Works.

Sharpe, C. K. A historical account of the beliefs in witch-craft in Scot-land. Glasgow, 1884.

Shchukin, N. Shamanism among the tribes of arctic Asia (Russ.).

Sheane, J. H. W. Some aspects of the Awemba religion and superstitious observances. JAI, XXXVI.

Shelford, R. On two medicine-baskets from Sarawak. JAI, XXXIII.

Sholapur, Collector of. On the Wadar caste, in the Pandurpur Taluka, Sholapur district. JASB, V.

Shonle, R. Peyote, the giver of vi-sions. AA, XXVII.

Shooter, J. The Kafirs of Natal and the Zulu country. London, 1857.

Showerman, G. The Great Mother of the gods. Madison (Wisc.), 1901.

Shufeldt, R. W. A maid of Wolpai. Proceedings of the USNM, 1892.

——Notes on Bhils, Burmese and Battaks. PSM, L.

Sibree, J. Curious words and customs connected with chieftainship and royalty among the Malagasy. JAI, XXI. •

——*The great African island. London, 1880.

Sienkiewicz, H. Works.

Sieroshevski, V. L. Dawn. (Russ.) Warsaw, 1900.

——*The Yakuts. (Russ.) St. Petersburg, 1896.

——The Polish version of the same work with revision and additions, under title, "Twelve years in the country of the Yakuts." Warsaw, 1900.

——The same work, translated and abridged from the Russian by Sumner, W. G. JAI, XXXI.

Sievers, W. Des Grafen Josef de Brettes Reisen im nordlichen Colombia. Globus, LXXIII.

Simkhovitsch, V. G. *Die Feldgemeinschaft in Russland. Jena, 1898.

——Toward the understanding of Jesus. New York, 1921.

Simmel, M. Comment les formes sociales se maintiennent. L'Année Sociologique I (1897).

Simms, S. C. Oath by the arrow. Anthr. Misc. AA, V.

Sinclair, A. T. Tattooing—Oriental and Gypsy. AA, X.

Sinclair, U. B. The Jungle. New York, 1906.

Singer, H. Hauptmann Merkers Monographie über die Massai. Globus, LXXXVI.

Sitzungsberichte der Philosophisch-philologischen und Historischen Classe der Königlichen Bayerischen Akademie zu München. München, 1871-1925.

Skeat, W. W. *†Malay Magic: being an introduction to the folklore and popular religion of the Malay peninsula. New York, 1900. Review in Folk-Lore, XI by J. Abercromby.

Skeat, W. W and Blagden, O. O. *Pagan races of the Malay Peninsula. 2 vols. London, 1906.

Skene, R. Arab and Swahili dances and ceremonies. JAI, XLVII.

Skene, W. F. The Highlanders of Scotland, their origin, history, and antiquities; with a sketch of their manners and customs, and an account of the clans into which they were divided and of the state of society which existed among them. London, 1837.

Skertchly, B. J. On the occurrence of stone mortars in the ancient river gravels of Butte County, California. JAI, XVII.

Skinner, A. A comparative sketch of the Menomini. AA, XIII.

——The cultural position of the Plains Ojibway. AA, XVI.

——Notes on the Florida Seminole. AA, XV.

——Notes on the Plains Cree. AA, XVI.

——A sketch of eastern Dakota ethnology. AA, XXI.

——War customs of the Menomini Indians. AA, XIII.

Smend, Oberleutnant von. Eine Reise durch die Nordostecke von Togo. Globus, XCII.

Smith, A. H. *†Chinese characteristics. New York, 1894.

Smith, C. M. A sketch of Flint Ridge, Licking Co., Ohio. Smithson. Rep., 1884, pt. I.

Smith, E. A. Myths of the Iroquois. BAE, II.

Smith, E. R. The Araucanians. New York, 1855.

Smith, H. I. Sympathetic magic and witchcraft among the Bellacoola. AA, XXVII.

Smith, S. P. Habits or mannerisms of the Polynesians. 1904.

Smith, W., Wayte, W. and Marindin, G. E. A dictionary of Greek and

Roman antiquities. 2 vols. London, 1891.

Smith, W. R. Australian conditions and problems. AAAS, 1913.

Smith, W. Robertson. *Kinship and marriage in early Arabia. Cambridge, 1885.

——*Religion of the Semites. London, 1894.

Smithsonian Institution. Annual report of the board of regents. Report of the Smithsonian Institution. I-LXXX. Washington, 1846-1926.

——Contributions to Knowledge. I-XXXV. Washington, 1848-1916.

Smyth, R. B. *The aborigines of Victoria. 2 vols. Melbourne, 1878.

Snouck-Hurgronje, C. *De Atjèhers. Leyden, 1894-1895.

——Mekkanische Sprichwörter und Redensarten. Bijd., XXXV.

——Twee populaire dwalingen. Bijd., XXXV.

Snyder, W. L. The geography of marriage. New York, 1889.

Social Forces (The Journal of Social Forces). I-IV. Chapel Hill (N. C.), 1922-6.

Solomon, V. Extracts from diaries kept in Car Nicobar. JAI, XXXII.

Somers, A. N. Prehistoric cannibalism in America. PSM, XLVII.

Somerville, B. Prehistoric monuments in the Outer Hebrides, and their astronomical significance. JAI, XLII.

Somerville, B. T. *Ethnographical notes in New Georgia, Solomon Islands. JAI, XXVI.

——*Notes on some islands of the New Hebrides. JAI, XXIII.

Sophocles. The text of the seven plays. Ed. by R. Jebb. Cambridge, 1906.

Southey, R. History of Brazil. 3 vols. London, 1822.

Spears, J. R. The end of the continent. Scribner's Magazine, XVII.

Speck, F. G. Game totems among the northeastern Algonkians. AA, XIX.

——Some outlines of aboriginal cul-

ture in the southeastern states. AA, IX.

——Yuchi. HAI, pt. II.

Spectator, The. I-CXXXVII. London, 1828-1926.

Spencer, B. Totemism in Australia. AAS, 1904.

Spencer, B. and Gillen, F. J. *Native tribes of central Australia. New York, 1899.

——*The northern tribes of Central Australia. New York, 1904.

——Remarks on totemism as applied to Australian tribes. JAI, XXVIII.

Spencer, H. *Descriptive sociology. Vol. No. I-No. VIII. New York.

——*Principles of sociology. 3 vols. New York, 1904-07.

——Social statics. New York, 1892.

——*†The study of sociology. New York, 1874.

Spencer, O. M. Picturesque Papua. Cosmop. Mag., XVIII.

Spiegel, F. Erânische Alterthumskunde. Leipzig, 1878.

Spiess, C. Die Schmiedekunst in Evhelande. Globus, LXXV.

Spinden, Herbert J. A great American emperor revealed. N. Y. Times, May 10, 1925.

Spire, F. Rain-making in equatorial Africa. Jr. Afric. Soc., Lond., V, 15-21.

Spix, J. B. von, und Martius, C. F. P. von. *Reise in Brasilien, 1817-1820. München, 1831.

——Travels in Brazil in the years 1817-20. Trans. by H. E. Lloyd. London, 1824.

Stack, J. W. Notes on "Maori literature." AAAS, 1891.

Stade, B. Geschichte des Volkes Israel. Berlin, 1887.

Staehr, G. Über Ursprung, Geschichte, Wesen und Bedeutung des russischen Volkes. Dorpat, 1890-91.

Stallybrass, J. S., see J. L. K. Grimm.

Stammler, C. Ueber die Stellung der Frauen im alten deutschen Recht. Berlin, 1877.

Stanard, Mrs. M. M. P. N. Colonial

Virginia, its people and customs. Philadelphia and London, 1917.

Stannus, H. S. Notes on some tribes of British Central Africa. JAI, XL.

Stannus, H. S. and Davey, J. B. The initiation ceremony for boys among the Yao of Nyasaland. JAI, XLIII.

Stärbäck, C. G. Guldhalsbaandet. (Danish trans.) Kristiania.

Starcke, C. N. *The primitive family. New York, 1889.

——*Samvittighedslivet, en fremstilling af principerne for menneskeligt samfundsliv. Vol. I. København. 1894.

Stark, L. Devil dancers. N. Y. Times, Sept. 3, 1922.

Starr, H. E. William Graham Sumner. New York, 1925.

Stationmaster, Powell's Creek. Telegraph Station. On the habits, etc., of the aborigines in the district of Powell's Creek, Northern Territory of South Australia. JAI, XXIV.

Statutes of the realm printed by command of his Majesty King George III . . . from original records and authentic manuscripts. Edition of 1817.

Stauf von der March, O. Völkerideale, I. Germanen und Griechen. Leipzig, 1902.

Stearns, R. E. C. Ethno-conchology, a study of primitive money. USNM, 1887.

Steen, R H. Paper on hallucinations of the sane, in British Medical Journal. (Summary in N. Y. Times, Aug. 16, 1917.)

Stegelmann, F. Die Indianer des Rio Envira. Globus, LXXXIII.

Stegelmann, F., see also Reich, A.

Steinbach, Dr. Note about Micronesia in PSM, XLIX.

Steindorff, G. The religion of the ancient Egyptians. New York and London, 1905.

*Steinen, K. von den. Bei den Indianern des Urubamba und des Envira. Globus, LXXXIII.

——Durch Central-Brasilien. Leipzig, 1886.

——Die Sammlung der Schingú-Expedition. Orig.-Mitt. aus d. K. Museen zu Berlin, 1885.

——Shingu tribes. Berlin Mus., 1888.

——Unter den Naturvölkern Zentral-Brasiliens. Berlin, 1894.

Steinmetz, S. R. Endokannibalismus. Mitt. d. Anthrop. Gesell. Wien, XXVI.

——Ethnologische Studien zur ersten Entwicklung der Strafe, nebst einer psychologischen Abhandlung über Grausamkeit und Rachsucht. 2 vols. Leiden, 1894.

——Suicide among primitive people. AA, VII. (o.s.)

Stengel, P. Die Griechischen Kultusalterthümer. München, 1898.

Stenin, P. von. Die Hochzeitsbräuche der Kasaner Tataren. Aus allen Weltteilen, XXIX.

——Jochelsons Forschungen unter den Jukagiren am Jassatschnaja und Korkodon. Globus, LXXVI.

——Die neuen Forschungen über die Baschkiren. Globus, LXXX.

Stephenson, N. W. Lincoln, an account of his personal life. Indianapolis, 1922.

Stern, B. Die Geschichte der öffentlichen Sittlichkeit in Russland. Berlin, 1907-08.

Stetson, G. R. The animistic vampire in New England. AA, IX. (o.s.)

Stevens, C. W. On explorations in the Vedirata of Ceylon. JASB, I.

Stevens, E. T. Flint chips. London, 1870.

Stevens, H. V. Materialien zur Kenntniss der Wilden Stämme auf der Halbinsel Maláka. Veröffentlichungen aus dem Königlichen Museum für Völkerkunde. Staatliche Museen zu Berlin, 1892.

——Mittheilungen aus dem Frauenleben der Ôrang Bëlendas, der Ôrang-Djâkun und der Ôrang Lâut. Bearbeitet von M. Bartels. Ztsft. f. Eth., XXVIII. (See estimate of this writer by Skeat and Blagden, Malay Peninsula, I, xxvi, xxvii.)

Stevenson, J. Ceremonial of Hasjelti Dailjis and mythical sand painting of the Navajo Indians. BAE, VIII.

Stevenson, M. C. Ethnobotany of the Zuñi Indians. BAE, XXX.

——*The Sia. BAE, XI.

——Zuñi ancestral gods and masks. AA, XI (o.s.).

——*The Zuñi Indians: their mythology, esoteric fraternities, and ceremonies. BAE, XXIII.

Stevenson, S. Y. Ancient Egyptian rites. Int. Cong. Anthrop., 1893.

Stevenson, T. E. The religious life of the Zuñi child. BAE, V.

Stieda, L. Die Anbetung der Ringelnatter. Globus, LXXV.

——Jaworskis anthropologische Skizze der Turkmenen. Globus, LXXIV.

Stigand, C. H. †Hunting the elephant in Africa, and other recollections of thirteen years' wanderings. New York, 1913.

——Notes on the natives of Nyassaland, N.E. Rhodesia, and Portuguese Zambesia, their arts, customs, and modes of subsistence. JAI, XXXVII.

——Notes on the tribes in the neighbourhood of Fort Manning, Nyassaland. JAI, XXXIX.

Stiles, H. R. Bundling, its origin, progress and decline in America. Albany, 1869.

Stobæus, J. Florilegium. 3 vols. in 2. Lipsiæ, 1838.

Stoddart, W. H. B. Mind and its disorders. Philadelphia, 1922.

Stoll, O. Das Geschlechtsleben in der Völkerpsychologie. Leipzig, 1908.

——Suggestion und Hypnotismus in der Völkerpsychologie. Leipzig, 1904.

Stow, G. W. Bantu Totemism. FolkLore, XV.

Strabo. The geography of Strabo. (Trans. by Hamilton and Falconer.) London, 1887.

Strack, H. L. Der Blutaberglaube in

d. Menschheit, Blutmorde u. Blutritus. (Inst. Judaicum in Berlin. Schriften, 14. P. 1267.) München, 1892.

Strange, W. T. Hindu law. London, 1830.

Strauss, A. Die Bulgaren. Leipzig, 1898.

Strong, W. M. Some personal experiences in British New Guinea. JAI, XLIX.

Struck, B. Pockenschutzmittel der Gäer (Goldküste). Globus, XCII.

Stuart, T. P. A. The "Mika" or "Kulpi" Operation of the Australian Aboriginals. Jr. and Proc. Roy. Soc. N.S. Wales. XXX.

Stuhlmann, F. *Mit Emin Pascha ins Herz von Afrika. Berlin, 1894.

Sturlason, S., see Laing, S., also Brodeur, A. G.

Suchier, H., Editor. Aucassin et Nicolette. Paderborn, 1899.

Suetonius. Works.

Sugenheim, S. Geschichte der Aufhebung der Leibeigenschaft und Hörigkeit in Europa bis um die Mitte des Neunzehnten Jahrhunderts. St. Petersburg, 1861.

Sukthankar, S. V. Discussion. JASB, I.

Summerhayes, W. Discussion. JAI, XX.

Sumner, W. G. Collected Essays. Vol. I. War and other essays, 1911. Vol. II. Earth hunger and other essays, 1913. Vol. III. The challenge of facts and other essays, 1914. Vol. IV. The forgotten man and other essays, 1919. (Referred to under these numbers, though not published under such designation.)

——Folkways, a study of the Sociological Importance of Usages, Manners, Customs, Mores, and Morals. Boston, 1906.

——Modern marriage. Yale Rev., XIII.

——Review of Simkhovitch, Feldgemeinschaft in Russland, in Yale Rev., VIII (o.s.).

——What social classes owe to each other. New York, 1920.

——The Yakuts. JAI, XXXI. Abridged from the Russian of Siero-shevski.

Supan, A. Die Bevölkerung der Erde. Petermann's Mittheilungen, XXIX, Ergänzungsheft 135.

Survey, The. I-LVI. New York, 1897-1926.

Sutherland, A. The origin and growth of the moral instinct. New York, 1898.

Svoboda, W. Die Bewohner des Niko-baren-Archipels. Internationales Archiv für Ethnographie, V.

——Ein kurzer Besuch auf den Nico-baren. Wien, 1888.

Swanton, J. R. Articles: Captives; Haida; Money; The name; Ordeal; Puberty customs; Sacrifice; Secret societies; Shamans and priests; Social organization; Witchcraft. HAI.

——The development of the clan system and of secret societies among the northwestern tribes. AA, VI.

——Tlingit Indians. BAE, XXVI.

Swanton, J. R. and Mooney, J. Hainai. HAI, pt. I.

Swanton, J. R. and Thomas, C. Choc-taw. HAI, pt. I.

Swanton, J. R., see also Goddard, P. E., also Henshaw, H. W., also Hewitt, J. N. B.

Symonds, J. A. The Catholic reaction. London, 1886.

——Renaissance in Italy: the age of the despots. London, 1875.

Synge, J. M. Letters to Max Meyer-feld in Meyerfeld, M., Letters of John Millington Synge. Yale Rev., XIII.

Tacitus. Works.

Taine, H. A. Les origines de la France contemporaine. Paris, 1887.

Tamura, N. Warum heiraten wir? Aus d. Japanischen von Auguste Beckel. Wiesbaden, 1898.

Tarde, G. L'opposition universelle, essai d'une théorie des contraires.

Review in L'Année Sociologique, I. Paris, 1897.

Tate, H. R. Notes on the Kikuyu and Kamba tribes of British East Africa. JAI, XXXIV.

Taubner, Herr. Vorchristliche recht-winkligen Kreuzzeichen. Verhandlungen der Berliner Gesellschaft f. Anthr., 1888.

Tavenner, E. Studies in magic from Latin literature. New York, 1916.

Taylor, R. *Te ika a maui; New Zealand and its inhabitants. London, 1870.

Technical World Magazine, The. (Later called Illustrated World.) I-XXXIX. Chicago, 1904-23.

Temesváry, R. *Volksbräuche und Aberglaube in der Geburtshilfe. Leipzig, 1900.

Temple, Capt. Formation and use of a museum of anthropology. JASB, I.

Tennyson, A. Works.

Terence. Works.

Tertullian. Works.

*Tetzner, F. Die Kroaten. Globus, LXXXV.

——Die Kuren in Ostpreussen. Globus, LXXV.

——Die Polaben im hannoverschen Wendland. Globus, LXXVII.

——Die Tschechen und Mährer in Schlesien. Globus, LXXVIII.

——Zur Volkskunde der Serben. Globus, XXXVI.

Th. S. Die Singhalesischen Teufels-tänzer auf Ceylon. Globus, LXXIV.

Thayer, A. W. The life of Ludwig van Beethoven. Edited, revised, and amended from the original English manuscript and the German editions of H. Deiters and H. Riemann, concluded and all the documents newly translated by H. E. Krehbiel. 3 vols. New York, 1921.

Thayer, W. M. Marvels of the New West. Norwich, Conn. 1888.

Theal, G. M. Kaffir folklore. London, 1882.

Theinert, A. Eine Blumenlese aus

Griechischen und Römischen Grab-
inschriften. Umschau, VI.

Theocritus. Works.

Theodosius II. Codex Theodosianus.

Thevenot, J. de. Voyages de Monsieur
de Thevenot en Europe, Asie, et
Afrique. Première partie contenant
le Voyage du Levant. 5 tomes. Amsterdam, 1727.

Thilenius, G. Alfred C. Haddons
Forschungen auf den Inseln der
Torresstrasse und in Neu-Guinea.
Globus, LXXXI.

——Kröte und Gebärmutter. Globus,
LXXXVII.

——Die Tätowierung der Frauen auf
den Laughlaninseln. Globus, LXXXI.

Thomas Aquinas. Works.

Thomas, C. Articles: Agriculture;
Canasatego; Mortuary customs;
Nanepashemet; Quapaw, a south-
western Siouan tribe. HAI.

——Burial mounds of the northern
sections of the United States. BAE,
V.

——Numerical systems of Mexico and
Central America. BAE, XIX.

——Vigesimal systems of enumeration. AA, IX.

Thomas, C., see also Dorsey, J. O.,
also Mooney, J., also Swanton, J. R.

Thomas, N. Burial ceremonies of the
Hurons. Trans. from Relations des
Jésuites, 1636, pp. 128-139. BAE, V.

Thomas, N. W. Animal superstitions
and totemism. Folk-Lore, XI.

——Birth customs of the Edo-speaking peoples. JAI, LII.

——Notes on Edo burial customs.
JAI, L.

——Some Ibo burial customs. JAI,
XLVII.

Thomas, W. I. Relation of sex to
primitive social control. Am. Jr.
Soc., III.

——Sex and society: studies in the social psychology of sex. Chicago,
1907.

——Source book for social origins.
Chicago, 1909.

Thompson, J. A., see Geddes, P.

Thomson, B. H. Ancestor-worship
among the Fijians. PSM, XLVII.

——*Concubitancy in the classificatory system of relationship. JAI,
XXIV.

——*The Kalou-Vu (Ancestor-Gods)
of the Fijians. JAI, XXIV.

Thomson, J. P. Exploration and discoveries in British New Guinea
since the proclamation of sovereignty. AAAS, 1892.

Thomson, J. Through the Masai country to Victoria Nyanza. Proceedings
of the Royal Geographical Society,
VI.

——Through Masái land: a journey of
exploration among the snowclad volcanic mountains and strange tribes
of Eastern equatorial Africa. Boston, 1885.

Thomson, W. J. *The Pito Te Henna,
or Easter Island. USNM, 1889.

Thonner, F. Das Gebiet des Mongala-
flusses in Centralafrika. Globus,
LXXII.

——Im Afrikanischen Urwald. Meine
Reise nach dem Kongo und der
Mongalla im Jahre 1896. Berlin,
1898.

Thorndike, L. A history of magic and
experimental science during the
first thirteen centuries of our era.
2 vols. New York, 1923.

Thruston, G. P. Antiquities of Tennessee. Cincinnati, 1890.

Thucydides. History.

Thurston, E. *Ethnographic notes in
Southern India. Madras, 1906.

Thurston, Father H. Celibacy of the
clergy. In Catholic Encyclopedia,
III.

Tiele, C. P. Babylonisch-Assyrische
Geschichte. Gotha, 1886-88.

——Elements of the science of religion. New York, 1897.

——Geschichte der Religion im Alter-
thume. 2 Bde. Ausgabe von G. Geh-
rich. Gotha, 1896.

Tietz, S. Folgen, Bedeutung, und
Wesen der Blutsverwandtschaft

(Inzucht) im Menschen-, Tier-, und Pflanzenleben. Leipzig, 1892.

Tikhomirov, L. A. Russia, political and social. Trans. from the French by E. Aveling. 2 vols. London, 1888.

Titelbach, V. Das "Heilige Feuer" bei den Balkenslaven. Intern. Archiv f. Ethnog., XIII.

Todd, A. J. The primitive family as an educational agency. New York, 1913.

Todd, J. H. Life of St. Patrick. Dublin, 1864.

Tolstoi, L. N. Bethink yourselves. N. Y. Times, July 10, 1904.

Tooker, W. W. Some Powhatan names. AA, VI.

Topinard, P. Éléments d'anthropologie générale. Paris, 1885.

——Trépanation dans les temps néolithiques. Rev. d'Anthr., III.

Torday, E. Culture and environment: cultural differences among the various branches of the Batetela. JAI, LI.

Torday, E. and Joyce, T. A. *Notes on the ethnography of the Ba-Huana. JAI, XXXVI.

——*Notes on the ethnography of the Ba-Mbala. JAI, XXXV.

——*Notes on the ethnography of the Ba-Yaka. JAI, XXXVI.

——*On the ethnology of the South-Western Congo Free State. JAI, XXXVII.

Tornauw, N. E. Das Moslemische Recht aus den Quellen dargestellt. Leipzig, 1855.

Tout, C. H., see Hill-Tout, C.

Towle, H. L. The motor menace. Atl. Mo., CXXXVI.

Train, A. On the trail of the bad men. New York, 1925.

Transactions and Collections of the American Antiquarian Society. I-XI. Worcester (Mass.), 1820-1909.

Transactions of the China Branch of the Royal Asiatic Society. I-VI. Hongkong, 1847-59.

Transactions of the Ethnological So-

ciety of London. I-VII. London, 1861-9.

Transactions of the International Congress of anthropology and pre-historic archeology. II-XIII. 1868-1906.

Transactions of the Royal Historical Society. 1st ser., I-X, 1869-81. 2d ser., I-XX, 1883-1906. 3d ser., I-XI, 1907-17. 4th ser., I-IX, 1918-26. London, 1869-1926.

Traquair, R. Women and civilization, an estimate of woman's usefulness. Atl. Mo., CXXXII.

Tregear, E. *The Maoris of New Zealand. JAI, XIX.

Tremearne, A. J. N. Bori beliefs and ceremonies. JAI, XLV.

——Notes on the Kagoro and other Nigerian Head-hunters. JAI, XLII.

Treon, Dr. Regarding Sioux women and their confinements. Cincinnati Lancet Clinic, Jan. 4, 1890.

Trevelyan, G. M. England in the age of Wycliffe. New York and London, 1899.

Trilles, R. P. H. Le totémisme chez les Fân. Münster i. W., 1912.

Troeltsch, E. Die Bedeutung des Protestantismus für die Entstehung der modernen Welt. Historische Zeitschrift, Folge 3, Bd. I.

Truhelka, C. Der vorgeschichtliche Pfahlbau von Dolnja Dolina. Globus, LXXXI.

Tsanoff, C. and R. The shoulders of Atlas. Atl. Mo., CXIX.

Tuck, H. N., see Carey, B. S.

Tuckerman, B. Peter Stuyvesant. New York, 1893.

Tudor, J. R. The Orkneys and Shetland; their past and present state. London, 1883.

Turner, G. *†Samoa, a hundred years ago and long before. London, 1884.

Turner, L. M. *Ethnology of the Ungava district, Hudson Bay Territory. BAE, XI.

Turner, O. The History of the pioneer settlement of Phelps and Gorham's purchase and Morris's reserve. Rochester, 1851.

Turner, W. Y. The ethnology of the Motu. JAI, VII.

Tyler. In Ill. Afr., Dec., 1895.

*†Tylor, E. B. Anthropology, an introduction to the study of man and civilization. New York, 1893.

——The limits of savage religion. JAI, XXI.

——The matriarchal family system. Nineteenth Century, XL.

——Note on the Haida totem-post lately erected in the Pitt Rivers Museum at Oxford. Man, II.

——On a method of investigating the development of institutions; applied to laws of marriage and .descent. JAI, XVIII.

——On the geographical distribution of games. JAI, IX.

——On the Tasmanians as representatives of Palæolithic man. JAI, XXIII.

——Primitive culture; researches into the development of mythology, philosophy, religion, language, art and custom. London, 1903.

——Remarks on totemism. JAI, XXVIII.

——Researches into the early history of mankind and the development of civilization. London, 1865.

——Totem-Post from the Haida Village of Masset, Queen Charlotte Islands. JAI, XXVIII.

Tyndall, J. †Fragments of Science for unscientific people. New York, 1879.

Uhland, L. Werke.

Umschau, Die. Übersicht über die Fortschritte und Bewegungen auf dem Gesamtgebiet der Wissenschaft, Technik, Litteratur, und Kunst. I-XVI. Frankfurt a.M., 1897-1912.

United States Exploring Expedition. 18 vols. Philadelphia, 1844-74.

United States National Museum (USNM). *Annual report of the board of regents of the Smithsonian Institution. Report of the United States National Museum. Washington, 1881 and following years.

Unpopular Review, The. I-XI. New York, 1914-19.

Urquhart, F. C. Legends of the Australian aborigines. JAI, XIV.

Usener, H. Mythologie. Archiv f. Religw., VII.

Usher, L. W. The origin of the sneezing formula. Pop. Sci. News, XXII.

Utiešenović, O. M. Die Haus-Kommunionen der Südslaven. Wien, 1859.

Vaca, *see* Nuñez Cabeça de Vaca.

Valerius Maximus. Decem Libri Dictorum et Factorum Memorabilium in Epitomem Redacti a Iulio Paride. Lipsiae, 1888.

Vámbéry, Arminius (Sometimes written Hermann). *Sittenbilder. aus dem Morgenlande. Berlin, 1877.

Vance, L. J. The study of folk-lore. Forum, XXII.

Vancouver, G. A voyage of discovery to the North Pacific ocean and round the world. London, 1798.

Van den Berg, L. W. C. De Afwijkingen van het Mohammedaansche Familie- en Erfrecht op Java en Madoera. Bijd., XLI.

——Rechtsbronnen van Zuid-Sumatra. In Bijd., XLIII.

Vandervelde, E., *see* Demoor, J.

Van Eck, R. Schetsen uit het Volksleven in Nederl. Oost-Indië. De Indische Gids, 1881, pt. II; 1882, pt. I.

Van Gennep, A. Le rite du refus. Archiv f. Religionsw. XI.

Van Hien, A. Totemism on the Gold Coast. JAI, XXXVI.

Vannutelli, L., e Citerni, C., L'Omo. Milano, 1899.

Van Ossenbruggen, F. D. E., Editor of Wilken's Verspreïde Geschriften. *See* Wilken.

Van Wagenen, J. V., Jr. A farmer on his own business. Atl. Mo., CXXVII.

Varney, G. J. Kite-Flying in 1897. In PSM, LIII.

Varnhagen, F. A. de. *Historia geral

do Brazil. Por um socio do Instituto Historico do Brazil. 2 vols. Rio de Janeiro, 1854 and 1857.

Vega, G. de la. First part of the royal commentaries of the Yncas. In 2 vols. London, 1869.

Vendidad. Part I of the Zend-Avesta. In the Sacred Books of the East. Oxford, 1880. See Müller, M.

Vergil. Æneid.

Verhandlungen der Berliner Gesellschaft für Anthropologie, Ethnologie, und Urgeschichte. (In Zeitschrift für Ethnologie,. III-XXXIV). Berlin, 1870-1902.

Verneau, R., see Malbot, H.

Veröffentlichungen aus den Königlichen Museum für Völkerkunde, Berlin, Staatliche Museen. I-X. Berlin, 1889-1919.

Vestnik Evropi (Russ.) (The European Messenger). Moscow, 1802-30. St. Petersburg, 1866-1914.

Veth, P. J. *Borneo's Wester-Afdeeling. Zaltbommel, 1856.

——Multatuli vs. Droogstoppel, Slijmering en Co. De Gids, 1860, II.

Videnskabs-Selskabet in Christiania, Forhandlinger i Christiania, 1858-94.

Vierkandt, A. Die Anfänge der Religion und Zauberei. Globus, XCII.

——Die Entstehungsgründe neuer Sitten. Braunschweig, 1897.

——Naturvölker und Kulturvölker. Leipzig, 1896.

Vigfússon, G. (editor) and Dasent, G. W. (translator). *Icelandic sagas and other historical documents relating to the settlements and descents of the Northmen on the British Isles. 4 vols. London, 1887-94.

Vigfússon, G. and Powell, F. Y., Editors. *Corpus Poeticum Boreale. 2 vols. Oxford, 1883.

——*Origines Islandicae, 2 vols. Oxford, 1905.

Vinci, Leonardo da. See McCurdy, E.

Vinogradoff, P. G. The growth of the manor. New York, 1905.

——*Outlines of historical jurispru-

dence. Vol. I. Introduction and tribal law. London, 1920.

——Villainage in England: essays in English mediaeval history. Oxford, 1892.

Vishwanath, Pandit. Notes by H. J. Rose. Ancient royal and Hindu marriage customs. JAI, XLVII.

Vogt, J. G. Die historische Bedeutung der natürlichen Rassenanlagen. Politisch-anthropologische Revue, I.

Voice for South America, A. X-XIII. London, 1863-66.

Volkens, G. Der Kilimandscharo. Berlin, 1897.

Volz, W. Die Bevölkerung Sumatras. Globus, XCV.

Vortisch, H. Die Neger der Goldküste. Globus, LXXXIX.

Vuillier, G. *†The forgotten isles. Impressions of travel in the Balearic Isles, Corsica, and Sardinia. New York, 1896.

W., R. Die Hochzeitsgebräuche der Setud. Globus, LXXXIX.

Wack, H. W. The story of the Congo free state. New York, 1905.

Waddell, L. A. Among the Himalayas. New York, 1899.

——*The Buddhism of Tibet; or Lamaism with its mystic cults, symbolism and mythology, and in its relation to Indian Buddhism. London, 1895.

Wadenstjerna, S. von. Die nordischen Festgebäck-formen. Globus, LXXII.

Waitz, T. and Gerland, G. E. *Anthropologie der Naturvölker. 6 Bde. Leipzig, 1859-72.

Wake, C. S. The nature and origin of group-marriage. JAI, XIII.

——Notes on the origin of the Malagasy. JAI, XI.

——The primitive human horde. JAI, XVII.

——The suastika and allied symbols. Amer. Antiq. and Or. Jour., XVI.

Walhouse, M. J. Some vestiges of girl sacrifices, jar burial, and contracted interments in India and the East. JAI, XI.

Wallace, A. R. *†The Malay archipelago; the land of the orang-utan and the bird of paradise. London, 1872.

Wallace, D. M. Russia. New York, 1905.

Wallace, L. The fair god; or, the last of the 'Tzins; a tale of the conquest of Mexico. Boston and New York, 1894.

Wallaschek, R. Primitive music. London and New York, 1893.

Wallis, W. D. Individual initiative and social compulsion. AA, XVII.

——"The intermarriage regulation of the Arunta and the Urabunna." Under Discussion and Correspondence. AA, XV.

——"The totem-centers and some possible relationships." Under Discussion and Correspondence. AA, XV.

Walsh, J. J. The story of cures that fail. Rev. in N. Y. Times, Aug. 19, 1923.

Walton, E. L. and Waterman, T. T. American Indian poetry. AA, XXVII.

Ward. In Am. Jour. Sem. Lang., XIX, 33. Quoted in Globus, LXXXVI.

Ward, Henshaw. †Thobbing. Indianapolis, 1926.

Ward, H. Ethnographical notes relating to the Congo tribes. JAI, XXIV.

Warner, G. H. The Jewish spectre. New York, 1905.

Warnshuis, A. L. Slavery in 1926. Survey, LVI.

Washington, B. T. Up from slavery. New York, 1901.

Waterloo, S. The story of Ab. New York, 1901.

Waterman, T. T. Religious practices of the Diegueño Indians. Book review. AA, XII.

Watermann, T. T., see also Walton, E. L.

Watson, J. (Ian Maclaren). Beside the bonnie brier bush. New York, 1895.

Watt, G. The aboriginal tribes of Manipur. JAI, XVI.

Wayte, W., see Smith, W.

Webb, A. J. Hill tribes of Navitilevu, Fiji. AAAS, 1890.

Webster, H. *†Primitive secret societies: a study in early politics and religion. New York, 1908.

——*†Rest days. A study in early law and morality. New York, 1916.

——Totem clans and secret associations in Australia and Melanesia. JAI, XLI.

Weeden, W. B. Economic and social history of New England, 1620-1789. 2 vols. New York, 1890.

Weeks, J. H. *Anthropological notes on the Bangala of the Upper Congo River. pts. I and II. JAI, XXXIX.

——Anthropological notes on the Bangala of the Upper Congo River (pt. III). JAI, XL.

——Notes from the Upper Congo. Folk-Lore, XV.

Weinhold, K. Altnordisches Leben. Berlin, 1856.

——*Die Deutschen Frauen in dem Mittelalter. Wien, 1882.

Weir, T. S. Sacrifices in India. JASB, I.

Weis, A. Die Kulturverhältnisse Lappmarkens. Globus, LXXVIII.

Weismann, A. The evolution theory. Trans. from German by J. A. and M. R. Thomson. 2 vols. London, 1904.

Weiss, B. *Mehr als fünfzig Jahre auf Chatham Island. Berlin, 1901.

Weiss, M. Land und Leute von Mpororo. Globus, XCI.

Weissenberg, S. Die Karäer der Krim. Globus, LXXXIV.

——Kinderfreud und Leid bei den südrussischen Juden. Globus, LXXXIII.

——*Krankheit und Tod bei den südrussischen Juden. Globus, XCI.

Weld, L. G. Among the cannibal islands. PSM, XLVIII.

Wellby, M. S. Through unknown Tibet. Philadelphia, 1898.

Wellhausen, J. Die Ehe bei den Arabern. Nachrichten von der Königlichen Gesellschaft der Wissenschaften und der Georg-Augusts-Universität zu Göttingen, 1893.
——Prolegomena to the history of Israel. Edinburgh, 1885.
——*Skizzen und Vorarbeiten. Berlin, 1877.

Welling, J. C. The law of Malthus. AA, I.

Wells, F. H. Aboriginals on the Diamentina, Herbert, and Eleanor rivers, in East Central Australia. AAAS, 1893.

Wells, H. G. The so-called science of sociology. Sociological Papers, III. London, 1907.

Werner, A. The natives of British Central Africa. London, 1906.

Wereschagin, B. In Tashkend, der Hauptstadt des russischen Turkestan. Globus, XXIV.
——Aus Wereschagin's Wanderungen in Turkestan. Anon. Globus, XXIV.

West, M. G. The symbolism of salt. PSM, LII.

Westermarck, E. The history of human marriage. London and New York, 1891.
——*†The same work, rewritten and enlarged. 3 vols. London, 1921.
——The magic origin of Moorish designs. JAI, XXXIV.

Westminster Review, The. I-CLXXXI. London, 1824-1914.

Weston, W. Customs and superstitions in Japanese highlands. JAI, XXVI.

Westropp, H. M. Primitive symbolism as illustrated in phallic worship of the reproductive principle. London, 1885.

Weygold, F. Das Indianische Lederzelt im Königlichen Museum für Völkerkunde zu Berlin. Globus, LXXXIII.

Wheelright, C. A. Native circumcision lodges in the Zoutpansberg District. JAI, XXXV.

White, A. D. *†A history of the warfare of science with theology in Christendom. 2 vols. New York, 1903.

White, E. L. El Supremo; a romance of the great dictator of Paraguay. New York, 1916.
——The unwilling vestal; a tale of Rome under the Cæsars. New York, 1918.

White, J. A chapter from Maori mythology. AAAS, 1891.

White, R. B. Notes on the aboriginal races of the N.W. provinces of S. America. JAI, XIII.

Whiteway, R. S. The rise of the Portuguese power in India, 1497-1550. Westminster, 1899.

Whitman, W. Leaves of grass.

Whitmarsh, H. P. The world's rough hand. New York, 1898.

Whitney, C. W. On snow-shoes to the barren grounds. Harper's Mag., XCII.

Whitney, W. D. Language and the study of language. New York, 1867.
——The life and growth of language. New York, 1875.

Whitney, W. D. and Lanman, C. R. Atharva-Veda Samhita. Rev. in Nation, LXXXII.

Whittlesey, C. The cross and the crucifix. Montreal, 1882.

Wickham, H. A. Notes on the Soumoo or Woolwa Indians, of Blewfields River, Mosquito territory. JAI, XXIV.

Wide World Magazine. An illustrated monthly of true narrative, adventure, travel, customs, and sport. London, 1898 and years following.

Wied-Neuwied, M. A. P., Prinz von. Reise nach Brasilien in den Jahren 1815 bis 1817. Frankfurt, 1831.

Wiener, L. Africa and the discovery of America. Philadelphia, 1920, 1922.

Wiklund, K. B. Om Lapparna i Sverige. Stockholm, 1899.

Wilde, Oscar. The picture of Dorian Gray. Complete works of Oscar Wilde. Ed. by Robert Ross. Boston.

Wilken, G. A. Vergelijkende Volkenkunde van Nederlandsch-Indie. Leiden, 1893.

——*Verspreïde Geschriften. Semarang, Soerabaja, 'sGravenhage, 1912, comprising
Part I. Bijdrage tot de kennis der Alfoeren van het eiland Boeroe (25-98); Iets over naamgeving en eigennamen bij de Alfoeren van de Minahasa (99-120); Over de primitieve vormen van het huwelijk en den oorsprong van het gezin (121-285); Over de verwantschap en het huwelijks- en erfrecht bij de volken van het Maleische ras (287-406); Het erfrecht op Nias (407-410); Over de verwantschap en het huwelijks- en erfrecht bij de volken van den Indischen Archipel, etc. (411-444); Plechtigheden en gebruiken bij verlovingen en huwelijken bij de volken van den Indischen Archipel (445-609); Verkrachting in kinderhuwelijk (611-628).
Part II. Het matriarchaat bij de oude Arabieren (1-82); Oostersche en westersche rechtsbegrippen (111-132); De couvade bij de volken van den Indischen Archipel (141-159); De verbreiding van het matriarchaat op Sumatra (161-216); Over het huwelijks- en erfrecht bij de volken van Zuid-Sumatra (217-308); Huwelijken tusschen bloedverwanten (309-352); Het landbezit in de Minahasa (353-387); Het pandrecht bij de volken van den Indischen Archipel (389-445); Het strafrecht bij de volken van het Maleische ras (447-514).
Part III. Het animisme bij de volken van den Indischen Archipel (1-287); De betrekking tusschen menschen-, dieren-, en plantenleven naar het volksgeloof (289-309); Iets over de beteekenis van de ithyphallische beelden bij de volken van den Indischen Archipel (311-322); Het shamanisme bij de volken van den Indischen Archipel (323-397); Über das Haaropfer und einige andere Trauergebräuche bei den Völkern Indonesiens (399-550); De Simsonsage (551-579).
Part IV. Iets over de mutilatie der tanden bij de volken van den Indischen Archipel (1-36); Iets over de schedelvereering bij de volken van den Indischen Archipel (37-81); Iets over de Papoewas van de Geelvinksbaai (83-121); De hagedis in het volksgeloof der Malayo-Polynesiërs (123-156); Eene nieuwe theorie over den oorsprong der offers (157-195); Het afplatten van het voorhoofd bij de Alfoeren van de Minahasa (197-201); De besnijdenis bij de volken van den Indischen Archipel (203-246); Het tellen bij nachten bij de volken van het Maleisch-Polynesische ras (247-263); Albino's in den Indischen Archipel (265-285); Struma en cretinisme in den Indischen Archipel (283-362).

Wilkens, D. Concilia Magnae Brittanniae et Hiberniae, 446-1717 A.D. (Contains the Laws of Canute). 4 vols. London, 1737.

Wilkes, C. Narrative of the U.S. exploring expedition during the years 1838, 1839, 1840, 1841, 1842. Philadelphia, 1845.

Wilkins, W. J. *Modern Hinduism. London, 1887.

Williams, F. E. The Pairama ceremony in the Purari Delta, Papua. JAI, LIII, 1923.

†Williams, J. H. The mountain that was "God," being a little book about the great peak which the Indians named "Tacoma" but which is officially called "Rainier." New York, 1911.

Williams, R. A key into the language of America. Collections of the Mass. Historical Society for the year 1794. Vol. III. Munroe and Francis, No. 7, Cornhill, 1810.

——Key to the Indian language. Collections of the R. I. Historical Society, I.

Williams, S. W. *The middle kingdom. 2 vols. London, 1883.

Williams, W. J. Notes on the Chatham Islands. JAI, XXVII.

Williamson, R. W. Some unrecorded customs of the Mekeo people of British New Guinea. JAI, XLIII.

——*The social and political systems of Central Polynesia. 3 vols. Cambridge, 1924.

Willoughby, C. Indians of the Quinaielt agency. Washington territory. Smithson. Rep., 1886, pt. I.

Willoughby, W. C. Notes on the initiation ceremonies of the Becwana. JAI, XXXIX.

——Notes on the totemism of the Becwana. JAI, XXXV.

Wilson, C. T. and Felkin, R. W. Uganda and the Egyptian Soudan. London, 1882.

Wilson, E., see Book of the Dead.

Wilson, T. Arrowpoints, spearheads, and knives of prehistoric times. USNM, 1897, pt. I.

——Prehistoric art. USNM, II, pt. 2.

——The swastika. USNM, 1894.

Wilutzky, P. Mann und Weib. Breslau, 1903. (Vol. I of Vorgeschichte des Rechts.)

Winchester Cathedral, Handbook to. Winchester, 1887. Warren, printer.

Winckler, H. Die Gesetze Hammurabis. Leipzig, 1902.

Wines, F. H. Punishment and reformation. New York, 1919.

Winship, G. P. The Coronado expedition, 1540-1542. RAE, XIV, pt. I.

Winslow, E. Good news from New England: or a relation of things remarkable in that plantation. In Coll. of Mass. Hist. Soc., VIII (1801).

Winter, A. C. Eine Bauernhochzeit in Russisch-Karelien. Globus, LXXVI.

Wirth, A. *The aborigines of Formosa and the Liu-Kiu islands. AA, X.

Wisen, T. *Om Qvinnan i Nordens Forntid. Lund, 1870.

Wissowa, G. Religion und Kultus der Römer. München, 1902.

Wittich, J. Bericht von den wunderbaren Bezoarischen Steinen. Leipzig, 1592.

Wobbermin, G. *Beeinflussung des Urchristenthums durch das Mysterienwesen. Berlin, 1896.

Wolff, A. Volksseuchen in Vergangenheit und Gegenwart. Umschau, V.

Woman resident in Russia, A. The Russian effort to abolish marriage. Atl. Mo., CXXXVIII.

Wönig, F. Die Pflanzen in alten Aegypten. Leipzig, 1886.

Wood, W. Wood's New England's Prospect. Boston, 1865.

Woodford, C. M. A naturalist among the headhunters. London, 1890.

Woods, F. A. and Baltzly, A. Is war diminishing? A story of the prevalence of war in Europe from 1450 to the present day. Boston, New York, 1915.

Woodthorpe, R. G. Notes on the wild tribes inhabiting the so-called Naga Hills, on our north east frontier of India. JAI, XI.

——*Some account of the Shans and hill tribes of the states on the Mekong. JAI, XXVI.

Worcester, D. C. *†The Philippine islands and their people. New York, 1898.

Worsaae, J. J. A. Fra steen- og bronzealderen i den gamle og den nye verden. Aarbøger, 1879.

——Nordens Forhistorie. Kjøbenhavn, 1881.

Wray. Ipoh poison of the Malay peninsula. Anthr. Misc. JAI, XXI.

Wünsch, R. Amuletum, in Glotta II.

Wuttke, A. Der deutsche Volksaberglaube. Berlin, 1869.

Xenophon. Works.

Yale Law Journal, The. 1-XXXV. New Haven (Conn.), 1891-1926.

Yale Review, The. I-XIX, 1892-1911 (o.s.). I-XIV, 1911-27 (n.s.).

Yamasaki, N. Ein Besuch in den Kopfjägerdörfern auf Formosa. Mittheil. d. Anthrop. Gesell. in Wien, XXXI.

Yarrow, H. C. *A further contribution to the study of the mortuary customs of the North American Indians. BAE, I.

Yates, L. E. Charm stones or plummets. Smithson. Rep., 1886, pt. I.

Yriarte, C. É. La vie d'un patricien de Venise au 16e siècle. Paris, 1874.

Yule, H. *The book of Ser Marco Polo, the Venetian, concerning the kingdoms and marvels of the east. 2 vols. London, 1875.

——Cathay and the way thither. London, 1866.

——A narrative of the mission sent by the Governor General of India to the Court of Ava in 1855. London, 1858.

Zachariae, T. Die weissagende indische Witwe. Ztsft. d. Vereins f. Volksk., XVIII. Berlin, 1908.

Zacharias, O. Bevölkerungs-Frage in ihrer Beziehung zu den socialen Nothständen der Gegenwart. Jena, 1883.

Zangwill, I. †Children of the Ghetto: a study of a peculiar people. London, 1895.

Zapletal, V. Der Totemismus und die Religion Israels. Freiburg, 1901.

Zeitschrift des Vereins für Volkskunde, Berlin. I-XXXIV. Berlin, 1891-1924.

Zeitschrift für Erdkunde. Continuation of Zeitschrift für vergleichende Erdkunde. V-X. Magdeburg, 1846-50.

Zeitschrift für Ethnologie. Organ der Berliner Gesellschaft für Anthropologie, Ethnologie, und Urgeschichte. I-LVI. Berlin, 1869-1924.

Zeitschrift für vergleichende Rechtswissenschaft; einschliesslich der ethnologischen Rechts und der Gesellschaftsforschung. I-XLI. Stuttgart, 1878-1925.

Zeitschrift für wissenschaftliche Theologie. I-LV. Jena, Halle, etc., 1858-1914.

Zelenin, A. V. Journeys of N. M. Prjevalski (Russ.). St. Petersburg, 1900.

Zeltner, F. de. Les Touareg du Sud. JAI, XLIV.

——Traitement d'une ophtalmie du Sahel soudanais. Bull. Soc. d'Anthr. de Paris, VIII (1907).

Zenker, E. V. Die Gesellschaft. Band I. Berlin, 1899.

Zichy, E. G. von. Aus Urga in der Mongolei. Globus, LXXIV.

Zimmer, H. *Altindisches Leben. Berlin, 1879.

Zimmern, H. Beiträge zur Kenntnis der babylonischen Religion. Die Beschwörungstafeln Surpu, Ritualtafeln für den Wahrsager, Beschwörer und Sänger. Leipzig, 1901.

Zimmermann, A. Die Europäischen Kolonien. Vol. I. Die Kolonialpolitik Portugals und Spaniens. Berlin, 1896.

Zmingrodzki, M. von. Zur Geschichte der Suastika. Archiv f. Anthr., XIX.

Zöller, H. Forschungsreisen in der deutschen Colonie Kamerun. Berlin u. Stuttgart, 1885.

Zumpt, C. G. Über den Stand der Bevölkerung und die Volksvermehrung im Alterthum. Berlin, 1841.

Zürcher, J. Jeanne d'Arc. Zürich, 1895.

Zwemer, S. M. The influence of animism on Islam. Reviewed in N. Y. Times, July 4, 1920.

NOTE TO INDEX

THE following index is part of the apparatus of this book; it has been constructed on lines calculated to realize the authors' purpose of exhibiting perspective, interrelations, and cross-sections, rather than to secure exhaustiveness. It reinforces the numerous cross-references in the footnotes. It is an index of topics rather than of words and names. Major topics can, with its aid, be followed throughout the volumes.

An index of such sort may, at least to some extent, repair the inevitable misrepresentation produced by any selected classification of societal phenomena, by bringing together elements common to many topics but not so capable of forming topics by themselves. A certain arrangement of topics and materials has to be adopted for purposes of exposition, and that arrangement necessarily excludes or subordinates others which will seem to many better and more logical. The index may suggest several cross-classifications, as well as the innumerable interrelations of topics which are the despair of any classifier of evolutionary phenomena, but which must needs be indicated unless violence is to be done to the truth.

It is as impossible, in this book, constructed as it is upon evolutionary lines, to index evolutionary factors and their action, as it would be to list all cases of the mores. The text of this treatise is adjustment, as resulting from the factors of variation, selection, and transmission. Such entries as "survival-value," "rationality," "maladjustment," offer some special indication of the results of the evolutionary process; and the topic of "correlations" assembles cases of adjustment of mores and institutions to one another, illustrative of "the strain toward consistency" in the mores. Samples of such correlations have been brought together under the key-word, "correlations," and many others are to be found under headings such as "property," "religion," "marriage." Here again, the impossibility of exhaustive indexing simply reflects the salient fact about human society, that it is a living whole whose parts are endlessly interrelated.

An index constructed along such lines presents no proper names, either of authorities or of tribes. It was at one time intended to attach to this book a register of tribes mentioned and also ethnographical maps. This project may sometime be realized but has been impossible of accomplishment prior to publication. In respect to the tribes, however, it should be noted by anyone who may wish to find the practice of any particular people with respect to a certain usage, that our instances are regularly presented, both in text and *Case-Book*, in a certain order.

We begin with the Eastern Branch of the Black Race (Australia and Melanesia), thence passing to Africa, which is traversed, usually, from south to north. Asia follows, beginning at the north and working in a southeasterly direction. Then come the Malay Archipelago and the islands of the Pacific (Micronesia and Polynesia). America is next, beginning with the Eskimo and working southward to the southern tip of South America. From this point we usually shift to the seats of ancient Eurasian culture (Assyria, Egypt, etc.) and end with contemporary but backward European peoples and with survivals in historical and contemporary periods. A slight familiarity with this

arrangement, which is based upon a rough combination of geographical and
cultural criteria, will enable anyone whose interest lies in certain regions to
find such relevant instances as our text and *Case-Book* contain.

The *Case-Book* is not as exhaustively indexed as is the text. It is understood
that an asterisk following a topic-number in the text indicates that there is a
corresponding topic in the *Case-Book*. When, therefore, an index-entry covers
an asterisked topic, there is no page-reference to the corresponding topic in
the *Case-Book*, but the one entry carries both text and *Case-Book* topics.

All references to the *Case-Book* are indicated by *italicized figures*, following the entries having to do with the text.

A. G. KELLER.

INDEX

Language of. 2101-2.

Drunkenness. 1192; *v.* intoxicants; possession; inspiration.

Dual organization. 428-9, 1960 ff. (always matrilineal), 1972, 2013, 2021-2, *152 ff., 157 ff., 864, 1096, 1138,* 1143; *v.* division; terms of address.

Dual standard of morality. 116, 117, 1674, 1680, 1775-6, 1822, 2054-5, *1012; v.* sex-differences; infidelity; divorce.

Dualism. 966, 969-70, 1067, 1144, 1215, 1219, 1314, *426, 432 ff., 729; v.* devil; fire-worship.

Duel. 371, 379, 385, 681-2, 684-6, *98, 117, 126, 128, 174, 292, 403; v.* champion; ordeal; test of man.

Duty. 348, 589-90, 1933-5, 2228, *647; v.* rights.

Ear-boring. *1069-1074, 1082 (on image, before birth), 1105, 1186; v.* sacrifice, exuvial; cult-mark.

Earth-eating; *v.* geophagy.

Earth-fetish. 986, 1021, 1162, *487; v.* nature-spirit; deity; fetish.

Earth-hunger. 361, 2153.

Earthquake. 761, 1253, *959.*

Eating; *v.* taboo on food and eating; totemism *(522 ff.)*; oath.
Ceremonial. *72, 651, 654.*
In spirit-world. *591.*

Eating in common. 446 ff., 453, 558, 1701, 1747-8, 2075-6, *148, 152 ff., 106, 956, 991, 1121; v.* guestfriendship; communion; redemption; covenant; sacrament; wedding; betrothal; proposal; *confarreatio;* relationship-mores; family-life.

Eclipse. 742, 1378, 1409, *74, 318, 423-4, 496, 562, 573, 597, 606-8, 709, 773, 958, 1061, 1069.*

Economic factors basic; *v.* maintenance basic.

Economics. 109, 695, 2214.

Economy, survival-value of. 149; *v.* thrift; forethought.

Ecstasy. 559, 1041 ff.; *v.* illusion; inspiration; narcotics; intoxicants.

Education. 521 ff., 1366-8, 1416, 1473-4, 1479-81, 1558, 1711-2, 1929 ff., 2006, 2068-9, 2111, *57, 223-4, 231 ff., 297 ff., 742, 745, 761-2, 993, 1079-80, 1082; v.* discipline; initiation, shaman, social position; games; dance; test of man and woman; secret societies; club; trade; fire-keeping.

Eel. 1116, 1275, *434, 442, 454, 498, 505, 548, 584 ff., 644; v.* fetish, animal.

Egg. 1034, 1092, 1129, 1134, 1154, 1257, 1397, *329, 442, 502, 561, 584 ff., 604, 606-7, 652, 655, 688, 712, 792, 968; v.* fetish; bird; reptile; food-taboo.

Eidolism. 827 ff., 833, 931, 932, 940-1, 1007-8, 1064, 2033; *v.* blood-vengeance; initiation; secret societies.
And fetishism. 985.

Eidolon. 796, 831, 984.

Eirenicism. 393; *v.* peace.

Elders. 534, 664, 673, 674, 686, 720, 1160, 1164, 1343, 1460, 1666, 1782, 1886, *154, 156-7, 210 ff., 356, 600, 1133; v.* family-head; council; law, procedure; gerontocracy; secret societies; club; government, embryonic; old, treatment of.

Election. 732 ff., 1052; *v.* chieftainship, succession to.

Elimination. 611.

Elopement. 689, 1629, 1631 ff., 1644, 1749, 1971, 1973, 1984, 1993, *889, 895 ff.; v.* mock capture; abduction.

Emetic. 1391, 1393, 1403, 1406, *316, 359-60, 601, 794, 814-5, 1170; v.* healing.

Emplacement. 57, 257, 280 ff., 323, *373; v.* grave.

Endocannibalism. 456, 1237.

Endogamy. 1271, 1491, 1568 ff., 1595 ff., 1614 ff., 1640, 1835, 1953, 1995, 2011, 2202, *869 ff.; v.* chosen people; incest; consanguine marriage; clan; cousin-marriage; cross-cousin; caste.
Divisional and tribal. 1569, 1595 ff., 1608 ff.
Return to. 1599, 1600.

Energies, appropriation of. 185 ff., 244-5; *v.* fire; domestication; slavery.

1988 ff., *881; v.* atomism; ostracism; endogamy; competition.

Jargon; *v.* word (fetish); language, secret; mystery.

Jealousy, 1497, 1528, 1551, 1554, 1599, 1766-8, 1771, 1775, 1808, 1838, 1873-5, 1880, 2031, *122-4, 339, 852, 857, 887, 977, 980-1, 1004, 1007, 1059, 1094, 1098, 1161; v.* infidelity; polyandry; polygyny; evil eye.

Jettatura; v. evil eye.

Jibes. 1719-20; *v.* vituperation; disparagement; deception of spirits.

Joint-family. 270, 276, 426, 1560-1, 1944, 1948, 1977, 1987, 2029, *102-3, 1083-6, 1100, 1105, 1110, 1114; v.* family.

Jokes, coarse; *v.* jibes.

Jubilee. 663, 1113, *89.*

Judge; *v.* justice, administration of; chieftainship, functions; elders.
　Immunity of. 639.
　God as. 1206, *284; v.* ordeal.

Jugglery. 1362-3, *772; v.* shaman; sleight of hand.

Jujur (bride-price). 1654 ff., *916 ff.*

Junshi. 902; *v.* suicide; grave-escort.

Jurisprudence. 2214.

Jus primæ noctis. 1550-1551, 1675-6, *847-8; v.* defloration.

Justice (fairness). 117, 127, 140, 148, 316, 321, 326, 606, 709, 1477, 1784, 2242; *v.* force; rights, "natural"; dual standard of morality; woman, disqualifications of.

Justice (legal). 423, 432, 1386, 1799, 2054-5.
　Administration of. 513, 629 ff., 651 ff., *190-1; v.* punishment; chieftainship, functions; secret societies, regulative function; group-solidarity; retaliation; blood-vengeance; law, procedure; rights (651).
　Retributive, distributive, reparatory. 652-3, 2242.
　As adjustment. 651-2.

Justification. 1168, 1208, *647; v.* redemption; covenant; religion and morals.

Kidnapping; *v.* abduction; elopement.

Kidney, kidney-fat. 623, 815, 859, 922, *498, 664, 714; v.* soul, location of.

"Killing" inanimate things. 882, 912-5, *331, 354, 395 ff., 1007; v.* soul, all things have.

Killing the old; *v.* old, treatment of.

King; *v.* chief.
　A slave. 564, *80.*
　A fetish-man. 1173; *v.* fetish-man.
　Divine right of; *v.* divine right.
　Can do no wrong. 1051; *v.* fetish-man; infallibility.

"King's evil." *458.*

"King's touch"; *v.* fetish-man, chief as; chief.

King's peace. 496; *v.* peace-group; war, amelioration of; taboo.

Kin-group. 1571, 1596 ff., 1623, *61; v.* endogamy; exogamy; syngenism; terms of address; kinship; blood-bond.

Kinship. 419 ff., 424 ff., 432, 439-40, 563 ff., 699, 1499, 1527, 1940 ff., 2011-2, *149, 1137; v.* family; clan; nobility; blood-bond; descent; kin-group; cannibalism; endocannibalism.
　By marriage of the dead. 1540.

Kinship-bond. 449 ff.; *v.* blood-bond; group-solidarity; organization, social and local.

Kiss, kissing. 797, 1303, 1308, 1770, 1787, 2029, 2073, 2120, *204, 403, 568, 570, 610, 628, 708, 937, 939-40, 974, 1015; v.* sniff.

Kite. *612-3.*

Knife, called "go-to-hell." 865.

Knot. 1300, 1394, 1718-9, *712; v.* exorcism; evil eye.

Knowledge. 2218 ff., 2221-2; *v.* science.

Label; *v.* allocation; terms of address.

Labor. 99-100, 108 ff., 111 ff., 1476, 2064; *v.* science, pure.
　"Creative." 103-4; *v.* land, not "made."
　Specialization. 141 ff., 150 ff., 229-30; *v.* sex-specialization.
　Incentives to. 2152; *v.* incentive.

Old and evil deities are female. 1402, 1817; *v.* woman, status of.

Transition to. *1127-9, 1136-7.*

Transition to father-family. 1911, 1971 ff., 1984-5; 1992 ff., *154, 160, 240 (symbolized by initiation), 323, 895, 1011, 1138; v.* cross-cousin; couvade; herding; clan; abduction.

Authority in. 1964 ff., 1968-9, 1990 ff., *1135; v.* uncle, maternal; sister and brother.

Individual initiative as a solvent of. 1974; *v.* individual initiative.

Compared with father-family; as adjustment and maladjustment. 715 ff., 1983 ff., 1988 ff., *1098, 1123-4.*

Legends of. *1102-4.*

Survivals of. *1130 ff.; v.* mother-in-law.

Mother-in-law. 1414, 1791, 1952, 1960, 2009, 2017 ff., 2023, 2030-1, 2045, 2142, *1004, 1090 ff., 1100 ff., 1130, 1143 ff., 1160; v.* relationship-mores.

Mother-love. 23, 1497, 1511 ff., 1937, 2030-1.

"Mother-right." 1942; *v.* mother-family.

Motive; *v.* purpose.

Mountain. *737; v.* fetish.

Sleep on. *754.*

Mourning. 528, 829, 863, 868-79, 920-2, 927, 1113, 1505, 1718, 1844 ff., 2031, *127, 403 ff., 663, 835, 972 (not for married daughter), 974 (not for wife); v.* mortuary; dead, disposal of; disguise; ritual; taboo, industrial; initiation as funeral; widow.

Of bride; *v.* bride's complaints.

Forbidden as punishment. *292.*

Mummification. 927, *399 ff., 468; v.* dead, disposal of; head-hunting; *tsantsa.*

Murder; *v.* homicide.

Attack soul. 798, 802, 806.

As qualification for majority. *235; v.* initiation.

Detection. 1319 ff.

Music. 2102-3, 2108; *v.* drama; singing.

"Must" and "ought." 619, 622; *v.* moral judgment; deduction.

Mutilation. *283, 391 ff., 688-90, 719; v.* deformation; sacrifice, exuvial; mourning; punishment; adultery.

Mutual aid; *v.* group-solidarity; communalism; humanitarianism.

Mysteries. 453, 527, 1217, *634-6, 684; v.* cult-bond.

Mystery. 558, 825, 1466-7, 2174, *1168-9; v.* aleatory element; doctrine of mystery.

Myth, mythology. 1427; *v.* legend.

Nagualism. 537, *436-7.*

Nails. 816, 818, 888, 995, 999, 1070, 1079, 1084, 1361, 1627, 2138, *59, 146, 283, 344, 372, 462-3, 477, 577, 603, 612, 714, 726, 733-4, 819, 1014, 1063; v.* soul, location of; magic, exuvial; onychomancy.

Nakedness; *v.* nudity.

Name. 810 ff., 904, 997, 1305, 1345, 1393, 1753, 1816, 1994, 2025, *91-2, 154, 157, 161, 313, 318 ff., 322, 410, 540 ff., 742, 876, 950, 952, 958, 975, 1056, 1074-5, 1091, 1099, 1103, 1106, 1108-9, 1117-8, 1124, 1126, 1129, 1154; v.* soul; fetish, name; terms of address; word-fetish.

Exchange of. 445; *v.* guestfriendship.

New, change of. 529, 531, 550 ff., 554, 712, 810, 812, 814, 864-5, 1072, 1149, 1150, 1367, 1693, 1886, *221, 223, 314, 319 ff., 331, 358, 375, 432-3, 563, 566-7, 947, 961 (wedding); v.* secret societies; initiation; re-birth; teknonymy; redemption.

Taboo on. 863 ff., 866-7, 876, 963-4, 971, 1026, 1071, 1086, 1205, 1922, 2001, 2006-7, 2016 ff., *60, 204, 232, 318 ff., 360, 368-70, 431, 453, 558, 579-80, 783, 785, 972, 974, 978, 990, 1013, 1020, 1051, 1088, 1137, 1145, 1149 ff., 1155-6, 1159; v.* deception; disparagement; avoidance; silence; word; terms of address; relationship-mores; marriage; taboos on betrothed and newly wed.